Touring Europ[...]
Central and South East E[...]
Benelux and Scandinavia

Also available:

©The Caravan Club Limited 2016
Published by The Caravan Club Limited
East Grinstead House, East Grinstead
West Sussex RH19 1UA

General Enquiries: 01342 326944
Travel Service Reservations: 01342 316101
Red Pennant Overseas Holiday Insurance:
01342 336633
Website: www.caravanclub.co.uk
Email: enquiries@caravanclub.co.uk

Editor: Kate Walters
Email: kate.walters@caravanclub.co.uk

Printed by Stephens & George Ltd
Merthyr Tydfil

ISBN 978-0-9932781-1-2

Maps and distance charts generated from Collins
Bartholomew Digital Database
Maps ©Collins Bartholomew Ltd 2015, reproduced by
permission of HarperCollins Publishers.

Except as otherwise permitted under Copyright, Design
and Patents Act, 1998, this publication may only be
reproduced, stored or transmitted in any form, or by
any means, with the prior permission in writing of the
publisher.

The contents of this publication are believed to be
correct at the time of printing. Nevertheless, the
publisher and copyright owner(s) can accept no
responsibility for errors or omissions, changes in the
detail given, or for any expense or loss thereby caused.

Cover: Venice ©Iakov Kalinin

Go further with The Caravan Club

Join The Caravan Club and experience the best of overseas touring.

- Preferential ferry rates on crossings from a variety operators

- Over 200 campsites in 16 countries across Europe

- Specially designed travel insurance for caravanners and motorhomers

GUARANTEED
BEST FERRY & CAMPSITE
PACKAGE RATES

Bonterra Park, Spain

Campsite De Haro, Spain

Visit caravanclub.co.uk/jointotravel
or call 01342 488106

THE
CARAVAN
CLUB

Main image: Cartagena Cala Cortina beach.

Welcome
to Touring Europe 2016

The fantastic thing about touring in your own 'home-from-home', whether that be a caravan, motorhome, trailer tent or tent, is that you really do have the freedom to make your holiday exactly what you want it to be.

You can pitch up in one place for a long stay, discover everything the area has to offer, find hidden gems and get to know the locals. Or you can move around to explore a wider area, covering countryside, towns and the coast in one trip. If you turn up to a site and it isn't your cup of tea you can simply move on; you can extend your stay if you find your own personal paradise.

Touring Europe is designed to be the ultimate aide to enjoying the freedom that touring offers. This guide, like sister titles *Touring France* and *Touring Spain and Portugal*, lists thousands of sites, including helpful comments from previous visitors, and offers basic information on a vast number of touring-related subjects. You will be able to find the information you need without an internet connection – sometimes an elusive thing if you're pitched in the middle of nowhere!

So as you start another year of touring adventures I would like to thank you for continuing to buy and contribute to these unique guides. If you can, please spare five minutes to fill in one of the forms at the back of this book or visit www.caravanclub.co.uk/europereport to let us know what you think about the sites you've stayed on this year. The more site reports we receive, the more people we can help to enjoy the freedom of independent touring in Europe. Happy touring!

Kate Walters

Kate Walters, Editor

Contents

How To Use This Guide

Planning your trip

Motoring advice

During your stay

How to use this guide

The information contained within *Touring Europe* is presented in the following categories:

The Handbook

This includes general information about touring in Europe, such as legal requirements, advice and regulations. The Handbook chapters are at the front of the guide and are separated as follows:

Planning Your Trip	Information you'll need before you travel including information on the documents and insurance you'll need, advice on money, customs regulations and planning your channel crossings.
Motoring Advice	Advice on motoring overseas, essential equipment and roads in Europe including mountain passes and tunnels.
During Your Stay	Information for while you're away including telephone, internet and TV advice, medical information and advice on staying safe.
Continental Campsites	Advice on choosing your site and the differences you might find overseas.

Country Introduction

Following on from the Handbook chapters you will find the Country Introductions containing information, regulations and advice specific to each country. You should read the Country Introduction in conjunction with the Handbook chapters before you set off on your holiday.

Campsite Entries

After the Country Introduction you will find the campsite entries listed alphabetically under their nearest town or village. Where several campsites are shown in and around the same town they will be listed in clockwise order from the north.

To find a campsite all you need to do is look for the town or village of where you would like to stay, or use the maps at the back of each site section to find a town where sites are listed. Where there are no sites listed in a relatively large or popular town you may find a cross reference, directing you to the closest town which does have sites.

In order to provide you with the details of as many site as possible in *Touring Europe* we use abbreviations in the site entries.

For a full and detailed list of these abbreviations please see the following pages of this section.

We have also included some of the most regularly used abbreviations, as well as an explanation of a campsite entry, on the fold-out on the back cover.

Campsite Fees

Campsite entries show high season fees per night for an outfit plus two adults, as at the year of the last report. Prices given may not include electricity or showers, unless indicated. Outside of the main holiday season many sites offer discounts on the prices shown and some sites may also offer a reduction for longer stays.

Campsite fees may vary to the prices stated in the site entries, especially if the site has not been reported on for a few years. You are advised to always check fees when booking, or at least before pitching, as those shown in site entries should be used as a guide only.

Site Maps

Each town and village listed alphabetically in the site entry pages has a map grid reference

number, e.g. 3B4. The map grid reference number is shown on each site entry. The maps can be found at the end of each country's site entry pages. The reference number will show you where each town or village is located, and the site entry will tell you how far the site is from that town. Place names are shown on the maps in two colours:

Red where we list a site which is open all year (or for at least eleven months of the year)

Black where we only list seasonal sites which close in winter.

These maps are intended for general campsite location purposes only; a detailed road map or atlas is essential for route planning and touring.

Town names in capital letters (**RED**, **BLACK** or in *ITALICS*) correspond with towns listed on the Distance Chart.

The scale used for the map means that it is not possible to pinpoint every town or village where a campsite exists, so some sites in small villages may be listed under a nearby larger town instead.

Satellite Navigation

Most campsite entries now show a GPS (sat nav) reference. There are several different formats of writing co-ordinates, and in this guide we use decimal degrees, for example 48.85661 (latitude north) and 2.35222 (longitude east).

Minus readings, shown as -1.23456, indicate that the longitude is west of the Greenwich meridian. This will only apply to sites in the west of France, most of Spain and all of Portugal as the majority of Europe (including all countries covered in this edition of the guide) are east of the Greenwich meridian.

Manufacturers of Sat Navs all use different formats of co-ordinates so you may need to convert the co-ordinates before using them with your device. There are plenty of online conversion tools which enable you to do this quickly and easily - just type 'co-ordinate converter' into your search engine.

Please be aware if you are using a sat nav device some routes may take you on roads that are narrow and/or are not suitable for caravans or large outfits.

The GPS co-ordinates given in this guide are provided by members and checked wherever possible, however we cannot guarantee their accuracy due to the rural nature of most of the sites. The Caravan Club cannot accept responsibility for any inaccuracies, errors or omissions or for their effects.

Site Report Forms

With the exception of campsites in The Club's Overseas Site Booking Service (SBS) network, The Caravan Club does not inspect sites listed in this guide. Virtually all of the sites listed in *Touring Europe* are from site reports submitted by users of these guides. You can tell us about great sites you have found or update the details of sites already within the books.

> **We rely on you, the users of this guide, to tell us about campsites you have visited**

Sites which are not reported on for five years are deleted from the guide, so even if you visit a site and find nothing different from the site listing we'd appreciate a update to tell us as much.

You will find site report forms towards the back of this guide which we hope you will complete and return to us by freepost (please post when you are back in the UK). Use the abbreviated site report form if you are reporting no changes, or only minor changes, to a site entry. The full report form should be used for new sites or sites which have changed a lot since the last report.

You can complete both the full and abbreviated versions of the site report forms by visiting www.caravanclub.co.uk/europereport.

Complete site report forms online – www.caravanclub.co.uk/europereport

Please submit reports as soon as possible. Information received by **mid August 2016** will be used wherever possible in the next edition of *Touring Europe*. Reports received after that date are still very welcome and will appear in the following edition. The editor is unable to respond individually to site reports submitted due to the large quantity that we receive.

Tips for Completing Site Reports

- If possible fill in a site report form while at the campsite. Once back at home it can be difficult to remember details of individual sites, especially if you visited several during your trip.
- When giving directions to a site, remember to include the direction of travel, e.g. 'from north on D137, turn left onto D794 signposted Combourg' or 'on N83 from Poligny turn right at petrol station in village'. Wherever possible give road numbers, junction numbers and/or kilometre post numbers, where you exit from motorways or main roads. It is also helpful to mention useful landmarks such as bridges, roundabouts, traffic lights or prominent buildings.

We very much appreciate the time and trouble you take submitting reports on campsites that you have visited; without your valuable contributions it would be impossible to update this guide.

Acknowledgements

The Caravan Club's thanks go to the AIT/FIA Information Centre (OTA), the Alliance Internationale de Tourisme (AIT), the Fédération International de Camping et de Caravaning (FICC) and to the national clubs and tourist offices of those countries who have assisted with this publication.

Every effort is made to ensure that information contained in this publication is accurate and that the details given in good faith in the site report forms are accurately reproduced or summarised. The Caravan Club Ltd has not checked these details by inspection or other investigation and cannot accept responsibility for the accuracy of these reports as provided by members and non-members, or for errors, omissions or their effects. In addition The Caravan Club Ltd cannot be held accountable for the quality, safety or operation of the sites concerned, or for the fact that conditions, facilities, management or prices may have changed since the last recorded visit. Any recommendations, additional comments or opinions have been contributed by caravanners and people staying on the site and are not generally those of The Caravan Club.

The inclusion of advertisements or other inserted material does not imply any form of approval or recognition, nor can The Caravan Club Ltd undertake any responsibility for checking the accuracy of advertising material.

Explanation of a Campsite Entry

The town under which the campsite is listed, as shown on the relevant Sites Location Map at the end of each country's site entry pages

Distance and direction of the site from the centre of the town the site is listed under in kilometres (or metres), together with site's aspect

Site Location Map grid reference

Indicates that the site is open all year

Campsite name

Telephone and fax numbers including national code where applicable

Description of the campsite and its facilities

⊞ **MUNSTERTAL** *03B4 (1.5km W Rural)* **47.85995, 7.76370 Feriencamping Münstertal, Dietzelbachstrasse 6, 79244 Münstertal** [(07636) 7080; fax (07636) 7448; info@ camping-muenstertal.de; www.camping-muenstertal. de] Exit A5 junc 64a at Bad Krozingen-Staufen-Münstertal. By-pass Staufen & foll Münstertal sps. Site on L 1.5km past Camping Belchenblick off rd L123. Lge, mkd pitch, shd; wc; chem disp; mv service pnt; serviced pitches; sauna; steam rm; solarium; private bathrms avail; shwrs inc; el pnts (16A) metered; gas; lndtte; shop; rest; snacks; adventure playgrnd; 2 htd pools (1 covrd); fishing; wintersports nr; skilift 10km; tennis; horseriding; games area; games rm; beauty treatments avail; wifi; entmnt; cab TV; some statics; dogs €3.50; phone; rlwy stn 200m; gates clsd 1300-1430 & 2200-0730; m'van o'night area; adv bkg rec school hols; quiet; red long stay. CCI. "Superb, well-managed site; luxurious, clean facs; many activities for all family; gd walking; vg rest; conv Freiburg & Black Forest." ♦ € 31.55 2011*

Contact email and website address

Directions to the campsite

Unspecified facilities for disabled guests. If followed by 'ltd' this indicates that the facilities are limited.

The year in which the site was last reported on by a visitor

Campsite address

BALATONSZEPEZD *C1 (4km SW Rural)* **46.82960, 17.64014** **Balatontourist Camping Napfény, Halász út 5, 8253 Révfülöp** [(87) 563031; fax 464309; napfeny@balatontourist.hu; www. balatontourist.hu] Take m'way E71/M7 & exit junc 90 along N shore of lake, passing Balatonalmádi & Balatonfüred to Révfülöp. Site sp. Lge, mkd pitch, pt shd; wc; chem disp; mv service pnt; baby facs; private san facs avail; shwrs inc; el pnts (6A) inc; lndtte (inc dryer); shop; supmkt 500m; tradsmn; rest; snacks; bar; BBQ; playgrnd; paddling pool; lake sw & beach adj; fishing; watersports; cycle & boat hire; tennis 300m; horseriding 5km; games area; games rm; wifi; entmnt; TV rm; 2% statics; dogs HUF900; twin-axles acc (rec check in adv); phone; adv bkg; quiet; ccard acc; red low ssn. "Warm welcome; excel, well-organised lakeside site; gd pitches; gd for families; fees according to pitch size & location." ♦ 27 Apr-30 Sep. HUF 7150 (CChq acc) SBS - X06 2011*

GPS co-ordinates – latitude and longitude in decimal degrees. Minus figures indicate that the site is west of the Greenwich meridian

Comments and opinions of caravanners who have visited the site (within inverted commas)

Charge per night in high season for car, caravan + 2 adults as at year of last report

Opening dates

Booking reference for a site the Club's Overseas Travel Service work with, i.e. bookable via The Club.

The site accepts Camping Cheques, see the **Continental Campsites** chapter for details

Site Description Abbreviations

Each site entry assumes the following unless stated otherwise:

Level ground, open grass pitches, drinking water on site, clean wc unless otherwise stated (own sanitation required if wc not listed), site is suitable for any length of stay within the dates shown.

aspect
urban – within a city or town, or on its outskirts
rural – within or on edge of a village or in open countryside
coastal – within one kilometre of the coast

size of site
sm – max 50 pitches
med – 51 to 150 pitches
lge – 151 to 500 pitches
v lge – 501+ pitches

pitches
hdg pitch – hedged pitches
mkd pitch – marked or numbered pitches
hdstg – some hard standing or gravel

levels
sl – sloping site
pt sl – sloping in parts
terr – terraced site

shade
shd – plenty of shade
pt shd – part shaded
unshd – no shade

Site Facilities

adv bkg
Advance booking accepted;
adv bkg rec – advance booking recommended

baby facs
Nursing room/bathroom for babies/children

beach
Beach for swimming nearby;
1km – distance to beach
sand beach – sandy beach
shgl beach – shingle beach

bus/metro/tram
Public transport within an easy walk of the site

chem disp
Dedicated chemical toilet disposal facilities;
chem disp (wc) – no dedicated point; disposal via wc only

CKE/CCI
Camping Key Europe and/or Camping Card International accepted

CL-type
Very small, privately-owned, informal and usually basic, farm or country site similar to those in the Caravan Club's network of Certificated Locations

dogs
Dogs allowed on site with appropriate certification (a daily fee may be quoted and conditions may apply)

el pnts
Mains electric hook-ups available for a fee;
inc – cost included in site fee quoted
10A – amperage provided
conn fee – one-off charge for connection to metered electricity supply
rev pol – reversed polarity may be present

(see *Electricity and Gas* in the section *DURING YOUR STAY*)

Eng spkn
English spoken by campsite reception staff

entmnt
Entertainment facilities or organised entertainment for adults and/or children

fam bthrm
Bathroom for use by families with small children

gas
Supplies of bottled gas available on site or nearby

internet
Internet point for use by visitors to site;
wifi – wireless local area network available

lndtte
Washing machine(s) with or without tumble dryers, sometimes other equipment available, eg ironing boards;
lndtte (inc dryer) – washing machine(s) and tumble dryer(s)
lndry rm – laundry room with only basic clothes-washing facilities

Mairie
Town hall (France); will usually make municipal campsite reservations

mv service pnt
Special low level waste discharge point for motor caravans; fresh water tap and rinse facilities should also be available

NH

Suitable as a night halt

noisy

Noisy site with reasons given;
quiet – peaceful, tranquil site

open 1 Apr-15 Oct

Where no specific dates are given, opening
dates are assumed to be inclusive, ie Apr-Oct –
beginning April to end October
(NB: opening dates may vary from those shown;
check before travelling, particularly when
travelling out of the main holiday season)

phone

Public payphone on or adjacent to site

playgrnd

Children's playground

pool

Swimming pool (may be open high season only);
htd – heated pool
covrd – indoor pool or one with retractable
cover

poss cr

During high season site may be crowded or
overcrowded and pitches cramped

red CCI/CCS

Reduction in fees on production of a Camping
Card International or Camping Card Scandinavia

rest

Restaurant;
bar – bar
BBQ – barbecues allowed (may be restricted to a
separate, designated area)
cooking facs – communal kitchen area
snacks – snack bar, cafeteria or takeaway

SBS

Site Booking Service (pitch reservation can be
made through the Caravan Club's Travel Service)

serviced pitch

Electric hook-ups and mains water inlet and grey
water waste outlet to pitch;
all – to all pitches
50% – percentage of pitches

shop(s)

Shop on site;
adj – shops next to site
500m – nearest shops
supmkt – supermarket
hypmkt – hypermarket
tradsmn – tradesmen call at the site, eg baker

shwrs

Hot showers available for a fee;
inc – cost included in site fee quoted

ssn

Season;
high ssn – peak holiday season
low ssn – out of peak season

50% statics

Percentage of static caravans/mobile homes/
chalets/fixed tents/cabins or long term seasonal
pitches on site, including those run by tour
operators

sw

Swimming nearby;
1km – nearest swimming
lake – in lake
rv – in river

TV

TV available for viewing by visitors (often in
the bar);
TV rm – separate TV room (often also a games
room)
cab/sat – cable or satellite connections to pitches

wc

Clean flushing toilets on site;
(cont) – continental type with floor-level hole
htd – sanitary block centrally heated in winter
own san – use of own sanitation facilities
recommended

Other Abbreviations

AIT	Alliance Internationale de Tourisme
a'bahn	Autobahn
a'pista	Autopista
a'route	Autoroute
a'strada	Autostrada
adj	Adjacent, nearby
alt	Alternative
app	Approach, on approaching
arr	Arrival, arriving
avail	Available
Ave	Avenue
bdge	Bridge
bef	Before
bet	Between
Blvd	Boulevard
C	Century, eg 16thC
c'van	Caravan
CC	Caravan Club
ccard acc	Credit and/or debit cards accepted (check with site for specific details)
CChq acc	Camping Cheques accepted

cent	Centre or central	o'look(ing)	Overlook(ing)
clsd	Closed	o'night	Overnight
conn	Connection	o'skts	Outskirts
cont	Continue or continental (wc)	PO	Post office
conv	Convenient	poss	Possible, possibly
covrd	Covered	pt	Part
dep	Departure	R	Right
diff	Difficult, with difficulty	rd	Road or street
dir	Direction	rec	Recommend/ed
dist	Distance	recep	Reception
dual c'way	Dual carriageway	red	Reduced, reduction (for)
E	East	reg	Regular
ent	Entrance/entry to	req	Required
espec	Especially	RH	Right-hand
ess	Essential	rlwy	Railway line
excel	Excellent	rm	Room
facs	Facilities	rndabt	Roundabout
FIA	Fédération Internationale de l'Automobile	rte	Route
FICC	Fédération Internationale de Camping & de Caravaning	RV	Recreational vehicle, ie large motor caravan
FFCC	Fédération Française de Camping et de Caravaning	rv/rvside	River/riverside
		S	South
FKK/FNF	Naturist federation, ie naturist site	san facs	Sanitary facilities ie wc, showers, etc
foll	Follow	snr citizens	Senior citizens
fr	From	sep	Separate
g'ge	Garage	sh	Short
gd	Good	sp	Sign post, signposted
grnd(s)	Ground(s)	sq	Square
hr(s)	Hour(s)	ssn	Season
immac	Immaculate	stn	Station
immed	Immediate(ly)	strt	Straight, straight ahead
inc	Included/inclusive	sw	Swimming
indus est	Industrial estate	thro	Through
INF	Naturist federation, ie naturist site	TO	Tourist Office
int'l	International	tour ops	Tour operators
irreg	Irregular	traff lts	Traffic lights
junc	Junction	twd	Toward(s)
km	Kilometre	unrel	Unreliable
L	Left	vg	Very good
LH	Left-hand	vill	Village
LS	Low season	W	West
ltd	Limited	w/end	Weekend
mkd	Marked	x-ing	Crossing
mkt	Market	x-rds	Cross roads
mob	Mobile (phone)		
m'van	Motor caravan		
m'way	Motorway		
N	North		
narr	Narrow		
nr, nrby	Near, nearby		
opp	Opposite		
o'fits	Outfits		

Symbols Used

◆ Unspecified facilities for disabled guests check before arrival

⊞ Open all year

* Last year site report received (see Campsite Entries in Introduction)

Documents

Camping Card Schemes

Camping Key Europe (CKE) is a useful companion for touring in Europe. Not only does it serve as a valid ID at campsites, meaning that you don't have to leave your passport with the site reception, it also entitles you to discounts at over 2200 sites.

CKE also offers third-party liability insurance for families including up to three children, which provides cover for loss or damage that occurs while on site. Full details of the levels of cover are provided with the card. For more information on the scheme and all its benefits visit www.campingkey.com.

You can purchase the CKE from The Club by calling 01342 336633, or it is provided free for Red Pennant Overseas Holiday Insurance customers taking out the 'Motoring' level of cover.

An alternative scheme is Camping Card International (CCI) - to find out more visit www.campingcardinternational.com.

If you are using a CKE or CCI card as a method of ID at a site, make sure that you collect your card when checking out. Also check that you have been given your own card instead of someone else's.

Driving Licence

A full (not provisional), valid driving licence should be carried at all times when driving abroad. You must produce it when asked to do so by the police and other authorities, or you may be liable for an immediate fine and confiscation of your vehicle(s).

If your driving licence is due to expire while you are away it can normally be renewed up to three months before the expiry date - contact the DVLA if you need to renew more than three months ahead.

All European Union countries recognise the pink EU-format driving licence introduced in the UK in 1990, subject to the minimum age requirements (normally 18 years for a vehicle with a maximum weight of 3,500 kg carrying no more than eight people). However, there are exceptions in some European Countries and the Country Introductions contain specific details.

Old-style green UK paper licences or Northern Irish licences issued before 1991 should be updated to a photocard licence before travelling as they may not be recognised by local authorities.

Selected post offices and DVLA local offices offer a premium checking service for photocard applications but the service is not available for online applications.

MOT Certificate

Carry your vehicle's MOT certificate (if applicable) when driving on the Continent. You may need to show it to the authorities if your vehicle is involved in an accident, or in the event of random vehicle checks. If your MOT certificate is due to expire while you are away you should have the vehicle tested before you leave home.

Passport

Many countries require you to carry your passport at all times. Enter next-of-kin details in the back of your passport and keep a separate photocopy or record of your passport details. It's also a good idea to leave a photocopy of it with a relative or friend at home.

The following information applies to British passport holders only. For information on passports issued by other countries you should contact the local embassy.

Applying for a Passport
Each person travelling out of the UK (including babies) must hold a valid passport - it is no longer possible to include children on a parent's passport. A standard British passport is valid for 10 years, or five years for children under 16.

All newly issued UK passports are now biometric, also known as e-passports, which contain a microchip with information which can be used to authenticate the holder's identity.

Full information and application forms are available from main post offices or from the Identity & Passport Service's website, www.gov.uk where you can complete an online application. Allow at least six weeks for first-time passport applications, for which you may need to attend an interview at your nearest Identity and Passport Service (IPS) regional office. Allow three weeks for a renewal application or replacement of a lost, stolen or damaged passport.

Post offices offer a 'Check & Send' service for passport applications which can prevent delays due to errors on your application form. To find your nearest 'Check & Send' post office call 0345 611 2970 or see www.postoffice.co.uk.

Passport Validity
Most countries in the EU only require your passport to be valid for the duration of your stay. However, in case your return home is delayed it is a good idea make sure you have six month's validity remaining. Any time left on a passport (up to a maximum of nine months) will be added to the validity of your new passport on renewal.

Schengen Agreement
The Schengen Agreement allows people and vehicles to pass freely without border checks from country to country within the Schengen area (a total of 26 countries). Where there are no longer any border checks you should still not attempt to cross land borders without a full, valid passport. It is likely that random identity checks will continue to be made for the foreseeable future in areas surrounding land borders.

The United Kingdom and Republic of Ireland do not fully participate in the Schengen Agreement.

Pet Travel Scheme (PETS)

The Pet Travel Scheme (PETS) allows owners of dogs, cats and ferrets from qualifying European countries to bring their pets into the UK (up to a limit of five per person) without quarantine. The animal must have an EU pet passport, be microchipped and be vaccinated against rabies. Dogs must also have been treated for tapeworm. It also allows pets to travel from the UK to other EU qualifying countries. Some countries may not allow entry to certain breeds of dogs and may have rules relating to muzzling and transporting dogs in cars – check the Country Introductions for any specific details or see www.caravanclub.co.uk/pets for more details.

Pets resident anywhere in the British Isles (excluding the Republic of Ireland) are able to travel freely within the British Isles and are not subject to PETS rules. For details of how to obtain a Pet Passport visit www.defra.gov.uk of call 0370 241 1710.

On your return to the UK with your pet you will need to visit a vet between 24 and 120 hours prior to your return journey in order for your pet to be treated for tapeworm. The vet will need to sign your pet passport - ensure that they put the correct date against their signature or you may not fall within the correct time range for travel. Ask your campsite to recommend a local vet.

Travelling with Children

Some countries require evidence of parental responsibility for people travelling alone with children, especially those who have a different surname to them (including single parents, grandchildren etc.). The authorities may want to see a birth certificate, a letter of consent from the child's parent (or other parent if you are travelling alone with your own child) and some evidence as to your responsibility for the child.

For further information on exactly what will be required at immigration contact the Embassy or Consulate of the countries you intend to visit.

Vehicle Tax

While driving abroad you still need to have current UK vehicle tax. If your vehicle's tax is due to expire while you are abroad you may apply to re-license the vehicle at a post office, by post, or in person at a DVLA local office, up to two months in advance.

Since October 2014 the DVLA have no longer issued paper tax discs - EU Authorities are aware of this change.

Vehicle Registration Certificate

You must always carry your Vehicle Registration Certificate (V5C) when taking your vehicle abroad. If yours has been lost, stolen or destroyed you should apply to a DVLA local office on form V62. Call DVLA Customer Enquiries on 0300 790 6802 for more information.

Caravan – Proof of Ownership (CRIS)

In Britain and Ireland, unlike most other European countries, caravans are not formally registered in the same way as cars. This may not be fully understood by police and other authorities on the Continent. You are strongly advised, therefore, to carry a copy of your Caravan Registration Identification Scheme (CRIS) document.

Hired or Borrowed Vehicles

If using a borrowed vehicle you must obtain a letter of authority to use the vehicle from the registered owner. You should also carry the Vehicle Registration Certificate (V5C).

In the case of hired or leased vehicles, including company cars, when the user does not normally possess the V5C, ask the company which owns the vehicle to supply a Vehicle On Hire Certificate, form VE103, which is the only legal substitute for a V5C. The BVRLA, the trade body for the vehicle rental and leasing sector, provide advice on hired or leased vehicles - see www.bvrla.co.uk or call them on 01494 434747 for more information.

If you are caught driving a hired vehicle abroad without this certificate you may be fined and/or the vehicle impounded.

Visas

British citizens holding a full UK passport do not require a visa for entry into any EU countries, although you may require a permit for stays of more than three months. Contact the relevant country's UK embassy before you travel for information.

British subjects, British overseas citizens, British dependent territories citizens and citizens of other countries may need visas that are not required by British citizens. Again check with the authorities of the country you are due to visit at their UK embassy or consulate. Citizens of other countries should apply to their own embassy, consulate or High Commission.

Insurance

Car, Motorhome and Caravan Insurance

It is important to make sure your outfit is covered whilst you are travelling abroad. Your car or motorhome insurance should cover you for driving in the EU or associated countries, but you should check what you are covered for before you travel. If you are travelling outside the EU or associated countries you'll need to inform your insurer and may have to pay an additional premium.

Make sure your caravan insurance includes travel outside of the UK, speak to your provider to check this. You may need to notify them of your dates of travel and may be charged an extra premium dependent on your current levels of cover.

The Caravan Club's Car, Caravan and Motorhome Insurance schemes extend to provide policy cover for travel within the EU free of charge, provided the total period of foreign travel in any one year does not exceed 270 days for Car and Motorhome Insurance and 182 for Caravan Insurance. It may be possible to extend this period, although a charge may apply.

Should you be delayed beyond these limits notify your broker or insurer immediately in order to maintain your cover until you can return to the UK.

If your outfit is damaged during ferry travel (including while loading or unloading) it must be reported to the carrier at the time of the incident. Most insurance policies will cover short sea crossings (up to 65 hours) but check with your insurer before travelling.

Visit www.caravanclub.co.uk/insurance or call 01342 336610 for full details of The Caravan Club's Caravan Insurance or for Car or Motorhome Insurance call 0345 504 0334.

European Accident Statement
Your car or motorhome insurer may provide you with a European Accident Statement form (EAS), or you may be given one if you are involved in an accident abroad. The EAS is a standard form, available in different languages, which gives all parties involved in an accident the opportunity to agree on the facts. Signing the form doesn't mean that you are accepting liability, just that you agree with what has been stated on the form. Only sign an EAS if you are completely sure that you understand what has been written and always make sure that you take a copy of the completed EAS.

Vehicles Left Behind Abroad

If you are involved in an accident or breakdown abroad which prevents you taking your vehicle home, you must ensure that your normal insurance will cover your vehicle if left overseas while you return home. Also check if you're covered for the cost of recovering it to your home address.

In this event you should remove all items of baggage and personal belongings from your vehicles before leaving them unattended. If this isn't possible you should check with your insurer if extended cover can be provided. In all circumstances, you must remove any valuables and items liable for customs duty, including wine, beer, spirits and cigarettes.

Legal Costs Abroad

If an accident abroad leads to you being taken to court you may find yourself liable for legal costs – even if you are not found to be at fault. Most UK vehicle insurance policies include cover for legal costs or have the option to add cover for a small additional cost – check if you are covered before you travel.

Holiday Travel Insurance

A standard motor insurance policy won't cover you for all eventualities, for example vehicle breakdown, medical expenses or accommodation so it's important to also take out adequate travel insurance. Make sure that the travel insurance you take out is suitable for a caravan or motorhome holiday.

Remember to check exemptions and exclusions, especially those relating to pre-existing medical conditions or the use of alcohol. Be sure to declare any pre-existing medical conditions to your insurer.

The Caravan Club's Red Pennant Overseas Holiday Insurance is designed specifically for touring holidays and can cover both motoring and personal use. Depending on the level of cover chosen the policy will cover you for vehicle recovery and repair, holiday continuation, medical expenses and accommodation.

Visit www.caravanclub.co.uk/redpennant for full details or call us on 01342 336633.

Holiday Insurance for Pets
Taking your pet with you? Make sure they're covered too. Some holiday insurance policies, including The Club's Red Pennant, can be extended to cover pet expenses relating to an incident normally covered under the policy – such as pet repatriation in the event that your vehicle is written off.

However in order to provide cover for pet injury or illness you will need a separate pet insurance policy which covers your pet while out of the UK. For details of The Club's Pet Insurance scheme visit www.caravanclub.co.uk/petins or call 0345 504 0336.

Home Insurance

Your home insurer may require advance notification if you are leaving your home unoccupied for 30 days or more. There may be specific requirements, such as turning off mains services (except electricity), draining water down and having somebody check your home periodically. Read your policy documents or speak to your provider.

The Caravan Club's Home Insurance policy provides full cover for up to 90 days when you are away from home (for instance when touring) and requires only common sense precautions for longer periods of unoccupancy. See www.caravanclub.co.uk/homeins or call 0345 504 0335 for details.

Personal Belongings
The majority of travellers are able to cover their valuables such as jewellery, watches, cameras, laptops, and bikes under a home insurance policy. This includes The Caravan Club's Home Insurance scheme.

Specialist gadget insurance is now commonly available and can provide valuable benefits if you are taking smart phones, tablets, laptops or other gadgets on holiday with you. The Club offers a Gadget Insurance policy - visit www.caravanclub.co.uk/gadget or call 01342 779413 to find out more

Customs Regulations

Caravans and Vehicles

You can temporarily import a caravan, trailer tent or vehicle from one EU country to another without any Customs formalities. Vehicles and caravans may be temporarily imported into non-EU countries generally for a maximum of six months in any twelve month period, provided they are not hired, sold or otherwise disposed of in that country.

If you intend to stay longer than six months, dispose of a vehicle while in another country or leave your vehicle there in storage you should seek advice well before your departure from the UK.

Borrowed vehicles
If you are borrowing a vehicle from a friend or relative, or loaning yours to someone, you should be aware of the following:

- The total time the vehicle spends abroad must not exceed the limit for temporary importation (generally six months).
- The owner of the caravan must provide the other person with a letter of authority.
- The owner cannot accept a hire fee or reward.
- The number plate on the caravan must match the number plate on the tow car.

- Both drivers' insurers must be informed if a caravan is being towed and any additional premium must be paid.

Currency

You must declare cash of €10,000 (or equivalent in other currencies) or more when travelling between the UK and a non-EU country. The term 'cash' includes cheques, travellers' cheques, bankers' drafts, notes and coins. You don't need to declare cash when travelling within the EU.

For further information contact HMRC Excise & Customs Helpline on 0300 200 3700.

Customs Allowances

Travelling within the European Union
If you are travelling to the UK from within the EU you can bring an unlimited amount of most goods without being liable for any duty or tax, but certain rules apply. The goods must be for your own personal use, which can include use as a gift (if the person you are gifting the goods to reimburses you this is not classed as a gift), and you must have paid duty and tax in the country where you purchased the

goods. If a customs official suspects that any goods are not for your own personal use they can question you, make further checks and ultimately seize both the goods and the vehicle used to transport them. Although no limits are in place, customs officials are less likely to question you regarding your goods if they are under the following limits:

- 800 cigarettes
- 400 cigarillos
- 200 cigars
- 1kg tobacco
- 10 litres of spirits
- 20 litres of fortified wine (e.g. port or sherry)
- 90 litres of wine
- 110 litres of beer

The same rules and recommended limits apply for travel between other EU countries.

Travelling outside the EU
There are set limits to the amount of goods you bring back into the UK from countries outside of the EU. All goods must be for your own personal use. Each person aged 17 and over is entitled to the following allowance:

- 200 cigarettes, or 100 cigarillos, or 50 cigars, or 250g tobacco

- 1 litre of spirits or strong liqueurs over 22% volume, or 2 litres of fortified wine, sparkling wine or any other alcoholic drink that's less than 22% volume
- 4 litres of still wine
- 16 litres of beer
- £390 worth of all other goods including perfume, gifts and souvenirs without having to pay tax and/or duty
- For further information contact HMRC National Advice Service on 0300 200 3700.

Medicines

There is no limit to the amount of medicines you can take abroad if they are obtained without prescription (i.e. over the counter medicines). Medicines prescribed by your doctor may contain controlled drugs (e.g. morphine), for which you will need a licence if you're leaving the UK for 3 months or more. Visit www.gov.uk/travelling-controlled-drugs or call 020 7035 0771 for a list of controlled drugs and to apply for a licence.

You don't need a licence if you carry less than 3 months' supply or your medication doesn't contain controlled drugs, but you should carry a letter from your doctor stating your name, a list of your prescribed drugs and dosages for each drug. You may have to show this letter when going through customs.

Personal Possessions

Visitors to countries within the EU are free to carry reasonable quantities of any personal possessions such as jewellery, cameras, and electrical equipment required for the duration of their stay. It is sensible to carry sales receipts for new items in case you need to prove that tax has already been paid.

Prohibited and Restricted Goods
Regardless of where you are travelling from the importation of some goods into the UK is restricted or banned, mainly to protect health and the environment. These include:

- Endangered animals or plants including live animals, birds and plants, ivory, skins, coral, hides, shells and goods made from them such as jewellery, shoes, bags and belts.
- Controlled, unlicensed or dangerous drugs.
- Counterfeit or pirated goods such as watches, CDs and clothes; goods bearing a false indication of their place of manufacture or in breach of UK copyright.
- Offensive weapons such as firearms, flick knives, knuckledusters, push daggers, self-defence sprays and stun guns.

- Pornographic material depicting extreme violence or featuring children

This list is not exhaustive; if in doubt contact HMRC on 0300 200 3700 (+44 2920 501 261 from outside the UK) or go through the red Customs channel and ask a Customs officer when returning to the UK.

Plants and Food

Travellers from within the EU may bring into the UK any fruit, vegetable or plant products without restriction as long as they are grown in the EU, are free from pests or disease and are for your own consumption. For food products Andorra, the Channel Islands, the Isle of Man, San Marino and Switzerland are treated as part of the EU.

From most countries outside the EU you are not allowed to bring into the UK any meat or dairy products. Other animal products may be severely restricted or banned and it is important that you declare any such products on entering the UK.

For up to date information contact the Department for Environment, Food and Rural Affairs (Defra) on 0345 33 55 77 or +44 20 7238 6951 from outside the UK. You can also visit www.defra.gov.uk to find out more.

Money

Being able to safely access your money while you're away is a necessity for you to enjoy your break. It isn't a good idea to rely on one method of payment, so always have a backup plan. A mixture of a small amount of cash plus one or two electronic means of payment are a good idea.

Traveller's cheques have become less popular in recent years as fewer banks and hotels are willing or able to cash them. There are alternative options which offer the same level of security but are easier to use, such as prepaid credit cards.

Local Currency

It is a good idea to take enough foreign currency for your journey and immediate needs on arrival, don't forget you may need change for tolls or parking on your journey. Currency exchange facilities will be available at ports and on ferries but rates offered may not be as good as you would find elsewhere. The Post Office, banks, exchange offices and travel agents offer foreign exchange. All should stock Euros but

during peak holiday times or if you need a large amount it may be sensible to pre-order your currency. You should also pre-order any less common currencies. Shop around and compare commission and exchange rates, together with minimum charges.

Banks and money exchanges in central and eastern Europe won't usually accept Scottish and Northern Irish bank notes and may be reluctant to change any sterling which has been written on or is creased or worn.

Foreign Currency Bank Accounts

Frequent travellers or those who spend long periods abroad may find a Euro bank account useful. Most such accounts impose no currency conversion charges for debit or credit card use and allow fee-free cash withdrawals at ATMs. Some banks may also allow you to spread your account across different currencies, depending on your circumstances. Speak to your bank about the services they offer.

Prepaid Travel Cards

Prepaid travel money cards are issued by various providers including the Post Office, Travelex, Lloyds Bank and American Express.

They are increasingly popular as the PIN protected travel money card offers the security of Traveller's Cheques, with the convenience of paying by card. You load the card with the amount you need before leaving home, and then use cash machines to make withdrawals or use the card to pay for goods and services as you would a credit or debit card. You can top the card up over the telephone or online while you are abroad. However there can be issues with using them with some automated payment systems, such as pay-at-pump petrol stations and toll booths, so you should always have an alternative payment method available.

These cards can be cheaper to use than credit or debit cards for both cash withdrawals and purchases as there are usually no loading or transaction fees to pay. In addition, because they are separate from your bank account, if the card is lost or stolen you bank account will still be secure.

Credit and Debit Cards

Credit and debit cards offer a convenient way of spending abroad. For the use of cards abroad most banks impose a foreign currency conversion charge of up to 3% per transaction. If you use your card to withdraw cash there will be a further commission charge of up to 3% and you will be charged interest (possibly at a higher rate than normal) as soon as you withdraw the money.

There are credit cards available which are specifically designed for spending overseas and will give you the best available rates. However they often have high interest rates so are only economical if you're able to pay them off in full each month.

If you have several cards, take at least two in case you encounter problems. Credit and debit 'Chip and PIN' cards issued by UK banks may not be universally accepted abroad so check that your card will be accepted if using it in restaurants or other situations where you pay after you have received goods or services

Contact your credit or debit card issuer before you leave home to let them know that you will be travelling abroad. In the battle against card fraud, card issuers frequently query transactions which they regard as unusual or suspicious, causing your card to be declined or temporarily stopped. You should always carry your card issuer's helpline number with you so that you can contact them if this happens. You will also need this number should you need to report the loss or theft of your card.

Dynamic Currency Conversion

When you pay with a credit or debit card, retailers may offer you the choice of currency for payment, e.g. a euro amount will be converted into sterling and then charged to your card account. This is known as a 'Dynamic Currency Conversion' but the exchange rate used is likely to be worse than the rate offered by your card issuer, so will work out more expensive than paying in the local currency.

Emergency Cash

If an emergency or theft means that you need cash in a hurry, then friends or relatives at home can send you emergency cash via money transfer services.

The Post Office, MoneyGram and Western Union all offer services which allows the transfer of money to over 233,000 money transfer agents around the world. Transfers take approximately ten minutes and charges are levied on a sliding scale.

Ferries & the Channel Tunnel

Booking Your Ferry

If travelling at peak times, such as Easter or school holidays, make reservations as early as possible. Each ferry will have limited room for caravans and large vehicles so spaces can fill up quickly, especially on cheaper crossings. If you need any special assistance or arrangements request this at the time of booking.

When booking any ferry crossing, make sure you give the correct measurements for your outfit including bikes, roof boxes or anything which may add to the length or height of your vehicle - if you underestimate your vehicle's size you may be turned away at boarding.

The Caravan Club is an agent for most major ferry companies operating services. Call The Club's Travel Service on 01342 316 101 or see www.caravanclub.co.uk/ferries to book.

The table at the end of this section shows current ferry routes from the UK to the Continent and Ireland. Some ferry routes may not be operational all year, and during peak holiday periods the transportation of caravans or motorhomes may be restricted. For the most up-to-date information on ferry routes and prices visit www.caravanclub.co.uk/ferries or speak to The Club's Travel Services team.

On the Ferry

Arrive at the port with plenty of time before your boarding time. Motorhomes and car/caravan outfits will usually either be the first or last vehicles boarded onto the ferry. Almost all ferries are now 'drive on – drive off' so you won't be required to do any complicated manoeuvres. You may be required to show ferry staff that your gas is switched off before boarding the ferry.

Be careful using the ferry access ramps, as they are often very steep which can mean there is a risk of grounding the tow bar or caravan hitch. Drive slowly and, if your ground clearance is low, consider whether removing your jockey wheel and any stabilising devices would help.

Vehicles are often parked close together on ferries, meaning that if you have towing extension mirrors they could get knocked or damaged by people trying to get past your vehicle. If you leave them attached during the ferry crossing then make sure you check their position on returning to your vehicle.

Channel Tunnel

The Channel Tunnel operator, Eurotunnel, accepts cars, caravans and motorhomes (except those running on LPG) on their service between Folkestone and Calais. You can just turn up and see if there is availability on the day, however prices increase as it gets closer to the departure time so if you know your plans in advance it is best to book as early as possible.

On the Journey

You will be asked to open your roof vents prior to travel and you will also need to apply the caravan brake once you have parked your vehicle on the train. You will not be able to use your caravan until arrival.

Pets

It is possible to transport your pet on a number of ferry routes to the Continent and Ireland, as well as on Eurotunnel services from Folkestone to Calais. Advance booking is essential as restrictions apply to the number of animals allowed on any one crossing. Make sure you understand the carrier's terms and conditions for transporting pets.

Once on board pets are normally required to remain in their owner's vehicle or in kennels on the car deck and you won't be able to access your vehicle to check on your pet while the ferry is at sea. On longer crossings you should make arrangements at the on-board information desk for permission to visit your pet in order to check its well-being. You should always make sure that ferry staff know your vehicle has a pet on board.

Information and advice on the welfare of animals before and during a journey is available on the website of the Department for Environment, Food and Rural Affairs (Defra), www.defra.gov.uk.

Gas

UK based ferry companies usually allow up to three gas cylinders per caravan, including the cylinder currently in use, however some may restrict this to a maximum of two cylinders. Some operators may ask you to hand over your gas cylinders to a member of the crew so that they can be safely stored during the crossing. Check that you know the rules of your ferry operator before you travel.

Cylinder valves should be fully closed and covered with a cap, if provided, and should remain closed during the crossing. Cylinders should be fixed securely in or on the caravan in the position specified by the manufacturer.

Gas cylinders must be declared at check-in and the crew may ask to inspect each cylinder for leakage before travel.

The carriage of spare petrol cans, whether full or empty, is not permitted on ferries or through the Channel Tunnel.

LPG vehicles

Vehicles fully or partially powered by LPG can't be carried through the Channel Tunnel. Gas for domestic use (e.g. heating, lighting or cooking) can be carried, but the maximum limit is 47kg for a single bottle or 50kg in multiple bottles. Tanks must be switched off before boarding and must be less than 80% full; you will be asked to demonstrate this before you travel.

Most ferry companies will accept LPG-powered vehicles but you must let them know at the time of booking. During the crossing the tank must be no more than 75% full and it must be turned off. In the case of vehicles converted to use LPG, some ferry companies also require a certificate showing that the conversion has

been carried out by a professional - before you book speak to the ferry company to see what their requirements are.

Caravan Club Sites Near Ports

If you've got a long drive to the ferry port, or want to catch an early ferry then an overnight stop near to the port gives you a relaxing start to your holiday. The following table lists Caravan Club sites which are close to ports.

Caravan Club Members can book online at www.caravanclub.co.uk or call 01342 327490. Non-members can book by calling the sites directly on the telephone numbers below when the sites are open.

Please note that Commons Wood, Daleacres, Fairlight Wood, Hunter's Moon, Mildenhall, Old Hartley and Rookesbury Park are open to Caravan Club members only. Non-members are welcome at all other sites listed below.

Port	Nearest Club Site	Tel No.
Cairnryan, Stranraer	New England Bay	01776 860275
Dover, Folkestone, Channel Tunnel	Bearsted	01622 730018
	Black Horse Farm*	01303 892665
	Daleacres	01303 267679
	Fairlight Wood	01424 812333
Fishguard, Pembroke	Freshwater East	01646 672341
Harwich	Cambridge Cherry Hinton*	01223 244088
	Commons Wood*	01707 260786
	Mildenhall	01638 713089
Holyhead	Penrhos	01248 852617
Hull	York Beechwood Grange	01904 424637
	York Rowntree Park	01904 658997
Newcastle upon Tyne	Old Hartley	0191 237 0256
Newhaven	Brighton*	01273 626546
Plymouth	Plymouth Sound	01752 862325
Poole	Hunter's Moon*	01929 556605
Portsmouth	Rookesbury Park	01329 834085
Rosslare	River Valley	00353 (0)404 41647
Weymouth	Crossways	01305 852032

* *Site open all year*

Ferry routes and Operators

Route	Operator	Approximate Crossing Time	Maximum Frequency
Belgium			
Hull – Zeebrugge	P & O Ferries	12½ hrs	1 daily
France			
Dover – Calais	P & O Ferries	1½ hrs	22 daily
Dover – Calais	DFDS Seaways	1½ hrs	10 daily
Dover – Dunkerque	DFDS Seaways	2 hrs	12 daily
Folkestone – Calais	Eurotunnel	35 mins	3 per hour
Newhaven – Dieppe	DFDS Ferries	4 hrs	2 daily
Plymouth – Roscoff	Brittany Ferries	6 hrs	2 daily
Poole – Cherbourg	Brittany Ferries	4½ hrs	1 daily
Poole – St Malo (via Channel Islands)	Condor Ferries	5 hrs	1 daily (May to Sep)
Portsmouth – Caen	Brittany Ferries	6 / 7 hrs	3 daily (maximum)
Portsmouth – Cherbourg	Brittany Ferries	3 hrs	2 daily (maximum)
Portsmouth – Cherbourg	Condor Ferries	5½ hrs	1 weekly (May to Sep)
Portsmouth – Le Havre	Brittany Ferries	3¼ / 8 hrs	1 daily (minimum)
Portsmouth – St Malo	Brittany Ferries	9 hrs	1 daily
Ireland – Northern			
Cairnryan/Troon – Larne	P & O Irish Sea	1 / 2 hrs	11 daily
Liverpool (Birkenhead) – Belfast	Stena Line	8 hrs	2 daily
Cairnryan – Belfast	Stena Line	2 / 3 hrs	7 daily
Ireland – Republic			
Cork – Roscoff†	Brittany Ferries	14 hrs	1 per week
Fishguard – Rosslare	Stena Line	2 / 3½ hrs	3 daily
Holyhead – Dublin	Irish Ferries	1¾ / 3¼ hrs	4 daily
Holyhead – Dublin	Stena Line	3¼ hrs	4 daily
Liverpool – Dublin	P & O Irish Sea	8 hrs	2 daily
Pembroke – Rosslare	Irish Ferries	4 hrs	2 daily
Rosslare – Cherbourg*	Irish Ferries	19½ hrs	3 per week
Rosslare – Cherbourg	Stena Line	19 hrs	3 per week
Rosslare – Roscoff†	Irish Ferries	19½ hrs	4 per week
Netherlands			
Harwich – Hook of Holland	Stena Line	6½ hrs	2 daily
Hull – Rotterdam	P & O Ferries	10¼ hrs	1 daily
Newcastle – Ijmuiden (Amsterdam)	DFDS Seaways	15½ hrs	1 daily
Spain			
Portsmouth – Bilbao	Brittany Ferries	24 / 32 hrs	1 - 3 per week
Portsmouth or Plymouth – Santander	Brittany Ferries	20 / 32 hrs	4 per week

Not bookable through the Club's Travel Service.
Note: Services and routes correct at time of publication but subject to change.

Motoring Advice

Preparing for Your Journey

The first priority in preparing your outfit for your journey should be to make sure it has a full service. Make sure that you have a fully equipped spares kit, and a spare wheel and tyre for your caravan – it is easier to get hold of them from your local dealer than to have to spend time searching for spares where you don't know the local area.

Club members should carry their UK Sites Directory & Handbook with them, as it contains a section of technical advice which may be useful when travelling. The Club also has a free advice service covering a wide range of technical topics – download free information leaflets at www.caravanclub.co.uk/advice or contact the team by calling 01342 336611 or emailing technical@caravanclub.co.uk.

For advice on issues specific to countries other than the UK, Club members can contact the Travel Service Information Officer, email: travelserviceinfo@caravanclub.co.uk or call 01342 336766.

Weight Limits

From both a legal and a safety point of view, it is essential not to exceed vehicle weight limits. It is advisable to carry documentation confirming your vehicle's maximum permitted laden weight - if your Vehicle Registration Certificate (V5C) does not state this, you will need to produce alternative certification, e.g. from a weighbridge.

If you are pulled over by the police and don't have certification you will be taken to a weighbridge. If your vehicle(s) are then found to be overweight you will be liable to a fine and may have to discard items to lower the weight before you can continue on your journey.

Some Final Checks

Before you start any journey make sure you complete the following checks:

- All car and caravan or motorhome lights are working and sets of spare bulbs are packed
- The coupling is correctly seated on the towball and the breakaway cable is attached
- Windows, vents, hatches and doors are shut

- On-board water systems are drained
- Mirrors are adjusted for maximum visibility
- Corner steadies are fully wound up and the brace is handy for your arrival on site
- Any fires or flames are extinguished and the gas cylinder tap is turned off. Fire extinguishers are fully charged and close at hand
- The over-run brake is working correctly
- The jockey wheel is raised and secured, the handbrake is released.

Driving in Europe

Driving abroad for the first time can be a daunting prospect, especially when towing a caravan. Here are a few tips to make the transition easier:

- Remember that Sat Navs may take you on unsuitable roads, so have a map or atlas to hand to help you find an alternative route.

- It can be tempting to try and get to your destination as quickly as possible but we recommend travelling a maximum of 250 miles a day when towing.

- Share the driving if possible, and on long journeys plan an overnight stop.

- Remember that if you need to overtake or pull out around an obstruction you will not be able to see clearly from the driver's seat. If possible, always have a responsible adult in the passenger seat who can advise you when it is clear to pull out. If that is not possible then stay well back to get a better view and pull out slowly.

- If traffic builds up behind you, pull over safely and let it pass.

- Driving on the right should become second nature after a while, but pay particular attention when turning left, after leaving a rest area, petrol station or site or after a one-way system.

- Stop at least every two hours to stretch your legs and take a break.

Fuel

Grades of petrol sold on the Continent are comparable to those sold in the UK; 95 octane is frequently known as 'Essence' and 98 octane as 'Super'. Diesel may be called 'Gasoil' and is widely available across Europe.

E10 petrol (containing 10% Ethanol) can be found in certain countries in Europe. Most modern cars are E10 compatible, but those which aren't could be damaged by filling up with E10. Check your vehicle handbook or visit www.acea.be and search for 'E10' to find the publication 'Vehicle compatibility with new fuel standards'.

Members of The Caravan Club can check current average fuel prices by country at www.caravanclub.co.uk/overseasadvice.

Away from major roads and towns it is a good idea not to let your fuel tank run too low as you may have difficulty finding a petrol station, especially at night or on Sundays. Petrol stations offering a 24-hour service may involve an automated process, in some cases only accepting credit cards issued in the country you are in.

Automotive Liquefied Petroleum Gas (LPG)

The increasing popularity of dual-fuelled vehicles means that the availability of LPG – also known as 'autogas' or GPL – has become an important issue for more drivers.

There are different tank-filling openings in use in different countries. Currently there is no common European filling system, and you might find a variety of systems. Most Continental motorway services will have adaptors but these should be used with care – see www.autogas.ltd.uk for more information.

Low Emission Zones

Many cities in countries around Europe have introduced 'Low Emission Zones' (LEZ's) in order to regulate vehicle pollution levels. Some schemes require you to buy a windscreen

sticker, pay a fee or register your vehicle before entering the zone. You may also need to provide proof that your vehicle's emissions meet the required standard. Before you travel visit www.lowemissionzones.eu for maps and details of LEZ's across Europe. Also see the Country Introductions later in this guide for country specific information.

Motorhomes Towing Cars

A motorhome towing a small A-frame or towing dolly is illegal in most European countries. Motorhome users towing a small car should transport it on a braked trailer so that all four of the car's wheels are off the ground.

Priority and Roundabouts

When driving on the Continent it can be difficult to work out which vehicles have priority in different situations. Watch out for road signs which indicate priority and read the Country Introductions later in this guide for country specific information.

Take care at intersections – you should never rely on being given right of way, even if you have priority; especially in small towns and villages where local traffic may take right of way. Always give way to public service and military vehicles and to buses and trams.

In some countries in Europe priority at roundabouts is given to vehicles entering the roundabout (i.e. on the right) unless the road signs say otherwise.

Public Transport

In general in built-up areas be prepared to stop to allow a bus to pull out from a bus stop when the driver is signalling his intention to do so.

Take particular care when school buses have stopped and passengers are getting on and off.

Overtaking trams in motion is normally only allowed on the right, unless on a one way street where you can overtake on the left if there is not enough space on the right. Do

not overtake a tram near a tram stop. These may be in the centre of the road. When a tram or bus stops to allow passengers on and off, you should stop to allow them to cross to the pavement. Give way to trams which are turning across your carriageway. Don't park or stop across tram lines; trams cannot steer round obstructions!

Pedestrian Crossings

Stopping to allow pedestrians to cross at zebra crossings is not always common practice on the Continent as it is in the UK. Pedestrians expect to wait until the road is clear before crossing, while motorists behind may be taken by surprise by your stopping. The result may be a rear-end shunt or vehicles overtaking you at the crossing and putting pedestrians at risk.

Traffic Lights

Traffic lights may not be as easily visible as they are in the UK, for instance they may be smaller or suspended across the road with a smaller set on a post at the roadside. You may find that lights change directly from red to green, bypassing amber completely. Flashing amber lights generally indicate that you may proceed with caution if it is safe to do so but you must give way to pedestrians and other vehicles.

A green filter light should be treated with caution as you may still have to give way to pedestrians who have a green light to cross the road. If a light turns red as approached, continental drivers will often speed up to get through the light instead of stopping. Be aware that if you brake sharply because a traffic light has turned red as you approached, the driver behind might not be expecting it.

Motoring Equipment

Essential Equipment

The equipment that you legally have to carry differs by country. For a full list see the Essential Equipment table at the end of this chapter, or see the Country Introductions of this book for country specific information. Please note equipment requirements and regulations can change frequently. To keep up to date with the latest equipment information please visit www.caravanclub.co.uk/overseasadvice.

Fire Extinguisher

As a safety precaution, an approved fire extinguisher should be carried in all vehicles. This is a legal requirement in several countries in Europe.

Glasses

In some countries it is a legal requirement for residents to carry a spare pair of glasses if they are needed for driving, and it is recommended that visitors also comply. Elsewhere, if you do not have a spare pair, you may find it helpful to carry a copy of your prescription.

Lights

When driving on the Continent headlights need to be adjusted to deflect to the right if they are likely to dazzle other road users. You can do this by applying beam deflectors, or some newer vehicles have a built-in adjustment system. Some modern high-density discharge (HID), xenon or halogen-type lights, may need to be taken to a dealer to make the necessary adjustment. Remember also to adjust headlights according to the load being carried and to compensate for the weight of the caravan on the back of your car. Even if you do not intend to drive at night, it is important to ensure that your headlights are correctly adjusted as you may need to use them in heavy rain, fog or in tunnels. If using tape or a pre-cut adhesive mask remember to remove it on your return home.

Dipped headlights should be used in poor weather conditions and in a tunnel even if it is well lit. You may find police waiting at the end of a tunnel to check vehicles. In some countries the use of dipped headlights is compulsory at all times and in others they must be used in built-up areas, on motorways or at certain times of the year.

Headlight-Flashing

On the Continent headlight-flashing is used as a warning of approach or as an overtaking signal at night, and not, as is commonly the case in the UK, an indication that you are giving way. Be more cautious with both flashing your headlights and when another driver flashes you.

Hazard Warning Lights

Hazard warning lights should not be used in place of a warning triangle, but they may be used in addition to it.

Nationality Plate (GB/IRL)

A nationality plate must be fixed to the rear of both your car or motorhome and caravan. Checks are made and a fine may be imposed for failure to display a nationality plate correctly. If your number plates have the Euro-Symbol on them there is no requirement to display an additional GB sticker within the EU and Switzerland. If your number plate doesn't have the EU symbol or you are planning to travel outside of the EU you will need a GB sticker.

GB is the only national identification code allowed for cars registered in the UK. Registration plates displaying the GB Euro-Symbol must comply with the appropriate British Standard.

Reflective Jackets/Waistcoats

If you break down outside of a built-up area it is normally a legal requirement that anyone leaving the vehicle must be wearing a reflective jacket or waistcoat. Make sure that your jacket is accessible from inside the car as you will need to put it on before exiting the vehicle. Carry one for each passenger as well as the driver.

Route Planning

It is always a good idea to carry a road atlas or map of the countries you plan to visit, even if you have Satellite Navigation. You can find information on UK roads from Keep Moving – www.keepmoving.co.uk or call 09003 401100. Websites offering a European route mapping service include www.google.co.uk/maps, www.mappy.com or www.viamichelin.com.

Satellite Navigation/GPS

Continental postcodes don't cover just one street or part of a street in the same way as UK postcodes. A French five-digit postcode, for example, can cover a very large area.

GPS co-ordinates and full addresses are given for site entries in this guide wherever possible, so that you can programme your device as accurately as possible.

It is important to remember that sat nav devices don't usually allow for towing or driving a large motorhome and may try to send you down unsuitable roads. Always use your common sense, and if a road looks unsuitable find an alternative route.

Use your sat nav in conjunction with the directions given in the site entries, which have been provided by members who have actually visited. Please note that the directions given in site entries have not been checked by The Caravan Club.

In nearly all European countries it is illegal to use car navigation systems which actively search for mobile speed cameras or interfere with police equipment (laser or radar detection). Car navigation systems which give a warning of fixed speed camera locations are legal in most countries with the exception of France, Germany, and Switzerland where this function must be de-activated.

Seat Belts

The wearing of seat belts is compulsory throughout Europe. On-the-spot fines will be incurred for failure to wear them and, in the event of an accident failure to wear a seat belt may reduce any claim for injury. See the country introductions for specific regulations on both seat belts and car seats.

Spares

Caravan Spares

It will generally be much harder to get hold of spare parts for caravans on the continent, especially for UK manufactured caravans. It is advisable to carry any commonly required spares (such as light bulbs) with you.

Take the contact details of your UK dealer or manufacturer with you, as they may be able to assist in getting spares delivered to you.

Car Spares Kits

Some car manufacturers produce spares kits; contact your dealer for details. The choice of spares will depend on the vehicle and how long you are away, but the following is a list of basic items which should cover the most common causes of breakdown:

- Radiator top hose
- Fan belt
- Fuses and bulbs
- Windscreen wiper blade
- Length of 12V electrical cable
- Tools, torch and WD40 or equivalent water repellent/ dispersant spray

Spare Wheel

Your local caravan dealer should be able to supply an appropriate spare wheel. If you have any difficulty in obtaining one, The Caravan Club's Technical Department can provide Club members with a list of suppliers on request.

Tyre legislation across Europe is more or less consistent and, while the Club has no specific knowledge of laws on the Continent regarding the use of space-saver spare wheels, there should be no problems in using such a wheel provided its use is in accordance with the manufacturer's instructions. Space-saver spare wheels are designed for short journeys to get your vehicle to a place where it can be repaired and there will usually be restrictions on the distance and speed at which the vehicle should be driven.

Towbar

The vast majority of cars registered after 1 August 1998 are legally required to have a European Type approved towbar (complying with European Directive 94/20) carrying a plate giving its approval number and various technical details, including the maximum noseweight. Your car dealer or specialist towbar fitter will be able to give further advice.

From 2011 for brand new motorhome designs (launched on or after that date) and 2012 for existing designs (those already being built before 29 April 2011), all new motorhomes will need some form of type approval before they can be registered in the UK and as such can only be fitted with a type approved towbar. This change will not affect older vehicles, which can continue to be fitted with non-approved towing brackets.

Tyres

Tyre condition has a major effect on the safe handling of your outfit. Caravan tyres must be suitable for the highest speed at which you can legally tow, even if you choose to drive slower.

Most countries require a minimum tread depth of 1.6mm but motoring organisations recommend at least 3mm. If you are planning a long journey, consider if they will still be above the legal minimum by the end of your journey.

Tyre Pressure

Tyre pressure should be checked and adjusted when the tyres are cold; checking warm tyres will result in a higher pressure reading. The correct pressures will be found in your car handbook, but unless it states otherwise add an extra 4 - 6 pounds per square inch to the rear tyres of a car when towing to improve handling. Make sure you know what pressure your caravan tyres should be. Some require a pressure much higher than that normally used for cars. Check your caravan handbook for details.

Tyre Sizes

It is worth noting that some sizes of radial tyre to fit the 13" wheels commonly used on older UK caravans are virtually impossible to find in stock at retailers abroad, e.g. 175R13C.

After a Puncture

A lot of new cars now have a liquid sealant puncture repair kit instead of a spare wheel. These sealants should not be used to achieve a permanent repair and in some cases have been known to make repair of the tyre impossible. If you need to use a liquid sealant you should get the tyre repaired or replaced as soon as possible.

Following a caravan tyre puncture, especially on a single-axle caravan, it is advisable to have the opposite side (non-punctured) tyre removed from its wheel and checked inside and out for signs of damage resulting from overloading during the deflation of the punctured tyre.

Winter driving

Winter tyres should be used in severe winter climates and in some countries they are a legal requirement. Winter tyres minimise the hardening effect of low temperatures which can lead to less traction on the road, and to provide extra grip on snow, ice or wet conditions.

Snow chains may be necessary on some roads in winter. They are compulsory in some countries, indicated by a road sign. They are not difficult to fit but it's a good idea to carry sturdy gloves to protect your hands when handling the chains in freezing conditions. Polar Automotive Ltd sells and hires out snow chains, tel 01892 519933 www.snowchains. com, email: polar@snowchains.com.

Warning Triangles

In almost all European countries it is a legal requirement to use a warning triangle in the event of a breakdown or accident.

A warning triangle should be placed on the road approximately 30 metres (100 metres on motorways) behind the broken down vehicle on the same side of the road. Always assemble the triangle before leaving your vehicle and walk with it so that the red, reflective surface is facing oncoming traffic. If a breakdown occurs round a blind corner, place the triangle in advance of the corner. Hazard warning lights may be used in conjunction with the triangle but they do not replace it.

Essential Equipment Table

The table on the following page shows the essential equipment required for each country. The Country Introduction chapters also include details of specific rules for each country. Please note that this information was correct at the time of going to print but is subject to change. For up to date equipment requirements visit www.caravanclub.co.uk/overseasadvice.

Country	Warning Triangle	Spare Bulbs	First Aid Kit	Reflective Jacket	Additional Equipment to be Carried/Used
Andorra	Yes (2)	Yes	Rec	Yes	Dipped headlights in poor daytime visibility. Winter tyres recommended; snow chains when road conditions or signs dictate.
Austria	Yes	Rec	Yes	Yes	Winter tyres from 1 Nov to 15 April.*
Belgium	Yes	Rec	Rec	Yes	Dipped headlights in poor daytime visibility.
Croatia	Yes (2 for vehicle with trailer)	Yes	Yes	Yes	Dipped headlights at all times from last Sunday in Oct - last Sunday in Mar. Spare bulbs compulsory if lights are xenon, neon or LED. Snow chains compulsory in winter in certain regions.*
Czech Rep	Yes	Yes	Yes	Yes	Dipped headlights at all times. Replacement fuses. Winter tyres or snow chains from 1 Nov - 31st March.*
Denmark	Yes	Rec	Rec	Rec	Dipped headlights at all times. On motorways use hazard warning lights when queues or danger ahead.
Finland	Yes	Rec	Rec	Yes	Dipped headlights at all times. Winter tyres Dec - Feb.*
France	Yes	Rec	Rec	Yes	Dipped headlights recommended at all times. Legal requirement to carry a breathalyser, but no penalty for non-compliance.
Germany	Rec	Rec	Rec	Rec	Dipped headlights recommended at all times. Winter tyres to be used in winter weather conditions.*
Greece	Yes	Rec	Yes	Rec	Fire extinguisher compulsory. Dipped headlights in towns at night and in poor daytime visibility.
Hungary	Yes	Rec	Yes	Yes	Dipped headlights at all times outside built-up areas and in built-up areas at night. Snow chains compulsory on some roads in winter conditions.*
Italy	Yes	Rec	Rec	Yes	Dipped headlights at all times outside built-up areas and in poor visibility. Snow chains from 15 Oct - 15 April.*
Luxembourg	Yes	Rec	Rec	Yes	Dipped headlights at night and daytime in bad weather.
Netherlands	Yes	Rec	Rec	Rec	Dipped headlights at night and in bad weather and recommended during the day.
Norway	Yes	Rec	Rec	Rec	Dipped headlights at all times. Winter tyres compulsory when snow or ice on the roads.*
Poland	Yes	Rec	Rec	Rec	Dipped headlights at all times. Fire extinguisher compulsory.
Portugal	Yes	Rec	Rec	Rec	Dipped headlights in poor daytime visibility, in tunnels and in lanes where traffic flow is reversible.
Slovakia	Yes	Rec	Yes	Yes	Dipped headlights at all times. Winter tyres compulsory when compact snow or ice on the road.*
Slovenia	Yes (2 for vehicle with trailer)	Yes	Rec	Yes	Dipped headlights at all times. Hazard warning lights when reversing. Use winter tyres or carry snow chains 15 Nov - 15 Mar.
Spain	Yes (2 Rec)	Rec	Rec	Yes	Dipped headlights at night, in tunnels and on 'special' roads (roadworks).
Sweden	Yes	Rec	Rec	Rec	Dipped headlights at all times. Winter tyres 1 Dec to 31 March.
Switzerland (inc Liechtenstein)	Yes	Rec	Rec	Rec	Dipped headlights recommended at all times, compulsory in tunnels. Snow chains where indicated by signs.

NOTES:
1) All countries: seat belts (if fitted) must be worn by all passengers.
2) Rec: not compulsory for foreign-registered vehicles, but strongly recommended
3) Headlamp converters, spare bulbs, fire extinguisher, first aid kit and reflective waistcoat are strongly recommended for all countries.
4) In some countries drivers who wear prescription glasses must carry a spare pair.
5) Please check information for any country before you travel. This information is to be used as a guide only and it is your responsibility to make sure you have the correct equipment.

* For more information and regulations on winter driving please see the Country Introductions.

Route Planning North

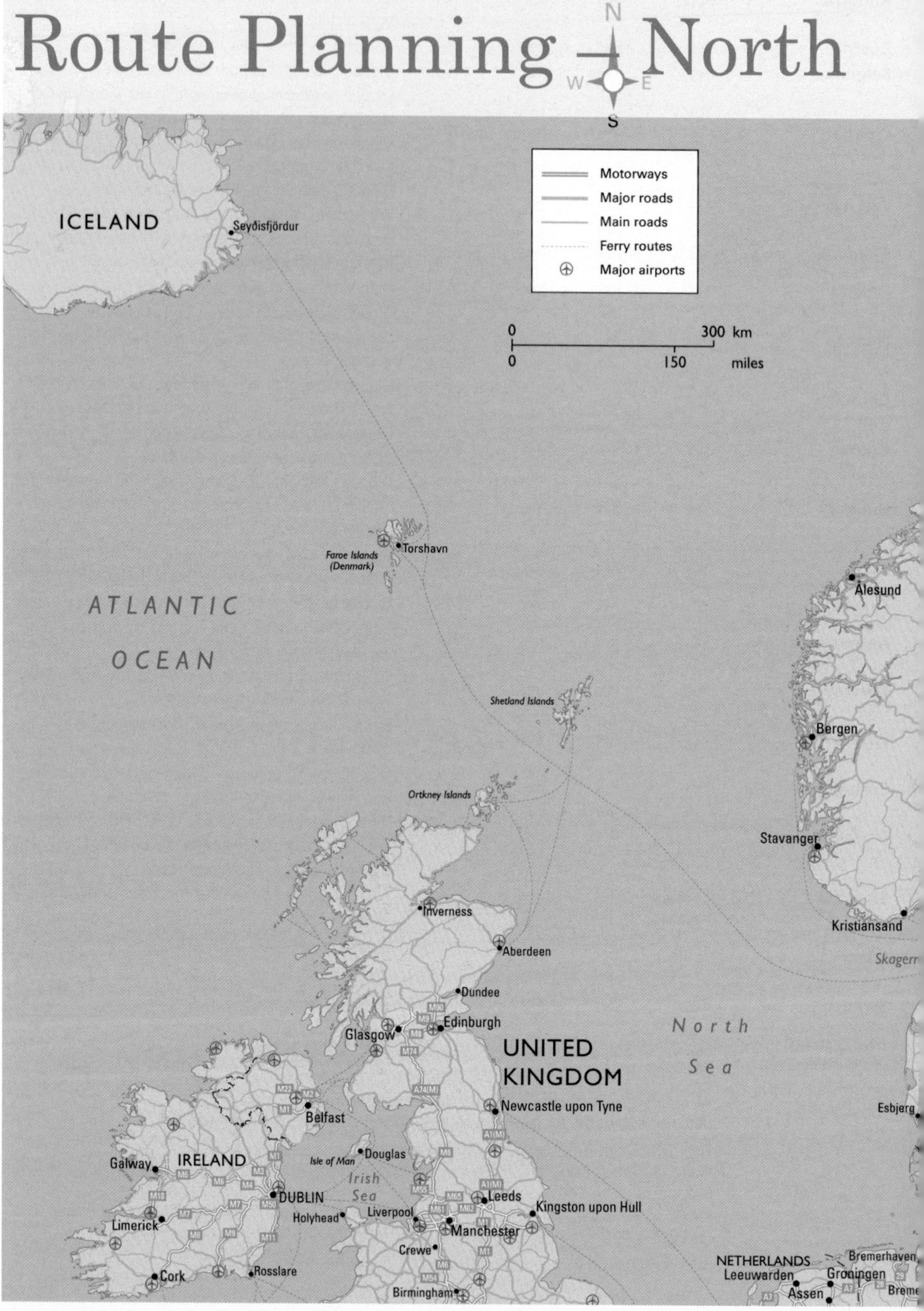

Legend:
- Motorways
- Major roads
- Main roads
- Ferry routes
- ⊕ Major airports

```
0                     300  km
0              150         miles
```

ICELAND
• Seyðisfjörður

ATLANTIC
OCEAN

Faroe Islands
(Denmark)
• Torshavn

Ålesund

Shetland Islands

Bergen

Ortkney Islands

Stavanger

Inverness

Kristiansand

Aberdeen

Skagerr

Dundee

North
Sea

Edinburgh
Glasgow

UNITED
KINGDOM

Belfast

Newcastle upon Tyne

Esbjerg

Galway • IRELAND

Isle of Man
• Douglas

Limerick

DUBLIN
Holyhead •

Irish
Sea

Leeds
Liverpool
Manchester

Kingston upon Hull

Crewe

Cork • Rosslare

Birmingham

NETHERLANDS
Leeuwarden

Bremerhaven
Groningen

Assen

Breme

Route Planning – Central

Bornholm Rønne
Baltic Sea
Kaliningrad · RUSSIA ⌐ LITHUANIA
·Gedser ·Sassnitz Sea
Kiel
·Rostock
·Gdańsk
·Olsztyn
Hrodna
Baranavichy·
Hamburg ·Schwerin ·Szczecin
Białystok N BELARUS
GERMANY
POLAND
·Bydgoszcz
annover Potsdam·
·Gorzów Wielkopolski
·Poznań
W ← E
·Magdeburg
Łódź·
S
·Leipzig
Motorways
Major roads
Erfurt
·Dresden
·Wrocław
Kielce·
Main roads
Ferry routes
⊕ Major airports
·Opole
Liberec
Katowice·
Kraków Rzeszów
L'viv
·Karlovy Vary
Hradec
Králové
Ostrava
Kraków Rzeszów
UKRAINE
PRAHA
Plzeň
CZECH
REPUBLIC
Olomouc
Zlín, Žilina
Prešov
·Ivano-Frankivs'k
ürnberg
České
Budějovice·
Brno
Trenčín
Košice ·Uzhhorod
Trnava Nitra
SLOVAKIA
·Linz WIEN
·München
·BRATISLAVA
Miskolc
·Nyíregyháza
Baia Mare
Bistrița·
·Salzburg
Sopron
Győr
Szombathely
Veszprém
BUDAPEST
·Debrecen
Zalău
·Szolnok ·Oradea
·Innsbruck AUSTRIA
Graz·
Kecskemét
·Békéscsaba Alba Iulia
ITENSTEIN
Klagenfurt·
·Maribor
Nagykanizsa
HUNGARY
Hódmezővásárhely
rt
Pécs
Szeged· ·Arad
Deva
Sibiu
·Bolzano
SLOVENIA
LJUBLJANA⊕
ZAGREB
Subotica·
ROMANIA
·Trento
Trieste·
Osijek· Novi
Sad·
Timişoara
Târgu Jiu
·Zrenjanin Reşiţa
Verona
·Venezia
Rijeka
Karlovac
Slavonski
Brod
⊕BEOGRAD
Drobeta-
Turnu Severin
·Pula
CROATIA
Banja Luka Tuzla· ·Šabac
SERBIA
·Bologna
BOSNIA AND
HERZEGOVINA
Zenica·
Kragujevac·
BULGARIA
SAN MARINO
·Firenze
·Ancona
Zadar
·SARAJEVO
Kraljevo·
Kruševac·
Niš·
no·
Perugia
Split
Mostar
·Mitrovicë
SOFIYA
PRISHTINË·
Kyustendil
·Blagoevgrad
MONTENEGRO
·Nikšić,
Peję·
KOSOVO
ITALY
L'Aquila·
·Pescara
Dubrovnik·
PODGORICA
Prizren·
Shkodër·
Kumanovo·
SKOPJE ·Veles
MACEDONIA
·ROMA
Campobasso
Durrës·
TIRANË Prilep·
Bitola·
Bari
Elbasan·
ALBANIA Korçë GREECE
Tyrrhenian
Sea
© Collins Bartholomew Ltd 2015
Napoli·
Vlorë·

FRANCE
Basel
A36
Zürich
A2
A1
A4
A7
Innsbruck
A12
AUSTRIA
Szombathely
Veszprén
BERN
Luzern
A3
LIECHTENSTEIN
A13
Graz
A2
A1
A14
A12
A13
Graz
Nagyl

SWITZERLAND
Klagenfurt
Maribor

Genève
A10
Bolzano
Trento
LJUBLJANA
ZAGREB
Lausanne

Geneve

A5
Milano
A9
A4
A22
A31
A27
A4
Trieste
A1/6
Slav
Verona
A4
Venezia
A9
A8
Rijeka
Karlovac
A3
B
A43
A26
A7
A35
A4
A1
A21
Pula
CROATIA
Ba
Torino
A32
A21
A21
A22
A13
A1
BOS
HERZ
A33
A26
Genova
A15
Bologna
A1
A14
Zadar
Z

Nice
A11
Firenze
SAN MARINO
Ancona
Split
A1
A6
MONACO
A12
Perugia
A14
A8
Livorno
2
A1
Dub
E67
Bastia
ITALY
A1
L'Aquila
A24
Pescara

Corse
(Corsica)
(France)
A12
A25
A14
Ajaccio
ROMA
Campobasso
A24
A1
A16
B

Olbia
Napoli
A14
Sassari
A3
Potenza

Sardegne
(Sardinia)
(Italy)
N
W E
S

T y r r h e n i a n
S e a
Nicastro
C
Cagliari

	Motorways
	Major roads
	Main roads
	Ferry routes
⊕	Major airports

Messina
Palermo
A29
A19
A20
A18
Reggio di C
Sicilia
(Sicily)
A19
A29
A3
Catania

M e d i t e r r a n
Nicastro
Siracusa
A18

Skikda
Annaba
Menzel
Bourguiba
Bizerte
L'Ariana
Ben Arous
Tunis
Guelma
Constantine
Souk
Ahras
TUNISIA
ALGERIA
Sousse
MALTA ⊕ VALLETTA

HUNGARY

Kecskemét
Békéscsaba
Hódmezővásárhely
Szeged
Arad
Subotica
Timișoara
Deva

zsa

Subotica

Isijek
Novi
Sad
Zrenjanin
Reșița
Târgu Jiu

Luka
Tuzla
Šabac
BEOGRAD

AND
OVINA

SARAJEVO
Kragujevac
Kraljevo
Kruševac
Niš

Mostar

MONTENEGRO
Nikšić
Pejë
PRIŠHTINE
KOSOVO
Prizren
Mitrovicë
SOFIYA
Kumanovo

nik
PODGORICA
Shkodër
SKOPJE
Veles

Durrës
TIRANË
Prilep
Bitola
Elbasan
ALBANIA
Korçë

Vlorë

Kerkyra
(Corfu)

Ioannina

Larisa

a

Târgu Mureș
Alba Iulia
Sibiu
Sfântu
Gheorghe
Focșani
Brașov
Tulcea
ROMANIA
Buzău

Ploiești
Slobozia
Constanța
Pitești
BUCUREȘTI
Călărași
Drobeta-
Turnu Severin
Silistra
Craiova

Ruse
Dobrich
Razgrad
Varna
Pleven
Shumen
Vratsa
Veliko Tŭrnovo
Gabrovo
Sliven
Burgas
BULGARIA
Stara Zagora

Kyustendil
Blagoevgrad
KŬrdzhali

Edirne
Kırklareli

Tekirdağ

MACEDONIA

TURKEY

Çanakkale

Thessaloniki

Limnos

Mytilini
Lesvos
(Lesbos)

İzmir

Evvoia
Chios
Chios

GREECE
Aegean
Sea

ATHINA
Andros
Tinos

Keffalonia
(Cephalonia)
Patra
Agios Dimitrios

Naxos
Naxos

Zakynthos
(Zante)

Ionian

Sea

Gytheio

Kriti
(Crete)

Chania
Irakleio
(Iraklion)

0   300 km
0   150   miles

© Collins Bartholomew Ltd 2015

Mountain Passes & Tunnels

Advice for Drivers

Mountain Passes

Mountain passes can create difficult driving conditions, especially when towing or driving a large vehicle. You should only use them if you have a good power to weight ratio and in good driving conditions. If in any doubt as to your outfit's suitability or the weather then stick to motorway routes across mountain ranges if possible.

The tables on the following pages show which passes are not suitable for caravans, and those where caravans are not permitted. Motorhomes aren't usually included in these restrictions, but relatively low powered or very large vehicles should find an alternative route. Road signs at the foot of a pass may restrict access or offer advice, especially for heavy vehicles. Warning notices are usually posted at the foot of a pass if it is closed, or if chains or winter tyres must be used.

Caravanners are particularly sensitive to gradients and traffic/road conditions on passes. The maximum gradient is usually on the inside of bends but exercise caution if it is necessary to pull out. Always engage a lower gear before taking a hairpin bend and give priority to vehicles ascending. On mountain roads it is not the gradient which puts strain on your car but the duration of the climb and the loss of power at high altitudes: approximately 10% at 915 metres (3,000 feet) and even more as you get higher. To minimise the risk of the engine overheating, take high passes in the cool part of the day, don't climb any faster than necessary and keep the engine pulling steadily. To prevent a radiator boiling, pull off the road safely, turn the heater and blower full on and switch off air conditioning. Keep an eye on water and oil levels. Never put cold water into a boiling radiator or it may crack. Check that the radiator is not obstructed by debris sucked up during the journey.

A long descent may result in overheating brakes; select the correct gear for the gradient and avoid excessive use of brakes. Even if you are using engine braking to control speed, caravan brakes may activate due to the overrun mechanism, which may cause them to overheat.

Travelling at altitude can cause a pressure build up in tanks and water pipes. You can prevent this by slightly opening the blade valve of your portable toilet and opening a tap a fraction.

Tunnels

Long tunnels are a much more commonly seen feature in Europe than in the UK, especially in mountainous regions. Tolls are usually charged for the use of major tunnels.

Dipped headlights are usually required by law even in well-lit tunnels, so switch them on before you enter. Snow chains, if used, must be removed before entering a tunnel in lay-bys provided for this purpose.

'No overtaking' signs must be strictly observed. Never cross central single or double lines. If overtaking is permitted in twin-tube tunnels, bear in mind that it is very easy to underestimate distances and speed once inside. In order to minimise the effects of exhaust fumes close all car windows and set the ventilator to circulate air, or operate the air conditioning system coupled with the recycled air option.

If you break down, try to reach the next lay-by and call for help from an emergency phone. If you cannot reach a lay-by, place your warning triangle at least 100 metres behind your vehicle. Modern tunnels have video surveillance systems to ensure prompt assistance in an emergency. Some tunnels can extend for miles and a high number of breakdowns are due to running out of fuel so make sure you have enough before entering the tunnel.

Mountain Pass Information

The dates of opening and closing given in the following tables are approximate. Before attempting late afternoon or early morning journeys across borders, check their opening times as some borders close at night.

Gradients listed are the maximum which may be encountered on the pass and may be steeper at the inside of curves, particularly on older roads.

Gravel surfaces (such as dirt and stone chips) vary considerably; they can be dusty when dry and slippery when wet. Where known to exist, this type of surface has been noted.

In fine weather winter tyres or snow chains will only be required on very high passes, or for short periods in early or late summer. In winter conditions you will probably need to use them at altitudes exceeding 600 metres (approximately 2,000 feet).

Converting Gradients

20% = 1 in 5	11% = 1 in 9
16% = 1 in 6	10% = 1 in 8
14% = 1 in 7	8% = 1 in 12
12% = 1 in 8	6% = 1 in 16

Tables and maps

Much of the information contained in the following tables was originally supplied by The Automobile Association and other motoring and tourist organisations. The Caravan Club haven't checked this information and cannot accept responsibility for the accuracy or for errors or omissions to these tables.

The mountain passes, rail and road tunnels listed in the tables are shown on the following maps. Numbers and letters against each pass or tunnel in the tables correspond with the numbers and letters on the maps.

Abbreviations

MHV	Maximum height of vehicle
MLV	Maximum length of vehicle
MWV	Maximum width of vehicle
MWR	Minimum width of road
OC	Occasionally closed between dates
UC	Usually closed between dates
UO	Usually open between dates, although a fall of snow may obstruct the road for 24-48 hours.

Major Alpine Mountain Passes

	Pass Height In Metres (Feet)	From To	Max Gradient	Conditions and Comments
①	**Achenpass** (Austria – Germany) 941 (3087)	Achenwald Glashütte	4%	UO. Well-engineered road, B181/307. Gradient not too severe.
②	**Albula** (Switzerland) 2312 (7585)	Tiefencastel La Punt	10%	UC Nov-early Jun. MWR 3.5m (11'6") MWV 2.25m (7'6") Inferior alternative to the Julier; fine scenery. **Not recommended for caravans.** Alternative rail tunnel. See *Rail Tunnels* in this section.
③	**Allos** (France) 2250 (7382)	Colmars Barcelonette	10%	UC early Nov-early Jun. MWR 4m (13'1") Very winding, narrow, mostly unguarded pass on D908 but not difficult otherwise; passing bays on southern slope; poor surface, MWV 1.8m (5'11"). **Not recommended for caravans.**
④	**Aprica** (Italy) 1176 (3858)	Tresenda Edolo	9%	UO. MWR 4m (13'1") Fine scenery; good surface; well-graded on road S39. Narrow in places; watch for protruding rock when meeting oncoming traffic. Not recommended for caravanners to attempt this pass E or W. Poor road conditions, repairs reduce width drastically.
⑤	**Aravis** (France) 1498 (4915)	La Clusaz Flumet	9%	OC Dec-Mar. MWR 4m (13'1"). Fine scenery; D909, fairly easy road. Poor surface in parts on Chamonix side. Some single-line traffic.
⑥	**Arlberg** (Austria) 1802 (5912)	Bludenz Landeck	13%	OC Dec-Apr. MWR 6m (19'8"). Good modern road B197/E60 with several pull-in places. Steeper fr W easing towards summit; heavy traffic. **Caravans prohibited.** Parallel road tunnel (tolls) available on E60 (poss long queues). See *Road Tunnels* in this section.
⑦	**Ballon d'Alsace** (France) 1178 (3865)	Giromagny St Maurice-sur-Moselle	11%	OC Dec-Mar. MWR 4m (13'1") Fairly straightforward ascent/descent; narrow in places; numerous bends. On road D465.
⑧	**Bayard** (France) 1248 (4094)	Chauffayer Gap	14%	UO. MWR 6m (19'8") Part of the Route Napoléon N85. Fairly easy, steepest on the S side with several hairpin bends. Negotiable by caravans from N-to-S via D1075 (N75) and Col-de-la-Croix Haute, avoiding Gap.
⑨	**Bernina** (Switzerland) 2330 (7644)	Pontresina Poschiavo	12.50%	OC Dec-Mar. MWR 5m (16'5") MWV 2.25m (7'6") Fine scenery. Good with care on open narrow sections towards summit on S-side; on road no. 29.
⑩	**Bracco** (Italy) 613 (2011)	Riva Trigoso Borghetto di Vara	14%	UO. MWR 5m (16'5") A two-lane road (P1) more severe than height suggests due to hairpins and volume of traffic; passing difficult. Rec cross early to avoid traffic. Alternative toll m'way A12 available.

Before using any of these passes, PLEASE READ CAREFULLY THE ADVICE AT THE BEGINNING OF THIS CHAPTER

	Pass Height in Metres (Feet)	From To	Max Gradient	Conditions and Comments
11	**Brenner (Europabrücke)** (Austria – Italy) 1374 (4508)	Innsbruck *Vipiteno/Sterzing*	14%	UO. MWR 6m (19'8") On road no. 182/12. Parallel toll m'way A13/A22/E45 (6%) suitable for caravans. Heavy traffic may delay at Customs. **Pass road closed to caravans/trailers**
12	**Brouis** (France) 1279 (4196)	Nice *Col-de-Tende*	12.50%	UO. MWR 6m (19'8") Good surface but many hairpins on D6204 (N204)/S20. Steep gradients on approaches. Height of tunnel at Col-de-Tende at the Italian border is 3.8m (12'4") **Not recommended for caravans.**
13	**Brünig** (Switzerland) 1007 (3340)	Brienzwiler Station *Giswil*	8.50%	UO. MWR 6m (19'8") MWV 2.5m (8'2") An easy but winding road (no. 4); heavy traffic at weekends; frequent lay-bys. On-going road improvement (2009) may cause delays – check before travel.
14	**Bussang** (France) 721 (2365)	Thann *St Maurice-sur-Moselle*	7%	UO. MWR 4m (13'1") A very easy road (N66) over the Vosges; beautiful scenery.
15	**Cabre** (France) 1180 (3871)	Luc-en-Diois *Aspres-sur-Buëch*	9%	UO. MWR 5.5m (18') An easy pleasant road (D93/D993), winding at Col-de-Cabre.
16	**Campolongo** (Italy) 1875 (6152)	Corvara-in-Badia *Arabba*	12.50%	OC Dec-Mar. MWR 5m (16'5") A winding but easy ascent on rd P244; long level stretch on summit followed by easy descent. Good surface, fine scenery.
17	**Cayolle** (France) 2326 (7631)	Barcelonnette *Guillaumes*	10%	UC early Nov-early Jun. MWR 4m (13'1") Narrow, winding road (D902) with hairpin bends; poor surface, broken edges with steep drops. Long stretches of single-track road with passing places. **Caravans prohibited.**
18	**Costalunga (Karer)** (Italy) 1745 (5725)	Bolzano *Pozza-di-Fassa*	16%	OC Dec-Apr. MWR 5m (16'5") A good well-engineered road (S241) but mostly winding with many blind hairpins. **Caravans prohibited.**
19	**Croix** (Switzerland) 1778 (5833)	Villars-sur-Ollon *Les Diablerets*	13%	UC Nov-May. MWR 3.5m (11'6") A narrow, winding route but extremely picturesque. **Not recommended for caravans.**
20	**Croix Haute** (France) 1179 (3868)	Monestier-de-Clermont *Aspres-sur-Buëch*	7%	UO on N75. MWR 5.5m (18') Well-engineered road (D1075/N75); several hairpin bends on N side.
21	**Falzárego** (Italy) 2117 (6945)	Cortina-d'Ampezzo *Andraz*	8.50%	OC Dec-Apr. MWR 5m (16'5") Well-engineered bitumen surface on road R48; many blind hairpin bends on both sides; used by tour coaches.

Pass / Height In Metres (Feet)	Max Gradient	From / To	Conditions and Comments
(22) **Faucille** (France) 1323 (4341)	10%	Gex / *Morez*	UO. MWR 5m (16'5") Fairly wide, winding road (N5) across the Jura mountains; negotiable by caravans but probably better to follow route via La Cure-St Cergue-Nyon.
(23) **Fern** (Austria) 1209 (3967)	8%	Nassereith / *Lermoos*	UO. MWR 6m (19'8") Obstructed intermittently during winter. An easy pass on road 179 but slippery when wet; heavy traffic at summer weekends. Connects with Holzleiten Sattel Pass at S end for travel to/from Innsbruck – see below.
(24) **Flexen** (Austria) 1784 (5853)	10%	Lech / *Rauzalpe (nr Arlberg Pass)*	UO. MWR 5.5m (18') The magnificent 'Flexenstrasse', a well-engineered mountain road (no. 198) with tunnels and galleries. The road from Lech to Warth, N of the pass, is usually closed Nov-Apr due to danger of avalanche. Not recommended for caravans.
(25) **Flüela** (Switzerland) 2383 (7818)	12.50%	Davos-Dorf / *Susch*	OC Nov-May. MWR 5m (16'5") MWV 2.3m (7'6") Easy ascent from Davos on road no. 28; some acute hairpin bends on the E side; bitumen surface.
(26) **Forclaz** (Switzerland – France) 1527 (5010)	8.50%	Martigny / *Argentière*	UO Forclaz; OC Montets Dec-early Apr. MWR 5m (16'5") MWV 2.5m (8'2") Good road over the pass and to the French border; long, hard climb out of Martigny; narrow and rough over Col-des-Montets on D1506 (N506).
(27) **Foscagno** (Italy) 2291 (7516)	12.50%	Bormio / *Livigno*	OC Nov-May. MWR 3.3m (10'10") Narrow and winding road (S301) through lonely mountains, generally poor surface. Long winding ascent with many blind bends; not always well-guarded. The descent includes winding rise and fall over the Passo-d'Eira 2,200m (7,218). **Not recommended for caravans.**
(28) **Fugazze** (Italy) 1159 (3802)	14%	Rovereto / *Valli-del-Pasubio*	UO. MWR 3.5m (11'6") Very winding road (S46) with some narrow sections, particularly on N side. The many blind bends and several hairpin bends call for extra care. **Not recommended for caravans.**
(29) **Furka** (Switzerland) 2431 (7976)	11%	Gletsch / *Realp*	UC Oct-Jun. MWR 4m (13'1") MWV 2.25m (7'6") Well-graded road (no. 19) with narrow sections (single track in place on E side) and several hairpin bends on both ascent and descent. Fine views of the Rhône Glacier. Beware of coaches and traffic build-up. **Not recommended for caravans.** Alternative rail tunnel available. See *Rail Tunnels* in this section.
(30) **Galibier** (France) 2645 (8678)	12.50%	La Grave / *St Michel-de-Maurienne*	UC Oct-Jun. MWR 3m (9'10") Mainly wide, well-surfaced road (D902) but unprotected and narrow over summit. From Col-du-Lautaret it rises over the Col-du-Telegraphe then 11 more hairpin bends. Ten hairpin bends on descent then 5km (3.1 miles) narrow and rough; easier in N to S direction. Limited parking at summit. **Not recommended for caravans.** (There is a single-track tunnel under the Galibier summit, controlled by traffic lights; caravans are not permitted).
(31) **Gardena (Grödner-Joch)** (Italy) 2121 (6959)	12.50%	Val Gardena / *Corvara-in-Badia*	OC Dec-Jun. MWR 5m (16'5") A well-engineered road (S243), very winding on descent. Fine views. **Caravans prohibited.**

	Pass Height In Metres (Feet)	From To	Max Gradient	Conditions and Comments
32	**Gavia** (Italy) 2621 (8599)	Bormio *Ponte-di-Legno*	20%	UC Oct-Jul. MWR 3m (9'10") MWV 1.8m (5'11") Steep, narrow, difficult road (P300) with frequent passing bays; many hairpin bends and gravel surface; not for the faint-hearted; extra care necessary. **Not recommended for caravans.** Long winding ascent on Bormio side.
33	**Gerlos** (Austria) 1628 (5341)	Zell-am-Ziller *Wald im Pinzgau*	9%	UO. MWR 4m (13'1") Hairpin ascent out of Zell to modern toll road (B165); the old, steep, narrow and winding route with passing bays and 14% gradient is not rec but is negotiable with care. Views of Krimml waterfalls. **Caravans prohibited.**
34	**Gorges-du-Verdon** (France) 1032 (3386)	Castellane *Moustiers-Ste Marie*	9%	UO. MWR probably 5m (16'5") On road D952 over Col-d'Ayen and Col-d'Olivier. Moderate gradients but slow, narrow and winding. Poss heavy traffic.
35	**Grand St Bernard** (Switzerland – Italy) 2469 (8100)	Martigny *Aosta*	11%	UC Oct-Jun. MWR 4m (13'1") MWV 2.5m (8' 2") Modern road to entrance of road tunnel on road no. 21/E27 (UO), then narrow but bitumen surface over summit to border; also good in Italy. Suitable for caravans using tunnel. Pass road feasible but not recommended. *See Road Tunnels* in this section.
36	**Grimsel** (Switzerland) 2164 (7100)	Innertkirchen *Gletsch*	10%	UC mid Oct-late Jun. MWR 5m (16'5") MWV 2.25m (7'6") A fairly easy, modern road (no. 6) with heavy traffic at weekends. A long winding ascent, finally hairpin bends; then a terraced descent with six hairpins (some tight) into the Rhône valley. Good surface; fine scenery.
37	**Grossglockner** (Austria) 2503 (8212)	Bruck-an-der-Grossglocknerstrasse *Heiligenblut*	12.50%	UC late Oct-early May. MWR 5.5m (18') Well-engineered road (no. 107) but many hairpins; heavy traffic, moderate but very long ascent/descent. Negotiable preferably S to N by caravans. Avoid side road to highest point at Edelweissespitze if towing, as road is very steep and narrow. Magnificent scenery. Tolls charged. Road closed from 2200-0500 hrs (summer). Alternative Felbertauern road tunnel between Lienz and Mittersil (toll). *See Road Tunnels* in this section.
38	**Hahntennjoch** (Austria) 1894 (6250)	Imst *Elmen*	15%	UC Nov-May. A minor pass. **Caravans prohibited.**
39	**Hochtannberg** (Austria) 1679 (5509)	Schröcken *Warth (nr Lech)*	14%	OC Jan-Mar. MWR 4m (13'1") A reconstructed modern road (no. 200). W to E long ascent with many hairpins. Easier E to W. **Not recommended for caravans.**
40	**Holzleiten Sattel** (Austria) 1126 (3694)	Nassereith *Obsteig*	12.50%	(12.5%), UO. MWR 5m (16'5") Road surface good on W side; poor on E. Light traffic; gradients no problem. **Not recommended for caravans.**
41	**Iseran** (France) 2770 (9088)	Bourg-St Maurice *Lanslebourg*	11%	UC mid Oct-late Jun. MWR 4m (13'1") Second highest pass in the Alps on road D902. Well-graded with reasonable bends, average surface. Several unlit tunnels on N approach. **Not recommended for caravans.**

Pass / Height In Metres (Feet)	From / To	Max Gradient	Conditions and Comments
42 **Izoard** (France) 2360 (7743)	Guillestre / Briançon	12.50%	UC late Oct-mid Jun. MWR 5m (16'5") Fine scenery. Winding, sometimes narrow road (D902) with many hairpin bends; care required at several unlit tunnels near Guillestre. **Not recommended for caravans.**
43 **Jaun** (Switzerland) 1509 (4951)	Bulle / Reidenbach	14%	UO. MWR 4m (13'1") MWV 2.25m (7'6") A modern but generally narrow road (no. 11); some poor sections on ascent and several hairpin bends on descent.
44 **Julier** (Switzerland) 2284 (7493)	Tiefencastel / Silvaplana	13%	UO. MWR 4m (13'1") MWV 2.5m (8'2") Well-engineered road (no. 3) approached from Chur via Sils. Fine scenery. Negotiable by caravans, preferably from N to S, but a long haul and many tight hairpins. Alternative rail tunnel from Thusis to Samedan. See *Rail Tunnels* in this section.
45 **Katschberg** (Austria) 1641 (5384)	Spittal-an-der-Drau / St Michael	20%	UO. MWR 6m (19'8") Good wide road (no. 99) with no hairpins but steep gradients particularly from S. Suitable only light caravans. Parallel Tauern/Katschberg toll motorway A10/E55 and road tunnels. See *Road Tunnels* in this section.
46 **Klausen** (Switzerland) 1948 (6391)	Altdorf / Linthal	10%	UC late Oct-early Jun. MWR 5m (16'5") MWV 2.30m (7'6") Narrow and winding in places, but generally easy in spite of a number of sharp bends. **Caravans prohibited** between Unterschächen and Linthal (no. 17).
47 **Larche (della Maddalena)** (France – Italy) 1994 (6542)	La Condamine-Châtelard / Vinadio	8.50%	OC Dec-Mar. MWR 3.5m (11'6") An easy, well-graded road (D900); long, steady ascent on French side, many hairpins on Italian side (S21). Fine scenery; ample parking at summit.
48 **Lautaret** (France) 2058 (6752)	Le Bourg-d'Oisans / Briançon	12.50%	OC Dec-Mar. MWR 4m (13'1") Modern, evenly graded but winding road (D1091), and unguarded in places; very fine scenery; suitable for caravans but with care through narrow tunnels.
49 **Leques** (France) 1146 (3760)	Barrême / Castellane	8%	UO. MWR 4m (13'1") On Route Napoléon (D4085). Light traffic; excellent surface; narrow in places on N ascent. S ascent has many hairpins.
50 **Loibl (Ljubelj)** (Austria – Slovenia) 1067 (3500)	Unterloibl / Kranj	20%	UO. MWR 6m (19'8") Steep rise and fall over Little Loibl pass (E652) to 1.6km (1 mile) tunnel under summit. **Caravans prohibited.** The old road over the summit is closed to through-traffic.
51 **Lukmanier (Lucomagno)** (Switzerland) 1916 (6286)	Olivone / Disentis	9%	UC early Nov-late May. MWR 5m (16'5") MWV 2.25m (7'6") Rebuilt, modern road.
52 **Maloja** (Switzerland) 1815 (5955)	Silvaplana / Chiavenna	9%	UO. MWR 4m (13'1") MWV 2.5m (8'2") Escarpment facing south; fairly easy, but many hairpin bends on descent; negotiable by caravans but possibly difficult on ascent. On road no. 3/S37.

Before using any of these passes, PLEASE READ CAREFULLY THE ADVICE AT THE BEGINNING OF THIS CHAPTER

	Pass / Height In Metres (Feet)	From / To	Max Gradient	Conditions and Comments
53	**Mauria** (Italy) 1298 (4258)	Lozzo di Cadore / Ampezzo	7%	UO. MWR 5m (16'5") A well-designed road (SS2) with easy, winding ascent and descent.
54	**Mendola** (Italy) 1363 (4472)	Appiano/Eppan / Sarnonico	12.50%	UO. MWR 5m (16'5") A fairly straightforward but winding road (S42) well-guarded, many hairpins. Take care overhanging cliffs if towing. The E side going down to Bolzano is not wide enough for caravans, especially difficult on busy days, not recommended for caravans.
55	**Mont Cenis** (France – Italy) 2083 (6834)	Lanslebourg / Susa	12.50%	UC Nov–May. MWR 5m (16'5") Approach by industrial valley. An easy highway (D1006/S25) with mostly good surface; spectacular scenery; long descent into Italy with few stopping places. Alternative Fréjus road tunnel available. See *Road Tunnels* in this section.
56	**Monte Croce-di-Comélico (Kreuzberg)** (Italy) 1636 (5368)	San Candido / Santo-Stefano-di-Cadore	8.50%	UO. MWR 5m (16'5") A winding road (SS2) with moderate gradients, beautiful scenery.
57	**Montgenèvre** (France – Italy) 1850 (6070)	Briançon / Cesana-Torinese	9%	UO. MWR 5m (16'5") An easy, modern road (N94/S24) with some tight hairpin bends and with good road surface on French side; road widened & tunnels improved on Italian side, in need of some repair but still easy. Much used by lorries; may be necessary to travel at their speed and give way to oncoming large vehicles on hairpins.
58	**Monte Giovo (Jaufen)** (Italy) 2094 (6870)	Merano / Vipiteno/Sterzing	12.50%	UC Nov–May. MWR 4m (13'1") Many well-engineered hairpin bends on S44; good scenery. **Caravans prohibited.**
	Montets (See Forclaz)			
59	**Morgins** (France – Switzerland) 1369 (4491)	Abondance / Monthey	14%	UO. MWR 4m (13'1") A lesser used route (D22) through pleasant, forested countryside crossing French/Swiss border. **Not recommended for caravans.**
60	**Mosses** (Switzerland) 1445 (4740)	Aigle / Château-d'Oex	8.50%	UO. MWR 4m (13'1") MWV 2.25m (7'6") A modern road (no. 11). Aigle side steeper and narrow in places.
61	**Nassfeld (Pramollo)** (Austria – Italy) 1530 (5020)	Tröpolach / Pontebba	20%	OC Late Nov–Mar. MWR 4m (13'1") The winding descent on road no. 90 into Italy has been improved but not rec for caravans.
62	**Nufenen (Novena) (Switzerland)** 2478 (8130)	Ulrichen / Airolo	10%	UC Mid Oct–mid Jun. MWR 4m (13'1") MWV 2.25m (7'6") The approach roads are narrow, with tight bends, but the road over the pass is good; negotiable with care. Long drag from Ulrichen.
63	**Oberalp** (Switzerland) 2044 (6706)	Andermatt / Disentis	10%	UC Nov–late May. MWR 5m (16'5") MWV 2.3m (7'6") A much improved and widened road (no. 19) with modern surface but still narrow in places on E side; many tight hairpin bends, but long level stretch on summit. Alternative rail tunnel during the winter. See *Rail Tunnels* in this section. **Not recommended for caravans.**

Pass / Height In Metres (Feet)	From / To	Max Gradient	Conditions and Comments
64 **Ofen (Fuorn)** (Switzerland) 2149 (7051)	Zernez / Santa Maria-im-Münstertal	12.50%	UO. MWR 4m (13'1") MWV 2.25m (7'6") Good road (no. 28) through Swiss National Park.
65 **Petit St Bernard** (France – Italy) 2188 (7178)	Bourg-St Maurice / Pré-St Didier	8.50%	UC mid Oct-Jun. MWR 5m (16'5") Outstanding scenery, but poor surface and unguarded broken edges near summit. Easiest from France (D1090); sharp hairpins on climb from Italy (S26). **Caravans prohibited.**
66 **Pillon** (Switzerland) 1546 (5072)	Le Sépey / Gsteig	9%	OC Jan-Feb. MWR 4m (13'1") MWV 2.25m (7'6") A comparatively easy modern road.
67 **Plöcken (Monte Croce-Carnico)** (Austria – Italy) 1362 (4468)	Kötschach / Paluzza	14%	OC Dec-Apr. MWR 5m (16'5") A modern road (no. 110) with long, reconstructed sections; OC to caravans due to heavy traffic on summer weekends; delay likely at the border. Long, slow, twisty pull from S, easier from N.
68 **Pordoi** (Italy) 2239 (7346)	Arabba / Canazei	10%	OC Dec-Apr. MWR 5m (16'5") An excellent modern road (S48) with numerous blind hairpin bends; fine scenery; used by tour coaches. Long drag when combined with Falzarego pass.
69 **Pötschen** (Austria) 982 (3222)	Bad Ischl / Bad Aussee	9%	UO. MWR 7m (23'). A modern road (no. 145). Good scenery.
70 **Radstädter-Tauern** (Austria) 1738 (5702)	Radstadt / Mauterndorf	16%	OC Jan-Mar. MWR 5m (16'5") N ascent steep (road no. 99) but not difficult otherwise; but negotiable by light caravans using parallel toll m'way (A10) through tunnel. See *Road Tunnels* in this section.
71 **Résia (Reschen)** (Italy – Austria) 1504 (4934)	Spondigna / Pfunds	10%	UO. MWR 6m (19'8") A good, straightforward alternative to the Brenner Pass. Fine views but no stopping places. On road S40/180.
72 **Restefond (La Bonette)** (France) 2802 (9193)	Barcelonnette / St Etienne-de-Tinée	16%	UC Oct-Jun. MWR 3m (9'10") The highest pass in the Alps. Rebuilt, resurfaced road (D64) with rest area at summit – top loop narrow and unguarded. Winding with hairpin bends. **Not recommended for caravans.**
73 **Rolle** (Italy) 1970 (6463)	Predazzo / Mezzano	9%	OC Dec-Mar. MWR 5m (16'5") A well-engineered road (S50) with many hairpin bends on both sides; very beautiful scenery; good surface.
Rombo (See Timmelsjoch)			
74 **St Gotthard (San Gottardo)** (Switzerland) 2108 (6916)	Göschenen / Airolo	10%	UC mid Oct-early Jun. MWR 6m (19'8") MHV 3.6m (11'9") MWV 2.5m (8'2") Modern, fairly easy two- to three-lane road (A2/E35). Heavy traffic. Alternative road tunnel. See *Road Tunnels* in this section.

Before using any of these passes, **PLEASE READ CAREFULLY THE ADVICE AT THE BEGINNING OF THIS CHAPTER**

Pass Height In Metres (Feet)	From To	Max Gradient	Conditions and Comments
⑦⑤ **San Bernardino** (Switzerland) 2066 (6778)	Mesocco *Hinterrhein*	10%	UC Oct-late Jun. MWR 4m (13'1") MWV 2.25m (7'6") Easy modern road (A13/E43) on N and S approaches to tunnel, narrow and winding over summit via tunnel suitable for caravans. See *Road Tunnels* in this section.
⑦⑥ **Schlucht** (France) 1139 (3737)	Gérardmer *Munster*	7%	UO. MWR 5m (16'5") An extremely picturesque route (D417) crossing the Vosges mountains, with easy, wide bends on the descent. Good surface.
⑦⑦ **Seeberg (Jezersko)** (Austria – Slovenia) 1218 (3996)	Eisenkappel *Kranj*	12.50%	UO. MWR 5m (16'5") An alternative to the steeper Loibl and Wurzen passes on B82/210; moderate climb with winding, hairpin ascent and descent. **Not recommended for caravans.**
⑦⑧ **Sella** (Italy) 2240 (7349)	Selva *Canazei*	11%	OC Dec-Jan. MWR 5m (16'5") A well-engineered, winding road; exceptional views of Dolomites. **Caravans prohibited.**
⑦⑨ **Sestriere** (Italy) 2033 (6670)	Cesana-Torinese *Pinarolo*	10%	UO MWR 6m (19'8") Mostly bitumen surface on road R23. Fairly easy; fine scenery.
⑧⓪ **Silvretta (Bielerhöhe)** (Austria) 2032 (6666)	Partenen *Galtur*	11%	UC late Oct-early Jun. MWR 5m (16'5") Mostly reconstructed road (188); 32 easy hairpin bends on W ascent; E side more straightforward. Tolls charged. **Caravans prohibited.**
⑧① **Simplon** (Switzerland – Italy) 2005 (6578)	Brig *Domodóssola*	11%	OC Nov-Apr. MWR 7m (23") MWV 2.5m (8'2") An easy, reconstructed, modern road (E62/S33), 21km (13 miles) long, continuous ascent to summit; good views, many stopping places. Surface better on Swiss side. Alternative rail tunnel fr Kandersteg in operation from Easter to September. See *Rail Tunnels* in this section.
⑧② **Splügen** (Switzerland – Italy) 2113 (6932)	Splügen *Chiavenna*	13%	UC Nov-Jun. MWR 3.5m (11'6") MHV 2.8m (9'2") MWV 2.3m (7'6") Mostly narrow, winding road (S36), with extremely tight hairpin bends, not well guarded; care also required at many tunnels/galleries. **Not recommended for caravans.**
⑧③ **Stelvio** (Italy) 2757 (9045)	Bormio *Spondigna*	12.50%	UC Oct-late Jun. MWR 4m (13'1") MLV 10m (32') Third highest pass in Alps on S38; 40-50 acute hairpin bends either side, all well-engineered; good surface, traffic often heavy. Hairpin bends too acute for long vehicles. **Not recommended for caravans.**
⑧④ **Susten** (Switzerland) 2224 (7297)	Innertkirchen *Wassen*	9%	UC Nov-Jun. MWR 6m (19'8") MWV 2.5m (8'2") Very scenic and well-guarded road (no. 11); easy gradients and turns; heavy traffic at weekends. Eastern side easier than west. Negotiable by caravans (recommended for small/medium sized only) with care, but not for the faint-hearted. Large parking area at summit.

Before using any of these passes, PLEASE READ CAREFULLY THE ADVICE AT THE BEGINNING OF THIS CHAPTER

	Pass Height In Metres (Feet)	From To	Max Gradient	Conditions and Comments
85	**Tenda (Tende)** Italy – France 1321 (4334)	Borgo-San Dalmazzo Tende	9%	UO. MWR 6m (19'8") Well-guarded, modern road (S20/ND6204) with several hairpin bends; road tunnel (height 3.8m) at summit narrow with poor road surface. Less steep on Italian side. **Caravans prohibited during winter.**
86	**Thurn** (Austria) 1274 (4180)	Kitzbühel Mittersill	8.50%	UO. MWR 5m (16'5") MWV 2.5m (8' 2") A good road (no. 161) with narrow stretches; N approach rebuilt. Several good parking areas.
87	**Timmelsjoch (Rombo)** (Austria – Italy) 2509 (8232)	Obergurgl Moso	14%	UC mid Oct-Jun. MWR 3.5m (11'6") Border closed at night 8pm to 7am. On the pass (road no 186/S44b) **caravans are prohibited.** (toll charged), as some tunnels on Italian side too narrow for larger vehicles. Easiest N to S.
88	**Tonale** (Italy) 1883 (6178)	Edolo Dimaro	10%	UO. MWR 5m (16'5") A relatively easy road (S42); steepest on W; long drag. Fine views.
89	**Tre Croci** (Italy) 1809 (5935)	Cortina-d'Ampezzo Auronzo-di-Cadore	11%	OC Dec-Mar. MWR 6m (19'8") An easy pass on road R48; fine scenery.
90	**Turracher Höhe** (Austria) 1763 (5784)	Predlitz Ebene-Reichenau	23%	UO. MWR 4m (13'1") Formerly one of the steepest mountain roads (no. 95) in Austria; now improved. Steep, fairly straightforward ascent followed by a very steep descent; good surface and mainly two-lane; fine scenery. **Not recommended for caravans.**
91	**Umbrail** (Switzerland – Italy) 2501 (8205)	Santa Maria-im-Münstertal Bormio	9%	UC Nov-early Jun. MWR 4.3m (14'1") MWV 2.3m (7'6") Highest Swiss pass (road S38); mostly tarmac with some gravel surface. Narrow with 34 hairpin bends. **Not recommended for caravans.**
92	**Vars** (France) 2109 (6919)	St Paul-sur-Ubaye Guillestre	9%	OC Dec-Mar. MWR 5m (16'5") Easy winding ascent and descent on D902 with 14 hairpin bends; good surface.
93	**Wurzen (Koren)** (Austria – Slovenia) 1073 (3520)	Riegersdorf Kranjska Gora	20%	UO. MWR 4m (13'1") Steep two-lane road (no. 109), otherwise not particularly difficult; better on Austrian side; heavy traffic summer weekends; delays likely at the border. **Caravans prohibited.**
94	**Zirler Berg** (Austria) 1009 (3310)	Seefeld Zirl	16.50%	UO. MWR 7m (23') South facing escarpment, part of route from Garmisch to Innsbruck; good, modern road (no. 171). Heavy tourist traffic and long steep descent with one hairpin bend into Inn Valley. Steepest section from hairpin bend down to Zirl. **Caravans not permitted northbound and not recommended southbound.**

Technical information by courtesy of the Automobile Association. Additional update and amendments supplied by caravanners and tourers who have themselves used the passes and tunnels. The Caravan Club has not checked the information contained in these tables and cannot accept responsibility for their accuracy, or for any errors, omissions, or their effects.

Major Alpine Rail Tunnels

	Tunnel	Route	Journey Time	General Information and Comments	Contact
Ⓐ	**Albula** (Switzerland) 5.9 km (3.5 miles)	**Chur – St Moritz** Thusis to Samedan	80 mins	MHV 2.85m + MWV 1.40m or MHV 2.50m + MWV 2.20 This tunnel no longer operates a car transport service, but there are regular passenger transport services.	Thusis (081) 2884716 Samedan (081) 2885511 www.rhb.ch
Ⓑ	**Furka** (Switzerland) 15.4 km (9.5 miles)	**Andermatt – Brig** Realp to Oberwald	15 mins	Hourly all year from 6am to 9pm weekdays; half-hourly weekends. MHV 3.5m Saturdays in February and March are exceptionally busy.	(027) 9277777 www.mgbahn.ch
Ⓒ	**Oberalp** (Switzerland) 28 km (17.3 miles)	**Andermatt – Disentis** Andermatt to Sedrun	60 mins	MHV 2.50m 2-6 trains daily when the Oberalp Pass is closed for winter.. Advance booking is compulsory.	(027) 9277777 www.mgbahn.ch
Ⓓ	**Lötschberg** (Switzerland) 14 km (8.7 miles)	**Bern – Brig** Kandersteg to Goppenstein	15 mins	MHV 2.90m Frequent all year half-hourly service. Journey time 15 minutes. Advance booking unnecessary; extension to Hohtenn operates when Goppenstein-Gampel road is closed.	Kandersteg (0)900 553333 www.bls.ch/autoverlad
Ⓔ	**Simplon** (Switzerland – Italy)	**Brig – Domodossola** Brig to Iselle	20 mins	10 trains daily, all year.	(0)900 300300 http://mct.sbb.ch/mct/autoverlad
Ⓕ	**Lötschberg/ Simplon** Switzerland – Italy	**Bern – Domodossola** Kandersteg to Iselle	75 mins	Limited service Easter to mid-October up to 3 days a week (up to 10 times a day) and at Christmas for vehicles max height 2.50m, motor caravans up to 5,000 kg. Advance booking compulsory.	(0)900 553333 www.bls.ch
Ⓕ	**Tauerbahn** (Austria)	**Bad Gastein – Spittal an der Drau** Böckstein to Mallnitz	11 mins	East of and parallel to Grossglockner pass. Half-hourly service all year.	(05) 1717 http://autoschleuse.oebb.at
Ⓖ	**Vereina** (Switzerland) 19.6 km (11.7 miles)	**Klosters – Susch** Selfranga to Sagliains	18 mins	MLV 12m Half-hourly daytime service all year. Journey time 18 minutes. Restricted capacity for vehicles over 3.30m high during winter w/ends and public holidays. Steep approach to Klosters.	(081) 2883737 www.rhb.ch

NOTES: *Information believed to be correct at time of publication. Detailed timetables are available from the appropriate tourist offices. Always check for current information before you travel.*

Major Alpine Road Tunnels

	Tunnel	Route and Height above Sea Level	General Information and Comments
(H)	**Arlberg** (Austria) 14 km (8.75 miles)	**Langen to St Anton** 1220m (4000')	On B197 parallel and to S of Arlberg Pass which is closed to caravans/trailers. Motorway vignette required; tolls charged. www.arlberg.com
(I)	**Bosruck** (Austria) 5.5 km (3.4 miles)	**Spital am Pyhrn to Selzthal** 742m (2434')	To E of Pyhrn pass; with Gleinalm Tunnel (see below) forms part of A9 a'bahn between Linz & Graz. Max speed 80 km/h (50 mph). Use dipped headlights, no overtaking. Occasional emergency lay-bys with telephones. Motorway vignette required; tolls charged.
(J)	**Felbertauern** (Austria) 5.3 km (3.25 miles)	**Mittersill to Matrei** 1525m (5000')	MWR 7m (23'), tunnel height 4.5m (14'9"). On B109 W of and parallel to Grossglockner pass; downwards gradient of 9% S to N with sharp bend before N exit. Wheel chains may be needed on approach Nov-Apr. Tolls charged.
(K)	**Frejus** (France – Italy) 12.8 km (8 miles)	**Modane to Bardonecchia** 1220m (4000')	MWR 9m (29'6"), tunnel height 4.3m (14'). Min/max speed 60/70 km/h (37/44 mph). Return tickets valid until midnight on 7th day after day of issue. Season tickets are available. Approach via A43 and D1006; heavy use by freight vehicles. Good surface on approach roads. Tolls charged. www.sftrf.fr
(L)	**Gleinalm** (Austria) 8.3 km (5 miles)	**St Michael to Fiesach (nr Graz)** 817m (2680')	Part of A9 Pyhrn a'bahn. Motorway vignette required; tolls charged.
(M)	**Grand St Bernard** (Switzerland – Italy) 5.8 km (3.6 miles)	**Bourg-St Pierre to St Rhémy (Italy)** 1925m (7570')	MHV 4m (13'1"), MVV 2.55m (8'2.5"), MLV 18m (60'). Min/max speed 40/80 km/h (24/50 mph). On E27. Passport check, Customs & toll offices at entrance; breakdown bays at each end with telephones; return tickets valid one month. Although approaches are covered, wheel chains may be needed in winter. Season tickets are available. Motorway vignette required; tolls charged. For 24-hour information tel: (027) 7884400 (Switzerland) or 0165 780902 (Italy). www.letunnel.com
(N)	**Karawanken** (Austria – Slovenia) 8 km (5 miles)	**Rosenbach to Jesenice** 610m (2000')	On A11. Motorway vignette required; tolls charged.
(O)	**Mont Blanc** (France – Italy) 11.6 km (7.2 miles)	**Chamonix to Courmayeur** 1381m (4530')	MHV 4.7m (15'5"), MWV 6m (19'6") On N205 France, S26 (Italy). Max speed in tunnel 70 km/h (44 mph) – lower limits when exiting; min speed 50 km/h. Leave 150m between vehicles; ensure enough fuel for 30km. Return tickets valid until midnight on 7th day after issue. Season tickets are available. Tolls charged. www.tunnelmb.net

Before using any of these tunnels, PLEASE READ CAREFULLY THE ADVICE AT THE BEGINNING OF THIS CHAPTER

	Tunnel	Route and Height above Sea Level	General Information and Comments
(P)	**Munt La Schera** (Switzerland – Italy) 3.5 km (2 miles)	**Zernez to Livigno** 1706m (5597')	MHV 3.6m (11'9"), MWV 2.5m (8'2"). Open 24 hours; single lane traffic controlled by traffic lights; roads from Livigno S to the Bernina Pass and Bormio closed Dec-Apr. On N28 (Switzerland). **Tolls charged.** Tel: (081) 8561888, www.livigno.eu
(Q)	**St Gotthard** (Switzerland) 16.3 km (10 miles)	**Göschenen to Airolo** 1159m (3800')	Tunnel height 4.5m (14'9"), single carriageway 7.5m (25') wide. Max speed 80 km/h (50 mph). No tolls, but tunnel is part of Swiss motorway network (A2). **Motorway vignette required.** Tunnel closed 8pm to 5am Monday to Friday for periods during June and September. Heavy traffic and delays high season. www.gotthard-strassentunnel.ch
-	**Ste Marie-aux-Mines** 6.8 km (4.25 miles)	**St Dié to Ste-Marie-aux Mines** 772m (2533')	Re-opened October 2008; the longest road tunnel situated entirely in France. Also known as Maurice Lemaire Tunnel, through the Vosges in north-east France from Lusse on N159 to N59. **Tolls charged.** Alternate route via Col-de-Ste Marie on D459.
(R)	**San Bernardino** (Switzerland) 6.6 km (4 miles)	**Hinterrhein to San Bernardino** 1644m (5396')	Tunnel height 4.8m (15'9"), width 7m (23'). On A13 motorway. No stopping or overtaking; keep 100m between vehicles; breakdown bays with telephones. Max speed 80 km/h (50 mph). **Motorway vignette required.**
(S)	**Tauern and Katschberg** (Austria) 6.4 km (4 miles) & 5.4km (3.5 miles)	**Salzburg to Villach** 1340m (4396') & 1110m (3642')	The two major tunnels on the A10, height 4.5m (14'9"), width 7.5m (25'). **Motorway vignette required; tolls charged.**

NOTES:

Dipped headlights should be used (unless stated otherwise) when travelling through road tunnels, even when the road appears well lit. In some countries police make spot checks and impose on-the-spot fines. During the winter wheel chains may be required on the approaches to some tunnels. These must not be used in tunnels and lay-bys are available for the removal and refitting of wheel chains.

Much of the information contained in the table was originally supplied by The Automobile Association and other motoring and tourist organisations. Updates and amendments are supplied by caravanners and tourers who have themselves used the passes and tunnels. The Caravan Club has not checked the information contained in these tables and cannot accept responsibility for their accuracy or for any errors, omissions, or for their effects.

Alpine Countries – East

Alpine Countries – West

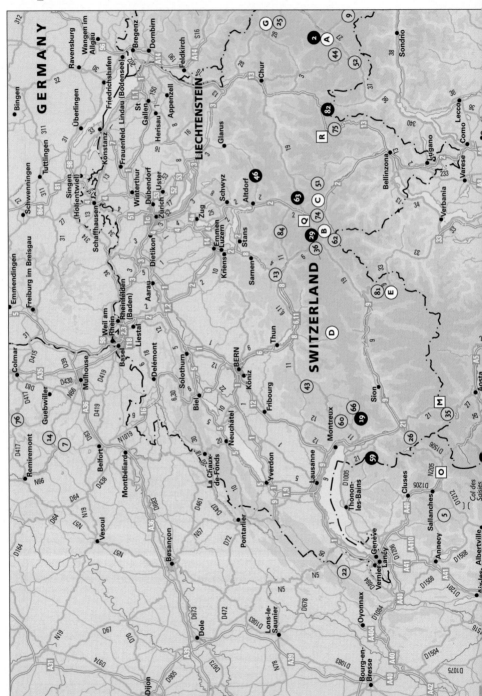

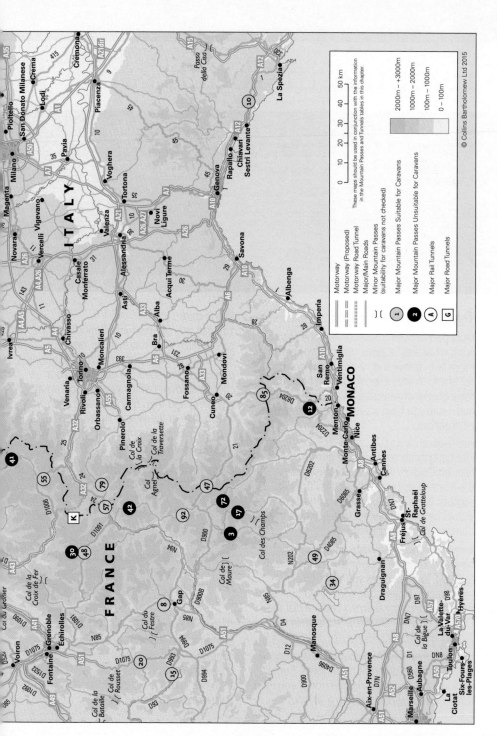

Keeping in Touch

Telephones and Calling

Most people need to use a telephone at some point while they're away, whether to keep in touch with family and friends back home or call ahead to sites. Even if you don't plan to use a phone while you're away, it is best to make sure you have access to one in case of emergencies.

International Direct Dial Calls
International access codes are given in the relevant Country Introduction - first dial the international access code then the local number. If the area code starts with a zero this should be omitted (except in Italy where the full number should be dialled).

Some countries' telephone numbers do not have area codes (e.g. Denmark, Luxembourg, Norway). In these cases you should dial the international access code and the number in full. The international access code to dial the UK from anywhere in the world is 0044.

Ringing Tones
Ringing tones vary from country to country, so may sound very different to UK tones. Some ringing tones sound similar to error or engaged tones that you would hear on a UK line.

Phone cards
You can buy pre-paid international phone cards which offer much lower rates for international calls than most mobile phone providers. You load the card with your chosen amount (which you can top up at any time) and then dial an access code from any mobile or landline to make your call. See www.planetphonecards.com or www.thephonecardsite.com for more details.

Using Mobile Phones Abroad
Mobile phones have an international calling option called 'roaming' which will automatically search for a local network when you switch your phone on. You should contact your service provider to ask about their roaming charges as these are partly set by the foreign networks you use and fluctuate with exchange rates. Most network providers offer added extras or 'bolt-ons' to your tariff to make the cost of calling to/from abroad cheaper.

Storing telephone numbers in your phone's contact list in international format (i.e. use the prefix of +44 and omit the initial '0') will mean that your contacts will automatically work abroad as well as in the UK.

Global SIM Cards

If you're planning on travelling to more than one country consider buying a global SIM card. This will mean your mobile phone can operate on foreign mobile networks, which will be more cost effective than your service provider's roaming charges. For details of SIM cards available, speak to your service provider or visit www.0044.co.uk or www.globalsimcard.co.uk.

You may find it simpler to buy a SIM card or cheap 'pay-as-you-go' phone abroad if you plan to use a mobile phone a lot for local calls, e.g. to book campsites or restaurants. Buying a local SIM or pay-as-you-go mobile may mean that you still have higher call charges for international calls (such as calling the UK). Before buying a different SIM card, check with your provider whether your phone is locked against use on other networks.

Hands-Free

Legislation in Europe forbids the use of mobile or car phones while driving except when using hands-free equipment. If you are involved in an accident whilst driving and, at the same time, you were using a hand-held mobile phone, your insurance company may refuse to honour the claim.

Accessing the Internet

Mobile Internet Costs - Data Roaming

Accessing the internet via your mobile while outside of the UK can be very expensive. It is recommended that you disable your internet access by switching 'data roaming' to off to avoid a large mobile phone bill.

Internet Access

Wi-Fi is available on lots of campsites in Europe, sometimes the cost in included in your pitch fee and other sites charge extra for access. Most larger towns may have internet cafés or libraries where you can access the internet, however lots of fast food restaurants and coffee chains now offer free Wi-Fi for customers and visiting them for a cup of coffee or bite to eat is often the most economical way if you only need access for a short time.

Many people now use their smartphones for internet access or have a dongle – a device which, when connected to your laptop or tablet, allows you to access the internet using a mobile phone network. While these methods are economical in the UK, if you do the same abroad you will be charged data roaming charges which can run into hundreds or thousands of pounds depending on how much data you use. If you plan on using your smartphone or a dongle abroad speak to your service provider before you leave the UK to make sure you understand the costs. There may even be an overseas package that you can add to your plan to make data roaming cheaper.

Making Calls from your Laptop

If you download Skype to your laptop you can make free calls to other Skype users anywhere in the world using a Wi-Fi connection. Rates for calls to non-Skype users (landline or mobile phone) are also very competitively-priced. You will need a computer with a microphone and speakers, and a webcam is handy too. It is also possible to download Skype to an internet-enabled mobile phone to take advantage of the same low-cost calls – see www.skype.com.

Club Together

If you want to chat to other members either at home or while you're away, you can do so on The Club's online community Club Together.

You can ask questions and gather opinions on the forums. Just visit www.caravanclub.co.uk/together.

Radio and Television

Radio

The BBC World Service broadcasts radio programmes 24 hours a day worldwide and you can listen on a number of platforms: online, via satellite or cable, DRM digital radio, internet radio or mobile phone. You can find detailed information and programme schedules at www.bbc.co.uk/worldservice.

Listeners in northern France can currently listen to BBC Radio 5 Live on either 693 or 909 kHz medium wave or BBC Radio 4 on 198 kHz long wave. Whereas analogue television signals were switched off in the UK during 2012, no date has yet been fixed for the switch off of analogue radio signals.

Digital Terrestrial Television

As in the UK, television transmissions in most of Europe have been converted to digital. The UK's high definition transmission technology may be more advanced than any currently implemented or planned in Europe. This means that digital televisions intended for use in the UK might not be able to receive HD terrestrial signals in some countries.

Satellite Television

For English-language TV programmes the only realistic option is satellite, and satellite dishes are a common sight on campsites all over Europe. A satellite dish mounted on the caravan roof or clamped to a pole fixed to the drawbar, or one mounted on a foldable free-standing tripod, will provide good reception and minimal interference. Remember however that obstructions to the south east (such as tall trees or even mountains) or heavy rain, can interrupt the signals.

A specialist dealer will be able to advise you on the best way of mounting your dish. You will also need a satellite receiver and ideally a satellite-finding meter.

The main entertainment channels such as BBC1, ITV1 and Channel 4 can be difficult to pick up in mainland Europe as they are now being transmitted by new narrow-beam satellites. A 60cm dish should pick up these channels in most of France, Belgium and the Netherlands but as you travel further afield, you'll need a progressively larger dish. See the website www.satelliteforcaravans.co.uk (created and operated by a Caravan Club member) for the latest changes and developments, and for information on how to set up your equipment.

Medical Matters

You can find country specific medical advice, including details of any vaccinations you may need from the NHS choices website, www.nhs.uk/healthcare abroad. Your GP surgery should also be able to give you advice on vaccinations and precautions. For general enquiries about medical care abroad you can contact NHS England on 0300 311 22 33 or email england.contactus@nhs.uk.

If you have any pre-existing medical conditions you should check with your GP that you are fit to travel. Ask your doctor for a written summary of any medical problems and a list of medications currently used. This is particularly important for travellers whose medical conditions require them to use controlled drugs or hypodermic syringes, in case customs officers question why you are carrying them.

Always make sure that you have enough of your medication to last the duration of your holiday and some extra in case you are delayed in returning to the UK. Ask your doctor for the generic name of any drugs you use, as brand names may be different abroad. If possible carry a card giving your blood group and details of any allergies or dietary restrictions (translations may be useful for restaurants).

An emergency dental kit is available from High Street chemists which will allow you temporarily to restore a crown, bridge or filling or to dress a broken tooth until you can get to a dentist.

A good website to check before you travel is www.nathnac.org/travel. This website gives general health and safety advice and reports of disease outbreaks, as well as highlighting potential health risks by country.

European Heath Insurance Card (EHIC)

Before leaving home apply for a European Health Insurance Card (EHIC). British residents temporarily visiting another EU country, as well Norway and Switzerland, are entitled to receive state-provided emergency treatment during their stay on the same terms as residents of those countries, but you must have a valid EHIC to claim these services.

To apply for your EHIC visit www.ehic.org.uk, call 0300 330 1350 or pick up an application form from a post office. An EHIC is required by each individual family member - children under 16 must be included in a parent or guardian's application.

The EHIC is free of charge, is valid for up to five years and can be renewed up to six months before its expiry date. Before you travel remember to check that your EHIC is still valid.

Private treatment is generally not covered by your EHIC, and state-provided treatment may not cover everything that you would expect to receive free of charge from the NHS. If charges are made, these cannot be refunded by the British authorities but may be refundable under the terms of your travel insurance policy.

An EHIC is not a substitute for travel insurance and it is strongly recommended that you arrange full travel insurance before leaving home regardless of the cover provided by your EHIC. Some insurance companies require you to have an EHIC and some will waive the policy excess if an EHIC has been used.

If your EHIC is stolen or lost while you are abroad contact 0044 191 2127500 for help. If you experience difficulties in getting your EHIC accepted, telephone the Department for Work & Pensions for assistance on the overseas healthcare team line 0044 (0)191 218 1999 between 8am to 5pm Monday to Friday. Residents of the Republic of Ireland, the Isle of Man and Channel Islands, should check with

their own health authorities about reciprocal arrangements with other countries.

Holiday Travel Insurance

Despite the fact that you have an EHIC you may incur thousands of pounds of medical costs if you fall ill or have an accident. The cost of bringing a person back to the UK, in the event of illness or death, is never covered by the EHIC. You may also find that you end up with a bill for treatment as not all countries offer free healthcare.

Separate additional travel insurance adequate for your destination is essential, such as The Caravan Club's Red Pennant Overseas Holiday Insurance, available to Club members – see www.caravanclub.co.uk/redpennant.

First Aid

A first aid kit containing at least the basic requirements is an essential item, and in some countries it is compulsory to carry one in your vehicle (see the Essential Equipment Table in the chapter Motoring – Equipment). Kits should contain items such as sterile pads, assorted dressings, bandages and plasters, antiseptic wipes or cream, cotton wool, scissors, eye bath and tweezers. Also make sure you carry something for upset stomachs, painkillers and an antihistamine in case of hay fever or mild allergic reactions.

If you're travelling to remote areas then you may find it useful to carry a good first aid manual. The British Red Cross publishes a comprehensive First Aid Manual in conjunction with St John Ambulance and St Andrew's Ambulance Association.

Vaccinations

The Department of Health advises long stay visitors to some eastern European countries to consider vaccination against hepatitis A. Your GP surgery can advise you if this or any other vaccinations are required.

Accidents and Emergencies

If you are involved in or witness a road accident the police may want to question you about it. If possible take photographs or make sketches of the scene, and write a few notes about what happened as it may be more difficult to remember the details at a later date.

The telephone numbers for police, fire brigade and ambulance services are given in each Country Introduction, however in all EU member states the number 112 can be used from landlines or mobile phones to call any of the emergency services.

Sun Protection

Never under-estimate how ill exposure to the sun can make you. If you are not used to the heat it is very easy to fall victim to heat exhaustion or heat stroke. Avoid sitting in the sun between 11am and 3pm and cover your head if sitting or walking in the sun. Use a good quality sun-cream with high sun protection factor (SPF) and re-apply frequently. Make sure you drink plenty of fluids.

Tick-Borne Encephalitis (TBE) and Lyme Disease

Hikers and outdoor sports enthusiasts planning trips to forested, rural areas in some parts of central and Eastern Europe should be aware

of tick-borne encephalitis, which is transmitted by the bite of an infected tick. If you think you may be at risk, seek medical advice on prevention and immunisation before you leave the UK.

There is no vaccine against Lyme disease, an equally serious tick-borne infection, which, if left untreated, can attack the nervous system and joints.

You can minimise the risk by using an insect repellent containing DEET, wearing long sleeves and long trousers, and checking for ticks after outdoor activity. Avoid unpasteurised dairy products in risk areas. See www.tickalert. org or telephone 01943 468010 for more information.

Water and Food

Water from mains supplies throughout Europe is generally safe, but may be treated with chemicals which make it taste different to tap water in the UK. If in any doubt, always drink bottled water or boil it before drinking. Food poisoning is potential anywhere, and a complete change of diet may upset your stomach as well. In hot conditions avoid any food that hasn't been refrigerated or hot food that has been left to cool. Be sensible about the food that you eat – don't eat unpasteurised or undercooked food and if you aren't sure about the freshness of meat or seafood then it is best avoided.

Returning Home

If you become ill on your return home tell your doctor that you have been abroad and which countries you have visited. Even if you have received medical treatment in another country, always consult your doctor if you have been bitten or scratched by an animal while on holiday.

If you were given any medicines in another country, it may be illegal to bring them back into the UK. If in doubt, declare them at Customs when you return.

Electricity and Gas

Electricity – General Advice

The voltage for mains electricity is 230V across the EU, but varying degrees of 'acceptable tolerance' mean you may find variations in the actual voltage. Most appliances sold in the UK are 220-240V so should work correctly. However, some high-powered equipment, such as microwave ovens, may not function well – check your instruction manual for any specific instructions. Appliances marked with 'CE' have been designed to meet the requirements of relevant European directives.

The table below gives an approximate idea of which appliances can be used based on the amperage which is being supplied (although not all appliances should be used at the same time). You can work it out more accurately by making a note of the wattage of each appliance in your caravan. The wattages given are based on appliances designed for use in caravans and motorhomes. Household kettles, for example, have at least a 2000W element. Each caravan circuit will also have a maximum amp rating which should not be exceeded.

Electrical Connections – EN60309-2 (CEE17)

EN60309-2 (formerly known as CEE17) is the European Standard for all newly fitted connectors. However there is no requirement

Amps	Wattage (Approx)	Fridge	Battery Charger	Air Conditioning	LCD TV	Water Heater	Kettle (750W)	Heater (1kW)
2	400	✓	✓					
4	900	✓	✓		✓	✓		
6	1300	✓	✓	*	✓	✓	✓	
8	1800	✓	✓	✓**	✓	✓	✓	✓**
10	2300	✓	✓	✓**	✓	✓	✓	✓**
16	3600	✓	✓	✓	✓	✓	✓	✓**

*   *Usage possible, depending on wattage of appliance in question*
**   *Not to be used at the same time as other high-wattage equipment*

for sites to replace connectors which were installed before this was standardised so you may still find some sites where your UK 3 pin connector doesn't fit. For this reason it is a good idea to carry a 2-pin adapter. If you are already on site and find your connector doesn't fit, ask campsite staff to borrow or hire an adaptor. You may still encounter a poor electrical supply on site even with an EN60309-2 connection.

Other Connections

French – 2-pin, plus earth socket. Adaptors available from UK caravan accessory shops. German – 2-pin, plus 2 earth strips, found in Norway and Sweden and possibly still Germany. Switzerland - 3-pin, but not the same shape as UK 3-pin. Adapters available to purchase in Switzerland. Most campsites using the Swiss 3-pin will have adaptors available for hire or to borrow.

If the campsite does not have a modern EN60309-2 (CEE17) supply, ask to see the electrical protection for the socket outlet. If there is a device marked with IDn = 30mA, then the risk is minimised.

Hooking Up to the Mains

Connection

Connection should always be made in the following order:

- Check your outfit isolating switch is at 'off'.
- Uncoil the connecting cable from the drum. A coiled cable with current flowing through it may overheat. Take your cable and insert the connector (female end) into your outfit inlet.
- Insert the plug (male end) into the site outlet socket.
- Switch outfit isolating switch to 'on'.
- Use a polarity tester in one of the 13A sockets in the outfit to check all connections are correctly wired. Never leave it in the socket. Some caravans have these devices built in as standard.

It is recommended that the supply is not used if the polarity is incorrect (see Reversed Polarity overleaf).

Warnings:
If you are in any doubt of the safety of the system, if you don't receive electricity once connected or if the supply stops then contact the site staff.

If the fault is found to be with your outfit then call a qualified electrician rather than trying to fix the problem yourself.

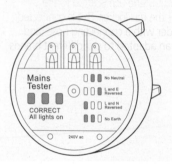

To ensure your safety you should never use an electrical system which you can't confirm to be safe. Use a mains tester such as the one shown above to test the electrical supply. Always check that a proper earth connection exists before using the electrics. Please note that these testers may not pick up all earth faults so if there is any doubt as to the integrity of the earth system do not use the electrical supply.

Disconnection

- Switch your outfit isolating switch to 'off'.
- At the site supply socket withdraw the plug.
- Disconnect the cable from your outfit.

Motorhomes – if leaving your pitch during the day, don't leave your mains cable plugged into the site supply, as this creates a hazard if the exposed live connections in the plug are touched or if the cable is not seen during grass-cutting.

Reversed Polarity

Even if the site connector meets European Standard EN60309-2 (CEE17), British caravanners are still likely to encounter the problem known as reversed polarity. This is where the site supply 'live' line connects to the outfit's 'neutral' and vice versa. You should always check the polarity immediately on connection, using a polarity tester available from caravan accessory shops. If polarity is reversed the caravan mains electricity should not be used. Try using another nearby socket instead. Frequent travellers to the Continent can make up an adaptor themselves, or ask an electrician to make one for you, with the live and neutral wires reversed. Using a reversed polarity socket will probably not affect how an electrical appliance works, however your protection is greatly reduced. For example, a lamp socket may still be live as you touch it while replacing a blown bulb, even if the light switch is turned off.

Shaver Sockets

Most campsites provide shaver sockets with a voltage of 220V or 110V. Using an incorrect voltage may cause the shaver to become

Site Hooking Up Adaptor
ADAPTATEUR DE PRISE AU SITE (SECTEUR)
CAMPINGPLATZ-ANSCHLUSS (NETZ)

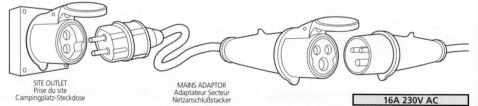

EXTENSION LEAD TO CARAVAN
Câble de rallonge à la caravane
Verläengerungskabel zum wohnwagen

SITE OUTLET
Prise du site
Campingplatz-Steckdose

MAINS ADAPTOR
Adaptateur Secteur
Netzanschlußstacker

16A 230V AC

hot or break. The 2-pin adaptor available in the UK may not fit Continental sockets so it is advisable to buy 2-pin adaptors on the Continent. Many modern shavers will work on a range of voltages which make them suitable for travelling abroad. Check you instruction manual to see if this is the case.

Gas – General Advice

Gas usage can be difficult to predict as so many factors, such as temperature and how often you eat out, can affect the amount you need. As a rough guide allow 0.45kg of gas a day for normal summer usage.

With the exception of Campingaz, LPG cylinders normally available in the UK cannot be exchanged abroad. If possible, take enough gas with you and bring back the empty cylinders. Always check how many you can take with you as ferry and tunnel operators may restrict the number of cylinders you are permitted to carry for safety reasons.

The wide availability of Campingaz across Europe means it is worth considering using it while touring overseas. However, prices can vary from country to country, and maximum cylinder sizes are quite limited (2.75kg of gas in a 907 cylinder), making it less practical for routine use in larger vehicles with several gas appliances. A Campingaz adapter is relatively inexpensive, though, and is widely available in the UK.

If you are touring in cold weather conditions use propane gas instead of butane. Many other brands of gas are available in different countries and, as long as you have the correct regulator,

adaptor and hose and the cylinders fit in your gas locker these local brands can also be used.

Gas cylinders are now standardised with a pressure of 30mbar for both butane and propane within the EU. On UK-specification caravans and motorhomes (2004 models and later) a 30mbar regulator suited to both propane and butane use is fitted to the bulkhead of the gas locker. This is connected to the cylinder with a connecting hose (and sometimes an adaptor) to suit different brands or types of gas. Older outfits and some foreign-built ones may use a cylinder-mounted regulator, which may need to be changed to suit different brands or types of gas.

Warnings:

- Refilling gas cylinders intended to be exchanged is against the law in most countries, however you may still find that some sites and dealers will offer to refill cylinders for you. Never take them up on this service as it can be dangerous; the cylinders haven't been designed for user-refilling and it is possible to overfill them with catastrophic consequences.

- Regular servicing of gas appliances is important as a faulty appliance can emit carbon monoxide, which could prove fatal. Check your vehicle or appliance handbook for service recommendations.

- Never use a hob or oven as a space heater.

The Caravan Club publishes a range of technical leaflets for its members including detailed advice on the use of electricity and gas – you can request copies or see www.caravanclub.co.uk/advice-and-training.

Safety and Security

EU countries have good legislation in place to protect your safety wherever possible. However accidents and crime will still occur and taking sensible precautions can help to minimise your risk of being involved.

Beaches, Lakes and Rivers

Check for any warning signs or flags before you swim and ensure that you know what they mean. Check the depth of water before diving and avoid diving or jumping into murky water as submerged objects may not be visible. Familiarise yourself with the location of safety apparatus and/or lifeguards.

Use only the designated areas for swimming, watersports and boating and always use life jackets where appropriate. Watch out for tides, undertows, currents and wind strength and direction before swimming in the sea. This applies in particular when using inflatables, windsurfing equipment, body boards, kayaks or sailing boats. Sudden changes of wave and weather conditions combined with fast tides and currents are particularly dangerous.

Campsite Safety

Once you've settled in, take a walk around the site to familiarise yourself with its layout and locate the nearest safety equipment. Ensure that children know their way around and where your pitch is.

Natural disasters are rare, but always think about what could happen. A combination of heavy rain and a riverside pitch could lead to flash flooding, for example, so make yourself aware of site evacuation procedures.

Be aware of sources of electricity and cabling on and around your pitch – electrical safety might not be up to the same standards as in the UK.

Poison for rodent control is sometimes used on sites or surrounding farmland. Warning notices are not always posted and you are strongly advised to check if staying on a rural site with dogs or children.

Incidents of theft on campsites are rare but when leaving your caravan unattended make sure you lock all doors and shut windows. Conceal valuables from sight and lock up any bicycles.

Children

Watch out for children as you drive around the site and don't exceed walking pace. Children's play areas are generally unsupervised, check which are suitable for your children's ages and abilities. Read and respect the displayed rules. Remember it is your responsibility to supervise your children at all times.

Be aware of any campsite rules concerning ball games or use of play equipment, such as roller blades and skateboards. When your children attend organised activities, arrange when and where to meet afterwards.

Make sure that children are aware of any places where they should not go and never leave children alone inside a caravan.

Fire

Fire prevention is important on sites, as fire can spread quickly between outfits. Never use paraffin or gas heaters inside your caravan. Gas heaters should only be fitted when air is taken from outside the caravan. Don't change your gas cylinder inside the caravan. If you smell gas turn off the cylinder immediately, extinguish all naked flames and seek professional help.

Make sure you know where the fire points and telephones are on site and know the site fire drill. Make sure everyone in your party knows how to call the emergency services.

Where site rules permit the use of barbecues, take the following precautions to prevent fire:

- Never locate a barbecue near trees or hedges.
- Have a bucket of water to hand in case of sparks.
- Only use recommended fire-lighting materials.
- Don't leave a barbecue unattended when lit and dispose of hot ash safely.
- Never take a barbecue into an enclosed area or awning – even when cooling they continue to release carbon monoxide which can lead to fatal poisoning.

Swimming Pools

Familiarize yourself with the pool area before you venture in for a swim, especially if you're travelling with children. Check the pool layout – identify shallow and deep ends and the location of safety equipment. Check the gradient of the pool bottom as pools which shelve off sharply can catch weak or non-swimmers unawares.

Never dive or jump into a pool without knowing the depth – if there is a no diving rule it usually means the pool isn't deep enough for safe diving.

For pools with a supervisor or lifeguard, note any times or dates when the pool is not supervised, e.g. lunch breaks or in low season. Read safety notices and rules posted around the pool.

On the Road

Do not leave valuables on car seats or on view in caravans, even if they are locked. Ensure that items on roof racks or cycle carriers are locked securely.

Beware of a 'snatch' through open car windows at traffic lights, filling stations or in traffic jams. When driving through towns and cities keep your doors locked. Keep handbags, valuables and documents out of sight at all times.

If flagged down by another motorist for whatever reason, take care that your own car is locked and windows closed while you check outside, even if someone is left inside.

Be particularly careful on long, empty stretches of motorway and when you stop for fuel. Even if the people flagging you down appear to be officials (e.g. wearing yellow reflective jackets or dark, 'uniform-type' clothing) lock your vehicle doors immediately. They may appear to be friendly and helpful, but could be opportunistic thieves. Have a mobile phone to hand and, if necessary, be seen to use it.

Road accidents are a significant risk in some countries where traffic laws may be inadequately enforced, roads may be poorly maintained, road signs and lighting inadequate, and driving standards poor. It's a good idea to keep a fully-charged mobile phone with you in your car with the number of your breakdown organisation saved into it.

On your return to the UK there are increasing issues with migrants attempting to stowaway in vehicles, especially if you're travelling from Calais. The UK government have issued the following instructions to prevent people entering the UK illegally:

- Where possible all access to vehicles or storage compartments should be fitted with locks.

- All locks must be engaged when the vehicle is stationary or unattended

- Immediately before boarding your ferry or train check that the locks on your vehicle haven't been compromised.

- If you have any reason to suspect someone may have accessed your outfit speak to border control staff or call the police. Do not board the ferry or train or you may be liable for a fine of up to £2000.

Overnight Stops

Overnight stops should always be at campsites and not at motorway service areas, ferry terminal car parks, petrol station forecourts or isolated 'aires de services' or 'aires de repos' on motorways where robberies and muggings are occasionally reported. If you decide to use these areas for a rest then take appropriate precautions, for example, shutting all windows, securing locks and making a thorough external check of your vehicle(s) before departing. Safeguard your property, e.g. handbags, while out of the caravan and beware of approaches by strangers.

For a safer place to take a break, there is a wide network of 'Stellplätze', 'Aires de Services', 'Aree di Sosta' and 'Áreas de Servicio' in cities, towns and villages across Europe, many specifically for motorhomes with good security and overnight facilities. It is rare that you will be the only vehicle staying on such areas, but avoid any that are isolated, take sensible precautions and trust your instincts. For example, if the area appears run down and there are groups of people hanging around who seem intimidating, then you are probably wise to move on.

Personal Security

Petty crime happens all over the world; however as a tourist you are more vulnerable to it. This shouldn't stop you from exploring new horizons, but there are a few sensible precautions you can take to minimise the risk.

- Leave valuables and jewellery at home. If you do take them, fit a small safe in your caravan or lock them in the boot of your car. Don't leave money or valuables in a car glovebox or on view. Don't leave bags in full view when sitting outside at cafés or restaurants, or leave valuables unattended on the beach.

- When walking be security-conscious. Avoid unlit streets at night, walk away from the kerb edge and carry handbags or shoulder bags on the side away from the kerb. The less of a tourist you appear, the less of a target you are.

- Keep a separate note of your holiday insurance details and emergency telephone numbers.

- Beware of pickpockets in crowded areas, at tourist attractions and in cities, and be cautious of bogus plain-clothes policemen who may ask to see your foreign currency or credit cards and passport. If approached, decline to show your money or to hand over your passport but ask for credentials and offer instead to go to the nearest police station.

- Laws and punishment vary from country to country so make yourself aware of anything which may affect you before you travel. Be especially careful on laws involving alcohol consumption (such as drinking in public areas), and never buy or use illegal drugs abroad.

- Respect customs regulations - smuggling is a serious offence and can carry heavy penalties. Do not carry parcels or luggage through customs for other people and do not cross borders with people you do not know in your vehicle, such as hitchhikers

The Foreign & Commonwealth Office produces a range of material to advise and inform British citizens travelling abroad about issues affecting their safety - www.gov.uk/foreign-travel-advice has country specific guides.

Money Security

We would rarely walk around at home carrying large amounts of cash, but as you may not have the usual access to bank accounts and credit cards you are more likely to do so on holiday. You are also less likely to have the same degree of security when online banking as you would in your own home. The following precautions are sensible to keep your money safe:

- Carry only the minimum amount of cash and don't rely on one person to carry everything. Never carry a wallet in your back pocket. Moneybelts are the most secure way to carry cash and passports.

- Keep a separate note of bank account and credit/debit card numbers. Carry your credit card issuer/bank's 24-hour UK contact number with you.

- Be careful when using cash machines (ATMs) – try to use a machine in an area with high footfall and don't allow yourself to be distracted. Put your cash away before moving away from the cash machine.
- Always guard your PIN number, both at cash machines and when using your card to pay in shops and restaurants. Never let your card out of your sight while paying.
- If using internet banking do not leave the PC or mobile device unattended and make sure you log out fully at the end of the session.

British Consular Services Abroad

British Embassy and Consular staff offer practical advice, assistance and support to British travellers abroad. They can, for example, issue replacement passports, help Britons who have been the victims of crime, contact relatives and friends in the event of an accident, illness or death, provide information about transferring funds and provide details of local lawyers, doctors and interpreters. But there are limits to their powers and a British Consul cannot, for example, give legal advice, intervene in court proceedings, put up bail, pay for legal or medical bills, or for funerals or the repatriation of bodies, or undertake work more properly done by banks, motoring organisations and travel insurers.

If you are charged with a serious offence, insist on the British Consul being informed. You will be contacted as soon as possible by a Consular Officer who can advise on local procedures, provide access to lawyers and insist that you are treated as well as nationals of the country which is holding you. However, they cannot get you released as a matter of course.

British and Irish embassy contact details can be found in the Country Introduction chapters.

Continental Campsites

The quantity and variety of sites across Europe means you're sure to find one that suits your needs – from full facilities and entertainment to quiet rural retreats. If you haven't previously toured outside of the UK you may notice some differences, such as pitches being smaller or closer together. In hot climates hard ground may make putting up awnings difficult.

In the high season all campsite facilities are usually open, however bear in mind that toilet and shower facilities may be busy. Out of season some facilities such as shops and swimming pools may be closed and office opening hours may be reduced. If the site has very low occupancy the sanitary facilities may be reduced to a few unisex toilet and shower cubicles.

Booking a Campsite

To save the hassle of arriving to find a site full it is best to book in advance, especially in high season. If you don't book ahead arrive no later than 4pm (earlier at popular resorts) to secure a pitch, after this time sites fill up quickly. You also need to allow time to find another campsite if your first choice is fully booked.

You can often book directly via a campsite's website using a credit or debit card to pay a deposit if required. Please be aware that some sites regard the deposit as a booking or admin fee and will not deduct the amount from your final bill.

Overseas Travel Service

The Caravan Club's Overseas Travel Service offers members an overseas site booking service to over 250 campsites in Europe. Full details of these sites plus information on Ferry special offers and Red Pennant Overseas Holiday Insurance can be found in the Club's Venture Abroad brochure – call 01342 327410 to request a copy or visit www.caravanclub.co.uk/overseas.

Overseas Site Booking Service sites are marked 'SBS' in the site listings. Many of them can be booked at www.caravanclub.co.uk. The Caravan Club cannot make advance reservations for any other campsites listed in this guide. Only those sites marked SBS have been inspected by Caravan Club staff.

Camping Cheques

The Caravan Club operates a low season scheme in association with Camping Cheques,

offering flexible holidays. The scheme covers approximately 635 sites in 29 countries.

Camping Cheques are supplied as part of a package which includes return ferry fare and a minimum of seven Camping Cheques. Those sites which feature in the Camping Cheques scheme and which are listed in this guide are marked 'CChq' in their site entries. For full details of the Camping Cheque scheme visit www.caravanclub.co.uk/campingcheques.

Caravan Storage Abroad

Storing your caravan on a site in Europe can be a great way to avoid a long tow and to save on ferry and fuel costs. Even sites which don't offer a specific long-term storage facility may be willing to negotiate a price to store your caravan for you.

Before you leave your caravan in storage abroad always check whether your insurance covers this, as many policies don't.

If you aren't covered then look for a specialist policy - Towergate Insurance (tel: 01242 538431 or www.towergateinsurance.co.uk) or Look Insurance (tel: 0333 777 3035 or www.lookinsuranceservices.co.uk) both offer insurance policies for caravans stored abroad.

Facilities and Site Description

All of the site facilities shown in the site listings of this guide have been taken from member reports, as have the comments at the end of each site entry. Please remember that opinions and expectations can differ significantly from one person to the next.

The year of report is shown at the end of each site listing – sites which haven't been reported on for a few years may have had significant changes to their prices, facilities, opening dates and standards. It is always best to check any specific details you need to know before travelling by contacting the site or looking at their website.

Sanitary Facilities

Facilities normally include toilet and shower blocks with shower cubicles, wash basins and razor sockets. In site listings the abbreviation 'wc' indicates that the site has the kind of toilets we are used to in the UK (pedestal style). Some sites have footplate style toilets and, where this is known, you will see the abbreviation 'cont', i.e. continental. European sites do not always provide sink plugs, toilet paper or soap so take them with you.

Waste Disposal

Site entries show (when known) where a campsite has a chemical disposal and/or a motorhome service point, which is assumed to include a waste (grey) water dump station and toilet cassette-emptying point. You may find fewer waste water disposal facilities as on the continent more people use the site sanitary blocks rather than their own facilities.

Chemical disposal points may be fixed at a high level requiring you to lift cassettes in order to empty them. Disposal may simply be down a toilet. Wastemaster-style emptying points are not very common in Europe. Formaldehyde chemical cleaning products are banned in many countries. In Germany the 'Blue Angel' (Blaue Engel) Standard, and in the Netherlands the 'Milieukeur' Standard, indicates that the product has particularly good environmental credentials.

Finding a Campsite

Directions are given for all campsites listed in this guide and most listings also include GPS co-ordinates. Full street addresses are also given where available. The directions have been supplied by member reports and haven't been checked in detail by The Club.

For information about using satellite navigation to find a site see the Motoring Equipment section.

Overnight Stops

Many towns and villages across Europe provide dedicated overnight or short stay areas specifically for motorhomes, usually with security, electricity, water and waste facilities. These are known as 'Aires de Services', 'Stellplatz' or 'Aree di Sosta' and are usually well signposted with a motorhome icon. Facilities and charges for these overnight stopping areas will vary significantly.

Many campsites in popular tourist areas will also have separate overnight areas of hardstanding with facilities often just outside the main campsite area. There are guidebooks available which list just these overnight stops, Vicarious books publish an English guide to the Aires including directions, GPS co-ordinates and photographs. Please contact 0131 208 3333 or visit their website www.vicarious-shop.co.uk.

For security reasons you shouldn't spend the night on petrol station service areas, ferry terminal car parks or isolated 'Aires de Repos' or 'Aires de Services' along motorways.

Municipal Campsites

Municipal sites are found in towns and villages all over Europe, in particular in France. Once very basic, many have been improved in recent years and now offer a wider range of facilities. They can usually be booked in advance through the local town hall or tourism office. When approaching a town you may find that municipal sites are not always named and signposts may simply state 'Camping' or show a tent or caravan symbol. Most municipal sites are clean, well-run and very reasonably prices but security may be basic.

These sites may be used by seasonal workers, market traders and travellers in low season and as a result there may be restrictions or very high charges for some types of outfits (such as twin axles) in order to discourage this. If you may be affected check for any restrictions when you book.

Naturist Campsites

Some naturist sites are included in this guide and are shown with the word 'naturist' after their site name. Those marked 'part naturist' have separate areas for naturists. Visitors to naturist sites aged 16 and over usually require an INF card or Naturist Licence - covered by membership of British Naturism (tel 01604 620361, visit www.british-naturism.org.uk or email headoffice@british-naturism.org. uk) or you can apply for a licence on arrival at any recognised naturist site (a passport-size photograph is required).

Opening Dates and times

Opening dates should always be taken with a pinch of salt - including those given in this guide. Sites may close without notice due to refurbishment work, a lack of visitors or bad weather. Outside the high season it is always best to contact campsites in advance, even if the site advertises itself as open all year.

Most sites will close their gates or barriers overnight – if you are planning to arrive late or are delayed on your journey you should call ahead to make sure you will be able to gain access to the site. There may be a late arrivals area outside of the barriers where you can pitch overnight. Motorhomers should also consider barrier closing times if leaving site in your vehicle for the evening.

Check out time is usually between 10am and 12 noon – speak to the site staff if you need to leave very early to make sure you can check out on departure. Sites may also close for an extended lunch break, so if you're planning to arrive or check out around lunchtime check that the office will be open.

Pets on Campsites

Dogs are welcome on many sites, although you may have to prove that all of their vaccinations are up to date before they are allowed onto the site. Certain breeds of dogs are banned in some countries and other breeds will need to be muzzled and kept on a lead at all times. A list of breeds with restrictions by country can be found at www.caravanclub.co.uk/pets.

Sites usually charge for dogs and may limit the number allowed per pitch. On arrival make yourself aware of site rules regarding dogs, such as keeping them on a lead, muzzling them or not leaving them unattended in your outfit.

In popular tourist areas local regulations may ban dogs from beaches during the summer. Some dogs may find it difficult to cope with changes in climate. Also watch out for diseases transmitted by ticks, caterpillars, mosquitoes or sandflies - dogs from the UK will have no natural resistance. Consult your vet about preventative treatment before you travel.

Visitors to southern Spain and Portugal, parts of central France and northern Italy should be aware of the danger of Pine Processionary Caterpillars from mid-winter to late spring. Dogs should be kept away from pine trees if possible or fitted with a muzzle that prevents the nose and mouth from touching the ground. This will also protect against poisoned bait sometimes used by farmers and hunters.

In the event that your pet is taken ill abroad a campsite should have information about local vets.

Most European countries require dogs to wear a collar identifying their owners at all times. If your dog goes missing, report the matter to the local police and the local branch of that country's animal welfare organisation.

See the Documents section of this book for more information about the Pet Travel Scheme.

Prices and Payment

Prices per night (for an outfit and two adults) are shown in the site entries. If you stay on site after midday you may be charged for an extra day. Many campsites have a minimum amount for credit card transactions, meaning they can't be used to pay for overnight or short stays. Check which payment methods are accepted when you check in.

Sites with automatic barriers may ask for a deposit for a swipe card or fob to operate it.

Extra charges may apply for the use of facilities such as swimming pools, showers or laundry rooms. You may also be charged extra for dogs, Wi-Fi, tents and extra cars.

A tourist tax, eco tax and/or rubbish tax may be imposed by local authorities in some European countries. VAT may also be added to your campsite fees.

Registering on Arrival

Local authority requirements mean you will usually have to produce an identity document on arrival, which will be retained by the site until you check out. If you don't want to leave your passport with reception then most sites will accept a camping document such as the Camping Key Europe (CKE) or Camping Card International (CCI) - if this is known site entries are marked CKE/CCI.

CKE are available for Caravan Club members to purchase by calling 01342 336633 or are free to members if you take out the 'motoring' level of cover from the Club's Red Pennant Overseas Holiday Insurance.

General Advice

If you've visiting a new site ask to take a look round the site and facilities before booking in. Riverside pitches can be very scenic but keep an eye on the water level; in periods of heavy rain this may rise rapidly.

Speed limits on campsites are usually restricted to 10 km/h (6 mph). You may be asked to park your car in a separate area away from your caravan, particularly in the high season.

The use of the term 'statics' in the campsite reports in this guide may to any long-term accommodation on site, such as seasonal pitches, chalets, cottages, fixed tents and cabins, as well as static caravans.

Complaints

If you want to make a complaint about a site issue, take it up with site staff or owners at the time in order to give them the opportunity to rectify the problem during your stay.

The Caravan Club has no control or influence over day to day campsite operations or administration of the sites listed in this guide. Therefore we aren't able to intervene in any dispute you should have with a campsite, unless the booking has been made through our Site Booking Service - see listings marked 'SBS' for sites we are able to book for you.

Campsite Groups

Across Europe there are many campsite 'groups' or 'chains' with sites in various locations.

You will generally find that group sites will be consistent in their format and the quality and variety of facilities they offer. If you liked one site you can be fairly confident that you will like other sites within the same group.

If you're looking for a full facility site, with swimming pools, play areas, bars and restaurants on site you're likely to find these on sites which are part of a group. You might even find organised excursions and activities such as archery on site.

Austria
Country Introduction

Salzburg

Welcome to Austria

From bustling, cosmopolitan cities, packed with culture, to stunning natural landscapes that will take your breath away, Austria is a rich and varied country that caters to every taste.

The Alps offer endless appeal for those looking to enjoy an active, outdoor holiday while the picturesque towns and villages that punctuate the landscape are ideal for relaxing and soaking up the local culture.

Country highlights

Austria is an important centre for European culture, in particular, music. As the birthplace of many notable composers – such as Mozart, Strauss and Haydn to name just a few – Austria is a magnet for classical music fans.

When it comes to food, one of Austria's most famous dishes is strudel, and there are many different varieties of flavours and types available. The oldest strudel recipes can be found in a handwritten cookbook from 1696 at the Vienna City Library.

Major towns and cities

- Vienna – enjoy a slice of sachertorte in this historic capital.
- Linz – a city of arts and music on the banks of the Danube.
- Graz – the old town is filled with sights and is on the UNESCO World Heritage List.
- Salzburg – this fairytale city was the birthplace of Mozart.

Attractions

- Schönbrunn Palace – this Baroque palace is a former imperial residence in the heart of Vienna.
- Hallstatt – this Alpine village has a fascinating history as well as picturesque views.
- Grossglockner Alpine Road – the highest road in Austria with unparalleled mountain views.
- Innsbruck – a renowned winter sports centre packed with historical sights.

Find out more

www.austria.info

Tel: 0043 (0)1 58 86 60 Austrian National Tourist Office

Country Information

Population (approx): 8.2 million

Capital: Vienna (population approx 1.7 million)

Area: 83,870 sq km

Bordered by: Czech Republic, Germany, Hungary, Italy, Liechtenstein, Slovakia, Slovenia, Switzerland

Terrain: Mountainous in south and west; flat or gently sloping in extreme north and east

Climate: Temperate; cold winters with frequent rain in the lowlands and snow in the mountains; moderate summers, sometimes very hot

Highest Point: Grossglockner 3,798m

Language: German

Local Time: GMT or BST + 1, i.e. 1 hour ahead of the UK all year

Currency: Euros divided into 100 cents £1 = €1.42, €1 = £0.71 (September 2015)

Telephoning: From the UK dial 0043 for Austria and omit the initial zero of the area code of the number you are calling.

Emergency numbers: Police 133; Fire brigade 122; Ambulance 144, or dial 112 for any service (operators speak English).

Public Holidays 2016: Jan 1, 6; Mar 28; May 1, 5, 16, 26; Aug 15; Oct 26 (National Day); Nov 1; Dec 8, 25, 26.

School summer holidays last the whole of July, August and early September

Camping and Caravanning

There are approximately 500 campsites in Austria around 150 campsites of which are open all year, mostly in or near to ski resorts.

Casual/wild camping is not encouraged and is prohibited in Vienna, in the Tyrol and in forests and nature reserves. Permission to park a caravan should be obtained in advance from the owners of private land, or from the local town hall or police station in the case of common land or state property.

Cycling

There is an extensive network of cycle routes, following dedicated cycle and footpaths, such as the 360 km cycle lane that follows the Danube.

Many cities encourage cyclists with designated cycle lanes. A Citybike hire scheme operates in Vienna from more than 60 rental offices situated close to underground/metro stations. See www.citybikewien.at for more information or email kontakt@citybikewien.at. There are eight signposted mountain bike routes between 10 and 42 kilometres long in the Vienna woods. Cycle helmets are compulsory for children under 12 years, or 15 years in Lower Austria (Niederösterreich).

Bikes may be carried on the roof or rear of a car. When carried at the rear, the width must not extend beyond the width of the vehicle, and the rear lights and number plate must be visible.

Electricity and Gas

Current on campsites varies from 4 - 16 amps. Plugs have two round pins and most campsites have CEE connections. Electricity points tend to be in locked boxes, so you will need to check polarity on arrival before the box is locked. Arrangements also need to be made for the box to be unlocked if making an early departure.

Some sites in Austria make a one-off charge for connection to the electricity supply, which is then metered at a rate per kilowatt hour (kwh) The full range of Campingaz cylinders is widely available.

Entry Formalities

There are no identity checks at the borders with EU countries or Switzerland nor are there Customs controls with EU countries. Random checks on goods and ID may still be carried out at the border with Switzerland.

British and Irish passport holders may stay in Austria for up to three months without a visa. Visitors arriving at a campsite or hotel must complete a registration form.

Medical Services

Minor matters can be dealt with by staff at pharmacies (apotheke). Pharmacies operate a rota system for out of hours access; when closed a notice is often displayed giving the addresses of the nearest open pharmacies.

Free treatment is available from doctors and hospital outpatient departments as long as the doctor is contracted to the local health insurance office (Gebietskrankenkasse). To be covered for hospital treatment you will need a doctor's referral. In-patient treatment will incur a daily non-refundable charge for the first 28 days.

Only a limited amount of dental treatment is covered under the state healthcare system. You will need to present your European Health Insurance Card (EHIC) to receive treatment.

Opening Hours

Banks – Mon-Fri 8am-12.30pm & 1.30pm-3pm (5.30pm Thu), main branches don't close for lunch; closed Sat/Sun. (Hours may vary).

Museums – Mon-Fri 10am-6pm (summer), 9am-4pm (winter); Sat, Sun & public holidays 9am-6pm.

Post Offices – Mon-Fri 8am-12pm & 2pm-6pm; city post offices don't close for lunch; in some towns open Sat 9am-12pm.

Shops – Mon-Fri 8am-6pm; some open until 7.30pm Thu; some close 12pm-2pm for lunch; Sat 8am-5pm; some open Sun and public holidays.

Safety and Security

Most visits to Austria are trouble-free, but visitors should take sensible precautions to avoid becoming a victim of crime at crowded tourist sites and around major railway stations and city centre parks after dark. Pickpockets and muggers operate in and around the city centre of Vienna.

Drivers, especially on the autobahns in Lower Austria, should be wary of bogus plain clothes police officers. In all traffic-related matters police officers will be in uniform and unmarked vehicles will have a flashing sign in the rear window which reads 'Stopp –Polizei – Folgen'. If in any doubt contact the police on the emergency number 133 or 112 and ask for confirmation. The winter sports season lasts from December to March, or the end of May in higher regions. If you plan to ski contact the Austrian National Tourist Office in London for advice on conditions before travelling, and take local advice throughout your stay.

In most areas children under the age of 15 are legally required to wear a helmet when skiing while in some areas the age is raised to 16.

British Embassy
JAURESGASSE 12
1030 VIENNA
Tel: (01) 716130
www.ukinaustria.fco.gov.uk/en/
viennaconsularenquiries@fco.gov.uk

Irish Embassy
ROTENTURMSTRASSE 16-18, 5th FLOOR
1010 VIENNA
Tel: (01) 7154246
www.embassyofireland.at
vienna@dfa.ie

Documents

Driving Licence
If you hold a UK driving licence which does not bear your photograph you should carry your passport as further proof of identity, or obtain a photocard licence.
Passport
You are advised to carry your passport or photocard licence at all times.
Vehicle(s)
You should carry your vehicle registration certificate (V5C), insurance details and MOT certificate.

Money

Cash dispensers (Bankomaten) have instructions in English. Major credit cards are widely accepted in large cities although a number of small hotels, shops and restaurants may refuse. Visa and Mastercard are more readily accepted than American Express and Diner's Club.

Motoring in Austria
Alcohol

The maximum permitted level of alcohol in the bloodstream is 0.049%, i.e. lower than that permitted in the UK. Penalties for exceeding this limit are severe. A lower limit of virtually zero (0.01%) applies to drivers who have held a full driving licence for less than two years.

Breakdown Service

The motoring organisation, ÖAMTC, operates a breakdown service 24 hours a day on all roads. The emergency number is 120 throughout the country from a land line or mobile phone. Motorists pay a set fee, which is higher at night; towing charges also apply. Payment by credit card is accepted.

Members of AIT and FIA affiliated clubs, such as The Caravan Club, qualify for reduced charges on presentation of a valid Club membership card.

Prohibited Equipment

Dashboard cameras are not allowed in Austria.

Essential Equipment

First aid kit
All vehicles must carry a first aid kit kept in a strong, dirt-proof box.

Warning Triangle
An EU approved warning triangle must be used if the vehicle breaks down, has a puncture or is involved in an accident.

Lights
Dipped headlights must be used in poor visibility or bad weather. Headlight flashing is used as a warning of approach, not as an indication that a driver is giving way.

Reflective Jackets/Waistcoats
If your vehicle breaks down or you are in an accident you must wear a reflective jacket or waistcoat when getting out of your vehicle (compliant with EU Standard EN471). This includes when setting up a warning triangle. It is also recommended that a passenger who leaves the vehicle, for example, to assist with a repair, should also wear one. Keep the jackets within easy reach inside your vehicle, not in the boot.

Child Restraint System
Children under 14 years of age and less than 1.5 metres in height must use a suitable child restraint system for their height and weight when travelling in the front and rear of a vehicle. Children under 14 years aren't allowed to travel in two seater sports cars.

Children under 14 years of age but over 1.35 metres are allowed to use a 3-point seat belt without a special child seat, as long as the seat belt does not cut across the child's throat or neck.

Winter Driving
From 1 November to 15 April vehicles, including those registered abroad, must be fitted with winter tyres marked M&S (mud & snow) on all wheels when there is snow or ice on the road. Snow chains are allowed on roads fully covered by snow or ice, as long as road surfaces will not be damaged by the chains. The maximum recommended speed for vehicles with snow chains is generally 50 km/h.

Between 15 November to 15 March vehicles weighing over 3500kg are required to have winter tyres on at least one of the driving axles, regardless of the road conditions. They must also carry snow chains, and use them where road signs indicate that they are compulsory.

It is the driver's legal responsibility to carry the required winter equipment; therefore, it is essential to check that it is included in any hire car.

Fuel

Most petrol stations are open from 8am to 8pm. Motorway service stations and some petrol stations in larger cities stay open 24 hours. Fuel is normally cheaper at self-service filling stations.

LPG (flüssiggas) is available at a limited number of outlets – a list should be available on www.oeamtc.at.

Parking

Regulations on the parking of motorhomes and caravans vary according to region, but restrictions apply in areas protected for their natural beauty or landscape and beside lakes. If in doubt, ask the local municipality. You cannot leave a caravan without its towing vehicle in a public place.

A zigzag line marked on the road indicates that parking is prohibited. Blue lines indicate a blue zone (Kurzparkzone) where parking is restricted to a period for up to two hours and you need to purchase a voucher (Parkschein) from a local shop, bank or petrol station.

Most cities have 'Pay and Display' machines, parking meters or parking discs, and in main tourist areas the instructions are in English. Illegally-parked cars may be impounded or clamped. Large areas of Vienna are pedestrianised and parking places are limited. However, there are several underground car parks in Vienna District 1.

AUSTRIA

Priority

Outside built-up areas, road signs on main roads indicate where traffic has priority or if there are no signs priority is given to traffic from the right.

Buses have priority when leaving a bus stop. Do not overtake school buses with flashing yellow lights which have stopped to let children on and off. Trams have priority even if coming from the left.

In heavy traffic, drivers must not enter an intersection unless their exit is clear, even if they have priority or if the lights are green.

Roads

Austria has a well developed and engineered network of roads classified as: federal motorways (A roads), expressways (S' roads), provincial (B roads) and local (L roads). There are over 2180km of motorways and expressways.

Road Signs and Markings

Most signs conform to international usage. The following are exceptions:

Diversions

Street lights not on all night

Tram turns at yellow or red

You may be stopped and fined in Austria for using roads that prohibit trailers and caravans. This is indicated by the below sign:

If there is an additional sign which shows a weight limit, then this indicates the maximum gross vehicle weight of the trailer. You can also find these signs with a length limit.

Some other signs that are also in use which you may find useful Include:

Austrian	English Translation
Abblendlicht	Dipped headlights
Alle richtungen	All directions
Bauarbeiten	Roadworks
Durchfahrt verboten	No through traffic
Einbahn	One-way street
Fussgänger	Pedestrians
Beschrankung für halten oder parken	Stopping or parking restricted
Lawinen gefahr	Avalanche danger
Links einbiegen	Turn left
Raststätte	Service area
Raststätte Rechts einbiegen	Turn right
Strasse gesperrt	Road closed
Überholen verboten	No passing
Umleitung	Detour

Speed Limits

	Open Road (km/h)	Motorway (km/h)
Car Solo	100	130
Car towing caravan/trailer	80	100
Motorhome under 3500kg	100	130
Motorhome 3500-7500kg	70	80

Exceptions

If the total combined weight of a car and caravan outfit or a motorhome exceeds 3,500 kg the speed limit on motorways is reduced to 80 km/h (50 mph) and on other roads outside built-up areas to 70 km/h (43 mph).

On motorways where the speed limit for solo vehicles is 130 km/h (81 mph) overhead message signs may restrict speed to 100 km/h (62 mph). Between 10pm and 5am solo cars are restricted to 110 km/h (68 mph) on the A10 (Tauern), A12 (Inntal), A13 (Brenner) and A14

(Rheintal). There is a general speed limit of 60 km/h (37 mph) on most roads in the Tyrol, unless indicated otherwise. There is a speed limit of 50km/h in build up areas unless otherwise indicated by road signs. A built-up area starts from the road sign indicating that place name as you enter a town or village.

Some sections of the A12 and A13 are limited to 100km/h, day and night.

The minimum speed on motorways, as indicated by a rectangular blue sign depicting a white car, is 60 km/h (37 mph). A number of towns have a general speed limit of 30 km/h (18 mph), except where a higher speed limit is indicated.

Traffic Lights

At traffic lights a flashing green light indicates the approach of the end of the green phase. An orange light combined with the red light indicates that the green phase is imminent.

Traffic Jams

In recent years traffic has increased on the A1 from Vienna to the German border (the West Autobahn). There are usually queues at the border posts with Czech Republic, Slovakia and Hungary. As a result, traffic has also increased on the ring road around Vienna and on the A4 (Ost Autobahn).

Other bottlenecks occur on the A10 (Salzburg to Villach) before the Tauern and Katschberg tunnels, the A12 (Kufstein to Landeck) before the Perjen tunnel and before Landeck, and the A13 (Innsbruck to Brenner) between Steinach and the Italian border. Busy sections on other roads are the S35/S6 between Kirchdorf or Bruck an der Mur and the A9, the B320/E651 in the Schladming and Gröbming areas, and the B179 Fern Pass.

Violation of Traffic Regulations

Police can impose and collect on-the-spot fines of up to €90 from drivers who violate traffic regulations. For higher fines you will be required to pay a deposit and the remainder within two weeks. An official receipt should be issued. A points system operates which applies to drivers of Austrian and foreign-registered vehicles.

Motorways

Orange emergency telephones on motorways are 2 km to 3 km apart. A flashing orange light at the top of telephone posts indicates danger ahead.

Whenever congestion occurs on motorways and dual carriageways drivers are required to create an emergency corridor. Drivers in the left-hand lane must move as far over to the left as possible, and drivers in the central and right-hand lanes must move as far over to the right as possible to provide access for emergency vehicles.

Motorway Tolls – Vehicles under 3,500 kg
Drivers of vehicles under 3,500 kg using motorways and expressways (A and S roads) must purchase a motorway vignette (sticker). One vignette covers your caravan as well. Vignettes may be purchased at all major border crossings into Austria and from OeAMTC offices, larger petrol stations and post offices in Austria. A two-month vignette is available for a car (with or without a trailer) or a motorhome at a cost of €25.30. Also available are a 10 day vignette at €8.70 and a one year vignette at €84.40 (2015 tariffs).

Failure to display a vignette incurs a fine of at least €120, plus the cost of the vignette. Credit cards or foreign currency may be used in payment. If you have visited Austria before, make sure you remove your old sticker.

There are special toll sections in Austria which are excluded from the vignette and where the toll needs to be paid at respective toll points. These include A10 Tauern tunnel, A13 Brenner motorway and S16 Alberg tunnel.

Motorway Tolls – Vehicles over 3,500 kg
Tolls for vehicles over 3,500 kg are calculated according to the number of axles and EURO emissions category and are collected electronically by means of a small box (called the GO-Box) fixed to your vehicle's windscreen. They are available for a one-off handling fee of €5 from around 220 points of sale – mainly petrol stations – along the primary road network in Austria and neighbouring countries, and at all major border crossing points.

You can pre-load a set amount onto your Go box or pay after you have travelled. Tolls are calculated according to the number of axles on a vehicle; those with two axles are charged between €0.156 and €0.211 per kilometre +

20% VAT, according to the vehicle's emissions rating. Visit www.go-maut.at to register for the scheme. Telephone 0043 19551266 or email info@go-maut.at for help before you travel. Operators speak English.

This distance-related toll system does not apply to a car/caravan combination even if its total laden weight is over 3,500 kg, unless the laden weight of the towing vehicle itself exceeds that weight.

Korridor Vignette

A special vignette, the 'Korridor Vignette' is required on the A14 in the region of Bregenz. Vehicles up to 3,500 kg without a standard motorway vignette need this special vignette to drive along the 23 km stretch (corridor) between Hohenems (junction 23 on the A14) and Hörbranz (junction 1) at the German border. The vignette is available from petrol stations in the area and at the border and costs €2 for a single journey, €4 return. In addition, separate tolls are payable on many roads and tunnels in mountainous regions.

Touring

Austria is divided into nine federal regions, namely Burgenland, Carinthia (Kärnten), Lower Austria (Niederösterreich), Salzburg, Styria (Steiermark), Tyrol (Tirol), Upper Austria (Oberösterreich), Vienna (Wien) and Voralberg.

A 10-15% service charge is included in restaurant bills, but it is customary to add a further 5% tip if satisfied with the service.

The Vienna Card offers unlimited free public transport and discounts at museums, restaurants, theatres and shops. The Card is valid for three days and is available from hotels, tourist information and public transport offices; see www.wienkarte.at.

A Salzburg Card and an Innsbruck Card are also available – see www.austria.info/uk or contact the Austrian National Tourist Office for more information.

Public Transport & Local Travel

All major cities have efficient, integrated public transport systems including underground and light rail systems, trams and buses. Two to five people travelling as a group by train can buy an Einfach-Raus-Ticket (ERT), which is good for a day's unlimited travel on all Austrian regional trains – see www.oebb.at (English option) for more information or ask at any station.

In Vienna there are travel concessions on public transport for senior citizens (show your passport as proof of age). Buy a ticket from a tobacconist or from a ticket machine in an underground station. Otherwise single tickets are available from vending machines in the vehicles themselves – have plenty of coins ready. Tickets are also available for periods of 24 and 72 hours. Children under six travel free and children under 15 travel free on Sundays, public holidays and during school holidays.

Car ferry services operate throughout the year on the River Danube, and hydrofoil and hovercraft services transport passengers from Vienna to Bratislava (Slovakia) and to Budapest (Hungary).

ABERSEE *B3* (3km N Rural) *47.74040, 13.40665* **Seecamping Primus, Schwand 39, 5342 Abersee [06227 3228; fax 32284; seecamping.primus@aon.at]** B158 fr St Gilgen to Strobl. After 3 km turn L. Camp is last but one. Med, mkd pitch, pt shd; wc; chem disp; baby facs; shwrs inc; EHU (10A); lndry (inc dryer); shops 300m; playgrnd; beach; sw; games area; wifi; bus 1km; twin axles; Eng spkn; quiet; CCI. "Very helpful owner; beautiful area nr shipping on lake; excel." 26 Apr-30 Sep. € 30.00   2014*

ABERSEE *B3* (3km SE Rural) *47.71336, 13.45138* **Camping Schönblick, Gschwendt 33, 5342 Abersee [(06137) 7042; fax 704214; laimer.schoenblick@aon.at; www.camping-schoenblick.at]** Fr B158 at km 36 dir Schiffstation & site in 1km on L. Med, mkd pitch, pt sl, terr, some hdstg, pt shd; wc; chem disp; shwrs €0.80; EHU (10A) €1.80; gas; lndry; shop & 1km; rest, snacks 300m; lake sw adj; 40% statics; dogs €2; quiet; ccard acc; CKE/CCI. "Beautiful, friendly, family-run site nr lakeside opp St Wolfgang town; ferry stn; excel san facs but stretched at busy times; walks & cycle path fr site; vg site." 1 May-15 Oct. € 29.00   2014*

ABERSEE *B3* (1.5km NW Rural) *47.73656, 13.43250* **Camping Wolfgangblick, Seestrasse 115, 5342 Abersee [(06227) 3475; fax 3218; camping@wolfgangblick.at; www.wolfgangblick.at]** Fr B158 fr St Gilgen, on ent Abersee turn L at km 34 twds lake. Site in 1km foll sp to site. Med, mkd pitch; hdstg, pt shd; wc; chem disp; shwrs €0.70; EHU (12A) metered; lndry; shop; rest, snacks; bar; playgrnd; lake beach adj; 50% statics; dogs €2.90; poss cr; Eng spkn; quiet; ccard acc. "Pleasant site; gd, friendly family run site by lake; helpful owners; beautiful scenery; excel for walking & cycling; on bus rte to Salzburg and local vills; poss cr, adv bkg advised." 1 May-30 Sep. € 20.00   2012*

ABERSEE *B3* (2.5km NW Rural) *47.73910, 13.40065* **Camping Wolfgangsee Birkenstrand, Schwand 4, 5342 Abersee [tel/fax (06227) 3029; camp@birkenstrand.at; www.birkenstrand.at]** Fr B158 fr St Gilgen, on ent Abersee turn L at km 32 twds lake. Site on both sides of rd in 1km. Med, mkd pitch, pt sl, unshd; wc; chem disp; shwrs €0.70; EHU (10A) metered; lndry (inc dryer); shop 100m; rest, bar 100m, snacks; BBQ; playgrnd; lake sw adj; boat & bike hire; golf 15km; entmnt; TV rm; 20% statics; dogs €3.40; Eng spkn; adv bkg; quiet. "Excel area for walking, cycling; lovely situation; immac site; ACSI card acc." 1 Apr-31 Oct. € 26.60   2013*

ABERSEE *B3* (3km NW Rural) *47.73945, 13.40245* **Romantik Camping Wolfgangsee Lindenstrand, Schwand 19, 5342 St Gilgen [(06227) 32050; fax 320524; camping@lindenstrand.at; www.lindenstrand.at]** Fr St Gilgen take B158 dir Bad Ischl. In 4km at km 32 foll sp Schwand, site on L on lakeside. Lge, mkd pitch, hdstg, pt shd; htd wc; chem disp; serviced pitches; shwrs inc; EHU (10A) metered; shop; rest 1km; playgrnd; lake adj; watersports; 10% statics; dogs €3.20; phone; bus & boat to local towns & Salzburg; Eng spkn; adv bkg; quiet; ccard acc; red LS; CKE/CCI. "Lovely site; rec adv bkg for lakeside pitches; elec conn by staff; poss req long leads; continental plugs high ssn." 1 Apr-31 Oct. € 25.00   2014*

AFRITZ AM SEE *D3* (2km NW Rural) *46.73701, 13.76874* **Camping Bodner, Seestrasse 27, 9542 Afritz-am-Zee (Kärnten) [(04247) 2579; fax 29990; office@camping-bodner.at; www.camping-bodner.at]** Fr Villach, take B94 twd Feldkirchen, turn L after 4km onto B98 sp Radenthein. N of Afritz, after Gassen, turn L, site sp. Med, some hdstg, pt sl, pt shd; wc; chem disp; mv service pnt; shwrs €1; EHU (4-6A) inc; gas; lndry; shop 1.5km; rest, snacks; bar; BBQ; playgrnd; lake sw adj; sailing; dogs €1.50; quiet. "Family-run site; gd walking country - both mountains & flat." 1 May-30 Sep. € 20.00   2010*

ALTAUSSEE *C3* (2km SE Rural) *47.62843, 13.77380* **Bauernhofcamping Temel, Puchen 39, 8992 Altaussee [(03622) 71968]** N fr Bad Aussee dir Altausseer See, site sp. Sm, hdstg, pt sl, unshd; wc; chem disp; mv service pnt; shwrs €0.50; EHU €2; shop 1.5km; rest 800m; lake sw 800m; dogs €1; quiet. "Well-kept, peaceful site amidst beautiful scenery; friendly owner; idyllic." 1 May-30 Sep. € 13.60   2009*

⊞ **ALTENMARKT IM PONGAU** *C3* (1km S Rural) *47.37145, 13.41915* **Camping Passrucker, Zauchenseestrasse 341, 5541 Altenmarkt [(06452) 7328; fax 7821; camping.passrucker@sbg.at; www.camping-passrucker.at]** Exit A10 junc 63 onto B99 to Altenmarkt. In town cent turn R & foll site sp. Med, pt shd; htd wc; chem disp; mv service pnt; baby facs; sauna; solarium; shwrs inc; EHU (13A) metered; lndry; shop high ssn; playgrnd; sm pool; fitness rm; skibus; TV rm; 50% statics (sep area); dogs €1.50; Eng spkn; adv bkg; quiet; red long stay; CKE/CCI. "Pretty town in lovely area; gd walking; higher prices in winter; excel san facs; friendly owner." ♦ € 21.00   2010*

ASCHACH AN DER DONAU *B3* (16km N Rural) *48.42026, 13.98400* **Camping Kaiserhof, Kaiserau 1, 4082 Aschach-an-der-Donau [(07273) 62210; fax 622113; kaiserhof@aschach.at; www.pension-kaiserhof.at]** Fr town cent foll site sp. Site adj rv & Gasthof Kaiserhof. Sm, pt shd; htd wc; chem disp; mv service pnt; shwrs; EHU; lndry; shop 6km; rest, snacks; bar; playgrnd; 80% statics; poss cr; Eng spkn; ccard acc; red long stay/CKE/CCI. "Beautiful location on Danube." ♦ 15 Apr-30 Sep. € 19.00   2010*

ATTERSEE *B3* (16km S Rural) *47.80100, 13.48266* **Inselcamping, Unterburgau 37, 4866 Unterach-am-Attersee [(07665) 8311; fax 7255; camping@inselcamp.at; www.inselcamp.at]** Leave A1 at junc 243 St Georgen/Attersee, foll B151 to Unterach fr Attersee vill. Site sp on app to Unterach. Med, pt shd; wc; chem disp; mv service pnt; shwrs €1; EHU (6A) €2; gas; shop; supmkt nr; snacks; lake sw; shgl beach; 25% statics; dogs €2; clsd 1200-1400; poss v cr; Eng spkn; adv bkg; quiet; CKE/CCI. "Excel site; helpful owner; 5 min walk to attractive town; conv Salzburg & Salzkammergut; lots to see locally; gd boat trips; extra for lakeside pitches - some with boat mooring." 1 May-15 Sep. € 21.00   2013*

AUSTRIA

ATTERSEE *B3* (700m S Rural) *47.91420, 13.52925*
Camping Wimroither Mühle, Mühlbach 5, 4864 Attersee
[tel/fax (07666) 7749] Exit A/E60/E551 junc 243 twd Attersee.
In 2km at town sp turn R to site down unclass rd in 200m.
Narr lane. Med, pt sl, pt shd; wc; chem disp; shwrs €1; EHU
(16A) €3; lndry; sm shop & 300m; rest 300m; snacks; lake
sw 250m; 60% statics; dogs; poss cr; adv bkg; quiet. "Conv
Salzkammergut & Dachstein with lovely scenery."
1 Apr-31 Oct. € 16.00   2013*

⊞ **AU** *C1* (1km SE Rural) *47.31604, 9.99881* **Camping Köb,
Neudorf 356, 6883 Au-im-Bregenzerwald [(05515) 2331;
fax 23314; info@campingaustria.at; www.axtres.net/
campingaustria]** Fr W on B200 fr Dornbirn sp Bregenzerwald,
take 2nd turn R after tunnel at end of Au. Site immed on L.
NB B200 not open to c'vans Au to Warth. Sm, pt shd; htd wc;
chem disp; mv service pnt; shwrs €0.70; EHU (6A) metered;
lndry; shop 100m; rest, bar 300m; pool 200m; internet;
10% statics; no dogs; phone adj; bus 100m; poss cr; adv bkg;
quiet; CKE/CCI. "Mountain scenery; excel, secluded, well-run,
family site; helpful owner." € 22.00   2009*

BAD AUSSEE *C3* (11km E Rural) *47.63783, 13.90365*
**Campingplatz Gössl, Gössl 201, 8993 Grundlsee
[(03622) 81810; fax 81814; office@campinggoessl.com;
www.campinggoessl.com]** Fr B145 foll sp to Grundlsee, then
along lake to Gössl at far end. Ent adj gasthof off mini-rndbt,
site on L. Med; wc; shwrs inc; EHU (10A) metered + conn fee;
lndry; shop adj; shop, rest, snacks, bar 500m; playgrnd adj;
sand beach & lake sw adj; fishing; boating (no motor boats);
dogs €1; bus; adv bkg; quiet. "Excel walking cent; scenery v
beautiful; local gasthofs vg; daily bus & ferry services; v clean
facs." ♦ 1 May-31 Oct. € 27.50   2014*

⊞ **BAD GASTEIN** *C2* (6km N Rural) *47.13421, 13.13137*
**Kur-Camping Erlengrund, Erlengrundstrasse 6, 5640 Bad
Gastein [(06434) 30205; fax 30208; office@kurcamping-
gastein.at; www.kurcamping-gastein.at]** Exit A10/E55 at
junc 46 onto B311 thro St Johann to Lend, then S on B167
thro Bad Hofgastein. On N o'skts of Bad Gastein turn L 300m
after BP g'ge to avoid narr town rds. Lge, mkd pitch, some
hdstg, pt shd; htd wc; chem disp; mv service pnt; serviced
pitches; baby facs; shwrs; EHU (16A) metered; mains gas conn
to some pitches; lndry (inc dryer); shop; rest adj; playgrnd; htd
pool; tennis; golf; fishing; ski bus; ski lift 4km; wifi; cab TV;
30% statics; dogs €2.50; adv bkg; quiet; ccard acc; red CKE/
CCI. "Excel ski area with over 50 ski lifts & 9 x-country trails."
€ 25.50   2011*

⊞ **BAD GLEICHENBERG** *C4* (3km E Rural) *46.87470,
15.93360* **Camping Feriendorf in Thermenland, Haus Nr
240, 8344 Bairisch-Kölldorf [(03159) 3941; fax 288411;
camping.bk@aon.at; www.bairisch-koelldorf.at]**
Exit A2 at Gleisdorf Süd onto B68 dir Feldbach. Take B66 dir
Bad Gleichenberg & at 2nd rndabt turn L, site sp. Med, unshd;
htd wc; chem disp; mv service pnt; baby facs; shwrs; EHU
(16A) metered; gas; lndry (inc dryer); rest, snacks; bar; BBQ;
playgrnd; covrd pool; lake sw; tennis 600m; bike hire; games
area; golf 3km; 10% statics; dogs €0.70; adv bkg; quiet. ♦
€ 20.00   2009*

BLUDENZ *C1* (2km N Rural) *47.16990, 9.80788*
**Terrassencamping Sonnenberg, Hinteroferstrasse 12,
6714 Nüziders [(05552) 64035; fax 33900; sonnencamp@
aon.at; www.camping-sonnenberg.com]** Exit A14/E60 junc
57 onto B190 N, foll sp Nüziders & foll site sp thro Nüziders
vill. Med, mkd pitch, hdstg, terr, pt shd; htd wc; chem disp;
mv service pnt; shwrs inc; EHU inc (5-13A) inc; lndry (inc dryer);
shop 500m; rest, snacks 300m; bar; playgrnd; wifi; entmnt;
TV rm; dogs €3.50; phone; sep car park; poss cr; Eng spkn; adv
bkg; quiet; ccard not acc; red LS/long stay. "Friendly, v helpful
owners; superb facs; beautiful scenery - extra for Panorama
pitches at top of site; excel mountain views; excel walking; lifts
to mountains; ltd opening hrs for recep - use phone at bldg on
L at main ent; no arr after 2200 hrs but sep o'night area; rec
bk in adv in high ssn; gd for m'vans; highly rec; excel site; gd
value." 27 Apr-6 Oct. € 37.00   2013*

⊞ **BLUDENZ** *C1* (12km E Rural) *47.14110, 9.92716* **Walch's
Camping & Landhaus, Arlbergstrasse 101, 6751 Innerbraz
[(05552) 281020; info@landhauswalch.at; www.landhaus
walch.at]** Fr A14/S16 E fr Feldkirch dir Arlberg, exit Braz. Site
further 2km on L, sp. Med, unshd; wc; chem disp; mv service
pnt; baby facs; sauna/solarium; shwrs inc; EHU (16A) metered +
conn fee; lndry (inc dryer); shop, rest; bar; playgrnd; pool 1km;
games rm; wifi; dogs €3.50; bus nr; site clsd Nov; Eng spkn;
adv bkg; quiet; CKE/CCI. "Mountain activities & golf avail nrby;
vg site; excel facs." ♦ € 25.00   2010*

Experience magic moments.

Those who like camping in the open air are in the right place here, as well as those who are looking for the comfort of a 4-star hotel!

At Woferlgut in Austria you
will find an own little world
with well-kept facilities and a
big swimming lake amidst the
splendid nature of the national
park Hohe Tauern.

A-5671 Bruck/Großglockner, Krössenbach 40
Tel.: +43(0)6545 7303-0, Fax: +43(0)6545 7303-3
Mail: info@sportcamp.at, www.sportcamp.at

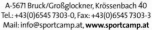

⊞ **BLUDENZ** *C1* (10km ESE Rural) *47.14628, 9.90236*
**Camping Gasthof Traube, Klostertalerstrasse 12, 6751
Braz [(05552) 28103; fax 2810340; office@traubebraz.at;
www.traubebraz.at]** Site behind Gasthof Traube in middle
of Braz vill, which is sp off dual c'way S16. Med, some hdstg,
sl, pt shd; htd wc; chem disp; baby facs; sauna; shwrs inc;
EHU (6A) inc (rev pol); lndry (inc dryer); shop 1km; rest, snacks
in gasthof; playgrnd; 2 htd pools (1 covrd); paddling pool;
tennis; solarium; ski lift 6km; skibus; golf 1.5km; wifi; entmnt;
40% statics; no dogs; poss v cr; quiet but some rlwy noise;
ccard acc; red CKE/CCI. "Clean & tidy, family-run site; poss
muddy pitches; conv Liechtenstein." € 25.60   2010*

⊞ **BLUDENZ** *C1* (3km S Rural) *47.14651, 9.81630* **Auhof
Camping, Aulandweg 5, 6706 Bürs [(05552) 67044; fax
31926; auhof.buers@aon.at; www.buers.at]** Exit A14/E60
junc 59 dir Bludenz/Bürs, then Brand. Site sp in 300m at Zimba
Park shopping cent on edge of sm indus est. Med, unshd; htd
wc; shwrs inc; EHU (4A); gas; lndry; shop & 300m; rest, snacks
300m; some rd noise. "Friendly, tidy, clean site on working
farm; conv Arlberg Tunnel, Liechtenstein & mountain resorts;
muddy in wet; conv NH for m'way." € 19.50   2011*

⊞ **BLUDENZ** *C1* (5km SW Rural) *47.14268, 9.77875* **Heidi's
Camping, Boden 7, 6707 Bürserberg [(05552) 65307;
fax 053074; info@burtschahof.at; www.burtschahof.at]**
Exit A14 at junc 59 twd Bürs/Brand. Site in 4km on
L - 10% climb with bends. Sm, mkd pitch, some hdstg, terr,
pt shd; htd wc; chem disp; baby facs; fam bthrm; shwrs inc;
EHU (16A) €1.50; lndry (inc dryer); shop, rest, bar 200m; BBQ;
playgrnd; pool; 25% statics; dogs; bus 200m; phone; poss
cr; adv bkg; quiet. "CL-type site in lovely situation - worth
the climb; sm/med o'fits only - manhandling poss req."
€ 23.50   2010*

BRAZ see Bludenz *C1*

BREITENWANG see Reutte *C1*

BRIXEN IM THALE see Kitzbühel *C2*

⊞ **BRUCK AN DER GROSSGLOCKNERSTRASSE** *C2*
(900m SW Urban) *47.28386, 12.81736* **Sportcamp
Woferlgut, Krössenbach 40, 5671 Bruck-an-der-
Grossglocknerstrasse [(06545) 73030; fax 73033; info@
sportcamp.at; www.sportcamp.at]** Exit A10 junc 47 dir
Bischofshofen, B311 dir Zell-am-See. Take 2nd exit to Bruck,
site sp fr by-pass, & foll sps thro town to site. Lge, pt shd; wc;
chem disp; mv service pnt; serviced pitches; baby facs; sauna;
shwrs inc; EHU (10-16A) €2.80 metered + conn fee; lndry;
rest; snacks; bar; farm produce; playgrnd; htd pool; lake sw
adj; tennis; indoor play area; games rm; gym & fitness cent;
ski cent; wifi; entmnt; TV; many statics; dogs €4.50; phone;
bus to Zell-am-Zee & glacier; poss cr; Eng spkn; adv bkg;
some rd & rlwy noise; red long stay; ccard acc. "Extended
facs area with R numbered pitches preferable; excel site
for sh or long stay; big pitches; excel mntn walking, local
horse riding; helpful recep; tour ops tents & statics; excel
for young/teenage families; vg san facs; warm welcome;
sm supmkt nrby & plenty of rests & cafes; excel." ♦ € 35.00
SBS - G06   2012*

See advertisement opposite

BRUCK AN DER MUR *C4* (4km W Urban) *47.40311, 15.22755*
**Camping Raddörf'l, Bruckerstrasse 110, 8600 Oberaich
[(03862) 51418; fax 59940; info@gasthofpichler.at;
www.gasthofpichler.at]** Fr S6 take Oberaich exit 4km W of
Bruck, Foll site sp (in opp dir to vill of Oberaich), go under rlwy
bdge, turn L at T-junc. Site is 300m on L at Gasthof Pichler, ent
thro car park. Sm, pt shd; wc; shwrs inc; EHU (10A) inc; lndry;
shop 3km; rest, snacks; bar; playgrnd; dogs €2; poss cr; some rlwy
noise; CKE/CCI. "Gd NH; site (10 o'fits max) in orchard at rear of
Gasthof; gd rest; cramped." 1 May-1 Oct. € 21.00   2015*

⊞ **DELLACH IM DRAUTAL** *D2* (1km S Rural) *46.73085,
13.07846* **Camping Waldbad, 9772 Dellach-im-Drautal
(Kärnten) [(04714) 234-18 or (04714) 288; info@camping-
waldbad.at; www.camping-waldbad.at]** Clearly sp on B100
& in vill of Dellach on S side or Rv Drau. Med, hdg/mkd pitch,
pt shd; wc; chem disp; mv service pnt; baby facs; shwrs inc;
EHU (6A) inc; gas; lndry; shop; rest, snacks; bar; playgrnd; htd
pool complex adj inc paddling pool, waterslide etc; games area;
games rm; entmnt; internet; 5% statics; dogs €2.50; poss cr;
adv bkg; quiet; ccard acc. "Peaceful, wooded site; vg leisure
facs adj." ♦ 1 May-30 Sep. € 37.50   2013*

⊞ **DOBRIACH** *D3* (2km S Rural) *46.77020, 13.64788*
**Komfort Campingpark Burgstaller, Seefeldstrasse 16,
A-9873 Döbriach (Kärnten) [04246 7774; fax 7774426;
info@burgstaller.co.at; www.burgstaller.co.at]**
Fr on A10/E55/E66 take exit Millstätter See. Turn L at traff lts
on B98 dir Radenthein. Thro Millstatt & Dellach, turn R into
Döbriach, sp Camping See site on L by lake after Döbriach.
V lge, hdg/mkd pitch, pt shd; wc; chem disp; mv service pnt;
baby facs; sauna; private san facs avail; shwrs inc; EHU (6-10A)
inc; gas; lndry; shop; rest, snacks; bar adj; playgrnd; htd pool;
lake sw; boating; solarium; games area; horseriding; bike hire;
cinema; golf 8km; entmnt; internet; TV; 10% statics; dogs €4;
poss cr; Eng spkn; adv bkg; quiet; red snr citizens/LS; CKE/CCI.
"Organised walks & trips to Italy; excel rest; some pitches tight;
fantastic facs." ♦ € 35.00   2013*

⊞ **DOBRIACH** *D3* (2km SW Urban) *46.76811, 13.64809*
**Camping Brunner am See, Glanzerstrasse 108, 9873
Döbriach [(04246) 7189 or 7386; fax 718914; office@
camping-brunner.at; www.camping-brunner.at]**
Fr Salzburg on A10 a'bahn take Seeboden-Millstatt exit bef
Spittal. Foll rd 98 N of Millstattersee to camping sp. Med,
pt shd; wc; chem disp; mv service pnt; fam bthrm; baby facs;
shwrs inc; EHU (6A) inc; rest, snacks; bar; shop; pool 300m;
playgrnd; tennis; watersports; poss cr; dogs €4.50; adv bkg;
ccard acc; CKE/CCI. "Great site with excel, clean san facs;
gd size pitches; lakeside location; supmkt nrby & rests in
vicinity; superb scenery." ♦ € 55.00   2013*

⊞ **DORNBIRN** *C1* (2km SE Rural) *47.39931, 9.75645* **Camping
in der Enz, Gütlestrasse, 6850 Dornbirn [(05572) 29119;
camping@camping-enz.at; www.camping-enz.at]**
Exit A14/E60 for Dornbirn-Sud, foll dir Ebnit-Rappenlochschlucht
gorge for 1.2km, camp sp beyond cable car base. Med, pt shd;
wc; chem disp; shwrs inc; EHU (6A) €2.50; lndry; shop; rest,
snacks; playgrnd; lge pool 200m; cable car stn opp; adv bkg;
ccard acc; red CKE/CCI. "Nice site in attractive location; conv
Lake Constance, Bregenz, Lindau; sep o'night area."
1 Apr-30 Sep. € 17.00   2009*

DROBOLLACH see Villach *D3*

AUSTRIA

⊞ **EBEN IM PONGAU** *C3* (1.5km S Rural) *47.39932, 13.39566* **See-Camping Eben, Familie Schneider, Badeseestraße 54, 5531 Eben I Pg [06458 8231 or 0664 450 2000; fax 8231; info@seecamping-eben.at; www.seecamping-eben.at]** Head E on A10, take exit 60 - Eben. Turn L onto B99. R onto Badeseestr. Campsite 800m on the L. Med, pt shd; htd wc; mv service pnt; baby facs; shwrs inc; EHU (16A) inc; lndry (inc dryer); bar; lake adj; games area; wifi; dogs; train 800km; adv bkg; quiet. "Helpful owners; saunas; steam rm; direct access fr mountains; clean & well organise; gd site." € 25.00   2014*

EBERNDORF see Völkermarkt *D3*

⊞ **EHRWALD** *C1* (1.5km NE Rural) *47.41142, 10.92360* **Comfort Camping Dr Lauth, Zugspitzstrasse 34, 6632 Ehrwald-Eben [(05673) 2666; fax 26664; info@camping ehrwald.at; www.campingehrwald.at]** On ent Ehrwald, foll sps Tiroler Zugspitz Camping, turn R immed bef rlwy bdge (R turn nearest rlwy; do not go under rlwy bdge). Sp on R 1.5km fr Ehrwald, same rd as for Zugspitzbahn Camping. Fr Lermoos take 1st L after rlwy bdge. Med, pt sl, pt shd; htd wc; chem disp; baby facs; shwrs inc; EHU (4A) metered; gas; lndry (inc dryer); shop; rest, snacks; bar; BBQ; playgrnd; pool 4km; wifi; 50% statics; dogs €2.20; poss cr; Eng spkn; adv bkg; quiet; red long stay; CKE/CCI. "Excel san facs; mountain walks, skiing & cycling; conv Innsbruck & Fern Pass; v beautiful; vg bistro." € 26.00   2010*

⊞ **EHRWALD** *C1* (4km NE Rural) *47.42689, 10.94093* **Tiroler Zugspitz Camp, Obermoos 1, 6632 Ehrwald [(05673) 2309; fax 230951; camping@zugspitze-resort.at; www.zugspitze-resort.at]** Foll sp fr Ehrwald to Obernoos & Zugspitzbahn. Med, mkd pitch, pt terr, pt shd; wc; chem disp; mv service pnt; baby facs; sauna; shwrs inc; EHU (16A) metered; gas; lndry (inc dryer); shop; rest; playgrnd; 2 pools (1 htd, covrd); paddling pool; games rm; 60% statics; dogs €4; phone; Eng spkn; adv bkg; quiet; ccard acc; red CKE/CCI. "Excel site in beautiful location; some awkward, sm pitches; vg facs; adj cable car to summit Zugspitz." ◆ ltd. € 32.00   2010*

⊞ **EHRWALD** *C1* (3km W Rural) *47.40250, 10.88893* **Happy Camp Hofherr, Garmischerstrasse 21, 6631 Lermoos [(05673) 2980; fax 29805; info@camping-lermoos.com; www.camping-lermoos.com]** On ent Lermoos on B187 fr Ehrwald site located on R. Med, pt sl, pt shd; htd wc; chem disp; mv service pnt; shwrs inc; EHU (16A) metered; gas (metered); lndry (inc dryer); shops 200m; rest; playgrnd; htd pool 200m; tennis; ski lift 300m; wifi; cab TV; 40% statics; dogs; phone; site clsd 1 Nov-mid Dec; adv bkg; quiet; ccard acc. "Ideal for walks/cycling; v picturesque; adj park; ask for guest card for discount on ski lifts etc; excel san facs; superb rest (clsd Mon & Tue eve); family run site." € 28.00   2014*

⊞ **EISENSTADT** *B4* (14km E Rural) *47.84401, 16.68720* **Campingplatz Oggau, 7063 Oggau-am-Neusiedlersee (Burgenland) [(02685) 7271; fax 72714; office@camping oggau.at; www.campingoggau.at]** Fr N or S exit A2 at Neustadt Süd, S4 sp Eisenstadt. Foll sps Eisenstadt on S4/S31, exit at Eisenstadt Süd & foll sps to Rust & Oggau; site sp thro vill. Lge, hdg pitch, shd; wc; chem disp; mv service pnt; shwrs €0.80; EHU (16A) €2; gas; shop; rest, snacks; bar; playgrnd; pool adj; wifi; 60% statics; dogs; poss cr; adv bkg; ccard acc. ◆ 1 Apr-31 Oct. € 19.00   2009*

⊞ **EISENSTADT** *B4* (16km SE Rural) *47.80132, 16.69185* **Storchencamp Rust, Ruster Bucht, 7071 Rust-am-Neusiedlersee (Burgenland) [(02685) 595; fax 5952; office@gmeiner.co.at; www.gmeiner.co.at]** Fr Eisenstadt take rd to Rust & Mörbisch. In Rust foll sps to site & Zee; lakeside rd to ent. Lge, pt shd; wc; chem disp; shwrs inc; EHU (16A) €2.30; lndry; shop; rest, snacks; pool 200m; lake sw 500m; boating; 60% statics; dogs €2.90; poss cr; quiet. "Nr Hungarian border; attractive vill with nesting storks." ◆ 1 Apr-31 Oct. € 20.00   2012*

EMMERSDORF AN DER DONAU see Melk *B4*

ENGELHARTSZELL *B3* (950m NW Rural) *48.51238, 13.72428* **Camp Municipal an der Donau, Nibelungenstrasse 113, 4090 Engelhartszell [(0664) 8708787; tourismus@ engelhartszell.ooe.gv.at; www.engelhartszell.at]** Fr Passau (Germany) exit SE on B130 along Rv Danube. Site on L in approx 28km just bef Engelhartszell adj municipal pool complex. Sm, unshd; wc; chem disp; shwrs; EHU (6A) metered; lndry; snacks; bar; playgrnd; pool adj; 50% statics; bus nr; poss cr; quiet. "Excel, clean, friendly site on rvside; Danube cycleway passes site." ◆ 15 Apr-15 Oct. € 15.00   2009*

FAAK/FAAK AM SEE see Villach *D3*

FEICHTEN IM KAUNERTAL see Prutz *C1*

FELDKIRCH *C1* (3km N Urban) *47.25880, 9.58336* **Waldcamping Feldkirch, Stadionstrasse 9, 6803 Feldkirch [(05522) 76001-3190; waldcamping@feldkirch.at; www.waldcamping.at]** Exit A14 at Feldkirch Nord, strt over next 2 rndabts sp Nofels. Cont to foll sp Nofels/Gisingen, then site sp. Site adj open air pool & leisure cent. Med, mkd pitch, pt shd; htd wc; chem disp; shwrs inc; EHU (6A) €2.20; (poss rev pol); lndry rm; rest 800m; BBQ; playgrnd; htd pool adj, TV rm; 50% statics; dogs €2.75; bus 200m; poss cr; adv bkg; noise fr adj leisure cent; red CKE/CCI. "Vg." 1 Apr-31 Oct. € 22.00   2009*

⊞ **FERLACH** *D3* (500m SW Urban) *46.52166, 14.29222* **Messeparkplatz Schloss Ferlach, 9170 Ferlach (Kärnten) [(04227) 4920; office_schloss@ferlach.net; www.ferlach.at]** Fr B85 foll sp Ferlach, parking sp adj rv (top half of car park). Sm, hdstg, pt shd; own san rec; chem disp €1; mv service pnt (water) €1; shop, rest, snacks, bar 500m; quiet. "Free to stay but €4 parking charge; vg, conv NH for Loibl pass; c'vans & m'vans acc; pleasant town." € 4.00   2011*

FIEBERBRUNN see St Johann in Tirol *C2*

FRAUENKIRCHEN *B4* (8km S Rural) *47.79160, 16.91619* **Camping Zicksee, 7161 St Andrä-am-Zicksee (Burgenland) [tel/fax (02176) 2144; info@st.andrae-tourism.or.at; www.tiscover.com/st.andrae.zicksee]** Fr B51 site sp on lake 1.5km W of vill of St Andrä. Fr St Andrä foll sp Zicksee, fork R at junc after rlwy x-ing, site on L. Lge, mkd pitch, some hdstg, shd; htd wc; chem disp; mv service pnt; baby facs; shwrs €0.50; EHU (10A) €1.80 (long cable poss req); gas; lndry (inc dryer); shop; rest adj; snacks; playgrnd; lake sw; fishing; watersports; phone; no dogs; poss cr; quiet; CKE/CCI. "Excel facs; gd cycling & birdwatching E of lake; remote pt of Austria; height restriction on ent of 3.2m." ◆ 1 Apr-30 Sep. € 18.00   2011*

FRAUENKIRCHEN *B4* (9km W Urban) *47.85424, 16.82665*
**Strandcamping Podersdorf-am-See, Strandplatz 19, 7141
Podersdorf-am-See (Burgenland) [(02177) 2279;
fax 227916; strandcamping@podersdorfamsee.at;
www.podersdorfamsee.at]** Foll sp fr cent of Podersdorf on
shore Neusiedlersee. Lge, mkd pitch, hdstg, pt shd; wc; chem
disp; mv service pnt; shwrs €0.50; EHU (12A) inc; shop; lndry;
rest, snacks; playgrnd; lake sw adj; sand beach; windsurfing;
boating; internet; poss cr at w/end; 25% statics; dogs €4.90;
quiet; red CKE/CCI. "Nature reserves & birdwatching lakes to
S; many cycle paths in flat region; gd views fr site; bread baked
daily." ♦ ltd. 1 Apr-1 Nov. € 27.00   2009*

⊞ **FUGEN** *C2* (2km N Rural) *47.35949, 11.85223*
**Campingplatz Hell, Gageringerstrasse 1, 6263 Fügen/
Zillertal [(05288) 62203; fax 64615; info@zillertal-camping.
at; www.zillertal-camping.at]** On A12/E45/E60 exit junc
39 exit onto B169. Site well sp. Med, mkd pitch, some hdstg,
terr, pt shd; wc; chem disp; mv service pnt; sauna; fam bthrm;
shwrs inc; EHU (10A) metered (long lead poss req); gas; lndry
(inc dryer); shop; supmkt 500m; rest; snacks high ssn; bar;
playgrnd; htd pool; paddling pool; bike hire; games rm; golf
10km; wifi; entmnt; dogs €2.50 (not acc Jul/Aug); Eng spkn;
adv bkg; some rd noise daytime only; red 8+ days; CKE/CCI.
"Wonderful site; superb san facs; lge pitches; friendly, helpful
staff; excel." € 34.00   2011*

FURSTENFELD *C4* (2km NW Rural) *47.05631, 16.06255*
**Thermenland Camping, Campingweg 1, 8280 Fürstenfeld
[(03382) 54940; fax 51671; camping.fuerstenfeld@
chello.at; www.camping-fuerstenfeld.at]** Exit A2/E59 sp
Fürstenfeld onto B65. Site well sp fr town cent. Med, pt sl,
pt shd; wc; chem disp; shwrs inc; EHU (10A) €2.30 (poss long
lead req); lndry (inc dryer); shop 500m; rest 1.5km; snacks; bar;
pool; paddling pool; waterslide; rv fishing; golf 5km; entmnt;
25% statics; dogs €2; phone; quiet; rec CKE/CCI. "Pleasant
rvside site; ltd facs but clean; conv Hungarian border."
15 Apr-15 Oct. € 20.00   2010*

FUSCH AN DER GLOCKNERSTRASSE *C2* (80m S
Rural) *47.22452, 12.82658* **Camping Lampenhäusl,
Grossglocknerstrsse 15, 5672 Fusch-an-der-
Glocknerstrasse [(06546) 2150; fax 215302; gasthof@
lampenhaeusl.at; www.lampenhaeusl.at]** E of rd, on S
o'skts of Fusch. Sm, pt shd; wc; shwrs inc; EHU (16A) €3.80
or metered; lndry (inc dryer); shop & 100m; rest, snacks; bar;
playgrnd; htd pool 100m; TV rm; 50% statics; phone; bus; Eng
spkn; adv bkg; quiet; ccard acc; red long stay; CKE/CCI. "Vg,
clean facs but stretched if site full; vg site." 10 May-26 Oct.
€ 17.50   2010*

FUSCHL AM SEE *B3* (1km SW Rural) *47.79230, 13.29682*
**Camping Seeholz, Dorfsrtrasse 36, 5330 Fuschl-am-See
[tel/fax (06226) 8310; camping-fuschl@aon.at]**
Exit A1 at junc 274 onto B158 dir Hof & St Gilgen. Foll sp to
Fuschl & site. Med, shd; wc; chem disp; shwrs inc; EHU (8A)
inc (long lead poss req); gas; lndry; shop; rest, snacks; lake sw
& shgl beach adj; 25% statics; dogs; poss cr; adv bkg; some rd
noise. "Helpful staff; basic, gd san facs; beautiful lake."
1 Apr-31 Oct. € 23.00   2009*

GMUND (KARNTEN) *C3* (6km NW Rural) *46.94950,
13.50940* **Terrassencamping Maltatal, Malta 6, 9854
Malta [(04733) 234; fax 23416; info@maltacamp.at;
www.maltacamp.at]** Exit A10/E14 onto B99 to Gmünd.
Foll sp Malta & after 6km site sp, on R next to filling stn.
Lge, mkd pitch, terr, pt shd; htd wc; chem disp; mv service
pnt; 20% serviced pitches; sauna; shwrs inc; EHU (10A) inc;
lndry (inc dryer); sm supmkt; rest, snacks; pizzeria; bar; BBQ;
playgrnd; htd pool; paddling pool; canoeing; trout-fishing;
games area; games rm; tennis; guided walks; children's
mini-farm; wifi; 5% statics; dogs €2.90; phone; poss cr;
adv bkg; quiet; CKE/CCI. "Gmund & Spittal gd shopping
towns; Millstättersee 15km, Grossglocknerstrasse 1hr's drive;
magnificent area with rvs, waterfalls, forests & mountains; vg
rest; excel site." ♦ 1 Apr-31 Oct. € 30.00   2012*

GNESAU *D3* (1km W Rural) *46.77966, 13.95062* **Camping
Hobitsch, Sonnleiten 24, 9563 Gnesau (Kärnten)
[(04278) 368; fax 3684; office@camping-hobitsch.at;
www.camping-hobitsch.at]** Site sp on B95. Sm, pt shd; wc;
chem disp; shwrs inc; EHU €2.80; lndry; shop, rest 2km; snacks;
bar; playgrnd; pool; tennis; games area; dogs €1.50; Eng spkn;
quiet. "Beautiful setting in meadow; excel san facs; adj to cycle
path." 1 May-30 Sep. € 13.00   2010*

GRAN *C1* (6km W Rural) *47.50825, 10.49468*
**Panoramacamp Alpenwelt, Kienzerle 3, 6675 Tannheim
[(05675) 43070; fax 430777; alpenwelt@tirol.com;
www.tannheimertal-camping.com]** Fr N leave A7 junc 137
Oy-Mittelberg onto B310 to Oberjoch, then B199 to Tannheim.
Fr S on B198 dir Reutte, turn onto B199 at Weissenbach to
Tannheim. Med, mkd pitch, hdstg, terr, unshd; htd wc; chem
disp; some serviced pitches; baby facs; sauna; shwrs inc; EHU
(16A) metered; lndry; shop; rest; bar; playgrnd; pool 4km; lake
sw 4km; entmnt; internet; cab TV; 30% statics; dogs €3.50;
ski bus; ski lift 2km; adv bkg; quiet; CKE/CCI. "Excel site; gd
walking, cycling area." ♦ 20 Dec-19 Apr & 1 May-30 Oct.
€ 22.00   2010*

GRAZ *C4* (7km SW Urban) *47.02447, 15.39719* **Stadt-
Camping Central, Martinhofstrasse 3, 8054 Graz-
Strassgang [(0316) 697824 or 0676 3785102 (mob);
guenther_walter@utanet.at; www.tiscover.at/camping
central]** Fr A9/E57 exit Graz-Webling, then dir Strassgang onto
B70, site sp on R after Billa supmkt & filling stn. Med, mkd
pitch, some hdstg, pt shd; wc; chem disp;
mv service pnt; shwrs inc; EHU (6A) inc; gas; lndry (inc dryer);
supmkt 200m; rest, snacks adj; bar; BBQ; playgrnd; pool,
paddling pool adj; tennis; 80% statics; dogs free; bus to city;
poss v cr; quiet; wifi. "Pleasant, conv site; reg bus service fr the
nrby main rd (no traff noise); free ent superb lido (pt naturist);
site manager v helpful." ♦ 1 Apr-31 Oct. € 30.00   2012*

⊞ **GREIFENBURG** *D2* (2km E Rural) *46.74744, 13.19448*
**Fliergercamp am See, Seeweg 333, 9761 Greifenburg
(Kärnten) [(04712) 8666; info@fliegercamp.at;
www.fliegercamp.at]** Leave A10 onto J139 onto 100 dir Lienz.
Site on L after 15km, mkd & visible fr rd. Med, hdg/mkd pitch,
pt shd; htd wc; chem disp; mv service pnt; fam bthrm; shwrs
inc; EHU (16A) inc; gas; lndry; shop 3km; rest, snacks, bar adj;
pool adj; lake sw adj; games area; 20% statics; dogs; twin
axles; poss cr; Eng spkn; quiet; ccard acc; CCI. "Gd cycling; vg
site; well run." ♦ ltd. € 24.00   2015*

AUSTRIA

GREIFENBURG *D2* (1.6km W Rural) *46.74805, 13.16416*
Familien-Camping Reiter, Hauzendorf 3, 9761 Greifenburg (Kärnten) [tel/fax (04712) 389; campingreiter@gmx.at; www.camping-reiter.at] Fr Greifenburg on B100, site on L. Sm, pt shd; htd wc; chem disp; baby facs; shwrs €1; EHU (10A) metered; lndry (inc dryer); shop; rest, snacks; bar; BBQ; playgrnd; htd pool; dogs €1; quiet. "Beautiful area."
1 Apr-15 Nov. € 21.00   2011*

GREIN *B3* (700m SW Urban) *48.22476, 14.85428*
Campingplatz Grein, Donaulände 1, 4360 Grein [(07268) 21230; fax 2123013; office@camping-grein.at; www.camping-grein.net] Sp fr A1 & B3 on banks of Danube. Med, pt shd; wc; chem disp; shwrs inc; EHU (6-10A) €3; gas; lndry; shop adj; rest in vill; snacks; bar; playgrnd; htd, covrd pool 200m; open air pool 500m; fishing; canoeing; wifi; 10% statics; dogs €1.50; poss cr; some rd/rlwy noise; red long stay; CKE/CCI. "Friendly, helpful owner lives on site; recep in café/bar; vg, modern san facs; lovely scenery; quaint vill; gd walking; excursions; conv Danube cycle rte & Mauthausen Concentration Camp." 1 Mar-31 Oct. € 32.50   2014*

GRUNDLSEE see Bad Aussee *C3*

HALL IN TIROL *C2* (6km E Rural) *47.28711, 11.57223*
Schlosscamping Aschach, Hochschwarzweg 2, 6111 Volders [tel/fax (05224) 52333; info@schlosscamping.com; www.schlosscamping.com] Fr A12 leave at either Hall Mitte & foll sp to Volders, or leave at Wattens & travel W to Volders (easiest rte). Site well sp on B171. Narr ent bet lge trees. Lge, mkd pitch, pt sl, pt shd; wc; chem disp; mv service pnt; shwrs inc; EHU (16A) €2.70 (long cable req some pitches; adaptor lead avail); gas; lndry; shop; 2 supmkts 500m; rest, snacks; bar; BBQ; playgrnd; htd pool; horseriding; tennis; TV rm; dogs €2.50; phone; bus 250m; Eng spkn; adv bkg; quiet but church bells, clock & some rlwy noise at night; red long stay; ccard acc (for 4+ days); CKE/CCI. "Well-run, clean site with vg, modern facs & helpful management; few water & waste points; grassy pitches; beautiful setting & views; gd walking/touring; arr early to ensure pitch." 1 May-12 Sep. € 22.00   2010*

HALL IN TIROL *C2* (1km NW Urban) *47.28423, 11.49658*
Schwimmbad-Camping, Scheidensteinstrasse 26, 6060 Hall-in-Tirol [(05223) 5855550; h.niedrist@hall.at; www.hall.ag] Exit A12/E45/E60 at junc 68 at Hall-in-Tirol. Cross rv strt into town & foll camp sp fr 2nd turn L; site on B171. Diff ent. Med, pt shd; wc; chem disp; mv service pnt; shwrs inc; EHU (6A) €2.50; lndry; shop high ssn; supmkt 500m; rest; playgrnd; htd pool adj; tennis; minigolf adj; wifi; 15% statics; dogs; bus; poss cr; Eng spkn; adv bkg; some rd noise & church bells; red long stay/CKE/CCI. "Well-cared for site; friendly welcome; vg, modern facs, poss stretched high ssn; local excursions, walking; pt of sports complex; Hall pretty, interesting medieval town; frequent music festivals; less cr than Innsbruck sites; no twin-axles; walk to town; conv for m'vans; NB m'vans only 1 Oct-30 Apr for €7.50 per night." ♦
1 May-30 Sep. € 28.00   2015*

HALLEIN *B2* (5km NW Rural) *47.70441, 13.06868* **Camping Auwirt, Salzburgerstrasse 42, 5400 Hallein [(06245) 80417; fax 84635; info@auwirt.com; www.auwirt.com]** Exit A10/E55 junc 8 onto B150 sp Salzburg Süd, then B159 twd Hallein. Site on L in 4km. Med, pt shd; wc; chem disp; mv service pnt; shwrs €2; EHU (10A) €3; lndry; rest, snacks; bar; playgrnd; paddling pool; wifi; dogs €2; bus to Salzburg at site ent; poss cr; Eng spkn; adv bkg; CKE/CCI. "Mountain views; cycle path to Salzburg nr; helpful staff; v friendly site; gd san facs & rest; conv salt mines at Hallein & scenic drive to Eagles' Nest; conv for Berchtesgaden; friendly family owners." ♦
Easter-15 Oct & 1 Dec-7 Jan. € 34.00   2014*

"I like to fill in the reports as I travel from site to site"

You'll find report forms at the back of this guide, or you can fill them in online at www.caravanclub.co.uk/europereport.

HALLSTATT *C3* (4km SE Rural) *47.54874, 13.67779*
Campingplatz am See, Winkl 77, 4831 Obertraun [(06131) 265; camping-am-see@chello.at; www.camping-am-see.at] Fr Hallstatt foll sps for Obertraun. Site immed on L on ent vill of Winkl. Med, some hdstg, pt shd; wc; chem disp; mv service pnt; baby facs; shwrs inc; EHU (10A) €3 (long lead req); lndry (inc dryer); shop; supmkt 1.5km; snacks; bar; BBQ; lake sw & shgl beach adj; wifi; dogs €1.50; Eng spkn; adv bkg; quiet; ccard acc; red CKE/CCI. "Nr Dachstein ice caves, Hallstatt salt mines, Gosau valley." 1 May-30 Sep. € 31.50   2010*

HALLSTATT *C3* (1km S Rural) *47.55296, 13.64786*
Camping Klausner-Höll, Lahnstrasse 201, 4830 Hallstatt [(06134) 6134 or 8322; fax 83221; camping@hallstatt.net; http://camping.hallstatt.net/home] On exit tunnel 500m thro vill, site on R nr lge filling stn. Med, pt shd; wc; chem disp; shwrs inc; EHU (16A) €3; lndry; shop; rest adj; snacks; bar; playgrnd; pool adj; lake sw; boat trips; dogs; poss cr; Eng spkn; ccard acc; red long stay/CKE/CCI. "Excel, level site; gd, clean san facs; chem disp diff to use; conv Salzkammergut region, Hallstatt salt mines, ice caves; pretty town 10 mins walk; family run site; relaxed & friendly; walks; idyllic quiet setting with mountains all around; cycle path around lake; supmkt 300m."
15 Apr-15 Oct. € 27.00   2014*

⊞ **HASELGEHR** *C1* (1km NE Rural) *47.31527, 10.49722*
Freien-Camping Rudi, Luxnach 122, 6651 Häselgehr [(05634) 6425; info@lechtal-camping-rudi.at; www.lechtal-camping-rudi.at] On rd B198 fr Reutte (N), in Häselgehr cross rv bdge, turn R bef church. In 100m take R fork, site on R in 500m. Med, hdstg, unshd; htd wc; chem disp; mv service pnt; shwrs inc; EHU (13A) metered; lndry (inc dryer); shop 5km; rest 500m; pool 500m; ski lift 5km; skibus; few statics; dogs €1.50; bus 400m; Eng spkn; adv bkg; quiet; red long stay; CKE/CCI. "Cycling & x-country skiing fr site; rafting cent on site; gd." € 20.40   2010*

HEILIGEN GESTADE see Ossiach *D3*

HEILIGENBLUT *C2* (3km S Rural) *47.02164, 12.86244*
**Camping Möllfuss, Pockhorn 25, 9844 Heiligenblut
(Kärnten) [tel/fax (04824) 24645; hoopfnstuben@gmx.at]**
On B107 at S end of Grossglockner Pass. Med, pt shd; htd wc;
chem disp; mv service pnt; shwrs inc; EHU (16A) metered; gas;
lndry; shop; rest, snacks; bar; playgrnd; pool; dogs; quiet; ccard
acc; red CKE/CCI. "Conv NH bef x-ing Grossglockner Pass."
1 Jun-15 Oct & 1 Dec-15 Apr. € 16.40   2009*

⊞ **HEILIGENBLUT** *C2* (8km S Rural) *46.97908, 12.88574*
**Camping Zirknitzer, Döllach 107, 9843 Grosskirchheim
(Kärnten) [tel/fax (04825) 451; camping.zirknitzer@
utanet.at; http://web.utanet.at/zirknitp]**
B107 fr Grossglockner Pass, S thro Heiligenblut dir Winklern &
Lienz, site sp. Sm, pt shd; wc; sauna; shwrs; EHU (16A) €2.60;
lndry; shop 500m; rest; bar; playgrnd; pool, tennis 500m;
fitness rm; site clsd Nov & end Apr; adv bkg; quiet. "Well-run,
scenic site; friendly & helpful; gd, modern san facs; gd walking;
conv Grossglockner & Italian border." € 15.00   2009*

⊞ **HEILIGENBLUT** *C2* (2km SW Rural) *47.03682, 12.83887*
**Nationalpark-Camping Grossglockner, Hadergasse 11,
9844 Heiligenblut (Kärnten) [(04824) 2048; fax 24622;
nationalpark-camping@heiligenblut.at; www.heiligenblut.
at/nationalpark-camping]** At S end Grossglockner. Keep R in
Heiligenblut, down hill & foll sp to site. Med, pt sl, unshd; wc;
shwrs inc; EHU (16-20A) €2.50; gas; lndry; shop 500m; rest,
snacks; bar; playgrnd; pool 200m; dogs €2; site clsd mid-Oct to
end Nov; Eng spkn; quiet; CKE/CCI. "In Hohe Tauern National
Park; sh, single walk to vill; gd NH bef/after Grossglockner Pass;
v ltd facs LS." € 19.70   2009*

HEITERWANG see Reutte *C1*

⊞ **HIRSCHEGG** *C3* (500m N Rural) *47.02300, 14.95325*
**Campingplatz Hirschegg, Haus No. 53, 8584 Hirschegg
[info@camping-hirschegg.at; www.camping-hirschegg.at]**
Exit A2 junc 224 Modriach N. At T-junc foll sp to Hirschegg &
in cent of vill turn R at petrol stn. Site in 300m on L by fire stn.
Med, hdg/mkd pitch, pt shd; wc; chem disp; shwrs inc; EHU
(10A) €2; lndry; shop, rest, bar in vill; playgrnd; pool; lake sw
adj; wifi; 30% statics; dogs €1; adv bkg; quiet. "Excel, family-
run site." € 16.00   2009*

HOPFGARTEN see Wörgl *C2*

IMST *C1* (1km E Rural) *47.23972, 10.7450* **International
Camping am Schwimmbad, Schwimmbadweg 10, 6460
Imst [(05412) 66612; camp1@gmx.at; http://members.
aon.at/camp1]** Exit A12/E60 at Imst onto B171 N dir Imst;
then exit B171 onto B189; in 500m turn R, then immed L
into Schwimmbadweg. Foll camp sps fr by-pass to avoid Imst
town & narr rds. Poss easier to foll Schwimbad (sw pool) sps.
Med, mkd pitch, pt sl, pt shd; wc; chem disp; shwrs inc; EHU
(6A) €2; gas; lndry (inc dryer); shop; pool adj; bike hire; wifi;
dogs €1.50; poss cr; Eng spkn; red long stay. "V pleasant in
mountain setting; gd walking; helpful owner; ltd san facs LS."
1 May-15 Sep. € 18.00   2009*

⊞ **IMST** *C1* (1.5km S Rural) *47.22861, 10.74305*
**Caravanpark Imst-West, Langgasse 62, 6460 Imst
[(05412) 66293; fax 662319; info@imst-west.com;
www.imst-west.com]** Fr A12/E60 exit Imst-Pitztal onto B171
N dir Imst. In 1km at rndabt take last exit heading W then
immed sharp L opp Citroën dealer into Langgasse. In 750m
turn L, site on R. Med, mkd pitch, pt sl, pt shd; wc; chem
disp; mv service pnt; shwrs inc; EHU (6-10A) €3; gas; lndry;
shop 200m; rest 200m; snacks; bar; playgrnd; pool 1.5km;
ski lift 2km; free skibus; dogs (€1.80-€2); Eng spkn; quiet.
"Gd cent for Tirol, trips to Germany & en rte for Innsbruck;
lovely views; clean facs; gd; new san facs being built (2015)."
€ 26.00   2015*

INNSBRUCK *C1* (11km SE Rural) *47.26002, 11.50509*
**Campingplatz Judenstein, Judenstein 42, 6074 Rinn-bei-
Innsbruck [(05223) 78098; fax 7887715; camping@kbrinn.
at; www.kbrinn.at/camping]** Exit A12/E45/E60 junc 68 & foll
Tulfes sp. Thro Tulfes & 2km onto Rinn, site sp, just bef church
with clock. App rd narr & steep in places. Med, hdg/mkd pitch,
pt sl, pt shd; wc; chem disp; mv service pnt; shwrs inc; EHU
(6A) €2; gas; lndry; shop adj; rest, bar adj; lake sw 5km; golf
1km; cab TV; 50% statics; dogs; Eng spkn; quiet but church
bells adj; CKE/CCI. "Gd, clean, well-run site; site yourself; office
open evenings; helpful, friendly staff; ample pitches; bus service
to area & city cent." 1 May-30 Sep. € 13.00   2011*

⊞ **INNSBRUCK** *C1* (9.5km SW Rural) *47.23724, 11.33865*
**Camping Natterersee, Natterer See 1, 6161 Natters
[(0512) 546732; fax 54673216; info@natterersee.com;
www.natterersee.com]** App Innsbruck fr E or W on A12
take A13/E45 sp Brenner. Leave at 1st junc sp Innsbruck Süd,
Natters. Foll sp Natters - acute R turns & severe gradients (care
across unguarded level x-ing), turn sharp R in vill & foll sp to
site. Take care on negotiating ent. Narr rds & app. Fr S on
A13 Brennerautobahn exit junc 3 & foll dir Mutters & Natters.
Med, pt shd, sl, terr; htd wc; chem disp; mv service pnt; baby
facs; shwrs inc; EHU (6A)€3.75; gas; lndry (inc dryer); shop;
rest, snacks; bar; BBQ; playgrnd; lake sw; watersilde; tennis;
bike hire; games area; games/TV rm; wifi; entmnt; no dogs
Jul/Aug, otherwise €4.50; bus to Innsbruck; train 2.5km; sep
car park high ssn; guided hiking; clsd 1 Nov-mid Dec; poss v
cr; Eng spkn; adv bkg; ccard acc; red LS; CKE/CCI. "Well-kept
site adj local beauty spot; lakeside pitches gd views (extra
charge); gd, scenic cent for walking & driving excursions; gd for
children; friendly, helpful staff; excel modern san facs; some sm
pitches & narr site rds diff lge o'fits; fantastic setting; special
shwr for dogs." ♦ € 48.40 SBS - G01   2013*

⊞ **INNSBRUCK** *C1* (7km W Rural) *47.26339, 11.32629*
**Camping Kranebittehof, Kranebitter Allee 216, 6020
Innsbruck-Kranebitten [(0512) 279558; fax 579558140;
info@camping-kranebitterhof.at; www.camping-
kranebitterhof.at]** Fr W fork L after Zirl bef main rd rv bdge,
sp Innsbruck & foll B171 for 3km. Fr S on A13 fr border foll
dir Bregenz on A12 exit Kranebitten & foll sp to site. Sharp ent
on R. Med, mkd pitch, some hdstg, terr, pt sl, pt shd; htd wc;
chem disp; mv service pnt; shwrs inc; EHU (6-10A) inc; lndry;
shop; pizzeria; hiking; ski lift 5km; wifi; 20% statics; dogs;
bus; poss cr; Eng spkn; some m'way & airport noise; ccard
acc; red LS/long stay/CKE/CCI. "Excel, refurbished site in lovely
situation; vg, modern san facs; friendly, helpful staff; site easy
to find fr m'way, excel rest on site." ♦ € 37.00   2013*

⊞ **INNSBRUCK** *C1* (7.5km W Urban) *47.25307, 11.32661*
**Campingplatz Pizzeria Stigger, Bahnhofstraße 10,
6176 Völs [(0512) 303533; campingvoels@aon.at;
www.camping-stigger.at]** Exit A12/E60 at Völs exit & foll site
sp. Sm, pt shd; wc; chem disp; mv service pnt; shwrs inc; EHU
inc; lndry; shop 100m; rest (pizzeria); snacks; bar; pool 200m;
bus adj; Eng spkn; ccard acc; CKE/CCI. "Gd; conv Innsbruck."
€ 28.00   2010*

⊞ **INNSBRUCK** *C1* (14km W Rural) *47.2605, 11.25575*
**Farmcamping Branger Alm, Haus Nr 32, 6175 Unterperfuss
[(05232) 2209; fax 22094; brangeralm@aon.at;
www.brangeralm.at]** Fr A12/E60 exit at Zirl-West, junc 91
& turn R at T-junc on m'way exit & foll sp Unterperfuss. Turn
L at next T-junc. Site on R in 2km at ent to vill, immed after
church on R. Med, pt shd; htd wc; chem disp; shwrs inc; EHU
(6A) metered; gas; lndry; snacks; rest adj; bar 1km; pool 3km;
ski lift 4km; 90% statics; dogs €1; bus to Innsbruck; Eng spkn;
quiet but some rlwy & rd noise. "Excel clean, modern facs; site
poss untidy LS; if recep not in office, go to rest; vg rest." ♦
€ 20.00   2009*

ITTER BEI HOPFGARTEN see Wörgl *C2*

⊞ **JENBACH** *C2* (6.5km NW Rural) *47.42156, 11.74043*
**Camping Karwendel, 6212 Maurach [(05243) 6116;
fax 20036; info@karwendel-camping.at; www.karwendel-
camping.at]** Exit A12/E45/E50 junc 39 onto B181. Foll sp
Pertisau & Maurach. In 8km (climbing fr a'route turn L at
Maurach. Foll rd thro vill, turn L at T-junc, then strt across
rndabt twd lake. Site sp past recycling cent. Med, unshd; htd
wc; chem disp; shwrs €1; EHU (10A) €2; lndry; shop 500m;
rest, snacks; bar; playgrnd; lake sw 500m; golf 4km; internet;
TV; 80% statics; dogs €2; site clsd Nov; poss cr; quiet. "In open
country, glorious views of lake & mountains; diff access lge
o'fits; site neglected & rundown." € 35.00   2014*

KALS AM GROßGLOCKNER *C2* (3km N Rural) *47.01912,
12.63680* **National Park Camping, Berg 22, A9981 Kals
am Großglockner [(043) 4852 67389; info@nationalpark-
camping-kals.at; www.nationalpark-camping-kals.at]**
Fr 108 (Leinz - Millersill) take L26 to Kals am Großglockner.
Site thro vill in abt 2km well sp. Care needed at 3 way rd junc
at end of vill, take ctr rd. Med, mkd pitch, terr, unshd; htd wc;
chem disp; mv service pnt; shwrs; EHU 10A; lndry; CKE/CCI.
"Excel, brand new purpose built site in Hohe Tauren Nat Park
at 1460m; superb san facs." 1 April - 31 Oct. € 30.00   2015*

KAUMBERG *B4* (5km E Rural) *48.01958, 15.94335*
**Campingplatz Paradise Garden, Höfnergraben 2, 2572
Kaumberg [0676 4741966 (mob); fax (02765) 3883;
grandl@camping-noe.at; www.camping-noe.at]**
B18 Hainfeld-Berndorf rd, site sp. Med, unshd; htd wc; chem
disp; mv service pnt; baby facs; shwrs inc; EHU (12A) €2;
gas; lndry (inc dryer); shop & 4km; rest 1.5km; snacks; bar;
playgrnd; bike hire; games rm; 60% statics; dogs free; phone;
Eng spkn; adv bkg; quiet; red long stay; CKE/CCI. "Gd walking,
helpful owner; superb san facs; easy access Vienna; lovely rural
area." ♦ 1 Apr-31 Oct. € 22.00   2011*

KEUTSCHACH AM SEE *D3* (3km E Rural) *46.58673, 14.22778*
**Camping Reautschnighof, Reauz 4, 9074 Keutschach-am-
See [tel/fax (0463) 281106; camping-reautschnighof@
gmx.at; www.camping-reautschnighof.at]**
Exit A2 at Klagenfurt West S to Viktring on S side of
Wörthersee. Foll sp Keutschach & site. Sm, mkd pitch, pt sl,
terr, unshd; wc; chem disp; shwrs €0.50; EHU (6A) inc; shop
3km; rest 600m; pool 8km; lake sw 200m; dogs €1.50; quiet;
"Lovely rural walks fr area." 1 May-30 Sep. € 20.50   2011*

KEUTSCHACH AM SEE *D3* (4km E Rural) *46.58348, 14.22878*
**Camping Reichmann, Reauz 5, 9074 Keutschach-am-See
[(0699) 1500057; info@camping-reichmann.at;
www.camping-reichmann.at]** Exit A2 at Klagenfurt W onto
B91 S to Viktring. Foll sp Keutschach-am-See, site sp. Lge, pt
sl, pt shd; wc; chem disp; shwrs inc; EHU (6A) inc; lndry (inc
dryer); shops 2km; rest, snacks; bar; BBQ; playgrnd; lake sw
adj; fishing; games rm; internet; dogs €1.50; phone; poss cr;
Eng spkn; quiet; ccard acc; red LS; CKE/CCI. "Excel." ♦
1 May-20 Sep. € 26.00   2009*

KEUTSCHACH AM SEE *D3* (4km SW Rural) *46.58472,
14.17225* **Strandcamping Sud, Dobeinitz 30a, 9074
Keutschach-am-See [(04273) 2773; fax 27734; info@
strandcampingsued.at; www.keutschachsued.at]**
Fr Klagenfurt (N) take rd 91 (E94) sp Loibl Pass & turn R for
Viktring & bypass Keutschach. At Keutschach See turn L off
main rd at rndabt & foll sp past Strandcamping North. Lge,
mkd pitch, some hdstg, pt sl, pt shd; wc; chem disp; mv service
pnt; shwrs inc; EHU (10A) inc; gas; lndry (inc dryer); shop; rest,
snacks; bar; BBQ; playgrnd; beach; lake sw adj; 80% statics;
dogs €2.30; poss cr; Eng spkn. "Gd walking, sw, cycling &
views." 1 May-30 Sep. € 27.50   2010*

KEUTSCHACH AM SEE *D3* (6km SW Rural) *46.57796,
14.14821* **FKK Camping Müllerhof (Naturist), Dobein
10, 9074 Keutschach-am-See [(04273) 2517; fax 25175;
muellerhof@fkk-camping.at; www.fkk-camping.at]**
Exit fr A2 junc 335 sp Velden West dir Velden. In 1km at
rndabt foll sp Keutschach; in 3km turn L at site sp. Or fr Villach,
take B83 E twd Velden. Turn R approx 3km bef Velden sp
Keutschach & foll site sp. Fr Klagenfurt, take B91 S, turn W to
Keutschach. Cont on main rd past vill & foll site sp. Lge, mkd
pitch, some hdstg, pt shd; htd wc; chem disp; mv service pnt;
sauna; baby facs; shwrs inc; EHU (6A) inc; lndry (inc dryer);
shops adj; rest, snacks; bar; playgrnd; sw in lake; games area;
games rm; wifi; entmnt; TV; 10% statics; no dogs; phone;
adv bkg; quiet. "Gd for lakes, walks, sailing." 15 Apr-30 Sep.
€ 30.00   2011*

KEUTSCHACH AM SEE *D3* (3km W Rural) *46.59080,
14.16490* **Camping Brückler Nord, Keutschachsee 5,
9074 Keutschach-am-See [tel/fax (04273) 2384; camp.
brueckler@aon.at; www.brueckler.co.at]**
On N point of Keutschacher See at exit of Reifnitz rd fr Velden-
Viktring rd. Med, pt shd; wc; chem disp; mv service pnt;
shwrs inc; EHU (6A) €4; lndry; shop, rest adj; snacks; BBQ;
playgrnd; lake sw; fishing; bike hire; wifi; 25% statics; dogs
€2.50; quiet. "Excel facs for children." 1 May-30 Sep. € 28.00
(CChq acc)   2009*

⊞ **KITZBUHEL** *C2* (3km NW Rural) *47.45906, 12.3619*
**Campingplatz Schwarzsee, Reitherstrasse 24, 6370
Kitzbühel [(05356) 62806 or 64479; fax 6447930; office@
bruggerhof-camping.at; www.bruggerhof-camping.at]**
Site sp fr Kitzbühel dir Kirchberg-Schwarzsee. Lge, pt sl, pt
shd; htd wc; chem disp; mv service pnt; fam bthrm; sauna;
shwrs inc; EHU (16A) metered; mains gas conn some pitches;
lndry; shop; rest adj; snacks; bar; playgrnd; pool 2km; lake
sw 300m; cab TV; 80% statics; dogs €5.50; phone; bus; poss
cr; Eng spkn; adv bkg; ccard acc; CKE/CCI. "Gd walks, cable
cars & chair lifts; vg, well-maintained site; poss mosquito &
vermin prob; some pitches in statics area; friendly owner." ◆
€ 46.00   2015*

KLAGENFURT *D3* (5km W Rural) *46.61826, 14.25641*
**Camping Wörthersee, Metnitzstrand 5, 9020 Klagenfurt
am wörthersee (Kärnten) [(0463) 287810; fax 287810;
info@campingfreund.at; www.camping-woerthersee.at]**
Fr A2/E66 take spur to Klagenfurt-West, exit at Klagenfurt-
Wörthersee. Turn R at traff lts & immed L at rd fork (traff lts),
then foll sp to site. Lge, shd; wc; chem disp; sauna; shwrs inc;
EHU (10A) inc; lndry; shop; rest; playgrnd; sand beach adj;
bike hire; entmnt; dogs €3.20; 10% statics; bus; quiet; ccard
acc. "V clean facs; local tax €3.50 per visit." ◆ 1 May-30 Sep.
€ 31.00   2013*

KLOSTERNEUBURG *B4* (650m N Rural) *48.31097, 16.32810*
**Donaupark Camping Klosterneuburg, In der Au, 3402
Klosterneuburg [(02243) 25877; fax 25878; camp
klosterneuburg@oeamtc.at; www.camping klosterneuburg.
at]** Fr A22/E59 exit junc 7 onto B14, site sp in cent of town
behind rlwy stn. After passing Klosterneuburg Abbey on L turn
1st R (sharp turn under rlwy). Site immed ahead. Med, mkd
pitch, pt shd; htd wc; chem disp; mv service pnt; shwrs inc;
EHU (6-12A) €3; gas; lndry (inc dryer); shop; rest 200m; snacks;
BBQ; cooking facs; playgrnd; leisure cent & htd pools adj; bike
& boat hire; tennis; wifi; TV rm; 5% statics; dogs free; phone;
bus; train to Vienna; poss cr; quiet; ccard acc; red CKE/CCI.
"Well-organised, popular site; vg san facs; helpful staff; sm
pitches; conv Danube cycle path & Vienna; church & monastery
worth visit." ◆ 15 Mar-31 Oct. € 26.00   2012*

⊞ **KOSSEN** *B2* (3km SE Rural) *47.65388, 12.41544*
**Eurocamping Wilder Kaiser, Kranebittau 18, 6345 Kössen
[(05375) 6444; fax 2113; info@eurocamp-koessen.com;
www.eurocamp-koessen.com]** Leave A12 at Oberaudorf/
Niederndorf junc, head E on 172 thro Niederndorf & Walchsee
to Kössen. Strt across at rndabt, in 1km turn R sp Hinterbarg
Lift. At next junc turn R & site located after 400m. Lge, mkd
pitch, pt shd; htd wc; chem disp; mv service pnt; serviced
pitches; sauna; solarium; baby facs; shwrs inc; EHU (6A)
metered + conn fee; gas; lndry; shop high ssn; rest, snacks high
ssn; bar; playgrnd; htd pool adj; tennis; games area; golf 2km;
entmnt; internet; cab TV; 50% statics; dogs €4; poss cr; Eng
spkn; adv bkg; ccard acc; CKE/CCI. "Lovely site; excel play area
& organised activities; rafting, hang-gliding & canoeing 1km;
excel." € 23.50   2012*

⊞ **KOTSCHACH** *D2* (1km SW Rural) *46.66946, 12.99153*
**Alpencamp, Kötschach 284, 9640 Kötschach-Mauthen
[tel/fax (04715) 429; info@alpencamp.at;
www.alpencamp.at]** At junc of rds B110 & B111 in
Kötschach turn W onto B111, foll camp sps to site in 800m on
L. Med, mkd pitch, pt shd; htd wc; chem disp; mv service pnt;
sauna; shwrs inc; EHU (16A) inc; lndry (inc dryer); sm shop;
supmkt 400m; rest 100m; snacks; playgrnd; 2 pools (1 htd,
covrd); waterslide; tennis; games area; games rm; boat & bike
hire; tennis 400m; wifi; TV; dogs €2.50; phone; site clsd 1 Nov-
14 Dec; poss cr; Eng spkn; quiet; ccard acc. "Useful for Plöcken
Pass; cycle tracks on rv bank nrby; vg san facs; friendly, helpful
owner; vg site." ◆ € 27.00   2010*

KRAMSACH AM REINTALERSEE see Rattenberg *C2*

KREMS AN DER DONAU *B4* (2km SW Urban) *48.40305,
15.59194* **Donaupark-Camping, Yachthafenstrasse 19,
3504 Krems-Stein [tel/fax (02732) 84455; donaucamping
krems@aon.at; www.donauparkcamping-krems.at]**
Fr B3 along N of Danube in Stein, foll site & 'Schiffstation' &
camping sps to site on rvside. Med, unshd; htd wc; chem disp;
mv service pnt; shwrs inc; EHU (16A) €2; gas; lndry (inc dryer);
shop 500m; rest adj; snacks; bar; playgrnd 200m; pool 500m;
bike hire; 5% statics; phone; poss v cr; Eng spkn; adv bkg rec
high ssn & pub hols; some rd & rv traffic noise; ccard acc; CKE/
CCI. "Well-run site; excel, clean facs; office open 0730-1000 &
1630-1900; sm pitches; conv Danube cycle rte." 1 Apr-31 Oct.
€ 17.60   2009*

KREMS AN DER DONAU *B4* (9km SW Rural) *48.38998,
15.51678* **Campingplatz Rossatzbach, Rossatzbach 21,
3602 Rossatz [(02714) 6317; fax 6249; gemeinde@rossatz-
arnsdorf.at; www.rossatz-arnsdorf.at]** Exit A1 junc 80
sp Melk & Donau Brücke. Cross Rv Danube & turn R along
Danube L bank. After Dürnstein re-cross Danube on metal box
bdge & turn R sp Melk & Rossatzbach. In 3km turn 1st R in
Rossatzbach vill & foll sp to site in 200m. Sm, pt shd; htd wc;
chem disp; shwrs inc; EHU (16A) metered; lndry; shop 1km;
rest, snacks; bar; playgrnd; games area; 20% statics; dogs;
poss cr; adv bkg; quiet; CKE/CCI. "Pleasant site on opp site of
Danube to Dürnstein; most pitches on rvside; interesting area."
Easter-31 Oct. € 17.00   2009*

⊞ **LANDECK** *C1* (500m W Urban) *47.14263, 10.56147*
**Camping Riffler, Bruggfeldstrasse 2, 6500 Landeck
[(05442) 64898; fax 648984; info@camping-riffler.at;
www.camping-riffler.at]** Exit E60/A12 at Landeck-West,
site in 1.5km, 500m fr cent on L. Sm, pt shd; wc; chem disp;
shwrs inc; EHU (10A) €2.70 (poss rev pol); gas; lndry; shop adj;
snacks, rest adj; playgrnd; pool 500m; bike hire; dogs free; poss
cr; site clsd May; ccard acc; red CKE/CCI. "Well-kept, clean,
friendly site; sm pitches; narr rds; recep open 1800-2000 LS -
site yourself & pay later; excel NH." € 23.50   2011*

AUSTRIA

⊞ **LANGENFELD** *C1* (550m W Rural) *47.07228, 10.96450*
Camping Ötztal, Unterlängenfeld 220, 6444 Längenfeld
[(05253) 5348; fax 5909; info@camping-oetztal.com;
www.camping-oetztal.com] Exit A12 junc 123 at Ötztal
onto B186 dir Sölden. On ent Längenfeld foll sp sports cent,
site on R immed bef bdge over Rv Fischbach. Med, some hdstg,
pt shd; wc; chem disp; mv service pnt; baby facs; solarium;
sauna; shwrs; EHU inc (6A) metered; gas; lndry; shop adj; rest;
bar; playgrnd; htd pool adj; rafting; tennis 500m; wifi; sat TV;
15% statics; dogs €3.10; poss cr; Eng spkn; quiet. "Gd rest
& bar; mountain views; thermal springs, open air museum &
Tirolean folk museum nr; vg site." ◆ € 22.50   2011*

⊞ **LANGENWANG** *C4* (260m N Rural) *47.56875, 15.62008*
Europa Camping, Siglstrasse 5, 8665 Langenwang
[(03854) 2950; fax (02143) 380982394; europa.camping.
stmk@aon.at; www.campsite.at/europa.camping.
langenwang] Exit S6 sp Langenwang, site sp in town cent.
Sm, hdg pitch, pt shd; htd wc; chem disp; shwrs €0.80; EHU
(16A) metered; lndry; shop, rest, snacks, bar 100m; playgrnd
adj; htd, covrd pool 7km; lake sw 4km; ski facs; 30% statics;
dogs; bus; Eng spkn; adv bkg; quiet. "Pleasant,
friendly site; family atmosphere; excel facs; peaceful site."
€ 15.00   2013*

LEIBNITZ *D4* (6.5km SW Urban) *46.77864, 15.52891*
Camping Leibnitz, Rudolf-Hans-Bartsch-Gasse 33, 8430
Leibnitz [(03452) 82463; fax 71491; leibnitz@camping-
steiermark.at; www.camping-steiermark.at] Fr A9 take exit
Leibnitz onto B74, site not well sp, but nr sw pool, on rvside.
Med, hdg/mkd pitch, pt shd; wc; chem disp; mv service pnt;
fam bthrm; shwrs €1; EHU (10-16A) €1.80; lndry (inc dryer);
shop 700m; rest, snacks; bar; playgrnd; pool adj; waterslide; rv
sw adj; tennis; no statics; dogs; Eng spkn; ccard acc; CKE/CCI.
"Gd NH; excel san facs; gd sports & leisure facs; interesting
town." ◆ 1 May-15 Oct. € 4.70   2009*

LERMOOS see Ehrwald *C1*

LEUTASCH see Seefeld in Tirol *C1*

LIENZ *C2* (1km SE Urban) *46.82255, 12.77111* **Comfort-**
Camping Falken, Falkenweg 7, 9900 Lienz [(04852) 64022;
fax 640226; camping.falken@tirol.com; www.camping-
falken.com] On B100 to town cent, foll sp Tristacher See, site
sp adj leisure cent. Med, pt shd; htd wc; chem disp; mv service
pnt; baby facs; shwrs €0.75; EHU (6A) inc; gas; lndry (inc dryer);
sm shop; rest, snacks, bar high ssn; playgrnd; htd, covrd pool
500m; ski lift 2km; ski bus; golf 4km; wifi; TV; 30% statics;
dogs €3.50; poss cr; quiet; ccard acc; red long stay. "Gate
closes 1300-1500; easy walk to vill with beautiful scenery -
nearest site to Lienz; sm pitches; vg site." ◆ 20 Dec-20 Oct.
€ 27.50   2010*

LIENZ *C2* (6km SE Rural) *46.80730, 12.80350* **Camping**
Seewiese, Tristachersee 2, 9900 Tristach [tel/fax
(04852) 69767; seewiese@hotmail.com; www.campingtirol.
com] On B100 to Lienz dir Tristach, turn sharp L after rlwy
underpass & rv bdge to by-pass Trisach. Turn R after 4km opp
golf course. Steep (11%) climb to site. Sp. Med, some hdstg, sl,
pt shd; wc; chem disp; mv service pnt; shwrs inc; EHU (6-16A)
€2.70; gas; lndry (inc dryer); sm shop & 5km; rest & 500m;
bar; playgrnd; htd pool 5km; lake sw 200m; tennis; bike hire;
wifi; TV rm; dogs €3; bus high ssn to Tristach; phone; poss cr;
Eng spkn; quiet; red LS; CKE/CCI. "Fairly secluded, relaxing
site; mountain views; gd walks; gd san facs; helpful owner."
15 May-14 Sep. € 36.00   2015*

"We must tell The Club about that great site we found"

Get your site reports in by mid-August
and we'll do our best to get your updates
into the next edition.

LIENZ *C2* (2km S Rural) *46.81388, 12.76388* **Dolomiten-**
Camping Amlacherhof, Lake rd 20, 9908 Amlach Lienz
[(04852) 62317 or 69917 62317-1 (mob); fax 62317-12;
info@amlacherhof.at; www.amlacherhof.at] S fr Lienz on
B100, foll sp in 1.5km to Amlach. In vill, foll site sp. Med, hdg/
mkd pitch, pt shd; htd wc; chem disp; mv service pnt; baby
facs; shwrs €0.80; EHU (16A) metered inc; lndry (inc dryer); rest
500m; snacks; bar; BBQ; playgrnd; htd pool; tennis; bike hire;
games rm; golf 7km; wifi; TV rm; 5% statics; dogs €2.90; bus
adj; site clsd 1 Nov-15 Dec; poss cr; Eng spkn; adv bkg; quiet.
"Excel touring cent; many mkd walks & cycle rtes; cable cars,
ski lifts 3km; attractive, historic town; excel, scenic site; local
taxes €5." ◆ 1 Mar-31 Oct. € 35.40 (CChq acc)   2014*

LIEZEN *C3* (11km SW Rural) *47.52061, 14.13080*
Camping Putterersee, Hohenberg 2A, 8943 Aigen [tel/
fax (03682) 22859; camping.putterersee@aon.at; www.
camping-putterersee.at] S on A10 fr Salzburg, exit 63 for
E651/B320 twds Hohenberg. Foll sp. Med, pt sl, pt shd, htd wc;
chem disp; shwrs inc; EHU (13A); gas; lndry (inc dryer); shop
1km; rest; snacks; bar; BBQ; playgrnd; sw lake, beach; fishing;
bike hire; boat hire; games rm; wifi; dogs €2.20; twin axles;
poss cr; Eng spkn; adv bkg; quiet; red LS; CKE/CCI. "Excel san
facs; gd views, walking & cycling; v helpful staff; vg." ◆ ltd.
15 Apr-31 Oct. € 21.00   2015*

LINZ *B3* (14km SE Rural) *48.23527, 14.37888* **Camping-**
Linz am Pichlingersee, Wienerstrasse 937, 4030 Linz
[(0732) 305314; fax 3053144; office@camping-linz.at;
www.camping-linz.at] Exit A1/E60 junc 160; take Enns dir;
go L on 1st rndabt; do not go under rndabt thro underpass;
site is sp on R. Med, mkd pitch, pt shd; htd wc; chem disp;
mv service pnt; shwrs inc; EHU (6A) inc; gas; lndry; sm shop
& 2km; rest, snacks, bar; cooking facs; lake sw adj; tennis;
internet; 40% statics; dogs €1.90; bus; site clsd 1300-1500;
poss cr; Eng spkn; adv bkg; some noise fr m'way; red long stay.
"Excel modern san facs, well-run, family-run site; friendly staff;
gd walks around lake; monastery at St Florian worth visit; conv
NH; gd." ◆ ltd. 15 Mar-15 Oct. € 22.50   2014*

LOFER C2 (2km SE Rural) 47.57500, 12.70804 **Camping Park Grubhof, St Martin 39, 5092 St Martin-bei-Lofer [(06588) 82370; fax 82377; home@grubhof.com; www.grubhof.com]** Clear sps to camp at ent on rd B311 Lofer to Zell-am-See. Site on L after garden cent. Lge, pt shd; htd wc; chem disp; mv service pnt; baby facs; serviced pitches; shwrs inc; EHU (10A) €2; lndry (inc dryer); supmkt 700m; rest; bar; pool 1km; fitness cent; playgrnd; wifi; dogs €3; phone; adv bkg; bus to Salzburg; quiet; ccard not acc; CKE/CCI. "Beautiful scenery; roomy, peaceful site; excel san facs; adult only & dog free areas; sh walk to vill; highly rec; mountain views; some meadowside and rvside pitches; delightful rest/ bar." ♦ 1 Jan-23 Mar, 11 Apr-2 Nov, 6 Dec-31 Dec. € 36.00 SBS - G04 2015*

⊞ **LUNZ AM SEE** B4 (900m E Urban) 47.86194, 15.03638 **Ötscherland Camping, Zellerhofstrasse 23, 3293 Lunz-am-See [tel/fax (07486) 8413; info@oetscherlandcamping.at; www.oetscherlandcamping.at]** Fr S on B25 turn R into Lunz-am-See. In 300m turn L, cross rv & take 1st L, site on L on edge of vill. Sm, hdstg, pt shd; htd wc; chem disp; mv service pnt; shwrs €1; EHU (16A) inc; lndry; shop, rest in vill; lake sw 500m; winter skiing; 80% statics; dogs €1; Eng spkn; quiet. "Excel walking; immac facs; vg site on Rv Ybbs & Eisenstrasse." € 15.00 2009*

MAISHOFEN see Zell am See C2

MALTA see Gmünd (Kärnten) C3

MARBACH AN DER DONAU B4 (1km W Rural) 48.21309, 15.13828 **Campingplatz Marbacher, Granz 51, 3671 Marbach-an-der-Donau [tel/fax (07413) 20733; info@marbach-freizeit.at; www.marbach-freizeit.at]** Fr W exit A1 junc 100 at Ybbs onto B25. Cross Rv Danube & turn R onto B3. Site in 7km. Fr E exit A1 junc 90 at Pöchlarn, cross rv & turn L onto B3 to Marbach, site sp. Med, mkd pitch, pt shd; htd wc; chem disp; mv service pnt; shwrs inc; EHU (16A) €2.50; lndry (inc dryer); shop 500m; rest 500m; BBQ; rv sw; watersports; tennis 800m; boat & bike hire; internet; entmnt; 5% statics; Eng spkn; adv bkg; rlwy & rv noise; ccard acc; red CKE/CCI. "Beautiful, well-managed site; sm, narr pitches; excel facs & staff; gd rst & bar; gd cycling & watersports; v clean facs; gd nh fr m'way or longer stay for touring." ♦ 1 Apr-31 Oct. € 28.00 (CChq acc) 2014*

MARIAZELL B4 (4km NW Rural) 47.79009, 15.28221 **Campingplatz am Erlaufsee, Erlaufseestrasse 3, 8630 St Sebastien-bei-Mariazell [(03882) 4937; fax 214822; gemeinde@st-sebastian.at; www.st-sebastian.at]** On B20 1km N of Mariazell turn W sp Erlaufsee. Site in 3km on app to lake, turn L thro car park ent to site. Med, pt sl, pt shd; wc; chem disp; shwrs €0.50; EHU (12A) metered; lndry; shop 3km; rest, snacks adj; beach nr; bus high ssn; dogs €1.90; quiet. "Cable car in Mariazell; pilgrimage cent; all hot water by token fr owner." 1 May-15 Sep. € 16.30 2011*

MATREI IN OSTTIROL C2 (500m S Rural) 46.99583, 12.53906 **Camping Edengarten, Edenweg 15a, 9971 Matrei-in-Osttirol [tel/fax (04875) 5111; info@campingedengarten.at; www.campingedengarten.at]** App fr Lienz on B108 turn L bef long ascent (by-passing Matrei) sp Matrei-in-Osttirol & Camping. App fr N thro Felbertauern tunnel, by-pass town, turn R at end of long descent, sps as above. Med, pt shd; wc; chem disp; mv service pnt; shwrs €0.50; EHU (10A); gas; lndry; supmkt, rest, snacks adj; bar; playgrnd; pool 300m; 10% statics; dogs; bus; poss cr. "Gd mountain scenery; helpful owner; beautiful views; pretty town; some rd noise during daytime." 1 Apr-31 Oct. € 29.00 2014*

MATREI IN OSTTIROL C2 (23km W Rural) 47.01912, 12.63695 **Camping Kals Am Großglockner, Burg 22, 9981 Kals am Großglockner [04852 67389; info@nationalpark-camping-kals.at; www.nationalpark-camping-kals.at]** Fr 108 Matrei in Osttirol to Lienz, exit at Huben onto L26 to Kals. 3km after vill foll sp to Dorfertal. National Park campsite on L. Med, unshd; htd wc; chem disp; mv service pnt; baby facs; shwrs inc; lndry (inc dryer); shop; rest; wifi; dogs €2.50; ski bus; twin axles acc; Eng spkn; quiet; ccard acc; CCI. "Excel site; excel walking & climbing." ♦ 17 May-13 Oct. € 21.00 2014*

MAURACH see Schwaz C2

MAYRHOFEN C2 (1km N Rural) 47.17617, 11.86969 **Camping Mayrhofen, Laubichl 125, 6290 Mayrhofen [(05285) 6258051; fax 6258060; camping@alpenparadies.com; www.alpenparadies.com]** Site at N end of vill off B169. Lge, mkd pitch, hdstg, pt shd; wc; chem disp; mv service pnt; sauna; shwrs inc; EHU (10A) €2.50 or metered; gas; lndry; shop 1km; rest, snacks; playgrnd; pool; bike hire; wifi; 50% statics; dogs €3; site clsd 1 Nov-15 Dec; adv bkg; poss cr; some factory noise; CKE/CCI. "Modern san facs; diff for lge o'fits, narr rds; gd rest." ♦ 1 Jan-31 Oct & 10 Dec-31 Dec. € 25.00 2012*

MELK B4 (3km N Urban) 48.24298, 15.34040 **Donau Camping Emmersdorf, Bundesstrasse 133, 3644 Emmersdorf-an-der-Donau [(02752) 71707; fax (2752) 7146930; office@emmersdorf.at; www.emmersdorf.at]** Fr A1 take Melk exit. Turn R, foll sp Donaubrücke, cross rv bdge. Turn R, site 200m on L, well sp. Sm, mkd/hdg pitch, pt shd; wc; chem disp; baby facs; shwrs inc; EHU (6A) inc; lndry (inc dryer); shops 300m; supmkt 3km; rest 300m; BBQ; pool 13km; fishing; tennis; bike hire; games rm; dogs; phone; noise fr rd & disco w/end; ccard acc; CKE/CCI. "Liable to close if rv in flood; clean facs; attractive vill; vg." ♦ 1 May-30 Sep. € 19.00 2014*

MELK B4 (6km NE Rural) 48.25395, 15.37115 **Campingplatz Stumpfer, 3392 Schönbühel [(02752) 8510; fax 851017; office@stumpfer.com; www.stumpfer.com]** Exit A1 junc 80. Foll sp for Melk on B1 as far as junc with B33. Turn onto B33 (S bank of Danube) for 2km to Schönbühel. Site on L adj gasthof, sp. Sm, pt shd; wc; chem disp; shwrs €0.50; EHU (10-16A) €2.40 or metered; gas; lndry; shops 5km; rest, snacks; rv adj; dogs; poss v cr; Eng spkn; adv bkg; ccard acc; red long stay/CKE/CCI. "On beautiful stretch of Danube; arr early for rvside pitch; abbeys in Melk & Krems worth visit; lower end site unrel in wet; helpful staff; vg facs but poss stretched high ssn; cycle path adj." 1 Apr-31 Oct. € 17.40 2010*

MELK *B4* (3.6km NW Rural) *48.23347, 15.32888* **Camping Fährhaus Melk, Kolomaniau 3, 3390 Melk [tel/fax (02752) 53291; jensch@brauhof-wieselburg.at]** Skirt Melk on B1, immed after abbey at traff lts, turn N on bdge over rv (sp). Site in 700m. Sm, pt shd; wc; shwrs; EHU (6A) inc; shop & 1km; rest at Gasthaus; snacks; bar; BBQ; playgrnd; fishing; quiet. "Basic site but adequate; abbey adj & boating on Danube; NB all sites on banks of Danube liable to close if rv in flood." 1 Apr-31 Oct. € 17.60   2010*

MILLSTATT *D3* (3km SE Rural) *46.79581, 13.59768* **Terrassencamping Pesenthein (Part Naturist), Presenthein, 9872 Millstatt [(04766) 2665; fax 202120; camping-pesenthein@aon.it; www.pesenthein.at]** Exit A10/E55 dir Seeboden & Millstaff. Lake lakeside rd B98 fr Millstatt to Dellach. Site on L just beyond Pesenthein. Lge, mkd pitch, terr, pt shd; htd wc; chem disp; mv service pnt; baby facs; shwrs inc; EHU (6A) €1.75; lndry; shop; rest; playgrnd; lake sw & beach adj (via tunnel); TV; 17% statics; dogs free; phone; Eng spkn; adv bkg; quiet; CKE/CCI. "Lovely views over lake; excel facs." 1 Apr-30 Sep. € 25.00   2010*

MILLSTATT *D3* (4km SE Rural) *46.78863, 13.61418* **Camping Neubauer, Dellach 3, 9872 Millstatt-am-See [(04766) 2532; fax 25324; info@camping-neubauer.at; www.camping-neubauer.at]** Exit A10/E55 dir Seeboden & Millstatt. Take lakeside rd B98 fr Millstatt to Dellach, R turn & foll sp camping sp. Med, mkd pitch, some hdstg, terr, pt shd; htd wc; chem disp; baby facs; shwrs inc; EHU (6A) inc; gas; lndry (inc dryer); shop; rest adj; snacks; bar; BBQ; playgrnd; lake sw; watersports; tennis; bike hire; golf 6km; wifi; entmnt; 10% statics; dogs €2; poss cr; no adv bkg; quiet; ccard acc. "Gd touring base; easy access to Italy; superb scenery with lakes & mountains; gd walks; excel facs; boat trips nr; gd rest; steep narr rd's to pitches, tractor avail to help; pt shd on lake pitches." 1 May-15 Oct. € 33.00   2013*

MITTERSILL *C2* (1km E Rural) *47.27761, 12.49267* **Camping Schmidl, Museumstrasse 6, 5730 Mittersill [(06562) 6158]** Fr Zell-am-See or Kitzbühel, exit to Mittersill, fr town sq foll camping sp past hospital. Sm, pt shd; wc; chem disp; shwrs €0.60; EHU (15A) inc; shop 1km; dogs; poss cr; quiet. "Friendly & welcoming; useful stop bef Felbertauern tunnel; conv Krimml waterfall & Grossglockner; large CL type with pitches for 10 o'fits; gd for NH." 1 May-30 Sep. € 12.00   2015*

MONDSEE *B3* (5km SE Rural) *47.82956, 13.36554* **Austria Camp, Achort 60, 5310 St Lorenz [(06232) 2927; fax 29274; office@austriacamp.at; austriacamp.at]** Exit A1/E55/E60 junc 265 onto B154. In 4km at St Lorenz at km 21.4 turn L onto unclassified rd to site in 600m at lakeside. Fr SW via Bad Ischl, at St Gilgen take Mondsee rd; 500m after Plomberg turn R at St Lorenz; Austria Camp sps clear. Med, shd; wc; chem disp; mv service pnt; sauna; baby facs; shwrs inc; EHU (6A) €2.90; lndry (inc dryer); rest, snacks; bar; shop; playgrnd; lake sw; fishing; boat-launch; tennis; bike hire; golf nr; entmnt; 45% statics; dogs €2.90; poss cr (Jul-Aug); adv bkg; quiet; 10% red CKE/CCI. "Gd, clean san facs; gd rest; friendly, family-run site; no arrivals bet 1200 & 1500." ♦ 1 Apr-30 Sep. € 30.00   2015*

MONDSEE *B3* (4km NW Rural) *47.86640, 13.30621* **Camping Mond-See-Land, Punz Au 21, 5310 Tiefgraben [(06232) 2600; fax 27218; austria@campmondsee.at; www.campmondsee.at]** Exit A1/E60/E55 junc 265 for Mondsee, turn N on B154 dir Strasswalchen. After 1.5km turn L dir Haider-Mühle on narr country rd to site in 2km. Site sp fr B154. Med, mkd pitch, pt sl, pt shd; htd wc; chem disp; shwrs inc; EHU (16A) €3.20; gas; lndry (inc dryer); shop; rest, snacks; bar; BBQ; playgrnd; pool; boating; internet; entmnt; dogs €2.90; phone; adv bkg; quiet; red long stay; "Beautiful mountain scenery; spacious pitches; excel new san facs; lovely countryside; serviced pitches avail for extra charge; somewhat isolated & away fr main rd." ♦ 1 Apr-31 Oct. € 20.00   2011*

⊞ **MURAU** *C3* (3km W Rural) *47.10791, 14.13883* **Camping Olachgut, Kaindorf 90, 8861 St Georgen-ob-Murau [(03532) 2162 or 3233; fax 21624; office@olachgut.at; www.olachgut.at]** Site sp on rd B97 bet Murau & St Georgen. Med, pt shd; wc; chem disp; mv service pnt; baby facs; sauna; shwrs inc; EHU (16A) metered; gas conn; lndry (inc dryer); shop 2.5km; rest, snacks; bar; playgrnd; lake sw; games area; bike hire; ski lift 2.5km; horseriding; entmnt; internet; 40% statics; dogs €2.20; adv bkg; quiet. "Rural site nr rlwy." ♦ € 25.00   2012*

MURECK *D4* (700m S Rural) *46.70491, 15.77240* **Campingplatz Mureck, Austrasse 10, 8480 Mureck [(03472) 210512; fax 21056; m.rauch@mureck.steiermark.at]** Fr Graz on A9, turn E at junc 226 onto B69 sp Mureck. NB: Low archway in Mureck. Med, mkd pitch, some hdstg, shd; wc; chem disp; shwrs €0.50; EHU (10A) inc; lndry (inc dryer); shops adj; rest, snacks; bar; BBQ; playgrnd; htd pool complex inc waterslide adj; fishing; tennis; bike hire; games area; wifi; 30% statics; dogs €3.50; phone; adv bkg; quiet; red long stay; ccard acc; red CKE/CCI. "Off beaten track in pleasant country town; pt of leisure complex; gd, modern san facs." ♦ 1 May-15 Sep. € 23.00   2010*

⊞ **MURECK** *D4* (7km W Rural) *46.71611, 15.68277* **Gasthof Dorfheuriger, Unterschwarza 1, 8471 Unterschwarza-Murfeld [(03453) 21001; dorfheuriger@gmx.net; www.dorfheuriger.eu]** On B69 fr Mureck or exit A9 junc 226 at Gersdorf & take B69 E for 2km. Sm, mkd pitch, unshd; wc; chem disp; mv service pnt; EHU; rest, bar adj; tennis; wifi; quiet. "Vg NH for m'vans only."   2010*

NASSEREITH *C1* (3km N Rural) *47.34043, 10.81585* **Romantik-Camping Schloss Fernsteinsee, Fernsteinsee, 6465 Nassereith [(05265) 5210157; fax 52016; camping@fernsteinsee.at; www.fernsteinsee.at/camping]** 5km S of Fern pass. Immed prior to rd bdge. Ent sp by Hotel - use S ent, not ent by bdge/hotel. Med, pt sl, shd; htd wc; chem disp; sauna; solarium; some serviced pitches; shwrs inc; EHU (6A) inc; lndry; shop & 4km; rest 400m; snacks; playgrnd; sw in lake adj; boating; sat TV; dogs €2; quiet; ccard acc. "Immac facs; excel rest; stunning scenery for walking/cycling." ♦ Easter-31 Oct. € 31.00   2011*

AUSTRIA

⊞ **NASSEREITH** *C1* (2.5km SE Rural) *47.30975, 10.85466*
Camping Rossbach, Rossbach 325, 6465 Nassereith
[tel/fax (05265) 5154; rainer.ruepp@gmx.at;
www.campingrossbach.com] On ent vill of Nassereith turn
E & foll dir Rossbach/Dormitz, site in 1.5km. Foll sm green
sps. Narr app. Med, mkd pitch, pt shd; htd wc; chem disp; mv
service pnt; baby facs; shwrs inc; EHU (6A) inc; lndry (inc dryer);
shop; rest, snacks; bar; BBQ; playgrnd; htd pool; paddling pool;
fishing; games rm; ski lift 500m; skibus; TV; 5% statics; dogs
€1.50; phone; adv bkg; quiet; CKE/CCI. "Mountain views." ♦
€ 21.50   2015*

NATTERS see Innsbruck *C1*

⊞ **NAUDERS** *C1* (4km S Rural) *46.85139, 10.50472*
Alpencamping, Bundestrasse 279, 6543 Nauders
[(05473) 87217; fax 8721750; info@camping-nauders.at;
www.camping-nauders.at] On W side of B180 just bef
Italian border. Sm, some hdstg, unshd; htd wc; chem disp;
baby facs; shwrs €0.50; EHU €1.90; gas conn; lndry; shop &
2km; rest, snacks; bar; no statics; dogs €2; phone; site clsd
1 Nov-19 Dec; poss cr; ccard acc; CKE/CCI. "Conv NH for
Reschen pass; gd touring base; excel cycling, walking; excel san
facs." € 18.00   2009*

⊞ **NENZING** *C1* (2.6km WSW Rural) *47.18313, 9.68238*
Alpencamping Nenzing, Garfrenga 1, 6710 Nenzing
[(05525) 624910; fax 624916; office@alpencamping.at;
www.alpencamping.at] Exit A14/E60 or B190 at Nenzing,
foll camping sps thro Nenzing for 3km up Gurtis rd, narr &
winding in parts, camp on L sp. When leaving site, vehicles
routed away fr Nenzing on sp country rds for 10km back to
B190. Lge, mkd pitch, hdstg; terr, pt sl, pt shd; wc; chem
disp; mv service pnt; baby facs; sauna; shwrs inc; EHU
(4-12A) metered; gas; lndry; shop; rest, snacks; bar; playgrnd;
htd pool; paddling pool; ski lift 1.5km; games rm; wifi;
entmnt; TV; many statics; dogs €4.50; clsd 31 Mar-24 Apr;
skibus; poss cr; Eng spkn; adv bkg ess; quiet; 10% red LS.
"Close to ski school & lifts; gd views & beautiful walks; excel
san facs; gd rest; recep poss unmanned in winter - phone
box adj; excel." ♦ ltd. € 31.00   2011*

See advertisement inside the front cover

⊞ **NEUSTIFT IM STUBAITAL** *C1* (500m NE Rural) *47.10977,*
11.30770 **Camping Stubai, Stubaitalstrasse 94, 6167**
Neustift-im-Stubaital [(05226) 2537; fax 29342; info@
campingstubai.at; www.campingstubai.at]
S fr Innsbruck on B182 or A13, take B183 dir Fulpmes &
Neustift. Site sp, in vill opp church & adj Billa supmkt. If app via
A13 & Europabrucke, toll payable on exit junc 10 into Stubaital
Valley. Med, some mkd pitch, pt sl, pt terr, pt shd; htd wc;
chem disp; mv service pnt; baby facs; fam bthrm; sauna; shwrs
inc; EHU (6A) €2.90; lndry; shops adj; rest, bar adj; playgrnd;
htd pool 500m; games rm; 50% statics; dogs €2.60; Eng spkn;
adv bkg; quiet but church bells (not o'night) & rd noise fr
some pitches; debit cards acc; CKE/CCI. "Friendly, family-run
site; pitches nr rv poss flood; recep open 0900-1100 & 1700-
1900 - barrier down but can use farm ent & find space; excel
mountain walking & skiing." € 33.60   2013*

⊞ **NEUSTIFT IM STUBAITAL** *C1* (6km SW Rural) *47.06777,*
11.25388 **Camping Edelweiss, Volderau 29, 6167 Neustift-**
im-Stubaital [tel/fax (05226) 3484; info@camping-
edelweiss.at; www.camping-edelweiss.com]
Fr B182 or A13 exit junc 10 take B183 to Neustift, site on R at
Volderau vill. Med, hdstg, unshd; htd wc; chem disp; mv waste;
shwrs inc; EHU (4A) €2; gas; lndry; shop 6km; rest, snacks;
30% statics; dogs €1.50; phone; bus; quiet. "Excel peaceful
site in scenic valley; vg, modern san facs; haphazard mix of
statics & tourers; winter skiing." € 20.00   2012*

NUZIDERS see Bludenz *C1*

⊞ **OBERNBERG AM INN** *B3* (1km SW Rural) *48.31506,*
13.32313 **Panorama Camping, Saltzburgerstrasse 28,**
4982 Obernberg-am-Inn [tel/fax (07758) 30024 or
173 2306 571 (mob); obernberg-panoramacamping@
aon.at; http://obernberg-panoramacamping.jimdo.com]
Exit A8/E56 junc 65 to Obernberg. Then take dir Braunau, site
well sp. Sm, hdg pitch, pt sl, pt shd; wc; chem disp; serviced
pitches; shwrs inc; EHU (10A) metered or €2 (poss rev pol);
lndry; shop 200m; rest 400m; pool, tennis 800m; o'night area
for m'vans; Eng spkn; adv bkg; quiet. "Friendly, excel sm site;
site yourself if office clsd; nr to border; spectacular views; san
facs clean; gd walking, birdwatching; network of cycle paths
around vills on other side of rv; pleasant walk to town past rv
viewpoint." € 29.00   2015*

OBERSAMMELSDORF see Völkermarkt *D3*

OBERTRAUN WINKL see Hallstatt *C3*

OBERWOLZ *C3* (2km E Rural) *47.20076, 14.29296* **Camping**
Rothenfels (Part Naturist), Bromach 1, 8832 Oberwölz
[tel/fax (03581) 76980 or 0664 1412514 (mob); camping@
rothenfels.at; www.rothenfels.at]
Fr E on B96 to Niederwölz, then B75 to Oberwölz. Site sp
on edge of town. Med, terr, pt shd; htd wc; chem disp; mv
service pnt; shwrs inc; EHU (6A) inc; lndry (inc dryer); shop
1km; rest, snacks; bar; BBQ; playgrnd; rv fishing; games rm;
15% statics; dogs €1; Eng spkn; no adv bkg; quiet; ccard acc;
red long stay. "Magnificent setting; Oberwölz worth visit -
m'vans use car parks outside gates; clean facs." 1 Apr-31 Oct.
€ 18.50   2010*

⊞ **OETZ** *C1* (10km S Rural) *47.13533, 10.9316* **Ötztal**
Arena Camp Krismer, Mühlweg 32, 6441 Umhausen
[tel/fax (05255) 5390; www.oetztalcamping.com;
www.oetztal-camping.at] Fr A12 exit junc 123 S onto B186
sp Ötztal. S of Ötztal turn L into Umhausen vill & foll site sp.
Med, mkd pitch, pt sl, pt shd; wc; chem disp; shwrs €0.75;
EHU (10A) metered (poss rev pol); gas; lndry; shop 200m;
rest; snacks 200m; bar; BBQ; playgrnd; pool 200m; lake sw;
internet; dogs €2.60; phone; Eng spkn; adv bkg (dep); quiet.
"Well-run site; immac facs; lots of local info given on arr;
friendly owners; poss diff pitching on some sh pitches; excel
cent for Stuibenfal waterfall (illuminated Wed night high ssn)
& Ötztaler Valley; pool & lake sw 200m; wonderful scenery; gd
walking fr site; narr app rd; v cr in high ssn." € 25.00   2015*

OGGAU AM NEUSIEDLERSEE see Eisenstadt *B4*

OSSIACH *D3* (3km NE Rural) *46.68558, 14.01233* **Familien-Camping Jodl, Alt-Ossiach 6, 9570 Ossiach [(04243) 8779; fax 87794; info@camping-jodl.at; www.camping-jodl.at]** Site on S shore of Ossiachersee at E end, fr Feldkirchen take B94 rd in 6km turn S sp Ossiach-Villach, at rd junc turn W, site on R in 1km (approx). Sp at site ent. Fr W on B94 thro Bodensdorf & Steindorf turn S as above. Med, mkd pitch, terr, pt shd; wc; chem disp; mv service pnt; shwrs inc; EHU inc (16A) inc; lndry; shop high ssn; supmkt 2km; rest, snacks; playgrnd; shgle beach adj; lake sw; watersports; dogs €3; o'night facs for m'vans; Eng spkn; adv bkg; quiet; red snr citizens; CKE/CCI. "Excel site; beautiful scenery; friendly owners; facs for sm boats; oldest established site on Ossiachersee." 11 Apr-30 Sep. € 26.00   2009*

OSSIACH *D3* (1km SW Rural) *46.66388, 13.97500* **Terrassen Camping Ossiacher See, Ostriach 67, 9570 Ossiach [(04243) 436; fax 8171; martinz@camping.at; www.terrassen.camping.at]** Leave A10/E55/E66 at exit for Ossiachersee, turn L onto B94 twd Feldkirchen & shortly R to Ossiach Süd. Site on lake shore just S of Ossiach vill. Lge, mkd pitch, terr, pt shd; htd wc; chem disp; mv service pnt; baby facs; fam bthrm; shwrs inc; EHU (4-10A) €3; gas; lndry; shop; rest, snacks; bar; BBQ; playgrnd; lake sw & beach; watersports; windsurfing; fishing; horse riding; tennis; games area; bike hire; games rm; cash machine; wifi; entmnt; TV rm; dogs €3; twin-axles acc (rec check in adv); poss cr; clsd 1200-1500 LS, parking adj; quiet; ccard acc; red long stay/LS; CKE/CCI. "Ideal Carinthian lakes, Hochosterwitz castle & excursions into Italy; beautiful scenery; many activities; excel san facs." ♦ 1 May-29 Sep. € 31.00 SBS - G05   2011*

OSSIACH *D3* (4km SW Rural) *46.65551, 13.93976* **Seecamping Plörz, Süduferstrasse 289, 9523 Heiligen-Gestade [(04242) 41286 or 0676-3221494 (mob); info@camping-ploerz.at; www.camping-ploerz.at]** Fr A10/E55/E65 turn N onto B94 twd Feldkirchen. Almost immed turn R sp Ossiach, site on R just past Camping Mentl. Sm, pt sl, pt shd; htd wc; chem disp; mv service pnt; baby facs; shwrs inc; EHU (16A) inc; lndry; shop, rest, snacks, bar nrby; play equipment; lake sw adj; TV rm; dogs €2; phone; Eng spkn; quiet. "Excel sm farm site with gd facs; friendly helpful owners; quiet alt to other busy lakeside sites; lge pitches; v clean facs; cycle paths & gd walks; bus stop at gate; ltd facs for children." Apr-25 Sep. € 25.00   2013*

OSSIACH *D3* (5km SW Rural) *46.65321, 13.93344* **Seecamping Berghof, Ossiachersee Süduferstrasse 241, 9523 Heiligengestade [(04242) 41133; fax 4113330; office@seecamping-berghof.at; www.seecamping-berghof.at]** Exit Villach on rd sp Ossiachersee; take R turn Ossiachersee Süd, site on L bet rd & lake. Lge, terr, pt sl, pt shd; htd wc; chem disp; mv service pnt; serviced pitches; fam bthrm; baby rm; private bthrms avail; shwrs inc; EHU (10A) inc; gas; lndry (inc dryer); shop, rest; snacks high ssn; bar; playgrnd; lake beach & sw; sailing; fishing; tennis; games area; bike hire; golf 10km; wifi; entmnt; 10% statics; dogs €3 (in sep area); phone; poss cr; adv bkg; quiet; red snr citizens/long stay/LS. "Excel site; gd cent for excursions to castles & lakes; many sports & activities; extra for lge/lakeside pitches; muddy when wet." ♦ 4 Apr-18 Oct. € 38.00   2014*

OSSIACH *D3* (5km SW Rural) *46.65376, 13.93735* **See-Camping Mentl, Süderstrasse 265, 9523 Heiligen-Gestade [(04242) 41886; fax 43850; camping@mentl.at; www.mentl.at]** Fr A10/E55/E65 turn N onto B94 twd Feldkirchen. Almost immed turn R sp Ossiach, site on L adj lake in 4km. Lge, mkd pitch, terr, pt shd; wc; chem disp; some serviced pitches; baby facs; shwrs inc; EHU (6A) inc (check pol); lndry (inc dryer); shops adj; snacks; rest adj; playgrnd; lake sw; watersports; bike hire; entmnt; no dogs high ssn; poss cr; Eng spkn; adv bkg; quiet; red long stay. "Beautiful setting; gd facs & entmnt for children; helpful staff; excel, modern, clean san facs." ♦ 1 Apr-15 Oct. € 29.00   2010*

PETTNAU *C1* (350m E Rural) *47.29020, 11.16453* **Camping Tiefental "Roppnerhof", Tiroler Strasse 121, 6408 Pettnau [(0664) 4663003 (mob); tiefental@aon.at; www.camping-tiefental.at]** Leave A12 autoban at junc 171 going E twds Zirl and Innsbruck. Site on Tiroler Strabe E end of Unter Pettnau vill. Sm, med pitches, open plan grassy, mkd, pt shd; wc, chem disp, mv service pnt, shwrs; EHU (13A) €3; lndry; BBQ; dog €2; twin axle acc; Eng spkn; adv bkg acc; CKE/CCI. "Superb views; walking and cycling in the Inn valley; Innsbruck 25km; excel." ♦ 1 May-30 Sep. € 26.00   2013*

PETTNEU AM ARLBERG see St Anton am Arlberg *C1*

PODERSDORF AM SEE see Frauenkirchen *B4*

POYSDORF *A4* (1km W Urban) *48.66454, 16.61168* **Veltlinerland Camping, Laaerstrasse 106, 2170 Poysdorf [(02552) 20371; fax 37131; veltlinerlandcamping.poysdorf@gmx.at; www.poysdorf.at]** Fr rd 7/E461 at traff lts in Poysdorf turn W onto rd 219 dir Laa an der Thaya. Site sp on R in approx 1km on edge of park. Sm, mkd pitch, some hdstg, terr, unshd; htd wc & shwrs at park adj (key issued); chem disp; mv service pnt; EHU (6A) €2.20; lndry; shop 1km; rest; playgrnd; rv sw adj; tennis; 50% statics in sep area; dogs; Eng spkn; quiet. "Gd, under-used site 1hr N of Vienna; no other site in area; conv Czech border." 1 May-31 Oct. € 12.00   2010*

⊞ **PRUTZ** *C1* (550m NE Rural) *47.07955, 10.6588* **Aktiv-Camping Prutz, Pontlatzstrasse 22, 6522 Prutz [(05472) 2648; fax 26484; info@aktiv-camping.at; www.aktiv-camping.at]** Fr Landeck to Prutz on rd B180 turn R at Shell stn over rv bdge, site sp. Med, hdg/mkd pitch, pt shd; htd wc; chem disp; mv service pnt; baby facs; shwrs inc; EHU (16A) inc; gas; lndry; shop high ssn; rest, snacks high ssn; bar; playgrnd adj; pool complex in vill; lake sw 1km; bike hire; internet; TV rm; 20% statics; dogs €3; o'night area for m'vans; site clsd Nov; poss cr; Eng spkn; adv bkg; some rd noise; ccard acc; red LS/long stay/snr citizens; CKE/CCI. "Excel, clean facs; gd views; office clsd 1000-1630 - find pitch & pay later; walks & cycle rtes; conv NH en rte Italy & for tax-free shopping in Samnaun, Switzerland; gd site; cards given for free bus travel." ♦ € 32.00   2015*

AUSTRIA

PURBACH AM NEUSIEDLERSEE *B4* (1km SE Rural) *47.90958, 16.70580* **Storchencamp Purbach, Türkenhain, 7083 Purbach-am-Neusiedlersee (Burgenland) [(02683) 5170; fax 517015; office@gmeiner.co.at; www.gmeiner.co.at]** Exit A4/E6 junc 43 onto B50 at Neuseidl-am-See to Purbach. Site sp in town nr pool complex. Sm, pt shd; htd wc; chem disp; mv service pnt; baby facs; shwrs inc; EHU (6A) €2.30; lndry; shop; rest; bar; BBQ; playgrnd; pools, waterslide adj; games area; 80% statics; dogs €2.90; bus/train 1km; Eng spkn; quiet. "Open field for tourers; excel sw complex adj free with local visitor card + free public transport & red ent to museums etc; modern facs; conv NH." 1 Apr-31 Oct. € 17.50   2010*

⊞ **RADSTADT** *C3* (300m N Rural) *47.38751, 13.46108* **Tauerncamping, Schloss-strasse 17, 5550 Radstadt [(06452) 4215; fax 42154; info@tauerncamping.at; www.tauerncamping.at]** Exit A10 junc 63 onto B99, site sp in Radstadt. Med, some hdstg, terr, pt shd; htd wc; chem disp; mv service pnt; baby facs; shwrs €1; EHU (10A) metered; gas; lndry (inc dryer); shop adj; rest, snacks; bar; BBQ; playgrnd; htd pool; tennis 200m; 50% statics; dogs; poss cr; adv bkg; quiet except church bells. "Conv NH." € 25.00   2010*

"I need an on-site restaurant"

We do our best to make sure site information is correct, but it is always best to check any must-have facilities are still available or will be open during your visit.

⊞ **RATTENBERG** *C2* (4.5km N Rural) *47.45670, 11.88084* **Seen-Camping Stadlerhof, Seebühel 15, 6233 Kramsach-am-Reintalersee [(05337) 63371; fax 65311; camping.stadlerhof@chello.at; www.camping-stadlerhof.at]** Exit A12/E45/E60 junc 32 Rattenberg dir Kramsach. At rndabt turn R, then immed L & foll sp 'Zu den Seen' & site sp. Site on L at Lake Krumsee. Lge, mkd pitch, some hdstg, pt sl, pt shd; htd wc; chem disp; sauna; baby facs; shwrs inc; EHU (10A) inc; gas; lndry (inc dryer); shops 2km; rest, snacks; bar; BBQ; playgrnd; htd pool; paddling pool; lake sw 200m; fishing; tennis; bike hire; games rm; wifi; cab TV; 50% statics; dogs €3.50; phone; adv bkg; quiet. "Beautiful, well laid-out site in lovely setting; excel san facs." ◆ € 44.00   2014*

⊞ **RATTENBERG** *C2* (4km NE Rural) *47.46198, 11.90708* **Camping Seehof, Moosen 42, 6233 Kramsach-am-Reintalersee [(05337) 63541; fax 6354120; info@camping-seehof.com; www.camping-seehof.com]** Exit A12/E45/E60 junc 32 sp Kramsach, foll sp 'Zu den Seen' for 5km. Site immed bef Camping Seeblick-Toni Brantlhof. Med, mkd pitch, pt shd; htd wc; chem disp; mv service pnt; baby facs; shwrs inc; EHU (6-13A) €2.80; lndry; shop; rest, snacks; bar; BBQ; playgrnd; pool; lake sw; bike hire; gym; solarium; horseriding nr; internet; cab TV; 30% statics; dogs €3.50; phone; poss cr; Eng spkn; adv bkg; quiet; ccard acc; red long stay; CKE/CCI. "Friendly staff; gd views fr some pitches; gd, modern san facs; gd rest; Excel site, local walks, excel museum next door; local taxes €2." ◆ € 41.50   2014*

⊞ **RATTENBERG** *C2* (4.5km NE Rural) *47.46121, 11.9066* **Camping Seeblick Ton, Moosen 46, 6233 Kramsach-am-Reintalersee [(05337) 63544; fax 63544305; info@camping-seeblick.at; www.camping-seeblick.at]** Exit A12/E45/E60 junc 32 sp Kramsach. Foll sps 'Zu den Seen' for about 5km. Drive past Camping Seehof site to Brantlhof site, 3rd site on Reintalersee. Med, mkd pitch, pt shd; wc; chem disp; mv service pnt; baby facs; sauna; serviced pitches; private bthrms avail; shwrs inc; EHU (10A) €3.50 + conn fee; mains gas conn; lndry (inc dryer); shop; rest, snacks; bar; playgrnd; lake sw; fishing; bike hire; games area; games rm; fitness rm; guided walks; x-country skiing; wifi; entmnt; TV rm; 10% statics; dogs €5.50; adv bkg; quiet; ccard acc. "Excel site, lovely lakeside setting; superb san facs, inc for children; excel meals; gd for ski & walking; conv NH fr a'bahn." ◆ € 27.00 (CChq acc)   2009*

REISACH *D2* (1.5km N Rural) *46.65467, 13.14906* **Alpenferienpark Reisach, Schönboden 1, 9633 Reisach [(04284) 301; fax 302; info@alpenferienpark.com; www.alpenferienpark.com]** Turn E in Kötschach to Hermagor. At Reisach turn L immed past bdge. Foll sps up hill & across bdge & cont. Bear R up long 1 in 8 slope into wood. Site on L at sp Schonboden. Med, mkd pitch, pt sl, pt shd; htd wc; chem disp; fam bthrm; shwrs inc; EHU (10A) €2.50; gas; lndry; shop & 4km; rest, snacks; bar; playgrnd; pool; tennis; some statics; dogs €2; Eng spkn; adv bkg; v quiet. "Friendly site; only suitable sm o'fits." 15 Dec-31 Oct. € 20.00   2009*

REUTTE *C1* (6km ESE Rural) *47.47448, 10.78511* **Camping Seespitze, Planseestrasse 68, 6600 Breitenwang [(05672) 78121; fax 63372; agrar.breitenwang@aon.at]** S fr Reutte on by-pass turn L outside town sp Oberammergau/Plansee. Site on L in 5km. Med, pt sl, terr, pt shd; wc; chem disp; shwrs €1; EHU (12A) metered (long lead poss req) + conn fee; lndry; shop; rest adj; snacks; bar; playgrnd; lake sw; 10% statics; dogs €2.50; Eng spkn; adv bkg; quiet; CKE/CCI. "Beautiful position, mountain scenery; gd walks; v clean san facs; well-maintained site." 1 May-15 Oct. € 24.00   2009*

⊞ **REUTTE** *C1* (9km SE Rural) *47.45547, 10.75937* **Camping Heiterwangersee, Fischer-am-See, 6611 Heiterwang [(05674) 5116; fax 5260; hotel@fischeramsee.at; www.fischeramsee.at]** Fr Reutte on B179 dir Ehrwald turn R to Heiterwang, foll sp to Hotel Fischer & to lakeside (1.5km). Med, some hdstg, pt shd; htd wc; chem disp; mv service pnt; sauna; shwrs inc; EHU (10-16A) metered; lndry (inc dryer); shop; rest, snacks; bar; lake sw; fishing; boating; ski lift 2km; 70% statics; dogs €2; skibus; poss cr; adv bkg rec high ssn; quiet; ccard acc. "Lovely location; vg san facs." € 29.00   2010*

⊞ **REUTTE** *C1* (1km S Rural) *47.47763, 10.72258* **Camping Reutte, Ehrenbergstrasse 53, 6600 Reutte [(05672) 62809 or (06641) 858279 (mob); fax 628094; camping-reutte@aon.at; www.camping-reutte.com]** Foll B179 (Fern pass rd), exit at Reutte Süd. Site sp in 1.5km on L. Med, mkd pitch, some hdstg, pt shd; wc; chem disp; mv service pnt; shwrs €1; EHU (16A) €2.40; lndry; shop; rest, snacks; pool adj; ski lift 500m; cab TV; dogs €2; phone; Eng spkn; adv bkg; quiet; ccard acc; CKE/CCI. "Conv for Fern Pass; adj Neuschwanstein Castle; barriers clsd 2100; clean, popular site; excel; free guest cards for facs & transport." € 29.00   2015*

AUSTRIA

⊞ **RIED IM OBERINNTAL** *C1* (600m E Rural) *47.05480, 10.65630* **Camping Dreiländereck, Gartenland 37, 6531 Ried Im Oberinntal [05472 6025; fax 60254; info@ tirolcamping.at; www.tirolcamping.at]** Fr Landeck take 180 twd Reschenpass. Exit at Ried & foll sp. Sm, unshd; htd wc; chem disp; mv service pnt; baby facs; shwrs €0.50; EHU (15A); lndry (inc dryer); shop 0.1km; snacks; bar; sw adj; wifi; TV rm; dogs €2; bus adj; twin axles; poss cr; Eng spkn; adv bkg; quiet; CCI. "Wellness cent; conv to vill shops; bike hire; helpful owners; gd clean san facs; adventure sports fac nrby; gd site." € 39.00 2014*

RINN BEI INNSBRUCK see Innsbruck *C1*

RUST AM NEUSIEDLERSEE see Eisenstadt *B4*

ST ANDRA AM ZICKSEE see Frauenkirchen *B4*

ST ANTON AM ARLBERG *C1* (2km E Rural) *47.14505, 10.33890* **Camping Arlberg, Strohsack 235c, 6574 Pettneu-am-Arlberg (Tirol) [(05448) 222660; fax 2226630; info@ camping-arlberg.at; www.camping-arlberg.at]** Fr W on S16/E60, thro Arlberg tunnel, then take Pettneu exit after St Anton to N; site sp in 200m. Lge, mkd/hdg pitch; pt shd; wc; chem disp; mv service pnt; htd private bathrms & sat TV each pitch; sauna; shwrs inc; EHU (16A) metered; lndry (inc dryer); rest; bar; playgrnd; htd, covrd pool; paddling pool; fishing; ski & boot rm; ski bus; ski lift 1km; 10% statics; dogs; phone; bus; twin-axles; o'night area for m'vans; Eng spkn; adv bkg; quiet. "Mountain views; beauty treatments avail; excel site; wellness ctr adj with pool." ◆ ltd. 1 Jan-30 Apr & 1 Jun-31 Dec. € 26.00 2015*

⊞ **ST ANTON AM ARLBERG** *C1* (7km E Rural) *47.14809, 10.34668* **Arlberg Panoramacamping, Sportranch 45a, 6574 Pettneu-am-Arlberg [(05448) 8352; fax 83524; info@arlberg-panormacamping.at; www.arlberg-panoramacamping.at]** Fr S16 exit at E end Arlberg Tunnel sp St Anton. Turn L (E) onto B197/B316 to Pettneu. After 3km at ent to vill, keep R skirting vill. Sportranch 1km on R, ent downhill to L of fire stn. Access only suitable sm/med o'fits. Sm, mkd pitch, pt shd; wc; chem disp; mv service pnt; all serviced pitches; shwrs €1; EHU (10-13A) €2.50 or metered; lndry; shop 1km; snacks; rest 500m; bar; games rm; horseriding; Wellness-Park nrby; TV; dogs free; bus; adv bkg; quiet but some rd/rlwy noise; ccard acc; red LS/long stay/CKE/CCI. "Clean facs; friendly owner; owner prefers long stay (significant red); geared for winter ssn; gd cent walking, skiing." € 26.00 2010*

ST GILGEN see Abersee *B3*

⊞ **ST JOHANN IM PONGAU** *C2* (1km S Urban) *47.34141, 13.19793* **Camping Kastenhof, Kastenhofweg 6, 5600 St Johann-im-Pongau [tel/fax (06412) 5490; info@kastenhof.at; www.kastenhof.at]** Take A10 S fr Salzburg onto B311 for Alpendorf. Go over rv & turn L into Liechtensteinklamm twd St Johann, site on L, sp. Med, unshd; htd wc; chem disp; mv service pnt; sauna; shwrs €1; EHU (15A) metered + €2 conn fee; lndry (inc dryer); shop; rest, snacks 500m; playgrnd; paddling pool; bus; cab TV; some statics; dogs free; adv bkg; quiet; CKE/CCI. "Conv Tauern tunnel, Grossglockner Hochalpenstrasse, Zell-am-See; gd clean site." € 20.00 2010*

⊞ **ST JOHANN IM PONGAU** *C2* (3km W Urban) *47.34605, 13.19276* **Camping Wieshof, Wieshofgasse 8, 5600 St Johann-im-Pongau [(06412) 8519; fax 8292; info@ camping-wieshof.at; www.camping-wieshof.at]** On rd B163 dir Zell-am-Zee, past Agip petrol stn, above rd. Med, terr, unshd; htd wc; chem disp; mv service pnt; shwrs €1; EHU (15A) metered; lndry; shop 500m; rest adj; playgrnd; golf 6km; 80% statics; dogs; poss cr; Eng spkn; quiet. "Pleasant site; gd views; vg san facs; friendly & helpful owners." € 18.00 2011*

ST JOHANN IN TIROL *C2* (12km SE Rural) *47.46845, 12.55440* **Tirol Camp, Lindau 20, 6391 Fieberbrunn (Tirol) [(05354) 56666; fax 52516; office@tirol-camp.at; www.tirol-camp.at]** Fr St Johann thro vill of Fieberbrunn, site sp at end of vill. Turn R up to Streuböden chair lift, site 200m on L. Lge, terr, pt shd; htd wc; chem disp; mv service pnt; baby facs; fam bthrm; sauna; shwrs inc; EHU (6A) metered; lndry (inc dryer); shop; rest, snacks, bar high ssn; playgrnd; 2 htd pools (1 covrd); waterslide; lake sw; games area; tennis; wellness cent; internet; entmnt; TV rm; 30% statics; dogs €8; phone; train; poss cr; adv bkg; quiet; red snr citizens; ccard acc; red LS/snr citizens. "Superb site & facs; gd base for skiing, gd walking; trips to Innsbruck & Salzburg; noise fr adj farm." 1 Jan-12 Apr, 11 May-1 Nov & 9 Dec-31 Dec. € 38.00 2015*

⊞ **ST JOHANN IN TIROL** *C2* (2.5km SW Rural) *47.51078, 12.40888* **Sonnencamping Michelnhof, Weiberndorf 6, 6380 St Johann-in-Tirol [(05352) 62584; fax 625844; camping@michelnhof.at; www.camping-michelnhof.at]** On L of B161 St Johann-Kitzbühel, heading S. Turn L in 2km at sp, follow L after level x-ing. Site on R in 500m. Med, mkd pitch, hdstg, sl, pt shd; htd wc; chem disp; mv service pnt; baby facs; shwrs inc; EHU (10A) €2.70; lndry; supmkt 1.5km; rest, snacks; playgrnd; pool 2km; golf 4km; 50% statics; dogs €4; phone; Eng spkn; quiet; CKE/CCI. "Friendly warden; higher prices in winter; vg." ◆ € 18.40 2009*

⊞ **ST MICHAEL IM LUNGAU** *C3* (190m S Rural) *47.09685, 13.63706* **Camping St Michael, Waaghausgasse 277, 5582 St Michael-im-Lungau [tel/fax (06477) 8276; camping-st. michael@sgb.at]** Exit junc 104 fr A10/E55, site sp at turn into vill, then on L after 200m bef hill. Sm, pt shd; wc; chem disp; mv service pnt; shwrs inc; EHU (16A) €3.50 (poss rev pol); gas; lndry; shop adj; rest, snacks adj; playgrnd; pool adj; ski lift 1km; dogs; poss cr; adv bkg; ccard acc; red CKE/CCI. "Delightful site adj vill; excel san facs (shared with adj sports club); poss full if arr after 6pm, but o'flow area avail." € 20.00 2010*

ST PETER AM KAMMERSBERG *C3* (3km ESE Rural) *47.17905, 14.21671* **Camping Bella Austria, Peterdorf 100, 8842 St Peter-am-Kammersberg [(03536) 73902; fax 73912; info@ camping-bellaustria.com; www.camping-bellaustria.com]** Fr B96 turn N onto L501 into Katschtal Valley dir Oberdorf, Althofen & St Peter-am-Kammersberg. Site sp. Lge, some hdstg, pt shd; wc; chem disp; mv service pnt; baby facs; sauna; hot shwrs; EHU (16A) inc; lndry; shop; rest, snacks; bar; playgrnd; htd pool; lake sw; games area; bike hire; wifi; entmnt; TV rm; 70% statics; dog €2; Eng spkn; adv bkg; quiet. "Superb walking area; excel." ◆ 12 Apr-28 Sep. € 30.00 2014*

ST PRIMUS *D3* (800m N Rural) *46.58569, 14.56598*
Strandcamping Turnersee Breznik, Unternarrach 21,
9123 St Primus [(04239) 2350; fax 235032; info@breznik.at;
www.breznik.at] Exit A2 at junc 298 Grafenstein onto
B70. After 4km turn R & go thro Tainach, St Kanzian twd
St Primus. Site is on W side of Turnersee. Lge, mkd pitch, pt
shd; htd wc; chem disp; mv service pnt; serviced pitches; baby
facs; shwrs inc; EHU (6A) inc; lndry (inc dryer); shop; rest;
bar; BBQ; playgrnd; lake sw; fishing; tennis 500m; games
rm; games area; bike hire; golf 2km; wifi; entmnt; cinema
rm; TV rm; 30% statics; dogs €3.30; adv bkg; quiet; CKE/
CCI. "Lovely situation; excel site." ♦ 16 Apr-2 Oct. € 26.60
(CChq acc)   2009*

ST VEIT IM PONGAU see St Johann im Pongau *C2*

⊞ **ST WOLFGANG IM SALZKAMMERGUT** *B3* (3km SE
Rural) *47.73063, 13.47795* **Komfortcamping Berau,**
Schwarzenbach 16, 5360 St Wolfgang-im-Salzkammergut
[(06138) 2543; fax 254355; camping@berau.at;
www.berau.at] Turn N off B158 at Strobl at sp for
St Wolfgang & foll sps. Easy to miss - look for Gasthaus/Hotel
Berau just after soccer field on L. Med, mkd pitch, pt shd;
wc; chem disp; mv service pnt; sauna; baby facs; shwrs inc;
EHU (6A) inc; gas; lndry (inc dryer); shop; rest, snacks; bar;
BBQ; playgrnd; lake sw; watersports; bike hire; wifi; entmnt;
dogs €3.10; phone; poss cr; Eng spkn; adv bkg; quiet; ccard
acc; red long stay; CKE/CCI. "Immac san facs; excel site." ♦
€ 29.00   2010*

ST WOLFGANG IM SALZKAMMERGUT *B3* (1km W Rural)
47.74277, 13.43361 **Seeterrassen Camping Reid, Ried 18,**
5360 St Wolfgang/Salzkammergut [tel/fax (06138) 3201;
camping-ried@aon.at; www.members.aon.at/camping-
ried] Fr Salzburg take B158 thro St Gilgen dir Bad Ischl. Exit at
sp Strobl & foll sp St Wolfgang. Go thro tunnel to avoid town
cent, foll rd along lake to site. Sm, pt sl, terr, pt shd; htd wc;
chem disp; mv service pnt; baby facs; shwrs €0.80; EHU (16A)
metered; gas; lndry; shop; rest, snacks; bar; playgrnd; lake sw,
fishing, watersports adj; tennis nr; TV rm; 10% statics; dogs
€1.80; phone; poss cr; Eng spkn; poss rd noise; ccard not acc;
CKE/CCI. "Mountain rlwy stn nr; lake views; gd touring base;
easy walk into town; friendly site; v clean san facs."
16 Apr-31 Oct. € 34.00   2014*

SALZBURG *B2* (2km N Urban) *47.82683, 13.06296* **Camping**
Nord-Sam, Samstrasse 22a, 5023 Salzburg Nord
[tel/fax (0662) 660494; office@camping-nord-sam.com;
www.camping-nord-sam.com] Heading E on A1/E55/E69
exit junc 288 Salzburg Nord exit & immed take slip rd on R;
then over to L-hand lane for L-hand turn at 2nd traff lts, up
narr rd to site, sp. If thro Salzburg foll Wien-Linz sps thro city;
turn onto B1 on exit o'skts, camp site posted on L. Med, hdg
pitch, hdstg, pt sl, pt shd; htd wc; chem disp; mv service pnt;
baby facs; shwrs inc; EHU (10A) €3; lndry (inc dryer); shop;
supmkt 10m; snacks; playgrnd; htd pool; dogs €3; bus adj;
poss cr; Eng spkn; adv bkg ess; rlwy noise; ccard not acc; red
long stay/CKE/CCI. "Sm pitches & high hdgs; san facs clean but
old & stretched when site full; friendly staff; many attractions
nrby; site sells Salzburg Card; cycle track to city cent; recep
open 0800-1200 & 1600-2030 high ssn." ♦ 1 Jan-6 Jan,
23 Mar-13 Oct, 26 Dec- 31 dec. € 40.00   2013*

SALZBURG *B2* (3km N Rural) *47.82843, 13.05221* **Panorama**
Camping Stadtblick, Rauchenbichlerstrasse 21, 5020
Salzburg [(0662) 450652; fax 458018; info@panorama-
camping.at; www.panorama-camping.at]
Fr A1/E55/E60 exit 288 Salzburg Nord/Zentrum & at end of slip
rd turn R & sharp R at traff lts, site sp. If coming fr S, foll ring
rd to W then N. Med, mkd pitch, hdstg, terr, pt shd; htd wc;
chem disp; mv service pnt; shwrs inc; EHU (4A) inc (long lead
req some pitches); gas; lndry; shop; rest/café high ssn; bar;
wifi; dogs €2; phone; bus to town nr (tickets fr recep); poss cr;
Eng spkn; adv bkg; rd noise; ccard not acc - cash only; red 3+
days; CKE/CCI. "Conv a'bahn; views of Salzburg; cycle track
by rv to town; Salzburg card avail fr recep; sm pitches - rec
phone ahead if lge o'fit; v helpful family owners; vg rest; excel,
modern san facs; rec arr early; also open some dates in Dec
& Jan; excel; 'Sound of Music' Tour; v conv for Salzburg; gd
views; beautiful city; cash only; helpful owner."
1 Jan-8 Jan, 20 Mar-5 Nov,5 Dec-10 Dec. € 41.00   2014*

SALZBURG *B2* (5km SE Urban) *47.78058, 13.08985* **Camping**
Schloss Aigen, Weberbartlweg 20, 5026 Salzburg-Aigen
[tel/fax (0662) 622079; camping.aigen@elsnet.at;
www.campingaigen.com] Fr S leave A10/E55 at junc 8
Salzburg-Süd & take B150 twds Salzburg on Alpenstrasse. Turn
R at rndabt dir Glasenbach, then L into Aignerstrasse. 1km S
of Aigen stn turn R into Glasenstrasse & foll sps to site. Lge,
pt sl, pt shd; wc; chem disp; shwrs inc; EHU (6-16A) €2; gas;
washing machine avail; shop; rest, snacks; bar; bus to town
700m; poss cr; adv bkg; quiet except nr bar/rest; red long stay/
CKE/CCI. "Friendly, family-run site; sl pitches v slippery & boggy
when wet; excel rest; conv for city; gd walks." 1 May-30 Sep.
€ 28.00   2014*

SCHARNSTEIN *B3* (2.5 km NE Rural) *47.91580, 13.97372*
Almcamp Schatzlmühle, Viechtwang 1A, 4644 Scharnstein
[07615 20269; fax 20279; office@almcamp.at;
www.almcamp.at] Fr A1 take exit 207 Vorchtdorf to
Pettenbach on the L536. Head twd Scharnstein on 120. Turn
R 2km bef vill (dir Viechtwang). Foll sp. Alt take A9, exit 5, dir
Scharnstein. Sm, hdg/mkd pitch, hdstg, pt shd; wc; chem disp;
mv service pnt; baby facs; shwrs; EHU (16A); lndry (inc dryer);
shop; rest; bar; BBQ; playgrnd; games area; games rm; wifi;
tv; 10% statics; dogs €1.50; phone; twin-axles acc; Eng spkn;
adv bkg; quiet; CCI. "Child friendly; family run site; site by rv,
scenic location; gd cycling & walking rtes; htd, excel site & san
facs." ♦ 12 Mar-31 Oct. € 30.00   2014*

SCHONBUHEL see Melk *B4*

⊞ **SCHRUNS** *C1* (1.6km S Rural) *47.06760, 9.91615*
Camping Zelfen, Zelfenstrasse 79, 6774 Tschagguns
[(0664) 2002326; kunsttischlerei.tschofen@utanet.at;
www.camping-zelfen.at] Fr Bludenz to Schruns. After x-ing
rlwy turn R at traff lts, foll rd L in front of Spar. Site on L in
1.6km, sp. Med, pt shd; htd wc; chem disp; shwrs €1; EHU (6A)
inc; lndry, shop & 1.6km; rest, snacks, bar 1.6km; playgrnd;
pool 200m; 50% statics; dogs; phone; poss cr; Eng spkn; adv
bkg; quiet; ccard acc; CKE/CCI. "Free sw & children's activities
at nrby Activpark; site conv Montafon valley; office open
0800-0900 & 1800-1900 - other times use freephone by office
door." € 22.00   2009*

SCHWAZ *C2* (7km SW Rural) *47.30613, 11.64926*
Alpencamping Mark, Bundesstrasse 12, 6114 Weer
[(05224) 68146; fax 681466; alpcamp.mark@aon.at;
www.alpencampingmark.com] Exit A12/E45/E60 junc 61;
cont E on B171. Site on R after Weer vill. Ent mkd by flags.
Med, hdg pitch, pt shd; htd wc; chem disp; mv service pnt;
baby facs; shwrs inc; EHU (6-10A) €2.70; lndry (inc dryer); shop
500m; rest, snacks; bar; BBQ; playgrnd; htd pool; lake sw 2km;
tennis; horseriding; bike hire; dogs €3; Eng spkn; adv bkg;
quiet; ccard acc; red long stay/CKE/CCI. "Well-maintained site
in scenic location; clean pleasant site with nice rest; friendly,
welcoming owners & staff; lavish sports facs; gd san facs; nr
town of Weer; many local attractions; rec." ♦ 1 Apr-31 Oct.
€ 21.00   2011*

⊞ **SEEFELD IN TIROL** *C1* (11km N Rural) *47.39832,*
11.17941 **Holiday Camping, Reindlau 230B, 6105 Leutasch**
[(05214) 65700; fax 657030; info@holiday-camping.at;
www.holiday-camping.at] Fr B2 fr Germany & passing S thro
Scharnitz on B177 & take minor rd W in 4km sp Leutasch. Foll
sps to site approx 11km. Do not use Mittenwald-Leutasch rd,
v narr & steep gradients. Rte fr S fr A12 via Telfs not rec for
c'vans. Med, unshd; htd wc; chem disp; mv service pnt; private
bthrms avail; serviced pitches; sauna; baby facs; shwrs inc; EHU
(12A) €3.20 or metered; gas; lndry (inc dryer); drying rm; shop;
rest; snacks; bar; htd; covrd pool; paddling pool; fishing; tennis;
golf driving range; golf 10km; ski lift 3km; skibus; wifi; sat TV
each pitch; dogs €3; site clsd 11 Nov-6 Dec; adv bkg; quiet;
ccard acc. "Gd walking & skiing cent; immac facs; superb
location; gd walking, cycling; excel." ♦ € 28.00   2010*

⊞ **SEEFELD IN TIROL** *C1* (1.6km NW Rural) *47.33661,*
11.17756 **Alpin Camp, Leutascherstrasse 810, 6100**
Seefeld [(05212) 4848; fax 4848 10; info@camp-alpin.at;
www.camp-alpin.at] Fr N on B177/E533 turn W into Seefeld.
Thro main rd, turn R sp Leutasch, site on L in 2km. Apps fr SE
& SW via v steep hills/hairpins, prohibited to trailers. Med,
hdstg, pt sl, terr, pt shd; wc; chem disp; mv service pnt; sauna
& steambath inc; shwrs inc; EHU (16A) €2.80 or metered; gas
(metered); lndry; shop & 2km; rest adj; playgrnd; htd, covrd
pool, golf 1.5km; bike hire; wifi; 10% statics; dogs €3; bus to
town; site clsd Nov; adv bkg; Eng spkn; quiet; red snr citizens.
"Excel site; excel facs; friendly owners; vg walking; delightful
setting; ski tows at gate; lovely vill." ♦ € 32.00   2015*

⊞ **SILLIAN** *D2* (4km E Rural) *46.74583, 12.46315* **Camping**
Lienzer Dolomiten, Tassenbach 191, 9918 Strassen-bei-
Sillian [(04842) 5228; fax 522815; camping-dolomiten@
gmx.at; www.camping-tirol.at] B100 fr Sillian dir Lienz,
turn R after filling stn, over level x-ing, then immed R; site sp.
Med, mkd pitch, some hdstg, pt sl, unshd; wc; chem disp; mv
service pnt; shwrs inc; EHU (6A) €2; lndry; shop, rest 3km; bar;
lake sw; ski lift 3km; wifi; 25% statics; dogs €2; red long stay.
"Informal, peaceful site; clean facs; helpful staff; mountain
views." € 27.50   2015*

SOLDEN *C1* (1km S Rural) *46.95786, 11.01193* **Camping**
Sölden, Wohlfahrtstrasse 22, 6450 Sölden [(05254) 26270;
fax 26725; info@camping-soelden.com; www.camping-
soelden.com] Turn L off main rd at cable car terminal. Turn
R at rv & foll narr track on rv bank for about 200m, turn R
into site. Med, mkd pitch, pt sl, terr, pt shd; wc; chem disp;
mv service pnt; serviced pitches; sauna; shwrs inc; EHU (10A)
metered; gas; lndry; shop 200m; snacks 500m; rest 20m;
playgrnd; gym; wifi; dogs €3; dog-washing facs; site clsd mid-
Apr to mid-Jun approx; adv bkg; quiet; Eng spkn; ccard acc.
"Excel for touring or climbing in upper Ötz Valley; pitches tight
for lge o'fits; superb site; excel san facs." ♦
1 Jan-12 Apr & 27 Jun-31 Dec. € 33.00   2015*

⊞ **SPITAL AM PYHRN** *C3* (3km N Rural) *47.6912, 14.3260*
Campingplatz Pyhrn-Priel, Gleinkerau 34, 4582 Spital-
am-Pyhrn [(07562) 7066; pyhrn-priel@aon.at;
www.pyhrn-priel.at] Exit A9 junc 52 - Gleinkerau; cross
rndabt on m'way access rd & turn L at T junc; foll sp for approx
500m & turn R to site. Med, unshd; wc; chem disp; shwrs; EHU
(10A) €2.50; lndry; shop 3km; rest, snacks; bar; playgrnd; pool
3km; 60% statics; dogs €2.20; Eng spkn; adv bkg; quiet; ccard
acc; CKE/CCI. "Gd views; walking; para/hang-gliding school;
summer toboggan run; pleasant owners." ♦ € 18.00   2011*

SPITTAL AN DER DRAU *D3* (5.6km NE Urban) *46.81510,*
13.52001 **Strandcamping Winkler, Seepromenade 33,**
9871 Seeboden [04 76 28 19 27; fax 76 28 18 22;
www.campsite.at] Leave A10 Villach-Salzburg at junc 139
twd Seeboden. Cont along main st across 2 rndabts & turn R
down narr rd sp Strandcamping Winkler. Sm, mkd pitch, pt sl,
pt shd; wc; chem disp; mv service pnt; shwrs €1; EHU (16A);
lndry; playgrnd; sw 40m; dogs; twin axles; poss cr; Eng spkn;
adv bkg; CCI. "Cycling & walking rtes rnd beautiful Millstätter;
gd site." 1 May-1 Oct. € 41.50   2014*

SPITTAL AN DER DRAU *D3* (2km S Rural) *46.78513,*
13.48669 **Camping Draufluss, Schwaig 10, 9800 Spittal-an-**
der-Drau [(04762) 2466; fax 36299; drauwirt@aon.at;
www.drauwirt.com] Exit A10 Salzburg-Villach junc 146
Spittal-Ost. In Spittal foll site & 'Goldeckbahn' sp. Cross bdge
& site on L - book in at hotel recep. Site on rvside. Med, pt
shd; htd wc; chem disp; shwrs inc; EHU (10-16A) €3; lndry (inc
dryer); shop in town; rest, bar at hotel; htd, covrd pool 800m;
rv fishing adj; boating; tennis; games/TV rm; dogs €1.30;
Eng spkn; quiet; red CKE/CCI. "Modern san facs; conv NH."
15 Apr-1 Oct. € 23.00   2011*

STAMS see Telfs *C1*

STEYR *B3* (4.5km NE Urban) *48.06117, 14.43764* **Camping**
Forelle, Kematmüllerstrasse 1a, 4400 Steyr-Münichholz
[tel/fax (07252) 78008 or 06764 729445 (mob);
forellesteyr@gmx.at] Fr W on B122 foll camping sp to
Amstetten on B115/309 & then 122a to Steyr-Münichholz. Site
on Rv Enns. Sm, hdstg, pt shd, unshd; htd wc; chem disp (wc);
shwrs inc; EHU (10A); lndry; shop 500m; rest, snacks, bar 1km;
BBQ; playgrnd; pools 1km; watersports, tennis nr; bike hire;
dogs €2.20; phone; quiet; red long stay; CKE/CCI. "Pleasant
rvside site; Steyr interesting, historic town." ♦ 1 Apr-31 Oct.
€ 31.60   2014*

AUSTRIA

SULZ IM WIENERWALD *B4* (1km N Rural) *48.10510,
16.13348* **Camping Wienerwald, Leopoldigasse 2, 2392
Sulz-im-Wienerwald [(0)664 4609796; fax (02238) 8855;
ww-camp@aon.at; www.camping-wienerwald.at]**
Leave A21/E60 at junc 26 dir Sittendorf, Foll sp to site at Sulz
(7km fr m'way). Sm, mkd pitch, pt sl, pt shd; wc; chem disp;
mv service pnt; shwrs inc; EHU (6A) €1.90 (poss long lead
req); lndry; shop, rest in vill; wifi; few statics; dogs €1.20; poss
cr; quiet. "Conv Vienna - 25km; gd walks." 15 Apr-15 Oct.
€ 14.00   2010*

⊞ **TELFS** *C1* (9km SW Rural) *47.27510, 10.98661* **Camping
Eichenwald, Schiess-Standweg 10, 6422 Stams
[tel/fax (05263) 6159; info@camping-eichenwald.at or
info@tirol-camping.at; www.tirol-camping.at]**
Exit A12 at exit Stams-Mötz, foll B171 sp Stams. Turn R into
vill, site behind monastery nr dry ski jump; steep app. Med,
terr, pt shd; htd wc; chem disp; mv service pnt; baby facs;
private bthrms some pitches; shwrs inc; EHU (6A) €2.70; gas;
lndry (inc dryer); shop 400m; rest, snacks; bar; playgrnd; sm htd
pool high ssn; tennis 500m; games area; games rm; bike hire;
wifi; TV rm; statics in sep area; dogs €2.50; Eng spkn; adv bkg;
quiet but monastery bells & rlwy noise; CKE/CCI. "Beautiful
views; friendly owner; vg site; gd rest; san facs v clean." ♦
€ 45.00   2013*

TRISTACH see Lienz *C2*

TULLN *B4* (1km E Urban) *48.33277, 16.07194* **Donaupark-
Camping Tulln, Donaulände 76, 3430 Tulln-an-der-Donau
[(02272) 65200; fax 65201; camptulln@oemtc.at;
www.campingtulln.at]** Fr S on A1 take exit 41 sp
St Christopher & foll B19 to o'skts of Tulln, then turn R onto
B14 Südring. Foll B14 round past commercial areas, eventually
over rlwy bdge to T-junc. Turn L into Langenlebarnerstrasse,
site on R (if reach BP g'ge you have overshot). Fr N foll B19
across rv on Rosenbrucke (bdge) & cont on B19 to B14 Südring,
then as above. Site sp (Camping des ÖAMTC) often shown on
local sp or on green sports complex sp. Med, some hdg/mkd
pitch, pt shd; htd wc; chem disp; mv service pnt; baby facs;
sauna; shwrs inc; EHU (6A) €3; gas; lndry (inc dryer); shop;
supmkt 1km; rest, snacks; bar; BBQ; playgrnd; pool 400m;
fishing, lake sw, water skiing nrby; horseriding 2km; bike hire;
tennis; games rm; wifi; entmnt; recep 0730-1930 high ssn;
20% statics; dogs; bus/train to Vienna; Eng spkn; adv bkg;
quiet; ccard acc; red LS/CKE/CCI. "Welcome pack; helpful staff;
gd base for area; gd walks, cycling, birdwatching; bus/train
to Vienna; poss cr & sm pitches; 15 mins walk to town." ♦
15 Apr-15 Oct. € 26.50   2011*

UNTERACH AM ATTERSEE see Attersee *B3*

UNTERPERFUSS see Innsbruck *C1*

UNZMARKT *C3* (1.5km W Rural) *47.19847, 14.44121*
**Camping im Freizeitpark, Am Sportplatz 27, 8800
Unzmarkt [(03583) 2956; www.unzmarkt-frauenburg.at]**
W fr Judenburg on B317, site sp opp Agip petrol stn. Sm, terr,
pt shd; wc; shwrs inc; EHU €1.10 (long lead poss req); lndry;
shop 200m; rest; bar; playgrnd; sports field adj; quiet, some
rlwy noise. "Gd site, pt of lge leisure complex; recep in café."
1 May-30 Sep. € 10.00   2009*

VELDEN AM WORTHERSEE *D3* (8km E Rural) *46.61890,
14.10565* **Camping Weisses Rössl, Auenstrasse 47,
Schiefling-am-See, 9220 Velden-Auen [(04274) 2898;
fax 28984; weisses.roessl@aon.at; http://members.aon.at/
weisses.roessl]** Fr A2 exit 335 dir Velden. At rndabt bef town
fol sp twd Maria Wörth for 9km on S side of Wörthersee. Site
on R up hill. Lge, some hdstg, terr, pt sl, pt shd; htd wc; chem
disp; mv service pnt; baby facs; shwrs inc; EHU (16A) inc; gas;
lndry (inc dryer); shop; rest; bar; BBQ; playgrnd; pool; beach &
lake sw nrby; TV; dogs; phone; poss cr; Eng spkn; some rlwy
noise; CKE/CCI. "Gd." 1 May-30 Sep. € 27.60   2010*

> ## "Satellite navigation makes touring much easier"
> Remember most sat navs don't know if
> you're towing or in a larger vehicle – always
> use yours alongside maps and site directions.

VIENNA see Wien *B4*

VILLACH *D3* (7km NE Rural) *46.65641, 13.89196* **Camping
Bad Ossiacher See, Seeuferstrasse 109, 9520 Annenheim
[(04248) 2757; fax 275757; office@camping-ossiachersee.
at; www.camping-ossiachersee.at]** Fr A10/E55/E66 exit sp
Villach/Ossiacher See onto B94. Turn R for St Andrä sp Süd
Ossiacher See. Site on L in 300m. Lge, pt shd; htd wc; baby
facs; chem disp; mv service pnt; shwrs inc; EHU (10-16A) inc;
lndry; shop; rest, snacks; bar; playgrnd; lake sw adj; sailing;
waterskiing; tennis; games area; 5% statics; phone; no dogs;
barrier clsd 1200-1400; poss cr; adv bkg; quiet; ccard acc.
"Well-kept site; handy NH even when wet; Annenheim cable
car; lge level grass pitches; excel." ♦ 1 Jan-22 Feb &
28 Mar-26 Oct. € 33.00   2015*

⊞ **VILLACH** *D3* (4km SE Rural) *46.59638, 13.89333*
**Camping Mittewald, Fuchsbichlweg 9, 9580 Drobollach
[(04242) 37392; fax 373928; camp.mittewald@gmail.com]**
Exit A2/E55 sp Villach/Faakersee. At end slip rd turn R onto B84
to Faakersee, site sp on L. Sm, pt sl, pt shd; htd wc; chem disp;
shwrs; EHU (10A); gas; lndry; shop 3km; rest; bar; playgrnd;
some statics; dogs; some Eng spkn; quiet. "Lovely location;
extensive grass pitches; excel san facs." ♦ € 29.00   2011*

VILLACH *D3* (7km SE Urban) *46.58953, 13.91483*
**Wisencamping Marhof, Greutherweg 19, A-9580
Drobollach-Faaker See [(4254) 2888; office@marhof.at;
www.marhof.at]** Foll sps in Villach mkd Faaker Nord. Site on
N side of rd at vill of Greuth. Sm, pt sl, pt shd; wc htd; chem
disp; mv waste; shwrs; EHU (metered); lndry; BBQ; playgrnd;
pool; dogs €0.70; quiet. "Delightful site; beautiful views; conv
for lakes; excel facs; gd cycling/walking area; v peaceful; Eng
not spkn; v helpful & friendly owners; excel." 1 Mar-30 Nov.
€ 28.00   2011*

AUSTRIA

VILLACH *D3* (10km SE Rural) *46.56986, 13.90701*
Familiencamping Poglitsch, Kirchenweg 19, 9583 Faak-am-See [(04254) 2718; fax 4144; poglitsch@net4you.at; www.kindercamping.at] Exit A11/E61 junc 3 & foll sp for Faakersee. Site in vill, bet church & lake. Med, mkd pitch, pt shd; wc; chem disp; mv service pnt; some serviced pitches; baby facs; shwrs inc; EHU (10-16A) inc; gas; lndry (inc dryer); shop; rest, snacks; bar; playgrnd; lake beach & sw; watersports; bike hire; games area; golf 1km; wifi; entmnt; TV; 15% statics; dogs €3.50; phone; Eng spkn; adv bkg; quiet; CKE/CCI. "Excel, well-run site; friendly owner; quiet imposed after 2300." ♦
1 Apr-15 Oct. € 27.00   2010*

VILLACH *D3* (10km SE Rural) *46.57416, 13.93694*
Strandcamping Arneitz, Seeuferlandesstrasse 53, 9583 Faak-am-See [(04254) 2137; fax 3044; camping@arneitz.at; www.camping-arneitz.at] On B83 Klagenfurt to Villach at Velden, foll sp to Faakersee. Thro Egg to site on R. Fr Villach foll sp to Faakersee. Clearly sp. Lge, mkd pitch, shd; wc; shwrs inc; EHU (16A) inc; gas; lndry (inc dryer); shop; rest, snacks; bar; BBQ; playgrnd; lake sw; tennis; entmnt; internet; TV; dogs free; adv bkg; quiet. "Excel facs, but ltd LS." ♦ 1 May-30 Sep. € 32.00   2010*

VILLACH *D3* (10km SE Rural) *46.57266, 13.93268*
Strandcamping Gruber, 9583 Faak-am-See [(04254) 2298; fax 22987; gruber@strandcamping.at; www.strandcamping. at] When app down Drau Valley fr Lienz foll sp round Villach to Faakersee. This will bring round N of lake to Egg. Site 800m beyond on R. Fr A11/E61 exit junc 3 & foll sps to Faakersee/Egg. Med, shd; wc; chem disp; shwrs inc; EHU (10A) €2.50; gas; lndry (inc dryer); shop; rest; playgrnd; lake sw; golf 2km; wifi; 10% statics; dogs €2; poss cr; adv bkg; quiet; ccard acc. "Excel for touring Carinthian Lake District; gd for children; v beautiful situation on lakeside; friendly staff." ♦
1 May-20 Sep. € 31.00   2010*

VILLACH *D3* (10km SE Rural) *46.56828, 13.9293*
Strandcamping Sandbank, Badeweg 3, 9583 Faak-am-See [(04254) 2261; fax 3943; info@camping-sandbank.at; www.camping-sandbank.at] Exit A11/E61 junc 3 & foll sp to Faakersee. Site last on R on E side of lake. Med, pt shd; wc; chem disp; serviced pitches; shwrs inc; EHU (12A) €2.20; lndry (inc dryer); supmkt 1km; rest adj; snacks; playgrnd; lake sw; tennis adj; games area; golf 15km; entmnt; TV; 10% statics; dogs €1.80; rd/rlwy noise; red snr citizens. "Surcharge for lakeside pitch; boats & surfboards for hire." 1 May-30 Sep.
€ 26.00   2010*

⊞ **VILLACH** *D3* (6km NW Urban) *46.61503, 13.80684*
Camping Gerli, Badstrasse 23, 9500 Villach [(04242) 57402; fax 582909; gerli.meidl@utanet.at; www.campgerli.com] Fr A10/E55/E66 exit junc 172. Fr rndabt at end of slip rd foll campsite sps. Med, pt shd; wc; some serviced pitches; baby facs; shwrs €0.75; EHU (4-16A) metered or €2; lndry (inc dryer); sm shop; rest; playgrnd; paddling pool; lake sw nr; solarium; tennis; entmnt; 20% statics; dogs €1.10; phone; poss cr high ssn; adv bkg; poss noisy; 10% red CKE/CCI. "Ski lift closeby."
€ 16.00   2009*

VOLDERS see Hall in Tirol *C2*

⊞ **VOLKERMARKT** *D3* (10km S Rural) *46.58376, 14.62621*
Rutar Lido FKK See-Camping (Naturist), Lido 1, 9141 Eberndorf [(04236) 22620; fax 2220; fkkurlaub@rutarlido. at; www.rutarlido.at] Take B82 S fr Völkermarkt to Eberndorf. At rndbt on vill by-pass turn R. Site sp on L. Camp ent in 700m down rd. Lge, pt shd; wc; chem disp; mv service pnt; sauna; shwrs inc; EHU (10A) inc; gas; lndry; shop; rest, snacks; playgrnd; 4 pools (1 htd, covrd); paddling pool; shgl beach & lake sw 2km; tennis adj; games area; 30% statics; dogs; o'night area for m'vans; adv bkg; quiet; ccard acc; red CKE/CCI. "Gd family site; v helpful staff; ltd Eng spkn." ♦
€ 49.00   2013*

VOLKERMARKT *D3* (13km SW Rural) *46.58613, 14.58080*
Terrassencamping Turnersee, 9122 Obersammelsdorf [(04239) 2285; fax 22854; ferienparadies@ilsenhof.at; www.ilsenhof.at] Turn off B82 dir Klopeinersee & St Kanzian. Just bef Turnersee foll sp L for site. Med, mkd pitch, some hdstg, terr, pt shd; wc; chem disp; mv service pnt; baby facs; shwrs; EHU (10A) inc; gas; lndry (inc dryer); shop 1km; rest 300m; snacks; bar; BBQ; playgrnd; pool; covrd pool 8km; shgl beach & lake sw 500m; 20% statics; dogs €2.90; v quiet; red CKE/CCI. "Excel views of mountains beyond Turnersee." ♦
1 May-10 Sep. € 28.00   2011*

VOLS see Innsbruck *C1*

WAIDHOFEN AN DER THAYA *A4* (1km SE Rural) *48.81113, 15.28839* **Campingplatz Thayapark, Badgasse, 3830 Waidhofen-an-der Thaya [(02842) 50356 or 0664 5904433 (mob); stadtamt@waidhofen-thaya.gv.at; www.waidhofen-thaya.at]** Site sp fr town cent. Med, pt shd; wc; chem disp; mv service pnt; baby facs; shwrs €0.50; EHU (10A) €2.30; lndry; shop, rest, snacks, bar 500m; playgrnd; pool 300m; cab TV; 5% statics; no adv bkg; quiet; CKE/CCI. "Quiet site nr attractive town; recep open 0800-1000 & 1600-1800." ♦ 1 May-30 Sep. € 11.00   2010*

⊞ **WALCHSEE** *B2* (750m SW Rural) *47.64881, 12.31433* **Sonnencamping Seespitz, Seespitz 1, 6344 Walchsee [(05374) 5359; fax 5845; info@camping-seespitz.at; www.camping-seespitz.at]** Exit A93/E45/60 junc 59 onto B172 thro Niederndorf to Walchsee (11km). Site on R by lake after rd on R to Südsee at beginning of Walchsee vill. Lge, pt shd; htd wc; chem disp; mv service pnt; serviced pitches; extra for lakeside pitches; baby facs; shwrs inc; EHU (6A) €3; gas; lndry (inc dryer); sm shop; supmkt adj; rest, snacks; bar; playgrnd; lake sw; fishing; boating; games area; 60% statics; dogs €3.50; poss cr; adv bkg; quiet; red CKE/CCI. "Excel; attractive lakeside setting with mountain views; vg san facs." ♦
€ 21.00   2010*

⊞ **WALD IM PINZGAU** *C2* (1km W Rural) *47.24343, 12.21071* **SNP Camping, Lahn 65, 5742 Wald-im-Pinzgau [(06565) 84460; fax 84464; info@snp-camping.at; www.snp-camping.at]** Sp fr both dir on B165 Gerlos-Mittersill rd. Sm, unshd, mkd pitch; wc; chem disp; mv service pnt; shwrs €1; EHU (10A) €4; gas; lndry; shop 1km; snacks; bar; playgrnd; pool 1km; site clsd Nov; Eng spkn; adv bkg ess; quiet; ccard acc; red long stay/CKE/CCI. "Gd walks; friendly, helpful owner; gd san facs, bus nrby for Krimul waterfalls."
€ 31.00   2011*

WEER see Schwaz *C2*

WERFEN C2 (4km S Rural) 47.44501, 13.21165 **Camping Vierthaler, Reitsam 8, 5452 Pfarrwerfen [(06468) 57570; fax 56574; vierthaler@camping-vierthaler.at; www.camping-vierthaler.at]** Fr A10 exit 43 or 44 sp Werfen/ Pfarrwerfen. Turn S onto B159 twd Bischofshofen. After 2km site on L bet rd & rv. Sm, pt shd; wc; chem disp; mv service pnt; shwrs €1.30; EHU (10-16A) €2; gas; lndry; shop; rest, snacks; playgrnd; htd pool 2km; walking; fishing; rafting; wifi; few statics; dogs free; quiet but some rd & rlwy noise; ccard acc. "Scenic site; friendly owners; Werfen castle & ice caves worth a visit; cycle path; ltd san facs, sometimes stretched." 15 Apr-30 Sep. € 18.50   2015*

WESTENDORF see Kitzbühel C2

"There aren't many sites open at this time of year"

If you're travelling outside peak season remember to call ahead to check site opening dates – even if the entry says 'open all year'.

WIEN B4 (9km E Urban) 48.20861, 16.44722 **Aktiv-Camping Neue Donau, Am Kleehäufel, 1220 Wien-Ost [(01) 2024010; fax 2024020; neuedonau@campingwien.at; www.campingwien.at]** Take A21-A23, exit sp Olhafen/ Lobau. After x-ing Rv Danube turn R, sp Neue-Donau Sud. In 150m turn L at traff lts after Shell g'ge; site on R. Fr E on A4 turn R onto A23 & take 1st slip rd sp N-Donau after x-ing rv Danube. Lge, unshd; htd wc; chem disp; mv service pnt; 20% serviced pitches (extra charge); shwrs inc; EHU (16A) €4 (poss rev pol); lndry; shop; rest, snacks; sm playgrnd; rv 1km; tennis; games area; wifi; dogs €4.50; bus/metro to city 1km; Eng spkn; adv bkg; rd & rlwy noise; ccard acc; red CKE/CCI. "Conv Vienna; lovely site; excel facs but poss stretched high ssn; poss v cr due bus tours on site; cycle track to city cent (map fr recep); 3 classes of pitch (extra charge for serviced); recep clsd 1200-1430; standard san facs." ♦ 15 Apr-30 Sep. € 44.00   2014*

WIEN B4 (11km SW Urban) 48.15065, 16.30025 **Camping Wien-Süd, Breitenfurterstrasse 269, 1230 Wien [(01) 8673649; fax 8675843; sued@campingwien.at; www.campingwien.at]** A1 fr Linz/Salzburg take A21 at Steinhausl (35km W of Vienna), merges with A2 dir Wien sp A23 Altmansdorf. At end a'bahn turn L dir Eisenstadt/ Vösendorf, in 500m turn R at 1st set traff lts into Anton Baumgartnerstrasse. Then turn R at 6th traff lts into Breitenfurterstrasse. Fr N on A22 foll A23 to m'way A2 dir Graz. At junc 5 (Vösendorf) take A21 to junc 36 (Brunn am Gebirge & foll 'Zentrum' sp for 5km. At Merkur supmkt on R, turn R to site. Med, mkd pitch, pt shd; htd wc; chem disp; shwrs inc; EHU (16A) €4; lndry; supmkt adj; snacks; playgrnd; dogs €4.50; bus; metro; Eng spkn; adv bkg; quiet; ccard acc; CKE/CCI. "Gd bus & metro conns to city; sep tent area; v pleasant, friendly, busy site; gd san facs; conv for Wien; recep open 0800-1600." ♦ 1 Jun-31 Aug. € 39.00   2013*

⊞ **WIEN** B4 (13km W Urban) 48.21396, 16.2505 **Camping Wien-West, Hüttelbergstrasse 80, 1140 Wien [(01) 9142314; fax 9113594; west@campingwien.at; www.campingwien.at/ww]** Fr Linz, after Auhof enter 3 lane 1-way rd. On app to traff lts get into L hand (fast) lane & turn L at traff lts. At next lts (Linzerstrasse) go strt over into Hüttelburgstrasse & site is uphill. Fr Vienna, foll sp A1 Linz on W a'bahn & site sp to R 100m bef double rlwy bdge. After this turn L on rd with tramlines & foll to v narr section, R at traff lts. Lge, mkd pitch, hdstg, pt shd; wc; chem disp; mv service pnt; shwrs inc; EHU (16A) €4; lndry; shop & 2km; snacks; playgrnd; wifi; some statics; dogs €4.50; bus; sep car park; site clsd Feb; poss v cr; Eng spkn; adv bkg; noisy in day but quiet at night; ccard acc; red CKE/CCI. "Rec arr early; gd bus service to U-Bahn & city cent - tickets fr recep + Vienna Card; clean facs, but poss stretched high ssn & ltd LS; poss travellers; site poss unkempt LS; sm pitches." € 41.50   2014*

WILDALPEN C3 (500m N Rural) 47.66673, 14.98692 **Camping Wildalpen, Hopfgarten 239, 8924 Wildalpen [(03636) 342; fax 313; camping@wildalpen.at; www.wildalpen.at]** On B24 in Wildalpen turn down hill by church, site 500m on R by rv. Med, pt shd; wc; chem disp; mv service pnt; shwrs €0.85; EHU (12A) inc; rest, snacks & shop in vill; pool 1.5km; tennis; 40% statics; dogs €1; poss cr; adv bkg. "Remote site, cent for white water canoeing instruction; excel for walking, photography, botany, bird life." ♦ 15 Apr-31 Oct. € 17.00   2009*

⊞ **WORGL** C2 (8km SE Rural) 47.46627, 12.13950 **Terrassencamping Schlossberg-Itter, Brixentalerstrasse 11, 6305 Itter-bei-Hopfgarten [(05335) 2181; fax 2182; info@camping-itter.at; www.camping-itter.at]** E fr Wörgl on B170 twd Kitzbühel. Site sp on L (N) side of rd in 7km, below castle & by rv opp Peugeot g'ge. Fr A12/E45 exit at Wörgl Ost & turn L at 1st T-junc sp Brixental for 4km. Turn R onto B178 at sp Brixental, then L on B170 for Hopfgarten. Med, mkd pitch, terr, pt sl, pt shd; htd wc; chem disp; mv service pnt; baby facs; fam bthrm; sauna; shwrs inc; EHU (8-10A) €2.80; gas; lndry (inc dryer); sm shop; rest, snacks; bar; BBQ; playgrnd; htd pool; paddling pool; solarium; canoeing; golf 15km; wifi; cab/sat TV; 25% statics; dogs €3.50; site clsd 15-30 Nov; poss cr; Eng spkn; adv bkg; quiet, but some rlwy noise; ccard not acc; CKE/CCI. "Superb site; highly rec, espec for children; immac pool; easy pitching on flat area but tractor assistance on steep terrs; luxury san facs; gd winter ski cent with drying rm; practice ski-run on site; gd walks; excursions arranged." ♦ € 26.00   2011*

⊞ **WORGL** C2 (13km SE Rural) 47.43068, 12.14990 **Camping Reiterhof, Kelchsauerstrasse 48, 6361 Hopfgarten [(05335) 3512; fax 4145; info@campingreiterhof.at; www.campingreiterhof.at]** Fr Wörgl S on B170, thro Hopfgarten, site sp on R dir Kelchsau. Med, mkd pitch, pt shd; htd wc; chem disp; mv service pnt; baby facs; shwrs €1; EHU (10A) €2.80; lndry (inc dryer); shop 2km; rest, snacks, bar adj; playgrnd; htd pool 200m; ski lift 2km; free ski bus; wifi; 45% statics; dogs €2.20; poss cr; Eng spkn; adv bkg; quiet but some rd noise; CKE/CCI. "V friendly, v welcoming, helpful staff; immac san facs; excel for families or couples; lge recreation park adj; excel walking & cycling area; excel." ♦ € 18.00   2011*

AUSTRIA

⊞ **ZELL AM SEE** *C2* (7km N Rural) *47.37740, 12.79583*
Campingplatz Bad Neunbrunnen, Neunbrunnen 56, 5751 Maishofen [(06542) 68548 or (0664) 3512282 (mob); camping@neunbrunnen.at; www.camping-neunbrunnen. at] Foll B311 N fr Zell-am-See dir Saalfelden; 500m after Maishofen turn L bef tunnel & foll site sp. Med, mkd pitch, some hdstg, unshd; wc; chem disp; mv service pnt; shwrs inc; EHU (10A) €2.20; lndry (inc dryer); shop; rest, snacks; bar; playgrnd; lake sw; fishing; games rm; winter sports area; wifi; dogs; quiet; ccard acc;. "Vg, scenic site; cycle & walking tracks fr site; vg rest." € 19.50   2015*

⊞ **ZELL AM SEE** *C2* (3km NE Rural) *47.33975, 12.80896*
Seecamp, Thumersbacherstrasse 34, 5700 Zell-am-See [(06542) 72115; fax 7211515; zell@seecamp.at; www.seecamp.at] Fr S end Zellersee take B311 N thro tunnel sp Zell-am-See Centrum. Cont thro town cent & in 500m turn R over rlwy x-ing sp Thumersbach. Site on R past yacht club. Med, pt shd, mkd pitch, hdstg; wc; chem disp; mv service pnt; shwrs inc; EHU (16A) metered + conn fee €2.50; metered gas; lndry; shop (high ssn); rest, snacks; bar; playgrnd; sand beach adj; lake sw; sailing; watersports; fishing (free); bike hire; wifi; dogs €4.30; bus at site ent; poss cr; Eng spkn; quiet but some rd & rlwy noise; ccard acc; red LS; CKE/CCI. "Lge sports cent nr; lger 'Komfort' pitch avail for extra; gd, clean san facs; gd walk town cent; site clsd 1100-1600; ltd pitch care LS; mountain views." ♦ € 29.40   2010*

"That's changed – Should I let The Club know?"

If you find something on site that's different from the site entry, fill in a report and let us know. See www.caravanclub.co.uk/europereport.

⊞ **ZELL AM SEE** *C2* (6km SE Rural) *47.30133, 12.8150*
Panorama Camp Zell am See, Seeuferstrasse 196, 5700 Zell am See [(06542) 56228; fax 562284; info@panoramacamp.at; www.panoramacamp.at] S fr Zell on B311 sp Salzburg (using tunnel). At 3rd rndabt turn L dir Thumersbach, site on L in 1.5km, sp. Med, hdg pitch, pt shd, 50% serviced pitch; mv service pnt; wc; chem disp; baby facs; shwrs inc; EHU (16A) metered + conn fee; lndry; shop; playgrnd; lake 300m; wifi; TV; 30% statics; dogs €3.50; bus; Eng spkn; adv bkg; quiet; red long stay; CKE/CCI. "Conv Salzburg & Krimml falls; clsd 1200-1330; cycle & footpaths round lake adj; helpful owners; excel facs; peaceful site; nicely laid out site with adequate pitches; owners take you to pitch and make elec conn; shops & rest 500m; pizzas & rolls fr recep; lovely view of mountains; easy access." € 31.00   2014*

⊞ **ZELL AM ZILLER** *C2* (4.6km N Rural) *47.26326, 11.8995*
Erlebnis Camping Aufenfeld, Aufenfeldweg 10, 6274 Aschau-im-Zillertal [(05282) 2916; fax 291611; info@ camping-zillertal.at; www.camping-zillertal.at] Fr A12 turn S at junc 39 Wiesing onto B169. At Kaltenbach take rd to Aschau, site sp. Lge, mkd pitch, terr, pt shd; htd wc; chem disp; mv service pnt; serviced pitches; baby rm; fam bthrm; sauna; shwrs inc; EHU (6A) €2.30; gas; lndry (inc dryer); shop; rest, snacks; bar; playgrnd; htd, covrd pool; padding pool; lake sw; boating; tennis; games area; skiing; bike hire; wifi; entmnt; TV; car wash; 30% statics; dogs €3.50; phone; train 500m; site clsd Nov; adv bkg rec public hols & high ssn; quiet; ccard acc. "Excel site; wonderful facs for children." ♦ € 31.00   2011*

See advertisement inside the front cover

⊞ **ZELL AM ZILLER** *C2* (700m SE Rural) *47.22830, 11.88590*
Camping Hofer, Gerlosstrasse 33, 6280 Zell-am-Ziller [(05282) 2248; fax 22488; info@campingdorf.at; www.campingdorf.at] Fr A12/E45/E60 exit junc 39 onto B169 dir Zell-am-Ziller. In vill, site on R, sp. Med, mkd pitch, pt shd; htd wc; chem disp; mv service pnt; baby facs; shwrs inc; EHU (10A) €3.50 or metered; gas; lndry (inc dryer); shops adj; rest, snacks; bar; BBQ; playgrnd; htd pool; bike hire; games rm; wifi; entmnt; dogs €2.50; phone; poss cr; quiet but rd noise; Eng spkn; adv bkg; debit cards acc; red long stay; CKE/CCI. "Excel site; clean, well-equipped facs; poss fly problem high ssn; friendly, welcoming family; some pitches tight for lge o'fits; gd walking & cycling; owner arranges guided walks; site discount for funicular." € 48.00   2013*

ZWETTL *A4* (12km E Rural) *48.58956, 15.31805*
Campingplatz Lichtenfels, Friedersbach 69, 3533 Friedersbach [(02826) 7492 or 0664 5746866 (mob); forstverwaltung@thurnforst.at; www.thurnforst.at] Fr E on B38 fr Zwettl on app Rastenfeld look for rv bdge & ruins of castle. Site sp on L. Med, pt shd; wc; chem disp; shwrs; no EHU; bar; BBQ; lake sw & shgl beach 100m; games area; 40% statics; dogs; quiet. "Pretty lake setting; open air concerts in ruins of castle high ssn; friendly, v clean facs." 1 May-10 Oct. € 15.50   2011*

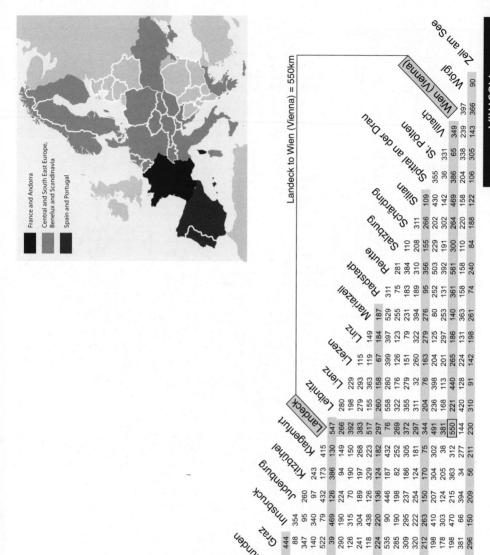

France and Andorra

Central and South East Europe, Benelux and Scandinavia

Spain and Portugal

Landeck to Wien (Vienna) = 550km

Site report forms at back of guide

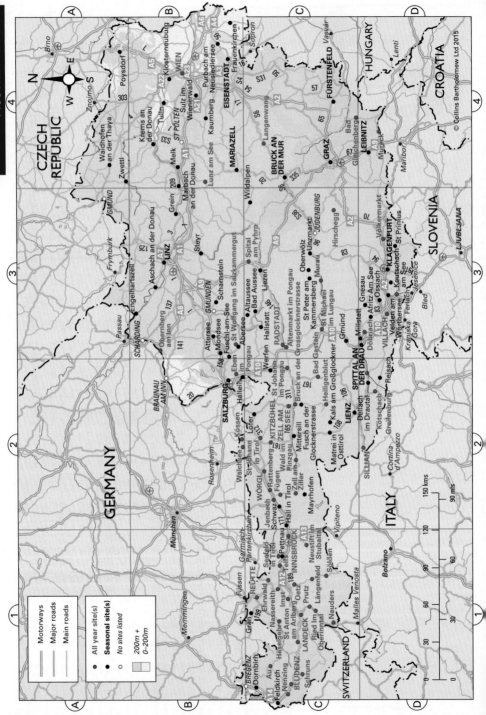

CZECH REPUBLIC

GERMANY

HUNGARY

CROATIA

SLOVENIA

ITALY

SWITZERLAND

© Collins Bartholomew Ltd 2015

Motorways
Major roads
Main roads

All year site(s)
Seasonal site(s)
No sites listed

200m +
0–200m

N
W E
S

0   30   60   90   120   150 kms
0   30   60   90 mls

Belgium
Country Introduction

Ghent

Welcome to Belgium

Although a country of two halves, with French-speaking Wallonia making up the southern part of the country, and Dutch-speaking Flanders the north, Belgium is very much united when it comes to delicious cuisine, fascinating historic attractions and breathtaking modern architecture.

With several UNESCO world heritage sites, a diverse landscape and a range of museums and art galleries, you will be spoilt for choice when deciding how best to spend your time in this delightful country.

Country highlights

Most people associate Belgium with chocolate, mussels and beer, but there are other products which share an equal amount of tradition. Lace making has been practiced in Belgium for centuries, Bruges still renowned for the intricate designs and delicacy of its product.

Belgium has also played an important role in the development of comics, and can boast Georges Remi (Hergé), the creator of Tintin, and Pierre Culliford (Peyo) the man behind the smurfs amongst its talented celebrities.

Major towns and cities

- Brussels – this historic city is Belgium's capital.
- Ghent – a city filled with beautiful buildings and important museums.
- Antwerp – Belgium's largest city is filled with stunning landmarks.
- Liège – famous for its folk festivals and for hosting a large annual Christmas Market.

Attractions

- Grand-Place, Brussels – this opulent central square is a UNESCO World Heritage site.
- Gravensteen Castle, Ghent – a magnificent 12th century castle that houses a museum.
- Historic Centre, Bruges – the medieval architecture of the city centre is a must-see.
- Ypres – an ancient town filled with historic monuments, including the Menin Gate.

Find out more

www.visitbelgium.com

Tel: 0032 (0) 70 22 10 21 Bruxelles Tourist Office

Country Information

Population (approx): 11.2 million
Capital: Brussels (population approx 1 million)
Area: 30,528 sq km
Bordered by: France, Germany, Luxembourg, Netherlands
Terrain: Flat coastal plains in north-west; central rolling hills; rugged Ardennes hills and forest in south-east; south and west criss-crossed by canals
Climate: Mild winters but snow likely in the Ardennes, cool summers, rain any time of the year; coast can be windy
Coastline: 66km
Highest Point: Signal de Botrange 694m
Languages: Flemish, French, German
Local Time: GMT or BST + 1, i.e. 1 hour ahead of the UK all year
Currency: Euros divided into 100 cents
£1 = €1.42, €1 = £0.71 (September 2015)
Emergency numbers: Police 112, Fire Brigade 112, Ambulance 112.
Public Holidays 2016: Jan 1; Mar 27, 28; May 1, 5, 15; Jul 21 (National Day); Aug 15; Nov 1, 11 (Armistice Day); Dec 25.

School summer holidays extend over July and August.

Camping and Caravanning

There are more than 900 campsites in Belgium, most of which are near the coast or in the Ardennes. Coastal sites tend to consist largely of mobile homes/statics and can be very crowded at the height of the holiday season. A local tourist tax is usually included in the rates charged.

Twin-axle caravans are not permitted on municipal sites in and around Antwerp. Caravans and vehicles longer than 6 metres are prohibited from Liège city centre.

Casual/wild camping is prohibited in Flanders. Elsewhere permission must first be sought from the landowner or police. Camping is not permitted alongside public highways for more than a 24-hour period, nor is it permitted in lay-bys, in state forests or along the seashore, or within a 100 metre radius of a main water point, or on a site classified for the conservation of monuments.

Cycling

Belgium is well equipped for cyclists, with an extensive network of signposted cycling routes. Cycle lanes are marked on the carriageway by means of a broken double white line or by circular signs depicting a white bicycle on a blue or black background.

Bikes may be carried at the rear of a vehicle as long as its width doesn't extend beyond the width of the vehicle or more than one metre from the rear, and providing the rear lights and number plate remain visible.

Electricity and Gas

The current on most campsites varies from 4 - 16 amps although on some it is as low as 2 amps. Plugs have two round pins. CEE connections are not yet available at all sites.

Use a mains tester to test a connection before hooking up as problems are more common in Belgium than other EU countries. Issues may include reversed polarity, no earth and/or incorrectly alternating current.

The full range of Campingaz cylinders are available.

Entry Formalities

British and Irish passport holders may visit Belgium for up to three months without a visa. Passports must be valid for at least 3 months after your departure.

Medical Services

The standard of health care is high. Emergency medical and hospital treatment is available at a reduced cost on production of a European Health Insurance Card (EHIC). Check whether a doctor you wish to see is registered with the national health service (conventionné/geconventioneerd) or offers private healthcare. You will have to pay for services provided but 75% of the cost of treatment and approved medicines will be refunded if you apply to a local Sickness Fund Office with your EHIC.

At night and at weekends at least one local pharmacy will remain open and its address will be displayed in the window of all local pharmacies.

Opening Hours

Banks - Open hours vary from one bank to another, however usual open hours are – Mon-Fri 9am-12pm & 2pm-4pm; Sat 9am-12pm (some banks).

Museums – Tue-Sun 10am-5pm; most museums close Monday.

Shops – Mon-Sat 10am-6pm or 8pm (supermarkets); some close 12pm-2pm; most shops closed Sunday.

Safety and Security

Belgium is relatively safe for visitors but you should take the usual sensible precautions to avoid becoming a victim of muggers, bag-snatchers and pickpockets, especially at major railway stations and on the public transport in Antwerp and Brussels.

Belgium shares with the rest of Europe an underlying threat from terrorism. Attacks could be indiscriminate and against civilian and tourist targets. The area around Brussels hosts a number of international institutions (EU, NATO) which are sensitive locations where you should be vigilant.

British Embassy
AVENUE D'AUDERGHEM 10
1040 BRUXELLES
Tel: (02) 2876211
www.ukinbelgium.fco.gov.uk/en/
public.brussels@fco.gov.uk

Irish Embassy
CHAUSEE D'ETTERBEEK 180
1040 BRUXELLES
Tel: (02) 2823400
www.embassyofireland.be
brusselsembassy@dfa.ie
There is also an Honorary Consulate in Antwerp

Documents

Passport
Belgian law requires everyone to carry some form of identification so you should carry your passport or photocard driving licence at all times.

Vehicle(s)
You should carry your vehicle registration certificate (V5C), insurance details and MOT certificate (if applicable).

Money

Major credit cards are widely accepted by shops, hotels, restaurants and petrol stations.

Carry your credit card issuer or bank's 24-hour UK contact numbers in case of loss or theft of your cards. If you have difficulty reporting the theft of your card(s) to your UK bank or credit card company, ask the Belgian group 'Card Stop' to send a fax to your UK company to block your card. Card Stop's telephone number is (070) 344344.

Motoring in Belgium
Accidents

The police must be called after an accident if an unoccupied stationary vehicle is damaged or if people are injured. If it isn't necessary to call the police to the scene of the accident you must still report it at the local police station within 24 hours.

Alcohol

The maximum permitted level of alcohol is 49 milligrams in 100 millilitres of blood, i.e. lower than in the UK (80 milligrams). Penalties for exceeding this limit are severe including suspension of driving licence and a possible jail sentence.

Breakdown Service

The Touring Club Royal de Belgique (TCB) operates a breakdown service 24 hours a day throughout the country, tel (070) 344777. On motorways, use the roadside telephones called 'telestrade' which are controlled by the police and are situated approximately every 2km. Ask for 'Touring Secours' or, when in the north of the country, 'Touring Wegenhulp'. It will be necessary to pay a fee which is variable depending on the time of day.

Essential Equipment

First aid kit
It is not compulsory for foreign registered vehicles to carry a first aid kit, but it is still recommended.

Warning Triangle
An EU approved warning triangle must be used if the vehicle breaks down, has a puncture or is involved in an accident.

Reflective Jacket/Waistcoat
If you have broken down or are in an accident where stopping or parking is prohibited, you must wear a reflective jacket or waistcoat when getting out of your vehicle. Anyone leaving the vehicle should also wear one. Keep the jacket(s) to hand in your vehicle, not in the boot.

Child Restraint System
Children under 1.35m must be seated in a child seat or child restraint when travelling in the front or rear seat of a vehicle. If a child seat/restraint is not available, i.e. when two child restraint systems are being used on rear seats and there isn't enough space for a third to be placed, a child must travel in the back of the vehicle using an adult seat belt. If the child is three years or under they must not travel in a vehicle without being seated in a child seat/restraint.

The child restraint must correspond to the child's weight and be of an approved type. A rear facing child restraint must not be used on a front seat with a frontal airbag unless it is deactivated.

Fuel

Petrol stations on motorways and main roads are open 24 hours and credit cards are generally accepted. Others may close from 8pm to 8am and often all day Sunday.

LPG, also known as GPL, is widely available at many service stations.

Parking

Blue zones indicating limited parking are used to denote where vehicles must display a parking disc on Monday to Saturday, from 9am to 6pm. Discs are available from police stations, petrol stations and some shops. Outside blue zones a parking disc must also be used where the parking sign has a panel showing the disc symbol. Parking areas are also regulated by parking meters and if these exist inside a blue zone parking discs must not be used, except if the parking meter or ticket machine is out of action. Illegally parked vehicles may be towed away or clamped.

Do not park in a street where there is a triangular sign 'Axe Rouge/Ax Rode'.

Pollution

From 1 November to 31 March during levels of high pollution, known as pollution peaks, restrictions are imposed on driving in the Brussels area. There are different levels of restriction, from reduced speed limits to a total ban on driving , depending on the severity of the pollution. When in place restrictions are announced on local media and an electronic sign boards around the city. For more information visit www.brussels.be and search for 'pollution peak'.

Priority

You should take great care to obey the 'priority to the right' rule which is designed to slow traffic in built-up areas. Drivers must give priority to vehicles joining from the right, even if those vehicles have stopped at a road junction or stopped for pedestrians or cyclists, and even if you are on what appears to be a main road. Exemptions to this rule apply on motorways, roundabouts and roads signposted with an orange diamond on a white background.

Trams have priority over other traffic. If a tram or bus stops in the middle of the road to allow passengers on or off, you must stop.

From 2014 a 'Zip Merging' rule has been in place in Belgium. Where a lane is ending or closed, drivers in that lane must continue to where that lane starts to close up before merging into the open lane. Drivers in the lane which remains open must give way in turn to the drivers merging into their lane.

Roads

Roads are generally in good condition and well lit, however, some stretches of motorways have poor quality surfacing and signs to advise drivers to slow down. Traffic is fast and the accident rate is high, especially at weekends, mainly due to speeding.

Road Signs and Markings

Roads signs and markings conform to international standards. A sign has been introduced prohibiting the use of cruise control. This sign will normally only be encountered on motorways where there is a risk of multiple crashes due to congestion or road works. Where this particular sign shows a weight limit, the prohibition applies to drivers of vehicles with a higher maximum permitted weight.

Destination road signs can be confusing to foreigners because a town may be signposted either by its French or its Flemish name, according to the predominant language in that particular area. The most important of these towns are listed below:

Flemish	French
Aalst	Alost
Aken (Aachen)	Aix-la-Chapelle (Germany)
Antwerpen	Anvers
Bergen	Mons
Brugge	Bruges
Brussel	Bruxelles
Doornik	Tournai
Gent	Gand
Geraardsbergen	Grammont
Ieper	Ypres
Kortrijk	Courtrai
Leuven	Louvain
Luik	Liège
Mechelen	Maline
Namen	Namur
Rijsel	Lille (France)
Roeselare	Roulers
Tienen	Tirlemont
Veurne	Furnes

Generally signposts leading to and on motorways show foreign destination place names in the language of the country concerned. e.g. German. Exceptions do occur, particularly on the E40 and E314 where city names may be given in Flemish or French.

Roads with the prefix N are regional roads; those with numbers 1 to 9 radiate from Brussels. Motorways have the prefix A and have blue and white signs. When route planning through Belgium follow the green European road numbers with the prefix E which may be the only road numbers displayed.

Road signs you may see include the following:

You may pass
right or left

Cyclists have priority
over turning traffic

Cyclists have
priority at junction

Use of Cruise
Control prohibited

Speed Limits

	Open Road (km/h)	Motorway (km/h)
Car Solo	90	120
Car towing caravan/trailer	90	120
Motorhome under 3500kg	90	120
Motorhome 3500-7500kg	90	90

Whilst the general speed limit in built-up areas is 50 km/h (31mph), lower limits of 30 km/h (18 mph) or 20 km/h (12mph) may be imposed and indicated by signs in residential areas, town centres and near schools. Brussels city centre is a 30 km/h (18mph) speed limit zone. The start and finish points of these zones are not always clearly marked.
Vehicles over 3,500 kg in weight are restricted to 90 km/h (56mph) outside built-up areas and on motorways.

Traffic Jams

During periods of fine weather roads to the coast, the Ardennes and around Brussels and Antwerp are very busy on Friday afternoons and Saturday mornings, and again on Sunday evenings.

Other busy routes are the E40 (Brussels to Ostend), the E25 (Liège to Bastogne and Arlon), the E411 (Brussels to Namur and Luxembourg), and the N4 from Bastogne to Arlon around the border town of Martelange caused by motorists queuing for cheap petrol in Luxembourg. Avoid traffic on the E40 by taking the R4 and N49, and on the E411 by taking the N4 Bastogne to Marche-en-Famenne and Namur.

These routes are heavily used and consequently the road surface can be poor.

Traffic Lights

A green light (arrow) showing at the same time as a red or amber light means that you can turn in the direction of the green arrow providing you give way to other traffic and to pedestrians. An amber light, possibly flashing, in the form of an arrow inclined at an angle of 45 degrees to the left or to the right, shows that the number of traffic lanes will be reduced.

Tunnels

Three road tunnels go under the River Scheldt at Antwerp. In the Liefkenhoeks tunnel on road R2 to the north of the city a toll of €17.60-19.00 (2015) for vehicles over 2.75m in height. Vehicles under 2.75m are charged €4.95-6.00. If you're towing your caravan will be included within this height categorisation. The Kennedy Tunnel on road R1 to the south of the city is toll-free but is heavily congested in both directions for much of the day. The smallest tunnel, the Waasland Tunnel is part of the N59a and is also toll-free.

Violation of Traffic Regulations

The police may impose on-the-spot fines on visitors who infringe traffic regulations such as speeding and parking offences. Penalties may be severe and if you are unable to pay on the spot your vehicle(s) may be impounded or your driving licence withdrawn. Fines can be paid in cash or with a debit or credit card. An official receipt must be issued.

In an effort to improve road safety the authorities have increased the number of speed traps throughout the country in the form of cameras and unmarked police vehicles.

Vehicles of 3,500 kg or over are not allowed to use the left lane on roads with more than three lanes except when approaching a fork in a motorway when vehicles have to move to the left or right lane, depending on their destination.

Motorways

Belgium has an extensive network of approximately 1,750km of motorways (A roads). Although Belgian motorways are toll free, the introduction of a motorway toll for vehicles over 3,500kg is planned during 2016.

Service areas usually have a petrol station, restaurant, shop, showers and toilets. Rest areas have picnic facilities. For detailed information about the motorway network see www.autosnelwegen.net.

Some motorways are so heavily used by lorries that the inside lane may become heavily rutted and/or potholed. These parallel ruts are potentially dangerous for caravans travelling at high speed. It is understood that parts of the A2/E314 and A3/E40 are particularly prone to this problem.

Touring

Flemish is spoken in the north of Belgium, whilst French is spoken in the south. Brussels is bi-lingual. English is widely spoken.

Prices in restaurants are quoted 'all inclusive' and no additional tipping is necessary. Smoking is severely restricted in public places including restaurants and cafés.

Carrier bags are generally not provided in supermarkets, so take your own.

When visiting Brussels visitors may buy a Brussels Card, valid for 24, 48 or 72 hours, which offers free access to virtually every major museum in the city and unlimited use of public transport, together with discounts at a number of other attractions. The pass is available from the tourist information office in the Hotel de Ville and from many hotels, museums and public transport stations, or visit www.brusselscard.be to buy online.

Public Transport

Anyone under the age of 25 years is entitled to free or reduced price travel on public transport in the Brussels region. During periods of severe air pollution public transport in that region is free to all passengers.

Brussels and Antwerp have metro systems together with extensive networks of trams and buses. Tram and bus stops are identified by a red and white sign and all stops are request stops; hold out your arm to signal an approaching bus or tram to stop. Tickets, including 10-journey and one-day travel cards, are available from vending machines at metro stations and some bus stops, newsagents, supermarkets and tourist information centres.

Most of Belgium is well connected by train and most main routes pass through Antwerp, Brussels or Namur. Trains are modern, comfortable and punctual and fares are reasonably priced. Buy tickets before boarding the train or you may be charged a supplement. Eurostar tickets to Brussels allow free, same day transfers to domestic Belgian stations.

Bikes are allowed on some buses in the Flanders area of the country.

Plans are in hand to introduce a unified smart card ticketing system covering all public transport, irrespective of company or mode of transport. This system will use chip cards, card readers and on-board computers.

Bruges

ADINKERKE see De Panne *A1*

AISCHE EN REFAIL *B3* (350m E Rural) *50.59977, 4.84335*
**Camping du Manoir de Là-Bas, Route de Gembloux 180,
5310 Aische-en-Refail [(081) 655353; europa-camping.sa@
skynet.be; www.camping-manoirdelabas.be]**
Fr E411/A4 exit junc 12 & foll sps to Aische-en-Refail. Site on
o'skts of vill. Lge, pt sl, pt shd; wc; chem disp; mv service pnt;
shwrs €1; EHU (6A) inc; gas; lndry; shop 0.5km; rest; snacks;
bar; BBQ; htd pool; paddling pool; fishing; tennis; games rm;
entmnt; 80% statics; dogs €3; poss cr; Eng spkn; adv bkg; quiet;
CKE/CCI. "Friendly staff; site little run down; EHU & water; poor
san facs, dated & long way fr pitches; some site rds are narr;
recep far side of chateau; gd rest & bar (clsd in Sep); site needs
updating (2014); poor." ♦ 1 Apr-31 Oct. € 21.00   2015*

AMBERLOUP/STE ODE see Tenneville *C3*

ANTWERPEN *A3* (20km NE Urban) *51.30548, 4.58536*
**Camping Floreal Club Het Veen, Eekhoornlaan 1, 2960
Sint Job-in't-Goor [(03) 6361327; fax 6362030; het.veen@
florealclub.be; www.florealclub.be]** Fr A1/E19 exit junc 4
to Sint Job in't Goor. Strt over traff lts & immed after canal
bdge turn L, 1.5km to site alongside canal. Lge, hdg/mkd pitch,
pt shd; htd wc; chem disp; mv service pnt; baby facs; shwrs
inc; EHU (10A) inc; lndry (inc dryer); shop; rest; snacks; bar;
playgrnd; tennis; games rm; 80% statics; dogs €3.40; phone;
bus 1.5km; Eng spkn; adv bkg; CKE/CCI. "V helpful recep;
pleasant site & town; gd cycling along canal; gd NH."
1 Mar-31 Oct. € 25.00   2010*

> # "I like to fill in the reports as I travel from site to site"
> You'll find report forms at the back of this guide, or you can fill them in online at www.caravanclub.co.uk/europereport.

⊞ **ANTWERPEN** *A3* (6km NW Urban) *51.23347, 4.39261*
**Camping De Molen, Thonelaan - Jachthavenweg 6, St
Annastrand, 2020 Antwerpen [tel/fax (03) 2198179; info@
camping-de-molen.be; www.camping-de-molen.be]**
Clockwise on ring rd, take 1st exit after Kennedy tunnel, exit
6. R at traff lts, 3rd L where cannot go strt on (rv on R), site
on R in 1km on bank of Rv Schelde. Or on ent Antwerp foll sp
Linkeroever, go strt on at 3 traff lts, then turn L & foll camping
sp. Fr A14/E17 exit junc 7 & foll sp for Linkeroever Park &
Ride until site sp appear, then foll sp. Med, pt shd; wc; chem
disp; shwrs; EHU (10A) €2.50 (poss rev pol) - €25 deposit for
adaptor/cable; shops 1km; supmkt by metro; rest adj; pool
nr; wifi; bus nrby; metro 1km; poss cr; Eng spkn; adv bkg rec;
quiet, but some rv traff noise & poss noise fr local bar; ccard
not acc; red LS. "Popular site; max 14 nt stay; pedestrian/cycle
tunnel to city cent 1km; gd for rollerblading, cycling; friendly,
helpful staff; mosquitoes poss a problem; san facs satisfactory;
30 min walk to city cent." ♦ € 27.00   2015*

⊞ **ARLON** *D3* (2km N Urban) *49.70215, 5.80678* **Camping
Officiel Arlon, 373 Rue de Bastogne, Bonnert, 6700 Arlon
[tel/fax (063) 226582; campingofficiel@skynet.be;
www.campingofficielarlon.be]** Fr E411 exit junc 31 onto
N82 Arlon for 4km, turn twd Bastogne on N4. Site sp on R.
Med, pt sl, pt shd; wc; chem disp; fam bthrm; shwrs inc; EHU
(6A) €2.40 (check earth); gas; lndry (inc dryer); shop 2km; rest,
snacks; bar; BBQ; playgrnd; pool; wifi; TV rm; dogs €2; Eng
spkn; poss cr; adv bkg; some rd noise; red long stay; CKE/CCI.
"Charming, clean, well laid out, pretty site; levelling blocks/
ramps req - supplied by site; c'vans tight-packed when site
busy; 5km approx to Luxembourg for cheap petrol; Arlon
interesting town; vg NH & longer stay; thoroughly rec for stop
over; payment cash only; 3 hdstgs for m'van; new pool (2014);
san facs updated, v clean (2015); busy but organised." ♦
€ 22.00   2015*

ARLON *D3* (7.6km N Rural) *49.74833, 5.78697* **Camping
Sud, 75 Voie de la Liberté, 6717 Attert [(063) 223715;
fax 221554; info@campingsudattert.com; www.camping
sudattert.com]** Off N4 Arlon rd on E side of dual c'way.
Sp to site fr N4 (500m). U-turn into site ent. Med, hdg/mkd
pitch, some hdstg, pt shd; htd wc; chem disp; shwrs €0.50
(high ssn); EHU (5-10A) €2.50 (check earth); lndry; shop; rest,
snacks; bar; BBQ; playgrnd; pool; dogs €2; phone; bus; adv
bkg; Eng spkn; quiet, some rd noise; red long stay; CKE/CCI.
"Vg, well-organised site; special NH pitches; fishing & walking;
peaceful site; v friendly staff; highly rec." 1 Apr-15 Oct.
€ 25.00   2014*

ATTERT see Arlon *D3*

AVE ET AUFFE see Han sur Lesse *C3*

⊞ **AYWAILLE** *C3* (1km E) *50.47633, 5.68916* **Domaine
Chateau de Dieupart, Route de Dieupart 37, 4920
Aywaille [(042) 631238; fax 462690; info@dieupart.be;
www.dieupart.be]** Leave E25 at exit 46 Remouchamps/
Aywaille. Turn R at traff lts dir Aywaille, and R by church.
Immed L and Rt at Delhaise car park, take ave up to the castle.
Site SP. Med, pt sh; wc; chem disp; mv service pnt; shwrs;
EHU (6A) inc; rest; bar; BBQ; playgrnd; wifi; 50% statics; bus
500m, train 1.5Km, Eng spkn, adv bkg acc; CKE/CCI, red LS.
"Nice site by rv; gd walking and cycling; supmkt 300m." ♦
€ 23.00   2013*

BASTOGNE *C3* (1.6km WNW Urban) *50.00340, 5.69525*
**Camping de Renval, 148 Route de Marche, 6600 Bastogne
[tel/fax (061) 212985; www.campingderenval.be]**
Fr N leave A26 exit 54, foll Bastogne sp. Fr Marche-en-Famenne
dir, exit N4 at N84 for Bastogne; site on L in 150m opp petrol
stn. Fr E foll Marche, in 1km site on R opp petrol stn. Med,
hdstg, pt sl, terr, pt shd; htd wc; chem disp; baby facs; shwrs
inc; EHU (10A) inc (poss rev pol); lndry (inc); shops 1km; snacks;
BBQ; playgrnd; tennis; games area; wifi; entmnt; 95% statics;
dogs €3; site clsd Jan; quiet; ccard acc; red LS. "Take care
speed bumps; helpful staff; clean san facs but long walk fr
tourers' pitches; gd security; facs ltd LS; gd NH." 1 Feb-31 Dec.
€ 24.00   2014*

BELGIUM

⊞ **BERLARE** *A2* (4km NNW Rural) *51.04350, 3.98960*
Camping Roosendael, Schriekenstraat 27, 9290 Berlare-Overmere [(09) 3678742; fax 3657355; hugoscalafilm@skynet.be; www.ideal-caravans.be] Fr A14/E17 junc 11 onto N449 dir Laarne. At T-junc turn L onto N445 past Overmere & Donk. Approx 2.5km after Overmere at rndabt with Shell g'ge turn R onto N467 past Donkmeer to Berlare. After 1.5km turn L in front of 'Café de Kalvaar', site at end of rd. Med, hdg/mkd pitch, pt shd; htd wc; chem disp; shwrs; EHU (6A) inc; lndry; shop, rest, snacks, bar 500m; BBQ; playgrnd; lake beach & sw 500m; fishing 500m; games rm; tennis 500m; many statics; phone; quiet; Eng spkn. "Nice site; lge pitches, mainly sandy soil; warm welcome; clean, modern san facs, but ltd; poss under-used LS; local vet comes to site; gd NH." ♦
€ 17.00   2011*

BERTRIX *D3* (2km S Rural) *49.83942, 5.25360* **Ardennen Camping Bertrix, Route de Mortehan, 6880 Bertrix [(061) 412281; fax 412588; info@campingbertrix.be; www.campingbertrix.be]** Exit A4/E411 junc 25 onto N89 for Bertrix & foll yellow sps to site. Lge, mkd pitch, terr, pt shd; htd wc; chem disp; mv service pnt; baby facs; fam bthrm; some serviced pitches; sauna; shwrs inc; EHU (10A) €4; gas; lndry (inc dryer); shop high ssn; rest, snacks, bar; playgrnd; htd pool high ssn; paddling pool; tennis; bike hire; internet; TV rm; 35% statics; dogs €5; poss cr; Eng spkn; adv bkg; quiet; ccard acc; red LS/snr citizens; red LS/CKE/CCI. "Excel site; scenic location; friendly, helpful owners; gd for families; excel clean facs; gd rest; lg pitches; big pool." ♦ 26 Mar-11 Nov. € 43.00 (CChq acc)   2013*

BOUILLON *D3* (2km SW Rural) *49.78247, 5.06212* **Camping Moulin de la Falize, Vieille Route de France 62, 6830 Bouillon [(061) 466200; fax 467275; moulindelafalize@swing.be; www.moulindelafalize.be]** Fr A4 exit junc 25 & foll N89. Turn R dir Bouillon. At end of town 1-way system turn R then immed L up hill, site on L in 800m. Med, pt sl, terr, unshd; wc; chem disp; sauna; shwrs inc; EHU (6A) inc; lndry; shop 1km; rest, snacks, bar; BBQ; playgrnd; pool; rv 1km; tennis; fitness cent; entmnt; 95% statics; phone; dogs; quiet; Eng spkn; ccard acc; CKE/CCI. "V ltd touring pitches; steep inclines; conv Orval Abbey, brewery; NH only." 1 Apr-31 Dec. € 17.50   2009*

BOUILLON *D3* (6km W Rural) *49.79479, 5.01352* **Camp Municipal Halliru, 1 Route de Corbion, 6830 Bouillon [(061) 466009; fax 468048; halliru@bouillon.be; www.bouillon.be]** Fr Bouillon pass under castle, turn L twd Corbion on N810; site on R in 6km. Steep descent into site. Med, pt shd; wc; shwrs €1; shops 1.5km; EHU (10A) €2.08 (long lead poss req); playgrnd; fishing; 50% statics; dogs; poss cr; phone; quiet. "Peaceful rvside site; conv historic town; fair." ♦
1 Apr-30 Sep. € 10.40   2011*

BREDENE see Oostende *A1*

BRUGES see Brugge *A2*

BRUGGE *A2* (13km NE Rural) *51.28937, 3.33332* **Camping Hoeke, Damse Vaart Oost 10, 8340 Damme [(050) 500496; www.campinghoeke.be]** Fr Brugge ring rd, take minor rd to NE, sp Damme on S side of canal. At Damme, cont by canal to Siphon. Cross canal, turn L in front of cafe, R & cont 4km by canal to Hoeke. Site behind pub building on R bef bdge at Hoeke. Or fr N fr junc N49 & N376 take N49 dir Maldagem for 3.5km. Site sp both sides of canal in Hoeke. Keep canal on R twd Damme, site 300m on L, sp on building. Sm, hdg/mkd pitch, pt shd; wc; chem disp; 10% serviced pitches; shwrs €1; EHU (6A) inc; gas; shops 4km; rest; bar; BBQ; playgrnd; sand beach 8km; 90% statics; phone; quiet; CKE/CCI. "Picturesque town, conv Bruges fishing in canal; tight access to pitches; charge for all hot water; NH/sh stay only." ♦ ltd.
1 Mar-15 Nov. € 16.00   2010*

⊞ **BRUGGE** *A2* (5km E Urban) *51.20722, 3.26305* **Camping Memling, Veltemweg 109, 8310 Sint Kruis [(050) 355845; fax 357250; info@camping-memling.be or info@bruges camping.be; www.camping-memling.be or www.brugescamping.be]** Exit A10 junc 8 Brugge. In 2km turn R onto N397 dir St Michiels & cont 2km to rlwy stn on R. Turn R under rlwy tunnel & at 1st rndbt take dir Maldegem onto ring rd & in a few kms take N9 sp Maldegem & St Kruis. After 3km at traff lts adj Macdonalds, turn R & immed L sp Camping to site on R in 400m past sw pool. Fr Gent exit E40 sp Oostkamp & foll Brugge sp for 7km to N9 as above. Med, mkd pitch, some hdstg, pt shd; htd wc; chem disp; mv service pnt; shwrs inc; EHU (6A) inc (poss rev pol); lndry; shops 500m; 3 supmkts nrby; rest, snacks, bar 500m; htd pool adj; bike hire; wifi; 13% statics; dogs €2; bus 200m; poss v cr; Eng spkn; adv bkg ess high ssn; poss noisy at w/ends & rd noise; ccard acc; red LS/long stay. "Busy site; conv Brugge & ports; red LS as no shwrs/rest/bar; friendly, helpful owners; recep open 0800-2200 (all day to 2200 high ssn); arr early high ssn to ensure pitch; LS site yourself & report to recep; conv Zeebrugge ferry (30mins) & allowed to stay to 1500; bus svrs every 20 mins to Bruges; adv bkgs taken but no pitch reserved; m'van pitches sm, rec pay extra for standard pitch; clean san facs refurbished 2012; cycle rte to Bruges; 35 min walk to Brugge cent; conv bus; nice site; rec." € 35.00   2014*

"We must tell The Club about that great site we found"

Get your site reports in by mid-August and we'll do our best to get your updates into the next edition.

⊞ **BRUGGE** *A2* (4km S Urban) *51.19634, 3.22573* **Motorcaravan Park, Off ring rd R30, Buiten Katelijnevest, Brugge** Exit A10 at junc 7 twd Brugge. After going under rlwy bdge, turn R under ring rd after old bus stn to dedicated mv parking adj coach parking, nr marina. Sm, hdstg, pt shd; chem disp €0.50; EHU (10A) inc; washrm nr; water €0.50; shop 500m; dogs; noisy; m'vans only; red LS. "In great location - gd view of canal, sh walk to town cent thro park; rec arr early high ssn; if full, take ticket & park in coach park opp; NH only." € 22.50   2015*

BELGIUM

DON'T LOOK ANY FURTHER
LARGE PITCHES, ALL FACILITIES!

He likes Klein Strand, so will you!

IN THE MIDDLE OF EVERYWHERE!
Varsenareweg 29, Jabbeke
only 9 km from Bruges (good bus connection)
near Ostend, Ypres & Ghent
www.kleinstrand.be

⊞ **BRUGGE** *A2* (13km SW Urban) *51.18448, 3.10445* **Recreatiepark Klein Strand, Varsenareweg 29, 8490 Jabbeke [(050) 811440; fax 814289; info@kleinstrand.be; www.kleinstrand.be]** Fr W leave A10/E40 at Jabbeke exit, junc 6; turn R at rndabt & in 100m turn R into narr rd. Foll site to statics car pk on L & park - walk to check-in at recep bef proceeding to tourer site in 400m. Fr E leave A10/E40 at junc 6 (Jabbeke) turn L at 1st rndabt. Drive over m'way twd vill. Turn L at next rndabt & foll site sp into site car pk as above. V lge, hdg/mkd pitch, pt shd; wc; chem disp; mv service pnt; baby facs; shwrs €0.75; EHU (10A) inc; gas; lndry (inc dryer); shop & 1km; 2 rests (1 open all yr); snacks; 3 bars; BBQ; playgrnd; paddling pool; direct access to lake sw adj; tennis; fishing; watersports; bike hire; games rm; wifi; entmnt; TV; 75% statics; dogs €2; no o'fits over 12m; bus to Brugge; poss cr with day visitors; Eng spkn; quiet but backgrnd m'way noise; ccard acc; red LS/CKE/CCI. "Busy site; vg touring base; lge pitches; wide range of entmnt & excursions; bus to Bruges every 20 mins." ♦ € 38.00 (up to 4 persons) SBS - H15   2014*

See advertisement

BRUSSELS see Bruxelles *B2*

BRUXELLES *B2* (13km N Rural) *50.93548, 4.38226* **Camping Grimbergen, Veldkantstraat 64, 1850 Grimbergen [(0479) 760378 or (02) 2709597; fax (02) 2701215; camping-grimbergen@webs.com]** Fr Ostend on E40/A10 at ringrd turn E & foll sp Leuven/Luik (Liège)/Aachen. Exit junc 7 N sp Antwerpen/Grimbergen N202. At bus stn traff lts turn R twd Vilvourde N211. Turn L at 2nd traff lts (ignore no L turn - lorries only). Site sp 500m on R. Ent via pool car pk. Med, hdg pitch, pt sl, pt shd; wc; chem disp; shwrs inc; EHU (10A) €2.50; lndry; shops 500m; rest adj; pool adj; bike hire; dogs €1; phone; hourly bus to city 200m; Eng spkn; adv bkg; quiet but some aircraft noise & cock crowing; CKE/CCI. "Well-run, popular site - rec arr early; gd, clean, modern san facs; helpful staff; sh walk to town; train to Brussels fr next vill; red facs LS; gates clsd 1130-1400 and 2000 onwards; gd rest by bus stop; conv Brussels; excel san facs; rec; gd NH." ♦ 1 Apr-25 Oct. € 26.00   2014*

BRUXELLES *B2* (12km E Urban) *50.85720, 4.48506* **RCCC de Belgique, Warandeberg 52, 1970 Wezembeek [(02) 7821009; camping.wezembeek@hotmail.com; www.rcccb.com]** Leave ringrd RO at junc 2 sp Kraainem turning E. In 140m 1st intersection on dual c'way (by pedestrian x-ing) turn L into Wezembeek. Foll orange camping sp taking rd to the R around church. Foll rd to crest of hill. Site on L between houses. Narr ent, easy to miss. Med, mkd pitch, hdstg, terr, pt sl, pt shd; wc; chem disp; shwrs inc; EHU (6A) inc (poss rev pol & no earth); gas 3km; lndry rm; shop, rest, snacks 1km; bar; playgrnd; 65% statics; dogs €1; metro nr; gates clsd 1200-1400 & 2200-0800; Eng spkn; adv bkg; some rd noise; aircraft noise; ccard acc; CKE/CCI. "Poss diff for lge o'fits due narr site ent, v tight corners, raised kerbs; unkempt & poor san facs (2011); gd for metro into Brussels fr Kraainem; welcoming wardens." 1 Apr-30 Sep. € 20.00   2015*

BURE/TELLIN see Tellin *C3*

DAMME see Brugge *A2*

DE HAAN *A1* (2.6km ENE Coastal) *51.28330, 3.05610* **Camping Ter Duinen, Wenduinesteenweg 143, Vlissegem, 8421 De Haan [(050) 413593; fax 416575; lawrence.sansens@scarlet.be; www.campingterduinen.be]** Exit A10/E40 junc 6 Jabbeke onto N377 dir De Haan. Go thro town dir Wenduine, site on R in 4km. Med, mkd pitch, pt shd; pt terr; htd wc; chem disp; mv service pnt; baby facs; shwrs €1.20; EHU (6A) inc; lndry (inc dryer); shop; snacks; bar; BBQ; playgrnd; htd pool 200m; water complex 1km; sand/shgl beach 500m; lake sw adj; fishing; bike hire 200m; horseriding 1km; golf 4km; wifi; 85% statics; dogs €5.75; phone; tram nrby; poss cr; Eng spkn; adv bkg ess; fairly quiet; CKE/CCI. "Neat, clean, well-managed site; friendly staff; poss long walk to excel san facs inc novelty wcs!; conv ferries, Bruges; excel; hot dish water req tokens; mkt in nrby towns." ♦ 15 Mar-15 Oct. € 40.00 (CChq acc)   2013*

DE HAAN *A1* (5km SW Urban/Coastal) *51.25698, 2.99150*
**Camping 't Rietveld, Driftweg 210, 8420 De Haan
[(0475) 669336; camping.rietveld@telenet.be;
www.campingrietveld.be]** Fr Ostend on N34; fork R onto
Driftweg bef golf club dir Vosseslag & Klemskerke, site sp.
Sm, unshd, mkd pitch; htd wc; chem disp; baby facs; shwrs
€1.20; EHU (16A) €1.95; lndry; shop, rest, snacks, bar in town;
playgrnd; sand beach 1km; 80% statics; dogs €1.85; poss cr;
Eng spkn; quiet; CKE/CCI. "Friendly, helpful staff; clean san
facs."
1 Apr-15 Oct. € 20.50   2013*

⊞ **DE PANNE** *A1* (3km S Rural) *51.08288, 2.59094* **Camping
Ter Hoeve, Duinhoekstraat 101, 8660 Adinkerke
[(058) 412376; camping.terhoeve@skynet.be;
www.camping-terhoeve.be]** Leave Calais-Ostend m'way at
junc 1 (ignore junc 1a) dir De Panne. Foll rd past theme park
(Plopsaland), L at filling stn, site 1km on L. Lge, hdg pitch, pt
shd; wc; chem disp; mv service pnt; shwrs inc; EHU (4A) €2
(poss no earth); lndry (inc dryer); shop; supmkt 1km; snacks;
playgrnd; beach 2km; 60% statics; no dogs; tram 1km; poss
cr; some daytime noise fr nrby theme park; ccard not acc.
"Nice pitches; friendly, helpful owner; gd, modern san facs;
lge grassed area for tourers & hdstg area for late arr/early
dep; barrier clsd 2200-0800 - go to visitors' car park on R bef
booking in; san facs clsd 1100-1600 LS; v busy site high ssn;
phone to check opening times LS; conv Dunkerque ferries &
Plopsaland park; tram tickets avail at filling stn; coin operated
dishwash water." € 14.00   2015*

⊞ **DE PANNE** *A1* (4km S Rural) *51.07666, 2.58663*
**Familie Camping Kingervreugde, Langgeleedstraat
1, 8660 Adinkerke [(050) 811440; fax 814289; info@
kindervreugde.be; www.familiecamping.net]**
Leave Calais-Ostend m'way at junc 1 (ignore junc 1a) dir De
Panne. Foll rd past theme park (Plopsaland), L at filling stn,
site 1.3km on L. Med, hdg pitch, pt shd; htd wc; chem disp;
shwrs inc; EHU (6A) €2.50; lndry; shop, rest, snacks, bar 1km;
BBQ; playgrnd; dogs; 50% statics; phone; bus 800m; Ltd
Eng spkn; adv bkg; quiet; ccard not acc; red CKE/CCI. "Conv
Dunkerque/Calais ferries; final appraoch diff for o'fits over
12ft." ♦ ltd. 29 Apr-1 Oct. € 28.00 (3 persons)   2013*

DEINZE see Ghent *A2*

⊞ **DINANT** *C3* (2km N Urban) *50.27722, 4.89694* **Camping
Communal Devant-Bouvignes, 1 Quai de Camping, 5500
Dinant [(082) 224002 or (477) 619873 (mob); fax 224132;
devantbouvignes.dinant@gmail.com; www.dinant.be]**
Exit E11 junc 20 onto N936; drive to cent of Dinant (steep
descent) to T-junc; turn R onto N92; cont along rv for 1.5km;
site on L after bend. Med, mkd pitches, pt shd; htd wc; chem
disp; mv service pnt; baby facs; shwrs €1; EHU (16A) €3; lndry
rm; supmkt 1km; drinks avail; playgrnd; rv sw; 50% statics;
dogs free; bus at ent; adv bkg; quiet, but some rd & rlwy noise;
ccard not acc. "Excel situation on rv bank; nice modern san fac
(2015); 25 min walk to interesting town." € 17.00   2015*

⊞ **DINANT** *C3* (14km NE Rural) *50.33557, 4.99534* **Camping
de Durnal - Le Pommier Rustique, Rue de Spontin, 5530
Durnal [tel/fax (083) 699963 or (0475) 407827 (mob);
info@camping-durnal.net; www.camping-durnal.net]**
Leave E411 at junc 19. Turn S dir Spontin onto D946, then
N937, foll site sp. Sm, mkd pitch, terr, unshd; wc; chem disp;
fam bthrm; sauna; shwrs inc; EHU (10A) inc (check rev pol);
lndry (inc dryer); shop; rest, snacks; playgrnd; games area;
child entmnt high ssn; cab TV; wifi; mainly statics; dogs free;
4 nights for price of 3; Eng spkn; quiet; ccard acc. "Friendly,
helpful owner; well-run, well-maintained site; ltd touring
pitches; sm pitches; conv NH fr m'way; v quiet LS; modern san
facs." ♦ 1 Mar-31 Dec. € 27.00   2013*

DINANT *C3* (18km SE Rural) *50.19094, 5.00611* **Camping de
la Lesse, Rue du Camping 1, 5560 Houyet [(82) 666100;
fax 667214; lafamiliale@coolweb.be; www.camping
delalesse.be]** S on N95 fr Dinant for about 13km; turn L
onto D929 sp Houyet. Cross rlwy & immed turn L along Rv
Lesse. Lge, pt shd; htd wc; chem disp; shwrs; EHU (15A) inc;
lndry; shop 500m; rest, snacks; bar; playgrnd; pool adj; tennis;
kayaking; fishing; 50% statics; dogs €2; train; poss noisy; CKE/
CCI. "Pleasant area for walking/cycling; caves at Han-sur-Lesse
worth visit; basic san facs." 1 Apr-31 Oct. € 20.00   2012*

DINANT *C3* (5.6km S Rural) *50.22726, 4.90945* **Camping
Parc de Vacances Villatoile, Ferme de Pont-à-Lesse, Route
de Walzin, 5500 Anseremme [(082) 222285; fax 227151;
info@villatoile.be; www.villatoile.be]** Leave E11 at junc
20 onto N97 dir Philippeville, then onto N94 dir Dinant. At
T-junc facing rv turn L onto N95 to Anseremme. Go thro vill &
turn L just bef rv bdge, site 1.5km on L. NB App rd has v lge,
brick-built speed ramp. Med, pt shd; wc; chem disp; mv service
pnt; shwrs €1.20; EHU (10A) inc (poss rev pol); gas; lndry (inc
dryer); rest, snacks; high ssn; bar; playgrnd; pool 300m;
rv sw adj; canoeing; games area; wifi; entmnt; 40% statics;
dogs; phone; Eng spkn; adv bkg (winter); quiet; ccard acc;
CKE/CCI. "On loop of Rv Lesse; busy, not particularly clean
site used by canoeists, rock climbers & hikers; extra for rvside
pitch; scenic area; gd san facs; gd walks; hign ssn music Sat
nights; gates locked 2200-0800; poss lge, noisy youth groups;
gd fun for older children otherwise NH only." 1 Apr-15 Oct.
€ 18.00   2010*

⊞ **DOCHAMPS** *C3* (700m ESE Rural) *50.23080, 5.63180*
**Panorama Campsite Petite Suisse, Al Bounire 27, 6960
Dochamps [(084) 444030; fax 444455; info@petitesuisse.
be; www.petitesuisse.be]** Fr E25, take N89 (La Roche) at
Samrée turn R onto N841 headed twrds Dochamp. Turn R
into rd sp Al Bounire and foll sp to site. Lge, various sizes, mkd
pitch, some hdstg, pt sl, terr, pt shd; htd wc; chem disp; mv
service pnt; shwrs; baby facs; fam bthrm; EHU (10A) inc; gas;
lndry (inc dryer); shop; rest, snacks; bar; BBQ; playgrnd; htd
pool; paddling pool; waterslide; tennis; games area; games rm;
wifi; TV rm; adv bkg; 50% statics; dogs €5; bus 8km; phone;
quiet; poss cr; ccard acc; red LS/snr citizens; CKE/CCI. "Gd facs;
beautiful spot; busy, popular, excel site." ♦ € 50.00 2014*

EEKLO

⊞ **EEKLO** *A2* (7km E Rural) *51.18093, 3.64180* **Camping Malpertuus, Tragelstraat 12, 9971 Lembeke [(09) 3776178; fax 3270036; campingmalpertuus@telenet.be; www.vkt. be]** Exit A10/E40 junc 11 onto N44 dir Aalter & Maldegem. Foll sp Eekloo onto N49 & then foll sp Lembeke, site sp. Med, pt shd; htd wc; chem disp; mv service pnt; shwrs €1; EHU (4A) €3; gas; lndry rm; shop 2km; rest 200m; snacks; bar; 85% statics; dogs; phone; bus 300m; Eng spkn; adv bkg; quiet; 10% red CKE/CCI. "Gd site in lovely area; friendly staff; entmnt/events at w/end; gd size pitches; gd site." ◆ ltd. € 15.50   2011*

"I need an on-site restaurant"

We do our best to make sure site information is correct, but it is always best to check any must-have facilities are still available or will be open during your visit.

⊞ **EREZEE** *C3* (3km SW Rural) *50.27923, 5.54779* **Camping Le Val de l'Aisne, Rue du TTA, 6997 Blier-Erezée [(086) 470067; fax 470043; info@levaldelaisne.be; www. levaldelaisne.be]** Fr Marche-en-Famenne take N86 dir Hotton. In Hotton cross Rv Ourthe & immed turn R dir Soy & Erezée. In 9km at lge rndabt foll sp La Roche-en-Ardenne, site in 900m on L. Med, hdg/mkd pitch, pt shd; htd wc; chem disp; baby facs; shwrs; EHU (16A) €3; gas; lndry (inc dryer); shop 1.5km; rest, snacks; bar; BBQ; playgrnd; htd, covrd pool 10km; lake beach & sw adj; fishing; kayaking; tennis; games area; wifi; entmnt; cab/sat TV; 70% statics; dogs €3; train 8km; phone; poss cr; Eng spkn; adv bkg; quiet; ccard acc; red long stay/ LS/CKE/CCI. "Beautiful situation; excel, well-maintained facs; friendly, helpful staff; vg, peaceful site." ◆ ltd. € 18.00   2010*

⊞ **ESNEUX** *C3* (3km N Rural) *50.53941, 5.56986* **Camping Les Murets, Chemin d'Enonck 57, 4130 Hony-Esneux [tel/fax (041) 3801987; lesmurets@skynet.be; www.lesmurets.be]** On rd A26/E25 take exit 41 or 42 dir Esneux. In vill of Méry, directly after green bottle bank turn R over bdge & immed L at end of bdge sp Hony/Hôni. Foll sp Les Murets, under rlwy bdge Les Murets on L. Med, pt shd wc; chem disp; shwrs €0.90; EHU (4A) inc; gas; shops, rest 500m; supmkt in Méry; BBQ; playgrnd; pool 5km; TV rm; dogs; phone; poss cr; Eng spkn; adv bkg rec high ssn; quiet but some rlwy noise. "Friendly; facs basic but clean; conv touring base." 1 Apr-31 Oct. € 17.00   2009*

⊞ **EUPEN** *B4* (3km SW Rural) *50.61457, 6.01686* **Camping Hertogenwald, Oestraat 78, 4700 Eupen [(087) 743222; fax 743409; info@camping-hertogenwald.be; www.camping-hertogenwald.be]** Fr German border customs on E40 a'bahn for Liège, take 2nd exit for Eupen. In Eupen L at 3rd traff lts & 1st R in 100m. Drive thro Eupen cent, foll sp to Spa. Camping sp immed at bottom of hill, sharp hairpin R turn onto N629, site on L in 2km. Med, unshd; htd wc; chem disp; shwrs inc; EHU (6A) inc (long lead req & poss no earth); lndry; rest, snacks; bar; playgrnd; htd, covrd pool 3km; games area; 90% statics; dogs €1.60; phone; poss cr; Eng spkn; quiet. "Sm tourer area; clean site adj rv & forest; muddy after rain; gd walking & cycling beside rv; conv Aachen." ◆ € 18.00   2011*

⊞ **EUPEN** *B4* (3.4km SW Rural) *50.61250, 6.01128* **Camping Wesertal, Rue de l'Invasion 66-68, 4837 Membach-Baelen [(087) 555961 or 555076; fax 556555; info@wesertal.com; www.wesertal.com]** Fr E40 junc 38 onto N67, turn R at 1st rndabt & foll sp Baelen & Membach, site sp in 7km. Med, shd; htd wc; chem disp; sauna; baby facs; shwrs €1; EHU (16A) inc (check pol & poss no earth); lndry; shops 3km; playgrnd; pool 2km; 90% statics; dogs €2; poss cr; Eng spkn; adv bkg; quiet; CKE/CCI. "Site adj rv & forest; friendly welcome; poss run down, scruffy; ltd space for tourers; some pitches well away fr (poss grubby) san facs; gd walks; NH only." € 19.60   2009*

FLORENVILLE *D3* (8km E Rural) *49.69208, 5.40866* **Camping du Faing, Rue du Faing 16, 6810 Jamoigne [(061) 320272; fax 464867]** Exit A4/E25 junc 30 onto N83 W or junc 29 onto N87/N83 thro Tintigny. Site at W end of Jamoigne - track to site adj lge concrete materials depot. Sp diff to spot. Med, pt shd; wc; chem disp; shwrs inc; EHU inc; lndry; supmkt in vill; bar; rest; playgrnd; covrd pool & sports adj nr; 80% statics; dogs; phone; quiet; ccard acc. "NH only; san facs need refurb - more facs avail in recep/rest/bar building at site ent." ◆ Mar-Dec. € 22.00   2009*

FLORENVILLE *D3* (17km E Rural) *49.68499, 5.52058* **Camping Chênefleur, Norulle 16, 6730 Tintigny [(063) 444078; fax 445271; info@chenefleur.be; www.chenefleur.be]** Fr Liège foll E25 dir Luxembourg. Exit junc 29 sp Habay-la-Neuve to Etalle, then N83 to Florenville. Site sp off N83 at E end of Tintigny vill. Med, pt shd; htd wc; chem disp; shwrs inc; baby facs; EHU (6-8A) inc; gas; lndry (inc dryer); shop; rest, snacks; bar; playgrnd; htd pool; paddling pool; games area; bike hire; wifi; entmnt; dogs €4; Eng spkn; adv bkg; quiet; ccard acc. "Orval Abbey, Maginot Line worth visit; friendly staff; gd, clean site & modern san facs; well kept site." ◆ 1 Apr-30 Sep. € 32.00   2012*

GEDINNE *C3* (1km SW Rural) *49.97503, 4.92719* **Camping La Croix Scaille, Rue du Petit Rot 10, 5575 Gedinne [(061) 588517; fax 588736; camping.croix-scaille@skynet. be; www.campingcroixscaille.be]** Fr N95 turn W to Gedinne on N935. Site sp S of vill on R after 1km. Lge, mkd pitch, some hdstg, terr, pt shd; htd wc; chem disp; shwrs inc; EHU (16A) €1.60; gas; lndry (inc dryer); snacks; bar; playgrnd; TV; pool; tennis, fishing adj; bike hire; 75% statics; dogs; poss cr; quiet; ccard acc; CKE/CCI. 1 Apr-15 Nov. € 13.40   2013*

⊞ **GEEL** *A3* (8km N Rural) *51.22951, 4.97836* **Camping Houtum, Houtum 51, 2460 Kasterlee [(014) 859216; fax 853803; info@campinghoutum.be; www.camping houtum.be]** On N19 Geel to Turnhout rd 1km bef Kasterlee site sp on R at windmill opp British WW2 cemetery. Foll sp to site 500m on rd parallel to N19, cross next rd, site in 300m. Lge, mkd pitch, pt shd; htd wc; chem disp; shwrs €1; EHU (4-6A) €2; lndry; shops adj; snacks; lge playgrnd; pool 2km; adj to rv with boating, canoeing, fishing; tennis & mini-golf 300m; bike hire; nature trails adj; 60% statics; phone; poss v cr; adv bkg; v quiet; ccard acc; red long stay/CKE/CCI. "Orderly, attractive site; lots for children all ages." € 20.70   2013*

⊞ **GERAARDSBERGEN** *B2* (6.4km NE Urban) *50.78990, 3.92351* **Camping Domein De Gavers, Onkerzelestraat 280, 9500 Geraadsbergen [(054) 416324; fax 410388; gavers@oost-vlanderen.be; www.degavers.be]** Fr N on A10 exit junc 17; S for 26km on N42 to Geraardsbergen. After level x-ing turn L at traff lts, L at rndabt & foll sp De Gavers for 4.3km. Fr S on N42 foll sp Geraardsbergen to rndabt, turn L then turn R at 2nd traff lts sp De Gavers. Lge, hdg pitch, pt shd; htd wc; chem disp; mv service pnt; baby facs; shwrs €0.50; EHU (10A) inc (long lead req); lndry; shop, rest, bar 400m; playgrnd; lake sw & sand beach adj; TV; 80% statics; dogs; phone; train 4km; poss cr; Eng spkn; adv bkg; quiet but some rd noise; ccard acc; red long stay/CKE/CCI. "Sep area for tourers; many leisure facs; excel touring region." € 25.00   2010*

GHENT *A2* (14km SW Rural) *51.00508, 3.57228* **Camping Groeneveld, Groenevelddreef 14, Bachte-Maria-Leerne, 9800 Deinze [(09) 3801014; fax 3801760; info@ campinggroeneveld.be; www.campinggroeneveld.be]** E or W E40/E10 on Brussels to Ostend m'way exit junc 13 at sp Gent W/Drongen. Take N466 sp Dienze. Approx 1km beyond junc with N437, turn L just after 2nd 70 km/h sp down narr side rd - house on corner has advert hoarding. Site on L opp flour mill. Sm sp at turning. Med, some hdg pitch, pt shd; htd wc; chem disp; mv service pnt; shwrs inc; EHU (10A) inc (poss no earth); shops 2km; rest (bkg ess), snacks, bar (w/end only LS); playgrnd; fishing; entmnt; TV; 40% statics; dogs €2; phone; poss cr; Eng spkn; adv bkg; quiet; red LS/long stay; CKE/CCI. "Gd welcome; additional san facs at lower end of site; office open 1900-2000 LS but staff in van adj san facs, or site yourself; barrier clsd until 0800; do not arr bef 1400; 1km fr Ooidonk 16th Castle; ok NH; gd site; bus to vill; some pitches tight." 1 Apr-31 Oct. € 23.00   2015*

GHENT *A2* (4km W Urban) *51.04638, 3.68083* **Camping Blaarmeersen, Zuiderlaan 12, 9000 Gent [(09) 2668160; fax 2668166; camping.blaarmeersen@gent.be; www.blaarmeersen.be]** Exit A10/E40 Brussels-Ostend m'way at junc 13 sp Gent W & Drongen. At T-junc turn onto N466 twd Gent. In 4km cross canal then turn R to site, sp (3 rings) Sport & Recreatiecentrum Blaarmeersen. Fr Gent cent foll N34 twd Tielt for 1km past city boundary & turn L to site; adj lake & De Ossemeersen nature reserve. NB Due to rd layout, rec foll camping sp on app to site rather than Sat Nav. Lge, hdg/mkd pitch, pt shd; htd wc; chem disp; mv service pnt; serviced pitch; shwrs inc; EHU (10A) metered + conn fee €1.25 (poss rev pol); lndry (inc dryer); shop; rest, snacks; bar; playgrnd; pool & full sports facs adj; lake sw adj; watersports; tennis; frequent bus to Gent; 5% statics; dogs €1.25; phone; bus to town nr; no dep bef 0815 hrs; Eng spkn; rd/rlwy noise; ccard acc; passport req. "Clean, well-organised, busy site; beautiful lake with path around; helpful staff; rest gd value; gd cycle track fr site; cycle into cent avoiding main rd; gd location for walks & activities; poss travellers LS; pitches muddy when wet; some m'van pitches sm & v shd; excel." 1 Mar-3 Nov. € 31.00   2015*

GODARVILLE *B2* (2km S Rural) *50.48794, 4.29318* **Camping Domaine Claire-Fontaine, 11 Ave Clémenceau, 7160 Godarville [(064) 443675; sites.voiesdeau@hainaut.be]** Exit A15/E42 junc 18 onto N59 to Godarville, site sp. Lge, unshd; wc; chem disp; shwrs inc; EHU (6A) inc; lndry rm; shop 1km; snacks; bar; BBQ; playgrnd; lake sw; games area; 85% statics; dogs; phone; ccard acc; CKE/CCI. "Facs better than 1st impression but avoid san facs nr touring area & avoid area outside barrier; helpful warden; NH only." 1 Mar-31 Oct. € 22.00   2010*

GRIMBERGEN see Bruxelles *B2*

⊞ **HAN SUR LESSE** *C3* (350m N Urban) *50.12727, 5.18773* **Camping Aire Gite d'Etape, Rue du Gite 10, 5580 Han-sur-Lesse [(084) 377441; gite.han@gitesdetape.be]** Exit A4/E411 junc 23 sp Ave-et-Auffe & Rochefort. Go over 2 rv bdges then immed L & 1st R. Site on L. Sm, hdstg, unshd; wc; mv service pnt; shops, rests etc nr; playgrnd nrby; games area; entmnt; m'van only. "Gd; attendant calls." € 5.00   2009*

HAN SUR LESSE *C3* (260m S Rural) *50.12330, 5.18587* **Camping de la Lesse, Rue du Grand Hy, 5580 Han-sur-Lesse [(084) 377290; fax 377576; han.tourisme@skynet.be; www.valdelesse.be or www.campingshansurlesse.be]** Site 500m off Han-sur-Lesse main sq adj Office de Tourisme. If app fr Ave-et-Auffe, turn R at Office du Tourisme, take care over rlwy x-ing to site on R in 150m. Med, mkd pitch; pt shd; htd wc; chem disp; shwrs inc; EHU (3-6A) inc; gas; lndry; shops, rests 200m; playgrnd; canoeing adj; rv adj; 50% statics; dogs; phone; poss cr; adv bkg ess high ssn via TO; phone adj; noisy; ccard not acc; CKE/CCI. "Gd touring base; undergrnd grotto trip; take care on narr rds to site - v high kerbs; excel; san facs immac; pleasant LS." 1 Apr-15 Nov. € 29.00   2013*

⊞ **HAN SUR LESSE** *C3* (5km SW Rural) *50.11178, 5.13308* **Camping Le Roptai, Rue Roptai 34, 5580 Ave-et-Auffe [(084) 388319; fax 387327; info@leroptai.be; www.leroptai.be]** Fr A4 exit 23 & take N94 dir Dinant. At bottom of hill turn R onto N86. Turn L in vill of Ave, foll sp, 200m to L. Med, mkd pitch, hdstg, pt sl, terr, pt shd; wc; chem disp; mv service pnt; shwrs €0.90; EHU (6A) €1.80; gas; shop & 5km; snacks; bar; playgrnd; htd pool; TV; 80% statics; dogs €1.50; site clsd Jan; poss cr; Eng spkn; adv bkg; quiet; CKE/CCI. "Some pitches awkwardly sl; generally run down & poor facs; ltd facs LS; NH only." € 25.00   2014*

HAN SUR LESSE *C3* (230m NW Urban) *50.12632, 5.18478* **Camping Le Pirot, Rue Joseph Lamotte 3, 5580 Han-sur-Lesse [(084) 377280; fax 377576; han.tourisme@skynet.be; www.valdelesse.be]** Exit A4/E411 junc 23 sp Ave-et-Auffe & Rochefort. Go over 1st bdge then L immed bef 2nd bdge in Han cent; sh, steep incline. Sm, unshd; wc; shwrs inc; EHU (10A) inc (poss rev pol); shop nr; rest, snacks, bar 200m; dogs; bus adj; poss cr; adv bkg; quiet; ccard acc; CKE/CCI. "Excel position on raised bank of rv; adj attractions & rests; interesting town; helpful staff; basic, dated san facs; conv NH or sh stay in attractive town." 1 Apr-15 Nov. € 20.00   2015*

BELGIUM

HASSELT *B3* (12km NE Rural) *50.99775, 5.42537* **Camping Holsteenbron, Hengelhoefseweg 9, 3520 Zonhoven [tel/fax 011 817140; camping.holsteenbron@skynet.be; www.holsteenbron.be]** Leave A2 junc 29 twd Hasselt; turn L at 1st traff lts in 1km, foll sp thro houses & woods for 3km. Site is NE of Zonhoven. Med, hdg/mkd pitch, hdstg, pt shd; htd wc; chem disp; shwrs €1; EHU (6A) inc; lndry rm; snacks; bar; playgrnd; games area; TV; 30% statics; dogs €1; phone; Eng spkn; quiet; CKE/CCI. "Pleasant, happy site in woodland; gd touring base; friendly owners." 1 Apr-13 Nov. € 22.00   2011*

HOTTON *C3* (900m NW Urban) *50.27085, 5.43833* **Camping Eau Zone, rue des Fonzays 10, 6990 Hotton [(084) 477715; campingeauzone@hotmail.be; www.campingeauzone.be]** E411 exit 18 to Marche then N86 to Hotton, over bdge in Hotton, turn L twds Melreux, foll rv and sp. Sm, pt shd; wc; chem disp; shwrs €2.50; EHU (10A); snacks; bar; BBQ; wifi; 20% statics; dogs; phone; public transport 1km; twin axles; Eng spkn; adv bkgs; CKE/CCI. "Site conv for Hotton caves; easy walk to town; gd NH." ♦ ltd. 1 Mar-30 Nov. € 20.00   2015*

HOUTHALEN *B3* (4km E Rural) *51.03222, 5.41613* **Camping Kelchterhoef, Binnenvaartstraat, 3530 Houthalen-Helchteren [(011) 492140]** Exit A2/E314 junc 30 N. In 2km at x-rds turn L, in 2km at rndabt turn R into Binnenvaartstraat, then foll site sp. Lge, mkd pitch, pt shd; htd wc; chem disp; shwrs; EHU (6A) inc; lndry; shop; snacks; playgrnd; lake sw adj; entmnt; internet; TV; 40% statics; adv bkg; Eng spkn; quiet. "Use ent phone for access; fair site; facs being updated (2015)." 1 Apr-1 Nov. € 22.00   2015*

HOUYET see Dinant *C3*

HUY *B3* (3km NE Urban) *50.53293, 5.25897* **Camping Mosan, Rue de la Paix 3, 4500 Tihange [(085) 231051; fax 251853; ces.huy@skynet.be]** Exit A15 junc 8 & proceed to Huy town cent, then along S bank of Rv Meuse dir Liège for 2km (past bdge on L) beyond town cent. Immed bef lge cooling towers on L, turn R (unmkd). In approx 200m sharp L turn into Rue de la Paix. Site recep at house beyond community cent. Sm, pt shd; wc; chem disp; mv service pnt; shwrs; EHU inc; shop 1km; adv bkg; ccard not acc. "Fair site; easy access to town; recep opens 1630 - site yourself." 1 Apr-30 Sep. € 15.00   2009*

JABBEKE see Brugge *A2*

KASTERLEE see Geel *A3*

KEMMEL/HEUVELLAND see Ypres/Ieper *B1*

KNOKKE HEIST *A2* (1.6km S Urban) *51.33530, 3.28959* **Camping Holiday, Natiënlaan 70-72, 8300 Knokke-Heist [(050) 601203; fax 613280; info@camping-holiday.be; www.camping-holiday.be]** On N49/E34 opp Knokke-Heist town boundary sp. Site ent at side of Texaco g'ge. Med, unshd; wc; chem disp; shwrs inc; EHU (6A) €1.90 (poss rev pol); supmkt opp; rest, snacks 500m; playgrnd; beach 1.5km; bike hire; phone; 60% statics; poss cr; quiet but rd noise. "V clean, tidy site but ltd san facs and waste disp pnts; may need to manhandle c'van onto pitch." ♦ ltd. Easter-30 Sep. € 27.00   2012*

KOKSIJDE *A1* (1.2km N Urban) *51.11105, 2.65215* **Camping De Blekker, Jachtwakersstraat 12, 8670 Koksijde ann Zee [(058) 511633; fax 511307; camping.deblekker@skynet.be; www.deblekker.be]** Fr E40 Brugge-Calais exit dir Veurne & foll sp Koksijde. At rndabt turn R for Koksijde then Koksijde ann Zee. Site sp on R. Lge, hdg/mkd pitch, pt shd; htd wc; chem disp; mv service pnt; serviced pitches; mv service pnt; baby facs; shwrs €1; EHU (10A) inc; gas; lndry (inc dryer); shop 300m; rest, snacks; bar; BBQ; playgrnd; htd, covrd pool 400m; sand beach 1.8km; games rm; TV; 80% statics; no dogs; phone; poss cr; adv bkg; quiet; Eng spkn; ccard acc; CKE/CCI. "Warm welcome; relaxing site; modern san facs but insufficient for size of site." ♦ 15 Mar-15 Nov. € 30.00   2010*

KOKSIJDE *A1* (1.6km NE Rural) *51.11114, 2.67082* **Camping Amazone, Westhinderstraat 2, 8670 Koksijde ann Zee [(058) 513363; fax 522512; info@camping-amazone.com; www.camping-amazone.com]** Fr A18/E40 exit junc 1A dir De Panne, foll sp Koksijde on N8. Pass airfield & turn R to Koksijde, site on L in 500m. Med, mkd pitch, unshd; wc; own san; chem disp; shwrs €1; EHU (6A) €2; sand beach 1.2km; 80% statics; Eng spkn; quiet. "Ltd touring pitches, but conv NH Dunkerque/Ostend ferries." 1 Apr-30 Sep. € 18.00   2009*

⊞ **KOKSIJDE** *A1* (2km W Rural) *51.10287, 2.63066* **Camping Noordduinen, Noordduinen 12, 8670 Koksijde aan Zee [(058) 512546; fax 512618; roos@campingbenelux.be; www.campingnoordduinen.be]** Exit A18/E40 junc 1A onto N8. Foll sp Koksijde to rndabt, strt over into Leopold III Laan, site on L. Sm, hdg pitch, hdstg, pt shd; wc; shwrs €1; EHU €2.50; lndry; supmkt 300m; sand beach 3km; wifi; 80% statics; dogs €2.50; bus 500m; Eng spkn; adv bkg; quiet; CKE/CCI. "Gd site; adj cycle rte to Veurne - attractive, historic town; new san facs closer to pitches (2012)." € 25.00   2012*

LEMBEKE see Eeklo *A2*

LIEGE *B3* (12km S Rural) *50.56770, 5.58826* **Camping du Syndicat d'Initiative de Tilff, Rue du Chera 5, 4040 Tilff-sur-Ourthe [(04) 3881883]** Exit m'way at Tilff junc 41 or 42 & foll sp to site. Sm, v sl, pt shd; wc; chem disp; shwrs; EHU (4A) €2.48; lndry; shops 500m; playgrnd; pool 2m; poss cr; 95% statics; dogs; quiet; CKE/CCI. "Basic site; ltd space for tourers; NH only." ♦ 1 Apr-31 Oct.   2009*

LILLE-GIERLE see Turnhout *A3*

⊞ **LONDERZEEL** *B2* (3.6km NNE Rural) *51.02041, 4.31936* **Camping Diepvennen, Molenhoek 35, 1840 Londerzeel [(052) 309492; fax 305716; info@camping-diepvennen.be; www.camping-diepvennen.be]** On A12 exit at Londerzeel, foll sp Industrie Zone & Diepvennen. Foll Diepvennen sp to site. Site on W side of A12. Lge, pt shd; wc; shwrs €1; EHU €3; lndry; shop; rest, snacks; playgrnd; pool; fishing pond; tennis; games area; 95% statics; rd noise; red long stay. "Long walk to san facs block; easy access by train to Antwerp & Brussels." ♦ € 18.00   2013*

⊞ **MALMEDY** *C4* (4km E Rural) *50.42008, 6.07059* **Familial Camping, Rue des Bruyères 19, 4960 Arimont-Malmédy [tel/fax (080) 330862; info@campingfamilial.be; www.campingfamilial.be]** Take St Vith rd (N62) out of Malmédy; in 2km over level x-ing turn L in 300m at sp Arimont & 2nd camping sp. Site on L, 1.5km up winding (but easy) hill. Med, pt sl, terr, pt shd; htd wc (some cont); chem disp; mv service pnt; shwrs €1; EHU inc (4-6A) €2; gas; lndry (inc dryer); sm shop; rest, snacks; bar; sm pool; playgrnd; games rm; wifi; entmnt; TV; bus 1km; 50% statics; dogs free; phone; site clsd last week Oct to 2nd week Dec; Eng spkn; adv bkg; ccard not acc; CKE/CCI. "Pleasant but untidy site with excel views over hills; gd facs; conv Ardennes, Spa motor racing circuit; lorry noise fr rd to quarry behind site." € 17.50   2011*

MALONNE see Namur *C3*

⊞ **MARCHE EN FAMENNE** *C3* (6.5km NW Rural) *50.24911, 5.27978* **Camping Le Relais, 16 Rue de Serinchamps, 5377 Hogne [(0475) 423049; info@campinglerelais.com; www.campinglerelais.com]** Sp fr N4 bet Marche-en-Famenne & Namur. Fr Namur ent immed R under new bdge. Med, pt sl, unshd; htd wc; chem disp; baby facs; shwrs inc; EHU (10A) €2.50; lndry; rest, snacks; playgrnd; lake adj; TV; 30% statics; dogs free; adv bkg; some rd noise; CKE/CCI. "V pleasant; gd, clean facs but dated (2015); conv for N4." € 20.50   2015*

MEMBACH-BAELEN see Eupen *B4*

MOL *A3* (5km E Rural) *51.20945, 5.17181* **Camping Zilverstrand, Kiezelweg 17, 2400 Mol [(014) 810098; fax 816685; info@zilverstrand.be; www.zilverstrand.be]** Exit A13 junc 23 dir Geel onto N19 then N71 to Mol, site sp on N712 twd Lommel. Lge, pt shd; htd wc; chem disp; mv service pnt; baby facs; fam bthrm; EHU (6A) inc; lndry (inc dryer); shop; rest, snacks; bar; BBQ; playgrnd; htd covrd pool; paddling pool; waterslides; lake sw & beach; tennis 1km; bike hire; golf 1km; wifi; 60% statics; dogs; adv bkg; quiet. ♦ 22 Apr-31 Oct. € 30.50   2011*

⊞ **MUNKZWALM** *B2* (700m E Rural) *50.87573, 3.74058* **Camping Canteclaer, Rekegemstraat 12, 9630 Munkzwalm [(055) 499688; fax 316150; camping. canteclaer@telenet.be; www.campingcanteclaer.be]** Fr A10 exit junc 17 onto N42 S. At junc with N46 turn R & in 7km turn L to Munkzwalm on N415 Noordlaan which becomes Zuidlaan. Turn L again into Zwalmlaan, site by rlwy. Lge, pt shd; wc; chem disp; shwrs €0.75; EHU (6A) inc; lndry; shops 1km; rest, snacks; bar; playgrnd; statics; phone; adv bkg; quiet, some rlwy noise; 80% statics. "Sm touring area." € 13.00   2009*

NAMUR *C3* (13km S Rural) *50.37233, 4.86966* **Camping La Douaire, 43 Rue du Herdal, 5170 Profondeville [(081) 412149]** Fr Namur take N92 S twds Dinant. At approx 8km 100m after rndabt take slip rd sp Profondeville. In 100m turn R into Chemin du Herdal, site on L, narr ent. Med, mkd pitch, sl, pt shd; wc; chem disp; shwrs €1.25; EHU €3; gas; shop, rest 300m; playgrnd; pool 4km; 95% statics; dogs; quiet. "Conv Namur & Dinant; not suitable twin-axles; only 2 (poor) touring pitches, no hdstg." 1 Apr-15 Oct. € 9.00   2009*

NAMUR *C3* (9km SW Rural) *50.44164, 4.80182* **Camping Les Trieux, 99 Rue Les Tris, 5020 Malonne [tel/fax (081) 445583 or 473 810742 (mob); camping.les.trieux@ skynet.be; www.campinglestrieux.be]** Fr Namur take N90 sp Charleroi, after 8km take L fork sp Malonne (camp sp at junc). After 400m turn L at camp sp & site at top of 1 in 7 (13%) hill, approx 200m. To miss steep hill, fr Namur take Dinant (N92) S. In 2km R at camping sp. Take care at hairpin in 200m. Foll site sps. Located up steep, but surfaced rd. Med, mkd pitch, terr, pt shd; htd wc; chem disp; mv service pnt; shwrs €1; EHU (10A) €2; lndry; shop; snacks; playgrnd; TV; 50% statics; phone; Eng spkn; quiet; ccard not acc; red LS; CKE/CCI. "Friendly owners; pretty site, but steep - take care ent pitch; pitches diff for lge o'fits; basic san facs but clean; NH only." 1 Apr-31 Oct. € 21.00   2015*

⊞ **NEUFCHATEAU** *D3* (2km SW Rural) *49.83502, 5.41640* **Camping Val d'Emeraude, Route de Malome 1-3, 6840 Neufchâteau [tel/fax (061) 511952; valdemeraude@ skynet.be; www.valdemeraude.be]** Take Florenville rd out of town. In 2km site at lge cream hse on L. Sm, pt sl, unshd; mkd pitch; wc; chem disp; shwrs; EHU €3 (poss rev pol); lndry rm; shop 3km; rest, snacks, bar 1km; BBQ; playgrnd; fishing 500m; pool (child); sw; tv rm; wifi; 25%; 70% statics; dogs €1.50; phone; bus adj; Eng spkn; adv bkg; quiet but some rd noise; CKE/CCI. "Beautiful setting; gd walks; helpful owner; well-kept, flat pitches; basic, ltd san facs; attractive location; gd NH." ♦ 1 Apr-31 Oct. € 28.00   2013*

"Satellite navigation makes touring much easier"

Remember most sat navs don't know if you're towing or in a larger vehicle – always use yours alongside maps and site directions.

⊞ **NEUFCHATEAU** *D3* (2.5km SW Rural) *49.83305, 5.41721* **Camping Spineuse, Rue de Florenville, 6840 Neufchâteau [061 27 73 20; fax 27 71 04; info@camping-spineuse.be; www.camping-spineuse.be]** Fr A4/E411 exit junc 26 or junc 27 fr E25 to Neufchâteau. Take N85 dir Florenville, site is 3rd on L. Ent easy to miss. Med, pt shd; htd wc; chem disp; mv service pnt; shwrs free; EHU (16A) €3; lndry; shops 1km; rest, snacks; bar; playgrnd; sm pool; wifi; TV; 30% statics; dogs €1.25; phone; Eng spkn; quiet; ccard acc; red LS/snr citizens. "Pleasant, pretty site; poss diff lge o'fits if site full; vg san facs; some flooding after heavy rain." € 21.50   2015*

⊞ **NIEUWPOORT** *A1* (1.5km NE Rural) *51.13324, 2.76031* **Parking De Zwerver, Brugsesteenweg 18, 8620 Nieuwpoort [(0474) 669526; de_zwerver@telenet.be]** Nr Kompass Camping - see dirs under Kompass Camping. Site behind De Zwerver nursery. Sm, mkd pitch, all hdstg, unshd; wc; mv service pnt €2.50; shwrs & hot water; lndry; BBQ; playgrnd; m'vans only. "Coin & note operated facs; modern & efficient; walking/cycling dist to town cent & port." ♦ € 0.50 (per hour)   2010*

BELGIUM

NIEUWPOORT *A1* (3km E Rural) *51.12960, 2.77220*
Kompascamping Nieuwpoort, Brugsesteenweg 49, 8620 Nieuwpoort [(058) 236037; fax 232682; nieuwpoort@ kompascamping.be; www.kompascamping.be] Exit E40/A18 at junc 3 sp Nieuwpoort; in 500m turn R at full traff lts; after 1km turn R at traff lts; turn R at rndabt & immed turn L over 2 sm canal bdgs. Turn R to Brugsesteenweg, site on L approx 1km. Fr Ostende on N34 (coast rd) turn L at rndabt after canal bdge as above. V lge, hdg/mkd pitch, some hdstg, pt shd; htd wc; chem disp; baby facs; shwrs inc; EHU (10A) €2.20; gas; lndry (inc dryer); shop & 2km; rest, snacks; bar; playgrnd; 2 pools (1 htd, covrd); paddling pool; waterslide; tennis; sports/games area adj; bike hire; golf 10km; wifi; entmnt; 90% statics; dogs €2.30; poss cr; adv bkg; quiet; red long stay/CKE/CCI. "Well-equipped site; helpful staff; boat-launching facs; sep area for sh stay tourers; v busy w/ends; excel cycle rtes; conv Dunkerque ferry." 1 Apr-14 Nov. € 34.50 (4 persons) (CChq acc) 2012*

See advertisement

⊞ **OLLOY SUR VIROIN** *C3* (1km SW Rural) *50.06876, 4.59643* **Camping Try des Baudets, Rue de la Champagne, 5670 Olloy-sur-Viroin [tel/fax (060) 390108; masson_p@ yahoo.fr]** Fr N99 turn to Olloy-sur-Viroin sp Fumay. At end of main st (where Fumay rd turns L) cont strt then R, site sp up fairly steep, narr rd with passing places. Lge, mkd pitch, sl, unshd; wc; chem disp; shwrs inc; EHU (6A) inc; lndry; shop, bar 1km; playgrnd; fishing; 80% statics; dogs; bus; Eng spkn; adv bkg; quiet; CKE/CCI. "Gd walking, cycling; steam rlwy in valley; friendly proprietor; vg." ♦ € 18.00 2009*

⊞ **OOSTENDE** *A1* (5km NE Coastal) *51.24882, 2.96710* **Camping 17 Duinzicht, Rozenlaan 23, 8450 Bredene [(059) 323871; fax 330467; info@campingduinzicht.be; www.campingduinzicht.be]** Fr Ostend take dual c'way to Blankenberge on N34. Turn R sp Bredene, L into Driftweg which becomes Kappelstraat & turn R into Rozenlaan. Site sp. Lge, mkd pitch, hdstg, unshd; htd wc; chem disp; mv service pnt; serviced pitches; baby facs; shwrs €1; EHU (10A) inc (poss no earth); gas; lndry (inc dryer); shop 500m; rest; snacks, bar adj; BBQ; playgrnd; sand beach 500m; wifi; 60% statics; dogs; phone; security barrier; poss cr; Eng spkn; adv bkg; quiet; ccard acc; red LS; CKE/CCI. "Excel site; poss long walk to san facs; take care slippery tiles in shwrs; Bredene lovely, sm seaside town." € 24.00 (4 persons) 2012*

⊞ **OOSTENDE** *A1* (6km NE Rural) *51.24366, 2.98002* **Camping T Minnepark, Zandstraat 105, 8450 Bredene-Dorp [(059) 322458; fax 330495; info@minnepark.be; www.minnepark.be]** Fr Ostend take N34 sp Blankenberge. After tunnel under rlwy turn R sp Brugge. Cross canal & in 300m turn L at filter sp Bredene-Dorp. In 2km immed after blue/white water tower on R, turn L at x-rds. At mini-rndabt turn R passing Aldi supmkt. Site on L after Zanpolder site. Fr A18 exit junc 6 & take N37 sp De Haan. In 5km turn L at rndabt onto N9 sp Oostende. In 5km turn R sp Bredene-Dorp, then R in 2.5km at rndabt into Zandstraat, then as above. V lge, unshd; wc; chem disp; shwrs €1; EHU (16A) €1 (poss rev pol); lndry (inc dryer); shops 1km; playgrnd; sand beach 2km; wifi; cab TV; 75% statics; dogs €3; Eng spkn; adv bkg; quiet. "Lge pitches; friendly, helpful staff; warm welcome; excel, well-run site; vg san facs; conv ferries, Bruges & coast." € 30.00 2013*

⊞ **OOSTENDE** *A1* (5km E Urban/Coastal) *51.24970, 2.96834* **Camping Astrid, Koning Astridlaan 1, 8450 Bredene [(059) 321247; fax 331470; info@camping-astrid.be; www.camping-astrid.be]** Foll tourist sp. Med, unshd; wc; chem disp; serviced pitch; shwrs; EHU (10A) inc; shops 100m; sand beach adj; cab/sat TV; 80% statics; phone; poss cr; Eng spkn; ccard not acc. "Most sites nrby are statics only; friendly, helpful owners; rec NH; barrier for new arr." ♦ € 29.00 2013*

⊞ **OPGLABBEEK** *B3* (2km SE Rural) *51.02825, 5.59745* **Camping Wilhelm Tell, Hoeverweg 87, 3660 Opglabbeek [(089) 854444; fax 810010; receptie@wilhelmtell.com; www.wilhelmtell.com]** Leave A2/E314 at junc 32, take rd N75 then N730 N sp As. In As take Opglabbeek turn, site sp in 1km. Med, mkd pitch, pt shd; wc; chem disp; mv service pnt; shwrs €0.90; EHU (10A) inc; gas; lndry (inc dryer); shop high ssn; rest, snacks; bar; BBQ; playgrnd; 2 htd pools (1 covrd); paddling pool; waterslide; tennis; bike hire; golf 10km; wifi; entmnt; TV rm; 55% statics; dogs €4; phone; adv bkg; red long stay/LS; quiet; CKE/CCI. "Nice site; narr ent; superb pools, wave machine; site in nature reserve; helpful staff; san facs dist; bit expensive; not suitable for lge o'fits." ♦ € 32.00 2012*

Amidst Flanders battlefields and significant sites and monuments of the Great War

BELGIAN COAST ◆ **WESTENDE** ● **NIEUWPOORT** ◆ **KOMPAS** camping

TEL. WESTENDE: +32 (0)58-22 30 25
TEL. NIEUWPOORT: +32 (0)58-23 60 37

HOLIDAY ... EXPERIENCE IT AT KOMPAS CAMPING

WWW.KOMPASCAMPING.BE

OTEPPE *B3* (500m N Rural) *50.58239, 5.12455* **Camping L'Hirondelle Château, Rue de la Burdinale 76A, 4210 Oteppe [(085) 711131; fax 711021; info@lhirondelle.be; www.lhirondelle.be]** App fr E A15/E42 at exit 8; turn W on N643 for 1.5km; turn at sp on R for Oteppe. In vill 3km pass church to x-rds & R by police stn: site 150m on L. Fr W exit A15 at exit 10 onto N80, turn R onto N652 at Burdinne for Oteppe - easier rte. V lge, pt sl, shd; wc; shwrs €1; EHU (6A) inc; gas; lndry; shop; rest, snacks; bar; BBQ; playgrnd; 2 pools; waterslide; tennis; games area; internet; 75% statics; dogs €2.50; poss cr; quiet; ccard acc; red CKE/CCI. "Site in grnds of chateau; excel facs for children; touring pitches at top of site poss diff (steep); gd area for walking, fishing; conv NH; v quiet LS." 1 Apr-31 Oct. € 29.00   2013*

OUDENAARDE *B2* (15km SW Urban) *50.76250, 3.48719* **Panorama Camping, Boskouter 24, Ruien, 9690 Kluisbergen [(032) 55 38 86 68; info@campingpanorama. be; www.campingpanorama.be]** Fr N8 (Oudenaarde - Berchem) foll sp to Kluisbergen, Ruien. Cont thro Ruien, past church on L turn into Wuipelstraat, then R at rndabt, then L into Boskouter foll sp to site. Med, mkd pitch, pt sl, terr, pt shd; wc; chem disp; shwrs, EHU; rest, snacks; bar; playgrnd; 90% statics; adv bkg; Eng spkn; CKE/CCI. "Gd site; v sm touring area; helpful owner; excel cycling and walking fr site." 1 Feb - 30 Nov. € 25.00   2012*

OVERIJSE see Bruxelles *B2*

PROFONDEVILLE see Namur *C3*

⊞ **ROCHE EN ARDENNE, LA** *C3* (2km E Rural) *50.17697, 5.59847* **Camping Floréal La Roche, 18 Route de Houffalize, 6980 La Roche-en-Ardenne [(084) 219467; camping.laroche@florealclub.be; www.florealclub.be]** Outside town on N860 dir Houffalize on rvside, sp. V lge, mkd pitch, unshd; htd wc; chem disp; mv service pnt; baby facs; shwrs inc; EHU (10A) inc; gas; lndry (inc dryer); shop; rest, snacks; bar; playgrnd; htd pool, paddling pool nr; fishing; tennis; bike hire; games area; wifi; TV rm; 70% statics; dogs; bus; poss cr; Eng spkn; adv bkg; some rd noise; ccard acc; red long stay/CCI. "La Roche interesting town; vg, well-run, friendly site; lge pitches." ♦ € 20.60   2010*

ROCHE EN ARDENNE, LA *C3* (800m S Rural) *50.17465, 5.57774* **Camping Le Vieux Moulin, Rue Petite Strument 62, 6980 La Roche-en-Ardenne [(084) 411507; fax 411080; info@strument.com; www.strument.com]** Off N89 site sp fr La Roche town cent (dir Barrièr-de-Champlon), site in 800m. Med, some hdg pitch, pt sl, shd; htd wc; chem disp; shwrs €2; EHU (6A) €2.50 (poss no earth); gas 800m; lndry; shops 800m; fishing; canoeing; 70% statics in sep area; dogs €2; poss cr; Eng spkn; adv bkg; quiet;CKE/CCI. "Beautiful site; gd pitches; poss unclean san facs & dishwashing (7/09); poss youth groups; poor security; gd walking (map avail)." Easter-Nov. € 14.00   2012*

ROCHEFORT *C3* (500m E Rural) *50.15947, 5.22609* **Camping Communal Les Roches, 26 Rue du Hableau, 5580 Rochefort [(084) 211900; fax 312403; campingrochefort@ lesroches.be; www.lesroches.be]** Fr Rochefort cent on N86 & turn L at rndabt, then 1st R. Site well sp. Lge, hdg/ mkd pitch, hdstg, pt sl, unshd; htd wc; chem disp; mv service pnt; baby facs; serviced pitches; shwrs inc; EHU (6A) metered; lndry (inc dryer); shop, rest, bar nrby; BBQ; playgrnd; pool high ssn adj; tennis; games area; internet; entmnt; TV; 50% statics; dogs; phone; bus 250m; train 2km; Eng spkn; quiet; ccard acc. "Vg, well-managed, pleasant, refurbished site; gd walking; sh walk to charming town; gd clean san facs." ♦ 1 Apr-31 Oct. € 25.00   2012*

ST VITH *C4* (5km SW Rural) *50.24229, 6.09402* **Camping Hohenbusch, Grufflingen 44, B-4791 Burg Reuland [80 22 75 23; info@hohenbusch.be; www.camping hohenbusch.be]** Fr St Vith take the E421 twds Grüfflingen; site on R of the rd sp. Med, hdg pitch, pt shd; htd wc; chem disp; mv service pnt; baby facs; shwrs (metered); EHU (6A) €2.50; lndry; rest; playgrnd; pool; games rm; entmnt; wifi; dogs €2.50. "Eng spkn; v helpful owner; v lge pitches; fully serviced immac modern san facs." 1 Apr-6 Nov. € 22.00   2011*

SART LEZ SPA see Spa *C4*

SINT JOB IN'T GOOR see Antwerpen *A3*

SINT KRUIS see Brugge *A2*

SINT MARGRIETE *A2* (2.6km NW Rural) *51.2860, 3.5164* **Camping De Soetelaer, Sint Margrietepolder 2, 9981 Sint Margriete [(09) 3798151; fax 3799795; camping. desoetelaer@telenet.be; www.desoetelaer.be]** Fr E on N49/E34 to Maldegem or fr W on N9 or N49 turn N onto N251 to Aardenburg (N'lands), then turn R twd St Kruis (N'lands) - site situated 1.5km strt on fr St Margriete (back in Belgium). Med, mkd pitch, pt shd; wc; chem disp; all serviced pitches; shwrs inc; EHU (6A) inc; lndry rm; shops 3km; no dogs; Eng spkn; adv bkg; quiet; ccard not acc; CKE/CCI. "Vg, clean site; excel, modern san facs; peace & quiet, privacy & space; highly rec for relaxation; o'fits pitched v close end to end." Easter-15 Oct. € 30.00   2014*

⊞ **SOUMAGNE** *B3* (3.5km S Rural) *50.61099, 5.73840* **Domaine Provincial de Wégimont, Chaussée de Wégimont 76, 4630 Soumagne [(04) 2372400; fax 2372401; wegimont@prov-liege.be; www.prov-liege. be/wegimont]** Exit A3 at junc 37 onto N3 W twd Fléron & Liège. In 500m at traff lts turn L sp Soumagne. In Soumagne at traff lts form R dir Wégimont, site on top of hill on R directly after bus stop. Med, hdg pitch, pt sl, pt shd; htd wc; chem disp; baby facs; shwrs inc; EHU (16A) inc poss rev pol; shop; rest; bar; communal BBQ; playgrnd; pool adj high ssn; tennis; games area; some entmnt; 70% statics; dogs; bus; site clsd Jan; poss cr; some rd noise; CKE/CCI. "Welcoming site in chateau grnds (public access); clean facs; conv sh stay/NH nr m'way." € 13.50   2011*

BELGIUM

SPA *C4* (6km NE Rural) *50.50806, 5.91928* **Camping Spa d'Or (TCB), Stockay 17, 4845(B) Sart-lez-Spa [087 47 44 00; fax 47 52 77; info@campingspador.be; www.camping spador.be]** App fr N or S on m'way A27/E42, leave at junc 9, foll sp to Sart & Spa d'Or. Lge, pt sl, pt shd; htd wc; chem disp; baby facs; shwrs & bath inc; EHU (10A) €4. (check earth); gas; Indry; shop high ssn; rest, snacks; BBQ; playgrnd; htd pool; bike hire; entmnt; 60% statics; dogs €5; poss cr; quiet; ccard acc; red CKE/CCI. "Conv F1 Grand Prix circuit Francorchamps & historic town Stavelot; vg; gd NH." 1 Apr-14 Nov. € 27.50 (CChq acc)   2013*

SPA *C4* (1.5km SE Rural) *50.48559, 5.88385* **Camping Parc des Sources, Rue de la Sauvenière 141, 4900 Spa [(087) 772311; fax 475965; info@parcdessources.be; www.parcdessources.be]** Bet Spa & Francorchamps on N62, sp on R. Med, mkd pitch, pt sl, pt shd; htd wc; chem disp; mv service pnt; baby facs; shwrs €1; EHU (10A) €2.75; gas; Indry; shops 1.5km; snacks; bar; playgrnd; pool; dogs €2; 60% statics; phone; poss cr; quiet. "Excel facs, modern Indry, beautiful location, nr forest; friendly & helpful staff." ♦ ltd. 1 Apr-31 Oct. € 30.00   2013*

⊞ **STAVELOT** *C4* (3km N Rural) *50.41087, 5.95351* **Camping L'Eau Rouge, Cheneux 25, 4970 Stavelot [(080) 863075; fb220447@skynet.be; www.eaurouge.eu]** Exit A27/E42 junc 11 onto N68 twd Stavelot. Turn R at T-junc, then 1st R into sm rd over narr bdge. Med, mkd pitch, pt sl, pt shd; htd wc; chem disp; mv service pnt; baby facs; shwrs €0.50; EHU (6-10A) €3 rev polarity; Indry (inc dryer); shop 2km; snacks; bar; BBQ; playgrnd; games area; archery; wifi; TV; 50% statics; dogs €1; poss cr; Eng spkn; quiet. "Vg rvside site; friendly, helpful owners; twin-axles not acc; conv Francorchamps circuit." ♦ € 25.00   2013*

⊞ **STEKENE** *A2* (4km SW Rural) *51.18366, 4.00730* **Camping Vlasaard, Heirweg 143, 9190 Stekene [(03) 7798164; fax 7899170; info@camping-vlasaard.be; www.camping-vlasaard.be]** Fr N49 Antwerp-Knokke rd, exit sp Stekene. In Stekene, take dir Moerbeke, site on L in 4km. V lge, mkd pitch, unshd; htd wc; chem disp; serviced pitches; shwrs €1.25; EHU (16A); Indry; supmkt adj; rest, snacks; bar; playgrnd; pool; games area; 75% statics; poss cr; Eng spkn; poss noisy; ccard acc. ♦ € 16.00   2009*

⊞ **TELLIN** *C3* (5km NE Rural) *50.09665, 5.28579* **Camping Parc La Clusure, 30 Chemin de la Clusure, 6927 Bure-Tellin [(084) 360050; fax 366777; info@parclaclusure.be; www.parclaclusure.be]** Fr N on A4 use exit 23A onto N899, fr S exit junc 24. Foll sp for Tellin & then take N846 thro Bure dir Grupont vill. At rndabt at junc N803 & N846 take 2nd exit to site, sp. Lge, mkd pitch, pt shd; htd wc; chem disp; mv service pnt; baby facs; shwrs inc; EHU (16A) inc (check rev pol); Indry (inc dryer); shop; rest, snacks; bar; playgrnd; htd pool; paddling pool; rv fishing; tennis; bike hire; games area; games rm; wifi; entmnt; TV rm; 35% statics; dogs €5; phone; poss cr; Eng spkn; adv bkg; some rlwy noise; ccard acc; red LS/CKE/CCI. "V pleasant, lovely, popular rvside site; conv m'way; conv for limestone caves at Han-sur-Lesse & gd touring base Ardennes; friendly owners; clean facs; wild beavers in adj rv; excel site." ♦ € 55.00 SBS - H09   2013*

See advertisement inside the front cover

⊞ **TENNEVILLE** *C3* (4km SE Rural) *50.07644, 5.55529* **Camping Pont de Berguème, Berguème 9, 6970 Tenneville [(084) 455443; fax 456231; info@pontbergueme.be; www.pontbergueme.be]** Fr N4 Brussels-Luxembourg fr NW; twd end of Tenneville past g'ge turn R sp Berguème. Almost immed turn L & foll sp to Berguème. Fr SE turn R off N4 50m after x-ing Rv Ourthe & foll sp to Berguème & site in 1.5km. Well sp fr N4. Med, unshd; htd wc; chem disp; baby facs; shwrs; EHU (4A) inc (poss rev pol &/or earth prob); gas; Indry; shop; snacks; playgrnd; pool; fishing; canoeing (winter only); wifi; 40% statics; dogs €1.75; phone; Eng spkn; adv bkg; quiet; red CKE/CCI. "Excel site; clean, modern facs." € 16.00 2010*

TENNEVILLE *C3* (12km S Rural) *50.02637, 5.51292* **Camping Tonny, Tonny 35, 6680 Amberloup/Ste Ode [(061) 688285; camping.tonny@skynet.be; www.campingtonny.be]** Fr N4 take N826 S; in 4km turn R to Tonny. Site on L. Med, mkd pitch, shd; htd wc; chem disp; mv service pnt; baby facs; shwrs €0.50; EHU (4-6A) €2.50-3.50; gas; Indry (inc dryer); ice; rest, snacks; bar; BBQ; playgrnd; fishing; games area; games rm; entmnt; TV; 10% statics; dogs €2; bus adj; poss cr; Eng spkn; adv bkg; quiet; CKE/CCI. "Friendly, helpful owners; excel walking & cycling." 15 Feb-15 Nov. € 17.50   2010*

TILFF SUR OURTHE see Liège *B3*

⊞ **TOURINNES LA GOSSE** *B3* (500m SW Rural) *50.77952, 4.73657* **Camping au Val Tourinnes, Rue du Grand Brou 16A, 1320 Tourinnes-la-Grosse [(010) 866642; info@ campingauvaltourinnes.com; www.campingauvaltourinnes. com]** Fr N on E40/A3 m'way exit junc 23 onto N25 S dir Hamme-Mille. In Hamme-Mille turn L at traff lts, site on R in 2km. Or fr S on E411/A4 exit junc 8 onto N25 to Hamme-Mille & turn R at traff lts, then as above. Sm, hdg/mkd pitch, shd; htd wc; chem disp; mv service pnt; baby facs; shwrs €0.50; EHU (10A) €5; Indry (inc dryer); rest; bar; playgrnd; lake fishing; wifi; some statics; dogs €2.50; Eng spkn; quiet. "Pleasant touring pitches on lakeside (take care goose droppings!); friendly owners; vg, modern san facs; access tight for lge o'fits; airshow 1st w/end July." € 18.00   2010*

⊞ **TOURNAI** *B2* (2km SE Urban) *50.59967, 3.41349* **Camp Municipal de l'Orient, Jean-Baptiste Moens 8, 7500 Tournai [(069) 222635; fax 890229; campingorient@ tournai.be]** Exit E42 junc 32 R onto N7 twd Tournai. L at 1st traff lts, foll sp Aquapark, L at rndabt, site immed on L (no sp). Med, hdg pitch, some hdstg, pt shd; htd wc; chem disp; some serviced pitches; shwrs inc; EHU (10A) inc (poss rev pol/no earth) or metered; gas; Indry (inc dryer); shops 1km; rest, bar & playgrnd at leisure complex; htd indoor pool adj; leisure cent/ lake adj (50% disc to campers); poss cr; Eng spkn; adv bkg ess high ssn; some rd noise daytime & fr leisure cent adj; ccard not acc; CKE/CCI. "Well-kept site in interesting area & old town; facs stretched high ssn, but excel site; take care raised kerbs to pitches; max length of c'van 6.5m due narr site rds & high hdgs; helpful wardens; E side of site quietest; EHU had no earth on a nbr of pitches; handy for Lille and Dunkerque ferries." € 16.00   2015*

⊞ **TURNHOUT** *A3* (9.6km SW Rural) *51.28253, 4.83750* **Recreatie de Lilse Bergen, Strandweg 6, 2275 Lille-Gierle [(014) 557901; fax 554454; info@lilsebergen.be; www.lilsebergen.be]** Exit A21/E34 junc 22 N dir Beerse; at rndabt foll sp Lilse Bergen. Site in 1.5km. Lge, mkd pitch, shd; htd wc; chem disp; mv service pnt; baby facs; shwrs €0.20 per min; EHU (10A) inc; lndry (inc dryer); shop; rest, snacks; bar; BBQ; playgrnd; pool; lake sw; watersports; tennis; bike hire; games area; wifi; entmnt; 60% statics; dogs €5; phone; sep car park; poss cr; Eng spkn; adv bkg; poss noisy; ccard acc; red LS/ CKE/CCI. "Site sep pt of lge leisure complex; pitches amongst pine trees; modern san facs, poss stretched high ssn; excel for children/teenagers." € 26.50 (4 persons)   2011*

"There aren't many sites open at this time of year"

If you're travelling outside peak season remember to call ahead to check site opening dates – even if the entry says 'open all year'.

⊞ **VEURNE** *A1* (500m S Urban) *51.07056, 2.66535* **Aire Naturelle, Kaaiplaats, 8630 Veurne [stadsbestuur@ veurne.be; www.veurne.be]** M'van parking area sp on inner ring rd, nr canal quay. No facs & no fee; shops, rest, nrby; busy in day, quiet at night.   2009*

⊞ **VIELSALM** *C4* (17km SW Rural) *50.24013, 5.75396* **Camping aux Massotais, 20 Petites Tailles, Baraque de Fraiture, 6690 Vielsalm [(080) 418560; info@auxmassotais. com; www.auxmassotais.com]** Exit A26/E25 junc 50 onto N89 dir Vielsalm. At 1st rndabt turn R onto N30 dir Houffalize. Site on L in 1km behind hotel. Med, some hdstg, pt sl, pt shd; htd wc; chem disp; shwrs inc; EHU (6-16A) inc; lndry (inc dryer); rest, snacks; bar; playgrnd; htd pool; internet; TV; 5% statics; dogs; Eng spkn; quiet, but some rd noise; CKE/CCI. "Special pitches for NH (don't need to unhitch); fair." € 15.00   2013*

⊞ **VIRTON** *D3* (3km NE Rural) *49.57915, 5.54892* **Camping Colline de Rabais, 1 Rue Clos des Horlès, 6760 Virton [(063) 571195; fax 583342; info@collinederabais.be; www.collinederabais.be]** Take junc 29 fr A4/E411 onto N87, 2km fr Virton turn into wood at site sp. At end of rd bef lge building turn R, then 3rd turn R at phone box. Lge, pt sl, terr, pt shd; htd wc; chem disp; mv service pnt; baby facs; shwrs inc; EHU (16A) €3; lndry; shop; rest, snacks; bar; playgrnd; pool; lake sw; fishing 1km; tennis 1km; bike hire; cab TV; 20% statics; dogs €2.50; phone; Eng spkn; adv bkg; quiet; ccard acc; CKE/CCI. "Pleasant site; gd facs." ♦ € 24.00   2009*

⊞ **WAASMUNSTER** *A2* (2.4km N Rural) *51.12690, 4.08455* **Camping Gerstekot, Vinkenlaan 30, 9250 Waasmunster [(0323) 7723424; fax 7727382; maria-lyssens@telenet.be]** Exit A14/E17 at junc 13 Waasmunster onto N446 S; take 1st L in 100m into Patrijzenlaan & L again into Vinkenlaan, foll camp sp. Med, mkd pitch, pt shd; htd wc; chem disp; mv service pnt; baby facs; shwrs; EHU (16A) inc; lndry (inc dryer); shop; snacks; bar; BBQ; playgrnd; games area; games rm; wifi; TV; 95% statics; phone; poss cr; adv bkg; quiet; ccard acc; CKE/ CCI. "Busy at w/end; water use metered; key req for shwrs; gd." ♦ € 18.00   2011*

⊞ **WESTENDE** *A1* (1km SW Coastal) *51.15423, 2.76046* **KACB Camping Duinendorp, Bassevillestraat 81, 8434 Westende [(058) 237343; fax 233505; campingkacbwestende@pi.be; www.kacbcamping.be]** Site clearly sp off N318 in Westende vill. Fr cent turn R dir Lombardsijde (Beukenstraat). Turn almost opp TCB site. Lge, unshd; htd wc; chem disp; baby facs; shwrs inc; EHU (10A) inc; gas; lndry (inc dryer); rest, snacks; bar; playgrnd; sand beach 600m; games area; golf adj; TV; 60% statics; poss cr; adv bkg; quiet; ccard acc; red long stay/CKE/CCI. ♦ € 28.00   2010*

WESTENDE *A1* (350m SW Coastal) *51.15728, 2.76561* **Camping Westende, Westendelaan 341, 8434 Westende [(058) 233254; fax 230261; info@campingwestende.be; www.campingwestende.be]** Fr Middelkerke foll N318; just after Westende vill church take dir Nieuwpoort, site on L in 150m. Lge, mkd pitch, unshd; htd wc; chem disp; mv service pnt; shwrs inc; EHU (10A) inc; gas; lndry; shops adj; rest, snacks; playgrnd; htd pool; sand beach 1km; wifi; 90% statics; dogs €2; bus adj; tram 1km; phone; poss cr; Eng spkn; quiet; ccard not acc; CKE/CCI. "Sm but tidy touring area; friendly owners; beach nr; excel cycling; gd." ♦ ltd. 1 Apr-14 Nov. € 34.00   2011*

WESTENDE *A1* (800m SW Coastal) *51.15787, 2.76060* **Kompascamping Westende, Bassevillestraat 141, 8434 Westende [(058) 223025; fax 223028; westende@ kompascamping.be; www.kompascamping.be]** Exit A18/ E40 junc 4 onto N369/325 dir Middelkerke. Fr Westender Dorp cent (Hovenierstraat church) turn R in approx 750m into Beukenstraat, site in 200m, sp. Lge, hdg/mkd pitch, some hdstg, pt shd; htd wc; chem disp; baby facs; fam bthrm; shwrs inc; EHU (10A) €2; gas; lndry (inc dryer); shop; rest, snacks; bar; playgrnd; sand beach 500m; tennis; games area; covrd play area; wifi; TV rm; 60% statics; dogs; adv bkg; quiet; ccard acc. ♦ 1 Apr-14 Nov. € 33.50 (CChq acc)   2009*

⊞ **WESTOUTER** *B1* (2km S Urban) *50.78222, 2.74249* **Douve Camping, Bellestraat 58, 8954 Westouter [(057) 444546; info@douve.be; www.douve.be]** Fr Ypres take rd SW thro Dikkebus & cont to Mont Noir on Belgium/France border. Site on L behind Douve Rest & household shop, at end of main high street. Sm, hdg pitch, sl, pt shd; wc; own san rec in winter; shwrs €1; EHU inc (long lead poss req); rest, snacks; playgrnd; dogs; bus; Eng spkn; quiet. "Conv for Ypres (14km) & Mont Noir military cemetary; pitch on car pk in winter (no water avail at this time of year); access to pitches v steep & narr in parts; rough path & 36 steps to facs & chem disp point; forest walks; gd." € 12.00   2010*

WEZEMBEEK see Bruxelles *B2*

YPRES/IEPER *B1* (3km SE Urban) *50.8467, 2.8994* **Camping Jeugdstadion, Bolwerkstraat 1, 8900 Leper, Ypres [(057) 217282; fax 216121; info@jeugdstadion.be; www.jeugdstadion.be]** Fr S ent town cent on N336, after rlwy x-ing turn R at rndabt onto ring rd & L at 2nd rndabt (lge, gushing tap in cent). Site in 300m on L, sp fr ring rd. If app town cent fr N on N8 fr Veurne take ring rd N37; at gushing tap rndabt turn L, site in 300m on L, well sp. Fr N38 in Ypres turn off at gushing tap rndabt sp Industrie/Jeugdstadion, take 2nd L, site at end. NB site open all year for m'vans. Med, hdg/mkd pitch, some hdstg, pt sl, pt shd; htd wc; chem disp; mv service pnt; shwrs inc; EHU (10A) inc (poss rev pol); shop 500m; playgrnd; bike hire; sports park & pool adj; wifi; statics; dogs €1; poss v cr; Eng spkn; adv bkg rec; quiet but some noise until evening fr indus unit & fr sports complex adj; ccard acc. "Automatic registration/check out avail when office clsd; peaceful, well-refurbished site conv WW1 battle fields & museums; 10 min walk to Menin Gate for daily Last Post Ceremony; helpful staff; gd, modern san facs; soft grass pitches - ask for one with 'rubber tracks' to avoid sinking; hdstg m'van (OAY with own san facs only) pitches in sep area like an Aire; site poss v full local public hols; site not fully enclsd; excel, clean, tidy, well run site; rec." 1 Mar-12 Nov. € 15.00   2015*

"That's changed – Should I let The Club know?"

If you find something on site that's different from the site entry, fill in a report and let us know. See www.caravanclub.co.uk/europereport.

YPRES/IEPER *B1* (10km SW Rural) *50.78643, 2.82035* **Camping Ypra, Pingelaarstraat 2, 8956 Kemmel-Heuvelland [(057) 444631; fax 444881; camping.ypra@ skynet.be; www.camping-ypra.be]** On N38 Poperinge ring rd turn S at rndabt onto N304. Foll sp Kemmel. Site on R in 12km on N edge of Kemmel. Med, mkd pitch, some hdstg, pt sl, pt shd; htd wc; chem disp; shwrs inc; EHU (6A) inc (poss rev pol); lndry (inc dryer); sm shop & 1km; rest 1km; bar; playgrnd; 90% statics in sep area; dogs €1.90; Eng spkn; adv bkg; quiet; red CKE/CCI. "Clean, well-maintained site; gd, modern san facs, but ltd; helpful, friendly staff; access to some pitches poss diff; interesting rest in vill; conv for WW1 battlefields; pitches varied sizes; poss noise fr club hse & bar." 1 Mar-30 Nov. € 22.00   2015*

ZELE *A2* (6.5km SW Rural) *51.05273, 3.97996* **Camping Groenpark, Gentsesteenweg 337, 9240 Zele [tel/fax (09) 3679071; Groenpark@scarlet.be; www.campinggroenpark.be]** Fr W (Ghent) exit A14 junc 11 onto N449 S & in 2km turn L onto N445. Site in 6km at ent sp to Zele. Sm, mkd pitch, pt shd, htd wc; chem disp; mv service pnt; baby facs; shwrs inc; EHU (10A) inc; lndry (inc dryer); shop, rest, bar 1km; snacks; playgrnd; lake sw & sand beach 2km; TV rm; some statics; tram; Eng spkn; adv bkg; quiet; CKE/CCI. "Nr Park & Ride to Ghent; wooded area for tourers; gd; Pleasant site; nice walk around lake." 1 Mar-4 Nov. € 29.00   2013*

ZONHOVEN see Hasselt *B3*

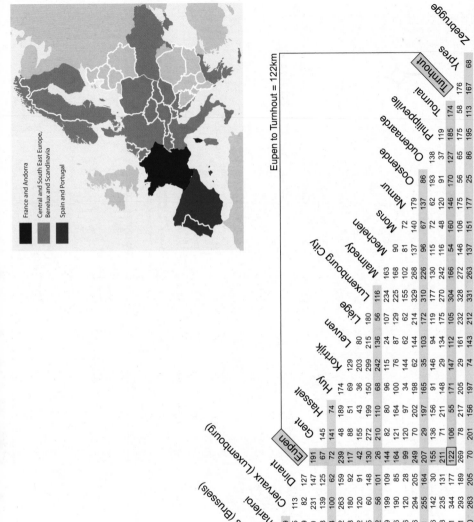

Map legend:
- France and Andorra
- Central and South East Europe, Benelux and Scandinavia
- Spain and Portugal

Eupen to Turnhout = 122km

Eupen · Turnhout

A distance chart (in km) between Belgian cities, with cities arranged along the diagonal:

Aalst, Aalter, Antwerpen, Arlon, Ath, Bastogne, Brugge, Bruxelles (Brussels), Charleroi, Clervaux (Luxembourg), Dinant, Eupen, Gent, Hasselt, Huy, Kortrijk, Leuven, Liège, Luxembourg City, Malmedy, Mechelen, Mons, Namur, Oostende, Oudenaarde, Philippeville, Tournai, Turnhout, Ypres, Zeebrugge.

Worked example: Eupen to Turnhout = 122

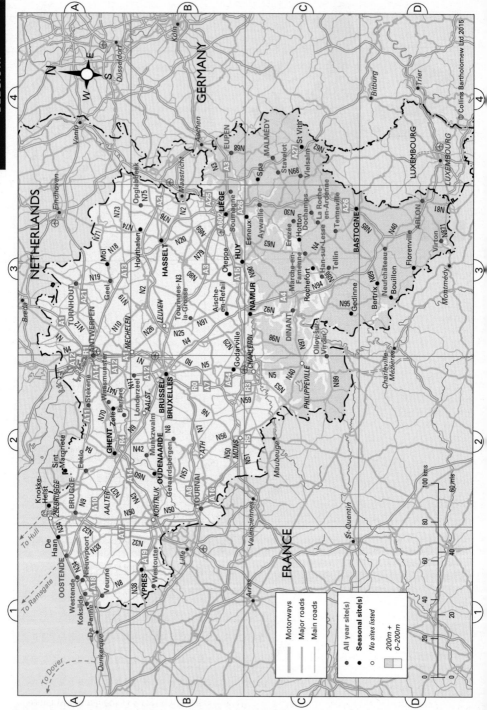

Croatia
Country Introduction

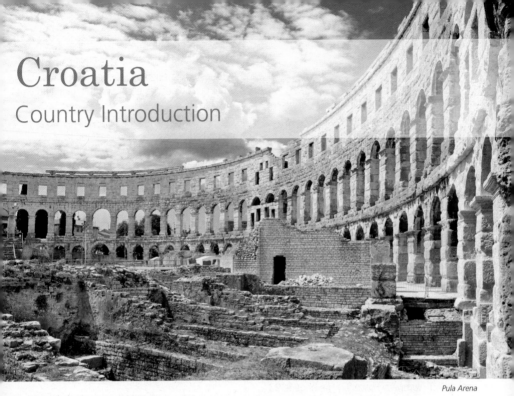

Pula Arena

Welcome to Croatia

Croatia's Adriatic coast is a land of sun, beauty and history. Soaked in culture going back thousands of years, there are so many different sights to see, from the 16th century walls of Dubrovnik to the Roman amphitheatre in Pula. With countless galleries, museums and churches to discover, as well as an exquisite natural landscape to explore, there truly is something for everyone.

Country highlights

Licitars are brightly decorated biscuits made of sweet honey dough. Often given as a gift at celebrations such as Christmas or weddings, they are an integral part of Croatian identity dating from the 16th century.

Croatia is well known for its carnivals, festivals and celebrations, which take place throughout the year. Some of the most important are the Spring Procession of Queens from Gorjani, the Bell Ringer's Pageant from the Kastav Area and the Festivity of St. Blaise, Dubrovnik's patron saint.

Major towns and cities

- Zagrab – the capital of Croatia has a rich history that dates from Roman times.
- Rijeka – Croatia's principal port city overlooking the Adriatic.
- Split – the centre of the city is built around an ancient Roman palace.
- Osijek – a gastronomic centre, and the best place to try a traditional dish.

Attractions

- Dubrovnik – a wonderfully-preserved medieval walled city with plenty to see.
- Plitvice Lakes - a stunning series of lakes and waterfalls set in an enchanting woodland.
- Pula Arena – this ancient Roman amphitheatre is one of the best preserved in the world.
- Diocletian's Palace – an ancient monument that makes up the heart of Split.

Find out more

www.croatia.hr
Tel: 0038 5 14 69 93 33 Croatian Tourist Office

Country Information

Population (approx): 4.4 million

Capital: Zagreb (population approx 690,000)

Area: 56,540 sq km, divided into 20 counties

Bordered by: Bosnia-Herzegovina, Hungary, Serbia, Montenegro and Slovenia

Terrain: Flat plains along border with Hungary; low mountains and highlands near Adriatic coast and islands

Climate: Mediterranean climate along the coast with hot, dry summers and mild, wet winters; continental climate inland with hot summers and cold winters

Coastline: 5,835km (inc 4,058km islands)

Highest Point: Dinara 1,830m

Language: Croatian

Local Time: GMT or BST + 1, i.e. 1 hour ahead of the UK all year

Currency: Kuna (HRK) divided into 100 lipa; £1 = HRK 10.72, HRK 10 = £0.93 (September 2015)

Emergency Numbers: Police 92; Fire brigade 93; Ambulance 94. Or dial 112 and specify the service you need.

Public Holidays in 2016: Jan 1, 6; Mar 27, 28; May 1, 26; Jun 22, 25 (National Day); Aug 5 (Thanksgiving Day), 15; October 8 (Independence Day); Nov 1; Dec 25, 26.

Some Christian Orthodox and Muslim festivals are also celebrated locally. School summer holidays take place from the last week in June to the end of August.

Camping and Caravanning

There are more than 150 campsites in Croatia including several well-established naturist sites, mainly along the coast. Sites are licensed according to how many people they can accommodate, rather than by the number of vehicles or tents, and are classed according to a grading system of 1 to 4 stars. There are some very large sites catering for up to 10,000 people at any one time but there are also many small sites, mainly in Dalmatia, situated in gardens, orchards and farms.

Many sites open from April to October; few open all year. They are generally well-equipped.

A tourist tax is levied of between HRK 4 and HRK 7 per person per day according to region and time of year.

Casual/wild camping is illegal and is particularly monitored at beaches, harbours and rural car parks. Most campsites have overnight areas for late arrivals and there are a number of rest areas established along main roads for overnight stays or brief stopovers.

Electricity and Gas

Current on campsites ranges from 10 to 16 amps. Plugs have 2 round pins. There may not be CEE connections and a long cable might be required.

Campingaz cylinders are not available, so take a good supply of gas with you.

Entry Formalities

British and Irish passport holders may visit Croatia for up to three months without a visa.

Unless staying at official tourist accommodation (hotel or campsite) all visitors are obliged to register at the nearest police station or town tourist agency within 24 hours of arrival in the country. Campsites and other tourist accommodation should carry out this function for their guests but make sure you check this with them. If you fail to register you may receive a fine or you may even have to leave Croatia.

British citizens intending to stay for an extended period should seek advice from the Croatian Embassy.

Medical Services

For minor ailments, first of all consult staff in a pharmacy (ljekarna).

Emergency hospital and medical treatment is available at a reduced cost on production of a valid EHIC. You will be expected to pay a proportion of the cost (normally 20%). Only basic health care facilities are available in outlying areas and islands

Opening Hours

Banks – Mon-Fri 7am-7pm; Sat 7am-1pm.

Museums – Tue-Sun 10am-5pm; most close Mon and some close Sun afternoons.

Post Offices – Mon-Fri 7am-7pm (2pm in small villages). In major towns or tourist places, post offices on duty are open until 9pm.

Shops – Mon-Fri 8am-8pm; Sat & Sun 8am-2pm.

Safety and Security

The level of street crime is low, but you should be aware of pickpockets in major cities, coastal areas (pavement cafés are particularly targeted), and on trains, and take sensible precautions when carrying money, credit cards and passports.

Incidents have been reported of gangs robbing car occupants after either indicating that they are in trouble and require assistance, or pulling alongside a car and indicating that something is wrong with the vehicle. Be extremely cautious should something similar occur.

If you are planning to travel outside the normal tourist resorts you should be aware that there are areas affected by the war, which ended in 1995, where unexploded mines remain. These include Eastern Slavonia, Brodsko-Posavska County, Karlovac County, areas around Zadar County and in more remote areas of the Plitvice Lakes National Park. See the Croatian Mine Action Centre's website at www.hcr.hr/en/protuminUvod.asp for more specific information about mine-affected areas.

Croatia shares with the rest of Europe an underlying threat from terrorism. Attacks could be indiscriminate and against civilian targets, including places frequented by tourists.

British Embassy

UL IVANA LUČIĆA 4
HR-10000 ZAGREB
Tel: (01) 6009100
www.british.embassyzagreb@fco.gov.uk

Irish Honorary Consulate

MIRAMARSKA 23 (EUROCENTER)
10000 ZAGREB
Tel: (01) 6310025
irish.consulate.zg@inet.hr

TRUMBICEVA OBALA 3
21000 SPLIT
Tel: (021) 343715
9csain@cpad.hr

Customs Regulations

Customs Posts

Main border crossings are open 24 hours a day.

Foodstuffs

Up to 10kg of meat and meat products and 10kg of dairy products may be imported into Croatia from EU countries. If you are entering from outside the EU, you can bring 2kg of meat products as long as they are in sealed packages.

Documents

Driving Licence

All types of full, valid British driving licence are recognised but if you have an old-style green licence then it is advisable to change it for a photocard licence in order to avoid any local difficulties.

Passport

You must be able to show some form of identification if required by the authorities and, therefore, should carry your passport or photocard driving licence at all times.

Vehicle(s)

Carry your vehicle registration certificate (V5C), insurance details and MOT certificate (if applicable).

Green Card

While an International Motor Insurance Certificate (Green Card) is not necessary, you should ensure that your vehicle insurance includes cover for Croatia.

If you are driving to or through Bosnia and Herzegovina (for example, along the 20 km strip of coastline at Neum on the Dalmatian coastal highway to Dubrovnik) you should ensure that you have obtained Green Card cover for Bosnia and Herzegovina. For Club members insured under The Caravan Club's Motor Insurance schemes full policy cover is available for this 20km strip, however you must ask at the time of taking out or renewing your insurance policy for one that specifically covers Bosnia. If you have difficulties obtaining this cover before departure Club members can contact the Club's Travel Service Information Officer for advice, email travelserviceinfo@caravanclub.co.uk. Alternatively, temporary third-party insurance can be purchased at the country's main border posts, or in Split and other large cities. It is not generally obtainable at the Neum border crossing itself.

As an alternative, you can take the ferry from Ploče to Trpanj on the Pelješac peninsula and avoid the stretch of road in Bosnia and Herzegovina altogether. There are frequent ferries during summer months, but be aware that motorhome drivers are sometimes requested to reverse onto them.

Money

Visitors may exchange money in bureaux de change, banks, post offices, hotels and some travel agencies but you are likely to get the best rates in banks. Exchange slips should be kept in order to convert unspent kuna on leaving the country. Many prices are quoted in both kuna and euros, and euros are widely accepted.

Most shops and restaurants accept credit cards. There are cash machines in all but the smallest resorts.

The police are warning visitors about a recent increase in the number of forged Croatian banknotes in circulation, especially 200 and 500 kuna notes. Take care when purchasing kuna and use only reliable outlets, such as banks and cash points.

Motoring in Croatia
Accidents

Any visible damage to a vehicle entering Croatia must be certified by the authorities at the border and a Certificate of Damage issued, which must be produced when leaving the country. In the event of a minor accident while in Croatia resulting in material damage only, the police must

be called and they will assist, if necessary, with the exchange of information between drivers and will issue a Certificate of Damage to the foreign driver. You should not try to leave the country with a damaged vehicle without this Certificate as you may be accused of a 'hit and run' offence.

Confiscation of passport and a court appearance within 24 hours are standard procedures for motoring accidents where a person is injured.

The Croatian Insurance Bureau in Zagreb can assist with Customs and other formalities following road accidents, tel: (01) 4696600, email: huo@huo.hr or see www.huo.hr.

Alcohol

The general legal limit of alcohol is 50 milligrams in 100 millilitres of blood, i.e. less than the level in the UK (80 milligrams). For drivers of vehicles over 3,500 kg and for drivers under 24 years of age the alcohol limit is zero. The general legal limit also applies to cyclists.

It is prohibited to drive after having taken any medicine whose side-effects may affect the ability to drive a motor vehicle.

Breakdown Service

The Hrvatski Auto-Klub (HAK) operates a breakdown service throughout the country, telephone 987 (or 01987 from a mobile phone) for assistance. On motorways use the roadside emergency phones which are placed at 2km intervals. Towing and breakdown services are available 24 hours a day in and around most major cities and along the coast in summer (6am to midnight in Zagreb).

Essential Equipment

First aid kit
All vehicles, including those registered abroad, must carry a first aid kit.

Lights
Dipped headlights are compulsory at all times, regardless of weather conditions, from the end of October to the end of March and in reduced visibility at other times of the year. It is compulsory to carry spare bulbs, however this rule does not apply if your vehicle is fitted with xenon, neon, LED or similar lights.

Reflective Jacket/Waistcoat
It is obligatory to carry a reflective jacket inside your car (not in the boot) and you must wear it if you need to leave your vehicle to attend to a breakdown, e.g. changing a tyre. It is also common sense for any passenger leaving the vehicle to also wear one.

Warning Triangle(s)
All motor vehicles must carry a warning triangle. If you are towing a caravan or trailer you must have two warning triangles.

Child Restraint Systems
Children under the age of 12 are not allowed to travel in the front seats of vehicles, with the exception of children under 2 years of age who can travel in the front if they are placed in a child restraint system adapted to their size. It must be rear-facing and the airbag must be de-activated.

Children up to 5 years old must be placed in a seat adapted to their size on the back seat. Children between the ages of 5 and 12 must travel on the back seat using a 3 point seat belt with a booster seat if necessary for their height.

Winter Driving
It is compulsory to carry snow chains in your vehicle and they must be used if required by the weather conditions (5cm of snow or black ice). The compulsory winter equipment in Croatia consists of a shovel in your vehicle and a set of snow chains on the driving axel.

Fuel

Petrol stations are generally open from 7am to 7 or 8pm, later in summer. Some of those on major stretches of road stay open 24 hours a day. Payment by credit card is widely accepted. LPG (Autogas) is fairly widely available.

Parking

Lines at the roadside indicate parking restrictions. Traffic wardens patrol roads and impose fines for illegal parking. Vehicles, including those registered outside Croatia, may be immobilised by wheel clamps.

Roads

In general road conditions are good in and around the larger towns. The Adriatic Highway or Jadranksa Magistrala (part of European route E65) runs the whole length of the Adriatic coast and is in good condition, despite being mostly single-carriageway. Minor road surfaces may be uneven and, because of the heat-resisting material used to surface them, may be very slippery when wet. Minor roads are usually unlit at night.

Motorists should take care when overtaking and be aware that other drivers may overtake unexpectedly in slow-moving traffic. The standard of driving is generally fair.

Road Signs and Markings

Road signs and markings conform to international standards. Motorway signs have a green background; national road signs have a blue background.

Speed Limits

	Open Road (km/h)	Motorway (km/h)
Car Solo	90-110	130
Car towing caravan/trailer	80	90
Motorhome under 3500kg	90-110	130
Motorhome 3500-7500kg	80	90

In addition to complying with other speed limits, drivers under the age of 25 must not exceed 80 km/h (50 mph) on the open road, 100 km/h (62 mph) on expressways and 120 km/h (74 mph) on motorways.

Traffic Jams

During the summer, tailbacks may occur at the border posts with Slovenia at Buje on the E751 (road 21), at Bregana on the E70 (A3) and at Donji Macelj on the E59 (A1). During July and August there may be heavy congestion, for example at Rupa/Klenovica and at other tourist centres, and on the E65 north-south Adriatic Highway. This is particularly true on Friday evenings, Saturday mornings, Sunday evenings and holidays. Queues form at ferry crossings to the main islands.

Road and traffic conditions can be viewed on the HAK website (in English), www.hak.hr or tel: (01) 4640800 (English spoken) or (072) 777777 while in Croatia for round-the-clock recorded information.

Violation of Traffic Regulations

The police may impose on-the-spot fines for parking and driving offences. If you are unable to pay the police may confiscate your passport. Motoring law enforcement, especially for speeding offences, is strictly observed.

Motorways

There is just over 1250km of motorways, with the major stretches being shown in the table below. Tolls (cestarina) are levied according to vehicle category. Electronic display panels above motorways indicate speed limits, road conditions and lane closures. Information on motorways can be found on www.hac.hr.

Motorway Tolls

Class 1 Vehicle with 2 axles, height up to 1.3m (measured from front axle) excluding vans

Class 2 Vehicle with 2 or more axles, height up to 1.3m (measured from front axle), including car + caravan or trailer, motorhomes and vans.

Class 3 Vehicle with 2 or 3 axles, height over 1.3m (measured from front axle), including van with trailer

Class 4 Vehicle with 4 or more axles, height over 1.3m (measured from front axle)

Tolls can be paid in cash or by credit card. Details of toll prices can be found in English at www.hac.hr.

Touring

There are a number of national parks and nature reserves throughout the country, including the World Heritage site at the Plitvice lakes, the Paklenica mountain massif, and the Kornati archipelago with 140 uninhabited islands, islets and reefs. Dubrovnik, itself a World Heritage site,

is one of the world's best-preserved medieval cities, having been extensively restored since recent hostilities.

While Croatia has a long coastline, there are few sandy beaches; instead there are pebbles, shingle and rocks with man-made bathing platforms.

The Croatian National Tourist Board operates 'Croatian Angels', a multi-lingual tourist information and advice service available from the end of March to mid-October, tel: 062 999 999 or 00385 62 999 999 from outside Croatia.

Croatia originated the concept of commercial naturist resorts in Europe and today attracts an estimated 1 million naturist tourists annually. There are approximately 20 official naturist resorts and beaches and numerous other unofficial or naturist-optional 'free' beaches. Smoking is prohibited in restaurants, bars and public places. A service charge is general included in the bill. English is widely spoken.

Public Transport

Many important rail routes are still not electrified and allow only single-track travel, making rail travel slow. By contrast the bus network offers the cheapest and most extensive means of public transport. Buy bus tickets when you board at the front of the vehicle or beforehand from kiosks, and ensure that you validate your ticket once on board. Trams operate in Zagreb and you can buy tickets from kiosks.

Coastal towns and cities have regular scheduled passenger and car ferry services. Most ferries are drive-on/drive-off – see www.jadrolinija.hr for schedules and maps.

Car ferries operate from Ancona, Bari, Pescara and Venice in Italy to Dubrovnik, Korèula, Mali Lošinj, Poreè, Pula, Rijecka, Rovinj, Sibenik, Split, Starigrad, Vis and Zadar. Full details from:

VIAMARE LTD
SUITE 108, 582 HONEYPOT LANE
STANMORE
MIDDX HA7 1JS
Tel: 020 8206 3420
Email: ferries@viamare.com
www.viamare.com

BANJOLE see Pula *A3*

BIOGRAD NA MORU *B3* (3km N Coastal) *43.96083, 15.42472*
Camping Đardin, 23207 Sveti Filip i Jakov [(023) 388960;
info@camping-croatia.com; www.camping-croatia.com]
S fr Zadar (approx 23km) on E65/rd 8 turn R immed bef lge
blue hotels/site sp twd sea. Site on L just bef lane narr. Lge, pt
sl, shd; wc; chem disp; shwrs inc; EHU (10A); gas 500m; lndry
rm; shop adj; rest, snacks, bar adj; playgrnd; sand beach adj;
watersports; boating; 80% statics; bus; poss cr; Eng spkn; adv
bkg; quiet; red CKE/CCI. "In superb position on edge of resort
vill; friendly, helpful staff; gd, clean facs." 15 Apr-15 Oct.
HRK 138   2010*

⊞ **BIOGRAD NA MORU** *B3* (3km N Coastal) *43.96015,
15.42849* Camping Filip, Put Primorja 10a, 23207 Sveti Filip
i Jakov [tel/fax (023) 389196; auto.kamp.filip@zd.t-com.hr;
www.camping-filip-kroatien.de] S fr Zadar (approx 23km)
turn R immed bef lge blue hotels/site sp twd sea. Site on L
just past Autocamp Đardin. Sm, hdg pitch, hdstg, pt sl, shd;
wc; chem disp; shwrs inc; EHU HRK23; lndry (inc dryer); shop
500m; rest, snacks, bar adj; BBQ; cooking facs; playgrnd; beach
adj; games area; dogs HRK16; phone; bus nr; Eng spkn; quiet;
red long stay. "San facs luxurious & clean; friendly owners;
private gate to beach; sh walk to town; excel." 1 May-30 Sep.
HRK 148   2010*

BIOGRAD NA MORU *B3* (500m N Coastal) *43.96064,
15.42963* Camping Moče, Put Primorja 8, 23207 Sveti
Filip i Jakov [tel/fax (023) 388436; info@camping-moce.
com; www.camping-moce.com] Sp fr rd 8/E65. Sm, pt shd;
wc; chem disp; serviced pitches; shwrs inc; EHU (16A) HRK20;
lndry; shop 100m; rest, bar 200m; playgrnd; shgl beach adj;
cab/sat TV; dogs; phone adj; poss cr; Eng spkn; adv bkg; red
long stay; CKE/CCI. "CL-type site in garden; excel clean facs;
friendly welcome fr owners; beach thro back gate - locked at
night." ♦ ltd. 1 Apr-15 Oct. HRK 135   2009*

BIOGRAD NA MORU *B3* (10km NE Coastal) Autocamp
Martin, Sveti Petar na Moru, 23207 Sveti Filip i Jakov
[tel/fax (023) 391104] Fr Zadar on rd 8/E65, lge yellow sp to
site. Sm, pt shd; htd wc; chem disp; mv service pnt; shwrs inc;
EHU (16A) inc; supmkt 9km; rest 100m; BBQ; beach adj; dogs
HRK10; poss cr; Eng spkn; adv bkg; quiet; CKE/CCI. "Family-
run site in unique position - some pitches on purpose-built
promontory into sea; friendly welcome; excel, unisex facs;
highly rec." HRK 130   2010*

⊞ **BIOGRAD NA MORU** *B3* (612km NW Coastal) *44.00532,
15.36748* Autokamp Filko, Aleksandar Colic 23207 Sveti
Petar Na Moru [tel/fax 02 33 91 177; info@autokamp-
filko.hr; www.autokamp-filko.hr] On D8 bet Zadar &
Biograd Na Moru at Sv Petar NM. 1st camp on the R by sea.
Sm, pt shd; wc; chem disp; mv service pnt; shwrs; lndry;
rest; bar; shingle beach; wifi; 30% statics; dogs; poss cr;
Eng spkn; some rd noise. "Some pitches by water on hdstg
with views across to islands; dir access fr rd; ideal LS; gd."
HRK 170   2014*

BRAC ISLAND *C4* Sites on Brač Island are listed together
at the end of the Croatia site entry pages.

CRES ISLAND *A3* Sites on Cres Island are listed together at
the end of the Croatia site entry pages.

DRASNICE see Drvenik *C4*

DRVENIK *C4* (12km NW Coastal) *43.17086, 17.1965* Camping
Dole, 21331 Živogošće [(021) 628749; fax 628750; auto-
camp-dole@st.hinet.hr; www.hotelizivogosce.com]
Ent at km post 679 on Adriatic Highway, rd 8/E65, sp. V lge,
some hdstg, pt sl, terr, pt shd; wc; chem disp; shwrs; EHU
(10A) HRK32; lndry rm; shop; rest, snacks; bar; BBQ; shgl
beach adj; tennis; wifi; dogs HRK19; Eng spkn; some rd noise;
ccard acc; red CKE/CCI. "Beach slopes steeply; used by school
groups; vg." ♦ 1 May-30 Sep. HRK 247   2011*

DUBROVNIK *C4* (6km S Rural/Coastal) *42.6240, 18.18856*
Autocamp Kupari, Kupari b.b, 20207 Mlini [(020) 485548;
fax 487344; info@campkupari.com; www.campkupari.
com] Fr Dubrovnik along coast rd sp airport & Mlini. Well sp
on inland side of rd on ent vill. V lge, hdg/mkd pitch, shd; wc
(cont); chem disp; shwrs inc; EHU (10A) inc; lndry; shop 200m;
rest, snacks, bar, BBQ; shgl beach 400m; internet; entmnt;
some statics; dogs HRK23; Eng spkn; adv bkg; some rd noise;
ccard acc; CKE/CCI. "San facs need update (2009)."
1 Apr-31 Oct. HRK 136   2009*

> ## "I like to fill in the reports as I travel from site to site"
> You'll find report forms at the back of
> this guide, or you can fill them in online
> at www.caravanclub.co.uk/europereport.

DUBROVNIK *C4* (7km S Coastal) *42.62471, 18.20801*
Autocamp Kate, Tupina 1, 20207 Mlini [(020) 487006;
fax 487553; info@campingkate.com; www.campingkate.
com] Fr Dubrovnik on rd 8 foll sp Cavtat or Čilipi or airport into
vill of Mlini. Fr S past Cavtat into Mlini. Site well sp fr main rd.
Sm, hdstg, pt sl, terr, pt shd; wc; chem disp; shwrs inc; EHU
(10-16A) inc; lndry; shop adj; rest, bar adj; BBQ; shgl beach
200m; phone; wifi; bus to Dubrovnik 150m; dogs HRK4;
Eng spkn; adv bkg; some rd noise; red long stay/LS; CKE/
CCI. "Family-run site in lovely setting; helpful, hard-working,
welcoming owners; vg clean facs; boats fr vill to Dubrovnik;
long, steep climb (steps) down to beach." 1 Apr-1 Nov.
HRK 143   2012*

⊞ **DUBROVNIK** *C4* (10km S Coastal) Autocamp
Matkovica, Srebreno 8, 20207 Dubrovnik [(020) 485867;
u.o.matkovica@hotmail.com] Fr Dubrovnik S on coast rd.
At Kupari foll sp to site behind Camping Porto. Sm, mkd pitch,
shd; wc; chem disp; shwrs inc; EHU (6A) inc; lndry; supmkt,
rest, snacks, bar 200m; shgl beach adj; wifi; dogs; Eng spkn;
phone; bus 200m; Eng spkn; no ccard, cash only; poss traff
noise; red LS. "Well-kept site; friendly, helpful owners; san facs
old but clean; water bus to Dubrovnik 1km." HRK 135   2014*

CROATIA

DUBROVNIK *C4* (5km NW Urban/Coastal) *42.66191, 18.07050* **Autocamp Solitudo, Vatroslava Lisinskog 17, 20000 Dubrovnik [(052) 465010; fax 460199; camping-dubrovnik@valamar.com; www.camping-adriatic.com/solitudo-camp-dubrovnik]** S down Adriatic Highway to Tuđjman Bdge over Dubrovnik Harbour. Turn L immed sp Dubrovnik & in 700m take sharp U-turn sp Dubrovnik & carry on under bdge. Site on Babin Kuk across harbour fr bdge. Lge, mkd pitch, hdstg, pt sl, pt terr, pt shd; htd wc; chem disp; mv service pnt; baby facs; shwrs inc; EHU (10A) inc (long lead poss req); lndry (inc dryer); shop; rest, snacks, bar; BBQ; pool, paddling pool 200m; shgl beach 500m; fishing; tennis; bike hire; wifi; dogs HRK46; twin-axles acc (rec check in adv); phone; bus 150m; poss cr; Eng spkn; adv bkg; quiet; ccard acc; red LS/CKE/CCI.; "Friendly, clean, well-run, v busy site; sm pitches poss stony &/or boggy; some lge pitches; levelling blocks poss req; san facs poss stretched high ssn & dated; nearest site to city cent; conv Bari ferry; Sat Nav/map advised as few sp; site in two parts, upper numbered but not mrkd and informal, lower numbered and mkd." ♦ 1 Apr-30 Oct. HRK 366 (CChq acc) SBS - X01   2013*

See advertisement on page 151

DUGA RESA see Karlovac *B2*

"We must tell The Club about that great site we found"

Get your site reports in by mid-August and we'll do our best to get your updates into the next edition.

FAZANA *A3* (500m S Coastal) *44.91717, 13.81105* **Camping Bi-Village, Dragonja 115, 52212 Fažana [(052) 300300; fax 380711; info@bivillage.com; www.bivillage.com]** N fr Pula on rd 21/A9/E751 at Vodnjan turn W sp Fažana. Foll sp for site. V lge, mkd pitch, pt shd; htd wc; chem disp; mv service pnt; shwrs inc; EHU (10A) inc; gas; lndry (inc dryer); supmkt; rest, snacks, bar; BBQ; playgrnd; 3 pools; waterslide; shgl/rocky beach adj; watersports; tennis 1km; games area; bike & boat hire; golf 2km; wifi; entmnt; 30% statics/apartments; dogs HRK37; phone; bus; poss cr; Eng spkn; adv bkg; quiet; ccard acc; red LS/snr citizens; CKE/CCI. "Excel, modern, clean san facs; private bthrms avail; site surrounded by pine trees; some beachside pitches; conv Brijuni Island National Park; excel leisure facs for families; vg cycle paths; no emptying point for Wastermaster; vg." ♦ 1 Apr-13 Nov. HRK 263 (5 persons) (CChq acc)   2010*

FUNTANA see Poreč *A2*

HVAR ISLAND *B4* Sites on Hvar Island are listed together at the end of the Croatia site entry pages.

ICICI see Opatija *A2*

KARLOVAC *B2* (12km SW Rural) *45.41962, 15.48338* **Autocamp Slapić, Mrežničke Brig, 47250 Duga Resa [tel/fax (098) 860601; autocamp@inet.hr; www.campslapic.hr]** Exit A1/E65 junc 3 for Karlovac; strt over traff lts immed after toll booth sp Split & Rijecka.Take D23 to Duga Resa; turn L by church in Duga Resa; cont over bdge & turn R; foll rd keeping rv on your R; cont thro vill of Mrnžnički Brig in 3km; site sp in another 1km. NB new bdge at Belavici. Site well sp fr Duga Resa. Sm, mkd pitch, pt shd; wc; chem disp; shwrs inc; EHU (16A) HRK20; lndry (inc dryer); shop 500m; rest, snacks, bar adj; BBQ; playgrnd; rv sw & beach adj; fishing; canoeing; tennis; games area; bike hire; wifi; dogs HRK15; phone; train to Zagreb 500m; Eng spkn; adv bkg; poss noise fr daytrippers; ccard acc. "Friendly, pleasant, family-owned site in gd location on rv; lovely area; gd bar/rest; gd clean facs; lge pitches; long hoses req LS; easy drive into Zagreb; excel; new, superb sans block (2014); rds to site narr." ♦ 1 Apr-31 Oct. HRK 220   2014*

KASTEL STARI *B4* (Coastal) *43.55305, 16.34666* **Camping Hrabar, Obala Kralja Tomislava 43, 21216 Kaštel-Stari [(091) 8998526; ihrabar77@yahoo.com]** Fr coast rd 8 turn twds coast at Kaštel-Stari, site sp. Site approx 18km fr Split. Med, mkd pitch, pt shd; wc; chem disp; shwrs inc; EHU; lndry; rest, snacks; bar; BBQ; shgl beach adj; dogs; bus 500m; poss cr; Eng spkn; adv bkg. "Helpful staff; gd cent location for Split & Trogir; Kaštela area worth exploring." 1 May-30 Sep.   2010*

KORENICA *B3* (1.5km NW Urban) *44.76527, 15.68833* **Camping Borje, Vranovaca bb, 53230 Korenica [(053) 751790; fax 751791; info@np-plitvicka-jezera.hr; www.np-plitvicka-jezera.hr]** Exit A1/A6 at Karlovac & take rd 1/E71 S dir Split. Site on R approx 15km after Plitvička Jezera National Park, well sp. Med, mkd pitch, sl, pt shd; htd wc; chem disp; mv service pnt; baby facs; fam bthrm; shwrs inc; EHU (10A) inc; gas (1km); lndry (inc dryer); supmkt 2km; rest, snacks; bar; BBQ; playgrnd; lake sw nr; TV in adj rest; wifi; dogs HRK20; twin axles; poss cr; Eng spkn; adv bkg; ccard acc; quiet; excel; CKE/CCI. "Vg, clean, well-kept, spacious, sloping site - levelling poss tricky; gd, modern, immac facs; helpful staff; well run by Plitvicka National Park; excel for visiting the Lakes & waterfalls; free bus runs to park at 1030 and returns at 1730; mountain views." ♦ 1 Apr-15 Oct. HRK 255   2014*

KRK ISLAND *A3* Sites on Krk Island are listed together at the end of the Croatia site entry pages.

KRUSCICA *B3* (5km SE Coastal) **Autocamp Punta Šibuljina, 23245 Trbanj-Šibuljina [tel/fax (023) 658004; info@camp sibuljina.com; www.campsibuljina.com]** On seaward side of E65 in vill. Med, pt sl, shd; wc; chem disp; mv service pnt; shwrs inc; EHU (10A) HRK16; lndry; shop 2km; rest 200m; snacks; bar; BBQ; playgrnd; shg beach adj; games area; entmnt; 60% statics; dogs HRK12; phone; bus adj; poss cr; Eng spkn; adv bkg; CKE/CCI. "V friendly welcome; view of Pag & bay; poss untidy site; tired san facs; quiet LS; gd." 15 Apr-15 Oct. HRK 106   2010*

KUCISTE see Orebič *C4*

LANTERNA see Poreč *A2*

LOSINJ ISLAND A4 Sites on Lošinj Island are listed together at the end of the Croatia site entry pages.

LOVISTE C4 (500m N Coastal) 43.02500, 17.03500 **Autokamp Đenka, 20269 Lovište [(020) 718069; fax 321160; autocamp.denka@hi.t-com.hr; www.denka.info]** Fr Orebič W to Lovište. In vill turn R at T-junc, site along sm rd which runs round bay. Sm, hdstg, terr, pt shd; wc; chem disp; shwrs inc; EHU (16A); shop, rest, snacks, bar 500m; BBQ; shgl beach adj; dogs; adv bkg; quiet. "Beautiful bay for sw & watersports; gd walks & historical sites; warm welcome; well-maintained site." 1 May-30 Oct. HRK 191   2009*

LOVRECICA see Umag A2

LOZOVAC see Sibenik B3

MEDULIN A3 (1km S Coastal) 44.80694, 13.95194 **Camp Kažela (Part Naturist), Kapovica 250, 52203 Medulin [(052) 576050; fax 577460; info@campkazela.com]** Fr Pula foll sp to Medulin. In Medulin site on R in 1.5km, sp. V lge, mkd pitch, pt sl, pt shd; wc (some cont) chem disp; mv service pnt; baby facs; shwrs inc; EHU (10A) inc; gas; lndry; shop; rest, snacks; bar; playgrnd; paddling pool; rocky beach; tennis; bike hire; internet; entmnt; TV; 10% statics; dogs HRK31; phone; adv bkg; v quiet; ccard acc; red snr citizens/CKE/CCI. "Well-maintained site with views; sep naturist site & beach." ♦ 3 Apr-9 Oct. HRK 208 (CChq acc)   2009*

MEDVEJA A2 (2.5km N Coastal) 45.27080, 14.26897 **Autocamp Medveja, Medveja bb, 51416 Lovran [(051) 291191; fax 292471; medveja@liburnia.hr; www.liburnia.hr or www.camping.hr]** Site Pula-Rijeka rd 21/E751, 2km S of Lovran, well sp. Lge, hdg/mkd pitch, pt shd; wc; chem disp; mv service pnt; baby facs; shwrs; EHU (10-16A) inc; gas; lndry (inc dryer); shop adj; rest; snacks adj; bar; playgrnd; shgl beach adj; scuba-diving; games area; wifi; entmnt; 20% statics; dogs; bus adj; poss cr; Eng spkn; adv bkg; quiet, a little rd noise; ccard acc; red LS/long stay/CKE/CCI. "Excel for sw & visiting local area - Lovran lovely town; conv for ferry to Cres; gd, modern san facs; various pitch prices." ♦ 1 Apr-15 Oct. HRK 253 (CChq acc)   2011*

MLINI see Dubrovnik C4

⊞ **MOLUNAT** D4 (500m N Coastal) 42.45298, 18.4276 **Autokamp Monika, Molunat 28, 20219 Molunat [tel/fax (020) 794557; info@camp-monika.hr; www.camp-monika.hr]** Site well sp in Molunat off Adriatic Highway E65. Sm, terr, pt shd; wc (some cont); chem disp; mv service pnt; shwrs inc; EHU (6A) HRK27; lndry; rest, snacks; bar; BBQ; sand beach adj; internet; dogs HRK8; poss cr; Eng spkn; quiet; red LS. "Gd site close to Montenegro border & in quiet cove; sea view fr all pitches; owner's wine & olive oil for sale; beautiful views, v quiet LS; v friendly & helpful owner; highly rec." HRK 248   2014*

MURTER see Jezera (Murter Island) B3

MURTER ISLAND B3 Sites on Murter Island are listed together at the end of the Croatia site entry pages.

NOVIGRAD (DALMATIA) B3 (N Coastal) 44.18472, 15.54944 **Camping Adriasol, 23312 Novigrad [(023) 375618; fax 375619; info@adriasol.com or office@adriasol.com; www.adriasol.com]** Exit A1 at Posedarje & foll sp Novigrad. Site sp at end of vill. Med, pt shd; wc; chem disp; mv service pnt; baby facs; shwrs inc; EHU (16A) HRK31; lndry; shop 500m; rest, snacks, bar adj; cooking facs; playgrnd; beach adj; watersports; bike hire; games area; internet; some statics; dogs HRK23; TV; adv bkg; quiet; red CKE/CCI. "Well-positioned site - poss windy; gd facs; friendly staff; popular level pitches by beach cost more; freezer avail for camper use; v helpful staff." ♦ 1 May-30 Sep. HRK 234   2013*

NOVIGRAD (ISTRIA) A2 (4km NW Coastal) 45.34333, 13.54805 **Autocamp Mareda, Škverska bb, 52466 Novigrad [(052) 735291; fax 757035; camping@laguna-novigrad. hr; www.laguna-novigrad.hr]** Fr Novigrad foll coast rd dir Umag, in 4km foll sp to L. Lge, mkd pitch, pt shd; wc (some cont); chem disp; mv service pnt; shwrs inc; EHU (10-16A) HRK23; lndry; shop; rest; bar; BBQ; playgrnd; shgl beach adj; boat lauch; tennis; entmnt; 50% statics; dogs HRK35; poss cr; Eng spkn; quiet; ccard acc; red CKE/CCI. "Peaceful site amongst vineyards; modern, clean san facs; cheaper, unmkd pitches avail." ♦ 1 Apr-30 Sep. HRK 194   2009*

⊞ **OMIS** C4 (8km S Coastal) 43.40611, 16.77777 **Autocamp Sirena, Četvrt Vrilo 10, 21317 Lokva Rogoznica [tel/fax (021) 870266; autocamp-sirena@st.t.hr; www.autocamp-sirena.com]** Thro Omiš S'wards on main coastal rd, site up sm lane on R immed bef sm tunnel. Med, hdstg, sl, terr, pt shd; wc; chem disp; mv service pnt; shwrs inc; EHU (16A) HRK15; gas; lndry; shop; rest, snacks; bar; BBQ; shgl beach adj; watersports; internet; dogs HRK15; phone; bus; poss cr; Eng spkn; adv bkg; quiet; CKE/CCI. "Enthusiastic, welcoming staff; improving site; easy access lge o'fits; stunning location above beautiful beach; excel stop bet Split & Dubrovnik; excel rest." HRK 206   2014*

⊞ **OMIS** C4 (1.5km W Coastal) 43.44040, 16.67960 **Autocamp Galeb, Vukovarska bb, 21310 Omiš [tel/fax (021) 864430; camping@galeb.hr; www.camp.galeb.hr]** Site sp on rd 2/E65 fr Split to Dubrovnik. Lge, mkd pitch, pt shd; wc; chem disp; mv service pnt; baby facs; serviced pitches; private bthrms avail; shwrs; EHU (16A) inc; gas; lndry; supmkt adj; rest, snacks; bar; BBQ (gas, elec); playgrnd; sand beach; watersports; white water rafting; sports area; bike hire; tennis; wifi; entmnt;. 50% statics; dogs HRK33; bus; poss cr; noisy high ssn; ccard acc; red LS/CKE/CCI. "Excel, well-maintained site in gd position; extra for waterside pitch; clean san facs; suitable young children; easy walk or water taxi to town." ♦ ltd. HRK 289 (CChq acc) SBS - X02   2012*

OPATIJA A2 (5km S Coastal) 45.30633, 14.28354 **Autocamp Opatija, Liburnijska 46, 51414 Ičići [(051) 704387; tz-icici@ri.t-com.hr]** Fr Opatija take Pula rd 66. Site sp on R of rd 5km after Opatija. Sp fr Ičići. Med, terr, pt shd; wc; chem disp; mv service pnt; shwrs inc; EHU (10A); rest, snacks 1km; shgl beach adj; tennis; dogs; Eng spkn; quiet. "Gd site nr coastal promenade; diff for lge o'fits without motor mover." 1 May-30 Sep. HRK 247   2013*

ORASAC *C4* (500m S Coastal) **Autocamping Peča, Na Przini 38, 20234 Orašac [(020) 891161; info@peca.hr; www.peca. hr]** Site on L of Split to Dubrovnik rd, on S edge vill Orašac. Sm, pt shd; wc; chem disp; shwrs inc; EHU (16A) HRK15; lndry rm; shop 300m; snacks, bar 600m; shgl beach 600m; dogs; phone; poss cr; Eng spkn; adv bkg; quiet; ccard not acc; CKE/ CCI. "Excel, well-run, friendly site; clean, modern facs; bus to Dubrovnik; gd bar/rest at beach - steep climb down."
1 Jun-30 Sep. HRK 108   2010*

ORASAC *C4* (900m S Coastal) *42.69919, 18.00578* **Autocamp Pod Maslinom, Na Komardi 23, 20234 Orašac [(020) 891169; orasac@orasac.com; www.orasac.com]** On main coast rd, on seaward side. Sp. Sm, hdstg, pt sl, terr, pt shd; wc; chem disp; shwrs inc; EHU HRK15; sm shop; rest, bar 200m; BBQ; shgl beach 200m; wifi; dogs; bus; Eng spkn; quiet. "Pleasant site, clean facs; vg value for money." 1 May-20 Oct. HRK 87   2010*

⊞ **OREBIC** *C4* (1km E Coastal) *42.9810, 17.1980* **Nevio Camping, Dubravica bb, 20250 Orebič [(020) 713100; fax 713950; info@nevio-camping.com; www.nevio-camping.com]** Fr N take ferry fr Ploče to Trpanj & take rd 415 then 414 dir Orebič, site sp. Fr S on rd 8/E65 turn W at Zaton Doli onto rd 414 to site. Site ent immed after lge sp - not 100m further on. Sm, terr, pt shd; htd wc; chem disp; mv service pnt; some serviced pitches; baby facs; shwrs inc; EHU (16A) inc; lndry (inc dryer); shop 300m; rest, snacks; beach bar; BBQ; cooking facs; pool; dir access to shgl beach; tennis; bike hire; wifi; TV rm; 40% statics; dogs HRK15-38; Eng spkn; adv bkg; quiet; red LS/snr citizens. "Excel new site in gd location; friendly, helpful, welcoming staff; gd views; gd, clean facs; not suitable lge o'fits." ◆ HRK 282   2013*

⊞ **OREBIC** *C4* (5km W Coastal) *42.97750, 17.12950* **Camping Palme, Kučište 45, 20267 Kučište [tel/fax (020) 719164; info@kamp-palme.com; www.kamp-palme.com]** Fr E thro Orebič on rd 414, site sp. Med, pt sl, terr, pt shd; htd wc; chem disp; mv service pnt; shwrs inc; EHU (10A) HRK30; gas; lndry; shop 100m; rest adj high ssn; snacks, bar high ssn; BBQ; shgl beach adj; watersports; boat hire; internet; TV rm; 10% statics; dogs HRK22; bus; poss cr; quiet; red CKE/CCI. "Nice, busy family-run site; beautiful wooded location on coast; friendly owners; excel rest; gd walking; ferry to Korčula; not suitable lge o'fits." HRK 163   2011*

PAKOSTANE *B3* (4km SE Coastal) *43.88611, 15.53305* **Autocamp Oaza Mira, Ul. Dr. Franje Tudmana 2, 23211 Drage [023 635419; info@oaza-mira.hr; www.oaza-mira.hr]** A1 Karlovac-Split past Zadar, exit Biograd dir Sibenik on coast rd; sp on coastal side of rd; foll sp site after bay. Med, hdstg, terr, pt shd; wc; chem disp; mv serv pnt; baby facs; fam bthrm; shwr; EHU inc; lndry rm; shop; rest; bar; BBQ; playgrnd; pool; beach adj; games rm; wifi; dogs HRK61; Eng spkn; adv bkg; quiet. "Excel new lovely site in beautiful location; generous pitches; rec using ACSI card; 2 beautiful bays adj to site; highly rec." 1 Apr-31 Oct. HRK 427   2012*

PAKOSTANE *B3* (500m S Coastal) *43.90547, 15.51616* **Autocamp Nordsee, Alojzija Stepinca 68, 23211 Pakoštane [tel/fax (023) 381438; info@autocamp-nordsee.com; www.autocamp-nordsee.com]** Site sp in Pakoštane on rd 8/E65. Med, mkd pitch, terr, pt shd; htd wc; chem disp; mv service pnt; baby facs; shwrs inc; EHU (16A) HRK23; lndry (inc dryer); shop 400m; rest, snacks; bar; dir access to beach adj; wifi; 10% statics; dogs HRK23; adv bkg; quiet. "Pleasant, family site." 1 Mar-31 Oct. HRK 196   2010*

"I need an on-site restaurant"

We do our best to make sure site information is correct, but it is always best to check any must-have facilities are still available or will be open during your visit.

PIROVAC *B3* (1km N Coastal) *43.82341, 15.65818* **Autocamp Miran, Zagrebačka bb, 22213 Pirovac [(022) 467064; fax 467022; reservations@rivijera.hr; www.rivijera.hr]** Sp on main coast rd NW Šibenik. Site 300m off Adriatic highway. Med, mkd pitch, some hdstg, pt sl, pt shd; wc; shwrs; EHU (16A) inc; lndry rm; shops & 2km; rest; playgrnd; pool nr; shgl beach; tennis; bike hire; entmnt; TV; some statics; dogs HRK34; poss cr; quiet; ccard acc. "Ideal for watersports; sm pitches on water's edge." 23 Apr-30 Sep. HRK 206   2011*

POREC *A2* (10km N Coastal) *45.29728, 13.59425* **Camping Lanterna, Lanterna 1, 52465 Tar [(052) 404 500; fax 404591; lanterna@valamar.com; www.camping-adriatic. com/camp-lanterna]** Site sp 5km S of Novigrad (Istria) & N of Poreč on Umag-Vrsar coast rd. V lge, hdg/mkd pitch, hdstg, pt sl, terr, pt shd; wc; chem disp; mv service pnt; fam bthrm; baby facs; shwrs inc; EHU (10A); gas; lndry; supmkts; rest, snacks; bar; BBQ; playgrnd; pool; 2 hydro-massage pools; paddling pool; shgl beach adj; watersports; boat launch; tennis; games area; bike hire; wifi; entmnt; 10% statics; dogs €5; phone; adv bkg (fee); noise fr ships loading across bay; ccard acc; red CKE/CCI (cash payments only). "V busy, well-run site; excel san facs & leisure facs; although many san facs they may be a long walk; variety of shops; gd sightseeing; extra for seaside/hdg pitch; vg." ◆
12 Apr-10 Oct. HRK 298 SBS - X10   2014*

See advertisement opposite

POREC *A2* (5km S Coastal) *45.19313, 13.59670* **Autocamp Bijela Uvala (Part Naturist), Zelena Luguna, 52440 Poreč [(052) 410551 or 410552; fax 410600; reservations@plavalaguna.hr; www.plavalaguna.hr]** Fr Poreč, take coast rd S to Vrsar, site sp on R. V lge, mkd pitch, some hdstg, pt sl, pt terr, pt shd; wc (some cont); chem disp; mv service pnt; baby facs; fam bthrm; shwrs; EHU (10A) HRK24; gas; lndry (inc dryer); shop; rest, snacks; bar; playgrnd; pools; paddling pool; rocky beach; sep naturist beach; watersports; games area; tennis; wifi; entmnt; TV; dogs HRK46; poss cr; Eng spkn; adv bkg; quiet; ccard acc. "Excel touring base Istrian peninsula; clean, tidy, well-run site; friendly staff." ◆ Easter-30 Sep. HRK 230   2011*

camping adriatic
by Valamar

Naturist Resort Solaris 3*

Camping Lanterna 4*

Camping Krk 5*

Camping Marina 4*

Your first choice for Camping in Croatia

> Tranquil oases by the sea

> Superb pitches, premium mobile homes

> International Valamar service standards

> Respect for nature at all times

> Great sports and entertainment options + free Wi-Fi

> Maro Clubs – kids own kingdom

> Pets are welcome

Istria
Camping Lanterna 4*
Camping Marina 4*
Camping Orsera 3*
Naturist Resort Solaris 3*
Naturist Camping Istra 2*
Camping Brioni 2*

Island Krk
Camping Krk 5*
Camping Ježevac 4*
Naturist Camping Bunculuka 4*
Camping Zablaće 3*
Camping Škrila 1*

Dubrovnik
Camping Solitudo 3*

T +385 52 465 010
www.camping-adriatic.com

Book online!

Find us on
Facebook

POREC *A2* (5km S Coastal) *45.19193, 13.58916* **Camping Zelena Laguna, 52440 Poreč [(052) 410700; fax 410601; reservations@plavalaguna.hr; www.plavalaguna.hr]** Fr Poreč take rd to Vrsar, site sp on R. V lge, some mkd pitch, hdstg, pt shd; wc; serviced pitches; chem disp; shwrs; EHU (10A) HRK27; lndry; shop, supmkt adj; rest, snacks; bar; playgrnd; pool; rocky shgl beach; sep naturist beach; entmnt; dogs HRK46; poss cr; adv bkg; quiet but noisy disco; ccard acc; red long stay/CKE/CCI. "A gd resort site with excel & spotless facs & lge, mainly terr, pitches; gd for touring Istrian peninsula; extra charge if stay fewer than 3 days Jul/Aug; footpath/cycle path to town." ♦ 27 Mar-4 Oct. HRK 203   2011*

POREC *A2* (7km S Coastal) *45.17693, 13.60053* **Autocamp Puntica, 52452 Funtana [(052) 410102; fax 451044; reservations@plavalaguna.hr; www.plavalaguna.hr]** Fr Koper on rte 2 foll sp to Poreč & Vrsar. 7km S of Poreč, turn R (care needed) 200m past Funtana sp. Site on R in 500m. Narr ent. Lge, sl, pt shd; wc (cont); chem disp; mv service pnt; shwrs inc; EHU (10A) HRK27; lndry; shop; rest adj; playgrnd; beach adj; watersports; wifi; 50% statics; dogs HRK32; quiet; red CKE/CCI. "Sep beach for naturists; located on peninsula nr Funtana complex; extra charge if stay fewer than 3 days." ♦ 24 Apr-3 Oct. HRK 171   2010*

POREC *A2* (7km S Coastal) *45.17453, 13.59213* **Camping Istra Naturist Funtana (Naturist), Ul Grgeti 35, 52450 Funtana [(052) 445123; fax 445306; camping@valamar. com; www.valamar.com or www.camping-adriatic.com]** Fr Poreč S sp Vrsar-Rovinj. After 6km turn R at sp Istra bef Funtana vill. Foll sp to camp in 1km. V lge, hdg/mkd pitch, pt sl, pt shd; wc (some cont); chem disp; mv service pnt; baby facs; fam bthrm; shwrs inc; EHU (16A) inc; gas; lndry; shop; rest, snacks; bar; BBQ; playgrnd; shgl beach adj; tennis; games area; boat & bike hire; wifi; entmnt; TV rm; 10% statics; dogs HRK42; poss cr; Eng spkn; quiet; ccard acc; red LS/INF/CKE/CCI. "Excel site; beaches v rocky." ♦ ltd. 16 Apr-3 Oct. HRK 225   2011*

POREC *A2* (8km NW Coastal) *45.2568, 13.5835* **Naturist-Center Ulika (Naturist), 52440 Poreč (Istra) [(052) 436325; fax 436352; reservations@plavalaguna.hr; www.laguna porec.com]** Site sp on rd fr Poreč to Tar & Novigrad. V lge, pt sl, shd; wc; shwrs; EHU (6A) HRK23; lndry; shop; rest, snacks; bar; playgrnd; pool; shgl & rocky beach; tennis; watersports; entmnt; 9% statics; dogs HRK48; adv bkg; quiet; ccard acc; red INF card/long stay; "Excel site." ♦ 28 Mar-6 Oct. HRK 199   2013*

PREMANTURA see Medulin *A3*

PRIMOSTEN *B4* (2km N Coastal) *43.60646, 15.92085* **Camp Adriatic, Huljerat b.b, 22202 Primošten [(022) 571223; fax 571360; info@camp-adriatic.hr; www.camp-adriatic.hr]** Off Adriatic Highway, rd 8/E65, sp. V lge, all hdstg, pt sl, pt terr, unshd; wc; chem disp; mv service pnt; fam bthrm; baby facs; shwrs inc; EHU (16A) inc; gas; lndry (inc dryer); shop & 2km; rest, snacks; bar; rocky beach adj; boat hire; watersports; diving cent; tennis; games area; wifi; entmnt; dogs HRK32; Eng spkn; quiet; red CKE/CCI. "Gd sea views; excel san facs; some pitches poss diff to get onto; beautiful views fr beach." ♦ 1 May-15 Oct. HRK 305   2010*

PULA *A3* (7km S Coastal) *44.82290, 13.85080* **Camping Peškera, Indije 73 52100 Banjole/Pula (Istra) [052 573209; fax 573189; info@camp-peskera.com; www.camp-peskera. com]** Fr N take A9 to Pula. Cont on m'way twd Premantura. Exit at Banjole, cont twd Indije. Campsite is 100m after Indije. Sm, pt sl, pt shd; wc; cont; chem disp; mv service pnt; shwrs; supmkt 2km; rest 1km; snacks; bar; shingle beach adj; wifi; dogs HRK15; bus 0.5km; poss cr; Eng spkn; adv bkg; quiet; ccard acc; red LS; CCI. "Beautiful situation; helpful & friendly owners; gd clean san facs; vg." ♦ ltd. 1 Apr-31 Oct. HRK 212   2014*

PULA *A3* (8km S Coastal) *44.82012, 13.90252* **Autocamp Pomer, Pomer bb, 52100 Pula [(052) 573128; fax 573062; camp-pomer@camp-pomer.com; www.camp-pomer.com]** Fr N on A9 to Pula, take exit to Pula. At bottom of hill turn L after filling stn & foll dir Medulin/Premantura. In Premantura turn L by Consum supmkt & foll sp to Pomer & site. Med, mkd pitch, terr, shd; wc; chem disp; shwrs; EHU (16A) HRK21 (long lead poss req); lndry rm; shop; rest, snacks; bar; BBQ; playgrnd; rocky beach adj; fishing; watersports; games area; entmnt; some statics; dogs HRK23; phone; Eng spkn; adv bkg; quiet; red CKE/CCI. "Clean san facs poss stretched high ssn; friendly owner; quiet, relaxing site." 1 Apr-15 Oct. HRK 147   2009*

PULA *A3* (8km S Rural) *44.82472, 13.85885* **Camping Diana, Castagnes b b, 52100 Banjole [(052) 505630; booking@ camp-diana.com; www.camp-diana.com]** Fr Pula ring rd foll sp Premantura & Camping Indije. Site 1km bef Cmp Indije. Sm, pt sl, pt shd; wc; chem disp (wc); shwrs inc; EHU (16A) inc; shop 200m; bar; playgrnd; pool; paddling pool; tennis; games area; wifi; no dogs; adv bkg; quiet. "Pleasant site in garden setting; gd range of facs; immac san facs; welcoming family owners." 1 May-1 Oct. HRK 206   2010*

PUNAT see Krk (Krk Island) *A3*

"Satellite navigation makes touring much easier"

Remember most sat navs don't know if you're towing or in a larger vehicle – always use yours alongside maps and site directions.

RAB ISLAND *A3* **Sites on Rab Island are listed together at the end of the Croatia site entry pages.**

RABAC *A3* (500m W Coastal) *45.08086, 14.14583* **Camping Oliva, 52221 Rabac [tel/fax (052) 872258; olivakamp@ maslinica-rabac.com; www.maslinica-rabac.com]** On ent Rabac fr Labin, turn R at sp Autocamp; site ent in 500m. V lge, mkd pitch, pt shd; wc (mainly cont); baby facs; shwrs; EHU (10A) inc (long lead poss req); gas; lndry (inc dryer); shop 100m; rest, snacks; bar; playgrnd; shgl beach; watersports; boat-launching; sports complex; 30% statics; dogs HRK22; phone; poss cr; adv bkg Aug ess; quiet; ccard acc; red CKE/CCI. "Conv historic walled town Labin; walk along beach to shops & rest." ♦ ltd. 21 Apr-6 Oct. HRK 402 (CChq acc)   2013*

RAKOVICA *B3* (3km S Rural) *44.97340, 15.64789* **Turist Grabovac Camping**, Grabovac 102, 47245 Rakovica [(047) 784192; fax 784189; info@kamp-turist.hr; www.kamp-turist.hr] On main rd 1/E71 S fr Karlovac, site on R, well sp opp Ina petrol stn. Med, hdg/mkd pitch, hdstg, pt sl, pt shd; wc; shwrs inc; EHU (6-16A) inc (long lead req); shop, rest adj; bike hire; 20% statics; dogs; bus to National Park adj; Eng spkn; adv bkg; some rd noise; ccard acc; CKE/CCI. "Gd views fr higher pitches; friendly staff; well-maintained site; insufficient facs stretched high ssn; excursions arranged." ♦ 1 Apr-30 Sep. HRK 166   2010*

RAKOVICA *B3* (7km SW Rural) *44.95020, 15.64160* **Camp Korana**, Plitvička Jezera, 47246 Drežnik Grad [(053) 751888; fax 751882; autokamp.korana@np-plitvicka-jezera.hr; www.np-plitvicka-jezera.hr] On A1/E59 2km S of Grabovac, site on L. Site is 5km N of main ent to Plitvička Nat Park, sp. Lge, some hdstg, pt sl, pt shd; wc; fam bthrm; own san; chem disp; mv service pnt; shwrs inc; EHU (16A) inc (poss long lead req); lndry rm; shop; rest, snacks; bar; BBQ; wifi; 10% statics; dogs HRK23; Eng spkn; no adv bkg; ccard acc; CKE/CCI. "Lovely site, v busy; poss long way fr facs; gd san facs but inadequate for size of site; efficient, friendly site staff; poss muddy in wet; bus to National Park (6km) high ssn; new san facs; gd rest." 1 Apr-31 Oct. HRK 259 (CChq acc)   2014*

RIJEKA *A2* (9km W Coastal) *45.35638, 14.34222* **Camping Preluk**, Preluk 1, 51000 Rijeka [(051) 662185; fax 622381; camp.preluk@gmail.com] On Rijeka to Opatija coast rd. Sm, shd; wc (some cont); own san; chem disp; shwrs; EHU (10A) inc; shop; snacks; mainly statics; dogs; bus; poss cr; Eng spkn; rd noise. "NH only; Many statics; facs recently renovated (2012); bus to town; sm beach on site; gd windsurfing." 1 May-30 Sep. HRK 158   2012*

RIZVANUSA *B3* (10km W Rural) *44.49580, 15.29165* **Eco Camp Rizvan City**, Rizvanuša 1, 53000 Gospić [053 57 33 33; info@adria-velebitica.hr; www.camp-rizvancity.com] Fr A1 take exit 12 (Gospic). Head 10km E twd Karlobag on highway 25. Turn L off main rd into Vill Rizvanusa. Camp 500m. Sm, pt shd; wc; chem disp; mv service pnt; fam bthrm; shwrs; EHU (16A); lndry (inc dryer); BBQ; playgrnd; beach 30km; games area; wifi; dogs; twin axles; Eng spkn; adv bkg; quiet. "Walks, high rope course; quad & jeep safari; archery; paintball; zip line; wall climbing; giant swing; bike trails; vg." ♦ ltd. 1 Mar-1 Nov. HRK 163   2014*

ROVINJ *A2* (5km N Coastal) *45.10444, 13.62527* **Camping Valdaliso**, Monsena b.b, 52210 Rovinj [(052) 805505; fax 811541; ac-valdaliso@maistra.hr; www.camping rovinjvrsar.com] N fr Rovinj dir Valalta for 2km, turn W to coast, site sp. Lge, hdg/mkd pitch, some hdstg, pt sl, pt shd; htd wc; chem disp; mv service pnt; baby facs; fam bthrm; shwrs; EHU (10A) inc; gas; lndry; shop; rest, snacks; bar; BBQ; playgrnd; shgl beach adj; waterslide; tennis; bike hire; games area; games rm; wifi; entmnt; sat TV; 10% statics; no dogs; phone; bus; water taxi; Eng spkn; adv bkg; quiet; ccard acc; CKE/CCI. "Pretty site in olive trees; use of all amenities in hotel adj; excel modern san facs; poss waterlogged after heavy rain; excel; facs stretched if site full; pitches uneven; closing in Sep 2015 for redevelopment." ♦ 12 Apr-26 Sep. HRK 288   2015*

ROVINJ *A2* (6.9km N Coastal) *45.12287, 13.62970* **Campsite Valalta Naturist (Naturist)**, Cesta Za Valaltu-Lim 7, 52210 Rovinj (Istra) [052 804800; fax 821004; valalta@valalta.hr; www.valalta.hr] 7km NW fr Rovinj. Foll signs to Valalta. V lge, hdg/mkd pitch, hdstg, pt shd; wc; chem disp; mv service pnt; baby facs; fam bthrm; shwrs; EHU (16A); lndry (inc dryer); shop; rest; snacks; bar; BBQ; playgrnd; pool; waterslide; paddling pool; beach; games area; games rm; bike hire; entmnt; wifi; tv; phone; twin axles; Eng spkn; adv bkg; quiet. "Excel site." ♦ ltd. 1 May-1 Oct. HRK 408   2014*

ROVINJ *A2* (5km SE Coastal) *45.05611, 13.68277* **Camping Veštar**, 52210 Rovinj [(052) 829150; fax 829151; vestar@maistra.hr; www.campingrovinjvrsar.com] Clearly sp on ent/exit Rovinj dir Pula. V lge, mkd pitch, pt sl, pt shd; wc; chem disp; mv service pnt; baby facs; shwrs inc; EHU (16A) inc (poss rev pol); gas; lndry; supmkt; rest, snacks; bar; playgrnd; pool; paddling pool; shgl beach adj; boat & bike hire; watersports; tennis; internet; entmnt; TV; 20% statics; dogs HRK47; phone; sep naturist beach adj; cash machine; poss cr; Eng spkn; adv bkg; ccard acc; red long stay/snr citizens/ CKE/CCI. "Well-run, clean site on beautiful sm bay; coastal cycle track to Rovinj; gd touring base; friendly staff; some lge pitches; ltd EHU high ssn; extra charge for stay fewer than 3 days." ♦ 25 Apr-3 Oct. HRK 232   2009*

ROVINJ *A2* (4km NW Coastal) *45.10909, 13.61974* **Camping Amarin**, Monsena bb, 52210 Rovinj [(052) 802000; fax 813354; ac-amarin@maistra.hr; www.campingrovinj vrsar.com] Fr town N in dir Valalta, turn L & foll site sp. V lge, mkd pitch, pt sl, pt shd; wc (some cont); chem disp; mv service pnt; shwrs inc; EHU (10A) inc; lndry; shop; rest, snacks; bar; playgrnd; htd pool; paddling pool; waterslide; shgl beach adj; sports facs; tennis; bike hire; entmnt; internet; TV; 30% statics; dogs HRK47; phone; poss cr; Eng spkn; adv bkg; quiet; ccard acc; red LS/CKE/CCI. "Excel site; clean, well-maintained san facs & pool; gd entmnt; views of town & islands; lovely situation in pine & olive trees; water taxi to town." ♦ 25 Apr-3 Oct. HRK 238   2011*

ROVINJ *A2* (700m NW Coastal) *45.09472, 13.64527* **Autocamp Porton Biondi**, Aleja Porton Biondi 1, 52210 Rovinj [(052) 813557; fax 811509; portonbiondi@web.de; www.portonbiondi.hr] Site sp on ent Rovinj. Lge, pt sl, terr, shd; wc; shwrs inc; EHU inc; shop adj; rest, snacks; rocky beach nr; watersports; entmnt; dogs HRK24; adv bkg; quiet; ccard acc; red LS/ long stay/CKE/CCI. "Gd site within walking dist Rovinj old town; beautiful views; new san facs; sm pitches not suitable lge o'fits; excel rest; 2nd & subsequent nights at red rate." ♦ ltd. 15 Mar-31 Oct. HRK 170   2012*

SELCE *A2* (1.3km SE Coastal) *45.15361, 14.72488* **Autocamp Selce**, Jasenová 19, 51266 Selce [(051) 764038; fax 764066; autokampselce@jadran-crikvenica.hr; www.jadran-crikvenica.hr] Thro Selce town cent, site is 500m SE of town, sp. Lge, hdstg, pt sl, terr, pt shd; wc (some cont) chem disp; mv service pnt; shwrs; EHU (10A) HRK27; lndry; shop; rest, snacks; bar; playgrnd; shgl beach adj; TV; statics; dogs HRK17; phone; poss cr; quiet; ccard acc; red long stay/CKE/CCI. "Wooded site; seaside location; helpful staff; long stay; blocks & wedges ess; san facs run down & neglected; long lead rec; door security." ♦ 1 Apr-15 Oct. HRK 247   2014*

CROATIA

Camping Resort SOLARIS ★★★★

Great Resort for a Great Vacation

Solaris Camping Beach Resort
Šibenik - CROATIA
T. +385 22 361 017
camping@solaris.hr
www.campingsolaris.com

SENJ *A3* (3km N Urban/Coastal) **Autokamp Skver, Skver bb,** 53270 Senj [tel/fax (053) 885266; kamp_skver@yahoo. com] Fr N on rd 8/E65 on ent town turn R opp petrol stn & cont down narr lane to sea. Site sp bef marina. Sm, mkd pitch, hdstg, unshd; wc; chem disp; shwrs inc; EHU inc; shops 500m; rest; bar; shgl beach adj; phone; poss cr; Eng spkn; adv bkg; rd noise. "Gd views; harbour & rest nrby."   2009*

SENJ *A3* (11km S Coastal) *44.98763, 14.91132* **Eurocamp Rača,** Rača bb, 53284 Sveti Juraj [tel/fax (053) 883209; info@sojat.net] On rte 2 Rjeka-Split, well sp fr Senj. Lge, hdstg, pt sl, terr, pt shd; wc; chem disp (wc); shwrs; EHU; sm shop; rest adj; snacks; bar; shgle beach adj; boat-launching; watersports; diving school; tennis; games area; entmnt; poss cr; some rd noise; CKE/CCI. "In ravine with own beach; beautiful location; ltd facs; conv NH."   2010*

SENJ *A3* (6km NW Coastal) *45.04403, 14.87817* **Autocamp Sibinj,** Sibinj 9, 51252 Klenovica [(051) 796916; milieijko. tomijanovic@ri.hinet.hr] Fr Novi Vinodolski, take rd S. In approx 12km site sp. Med, sl, terr, pt shd; wc (male cont); shwrs inc; EHU (10A); shops, sm bar & rest; private shgl beach adj; some rd noise. "Well-run site; clean facs but in need of modernising; magnificent views; poss open all yr; noisy rd; NH only." 1 May-31 Oct. HRK 152   2011*

SIBENIK *B3* (10km NE Rural) *43.80063, 15.94210* **Camp Krka,** Skocici 21, 22221 Lozovac [(022) 778495; goran.skocic@ si.t-com.hr; www.camp-krka.hr] Exit A1 at junc 22 Šibenik, turn E at T-junc, thro tunnel & site in approx 4km. Fr main coast rd at Sibenik turn N onto rte 33 twd Drniš. After 15km turn L dir Skradin, site sp on L. Med, hdstg, pt shd; wc; chem disp; shwrs; EHU (16A) HRK23 (poss rev pol; check earth); lndry; shop 4km; bar; some statics & B&B; Eng spkn; quiet; red LS/CKE/CCI. "Pleasant, basic site in orchard; friendly owner; gd modern san facs; conv Krka National Park & Krka gorge; gd; clean new shwr/wc facs (2014); rest, cheap basic food." 1 Apr-30 Oct. HRK 151   2014*

SIBENIK *B3* (4km S Coastal) *43.69925, 15.87942* **Camping Solaris,** Hotelsko Naselje Solaris, 22000 Šibenik [(022) 364000; fax 364450; info@solaris.hr; www.solaris.hr] Sp fr E65 Zadar-Split rd, adj hotel complex. V lge, hdg/mkd pitch, pt shd; htd wc; chem disp; mv service pnt in adj marina; sauna; serviced pitches; shwrs inc; EHU (6A) inc; lndry; shop adj; rest, snacks; bar; BBQ; playgrnd; pool; paddling pool; waterslide; watersports; tennis; bike hire; wifi; entmnt; TV; dogs; bus; poss v cr; some rd noise; ccard acc; red long stay/LS/CKE/CCI. "Well-situated in olive & pine trees; some pitches adj marina; excel, modern san facs." ♦ 15 Apr-31 Oct. HRK 225   2012*

"There aren't many sites open at this time of year"

If you're travelling outside peak season remember to call ahead to check site opening dates – even if the entry says 'open all year'.

SIBENIK *B3* (10km S Coastal) *43.65238, 15.95066* **Camping Jasenovo,** Uvala Jasenovo, 22010 Žaborić-Brodarica [(022) 350550; fax 350953; kamp@jasenovo.hr; www.jasenovo.hr] Fr Šibinik S on E65, site well sp on R. Sm, hdstg, pt sl, shd; wc; chem disp; shwrs inc; EHU HRK23; lndry rm; shop 2km; snacks; bar; shgl beach adj; wifi; dogs HRK31; bus adj; poss cr; Eng spkn; adv bkg; quiet; CKE/CCI. "Vg, family-run site in pine & olive trees; helpful staff; plans to extend." ♦ ltd. 1 May-1 Oct. HRK 168   2010*

⊞ **SPLIT** *B4* (7.9km E Coastal) *43.50451, 16.52598* **Camping Stobreč-Split,** Sv Lovre 6, 21311 Stobreč [(021) 325426; fax 325452; camping.split@gmail.com; www.campingsplit. com] Fr N foll E65 & m'way thro Split to sp Stobreč. Site sp R off E65 at traff lts in Stobreč. Lge, mkd pitch, hdstg, pt sl, shd; wc; chem disp; mv service pnt; shwrs; EHU (16A) inc (long lead poss req); lndry (inc dryer); shop; rest, snacks; bar; playgrnd; sand beach; games area; wifi; dogs HRK45; bus to Split; poss cr; Eng spkn; some rd noise. "Superb, well-run site in lovely setting with views; friendly, welcoming staff; gd facs; own sandy beach; public footpath thro site; rec arr early to secure pitch; gd value for money; highly rec; free bus into cent Split; Diocletian's Palace worth a visit." ♦ HRK 268   2014*

Belvedere
CAMPING & APARTMENTS
TROGIR
★★★★

Kralja Zvonimira 62
21218 Seget Vranjica
TROGIR-CROATIA
www.vranjica-belvedere.hr
info@vranjica-belvedere.hr
T.+385 21 798 222

BELVDERE Camping & Apartments _ is located 5 km from Trogir, town museum protected by UNESCO, 8 km from Split airport and cca 30 km from old dalmatian town Split. 66 apartments, mobile homes & camping are situated in cascades with a beautiful sea view. There is a lot of different offer & facilities for all generations such as restaurant & bar right on the beach, sport & recreation facilities, animation program, excursions offer, Wifi, safe & exchange office, ATM, Supermarket, laundry service.

STARIGRAD PAKLENICA *B3* (1km S Coastal) *44.28713, 15.44761* **Autocamp Nacionalni Park Paklenica, Dr Franje Tudmana 14, 23244 Starigrad-Paklenica [(023) 369202 or 369155; fax 359133; alan@bluesunhotels.com; www.bluesunhotels.com]** On seaward side of rd 8/E65 adj Hotel Alan. Sm, gravel, pt shd; wc (some cont); chem disp; shwrs inc; EHU (10-15A) HRK16-22; shop adj; rest, snacks adj & 700m; bar; shgl beach; boating; dogs HRK15; phone; bus; poss cr; ccard acc. "Ent to National Park 2km; hiking; rock-climbing; v pleasant staff; lack of privacy in shwrs." ♦ ltd. 1 Apr-15 Nov. HRK 160   2010*

STARIGRAD PAKLENICA *B3* (300m S Coastal) *44.28694, 15.44666* **Autocamp Paklenica, Dr Franje Tuđmana 14, 23244 Starigrad-Paklenica [(023) 209050; fax 209073; camping.paklenica@bluesunhotels.com or alan@bluesun hotels.com; www.bluesunhotels.com]** On rd 8/E65 Adriatic H'way at ent to Paklenica National Park in Zidine vill. Hotel Alan is lge, 10-storey block - ent & cont to site. Lge, pt sl, shd; wc; chem disp; shwrs inc; EHU (16A) inc (long lead poss req); lndry; shop; rest; bar; playgrnd; pool adj; paddling pool; beach adj; tennis; games area; bike hire; wifi; entmnt; TV; 5% statics; dogs HRK37; phone; Eng spkn; poss cr nr shore; adv bkg; ccard acc; red long stay/LS/CKE/CCI. "Gd clean facs; conv National Park; excel walking & rockclimbing; use of facs at adj hotel; site muddy when wet; gd res, pleasant helpful staff, san facs being enlarged (2013)." ♦ 1Apr-15 Nov. HRK 329   2013*

⊞ **STARLGRAD PAKLENICA** *B3* (1km N Coastal) *44.31340, 15.43579* **Auto-Kamp Plantaža, Put Plantaza 2, 23244 Starigrad Paklenica [(038) 23 369131; fax 23 359159; plantaza@hi.t-com.hr; www.plantaza.com]** Fr Rijeka foll M2/E27 coast rd until 1 km N of Steligrad. V Steep pull out of site. Sm, mkd pitch, hdstg, terr, shd; htd wc; chem disp; mv service pnt; baby facs; shwrs; EHU 10A; rest; BBQ; beach; Eng spkn; poss cr; quite; ACSI; CKE/CCI. "Vg site; excel new facs; handy for NP; shopping for fresh food v ltd locally." HRK 114   2012*

STOBREC see Split *B4*

STON *C4* (3km S Coastal) *42.81775, 17.67591* **Autocamp Prapratno, Dubrovačko Primorje, 20230 Ston [(020) 754000; fax 754344; dubrovacko-primorje.dd@inet. hr]** SE on Adriatic highway thro Neum. Take R turn after 15km for Ston & Pelješac Island, skirt Ston, up winding hill & after 8.5km turn L on sharp bend, site sp. Easy access due improved rd. Site adj ferry to Korčula. Lge, pt shd; wc; chem disp; mv service pnt; shwrs inc; EHU (6A) HRK23; shop; rest, snacks; bar; playgrnd; sand beach; tennis; games area; TV; dogs HRK21; poss cr; quiet; ccard acc; red CKE/CCI. "Beautiful setting on gd sand beach; ideal for sailing & watersports; gd san facs; welcoming owner." 15 May-30 Sep. HRK 191   2010*

SVETI JURAJ see Senj *A3*

TROGIR *B4* (2km S Coastal) *43.50510, 16.25833* **Camping Rožac, Okrug Gornji, 21220 Trogir [(021) 806105; booking@camp-rozac.hr; www.camp-rozac.hr]** Fr A8 foll sp Trogir. Cross bdge onto Trogir Island, keep L & cross 2nd bdge to Čiovo Island. Turn R & foll sp Okrug Gornji, site in 1.5km on R. NB Narr app rd to site poss diff lge o'fits. Lge, hdg/mkd pitch, shd; wc; chem disp; mv service pnt; baby facs; shwrs inc; EHU (16A) HRK27; lndry (inc dryer); shop 200m; rest, snacks; bar; beach adj; watersports; wifi; entmnt; 5% statics; dogs HRK16; bus to Trogir; adv bkg; quiet, but poss noise fr nrby beach resort; red LS/snr citizens. "Pleasant, wooded site on headland; narr app rds - not rec for lge o'fits; gd, modern facs; excel." ♦ 1 Apr-31 Oct. HRK 205 (CChq acc)   2011*

TROGIR *B4* (2km W Coastal) *43.51910, 16.22442* **Camping Seget, Hrvatskih Žrtava 121, 21218 Seget-Donji [(021) 880394; kamp@kamp-seget.hr; www.kamp-seget. hr]** Exit A1 at junc Prgomet & foll sp Trogir twd coast. Pass under coast rd at Trogir-Seget rd, turn R & site in 300m on L. Fr coast rd going SE take minor rd that runs thro Trogir & Seget Donji. Med, pt sl, pt shd; wc; chem disp; shwrs; EHU (10A) HRK23; shop on site & 300m; rest 300m; shgl beach adj; dogs HRK12; bus 300m; poss cr; Eng spkn; poss noisy high ssn. "Busy site; old, poor san facs; friendly staff; public access to beach via site; water bus to Trogir fr site; pleasant vill with excel seafood rests etc; mkt in Trogir every day except Sun." ♦ 1 May-31 Oct. HRK 214   2010*

CROATIA

TROGIR *B4* (5km W Coastal) *43.51150, 16.19430* **Camping Vranjica-Belvedere, Seget Vranjica bb, 21218 Seget Donji [(021) 798222; fax 894151; info@vranjica-belvedere.hr; www.vranjica-belvedere.hr]** Site clearly sp on coast rd, W of Trogir, 100m bef start of by-pass. Lge, mkd pitch, terr, pt sl, pt shd; wc (some cont); chem disp; mv service pnt; baby facs; private san facs avail; shwrs inc; EHU (16A) HRK36; lndry (inc dryer); supmkt; rest, snacks; bar; BBQ; playgrnd; shgl beach adj; watersports; tennis; games area; wifi; entmnt; TV rm; 30% statics; dogs HRK25; phone; bus, water taxi; poss cr; Eng spkn; adv bkg; quiet; ccard acc; red lw ssn/long stay/CKE/CCI. "Beautiful position with views of bay; lovely town; gd facs; vg site; site OK, bit scruffy but clean san facs; v helpful staff." 15 Apr-15 Oct. HRK 303 (CChq acc) 2013*

See advertisement on previous page

TUHELJSKE TOPLICE *B2* (Urban) *46.06583, 15.78513* **Camping Terme Tuhelj, Ljudevita Gaja 4, 49215 Tuhelj [(049) 203000; info@terme-tuhelj.hr; www.terme-tuhelj.hr]** N fr Zagreb on A2 for approx 24km, exit junc 5 Zabok & foll rds 24/301/205 to sp Tuheljske Toplice. Check in at Hotel Toplice. Sm, pt shd; wc; chem disp; mv service pnt; shwrs inc; EHU (6A) HRK25; lndry rm; rest, snacks; bar; playgrnd; htd pool; waterslide; paddling pool; thermal spa adj; games area; games rm; wifi; TV; no dogs; phone; bus; Eng spkn; adv bkg; quiet. "Gd, new site (2010); conv Zagreb & gd alt to Zagreb site where poss security probs." ◆ ltd. 1 Apr-31 Oct. HRK 200 2010*

UMAG *A2* (2.5km N Coastal) *45.45055, 13.52265* **Camping Stella Maris, Savudrijska Cesta b.b, 52470 Umag [(052) 710900; fax 710909; camp.stella.maris@istraturist.hr; www.istracamping.com]** Site sp on o'skts of Umag. Lge, pt shd; wc; chem disp; mv service pnt; shwrs inc; EHU (10A) inc; gas; lndry; shop; rest, snacks adj; playgrnd; pool 200m; shgl beach; watersports; bike hire; entmnt; 25% statics; dogs HRK27; m'van o'night area; Eng spkn; adv bkg; ccard acc; red long stay/CKE/CCI. "Gd for touring Istrian peninsula; helpful staff; lge pitches; gd, modern san facs; use of amenities in hotel adj." ◆ ltd. 26 Mar-31 Oct. HRK 233 2010*

UMAG *A2* (10km N Coastal) *45.48550, 13.56523* **FKK Camping Kanegra (Naturist), Kanegra b.b, 52470 Umag [(052) 709000; fax 709499; camp.kanegra@istraturist.hr; www.istracamping.com]** Fr Trieste foll sp Slovenia, then Umag. Bef Umag foll sp Savudrija, site well sp. Lge, mkd pitch, pt shd; htd wc; chem disp (wc); mv service pnt; baby facs; shwrs; EHU (10A) inc; gas; lndry; shop; rest, snacks; bar; playgrnd; beach adj; tennis; watersports; tennis; bike hire; games area; internet; entmnt; TV; 40% statics; dogs HRK27; phone; poss cr; Eng spkn; adv bkg; quiet; ccard acc; red CKE/CCI. "Clean san facs; excel." ◆ 23 Apr-26 Sep. HRK 233 2010*

UMAG *A2* (6km S Coastal) *45.39271, 13.54193* **Autocamp Finida, Križine br 55A, 52470 Umag [(052) 756296; fax 756295; camp.finida@instraturist.hr; www.istracamping. com]** Site clearly sp. Lge, mkd pitch, pt sl, pt shd; wc; chem disp; mv service pnt; baby facs; shwrs inc; EHU (10A) inc; lndry; shop; rest, snacks; bar; playgrnd; shgl beach adj; bike hire; TV; 50% statics; dogs HRK25; phone; bus; poss cr; Eng spkn; adv bkg; quiet; ccard acc; red long stay/CKE/CCI. "Gd base for touring Istria; gd, clean, modern facs; lovely site amongst oak trees; friendly staff." 23 Apr-30 Sep. HRK 213 2009*

UMAG *A2* (8km S Coastal) *45.36540, 13.54473* **Camping Park Umag, Karigador b.b, 52466 Lovrečica [(052) 725040; fax 725053; camp.park.umag@istraturist.hr; www.istracamping.com]** Fr Novigrad, take coast rd N twd Umag. Site in 6km twd sea. V lge, mkd pitch, pt sl, pt shd; wc; chem disp; mv service pnt; baby facs; fam bthrm; shwrs inc; EHU (6A) inc; gas; lndry; supmkt; rest, snacks; bar; playgrnd; pools; paddling pool; boat anchorage & own rocky beach adj; tennis; games area; wifi; entmnt; TV; 20% statics; dogs HRK25; m'van o'night area; Eng spkn; adv bkg; ccard acc; red long stay/CKE/CCI. "Excel site for beach holiday; many leisure facs inc dog shwrs! immac san facs; narr site rds; sm pitches & v muddy after rain." ◆ 10 Apr-4 Oct. HRK 293 2010*

VODICE *B3* (2.5km E Coastal) *43.75268, 15.78981* **Camping Imperial, Vatroslava Lisinskog 2, 22211 Vodice [tel/fax (022) 454412 or (022) 454488 (LS); reservations@rivijera. hr; www.rivijera.hr]** Fr N on E65 pass INA service stn in Vodice, then at rndabt foll Hotel Imperial & site sps. Fr S site sp at ent to town. Med, mkd pitch, terr, pt shd; wc; chem disp; baby facs; shwrs inc; EHU (16A) inc; shop; rest, snacks; bar; BBQ; playgrnd; 2 pools (1 htd covrd); waterslide; paddling pool; shgl beach adj; fishing; watersports; tennis; bike hire; games rm; entmnt; internet; wifi; 8% statics; dogs HRK54; bus; poss cr; Eng spkn; noisy entmnt; ccard acc; red LS/long stay; CKE/CCI. "Vg site." ◆ 22 Mar-9 Nov. HRK 274 2011*

VRSAR *A2* (2km N Coastal) *45.16505, 13.60796* **Camping Valkanela, Petalon 1, 52450 Vrsar [(052) 800200; fax 800215; info@maistra.hr; www.campingrovinjvrsar. com]** Site sp N of town fr coast rd. V lge, pt sl, terr, pt shd; wc (some cont); chem disp; mv service pnt; fam bthrm; baby rm; shwrs inc; EHU (6A) inc; gas 1km; lndry; supmkt; shops; 2 rests; snacks; bar; playgrnd; rocky beach; watersports; tennis; games area; bike hire; entmnt; TV; 40% statics; dogs HRK50; phone; poss cr; Eng spkn; adv bkg; quiet; ccard acc; red CKE/ CCI. "Excel for watersports; vg san facs; vg site for children." ◆ 25 Apr-3 Oct. HRK 275 2013*

VRSAR *A2* (500m N Urban/Coastal) *45.15555, 13.61055* **Camping Orsera, 52450 Vrsar [(052) 441330; fax 441010; camping@valamar.com; www.valamar.com]** S fr Poreč pass Autocamp Funtana, site on R. V lge, hdg/mkd pitch, pt sl, pt shd; wc; chem disp; mv service pnt; baby rm; fam bthrm; shwrs inc; EHU (10A) inc; gas; lndry; shop; rest, snacks; bar; playgrnd; shgl/rocky beach adj; waterslide; boat slipway; watersports; games area; games rm; 15% statics; dogs HRK39; phone; money exchange; poss v cr; Eng spkn; adv bkg rec high ssn; quiet; ccard acc; red CKE/CCI. "Gd situation nr Vrsar vill & harbour; clean san facs; muddy in rain; conv for town; vg." ◆ ltd. 1 Apr-3 Oct. HRK 224 2010*

Tell us about the sites you visit

CROATIA

VRSAR *A2* (1km SE Coastal) *45.14144, 13.60196* **Camping Porto Sole**, Petalon 1, 52450 Vrsar [(052) 441198; fax 441830; portosole@maistra.hr; www.campingrovinj vrsar.com] Site sp in dir Koversada. V lge, mkd pitch, hdstg, pt shd; wc (some cont); chem disp; mv service pnt; fam bthrm; baby facs; shwrs inc; EHU (10A) inc; gas; lndry (inc dryer); supmkt; rest, snacks; bar; playgrnd; pool; paddling pool; rocky beach adj; watersports; diving school; tennis; games area; bike hire; wifi; entmnt; TV rm; 20% statics; dogs HRK50; adv bkg req high ssn; quiet; ccard acc; red long stay/CKE/CCI. "Lovely area & site; excel sports facs; easy walk to town cent; vg." ♦ 24 Apr-1 Oct. HRK 239   2010*

VRSAR *A2* (1km SE Coastal) *45.14233, 13.60541* **Naturist-Park Koversada (Naturist)**, Petalon 1, 52450 Vrsar [(052) 441378; fax 441761; koversada-camp@maistra.hr; www.campingrovinjvrsar.com] Site sp fr Vrsar in dir Koversada. V lge, hdg/mkd pitch, pt sl, terr, pt shd; wc (some cont); chem disp; mv service pnt; baby facs; fam bthrm; shwrs inc; EHU (10-16A) inc; gas 500m; lndry; supmkt; shops; rests; snacks; bar; playgrnd; rocky/sandy beach; tennis; games area; diving school; watersports; bike hire; entmnt; internet; TV rm; 50% statics; dogs HRK46; phone; poss cr; Eng spkn; adv bkg; quiet; ccard acc; red long stay/CKE/CCI. "Vg, modern san facs; excel leisure facs; peaceful situation; excel; busy noisy hilly site." ♦ 26 Apr-28 Sep. HRK 214   2013*

ZADAR *B3* (3.5km N Coastal) *44.13485, 15.21599* **Autocamp Borik**, Majstora Radovana 7, 23000 Zadar [(023) 332074; fax 332065; camp@hoteliborik.hr; www.hoteliborik.hr] On ent Zadar foll sps to Borik. Site poorly sp. V lge, shd; wc; own san; chem disp; mv service pnt; shwrs; EHU (10A) inc; shop; rest, snacks; bar; playgrnd; 2 pools (1 htd, covrd) nrby; shgl beach; watersports; tennis; no dogs; phone; bus 450m; Eng spkn; no adv bkg; ccard acc; 10% red CKE/CCI. "Pt of resort complex of 6 hotels; facs poor & some cold water only; poor security; gd sw beach; gd rests nrby; site run down; NH only." ♦ 1 May-30 Sep. HRK 229   2010*

ZAGREB *B2* (12km SW Urban) *45.77389, 15.87778* **Camping Motel Plitvice**, Lučko, 10090 Zagreb [(01) 6530444; fax 6530445; motel@motel-plitvice.hr] Site at motel attached to Plitvice services on A3/E70. Access only fr m'way travelling fr N, otherwise long m'way detour fr S. Lge, pt shd; htd wc; chem disp; shwrs inc; EHU (16A) inc; lndry rm; shop; rest, snacks; bar; tennis; TV; phone; bus to town fr site; m'way noise; ccard acc; red CKE/CCI. "Ask at motel recep (excel Eng) for best way back fr city &/or details minibus to city; Zagreb well worth a visit; site shabby but facs clean & adequate - stretched when site full & in need of update." 1 May-30 Sep. HRK 199   2010*

ZAOSTROG *C4* (Centre SE Coastal) *43.13925, 17.28047* **Camp Viter**, Obala A.K. Miosica 1, 21334 Zaostrog (Dalmatija) [098 704018; fax 021 629190; info@camp-viter.com; www.camp-viter.com] Foll Camp Viter signs 600m on R after Zaostrog sign. Sm, pt shd; hdstg; ww; chem disp; mv service pnt; shwrs inc; EHU (16A) HRK25; lndry (inc dryer); shop, rest, snacks & bar 0.25km; BBQ; beach; wifi; dogs HRK25; twin axles; Eng spkn; adv bkg; Quiet; red LS; CCI. "Very helpful, friendly owners; vg." 1 Apr-31 Oct. HRK 237   2014*

ZAOSTROG *C4* (1km S Coastal) *43.13133, 17.28751* Campsite Uvala Borova, Lucica 23, 21335 Zaostrog [tel/fax 021 629 111 or 099 253 4229 (mob); camp.uvala. borova@gmail.com; www.uvala-borova.com] On rte 8 fr Split, 1km after Zaotrog on the R. Med, mkd pitch, hdstg, terr, shd; wc; chem disp; mv service pnt; shwrs; EHU (16A) HRK25; lndry; rest; bar; BBQ; pool; beach adj; games rm; wifi; tv rm; dogs HRK20; phone; bus; twin axles; Eng spkn; adv bkg; CCI. "Peaceful site with beautiful views of the Croatian coast & mountains; easy walk/cycle into Zaotrog along minor rd; friendly, helpful ownersl vg." ♦ 1 Apr-30 Sep. HRK 215   2014*

ZATON *B3* (1.5km N Coastal) *44.22960, 15.17320* **Autocamp Peroš**, Put Petra Zoranica 14, 23232 Zaton [(023) 265830; fax 265831; info@autocamp-peros.hr; www.autocamp-peros.hr] Site sp 16km N of Zadar fr rd 306 dir Nin. Foll sp to Zaton Holiday Vill & fork R to site. Sm, mkd pitch, hdstg, pt shd; wc; chem disp; mv service pnt; shwrs inc; EHU (16A) inc; lndry; shop 1.5km; snacks; bar; cooking facs; htd pool; paddling pool; watersports; shgl beach 300m; bike hire; wifi; TV rm; dogs HRK39 (no Rottweillers or Dobermans); phone; bus 1.5km; Eng spkn; adv bkg; quiet; ccard acc; red LS/long stay. "Excel, peaceful, pleasant, family-run site; vg gd new facs; helpful staff; cycle rtes to local areas of interest; close to sea & gd access to Zadar; friendly owners." 1 Mar-30 Nov. HRK 229 (CChq acc)   2011*

ZATON *B3* (1.5km N Coastal) *44.23434, 15.16605* **Camping Zaton Holiday Resort**, Široka ulica bb, 23232 Zaton [023 280215; fax 280310; camping@zaton.hr; www.zaton.hr] Site 16km NW of Zadar on Nin rd. Pt of Zaton holiday vill. Wel sp. V lge, pt shd; htd wc; chem disp; mv service pnt; shwrs inc; EHU (10A) inc; gas; lndry; supmkt; 3 rest, snacks; bar; playgrnd; pool; paddling pool; sand beach adj; boat hire; watersports; tennis; games area; entmnt; internet; 15% statics; dogs HRK65; phone; adv bkg; quiet; ccard acc; red LS; CKE/CCI. "Excel, well-run, busy site; own beach; excel, modern san facs; cent of site is 'vill' with gd value shops & rests; gd for all ages; nr ancient sm town of Nin, in walking dist; conv National Parks; v expensive outside ACSI discount period but has first class facs & nrby town well worth a visit; Croatia's best campsite; superbly laid out & equipped." ♦ 1 May-30 Sep. HRK 480   2014*

See advertisement inside the front cover

BRAC ISLAND

⊞ **BOL** *C4* (500m W Urban/Coastal) *43.26373, 16.64799* **Camping Konoba Kito**, Braćke Ceste bb, 21420 Bol [(021) 635551; www.bol.hr] Take ferry fr Makarska to Brač & take rd 113/115 to Bol (37km). On o'skrts do not turn L into town but cont twd Zlatni Rat. Pass Studenac sup'mkt on R, site on L. Sm, pt shd; wc; chem disp; shwrs inc; EHU (16A) HRK20; gas; lndry; rest; BBQ; beach 500m; TV; some statics; dogs; poss cr; Eng spkn; adv bkg; quiet. "Excel for beaches & boating; gd local food in rest; vg, friendly, family-run site; clean, well-equipped; well worth effort to get there." HRK 141   2010*

CRES ISLAND

CRES *A3* (1km N Coastal) *44.96277, 14.39694* **Camping Kovačine (Part Naturist), Melin 1/20, 51557 Cres [(051) 573150; fax 571086; campkovacine@kovacine. com; www.camp-kovacine.com]** Fr N, foll sp bef Cres on R. Fr S app thro vill of Cres. V lge, mkd pitch; wc; chem disp; baby facs; shwrs inc; EHU (12A) inc; lndry; shop; rest, snacks; playgrnd; beach; watersports; tennis; games area; sep area for naturists; wifi; dogs HRK23; Eng spkn; quiet; ccard acc; red long stay/CKE/CCI. "Site in olive grove; rocky making driving diff, but amenities gd & well-run; welcoming staff; delightful walk/cycle rte to sm vill of Cres; excel site." ♦ 4 Apr-15 Oct. HRK 276   2013*

MARTINSCICA *A3* (500m NW Coastal) *44.82108, 14.34298* **Camping Slatina, 51556 Martinščica [(051) 574127; fax 574167; info@camp-slatina.com; www.camp-slatina. com]** Fr Cres S on main rd sp Mali Lošinj for 17km. Turn R sp Martinščica, site in 8km at end of rd. V lge, hdg pitch, hdstg, terr, shd; wc; chem disp; mv service pnt; baby facs; fam bthrm; shwrs inc; EHU (10A) inc (long lead req); lndry; shop; rest, snacks; bar; playgrnd; shgl beach adj; boat launching; entmnt; internet; 20% statics; dogs HRK23; phone; poss cr; Eng spkn; adv bkg; quiet; cc acc. "Site on steep slope; newest san facs superb; beautiful island." ♦ 23 Mar-1 Oct. HRK 241   2013*

HVAR ISLAND

HVAR *B4* (4km N Coastal) *43.18970, 16.42990* **Autocamp Vira, Mala Vira b.b, 21450 Hvar [(021) 741803; info@ campvira.com; www.campvira.com]** N fr Hvar town (cent parking area on L) dir Vira, site sp. Med, mkd pitch, hdstg, pt shd; htd wc; chem disp; mv service pnt; baby facs; shwrs inc; EHU (10A); gas; lndry (inc dryer); shop; rest, snacks, bar; BBQ; playgrnd; shgl beach; bike hire; games area; wifi; entmnt; dogs HRK39; bus; phone; adv bkg; quiet; red LS/long stay. "Excel site; sea views all pitches; vg san facs; ltd water pnts; rest & bar o'look private beach; highly rec." 20 Apr-30 Sep. HRK 267   2011*

JELSA *C4* (500m E Coastal) *43.16396, 16.70306* **Camping Mina, 21465 Jelsa [(021) 761210; fax 761227; www.tzjelsa.hr]** Fr W take main rd 116. After main town junc ignore sp Hotel Mina & shortly after Autocamp Holiday turn L (rd passes thro pt of this site) & cont round bay. Site on R on promontory, sp. Lge, mkd pitch, terr, pt shd; wc; shwrs; EHU; lndry; shop; bar; playgrnd; sand beach adj; tennis nr; games area; bike hire; adv bkg; quiet. "Excel location & lovely vill, but poor facs." 1 May-30 Sep.   2009*

STARIGRAD *B4* (SW Coastal) *43.18688, 16.58655* **Camping Jurjevac, Njiva b b, 21460 Starigrad [(021) 765843; fax 765128; info@hoteli-helios.hr; www.hoteli-helios.hr]** Ferry fr Split to Starigrad, fr dock dir Starigrad, site on L in 1km on SW town o'skts. Med, pt shd; chem disp (wc); shwrs inc; EHU (10A) HRK23; shop 100m; BBQ; rocky beach 300m; watersports; bike hire; 25% statics; dogs HRK23; phone; bus 500m; poss cr; Eng spkn; adv bkg; quiet; red CKE/CCI. "Gd." 1 May-30 Sep. HRK 115   2010*

ZIVOGOSCE see Drvenik *C4*

KRK ISLAND

KRK *A3* (4km SE Coastal) *45.01638, 14.62833* **Autocamp Pila, Šetalište Ivana Brusića 2, 51521 Punat [tel/fax (051) 854020; pila@hoteli-punat.hr; www.hoteli-punat.hr]** Take coast rd, rte 2 twd Split. At Kraljevica, turn R onto rd 103 over Krk toll bdge. Foll sp for Krk, Punat. Site sp at T-junc after Punat Marina & vill. Lge, pt shd; wc; chem disp; mv service pnt; baby facs; some serviced pitches; shwrs inc; EHU (10-16A) inc; lndry (inc dryer); shops adj; rest, snacks, cooking facs; playgrnd; beach adj; fishing; watersports; wifi; entmnt; TV; 80% statics; dogs HRK32; quiet; ccard acc; red CKE/CCI. "Well-run, big site; clean facs; gd for families with sm children; boat hire; boat trips; sm picturesque vill; lots to do; poss cr." ♦ 12 Apr-18 Oct. HRK 347   2014*

KRK *A3* (5km SE Coastal) *44.98972, 14.62805* **FKK Camp Konobe (Naturist), Obala 94, 51521 Punat [(051) 854049; fax 854036; konobe@hoteli-punat.hr; www.hoteli-punat. hr]** Site is approx 30km fr Krk Bdge, sp fr Krk-Baska rd. Lge, pt shd; wc; mv service pnt; baby facs; shwrs inc; EHU (16A) inc; lndry (inc dryer) shop; rest, snacks; BBQ; playgrnd; rocky beach adj; watersports; tennis; wifi; entmnt; 10% statics; dogs HRK23; sep car park; adv bkg; ccard acc; red CKE/CCI. "Vg san facs; beach with crystal clear water." ♦ Easter-30 Sep. HRK 225   2010*

KRK *A3* (16km SE Coastal) *44.96048, 14.68402* **Autocamp Škrila, Stara Baška, 51521 Punat [(051) 844678; fax 844705; skrila@valamar.com; www.skrila.hr]** Fr Krk E on rd 102, turn S dir Punat & Stara Baška. Site on R at bottom of hill approx 8km after Punat. Lge, hdstg, terr, unshd, mkd pitch; wc; chem disp; shwrs inc; EHU HRK27; shop; rest; bar; shg beach adj; statics; dogs €2; poss cr; Eng spkn; quiet. "Approx 50 touring pitches; friendly, helpful staff; gd security; lovely, isolated position; new excel san facs (2014)." 13 Apr-7 Oct. HRK 316   2014*

See advertisement on page 151

KRK *A3* (2km S Coastal) *45.02444, 14.59222* **FKK Camp Politin (Naturist), 51500 Krk [(051) 221351; fax 221246; politin@valamar.com; www.valamar.com]** Site S of Krk town on Baška rd, sp. Lge, unshd; wc; chem disp; shwrs inc; EHU (6A) inc; gas; lndry; shop; rest; playgrnd; shgl beach; watersports; boat-launching; tennis; entmnt; dogs HRK33; poss cr; quiet; ccard acc; red INF/CKE/CCI. "Hilly walk to town; gd renovated san facs." ♦ 24 Apr-9 Oct. HRK 221   2009*

⊞ **KRK** *A3* (800m SW Rural/Coastal) *45.02246, 14.56210* **Autocamp Bor, Crikvenička 10, 51500 Krk [(051) 221581; fax 222429; info@camp-bor.hr; www.camp-bor.hr]** Foll sp to Krk cent. At bottom of hill turn R at rndabt, site well sp up hill. Med, mkd pitch, hdstg, pt sl, terr, pt shd/unshd; wc; mv service pnt; shwrs inc; EHU (10A) HRK33; lndry; rest, snacks; bar; shgl beach 800m; bike hire; many statics; dogs HRK28; poss cr; Eng spkn; adv bkg; quiet. "Well-maintained, family-run site, but some pitches bare earth; close to lovely town & harbour; choice of gd beaches." HRK 172   2011*

KRK *A3* (300m W Urban/Coastal) *45.01875, 14.56701*
Autocamp Ježevac, Planicka bb, 51500 Krk
[(051) 221081; fax 221137; jezevac@valamar.com;
www.valamar.com] Fr main island rd heading S, app Krk,
take 1st rd on R (W) sp Centar. At rndabt take 2nd exit sp
Autocamp. App to site thro housing estate. V lge, hdstg, pt
sl, pt shd; wc; chem disp (wc); mv service pnt; some serviced
pitches; shwrs inc; EHU (10-16A) inc; lndry (inc dryer); shop;
rest, snacks; bar; playgrnd; shgl beach adj; watersports; tennis;
games area; wifi; entmnt; dogs HRK34; phone; poss cr; Eng
spkn; poss noisy high ssn; ccard acc; red CKE/CCI. "Conv for
touring Krk Island; pleasant, gd value rest with view of old
town; registration fee payable 1st night; busy site; levelling
poss diff for m'vans." ♦ 1 Apr-10 Oct. HRK 229   2010*

See advertisement on page 151

NJIVICE *A2* (400m N Coastal) *45.16971, 14.54701* **Autocamp
Njivice**, 51512 Njivice [(051) 846168; fax 846185; anton.
bolonic@finvestcorp.hr; www.hoteli-njivice.hr]
8km S of Krk Bdge on rd 102 turn R to Njivice. Site not well sp
but foll sp to hotel area N of town cent. V lge, shd; wc (mainly
cont); chem disp; mv service pnt; shwrs inc; EHU (6-10A)
HRK28; shop; rest; bar; shgl/rocky beach adj; playgrnd nr; wifi;
60% statics; dogs HRK24; phone; bus; poss cr; Eng spkn; no
adv bkg; ccard acc; red CKE/CCI. "Less cr than other Krk sites;
gd facs." ♦ 1 May-30 Sep. HRK 155 (CChq acc)   2010*

"That's changed – Should I let The Club know?"

If you find something on site that's different from
the site entry, fill in a report and let us know. See
www.caravanclub.co.uk/europereport.

LOSINJ ISLAND

MALI LOSINJ *A3* (2km SW Coastal) *44.53599, 14.45064*
Camping Čikat, Drazica 1, 51550 Mali Lošinj [(051) 232125;
fax 231708; info@camp-cikat.com; www.camp-cikat.com]
Sp fr town. V lge, hdstg, terr, shd; wc (some cont); chem disp;
mv service pnt; baby facs; shwrs inc; EHU (16A); lndry; shop;
rest, snacks; bar; playgrnd; shgl beach adj; bike hire; entmnt;
many statics; dogs HRK21; poss cr; adv bkg; quiet; ccard acc;
CKE/CCI. "Touring pitches on terr with sea views; gd san facs;
easy walk/cycle to attractive town; boat trips & ferry to Zadar
daily fr mid-Jun." ♦ 4 Apr-20 Oct. HRK 171   2009*

MALI LOSINJ *A3* (500m W Coastal) *44.53397, 14.45461*
Kredo Camping & Hotel, Šet. Dr Von M-Montesole 5,
Čikat, 51550 Mali Lošinj [(051) 233595; fax 238274; info@
kre-do.hr; www.kre-do.hr] Hotel & site sp on Čikat rd. Med,
shd; htd wc; chem disp; mv service pnt; some private bthrms
avail; sauna; baby facs; shwrs; EHU HRK11; lndry (inc dryer);
shop; supmkt 1.5km; rest, snacks; bar; playgrnd; beach adj;
watersports; boat hire; bike hire; tennis 400m; fitness rm; wifi;
TV; some statics; dogs HRK30; adv bkg; quiet. 1 Mar-1 Dec.
HRK 217   2010*

MALI LOSINJ *A3* (4km NW Coastal) *44.55555, 14.44166*
Camping Village Poljana, Privlaka 19, 51550 Mali Lošinj
[(051) 231726; fax 231728; info@poljana.hr info@baia
holiday.com; www.baiaholiday.com] On main island rd
1km bef vill of Lošinj, sp. Two ferries a day fr Rijeka take car
& c'van on 2hr trip to island. V lge, pt sl, terr, shd; wc (some
cont); chem disp; mv service pnt; baby facs; private washrms
avail; shwrs; EHU (6-16A) inc; gas; lndry (inc dryer); shop; rest,
snacks; bar; playgrnd; shgl beach; watersports; sep naturist
beach; tennis; games area; boat & bike hire; wifi; entmnt;
50% statics; dogs 61; phone; poss cr; adv bkg; quiet; ccard
acc; CKE/CCI. "Site in pine forest; sw with dolphins nrby." ♦
24 Mar-31 Oct. HRK 312   2011*

MURTER ISLAND

JEZERA *B3* (800m NW Coastal) *43.79313, 15.62734*
Holiday Village Jezera Lovišća, Zaratic 1, 22242 Jezera
[(022) 439600; fax 439215; info@jezera-kornati.hr;
www.jezera-kornati.hr] S on main coast rd turn R 4km SE of
Pirovac sp Murter. Foll winding rd into vill & over swing bdge
on island. Foll rd round to R. Site on R in 2km. V lge, pt sl, pt
shd; wc; chem disp; shwrs inc; EHU (10A) HRK29; shop, rest,
snacks high ssn; bar; playgrnd; shgl beach adj; watersports;
tennis; entmnt; internet; TV rm; 50% statics; dogs HRK46;
quiet; ccard acc; red long stay/CKE/CCI. "Excel site; boat trips
organised fr site; excel rest; lots to do in area." ♦
26 Apr-9 Oct. HRK 212   2009*

RAB ISLAND

LOPAR *A3* (3km E Coastal) *44.82345, 14.73735* **Hotel Village
San Marino**, 51281 Lopar [(051) 775133; fax 775290;
ac-sanmarino@imperial.hr; www.rab-camping.com]
Fr Rab town N to Lopar, sp ferry. At x-rds turn R sp San Marino,
site sp. V lge, mkd pitch, some hdstg, terr, shd; wc (some
cont); chem disp; mv service pnt; baby facs; fam bthrm; shwrs
inc; EHU (16A) inc; lndry (inc dryer); shop; rest, snacks; bar;
playgrnd; sand beach adj; watersports; tennis; games area;
entmnt; TV; 10% statics; dogs HRK29; phone; bus; poss cr;
Eng spkn; adv bkg; ccard acc; red CKE/CCI. "Superb, family site
on delightful island; pitches on sandy soil in pine woods." ♦
1 Apr-30 Sep. HRK 187   2011*

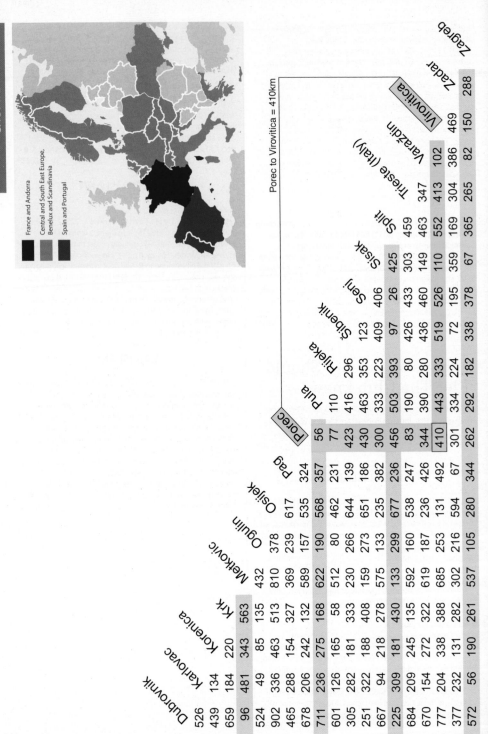

CROATIA

Legend:
- France and Andorra
- Central and South East Europe, Benelux and Scandinavia
- Spain and Portugal

Porec to Virovitica = 410km

Distance chart (km):

From \ To	Karlovac	Korenica	Krk	Metković	Ogulin	Osijek	Pag	Porec	Pula	Rijeka	Šibenik	Senj	Sisak	Split	Trieste (Italy)	Varaždin	Virovitica	Zadar	Zagreb
Dubrovnik	526	439	659	96	524	902	465	678	711	601	305	251	667	225	684	670	777	377	572
Karlovac		134	184	481	49	336	288	206	236	126	282	322	94	309	209	154	204	232	56
Korenica			220	343	85	353	154	242	275	165	181	188	218	181	245	272	338	131	190
Krk				563	135	513	327	132	168	58	333	408	278	430	135	322	388	282	261
Metković					432	810	369	589	622	512	230	159	575	133	592	619	685	302	537
Ogulin						378	239	157	190	80	266	273	133	299	160	187	253	216	105
Osijek							617	535	568	462	644	651	235	677	538	236	131	594	280
Pag								324	357	231	139	186	382	236	247	426	492	67	344
Porec									56	77	423	430	300	456	83	344	410	301	262
Pula										110	416	463	333	503	190	390	443	334	292
Rijeka											296	353	223	393	80	280	333	224	182
Šibenik												123	409	97	426	436	519	72	338
Senj													406	26	433	460	526	195	378
Sisak														425	303	149	110	359	67
Split															459	463	552	169	365
Trieste (Italy)																347	413	304	265
Varaždin																	102	386	82
Virovitica																		469	150
Zadar																			288

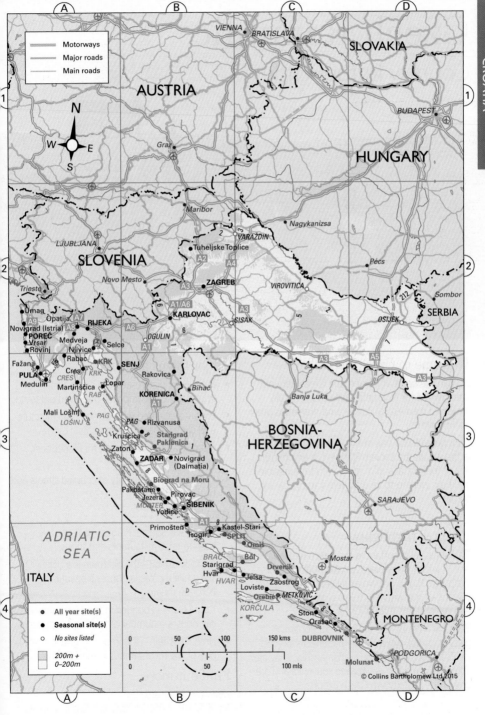

Motorways
Major roads
Main roads

VIENNA BRATISLAVA
SLOVAKIA

N
W E
S

AUSTRIA

BUDAPEST

Graz

HUNGARY

Maribor

Nagykanizsa

VARAŽDIN

LJUBLJANA

Tuheljske Toplice

Pécs

SLOVENIA

Novo Mesto

A2

A4

ZAGREB

Trieste

VIROVITICA

Sombor

Umag
Opatija
Novigrad (Istria)
POREČ
Vrsar
Rovinj
Fažana
PULA
Medulin

A9
A8

RIJEKA

Medveja
Njivice
Rabac
Cres
Martinšcica

A7

A6

A1/A6
KARLOVAC

A3

SISAK

OGULIN

A1

Selce

KRK

SENJ

Rakovica

Bihać

SERBIA
OSIJEK

A3

A5

A3

CRES
KRK

Lopar

RAB

KORENICA

A1

Banja Luka

Mali Lošinj
LOŠINJ

PAG

PAG

Rizvanusa

Kruščica

Starigrad
Paklenica

BOSNIA-
HERZEGOVINA

Zaton

ZADAR

Novigrad
(Dalmatia)

Biograd na Moru

Pakoštane
Jezera
MURTER

Pirovac

Vodice

ŠIBENIK

SARAJEVO

Primošten

A1

Kaštel-Stari

Trogir

SPLIT

ADRIATIC
SEA

ITALY

Omiš

BRAC

Bol

Mostar

Starigrad

Hvar

HVAR

Jelsa

Drvenik

Zaostrog

Lovište

Orebić

KORČULA

METKOVIC

All year site(s)
Seasonal site(s)
No sites listed

200m +
0–200m

Ston

Orašac

MONTENEGRO

0   50   100   150 kms

0   50   100 mls

DUBROVNIK

Molunat

PODGORICA

© Collins Bartholomew Ltd 2015

Czech Republic
Country Introduction

Hrad Karlšstejn

Welcome to Czech Republic

Lying in the heart of Europe, the Czech Republic is renowned for its ornate castles, fantastically preserved medieval buildings, and numerous other cultural sights.

Considered to be one of the most beautiful cities in the world, the capital, Prague, is a wonderful mix of traditional and modern with treasures old and new waiting to be discovered around every corner.

Country highlights

Traditions are important in the Czech Republic, one of which takes places on the 30th of April – Walpurgis Night. Known as pálení čarodějnic (the burning of the witches), this is a night of bonfires and celebrations throughout the country.

The Czech Republic is the home of Bohemian glass or crystal, which is international renowned for its beauty, quality and craftsmanship. They are immensely popular as gifts and souvenirs and are one of the best known Czech exports.

Major towns and cities

- Prague – a picturesque city home to an impressive castle and well-preserved old town.

- Brno – a city filled with gorgeous architecture and captivating historical sights.

- Plzeň – famous worldwide for Pilsner beer, created here in 1842.

- Olomouc – a quaint city of cobbled streets and historic buildings.

Attractions

- Wenceslas Square, Prague – bursting with monuments, restaurants and shops.

- Český Krumlov – the old town is a UNESCO site while the castle houses a beautiful baroque theatre.

- Kutná Hora – Founded in the 12th century, this city houses a number of spectacular churches.

- Hrad Karlšstejn – this imposing gothic castle is one of the most famous in the country.

Find out more

www.czechtourism.com
Tel:0042 (0)22 4861 578 Czech Republic Tourism

Country Information

Population (approx): 10.6 million

Capital: Prague (population approx 1.23 million)

Area: 78,864 sq km

Bordered by: Austria, Germany, Poland, Slovakia

Terrain: Diverse landscape with rolling hills and plains in the west (Bohemia) surrounded by low mountains; higher hills and heavily forested mountains in the east (Moravia)

Climate: Temperate continental with warm, showery summers and cold, cloudy, snowy winters

Highest Point: Snezka 1,602m

Language: Czech

Local Time: GMT or BST + 1, i.e. 1 hour ahead of the UK all year

Currency: Czech crown (CZK) £1 = CZK 38, CZK 100 = £2.62 (September 2015)

Emergency numbers: Police 158; Fire brigade 150; Ambulance 155 (operators speak English) or 112.

Public Holidays 2016: Jan 1; Mar 28; May 1, 8 (National Liberation Day); Jul 5, 6; Sep 28 (St Wenceslas), Oct 28 (Independence Day); Nov 17; Dec 24, 25, 26.

School summer holidays are from the beginning of July to the end of August.

Camping and Caravanning

Campsites are divided into four categories from 1 to 4 stars. Normally campsites are open from May to mid September, although some campsites stay open all year. They usually close at night between 10pm and 6am.

Campsites are generally good value and in recent years many have upgraded their facilities. Privacy in the showers may be a problem due to a shortage of, or lack of, shower curtains and only a communal dressing area.

Some sites have communal kitchen facilities which enable visitors to make great savings on their own gas supply.

Motorhomes are recommended to carry a very long hose with a variety of tap connectors. Refill the onboard tank whenever possible as few sites have easily accessible mains water.

Casual/wild camping is not permitted and fines are imposed for violation of this law, especially in national parks. It is prohibited to sleep in a caravan or motorhome outside a campsite.

Cycling

There are around 2,500km of cycle tracks, known as Greenways, in tourist areas. A long-distance cycle track links Vienna and Prague and there are many tracks linking the Czech Republic to Austria and Poland. Helmets are compulsory for cyclists under the age of 18.

Electricity and Gas

Current on campsites varies between 6 and 16 amps. Plugs have two round pins. A few campsites have CEE connections but not many. Reversed polarity may be encountered.

You may find that Campingaz 907 cylinders are available from large DIY warehouses.

Entry Formalities

British and Irish passport holders may visit the Czech Republic for up to three months without a visa. If intending to stay longer, visitors must register with the police. There are no identity checks at the borders with neighbouring countries and normally it is not necessary for a driver to stop when crossing the border. However, random identity checks may be made at any time at the border or inside the country itself.

Medical Services

For minor ailments first consult staff at a pharmacy (lékárna) who are qualified to give advice and are sometimes able to sell drugs which are normally only available on prescription in the UK. Language may be a problem outside Prague; if you need particular drugs or a repeat prescription, take an empty bottle or remaining pills with you. For more serious matters requiring a visit to a doctor go to a medical centre (poliklinika) or hospital (nemocnice).

British nationals may obtain emergency medical and hospital treatment and prescriptions on presentation of a European Health Insurance Card

(EHIC). You may have to make a contribution towards costs. Make sure that the doctor or dentist you see is contracted to the public health insurance service, the CMU (most are), otherwise you will have to pay in full for private treatment and for any prescription medicines and the Czech insurance service will not reimburse you. See www.cmu.cz, email info@cmu.cz for advice on healthcare in the Czech Republic.

In parts of the country where few foreign visitors venture, medical staff may not be aware of the rights conferred on you by an EHIC. If you have difficulties contact the British Embassy in Prague.

Outbreaks of hepatitis A occur sporadically, particularly in the Prague and Central Bohemia areas, and immunisation is advised for long-stay visitors to rural areas and those who plan to travel outside tourist areas. Take particular care with food and water hygiene.

Opening Hours

Banks – Mon-Fri 9am-5pm. Some foreign exchange bureaux in Prague are open 24 hours.

Museums – Tue-Sun 10am-6pm; closed Monday

Post Offices – Mon-Fri 8am-6pm, some open on Saturday morning; main post office in Prague (Jindrisska Street 14) is open 2am-12am

Shops – Mon-Fri 9am-6pm, small shops usually close at lunchtime; Sat 9am-1pm; some food shops open on Sundays

Safety and Security

There is a high incidence of petty theft, particularly in major tourist areas in Prague, and pickpocketing is common at popular tourist attractions. Particular care should be taken around the main railway station and on trains and trams, particularly routes to and from Prague Castle where pickpockets may operate.

Beware of fake plain-clothes police officers asking to see your foreign currency and passport. If approached, don't get out your passport. You can call 158 or 112 to check if they are genuine officers, or offer to go to the nearest police station or find a uniformed officer. No police officer has the right to check your money or its authenticity.

If your passport, wallet or other items are lost or stolen you should report the incident immediately to the nearest police station and obtain a police report. A police station that is used to dealing with foreign travellers and is open 24 hours, is at Jungmannovo Námistí 9, Praha 1, 24 hour telephone number 974 851 750; nearest metro: Müstek. Any theft of property must be reported in person to the police within 24 hours in order to obtain a crime number.

Seasonal flooding, usually in spring, occurs occasionally.

The Czech Republic shares with the rest of Europe an underlying threat from terrorism. Attacks could be indiscriminate and against civilian targets, including tourist attractions.

British Embassy
THUNOVSKÁ 14
118 00 PRAGUE 1
Tel: 257402111
www.ukinczechrepublic.fco.gov.uk
Email: ukinczechrepublic@fco.gov.uk

Irish Embassy
VELVYSLANECTVÍ IRSKA
TRŽIŠTĚ 13, 118 00 PRAHA 1
Tel: 257011280
www.embassyofireland.cz
Email: pragueembassy@dfa.ie

Documents

Driving Licence
The Czech Republic authorities require foreign drivers to carry a photocard driving licence. If you still have an old-style driving license you should update it to a photocard before you travel, or obtain an International Driving Permit to accompany your old-style licence. The minimum driving age is 18.

Passport
You must have a valid passport to enter Czech Republic. It is recommended that your passport is valid after your planned departure date in case of an unforeseen emergency, which may prevent you from leaving.

British nationals with passports in poor condition have been refused entry so you should ensure that your passport is in an acceptable state.

If you hold a British passport where your nationality is shown as anything other than British Citizen contact the Czech Embassy in London to determine whether you require a visa for entry.

Vehicle(s)

Carry your vehicle registration certificate (V5C), insurance details and MOT certificate (if applicable). If you are not the owner of the vehicle you are advised to carry a letter of authority from the owner permitting you to drive it.

Money

The best place to exchange foreign currency is at banks, where commission rates are generally lower. In Prague some foreign exchange bureaux are open

24 hours. Scottish and Northern Irish bank notes will not be changed. Never exchange money with vendors on the street as notes are often counterfeit.

Credit cards are often accepted in tourist areas. Cash points are widely available but take care using them from a personal security point of view. Many retail outlets accept payment in euros.

Motoring in the Czech Republic

Accidents

If an accident causes injury or damage in excess of CZK 100,000 it must be reported to the police immediately. You should wait at the scene of the accident until the police arrive and then obtain a police report. If your vehicle is only slightly damaged it is still a good idea to report the accident to the police as they will issue a certificate which will facilitate the exportation of the vehicle.

Alcohol

It is prohibited to drink alcohol before or whilst driving. No degree of alcohol is permitted in the blood and driving under the influence of alcohol is considered a criminal offence. This rule also applies to cyclists and horse riders. Frequent random breath-testing takes places and drivers are likely to be breathalysed after an accident, even a minor one.

Breakdown Service

The motoring organisation ÚAMK provides roadside assistance and towing services 24 hours a day, telephone 1230 or 261104123. Emergency operators speak English. Breakdown assistance is provided for all motorists at a basic cost of approximately CZK 400 for 30 minutes + CZK 24 per kilometre travelled, payable in cash (2015). Extra charges apply at night, at weekends and for towing.

The vehicles used for road assistance are yellow Skodas, bearing the ÚAMK and/or ARC Transistance logos or the words 'Silnični Služba', together with the telephone number of the emergency centre. ÚMAK also uses the services of contracted companies who provide assistance and towing. These vehicles are also marked with the ÚAMK logo and the telephone number of the emergency centre.

Essential Equipment

First aid kit

You are required to carry a basic first aid kit in your vehicle.

Lights

Dipped headlights are compulsory at all times, regardless of weather conditions. Bulbs are more likely to fail with constant use and it is recommended that you carry a complete set of spares.

Drivers are required to signal when leaving a roundabout and when overtaking cyclists.

Reflective Jacket/Waistcoat

If your vehicle has broken down, or in the event of an emergency, you must wear a reflective jacket or waistcoat on all roads, carriageways and motorways when getting out of your vehicle. Passengers who leave the vehicle, for example to assist with a repair, should also wear one. Jackets should, therefore, be kept inside your vehicle, and not in the boot. These must be of an EU standard EN471.

Child Restraint System

Children under 1.5m in height must use a suitable child restraint conforming to ECE standard 44/03 or 44/04. If in the front seat, the restraint must be rear facing with any airbag deactivated.

If there are no seatbelts fitted in the vehicle children over the age of 3 may travel in the rear of the vehicle without a child restraint.

Warning Triangles

You must carry a warning triangle, which must be placed at least 100m behind the vehicle on motorways and highways and 50m behind on other roads. Drivers may use Hazard Warning lights in conjunction with the warning triangle.

Winter Driving

Winter tyres are compulsory from 1 November to 31 March on all wheels of vehicles up to 3.5 tonnes when there is compacted snow or ice on the road. They are also compulsory whenever the temperature is lower than 4°C and there is a possibility of snow or ice on the road. On roads where there are winter tyres signs (see below) , the regulations apply even if the road surface is free of snow and ice, regardless of the weather.

Sign for winter tyres (if shown with a line through indicates the end of restriction)

Vehicles over 3,500 kg must be fitted with winter tyres on the driving wheels or carry snow chains. A full list of roads where this rule applies can be found on www.uamk.cz.

Fuel

Some petrol stations on main roads, international routes and in main towns are open 24 hours a day. Most accept credit cards.

Diesel pumps are marked 'Nafta'. LPG is called 'Autoplyn' or 'Plyn' and is widely available at many filling stations. A list of these is available from the ÚAMK and a map is available from filling stations, or see www.lpg.cz and click on 'Čerpací stanice'.

Parking

Vehicles may only be parked on the right of the road. In a one-way road, parking is also allowed on the left.

Continuous or broken yellow lines along the carriageway indicate parking prohibitions or restrictions. Visitors are advised to park only in officially controlled and guarded parking areas since cars belonging to tourists may be targeted by thieves. Illegally-parked vehicles may be clamped or towed away.

Prague city centre is divided into three parking zones: the orange and green zones are limited to two and six hours respectively between 8am and 6pm, and the blue zones are for residents only. Parking meters have been introduced in both Prague and Brno.

Priority

At uncontrolled intersections which are not marked by a priority road sign, priority must be given to vehicles coming from the right. Where there are priority signs, these may easily be missed and care is therefore needed at junctions which, according to recent visitors, may have no road markings.

Trams turning right have priority over traffic moving alongside them on the right. Drivers must slow down and, if necessary, stop to allow buses and trams to merge with normal traffic at the end of a bus lane. On pedestrian crossings pedestrians have right of way, except if the vehicle approaching is a tram.

Roads

Czech drivers are sometimes described as reckless (particularly when overtaking). Speeding is common and the law on the wearing of seat belts is sometimes ignored.

In general roads are in a good condition and well-signposted. Roads are being upgraded and many have new numbers. It is essential, therefore, to have an up-to-date road map or atlas.

Care is required where roads follow an old route through a village when there may be sudden bends in an otherwise straight road.

Road Signs and Markings

Road signs and markings conform to international standards. Continuous white lines indicate no overtaking, but are often ignored.

The following road signs may be encountered:

Czech	English Translation
Bez poplatků	Free of charge (some motorway or express roads)
Chod'te vlevo	Pedestrians must walk on the left
Dálkový provoz	By-pass
Nebezpečí smyku	Danger of skidding
Nemocnice	Hospital
Objizdka	Diversion
Pozor děti	Attention children
Průjezd zakázán	Closed to all vehicles
Rozsvit' světla	Lights needed
Úsek častých nehod	Accident blackspot
Zákaz zastavení	Stopping prohibited

Traffic Lights

A traffic light signal with a green arrow shows that drivers may turn in the direction indicated by the arrow. If a yellow light in the form of a walking figure accompanies the signal, this means that pedestrians may cross the road and drivers must give them right of way. A green light lit at the same time as a red or yellow light means that drivers may turn in the direction indicated by the arrow on condition that they give way to other traffic and to pedestrians.

An illuminated speed signal indicates the speed at which to travel in order to arrive at the next set of traffic lights when they are green.

Speed Limits

	Open Road (km/h)	Motorway (km/h)
Car Solo	90	130
Car towing caravan/trailer	80	80
Motorhome under 3500kg	90	130
Motorhome 3500-7500kg	80	80

Motorhomes over 3,500 kg and cars towing a caravan or trailer are restricted to 80 km/h (50 mph) on motorways and main roads and lower limits in urban areas. Speed limits are strictly enforced and drivers exceeding them may be fined on the spot. Police with radar guns are much in evidence.

The use of radar detectors is prohibited and GPS systems which indicate the position of fixed speed cameras must have that function deactivated.

Traffic Jams

The volume of traffic has increased considerably in recent years, particularly in and around Prague, including its ring road. Traffic jams may also occur on the E50/D1 (Prague-Mirošovice), the E48/R6 (Prague-Kladno), the E50/D5 (Plzeň-Rozvadov) and on the E50/D1 (Prague-Brno).

Traffic may be heavy at border crossings from Germany, Austria and Slovakia, particularly at weekends, resulting in extended waiting times. Petrol is cheaper than in Germany and you may well find queues at petrol stations near the border. Traffic information can be obtained from the ÚAMK Information Centre, tel 261104333, or from their website www.uamk.cz.

Violation of Traffic Regulations

The police are authorised to impose and collect on-the-spot fines up to CZK 5,000 and to withdraw a driving licence in the case of a serious offence. An official receipt should be obtained. Efforts are under way to improve enforcement of traffic regulations and a points system has been introduced, together with stricter penalties.

Motorways

There are approximately 1240 km of motorways and express roads. New sections of motorways are being built and on some motorways junctions are being renumbered to correspond with kilometre markers.

There is a good network of service areas with petrol stations, restaurants and shops, together with rest areas with picnic facilities. Emergency telephones connected to the motorway police are placed at 2 km intervals.

Emergency corridors are compulsory on motorways and dual carriageways. Drivers are required to create a precautionary emergency corridor at least 3m wide to provide access for emergency vehicles whenever congestion occurs. Drivers in the left-hand lane must move as far over to the left as possible, and drivers in the central and right-hand lanes must move as far over to the right as possible.

Motorway Tolls – Vignette

To use motorways and express roads you must purchase a vignette (windscreen sticker) which must be displayed on the right hand side of your windscreen. This is available from post offices, ÚAMK branch offices, petrol stations and border posts where euros may be used in payment. If you have been to the Czech Republic before, make sure you remove your old sticker.

Charges in 2015 (subject to change) are CZK 1,500 for an annual vignette, CZK 440 for one month and CZK 310 for 10 consecutive days. For more information please visit www.motorway.cz/stickers.

Vehicles over 3,500 kg

Vehicles over 3,500 kg are subject to an electronic toll (mýto) and vehicle owners must register with the toll-collection service to obtain an on-board device called a Premid which must be fixed on your windscreen inside the vehicle and for which a deposit is required.

Tolls vary according to the emissions category and weight of the vehicle and distance driven. You must be able to show your vehicle documentation when obtaining the device but if your vehicle registration certificate (V5C) does not give an emissions category, then your vehicle will be classified in category Euro 2 for the purposes of this system. For more information please visit www.premid.cz before you travel.

Touring

It is not necessary to tip in restaurants but if you have received very good service add 10% to the bill or round it up.

Smoking is not permitted in public places (public transport, places of entertainment, etc) and restaurant owners must provide an area for non-smokers.

A Prague Card offers entrance to over 50 tourist attractions and discounts on excursions and activities. It is available from tourist offices, main metro stations, some travel agents and hotels or order online from www.praguecard.com.

German is the most widely spoken foreign language and a basic understanding is particularly helpful in southern Bohemia. However, many young people speak English.

Public Transport

Prague city centre is very congested, so park outside and use buses, trams or the metro which are efficient and cheap. There are guarded Park and Ride facilities at a number of metro stations around Prague.

Public transport tickets must be purchased before travelling and are available from newspaper stands ('Trafika'), tobacconists, convenience stores and from vending machines at stations. Special tourist tickets are available for one or three days. Tickets must be validated before the start of your journey at the yellow machines at metro stations or on board trams and buses, including before boarding the funicular tram at Petřín. Failure to do so may result in an on-the-spot fine.

Take extra care when in the vicinity of tram tracks and make sure you look both ways. Trams cannot stop quickly nor can they avoid you if you are on the track.

As a pedestrian you may be fined if you attempt to cross the road or cross tram tracks within 50 metres of a designated crossing point or traffic lights. You may also be fined if you cross at a pedestrian crossing if the green pedestrian light is not illuminated.

For reasons of safety and economy use major taxi companies wherever possible. If you telephone to order a taxi these companies are usually able to tell you in advance the type, number and colour of the car allocated to you. If you do pick up a taxi in the street always check the per kilometre price before getting in. The price list must be clearly displayed and the driver must provide a receipt if requested.

BEROUN *B2* (10km NE Rural) *50.0115, 14.1505*
Camping Valek, Chrustenice 155, 267 12 Chrustenice
[tel/fax 311 672 147; info@campvalek.cz; www.campvalek.
cz] SW fr Prague on E50; take exit 10 twd Loděnice then N to
Chrustenice. Foll sp. Lge, pt shd; wc; chem disp; mv service
pnt; shwrs inc; EHU (10A) CZK110; lndry; sm shop & 4km; rest,
snacks; bar; BBQ; playgrnd; pool; tennis; entmnt at w/end; TV;
10% statics; dogs CZK45; phone; Eng spkn; adv bkg; quiet; red
long stay/CKE/CCI. "Vg location; money change on site; excel
rest; metro to Prague at Zličín (secure car park adj)."
1 May-30 Sep. CZK 460   2010*

BEROUN *B2* (1.6km W Urban) *49.96910, 14.07563*
Autocamping Na Hrázi, Závodí, 266 01 Beroun
[tel/fax 311 623 294] On NE bank of rv, 200m upstream
fr bdge dir Krivoklát. Exit D5/E50 junc 14, turn R after uneven
level x-ing opp factory, then in 100m L down ul Mostnikovska
(turn easy to miss). Med, pt shd; htd wc; shwrs; EHU (4A) inc
(rev pol); lndry; shop 500m; playgrnd; pool 1.5km; phone;
quiet; ccard not acc; CKE/CCI. "Basic san facs; walking dist to
rlwy stn to Prague; excel base for Prague & Karlstein; waymkd
walks fr Beroun." CZK 180   2009*

⊞ **BESINY** *C1* (500m SW Rural) *49.29533, 13.32086* **Eurocamp
Běšiny, Běšiny 150, 339 01 Běšiny** [tel/fax 376 375 0011;
eurocamp@besiny.cz; www.eurocamp.besiny.cz]
Fr E53/rd 27 take rd 171 twd Sušice. Site just outside vill on L.
Med, unshd; htd wc; chem disp; shwrs; EHU (6A) inc; lndry;
shop 500m; rest; bar; BBQ; cooking facs; pool; paddling pool;
tennis; games area; wifi; 50% statics; dogs; poss cr; adv bkg;
quiet; ccard acc; CKE/CCI. "Pleasant setting; nrby vill drab." ♦
CZK 303   2011*

BOJKOVICE see Uherský Brod *C4*

BOSKOVICE *C3* (12km NE Urban) *49.50980, 16.77308*
Camping de Bongerd, Benešov U Boskovic C.P. 104. 67953
[tel 516 467 233; campingbenesov@hetnet.nl;
www.camping-benesov.nl] Foll sp fr 373 at E end of Benešov
on L. Sm, med, sl, terr, pt shd; wc; chem disp; shwrs; playgrnd;
pool; games area; Eng spkn; quiet; CKE/CCI. "Vg site run by
helpful talkative Dutch couple; ent narr, unsuitable for lge
o'fits." 1 May-20 Sept. CZK 300   2012*

BOSKOVICE *C3* (15km SE Rural) *49.42296, 16.73585* **Camping
Relaxa, 679 13 Sloup** [tel 516 435 291; info@staraskola.cz;
www.camprelaxa.cz] Fr Boskovice take dir Valchov; at
Ludikov head S & onto rte 373 to Sloup. Site sp up track on R.
Sm, pt sl, unshd; htd wc; chem disp; shwrs inc; EHU (6A) inc
(poss rev pol); lndry rm; shop, rest 1km; bar; pool 250m; dogs;
bus 1km; poss cr; quiet; CKE/CCI. "Conv Moravski Kras karst
caves; immed access walking/cycling trails." 1 May-20 Sep.
CZK 400   2012*

BRECLAV *D3* (6km NW Rural) *48.78549, 16.82663*
Autocamp Apollo, Charvátská Nová Ves, 691 44 Břeclav
[tel 519 340 414; info@atcapollo.cz; www.atcapollo.cz]
Fr Breclav take Lednice rd. Site is 3km S of Lednice vill. Lge,
pt sl, pt shd; wc; chem disp; shwrs inc; EHU CZK30; shops
3km; rest adj; lake sw 500m; dogs CZK30; bus; poss cr; noisy;
CKE/CCI. "Fair sh stay; site in beautiful area; excel cycling &
walking; Lednice Castle worth a visit; poss school parties."
1 May-30 Sep. CZK 280   2009*

BRNO *C3* (19km W Rural) *49.20640, 16.41565* **Camping
Alpa, Osvobození, 664 81 Ostrovačice** [tel 602 715 674 or
728 066 609 (mob); sitar@campalpa.cz; www.campalpa.cz]
Leave E65/E50/D1 exit 178 to Ostrovačice, site well sp. Med,
hdg pitch, pt shd; wc; chem disp; shwrs inc; EHU CZK60; shop,
rest 200m; cooking facs; playgrnd; htd, covrd pool 500m;
10% statics; dogs free; phone; Eng spkn; adv bkg; quiet; some
rd noise; ccard not acc; CKE/CCI. "If site unattended, site
van yourself - owner calls eves; clean facs." 15 Apr-15 Oct.
CZK 390   2010*

BRNO *C3* (21km W Rural) *49.21182, 16.40745* **Camping
Oáza, Náměstí Viléma Mrštíka 10, 66481 Ostrovačice**
[tel 606 457 448 or 546 427 552; info@kempoaza.cz;
www.kempoaza.cz] Leave E65/E50 Prague-Brno at junc 178
for Ostrovačice. At T-junc in vill turn L, site on R 100m. Sm, pt
sl, pt shd; wc; chem disp (wc); shwrs inc; EHU (10A) inc; lndry;
shop & 500m; rest 500m; sm pool; playgrnd; phone 500m;
quiet; CKE/CCI. "Excel CL-type site, v clean facs; friendly,
helpful lady owner; narr, uneven ent poss diff lge o'fits; poss
unrel opening dates." 1 May-31 Oct. CZK 310   2013*

BRNO *C3* (24km NW Rural) *49.27618, 16.4535* **Camping Hana,
Dlouhá ul 135, 664 71 Veverská Bítýška** [tel 549 420 331 or
607 905 801 (mob); camping.hana@seznam.cz;
www.campinghana.com] On E50 Prague-Brno m'way, exit
junc 178 at Ostrovačice & turn N on 386 for 10km to Veverská
Bítýška. Site sp bef & in vill. Med, mkd pitch, pt shd; wc; chem
disp; shwrs CZK10; EHU (10A) CZK60; lndry (inc dryer); shop;
rest in vill 1km; snacks adj; BBQ; cooking facs; wifi; dogs
CZK40; Eng spkn; quiet; twin-axles extra; CKE/CCI. "Peaceful,
well-run site; family owned; clean, dated san facs; hot water
runs out by evening if site full; gd security; interesting caves
N of town; bus/tram/boat to Brno; excel rest in vill; flexible
open-closing dates if reserved in adv; helpful, friendly owners;
pleasant walk along rv to vill; gd NH; gd site; lg shwrs but
communal chnge rm." 1 May-30 Sept. CZK 518   2013*

BUCHLOVICE see Uherské Hradiště *C4*

BUDISOV NAD BUDISOVKOU *B4* (800m SE Urban) *49.79089,
17.63668* **Autokemp Budišov, Nábřeží č. 688, 747 87,
Budišov nad Budišovkou** [tel 556 305 283; autokemp@
budisov.cz; www.autokemp.budisov.cz] Ent town fr E on
rd 443; at T junc turn L sp; foll rd which will take you under
rlwy; site on R in 100m. Sm, sl, unshd; wc; shwrs; EHU (6A)
CZK80; shop 500m; rest, snacks; bar; BBQ; playgrnd; pool; wifi;
50% statics; dogs CZK30 (valid vaccination card req); quiet;
CKE/CCI. "Space for 20 vans only, with 4 elec pnts; mini-golf
onsite & bike hire avail." 1 May-30 Sep. CZK 240   2011*

CERNA V POSUMAVI see Horni Plana *C2*

CESKA SKALICE see Náchod *B3*

CESKE BUDEJOVICE *C2* (10km N Rural) *49.07305, 14.41155* **Autocamping Křivonoska, Munice 75, 373 41 Hluboká nad Vltavou [tel/fax 387 965 285; info@krivonoska.cz; www.krivonoska.cz]** Fr E49, turn N 5km fr České Budějovice (avoid minor rd thro woods). Site sp fr rte 105 (České Budějovice) 2km N of vill of Hluboká nad Vltavou on L. Lge, pt shd; wc; chem disp; cold shwrs; EHU (16A) CSK60; lndry; shop; rest, snacks; playgrnd; lake sw; beach adj; dogs CSK40; quiet; red CKE/CCI. "Walk thro pinewoods to facs; castle (copy of Windsor Castle) open in vill." ◆ 1 May-30 Sep. CZK 225   2008*

CESKE BUDEJOVICE *C2* (22km N Rural) *49.13701, 14.47413* **Camping Kostelec, Kostelec 8, 373 41 Hluboká nad Vltavou [tel 731 272 098; info@campingkostelec.nl; www.campingkostelec.nl]** Fr České Budějovice N twd Hluboká nad Vltavou, then foll unnumbered rd thro forest to Poněšice & Kostelec for approx 14km. Med, pt sl, terr, pt shd; wc; chem disp; shwrs inc; EHU (10A) inc; gas; lndry (inc dryer); shop & 14km; rest, snacks; BBQ (gas/elec); playgrnd; sm pool; fishing; games rm; wifi; entmnt; dogs free; bus adj; poss cr; Eng spkn; adv bkg; quiet; red LS; CKE/CCI. "Remote, peaceful site; gd walking; conv Prague, České Budějovice & Český Krumlov." ◆ 30 Apr-15 Sep. CZK 570   2011*

⊞ **CESKE BUDEJOVICE** *C2* (3km SW Urban) *48.96743, 14.46014* **Autocamping-Motel Dlouhá Louka, Stromokva 8, 370 01 České Budějovice [tel 387 203 601; fax 387 203 595; motel@dlouhalouka.cz; www.dlouhalouka.cz]** On Ceske Budějovice to Cesky. Krumlov/Linz rd. Site sp on R on o'skts of town. Fr town foll sp for C. Krumlov; after exit ring rd turn R in 300m at motel sp, 60m bef Stromovka site. Can take new ring rd round town. Site next to Interhotel Autocamping Stomovka - foll sp. Med, some hdstg, pt shd; htd wc; serviced pitches; chem disp; shwrs inc; EHU (10A) inc (rev pol); lndry (inc dryer); supmkt 1km; rest, snacks, bar high ssn; cooking facs; playgrnd; 10% statics; dogs CZK30; phone adj; poss cr; some Eng spkn; quiet; red LS; ccard not acc; CKE/CCI. "Clean facs; supmkt nr; easy walk to interesting town or gd bus service; grassy area rough & uneven - poss diff wet weather; conv Český Krumlov & area; gd cycle paths along rd; gd site; no facs for waste water disp; no curtain or doors on shwrs." 1 Apr-30 Oct. CZK 561   2013*

CESKY KRUMLOV *C2* (5km W Rural) *48.81888, 14.26645* **Caravan Camp Petráškuv Dvur, Topolová 808, 383 01 Prachatice [tel 602 130 418; fax 388 314 125; milan. sebesta@seznam.cz; www.petraskuv-dvur.cz]** Fr Český Krumlov on rd 39 dir Černá for 3km. Take 2nd R after Motorest Krumlov at site sp, then 300m R again for site. Med, pt sl, pt shd; wc; chem disp; shwrs CZK10; EHU (16A) CZK70; lndry; shop 3km; rest; bar; games area; wifi; dogs CZK50; Eng spkn; quiet; red long stay; CKE/CCI. "Site yourself if recep clsd; vg san facs; gd & clean; pleasant walk to town, or cycle path." ◆ 1 May-30 Sep. CZK 320   2011*

CHEB *B1* (6km SE Rural) *50.05108, 12.41189* **Camping am See Václav, Jesenická Přehrada, 350 02 Podhrad [tel/fax 354 435 653; info@kempvaclav.cz; www.kempvaclav.cz]** E fr Cheb on rte 606 sp Praha & Karlovy Vary. After 3km take minor rd to R (150m bef petrol stn) to Podhrad. At Podhrad under rlwy bdge take immed L fork & cont thro houses for 2km (rlwy on R). Site sp fr town on NW shore Lake Jesenice. Fr N on E48/6 exit junc 164 onto rd 606 & foll sp Cheb. Turn L at site sp 150m after petrol stn, foll site sp. Med, pt sl, terr, pt shd; wc; chem disp; shwrs inc; EHU (16A) inc; lndry; shop; rest, snacks; bar; playgrnd; beach & lake sw adj; fishing; watersports; games area; TV; wifi; dogs CZK60; poss cr; Eng spkn; adv bkg; quiet but some rlwy noise; red long stay/LS; CKE/CCI. "Friendly, improving, spacious, family-run site; well managed & scenic; choose own pitch; gd, clean, modern san facs; boats, pedalos for hire; scenic area; conv Mariánské Lázně, Karlovy Vary, hot springs at Soos." 25 Apr-25 Sep. CZK 735   2011*

⊞ **CHEB** *B1* (10km W Rural) *50.05258, 12.16572* **Camping Bříza, Bříza 19, 350 02 Briza, Cheb 2 [tel (0420) 773 570 196; campingbriza@gmail.com; www.camping bohemen.com]** Fr W on 303/E48 thro border take the 2nd exit to Leba, travel back down E48 to Bříza, foll sp to site. Sm, various size pitches; wc; green chem disp; shwrs; rest, bar; sw lake; Eng spkn; quiet. "Excel site; lakeside fishing; boat trips; cycling." CZK 500   2012*

⊞ **CHEB** *B1* (8km NW Rural) *50.11715, 12.38808* **Hotel Jadran Autocamping, Jezerní 84/12, 351 01 Františkovy Lázně [tel/fax 354 542 412 or 603 845 789 (mob); info@ atcjadran.cz; www.atcjadran.cz]** Fr rte 6 turn N dir Libá. After 2km, immed N of new by-pass over bdge, fork L to vill; on o'skirts turn L & foll site/hotel sp, then R in 100m onto narr lane. In 700m turn R. Site in 400m, well sp. Lge, pt shd; wc; mv service pnt; shwrs inc; EHU (16A) inc (rev pol & long cable req); shop 2km; rest; bar; sw lake; bike hire; many statics; dogs CZK60; poss noisy w/end; red long stay; CKE/CCI. "Delightful site beside sm lake; many places of interest nr; walk thro woods to beautiful spa town; supmkt on rd to Cheb; run down facs clean, being rebuilt; rec NH only." CZK 550   2012*

CHOMUTOV *B1* (1km NE Rural) *50.46899, 13.42278* **Autokemp Kamencové Jezero, Tomáše ze Štítného, 430 01 [tel (420) 474 688 029; autocamping@kamencove jezero.cz; www.kamencovejezero.cz]** Foll site sps in town, look for camp sp on L bet flats. Next sp on R bet more flats. Lge, sl, pt shd; htd wc; snacks; shwrs inc; shop adj; EHU; beach; lake sw; poss cr; fairly quiet; little Eng spkn. "Site on edge of town with gd bathing facs; gd site based in N Czech Rep in v interesting area." 1 May-30 Sept. CZK 160   2012*

CHRUSTENICE see Beroun *B2*

CHVALSINY see Český Krumlov *C2*

⊞ **DECIN** *A2* (10km ENE Rural) *50.80101, 14.33389*
Rosalka, Stará Oleška 35, Huntířov, 405 02 Děčin II
[tel 0420 412 513 484; fax 0420 412 512 102; info@rosalka.eu;
www.rosalka.eu] On the E442/13 fr Decin turn L at x-rds in
vill of Huntirov, in dir of Stara Oleska, site on R within 2km.
Sm, unshd; htd wc; EHU (16A); chem disp; shwrs; lndry; rest;
bar; BBQ; wifi; dogs €1; bus adj; twin axles; Eng spkn; adv bkg;
quiet; ccard not acc; no smoking on site; CKE/CCI. "Excel site
nr NP attraction; numerous walks & attractions; welcoming
owners; immac facs." ♦ CZK 688   2013*

DOLNI BREZANY see Praha *B2*

DOMAZLICE *C1* (11km SE Rural) *49.40314, 13.05763*
Autocamping Hájovna, Na Kobyle 209, 345 06 Kdyně
[tel 379 731 233; fax 379 731 595; automotoklub@kdyne.cz;
www.camphajovna.cz] In Kdyně going twd Klatovy on rd 22,
turn L at end of town sq; then 1st R twd cobbled rd (for 300m);
site on L in 2km. Med, some hdstg, pt sl, pt shd; wc; shwrs
CZK10; EHU (10A) inc (poss rev pol); lndry; shop; rest adj;
playgrnd; pool; TV; some statics; dogs CZK35; phone; quiet;
CKE/CCI. "Hořovský Týn & Domažlice interesting towns; gd
walking; friendly owner; ltd level pitches." 1 May-30 Sep.
CZK 250   2009*

FRANTISKOVY LAZNE see Cheb *B1*

"I like to fill in the reports as I travel from site to site"

You'll find report forms at the back of this guide, or you can fill them in online at www.caravanclub.co.uk/europereport.

FRYDEK MISTEK *B4* (5km SW Rural) *49.66459, 18.31161*
Autokemp Olešná, Nad Přehradou, 738 02 Frýdek-Místek
[tel 558 434 806; fax 558 431 195; olesna@tsfm.cz;
www.katalog-kempu.cz/autokemp-olesna/]
Nr Tesco on S side of E462/rte 48 on lakeside. Sm, sl, unshd;
wc; chem disp; shwrs; EHU (10A); shop; rest; bar; cooking facs;
fishing; dogs; Eng spkn; quiet. "Unisex san facs; individual shwr
cabins." 1 May-30 Sep. CZK 200   2009*

FRYDLANT *A2* (6km SE Urban) *50.90116, 15.14147*
Rekreační a sportovní areál, Raspenava, U Stadionu 181,
46361 [tel 482 360 431; mesto.raspenava@raspenava.cz;
www.raspenava.cz] Ent Raspenava fr E on rd 290, do not
cross rv; turn R round filling stn (dir Nove Mesto Pod Smrkem)
& immed L along R side of rv for approx 500m; site sp on the
R. Sm, pt shd; wc; shwrs inc; EHU; shop 1km; rest; snacks, bar;
playgrnd; pool; games area; games rm; 50% statics; bus 500m;
train 500m; quiet; CKE/CCI. "In Jizerske Hory mountains area &
close to Polish border; Frydlant has chateau/castle & interesting
cent; sm campsite on a sports cent with pool & hall; only 8 elec
pnts." 1 May-30 Sep. CZK 200   2011*

FRYMBURK *D2* (1km S Rural) *48.65556, 14.17008*
Camping Frymburk, Frymburk 20/55, 382 79 Frymburk
[tel 380 735 284; fax 380 735 283; info@campingfrymburk.
cz; www.campingfrymburk.cz] Fr Černa on lake, take rd
163 dir Loucovice to site. Fr Český Krumlov take Rožmberk nad
Vltavou rd, turn R at Větřni on rd 162 sp Světlik. At Frymburk
turn L to Lipno then site 500m on R on lake shore. Med, v
sl, terr, pt shd; wc; chem disp; private san facs some pitches;
shwrs CZK15; EHU (6A) inc; lndry; shop & 600m; rest 200m;
snacks; playgrnd; lake sw; fishing; boating; bike & boat hire;
entmnt & child entmnt high ssn; wifi; TV rm; some statics;
dogs CZK60; poss v cr; adv bkg; quiet. "Beautiful lakeside site;
modern, clean san facs; some pitches poss tight for lge o'fits;
gd rest nrby; helpful Dutch owners; gd walking; adv bkg rec
bef 1st Apr." 25 Apr-1 Oct. CZK 640   2012*

HLUBOKA NAD VLTAVOU see České Budějovice *C2*

HLUBOKE MASUVKY see Znojmo *C3*

HORNI PLANA *C2* (9km ESE Rural) *48.74617, 14.11945*
Autocamp Olšina Lipno, Čkyně 212, 382 23 Černá v
Pošumaví [tel 608 029 982 (mob); info@campingolsina.cz;
www.campingolsina.cz] Fr Horní Planá E to Černá v
Pošumaví on rd 39. Cont on this rd 1.5km N to site on
lakeside. Sm, pt shd; wc; chem disp; mv service pnt; shwrs
CZK20; EHU (6A) CZK80; lndry; rest, snacks; playgrnd; lake
sw adj; watersports; windsurfing 1.5km; boat & bike hire;
wifi; 25% statics; dogs CZK60; quiet; CKE/CCI. "Vg; lovely
countryside; welcoming owner; lovely site." ♦ 2 Apr-31 Oct.
CZK 370   2011*

HRANICE *C4* (2km S Rural) *49.54178, 17.74196*
Autocamp Hranice, Pod Hůrkou 2103, 753 01 Hranice
[tel/fax 581 601 633; autokemphranice@seznam.cz]
Fr Olomouc head E on rd 35/E442/E462 to Hranice. On app
to town turn R onto E442 sp Valašské-Meziřiči for 2km thro
town, sp to site on R. Site in 500m, turn R then L up steep
hill & under rlwy bdge (3.2m high) to site. Sm, pt sl, pt shd;
wc; chem disp; shwrs; EHU (10A); lndry; shops 500m; rest,
snacks; bar; cooking facs; playgrnd; htd pool 1.5km; dogs;
poss cr; some rlwy noise; red CKE/CCI. "Gd 24hr security;
lovely site; conv for Helfstýn Castle & Zbrašov Caves."
1 May-30 Sep.   2011*

JEDOVNICE *C3* (2km SE Rural) *49.33350, 16.76299*
Autokemp Olšovec, Havlíčkovo Náměstí 71, 679 06
Jedovnice [tel/fax 516 442 216; kemp@olsovec.cz;
www.olsovec.cz] Fr S on rd 373 or fr N on rd 379, site sp on
W side of lake. Med, pt shd; htd wc; chem disp; mv service pnt;
shwrs; EHU (10A) CZK50; lndry; rest, snacks; bar; BBQ;
playgrnd; lake sw adj; fishing; TV rm; 25% statics; dogs CZK50;
bus 1km; poss cr; noisy due fairgrnd adj; red CKE/CCI. "Conv
Moravský Kra karst show caves; gd walking/cycling; lively site."
1 May-30 Sep. CZK 320   2010*

JICIN *B2* (8km NW Rural) *50.47236, 15.31161* **Chatový tábor**
Jinolice, Jičín Jinolice, 50601 [tel (0420) 493 591 929;
jinol.kemp@seznam.cz; www.kempy-ceskyraj.cz]
Fr Jicin foll rte 35 twrds Turnov. After 6km turn L to Jinolice
and foll sp thro vill. Lge, pt sl; htd wc; shwrs; rest; sw; dogs;
TV; sport; boating; cycling. "In cent of Bohemian Tourist area."
1 May-30 Sept. CZK 355   2012*

JIHLAVA *C3* (8km S Rural) *49.44732, 15.59911* **Autocamping Pávov, Pávov 90, 586 01 Jihlava [tel 567 210 295; fax 567 210 973; atcpavov@volny.cz; www.pavov.com]** Fr D1/E50/E65 exit junc 112 sp Jihlava. Foll sp Pávov & site for 2km. Fr N/S on rte 38, nr a'bahn pick up sp for Pávov. Recep in adj pension/rest. Med, mkd pitch, unshd; wc; shwrs CZK14; EHU (6A); lndry; shop; rest, snacks; playgrnd; lake sw & beach adj; fishing; tennis; 30% statics; dogs; m'way noise. "Grand Hotel in Jihlava gd, friendly rest." 1 May-30 Sep. CZK 135   2011*

KARLOVY VARY *B1* (5.5km NNE Rural) *50.26450, 12.90013* **Autokamp Sasanka, Sadov 7, 360 01 Sadov [tel/fax 353 590 130 or 603 202 051 (mob); campsadov@seznam.cz]** Fr Karlovy Vary on rd 13/E442 to Bor, exit to Sadov, site sp. Med, pt sl, pt shd; wc; chem disp; mv service pnt; shwrs inc; EHU (16A) CZK60 (poss rev pol); lndry; shops 200m; snacks; bar; playgrnd; wifi; dogs CZK50; poss cr; no adv bkg; quiet but some rlwy noise; red long stay/CKE/CCI. "Lovely, well-run site; friendly, helpful staff; modern, clean san facs; picturesque vill of Loket a must; gd bus service fr vill to Karlovy Vary; take care height restriction on app to Tesco fr m'way; rec." 1 Apr-31 Oct. CZK 380   2011*

KARLOVY VARY *B1* (8km S Rural) *50.19558, 12.86282* **Camping Březová Háj, Staromlýnská 154, 362 15 Březová [tel/fax 353 222 665; info@brezovy-haj.cz; www.brezovy-haj.cz]** Fr Cheb-Karlovy Vary R6/E48, turn R on edge of town onto rd 20/E49, turn R goes across dam, site on R. Med, wc; shwrs; EHU (6A) inc; rest, bar at hotel adj; games area; adv bkg; quiet. "Ltd space for c'vans; poss lge, noisy youth groups; some barrack-like buildings; NH/sh stay only." 1 Apr-30 Sep. CZK 300   2010*

KDYNE see Domažlice *C1*

KLATOVY *C1* (19km S Rural) *49.28177, 13.24003* **Camping U dvou Orecha, Splz 13 Strážov na Sumava 34024 [tel (0420) 376 382 421; info@camping-tsjechie.nl; www.camping-tsjechie.nl]** Fr Klatovy twrds Nýrsko on 191, after Janovice turn L twrds Strážov dir Dešenice, after 3km turn L twrds Splz -Hajey, site on L. Sm lge pitches, terr, pt shd; wc; shwrs; lndry rm; shop 4km; bar; wifi; Eng spkn; adv bkg; quiet; 10% disc, CKE/CCI. "Delightful, vg CL type site; warm welcome fr friendly, helpful Dutch owners." 1 May-1 Oct. CZK 395   2012*

KONSTANTINOVY LAZNE *B1* (1km NNW Rural) *49.8869, 12.97168* **Camping La Rocca, 349 52 Konstantinovy Lázně [tel/fax 374 625 287; laroccacamp@seznam.cz; www.larocca.cz]** Fr rd 230 turn onto rd 201 to Konstantinovy Lázně in 18km, site sp. Med, mkd pitch, pt shd; wc; chem disp; mv service pnt; shwrs; EHU (4-10A) CZK100; shop adj; rest; bar; playgrnd; htd pool 100m; paddling pool; games area; bike hire; entmnt; 30% statics; dogs CZK50; adv bkg; quiet. "Friendly, spacious site; conv for spa towns, Pilzen & Tepla Monastery." ♦ 1 May-30 Sep. CZK 320   2010*

KUTNA HORA *B2* (3km NE Urban) *49.96416, 15.30250* **Autocamp Transit, Malín 35, 284 05 Kutná Hora [tel 327 523 785; egidylada@seznam.cz; www.transit.zde.cz]** Fr N on rd 38 fr Kolín, turn R immed after flyover onto rd No 2 then turn L twrds town, ln 1km turn L immed bef rlwy bdge. Sm, pt shd; wc; chem disp (wc); shwrs inc; EHU (16A); shop 1.2km; rest 1km; cooking facs; wifi; TV; dogs free; phone; bus 800m; Eng spkn; CKE/CCI. "Poss noise fr nrby rlwy; sw high ssn; family run; lnt UNESCO World Heritage Town; clean, well-kept, CL-type site with garden area." 1 Apr-30 Sep. CZK 390   2013*

KUTNA HORA *B2* (500m NW Urban) *49.95444, 15.26003* **Camping Santa Barbara, Česká 988, 284 01 Kutná Hora [tel 327 512 051 or 602 361 330 (mob); info@santabarbara.cz; www.santabarbara.cz]** Site off minor ring rd to NW of town, turn uphill (NW) into Ceska Ulice just below crest, site 200m on on L. Site sp is set back (not easy to see). Sm, hdg/mkd pitch, pt shd; wc; chem disp; shwrs CZK25; EHU (6A) CZK80; lndry; shop 200m; snacks; bar; htd pool nr; dogs CZK50; Eng spkn; adv bkg; ccard acc; CKE/CCI. "Nice shady site; welcoming owner; vg, modern san facs; 5 min walk to historic cent of Kutná Hora with many attractions; site locked at night, if locked on arr call for owner." ♦ 1 Apr-31 Oct. CZK 370   2010*

⊞ **KYSELKA** *B1* (1km N Rural) *50.27038, 12.99445* **Camping Na Špici, Radošov 87, 362 72 Kyselka [tel 353 941 152 or 777 145 710 (mob); fax 353 941 285; naspici@quick.cz; http://naspici.sweb.cz/naspiciAN.htm]** Fr Karlovy Vary N on rd 222 along Rv Ohře. Site nr hotel, S of Radošov. Or take rd 13/E442 fr Karlovy Vary & turn R to Bor. Cont on rd & cross wooden bdge (max height 3m) & turn R. Site in 500m on R. Site behind Na Špici Hotel. Med, terr, pt shd; wc; chem disp; shwrs inc; EHU (10A); lndry; shop 500m; rest, snacks; bar; playgrnd; rv sw adj; rv sports; wifi; TV; 25% statics; dogs CZK70; phone; bus; site poss clsd mid Jan to mid-Mar & Xmas, rec phone in adv; Eng spkn; adv bkg; quiet; red long stay; CKE/CCI. "Vg site in beautiful valley; rest gd value; gd walking & rv sports; conv Karlovy Vary." ♦ ltd. CZK 410   2011*

⊞ **LIBEREC** *A2* (3km N Rural) *50.78527, 15.04409* **Autocamping Liberec-Pavlovice, ul Letná, 460 01 Liberec [tel/fax 485 123 468; info@autocamp-liberec.cz; www.autocamp-liberec.cz]** App fr W on rte 13, take 1st exit sp town cent. Foll to rndabt; sp ahead to Pavlovice (site sp after rndabt). Site on L immed after footbdge. Med, pt shd; wc; shwrs CZK10; EHU (10A) CZK80; lndry; shop 200m; rest; snacks 200m; playgrnd; pool high ssn; tennis; karting track adj; dogs CZK50; quiet; red CKE/CCI. "Conv Jizerské Hory mountains." CZK 290   2009*

LIPNO NAD VLTAVOU *D2* (3km W Rural) *48.63891, 14.20880* **Autocamp Lipno Modřín, 382 78 Lipno nad Vltavou [tel 380 736 272; camp@lipnoservis.cz]** Site sp on rd 163 on lakeside. Lge, mkd pitch, unshd; wc; chem disp; shwrs CZK20; EHU (6A); lndry (inc dryer); shop 500m; rest, snacks; bar; playgrnd; htd pool complex 500m; lake beach & sw; boat & bike hire 500m; tennis; games area; wifi; some statics; dogs CZK41; adv bkg; quiet. "Pleasant, popular site." ♦ 1 Apr-30 Sep. CZK 450 (CChq acc)   2009*

LITOMERICE A2 (2km SE Urban) 50.53185, 14.13899
Autocamping Slavoj, Střelecký Ostrov, 412 01 Litoměřice
[tel 416 734 481; kemp.litomerice@post.cz; www.autokemp
slavojlitomerice.w1.cz] Fr N on rd 15 N of rv make for bdge
over Rv Elbe (Labe) sp Terezín; R down hill immed bef bdge
(cobbled rd), L under rlwy bdge, L again, site 300m on R
bef tennis courts at sports cent beside rv. Fr S on rd 15 turn
L immed after x-ing rv bdge to cobbled rd. Sm, pt shd; wc;
chem disp; shwrs inc; EHU (8-16A) CZK75; supmkt 1.5km;
rest; pool; tennis; some statics; dogs CZK30; poss cr; Eng spkn;
quiet but rlwy noise; CKE/CCI. "Friendly, family-run site; gd,
modern san facs; vg rest; 10 mins walk town cent; Terezín
ghetto & preserved concentration camp." 1 May-30 Sep.
CZK 300   2012*

LITOMERICE A2 (4.5km S Rural) 50.50769, 14.14452
Autocamping Kréta, Kréta 322, 411 55 Terezín
[tel 416 782 473; camp@terezin-camp.cz; http://autocamp.
kreta.sweb.cz] Fr rd 8 (E55) Prague to Lovosice. In Terezín at
L-hand bend turn R at museum & ghetto sp. Take 4th turning
on R (with caution), foll camp sp at T-junc, turn L & immed R,
site on R. Sm, pt shd; wc; own san; shwrs inc; EHU CZK80;
shop 200m; rest; playgrnd; watersports; some statics; dogs
CZK50; quiet; CKE/CCI. "Basic site & tired facs; no privacy in
unisex san facs; gd rest; ltd space for tourers; historic forts &
Jewish museum in town; fair NH/sh stay when not full."
1 Apr-30 Sep. CZK 390   2010*

LITOMYSL B3 (1.5km E Urban) 49.86776, 16.32440 **ATC**
Primátor Camping, Strakovská, 570 01 Litomyšl
[tel/fax 461 612 238 or 732 148 723 (mob); primator@
camplitomysl.cz; www.camplitomysl.cz] Fr S on E442/35
turn R at sp on edge of town, site on L in 500m. Sm, some
hdstg, sl, pt shd; wc; shwrs CZK10; EHU (6A) CZK60; lndry;
shop, rest in town; playgrnd; pool & sports facs 300m; TV;
80% statics; dogs CZK45; Eng spkn; quiet but some rd noise;
CKE/CCI. "Worth visit to Litomyšl - steep walk; easy (paid)
parking in town sq; vg san facs; v sloping site; friendly owner."
1 May-30 Sep. CZK 230   2010*

MARIANSKE LAZNE B1 (1.5km SE Rural) 49.94419, 12.72797
Camping Stanowitz-Stanoviště, Stanoviště 9, 35301
Mariánské Lázně [tel/fax 354 624 673; info@stanowitz.
com; www.stanowitz.com] Fr Cheb on rd 215, then rd 230
dir Karlovy Vary/Bečov. Site sp on R after passing under rlwy
bdge. Sm, pt sl, pt shd, some hdstg; htd wc; chem disp; mv
service pnt; shwrs inc; EHU (16A) CZK90; lndry; shop & 3km;
rest, snacks; bar; BBQ; TV; dogs CZK30; phone; Eng spkn;
ccard not acc; CKE/CCI. "Excel CL-type site with gd rest; conv
spa towns & Teplá Monastery; mkd walks in woods; helpful
staff." ◆ 1 Apr-31 Oct. CZK 539   2013*

MARIANSKE LAZNE B1 (5km SW Rural) 49.95238, 12.66799
Autocamping Luxor, Plzeňská ul, 354 71 Velká Hleďadie
[tel 354 623 504; autocamping.luxor@seznam.cz;
www.luxor.karlovarsko.com] Site on E side of rd 21
fr Cheb-Stříbro at S end of vill. Med, hdstg, pt sl, unshd; wc;
chem disp; shwrs inc; EHU (10A) inc; shops 1km; rest, snacks;
bar; cooking facs; sm lake 100m; some statics; dogs free; poss
cr; quiet; ccard not acc; CKE/CCI. "Site in woodland clearing;
gd, modern san facs; gd walking; delightful town; grnd poss
unrel in wet." 1 May-30 Sep. CZK 360   2009*

MLADA BOLESLAV B2 (5km N Urban) 50.44432, 14.91561
Autocamp Škoda, Pod Oborou, 293 06 Kosmonosy
[tel 326 724 134; fax 326 321 344; camp@skskoda.cz;
www.akskoda.cz] Fr Mladá Boleslav head N to Kosmonosy.
Turn W off main rd in vill cent & foll site sp. Sm, pt sl, pt
shd; wc; shwrs; EHU inc; lndry rm; rest; cooking facs; games
area; tennis; 70% statics; dogs; quiet. "Fair site; conv Škoda
museum." 1 May-30 Sep.   2010*

"We must tell The Club about that great site we found"

Get your site reports in by mid-August
and we'll do our best to get your updates
into the next edition.

⊞ **NACHOD** B3 (8km SW Rural) 50.39866, 16.06302
Autocamping Rozkoš, Masaryka 836, 552 03 Česká
Skalice [tel 491 451 112 or 491 451 108; fax 491 452 400;
atc@atcrozkos.com; www.atcrozkos.com] On rd 33/E67
fr Náchod dir Hradec Králové, site sp 2km bef Česká Skalice on
lakeside. V lge, wc; sauna; baby facs; shwrs; EHU (16A) CZK60;
lndry; shop; rest, snacks; playgrnd; paddling pool; lake sw &
beach adj; watersports; windsurfing school; bike hire; entmnt;
10% statics; dogs CZK30; poss cr; no adv bkg; ccard acc.
"Lovely countryside." ◆ CZK 290   2010*

NEPOMUK C2 (4km W Rural) 49.48757, 13.53498
Autokemping Nový Rybník, Plzeňská 456, 335 01
Nepomuk [tel 371 591 336; kemp@novyrybnik.cz;
www.novyrybnik.cz] Fr Plzeň foll E49/rd 20 twd Písek. At
o'skirts of Nepomuk turn R onto rd 191 & foll sp. Med, unshd;
wc; chem disp; shwrs; EHU (10A) CZK70; lndry; shop; rest,
snacks; playgrnd; lake sw; tennis; boating; bike hire; wifi; poss
noisy; adv bkg; CKE/CCI. "Gd forest walks." 15 May-30 Sep.
CZK 220   2010*

NETOLICE C2 (2km SW Rural) 49.03767, 14.18457
Autocamping Podroužek, Tyřsova 226, 384 11 Netolice
[tel 338 324 315; post@autocamp-podrouzek.cz;
www.autocamp-podrouzek.cz] Fr Netolice cent take rd 122
dir Český Krumlov, site sp on R in 1km adj lake. Med, pt shd;
wc; shwrs CZK5; EHU CZK85; shop; lndry; rest; snacks high
ssn & in vill; playgrnd; lake sw; tennis; games area; internet;
some statics; dogs CZK25; quiet; CKE/CCI. "V quiet site; poss /
problematic EHU; modern san facs; conv Kratochvile & museum
of animated film - delightful." 1 May-30 Oct. CZK 220 2010*

NOVE STRASECI B2 (6km NW Rural) 50.17221, 13.83951
Camping Bucek, Trtice 170, 271 01 Nové Strašecí
[tel 313 564 212; info@campingbucek.cz; www.camping
bucek.cz] Site sp fr E48/rd 6, 2km S of Řevničov on lakeside
& approx 40km fr Prague. Med, mkd pitch, pt sl, pt shd; wc;
chem disp; mv service pnt; shwrs inc; EHU (6A) inc; lndry (inc
dryer); shop 2km; rest, snacks; bar; BBQ; playgrnd; htd pool;
sw & boating on adj lake; wifi; TV; dogs CZK60; Eng spkn; no
adv bkg; quiet. "Helpful owner; modern san facs; gd walks in
woods." 25 Apr-15 Sep. CZK 400   2009*

NYRSKO see Klatovy C1

OPATOV C3 (2km S Rural) 49.20888, 15.65611 **Camping Vidlák, Jur en Lilian Vinke, C.p. 322, 675 28 Opatov na Morave [tel 736 678 687; campingvidlak@tiscali.cz; www.campingvidlak.cz]** Fr Prague foll dir Brno (E50, E55, E65), take exit 112 dir Jihlava; in Jihlava foll E59 (rd no. 38) dir Znojmo/Vienna for approx 20km; in Dlouhá Brtnice turn L after first few houses sp Opatov; in Opatov foll sp for camping. Fr S (Vienna) drive via Znojmo on the E59 (rd no. 38) dir Jihlava for approx 50km; turn R dir Třebíč (rd no. 23); in Předin turn L sp Opatov; in Opatov foll sp for camping. Sm, pt sl, pt shd; htd wc; chem disp; mv service point; shwrs inc; EHU (10A) CZK110; lndry; BBQ; playgrnd; lake sw; games area; internet; TV rm; dogs CZK30; bus 1.5km; Eng spkn; adv bkg; quiet; red LS/CKE/CCI. "Well-kept site in picturesque location nr lake; friendly, helpful Dutch owners; spacious pitches; 1st class san facs; bread order during summer months; special m'van pitches avail; forest walks; cycle rtes for mountain bikes; site is exceptional." ♦ 15 Apr-15 Sep. CZK 415   2011*

ORLIK NAD VLTAVOU C2 (5km S Rural) 49.52458, 14.15563 **Camping Velký Vír, Kožlí 23, 398 07 Oriik nad Vltavou [tel 382 275 192; fax 382 275 171; obec.kozli@seznam.cz; www.velkyvir.cz]** Fr Milevsko head W on rte 19; turn N to Orlík vill; foll camp sp 7km N to Velký Vír. Med, pt sl, unshd; wc; chem disp; shwrs CZK10; EHU (6A) CZK60; shop; rest, snacks; playgrnd; rv sw adj; tennis; some statics; dogs CZK60; poss v cr; adv bkg; quiet; CKE/CCI. "V quiet site by rv; few EHU & may not work." 1 May-30 Sep. CZK 310   2009*

OSECNA A2 (1km NE Rural) 50.70428, 14.93898 **Camping 2000, Junův Důl 15, 463 52 Janův Důl [tel/fax 485 179 621; camping2000@wanadoo.nl; www.camping2000.com]** Fr Liberec on rd 35/E442 turn W sp Ještěd then Osečná. Med, mkd pitch, unshd; chem disp; mv service pnt; wc; shwrs inc; EHU (6A) inc; lndry (inc dryer); rest, snacks; bar; cooking facs; playgrnd; pool; paddling pool; waterslide; tennis; horseriding; bike hire; wifi; TV rm; 5% statics; dogs €2.50; Eng spkn; adv bkg; quiet. "Pleasant site; conv Ještěd Mountains." ♦ 15 Apr-15 Sep. CZK 710   2011*

OSTROVACICE see Brno C3

PASOHLAVKY C3 (2km E Rural) 48.89914, 16.56738 **Autocamp Merkur, 691 22 Pasohlávky [tel 519 427 714; fax 519 427 501; camp@pasohlavky.cz; www.pasohlavky.cz]** S fr Brno on E461/rd 52. After Pohořelice site 5km on R, sp. V lge, hdg/mkd pitch, pt shd; wc; chem disp; mv service pnt; shwrs; EHU inc; lndry; shop; rest, snacks; bar; BBQ; cooking facs; playgrnd; lake sw & beach adj; watersports; tennis; games area; bike hire; entmnt; TV rm; some statics; dogs CZK60; phone; poss cr; Eng spkn; adv bkg; ccard acc; CKE/CCI. "Vg; secure, pleasant site." ♦ 1 Apr-31 Oct. CZK 519   2013*

PLANA B1 (7km S Rural) 49.82043, 12.75463 **Camping Karolina, Brod nad Tichou, 348 15 Planá [tel 777 296 990; camping@campingkarolina.com; www.campingkarolina. com]** S fr Planá on rd 21 to Brod nad Tichou, site sp 1km SE of Brod. Narr app rd. Med, pt shd; wc; chem disp; shwrs; EHU (10A) €2.50; lndry; snacks; bar; BBQ; playgrnd; sm pool; games area; TV; some statics; adv bkg; quiet. "Pretty site; gd walking." 1 May-15 Oct. CZK 413   2009*

PLUMLOV see Prostějov C3

PLZEN B1 (6km N Rural) 49.77747, 13.39047 **Autocamping Ostende, 315 00 Plzeň-Malý Bolevec [tel/fax 377 520 194; atc-ostende@cbox.cz; www.cbox.cz/atc-ostende]** Head N fr Plzeň on rd 27 dir Kaznějov; site sp R on o'skts Plzeň. Foll minor rd over rlwy bdge & sharp R bend to site on L. Beware earlier turning off rd 27 which leads under rlwy bdge with height restriction. Med, pt sl, shd; wc; shwrs CZK20; EHU (10A) poss rev pol CZK140; gas; lndry; shop; rest, snacks; playgrnd; lake sw; beach adj; entmnt; dogs CZK70; bus to town; poss cr; Eng spkn; no adv bkg; red CKE/CCI. "Pretty, well-run site; bar/rest area untidy - needs upgrade (2009); facs poss gd walk fr c'van area - no shwr curtains; gates not locked at night (2011); cycle rte & walk around lake, site is shabby needs upgrading and thorough cleaning (2011)." 1 May-30 Sep. CZK 719   2013*

PODEBRADY B2 (2km SE Rural) 50.13549, 15.13794 **Autocamping Golf, U Nové Vodárny 428, 290 01 Poděbrady [tel 325 612 833; ATCAutokemp@gmail.com; www.kemp-golf.cz]** Fr D11/E67 (Prague/Poděbrady) take Poděbrady exit N onto rd 32 for 3km; at junc with rte 11/E67 turn W sp Poděbrady (care needed, priority not obvious); site sp on L on E edge of town; site opp town name sp 400m down lane; app fr E if poss. Med, pt shd; wc (own san rec); chem disp; shwrs inc; EHU (long cable req); snacks; bar; lake 2km; statics; quiet; CKE/CCI. "Conv for touring area; gd supmkt with parking in town; basic site." 1 May-31 Sep. CZK 260   2010*

PRAGUE (SEE PRAHA) see Praha B2

⊞ **PRAHA** B2 (6km N Urban) 50.11715, 14.42775 **Autocamp Trojská, Trojská 157/375, 171 00 Praha 7 [tel 233 542 945; autocamp-trojska@iol.cz; www.autocamp-trojska.cz]** Fr Plzeň (E50/D5) head into cent to rte D8/E55 sp Treplice. Foll sp N to c sp. Immed after rv x-ing take exit under rte 8 & foll camp sp & site on L. Fr Dresden on E55/D8 foll sp to Centrum. Exit just N of Vltava Rv sp Troja & zoo. R (W) fr exit ramp twd Troja & zoo, turn L at traff lts, site on L in 400m. NB: There are 5 sites adj to each other with similar names. Sm, mkd pitch, shd; wc; chem disp (wc); shwrs inc; EHU (16A) inc; lndry; shop; rest, snacks; cooking facs; BBQ; TV; some statics; dogs CZK50; bus for city at ent; tram stop 500m; poss cr; adv bkg; quiet. "Friendly & welcoming; poss diff lge o'fits due trees on site; peaceful, clean & conv site; gd security." CZK 600   2010*

PRAHA B2 (6km N Urban) 50.11745, 14.42528 **Camping Sokol, Národnich Hrdinů 290, 190 12 Dolní Počernice [tel/fax 281 931 112; info@campingsokol.cz; www.campingsokol.cz]** Site sp 400m off main rd 12 to Koīn in vill of Dolní Počernice. Med, pt shd; wc; shwrs inc; EHU (16A) €4; lndry (inc dryer); shop; rest, snacks; bar; cooking facs; playgrnd; paddling pool; bike hire; wifi; some statics; dogs €2; poss cr; Eng spkn; adv bkg; some rd noise; red long stay; ccard acc; CKE/CCI. "Friendly owners; gd, clean facs; excel meals; 1 hr to Prague by public transport." ♦ 1 Apr-31 Oct. CZK 688   2010*

⊞ **PRAHA** *B2* (6km N Urban) *50.11694, 14.42361*
Camping Sokol Trója, Trojská 171a, 171 00 Praha 7
[tel/fax 233 542 908 or 283 850 486; tj.sokol.troja@quick.cz
or info@camp-sokol-troja.cz; www.camp-sokol-troja.cz]
Fr Pilsen (E50/D5) head into cent to rte D8/E55 sp Treplice. Foll
N to Trója sp. Immed after rv x-ing take exit under rte 8 & foll
camp sp & site on L 100m past Autocamp Trojská. Fr Dresden
on E55/D8 foll sp to Centrum to Trója exit on R, foll camping
sp. NB: There are 5 sites adj to each other with similar names.
Best app fr Treplice. Med, some hdstg, pt shd; wc; shwrs inc;
EHU (10A) CZK100; lndry service; shop high ssn; rest, snacks;
bar; internet; dogs CZK50; poss cr; ccard acc; noise fr bar; red
CKE/CCI. "Easy tram transport to city; Trója Palace & zoo 1km;
v helpful owner; bar & rest gd value." CZK 590   2013*

⊞ **PRAHA** *B2* (12km N Rural) *50.15277, 14.4506* **Camping
Triocamp, Ústecká ul, Dolní Chabry, 184 00 Praha 8
[tel/fax 283 850 793; triocamp.praha@telecom.cz;
www.triocamp.cz]** Fr N on D8/E55 take junc sp Zdiby, strt
on at x-rds to rd 608 dir Praha. Camp sp in 2km on R just
after city boundary. Med, pt sl, pt shd; wc; chem disp; mv
service pnt; baby facs; shwrs inc; EHU (6-10A) CZK90; gas;
lndry; shop; rest, snacks; bar; cooking facs; playgrnd; sw 4km;
internet; 30% statics; dogs CZK80; phone; bus/tram to city
(tickets fr recep); barrier clsd at 2200; poss cr; Eng spkn; rd
noise & daytime aircraft noise; ccard acc; red CKE/CCI. "Well-
organised, clean, family-run site; excel facs; rec arr early; free
cherries in ssn; helpful staff." ◆ CZK 1111   2013*

PRAHA *B2* (4.5km NE Urban) *50.09210, 14.47356*
**Camp Žižkov, Nad Ohradou 2667/17 Praha 3
[tel (0420) 607 296 507; camp.zizkov@gmail.com;
www.praguecamping.com]** Fr city cent pass main rl'wy stn
head E on Husitska then Koněvova, site on L sp. Sm, mkd pitch,
pt shd; htd wc; own san rec; mv service pnt; shwrs; EHU (16A);
lndry; shop 500m; snacks; bar; playgrnd under 5's; games area;
wifi; youth hostel; bus/tram adj; Eng spkn; no ccard acc; CKE/
CCI. "Close to city; cycle path; sports facs." 1 June-30 Sept.
CZK 550   2014*

PRAHA *B2* (22km E Urban) *50.09833, 14.68472* **Camping
Praha Klánovice, V Jehličině 391, 190 14 Klánovice
[tel 774 553 542; info@campingpraha.cz; www.camping
praha.cz]** Fr Prague ring rd exit at Běchovice onto rd 12 dir
Kolin. At Újezd nad Lesy turn L at x-rds twd Klánovice & in
approx 3km turn R into Šlechtitelská, site on R in approx 1km.
Med, mkd pitch, pt shd; wc; chem disp; mv service pnt; sauna;
shwrs inc; EHU (16A) €4; gas; lndry (inc dryer); shop; supmkt
3km; rest, snacks; bar; BBQ; playgrnd; pool; paddling pool;
bike hire; games area; games rm; wifi; TV; 50% statics; dogs
€2; phone; bus to Prague; poss cr; Eng spkn; adv bkg; quiet;
ccard acc. "New site 2010; gd public transport to city; excel
site, lge woods for walks & cycling." ◆ 9 Apr-22 Oct. CZK 688
(CChq acc)   2012*

PRAHA *B2* (11km SE Urban) *50.01271, 14.51183*
**Camp Prager, V Ladech 3, Šeberov, 149 00 Praha 4
[tel 244 912 854, 244 911 490 or 603 418 391 (mob);
fax 244 912 854; petrgali@login.cz; www.pensioncamp
prague.com]** Fr W on D1/E50 fr Prague exit 2 sp Praha-
Šeberov, turn L at rndabt. Fr SE fr Brno take exit 2A. After traff
lts take outside lane & at go strt over at next rndabt & in 700m
turn R into V. Ladech. Site L in 100m. Ring bell if gate shut.
Site well sp. Sm, pt shd; wc; chem disp; shwrs inc; EHU (10A)
CZK80; shops 500m; games area; games rm; wifi; dog CZK30;
bus 100m; metro 1km; Eng spkn; adv bkg; quiet; CKE/CCI.
"Gd, secure site in orchard; facs impeccable; helpful & friendly
owner; phone ahead to check if open LS; flexible opening
dates with adv notice; guarded park & ride facs adj Opatov
metro stn; bus/metro tickets fr recep; lge o'fits not acc as diff
access; excel security; cash payment only." 1 May-30 Sep.
CZK 400   2012*

PRAHA *B2* (18km S Rural) *49.95155, 14.47455* **Camping
Oase, Zlatníky 47, 252 41 Dolní Břežany [tel 241 932 044;
info@campingoase.cz; www.campingoase.cz]**
Fr Prague on D1 (Prague-Brno). Exit 12 (Jesenice). Head twd
Jesenice on rd 101. In vill turn R then immed L at rndabt dir
Zlatníky. At Zlatníky rndabt turn L dir Libeň, site in 500m.
Beware 'sleeping policemen' on final app. Med, hdg pitch, pt
shd; htd wc; chem disp; mv service pnt; fam bthrm; serviced
pitches; sauna; shwrs inc; EHU (6A) inc (poss rev pol); gas;
lndry (inc dryer); shop; rest, snacks; bar; cooking facs; BBQ;
playgrnd; 2 pools (1 htd covrd); paddling pool; fishing lake
1km; horseriding; bike hire; games area; games rm; wifi;
entmnt; sat TV rm; dogs CZK50; no o'fits over 12m high ssn;
phone; bus, tram to city; metro 10km; Eng spkn; adv bkg;
quiet; ccard acc (discount for cash); red LS/snr citizens. "Lovely
site; v helpful owners; excel, clean san facs; vg pool; swipe
card for barrier & all chargeable amenities; well-guarded; bus/
train/metro tickets fr recep; rec use metro Park & Ride to city;
lge well maintained pitches; excel security." ◆ 25 Apr-14 Sep.
CZK 750 SBS - X07   2013*

PRAHA *B2* (20km S Rural) *49.93277, 14.37294* **Camp
Matyáš, U Elektrárny, 252 46 Vrané nad Vltavou
[tel 257 761 228 or 777 016073 (mob); fax 257 761 154;
campmatyas@centrum.cz; www.camp-matyas.com]**
Exit D1 junc 11 onto rd 101 to Dolní Břežany. Turn S thro
Ohrobec & foll sp Vrané nad Vltavou, site sp on rvside. Or S
fr Prague on rd 4/102, cross Rv Vltava at Zbraslav to Dolní
Břežany, then as above. Med, pt shd; wc; chem disp; mv service
pnt; shwrs inc; EHU (10A) CZK120; lndry; shop & 800m; rest,
snacks; bar; cooking facs; playgrnd; paddling pool; rv sw &
fishing adj; wifi; dogs free; bus, train to city; Eng spkn; adv bkg;
quiet; red LS; CKE/CCI. "In lovely location; friendly owners;
train & tram service to Prague (1 hr); boat trips on Rv Vltava."
20 Apr-30 Sep. CZK 550   2013*

PRAHA *B2* (8km SW Rural) *50.03254, 14.40421* **Intercamp
Kotva Braník, ul Ledáren 55, 147 00 Praha 4
[tel 244 461 712; fax 244 466 110; kotva@kotvacamp.cz;
www.kotvacamp.cz]** Site well sp fr main rd fr Plzeň & fr S
ring rd. Med, unshd; wc; shwrs inc; EHU (10A) inc; lndry; shop
& 500m; snacks; cooking facs; boating; fishing; tennis; games
area; wifi; some statics; poss cr; Eng spkn; adv bkg; some rlwy/
rd/airport noise; no ccard acc; red CKE/CCI. "Conv Prague -
buy tram tickets fr recep; tents & vans pitched v close; 26 steps
to wc; site guarded." 1 Apr-31 Oct. CZK 257   2009*

⊞ **PRAHA** *B2* (10km SW Urban) *50.05583, 14.41361*
Caravan Camping Praha, Císařská Louka 162, Smíchov,
150 00 Praha 5 [tel 257 317 555; fax 257 318 763; info@
caravancamping.cz; www.caravancamping.cz]
Foll dir as for Prague Yacht Club C'van Park. This site just bef
on R, look for lge yellow tower. Sm, unshd; wc; chem disp;
shwrs inc; EHU CZK95; lndry; shop; rest, snacks; poss v cr;
Eng spkn; quiet; CKE/CCI. "V helpful gd staff; busy sh stay
site on island; conv for Prague cent metro - St Wenceslas Sq
15/20mins; no privacy in shwrs; san fanc modernised & v clean
(2015); v busy." CZK 600   2015*

⊞ **PRAHA** *B2* (10km SW Urban) *50.06233, 14.41331* **Praha
Yacht Club Caravan Park, Cisařská Louka 599, Smíchov,
150 00 Praha 5 [tel 257 318 387 or 060 2343701 (mob);
fax 257 318 387; caravanpark.cl@gmail.com; www.volny.
cz/convoy]** Fr E50 access only poss fr S by travelling N on
W side of rv. After complex junc (care needed), turn sharp R
bef Shell petrol stn to Cisařská Island, foll rd to end. Nr C'van
Camping CSK. Diff app fr N due no L turns on Strakonická. Sm,
pt shd; wc; chem disp; shwrs CZK20; EHU (16A) CZK95.; shops
1.5km across rv; pool 1km; tennis 100m; dogs CZK57; poss v
cr; adv bkg; quiet; ccard acc. "Boats for hire; launch trips on rv;
1 min to ferry & metro to Prague; water taxi fr Prague, book at
site recep; helpful staff; friendly, secure site; v basic san facs;
excel location; views of city; milk etc avail fr Agip petrol stn on
Strakonická." CZK 484   2013*

⊞ **PRAHA** *B2* (12km SW Rural) *50.01984, 14.35579*
**Camping Auto Servis Slivenic, Ke Smíchovu 25, 154 00
Slivenec-Praha 5 [tel/fax 251 817 442; info@camp-
autoservis.cz; www.camp-autoservis.cz]** App Prague fr E
on E50, turn R into Slivenec, Turn R in vill after pond immed
bef shop. Sm, sl, shd; htd wc; chem disp; shwrs; EHU (10A) inc;
lndry; rest; tram to city; quiet. "Site in garden - recep at back
of hse; facs old/sparse but clean; sm pitches; conv city cent."
CZK 380   2012*

PRAHA *B2* (14km SW Rural) *50.04388, 14.28416* **Camp
Drusus, Třebonice 4, 155 00 Praha 5 [tel/fax 235 514 391;
drusus@drusus.com; www.drusus.com]** Fr Plzeň take E50/
D5 to exit 1/23 Třebonice, then E50 dir Brno. Fr Brno exit E50/
D5 at junc 19 sp Řeporyje, site in 2km, sp. Sm, sl, unshd; wc;
chem disp; mv service pnt; shwrs CZK20; EHU (10A) CZK90;
gas; lndry (inc dryer); shop 1.5km; rest; bar; playgrnd; internet;
TV; dogs free; 10% statics; bus; Eng spkn; adv bkg; ccard acc;
red LS/CKE/CCI. "Reg bus service to Prague nrby - tickets fr
site; owner v helpful." 1 Apr-15 Oct. CZK 540   2011*

PRAHA *B2* (12km NW Rural) *50.09890, 14.33569* **Camping
Džbán, Nad Lávkou 5, Vokovice, 160 05 Praha 6
[tel 235 359 006; fax 235 351 365; info@campdzban.eu;
www.campdzban.eu]** Exit 28 off ring rd onto rd 7
Chomutov-Prague; site approx 4km after airport twd Prague;
at traff lts on brow of hill just bef Esso stn on L turn L; take
2nd L & strt on for 600m; site adj go-kart racing. Lge, pt sl,
unshd; wc; chem disp; shwrs inc; EHU (10A) CZK90; lndry;
shop & 2km; rest, snacks; bar; pool & lake 500m; tennis; games
area; wifi; dogs CZK60; tram 200m; poss cr; some Eng spkn;
ccard acc; red CKE/CCI. "Tram direct to Prague (Republic Sq)
25 mins, tickets at bureau; gd security; long way bet shwrs
& wcs; san facs old but clean; communal male shwrs; narr
pitches." 1 May-30 Sep. CZK 550   2010*

PROSTEJOV *C3* (8km W Rural) *49.46123, 17.01154*
Autocamping Žralok, Rudé Armády 302, 798 03 Plumlov
[tel/fax 582 393 224 or 775 568 378 (mob); atczralok@
seznam.cz; www.camp-zralok.cz] Fr cent of Prostějov foll sp
to Boskovice & thro Čechovice & Plumlov, site clearly sp. Down
steep narr lane, cross dam & R to site. Med, sl, unshd; wc;
shwrs inc; EHU (10A) CZK90; long cable req; shop; rest, snacks;
paddling pool; 20% statics; dogs CZK35.; quiet; CKE/CCI.
"O'looking lake; facs basic but clean, needs upgrading; ccards
not acc." 1 May-30 Sep. CZK 340   2013*

PROTIVIN *C2* (1km S Rural) *49.19038, 14.21723* **Camping
Blanice, Celčického 889, 398 11 Protivín [tel 721 589 125;
info@campingblanice.nl; www.campingblanice.nl]**
Fr E49 take 1st exit Protivin going N or 2nd exit going S. Site
sp bef town cent. Sm, mkd pitch, pt shd; wc; chem disp; mv
service pnt; shwrs inc; EHU (8-16A) €3-4.50; lndry (inc dryer);
shop 500m; rest, snacks; bar; rv sw adj; wifi; 5% statics; dogs
free; train 1km; Eng spkn; adv bkg; quiet but some rlwy noise.
"Friendly, peaceful Dutch-run site; easy walk thro fields beside
rv into town." 1 Apr-1 Nov. CZK 537   2010*

"I need an on-site restaurant"

We do our best to make sure site
information is correct, but it is always best
to check any must-have facilities are still
available or will be open during your visit.

⊞ **REJSTEJN** *C1* (300m NW Rural) *49.14222, 13.51344*
**Camping Klášterský Mlýn, Klášterský Mlýn 9, 341 92
Rejštejn [tel 376 582 833; info@klasterskymlyn.nl;
www.klasterskymlyn.nl]** S fr Susice on rd 169 dir Kašperské
Hory for 12 km. In Kašperské Hory turn L onto rd 145 to
Rejštejn. In Rejštejn take 1st R, cross bdge & foll site sp. Med,
mkd pitch, pt shd; htd wc; chem disp; baby facs; fam bthrm;
sauna; shwrs; EHU (6-16A) CZK100; lndry; shop; rest, snacks;
bar; cooking facs; playgrnd; tennis; games area; bike hire;
fitness rm; wifi; some statics; dogs CZK50; quiet. "Friendly,
family-run, renovated site; gd, modern facs; gd touring base."
CZK 300 (CChq acc)   2009*

ROZNOV POD RADHOSTEM *C4* (2km NE Rural) *49.46654,
18.16376* **Camping Rožnov, Radhoštská 940, 756 61
Rožnov pod Radhoštěm [tel 571 648 001; fax 571 620 513;
info@camproznov.cz; www.camproznov.cz]**
On rd 35/E442; on E o'skts of Rožnov on N of rd 200m past ent
to Camping Sport, take L fork opp Benzina petrol stn (site sp
obscured by lamp post). Med, pt shd; htd wc; chem disp; shwrs
inc; EHU (16A) inc; lndry (inc dryer); shop; rest 300m; snacks;
playgrnd; htd pool; tennis; 60% statics; phone; some Eng spkn;
no adv bkg; quiet; ccard acc; red CKE/CCI. "Welcoming; gd
cooking & washing facs; pitches v close together, but annexe
has more space (extra charge); basic, worn san facs; nr open-air
museum (clsd Mon); gd walking cent; cycle to town thro park."
1 Apr-15 Oct. CZK 453 (CChq acc)   2011*

SADOV see Karlovy Vary *B1*

SLOUP see Boskovice *C3*

SOBESLAV *C2* (4km S Rural) *49.22988, 14.72062* **Autocamp Karvánky, Jirásková 407/2, 392 01 Soběslav [tel 381 521 003; fax 381 522 011; karvanky@post.cz; www.karvanky.cz]** Site well sp on rte 3/E55. Lge, pt sl, pt shd; wc; shwrs CZK25; EHU (10A) CZK90; snacks; playgrnd; lake sw; bike hire; TV; 10% statics; dogs CZK60; phone; rd noise; ccard acc. "Conv NH." 15 May-27 Sep. CZK 170   2009*

STERNBERK *B3* (2km N Rural) *49.74800, 17.30641* **Autocamping Šternberk, Dolní Žleb, 785 01 Šternberk [tel 585 011 300; info@campsternberk.cz; www.campsternberk.cz]** Fr Olomouc take rte 46 to Šternberk. At Šternberk go thro town cent & foll sp Dalov, site just bef vill of Dolní Žleb. Or circumnavigate to W on rds 444 & 445, site sp. Med, pt shd; wc; chem disp; shwrs inc; EHU (10A) CZK60 (poss rev pol); lndry; shop & 500m; rest 500m; snacks; bar; cooking facs; playgrnd; lake 1km; TV; phone; 30% statics; dogs CZK30; poss cr; adv bkg; quiet; red CKE/CCI. "Gd, clean facs even when full; helpful staff." 15 May-15 Sep. CZK 190   2010*

STRIBRO *B1* (16km NE Rural) *49.79073, 13.16869* **Transkemp Hracholusky, 330 23 Hracholusky [tel 420 337 914 113 or 420 728 470 650; info@hracholusky.com; www.hracholusky.com]** Fr Ulice bet Stribro & Plzen on rte 5/E50 turn N, sp Plesnice, & foll vill sp to site in 4km at E end of lake. Med, pt sl, unshd; wc; chem disp; shwrs CZK10; EHU inc (adaptor for hire); rest, snacks; shop 3km; lndry; shgl beach adj; lake sw; boating; waterskiing; 25% statics; adv bkg; Eng spkn. "Lake steamer trips; gd sh stay/NH; gd location on lakeside; fair site; facs basic." 1 May-31 Dec. CZK 270   2014*

STRMILOV *C2* (2km SE Rural) *49.14956, 15.20890* **Autokemp Komorník, 378 53 Strmilov [tel 384 392 468; recepce@ autokempkomornik.cz; www.autokempkomornik.cz]** Sp fr rd 23 at Strmilov. Lge, pt sl, pt shd; wc; chem disp (wc); shwrs CZK20; EHU (10A) CZK60 (long lead rec); shop; rest, snacks; bar; BBQ; playgrnd; lake & sand beach adj; 20% statics; quiet; CKE/CCI. "V pleasant setting by lake; clean, modern san facs; gd rest & bar; conv Telč & Slavonice historic towns." ♦ ltd. 1 Jun-15 Sep. CZK 300   2009*

⊞ **TABOR** *C2* (6km E Rural) *49.40985, 14.73157* **Autocamping & Hotel Knížecí Rybník, Měsice 399, 39156 Tábor [tel 381 252 546; knizecak@seznam.cz; www.knizecirybnik.cz]** On N side of rd 19 fr Tábor to Jihlava, in woods by lake adj hotel. Lge, hdg/mkd pitch, pt shd; wc; shwrs CZK20; EHU (6-10A) inc; lndry; shop & 3km; rest, snacks; bar; lake sw & beach adj; fishing; tennis; some statics; dogs; poss cr; rd noise; ccard acc; CKE/CCI. "Pleasant, lakeside site; modern san facs." CZK 280   2010*

⊞ **TANVALD** *A2* (3km W Rural) *50.74205, 15.28269* **Camping Tanvaldská Kotlina (Tanvald Hollow), Pod Špičákem 650, 46841 Tanvald [tel 483 311 928; kotlina@ tanvald.cz; www.tanvald.cz]** Fr S on rte 10, in cent Tanvald at rndabt turn foll sp Desnou & Harrachov. In 500m take L fork under rlwy bdge, then immed turn L & foll rd past hospital. Turn R bef tennis courts, site in 600m. Sm, pt shd; wc; chem disp; mv service pnt; shwrs; EHU CZK30 + metered; lndry; rest; BBQ; cooking facs; playgrnd; pool in town; games area; entmnt; wifi; dogs CZK20; quiet - occasional motor cycle trials nrby. "Excel." CZK 230   2012*

⊞ **TELC** *C2* (10km NW Rural) *49.22785, 15.38442* **Camp Velkopařezitý, Řásná 10, 58856 Mrákotín [tel 567 379 449; fax 567 243 719; campvelkoparezity@tiscali.cz; www.campvelkoparezity.cz]** Exit Telč on Jihlava rd; turn L in 300m (sp) & foll sp to site beyond Rásná. Well sp fr Telč. Steep site ent. Sm, pt sl, pt shd; wc; chem disp; shwrs; EHU CZK100; rest; shop; beach 1km; some statics; dogs CZK30; poss cr. "Friendly atmosphere; poor san facs; gd walking & cycling; Telč wonderful World Heritage site." CZK 270   2010*

TEREZIN see Litoměřice *A2*

TREBIC *C3* (3km W Urban) *49.21671, 15.85904* **Autocamping Třebíč-Poušov, Poušov 849, 67401 Třebíč [tel 568 850 641]** Foll sp for Telč fr town cent. After 3km turn R after 2nd rlwy x-ing, site at bottom of hill. Sm, pt shd; own san rec; shwrs CZK20; EHU inc; lndry rm; shop 1km; snacks; bar; cooking facs; some statics; dogs; adv bkg; quiet, some rd noise; CKE/CCI. "Excel san facs; cycle rte to town along rv." 1 Jun-30 Sep. CZK 300   2009*

TREBON *C2* (19km ESE Rural) *48.96432, 14.93705* **Camping Sever, 37804 Chlum u Třeboně [tel/fax 384 797 189; post@campsever.cz; www.campsever.cz]** S fr Třeboň on E49 dir Vienna, turn L in 5km to Chlum u Třeboně. Site sp thro vill on N side of lake. Med, pt sl, pt shd; wc; chem disp; mv service pnt; shwrs CZK10; EHU (6A) CZK60; lndry; shop 300m; rest 300m; snacks; bar; playgrnd; lake sw; fishing; canoeing; games area; bike hire; golf 15km; wifi; 20% statics; dogs CZK20; phone; bus; adv bkg; quiet; ccard acc; red CKE/CCI. "Lovely situation; excel value site; basic san facs; gd touring base; excel cycling, walking." 9 Apr-31 Oct. CZK 280   2010*

⊞ **TURNOV** *A2* (6km SSE Rural) *50.5580, 15.1867* **Autocamping Sedmihorky, Sedmihorky 72, 51101 Turnov [tel 481 389 162; fax 481 389 160; camp@campsedmihorky.cz; www.campsedmihorky.cz]** Fr rte 35/E442 fr Turnov. Turn SW over rlwy x-ing at camping sp S of Sedmihorky. 300m along ave take 1st R. Lge, pt sl, pt shd; wc; chem disp; shwrs CZK10; EHU (16A) CZK60; lndry; shop, rest, snacks; bar; playgrnd; lake sw; bike hire; dogs CZK50; phone; poss cr; Eng spkn; quiet; ccard acc; CKE/CCI. "V beautiful site in National Park, sometimes called Bohemian Paradise; v busy site high ssn; dep bef 1000 otherwise charge for extra day; excel site." ♦ CZK 410   2012*

UHERSKE HRADISTE *C4* (16km SSE Rural) *48.95488, 17.55338* **Camping Babě hora, Hluk 68725 [tel 581 180; babihora@quick.cz; www.camping-babihora.com]** Site is 4.5km SE of Hluk on R of minor rd to Boršice u Blantniste. Sm, open grass no mkd pitches, pt sl, unshd; wc; chem disp; shwrs; 50% statics; playgrnd; Eng spkn; quiet. 15 May-31 Aug. CZK 210   2012*

UHERSKE HRADISTE *C4* (12km NW Rural) *49.1186, 17.38038* **Autocamping Velehrad, Velehrad 31, 68706 Velehrad [tel 572 571 183]** Foll rd 428 to Velehrad, site 1km N of vill. Sm, pt sl, pt shd; wc; shwrs inc; EHU (10A) CZK30; lndry; shop 1km; rest; bar; playgrnd; tennis; dogs CZK10; adv bkg; CKE/CCI. "Well sp cycle & hiking rtes; Velehrad interesting vill; NH only." 1 May-30 Sep. CZK 200   2009*

UHERSKY BROD *C4* (14km E Urban) *49.04034, 17.79993*
Eurocamping Bojkovice, Stefánikova, 68771 Bojkovice
[tel/fax 572 641 717; info@eurocamping.cz;
www.eurocamping.cz] Off E50 at Uherský Brod turn onto
rd 495. Find rlwy stn at Bojkovice on rd 495 at SW end of
town. Cross rlwy at NE (town) end of stn & foll sp round L & R
turns to site. Med, pt sl, terr, pt shd; wc; chem disp; shwrs inc;
EHU (6A) inc; lndry rm; shop; rest, snacks; bar; cooking facs;
playgrnd; pool high ssn; paddling pool; games area; entmnt;
dogs CZK50; adv bkg; poss noisy. "Gd walking area." 1 May-
30 Sep. CZK 520   2012*

VELEHRAD see Uherské Hradiště *C4*

VRANE NAD VLTAVOU see Praha *B2*

⊞ **VRCHLABI** *A3* (3km NE Rural) *50.62406, 15.64056* **Euro Air
Camp, 54311 Vrchlabí [tel 499 421 292 or 603 235 743 (mob);
fax 499 422 179; info@euro-air-camp.cz; www.euro-air-camp.
cz]** E of Vrchlabí on rd 14, site close to airfield. Med, mkd pitch,
pt sl, pt shd; htd wc; chem disp; mv service pnt; baby facs;
shwrs inc; EHU (16A) inc; lndry; shop; rest, snacks; bar; cooking
facs; playgrnd; pool high ssn; lake fishing; tennis 200m; wifi;
dogs; Eng spkn; adv bkg; quiet; ccard acc; red LS/CKE/CCI.
"Nr Giant Mountains & Polish border; facs dated but clean;
friendly, helpful owners; gd walking; gliding fr adj grass strip."
♦ ltd. CZK 453   2010*

⊞ **VRCHLABI** *A3* (1km S Rural) *50.61036, 15.60263* **Holiday
Park Liščí Farma, Dolní Branná 350, 54362 Vrchlabí
[tel 499 421 473; fax 499 421 656; info@liscifarma.cz;
www.liscifarma.cz]** S fr Vrchlabí on rd 295, site sp. Lge, mkd
pitch, pt shd; htd wc; chem disp; mv service pnt; sauna; private
bthrms avail; shwrs inc; EHU (6A) inc; lndry; shop 500m; rest;
bar; cooking facs; playgrnd; pool high ssn; canoeing; tennis;
games area; bike hire; horseriding 2km; golf 5km; entmnt; TV;
dogs CZK90; adv bkg; quiet; ccard acc. ♦ CZK 640   2009*

ZAMBERK *B3* (1km E Urban) *50.08638, 16.47527*
**Autocamping Jan Kulhanek, U koupaliště, 564 01
Žamberk [tel 465 614 755; kemp@orlicko.cz;
www.autocamping.cz]** Fr Zamberk centre on rd 11, foll sp.
Sm, pt shd; wc; shwrs; EHU (16A) CZK70; lndry; shop 1km;
rest, snacks & bar 200m at sports cent; cooking facs; playgrnd,
pool, games area, games rm at sports cent; TV rm; 50% statics;
wifi; dogs CZK50; phone; bus adj; train 1km; Eng spkn; quiet;
CKE/CCI. "Site is pt of sports cent & aqua park with many
diff facs inc mini-golf, volleyball & bowling; site leaflet avail at
recep showing town plans with supmkts & info office; gd site."
1 Apr-31 Oct. CZK 241   2011*

"Satellite navigation makes touring much easier"

Remember most sat navs don't know if
you're towing or in a larger vehicle – always
use yours alongside maps and site directions.

ZNOJMO *C3* (8km N Rural) *48.92018, 16.02588* **Camping
Country, 67152 Hluboké Mašůvky [tel/fax 515 255 249;
camping-country@cbox.cz; www.camp-country.com]**
N fr Znojmo on E59/38 4km; turn E on 408 to Přímětice; then
N on 361 4km to Hluboké Mašůvky. Sharp turn into site fr S.
Med, sl, pt shd; wc; chem disp; shwrs inc; EHU (16A) CZK80
(long lead poss req); lndry; shop 500m; rest in ssn; playgrnd;
sm pool; tennis; lake sw 1km; bike hire; horseriding; TV rm;
20% statics; dogs CZK50; phone 500m; Eng spkn; quiet;
no ccard acc; red CKE/CCI. "Gd, clean, well-manicured site;
v helpful owner & family; not easy to find level pitch; excel
meals." ♦ 1 May-30 Oct. CZK 410   2009*

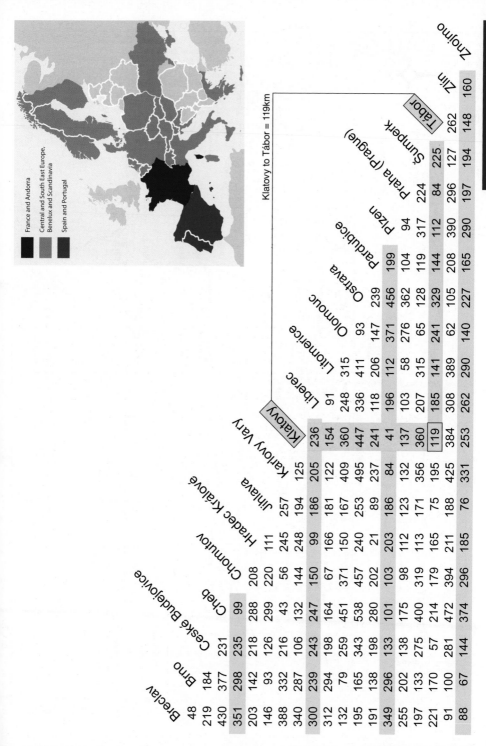

Klatovy to Tábor = 119km

France and Andorra
Central and South East Europe, Benelux and Scandinavia
Spain and Portugal

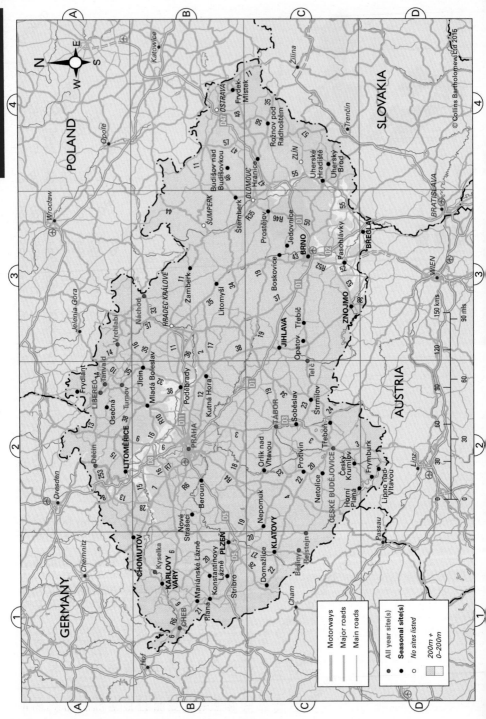

© Collins Bartholomew Ltd 2015

Motorways
Major roads
Main roads

All year site(s)
Seasonal site(s)
No sites listed

200m +
0–200m

Denmark
Country Introduction

Copenhagen

Welcome to Denmark

Regularly found high on the list of the happiest nations on earth, Denmark is a friendly country that welcomes everyone. You can enjoy a charming, fairytale atmosphere working together with modern cities at the forefront of design and sustainability,

The landscape, too, is enchanting, and the beautiful sandy beaches, lakes, river and plains are a delight to explore, and ideal for cyclists.

Country highlights

The smørrebrød, a traditional open sandwich made with rye bread, salad and meat or fish, is perhaps one of Denmark's most famous dishes. Equally renowned is the Danish pastry - known locally as Vienna bread or wienerbrød. You'll find these at bakeries throughout the country.

A traditional Scandinavian drink, Akvavit is believed to have originated in Denmark in the 16th century. The spirit takes its distinct flavour from herbs and spices and is often sipped slowly from a small shot glass.

Major towns and cities

- Copenhagen – Denmark's bustling capital city is a perfect mix of old and new.

- Aarhus – this compact city is well known for its musical heritage.

- Odense – one of the country's oldest cities, and the birthplace of Hans Christian Anderson.

- Aalborg – a vibrant city with an atmospheric waterfront.

Attractions

- Tivoli Gardens, Copenhagen – one of the oldest amusement parks in the world.

- Kronborg Castle, Helsingør – This renaissance castle is a UNESCO site and was the inspiration for Elsinore Castle in Shakespeare's Hamlet.

- Frederiksborg Castle, Hillerød – a palatial residence that now houses a museum.

- Skagen Beaches – 60km of white, sandy beaches and stunning, rugged coastline.

Find out more

www.visitdenmark.com

Tel: 0045 (0) 32 88 99 00 Denmark Tourist Office

Country Information

Population (approx): 5.5 million

Capital: Copenhagen (population approx 1.2 million)

Area: 43,094 sq km (excl Faroe Islands and Greenland)

Bordered by: Germany

Terrain: Mostly fertile lowland, undulating hills, woodland, lakes and moors

Climate: Generally mild, changeable climate without extremes of heat or cold; cold winters but usually not severe; warm, sunny summers; the best time to visit is between May and September

Coastline: 7,400km

Highest Point: Ejer Bavnehøj 173m

Languages: Danish

Local Time: GMT or BST + 1, ie 1 hour ahead of the UK all year

Currency: Krone (DKK) divided into 100 øre; £1 = DKK 10.53, DKK 10 = £0.95 (September 2015)

Emergency numbers: Police 112 (114 for non-urgent calls); Fire brigade 112; Ambulance 112 (operators speak English).

Public Holidays 2016: Jan 1; Mar 24, 25, 27, 28; Apr 22; May 5, 15, 16; Dec 25, 26.

School summer holidays extend from end June to mid August.

Camping and Caravanning

Denmark has approximately 500 approved, well-equipped, annually inspected campsites. A green banner flies at each campsite entrance, making it easy to spot. Campsites are graded from 1 to 5 stars, many having excellent facilities including baby-changing areas, private family bathrooms, self-catering cooking facilities and shops. Prices are regulated and there is very little variation.

All except the most basic 1-star sites have water and waste facilities for motorhomes and at least some electric hook-ups. You may find it useful to take your own flat universal sink plug. During the high season it is advisable to book in advance as many Danish holidaymakers take pitches for the whole season for use at weekends and holidays resulting in minimal space for tourers.

A Camping Key Europe (CKE) or Camping Card International (CCI) is required on all classified campsites.

Approximately 190 campsites have a 'Quick Stop' amenity which provides safe, secure overnight facilities on or adjoining campsites, including the use of sanitary facilities. Quick Stop rates are about two thirds of the regular camping rate but you must arrive after 8pm and leave by 10am next morning. A list of Quick Stop sites may be obtained from local tourist offices or downloaded from DK-Camp www.dk-camp.dk.

Wild camping is prohibited on common or State land, in stopping bays and parking sites, in the dunes, or on the beaches, unless there is an organised camp site. Farmers or landowners may allow you to pitch on their land, but you must always seek permission from them is advance.

Cycling

Although not as flat as the Netherlands, Denmark is very cyclist-friendly and many major and minor roads, including those in all major towns, have separate cycle lanes or tracks. They have their own traffic lights and signals. Cyclists often have the right of way and, when driving, you should check cycle lanes before turning left or right.

In Åarhus and Copenhagen city centre bicycles are free to use between mid-April and November - you will need to pay a refundable deposit. Simply look for one of the many bicycle racks around the central area; see www.visitcopenhagen.com for more information.

There are many separate cycle routes, including eleven national routes, which may be long distance, local or circular, mainly on quiet roads and tracks. Local tourist offices can provide information. When planning a route, take the (often strong) prevailing westerly winds into account.

Transportation of Bicycles

Bicycles may be carried on the roof of a car as well as at the rear. When carried at the rear, the lights and number plate must remain visible.

Electricity and Gas

Current on campsites varies between 6 and 16 amps, a 10 amp supply being the most common. Plugs have 2 round pins. Some sites have CEE17 electric hook-ups or are in the process of converting. If a CEE17 connection is not available site staff will usually provide an adaptor. Visitors report that reversed polarity is common.

Campingaz 904 and 907 butane cylinders are readily available from campsites, or some Statoil service stations and at camping or hardware shops. If travelling on to Norway, Statoil agencies there will exchange Danish propane cylinders.

Entry Formalities

Visas are not required by British or Irish passport holders for a stay of up to three months. Visitors planning to stay longer should contact the Danish Embassy in London before they travel - find contact details at www.denmark.org.uk.

Regulations for Pets

Between April and September all dogs must be kept on a lead. This applies not only on campsites but throughout the country in general.

Medical Services

The standard of healthcare is high. Citizens of the UK are entitled to the same emergency medical services as the Danish, including free hospital treatment, on production of a European Health Insurance Card (EHIC). Tourist offices and health offices (kommunes social og sundhedforvaltning) have lists of doctors and dentists who are registered with the public health service. For a consultation with a doctor you may have to pay the full fee but you will be refunded if you apply to a local health office if they are registered with the Danish Public Health Service. Partial refunds may be made for dental costs and approved medicines. Prescriptions are dispensed at pharmacies (apotek).

Opening Hours

Banks: Mon-Fri 10am-4pm (Thu to 6pm). In the Provinces opening hours vary from town to town.

Museums: Tue-Sun 9am/10am-5pm; most close Mon.

Post Offices: Mon-Fri 9am/10am-5pm/6pm, Sat 9am/10am-12pm/1pm/2pm or closed all day.

Shops: Mon-Fri 9am-5.30pm (Fri to 7pm); Sat 9am-1pm/2pm; supermarkets open Mon-Fri 9am-7pm & Sat 9am-4pm/5pm; open on first Sunday of the month 10am-5pm. Most shops close on public holidays but you may find some bakers, sandwich shops, confectioners, kiosks and florists open.

Safety and Security

Denmark has relatively low levels of crime and most visits to the country are trouble-free. The majority of public places are well lit and secure, most people are genuinely friendly and the police are courteous, helpful and often speak good English. Visitors should, however, be aware of the risk of pickpocketing or bag-snatching in Copenhagen, particularly around the central station and in the Christiania and Nørrebro areas, as well as in other large cities and tourist attractions, and should take the usual common-sense precautions. Car break-ins have increased in recent years; never leave valuables in your car.

Denmark shares with the rest of Europe a general threat from terrorism. Attacks could be indiscriminate and against civilian targets in public places, including tourist sites.

British Embassy
KASTELSVEJ 36-40
DK-2100 Copenhagen Ø
Tel: 35 44 52 00
www.ukindenmark.fco.gov.uk/en

There are also Honorary Consulates in Aabenraa, Aarhus, Fredericia and Herning

Irish Embassy
ØSTBANEGADE 21
DK-2100 Copenhagen Ø
Tel: 35 47 32 00
www.embassyofireland.dk

Documents

Passport
Your passport must be valid for the proposed duration of your stay, however in case of any unforeseen delays it is strongly recommended to have a period of extra validity on your passport.

Vehicle(s)
Carry your vehicle documentation, including vehicle registration certificate (V5C), certificate of insurance and MOT certificate (if applicable). You may be asked to produce your V5C if driving a motorhome over the Great Belt Bridge between Funen and Zealand in order to verify the weight of your vehicle. For more information see the 'Motorways' section of this introduction.

The minimum age you can drive, with a valid driver's licence, is 17.

Money

Some shops and restaurants, particularly in the larger cities, display prices in both krone and euros and many will accept payment in euros.

Travellers' cheques are no longer recommended as it is increasingly difficult to find somewhere to cash them. A prepaid currency card is an alternative - see www.caravanclub.co.uk/travelmoney for details of the Moneycorp Explorer card.

The major credit cards are widely, but not always, accepted. Credit cards are not normally accepted in supermarkets. Cash machines are widespread. A 5% surcharge is usually applied to credit card transactions. Some banks and/or cash machines may not accept debit cards issued by non-Danish banks.

It is advisable to carry your passport or photocard driving licence if paying with a credit card as you may well be asked for photographic proof of identity. Carry your credit card issuers'/banks' 24-hour UK contact numbers in case of loss or theft of your cards.

Motoring in Denmark

Alcohol

The level of alcohol cannot exceed 50 milligrams (0.05%) in 100 millilitres of blood which is lower than in the UK. Drivers caught over this limit will be fined and their driving licence withdrawn. Police carry out random breath tests.

Breakdown Service

24 hours assistance is available from SOS Dansk Autohjaelp (Danish Automobile Assistance) call Tel: 70 10 80 90.

The hourly charge between Monday and Friday is DKK 638 + VAT and an administration charge; higher charges apply at night and at weekends and public holidays. On-the-spot repairs and towing must be paid for in cash.

On motorways use the emergency telephones, situated every 2 km, to call the breakdown service. The telephone number to dial in case of an accident is 112.

Essential Equipment

Warning Triangle
An EU approved red warning triangle must be used if the vehicle breaks down, punctures or is involved in an accident.

Lights and Indicators
Dipped headlights are compulsory at all times, regardless of weather conditions. Bulbs are more likely to fail with constant use and you are recommended to carry spares.

On motorways drivers must use their hazard warning lights to warn other motorists of sudden queues ahead or other dangers such as accidents.

By law indicators must be used when overtaking or changing lanes on a motorway and when pulling out from a parked position at the kerb.

Child Restraint System
Children under three years of age must be seated in an approved child restraint system adapted to their size. Children over three years old and under 1.35 metres in height must be seated in an approved child restraint suitable for both their height and weight. If the vehicle is fitted with an active airbag children must not be placed in the front seat in a rear-facing child seat.

Fuel

Some petrol stations in larger towns stay open 24 hours a day and they are increasingly equipped with self-service pumps which accept DKK 50, 100 and occasionally DKK 200 notes. Few display instructions in English and it is advisable to fill up during normal opening hours when staff are on hand.

Unleaded petrol pumps are marked 'Blyfri Benzine'. Leaded petrol is no longer available and has been replaced by Lead Replacement Petrol, called Millennium, which contains an additive. The major credit cards are normally accepted.

LPG (Autogas or Bilgas) is available from a handful of BP, OK, Q8, Uno-X, YX, Shell and Statoil service stations – the Danish Tourist Board publishes a list of outlets on its website www.visitdenmark.com.

Low Emission Zones

Low Emission zones are in operation in many large cities. The rules affect all diesel powered vehicles over 3,500kg, which must meet European Emission Standard 4 (EURO 4). All vehicles over 3,500kg must display an Environmental Zone sticker (Eco-label) You can order the Eco-label online from www.applusbilsyn.dk for DKK 93 or visit a car inspection station in Denmark where the Eco-label will cost DKK 165.

Vehicles which do not meet European Emission Standard 4 are not allowed into the Low Emission Zone. A fine of DKK 20,000 (Approximately £1900 in 2015) is payable for non-compliance.

Parking

Parking prohibitions and limitations are indicated by signs. Hours during which parking is not allowed are displayed in black for weekdays, with brackets for Saturdays and in red for Sundays and public holidays. Parking meters and discs are used and discs are available free of charge from post offices, banks, petrol stations and tourist offices. The centre of Copenhagen is divided into red, green and blue zones and variable hourly charges apply round the clock Monday to Friday (Saturday to 5pm; Sunday and public holidays free). 'Pay and display' tickets may be bought from machines with cash or a credit card. Cars must be parked on the right-hand side of the road (except in one-way streets). An illegally parked vehicle may be removed by the police.

Priority

At intersections where there are 'give way' or 'stop' signs and/or a transverse line consisting of triangles (shark's teeth) with one point facing towards the driver, drivers must give way to traffic at an intersection. If approaching an intersection of two roads without any signs you must give way to vehicles coming from the right. Give way to cyclists and to buses signalling to pull out. Motorists should take special care on the Danish islands where many people travel by foot, bicycle or on horseback.

Roads

Roads are generally in good condition, well-signposted and largely uncongested and driving standards are fairly high.

Caravanners should beware of strong crosswinds on exposed stretches of road. Distances are short; it is less than 500 km (310 miles) from Copenhagen on the eastern edge of Zealand, to Skagen at the tip of Jutland, and the coast is never more than an hour away.

Road Signs and Markings

Signs directing you onto or along international E-roads are green with white lettering. E-roads, having been integrated into the Danish network, usually have no other national number.

Signs above the carriageway on motorways have white lettering on a blue background. Signs guiding you onto other roads are white with red text and a hexagonal sign with red numbering indicates the number of a motorway exit.

Primary (main roads) connecting large towns and ferry connections have signs with black numbers on a yellow background. Secondary (local) roads connecting small towns and primary routes are indicated by signs with black numbers on a white background. Signs of any colour with a dotted frame refer you to a road further ahead. Road signs themselves may be placed low down and, as a result, may be easy to miss.

'Sharks teeth' markings at junctions indicate stop and give way to traffic on the road you are entering.

General roads signs conform to international standards. You may see the following:

| Place of interest | Recommended speed limits | Dual Carriage-way ends |

The following are some other common signs:

Danish	English Translation
Ensrettet kørsel	One-way street
Fare	Danger
Farligt sving	Dangerous bend
Fodgægerovergang	Pedestrian crossing
Gennemkørsel forbudt	No through road
Hold til hojre	Keep to the right
Hold til venstre	Keep to the left
Omkørsel	Diversion
Parkering forbudt	No parking
Vejen er spærret	Road closed

Speed Limits

	Open Road (Km/h)	Motorway (Km/h)
Car Solo	80-90	110-130
Car towing caravan/trailer	70	80
Motorhome under 3500kg	80-90	110-130
Motorhome 3500-7500kg	70	70

Vehicles over 3,500 kg are restricted to 70 km/h (44 mph) on the open road and on motorways. It is prohibited to use radar detectors.

Traffic Jams

British drivers will enjoy the relatively low density of traffic. At most, traffic builds up during the evening rush hours around the major cities of Copenhagen, Århus, Aalborg and Odense.

During the holiday season traffic jams may be encountered at the Flensburg border crossing into Germany, on the roads to coastal areas, on approach roads to ferry crossings and on routes along the west coast of Jutland.

Violation of Traffic Regulations

The police are authorised to impose and collect on-the-spot fines for traffic offences. Driving offences committed in Denmark are reported to the UK authorities.

Motorways

There are approximately 1,000 km of motorways, mainly two-lane and relatively uncongested. No tolls are levied except on bridges. Lay-bys with picnic areas and occasionally motorhome service points are situated at 25 km intervals. These often also have toilet facilities. Service areas and petrol stations are situated at 50 km intervals and are generally open from 7am to 10pm.

Toll Bridges

The areas of Falster and Zealand are linked by two road bridges, 1.6 km and 1.7 km in length respectively.

The areas of Funen and Zealand are linked by an 18 km suspension road bridge and rail tunnel known as the Great Belt Link (Storebæltsbroen), connecting the towns of Nyborg and Korsør. The toll road is part of the E20 between Odense and Ringsted and tolls for single journeys on the bridge are shown in Table 1 below (2015 prices subject to change).

Table 1 – Great Belt Bridge

Vehicle(s)	Price
Solo Car up to 6 metres	DKK 235
Car + trailer/caravan	DKK 360
Motorhome (under 3,500 kg) under 6 metres	DKK 235
Motorhome (under 3,500kg) over 6 metres	DKK 360
Motorhome (over 3,500 kg) up to 10 metres	DKK 710
Motorhome (over 3,500 kg) over 10 metres	DKK 1,125

You may be asked to produce your Vehicle Registration Certificate (V5C) to verify the weight of your vehicle. Day return and weekend return tickets are also available. For more information see www.storebaelt.dk/english.

The 16 km Øresund Bridge links Copenhagen in Denmark with Malmö in Sweden and means that it is possible to drive all the way from mainland Europe to Sweden by motorway. The crossing is via a 7.8 km bridge to the artificial island of Peberholm, and a 4 km tunnel. Tolls for single journeys (payable in cash, including euros, or by credit card) are levied on the Swedish side, and are shown in Table 2 below (2015 prices subject to change).

Table 2 – Øresund Bridge

Vehicle(s)	Price
Solo Car or motorhome up to 6 metres	€ 47
Car + caravan/trailer or motorhome over 6 metres	€ 94

Speed limits apply, and during periods of high wind the bridge is closed to caravans. Bicycles are not allowed. Information on the Øresund Bridge can be found on www.oeresundsbron.com.

On both the Øresund and Storebælts bridges vehicle length is measured electronically and even a slight overhang over six metres, e.g. towbars, projecting loads and loose items, will result in payment of the higher tariff.

Touring

The peak holiday season and school holidays are slightly earlier than in the UK and by mid-August some attractions close or operate reduced opening hours.

Service charges are automatically added to restaurant bills although you may round up the bill if service has been good, but it is not expected. Tips for taxi drivers are included in the fare. Smoking is not allowed in enclosed public places, including restaurants and bars.

The 3,500 km Marguerite Route, marked by brown signs depicting a flower (see below), takes motorists to the best sights and scenic areas in Denmark.

Tourist Route

A route map and guide (in English) are available from bookshops, tourist offices and Statoil service stations all over Denmark. Stretches of the route are not suitable for cars towing caravans as some of the roads are narrow and twisting.

The capital and major port, Copenhagen, is situated on the island of Zealand. Grundtvig Cathedral, Amalienborg Palace and the Viking Museum are well worth a visit, as are the famous Tivoli Gardens open from mid April to the third week in September and again for a few days in October and from mid November to the end of December (excluding Christmas). The statue of the Little Mermaid, the character created by Hans Christian Andersen, can be found at the end of the promenade called Langelinie. Copenhagen is easy to explore and from there visitors may travel to the north of Zealand along the 'Danish Riviera' to Hamlet's castle at Kronborg, or west to Roskilde with its Viking Ship Museum and 12th century cathedral.

A Copenhagen Card (CPH Card) offers unlimited use of public transport throughout Greater Copenhagen and North Zealand, free entry to over 60 museums and attractions and discounts at restaurants and other attractions. Cards are valid for 24 or 72 hours and may be purchased from selected tourist offices, travel agents, hotels and railway stations or online from www.visitcopenhagen.com. Two children up to the age of nine are included free of charge on an adult card. The Copenhagen Card is also available to buy and use via a free mobile app.

National Parks in the country include Thy National Park near Thisted along Jutland's north-west coast, Mols Bjerge National Park in eastern Jutland and Wadden Sea National Park in the south-west of the country.

English is widely spoken throughout the country.

Public Transport

Public transport is excellent and you can buy a variety of bus, train and metro tickets at station kiosks and at some supermarkets. Children under the age of 12 travel free on buses and metro trains in the Greater Copenhagen area when accompanied by an adult. Tickets must be purchased for dogs and bicycles.

Numerous car ferry connections operate daily between different parts of the country. The ferry is a common mode of transport in Denmark and there may be long queues, especially at weekends in summer. The most important routes connect the bigger islands of Zealand and Funen with Jutland using high-speed vessels on day and night services. Vehicle length and height restrictions apply on routes between Odden (Zealand) and Århus and Æbeltoft (Jutland) and not all sailings transport caravans – check in advance. The Danish Tourist Board can provide general information on car ferry services or contact Scandlines for information on inter-island services including timetables and prices - www.scandlines.dk, email scandlines@scandlines.com or telephone 0045 (0) 33 15 15 15.

International ferry services are particularly busy during July and August and it is advisable to book in advance. Popular routes include Frederikshavn to Gothenburg (Sweden), Helsingør to Helsingborg (Sweden), Copenhagen to Oslo (Norway), and Rødby to Puttgarden in Germany (this route involves a road bridge which is occasionally closed to high-sided vehicles because of high winds). The ferry route from Copenhagen to Hamburg is a good alternative to the busy E45 motorway linking Denmark and Germany.

Tivoli Gardens

SITES IN DENMARK

AABENRAA B3 (2.7km S Coastal) 55.02490, 9.41461
Fjordlyst Aabenraa City Camping, Sønderskovvej 100,
6200 Aabenraa [tel 45 74 62 26 99; fax 45 74 62 29 39;
mail(ad)fjordlyst.dk; www.fjordlyst.dk] Fr S take E45 &
exit at junc 72 to Aabenraa. Foll Rd 42 then turn L onto Rd 24.
Site sp on R. Med, mkd pitch, sl, terr, pt shd; wc; chem disp;
mv service pnt; baby facs; shwrs; EHU (16A) 35DKK; lndry (inc
dryer); shop; bar; BBQ; playgrnd; beach 500m; games area;
wifi; tv; 10% statics; dogs 10DKK; bus adj; twin axles; poss cr;
Eng spkn; adv bkg; quiet; CCI. "Scenic location with views over
the bay; excel facs; friendly staff; some steep slopes on site rds;
vg." ◆ ltd. 1 Apr-31 Oct. DKK 300   2014*

AALBORG B1 (3km W Urban) 57.05500, 9.88500
Strandparken Camping, Skydebanevej 20, 9000 Aalborg
[tel 98 12 76 29; fax 98 12 76 73; info@strandparken.dk;
www.strandparken.dk] Turn L at start of m'way to Svenstrup
& Aalborg W, foll A180 (Hobrovej rd) twd town cent. Turn L
bef Limfjorden bdge onto Borgergade for 2km, site on R. Fr N
turn R after bdge onto Borgergade. Med, shd; wc; chem disp;
mv service pnt; baby rm; shwrs DKK10; EHU (10A) DKK30 (poss
rev pol); kiosk & shops 500m; cooking facs; playgrnd; pool adj;
TV; some statics; dogs DKK10; phone; bus nr; Eng spkn; adv
bkg; poss noisy tent campers high ssn; ccard acc; CKE/CCI. "Gd
cent for town & N Jutland; gd security; facs block excel; card
for elec." ◆ 1 Apr-13 Sep. DKK 245   2015*

"I like to fill in the reports
as I travel from site to site"
You'll find report forms at the back of
this guide, or you can fill them in online
at www.caravanclub.co.uk/europereport.

AALESTRUP B2 (1km E Rural) 56.69166, 9.49991 Aalestrup
Camping, Parkvænget 2, 9620 Aalestrup [tel 98 64 23 86;
pouledb@ofir.dk; www.rosenparken.dk] Fr E45 turn W
onto rd 561 to Aalestrup; 500m after junc with rd 13 turn
L into Borgergade, cross rlwy line. Site sp. Med, pt shd; wc;
shwrs; chem disp; mv service pnt; EHU DKK25; shop nr; rest,
snacks; playgrnd; quiet. "Free ent beautiful rose garden; gd
touring base; friendly staff." 1 Mar-1 Nov. DKK 120   2010*

⊞ **AARHUS** C2 (8km N Rural) 56.22660, 10.16260 Åarhus
Camping, Randersvej 400, Lisbjerg, 8200 Åarhus Nord
[tel 86 23 11 33; fax 86 23 11 31; info@aarhuscamping.dk;
www.aarhuscamping.dk] Exit E45 junc 46 Århus N, then to
Ikea rndabt. Then foll sp Lisbjerg & head for smoking factory
chimney. Site 400m N of Lisbjerg. Med, pt sl, pt shd; wc;
chem disp; mv service pnt; baby facs; fam bthrm; shwrs DKK5;
EHU (16A) metered; gas; lndry (inc dryer); shop; snacks; BBQ;
cooking facs; playgrnd; htd pool; paddling pool; beach 9km;
games area; golf 10km; wifi; TV rm; 10% statics; dogs DKK10;
phone; poss cr; adv bkg; rd noise; red CKE/CCI. "Conv Århus;
gd, tidy site; modern san facs; conv for bus into Aarhus, helpful
owner; elec cards for shwrs." ◆ DKK 203   2015*

AARHUS C2 (8km S Coastal) 56.11030, 10.23209
Blommehaven Camping, Ørneredevej 35, 8270 Højbjerg
[tel 86 27 02 07; fax 86 27 45 22; info@blommenhaven.dk;
www.blommehaven.dk] Fr S on E45 at junc 50 take rd
501 twd Århus. In 10km this becomes 01 ring rd. Take 2nd R
Dalgas Ave, at T-junc turn L & immed R into Strandvejen. Site
3km on L in Marselisborg Forest. Lge, hdg/mkd pitch, terr,
pt shd; wc; chem disp; mv service pnt; fam bthrm; baby facs;
shwrs; EHU DKK35; lndry; shop; BBQ; cooking facs; playgrnd;
sand beach adj; TV rm; 4% statics; dogs DKK10; phone; bus;
Quickstop o'night facs; poss cr; Eng spkn; adv bkg; quiet.
"Some pitches sm & bare earth; helpful staff; clean facs; easy
reach woods, cliffs & beach; conv for open-air museum." ◆
21 Mar-18 Oct. DKK 180   2011*

AARS B2 (2km N Rural) 56.81530, 9.50695 Aars Camping,
Tolstrup Byvej 17, 9600 Aars [tel 98 62 36 03;
fax 98 62 52 99; camping@aars.dk; www.aarscamping.dk]
Fr E45 exit junc 33 W to Aars on rd 535. Turn N onto rd 29
(Aggersundvej), site sp. Med, pt sl, pt shd; htd wc; chem disp;
mv service pnt; shwrs DKK5; EHU (16A) DKK30; gas; lndry;
shop; rest, snacks; bar & 1km; BBQ; cooking facs; playgrnd;
tennis; horseriding; internet; TV; some statics; dogs; poss cr;
Eng spkn; adv bkg; quiet; ccard acc; CKE/CCI. "Vg." ◆
1 Apr-1 Nov. DKK 150   2011*

AERO ISLAND C3 Sites on Aerø Island are listed together
at the end of the Denmark site entry pages.

ALBAEK C1 (9.6km N Coastal) 57.64433, 10.46179 Bunken
Camping, Ålbækvej 288, Bunken Klitplantage, 9982
Ålbæk [tel 98 48 71 80; fax 98 48 89 05; dancamp@mail.
tele.dk; www.dancamp.dk] Site in fir plantation E of A10. V
lge, hdg pitch, pt shd; wc; chem disp; mv service pnt; baby rm;
fam bthrm; shwrs DKK5; EHU DKK25 (adaptor on loan fr recep)
(poss rev pol); gas; lndry; shop; cooking facs; playgrnd; sand
beach 150m; fishing; boating; TV; dogs DKK15; phone; adv
bkg; some rd noise. "Beautiful site in trees; spacious pitches."
◆ 3 Apr-18 Oct. DKK 158   2009*

ALSGARDE see Helsingør D2

ASAA C1 (350m S Urban/Coasal) 57.1460, 10.4023 Asaa
Camping, Vodbindervej 13, 9340 Aså [tel 98 85 13 40;
fax 98 85 00 38; info@asaacamping.dk; www.asaacamping.
dk] Fr Aalborg take E45 NE for approx 20km, turn E to Aså
at junc 16 onto rd 559, then R onto rd 541, site sp. Lge,
pt shd; wc; chem disp; mv service pnt; shwrs; fam bthrm;
baby facs; EHU DKK30; lndry; shop; snacks; cooking facs;
playgrnd; pool; sw 2km; games area; fishing; TV; some statics;
dogs free; phone; Eng spkn; adv bkg; red LS; quiet; CKE/
CCI. "Pleasant location; facs for anglers." ◆ 15 Mar-28 Sep.
DKK 180   2011*

ASSENS *B3* (12km N Coastal) *55.33400, 9.89002* **Sandager Naes Camping, Strandgårdsvej 12, DK 5610 Assens [tel 45 64 79 11 56; info@sandagernaes.dk; www.sandagernaes.dk]** Fr E20, take exit 57 dir Assens. R at Sandager & foll sp. Med, hdg/mkd pitch, pt sl, pt shd; wc; chem disp; mv service pnt; baby facs; fam bthrm; shwrs DKK5; EHU (13A); lndry (inc dryer); shop; snacks; bar; BBQ; cooking facs; playgrnd; htd pool; waterslide; paddling pool; beach 0.5km; games area; games rm; wifi; tv rm; 50% statics; dogs; phone; Eng spkn; adv bkg; CCI. "Excel site". ♦ 23 Mar-15 Sep. DKK 330   2014*

ASSENS *B3* (1.6km W Urban/Coastal) *55.26569, 9.88390* **Camping City Camping, Næsvej 15, 5610 Assens [tel 64 71 15 43; fax 64 71 15 83; info@camping-willemoes.dk; www.camping-willemoes.dk]** Site on beach at neck of land W of town adj marina. Med, pt shd; wc; chem disp; mv service pnt; fam bthrm; baby facs; shwrs DKK5; EHU (10A) DKK30; gas; lndry; shop; playgrnd; sand beach adj; fishing; watersports; TV; 20% statics; phone; adv bkg; red LS. "Pleasant site on beach." ♦ Easter-13 Sep. DKK 155   2009*

AUGUSTENBORG see Sønderborg *B3*

⊞ **BILLUND** *B3* (2.6km ENE Rural) *55.73131, 9.13565* **FDM Billund Camping, Ellehammers Allé 2, 7190 Billund [tel 75 33 15 21; fax 75 35 37 36; c-billund@fdm.dk; www.billund.fdmcamping.dk]** In vill of Billund take rd twd Grindsted & Vejle. In 1km turn N foll sp to Legoland, site on R. V lge, pt shd; wc; chem disp; mv service pnt; shwrs inc; EHU (10A) DKK32; gas; lndry; shop & 2km; rest; bar; playgrnd; pool 500m; games area; internet; TV; some statics; dogs DKK12; phone; Quickstop o'night facs; poss cr; Eng spkn; adv bkg; some aircraft noise; ccard acc; red long stay/CKE/CCI. "Impersonal but excel; open 24 hrs; sh walk to Legoland (free ent for last 90 mins of day)." ♦ DKK 162   2010*

⊞ **BILLUND** *B3* (12km SE Rural) *55.68877, 9.26864* **Randbøldal Camping, Dalen 9, 7183 Randbøl [tel 75 88 35 75; fax 75 88 34 38; info@randboldalcamping.dk; www.randboldalcamping.dk]** Fr Vejle take Billund rd. After approx 18km take L turn to Randbol & Bindebolle. Foll sp, site located approx 5km on L. Med, pt sl, shd; htd wc; chem disp; mv service pnt; baby facs; fam bthrm; shwrs inc; EHU (10A) DKK30; lndry; shop; snacks; cooking facs; playgrnd; lake sw, waterslide & fishing nr; TV; 15% statics; dogs DKK10; phone; poss cr; Eng spkn; adv bkg; quiet; ccard acc. "Wooded site nr rv & trout hatchery; facs stretched high ssn; conv Legoland & Lion Park." ♦ DKK 175   2009*

BINDSLEV *C1* (6km N Coastal) *57.58994, 10.18716* **Tannisby Camping, Tannisbugtvej 86, 9881 Tversted/Bindslev [tel 98 93 12 50; info@tannisbycamping.dk; www.tannisbycamping.dk]** Fr S on E39 dir Hirtshals, turn R dir Ålbæk & foll sp to Tversted & site. Med, mkd pitch, some hdstg, pt shd; htd wc; chem disp; mv service pnt; baby facs; fam bthrm; private san facs avail; sauna; shwrs inc; EHU (13A) DKK30; lndry (inc dryer); shop; BBQ; cooking facs; playgrnd; sand beach 500m; wifi; TV rm; some statics; dogs DKK5; Quickstop o'night facs; Eng spkn; adv bkg; quiet. "Peaceful, friendly site." 1 Apr-26 Sep. DKK 180   2010*

⊞ **BJERGE** *C3* (4km SW Coastal) *55.56295, 11.16500* **FDM Camping Bjerge Sydstrand, Osvejen 30, Bjerge Sydstrand, 4480 Store Fuglede [tel 59 59 78 03; fax 59 59 37 20; c-bjerge@fdm.dk; www.bjerge.fdmcamping.dk]** E22 to Bjerge. Foll sp Bjerge Systrand on Filipsdalsvej rd, then onto Osvejen rd, site sp. Med, hdg/mkd pitch, pt shd; htd wc; mv service pnt; fam bthrm; shwrs inc; EHU (6A) DKK30; lndry; shop; rest 6km; snacks 300m; playgrnd; sand beach adj; watersports; fishing; internet; TV rm; 50% statics; dogs DKK15; adv bkg; quiet; ccard acc. "Pleasant, peaceful site." DKK 189   2009*

BLOKHUS *B1* (8km NE Rural) *57.27855, 9.66133* **Jambo Feriepark, Solvejen 60, 9493, Saltum [tel 98 88 16 66]** Take A17/A11 fr Aalborg, L at Saltum Kirke, approx 1.5km, sp on L. Lge, pt shd; wc; chem disp; snacks; shwrs; gas; shops; EHU; sand beach 1.5km; pool; quiet; lndry; cook facs; playgrnd; sauna; tennis. ♦ May-15 Sep. DKK 110   2013*

See advertisement inside the front cover

BLOMMENSLYST see Odense *C3*

BOESLUNDE see Korsor *C3*

BOGENSE *C3* (1.9km SW Coastal/Urban) *55.56144, 10.08530* **Bogense Strand Camping, Vestre Engvej 11, 5400 Bogense [tel 64 81 35 08; fax 64 81 27 17; info@ bogensecamp.dk; www.bogensecamp.dk]** Fr E20 at junc 57 & take 317 NE to Bogense. At 1st traff lts turn L for harbour, site sp at side of harbour. Lge, pt shd; wc; chem disp; mv service pnt; baby facs; fam bthrm; shwrs DKK5; EHU (12A) DKK35; lndry; shop on site & 200m; cooking facs; playgrnd; pool; paddling pool; shgl beach adj; TV; some statics; dogs DKK17; phone; adv bkg; quiet; red LS; CKE/CCI. "Well-run site; excel facs; interesting sm town 5 mins walk." ♦ 3 Apr-18 Oct. DKK 250   2009*

⊞ **BOGENSE** *C3* (1.2km W Coastal/Urban) *55.56770, 10.08336* **Kyst Camping Bogense, Østre Havnevej 1, 5400 Bogense [tel 64 81 14 43; info@kystcamping.dk; www.kystcamping.dk]** Fr E20 at junc 57 take 317 NE to Bogonense, foll sp for harbour, site sp. Lge, mkd/hdg pitch, unshd pitch; wc; chem disp; mv service pnt; baby facs; shwrs DKK6; EHU (16A) DKK35; lndry; BBQ; cooking facs; playgrnd; pool; beach 200m; games area; games rm; wifi; TV; dogs DKK10; bus 200m. "Vg site; friendly, helpful owners; nice sm town and harbour; ideal cycling." ♦ DKK 285   2012*

BOJDEN see Faaborg *C3*

BORK HAVN *A2* (2.3km S Coastal) *55.84822, 8.28333* **Bork Havn Camping, Kirkehøjvej 9a, 6893 Bork Havn/Hemmet [tel 75 28 00 37; mail@borkhavncamping.dk; www.borkhavncamping.dk]** Fr Tarm take rd 423 thro Hemmet; 500m bef Nørre Bork turn R to Bork Havn, site on L in town just bef harbour. Lge, mkd pitch, pt shd; htd wc; chem disp; mv service pnt; baby facs; shwrs; EHU (10A) DKK22; lndry (inc dryer); shop, rest, snacks, bar adj; cooking facs; playgrnd; htd, cov'rd pool in Tarm; shgl beach 200m; watersports nr; fishing; games rm; TV rm; 25% statics; dogs; Eng spkn; adv bkg; quiet; red LS; CKE/CCI. "Conv Esbjerg ferry to UK; excel." 1 Apr-1 Nov. DKK 144   2010*

DENMARK

BORNHOLM ISLAND *A1* **Sites on Aerø Island are listed together at the end of the Denmark site entry pages.**

BORRE *D3* (6km SE Rural) *54.97971, 12.52198* **Camping Møns Klint, Klintevej 544, 4791 Magleby [tel 55 81 20 25; fax 55 81 27 97; camping@klintholm.dk; www.camping moensklint.dk]** Site nr end of metalled section of rd 287 fr Stege to E of Magleby, site sp. Lge, pt sl, pt shd; wc; chem disp; mv service pnt; shwrs DKK7; EHU (10A) DKK40; lndry; gas; shop; rest, snacks; cooking facs; playgrnd; pool; shgl beach 3km; fishing; boating; tennis; games area; bike hire; wifi; TV; 20% statics; dogs; phone; poss cr; Eng spkn; adv bkg; quiet; ccard acc; red LS; CKE/CCI. "150m chalk cliffs adj - geological interest; much flora, fauna, fossils; gd walks; friendly staff; excel facs." 1 Apr-31 Oct. DKK 195   2009*

BOSORE *C3* (1.5km N Coastal) *55.19295, 10.80633* **Bøsøre Strand Feriepark, Bøsørevej 16, 5874 Hesselager [tel 62 25 11 45; fax 62 25 11 46; info@bosore.dk; www.bosore.dk]** Fr Hesselager N on rd 163, site sp. Lge, mkd pitch, pt shd; htd wc; mv service pnt; chem disp; baby facs; fam bthrm; serviced pitches; sauna; shwrs DKK4; EHU (10A) DKK35; lndry (inc dryer); shop; rest, snacks; bar; cooking facs; playgrnd; htd, covrd pool; sand beach adj; games area; bike hire; golf 18km; wifi; entmnt; TV rm; 15% statics; dogs DKK20; phone; poss cr high ssn; red LS/snr citizens; Quickstop o'night facs. "Superb san facs; gd facs young children; on-site bakery; swipe card for facs - settle on dep." ♦ 26 Mar-23 Oct. DKK 236   2011*

BRAEDSTRUP *B2* (6.3km SSE Rural) *55.93552, 9.65314* **Gudenå Camping Brædstrup, Bolundvej 4, 8740 Brædstrup [tel 75763070; info@gudenaacamping.dk; www.gudenaacamping.dk]** Fr Silkeborg take rd 52 twds Horsens; site sp R off rd 52 approx 4km fr Braedstrup. Sm, mkd pitch, unshd; htd wc; chem disp; MV service pnt; baby facs; fam bthrm; shwrs metered; EHU (10A) metered; lndry; rest, snacks; bar; BBQ; playgrnd; pool; games rm; wifi; TV rm; 25% statics; dogs DKK10; adv bking; quiet; CKE/CCI. "Sm, attractive site beside River Gudenå; v well run fam site; fishing fr site; excel san facs." ♦ 29 Apr-27 Sep. DKK 223   2015*

⊞ BREDERBRO *B3* (15km W Rural/Coastal) *55.06877, 8.66012* **Ballum Camping, Kystvej 37, 6261 Ballum [tel 74 71 62 63; ballum.camping@bbsyd.dk; www.ballum-camping.dk]** At Bredebro on rd 11 turn W on rd 419 twd coast. Site sp 2km S of Ballum. Med, pt shd; htd wc; chem disp; mv service pnt; shwrs DKK1/min; EHU (10A) DKK30; lndry (inc dryer); shop & 2km; rest 1km; playgrnd; sand beach 1km; games area; bike hire; wifi; 50% statics; dogs DKK10; quiet; CKE/CCI. "Close German border; conv Rømø Island with v lge sand beach; gd birdwatching; immac facs." DKK 136   2010*

CHARLOTTENLUND see København *D3*

COPENHAGEN see København *D3*

⊞ EBELTOFT *C2* (2km N Coastal) *56.20997, 10.67838* **Ebeltoft Strand Camping, Nordre Strandvej 23, 8400 Ebeltoft [tel 86 34 12 14; fax 86 34 55 33; info@ ebeltoftstrandcamping.dk; www.ebeltoftstrandcamping. dk]** Fr N site on R of rd 21 as ent Ebeltoft. Lge, pt shd; wc; chem disp; mv service pnt; fam bthrm; baby facs; shwrs inc; EHU (10A) DKK30; lndry; gas; shop; rest 200m; snacks; playgrnd; sand beach adj; wifi; TV; some statics; phone; Eng spkn; quiet; ccard acc; red snr citizens; CKE/CCI. "Adv bkg ess 1 Nov-1 Apr as facs open/htd by arrangment only; gd location; 10 mins walk to interesting old town cent; conv Mols Peninsula; excel." ♦ DKK 210   2009*

EBELTOFT *C2* (5.2km SE Coastal) *56.16775, 10.73085* **Blushøj Camping, Elsegårdevej 55, 8400 Ebeltoft [tel 86 34 12 38; blushoj@mail.dk; http://blushojcamping. dk-camp.dk]** Head Sw on Rte 21 twds Nørrealle. Turn L onto Nørrealle, go thro 1st rndabt, cont ontosteralle, turn L onto Elsegardevej, turn L then R to stay on same rd. Site will be on R. Lge, mkd pitch, ter, pt shd; htd wc; chem disp; mv service pnt; child/baby facs; fam bthrm; shwrs; EHU (10A) DKK5; gas; lndry inc dryer; shop on site & 4km; rest, snacks, bar; BBQ; playgrnd; pool; beach pebble; games rm; internet; wifi; tv rm; dogs free; bus 0.1Km; twin axles; Eng spkn; adv bkg acc; ccard acc; CKE; red LS. "Fantastic location; number of pitches with sea view; immac facs; friendly owner; highly rec." ♦ ltd. 23 Mar-15 Sep. DKK 306   2013*

> ## "We must tell The Club about that great site we found"
>
> Get your site reports in by mid-August and we'll do our best to get your updates into the next edition.

⊞ EGTVED *B3* (3.8km SW Rural) *55.60670, 9.27873* **Egtved Camping, Verstvej 9, 6040 Egtved [tel 75 55 18 32; fax 75 55 08 32; post@egtvedcamping.dk; www.egtvedcamping.dk]** Fr junc 63 E20/E45 (Kolding) take rd 176. At Egtved L onto rd 417, site sp on L. Lge, mkd pitch, pt sl, pt shd; wc; chem disp; mv service pnt; baby facs; fam bthrm; shwrs; EHU (10A) DKK25; gas; lndry (inc dryer); shop; rest, snacks; cooking facs; playgrnd; htd pool; fishing; games rm; wifi; 60% statics; phone; poss cr; Eng spkn; adv bkg; quiet; ccard acc; CKE/CCI. "Clean san facs; conv Legoland, 20km." ♦ DKK 155   2010*

ENGESVANG *B2* (3km N Rural) *56.18736, 9.35627* **Bøllingsø Camping, Kragelundvej 5, 7442 Engesvang [tel 86 86 51 44; fax 86 86 41 71; post@bollingso-camping.dk; www.bollingso-camping.dk]** Fr A13 dir Viborg, turn E to N of Engesvang & foll minor rd so Kragelund. Site on L 1km after museum. Med, mkd pitch, pt sl, pt shd; htd wc; chem disp; mv service pnt; fam bthrm; baby facs; shwrs; EHU (16A) DKK25; lndry (inc dryer); shop; snacks; rest 3km; cooking facs; playgrnd; pool; paddling pool; games area; lake fishing 250m; TV; 2% statics; dogs DKK10; phone; poss cr; adv bkg; red LS; quiet; CKE/CCI. "Conv NH for A13; well-kept family site; clean, dated facs; nr Danish lake district." ♦ 1 Apr-1 Oct. DKK 135   2010*

DENMARK

ERSLEV *B2* (7km W Coastal) *56.81754, 8.67203* **Dragstrup Camping, Dragstrupvej 87, 7950 Erslev [tel 97 74 42 49; fax 97 74 45 49; dragstrup.camping@mail.dk; www.dk-camp.dk/dragstrup]** Fr Nykøbing (Mors) head NW along rte 26. Turn L level with Øster Jolby sp Hvidberg, foll sp Dragstrup & site - well sp fr rte 26. Lge, mkd pitch, pt sl, pt shd; wc; chem disp; mv service pnt; baby facs; fam bthrm; shwrs DKK5; EHU (10A) DKK26; lndry; shop & 5km; BBQ; cooking facs; playgrnd; sand beach 200m; fishing; 20% statics; dogs DKK10; phone; Quickstop o'night facs; Eng spkn; adv bkg; quiet; CKE/CCI. "V attractive site; gd touring base; trout-fishing on site." ♦ 1 Apr-30 Sep. DKK 189   2011*

ERTEBOLLE see Farsø *B2*

⊞ **ESBJERG** *A3* (6km NW Coastal) *55.51180, 8.39350* **Ådalens Camping, Gudenåvej 20, Sædding, 6710 Esbjerg Vest [tel 75 15 88 22; fax 75 15 97 93; info@adal.dk; www.adal.dk]** Exit E20 junc 75 & at rndabt take 2nd exit twd Esjberg N. In 5km turn R at major x-rds with traff lts. Turn L at 1st rndabt into Gudenåvej, site sp. Site on R in 300m. Lge, hdg pitch, pt shd; htd wc; chem disp; mv service pnt; serviced pitches; baby facs; fam bthrm; shwrs; EHU (10A) DKK30; lndry (inc dryer); shop; cooking facs; playgrnd; htd pool; paddling pool; waterslide; beach 500m; golf 10km; internet; some statics; dogs DKK10; phone; Eng spkn; CKE/CCI. "Gd, clean site & modern facs; excel play areas; friendly, helpful recep; conv ferry to Harwich; worth more than a nights stay, ideal for cycling, lovely quiet site, free dog wash." ♦ DKK 200   2011*

ESBJERG *A3* (13km NW Rural/Coastal) *55.54359, 8.33921* **Sjelborg Camping, Sjelborg Standvej 11, Hjerting, 6710 Esbjerg Vest [tel 75 11 54 32; fax 76 13 11 32; info@ sjelborg.dk; www.sjelborg.dk]** Fr Esbjerg take coast rd N twds Hjerting & Sjelborg. At T-junc, Sjelborg Vej, turn L & in 100m turn R onto Sjelborg Kirkevej (camping sp); in 600m turn L into Sjelborg Strandvej (sp); site on R in 600m. Lge, hdg/ mkd pitch, pt shd; wc; chem disp; mv service pnt; shwrs inc; fam bthrm; EHU (10A)€4.50; lndry (inc dryer); shop; sand/ shgl beach nr; lake adj; fishing; golf 5km; bus to town; phone; adv bkg; quiet. "Excel, well maintained site in a quiet country setting; superb facs & activities all ages; spacious on edge of conservation area; mkd walks & bird sanctuary; v welcoming & friendly." ♦ 11 Apr-20 Sep. DKK 190   2015*

FAABORG *C3* (6.6km NE Rural) *55.10987, 10.29592* **Diernæs Camping, Bjerregardsvej 1, Diernæs, 5600 Faaborg [tel 62 61 13 76; fax 62 61 13 74; diernaes@dk-camp.dk; www.dk-camp.dk/diernaes]** Fr Faaborg foll sp Diernæs, then site. Med, pt sl, pt shd; wc; chem disp; mv service pnt; baby facs; fam bthrm; shwrs DKK2; EHU (10A) DKK27; lndry; shop; cooking facs; playgrnd; pool; TV; quiet. "Faaborg pretty town conv for ferries to nrby islands; site in quiet, isolated area." ♦ 1 May-5 Sep. DKK 150   2009*

FAABORG *C3* (10km SE Coastal) *55.06405, 10.31373* **Nab Camping, Kildegårdsvej 8, Åstrup, 5600 Faaborg [tel 62 61 67 79; fax 62 61 67 69; info@nabcamping.dk; www.nabcamping.dk]** Fr Faaborg SE on rd 44 dir Svendborg, turn R after 5km at centre bollards; after 1km turn R onto gravel rd, cont 500m to site. Med, sl, pt shd; wc; chem disp; mv service pnt; baby facs; fam bthrm; shwrs DKK2; EHU (10A) DKK25; gas; lndry; shop; rest 1km; snacks; BBQ; playgrnd; sand beach 1km; boating; wifi; some statics; dogs free; phone; Eng spkn; quiet; ccard acc; red long stay; CKE/CCI. "Superb views over archipelago; conv Egeskov Castle & Gardens; excel site; gd cycling & bird watching nrby; m'vans will need levelling blocks; v quiet, views you dream about." 30 Apr-31 Aug. DKK 190   2011*

FAABORG *C3* (8.5km W Coastal) *55.10568, 10.10776* **Bøjden Strandcamping, Bøjden Landevej 12, 5600 Bøjden [tel 63 60 63 60; fax 63 60 63 63; info@bojden.dk; www.bojden.dk]** Rd 8 W fr Fåborg dir Bøjden/Fynshav, site sp nr ferry. Lge, some hdg/mkd pitch, pt sl, terr, pt shd; htd wc; chem disp; mv service pnt; serviced pitches; baby facs; fam bthrm; shwrs DKK5; EHU (16A) DKK31; lndry; shop; rest adj; cooking facs; playgrnd; htd pool & paddling pool; sand beach adj; bike & boat hire; games rm; golf 12km; entmnt; internet; TV rm; 80% statics; dogs DKK15; sep car park; Eng spkn; adv bkg; ccard acc. "Excel family site with activity cent; blue flag beach; sea views fr pitches; interesting area." ♦ 12 Apr-20 Oct. DKK 460   2014*

⊞ **FAKSE** *D3* (12km E Coastal) *55.23913, 12.23964* **Vemmetofte Strand Camping, Ny Strandskov 1, Vemmetofte, 4640 Fakse [tel 53 71 02 26; fax 53 71 02 59; camping@vemmetofte.dk; www.vemmetofte.dk/camping]** Fr rd E47/E55 turn E on rd 154 to Faske & onto Faske Ladeplads. Head NE for 7km, R for Vemmeltofte-Strand to site in 1.5km. Lge, hdg/mkd pitch, pt shd; wc; chem disp; mv service pnt; baby facs; fam bthrm; sauna; shwrs DKK5; EHU (10A) DKK30; gas; lndry (inc dryer); shop; rest, snacks 100m; BBQ; playgrnd; sand beach adj; bike hire; wifi; 50% statics; dogs DKK20; poss cr; Eng spkn; adv bkg; ccard acc. "Quiet site; Copenhagen 50km; ferry port at Rødby 90km." DKK 159   2010*

FARSO *B2* (9km W Rural/Coastal) *56.75751, 9.24267* **Farsø Fjord Camping, Gamle Viborgvej 13, Stistrup, 9640 Farsø [tel 98 63 61 76; fax 98 63 61 73; info@farso-fjordcamping.dk; www.farso-fjordcamping.dk]** Fr Viborg take rd 533 N dir Løgstør. 5km N of junc with 187 turn R, site sp on R in 300m. Med, mkd pitch, unshd; htd wc; chem disp; mv service pnt; fam bthrm; baby facs; shwrs DKK5; EHU (10A) DKK30; gas; lndry (inc dryer); sm shop; rest, snacks; playgrnd; sm htd pool; shgl beach adj; TV; some statics; dogs free; phone; Eng spkn; adv bkg; quiet; CKE/CCI. "Gd, clean san facs; well-kept; friendly staff; site only 500m fr fjord edge." ♦ ltd. 27 Mar-24 Sep. DKK 128   2010*

FERRING see Lemvig *A2*

FJELLERUP *C2* (3km W Coastal) *56.51209, 10.54980* **FDM Camping Hegedal Strand, Ravnsvej 3, 8585 Glesborg [tel 86 31 77 50; fax 86 71 77 40; c-hegedal@fdm.dk; www.hegedal.fdmcamping.dk]** Fr rd 16 turn N onto rd 547 dir Fjellerup. Cont W of Fjellerup to Hegedal, site sp. Med, hdg/mkd pitch, pt shd; htd wc; chem disp; mv service pnt; shwrs; EHU (6A) DKK32; lndry; shop; rest 3km; BBQ; cooking facs; playgrnd; sand beach adj; watersports; golf 10km; internet; TV rm; some statics; dogs DKK15; adv bkg; quiet; ccard acc. "Well-maintained family site; gd walking, cycling." ♦ 26 Mar-12 Sep. DKK 184   2010*

⊞ **FJERRITSLEV** *B1* (10km W Rural) *57.10912, 9.09998* **Jammerbugt Camping, Thistedvej 546, 9690 Fjerritslev [tel 98 22 51 36; fax 98 22 55 12; kj@jamcamp.dk; www.jammerbugtcamping.dk]** Fr Ferritslev take rd 569 thro Klim & Vester Torup, site on R 1km beyond Vester Torup. Lge, hdg/mkd pitch, pt shd; htd wc; chem disp; mv service pnt; baby facs; fam bthrm; shwrs; EHU (16A) DKK32; lndry; ice; shop; rest, snacks; bar; BBQ; cooking facs; playgrnd; htd pool; paddling pool; sand beach 4km; games area; games rm; internet; entmnt; TV; 80% statics; dogs; phone; bus adj; poss cr; Eng spkn; adv bkg; quiet; CKE/CCI. "Vg; friendly owners." ♦ DKK 144   2010*

⊞ **FREDERICIA** *B3* (6km NE Coastal) *55.62457, 9.83351* **Trelde Næs Camping, Trelde Næsvej 297, Trelde Næs, 7000 Fredericia [tel 75 95 71 83; fax 75 95 75 78; trelde@mycamp.dk; www.mycamp.dk]** Route 28 (Vejle-Fredericia). Fr Vejle take Egeskov exit, then Trelde and Trelde-Næs. Fr Fredericia to Trelde, then Trelde Næs. Lge, pt sl, unshd; htd wc; chem disp; mv service pnt; baby facs; fam bthrm; sauna; shwrs DKK4; EHU (10A) DKK32; lndry (inc dryer); shop; snacks; BBQ; cooking facs; playgrnd; htd pool; waterslide; sand beach adj; wifi; TV rm; 10% statics; dogs DKK16; phone; poss cr; adv bkg; quiet; ccard acc; red LS. "Vg; friendly; fine views over fjord; conv Legoland & island of Fyn; swipecard for all services - pay on dep." ♦ DKK 405   2013*

GILLELEJE *D2* (12km SW Coastal) *56.09051, 12.14977* **DCU Rågeleje Strand Camping, Hostrupvej 2, 3210 Rågeleje [tel 48 71 56 40; fax 48 71 56 85; raageleje@dcu.dk; www.camping-raageleje.dk]** Fr Gilleleje foll sp to Rågeleje on rd 237. Site on coast rd 2km SW of Rågeleje dir Vejby. Lge, hdg pitch, unshd; wc; chem disp; mv service pnt; shwrs; baby facs; fam bthrm; EHU (10A) DKK30; gas; lndry (inc dryer); supmkt; rest 1km; cooking facs; playgrnd; sand beach 300m; wifi; TV; dogs DKK20; phone; poss cr; adv bkg; ccard acc; quiet. ♦ 27 Mar-19 Oct. DKK 193   2010*

GIVE see Jelling *B3*

⊞ **GRAM** *B3* (7km W Rural) *55.28884, 8.94758* **Enderupskov Camping, Ribe Landevej 30, Enderupskov, 6510 Gram [tel 74 82 17 11; fax 74 82 07 82; info@enderupskov.dk; www.enderupskov.dk]** Fr Ribe on rd 24 E twds Gram; site on L of main rd (sp) just bef L turn to Fole. Sm, hdg pitch, pt sl, pt shd; wc; chem disp; mv service pnt; shwrs DKK5; EHU (10A) DKK20; lndry (inc dryer); shop & 5km; rest, snacks; bar; playgrnd; fishing; some statics; dogs free; phone; Eng spkn; adv bkg; quiet; CKE/CCI. "Conv stop after Esbjerg for Ribe & sw coast; woodland walks; friendly owner." ♦ ltd. DKK 125   2009*

GRENAA *C2* (4km S Coastal) *56.38957, 10.91213* **Grenaa Strand Camping, Fuglsangsvej 58, 8500 Grenå [tel 86 32 17 18; fax 86 30 95 55; info@grenaastrandcamping. dk; www.grenaastrandcamping.dk]** Fr Grenå harbour foll coast rd due S foll sp. V lge, unshd; wc; chem disp; mv service pnt; fam bthrm; baby facs; shwrs; EHU (10A) DKK35; gas; lndry; shop; snacks; playgrnd; pool; solarium; sand beach 250m; entmnt; TV; some statics; dogs DKK30; phone; poss cr; adv bkg; red LS; poss noisy high ssn. "Conv for ferries to Sweden; busy site." ♦ 1 Apr-16 Sep. DKK 264   2011*

⊞ **GREVE** *D3* (9km E Urban/Coastal) *55.59434, 12.34315* **Hundige Strand Familiecamping, Hundige Strandvej 72, 2670 Greve [tel 43 90 31 85; info@hsfc.dk; www.hsfc.dk]** Leave E20/47/55 at junc 27 & foll sp Hundige, cont strt ahead until T-junc with rd 151. Turn L, ent 200m on L. Or leave at junc 22 & foll rd 151 down coast to site on R in 8km. Med, some mkd pitch, terr, pt shd; wc; chem disp; mv service pnt; shwrs; EHU inc; gas; lndry; shop, hypmkt 1km; rest, snacks; bar adj; BBQ; cooking facs; playgrnd; sand beach 1km; lge sw stadium 5km; TV; 25% statics (sep area); dogs free; phone; site clsd Xmas & New Year; poss cr; Eng spkn; adv bkg; quiet but some rd noise; ccard acc (surcharge); CKE. "Sh walk to rlwy stn & 15 mins to Copenhagen; friendly, helpful staff; office open morning & eves only LS; site in two parts; v scenic; excel, clean facs." DKK 339   2013*

GRINDSTED *B3* (1.5km SW Rural) *55.75005, 8.91740* **Grindsted Aktiv Camping, Søndre Boulevard 15, 7200 Grindsted [tel 75 32 17 51; fax 75 32 45 75; grindsted@dk-camp.dk; www.dk-camp.dk/grindsted]** Foll sp on Varde-Vejle rd to site on SW o'skts of town nr open-air pool. Med, hdg pitch, pt shd; wc; chem disp; mv service pnt; fam bthrm; baby facs; shwrs DKK5; EHU (10A) DKK28; lndry; kiosk; shops 1km; rest 100m; bar; playgrnd; pool 600m; tennis adj; bike hire; TV; some statics; dogs DKK15; phone; poss cr w/end; adv bkg; quiet. "Sports complex adj with golf & tennis; clean facs; friendly staff; conv Legoland; gd walking & cycle rtes; nh only, site untidy, rd noise." ♦ 1 Apr-1 Oct. DKK 152   2011*

HADERSLEV *B3* (13.6km S Coastal) *55.15313, 9.49424* **Vikaer Strand Camping, Dundelum 29, Djernaes, 6100 Haderslev [tel 74 57 54 64; info@vikaercamp.dk; www.vikaercamp.dk]** S on Katsund twd Lille Klingbjerg, turn R onto Lille Klingbjerg, L onto Højgade, R onto Møllepladsen, L to stay on Møllepladsen then take rte 170 to Diernæs Strandvej for 10.9km, then take 1st R onto Ny Erlevvej for 450m, turn L onto Omkørselsvejen/Rte 170, cont to foll Rte 170 for 8.1km, go thro 1 rndbt, turn L onto Diernæsvej Strandvej for 2.3km foll Diernæs Strandvej to Dundelum, L onto Diernæs Strandvej, R to stay on same rd, R onto Dundelum, L to stay on Dundelum and site on R. Lge, mkd pitch, pt sl, unshd; wc; chem disp; mv service pnt; shwrs; EHU (10-16 A); lndry facs; shop; snacks; playgrnd; dogs 12DKK; Eng spkn; quiet; CCI. "Super site, many outlets for children; lovely beach; immac san facs." ♦ ltd. Easter-31 Oct. DKK 300   2014*

DENMARK

HADERSLEV *B3* (1km W Urban) *55.24431, 9.47701*
**Haderslev Camping, Erlevvej 34, 6100 Haderslev [tel
74 52 13 47; fax 74 52 13 64; info@haderslev-camping.dk;
www.haderslev-camping.dk]** Turn of E45 at junc 68 sp
Haderslev Cent; turn R onto rd 170. On ent town, cross lake &
turn R at traff lts. Site on R at rndabt in 500m. Med, mkd pitch,
hdstg, pt sl, pt shd; htd wc; chem disp; mv service pnt; fam
bthrm; shwrs; EHU (16A) DKK25; lndry (inc dryer); shop 1km;
rest, snacks; bar; BBQ; cooking facs; playgrnd; pool 1km; lake
sw 1km; games rm; internet; TV; some statics; phone; bus 1km;
Eng spkn; adv bkg; quiet; ccard acc (surcharge); CKE/CCI. "Gd,
well-kept site conv E45; all facs to high standard; attractive old
town." 15 Mar-31 Oct. DKK 34   2013*

⊞ **HAMPEN** *B2* (700m SE Rural) *56.01433, 9.36365*
**Hampen Sø Camping, Hovedgaden 31, 7362 Hampen
[tel 75 77 52 55; fax 75 77 52 66; info@hampen-soe-camping.
dk; www.hampencamping.dk]** Fr Vejle leave E45 at junc 59
onto rd 13. After approx 35km turn L when app Hampen at
site sp, site on R in 1km. Lge, mkd pitch, pt shd; htd wc; chem
disp; mv service pnt; baby rm; shwrs DKK5; EHU (16A) DKK30;
gas; lndry (inc dryer); shop; rest, snacks; bar; playgrnd; pool
high ssn; lake sw 1km; fishing 4km; games area; wifi; entmnt;
TV rm; phone; dogs DKK10; Eng spkn; adv bkg; quiet; ccard
acc; CKE/CCI. "Surrounded by moorland; forests & lakes; conv
Legoland (tickets sold) & lake district; welcoming & friendly." ◆
DKK 149 (CChq acc)   2009*

⊞ **HANSTHOLM** *B1* (4km E Coastal) *57.10913, 8.66731*
**Hanstholm Camping, Hamborgvej 95, 7730 Hanstholm
[tel 97 96 51 98; fax 97 96 54 70; info@hanstholm-
camping.de; www.hanstholm-camping.dk]** Ent town fr S
on rte 26. At rndabt turn R onto coast rd sp Vigsø. Site on L
in about 4km. Lge, hdg/mkd pitch, pt sl, pt shd; htd wc; chem
disp; mv service pnt; baby facs; fam bthrm; sauna; shwrs DKK5;
EHU (10A) DKK35; gas; lndry (inc dryer); shop; snacks; BBQ;
playgrnd; htd pool; paddling pool; sand beach 1km; fishing;
horseriding; wifi; TV rm; 30% statics; dogs DKK10; phone; Eng
spkn; adv bkg; ccard acc; CKE/CCI. "Fine view of North Sea
coast; nr wildlife area; gd cycling/walking on coast path; excel,
busy, well-maintained site." ◆ DKK 226   2010*

HEJLSMINDE *B3* (2km NW Coastal) *55.36847, 9.60097*
**Hejlsminde Strand Camping, Gendarmvej 3, Hejlsminde,
6094 Hejls [tel 75 57 43 74; fax 75 57 46 26; info@
hejlsmindecamping.dk; www.hejlsmindecamping.dk]**
14km NE of Haderslev & 8km E of Christiansfeld. Only site 1km
fr harbour at Hejlsminde. Med, mkd pitch, terr, pt shd; wc;
chem disp; mv service pnt; shwrs DKK5; fam bthrm; baby facs;
EHU (10A) DKK35; gas; lndry (inc dryer); shop & 1km; rest 1km;
playgrnd; htd, covrd pool; sand/shgl beach 500m; bike hire;
wifi; TV; 40% statics; dogs free; phone; Eng spkn; adv bkg;
quiet; ccard acc; CKE/CCI. "Well-equipped; friendly owner;
excel." ◆ ltd. 27 Mar-19 Sep. DKK 209   2010*

HELNAES BY *B3* (2km SE Coastal) *55.13253, 10.0357* **Helnæs
Camping, Strandbakken 21, Helnæs, 5631 Ebberup
[tel 64 77 13 39; fax 64 77 13 54; info@helnaes-camping.dk;
www.helnaes-camping.dk]** Fr Assens to Ebberup on rd 323,
in town cent foll sp Helnæs island, site sp. Med, hdg/mkd
pitch, htd wc; chem disp; mv service pnt; fam bthrm; private
san facs some pitches; shwrs inc; EHU (6A) DKK30; lndry;
shop; rest 900m; snacks; bar; BBQ; cooking facs; playgrnd;
sand beach 300m; fishing; watersports; games area; wifi; TV
rm; 50% statics; dogs free; adv bkg; quiet. 1 Apr-30 Sep.
DKK 166   2010*

⊞ **HELSINGOR** *D2* (3km NE Urban/Coastal) *56.04393,
12.60433* **Helsingør Camping Grønnehave, Strandalleen 2,
3000 Helsingør [tel 49 28 49 50 or 25 31 12 12;
fax 49 28 49 40; campingpladsen@helsingor.dk;
www.helsingorcamping.dk]** Site in NE o'skts of town, twd
Hornbæk. Site nr beach o'looking channel to Sweden on E
side of rd. Foll sps on app or in town (beware: sp are sm &
low down). Med, pt shd; wc; chem disp; mv service pnt; shwrs
DKK5; EHU (10A) DKK30; lndry; shop; cooking facs; playgrnd;
htd pool nr; beach; 25% statics; phone; poss v cr. "10 min
walk to Hamlet's castle; 20 min walk to town & stn; gd train
service to Copenhagen; max stay 14 days 15 Jun-15 Aug; Baltic
ships w/end mid-Aug; v busy/cr high ssn." ◆ DKK 217   2014*

HELSINGOR *D2* (13km SSW Coastal) *55.93949, 12.51643*
**Niva Camping, Sølyst Allé 14, 2290 Nivå [tel 49 14 52 26;
fax 49 14 52 40; nivaacamping@post8.tele.dk;
www.nivaacamping.dk]** Take coast rd bet Copenhagen &
Helsingør. Fr N foll sp to Nivå, & site 500m fr main rd, sp. Fr S
site 2km after vill. Lge, mkd pitch, hdstg, pt sl, pt shd; htd wc;
chem disp; mv service pnt; baby facs; fam bthrm; shwrs; EHU
(16A); lndry (inc dryer); shop; rest 500m, snacks 500m; BBQ;
cooking facs; playgrnd; sw beach 800m; fishing adj; games rm;
wifi; tv rm; 10% statics; dogs; twin axles; poss cr; Eng spkn;
adv bkg; quiet but nr busy rlwy; red snr citizens; ccard acc;
CKE/CCI. "Conv Helsingborg ferry, Copenhagen, Kronborg
Castle (Hamlet); excel san facs; vg location; v quiet; best site
in Zealand; excel help; upper level pitches quietest & coolest if
hot." 31 Mar-30 Sep. DKK 240   2014*

HELSINGOR *D2* (12km SW Rural) *55.96777, 12.45611*
**Højsager Camping, Humlebækvej 31; 3480 Fredensborg
[tel 4919 44 48; hojsager@dk-camp.dk; www.hojsager.
dk-camp.dk]** Leave E47 at junc 5 sp fredensborg; cont along
Humleboekvej Rd; site sp on R. Med, hdg pitch, pt shd; wc;
chem disp; shwrs DKK10; EHU (10A) DKK25; gas; lndry; shop;
BBQ; wifi (ltd); 50% statics; dogs; Eng spkn; adv bkg; quiet.
"V conv for Helsingborg-Helsingor ferry & Fredensborg Palace;
gd cycle paths adj; basic CL type site; NH/sh stay only; helpful,
friendly owner." 1 Apr-30 Sep. DKK 155   2011*

HELSINGOR *D2* (10km NW Urban) *56.08104, 12.51348*
**Skibstrup Camping, Stormlugen 20, 3140 Ålsgårde [tel
49 70 99 71; fax 49 70 99 61; info@skibstrup-camping.dk;
www.skibstrup-camping.dk]** Fr Helsingør take N coast rd to
Ålsgårde; then foll site sp. Lge, shd; wc; chem disp; mv service
pnt; baby facs; fam bthrm; shwrs; EHU (10A) DKK35; lndry (inc
dryer); shop 1km; cooking facs; playgrnd; pool; paddling pool;
beach 500m; wifi; TV; some statics; dogs free; phone; adv bkg;
ccard acc; quiet. "Pleasant site amongst trees; conv for ferry &
Copenhagen." ◆ 1 Apr-31 Oct. DKK 150   2015*

HENNE *A3* (2.7km NNW Rural) *55.73258, 8.22189* **Henneby Camping, Hennebysvej 20, 6854 Henne [tel 75 25 51 63; fax 75 25 65 01; info@hennebycamping.dk; www.henneby camping.dk]** Fr Varde on rd 181 & 465 foll sp Henne Strand. Turn R after Kirkeby. Site sp. Lge, hdg pitch, pt shd; htd wc; chem disp; mv service pnt; baby facs; fam bthrm; shwrs DKK2; EHU (10A) DKK32; gas; Indry; shop; rest; cooking facs; playgrnd; pool 2.5km; beach 2km; bike hire; TV rm; some statics; dogs DKK15; poss cr; Eng spkn; quiet; ccard acc; CKE/CCI. "Superb facs; gd, clean site." ♦ 22 Mar-20 Oct. DKK 349   2013*

HILLEROD *D2* (1km SW Urban) *55.9246, 12.2941* **Hillerød Camping, Blytækkervej 18, 3400 Hillerød [tel 48 26 48 54; info@hillerodcamping.dk; www.hillerodcamping.dk]** Fr Roskilde or Copenhagen on A16 twd Hillerød, take 1st L at traff lts sp Hillerød & Frederiksborg Slot Rv233. Site in town cent, not well sp. Med, pt sl, pt shd; wc; chem disp; mv service pnt; fam bthrm; baby facs; shwrs inc; EHU (10A) DKK35 (long lead poss req); gas; Indry; shop, rest nrby; snacks; cooking facs; common/dining rm; playgrnd; bike hire; TV; phone; bus, train nr; poss cr; Eng spkn; adv bkg; quiet; ccard acc; CCI. "Frederiksborg castle in town cent; gd base for N Seeland; 30 min by train to Copenhagen; v helpful, charming owner; pleasant, well-run site; excel, new san facs 2010; no mkd pitch, but owner positions o'fits carefully; many personal touches - eg courtyard with herbs, fruit trees, candles & torches; best site." 12 Apr-19 Oct. DKK 340   2014*

HIRTSHALS *C1* (5km SW Coastal) *57.55507, 9.93254* **Tornby Strand Camping, Strandvejen 13, 9850 Tornby [tel 98 97 78 77; fax 98 97 78 81; mail@tornbystrand.dk; www.tornbystrand.dk]** Take rd 55 fr Hjørring twd Hirtshals. In 12km turn L sp Tornby Strand & Camping, site on L in 200m. Lge, pt shd; wc; chem disp; mv service pnt; baby facs; fam bthrm; shwrs; EHU (10A) DKK30; gas; Indry; shops adj; snacks; playgrnd; pool 2km; sand beach 1km; TV; dogs DKK5; phone; some statics; Eng spkn; poss cr; adv bkg; quiet; CKE/CCI. "Useful for ferries to Kristiansand & Arendal." ♦ 1 Apr-1 Oct. DKK 170   2009*

"I need an on-site restaurant"

We do our best to make sure site information is correct, but it is always best to check any must-have facilities are still available or will be open during your visit.

HIRTSHALS *C1* (1.5km W Urban) *57.58650, 9.94583* **Hirtshals Camping, Kystvejen 6, 9850 Hirtshals [tel 98 94 25 35; fax 98 94 33 43; info@hirtshals-camping.dk; www.dk-camp.dk/hirtshals]** Located 16km N of Hjørring. Turn L off rd 14 3km SW of Hirtshals & site on L. Fr ferry foll sp town cent, then site sp. Med, terr, unshd; wc; chem disp; mv service pnt; baby facs; fam bthrm; shwrs DKK5; EHU (10A) DKK30; kiosk; rest 500m; snacks 300m; playgrnd; beach 200m; fishing & sw 200m; bike hire; TV; dogs DKK10; phone; quiet; red LS. "Open site on cliff top; san facs dated; friendly staff; conv ferries; on coastal cycle path; late arr area; busy but efficient; conv for NH." ♦ 25 Apr-14 Sep. DKK 230   2015*

HJORRING *C1* (14km W Urban) *57.47375, 9.80100* **Lønstrup Camping, Møllebakkevej 20, Lonstrup, 9800 Hjørring [tel 45 21 44 56 37; loenstrupcamping@mail.dk; www.campingloenstrup.dk]** Fr E39 take Exit 3 dir Hjørring for Rte 35 twd Rte 55. Turn R onto Lonstrupvej. Foll sp to site. Med, mkd pitch, pt shd; htd wc; chem disp; mv service pnt; fam bthrm; shwrs inc; EHU (10A) 25DKK; Indry (inc dryer); BBQ; cooking facs; playgrnd; beach 500m; wifi; 30% statics; dogs 15DKK; bus 200m; twin axles; Eng spkn; adv bkg; quiet; CCI. "Vg site; friendly, helpful family owned; lge units may be tight access; close to sm vill & coast." ♦ ltd. 28 Mar-29 Sep. DKK 225   2014*

"Satellite navigation makes touring much easier"

Remember most sat navs don't know if you're towing or in a larger vehicle – always use yours alongside maps and site directions.

HOBRO *B2* (9km ENE Rural) *56.65161, 9.86876* **Camping Bramslev Bakker, Valsgård, 9500 Hobro [tel 40 29 52 53; mail@bramslevbakker.dk; www.bramslevbakker.dk]** Fr E45 turn E at junc 34 onto rd 541 dir Hadsund. Foll sp fr Valsgaard, site above fjord at end of rd. Med, hdg/mkd pitch, pt sl, unshd; htd wc; chem disp; mv service pnt; shwrs inc; EHU (10-16A) DKK23; Indry (inc dryer); shop 3km; rest adj; BBQ; cooking facs; playgrnd; lake sw & beach 300m; fishing, watersports adj; 80% statics; dogs; phone; poss cr; Eng spkn; quiet; red long stay; CKE/CCI. "In nature reserve." ♦ 15 Apr-2 Oct. DKK 112   2011*

HOBRO *B2* (2km SW Urban/Coastal) *56.63589, 9.78109* **Hobro Camping Gattenborg, Skivevej 35, 9500 Hobro [tel 98 52 32 88; fax 98 52 56 61; hobro@dk-camp.dk; www.hobrocamping.dk]** Exit E45 junc 35 dir Hobro. Site sp in 3km. Med, mkd pitch, terr, pt shd; htd wc; chem disp; mv service pnt; baby facs; fam bthrm; shwrs DKK5; EHU (10A) DKK28; Indry; shop; snacks; cooking facs; playgrnd; pool; games area; TV; 5% statics; Quickstop o'night facs; Eng spkn; quiet; CKE/CCI. "Excel, clean site; easy walk to town; views over fjord; friendly site; vg playgrnd; Viking sites in area." ♦ 1 Apr-30 Sep. DKK 280   2011*

HOJBJERG see Århus *C2*

HOJER *A3* (4km NW Coastal) *54.98713, 8.66325* **Vadehavs Camping, Emmerlev Klev 1, 6280 Højer [tel 74 78 22 38; fax 74 78 20 58; vadehavscamping@mail.dk; www.vadehavscamping.dk]** Take rd 419 W fr Tønder; on ent Højer turn R sp Emmerlev. In 1.5km turn L at campsite sp to end of rd. Med, hdg/mkd pitch, pt shd; wc; chem disp; mv service pnt; baby facs; shwrs inc; EHU (10A) DKK25; Indry (inc dryer); shop high ssn; rest 100m; snacks high ssn; BBQ; playgrnd; pool; beach 200m; fishing; bike hire; wifi; 30% statics; dogs DKK10; Eng spkn; quiet; CKE/CCI. 26 Mar-24 Oct. DKK 146   2010*

⊞ **HOLBAEK** D3 (4km E Coastal) 55.71799, 11.76020 **FDM Holbæk Fjord Camping, Sofiesminde Allé 1, 4300 Holbæk [tel 59 43 50 64; fax 59 43 50 14; c-holbaek@fdm.dk]** Fr Rv21 exit junc 20 (fr N) or junc 18 (fr S) & foll sp to harbour. Turn R (E) at harbour - Munkholmvej. Approx 1.5km along Munkholmvej, after traff lts, turn L into Sofiesminde Allé dir marina. Site on R, close to marina. Lge, hdg/mkd pitch, pt shd; htd wc; chem disp; mv service pnt; baby facs; fam bthrm; sauna; shwrs inc; EHU (10A) inc; gas; lndry (inc dryer); shop; rest, snacks; cooking facs; BBQ; playgrnd; htd pool; paddling pool; whirlpool; spa; watersports; fishing; golf nr; bike hire; games area; games rm; wifi; TV rm; 80% statics; dogs DKK15; no o'fits over 10m high ssn; phone; adv bkg; quiet; ccard acc; red LS. "Well-run site in attractive position; helpful staff; pitches poss tight lge o'fits; clean san facs; gd walks & cycle tracks." ♦ DKK 328 SBS - H17   2015*

HOLSTEBRO B2 (3.6km SE Rural) 56.34930, 8.64496 **Mejdal Camping, Birkevej 25, 7500 Holstebro [tel 97 42 20 68; fax 97 41 24 92; mejdal@dcu.dk; www.camping-mejdal.dk]** Sp off ring rd A11 & A16, SE of town, sp at km 44. Med, pt sl, pt shd; wc; chem disp; mv service pnt; shwrs inc; fam bthrm; baby facs; EHU (10A) DKK25; gas; lndry; shop; rest 2km; playgrnd; fishing; boating; golf 5km; TV; dogs DKK15; phone; adv bkg; ccard acc. "Site adj to lge lake in quiet surroundings, but v cr high ssn; open air museum adj." ♦ 21 Mar-22 Sep. DKK 158   2009*

⊞ **HORSENS** B2 (6km W Rural/Coastal) 55.85928, 9.91747 **Husodde Strand Camping, Husoddevej 85, 8700 Horsens [tel 75 65 70 60; fax 75 65 50 72; camping@husodde.dk; www.husodde-camping.dk]** Site sp to R of Horsens-Odder rd (451), foll rd to fjord, site sp. Med, mkd pitch, pt sl, pt shd; wc; chem disp; mv service pnt; baby facs; fam bthrm; shwrs DKK5; EHU (10A) DKK35; lndry; kiosk & shops 500m; rest, snacks, bar 5km; cooking facs; BBQ; playgrnd; pool 3km; sand beach & fishing adj; TV; 10% statics; dogs DKK10; phone; Eng spkn; quiet; CKE/CCI. "Lovely location; lge pitches; well-maintained, well-managed site; friendly welcome; cycle tracks." ♦ DKK 238   2015*

> ## "There aren't many sites open at this time of year"
> If you're travelling outside peak season remember to call ahead to check site opening dates – even if the entry says 'open all year'.

⊞ **HOVBORG** B3 (700m NW Rural) 55.60900, 8.93267 **Holme A Camping, Torpet 6, 6682 Hovborg [tel 75 39 67 77 or 60 91 86 65 (mob); holmeaacamping@ mail.dk; www.holmeaacamping.dk]** Campsite located besides the 425 Grindsted-Ribe. Well sp after Hovborg. Med, mkd pitch, pt shd; htd wc; chem disp; mv service pnt; child/baby facs; fam bthrm; shwrs inc; EHU DKK32; gas; lndry (inc dryer); shop 0.5km; rest, snacks, bar 300m; playgrnd; pool; entmnt; wifi; tv rm; dog DKK10; bus 0.5km; twin axles; Eng spkn; ccard acc; CKE; red LS. "Gd cycling; walking; fishing lakes; 20 min fr Legoland; lovely quiet site; immac facs; friendly helpful owner." DKK 165   2013*

HVIDE SANDE A2 (6.5km S Coastal) 55.96253, 8.14221 **Camping Holmsland Klit, Tingodden 141, Årgab, 6960 Hvide Sande [tel 97 31 13 09; fax 97 31 35 20; c-holmsland@fdm.dk; www.holmsland.fdmcamping.dk]** Fr Ringkøbing rd 15 then rd 181 twd Søndervig, Hvide Sande & Årgab. Site on R. Med, hdstg, pt sl, unshd; wc; chem disp; mv service pnt; fam bthrm; baby facs; shwrs; EHU (6-10A) DKK30; gas; lndry (inc dryer); rest 4.5km; beach adj; playgrnd; fishing; wifi; TV; 20% statics; dogs DKK12; phone; Eng spkn; adv bkg; quiet; ccard acc; red CKE/CCI. "Superb beach; next to 40km cycle track; excel for sm children; Legoland 1 hr; friendly." ♦ Easter-26 Sep. DKK 187 (CChq acc)   2010*

HVIDE SANDE A2 (7.6km S Coastal) 55.94975, 8.15030 **Nordsø Camping & Badeland, Tingodden 3, Årgab, 6960 Hvide Sande [tel 96 59 17 22; fax 96 59 17 17; info@ nordsoe-camping.dk; www.nordsoe-camping.dk]** Fr E20 take exit 73 onto rd 11 to Varde. Then take rd 181 twd Nymindegab & Hvide Sande. Lge, some hdstg, unshd; htd wc; chem disp; mv service pnt; baby facs; fam bthrm; serviced pitches; sauna; private san facs avail; shwrs inc; EHU (10A) DKK30; lndry (inc dryer); shop; rest, snacks; bar; playgrnd; 2 pools (1 htd, covrd); paddling pool; waterslides; sand beach 200m; fishing; tennis; wifi; entmnt; TV rm; 10% statics; dogs DKK20; phone; adv bkg; quiet. "Well-maintained facs; extra charge seaview pitches; vg." ♦ 15 Apr-31 Oct. DKK 199 (CChq acc)   2011*

IDESTRUP see Nykøbing (Falster) D3

ISHOJ HAVN see København D3

JELLING B3 (13km NW Rural) 55.83138, 9.29944 **Topcamp Riis & Feriecenter, Østerhovedvej 43, Riis 7323 Give [tel 75 73 14 33; fax 75 73 58 66; info@riisferiepark.dk or info@topcampriis.dk; www.riisferiepark.dk]** Fr S exit E45 at junc 61, turn L & foll rd 28 for approx 8km. Turn R onto rd 441 for 15km, then turn R into Østerhovedvej for 2km & turn L into site. Or fr N on E45 exit junc 57, turn R & foll rd for 25km; turn L & foll 442 for 500m; turn R into Østerhovedvej & cont for 1.5km; turn R into site. Med, pt shd; hdg; mkd; hdstg; wc; chem disp; mv service pnt; serviced pitch; baby facs; fam bthrm; jacuzzi; sauna; shwrs DKK5; EHU (13A) inc; gas; lndry (ind dryer); shop; rest; bar; BBQ; playgrnd; htd pool; waterslide; paddling pool; jacuzzi; fitness cent; fishing 3.5km; bike hire; games rm; child entmnt high ssn; golf 4km; wifi; TV rm; 60% statics; dogs DKK20; no o'fits over 15m high ssn; phone; recep 0800-2200; poss cr; adv bkg; quiet; ccard acc; red LS; CKE/CCI. "Attractive, well laid-out, well-run site in beautiful countryside; vg san facs; conv for Legoland, Safari Park, Center Mobilium museum in Billund, lakes & E coast; excel." ♦ 12 Apr-27 Sep. DKK 430 SBS - H11   2014*

JUELSMINDE *B3* (1.6km ENE Urban) *55.71330, 10.01562*
Juelsminde Strand Camping, Rousthøjs Allé 1, 7130
Juelsminde [tel 75 69 32 10; fax 75 69 32 28; juelsmin@
image.dk; www.juelsmindecamping.dk] Nr beach in SE
corner of town; site sep fr public beach. Nr ferry terminal to
Kalundborg. Lge, hdg/mkd pitch, pt shd; htd wc; chem disp; mv
service pnt; baby facs; fam bthrm; shwrs; EHU (10A) DKK15;
lndry (inc dryer); shop, rest, snacks & bar; cooking facs; playgrnd;
sand beach 200m; fishing; boating; wifi; TV; phone; poss cr;
dogs DKK10; Eng spkn; adv bkg; quiet; CKE/CCI. "Conv to town
& harbour; poss cr." ♦ 1 Apr-27 Sep. DKK 258   2011*

JYDERUP *C3* (2km SW Rural) *55.65251, 11.39555* **Skarresø**
Camping, Slagelsevej 40, 4450 Jyderup [tel 59 24 86 80;
fax 59 24 86 81; info@skarresoecamping.dk;
www.skarresoecamping.dk] Approx 25km fr Kalundborg dir
Copenhagen rte 23 turn L dir Jyderup. Fr town cent foll sp to
site on RV225 dir Slagelse, site on R in 1km. Med, pt sl, pt shd;
htd wc; chem disp; mv service pnt; baby facs; fam bthrm; shwrs
DKK2; EHU (10A) metered or DKK30; gas; lndry (inc dryer);
shop; rest 1km; BBQ; cooking facs; playgrnd; lake adj; fishing;
bike hire; games area; wifi; TV rm; 25% statics; dogs free; Eng
spkn; adv bkg; quiet. "Pleasant site; gd walks round lake fr site;
tourist info fr site office." ♦ 26 Mar-26 Sep. DKK 140   2010*

⊞ **KARISE** *D3* (5km S Rural) *55.27086, 12.22281* **Lægårdens**
Camping, Vemmetoftevej 2A, Store Spjellerup,
4653 Karise [tel 56 71 00 67; fax 56 71 00 68; info@
laegaardenscamping.dk; www.laegaardenscamping.dk]
Turn S off rd 209 in Karise, site sp. Med, hdg/mkd pitch, pt
shd; htd wc; chem disp; mv service pnt; shwrs DKK5; EHU
DKK30; lndry; rest, snacks 1km; playgrnd; beach 3km; TV;
60% statics; dogs DKK10; Eng spkn; adv bkg; CKE/CCI.
DKK 150   2011*

KARREBAEKSMINDE see Næstved *D3*

KERTEMINDE *C3* (2km NE Coastal) *55.46348, 10.67077*
Kerteminde Camping, Hindsholmvej 80, 5300 Kerteminde
[tel 65 32 19 71; fax 65 32 18 71; kerteminde@mycamp.dk;
www.kertemindecamping.dk] On L of coast rd on N o'skts
of town on rd 315. Lge, pt shd; htd wc; chem disp; mv service
pnt; shwrs DKK6; fam bthrm; baby facs; EHU (10A) DKK30;
lndry; gas; kiosk; rest 2km; BBQ; cooking facs; playgrnd; beach
100m; watersports; bike hire; wifi; TV rm; 10% statics; dogs
DKK15; phone; poss cr; adv bkg; quiet; ccard acc (surcharge);
CKE/CCI. "Excel facs; Viking burial ship in cave nrby." ♦
27 Mar-24 Oct. DKK 173   2010*

KOBENHAVN *D3* (10km N Coastal) *55.74536, 12.58331*
Camping Charlottenlund Fort, Strandvejen 144B,
2290 Charlottenlund [tel 39 62 36 88; fax 39 61 08 16;
camping@gentofte.dk; www.campingcopenhagen.dk]
Take København-Helsingør coast rd O2/152, site on seaside
2km N of Tuborg factory. Sm, mkd pitch, few hdstg, shd; wc;
chem disp; mv service pnt; shwrs DKK5; EHU (10A) metered;
lndry (inc dryer); shops 500m; rest, bar adj; cooking facs;
sand beach; bus; poss v cr; wifi; Eng spkn; adv bkg rec; quiet
but noisy during mid-summer festivities; ccard acc; CKE/CCI.
"Experimentarium Science Park at Tuborg brewery; in grnds
of old moated fort; conv Copenhagen & Sweden; gd facs
but inadequate high ssn; friendly staff." ♦ 30 Apr-6 Sep.
DKK 260   2014*

KOBENHAVN *D3* (20km N Rural) *55.80896, 12.53062*
Nærum Camping, Langebjerg 5, Ravnebakken, 2850
Nærum [tel 42 80 19 57; fax 45 80 11 78; naerum@dcu.dk;
www.camping-naerum.dk] Fr Copenhagen take E47/E55/
rd 19 N for 16km, turn W to Nærum at junc 14, over bdge
x-ing m'way & sharp L. Lge, pt sl, pt shd; wc; chem disp; mv
service pnt; shwrs inc; EHU (10A); gas; lndry; shop; playgrnd;
pool 10km; TV rm; train/bus 500m; poss cr; Eng spkn; adv
bkg; some rlwy & m'way noise; ccard acc; CKE/CCI. "Popular
nr woods; conv Copenhagen & Helsingor; shopping cent nrby
over m'way bdge; gd cycle paths; path fr site for suburban rlwy
to Copenhagen; if arr bet 1200 & 1400 select pitch & report to
office after 1400; facs stretched in high ssn; excel bus service to
Copenhagen." ♦ 21 Mar-19 Oct. DKK 331   2014*

KOBENHAVN *D3* (2.7km S Urban) *55.65903, 12.55785*
City Camp, Fisketorvet/Vasbygade, 1560 København
[tel 45 21 42 53 84; reservation@citycamp.dk]
Fr S on E20, cont over O2 over 'Sjællandsbroen' to R on
Scandiagade, cont on Vasbygade, turn R at 1st traff lts. Site
is behind Fisketorv shopping cent on 'brown field' site - looks
like car park - S of rlwy line by canal. Suggest phone for dirs.
M'vans only. Med, hdstg, unshd; wc; shwrs inc; chem disp; mv
service pnt; EHU (16A) DKK35; shops nr; dogs; open 0800 to
2200; poss cr; Eng spkn; poss noisy. "Conv city cent & Tivoli;
boat ride to cent; facs sufficient but simple; friendly."
29 May-30 Aug. DKK 225   2009*

⊞ **KOBENHAVN** *D3* (9km W Urban) *55.67055, 12.43353*
DCU Absalon Camping, Korsdalsvej 132, 2610 Rødovre
[tel 36 41 06 00; fax 36 41 02 93; absalon@dcu.dk;
www.camping-absalon.dk] Fr E55/E20/E47 exit junc 24 dir
København, site on L in 1km, sp. Or fr København foll A156 W
for 9km. Sp Rødovre then Brøndbyøster, shortly after this site
sp to R at traff lts; ent on L after 100m down side rd, sp. V lge,
mkd pitch, pt shd; htd wc; chem disp; mv service pnt; baby
facs; fam bthrm; shwrs inc; EHU (10-16A) DKK30 or metered
+ conn fee; gas; lndry (inc dryer); shop & 500m; rest 2km;
BBQ; cooking facs; playgrnd; htd pool 300m; golf 10km; wifi;
TV rm; 10% statics; dogs DKK21; bus/train nr; poss cr; ccard
acc (surcharge). "Well located nr Brøndbyøster rlwy stn & bus
Copenhagen (rail tickets fr recep); some pitches unrel in wet &
dusty when dry; vg, modern san facs; office clsd 1200-1400 LS;
sep area for c'vans & m'vans; helpful staff; cycle rte to city; vg;
nice site; gd cooking facs; well run." ♦ DKK 331   2014*

⊞ **KOGE** *D3* (14km SE Coastal) *55.39793, 12.29022* **Stevns**
Camping, Strandvejen 29, 4671 Strøby [tel 60 14 41 54;
info@stevnscamping.dk; www.stevnscamping.dk]
Exit E20/E55 junc 33 twd Køge. In Køge take rd 209 & 260
to Strøby. In Strøby turn L onto Strandvejen. Lge, mkd pitch,
unshd; htd wc; chem disp; mv service pnt; fam bthrm; baby
facs; shwrs inc; EHU (10A) inc; lndry (inc dryer); shop; rest, bar
400m; BBQ; cooking facs; playgrnd; htd pool; paddling pool;
shgl beach 400m; wifi; some statics; dogs DKK10; phone;
Eng spkn; quiet; CKE/CCI. "Gd site nr coast & Koge; access to
Copenhagen by public transport." ♦ DKK 240   2013*

DENMARK

KOGE *D3* (2km S Coastal) *55.44561, 12.19280* **Vallø Camping,
Strandvejen 102, 4600 Køge [tel 56 65 28 51; fax 56 65 10 25;
vallo.camp@mail.dk; www.valloecamping.dk]**
Exit Køge head SE on rd 261, sp Store Heddinge for 500m.
Site on R on o'skts of town. Lge, pt sl, pt shd; wc; chem disp;
mv service pnt; shwrs; fam bthrms; baby facs; EHU (10A)
DKK34; gas; lndry; shop; cooking facs; playgrnd; sand beach
500m; TV; phone; poss cr; adv bkg; quiet. "Poss some traff
noise fr boundary rd; DKK100 deposit for card to use facs -
automatically deducted; pitches & san facs run down (Jun 09);
excel rlwy links to Copenhagen, Roskilde & Helsingør 15 mins
walk fr site." ♦ 1 Apr-30 Sep. DKK 168   2009*

⊞ **KOLDING** *B3* (16km E Coastal) *55.46777, 9.67972*
**Gammel Ålbo Camping, Gammel Aalbovej 30, 6092
Sønder Stenderup [tel 75 57 11 16; camping@gl-aalbo.dk;
www.gl-aalbo.dk]** Foll rd SE fr Kolding to Agtrup then on
to Sønder Bjert & Sønder Stenderup. Foll site sp thro vill twd
coast, site at end of rd. Med, hdg pitch, some hdstg, terr, pt
shd; htd wc; chem disp; mv service pnt; fam bthrm; shwrs
inc; EHU (16A) DKK38.50; lndry rm; shop; cooking facs; shgl
beach adj; fishing; boat hire; skindiving; dogs free; 10% statics;
poss cr; Eng spkn; quiet; CKE/CCI. "Well-kept, relaxing site
o'looking Lillebælt; v cr in high ssn." DKK 224   2015*

⊞ **KOLDING** *B3* (5km S Urban) *55.46290, 9.47290* **Kolding
City Camp, Vonsildvej 19, 6000 Kolding [tel 75 52 13 88;
fax 75 52 45 29; info@koldingcitycamp.dk; www.kolding
citycamp.dk]** E45 (Flensbury-Frederikshavn) take exit 65 at
Kolding Syd twrds Kolding; at 1st traff lts turn R site 800m on
L. Lge, pt sl, pt shd; htd wc; chem disp; mv service pnt; baby
facs; fam bthrm; private san facs avail; shwrs inc; EHU (10A)
DKK30; gas; lndry (inc dryer); shop high ssn; supmkt 800m; rest
3km; BBQ; cooking facs; playgrnd; htd, covrd pool 3km; lake
beach & fishing 5km; tennis; wifi; TV rm; dogs DKK10; phone;
bus to town; poss cr; Eng spkn; adv bkg; some rd noise; ccard
acc; 10% red CKE/CCI. "Friendly & v quiet; conv NH Legoland;
vg san facs; gd site; level pitches; full kitchen facs." ♦ ltd.
DKK 294 (CChq acc)   2014*

KOLLUND see Kruså *B3*

KORSOR *C3* (5km N Coastal) *55.34951, 11.1064* **Storebælt
Camping & Feriecenter, Storebæltsvej 85, 4220 Korsør
[tel 58 38 38 05; fax 58 38 38 65; info@storebaeltferiecenter.
dk; www.storebaeltferiecenter.dk]** Exit E20 junc 43 & foll sp
to site on S side of bdge. Lge, mkd pitch, unshd; htd wc; chem
disp; mv service pnt; baby facs; fam bthrm; serviced pitches;
shwrs DKK5; EHU (10A) metered + conn fee; lndry; shop;
snacks; bar; cooking facs; playgrnd; pool; beach adj; games
area; games rm; wifi; some statics; dogs free; bus 1km; Eng
spkn; adv bkg; quiet; ccard acc (surcharge); CKE/CCI. "Some
m'way noise; sea views; exposed site poss v windy." ♦ ltd.
1 Mar-31 Oct. DKK 170   2009*

KORSOR *C3* (10km SE Rural) *55.28991, 11.2649*
**Campinggaarden Boeslunde, Rennebjergvej 110, 4242
Boeslunde [tel 58 14 02 08; fax 58 14 03 40; info@camping
gaarden.dk; www.campinggaarden.dk]** Take rd 265 S out
of Korsør & in 8km, bef Boeslunde at camping sp, turn R. Site
on L in 2km. Lge, pt sl, shd; wc; chem disp; mv service pnt;
shwrs inc; fam bthrm; baby facs; EHU DKK30 (long lead poss
req); gas; lndry; shop; bar; playgrnd; paddling pool; beach
1.5km; sat TV; dogs DKK10; phone; poss cr w/ends; adv bkg;
quiet; red CKE/CCI. "Gd size, grassy pitches." ♦
1 Apr-30 Sep. DKK 190   2009*

⊞ **KRUSA** *B3* (600m N Rural) *54.85370, 9.40220* **Kruså
Camping, Åbenråvej 7, 6340 Kruså [tel 74 67 12 06;
fax 74 67 12 05; info@krusaacamping.dk; www.krusaa
camping.dk]** S on E45, exit junc 75 twd Kruså. Turn L onto rd
170, site on L. Lge, pt shd, pt sl; wc; chem disp; mv service pnt;
fam bthrm; baby facs; shwrs DKK5; EHU (10A) DKK30; gas;
lndry (inc dryer); shop; rest, snacks; bar; cooking facs; playgrnd;
htd pool; TV; dogs; phone; rd noise; CKE/CCI. "Gd NH; bus
to Flensburg (Germany) 1km fr site; new san facs 2010." ♦
DKK 338   2013*

⊞ **KRUSA** *B3* (5km E Coastal) *54.84231, 9.45896* **Frigård
Camping, Kummelefort 14, 6340 Kollund [tel 74 67 88 30;
fax 74 67 88 72; fricamp@fricamp.dk; www.fricamp.dk]**
Take coast rd 8 fr Kruså dir Sønderborg. Turn R at 2nd set traff
lts dir Kollund, site sp on L after 3km. V lge, pt sl, pt shd; htd
wc; chem disp; mv service pnt; baby facs; fam bthrm; sauna;
shwrs DKK5; EHU (16A) DKK35; lndry (inc dryer); shop; snacks;
cooking facs; playgrnd; htd pool; paddling pool; games area;
bike hire; wifi; 50% statics; dogs free; phone; poss cr; no adv
bkg; quiet. "Conv Sønderborg & fjord." ♦ DKK 241   2010*

KRUSA *B3* (6.6km E Coastal) *54.84538, 9.46715*
**DCU Camping Kollund, Fjordvejen 29A, 6340 Kollund
[tel 74 67 85 15; fax 74 67 83 62; c-kollund@fdm.dk]**
Take coastal rd E fr Kruså dir Sønderborg; site on L 500m after
Kollund. Med, mkd pitch, pt sl, unshd; wc; chem disp; mv
service pnt; shwrs DKK5; EHU (6A) DKK45; lndry; shop; rest
adj; cooking facs; playgrnd; internet; 40% statics; dogs DKK15;
phone; Eng spkn; adv bkg; ccard acc. "Friendly owners; gd." ♦
Easter-14 Oct. DKK 175   2009*

KULHUSE *D2* (750m S Coastal) *55.93168, 11.90907*
**DCU Camping Kulhuse, Kulhusevej 199, 3630 Kulhuse
[tel 47 53 01 86; fax 47 53 51 28; kulhuse@dcu.dk;
www.camping-kulhuse.dk]** Fr Jægerspris on rd 207 N sp
Kulhuse. Well sp on L 1km bef vill. Lge, pt sl, terr, pt shd; htd
wc; chem disp; mv service pnt; fam bthrm; baby facs; shwrs
inc; EHU (4A) DKK30; lndry; shop & 1km; rest 1km; snacks;
bar 1km; BBQ; cooking facs; playgrnd; sand beach 500m; TV;
20% statics; dogs DKK20; phone; poss cr; Eng spkn; adv bkg;
quiet; CKE/CCI. "Gd children's playgrnd facs; pleasant site." ♦
24 Mar-21 Oct. DKK 194   2011*

LANGELAND ISLAND *C3* Sites on Langeland Island are
listed together at the end of the Denmark site entry
pages.

LAVEN see Ry *B2*

LEMVIG *A2* (12km W Coastal) *56.52608, 8.12633* **Bovbjerg Camping, Julsgårdvej 13, 7620 Ferring [tel 97 89 51 20; fax 97 89 53 43; bc@bovbjergcamping.dk; www.bovbjerg camping.dk]** Fr Lemvig foll rd 181 past Nissum Fjord, take rd to L for Ferring. Site to N of vill. Med, hdg/mkd pitch, pt shd; wc; chem disp; mv service pnt; baby facs; fam bthrm; shwrs DKK2; EHU (10A) DKK29; lndry; shop; rest 400m; cooking facs; htd pool; paddling pool; sand beach 300m; bike hire; golf 13km; TV rm; 30% statics; dogs; phone; Eng spkn; adv bkg; quiet; red long stay/snr citizens; CKE/CCI. "Lge pitches with view." 20 Mar-18 Oct. DKK 178 **2009***

LEMVIG *A2* (4km NW Coastal) *56.56733, 8.29399* **Lemvig Strand Camping, Vinkelhagevej 6, 7620 Lemvig [tel 97 82 00 42; fax 97 81 04 56; lemvig@dk-camp.dk; www.lemvigstrandcamping.dk]** Foll camping sps in Lemvig to site. Med, mkd pitch, unshd; wc; chem disp; mv service pnt; baby facs; fam bthrm; sauna; shwrs DKK2; EHU (10A) DKK35; lndry; shop; rest adj; cooking facs; playgrnd; htd, covrd pool; beach 300m; games area; games rm; internet; TV rm; 30% statics; dogs DKK10; phone; adv bkg; ccard acc. "Vg sailing cent; pretty area." ♦ 30 Mar-16 Sep. DKK 359 **2013***

LOKKEN *B1* (2km N Rural) *57.38580, 9.72580* **Løkken Strandcamping, Furreby Kirkevej 97, 9480 Løkken [tel 45 98 99 18 04; info@loekkencamping.dk]** Head NE on Lokkensvej/Rte 55. At rndabt take 3rd exit onto Harald Fischers Vej. Turn R onto Furreby Kirkevej. Site 1.3km on the L. Med, pt shd; htd wc; chem disp; mv service pnt; fam bthrm; shwrs; lndry (inc dryer); shops 2km; cooking facs; sand beach adj; TV rm; dogs DKK11; twin axles; Eng spkn; adv bkg; quiet; ccard acc. "Vg site; pitches separated by fences; direct access to sand dunes." 1 May-7 Sep. DKK 312 **2014***

LOKKEN *B1* (8km SW Coastal) *57.32070, 9.67760* **Grønhøj Strand Camping, Kettrupvej 125, Ingstrup, 9480 Løkken [tel 98 88 44 33; fax 98 88 36 44; info@gronhoj-strand-camping.dk; www.gronhoj-strand-camping.dk]** S fr Løkken on rd 55, sp on rd Grønhøj Strandvej. Lge, unshd; htd wc; chem disp; mv service pnt; serviced pitches; sauna; baby facs; fam bthrm; shwrs DKK5; EHU (13A) DKK30; lndry (inc dryer); shop; rest 2km; BBQ; cooking facs; playgrnd; sand beach 700m; tennis adj; games area; wifi; TV rm; 30% statics; dogs; phone; Eng spkn; adv bkg; quiet; ccard acc; red snr citizens. ♦ 15 Apr-18 Sep. DKK 158 (CChq acc) **2011***

LUNDEBORG *C3* (450m N Coastal) *55.14560, 10.78136* **Lundeborg Strand-Camping, Gammel Lundeborgvej 46, 5874 Hasselager [tel 62 25 14 50; fax 62 25 20 22; ferie@lundeborg.dk; www.lundeborg.dk]** Fr rd 163 turn E at Oure, site sp fr Lundeborg. Med, pt sl, unshd; wc; chem disp; mv service pnt; shwrs DKK5; fam bthrm; baby facs; EHU (6A) DKK35; lndry; shop; cooking facs; playgrnd; beach adj; boat-launching; TV; some statics; dogs DKK15; phone; poss cr; adv bkg; quiet. "Attractive sm fishing vill; pay in adv on arr." Easter-13 Sep. DKK 192 **2009***

MALLING *C2* (4km E Coastal) *56.04122, 10.26390* **Ajstrup Strand Camping, Ajstrup Strandvej 81, Ajstrup Strand, 8340 Malling [tel 86 93 35 35; fax 86 93 15 84; info@ ajstrupcamping.dk; www.ajstrupcamping.dk]** Fr S turn R in Odder off rd 451 sp Sakslid. Foll rd for 8km thro Norsminde, then turn R & foll site sp. Lge, mkd pitch, pt shd; htd wc; chem disp; mv service pnt; baby facs; fam bthrm; private san facs avail; shwrs; EHU (6A) DKK30; lndry (inc dryer); shop; snacks; BBQ; cooking facs; playgrnd; beach adj; bike & canoe hire; wifi; 6% statics; dogs DKK10; Eng spkn; CKE/CCI. "Adj to excel cycle track thro forest to Århus." ♦ 15 Apr-23 Oct. DKK 164 (CChq acc) **2009***

MARIAGER *B2* (750m N Coastal) *56.65424, 9.97500* **Mariager Camping, Ny Havnevej 5A, 9550 Mariager [tel 98 54 13 42; fax 98 54 25 80; info@mariagercamping.dk; www.mariagercamping.dk]** E fr Hobro on rd 555, do not take R sp Mariager, but on to bottom of hill, turn L at camp sp. Med, mkd pitch, unshd; wc; chem disp; mv service pnt; baby facs; fam bthrm; shwrs DKK2; EHU (16A) DKK25; gas; lndry; shop; snacks; playgrnd; sand/shgl beach adj; sea & rv fishing; boat launch; 50% statics; dogs free; phone; Eng spkn; adv bkg; quiet; CKE/CCI. "Beautiful vill with museum & abbey; fjord views fr site; vg facs." ♦ 5 Apr-23 Sep. DKK 178 **2009***

MARIBO *C3* (2km SW Rural) *54.77260, 11.49463* **Maribo Sø Camping, Bangshavevej 25, 4930 Maribo [tel 54 78 00 71; fax 54 78 47 71; camping@maribo-camping.dk; www.maribo-camping.dk]** Exit E47 junc 48 at Maribo. At rndabt take rd to 'Centrum' strt on into Vesterbrogade; turn R into Bangshavevej & foll site sp. Lge, pt shd; wc; chem disp; mv service pnt; baby facs; fam bthrm; shwrs inc; EHU (6A) DKK32; lndry; shop; cooking facs; playgrnd; sand beach & lake adj; internet; TV rm; 30% statics; phone; poss cr; Eng spkn; adv bkg; quiet; CKE/CCI. "Clean facs; 5 mins walk into Maribo; museum adj; helpful staff; useful as NH after ferry fr Puttgarden, Germany; site clsd 1300-1500, site yourself; late arr area avail at night." ♦ 30 Mar-21 Oct. DKK 177 **2011***

MIDDELFART *B3* (11km NE Coastal) *55.51948, 9.85025* **Vejlby Fed Camping, Rigelvej 1, 5500 Vejlby Fed [tel 64 40 24 20; fax 64 40 24 38; mail@vejlbyfed.dk; www.vejlbyfed.dk]** Exit E20 junc 57 or 58. Site sp in Vejlby Fed, NE fr Middelfart dir Bogense, on coast. Lge, mkd pitch, pt shd; wc; chem disp; mv service pnt; fam bthrm; baby facs; sauna; shwrs DKK6; EHU (10A) DKK28; lndry; shop; snacks; bar; cooking facs; playgrnd; htd pool; paddling pool; sand beach adj; boating; fishing; tennis; wifi; 30% statics; dogs DKK15; phone; Eng spkn; adv bkg; CKE/CCI. ♦ 15 Mar-14 Sep. DKK 430 **2014***

MIDDELFART *B3* (11km SE Rural/Coastal) *55.43995, 9.82464* **Ronæs Strand Camping, Ronæsvej 10, Ronæs Strand, 5580 Nørre Aaby [tel 64 42 17 63; fax 64 42 17 73; campingferie@hotmail.com; www.camping-ferie.dk]** Leave E20 at Nørre Aaby junc 57, take 313 S twd Assens. In 5km turn R (NW) to Udby. In Udby turn L to Ronaes, turn R in vill. Site on L, sp. Med, mkd pitch, terr, pt sl, pt shd; wc; chem disp; mv service pnt; baby facs; fam bthrm; shwrs DKK6; EHU (10A) DKK30; gas; lndry (inc dryer); shop; rest 6km; snacks high ssn; playgrnd; sand beach adj; fishing; boat hire & launching facs; bike hire; wifi; TV; 10% statics; dogs DKK15; phone; Eng spkn; adv bkg; quiet; ccard acc; CKE/CCI. "Gd for families; vg facs." ♦ Easter-19 Sep. DKK 200 **2010***

DENMARK

MIDDELFART *B3* (5km NW Rural) *55.51694, 9.68225* **Gals Klint Camping, Galsklintvej 11, 5500 Middelfart [tel 64 41 20 59; fax 64 41 81 59; mail@galsklint.dk; www.galsklint.dk]** Fr W on E20 take rd 161. At traff lts turn L & cross Little Belt Bdge. In 300m turn R into Galsklintvej & foll sp. Lge, hdg/mkd pitch, pt shd; htd wc; chem disp; mv service pnt; baby facs; fam bthrm; shwrs DKK3; EHU (16A) DKK28; lndry; shop; rest, snacks; BBQ; cooking facs; playgrnd; shgl beach adj; fishing; boat hire; 10% statics; dogs; Eng spkn; adv bkg; quiet; ccard acc (surcharge); CKE/CCI. "Site surrounded by forest; gd cycling/walking; vg; well run mod facs shoreside next woodland." ♦ Easter-2 Oct. DKK 200   2012*

NAERUM see København *D3*

NAESTVED *D3* (9km SW Rural/Coastal) *55.20051, 11.66438* **De Hvide Svaner Camping, Karrebækvej 741, 4736 Karrebæksminde [tel 55 44 24 15; svaner@mail.dk; www.dehvidesvaner.dk]** Fr Næstved take Karrebæksminde rd 265. Site on L 200m after turn for Skælskør. Lge, hdg/ mkd pitch, pt sl, pt shd; wc; chem disp; mv service pnt; baby facs; fam bthrm; shwrs inc; EHU (10A) DKK30; gas; lndry; sm shop; rest; playgrnd; htd pool; paddling pool; beach nrby; bike hire; games area; wifi; TV; many statics; dogs DKK10; phone; Quickstop o'night facs; Eng spkn; adv bkg; quiet. "Excel, modern san facs; friendly staff; well situated nr lake." ♦ Easter-16 Oct. DKK 192   2009*

NAKSKOV *C3* (15km SW Coastal) *54.79180, 10.98110* **Albuen Strand Camping, Vesternæsvej 70, Ydø, 4900 Nakskov [tel 54 94 87 62; fax 54 94 90 27; mail@albuen.dk; www.albuen.dk]** S fr Nakskov dir Langø. In approx 10km at Ydø, foll sp to site. Lge, unshd; htd wc; chem disp; mv service pnt; baby facs; fam bthrm; shwrs DKK2; EHU (10A) DKK30; lndry (inc dryer); shop; cooking facs; playgrnd; htd pool; paddling pool; sand beach adj; bike hire; games area; wifi; TV rm; 15% statics; dogs DKK20; phone; adv bkg; quiet. ♦ 17 Apr-25 Sep. DKK 200   2010*

NAKSKOV *C3* (4km W Coastal) *54.83303, 11.09083* **Hestehoved Camping, Hestehovedet 2, 4900 Nakskov [tel 54 95 17 47; fax 54 95 69 20; hestehovedet@tdcadsl.dk]** Cont on main rd fr Tårs after exit ferry fr Spodsbjerg. Site sp R after passing town boundary. Med, mkd pitch, pt shd; wc; chem disp; mv service pnt; baby facs; fam bthrm; shwrs DKK2; EHU (10A) DKK27; lndry; shop 3km; rest 200m; playgrnd; marina adj; sand beach 250m; bike hire; TV; 70% statics; phone; adv bkg; quiet. "Conv for ferry Spodsbjerg-Tårs." ♦ 7 Apr-30 Sep. DKK 140   2009*

⊞ **NORDBORG** *B3* (5km N Rural/Coastal) *55.07762, 9.71482* **Augustenhof Strand Camping, Augustenhofvej 30, 6430 Nordborg [tel/fax 74 45 03 04; augustenhof@dk-camp.dk; www.dk-camp.dk/augustenhof]** Take rd N out of Nordborg to Købingsmark. In 1km turn W to Stærbækvej. Cont twd Augustenhofvej. Turn NW & foll rd to camp nr lighthouse. Med, mkd pitch, pt shd; htd wc; chem disp; mv service pnt; baby facs; fam bthrm; shwrs DKK2; EHU (6-13A) DKK26.50; gas; lndry; shop; rest, bar 4km; playgrnd; pool 5km; beach; boat-launching; TV; 60% statics; dogs DKK9; phone; Quickstop o'night facs; adv bkg; quiet. "Conv for Nordberg Castle; adv bkg rec LS." DKK 167 (CChq acc)   2009*

⊞ **NORDSKOV** *C3* (1km N Coastal) *55.60648, 10.62190* **Fyns Hoved Camping, Fynshovedvej 748, Nordskov, 5390 Martofte [tel 65 34 10 14; fax 65 34 25 14; fynshoved@ dk-camp.dk; www.fynshovedcamping.dk]** Fr E20 foll sp N to Kerteminde then take 315 dir Martofte & Nordskov. Or fr Odense/Nyborg take 165 N to Kerteminde, then as above. Lge, mkd pitch, pt shd; wc; chem disp; 50% serviced pitches; mv service pnt; baby facs; fam bthrm; shwrs; EHU (10A) DKK30 (long lead poss req); gas; lndry; shop; rest, snacks; bar; BBQ; cooking facs; playgrnd; shgl beach adj; entmnt; TV rm; some statics; dogs; poss cr; Eng spkn; adv bkg; quiet; ccard acc; CKE/CCI. "Excel scenic, rural area; ideal for cycling; vg." ♦ DKK 165   2010*

NORRE AABY see Middelfart *B3*

NORRE NEBEL *A2* (8km NW Rural) *55.82675, 8.21552* **Vesterlund Camping & Café, Vesterlundvej 101, 6830 Nørre Nebel [tel 86 85 56 65; mai-britt.schulze@teliamail. dk; www.vesterlundcamping.dk]** Fr rte 181 thro Nørre Nebel dir Hvide Sande, turn R at site sp in approx 5km, site in 1km on L. Recep in site rest. Med, hdg pitch, pt shd; htd wc; chem disp; mv service pnt; fam bthrm; shwrs; lndry rm; rest; cooking facs; playgrnd; few statics; Eng spkn; quiet; CKE/CCI. "Peaceful, relaxing, well-kept site; helpful owner." 27 Mar-24 Oct. DKK 150   2010*

NYBORG *C3* (4km N Coastal) *55.35853, 10.78660* **Gronnehave Strand, Regstrupvej 83, 5800 Nyborg [tel 65 36 15 50; info@gronnehave.dk; www.gronnehave.dk]** 10 mins N fr E20 on Skaboeshusevej. Med, mkd pitch, terr, unshd; htd wc; chem disp; mv service pnt; baby facs; fam bthrm; shwrs; EHU (10A) DKK36; lndry (inc dryer); shop 3km; playgrnd; beach adj; games area; wifi; tv rm; dogs; bus 2km; Eng spkn; quiet. "Friendly owner; gd views; bdge to Zeeland; vg." 12 Apr-19 Oct. DKK 244   2015*

NYBORG *C3* (3km SE Coastal) *55.30457, 10.82453* **Nyborg Strandcamping, Hjejlevej 99, 5800 Nyborg [tel 65 31 02 56; mail@strandcamping.dk; www.strandcamping.dk]** Exit E20 at junc 44. Turn N, site sp in 1km. Lge, mkd pitch, pt shd; wc; chem disp; mv service pnt; fam bthrm; baby facs; shwrs DKK9; EHU (10A) metered; gas; lndry; shop; rest 500m; snacks; playgrnd; sand beach adj; fishing; golf 1km; internet; TV; 50% statics; dogs; phone; Eng spkn; adv bkg; CKE/CCI. "Conv m'way, rlwy & ferry; excel views of bdge; gd facs; gd site; well difined pitches next to beach." ♦ 13 Apr-21 Sep. DKK 256   2014*

NYBORG *C3* (13km S Rural) *55.23693, 10.8080* **Tårup Stand Camping, Lersey Allé 25, Tårup Strand, 5871 Frørup [tel 65 37 11 99; fax 65 37 11 79; mail@taarupstrandcamping. dk; www.taarupstrandcamping.dk]** S fr Nyborg take 163 twds Svendborg; after 6.5km turn L sp Tårup. In 2.7km turn L sp Tårup Strand. Site 1.5km on R. Med, mkd pitch, terr; htd wc; chem disp; mv service pnt; fam bthrm; baby facs; shwrs DKK5; EHU (6-10A) DKK26; lndry; kiosk; playgrnd; shgl beach; lake; TV; 70% statics; games rm; wifi; phone; dogs; adv bkg; quiet; poss cr high ssn; Ccard acc; CKE/CCI. "Quiet family site; excel views of bdge; fishing; excel site." 4 Apr-21 Sep. DKK 222   2014*

DENMARK

NYKOBING (FALSTER) *D3* (14km E Coastal) *54.74057, 12.02801* **Campinggården Ulslev Strand, Strandvejen 3, Ulslev Strand, 4872 Idestrup [tel 54 14 83 50; fax 54 14 83 47; ulslev@dk-camp.dk; www.campinggaarden-ulslev.dk]** Foll E55 around Nykøbing to E, at rndabt turn L twd Horbelev. In 2km turn R & foll sp Ulslev Strand. Fr Gedser ferry turn R (E) at rndabt on app Nykøbing, then as above. Lge, mkd pitch, pt sl, pt shd; wc; chem disp; mv service pnt; fam bthrm; baby facs; sauna; shwrs; EHU (10A) DKK30; gas; lndry; shop; rest; playgrnd; sand beach adj; games area; TV; 20% statics; dogs free; phone; Eng spkn; adv bkg; quiet; ccard acc; CKE/CCI. "Gd beaches; gd cycling; nr several theme parks; day ferry to Rostok fr Gedser." 20 Mar-3 Oct. DKK 174   2010*

NYKOBING (MORS) *B2* (5km SW Coastal) *56.76435, 8.81474* **Jesperhus Camping, Legindvej 30, 7900 Nykøbing [tel 96 70 14 00; fax 96 70 14 17; jesperhus@jesperhus.dk; www.jesperhus.dk]** Exit rd 26 at sp Nykøbing Syd (S) & foll sp to Salling Sund for 1km; foll sp for Billund. Site on R 200m past Jesperhus Blomsterpark (Flower Park). V lge, hdg pitch, terr, pt shd; wc; chem disp; mv service pnt; fam bthrm; baby facs; sauna; shwrs inc; EHU (6A) DKK40; lndry (inc dryer); shop; rest, snacks; bar; cooking facs; playgrnd; htd pools (1 covrd); waterpark; beach 1km; fishing; tennis; games area; entmnt; TV; 50% statics; dogs DKK30; phone; adv bkg; quiet. "Jesperhus Blomsterpark (open May-Oct) excel; site vg for families; many activities." ♦ 26 Mar-25 Oct. DKK 260   2010*

"That's changed – Should I let The Club know?"

If you find something on site that's different from the site entry, fill in a report and let us know. See www.caravanclub.co.uk/europereport.

NYMINDEGAB *A2* (600m S Rural) *55.81263, 8.20001* **Nymindegab Familie Camping, Lyngtoften 12, 6830 Nymindegab [tel 75 28 91 83; fax 75 28 94 30; info@ nycamp.dk; www.nycamp.dk]** Clear sp on L of rd 181 at ent to vill fr Esbjerg & SE via Nørre Nebel. If app fr N, thro vill & look for Int'l sp on R. Lge, mkd pitch, pt shd; wc; chem disp; mv service pnt; baby facs; fam bthrm; sauna; shwrs DKK2; EHU (16A) DKK25; gas; lndry; shop; rest 500m; bar; playgrnd; pool; paddling pool; sand beach 2km; games area; TV; internet; dogs; phone; adv bkg; poss cr; quiet; ccard acc; red LS. "Adj army firing ranges troublesome at times; helpful warden." ♦ 1 Apr-27 Sep. DKK 151   2009*

NYSTED *D4* (2km SE Coastal) *54.65426, 11.73167* **Nysted Camping, Skansevej 38, 4880 Nysted [tel 54 87 09 17; fax 54 87 14 29; nystedcamping@post.tele.dk; www.nysted-camping.dk]** Foll sp for site in Nysted. Med, mkd pitch, pt shd; htd wc; chem disp; mv service pnt; baby facs; fam bthrm; shwrs; EHU (10A) DKK30; gas; lndry; shop; snacks; cooking facs; playgrnd; sand beach adj; bike hire; games area; TV; wifi; 10% statics; dogs; site open in winter on request; adv bkg; ccard acc; red CKE/CCI. "Noisy at w/end; conv for Rødbyhavn-Puttgarden ferry; castle & vintage car museum in 4km." ♦ Easter-19 Oct. DKK 150   2009*

ODENSE *C3* (5km S Rural) *55.36966, 10.39316* **DCU Camping Odense, Odensevej 102, 5260 Odense [tel 66 11 47 02; fax 65 91 73 43; odense@dcu.dk; www.camping-odense.dk]** Exit E20 junc 50 foll sp 'centrum' (Stenlosevej). After rndabt site on L just after 3rd set traff lts. Ent to R of petrol stn. Lge, pt shd; mkd pitch; htd wc; chem disp; mv service pnt; fam bthrm; baby facs; shwrs inc; EHU (10A) DKK30; gas; lndry; shop; rest 1.5km; playgrnd; pool; TV rm; dogs DKK15; phone; bus; Eng spkn; adv bkg; quiet; ccard acc (surcharge); CKE/CCI. "Hans Christian Andersen's house; many attractions; excel, friendly, family-run site; busy high ssn & facs stretched; easy bus access to town cent; lovely, easy cycle rte into town cent; gd san fac; pitches tight for larger units." ♦ DKK 240   2014*

ODENSE *C3* (11km W Rural) *55.3894, 10.2475* **Campingpladsen Blommenslyst, Middelfartvej 494, 5491 Blommenslyst [tel/fax 65 96 76 41; info@blommelyst-camping.dk; www.blommenslyst-camping.dk]** Exit E20 onto 161 (junc 53); sp 'Odense/Blommenslyst', site on R after 2km; lge pink Camping sp on side of house. Sm, pt sl, shd; htd wc; chem disp; mv service pnt; shwrs DKK5; EHU (4A) DKK30; lndry; shop; café 500m; playgrnd; sm lake; some statics; dogs DKK10; bus; Eng spkn; adv bkg; some rd noise; CKE/CCI. "Picturesque setting round sm lake; gd, clean facs; welcoming owners; frequent bus to town outside site; excel." ♦ 5 Jan-20 Dec. DKK 206   2013*

OKSBOL *A3* (1km N Rural) *55.64048, 8.28204* **Camp West, Baunhøjvej 34, 6840 Oksbøl [tel 75 27 11 30; fax 75 27 11 31; info@campwest.dk; www.campwest.dk]** N fr Oksbøl dir Øster Vrøgum & Henne, site sp. Med, hdg pitch, pt shd; wc; chem disp; mv service pnt; fam bthrm; baby facs; shwrs inc; EHU (10A) DKK30; gas; lndry; shop; playgrnd; sand beach 12km; TV; dogs free; phone; Quickstop o'night facs; adv bkg; ccard acc; quiet; CKE/CCI. "Pleasant, rural site; less cr than beach sites." DKK 174   2011*

OTTERUP *C3* (6km NE Coastal) *55.56295, 10.45390* **Hasmark Strand Camping, Strandvejen 205, Hasmark Strand, 5450 Otterup [tel 64 82 62 06; fax 64 82 55 80; info@hasmark. dk; www.hasmark.dk]** Exit rd 51 thro Odense onto rd 162 & foll sp Havn Otterup, then dir Hasmark. Site sp. Lge, pt shd; htd wc; chem disp; mv service pnt; fam bthrm; private san facs avail; shwrs; EHU (10A) DKK35; lndry; shop; rest, snacks; bar; cooking facs; playgrnd; pool complex; sand beach adj; games area; bike hire; golf 15km; wifi; TV rm; 25% statics; dogs DKK10; adv bkg; quiet. "Pleasant site on superb beach." ♦ 1 Apr-25 Sep. DKK 175 (CChq acc)   2009*

RAGELEJE see Gilleleje *D2*

RANDERS *B2* (8km SW Rural) *56.44984, 9.95287* **Randers City Camp, Hedevej 9, Fladbro, 8900 Randers [tel/fax 86 42 93 61; info@randerscitycamp.dk; www.randerscitycamp.dk]** Take exit 40 fr E45 & turn twd Randers. Approx 100m fr m'way turn R at traff lts dir Langå. Site clearly sp in 3km & also sp fr rd 16. Lge, pt shd; wc; chem disp; mv service pnt; baby facs; fam bthrm; shwrs inc; EHU (10A) DKK30; lndry (inc dryer); shop 2km; cooking facs; playgrnd; htd pool; fishing; games rm; golf adj; TV; some statics; dogs DKK10; phone; Eng spkn; ccard acc. "On heather hills with view of Nørreå valley; rec arr early for pitch with view; golf course." ♦ DKK 164   2010*

⊞ **RIBE** *B3* (2km SE Rural) *55.34115, 8.76506* **Parking Storkesøen, Haulundvej 164, 6760 Ribe [tel 75 41 04 11; fax 41 08 57; info@storkesoen.dk; www.storkesoen.dk]** Fr S on rte 11, turn R at 1st rndabt onto rte 24 & R at next rndabt. Site 100m on R, sp fishing. Fr S on rte 24, at 1st rndabt after rlwy turn L, site 200m on R. M'vans only - check in at fishing shop on R. Sm, all hdstg, unshd; wc; own san; chem disp; shwrs inc; EHU (5A/16A) inc; fishing shop; snacks; lake fishing. "Picturesque, quiet site o'looking fishing lakes; walking dist Denmark's oldest city; m'vans & c'vans acc, ideal NH." DKK 140   2014*

⊞ **RIBE** *B3* (2.4km NNW Rural) *55.34115, 8.76506* **Ribe Camping, Farupvej 2, 6760 Ribe [tel 75 41 07 77; fax 75 41 00 01; info@ribecamping.dk; www.ribecamping.dk]** Fr S foll A11 by-pass W of Ribe to traff lts N of town; turn W off A11 at traff lts; site 500m on R. Fr N (Esbjerg ferry) to Ribe, turn R at traff lts sp Farup. Site on R, sp. Lge, pt shd; htd wc; chem disp; mv service pnt; baby rm; fam bthrm; some serviced pitches; shwrs DKK8; EHU (10A) DKK35; gas; lndry; shop; snacks; cooking facs; playgrnd; htd pool; games rm; internet; TV; 10% statics; dogs DKK15; phone; Quickstop o'night facs; poss cr; adv bkg; quiet; ccard acc (transaction charge); CKE/CCI. "Ribe oldest town in Denmark; much historical interest; helpful staff; well-run, friendly site; excel, modern san facs; conv Esbjerg ferry." ♦ DKK 253   2014*

RINGE *C3* (1km NNW Urban) *55.24024, 10.47439* **Midtfyns Camping, Søvej 30-34, 5750 Ringe [tel 62 62 21 51; fax 62 62 21 54; mfc@midtfyns-frididscenter.dk; www.midtfyns-fritidscenter.dk]** Exit A9 Odense-Svendborg at Ringe N & foll site sp. Register at recep adj sports cent. Med, hdg/mkd pitch, pt sl, pt shd; wc; chem disp; mv service pnt; shwrs; EHU DKK24; lndry; shops 500m; rest, snacks; playgrnd; pool; sand beach 20km; tennis; some statics; phone; Quickstop o'night facs; quiet; ccard acc;CKE/CCI. "Egeskov Castle 10km, worth a visit." ♦ 1 May-30 Sep. DKK 157   2009*

RINGKOBING *A2* (5km E Rural) *56.08856, 8.31659* **Ringkøbing Camping, Herningvej 105, 6950 Ringkøbing [tel/fax 97 32 04 20; info@ringkobingcamping.dk; www.ringkøbingcamping.dk]** Take rd 15 fr Ringkøbing dir Herning, site on L. Med, hdg/mkd pitch, pt shd; wc; chem disp; mv service pnt; shwrs DKK2; EHU (10A) DKK29; gas; lndry; shop; sand beach 3km; playgrnd; TV; phone; dogs DKK10; Quickstop o'night facs; poss cr; adv bkg; quiet. "Beautiful site in mixed forest; friendly welcome; excel facs; gd walks; 3km to fjord; 14km to sea." ♦ 1 Apr-30 Sep. DKK 226   2011*

RINGSTED *D3* (10km NE Rural) *55.49644, 11.85796* **Camping Skovly, Nebs Møllevej 65, Ortved, 4100 Ringsted [tel 57 52 82 61; fax 57 52 86 25; info@skovlycamping.dk; www.skovlycamping.dk]** Take junc 35 off E20 onto rd 14 N. Turn W at sp in Ortved. Med, hdg/mkd pitch, pt sl, shd; wc; chem disp; mv service pnt; fam bthrm; baby facs; shwrs DKK6; EHU (6A) metered + DKK15; lndry (inc dryer); shop; cooking facs; playgrnd; htd pool; paddling pool; games rm; wifi; TV; 50% statics; dogs DKK15; phone; Eng spkn; adv bkg; quiet; ltd facs LS; ccard acc (surcharge);CKE/CCI. "Pleasant, wooded site; friendly, family-run, well-organised site; clean san facs; conv Viking Cent & other attractions." 1 Apr-1 Oct. DKK 182   2010*

⊞ **RODBYHAVN** *C4* (5km NE Urban) *54.69873, 11.39218* **Camping Rødby Lystskov, Strandvej 3, 4970 Rødby [tel 54 60 12 16; info@rodbycamping.dk; www.rodby camping.dk]** Fr N Zeeland or Rødby ferries, foll sps for site in Rødby, NE of town cent. Med, pt shd; wc; chem disp; mv service pnt; baby facs; shwrs inc; EHU (16A) DKK25; gas; lndry (inc dryer); shop; cooking facs; playgrnd; beach 4km; TV; 20% statics; dogs free; poss cr; Eng spkn; adv bkg;CKE/CCI. "Clean facs; helpful owner; liable to flooding; sh walk to town cent; conv for ferries." ♦ DKK 150   2010*

RODOVRE see København *D3*

ROMO ISLAND *A3* Sites on Rømø Island are listed together at the end of the Denmark site entry pages.

ROSKILDE *D3* (4km N Rural) *55.67411, 12.07955* **Roskilde Camping, Baunehøjvej 7-9, 4000 Veddelev [tel 46 75 79 96; fax 46 75 44 26; mail@roskildecamping.dk; www.roskilde camping.dk]** Leave rd 21/23 at junc 11 & turn N on rd 6 sp Hillerød. Turn R onto rd 02 (E ring rd); then rejoin 6; (watch for camping sp). At traff lts with camping sp turn L twds city & foll site sp. Lge, mkd pitch, pt sl, pt shd; htd wc; own san; chem disp; baby facs; shwrs DKK6; EHU (10A) DKK30; gas; lndry; shop; rest; playgrnd; shgl beach; watersports; games rm; TV; wifi; poss cr high ssn; Eng spkn; adv bkg; quiet; ccard acc (surcharge); CKE/CCI. "Beautiful views over fjord; nr Viking Ship Museum (a must) - easy parking; beautiful Cathedral; excel rest & shop open 0800-2000; bus service to stn, frequent trains to Copenhagen; ltd flat pitches; lovely site; immac, new state of the art san facs block with card for ent (2014); v welcoming & helpful staff." 31 Mar-23 Sep. DKK 225   2014*

ROSLEV *B2* (10km NW Rural/Coastal) *56.74333, 8.86884* **Glyngøre Camping, Sundhøj 20A, Glyngøre, 7870 Roslev [tel 97 73 17 88; fax 97 73 17 99; post@glyngore-camping. dk; www.glyngore-camping.dk]** Site sp fr rd 26 dir Glyngøre, immed S of Sallingsund bdge. Lge, hdg/mkd pitch, pt sl, pt shd; htd wc; chem disp; mv service pnt; baby facs; fam bthrm; shwrs metered; EHU (16A) inc; lndry (inc dryer); ice; shop; rest, snacks; bar; BBQ; cooking facs; playgrnd; htd, covrd pool; sand beach 1km; games area; games rm; internet; TV; 30% statics; dogs; phone; Eng spkn; adv bkg; quiet; ccard acc; CKE/CCI. "Excel, welcoming, spacious site in attractive position; gd touring base." ♦ 1 Apr-12 Oct. DKK 202   2010*

RY *B2* (2km S Rural) *56.07692, 9.76527* **Holmens Camping, Klostervej 148, 8680 Ry [tel 86 89 17 62; fax 86 89 17 12; info@holmens-camping.dk; www.holmens-camping.dk]** Exit Skanderborg on 445 sp Ry & Silkeborg. In Ry immed after level x-ing turn L on rd sp Øm-Kloster & camping sp. Site on R in 2km. Lge, mkd pitch, pt sl, pt shd; wc; chem disp; mv service pnt; baby facs; fam bthrm; shwrs DKK7; EHU (6A) DKK28; gas; lndry; shops 2km; rest 2km; snacks; cooking facs; playgrnd; lake sw, fishing, caneoing & watersports (no windsurfing); TV; 25% statics; phone; Eng spkn; adv bkg; quiet; ccard acc; red long stay. "Ry cent of Danish lake district; vg, well organised site." 1 Apr-15 Sep. DKK 175   2009*

RY *B2* (4km NW Rural) *56.10388, 9.74555* **Birkede Camping, Lyngvej 14, 8680 Ry [tel 86 89 13 55; fax 86 89 03 13; info@birkhede.dk; www.birkhede.dk]** Fr S on rd 52 exit onto rd 445 to Ry, then foll sp N on rd dir Laven. Turn R in 1km to site on lakeside. Clearly sp in cent of Ry. Lge, mkd pitch, pt sl, pt shd; wc; chem disp; mv service pnt; baby facs; shwrs DKK6; EHU (10A) metered + conn fee; gas; lndry (inc dryer); shop; rest; bar; cooking facs; playgrnd; htd pool; bike & boat hire; fishing; games rm; golf 10km; wc; dogs; phone; poss cr; Eng spkn; adv bkg; CKE/CCI. "Gd site." ♦ 11 Apr-21 Sep. DKK 260   2014*

RY *B2* (7km NW Rural) *56.12421, 9.71055* **Terrassen Camping, Himmelbjergvej 9a, 8600 Laven [tel 86 84 13 01; fax 86 84 16 55; info@terrassen.dk; www.terrassen.dk]** In Silkeborg take Århus rd 15 to Linå. In Linå turn R for Laven. In Laven turn R parallel to lake; site up hill on R in 300m. Sharp turn R into ent. Lge, terr, pt shd; wc; chem disp; mv service pnt; baby facs; fam bthrm; sauna; shwrs DKK7; EHU (10A) DKK32; gas; lndry (inc dryer); rest adj; snacks 1.5km; shops adj; playgrnd; htd pool; fishing; lake sw; games area; pet zoo; wifi; entmnt; TV rm; 15% statics; dogs DKK15; phone; poss cr; adv bkg; ccard acc; quiet. "Excel views of lake & woods; British owner; Jutland's lake district." ♦ 11 Apr-14 Sep. DKK 268   2014*

RY *B2* (9km NW Rural) *56.13603, 9.68978* **Askehøj Camping, Askehøjvej 18, 8600 Laven [tel 86 84 12 82; fax 86 84 12 80; askehoj@dk-camp.dk; www.askehoj.dk]** Fr Silkeborg take rte 15 twd Århus. In approx 5km site is sp. Lge, mkd pitch, pt sl, terr, pt shd; wc; chem disp; mv service pnt; shwrs inc; EHU (10A) DKK30; lndry; shop & 8km; rest 3km; playgrnd; htd pool; paddling pool; waterslide; some statics; dogs DKK5; poss v cr; Eng spkn; adv bkg; quiet; ccard acc; CKE/CCI. "Excel site in scenic location; rec." ♦ Easter-27 Sep. DKK 185   2009*

SAEBY *C1* (3km N Coastal) *57.35498, 10.51026* **Hedebo Strandcamping, Frederikshavnsvej 109, 9300 Sæby [tel 98 46 14 49; fax 98 40 13 13; hedebo@dk-camp.dk; www.hedebocamping.dk]** Sp on rd 180. Lge, hdg/mkd pitch, unshd; htd wc; chem disp; mv service pnt; baby facs; fam bthrm; shwrs DKK5; EHU (10A) inc; lndry (inc dryer); shop; rest, snacks; bar; BBQ; cooking facs; playgrnd; htd pool; beach adj; wifi; 60% statics; dogs; phone; bus adj; poss cr; Eng spkn; adv bkg; quiet; CKE/CCI. 7 Apr-7 Sep. DKK 240   2009*

SAKSKOBING *C3* (750m W Urban) *54.79840, 11.64070* **Sakskøbing Camping, Saxes Allé 15, 4990 Sakskøbing [tel 45 54 70 45 66 or 45 54 70 47 57; fax 54 70 70 90; sax@sport.dk; www.saxcamping.dk]** N fr Rødby exit E47 at Sakskøbing junc 46, turn L twd town: at x-rds turn R. In 300m turn R into Saxes Allé, site sp. Med, hdg/mkd pitch, pt shd; wc; mv service pnt; fam bthrm; baby facs; shwrs; EHU (6A) DKK30; gas; lndry; shop; rest adj; cooking facs; sand beach 15km; pool 100m; fishing; phone; adv bkg; quiet. "Conv for Rødby-Puttgarden ferry; gd touring base; excel site in pretty area; v welcoming & friendly." 15 Mar-28 Sep. DKK 194   2014*

SILKEBORG *B2* (11km SE Rural) *56.12468, 9.64015* **Skyttehuset's Camping, Svejbækvej 3, Virklund, 8600 Silkeborg [tel 86 84 51 11; fax 86 84 50 38; mail@skyttehusetscamping.dk; www.skyttehusetscamping.dk]** Fr S on rd 52 dir Silkeborg turn R onto rd 445 dir Ry. In 5km turn L twd lake, site in 6km, sp. Med, mkd pitch, hdstg, terr, shd; htd wc; chem disp; baby facs; fam bthrm; shwrs DKK6; EHU (10A) DKK31; lndry (inc dryer); shop; rest, snacks; bar; playgrnd; lake sw 500m; fishing; canoe & bike hire; crazy golf; TV; dogs DKK10; phone; Eng spkn; quiet; ccard acc; CKE/CCI. "Campsite marina; sh walk to Denmark's cleanest lake; forest location; vg." ♦ 27 Mar-12 Sep. DKK 183   2010*

SILKEBORG *B2* (3km S Rural) *56.15716, 9.56395* **Gudenåens Camping Silkeborg, Vejlsøvej 7, 8600 Silkeborg [tel 86 82 22 01; fax 86 80 50 27; mail@gudenaaenscamping.dk; www.gudenaaenscamping.dk]** Fr S on Rv52 at rndabt at beg of Silkeborg bypass take rd sp 'Centrum'. Take 1st R to site, sp. Med, mkd pitch, pt sl, shd; htd wc; chem disp; mv service pnt; baby facs; fam bthrm; EHU (16A) DKK28; lndry; shop; rest, snacks 500m; BBQ; cooking facs; playgrnd; internet; TV; many statics; dogs free; Eng spkn; adv bkg; ccard acc; CKE/CCI. "Vg site; heavily wooded; easy walk/cycle to Silkeborg; steamer to Himmelbjerget 5 mins fr site." 3 Apr-18 Oct. DKK 283   2009*

⊞ **SILKEBORG** *B2* (12km W Rural) *56.14869, 9.39697* **DCU Hesselhus Camping, Moselundsvej 28, Funder, 8600 Silkeborg [tel 86 86 50 66; fax 86 86 59 49; hesselhus@dcu.dk; www.camping-hesselhus.dk]** Take rd 15 W fr Silkeborg twd Herning; after 6km bear R, sp Funder Kirkeby, foll camping sps for several km to site. Lge, mkd pitch, pt shd; wc; chem disp; mv service pnt; shwrs inc; fam bthrm; baby facs; shwrs; EHU DKK35; gas; lndry; supmkt; snacks; playgrnd; htd pool; TV; 40% statics; dogs DKK20; phone; adv bkg; quiet; 10% red CKE/CCI. "Great family site; beautiful natural surroundings; 1 hr fr Legoland; busy at w'ends." ♦ DKK 144   2011*

⊞ **SINDAL** *C1* (2km W Rural) *57.46785, 10.17851* **Sindal Camping, Hjørringvej 125, 9870 Sindal [tel 98 93 65 30; fax 98 93 69 30; info@sindal-camping.dk; www.sindal-camping.dk]** On rte 35 due W of Frederikshavn on S side of rd. Lge, hdg pitch, pt shd; wc; chem disp; mv service pnt; baby facs; fam bthrm; shwrs; EHU (16A) metered; gas; lndry; shop; playgrnd; pool; paddling pool; sand beach 11km; golf 3km; TV; dogs DKK10; phone; poss cr; Eng spkn; adv bkg; quiet; CKE/CCI. "Train & bus v conv; lovely beaches 30 mins; excel modern san facs; vg site; helpful owners." ♦ DKK 260   2013*

⊞ **SKAELSKOR** *C3* (1km NW Rural) *55.25648, 11.28461* **Skælskør Nør Camping, Kildehusvej 1, 4230 Skælskør [tel 58 19 43 84; fax 58 19 25 50; kildehuset@cafeer.dk; www.campnor.dk]** Exit E20 junc 42 sp Korsør. Take rd 265 S sp Skælskør, site on L just bef town, nr Kildehuset Rest. Med, mkd pitch, unshd; wc; chem disp; baby facs; fam bthrm; shwrs DKK5; EHU DKK35; lndry; shop 1km; rest; bar; cooking facs; playgrnd; shgl beach 2km; TV; phone; Eng spkn; adv bkg; rd noise; ccard acc (surcharge); CKE/CCI. "Lovely location by lake in nature reserve; woodland walks; excel facs; helpful owners." ♦ DKK 150   2009*

DENMARK

⊞ **SKAERBAEK** *B3* (2km NE Rural) *55.16776, 8.78326*
**Skærbæk Familie Camping, Ullerupvej 76, 6780
Skærbæk [tel 74 75 22 22; fax 74 75 25 70; skaerbaek
familiecamping@c.dk; www.skaerbaekfamiliecamping.dk]**
On rd 11 fr Ribe to Tønder, site well sp. Med, hdg/mkd
pitch, pt shd; htd wc; chem disp; mv service pnt; fam bthrm;
shwrs inc; EHU DKK25; BBQ; cooking facs; playgrnd; games
area; wifi; 50% statics; phone; Eng spkn; quiet; CKE/CCI.
"Helpful owner; gd tourist info; conv Rømø Island." ♦ ltd.
DKK 140   2010*

SKAGEN *C1* (3km N Coastal) *57.7319, 10.61458* **Grenen
Camping, Fryvej 16, 9990 Skagen [tel/fax 98 44 25 46;
info@grenencamping.dk; www.grenencamping.dk]**
Site on rd 40, sp 500m after white lighthouse. Lge, hdg/mkd
pitch, pt shd; htd wc; chem disp; mv service pnt; baby facs;
fam bthrm; shwrs DKK5; EHU (16A) DKK35; lndry; shop; rest,
snacks, bar 1km; cooking facs; playgrnd; sand/shgl beach adj;
bike hire; TV rm; 50% statics; dogs DKK15; phone; poss cr; Eng
spkn; quiet; ccard acc; CKE/CCI. "Immac site nr pretty town;
conv Grenen Point where Baltic & North Seas meet; gd cycling;
friendly, helpful staff." ♦ 1 Apr-19 Sep. DKK 240   2010*

SKAGEN *C1* (3km NE Coastal) *57.73448, 10.60412* **Poul Eeg
Camping, Bøjlevejen 21, 9990 Skagen [tel 98 44 14 70;
fax 98 45 14 60; info@pouleegcamping.dk;
www.pouleegcamping.dk]** Take rd 40 thro Skagen twd
Grenen; by hexagonal white tower on N o'skts turn L; site sh
dist on L. Lge, pt shd; htd wc; chem disp; mv service pnt; baby
facs; fam bthrm; shwrs DKK5; EHU (10A) DKK35; lndry (inc
dryer); shop; rest 1km; snacks; cooking facs; playgrnd; beach
1km; bike hire; wifi; TV rm; some statics; dogs DKK15; phone;
poss cr; Eng spkn; adv bkg; quiet; ccard acc (surcharge); CKE/
CCI. "Excel, well-run, peaceful site & facs; friendly, helpful
staff; gd sea fishing & cycling; conv touring base." ♦
20 Apr-4 Sep. DKK 195   2010*

SKAGEN *C1* (3km S Rural) *57.71987, 10.53991*
**Øster Klit Camping, Flagbakkevej 55, 9990 Skagen
[tel/fax 98 44 31 23; skagen-camping@mail.dk]**
Fr Albæk on rte 40, site sp to R of rd. Med, mkd pitch, pt
shd; wc; chem disp; mv service pnt; baby facs; fam bthrm;
shwrs; EHU; lndry; shop; rest, snacks; cooking facs; playgrnd;
pool; sand beach 2km; TV; 10% statics; phone; Eng spkn; adv
bkg; quiet; ccard acc. "Well-run site; clean facs; friendly staff;
Skagen worth visit." ♦ Easter-12 Sep. DKK 200   2009*

SKAGEN *C1* (13km SW Rural) *57.65546, 10.45008* **Råbjerg Mile
Camping, Kandestedvej 55, 9990 Skagen [tel 98 48 75 00;
fax 98 48 75 88; info@raabjergmilecamping.dk; www.990.dk]**
Fr rd 40 Frederikshavn-Skagen, foll sp Hulsig-Råbjerg Mile,
site sp. Lge, hdg/mkd pitch, unshd; wc; chem disp; fam bthrm;
shwrs DKK2; EHU (10A) DKK30; lndry; shop; rest 1km; snacks;
bar; cooking facs; playgrnd; htd pool; paddling pool; beach
1.5km; tennis; bike hire; golf 1.5km; TV; 25% statics; dogs
DKK10; phone; poss cr; Eng spkn; adv bkg; ccard acc; CKE/CCI.
"Gd touring base N tip of Denmark; gd cycling." ♦
24 Mar-30 Sep. DKK 354 (CChq acc)   2013*

SKANDERBORG *B2* (4km SW Rural) *56.02088, 9.89023*
**Skanderborg Sø Camping, Horsensvej 21, 8660
Skanderborg [tel 86 51 13 11; fax 86 51 17 33; info@
campingskanderborg.dk; www.campingskanderborg.dk]**
N on E45 approx 10km beyond Horsens exit junc 54 to
Trebstrup on rd 170 to site on R in 5km. Camping sp on R at
top of hill after passing lake. Med, pt sl, pt shd; wc; chem disp;
mv service pnt; fam bthrm; baby facs; shwrs DKK8; EHU (6A)
DKK25; gas & 5km; lndry; shop; rest 1km; snacks; cooking
facs; playgrnd; lake sw; boating; fishing; TV; some statics;
dogs DKK10; phone; poss cr; adv bkg; Eng spkn; quiet; ccard
acc. "In Jutland's lake district; clean, pleasant, well-spaced site
in former orchard; friendly, helpful owner; gd touring base."
♦ ltd. 16 Apr-26 Sep. DKK 188   2010*

⊞ **SONDER FELDING** *B2* (300m S Rural) *55.93960, 8.78418*
**Sønder Felding Camping & Hytteby, Søndergade 7, 7280
Sønder Felding [tel/fax 97 19 81 89; http://sdrfelding.
dk-camp.dk]** Fr rd 12 turn W onto rd 439, site sp. Call at
Q8 filling stn to check in. Sm, pt shd; htd wc; chem disp;
mv service pnt; shwrs DKK5; EHU (10A) inc (long lead req);
lndry; shop; rest, snacks; cooking facs; playgrnd; quiet; CKE/
CCI. "If not staffed - pay at petrol stn; rvside walk; gd."
DKK 126   2010*

SONDER STENDERUP see Kolding *B3*

SONDERBORG *B3* (4.5km NE Rural) *54.93518, 9.84591*
**Madeskov Camping, Madeskov 9, 6400 Sønderborg
[tel 74 42 13 93]** Exit E45 at junc 75 onto rd 8 to Sønderborg.
Turn L at rndabt with tent sp. Med, unshd; wc; chem disp;
mv service pnt; baby facs; shwrs DKK4; EHU (10A) DKK20;
lndry; shop; rest 5km; playgrnd; sw 300m; bike hire; TV rm;
20% statics; phone; poss cr; Eng spkn; aircraft noise during
day; CKE/CCI. "On shores of Augustenborg fiord; under airport
flight path." ♦ 15 Mar-18 Oct. DKK 130   2009*

SONDERVIG *A2* (500m S Coastal) *56.11179, 8.11680*
**Søndervig Camping, Solvej 2, 6950 Søndervig
[tel/fax 97 33 90 34; post@soendervigcamping.dk;
www.soendervigcamping.dk]** Fr Ringkøbing E on rd 15.
At traff lts in Søndervig turn L, site on R in 600m. Lge, hdg/
mkd pitch, unshd; htd wc; chem disp; mv service pnt; baby
facs; shwrs DKK6; EHU (10A) DKK30 or metered + conn fee;
lndry (inc dryer); shop; rest, snacks 600m; playgrnd; htd, covrd
pool 700m; bike hire 600m; wifi; TV rm; 10% statics; dogs
DKK15; phone; bus 600m; poss cr; Eng spkn; adv bkg; quiet;
CKE/CCI. "Excel; gd, modern san facs." ♦ Easter 31 Oct.
DKK 177   2010*

SORO *C3* (2km NW Urban) *55.44673, 11.54628* **Sorø Camping,
Udbyhøjvej 10, 4180 Sorø [tel 57 83 02 02; fax 57 82 11 02;
info@soroecamping.dk; www.soroecamping.dk]**
On rd 150 fr Korsør, 300m bef town name board turn L at
camping sp, site in 100m on lakeside. Med, pt sl, pt shd; wc;
chem disp; mv service pnt; fam bthrm; baby facs; shwrs DKK2
per min; EHU (10A) DKK30; lndry; shop; rest 500m; snacks
1km; cooking facs; playgrnd; lake sw adj; fishing; boating; TV;
some statics; dogs free; phone; Eng spkn; adv bkg; quiet; ccard
acc; CKE or CCI ess. "Conv Copenhagen, friendly owners;
busy site; clean facs - up to CC standards." ♦ 1 Mar-31 Oct.
DKK 180   2013*

STENBJERG A2 (500m SE Rural) 56.91835, 8.36483
Krohavens Familie Camping, Stenbjerg Kirkevej 21, 7752 Stenbjerg [tel 97 93 88 99; fax 97 93 86 55; stenbjerg@ kh-camp.dk; www.kh-camp.dk] On rd 571 fr Snedsted, site sp on ent vill. Med, hdg pitch, unshd; htd wc; chem disp; mv service pnt; fam bthrm; shwrs; EHU DKK25; lndry; shop; rest; bar; cooking facs; playgrnd; sand beach 2km; games area; TV; some statics; dogs free; Eng spkn; quiet; CKE/CCI. 1 Apr-1 Oct. DKK 160   2011*

STOUBY B3 (4.5km E Rural) 55.70761, 9.84385 **Løgballe Camping, Løgballevej 12, 7140 Stouby [tel/fax 75 69 12 00; camping@logballe.dk; www.logballe.dk]** N of Vejle turn onto rd 23 dir Juelsminde, thro vill of Stouby, site on R. Med, hdg/mkd pitch, pt sl, pt terr, pt shd; wc; chem disp; mv service pnt; baby facs; fam bthrm; shwrs DKK5; EHU (6-10A) DKK27; lndry; shop; snacks; bar; BBQ; cooking facs; playgrnd; pool; paddling pool; beach 6km; bike hire; games area; TV rm; some statics in sep area; dogs; phone; bus 500m; poss cr; adv bkg; quiet; CKE/CCI. "Excel facs for children." ◆ Easter-4 Oct. DKK 140   2009*

STOUBY B3 (4km S Coastal) 55.67674, 9.81319 **Rosenvold Camping, Rosenvoldvej 19, 7140 Stouby [tel 75 69 14 15; info@rosenvoldcamping.dk; www.rosenvoldcamping.dk]** Exit E45 at junc 59 E twd Daugard & Juelsminde on rd 23. Watch for site sp in approx 20km & turn R to coast, site sp. Med, mkd pitch, unshd; wc; chem disp; mv service pnt; baby facs; fam bhtrm; shwrs DKK6; EHU (10A) DKK30; lndry (inc dryer); shop; snacks; BBQ; cooking facs; playgrnd; beach adj; fishing at marina; games area; entmnt; 80% statics; Eng spkn; quiet; ccard acc; CKE/CCI. "Vg site." ◆ 1 Apr-30 Sep. DKK 225   2009*

STROBY see Koge D3

SVENDBORG C3 (7km SE Coastal) 55.0537, 10.6304
Svendborg Sund Camping (formerly Vindebyøre), Vindebyørevej 52, Tåsinge, 5700 Svendborg [tel 21 72 09 13 or 62 22 54 25; fax 62 22 54 26; maria@ svendborgsund-camping.dk; www.svendborgsund-camping.dk] Cross bdge fr Svendborg (dir Spodsbjerg) to island of Tåsinge on rd 9; at traff lts over bdge turn L, then immed 1st L to Vindeby, thro vill, L at sp to site. Med, pt sl, pt shd; htd wc; chem disp; mv service pnt; fam bthrm; baby facs; shwrs; EHU DKK30; lndry; shop; snacks; cooking facs; BBQ; playgrnd; sand beach; bike & boat hire; entmnt; internet; TV; some statics; dogs DKK10; phone; o'night area; poss cr; adv bkg; quiet; ccard acc; CKE/CCI. "V helpful owners; swipe card for facs; excel touring base & conv ferries to islands; beautiful views; immac, excel site; narr sandy beach." ◆ 18 Mar-27 Sep. DKK 225   2015*

SVENDBORG C3 (5km S Rural) 55.03336, 10.61403 **Carlsberg Camping, Sundbrovej 19, Tåsinge, 5700 Svendborg [tel 62 22 53 84; fax 62 22 58 11; mail@carlsberg-camping.dk; www.carlsberg-camping.dk]** Fr Svendborg cross bdge on A9 S to Rudkøbing. After traffic lts in approx 4km sp camping on E side of rd. Enter sm rd & up steep hill for 300m. Steep & narr app. Med, pt shd; wc; chem disp; mv service pnt; fam bthrm; baby facs; shwrs inc; EHU (6A) DKK30; gas; lndry (inc dryer); shop; snacks; playgrnd; htd pool inc; beach 4km; games area; games rm; TV; poss cr; quiet; ccard acc; red LS. "Gd facs; scenic area." ◆ 1 Apr-25 Sep. DKK 184   2010*

⊞ **TAPPERNOJE** D3 (500m NE Urban) 55.16568, 11.98195 **Heino's Camping, Hovedvejen 47B, Lille Røttinge, 4733 Tappernøje [tel 55 96 53 22; fax 55 96 01 22; www.heinoscamping.dk]** Fr E47/55 exit 38 twd coast. Site sp. Med, hdg pitch, pt shd; wc; chem disp; shwrs; EHU DKK20; lndry rm; shop, rest 500m; playgrnd; sand beach 2km; bike hire; 10% statics; quiet; CKE/CCI. "Gd size pitches." DKK 100   2009*

TARM A2 (1.5km S Rural) 55.89309, 8.51278 **Tarm Camping, Vardevej 79, 6880 Tarm [tel 30 12 66 35; fax 97 37 30 15; tarm.camping@pc.dk; www.tarm-camping.dk]** Fr rd 11 S of Tarm take exit twds Tarm; immed turn R, site on L in 500m, sp. Med, mkd pitch, pt shd; wc; chem disp; mv service pnt; fam bthrm; baby facs; shwrs DKK2; EHU (10A) DKK30; gas; lndry; snacks; cooking facs; playgrnd; pool; some statics; dogs; phone; Eng spkn; adv bkg; some rd noise; CKE/CCI. "Friendly & helpul staff; vg." ◆ 27 Mar-4 Oct. DKK 168   2015*

> ## "I like to fill in the reports as I travel from site to site"
> You'll find report forms at the back of this guide, or you can fill them in online at www.caravanclub.co.uk/europereport.

THISTED B2 (1km SE Coastal) 56.95226, 8.71286 **Thisted Camping, Iversensvej 3, 7700 Thisted [tel 97 92 16 35; fax 97 92 52 34; mail@thisted-camping.dk; www.thisted-camping.dk]** On side of fjord on o'skts of Thisted, sp fr rd 11. Med, pt sl, unshd; wc; chem disp; mv service pnt; baby facs; fam bthrm; shwrs DKK5; EHU (16A) DKK30; gas; lndry; shop; rest; cooking facs; playgrnd; pool; TV; Eng spkn; adv bkg; quiet; CKE/CCI. "Attractive views fr some pitches; nice site; well run." ◆ 23 Mar-1 Oct. DKK 280   2013*

THORSMINDE A2 (500m N Coastal) 56.37626, 8.12251 **Thorsminde Camping, Klitrosevej 4, 6990 Thorsminde [tel 97 49 70 56; fax 97 49 72 18; mail@thorsmindecamping. dk; www.thorsmindecamping.dk]** On rd 16/28 to Ulfborg, turn W twd coast & Husby Klitplantage. Turn N onto rd 181 to Thorsminde, 1st turn R past shops, site sp. Lge, unshd; wc; chem disp; mv service pnt; fam bthrm; baby facs; sauna; shwrs; EHU (10A) DKK30; lndry; shop; rest; cooking facs; playgrnd; covrd pool; beach 300m; TV; few statics; phone; poss cr; adv bkg; quiet. "Pleasant site; helpful staff; excel sea fishing." ◆ 8 Apr-23 Oct. DKK 200   2011*

TONDER B3 (2km E Rural) 54.93409, 8.87957 **Tønder Campingplads, Sønderport 4, 6270 Tonder [tel/fax 74 72 35 00; tonder@danhostel.dk; www.tondercamping. dk]** W fr junc A8 & A11 twd town, in 800m turn R at camping sp. Ent on L in 100m. Med, hdg/mkd pitch, unshd; wc; chem disp; mv service pnt; shwrs; baby facs; EHU (10A) DKK30; lndry; shop 1km; bar; playgrnd; sand beach 10km; TV; 50% statics; dogs DKK10; phone; poss cr; Eng spkn; adv bkg; quiet; CKE/ CCI. "Pleasant old town with gd shopping cent; gd site with modern san facs; helpful recep." ◆ 26 Mar-24 Oct. DKK 150   2011*

DENMARK

DENMARK

⊞ **TONDER** *B3* (5km W Rural) *54.93746, 8.80008* **Møgeltønder Camping, Sønderstrengvej 2, Møgeltønder, 6270 Tønder [tel 74 73 84 60; fax 74 73 80 43; www.mogeltondercamping.dk]** N fr Tønder thro Møgeltønder (avoid cobbled main rd by taking 2nd turning sp Møgeltønder) site sp on L in 200m outside vill. Lge, mkd pitch; pt shd; htd wc; chem disp; mv service pnt; baby facs; fam bthrm; shwrs DKK2 (per 2 mins); EHU (10A) DKK25; lndry (inc dryer); shop; snacks; BBQ; cooking facs; playgrnd; htd pool; sand beach 10km; internet; TV rm; 25% statics; dogs DKK10; phone; poss v cr; Eng spkn; adv bkg; quiet; ccard not acc; CKE/CCI. "Gd cycle paths; beautiful & romantic little vill adj; Ribe worth visit (43km); friendly owner." ♦ DKK 219   2014*

ULFBORG *A2* (13km W Coastal) *56.25961, 8.14625* **Vedersø Klit Camping, Øhusevej 23, Vedersø Klit, 6990 Ulfborg [tel 97 49 52 02; fax 97 49 52 01; vedersoklit@dk-camp.dk; www.dk-camp.dk/vedersoklit]** W fr Ulfborg on rd 537, turn S onto rd 181 & foll site sp. Lge, mkd pitch; pt shd; wc; chem disp; mv service pnt; fam bthrm; baby facs; shwrs inc; EHU (10A) DKK25; lndry (inc dryer); shop; snacks; cooking facs; playgrnd; pool; paddling pool; beach 500m; games area; TV; some statics; dogs DKK10; phone; adv bkg; quiet. ♦ 27 Mar-26 Sep. DKK 190   2010*

"We must tell The Club about that great site we found"

Get your site reports in by mid-August and we'll do our best to get your updates into the next edition.

ULSTRUP *B2* (2km W Rural) *56.38678, 9.76341* **Bamsebo Camping ved Gudenåen, Hagenstrupvej 28, Hvorslev, 8860 Ulstrup [tel 86 46 34 27; fax 86 46 37 18; bamsebo@ dk-camp.dk; www.bamsebo.dk]** Fr W twd Ulstrup on rd 525, turn R at traff lts to Ulstrop, take 1st exit at rndabt at top of Ulstrup dir Busbjerg, site sp on R in 2km on rv. Med, hdg pitch; pt sl, pt shd; htd wc; chem disp; mv service pnt; baby facs; fam bthrm; shwrs; EHU (16A) DKK30; lndry rm; shop on site & 2.5km; snacks; playgrnd; htd pool; canoes for hire; tennis; games area; TV rm; 60% statics; dogs DKK15; poss cr; Eng spkn; adv bkg; CKE/CCI. ♦ 17 Apr-2 Oct. DKK 184   2011*

VAMMEN see Viborg *B2*

⊞ **VEJERS STRAND** *A3* (400m SE Urban) *55.61916, 8.13650* **Vejers Familie Camping, Vejers Havvej 15, 6853 Vejers Strand [tel 75 27 70 36; fax 75 27 72 75; ftj@vejersfamiliecamping.dk; www.vejersfamiliecamping.dk]** Well sp in Vejers Strand on coast. Lge, hdg/mkd pitch; pt shd; wc; chem disp; mv service pnt; fam bthrm; baby facs; shwrs DKK6; EHU (8A) DKK30; lndry (inc dryer); shop; rest, snacks; cooking facs; BBQ; playgrnd; pool; paddling pool; sand beach 1km; fishing; wifi; TV rm; some statics; dogs DKK13; phone; Eng spkn; some noise fr adj military firing range; CKE/CCI. "Site open all yr but in winter telephone ahead; gd, modern facs." DKK 188 (CChq acc)   2010*

VEJERS STRAND *A3* (12km S Coastal) *55.54403, 8.13386* **Hvidbjerg Strand Feriepark, Hvidbjerg Strandvej 27, 6857 Blåvand [tel 75 27 90 40; fax 75 27 80 28; info@hvidbjerg.dk; www.hvidbjerg.dk]** Exit rd 11 at Varde on minor rd, sp Blåvand, turn L at sp to Hvidbjerg Strand 2km; site 1km on L. V lge, hdg pitch, pt shd; wc; chem disp; mv service pnt; baby facs; fam bthrm; serviced pitches; shwrs inc; EHU (6A) inc; gas; lndry; supmkt; rest, snacks; bar; cooking facs; playgrnd; htd, covrd pool; sand beach; tennis; games area; entmnt; TV; 10% statics; dogs DKK30; phone; adv bkg; quiet; ccard acc. "Superb facs; excel family site; young groups not acc." ♦ 7 Apr-22 Oct. DKK 453   2014*

See advertisement inside the front cover

VEJERS STRAND *A3* (1km W Coastal) *55.61998, 8.11931* **Vejers Strand Camping, Vejers Sydstrand 3, 6853 Vejers Strand [tel 75 27 70 50; fax 75 27 77 50; info@ vejersstrandcamping.dk; www.vejersstrandcamping.dk]** Site at end of rd 431 fr Varde (23km). Lge, unshd; htd wc; chem disp; mv service pnt; fam bthrm; baby facs; shwrs; EHU (10A) DKK28; lndry (inc dryer); shop; rest, snacks; bar; cooking facs; playgrnd; beach 250m; TV; phone; 50% statics; dogs DKK15; adv bkg; quiet but some aircraft noise; ccard acc. "Pt sheltered in dunes; fine beach." ♦ 1 Apr-16 Sep. DKK 180   2009*

VEJLE *B3* (2km ENE Urban) *55.7151, 9.5611* **Vejle City Camping, Helligkildevej 5, 7100 Vejle [tel 75 82 33 35; fax 75 82 33 54; vejlecitycamping@mail.dk; www.vejlecity camping.dk]** Exit E45 m'way at Vejle N. Turn L twd town. In 250m turn L at camping sp & 'stadion' sp. Med, pt sl, pt shd; wc; chem disp; mv service pnt; fam bthrm; baby facs; shwrs DKK5; EHU (6-10A) DKK30; lndry; shop on site & 1km; snacks; cooking facs; playgrnd; sand beach 2km; TV; dogs DKK5; phone; poss cr; Eng spkn; adv bkg; quiet; 25% med long stays; ccard acc; red snr citizens. "Site adj woods & deer enclosure; Quickstop o'night facs; walk to town; conv Legoland (26km)." ♦ 17 Apr-14 Sep. DKK 150   2009*

⊞ **VIBORG** *B2* (15km N Rural/Coastal) *56.53452, 9.33117* **Hjarbæk Fjord Camping, Hulager 2, Hjarbæk, 8831 Løgstrup [tel 86 64 23 09; fax 86 64 25 91; info@hjarbaek.dk; www.hjarbaek.dk]** Take A26 (Viborg to Skive) to Løgstrup, turn R (N) to Hjarbæk, keep R thro vill, site sp. Lge, mkd pitch, terr, pt shd; htd wc; chem disp; baby facs; fam bthrm; shwrs inc; EHU metered; gas; lndry (inc dryer); shop; rest; bar; cooking facs; BBQ; playgrnd; pool; sand beach adj; lake fishing; wifi; TV; 3% statics; phone; dogs DKK10; quiet; Eng spkn; adv bkg; ccard acc; red snr citizens; CKE/CCI. "Friendly & well-run; gd views; close to attractive vill & harbour." ♦ DKK 299 (CChq acc)   2014*

VINDERUP *B2* (6.7km ESE Rural) *56.45901, 8.86918* **Sevel Camping, Halallé 6, Sevel, 7830 Vinderup [tel 97 44 85 50; fax 97 44 85 51; mail@sevelcamping.dk; www.sevelcamping.dk]** Fr Struer on rd 513. In Vinderup L nr church then R past Vinderup Camping. Site sp on R on edge of vill. Sm, hdg pitch, pt sl, pt shd; htd wc; chem disp; mv service pnt; baby facs; fam bthrm; shwrs DKK5; EHU (16A) DKK27; lndry; shop 100m; cooking facs; rest 1km; snacks; playgrnd; 10% statics; dogs DKK6; Eng spkn; adv bkg; quiet; ccard acc; CKE/CCI. "Family-run site; pleasant, helpful owners; picturesque, historic area." ♦ 1 Apr-30 Sep. DKK 142   2009*

VIPPEROD see Holbæk *D3*

⊞ **VORDINGBORG** *D3* (3.6km W Urban/Coastal) *55.00688, 11.87509* **Ore Strand Camping, Orevej 145, 4760 Vordingborg [tel 55 77 8822; mail@orestrandcamping.dk; www.orestrandcamping.dk]** Fr E55/47 exit junc 41 onto rd 59 to Vordingborg 7km. Rd conts as 153 sp Sakskøbing alongside rlwy. Turn R at site sp into Ore, site on L. Med, pt shd; wc; chem disp; mv service pnt; baby facs; shwrs; EHU (6A) DKK30; lndry; shop; cooking facs; playgrnd; shgl beach adj; phone; adv bkg; poss cr; quiet; Eng spkn; ccard acc. "Gd touring cent; fine views if nr water; interesting old town." DKK 140   2015*

AERO ISLAND

⊞ **MARSTAL** *C3* (2km S Urban/Coastal) *54.84666, 10.51823* **Marstal Camping, Eghovedvej 1, 5960 Marstal [tel 63 52 63 69; fax 62 53 36 40; marstal.camping@mail.tele. dk; www.marstalcamping.dk]** Fr Ærøskobing ferry to E end of Ærø Island, thro town of Marstal & turn R at harbour twd sailing club; site adj to club. Med, mkd pitch, pt shd; wc; chem disp; mv service pnt; baby facs; fam bthrm; shwrs DKK5; EHU (16A) DKK28; lndry (inc dryer); shop; rest, snacks, bar 500m; BBQ; playgrnd; TV; 10% statics; dogs DKK15, phone; poss cr; adv bkg; poss noisy; ccard acc; red LS/CKE/CCI. ♦ DKK 163 (CChq acc)   2009*

BORNHOLM ISLAND

GUDHJEM *A1* (2km S Coastal) *55.19566, 14.98602* **Sannes Familiecamping, Melstedvej 39, 3760 Melsted [tel 56 48 52 11; fax 56 48 52 52; sannes@familiecamping.dk; www.familiecamping.dk]** SW fr Gudhjem on rd 158, in 2km site on L. Pass other sites. NB: Bornholm Is can be reached by ferry fr Sassnitz in Germany or Ystad in Sweden. Med, mkd pitch, hdstg, terr, pt shd; wc; chem disp; mv service pnt; sauna; shwrs; EHU (6A) DKK30; gas; lndry; shop & supmkt 1km; rest 500m; playgrnd; htd pool; paddling pool; sand beach adj; fishing; fitness rm; bike hire; wifi; TV rm; 10% statics; dogs; phone; Eng spkn; adv bkg; quiet; ccard acc; CKE/CCI. "Friendly & helpful staff; gd cycle paths in area; bus service fr site." ♦ 1 Apr-18 Sep. DKK 270   2011*

NEXO *A1* (5.5km S Coastal) *55.02895, 15.11130* **FDM Camping Balka Strand, Klynevej 6, Snogebæk, 3730 Nexø [tel 56 48 80 74; fax 56 48 86 75; c-balka@fdm.dk; www.balka.fdmcamping.dk]** Fr ferry at Rønne on rd 38 to Nexø, foll sp to site N of Snogebæk. Lge, mkd pitch, pt shd; htd wc; chem disp; mv service pnt; baby facs; shwrs inc; EHU (6A) DKK30; lndry; shop; supmkt 500m; rest, snacks 500m; BBQ; cooking facs; playgrnd; sand beach 200m; fishing 500m; windsurfing 1km; bike hire; games area; golf 5km; internet; TV; some statics; dogs DKK15; adv bkg; quiet; ccard acc. "Superb beach; vg touring base Bornholm Is." ♦ 25 Apr-13 Sep. DKK 189   2009*

RONNE *A1* (1km S Coastal) *55.08978, 14.70565* **Galløkken Camping, Strandvejen 4, 3700 Rønne [tel 56 95 23 20; info@gallokken.dk; www.gallokken.dk]** Fr Rønne cent foll dir airport, site well sp. Med, hdg/mkd pitch, pt shd; htd wc; chem disp; mv service pnt; baby facs; fam bthrm; private san facs avail; shwrs; EHU (13A) DKK25; lndry (inc dryer); shop; supmkt 500m; rest 600m; BBQ; cooking facs; playgrnd; sand beach 200m; tennis 1km; bike hire; games rm; wifi; TV; some statics; dogs; adv bkg; quiet. "Lovely location; gd, modern san facs." ♦ 1 May-31 Aug. DKK 168   2010*

LANGELAND ISLAND

⊞ **LOHALS** *C3* (400m W Urban) *55.13383, 10.90578* **Lohals Camping, Birkevej 11, 5953 Lohals [tel 58 37 50 80; info@ lohalscamping.dk; www.lohalscamping.dk]** On island of Langeland. Cross to Rudkøbing, fr island of Tåsinge, then 28km to N of island (only 1 main rd); site in middle of vill nr ferry to Sjælland Island. Med, shd; wc; chem disp; mv service pnt; baby facs; fam bthrm; shwrs; EHU (10A) DKK30; gas in vill; lndry; shop; rest, snacks 200m; playgrnd; htd pool; paddling pool; sand beach 1km; boat & bike hire; fishing; tennis; games area; TV; some statics; dogs free; phone; adv bkg; quiet. "Conv ferry (Lohals-Korsor) 500m." ♦ DKK 178   2009*

SPODSBJERG *C3* (2km NE Rural/Coastal) *54.92317, 10.80479* **Billevænge Camping, Spodsbjergvej 182, 5900 Spodsbjerg [tel 62 50 10 06; fax 62 50 10 46; info@billevaenge-camping.dk; www.billevaenge-camping.dk]** Fr Spodsbjerg ferry turn L into town. Site on L in approx 2km. Med, mkd pitch, pt terr, pt shd; wc; chem disp; mv service pnt; baby facs; shwrs DKK5; EHU (16A) inc; gas; lndry; shop; cooking facs; playgrnd; sand/shgl beach 500m; games area; internet; dogs DKK10; Eng spkn; adv bkg; quiet; ccard acc; CKE/CCI. "Helpful owner; gd, clean beach." 1 Apr-21 Oct. DKK 169   2011*

ROMO ISLAND

⊞ **HAVNEBY** *A3* (2km N Coastal) *55.09883, 8.54395* **Kommandørgårdens Camping, Havnebyvej 201, 6792 Rømø [tel 74 75 51 22; fax 74 75 59 22; info@ kommandoergaarden.dk; www.kommandoergaarden.dk]** Turn S after exit causeway fr mainland onto rd 175 sp Havneby. Site on L in 8km. V lge, mkd pitch, pt shd; htd wc; chem disp; mv service pnt; baby facs; fam bthrm; shwrs; EHU (10A) DKK25; gas; lndry; shop; rest, snacks; playgrnd; htd pool; paddling pool; sand beach 1km; tennis; wellness & beauty cent on site; TV; 30% statics; dogs DKK15; phone; poss cr; adv bkg; quiet. "Family-owned site; ferry to German island of Sylt." ♦ DKK 180   2009*

TOFTUM *A3* (300m SW Rural/Coastal) *55.16267, 8.54768* **Rømø Familiecamping, Vestervej 13, 6792 Toftum [tel 74 75 51 54; fax 74 75 64 18; romo@romocamping.dk; www.romocamping.dk]** Cross to Rømø Island on rd 175, turn R at 1st traff lts & turn L in 1km to site, sp. Lge, hdg/mkd pitch, some hdstg, pt shd; htd wc; chem disp; mv service pnt; baby facs; fam bthrm; shwrs; EHU (10A) DKK30; lndry; shop; BBQ; cooking facs; playgrnd; sand beach, windsurfing 4km; games area; bike hire; wifi; TV rm; some statics; dogs; adv bkg; quiet. "Pleasant site." 15 Apr-23 Oct. DKK 152   2009*

DENMARK

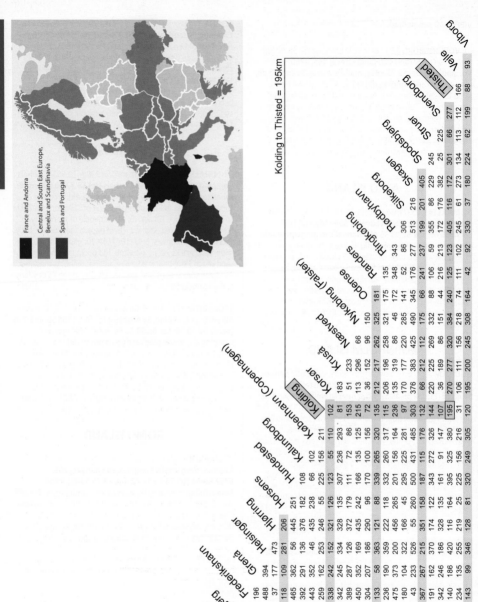

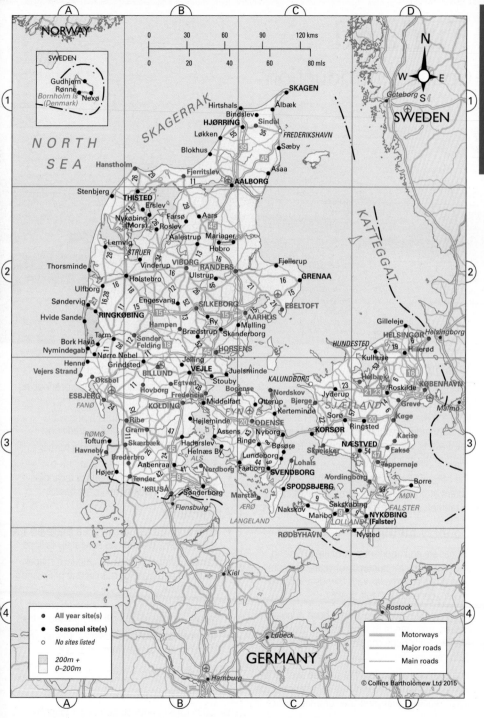

© Collins Bartholomew Ltd 2015

Finland
Country Introduction

Olavinlinna Castle, Savolinna

Welcome to Finland

Finland is a country filled with vast forests, crystal clear lakes and a diverse range of flora and fauna. With the Northern Lights visible from Lapland, the outstanding natural world is one of Finland's finest assets, with a vast, pristine wilderness that captures the imagination.

The cities of Finland are not to be missed, with vibrant atmospheres, museums, galleries, delicious restaurants and gorgeous architecture in spades.

Country highlights

Saunas are an important part of life in Finland, and have been for hundreds of years. They are used as a place to relax with friends and family and are generally sociable spaces.

Design and fashion have always been popular in Finland, with one of its most famous companies, Marimekko, a huge contributor to fashion in the 20th century.

Visit Svalbard to witness the unique spectacle of the Midnight Sun. This natural phenomenon occurs each year around the summer solstice.

Major towns and cities

- Helsinki – this capital city is a hub of shopping and architecture.

- Tempere – Finland's cultural home with theatrical, musical and literary traditions.

- Turku – Finland's oldest city and a former European City of Culture.

- Oulu – a quirky city where many technology companies, including Nokia, are based.

Attractions

- Olavinlinna Castle, Savolinna – a medieval stone fortress that houses several exhibitions.

- Kamppi Chapel, Helsinki – a modern chapel designed as a place of calm in one of Finland's busiest areas.

- Repovesi National Park – a stunning area of nature with plenty of walking and hiking trails.

- Temppeliaukio Kirkko, Helsinki – This amazing church is built directly into solid rock.

Find out more

www.visitfinland.com

Tel: 0035 (0) 82 94 69 56 50 Finnish Tourism

Country Information

Population (approx): 5.3 million

Capital: Helsinki (population approx 620,000)

Area: 338,145 sq km

Bordered by: Norway, Sweden, Russia

Terrain: Flat, rolling, heavily forested plains interspersed with low hills and more than 60,000 lakes; one third lies within the Arctic Circle

Climate: Short, warm summers; long, very cold, dry winters; the best time to visit is between May and September

Coastline: 1,250km (excluding islands)

Highest Point: Haltiatunturi 1,328m

Languages: Finnish, Swedish

Local Time: GMT or BST + 2, ie 2 hours ahead of the UK all year

Currency: Euros divided into 100 cents; £1 = €1.42, €1 = £0.71 (September 2015)

Emergency numbers: Police 112; Fire brigade 112; Ambulance 112 (operators speak English). *Public Holidays 2016:* Jan 1, 6; Mar 25, 27, 28; May 1, 5, 15; Jun 25 (Midsummer's Day); Nov 5; Dec 6 (Independence Day), 25, 26.

School summer holidays from early June to mid-August.

Camping and Caravanning

There are around 500 campsites in Finland. Campsites are graded from 1 to 5 stars according to facilities available. Most have cabins for hire in addition to tent and caravan pitches, and most have saunas.

At some sites visitors who do not already have one must purchase a Camping Key Europe, which replaced the Camping Card Scandinavia (CCS) in 2012. The Camping Key is valid across Europe and you may purchase it for €16 (2015) on arrival at your first campsite or from local tourist offices - for more information visit www.camping.fi.

During the peak camping season from June to mid August it is advisable to make advance reservations. Prices at many campsites may double (or treble) over the midsummer holiday long weekend in June and advance booking is essential for this period. Approximately 70 campsites stay open all year.

Casual or wild camping may be allowed for a short period - one or 2 days. For longer periods, permission must be obtained from the landowner. Camping may be prohibited on public beaches and in public recreation areas where campers are often directed to special areas, many of which have facilities provided free of charge.

Cycling

Finland is good for cyclists as it is relatively flat. Most towns have a good network of cycle lanes which are indicated by traffic signs. In built up areas pavements are sometimes divided into two sections, one for cyclists and one for pedestrians. It is compulsory to wear a safety helmet.

Electricity and Gas

Current on campsites is usually between 10 and 16 amps. Plugs are round with two pins. Some sites have CEE connections.

Butane gas is not generally available and campsites and service stations do not have facilities for replacing empty foreign gas cylinders. You will need to travel with sufficient supplies to cover your needs while in Finland or purchase propane cylinders locally, plus an adaptor. The Club does not recommend the refilling of cylinders.

Entry Formalities

Holders of British and Irish passports are permitted to stay up to three months in any six month period in Finland before a visa is required. Campsites and hotels register foreign guests with the police within 24 hours of arrival.

Medical Services

The local health system is good and Finland generally has a high level of health and hygiene. British citizens are entitled to obtain emergency health care at municipal health centres on presentation of a European Health Insurance Card (EHIC). Treatment will either be given free or for a standard fee. Dental care is provided mainly by private practitioners.

There is a fixed non-refundable charge for hospital treatment, whether for inpatient or outpatient visits. Refunds for the cost of private medical treatment may be obtained from local offices of the Sickness Insurance Department, KELA, (www.kela.fi – English option) up to six months from the date of treatment.

Prescribed drugs can be obtained from pharmacies (apteekki), some of which have late opening hours. Some medicines that are available in stores and supermarkets in other countries, such as aspirin and various ointments, are only available in pharmacies in Finland.

Opening Hours

Banks – Mon-Fri 9.15am-4.15pm.

Museums – Check locally as times vary.

Post Offices – Mon-Fri 9am-5pm. During winter some post offices may stay open until 6pm.

Shops – Mon-Fri 7am/8am/9am-9pm; Sat 7am/8am/9am/10am-6pm; Sun noon-6pm (some supermarkets until 11pm). On the eve of a public holiday some shops close early.

Safety and Security

The crime rate is relatively low in Finland although the tourist season attracts pickpockets in crowded areas. You should take the usual commonsense precautions to safeguard your person and property.

There is a low threat from international terrorism but you should be aware of the global risks of indiscriminate terrorist attacks which could be against civilian targets in public places, including tourist sites.

British Embassy
ITÄINEN PUISTOTIE 17, 00140 HELSINKI
Tel: (09) 22865100 Fax: (09) 22865262
www.ukinfinland.fco.gov.uk
info.helsinki@fco.gov.uk

There are also Honorary Consulates in Åland Islands, Jyväskylä, Kotka, Kuopio, Oulu, Rovaniemi, Tampere, Turku and Vaasa.

Irish Embassy
EROTTAJANKATU 7A, FIN-00130 HELSINKI
Tel: (09) 6824240
www.embassyofireland.fi

Border Posts

The main border posts with Sweden are at Tornio, Ylitornio and Kaaresuvanto. Those with Norway are at Kilpisjärvi, Kivilompolo, Karigasniemi, Utsjoki Ohcejohka and Nuorgam. Border posts are open day and night. The Finnish-Russian border can only be crossed by road at certain official points – contact the Finnish Tourist Board for details.

In order to deter illegal immigrants border guards patrol the area close to the Russian border and it is important, therefore, to carry identification at all times when visiting the region.

Documents

Driving Licence/Vehicle(s)
When driving you should carry your driving licence, vehicle registration certificate (V5C), insurance certificate plus MOT certificate (if applicable).

Passport
You should also carry your passport at all times.

Money

Currency may be exchanged at banks and at bureaux de change.

Major credit cards are widely accepted and cash machines are widespread.

Carry your credit card issuers'/banks' 24-hour UK contact numbers in case of loss or theft of your cards.

Motoring in Finland
Accidents

Accidents must be reported to the police and if a foreign motorist is involved the Finnish Motor Insurers Bureau (Liikennevakuutuskeskus) should also be informed. Their address is Bulevardi 28, FIN-00120 Helsinki, tel (09) 40 450 4700/4750, www.lvk.fi./en. At the site of an accident other road users must be warned by the use of a warning triangle.

Alcohol

The maximum permitted level of alcohol is 50 milligrams in 100 millilitres of blood, i.e. lower than that permitted in the UK (80 milligrams). It is advisable to adopt the 'no drink and drive' rule at all times as anyone exceeding this limit will be arrested immediately and could face a prison sentence. Breath tests and blood tests may be carried out at random.

Breakdown Service

The Automobile & Touring Club of Finland, Autoliitto, has approximately 300 roadside patrols manned by volunteers and these can be called out at weekends and on public holidays. At other times, or if the Autoliitto patrol cannot be reached, contracted partners will provide assistance. For 24-hour assistance telephone (0)200 8080. Charges are made for assistance and towing, plus a call-out fee.

Emergency telephone boxes are installed around Helsinki, Kouvola, Jamsa, and Rovaniemi, and on the roads Kouvola-Lappeenranta-Imatra-Simpele and Rovaniemi-Jaatila. Drivers are connected to the national breakdown service.

Essential Equipment

Lights
Dipped headlights are compulsory at all times, regardless of weather conditions. Bulbs are more likely to fail with constant use and you are recommended to carry spares.

Reflective Jacket/Waistcoat
Pedestrians must wear reflective devices during the hours of darkness (any type of reflector is acceptable). If you get out of your vehicle you are required to wear one and the standard reflective jacket is probably the best option for driver and passengers.

Child Restraint System
Children under the height of 1.35m must be seated in a suitable child restraint.

If there is not a child restraint/seat available children of 3 years or older must travel in the rear seat using a seat belt or other safety device attached to the seat. Unless in a taxi a child under the age of 3 must not travel in a vehicle without a child restraint. It is the responsibility of the driver to ensure all children under the age of 15 years old are correctly and safely restrained.

Warning Triangles
All vehicles must carry a warning triangle and use it when broken down.

Winter Driving
Winter tyres are compulsory from 1 December to 28 February. Snow chains may be used temporarily when conditions necessitate.

The main arctic road leads from Kemi on the Gulf of Bothnia through Rovaniemi to the Norwegian border. During the winter, all high volume, main roads are kept open including routes to Norway and Sweden. In total between 6,000 and 7,000km of roads are mainly kept free of ice and snow by the use of salt. Other roads will consist of compacted snow. Drivers should expect winter conditions as early as October.

Fuel

Petrol stations are usually open from 7am to 9pm on weekdays and for shorter hours at weekends, although a few stay open 24 hours. Their frequency reduces towards the north, so it is advisable not to let your tank run low. Credit cards are accepted at most manned petrol stations. There are many unmanned stations, which have automatic petrol pumps operated with bank notes or credit cards.

It is understood that automatic payment machines at petrol pumps do not accept cards issued outside Finland.

LPG is not available.

Parking

A vehicle that has been illegally or dangerously parked may be removed by the police and the owner fined. Parking fines may be enforced on the spot, the minimum charge being €10. Parking meters operate for between 15 minutes and four hours; the free use of unexpired time is allowed. In some built-up areas you will need a parking disc obtainable from petrol stations or car accessory shops.

8 - 17	(8-13)	8 - 14
Restriction applies 8-17 hrs (Mon-Fri)	Restriction applies 8-13 hrs (Sat)	Restriction applies 8-14 hrs (Sun)

In some towns streets are cleaned on a regular basis and road signs indicate which day the cleaning takes place and, therefore, when the street should be kept clear of parked vehicles. Vehicles which cause an obstruction will be removed and drivers fined.

If you have a low emission car you may be entitled to 50% off parking fees in Helsinki. To qualify for this reduction the parking fees must be made by mobile phone and you will need to have obtained a green sticker with the letter 'P' from the Helsinki town authorities, which then needs to be attached to the windscreen. For further information visit www.easypark.fi or www.nextpark.com.

Priority

At intersections, vehicles coming from the right have priority, except when otherwise indicated. The approach to a main road from a minor road is indicated by a sign with a red triangle on a yellow background. When this sign is supplemented by a red octagon with STOP in the centre, vehicles must stop before entering the intersection. Trams and emergency vehicles, even coming from the left, always have priority. Vehicles entering a roundabout must give way to traffic already on the roundabout, i.e. on the left.

Roads

In general there is a good main road system, traffic is light and it is possible to cover long distances quickly, but there are still some gravelled roads in the countryside which have speed restrictions to avoid windscreens being broken by loose stones. During the spring thaw and during the wet season in September, gravelled roads may be in a poor condition. Roadworks take place during the summer months and sections under repair can extend for many miles.

There are large numbers of elk in Finland and they often wander across roads, especially at dawn and dusk. The same applies to reindeer in Lapland. Warning signs showing approximate lengths of danger zones are posted in these areas. If you collide with an elk, deer or reindeer you must notify the police.

The Finnish Transport Agency operates an information service on weather and road conditions, recommended driving routes and roadworks, tel 0295 020 600 or visit www.liikennevirasto.fi.

Road Signs and Markings

Road markings are generally white. Road signs conform to international conventions. Signs for motorway and end of motorway are on a green background while those for main roads are on a blue background. The following signs may also be found:

Finnish	English Translation
Aja hitaasti	Drive slowly
Aluerajoitus	Local speed limit
Kelirikko	Frost damage
Kokeile jarruja	Test your brakes
Kunnossapitotyö	Roadworks (repairs)
Lossi färja	Ferry
Päällystetyötä	Roadworks (resurfacing)
Tulli	Customs
Tie rakenteilla	Roadworks (road under construction)
Varo irtokiviä	Beware of loose stones

Speed Limits

	Open Road (km/h)	Motorway (km/h)
Car Solo	80-100	120
Car towing caravan/trailer	80	80
Motorhome under 3500kg	100	100
Motorhome 3500-7500kg	80	80

On all roads outside built-up areas throughout the country, other than motorways, differing speed limits between 70 and 100 km/h (44 and 62 mph) apply – except where vehicles are subject to a lower limit – according to the quality of the road and traffic density. Where there is no sign, the basic speed limit is usually 80 km/h (50 mph) on main roads and 70 km/h (44 mph) on secondary roads, whether solo or towing. The road sign which indicates this basic limit bears the word 'Perusnopeus' in Finnish, and 'Grundhastighet' in Swedish.

Reduced speed limits apply during the winter from October to March and these are generally 20 km/h (13 mph) lower than the standard limits. At other times temporary speed limits may be enforced locally.

The maximum speed limit for motorhomes up to 3,500kg is 100 km/h (62 mph).

Recommended maximum speed limits are indicated on some roads by square or rectangular signs bearing white figures on a blue background. The maximum speed limit in residential areas is 20 km/h (13 mph).

Slow moving vehicles must let others pass wherever possible, if necessary by moving onto the roadside verge. Maintain a sufficient distance behind a slow moving vehicle to allow an overtaking vehicle to pull in front.

Radar detectors are prohibited.

Violation of Traffic Regulations

The police can impose, but not collect, fines when road users violate traffic regulations. Fines should be paid at banks.

Motorways

There are 700km of motorway (moottoritie) in Finland linking Helsinki, Tampere and Turku. No tolls are levied. There are no emergency phones located on motorways. In the case of breakdown on a motorway drivers of all vehicles must use a warning triangle.

Touring

Both Finnish and Swedish are official languages. As a result, many towns and streets have two names, e.g. Helsinki is also known as Helsingfors, and Turku as Åbo. Finnish street names usually end 'katu', while Swedish street names usually end 'gatan' or 'vägen'. Swedish place names are more commonly used in the south and west of the country.

Smoking is not permitted in public buildings, restaurants or bars, except in designated smoking zones, nor on public transport.

The Helsinki Card offers free entry to several major museums and other attractions, and unlimited travel for 24, 48 or 72 hours on public transport, plus discounts for sightseeing, restaurants, shopping, concert tickets, sports, etc. For more information see www.helsinkicard.fi.

The sale of wine and spirits is restricted to Alko shops which are open Monday to Friday until 6pm or 8pm, Saturday until 4pm or 6pm, and closed on Sunday and public holidays. Medium strength beer is also sold in supermarkets and other stores.

A service charge is generally included in most restaurant bills and tips are not expected, but if the service has been good it is customary to round up the bill.

Most lakes are situated in the south east of the country and they form a web of waterways linked by rivers and canals, making this a paradise for those who enjoy fishing, canoeing and hiking. In Lapland the vegetation is sparse, consisting mostly of dwarf birch. Reindeer roam freely so motorists must take special care and observe the warning signs. Rovaniemi is the biggest town in Lapland, just south of the Arctic Circle. It has a special post office and 'Santa Claus Land'.

A number of 'Uniquely Finnish' touring routes have been established including the King's Road along the south coast which takes you through many places of interest including Porvoo, a small town with well-preserved, old, wooden houses, Turku, the former capital, and the famous Imatra waterfall near the southern shore of Lake Saimaa. Swedish influence is evident in this area in local customs, place names and language. These 'Uniquely Finnish' touring routes are marked with brown sign posts; contact the Finnish Tourist Board for more information.

Southern and central Finland are usually snow covered from early December to mid or late April, although in recent years the south coast has had little or no snow. Northern Finland has snow falls from October to May and temperatures can be extremely low. Thanks to the Gulf Stream and low humidity, Finland's winter climate does not feel as cold as temperature readings might indicate but if you plan a visit during the winter you should be prepared for harsh weather conditions.

In the summer many Finnish newspapers have summaries of main news items and weather forecasts in English and radio stations have regular news bulletins in English. English is taught in all schools and is widely spoken.

The Midnight Sun and Northern Lights

Areas within the Arctic Circle have 24 hours of daylight in the height of summer and no sun in winter for up to two months. There are almost 20 hours of daylight in Helsinki in the summer.

The Northern Lights (Aurora Borealis) may be seen in the arctic sky on clear dark nights, the highest incidence occurring in February/March and September/October in the Kilpisjärvi region of Lapland when the lights are seen on three nights out of four.

The Order of Bluenosed Caravanners

Visitors to the Arctic Circle from anywhere in the world may apply for membership of the Order of Bluenosed Caravanners which will be recognised by the issue of a certificate by the International Caravanning Association (ICA).

For more information contact David Hirst on tel: 01422 372390, or email: david.hirst118@gmail.com and attach a photograph of yourselves and your outfit under any Arctic Circle signpost, together with the date and country of crossing and the names of those who made the crossing.

This service is free to members of the ICA (annual membership £20); the fee for non-members is £5. Coloured plastic decals for your outfit, indicating membership of the Order, are also available at a cost of £4. Cheques should be payable to the ICA. Visit www.icacaravanning.org for more information.

Public Transport & Local Travel

The public transport infrastructure is of a very high standard and very punctual. You can buy a variety of bus, train, tram and metro tickets at public transport stations, HKL service points, newspaper kiosks and shops all over the country.

Single tickets, which are valid for 60 minutes, can be purchased from ticket machines, bus and tram drivers or train conductors. Tourist tickets valid for one, three or five days can also be purchased from kiosks, ticket machines and bus and tram drivers and are valid on all forms of public transport including the Suomenlinna ferry.

Within the Helsinki city area you may hire city bicycles in the summer for a token fee (refundable) from one of 26 Citybike stands.

Vehicle ferries operate all year on routes to Estonia, Germany and Russia and it is now possible to enjoy a visa free ferry trip to St Petersburg for up to 72 hours from Helsinki; see www.visitfinland.com for a link to more information or contact the Finnish Tourist Board.

Internal ferry services (in Finnish 'lossi') transport motor vehicles day and night. Those situated on the principal roads, taking the place of a bridge, are state-run and free of charge. There are regular services on Lake Paijanne, Lake Inari and Lake Pielinen, and during the summer vessels operate daily tours as well as longer cruises through Finland's lake region. Popular routes are between Hameenlinna and Tampere, Tampere and Virrat, as well as the Saimaa Lake routes. Full details are available from the Finnish Tourist Board.

ALAND ISLANDS Campsites in towns in the Aland Islands are listed together at the end of the Finnish site entry pages.

HAMEENLINNA *B4* (7km NE Rural) *61.03263, 24.47209* **Camping Aulangon Lomäkylä, Heikkiläntie 168, 13990 Hämeenlinna [(03) 6759772; myynti@aulangonlomakyla.fi; www.aulangonlomakyla.fi]** E12 exit Hämeenlinna onto rd. Site clearly sp fr Hämeenlinna in Aulanko. Lge, terr, shd; wc; chem disp; mv service pnt; sauna; shwrs inc; EHU (10A) €5; gas; lndry; shop; rest, snacks; bar; playgrnd; lake sw & sand beach; bike hire; tennis; golf course adj; wifi; some statics; poss cr; quiet; ccard acc; red CKE/CCI. "Beautiful location." 1 May-17 Aug. € 20.00   2010*

HANKO/HANGO *B4* (4km NE Coastal) *59.85271, 23.01716* **Camping Silversand, Hopeahietikko, 10960 Hanko Pohjoinen [(019) 2485500; fax 713713; info@silversand.fi; www.silversand.fi]** Site sp fr rd 25. Lge, shd; wc; chem disp; mv service pnt; sauna; shwrs inc; EHU (16A) €5; lndry; shop & 1km; rest 3km; snacks; cooking facs; playgrnd; fishing; boat & bike hire; games rm; wifi; TV; 10% statics; poss cr; Eng spkn; no adv bkg; ccard acc; red CKE. "Beautiful location on edge of sea in pine forest." ♦ 25 Apr-30 Sep. € 20.00   2009*

⊞ **HELSINKI/HELSINGFORS** *C4* (13km E Coastal/Urban) *60.20668, 25.12116* **Rastila Municipal Camping, Karavaanikatu 4, Vuosaari, 00980 Helsinki [(09) 31078517; fax 31036659; rastilacamping@hel.fi; www.hel.fi/rastila]** E fr Helsinki on rte 170, over Vuosaari bdge; or get to ring rd 1, turn E dir Vuosaari, site sp. Also sp fr Silja & other ferry terminals & fr rte 170 to Porvoo. Also sp on rte 167. V lge, hdstg, pt shd; wc; chem disp, mv service pnt; sauna, shwrs inc; EHU (16A) €4.50; lndry; shops 100m; supmkt 400m; rest, snacks; cooking facs; playgrnd; sand beach 1.2km; wifi; TV & games rm; 10% statics; metro nr; poss cr; Eng spkn; quiet; ccard acc; red long stay/CKE. "Conv Helsinki & district; pleasant site; gd san facs; helpful staff; poss itinerant workers but site clean & tidy; weekly rates avail; best place we stayed at." ♦ € 37.00   2014*

⊞ **HOSSA** *C2* (500m NW Rural) *65.44293, 29.55108* **Erä-Hossa Camping, Hossantie 278B, 89220 Ruhtinansalmi [(08) 732310; fax 732316; era-hossa@luukku.com; www.hossa.fi]** At Peranka on rd 5/E63 Kuusamo to Suomussalmi, turn E onto 9190; at T-junc after 29km turn N on rd 843/9193 sp Hossa; site on L 3km. Med, hdstg, pt shd; wc; chem disp; sauna; shwrs inc; EHU (10A) inc; lndry; rest; bar; cooking facs; playgrnd; lake sw adj; boating; fishing; bike hire; quiet; ccard acc; red CKE/CCI. "Deep in Karelian Forest; lakeside site in holiday cabin complex with cent facs; many hiking & ski trails 4km in National Park." € 21.00   2009*

IISALMI *C3* (5km N Rural) *63.5947, 27.16165* **Camping Koljonvirta, Ylemmäisentie 6, 74120 Iisalmi [(017) 825252; fax 822559; info@campingkoljonvirta.fi; www.camping koljonvirta.fi]** Fr S on rd 5/E63 past Iisalmi, take rd 88 twd Oulu, strt over rndabt, site in 1km on L. Lge, mkd pitch pt sl, pt shd; htd wc; chem disp; mv service pnt; sauna, shwrs inc; EHU (10A) €5; lndry; shops adj; rest, snacks; sand beach adj; boating & fishing; poss cr; Eng spkn; quiet; ccard acc; red CKE/ CCI. "Vg." ♦ ltd. 20 May-30 Sep. € 20.00   2011*

IKAALINEN *B4* (1.2km NW Rural) *61.77872, 23.0445* **Camping Toivolansaari, Toivolansaarentie 3, 39500 Ikaalinen [(03) 4586462; fax 4501206; kylpylakaupunki@ ikaalinen.fi; www.kylpylakaupunki.fi]** Fr rd 3/E12 exit twd Ikaalinen cent onto rd 2595 Silkintie. Take 4th L in approx 1km sp Keskusta & foll Vanha Tampereentie thro town cent to lake, site sp on tip of promontory on Kyrösjärvi Lake. Med, pt shd; wc; chem disp; mv service pnt; sauna, shwrs inc; EHU (16A) €4; lndry; shops 1km; rest; BBQ; playgrnd; pool nr; sand beach & lake sw; boat hire; tennis nr; games rm; entmnt; TV rm; 5% statics; dogs; boat to hotel 800m; poss cr; Eng spkn; adv bkg; quiet; CKE/CCI. "Vg, attractive lakeside site; friendly, accommodating staff." ♦ 1 Jun-31 Aug. € 18.00   2009*

INARI *B1* (2km E Rural) *68.90216, 27.07141* **Uruniemi Camping, Uruniementie 7, 99870 Inari [(050) 3718826; pentti.kangasniemi@uruniemi.inet.fi; www.uruniemi.com]** N on rte 4/E74, site S of Inari on R, sp. Sm, pt sl, pt shd; wc; sauna; shwrs €0.20; EHU (10A) €4.50; lndry; shop on site & 2km; snacks; cooking facs; playgrnd; lake adj; fishing & boating; bike hire; TV; 10% statics; quiet; ccard acc. "Vg for viewing midnight sun; boggy in wet; slightly makeshift facs." 1 Jun-20 Sep. € 19.00   2010*

⊞ **INARI** *B1* (500m SE Rural) *68.90233, 27.0370* **Holiday Village/Lomakylä Inari, Inarintie 26, 99780 Inari [(016) 671108; fax 671480; info@lomakyla-inari.fi; www.saariselka.fi/lomakylainari]** Fr S on rte 4/E75, site on R app Inari, clearly sp. Fr N on E75 500m past town cent, site on L, sp. Sm, some hdstg, unshd; wc; chem disp; mv service pnt; sauna; shwrs inc; EHU (16A) inc (long lead poss req); lndry; shops, rest 500m; snacks; playgrnd; lake sw adj; sand beach adj; motorboat & canoe hire; 40% statics; dogs free; poss cr; no adv bkg; some rd noise; ccard acc; red CKE/ CCI. "Gd for walking; midnight sun cruises on Lake Inari; excel Lapp museum; poss boggy in wet; poss low voltage if site full; some lge pitches suitable RVs & lge o'fits; clean & tidy." € 22.00 (4 persons)   2009*

IVALO *B1* (2km S Rural) *68.64369, 27.52714* **Holiday Village Näverniemi, 99800 Ivalo [(016) 677601; fax 677602]** Sp on W side of rte 4/E75. Lge, unshd; wc; chem disp; sauna; shwrs inc; EHU (10A) €2.50; lndry; shop; rest, snacks; playgrnd; lake sw adj; entmnt; TV; adv bkg; quiet; ccard acc.; red CKE/ CCI "Gd cent for birdwatchers; rvside site; reindeer herds nr site; insufficient el hook-ups; helpful, friendly owner; phone ahead early ssn to check open - poss flooding during spring thaw." 1 May-31 Oct. € 26.00   2009*

JUUKA C3 (6km SE Rural) 63.22607, 29.34165
Piitterin Lomakylä Camping, Piitterintie 144, 83900 Juuka
[(013) 472000; fax 673220; piitteri@piitteri.fi;
www.piitteri.fi] Turn E off R6 just S of Juuka; site in 5km;
sp. Med, hdstg, pt shd; wc; chem disp; sauna; shwrs inc; EHU
(15A) inc; lndry; snacks; BBQ; cooking facs; playgrnd; sand
beach adj; lake sw & boating; tennis; some statics; Eng spkn;
ccard acc; red CKE. ♦ 1 Jun-15 Aug. € 20.00   2010*

JUVA C4 (3km W Rural) 61.89444, 27.82138 **Juva Camping,**
Hotellitie 68, 51900 Juva [(015) 451930; camping@
juvacamping.com; www.juvacamping.com] Sp fr x-rds of
rds 5 and 14. Sm, hdstg, shd; htd wc; chem disp; mv service
pnt; baby facs; EHU €3; lndry; shop on site & 700m; rest,
snacks; bar 700m; playgrnd; sand beach adj; boat/canoe hire;
games area; internet; some statics; dogs free; Eng spkn; adv
bkg; quiet; ccard acc; red CKE. "Vg, well-kept site on lakeside;
friendly, helpful staff." ♦ 1 May-31 Oct. € 18.00   2009*

⊞ **JYVASKYLA** C3 (4km N Urban) 62.25536, 25.6983
Laajis Camping, Laajavuorentie 15, 40740 Jyväskylä
[207 436 436; fax (014) 624888; gasthaus@laajis.fi;
www.laajavuori.com] Well sp fr N on E75 & E63 fr S, site sp
adj youth hostel. Med, mkd pitch, hdstg, unshd; htd wc; chem
disp; mv service pnt; sauna; shwrs inc; EHU (16A) inc; lndry;
shop 500m; rest, snacks; cooking facs; htd pool 3km; lake
2km; ski lift/jumps adj; wifi; entmnt; cab TV; dogs; Eng spkn;
quiet; red long stay; CKE/CCI. "Facs stretched if site full; c'vans
only." ♦ € 29.00   2011*

"I like to fill in the reports
as I travel from site to site"
You'll find report forms at the back of
this guide, or you can fill them in online
at www.caravanclub.co.uk/europereport.

KAMMENNIEMI B4 (7km NW Rural) 61.65423, 23.77748
Camping Taulaniemi, Taulaniementie 357, 34240
Kämmenniemi [(03) 3785753; taulaniemi@yritys.soon.fi;
www.taulaniemi.fi] Fr Tampere take rte 9/E63 dir Jyvaskyla.
In 10km take rte 338 thro Kämmenniemi. Foll sp Taulaniemi on
unmade rd to lakeside site. Sm, pt sl, terr, unshd; htd wc; chem
disp; mv service pnt; sauna; shwrs inc; EHU (16A) €3; lndry;
shop; rest, snacks; cooking facs; playgrnd; sandy beach/lake on
site; boat hire; TV; adv bkg; v quiet; CKE/CCI. "Beautiful site."
21 May-13 Sep. € 20.00   2009*

KARIGASNIEMI B1 (850m NW Rural) 69.39975, 25.84278
Camping Tenorinne, Ylätenontie 55, 99950 Karigasniemi
[(016) 676113; camping@tenorinne.com; www.tenorinne.
com] N of town cent on rd 970 Karigasniemi to Utsjoki. Sm, pt
shd; htd wc; chem disp; sauna; shwrs inc; EHU (16A) €4; lndry;
shop, rest 200m; playgrnd; TV; some statics; no adv bkg; quiet;
ccard acc; red CKE/CCI. 5 Jun-20 Sep. € 18.00   2010*

KEMIJARVI C2 (700m NW Urban) 66.71689, 27.41908
Camping Hietaniemi, Hietaniemenkatu, 98100 Kemijärvi
[tel/fax (016) 813640; sales@hietaniemicamping.info;
www.hietaniemicamping.info] In cent of town on lake. Nr
x-rds of rte 5 & rte 82, sp. Med; htd wc; chem disp; sauna;
shwrs inc; EHU (16A) inc; lndry; shop 500m; snacks; bar;
playgrnd; pool 1km; fishing; TV; ccard acc; red CKE. "Gd site;
helpful staff." ♦ ltd. 25 May-31 Aug. € 24.00   2010*

KESALAHTI D4 (19km NNW Rural) 62.01883, 29.68420
Karjalan Lomakeskus Camping, Vääramäentie 147A,
59800 Kesälahti [(013) 378121; fax 378130; info@karjalan-
lomakeskus.fi; www.karjalan-lomakeskus.fi] Fr Kesälähti
N on rd 6 to Aittolahti then on rd 4800 for 14km, site sp. Last
400m on narr rd. Med, pt shd; wc; chem disp; mv service pnt;
sauna; shwrs inc; EHU (10A) €3 or metered; lndry (inc dryer);
shop 10km; rest, snacks high ssn; bar; playgrnd; lake sw & sand
beach; fishing; tennis; games area; TV; some statics; dogs; no
adv bkg; red CKE. 1 May-30 Sep. € 19.00   2009*

KEURUU B4 (3km S Rural) 62.24435, 24.70893
Camping Nyyssänniemi, Nyyssänniementie 10, 42700
Keuruu [(040) 7002308; leena.ikalainen@nic.fi;
www.nyyssanniemi.fi] Clearly sp W of rd 58 on S o'skirts of
Keuruu. Med, some hdstg, pt shd; wc; chem disp; sauna; shwrs
inc; EHU (16A) €5; lndry; shops in town; snacks; cooking facs;
playgrnd; lake sw; boating; wifi; TV; Eng spkn; adv bkg; quiet;
ccard acc; red CKE. 20 May-11 Sep. € 21.00   2011*

⊞ **KILPISJARVI** A1 (4.6km SSE Rural) 69.01413, 20.88235
Kilpisjärvi Holiday Village, Käsivarrentie 14188, 99490
Kilpisjärvi [(016) 537801; fax 537803; info@kilpisjarvi.
net; www.kilpisjarvi.net] On main rd 21 almost opp g'ge,
in middle of vill, sp. Lge, hdstg, unshd; htd wc; chem disp;
baby facs; shwrs €2; EHU (10A) inc; lndry; supmkt 100m;
rest, snacks; bar; BBQ; cooking facs; bus adj; Eng spkn; quiet.
"Gd NH to/fr N Norwegian fjords; access to Saana Fells for gd
walking/trekking; winter sports cent." ♦ € 20.00   2011*

KOKKOLA B3 (2.5km N Coastal) 63.85500, 23.11305
Kokkola Camping, Vanhansatamanlahti, 67100 Kokkola
[tel/fax (06) 8314006; info@kokkola-camping.fi;
www.kokkola-camping.fi] Exit A8 at Kokkola onto rte
749. Site on R, sp fr town. Sm, pt shd; wc; chem disp; mv
service pnt; sauna; baby facs; shwrs inc; EHU €4; shop; snacks;
cooking facs; playgrnd; sand beach adj; games area; poss cr;
quiet; red CKE. "New owner 2008 - improvements ongoing."
1 Jun-31 Aug. € 20.00   2009*

KOLI D3 (7km NE Rural) 63.15028, 29.84301 **Loma-Koli**
Camping, Merilänrannantie 65, 83960 Koli [(013) 673212;
fax 223337; info@lomakolicamping.fi; www.
lomakolicamping.fi] Site 16km off rte 6, down rte 504. 64km
N of Joensuu. Lge, pt shd; wc; chem disp; sauna; shwrs inc;
EHU (16A) €3; lndry; shop; snacks; rest 1km; BBQ; playgrnd;
lake sw & sand beach; bike hire; games rm; TV; some statics;
dogs; poss cr; no adv bkg; quiet; ccard acc; red CKE/CCI.
1 Jun-12 Aug. € 12.00   2009*

FINLAND

KUOPIO C3 (9km SW Rural) 62.86432, 27.64165
Rauhalahti Holiday Centre, Kiviniementie, 70700 Kuopio
[(017) 473000; fax 473099; rauhalahti.camping@kuopio.fi;
www.rauhalahti.com] Well sp fr rte 5 (E63). Site 1.5km
fr E63 dir Levänen, on Lake Kallavesi. Lge, hdstg, pt sl, pt shd;
htd wc; chem disp; mv service pnt; baby facs; sauna; shwrs inc;
EHU (16A) €5; gas; lndry; shop; rest, snacks; bar; cooking facs;
playgrnd; lake sw; boat trips; watersports; TV rm; ccard acc; red
CKE/CCI. "Hdstg for cars, grass for van & awning." ♦
30 May-31 Aug. € 20.00   2009*

⊞ **KUUSAMO** C2 (5km N Rural) 66.00143, 29.16713
Camping Rantatropiikki, Kylpyläntie, 93600 Kuusamo/
Petäjälampi [(08) 8596000; fax 8521909; myyntipalvelu.
tropiikki@holidayclub.fi] Three sites in same sm area on rd
5/E63, sp. Med, pt shd; htd wc; chem disp; mv service pnt;
sauna; shwrs inc; EHU (10A) inc; lndry; pool in hotel adj; sand
beach; lake sw; tennis; bike hire; internet; dogs; no adv bkg;
quiet; ccard acc; CKE/CCI. "Conv falls area; LS site recep at
hotel 500m past site ent." € 20.00   2009*

⊞ **LAHTI** C4 (5km N Rural) 61.01599, 25.64855 Camping
Mukkula, Ritaniemenkatu 10, 15240 Lahti [(03) 7535380;
fax 7535381; tiedustelut@mukkulacamping.fi;
www.mukkulacamping.fi] Fr S on rte 4/E75 foll camping
sps fr town cent. Med, pt shd; htd wc; chem disp; mv service
pnt; baby facs; sauna; shwrs inc; EHU (10A) inc; lndry; shop
1km; rest, snacks, bar 1km; cooking facs; playgrnd; lake sw;
fishing; tennis; bike hire; internet; TV; no dogs; no adv bkg;
quiet; ccard acc; red CKE. "Beautiful lakeside views." ♦
€ 22.00   2009*

LIEKSA D3 (3km SW Rural) 63.30666, 30.00532
Timitranniemi Camping, Timitra, 81720 Lieksa
[(013) 521780; fax 525486; loma@timitra.com;
www.timitra.com] Rte 73, well sp fr town on Lake Pielinen.
Med, pt sl, pt shd; wc; chem disp; sauna; shwrs inc; EHU (16A)
€4; lndry; shop; rest 2km; snacks; cooking facs; playgrnd; lake
sw; fishing; boat & bike hire; internet; TV; ccard acc; red CKE/
CCI. "Pt of recreational complex; Pielinen outdoor museum
worth visit." 15 May-20 Sep. € 20.00   2010*

MERIKARVIA B4 (3km SW Coastal) 61.84777, 21.47138
Mericamping, Palosaarentie 67, 29900 Merikarvia
[tel/fax (02) 5511283; mericamping.merikarvia@luukka.com;
www.mericamping.fi] Fr E8 foll sp to Merikarvia, site sp 2km
W beyond main housing area. Med, mkd pitch, unshd; wc;
chem disp; mv service pnt; shwrs inc; EHU €3.50; rest, snacks;
beach adj; wifi; some cottages; Eng spkn; quiet; ccard acc; red
CKE. "Vg site on water's edge; friendly, helpful staff."
1 Jun-31 Aug. € 12.00   2009*

⊞ **MUONIO** B1 (3km S Rural) 67.93333, 23.6575 Harrinivan
Lomakeskus, Harrinivantie 35, 99300 Muonio [016 5300 300;
fax 532 750; info@harriniva.fi; www.harriniva.fi]
On E8 5km S of Muonio, well sp on R going S. Sm, some
hdstg, pt sl, pt shd; htd wc; chem disp; shwrs inc; en pnts (16A)
€4; shop 5km; rest; bar; BBQ; playgrnd; shingle rv; wifi; twin
axles; Eng spkn; adv bkg; quiet; ccard acc; CCI. "Canoe hire for
white water rafting; huskies; san facs stretch in high ssn; fair."
€ 22.00   2014*

⊞ **NOKIA** B4 (5km S Rural) 61.44798, 23.49247 Camping
Viinikanniemi, Viinikanniemenkatu, 37120 Nokia
[(03) 3413384; fax 3422385; info@viinikanniemi.com;
www.viinikanniemi.com] SW fr Tampere on rd 12, site well
sp. Med, mkd pitch, hdstg, pt sl, pt shd; htd wc; chem disp;
mv service pnt; fam bathrm; shwrs inc; EHU (16A) €5.90-10;
gas; lndry; shop; rest, snacks; bar; BBQ; playgrnd; sand beach
& lake sw adj; boat hire; fishing; bike hire; games area; entmnt;
internet; some statics; dogs; Eng spkn; adv bkg; quiet; ccard
acc; CKE/CCI. "Excel site; conv Tampere." ♦ € 21.00   2011*

NURMES C3 (4km SE Rural) 63.53274, 29.19889 Hyvärilä
Camping, Lomatie 12, 75500 Nurmes [(013) 6872500;
fax 6872510; hyvarila@nurmes.fi; www.hyvarila.com]
On rte 73 to Lieksa, turn R 4km fr rte 6/73 junc. Well sp on
Lake Pielinen. Check in at hotel. Lge, unshd; wc; chem disp;
mv service pnt; sauna; shwrs inc; EHU (16A) €5; lndry; shop
2km; rest, snacks; playgrnd; lake sw; tennis; games area; some
statics; dogs; quiet; ccard acc; red long stay/CKE/CCI. "Gd base
for N Karelia; pt of recreational complex." 15 May-15 Sep.
€ 19.00   2009*

⊞ **OULU/ULEABORG** B2 (6km NW Coastal) 65.0317,
25.4159 Camping Nallikari, Leiritie 10, Hietasaari, 90500
Oulu/Uleåborg [(08) 55861350; fax 55861713; nallikari.
camping@ouka.fi; www.nallikari.fi] Off Kemi rd. Sp fr town
& rte 4/E75 fr Kemi. (Do not take Oulu by-pass app fr S). Lge,
pt shd; htd wc; chem disp; mv service pnt; sauna; shwrs inc;
EHU (16A) €4.50; lndry; shop; rest 300m; snacks; bar; BBQ;
cooking facs; playgrnd; pool & spa adj; sw 500m; bike hire;
games area; child entmnt high ssn; wifi; TV; 20% statics; dogs;
poss cr; no adv bkg; quiet; ccard acc; red CKE/CCI. "Gd cycling;
excel modern services block." ♦ € 23.00   2009*

PELLO B2 (1km NW Rural) 66.78413, 23.94540 Camping
Pello, Nivanpääntie 58, 95700 Pello [(016) 512494;
fax 515601; era.ahjo@oy.inet.fi] Foll site sp fr town cent.
Med, hdstg, pt shd; htd wc; chem disp; mv service pnt;
sauna; shwrs; EHU (16A) inc; lndry; shop, rest 1km; snacks;
playgrnd; rv adj; fishing; boat hire; 30% statics; Eng spkn;
quiet; ccard acc. "Rvside pitches avail - insects!" 1 Jun-20 Sep.
€ 21.00   2009*

PERANKA C2 (2km E Rural) 65.39583, 29.07094 Camping
Piispansaunat, Selkoskyläntie 19, 89770 Peranka
[(040) 5916784] Take rte 5/63 N or S; at Peranka turn E on
rd 9190 for 2km; site on R in trees. Sm, hdstg, pt sl, shd; wc;
chem disp; sauna; shwrs inc; EHU (10A) €4; lndry; shop 2km;
snacks; BBQ; cooking facs; playgrnd; lake sw & sand beach
adj; fishing; dogs; Eng spkn; quiet; red CKE/CCI. 1 Jun-31 Aug.
€ 25.00   2011*

PORVOO/BORGA C4 (2km S Rural) 60.3798, 25.66673
Camping Kokonniemi, Uddaksentie 17, 06100 Porvoo
[(019) 581967; myynti@suncamping.fi; www.fontana.fi]
Fr E on rte 7/E18 m'way ignore 1st exit Porvoo, site sp fr 2nd
exit. Med, some hdstg, pt sh; wc; chem disp; mv service
pnt; sauna; shwrs inc; EHU (16A) €5; lndry rm; shop, rest 2km;
snacks; playgrnd; poss cr; Eng spkn; no adv bkg; quiet; ccard
acc; red CKE. "Access to old town & rv walk; conv Helsinki &
ferry." 4 Jun-22 Aug. € 19.00   2010*

⊞ **PUNKAHARJU** *D4* (9km NW Rural) *61.80032,
29.29088* **Punkaharjun Camping, Tuunaansaarentie 4,
58540 Punkaharju [(020) 7529800; fax (015) 441784;
punkaharju@fontana.fi]** 27km SE of Savonlinna on rte 14 to
Imatra, sp on R. V lge, pt shd; wc; chem disp; mv service pnt;
sauna; shwrs inc; EHU (16A) €5; lndry; shop; rest, snacks; bar;
playgrnd; lake sw; waterslide; fishing; tennis; games area; TV;
poss cr; no adv bkg; quiet but noise fr bar; ccard acc; red CKE/
CCI. "Theme park nrby (closes 15/8); Kerimäki, world's largest
wooden church; Retretti Art Cent adj." € 19.00   2009*

RAUMA *B4* (3km NW Coastal) *61.13501, 21.47085*
**Poroholma Camping, Poroholmantie, 26100 Rauma
[(02) 83882500; fax 83882400; poroholma@kalliohovi.fi;
www.visitrauma.fi]** Enter town fr coast rd (8) or Huittinen
(42). Foll campsite sp around N pt of town to site on coast.
Site well sp. Lge, pt sl, shd; wc; chem disp; sauna; shwrs inc;
EHU (16A) €3; lndry; shop; snacks; bar; playgrnd; pool 250m;
sand beach; dogs; no adv bkg; quiet; ccard acc; red CKE/CCI.
"Attractive, peaceful location on sm peninsula in yacht marina
& jetty for ferry (foot passengers only) to outlying islands; excel
beach; warm welcome fr helpful staff; clean facs."
15 May-31 Aug. € 18.00   2009*

ROVANIEMI *B2* (1km E Urban) *66.49743, 25.74340*
**Ounaskoski Camping, Jäämerentie 1, 96200 Rovaniemi
[tel/fax (016) 345304]** Exit rte 4 onto rte 78 & cross rv. Over
bdge turn S on rvside along Jäämerentie. Site on R in approx
500m immed bef old rd & rail bdge, sp. Med, mkd pitch, pt
shd, some hdstg; htd wc; chem disp; mv service pnt; baby facs;
sauna; shwrs inc; EHU (16A) €4.90; lndry; shop; rest 400m;
snacks; cooking facs; playgrnd; pool 1km; rv sw & sand beach;
wifi; TV rm; poss v cr; Eng spkn; adv bkg; quiet; ccard acc;
red CKE/CCI. "Helpful staff; excel site beside rv in parkland;
gd facs; suitable RVs & twin-axles; 9km fr Arctic Circle; 6km
to Santa Park, 'official' home of Santa; Artikum Museum
worth visit; easy walk to town cent." ♦ 25 May-15 Sep.
€ 24.00   2010*

ROVANIEMI *B2* (7km E Rural) *66.51706, 25.84678* **Camping
Napapiirin Saarituvat, Kuusamontie 96, 96900 Saarenkylä
[tel/fax (016) 3560045; reception@saarituvat.fi;
www.saarituvat.fi]** Fr town cent take rd 81, site on R at side
of rd on lakeside. NB ignore 1st campsite sp after 2km. Sm,
terr, pt shd; htd wc; chem disp; sauna; shwrs inc; EHU (16A)
€5.50; lndry; shop 4km; rest; bar; BBQ; playgrnd; dogs; Eng
spkn; adv bkg; quiet; red CKE/CCI. "Excel; friendly staff; vg
base for Santa Park & Vill." 20 May-9 Sep. € 32.50   2014*

SALO *B4* (7km SW Rural) *60.36359, 23.06626* **Vuohensaari
Camping, 24100 Salo [(02) 7312651; fax 7784810]**
N fr Lahti, foll sp on rd 101 at edge of town. Med, pt sl, pt
shd; htd wc; chem disp (wc); shwrs inc; EHU (16A) inc; lndry
rm; shop on site & 4km; snacks; cooking facs; playgrnd; quiet;
CKE/CCI. "Lge mkt on Thurs in town." ♦ 1 Jun-30 Sep.
€ 18.50   2009*

SIMO *B2* (850m SE Rural) *65.65902, 25.06655* **Lapin Rinki
Camping, Lohitie 14, 95200 Simo [(016) 266444;
fax 266044]** Fr S just off E75/rd 4 on L, well sp. Sm, pt shd; htd
wc; shwrs inc; some EHU; 50% statics; dogs; poss cr; Eng spkn;
quiet; CKE/CCI. "Super NH or longer stay for salmon fishing -
rv adj, licence avail." ♦ ltd. 20 May-25 Sep. € 14.00   2009*

⊞ **SIRKKA LEVI** *B1* (1km W Rural) *67.80407, 24.78827*
**Muumari Huoneistot & Caravan, Konttisentie 1, 99130
Sirkka-Levi [(016) 644240; www.peak.fi]** Fr rd 79 at rndabt
in Sirkka take exit W sp for tourist info, then foll site sps. Recep
in kiosk by lake. Sm, mkd pitch, pt shd; htd wc; chem disp;
shwrs inc; EHU (10A) inc; lndry (inc dryer); snacks; bar; BBQ;
lake sw 150m; 20% statics; dogs; Eng spkn; quiet; rec CKE.
"Gd, friendly site." € 25.00   2009*

TAMPERE *B4* (6km SW Rural) *61.47183, 23.7390* **Camping
Härmälä, Leirintäkatu 8, 33900 Tampere [(03) 2651355;
fax (09) 7141733; myyntipalvelu@lomaliitto.fi;
www.lomaliitto.fi]** Foll camping sp fr Tampere cent to site on
Lake Pyhäjärvi. Lge, pt shd; wc; chem disp; baby facs; sauna;
shwrs inc; EHU (16A) €5.50; lndry; shop 4km; snacks; playgrnd;
sand beach; bike & boat hire; TV; poss cr; adv bkg; quiet; ccard
acc; red long stay; CKE. 13 May-18 Sep. € 24.00   2011*

TORNIO *B2* (3km SE Rural) *65.83211, 24.19953* **Camping
Tornio, Matkailijantie, 95420 Tornio [(016) 445945;
fax 445030; camping.tornio@co.inet.fi; www.camping
tornio.com]** App Tornio on E4 coast rd fr Kemi sp on L of dual
c/way; turn L at traff lts then immed R. Site well sp. Lge, pt
shd; wc; chem disp; sauna; shwrs inc; EHU (16A) €4; lndry (inc
dryer); shop 3km; snacks; cooking facs; playgrnd; tennis; bike
hire; TV; quiet; ccard acc; red CKE/CCI. "Poss boggy in wet."
♦ ltd. 15 May-30 Sep. € 22.00   2013*

⊞ **TURKU/ABO** *B4* (12km SW Rural) *60.42531, 22.10258*
**Ruissalo Camping (Part Naturist), Saaronniemi, 20100
Turku [(02) 2625100; fax 2625101; ruissalocamping@
turku.fi]** Well sp fr m'way & fr Turku docks; recep immed
after sharp bend in a layby. Med, pt shd, some hdstg; htd
wc; chem disp; mv service pnt; sauna; shwrs inc; EHU (16A)
inc; lndry; shop; rest 200m; snacks; playgrnd; sand beach adj;
watersports; games area; wifi; TV; some statics; sep area for
naturists; bus; Eng spkn; quiet; ccard acc; red CKE/CCI. "Conv
for ferry; modern, clean san facs; ltd EHU some parts." ♦ ltd.
€ 35.00   2014*

⊞ **UUKUNIEMI** *D4* (3km NW Coastal) *61.80222,
29.96538* **Papinniemi Camping, Papinniementie 178,
Uukuniemi Parikkala 59730, Suomi [(40) 7369852; info@
papinniemicamping.net; www.papinniemicamping.net]**
Fr Karelia rd foll sp. Fr S take R Niukkalantie. Fr N take L
Uukuniementie. Sm, pt shd; wc; shwrs; EHU (16A) €4; games
area; sauna €15; rest, snacks; BBQ; wifi; bicycles; rowing boats
& canoes; "Amazing nature; peaceful beautiful place; lake
water so clean." € 33.00   2013*

VAASA/VASA *B3* (3km NW Coastal) *63.1008, 21.57618*
**Top Camping Vaasa, Niemeläntie 1, 65170 Vaasa
[(06) 2111255; fax 2111288; info.topcampingvaasa@
aspro-ocio.es; www.topcamping.fi/vaasa]** Fr town cent foll
sp to harbour (Satama), site sp. Lge, pt shd; htd wc; chem disp;
mv service pnt; baby facs; sauna; shwrs inc; EHU (10A) €5;
lndry; shop; snacks; bar; playgrnd; bike hire; TV; 10% statics;
dogs; no adv bkg; ccard acc; red long stay/CKE/CCI. ♦
25 May-10 Aug. € 22.00   2009*

VARKAUS *C3* (4km SE Rural) *62.29914, 27.92244* **Taipale Camping, Leiritie 1, 78250 Varkaus [tel/fax (017) 5526644]** Fr rd 5 foll sp Joensuu, site sp on lakeside. Med, pt shd; htd wc; chem disp; mv service pnt; sauna; shwrs inc; EHU (16A) €3.50; lndry; shop 1.5km; rest 3km; snacks; playgrnd; lake sw; fishing; games area; bike hire; TV; adv bkg; quiet; ccard acc. ♦ Jun-Aug. € 16.00   2009*

VIRRAT *B4* (6km SE Rural) *62.20883, 23.83501* **Camping Lakarin Leirintä, Lakarintie 405, 34800 Virrat [(03) 4758639; fax 4758667; virtain.matkailu@phpoint.net; www.virtainmatkailu.fi]** Fr Virrat on rte 66 twd Ruovesi. Fr Virrat pass info/park & take 2nd L, then 1st L. Site 1.7km on R (poor surface), sp. Med, pt sl, pt shd; htd wc; chem disp; sauna; shwrs inc; EHU (16A) €3.40; lndry rm; shop in Virrat; snacks; playgrnd; lake sw adj; boating; fishing; 50% statics; Eng spkn; quiet; red CKE. "Beautiful lakeside pitches." 1 May-30 Sep. € 20.00   2011*

⊞ **VUOSTIMO** *C2* (2km SW Rural) *66.95783, 27.50350* **Camping Kuukiurun, Sodankyläntie, 98360 Vuostimo [(016) 882535; fax 882540; kuukiuru@webinfo.fi; www.kuukiuru.fi]** N fr Kemijarvi on rd 5, site on R of rd leaving Vuostimo adj rv. Sm, mkd pitch, pt sl, unshd; wc; chem disp; sauna; shwrs; EHU inc; snacks; fishing; boat hire; x-country skiing; TV; many statics; dogs; quiet. "Beautiful, peaceful site; friendly owners." € 20.00   2009*

ALAND ISLANDS

ECKERO *A4* (7km SE Coastal) *60.19351, 19.62164* **Notvikens Camping, Södra Överbyvägen 239, 22270 Eckerö/Överby [(018) 38020; fax 38329; info@notviken.aland.fi; www.notviken.aland.fi]** Fr Eckerö ferry take rd 1 E & turn R at site sp in hamlet of Överby. Site in 2km. Med, pt sl, pt shd; wc, chem disp, mv service pnt; shwrs €1; EHU (10A) inc; lndry; sm shop; rest, snacks; bar; BBQ; cooking facs; playgrnd; sand beach adj; games area; 5% statics; dogs; phone; bus 2km; Eng spkn; adv bkg; quiet; CKE/CCI. "Well-maintained, family-run site in lovely location by long inlet; facs rustic but clean & well-equipped." ♦ ltd. 15 May-31 Aug. € 18.00   2009*

FOGLO *A4* (10km NE Coastal) *60.05981, 20.51586* **CC Camping, Finholmavägen, 22270 Föglö [(018) 51440; fax 51455; cc.camp@aland.net; http://home.aland. net/cc.camp]** Fr ferry at Degerby on Föglö Island foll main island rd E then N. Site sp fr ferry. Sm, pt sl, unshd; htd wc; chem disp; baby facs; shwrs €1; EHU €3.50; lndry; shop 10km; rest, snacks; bar; BBQ; cooking facs; playgrnd; shgl beach adj; no statics; dogs; phone; no twin axles; Eng spkn; adv bkg; quiet; CKE/CCI. "Beautiful, quite site on attractive island; gd birdwatching & walks fr site." ♦ 1 Jun-31 Aug. € 10.00   2009*

MARIEHAMN/MAARIANHAMINA *A4* (2km SE Coastal) *60.09079, 19.95038* **Gröna Uddens Camping, Österinäsvägen, 22100 Mariehamn/Maarianhamina [(018) 21121; fax 19041; gronaudden@aland.net; www.gronaudden.com]** Sp fr ferry. Lge, sl, pt shd; wc; chem disp; baby facs; sauna; shwrs; EHU (10A) inc (long lead req); lndry; shop; rest 1km; snacks; bar; playgrnd; sand beach; watersports; games area; bike hire; quiet; ccard acc. "Superb natural scenery, worth long haul; unrel in wet; modern san facs but poss long walk." 1 May-17 Sep. € 23.50   2009*

"We must tell The Club about that great site we found"

Get your site reports in by mid-August and we'll do our best to get your updates into the next edition.

SUND *A4* (12km SE Coastal) *60.21252, 20.23508* **Puttes Camping, Bryggvägen 40, Bomarsund, 22530 Sund [(018) 44040; fax 44047; puttes.camping@aland.net; www.visitaland.com/puttescamping]** N fr Mariehamn on rd 2 for 40+ km, site at Bomarsund fortress ruins. Med, pt sl, pt shd; wc; chem disp; mv service pnt; shwrs €1; EHU (10A) inc; lndry; shop; rest, snacks; bar; BBQ; cooking facs; shgl beach adj; bike hire; games area; 5% statics; dogs; phone; bus adj; Eng spkn; adv bkg; quiet; CKE/CCI. "Basic, but clean & welcoming; vg." ♦ ltd. 15 May-11 Sep. € 12.00   2009*

VARDO *A4* (4km N Coastal) *60.27073, 20.38819* **Sandösunds Camping, Sandösundsvägen, 22550 Vårdö [tel/fax (018) 47750; info@sandocamping.aland.fi; www.sandocamping.aland.fi]** Site sp fr ferry at Hummelvik & fr rd 2. Med, pt sl, pt shd; htd wc; chem disp; mv service pnt; baby facs; shwrs inc; EHU (10A) €3.50 (long lead poss req); lndry; shop; rest, snacks; bar; BBQ; cooking facs; playgrnd; sand beach adj; bike & kayak hire; games area; wifi; 5% statics; dogs; phone; Eng spkn; adv bkg; quiet; CKE/CCI. "Well-run site in beautiful location; excel facs." ♦ ltd. 15 Apr-31 Oct. € 14.00   2009*

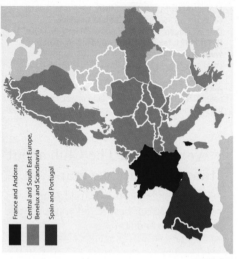

France and Andorra

Central and South East Europe, Benelux and Scandinavia

Spain and Portugal

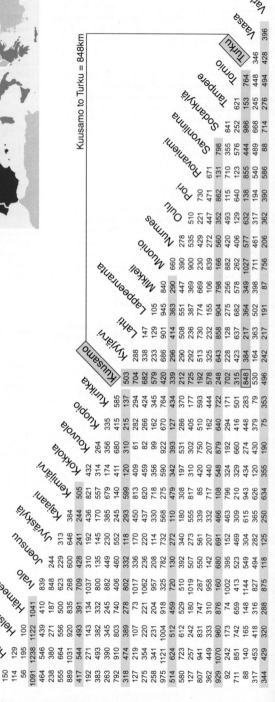

Kuusamo to Turku = 848km

Cities (chart axes): Forssa, Hanko, Helsinki, Hämeenlinna, Ivalo, Joensuu, Jyväskylä, Kajaani, Kemijärvi, Kokkola, Kouvola, Kuopio, Kurikka, **Kuusamo**, Kyyjärvi, Lahti, Lappeenranta, Mikkeli, Muonio, Nurmes, Oulu, Pori, Rovaniemi, Savonlinna, Sodankylä, Tampere, Tornio, **Turku**, Vaasa, Varkaus

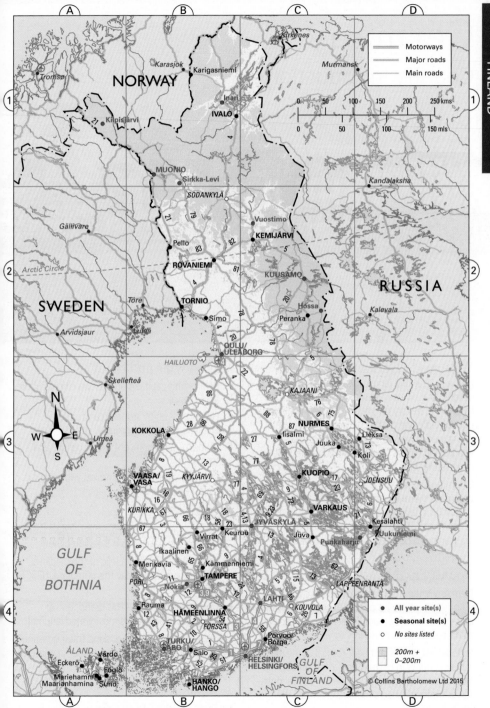

Germany
Country Introduction

Lindau Harbour

Welcome to Germany

Home to beautiful landscapes, architectural delights and diverse cities, Germany has a rich culture and history for you to discover. Berlin is undoubtedly one of the culture and arts capitals of the world, while the picturesque timbered villages and castles have inspired countless works of literature, film and art.

Often thought of as the home of beer and bratwurst, Germany has much more to offer on a gastronomic level, with Riesling wine, Black Forest Gateaux and Stollen just some of the treats that are waiting to be discovered and enjoyed.

Country highlights

Germany is the home of the modern car, and its automobile industry is one of the most innovative in the world. BMW, Audi, Porsche and Mercedes all have interesting museums to visit.

Oktoberfest, the largest beer festival in the world, is held annually in Munich and attracts people from around the globe. This 17-day festival only serves traditional beers that are brewed within Munich city limits.

Major towns and cities

- Berlin – this capital is an exciting city of culture and science.
- Hamburg – enjoy stunning and varied architecture in this gorgeous city.
- Munich – a magnificent city of culture and technology.
- Cologne – this city is brimming with bars, restaurants and pubs.

Attractions

- Neuschwanstein, Füssen – this fairytale castle inspired the palace from Sleeping Beauty.
- Holstentor, Lübeck – a relic of the medieval city fortifications, today this gate has UNESCO status.
- Cologne Cathedral – This grand, gothic cathedral is Germany's most visited landmark.
- Lindau – an enchanting island town boasting beautiful architecture and wonderful gardens.

Find out more

www.germany.travel

Tel: 0049 (0) 69 97 46 40 German Tourism Board

Country Information

Population (approx): 81million

Capital: Berlin (population approx 3.4 million)

Area: 357,050 sq km

Bordered by: Austria, Belgium, Czech Republic, Denmark, France, Luxembourg, Netherlands, Poland, Switzerland

Terrain: Lowlands in north; uplands/industrialised belt in the centre; highlands, forests and Bavarian Alps in the south

Climate: Temperate throughout the year; warm summers and cold winters; rain throughout the year

Coastline: 2,389km

Highest Point: Zugspitze 2,962m

Language: German

Local Time: GMT or BST + 1, i.e. 1 hour ahead of the UK all year

Currency: Euros divided into 100 cents; £1 = €1.42, €1 = £0.71 (September 2015)

Emergency numbers: Police 112; Fire brigade 112; Ambulance 112. Operators speak English

Public Holidays 2016: Jan 1; Mar 28; May 1, 5, 16; Aug 15; Oct 3, 31; Nov 1, 16; Dec 25, 26.

Public holidays vary according to region. The dates shown here may not be celebrated throughout the country. School summer holidays also vary by region but are roughly July to mid/end Aug or Aug to mid Sept.

Camping and Caravanning

There are approximately 3,500 campsites in Germany, which are generally open from April to October. Many (mostly in winter sports areas) stay open in winter and have all the necessary facilities for winter sports enthusiasts. Sites may have a very high proportion of statics, usually in a separate area. In the high summer season visitors should either start looking for a pitch early in the afternoon or book in advance.

Campsites are usually well equipped with modern sanitary facilities, shops and leisure amenities, etc. Some sites impose a charge for handling rubbish, commonly €1 to €2 a day. Separate containers for recycling glass, plastic, etc, are now the norm.

A daily tourist tax may also be payable of up to €2 or €3 per person per night.

Naturism is popular, particularly in eastern Germany, and sites which accept naturists will generally display a sign 'FKK'.

Many sites close for a two hour period between noon and 3pm (known as Mittagsruhe) and you may find barriers down so that vehicles cannot be moved on or off the site during this period. Some sites provide a waiting area but where a site entrance is off a busy road parking or turning may be difficult.

For a list of small sites (up to 150 pitches) see www.kleincamp.de.

Casual/wild camping is discouraged and is not allowed in forests and nature reserves. In the case of private property permission to pitch a tent or park a caravan should be obtained in advance from the owners, or on common land or state property, from the local town hall or police station.

Cycling

There is an extensive network of over 70,000 km of cycle routes across all regions. Children under eight years are not allowed to cycle on the road. Up to the age of 10 years they may ride on the pavement but must give way to pedestrians and dismount to cross the road. Bicycles must have front and rear lights and a bell.

Cyclists can be fined €25 for using a mobile phone while cycling and €10 for using earphones.

Electricity and Gas

Current on campsites varies between 2 and 16 amps, 6 to 10 amps being the most common. Plugs have two round pins. Most campsites have CEE connections.

Many sites make a one-off charge – usually €1 or €2 however long your stay – for connection to the electricity supply, which is then metered at a rate per kilowatt hour (kwh) of approximately €0.50-€0.70, with or without an additional daily charge. This connection charge can make one night stays expensive. During the summer you may find only a flat, daily charge for electricity of €2-€5, the supply being metered during the rest of the year.

Campingaz is available and the blue cylinders in general used throughout Europe may be exchanged for German cylinders which are green-grey. At some campsites in winter sports areas a direct connection with the gas mains ring is available and the supply is metered.

Entry Formalities

British and Irish passport holders may stay in Germany for up to three months without a visa. While there are no Customs controls at Germany's borders into other EU countries, when you enter or leave the Czech Republic and Poland you may still have to show your passport.

Regulations for Pets

Certain breeds of dogs, such as pit bull terriers and American Staffordshire terriers, are prohibited from entering Germany. There is an exception to this rule, whereby these dogs can be imported for up to 4 weeks with a Certificate of Personality Test, which must be given by a vet on entering Germany. Other large dogs and breeds such as Dobermann, Mastiff and Rottweiler may need to be kept on a lead and muzzled in public, which also means in your car. You are advised to contact the German embassy in London before making travel arrangements for your dog and check the latest available information from your vet or from the PETS Helpline on 0370 241 1710

Medical Services

Local state health insurance fund offices offer assistance round-the-clock and telephone numbers can be found in the local telephone directory. EU citizens are entitled to free or subsidised emergency care from doctors contracted to the state health care system on presentation of a European Health Insurance Card (EHIC). Private treatment by doctors or dentists is not refundable under the German health service. You will be liable for a percentage of prescribed medication charges at pharmacies and this is also non-refundable. Pharmacies offer an all-night and Sunday service and the address of the nearest out-of-hours branch will be displayed on the door of every pharmacy.

There is a fixed daily charge for a stay in hospital (treatment is free for anyone under 18 years of age) which is not refundable. If you are required to pay an additional patient contribution for treatment then reduced charges apply to holders of an EHIC. For refunds of these additional charges you should apply with original receipts to a local state health insurance fund office.

Opening Hours

Banks – Mon-Fri 8.30am-12.30pm & 1.30pm-3.30pm (to 5pm or 6pm on Thurs).

Museums – Check locally as times vary.

Post Offices – Mon-Fri 7/8am-6/8pm; Sat 8am-12pm.

Shops – Mon-Fri 8/9am-6pm/8pm. Sat 8/9am-12/4pm; in some places bakers are open Sun mornings.

Safety and Security

Most visits to Germany are trouble free but visitors should take the usual commonsense precautions against mugging, pickpocketing and bag snatching, particularly in areas around railway stations, airports in large cities and at Christmas markets. Do not leave valuables unattended.

Germany shares with the rest of Europe a general threat from terrorism. Attacks could be indiscriminate and against civilian targets in public places, including tourist sites. You should maintain a high level of vigilance at all times.

British Embassy
WILHELMSTRASSE 70, D-10117 BERLIN
Tel: (030) 204570,
www.ukingermany.fco.gov.uk/en/

British Consulates-General
Oststraße 86, 40210 DÜSSELDORF
Tel: (0211) 94480
MÖHLSTRASSE 5, 81675 MÜNCHEN
Tel: (089) 211090

Irish Embassy
JÄGERSTRASSE 51, 10117 BERLIN
Tel: (030) 220720
www.embassyofireland.de
There are also Irish Honorary Consulates in
Frankfurt, Hamburg, Köln (Cologne) and
München (Munich).

Documents

Passport

It is a legal requirement to carry your passport at
all times. German police have the right to ask to
see identification and for British citizens the only
acceptable form of ID is a valid passport.

Vehicle(s)

Carry your valid driving licence, insurance and
vehicle documents with you in your vehicle at
all times. It is particularly important to carry your
vehicle registration document V5C, as you will
need it if entering a low emission zone (see later
in this chapter for more information).

If you are driving a hired or borrowed vehicle, you
must be in possession of a letter of authorisation
from the owner or a hire agreement.

Money

The major debit and credit cards, including American
Express, are widely accepted by shops, hotels,
restaurants and petrol stations. However, you may
find that credit cards are not as widely accepted
in smaller establishments as they are in the UK,
including many shops and campsites, due to the
high charges imposed on retailers, and debit cards
are preferred. Cash machines are widespread and
have instructions in English.

British visitors have been arrested for possession
of counterfeit currency and the authorities advise
against changing money anywhere other than at
banks or legitimate bureaux de change.

Carry your credit card issuers'/banks' 24-hour UK
contact numbers in case of loss or theft of your
cards.

Motoring in Germany

Roads in Germany are of an excellent standard
but speed limits are higher than in the UK and the
accident rate is greater. Drivers undertaking long
journeys in or through Germany should plan their
journeys carefully and take frequent breaks.

Accidents

In the event of a road accident the police must
always be called even if there are no injuries.

Alcohol

The maximum permitted level of alcohol is
50 milligrams per 100 millilitres of blood, i.e.
lower than that in the UK (80 milligrams). For
novice drivers who have held a driving licence for
less than two years, and for drivers under the age
of 21, no alcohol is permitted in the bloodstream.
Penalties for driving under the influence of alcohol
or drugs are severe.

Breakdown Service

The motoring organisation Allgemeiner Deutscher
Automobil-Club (ADAC) operates road patrols
on motorways and in the event of a breakdown,
assistance can be obtained by calling from
emergency phones placed every 2 km. Members
of clubs affiliated to the AIT or FIA, such as The
Caravan Club, must ask specifically for roadside
assistance to be provided by ADAC as they should
be able to receive assistance free of charge. You
must pay for replacement parts and towing.
ADAC breakdown vehicles are yellow and marked
'ADAC Strassenwacht'.

If ADAC Strassenwacht vehicles are not available,
firms under contract to ADAC provide towing and
roadside assistance, against payment. Vehicles
used by firms under contract to ADAC are marked
'Strassendienst im Auftrag des ADAC'.

On other roads the ADAC breakdown service
can be reached 24 hours a day by telephoning
01802-22 22 22 (local call rates) or 22 22 22 from
a mobile phone.

Essential Equipment

First Aid Kit

Drivers of German registered vehicles must carry
a first aid kit but this is not a legal requirement
for foreign visitors.

Lights

Dipped headlights are recommended at all times and must always be used in tunnels, as well as when visibility is poor and during periods of bad weather. Bulbs are more likely to fail with constant use and you are recommended to carry spares.

Child Restraint Systems

Children under three years of age must be placed in an approved child restraint and cannot be transported in a vehicle otherwise. Children of three years and over must travel in the rear of vehicles. Children under 12 years old and 1.5 metres in height must be seated in an approved child restraint. If a child restraint won't fit into the vehicle because other children are using a child restraint, then children of three years and over must use a seat belt or other safety device attached to the seat.

Winter Driving

All vehicles, including those registered outside Germany, must be fitted with winter tyres (or all season tyres) during winter conditions, bearing the mark 'M+S' (Mud + Snow) or the snowflake symbol. Failure to use them can result in a fine and penalty points. There must also be anti-freeze in the windscreen cleaning fluid.

The use of snow chains is permitted and for vehicles fitted with them there is a maximum speed limit of 50 km/h (31 mph). In mountainous areas the requirement for chains is indicated by signs. The use of spiked tyres is not authorised.

Fuel

Most petrol stations are open from 8am to 8pm. In large cities many are open 24 hours. In the east there are fewer petrol stations than in the south and west. Some have automatic pumps operated using credit cards.

LPG (autogas or flussiggas) is widely available. You can view a list of approximately 800 outlets throughout the country, including those near motorways, from the website www.autogastanken.de (follow the links under 'Tanken' and 'Tankstellan-Karte).

On some stretches of motorway petrol stations may be few and far between, e.g. the A45, A42 and A3 to the Dutch border, and it is advisable not to let your fuel tank run low.

Low Emission Zones

A large number of German cities and towns now require motorists to purchase a 'Pollution Badge' (Umwelt Plakette) in the form of a windscreen sticker in order to enter city centre 'Umwelt' or green zones. The areas where restrictions apply are indicated by signs showing coloured vignettes, the colour of the vignette issued (red, yellow or green) depending on your vehicle's engine type and its Euro emission rating.

You must present your vehicle registration document, V5C, at an 'Umwelt Plakette' sales outlet, which can be found at vehicle repair centres, car dealers, MOT (Tüv) stations and vehicle licensing offices and it is understood that badges are also available from ATU motoring supplies shops. The cost varies between €5 and €10 + VAT and postage.

Failure to display a badge could result in a fine of €40. Enforcement is managed by the police, local authorities and traffic wardens. Older vehicles without a catalytic converter or a particulate filter (generally emission-rated Euro 1) will not be issued with a badge and will not be permitted to enter the centres of those cities and towns participating in the scheme.

Visit www.lowemissionzones.eu or www.umwelt-plakette.de (you may also be able to purchase your badge here before you travel to Germany). Alternatively contact The Club's Travel Service Information Officer (Club members only), email: travelserviceinfo@caravanclub.co.uk.

Parking

Zigzag lines on the carriageway indicate a stopping (waiting) and parking prohibition, e.g. at bus stops, narrow roads and places with poor visibility, but double or single yellow lines are not used. Instead look out for 'no stopping', 'parking prohibited' or 'no parking' signs.

Except for one-way streets, parking is only permitted on the right-hand side. Do not park in the opposite direction to traffic flow. Parking meters and parking disc schemes are in operation and discs may be bought in local shops or service stations.

Priority

At crossroads and junctions, where no priority is indicated, traffic coming from the right has priority. Trams do not have absolute priority over other vehicles but priority must be given to passengers getting on or off stationary trams. Trams in two-way streets must be overtaken on the right. Drivers must give way to a bus whose driver has indicated his intention to pull away from the kerb. Do not overtake a stationary school bus which has stopped to let passengers on or off. This may be indicated by a red flashing light on the bus.

Traffic already on a roundabout has right of way, except when signs show otherwise. Drivers must use their indicators when leaving a roundabout, not when entering.

Always stop to allow pedestrians to cross at marked pedestrian crossings. In residential areas where traffic-calming zones exist, pedestrians are allowed to use the whole street, so drive with great care.

Road Signs and Markings

Most German road signs and markings conform to the international pattern. Other road signs that may be encountered are:

Keep distance shown

Street lights not on all night

Lower speed limit applies in the wet

Recommended route on motorways

One way street

Tram or bus stop

German	English Translation
Einsatzfahrzeuge Fre	Emergency vehicles only
Fahrbahnwechsel	Change traffic lane
Freie Fahrt	Road clear
Frostchaden	Frost damage
Gefährlich	Danger
Glatteisgefahr	Ice on the road
Notruf	Emergency roadside telephone
Radweg Kreuzt	Cycle-track crossing
Rollsplitt	Loose grit
Stau	Traffic jam
Strassenschaden	Road damage
Umleitung	Diversion
Vorsicht	Caution

Road signs on motorways are blue and white, whereas on B roads (Bundesstrasse) they are orange and black. If you are planning a route through Germany using E road numbers, be aware that E roads may be poorly signposted and you may have to navigate using national A or B road numbers.

Speed Limits

	Open Road (kmph)	Motorway (kmph)
Solo Car	100	130
Car towing caravan/trailer	80*	80
Motorhome under 3500kg	100	130
Motorhome 3500-7500kg	80	100

* 100 km/h (62 mph) if your car and caravan passes a TUV test in Germany (test costs €70 and takes 2 hours to complete)

There is a speed limit of 50 km/h (31 mph) in built-up areas for all types of motor vehicles, unless otherwise indicated by road signs. A built-up area starts from the town name sign at the beginning of a town or village.

The number of sections of autobahn with de-restricted zones, i.e. no upper speed limit, is diminishing and the volume of traffic makes high speed motoring virtually impossible. Regulations on many stretches of two-lane motorway restrict lorries, together with cars towing caravans, from overtaking.

Speed cameras are frequently in use but they may be deliberately hidden behind crash barriers or in mobile units. A GPS navigation system which indicates the location of fixed speed cameras must have the function deactivated. The use of radar detectors is prohibited.

A car towing a caravan or trailer is prohibited to 80km/h (50 mph) on motorways and other main roads. You may occasionally see car/caravan combinations displaying a sign indicating that their maximum permitted speed is 100 km/h (62 mph). This is only permitted for vehicles that have passed a TUV test in Germany, who will then need to apply for a sticker at a Zulassungsstelle. The application process can be complicated as some Zulassungsstelles will insist they see a registration certificate for your caravan. Obtaining a 100km/h sticker without a registration certificate is best done in Aachen as they are the only Zulassungsstelle familiar with this process. If you are having difficulty at a different Zulassungsstelle ask them to call the Zulassungsstelle in Aachen to confirm that a registration document is not required.

In bad weather when visibility is below 50 metres, the maximum speed limit is 50 km/h (31 mph) on all roads.

Towing

Drivers of cars towing caravans and other slow-moving vehicles must leave enough space in front of them for an overtaking vehicle to get into that space, or they must pull over from time to time to let other vehicles pass.

Motorhomes are prohibited from towing a car using an 'A-Frame'. Anyone wishing to do this should put the car on a trailer so that all four wheels of the car are off the ground. Outside built-up areas the speed limit for such vehicle combinations is 80 km/h (50 mph) or 60 km/h (37 mph) for vehicles over 3,500 kg.

Traffic Jams

Roads leading to popular destinations in Denmark, the Alps and Adriatic Coast become very congested during the busy holiday period of July and August and on public holidays. In those periods traffic jams of up to 60 km are not unheard of.

Congestion is likely on the A3 and A5 north-south routes. Traffic jams are also likely to occur on the A7 Kassel-Denmark, the A8 Stuttgart-Munich-Salzburg and on the A2 and A9 to Berlin. Other cities where congestion may occur are Würzburg, Nürnberg (Nuremberg), Munich and Hamburg. Alternative routes, known as U routes, have been devised; those leading to the south or west have even numbers and those leading to the north or east have odd numbers. These U routes often detour over secondary roads to the following motorway junction and the acquisition of a good road map or atlas is recommended.

ADAC employs 'Stauberater' (traffic jam advisors) who are recognisable by their bright yellow motorbikes. They assist motorists stuck in traffic and will advise on alternative routes.

Upgrading of motorways to Berlin from the west and improvements to many roads in the old east German suburbs may result in diversions and delays, and worsened traffic congestion.

Violation of Traffic Regulations

Police are empowered to impose and collect small on-the-spot fines for contravention of traffic regulations. Fines vary according to the gravity of the offence and have in recent years been increased dramatically for motorists caught speeding in a built-up area (over 50 km/h – 31 mph). A deposit may be required against higher fines and failure to pay may cause the vehicle to be confiscated.

It is an offence to use abusive language, or make rude gestures in Germany, including to other drivers while driving. It is also an offence to stop on the hard shoulder of a motorway except in the case of mechanical failure - please note that running out of fuel is not classed as a mechanical failure so you may be liable for a fine of up to €20 if you do run out of fuel and stop on the hard shoulder.

It is illegal for pedestrians to cross a road when the red pedestrian light is displayed, even if there is no traffic approaching the crossing. Offenders could be fined and will find themselves liable to all costs in the event of an accident.

Motorways

With around 12,845 toll free kilometres, Germany's motorways (autobahns) constitute one of the world's most advanced and efficient systems. For a complete list of autobahns, including the location of all junctions and roadworks in progress, see www.autobahn-online.de.

Some motorways are so heavily used by lorries that the inside lane has become heavily rutted. These parallel ruts are potentially dangerous for caravans travelling at high speed and vigilance is necessary. It is understood that the A44 and A7 are particularly prone to this problem. Caution also needs to be exercised when driving on the concrete surfaces of major roads.

On motorways emergency telephones are placed at 2 km intervals; some have one button to request breakdown assistance and another to summon an ambulance. Other telephones connect the caller to a rescue control centre. A vehicle that has broken down on a motorway must be towed away to the nearest exit.

There are hundreds of motorway service areas offering, at the very least, a petrol station and a restaurant or cafeteria. Tourist information boards are posted in all the modern motorway service areas. Recent visitors have reported an increase in service facilities just off Autobahn exit ramps, in particular with 'Autohof' (truck stops). The facilities at Autohofs are reported to be comparable to service areas, but usually with considerably lower prices.

Touring

German food is generally of high quality and offers great regional range and diversity. In the country there is at least one inn – 'gasthof' or 'gasthaus' – in virtually every village. A service charge is usually included in restaurant bills but it is usual to leave some small change or round up the bill by 5-10% if satisfied with the service.

Smoking is generally banned on public transport and in restaurants and bars, but regulations vary from state to state.

The German National Tourist Board (GNTB) produces guides to walking and cycle paths throughout the country, as well an extensive range of other brochures and guides. The individual tourist offices for the 16 federal states can also supply a wealth of information about events, attractions and tourist opportunities within their local regions. Obtain contact details from the GNTO.

Christmas markets are an essential part of the run-up to the festive season and they range in size from a few booths in small towns and villages, to hundreds of stalls and booths in large cities. The markets generally run from mid November to 22 or 23 December.

There are 32 UNESCO World Heritage sites in Germany, including the cities of Lübeck, Potsdam and Weimar, the cathedrals of Aachen, Cologne and Speyer, together with numerous other venues of great architectural and archaeological interest.

The Berlin Welcome Card is valid for 2, 3 or 5 days and includes free bus and train travel (including free travel for three accompanying children up to the age of 14), as well as discounted or free entrance to museums, and discounts on tours, boat trips, restaurants and theatres. It can be extended to include Potsdam and the Museuminsel and is available from tourist information centres, hotels and public transport centres or from www.visitberlin.de. A 3 day museum card – SchauLUST-MuseenBERLIN – is also available, valid in more than 60 national museums in and around the city.

Other cities, groups of cities or regions also offer Welcome Cards, including Bonn, Cologne, Dresden, Düsseldorf, Frankfurt, Hamburg, Heidelberg and Munich. These give discounts on public transport, museums, shopping, dining and attractions. Enquire at a local tourist office or at the German National Tourist Office in London.

Public Transport

Most major German cities boast excellent underground (U-bahn), urban railway (S-bahn), bus and tram systems whose convenience and punctuality are renowned. On public transport services, pay your fare prior to boarding the vehicle using the automated ticketing machines. Your ticket must then be date stamped separately using the machines onboard the vehicle or at the entry gates at major stops. Daily tickets permit the use of trains, buses and trams. Berlin's integrated transport system extends as far as Potsdam.

A number of car ferries operate across the Weser and Elbe rivers which allow easy touring north of Bremen and Hamburg. Routes across the Weser include Blexen to Bremerhavn, Brake to Sandstedt and Berne to Farge. The Weser Tunnel (B437) connects the villages of Rodenkirchen and Dedesdorf, offering an easy connection between the cities of Bremerhaven and Nordenham. Across the Elbe there is a car ferry route between Wischhafen and Glückstadt. An international ferry route operates all year across Lake Constance (Bodensee) between Konstanz and Meersburg. There is also a route between Friedrichshafen and Romanshorn in Switzerland.

Holstentor, Lübeck

⊞ **AACHEN** *1A4* (3.5km SE Urban) *50.76140, 6.10285*
Aachen Platz für Camping, Branderhoferweg 11, 52066
Aachen-Burtscheid [(0241) 6088057; fax 6088058; mail@
aachen-camping.de; www.aachen-camping.de]
Exit A44 junc 2 onto L233 Monschauerstrasse dir Aachen. In
3.8km at outer ring rd Adenauer Allee L260 turn R, then in
800m L at 2nd traff lts onto Branderhoferweg twd Beverau.
Site on R at bottom of hill. Sm, mkd pitch, hdstg, pt shd; htd
wc; chem disp; mv service pnt; EHU (16A) inc; shwr; dogs; bus
500m; poss cr; Eng spkn; no adv bkg; quiet, but poss noise fr
bar. "Nice, clean, well-run municipal site; gd, modern san facs;
max stay 5 nights; excel o'night stop; rec arr bef 1600 high ssn;
ideal Xmas mkts; gd conv site; close to city ctr; open access
site; fair." ♦ ltd. € 15.00   2015*

⊞ **AACHEN** *1A4* (18km SE Rural) *50.69944, 6.22194*
Camping Vichtbachtal, Vichtbachstrasse 10, 52159
Roetgen-Mulartshütte [tel/fax (02408) 5131; camping@
vichtbachtal.de; www.vichtbachtal.de]
On E40/A44 exit junc 3 Aachen/Brand onto B258 dir
Kornelimünster. In 5km at R-hand bend turn L sp Mulartshütte.
Thro Venwegen. Site ent on L 50m bef T-junc app
Mulartshütte, site sp. Med, pt sl, shd; wc; chem disp; mv service
pnt; shwrs inc; EHU (16A) €1.50 or metered; lndry; shop; rest
150m; playgrnd; 80% statics; site clsd Nov; poss cr; quiet; CKE/
CCI. "Sm area for tourers; v friendly Eng spkn owners; gd site
for visiting Aachen; gd walks adj." € 20.50   2014*

⊞ **AALEN** *3D3* (13km SW Rural) *48.78583, 9.98218*
Camping Hirtenheich, Hasenweide 2, 73457 Essingen-
Lauterburg [(07365) 296; fax 251; camphirtenteich@aol.
com; www.campingplatz-hirtenteich.de]
Exit A7/E43 at Aalen onto B29. Site sp beyond Essingen dir
Lauterburg. Med, pt sl, unshd; wc; chem disp; mv service
pnt; sauna; shwrs inc; EHU (16A) metered; lndry; shop; rest;
playgrnd; pool; wintersports; ski lift 300m; 70% statics; dogs;
Eng spkn; quiet; debit cards acc. "Clean facs; pleasant site." ♦
€ 17.50   2009*

ABTSGMUND *3D3* (9km NW Rural) *48.94650, 9.97628*
Camping Hammerschmiede-See, Hammerschmiede
2, 73453 Abtsgmünd [(07963) 369; fax 840032; hug.
hammerschmiede@t-online.de; http://camping.hug-
hammerschmiede.de] Exit B19 (Aalen-Schwabisch Hall) at W
end of Abtsgmünd by-pass dir Pommertsweiler. Site sp on lake.
Lge, terr, pt sl, pt shd; wc; shwrs €0.50; EHU (10A) metered
+ conn fee; gas; shop, rest, snacks 2km; playgrnd; games
area; 60% statics; dogs €1.60; no adv bkg; quiet. "Direct rd
fr Schwabisch Hall, not suitable for lge o'fits; lakeside pitches
long walk to san facs." 1 May-30 Sep. € 12.00   2009*

⊞ **ACHERN** *3C3* (5km NW Rural) *48.64578, 8.03728*
Camping am Achernsee, Oberacherner Strasse 19, 77855
Achern [(07841) 25253; fax 508835; camping@achern.de;
www.achern.de] Exit A5/E35/E52 junc 53 to Achern, site sp
in 1km. Med, mkd pitch, shd; wc; shwrs €0.50; chem disp; mv
service pnt; EHU (10A) €2.50; lndry (inc dryer); shop 2km; rest
adj; BBQ; playgrnd; fishing; lake sw; 80% statics; dogs €3.50;
quiet, but noise nr m'way. "Useful stop for Strasbourg' gd
NH". ♦ € 30.00   2014*

ADELBERG see Göppingen *3D3*

AEGIDIENBERG see Bad Honnef *1B4*

AICHELBERG see Göppingen *3D3*

AITRACH see Memmingen *3D4*

AITRANG see Marktoberdorf *4E4*

ALLENSBACH see Radolfzell am Bodensee *3C4*

⊞ **ALPIRSBACH** *3C3* (2km N Rural) *48.35576, 8.41224*
Camping Alpirsbach, Grezenbühler Weg 18-20, 72275
Alpirsbach [(07444) 6313; fax 917815; info@camping-
alpirsbach.de; www.camping-alpirsbach.de]
On B294 leave Alpirsbach twds Freudenstadt. 1st site sp on
L. Med, pt shd, serviced pitch; wc; chem disp; mv service pnt;
shwrs inc; EHU (16A) metered; gas; lndry; shop; rest, snacks;
bar; playgrnd; tennis; golf 5km; 10% statics; dogs €1; o'night
area for m'vans €10; poss cr; Eng spkn; quiet; ccard not
acc; red long stay/CKE/CCI. "Excel site; helpful, informative
& friendly owner; vg welcome, free bottle of local beer per
person; immac san facs; gd rest; gd walking; guest card for free
transport on some local transport; some rvside pitches (v shd)."
♦ € 30.00   2014*

ALSFELD *1D4* (11km W Rural) *50.73638, 9.15222* Camping
Heimertshausen, Ehringshäuserstrasse, 36320 Kirtorf-
Heimertshausen [(06635) 206; fax 918359; info@
campingplatz-heimertshausen.de; campingplatz-
heimertshausen.de] Exit A5 junc 3 Alsfeld West onto B49
dir Frankfurt. Turn R in vill of Romrod to Heimertshausen &
L to site. Site also sp fr B62. Med, shd; wc; chem disp; shwrs
€0.55; EHU (10-16A) €2 or metered; lndry; shop; rest, snacks;
playgrnd; htd pool adj; dogs €1; 65% statics; clsd 1300-1500
& 2200-0800; o'night area for m'vans; Eng spkn; adv bkg;
quiet; red CKE/CCI. "Beautiful, wooded area; lovely 'hunting
lodge' type cosy rest; bar/food open Jul/Aug; site run down
(2015); facs dated but clean & adequate." 1 Apr-30 Sep.
€ 27.50   2015*

ALTENAHR *3B1* (2km S Rural) *50.51328, 6.98637*
Campingplatz Altenahr, Im Pappelauel, 53505 Altenahr-
Altenburg [(02643) 8503; fax 900764; info@camping-
altenahr.de; www.camping-altenahr.de]
Foll B257 thro narr town cent; site visible on R, on opp bank
of Rv Ahr; care needed for lge o'fits over bdge. Lge, wc; shwrs
€0.50; EHU (6A) €3.50; lndry (inc dryer); shop & 500m; rest,
snacks; bar; playgrnd; 30% statics; dogs €1.50; bus; poss cr;
some rd & rlwy noise; ccard acc; CKE/CCI. "Clean, friendly,
well-kept site amongst vineyards; excel facs; conv for x-country
rte Koblenz/Aachen; sh walk to pretty vill." ♦ 1 Apr-31 Oct.
€ 17.00   2010*

ALTENAU see Goslar *1D3*

⊞ **ALTENBERG** 4G1 (1km W Rural) 50.76666, 13.74666
Camping Kleiner Galgenteich (Naturist), Galgenteich 3, 01773 Altenberg [(035056) 31995; fax 31993; mail@camping-erzgebirge.de; www.camping-erzgebirge.de] Leave A4 at Dresden-Nord onto B170 sp Zinnwald then Altenberg. On SW side of B170; clearly sp. Lge, pt sl, pt shd; wc; chem disp; mv service pnt; shwrs €0.50; EHU (10A) metered + conn fee; lndry; shop; rest; snacks adj; playgrnd; lake sw & sailing adj; ski lift 500m; 50% statics; dogs €1; poss cr; quiet. "Sep area for naturists." € 18.50   2009*

"I like to fill in the reports as I travel from site to site"

You'll find report forms at the back of this guide, or you can fill them in online at www.caravanclub.co.uk/europereport.

ALTENKIRCHEN 2F1 (3km E Coastal) 54.63157, 13.37250
Campingplatz Drewoldke, Zittkower Weg 27, 18556 Altenkirchen [038391 12965; info@camping-auf-ruegen.de; www.camping-auf-ruegen.de] Take rd fr Sassnitz to Altenkirchen (L30), site sp on R bef you reach Altenkirchen. Lge, pt shd; htd wc; chem disp; MV service pnt; baby facs; shwrs (metered); EHU (16A) €2.50; lndry; shop; rest, snacks; bar; playgrnd; beach adj; dogs €4.50; phone. "Site being updated & has gd modern san facs; site located just outside of Altenkirchen on the Baltic Sea clse to ferry point Sassnitz (plse note there is another place in Germany named Altenkirchen, do not get this confused); gd site." 1 Apr-31 Oct. € 25.40   2011*

ALVERN see Celle 1D3

AMORBACH 3D2 (7km SW Rural) 49.60730, 9.15876
Azur Campingpark Odenwald, Siegfriedstrasse 2, 63931 Kirchzell [(09373) 566; fax 7375; kirchzell@azur-camping.de; www.azur-camping.de] Exit A81 at junc 3 Tauberischofsheim onto B27 dir Mosbach. At Walldürn take B47 to Amorbach & turn L dir Kirchzell. Site sp 1km S of Kirchzell dir Amorbach. Lge, hdg pitch, pt shd; wc; mv service pnt; sauna; shwrs; EHU (10A) €2.80; lndry (inc dryer); shop; rest, snacks; playgrnd; htd, covrd pool; games area; 60% statics; dogs €3; Eng spkn; adv bkg; quiet; CKE/CCI. ♦ 1 Apr-31 Oct. € 24.00   2010*

⊞ **ANNABERG BUCHHOLZ** 4G1 (15km NW Rural) 50.64291, 12.91496 Camping Greifensteine, 09427 Ehrenfriedersdorf [(037346) 1454; fax 1218; webmaster@greifenbachstauweiher.de; www.greifenbachstauweiher.de] On B95 S fr Chemnitz turn W at Thum sp Jahnsbach; after 2km at Jahnsbach turn S & site on R after 3km, sp. V lge, pt sl, pt shd; wc; shwrs €0.50; EHU (10A) €2; lndry; shop, rest, snacks; bar; playgrnd; pool; lake; boating; windsurfing; bike hire; 60% statics; dogs €3; Eng spkn; red long stay; CKE/CCI. "Conv for Ore mountains or en rte to Czech Republic; woodland surroundings; friendly staff; excel value." ♦ € 14.00   2009*

ANNWEILER AM TRIFELS see Landau in der Pfalz 3C3

ASBACHERHUTTE see Idar Oberstein 3B2

⊞ **ATTENDORN** 3C1 (5km E Rural) 51.13694, 7.93969
Campingplatz Hof Biggen, Finnentroperstrasse 131, 57439 Attendorn [(02722) 95530; info@biggen.de; www.biggen.de] Exit A55 junc 16 Meinerzhagen onto L539 E dir Attendorn. Thro Attendorn, site sp on Ahauser Stausee, 4km fr Biggesee. Lge, some hdstg, terr, unshd; htd wc (some cont); chem disp; mv service pnt; EHU (16A); lndry (inc dryer); shop; rest, snacks; bar; BBQ; playgrnd; games area; games rm; wifi; entmnt; TV; 75% statics; dogs; adv bkg; quiet. "Excel, scenic site." ♦ € 23.00 (CChq acc)   2011*

⊞ **AUGSBURG** 4E3 (7km N Rural) 48.41168, 10.92371
Camping Bella Augusta, Mühlhauserstrasse 54B, 86169 Augsburg-Ost [(0821) 707575; fax 705883; info@caravaningpark.de; www.caravaningpark.de] Exit A8/E52 junc 73 dir Neuburg to N, site sp. Lge, pt shd; wc; chem disp; mv service pnt; shwrs inc; EHU (10A) inc; lndry rm; shop; supmkt 4km; rest; snacks & bar adj; playgrnd adj; lake sw & shgl beach adj; boating; 80% statics; dogs €2.55; noise fr a'bahn; ccard acc. "V busy NH; excel rest; camping equipment shop on site; vg san facs but site looking a little run down; cycle track to town (map fr recep); vg; nice lake." € 31.00   2014*

AUGSBURG 4E3 (8km N Rural) 48.43194, 10.92388 Camping Ludwigshof am See, Augsburgerstrasse 36, 86444 Mühlhausen-Affing [(08207) 961724; fax 961770; info@bauer-caravan.de; www.bauer-caravan.de] Exit A8/E52 junc 73at Augsburg Ost/Pöttmes exit; foll sp Pöttmes; site sp on L on lakeside. Lge, unshd; wc; chem disp; mv service pnt; shwrs inc; EHU (6-16A) €3.50 (long cable req); lndry; supmkt 500m; bar; rest; playgrnd; lake sw; 70% statics sep area; dogs €2; bus; clsd 1300-1500; poss cr; Eng spkn; quiet; 10% red 3+ days; ccard not acc; CKE/CCI. "Pleasant site; lge unmkd field for tourers, close to san facs but long walk to recep; both 6A panel & 16A panels for EHU -16A only accepts German type of plug; beautiful clean, modern facs; nr A8 m'way; conv NH on way to E Italy; gd for long stay, special rates can be negotiated." 1 Apr-31 Oct. € 22.00   2014*

AUGSBURG 4E3 (9km NE Rural) 48.4375, 10.92916
Lech Camping, Seeweg 6, 86444 Affing-Mühlhausen [(08207) 2200; fax 2202; info@lech-camping.de; www.lech-camping.de] Exit A8/E52 at junc 73 Augsburg-Ost; take rd N sp Pöttmes; site 3km on R. Sm, mkd pitch, pt shd; htd wc; chem disp; mv service pnt; shwrs inc; EHU (16A) €3.60 or metered + conn fee (poss rev pol); lndry; shop 300m; supmkt opp; rest; snacks; bar; playgrnd; lake sw adj; boating; wifi; adv bkg rec; statics sep area; dogs €3; bus to Augsburg; train Munich; Eng spkn; some rd noise; ccard acc. "Lovely, well-ordered site; friendly, helpful owners; excel san facs; gd play area; deposit for san facs key; camping accessory shop on site; cycle rte to Augsburg; excel NH for A8; excel site espec lakeside pitch." ♦ 15 Apr-4 Oct. € 31.50 SBS - G19   2015*

BACHARACH see Oberwesel 3B2

BAD ABBACH 4F3 (6km W Rural) 48.93686, 12.01992
Campingplatz Freizeitinsel, Inselstraße 1a, D93077 Bad
Abbach [(09405) 9570402; fax 940348; alois.schmidbauer@
web.de; www.campingplatz-freizeitinsel.de]
A93 Regensburg, exit Pentling B16 dir twrds Kelheim. Cont on
B16 past Bad Abbach and take next exit R to Poikam/Inselbad.
Over rv and foll rd round to R past Poikam sp. At junc turn R
sp Inselbad. Site on R. Med, mkd pitches; terr; wc; chem disp;
mv service pnt; baby facs; shwrs; EHU; lndry (inc dryer); café;
snacks; bar; bbq; cooking facs; playgrnd; sw 400m; bike hire;
wifi; 20% statics; twin axles; Eng spkn; adv bkg; quiet; CKE/
CCI. "New (2014) family run developing site; vg modern facs;
some deluxe serviced pitches avail with supp; gd area for
touring, cycling & walking; nrby lake, sw & thermal baths; gd
rest in vill 1km; train to Regensburg 1km; excel site." ♦
1 Apr-23 Dec. € 37.00   2014*

⊞ **BAD BEDERKESA** 1C2 (1km S Rural) 53.62059, 8.84879
Regenbogen-Camp Bad Bederkesa, Ankeloherstrasse 14,
27624 Bad Bederkesa [(04745) 6487 or (0431) 2372370;
fax 8033; badbederkesa@regenbogen-camp.de;
www.regenbogen-camp.de] Exit A27 junc 5 Debstedt, dir
Bederkesa, site sp. V lge, pt shd; wc; chem disp; mv service
pnt; shwrs inc; EHU (16A) metered + conn fee; lndry (inc dryer);
shop 800m; rest, snacks; bar; playgrnd; games area; golf 4km;
wifi; TV; 60% statics; dogs €4; clsd 1300-1500; o'night area
for m'vans; adv bkg; quiet; ccard acc; red long stay/CKE/CCI. ♦
€ 27.00   2013*

BAD BELLINGEN see Lörrach 3B4

BAD BENTHEIM 1B3 (3km E Rural) 52.29945, 7.19361
Campingplatz am Berg, Suddendorferstrasse 37, 48455
Bad Bentheim [(05922) 990461; fax 990460; info@
campingplatzamberg.de; www.campingplatzamberg.de]
Exit A30 ad junc 3 onto B403, foll sp to Bad Bentheim. After sh
incline, passing g'ge on R at traff lts, at next junc turn R round
town to hospital (sp Orthopäde). Turn L & cont past hospital to
rndabt, strt over then 1.5km on L. Sm, mkd pitch, pt shd; htd
wc; chem disp; shwrs inc; EHU (16A) €2.50; gas; lndry; shop
2.5km; rest; bar; cooking facs; playgrnd; 50% statics in sep
area; dogs; phone; site clsd 24 Dec-26 Jan; poss v cr; Eng spkn;
adv bkg; quiet; CKE/CCI. "Friendly, helpful owners; easy drive
to Europort & ferries; rlwy museum on Dutch side of border."
♦ 4 Mar-24 Dec. € 24.50   2013*

BAD BREISIG see Remagen 3B1

BAD DOBERAN 2F1 (10km N Coastal) 54.15250, 11.89972
Ferien-Camp Borgerende (Part Naturist), Deichstrasse 16,
18211 Börgerende [(038203) 81126; fax 81284; info@
ostseeferiencamp.de; www.ostseeferiencamp.de]
In Bad Doberan, turn L off B105 sp Warnemunde. In 4km in
Rethwisch, turn L sp Börgerende. In 3km turn R at site sp. V
lge, hdg pitch, unshd; wc; chem disp; mv service pnt; baby
facs; fam bthrm; sauna; shwrs inc; EHU (10-16A) €3; lndry
(inc dryer) shop; rest, snacks; bar; cooking facs; playgrnd; shgl
beach adj; sep naturist beach; bike hire; games area; internet;
child entmnt; 10% statics; dogs €4; bus 500m; phone; o'night
area for m'vans; Eng spkn; quiet; red LS/snr citizens; CKE/
CCI. "Excel beaches; cycle paths; excel site." ♦ 1 Apr-31 Oct.
€ 28.00   2010*

⊞ **BAD DURKHEIM** 3C2 (3km NE Rural) 49.47361, 8.19166
Knaus Campingplatz Bad Dürkheim, In den Almen 3,
67098 Bad Dürkheim [(06322) 61356; fax 8161;
badduerkheim@knauscamp.de; www.knauscamp.de]
Fr S on A61/E31 exit junc 60 onto A650/B37 twds Bad
Dürkheim. At 2nd traff lts turn R, site sp nr local airfield. Fr N
on A6 exit junc 19 onto B271 to Bad Dürkheim. At traff lts
after Ungstein turn L dir Lugwigshafen, at next traff lts turn
L, then 1st R. Site at end of rd. Ent strictly controlled. Site
well sp fr all dir on town o'skts. V lge, mkd pitch, pt shd; htd
wc; chem disp; mv service pnt; child/baby facs; sauna; shwrs
inc; EHU (16A) €2.50; gas; lndry (inc dryer); shop; BBQ; rest;
playgrnd; sand beach adj; lake sw adj; tennis; games area;
solarium; TV rm; bike hire; golf 8km; 45% statics; phone; bus;
m'van o'night facs; poss v cr; quiet but some daytime noise
fr adj sports airfield; poss cr; Eng spkn; no ccard acc; red long
stay; CKE/CCI. "Well-equipped, busy site in vineyards; sm,
well-worn pitches; some modern san facs - all clean; no access
1300-1500; gd pool in Bad Dürkheim; wine-fest & wurst-fest
Sep excel; conv NH Bavaria & Austria." ♦ € 36.50   2015*

BAD DURKHEIM 3C2 (3km S Rural) 49.43741, 8.17036
Campingplatz im Burgtal, Waldstrasse 105, 67157
Wachenheim [(06322) 9580-801; fax 9580-899;
touristinfo@vg-wachenheim.de; www.wachenheim.de]
Fr Bad Dürkheim, take B271 S dir Neustadt for approx 2km.
After passing Villa Rustica rest area, turn L for Wachenheim,
then R. Go strt at traff lts, up hill thro vill (narr). Site on L.
Med, hdg/mkd pitch, hdstg; pt shd; wc; chem disp; mv service
pnt; serviced pitches; shwrs inc; EHU (16A) inc; lndry (inc
dryer); shop & 1.5km; rest; bar; playgrnd; tennis; golf 12km;
50% statics; dogs €1; poss cr; quiet; CKE/CCI. "Forest walks
in Pfalz National Park; in heart of wine-tasting country; v busy
during wine festival - adv bkg rec; helpful owners; gd facs."
♦ ltd. 1 Mar-30 Nov. € 31.00 (3 persons)   2013*

BAD EMS 3B2 (7km E Rural) 50.32773, 7.75483
Camping Lahn-Beach, Hallgarten 16, 56132 Dausenau
[(02603) 13964; fax 919935; info@canutours.de;
www.campingplatz-dausenau.de] Foll rv E fr Bad Ems twd
Nassau on B260/417. At ent to vill of Dausenau turn R over
bdge, site visible on S bank of Lahn Rv. Med, pt shd; wc; chem
disp; mv service pnt; shwrs €1; EHU (6-16A) metered + conn
fee; lndry; shop 400m; rest, snacks; playgrnd; boat-launching;
bike hire; wifi; 40% statics; dogs; sep car park; poss v cr; adv
bkg; rd noise. "Pleasant situation; interesting rv traffic &
sightseeing around Lahn Valley; liable to flood at v high water;
gd san facs." 1 Apr-31 Oct. € 23.50   2015*

⊞ **BAD FALLINGBOSTEL** 1D2 (3km NE Rural) 52.87686,
9.73147 DCC Camping Bohmeschlucht, Vierde 22,
D 29683 Fallingbostel-Vierde [(05162) 5604; fax 5160;
campingplatz-hoehmeschlucht@t-online.de;
www.boehmeschlucht.de] A7 junc 47 Bad Fallingbostel. Foll
sp Dorfmark/Soltau. On leaving Fallingbostel, go strt at rndabt
and cont for approx 1 km. Site sp on R. Med, mkd, pt shd;
wc; chem disp; mv service pnt; baby facs; shwrs; EHU (16A)
- €2; lndry (inc dryer); shops 3km; rest; bar; BBQ; playgrnd;
rvside sw; games rm; internet; 60% statics; dogs; Eng spkn;
acc adv bkg; quiet. "Excel walking, cycling & boat/canoe
tours fr site; vg rest; library; helpful staff; excel for exploring
Luneburger Heide, Hamburg or Walsrode Bird Park; excel site."
€ 21.00   2014*

BAD FEILNBACH see Rosenheim *4F4*

⊞ **BAD FUSSING** *4G3* (3km S Urban) *48.33236, 13.31577*
Fuchs Kur Camping, Falkenstraße 14, 94072 Bad Fussing
[(0853) 7356; fax (08537) 912083; info@kurcamping-fuchs.
de; www.kurcamping-fuchs.de] Fr A3 Nurnberg-Passau,
take exit 118 dir Egglfing. Foll sp. Med, mkd pitch, hdstg;
wc; chem disp, dedicated pnt; shwrs inc; EHU inc; lndry;
rest; playgrnd; 10% statics; dogs €2; poss cr; Eng spkn;
adv bkg; quiet; ccard acc; CKE/CCI. "Gd NH; gd value; vg."
€ 23.00   2015*

⊞ **BAD FUSSING** *4G3* (3km S Rural) *48.33255, 13.31440*
Kur & Feriencamping Max I, Falkenstrasse 12, 94072
Egglfing-Bad Füssing [(08537) 96170; fax 961710; info@
campingmax.de; www.campingmax.de]
Across frontier & bdge fr Obernberg in Austria. Site sp in
Egglfing. On B12 Schärding to Simbach turn L immed bef vill
of Tutting sp Obernberg. Site on R after 7km, sp. Med, pt shd;
htd wc; chem disp; mv service pnt; private san facs avail; shwrs
inc; EHU (16A) metered + conn fee; lndry (inc dryer); shop;
rest 300m; snacks; bar; cooking facs; playgrnd; pool 3km; lake
sw; fishing; thermal facs in Bad Füssing; tennis 2km; bike hire;
wellness cent; golf 2km; wifi; entmnt; TV; 20% statics; dogs
€2; quiet; red CKE/CCI "Gd rest for snacks & meals on site;
well managed site; excel clean facs; new indoor thermal bath &
outdoor sw pool (2014)." ♦ € 22.60   2014*

⊞ **BAD FUSSING** *4G3* (900m NW Rural) *48.35801, 13.30661*
Camping Holmernhof, Am Tennispark 10, 94072 Bad
Füssing [(08531) 24740; fax 2474360; info@holmernhof.de;
www.holmernhof.de] Exit A8/E56 junc 118 Pocking. Foll
sp Bad Füssing, then sp 'Freibad' & 'Tenniszentrum', site sp.
Med, mkd pitch, hdstg, pt shd; wc; chem disp; mv service pnt;
baby facs; private bthrms avail; sauna; shwrs inc; EHU (16A)
metered; gas; lndry (inc dryer); shop; rest adj; snacks; bar;
playgrnd; htd pool, tennis 200m; games area; golf 2km; wifi;
entmnt; TV; no dogs; phone; o'night area for m'vans; Eng
spkn; quiet; CKE/CCI. "Excel site." ♦ € 23.00   2010*

⊞ **BAD GANDERSHEIM** *1D3* (2km E Rural) *51.86694,
10.04972* DCC-Kur-Campingpark, 37581 Bad Gandersheim
[(05382) 1595; fax 1599; info@camping-bad-gandersheim.
de; www.camping-bad-gandersheim.de]
Exit A7/E45 at junc 67 onto B64 dir Holzminden & Bad
Gandersheim. Site on R shortly after Seboldshausen. Lge, pt
shd; wc; chem disp; mv service pnt; shwrs €0.50; EHU (10A)
metered + conn fee; lndry; shop; rest, snacks; playgrnd; pool
1.5km; bike hire; 40% statics; dogs €1; sep o'night area; poss
cr; quiet. "Excel; always plenty of space." ♦ € 28.00   2014*

⊞ **BAD HARZBURG** *2E3* (3.5km W Rural) *51.89158,
10.51100* Freizeitoase-Harz Camp, Kreisstrasse 66, 38667
Bad Harzburg-Göttingerode [(05322) 81215; fax 877533;
harz-camp@t-online.de; www.harz-camp.de]
Fr A395 to Bad Harzburg, foll sp Oker & Goslar. Site on L
at traff lts. Lge, hdstg, pt sl, terr, pt shd; wc; chem disp;
mv service pnt; fam bthrm; sauna; shwrs €0.50; EHU (10A)
metered + conn fee; gas; lndry; shop; rest; bar; cooking
facs; playgrnd; pool; solarium; games area; entmnt; sat TV;
40% statics in sep area; dogs €2; phone; bus 100m; Eng spkn;
no adv bkg; quiet; CKE/CCI. "Friendly owners; excel facs; conv
walk to town." ♦ € 18.00   2009*

BAD HERRENALB see Bad Wildbad im Schwarzwald *3C3*

⊞ **BAD HONNEF** *1B4* (9km E Rural) *50.65027, 7.30166*
Camping Jillieshof, Ginsterbergweg 6, 53604 Bad Honnef-
Aegidienberg [(02224) 972066; fax 972067; information@
camping-jillieshof.de; www.camping-jillieshof.de]
Exit E35/A3 junc 34 & foll sp Bad Honnef. In Himburg bef
pedestrian traff lts turn L, then R. Site in 300m. Lge, mkd pitch,
sl, pt shd; wc; chem disp; mv service pnt; shwrs inc; EHU (16A)
€2 or metered; shop; playgrnd; pool 9km; fishing; 85% statics;
dogs €2; Eng spkn; quiet; red LS. "Excel facs; gated."
€ 17.50   2012*

BAD KISSINGEN *3D2* (1.6km S Urban) *50.18972, 10.07194*
Campingpark Bad Kissingen, Euerdorferstrasse 1,
97688 Bad Kissingen [(0971) 5211; info@campingpark-
badkissingen.de; www.campingpark-badkissingen.de]
Exit A7/E45 junc 96 dir Bad Kissingen onto B286. After Garitz
take major turn L turn onto B287 immed bef Südbrücke
(bdge) - caution tight R-hand bend - take L-hand lane & turn
L in cent of this bend. Site on R. Med, pt shd; wc; chem disp;
mv service pnt; some serviced pitches; baby facs; shwrs €0.50;
EHU (16A) €2.80; gas; lndry (inc dryer); shop; rest; playgrnd;
adj rv in park; fishing; golf 1km; wifi; some statics; dogs €2.50;
adv bkg; quiet; red long stay/CKE/CCI. "Site immac; excel facs;
some daytime rd noise; pleasant spa town." ♦ 1 Apr-31 Oct.
€ 24.50   2010*

BAD KOSEN *2E4* (1.5km S Rural) *51.12285, 11.71743*
Camping an der Rudelsburg, 06628 Bad Kösen
[(034463) 28705; fax 28706; campkoesen@aol.com;
www.campingbadkoesen.de] Site sp fr town. Med, pt shd;
wc; chem disp; baby facs; shwrs €1; EHU (16A) metered + conn
fee; gas; lndry; shop 1.5km; rest 1.5km; snacks; bar; playgrnd;
10% statics; dogs €2; o'night area for m'vans; quiet; CKE/CCI.
♦ 1 Apr-1 Nov. € 17.00   2009*

BAD KREUZNACH *3C2* (8km N Rural) *49.88383, 7.85712*
Campingplatz Lindelgrund, Im Lindelgrund 1, 55452
Guldental [(06707) 633; fax 8468; info@lindelgrund.de;
www.lindelgrund.de] Fr A61 exit junc 47 for Windesheim.
In cent immed after level x-ing, turn L & pass thro Guldental.
Site sp on R in 500m. Sm, some hdstg, terr, pt shd; wc; chem
disp; shwrs €0.50; EHU (10-16A) €2 or metered; rest, snacks;
playgrnd; htd, covrd pool 2km; tennis; golf 12km; 60% statics
in sep area; dogs €1.50; poss cr; no adv bkg; quiet; red long
stay. "Lovely, peaceful site; friendly owner; wine sold on site;
narr gauge rlwy & museum adj; gd NH; new san facs (2012) nr
touring pitches." 1 Mar-31 Dec. € 19.50   2015*

BAD KREUZNACH *3C2* (7km S Rural) *49.80542, 7.84236*
Camping Nahe-Alsenz-Eck, Auf dem Grün, 55583 Bad
Münster-am-Stein-Ebernburg [(06708) 2453; cnae@gmx.
de; www.campingplatz-nahe-alsenz-eck.de]
Exit A61 junc 51 for Bad Kreuznach, take B48 dir Kaiserslauten
thro town. Site well sp on rvside. Med, mkd pitch, pt shd; wc;
chem disp; shwrs €0.50; EHU (10A) metered + conn fee; lndry
(inc dryer); shop 200m; rest 300m; snacks; bar; playgrnd; htd
pool 300m; 80% statics; dogs €2.10; clsd 1300-1500; poss cr;
quiet; CKE/CCI. "Pleasant spa town; gd facs; sm pitches; gd
atmosphere; many long stay residents; site poss muddy in wet
& liable to flood." 1 Apr-15 Oct. € 16.00   2010*

BAD LIEBENZELL see Calw *3C3*

GERMANY

⊞ **BAD MERGENTHEIM** *3D2* (3km SE Rural) *49.46481, 9.77673* Campingplatz Bad Mergentheim, Willinger Tal 1, 97980 Bad Mergentheim [(07931) 2177; fax 5636543; info@camping-mgh.de; www.camping-mgh.de]
Fr Bad Mergentheim foll B19 S, sp Ulm. After 1km take rd to L (sps). Ent 2.7m. Med, sl, pt shd; wc; chem disp; shwrs inc; EHU (10A) metered + conn fee or €1.90; gas; lndry; shop; snacks; playgrnd; htd, covrd pool; paddling pool; tennis; 20% statics; dogs €2.50; bus nr; sep o'night area; quiet; ccard not acc; CKE/CCI. "Nice site; friendly, helpful owner." € 17.00   2013*

⊞ **BAD NEUENAHR AHRWEILER** *3B1* (2km W Urban) *50.53892, 7.09612* Camping Ahrtor, Am Ahrtor, Kalvarienbergstrasse 1, 53474 Bad Neuenahr-Ahrweiler [(02461) 26539; camping-ahrweiler@online.de; www.camping-ahrweiler.de] Exit A9 B266 W bet Remagen & Sinzig; then take L84 S to Ahrweiler. Site on S side of city wall sp Nürburgring; after x-ing bdge, sharp R into site on rv bank. Sm, pt shd; wc; shwrs €1; EHU (16A) €2.50; lndry (inc dryer); shop, rest, bar 500m; 50% statics on rv bank pitches (rv fast flowing & unfenced); dogs free; o'night m'van area; Eng spkn; adv bkg; quiet; CKE/CCI. "Excel, modern san facs; interesting walled city; conv for m'way." € 16.50   2010*

BAD NEUENAHR AHRWEILER *3B1* (8km W Rural) *50.53400, 7.04800* Camping Dernau, Ahrweg 2, 53507 Dernau [(02643) 8517; www.camping-dernau.de]
Exit A61 junc 30 for Ahrweiler. Fr Ahrweiler on B267 W to Dernau, cross rv bef Dernau & turn L into Ahrweg, site sp. Sm, some hdstg, shd; htd wc; chem disp; mv service pnt; shwrs €1; EHU (16A) €2; shops 500m; playgrnd; dogs €1; bus; train; some rlwy noise. "In beautiful Ahr valley - gd wine area; train to Ahrweiler Markt rec; immac, modern san facs; v nice." ♦ 1 Apr-31 Oct. € 17.40   2014*

BAD PETERSTAL *3C3* (2km W Rural) *48.42944, 8.18166* Kurcamping Traiermühle, Renchtalstrasse 53a, 77740 Bad Peterstal-Griesbach [(07806) 8064; fax 910528; camping@traiermuehle.de; www.traiermuehle.de]
Fr French border at Strasbourg take B28 to Bad Peterstal, site sp after Löcherberg site. Sm, unshd; wc; chem disp; shwrs €0.20; EHU (10-16A) €2 or metered; lndry (inc dryer); rest 300m; playgrnd; 70% statics; dogs; train 2km; Eng spkn; quiet, but some daytime rd noise; CKE/CCI. "Excel, peaceful site; walking dist to town with rests, shops etc." 1 Apr-31 Oct. € 11.00   2009*

⊞ **BAD PYRMONT** *1D3* (10km S Rural) *51.89800, 9.25533* Camping Eichwald, Obere Dorfstrasse 80, 32676 Lügde-Elbrinxen [(05283) 335; fax 640; info@camping-eichwald.de; www.camping-eichwald.de]
Fr W 7km after Schwalenberg in dir Höxter turn L at sp Bad Pyrmont & Lügde. In 2km site sp bef vill of Elbrinxen. Fr N take Bad Pyrmont rd to Lugde & foll camp sps. Med, mkd pitch, pt sl, pt shd; wc; chem disp; mv service pnt; sauna; shwrs €1; EHU (16A) €1.50; gas; lndry; shop 500m; rest; playgrnd; htd pool 400m; 60% statics; dogs €1.30; o'night area for m'vans; poss cr; quiet; ccard acc; CKE/CCI. "Gd for country lovers; pretty site." ♦ € 14.40   2009*

BAD PYRMONT *1D3* (13km W Rural) *51.98671, 9.10833* Ferienpark Teutoburgerwald, Badeanstaltsweg 4, 32683 Barntrup [(05263) 2221; info@ferienparkteutoburgerwald.de; www.ferienparkteutoburgerwald.de]
On B1 bet Blomberg & Bad Pyrmont turn W for 1km to Barntrup & foll sp fr vill cent. Med, some hdstg, terr, pt shd; wc; chem disp; mv service pnt; shwrs inc; EHU (16A) inc; gas; lndry (inc dryer); shop, rest, snacks 500m; playgrnd; pool, tennis adj; wifi; 10% statics; dogs €2.25; sep m'van area; adv bkg; quiet; red long stay. "Excel site; vg san facs but poss stretched in high ssn; conv Hameln (Hamelin)." 1 Apr-31 Oct. € 26.50   2010*

BAD REICHENHALL *4G4* (6km N Rural) *47.74645, 12.8958* Campingplatz Staufeneck, Streilachweg, 83451 Piding [(08651) 2134; fax 710450; info@camping-berchtesgadener-land.de; www.camping-berchtesgadener-land.de] Exit A8/E52/E60 junc 115 onto B20 for approx 3km, site sp. Cannot ent site fr S, so if coming fr S, turn at m'way junc & return on B20, as above. Med, mkd pitch, some hdstg, pt shd; wc; chem disp; mv service pnt; shwrs €0.50; EHU (16A) €3 or metered + conn fee; lndry (inc dryer); shop; supmkt 500m; rest 300m; playgrnd; 30% statics; dogs €1.50; bus; Eng spkn; quiet; red CKE/CCI. "Excel views; site clsd 2200-0700; office open am & evenings, site yourself if office clsd; Bad Reichenhall v pleasant; conv Salzburg, Berchtesgaden & Tirol - gd bus service; clean, dated facs; excel walking/cycle tracks; v welcoming - nothing too much trouble; pitches on gravel; fast-flowing rv adj; excel site." 1 Apr-30 Oct. € 20.00   2010*

⊞ **BAD RIPPOLDSAU** *3C3* (7km S Rural) *48.38396, 8.30168* Schwarzwaldcamping Alisehof, Rippoldsauerstrasse 8, 77776 Bad Rippoldsau-Schapbach [(07839) 203; fax 1263; camping@alisehof.de; www.alisehof.de]
Exit A5/E35 junc 55 Offenburg onto B33 dir Gengenbach & Hausach to Wolfach. At end of Wolfach vill turn N dir Bad Rippoldsau. Site on R over wooden bdge after vill of Schapbach. 2 steep passes fr other dir. Med, mkd pitch, pt sl, pt shd; htd wc; chem disp; mv service pnt; 30% serviced pitches; baby facs; fam bthrm; shwrs inc; EHU (16A) metered + conn fee; gas; lndry; shop, rest, snacks; bar; playgrnd; pool 2km; entmnt; 20% statics; dogs €2.30; phone; site clsd 1230-1430; poss cr; Eng spkn; adv bkg; quiet; red 7+ nts/CKE/CCI. "Highly rec; clean, friendly site; many gd walks in area; not a NH." ♦ € 35.70   2014*

BAD SCHANDAU *2G4* (5km NE Rural) *50.93503, 14.21165* Panorama-Camping Kleine Bergoase, Oberestrasse 19, 01855 Kirnitzschtal (OT Mittelndorf) [0176 22906538 (mob); fax (035971) 809891; berg-oase@t-online.de; www.panorama-camping.de]
Fr Bad Schandau take rd 154 dir Sebnitz. In 5km at Mittelndorf turn R at end of vill, site sp. Sm, mkd pitch, terr, pt shd; htd wc; chem disp; shwrs €0.50; EHU (10) metered; shop 5km; rest, snacks, bar 5km; BBQ; pool 5km; spa; wifi; dogs €1.50; bus adj; poss cr; Eng spkn; adv bkg; quiet; CKE/CCI. "Vg site, new in 2009; spectacular views; gd hiking; adv bkg rec - not many pitches; close Czech border, Dresden." Mar-Oct. € 20.00   2011*

⊞ **BAD SCHANDAU** 2G4 (3km E Rural) 50.92996, 14.19301
Campingplatz Ostrauer Mühle, Im Kirnitzschtal, 01814
Bad Schandau [(035022) 42742; fax 50352; info@ostrauer-
muehle.de; www.ostrauer-muehle.de] SE fr Dresden on
B172 for 40km (Pirna-Schmilka). In Bad Schandau turn E twds
Hinterhermsdorf; site in approx 3km. Med, terr, pt shd; wc;
chem disp; mv service pnt; shwrs €0.50; EHU (10A) €1.75 +
conn fee; lndry; shop; supmkt 4km; rest; sm playgrnd; dogs €2;
sep car park; quiet; CKE/CCI. "In National Park; superb walking
area; rec arr early high ssn; site yourself if office clsd on arr."
♦ ltd. € 18.50   2012*

⊞ **BAD SEGEBERG** 1D2 (5km NE Rural) 53.96131, 10.33685
Klüthseecamp Seeblick, Stripdorfer Weg, Klüthseehof 2,
23795 Klein Rönnau [(04551) 82368; fax 840638; info@
kluethseecamp.de; www.kluethseecamp.de]
Exit A21 junc 13 at Bad Sedgeberg Süd onto B432; turn L sp
Bad Sedgeberg; cont on B432 dir Scharbeutz & Puttgarden
thro Klein Rönnau, then turn R for site. V lge, pt shd; wc; chem
disp; mv service pnt; some serviced pitches; baby facs; sauna;
steam rm; shwrs inc; EHU (16A) inc; gas; lndry (inc dryer); shop;
rest, snacks; BBQ; playgrnd; htd pool; lake sw 200m; fishing;
horseriding; tennis; bike hire; spa; golf 6km; internet; games/
TV rm; bus adj; wifi; 75% statics (sep area); dogs €2; twin-axles
acc (rec check in adv); train to Hamburg, Lübeck; site clsd Feb;
poss cr; Eng spkn; adv bkg; quiet; ccard acc; red LS/CKE/CCI.
"Spacious, well-kept nr lakeside site; relaxing atmophere; lge
pitches; helpful staff; gd facs & pool; wide range of activities;
gd cycling, walking; conv Hamburg, Lübeck; excel; peaceful 50
min lakeside walk to town." ♦ € 31.60 SBS - G12   2014*

⊞ **BAD SOBERNHEIM** 3B2 (1km S Urban) 49.77861,
7.65861 **Reisemobilplatz Am Nohfels, Hömigweg 1, 55566
Bad Sobernheim [(06751) 854611; fax 854626; info@
amnohfels.de; www.amnohfels.de]** Exit A6/E31 junc 51
onto B41 Bad Kreuznach-Saarbrücken to Sobernheim. Foll sp
'Freilichtmuseum' & sp with m'van symbol. M'vans only. Sm, pt
shd; wc; shwrs inc; EHU (12A) €2; rest 200m; pool 800m; dogs;
adv bkg; quiet. € 7.00   2009*

⊞ **BAD SOBERNHEIM** 3B2 (6km W Rural) 49.79505, 7.57786
Camping Nahemühle, 55569 Monzingen [(06751) 7475;
fax 7938; info@campingplatz-nahemuehle.de;
www.campingplatz-nahemuehle.de] On B41 W fr Bad
Kreuznach cross rlwy at traff lts & turn R to stadium, site sp.
Sm, unshd; wc; chem disp; mv service pnt; sauna; shwrs inc;
EHU (16A) metered + conn fee; lndry; shop 1.2km; rest, snacks;
bar; playgrnd; fishing; horseriding; 60% statics; dogs; Eng
spkn; adv bkg; quiet; red CKE/CCI. "Gd cycling area; wine
vills." ♦ € 15.00   2009*

⊞ **BAD TOLZ** 4E4 (7km S Rural) 47.70721, 11.55023 Alpen-
Camping Arzbach, Alpenbadstrasse 20, 83646 Arzbach
[(08042) 8408; fax 8570; campingplatz-arbach@web.de;
www.arzbach.de] S fr Bad Tölz on B13. Exit Lenggries, turn
R to cross rv & R on Wackersburgerstrasse twds Arzbach; in
5km on ent Arzbach turn L. Site ent past sw pool. Med, pt
shd; wc; chem disp; shwrs €1; EHU (16A) inc; gas; lndry; shop
4km; rest; snacks 300m; playgrnd; covrd pool; tennis 100m;
60% statics; no dogs €1; bus 300m; poss cr; no adv bkg;
quiet; CKE/CCI. "Gd walking, touring Bavarian lakes, excel facs
& rest; care needed with lge c'vans due trees & hedges." ♦
€ 20.00   2012*

⊞ **BAD URACH** 3D3 (3.5km NE Rural) 48.50333, 9.42388
Camping Pfählhof, Pfählhof 2, 72574 Bad Urach
[(07125) 8098; fax 8091; camping@pfaehlhof.de;
www.pfaehlhof.de] Fr Stuttgart or Reutlingen to Bad Urach &
on twd Blaubeuren. 1km after Bad Urach cent nr town exit sp
turn L bef long steep climb sp Oberlenningen & Grebenstetten
to site on L in 1.6km. Lge, mkd pitch, pt shd; wc; shwrs; chem
disp; baby facs; shwrs €0.50; EHU (16A) metered + conn fee;
lndry; shop 2km; rest; cooking facs; playgrnd; pool 2km; ski lift
8km; 80% statics; dogs €1.65; adv bkg in high ssn rec; quiet;
CKE/CCI. "Site admission gives red fees at spa facs; gd rest on
site; picturesque sm town; gd walking area; gates close 1300-
1500 & 2200-0700; helpful staff." € 16.60   2011*

"We must tell The Club about that great site we found"

Get your site reports in by mid-August
and we'll do our best to get your updates
into the next edition.

⊞ **BAD URACH** 3D3 (11km E Rural) 48.48598, 9.50761
Camping Lauberg, Hinter Lau 3, 72587 Römerstein-
Böhringen [(07382) 1509; fax 1074; info@lauberg.de;
www.lauberg.de] Fr Bad Urach, take rd twd Grabenstetten
& foll sp to Böhringen, then sp to site. NB Rd to Grabenstetten
avoids long, steep climb on B28. Med, mkd pitch, terr, unshd;
htd wc; chem disp; 90% serviced pitch; shwrs inc; EHU (16A)
metered + conn fee; lndry; shop, rest high ssn; supmkt 1.5km;
bar; BBQ; playgrnd; htd pool 9km; wintersports; ski lift 5km;
80% statics; dogs €1.50; poss cr; quiet; adv bkg; 10% red 10+
days. "Ideal walking area, castles, caves, Bad Urach baths."
♦ ltd. € 16.50   2015*

⊞ **BAD WILDBAD IM SCHWARZWALD** 3C3 (9km E Rural)
48.73745, 8.57623 **Camping Kleinenzhof, Kleinenzhof
1, 75323 Bad Wildbad [(07081) 3435; fax 3770; info@
kleinenzhof.de; www.kleinenzhof.de]** Fr Calmbach foll
B294 5km S. Site sp on R, in rv valley. Fr Bad Wildbad site
is on L. Lge, pt sl, pt shd; wc; chem disp; mv service pnt;
serviced pitches; sauna; shwrs inc; EHU (16A) metered +
conn fee; gas; lndry; shop; rest, snacks; playgrnd; 2 pools
(1 htd & covrd); bike hire; ski lift 8km; entmnt; 80% statics;
dogs €2.10; o'night area for m'vans; clsd 1300-1500;
poss cr; adv bkg; quiet; red long stay. "Nature trails fr site;
mountain views; distillery on site; modern san facs; sm
pitches." ♦ € 26.40   2012*

See advertisement opposite

⊞ **BAD WILDBAD IM SCHWARZWALD** 3C3 (7km
S Rural) 48.69777, 8.52027 **Camping Kälbermühle,
Kälbermühlenweg 57, 75323 Bad Wildbad [(07085) 7322
or 7353; fax 1043; information@kaelbermuehle.de]**
Take Enzklösterle rd S fr Bad Wildbad, site sp on rv bank. Med,
pt shd; wc; chem disp (wc); shwrs €0.50; EHU (16A) metered
+ conn fee; lndry (inc dryer); playgrnd; 60% statics; dogs
€0.80; bus; adv bkg; quiet. "Friendly owners; beautifully kept,
peaceful site; superb rest; mkd forest walks; gd; no cc/debit
cards." € 23.00   2015*

⊞ **BAD WILDBAD IM SCHWARZWALD** *3C3* (12km SW Rural) *48.66641, 8.46820* **Campingplatz Müllerwiese, Hirschtalstrasse 3, 75337 Enzklösterle [tel/fax (07085) 7485; info@muellerwiese.de; www.muellerwiese.de]** Fr Bad Wildbad take tunnel S; site well sp in vill. Med, hdg/mkd pitch, pt shd; wc; chem disp; mv service pnt; shwrs €0.50; EHU (10-16A) €2.50 or metered; gas; lndry; shop, rest in vill; playgrnd; cab/sat TV; 75% statics; dogs €2; bus; site clsd mid-Nov to 19 Dec; Eng spkn; adv bkg; quiet; CKE/CCI. "Gd walking, cycling in heart of Black Forest; gd local entmnt high ssn; friendly owners; clean but dated facs; vg." € 16.50   2009*

BAD WILDBAD IM SCHWARZWALD *3C3* (20km NW Urban) *48.79268, 8.42908* **Campingplatz Jungbrunnen, Schwimmbadstrasse 29, 76332 Bad Herrenalb [(07083) 932970; fax 932971; info@camping-jungbrunnen. de; www.camping-jungbrunnen.de]** On S o'skirts Bad Herrenalb on L564 to Gernsbach & Baden-Baden. Foll sp on L down slope. NB: Rd dist fr Bad Wildbad is much more than crow flies due to no direct rds & inclines. If app fr Gernsbach, pass site & proceed into Bad Herrenalb to rndabt, then return. This avoids diff turn. Med, terr, pt shd; wc; chem disp; shwrs €0.50; EHU (16A) metered; gas; lndry; shop; snacks; bar; cooking facs; pool; paddling pool; 60% statics; dogs €1.50; bus; Eng spkn; adv bkg; quiet; "Friendly owner; easy walk into interesting sm town; san facs tired but clean." 1 Apr-31 Oct. € 22.30   2013*

"I need an on-site restaurant"

We do our best to make sure site information is correct, but it is always best to check any must-have facilities are still available or will be open during your visit.

⊞ **BADEN BADEN** *3C3* (1km NW Urban) *48.7720, 8.2215* **Stellplatz, Aumattstrasse, 76530 Baden-Baden [(07221) 275200; info@baden-baden.com]** Exit A5/E35/E52 at junc 51 for Baden-Baden & foll B500 twd cent. Turn R at traff lts into Aumattstrasse, dir 'stadion' (stadium). Make for coach/bus park, site sp. Free, sm parking place for m'vans only; wc; shop 800m; no other facs.   2010*

BADENWEILER see Neuenburg am Rhein *3B4*

⊞ **BAMBERG** *4E2* (5km S Rural) *49.86138, 10.91583* **Camping Insel, Am Campingplatz 1, 96049 Bamberg-Bug [(0951) 56320; fax 56321; buero@campinginsel.de; www.campinginsel.de]** Exit A70/E48 junc 16 or A73 exit Bamberg-Süd onto B22 dir Würzburg. Site on L of rd along Rv Regnitz. Bug sm vill suburb of Bamburg to S of rv. Fr S on A3 exit junc 79 dir Bamberg. In 12km turn L dir Pettstadt; turn R at rndabt, site in 2km. Lge, pt shd; htd wc; baby facs; shwrs inc; chem disp; mv service pnt; EHU (16A) metered (long lead poss req); gas; lndry; supmkt 4km; shop; snacks; playgrnd; TV; 20% statics; dogs €1.10; clsd 1300-1500 & 2300-0700; bus to Bamburg; Eng spkn; quiet; cash only; red long stay/CKE/CCI. "Lovely historic town, Unesco; rvside site; excel cycle facs to town; bus to town €1.50; excel, modern san facs; family run site; gd rest; beautiful walk thro park by rvside; UNESCO World Heritage town; new lgr san facs for 2015." ◆ € 29.50   2015*

BAUTZEN *2G4* (4.5km NE Rural) *51.20194, 14.46083* **Natur & AbenteuerCamping am Stausee Bautzen, Nimschützerstrasse 41, 02625 Bautzen [(03591) 271267 or (035828) 76430; fax 271268; camping-bautzen@web.de; www.camping-bautzen. de]** Exit A4 junc 90 onto B156. Site sp on lakeside. Med, hdstg, pt shd; htd wc; chem disp; mv service pnt; all serviced pitches; baby facs; shwrs inc; EHU (16A) €2.50 (poss rev pol); lndry (inc dryer); shop & 2km; BBQ; cooking facs; playgrnd; lake sw & beach adj; watersports; games rm; entmnt; internet; TV; dogs €2.50; phone; bus adj; Eng spkn; adv bkg; quiet; ccard acc; CKE/CCI. "V high quality site; lovely location; Bautzen interesting town; gd cycling & walking; excel." 1 Apr-31 Oct. € 24.50   2010*

⊞ **BERCHTESGADEN** *4G4* (5km NE Rural) *47.64742, 13.03993* **Camping Allweglehen, Allweggasse 4, 83471 Berchtesgaden-Untersalzberg [(08652) 2396; camping@allweglehen.de; www.allweglehen.de]** On R of rd B305 Berchtesgaden dir Salzburg, immed after ent Unterau; sp. App v steep in places with hairpin bend; gd power/weight ratio needed. Lge, pt sl, terr, pt shd, some hdstg; htd wc; serviced pitches; chem disp; mv service pnt; baby facs; shwrs inc; EHU (16A) metered + conn fee; lndry (inc dryer); shop; rest; bar; playgrnd; htd pool; cycles; wifi; entmnt; 20% statics; dogs €2.95; bus 500m; ski lift; phone; poss cr; adv bkg rec high ssn; quiet; ccard acc; 10% red CKE/CCI. "Gd touring/walking cent; wonderful views some pitches; beautiful scenery; Hitler's Eagles' Nest worth visit (rd opens mid-May) - bus fr Obersalzburg; site rds poss o'grown & uneven; steep app some pitches - risk of grounding for long o'fits; friendly, family-run site; excel rest." ◆ € 45.50   2014*

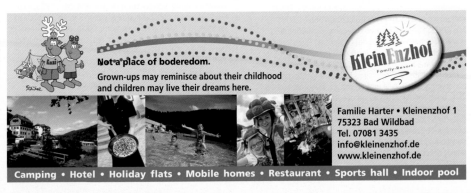

Not a place of boderedom.

Grown-ups may reminisce about their childhood and children may live their dreams here.

KleinEnzhof
Family-Resort

Familie Harter • Kleinenzhof 1
75323 Bad Wildbad
Tel. 07081 3435
info@kleinenzhof.de
www.kleinenzhof.de

Camping • Hotel • Holiday flats • Mobile homes • Restaurant • Sports hall • Indoor pool

GERMANY

⊞ **BERCHTESGADEN** 4G4 (9km NW Rural) 47.67666, 12.93611 **Camping Winkl-Landthal, Klaushäuslweg 7, 83483 Bischofswiesen [(08652) 8164; fax 979831; camping-winkl@t-online.de; www.camping-winkl.de]** Fr Munich-Salzburg m'way take rd 20 sp Bad Reichenhall. Where rd turns L, foll rd 20 twd Berchtesgaden. Site on R in 9km. Med, mkd pitch, pt shd; wc; chem disp; some serviced pitches with sat TV; shwrs inc; EHU (10A) metered + conn fee (poss rev pol); gas; lndry; shop & 500m; rest; playgrnd; htd pool 3.5km; golf 15km; wifi; 50% statics; dogs €1.50; site clsd Nov; Eng spkn; adv bkg; some rd & rlwy noise; red long stay/CKE/CCI. "Some pleasant, shd pitches adj sm rv; clean san facs." € 21.00   2009*

⊞ **BERGEN** 1D3 (9km E Rural) 52.80443, 10.10376 **Camping am Örtzetal, Dicksbarg 46, 29320 Oldendorf [(05052) 3072; www.campingplatz-oldendorf.de]** Fr S, exit A7/E45 junc 52 dir Celle, in 5km turn L sp Winsen, Belsen & Bergen. Fr N exit A7/E45 at junc 45 onto B3 to Bergen. Foll rd to Bergen. In Bergen foll sp Hermannsburg. In about 7km at T-junc turn R, then 1st L sp Eschede & Oldendorf. In Oldendorf turn L at 2nd x-rds. Site on R in 1km. Lge, pt shd; wc; chem disp; shwrs €0.80; EHU (6A) metered + conn fee; lndry (inc dryer); shop 4km; rest 500m; snacks; bar; htd pool 4km; lake 4km; playgrnd; bike hire; 40% statics; dogs €1.50; phone; quiet; CKE/CCI. "Ideal for walking & cycling on Lüneburg Heath; conv Belsen memorial; welcoming, friendly owner; peaceful site; barrier clsd 1300-1500." € 15.50   2009*

BERGWITZ see Lutherstadt Wittenberg 2F3

⊞ **BERLIN** 2G3 (23km SW Rural) 52.4650, 13.16638 **DCC Campingplatz Gatow, Kladower Damm 207-213, 14089 Berlin-Gatow [(030) 3654340; fax 36808492; gatow@ dccberlin.de; www.dccberlin.de]** Fr A10 to W of Berlin turn E on rd 5 sp Spandau/Centrum. Go twd city cent & after 14km turn R onto Gatowerstrasse (Esso g'ge) sp Kladow/Gatow. Site 6.5km on L almost opp Kaserne (barracks). Med, pt shd; htd wc; chem disp; mv service pnt; shwrs inc; fam bthrm; EHU (10-16A) metered + conn fee; gas; lndry (inc dryer); supmkt 2km; snacks; bar; playgrnd; sand beach 1km; 60% statics; dogs €2; bus at gate; poss cr; Eng spkn; rd noise; red CKE/CCI. "Excel site; bus tickets fr recep; frequent bus to Berlin cent at gate; highly rec; excel, clean san facs; bicycles can be taken on nrby Kladow ferry to Wannsee S. Bahn; gates close bet 1300 & 1500 and at 2200; rec." ♦ € 26.50   2015*

⊞ **BERLIN** 2G3 (26km SW Rural) 52.40027, 13.18055 **City Campingplatz Hettler & Lange, Bäkehang 9a, 14532 Kleinmachnow-Dreilinden [(033203) 79684; fax 77913; kleinmachnow@city-camping-berlin.de; www.city-camping-berlin.de]** Fr S exit A115/E51 junc 5 sp Kleinmachnow, turn L at T-junc & cont to rndabt. Turn L & foll site sp in 800m. Lge, pt sl, pt shd; htd wc; chem disp; mv service pnt; baby facs; shwrs inc; EHU (6A) €2.50; gas; lndry (inc dryer); sm shop & 5km; rest, snacks; playgrnd; lake sw 2km; boats for hire; dogs €2; phone; bus nr; poss v cr; some Eng spkn; adv bkg; quiet but some barge & rd noise; CKE/ CCI. "Excel location on canal side; immac, modern san facs; twin-axles by arrangement; gd walking in woods; gd public transport conv Berlin 45 mins - parking at Wannsee S-bahn (family ticket avail for bus & train); vg." € 23.00   2013*

⊞ **BERLIN** 2G3 (13km NW Urban) 52.54861, 13.25694 **City-Camping Hettler & Lange, Gartenfelderstrasse 1, 13599 Berlin-Spandau [(030) 33503633; fax 33503635; spandau@ city-camping-berlin.de; www.hettler-lange.de]** Fr N on A111/A115/E26 exit junc 10 sp Tegel Airport & head W on Saatwinkler Damm. Fr S on A100 exit junc 11 onto Saatwinkler Damm. Cont 3.2km to traff lts, turn R, then R again immed bef 2nd bdge. Site on island in rv. Med, pt sl, shd; wc; chem disp; shwrs €1; EHU (16A) €2; lndry; shop 2km; rest; bar; dogs €2; Eng spkn; no adv bkg; aircraft noise; ccard acc; CKE/CCI. "Conv Berlin; 15 min walk to bus stn; gd location beside a canal but aircraft noise; gd san facs; NH/sh stay only; poss to cycle along canal to Potsdam." € 22.50   2014*

BERNKASTEL KUES 3B2 (20km NE Rural) 49.96556, 7.10475 **Camping Rissbach, Rissbacherstrasse 155, 56841 Traben-Trarbach [(06541) 3111; info@moselcampings.de; www.moselcampings.de]** Fr Bernkastel on B53, after Kröv do not cross Mosel bdge but cont strt on twd Traben, site on R in 1km. NB 20km by rd fr Bernkastel to site. Med, mkd pitch, pt sl, shd; htd wc; chem disp; mv service pnt; shwrs €0.25/ min; EHU (16A) €2.50; gas 500m; lndry; shop & 2km; rest 1km; snacks; BBQ; playgrnd; htd pool adj; boat-launch; wifi; 30% statics; dogs €3.50; phone; quiet. "In lovely position nr rv; extra for pitches nr rv; well-run site; excel san facs; vg sw pools in town; poss flooding at high water; Sept wine fest." ♦ 1 Apr-31 Oct. € 16.00   2012*

BERNKASTEL KUES 3B2 (2km SW Rural) 49.90883, 7.05600 **Kueser Werth Camping, Am Hafen 2, 54470 Bernkastel-Kues [(06531) 8200; fax 8282; camping-cueser-werth@ web.de; www.camping-kueser-werth.de]** A'bahn A1/48 (E44) exit Salmtal; join rd sp Bernkastel. Bef rv bdge turn L sp Lieser, thro Lieser cont by rv to ent on R for boat harbour, foll camping sp to marina. Diff access via narr single-track rd. Lge, pt shd; wc; chem disp; mv service pnt; shwrs inc; EHU (16A) metered; lndry; sm shop; rest, snacks; playgrnd; bike hire; TV rm; 20% statics; dogs €2; bus 1km; poss cr; Eng spkn; adv bkg; some rd noise & rv barges; 5% red CKE/CCI. "Excel cent for touring Mosel Valley; Bernkastel delightful sm town with gd parking, sailing, boat excursions, wine cent; cycle lanes; site low on rv bank - poss flooding in bad weather; efficient staff; gd site with excel facs; not rec for NH/sh stay high ssn as pitches & position poor." ♦ 1 Apr-31 Oct. € 18.00   2009*

BERNKASTEL KUES 3B2 (3km NW Rural) 49.93736, 7.04853 **Camping Schenk, Hauptstrasse 165, 54470 Bernkastel-Wehlen [(06531) 8176; fax 7681; info@camping-schenk.de; www.camping-schenk.com]** On Trier/Koblenz rd B53, exit Kues heading N on L bank of rv & site on R in 4km at Wehlen, sp. Steep exit. Med, mkd pitch, some hdstg, pt sl, some terr, pt shd; htd wc; chem disp; mv service pnt; some serviced pitches; shwrs €0.50; EHU (16A) metered + conn fee; gas; lndry; shops 1km; rest adj; snacks; bar; playgrnd; pool; 40% statics; dogs; phone; bus; poss cr; Eng spkn; adv bkg; quiet; CKE/CCI. "In apple orchard on Rv Mosel; price according to pitch size; friendly owners; debit cards acc; pool deep - not suitable non-swimmers; poorly ventilated san facs; rv walks & cycle path to town." ♦ ltd. 27 Mar-31 Oct. € 25.40   2011*

BERNKASTEL KUES *3B2* (10km NW Rural) *49.97972, 7.0200* Camping Erden, Moselufer 1, 54492 Erden [(06532) 4060; fax 5294; schmitt@campingplatz-erden.de; www.campingplatz-erden.de] Exit A1/48 junc 125 onto B50 to Zeltingen. Cross bdge over Mosel, turn L to Erden, site sp. Med, pt sl, shd; htd wc; chem disp; mv service pnt; shwrs; EHU (16A) metered + conn fee; gas; lndry; shop nr; rest, snacks; bar; playgrnd; pool 5km; TV; 90% statics in sep area; dogs €2; phone; bus; poss cr; adv bkg; rd noise; ccard acc; red long stay. "Pleasant, less cr site on opp side of rv to main rd; wonderful setting in scenic area; water point & san facs long way fr tourer pitches; barrier locked 1300-1500 & o'night." ♦ 1 Apr-31 Oct. € 18.00   2013*

BERNRIED see Deggendorf *4G3*

BIELEFELD *1C3* (8km SW Rural) *52.00624, 8.45681* Campingpark Meyer Zu Bentrup, Vogelweide 9, 33649 Bielefeld [(0521) 4592233; fax 459017; bielefeld@meyer-zu-bentrup.de; www.camping-bielefeld.de] Fr N or S on A2 - At interchange 21 take A33 Osnabruck. Cont till m'way ends, cont onto A61 dir Bielefeld. After 2km take A68 exit, dir Osnabruck/Halle West. Site on L after 3km. Lge, pt sl, unshd; wc; chem disp; mv service pnt; shwrs €0.30/min; EHU (10-16A) €1.50; lndry (inc dryer); farm shop; bar; cooking facs; playgrnd; games area; games rm; wifi; 70% statics; dogs €2; quiet; red CKE/CCI. "Vg; immac but dated san facs (2015); conv for Bielefeld; well maintained; warm welcome; excel shop at adj fruit farm." ♦ 1 Mar-30 Nov. € 25.00   2015*

BINGEN *3C2* (3km E Urban) *49.97029, 7.93916* Camping Hindenburgbrucke, Bornstrasse 22, 55411 Kempton-Bingen [(06721) 17160; fax 16998; bauer@bauer-schorsch.de; www.bauer-schorsch.de] Foll rd on Rhine twd Mainz, site on L bef traff lts. Turn into tarmac rd, bear R, L under rlwy bdge, strt to site ent by Rhine. Lge, some hdg, unshd; wc; chem disp; shwrs; EHU (watch rev pol); rest; snacks; bar; BBQ; playgrnd; 40% statics (adj area); bus/train adj; twin axles; poss cr; quiet (apart fr barges). "Open site on W bank of Rhein; staff conn elec pnts; lovely position for sh stay; mosquitoes abound; close to R desheim-Bingen ferry, vineyards, castles, cruising." ♦ ltd. 1 May-31 Oct. € 19.00   2014*

BINZ *2G1* (6km NW Coastal) *54.44817, 13.56152* Wohnmobil-Oase Rügen, Proraer Chaussee 60, 18609 Ostseebad Binz OT Prora [(01577) 428 3715; info@.wohnmobilstellplatz-ruegen.de; www.wohnmobil stellplatz-ruegen.de] Fr Binz foll coast rd to Prora, site on L past traff lts. Med, hdstg, pt shd; htd wc; chem disp; mv service pnt; shwrs, EHU (16A); lndry; gas; snacks; dogs; bus/tram adj; Eng spkn; m'vans only. "Vg site; track to beach." 23 Mar-20 Oct. € 15.00   2012*

BIRKENFELD *3B2* (2km E Rural) *49.65501, 7.18211* Campingpark Waldwiesen (Naturist), 55765 Birkenfeld [(06782) 5215; fax 5219; info@waldwiesen.de; www.waldwiesen.de] Exit A62 junc 4 N to Birkenfeld. Site sp off rd B41. Med, hdg pitch, pt sl, pt shd; wc; chem disp; mv service pnt; shwrs inc; EHU 16A) metered + conn fee; gas; lndry; shops 500m; rest 600m; snacks 1km; playgrnd; lake sw adj; bike hire; 10% statics; dogs €2.50; adv bkg; quiet; ccard acc; CKE/CCI. "Sep area for naturists; excel facs for children; gd base for Saar-Hunsruck area." Easter-14 Oct. € 22.00   2009*

BISCHOFSHEIM AN DER RHON *3D2* (1km SE Rural) *50.39558, 10.02011* Camping am Schwimmbad, Kissingerstrasse 53, 97653 Bischofsheim [(09772) 1350; fax 931350; info@rhoencamping.de; www.rhoencamping.de] Fr A7 exit junc 93 at Fulda onto B279 E to Bischofsheim, site sp 1km down minor rd dir Bad Kissingen. Fr A71 exit junc 25 Bad Neustadt onto B279 W. Med, hdg/mkd pitch, hdstg, pt shd; wc; chem disp; mv service pnt; shwrs €0.50; EHU (16A) metered; gas; lndry; shop & 500m; rest, bar 500m; BBQ; playgrnd; 2 htd pools (1 covrd); paddling pool; waterslide; tennis; solarium; bike hire; 30% statics; dogs €1; sep m'van area; adv bkg; quiet; red CKE/CCI. "In cent of Rhon Nature Park, ideal for walking; ski adj in winter; office hrs 0800-1230 & 1430-1800; if arr after 1800 phone in adv & ent key will be left for you." ♦ € 19.50   2011*

> ## "Satellite navigation makes touring much easier"
>
> Remember most sat navs don't know if you're towing or in a larger vehicle – always use yours alongside maps and site directions.

BITBURG *3B2* (12km NE Urban) *50.03750, 6.59111* Camping Kyllburg, Karl-Kaufmann-Weg 5, D-54655 Kyllburg [65 63 81 33; info@campingkyllburg.de; www.camping kyllburg.de] Site on E o'skts of Kyllburg on banks of rv Kyll. App fr W turn R immed after x-ing rv. Ent down hill on R immed bef sharp LH bend. Steep & narr descent. Med, unshd; htd wc; chem disp; mv service pnt; baby facs; shwrs inc; EHU (16A) €0.80; gas; lndry; shop 500m; rest, snacks; bar; BBQ; playgrnd; pool; rv adj; wifi; 30% statics; dogs €1.80; bus 500m; train 500m; Eng spkn; adv bking; quiet; cc acc; red LS; CKE/CCI. "Gd for sh stays; 5 sw pool with waterslide; cycling & walking paths; vg site." ♦ Mar-Oct. € 18.60   2011*

⊞ **BITBURG** *3B2* (10km W Rural) *49.95895, 6.42454* Prümtal Camping, In der Klaus 5, 54636 Oberweis [(06527) 92920; fax 929232; info@pruemtal.de; www.pruemtal.de] On B50 Bitburg-Vianden rd. On ent Oberweis sharp RH bend immed L bef rv bdge - sp recreational facs or sp Köhler Stuben Restaurant-Bierstube. V lge, pt shd; htd wc; chem disp; shwrs inc; EHU (16A) €2.75 or metered; lndry; shop; rest, snacks; bar; playgrnd; pool; bike hire; internet; entmnt; 60% statics; dogs €2.10; Eng spkn; poss v cr high ssn; adv bkg; ccard acc; CKE/CCI. "Excel facs; san facs stretched high ssn; vg rest." ♦ € 26.00   2012*

⊞ **BONN** *1B4* (13km SE Rural) *50.65388, 7.20111* Camping Genienau, Im Frankenkeller 49, 53179 Bonn-Mehlem [(0228) 344949; fax 3294989; genienau@freenet.de] Fr B9 dir Mehlem, site sp on Rv Rhine, S of Mehlem. Med, pt shd; wc; chem disp; shwrs €1; EHU (6A) €3 or metered; lndry; rest & shop 600m; rest, snacks 1km; 60% statics; dogs €2; bus; Eng spkn; no adv bkg; some rv & rlwy noise; CKE/CCI. "Excel site on rv bank; liable to flood when rv v high; nr ferry to cross Rhine; late arr no problem; san facs up steps but disabled facs at grnd level; lots to see & do." ♦ € 28.00   2013*

BOPPARD 3B2 (6km NE Rural) 50.24888, 7.62638 **Camping Sonneneck, 56154 Boppard [(06742) 2121; fax 2076; kontakt@camping-sonneneck.de; www.campingpark-sonneneck.de]** On Koblenz-Mainz rd B9, on W bank of Rhine, in vill of Spay. Lge, mkd pitch, pt shd; wc; chem disp; mv service pnt; serviced pitches; sauna; shwrs inc; EHU (4A) €2.50; gas; lndry; shop; rest, snacks; bar; playgrnd; pool high ssn; shgl beach nr; fishing; crazy-golf; 18-hole golf 2km; 10% statics; dogs €2.40; phone; night watchman; poss cr; Eng spkn; rlwy & barge noise; CKE/CCI. "V pleasant staff; clean san facs, poss long way fr pitches; ltd waste water points; extra fr rvside pitch; site poss liable to flood; gd cycle path along Rhine; gd NH." ♦ 1 Apr-31 Oct. € 25.00   2015*

BORGERENDE see Bad Doberan 2F1

⊞ **BRANDENBURG AN DER HAVEL** 2F3 (9km E Rural) 52.39833, 12.43665 **Camping und Ferienpark am Plauer See, Plauer Landstrasse 200, 14774 Brandenburg [33 81 80 45 44; fax 81 80 46 44; info@camping-plauersee. de; www.camping-plauersee.de]** Fr A2 take 102 to Brandenburg. L onto 1, cont 4km. Just after sign for Plauerhof is a campsite sign. Turn L & foll rd for 1.5km to site on the side of lake. Med, mkd pitch, pt sl, pt shd; wc; chem disp; mv service pnt; fam bthrm; shwrs €1.40; EHU (10A) €1.90; lndry (inc dryer); rest; snacks; bar; BBQ; playgrnd; games area; bike hire; 75% statics; dogs; bus 1.5km; Eng spkn; adv bkg; quiet; CCI. "Next to sm lake; boat, cycles & BBQ hire; nr historic town of Brandenburg; vg site." € 18.00   2014*

BRAUBACH see Lahnstein 3B2

⊞ **BRAUNEBERG** 3B2 (900m W Rural) 49.90564, 6.97603 **Wohnmobilstellplatz Brauneberger Juffer, Moselweinstraße 101, 54472 Brauneberg [6534 933 333; mfrollison@yahoo.co.uk or info@brauneberg.de]** Fr NE of A1 take exit 127-Klausen onto L47 twds Mulheim. Cont onto L158, then turn L onto B53. Supermkt 20m fr site ent which is down side rd twds rv. Sm, hdg/mkd pitch, hdstg, pt shd; chem disp; mv service pnt; EHU (16A); BBQ; sw 500m; dogs; bus 100m; Eng spkn; quiet. "Gd cycle paths along rv; vg site." € 8.00   2014*

⊞ **BRAUNLAGE** 2E4 (8.6km N Rural) 51.75713, 10.68345 **Campingplatz am Schierker Stern, Hagensnasse, 38879 Schierke [(039455) 58817; fax 58818; info@harz-camping. com; www.harz-camping.com]** Fr W on B27 fr Braunlage for 4km to Elend. Turn L & cross rlwy line. Site on L in 2km at x-rds. Med, hdstg, pt sl, pt shd; htd wc; chem disp; mv service pnt; shwrs inc; EHU (6A) €2.60; lndry; sm shop & 8km; rest 200m; snacks 1km; BBQ; cooking facs; TV rm; dogs €1.60; bus at site ent; train 1km; adv bkg; quiet. "Conv & pleasant site in Harz mountains; excel san facs; friendly, helpful owners live on site; sm pitches; vg." € 24.00   2013*

⊞ **BRAUNLAGE** 2E4 (12km SE Rural) 51.65697, 10.66786 **Campingplatz am Bärenbache, Bärenbachweg 10, 38700 Hohegeiss [(05583) 1306; fax 1300; campingplatz-hohegeiss@t-online.de; www.campingplatz-hohegeiss.de]** Fr Braunlage S on B4 thro Hohegeiss; site sp on L downhill (15%) on edge of town. Med, hdg/mkd pitch, terr; pt shd; htd wc; chem disp; mv service pnt; baby facs; shwrs inc; EHU (10A); lndry (inc dryer); shops 500m; rest, snacks; bar; cooking facs; BBQ; playgrnd; htd pool; paddling pool; bike hire; some statics; wifi; dogs €1.50; Eng spkn; adv bkg; quiet; red snr citizens. "Gd walking; friendly; walking dist to vill; vg." ♦ ltd. € 22.50 (CChq acc)   2014*

⊞ **BRAUNLAGE** 2E4 (2km SW Rural) 51.71322, 10.59780 **Camping Hohe Tannen, Am Campingplatz 1, 38700 Braunlage [(05520) 413; fax 950065; campingplatz.hohe tannen@t-online.de]** Take B27 fr Braulage dir Bad Lauterberg, site sp. Med, mkd pitch, terr, pt shd; htd wc; shwrs inc; chem disp; mv service pnt; EHU (16A) metered + conn fee; lndry; shop; rest; snacks 1km; playgrnd; pool; 50% statics; dogs €1.20; bus; adv bkg; quiet; red CKE/CCI. "Excel facs, ltd LS." € 15.00   2009*

BREISACH AM RHEIN 3B4 (7km E Rural) 48.03104, 7.65781 **Kaiserstuhl Camping, Nachwaid 5, 79241 Ihringen [(07668) 950065; fax 950071; info@kaiserstuhlcamping.de; www.kaiserstuhlcamping.de]** Fr S exit A5/E35 junc 64a, foll sp twds Breisach, then camping sp to Ihringen. At Ihringen site sp dir Merdingen. Fr N exit junc 60 & foll sp. Med, unshd; wc; chem disp; mv service pnt; baby facs; shwrs €0.50; EHU (16A) metered + conn fee; lndry; shop 800m; rest adj; snacks; bar; playgrnd; htd pool, tennis adj; golf 8km; 10% statics; dogs €2.50; poss cr; quiet; 10% red long stay/CKE/CCI."Can get cr in high ssn." ♦ 15 Mar-31 Oct. € 32.00   2014*

BREISACH AM RHEIN 3B4 (2km S Rural) 48.01972, 7.60861 **Campingplatz Münsterblick Breisach, Hochstetterstrasse 11, 79206 Breisach-Hochstetten [(07667) 93930; fax 939393; adler-hochstetten@t-online.de; www.adler-hochstetten.de]** Fr E5/A5 exit 63 sp Breisach. Site sp off B31 rd app Breisach, adj to Gasthof Adler in Hochstetten. Or cross Rv Rhine fr France at Neuf-Brisach on D415. Site sp at Breisach in approx 1km (L of rd). Sm, pt shd; wc; shwrs inc; chem disp; shwrs €0.50; EHU (10A) metered + conn fee; lndry; shop 2km; rest; bar; 10% statics; dogs €1.20; poss cr; adv bkg; quiet; red CKE/CCI. "Excel NH; modern, clean san facs; gates clsd 2100." 27 Mar-2 Nov. € 16.00   2009*

⊞ **BREMEN** 1C2 (16km SW Rural) 53.01055, 8.68972 **Camping Wienberg, Zum Steller See 83, 28816 Stuhr-Gross Mackenstedt [(04206) 9191; fax 9293; info@ camping-wienburg.de; www.camping-wienberg.de]** Exit A1/E37 junc 58a onto B322 sp Stuhr/Delmenhorst. Foll Camping Steller See sp. Lge, mkd pitch, pt sl, hdstg, pt shd; htd wc; chem disp; mv service pnt; baby facs; shwrs €1; EHU (16A) metered or €3; lndry (inc dryer); shop; rest, snacks; bar; playgrnd; pool; bike hire; entmnt; TV; 50% statics; dogs €2; some Eng spkn; adv bkg; rd noise; ccard acc; CKE/CCI. "Helpful staff; basic facs; gd." € 23.70   2011*

GERMANY

BREMEN *1C2* (17km SW Rural) *53.00694, 8.69277*
Campingplatz Steller See, Zum Stellersee 15, 28817 Stuhr-
Gross Mackenstedt [(04206) 6490; fax 6668; steller.see@t-
online.de; www.steller-see.de] Exit A1/E37 junc 58a onto
B322 sp Stuhr/Delmenhorst. Foll site sp. Lge, unshd; htd wc;
chem disp; mv service pnt; baby facs; shwrs €0.50; EHU (10-
16A) metered or €2.50; gas; lndry (inc dryer); rest, snacks; bar;
BBQ; playgrnd; lake sw adj; games area; entmnt; 80% statics in
sep area; phone; wifi; poss cr at w/end; adv bkg; poss noisy; no
ccard acc; red long stay/CKE/CCI. "Site officially clsd but owner
may accommodate you; well-appointed, clean, lakeside site;
immac san facs; friendly owners; conv NH fr m'way & for trams
to Bremen; some m'way noise; gd space, easy to position; vg."
♦ 1 Apr-30 Sep. € 25.50   2014*

⊞ BREMEN *1C2* (5km NW Rural) *53.11483, 8.83263*
Camping am Stadtwaldsee, Hochschulring 1, 28359
Bremen [(0421) 8410748; fax 8410749; contact@camping-
stadtwaldsee.de; www.camping-stadtwaldsee.de]
Fr A27 exit junc 18 onto B6. At 1st junc turn R sp University,
site on R in approx 2km. Foll 'Campingplatz' sp. Lge, mkd pitch,
hdstg, pt shd; htd wc; chem disp; mv service pnt; baby facs;
fam bthrm; shwrs inc; EHU (16A) metered; gas; lndry (inc dryer);
shop, rest, snacks; bar; cooking facs; BBQ; playgrnd; lake sw adj;
wifi; some statics; dogs €4; phone; bus 100m; poss cr; Eng spkn;
adv bkg; some rd noise; ltd ccard acc; red long stay; CKE/CCI.
"Excel, spacious lakeside site; vg san & kitchen facs; cycle path to
beautiful city; gd bus service." ♦ € 47.00   2014*

"There aren't many sites open at this time of year"

If you're travelling outside peak season
remember to call ahead to check site opening
dates – even if the entry says 'open all year'.

⊞ BRETTEN *3C3* (11km E Rural) *49.03478, 8.83352*
Stromberg Camping, Diefenbacherstrasse 70, 75438
Knittlingen-Freudenstein [(07043) 2160; fax 40405; info@
strombergcamping.de; www.strombergcamping.de]
Take B35 E fr Bretten, foll sp Knittlingen then Freudenstein, site
sp in approx 1lm on L. V lge, mkd pitch, pt shd; wc; chem disp;
mv service pnt; shwrs inc; EHU (16A) €1.50 (rev pol); lndry (inc
dryer); shop, rest high ssn; snacks; bar; cooking facs; playgrnd;
pool; paddling pool; pony riding; games area; entmnt;
90% statics; dogs €2.50; poss cr; quiet; red long stay; CKE/
CCI. "Clsd to vehicles 1300-1500 & 2200-0700; gd touring
base for Black Forest; ltd number touring pitches cr nr ent." ♦
€ 17.00   2010*

⊞ BRIESELANG *2F3* (5km W Rural) *52.57138,
12.96583* Campingplatz Zeestow im Havelland, 11
Brieselangerstrasse, 14665 Brieselang [(033234) 88634;
fax 22863; info@campingplatz-zeestow.de;
www.campingplatz-zeestow.de] Exit A10/E55 junc 27; turn
W dir Wustermark; site on L after canal bdge in 500m. Lge, pt
sl, unshd; wc; chem disp; shwrs €1; EHU (16A) metered; gas;
lndry; shop; rest; bar; 75% statics; dogs €2; bus; poss cr; CKE/
CCI. "Gd NH nr a'bahn; facs dated but clean; 13km fr Berlin &
25km fr Potsdam; fair." ♦ ltd. € 14.00   2011*

⊞ BRUGGEN *1A4* (2km SE Rural) *51.23416, 6.19815*
Camping-Forst Laarer See, Brüggenerstrasse 27, 41372
Niederkrüchten [(02163) 8461 or 0172 7630591 (mob);
info@campingforst-laarersee.com; www.campingforst-
laarersee.com] Fr A52 junc 3 or A61 junc 3 - take B221 to
Brüggen. Foll sp Laarer See & site. Sm sp on R. Lge, pt sl, pt
shd; htd wc; chem disp; mv service pnt; baby facs; fam bthrm;
shwrs €1; EHU (16A) inc; lndry; shop 2km; rest, snacks; bar;
BBQ; playgrnd; games area; 80% statics; dogs €1; Eng spkn;
adv bkg; quiet; CKE/CCI. "Unspoilt area nr pretty town; many
leisure amenities nr site - gd for children; vg site; ltd touring
pitches; pleasant site with lake; walking/bike paths." ♦
€ 13.00   2015*

BRUNNEN see Füssen *4E4*

⊞ BUHL *3C3* (7km NW Rural) *48.72719, 8.08074* Ferienpark
& Campingplatz Adam, Campingstrasse 1, 77815 Bühl-
Oberbruch [(07223) 23194; fax 8982; info@campingplatz-
adam.de; www.campingplatz-adam.de] Exit A5 at Bühl
take sp Lichtenau & foll sp thro Oberbruch, then L twd Moos
to site in 500m. If app on rd 3 take rd sp W to Rheinmünster
N of Bühl. Site sp to S at W end of Oberbruch. Lge, mkd pitch,
hdstg, pt shd; serviced pitches; wc; chem disp; mv service pnt;
shwrs €0.50; EHU (10A) €2.20; lndry; shop; supmkt 1km; rest,
snacks; bar; playgrnd; tennis; lake sw; boating; sailing; fishing;
entmnt; 60% statics; dogs €2.50; o'night area tarmac car park;
extra for lakeside pitches; poss cr; Eng spkn; adv bkg; quiet;
ccard acc; red long stay/LS; CKE/CCI. "Facs gd, clean; conv for
Strasbourg, Baden-Baden & Black Forest visits; if recep clsd
use area outside gate; vg; excel camp with own lake; gd rest;
friendly staff; handy for m'way but still quiet; o'night tarmac
area excel for NH but worth a longer stay." ♦ € 34.50 2014*

BULLAY see Zell *3B2*

BURGEN *3B2* (600m N Rural) *50.21457, 7.38976* Camping
Burgen, 56332 Burgen [(02605) 2396; fax 4919; info@
camping-burgen.de; www.camping-burgen.de]
Leave A61 at J39; foll B411 twds Dieblich to reach S bank of
Mosel; turn L and foll B49 for approx 12km; site on L bet rd
and rv bef vill. SatNav uses rte thro vill, not suitable. Med, mkd
pitch, unshd; wc; mv service pnt; shwrs inc; EHU (10A) metered
+ conn fee (poss rev pol); lndry; gas; shop; rest 200m; snacks
adj; playgrnd; pool; boat-launching; entmnt; 30% statics; dogs
€2; Eng spkn; some rd, rlwy & rv noise; red CKE/CCI. "Scenic
area; ideal for touring Mosel, Rhine & Koblenz areas; gd shop;
poss liable to flood; lovely, clean site; gd san facs; rec."
11 Apr-19 Oct. € 30.00 (CChq acc)   2014*

⊞ CALW *3C3* (8km N Rural) *48.77884, 8.73130*
Campingpark Bad Liebenzell, Pforzheimerstrasse 34,
75378 Bad Liebenzell [(07052) 935680; fax 935681;
campingpark@abelundneff.de] N fr Calw on B463 twd
Pforzheim. Site on N edge of Bad Liebenzell on R sp & visible
fr rd. Lge, hdg pitch, shd; wc; chem disp; mv service pnt; shwrs
inc; EHU (16A) metered or €2.40; gas; lndry; shop & 500m;
rest, snacks; bar; playgrnd; htd pool adj; waterslide; tennis;
50% statics; dogs €1.50; phone; m'van o'night area; poss
cr; adv bkg; poss noisy; ccard acc; red CKE/CCI. "Excel pool
complex adj; ltd san facs & site slightly scruffy; popular with
young families; lovely area; gd walking." ♦ € 18.00   2009*

GERMANY

⊞ **CALW** *3C3* (12km SW Rural) *48.67766, 8.68990* **Camping Erbenwald, 75387 Neubulach-Liebelsberg [(07053) 7382; fax 3274; info@camping-erbenwald.de; www.camping-erbenwald.de]** On B463 S fr Calw, take R slip rd sp Neubulach to go over main rd. Foll Neubulach sp until camping sp at R junc. Site well sp. Lge, hdg/mkd pitch, pt shd; wc; chem disp; mv service pnt; baby facs; shwrs €0.50; EHU (10A) metered; lndry; shop; rest, snacks; bar; playgrnd; htd pool; paddling pool; games area; internet; 60% statics; dogs €2; phone; Eng spkn; adv bkg; quiet. "Gd size pitches; child-friendly site; no vehicles in or out fr 1300-1500; excel; cash only." ♦ € 22.00   2014*

⊞ **CANOW** *2F2* (2km E Rural) *53.19636, 12.93116* **Camping Pälitzsee, Am Canower See 165, 17255 Canow [(039828) 20220; fax 26963; info@mecklenburg-tourist.de; www.mecklenburg-tourist.de]** Fr N on B198 turn S dir Rheinsberg to Canow vill, site sp. Lge, pt shd; wc; chem disp; shwrs €1; EHU (16A) metered or €3; lndry; shop high ssn; supmkt 2km; rest 2m; snacks; bar; playgrnd; lake sw & boating; 50% statics; dogs €2; adv bkg; quiet. "Canow charming vill; vg touring base for lakes." ♦ € 19.50   2009*

⊞ **CELLE** *1D3* (10km NE Rural) *52.65305, 10.19361* **Camping Alvern, Beedenbostelerweg 7, 29229 Celle-Alvern [(05145) 6000; schaefer@alvern.com]** NE fr Celle on B191. After 5km at Garssen turn R onto K29 & foll sp thro Alvern. Site sp. Med, pt shd; wc; chem disp; shwrs €0.50; EHU (10A) inc; lndry (inc dryer); shop; BBQ; playgrnd; games area; 80% statics; quiet; CKE/CCI. "Gd site; gd cycling tracks." € 14.00   2009*

⊞ **CHEMNITZ** *2F4* (10km SW Rural) *50.76583, 13.01444* **Waldcampingplatz Erzgebirgsblick, An der Dittersdorfer Höhe 1, 09439 Amtsberg [(0371) 7750833; fax 7750834; info@waldcamping-erzgebirge.de; www.waldcamping-erzgebirge.de]** Fr A4 take A72 S & exit junc 15. Foll sp 'Centrum' & join 'Südring' ring rd. Turn onto B174 & foll sp Marienberg twd junc with B180. Site sp 500m fr junc. Med, mkd pitch, pt shd; htd wc; chem disp; mv service pnt; baby facs; shwrs €0.50; EHU (16A) metered; gas; lndry; shop; supmkt 4km; playgrnd; games area; TV rm; dogs free; bus 800m; site clsd 6-27 Nov; Eng spkn; red long stay; ccard not acc; red long stay/snr citizens/CKE/CCI. "Gd san facs; relaxing site; gd walking; vg standard of site." € 17.00   2009*

⊞ **CLAUSTHAL ZELLERFELD** *1D3* (4km SE Rural) *51.78490, 10.35060* **Campingplatz Prahljust, An den Langen Brüchen 4, 38678 Clausthal-Zellerfeld [(05323) 1300; fax 78393; camping@prahljust.de; www.prahljust.de]** Fr Clausthal turn onto B242 dir Braunlage, in 3km turn R, site sp. V lge, terr, pt shd; htd wc; chem disp; mv service pnt; baby facs; sauna; shwrs inc; EHU (10-16A) metered; gas; lndry (inc dryer); shop; rest, snacks; bar; cooking facs; playgrnd; htd pool; lake sw adj; bike hire; ski lift 8km; wifi; TV rm; 30% statics; dogs €2; phone; bus 1km; Eng spkn; adv bkg; CKE/CCI. "Beautiful wooded location adj lake; gd hiking & cycling; vg." ♦ € 17.40 (CChq acc)   2010*

⊞ **COBURG** *4E2* (9km SW Rural) *50.19433, 10.83809* **Campingplatz Sonnland, Bahnhofstrasse 154, 96145 Sesslach [(09569) 220; fax 1593; info@camping-sonnland.de; www.camping-sonnland.de]** Exit A73 junc 10 Ebersdorf onto B303 W. Then at Niederfüllbach turn S onto B4, then turn W dir Sesslach. Site sp N of Sesslach dir Hattersdorf; turn R at sp opp filling stn, site in 150m. Med, mkd pitch, some hdstg, terr, pt shd; htd wc; chem disp; mv service pnt; serviced pitches; shwrs €1.50; EHU (16A) metered; lndry (inc dryer); shop 300m; rest 400m; BBQ; playgrnd; lake sw; 70% statics; dogs €1.50; adv bkg; CKE/CCI. "Sesslach unspoilt, medieval, walled town; site well laid-out." € 18.00   2012*

⊞ **COCHEM** *3B2* (1.5km N Rural) *50.15731, 7.17360* **Campingplatz am Freizeitzentrum, Moritzburgerstrasse 1, 56812 Cochem [(02671) 4409; fax 910719; info@camping platz-cochem.de; www.campingplatz-cochem.de]** On rd B49 fr Koblenz, on ent town go under 1st rv bdge then turn R over same bdge. Foll site sp. Lge, mkd pitch, pt sl, pt shd; wc; chem disp; mv service pnt; shwrs €0.90; EHU (10-16A) €2.50 + conn fee (some rev pol); gas; lndry (inc dryer); snacks; shops/supmkt, rest nrby; playgrnd; bike hire; dogs €3; poss cr; some rd/rlwy/rv noise; red LS; CKE/CCI. "Gd, clean site adj Rv Mosel; pitches tight & poss diff access fr site rds; gd for children; easy walk along rv to town; train to Koblenz, Trier, Mainz." 1 Apr-31 Oct. € 17.00   2010*

⊞ **COCHEM** *3B2* (5km NE Rural) *50.16861, 7.26555* **Camping Pommern, Moselweinstrasse 12, 56829 Pommern [(02672) 2461; fax 912173; campingpommern@netscape.net; www.campingplatz-pommern.de]** On W edge of vill of Pommern bet B49 & Rv Mosel. Med, pt shd; htd wc; chem disp; mv service pnt; baby facs; shwrs; EHU (16A) metered + conn fee; gas; lndry; shop; rest, snacks; bar; BBQ; cooking facs; playgrnd; htd pool; watersports; games area; internet; 30% statics; dogs €1.60; bus; train adj; poss cr; adv bkg; rd noise. "Well-kept, friendly site in lovely location; clean, modern san facs." 1 Apr-31 Oct. € 14.00   2010*

⊞ **COCHEM** *3B2* (10km E Rural) *50.17056, 7.29285* **Camping & Watersports Mosel-Islands, Yachthafen, 56253 Treis-Karden/Mosel [(02672) 2613; fax 912102; campingplatz@mosel-islands.de; www.mosel-islands.de]** Fr Cochem take B49 to Treis-Karden (11km), cross Mosel bdge bear L then 1st sharp L back under Mosel bdge & parallel with rv. After 300m at bdge over stream turn R then thro allotments. Site over bdge by boating cent. Fr A61 Koblenz/Bingen a'bahn descend to rv level by Winningen Valley Bdge, turn L onto B49 (Moselweinstrasse). Do not descend thro Dieblich as c'vans are prohibited. After 25km; turn R immed bef Mosel bdge & then as above. Avoid Treis vill (narr with thro traffic priorities). Med, mkd pitch, pt shd; wc; serviced pitches; shwrs €0.80; EHU (6A) metered & conn fee; gas; lndry; shops 200m; rest; BBQ; pool 1km; tennis 300m; 50% statics; dogs €4; adv bkg; some rv & rlwy noise. "Ideal for touring Mosel valley; rv cruising & historical sites; vg san facs 1st floor; poss midges; gd site." ♦ 1 Apr-31 Oct. € 20.00   2013*

GERMANY

COCHEM *3B2* (6km SE Rural) *50.10999, 7.23542*
Campingplatz Happy-Holiday, Moselweinstrasse, 56821
Ellenz-Poltersdorf [(02673) 1272; fax 962367;
www.camping-happy-holiday.de] Fr Cochem, take B49 S
to Ellenz; site sp on bank of Rv Mosel. Med, pt sl, shd; htd wc;
chem disp; shwrs €1; EHU (6A) metered; gas; lndry (inc dryer);
sm shop; rest, snacks; bar; pool 300m; fishing; watersports;
wifi; 70% statics; dogs €1; poss cr; Eng spkn; quiet but rd &
rv noise. "Pleasant situation; gd value rest; clean facs; conv
touring base." 1 Apr-31 Oct. € 15.00   2014*

COCHEM *3B2* (7km SE Rural) *50.08231, 7.20796* **Camping
Holländischer Hof, Am Campingplatz 1, 56820 Senheim
[(02673) 4660; fax 4100; holl.hof@t-online.de;
www.moselcamping.com]** Fr Cochem take B49 twd Traben-
Trarbach; after approx 15km turn L over rv bdge sp Senheim;
site on rv island. Med, mkd pitch, pt shd; wc; chem disp; mv
service pnt; baby facs; shwrs €0.85; EHU (6-10A) metered;
lndry; gas; shop & 1km; rest, snacks; bar; playgrnd; rv sw adj;
tennis; wifi at office; 20% statics; no dogs; phone; poss cr;
Eng spkn; adv bkg; quiet; debit card acc; red long stay; CKE/
CCI. "Pleasant, well-run site; beautiful location; helpful staff;
sm pitches on loose pebbles; excel cycle paths; poss flooding
when wet weather/high water; poss overcr." ♦ 15 Apr-1 Nov.
€ 16.00   2012*

COCHEM *3B2* (8km SE Rural) *50.13253, 7.23029*
Campingplatz Bruttig, Am Moselufer, 56814 Bruttig-
Fankel [(02671) 915429; www.campingplatz-bruttig.
de] Leave Cochem on B49 twd Trier. In 8km turn L over bdge
to Bruttig-Fankel. Thro vill, site on R on banks Rv Mosel. Sm,
mkd pitch, pt shd; htd wc; chem disp; shwrs €0.50; EHU (16A)
metered; lndry; snacks; bar; playgrnd; rv sw adj; 50% statics;
phone; Eng spkn; quiet. "Pleasant site in pretty vill; gd walking,
cycling." Easter-31 Oct. € 14.00   2009*

COCHEM *3B2* (6km S Rural) *50.0804, 7.19298* **Campingplatz
Nehren, Moselufer 1, 56820 Nehren [(02673) 4612;
fax 962825; info@campingplatz-nehren.de;
www.campingplatz-nehren.de]** Fr Cochem take B49 twd
Bernkastel-Kues site on rv bank at ent to Nehren - 15km by
rd. Lge, mkd pitch, pt sl, pt shd; htd wc; chem disp; mv service
pnt; shwrs inc; EHU (6A) €2.20; lndry (inc dryer); shop; rest
100m; snacks; bar; boat-launching; 40% statics; dogs €1.20;
bus adj; poss cr; Eng spkn; adv bkg; quiet; red CKE/CCI. "V
pleasant setting; san facs up 2 flights stairs; helpful owners;
poss flooding at high water; poss midges; excel cycle paths
along Mosel." 1 Apr-24 Oct. € 20.00   2011*

COCHEM *3B2* (7km S Rural) *50.09162, 7.16319*
Campingplatz zum Feuerberg, 56814 Ediger-Eller
[(02675) 701; fax 911211; prokop@zum-feuerberg.de;
www.zum-feuerberg.de] On A49 fr Cochem to Bernkastel
Kues, just bef vill of Ediger on L - 17km by rd. Lge, hdg/mkd
pitch, pt shd; wc; chem disp; mv service pnt; shwrs €0.90; EHU
(16A) metered + conn fee; gas; lndry; shop adj; snacks; bar;
playgrnd; pool; boat mooring; bike hire; internet; 40% statics;
dogs €2; phone; bus, train to Cochem; Eng spkn; adv bkg;
quiet; CKE/CCI. "Well-kept site in lovely area; charming vill;
helpful staff; facs at 1st floor level; gd selection of rests &
pubs; rv bus high ssn; gd touring base; gd." 1 Apr-31 Oct.
€ 16.50   2010*

⊞ **COLBITZ** *2E3* (3km NE Rural) *52.33158, 11.63123*
Campingplatz Heide-Camp, Angerschestrasse, 39326
Colbitz [(039207) 80291; fax 80593; info@heide-camp-
colbitz.de; www.heide-camp-colbitz.de] Exit A2/E30 junc
70 onto B189 N dir Stendal. In Colbitz foll sp Angern. Site in
2km. Lge, mkd pitch, pt shd; wc; chem disp; mv service pnt;
shwrs inc; EHU (6-16A) metered + conn fee; gas; lndry; shop,
rest adj; snacks; playgrnd; games area; 20% statics; dogs
€2.80; Eng spkn; adv bkg; quiet; ccard acc, red CKE/CCI. "Site
on woodland, lge pitches." ♦ € 19.00   2014*

COLDITZ *2F4* (4km E Rural) *51.13083, 12.83305*
Campingplatz am Waldbad, Im Tiergarten 5, 04680
Colditz [tel/fax (034381) 43122; info@campingplatz-
colditz.de; www.campingplatz-colditz.de] Fr Leipzig A14
to Grimma, foll B107 to Colditz. Cross rv, foll B176 sp Dobeln.
Turn L immed bef town exit sp. After 1km turn R at camping
sp. Foll track thro woods for 500m, site on R immed after
sw pool. Med, pt sl, pt shd; wc; chem disp; sauna; shwrs €2;
EHU (10A) inc; shop 1km; sm rest & 500m; leisure cent/pool
adj; 30% statics; dogs €1; phone; quiet but some daytime
noise fr leisure cent adj; some Eng spkn; red CKE/CCI. "V
nice peaceful site; gd clean facs; gd value; tight turn into site
fr narr rd; helpful, friendly manager & staff; 30 mins walk to
Colditz Castle; sm rest 200m; new chem point." 1 Apr-30 Sep.
€ 19.00   2015*

COLOGNE see Köln *1B4*

COSWIG *2G4* (1km W Rural) *51.12055, 13.56388*
Campingplatz am Badesee Coswig-Kötitz,
Brockwitzerstrasse 33, 01640 Coswig-Kötitz
[(03523) 700220; camping@tw-coswig.de;
www.campingplatz-coswig.de] Exit A4 junc 79 onto S82
dir Meissen for 9km. Pass Autocentre Coswig & under rlwy
bdge then in 400m turn L into Brockwitzerstrasse. Foll sp to
site. Med, hdg pitch, pt shd; htd wc; chem disp; mv service pnt;
serviced pitches; shwrs inc; EHU (10A) €2.20; lndry (inc dryer);
shop 2km; rest, snacks; bar; BBQ; playgrnd; pool; paddling
pool; lake sw adj; games area; 10% statics; dogs €1.70; bus
2km; Eng spkn; quiet; CKE/CCI. "Adj Rv Elbe & cycle path
to Dresden & Meissen; gd touring area; easy access to lge
pitches." ♦ 1 Apr-31 Oct. € 15.60   2010*

CREGLINGEN *3D2* (3.5km S Rural) *49.43945, 10.04210*
Campingpark Romantische Strasse, Münster 67, 97993
Creglingen-Münster [(07933) 20289; fax 990019; camping.
hausotter@web.de; www.camping-romantische-strasse.
de] Fr E43 exit A7/junc 105 at Uffenheim. At edge of
Uffenheim turn R in dir of Bad Mergentheim; in approx 17km
at T-junc turn L for Creglingen, thro vill & then R sp Münster
with camping sp - approx 8km further. Site on R after Münster.
(Avoid rte bet Rothenburg & Creglingen as includes some v
narr vills & coaches). Med, pt shd; 10% serviced pitches; htd
wc; chem disp; mv service pnt; baby facs; sauna; shwrs inc;
EHU (6A) €2.20; lndry (inc dryer); shop; rest, snacks; bar; BBQ;
playgrnd; htd, covrd pool; paddling pool; lake fishing; bike
hire; wifi; 20% statics; dogs €1; phone; clsd 1300-1500; poss
cr; quiet; debit card acc (surcharge); red CKE/CCI. "Site ent
needs care; helpful owner; lovely welcome; excel rest & facs;
Romantische Strasse with interesting medieval churches locally;
gd cent for historic towns; gd value; facs stretched high ssn;
poss long walk fr facs." ♦ ltd. 15 Mar-15 Nov. € 24.00   2014*

DAHME *2E1* (1.5km N Coastal) *54.24254, 11.08030*
Camping Stieglitz, Im Feriengebiet Zedano, 23747 Dahme
[(04364) 1435; fax 470401; info@camping-stieglitz.de;
www.camping-stieglitz.de] Exit A1/E47 junc 12 at Lensahn
E twd coast. Fr B501 foll sp Dahme-Nord to sea wall, site sp.
Lge, mkd/hdg pitch; pt shd; htd wc; chem disp; mv service pnt;
baby facs; shwrs €0.50; EHU (16A) €2.60 or metered; lndry
(inc dryer); shop; rest; playgrnd; sand beach 200m; fishing;
watersports; bike hire; wifi; entmnt; TV rm; 50% statics; dogs
(not Jul-Aug) €5; adv bkg; ccard acc; quiet. "Excel site." ♦
26 Mar-24 Oct & 5-31 Dec. € 32.50   2013*

DAHN *3B3* (500m W Rural) *49.14416, 7.76805*
Campingplatz Büttelwoog, Am Campingplatz 1, 66994
Dahn [(06391) 5622; fax 5326; buettelwoog@t-online.de;
www.camping-buettelwoog.de] Fr rte 10 Pirmasens-
Karlsruhe turn S at traff lts at Hinterweidenthal onto B427 to
Dahn. In Dahn cent turn R, foll Youth Hostel sp; over single
track rlwy & up hill; site on R in 500m, clearly sp opp Youth
Hostel (Jugendherberge). Med, terr, pt shd; wc; chem disp;
mv service pnt; shwrs inc; EHU (4A) inc (rev pol); gas; lndry;
shop; sm rest, snacks; bar; playgrnd; covrd pool adj; bike hire;
10% statics; dogs €3; Quickstop o'night facs; poss cr; Eng
spkn; adv bkg; quiet; red CKE/CCI. "Welcoming, informal site;
clsd to arr 1200-1400 & 2200-0800; facs dated & stretched
high ssn; picturesque area; gd walks fr site." ♦ 15 Mar-4 Nov.
€ 31.00   2013*

⊞ **DAUN** *3B2* (7km SE Rural) *50.13540, 6.92219* **Feriendorf
Pulvermaar, Auf der Maarhöhe, Vulkanstrasse, 54558
Gillenfeld [(06573) 287; info@feriendorf-pulvermaar.de;
www.feriendorf-pulvermaar.de]** Fr A1/A48/E44 exit junc
121 onto B421 dir Zell/Mosel. After approx 5km turn R to
Pulvermaar, site sp nr lakeside. Med, sl, pt shd; wc; chem disp;
shwrs inc; EHU (16A) metered + conn fee; lndry; shop; snacks;
BBQ; playgrnd; pool; fishing adj; games area; 60% statics; dogs
€1; Eng spkn; adv bkg; quiet; CKE/CCI. "Conv Mosel valley &
Weinstrasse; attractive site." € 17.00   2010*

⊞ **DAUN** *3B2* (9km NW Rural) *50.25483, 6.77946*
Campingpark Zur Oberen Mühle, Mühlenweg,
54552 Dockweiler [(06595) 961130; fax 961131; info@
campingpark-dockweiler-muehle.de; www.campingpark-
dockweiler-muehle.de] Exit A1/A48 at junc 121 onto B421
dir Daun & Gerolstein. Site sp at ent to Dockweiler vill. Lge,
terr, unshd; wc; chem disp; mv service pnt; shwrs €0.50; EHU
(16A) inc; lndry; gas; shop 500m; rest high ssn; BBQ; playgrnd;
covrd pool; 60% statics; dogs €2; sep car park; ccard acc; red
long stay/snr citizens; quiet. ♦ € 23.50   2009*

DAUSENAU see Bad Ems *3B2*

DEGGENDORF *4G3* (1.5km W Rural) *48.83083, 12.94611*
Camping Donaustrandhaus, Egingerstrasse 42, 94469
Deggendorf [(0991) 4324; fax 4349; hirt.hj@t-online.de]
Exit A3 junc 110 onto A92. Exit junc 25 Deggendorf. At N end
of bdge bear R sp Stadtmitte & foll sp 'Festplatz'. Sm, pt shd;
wc; chem disp; shwrs €0.50; EHU (16A) €1.50; lndry; rest,
snacks; htd pool 1km; sw 5km; fishing; boating; tennis adj;
60% statics; dogs €1.50; bus; poss cr; some noise fr barges &
rlwy; CKE/CCI. "Gd NH; check earth on EHU." 1 Mar-31 Oct.
€ 14.50   2009*

⊞ **DEGGENDORF** *4G3* (8km NW Rural) *48.91533, 12.8860*
Campingland Bernrieder Winkl, Grub 6, 94505 Bernried
[tel/fax (09905) 8574; campingland.bernried@vr-web.de;
www.camping-bernried.de] Exit A3/E56 junc 108 or 109 &
foll sp Bernried. Site at S ent to vill. Sm, hdg/mkd pitch, hdstg,
terr, pt shd; htd wc; chem disp; mv service pnt; fam bthrm;
serviced pitches; shwrs; EHU (10A) metered + conn fee; lndry
(inc dryer); shop 1km; rest, snacks; bar; BBQ; playgrnd; tennis;
50% statics; dogs €2.50; adv bkg; quiet; red long stay. "Excel,
well-organised, attractive site in National Park; gd walking,
cycling, skiing; conv Passau, Regensburg; helpful owner." ♦
€ 19.50   2011*

"That's changed – Should I let The Club know?"

If you find something on site that's different from
the site entry, fill in a report and let us know. See
www.caravanclub.co.uk/europereport.

⊞ **DESSAU** *2F3* (5km E Rural) *51.81206, 12.30973*
Campingplatz Adria, Waldbad Adria 1, 06842 Dessau-
Mildensee [(0340) 2304810; fax 2508774; info@cuct.
de; www.cuct.de] Exit A9 junc 10 Dessau-Ost onto B185
dir Oranienbaum, site sp almost immed on R; down track,
on lakeside. Sm, pt shd; htd wc; chem disp; shwrs €1; EHU
(16A) €2.50; lndry; snacks; bar; sand beach & lake sw 150m;
90% statics; no dogs; sep car park; little rd noise. "Excel
touring base; vg." ♦ € 16.00   2009*

DETTELBACH *3D2* (6km S Rural) *49.82603, 10.20083*
Camping Katzenkopf, Am See, 97334 Sommerach
[(09381) 9215; fax 6028; www.camping-katzenkopf.de]
Fr A7/E45 junc 101 dir Volkach. Cross rv & foll sp S to
Sommerach, site sp. Fr S exit A3/E43 junc 74 dir Volkach &
foll sp. NB Town unsuitable c'vans; foll site sps bef town ent
(beware - Sat Nav rte poss thro town). Lge, pt shd; wc; chem
disp; mv service pnt; baby facs; shwrs inc; EHU (16A) €2.50
or metered; gas; lndry; shop; rest, snacks; playgrnd; lake sw &
beach; fishing & boating; golf 10km; dogs €2; poss v cr; no adv
bkg; quiet; ccard acc; red LS/CKE/CCI. "Beautiful surroundings;
sm pitches; clean, modern facs; m'van o'night area outside site;
barrier clsd 1300-1500; easy walk to wine-growing vill; gd rest;
gd NH nr A3." ♦ 1 Apr-25 Oct. € 21.60   2012*

DIERHAGEN STRAND see Ribnitz Damgarten *2F1*

DIESSEN *4E4* (1.5km N Rural) *47.96528, 11.10308* **Camping
St Alban am Ammersee, Seeweg Süd 85, 86911 St Alban
[(08807) 7305; fax 1057; ivian.pavic@t-online.de;
www.camping-ammersee.de]** Exit A96 junc 29 & foll rd S
to Diessen; site on L 150m after Diessen town sp. Med, unshd;
wc; chem disp; baby facs; shwrs inc; EHU (16A) inc; lndry;
rest; lake sw; shgl beach; boating; windsurfing; games rm;
60% statics; dogs €1; train nr; Eng spkn; adv bkg; ccard acc.
"Friendly helpful staff; excel rest; clsd 1200-1400; gd, immac
san facs." ♦ 15 Mar-15 Oct. € 34.00   2013*

DINGELSDORF see Konstanz *3D4*

GERMANY

⊞ **DINKELSBUHL** *3D3* (2km NNE Rural) *49.08194, 10.33416* DCC Campingpark Romantische Strasse, Kobeltsmühle6, 91550 Dinkelsbühl [(09851) 7817; fax 7848; campdinkelsbuehl@aol.com; www.campingplatz-dinkelsbuehl.de] On Rothenburg-Dinkelsbühl rd 25. Turn sharp L at camp sp immed bef rlwy x-ing (at Jet petrol stn) at N end of town. Site on R in 1km on lakeside. Or exit A7/E43 junc 112; turn R at T-junc. Site well sp. Lge, mkd pitch, terr, pt shd; wc; chem disp; mv service pnt; baby facs; shwrs inc; EHU (16A) metered; gas; lndry; sm shop; rest, snacks; bar; playgrnd; lake sw; boating; internet; 40% statics; dogs €1; phone; dog-washing facs; site clsd 1300-1500 & 2200-0800; m'van o'night area with EHU; adv bkg; quiet; 10% red CKE/CCI. "Pitches poss long way fr san facs; gd, modern san facs; NH area with easy access; m'van o'night area; close to beautiful medieval town; quiet, peaceful, well-equipped & well-managed site; excel rest; gd cycle paths in area; gd." ♦ € 23.00   2014*

DOCKWEILER see Daun *3B2*

⊞ **DONAUESCHINGEN** *3C4* (2km SE Rural) *47.93754, 8.53422* Riedsee-Camping, Am Riedsee 11, 78166 Donaueschingen [(0771) 5511; fax 15138; info@riedsee-camping.de; www.riedsee-camping.de] Fr Donaueschingen on B31 to Pfohren vill, site sp. Lge, mkd pitch, pt shd; wc; chem disp; mv service pnt; shwrs inc; EHU (16A) metered (check fr rev pol); lndry; shop (poss ltd opening); rest, snacks; bar; lake sw; boating; tennis; bike hire; golf 9km; entmnt; 90% statics; dogs €3.50; Eng spkn; ccard acc; CKE/CCI. "Vg facs; clean, well-run site; sm pitches; site busy at w/end; office clsd Mon (poss LS only); gd value rest; conv Danube cycle way." ♦ ltd. € 19.50   2011*

⊞ **DONAUWORTH** *4E3* (5km SE Rural) *48.67660, 10.84100* Donau-Lech Camping, Campingweg 1, 86698 Eggelstetten [tel/fax (09090) 4046; info@donau-lech-camping.de; www.donau-lech-camping.de] Fr B2 take Eggelstetten exit & foll sp to vill. Site immed bef vill on R, foll 'Int'l Camping' sp. Med, hdg/mkd pitch, hdstg, pt shd; htd wc; chem disp; mv service pnt; shwrs inc; EHU (16A) inc (some rev pol); gas; lndry; shop adj; rest 200m; bar; playgrnd; lake sw; boat hire; golf, horseriding & fishing nr; archery; wifi; 80% statics; dogs €2.20; phone; site clsd Nov; Eng spkn; adv bkg; v quiet; no ccard acc; CKE/CCI. "Superb, well-maintained, site but poss unkempt & boggy LS; ltd area for tourers; friendly, helpful staff & owner; facs clean but update req; owner sites vans; conv base for touring Danube & Romantic Rd; nr Danube cycle way." € 24.00   2014*

DORNSTETTEN HALLWANGEN see Freudenstadt *3C3*

⊞ **DORSEL** *3B2* (1km W Rural) *50.37708, 6.79768* Camping Stahlhütte an der Ahr, 53533 Dorsel [(02693) 438; fax 511; www.campingplatz-stahlhuette.de] Take B258 SE fr Blankenheim dir Nürburgring for approx 12km to Dorsel vill. Site on W side of rd. Med, hdg shd; wc; chem disp; serviced pitch; shwrs €0.75; EHU (16A) metered; lndry; shop; rest, snacks; bar; playgrnd; bike hire; golf 10km; 60% statics; dogs €2.50; barrier clsd 1300-1500 & 2130-0730; ccard not acc; red CKE/CCI. € 20.00   2009*

⊞ **DORTMUND** *1B4* (10km SE Rural) *51.42078, 7.49514* Camping Hohensyburg, Syburger Dorfstrasse 69, 44265 Dortmund-Hohensyburg [(0231) 774374; fax 7749554; info@camping-hohensyburg.de; www.camping-hohensyburg.de] Exit Dortmund a'bahn ring at Dortmund Sud onto B54 sp Hohensyburg. Foll dual c'way S & strt at next traff lts. Turn L twd Hohensyburg, up hill to Y junc. Turn L (camping sp) & cont over hill to Gasthof. Turn R immed bef Gasthof down narr, steep rd (sharp bends) to site in 100m. Lge, pt sl, pt shd; wc; chem disp; mv service pnt; shwrs inc; EHU (10A) €2.50 or metered; lndry; shop; rest; playgrnd; boat launch adj; golf 3km; 80% statics; dogs €3; poss cr; adv bkg; quiet, but some aircraft noise; "Lovely, friendly site; narr lane at ent not suitable lge o'fits; excel, clean san facs; gd." € 23.00   2011*

DORUM *1C2* (6km NE Coastal) *53.73938, 8.51680* Knaus Campingpark Dorum, Am Kuterhafen, 27632 Dorum/Neufeld [0049 4741 5020; dorum@knauscamp.de; www.knauscamp.de] Fr A27 Bremerhaven-Cuxhaven, take exit 4 to Dorum. Then foll signs to Dorum-Neufeld. Cont over dyke to harbour, campsite on R. Lge, unshd; wc; chem disp; mv service pnt; shwrs; EHU (6A); lndry (inc dryer); snacks; playgrnd; grass beach adj; bike hire; 40% statics; dogs; bus 0.5km; twin axles; Eng spkn; adv bkg; CCI. "Vg; temporary ssnal site; scenic fishing port." 1 Apr-30 Sep. € 41.00 (CChq acc)   2014*

DRAGE see Geesthacht *1D2*

⊞ **DRANSFELD** *1D4* (1km S Rural) *51.49177, 9.76180* Camping am Hohen Hagen, Hoher-Hagenstrasse 12, 37127 Dransfeld [(05502) 2147; fax 47239; camping.lesser@t-online.de; www.campingplatz-dransfeld.de] Exit A7 junc 73 onto B3 to Dransfeld; foll sp to S of town & site. Lge, mkd pitch, terr, pt shd; htd wc; chem disp; mv service pnt; baby facs; sauna; shwrs inc; EHU (16A) metered + conn fee; gas; lndry (inc dryer); shop; rest, snacks; BBQ; cooking facs; playgrnd; htd pool; paddling pool; waterslide; tennis 100m; games area; wifi; entmnt; 95% statics; dogs €1.50; o'night area for m'vans; Eng spkn; quiet; ccard acc. "Beautiful area; gd san facs; diff after heavy rain; helpful staff." ♦ € 17.00   2009*

DRESDEN *2G4* (7km N Rural) *51.13833, 13.71861* Campingplatz Oberer Waldteich - Dresden Nord, Sandweg, 01471 Volkersdorf [(035207) 81469; fax 81499; kontakt@dresden-camping.com] Exit A4/E40 junc 81A (Dresden-Flughafen) onto S81 W - Wilschdorfer Landstrasse. In approx 600m turn R at x-rds dir Volkersdorf, then L to site on lakeside, sp. Med, hdg pitch, pt sl, shd; wc; chem disp; shwrs inc; EHU (16A) or mtrd (poss rev pol); lndry (inc dryer); shop; snacks; bar; BBQ; playgrnd; lake sw; 60% statics; dogs €1; adv bkg; quiet; CKE/CCI. "Gd; poss cr at w/end; touring pitch at lake v attractive; san facs v clean but poss a bit distant; little Eng spkn." 1 Apr-31 Oct. € 21.50   2014*

Check any essential information with the site before you travel   *Last year of report   **247**

DRESDEN *2G4* (17km NE Rural) *51.12027, 13.98000*
**Camping- und Freizeitpark Lux Oase, Arnsdorferstrasse
1, 01900 Kleinröhrsdorf [(035952) 56666; fax 56024;
info@luxoase.de; www.luxoase.de]** Leave A4/E40 at junc
85 dir Radeberg. S to Leppersdorf, Kleinröhrsdorf. Sp on L
end vill, well sp fr a'bahn. Lge, mkd pitch, pt shd; wc; chem
disp; mv service pnt; fam bthrm; some serviced pitches; baby
facs; sauna; shwrs; EHU (10A) inc; gas; lndry (inc dryer);
shop; rest, snacks; bar; BBQ; playgrnd; covrd pool; fitness
cent; beach adj; lake sw adj; fishing; horseriding; bike hire;
games area; wifi; entmnt; games/TV rm; 30% statics; dogs
€3.50; twin-axles acc (rec check in adv); bus to city; trains
3km; poss v cr w/end; Eng spkn; quiet; ccard acc; red LS/long
stay/CKE/CCI. "Excel site by lake; vg san facs; new luxury san
facs 2011; v helpful staff; gd rest; site bus to Dresden Tues -
15 mins walk to reg bus; weekly bus to Prague fr site & other
attractions in easy reach; new spa 2013." ♦ 1 Jan-31Dec.
€ 33.60 SBS - G14   2014*

See advertisement inside the front cover

DRESDEN *2G4* (16km SE Rural) *50.99839, 13.86919*
**Campingplatz Wostra, At 7 Wostra, 01259 Dresden
[(351) 201 3254; cp-wostra@freenet.de; www.dresden.de]**
Take exit 6 fr E55 Prague-Dresden in dir of Pirna, then take
B172 Dresden-Pirna to Heidenau, foll sp to site. Med, pt shd;
htd wc; chem dis; shwrs; EHU (16A); lndry; BBQ; cooking facs;
htd pool; games rm; bus/tram adj; twin axles; Eng spkn; ccard
acc; red LS; CKE/CCI. "Excel quiet site." ♦ ltd. 1 Apr-31 Oct.
€ 20.00   2012*

DRESDEN *2G4* (4.5km S Urban) *51.01416, 13.7500*
**Campingplatz Mockritz, Boderitzerstrasse 30, 01217
Dresden-Mockritz [(0351) 4715250; fax 4799227; camping-
dresden@t-online.de; www.camping-dresden.de]**
Exit E65/A17 junc 3 onto B170 N sp Dresden. In approx 1.5km
turn E at traff lts sp Zschernitz, site sp. Med, mkd pitch, pt sl, pt
shd; htd wc; chem disp; mv service pnt; baby facs; shwrs €0.50;
EHU (10A) €2.70; lndry; shop; rest, snacks; bar; pool; wifi;
bus; quiet; 5% statics; dogs €1; site clsd Christmas to end Jan;
poss cr w/ends; Eng spkn; CKE/CCI. "V conv city cent & buses;
poss muddy after rain; helpful staff; excel; office clsd 1300-
1600 find a pitch and inform recep." ♦ ltd. 30 Jan-22 Dec.
€ 25.00   2013*

DROLSHAGEN see Olpe *1B4*

DULMEN *1B3* (3km S Rural) *51.78757, 7.27186* **Camping
Tannenwiese, 217 Borkenbergstrasse, 48249 Dülmen
[(02594) 991759; www.camping-tannenwiese.de]**
Fr A43 take junc 7 Haltern/Lavesum dir Dülmen. In Hausdülmen
foll sp Flugplatz Borkenberge to site in approx 3km. Med, hdg/
mkd pitch, pt shd; wc; chem disp; shwrs €0.50; EHU (10A)
€2.10 or metered; gas; lndry (inc dryer); shop & 3km; rest 2km;
playgrnd; 80% statics; dogs free; CKE/CCI. "Tidy & tranquil; lge
pitches; gd for families with sm children; away fr main rds; sep
area for tourers." 1 Mar-31 Oct. € 13.00   2010*

DUSSELDORF *1B4* (10km SE Rural) *51.19921, 6.88630*
**Campingplatz Unterbacher See/Nord, Kleiner Torfbruch
31, 40627 Düsseldorf [(0211) 8992038; fax 8929132;
service@unterbachersee.de; www.unterbachersee.de]**
Fr A3 turn W onto A46 dir Düsseldorf/Neuss & exit junc 27
to Erkrath/Unterbach. Foll sp Unterbacher See Nordufer to
harbour, site sp. Lge, pt shd; wc; chem disp; mv service pnt;
sauna; shwrs; EHU (6A) €2; gas; lndry; shop 500m; rest 200m;
snacks; gas BBQ only; playgrnd; boating & sw in adj lake;
games area; bike hire; 60% statics; no dogs; poss cr; adv bkg.
"Gd NH; pitches close together & poss cr; gd san facs; gd rest
& lake nrby." ♦ 3 Apr-24 Oct. € 23.50   2009*

⊞ **DUSSELDORF** *1B4* (1.5km NW Rural) *51.25225, 6.72813*
**Campingplatz Nord, Niederkasseler Deich 305, 40547
Düsseldorf-Lörick [tel/fax (0211) 591401; duesselcamp@
web.de; www.duesselcamp.de]** Fr city take rd 52 to
Monchengladbach & turn R at sp Düsseldorf-Oberkassel &
Düsseldorf-Lörick. Turn L at traff lts, then strt on at next traff
lts. In 1.5km turn R at traff lts (camping sp). Foll cobbled rd to
site. Fr E, cross Theodor Heuss Brücke (bdge) & immed after
bdge fork R then in 1.5km turn R at traff lts, then as above.
Med, shd; wc; snacks; shwrs €1; EHU (4A) €3; lndry; shop
2km; 2 pools & lake adj; bus to city nr; poss cr; 10% statics;
dogs €3; noise fr adj airport; CKE/CCI. "Conv NH; ltd facs LS."
€ 16.00   2011*

DUSSELDORF *1B4* (19.5km NNW Urban) *51.30180, 6.72560*
**Rheincamping Meerbusch (formerly Azur Campingplatz),
Zur Rheinfähre 21, 40668 Meerbusch [(02150) 911817;
fax 707571; info@rheincamping.com; www.
rheincamping.com]** Exit A44 junc 28, turn R twd Strümp.
Thro vill, turn L at sp for Kaiserswerth ferry, site on rv. Lge,
pt shd; htd wc; chem disp; mv service pnt; baby facs; shwrs
inc; EHU (10A) €3.20; gas; lndry; shop; rest adj; snacks; bar;
BBQ; playgrnd; boat slipway; wifi; 40% statics; dogs €2.80;
ferry/tram; site may flood when rv at v high level; poss cr;
Eng spkn; adv bkg; some rv noise; CKE/CCI. "Pleasant, busy,
well-organised, open site with gd views of Rv Rhine; all facs up
steps; ferry x-ring rv, then tram/train to Dusseldorf; long lead
req'd; gd NH."
4 Apr-12 Oct. € 25.00   2014*

EBERBACH *3C2* (9km SW Rural) *49.45241, 8.87816*
**Odenwald Camping Park, Langenthalerstrasse 80, 69434
Hirschhorn-am-Neckar [(06272) 809; fax 3658; odenwald-
camping-park@t-online.de; www.odenwald-camping-
park.de]** Fr Eberbach or Neckargemünd leave B37/45 for
Hirschorn; foll Int'l Camping sps at Hirschhorn Cent (not
Hirschhorn Ost); site on L in 2km NW of town on Heddesbach
rd L3105. Med, mkd pitch, pt shd; wc; chem disp; mv service
pnt; sauna; shwrs inc; EHU (6A) €2.50 or metered; gas; lndry;
shop; rest; bar; playgrnd; htd pool; tennis; bike hire; cab
TV; 50% statics; dogs €2.50; quiet; ccard not acc; CKE/CCI.
"Friendly, helpful staff; sep area for 20 tourers." ♦
1 Apr-4 Oct. € 18.50   2009*

EBERBACH *3C2* (W Urban) *49.46068, 8.98241* **Campingpark Eberbach, Alte Pleutersbacherstrasse 8, 69412 Eberbach [(06271) 1071; fax 942712; info@campingpark-eberbach. de; www.campingpark-eberbach.de]** Fr Heidelberg-Heilbronn rd B37, ent Eberbach & cross Rv Neckar, turn R at end of bdge. Site 100m on rv bank, sp. Med, pt sl, pt shd; htd wc; chem disp; shwrs €0.50; EHU (6A) €2.50; lndry (inc dryer); shops adj; rest; playgrnd; htd pools adj; 10% statics; dogs €2; poss cr w/end; adv bkg; some rd & rlwy noise at night; CKE/CCI. "Rv cruises fr opp bank; ferry adj; annual fair last week Aug; excel cycling; NB - cash only."
1 Apr-31 Oct. € 16.70   2011*

ECHTERNACHERBRUCK *3A2* (500m E Rural) *49.81240, 6.43160* **Camping Freibad Echternacherbrück, Mindenerstrasse 18, 54668 Echternacherbrück [(06525) 340; fax 93155; info@echternacherbrueck.de; www.echternacherbrueck.de]** Fr Bitburg on B257/E29 site is at Lux'burg border, sp. Fr Trier take A64 dir Luxembourg; exit junc 15 onto N10 to Echternacherbrück; cross bdg dir Bitburg, then 1st L sp camping & foll sp. Lge, pt shd; htd wc; chem disp; mv service pnt; private bthrms avail; baby facs; shwrs inc; EHU (10A) €2.70 + conn fee; lndry (inc dryer); shop 100m; rest 100m; snacks; bar; playgrnd; 2 htd pools 400m (1 covrd); paddling pool; waterslide; rv sw & sandy beach adj; tennis 400m; boat & bike hire; horseriding 4km; games area; wifi; entmnt; TV rm; 30% statics; dogs €4.70; o'night m'van area; Eng spkn; quiet; CKE/CCI. "Poss flooding in v wet weather; excel facs; gd, well-organised site; gd bus service to Luxembourg and Trier; ACSI card acc." ♦ 1 Apr-15 Oct.
€ 35.00 (CChq acc)   2013*

"I like to fill in the reports as I travel from site to site"
You'll find report forms at the back of this guide, or you can fill them in online at www.caravanclub.co.uk/europereport.

ECKERNFORDE *1D1* (12km NE Coastal) *54.50280, 9.95802* **Ostsee-Camping Gut Ludwigsburg, Ludwigsburg 4, 24369 Waabs [(49043) 58370; fax 58460; info@ostseecamping-ludwigsburg.de; www.ostseecamping-ludwigsburg.de]** Fr Eckernforde take coastal rd NE, sp Ludwigsburg & Waabs. Site sp in approx 12km on R; turn R down single track rd. Site in 2km. Lge, mkd pitch, hdstg, pt shd; wc; chem disp; mv service pnt; baby facs; shwrs; EHU (16A) €2; lndry (inc dryer); supmkt; rest; snacks; bar; bbq; playgrnd; beach adj; games area; games rm; entmnt; wifi; tv rm; 60% statics; dogs €2-6 (depending on size); twin-axle; Eng spkn; red LS; CKE/CCI. "Fishing in lake adj; excel san facs; horseriding & watersports adj; gd walking and cycling rtes nrby; gd site." ♦ ltd.
28 Mar-1 Oct. € 26.00   2014*

EDIGER ELLER see Cochem *3B2*

EGGELSTETTEN see Donauwörth *4E3*

⊞ EGING AM SEE *4G3* (1km NE Rural) *48.72135, 13.26540* **Bavaria Kur-Sport-Campingpark, Grafenauerstrasse 31, 94535 Eging [(08544) 8089; fax 7964; info@bavaria-camping.de; www.bavaria-camping.de]** Exit A3 junc 113 at Garham dir Eging, site sp in 4.5km twd Thurmansbang. Med, hdg/mkd pitch, some hdstg, pt sl, terr, pt shd; htd wc; chem disp; mv service pnt; baby facs; shwrs inc; EHU (16A) €2.50; lndry (inc dryer); shop; rest; bar; htd pool 700m; lake sw 700m; fishing; tennis; games area; bike hire; golf 10km; wifi; TV rm; 20% statics; dogs €2.60; Eng spkn; quiet; ccard add; red LS/CKE/CCI. "Lovely site nr Bavarian National Park; gd walking/cycling fr site; Wild West theme town, Pullman City, 2.5km; vg NH & longer; adj to Danube llz cycleway and other cycleways."
♦ € 29.00 (CChq acc)   2015*

⊞ EHRENBERG *3D1* (500m N Rural) *50.50653, 10.01065* **Rhön Camping Park, An der Ulster 1, 36115 Ehrenberg-Wüstensachsen [(06683) 1268; fax 1269; info@rhoen-camping-park.de; www.rhoen-camping-park.de]** Exit A7 junc 93 at Fulda onto B27 dir Bad Brückenau. In Döllbach turn L to Gersfeld & Ehrenberg. Site on R immed bef vill, well sp. Med, mkd pitch, pt shd; htd wc; chem disp; mv service pnt; baby facs;100% serviced pitches; sauna; shwrs €0.50; EHU (16A) metered; lndry; shop; rest 300m; BBQ; playgrnd; sm water theme park; solarium; gym; ski lift 5km; gliding 5km; TV; 25% statics; dogs €2.50; phone; adv bkg; quiet; CKE/CCI. "Gd walking; excel." ♦ € 21.00   2009*

EHRENFRIEDERSDORF see Annaberg Buchholz *4G1*

EISENACH *1D4* (10km S Rural) *50.90888, 10.29916* **Campingpark Eisenach am Altenberger See, Am Altenberger See, 99819 Wilhelmsthal [(03691) 215637; fax 215607; campingpark-eisenach@t-online.de; www.campingpark-eisenach.de]** Leave E40/A4 at junc 39 Eisenach Ost onto B19 sp Meiningen; site 2km S of Wilhelmsthal, sp. Med, pt sl, pt hdstg, pt shd; wc; chem disp; mv service pnt; serviced pitches; sauna; shwrs metered; EHU (16A) inc; lndry; shop; rest, snacks; bar; sm playgrnd; lake adj; boating; 80% statics; dogs €2; bus to Eisenach nr; clsd 1300-1500; site clsd Nov; poss cr; quiet; ccard acc; CKE/CCI. "Helpful staff; conv Wartburg & Thuringer Wald, Bach & Luther houses in Eisenach." 1 Jan-31 Oct & 1 Dec-31 Dec. € 28.00   2013*

ELBINGERODE see Wernigerode *2E3*

ENGEHAUSEN *1D3* (160m Rural) *52.68916, 9.69774* **Camping Aller-Leine-Tal, Marschweg 1, 29690 Engehausen [(05071) 511549; camping@camping-aller-leine-tal.de; www.camping-aller-leine-tal.de]** Exit A7/E45 at 'Rasthof Allertal', keep R & at x-rds turn L twd Celle. Site in 800m. Med, mkd pitch, pt shd; htd wc; chem disp; mv service pnt; baby facs; shwrs inc; EHU (10A) €3; lndry (inc dryer); supmkt 7km; rest 4km; snacks; bar; playgrnd; rv sw & fishing; games area; games rm; wifi; TV rm; 20% statics; dogs €2.50; Quickstop o'night facs; adv bkg; quiet. "Peaceful site conv m'way." 1 Mar-31 Oct. € 16.50   2009*

ENZKLOSTERLE see Bad Wildbad im Schwarzwald *3C3*

EPPSTEIN NIEDERJOSBACH see Frankfurt am Main *3C2*

⊞ **ERFURT** *4E1* (10.3km NW) *51.03895, 10.97870*
Campingplatz "Erfurt am See", Steinfeld 4, 99189 Erfurt-Kühnhausen [(0176) 517 52386; mail@erfurtamsee.de; www.erfurtamsee.de] Fr A71 take exit 9 twds Kühnhausen. Turn L onto August-Röbling-Straße. Turn L onto Kühnhäuser Str, turn R onto Steinfeld, site on L. Med, pt sl, unshd; htd wc; chem disp; shwrs €0.50; EHU; lndtte (inc dryer); rest; bar; beach adj; train 1km; quiet; CKE/CCI. "Basic clean site bet angling & sw lakes; conv for visiting Erfurt; no laundry rm; gd site." € 23.00   2014*

⊞ **ERKNER** *2G3* (3km S Rural) *52.38530, 13.78160* **Camping Jägerbude, Jägerbude 3, 15537 Erkner [(03362) 888084; fax 888094; post@spreecamping.de; www.spreecamping. de]** A10/E55 E of Berlin exit junc 7 Freienbrink to Erkner. Site sp on W side of a'bahn. Lge, hdg/mkd pitch, pt shd; htd wc; chem disp; mv service pnt; sauna; shwrs €0.50; EHU (16A) €3 or metered; lndry (inc dryer); shop; rest; BBQ; cooking facs; playgrnd; rv sw; games rm; wifi; few statics; dogs €2; poss cr; CKE/CCI. "Conv Berlin; some pitches lake view; gd NH." ♦ € 18.00   2010*

ERLANGEN *4E2* (7km NW Rural) *49.63194, 10.9425* **Camping Rangau, Campingstrasse 44, 91056 Erlangen-Dechsendorf [(09135) 8866; fax 724743; infos@camping-rangau.de; www.camping-rangau.de]** Fr A3/E45 exit junc 81 & foll camp sp. At 1st traff lts turn L, strt on at next traff lts, then L at next traff lts, site sp. Med, pt shd; htd wc; shwrs inc; chem disp; EHU (6A) €3 (long lead poss req); lndry; shop 2km; rest, snacks; playgrnd; pool; lake sw; boat hire; dogs €2.50; gates clsd 1300-1500 & 2200 hrs; poss cr; Eng spkn; adv bkg; quiet; ccard acc; red long stay/CKE/CCI. "Gd site, espec for families; clean facs; welcoming & well-run; some sm pitches; popular NH - overflow onto adj sports field; vg, busy NH; arrive early; dog wash facs." ♦ ltd. 1 Apr-15 Oct. € 28.50   2014*

⊞ **ERNST** *3B2* (800m W Rural) *50.1425, 7.23194*
Wohnmobil Parkplatz, Weingartenstrasse 97, 56814 Ernst [(02671) 980310; fax 980312; info@mosella-schinkenstube.de; www.mosella-schinkenstube.de] Site on o'skts of vill behind winery, sp fr B49. Sm, mkd pitch, hdstg, pt sl, unshd; EHU inc, wc; chem disp; mv service pnt; rest, snacks, bar adj; bus; poss cr; no adv bkg; quiet. "Gd NH for m'vans only; drinking water & rubbish points; pay at nrby butchers (Metzgerei-Gaststatte). € 8.00   2011*

⊞ **ESSEN** *1B4* (8km S Urban) *51.38444, 6.99388*
DCC Campingpark Stadtcamping, Im Löwental 67, 45239 Essen-Werden [(0201) 492978; fax 8496132; Stadtcamping-Essen@t-online.de; www.dcc-stadt camping-essen-werden.de] Exit A52 junc 28 onto B224 S dir Solingen. Turn R bef bdge over Rv Ruhr at traff lts & immed sharp R into Löwental, site sp. Med, mkd pitch, hdstg, pt shd; wc; chem disp; mv service pnt; shwrs; EHU (16A) metered; gas; lndry; shop; rest; bar; playgrnd; games area; games rm; 95% statics; no dogs; phone; poss cr; Eng spkn; adv bkg; site clsd 1300-1500 & 2130-0700; car park adj; quiet; no ccard acc. "Rv trips; poss itinerant workers; gd." € 16.40   2009*

ETTENHEIM see Lahr (Schwarzwald) *3B3*

⊞ **ETTLINGEN** *3C3* (5km SE Rural) *48.91465, 8.45567*
Campingplatz Albgau, Kochmühle 1, 76337 Waldbronn-Neurod [tel/fax 07243 61849; erwilux@gmx.de; www.campingplatzstueble-albgau-waldbronn.de] Exit A8/E52 at junc 42 & foll sp Bad Herrenalb. When rlwy on R, site sp in 4km on R. Lge, pt shd; wc; own san rec; chem disp; shwrs €0.50; EHU (16A) €2.30; gas; lndry (inc dryer); shop; snacks; bar; playgrnd; 90% statics; dogs €3; gates locked 1300-1500 & 2200-0700; quiet but poss noisy at w/end & fr rlwy; ccard not acc. "On edge of Black Forest; footpath walks in vicinity; adj field for NH; modern san facs; helpful owner; ltd facs in high ssn." ♦ € 33.60   2014*

⊞ **EXTERTAL** *1C3* (3km SW Rural) *52.05118, 9.10223*
Camping Extertal, Eimke 4, 32699 Extertal-Eimke [(05262) 3307; info@campingpark-extertal.de; www.campingpark-extertal.de] Fr Rinteln on B238 S twd Barntrup; about 1.5km S Bösingfeld turn L at sp to site over level x-ing. Med, hdg/mkd pitch, pt sl, pt shd; htd wc; chem disp; mv service pnt; serviced pitches; baby facs; shwrs inc; EHU (16A) €1.50 or metered; gas; lndry (inc dryer); shop; rest 500m; snacks high ssn; bar; cooking facs; playgrnd; pool; lake sw; games rm; wifi; entmnt; 90% statics in sep area; dogs €1.50; bus adj; some Eng spkn; quiet; red long stay; CKE/CCI. "Gd site; dry & well-drained in v wet weather; all facs clean; forest walks & cycle paths fr site; 80 touring pitches; gd facs; some rd noise in day; clsd 1300-1500." ♦ € 15.50   2015*

⊞ **FASSBERG** *1D2* (6km E Rural) *52.87593, 10.22718*
Ferienpark Heidesee (Part Naturist), Lüneburger-Heidesee, 29328 Fassberg-Oberohe [(05827) 970546; fax 970547; heidesee@ferienpark.de; www.camping heidesee.com] Leave A7/E45 at exit 44 onto B71. Turn S to Müden, then dir Unterlüss. Foll site sp. V lge, terr, pt shd; htd wc; chem disp; mv service pnt; sauna; private bthrms avail; baby facs; shwrs inc; EHU (10A) €3; lndry (inc dryer); gas; shop; rest, snacks; playgrnd; pool 250m; lake sw; fishing; tennis; bike hire; horseriding; games rm; entmnt; 65% statics; dogs €2; ccard acc; Eng spkn; quiet; CKE/CCI. "Naturist camping in sep area; long leads maybe req; friendly helpful staff; places of interest nrby; gd mkd cycling and walking rtes fr site." ♦ € 21.00 (CChq acc)   2014*

FEHMARN ISLAND *2E1* Sites on Fehmarn Island are listed together at the end of the Germany site entry pages.

⊞ **FELDBERG** *2G2* (2km NE Rural) *53.34548, 13.45626*
Camping am Bauernhof, Hof Eichholz 1-8, 17258 Feldberg [(039831) 21084; fax 21534; scholverberg@feldberg.de; www.campingplatz-am-bauernhof.de] Fr B198 at Möllenbeck turn dir Feldburg, thro Feldburg dir Prenzlau, site sp. Med, mkd pitch, pt sl, unshd; wc; chem disp; shwrs inc; EHU (16A) metered + conn fee; lndry; shop; rest 800m; snacks; playgrnd; lake sw; fishing; 30% statics; dogs €3; quiet; CKE/CCI. "Well-situated, vg site among lakes; many cycle paths in area." ♦ € 18.00   2011*

FERCH *2F3* (3km N Rural) *52.33122, 12.93105* **Campingplatz Neue Scheune, Fercherstrasse 55, Schwielowsee, 14548 Ferch [(033209) 70957; fax 70958; Camping-Neue-Scheune-Ferch@t-online.de; www.camping-schwielowsee.de]** Exit A10/E55 Berlin ring rd junc 18 twd Ferch. In Ferch foll sp Petzow & Neue Scheune. Site on L after stretch of rough cobbles. Sm, pt shd; htd wc; chem disp; shwrs; EHU (13A) €2.50; shop 2km; BBQ (gas only); playgrnd; games area; some statics; dogs €1.10; poss cr; Eng spkn; adv bkg; quiet; CKE/CCI. "Site on edge woodland on W side Schwielowsee; helpful staff; conv Potsdam." Easter-31 Oct. € 15.00   2009*

⊞ FICHTELBERG *4F2* (2.5km N Rural) *50.01673, 11.85525* **Kur-Camping Fichtelsee, Fichtelseestrasse 30, 95686 Fichtelberg [(09272) 801; fax 909045; info@camping-fichtelsee.de; www.camping-fichtelsee.de]** Exit junc 39 fr A9/E51. Foll B303 twd Marktredwitz. After Bischofsgrün take R turn sp Fichtelberg, site on L in 1km. Lge, mkd pitch, hdstg, terr, pt sl, pt shd; wc (some cont); chem disp; mv service pnt; shwrs inc; EHU (16A) metered + conn fee (poss rev pol); lndry; shop 2km; rest 200m; playgrnd; pool 800m; entmnt; internet; TV; 20% statics; dogs €2.50; dog-washing facs; phone; site clsd 7 Nov-15 Dec; Eng spkn; ccard acc; CKE/CCI. "Gd cent for walking in pine forests round lake & wintersports; peaceful site; barrier clsd 1230-1430; excel san facs." ◆ ltd. € 22.00   2009*

⊞ FINSTERAU *4G3* (1km N Rural) *48.94091, 13.57180* **Camping Nationalpark-Ost, Buchwaldstrasse 52, 94151 Finsterau [(08557) 768; fax 1062; berghof-frank@berghof-frank.de; www.camping-nationalpark-ost.de]** Fr B12 turn N dir Mauth. Cont to Finsterau & site 1km adj parking for National Park. Sm, pt shd; wc; chem disp; shwrs €1; EHU (6-16A) metered + conn fee or €2.50; gas; lndry (inc dryer); shop 1km; wifi; TV rm; dogs €2; quiet; red CKE/CCI. "Gd walking & mountain biking; site in beautiful Bavarian forest." ◆ € 17.60   2009*

⊞ FLOSSENBURG *4F2* (1.5km N Rural) *49.74457, 12.34414* **Camping Gaisweiher, Gaisweiher 1, 92696 Flossenbürg [(09603) 644; fax 914666; kontakt@gaisweiher-camping.de; www.campingauer-hellas.de]** Exit A93 to Neustadt. Take minor rd E thro Floss to Flossenbürg, site sp. Lge, pt sl, pt shd; wc; shwrs €0.50; chem disp; mv service pnt; EHU (16A) metered + conn fee; lndry; shop; rest, snacks; bar; playgrnd; sw adj; bike hire; entmnt high ssn; TV rm; 50% statics; dogs €2; quiet; CKE/CCI. "Recep 0930-1130, site self other times; barrier clsd 1300-1500; facs old & dark; gd." € 15.50   2009*

FRANKFURT AM MAIN *3C2* (8KM NE Rural) *50.81700, 8.46550* **Campingplatz Mainkur, Frankfurter Landstraße 107, 63477 Maintal [(069)-412193; campingplatz-mainkur@t-online.de; www.campingplatz-mainkur.de]** Fr Frankfurt head NE B4 and Hanua cross over A661 and cont over 8 sets of traff lts pass car showrooms and Bauhaus on L. 100m aft flyover bear R into single track tarmac rd to site. Sp on B8/B4. Med, mkd pitch, pt shd; wc; shwrs; lndry; mv waste disp; basic shop; bar; BBQ; 35% statics; dogs; bus 3km; adv bkg; Eng spkn; boating; playgrnd. "Family run site o'looking rv; conv for Frankfurt; vg, rec." ◆ ltd. 1 Apr-30 Sept. € 28.00   2012*

⊞ FRANKFURT AM MAIN *3C2* (30km W Rural) *50.14758, 8.36173* **Taunuscamp Hubertushof, Bezirkstrasse 2, 65817 Eppstein-Niederjosbach [(06198) 7000; fax 7002; info@taunuscamp.de; www.taunuscamp.de]** Fr A3/E35 exit junc 46 dir Niedernhausen B455 & foll sp for Eppstein (Niederjosbach). Fr B455 take minor rd K792 x-ing rlwy bef vill, foll rd & take 1st R into Bezierkstrasse, site on L in 1km. Med, mkd pitch, terr, pt shd; htd wc; chem disp; mv service pnt; 50% serviced pitch; shwrs inc; EHU (16A) €2 or metered; gas; lndry; shop & 500m; rest 1km; snacks; playgrnd; pool nr; 60% statics; dogs free; barrier closes 1300-1500; poss cr; Eng spkn; adv bkg; quiet; ccard acc; red long stay/CKE/CCI. "Friendly, pleasant site; steep terr diff for underpowered or long twin-axle o'fits; some sm pitches; excursions arranged." ◆ ltd. € 21.00   2009*

⊞ FRANKFURT AM MAIN *3C2* (9km NW Urban) *50.16373, 8.65055* **City-Camp Frankfurt, An der Sandelmühle 35b, 60439 Frankfurt Am Main [(069) 570332; fax 57003604; info@city-camp-frankfurt.de; www.city-camp-frankfurt.de]** Exit A661 junc 6 dir Heddernheim, site in park, sp. Med, hdstg, pt shd; wc; chem disp; mv service pnt; shwrs €1.10; EHU (10A) €3; gas; lndry; shop 800m; snacks 800m; rest 500m; 30% statics; dogs €2.50; poss cr; Eng spkn; poss noisy; CKE/CCI. "Conv for city via adj U-Bahn (20 min to cent); clean but dated; v busy when trade fair on; vg for visiting Frankfurt." ◆ ltd. € 28.50   2013*

FREIBURG IM BREISGAU *3B4* (21km NE Rural) *48.02318, 8.03253* **Camping Steingrubenhof, Haldenweg 3, 79271 St Peter [(07660) 210; fax 1604; info@camping-steingrubenhof.de; www.camping-steingrubenhof.de]** Exit A5 junc 61 onto B294. Turn R sp St Peter. Steep hill to site on L at top of hill. Or fr B31 dir Donaueschingen, after 4km outside Freiburg turn N sp St Peter; by-pass vill on main rd, turn L under bdge 1st R. Fr other dir by-pass St Peter heading for Glottertal; site on R 200m after rd bdge on by-pass. Med, hdg/mkd pitch, hdstg, pt terr, unshd; wc; chem disp; mv service pnt; serviced pitches; shwrs €0.50; EHU (16A); lndry (inc dryer); shop & 1km; rest & bar adj; BBQ; playgrnd; wifi; 70% statics; dogs €2; phone; Eng spkn; adv bkg; quiet; ccard acc; 10% red long stay; CKE/CCI. "Peaceful site in heart of Black Forest; wonderful location; pleasant staff; immac facs; gate clsd 1200-1400 & 2200-0800; v diff to manoeuvre twin-axle vans onto pitches as narr access paths; pitches are sm & few for tourers; great site." ◆ ltd. 1 Jan-10 Nov & 15 Dec-31 Dec. € 25.00   2014*

⊞ FREIBURG IM BREISGAU *3B4* (4km E Rural) *47.99250, 7.87330* **Camping Hirzberg, Kartäuserstrasse 99, 79104 Freiburg-im-Breisgau [(0761) 35054; fax 289212; hirzburg@freiburg-camping.de; www.freiburg-camping.de]** Exit A5 at Freiburg-Mitte & foll B31 past town cent sp Freiburg, Titisee. Foll camping sp twd Freiburg-Ebnet, nr rocky slopes on R. Then approx 2.5km on narr, winding rd. Site on R just after start of blocks of flats on L. Med, pt sl, terr, pt shd; htd wc; chem disp; mv service pnt; shwrs inc; EHU (10A) €2.50; gas; lndry; sm shop; rest, snacks; bar; BBQ; playgrnd; pool 500m; bike hire; internet; 40% statics; dogs €1; bus 300m/tram; site clsd 1300-1500; poss v cr; Eng spkn; adv bkg; quiet; CKE/CCI. "Pleasant, v helpful owner; site clsd 2000 - ltd outside parking; gd cycle path & easy walk to town; busy in high ssn; excel, v clean & modern san facs; gd value rest." € 27.00   2015*

FREIBURG IM BREISGAU *3B4* (5km SE Urban) *47.98126, 7.88127* **Camping Möslepark, Waldseestrasse 77, 79117 Freiburg-im-Breisgau [(0761) 7679333; fax 7679336; information@camping-freiburg.com; www.camping-freiburg.com]** Fr A5 exit junc 62 onto B31 & foll sp Freiburg strt thro city sp Donauschingen. Bef ent to tunnel take L lane & foll site sp (do not go thro tunnel). Site nr Möselpark Sports Stadium. When sps run out, cross level x-ing and turn L. Med, pt sl, shd; wc; chem disp; mv service pnt; sauna; shwrs inc; EHU (16A) €2.50; lndry (inc dryer); shop 100m; supmkts 500m; rest adj; playgrnd; htd, covrd pool nr; tennis 1km; bike hire; wifi; dogs €1.90; tram to city nr; o'night m'van area; Eng spkn; no adv bkg; noise fr stadium adj; ccard acc; red CKE/CCI. "Conv Freiburg & Black Forest (footpath adj); wooded site easily reached fr a'bahn; clsd 1200-1430 & 2200-0800 - waiting area in front of site; excel, modern san facs; public transport tickets fr recep; parking nr tram stop; v helpful staff; red CC Members." 26 Mar-24 Oct. € 30.00   2013*

⊞ **FREIBURG IM BREISGAU** *3B4* (11km SE Rural) *47.96015, 7.95001* **Camping Kirchzarten, Dietenbacherstrasse 17, 79199 Kirchzarten [(07661) 9040910; fax 61624; info@ camping-kirchzarten.de; www.camping-kirchzarten.de]** Sp fr Freiburg-Titisee rd 31; into Kirchzarten; site sp fr town cent. Lge, mkd pitch, pt shd; htd wc; chem disp; mv service pnt; serviced pitches; baby facs; fam bthrm; shwrs inc; EHU (16A) €2.50 or metered; lndry; shops 500m; rest adj; snacks; bar; BBQ; playgrnd; 3 htd pools adj; tennis adj; wintersports area; entmnt; 20% statics; dogs €2.50 (not acc Jul/Aug); train 500m; office clsd 1300-1430; Quickstop o'night area; poss cr; Eng spkn; adv bkg (ess Jul/Aug); quiet; ccard acc; red long stay/red LS; CKE/CCI. "Gd size pitches; choose pitch then register at office; spacious, well-kept site; excel san facs; gd rest; site fees inc free bus & train travel in Black Forest region; helpful staff; call to inq about dogs late Aug." ♦ € 35.00   2015*

See advertisement opposite

"We must tell The Club about that great site we found"

Get your site reports in by mid-August and we'll do our best to get your updates into the next edition.

FREIBURG IM BREISGAU *3B4* (10km NW Rural) *48.06350, 7.81421* **Camping Tunisee, Seestrasse, 79108 Freiburg-Hochdorf [(07665) 2249; fax 95134; info@tunisee.de; www.tunisee.de]** Fr E35/A5 exit junc 61, keep to R lane at traff lts & foll camp sp under 2nd bdge. Site on L; awkward app rd. Lge, mkd pitch, pt shd; serviced pitches; wc; chem disp; mv service pnt; shwrs €0.55; EHU (16A) €2 or metered; lndry; shop, rest, snacks; bar; playgrnd; lake sw adj; 75% statics; dogs €1; Eng spkn; some rd noise; red long stay; ccard acc; CKE/CCI. "Pleasant site; conv Freiburg & Black Forest; gd san facs but quite far fr touring pitches; recep clsd 1300-1500." ♦ 1 Apr-31 Oct. € 17.00   2010*

⊞ **FREUDENSTADT** *3C3* (8km ENE Rural) *48.48011, 8.5005* **Höhencamping Königskanzel, Freizeitweg 1, 72280 Dornstetten-Hallwangen [(07443) 6730; fax 4574; info@camping-koenigskanzel.de; www.camping-koenigskanzel.de]** Fr Freudenstadt head E on rte 28 foll sp Stuttgart for 7km. Camping sp on R, sharp R turn foll sp, sharp L on narr, winding track to site in 200m. Fr Nagold on R28, 7km fr Freudenstadt fork L; sp as bef. NB: 1st sharp R turn is v sharp - take care. Med, some hdg pitch, pt sl, terr, pt shd; wc; chem disp; mv service pnt; serviced pitch; sauna; shwrs inc; EHU (10A) metered; gas; lndry (inc dryer); shop; sm rest, snacks; bar; BBQ; playgrnd; htd pool; bike hire; golf 7km; ski lift 7km; wifi; 60% statics sep area; dogs €2; phone; site clsd 3 Nov-15 Dec; Eng spkn; adv bkg (bkg fee); quiet; ccard not acc; red long stay/CKE/CCI. "Pleasant owners; friendly welcome; excel shwr facs, inc for dogs; well run family site; hill top location with gd views of Black Forest; recep clsd 1300-1400; excel value rest." ♦ € 25.00   2014*

FREUDENSTADT *3C3* (5km W Rural) *48.45840, 8.37255* **Camping Langenwald, Strassburgerstrasse 167, 72250 Freudenstadt-Langenwald [(07441) 2862; fax 2891; info@ camping-langenwald.de; www.camping-langenwald.de]** Foll sp fr town on B28 dir Strassburg. Med, terr, pt shd; htd wc; chem disp; mv service pnt; fam bthrm; serviced pitch; shwrs inc; EHU (16A) metered; gas; lndry; shop; rest, snacks; playgrnd; htd pool; bike hire; golf 4km; 10% statics; dogs €2; Eng spkn; noisy nr rd; ccard acc (not VISA); red long stay/LS/CKE/CCI. "Gd, clean san facs; woodland walks fr site; gd rest; friendly owners." ♦ 1 Apr-1 Nov. € 33.00   2014*

FRICKENHAUSEN AM MAIN *3D2* (1km W Rural) *49.66916, 10.07444* **Knaus Campingpark Frickenhausen, Ochsenfurterstrasse 49, 97252 Frickenhausen/Ochsenfurt [(09331) 3171; fax 5784; info@knauscamp.de; www.knauscamp.de]** Turn off B13 at N end of bdge over Rv Main in Ochsenfurt & foll camping sp. Lge, hdg/mkd pitch, pt shd; wc; serviced pitches; chem disp; mv service pnt; baby facs; shwrs inc; EHU (16A) €2.40 or metered; gas; lndry; shop; rest high ssn; bar; playgrnd; htd pool; bike hire; TV; wifi; 40% statics; dogs €3; site clsd 1300-1500; Eng spkn; adv bkg; quiet; red long stay/snr citizens. "Vg, well-managed site on rv island; excel facs; located on Romantischestrasse with many medieval vills; v clean, cared for site; gd rest; friendly staff." 31 Mar-5 Nov. € 35.00   2013*

FRIEDRICHSHAFEN *3D4* (8km W Rural) *47.66896, 9.40253* **Camping Fischbach, Grenzösch 3, 88048 Friedrichshafen-Fischbach [(07541) 42059; fax 401113; info@camping-fischbach.de; www.camping-fischbach.de]** Take B31 fr Friedrichshafen to Meersburg. Site sp on L at end of vill. Turning lane avail for easy access off busy rd. Med, mkd pitch, some hdstg, pt shd; wc; chem disp; mv service pnt; shwrs €0.50; EHU (10-16A) €2 (poss rev pol); lndry (inc dryer); shop; rest, snacks; bar; lake sw adj; sand beach adj; 40% statics; no dogs; phone; poss v cr; Eng spkn; no adv bkg; rd noise; CKE/CCI. "Tranquil, relaxing site; some lake view pitches - worth the extra; excel, clean, modern san facs; ferries to Konstanz nrby; Zeppelin/Dornier museums nrby; cr; site on Lake Constance cycle rte." 11 Apr-12 Oct. € 28.60   2014*

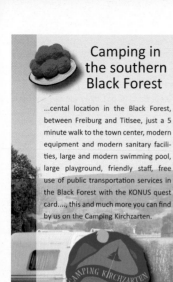

Camping in the southern Black Forest

...cental location in the Black Forest, between Freiburg and Titisee, just a 5 minute walk to the town center, modern equipment and modern sanitary facilities, large and modern swimming pool, large playground, friendly staff, free use of public transportation services in the Black Forest with the KONUS quest card...., this and much more you can find by us on the Camping Kirchzarten.

Camping Kirchzarten
Dietenbacher Str. 17
D-79199 Kirchzarten
Tel.: 0049 (0)7661 / 9040910
www.camping-kirchzarten.de
info@camping-kirchzarten.de

FRIEDRICHSHAFEN *3D4* (10km W Rural) *47.66583, 9.37694* **Campingplatz Schloss Helmsdorf, Friedrichshafenerstrasse, 88090 Immenstaad-am-Bodensee [(07545) 6252; fax 3956; campingplatz@schloss-helmsdorf.org; www.schloss-helmsdorf.org]** Site sp fr B31 bet Meersburg & Friedrichshafen at Immenstaad. Lge, pt sl, pt shd; htd wc; chem disp; mv service pnt; shwrs €0.50; EHU (6A) €2.50; lndry; shop; rest, snacks; lake beach & sw; boating; windsurfing; 80% statics; no dogs high ssn; poss cr; quiet. "Vg, well-run site; gd position on lakeside; gd, clean san facs; helpful owners; sh walk to lake ferry; gd but expensive." 30 Mar-14 Oct. € 24.50　　　　　　　　　　2013*

⊞ **FRIESOYTHE** *1C2* (13km SE Rural) *52.93703, 7.92923* **Campingplatz Wilken, Thülsfelder Str. 3, 26169 Friesoythe [04 49 52 61; info@camping-wilken.de; www.camping-wilken.de]** Fr B72 Cloppenburg-Friesoythe. After 13km turn L onto Thülsfelder Straße. Site next to Thülsfeld Reservoir on L. Lge, mkd pitch, hdstg, unshd; htd wc; chem disp; mv service pnt; shwrs inc; EHU (16A) inc; lndry rm; shop; playgrnd; dogs; quiet. "Excel site for long stay; spacious pitches; v clean san facs; would rec." € 13.50　　　　　　　　　　2014*

FURSTENBERG *2F2* (1.6km NW Rural) *53.18680, 13.13111* **Campingplatz am Röblinsee, Röblinsee Nord 1, 16798 Fürstenberg [(033093) 38278; fax 38613]** Fr S on E251/B96, L turn 500m N of Fürstenburg to N side of lake, site sp. Med, pt shd; wc; chem disp; mv service pnt; shwrs inc; EHU (16A) €1.50 or metered; lndry; shop 800m; rest 600m; snacks; lake sw; dogs €1; sep car park high ssn; CKE/CCI. "Conv for German Lake District & NH to Poland/Baltic Coast." 1 Apr-31 Oct. € 16.00　　2009*

⊞ **FUSSEN** *4E4* (2km N Urban) *47.58222, 10.70083* **Camper's Stop, Abt-Hafnerstrasse 9, 87629 Füssen [(08362) 940104; fax 925829; info@wohnmobilplatz.de]** Foll sp (mv symbol) fr town cent. Fr N or W after junc B310 & B16 turn R bef chapel (sp), then 2nd L. Fr B17 thro' town, turn L after chapel. Sm, hdstg, unshd; wc; own san rec; chem disp; mv service pnt; shwrs €1; EHU (16A) €2; lndry (inc dryer); supmkt 500m; sw adj; sports cent opp (free use of san facs); wifi; quiet. "Popular site open 24 hrs; warden attends 1700-2100 (site managed fr sports cent); sm pitches; chem disp & water fr machine during day; full facs open 1900-1000 for NH; conv Neuschwanstein Castle; sh walk to Füssen; m'vans only; excel." € 11.00　　　　　　　　　　2010*

⊞ **FUSSEN** *4E4* (2km N Urban) *47.58250, 10.70098* **Caravan Zentrum Allgäu/Wohnmobilstellplatz, Abt-Hafnerstrasse 1, 87629 Füssen [(08362) 9261097; fax 921291; info@caravanzentrum-allgaeu.de]** Foll sp (mv symbol) fr town cent. Fr N or W after junc B310 & B16 turn R bef chapel (sp), then 2nd L. Fr B17 thro' town, turn L after chapel. This site is 50m bef Camper's Stop. Med, hdstg, unshd; htd wc; chem disp; mv waste; shwrs €0.50; EHU (6A) €2; shop 200m; supmkt 500m; sw 500m; phone; poss cr; quiet. "M'vans only; excel, clean san facs; gd rest; cycle paths to town, castle & lake; gd value." € 14.00 (4 persons)　　　　2011*

GERMANY

FUSSEN 4E4 (6km N Rural) 47.61553, 10.7230 **Camping Magdalena am Forggensee, Bachtalstrasse 10, 87669 Osterreinen [(08362) 4931; fax 941333; campingplatz. magdalena@t-online.de; www.sonnenhof-am-forggensee.de]** Fr Füssen take rd 16 sp Kaufbeuren & Forggensee for 5km; R sp Osterreinen for 500m; L at T-junc foll site sp; site on R in 50m; app rd steep with sharp bends. Site well sp. Med, mkd/hdg pitch, terr, pt shd; wc; chem disp; shwrs €0.50; EHU (10A) metered + conn fee (poss rev pol); gas; lndry (inc dryer); shop; rest; bar; playgrnd; beach on lake; sailing; watersports; 40% statics; dogs €3; poss cr; Eng spkn; adv bkg rec; v quiet; CKE/CCI. "Ltd touring pitches; superb views over lake; peaceful; gd site; sm pitches; conv for Zugspitze, Royal Castles, Oberammergau; lakeside cycle track to Füssen & to Neuschwanstein Castle." 1 Apr-31 Oct. € 22.00   2014*

⊞ FUSSEN 4E4 (6km NE Rural) 47.59194, 10.77222 **Camping Bannwaldsee, Münchenerstrasse 151, 87645 Schwangau [(08362) 93000; fax 930020; info@camping-bannwaldsee. de; www.camping-bannwaldsee.de]** On side of B17 rd fr Füssen to Munich & on shore of Bannwaldsee 3km after Schwangau vill. Fr N on B17 5km after Buching vill. Site name only visible at site ent. V lge, mkd pitch, pt sl, pt shd; htd wc; chem disp; mv service pnt; shwrs inc; shop; EHU (16A) metered + conn fee; lndry; shop; rest, snacks; bar; playgrnd; lake sw, fishing, boat hire; wintersports area; wifi; entmnt; 30% statics; dogs €3.50; poss cr; poss noisy; red long stay. "Narr site rds & poss diff pitch access; some lge pitches; excel san facs; gd facs young children; gd cycle paths in area." ♦ € 23.00   2009*

"I need an on-site restaurant"

We do our best to make sure site information is correct, but it is always best to check any must-have facilities are still available or will be open during your visit.

⊞ FUSSEN 4E4 (6km NE Rural) 47.59638, 10.73861 **Camping Brunnen, Seestrasse 81, 87645 Brunnen [(08362) 8273; fax 8630; info@camping-brunnen.de; www.camping-brunnen.de]** S on rte 17 twd Füssen turn R in vill of Schwangau N to Brunnen; turn R at ent to vill at Spar shop, site clearly sp. Fr Füssen N on B17; turn L in Schwangau; well sp on lakeside. Lge, mkd pitch, hdstg, pt sl, pt shd; wc; chem disp; mv service pnt; serviced pitches; shwrs inc; EHU (10-16A) metered + conn fee; gas; lndry rm; sm shop; rest/bar adj; playgrnd; sw & yachting in Lake Forggensee adj; beach adj; bike hire; golf 3km; dogs €4; bus; site clsd 5 Nov-20 Dec; poss cr; Eng spkn; adv bkg; ccard acc; CKE/CCI. "Lovely location, next to lake; o'fits poss tightly packed; steel pegs ess; excel san facs; some pitches cramped; gd for Royal castles; gd cycle rtes; 10% red visits to Neuschwanstein Castle nrby; gates clsd 2200-0700; excel, busy, vg site; handy rest, supmkt & g'ge." ♦ € 32.00   2014*

FUSSEN 4E4 (5km NW Rural) 47.60198, 10.68333 **Camping Hopfensee, Fischerbichl 17/Uferstrasse, 87629 Hopfen-am-See [(08362) 917710; fax 917720; info@camping-hopfensee.de; www.camping-hopfensee.com]** Fr Füssen N on B16 twd Kaufbeuren in 2km L on rd sp Hopfen-am-See, site at ent to vill on L thro c'van car park. Lge, mkd pitch, hdstg, pt shd; wc; chem disp; mv service pnt; baby facs; all serviced pitches; sauna; shwrs inc; EHU (16A) metered; gas; lndry; shop; rest, snacks; bar; playgrnd; htd covrd pool; shgl beach & lake sw adj; boating & fishing; fitness cent; solarium; wintersports area; entmnt; dogs €4.15; internet; poss cr; Eng spkn; adv bkg rec high ssn; quiet; ccard not acc; red LS; CKE/CCI. "Gd location; excel facs; helpful staff; gd rest on site; no tents allowed except for awnings; tight squeeze in high ssn; vans need manhandling; gd walking & cycling; lakeside pitches rec; excel; highly rec; 5 star facs." ♦ 1 Jan-3 Nov & 17 Dec-31 Dec. € 38.00   2014*

See advertisement inside the front cover

FUSSEN 4E4 (6km NW Rural) 47.60883, 10.66918 **Haus Guggemos, Uferstrasse 42, 87629 Hopfen-am-See [(08362) 3334; fax 6765; haus.guggemos@t-online.de; www.haus-guggemos.de]** Fr Füssen take B16 N dir Kaufbeuren; in 2km turn L sp Hopfen-am-See. Drive thro vill; site on R opp lake. Sm, some hdstg, pt shd; terr; wc; chem disp; shwrs inc; EHU (10A) metered; lndry; shop 500m; rest, snack & bar 200m; playgrnd; lake sw adj; dogs €2; bus adj; Eng spkn; adv bkg; quiet; CKE/CCI. "Excel, family-run, farm site in beautiful area; views across lake to Alps." 1 Apr-31 Oct. € 16.00   2013*

GAIENHOFEN HORN see Radolfzell am Bodensee 3C4

⊞ GANDERKESEE 1C2 (7km W Rural) 53.04666, 8.46388 **Ferienpark Falkensteinsee, Am Falkensteinsee 1, 27777 Ganderkesee-Steinkimmen [(04222) 9470077; fax 9470079; camping@falkensteinsee.de; www.falkensteinsee.de]** Exit A28/E22 junc 18 dir Habbrügge. Site on R in 2km. Lge, pt shd; wc; sauna; shwrs inc; EHU (16A) €3.50 or metered; lndry; shop; rest 1km; snacks; playgrnd; lake sw adj; sep naturist beach; golf 8km; 70% statics; dogs €1.50; o'night m'van area; Eng spkn; quiet; ccard not acc; 5% red CKE/CCI. "Conv Oldenburg & Bremen; new owners; completely refurb (2015); sw lake with 2 sandy beaches; pleasant holiday park; well organised; friendly staff; new facs & v high quality; excel; sep sw area for dogs fr 2016." ♦ ltd. € 20.60   2015*

GARBSEN see Hannover 1D3

⊞ GARMISCH PARTENKIRCHEN 4E4 (3km N Rural) 47.50444, 11.10694 **Alpencamp am Wank, Wankbahnstrasse 2, 82467 Garmisch-Partenkirchen [(08821) 9677805; fax 76866; info@alpencamp-gap.de; www.alpencamp-gap.de]** A9/E533 exit onto B2 to Garmisch. Foll m'van symbol/sp to site. M'vans only. Med, hdstg, terr, unshd; htd wc; chem disp; mv service pnt; shwrs €1; EHU (16A) metered; gas; lndry; shop 2km; rest; wifi; dogs; bus to town; Eng spkn; quiet. "M'vans only; v clean facs; view fr all pitches of Zugspitze; excel for walking & winter sports; gd for NH or poss longer; disposal point/water coin operated." € 14.00   2011*

GARTOW *2E2* (4km NW Rural) *53.03972, 11.41583* **Camping Laascher See, Ortsteil Laasche 13, 29471 Gartow [(05846) 342; pewsdorf@campingplatz-laascher-see.de; www.campingplatz-laascher-see.de]** Fr S on B493 to Gartow, turn N on L256 (Rondelerstrasse) dir Gartower See & Laasche See, site sp on R. Or E fr Dennenberg on L256 dir Gorleben & Gartow, site sp approx 5km after Gorleben. Med, hdg pitch, pt sl, pt shd; wc; chem disp; mv service pnt; shwrs €0.80; EHU (6A) inc; lndry (inc dryer); shop, rest 2.5km; bar; playgrnd; lake sw 300m; 60% statics; dogs €1.50; adv bkg; quiet; CKE/CCI. "Pleasant owners; clean, modern san facs; vg." ◆ 1 Apr-31 Oct. € 16.00   2010*

⊞ **GEESTHACHT** *1D2* (9km SW Rural) *53.42465, 10.29470* **Campingplatz Stover Strand International, Stover Strand 10, 21423 Drage [(04177) 340; info@stover-strand.de; www.camping-stover-strand.de]** Fr N on A25 to Geesthacht, then B404 dir Winsen to Stove. Site at end Stover Strand on banks of Rv Elbe. Fr S on A7 to Maschen, then A250 to Winsen then B404, as above. V lge, mkd pitch, pt shd; htd wc; chem disp; mv service pnt; baby facs; shwrs €0.50; EHU (6-16A) €2 or metered; lndry (inc dryer); shop; rest, snacks; bar; BBQ; cooking facs; playgrnd; rv sw & beach; fishing; watersports; marina; bike hire; games area; wifi; entmnt; 80% statics; dogs €2; poss cr; adv bkg; quiet; ccard acc; CKE/CCI. "Excel rvside site; poss cr even LS; site clsd 1300-1500; Hamburg Card avail." ◆ € 20.00   2012*

⊞ **GELSENKIRCHEN** *1B4* (7km N Urban) *51.56081, 7.07114* **Mobilcamp Gelsenkirchen, Adenauerallee 100, 45891 Gelsenkirchen [tel/fax (0176) 78569829; mobilcamp@web.de; www.mobilcamp.de]** Fr W exit A2/E34 junc 6, at rndabt at end of sliprd turn R into Emil Zimmerman Allee, then R again. Site on R. M'vans only. Med, pt shd; wc; chem disp; mv service pnt; shwrs €1; EHU; gas; shop; rest; bar; dogs; Eng spkn; adv bkg; quiet. "Gd NH." € 7.00   2009*

> ## "Satellite navigation makes touring much easier"
>
> Remember most sat navs don't know if you're towing or in a larger vehicle – always use yours alongside maps and site directions.

GEMUNDEN AM MAIN *3D2* (5km W Rural) *50.05260, 9.65656* **Spessart-Camping Schönrain, Schönrainstrasse 4-18, 97737 Gemünden-Hofstetten [(09351) 8645; fax 8721; info@spessart-camping.de; www.spessart-camping.de]** Rd B26 to Gemünden, cross Rv Main & turn R dir Hofstetten, site sp. Lge, hdg/mkd pitch, some hdstg, terr, pt shd; htd wc; chem disp; mv service pnt; sauna; shwrs €0.50; EHU (10A) metered + conn fee €2.15; lndry (inc dryer); shop & 2km; rest, snacks; bar; playgrnd; children's pool; games area; bike hire; fitness rm; solarium; TV; 50% statics (sep area); dogs €2.80; phone; variable pitch sizes/prices; poss cr; Eng spkn; quiet; CKE/CCI. "Clean, well-kept, wooded site; interesting towns nrby; excel." ◆ 1 Apr-30 Sep. € 32.00   2014*

GEORGENTHAL see Ohrdruf *2E4*

GERBACH see Rockenhausen *3C2*

⊞ **GEROLSTEIN** *3B2* (5km NW Rural) *50.23910, 6.61477* **Campingplatz Oosbachtal, Müllenbornerstrasse 31, 54568 Gerolstein-Müllenborn [(06591) 7409; fax 3635; camping-oosbach@t-online.de; www.camping-oosbachtal.de]** Site well sp fr rte 410 Prüm to Gerolstein. Med, pt sl, hdstg, pt shd; wc; chem disp; mv service pnt; fam bthrm; shwrs inc; EHU (16A) metered or €1.50; lndry (inc dryer); shop; rest; bar; BBQ; playgrnd; 2 pools (1 htd, covrd); 60% statics; dogs €2; adv bkg; poss cr; Eng spkn; quiet; CKE/CCI. "Scenic area for touring Eifel region; owners friendly & helpful." ◆ € 16.50   2010*

⊞ **GERSFELD (RHON)** *3D2* (2.5km N Rural) *50.46223, 9.91953* **Camping Hochrhön, Schachen 13, 36129 Gersfeld-Schachen [tel/fax (06654) 7836; campinghochrhoen@aol.com; www.rhoenline.de/camping-hochrhoen]** Exit A7 exit Fulda-Süd S onto B27/B279 to Gersfeld, then B284 sp Ehrenberg, Turn L dir Schachen, foll sp to site. Med, hdg/mkd pitch, hdstg, pt shd; wc; chem disp; mv service pnt; shwrs €0.60; EHU (16A) metered; lndry; shops 1.5km; rest 500m; playgrnd; ski lift 3km; some statics (sep area); dogs free; poss cr; red CKE/CCI. "Conv for gliding & air sports at Wasswerkuppe; friendly." ◆ € 18.00   2012*

GETTORF *1D1* (12km NE Coastal) *54.47485, 10.02910* **Campingplatz Grönwohld, Kronshörn, 24229 Schwedeneck [(04308) 189972; fax 189973; info@groenwohld-camping.de; www.groenwohld-camping.de]** Fr A7 exit junc 6 or 8 to Eckernförde, then onto B503, site sp bet km 8.9 & 9. V lge, hdg/mkd pitch, hdstg, pt shd; wc; chem disp; mv service pnt; sauna; shwrs inc; EHU (10-16A) metered + conn fee; lndry; shop; rest; playgrnd; beach adj; fishing; sailing; entmnt; 75% statics; dogs €2.10; adv bkg; quiet; ccard not acc; CKE/CCI. "Conv NH; gd, modern facs." ◆ 1 Apr-31 Oct. € 14.00   2011*

GIESELWERDER *1D4* (6km S Rural) *51.56623, 9.59661* **Camping Weissehütte, Weissehütte 1, 34399 Oberweser-Weissehütte [(05574) 211939; info@camping-weser.de; www.camping-weser.de]** S fr Bad Karlshafen on B80 along W bank of Rv Weser. Site on L. Sm, hdg pitch, pt shd; wc; chem disp; shwrs; EHU (10A) €2.30; shop 5km; snacks; mainly statics; dogs €1.50; bus adj; Eng spkn; adv bkg; quiet; CKE/CCI. "Gd cycle rtes N & S." € 14.00   2011*

GIROD see Montabaur *3C2*

GLUCKSBURG (OSTSEE) *1D1* (6km NE Coastal) *54.85901, 9.59109* **Ostseecamp, An der Promenade 1, 24960 Glücksburg-Holnis [(04631) 622071; fax 622072; info@ostseecamp-holnis.de; www.ostseecamp-holnis.de]** Fr Flensburg on rd 199 turn off thro Glücksburg & further 6km to Holnis. Med, mkd pitch, some hdstg, pt shd; htd wc; chem disp; mv service pnt; baby facs; shwrs inc; EHU (16A) €3; lndry (inc dryer); shop; rest 200m; snacks; BBQ; cooking facs; playgrnd; pool; sand beach adj; fishing; windsurfing 1km; bike hire; wifi; entmnt; 30% statics; dogs €2.50; adv bkg; quiet; CKE/CCI. ◆ 1 Apr-15 Oct. € 20.00 (CChq acc)   2011*

GERMANY

⊞ **GOPPINGEN** *3D3* (13.5km SW Rural) *48.63946, 9.55508*
**Campingplatz Aichelberg, Bunzenberg 1, 73101
Aichelberg [(07164) 2700; fax 903029]** Exit E52/A8 junc 58
sp Aichelberg-Goppingen & foll sp to camp site in 1km. Med,
pt shd; wc; chem disp; shwrs inc; EHU (10A) €2; shop; rest
500m; bar; poss cr; adv bkg; 80% statics; dogs €2; poss cr;
quiet. "Fills up after 1600 hrs but gd overflow field with EHU
for NH; family-run site; new excel facs; owner helpful; nr A8."
€ 20.00   2015*

⊞ **GOSLAR** *1D3* (17km S Rural) *51.82166, 10.43722*
**Campingplatz Okertalsperre, Kornhardtweg 2, 38707
Altenau [(05328) 702; fax 911708; info@campingokertal.
de; www.campingokertal.de]** Fr Goslar B498 S, site on L of
N o'skts of Altenau. Med, hdg/mkd, pt shd; wc; chem disp; mv
service pnt; serviced pitches; shwrs inc; EHU (16A) metered +
conn fee; gas; lndry (inc dryer); shop; snacks; BBQ; playgrnd;
lake sw; shgl beach; watersports; wintersports; ski lift 2km;
games area; games rm; wifi; entmnt; 50% statics (sep area);
dogs €2; adv bkg; Eng spkn; quiet; ccard not acc; red CKE/
CCI. "Beautiful setting 20 mins walk fr cent of Altenau; gd
welcome; sm pitches; excel play area; excel cycle paths around
lake; ltd facs LS; excel." ♦ € 16.50   2010*

⊞ **GOSLAR** *1D3* (4km SW Rural) *51.88958, 10.39889*
**Campingplatz Sennhütte, Clausthalerstrasse 28, 38644
Goslar [(05321) 22498; sennhuette@campingplatz-goslar.
de; www.sennhuette-goslar.de]** Fr Goslar on B241 twd
Clausthal, Zellerfeld site on R in 2km. Ent thro car pk of Hotel
Sennhütte. Med, pt shd; wc; chem disp; shwrs €0.50; EHU
(16A) metered + conn fee (poss long lead req); lndry (inc dryer);
shop; rest; 30% statics; dogs; bus at ent to town; no adv bkg;
noisy nr rd; ccard acc. "Gd NH/sh stay nr beautiful town."
€ 15.50   2010*

⊞ **GOSLAR** *1D3* (13km W Rural) *51.90110, 10.32724*
**Camping am Krähenberg, Harzstrasse 8, 38685
Langelsheim [(05326) 969281; fax 969282; post@
campingplatz-Wolfshagen.de; www.campingplatz-
wolfshagen.de]** Foll rd 82 W fr Goslar twd Langelsheim. Turn
L to Wolfshagen 1km bef Langelsheim. In Wolfshagen foll site
sp, site in SE corner of vill uphill. Lge, mkd pitch, terr, pl sl,
pt shd; wc; chem disp; mv service pnt; shwrs inc; EHU (16A)
metered + conn fee; gas; lndry (inc dryer); shop; rest; playgrnd;
htd pool adj; tennis; horseriding 1km; internet; 75% statics;
dogs €1.20; ccard acc; red CKE/CCI. "Gate clsd 1300-1430;
shwrs remote (in rest block); lge pitches; charge for sw pool
poss automatically added to bill - check bef dep if not req; gd."
♦ € 14.00   2010*

⊞ **GRAFENDORF** *3D2* (11km SE Rural) *50.10678, 9.78241*
**Camping Rossmühle, 97782 Gräfendorf-Weickersgrüben
[(09357) 1210; fax 832; www.campingplatz-rossmuehle.
de]** Exit A7 junc 96 onto B27 sp Karlstadt. At Hammelburg
foll sps to Gräfendorf & site in 8km on rvside, beyond
Weickersgrüben. Lge, mkd pitch, terr, pt shd; wc; chem disp;
mv service pnt; shwrs €1; EHU (6-10A) €2; lndry; shop; rest
high ssn; bar; playgrnd; watersports; fitness rm; bike & canoe
hire; solarium; entmnt; TV; 50% statics; dogs €2; o'night area
for m'vans; adv bkg; quiet. "Poss liable to flooding after heavy
rain; clean san facs; excel; cycle rte tourers sep fr statics." ♦
€ 18.00   2012*

GRAMBIN *2G2* (500m N Coastal/Rural) *53.75944, 14.01000*
**Campingpark Oderhaff, Dorstrasse 661, 17375 Grambin
[tel/fax (039774) 20420; info@campingpark-oderhaff.de;
www.campingpark-oderhaff.de]** Exit A20 junc 28 onto
B110 dir Anklam. After approx 23km turn R onto B109 & in
15km turn L in Ducherow onto L31 & foll sp Grambin. Site
on L in 17km. Med, pt sl, pt shd; htd wc; chem disp; shwrs
€1; EHU (10-16A) €2.50; lndry (inc dryer); shop 700m; rest
200m; bar; BBQ; cooking facs; playgrnd; sand beach adj;
games area; 60% statics; dogs €2; bus nr; adv bkg; quiet. "Vg
site; conv day trips Poland & Peenemunde." ♦ 1 Apr-15 Oct.
€ 17.40   2010*

"There aren't many sites open at this time of year"

If you're travelling outside peak season
remember to call ahead to check site opening
dates – even if the entry says 'open all year'.

⊞ **GREFRATH** *1A4* (4km N Rural) *51.36492, 6.32328*
**Campingplatz Waldfrieden, An der Paas 13, 47929
Grefrath [(02158) 3855; fax 3685; ferienpark@
waldfrieden@t-online.de; www.ferienpark-waldfrieden.
de]** Fr A40-E34 S to Duisburg; turn S at exit 3 sp Grefrath; site
sp on L in 3km. Lge, hdg pitch, hdstg, pt shd; htd wc; chem
disp; mv service pnt; shwrs; EHU (10A) metered + conn fee;
gas; lndry; shop 1.2km; playgrnd; lake sw adj; sw pools 1.5km;
80% statics; dogs €2; poss cr; Eng spkn; quiet; CKE/CCI. "Conv
NH North Sea ports; WWII cemeteries at Reichswald; site over-
used & weary." € 17.50   2013*

GREIFSWALD *2G1* (16km NE Coastal) *54.12666, 13.52196*
**Campingplatz Loissin (Part Naturist), 17509 Loissin
[(038352) 243; fax 725; info@campingplatz-loissin.de;
www.campingplatz-loissin.de]** Fr Greifswald E to Kemnitz,
then head N twds Loissin; site on coast N, well sp fr the vill.
Lge, mkd pitch, pt shd; wc; chem disp; mv service pnt; shwrs
€0.50; EHU (16A) inc; lndry; shop; rest, snacks; bar; playgrnd;
sand beach adj; sep naturist beach; windsurfing; games area;
bike hire; internet; entmnt; 40% statics; dogs €2; clsd 1300-
1430 & 2200-0800; adv bkg; quiet; red CKE/CCI. "Vg site;
approx 40km to foot x-ing fr car park to Poland for shopping;
excelsan facs - no toilet paper, main attraction is immed
proximity to sea." ♦ Easter-31 Oct. € 21.00   2011*

⊞ **GREVEN** *1B3* (6km SW Rural) *52.08328, 7.55806*
**Campingplatz Westheide, Altenbergerstrasse 23,
48268 Greven [(02571) 560701; kontakt@campingplatz-
westheide.de; www.campingplatz-westheide.de]**
Exit A1 junc 76 onto B481 around E side of Greven, then turn
L onto B219 for 2km. Turn R onto L555 Nordwalderstrasse &
in 2km at Westerode turn L into Altenbergerstrasse, site on L in
1km. Med, hdg pitch, pt shd; htd wc; chem disp; fam bthrm;
shwrs €0.50; EHU (16A) metered; lndry; snacks; bar; playgrnd;
lake & sand beach adj; fishing; games rm; 80% statics; dogs
€1; quiet; ccard acc; CKE/CCI. "Gd for sh stay; walks around
lake." € 18.00   2009*

GERMANY

GROSS QUASSOW see Neustrelitz *2F2*

⊞ **GROSS-SEEHAM** *4F4* (1km SE Rural) *47.85166, 11.86222*
Camping Seehamer See, Hauptstrasse 32, 83629 Gross-
Seeham [(08020) 396; fax 1400; info@seehamer-see.de;
www.seehamer-see.de] Along W side of A8/E45/E52 a'bahn
bet juncs 98 Weyarn & 99 Irschenberg exit at km 37 into
parking layby; site sp. If fr S take Weyarn exit & in Weyarn turn
L opp maypole, site in 4km. Lge, pt sl, unshd; wc; chem disp;
mv service pnt; shwrs €1; EHU (16A) €2; lndry; shop; rest high
ssn; snacks; shop 500m; lake sw; shgl beach; mainly statics;
poss cr; no adv bkg; rd noise; red CKE/CCI. "V friendly owner;
sm, sep area for tourers." ♦ € 22.00   2009*

GRUNBERG *1C4* (1km E Urban) *50.59105, 8.97361* **Camping**
Spitzer Stein, 35305 Grünberg [(06401) 6553; s.moebus@
gruenberg.de; www.gruenberg.de] Exit A5/E40 junc 7 S to
Grünberg. At traff lts turn L onto B49; site in 1km on R. Lge, pt
sl, pt shd, some hdstg; wc; chem disp; shwrs €0.50; EHU (5A)
metered + conn fee; lndry; shop, rest & snacks adj; playgrnd;
htd pool adj; golf 8km; 95% statics; poss cr; adv bkg; poss
noisy; ccard acc; red CKE/CCI. "Site surrounded by pleasant
wooded hills; sm, unmkd area for tourers; interesting old town;
OK, busy NH." 1 Mar-31 Oct. € 12.00   2009*

GUNZBURG *3D3* (4km S Rural) *48.42688, 10.29842*
Legoland Feriendorf, Legoland Allee 2, 89312 Günzburg
[(08221) 700789; fax 700199; info@legoland-feriendorf.de;
www.legoland-feriendorf.de] Exit A8/E52 junc 67 S onto
B16. Foll sp Lego-Park & Feriendorf to site. Med, unshd;
htd wc; chem disp; mv service pnt; fam bthrm; shwrs; EHU
(16A) inc (long dryer); shop 2km; rest; playgrnd; pool
3km; entmnt; no dogs; adv bkg; ccard acc. "Opening dates/
times dependent on Legoland Deutschland adj - www.
legoland.de." ♦ 9 Apr-6 Nov. € 42.00 (inc Legoland tickets)
(CChq acc)   2009*

⊞ **GYHUM** *1D2* (4km SE Rural) *53.19308, 9.33638*
Waldcamping Hesedorf, Zum Waldbad 3, 27404 Gyhum-
Hesedorf [(04286) 2252; fax 924509; info@waldcamping-
hesedorf.de; www.waldcamping-hesedorf.de]
Exit A1/E22 junc 49 in dir Zeven. In 1km turn R sp Gyhum & foll
site sp to Hesedorf. Med, unshd; htd wc; chem disp; mv service
pnt; shwrs; EHU (16A) inc; lndry; shop 1km; rest; playgrnd;
htd pool 150m inc; wifi; 70% statics (sep area); dogs €0.50;
barrier clsd 1300-1500; Eng spkn; quiet; CKE/CCI. "Clean,
well-kept site; attractive area; gd rest; lge sep area for tourers."
€ 20.00   2010*

⊞ **HALBERSTADT** *2E3* (3km NE Rural) *51.90981, 11.0827*
Camping am See (Part Naturist), Warmholzberg 70, 38820
Halberstadt [(03941) 609308; fax 570791; info@camping-
am-see.de; www.camping-am-see.de]
Sp on B81 (Halberstadt-Magdeburg). Med, terr, unshd; wc;
chem disp; shwrs inc; EHU (10A) metered + conn fee €2.50
(poss rev pol); lndry; shop; snacks; pool adj; lake beach & sw
adj (sep naturist beach); 75% statics; dogs €2; sep car park;
quiet; red CKE/CCI. "Conv Harz mountains & Quedlinburg
(770 houses classified as historic monuments by UNESCO);
quiet, green site; some individual shwrs; clsd 1300-1500."
€ 34.00   2013*

⊞ **HAMBURG** *1D2* (7km NW Urban) *53.5900, 9.93083*
Campingplatz Buchholz, Keilerstrasse 374, 22525
Hamburg-Stellingen [(040) 5404532; fax 5402536; info@
camping-buchholz.de; www.camping-buchholz.de]
Exit A7/E45 junc 26 & foll dir 'Innenstadt' - city cent. Site sp in
600m on L. Sm, hdg/mkd pitch, all hdstg, pt shd; wc; shwrs
€1; chem disp; EHU (16A) €3; lndry; shop, rest, snacks 200m;
bar; 10% statics; dogs €3.80; bus, train nr; poss v cr; adv bkg;
rd noise; no ccard acc. "Fair NH nr a'bahn & Hamburg cent;
conv transport to city - tickets fr recep; friendly management;
sm pitches; busy site, rec arr early; diff access for lge o'fits." ♦
€ 34.00   2014*

⊞ **HAMBURG** *1D2* (9km NW Urban) *53.64916, 9.92970*
Knaus Campingpark Hamburg (formerly Camping
Schnelsen-Nord), Wunderbrunnen 2, 22457 Hamburg
[(040) 5594225; fax 5507334; service@campingplatz-
hamburg.de; www.campingplatz-hamburg.de]
Heading N on A7 exit junc 23 to Schnelsen Nord; L at traff lts,
foll sp Ikea & site behind Ikea. Med, pt shd, mkd pitch; wc;
chem disp; mv service pnt; shwrs inc; EHU (6A) €2.50; lndry rm;
shop; rest adj (in Ikea); snacks; bar; playgrnd; TV rm; no dogs;
phone; bus to city; stn adj; deposit for key to san facs & el box;
Eng spkn; quiet but some rd noise; ccard acc; CKE/CCI. "Useful
NH; helpful staff; gates clsd 2200 hrs & 1300-1600 LS; elec
pylons & cables cross site; 3-day Hamburg card excel value." ♦
€ 40.00   2014*

⊞ **HAMELN** *1D3* (2km S Urban) *52.09638, 9.35805*
Wohnmobilstellplatz Hannes-Weserblick, Ruthenstrasse
14, 31785 Hameln [(05151) 957810; fax 931099; hannes@
hwg-hameln.de; www.wohnmobilstellplatz-hameln.de]
Fr B1 to Hameln & foll sp Gewerbegebiet Süd & m'van park.
Sm, hdstg; mv service pnt; EHU (6A) €1; shop 700m; snacks;
quiet. "Situated bet buildings of Hameln Youth Training
Cent; footpath along Rv Weser to town; m'vans only."
€ 8.00   2011*

⊞ **HAMELN** *1D3* (2km W Urban) *52.10916, 9.3475*
Campingplatz zum Fährhaus, Uferstrasse 80, 31785
Hameln [(05151) 67489; fax 61167; info@campingplatz-
hameln.de; www.campingplatz-hameln.de]
Fr A2/E30 at Bad Eilsen junc 35 onto B83 to Hameln on NE
side of Rv Weser; in town foll sp Detmold/Paderborn; cross
bdge to SW side (use Thiewall Brücke); turn R on minor rd twd
Rinteln; foll site sp. Med, unshd; htd wc; chem disp; mv service
pnt; shwrs inc; EHU (10-16A) metered; lndry; supmkt 500m;
rest; bar; htd pool high ssn; 40% statics; dogs €1; phone; clsd
1300-1430; quiet; red CKE/CCI. "Picturesque & historic district;
open-air performance of Pied Piper in town on Sun to mid-Sep;
sm pitches & poss uneven; helpful staff; san facs being updated
(2015); site poss muddy & untidy; gd cycle paths by rv to
town." ♦ ltd. € 18.50   2015*

HAMELN *1D3* (8km W Rural) *52.10725, 9.29588* **Camping**
am Waldbad, Pferdeweg 2, 31787 Halvestorf
[tel/fax (05158) 2774; info@campingamwaldbad.de;
www.campingamwaldbad.de] Fr Hameln on B83 dir Rinteln.
In approx 10km turn L, cross rv & foll sp Halvestorf & site. Med,
pt sl, unshd; wc; chem disp; shwrs €0.50; EHU (16A) €; lndry
(inc dryer); shops 2km; snacks; playgrnd; htd pool; paddling
pool; 80% statics; dogs free; adv bkg; quiet. "Pleasant site -
better than site in Hameln." ♦ 1 Apr-31 Oct. € 15.00 2013*

GERMANY

⊞ **HAMM** *1B3* (13km E Rural) *51.6939, 7.9710* **Camping Uentrop, Dolbergerstrasse 80, 59510 Lippetal-Lippborg [(02388) 437; fax 1637; info@camping-helbach.de; www.camping-helbach.de]** Exit A2/E34 junc 19, site sp; behind Hotel Helbach 1km fr a'bahn. Lge, pt sl, pt shd; htd wc; chem disp; shwrs inc; EHU (16A) €2; gas; lndry; shops adj; rest adj; playgrnd; 90% statics; dogs €2; poss cr; Eng spkn; rd noise; ccard acc. "Friendly; gd security; barrier clsd 1300-1500 & 2200-0500; fair NH." € 18.00   2011*

HAMMELBACH *3C2* (600m S Rural) *49.63277, 8.83000* **Camping Park Hammelbach, Gasse 17, 64689 Grasellenbach/Hammelbach [(06253) 3831; info@ camping-hammelbach.de; www.camping-hammelbach. de]** Exit A5/E35 exit junc 31 onto B460 E. Turn S in Weschnitz to Hammelbach & foll site sp. Med, hdg pitch, pt shd; htd wc; chem disp; mv service pnt; baby facs; fam bthrm; sauna adj; shwrs inc; EHU (16A) metered; gas; lndry (inc dryer); shop 300m; rest, snacks, bar 300m; BBQ; htd pool 300m; wifi; 70% statics; dogs €1.50; bus 300m; poss cr; Eng spkn; adv bkg; quiet; ccard acc; red LS; CKE/CCI. "Excel family run site with views; v pleasant, helpful staff; red for seniors; conv Heidelberg; immac hotel like san facs; well up to CC standards." ◆ 1 Apr-31 Oct. € 20.00   2014*

HANNOVER *1D3* (14km NE Urban) *52.45383, 9.85611* **Campingplatz Parksee Lohne, Alter Postweg 12, 30916 Isernhagen [05139 88260; fax 891665; parksee-lohne@t-online.de; www.parksee-lohne.de]** Fr A2 take exit 46 to Altwarmbüchen. Cont onto K114, turn R onto Alter Postweg & foll sp to campsite. V lge, pt shd; htd wc; chem disp; mv service pnt; baby facs; fam bthrm; shwrs inc; lndry (inc dryer); rest; snacks; bar; cooking facs; 95% statics; dogs; Eng spkn; quiet. "Vg site; next to golf course; excel san facs; narr cobbled rd 1/2 m; under flight path, but quiet at night." ◆ 1 Apr-15 Oct. € 29.60   2014*

⊞ **HANNOVER** *1D3* (16km SE Rural) *52.30447, 9.86216* **Camping Birkensee, 30880 Laatzen [(0511) 529962; fax 5293053; birkensee@camping-laatzen.de; www.camping-laatzen.de]** Fr N leave A7 junc 59 dir Laatzen, turn R, then turn L & site well sp on L after traff lts. Fr S exit junc 60 twd Laatzen, site sp on L on lakeside. Lge, pt shd; wc; chem disp; mv service pnt; sauna; shwrs inc; EHU (10A) €2.50 (poss rev pol); lndry; snacks; bar; playgrnd; covrd pool; lake sw & fishing; games area; 60% statics; dogs €2.50; Eng spkn; rd noise; CKE/CCI. "Gd, clean facs; sm touring area; site needs TLC; v helpful staff." ◆ ltd. € 27.00   2014*

⊞ **HANNOVER** *1D3* (10km S Rural) *52.30133, 9.74716* **Campingplatz Arnumer See, Osterbruchweg 5, 30966 Hemmingen-Arnum [(05101) 3534; fax 85514999; info@ camping-hannover.de; www.camping-hannover.de]** Leave A7 junc 59 onto B443 dir Pattensen, then B3 dir Hannover. Site sp in Hemmingen dir Wilkenburg. Lge, hdg/ mkd pitch, pt shd; htd wc; chem disp; mv service pnt; baby facs; shwrs €0.50; EHU (16A) €2.50; gas; lndry (inc dryer); shop 500m; rest, snacks; bar; cooking facs; playgrnd; lake sw; fishing; tennis; bike hire; wifi; 95% statics; dogs €1.50; bus to Hannover 1.5km; quiet; CKE/CCI. "Friendly staff; excel, modern, clean san facs; sm area for tourers - gd size open pitches; gd lake sw & boating; insect repellent ess!" € 31.00   2014*

⊞ **HANNOVER** *1D3* (16km NW Rural) *52.42083, 9.54638* **Camping Blauer See, Am Blauen See 119, 30823 Garbsen [(05137) 89960; fax 899677; info@camping-blauer-see.de; www.camping-blauer-see.de]** Fr W exit A2 at junc 41 onto Garbsen rest area. Thro service area, at exit turn R, at T-junc turn R (Alt Garbson). All sp with int'l camp sp. Fr E exit junc 40, cross a'bahn & go back to junc 41, then as above. Lge, some hdstg, pt shd; htd wc; chem disp; mv service pnt; some serviced pitches; baby facs; shwrs €1; EHU (16A) €2.70; gas; lndry (inc dryer); shop; rest, snacks; bar; BBQ; lge playgrnd; lake sw & watersports adj; 90% statics; dogs €2.50; phone; bus to Hannover 1.5km; barrier clsd 2300-0500 & 1300-1500; poss cr; Eng spkn; rd noise; ccard acc; CKE/CCI. "Excel san facs; well-organised site; helpful staff; conv bus/train to Hannover; rec pitch by lake." ◆ ltd. € 29.00   2014*

⊞ **HANNOVERSCH MUNDEN** *1D4* (7km SE Rural) *51.39500, 9.72527* **Camping Zella im Werratal, Zella 1-2, 34346 Hannoversch-Münden [(05541) 904711; info@zella-im-werratal.de; www.zella-im-werratal.de]** Exit A7/E45 junc 75 onto B80 dir Hann-Münden. In 4km turn L over rv bdge, site in 1km. Med, pt shd; wc; shwrs €0.60; EHU (16A) inc; gas; lndry (inc dryer); shop; rest, bar adj; cooking facs; playgrnd; 30% statics; dogs €2; some train noise; red long stay/CKE/CCI. "Facs across rd; vg rest; gd NH." € 22.50   2009*

HANNOVERSCH MUNDEN *1D4* (2.5km W Rural) *51.41666, 9.64750* **Campingplatz Grüne Insel Tanzwerder, Tanzwerder 1, 34346 Hannoversch-Münden [(05541) 12257; fax 660778; info@busch-freizeit.de; www.busch-freizeit.de]** A7/E45 exit junc 76 onto B496 to Hann-Münden. Cross bdge & site sp on an island on Rv Fulda next to town cent. App over narr swing bdge. Fr junc 75 foll sp to Hann-Münden. At Aral g'ge in town take next L & foll sp to site (sp Weserstein). Med, mkd pitch, pt shd; wc; chem disp; mv service pnt; shwrs €1; EHU (16A) metered + conn fee; lndry; shops, rest, snacks, bar 1km; playgrnd; htd pool 1km; wifi; dogs €2; poss cr; Eng spkn; adv bkg; noisy bdge traff; red long stay; CKE/CCI. "Pleasant site on island bordered by rv both sides; historic old town." 30 Mar-15 Oct. € 21.00   2010*

⊞ **HARZGERODE** *2E4* (8km SW Rural) *51.60833, 11.08444* **Ferienpark Birnbaumteich, Birnbaumteich 1, 06493 Neudorf Harzgerode [(03948) 46243; info@ferienpark-birnbaumteich.de; www.ferienpark-birnbaumteich.de]** Fr Harzgerode on B242 dir Halle, after 1km turn R, dir Stolberg. In 4.3km after Neudorf turn R at camping sp. Site 1km on R. Med, pt sl, pt shd; wc; chem disp; mv service pnt; baby facs; sauna; shwrs; EHU (16A) €3; lndry (inc dryer); shop; rest; café; snacks; bar; BBQ; playgrnd; lake sw; games area; games rm; entmnt; wifi; 50% statics; dogs €4; phone; bus 1km, train 3km; twin axles; Eng spkn; adv bkg; CKE/CCI. "Forest walk & bike trails; steam rlwy 3km; interesting towns nrby; vg." ◆ ltd. € 24.00   2015*

HASSENDORF see Rotenburg (Wümme) *1D2*

HATTINGEN *1B4* (3km NW Urban) *51.40611, 7.17027*
Camping Ruhrbrücke, Ruhrstrasse 6, 45529 Hattingen
[(02324) 80038; info@camping-hattingen.de; www.
camping-hattingen.de] Fr A40 bet Essen & Bochum exit
junc 29 dir Höntrop & Hattingen. Foll sp Hattingen on L651
& B1, site sp bef rv bdge. Med, pt sl, unshd; htd wc; chem
disp; shwrs €1; EHU (16A) €3; shop 1km; rest, snacks 1km;
bar 800m; BBQ; rv sw adj; canoeing, windsurfing adj; dogs
€2; phone; bus, train adj; Eng spkn; adv bkg; quiet; CKE/CCI.
"Beautiful rvside setting; plentiful, clean facs; friendly owner;
excel cycle tracks." ◆ ltd. 1 Apr-10 Oct. € 18.00   2010*

HAUSBAY see Lingerhahn *3B2*

HAUSEN IM TAL *3C4* (100m E Rural) *48.08365, 9.04290*
Camping Wagenburg, Kirchstr. 24, 88631 Beuron /
i Tal Hausen [(07579) 559; fax 1525; info@camping-
wagenburg.de; www.camping-wagenburg.de]
Fr E on B32 stay on Sigmaringen bypass and take minor rd
L227 sp Gutenstein/Beuron to Hausen, site in vill beside Rv
Donau. Med, hdstg, pt shd; wc; chem disp; mv service pnt;
shwrs €0.50; EHU (16A) metered + conn fee; lndry; shop 50m;
rest adj; bar; playgrnd; rv sw adj; tennis 300m; TV; dogs €1.50;
poss cr; Eng spkn; adv bkg; red long stay. "Beautiful location in
Danube Gorge; friendly, helpful owner; clsd 1230-1430; poss
flooding in wet weather/high rv level; gd walking/cycling; vg;
excel site gd for walking cycling; rv canoeing." ◆ ltd.
10 Apr-3 Oct. € 26.00   2012*

⊞ **HECHTHAUSEN** *1D2* (4km SW Rural) *53.62525, 9.20298*
Ferienpark & Campingpark Geesthof, Am Ferienpark 1,
21755 Hechthausen-Klint [(04774) 512; fax 9178; info@
geesthof.de; www.geesthof.de] Site sp on B73 rd to
Lamstedt. Med, hdg/mkd pitch, pt shd; wc; chem disp; mv
service pnt; sauna; baby facs; shwrs inc; EHU (10A) €2; lndry
(inc dryer); shop; rest, snacks; playgrnd; 2 pools (1 htd, covrd);
paddling pool; waterslide; watersports; fishing; boat & bike
hire; wifi; entmnt; 60% statics; dogs €2; Eng spkn; quiet;
red 7+ nts. "Superb site with mature trees around pitches;
peaceful surroundings adj to rv, lake & woods; friendly staff."
◆ € 22.50 (CChq acc)   2015*

HEIDELBERG *3C2* (10km E Rural) *49.40175, 8.77916*
Campingplatz Haide, Ziegelhäuser Landstrasse 91, 69151
Neckargemünd [(06223) 2111; fax 71959; info@camping-
haide.de] Take B37 fr Heidelberg, cross Rv Neckar by Ziegelhausen
bdge by sliprd on R (avoid vill narr rd); foll site sp. Site on R
bet rv & rd 1km W of Neckargemünd on rvside. Lge, unshd;
wc; chem disp; mv service pnt; shwrs €1; EHU (6A) €2.50
(long lead req); lndry (inc dryer); shop 2km; rest, snacks; BBQ;
playgrnd; bike hire; wifi; 5% statics; dogs €2; bus 1.5km; Eng
spkn; some rd, rlwy (daytime) & rv noise; red CKE/CCI. "Conv
Neckar Valley & Heidelberg; NH/sh stay only." ◆ 1 Apr-31 Oct.
€ 18.00   2011*

HEIDELBERG *3C2* (12km E Urban) *49.39638, 8.79472*
Campingplatz an der Friedensbrücke, Falltorstrasse
4, 69151 Neckargemünd [tel/fax (06223) 2178;
j.vandervelden@web.de] Exit Heidelberg on S side of
rv on B37; on ent Neckargemünd site sp to L (grey sp)
mkd Poststrasse; site adj rv bdge. Fr S on B45 turn L sp
Heidelberg, then R at camping sp. Fr A6 exit junc 33 onto
B45 sp Neckargemünd, then as above. Foll sp - do not foll
Sat Nav. Lge, unshd; htd wc; chem disp; mv service pnt;
baby facs; shwrs €0.75; EHU (6-10A) €5 or metered (poss
rev pol); gas; lndry; shop; rest adj; snacks; bar; playgrnd nr;
pool adj; kayaking 500m; tennis; wifi; TV rm; dogs €1.50;
phone; transport to Heidelberg by boat, bus & train 10 mins
walk fr site; poss cr; Eng spkn; adv bkg; rd & rv noise; ccard
not acc. "Gd location by busy rv, poss liable to flood; immac,
well-run, relaxing site; ask for rvside pitch (sm) - extra charge;
owner will site o'fits; warm welcome; helpful staff; no plastic
grndsheets; 26 steps up to main san facs; gd rvside walks &
cycling; TO 500m; gd NH facs, nr ent." ◆ 29 Mar-25 Oct.
€ 24.00   2015*

⊞ **HEIDENAU** *1D2* (2.6km W Rural) *53.30851, 9.62038*
Ferienzentrum Heidenau, Minkens Fuhren, 21258
Heidenau [(04182) 4272 or 4861; fax 401130; info@
ferienzentrum-heidenau.de; www.ferienzentrum-
heidenau.de] Exit A1 Hamburg-Bremen m'way junc 46
to Heidenau; foll sp. Lge, pt shd; htd wc; chem disp; mv
service pnt; sauna; shwrs inc; EHU (16A) €2.50 (poss long
lead req); lndry; shop; rest, snacks; bar; BBQ (sep area);
playgrnd; htd pool; fishing lakes; gd cycling; tennis; games
area; internet; 75% statics; no dogs; phone; Eng spkn; quiet;
CKE/CCI. "Pleasant, wooded site; tourers on grass areas by
lakes; clean, modern facs; ltd shop; gd; visa ccards not acc."
€ 24.50   2015*

HEIDENBURG see Trittenheim *3B2*

HEINSEN see Holzminden *1D3*

HELLENTHAL see Schleiden *3B1*

HEMMINGEN ARNUM see Hannover *1D3*

HEMSBACH see Weinheim *3C2*

HENNSTEDT *1D1* (4km N Rural) *54.31351, 9.18953* Camping-
Ferienpark Eider, Eiderstrasse 20, 25779 Hennstedt-Horst
[tel/fax (04836) 611; eidercamping@t-online.de;
www.eidercamping.de] Fr B203 Rendsburg-Heide rd, turn N
in Tellingstedt to Hennstedt, then to Horst. Site sp on Rv Eider.
Med, hdg/mkd pitch, pt shd; wc; chem disp; shwrs €0.50; EHU
(6A) €1.60; lndry; shop; rest 4km; snacks; bar; cooking facs;
playgrnd; pool; fishing; boat-launching; golf 5km; 40% statics;
dogs €2; CKE/CCI. 1 Apr-31 Oct. € 14.50   2009*

HERBOLZHEIM *3B3* (2km E Rural) *48.21625, 7.78796*
**Terrassen-Campingplatz Herbolzheim, Laue-Dietweg
1, 79336 Herbolzheim [(07643) 1460; fax 913382;
s.hugoschmidt@t-online.de; www.laue-camp.de]**
Fr E35/A5 exit 58 to Herbolzheim. Turn R in vill. Turn L on
o'skts of vill. Site in 1km next to sw pool, sp. Med, terr, pt shd;
wc; chem disp; mv service pnt; shwrs inc; EHU (10A) €2; lndry;
shop; rest; playgrnd; pool & tennis nrby; 30% statics; dogs €2
(not acc mid-Jul to mid-Aug); o'nights facs for m'vans; clsd
1300-1500; adv bkg; quiet; ccard acc; red long stay; ACSI;
CKE/CCI. "Excel friendly, well-maintained site; conv Vosges,
Black Forest & Europapark; gd simple rest, spotless and supmkt
nrby, excel staff; immac grass on firm base." 23 Mar-3 Oct.
€ 30.00   2013*

HERSBRUCK *4E2* (6km E Rural) *49.51884, 11.49200* **Pegnitz
Camping, Eschenbacherweg 4, 91224 Hohenstadt
[(09154) 1500; fax 91200]** Exit A9 junc 49 onto B14 dir
Hersbruck & Sulzbach-Rosenberg. By-pass Hersbruck & after
8km turn L sp Hohenstadt. Bef vill, cross rv bdge & immed
turn R at site sp. Med, pt shd; wc; chem disp; mv service pnt;
shwrs inc; EHU (10A) inc; gas; lndry; shop & rest 1km; bike
hire; 10% statics; trains nrby; Eng spkn; adv bkg; quiet; CKE/
CCI. "Lovely, peaceful, friendly site; gd walking & cycling area;
helpful owner; vg san facs; train to Nuremberg; gd; stn 200m."
1 Mar-31 Oct. € 16.00   2014*

HERSBRUCK *4E2* (10km NW Rural) *49.53900, 11.37200*
**Berghof Glatzenstein M'van Parking, Jurastrasse 14,
91233 Weissenbach [(09153) 7906; fax 9229926]**
Exit A9/E51 junc 49 dir Hersbruck. In 2km turn L on minor rd sp
Speikern & Kersbach. Foll sp Weissenbach & Berg Glatzenstein,
up winding rd to Berghof. O'night parking area is opp hotel.
Sm (5 pitches); no facs, no fee on condition have meal in rest;
gd views; m'vans only. May-Sep. € 11.70   2009*

HIRSCHAU *4F2* (6km E Rural) *49.55608, 12.00634*
**Campingplatz am Naturbad, Badstrasse 13, 92253
Schnaittenbach [tel/fax (09622) 1722; info@campingplatz.
schnaittenbach.de; www.schnaittenbach.de]** On B14 bet
Rosenberg & Wernberg, clearly sp in vill. Med, sl, unshd; wc;
chem disp; shwrs inc; EHU (16A) €1.50 or metered + conn fee;
lndry (inc dryer); shop 1.5km; rest adj; playgrnd; pool; games
area; 80% statics; quiet; red CKE/CCI. "Gd NH; scenic area; v
pleasant site." ♦ ltd. 1 Apr-30 Sep. € 17.50   2013*

⊞ **HIRSCHAU** *4F2* (3km SE Rural) *49.53088, 11.96525*
**Camping Monte Kaolino, Wolfgang-Drossbach Strasse
115, 92242 Hirschau [(09622) 81502; fax 81555; info@
montekaolino.eu; www.montekaolino.eu]** Exit A93 junc 27
onto B14, site sp. Med, terr, pt sl, pt shd; wc; chem disp; baby
facs; shwrs; EHU (16A) metered + conn fee; lndry; shop 1.5km;
rest, snacks; playgrnd; htd pool; paddling pool; games area;
dry-ski & lift; 60% statics dogs €1.50; poss v cr; adv bkg; quiet;
red CKE/CCI. "Vg for children; poss diff access to pitches for
tourers; interesting area." ♦ ltd. 1 Apr-15 Sep. 2009*

HIRSCHHORN see Eberbach *3C2*

⊞ **HOF** *4F2* (10km NW Rural) *50.37494, 11.83804*
**Camping Auensee, 95189 Joditz-Köditz [(09295) 381;
fax (09281) 706666; rathaus@gemeinde-koeditz.de;
www.gemeinde-koeditz.de]** Exit A9 at junc 31 Berg/Bad
Steben. Turn R fr m'way & in 200m L to Joditz, foll site sp in vill
(1-way ent/exit to site). Med, terr, unshd; wc; mv service pnt;
shwrs; EHU (16A) €1.80 or metered; lndry; shops adj; rest high
ssn; playgrnd; lake sw; fishing; tennis; 75% statics; dogs €1.50;
clsd 1230-1500; quiet; red CKE/CCI. € 13.00   2010*

HOFHEIM AM RIEGSEE see Murnau am Staffelsee *4E4*

HOHENFELDE *2E1* (2km N Coastal) *54.38630, 10.49165*
**Camping Ostseestrand, Strandstrasse, 24257 Hohenfelde
[(04385) 620; fax 593846; info@campingostseestrand.de;
www.campingostseestrand.de]**
Fr Kiel on B502 dir Lütjenburg, foll sp to site in Hohenfelde.
Med, mkd pitch, unshd; htd wc; chem disp; mv service pnt;
shwrs €0.50; private san facs avail; EHU (10A); €2.50; lndry
(inc dryer); shop; rest, snacks, bar adj; playgrnd; sand beach
adj; watersports; horseriding 2km; golf 5km; internet; TV; 70%
statics; dogs €2; o'night facs for m'vans; adv bkg; quiet; ccard
acc. "Pleasant area of lakes & forests; ltd pitches for tourers;
gd, clean san facs; vg." ♦ 1 Apr-24 Oct. € 19.50   2009*

HOHENFELDEN see Kranichfeld *2E4*

HOHENSTADT see Hersbruck *4E2*

⊞ **HOHENSTADT** *3D3* (500m NE Rural) *48.54693, 9.66794*
**Camping Waldpark Hohenstadt, Waldpark 1, 73345
Hohenstadt [(07335) 6754; fax (7335) 184574; camping@
waldpark-hohenstadt.de; www.waldpark-hohenstadt.de]**
Exit A8/E52 junc 60 Behelfs & foll sp to Hohenstadt & site in
approx 5km. Med, some hdstg, pt sl, pt shd; htd wc; chem
disp; mv service pnt; baby facs; shwrs €0.50; EHU (16a) €2.50;
lndry (inc dryer); rest, snacks; bar; BBQ; playgrnd; htd pool;
wifi; 75% statics; dogs €1; Eng spkn; quiet; red LS; CKE/
CCI. "Gd, peaceful NH to/fr Austria; handy off A8 - conv for
mway; helpful & friendly staff; gd facs; long walk to shwrs
fr tourer parking; lovely site; area ideal for walking, cycling,
climbing, skiing and cross country skiing; excel." 1 Mar-31 Oct.
€ 27.50   2013*

HOLLE *1D3* (5km NW Rural) *52.10285, 10.13877* **Seecamp
Derneburg, 31188 Holle-Derneburg [(05062) 565;
fax 8785; info@campingplatz-derneburg.de;
www.seecamp-derneburg.de]** Exit A7/E45 junc 63 at
Derneberg onto B6, dir Hildesheim. Site in 300m. Med,
unshd; wc; chem disp; shwrs €0.50; EHU (16A) metered;
shop high ssn; rest; playgrnd; lake adj; bike hire; 50% statics;
dogs €2; Eng spkn; ccard acc. "Quiet site; locked at 2200,
barrier key ess after this time; helpful; gd rest." 1 Apr-15 Sep.
€ 18.40   2011*

HOLZMINDEN *1D3* (10km N Rural) *51.88618, 9.44335*
Weserbergland Camping, Weserstrasse 66, 37649 Heinsen
[(05535) 8733; fax 911264; info@weserbergland-camping.
de; www.weserbergland-camping.de] Fr Holzminden on
B83 twd Hameln, site sp in Heinsen cent twd rv bank. Med, pt
sl, pt shd; htd wc; chem disp; mv service pnt; baby facs; sauna;
shwrs €0.50; EHU (10A) €1.90; gas; lndry (inc dryer); shop
600m; rest; bar; playgrnd; htd pool; bike hire; games area;
entmnt in high ssn; wifi; 50% statics; dogs €3; twin axles; Eng
spkn; adv bkg; quiet; ccard acc; 10% red long stay/CKE/CCI.
"Beautiful site on rv bank; gd modern san facs (2015); gd area
for walking/cycling; gd local bus service; accomodating owner;
excel." 1 Apr-31 Oct. € 23.00   2015*

⊞ **HOLZMINDEN** *1D3* (11km SE Rural) *51.77086, 9.54873*
Campingplatz Silberborn, Glashüttenweg 4, 37603
Holzminden-Silberborn [tel/fax (05536) 664; info@
naturcamping-silberborn.de; www.naturcamping-
silberborn.de] S fr Holzminden on B497; turn L to Silberborn.
Lge, mkd pitch; pt shd; htd wc; chem disp; baby facs; shwrs
€0.50; EHU (16A) €2 or metered; gas; lndry (inc dryer); shop
500m; rest; bar; BBQ; playgrnd; pool; 50% statics; dogs €2;
phone & bus 500m; adv bkg; quiet; red long stay/CKE/CCI. "V
clean, well-kept site; popular with bikers; gd value rest; vg." ♦
€ 17.00   2010*

HOOKSIEL *1C2* (2km N Coastal) *53.64100, 8.03400* Nordsee
Camping Hooksiel (Part Naturist), Bäderstrasse, 26434
Wangerland [(04425) 958080; fax 991475; camp-
hooksiel@wangerland.de; www.wangerland.de]
Exit A29 at junc 4 sp Fedderwarden to N. Thro Hooksiel,
site sp 1.5km. V lge, some hdstg, unshd; wc; chem disp; mv
service pnt; baby facs; shwrs inc; EHU (6-10A) inc; gas; lndry
(inc dryer); shop; rest, snacks; playgrnd; muddy beach; fishing;
sailing; watersports; games area; bike hire; wifi; entmnt;
50% statics; dogs €3.10; naturist site adj with same facs; poss
cr; quiet. "Main san facs excel but up 2 flights steps - otherwise
facs in Portakabin." ♦ 25 Mar-17 Oct. € 21.40   2010*

⊞ **HORB AM NECKAR** *3C3* (4km W Rural) *48.44513,
8.67300* Camping Schüttehof, Schütteberg 7-9, 72160
Horb-am-Neckar [(07451) 3951; fax 623215; camping-
schuettehof@t-online.de; www.camping-schuettehof.de]
Fr A81/E41 exit junc 30; take Freudenstadt rd out of Horb site
sp. Med, mkd pitch, pt sl, pt shd; wc; chem disp; shwrs €0.50;
EHU (16A) metered + conn fee; gas; lndry; shop; rest; playgrnd;
htd pool; paddling pool; internet; entmnt; 75% statics; dogs
€2; poss cr; adv bkg; quiet. "Horb delightful Black Forest town;
site close to saw mill & could be noisy; steep path to town; site
clsd 1230-1430." € 17.00   2012*

HORSTEL *1B3* (5km N Rural) *52.32751, 7.60061*
Campingplatz Herthasee, Herthaseestrasse 70, 48477
Hörstel [(05459) 1008; fax 971875; contact@hertha-see.de;
www.hertha-see.de] Exit A30/E30 junc 10 to Hörstel, then
foll sp Hopsten. Site well sp fr a'bahn. V lge, pt sl, shd; wc;
chem disp; mv service pnt; baby facs; shwrs €0.50; EHU
(16A) €2.40 or metered + conn fee (poss long lead req); gas;
lndry; shop; rest 2km; snacks; bar; BBQ; playgrnd; lake sw &
beach adj; tennis; bike hire; TV; wifi; 70% statics; no dogs;
Eng spkn; quiet; CKE/CCI. "Excel site." ♦ 22 Mar-29 Sep.
€ 31.00   2013*

HOSSERINGEN *1D2* (2km N Rural) *52.86940, 10.42274*
Campingplatz am Hardausee, Am Campingplatz 1, 29556
Suderburg-Hösseringen [(05826) 7676; fax 8303; info@
camping-hardausee.de; www.camping-hardausee.de]
S fr Uelzen on B4/B191 for 9km to Suderburg & Hösseringen,
site sp. Med, pt shd; wc; chem disp; mv service pnt; shwrs
inc; EHU (16A) €2; lndry; shop (high ssn); rest 1km; snacks;
playgrnd; sw 300m; dogs €1.50; quiet. "Ltd touring pitches;
excel, clean facs; excel cycling & walking; conv Lüneberg."
€ 17.00   2009*

HOXTER *1D3* (2km S Rural) *51.76658, 9.38308*
Wesercamping Höxter, Sportzentrum 4, 37671 Höxter
[tel/fax (05271) 2589; info@campingplatz-hoexter.de;
www.campingplatz-hoexter.de] Fr B83/64 turn E over rv sp
Boffzen, turn R & site sp almost on rv bank. Turn R in 300m
at green sp, turn L in car park. Med, pt shd; wc; chem disp;
baby facs; shwrs €0.50; EHU (10-16A) €2; lndry (inc dryer);
shop; rest; playgrnd; internet; child entmnt; 60% statics; dogs
€1.50; quiet; red CKE/CCI. "Lge open area for tourers; clsd
1300-1500; spaces beside rv; easy walk along rv to town."
15 Mar-15 Oct. € 14.50   2014*

⊞ **HUCKESWAGEN** *1B4* (4km NE Rural) *51.15269,
7.36557* Campingplatz Beverblick, Grossberghausen
29, Mickenhagen, 42499 Hückeswagen [(02192) 83389;
info@beverblick.de; www.beverblick.de] Fr B237 in
Hückeswagen at traff lts take B483 sp Radevormwald. Over
rv & in 500m turn R sp Mickenhagen. In 3km strt on (no thro
rd), turn R after 1km, site on R. Steep app. Med, hdstg, pt
sl, unshd; htd wc; chem disp (wc); shwrs €1.10; EHU (10A)
metered; shop & 5km; rest; bar; 90% statics; dogs; quiet. "Few
touring pitches; helpful owners; gd rest & bar; gd touring base;
vg." € 15.00   2012*

⊞ **HUNFELD** *1D4* (5km SW Rural) *50.65333, 9.72388* Knaus
Campingpark Praforst, Dr Detlev-Rudelsdorff Allee 6,
36088 Hünfeld [(06652) 749090; fax 7490901; huenfeld@
knauscamp.de; www.knauscamp.de] Exit A7 junc 90 dir
Hünfeld, foll sp thro golf complex. Med, mkd pitch, pt sl, pt
shd; wc; shwrs; chem disp; mv service pnt; EHU (16A) metered
or €2.50; lndry; shop; playgrnd; pool; fishing; games rm; games
area; golf adj; wifi; 40% statics; dogs €2; quiet. "Excel san facs;
gd walking/cycling." ♦ € 22.00   2009*

HUSUM *1D1* (9km SW Coastal) *54.45557, 8.97224*
Nordseecamping Zum Seehund, Lundenbergweg 4,
25813 Simonsberg [(04841) 3999; fax 65489; info@
nordseecamping.de; www.nordseecamping.de] L off B5
Heide-Husum at Darigbull sp Simonberg. Site sp. Lge, unshd;
wc (htd); chem disp; mv service pnt; baby facs; shwrs inc; EHU
(16A) €2.50; gas; lndry (inc dryer); shop 6km; rest, snacks; bar;
BBQ; playgrnd; mud beach adj; lake sw 300m; wellness cent;
golf 10km; 60% statics; dogs €2; poss cr; Eng spkn; quiet;
CKE/CCI. "Superb family run site with excel facs; modern air-
con san facs; gd value for money; really gd for cycling & bikes
avail for hire on site." ♦ 1 Mar-15 Nov. € 22.00   2011*

GERMANY

IBBENBUREN *1B3* (4.6km S Rural) *52.24555, 7.69861*
Camping Dörenther Klippen, Münsterstrasse 419,
49479 Ibbenbüren [(05451) 2553; fax 9615; roesch-
ibbenbueren@freenet.de; www.doerenther-klippen.de]
Fr A30/E30 exit junc 11b on B219 dir Greven. Site sp in 1.7km.
Sm, hdg/mkd pitch, pt sl, pt shd; wc; chem disp; shwrs inc;
EHU (16A) €2.50 (rev pol); lndry; rest; bar; pool 5km; many
statics; dogs; Eng spkn; quiet but some rd noise; ccard acc;
CKE/CCI. "Friendly, gd walking; ltd space for tourers; barrier
clsd 2200-0700; site poss unkempt/untidy LS; NH only."
1 Mar-31 Oct. € 21.50 (4 persons)   2010*

⊞ **IBBENBUREN** *1B3* (9km SW Rural) *52.21829, 7.66502*
Camping Eichengrund, Im Brook 2, 49479 Ibbenbüren
[(05455) 521; fax 287] Exit A30/E30 junc 11b onto B219 dir
Greven for 5.8km; site sp on R 200m after x-ing canal bdge.
Lge, hdg pitch, pt shd; wc; chem disp; mv service pnt; private
bathrms avail; shwrs €0.50; EHU (16A) €1.50; gas; lndry;
shop; rest; playgrnd; 90% statics; quiet; CKE/CCI. "Excel
site; barrier & office clsd 1300-1500; ltd shwrs & san facs."
€ 14.00   2009*

⊞ **IDAR OBERSTEIN** *3B2* (15km N Rural) *49.80455,
7.26986* Camping Harfenmühle, 55758 Asbacherhütte
[(06786) 7076; fax 7570; mail@harfenmuehle.de;
www.camping-harfenmuehle.de] Fr rte 41 fr Idar twd Kirn,
turn L at traff lts at Fischbach by-pass sp Herrstein/Morbach,
site 3km past Herrstein vill. Sharp turn to site. Med, pt shd;
wc; chem disp; mv service pnt; sauna; shwrs €0.50; EHU (16A)
metered; lndry; gas; shop; rest, snacks; bar; playgrnd; lake sw
adj; fishing; tennis; games area; games rm; golf 10km; internet;
TV rm; 50% statics; dogs €2; phone; o'night area for m'vans;
adv bkg; Eng spkn; no ccard acc; 10% red CKE/CCI. "Vg rest;
gd san facs but poss inadequate in high ssn; sep area late arr;
barrier clsd 2200; gd site." ♦ ltd. € 25.00   2014*

IHRINGEN see Breisach am Rhein *3B4*

⊞ **ILLERTISSEN** *3D4* (11km S Rural) *48.14138, 10.10665*
Camping Christophorus Illertal, Werte 6, 88486 Kirchberg-
Sinningen [(07354) 663; fax 91314; info@camping-
christophorus.de; www.camping-christophorus.de]
Exit A7/E43 junc 125 at Altenstadt. In cent of town turn L,
then R immed after level x-ing. Foll site sp. Lge, pt shd; htd wc;
chem disp; sauna; shwrs; EHU (16A) €2.80 or metered; lndry;
shop high ssn; rest, snacks; playgrnd; covrd pool; lake sw adj;
fishing; bike hire; 80% statics; dogs €3.50; Eng spkn; adv bkg;
red CKE/CCI. "Gd site; sm sep area for tourers; excel san facs."
€ 29.00   2013*

ILLERTISSEN *3D4* (2km SW Rural) *48.21221, 10.08773*
Camping Illertissen, Dietenheimerstrasse 91, 89257
Illertissen [(07303) 7888; fax 2848; campingplatz-
illertissen@t-online.de; www.camping-illertissen.de]
Leave A7 at junc 124, twd Illertissen/Dietenheim; after rlwy
x-ing turn R then L foll site sp. Off main rd B19 fr Neu Ulm-
Memmingen fr N, turn R in Illertissen, foll sp. Sm, mkd pitch,
terr, pt shd; wc; chem disp; mv service pnt; shwrs inc; EHU
(16A) €2 or metered; gas; lndry; shop & 1.5km; snacks; rest in
hotel adj; playgrnd; pool; 65% statics; dogs €2; poss cr; quiet;
ccard acc; 10% red CKE/CCI. "Trains to Ulm & Kempten; 20
mins walk to town or cycle track; some pitches poss unrel in
wet; site clsd bet 1300-1500 & 2200-0700; obliging owner;
conv a'bahn; vg." ♦ 1 Apr-30 Oct. € 20.00   2015*

IMMENSTAAD AM BODENSEE see Friedrichshafen *3D4*

⊞ **IMMENSTADT IM ALLGAU** *3D4* (3km NW Rural)
47.57255, 10.19358 Buchers Alpsee Camping, Seestrasse
25, 87509 Bühl-am-Alpsee [(08323) 7726; fax 2956;
mail@alpsee-camping.de; www.alpsee-camping.de]
Fr Immenstadt, W on B308; turn R dir Isny & Missen. In 1.3km
turn L sp Bühl & site sp. Lge, unshd; wc; shwrs inc; EHU (16A)
€2.50 (poss rev pol); gas; lndry; shop; rest; playgrnd; pool 2km;
lake sw adj; ski lift 3km; dogs €3; poss cr; Eng spkn; adv bkg;
quiet. "Lake sm but pleasant; gd mountain walks; friendly
welcome; excel site, first class facs." € 45.00   2014*

⊞ **INGOLSTADT** *4E3* (4.5km E Rural) *48.75416, 11.46277*
Azur Campingpark Am Auwaldsee, 85053 Ingolstadt
[(0841) 9611616; fax 9611617; ingolstadt@azur-camping.
de; www.azur-camping.de] Exit A9/E45 junc 62 Ingolstadt
Süd, foll sp for camp site & Auwaldsee. V lge, pt shd; wc; shwrs
inc; chem disp; mv service pnt; EHU (16A) €2.80; gas; lndry
(inc dryer); shop 1.5km; rest, snacks; adj; bar; playgrnd; pool
1km; rv beach & sw; fishing & boating; wifi; 50% statics; dogs
€3.50; bus; clsd 1300-1500; poss cr; adv bkg. "Basic wooded
site by lake; useful NH nr m'way." ♦ ltd. € 24.00   2012*

⊞ **INZELL** *4F4* (800m SW Rural) *47.76722, 12.75341*
Camping Lindlbauer, Kreuzfeldstraße 44, 83334 Inzell
[08665 928 99 88; fax 928 99 86; info@camping-inzell.de]
Fr A8 exit 112 Traunstein-Siegsdorf. Take B306 twds Inzell. Foll
sp in vill to campsite. Med, mkd pitch, hdstg, terr, unshd; htd
wc; chem disp; mv service pnt; baby facs; shwrs inc; EHU (16A);
lndry (inc dryer); shop; rest, snacks; bar; playgrnd; htd covrd
pool; games area; wifi; dogs €4; phone adj; bus adj; twin axles;
Eng spkn; adv bkg; quiet; red LS; CCI. "Excel site; beautiful
views; friendly, family run site; excel location for walking &
cycling". ♦ € 44.70   2014*

⊞ **IRREL** *3A2* (700m S Urban) *49.84175, 6.45750*
Campingplatz Südeifel, Hofstraße 19, 54666 Irrel
[06525 510; info@camping-suedeifel.de; www.camping-
suedeifel.de] Take Irrel exit off B257; site sp. Lge, pt shd;
wc; shwrs; EHU (6A) €2; gas; lndry; rest; bar; BBQ; playgrnd;
wifi; dogs €2; quiet; CKE/CCI. "Cycling in area & walks fr site;
pleasant town; tourist info in town; gd site."   2011*

ISNY IM ALLGAU *3D4* (10km NW Rural) *47.75400, 10.00432*
Campingplatz am Badsee, Allmisried 1, 88316 Isny-Beuren
[(07567) 1026; fax 1092; campingbadsee@t-online.de;
www.campingbadsee.de] On Isny-Leutkirch rd turn W on N
side of Friesenhofen sp Beuren. In 4km at Beuren turn N onto
sm rd sp to site, Badsee & Winnis. Med, pt sl, pt terr, pt shd;
wc; chem disp; mv service pnt; baby facs; fam bthrm; shwrs
€1; EHU (16A) metered + €2.50; lndry; shop high ssn snacks;
rest; playgrnd; lake sw & beach; 80% statics; dogs €2.30;
clsd 1300-1500; adv bkg. "Isny interesting; excel facs; vg." ♦
15 Apr-15 Oct. € 18.50   2010*

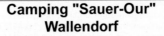

Camping "Ourtalidyll"
Gentingen ★★★★

QUALITÄT IST UNSERE NATUR

Q ServiceQualität DEUTSCHLAND EIFEL GASTGEBER

Camping "Sauer-Our"
Wallendorf

Eifelidyll
Camping und mehr...

Tel.: 0049 (0) 6566 352   www.eifelidyll.de   @eifelidyll.de

GERMANY

ISSIGAU 4F2 (450m S Rural) 50.37413, 11.72103
Camping Schloss Issigau, Altes Schloss 3, 95188 Issigau [(09293) 7173; fax 7050; info@schloss-issigau.de; www.schloss-issigau.de] Exit A9/E51 junc 31 dir Berg. In Issigau foll sp over bdge to site. Sm, pt sl, pt shd; wc; chem disp; mv service pnt; shwrs inc; EHU (16A) metered; gas; lndry; shop 300m; rest, snacks; bar; playgrnd; TV rm; dogs €1.50; phone; Eng spkn; adv bkg; quiet; ccard not acc; CKE/CCI. "Gd walking & cycling; friendly, helpful owners; delightful, well-kept site; vg facs & rest; visit to Mödlareuth worthwhile."
15 Mar-31 Oct & 17 Dec-6 Jan. € 17.50   2011*

⊞ **JENA** 2E4 (2km NE Rural) 50.93583, 11.60833
Campingplatz Unter dem Jenzig, Am Erlkönig 3, 07749 Jena [(03641) 666688; post@camping-jena.com; www.camping-jena.com] Exit A4/E40 junc 54 to Jena, then B88 for 4m N dir Naumberg. Turn R just outside Jena at campsite sp, R over blue bdge; site nr sports stadium/sw pool on L, sp. Med, unshd; wc; chem disp; mv service pnt; shwrs inc; EHU (10A) €2.50 or metered; lndry; rest 500m; snacks; bar; playgrnd; pool adj; dogs €1; phone; bus 1km; shop 1.5km; some Eng spkn; adv bkg; quiet. "Gd san facs in Portakabin; sh walk to interesting town; gd cycle paths." ♦ ltd.
€ 23.50   2014*

"That's changed – Should I let The Club know?"

If you find something on site that's different from the site entry, fill in a report and let us know. See www.caravanclub.co.uk/europereport.

JESTETTEN 3C4 (750m SW Urban) 47.64802, 8.56648
Campingplatz & Schwimmbad, Waldshuterstrasse 13, 79798 Jestetten [(07745) 1220; info@jestetten.de; www.jestetten.de] Site in town on B27 main rd, sp. Sm, pt sl, pt shd; htd wc; chem disp (wc); shwrs inc; EHU (10A) metered; lndry; shop, rest in town; snacks; playgrnd; htd pool; wifi; no dogs; bus at gate; train 500m; Eng spkn; adv bkg; quiet. "Gd for walk or train Rhine Falls & Switzerland; shwr token inc; friendly; site in Schwimmbad grnds." ♦ ltd. Mid May-Mid Sep.
€ 22.00   2015*

JODITZ KODITZ see Hof 4F2

⊞ **KALKAR** 1A3 (5km N Rural) 51.76100, 6.28483
Freitzeitpark Wisseler See, Zum Wisseler-See 15, 47546 Kalkar-Wissel [(02824) 96310; fax 963131; info@wisseler-see.de; www.wisseler-see.de] Fr A3 take junc 4 onto B67 dir Kalkar & Wissel. Fr Kleve take B57 SE for 8km twd Kalkar, E to Wissel & foll camp sp. V lge, hdg/mkd pitch, pt shd; serviced pitches; wc; chem disp; mv service pnt; shwrs inc; EHU (16A) inc; lndry; shop; rest, snacks; pool; playgrnd; beach; watersports; tennis; bike hire; games area; wifi; entmnt; 75% statics; dogs €2.50; Eng spkn; adv bkg;. "Commercialised & regimented but conv NH Rotterdam ferry; gd facs; gd for children & teenagers." ♦ € 24.00   2009*

⊞ **KAMENZ** 2G4 (7km NE Rural) 51.30465, 14.15272
Campingplatz Deutschbaselitz, Grossteichstrasse 30, 01917 Kamenz [(03578) 301489; fax 308098; info@campingplatz-deutschbaselitz.com; www.campingplatz-deutschbaselitz.com] Fr Kamenz N on rd S95 dir Wittichenau; at Schiedel turn R twd lake, site sp. Med, pt shd; htd wc; chem disp; mv service pnt; baby facs; fam bthrm; shwrs inc; EHU (16A) €3; lndry (inc dryer); shop; snacks; BBQ; cooking facs; playgrnd; lake sw & beach adj; watersports; bike hire; games area; games rm; 10% statics; dogs; adv bkg; quiet; CKE/CCI. ♦ € 16.00 (CChq acc)   2009*

⊞ **KAPPELN** 1D1 (7km SW Rural) 54.61945, 9.88402
Campingpark Schlei-Karschau, Karschau 56, 24407 Rabenkirchen-Faulück [(04642) 920820; fax 920821; info@campingpark-schlei.de; www.campingpark-schlei.de] Exit A7 junc 5 onto B201 dir Kappeln, site sp dir Faulück & Karschau. Lge, mkd pitch, pt sl, unshd; htd wc; mv service pnt; baby facs; shwrs €0.50; EHU (6A) inc; lndry (inc dryer); shop; rest, snacks; playgrnd; sand beach & private beach, rv sw adj; fishing; boat & bike hire; tennis; games area; golf 5km; 70% statics; dogs €2; adv bkg; quiet. "Gd, peaceful site." ♦ € 20.60   2011*

⊞ **KARLSHAGEN** 2G1 (2km E Coastal) 54.11769, 13.84477
Dünencamp, Zeltplatzstraße, 17449 Ostseebad; Karlshagen [038371 20291; camping@karlshagen.de; www.duenencamp.de] Site sp fr karlshagen along Zeltplatzstrasse. Lge, mkd pitch, pt sl, shd; htd wc; chem disp; MV service pnt; baby facs; fam bthrm; shwrs (metered); elec pnt (16A) €2 (or metered); lndry; playgrnd; beach adj; dogs €4; phone; Eng spkn; quiet. "Site has direct access to long clean sandy beach; long mains lead may be needed for some pitches; conv for visiting Peenemünde; gd site." € 26.00   2011*

GERMANY

KARLSRUHE *3C3* (9km E Rural) *49.00788, 8.48303* **Azur Campingpark Turmbergblick, Tiengenerstrasse 40, 76227 Karlsruhe-Durlach [(0721) 497236; fax 497237; karlsruhe@ azur-camping.de; www.azur-camping.de]** Exit A5/E35 junc 44 dir Durlach/Grötzingen onto B10 & foll sp to site 3km. Lge, mkd pitch, pt shd; htd wc; chem disp; mv service pnt; baby facs; shwrs inc; EHU (10A) €3 (long lead poss req); gas; lndry; shop; supmkt 500m; rest, snacks; bar; playgrnd; 2 pools nr; tennis; entmnt; internet; 20% statics; dogs €3.50; Eng spkn; adv bkg; some rd & rlwy noise; ccard acc; CKE/CCI. "NH conv to a'bahn; adequate san facs; clsd 1230-1400; expensive for average site." ♦ 1 Apr-31 Oct. € 26.50   2012*

⊞ **KASSEL** *1D4* (4km S Urban) *51.29055, 9.48777* **Wohnmobilstellplatz Kassel, Giesenallee, 34121 Kassel [(0561) 707707; strassenverkehrsamt@stadt-kassel.de]** Exit A49 junc 5; strt on at traff lts; 1st R sp camping. Site 80m beyond Fulda Camp. Sm, hdstg, unshd; chem disp; mv service pnt; EHU (10A) metered; dogs; bus adj. M'vans only. "Max stay 3 nights; excel stopover; nice walk along rv & lge park nrby." € 12.50   2014*

⊞ **KASTELLAUN** *3B2* (800m SE Rural) *50.06846, 7.45382* **Burgstadt Camping Park, Südstrasse 34, 56288 Kastellaun [(06762) 40800; fax 4080100; info@burgstadt.de; www.burgstadt.de]** Exit A61 junc 42 dir Emmelshausen onto L206/L213 for 1.2km; turn L onto B327; cont for 13.5km to Kastellaun. Site adj hotel on B237. Med, mkd pitch, hdstg, terr, unshd; htd wc; chem disp; mv waste; baby facs; sauna; solarium; shwrs inc; EHU (16A) metered; lndry; shop; rest, snacks; bar; BBQ; playgrnd; htd, covrd pool 300m; tennis, bike hire, riding & kayaking nrby; wifi; dogs €2; o'night m'van area; Eng spkn; adv bkg; quiet; ccard acc; CKE/CCI. "Lge pitches; clean site; excel, clean san facs; helpful staff; conv touring base; fitness & beauty cent in hotel adj; excel; v peaceful." ♦ € 24.00   2015*

KEHL *3B3* (12km ESE Rural) *48.54375, 7.93518* **Europa-Camping, Waldstrasse 32, 77731 Willstätt-Sand [tel/fax (07852) 2311; europa.camping@t-online.de; www.europa-camping-sand.de]** Exit A5/E35/E52 at junc 54 almost immed turn R at Int'l Camping sp; foll site sp. Med, some hdstg, pt shd; htd wc; shwrs inc; EHU (16A) €2.50 (long lead poss req); lndry (inc dryer); shop & 5km; rest; cooking facs; playgrnd; 30% statics; dogs €2; poss cr; Eng spkn; quiet but some rd noise; ccard acc; red long stay/CKE/CCI. "Easy reach Black Forest & Strasbourg; 1km fr a'bahn exit; well-managed, clean, tidy site; gd san facs; friendly helpful owner; cycle tracks fr site." 1 Feb-30 Nov. € 26.00   2013*

KEHL *3B3* (3km S Urban) *48.5615, 7.80861* **DCC Campingpark Kehl-Strassburg, Rheindammstrasse 1, 77694 Kehl-Kronenhof [(07851) 2603; fax 73076; CampingparkKehl@aol.com; www.campingplatz-kehl.de]** Fr A5/E35, take exit 54 onto B28 at Appenweier twd Kehl & foll site sp. Lge, pt shd; htd wc; chem disp; mv service pnt; shwrs €0.50; EHU (16A) metered + conn fee (long lead poss req); gas; lndry; shop & 1km; rest, snacks; bar; playgrnd; sw pool adj; wifi; 15% statics; dogs €1; bus 1km; poss cr; Eng spkn; adv bkg; quiet but noise fr adj stadium w/end; ccard acc; red CKE/ CCI. "Peaceful site adj Rv Rhine; excel rest & modern san facs; sm pitches; pleasant rv walk & cycle paths to town; barrier clsd 1300-1500." ♦ 15 Mar-31 Oct. € 23.50   2014*

⊞ **KELBRA** *2E4* (2km W Rural) *51.42551, 11.00307* **Seecamping Kelbra, Langestrasse 150, 06537 Kelbra [(034651) 45290; fax 45292; info@seecampingkelbra.de]** Exit A38 at Berga (bet junc 12 & 14); on app to town turn L at traff lts onto B85 to Kelbra; go thro chicane in vill, then R onto L234/L1040 dir Sonderhausen; site sp. L234 is Langestrasse. Lge, pt sl, unshd; htd wc; chem disp; mv service pnt; shwrs €0.50; EHU (16A) €2; lndry; shop; rest, snacks; bar; BBQ (gas/ elec); playgrnd; lake sw adj; sand beach 1km; games area; internet; TV; dogs adj; poss cr; Eng spkn; adv bkg; quiet; CKE/CCI. "Gd touring base & walking area; boat hire on site; vg; 2 toilet blocks now (2015); NH outside main gates." € 18.50   2015*

⊞ **KEMPTEN (ALLGAU)** *3D4* (25km E Rural) *47.80283, 10.55377* **Camping Platz Elbsee, Am Elbsee 3, 87648 Aitrang [08 34 32 48; fax 34 31 406; info@elbsee.de; www.elbsee.de]** S on A7. Take J134 dir Marktobedorf on B12. Take exit twd Unterthingau on OAL10. Turn L on OAL3, cont onto OAL 5. Turn R on Am Elbsee. Foll sp. Lge, hdg/mkd pitch, hdstg, pt shd; htd wc; chem disp; mv service pnt; baby facs; shwrs; EHU (16A) lndry (inc dryer); shop; rest; snacks; BBQ; cooking facs; playgrnd; lake adj; games rm; entmnt; wifi; dogs €4.50; bus 0.75km; twin axles; poss cr; Eng spkn; adv bkg; quiet; ccard acc; CCI. "Excel site; gd base; many local historical places & amazing architecture; camp has much to offer - peace & quiet, spa art, yoga." ♦ € 34.50   2014*

⊞ **KEMPTEN (ALLGAU)** *3D4* (7km S Rural) *47.67485, 10.33386* **Camping Öschlesee, 87477 Sulzberg [(08376) 93040; fax 93041; info@camping.oeschlesee.de; www.camping.oeschlesee.de]** Exit A7 at junc 136 Dreieck Allgäu onto rd 980 dir Lindau/Oberstdorf. Turn L to Sulzberg in 1.5km, site sp. Lge, some hdstg, pt sl, pt shd; wc; mv service pnt; shwrs inc; EHU (16A) €2; gas; lndry; shop; supmkt 1km; rest adj; snacks; bar; cooking facs; playgrnd; lake sw 300m; TV; 70% statics; dogs €2; bus 200m; poss cr; Eng spkn; quiet; CKE/ CCI. "Some pitches views of Alps; vg san facs; gd rest 300m; some pitches diff in wet; gd walks." ♦ € 22.00   2010*

KIEL *1D1* (13km N Coastal) *54.41198, 10.18388* **Campingplatz Kiel-Falckenstein, Palisadenweg 171, 24159 Kiel-Friedrichsort [tel/fax (0431) 392078; falckenstein1@ aol.com; www.campingkiel.de]** N fr Kiel foll sp to 'Flughafen' & Friedrichsort on B503. Foll 'Olympiazentrum', site sp. Access rd narr with bends, but ent gd. Lge, pt sl, unshd; wc; sauna; shwrs; EHU (16A) metered + conn fee; gas; lndry; shop; rest; bar; playgrnd; pool 1km; shgl beach adj; 60% statics; dogs €1.90; poss cr; quiet. "Poor san facs; NH only." ♦ 1 Apr-31 Oct. € 18.50   2011*

⊞ **KINDING** *4E3* (5km E Rural) *49.00328, 11.45200* **Camping Kratzmühle, Mühlweg 2, 85125 Kinding-Pfraundorf [(08461) 64170; fax 641717; info@kratzmuehle.de; www.kratzmuehle.de]** Exit A9/E45 junc 58, dir Beilngries. Site sp. Lge, pt shd; wc; chem disp; mv service pnt; baby facs; some serviced pitches; sauna; shwrs inc; EHU (16A) €2.50; gas; lndry; shop; rest; cooking facs; playgrnd; lake sw adj & shgl beach; games area; 40% statics; dogs €2; clsd 1300-1500; poss cr; adv bkg; 10% red 2+ days; quiet; ccard acc; CKE/ CCI. "Beautiful situation; conv NH for a'bahn; ideal boating & bathing, public access to lake; poss mosquito prob; helpful staff." ♦ € 23.50   2010*

KIPFENBERG *4E3* (800m W Rural) *48.9486, 11.38859* **Azur Campingpark Altmühltal, Campingstrasse 1, 85110 Kipfenberg [(08465) 905167; fax 3745; kipfenberg@azur-camping.de; www.azur-camping.de/kipfenberg]** Exit A9/E45 junc 58 or 59 & foll sp to Kipfenberg, site sp on rvside. Lge, pt shd; htd wc; mv service pnt; shwrs inc; chem disp; mv service pnt; baby facs; EHU (6A) €2.80; gas; lndry; shop, rest, snacks 100m; bar; cooking facs; playgrnd; tennis; fishing; excursions; wifi; TV rm; 20% statics; dogs €3.50; sep o'night area; quiet; red CKE/CCI. "On edge of attractive old vill; cent for walking, cycling & canoeing; charming site." ♦ 1 Apr-31 Oct. € 23.00   2009*

KIRCHBERG SINNINGEN see Illertissen *3D4*

⊞ **KIRCHHEIM** *1D4* (5km SW Rural) *50.81435, 9.51805* **Camping Seepark, Reimboldshäuserstraße, 36275 Kirchheim [(06628) 1525; fax 8664; info@campseepark.de; www.campseepark.de]** Exit A7 at Kirchheim junc 87, site clearly sp. Lge, mkd pitch, pt sl, terr, mkd pitch, pt shd; htd wc; chem disp; mv service pnt; sauna; shwrs €1; EHU (16A) €2.50; metered; gas; lndry; dishwashers; shop; rest, snacks; bar; playgrnd; covrd pool; lake sw & sand beach; tennis; games area; golf 3km; entmnt; 50% statics; dogs €2; bus 500m; phone; o'night area for m'vans; adv bkg; quiet but poss noisy high ssn; ccard acc; red long stay/CKE/CCI. "Gd walking; helpful owner; excel site - leisure facs pt of lge hotel complex." ♦ € 20.00 (6 people)   2009*

KIRCHZARTEN see Freiburg im Breisgau *3B4*

KIRCHZELL see Amorbach *3D2*

⊞ **KIRKEL** *3B3* (1km S Urban) *49.28175, 7.22860* **Caravanplatz Mühlenweiher, Unnerweg 5c, 66458 Kirkel-Neuhäusel [(06849) 1810555; fax 1810556; info@camping-kirkel.de; www.caravanplatz-kirkel.de]** Fr A6 junc 7 & fr A8 junc 28, take dir into town & foll sp for 'schwimmbad'. Site on L past pool, well sp. Med, mkd pitch, hdstg, pt shd; htd wc; chem disp; mv service pnt; baby facs; shwrs inc; EHU (10A) €3 or metered + conn fee (poss rev pol); gas; lndry (inc dryer); shop 1km; rest; bar; pool adj; wifi; TV cab/sat; 60% statics; dogs €1.15; phone; noise fr pool & church bells all night; CKE/CCI. "Gd welcome; excel area for cycling; site/office clsd 1230-1500." ♦ € 15.00   2010*

KIRTORF HEIMERTSHAUSEN see Alsfeld *1D4*

KITZINGEN *3D2* (3km E Urban) *49.73233, 10.16833* **Camping Schiefer Turm, Marktbreiterstrasse 20, 97318 Kitzingen-Hohenfeld [(09321) 33125; fax 384795; info@camping-kitzingen.de; www.camping-kitzingen.de]** Fr A3 take exit junc 74 sp Kitzingen/Schwarzach or exit 72 Würzburg-Ost, or fr A7 exit junc 103 Kitzingen. Site sp in town 'Schwimmbad'. Med, mkd pitch, pt shd; wc; chem disp; mv service pnt; shwrs €0.50; EHU (16A) €2 or metered; gas; lndry; shop; supmkt 200m; rest, snacks; pool adj; dogs €1.50; bus; poss cr w/end & high sn; ccard acc. "Bird reserve; pleasant town in evening; gd cycling; busy NH high ssn; san facs up steps; excel Lido adj." 1 Apr-15 Oct. € 18.00   2012*

KLAIS KRUN see Mittenwald *4E4*

KLEIN RONNAU see Bad Segeberg *1D2*

KLEINROHRSDORF see Dresden *2G4*

KOBLENZ *3B2* (2.8km NE Urban) *50.36611, 7.60361* **Camping Rhein-Mosel, Schartwiesenweg 6, 56070 Koblenz-Lützel [(0261) 82719; fax 802489; info@camping-rhein-mosel.de; www.camping-rhein-mosel.de]** Fr Koblenz heading N on B9 turn off dual c'way at sp for Neuendorf just bef Mosel rv bdge; foll sp to Neuendorf vill. Or heading S on B9 exit dual c'way at camping sp (2nd sp) bef Koblenz; fr Koblenz cent foll sp for 'Altstadt' until Baldwinbrücke (bdge); N over bdge instead of foll sp along S bank of Rv Mosel; R after bdge, then foll sp; site on N side of junc Rhine/Mosel rvs. Lge, some hdstg, pt sl, pt shd; wc; chem disp; mv service pnt; shwrs inc; EHU (6-16A) €2.05 or metered (long lead poss req); lndry (inc dryer); shop; supmkt 500m; cooking facs; rest, snacks; bar; dogs; poss v cr; Eng spkn; no adv bkg; heavy rv & rlwy noise; no ccard acc; CKE/CCI. "Pleasant, informal site in beautiful location; muddy in wet; staff helpful; no veh acc after 2200; adj ferry to city & easy cycle rte; mkt Sat; sep dog shwr; flea mkt Sun; 'Rhine in Flames' fireworks 2nd Sat in Aug - watch fr site; recently renovated (2013); mv stopover called Knaus Campingpark just outside main gates, basic price €12.50, both sites under same owner." ♦ 1 May-20 Oct. € 33.00   2014*

⊞ **KOBLENZ** *3B2* (8km SW Rural) *50.33194, 7.55277* **Camping Gülser Moselbogen, Am Gülser Moselbogen 20, 56072 Koblenz-Güls [(0261) 44474; fax 44494; info@moselbogen.de; www.moselbogen.de]** Fr A61/E31 exit 38 dir Koblenz/Metternich. After 400m turn R at rndabt dir Winningen. Stay on this rd to T-junc in Winningen, turn L dir Koblenz-Güls, site sp on R in 3km. Med, hdg/mkd pitch, pt shd; htd wc; chem disp; mv service pnt; baby facs; fam bthrm; shwrs €0.50; EHU (16A) €1.50 + conn fee; gas; lndry (inc dryer); shop 2km; rest 200m; playgrnd; bike hire - €5; cab/sat TV; 50% statics; dogs €2; phone; poss cr; Eng spkn; adv bkg; rd & rlwy noise; ccard acc; CKE/CCI. "High quality, high-tech san facs; no vehicles 1200-1400; poss subject to flooding; excel." ♦ € 27.00   2014*

KOBLENZ *3B2* (12km SW Urban) *50.30972, 7.50166* **Campinginsel Winningen (previously Campingplatz Ziehfurt), Raiffeisenstraße 16, 56333 Winningen [(02606) 357 or 1800; fax 2566; ferieninsel-winningen@t-online.de; www.mosel-camping.com]** Exit A61/E31 junc 38 to Winningen. In Winningen turn R twds Cochem B416, then L at sw pool. In approx 100m turn R and then in 700m turn L over bdge to site recep. Lge, pt shd; wc; chem disp; mv service pnt; shwrs €0.90; EHU (16A) €2.50; lndry; shop; rest, snacks; playgrnd; pool 300m; rv adj; 50% statics; dogs €3; poss v cr; Eng spkn; no adv bkg; some noise fr rd & rlwy. "Cent of wine-growing country; boat trips avail fr Koblenz; cycle rtes; scenic area; poss flooding if v high water; lively site when busy; gd, modern san facs up steep steps but poss stretched when busy; excel rest; excel site." Easter-1 Oct. € 20.50   2012*

GERMANY

KOCHEL AM SEE *4E4* (3km SW Rural) *47.63642, 11.34827*
Camping Kesselberg, Altjoch 2 ½, 82431 Kochel-am-See
[(08851) 464; mailto:campingplatz-kesselberg.de;
www.campingplatz-kesselberg.de] S fr Kochel on
Bundesstrasse 11. After 3km fork R for Walchensee Kraftwerk,
many hairpins, site 150m on R. Med, mkd pitch, pt sl, pt shd;
wc; chem disp; mv service pnt; child/baby facs; shwrs €0.50;
EHU (10A) metered; gas; lndry; shop; rest, snacks; bar; BBQ;
lake sw adj; sailing; wifi; 40% statics; dogs €3; poss cr; Eng
spkn; adv bkg; quiet; red 10+ days; CKE/CCI. "Friendly site;
beautifully situated by Kochelsee; attractive peaceful lakeside
site; clean san facs; friendly & helpful staff; vg."
22 Mar-15 Oct. € 29.50   2013*

⊞ **KOLN** *1B4* (4km NE Urban) *50.96305, 6.98361*
Reisemobilhafen Köln, An der Schanz, 50735 Köln
[017 84674591 (mob); info@reisemobilhafen-koeln.de]
Fr A1 Köln ring rd exit junc 100 dir Köln 'Zentrum' until reach
rv. Turn L & foll sp to site. M'vans only. Sm, mkd pitch, hdstg;
own san; mv service pnt; EHU (10A) €1 for 12 hrs; shop, rest,
snacks, bar 500m; dogs; bus, train nr. "Adj Rv Rhine; must
have change for elec, water (metered), parking etc; easy access
to city cent; site is unmanned." € 10.00   2014*

⊞ **KOLN** *1B4* (12km NE Rural) *50.99551, 7.06021* **Camping**
Waldbad, Peter Baum Weg, 51069 Köln-Dünnwald
[(0221) 603315; fax 608831; info@waldbad-camping.de;
www.waldbad-camping.de] Exit A3/E35 at junc 24. E for
2km on Willy Brandt ringrd, turn R onto B51 (Mülheimstrasse).
In 2.7km turn L into Odenthalerstrasse then foll site sp. Med, pt
sl, pt shd; wc; chem disp; mv service pnt; baby facs; shwrs inc;
EHU (10-16A) metered & conn fee; lndry; shop; rest adj; pool
adj; 75% statics; dogs €2; phone; metro to city 10 mins drive;
no adv bkg; v quiet. "Close to wildpark, pool & sauna; no ent/
exit for cars 1300-1500 & 2200-0700; friendly warden." ♦
€ 16.00   2012*

⊞ **KOLN** *1B4* (8km SE Rural) *50.8909, 7.02306*
Campingplatz Berger, Uferstrasse 71, 50996 Köln-
Rodenkirchen [(0221) 9355240; fax 9355246; camping.
berger@t-online.de; www.camping-berger-koeln.de]
Fr A4 turn S onto A555 at Köln-Sud exit 12. Leave A555
at Rodenkirchen exit 3. At 1st junc foll site sp to R. Fr A3
Frankfurt/Köln a'bahn, take A4 twd Aachen (Köln ring rd); exit
at Köln Sud; foll sp Bayenthal; at lge rndabt turn R sp Rheinufer
& R again at camp sp, under a'bahn. App rd narr & lined
with parked cars. Lge, pt shd; htd wc; chem disp; mv service
pnt; shwrs inc; EHU (4-10A) €1.50; gas; lndry; shop; supmkt
1km; rest, snacks; bar; cooking facs; playgrnd; bike hire; wifi;
80% statics; dogs €1; phone; bus 500m; poss v cr; Eng spkn;
no adv bkg; quiet but some noise fr Rhine barges; ccard acc;
red long stay; CKE/CCI. "Pleasant, popular, wooded site on
banks of Rhine; rvside pitches best; excel rest; helpful staff;
gd dog walking; cycle path to city cent; conv cathedral, zoo &
museums; don't arr early eve at w/end as narr app rd v busy;
pitches poss muddy after rain; san facs up steps - poss clsd
2300-0600; gd site; vr gd facs." ♦ € 30.40   2014*

KOLN *1B4* (6km S Urban) *50.90263, 6.99070* **Campingplatz**
der Stadt Köln, Weidenweg 35, 51105 Köln-Poll
[(0221) 831966; fax 4602221; info@camping-koeln.de;
www.camping-koeln.de] Exit fr A4 (E40) at junc 13 for
Köln-Poll-Porz at E end of bdge over Rv Rhine, 3km S of city. At
end of slip rd, turn L twd Poll & Köln. Cont about 500m turn L
at sp just bef level x-ing, then foll site sp. Narr lane to ent. Lge,
pt shd; wc; chem disp; mv service pnt; shwrs €0.50; EHU (10A)
€3.50 (some rev pol & long lead poss req); gas; lndry; basic
shop; snacks; rest 200m; cooking facs; dogs €2.50; phone;
trams 1.5km; clsd 1230-1430; poss cr at w/ends; Eng spkn;
no adv bkg; some rd & aircraft noise; CKE/CCI. "Tram to city
over rv bdge; rural site in urban setting on bank of Rv Rhine;
subject to flooding; gd undercover cooking facs; gd refurbished
san facs on 1st floor; friendly site; v busy at w/end; rvside cycle
track to city; cycle theft a problem (store in caged kitchen
o'night)." ♦ 28 Mar-15 Oct. € 33.00   2014*

KOLPIN see Storkow *2G3*

KONIGSSEE *4G4* (2km N Rural) *47.59445, 12.98583*
Camping Grafenlehen, Königsseer Fussweg 71, 83471
Königssee [(08652) 6554488; fax 690768; camping-
grafenlehen@t-online.de; www.camping-grafenlehen.de]
On B20 fr Berchtesgaden 5km to Königssee. Where car park
with traff lts is ahead, turn R sp Schönau, site on R. Lge, terr, pt
shd; htd wc; chem disp; mv service pnt; shwrs inc; EHU (16A)
metered; lndry; shop; rest, snacks; playgrnd; 10% statics; dogs
€2; site clsd Nov to mid-Dec; quiet; red CKE/CCI. "Pleasant
site; spectacular views; gd san facs; superb walking; cycle
path by rv; gd value rest; 30 mins drive Salzburg Park &
Ride; conv Berchtesgaden." 1 Jan-1 Nov & 15 Dec-31 Dec.
€ 31.00   2015*

⊞ **KONIGSSEE** *4G4* (2km N Rural) *47.5992, 12.98933*
Camping Mühlleiten, Königsseerstrasse 70, 83471
Königssee [(08652) 4584; fax 69194; info@muehlleiten.eu;
www.camping-muehlleiten.eu] On on R of B20
Berchtesgaden-Königssee. Med, unshd; wc; chem disp; shwrs
inc; EHU (16A) €3 or metered; gas; lndry; shop & 1km; rest adj;
snacks; bar; beach 1km; ski lift 500m; golf 6km; entmnt; dogs
€2.50; poss cr; quiet; red CKE/CCI. "Beautiful area; friendly
staff; excel san facs." € 17.50   2009*

KONIGSTEIN *2G4* (1km E Rural) *50.92222, 14.08833*
Camping Königstein, Schandauerstrasse 25e, 01824
Königstein [(035021) 68224; fax 60725; info@camping-
koenigstein.de; www.camping-koenigstein.de]
Foll B172 SE fr Dresden/Pirna. Site 500m past Königstein rlwy
stn. Turn L over rlwy x-ing & R into site ent on Rv Elbe. Med,
pt sl, unshd; wc; chem disp; mv service pnt; shwrs €0.80; EHU
(16A) €2.60; gas; lndry; shop 1km; rest; playgrnd; 15% statics;
dogs €3 (not acc Jul/Aug); sep car park; adv bkg; rlwy noise;
red 5+ days. "Gd san facs; lovely location nr national parks &
Czech border; on Elbe cycle path; frequent trains to Dresden;
boat trips; gates clsd 1300-1500; red for 7+ days." ♦
1 Apr-31 Oct. € 32.00   2013*

GERMANY

Camping-und Ferienpark
★ ★ ★ ★ TEICHMANN
34516 Vöhl-Herzhausen . Tel. 05635-245 . Fax 05635-8145
Internet: www.camping-teichmann.de . E-Mail: camping-teichmann@t-online.de

Our family-friendly campsite, in the heart of Germany
offers unforgettable holiday enjoyment.

young persons tent area . animation . tennis court . beach volleyball . minigolf
boat hire . motorhome friendly . swimming & fishing lake . barbecue hut
bicycle hire . restaurant . mini-market . sauna & solarium . holiday homes
at the nationalpark info centre . new: w-lan . wellness station . Internetroom

⊞ **KONIGSTEIN** *2G4* (3km E Rural) *50.91500, 14.10730*
Caravan Camping Sächsische Schweiz, Dorfplatz 181d,
01824 Kurort-Gohrisch [350 21 59107; caravan-camping@
web.de; www.caravan-camping-saechsischeschweiz.de]
Fr Königstein foll B172 E dir Bad Schandau. Fork R dir Gohrisch
for 2.5km, turn L into Dorfplatz & foll site sp. Med, hdg/mkd
pitch, hdstg, pt sl, pt shd; wc; chem disp; mv service pnt; baby
facs; fam bathrm; sauna; shwrs €0.50; EHU (16A) metered;
lndry (inc dryer); shop; rest; bar; BBQ; cooking facs; playgrnd;
htd, covrd pool 4km; padding pool; games area; bike hire;
wifi; sat/cable TV; 5% statics; dogs €2; bus 500m; Eng spkn;
adv bkg; quiet; red LS/long stay. "Excel site; gd touring base;
interesting area; guided walks." ♦ € 22.00   2012*

KONIGSWALDE see Annaberg Buchholz *4G1*

KONSTANZ *3D4* (13km N Rural) *47.74596, 9.14701* **Camping
Klausenhorn, Hornwiesenstrasse, 78465 Dingelsdorf
[(07533) 6372; fax 7541; info@camping-klausenhorn.de;
www.konstanz.de/tourismus/klausenhorn]** Site sp N of
Dingelsdorf on lakeside. Lge, mkd pitch, hdstg, pt shd; htd wc;
chem disp; baby facs; shwrs €0.50; EHU (10A) inc; lndry; shop
& 1.5km; rest 800m; snacks; bar; BBQ; playgrnd; shgl beach
& lake adj; boating; games area; wifi; entmnt; 50% statics;
no dogs; bus 500m; sep car park; poss cr; Eng spkn; adv
bkg; quiet; ccard acc; CKE/CCI. "Excel site." ♦ 1 Apr-4 Oct.
€ 25.50   2009*

KONSTANZ *3D4* (12km W Rural) *47.69871, 9.04603*
Camping Sandseele, Bradlengasse 24, 78479 Niederzell
[(07534) 7384; fax 98976; beyer@sandseele.de;
www.sandseele.de] Clearly sp off B33 Konstanz-Radolfzell
rd. Foll sp on island & sm multiple sp. Lge, pt shd; wc; chem
disp; mv service pnt; shwrs inc; EHU (16A) €3; gas; lndry;
shop; rest, snacks; playgrnd; lake sw & beach; watersports;
30% statics; no dogs; sep car park high ssn; poss v cr; poss
noisy. "Insect repellent rec, excel san facs; excel walking &
cycling all over island." ♦ 15 Mar-5 Oct. € 26.50   2013*

KONZ see Trier *3B2*

⊞ **KORBACH** *1C4* (14km S Rural) *51.17500, 8.89138*
Camping & Ferienpark Teichmann, Zum Träumen
1a, 34516 Vöhl-Herzhausen [(05635) 245; fax 8145;
camping-teichmann@t-online.de; www.camping-
teichmann.de] Fr Korbach, take B252 S. In 12m cross Rv
Eder. Site in 1km on R by lake. Lge, mkd pitch, pt shd, wc;
chem disp; mv service pnt; baby facs; sauna; shwrs inc;
EHU (10A) €2.60; lndry (inc dryer); shop; rest, snacks; bar;
playgrnd; lake sw & beach; boat & bike hire; tennis; games
area; horseriding 500m; wellness cent; winter sports; entmnt
high ssn; wifi; TV; 50% statics; dogs €3.60; sep car park;
o'night area for m'vans; adv bkg; ccard acc; red CKE/CCI.
"Excel family site in lovely situation; friendly, helpful staff; gd
walking in area." ♦ € 30.00   2011*

See advertisement

⊞ **KOTZTING** *4F3* (8km NE Rural) *49.20610, 12.92381*
Camping Hohenwarth Fritz-Berger, Ferienzentrum 3,
93480 Hohenwarth [(09946) 367; fax 477; info@
campingplatz-hohenwarth.de; www.campingplatz-
hohenwarth.de] Fr Cham, take B85 SW to Miltach, Kötzting
& site sp on L on Hohenwarth by-pass. Lge, mkd pitch, some
hdstg, unshd; wc; chem disp; mv service pnt; sauna; shwrs inc;
EHU (16A) metered + conn fee; gas; lndry; shop; rest, snacks;
bar; playgrnd; pool; lake sw; ski lift 7km; entmnt; internet;
10% statics; dogs €2; phone; site clsd 5 Nov-10 Dec; adv bkg;
quiet; ccard acc; CKE/CCI. "Gd walking & cycling area; office
clsd 1200-1400 & 1800-0800; conv NH for Bavaria & Czech
Rep." ♦ € 18.00   2011*

⊞ **KRANICHFELD** *2E4* (4km NW Rural) *50.87216, 11.17843*
Campingplatz Stausee Hohenfelden, 99448 Hohenfelden
[(036450) 42081; fax 42082; info@stausee-hohenfelden.de;
www.stausee-hohenfelden.de] Fr A4/E40 take exit 47a S
twd Kranichfeld. Site clearly sp by lake along rough rd. Lge,
sl, pt terr, pt shd; wc; chem disp; mv service pnt; shwrs €0.80;
EHU (10A) €2.60; lndry (inc dryer); supmkt 3km; snacks;
boating; bike hire; TV; 60% statics; dogs €2.50; no adv bkg;
ccard acc; CKE/CCI. "Woodland, lakeside walks; gates clsd
1300-1500 & 2200-0700; poss noisy, scruffy; poss lge youth
groups; gd san facs but diff access." ♦ € 17.40   2010*

GERMANY

KRESSBRONN AM BODENSEE *3D4* (10km NE Rural) *47.63395, 9.6477* **Gutshof-Camping Badhütten (Part Naturist), Badhütten 1, 88069 Laimnau [(07543) 96330; fax 963315; gutshof.camping@t-online.de; www.gutshof-camping.de]** Fr Kressbronn take B467 to Tettnang & Ravensburg. In 3km immed after x-ing Rv Argen turn R & site sp for approx 3km. V lge, hdg/mkd pitch, pt shd; wc; chem disp; mv service pnt; serviced pitches; baby facs; shwrs inc; EHU (16A) metered; gas; lndry; shop; rest; snacks; bar; playgrnd; pool; lake 7km; entmnt; 40% statics; dogs €2; adv bkg; quiet; red long stay; CKE/CCI. "Sep area for naturists; gd facs; v rural site; clean, quiet & pleasant; excel." ♦ 30 Mar-5 Nov. € 28.00   2011*

KRESSBRONN AM BODENSEE *3D4* (2km SW Rural) *47.58718, 9.58281* **Campingplatz Irisweise, Tunau 16, 88079 Kressbronn [(07543) 8010; fax 8032; info@camping platz-irisweise.de; www.campingplatz-iriswiese.de]** Fr E or W take exit off B31 bypass for Kressbronn, site well sp. Lge, hdg/mkd pitch, pt shd; htd wc; chem disp; mv service pnt; baby facs; shwrs inc; EHU (10A) metered + conn fee; gas; lndry; shop; rest; bar; BBQ; playgrnd; beach, lake sw adj (sep naturist beach); sailing; watersports; internet; 10% statics; dogs €2; phone; poss v cr; Eng spkn; no adv bkg; quiet; CKE/CCI. "Steamer trips on lake; no car access 2100-0700, park outside site; excel san facs but some dist fr touring pitches; gd." ♦ 22 Mar-21 Oct. € 30.00   2014*

KROV see Wittlich *3B2*

KRUMBACH *4E4* (7km SW Rural) *48.22720, 10.29280* **See Camping Günztal, Oberrieder Weiherstrasse 5, 86488 Breitenthal [(08282) 881870; info@see-camping-guenztal. de; www.see-camping-guenztal.de]** W fr Krumbach on rd 2018, in Breitenthal turn S twd Oberried & Oberrieder Weiher, site sp on lakeside. Med, mkd pitch, some hdstg; pt shd; htd wc; chem disp; mv service pnt; baby facs; shwrs inc; EHU (10A) inc; lndry (inc dryer); shop 800m; rest 1.5km; snacks; bar; BBQ; playgrnd; lake sw; watersports; fishing; games area; wifi; TV; 30% statics; dogs €2; adv bkg; quiet. ♦ 1 Apr-30 Oct. € 19.50 (CChq acc)   2010*

KUHLUNGSBORN *2E1* (2km W Coastal) *54.15137, 11.71947* **Campingpark Kühlungsborn, Waldstrasse 1b; 18225 Kühlungsborn [(038293) 7195; fax 7192; info@ topcamping.de; www.topcamping.de]** On rd B105 turn N in Neubukow sp Kühlungsborn. In 15km, at W Kühlungsborn stn, rd turns N; foll sp. V lge, pt sl, shd; wc; chem disp; mv service pnt; serviced pitches; baby facs; shwrs inc; EHU (16A) inc; lndry; shop adj; rest, snacks; rest; shop; playgrnd; htd pool 300m; beach (sep naturist beach); sailing; windsurfing; games area; bike hire; entmnt; TV; 20% statics; dogs €5; poss cr; quiet; ccard acc. "Excel site; upgraded & modernised facs, esp luxurious san facs (even has luxury dog wash!); v clean & well managed; town pleasant, old-fashioned holiday resort." ♦ 30 Mar-26 Oct. € 34.00   2011*

⊞ **KULMBACH** *4E2* (2km NE Urban) *50.11083, 11.46160* **Parkplatz am Schwedensteg, 95326 Kulmbach [(09221) 95880; fax 958844; touristinfo@stadt-kulmbach. de; www.stadt-kulmbach.de]** Exit A70/E48 junc 24 onto B289 dir Kulmbach Stadtmitte. Foll sp 'Festplatz am Schwedensteg' to area behind bus & truck park. Sm, hdstg, unshd; own san; chem disp; mv service pnt; water €1/100 litres; EHU (16A) metered; shop, rest, snacks, bar 500m; m'vans only. "Historic town cent." ♦ € 3.00   2009*

KULMBACH *4E2* (11km NE Rural) *50.16050, 11.51605* **Campingplatz Stadtsteinach, Badstrasse 5, 95346 Stadtsteinach [(09225) 800394; fax 800395; info@ campingplatz-stadtsteinach.de; www.campingplatz-stadtsteinach.de]** Fr Kulmbach take B289 to Untersteinach (8km); turn L to Stadtsteinach; turn R at camping sp & foll rd for 1km. Site also sp fr N side of town on B303. Or fr A9/E51 exit junc 39 onto B303 NW to Stadtsteinach. Med, pt shd; htd wc; chem disp; mv service pnt; shwrs inc; EHU (16A) €2.10; lndry; shop 600m; rest, snacks; bar; cooking facs; playgrnd; htd pool adj; paddling pool; rv fishing; tennis; bike hire; games area; 75% statics; dogs €2; Eng spkn; adv bkg; ccard acc; CKE/ CCI. "Excel site in beautiful countryside; excel, modern facs; highly rec." ♦ 1 Mar-30 Nov. € 29.50   2014*

"I like to fill in the reports as I travel from site to site"

You'll find report forms at the back of this guide, or you can fill them in online at www.caravanclub.co.uk/europereport.

LABOE *1D1* (3km NE Coastal) *54.41399, 10.24846* **Camping Fördeblick, Kreisstrasse 30, 24235 Stein [(04343) 7795; fax 7790; info@camping-foerdeblick.de; www. camping-foerdeblick.de]** Exit B76/B202 into Kiel & take sp Gaarden-Ost. Then turn L onto B502 dir Heikendorf. Foll sp Laboe & Stein. Lge, mkd pitch, pt sl, unshd; htd wc; chem disp; mv service pnt; baby facs; shwrs inc; EHU (10A) €2.60; gas; lndry; shop; rest, snacks; bar; playgrnd; sand/shgl beach adj; watersports nrby; games area; golf 5km; wifi; entmnt; 75% statics (sep area); no dogs; phone; bus 500m; poss cr; Eng spkn; adv bkg; CKE/CCI. "Facs dated but vg; site on cliffs, some pitches excel views; narr access lanes to pitches; pleasant walk into Laboe." ♦ 1 Apr-28 Oct. € 26.00   2011*

LABOE *1D1* (8km NE Coastal) *54.42698, 10.29646* **Camping Oase-Bonanza, Schleusenweg 25, 24235 Wendtorf [(04343) 9688; fax 9899; camping@camping-oase-bonanza.de; www.camping-oase-bonanza.de]** N fr Kiel on B502 sp Laboe take turning N sp Stein & Wendtorf. Drive to end past marina ignoring all sps, site on R behind dyke. Med, hdg/mkd pitch; pt shd; htd wc; chem disp; mv service pnt; shwrs €0.60; EHU (12A) €3; gas; lndry; shop; supmkt 1km; rest, snacks; bar; playgrnd; sand beach adj (inc naturist); 70% statics; dogs €3; phone; adv bkg; quiet; ccard acc; CKE/CCI. "Excel cycle paths; friendly owners; excel san facs; stunning beach." 1 Apr-30 Sep. € 20.50   2011*

LAHNSTEIN 3B2 (3km E Urban) 50.30565, 7.61313 **Kur-Campingplatz Burg Lahneck, Am Burgweg, 56112 Lahnstein-Oberlahnstein [(02621) 2765; fax 18290]** Take B42 fr Koblenz over Lahn Rv, if fr low bdge turn L immed after church & sp fr there; if fr high level bdge thro sh tunnel turn L at 1st rd on L sp to Burg-Lahneck - site sp on L. Med, pt sl, pt shd; wc; chem disp; mv service pnt; shwrs €0.50; EHU (16A) metered + conn fee; lndry; shop; rest; playgrnd; pool adj; 10% statics; dogs €1; poss cr; Eng spkn; quiet but distant rlwy noise at night; ccard not acc. "Gd views over Rhine; scenic area; delightful, helpful owner v particular about pitching; gd size pitches; immac, well-run site." 1 Apr-31 Oct. € 21.50   2012*

> ## "We must tell The Club about that great site we found"
>
> Get your site reports in by mid-August and we'll do our best to get your updates into the next edition.

LAHNSTEIN 3B2 (6km SE Urban) 50.27393, 7.64098 **Campingplatz Uferwiese, Am Campingplatz 1, 56338 Braubach [tel/fax (02627) 8762; uferwiese@web.de; www.campingplatz-braubach.de]** Take B42 S twd Rüdesheim. Site behind hotel opp church. Med, shd; wc; chem disp; shwrs €1; EHU (16A) €2 (poss rev pol); lndry; shop 300m; rest 200m; snacks; bar; wifi; 50% statics; dogs €1; bus; rd & rlwy noise; no ccard acc; CKE/CCI. "Scenic on Rv Rhine; poss flooding after heavy rain; gd san facs; no shd on rvside pitches." 15 Apr-25 Oct. € 21.50   2015*

⊞ **LAHR (SCHWARZWALD)** 3B3 (9km SE Rural) 48.29999, 7.94395 **Ferienparadies Schwarzwälder Hof, Tretenhofstrasse 76, 77960 Seelbach [(07823) 960950; fax 9609522; info@spacamping.de; www.campingplatz-schwarzwaelder-hof.de]** Fr A5 take exit 56 to Lahr. In 5km turn R twd Seelbach & Schuttertal. Thro town & site on S o'skts of Seelbach just after town boundary. Med, mkd pitch, some hdstg, pt sl, terr, pt shd; serviced pitches (extra charge); wc; chem disp; mv service pnt; shwrs inc; EHU (10A) metered + conn fee; gas; lndry; shop; rest; snacks 1km; bar; playgrnd; htd pool adj; lake adj; 10% statics; dogs €3.50; o'night area for m'vans; poss v cr; Eng spkn; adv bkg ess high ssn; quiet; ccard acc; red CKE/CCI. "Vg touring base; well-laid out pitches & excel facs; many gd mkd walks; gd programme of events in Seelbach; within easy reach of Strasbourg." ◆ € 37.00   2015*

LAHR (SCHWARZWALD) 3B3 (14km S Rural) 48.24739, 7.82804 **Terrassen-Campingpark Oase, Mühlenweg 34, 77955 Ettenheim [(07822) 445918; fax 445919; info@campingpark-oase.de; www.campingpark-oase.de]** Exit A5/E35 at junc 57a, foll site sp. Lge, shd; wc; shwrs; chem disp; mv service pnt; baby facs; shwrs €0.50; EHU (6A) €2; lndry; shop; rest, snacks; playgrnd; pool adj; tennis adj; bike hire; 30% statics; dogs €1.50; quiet; CKE/CCI. "Modern san facs; variable pitch size/price; sh walk/cycle track to attractive town; conv glassworks at Wolfach & House of 1000 clocks nr Triberg." ◆ ltd. 15 Mar-8 Oct. € 22.00   2009*

⊞ **LAICHINGEN** 3D3 (6km SE Rural) 48.47560, 9.7458 **Camping & Freizeitzentrum Heidehof, Heidehofstrasse 50, 89150 Laichingen-Machtolsheim [(07333) 6408; fax 21463; info@heidenhof.info; www.camping-heidehof.de]** Exit A8 junc 61 dir Merklingen. At T-junc turn R sp Laichingen. In 3km site sp to L. V lge, hdg/mkd pitch, hdstg, pt sl, pt shd; some hdstg; wc; chem disp; mv service pnt; baby facs; fam bthrm; sauna; shwrs inc; EHU (10-16A) €2 or metered; gas; lndry; shop; rest; playgrnd; htd pool; bike hire; 95% statics; adv bkg; red long stay/CKE/CCI. "Blaubeuren Abbey & Blautopf (blue pool of glacial origin) worth visit; sep area for o'nighters immed bef main camp ent - poss unrel when wet; hdstg pitches sm & sl; vg rest; gd NH; clean modern facs; lack of elec boxes; no water taps excep at facs; whole site on uneven sl; arr early to get nr elec." ◆ € 33.00   2014*

LAIMNAU see Kressbronn am Bodensee 3D4

LANDAU IN DER PFALZ 3C3 (13km W Rural) 49.20138, 7.97222 **Camping der Naturfreunde, Victor von Scheffelstrasse 18, 76855 Annweiler-am-Trifels [(06346) 3870; fax 302945; info@naturfreunde-annweiler.de; www.naturfreunde-annweiler.de]** Fr Landau take B10 dir Pirmasens, take 1st exit to Annweiler then turn L into vill along Landauerstrasse. Turn L immed after VW/Audi g'ge, site sp. Tight access at ent. Sm, hdstg, pt shd; htd wc; chem disp; mv service pnt; shwrs inc; EHU (10A) €2; lndry; shops 500m; rest adj; playgrnd; 80% statics; dogs €2; poss cr; quiet; CKE/CCI. "Friendly, helpful owner poss on site evenings only; immac, modern san facs; ltd space for tourers but adequate facs; vg views across valley & forest; Ent is up steep hill with acute L turn; advise use campingplatz on R." ◆ 1 Apr-31 Oct. € 16.00   2012*

⊞ **LANDSBERG AM LECH** 4E4 (4km SE Rural) 48.03195, 10.88526 **DCC Campingpark Romantik am Lech, Pössinger Au 1, 86899 Landsberg-am-Lech [(08191) 47505; fax 21406; campingparkgmbh@aol.com; www.camping platz-landsberg.de]** Not rec to tow thro Landsberg. If app fr S, get onto rd fr Weilheim & foll sp on app to Landsberg. Fr other dir, exit junc 26 fr a'bahn A96 Landsberg Ost, then app town via Muchenstrasse. Foll sp dir Weilheim, after 400m turn R & foll site sp. Lge, hdg/mkd pitch, pt sl, pt shd; wc; chem disp; mv service pnt; shwrs inc; EHU (16A) metered (some rev pol); gas; lndry; shop; rest 2km; snacks; bar; playgrnd; pool 3km; tennis; bike hire; 50% statics; dogs €1; adv bkg; Eng spkn; quiet; red CKE/CCI. "V pleasant site; excel, clean facs; nature reserve on 2 sides; gd walking & cycling; attractive old town; site clsd 1300-1500 & 2200-0700." ◆ € 19.00   2015*

LANDSHUT 4F3 (3km NE Urban) 48.55455, 12.1795 **Camping Landshut, Breslauerstrasse 122, 84028 Landshut [tel/fax (0871) 53366; www.landshut.de]** Fr A92/E53 exit junc 14 onto B299 dir Landshut N. After approx 5km turn L at int'l camping sp & foll site sp. Med, pt shd; wc; chem disp; mv service pnt; shwrs inc; EHU (16A) €2.50; lndry; shop 500m; rest 200m; snacks; bar; BBQ; htd pool 3km; 10% statics; dogs €1.50; poss cr; quiet; CKE/CCI. "Well-run, friendly site; gd san facs; beautiful medieval town & castle - easy cycle rte." ◆ 1 Apr-30 Sep. € 17.00   2009*

LANGELSHEIM see Goslar 1D3

LANGSUR METZDORF see Trier *3B2*

⊞ **LANGWEDEL** *1D1* (1km W Rural) *54.21465, 9.91825* Caravanpark am Brahmsee, Mühlenstrasse 30a, 24631 Langwedel [(04329) 1567; info@caravanpark-sh.de; www.caravanpark-sh.de] Exit A7 at junc 10 dir Tierpark Warder (animal park) & foll site sp to lakeside. Or exit A215 at Blumenthal onto L298 thro Langwedel dir Tierpark Warder, site sp. Med, hdg/mkd pitch, some hdstg, pt shd; htd wc; chem disp; mv service pnt; shwrs inc; EHU €2.50; lndry (inc dryer); shop 1km; rest 1km; cooking facs; BBQ; playgrnd; lake sw 100m; fishing; wifi; 80% statics; dogs; adv bkg; quiet. "Peaceful site in nature park; gd; diff access to some pitches for lge o'fits; excel san facs; dedicated hdstg area for campers." ♦ ltd. € 20.50 (CChq acc) 2013*

⊞ **LECHBRUCK** *4E4* (3km NE Rural) *47.71169, 10.81872* Via Claudia Camping (formerly DCC Campingpark Lechsee), Via Claudia 6, 86983 Lechbruck [(08862) 8426; fax 7570; info@camping-lechbruck.de; www.via-claudia-camping. de] A95 exit junc 10 Murnau/Kochel & then via Murnau, Saulgrub, Steingaden to Lechbruck. Then foll sps. V lge, mkd pitch, terr, pt shd; wc; chem disp; mv service pnt; baby facs; shwrs inc; EHU (10-16A) €2.65; gas; lndry (inc dryer); shop; rest; bar; playgrnd; pool 500m; lake beach & sw; watersports; minigolf; volleyball; archery; wifi; entmnt; 50% statics; dogs €3.50; o'night m'van area; Eng spkn; adv bkg; quiet; ccard acc; red CKE/CCI. "Pleasant, peaceful, lakeside site; fac to a high standard; gd welcome; v helpful; cont investment in site fr new owners." ♦ € 24.70 2011*

LEEDEN see Osnabrück *1C3*

⊞ **LEER (OSTFRIESLAND)** *1B2* (7km W Rural) *53.22416, 7.41891* Camping Ems-Marina Bingum, Marinastrasse 14-16, 26789 Leer-Bingum [(0491) 64447; fax 66405; into-camping-bingum@t-online.de; www.bingumcamper.de] Leave A32/E12 junc 12; site 500m S of Bingum; well sp. Lge, pt shd; wc; chem disp; mv service pnt; baby facs; shwrs €1; EHU (16A) €2.50 or metered; gas; lndry (inc dryer); shop 500m; rest, snacks; playgrnd; bike hire; 65% statics; dogs €3.50; gate clsd 1230-1500; adv bkg; quiet; red long stay/CKE/CCI. ♦ € 20.00 2010*

LEINATEL see Ohrdruf *2E4*

⊞ **LEIPHEIM** *3D3* (3.5km NNW Rural) *48.46566, 10.2035* Camping Schwarzfelder Hof, Schwarzfelderweg 3, Riedheim, 89340 Leipheim [(08221) 72628; fax 71134; info@schwarzfelder-hof.de; www.schwarzfelder-hof.de] Fr A8 exit junc 66 Leipheim onto B10. In Leipheim foll sp Langenau & Riedheim, site sp. Do not confuse with Laupheim 25km S of Ulm on B30. Sm, hdstg, pt shd; htd wc; chem disp (wc); serviced pitches; shwrs inc; EHU (16A) €2.10 or metered; lndry; shop 2km; rest 1.5km; snacks; bar; BBQ; playgrnd; 50% statics; dogs €3.20; train 1km; poss cr; Eng spkn; quiet. "Peaceful, delightful, farm-based site on site of old quarry; ideal for children & adults; welcoming, helpful owner; lge pitches; vg san facs but ltd; farm animals & riding for children; conv Ulm; recep open 0800-1000 & 1730-2000; poss noisy youth groups; conv NH for m'way." € 25.00 2014*

LEIPZIG *2F4* (21km W Rural) *51.38946, 12.15727* Campingplatz Elsteraue, Delitscherstrasse 68, 06184 Ermlitz [tel/fax (0341) 9121874; ccl-camping@web.de; www.campingplatzleipzig.de] Exit A9/E51 junc 16 Grosskugel dir Leipzig. Foll sp W to Erlmitz. Site sp (blue sp) at end of single track, unsurfaced but gd rd. Sm, pt shd; wc; chem disp; shwrs €0.50; EHU (16A) €1.50; lndry; shop 500m; dogs €1.50; Eng spkn; adv bkg; quiet; CKE/CCI. "Peaceful; v clean facs; charge for refilling water tanks & water/waste removal; gd security; cycle rte into Leipzig; pleasant site nr rv; conv to town." 15 May-15 Sep. € 17.00 2013*

⊞ **LEIPZIG** *2F4* (7km NW Urban) *51.37030, 12.31375* Campingplatz Auensee, Gustav-Esche Strasse 5, 04159 Leipzig [(0341) 4651600; fax 4651617; info@camping-auensee.de] www.camping-auensee.de] Fr A9/E51 exit junc 16 onto B6 two Leipzig. In Leipzig-Wahren turn R at 'Rathaus' sp Leutzsch (camping symbol), site on R in 1.5km, sp. Lge, mkd pitch, some hdstg, pt shd; htd wc; chem disp; mv service pnt; shwrs inc; EHU (16A) €3; lndry (inc dryer); supmkt 1.5km; rest, snacks; bar; BBQ; cooking facs; playgrnd; Lake Auensee 500m; TV; dogs €2; phone; bus; tram 1.5km; poss cr; Eng spkn; adv bkg; ccard acc; CKE/CCI. "Roomy, well-run, clean site; plentiful san facs; gd size pitches; vg rest; friendly, helpful staff; 10 mins walk to tram for city cent or bus stop at site ent, tickets avail fr recep; excel." ♦ € 23.50 2012*

⊞ **LEMGO** *1C3* (600m E Urban) *52.02503, 8.90874* Campingpark Lemgo, Regenstorstrasse 10, 32657 Lemgo [(05261) 14858; fax 188324; info@camping-lemgo.de; www.camping-lemgo.de] Exit A2 junc 28 onto L712N to Lemgo; at traff lts turn L following L712; at rnd abt take Bismarckstrasse exit; at traff lts turn R into Regenstorstrasse. Site sp. Med, pt shd; wc; shwrs €0.50; EHU (6A) metered + conn fee; lndry (inc dryer); shop 500m; rest 300m; snacks 500m; playgrnd; pool 200m; wifi; 25% statics; dogs €2; adv bkg. "Slightly scruffy site but in cent of lovely medieval town; o'night area for m'vans - modern san facs." € 19.50 2010*

⊞ **LENGERICH** *1C3* (5km W Rural) *52.18854, 7.80439* Campingplatz auf dem Sonnenhügel, Zur Sandgrube 40, 49525 Lengerich [(05481) 6216; fax 845829; info@ sonnenhuegel-camping.de; www.sonnenhuegel-camping.de] Leave A1 Lengerich/Tecklenburg, turn R at bottom of slip rd onto S ring rd; L into Ibbenbüren Str; R & immed R again into Antruper Str; foll rd under S ring; R into Sonnenhügeldamm; foll sp. Med, pt shd; wc; chem disp; shwrs €0.50; EHU €2 or metered; gas; lndry; rest 1km; bar; shop; playgrnd; lake sw adj; fishing; 80% statics; dogs €2; clsd 1300-1500; Eng spkn; adv bkg; a'bahn noise; ccard acc; CKE/CCI. "Immac facs; vg value." ♦ € 14.00 2011*

LENZEN *2E2* (5km E Rural) *53.11000, 11.54083* Naturcampingplatz am Rudower See, Leuengarten 9, 19309 Lenzen [(038792) 80075 or (030854) 4020 (winter); fax 80076; info@naturcampingplatz.de; www.natur campingplatz.de] Fr B195 turn N along S side of Rudower See, site sp. Site at E end of lake. Med, terr, pt shd; htd wc; chem disp; fam bthrm; shwrs inc; EHU (16A) €1.75; gas; lndry; shop 4km; rest & bar 2km; snacks; playgrnd; lake sw adj; boat hire; games area; 20% statics; dogs €2.50; phone; adv bkg; quiet. "Peaceful site in nature park; gd facs; helpful owners; gd walking, cycling, birdwatching; gd NH." ♦ 1 Apr-15 Oct. € 17.00 2010*

LIETZOW *2G1* (150m N Coastal) *54.48358, 13.50846*
Störtebecker Camp, Gästehaus Lietzow, Waldstraße 59a,
18528 Lietzow [038302 2166; info@lietzow.net;
www.lietzow.net] On rd 96, E22 fr Stralsund to ferry harbour
at Sassnitz; when you arr at Lietzow site sp 'Gästehaus Lietzow'
on RH side of rd; sh, steep incline fr main rd. Med, hdg pitch,
pt shd; wc; chem disp; MV waste; shwrs inc; EHU inc; gas;
lndry; rest, snacks; bar; playgrnd; beach 250m; dogs €2.50;
adv bking; CKE/CCI. "Pleasant, beautifully kept sm site in
woodland; cent for the island, sightseeing & useful stopover
nr ferry point; many mkd cycle rtes around island; charming
owners; excel san facs; sh walk to delightful coast." 29 Mar-
15 Oct. € 33.50   2015*

LIMBURG AN DER LAHN *3C2* (2km SSW Urban) *50.38916,
8.07333* Lahn Camping, Schleusenweg 16, 65549
Limburg-an-der-Lahn [(06431) 22610; fax 92013; info@
lahncamping.de; www.lahncamping.de] Exit A3/E35 junc
42 Limburg Nord, site sp. By Rv Lahn in town, easy access.
Lge, pt shd; wc; chem disp; mv service pnt; baby facs; shwrs
€1; EHU (6A) €2.60 (long lead poss req); gas; lndry; shop;
rest; playgrnd; htd pool 100m; rv sw & fishing; 20% statics;
dogs €1.50; bus; poss v cr; Eng spkn; rd & rlwy noise; red
CKE/CCI. "Busy, well-organised site; delightful location by rv;
sm pitches - some poss diff to manoeuvre; gd views; friendly
staff; poss flooding in wet weather; sh walk to interesting
town; gates clsd 1300-1500; useful NH." ♦ 28 Mar-27 Oct.
€ 25.00   2014*

LIMBURG AN DER LAHN *3C2* (9km SW Rural) *50.38151,
8.00046* Camping Oranienstein, Strandbadweg, 65582
Diez [(06432) 2122; fax 924193; info@camping-diez.de;
www.camping-diez.de] In Diez on L bank of Lahn. Exit A3
junc 41 Diez or junc 43 Limburg-Süd. Site sp 1km bef Diez,
8km fr a'bahn. Lge, pt shd; wc; chem disp; mv service pnt;
shwrs; EHU (6A) inc; gas; lndry; shop; rest; playgrnd; children's
pool; watersports; bike hire; 60% statics; dogs; adv bking; ccard
acc; CKE/CCI. "Pleasant vill; gd rests; hot water metered; gd
NH." ♦ 1 Apr-31 Oct. € 20.00   2015*

⊞ **LINDAU (BODENSEE)** *3D4* (5km NE Rural) *47.58509,
9.70667* Campingpark Gitzenweiler Hof, Gitzenweiler 88,
88131 Lindau-Gitzenweiler [(08382) 94940; fax 949415;
info@gitzenweiler-hof.de; www.gitzenweiler-hof.de]
Exit A96/E43/E54 junc 4 onto B12 sp Lindau. Turn off immed
after vill of Oberreitnau twd Rehlings. Site well sp fr all dirs.
Lge, mkd pitch, pt sl, pt shd; wc; chem disp; mv service pnt;
serviced pitches; baby facs; shwrs inc; EHU (6A) €2.50; gas;
lndry; shop; rest, snacks; playgrnd; pool; sm boating/fishing
lake; lake sw 6km; entmnt high ssn; TV; 50% statics; dogs
€2.50; bus 1km; o'night facs for m'vans; Eng spkn; adv bking;
poss noisy high ssn; red long stay; CKE/CCI. "Well-run, busy
site in scenic area; gd facs; friendly staff; excel site for children;
gd cycling; poss prone to flooding after v heavy rain; pitches
poorly maintained; poss cr." ♦ € 33.00 SBS - G18   2014*

LINDAU (BODENSEE) *3D4* (9km SE Rural) *47.53758, 9.73143*
Park-Camping Lindau am See, Fraunhoferstrasse 20,
88131 Lindau-Zech [(08382) 72236; fax 976106; info@
park-camping.de; www.park-camping.de]
On B31 fr Bregenz to Lindau, 200m after customs turn L
to site in 150m; ent could be missed; mini-mkt on corner;
ent rd crosses main rlwy line with auto barriers. B31
fr Friedrichshafen, site well sp fr o'skts of Lindau. Lge, mkd
pitch, hdstg, pt shd; wc; chem disp; mv service pnt; shwrs
inc; EHU (10A) €1 (long lead poss req); lndry (inc dryer); sm
shop; mini-mkt nr; rest, snacks; playgrnd; shgl beach; lake
sw; bike hire; golf 3km; wifi; entmnt high ssn; 20% statics;
dogs €3; m'van o'night area €10; poss cr; Eng spkn; rd & rlwy
noise. "Busy site; immac san facs; sh stay pitches poss diff to
manoeuvre (v cramped; office/gate clsd 1300-1400; helpful
staff; shwr rm for dogs; excel walking in Pfänder area; excel."
♦ 15 Mar-10 Nov. € 26.50   2010*

LINDENBERG IM ALLGAU *3D4* (2km SE Rural) *47.59789,
9.90047* Camping Alpenblick, Schreckenmanklitz 18,
88171 Weiler-Simmerberg [(08381) 3447; fax 942195;
info@camping-alpenblick.de; www.camping-alpenblick.
de] On S of B308 bet Lindau & Immenstadt. Turn off B308
opp hotels sp 'Schreckenmanklitz. Site in 200m on L, visible
fr rd. Diff ent - do not attempt to turn in fr dir Lindau - cont
200m to turning point (mkd 'wendelplatz') & return. Med,
mkd pitch, terr, pt shd; wc; chem disp; mv service pnt; shwrs
€0.20; EHU (10A) metered + conn fee; lndry; shops 700m; rest
800m; snacks; playgrnd; lake sw; 60% statics; dogs €3; adv
bkg; quiet; red CKE/CCI. "Pleasant site with gd views fr some
pitches; gd san facs; gd." 1 Mar-30 Oct. € 19.50   2011*

⊞ **LINGERHAHN** *3B2* (1km NE Rural) *50.09980, 7.57330*
Campingpark am Mühlenteich, Am Mühlenteich 1, 56291
Lingerhahn [(06746) 533; fax 1566; info@muehlenteich.
de; www.muehlenteich.de] Exit A61/E31 exit junc 44 to
Laudert & Lingerhahn. In Lingerhahn foll sp Pfalzfeld, site sp.
Lge, unshd; wc; chem disp; mv service pnt; serviced pitches;
baby facs; shwrs inc; EHU (6A) €2; lndry; shop; rest, snacks;
playgrnd; pool; tennis; entmnt; golf 12km; 75% statics; dogs
€3.50; ent clsd 1300-1500 & 2200; poss cr; adv bkg; quiet;
10% red CKE/CCI. "Delightful rest & beer garden; excel site."
€ 22.50   2012*

LIPPETAL LIPPBORG see Hamm *1B3*

LIPPSTADT *1C4* (8km NE Rural) *51.70095, 8.40808*
Campingparadies Lippstadter Seenplatte, Seeufer Straße
16, 59558 Lippstadt [02 948 22 53; fax 02948 28 94 14;
info@camping-lippstadt.de; www.camping-lippstadt.de]
Turn R off B55 to Lipperode. In town turn R onto
Niederdedinghauser. After 2.5km turn L onto Seeuferstraße.
Site 200m on R. Sm, mkd pitch, pt shd; wc; chem disp; mv
service pnt; baby facs; shwr; EHU (16A); lndry (inc dryer);
playgrnd; bike hire; 25% statics; dogs €2.50; bus 200m; twin
axles; adv bkg; quiet; CCI. " Vg site; fishing in adj lake". ♦
1 Mar-31 Oct. € 27.00   2014*

LOISSIN see Greifswald *2G1*

GERMANY

LORCH 3C2 (6km SE Rural) 50.01820, 7.85493 **Naturpark Camping Suleika, Im Bodenthal 2, 65391 Lorch-bei-Rüdesheim [(06726) 839402; fax 9440; info@suleika-camping.de; www.suleika-camping.de]** Site off B42 on E bank of Rv Rhine, 3km NW of Assmannshausen. 3km SE of Lorch foll sp over rlwy x-ing on narr winding, steep rd thro vineyards to site. App poss diff & dangerous for lge o'fits. Sm, pt sl, terr, pt shd; wc; mv service pnt; serviced pitches; shwrs inc; EHU (16A) metered + conn fee; lndry; shop; rest, snacks; playgrnd; bike hire; dogs €2; poss cr; quiet; sep car park; red CKE/CCI. "Vg site in magnificent setting; excursions by Rhine steamer, local places of interest, wine district; access & exit 1-way system; helpful staff; excel rest; environmentally friendly." 15 Mar-1 Nov. € 23.00   2015*

"I need an on-site restaurant"

We do our best to make sure site information is correct, but it is always best to check any must-have facilities are still available or will be open during your visit.

⊞ **LORRACH** 3B4 (2km N Rural) 47.62461, 7.66275 **Drei-Länder Camp, Grüttweg 8, 79539 Lörrach [(07621) 82588; fax 165034; info@dreilaendercamp.de; www.dreilaender camp.de]** Exit A98/E54 junc 5. Turn L at 1st traff lts after rv bdge on ent Lörrach & site 100m on L, sp. Med, unshd; wc; chem disp; mv service pnt; baby facs; shwrs €0.60; EHU (16A) metered + €3 conn fee; lndry; shop & 300m; rest, snacks; playgrnd; tennis; internet; 30% statics; dogs €3.50; Eng spkn; ccard acc; red CKE/CCI. "Gd facs; lge park adj; clsd 1300-1500; gd NH." ♦ € 24.60   2011*

⊞ **LOWENSTEIN** 3D3 (4km N Rural) 49.11697, 9.38321 **Camping Heilbronn Breitenauer See, 74245 Löwenstein [(07130) 8558; fax 3622; info@breitenauer-see.de; www.breitenauer-see.de]** Exit m'way A81 (E41) at J10, Weinsberg/Ellhofen & on B39 twd Löwenstein/Schwäbisch Hall; site in approx 8km. V lge, mkd pitch, pt shd; htd wc; chem disp; mv service pnt; baby facs; fam bthrm; shwrs inc; EHU (16A) €2 or metered + conn fee; gas; lndry; shop; rest, snacks; bar; playgrnd; lake sw adj; boating; watersports; golf 15km; dog-washing facs; child entmnt high ssn; 50% statics; dogs €5; poss cr; Eng spkn; adv bkg; quiet; ccard acc; 10% red long stay/LS; red CKE/CCI. "Lake walks; beautiful location; pleasant site close to A6 & A81; all facs highest quality & superb; some fully serviced pitches; excel." ♦ € 25.00   2015*

⊞ **LUBBEN** 2G3 (14km SE Rural) 51.86965, 13.9799 **Spreewald-Natur-Camping am Schlosspark, Schlossbezirk 20, 03222 Lübbenau [tel/fax (03542) 3533; info@ spreewaldcamping.de; www.spreewaldcamping.de]** Leave A13 at junc 9, foll rd 115 into Lübbenau. Site well sp. Med, hdstg, pt shd; wc; chem disp; mv service pnt; shwrs €1; EHU (16A) metered + conn fee; gas; lndry; shop; bar; snacks & rest adj; BBQ; canoe hire; bike hire; dogs €2; phone; poss cr; adv bkg; quiet; CKE/CCI. "Cent of Spreewald nature reserve; Lehde Vill open-air heritage museum 2km; boat trips on Rv Spree in punts; excel walking, cycling, canoeing; highly rec; excel site, gd san facs." ♦ € 19.50   2011*

LUBBEN 2G3 (1km S Urban) 51.93641, 13.89490 **Spreewald Camping, Am Burglehn 218, 15907 Lübben [(03546) 7053 or 3335 or 8874; fax 181815; info@spreewald-camping-luebben.de; www.spreewald-camping-luebben.de]** Fr N on A13 exit junc 7 at Freiwalde onto B115 twd Lübben. In town cent turn R to stay on B115 sp Lübbenau. Site on L - well sp. Or fr S exit junc 8 onto B87 to Lübben. Cross rlwy, cont along Luckauerstrasse. Turn R at traff lts into Puschkinstrasse, sp Cottbus. Site on L, well sp. Lge, pt shd; wc; chem disp; mv service pnt; shwrs €0.50; EHU (10A) metered; gas; lndry (inc dryer); shop 400m; rest; playgrnd; wifi; 20% statics; dogs free; adv bkg; quiet; CKE/CCI. "Excel location; modern, clean facs; excel cycle rtes; adj rv for boating; conv for Berlin." ♦ 15 Mar-31 Oct. € 27.00   2015*

⊞ **LUBECK** 2E2 (6km W Rural) 53.86943, 10.63086 **Campingplatz Lübeck-Schünböcken, Steinrader Damm 12, 23556 Lübeck-Schönböcken [tel/fax (0451) 893090; info@ camping-luebeck.de; www.camping-luebeck.de]** Fr A1 exit junc 23 on sh slip rd, stay in L lane, foll sp to Schönböcken & then camp sp (not v obvious); turn R at traff lts bef Dornbreite, site in 1km on L. Med, pt sl, unshd; wc; chem disp; mv service pnt; shwrs €0.50; EHU (6A) €2.50; gas; lndry; shop; playgrnd; dogs €1; bus to town; wifi; Eng spkn; quiet; CKE/CCI. "Helpful owners; busy site; gd san facs but poss stretched if site full; conv Travemünde ferries; Lübeck interesting town; cycle path to town; vg; some rd noise; nice place." € 21.00   2015*

⊞ **LUNEBURG** 1D2 (6km S Rural) 53.20303, 10.40976 **Camping Rote Schleuse, Rote Schleuse 4, 21335 Lüneburg [(04131) 791500; fax 791695; camproteschleuse@aol.com; www.camproteschleuse.de]** Exit A250 junc 4 onto Neu Häcklingen twd Lüneburg. Site sp to R in 300m. Med, pt shd; wc; chem disp; shwrs €0.50; EHU €2.50 or metered; lndry; shop; rest adj; snacks; bar; playgrnd; pool; bike hire; internet; 60% statics; dogs €1; bus fr site ent; clsd 1300-1500; poss cr; Eng spkn; adv bkg; quiet. "Pleasant owners; interesting town." € 19.00   2013*

⊞ **LUTHERSTADT WITTENBERG** 2F3 (5km S Rural) 51.85465, 12.64563 **Marina-Camp Elbe, Brückenkopf 1, 06888 Lutherstadt-Wittenberg [(03491) 4540; fax 454199; info@marina-camp-elbe.de; www.marina-camp-elbe.de]** Site on S side of Elbe bdge on B2 dir Leipzig; well sp. Med, pt shd; wc; chem disp; mv service pnt; serviced pitches; baby facs; sauna; shwrs inc; EHU (16A) metered + conn fee; gas; lndry (inc dryer); shop 1.5km; BBQ; cooking facs; snacks; marina adj; bike hire; wifi; TV; dogs €1.50; bus at gate; quiet; ccard acc; CKE/CCI. "Delightful rvside site; excel, modern san facs." ♦ € 23.00   2011*

⊞ **LUTHERSTADT WITTENBERG** 2F3 (14km S Rural) 51.79135, 12.56995 **Camping Bergwitzsee, Zeltplatz, 06773 Bergwitz [(034921) 28228; fax 28778; info@bergwitzee. de; www.bergwitzsee.de]** S fr Berlin on B2 thro Wittenberg, then thro Eutzsch, bear R onto B100 into Bergwitz; at cent site is sp, foll to lake, turn R & site ahead. Fr main rd to site thro vill 1.5km, cobbled. Site on lakeside. Lge, shd; wc; chem disp; mv service pnt; shwrs €0.50; EHU (10-16A) €2; lndry; shop; rest, snacks; bar; playgrnd; lake sw & sand beach; fishing; watersports; games area; bike hire; TV; 90% statics; dogs €3; adv bkg rec; red CKE/CCI. "Interesting town - Martin Luther Haus; gd cycling/walking area; quiet, restful site; Lakeside site nr Ferropolis, popular with families." ♦ € 16.00   2012*

MAGDEBURG 2E3 (15km N Rural) 52.21888, 11.65944
Campingplatz Barleber See, Wiedersdorferstrasse, 39126
Magdeburg [(0391) 503244; fax 2449692; campingplatz@
cvbs.de; www.cvbs.de] Exit A2/E30 junc 71 sp Rothensee-
Barleber See; site 1km N of a'bahn. Lge, mkd pitch, pt shd; wc;
chem disp; mv service pnt; shwrs inc; EHU (10A) €2; gas; lndry;
shop; rest, snacks; bar; playgrnd; pool; sand beach adj; lake sw;
bike hire; wifi; 60% statics; dogs €2; poss cr; Eng spkn; no adv
bkg; poss noisy w/end; fairly quiet; red long stay/CKE/CCI. "Gd
beach & watersports; pleasant site; helpful staff; gd sports facs;
gd touring base." ♦ ltd. 1 May-30 Sep. € 25.00   2014*

MAINZ 3C2 (8km NE Urban) 50.00296, 8.28556 Camping
Internationaler Mainz-Wiesbaden Maaraue, Maaraue
48, 55246 Mainz-Kostheim [(06134) 4383; fax 707137;
camping@camping-maaraue.de; www.krkg.de/camping]
App fr A671 exit 'Hochheim Süd' foll sp for Kostheim then Int'l
camping sp. Med, mkd pitch, pt shd; wc; chem disp; shwrs inc;
EHU (16A) inc; gas; lndry; shop; rest adj; bar; pool adj; tennis;
dogs €3; adv bkg; quiet; ccard not acc; red CKE/CCI. "Site on
island next to Rv Rhine/Maine junc; o'looks city on opp bank;
excel for Rhine cruises; gd NH." 1 Apr-31 Oct. € 23.00   2009*

⊞ MALCHOW 2F2 (5km NW Rural) 53.49216, 12.37412
Naturcamping Malchow am Plauer See, Am Plauser See
1, 17213 Malchow [(039932) 49907; fax 49908; malchow@
campingtour-mv.de; www.campingtour-mv.de]
Exit A19/E55 junc 16 onto B192 dir Schwerin. Turn L at
camping sp in 500m down narr lane. Lge, mkd pitch, pt shd;
wc; chem disp; mv service pnt; baby facs; shwrs metered;
EHU (10A) €2.50; gas; lndry; shop; rest; bar; BBQ; cooking
facs; playgrnd; sand beach & lake sw adj; 30% statics; dogs
€2.90; phone; poss cr; Eng spkn; adv bkg; quiet; CKE/CCI.
"Vg NH bet Rostock ferry & Berlin; excel, modern facs; all
hot water metered; Malchow swing bdge worth visit." ♦
€ 20.00   2011*

⊞ MALLISS 2E2 (2km SE Rural) 53.19596, 11.34046
Camping am Wiesengrund, Am Kanal 4, 19294 Malliss
[tel/fax (038750) 21060; sielaff-camping@t-online.de;
www.camping-malliss.m-vp.de] Sp in Malliss on rd 191
fr Ludwigslust to Uelzen. Sm, pt shd; wc; chem disp; mv
service pnt; shwrs €0.75; EHU (16A) €2; gas; lndry; shop &
2km; rest 2km; snacks; bar; playgrnd; rv sw adj; watersports;
bike hire; 30% statics; dogs €2.50; phone; m'van o'night facs;
quiet; red CKE/CCI. "Well-run, pleasant, family site; beautiful
surroundings; barrier clsd 1200-1400; visit Ludwigslust
Palace & Dömitz Fortress; vg; lovely site & v friendly staff."
€ 16.50   2012*

⊞ MALSCH 3C3 (4km S Rural) 48.86165, 8.33789
Campingpark Bergwiesen, Waldenfelsstrasse 1, 76316
Malsch [(07246) 1467; fax 5762; email@Campingpark-
Bergwiesen.eu; www.Campingpark-Bergwiesen.eu]
Fr Karlsruhe on B3 thro Malsch vill over level x-ing to
Waldprechtsweier. Foll site sp, take care tight L turn & steep
app thro residential area. Lge, hdg/mkd pitch, hdstg, terr, pt
shd; wc; chem disp; serviced pitches; shwrs inc; EHU (16A)
metered + conn fee; gas; lndry; shop 200m; rest; bar; playgrnd;
pool 1km; sw adj; 80% statics; dogs €2; Eng skn; adv bkg
(no fee); quiet; red CKE/CCI. "1st class facs; well-run site in
beautiful forest setting; v friendly site & owner; not rec for long
o'fits or lge m'vans; gd walks fr site." € 19.00   2011*

MANDERSCHEID see Wittlich 3B2

MANNHEIM 3C2 (8km S Urban) 49.44841, 8.44806 Camping
am Strandbad, Strandbadweg 1, 68199 Mannheim-
Neckarau [(0176) 55422268; fax (0621) 8619968; cfsm.
mannheim@googlemail.com; www.campingplatz-
mannheim-strandbad.de] Exit A6 Karlsruhe-Frankfurt at AB
Kreuz Mannheim (junc 27) L onto A656 Mannheim-Neckarau.
Exit junc 2 onto B36 dir Neckarau, site sp. Med, pt shd; wc;
mv service pnt; shwrs €1; EHU (16A) metered; gas; lndry; shop
2km; rest 300m; snacks; shgl beach & rv sw; wifi; 60% statics;
dogs €1.50; poss cr; quiet; CKE/CCI. "Some noise fr barges on
Rhine & factories opp; poss flooding at high water; interesting
area; barrier down & recep clsd 1200-1500." 1 Apr-31 Oct.
€ 20.00   2014*

MARBURG AN DER LAHN 1C4 (2km S Urban) 50.80000,
8.76861 Camping Lahnaue, Trojedamm 47, 35037
Marburg-an-der-Lahn [tel/fax (06421) 21331; info@
lahnaue.de; www.lahnaue.de] Site by Rv Lahn, app fr sports
cent. Exit a'bahn at Marburg Mitte & sp fr a'bahn. Med, mkd
pitch, pt shd; wc; chem disp; shwrs inc; EHU (10A) €2; lndry
(inc dryer); shops 1km; rest 1.5km; snacks; bar; pool adj; rv
canoeing; tennis; sw & boating nrby; 10% statics; dogs €2.50;
clsd 1300-1500; poss cr; Eng spkn; quiet but m'way & rlwy
noise; ccard acc; CKE/CCI. "Busy site; some pitches v narr; cycle
& footpath to interesting town; excel pool adj; gd." ♦
1 Apr-30 Oct. € 27.00   2013*

MARKDORF 3D4 (2km E Rural) 47.71503, 9.40925
Camping Wirthshof, Steibensteg 12, 88677 Markdorf
[(07544) 96270; fax 962727; info@wirthshof.de;
www.wirthshof.de] Take B33 Markdorf to Ravensburg; site
on R sp Camping/Schwimbad/Mini-Golf, in vill of Steibensteg.
Lge, pt shd; wc; mv service pnt; sauna; shwrs inc; EHU (6A)
inc; lndry; shop; rest; playgrnd; pool; bike hire; golf 10km;
entmnt; dogs €4 (reservation req Jul & Aug); clsd 1200-
1400; poss cr; debit cards acc. "Excel; activities for children
& teenagers; gd sightseeing; special pitches for m'vans in
quiet area with EHU; immac facs; excel rest; helpful owners;
Markdorf vill picturesque; gd walking/cycling rtes; Thurs
mkt; boat trips on Bodensee; gd tourist info; wonderful." ♦
1 Mar-30 Oct. € 27.70   2009*

See advertisement inside the front cover

⊞ MARKTHEIDENFELD 3D2 (5km S Rural) 49.81885,
9.58851 Camping Main-Spessart-Park, Spessartstrasse
30, 97855 Triefenstein-Lengfurt [(09395) 1079; fax 8295;
info@camping-main-spessart.de; www.camping-main-
spessart.de] Exit A3/E41 junc 65 or 66 sp Lengfurt. In Lengfurt
foll sp Marktheidenfeld; site in 1km. Lge, pt sl, terr, pt shd; wc;
chem disp; mv service pnt; serviced pitches; shwrs inc; EHU
(6-10A) €3; lndry; shop; rest; playgrnd; pool adj; watersports;
50% statics; dogs €2.50; Eng spkn; adv bkg; ccard acc; red
CKE/CCI. "Excel, high quality site; vg rest; vg san facs; easy
access A4; sep NH area; helpful owners; access diff parts of site
due steep terrs; busy site; gd facs." ♦ € 32.50   2014*

⊞ **MARKTOBERDORF** *4E4* (12km NW Rural) *47.80285, 10.55360* **Campingplatz Elbsee, Am Elbsee 3, 87648 Aitrang [(08343) 248; fax 1406; info@elbsee.de; www.elbsee.de]** W fr Marktoberdorf on B472 onto B12. Turn N foll sp to Elbsee. Fr Kempten E on B12 to Unterthingau N to Aitrang, site 2km S of vill. Lge, mkd pitch, pt sl, pt shd; htd wc; chem disp; mv service pnt; serviced pitches; sauna; shwrs inc; EHU (16A) metered + conn fee; lndry (inc dryer); shop; rest adj; BBQ; playgrnd; lake sw & boating adj; solarium; bike hire; wifi; TV rm; 60% statics; dogs €4.50; phone; o'night facs for m'vans; site clsd 4 Nov-16 Dec; Eng spkn; ccard acc; red CKE/CCI. "Excel, friendly, family-owned site; clean, modern facs; dog shwr rm + hairdryer; well mkd walk signs fr site." ♦ € 24.70   2011*

⊞ **MEDELBY** *1D1* (700m W Rural) *54.81490, 9.16361* **Camping Kawan Mitte, Sonnenhügel 1, 24994 Medelby [(04605) 189391; info@camping-mitte.de; www.camping kawanmitte.eu]** Exit A7 junc 2 onto B199 dir Niebüll to Wallsbüll, turn N dir Medelby, site sp. Lge, mkd pitch, pt shd; htd wc; chem disp; mv service pnt; baby facs; fam bthrm; sauna; shwrs inc; EHU (16A) metered; lndry (inc dryer); shop; supmkt 600m; rest 600m; snacks; BBQ; cooking facs; playgrnd; 2 htd pool; games area; fitness rm; bike hire; horseriding 600m; golf 12km; wifi; TV rm; 20% statics; dogs free; adv bkg; quiet; CKE/CCI. "Conv m'way & Danish border; vg." ♦ € 24.00 (CChq acc)   2015*

MEERBUSCH see Düsseldorf *1B4*

MEISSEN *2G4* (5km S Rural) *51.13942, 13.49883* **Camping Rehbocktal, Rehbocktal 4, 01665 Scharfenberg-bei-Meissen [(03521) 404827; fax 404828; info@camping-rehbocktal.de; www.camping-rehbocktal.de]** Exit E40/A4 at Dresden Altstadt; foll sp Meissen on B6 to Scharfenberg; site on L opp Rv Elbe. Med, pt sl, pt shd; wc; chem disp; shwrs inc; EHU (16A) €3; lndry; shop & 3km; rest adj; snacks; bar; playgrnd; 10% statics; dogs €2; bus; poss cr; no adv bkg; v quiet; CKE/CCI. "In wooded valley opp vineyard; friendly staff; conv Colditz; Meissen factory & museum worth visit; cycle path to Meissen nr." 15 Mar-31 Oct. € 26.00   2013*

MEISSENDORF see Winsen (Aller) *1D3*

⊞ **MELLE** *1C3* (8km NW Rural) *52.22428, 8.2661* **Campingplatz Grönegau-Park Ludwigsee, Nemdenerstrasse 12, 49326 Melle [(05402) 2132; fax 2112; info@ludwigsee.de; www.ludwigsee.de]** Exit A30/E30 junc 22 twd Bad Essen, site sp on lakeside. Lge, hdg/mkd pitch, pt shd; wc; chem disp; mv service pnt; shwrs €1; EHU (10A) inc; lndry; shop 1.5km; rest, snacks; bar; playgrnd; lake sw; games area; bike hire; internet; entmnt; 80% statics; dogs €2; sep car park; barrier clsd 1300-1500; adv bkg; quiet; ccard acc; red CKE/CCI. "Beautiful & pleasant site; helpful owners; sep area for tourers." € 30.00   2014*

MEMMINGEN *3D4* (10km SW Rural) *47.94871, 10.08578* **Park-Camping Iller, Illerstrasse 57, 88317 Aitrach [(07565) 5419; fax 5222; info@camping-iller.de; www.camping-iller.de]** Exit A96/E43/E54 junc 11, site in 3km, sp. Or fr Memmingen take rd dir Leutkirch. In Ferthofen vill look for camping sp & turn R after rv bdge. In Aitrach turn R, site 1km on L. Lge, pt shd; htd wc; chem disp; mv service pnt; serviced pitches; baby facs; fam bthrm; shwrs inc; EHU (10A) €2.50; gas; lndry (inc dryer); shop; rest 1.5km; snacks; bar; playgrnd; pool; paddling pool; tennis; games rm; internet; 75% statics; dogs €2; o'night area for m'vans; poss cr; adv bkg; quiet; Eng spkn; ccard acc; red snr citizens/CKE/CCI. "Gd family site; helpful staff; gd walking, cycling." ♦ 1 May-15 Oct. € 24.50   2011*

MENDIG *3B2* (6km N Rural) *50.42151, 7.26448* **Camping Laacher See, Am Laacher See, 56653 Wassenach [(02636) 2485; fax 929750; info@camping-laacher-see.de; www.camping-laacher-see.de]** Fr A61, exit junc 34 Mendig. Foll tents sp to Maria Laach. Site on Laacher See. Lge, hdg/mkd pitch, hdstg, pt sl, pt terr, pt shd; htd wc; chem disp; mv service pnt; baby facs; shwrs €0.50; EHU (16A) metered + conn fee; gas; lndry (inc dryer); shop; rest, snacks; bar; playgrnd; lake sw; sailing; fishing; wifi; 50% statics; dogs €4; bus 500m; Eng spkn; quiet; adv bkg; ccard acc; CKE/CCI. "Neat, clean, relaxing site; all pitches lake views; busy at w/end; modern, outstanding san facs; gd woodland walks, cycling & sw; excel sailing facs; excel site & rest; close to m'way; rec." ♦ ltd. 2 Apr-28 Sep. € 30.50   2014*

⊞ **MENDIG** *3B2* (2km NNW Rural) *50.38646, 7.27237* **Camping Siesta, Laacherseestrasse 6, 56743 Mendig [(02652) 1432; fax 520424; service@campingsiesta.de; www.campingsiesta.de]** Fr A61 exit junc 34 for Mendig dir Maria Laach; foll camp sps; site on R in 300m by ent to car park. Med, some hdg pitch, sl, pt terr, pt shd; htd wc; chem disp; shwrs inc; EHU (16A) €1.80; gas; lndry; rest; bar; playgrnd; sm pool; sw pool 500m; 60% statics; dogs €1.30; poss v cr; Eng spkn; noise fr nrby a'bahn; CKE/CCI. "Useful NH; easy access fr A61; owner helpful in siting NH o'fits; longest waterslide in Europe; gd base for region's castles & wines; friendly owners; spotless site; gd rest; site has so much more to offer than only a NH; v welcoming; vg refurbished; new san facs (2014)." € 24.00   2014*

⊞ **MESCHEDE** *1C4* (10km S Rural) *51.29835, 8.26425* **Knaus Campingpark Hennesee, Mielinghausen 7, 59872 Meschede [(0291) 952720; fax 9527229; hennesee@ knauscamp.de; www.knauscamp.de]** S fr Meschede on B55 for 7km; at sp for Erholungszentrum & Remblinghausen turn L over Lake Hennesee, site on L in 500m, sp. Lge, mkd pitch, terr, pt shd; wc; chem disp ltd; mv service pnt; sauna; serviced pitches; shwrs inc; EHU (6A) conn fee; gas; lndry; supmkt; rest, snacks; bar; playgrnd; lake sw 200m; bike hire; entmnt high ssn; internet; 60% statics; dogs €3.80; poss cr; adv bkg; Eng spkn; quiet; red CKE/CCI. "Conv Sauerland mountains & lakes; 50m elec cable advisable; vg." € 28.70 (CChq acc)   2012*

MESENICH see Trier *3B2*

You can now fill in site reports online

⊞ **METTINGEN** *1B3* (2km SW Rural) *52.31251, 7.76202*
Camping Zur Schönen Aussicht, Schwarzestrasse 73,
49497 Mettingen [(05452) 606; fax 4751; info@camping-
schoene-aussicht.de; www.camping-schoene-aussicht.de]
Exit A30 junc 12 dir Mettingen. Go thro town cent, uphill
turn L at traff lts, site sp. Med, hdg/mkd pitch, pt sl, pt shd;
wc; chem disp; mv service pnt; shwrs €1.30; EHU (10A) €3
or metered; lndry; shop; rest; bar; playgrnd; htd, covrd pool;
internet; 50% statics; no dogs; Eng spkn; adv bkg; quiet;CKE/
CCI. "Nice, friendly site; gd walking, cycling; easy walk to
town; gd facs." € 27.50   2015*

MILTENBERG *3D2* (600m N Urban) *49.70366, 9.25417*
Camping Mainwiese, 12 Steingasserstrasse, 63897
Miltenberg [(09371) 3985; fax 68723; info@campingplatz-
miltenberg.de; www.campingplatz-miltenberg.de]
On B469 to Miltenberg. Cross rv bdge dir Klingenberg. Ent
in 200m on R, sp. Lge, unshd; wc; chem disp; mv service
pnt; baby facs; shwrs inc; EHU (16A) €2; lndry; shop; rest
adj; playgrnd; golf 10km; 25% statics; dogs €2; quiet; red
long stay. "Poss long walk to san facs." 1 Apr-30 Sep.
€ 14.50   2009*

⊞ **MITTENWALD** *4E4* (4km N Rural) *47.47290, 11.27729*
Naturcamping Isarhorn, Am Horn 4, 82481 Mittenwald
[(08823) 5216; fax 8091; camping@mittenwald.de; www.
camping-isarhorn.de] E fr Garmisch-Partenkirchen on rd 2;
at Krün turn S on D2/E533 dir Mittenwald. Site on R in approx
2km at int'l camping sp. Ent on R fr main rd. NB: Rd thro to
Innsbruck via Zirlerberg improved & no longer clsd to c'vans
descending S; long & steep; low gear; not to be attempted N.
Lge, pt shd, unmkd, some hdstg; wc; chem disp; mv service
pnt; shwrs €0.50; EHU (16A) €2.80 or metered; lndry; shop;
snacks; rest; BBQ; htd, covrd pool 4km; canoeing (white water);
ski lift; tennis; wifi; dogs €2.90; bus adj; site clsd 1300-1500 &
2200-0700; site clsd 1 Nov-mid Dec; Eng spkn; quiet but some
rd noise; ccard acc; red LS; "Relaxed, secluded site in pines;
mountain views; excel base for walking; cycle track to attractive
town; poss some noise fr nrby military base; owner v keen on
recycling waste; facs gd but insufficient for size of site; highly
rec." € 27.50   2015*

⊞ **MITTENWALD** *4E4* (6km N Rural) *47.49040, 11.25438*
Alpen-Caravanpark Tennsee, Am Tennsee 1,82493 Klais-
Krün [(08825) 170; fax 17236; info@camping-tennsee.de;
www.camping-tennsee.de] N fr Mittenwald on main
Innsbruck-Garmisch rd turn off for Krun, foll Tennsee & site sp.
2km SE of Klais, not well sp. Lge, mkd pitch, hdstg, pt terr, pt
shd; htd wc; chem disp; mv service pnt; 50% serviced pitches;
family & baby facs; shwrs inc; EHU (16A) metered; gas; lndry;
shop & 2km; rest, snacks; bar; playgrnd; ski lift 2.5km; bike
hire; entmnt; dogs €3.30; phone; poss cr; Eng spkn; adv bkg;
ccard acc; CKE/CCI. "Excel area for Bavarian Alps, Tirol; site
clsd Nov-mid Dec; barrier clsd 1200-1500; gd size pitches; red
snr citizens; vg, clean, friendly, family-run site; price inc use of
tourist buses." ♦ € 49.00   2013*

⊞ **MITTERTEICH** *4F2* (3km NW Rural) *49.97311, 12.22497*
Campingplatz Großbüchlberg, Großbüchlberg 32, 95666
Mitterteich [09633 40 06 73; fax 40 06 77; camping@
freizeithugl.de; www.freizeithugl.de] Fr A93 Marktredwitz-
Mitterteich take exit 16 Mitterteich. At xrds in town cent foll
Freizeithugl signs. Turn L after 200m twds Grossbuchberg. Foll
sp. Med, hdg/mkd pitch, hdstg, pt sl, terr, pt shd; htd wc; chem
disp; mv service pnt; baby fasc; fam bthrm; shwrs inc; EHU
(16A); lndry (inc dryer); shop; rest; snacks; bar; playgrnd; wifi;
tv rm; dogs €1.50; phone adj; bus adj; twin axles; poss cr; Eng
spkn; adv bkg; quiet; ccard acc; CCI. "Excel site; superb htd san
facs; close to mini-golf, toboggan run, etc; extensive views;
v friendly." ♦ € 25.00   2014*

MOHNESEE see Soest *1C4*

MONSCHAU *3A1* (3km SW Rural) *50.54305, 6.23694*
Camping Perlenau, 52156 Monschau [(02472) 4136;
fax 4493; familie.rasch@monschau-perlenau.de;
www.monschau-perlenau.de] Fr N (Aachen) foll B258 past
Monschau dir Schleiden. Site on L just bef junc with B399 to
Kalterherberg. Steep & narr app. Fr Belgium, exit A3 junc 38 for
Eupen & foll rd thro Eupen to Monschau. Site on rvside. Med,
hdg/mkd pitch, hdstg, pt sl, terr, pt shd; htd wc; chem disp;
mv service pnt; baby facs; fam bthrm; shwrs; EHU (10-16A)
€2.60 or metered; gas; lndry; shop; rest, snacks; bar; BBQ;
cooking facs; playgrnd; 20% statics; dogs €2.60; phone; bus
500m; poss cr; Eng spkn; adv bkg; quiet; red long stay; CKE/
CCI. "Gd touring base for Eifel region; attractive site beside
stream; historic town in walking dist." ♦ 20 Mar-31 Oct.
€ 27.60   2013*

⊞ **MONTABAUR** *3C2* (8km E Rural) *50.43761, 7.90498*
Camping Eisenbachtal, 56412 Girod [(06485) 766;
fax 4938] S on A3/E35 exit junc 41 dir Montabaur; at Girod
turn L to site, well sp. Med, hdg/mkd pitch, some hdstg, pt
sl, pt shd; htd wc; chem disp; mv service pnt; some serviced
pitches; shwrs €0.50; EHU (10A) inc; (poss rev pol); gas; lndry;
2 x rest adj; playgrnd; sw 5km; 75% statics; dogs €2; poss cr;
Eng spkn; adv bkg; quiet; red long stay; CKE/CCI. "Beautiful,
well-equipped site in Naturpark Nassau; conv NH fr a'bahn
& worth longer stay; friendly, welcoming staff; gd for nature
lovers & children; gd walking & cycling; adj rest excel; site clsd
1300-1500 but car park opp; conv Rhine & Mosel valleys." ♦
€ 18.00   2015*

MORFELDEN *3C2* (9km S Rural) *49.94461, 8.60544*
Campingplatz Am Steinrodsee, Triftweg 33, 64331
Weiterstadt [06150 53593; fax 591345; rezeption.
koehres@t-online.de; www.camping-steinrodsee.de]
Leave A5 twds Darmstadt at exit 25. L at traff lts onto
L3113. Turn R in 5km & foll signs. Lge, hdg/mkd pitch, pt
shd; htd wc; chem disp; mv service pnt; baby facs; shwrs inc;
EHU (16A); lndry (inc dryer); rest; bar; BBQ; playgrnd; wifi;
60% statics; dogs; bus 2km; twin axles; quiet; CCI. "Vg site;
quiet with some aircraft & m'way noise; clean, tidy, well
regulated site; immac san facs; conv for Darmstadt." ♦
1 Jan-31 Oct. € 23.00   2015*

GERMANY

MORITZBURG 4G1 (3km S Rural) 51.1450, 13.67444
Campingplatz Bad Sonnenland, Dresdnerstrasse 115,
01468 Moritzburg [(0351) 8305495; fax 8305494; bad-
sonnenland@t-online.de; www.bad-sonnenland.de]
Leave A4/E40 exit 80. Turn R sp Moritzburg, foll site sp thro
Reichenberg. Site on L 3km bef Moritzburg. Lge, pt shd; wc;
chem disp; mv service pnt; shwrs (inc); EHU (16A) €2.50; gas;
lndry; shop; supmkt 2km; rest, snacks; bar; playgrnd; lake sw
adj; games rm; games area; statics in sep area; dogs €3; bus
to Dresden; Eng spkn; quiet; ccard acc; CKE/CCI. "Scenic area;
friendly staff; excel, immac facs; site clsd 1300-1500 & 2200-
0700; also holiday vill with many huts; conv Dresden, Meissen;
narr gauge steam train Dresden-Moritzburg; day trip to Prague;
many mkd walking & cycling rtes in area; Schloss Moritzburg in
vill; vg site; poss cr high ssn." 1 Apr-31 Oct. € 22.00   2015*

MOSCHWITZ see Plauen 4F1

MUDEN AN DER ORTZE see Fassberg 1D2

⊞ **MUHLBERG** 2E4 (1.6km NW Rural) 50.87516, 10.80843
Campingplatz Drei Gleichen, Am Gut Ringhofen,
99869 Mühlberg [(036256) 22715; fax 86801; service@
campingplatz-muehlberg.de; www.campingplatz-
muehlberg.de] Leave A4/E40 at junc 43 (Wandersleben) S
twds Mühlberg; site well sp in 2km on rd to Wechmar. Med,
hdg/mkd pitch, pt sl, unshd; wc; chem disp; mv service pnt;
shwrs €1; EHU (16A) €1.80 + conn fee; lndry; shop 3km; rest
adj; bar; playgrnd; sw adj; 50% statics; dogs €2.20; site clsd
1300-1500; adv bkg; quiet; CKE/CCI. "Gd facs; helpful staff;
conv a'bahn." ♦ € 16.00   2015*

MUHLHAUSEN see Augsburg 4E3

MUNCHEN 4E4 (7km S Urban) 48.09165, 11.54516 Camping
München-Thalkirchen, Zentralländstrasse 49, 81379
München [(089) 7231707; fax 7243177; campingplatz.
muenchen@web.de; www.muenchen.de] Fr S on A95/E533
at end of a'bahn keep strt on (ignore zoo sp). After tunnel exit
R at sp Thalkirchen. Turn L at traff lts & foll sp to camp. If app
fr S on A8/E45 turn L at traff lts at end twd Garmish & strt on
to tunnel, site sp. Fr NW at end of A8 in 200m turn R & foll sp
to zoo (Tierpark). Cont to foll zoo sp until in approx 10km pick
up sp to site. (Zoo on E side of Rv Isar, site on W side.) App
fr N not rec due v heavy traffic. V lge, mkd pitch, pt shd; htd
wc; chem disp; mv service pnt; many serviced pitches; shwrs
€1; EHU (10A) €2 (long lead req); lndry (inc dryer); shop; rest
500m; snacks; playgrnd; pool & rv 500m; internet; dogs inc;
phone; bus 100m; poss cr esp Oktoberfest; Eng spkn; quiet;
ccard not acc; CKE/CCI. "Busy site; some m'van/o'night pitches
v sm; bus/U-bahn tickets avail fr recep; cycle track/walk along
rv to town cent, avoiding traffic; helpful staff; san facs clean,
stretched when site full; gd site when visiting Munich." ♦
15 Mar-31 Oct. € 28.00   2013*

⊞ **MUNCHEN** 4E4 (12km NW Urban) 48.19888, 11.49694
Campingplatz Nord-West, Auf den Schrederwiesen
3, 80995 München-Moosach [(089) 1506936; info@
campingplatz-nord-west.de; www.campingplatz-nord-
west.de] Fr N exit A99 junc 10 Lugwigsfeld onto B304
S - Dachauerstrasse, sp München. Turn L in approx 800m at
traff lts. Turn R at T-junc to site on R. Med, hdstg, shd; htd wc;
chem disp; mv service pnt; shwrs €1.50; EHU (10-16A) €5 or
metered; lndry (inc dryer); shop & 1km; rest 3km; snacks; bar;
entmnt; 50% statics; dogs €2; phone; bus to city; poss cr; Eng
spkn; adv bkg; quiet; ccard acc; CKE/CCI. "Friendly, helpful
welcome; enquire about public transport tickets; ltd facs LS;
Dachau - pretty town 10km; gd." ♦ € 24.40   2014*

MUNCHEN 4E4 (14km NW Rural) 48.17421,
11.44645 Waldcamping München-Obermenzing,
Lochhausenerstrasse 59, 81247 München [(089) 8112235;
fax 8144807; campingplatz-obermenzing@t-online.de;
www.campingplatz-muenchen.de] Foll sp around
Munich ring rd to ent of A8 Munich/Stuttgart a'bahn;
passing m'way ent on L cont on Pippingerstrasse & site on
Lochhausenerstrasse; heavy traff to/fr S of site. Lge, hdg/mkd
pitch, pt shd; htd wc; chem disp; mv service pnt; serviced
pitches; shwrs €1; EHU (10A) metered; gas; lndry; shop; snacks;
bar; cooking facs; pool 3km; internet; 10% statics; dogs €1;
bus to city 1km, tram 2km; poss cr; Eng spkn; no adv bkg;
m'way noise; CKE/CCI. "Pleasant management; Park & Ride to
city 3km; variable size pitches, some narr, & poss overgrown; v
busy & noisy during beer festival & prices increased."
15 Mar-31 Oct. € 22.00   2009*

"Satellite navigation makes touring much easier"

Remember most sat navs don't know if
you're towing or in a larger vehicle – always
use yours alongside maps and site directions.

⊞ **MUNCHEN** 4E4 (17km NW Rural) 48.19821, 11.41161
Campingplatz am Langwieder See, Eschenriederstrasse
119, 81249 München-Langwied [(089) 8641566;
fax 8632342; info@camping-langwieder-see.de;
www.camping-langwieder-see.de] Exit A8 junc 80 at
Langwieder See & foll sp Dachau; site within 200m. Fr ring
rd A99 junc 8 join A8 to N, then as above. Med, hdstg, pt
shd; htd wc; chem disp; shwrs €0.50; EHU (10A) metered +
conn fee €1; gas; lndry; shop; snacks; rest; bar; lake sw adj;
95% statics; dogs €1.70; poss v cr; Eng spkn; no adv bkg;
m'way noise; CKE/CCI. "Pleasant owners; tourers in a row
outside recep area parked v close together; v sm pitches,
mostly on gravel; gd san facs; site used by workers; easy access
to Munich by train fr Dachau; lge free car park at stn; NH/sh
stay only." € 21.50   2011*

MUNCHSTEINACH see Neustadt an der Aisch 4E2

MUNICH see München 4E4

⊞ **MUNSTER** *1B3* (6km SE Rural) *51.94638, 7.69027*
Camping Münster, Laerer Wersuefer 7, 48157 Münster
[(0251) 311982; fax 3833985; campingplatz-muenster@t-
online.de; www.campingplatz-muenster.de] Fr A43 exit
junc 2 or A1/E37 exit junc 78 onto B51 dir Münster then
Bielefeld. On leaving built-up area, turn R after TV mast on R.
Cross Rv Werse & turn L at 1st traff lts, site sp. (Site is also sp
fr Münster S by-pass). Lge, mkd pitch, some hdstg, pt shd; htd
wc; chem disp; mv service pnt; serviced pitches; shwrs €0.50;
EHU (16A) inc; lndry; shop; rest, snacks; playgrnd; htd pool
adj; fishing; tennis; bike hire; wifi; 50% statics; dogs €3; bus
300m; o'night m'van area; barrier clsd 1300-1500; poss v cr
w/e; Eng spkn; adv bkg; quiet; red CKE/CCI. "Excel; quiet mid
wk; Münster v interesting; radio/tv mast useful landmark fr
S; gd cycle rtes; vg site, tokens for shwrs; sep motor parking
outside camp; excel for bus to Munster; helpful staff; clean facs
& plentiful." ♦ € 24.00   2015*

"There aren't many sites open at this time of year"

If you're travelling outside peak season
remember to call ahead to check site opening
dates – even if the entry says 'open all year'.

⊞ **MUNSTERTAL** *3B4* (2km W Rural) *47.85995, 7.76370*
Feriencamping Münstertal, Dietzelbachstrasse 6, 79244
Münstertal [(07636) 7080; fax 7448; info@camping-
muenstertal.de; www.camping-muenstertal.de]
Exit A5 junc 64a at Bad Krozingen-Staufen-Münstertal. By-pass
Stauffen & foll Münstertal sps. Site on L 1.5km past Camping
Belchenblick off rd L123. Lge, mkd pitch, shd; wc; chem disp;
mv service pnt; serviced pitches; sauna; steam rm; solarium;
private bathrms avail; shwrs inc; EHU (16A) metered; gas; lndry;
shop; rest, snacks; adventure playgrnd; 2 htd pools (1 covrd);
fishing; wintersports nr; ski lift 10km; tennis; horseriding;
games area; games rm; beauty treatments avail; wifi; entmnt;
cab TV; some statics; dogs €3.50; phone; rlwy stn 200m;
gates clsd 1300-1430 & 2200-0730; m'van o'night area; adv
bkg rec school hols; quiet; red long stay/CKE/CCI. "Superb,
well-managed site; luxurious, clean facs; many activities for all
family; gd walking; vg rest; conv Freiburg & Black Forest." ♦
€ 31.50   2011*

MURNAU AM STAFFELSEE *4E4* (5km N Rural) *47.70680,*
11.21821 **Camping Brugger am Riegsee, Seestrasse 1,**
82418 Hofheim-am-Riegsee [(08847) 728; fax 228; office@
camping-brugger.de; www.camping-brugger.de]
Fr A95/E533 exit 9 for Sindelsdorf, dir Habach. Foll sp Hofheim
& site. Med, hdg/mkd pitch, hdstg, terr, pt shd; htd wc; chem
disp; mv service pnt; serviced pitches; shwrs €0.50; EHU (16A)
€2.50 or metered; gas; lndry; shop; snacks; playgrnd; pool
5km; shgl beach & lake sw adj; boating; windsurfing; tennis
2km; games area; games rm; internet; entmnt; 60% statics;
dogs €2.50; m'van o'night area; clsd 1230-1430; Eng spkn; adv
bkg; quiet; red long stay; CKE/CCI. "Friendly/helpful owners;
beautiful lake & mountain views; gd, modern facs; excel site;
panoramic pitches get booked up early for the peak ssn."
1 May-1 Oct. € 25.00   2011*

MURNAU AM STAFFELSEE *4E4* (3.5km NW Rural) *47.68493,*
11.17918 **Camping Halbinsel Burg, Burgweg 41, 82418**
Murnau-Seehausen [(08841) 9870; fax 626071; info@
camping-staffelsee.de; www.camping-staffelsee.de]
Exit A95 junc 9 Sindelsdorf/Peissenberg to Murnau. Site sp at
traff lts in cent of Murnau, dir Seehausen. Med, pt shd; wc;
chem disp; mv service pnt; shwrs inc; EHU (16A) €1.80; lndry;
shop; rest; playgrnd; lake sw & beach; watersports; entmnt
high ssn; 20% statics; no dogs; no adv bkg; red CKE/CCI.
"Wonderful sw & boating; pleasant, lovely, well-equipped site
in superb location for alps, lakes & local amenities." ♦
6 Jan-25 Oct. € 26.00   2014*

MURNAU AM STAFFELSEE *4E4* (8km NW Rural) *47.69861,*
11.15833 **Campingplatz Aichalhof, Aichalehof 4, 82449**
Uffing-am-Staffelsee [(08846) 211; camping@aichalehof.
de; www.aichalehof.de] N fr Murnau dir Seehausen & Uffing
- Murnaustrasse. In Murnau turn L into Seestrasse to site in
2km. Site on L after sailing club. Or exit A95 junc 9 onto B472
W to Uffing, then as above. Med, pt sl, pt shd; wc; chem disp;
mv service pnt; baby facs; shwrs €0.50; EHU (10A) €2; lndry
(inc dryer); shop, rest 2km; snacks; bar; BBQ; playgrnd; lake sw
adj; watersports; fishing; 70% statics; dogs €2; Eng spkn; adv
bkg; quiet; CKE/CCI. "Excel, peaceful, scenic site, cycle/walking
path around lake, steamer on lake, trains and buses fr Uffing."
♦ 1 May-3 Oct. € 21.00   2011*

⊞ **NAUMBURG (HESSEN)** *1C4* (800m NW Rural) *51.25070,*
9.16060 **Camping in Naumburg (formerly Kneipp Kur**
Camping), Am Schwimmbad 12, 34311 Naumburg
[(05625) 9239670 or (mob) 0170 4418621; info@camping-
naumburg.de; www.camping-naumburg.de] Exit A44
junc 67 onto B251 thro Istha. At Bründersen foll sp Altenstadt
& Naumburg. Foll int'l camping sp, well sp. Med, mkd pitch,
terr, unshd; htd wc; chem disp; mv service pnt; baby facs;
shwrs; EHU (16A) €2 or metered (poss rev pol); lndry; bar;
BBQ; cooking facs; playgrnd; games area; pool adj; tennis;
horseriding 5km; golf 15km; spa treatments; 30% statics; dogs
€2.50; bus 500m; clsd 1300-1500; twin axles; Eng spkn; adv
bkg; quiet; red LS; CKE/CCI. "Charming site; excel, modern san
facs; spacious pitches; friendly, helpful staff; interesting town;
gd walks fr site; rec; nr pool, smkt, Dambusters Dam; new
management." ♦ € 22.00   2015*

NECKARGEMUND see Heidelberg *3C2*

⊞ **NECKARSULM** *3D3* (2km E Urban) *49.18734,*
9.24776 **Camping Reisachmühle, Reisachmühlweg 6,**
74172 Neckarsulm [(07132) 2169; fax 308633; info@
campingplatz-reisachmuehle.de; www.campingplatz-
reisachmuehle.de] Exit A6/E50 junc 37 onto B27 to
Neckarsulm, site well sp nr Aquatoll. Med, mkd pitch, unshd;
wc; chem disp; shwrs inc; EHU (16A) €2 or metered; gas; lndry;
shop; rest 500m; playgrnd; 40% statics; dogs €2; some Eng
spkn; CKE/CCI. "Conv NH nr a'bahn; rec arr early high ssn."
€ 16.00   2011*

NEEF *3B2* (500m N Rural) *50.09500, 7.13694*
Wohnmobilplatz Am Frauenberg, Am Moselufer, 56858
Neef [(06542) 21575] Exit A1/E44 junc 125 onto B49 to Neef.
In Neef cross rv bdge, site sp on L beside rv. M'vans only. Med,
pt shd; chem disp; mv service pnt; EHU (10A) inc; shop 400m;
rest 100m; some rlwy & rv noise. "Gd; owner calls am & pm for
payment; beautiful location." 1 Mar-30 Oct. € 5.00   2013*

GERMANY

NEEF *3B2* (4km S Urban) *50.05294, 7.13115* **Bären Camp Bullay, Am Moselufer 1+3, D-56859 Bullay (Mosel) [06542 900097; info@baeren-camp.de; www.baeren-camp.de]** Foll B49 to Alf, cross Moselle bdge to Bullay. Turn L and drive under the rlwy bdge, foll the rd. At the vill sq turn into Fährstrasse, drive across Moselle car park past the football grnd foll sp to site. Sm, mkd pitch, pt shd; htd wc; chem disp; shwrs; baby facs; lndry; playgrnd; shop; rest, bar; BBQ; dogs; Eng spk; poss noisy; CKE/CCI. "Fair site; handy for Mosel Cycle Rte; diff ent, barrier down rest time." 18 Apr-27 Aug. € 21.00   2012*

NEHREN see Cochem *3B2*

NENNIG *3A2* (1.6km N Rural) *49.54195, 6.37126* **Mosel-Camping Dreiländereck, Am Moselufer, 66706 Perl-Nennig [(06866) 322; fax 1005; info@mosel-camping.de; www.mosel-camping.de]** Site on bank of Mosel opp Remich (Luxembourg), access on R just bef bdge (fr German side). Fr Luxembourg cross rv bdge, turn L after former border post cont to rv & turn L under bdg; site is ahead. Med, unshd; htd wc; chem disp; mv service pnt; shwrs €1.40; EHU (16A) inc; lndry; shops 400m; rest, snacks; bar; BBQ; playgrnd; fishing; cycling; golf 15km; 65% statics; dogs €1; phone; poss cr; adv bkg; quiet; no ccard acc; Eng spkn; 10% red long stay; 5% red CKE/CCI. "Nice site; dishwashing & chem disp adj; ltd facs; conv vineyards, Roman mosaic floor in Nennig; cycle track along rv; sh walk to Remich; friendly welcome." 1 Apr-15 Oct. € 18.60   2015*

NENNIG *3A2* (1.8km N Rural) *49.54331, 6.37207* **Camping Mosella am Rothaus (formerly Moselplatz), Zur Moselbrücke 15, 66706 Perl-Nennig [(06866) 510 or 26660222 (Lux'bourg); fax 1486; info@mosel-camping.de]** Site on bank of Mosel opp Remich (Luxembourg), access on R just bef bdge. Fr Luxembourg cross rv bdge, turn L after former border post, site is ahead, opp Mosel-Camping Dreiländereck. Med, hdg pitch, pt shd; htd wc; chem disp; mv service pnt; shwrs inc; EHU (10A) inc; gas 1km; shop 500m; rest, snacks; bar; BBQ; 50% statics; dogs; bus 100m; poss cr; Eng spkn; quiet, some rd noise; CKE/CCI. "Lovely site by rv for sh or long stay; helpful, friendly owner; ltd facs, a bit tired; rest adj; rvside pitch sm extra charge; gd touring base; frequent bus to Luxembourg City." ♦ ltd. 1 Apr-15 Oct. € 22.60   2015*

NESSELWANG *4E4* (10km SE Urban) *47.56315, 10.57843* **Campingplatz Pfronten, Tirolerstrasse 109, 87459 Pfronten-Steinach [(08363) 377 or 8353]** Fr Nesselwang on B309/E532, go thro Pfronten, site on R by 'Osterreich 1km' sp. Med, pt sl, pt shd; wc; chem disp; mv service pnt; shwrs inc; EHU (10A) €1.40 (poss rev pol); lndry; shop & 1km; rest 300m; bar; pool 2km; dogs €0.50; phone; no adv bkg; quiet; CKE/CCI. "Gd mountain walks; castles & lakes adj; helpful & friendly staff; no grndsheets allowed, duckboards provided; immac facs." 15 May-27 Sep. € 17.00   2009*

⊞ **NESSLBACH** *4G3* (700m W Rural) *48.69400, 13.11638* **Donautal Camping, Schillerstrasse 14, 94577 Nesslbach-Winzer [(08545) 1233 or 0121 or 8225; fax 911562; info@camping-donautal.de; www.camping-donautal.de]** Exit A3/E56 junc 112 to Nesslbach. Site adj sports stadium, sp. Sm, mkd pitch, unshd; htd wc; chem disp; mv service pnt; shwrs inc; EHU (6A) inc; lndry; shop 100m; rest 300m; snacks 100m; games area; 20% statics; dogs free; quiet. "Adj Danube cycleway; lovely, open site; friendly staff; lge pitches - easy access lge o'fits; ltd san facs but clean; site yourself instructions if site not manned; vg." € 15.00   2013*

⊞ **NEUENBURG AM RHEIN** *3B4* (10km E Rural) *47.81000, 7.67694* **Feriencamping Badenweiler, Weilertalstrasse 73, 79410 Badenweiler [info@camping-badenweiler.de; www.camping-badenweiler.de]** Exit A5 junc 65 at Neuenburg onto B378 dir Müllheim, then L131. Site sp on L bef R turn to Badenweiler. Med, terr, pt shd; htd wc; chem disp; mv service pnt; fam bthrm; shwrs inc; EHU (16A) metered; lndry (inc dryer); shop; rest, snacks; bar; playgrnd nr; pool 500m; wifi; dogs €3; phone; bus 300m; site clsd mid-Dec to mid-Jan; Eng spkn; adv bkg; quiet; red LS; CKE/CCI. "Excel, well-managed site; strenuous cycle rides; thermal baths nr." ♦ € 29.00   2009*

NEUHAUSEN SCHELLBRONN see Pforzheim *3C3*

> ## "That's changed – Should I let The Club know?"
>
> If you find something on site that's different from the site entry, fill in a report and let us know. See www.caravanclub.co.uk/europereport.

NEUKLOSTER *2E2* (1km E Urban) *53.86597, 11.69792* **See-Camping Neukloster, Bützowerstrasse 27a, 23992 Neukloster [(038422) 20844; fax 20461; info@see-camping-neukloster.de; www.see-camping-neukloster.de]** Exit A20 junc 10 or 11 & foll sp Neukloster, then camping sp. Med, pt sl, shd; htd wc; chem disp; shwrs €0.80; EHU (10-16A) €1.50 (poss rev pol); lndry; shop 300m; rest 200m; playgrnd; lake adj; 50% statics; dogs €1.50; bus 500m; quiet; CKE/CCI. "Conv touring base; easy walk to town; sep site for m'vans sp in town." ♦ 1 Apr-31 Oct. € 13.50   2010*

NEUMAGEN DHRON see Trittenheim *3B2*

⊞ **NEUMARKT IN DER OBERPFALZ** *4E3* (8km N Rural) *49.32944, 11.42876* **Campingplatz Berg, Hausheimerstrasse 31, 92348 Berg [tel/fax (09189) 1581; campingplatz-herteis@t-online.de; www.camping-in-berg.de]** Exit A3 junc 91 & foll sp Berg bei Neumarkt. In cent of Berg, turn R, site on R in 800m, sp. On ent turn R to tourers area & walk to recep. Med, pt sl, unshd; wc; chem disp; mv service pnt; baby facs; shwrs €0.60; EHU (20A) €2.50; lndry (inc dryer); shop 400m; rest 400m; snacks; golf 8km; 60% statics (sep area); dogs €2; Eng spkn; quiet. "Well-run, friendly, family-owned site; excel san facs; sh walk to Berg cent; excel touring base; gd nh fr m'way; pleasant views of countryside; canal walk." € 27.00   2014*

⊞ **NEUMUNSTER** *1D1* (6km SW Rural) *54.04636, 9.92306*
**Familien-Camping Forellensee, Humboldredder 5, 24634
Padenstedt [(04321) 82697; fax 84341; info@familien-
campingplatz.de; www.familien-campingplatz.de]**
Exit A7 junc 14 for Padenstedt, join dual c'way for 1km & turn
L sp Centrum. In 1km turn L at traff lts sp Padenstedt for 3km,
under m'way. Site on L in vill. Lge, mkd pitch, pt shd; wc; chem
disp; mv service pnt; shwrs inc; EHU (16A) €3 or metered;
lndry; rest 500m; snacks; bar; playgrnd; lake sw; trout-fishing;
tennis; games area; 75% statics; phone; poss cr; Eng spkn;
some rd noise; CKE/CCI. "Gd NH; conv for trains to Hamburg/
Lübeck." ♦ € 26.50   2014*

NEUNKIRCHEN *3B2* (4km S Rural) *49.32777, 7.19416*
**Camping Volkssonnengarten, Kirkelerstrasse, 66539
Neunkirchen [(0160) 94753613; fax (06821) 24564]**
Leave A8 at junc 24; N twd Neunkirchen; 1st L (camping sp);
next L into Kirkelerstrasse sp Kirkel; sharp turn L immed after
passing under a'bahn into rd sp as no thro rd. Med, terr, pt
shd; wc; chem disp; shwrs inc; EHU (16A) metered + conn fee
or €1.50; lndry; shops 600m; rest, snacks; bar; playgrnd; pool
adj; paddling pool; tennis 200m;90% statics; dogs €2; phone;
clsd 1300-1500; poss cr; some Eng spkn; quiet but some rd
noise; red CKE/CCI. "V friendly, helpful staff; tight pitches;
adj pool free to campers; gd NH/sh stay." 1 Mar-31 Oct.
€ 14.50   2009*

NEUREICHENAU *4G3* (8km E Urban) *48.74861, 13.81694*
**Knaus Campingpark Lackenhäuser, Lackenhäuser
127, 94089 Neureichenau [(08583) 311; fax 91079;
lackenhaeuser@knauscamp.de; www.knauscamp.de]**
Leave A3/E56 at junc 14 (Aicha-vorm Wald) & go E for 50km
via Waldkirchen, Jandelsbrunn, Gsenget & Klafferstrasse to
Lackenhäuser. Lge, some hdg/mkd pitch, pt sl, terr, pt shd;
wc; chem disp; mv service pnt; some serviced pitches; baby
facs; sauna; shwrs inc; EHU (16A) €2.60 or metered; gas;
lndry; shop; rest, snacks; bar; BBQ; playgrnd; 2 pools (1 htd);
paddling pool; tennis 500m; bike hire; fishing; horseriding adj;
games rm; entmnt; solarium; hairdresser; internet; games/TV
rm; 40% statics; dogs €2.50; adv bkg; quiet; ccard acc; red LS/
long stay. "Lge site with little waterfalls & walkways; ski lift on
site - equipment for hire; mv service pnt diff to access; excel
shop; 2km to 3 point border with Austria & Czech Republic;
excursions booked; recep clsd 1200-1500 & after 1800." ♦
10 Jan-7 Nov. € 26.00   2010*

NEUSTADT *3C2* (10km SW Rural) *49.30083, 8.09027*
**Campingplatz Wappenschmiede, Talstrasse 60, 67487 St
Martin [(06323) 6435; cpwappenschmiede@hotmail.de;
www.campingplatz-wappenschmiede.beep.de]**
Exit A65 at junc 13 or 14 to Maikammer, then foll sp St Martin
& site (blue/white or yellow/brown sp). At end houses take 1st
L into touring area (do not go up hill to statics area). Sm, shd;
wc; chem disp; shwrs €1; EHU €2; lndry; supmkt 5km; rest; bar;
playgrnd; 50% statics; dogs; Eng spkn; adv bkg; quiet; red long
stay; CKE/CCI. "Poss long walk to facs; friendly site; St Martin
v picturesque; gd rests; gd walking area; gd site." 1 Apr-1 Nov.
€ 20.00   2015*

NEUSTADT AM MAIN *3D2* (4km S Rural) *49.91097,
9.58448* **Main-Spessart-Camping International, 97845
Neustadt-am-Main [(09393) 639; fax 1607; info@camping-
neustadt-main.de; www.camping-neustadt-main.de]**
Exit A3/E41 junc 65 sp Marktheidenfeld. Do not cross bdge
to Marktheidenfeld but turn L up rv sp Lohr. Site on R past
Rothenfels on W bank of Rv Main. Med, mkd pitch, pt shd; wc;
chem disp; mv service pnt; baby facs; shwrs €0.50; EHU (16A)
metered + conn fee; gas; lndry (inc dryer); shop; rest 2.5km;
snacks; playgrnd; htd pool; paddling pool; boating, waterskiing
& fishing; golf 10km; entmnt; 70% statics; dogs €2.50; clsd
1200-1400; Eng spkn; adv bkg; quiet but some rd noise; ccard
acc; red CKE/CCI. "Beautiful countryside; rvside cycle track
500m; sm pitches; excel." 1 Apr-30 Sep. € 18.50   2010*

⊞ **NEUSTADT AN DER AISCH** *4E2* (9km N Rural) *49.64058,
10.59975* **Campingplatz Münchsteinach, Badstrasse 10,
91481 Münchsteinach [(09166) 750; fax 278; gemeinde@
muenchsteinach.de; www.muenchsteinach.de]**
Turn NW fr rd 470 Neustadt-Höchstadt at camp sp 8km
fr Neustadt & thro Gutenstetten. Int'l camping in 5km turn
R, foll camp sp. Lge, unshd; wc; mv service pnt; chem disp;
shwrs inc; EHU (16A) metered; lndry (inc dryer); shop, snacks
500m; pool adj; 60% statics; dogs €2; quiet; red long stay;
CKE/CCI. "Sm touring area; clean facs; site muddy when wet."
♦ € 11.00   2010*

⊞ **NEUSTADT AN DER WALDNAAB** *4F2* (1km NW Urban)
49.73750, 12.17222 **Waldnaab Camping, Gramaustrasse
64, 92660 Neustadt-an-der-Waldnaab [(09602) 3608; fax
943466; pfoster@neustadt-waldnaab.de; www.neustadt-
waldnaab.de]** Exit A93 junc 21a onto B15 for 4km S into
Neustadt. Site sp fr N side of vill. Sm, hdg pitch, pt shd; htd wc;
chem disp; mv service pnt; shwrs €0.50; EHU (16A)inc; lndry;
supmkt 500m; rest 1km; snacks; bar; playgrnd; pool; games
area; dogs €1.50; quiet. "Helpful owners; clean facs; excel
value for money." € 17.00   2013*

NEUSTADT IN HOLSTEIN *2E1* (1.52km SE Coastal) *54.09286,
10.82583* **Camping am Strande, Sandbergweg 94, 23730
Neustadt-in-Holstein [(04561) 4188; fax (04361) 7125;
info@amstrande.de; www.amstrande.de]** Exit A1/E47 junc
13 or 14 for Neustadt; thro Neustadt twd Pelzerhaken for 2km,
site on R past hospital. Lge, hdg/mkd pitch, pt sl, pt shd; wc;
chem disp; mv service pnt; shwrs €0.50; EHU (10A) €2; gas;
lndry; shop 100m; rest 200m; playgrnd; sw & shgl beach adj;
watersports; bike hire; 70% statics; dogs €3; poss cr; Eng spkn;
adv bkg; quiet; ccard acc; CKE/CCI. "Gd area, gd beaches, &
cycling; v pleasant site." ♦ 1 Apr-30 Sep. € 18.00   2009*

⊞ **NEUSTADT/HARZ** *2E4* (2km NW Rural) *51.56897,
10.82836* **Campingplatz am Waldbad, An der Burg 3,
99762 Neustadt/Harz [036331 479891; fax 479892; info@
neustadt-harz-camping.de]** Fr A38, exit J10 for B243 to
Nordhausen. Turn B4 dir Niedersachswerfen. Turn R
onto L1037, L onto Osteroder Straße and R onto Klostergasse.
Foll sp to campsite. Med, hdg pitch, pt sl, pt shd; htd wc; chem
disp; mv service pnt; shwrs inc; EHU (10A); lndry (inc dryer);
snacks; bar; playgrnd; games area; 50% statics; bus/train 4km;
twin axles; adv bkg; quiet; CCI. "Gd site; conv for Harz; helpful
owners; vg san facs." ♦ € 31.00   2014*

GERMANY

⊞ **NEUSTRELITZ** *2F2* (10km SW Rural) *53.30895, 13.00305* **Camping- und Ferienpark Havelberge, An der Havelbergen 1, 17237 Gross Quassow [(03981) 24790; fax 247999; info@haveltourist.de; www.haveltourist.de]** Fr Neustrelitz foll sp to Userin on L25 & bef Userin turn L sp Gross Quassow. Turn S in vill at camping sp, cross rlwy line & rv, sm ent in 1.5km. Site 1.7km S of Gross Quassow twd lake, sp. Lge, pt sl, pt shd; wc; chem disp; mv service pnt; sauna; shwrs €0.90; EHU (10A) €2.90; lndry (inc dryer); shop adj; rest high ssn; snacks; bar; playgrnd; lake sw; watersports; bike hire; wifi; entmnt & 30% statics; dogs €4.40; quiet. "Lovely wooded area; poss diff lge o'fits; not rec as NH." ♦ € 24.60   2010*

⊞ **NIDEGGEN** *1A4* (2km SW Rural) *50.68530, 6.46966* **Campingplatz Hetzingen, Campingweg 1, 52385 Brück [(02427) 508; fax 1294; info@campingplatz-hetzingen.de; www.campingplatz-hetzingen.de]** Fr Nideggen take rd sp Schmidt/Monschau, ent 2km on L at R-hand bend on ascent fr level x-ing. Lge, pt sl, pt shd; wc; chem disp; sauna; baby facs; shwrs €0.80; EHU (10-16A) metered; gas; lndry; shop; rest, snacks; bar; playgrnd; bike hire; 75% statics; dogs €2.50; train 500m; poss cr; Eng spkn; adv bkg; some rlwy noise; red CKE/CCI. "C'van may need manhandling onto pitch; site in wildlife reservation." € 16.00   2009*

NIEDERAU see Meissen *2G4*

NIEDERZELL see Konstanz *3D4*

NIESKY *2H4* (3km W Rural) *51.30156, 14.80302* **Campingplatz Tonschächte (Part Naturist), Raschkestrasse, 02906 Niesky [(03588) 205771; camping_ tonschacht@gmx.de]** Leave A4/E40 at junc 93 onto B115 sp Niesky; cont on B115 site sp on L; do not go into Niesky but stay on B115. Lge, shd; wc; shwrs €0.75; EHU (10A); lndry; shop; rest 1km; snacks; playgrnd; games area; 50% statics; dogs; poss cr. "Conv Polish border x-ing & a'bahn; sep naturist area." ♦ 15 Apr-15 Oct. € 12.50   2011*

⊞ **NOHFELDEN** *3B2* (10km SW Rural) *49.56072, 7.06105* **Campingplatz Bostalsee, 66625 Nohfelden-Bosen [(06852) 92333; fax 92393; campingplatz@bostalsee.de; www.bostalsee.de]** Fr A62 exit junc 3 sp Nohfelden/ Türkismühle & Bostalsee. Turn R & foll camp sp. Site on R in 1.6km after passing thro vill of Bosen. V lge, mkd pitch, pt sl, unshd; htd wc; chem disp; mv service pnt; baby facs; fam bthrm; sauna; shwrs inc; EHU (16A) €2; lndry (inc dryer); shop 1km; rest; snacks adj; playgrnd; lake sw 800m; watersports; golf 7km; wifi; entmnt; 75% statics; dogs €2; clsd to vehicles 1300-1500 & 2200-0700; adv bkg; quiet. "Vg san facs; pleasant lakeside site but poss unrel in wet; spacious, hdstg pitches; conv NH." ♦ € 20.00   2012*

NORDEN *1B2* (5km W Coastal) *53.60471, 7.13863* **Nordsee-Camp Norddeich, Deichstrasse 21, 26506 Norden-Norddeich [(04931) 8073; fax 8074; www.Nordsee-Camp. de]** Off B70 N of Norden. Well sp. V lge, mkd pitch, pt shd; wc; chem disp; mv service pnt; baby facs; shwrs inc; EHU (6A) €2.20; lndry; shop; rest, snacks; playgrnd; beach 200m; fishing; bike hire; internet; entmnt; 25% statics; dogs; €3.80; ccard acc; red CKE/CCI. "Immac san facs; friendly atmosphere; day trips to Frisian Islands; excel rest; vg site." ♦ 8 Mar-25 Oct. € 20.80   2011*

NORDLINGEN *4E3* (8km SW Rural) *48.82622, 10.40933* **Campingplatz Ringlesmühle, 73469 Riesbürg-Utzmemmingen [(07362) 21377; fax 923516; info@ ringsmuehle.de; www.ringlesmuehle.de]** Exit Nördlingen on B466 dir Ulm. In approx 5km turn R in Holheim sp Utzmemmingen. Site sp fr B466 500m beyond Utzmemmingen. Med, pt sl, unshd; wc; chem disp; shwrs; EHU (6A) €1.50; BBQ; dogs; quiet. "Beautiful setting, cycle rte to Nördlingen; relaxed, friendly site; poss w/end rallies." Easter-31 Oct. € 12.00   2009*

⊞ **NORDLINGEN** *4E3* (1.6km NW Urban) *48.85529, 10.48162* **Nördlingen Wohnmobil Stellplatz, Würtzburger Strasse, Nördlingen** Fr Donauwörth foll B25 round Nördlingen. Site on R, NW of town. Sm, hdstg, unshd; chem disp; mv service pnt; EHU €2; dogs; bus/train adj; noisy. "Along main rd; mvs only, pt of car & coach park; grassy area alongside; services fr coin operated machines; notice in Eng; easy walk to cent of lovely town, built on site of ancient meteorite hit; NH only."   2014*

"I like to fill in the reports as I travel from site to site"

You'll find report forms at the back of this guide, or you can fill them in online at www.caravanclub.co.uk/europereport.

⊞ **NORTHEIM** *1D4* (4km N Rural) *51.72900, 9.98374* **Camping Sultmerberg, Am Sultmerberg 3, 37154 Northeim [(05551) 51559; fax 5656; campingplatzmajora@ web.de; www.campingplatzsultmerberg.de]** Exit 69 fr A7/E45 onto B3, site sp. Med, pt shd; wc; shwrs inc; EHU (10A) €3 or metered + conn fee; lndry; shop; rest 100m; snacks; playgrnd; sm pool; 30% statics; dogs €2; poss some rd & rlwy noise; clsd 1-14 Jan; ccard acc; red long stay/ CKE/CCI. "Delightful, well-kept, woodland site; gd, clean san facs; superb views Harz mountains; plenty space; conv NH." € 22.00   2010*

NUREMBERG see Nürnberg *4E2*

⊞ **NURNBERG** *4E2* (8km SE Urban) *49.42305, 11.12138* **Knaus Campingpark Nürnberg, Hans-Kalb-Strasse 56, 90471 Nürnberg [(0911) 9812717; fax 9812718; nuernberg@knauscamp.de; www.knauscamp.de]** Exit E45/A9 junc 52 or E50/A6 junc 59 dir Nürnberg-Langwasser heading N, or Nürnberg-Fischbach exit travelling S; foll sp to 'Stadion', turn L. Site ent off wide rd opp Nürnberg Conference Cent. Lge, pt mkd pitch, pt shd; htd wc; chem disp; mv service pnt; shwrs inc; EHU (6-16A) €3 (long cable rec); gas; lndry (inc dryer); shop; rest 1km; playgrnd; htd, pool adj; tennis; wifi; TV; 25% statics; dogs €5 (on request); tram/ metro 1.2km; poss cr; Eng spkn; adv bkg; noise fr rd & poss fr stadium; red long stay; ccard acc; CKE/CCI. "Friendly, helpful staff; peaceful; surrounded by trees; san facs poss stretched high ssn; v quiet midwk LS; gd security; office & access clsd 1300-1500 & 2200-0700; gd cycle rte to town; national rlwy museum in town worth visit; 1.2km to metro to town cent; red squirrels on site." ♦ € 40.00   2013*

NURNBERG *4E2* (12km W Rural) *49.43174, 10.92541*
Camping Zur Mühle, Seewaldstraße 75, 90513 Zirndorf/
Leichendorf [(0911) 693801; fax 9694601; camping.
walther@t-online.de; www.camping-zur-muehle.de]
Head W on Adlerstraße twd Stangengäßchen, cont onto
Josephspl, then Vordere Lederg. Cont onto Schlotfegerg then
onto Fürther Tor; Cont onto Dennerstraße then slight R onto
Am Plärrer. Cont onto Rothenburger Str, turn L to stay on
Rothenburger. Turn R twd Seewaldstraße, keep R. Site on L.
Med, mkd pitch, pt shd; htd wc; chem disp; baby facs; shwrs
€0.50; EHU metered; lndry (inc dryer); rest; snacks; bar; bbq;
playgrnd; wifi; dogs €2; quiet; ccard acc; CKE/CCI. "Mastercard
acc not Visa; local style rest in traditional building on site; conv
for visiting Nurnberg; vg site." 1 Apr-31 Dec. € 24.00   2014*

⊞ OBERAMMERGAU *4E4* (1km S Rural) *47.58988, 11.0696*
Campingpark Oberammergau, Ettalerstrasse 56B, 82487
Oberammergau [(08822) 94105; fax 94197; info@camping-
oberammergau.de; www.campingpark-oberammergau.
de]
Fr S turn R off B23, site on L in 1km. Fr N turn L at 2nd
Oberammergau sp. Do not ent vill fr N - keep to bypass. Med,
plenty hdstg, hdg/mkd pitch, pt shd; wc; chem disp; mv service
pnt; fam bthrm; baby facs; shwrs inc; EHU (16A) metered +
conn fee; gas; lndry (inc dryer); shop in vill; rest adj; playgrnd;
bike hire; wifi; entmnt; 25% statics; dogs €2; sep car park; bus;
poss cr; Eng spkn; adv bkg ess high ssn; red long stay/LS; CKE/
CCI. "Plenty of space; helpful recep; excel san facs; excel rest
adj; easy walk to vill; well run site, visitor tax does not apply to
one night stays." ♦ € 26.50   2015*

⊞ OBERSTDORF *3D4* (2km N Rural) *47.42370, 10.27843*
Rubi-Camp, Rubingerstrasse 34, 87561 Oberstdorf
[(08322) 959202; fax 959203; info@rubi-camp.de;
www.rubi-camp.de] Fr Sonthofen on B19, just bef Oberstdorf
at rndabt take exit sp Reichenbach, Rubi. Site in 1km over
level x-ing, 2nd site on R. Med, hdstg, unshd; htd wc; chem
disp; mv service pnt; baby facs; serviced pitches; shwrs inc;
EHU (8A) metered; lndry; shop 1km; rest, snacks; bar; BBQ;
playgrnd; skiift 1km; TV; 10% statics; dogs €2.70; phone; bus;
site clsd Nov; Eng spkn; adv bkg; quiet; CKE/CCI. "Well-run,
well-maintained site; immac facs; block paved paths to pitches;
block hdstg with grass growing thro; excel scenery; excel facs;
easy 20 min level walk to town." ♦ € 32.00   2014*

⊞ OBERSTDORF *3D4* (3km N Rural) *47.42300, 10.27720*
Campingplatz Oberstdorf, Rubingerstrasse 16, 87561
Oberstdorf [(08322) 6525; fax 809760; camping-
oberstdorf@t-online.de; www.camping-oberstdorf.de]
Fr B19 dir Oberstdorf, foll site sp. Med, hdstg, pt shd; wc;
chem disp; mv service pnt; serviced pitches; shwrs inc; EHU
(10A) metered; lndry (inc dryer); shops 1.5km; rest, snacks;
golf 5km; ski lift 3km; skibus; wifi; 45% statics (sep area); dogs
€0.50; Eng spkn; rd & rlwy noise. "Cable cars to Nebelhorn &
Fellhorn in town; Oberstdorf pedestrianised with elec buses fr
o'skirts; ask for Allgäu Walser card for free local buses & shop
discounts; vg." € 19.40   2010*

OBERWEIS see Bitburg *3B2*

⊞ OBERWESEL *3B2* (5km N Rural) *50.14188, 7.72101*
Camping Loreleyblick, An der Loreley 29-33, 56329 St
Goar-am-Rhein [(06741) 2066; fax 7233; info@camping-
loreleyblick.de; www.camping-loreleyblick.de]
Exit A61/E31sp Emmelshausen junc 42 & foll sp for St Goar;
site adj B9 1km S of St Goar opp Loreley rock on rv bank.
Or exit A48 junc 10 dir Koblenz, then B9 St Goar. Lge, pt sl,
unshd; htd wc; chem disp; mv service pnt; shwrs inc; EHU (6A)
€2.50; gas; lndry; shop & 500m; rest, snacks, bar adj (hotel
opp); pool 3km; 10% statics; dogs €1.70; phone adj; poss v
cr; wifi; Eng spkn; no adv bkg; much noise fr rlwy 24 hrs, plus
noise fr rd & rv barges; red long stay; CKE/CCI. "Lovely setting
in scenic area; friendly, helpful owner; excel modern san facs,
stretched when site full; pool complex in hills behind; conv
boat trips & car ferry across Rhine 500m; if office clsd site self
& report later; site clsd if rv in flood Dec-Feb; el voltage drops
when site v cr; easy walk to town; castles & museums; wine
cents; chair lift at Boppard; gd range of shops in St Goar." ♦
€ 19.00   2012*

⊞ OBERWESEL *3B2* (8km N Urban) *50.15995, 7.70875*
Camping Loreleystadt, Wellmicher Str 55, 56346 St
Goarshausen [(06771) 2592; info@camping-loreleyblick.
de; www.camping-loreleystadt.de] Site on B42, E side of
Rhine on N o'skts of St Goarshausen, sp, but take care not to
overshoot. Med, unshd; wc; chem disp; mv service pnt; shwrs
€0.75; EHU (10A) metered + conn fee €1.28; rest 200m;
snacks 100m; gas; shop; entmnt; sw in rv; poss cr; adv bkg;
few statics; quiet. "Poss flooding in heavy rain." ♦
20 Mar-31 Oct. € 24.00   2013*

OBERWESEL *3B2* (900m S Urban) *50.10251, 7.73664*
Camping Schönburgblick, Am Hafendamm 1, 55430
Oberwesel [(06744) 714501; fax 714413; camping-
oberwesel@t-online.de; www.camping-oberwesel.de]
Fr A61/E31 exit sp Oberwesel, site sp on L at ent to sports
stadium, on rvside. Sm, pt shd; wc; chem disp; mv service pnt;
shwrs inc; EHU (6A) €8.50; supmkt 200m; rest 200m; snacks;
bar; tennis adj; o'night area for m'vans; poss cr; adv bkg;
some rlwy noise; red long stay; CKE/CCI. "Clean, modern san
facs in Portacabins - stretched when site full; rv trips, cycling,
walking." 15 Mar-31 Oct. € 17.00   2011*

OBERWESEL *3B2* (9km NW Rural) *50.14976, 7.69478* Camping
Friedenau, Gründelbach 103, 56329 St Goar-am-Rhein
[tel/fax (06741) 368; info@camping-friedenau.de;
www.camping-friedenau.de] App on B9 fr Boppard or
Bingen; turn under rlwy bdge 1km N of St Goar; keep L; site
on L in 1km. NB - do not app fr J43 off m'way. Sm, pt sl, shd;
wc; chem disp; mv service pnt; shwrs inc; EHU (16A) €2.50;
gas; lndry; shops 1.5km; rest; bar; playgrnd; pool 1.5km; dogs
€1; bus; poss cr; Eng spkn; quiet; red CKE/CCI. "Quieter than
other sites in area - uphill fr busy Rhine & resorts; some pitches
uneven & poss diff after heavy rain; vg welcome; easy walk
or cycle to rv town; country walks fr site; relaxed atmosphere;
friendly staff; gd bar/rest; san fac adequate but needs
updating; great views fr Rheinfels Castle." ♦ 15 Mar-1 Nov.
€ 27.50   2014*

OHNINGEN WANGEN see Radolfzell am Bodensee *3C4*

GERMANY

⊞ **OHRDRUF** *2E4* (17km S Rural) *50.73363, 10.75671*
Oberhof Camping Lütschesee, Am Stausee 9, 99330
Frankenhain [(036205) 76518; fax 71768; info@
oberhofcamping.de; www.oberhofcamping.de]
Fr A4/E40 exit junc 42 onto B247 S twd Oberhof. After approx
25km at Gasthaus Wegscheide turn L onto forest rd to site.
Also accessible fr B88, sp in vill of Frankenhain via tarmac rd -
5km. Lge, shd; htd wc; chem disp; mv service pnt; shwrs inc;
EHU (10A) inc; gas; lndry (inc dryer); shop; rest 1.5km; rest,
snacks; bar; BBQ; playgrnd; lake sw; boat & bike hire; wifi; TV
rm; 60% statics; dogs €2; adv bkg; ccard acc; red long stay/
CKE/CCI. "Vg, busy site in heart of Thüringer Forest; excel san
facs; gd walking & cycling." ♦ € 22.00 (CChq acc)   2010*

⊞ **OHRDRUF** *2E4* (10km W Rural) *50.82452, 10.61060*
Campingplatz Paulfeld, Catterfeld, 99894 Leinatal
[(036253) 25171; fax 25165; info@paulfeld-camping.de;
www.paulfeld-camping.de] Fr E exit A4 junc 42 onto B88
sp Friedrichroda & foll sp Catterfeld & site on R. Or fr W exit
junc 41a at Gotha. Take B247 S twd Ohrdruf. After 6km bear
R sp Georgenthal. In Georgenthal vill, bear R onto B88. After
2km site sp L on app Catterfeld vill. Foll rd 2km thro forest to
site, sp. Site approx 12km fr A4. Lge, some hdg, pt shd; chem
disp; mv service pnt; wc; sauna; shwrs €0.80; EHU (16A) inc;
gas; lndry (inc dryer); shop; rest, snacks; bar; BBQ; playgrnd; sm
pets corner; lake sw & fishing; solarium; games area; bike hire;
games rm; internet; 40% statics in sep area; dogs €2; twin-
axles acc (rec check in adv); poss cr w/end; quiet; ccard not
acc; red LS/long stay; CKE/CCI. "Excel, well-kept site; gd access
to pitches; clean san facs; gd for families with young children;
woodland walks; conv stop en rte eastern Europe; happy family
site; helpful friendly owners." ♦ € 26.50   2013*

"We must tell The Club about that great site we found"

Get your site reports in by mid-August
and we'll do our best to get your updates
into the next edition.

OLDENDORF see Bergen *1D3*

⊞ **OLPE** *1B4* (8km N Rural) *51.0736, 7.8564* Feriencamp
Biggesee - Vier Jahreszeiten, Am Sonderner Kopf 3,
57462 Olpe-Sondern [(02761) 944111; fax 944141; info@
camping-sondern.de; www.camping-biggesee.de]
Exit A45/E41 junc 18 & foll sp to Biggesee. Pass both turnings
to Sondern. Take next R in 200m. Ent on R in 100m. NB:
Other sites on lake. Lge, mkd pitch, terr, pt shd; wc; chem
disp; mv service pnt; baby facs; sauna; shwrs inc; EHU (16A)
inc; gas; lndry; shop & 6km; rest, snacks; bar; cooking facs;
playgrnd; shgl beach & lake sw adj; watersports inc diving;
tennis; rollerskating rink; bike hire; solarium; entmnt; internet;
20% statics; dogs €2.50; poss cr; Eng spkn; adv bkg; quiet;
CKE/CCI. "Gd facs; well-organised site; barrier clsd 1300-1500
& 2200-0700; conv Panorama Theme Park & Cologne; vg
cycling area; footpaths." ♦ € 30.50   2014*

⊞ **ORTRAND** *2G4* (2km E Rural) *51.37265, 13.77956*
Ferienpark Dresden, Am Bad 1, 01990 Ortrand
[35 75 56 20 00; fax 75 56 20 09; ferienpark-dresden@
themencamping.de; www.themencamping.de] A13 Berlin-
Dresden. Take exit 18 - Ortrand. At rndabt take 2nd exit (L55)
& foll signs to camp site 2km. Note tight turn L after passing
thro indus units. Med, mkd pitch, unshd; wc; chem disp; mv
service pnt; baby facs; fam bthrm; shwrs; EHU (16A) €2.90;
lndry (inc dryer); shop; rest; bar; BBQ; cooking facs; playgrnd;
htd pool; waterslide; paddling pool; games area; games rm;
bike hire; entmnt; wifi; tv rm; 30% statics; dogs €2; phone;
bus/train 1.5km; twin axles; Eng spkn; adv bkg; quiet; CCI. "Vg
site; volleyball; fishing adj; cls to mkd cycle rtes; sep car park
with hook-ups for late arrs." ♦ € 35.00   2014*

⊞ **OSNABRUCK** *1C3* (6.5km NE Rural) *52.29181, 8.10593*
Camping Niedersachsenhof, Nordstrasse 109, 49084
Osnabrück [(0541) 77226; fax 70627; osnacamp@aol.
com; www.osnacamp.de] Exit A30/E30 junc 19 onto A11
sp Diepholz. At traff lts (end of m'way) at junc with B51/65
turn L sp Osnabrück & L again at next traff lts into minor
rd (Nordstrasse). Site on R in 600m - do not take 1st ent.
Fr Osnabrück, take B51/65 sp Diepholz, & turn R at traff lits
in approx 4km by TV tower. Sp throughout Osnabrück. Med,
mkd pitch, pt sl, pt shd, pt sl; wc; chem disp; shwrs €0.50; EHU
(16A) €2.80 or metered; lndry (inc dryer); supmkt 2km; rest
adj; snacks 1.5km; BBQ; playgrnd; entmnt; 30% statics; dogs;
phone; bus; Eng spkn; adv bkg; quiet but some rd noise; CKE/
CCI. "V friendly; spacious pitches with views; mv service pnt
outside site & diff to use; excel." € 18.50   2010*

⊞ **OSNABRUCK** *1C3* (14km SW Rural) *52.22944, 7.89027*
Regenbogen-Camp Tecklenburg, Grafenstrasse 31, 49545
Leeden [tel/fax (05405) 1007; tecklenburg@regenbogen-
camp.de; www.regenbogen-camp.de] Exit A1/E37 junc 73
or fr A30/E30 junc 13; foll sp to Tecklenburg, then Leeden &
foll site sp. V lge, pt sl, pt shd; wc; chem disp; mv service pnt;
serviced pitches; baby facs; shwrs; EHU (16A) €2.90; lndry;
shop, rest, snacks high ssn; playgrnd; htd, covrd pool; paddling
pool; games area; bike hire; entmnt; 45% statics; dogs €4;
o'night area for m'vans open all yr; site clsd 1 Nov-15 Dec; clsd
1300-1500; poss cr; adv bkg; quiet; ccard acc; red CKE/CCI.
"Gd views; excel san facs, poss sometimes unclean; gd rest." ♦
€ 37.00   2013*

⊞ **OSTERODE AM HARZ** *1D4* (2km E Rural) *51.72779,
10.28281* Camping Eulenburg, Scheerenbergstrasse 100,
37520 Osterode-am-Harz [(05522) 6611; fax 4654; ferien@
eulenburg-camping.de; www.eulenburg-camping.de]
Take B498 fr Osterode cent, cross by-pass at traff lts. Site on
R in 1.5km. Med, hdg/mkd pitch, hdstg, pt shd; htd wc; some
serviced pitches; chem disp; mv service pnt; baby facs; fam
bthrm; shwrs €0.70; EHU (6-16A) metered + conn fee; gas;
lndry; shop 2km; rest; snacks; bar; BBQ (charcoal, sep area);
playgrnd; pool & paddling pool; wifi; 50% statics; dogs €2; Eng
spkn; quiet; quiet; red long stay; CKE/CCI. "Beautiful old town;
gd cent for Harz mountains; walks to lake fr site; motorhome
stellplatze adj." ♦ € 21.00   2015*

OSTERREINEN see Füssen *4E4*

GERMANY

OSTRINGEN *3C3* (5km SE Rural) *49.20035, 8.76066*
Kraichgau-Camping Wackerhof, Schindelberg 10, 76684
Ostringen-Schindelberg [(07259) 361; fax 2431; info@
wackerhof.de; www.wackerhof.de] Exit A5 junc 41 Kronau;
E on B292 to cent Ostringen 9km; turn SE foll camp sp. Site
in 5km. Med, mkd pitch, pt sl, terr, pt shd; wc; chem disp; mv
service pnt; shwrs inc; EHU (16A) metered; gas; lndry; shop;
rest, snacks 5km; playgrnd; 60% statics; rd & rlwy noise;
some Eng spkn; 10% red CKE/CCI. "Friendly; gd, clean facs."
25 Mar-15 Oct. € 10.00   2011*

OTTERNDORF *1C2* (4km NE Coastal) *53.82524, 8.87613*
Campingplatz See Achtern Diek, Deichstrasse 14, 21762
Otterndorf [(04751) 2933; fax 3016; campingplatz.
otterndorf@ewetel.net; www.otterndorf.de]
Fr Cuxhaven W to Otterndorf on B73. Take 1st L after rlwy to
traff lts, turn L twd Müggendorf, foll site sp, site on Rv Elbe. V
lge, hdg/mkd pitch, hdstg; wc; chem disp; mv service pnt; baby
facs; serviced pitches; shwrs inc; EHU (16A) €1.80; gas; lndry;
shop 3.5km; rest, snacks, bar adj; playgrnd; pool; sand beach
& sw adj; entmnt; 40% statics; dogs €3.50; phone; adv bkg;
quiet; ccard acc; red CKE/CCI. "Friendly; efficiently run; easy
cycle rtes to town; gd touring cent; site clsd 1300-1500; conv
for ferry." ♦ 1 Apr-31 Oct. € 20.00   2009*

PAPENBURG *1B2* (1km S Rural) *53.06481, 7.42691*
Camping Poggenpoel, Am Poggenpoel, 26871 Papenburg
[(04961) 974026; fax 974027; campingpcp@aol.com;
www.papenburg-camping.de] Fr B70, site sp fr town.
Med, pt shd; htd wc; chem disp; mv service pnt; baby facs;
shwrs €2; EHU (10A) €2; lndry; shop; rest; snacks 1km; bar;
playgrnd; lake sw adj; games area; golf 1km; entmnt; cab TV;
40% statics; dogs €2; phone; o'night facs for m'vans; quiet;
red long stay/CKE/CCI. ♦ € 19.00   2009*

PAPPENHEIM *4E3* (1.8km N Rural) *48.93471, 10.96993*
Camping Pappenheim, Badweg 1, 91788 Pappenheim
[(09143) 1275; fax 837364; info@camping-pappenheim.de;
www.camping-pappenheim.de] B2 heading S, site sp after
passing thro Weissenburg, on edge of Pappenheim. Med, pt
shd; wc; shwrs; chem disp; mv service pnt; EHU (16A) €2; lndry;
shop; rest 500m; snacks; lake sw; 25% statics; dogs €1.50;
quiet. "Mountain views; excel site in historical town; castle
worth visiting." 1 Apr-25 Oct. € 16.50   2014*

PASSAU *4G3* (10km NW Rural) *48.60605, 13.34583* Drei-
Flüsse Campingplatz, Am Sonnenhang 8, 94113 Irring
[(08546) 633; fax 2686; dreifluessecamping@t-online.de;
www.dreifluessecamping.privat.t-online.de]
On A3/E56, junc 115 (Passau Nord); foll sps to site. Med, pt
sl, terr, pt shd; wc; chem disp; mv service pnt; 60% serviced
pitches; shwrs inc; EHU (16A) €2.50 or metered; gas; lndry;
shop; rest; BBQ; playgrnd; cov'rd pool May-Sep; dogs €1.50;
phone; bus 200m; poss cr; adv bkg; ccard acc; red 5+ days;
CKE/CCI. "Interesting grotto on site; gd rest; rec arr early;
facs need updating; poor surface drainage after heavy rain;
interesting town at confluence of 3 rvs; on Danube cycle way;
conv NH fr A3/E56." ♦ 1 Apr-31 Oct. € 35.00   2014*

PEINE *1D3* (11km NW Rural) *52.35158, 10.12657*
Camping Waldsee, Am Waldsee 1, 31275 Lehrte-
Hämelerwald [(05175) 4767; fax 929025] Exit A2 junc 51
dir Hämelerwald. Thro Hämelerwald, under rlwy bdge. Strt
over 1st traff lts, immed L after 2nd pedestrian x-ing in 300m.
Site sp. Med, shd; htd wc; chem disp; mv service pnt; shwrs
inc; EHU (10A) inc; lndry (inc dryer); shop 2km; rest high ssn;
snacks; bar; playgrnd; pool 3km; lake sw adj; 5% statics; dogs;
Eng spkn; rlwy noise; CKE/CCI. "Woodland site; rather run
down (2010) but conv NH." ♦ € 15.00   2014*

PFALZFELD *3B2* (1km SW Rural) *50.10612, 7.56804*
Country-Camping Schinderhannes, Hausbayerstrasse,
56291 Hausbay [(06746) 8005440; fax 80054414; info@
countrycamping.de; www.countrycamping.de]
Fr A61/E31 exit junc 43, foll sps for 3km to Pfalzfeld & onto
Hausbay, site sp. V lge, mkd pitch, pt sl, terr, pt shd; htd wc;
chem disp; mv service pnt; some serviced pitches; baby facs;
shwrs inc; EHU (8-16A) inc; lndry (inc dryer); shop; rest, snacks;
bar; BBQ; playgrnd; htd pool 8km; lake sw; fishing; tennis;
internet; entmnt; TV rm; internet; 60% statics; dogs €2; twin
axles; Eng spkn; sep NH area; adv bkg; quiet; red CKE/CCI.
"Pleasant, peaceful, clean site; spacious pitches, some far fr
san facs; helpful, friendly staff; excel, immac san facs; scenic
area close Rv Rhine; vg cycle track; nice area for walking; conv
m'way; excel NH with sep area to stay hitched-on; wonderful
touring area; excel." ♦ € 29.00   2014*

PFEDELBACH *3D3* (3.7km S Rural) *49.15356, 9.49894*
Camping Seewiese, 11 Seestrasse; 74629 Pfedelbach-
Buchorn [(07941) 61568; fax 33827; campingseewiese@t-
online.de; www.camping-seewiese.de] Exit A6 junc 40 at
Öhringen; foll sp Pfedelbach & Camping. Lge, pt sl, pt shd;
wc; chem disp; shwrs; EHU (10A) €2 or metered; gas; lndry
(inc dryer); ice; rest; sacks; bar; BBQ; playgrnd; htd pool; lake
fishing; games rm; TV; 90% statics; phone; dogs €1.50; Eng
spkn; adv bkg; quiet; CKE/CCI. "Mainly statics, ok NH." ♦ ltd.
€ 19.00   2009*

PFORZHEIM *3C3* (13km S Rural) *48.81800, 8.73400*
International Camping Schwarzwald, Freibadweg 4,
75242 Neuhausen-Schellbronn [(07234) 6517; fax 5180;
fam.frech@t-online.de; www.camping-schwarzwald.de]
Fr W on A8 exit junc 43 for Pforzheim; fr E exit junc 45. In
town cent take rd 463 sp Calw, immed after end of town sp
take minor rd L thro Huchenfeld up hill to Schellbronn. Site
in vill of Schellbronn on N side of rd to Bad Liebenzell - sp at
church on R. Lge, pt sl, pt shd; wc; chem disp; mv service pnt;
shwrs €0.50; EHU (17A) €2 or metered; gas; lndry; shop; rest;
snacks; bar; playgrnd; htd pool adj; dance & fitness cent; bike
hire; entmnt high ssn; internet; 80% statics; no dogs; bus; no
vehicle access after 2200; poss cr; adv bkg; quiet; red long stay;
CKE/CCI. "Scenic area; v clean, well-maintained site; vg san
facs; excel rest/takeaway; v rural." ♦ € 18.00   2011*

PFRONTEN STEINACH see Nesselwang *4E4*

PIDING see Bad Reichenhall *4G4*

GERMANY

⊞ **PIELENHOFEN** *4F3* (2km S Rural) *49.05896, 11.95820*
Campingplatz Naabtal, Distelhausen 2, 93188 Pielenhofen
[(09409) 373; fax 723; camping-pielenhofen@t-online.de;
www.camping-pielenhofen.de] Exit A3/E56 junc 97 onto
B8 dir Etterzhausen. Thro Etterzhausen turn L to Pielenhofen/
Amberg. In Pielenhofen turn R over bdge. Lge, mkd pitch,
pt shd; htd wc; chem disp; mv service pnt; sauna; shwrs
€0.50; EHU (10A) metered + conn fee €0.60; gas; lndry;
sauna/solarium; shop; rest; bar; playgrnd; tennis; bike hire;
skittle alley; summer curling rink; games area; dogs €2.20;
65% statics; Eng spkn; CKE/CCI. "In beautiful valley; helpful
warden; v nice site in gd location; liable to flooding; gd rv
access for boating; family-run site; lots of facs; spacious pitches;
gd rest; conv Regensburg; busy site." ♦ € 17.60   2015*

⊞ **PIRMASENS** *3B3* (21km NE Rural) *49.27546, 7.72121*
Camping Clausensee, 67714 Waldfischbach-Burgalben
[(06333) 5744; fax 5747; info@campingclausensee.de;
www.campingclausensee.de] Leave a'bahn A6 at junc 15
Kaiserslautern West; S onto B270 for 22km. E 9km on minor
rd sp Leimen, site sp. Lge, mkd pitch, pt shd; chem disp; htd
wc; mv service pnt; some serviced pitches; shwrs €0.50; EHU
(6-16A) inc; gas; lndry (inc dryer); shop; rest, snacks; bar; BBQ;
playgrnd; lake sw adj; fishing; boating; games/TV rm; quiet;
50% statics; dogs €4.20; no twin-axles; poss cr; Eng spkn; adv
bkg; quiet; ccard acc; red LS/long stay; CKE/CCI. "Peaceful
situation in Pfalzerwald Park; helpful staff; clean san facs; busy
at w/ends; gd walking & cycling; gd." ♦ € 23.50   2009*

PIRNA *4G1* (3km N Urban) *50.98169, 13.92508*
Waldcampingplatz Pirna-Copitz, Außere Pillnitzerstrasse 19,
01796 Pirna [(03501) 523773; fax 571855; waldcamping@
stadtwerke-pirna.de; www.waldcamping-pirna.de]
Fr B172 fr Dresden to Pirna-Copitz or fr A17/E55. Site well sp.
Med, mkd pitch, pt shd; htd wc; chem disp; mv service pnt;
baby facs; shwrs inc; EHU (10A) €3; lndry; shop 200m; rest
400m; snacks 700m; playgrnd; 20% statics; dogs €2.50; bus
200m; adv bkg; quiet. "Clean, well-run site; modern facs." ♦
1 Apr-31 Oct. € 31.00   2013*

⊞ **PLAU** *2F2* (4km SE Rural) *53.43832, 12.28699*
Campingpark Zuruf am Plauer See, Seestrasse 38d,
19395 Plau-Plötzenhöhe [(038735) 45878; fax 45879;
campingpark-zuruf@t-online.de; www.campingpark-
zuruf.de] N on B103, turn E at x-rds 200m after int'l camping
sp. Site on lakeside. Lge, pt shd; wc; chem disp; mv service pnt;
shwrs €0.80; EHU (10A) €2.20; lndry; shop; rest 1km; snacks;
playgrnd; lake sw & beach; watersports; bike hire; entmnt;
dogs €2.50; adv bkg; quiet; CKE/CCI. "Pleasant, friendly site;
sm pitches, tight access; muddy when wet." € 18.00   2010*

PLAUEN *4F1* (7km NE Rural) *50.53860, 12.18495* **Camping**
Gunzenberg Pöhl, 08543 Möschwitz [(037439) 6393;
fax 45013; tourist-info@poehl.de; www.camping-poehl.de]
Exit A72/E441 junc 7 & foll sp for Möschwitz & white sp for
Talsperre Pöhl. V lge, pt hdg/mkd pitch, terr, pt shd; wc; chem
disp; mv service pnt; shwrs inc; EHU (10A) €2 or metered +
conn fee; lndry (inc dryer); shop; rest, snacks; bar; playgrnd;
shgl beach & lake sw adj; golf 2km; wifi; entmnt; 60% statics;
dogs €3; clsd 1230-1400; poss cr; quiet; red CKE/CCI. "Excel,
v formal, clean site; helpful, friendly staff." ♦ 26 Mar-2 Nov.
€ 19.00   2012*

PLON *1D1* (7km SE Rural) *54.12855, 10.45510* **Campingpark**
Augstfelde, Am See, 24306 Augstfelde [(04522) 8128;
fax 9528; info@augstfelde.de; www.augstfelde.de]
Fr Plön on B76 twd Bosau, sp. Lge, mkd pitch, terr, pt shd; htd
wc; chem disp; mv service pnt; baby facs; sauna; private bthrms
avail; shwrs €0.75; EHU (10-16A) €2.50; gas; lndry (inc dryer);
shop; rest; snacks 3km; bar; playgrnd; lake sw & sand beach
adj; fishing; boat, canoe & bike hire; tennis; fitness cent; games
area; golf 100m; wifi; entmnt; 60% statics; dogs €2; o'night
area for m'vans; Eng spkn; adv bkg; ccard acc; red long stay;
CKE/CCI. "Lovely situation; superb sailing, windsurfing; gd for
families; excel." ♦ 1 Apr-24 Oct. € 20.00   2010*

PLON *1D1* (11km SW Rural) *54.11928, 10.33670* **Camping**
Seeblick, Dorfstrasse 59, 24326 Dersau [(04526) 1211; fax
1218; info@camping-dersau.de; www.camping-dersau.de]
Exit A21/B404 junc 8 dir Plöner See, turn R bef lake to Dersau,
site on L in 2km, sp. Lge, pt sl, unshd; wc; chem disp; mv
service pnt; shwrs inc; EHU (10-16A) €2 (poss rev pol); lndry
(inc dryer); shop; rest 200m; snacks; playgrnd; lake sw & sand
beach adj; boating; wifi; 75% statics; no dogs; adv bkg; quiet;
red long stay/LS; CKE/CCI. "Excel site bet vill & lake; gd walks;
gd site shop." 1 Apr-25 Oct. € 16.00   2010*

⊞ **PLOTZKY** *2E3* (1.5km N Rural) *52.06249, 11.79998*
Ferienpark Plötzky, Kleiner Waldsee 1, 39245 Plötzky
[(039200) 50155; fax 76082; info@ferienpark-ploetzky.de;
www.ferienpark-ploetzky.de] Exit A14 junc 7 onto B246a
dir Schönebeck & Gommern for 13km. Site on L immed
after vill of Plötzky, site sp. Lge, pt shd; htd wc; chem disp;
mv service pnt; private bthrms avail; baby facs; shwrs €1;
EHU (16A) €2 or metered; lndry (inc dryer); shop 1.5km;
rest 1.5km; snacks; bar; playgrnd; lake sw; boat & bike hire;
games area; horseriding; archery; entmnt; internet; TV rm;
70% statics; dogs €2; adv bkg; quiet; ccard acc. "Gd walking,
cycling in wooded area; peaceful, relaxing, well-run site." ♦
€ 17.00   2010*

POMMERN see Cochem *3B2*

PORSTENDORF see Jena *2E4*

⊞ **PORTA WESTFALICA** *1C3* (8km SW Rural) *52.22146,*
8.83995 **Camping Grosser Weserbogen, Zum Südlichen**
See 1, 32457 Porta Westfalica [(05731) 6188 or 6189;
fax 6601; info@grosserweserbogen.de;
www.grosserweserbogen.de] Fr E30/A2 exit junc 33, foll
sp to Vennebeck & Costedt. Site sp. Site 12km by rd fr Bad
Oeynhausen. Site sp fr m'way. Lge, mkd pitch, some hdstg,
pt shd; wc; chem disp; shwrs; EHU (10A) €2.90; lndry; shop
& 5km; rest, snacks; bar; playgrnd; lake sw adj (w/ends only);
fishing; watersports; dogs €1.50; some Eng spkn; adv bkg;
quiet, poss noisy w/end; debit card acc; 10% red CKE/CCI.
"Site in cent of wildlife reserve; v tranquil; gd base Teutoburger
Wald & Weser valley; barrier clsd 1300-1500 & o'night; many
statics; lge area for tourers; gd for families; excel san facs &
rest; shwrs charged to electronic card; level access; highly rec."
♦ Easter-31 Oct. € 25.50   2012*

GERMANY

POTSDAM 2F3 (7km SW Rural) 52.36055, 13.00722 **Camping Sanssouci, An der Pirschheide 41, 14471 Potsdam [tel/fax (0331) 9510988; info@camping-potsdam.de; www.camping-potsdam.de]** Fr A10 Berlin ring rd take exit 22 at Gross Kreutz onto B1 twd Potsdam cent for approx 17km, past Werder (Havel) & Geltow. Site sp approx 2km after Geltow immed bef rlwy bdge. Lge, shd; wc; chem disp; mv service pnt; 50% serviced pitches; baby facs; shwrs inc; EHU (6A) inc (poss rev pol); gas; lndry; shop; rest; bar; BBQ; playgrnd; covrd pool 200m; lake sw & sand beach adj; fitness cent; watersports; fishing; horseriding 8km; bike hire; games rm; wifi; 25% statics; dogs €4.90; mini-bus to stn; poss cr; Eng spkn; adv bkg; quiet; ccard not acc; CKE/CCI. "V helpful, friendly owners; lovely area; sandy pitches; poss diff lge o'fits manoeuvring round trees; excel clean facs inc music & underfloor heating in san facs; camp bus to/fr stn; gate clsd 1300-1500; gd security; conv Schlosses & Berlin by rail; excel site and rest; 5 star facs; sm pitches; site & rest cash only." ♦ 1 Apr-2 Nov. € 33.00 SBS - G16   2015*

POTSDAM 2F3 (10km SW Rural) 52.36088, 12.94663 **Camping Riegelspitze, Fercherstrasse, 14542 Werder-Petzow [(03327) 42397; fax 741725; info@campingplatz-riegelspitze.de; www.campingplatz-riegelspitze.de]** Fr A10/E55 Berlin ring a'bahn take exit 22 dir Glindow or Werder exits & foll sp to Werder; then foll B1 for 1.5km twd Potsdam, R after Strengbrücke bdge twd Petzow. Med, terr, pt shd; wc; chem disp; mv service pnt; shwrs (metered); EHU (16A) €1.80 (poss rev pol & long lead req); lndry; shop; lge supmkt 1km; rest, snacks; bar; playgrnd; lake sw & sand beach; watersports; bike hire; 50% statics; dogs €2.50, no dogs high ssn; bus; poss cr; adv bkg; quiet. "Friendly recep; haphazard pitching; transport tickets fr recep; recep clsd 1300-1500; bus outside site; Sanssouci visit a must." ♦ 1 Apr-25 Oct. € 23.00   2011*

POTSDAM 2F3 (10km SW Rural) 52.35278, 12.98981 **Naturcampingplatz Himmelreich, Wentorfinsel, 14548 Caputh [(033209) 70475; fax 20100; info@berlin-potsdam-camping.de; www.berlin-potsdam-camping.de]** Exit A10 junc 20 or 23 to Glindow. Take B1 to Geltow, turn L immed after rlwy x-ring & foll sp Caputh. Do not foll SatNav. Lge, shd; htd wc; chem disp; mv service pnt; shwrs €1; EHU (10A) €1.50 (poss rev-pol); lndry; shop; rest, snacks; bar; sand beach & lake adj; boat hire; 65% statics; dogs €2; phone; ferry 750m; poss cr; adv bkg; quiet - rlwy noise some pitches; CKE/CCI. "Lovely position on waterfront; modern san facs; poss haphazard pitching; cycle rtes & walks; 2 pin adaptor needed for some pitches." ♦ 1 Apr-31 Oct. € 30.00   2015*

⊞ **POTSDAM** 2F3 (15km W Rural) 52.36002, 12.91677 **Camping Glindowsee, Jahnufer 41, 14542 Glindow [(03227) 40855; info@hogab.de; www.hogab.de]** Fr A10/E55 a'bahn exit junc 23 dir Werder. In 4km at beginning of Glindow turn R (S). Thro Glindow, site sp on L. Med, pt shd; htd wc; chem disp; mv service pnt; shwrs inc; EHU (16A) €3; gas 3km; lndry; shop 1.5km; rest; bar; BBQ; playgrnd; sand beach & lake sw adj; 80% statics; dogs €1; poss cr; quiet; CKE/CCI. "Sm grassy area for tourers; gd, clean, modern facs." € 21.00   2010*

⊞ **POTTENSTEIN** 4E2 (3km NW Rural) 49.77942, 11.38411 **Feriencampingplatz Bärenschlucht, 12 Weidmannsgesees, 91278 Pottenstein [(09243) 206; fax 880; info@baerenschlucht-camping.de; www.baerenschlucht-camping.de]** Exit A9 junc 44 onto B470 dir Forchheim; cont past Pottenstein; site in 2km on R. Med, pt sl, pt shd; htd wc; chem disp; mv service pnt; baby facs; shwrs €0.50; EHU (8-16A) €1.90; gas; lndry; cooking facs; shops 2km; rest; bar; 40% statics; dogs €1.90; poss cr; quiet. "A naturalized quarry surrounded by trees & rocky cliffs; vg." ♦ € 19.00   2011*

PREETZ 1D1 (6km SE Rural) 54.21073, 10.31720 **Camp Lanker See, Gläserkoppel 3, 24211 Preetz-Gläserkoppel [(04342) 81513; fax 789939; camp-lanker-see@t-online.de; www.campingplatz-lanker-see.de]** Sp off B76 bet Preetz & Plön. Lge, mkd pitch, terr, pt shd; wc; chem disp; shwrs €0.50; EHU (6A) metered; lndry; shop; rest, snacks; bar; playgrnd; lake sw; boating; horseriding; some statics; dogs €1; phone; adv bkg; quiet; ccard acc; red LS; CKE/CCI. "Barrier clsd 1300-1500 & o'night; gd." 1 Apr-31 Oct. € 22.00   2009*

"I need an on-site restaurant"

We do our best to make sure site information is correct, but it is always best to check any must-have facilities are still available or will be open during your visit.

PRIEN AM CHIEMSEE 4F4 (4km SE Rural) 47.83995, 12.37170 **Panorama-Camping Harras, Harrasserstrasse 135, 83209 Prien-Harras [(08051) 904613; fax 904616; info@camping-harras.de; www.camping-harras.de]** Exit A8/E52/E60 junc 106 dir Prien. After 2.5km turn R at rndabt sp Krankenhaus & site. Lge, pt shd; htd wc; chem disp; mv service pnt; baby facs; fam bthrm; shwrs €0.80; EHU (6A) €2 (poss no earth); gas; lndry (inc dryer); shop; rest, snacks; bar; playgrnd; htd, covrd pool 3km; lake sw; canoeing; boat & bike hire; golf 3km; wifi; 20% statics; dogs €3.20; poss v cr; Eng spkn; quiet but poss noisy disco at w/end; ccard acc, not at w/ends; CKE/CCI. "Beautiful, scenic area; on Chiemsee lakeside (extra for lakeside pitches); 15% extra if staying fewer than 4 nights; sm pitches; popular, busy site - rec arr early; modern, clean facs; poor drainage after rain; site rather run down end of ssn." ♦ 1 Apr-31 Oct. € 33.00 (CChq acc)   2013*

PRIEN AM CHIEMSEE 4F4 (2.6km S Rural) 47.8387, 12.35078 **Camping Hofbauer, Bernauerstrasse 110, 83209 Prien [(08051) 4136; fax 62657; ferienhaus.campingpl.hofbauer@t-online.de; www.camping-prien-chiemsee.de]** Exit A8/E52/E60 junc 106 dir Prien. Site on L in 3km immed after rndabt. Med, mkd pitch, pt sl, pt shd; wc; chem disp; mv service pnt; shwrs inc; EHU (16A) metered + conn fee; shop; snacks; playgrnd; pool; lake sw 1km; bike hire; internet; 50% statics; dogs €2; some rd noise; ccard acc (surcharge); CKE/CCI. "Well-kept site; helpful owners; sm pitches - siting poss diff; pts of site flooded after heavy rain, but some raised pitches; solar htd water; gd." ♦ 1 Apr-30 Oct. € 19.00   2009*

PRORA see Binz 2G1

GERMANY

The NATURCAMP located in the north of Germany on the baltic Sea. In sept./oct. are many thousands common cranes in this region and also near the campsite.

NATURCAMP PRUCHTEN
★★★★

0049-38231-2045
-15%€ in the low season www.naturcamp.eu

PRUCHTEN *2F1* (1km W Rural/Coastal) *54.37960, 12.66181* Naturcamping Pruchten, Zeltplatzstrasse 30, 18356 Pruchten [(038231) 2045; fax 038231 66346; info@ naturcamp.de; www.naturcamp.eu] Fr Rostock on B105, at Löbnitz take L23 N sp Barth & Zingst to Pruchten & foll site sp. Lge, mkd pitch, pt shd; htd wc; chem disp; mv service pnt; baby facs; shwrs; EHU (16A) €2; lndry; shop; rest, snacks; bar; playgrnd; sand beach 500m; games area; horseriding 500m; wifi; 20% statics; dogs €2; m'van o'night area; adv bkg; quiet. "Gd birdwatching, surfing, fishing; vg." 1 Apr-31 Oct. € 26.00   2012*

See advertisement

⊞ **PRUM** *3A2* (2km NE Rural) *50.21906, 6.43811* Waldcamping Prüm, 54591 Prüm [(06551) 2481; fax 6555; info@waldcamping-pruem.de; www.waldcamping-pruem.de] Site sp fr town cent dir Dausfeld. Med, pt shd; wc; chem disp; mv service pnt; baby facs; shwrs inc; EHU (10-16A) inc; gas; lndry (inc dryer); shop; rest 1km; snacks; playgrnd; pool complex adj; tennis adj; bike hire; ski lift 2km; entmnt high ssn; internet; 60% statics; dogs €1.50; o'night facs for m'vans; poss cr; Eng spkn; adv bkg; quiet; ccard acc; red CKE/CCI. "Pleasant site in lovely surroundings; friendly staff; clean facs; m'van o'night facs; do not arr bef 1900 on Sundays due local rd closures for family cycling event." ♦ € 25.00   2014*

⊞ **QUEDLINBURG** *2E3* (10km SW Urban) *51.75614, 11.04956* Kloster Camping Thale, Burghardt Wilsdorf, Wendhusenstraße 3, 06502 Thale [(03947) 63185; info@ klostercamping-thale.de; www.klostercamping-thale.de] Head S twds Steinholzstraße. 1st R onto Steinholzstraße. Bear L onto Stauffenberg-Platz. Turn L onto Weststraße cont onto Wipertistraße for 1.4km then onto Unter der Altenburg. Cont onto K2356, turn L onto Thalenser Str. Cont onto L240 then turn L onto L92. After 1.4km turn L onto Schmiedestraße. Then R onto Breiteweg & bear R onto Wendhusenstraße. Site on LH side. Med, mkd pitch, pt hdstg, pt shd; htd wc; chem disp; mv service pnt; baby facs; shwrs €0.80; EHU (10A) €2.50; lndry; shop 0.5km; rest 0.5km; snacks; bar; playgrnd; 10% statics; bus 0.3km; quiet; no ccard acc; CKE/CCI. "San facs excel." € 23.00   2014*

⊞ **RADEVORMWALD** *1B4* (5km SW Rural) *51.18498, 7.31362* Camping-Ferienpark Kräwinkel, Kräwinkel 1, 42477 Radevormwald [(02195) 6887899; fax 689597; info@ferienpark.de] Exit A1 Remscheid onto B229 Radevormwald. In Radevormwald 1st mini island turn R, site on L in 4km. Sm, hdg pitch, terr, pt shd; htd wc; chem disp; shwrs inc; EHU (20A) inc; rest; bar; playgrnd; lake sw nr; 80% statics; dogs €2; Eng spkn; adv bkg; quiet; CKE/CCI. "Lge pitches; pleasant area; key needed for all facs €10 deposit." ♦ € 15.00   2013*

RADOLFZELL AM BODENSEE *3C4* (4km E Rural) *47.73888, 9.00305* Campingplatz Markelfingen, Unterdorfstrasse 19, 78315 Radolfzell-Markelfingen [(07732) 10611; fax 10727; info@campingplatz-markelfingen.de; www.campingplatz-markelfingen.de] Fr B33 turn twd Radolfzell. Turn L in 2km at traff lts sp Markelfingen then R at traff lts in Markelfingen. Site sp. Med, hdstg, pt shd; wc; chem disp; shwrs €1; EHU (10A) metered; lndry; shop; rest, snacks; bar; BBQ; lake sw & shgl beach; boat launch; 50% statics; dogs €2.30; phone; train adj; poss cr; Eng spkn; quiet; CKE/CCI. "Recep clsd 1230-1400; gd train service to Radolfzell & Konstanz; modern san facs." ♦ 1 Apr-3 Oct. € 19.00   2011*

> ## "Satellite navigation makes touring much easier"
>
> Remember most sat navs don't know if you're towing or in a larger vehicle – always use yours alongside maps and site directions.

RADOLFZELL AM BODENSEE *3C4* (11km S Rural) *47.68796, 8.99428* Campingdorf Horn, Strandweg 3-18, 78343 Gaienhofen-Horn [(07735) 685; fax 8806; campingdorf. horn@t-online.de] Fr Stein-am-Rhein take L192 along N of Untersee for approx 13km. Site on app to Horn vill, sp. Fr Radolfzell, take rd S on E bank of Zellersee, site on L exit Horn vill. Med, pt shd; wc; chem disp; some serviced pitches; shwrs €1; EHU (16A) metered + conn fee; lndry; shop; rest; snacks 200m; bar; playgrnd; lake sw; watersports; entmnt; 20% statics; no dogs; bus; phone; sep car park; adv bkg; quiet; ccard acc; red CKE/CCI. "Vg." ♦ 15 Mar-7 Oct. € 26.00   2011*

RADOLFZELL AM BODENSEE *3C4* (16km S Rural) *47.65972, 8.93388* **Campingplatz Wangen, Seeweg 32, 78337 Öhningen-Wangen [(07735) 919675; fax 919676; info@ camping-wangen.de; www.camping-wangen.de]** Site in Wangen vill, 5km E of Stein am Rhien. Med, hdstg, pt shd; wc; chem disp; mv service pnt; baby facs; shwrs inc; EHU (10A) metered + conn fee; lndry (inc dryer); shop 300m; rest, snacks; bar; BBQ; playgrnd; lake sw & sand beach adj; fishing; games area; wifi; 40% statics; dogs €2 (check with site bef arr to make sure they will acc); phone; twin axles; Eng spkn; adv bkg; quiet; CKE/CCI. "Lovely scenery; site in vill but quiet; helpful recep; gd cycling & sw; lake steamer trips; Stein-am-Rhein 5km; water sports in adj lake." ♦ ltd. 3 Apr-3 Oct.
€ 29.00   2014*

RADOLFZELL AM BODENSEE *3C4* (6km SW Urban) *47.72942, 9.02432* **Campingplatz William, 78315 Markelfingen [(049) 7533 6211; info@campingplatz-william.de; www.campingplatz-william.de]** Fr S on A81 at junc 40 take A98 for 9m, at end of m'way turn L, site ent on L in 0.75m. Lge, med mkd pitches, pt shd; wc; chem disp, shwrs; lndry; gas; rest, snacks, bar; BBQ; playgrnd; beach and sw adj; boat hire; Eng spkn; CKE/CCI and passport. "Gd site; cycle track; modern san facs; some noise fr rlwy." 1 Apr-3 Oct. € 18.00   2012*

RAVENSBURG *3D4* (13km SW Rural) *47.73935, 9.47187* **Camping am Bauernhof, St Georg Strasse 8, 88094 Oberteuringen-Neuhaus [(07546) 2446; fax 918106; kramer@camping-am-bauernhof.de; www.camping-am-bauernhof.de]** Fr Ravensburg twd Meersburg on B33. In Neuhaus foll sp on R; site bef chapel. Sm, pt shd; wc; chem disp; shwrs; EHU (10A) €2.50; lndry inc dryer; shop 300m; BBQ; playgrnd; lake sw, games rm, volleyball,; 20% statics; dogs €2; Eng spkn; quiet; CKE/CCI. "CL-type but with full facs inc shwrs for wheelchair users; vg, clean, modern san facs; relaxed atmosphere; gd cycling area; farm with animals, fruit, distillery, herb garden, barn; sm lake on site; pre order fresh rolls/bread daily; excel site; lots of interest for kids; sep park for m'van on hdstg; friendly, helpful owners." ♦ 28 Mar-15 Sep.
€ 22.50   2015*

⊞ **REGENSBURG** *4F3* (5km NW Urban) *49.02779, 12.05899* **Azur Campingpark Regensburg, Weinweg 40, 93049 Regensburg [(0941) 270025; fax 299432; regensburg@ azur-camping.de; www.azur-camping.de]** Fr A93/E50 exit junc 40 Regensburg W, dir Weiden; turn W away fr town onto dual c'way; R at traff lts, site sp fr next T-junc. Lge, some hdstg, pt shd; htd wc; chem disp; mv service pnt; shwrs inc; EHU (10A) €3 (poss long lead req); lndry; shop high ssn; supmkt 400m; rest high ssn; bar; playgrnd; covrd pool 300m; bike hire; 40% statics (sep area); dogs €3.50; phone; bus at site ent; o'night area for m'vans; poss cr; quiet; ccard not acc; red CKE/CCI. "Helpful owner; vg facs; gd, clean san facs, lge block unisex; sm pitches poss diff lge o'fits; dist bet units minimal; cycle path into town along Rv Danube; gates clsd 1300-1500 & 2200-0800; gd." ♦ € 31.00   2015*

REINSBERG *2G4* (1KM W Rural) *51.00381, 13.36012* **Campingplatz Reinsberg, Badstrasse 17, 19629 Reinsberg [(037324) 82268; fax 82270; campingplatz-reinsberg@ web.de; www.campingplatz-reinsberg.de]** Exit A4/E40 junc 75 Nossen. Take 1st R to Siebenlehn & foll sp Reinsberg. In Reinsberg take 1st R sp camping & 'freibad' to site. Med, pt shd; htd wc; chem disp (wc); shwrs inc; EHU (16A) €2; lndry; sm shop; rest, bar 500m; snacks; playgrnd; pool & sports facs adj; 40% statics; dogs €2; phone; Eng spkn; adv bkg; quiet. "Friendly, helpful owner; excel san facs; gd walking; conv Meissen, Dresden & Freiberg." ♦ 1 Apr-31 Oct.
€ 15.00   2010*

⊞ **REINSFELD** *3B2* (2km S Rural) *49.68612, 6.86781* **Azur Campingpark Hunsrück, Parkstrasse 1, 54421 Reinsfeld [(06503) 95123; fax 95124; reinsfeld@azur-camping.de; www.azur-camping.de/reinsfeld]** Fr A1 exit junc 132 Reinsfeld onto B407; site well sp. Lge, pt sl, pt shd; htd wc; chem disp; private bthrms avail; shwrs inc; EHU (10A) €3; gas; lndry; shop; rest, snacks; bar; playgrnd; htd pool 200m; paddling pool; sm lake; tennis; games area; entmnt; TV; 40% statics; dogs €3; clsd 1300-1500; poss cr; Eng spkn; adv bkg; no ccard acc; red CKE/CCI. "Aircraft exhib worthwhile; some pitches v muddy in wet weather; scenic area; conv Trier & Luxembourg." ♦ € 22.00   2010*

REIT IM WINKL *4F4* (6km E Rural) *47.65845, 12.54114* **Camping Seegatterl, Seegatterl 7, 83242 Reit-im-Winkl [(08640) 98210; fax 5150; info@camping-reit-im-winkl. com; www.camping-reit-im-winkl.com]** On B305, site sp behind lge car park. Camping sp obscured in vill. Med, pt sl, unshd; htd wc; chem disp; mv service pnt; sauna; shwrs inc; EHU (16A) metered; gas; lndry (inc dryer); shop; rest, snacks; BBQ; playgrnd; lake sw & beach 2km; bike hire; ski lift fr site; skibus 100m; golf 5km; internet; 50% statics; dogs €2; adv bkg; quiet. "Gd family site; friendly; excel skiing & walking; mainly for winter sport users." 1 Dec-31 Mar & 15 May-15 Oct.
€ 20.00   2009*

⊞ **REIT IM WINKL** *4F4* (16km NW Rural) *47.73556, 12.41565* **Camping Zellersee, Zellerseeweg 3, 83259 Schleching-Mettenham [(08649) 986719; fax 816; info@camping-zellersee.de; www.camping-zellersee.de]** Fr A8 exit junc 109 S sp Reit im Winkel. Just after Marquartstein turn R onto B307 sp Schleching, site sp just N of Schleching. Med, mkd pitch, pt sl, terr, pt shd; htd wc; chem disp; baby facs; shwrs inc; EHU (16A) metered; gas; lndry; shop 1.2km; rest, bar 600m; lake sw; tennis; 50% statics; no dogs; phone; Eng spkn; adv bkg; quiet; ccard acc; red long stay/CKE/CCI. "Excel, high quality facs; many footpaths fr site; mountain views; nr Alpenstrasse." ♦ ltd. € 23.00   2012*

REMAGEN *3B1* (9.6km N Rural) *50.64500, 7.20694* **Camping Siebengebirgsblick, Wickchenstrasse, 53424 Remagen-Rolandswerth [(02228) 910682; fax (02633) 472008; info@ siebengebirgsblick.de; www.siebengebirgsblick.de]** Site sp close to car ferry to Königswinter, opp Nonnewerth Is. Fr B9, foll sp to site on rvside. Lge, mkd pitch, unshd; wc; chem disp; shwrs €0.50; EHU (8A) metered or €2.50; sm shop 500m; rest, snacks; bar; playgrnd; TV; 40% statics; dogs €1; Eng spkn; quiet; red long stay; CKE/CCI. "Extra for pitches on rvside; facs in Portacabins; minimal rv & rlwy noise; cycle tracks along rv to Bonn & Remagen; gd NH." 15 Apr-20 Oct. € 17.00   2010*

⊞ **REMAGEN** *3B1* (1km ENE Urban) *50.57666, 7.25083*
Campingplatz Goldene Meile, Simrockweg 9-13, 53424 Remagen [(02642) 22222; fax 1555; info@camping-goldene-meile.de; www.camping-goldene-meile.de] Fr A61 exit dir Remagen onto B266; foll sp 'Rheinfähre Linz'; in Kripp turn L, site sp. Or fr B266 1km beyond Bad Bodendorf at rndabt take B9 (dir Bonn & Remagen); in 1km take exit Remagen Süd; foll sp to sports cent/camping. Site adj Luddendorf Bdge. Fr S on A48 exit junc 10 onto B9 twd Bonn. Site sp in 22km after junc with B266. Lge, hdg/mkd pitch, some hdstg, pt shd; wc; chem disp; mv service pnt; some serviced pitches; shwrs €0.75; EHU (16A) €2.60 (50m cable rec some pitches); gas; lndry; shop (ltd opening); rest high ssn; snacks; bar; playgrnd; pool adj; bike hire; wifi; entmnt; 50% statics; dogs €1.70; m'van o'night area adj; poss cr; Eng spkn; adv bkg; quiet but some noise fr rlwy across rv; red CKE/CCI. "Tourers on flat field away fr rvbank; sm pitches tightly packed in high ssn; gd rest; helpful staff; EHU up ladder; access to facs not gd; cycle path along Rhine; site clsd 1300-1500; vg, well-organised site; interesting old town." ♦ € 23.00   2014*

⊞ **RERIK** *2E1* (1km NE Urban) *54.11133, 11.63234*
Campingpark Ostseebad Rerik, Straße am Zeltplatz 18230 Ostseebad Rerik [038296 75720; fax 75722; info@campingpark-rerik.de; www.campingpark-rerik.de] Fr A20 junc 12 to Kröpelin on L12 thro Kröelin twrds Rerik then foll sps to site. Med, hdg/mkd pitch, pt shd; htd wc; chem disp; mv service pnt; child/baby facs; shwrs; EHU (16A); lndry; rest; snacks; bar; playgrnd; beach; internet; dogs-€3; Eng spkn; quiet; ccard acc. "Gd site; new modern facs." ♦ € 34.00   2014*

RETGENDORF *2E2* (4.6km N Rural) *53.75194, 11.49638*
Seecamping Flessenow, Am Schweriner See 1a, 19067 Flessenow [(03866) 81491; info@seecamping.de; www.seecamping.de] Exit A14 at junc 4 Schwerin-Nord onto B104 dir Schwerin. In 2km turn R along lakeside sp Retgendorf & Flessenow, site in approx 10km at end of surfaced rd. Med, mkd pitch, pt shd; htd wc; chem disp; mv service pnt; baby facs; shwrs €0.80; EHU (10A) €2.50; gas; lndry (inc dryer); shop; snacks; bar; playgrnd; sand beach & lake sw adj; watersports; games area; 35% statics; dogs free; phone; bus adj; quiet; CKE/CCI. "Fair site in gd location." ♦ 1 Apr-31 Oct. € 22.50   2009*

RETGENDORF *2E2* (400m N Rural) *53.72947, 11.50279*
Campingplatz Retgendorf, Seestrasse 7A, 19067 Retgendorf [(03866) 400040; fax 400041; info@camping-retgendorf.de; www.camping-retgendorf.m-vp.de] Exit A241 at junc 4 onto B104 dir Schwerin, in 2km turn N onto lakeside rd dir Retgendorf & Flessenow. On ent Retgendorf, site on L by bus stop. Med, mkd pitch, pt shd; wc; chem disp; shwrs €1; EHU (10A) €2; lndry; shop 1km; snacks; bar; lake sw & sand beach adj; fishing; 70% statics; dogs €1.50; phone; quiet. "Views of lake; conv beautiful towns of Schwerin & Wismar; gd cycling area; san facs clean & functional but dated; shwrs lack privacy; staff/ static owners friendly & helpful; lovely peaceful site if prepared to rough it a bit." ♦ ltd. 1 Apr-15 Oct. € 15.00   2013*

⊞ **RHEINMUNSTER** *3C3* (1km NW Rural) *48.77330, 8.04041* **Freizeitcenter Oberrhein, Am Campingpark 1, 77836 Rheinmünster-Stollhofen [(07227) 2500; fax 2400; info@freizeitcenter-oberrhein.de; www.freizeitcenter-oberrhein.de]** Exit A5 junc 51 at Baden Baden/Iffezheim sp to join B500. At traff lts turn L onto B36 dir Hügelsheim & Kehl. In 8km turn R at rndabt immed on ent Stollhofen & cont to end of lane. V lge, hdg/mkd pitch, pt shd; 60% serviced pitches; wc; chem disp; mv service pnt; fam bthrm; shwrs inc; EHU (16A) €2.50 + conn fee; gas; lndry; shop; 2 rests; snacks; bar; playgrnd; lake sw; watersports; windsurfing; fishing; tennis; golf 6km; bike hire; internet; entmnt; 70% statics (sep area); dogs €4.50; phone; clsd 1300-1500; m'van o'night area outside site; poss cr; Eng spkn; adv bkg; ccard acc; quiet. "Conv touring base Baden-Baden, Strasbourg; Black Forest; helpful, nice staff; excel san facs; highly rec; some lovely lakeside pitches; gd cycling by Rhine." ♦ € 32.00   2015*

⊞ **RIBNITZ DAMGARTEN** *2F1* (13km NE Coastal) *54.28194, 12.31250* **Camping in Neuhaus, Birkenallee 10, 18347 Dierhagen-Neuhaus [(038226) 539930; fax 539931; ostsee@camping-neuhaus.de; www.camping-neuhaus.de]** Exit E55/A19 junc 6 onto B105 N. At Altheide turn N thro Klockenhagen dir Dierhagen, then turn L at camping sp & foll site sp to sea. Med, pt hdg pitch, pt shd; htd wc; chem disp; baby facs; shwrs €0.50; EHU (16A) €3; lndry (inc dryer); shop; rest 1.5km; snacks; playgrnd; beach 100m; wifi; 40% statics; dogs €3; adv bkg; quiet; ccard not acc. "Friendly site; vg." ♦ € 26.00   2009*

"There aren't many sites open at this time of year"

If you're travelling outside peak season remember to call ahead to check site opening dates – even if the entry says 'open all year'.

RIBNITZ DAMGARTEN *2F1* (13km NW Coastal) *54.29188, 12.34375* **Ostseecamp Dierhagen, Ernst Moritz Arndt Strasse, 18347 Dierhagen-Strand [(038226) 80778; fax 80779; info@ostseecamp-dierhagen.de; www.ostseecamp-dierhagen.de]** Take B105 fr Rostock dir Stralsund. Bef Ribnitz, turn L sp Dierhagen & Wustrow & cont for 5km to traff lts & camp sp. Turn L to site on R in 300m. Lge, pt shd; wc; chem disp; mv service pnt; shwrs €0.50; EHU (6A) €3; gas; lndry; shop; supmkt 500m; rest 1km; snacks; playgrnd; sand beach 800m; bike hire; 20% statics; dogs €2.80; phone; adv bkg (fee); quiet. "Site low-lying, poss v wet after heavy rain; charge for chem disp." ♦ ltd. 15 Mar-31 Oct. € 21.50   2009*

RIEGEL AM KAISERSTUHL *3B4* (1.5km N Rural) *48.16463, 7.74008* **Camping Müller-See, Zum Müller-See 1, 79359 Riegel-am-Kaiserstuhl [(07642) 3694; fax 923014; info@muellersee.de; www.muellersee.de]** Exit A5/E35 at junc 59 dir Riegel, foll site sp. Med, unshd; htd wc; chem disp; mv service pnt; baby facs; shwrs €0.30; EHU (16A) €2; lndry; shop in vill; rest, snacks in vill; bar; playgrnd; lake sw adj; no dogs; phone; quiet; redCKE/CCI. "Excel cycle paths in area; excel san facs; gd NH." ♦ 1 Apr-31 Oct. € 16.00   2012*

⊞ **RIESTE** *1C3* (200m W Rural) *52.48555, 7.99003* **Alfsee Ferien- und Erholungspark, Am Campingpark 10, 49597 Rieste [(05464) 92120; fax 5837; info@alfsee.de; www.alfsee.de]** Exit A1/E37 junc 67; site in 10km, sp. V lge, mkd pitch, pt shd; htd wc; chem disp; mv service pnt; baby facs; fam bthrm; shwrs inc; EHU (16A) metered; lndry (inc dryer); shop; rest, snacks; bar; playgrnd; lake sw & sand beach adj; watersports; tennis; bike hire; 50% statics; dogs €3; phone; poss cr at w/end with day visitors; Eng spkn; poss noisy; ccard acc; 10% redCKE/CCI. "Site pt of lge watersports complex; modern san facs; gd for famiies, conv for Osnotbruk old town." ♦ € 39.40   2014*

See advertisement inside the front cover

⊞ **RINTELN** *1C3* (2km W Rural) *52.1865, 9.05988* **Camping Doktorsee, Am Doktorsee 8, 31722 Rinteln [(05751) 964860; fax 964888; info@doktorsee.de; www.doktorsee.de]** Exit A2/E30 a'bahn, junc 35; foll sp 'Rinteln' then 'Rinteln Nord'. Turn L at traff lts, foll 'Stadtmitte' sp over rv bdge. immed turn R, bear L at fork, site in 1km on R. V lge, pt shd; wc; chem disp; mv service pnt; shwrs inc; EHU (16A) €1.90; lndry; shop, rest, snacks; bar; playgrnd; lake sw adj; tennis; bike hire; entmnt high ssn; 60% statics; dogs €1.60; phone; poss cr; Eng spkn; adv bkg; quiet; ccard acc; redCKE/CCI. "NH on hdstg by ent; picturesque town with gd shops; 1 excel san facs block, other run down; pleasant staff." ♦ € 20.00   2012*

ROCKENHAUSEN *3C2* (7km NE Rural) *49.67000, 7.88666* **Azur Campingpark Pfalz, Kahlenbergweiher 1, 67813 Gerbach [(06361) 8287; fax 22523; gerbach@ azur-camping.de; www.azur-camping.de/gerbach]** Fr Rockenhausen take local rd to Gerbach then foll site sp on rd L385. Med, pt shd; wc; chem disp; mv service pnt; baby facs; shwrs inc; EHU (16A) metered or €2.80; gas; lndry; supmkt; rest, snacks; bar; cooking facs; playgrnd; pool; paddling pool; tennis; entmnt; 60% statics; dogs €2.80; adv bkg; quiet; redCKE/CCI. "Conv Rhein & Mosel wine regions; gd walking." 1 Apr-31 Oct. € 34.00   2013*

RODENKIRCHEN see Köln *1B4*

⊞ **ROSENHEIM** *4F4* (9km N Rural) *47.92518, 12.13571* **Camping Erlensee, Rosenheimerstrasse 63, 83135 Schechen [(08039) 1695; fax 9416; campingplatz-erlensee@t-online.de; www.camping-erlensee.de]** Exit A8 junc 102, avoid Rosenheim town cent by foll B15 sp Landshut. Site on E side of B15 at S end Schechen. Med, pt shd; wc; chem disp; some serviced pitches; shwrs €0.50; EHU (16A) €2; lndry; shop 1km; rest; lake sw; 60% statics; dogs €2; poss cr; Eng spkn; adv bkg; quiet; red CKE/CCI. "Pleasant, gd & simple site; helpful owners; excel facs; mosquito prob." ♦ € 19.40   2014*

⊞ **ROSENHEIM** *4F4* (14km SW Rural) *47.78978, 12.00575* **Kaiser Camping (formerly known as Tenda-Park), Reithof 2, 83075 Bad Feilnbach [(08066) 884400; fax 8844029; info@kaiser-camping.com; www.kaiser-camping.com]** Take exit 100 fr A8/E45/E52 & foll sp to Brannenburg. Site in 5km on R, 1km N of Bad Feilnbach. V lge, pt shd; wc; baby facs; shwrs inc; EHU (16A) €2. or metered + conn fee (poss rev pol); gas; lndry (inc dryer); shop; rest; playgrnd; htd pool; paddling pool; bike hire; ski lift 12km; entmnt high ssn; wifi; 80% statics; dogs €3; Eng spkn; adv bkg; quiet. "V busy, clean, well-run site; pleasant, wooded pitches; useful NH; pleasant helpful staff; some of the best san facs; discount vouchers for local shops/rest." ♦ € 35.00   2014*

⊞ **ROSSHAUPTEN** *4E4* (500m N Rural) *47.65800, 10.71900* **Wohnmobilstellplatz Rosshaupten, Augsburgerstrasse 23, 87672 Rosshaupten [(08367) 913877; fax 913876; info@womomi.de]** Fr N twd Forggensee on B16, site on R immed after taking Rosshaupten exit. Sm, mkd pitch, hdstg, pt shd; htd wc; chem disp; mv service pnt; shwrs €1; EHU (10A) €2; gas; lndry; shop, rest, bar 500m; sat TV; dogs; bus; Eng spkn; some rd noise; red long stay. "OK for m'vans but will acc cars/c'vans if site not busy; gd, modern san facs; helpful, friendly owners; c'van dealer/repair on site - can be like parking in a c'van sales yard!; gd location for castles, Forggensee & Austrian border." ♦ ltd. € 9.00 (4 persons)   2010*

⊞ **ROTENBURG (WUMME)** *1D2* (10km SE Rural) *53.06977, 9.49413* **Camping Ferienpark Hanseat, Am Campingplatz 4, 27386 Bothel [(04266) 335; fax 8424; info@campingpark-hanseat.de]** Exit A1 junc 50 Sottrum twd Rotenburg, then take B71 E dir Soltau. Site sp in Bothel. Med, unshd; htd wc; chem disp; mv service pnt; shwrs; EHU; lndry (inc dryer); shop; rest, snacks; BBQ; playgrnd; htd pool 100m; lake sw & fishing 1km; tennis; games area; TV rm; 60% statics; dogs €2; adv bkg; quiet. "Gd for NH, a bit run down." ♦ € 22.00   2013*

ROTENBURG (WUMME) *1D2* (10km W Rural) *53.12027, 9.27833* **Camping Stürberg, 27367 Hassendorf [(04264) 9124; fax 821440; campingpark-stuerberg@gmx. de; www.stuerberg.de]** Exit A1/E22 Ottersberg-Rotenburg at Sottrum exit, junc 50. Turn E on B75, site on N side of B75 3km after Sottrum. Fr Rotenburg, take B75 turn S sp Hassendorf; site well sp. Med, pt shd; wc; chem disp; mv service pnt; shwrs inc; EHU (10A) €2 & metered; gas; lndry (inc dryer); shop 3km; rest 200m; snacks; bar; playgrnd; pool 3km; 30% statics; dogs €2; Eng spkn; some rd noise; red long stay/CKE/CCI. "Grassy, open plan pitches; peaceful; pleasant staff; excel, clean facs." ♦ 15 Mar-31 Oct. € 15.00   2009*

ROTENBURG AN DER FULDA *1D4* (1km E Urban) *50.99348, 9.74303* **Camping der Stadt, Campingweg, 36199 Rotenburg-an-der-Fulda [(06623) 5556; petra.reinhardt@ rotenburg.de; www.rotenburg.de]** Fr A4/E40 junc 32 N to Bebra on B27 Kasselerstrasse. Thro Bebra twd Rotenburg on B83; site sp on N side of Rv Fulda. Med, hdstg, pt shd; wc; chem disp; mv service pnt; shwrs inc; EHU (16A) €2; lndry (inc dryer); shop; rest 600m; snacks; covrd pool 400m; bike hire; TV; dogs €0.70; quiet; red CKE/CCI. "Basic facs; few mins walk to town." 1 Apr-15 Oct. € 13.00   2010*

GERMANY

⊞ **ROTHENBURG OB DER TAUBER** *3D2* (2km S Urban) *49.37083, 10.18361* **Wohnmobil Park (P2), Bensenstrasse, 91541 Rothenburg-ob-der-Tauber [(09861) 404800; fax 404529; info@rothenburg.de]** Exit A7/E43 junc 108. Just S of Rothenburg, foll sp P2 (car park no. 2). M'vans only. Med, mkd pitch, hdstg, pt sl, unshd; wc; chem disp; mv service pnt & water €1; EHU (metered); shop 500m; rest opp; rd & rlwy noise. "M'vans only; clean, tidy o'night stop; wcs avail in car park; pay at machine; 5 min walk beautiful, interesting medieval town." € 10.00   2011*

ROTHENBURG OB DER TAUBER *3D2* (3km NW Rural) *49.38805, 10.16638* **Camping Tauber-Idyll, Detwang 28, 91541 Rothenburg-ob-der-Tauber [(09861) 3177 or 6463; fax 92848; camping-tauber-idyll@t-online.de; www.rothenburg.de/tauberidyll]** NW on Rothenburg-Bad Mergentheim rd in vill of Detwang. Sp. Site behind inn nr church. Care on tight R turn into ent. Sm, pt shd; htd wc; chem disp; mv service pnt; shwrs inc; EHU (6-16A) €2 or metered + conn fee; gas; lndry; shop; rest at inn; bike hire; dogs €1; bus; poss v cr; Eng spkn; adv bkg. "Church clock chimes each hr; clsd to vehicles 2200-0800; old walled town, gd cent for Romantische Strasse & Hohenlohe Plain; owners helpful; pleasant site; gd san facs; sm c'van pitches at busy times; gd cycle rte along valley." 22 Mar-1 Nov. € 25.60   2013*

ROTHENBURG OB DER TAUBER *3D2* (3km NW Rural) *49.38888, 10.16722* **Campingplatz Tauber-Romantik, Detwang 39, 91541 Rothenburg-ob-der-Tauber [(09861) 6191; fax 9368889; info@camping-tauberromantik.de; www.camping-tauberromantik.de]** NW on Rothenburg-Bad Mergentheim rd in vill of Detwang; turn L at camp sp & immed R; site sp fr Rothenburg. Sharp turn into site ent. Med, mkd pitch, some hdstg, pt sl, terr, pt shd; htd wc; chem disp; mv service pnt €1; shwrs inc; EHU (16A) €2.20; gas; lndry (inc dryer); sm shop; rest nr; snacks; bar; playgrnd; pool 2km; some statics; dogs €2; phone; bus adj; poss cr; Eng spkn; adv bkg; ccard acc; quiet, but constant church bells; CKE/CCI. "Pleasant, gd value site; excel, clean, vg facs; gd sized pitches; picturesque town; gd cycle rte; pleasant atmosphere; gd facs for children; conv NH for Rothenburg, Austria, Italy; busy over festival w/ends; vg; well managed." ♦ 15 Mar-4 Nov & 30 Nov-7 Jan. € 25.00   2015*

⊞ **ROTTENBUCH** *4E4* (500m S Rural) *47.72763, 10.96691* **Terrasencamping am Richterbichl, Solder 1, 82401 Rottenbuch [(08867) 1500; fax 8300; info@camping-rottenbuch.de; www.camping-rottenbuch.de]** S fr Schongau for 10km on B23 dir Oberammergau, site just S of Rottenbuch. Med, mkd pitch, terr, pt shd; wc; chem disp; mv service pnt; shwrs inc; EHU (10A) metered + conn fee; gas; lndry (inc dryer); shop; rest 300m; snacks; bar; playgrnd; lake sw adj; wifi; 40% statics; dogs €2; Eng spkn; adv bkg; quiet; ccard acc; red long stay/CKE/CCI. "Walks & cycle paths fr site; local castles, churches & interesting towns; excel facs; friendly, helpful owners." ♦ ltd. € 18.00   2012*

RUDESHEIM *3C2* (3km E Urban) *49.97944, 7.95777* **Camping Geisenheim Rheingau, Am Campingplatz 1, 65366 Geisenheim [tel/fax (06722) 75600; campingplatzgeisenheim@t-online.de; www.rheingau-camping.de]** Well sp fr B42, on rvside. Lge, mkd pitch, pt shd; htd wc; chem disp; baby facs; fam bthrm; shwrs inc; EHU (16A) inc; lndry (inc dryer); shop 2km; rest, snacks; bar; BBQ; playgrnd; htd pool 1km; games area; 50% statics; dogs €1.50; phone adj; bus adj; Eng spkn; adv bkg; quiet; CKE/CCI. "Vg site bet Rv Rhine & vineyards; walks and cycling by rv; lots to do." ♦ 1 March to 31 October. € 30.00   2013*

RUDESHEIM *3C2* (2km SE Urban) *49.97777, 7.94083* **Camping am Rhein, Auf der Lach, 65385 Rüdesheim-am-Rhein [(06722) 2528 or 49299 (LS); fax 406783; info@campingplatz-ruedesheim.de; www.campingplatz-ruedesheim.de]** Fr Koblenz (N) on B42 pass car ferry to Bingen on app to Rüdesheim; turn L & over rlwy x-ing, foll Rheinstrasse & rlwy E for 1km; cont under rlwy bdge, turn R sp to Car Park 6; turn R at T-junc, pass coach park; turn L at x-rds & foll rd to site on R. When arr via Bingen ferry turn R onto B42 & foll above dir fr level x-ing. Fr S on B42 ent Rüdesheim, turn L immed after o'head rlwy bdge (2.8m); foll camping sp. Lge, pt shd; htd wc; chem disp; mv service pnt; baby facs; shwrs €1; EHU (10A) inc (poss rev pol & poss long lead req); gas; lndry (inc dryer); rest 600m; bar; BBQ (gas/charcoal); playgrnd; htd pool, paddling pool, tennis adj; bike hire; horseriding 4km; dogs €3; no o'fits over 11m; bus 500m; recep 0800-2200; poss v cr; Eng spkn; adv bkg; quiet but rlwy & rv traff noise; ccard not acc; CKE/CCI. "Pleasant, busy, family-run site; busy, well-kept & well-run; gd facs; poss long walk to water supply; pleasant 1km walk/cycleway by rv to town; warden sites you & connects elec - no mkd pitches; perforated grnd sheets only allowed; rallies welcome; Harley Davidson w/end bike festival in June; shwrs far; pleasant loc by rv; shops conv; ladies san facs refurbished (2014)." ♦ 30 Apr-3 Oct. € 29.00 SBS - G08   2014*

RUGEN ISLAND *2G1* Sites on Rügen Island are listed together at the end of the Germany site entry pages.

⊞ **RUHPOLDING** *4F4* (3km S Rural) *47.7424, 12.66356* **Camping Ortnerhof, Ort 5, 83324 Ruhpolding [(08663) 1764; fax 5073; camping-ortnerhof@t-online.de; www.camping-ruhpolding.de]** Exit A8/E52/E60 junc 112, thro Ruhpolding, turn L onto B305 dir Berchtesgaden, site sp. Med, mkd pitch, some hdstg, unshd; htd wc; chem disp; mv service pnt; shwrs inc; EHU (10A) metered + conn fee; lndry; shop 1.5km; rest, snacks; playgrnd; pool 3km; ski lift 3km; skibus; internet; quiet; 30% statics; no dogs; poss cr; 10% red CKE/CCI 2+ nts. "Restful, friendly site in gd location; helpful recep; sep area for m'vans adj hotel; barrier clsd 1200-1400." € 18.50   2010*

SAALBURG *4F2* (2km N Rural) *50.51542, 11.73072* **Campingplatz Kloster, Klosterstrasse 1b, 07929 Saalburg-Kloster [tel/fax (036647) 22441; bb@saalburg-ebersdorf.de; www.saalburg-ebersdorf.de]** Exit A9/E51 junc 28 dir Saalburg. Site sp on lakeside. Lge, pt sl, unshd; wc; chem disp; mv service pnt; baby facs; shwrs €1; EHU (10-16A) €1.50; gas; lndry (inc dryer); shop 1km; rest, snacks; bar; playgrnd; lake sw adj; games area; 80% statics; dogs €2; sep car park; quiet. "Gd." ♦ 1 Apr-31 Oct. € 19.00   2010*

GERMANY

⊞ **SAARBURG** *3B2* (3km W Rural) *49.60083, 6.52833*
Campingplatz Waldfrieden, Im Fichtenhain 4,
54439 Saarburg [(06581) 2255; fax 5908; info@
campingwaldfrieden.de; www.campingwaldfrieden.de]
Fr B51/B407 bypass foll sp 'krankenhaus' (hospital). Site sp
off L132. Med, hdg pitch, some hdstg, pt sl, pt shd; wc;
chem disp; mv service pnt; some serviced pitches; shwrs inc;
EHU (16A) metered; gas; lndry; shop 600m; rest, snacks; bar;
BBQ; cooking facs; playgrnd; pool 1km; bike hire; wifi; TV rm;
60% statics; dogs €2; Eng spkn; adv bkg; quiet; red LS/long
stay/CKE/CCI. "Highly rec; helpful owners; warm welcome;
clean facs; pitches poss tight lge o'fits." ◆ € 24.00   2014*

SAARBURG *3B2* (4km NW Rural) *49.62010, 6.54274*
Camping Landal Warsberg, In den Urlaub, 54439 Saarburg
[(06581) 91460; fax 914646; warsberg@landal.de;
www.landal.de] Fr Trier foll B51 S and turn at rd sp
Saarbrücken at Konz, after 25km on leaving Ayl vill turn R sp
Saarburg. Cont over bdge turn R sp Centre. At rndabt turn L
thro cent, at rndabt L into rd sp Warsburg, after 300m turn
L uphill sp Landal. V lge, mkd pitch, pt sl, pt shd; wc; chem
disp; mv service pnt; baby facs; shwrs inc; EHU (6A) inc; gas;
lndry; shop; rest, snacks; bar; BBQ; playgrnd; htd, covrd pool;
tennis; bike hire; games rm; entmnt high ssn; dogs €3; site clsd
1300-1500; poss noisy, quiet at far end; ccard acc. "Excel;
gd san facs; chem disp diff to use; excel pool; chairlift to attractive
town cent; gd views; many activities all ages." ◆ 3 Apr-9 Nov.
€ 32.00   2012*

SAARLOUIS *3B2* (2km NW Urban) *49.31833, 6.73972*
Campingpark Saarlouis Dr Ernst Dadder, Marschall-Ney-
Weg 2, 66740 Saarlouis [(06831) 3691; fax 7648011; info@
campingplatz-saarlouis.de; www.campingplatz-saarlouis.
de] Exit A620/E29 junc 2. Foll sp to city cent. At 500m approx
turn L at traff lts sp 'Schiffanlegestelle'. At 500m approx site
on R. Med, pt shd; wc; mv service pnt; shwrs inc; EHU (16A)
€2.30 or metered; gas; lndry; shop 500m; rest, snacks; htd
pool 150m; 30% statics; dogs €0.60; Eng spkn; adv bkg;
quiet; ccard acc; red long stay/snr citizens/CKE/CCI. "Castles,
Roman remains, ruins & forest rds at Saarland & Saarbrücken;
beautifully situated; conv for A8; 10min walk to town; friendly,
helpful owner; gd rest." 15 Mar-31 Oct. € 19.00   2015*

SAARLOUIS *3B2* (11km NW Rural) *49.36732, 6.66043*
Camping Siersburg, Zum Niedwehr 1, 66780 Siersburg
[(06835) 2100; fax 2247; info@campingplatz-siersburg.de;
www.campingplatz-siersburg.de] Fr Saarlouis, leave A8 at
junc 7, foll Rehlingen, turn off to Siersburg. Foll sp in Siersburg
for site thro town to o'skirts. Lge, mkd pitch, pt shd; wc; chem
disp; shwrs €1; EHU (16A); lndry (inc dryer); rest; snacks; BBQ
playgrnd; games area; wifi; dogs €2; twin axles; Eng spkn;
quiet. "Spacious site in rv Nied; walking & cycling rtes nrby;
ruined castle in town; vg." 1 Apr-31 Oct. € 19.00   2015*

ST GOAR AM RHEIN see Oberwesel *3B2*

ST GOARSHAUSEN *3B2* (4km S Rural) *50.14021, 7.73469*
Campingplatz auf der Loreley, Auf de Loreley 5, 56346
Bornich [(06771) 802697; fax 802698; info@loreley-
camping.de; www.loreley-camping.de] Fr St Goarshausen
on E bank of Rhine, take minor, steep rd to Bornich for 2.5km.
Turn R twds Loreley rock, site on L 1km downhill. Med, mkd
pitch, pt sl, pt shd; htd wc; chem disp; shwrs inc; EHU (16A)
metered + conn fee; lndry (inc dryer); shop 2km; rest, snacks;
bar; BBQ; playgrnd; htd, covrd pool; wifi; 20% statics; dogs
€1.50; Eng spkn; quiet; CKE/CCI. "Lovely, peaceful, spacious
site with views of Rv Rhine; gd, clean san facs; gd bar & rest;
friendly, helpful owner with fund of local knowledge."
1 Mar-31 Oct. € 19.00   2010*

ST LEON ROT see Wiesloch *3C3*

ST MARTIN see Neustadt *3C2*

ST PETER see Freiburg im Breisgau *3B4*

SALEM *3D4* (2.6km NE Rural) *47.76926, 9.30693* **Gern-**
Campinghof Salem, Weildorferstrasse 46, 88682 Salem-
Neufrach [(07553) 829695; fax 829694; info@campinghof-
salem.de; www.campinghof-salem.de] Site well sp on all
app to Neufrach on rvside. Med, mkd pitch, pt sl, unshd; htd
wc; chem disp; baby facs; shwrs inc; EHU (16A) €2; gas; lndry
(inc dryer); rest, snacks 2km; bar; BBQ; cooking facs; playgrnd;
htd, covrd pool 4km; lake sw nr; tennis; games rm; internet;
cab/sat TV; 5% statics; dogs €2 (not Jul/Aug); phone; bus; poss
cr; Eng spkn; adv bkg; quiet; ccard acc; CKE/CCI. "Excel touring
base for Lake Constance away fr busy lakeside sites; barrier clsd
1230-1500 & 2200-0700; avoid pitches facing recep - noise &
dust; gd, clean san facs; friendly, helpful, young owners; gd for
families; vg." 1 Apr-31 Oct. € 17.50   2010*

⊞ **SALZHEMMENDORF** *1D3* (9km S Rural) *52.00390,*
9.64302 **Campingpark Humboldtsee, Humboldtsee 1,**
31020 Salzhemmendorf-Wallensen [(05186) 957140;
fax 957139; info@campingpark-humboldtsee.se;
www.campingpark-humboldtsee.de] E fr Hameln on B1,
at Hemmendorf turn S twd Salzhemmendorf & Wallensen, site
sp 2km SE of Wallensen. V lge, hdg/mkd pitch, pt shd; htd wc;
chem disp; mv service pnt; baby facs; shwrs €0.50; EHU (6A)
inc; lndry (inc dryer); shop & 2km; rest, snacks; cooking facs;
playgrnd; pool 3km; paddling pool; lake sw & beach; fishing;
boat hire; games rm; entmnt; 60% statics; dogs €2; adv bkg;
quiet; ccard acc; red snr citizens/CKE/CCI. "Gd facs for families;
Hameln (Hamlin) 30km." € 22.50   2011*

SCHIERKE see Braunlage *2E4*

⊞ **SCHILLINGSFURST** *3D3* (2km S Rural) *49.27353,*
10.26587 **Campingplatz Frankenhöhe, Fischhaus 2,**
91583 Schillingsfürst [(09868) 5111; fax 959699; info@
campingplatz-frankenhoehe.de; www.campingplatz-
frankenhoehe.de] Fr A7/E43 exit junc 109; fr A6/E50 exit junc
49. Site situated bet Dombühl & Schillingsfürst. Med, pt sl, pt
shd; htd wc; chem disp; mv service pnt; baby facs; shwrs inc;
EHU (16A) €2.50 or metered + conn fee; gas; lndry; shop; rest;
playgrnd; lake sw 200m; wifi; 40% statics; dogs €1.50; phone;
poss cr; adv bkg; red long stay/CKE/CCI. "Very clean facs;
barrier clsd 1300-1500 & 2100-0700; poss unkempt early ssn
(2009); gd cycle paths." ◆ € 16.50   2011*

SCHILTACH 3C3 (800m W Urban) 48.29061, 8.33746
Camping Schiltach, Bahnhofstrasse 6, 77761 Schiltach
[(07836) 7289; fax 7466; campingplatz-schiltach@t-online.
de] Site on B294 sp on ent to vill; short, steep ent & sharp
turns. Sm, mkd pitch, pt shd; htd wc; chem disp; mv service
pnt; shwrs inc; baby facs; EHU (16A) metered + conn fee;
lndry (inc dryer); shop 500m; rest 200m; snacks; bar; BBQ;
playgrnd; covrd pool 2km; shgl beach adj; 2% statics; no dogs;
phone; recep clsd 1230-1430; train 200m; Eng spkn; adv
bkg; quiet; CKE/CCI. "Vg, clean, tidy site on rv bank adj indus
est; picturesque vill; disused rlwy bdge over pt of site, 2.6m
headrm; friendly staff." ♦ ltd. 1 Apr-10 Oct. € 15.00   2010*

SCHLECHING METTENHAM see Reit im Winkl 4F4

⊞ **SCHLEIDEN** 3B1 (6km NW Rural) 50.52752, 6.41195
Camping Schafbachmühle, 53937 Schleiden-Harperscheid
[(02485) 268; info@schafbachmuehle.de;
www.schafbachmuehle.de] Fr Schleiden take B258 twd
Monschau. In 3.5km turn R sp Schafbachmühle. Site in 2.5km
on L. Med, mkd pitch, hdstg, terr, pt shd; htd wc; chem disp;
mv service pnt; baby facs; shwrs €1; EHU (10A) metered +
conn fee; lndry (inc dryer); shop 800m; rest, snacks; bar; BBQ;
playgrnd; games area; 60% statics; dogs €2.20; phone; Eng
spkn; adv bkg; quiet. "Tranquil site; gd for touring Eifel, Mosel
Valley, Rhine Valley." ♦ € 15.00   2010*

⊞ **SCHLESWIG** 1D1 (12km E Coastal) 54.52563, 9.71543
Campingplatz am Missunder Fährhaus, Missunder
Fährstrasse 33, 24864 Brodersby [(04622) 626; fax 2543;
missunder-faehrhaus@t-online.de; www.missunder-
faehrhaus.de] Exit A7 junc 5; take B201 sp Kappeln; in 10km
turn R sp Scholderup & Brodersby; foll sp Missunder ferry. Site
100m bef ferry x-ing. Sm, sl, unshd; wc; chem disp; shwrs €1;
EHU (16A) €2.50; rest, snacks & bar adj; sailing & canoeing;
dogs; quiet; gd. "Watersports; deposit for wc key; rest rec."
€ 12.00   2009*

SCHLESWIG 1D1 (6km S Rural) 54.50111, 9.57027 Wikinger
Camping Haithabu, 24866 Haddeby [(04621) 32450;
fax 33122; info@campingplatz-haithabu.de;
www.campingplatz-haithabu.de] Leave A7/45 N & S
junc 6. Travel E two Schleswig & turn R onto B76 sp Kiel &
Eckernförde. Site on L in 2km sp. Med, pt shd; wc; chem disp;
mv service pnt; shwrs €0.50; EHU (4A) €2; lndry; shop 3km;
rest, snacks; playgrnd; lake sw adj; boating facs; dogs €2; poss
cr; Eng spkn; adv bkg; some rd noise; CKE/CCI. "Lovely site on
rv with lovely views; foot & cycle paths to Schleswig (4.5km) &
ferry; gd area for children; Schloss Gottorf worth visit; vg Viking
museum adj; shwrs newly refurb (2015)." 22 Mar-31 Oct.
€ 20.00   2015*

⊞ **SCHLUCHSEE** 3C4 (2km NW Rural) 47.82236, 8.16273
Campingplatz Wolfsgrund, Sägackerweg, 79859
Schluchsee [(07656) 573; fax 7759; info@schluchsee.de;
www.camping-schluchsee.de] Site sp fr rd B500 - rec app
fr N only. Lge, hdg/mkd pitch, terr, pt sl, pt shd; wc; chem disp;
mv service pnt; shwrs inc; EHU (10A) metered; gas; lndry (inc
dryer); shop 500m; rest, snacks; playgrnd; shgl beach & lake
sw 200m; games area; wifi; dogs €1.50; site clsd 1300-1500 &
2200-0800; poss cr; Eng spkn; quiet; ccard acc; red CKE/CCI.
"Fishing & sailing on lake adj; wintersports area; gd walking &
cycling country with excel views." € 27.50   2011*

⊞ **SCHOMBERG** 3C3 (2km N Rural) 48.79820, 8.63623
Höhen-Camping, Schömbergstrasse 32, 75328
Langenbrand [(07084) 6131; fax 931435; info@
hoehencamping.de; www.hoehencamping.de] Fr N exit A8
junc 43 Pforzheim, take B463 dir Calw. Turn R sp Schömberg &
foll sp Langenbrand. Med, hdg/mkd pitch, pt sl, pt shd; htd wc;
chem disp; fam bthrm; shwrs €0.50; EHU (10-16A) €3; lndry;
shop 200m; playgrnd; TV; 70% statics; dogs €2; phone; adv
bkg; quiet; CKE/CCI. "Clean, well-maintained site in N of Black
Forest; vg san facs; no recep - ring bell on house adj site ent;
blocks req for sl pitches." € 19.00   2013*

⊞ **SCHONAU IM SCHWARZWALD** 3B4 (1km N Rural)
47.79127, 7.90076 Camping Schönenbuchen,
Friedrichstrasse 58, 79677 Schönau [(07673) 7610;
fax 234327; info@camping-schoenau.de; www.camping-
schoenau.de] Fr Lörrach on B317 dir Todtnau for approx
23km. Site thro Schönau main rd on R on rvside, ent thro car
park. Narr access diff for l'ge o'fits. Med, hdg pitch, pt shd;
wc; chem disp; mv service pnt; baby facs; sauna; shwrs; EHU
inc (16A) (poss rev pol); lndry; shop 400m; rest; bar; playgrnd;
htd pool; sw & watersports adj; tennis; horseriding; bike hire;
70% statics; dogs €1; adv bkg; quiet; red long stay; CKE/CCI.
"Friendly staff; site poss not well-kept; gd walking & cycling;
lovely old town." ♦ € 28.00   2014*

"That's changed – Should
I let The Club know?"

If you find something on site that's different from
the site entry, fill in a report and let us know. See
www.caravanclub.co.uk/europereport.

⊞ **SCHONENBERG KUBELBERG** 3B2 (2km E Rural) 49.41172,
7.40479 Campingpark Ohmbachsee, Miesauerstrasse,
66901 Schönenberg-Kübelberg [(0673) 4001; fax 4002;
jungfleisch@campingpark-ohmbachsee.de;
www.campingpark-ohmbachsee.de] Exit A6/E50 junc 10
or 11 twd Schönenberg, site sp on Lake Ohmbach. Lge, mkd
pitch, terr, pt shd; htd wc; chem disp; mv service pnt; baby
facs; sauna; shwrs inc; EHU (6A) €2.50 or metered; lndry (inc
dryer); shop; rest, snacks; bar; BBQ; cooking facs; playgrnd;
htd pool; paddling pool; canoeing; boat & bike hire; tennis;
games area; horseriding 7km; golf driving range; wifi; entmnt;
50% statics; dogs €3; adv bkg; quiet. "Lake views fr some
pitches (ltd); excel facs & rest." ♦ € 19.50   2009*

SCHORTENS 1C2 (2km N Rural) 53.55055, 7.93722
Friesland Camping, Am Schwimmbad 2, 26419 Schortens
[(04461) 758727; fax 758933; info@friesland-camping.de;
www.friesland-camping.de] Exit A29 junc 5 onto B210
dir Schortens & Jever. Site on L past Schortens vill. Med, mkd
pitch, shd; htd wc; chem disp; mv service pnt; baby facs;
serviced pitches; shwrs inc; EHU (16A) €2.40 or metered; lndry
(inc dryer); shop 800m; snacks; cooking facs; playgrnd; pool;
sand beach 15km; lake sw adj; golf 8km; wifi; 20% statics;
dogs €3; phone; bus 800m; Eng spkn; adv bkg; quiet; red long
stay. "V pleasant site; gd facs; aquapark at Schortens & Jever
worth visit; vg." ♦ Easter- 24 Oct. € 20.00   2010*

SCHUTTORF *1B3* (2km N Rural) *52.33960, 7.22617* **Camping Quendorfer See, Weiße Riete 3, 48465 Schüttorf** [05923 90 29 39; fax 90 29 40; info@camping-schuettorf. de; www.camping-schuettorf.de] A1/A30, exit J4 Schüttorf-Nord. Or A31 exit J28 Schüttorf-Ost twds town cent. Foll sp to site. Sm, hdg/mkd pitch, unshd; htd wc; chem disp; mv service pnt; baby facs; fam bthrm; shwrs inc; EHU (16A); lndry (inc dryer); shop 2km; snacks; bar; playgrnd; sw adj; games area; dogs €2; bus 2km; twin axles; adv bkg; quiet; ccard acc; CCI. "Excel site; immac san facs; mostly fully serviced pitches; conv NH for ferries fr Holland; flat cycling & walking." ◆ 1 Apr-31 Oct. € 25.00   2014*

SCHWAAN *2F2* (3.6km S Rural) *53.92346, 12.10688* **Camping Schwaan, Güstrowerstrasse 17/Sandgarten 17, 18258 Schwaan** [(03844) 813716; fax 814051; info@ campingplatz-schwaan.de; www.campingplatz-schwaan. de] Fr A20 exit junc 13 to Schwaan, site sp. Fr A19 exit junc 11 dir Bad Doberan & Schwaan. Site adj Rv Warnow. Lge, mkd pitch, pt shd; htd wc; mv service pnt; sauna; baby facs; shwrs inc; EHU (16A) €2.20 or metered; lndry (inc dryer); shop high ssn; supmkt 800m; rest, snacks; bar; cooking facs; playgrnd; canoeing; boat & bike hire; tennis 700m; games area; wifi; entmnt; TV; 30% statics; dogs €2; site clsd 21 Dec-4 Jan; adv bkg; quiet. "Pleasant rvside site; gd touring base; tight app thro Schwaan town (esp fr N)." ◆ 1 Mar-31 Oct. € 26.50   2014*

SCHWABISCH HALL *3D3* (2km S Urban) *49.09868, 9.74288* **Camping am Steinbacher See, Mühlsteige 26, 74523 Schwäbisch Hall-Steinbach** [(0791) 2984; fax 9462758; thomas.seitel@t-online.de; www.camping-schwaebisch-hall.de] Fr A6/E50 exit junc 43 fr W or junc 42 fr E & foll permanent diversion via new B19 rd. At x-rds at lge Lidl store, turn L twds town and foll sp S to Comburg & site. Med, mkd pitch, pt shd; htd wc; chem disp; mv service pnt; shwrs €0.50; EHU (10A) metered + conn fee; lndry; shop 3km; rest 200m; snacks; bar; BBQ; playgrnd; bike hire; 50% statics; dogs €2; clsd 1300-1500; poss cr; Eng spkn; adv bkg; red CKE/CCI. "Lovely well kept idiosyncratic site; friendly; walking dist to interesting medieval town; cycle track to town." ◆ 15 Mar-15 Oct. € 22.00   2015*

SCHWANGAU see Füssen *4E4*

SCHWEDENECK see Gettorf *1D1*

SCHWEICH *3B2* (1.6km S Urban) *49.81459, 6.75019* **Campingplatz zum Fährturm, Am Yachthafen, 54338 Schweich** [(06502) 91300; fax 913050; camping@kreusch. de; www.kreusch.de] Fr exit 129 or 130 fr A1/E44. Site by rv bank by bdge into town, sp. Lge, mkd pitch, pt shd; wc; chem disp; mv service pnt; baby facs; shwrs; EHU (16A) €1.60; gas; lndry (inc dryer); supmkt 0.5km; rest; snacks; bar; BBQ; playgrnd; sports cent with pool adj; watersports; bike hire; dogs; bus to Trier nr; twin axles; Eng spkn; adv bkg; quiet; red LS; CKE/CCI. "Poss long wait for conn to EHU; poss long walk to san facs - dated; m'van o'night area outside site - no EHU; on banks of Mosel with cycle rte; yacht/boating harbour adj; vg." ◆ 5 Apr-20 Oct. € 20.00   2014*

SCHWEPPENHAUSEN *3B2* (1km N Rural) *49.9340, 7.79180* **Campingplatz Aumühle, Naheweinstraße 65, 55444 Schweppenhausen** [06724 602392; fax 601610; info@camping-aumuehle.de] Fr A61 take exit 47 - Waldlaubersheim. Foll signs to Schweppenhausen. Sp to camp site. Med, mkd pitch, pt shd; htd wc; chem disp; baby facs; shwrs inc; EHU (10A); lndry; rest; snacks; bar; playgrnd; 50% statics; dogs; twin axles; Eng spkn; adv bkg; poss cr; quiet; CKE/CCI. "Gd site; cycle rtes fr site." 1 Apr-31 Oct. € 20.50   2015*

⊞ **SCHWERIN** *2E2* (10km N Rural) *53.69725, 11.43715* **Ferienpark Seehof, Am Zeltzplatz 1, 19069 Seehof** [(0385) 512540; fax 5814170; info@ferienparkseehof.de; www.ferienparkseehof.de] Take B106 N fr Schwerin for approx 5km: turn R at city boundary & site within 5km at end of vill, sp. Lge, pt sl, pt shd; wc; chem disp; mv service pnt; serviced pitches; shwrs €1; EHU (4A) inc (poss rev pol); gas; lndry; shop; rest, snacks; bar; playgrnd; lake sw & sand beach; windsurfing; sailing school; bike hire; entmnt; 30% statics; dogs €1; poss cr; adv bkg; quiet; ccard acc. "Lge pitches; vg." € 33.00   2015*

⊞ **SEEBURG** *2E4* (1km NW Rural) *51.49400, 11.69400* **Camping Seeburg am Süsser See, Nordstrand 1, 06317 Seeburg** [(034774) 28281; fax 41757; info@campingplatz-seeburg.de; www.campingplatz-seeburg.de] W fr Halle on B80 twd Eisleben, sp fr Seeburg. Site on N shore of Lake Süsser See. Lge, pt shd; wc; chem disp; shwrs €1; EHU (16A) €1.10; rest 500m; playgrnd; lake sw; fishing; 95% statics; dogs €1.20. "Attractive, busy site by lake; excel base for medieval towns nr & 'Martin Luther country'; gd; nice site by lake; not many pitches; new immac facs (2015)." ◆ € 19.60   2015*

⊞ **SEESHAUPT** *4E4* (4km E Rural) *47.82651, 11.33906* **Camping beim Fischer, Buchscharnstrasse 10, 82541 St Heinrich** [(08801) 802; fax 913461; info@camping-beim-fischer.de; www.camping-beim-fischer.de] Exit A95 junc 7 & foll sp Seeshaupt for 1.6km to T-junc. Turn R, site in 200m on R. Med, mkd pitch, unshd; htd wc; chem disp; baby facs; shwrs inc; EHU (16A) metered; gas; lndry; rest, snacks, bar 200m; playgrnd; lake sw adj; games area; TV; 45% statics; dogs free; bus adj; Eng spkn; adv bkg; quiet; CKE/CCI. "Well-maintained, friendly, lovely, honest family-run site; immac facs; conv Munich & Bavarian castles." ◆ € 23.50   2014*

SENHEIM see Cochem *3B2*

SESSLACH see Coburg *4E2*

⊞ **SIGMARINGEN** *3D4* (2km SW Urban) *48.08366, 9.20794* **Erlebnis-Camp Sigmaringen, Georg-Zimmererstrasse 6, 72488 Sigmaringen** [(07571) 50411; fax 50412; info@ outandback.de; www.erlebnis-camp.de] App town fr N or SW, ent town over Danube bdge, turn R into car pk (camp sp). To far end of car park, turn R in front of supmkt. Ent camp fr far end. Site adj to stadium by rv, sp fr town. Med, pt shd; wc; chem disp; mv service pnt; shwrs €0.50; EHU (6-16A) €3; lndry; shop 300m; rest; snacks 300m; playgrnd; htd pool 300m; bike hire; internet; 10% statics; dogs €1; CKE/CCI. "On Danube cycle way; gd outdoor activities; lovely site; clsd 12-1400; new facs; new ent." ◆ € 26.50   2015*

GERMANY

SIMMERATH *1A4* (8km E Rural) *50.61777, 6.37690* **Camping Rursee, Seerandweg 26, D 52152 Simmerath/Rurberg [(02473) 2365; info@camping-rursee.de; http://camping-rursee.de]** Fr Simmerath L166 to Kesternich; R on 266 for 1 km; then L on L166 twds Rurberg. L on L128 twds Woffelsbach then sp R to site. Sm, grassy, mkd pitch, unshd; wc; chem disp; shwr; EHU; lndry; shop; snacks; bar; games area. 1 Apr-Nov. € 21.00   2014*

⊞ **SIMMERATH** *1A4* (9km SE Rural) *50.56388, 6.33333* **Camping Hammer, An der Streng 7, 52152 Simmerath-Hammer [(02473) 929041; fax 937481; info@camp-hammer.de; www.camp-hammer.de]** Fr Monschau take B399 N for 5km to Imgenbroich, minor rd E to Hammer. Fr Simmerath take B399 SW for 2km L sp Hammer to site on R in vill. Med, pt shd; wc; chem disp; mv service pnt; shwrs €1; EHU (10A) €3; gas; lndry; shop & 5km; rest 800m; playgrnd; 60% statics; no dogs; quiet; cash only; CKE/CCI. "Excel rvside site; pleasant bistro; unique san facs! walking area, non-touristy." € 18.00   2011*

SIMONSBERG see Husum *1D1*

SIMONSWALD see Waldkirch *3C4*

SOEST *1C4* (12km S Rural) *51.47722, 8.10055* **Camping Delecke-Südufer, Arnsbergerstrasse 8, 59519 Möhnesee-Delecke [(02924) 8784210; fax 1771; info@campingplatz-moehnesee.de; www.campingplatz-moehnesee.de]** Exit A44/E331 at junc 56 onto B229 sp Arnsberg/Mohnesee. Cont to lake, cross bdge. At next junc turn L & site immed on L, sp. Med, hdg pitch, pt sl, unshd; wc; chem disp; mv service pnt; shwrs (inc); EHU (16A); snacks; bar; rest 800m; lndry; shop; playgrnd; lake sw & beach adj; boating; 50% statics; phone; no dogs; poss cr; quiet; clsd 1300-1500 & 2000-0800; Eng spkn; adv bkg; CKE/CCI. "Excel site on boating lake; san facs locked o'night; gd walking & sailing; v busy at w/ends; gd disable facs." ♦ 1 Apr-15 Oct. € 25.00   2015*

"I like to fill in the reports as I travel from site to site"

You'll find report forms at the back of this guide, or you can fill them in online at www.caravanclub.co.uk/europereport.

⊞ **SOLINGEN** *1B4* (6km S Rural) *51.13388, 7.11861* **Waldcamping Glüder, Balkhauserweg 240, 42659 Solingen-Glüder [(0212) 242120; fax 2421234; info@camping-solingen.de; www.camping-solingen.de]** Exit A1 junc 97 Burscheid onto B91 N dir Hilgen. In Hilgen turn L onto L294 to Witzhelden then R on L359 dir Solingen. Site sp in Glüder by Rv Wupper. Med, hdg/mkd pitch, some hdstg, unshd; htd wc; chem disp; shwrs inc; chem disp; EHU (6-10A) €3; gas; lndry; shop 3km; rest adj; snacks; bar; playgrnd; TV; 80% statics; dogs €2.30; bus; Eng spkn; quiet; CKE/CCI. "Beautiful location in wooded valley; clsd 1300-1500; resident owner; excel san facs; easy walk to Burg-an-der-Wupper Schloss - worth visit." € 27.40   2013*

⊞ **SOLTAU** *1D2* (3km N Rural) *53.00075, 9.8366* **Kur & Fereincamping Röders Park, Ebsmoor 8, 29614 Soltau [(05191) 2141; fax 17952; info@roeders-park.de; www.roeders-park.de]** Exit A7/E45 junc 45 onto B3 dir Soltau. Turn L onto B71 in Soltau cent, then R onto B3 sp Hamburg. Site sp on L at town boundary. Med, mkd pitch, pt shd; wc; chem disp; mv service pnt; some serviced pitches; shwrs inc; EHU (6A) metered + conn fee; gas; lndry; shop; rest, snacks; playgrnd; bike hire; 25% statics; dogs €2; office clsd 1300-1500; ccard acc; red CKE/CCI. "Delightful, family-run site; helpful staff; excel rest; vg san facs; gd walking nrby." ♦ € 23.50   2009*

SOLTAU *1D2* (13km SE Urban) *52.93487, 9.96786* **Südsee Camp, 29649 Wietzendorf [(5196) 345]** Exit a'bahn at Soltau Sud on rte 3 to Celle. After 3km turn L for Wietzendorf. Campsite on L, look for lge flag poles. Lge, pt shd; wc (cont); meals; snacks; shwrs; shop; EHU; sand beach; lake sw; poss cr; adv bkg; quiet. pony rides, gd walking, all watersports. 22 Dec-Oct. € 23.40   2011*

See advertisement inside the front cover

⊞ **SOLTAU** *1D2* (5km S Rural) *52.94801, 9.85403* **Freizeithof Imbrock, Imbrock 4, 29614 Soltau [(05191) 5202; fax 15960; www.camping-imbrock.de]** Exit A7/E45 junc 45 Soltau-Süd. Foll sp Soltau then Brock, site sp fr main rd. V lge, pt shd; wc; mv service pnt; baby facs; shwrs €0.50; EHU (10A) €2; lndry; shop; rest, snacks; playgrnd; lake sw; tennis; games area; 60% statics; dogs €1.50; quiet. "San facs poss stretched." € 16.00   2009*

SOMMERACH see Dettelbach *3D2*

⊞ **SONTHOFEN** *3D4* (1.5km SW Rural) *47.50636, 10.27353* **Camping an der Iller, Sinwagstrasse 2, 87527 Sonthofen [(08321) 2350; fax 68792; info@illercamping.de; www.illercamping.de]** Clearly sp fr Sonthofen Süd junc on B19; on Rv Iller. Med, mkd pitch, hdstg, unshd; wc; shwrs inc; chem disp; mv service pnt; EHU (16A) metered; gas; lndry; shop; rest 200m; snacks; bar; playgrnd; htd pool adj; dogs €2; clsd 1300-1500; some Eng spkn; adv bkg; quiet but some rlwy noise; CKE/CCI. "Scenic wintersports area; gd walking, cycling; excel, well-maintained facs; helpful owner; some rd noise; site quite bare; site designed on feng shui principles!" ♦ € 18.00   2011*

⊞ **SOTTRUM** *1D2* (5km SW Rural) *53.08335, 9.17697* **Camping-Paradies Grüner Jäger, Everinghauser Dorfstrsse 17, 27367 Sottrum/Everinghausen [(04205) 319113; fax 319115; info@camping-paradies.de; www.camping-paradies.de]** Exit A1 junc 50 at Stuckenborstel onto B75 dir Rotenburg. In approx 500m turn R & foll sp Everinghausen. Site in 4km. Med, mkd pitch, unshd; htd wc; chem disp; mv service pnt; baby facs; shwrs €0.15 per min; EHU (16A) €2.50; lndry; shop 6km; rest; bar; playgrnd; pool; paddling pool; 30% statics; dogs free; Eng spkn; some rd noise; CKE/CCI. "Excel NH." € 23.50   2011*

GERMANY

⊞ SPANGENBERG *1D4* (1km E Rural) *51.11373, 9.67391*
Campingplatz Municipal am Sportplatz, Jahnstrasse 23,
34286 Spangenberg [(05663) 222; fax 509026; service-
center@stadt-spangenberg.de; www.stadt-spangenberg.de]
Fr A7 exit sp Melsungen & take B487 to Spangenberg. Site
on SE of town, clearly visible fr rd. Narr app. Med, mkd pitch,
terr, unshd; htd wc; chem disp; shwrs inc; EHU (16A) metered;
lndry; supmkt 1km; cooking facs; playgrnd; pool & sports
complex adj; 60% statics; dogs; clsd 1300-1500; some rd
noise; CKE/CCI. "Historic old town; welcoming staff; gd clean
facs; gd walking/cycling; gd NH & longer." ♦ € 17.00   2010*

SPEYER *3C3* (3km N Rural) *49.33600, 8.44300* Camping
Speyer, Am Rübsamenwühl 31, 67346 Speyer
[(06232) 42228; fax 815174; info@camping-speyer.de;
www.camping-speyer.de] Fr Mannheim or Karlsruhe take
rd 9 to exit Speyer Nord dir Speyer. At 3rd traff lts turn L into
Auestrasse, then at 2nd rndabt L into Am Rübsamenwühl.
Site in 500m. Sm, some mkd pitch; shwrs €1; EHU €3; supmkt
500m; rest, snacks; bar; playgrnd; lake sw & sand beach;
90% statics; dogs €2; no adv bkg; quiet; red long stay. "Speyer
pleasant town, cathedral & Technik Museum worth visit; v basic
site; scruffy & not well-kept; fair NH/sh stay." 15 Mar-15 Oct.
€ 29.00   2014*

⊞ SPEYER *3C3* (1km SE Urban) *49.31250, 8.44916* Camping
Technik Museum, Am Technik Museum 1, Geibstrasse,
67346 Speyer [(06232) 67100; fax 6710 20; info@hotel-
speyer.de; www.hotel-speyer.de] Exit A61/E34 at junc
64, foll sp to museum. Med, unshd; htd wc; chem disp; mv
service pnt; shwrs inc; EHU inc (10A); shop 1km; rest, snacks,
bar adj; dogs free; phone (hotel); bus; poss cr; Eng spkn;
adv bkg. Ccard acc, 3 nights max stay; "Book in at hotel adj;
excel museum & IMAX cinema on site; conv Speyer cent and
cathedral; site unkept; excel san facs; 24hr CCTV controlled ent
gate." ♦ ltd. € 22.00   2015*

⊞ SPIEGELAU *4G3* (2km W Rural) *48.91737, 13.33150*
Camping am Nationalpark, Bergstrasse 44, 94518
Klingenbrunn [(08553) 727; fax 6930; info@camping-
nationalpark.de; www.camping-nationalpark.de]
Fr A3 exit 111 at Hengersberg onto B333 dir Schönberg, turn
N onto B85 (Regen-Passau) & foll sp Klingenbrunn. At T-junc
in vill cent R & bear L in 300m to site on R in 1km. Med,
mkd pitch, terr, pt shd; serviced pitches; mv service pnt; wc;
shwrs inc; chem disp; mv service pnt; EHU (16A) metered +
conn fee; lndry; shop 1km; rest; playgrnd; covrd pool; fishing;
horseriding 1km; ski lift 3km; entmnt; 15% statics; dogs €1;
site clsd 9 Nov-14 Dec; adv bkg; quiet; ccard acc; red CKE/CCI.
"Peaceful, family-run site." € 13.70   2010*

⊞ STADTKYLL *3B2* (1km S Rural) *50.33903, 6.53966*
Camping Landal Wirfttal, Wirftstrasse 81, 54589 Stadtkyll
[(06597) 92920; fax 929250; wirfttal@landal.de;
www.landal.de] Exit A1 onto B51 dir Prüm to Stadtkyll, site
well sp on minor rd to Schüller fr town cent. Fr SE app town on
B421 then foll sps. Lge, pt shd; htd wc; chem disp; mv service
pnt; baby facs; sauna; baby facs; shwrs inc; EHU (8A) inc; gas;
lndry (inc dryer); shop, rest, snacks; bar; playgrnd; htd pool adj;
paddling pool; waterslides; tennis; games area; horseriding
adj; bike hire; entmnt; TV; 30% statics; dogs €3; phone; adv
bkg; quiet; ccard acc. "Excel site; all facs htd & clean." ♦
€ 32.00   2009*

STADTSTEINACH see Kulmbach *4E2*

⊞ STAUFEN IM BREISGAU *3B4* (1.4km SE Rural)
47.87194, 7.73583 Ferien-Campingplatz Belchenblick,
Münstertälerstrasse 43, 79219 Staufen-im-Breisgau
[(07633) 7045; fax 7908; info@camping-belchenblick.de;
www.camping-belchenblick.de] Exit A5/E35 junc 64a
dir Bad Krozingen-Staufen-Münstertal. Avoid Staufen cent,
foll Münstertal sp. Camp on L 500m past Staufen. Visibility
restricted fr Münstertal dir. Lge, pt shd; wc; chem disp; mv
service pnt; baby facs; fam bthrm; sauna; shwrs inc; EHU (16A)
metered; gas; lndry (inc dryer); shop; rest 500m; snacks; bar;
BBQ area; sm htd indoor pool; playgrnd; public pool & tennis
nrby over unfenced rv via footbdge; bike hire; horseriding
500m; wifi; entmnt; games/TV rm; 60% statics; dogs €2.50;
no o'fits over 8m high ssn; phone; no veh access 1230-1500
& night time - parking area avail; poss cr; Eng spkn; adv bkg
rec high ssn; some rd & rlwy noise in day; no ccard acc; red LS/
CKE/CCI. "Well-run, family-owned site; some pitches sm; strict
pitching rules; beautiful area & Staufen pleasant town; beware
train app round blind corner at x-ing; gd walking, cycling,
horseriding; san facs tired, need refurbishing (2013); better
cheaper sites close by." ♦ € 30.00 SBS - G02   2015*

STECHOW *2F3* (6km N Rural) *52.65472, 12.42972*
Campingpark Buntspecht Ferchesar, Weg zum Zeltplatz 1,
14715 Stechow-Ferchesar [(03387) 490072; camping-park-
buntspecht@web.de; www.campingpark-buntspecht.de]
Fr Rathenow NE on B188 to Stechow, then turn L sp Ferchesar
& foll site sp to lakeside. Or fr A10 exit junc 26 sp Nauen &
take B5 for approx 25km to junc with B188 to Stechow. At
Stechow rurn R sp Ferchesar then as above. Lge, mkd pitch, pt
shd; htd wc; chem disp; mv service pnt; baby facs; private san
facs avail; shwrs inc; EHU (16A) €2; lndry (inc dryer); shop; rest,
snacks; BBQ; cooking facs; playgrnd; lake sw; fishing; boat,
canoe, bike hire; games area; wifi; 10% statics; dogs €3.50;
Eng spkn; adv bkg; quiet. "Pleasant, peaceful, family site; gd
walking/cycling in area." ♦ 1 Apr-31 Oct. € 23.00   2011*

STEINENSTADT *3B4* (200m W Urban) *47.76895, 7.55115*
Camping Vogesenblick, Eichwaldstrasse 7, 79395
Steinenstadt [(07635) 1846] Exit A5/E35 junc 65 Neuenburg-
am-Rhein. Turn S at traff lts for Steinenstadt, site sp. Sm, pt
shd; wc; chem disp; mv service pnt; shwrs €0.50; EHU (16A)
metered; lndry; shop, rest adj; bar; htd, covrd pool 5km;
20% statics; dogs €1.50; bus nr; poss cr; adv bkg; quiet.
"Peaceful, friendly site; gd cycling beside Rv Rhine; easy access
Black Forest, Freiburg etc; v quiet site and vill; petrol 2km."
15 Mar-31 Oct. € 20.50   2012*

STOCKACH *3C4* (7.5km SSW Rural) *47.80860, 8.97000*
Campinggarten Wahlwies, Stahringerstrasse 50, 78333
Stockach-Wahlwies [(07771) 3511; fax 4236; info@
camping-wahlwies.de; www.camping-wahlwies.de]
Exit A98 junc 12 Stockach West onto B313 to Wahlwies. In vill
turn L immed after level x-ing, site on R bef next level x-ing, sp.
Med, pt shd; wc; chem disp; mv service pnt; shwrs inc; EHU
(16A) €2; lndry; shop 1km; rest 1km; snacks; bar; lake sw 5km;
50% statics; dogs free; phone; poss cr; Eng spkn; adv bkg
rec bank hols; quiet; CKE/CCI. "Pleasantly situated, orchard
site 6km fr Bodensee; friendly, helpful staff; female san facs
inadequate; gd touring cent; gd local train service; excel cycle
tracks." 28 Mar-31 Dec. € 23.00   2014*

GERMANY

⊞ **STOCKACH** 3C4 (2.5km SW Urban) 47.84194, 8.99500
Camping Papiermühle, Johann Glatt Strasse 3, 78333
Stockach [(07771) 91651333; campingplatz@caramobil.de;
www.caramobil.de/stockach/freizeitpark]
Fr Stockach at junc rndabt of B31 & B313, turn L (E)
to Caramobil C'van Sales Depot. Site adj under same
management. Med, mkd pitch, some hdstg, pt sl, terr, pt shd;
htd wc; chem disp; mv service pnt; shwrs inc; EHU (6A) €2;
lndry (inc dryer); shop; rest adj; snacks; bar; BBQ; playgrnd;
50% statics; dogs €2.20; phone; bus 200m; poss cr; Eng spkn;
adv bkg; quiet; ccard acc; CKE/CCI. "Sep m'van area adj; v
clean facs; helpful staff; conv location for town; gd walking &
cycling; vg site." ♦ € 19.00   2013*

⊞ **STORKOW** 2G3 (6km NE Rural) 52.29194, 13.98638
Campingplatz Waldsee, 15526 Reichenwalde-Kolpin
[(033631) 5037; fax 59891; mail@campingplatz-waldsee.de;
www.campingplatz-waldsee.de] Fr A12/E30, exit junc 3
Storkow. Just bef ent Storkow, turn N twd Fürstenwalde. In
6km turn R leaving Kolpin, site sp. Med, pt sl, pt shd; wc; chem
disp; sauna; shwrs €0.50; EHU (16A) €2; lndry; shops 2km; rest
6km; rest 6km; snacks; bar; playgrnd; lake sw adj; bike hire;
60% statics; dogs €1; Eng spkn; adv bkg; quiet; ccard acc; red
CKE/CCI. "Gd san facs; haphazard pitching; conv NH en rte to/
fr Poland; gd cycling area; Bad Saarow lakeside worth visit; facs
dated (2012); staff friendly." € 16.00   2012*

STUHR see Bremen 1C2

⊞ **STUTTGART** 3D3 (15km NE Urban) 48.83111, 9.32222
Parkplatz am Hallenbad, An der Talaue, 71332
Waiblingen [(07151) 5001155; parkierungsgesellschaft@
waiblingen.de] Fr N exit A81/E41 junc 16 at Ludwigsburg
Süd, foll sp dir Remseck & Waiblingen. Fr S or E on B29 take
B14 to Waiblingen town cent. Foll sp sw pool, sports park &
parking. M'vans only. Sm, mkd pitch, hdstg, pt shd; wc; chem
disp; mv service pnt; water €1/80 litres; EHU €1/8 hrs; pool;
dogs; rd noise. "Fair NH." € 6.00   2010*

⊞ **STUTTGART** 3D3 (5km E Urban) 48.79395, 9.21911
Campingplatz Cannstatter Wasen, Mercedesstrasse
40, 70372 Stuttgart [(0711) 556696; fax 557454; info@
campingplatz-stuttgart.de; www.campingplatz-stuttgart.
de] Fr B10 foll sp for stadium & Mercedes museum & then
foll camping sp. Access poss diff when major events in park
adj. Lge, all hdstg, pt shd; htd wc; chem disp; mv service pnt;
serviced pitches; shwrs inc; EHU (16A) metered + conn fee;
lndry; shop 1.5km; rest; BBQ; playgrnd; pool 2km; dogs €3;
bus nr; stn 1.5km; poss v cr; Eng spkn; adv bkg; poss noise fr
local stadium; ccard acc; CKE/CCI. "Helpful staff; clean san facs
(2015); town cent best by train - tickets fr recep; cycle ride to
town thro park; Mercedes museum 15 mins walk; fr Sep site/
office open 0800-1000 & 1700-1900 only; site within low
emission zone; camping field for tents." ♦ € 22.00   2015*

SULZBERG see Kempten (Allgäu) 3D4

⊞ **SULZBURG** 3B4 (1.5km SE Rural) 47.83583, 7.72333
Terrassen-Camping Alte Sägemühle, Badstrasse 57, 79295
Sulzburg [(07634) 551181; fax 551182; info@camping-alte-
saegemuehle.de; www.camping-alte-saegemuehle.de]
Exit A5 junc 64b to Heitersheim & Sulzburg. Fr cent of
Sulzburg, foll camp sps SE past timber yard on rd to Bad
Sulzburg hotel. Sm, mkd pitch, terr, pt shd; htd wc; chem disp;
mv service pnt; shwrs inc; EHU (16A) metered + conn fee; gas
1km; lndry; shop; rest, snacks, bar 1.5km; BBQ; lake sw adj;
10% statics; dogs €2; Eng spkn; quiet; 10% red CKE/CCI.
"Excel san facs - poss long walk; v friendly, helpful owners site
van with tractor; restful site in beautiful hilly countryside; gd
walking, cycling." € 21.00   2011*

⊞ **SULZBURG** 3B4 (1km NW Rural) 47.84778, 7.69848
Camping Sulzbachtal, Sonnmatt 4, 79295 Sulzburg
[(07634) 592568; fax 592569; a-z@camping-sulzbachtal.de;
www.camping-sulzbachtal.de] Fr A5/E35 exit junc 64a Bad
Krozingen onto L120/L123 dir Staufen-in-Breisgau. Cont on
L125, site sp on L. Med, mkd pitch, hdstg, terr, pt shd; htd wc;
chem disp; mv service pnt; 65% serviced pitches; baby facs;
shwrs inc; EHU (16A) metered; lndry (inc dryer); shop 1km;
snacks; rest 1km; playgrnd; pool; tennis; wifi; 10% statics; dogs
€2.60; phone; m'van o'night facs; Eng spkn; adv bkg; quiet;
ccard acc; red long stay/CKE/CCI. "Gd base for S Black Forest
& Vosges; well laid-out site; clean facs; conv m'way; 45 mins to
Basel; helpful, pleasant owners; ask about bus/train pass; high
standards; well maintained; excel san facs; lge pitches; in wine
growing area; excel walks." ♦ € 38.00 (CChq acc)   2014*

SUTEL 2E1 (1km E Coastal) 54.33356, 11.06885
Campingplatz Seepark Sütel, 23779 Sütel [(04365) 7474;
fax 1027; info@camping-seekamp.de; www.seepark-
suetel.de] Fr B501 foll sp to Sütel; drive thro vill to beach &
site. V lge, mkd pitch, unshd; wc; chem disp; baby facs; shwrs
€0.50; EHU (16A) €2; lndry (inc dryer); shop, rest 500m; snacks;
bar; playgrnd; beach adj; 90% statics; dogs €1.50; quiet;
phone; adv bkg; CKE/CCI. "San facs poss inadequate if site full;
helpful owner." ♦ 1 Apr-3 Oct. € 14.00   2009*

SYLT ISLAND 1C1 Sites on Sylt Island are listed together
at the end of the Germany site entry pages.

⊞ **TENGEN** 3C4 (1km NW Rural) 47.82365, 8.65296 Hegau
Familien-Camping, An der Sonnenhalde 1, 78250 Tengen
[(07736) 92470; fax 9247124; info@hegau-camping.de;
www.hegau-camping.de] Exit A81 junc 39 thro Engen dir
Tengen, site sp. Lge, mkd pitch, hdstg, pt sl, pt shd; htd wc;
chem disp; mv service pnt; serviced pitches; baby facs; fam
bthrm; sauna; shwrs inc; EHU (16A) metered or €2; gas; lndry
(inc dryer); shop; supmkt 500m; rest, snacks; bar; playgrnd;
htd, covrd pool; paddling pool; lake sw; canoeing; tennis
adj; games area; games rm; bike hire; horseriding 2km; wifi;
entmnt; 40% statics; dogs €4 inc dog shwr; bus 500m; clsd
1230-1430; o'night area for m'vans; Eng spkn; adv bkg; quiet;
ccard acc; red long stay/LS/CKE/CCI. "Site of high standard;
fairly isolated; gd family facs; excel." ♦ € 35.00   2010*

⊞ **TIEFENSEE** *2G3* (1km E Rural) *52.68019, 13.85063*
Country-Camping Tiefensee, Schmiedeweg 1, 16259
Tiefensee [(033398) 90514; fax 86736; info@country-camping.de; www.country-camping.de] Site sp fr B158
on lakeside. Lge, hdg/mkd pitch, pt shd; htd wc; chem disp;
mv service pnt; sauna; baby facs; shwrs €0.50; EHU (16A)
metered or €2.50; lndry (inc dryer); shop; rest, snacks; bar;
BBQ; playgrnd; lake sw & beach adj (sep naturist area); fishing;
games area; internet; TV; 75% statics; dogs €1.50; sep car
park; o'night area for m'vans; clsd 1300-1500; poss cr; Eng
spkn; adv bkg; quiet; ccard acc; red long stay. "Family-owned
site; sep m'van pitches; gd cycling & walking; train to Berlin fr
Arensfeldt; working ship lift at Niederfinow; vg." ♦ € 20.00
(CChq acc) 2012*

⊞ **TITISEE NEUSTADT** *3C4* (7.6km SW Rural) *47.89516,
8.13789* Camping Bühlhof, Bühlhofweg 13, 79822 Titisee-
Neustadt [(07652) 1606; fax 1827; herta-jaeger@t-online.
de; www.camping-buehlhof.de] Take rd 31 out of Freiburg
to Titisee; R fork on ent Titisee; bear R to side of lake, site on
R after end of Titisee, up steep but surfaced hill, sharp bends.
Lge, mkd pitch, pt sl, terr, pt shd; wc; chem disp; mv service
pnt; serviced pitch; baby facs; shwrs €0.50; EHU (16A) €1.80;
gas; lndry (inc dryer); rest 300m; BBQ; playgrnd; htd pool
1km; tennis; 300m fr Lake Titisee (but no access); watersports;
wintersports area - ski lift 6km; boats for hire; horseriding;
wifi; 30% statics; dogs €2.30; recep 0700-2200; site clsd Nov
to mid-Dec; Eng spkn; ccard not acc; CKE/CCI. "Beautiful
situation on hillside above Lake Titisee; lower terr gravel &
50% statics; top terr for tents & vans without elec; pitches sm;
woodland walks; pleasant walk to town." € 17.00 2014*

TITISEE NEUSTADT *3C4* (8km SW Rural) *47.88996, 8.13273*
Natur-Campingplatz Weiherhof, Bruderhalde 26, 79822
Titisee-Neustadt [(07652) 1468; fax 1478; info@camping-
titisee.de; www.camping-titisee.de] Fr B31 Frieberg-
Donaueschingen, turn S into Titisee & fork R after car park on
R, foll sp Bruderhalde thro town. Site on L on lakeside. Lge,
shd; htd wc; chem disp; shwrs inc; EHU (10A) €2.50; lndry;
shop; rest, snacks; bar; playgrnd; pool 1km; lake sw adj; bike
hire; golf 2km; 20% statics; dogs €2; phone; poss cr; quiet;
CKE/CCI. "Site in woodland next to the lake; no mkd pitches
but ample rm; vg; trip to town along lakeside well worth a
visit." ♦ 1 May-15 Oct. € 23.00 2012*

⊞ **TITISEE NEUSTADT** *3C4* (8.6km SW Rural) *47.88633,
8.13055* Camping Bankenhof, Bruderhalde 31a, 79822
Titisee-Neustadt [(07652) 1351; fax 5907; info@camping-
bankenhof.de; www.camping-bankenhof.de]
Fr B31 Frieberg-Donaueschingen, turn S into Tittisee & fork R
after car park on R, foll sp Bruderhalde thro town. In 2.5km
fork L after youth hostel; foll sp to site in 200m. If app Titisee
fr Donauechingen (B31) do not take Titisee P sp exit but exit
with int'l camping sp only, then as above. Lge, mkd pitch,
hdstg, pt shd; wc; chem disp; mv service pnt; fam bthrm; shwrs
inc; EHU (10A) metered (poss rev pol); gas; lndry (inc dryer);
shop; rest; bar; playgrnd; lake sw adj; bike hire; wifi; entmnt
high ssn; boat-launching 200m; 20% statics; dogs €2.80 (free
in m'van area); shwr inc; o'night area for m'vans €12; poss cr;
Eng spkn; adv bkg; quiet; ccard acc; red CKE/CCI. "Gd walk to
town & in forest; lovely scenery; helpful staff; vg san facs; excel
rest; most pitches gravel; ask at recep for red/free tickets on
public transport; excel, well-run, clean site, some pitches narr."
♦ € 28.00 2015*

TITISEE NEUSTADT *3C4* (9km SW Rural) *47.88693, 8.13776*
Terrassencamping Sandbank, Seerundweg 9, 79822
Titisee-Neustadt [(07651) 8243 or 8166; fax 8286 or 88444;
info@camping-sandbank.de; www.camping-sandbank.de]
Fr rte 31 Freiberg-Donauschingen turn S into Titisee. Fork R
after car park on R, foll sp for Bruderhalde thro town. After
youth hostel fork L & foll sp at T junc. Gravel track to site. Lge,
mkd pitch, terr, mainly hdstg by lake; wc (htd); chem disp; mv
service pnt; baby facs; shwrs €0.50; EHU (16A) €1.40; lndry;
shop; rest, snacks; bar; playgrnd; lake sw; boating; bike hire;
50% statics; dogs €1.50; poss cr; Eng spkn; no adv bkg; quiet
but some rlwy noise; ccard acc; red long stay/CKE/CCI. "Ltd
touring pitches; steel pegs ess; clean, well-run, well laid-out
site in gd position; terr gives gd lake views; helpful owner; gd
welcome; larger pitches avail at extra cost; gd touring base
for Black Forest; gd walks round lake; lakeside walk into town
thru woods (approx 30 mins); ask for Konus card for free travel
on local buses; clsd 1200-1400; excel; rd to site tarmaced." ♦
1 Apr-19 Oct. € 32.40 2014*

⊞ **TODTNAU** *3C4* (6km NW Rural) *47.86400, 7.91670*
Feriencamping Hochschwarzwald, Oberhäuser Strasse 6,
79674 Todtnau-Muggenbrunn [(07671) 1288 or 530;
fax 95190; camping.hochscharzwald@web.de;
www.camping-hochschwarzwald.de]
Freiburg rd fr Todtnau past vill of Muggenbrunn; site ent at
top end of vill. Med, terr, pt sl, pt shd; htd wc; chem disp;
shwrs €0.50; EHU (10-16A) metered; gas; lndry; shop; rest,
snacks; playgrnd; htd, covrd pool 1km; tennis 1km; sm lake;
wintersports; 70% statics; dogs €1.50; sep car park winter ssn;
poss cr; quiet; red CKE/CCI. "Beautiful location; gd walking
area; sm pitches unsuitable lge o'fits; san facs stretched; helpful
staff." ♦ € 16.00 2011*

TORGAU *2F4* (2km S Rural) *51.54589, 12.98991*
Campingplatz am Grosser Teich, Turnierplatzweg, 04860
Torgau [(03421) 902875; SV_info@torgau.de;
www.torgau.de] S on B182 fr Torgau, turn R at site sp onto
Tunierplatzweg, site sp on L in 700m. Sm, pt shd; wc; shwrs;
EHU (10A) inc; shop 500m; pool; lake sw; quiet. "Sm, old san
facs block, but clean; pleasant hosts; lake famous for rare birds
& visiting beavers; conv Elbe cycle path." Mid-Apr to Mid-Oct.
€ 19.00 2009*

TRABEN TRARBACH see Bernkastel Kues *3B2*

⊞ **TRAUNSTEIN** *4F4* (8km SW Rural) *47.81116, 12.5890*
Camping Wagnerhof, Campingstrasse 11, 83346 Bergen
[(08662) 8557; fax 5924; info@camping-bergen.de;
www.camping-bergen.de] Exit A8/E52/E60 junc 110. On ent
Bergen take 2nd R turn (sp). Med, mkd pitch, pt shd; wc; chem
disp; mv service pnt; shwrs €0.50; EHU (16A) metered; lndry;
shop on site & 500m; rest 400m; playgrnd; htd pool adj; shgl
beach 10km; tennis; 30% statics; dogs €2; site clsd 1230-1500;
some Eng spkn; adv bkg; quiet; debit & euro card acc; red
long stay; CKE/CCI. "Excel, v clean, pleasant site in beautiful
location; helpful owner; when not full owner tries to offer
pitches with empty pitches adjoining; conv a'bahn; cable car to
Hockfelln." € 22.00 2014*

⊞ **TRAVEMUNDE** *2E2* (4km SW Rural) *53.94196, 10.84417*
Camping Ivendorf, Frankenkrogweg 2, 23570 Ivendorf
[(04502) 4865; fax 75516] Fr A1 exit junc 19 take B226 to
Ivendorf, then B75 dir Travemünde, site well sp. Med, mkd
pitch, pt shd; wc; chem disp; baby facs; shwrs inc; EHU €3.50
or metered; lndry (inc dryer); shop; rest 200m; playgrnd; pool
4km; 10% statics; dogs €2; train 2km; poss cr; CKE/CCI. "Sep
disabled pitches; conv ferries to/fr Sweden; easy access to
Lübeck, a beautiful city." ♦ € 23.00   2010*

TREIS KARDEN see Cochem *3B2*

⊞ **TRENDELBURG** *1D4* (1km S Rural) *51.57250, 9.42416*
**Campingplatz Trendelburg, Zur Alten Mühle, 34388
Trendleburg [(05675) 301; fax 5888; conradi-camping@t-
online.de; www.campingplatz-trendelburg.de]**
Enter Trendelburg fr Karlshafen on B83 turn R immed bef x-ing
Rv Diemel, site on L in 800m. Sm, pt shd; wc; chem disp; baby
facs; shwrs €0.50;; EHU (16A) metered + conn fee; gas; lndry;
shop; rest, snacks; bar; playgrnd; canoeing in adj rv; tennis;
40% statics; dogs €2.20; poss cr; adv bkg; quiet; 10% red
CKE/CCI. "Pleasant, rvside site." ♦ € 12.00   2011*

TRIER *3B2* (2km S Urban) *49.74385, 6.62523* **Camping
Treviris, Luxemburgerstrasse 81, 54290 Trier
[(0651) 8200911; fax 8200567; info@camping-treviris.de;
www.camping-treviris.de]** On E side of Rv Mosel
on A1/A603/B49/B51 cross to W side of rv on Konrad
Adenauerbrücke. Cont in R lane & foll sp Koln/Aachen -
Luxemburgerstrasse. In 500m turn R to site, site on R. Well
sp fr W bank of rv. Med, mkd pitch, pt shd; wc; chem disp;
mv service pnt; baby facs; shwrs inc; EHU (6A) €2.90; lndry
(inc dryer); shop 500m; rest, snacks; bar; BBQ; playgrnd; dogs
€1.30; bus 200m; poss cr; site clsd 1-10 Jan; quiet; ccard acc;
CKE/CCI. "Cycle/walk to town cent; m'van park adj open all
yr - ltd facs; clean, modern san facs; swipe card for all facs; elec
pylon in cent of site; gd touring base; gd sh stay/NH." ♦ ltd.
15 Mar-15 Nov. € 29.50   2014*

TRIER *3B2* (8.4km SW Rural) *49.70460, 6.57398* **Camping
Konz, Saarmünding, 54329 Konz [(06501) 2577; fax 947790;
camping@campingplatz-konz.de; www.campingplatz-
konz.de]** On B51 S of rv at rndabt just bef rv x-ing, go L & foll
sp Camping Konz (not Konz-Könen). Do not go into Konz. Med,
mkd pitch, pt shd; wc; mv service pnt; shwrs €1; EHU metered
+ conn fee; lndry rm; shops 500m; rest, snacks; playgrnd;
watersports; dogs €0.70; Eng spkn; some rd noise. "Conv NH/
sh stay for Trier - cycle rte or public transport; facs clean; poss
flooding; sm pitches." 15 Mar-15 Oct. € 15.00   2014*

TRIER *3B2* (9km SW Rural) *49.70555, 6.55333* **Campingplatz
Igel, Moselstrasse, 54298 Igel [(06501) 12944; fax 601931;
info@camping-igel.de; www.camping-igel.de]** SW on A49
Luxemburg rd fr Trier; in cent of Ige vill, turn L by Sparkasse
Bank, thro narr tunnel (3.6m max height); in 200m turn L along rv
bank; site 300m on L; café serves as recep. Med, pt shd; htd wc;
chem disp; mv service pnt; shwrs €1; EHU (6A) €2 (poss rev pol);
lndry; shop in vill; rest; bar; playgrnd; fishing lakes adj; 90% statics
(sep area); dogs €2; bus/train to Trier & Roman amphitheatre;
poss cr; quiet but some noise fr rlwy & rv barges; CKE/CCI. "Excel,
friendly, well-run site; immac san facs; gd rest; ltd touring pitches;
rv bank foot & cycle path to Trier; conv Roman amphitheatre in
Trier; close to Luxembourg border for cheap petrol; conv for bus
into Trier." 1 Apr-31 Oct. € 24.50   2014*

⊞ **TRIER** *3B2* (15km W Rural) *49.75416, 6.50333*
**Campingplatz Alter Bahnhof-Metzdorf, Uferstrasse 42,
54308 Langsur-Metzdorf [(06501) 12626; fax 13796; info@
camping-metzdorf.de; www.camping-metzdorf.de]**
Fr W leave A64/E44 junc 15 & foll sp Wasserbillig; at T-junc
in Wasserbillig turn L onto B49 sp Trier. Ignore campsite in
500m. On ent Germany at end of bdge turn sharp L onto
B418 sp Ralingen/Metternich. In 3km turn L sp Metzdorf; in
750m turn L, site in 750m. Fr N (Bitburg) join A64 at junc 3 sp
Luxembourg, then as above. Fr SE on A1/E422 join A602 (Trier)
& approx 1km past end of a'bahn turn R over Kaiser Wilhelm
Bdge sp A64 Lux'bourg) & immed L at end of bdge. In 9km
in Wasserbillig turn R under rlwy bdge & keep R on B418 sp
Ralingen/Mesenich. In 3km turn L sp Melzdorf, in 750m turn
L, site in 750m. Do not use SatNav as approaching from the E
Med, pt sl, pt shd; htd wc; chem disp; mv service pnt; shwrs
€0.50; EHU (6-16A) €2 or metered (10A); lndry; rest; bar;
playgrnd; wifi; 75% statics; dogs €1; phone; bus 500m; m'van
o'night €9; poss cr; Eng spkn; adv bkg; quiet; ccard not acc;
red long stay/LS; CKE/CCI. "Rvside location; gd san facs but
poss long walk & steep climb; cycle rte to Trier; vg NH." ♦ ltd.
€ 17.50   2015*

⊞ **TRIPPSTADT** *3B2* (3.8km S Rural) *49.35145, 7.78117*
**Camping Freizeitzentrum Sägmühle, Sägmühle 1, 67705
Trippstadt [(06306) 92190; fax 2000; info@saegmuehle.de;
www.saegmuehle.de]** Fr Kaiserslautern take B270 or B48 S
for 14km, foll sp Trippstadt. Cont thro vill in dir of Karstal; site
sp. Lge, mkt pitch, pt sl, pt terr, pt shd; htd wc; chem disp;
mv service pnt; baby facs; fam bthrm; shwrs inc; EHU (16A)
inc; lndry (inc dryer); shop; rest, snacks; bar; playgrnd; lake
fishing; boat & bike hire; tennis; games area; wifi; emtmnt;
TV rm; 50% statics; dogs €2.60; site clsd 1 Nov-13 Dec; poss
cr; adv bkg; quiet. "Excel walking area; san facs on edge of
site nr tents vg & under-used but long way fr pitches; san
facs in cent stretched; c'van spares shop/dealer on site." ♦
€ 25.70   2011*

⊞ **TRITTENHEIM** *3B2* (4km N Urban) *49.84933, 6.89283*
**Camping Neumagen-Dhron, Moselstrasse 100, 54347
Neumagen-Dhron [(06507) 5249; fax 703290; camping-
neumagen@t-online.de; www.campingneumagen.de]**
On B53 fr Trittenheim twd Piesport. Immed after x-ing rv turn
R, then R again sp Neumagen. Site sp in vill on rvside. Med,
mkd pitch, pt shd; wc; chem disp; baby facs; shwrs inc; EHU
(6-10A) metered + conn fee; lndry (inc dryer); shop; rest,
snacks; bar; BBQ; playgrnd; boating; 40% statics; dogs free;
phone adj; poss cr; Eng spkn; adv bkg; quiet; CKE/CCI. "Gd
site clsd if rv in flood." € 19.00   2010*

TRITTENHEIM *3B2* (400m E Urban) *49.82472, 6.90305*
**Reisemobil/Wohnmobilstellplatz (Motorhome Camping),
Am Moselufer, 54349 Trittenheim [(06507) 5331; info@
trittenheim.de; www.trittenheim.de]** Fr Trier foll B53 dir
Bernkastel Kues. Site sp in Trittenheim dir Neumagen-Dhron,
on rvside. Sm, hdstg, pt sl, unshd; own san req; chem disp;
mv service pnt; EHU (16A) €2.50; shop, rest, snacks nr; dogs;
poss cr; quiet. "M'vans only; pleasant site poss clsd if rv floods;
warden calls for payment." 1 Apr-31 Oct. € 5.00   2013*

TRITTENHEIM *3B2* (400m SE Rural) *49.82131, 6.90201*
Campingplatz im Grünen, Olkstrasse 12, 54349
Trittenheim [(06507) 2148; fax 992089; cp-trittenheim@t-
online.de; www.camping-trittenheim.de] Foll B53 along
Rv Mosel fr Trier dir Bernkastel Kues; turn R in Trittenheim
at camping symbol sp Leiwen as if to go over rv & site on R
immed bef x-ring rv. Sm, mkd pitch, pt shd; wc; chem disp;
fam bthrm; shwrs inc; EHU €2.60 or metered + conn fee; lndry;
shop, rest in vill; 20% statics in ssn; dogs €1.50; recep clsd
1200-1500; Eng spkn; some rv noise; no ccard acc; CKE/CCI.
"Lovely, quiet site by Rv Mosel o'looking vineyards; boat trips;
beautiful area; excel, clean san facs; mv service pnt point in adj
vills; friendly owner; gd cycle paths; close to vill; infrequent bus
to Trier; interesting area; adv bkg fr March; no plastic materials
on lawns; close to local rests and seasonal boat cruises."
15 Apr-15 Oct. € 36.00   2013*

TRITTENHEIM *3B2* (5km S Rural) *49.80305, 6.89111*
Ferienpark Landal Sonnenberg, 54340 Leiwen
[(06507) 93690; fax 936936; sonnenberg@landal.de;
www.landal.de] Fr Bernkastel Kues or Trier on B53 take bdge
over Rv Mosel to S bank at Thörnich & foll sp Leiwen. Turn R to
top of hill, site sp. Long, winding ascent. Med, mkd pitch, terr,
pt shd; wc; chem disp; mv service pnt; sauna; shwrs inc; EHU
(6A) inc; gas; lndry; shop, rest, snacks; playgrnd; htd, cov'rd
pool; tennis; games rm; fitness rm; internet; statics; dogs €3;
poss cr; adv bkg; quiet; red CKE/CCI. "Vg family site with rv
views; excel san facs." ♦ 15 Mar-15 Nov. € 46.00   2013*

⊞ **TRITTENHEIM** *3B2* (8km S Rural) *49.79956, 6.92715*
Campingplatz Moselhöhe, Bucherweg 1, 54426
Heidenburg [(06509) 99016; fax 99017; vandijk1968@
hotmail.com; www.moselhohe.de] Leave A1/E422 at junc
131, foll sp twd Thalfang. After 4km take 2nd L over bdge sp
Heidenburg (2 hairpin bends). Thro Büdlich to Heidenburg,
foll sp in vill. Med, mkd pitch, terr, unshd; htd wc; chem disp;
mv service pnt; serviced pitch; shwrs inc; EHU (16A) metered;
lndry; shops 1km; snacks; rest 200m; bar; games rm; playgrnd;
paddling pool; 25% statics; dogs €1.70; site clsd mid-Nov to
mid-Dec; Eng spkn; adv bkg; quiet; ccard acc; red long stay;
CKE/CCI. "Excel, clean, hilltop site surrounded by meadows;
well-maintained; generous terraces; excel san facs; water &
waste disposal points nr every pitch; wonderful views; v friendly
owner; conv Rv Mosel attractions 4km." ♦ € 19.00   2015*

TUBINGEN *3C3* (5km SW Rural) *48.51008, 9.03525*
Neckarcamping Tübingen, Rappenberghalde 61,
72070 Tübingen [(07071) 43145; fax 793391; mail@
neckarcamping.de; www.neckarcamping.de] B28 to
Tübingen, site well sp fr main rds. Site on N bank of Rv Neckar.
Med, pt shd; wc; chem disp; mv service pnt; shwrs inc; EHU
(6A) metered + conn fee (rev pol); lndry; shop, rest, snacks;
playgrnd; bike hire; 70% statics; dogs €1.50; clsd 1230-1430
& 2200-0800; noisy at w/end; red CKE/CCI. "Easy walk to
attractive old town & lge pool complex; Neckar cycle path rn;
cramped pitches; NH only; bus stop nr camp ent." ♦
1 Apr-30 Oct. € 27.00   2015*

UBERLINGEN *3D4* (3km SE Rural) *47.75186, 9.19315*
Campingplatz Nell, Zur Barbe 7, 88662 Überlingen-
Nussdorf [(07551) 4254; info@campingplatz-nell.de;
www.campingplatz-nell.de] Exit B31 to Nussdorf. In vill
cent turn L under rlwy bdge at 2nd campsite sp, site on R on
lakeside. Sm, pt shd; wc; chem disp; snacks; shwrs €0.50; EHU
(6A) metered; lndry rm; shop, rest, snacks, bar 200m; BBQ;
shgl beach & lake sw adj; no dogs; adv bkg; poss cr; quiet.
"Beautifully-kept site; friendly owner; all amenities nr; gd
cycling; excel; lge plots; ltd places for tourers so arrive early."
Easter-20 Oct. € 21.00   2014*

UBERLINGEN *3D4* (3km NW Rural) *47.77081, 9.13813*
Campingplatz Überlingen, Bahnhofstrasse 57, 88662
Überlingen [tel/fax (07551) 64583; info@campingpark-
ueberlingen.de; www.campingpark-ueberlingen.de]
Heading SE on B31, bef Überlingen turn R at sp Campingplatz
Goldbach down slip rd; after 1.75km turn R; foll rd parallel
with rlwy; after level x-ing site immed on R by lakeside. Lge,
pt sl, pt shd; htd wc; chem disp; mv service pnt; shwrs €0.50;
EHU (16A) metered; gas; lndry; shop, rest, snacks; bar; BBQ;
playgrnd; lake sw & boating adj; 30% statics; dogs €2.50; bus;
ltd Eng spkn; no adv bkg; rd & rlwy noise; red long stay/snr
citizens/LS; no ccard acc; CKE/CCI. "Extra for lake pitches; high
ssn poss diff for lge c'vans to manoeuvre; gd rest; strict rule no
vehicles in after 2230; rec arr early to secure pitch."
1 Apr-9 Oct. € 25.00   2011*

UBERLINGEN *3D4* (14km NW Rural) *47.81783, 9.03856*
Camping See-Ende, Radolfzellerstrasse 23, 78346
Bodman-Ludwigshafen [(07773) 937518; fax 937529;
info@see-ende.de; www.see-ende.de] Exit A98/E54 junc
12 onto B34, site sp. Med, pt sl, pt shd; wc; chem disp; mv
service pnt; shwrs inc; EHU (16A) metered + conn fee; gas;
lndry; shop; rest 1.5km snacks; gas; lake sw & shgl beach;
50% statics; no dogs; Eng spkn; quiet; ccard acc; CKE/CCI.
"Excel position on lake; poor san facs; fair NH." 1 May-30 Sep.
€ 19.50   2009*

UBERSEE *4F4* (4km N Rural) *47.8412, 12.47166* Chiemsee-
Campingplatz Rödlgries, Rödlgries 1, 83236 Übersee-
Feldwies [(08642) 470; fax 1636; info@chiemsee-camping.
de; www.chiemsee-camping.de] Exit A8/E52 junc 108
Übersee, foll sp Chiemseestrand, veer L at wooden sign of sites.
V lge, some hdstg, pt shd; 50% serviced pitch; htd
wc; chem disp; mv service pnt; shwrs inc; EHU (16A) metered
+ conn fee; gas; lndry; shop, rest, snacks; bar; playgrnd; sand/
shgl beach; lake sw; boating; entmnt & dogs €2.50 (July/Aug
by agreement only); phone; train 3km; poss cr w/end; adv bkg;
quiet but some rd noise. "Superb facs; vg for children; highly
rec; extra for lakeside/serviced pitches; vg touring base; v conv
nr A8; cycle track around lake; excel; lge level pitches." ♦
1 Apr-31 Oct. € 32.50   2015*

UCKERITZ *2G1* (2km E Coastal) *54.01666, 14.06833*
Naturcamping Ückeritz (Part Naturist), Strandstrasse,
17459 Ückeritz [(038375) 2520; fax 25218;
kv.campingplatz@ueckeritz.de; www.campingplatz-
ueckeritz.de] Sp fr B111. V lge, pt shd; wc; chem disp; mv
service pnt; shwrs €1; EHU (10A) metered + conn fee; lndry
(inc dryer); shop; rest, snacks; bar; playgrnd; sand beach (sep
naturist area); games area; bike hire; 60% statics; dogs €3;
phone; bus 500m; poss cr; adv bkg; poss noisy high ssn. ♦
Easter-31 Oct. € 21.00   2010*

GERMANY

UFFENHEIM *3D2* (1km W Urban) *49.54426, 10.2248*
Naturcamping am Freibad, Sportstrasse, 97215 Uffenheim
[(09842) 1568; fax (09381) 716821; maempel-volkach@t-online.de] Fr A7/E43 exit junc 105 onto B13 dir Uffenheim,
site sp. Med, hdg pitch, pt shd; wc; chem disp; shwrs inc;
EHU (16A) €3 or metered + conn fee; lndry; shops 1km; rest
300m; snacks; bar; pool adj; dogs €1; adv bkg; quiet; CKE/CCI.
"Charming town; excel site; quite, v friendly CL type site; gd
cycling area." 1 May-15 Sep. € 15.60   2011*

⊞ **UFFENHEIM** *3D2* (10km W Rural) *49.52277, 10.12583*
Camping Paradies Franken, Walkershofen 40, 97215
Simmershofen [(09848) 969633; camping-paradies-franken@web.de; www.camping-paradies-franken.de]
Fr N exit A7 junc 105 Gollhofen or fr on B13 to Uffenheim. In
Uffenheim turn W thro Adelhofen to Simmershofen, then turn
L twd Walkershofen, site sp. Med, mkd pitch, pt shd; htd wc;
mv service pnt; baby facs; shwrs; EHU inc; lndry (inc dryer);
shop; rest, snacks; bar; BBQ; playgrnd; htd pool nr; games
area; bike hire; wifi; some statics; dogs €1.50; adv bkg; quiet.
"Interesting area; gd touring base; gd rest, cycling gd." ♦
€ 23.00   2012*

"We must tell The Club about that great site we found"

Get your site reports in by mid-August and we'll do our best to get your updates into the next edition.

URNSHAUSEN *1D4* (2km NE Rural) *50.74308, 10.20200*
Camping Am Schönsee, Schönsee, 36457 Urnshausen
(Thüringen) [(036964) 7451] Exit B285 at Urnshausen; turn
L sp Schönesee; site in 2km at end of rd/track. Med, sl, pt
shd; wc; chem disp; shwrs €0.50; EHU inc; shop 2km; rest,
snacks; BBQ (charcoal); playgrnd; lake sw adj; 30% statics;
dogs; bus 2km; adv bkg; quiet. "Rustic site adj sm lakes; basic,
clean san facs; gd walking in woods; gd value; gd." May-Oct.
€ 12.00   2009*

URZIG see Wittlich *3B2*

⊞ **VLOTHO** *1C3* (5km NE Rural) *52.17388, 8.90666*
Camping Sonnenwiese, Borlefzen 1, 32602 Vlotho
[(05733) 8217; fax 80289; info@sonnenwiese.com;
www.sonnenwiese.com] Fr S exit A2 junc 31 to Vlotho;
cross rv bdge (Mindenerstrasse) & in 500m turn R into
Rintelnerstrasse to site - 2 sites share same access. Lge, some
hdstg, unshd; htd wc; chem disp; mv service pnt; baby facs;
some serviced pitches inc private san facs; shwrs inc; EHU (10A)
inc; lndry (inc dryer); shop; rest, snacks; bar; BBQ; playgrnd;
paddling pool; lake sw; games rm; wifi; entmnt; cab TV;
75% statics; dogs €2.20; phone; bus/train 4km; Eng spkn; adv
bkg; quiet; CKE/CCI. "Excel site." ♦ € 30.50   2014*

VOHL HERZHAUSEN see Korbach *1C4*

WAGING AM SEE *4F4* (2km NE Rural) *47.94333, 12.74741*
Strandcamping Waging-am-See, Am See 1, 83329
Waging-am-See [(08681) 552; fax 45010; info@
strandcamp.de; www.strandcamp.de] Exit A8 junc 112 to
Traunstein, then foll sp to Waging-am-See; in vill site sp on rd
to Tittmoning. V lge, hdg/mkd pitch, pt shd; wc; chem disp;
mv service pnt; some serviced pitches; baby facs; shwrs inc;
EHU (10A) metered + conn fee; gas; lndry; shop; rest, snacks;
bar; playgrnd; shgl beach & lake sw adj; sailing; windsurfing;
fishing; tennis; games area; bike hire; wifi; entmnt;
30% statics; dogs €2.90 (not acc Jul & Aug); site clsd 1200-1400; adv bkg; quiet; 10% red long stay; CKE/CCI. "Excel,
clean, family site; gd cycling country; well-equipped shop." ♦
1 Apr-31 Oct. € 23.60   2013*

WAHLHAUSEN see Witzenhausen *1D4*

WALDBREITBACH *3B1* (1.5km NE Rural) *50.55389, 7.42518*
Campingplatz Wiedhof, Wiedhof 1, 56588 Waldbreitbach
[(02638) 4258; camping@wiedhof.de; www.wiedhof.de]
Exit A3 junc 36 onto B256 W to Bonefeld, then take L257
Kurtscheiderstrasse to Niederbreitbach, then L255 to
Waldbreitbach, site sp on rvside. This rte avoids steep hills. Sm,
unshd; wc; chem disp; shwrs; EHU (10A) inc; lndry (inc dryer);
snacks; BBQ; playgrnd; fishing; TV; 80% statics; dogs; adv bkg;
quiet; CKE/CCI. "Conv A3 m'way; vg, peaceful site; gd walks,
quiet site next to local town." 1 Apr-31 Oct. € 13.00   2015*

WALDFISCHBACH BURGALBEN see Pirmasens *3B3*

WALDKIRCH *3C4* (4km NE Rural) *48.10256, 7.99045*
Camping Elztalblick, Biehlstrasse 10, 79183 Waldkirch-Siensbach [(07681) 4212; fax 4213; elztalblick@t-online.
de; www.camping-elztalblick.de] Exit Waldkirch by B294
NE; within 1km of town cent fork R, sp Siensbach & Camping
2km. After 2km Siensbach vill, turn R into narr rd (camping
sp), site at top of hill with 1 in 7 app. If app fr m'way do not
go into Waldkirch but foll sp to Waldkirch-Siensbach. Med,
hdstg, terr, pt shd; wc; chem disp; mv service pnt; shwrs inc;
EHU (10A) €2; lndry; shop; rest, snacks; bar; playgrnd; golf
2km; TV rm; 70% statics; dogs €1; Eng spkn; quiet; CKE/CCI.
"Wonderful views; friendly, family-run site." 1 Apr-20 Oct.
€ 18.00   2009*

WALDKIRCH *3C4* (10km E Rural) *48.10023, 8.05215* Camping
Schwarzwaldhorn, Ettersbachstrasse 7, 79263 Simonswald
[(07683) 477 or 1048; fax 909169; evers@schwarzwald-camping.de; www.schwarzwald-camping.de]
Exit Waldkirch by B294 NE twd Elzach. Turn E dir to Bleibach/
Simonswald onto L173. After 3km turn R at camping sp &
site on R. Sm, mkd pitch, pt sl, pt shd; htd wc; chem disp; mv
service pnt; shwrs €0.50; EHU (16A) metered or €1.50; lndry;
shop; rest adj; playgrnd; htd pool 200m; 40% statics; dogs
€2.50; phone; bus 500m; sep car park; adv bkg; quiet; CKE/
CCI. "Pleasant owners; vg site amongst fruit trees; excel base
for Black Forest, Freiburg; modern san facs."
1 Apr-20 Oct. € 31.00   2011*

⊞ **WALDMUNCHEN** *4F2* (3km N Rural) *49.39598, 12.69913*
Campsite Ferienpark Perlsee (formerly Camping am
Perlsee), Alte Ziegelhütte 6, 93449 Waldmünchen
[(09972) 1469; fax 3782; info@ferienpark-perlsee.de;
www.ferienpark-perlsee.de] N fr Cham on B22 to Schontal,
NE to Waldmünchen for 10km. Foll site sp 2km. Med, hdg/mkd
pitch, terr, pt shd; htd wc; chem disp; mv service pnt; baby
facs; shwrs inc; EHU (16A) metered; lndry (inc dryer); shop &
1km; rest, snacks; bar; BBQ; playgrnd; lake sw adj; watersports;
games area; 50% statics; dogs €2; quiet; CKE/CCI. "Vg san
facs; superb site; long leads poss req." ♦ € 22.00   2014*

⊞ **WALDSHUT** *3C4* (5.6km SW Urban) *47.61083, 8.22526*
Rhein Camping, Jahnweg 22, 79761 Waldshut-Tiengen
[(07751) 3152; fax 3252; info@rheincamping.de; www.
rheincamping.de] Site on rvside on E o'skts of vill. Fr N foll
rd 500 in dir Tiengen fr Switzerland, take 1st L after Koblenz
border x-ing & foll site sp. Med, mkd pitch, hdstg, pt shd; wc;
chem disp; mv service pnt; shwrs €0.50; EHU (16A) metered
+ conn fee €1; gas; lndry (inc dryer); shop; rest, snacks; bar;
pool 200m; paddling pool; rv adj; tennis 100m; wifi; TV;
40% statics; dogs €2; poss cr; Eng spkn; adv bkg; quiet;
debit cards acc; red long stay/CKE/CCI. "Nr Rhine falls at
Schaffhausen; boat for Rhine trips fr site; immac facs; sm,
tight pitches; helpful staff; gd rest; pleasant walk along Rhine;
excel; conv NH mobil park adj." ♦ ltd. € 30.40   2013*

⊞ **WALKENRIED** *2E4* (1km NE Rural) *51.58944, 10.62472*
Knaus Campingpark Walkenried, Ellricherstrasse 7,
37445 Walkenried [(05525) 778; fax 2332; walkenried@
knauscamp.de] A7, exit Seesen,
then B243 to Herzberg-Bad Sachsa-Walkenried, sp. Lge,
mkd pitch, terr, pt sl, pt shd; wc; chem disp; mv service pnt;
sauna; solarium; shwrs inc; EHU (6-10A) €2.40; gas; lndry;
shop; rest, snacks; bar; playgrnd; htd covrd pool; games area;
wintersports; entmnt; TV; 20% statics; dogs €3; site clsd
Nov; Eng spkn; adv bkg; quiet; ccard not acc; red long stay/
snr citizens. "Vg rest; lovely old vill; excel site." ♦ € 34.00
(CChq acc)   2013*

⊞ **WARBURG** *1C4* (2km E Rural) *51.48600, 9.16590*
Camping Eversburg, Zum Anger 1, 34414 Warburg
[(05641) 8668; www.camping-eversburg.de] Exit A44 junc
65 Warburg; turn R onto B7 twd Kassel; site in approx 4km on
R (tight turn) just aft bdge. Sm, pt sl, unshd; wc; chem disp; mv
service pnt; shwrs €1; EHU €1.50 or metered (poss long lead
req); gas; lndry; shops 1km; rest; pool 2km; dogs €1; adv bkg;
quiet; red long stay. "Pleasant town." ♦ € 19.50   2011*

⊞ **WAREN** *2F2* (4km S Rural) *53.50025, 12.66525*
Camping Ecktannen, Fontanestrasse 66, 17192 Waren
[(03991) 668513; fax 664675; camping-ecktannen@waren-
tourismus.de; www.camping-ecktannen.de]
Exit A19/E55 Berlin-Rostock dir Waren on B192; in Waren foll
site sp. Lge, pt sl, pt shd; wc; chem disp; mv service pnt; shwrs
inc; EHU (10A) €2.30 (long lead poss req); gas; lndry; shop;
supmkt 2km; rest, snacks; bar; playgrnd; sand beach & lake sw
adj; bike hire; internet; 10% statics; dogs €2.10; o'night area;
poss cr; quiet; ccard acc; CKE/CCI. "Open plan site amongst
trees; insects poss a problem in spring; gd for cycling; public
transport nrby." ♦ € 17.70   2011*

WARNITZ *2G2* (700m S Rural) *53.17754, 13.87400*
Camping Oberuckersee, Lindenallee 2, 17291 Warnitz
[(039863) 459; fax 78349; info@camping-oberuckersee.
de; www.camping-oberuckersee.de] Fr A11/E28 exit 7. Site
sp fr Warnitz on lakeside. Lge, pt sl, shd; wc; chem disp; mv
service pnt; shwrs €0.80; EHU (10A) €2; lndry rm; shop 500m;
rest 100m; snacks adj; playgrnd; lake sw & beach; fishing;
boating; bike hire; TV; 50% statics; dogs €2; clsd 1300-1500;
quiet. "Lovely site in pine trees on edge lge lake; conv NH en
rte to Poland; deposit for san facs key; gd cycle rte nrby." ♦
1 Apr-5 Oct. € 16.00   2011*

WASSENACH see Mendig *3B2*

WAXWEILER *3A2* (700m W Rural) *50.09270, 6.35866*
Eifel Ferienpark Prümtal, Schwimmbadstrasse 7, 54649
Waxweiler [(06554) 92000; fax 920029; info@ferienpark-
waxweiler.de; www.ferienpark-waxweiler.de]
Exit A60/E42/E29 junc 5 to B410 to Waxweiler. Site sp dir
Prüm on rvside. Med, hdg/mkd pitch, pt shd; htd wc; chem
disp; mv service pnt; sauna; shwrs inc; EHU (10A) inc; lndry
(inc dryer); shop; rest 800m; snacks; bar; BBQ; playgrnd;
htd pool adj; paddling pool; waterslide; fishing; tennis; bike
hire; games area; wifi; entmnt; 50% statics (sep area); dogs
€2.50; Eng spkn; adv bkg; quiet. "V nice site in the valley; v
warm welcome fr staff; lovely pool adj." ♦ 1 Apr-31 Oct.
€ 29.00   2012*

⊞ **WEBERSTEDT** *1D4* (1.4km SW Rural) *51.10186, 10.50806*
Campingplatz am Tor zum Hainich, Hainichstrasse,
99947 Weberstedt [(036022) 98690; fax (36022) 98691;
nh@camping-hainich.de; www.camping-hainich.de]
Leave B247 Mühlhausen to Bad Langensalza rd at Schönstedt
sp Weberstedt; on entering vill look for sp on L; 1km up
cobbled rd. Med, hdstg, unshd; wc; chem disp; mv service pnt;
baby facs; EHU (10A) metered; lndry; sm shop; shop, rest &
bar 1km; playgrnd; bike hire; horseriding nrby; TV rm; dogs
€1; quiet; ccard acc; CKE/CCI. "Close to Hainich National
Park; modern san facs; recep 0700-1300 & 1500-2200."
€ 14.40   2011*

WEHLEN see Bernkastel Kues *3B2*

WEIKERSHEIM *3D2* (4km S Rural) *49.45640, 9.92565*
Camping Schwabenmühle, Weikersheimer Straße 21,
97990 Weikersheim [07934 99 22 23; fax 99 24 08;
info@camping-schwabenmuehle.de; www.camping-
schwabenmuehle.de] Fr Weikersheim twd Laudenbach,
site on R in 3km. Med, hdg/mkd pitch, hdstg, pt shd; wc;
chem disp; mv service pnt; shwrs; EHU (16A); lndry (inc
dryer); bar; playgrnd; bike hire; wifi; dogs €1; twin axles; Eng
spkn; CCI. "Excel; bread can be ordered." ♦ 17 Apr-12 Oct.
€ 32.60   2014*

GERMANY

WEILBURG *3C1* (4km SW Rural) *50.4757, 8.23966*
Campingplatz Odersbach, Runkelerstrasse 5A, 35781
Weilburg-Odersbach [(06471) 7620; fax 379603; info@
camping-odersbach.de; www.camping-odersbach.de]
Fr Limburg exit B49 sp Weilburg & Bad Homburg, turn S (R)
opp Shell stn at top of hill at Weilburg o'skts. Site on L at foot
of hill in Odersbach. Lge, unshd; wc; shwrs €0.90; EHU (16A)
metered + conn fee; lndry; shops at ent; rest 100m; snacks;
bar; playgrnd; pool; paddling pool; boating; bike hire; golf
8km; 75% statics; dogs €1; poss cr; quiet; ccard acc; CKE/CCI.
♦ ltd. 1 Apr-31 Oct. € 23.00   2014*

WEIMAR *2E4* (12km S Rural) *50.92456, 11.34785* **Camping
Mittleres Ilmtal, Auf den Butterberge 1, 99438 Oettern
[(036453) 80264; fax 808519; weil-camping@freenet.de;
www.camping-oettern.de]** Exit A4/E40 junc 50 & foll B87
to SW to Oettern, take 1st L after narr rd, site on L in 600m
along narr rd, sp 'Camperbaude'. Med, some hdstg, pt sl, terr,
pt shd; wc; chem disp; shwrs €1; EHU (16A) €2; rest, snacks;
bar; 50% statics; dogs €2; phone; quiet. "Conv Weimar &
Buchenwald; recep open 0800-1000 & 1700-2000; welcoming;
gd NH/sh stay." 15 Apr-31 Oct. € 14.00   2011*

"I need an on-site restaurant"

We do our best to make sure site
information is correct, but it is always best
to check any must-have facilities are still
available or will be open during your visit.

⊞ **WEINHEIM** *3C2* (9km N Rural) *49.59776, 8.64013*
Camping Wiesensee, Ulmenweg 7, 69502 Hemsbach
[(06201) 72619; fax 493426; familie.herwig@camping-
wiesensee.de; www.camping-wiesensee.de]
Exit A5/E35 junc 32; foll sp Hemsbach. On ent vill strt at 1st
rndbt & traff lts, at 2nd rndabt turn L & foll camping sp about
1km. Lge, hdg pitch, pt shd; wc; chem disp; mv service pnt;
serviced pitches; shwrs €0.60; EHU (16A) €1.90 or metered
+ conn fee; gas; lndry (inc dryer); shop; rest high ssn; snacks;
playgrnd; htd pool 100m; lake sw; boating; tennis 100m; bike
hire; golf 12km; 75% statics; dogs €2; Eng spkn; adv bkg
rec high ssn; quiet but some rlwy noise. "Superb facs to CC
standard; friendly welcome; helpful staff; supmkt in walking
dist; gd NH for A5." ♦ € 30.00   2014*

WEISSENSEE *2E4* (1.5km N Rural) *51.20593, 11.06735*
Camping Weissensee, Grünstedterstrasse 4, 99631
Weissensee [(036374) 36936; fax 36937; info@
campingplatz-weissensee.de; www.campingplatz-
weissensee.de] App on B4 fr Erfurt, turn R after Straussfurt
onto B86. Site on R exit Weissensee past lake, clearly sp fr town
cent. Med, unshd; wc; chem disp; mv service pnt; shwrs inc;
EHU (10A) metered + conn fee; lndry (inc dryer); shop high
ssn; rest adj; snacks; playgrnd; pool & paddling pool; bike
hire; wifi; 50% statics; dogs €1; no adv bkg; quiet. 1 Apr-30 Sep.
€ 16.50   2009*

WENNINGSTEDT see Westerland (Sylt Island) *1C1*

WERDER PETZOW see Potsdam *2F3*

⊞ **WERNIGERODE** *2E3* (12km S Rural) *51.77586, 10.7965*
Camping am Brocken, Schützenring 6, 38875 Elbingerode
[(039454) 42589; hobittner@ngi.de; www.campingam
brocken.de] S on B244 fr Werningerode. Turn R at int'l
camping sp at bottom of hill ent Elbingerode. Foll sp for
1km - take care on app fr N. Lge, mkd pitch, some hdstg, pt
sl, unshd; wc; chem disp; mv service pnt; shwrs €0.50; EHU
(16A) metered + conn fee (poss rev pol); gas; lndry; shop;
rest, snacks 100m; playgrnd; pool 200m; dogs €2; poss cr;
adv bkg; quiet; 10% red CKE/CCI. "Lovely, friendly site; vg
facs; easy for c'vans; sep area for m'vans; highly rec; excel." ♦
€ 20.00   2011*

⊞ **WERTACH** *4E4* (1km NE Rural) *47.60861, 10.41750*
Camping Waldesruh, Bahnhofstrasse 19, 87497 Wertach
[(08365) 1004; fax 706369; info@camping-wertach.de;
www.camping-wertach.de] Fr A7 exit junc 137 at Oy & take
B310 dir Wertach; 2km bef Wertach turn R into Bahnhofstrasse
& foll site sp. Med, mkd pitch, pt sl, pt shd; htd wc; chem
disp; mv service pnt; baby facs; shwrs inc; EHU (16A) metered;
gas; lndry (inc dryer); shop, rest, snacks, bar 500m; BBQ;
playgrnd; lake sw 2km; games area; games rm; wifi; TV rm;
50% statics; dogs €2.50; phone; bus; Eng spkn; adv bkg; quiet;
red long stay; CKE/CCI. "V picturesque area; friendly site; gd
walks; winter sports site & conv NH in rte Austria/Italy." ♦
€ 22.50   2015*

⊞ **WERTACH** *4E4* (3km E Rural) *47.61030, 10.44618*
International Grüntensee-Camping, Grüntenseestrasse
41, 87497 Wertach [(08365) 375; fax 1221; info@
gruentensee.de; www.gruentensee.de] Exit A7 junc 137
to Nesselwang. Site on rd fr Nesselwang to Wertach, sp. Lge,
terr, pt shd; wc; chem disp; mv service pnt; baby facs; shwrs;
EHU (10-16A) metered + conn fee; lndry; shop 2km; playgrnd;
lake sw & beach; watersports; entmnt; golf 4km; ski lift nr; wifi;
40% statics; dogs €2.50; o'night m'van facs; adv bkg; quiet;
red CKE/CCI. "Excel location; extra charge for lakeside pitches;
gd walking." € 22.00   2009*

WERTHEIM *3D2* (3.6km N Urban) *49.77805, 9.50916*
Azur Campingpark Wertheim, An den Christwiesen 35,
97877 Wertheim-Bestenheid [(09342) 83111; fax 83171;
wertheim@azur-camping.de; www.azur-camping.de/
wertheim] Exit A3/E41 junc 66 onto L2310 thro Wertheim,
site on W bank of Rv Main sp dir Bestenheid. V lge, mkd pitch,
hdstg, pt shd; htd wc; chem disp; mv service pnt; baby facs;
shwrs inc; EHU (6A) €3; gas; lndry; shop; supmkt 1km; rest
1km; snacks; bar; cooking facs; playgrnd; htd pool; paddling
pool; waterslide; fishing; boat hire; tennis 500m; games
area; 30% statics; dogs €3; phone; bus 100m; train 1km;
poss cr; adv bkg; Eng spkn; rush hr rd noise; red LS/CKE/CCI.
"Interesting town in walking dist; helpful staff; gd pitches on
rv (extra charge); san facs OK (1 block needs upgrade); site clsd
2200; gd rvside cycle paths; gd." ♦ 1 Apr-31 Oct. € 22.50
(CChq acc)   2011*

WERTHEIM *3D2* (11km NE Rural) *49.78097, 9.56553*
Campingpark Wertheim-Bettingen, Geiselbrunnweg 31,
97877 Wertheim-Bettingen [(09342) 7077; fax 913077;
info@campingpark-wertheim-bettingen.de;
www.campingpark-wertheim-bettingen.de]
Fr A3/E41 exit junc 66 - 2nd Wertheim exit; then turn off to
vill of Bettingen; site sp. Med, pt sl, unmkd pitch, pt shd; wc;
chem disp; mv service pnt; shwrs €0.50; EHU (6A) €3.50 (long
lead req for rvside pitches); gas; lndry (inc dryer); shop; rest,
snacks; playgrnd; htd pool adj; paddling pool adj; waterslide
adj; boating; fishing; bike hire; 60% statics; dogs €1; poss v
cr; adv bkg; red long stay; Eng spkn; many statics; quiet; ccard
acc; red 3+ days; CKE/CCI. "On bank of Rv Main; conv, popular
NH for A3 - rec arr early; NH tourers on sep, lge, level meadow
outside main site (but within barrier); gd rest; san facs tired, req
upgrade (2014)." ♦ 1 Apr-31 Oct. € 20.50   2014*

WESEL *1B3* (3km W Rural) *51.66795, 6.55620*
Erholungszentrum Grav-Insel, 46487 Wesel-Flüren
[(0281) 972830; fax 972834; grav-insel@t-online.de;
www.grav-insel.com] Exit A3/E35 junc 6 dir Wesel. Then
foll sp Rees & Flüren, site sp. V lge, unshd; wc; chem disp;
mv service pnt; shwrs inc; EHU (10) €3; lndry; shop, rest,
snacks, bar high ssn; playgrnd; htd pool 3km; fishing; tennis
3km; watersports; boat hire; bike hire; golf 7km; games area;
internet; 65% statics; dogs €1; poss cr; Eng spkn;
quiet. "Rv Rhine adj; many activities; gd touring base; modern
san facs but pss far fr pitches; v lge site with comprehensive
facs & v well kept." ♦ € 15.50   2011*

WESTERHEIM *3D3* (2km SW Rural) *48.51055, 9.60933*
Alb-Camping Westerheim, Albstrasse, 72589 Westerheim
[(07333) 6197 or 6140; fax 7797; info@alb-camping.de;
www.alb-camping.de] Exit A8/E52 at junc 61 (Merklingen)
to Laichingen; turn R to Westerheim; foll camp sp (thro
housing estate) for 2km to top of hill. Or exit A8 junc 60 thro
Westerheim. V lge, mkd pitch, hdstg, pt sl, pt shd; wc; shwrs
inc; chem disp; EHU (16A) €2.50; gas; lndry; shop, rest, snacks;
playgrnd; 3 free pools; tennis 500m; games area; skibus;
entmnt; 80% statics; poss cr with long stay vans; Eng spkn;
adv bkg ess high ssn; quiet; no ccard acc; red long stay/CKE/
CCI. "Huge, holiday-camp style site; gd walking & touring area;
wintersports; ski lift adj; lge pitches; helpful staff; gd facs for
children; immac san facs; office clsd 1200-1300 (check-in at
bar)." € 20.60   2010*

WESTERSTEDE *1C2* (1km S Rural) *53.2508, 7.93506*
Camping Westerstede, Süderstrasse 2, 26655 Westerstede
[tel/fax (04488) 78234; camping@westerstede.de;
www.westerstede.de/camping] Exit E35/A28 junc 6 to
Westerstede; cont thro town dir Bad Zwischenahn on L815 for
1km; then foll L815 to L onto Oldenburgerstrasse (rd conts strt
on as L821); in 200m turn L to site. Med, mkd pitch, hdstg, pt
shd; htd wc; chem disp; mv service pnt; shwrs inc; EHU (9A)
inc; lndry; shop 300m; rest; playgrnd; bus; train 400m; poss
cr; Eng spkn; quiet; red CKE/CCI. "Pleasant, friendly, relaxing,
well-managed site; clsd 1300-1500; sm pitches; outer field
cheaper but rd noise & remote fr facs; o'night m'van facs; gd
touring base; many cycle paths; gd town for shopping." ♦
€ 15.50   2009*

WETTRINGEN *1B3* (10km N Rural) *52.27408,
7.3204* Campingplatz Haddorfer Seen, Haddorf 59,
48493 Wettringen [(05973) 2742; fax 900889; info@
campingplatz-haddorf.de; www.campingplatz-haddorf.
de] Exit A30 junc 7 at Rheine Nord dir Neuenkirchen. At end
city limits turn R dir Salzbergen then L in 4km & foll site sp.
V lge, mkd pitch, pt shd; htd wc; chem disp; mv service pnt;
shwrs inc; EHU (16A) metered + conn fee; lndry (inc dryer);
shop; supmkt 10km; rest, snacks; bar; playgrnd; lake sw;
fishing; watersports; boat hire; games area; 90% statics; dogs
€3; adv bkg; red CKE/CCI. "Family-friendly site; modern
san facs; gd bistro; gd walking/cycling." ♦ € 19.00   2010*

WETZLAR *3C1* (13.2km SW Rural) *50.51155, 8.38293*
Campingpark Braunfels, Am Weiherstieg 2, 35619
Braunfels [(06442) 4366; fax 6895; www.braunfels.de]
Take B49 fr Wetzlar to Braunfels. Site on R at S end of town.
Med, hdg/mkd pitch, pt sl, pt shd; wc; chem disp; shwrs €0.50;
EHU (16A) metered + conn fee; lndry (inc dryer); shop 300m;
rest, snacks; htd pool 200m, tennis 300m; horseriding 1km; 60%
statics; dogs €1; adv bkg; quiet. "Braunfels beautiful health resort
in easy reach Taunus mountains; fair NH." € 20.00   2015*

WIESLOCH *3C3* (11km W Rural) *49.28146,
8.58445* Camping St Leoner See, 68789 St Leon-Rot
[(06227) 59000; fax 880988; info@st.leoner-see.de;
www.st.leoner-see.de] Fr A5/E35 exit junc 39 & turn S onto
L 546 for 5km. Thro St Leon-Rot two Reilingen, site sp on R.
Avoid Walldorf & Wiesloch. V lge, pt shd; wc; chem disp; mv
service pnt; baby facs; shwrs inc; EHU (6-16A) €2; lndry; shop;
rest, snacks; playgrnd; lge watersports complex inc fishing,
windsurfing, waterskiing, skin-diving; lake sw; golf 4km;
entmnt; internet; 60% statics; no dogs; phone; sep car park;
gates clsd 1300-1500 & 2200-0700; poss cr; Eng spkn; adv
bkg; quiet except w/end; ccard acc; red CKE/CCI. "Touring
vans on hdstg in mkd bays at ent - no space for chairs, awning,
etc - NH only; otherwise gd family site; excel sports/water
facs." ♦ € 21.00   2009*

WIESLOCH *3C3* (8km NW Urban) *49.31643, 8.63481*
Campingplatz Walldorf-Astoria, Schwetzingerstrasse 98,
69190 Walldorf [tel/fax (06227) 9195] Fr A5, exit junc 39 for
Walldorf & Wiesloch; take B291/L598 N sp Walldorf Nord; in
2km turn R onto Schwetzingerstrasse; site sp in 250m. Med, pt
shd; wc; chem disp; mv service pnt; shwrs inc; EHU (16A) €2.50;
shop; rest; indoor pool 200m; 50% statics in sep area; no dogs;
Eng spkn; CKE/CCI. "Vg rest on site; sm zoo & sports complex
adj; bus to Heidelberg at gate; gates clsd 1200-1500; excel NH/
sh stay, busy; rec arr bef 1700 high ssn; conv for Hockenheim
Circuit; gd rest; hard working fam run site; Heidelberg & Speyer
worth visiting." ♦ 15 Apr-15 Oct. € 18.00   2015*

WILDBERG *3C3* (1.9km SSW Rural) *48.61248, 8.73507*
Camping Carpe Diem, Martinshölzle 6-8, 72218 Wildberg
[(07054) 931851; campingcarpedeum@live.de;
www.campingcarpediem.de] Take the A8, exit 43 Pforzheim-
West dir Calw. In Calw foll the B463 dir Nagold. Foll the rd in
Wildberg. Foll the camping signs. Med, hdg pitch, pt shd; wc;
chem disp; child/baby facs; shwrs €1, EHU (16A) inc; rest; take
away; bar; playgrnd; pool & paddling pool; bicycles for hire; wifi;
70% statics; dog €2.50 high ssn only; twin axles acc; Eng spkn;
adv bkgs; red LS. "Cycling and walks by rv Nagold; gd site."
29 Mar-20 Oct. € 26.00   2013*

⊞ **WILDESHAUSEN** *1C2* (8km N Rural) *52.93400, 8.40200*
Camping Aschenbake, Zum Sande 18, 27801 Dötlingen
[(04433) 333; fax 1531; aschenbeck@nwn.de;
www.aschenbeck-camping.de] Exit E37/A1 Osnabrück/
Bremen junc 60 dir Wildeshausen. Turn R in traff lts in 800m
+ foll sp to site in 4km. Single track for last km. Med, hdg/
mkd pitch, pt shd; wc; chem disp; shwrs €0.60; EHU (16A)
€2; lndry; shop; rest, snacks; playgrnd; lake sw & beach adj;
dogs €2; quiet. "Walks in woods; office clsd 1300-1500." ♦
€ 14.00   2009*

⊞ **WILDESHAUSEN** *1C2* (6km W Rural) *52.89916, 8.35444*
Camping Auetal, Aumühlerstrasse 75, 27793 Aumühle
[(04431) 1851; fax 2203] Exit a'bahn A1/E37 junc 61. Take
rd B213 E; site on L in 1.5km. Sm, pt shd; wc; shwrs inc; EHU
(16A) €1.50; lndry (inc dryer); rest; bar; BBQ; playgrnd; lake sw
adj; CKE/CCI. "Statics site but sm field for tourers; vg rest; NH
only." ♦ ltd. € 16.00   2015*

WILDESHAUSEN *1C2* (8km W Rural) *52.8995, 8.3281*
Camping Bürgerpark, Aumühle 78A, 27793 Oberhausen
[(04431) 7048812; camp.buergerpark@gmx.de;
www.wildeshausen.de] Exit A1/E37 junc 61 onto B213 dir
Cloppenburg. Site in 300m on R. Med, pt sl, pt shd; wc; chem
disp; shwrs; EHU (6A) inc; shops 500m; snacks; 50% statics;
Eng spkn; adv bkg; quiet but some rd noise. "Fair NH; pleasant,
wooded o'night area; conv for a'bahn; tourers in sep field, san
facs clean and adequate but dated; gd for NH." 1 Apr-30 Sep.
€ 14.00   2013*

WILHELMSTHAL see Eisenach *1D4*

WILLSTATT SAND see Kehl *3B3*

⊞ **WILSUM** *1B3* (7km S Rural) *52.51689, 6.87390*
Wilsumerberge Resort, Zum Feriengebiet 1, 49849 Wilsum
[(05945) 995590; fax 9955899; info@wilsumerberge.nl;
www.wilsumerberge.nl] Site sp on B403. V lge, pt shd; htd
wc; chem disp; mv service pnt; baby facs; shwrs inc; EHU (6A)
inc; lndry (inc dryer); shop; rest, snacks; bar; playgrnd; lake sw;
waterslide; fishing; tennis; bike hire; games area; games rm;
wifi; entmnt; 60% statics; dogs €3; adv bkg; ccard acc; red
LS. "Attractive site in forest; extra for serviced pitches; vg facs,
espec for youngsters." ♦ € 22.00   2010*

WINNINGEN see Koblenz *3B2*

⊞ **WINSEN (ALLER)** *1D3* (1.5km W Rural) *52.67506, 9.89968*
Campingplatz Winsen, Auf der Hude 1, 29308 Winsen
[(05143) 93199; fax 93144; info@camping-winsen.de;
www.camping-winsen.de] Fr A7/E45 exit junc 50 Wietze
onto B214Thro Wietze & in 6km turn L to Oldau & Winsen. Foll
site sp. Med, mkd pitch, pt shd; htd wc; chem disp; mv service
pnt; shwrs inc; EHU (10-16A) inc; gas; lndry (inc dryer); shop;
supmkt 1km; rest, snacks; bar; playgrnd; htd, covrd pool 200m;
rv beach adj; wifi; 50% statics; dogs €2; phone; bus 1km;
m'van o'night area; quiet; red CKE/CCI. "Attractive site; helpful
staff; some rvside pitches - poss liable to flood; easy walk to
picturesque town cent; lovely cycle paths." € 31.00   2013*

⊞ **WINSEN (ALLER)** *1D3* (9km NW Rural) *52.71983,
9.82521* Campingpark Hüttensee, Hüttenseepark 1,
29308 Meissendorf [(05056) 941880; fax 941881; info@
campingpark-huettensee.de; www.campingpark-
huettensee.de] Fr N on A27/A7 exit at Westenholz & cont
twd Westenholz/Ostenholz to Meissendorf, site sp. Fr S exit at
Allertal rest stop twd Celle/Winsen-Aller. Turn L at traff lts & L
again to Meissendorf. Lge, mkd pitch, pt shd; htd wc; chem disp;
mv service pnt; baby facs; shwrs €0.50; EHU (16A) inc; lndry (inc
dryer); shop; supmkt 800m; rest, snacks; bar; playgrnd; lake sw &
sand beach; fishing; tennis 500m; boat & bike hire; games area;
wifi; entmnt; 60% statics; dogs €2.50; clsd 1300-1500; adv bkg;
quiet; ccard acc; red CKE/CCI. ♦ € 25.00 (CChq acc)   2011*

⊞ **WINTRICH** *3B2* (30km NE Rural) *49.96541, 7.10537* Mosel
Stellplatz Wintrich, Rissbacherstraße 15, 56841 Traben-
Trarbach [06541 3111; info@moselstellplatz.de; www.
moselstellplatz.de] Fr S of A1 take exit 125 Wittlich-Mitte for
B50 twds Wittlich. Merge onto B49, cont onto L55 to Urzig,
then turn R onto B53 & foll sp to camp. Med, shd; wc; chem
disp; mv service pnt; shwr; EHU (6A); wifi; dogs; poss cr; quiet.
"Vg site." € 8.00   2014*

⊞ **WISMAR** *2E2* (400m S Urban) *53.89388, 11.45166*
Wohnmobilpark Westhafen, Schiffbauerdamm 12, 23966
Wismar [(03841) 706070; info@wohnmobilpark-wismar.de]
Exit A20/E22 junc 8 to cent of Wismar; foll sp to 'hafen', site sp.
Sm, hdstg, unshd; wc; shwrs €1; EHU (10A) €1 for 8 hrs; shop
adj; rest 200m; adv bkg; quayside noise. "Superb NH in stunning
town; m'vans only - no c'vans allowed." € 9.00   2011*

⊞ **WISMAR** *2E2* (9km NW Coastal) *53.93441, 11.37160*
Ostsee Camping, Sandstrasse 19c, 23968 Zierow
[(038428) 63820; fax 63833; info@ostsee-camping.de;
www.ostsee-camping.de] Fr Wismar-Lübeck rd B105/22 to
Gägelow, turn N to Zierow; thro vill to site at end of rd. V lge,
unshd; htd wc; chem disp; mv service pnt; sauna; baby facs;
shwrs €1; EHU (16A) €2.80; lndry (inc dryer); shop; rest, snacks;
playgrnd; beach adj; bike hire; games area; horseriding adj;
wifi; TV; 75% statics (sep area); dogs €2.70; CKE/CCI. "Busy
site in superb location; gd san facs; a first class campsite." ♦
€ 32.00   2011*

WITTENBERG see Lutherstadt Wittenberg *2F3*

WITTLICH *3B2* (10km E Urban) *49.97861, 7.00750*
Wohnmobilstellplatz (M'van Park), Moseluferstrasse,
54539 Ürzig [(06532) 954888; info@uerzig-mosel.de]
Foll B50 fr Wittlich, then B53 for 3km along rv bank to Ürzig.
M'vans only, sp. Sm, own san; chem disp; mv service pnt; EHU
€1.50 (16A); shop 200m; rest, bar 100m; dogs; adv bkg.
1 Apr-5 Nov. € 6.50   2009*

⊞ **WITTLICH** *3B2* (15km E Rural) *49.98986, 7.07780*
Camping Sportzentrum Kröverberg, 54536 Kröv
[(06541) 70040; fax 700444; www.kroeverberg.de]
Exit A1/A48 junc 125; then B49 dir Koblenz; then L62 Ürzig;
L in Ürzig sp Kröv-Bergstrecke up hill (10%) for 2km; foll sp
on this rd (do not go downhill into Mosel Valley). Med, hdg/
mkd pitch, terr, unshd; wc; shwrs inc; chem disp; mv service
pnt; EHU (10A) metered; gas; lndry; shop 4km; rest, snacks;
playgrnd; games area; statics; dogs €1.80; quiet; adv bkg.
"Friendly site high above Mosel; lovely scenery; boat trips on
Mosel; mkd walks thro vineyards; excel facs." € 14.00 2011*

WITTLICH *3B2* (22km NW Rural) *50.09680, 6.79797* **Natur-Camping Vulkaneifel, Feriendorf Moritz, Herbstwiese 1, 54531 Manderscheid [(06572) 92110; fax 921149; info@vulkan-camping.de; www.vulkan-camping.de]** Exit A1/E44 junc 122 dir Manderscheid, then foll sp Daun. Site sp. Med, mkd pitch, terr, pt shd; wc; chem disp; mv service pnt; shwrs inc; EHU (2A) €2.50; lndry; shop 2km; rest 700m; snacks; playgrnd; htd pool; games area; 10% statics; dogs €1.50; o'night m'van area; red CKE/CCI. "Gd walking, cycling; facs shared with football club." ♦ 1 Apr-31 Oct. € 20.00   2009*

WITZENHAUSEN *1D4* (2km N Rural) *51.3499, 9.86916* **Camping Werratal, Am Sande 11, 37213 Witzenhausen [(05542) 1465; fax 72418; info@campingplatz-werratal.de; www.campingplatz-werratal.de]** Exit A7/E45 junc 75 to Witzenhausen. Cross rv & immed R foll sp rte around town cent. Site nr rv, sp. Med, unshd; wc; chem disp; mv service pnt; shwrs €0.70; EHU (16A) €2.30; lndry (inc dryer); shop; rest, snacks adj; playgrnd; htd, covrd pool 200m; bike hire; wifi; 50% statics; dogs €2.30; red long stay. "Clean, pleasant, family-run site; poss flooding at high water; easy walk to town; some rd & rlwy noise." € 20.00   2015*

WITZENHAUSEN *1D4* (16km SE Urban) *51.28889, 9.97638* **Camping Oase, Kreisstrasse 32, 37318 Wahlhausen [tel/fax (036087) 98671; www.camping-oase.de]** Take B27 dir Wahlhausen, site sp bet Bad Sooden & Allendorf. Med, pt sl, pt shd; wc; chem disp; shwrs inc; EHU (16A) metered; lndry (inc dryer); shop adj; rest; playgrnd; Rv Werra nr; dogs €1; adv bkg; quiet. € 14.50   2010*

WOLFACH *3C3* (6km E Rural) *48.29083, 8.27805* **Trendcamping Wolfach (previously named Schwarzwald Camp Wolfach), Schiltacherstrasse 80, 77709 Wolfach-Halbmeil [(07834) 859309; fax 859310; info@trendcamping.de; www.trendcamping.de]** Fr Wolfach E 5km on B294 dir Schiltach. Site on L opp rv bdge. Med, hdstg, terr, unshd; wc; chem disp; mv service pnt; serviced pitches; shwrs; EHU (16A) metered + conn fee; gas; lndry; shop; rest, snacks; playgrnd; wifi; some sat TV; 30% statics; dogs €2; o'night m'van area; Eng spkn; adv bkg; quiet but some rd noise; red long stay. "Scenic views across valley; excel, modern, clean san facs; barrier clsd 1230-1430; NH area for m'vans; rock pegs req for awning; free bus & train pass for Black Forest; gd cycling & walking." € 25.00   2012*

WOLFACH *3C3* (5km S Rural) *48.26750, 8.23777* **Campingplatz zur Mühle, Talstrasse 79, 77709 Kirnbach [(07834) 775; fax 8670975; camping-kirnbach@t-online.de; www.camping-kirnbach.de]** Turn S off B294 dir Kirnbach, site sp. Steep access. Sm, hdg/mkd pitch, terr; pt sl, pt shd; htd wc; chem disp (wc); shwrs €0.50; EHU metered + conn fee; lndry; shop; snacks; bar; BBQ; rv 500m; TV rm; few statics; no dogs high ssn; phone; quiet. "Pleasant site but not suitable lge o'fits; poss boggy in wet weather; friendly owners help with van placing; gd touring base; gd views Black Forest; gd walks & rests nrby." € 18.00   2009*

WOLFSBURG *2E3* (3km NE Urban) *52.4316, 10.8158* **Camping am Allersee, In den Allerwiesen 5, 38446 Wolfsburg [(05361) 63395; fax 651271; allerseecamping@gmx.de; www.camping-allersee.de]** Exit A39 junc 5 twd Zentrum, foll sp VW Autostadt until start of flyover, keep R and foll sp. Med, mkd pitch, hdstg, pt shd; htd wc; chem disp; shwrs €0.50; EHU (10A) €2.50 or metered; lndry; shops 2km; rest; bar; cooking facs; playgrnd; beach adj; lake sw 100m; sailing & canoeing; entmnt; 80% statics; dogs €1; clsd 1300-1500 & 2200-0700; o'night area for m'vans; poss cr; Eng spkn; adv bkg; quiet, but poss noise fr pop concerts in VW stadium. "Vg, clean site beside lake; conv VW factory visits (not w/end or bank hols) - check time of tour in Eng; gd lake perimeter path adj; friendly, helpful owners; ice rink & indoor water cent other side of lake." ♦ ltd. € 19.00   2015*

WOLFSTEIN *3B2* (2km S Rural) *49.5803, 7.6187* **Azur Camping am Königsberg, Am Schwimmbad 1, 67752 Wolfstein [(06304) 4143; fax 7543; nfo@Camping Wolfstein.de; www.campingwolfstein.de]** Exit A61 at junc 15 Kaiserslauten West onto B270 dir Lauterecken, site on R 200m bef Wolfstein, sp. Sm, mkd pitch, hdstg, pt sl, unshd; wc; chem disp; serviced pitches; shwrs inc; EHU (16A) €3 + conn fee; lndry; ice shop 200m; rest; bar; playgrnd; htd pool adj; games area; wifi; 60% statics; dogs €2.30; poss cr; adv bkg; site clsd 1300-1500; Eng spkn; quiet; ccard acc; red snr citizens/CKE/CCI. "Gd." € 22.00   2011*

"Satellite navigation makes touring much easier"

Remember most sat navs don't know if you're towing or in a larger vehicle – always use yours alongside maps and site directions.

WURZBURG *3D2* (6km NE Urban) *49.83286, 9.99783* **Camping Estenfeld, Maidbronnerstrasse 38, 97230 Estenfeld [(09305) 228; fax 8006; cplestenfeld@freenet.de; www.camping-estenfeld.de]** Exit A7/E45 junc 101. Foll sp to Estenfeld & site sp. Sm, some hdstg, pt shd; wc; chem disp; shwrs €0.75; EHU (16A) €2.50 or metered & conn fee; lndry; shop; rest adj; snacks; bar; playgrnd; some statics; dogs €1.50; clsd 1300-1500; poss v cr high ssn; Eng spkn; quiet; red long stay; CKE/CCI. "Helpful owner; clean, tidy site; rec NH." 15 May-10 Nov. € 20.50   2014*

WURZBURG *3D2* (3.6km S Urban) *49.77973, 9.92636* **Kanu-Club Würzberg, Mergentheimerstrasse 13b, 97082 Würzburg [(09317) 72536; www.kc-wuerzburg.de]** Fr A3/E43 exit junc 70, Heidingsfeld. Turn L onto B19 & foll sp for Heidingsfeld. Turn R at site sp to cross tram line, sp Zeltplatz. Site L in 30m on W bank of rv, not well sp. Sm, mkd pitch, pt shd; wc; chem disp; shwrs €0.50; EHU €2; shop 1.5km; rest; bar; 80% statics; bus/tram adj; dogs €1.50; Eng spkn; adv bkg; CKE/CCI. "Site is private club with ltd touring pitches; gd access to lovely, historic city; gd cycling by rv; friendly staff; not suitable lge o'fits due rbts & restricted access; long walk to san facs; adv bkg ess holiday w/ends; attractive quiet site." Mar-Dec. € 13.00   2011*

GERMANY

⊞ **WURZBURG** *3D2* (8km S Rural) *49.74471, 9.98433*
**Camping Kalte Quelle, Winterhäuserstrasse 160, 97084
Würzburg-Heidingsfeld [(0931) 65598; fax 612611; info@
kalte-quelle.de; www.kalte-quelle.de]** Exit A3/E43 at
Heidingsfeld junc 70 onto A19 dir Würzburg. Take 1st exit &
foll sp Ochsenfurt + camping sp. Site on L in approx 5km. Med,
mkd pitch, pt shd; wc; chem disp; mv service pnt; shwrs €1;
EHU (16A) conn fee + €2; lndry; shop; rest; bar; playgrnd; bike
hire; 50% statics; dogs free; clsd 1330-1430; poss cr; Eng spkn;
adv bkg; some rd, rv & rlwy noise; ccard acc; CKE/CCI. "No
doors on shwrs & run down facs, but clean; pleasant situation
on rv; NH only; conv Würzburg & Nürnberg; bus to centrum
2km; no mkd pitches for NH." € 16.00   2014*

WUSTENWELSBERG *4E2* (500m SE Rural) *50.13750,
10.82777* **Camping Rückert-Klause, Haus Nr 16, 96190
Wüstenwelsberg [tel/fax (09533) 288]** Fr Coburg on
B4, turn W at Kaltenbrunn; site sp thro Untermerzbach &
Obermerzbach. Or fr B279 fr Bamberg to Bad Königshofen,
turn R just S of Pfarrweisch, sp. Sm, pt sl, pt shd; wc; chem
disp; shwrs inc; EHU (16A) metered + conn fee; lndry; shops
3km; snacks; bar; playgrnd; 50% statics; Eng spkn; adv bkg;
quiet; ccard not acc; CKE/CCI. "Many castles nrby; beautiful
countryside; super situation." 1 Apr-31 Oct. € 14.00   2009*

ZELL *3B2* (4km N Rural) *50.03375, 7.17365* **Campingplatz
Mosella, 56856 Zell-Kaimt [tel/fax (06542) 41241; info@
capingpark-zell.de; www.campingpark-zell.de]**
Fr Cochem S on B49, in Alf take B53 dir Bernkastel-Kues. In
Zell site sp to Kaimt. Med, mkd pitch, hdstg, unshd; wc; chem
disp; mv service pnt; shwrs; EHU (16A) inc; gas; lndry; snacks;
playgrnd; watersports; wifi; dogs €1; poss cr; quiet. "Scenic
area; v quiet at night; site soggy after rain; excel well kept site,
rest and bar being built (2012); cycles and boats for hire."
1 Apr-31 Oct. € 26.50   2012*

ZELL *3B2* (9km W Rural) *50.03305, 7.11527* **Camping
Moselland, Im Planters, 56862 Pünderich [(06542) 2618;
fax 960669; www.campingplatz-moselland.de]**
Foll Rv Mosel S fr Zell on B53. In 6km turn R sp Pünderich &
site. Turn immed L, then immed R & foll narr rd to site in 1km.
Med, mkd pitch, pt shd; wc; chem disp; shwrs €1; EHU (16A)
metered + conn fee; lndry; rest, snacks; bar; playgrnd; boat-
launching; 30% statics; dogs €2; phone; little Eng spkn; adv
bkg; quiet. "Pleasant rvside site in vineyards & orchards; vg;
various odd rules." 1 Apr-1 Nov. € 18.00   2015*

ZELL *3B2* (6km NW Rural) *50.05391, 7.13041* **Bären Camp,
Am Moselufer 1-3, 56859 Bullay [(06542) 900097; fax
900098; info@baeren-camp.de; www.baeren-camp.de]**
Exit A1 junc 125 at Wittlich onto B49 to Alf. At Alf cross rv
to Bullay & foll sp to site. Med, pt shd; wc; chem disp; mv
service pnt; baby facs; shwrs €1; EHU (16A) metered; lndry
(inc dryer); shop; BBQ; playgrnd; dogs €2; Eng spkn; quiet.
"Conv Cochem, Bernkastel-Kues; gd cycling along tow-path;
extra for rvside pitch; recep clsd 1230-1400; narr rd to recep;
friendly staff; gd location on the Mosel." ◆ ltd. 17 Apr-1 Nov.
€ 27.00   2014*

⊞ **ZEVEN** *1D2* (2km NE) *53.30401, 9.29793* **Campingplatz
Sonnenkamp Zeven, Sonnenkamp 10, 27404 Zeven
[(04281) 951345; fax 951347; info@campingplatz-
sonnenkamp.de; www.campingplatz-zeven.de]**
Fr A1 exit 47 or 49 to Zeven. Fr Zeven dir Heeslingen/Buxtehude
rd, site sp fr all dir twd stadium. Lge, mkd pitch, some hdstg,
unshd; htd wc; chem disp; mv service pnt; baby facs; sauna;
shwrs inc; EHU (16A) metered; gas; lndry (inc dryer); shop; rest,
snacks; bar; playgrnd; pool, paddling pool, waterslide & sports
facs adj; tennis; bike hire; games area; games rm; wifi; entmnt;
75% statics; dogs €0.50; phone; Eng spkn; poss cr; adv bkg;
ccard acc; quiet; red snr citizens; CKE/CCI. € 22.60   2011*

FEHMARN ISLAND

GROSSENBRODE *2E1* (1km S Coastal) *54.36035,
11.08743* **Camping Strandparadies, Südstrand 3, 23775
Grossenbrode [(04367) 8697; fax 999031; camping@
strandparadies-grossenbrode.de; www.camping-
strandparadies-grossenbrode.de]** Fr E47/B207 fr Lübeck dir
Puttgarden turn R to Grossenbrode & foll 'campingplatz' sp.
Turn L after sports hall, foll rd round & turn L into site in front
of yellow phone box. Lge, hdg pitch, unshd; wc; chem disp; all
serviced pitches; baby facs; shwrs €0.50; EHU (16A) inc; gas;
lndry; shop, rest, snacks 300m; playgrnd; sand beach 200m;
watersports; windsurfing; internet; 75% statics; dogs €2.50;
phone; bus; clsd 1300-1500; poss cr; adv bkg; quiet; red long
stay. "Superb beach; gd cycle paths; beach area well fenced for
special 1 night fee; conv ferries to Denmark & Fehmarn Island;
gd for wheelchair users; vg." ◆ 1 Apr-31 Oct. € 21.00   2011*

> ## "There aren't many sites open at this time of year"
> If you're travelling outside peak season
> remember to call ahead to check site opening
> dates – even if the entry says 'open all year'.

PETERSDORF *2E1* (4km NW Coastal) *54.48760, 11.01858*
**Strandcamping Wallnau (Part Naturist), 23769 Wallnau
[(04372) 456; fax 1829; wallnau@strandcamping.de;
www.strandcamping.de]** Site is to W of Fehmarn peninsula
4km W of Petersdorf, sp. V lge, mkd pitch, pt shd; htd wc;
mv service pnt; serviced pitches; sauna; baby facs; shwrs; EHU
(16A) €2.50; gas; lndry (inc dryer); shop; rest, snacks; bar; BBQ;
playgrnd; sand beach adj; sep naturist beach; bike hire; wellness
cent; games area; wifi; entmnt; 50% statics; dogs €5.50; poss cr;
adv bkg; quiet; red LS. "Nature reserve & bird sanctuary nr; excel
for families." ◆ 1 Apr-30 Oct. € 30.00 (CChq acc)   2011*

PUTTGARDEN *2E1* (500m N Coastal) *54.5029, 11.21635*
**Camping Puttgarden, Strandweg, 23769 Puttgarden
[tel/fax (04371) 3492 or 2185]** N on B207/E47, on app
Puttgarden ferry terminal take L turn & foll sp Strand to site
on R. Med, hdstg, unshd; wc; mv service pnt; shwrs €0.50;
EHU (16A) metered; lndry; shop; rest, snacks; playgrnd;
fishing; sailing; many statics; dogs €1; poss cr; adv bkg; quiet;
ccard acc. "Conv NH for ferry to Denmark." 1 Apr-15 Oct.
€ 18.00   2009*

GERMANY

PUTTGARDEN *2E1* (8km SE Coastal) *54.45806, 11.27203*
Camping Klausdorfer Strand, 23769 Klausdorf
[(04371) 2549; fax 2481; info@camping-klausdorferstrand.
de; www.camping-klausdorferstrand.de] Fr Puttgarden on
minor rd (not main E47) sp Burg, turn L after 6km sp Klausdorf.
Foll site sp thro Klausdorf to coast. Lge, hdg/mkd pitch, unshd;
htd wc; chem disp; mv service pnt; some serviced pitches; baby
facs; fam bthrm; shwrs inc; EHU (16A) metered or €2; lndry;
shop; rest; playgrnd; sand beach adj; bike hire; golf 10km;
entmnt; 50% statics; dogs €4; phone; poss cr; Eng spkn; adv
bkg; quiet; red CKE/CCI. "Conv for ferry to Denmark; excel
cycling area; bird sanctuary nr; gd access to pitches; excel."
1 Apr-15 Oct. € 23.00   2011*

⊞ **WULFEN** *2E1* (1km E Coastal) *54.40611, 11.1772*
Camping-und Ferienpark Wulfener Hals (Part Naturist),
Wulfener Hals Weg, 23769 Wulfen [(04371) 86280;
fax 3723; camping@wulfenerhals.de; www.wulfenerhals.
de] Turn off B207/E47 to Avendorf, site sp. V lge, mkd pitch,
shd; htd wc; chem disp; mv service pnt; serviced pitches;
sauna; baby rm; fam bthrm; shwrs; EHU (10A) €2.10; gas;
lndry; shop; rest; snacks; bar; playgrnd; pool; sand beach adj;
sailing; watersports; golf adj; wifi; entmnt; 60% statics; dogs
€7.50; phone; adv bkg; ccard acc; red CKE/CCI. "Excel." ♦
€ 39.50   2011*

See advertisement inside the front cover

⊞ **ZIERENBERG** *1D4* (1km E Rural) *51.36809, 9.31494*
Campingplatz Zur Warme, Im Nordbruch 2, 34289
Zierenberg [tel/fax (05606) 3966; campingplatz-
zierenberg@t-online.de; www.campingplatz-zierenberg.
de] Exit A44 at junc 67 to Zierenberg. In vill cent foll sp for
Freizeit Centrum. Site on R on leaving vill, well sp. Med, mkd
pitch, some hdstg, unshd; htd wc; chem disp; shwrs inc; EHU
(16A) €1.70 or metered; lndry (inc dryer); shop 500m; rest,
snacks; bar; playgrnd; covrd pool; fishing; TV; 75% statics;
dogs €1.50; poss v cr; Eng spkn; adv bkg; quiet. "Scenic, well-
kept site with stream & sm lake adj; clean, modern facs but
poss stretched if site full." ♦ € 16.50   2011*

ZIEROW see Wismar *2E2*

⊞ **ZINGST AM DARSS** *2F1* (3km W Coastal) *54.44055,
12.66031* Camping am Freesenbruch, Am Bahndamm 1,
18374 Zingst-am-Darss [(038232) 15786; fax 15710; info@
camping-zingst.de; www.camping-zingst.de]
On rd 105/E22 at Löbnitz take rd thro Barth to Zingst; site on
coast rd. Lge, mkd pitch, pt shd; wc; chem disp; mv service
pnt; shwrs inc; EHU (16A) metered + conn fee; lndry; shop;
rest, snacks; bar; playgrnd; beach adj; games area; bike hire;
entmnt; 20% statics; dogs €2; sep car park; o'night facs for
m'vans; poss cr; adv bkg; quiet; red CKE/CCI. "Well-
maintained site in National Park; sep fr beach by sea wall & rd;
well-maintained; card operated barrier." ♦ € 20.00   2009*

⊞ **ZISLOW** *2F2* (2km N Rural) *53.44555, 12.31083*
Naturcamping Zwei Seen, Waldchaussee 2, 17209 Zislow
[(039924) 2550; fax 2062; info@zwei-seen-naturcamping.
de; www.zwei-seen-naturcamping.de] A19/E55 exit 17 dir
Adamshoffnung. Turn R at x-rds in 4km. Site sp. Also sp fr W
of Stuer on B198. Lge, pt shd; wc; chem disp; mv service pnt;
shwrs €0.50; EHU (6A) €2; lndry (inc dryer); shop; rest, snacks;
bar; playgrnd; lake sw; watersports; games area; bike hire;
wifi; entmnt; 40% statics; dogs €2.50; phone; poss cr; Eng
spkn; adv bkg; quiet; ccard acc; red CKE/CCI. "Ideal for country
lovers; remote spot; vg lakeside pitches." ♦ € 17.50   2010*

⊞ **ZITTAU** *2H4* (3km W Rural) *50.8943, 14.77005* See-
Camping Zittauer Gebirge, Zur Landesgartenschau 2,
02785 Olbersdorf [(03583) 69629-2; fax 696293; info@
seecamping-zittau.com; www.seecamping-zittau.com]
Fr Zittau foll Olbersdorfer See sp, site on lakeside. Lge, sl,
unshd; wc; chem disp; shwrs €0.70; EHU (10A) €2; lndry
(inc dryer); shop; rest, snacks, bar adj; lake sw adj; entmnt;
10% statics; dogs €2; Eng spkn; quiet; ccard acc; CKE/CCI.
"Excel san facs; excel base for hill walking; close Polish & Czech
borders." ♦ € 19.00   2010*

⊞ **ZORGE** *2E4* (4km NE Urban) *51.64176, 10.65083*
Camping im Waldwinkel, Im Kunzental 2, 37449 Zorge
[(05586) 1048; fax 8113] Fr N via Bad Harzburg, Braunlage,
Hohegeiss, turn L at ent to Zorge vill, site sp dir 'Schwimmbad'.
Fr S on B243, turn N at Bad Sachsa, dir Walkenried & Zorge, turn
R in vill. Med, pt sl, unshd; wc; chem disp; mv service pnt; shwrs;
baby rm; EHU (16A) metered + conn fee; gas; lndry (inc dryer);
shop 1km; rest, snacks adj; playgrnd; htd pool 200m; tennis; ski
lift 4km; skibus; entmnt; TV; dogs €1; o'night area for m'vans; adv
bkg; quiet; red CKE/CCI. "Beautiful location." ♦ € 16.00   2010*

RUGEN ISLAND

⊞ **ALTEFAHR** *2F1* (1km NW Coastal) *54.33200,
13.12206* Sund Camp, Am Kurpark 1, 18573 Altefähr
[(038306) 75483; fax 60306; info@sund-camp.de;
www.sund-camp.de] Fr Stralsund, cross bdge on B96 to
Rügen Island. Foll sp to Altefähr. Site well sp fr vill. Med, mkd
pitch, pt shd; wc; chem disp; mv service pnt; shwrs inc; EHU
(16A) inc (poss rev pol); shops 500m; lndry; sm shop; rest 400m;
shgl beach 500m; bike hire; TV; 15% statics; dogs €2; poss cr;
phone; sep car park; quiet; red long stay. "Conv Rugen Is (walks,
cycle tracks, beaches, steam rlwy); easy walk to vill & harbour;
splendid, but busy island; well worth visit; ferry to Stralsund
Altstadt nrby; excel, friendly site; muddy when wet; excel, clean
san facs; ltd nbr of touring pitches." € 24.00   2015*

BINZ *2G1* (3km NW Coastal) *54.42315, 13.57808* Camping
Meier, Proraer Chaussee 30, 18609 Prora [(038393) 2085;
fax 32624; info@camping-meier-ruegen.de;
www.camping-meier-ruegen.de] On B96 Stralsund to
Bergen cont on 196 to Karow. Turn L on 196a to Prora, at
traff lts turn R onto L29 to Binz. After 1.5km at camp sp turn
R thro wood to site. Med, mkd pitch, pt shd; wc; chem disp;
mv service pnt; shwrs €0.50; EHU (6A) €2.50; gas 1km; lndry;
shops 1km; rest; bar; playgrnd; sand beach 500m; tennis; bike
hire; dogs €3.50; phone; Eng spkn; adv bkg (bkg fee); quiet;
red 7+ days; ccard acc (Visa only). "Gd location for touring
Rügen area; gd sandy beach thro woods; vg rest; vg san facs."
♦ 1 Apr-31 Oct. € 23.00   2011*

GERMANY

SCHAPRODE *2F1* (230m N Coastal) *54.51610, 13.16510*
Camping am Schaproder Bodden, Langestrasse 24, 18569 Schaprode [tel/fax (038309) 1234; camping.schaprode@t-online.de; www.camping-schaprode.de] Fr Stralsund on B96 to Rügen Island, N to Samtens then turn N thro Gingst; at Trent turn W to Schaprode; site sp on ent to vill. Lge, mkd pitch, pt shd; wc; chem disp; mv service pnt; shwrs €0.50; EHU (6A) €1.50; lndry; shop; rest, snacks; bar; BBQ; playgrnd; sand/shgl beach adj; watersports; bike hire; 20% statics; dogs €1.25; Eng spkn; adv bkg; quiet; CKE/CCI. "Pleasant beach position; some great pitches; cheerful, family-owned site; trips to island of Hiddensee (nature reserve) - unspoilt island; rec." 1 Apr-31 Oct. € 18.00   2011*

SYLT ISLAND

WESTERLAND *1C1* (5km N Coastal) *54.94251, 8.32685*
Camping Wenningstedt, Am Dorfteich, 25996 Wenningstedt [(04651) 944004; fax 44740; camp@wenningstedt.de; www.wenningstedt.de] Fr Westerland foll sp to Wenningstedt or List. Site app rd on sharp bend bef Wenningstedt. Lge, pt sl, unshd; wc; chem disp; mv service pnt; baby facs; shwrs inc; EHU (16A) metered; lndry (inc dryer); rest; playgrnd; htd, covrd pool; fishing 300m; wifi; entmnt; dogs €3.20; adv bkg; quiet. Easter-31 Oct. € 25.00   2010*

ZWEIBRUCKEN *3B3* (2km E Urban) *49.25368, 7.37736*
Campingplatz Zweibrücken, Geschwister-Scholl-Allee 11, 66482 Zweibrücken [(06332) 482984; info@campingplatz-zw.de; www.campingplatz-zw.de] Exit A8 junc 32 for Zweibrücken town cent. Sp infrequent so foll sp to Rosegarten site beyond show-jumping arena. Turn R at camping sp immed over bdge. Med, unshd; wc; chem disp; shwrs inc; EHU (10A) metered + conn fee; lndry; shop 300m; rest, snacks; playgrnd; htd pool 150m; rv & beach adj; bike hire; wifi; 50% statics; dogs €1; noisy at w/end; red CKE/CCI. "Poss diff access due parked cars for sw pool; 15 min walk to town cent; gd NH." ♦ 1 Apr-30 Sep. € 22.00   2009*

ZWEIBRUCKEN *3B3* (5km SW Rural) *49.20638, 7.33111*
Camping Hengstbacher-Mühle, Hengstbacher Mühle 1, 66482 Zweibrücken-Mittelbach [(06332) 18128; fax 904001] Fr A8 exit junc 33 onto B424 sp Zweibrücken-Ixheim & Mittelbach. At T-junc turn R dir Bitsch & in 50m turn R at camping sp. Site on L in 4km after end of Mittelbach vill. Sm, pt shd; wc; chem disp; mv service pnt; shwrs inc; EHU (15A) €2.50 or metered (poss rev pol); shops 4km; 70% statics in sep area; liable to flooding; Eng spkn; quiet. "Friendly owner; lovely setting; basic site but clean san facs; gd NH; CL type size." 15 Apr-31 Oct. € 13.50   2014*

"That's changed – Should I let The Club know?"
If you find something on site that's different from the site entry, fill in a report and let us know. See www.caravanclub.co.uk/europereport.

ZWEIBRUCKEN *3B3* (17km SW Rural) *49.15888, 7.24388*
Camping am Schwimmbad, Am Campingplatz 1, 66453 Gersheim-Walsheim [(06843) 1030; fax 80138; freizeitbetrieb@gersheim.de; www.gersheim.de] Fr A8/E50 exit junc 9 onto B423 dor Blieskastel. In Webenheim turn L twd Gersheim, after 11km turn L for Walsheim. Site on L beyond vill. Med, pt sl, pt shd; wc; chem disp; shwrs inc; EHU €2 or metered (10A); lndry (inc dryer); shop in vill; rest, bar adj; BBQ; htd pool adj; 85% statics; dogs €0.50; phone; poss cr; adv bkg; quiet; red CKE/CCI. "Helpful warden; sep area for tourers; pleasant countryside; walking & cycle paths nr; site barrier clsd 1300-1500 & 2200." ♦ 15 Mar-15 Oct. € 15.70   2014*

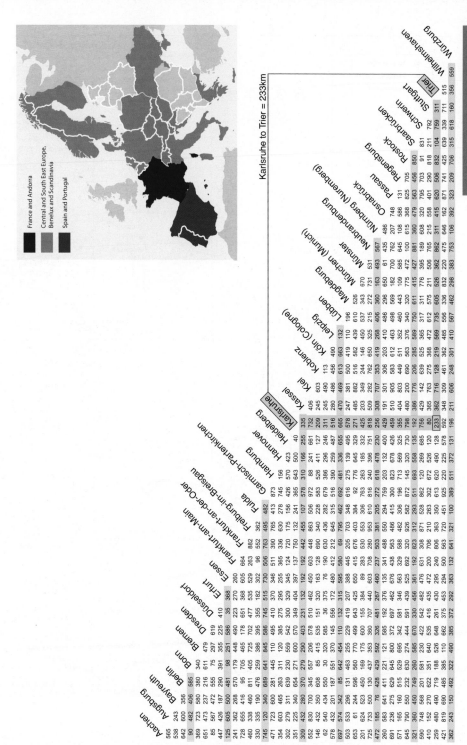

Map 1

Map 2

311

Map 3

Map 4

© Collins Bartholomew Ltd 2015

Motorways		
Major roads		
Main roads		

FEDERAL STATES OF GERMANY

SCHLESWIG-HOLSTEIN

MECKLENBURG-VORPOMMERN
(Mecklenburg-Western Pomerania)

Hamburg

HAMBURG

BREMEN · Bremen

NIEDERSACHSEN
(Lower Saxony)

Hannover

BERLIN

Berlin

BRANDENBURG

NORDRHEIN-WESTFALEN
(North Rhine-Westphalia)

Düsseldorf

Köln

Bonn

SACHSEN-ANHALT
(Saxony-Anhalt)

Leipzig

SACHSEN · Dresden
(Saxony)

HESSEN
(Hesse)

THÜRINGEN
(Thuringia)

Frankfurt-am-Main

RHEINLAND-PFALZ
(Rhineland-Palatinate)

SAARLAND

Nürnberg

Stuttgart

BADEN-WÜRTTEMBERG

BAYERN
(Bavaria)

München

Greece
Country Introduction

Cape Sounion, Greece

Welcome to Greece

Whether you want to marvel at ancient ruins, lay on an idyllic sandy beach or sample local dishes, Greece is undoubtedly the place to be.

From rugged hillsides to the sparkling blue waters of the Mediterranean, this is a country steeped in myths of gods and heroes. The country is also famed for the friendly and hospitable nature of its people, so you're sure to receive a warm welcome.

Country highlights

Music is an integral part of Greek society and laïkó is a modern folk music genre that boomed in the 1960s and 70s. There are now many different forms of this music and often generally refers to Greek popular music, but it still retains a sense of being a song of the people.

Greece can be considered the birthplace of wine, and the origins of wine-making in Greece go back well over 6000 years. Although not as well-known as other European nations for its wine, Greece has a thriving industry and the local varieties pair up well with food dishes from the same area.

Major towns and cities

- Athens – the cradle of Western civilization and one of the world's oldest cities.

- Thessalonika – a charming city filled with museums to explore.

- Patras – this amazing city is home to fascinating sites from ancient times.

- Larissa – surrounded by mountains and home to several ancient sites.

Attractions

- The Acropolis, Athens – an ancient citadel containing the remains of several ancient buildings, including the Parthenon.

- Meteora – a stunning series of Greek Orthodox monasteries built on natural sandstone pillars.

- Delphi – this site boasts some of Greece's most important ancient ruins as well as a museum with an impressive collection of artefacts.

- Cape Sounion – fantastic views over the Aegean and the ruins of an ancient temple.

Find out more

www.visitgreece.gr

Tel: 0030 (0) 21 03 31 05 29 Greece Tourist Board

Country Information

Population (approx): 10.8 million

Capital: Athens (population approx 3.7 million)

Area: 131,957 sq km

Bordered by: Albania, Bulgaria, Macedonia, Turkey

Coastline: 13,676km

Terrain: Mainly mountain ranges extending into the sea as peninsulas and chains of islands

Climate: Warm Mediterranean climate; hot, dry summers; mild, wet winters in the south, colder in the north; rainy season November to March; winter temperatures can be severe in the mountains

Highest Point: Mount Olympus 2,919m

Language: Greek

Local Time: GMT or BST + 2, i.e. 2 hours ahead of the UK all year

Currency: Euros divided into 100 cents; £1 = €1.42, €1 = £0.71 (September 2015)

Emergency numbers: Police 100; Fire brigade 199; Ambulance 166. Operators speak English. Dial 171 for emergency tourist police.

Public Holidays 2016: Jan 1, 6; Mar 14, 25; Apr 29; May 1, 2; Jun 20; Aug 15; Oct 28; Dec 25, 26.

School summer holidays run from the beginning of July to the first week in September.

Camping and Caravanning

There are over 340 campsites licensed by the Greek National Tourist Office. These can be recognised by a sign displaying the organisation's blue emblem. Most are open from April until the end of October, but those near popular tourist areas stay open all year. There are other unlicensed sites but visitors to them cannot be assured of safe water treatment, fire prevention measures or swimming pool inspection.

Casual/wild camping is not allowed outside official sites in Greece.

Electricity and Gas

Usually current on campsites varies between 4 and 16 amps. Plugs have two round pins. There are few CEE connections.

The full range of Campingaz cylinders are available from hypermarkets and other shops, but when purchasing a cylinder you may not be given a refundable deposit receipt.

Entry Formalities

Visas are not required by British or Irish passport holders for a stay of up to three months. Visitors planning to stay longer should contact the Greek Embassy in London before they travel www.greekembassy.org.uk.

Medical Services

For minor complaints seek help at a pharmacy (farmakio). Staff are generally well trained and in major cities there is usually one member of staff in a pharmacy who speaks English. You should have no difficulty finding an English speaking doctor in large towns and resorts.

Medications containing codeine are restricted. If you are taking any medication containing it, you should carry a letter from your doctor and take no more than one month's supply into the country.

There are numerous public and private hospitals and medical centres of varying standards. Wards may be crowded and the standards of nursing and after care, particularly in the public health sector, are generally below what is normally acceptable in Britain. Doctors and facilities are generally good on the mainland, but may be limited on the islands. The public ambulance service will normally respond to any accident but there are severe shortages of ambulances on some islands.

Emergency treatment at public medical clinics (yiatria) and in state hospitals registered by the Greek Social Security Institute, IKA-ETAM, is free on presentation of a European Health Insurance Card (EHIC) but you may face a long wait. You will be charged for prescriptions so keep the adhesive labels from the medicines packages in order to claim a refund at an IKA-ETAM office. See www.ika.gr for a list of local offices.

You may consult a doctor or dentist privately but you will have to present your EHIC and pay all charges up front. You can then claim back the charges later from the IKA-ETAM.

If staying near a beach, ensure that you have plenty of insect repellent as sand flies are prevalent. Do not be tempted to befriend stray dogs as they often harbour diseases which may be passed to humans.

Opening Hours

Banks – Mon-Fri 8am-2pm (1.30pm on Friday); 8am-6pm in tourist areas. During 2015, Greek banks were closed because of the economic crisis, and there is an ongoing possibility that banking services could be withdrawn or restricted at any time.

Museums – Check locally for opening hours. Normally closed on Mon or Tues and some bank holidays.

Post Offices – Mon-Fri 8am-2pm; 8am-7pm in tourist areas; many in Athens open Sat mornings in summer.

Shops – Mon-Fri 8am/8.30am/9am-2pm/4.30pm & on some days 5pm-8.30pm; Sat 8.30am-3pm; check locally as hours vary according to season.

Safety and Security

Normally visits to Greece are trouble-free, but the tourist season results in an increase in incidents of theft of passports, wallets, handbags, etc, particularly in areas or at events where crowds gather. Personal attacks are rare but visitors are advised to maintain the same level of personal security awareness as in the UK.

Take care when visiting well-known historical sites; they are the favoured haunts of pickpockets, bag-snatchers and muggers. Women should not walk alone at night and lone visitors are strongly advised never to accept lifts from strangers or passing acquaintances at any time.

Since banking services were restricted in 2015, the FCO has recommended that you take enough cash to cover your needs while you are in Greece. If you are carrying large amounts of cash, make sure you take safety precautions. Be aware that tourists are expected to be carrying larger amounts of money, making them potential targets for thieves.

Multi-lingual tourist police operate in most resorts offering information and help; they can be recognised by a 'Tourist Police' badge, together with a white cap band. There is also a 24-hour emergency helpline for tourists; dial 171 from anywhere in Greece.

Certain areas near the Greek borders are militarily sensitive and you should not take photographs or take notes near military or official installations. Seek permission before photographing individuals.

There is a general threat from domestic terrorism. Attacks could be indiscriminate and against civilian targets in public places. Public protests are a standard feature of Greek politics and it is wise to avoid public gatherings and demonstrations. Domestic anarchist groups remain active but their actions are primarily directed against the Greek state.

During especially hot and dry periods there is a danger of forest fires. Take care when visiting or driving through woodland areas. Ensure that cigarette ends are properly extinguished, do not light barbecues and do not leave rubbish or empty bottles behind.

Some motorists have encountered stowaway attempts while waiting to board ferries to Italy from Patras. Keep a watch on your vehicle(s).

In order to comply with the law, always ensure that you obtain a receipt for goods purchased. If you buy pirate CDs or DVDs you could be penalised heavily.

British Embassy

1 PLOUTARCHOU STREET
106 75 ATHENS
Tel: (210) 7272600
www.ukingreece.fco.gov.uk
There are also British Consulates/Vice-Consulates/Honorary Consulates in Corfu, Heraklion (Crete), Rhodes and Zakynthos.

Irish Embassy

7 LEOF.VAS
KONSTANTINOU, 106 74 ATHENA
Tel: (210) 7232771
www.embassyofireland.gr
There are also Honorary Consulates in Corfu, Crete, Rhodes and Thessaloniki.

Border Posts

Borders may be crossed only on official routes where a Customs office is situated. These are usually open day and night. Customs offices at ports are open from 7.30am to 3pm Monday to Friday.

Documents

Passport

Carry your passport at all times as a means of identification.

Vehicle(s)

Carry your vehicle registration certificate (V5C), insurance certificate and MOT certificate (if applicable) at all times.

Money

Major credit cards are accepted in hotels, restaurants and shops and at some petrol stations. They may not be accepted at shops in small towns or villages. There is an extensive network of cash machines in major cities.

Carry your credit card issuers'/banks' 24-hour UK contact numbers in case of loss or theft.

Motoring in Greece
Accidents

It is not essential to call the police in the case of an accident causing material damage only, however motorists are advised to call at the nearest police station to give a description of the incident to the authorities.

Whenever an accident causes physical injury, drivers are required to stop immediately to give assistance to the injured and to call the police. Drivers who fail to meet these requirements are liable to imprisonment for up to three years.

If a visiting motorist has an accident, especially one causing injuries, they should inform the motoring organisation, ELPA, preferably at its head office in Athens, on (210) 6068800, email: info@elpa.gr, as they should be able to offer you assistance.

Alcohol

The maximum permitted level of alcohol is 50 milligrams in 100 millilitres of blood, i.e. lower than that permitted in the UK (80 milligrams). A level of 20 milligrams in 100 millilitres of blood applies to drivers who have held a driving licence for less than two years and to motorcyclists. Police carry out random breath tests and refusal to take a test when asked by the police, and/or driving while over the legal limit, can incur high fines, withdrawal of your driving licence and even imprisonment.

Breakdown Service

The Automobile & Touring Club of Greece (ELPA) operates a roadside assistance service (OVELPA) 24 hours a day on all mainland Greek roads as well as on most islands. The number to dial from most towns in Greece is 10400.

Members of AIT/FIA affiliated clubs, such as The Caravan Club, should present their valid membership card in order to qualify for reduced charges for on-the-spot assistance and towing. Payment by credit card is accepted.

Essential Equipment
First Aid Kit

All vehicles must carry a first aid kit.
Fire Extinguisher

All vehicles must carry a fire extinguisher.
Warning Triangles

The placing of a warning triangle is compulsory in the event of an accident or a breakdown. It must be placed 100 metres behind the vehicle.
Child Restraint System

Children under three years of age must be seated in a suitable and approved child restraint. Children between the ages of 3 and 11 years old that are less than 1.35 metres in height must be seated in an appropriate child restraint for their size. From 12 years old children that are over 1.35 metres in height can wear an adult seat belt.

A rear facing child restraint can be placed in the front seat but only if the airbag is deactivated.

Fuel

Petrol stations are usually open from 7am to 7pm; a few are open 24 hours. Some will accept credit cards but those offering cut-price fuel are unlikely to do so. In rural areas petrol stations may close in the evening and at weekends, so keep your tank topped up. There are no automatic petrol pumps operated with either credit cards or bank notes.

LPG (autogas) is available from a limited number of outlets.

Parking

Parking is only permitted in the Athens 'Green Zone' where there are parking meters. Special parking sites in other areas are reserved for short-term parking for tourists.

There may be signs on the side of the road indicating where vehicles should be parked. Parking restrictions are indicated by yellow lines at the side of the road. The police are entitled to remove vehicles. They can also confiscate the number plates of vehicles parked illegally and, while this usually applies only to Greek-registered vehicles, drivers of foreign registered vehicles should nevertheless avoid illegal parking.

Parking is not permitted within three metres of a fire hydrant, five metres of an intersection, stop sign or traffic light, and fifteen metres of a bus stop, tram stop and level crossings.

Roads

The surfaces of all major roads and of the majority of other roads are in good condition. Some mountain roads, however, may be in poor condition and drivers must beware of unexpected potholes (especially on corners), precipitous, unguarded drops and single-carriageway bridges. Even on narrow mountain roads you may well encounter buses and coaches.

British motorists visiting Greece should be extra vigilant in view of the high incidence of road accidents. Driving standards are generally poorer than in the UK and you may well have to contend with dangerous overtaking, tailgating, weaving motorcycles and scooters, constant use of the horn, roaming pedestrians and generally erratic driving. Greece has one of the highest rate of road fatalities in Europe and overtaking and speeding are common causes of accidents, particularly on single lane carriageways. Drive carefully and be aware of other drivers at all times.

August is the busiest month of the year for traffic and the A1/E75 between Athens and Thessalonika is recognised as one of the most dangerous routes, together with the road running through the Erimanthos mountains south of Kalavrita. Mountain roads in general can be dangerous owing to narrow carriageways, blind bends and unprotected embankments, so keep your speed down.

You are strongly advised against hiring motorcycles, scooters and mopeds, as drivers of these modes of transport are particularly at risk. The wearing of crash helmets is a legal requirement. Never hand over your passport when hiring a vehicle.

Greece has a high level of pedestrian fatalities. Where there is a shortage of parking spaces drivers park on pavements so that pedestrians are forced to walk in the road. Collisions between pedestrians and motorcycles are common.

Road Signs and Markings

Road signs conform to international conventions. Motorway signs have white lettering on a green background, signs on other roads are on a blue background. All motorways, major and secondary roads are signposted in Greek and English.

Some open roads have a white line on the nearside, and slower-moving vehicles are expected to pull across it to allow vehicles to overtake.

Traffic Jams

There is heavy rush hour traffic in and around the major cities and traffic jams are the norm in central Athens any time of day. During the summer months traffic to the coast may be heavy, particularly at weekends. Traffic jams may be encountered on the A1/E75 Athens to Thessalonika road and on the A8/E65 Athens to Patras road. Traffic may also be heavy near the ferry terminals to Italy and you should allow plenty of time when travelling to catch a ferry. Delays can be expected at border crossings to Turkey and Bulgaria.

Speed Limits

	Open Road (Km/h)	Motorway (Km/h)
Car Solo	90-110	130
Car towing caravan/trailer	80	80
Motorhome under 3500kg	80	90
Motorhome 3500-7500kg	80	80

Violation of Traffic Regulations

The Greek police are authorised to impose fines in cases of violation of traffic regulations, but they are not allowed to collect fines on the spot. Motorists must pay fines within ten days, otherwise legal proceedings will be started.

Motorways

There are over 2,000 km of motorways in Greece. Service areas provide petrol, a cafeteria and shops. The main motorways are A1 Agean, A2 Egnatia, A6 Attiki, A7 Peloponissos, A8 Pathe, A29 Kastorias. For further information visit www.greek-motorway.net.

Motorway Tolls

Tolls are charged according to vehicle classification and distance travelled. By European standards the tolls are generally quite low. Cash is the preferred means of payment.

The Egnatia Highway

The 804 km Egnatia Highway (the A2), part of European route E90 linking the port of Igoumenitsa with the Turkish border at Kipoi, has undergone extensive upgrade and improvement in recent years. The route includes many bridges and tunnels with frequent emergency telephones for which the number to call from a landline or mobile phone is 1077. The road provides a continuous high speed link from west to east and will eventually connect with Istanbul. An electronic toll collection system is planned for the future.

Patras – Antirrio Bridge

A 2.8 km long toll suspension bridge between Rio (near Patras) and Antirrio links the Peloponnese with western central Greece and is part of the A8/E55 motorway. It has cut the journey time across the Gulf of Corinth – formerly only possible by ferry – to just five minutes. Tolls are charged.

Preveza – Aktio Tunnel

This undersea toll tunnel links Preveza with Aktio near Agios Nikolaos on the E55 along the west coast of mainland Greece and is part of a relatively fast, scenic route south from Igoumenitsa to central and southern regions.

Touring

Mainland Greece and most of the Greek islands that are popular with British tourists are in seismically active zones, and small earth tremors are common. Serious earthquakes are less frequent but can, and do, occur.

Smoking is prohibited in bars and restaurants. In restaurants, if the bill does not include a service charge, it is usual to leave a 10 to 20% tip. Taxi drivers do not normally expect a tip but it is customary to round up the fare.

The best known local wine is retsina but there is also a wide range of non-resinated wines. Beer is brewed under licence from German and Danish breweries; Ouzo is a popular and strong aniseed-flavoured aperitif.

The major Greek ports are Corfu, Igoumenitsa, Patras, Piraeus and Rhodes. Ferry services link these ports with Cyprus, Israel, Italy and Turkey. The routes from Ancona and Venice in Italy to Patras and Igoumenitsa are very popular and advance booking is recommended.

For further information contact:

VIAMARE LTD
SUITE 108
582 Honeypot Lane
STANMORE
MIDDX
HA7 1JY
Tel: 020 8206 3420,
www.viamare.com
Email: ferries@viamare.com

Some ferries on routes from Italy to Greece have 'camping on board' facilities whereby passengers are able to sleep in their caravan or motorhome. Mains hook-ups are available, together with showers and toilets.

There are several World Heritage Sites in Greece (with more under consideration), including such famous sites as the Acropolis in Athens, the archaeological sites at Olympia and Mistras, and the old towns of Corfu and Rhodes. See www.worldheritagesite.org for more information. When visiting churches and monasteries dress conservatively, i.e. long trousers for men and no shorts, sleeveless T-shirts or short skirts for women.

Public Transport

Greece has a modern, integrated public transport system, including an extensive metro, bus, tram and suburban railway network in and around Athens – see www.ametro.gr for a metro map.

A metro system is under construction in Thessaloniki that is not due for completion until 2018.

Buy bus/tram tickets from special booths at bus stops, newspaper kiosks or from metro stations. A ticket is valid for a travel time of 90 minutes.

Taxis are relatively cheap. All licensed taxis are yellow and are equipped with meters (the fare is charged per kilometre) and display a card detailing tariffs and surcharges. In certain tourist areas, you may be asked to pay a predetermined (standard) amount for a ride to a specific destination.

Taxis run on a share basis, so they often pick up other passengers on the journey.

There are many ferry and hydrofoil services from Piraeus to the Greek islands and between islands.

Meteora

⊞ **AGIOI THEODOROI** *B3* (12km E Coastal) *37.95212, 23.17868* **Camping Glaros, Kineta, 19100 Agioi Theodoroi [(22960) 62805; info@camping-glaros.gr; www.camping-glaros.gr]** E fr Korinthos on A8 dir Athens, site sp. Med, pt sl, pt shd; wc; chem disp; shwrs; EHU; lndry; shop; rest, snacks; bar; cooking facs; playgrnd; sand beach; internet; some statics; dogs; quiet. "Well-situated for archeological sites; pleasant." € 22.00 (CChq acc) 2011*

AGIOS KONSTANTINOS see Kamena Vourla *B2*

⊞ **ALEXANDROUPOLI** *C1* (2km W Coastal) *40.84679, 25.85614* **Camping Alexandroupolis Beach, Makris Ave, 68100 Alexandroupolis [tel/fax (25510) 28735; camping@ditea.gr; www.ditea.gr]** Site on coast - after drainage channel, at 2nd set traff lts close together. Lge, hdg/mkd pitch, pt hdstg, shd; wc (some cont); chem disp; shwrs inc; EHU (8A) €3.60; gas; shop; snacks; bar; playgrnd; sand beach adj; watersports; tennis; games area; wifi; 20% statics; phone; Eng spkn; quiet but cr & noisy high ssn; red CKE/CCI. "Spacious, secure, well-run site; clean, hot shwrs; easy walk to pleasant town cent." € 18.50 2011*

ALISSOS see Patra *A2*

ANTIRRIO see Nafpaktos *B2*

ASSINI see Nafplio *B3*

ATHENS see Athina *B3*

⊞ **ATHINA** *B3* (17km NE Urban) *38.09944, 23.79166* **Camping Nea Kifissia, Potamou 60, Adames, 14564 Athina [tel/fax (210) 8075579 or 6205646; camping@hol.gr; www.camping-neakifissia.gr]** Sp both dirs on E75 Athens-Lamia rd. Heading twd Athens exit at sp, to U-turn onto service rd then take 1st L & foll sp. Sm, hdg pitch, hdstg, terr, shd; wc; chem disp; shwrs inc; EHU (10A) €4; lndry rm; shop 800m; pool high ssn; TV; 50% statics; dogs; phone; bus to metro stn 200m; poss cr; Eng spkn; aircraft, rlwy & rd noise; red CCI. "Conv base for Athens - metro at Kifissia; pleasant, quiet, well-run site; excel pool; clean san facs but tired; helpful recep staff; san facs down 30+ steps." € 33.00 2015*

⊞ **ATHINA** *B3* (7km NW Urban) *38.00916, 23.67236* **Camping Athens, 198-200 Athinon Ave, 12136 Athens [(210) 5814114 or 5814101 winter; fax 5820353; info@campingathens.com.gr; www.campingathens.com.gr]** Fr Corinth on E94 m'way/highway, stay on this rd to Athens o'skts; site is approx 4km past Dafni Monastery, set back on L of multi-lane rd, sh dist beyond end of underpass. Go past site to next traff lts where U-turn permitted. Fr N use old national rd (junc 8 if on toll m'way). Med, pt shd; wc (some cont); chem disp; mv service pnt; shwrs inc; EHU (16A) €4; lndry; shop, rest high ssn; snacks; bar; internet; TV; dogs; frequent bus to Athens; poss v cr; rd noise; ccard acc; red LS. "V dusty but well-managed site; gd san facs but poss insufficient high ssn; helpful staff; bus tickets to Athens sold; visitors rec not to use Sat Nav to find site, as it misdirects!" € 42.00 2013*

CHRISSA see Delfi *B2*

CORINTH see Korinthos *B3*

DELFI *B2* (20km S Coastal) *38.42502, 22.45824* **Camping Ayannis, 33200 Itea-Kirra [(22650) 32555; fax 33870; m.anagnostakos@hotmail.com]** App Itea fr Delfi; 1km bef Itea take ring rd sp Desfina; site on R after 4km; ent site on rough track for 200m. Med, pt shd; wc (some cont); chem disp; 100% serviced pitches; shwrs inc; EHU (6A) inc; gas; lndry; shop; rest, snacks; bar; BBQ; sm shgl beach adj; Eng spkn; quiet; ccard acc; CKE/CCI. "Friendly owner; conv for Delphi; poss diff access lge o'fits; fair sh stay." 1 May-30 Oct. € 22.50 2010*

⊞ **DELFI** *B2* (2km W Rural) *38.4836, 22.4755* **Camping Apollon, 33054 Delfi [(22650) 82762 or 82750; fax 82888; apollon4@otenet.gr; www.apolloncamping.gr]** Site on N48 fr Delfi twd Itea & 1st of number of campsites on this rd. Site 25km fr Parnassus ski cent. Med, mkd pitch, pt sl, pt terr, pt shd; wc; chem disp; mv service pnt; shwrs inc; EHU (16A) €3; gas; lndry; shop; rest; bar; playgrnd; pool; TV; bike hire; 30% statics; dogs free; phone; Harmonie Group site; poss cr; adv bkg; ccard acc; red CKE/CCI. "Magnificent views over mountains & Gulf of Corinth; site cooler than some other sites due to its elevation; vg site; popular with groups of students; vg campsite." ♦ € 30.00 2015*

DELFI *B2* (5km W Rural) *38.47868, 22.47461* **Camping Delphi, Itea Road, 33054 Delfi [(22650) 82209; fax 82363; info@delphicamping.com; www.delphicamping.com]** App fr Itea-Amfissa rd or Levadia; well sp. Med, terr, shd; wc; chem disp; mv service pnt; shwrs inc; EHU (16A) €3.90; gas; lndry; shop, rest, snacks high ssn; bar; pool; tennis; wifi; TV; dogs free; phone; bus to Delfi; Sunshine Group site; poss cr; adv bkg; ccard acc; red CKE/CCI. "Visit grotto, refuge of Parnassus; Delfi archaeological sites 3km; friendly, helpful staff; magnificent views; gd pool; tired facs; 20% discount for Minoan Line ticketholders; delightful site; san facs bit tired but clean & tidy; excel site." 1 Apr-31 Oct. € 25.00 2014*

⊞ **DELFI** *B2* (8.5km W Rural) *38.47305, 22.45926* **Chrissa Camping, 33055 Chrissa [(22650) 82050; fax 83148; info@chrissacamping.gr; www.chrissacamping.gr]** 1st site on Itea to Delfi rd, sp. Med, pt sl, terr, shd; wc; chem disp; shwrs inc; EHU (10A) €4; gas; lndry; shop; rest, snacks; bar; playgrnd; pools; paddling pool; shgl beach 10km; tennis 300m; games area; wifi; TV rm; adv bkg; quiet; ccard acc; red CKE/CCI. "Excel, scenic site." € 26.00 (CChq acc) 2011*

DREPANO see Nafplio *B3*

⊞ **DREPANO** *B3* (12km E Coastal) *37.49710, 22.99028* **Iria Beach Camping, Iria Beach 21100, Nafplio [tel/fax 02 75 20 94 253; iriabeach@naf.forthnet.gr; www.iriabeach.com]** Fr Drepano head E on Epar. Od. Drepanou-Kantias. Cont onto Kantias-Irion. 800m after Iria Beach Hotel turn R. Site on L after 1.5km. Med, hdstg, shd; wc; chem disp; mv service pnt; baby facs; shwrs; EHU (16A); lndry; shop; snacks; bar; BBQ; cooking facs; playgrnd; beach adj; wifi; TV; 5% statics; dogs; twin axles; Eng spkn; adv bkg; quiet; CCI. "Opp beach; gd sw; site quiet & relaxing; helpful staff; vg site." ♦ ltd. € 33.50 2014*

⊞ **EGIO** *B2* (13km NW Coastal) *38.32078, 21.97195* **Tsoli's Camping, Lambíri Egion, 25100 Lambiri [(26910) 31469 or 31621; fax 32473]** Fr Athens: A8/E65 exit Kamaras, site clearly sp 1km W of Lambiri. Fr Patras: Leave A8/E65 at exit Longos, take the Old Nat. On L in 1.5km after Lampiri. Med, hdstg, shd; wc; chem disp; shwrs inc; EHU (16A) inc; gas; lndry; shop; rest high ssn; snacks; bar; BBQ; playgrnd; shgl beach adj; watersports; fishing; boat-launching; entmnt; TV; 10% statics; dogs; phone; bus; sep car park; Eng spkn; adv bkg; some rd & rlwy noise & noise fr bar; ccard acc; red LS; CKE/CCI. "Bus & train service to Athens & Patras; gd site with gd facs in delightful position; few shd pitches for tourers & poss diff for high o'fits." € 24.00   2015*

⊞ **FINIKOUNDAS** *A3* (1km W Coastal) *36.80555, 21.79583* **Camping Thines, 24006 Finikoundas [(27230) 71200; fax 71027; thines@otenet.gr; www.finikounda.com]** Fr Methoni dir Finikoundas, turn R 1km bef vill, site on L. Sm, hdg/mkd pitch, hdstg, pt shd; wc; chem disp; shwrs inc; EHU (6-10A); gas; lndry; shop & 1km; snacks; bar; BBQ; cooking facs; sand beach adj; boat-launching; wifi; TV; dogs; poss cr; Eng spkn; quiet; ccard acc; red winter long stay; CKE/CCI. "Excel facs; helpful, friendly management; wonderful scenery & beach; lovely vill in walking dist; beautiful site." ♦ € 26.50 (CChq acc)   2015*

"I like to fill in the reports as I travel from site to site"

You'll find report forms at the back of this guide, or you can fill them in online at www.caravanclub.co.uk/europereport.

GERAKINI *B2* (3km SE Coastal) *40.26464, 23.46338* **Camping Kouyoni, 63100 Gerakini [tel/fax (23710) 52052; info@kouyoni.gr; www.kouyoni.gr]** Take main rd S fr Thessaloniki to Nea Moudania, then turn E twd Sithonia. Site is 18km on that rd past Gerakini on R, past filling stn. Well sp. Med, hdg/mkd pitch, pt sl, shd; wc; chem disp; shwrs inc; EHU (16A) €3.30; lndry; shop & 1km; rest, snacks; bar; BBQ; playgrnd; pool; paddling pool; sand beach adj; games area; boat-launching; TV; 30% statics; dogs; phone; adv bkg; quiet; red long stay/CKE/CCI. "Gd touring base set in olive grove; friendly owner; gd facs; gd beach; influx of w/enders high ssn." 24 Apr-30 Sep. € 26.00   2009*

GIALOVA see Pylos *A3*

GIANNITSOCHORI see Kyparissia *A3*

GITHIO *B3* (5km SSW Coastal) *36.73055, 22.55305* **Camping Meltemi, Mavrovouni Gytheio Lakonias 23200 [(02733) 023260; fax 023833; info@campingmeltemi.gr; www.campingmeltemi.gr]** Site is approx 3km S of Githio on the L of the rd to Areopoli. Lge, mkd pitch, shd; wc; chem disp; mv service pnt; shwrs; EHU (16A); lndry; shop; rest; snacks; BBQ; cooking facs; playgrnd; pool; waterslide; beach 20m; games area; wifi; TV; dogs; phone; twin axles; Eng spkn; adv bkg; red LS; CKE/CCI. "Beach volleyball, tennis, table tennis & basketball court; vg." 1 Apr-31 Oct. € 26.00   2015*

⊞ **GITHIO** *B3* (5km SW Coastal) *36.72913, 22.54519* **Gythion Bay Camping, 23200 Githio [(27330) 22522; fax 23523; info@gythiocamping.gr; www.gythiocamping.gr]** Sp fr Githio town, on E of Githio-Areopolis rd. Med, shd; wc (some cont); chem disp; mv service pnt; shwrs inc; EHU (16A) inc; gas; lndry; shop; rest, snacks; bar; playgrnd; beach adj; surfing school; boating; games area; wifi; entmnt; TV; no dogs; poss cr; no adv bkg; quiet; Harmonie Group site; ccard acc; 10% red CKE/CCI. "Facs clean; mv service pnt up ramp - risk of grounding; site in orange grove; ferries to Crete in ssn." ♦ € 24.00 (CChq acc)   2009*

⊞ **GITHIO** *B3* (7km SW Coastal) *36.72847, 22.54215* **Camping Mani Beach, Mavrovouni, 23200 Githio [(27330) 23450; fax 25451; info@manibeach.gr; www.manibeach.gr]** Fr Githio dir Aeropolis, site sp on L on Mavrovouni beach. Lge, hdg/mkd pitch, hdstg, shd; htd wc; chem disp; shwrs inc; EHU (16A) €4; gas; lndry; shop; rest, snacks; bar; BBQ; playgrnd; shgl beach adj; games area; wifi; cab TV; 10% statics; dogs; phone; Eng spkn; adv bkg; ccard acc; red long stay/snr citizens/CKE/CCI. "Less cr & noisy than other sites along this rd; set in olive grove; lovely mountain views; conv ferries to Crete; vg." ♦ € 22.00   2011*

GREEK ISLANDS Campsites in towns on Greek Islands are listed together at the end of the Greek site entries.

IERISSOS *B2* (500m NW Coastal) *40.40369, 23.87608* **Camping Ierissos, 63075 Ierissos [(23770) 21130; fax 21132; desa@ierissos.gr]** Sp at major x-rds in town cent. Med, mkd pitch, unshd; wc; chem disp (wc); shwrs inc; EHU (10A) €3.15; lndry; shop, rest, snacks, bar in town/on beach; BBQ; sand beach adj; 80% statics; dogs; poss cr; Eng spkn; poss noisy high ssn. "Fair sh stay; a few dogs roaming site." 1 May-30 Sep. € 15.50   2009*

IGOUMENITSA *A2* (7km SE Coastal) *39.47437, 20.23919* **Camping Kalami Beach, 46100 Plataria [(26650) 71211; fax 71245; info@campingkalamibeach.gr; www.camping kalamibeach.gr]** S fr Igoumenitsa on coast rd, turn sharp R at camping sp down lane to sea & site. Site is 4km N of Platariá. Lge, terr, pt shd; wc; chem disp; mv service pnt; shwrs inc; EHU (10A) €3; gas; lndry (inc dryer); shop; rest, snacks; bar; BBQ; shgl beach; watersports; games rm; wifi; TV; some statics; dogs; phone; poss cr; adv bkg; quiet but some rd noise; Sunshine Group site. "Access diff for lge o'fits due tight corners & sm pitches; ltd lge pitches & some diff due to trees; pleasant, relaxing site; helpful staff; excel, clean san facs; 20% discount for Minoan Line ticketholders." 20 Mar-31 Oct. € 28.00   2011*

IGOUMENITSA *A2* (10km S Coastal) *39.46346, 20.26037* **Camping Elena's Beach, 46100 Platariá [(26650) 71031; fax 71414; bteo@altecnet.gr or info@campingelena.gr; www.epirus.com/campingelena]** Sp on Igoumenitsa-Preveza rd, 2km NW of Platariá. Med, hdstg, pt terr, pt shd; wc; chem disp; shwrs inc; EHU (5A) inc; gas; lndry; shop; rest, snacks; bar; BBQ; playgrnd; shgl beach adj; a few statics; dogs; phone; bus; adv bkg; quiet; red long stay; CKE/CCI. "Well-maintained, family-run, friendly site; clean, modern san facs; beautiful location with pitches next to sea; excel rest; conv ferries Corfu, Paxos." ♦ 1 Apr-31 Oct. € 33.50   2014*

IGOUMENITSA *A2* (16km S Coastal) *39.44390, 20.25813*
**Nautilos Camping, 46100 Plataria [(26650) 71416;
fax 71417; wassosf@otenet.gr]** S fr Igoumenitsa on coast
rd to Plataria; turn R at end of Plataria Beach; site at top of
hill with flags clearly visible, 2km SW of Plataria. Lge, mkd
pitch, some hdstg, terr, pt sl, shd; wc; chem disp; shwrs inc;
EHU (16A) inc; gas; lndry; shop; rest; bar; BBQ; cooking facs;
playgrnd; pool; private beach; tennis; wifi; some statics; dogs;
phone; Eng spkn; adv bkg; quiet; red CKE/CCI. "Helpful
staff; lovely quiet site; picturesque setting." 1 Apr-20 Oct.
€ 27.50   2011*

IOANINA *A2* (2km NW Urban) *39.67799, 20.84279* **Camping
Limnopoula, Kanari 10, 45000 Ioanina [(26510) 25265;
fax 38060]** At Ioanina Nautical Club on Igoumenitsa rd at W
o'skts of town on rd that runs along lake fr citadel; site well sp
fr all dirs. Med, pt shd; wc; chem disp; shwrs inc; EHU (10A)
inc; gas; lndry; shop; rest, snacks, bar adj; BBQ; playgrnd;
watersports; dogs free; phone; Eng spkn; quiet. "Beautiful
situation on lake, mountain views; excel touring base; helpful
staff; gd facs; clean; may close earlier; adv bkg acc 1-2 days
ahead only LS; popular with groups LS; vg." 1 Apr-15 Oct.
€ 27.00   2015*

KALAMBAKA *A2* (2km SE Rural) *39.69017, 21.64564*
**Camping International Rizos, Trikala Road, Meteora,
42200 Kalambaka [tel/fax (24320) 22239; info@
meteorarizoscamp.gr]** Site visible on S of E92 rd. Med, hdg/
mkd pitch, pt shd; htd wc; chem disp; shwrs inc; EHU (16A);
gas; lndry; shop; rest, snacks; bar; playgrnd; pool; paddling
pool; TV; bus to town; adv bkg; CKE/CCI. ♦
1 Apr-31 Oct.   2010*

KALAMBAKA *A2* (4km SE Rural) *39.68250, 21.65510*
**Camping Philoxenia, 42200 Kalambaka [(24320) 24466;
fax 24944; philoxeniacamp@ath.forthnet.gr]** Site on N side
of E92 Trikala rd, behind barrier. Med, some hdstg, shd; htd
wc; chem disp; mv service pnt; shwrs inc; EHU (6A) inc; gas;
lndry; shop; rest 1km; snacks; bar; BBQ; cooking facs; playgrnd;
pool; paddling pool; waterslide; bike hire; TV; 30% statics;
dogs free; poss cr; Eng spkn; adv bkg; quiet; ccard acc; red
CKE/CCI. "Interesting area particularly during Easter religious
festivals." ♦ ltd. 1 Mar-30 Nov. € 20.00 (CChq acc)   2011*

⊞ **KALAMBAKA** *A2* (2km NW Rural) *39.7120, 21.61625*
**Camping Vrachos, Meteoron Street, 42200 Kastraki
[(24320) 22293; fax 23134; campingkastraki@yahoo.com;
www.campingkastraki.gr]** Fr cent of Kalambaka take rd at
app to vill of Kastraki. Site is 2km N of E92. Med, hdg/mkd
pitch, pt sl, terr, shd; wc; chem disp; mv service pnt; shwrs
inc; EHU (16A) inc; gas; lndry; shop; rest, snacks; bar; BBQ;
cooking facs; playgrnd; pool; TV; internet (ltd); dogs free;
phone; poss cr; Eng spkn; adv bkg; Harmonie Group site; red
CKE/CCI. "Friendly management; clean san facs; vg views fr
some pitches; ltd facs open in winter; conv for monasteries." ♦
€ 18.00   2011*

KALIVIA VARIKOU see Plaka Litohorou *B2*

KAMENA VOURLA *B2* (10km NW Coastal) *38.82310,
22.71543* **Venezuela Camping, Paralia, Agios Serafeim;
35009 Malos [tel/fax (22350) 41691; camping@venezuela.
gr; www.venezuela.gr]** Fr Lamia on E75, turn L twd Skarfeia
& foll site sp. Fr Athens turn R sp Agios Serafeim, site sp. Med,
hdg/mkd pitch, some hdstg, shd; wc; chem disp; shwrs inc;
EHU (10A) €4; shop; rest, snacks; bar; cooking facs; beach
adj; wifi; TV; dogs; phone; Eng spkn; adv bkg; quiet; CKE/
CCI. "Conv NH bet Athens & N; peaceful." 1 May-30 Sep.
€ 20.00   2011*

KARDAMILI see Stoupa *B3*

⊞ **KASSANDRIA** *B2* (17km SW Coastal) *39.96416, 23.36472*
**Camping Kalandra, 63077 Possidi [(23740) 41345;
fax 41123]** Fr Thessaloniki foll sp to Nea Moudania, down
peninsula to Kalithea, W to Kassandria, S thro Fourka, W to
Kalandra, fork R to Possidi & foll sps to end of rd. Lge, pt shd;
wc; chem disp; shwrs; EHU (15A); gas; lndry; shop; rest, snacks;
bar; sand beach adj; no adv bkg; 40% statics; dogs; red CKE/
CCI. "Quiet but fills up end Jun for Greek hols."   2009*

KASTRAKI see Kalambaka *A2*

KATO ALISSOS see Patra *A2*

KATO GATZEA see Volos *B2*

⊞ **KAVALA** *C1* (4km SW Urban/Coastal) *40.91573, 24.37851*
**Camping Multiplex Batis, 65000 Kavala [(2510) 243051;
fax 245690; nfo@batis-sa.gr; www.batis-sa.gr]**
On W app to town on old coast rd, ent on a curving hill.
Med, hdg/mkd pitch, pt sl, shd; htd wc; chem disp; shwrs inc;
EHU (6A) €4; lndry rm; shop; rest, snacks; bar; pool; paddling
pool; sand beach adj; entmnt; phone; bus; poss cr; Eng spkn;
adv bkg; ccard acc; red CKE/CCI. "Beautiful location but v
developed; conv ferry to Thassos & archaeological sites; clean
facs but site poss unkempt LS; vg." ♦ € 26.00   2009*

KORINTHOS *B3* (7km W Coastal/Urban) *37.93470,
22.86543* **Blue Dolphin Camping, 20011 Lecheon Korinth
[(27410) 25766 or 25767; fax 85959; info@camping-blue-
dolphin.gr; www.camping-blue-dolphin.gr]**
Best app fr E to avoid town; Fr A8 exit sp Ancient Corinth, then
N (R) to T-junc end of rd, W (R) past pipe factory, sp 400m N
(R) at bottom of bdge sl. Fr W take exit sp Ancient Corinth after
toll point. Fr Old National rd turn N (L) immed over rlwy bdge
bef pipe factory. Fr Corinth foll old National rd twd Patras,
past pipe factory. Med, mkd pitch, hdstg, pt shd; wc; chem
disp; shwrs inc; EHU (6A) €3.50; gas; lndry; shop; rest, snacks;
bar; BBQ; playgrnd; shgl beach; games area; wifi; TV; dogs;
Sunshine Group site; Eng spkn; quiet; ccard acc; red CKE/CCI.
"V obliging, friendly owners; pleasant site; sm pitches; lovely
site by sea." ♦ 1 Apr-31 Oct. € 23.00   2015*

GREECE

KORONI *B3* (1km ESE Coastal) *36.79932, 21.95013* **Camping Koroni, 24004 Koroni [(27250) 22119; fax 22884; info@ koronicamping.com; www.koronicamping.com]** Sp on Kalamata to Koroni rd. Med, mkd pitch, pt sl, terr, shd; wc; shwrs inc; EHU (6A) €4; lndry; shop; rest, snacks; bar; cooking facs; pool; sand beach adj; wifi; TV; dogs; phone; site clsd Nov; Sunshine Group site; Eng spkn; red CKE/CCI. "Pleasant site; friendly owners; basic but adequate facs; gd pool; easy walk to lovely fishing vill; dusty in summer." 1 Mar-20 Oct. € 25.00   2009*

KYLLINI *A3* (10km S Coastal) *37.88539, 21.11175* **Campsite Melissa, 27050 Kastro Kyllinis Ilia [02 62 30 95 213; fax 62 30 95 453; camping_melissa@yahoo.gr]** S fr Patras twd Pygros on E55. Turn R twds Lehena after 58km marker. Foll signs to Kastro Kyllinis. Med, hdg pitch, shd; wc; chem disp; mv service pnt; shwrs; EHU (10A); lndry; shop; rest; bar; BBQ; cooking facs; playgrnd; beach; wifi; TV; 2% statics; dogs; twin axles; Eng spkn; adv bkg; quiet; CCI. "Great campsite to chill; excel rest, bar & shop; lovely sandy beach; excel sw; fabulous views across the bay." ♦ ltd. 1 Apr-31 Oct. € 31.00   2014*

⊞ **KYLLINI** *A3* (17km S Coastal) *37.83828, 21.12972* **Camping Aginara Beach, Lygia, 27050 Loutra Kyllinis [(26230) 96211; fax 96271; info@camping-aginara.gr; www.camping-aginara.gr]** S fr Patras on E55 twds Pyrgos; exit Gastouni & turn W thro Vartholomio twd Loutra Kyllinis; turn L about 3km bef Kyllinis then foll sps. Lge, hdg pitch, hdstg, pt sl, shd; wc; chem disp; mv service pnt; shwrs inc; EHU (10A); gas; lndry; shop; rest, snacks; bar; BBQ; playgrnd; sand/ shgl beach adj; watersports; wifi; TV; 25% statics; dogs; phone; Eng spkn; adv bkg; quiet; ccard acc; red CKE/CCI. "Friendly proprietor; excel, modern facs; site on lovely beach; beautiful views." ♦ € 36.00   2014*

KYLLINI *A3* (7km SW Coastal) *37.89944, 21.11666* **Camping Fournia Beach, 27050 Kastro-Kyllini [(26230) 95095; fax 95096]** W fr Patras on E55, for about 61 km, exit Kyllini/ Zakinthos, turn R & foll sp for 15km to Kastro-Kyllini. Site sp. Med, mkd pitch, pt shd; wc; chem disp; shwrs; EHU (16A) inc; lndry; shop; rest; bar; BBQ; playgrnd; sand beach adj; wifi; TV; some statics; dogs; phone; Eng spkn; adv bkg; ccard acc; CKE/ CCI. 1 Apr-1 Nov. € 21.00 (CChq acc)   2011*

KYPARISSIA *A3* (1km N Coastal) *37.25697, 21.67120* **Camping Kyparissia, 24500 Kyparissia [(27610) 23491; fax 24519; info@campingkyparissia.com; www.camping kyparissia.com]** S fr Pirgos take R fork on ent Kyparissia, foll sp via beach rd; site in view ahead; fr Pilos turn N on o'skts of town. Med, hdg pitch, pt sl, shd; wc; chem disp; mv service pnt; shwrs; EHU (16A) €3.50; lndry; shop & 1km; rest, snacks; bar; playgrnd; sand beach; watersports; wifi; TV; dogs free; phone; Eng spkn; Sunshine Group site; quiet; red long stay/CKE/CCI. "Excel, attractive site; friendly staff; ltd number of shd pitches for high o'fits." 1 Apr-20 Oct. € 19.50   2009*

KYPARISSIA *A3* (18km N Coastal) *37.39690, 21.67738* **Camping Apollo Village, 27054 Giannitsochori [tel/fax (26250) 61200]** Fr Pirgos S dir Kyparissia, 11km after Zaharo at sp for Giannitsochori, turn R, cross rlwy line & foll site sp. Lge, shd; wc; chem disp; shwrs inc; EHU (16A) inc; lndry; shop; rest, snacks; bar; BBQ; sand beach adj; games rm; TV; 10% statics; dogs; phone; quiet; red long stay; CKE/CCI. "Excel beach." 1 May-31 Oct. € 24.00   2010*

LECHEON see Korinthos *B3*

LEONIDI *B3* (23km N Coastal) *37.27566, 22.84054* **Camping Zaritsi, Paralia Tirou, 22300 Tiros [(27570) 41429; fax 41074; camping@zaritsi.gr; www.zaritsi.gr]** Foll main N-S rd down E coast; site immed off this rd on coast 4km N of Tirós, well sp. Steep rd down, but practical for lge o'fits. Site not sp fr S. Med, hdstg, pt shd; wc; chem disp; mv service pnt; shwrs inc; EHU (16A) inc; gas; lndry; shop; rest (high ssn); snacks; bar; playgrnd; shgl beach adj; watersports; TV rm; 50% statics; phone; Eng spkn; adv bkg; quiet; no ccard acc; CKE/CCI. "Fine site on exceptionally beautiful Arcadia coast rd; friendly owner; stunning mountain scenery; gd rest." 15 Apr-30 Sep. € 27.00   2009*

METHONI *A3* (1km ESE Coastal) *36.81736, 21.71515* **Camp Methoni, 24006 Methoni [(27230) 31228 or 0728 31455]** Fr Pylos on rd 9, strt thro Methoni to beach, turn E along beach, site sp. Med, hdstg, pt shd; wc (some cont); shwrs inc; EHU (10A) inc; lndry rm; rest, snacks; bar; BBQ; playgrnd; sand beach; dogs; phone; Eng spkn; adv bkg; some rd noise; ccard not acc; CKE/CCI. "Superb Venetian castle; close to pleasant vill; park away fr taverna & rd to avoid noise; excel sw; v dusty site; clean san facs; new owner & undergoing renovations (2013); quiet & gd site." 1 Jun-30 Sep. € 19.00   2014*

METHONI PIERIAS *B2* (3km S Coastal) *40.42712, 22.60401* **Hotel & Camping Agiannis, 60066 Methoni-Pierias [(23530) 41216; fax 51840]** Leave E75 Thessaloniki/Athens m'way dir Magrigialos/Methoni, foll sp Camping & Hotel. Med, hdg pitch, pt sl, terr, shd; wc (some cont); chem disp (wc); mv service pnt; shwrs inc; EHU (6-10A) €3.50 (poss no earth/rev pol); shop; rest high ssn; snacks; playgrnd; pool; sand beach adj; entmnt; TV; 80% statics; dogs free; Eng spkn; red long stay;CKE/CCI. "Friendly family-run site; clean facs; gd touring base; excel rest o'looking beach." 1 May-15 Oct. € 18.00   2009*

⊞ **MIKINES** *B3* (95m E Urban) *37.71922, 22.74676* **Camping Mikines/Mykenae, 21200 Mikines [(27510) 76247; fax 76850; dars@arg.forthnet.gr; www.ecogriek.nl]** In town of Mikines (Mycenae) nr bus stop. On R as heading to archeological site, sp. Sm, mkd pitch, hdstg, pt shd; wc; chem disp (wc); shwrs inc; EHU (10A) €4.50; lndry; shops 500m; meals served; dogs; Eng spkn; quiet; CKE/CCI. "Quaint family-run site; v warm welcome; conv ancient Mycenae; friendly staff; vg." ♦ ltd. € 21.00   2014*

⊞ **MIKINES** *B3* (500m W Rural) *37.71915, 22.74081* **Atreus Camping, Argolida, 21200 Mikines [(27510) 76221; fax 76760; atreus@otenet.gr]** Fr E65 twd Mycenae (Mikines), site on L when heading twd archeological site. Sm, pt shd; wc; chem disp; shwrs inc; EHU (10A) €4; lndry; shop; rest; bar; pool; paddling pool; wifi; TV; Sunshine Camping Group site; Eng spkn; CKE/CCI. "Sm pitches; poss noise fr barking dogs; san facs dated but clean; 2km fr archeological site." € 24.00   2010*

NAFPAKTOS B2 (10km SW Coastal) 38.34297, 21.77006
Camping Dounis Beach, Neromana, 30200 Antirrio
[(26340) 31565; fax 31131] Foll sp to Antirrio off E55
Mesolongi to Nafpaktos rd. Site situated 1.5km E of Antirrio.
Med, pt shd; wc; chem disp; mv service pnt; shwrs inc; EHU
(16A) €4; gas; lndry; shop; rest, snacks adj; playgrnd; shgl
beach; entmnt; no dogs; adv bkg; quiet; red CKE/CCI. "San
facs in need of upgrade; gd size pitches; ltd facs LS; rather run
down." 1 May-30 Oct. € 24.50   2010*

NAFPLIO B3 (7km ENE Coastal) 37.58280, 22.86725
Camping Lido, Sfakes Tolon, 21056 Tolon [(27520) 59396;
fax 59596; lidotolo@otenet.gr; www.camping-lido.com]
App Tolon fr Nafplio, site just bef vill on L. Med, pt sl, terr,
shd; wc; chem disp; shwrs inc; EHU (16A); gas; lndry; shop adj;
snacks; sand beach adj; watersports; TV; poss cr; quiet; ccard
acc; red CKE/CCI. "Excel beach; easy walk to town - many rests
& boat trips; sm pitches; some pitches excel views; newer san
facs block gd." 1 Apr-30 Oct. € 26.00   2010*

NAFPLIO B3 (10km SE Coastal) 37.53226, 22.89143
New Triton Camping, Plaka Drepano, 21060 Drepano
[(27520) 92128; fax 92121; campnewtriton@yahoo.gr]
E fr Nafplio to Epidhuros; in 5km turn R twds Drepano; in
Drepano cent turn R; in one block turn slight L; may not be sp
but foll sp for Camping Triton II which is 100m beyond New
Triton. Sm, hdg pitch, hdstg, well shd; wc (some cont); chem
disp; mv service pnt; serviced pitches; shwrs inc; EHU (16A)
inc; gas 1km; lndry; shop; rest, snacks; bar; BBQ; cooking facs;
beach adj; watersports; games area; wifi; TV; dogs free; poss
cr; Eng spkn; CKE/CCI. "Immac site & facs; wheelchair-friendly;
excel site." ♦ 1 Apr-31 Oct. € 25.00   2011*

⊞ **NAFPLIO** B3 (12km SE Coastal) 37.53173, 22.89056
Camping Triton II, Plaka Drepano, 21060 Drepano
[(27520) 92228; fax 92510; tritonii@otenet.gr;
www.tritonii.gr] Take rd E fr Nafplio dir Epidavros; after 5km
turn R for Drepano vill & foll site sps. Med, hdg/mkd pitch,
hdstg, pt shd; wc; chem disp; mv service pnt; baby facs; shwrs;
EHU (6A) inc; lndry (inc dryer); shop & 1km; rest, snacks; shgl
beach adj; tennis; games area; wifi; 30% statics; dogs; phone;
Eng spkn; adv bkg (Jul/Aug); ccard acc; red LS/long stay; CKE/
CCI. "Vg LS; excel, clean facs; all supplies in walking dist in
vill." € 25.00   2011*

NAFPLIO B3 (12km SE Coastal) 37.5287, 22.87553 **Kastraki**
Camping, Kastraki Assinis, 21100 Assini [(27520) 59386
or 59387; fax 59572; sgkarmaniola@kastrakicamping.gr;
www.kastrakicamping.gr] Fr Nafplio take rd to Tolon.
Immed after Assini, take L fork sp Ancient Assini. Site 3km on
L. Lge, shd; wc; chem disp; mv service pnt; baby facs; shwrs
€0.20; EHU (16A) shared €4; lndry; shop; rest, snacks; bar;
playgrnd; sand beach; tennis; games area; TV; dogs; quiet; red
facs LS; ccard acc. "Vg location with own private beach & excel
facs; day trips to several islands fr Tolón harbour; many pitches
too sm for lge m'vans." ♦ 1 Apr-30 Sep. € 35.00   2013*

NAFPLIO B3 (10km S Coastal) 37.53006, 22.86528 **Sunset**
Camping, 21056 Tolon [(27520) 59566; fax 59195; info@
camping-sunset.gr; www.camping-sunset.gr]
Visible on R as app Tolón fr Nafplio, approx 200m bef Tolon.
Med, hdstg, terr, pt shd; wc; chem disp; mv service pnt; shwrs
inc; EHU (16A) €4.50; lndry; shop; rest, snacks; bar; rest; BBQ;
cooking facs; playgrnd; sand beach 200m; games rm; wifi; TV
rm; some statics; dogs; Eng spkn; adv bkg; quiet; red CKE/CCI.
"Lovely seaside site; v friendly; pleasant town." 1 Apr-31 Oct.
€ 26.50   2010*

NEOS MARMARAS B2 (12km S Coastal) 40.04252, 23.81391
Camping Stavros, Agia Kyriaki, 63081 Neos Marmaras
[tel/fax (23750) 71375; info@campingstavros.gr]
Site on W side of Sithonia Peninsular. Fr Nikitas go S thro Neos
Marmaras & Porto Carrasi; sp on R on winding rd. Med, shd;
wc (some cont); chem disp; mv service pnt; EHU (10A) €4; gas;
lndry; shop; rest; bar; playgrnd; beach adj; watersports; games
area; TV; phone; Eng spkn; adv bkg; quiet. "Excel facs; friendly,
helpful management; gd rest & bar; clean, well-run, peaceful
site." 1 May-10 Oct. € 22.00   2009*

NEOS PANTELEIMONAS see Platamonas B2

⊞ **OLIMBIA** A3 (300m S Urban) 37.64518, 21.6228 **Camping**
Diana, 27065 Olimbia [(26240) 22314 or 22945; fax 22425;
harmocamp@europe.com; www.campingdiana.gr]
Fr E55 Pyrgos to Tripoli rd take exit sp 'Ancient Olympia' & foll
site sp. Sm, sl, terr, pt shd; wc; chem disp; shwrs inc; EHU (16A)
€5; gas; lndry rm; shop; snacks; bar; pool; TV; dogs; Eng spkn;
adv bkg; quiet but some rd noise; Harmonie Group site; red
CKE/CCI. "Pretty site; san facs clean & tidy; helpful & friendly
management; closest campsite to archaeological sites; noisy
roosters in morning!" € 23.00   2011*

OLIMBIA A3 (1km W Rural) 37.64337, 21.61943 **Camping**
Alphios, 27065 Olimbia [(26240) 22951; fax 22950;
alphios@otenet.gr; www.campingalphios.gr]
Fr E55 Pyrgos to Tripoli rd take exit sp 'Ancient Olympia' & foll
site sp. Med, hdg/mkd pitch, hdstg, terr, pt sl, pt shd; wc; chem
disp; mv service pnt; shwrs inc; EHU (16A) inc; gas; lndry; shop;
rest, snacks; bar; BBQ; cooking facs; playgrnd; pool; wifi; TV;
quiet; ccard acc. "Superb views fr some pitches; excel pool; v
friendly; walking dist to ancient Olympic site." 1 Apr-15 Oct.
€ 30.00   2013*

OLYMPIA see Olimbia A3

PALEA EPIDAVROS B3 (2km S Coastal) 37.61868,
23.15599 **Camping Bekas, Gialasi, 21059 Palea Epidavros**
[(27530) 41524; fax 41394; info@bekas.gr; www.bekas.gr]
S fr Korinthos past Nea (New) Epidavros. Do not take 1st sp
to Palea (Ancient) Epidavros but exit R 3km later & foll sp to
vill. On ent vill turn sharp R at Bekas sp, site in 1.5km. Med,
hdstg, terr, shd; wc; chem disp; mv service pnt; baby facs; fam
bthrm; shwrs inc; EHU (16A) €4; gas; lndry; ice; shop; supmkt
4km; rest, snacks; bar; BBQ; cooking facs; shgl beach adj;
tennis; wifi; TV; 10% statics; dogs free; phone; poss cr; Eng
spkn; adv bkg; quiet; ccard acc; red LS/long stay; CKE/CCI.
"Sheltered beach in beautiful bay; friendly, family-run site in
orange grove; some beachfront pitches; excel." 25 Mar-20 Oct.
€ 23.50   2009*

PARGA *A2* (4km E Coastal) *39.2822, 20.43478* **Enjoy Lichnos Camping, 48060 Lichnos-Parga [(26840) 31371 or 31171; fax 32076; holidays@enjoy-lichnos.net; www.enjoy-lichnos.net]** On Igoumenitsa-Preveza rd turn W at sp Parga; sp 3km bef vill, steep app down private rd. Lge, terr, shd; wc; chem disp; shwrs; EHU (16A) €3.80; lndry; shop, rest high ssn; snacks; bar; shgl beach; watersports; dogs free; wifi; sep car park; Sunshine Camping Group site; adv bkg; quiet; red CKE/CCI. "Vg facs, excel location; some pitches adj excel beach; water taxis to Parga." 1 May-15 Oct. € 22.00   2011*

PATRA *A2* (21km SW Coastal) *38.14986, 21.57740* **Camping Kato Alissos, 25002 Kato Alissos [(26930) 71249 or 71914; fax 71150; demiris-cmp@otenet.gr; www.camping-kato-alissos.gr]** W of Patra on old national rd turn R at Kato Alissos & foll site sp for 600m. Med, shd; wc; chem disp; shwrs inc; EHU (10A) €4.; lndry; shop; rest, snacks; bar; cooking facs; playgrnd; shgl beach adj (down 50 steps); watersports; wifi; 10% statics; dogs; phone; bus 1km; Sunshine Camping Group site; poss cr; Eng spkn; adv bkg; quiet; ccard acc; red snr citizens; CKE/CCI. "Clean ltd facs; gd NH." 1 Apr-25 Oct. € 19.00   2013*

> ## "We must tell The Club about that great site we found"
>
> Get your site reports in by mid-August and we'll do our best to get your updates into the next edition.

PATRA *A2* (22km SW Coastal) *38.14367, 21.58772* **Camping Golden Sunset Beach, 25002 Alissos [(26930) 71276; fax 71556; goldensunset@patrascamping.gr; www.patrascampings.gr]** 1st site on old national rd W of Patras to Pirgos-Olimbia, sp. Med, pt shd; wc; shwrs inc; EHU (6A) €4; gas; lndry; shop; rest, snacks; bar; playgrnd; 3 pools; waterslides; shgl beach; boating; tennis; games area; sat TV; 10% statics; poss cr; Eng spkn; adv bkg; quiet; ccard acc; red long stay; Harmonie Group site. "Helpful management; gd base for tours; site poss clsd Jun-Aug for exclusive use parties of students - phone ahead to check; excel." ♦ 1 May-30 Sep. € 28.00   2009*

PETALIDI *B3* (4km N Coastal) *36.98167, 21.92886* **Camping Petalidi Beach, 24005 Petalidi [(27220) 31154; fax 31690; info@campingpetalidi.gr; www.campingpetalidi.gr]** Turn L off Kalamata-Pylos rd at Rizomylos. Site sp in 2km. Lge, hdstg, pt shd; wc; chem disp; mv service pnt; shwrs inc; EHU (16A) inc; gas; lndry (inc dryer); shop; rest, snacks; bar; BBQ; playgrnd; shgl beach adj; watersports; games area; entmnt; TV; dogs; phone; Eng spkn; adv bkg; quiet; Harmonie Group site; red CKE/CCI. 1 Apr-30 Sep. € 23.50   2011*

⊞ **PLAKA LITOHOROU** *B2* (10km N Coastal) *40.18230, 22.55885* **Camping Stani, 60200 Kalivia Varikou [(23520) 61277]** Leave E75 (Athens-Thessaloniki) at N Efesos/Variko, foll sp Varikou & site. Lge, mkd pitch, shd; wc; chem disp; shwrs inc; EHU; lndry; shop; rest, snacks; bar; TV rm; dogs; phone; poss cr; CKE/CCI. "Ltd facs LS; conv Dion; fair site." € 22.00   2014*

PLATAMONAS *B2* (6km NW Coastal) *40.01291, 22.59053* **Camping Poseidon Beach, Paralia Pandeleimonas, 60065 Platamonas [(23520) 41654 or 41792; fax 41994; info@poseidonbeach.net; www.poseidonbeach.net]** Exit Katerini to Larissa toll rd 1/E75 & foll site sp over rlwy line (2km) & turn L (sp camping), use underpass, turn R at junc, site in 400m. Lge, hdg pitch, pt shd; wc; chem disp; shwrs inc; EHU (16A) €3.50; gas; lndry; shop; rest; bar; sand beach; TV; 80% statics; no dogs; bus 1km; poss cr; Eng spkn; quiet; red long stay/CKE/CCI. "Well-managed site; immac facs; sm pitches & narr rds may be diff for lge o'fits; vg beach; pleasant area." 1 Apr-15 Oct. € 23.50   2011*

PLATARIA see Igoumenitsa *A2*

POSSIDI see Kassandria *B2*

PREVEZA *A2* (4km NW Coastal) *38.97395, 20.7161* **Camping Kalamitsi Beach, 48100 Preveza [(26280) 23268; fax 28660; kalamitsi_camping@hotmail.com]** Fr Preveza on E55 twds Igoumenitsa on L of rd; clearly sp. Best app fr N. Med, shd; wc; chem disp; shwrs inc; EHU (16A); gas; lndry; shop; rest; bar; playgrnd; pool; beach adj; watersports; wifi; TV; Eng spkn; adv bkg; quiet; red long stay; CKE/CCI. "Attractive site; nr archaeological sites; friendly owner; poss diff to manoeuvre onto pitches high ssn." ♦ ltd. 15 Jun-1 Oct. € 26.00   2009*

⊞ **PYLOS** *A3* (7km N Coastal) *36.94784, 21.70635* **Camping Navarino Beach, 24001 Gialova [(27230) 22973; fax 23512; info@navarino-beach.gr; www.navarino-beach.gr]** Fr Pylos N twds Kiparissia for 5km around Navarino Bay, site at S end of Gialova vill; sp. Med, some hdstg, pt shd, wc; chem disp; mv service pnt; shwrs inc; EHU (16A) €4; gas; lndry; shop 300m; rest, snacks; BBQ; cooking facs; playgrnd; beach; windsurfing, boat-launch; internet; dogs; bus; Eng spkn; adv bkg; quiet; ccard acc; red long stay; CKE/CCI. "Management v helpful; gd, clean, modern facs; several rest & shops in easy walking dist; some pitches on beach; vg." € 32.50   2014*

PYLOS *A3* (9km N Coastal) *36.95291, 21.69565* **Camping Erodios, 24001 Gialova [(27230) 28240; fax 28241; info@erodioss.gr; www.erodioss.gr]** Fr N side of Gialova foll sp 'Golden Beach', site sp. Med, pt shd; wc; chem disp; mv service pnt; baby facs; shwrs; EHU (10A) €4.50; lndry; shop; rest, snacks; bar; cooking facs; playgrnd; beach adj; watersports; surfing; bike hire; wifi; sat TV; 10% statics; bus 500m; Eng spkn; adv bkg; quiet; ccard acc; red long stay/CKE/CCI. "Excel facs; welcoming; beautiful situation & sea views fr some pitches; some v lge pitches - can be pre-booked; friendly, helpful staff." ♦ 1 Apr-31 Oct. € 27.50   2011*

RAFINA *B3* (2km N Coastal) *38.03120, 23.99992* **Camping Kokkino Limanaki, 19009 Rafina [(22940) 31604; fax 31603; info@athenscampings.com; www.athenscampings.com]** On Marathon/Athens rd, 25km fr Athens turn L sp Rafina 3km; after 1.6km turn L; after 1.2km thro x-rds & turn L after 200m; site on R in 150m. Med, pt sl, terr, pt shd; wc (some cont); chem disp; shwrs inc; EHU (10A) inc; gas; lndry; shop; rest, snacks; bar; BBQ; sand beach; dogs; quiet LS; ccard acc. "Site on cliff 100m above sea with excel mountain & ocean views; some pitches sm & poss diff lge o'fits." 1 Apr-15 Oct. € 26.00   2010*

GREECE

⊞ **RIZA** *A2* (3km NW Coastal) *39.13493, 20.58415* **Camping Acrogiali, Mitos Apostolos, 48100 Riza [(26820) 56382; fax 56283; campacro@hol.gr; www.camping-acrogiali.com]** Fr S foll E44 N fr Preveza, site sp on L in approx 28km. Fr N approx 20km S of Igoumenitsa after x-ring rd bdge, start to climb & at sharp R-hand bend (sign for Riza to L) turn R onto winding, tarmac rd, downhill to coast. In approx 4km, site on L. Sm, mkd pitch, shd; wc; chem disp; mv service pnt; shwrs inc; EHU (16A) inc; lndry; shop; rest; bar; BBQ; shgl beach adj; wifi (in rest); TV rm; 50% statics; Eng spkn; adv bkg; quiet; ccard acc. "Gd facs & sw; excel, new, modern san facs; pitches poss a challenge but location of site on beach worth effort!" € 20.00 (CChq acc)   2011*

SARTI *B2* (13km NW Coastal) *40.15233, 23.91293* **Camping Armenistis, Akti Armenistis, 63072 Sarti [tel/fax (23750) 91487; info@armenistis.com.gr; www.armenistis.com.gr]** Fr Nikitas, turn E at junc down E side of Sithonia along coast rd sp Sarti/Sikia; site on E side 28km fr junc; last few km diff driving. Lge, mkd pitch, pt shd; wc; mv service pnt; shwrs inc; EHU (6A) €3.70; lndry; shop; rest, snacks; bar; BBQ; playgrnd; beach; games area; entmnt; 30% statics; Sunshine Camping Group site; ccard acc; red CKE/CCI. "Gd location with views of Mount Athos; excel for families." 1 May-15 Sep. € 26.40   2009*

⊞ **SOUNIO** *B3* (7km NE Coastal) *37.67620, 24.04884* **Camping Bacchus, Ave Lavrio, 19500 Sounio [tel/fax (22920) 39572; campingbacchus@hotmail.com; www.tggr.com/camping-bacchus]** Site sp on N89 coastal rd at km stone 71. Sm, pt shd; wc; chem disp; shwrs inc; EHU (6A) €4; gas; lndry; shop, rest (high ssn); snacks; bar; cooking facs; playgrnd; sand beach adj; fishing, windsurfing nr; TV; 50% statics; phone; Sunshine Group site; ccard acc; red LS. "Basic facs; solar water heating, open air wash basins with cold taps only, no privacy cubicles - not rec in winter (2009); rundown statics (2009); 4.5km fr Temple of Poseidon; easy access coastal walks & views." € 25.50   2009*

SPARTI *B3* (5km W Rural) *37.06941, 22.38163* **Camping Castle View, 23100 Mistras [(27310) 83303; fax 20028; info@castleview.gr]** Fr Kalamata take 1st turning to Mistras, past castle then thro vill dir Sparti. Site in approx 1km on L, well sp. Med, pt shd; wc; chem disp; shwrs inc; EHU (16A) inc; gas; lndry; shop; rest, snacks; bar; playgrnd; pool; wifi; TV; some statics; dogs; phone; Eng spkn; quiet; red CKE/CCI. "Gd clean facs; gd rest; close to archaeological remains; helpful owner." 1 Apr-20 Oct. € 26.00   2011*

STOUPA *B3* (1.6km N Coastal) *36.84934, 22.25877* **Camping Kalógria, Barbecer Nicda 29, 24024 Stoupa [(27210) 77319]** S fr Kalamata, turn R at site sp just bef Stoupa, site 200m on L. Med, some hdstg, pt sl, pt shd; wc; chem disp; mv service pnt; shwrs; EHU (16A) inc; lndry; shop; rest, snacks, bar 100m high ssn; BBQ; playgrnd; sand beach adj; phone; poss cr; Eng spkn; quiet; CKE/CCI. "Nice location; friendly staff; pitches on loose earth amongst trees; pleasant resort town." ♦ ltd. 5 May-31 Oct. € 24.00   2011*

STOUPA *B3* (2km N Coastal) *36.86071, 22.25220* **Camping Ta Delfinia, Neo Proastio, 24022 Kardamili [(27210) 77318; perdikeas@in.gr]** Site sp in lay-by; go thro gate & keep going. Sm, some hdstg, pt sl, shd; wc (some cont); chem disp; shwrs; ltd EHU (16A) inc; lndry; shop high ssn; rest 1.5km; snacks, bar high ssn; BBQ; playgrnd; sand/shgl beach adj; wifi; TV; poss cr; Eng spkn; red snr citizens; CKE/CCI. "Friendly welcome; ltd facs LS." 1 Mar-31 Oct. € 26.00   2010*

⊞ **STYLIDA** *B2* (4km SE Coastal) *38.89638, 22.65555* **Camping Interstation, Rd Athens-Thessalonika, Km 230, 35300 Stylida [(22380) 23827; fax 23828; interstation@ hotmail.com; www.tggr.com/interstation/]** Fr Lamia take rd E to Stylis; cont for further 3km & site situated to side of dual-c'way opp petrol stn. Med, shd; wc; chem disp; shwrs €0.30; EHU (16A) €3.60; gas; lndry; shop, rest high ssn; playgrnd; beach adj; tennis; watersports; TV; entmnt; some statics; no dogs; Eng spkn; adv bkg; quiet but some rd noise; red CKE/CCI. "Day visitors have access to beach via site; do not confuse with Cmp Paras adj - not rec; Sunshine Camping Group site; poss poor san facs LS; NH only." ♦ € 22.60   2009*

THERMISIA *B3* (350m SE Coastal) *37.41047, 23.32733* **Hydra's Wave Camping, Thermissia Argolidas, TK 21051 Greece [tel/fax (27540) 41095; info@hydraswave.gr; www.hydraswave.gr]** Fr Kranidi turn E on rd to Ermioni & then foll coast rd dir Póros. Site sp on R after 6km. Med, hdg pitch, shd; wc (some cont); chem disp; shwrs inc; EHU (16A) €4; lndry; shop; rest, snacks; bar; playgrnd; shgl beach adj; TV; dogs €2.50; bus 500m; Eng spkn; adv bkg; quiet; ccard acc; CKE/CCI. "Gd cent for Poros, Hydra, Spetses; helpful owner; dated facs but clean; area somewhat run down (2010); ok touring base." 1 Mar-30 Nov. € 21.00   2010*

TIROS see Leonidi *B3*

TOLON see Nafplio *B3*

⊞ **VARTHOLOMIO** *A3* (10km SW Coastal) *37.83555, 21.13333* **Camping Ionion Beach, 27050 Glifa [(26230) 96395; fax 96425; ioniongr@otenet.gr; www.ionion-beach.gr]** Fr E55 Patras-Pirgos rd turn W to Gastouni, Ligia & Glifa, then Glifa Beach. Site is 1km SW of Glifa. Med, hdg pitch, hdstg, pt shd; htd wc; chem disp; mv service pnt; serviced pitch; shwrs; EHU (16A); gas; lndry (inc dryer); shop in vill; rest, snacks; bar; BBQ; playgrnd; pool; paddling pool; beach adj; watersports; games area; wifi; TV; statics; dogs; Eng spkn; adv bkg; poss noisy; ccard acc; red LS; CKE/CCI. "Excel, well-run site; superb facs." ♦ € 27.00   2010*

VIVARI *B3* (1km E Coastal) *37.53421, 22.93179* **Camping Lefka Beach, 21100 Drepanon Vivari [tel/fax (27520) 92334; info@camping-lefka.gr; www.camping-lefka.gr]** On the Nafplio-Drepanon-Iria rd. About 1km on the R after vill of Vivari. Foll sp. Med, mkd pitch, hdstg, terr, shd; wc; chem disp; shwrs; EHU (16A); lndry; shop; rest; snacks; bar; BBQ; beach 20m; wifi; tv; dogs; twin axles; Eng spkn; adv bkg; CKE/CCI. "Beautiful views of bay fr site; close to antiquities; vg." ♦ ltd. 1 Apr-10 Nov. € 28.00   2015*

VLYCHO see Lefkada (Lefkas Island) *A2*

VOLOS *B2* (17km SE Coastal) *39.31105, 23.10922* **Camping Hellas International, 38500 Kato Gatzea [(24230) 22267; fax 22492; info@campinghellas.gr; www.campinghellas.gr]** Fr Volos take coast rd N34 to Kato Gatzea; sp on R immed bef & adj Sikia (Fig Tree) Camping. Med, shd; wc; chem disp; baby facs; shwrs inc; EHU (16A) inc; gas; lndry; shop high ssn; rest, snacks high ssn; BBQ; shgl beach adj; boating; bike hire; internet; 30% statics; dogs; phone; Harmonie Group site; Eng spkn; adv bkg; ccard acc; red LS; CKE/CCI. "Excel san facs - poss stretched with site full; friendly, helpful family-run site; great location; vg touring base." ♦ 15 Mar-31 Oct. € 27.50   2010*

VOLOS *B2* (18km SE Coastal) *39.31027, 23.10972* **Camping Sikia, 37300 Kato Gatzea [(24230) 22279 or 22081; fax 22720; camping-sikia.gr; www.camping-sikia.gr]** Fr Volos take coast rd S to Kato Gatzea site on R, sp immed next to Camping Hellas. Med, terr, shd; wc; chem disp; mv service pnt; shwrs inc; EHU (16A) €3; gas; lndry; shop; rest, snacks; shgl beach; internet; entmnt; 20% statics; dogs; phone; poss cr; Eng spkn; adv bkg; quiet; Sunshine Group site; ccard acc; red long stay/CKE/CCI. "Highly rec; some beautiful, but sm, pitches with sea views; excel, friendly family-run site; v clean; v helpful staff; take care o'hanging trees." ♦ 15 Mar-10 Nov. € 24.00   2015*

ZACHARO *A3* (8km S Coastal) *37.41068, 21.66850* **Camping Tholo Beach, Tholo, 27054 Zacharo [(26250) 61345 or 33454 (winter); campingtholo@hotmail.com]** S fr Pyrgos on E55 dir Kyparissia, 8km S of Zacharo turn R to Tholo. Site sp in 500m on L. Med, shd; wc; chem disp; mv service pnt; shwrs inc; EHU €4; lndry rm; shop; rest; bar; BBQ; playgrnd; sand beach adj; wifi; TV; dogs; Eng spkn; adv bkg; quiet; CKE/CCI, "Excel, quiet, clean site; gd, clean san facs; friendly staff; excel sandy beach where loggerhead turtles lay eggs; dolphins off shore; san facs need updating; great location; excel mkt on Tuesdays; Ancient Olympia about an hr's drive." 1 May-30 Oct. € 24.50   2015*

GREEK ISLANDS

⊞ **AGIA GALINI (CRETE)** *C4* (2km E Rural/Coastal) *35.10004, 24.69514* **Camping No Problem!, 74056 Agia Galini [(28320) 91386; www.agia-galini.com]** Site sp on Tympaki rd. Sm, mkd pitch, pt shd; wc; chem disp; mv service pnt; shwrs; EHU (6A) €4; lndry; shop; rest, snacks; bar; BBQ; pool; paddling pool; sand/shgl beach 500m; wifi; some statics; dogs free; bus 500m; poss cr; Eng spkn; adv bkg; quiet. "Vg, family-run site; gd walks." ♦ € 25.50   2010*

ERETRIA (EVIA) *B2* (11km NE Coastal) *38.39148, 23.77562* **Milos Camping, 34008 Eretria [(22290) 60420; fax 60360; info@camping-in-evia.gr; www.camping-in-evia.gr]** Fr Chalkida for 20km; ignore any previous sp for Milos Camping. Med, mkd pitch, terr, pt shd; wc; chem disp; mv service pnt; shwrs inc; EHU (16A) inc; gas; lndry; shop; rest, snacks; bar; BBQ; playgrnd; shgl beach adj; internet; TV; 70% statics; dogs; phone; Eng spkn; quiet but some rd noise; red CKE/CCI. "Friendly site; excel rest; rather scruffy (5/09) but gd san facs." ♦ 15 Apr-30 Sep. € 25.00   2015*

HANIA (CRETE) *C4* (5km W Coastal) *35.51183, 23.98482* **Camping Hania, Agii Apostoli, Kato Daratso, 73100 Hania [(28210) 31138; fax 33371; camhania@otenet.gr; www.camping-chania.gr]** W fr cent of Hania on main rd to Kissamos. Med, hdstg, pt sl, shd; wc (some cont); chem disp; mv service pnt; shwrs inc; EHU (16A) inc; gas; lndry; shop; rest, snacks; bar; BBQ; cooking facs; playgrnd; pool; paddling pool; sand beach 200m; bike hire; games rm; TV; some statics; dogs; bus; phone; poss cr; Eng spkn; adv bkg; quiet; ccard acc; red long stay; CKE/CCI. "Take care low olive trees; vg." 1 Apr-30 Oct. € 30.00   2011*

KOS (KOS) *D3* (3km E Coastal) *36.88428, 27.32338* **Kos Camping, 85300 Psalidi [(22420) 29886; fax 29887; grigoris70@hotmail.gr]** On Ag Fokas rd fr Kos town, site on R. Only site on island. Med, mkd pitch, pt shd; wc; shwrs inc; EHU; gas; shop; rest, snacks; playgrnd; shgl beach across rd; tennis; bike hire; 30% statics; phone; sep car park; poss cr; adv bkg; quiet. 1 May-5 Oct.   2009*

LEFKADA (LEFKAS) *A2* (26km SE Coastal) *38.67511, 20.71475* **Camping Santa Maura, Dessimi, 31100 Vlycho [(26450) 95007; fax 95493; www.lefkada.biz/ campingsantamavra/]** Take coast rd S fr Lefkada to Vlycho, turn L for Dessimi, site in 2.5km (after Camping Dessimi). Access via v steep hill - severe gradients both sides. Med, mkd pitch, terr, pt shd; wc; chem disp; mv service pnt; shwrs inc; EHU (12A) inc; gas; lndry; shop; rest, snacks; bar; BBQ; sand/ shgl beach adj; TV rm; phone; quiet; CKE/CCI. "Excel site & beach; gd, clean san facs; friendly owners." 20 Apr-20 Oct. € 25.00   2009*

PEFKARI (THASSOS) *C2* (250m W Coastal) *40.61630, 24.60021* **Camping Pefkari Beach, 64002 Pefkari [tel/fax (25930) 51190; info@camping-pefkari.gr; www.camping-pefkari.gr]** SW fr Thassos port approx 43km to Limenaria, Pefkari is next sm vill. Site well sp in vill. Med, hdstg, pt shd; own san; chem disp; shwrs inc; EHU (6A) €2.90; lndry rm; shop; rest, snacks; bar; BBQ; sand beach adj; 5% statics; bus 1km; Eng spkn; quiet; CKE/CCI. "Lovely spot; worth putting up with poor, dated san facs; gd local rest; vg; improving site; beautiful; easy walk to Pefkari and Potos; excel on site rest; lovely spot." 1 May-30 Sep. € 27.50   2014*

⊞ **RETHYMNO (CRETE)** *C4* (3km E Coastal) *35.36795, 24.51487* **Camping Elizabeth, Ionias 84 Terma, 74100 Missiria [tel/fax (28310) 28694; wallydewever@yahoo.gr; www.camping-elizabeth.com]** W fr Iraklio/Heraklion exit Platanes/Arkadi. Site 1km bef Platanes, on R on sh unsurfaced rd. Lge, hdg pitch, shd; wc; chem disp; mv service pnt; shwrs; EHU (12A) inc; lndry (inc dryer); shop; rest, snacks; bar; BBQ; cooking facs; beach adj; wifi; 3% statics; dogs; phone; bus 500m; poss cr; Eng spkn; adv bkg; quiet; red LS; CKE/CCI. "Gd walking on mkd rtes; gd cycling; excursion programme; vg." ♦ ltd. € 28.00   2010*

RODA (CORFU) *A2* (2km W Coastal) *39.78446, 19.78486*
Camping Roda Beach International, 49081 Roda
[(26630) 63120; fax 63081; info@rodacamping.gr;
www.rodacamping.gr] N fr port to join main rd to
Palaeokastlitsa. Turn R for Sidari & foll sp to Roda. Turn L 30m
bef rndabt, 200m on R, sp. Med, pt shd; wc; mv service pnt;
shwrs inc; EHU €3.80; lndry; shop; rest, snacks; bar; playgrnd;
pool; beach 700m; bike hire; entmnt; internet; TV; dogs free;
Eng spkn; some rd noise; red snr citizens/CCI. 15 Apr-15 Oct.
€ 22.50   2010*

ROVIES (EVIA) *B2* (5km N Coastal) *38.83276, 23.19886*
Camping Rovies Beach, 34005 Rovies [(22270) 71120;
info@campingevia.com; www.campingevia.com]
Fr N on ferry fr Glifa to Agiokampos foll coast rd S for 23 km.
Med, hdg pitch, hdstg, terr, pt shd; wc; chem disp; shwrs inc;
EHU (12A) inc; lndry rm; shop; BBQ; shgl beach adj; 5% statics;
CKE/CCI. "Delightful location; facs dated & plagued by moths
(May 09); many pitches diff for m'vans due low branches; gd."
1 Apr-30 Oct. € 29.00   2009*

SAMI (CEPHALONIA) *A2* (1km W Coastal) *38.25088,
20.63803* Camping Karavomilos Beach, 28080 Sami
[(26740) 22480; fax 22932; info@camping-karavomilos.gr;
www.camping-karavomilos.gr] Site sp. Lge, hdg/mkd pitch,
pt shd; wc; chem disp; mv service pnt; shwrs inc; EHU (16A)
inc; lndry (inc dryer); shop; rest, snacks; bar; playgrnd; pool;
paddling pool; shgl beach adj; wifi; TV rm; dogs; phone; poss
cr; Eng spkn; adv bkg; some rd noise; ccard acc; red CKE/
CCI. "Friendly owner; wonderful scenery; easy walk to town;
v lge o'fits ring ahead for easy access; excel." 1 May-30 Sep.
€ 28.50   2010*

SISI (CRETE) *C4* (1.5km W Coastal) *35.30371, 25.50858*
Sisi Camping, 72400 Sisi [tel/fax (28410) 71247; info@
sisicamping.gr; www.sisicamping.gr] E fr Iraklio/Heraklion
on E75, after Malia look for Sisi turn approx 5km after Malia.
Site sp. Sm, mkd/hdg pitch, pt shd; wc (cont); chem disp; mv
service pnt; shwrs inc; EHU (10A) €3.50; lndry; shop 800m; rest
250m; snacks; bar; BBQ; pool; paddling pool; sand beach 1km;
watersports; wifi; dogs free; phone; Eng spkn; adv bkg; quiet;
red LS; CKE/CCI. "Sisi pretty vill; gd touring base attractions
& archaeological sites; warm welcome; vg." 1 May-15 Oct.
€ 23.00   2010*

THASSOS (THASSOS) *C1* (12km SE Coastal) *40.72561,
24.7567* Camping Golden Beach, 64004 Panagia
[(25930) 61472; fax 61473; info@camping-goldenbeach.gr;
www.camping-goldenbeach.gr] S fr Thassos to Panagia.
Turn L to Hrissi Armoudia & site. Site sp in Panagia. Lge, hdg/
mkd pitch, pt shd; wc (some cont); shwrs inc; EHU €4.30;
lndry; shop; rest adj; snacks; bar; playgrnd; sand beach adj;
games area; entmnt; TV; 50% statics; poss cr; Eng spkn;
quiet. "Beautiful, long, sandy beach." ♦ 1 May-15 Oct.
€ 20.00   2011*

> ## "I need an on-site restaurant"
>
> We do our best to make sure site
> information is correct, but it is always best
> to check any must-have facilities are still
> available or will be open during your visit.

TINOS (TINOS) *C3* (500m E Coastal) *37.53994, 25.16377*
Tinos Camping, Louizas Sohou 5, 84200 Tinos
[(22830) 22344; fax 24373; tinoscamping@thn.forthnet.gr;
www.tinos-info.gr/tinoscamping] Clearly sp fr port. Sm,
hdg/mkd pitch, hdstg; shd; wc; chem disp (wc); shwrs inc; EHU
€4.50; lndry rm; shop; rest, snacks; BBQ; cooking facs; sand/
shgl beach 500m; dogs; phone; Eng spkn; adv bkg; ccard
acc; red long stay/CKE/CCI. "1,600 Venetian dovecots & 600
churches on island; monastery with healing icon." ♦
1 May-31 Oct. € 21.50   2009*

VASILIKI (LEFKAS) *A2* (500m NW Coastal) *38.63108,
20.60663* Camping Vasiliki Beach, 31082 Vasiliki
[(26450) 31308; fax 31458] On arr in Vasiliki, turn R in 300m,
site sp. Med, some hdstg, shd; wc; chem disp; mv service pnt;
shwrs; EHU (10A); gas; lndry; shop; rest, snacks; bar; BBQ;
playgrnd; beach adj; games rm; TV; dogs; phone; poss cr; Eng
spkn; red CKE/CCI. "Popular with windsurfers; easy walk to
town along beach." ♦ ltd. 15 Apr-15 Oct. € 36.00   2011*

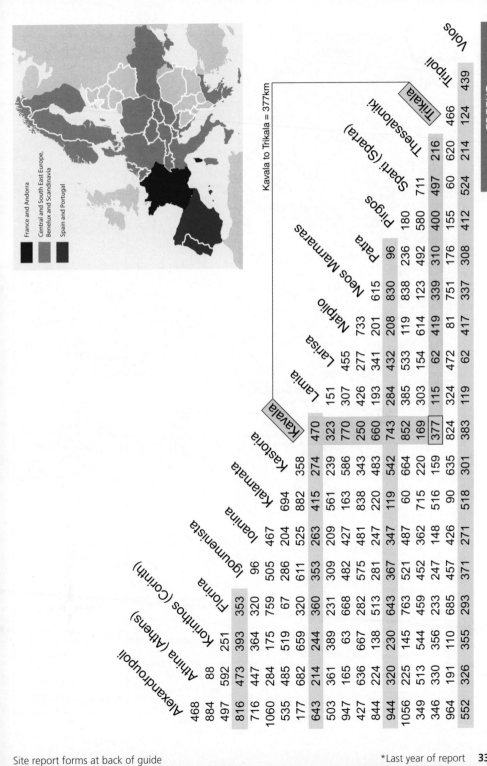

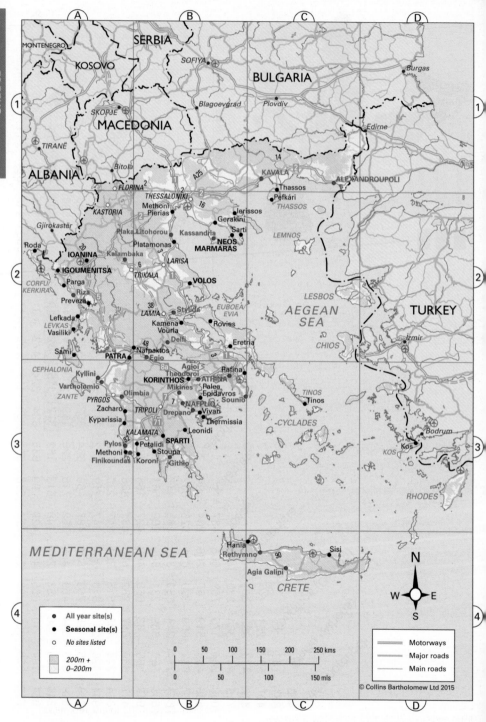

MONTENEGRO

SERBIA

KOSOVO

SOFIYA

Blagoevgrad

BULGARIA

Plovdiv

Burgas

SKOPJE

MACEDONIA

Edirne

TIRANE

Bitola

14

KAVALA

ALEXANDROUPOLI

FLORINA 2

Thassos

Pefkári

A25

THESSALONIKI

THASSOS

2

KASTORIA

16

Ierissos

Methoni

Gerakini

LEMNOS

Gjirokastër

Pierias

Kassandria

Sarti

8

Roda

Plaka Litohorou

NEOS

Platamonas

MARMARAS

20

IOANINA

Kalambaka

LARISA

LESBOS

IGOUMENITSA

6

AEGEAN

CORFU

TRIKALA

VOLOS

SEA

KERKIRA

Parga

Riza

TURKEY

Preveza

38

EUBOEA

LAMIA

Stylida

EVIA

Lefkada

Kamena

CHIOS

LEVKAS

Vourla

Rovies

Izmir

Vasiliki

Delfi

Eretria

Sami

48

Nafpaktos

CEPHALONIA

Egio

Agioi

PATRA

Theodoroi

Rafina

Kyllini

8a

KORINTHOS

ATHINA

ZANTE

Mikines

Palea

TINOS

Vartholomio

Olimbia

Epidavros

Tinos

PYRGOS

7

NAFPLIO

Sounio

Zacharo

TRIPOLI

Drepano

Vivari

CYCLADES

Kyparissia

Thermissia

Bodrum

71

KALAMATA

Leonidi

Petalidi

Kos

Pylos

SPARTI

KOS

3

Methoni

Stoupa

Finikoundas

Koroni

Githio

RHODES

MEDITERRANEAN SEA

Hania

Sisi

Rethymno

90

N

Agia Galipi

CRETE

W   E

S

© Collins Bartholomew Ltd 2015

● All year site(s)

● Seasonal site(s)

○ No sites listed

200m +

0–200m

0   50   100   150   200   250 kms

0   50   100   150 mls

Motorways

Major roads

Main roads

Hungary
Country Introduction

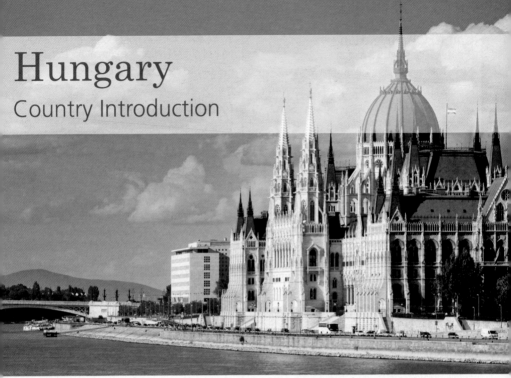

Hungarian Parliament Building, Budapest

Welcome to Hungary

Hungary is home to some of the most dramatic and exotic architecture found in Europe, with buildings spanning from the Art Nouveau era to Ancient Rome. Turkish, Slavic, Magyar and Roman influences entwine with its own unique culture to make Hungary a fascinating place.

There are more medicinal spas in Hungary than anywhere else in Europe and the spa culture is an important part both of the tourist industry and everyday life. You can enjoy spas that range from traditional bathhouses to modern wellness centres that cater for the whole family.

Country highlights

Many folk festivals are celebrated in Hungary throughout the year, the biggest of which is the Festival of Folk Arts/Crafts held every August in Buda Castle. Thousands of visitors attend to view the fantastic traditional crafts on offer.

One of the most renowned crafts is pottery making, with Hungary having a long tradition of creating both fine porcelain, such as Herend, and tiling and stoneware, such as Zsolnay produces.

Major towns and cities

- Budapest – an enchanting city full of galleries, theatres and museums.
- Debrecen – this former capital is one of Hungary's most important cultural centres.
- Pécs – an ancient city with countless things to see and do.
- Eger – a city famous for its fine red wines.

Attractions

- Fisherman's Bastion, Budapest – enjoy unmatched views over the city.
- Hungarian Parliament Building, Budapest – a magnificent structure on the banks of the Danube that houses the Hungarian Crown Jewels amongst other artefacts.
- Lake Hévíz – one of the largest thermal lakes in the world with its own unique ecosystem.
- Esztergom Basilica – a spectacularly enormous cathedral with Renaissance art.

Find out more

www.gotohungary.com

Tel: 0036 (0) 14 88 87 00 Tourist Information

Country Information

Population (approx): 9.9 million

Capital: Budapest (population approx 1.7 million)

Area: 93,000 sq km

Bordered by: Austria, Croatia, Romania, Serbia, Slovakia, Slovenia, Ukraine

Terrain: Mostly flat and rolling plains; hills and low mountains to the north

Climate: Temperate, continental climate; cold, cloudy winters; warm, sunny summers; changeable in spring and early summer with heavy rain and storms. The best times to visit are spring and autumn

Highest Point: Kekes 1,014m

Language: Hungarian

Local Time: GMT or BST + 1, i.e. 1 hour ahead of the UK all year

Currency: Forint (HUF); £1 = HUF 435, HUF 1000 = £2.30 (September 2015)

Emergency numbers: Police 107; Fire brigade 105; Ambulance 104. Operators speak English.

Public Holidays 2016: Jan 1; Mar 15, 27, 28; May 1, 16; Aug 20; Oct 23; Nov 1; Dec 25, 26.

School summer holidays are from mid-June to the end of August

Camping and Caravanning

There are approximately 100 organised campsites in Hungary rated from 1 to 4 stars. These are generally well signposted off main routes, with the site name shown below a blue camping sign. Most campsites open from May to September and the most popular sites are situated by Lake Balaton and the Danube. A Camping Key Europe (CKE) or Camping Card International (CCI) is essential.

Facilities vary from site to site, but visitors will find it useful to carry their own flat universal sink plug. There has been much improvement in recent years in the general standard of campsites, but communal changing areas for showers are not uncommon. Many sites have communal kitchen facilities which enable visitors to make great savings on their own gas supply.

Many campsites require payment in cash. Prices have risen sharply in recent years. Therefore, prices

in this guide for sites not reported on for some time might not reflect the current prices.

Casual/wild camping is prohibited.

Cycling

There are approximately 2,000km of cycle tracks, 100km of which are in Budapest and 200km around Lake Balaton. Tourinform offices in Hungary provide maps of cycling routes.

Children under 14 years are not allowed to ride on the road and all cyclists must wear a reflective jacket at night and in poor daytime visibility.

Electricity and Gas

Current on campsites varies between 6 and 16 amps.
Plugs have two round pins. There are some sites that do not have CEE connections.

Only non-returnable and/or non-exchangeable Campingaz cylinders are available.

Entry Formalities

British and Irish passport holders may stay for a period of three months without a visa. Your passport needs to be valid for the duration of your stay and it is always recommended when visiting a foreign country to have an additional period of validity on your passport in case of any unforeseen delays. Anyone planning to stay longer than three months should contact the Hungarian Embassy for further information

There are no immigration or Customs checks at borders with other EU countries, i.e. Slovakia, Slovenia and Austria. Border crossings with other countries are generally open 24 hours.

Medical Services

British nationals may obtain emergency medical and dental treatment from practitioners contracted to the national health insurance scheme, Országos Egészségbiztosítási (OEP), together with emergency hospital treatment, on presentation of a European Health Insurance Card (EHIC) and a British passport.

Fees are payable for treatment and prescribed medicines, and are not refundable in Hungary.

You may be able to apply for reimbursement when back in the UK.

Pharmacies (gyógyszertár) are well stocked. The location of the nearest all-night pharmacy is displayed on the door of every pharmacy.

Opening Hours

Banks – Mon-Thurs 8am-3pm. Fri 8am - 1pm. Hours may vary slightly.

Museums – Tue-Sun 10am-6pm; closed Mon.

Post Offices – Mon-Fri 8am-6pm; post office at Budapest open Mon-Sat 7am-9pm.

Shops – Mon-Fri 10am-6pm (supermarkets from 7am-7pm with some grocery stores open 24 hours); open half day Saturdays.

Safety and Security

Petty theft in Budapest is common in areas frequented by tourists, particularly on busy public transport, at markets and at popular tourist sites. Beware of pickpockets and bag snatchers.

Do not carry large amounts of cash. Take care when receiving bank notes and change as some that are no longer valid are still in circulation, e.g. HUF 200 notes were withdrawn in 2009. There has been a small number of instances of taxi drivers deliberately passing these notes to tourists. Be aware especially when paying with a HUF 10,000 or 20,000 bank note.

Theft of and from vehicles is common. Do not leave your belongings, car registration documents or mobile phones in your car and ensure that it is properly locked with the alarm on, even if leaving it for just a moment. Beware of contrived 'incidents', particularly on the Vienna-Budapest motorway, designed to stop motorists and expose them to robbery.

Visitors have reported in the past that motorists may be pestered at service areas on the Vienna to Budapest motorway by people insisting on washing windscreens and demanding money.

During the summer season in Budapest, uniformed tourist police patrol the most frequently visited areas of the city. Criminals sometimes pose as tourist police and ask for visitors' money, credit cards or travel documents in order to check them.

Always ensure that a uniformed police officer is wearing a badge displaying the word 'Rendörség' and a five-digit identification number, together with a separate name badge. Plain clothes police carry a badge and an ID card with picture, hologram and rank. If in doubt, insist on going to the nearest police station.

There are still occasional incidents of exorbitant overcharging in certain restaurants, bars and clubs in Budapest, accompanied by threats of violence. Individuals who have been unable to settle their bill have frequently been accompanied by the establishment's security guards to a cash machine and made to withdraw funds. Visitors are advised to ask for a menu and only order items which are priced realistically. A five digit price for one dish is too high. Never accept menus which do not display prices and check your bill carefully.

Taxi drivers are sometimes accomplices to these frauds, receiving 'commission' for recommending restaurants and bars which charge extortionate prices to visitors. Never ask a taxi driver to recommend a bar, club or restaurant. If a driver takes you to one or you are approached on the street with an invitation to an unfamiliar bar or restaurant, you should treat such advice with extreme caution.

Do not change money or get involved in any form of gambling in the street; these activities are illegal.

If you need help, go to the nearest police station or the Tourist Information Point open 8am - 8pm, Deák Ferenc Square, 1052 Budapest, Sütő Street 2 (1) 438 8080

There is a low threat from terrorism.

British Embassy

HARMINCAD UTCA 6, BUDAPEST 1051
Tel: (1) 2662888
www.ukinhungary.fco.gov.uk

Irish Embassy

SZABADSÁG TÉR 7,
BANK CENTRE, GRANIT TOWER, V. FLOOR
1054 BUDAPEST
Tel: (1) 3014960
www.embassyofireland.hu

Documents

Passport
Carry your passport at all times. A photocopy is not acceptable.

Vehicle(s)
Carry your vehicle registration certificate (V5C), vehicle insurance certificate and MOT certificate (if applicable) with you when driving.

Money

Hungarian currency is available from banks in Austria before crossing the border. For emergency cash reserves, it is advisable to have euros, rather than sterling. Foreign currency is best exchanged at banks as, by law, this is at the rate shown on the banks' currency boards and they are not permitted to charge commission. Private bureaux de change, however, do charge commission, but the rate of exchange may be better.

Credit cards are accepted at many outlets in large towns and cities and cash dispensers, 'bankomats', are widespread even in small towns. There is a high incidence of credit card fraud and payment in cash wherever possible is advisable. Carry your credit card issuers'/banks' 24 hour UK contact numbers separately in case of loss or theft of your cards.

Recent visitors report that some newer types of debit and credit cards issued in the UK do not work in certain cash machines in Hungary. The banks are working on a solution but, in the meantime, if you encounter this problem you should try a cash machine at a different bank. It is possible to obtain cash from post offices with a debit or credit card.

Euros are widely accepted in shops and restaurants frequented by tourists, but check the exchange rate.

When leaving Hungary on the MI motorway (Budapest-Vienna), it is important to change back your forints on the Hungarian side of the border by crossing the carriageway to the left at the designated crossing-point, as visitors report that there are no facilities on the right hand side and none on the other side in Austria.

Motoring in Hungary

Accidents

Accidents causing damage to vehicles or injury to persons must be reported to the nearest police station and to the Hungarian State Insurance Company (Hungária Biztositó) within 24 hours. The police will issue a statement which you may be asked to show when leaving the country.

If entering Hungary with a conspicuously damaged vehicle, it is recommended that you obtain a report confirming the damage from the police in the country where the damage occurred, otherwise difficulties may arise when leaving Hungary.

Alcohol

It is illegal to drive after consuming any alcohol whatsoever.

Breakdown Service

The motoring organisation, Magyar Autóklub (MAK), operates a breakdown service 24 hours a day on all roads. Drivers in need of assistance should telephone 188 or (1) 3451680. The number (1) is the area code for Budapest. On motorways emergency phones are placed at 2km intervals.

MAK road patrol cars are yellow and marked 'Segélyszolgálat'. Their registration numbers begin with the letters MAK.

The roadside breakdown service is chargeable, higher charges applying at night. There is a scale of charges by vehicle weight and distance for towing vehicles to a garage. Payment is required in cash.

Essential Equipment

First Aid Kit
It is a legal requirement that all vehicles should carry a first aid kit.

Lights
Outside built-up areas dipped headlights are compulsory at all times, regardless of weather conditions. Bulbs are more likely to fail with constant use and you are recommended to carry spares. At night in built-up areas dipped

headlights must be used as full beam is prohibited.

Headlight flashing often means that a driver is giving way, but do not carry out a manoeuvre unless you are sure that this is the case.

Reflective Jackets/Waistcoats
If your vehicle is immobilised on the carriageway outside a built-up area, or if visibility is poor, you must wear a reflective jacket or waistcoat when getting out of your vehicle. Passengers who leave the vehicle, for example, to assist with a repair, should also wear one. Keep the jackets inside your vehicle, not in the boot.

In addition, pedestrians and cyclists walking or cycling at night or in poor visibility along unlit roads outside a built-up area must also wear a reflective jacket.

Warning Triangles
In the event of accident, it is compulsory to place a warning triangle 100 metres behind the vehicle on motorways and 50 metres on other roads.

Child Restraint System
Children under the height of 1.5m must be seated in a suitable child restraint system appropriate for their size in the rear of the vehicle.

If no child restraint is available a child over 3 who is over 1.35m in height may travel in the rear seat with a seatbelt. Children younger or shorter than this may not ever travel without a suitable restraint system in the vehicle.

Winter Driving
The use of snow chains can be made compulsory on some roads when there is severe winter weather.

Fuel

Leaded petrol is no longer available. The sign 'Ólommentes üzemanyag' or 'Bleifrei 95' indicates unleaded petrol. LPG is widely available.

Most petrol stations are open from 6am to 8pm. Along motorways and in large towns they are often open 24 hours. Some petrol stations accept credit and debit cards but cash is the most usual means of payment.

Parking

Zigzag lines on the carriageway and road signs indicate a stopping/parking prohibition. Illegally-parked vehicles will be towed away or clamped. On two-way roads, vehicles must park in the direction of traffic; they may park on either side in one-way streets. In certain circumstances, parking on the pavement is allowed.

Budapest is divided into various time restricted parking zones (maximum three hours) where tickets must be purchased from Monday to Friday from a machine. For longer periods you are advised to use 'Park and Ride' car parks located near major metro stations and bus terminals.

Priority

Pedestrians have priority over traffic at pedestrian crossings and at intersections. They do not have priority on the roadway between central tram loading islands and pavements, and drivers must exercise care on these sections. Major roads are indicated by a priority road ahead sign. At the intersection of two roads of equal importance, where there is no sign, vehicles coming from the right have priority. Trams and buses have priority at any intersection on any road and buses have right of way when leaving bus stops after the driver has signalled his intention to pull out.

Roads

Hungary has a good system of well surfaced main roads and driving standards are higher than in many other parts of Europe. There are few dual carriageways and care is required, therefore, when overtaking with a right-hand drive vehicle. Extra care is required on provincial roads which may be badly lit, poorly maintained and narrow. In the countryside at night be on the alert for unlit cycles and horse drawn vehicles

Road Signs and Markings

Road signs and markings conform to international conventions. Square green road signs indicate the number of km to the next town. At traffic lights a flashing amber light indicates a dangerous intersection. Destination signs feature road numbers rather than the names of towns, so it is essential to equip yourself with an up-to-date road map or atlas. Signs for motorways have white lettering on a blue background; on other roads signs are white and green.

Speed Limits

	Open Road (km/h)	Motorway (km/h)
Car Solo	90-110	130
Car towing caravan/trailer	70	80
Motorhome under 3500kg	90-110	130
Motorhome 3500-7500kg	70	80

A speed limit of 30 km/h (18 mph) is in force in many residential, city centre and tourist resort areas.

Traffic Jams

Roads around Budapest are busy on Friday and Sunday afternoons. In the holiday season roads to Lake Balaton (M7) and around the lake (N7 and N71) may be congested. There are regular traffic hold ups at weekends at the border crossings to Austria, the Czech Republic and Serbia. Motorway traffic information (in English) is available on www.motorway.hu

Violation of Traffic Regulations

The police make spot vehicle document checks and are keen to enforce speed limits. They are permitted to impose on-the-spot fines of up to HUF300,000. Credit cards are accepted for the payment of fines in some circumstances.

Motorways

All motorways (autópálya) and main connecting roads run to or from Budapest. In recent years the road network has been extended and improved and there are now approximately 900 kilometres of motorway and dual carriageways or semi-motorways. However, most roads are still single carriageway, single lane and care is recommended. The M0 motorway is a 75km

ringroad around Budapest which links the M1, M7, M6, M5 and Highway 11. The recently built Megyeri Bridge on the Danube is part of the M0 and its opening has considerably reduced traffic congestion to the north of Budapest.

Emergency corridors are compulsory on motorways and dual carriageways. Drivers are required to create a precautionary emergency corridor to provide access for emergency vehicles whenever congestion occurs. Drivers in the left-hand lane must move as far over to the left as possible, and drivers in the central and right-hand lanes must move as far over to the right as possible.

Motorway Vignettes

Approximately 30% of motorways are toll-free; otherwise you must purchase an electronic vignette (matrica) or e-vignette (sticker) before entering the motorway.

They are available online, from motorway customer service offices and at large petrol stations near the motorways.
You can pay in forints or by credit card.

Leaflets are distributed to motorists at the border and a telephone information centre is available in Hungary – tel 36 58 75 00. Vignettes should only be purchased from outlets where the prices are clearly displayed at the set rates. For full details (in English), including how to buy online and toll-free sections, see www.motorway.hu

When purchasing an e-vignette a confirmation message will be sent or a coupon issued and this must be kept for a year after its expiry date. There is no need to display the vignette in your windscreen as the motorway authorities check all vehicles electronically (without the need for you to stop your vehicle) and verify registration number, category of toll paid and validity of an e-vignette. Charges in forints (2015 charges, subject to change) are shown below:

Category of Vehicle	Period of Validity	
	1 week	1 month
Vehicle up to 3,500kg with or without caravan or trailer	2,975	4,780
Motorhome	5,950	9,560

Since the beginning of 2013 Hungary's State Motorway Management company (AAK) have been imposing on-the-spot fines for motorists who do not have a vignette. Fines amount to HUF 14,875 (around £40) for vehicles under 3,500kg or HUF 66,925 (around £178) for vehicles between 3,500kg and 7,500kg if paid within 30 days. 78% of the motorists fined so far have been foreign nationals, so ensure you have a vignette before travelling on motorways.

Touring

Hungary boasts eight World Heritage sites including the national park at Aggtelek which contains Europe's largest cave network, the Christian cemetery at Pécs and the monastery at Pannonhalma. Lake Balaton, the largest lake in Central Europe, attracts lovers of bathing, sailing, fishing and windsurfing. With 200km of sandy shoreline and shallow warm waters, it is very popular with families and easily Hungary's favourite tourist area.

A Budapest Card is available, allowing unlimited travel on public transport for two or three consecutive days, free city walking tours, discounted entry to museums and other attractions, plus discounts on many guided tours, events, shops and restaurants. Cards are available from metro stations, tourist information offices, many travel agencies, hotels, museums and main Budapest transport ticket offices, as well as from the Hungarian National Tourist Office in London. A child under 14 travelling with the cardholder is included free of charge. You may also order online from www.budapest-card.com

A tip of 10-15% of the bill is expected in restaurants. Check your bill first to ensure that a service charge has not already been added.

Take your own supply of plastic carrier bags to supermarkets, as generally they are not supplied.

Hungarian is a notoriously difficult language for native English speakers to decipher and pronounce. English is not widely spoken in rural areas, but it is becoming increasingly widespread elsewhere as it is now taught in schools. German is widely spoken and a dictionary may be helpful.

Public Transport & Local Travel

Cars are not permitted within the Castle District and on Margaret Island in Budapest. It is advisable to use public transport when travelling into the city and there is an excellent network of bus, tram and metro routes (BKV). All public transport in Hungary is free for over 65s, and this also applies to foreign visitors with proof of age (passport).

There are a number of ticket options, including family tickets, 1, 3 and 7 day tickets, and they can be bought at metro stations, ticket machines, tobacconists and newsagents. Validate your bus and metro tickets before use at each stage of your journey and every time you change metro lines at the red machines provided. Tickets are often checked on vehicles or at metro station exits by controllers wearing arm bands and carrying photo ID. For further information on public transport in Budapest see www.bkv.hu

As a general rule, it is better to phone for taxis operated by reputable local companies, rather than flag them down in the street, and always ensure that fares are metered. A tip of approximately 10% of the fare is customary.

Mahart, the Hungarian Shipping Company, operates a regular hydrofoil service from April to October along the Danube between Budapest and Vienna. The journey lasts six hours and covers 288km.

Local companies Legenda (www.legenda.hu) and Mahart also offer city cruises between May and October, as well as regular trips to tourist attractions outside Budapest, such as Szentendre, Visegrád and Esztergom.

A ferry service takes cars across Lake Balaton from Szántód to Tihany. There are crossings every 10 minutes from June to September and every hour during the low season. Regular bus and train services link the towns and villages along the lakeside.

AGGTELEK *A3* (1km NW Rural) *48.47094, 20.49446* **Baradla Camping, Baradla Oldal 1, 3759 Aggtelek [tel/fax (48) 503000; szallas@anp.hu]** Fr Slovakia turn off E571/A50 at Plesivec onto rd 587 S via Dlha Ves to border x-ing. Cont S for approx 800m & hotel/campsite complex is on L. Fr Miskolc 45km N on rte 26, turn onto rte 27 sp Perkupa then foll sp Nemzeti National Park & Aggtelek. Site sp in vill. Med, pt sl, pt shd; wc; shwrs; EHU (16A) inc; rest, snacks, bar at motel; BBQ; cooking facs; playgrnd; some statics; quiet. "Gd NH to/fr Slovakia; ent to lge Barlang Caves system adj; facs poss stretched high ssn." 15 Apr-15 Oct. HUF 4359   2010*

ALSOORS see Balatonfüred *C2*

BALATONAKALI *C1* (1.5km E Rural) *46.8834, 17.76913* **Balatontourist Camping Strand-Holiday, Strand u 2, 8243 Balatonakali [(87) 544021; fax 544022; strand@ balatontourist.hu; www.balatontourist.hu]** Site sp on rte 71 at km 53.6 at E end of Balatonakali. Lge, hdg/mkd pitch, pt shd; wc; chem disp; mv service pnt; baby facs; private bthrms avail; shwrs inc; EHU (6-10A) inc; lndry; shop high ssn; rest & 500m; playgrnd; sand beach & lake sw; windsurfing; watersports; fishing; bike hire; games area; internet; entmnt; TV rm; some statics; dogs HUF900; adv bkg; daytime rlwy noise; ccard acc. "Excel san facs; some lakeside pitches; cycle track around lake adj." ♦ 2 Apr-10 Oct. HUF 8250 (CChq acc)   2010*

BALATONAKALI *C1* (1km SW Rural) *46.87939, 17.74190* **Balatontourist Camping Levendula (Naturist), Hókuli u 25, 8243 Balatonakali [(87) 544011; fax 544012; levendula@ balatontourist.hu; www.balatontourist.hu]** NE on rte 71 on N shore of Lake Balaton twds Tihany. Site sp on W app to Balatonakali. Turn R twds lake; go over level x-ing, site ent on R. Med, mkd pitch, pt shd; wc; chem disp; mv service pnt; sauna; shwrs inc; EHU (4A) inc; gas; lndry (inc dryer); shop; supmkt 1km; rest, snacks; bar; playgrnd; sand beach & lake sw; fishing; windsurf school; games area; bike hire; wifi; TV rm; dogs HUF950; adv bkg; Eng spkn; quiet at night, train noise fr early morning; ccard acc; CKE/CCI. "Superb site." ♦ 7 May-12 Sep. HUF 6800   2010*

BALATONALMADI *C2* (2km SW Rural) *47.0205, 18.00828* **Balatontourist Camping Yacht, Véghely Dezsö út 18, 8220 Balatonalmádi [(88) 584101; fax 584102; yacht@ balatontourist.hu; www.balatontourist.hu]** Fr rd 71, km post 25.5, site sp at lakeside. Lge, hdg/mkd pitch, pt shd; wc; chem disp; mv service pnt; shwrs inc; EHU (4A) inc (rev pol); lndry; shop; rest, snacks; bar; playgrnd; beach adj; watersports; bike hire; entmnt; TV; 10% statics; dogs HUF990; Eng spkn; adv bkg; ccard acc; CKE/CCI. "Excel san facs; excel rest; several sites in close proximity; great site with friendly owners." ♦ 1 May-15 Sep. HUF 9980   2013*

BALATONBERENY *C1* (1km NW Rural) *46.71340, 17.31080* **FKK Naturista Camping (Naturist), Hetvezer u.2, 8649 Balatonberény [tel/fax (85) 377299; bereny@balatontourist.hu]** Fr Keszthely foll rte 71 & rte 76 round SW end of lake. Lge sp indicates Balatonberény & site. Sps change fr Naturista Camping to FKK at turn off main rd. Med, hdg/mkd pitch, pt shd; wc; chem disp; shwrs inc; EHU (12-16A) inc; lndry; shop; rest, snacks; bar; BBQ; direct access lake sw adj; playgrnd; windsurfing; watersports; games area; wifi; entmnt; TV; few statics; dogs €2.60; phone; quiet; poss cr; adv bkg; red INF. "Vg site; gd sized pitches; excel san facs." 15 May-15 Sep. HUF 8695   2013*

⊞ **BALATONFURED** *C2* (9km NE Rural) *46.99184, 17.98698* **Présház Camping, Présház út 1, 8226 Alsóörs [(87) 447736]** Rd 71 fr Balatonfüred, site just past vill of Alsóörs on L. Sm, pt sl, pt shd; wc; chem disp; shwrs inc; EHU (10A) inc; lake sw 1km; games area; dogs; quiet. "Vg, lovely, CL-type site in orchard of wine shop; friendly owner; wine-tasting; paid in Euros but Forint preferred; sighting of wild boar nrby!" HUF 4360   2015*

BALATONFURED *C2* (2km SW Rural) *46.94660, 17.87590* **Balatontourist Camping Füred, Széchenyi út 24, 8230 Balatonfüred [(87) 580241; fax 580242; fured@ balatontourist.hu; www.balatontourist.hu]** Exit M3 or rte 70 on rte 71 sp Balatonfüred. Site sp 1km SW of Balatonfüred on SE side of rd 71 on N side of lake. V lge, pt shd; htd wc; chem disp; mv service pnt; baby facs; sauna; shwrs inc; EHU (4A) inc; lndry (inc dryer); shop; rest, snacks; bar; playgrnd; pool; paddling pool; waterslides; beach & lake sw; watersports; tennis; bike hire; wifi; entmnt; TV rm; 10% statics; no dogs; phone; bus; poss cr; adv bkg; quiet except nr rd; ccard acc; red LS. "Many attractions in this holiday area; lovely lakeside town; gd facs, but ltd LS; prices vary depending on pitch size; excel." ♦ 22 Apr-2 Oct. HUF 8700 (CChq acc)   2011*

BALATONKENESE *C2* (W Rural) **Romantik Camping, Gesztenye Fasor 1, 8174 Balatonkenese [tel/fax (88) 482360; romantikcamping@invitel.hu]** Off rte 71 on N shore of lake, sp. Med, pt terr, pt shd; wc; shwrs; EHU HUF400; lndry rm; shop; snacks; cooking facs; 250m to lake; quiet. "Reasonable facs; site has potential." Jun-Sep.   2009*

BALATONSZEPEZD *C1* (2km NE Rural) *46.8610, 17.67335* **Balatontourist Camping Venus, Halász út 1, 8252 Balatonszepezd [(87) 568061; fax 568062; venus@ balatontourist.hu; www.balatontourist.hu]** On rte 71; site sp at km post 61, over level x-ing into site. Med, pt shd; wc; chem disp; mv service pnt; shwrs inc; EHU (4-10A) inc; lndry; shop; rest, snacks; playgrnd; beach; watersports; fishing; games area; dogs HUF750; Eng spkn; noise fr rlwy; ccard acc. "Excel lakeside position; gd rest; gd value." ♦ 14 May-5 Sep. HUF 5400   2010*

BALATONSZEPEZD C1 (4km SW Rural) 48.82950, 17.64000 Balatontourist Camping Napfény, Halász út 5, 8253 Révfülöp [(87) 563031 or (88) 544444 (LS); fax 464309 or (88) 544455 (LS); napfenyj@balatontourist.hu; www.balatontourist.hu] Take m'way E71/M7 & exit junc 90 along N shore of lake, passing Balatonalmádi & Balatonfüred to Révfülöp. Site sp. Lge, mkd pitch, pt shd; wc; chem disp; mv service pnt; baby facs; private san facs avail; shwrs inc; EHU (6A) inc; lndry (inc dryer); shop; supmkt 500m; rest, snacks; bar; BBQ; playgrnd; paddling pool; lake sw & beach adj; fishing; watersports; bike & boat hire; spa; tennis 300m; horseriding 5km; games area; games rm; wifi; entmnt; TV rm; 2% statics; dogs HUF900; twin-axles acc (rec check in adv); phone; adv bkg; quiet; ccard acc; red LS. "Warm welcome; excel, well-organised lakeside site; gd pitches; gd for families; fees according to pitch size & location." ♦ 25 Apr-27 Sep. HUF 9449 (CChq acc) SBS - X06   2012*

BOLDOGASSZONYFA D2 (1km S Rural) 46.17807, 17.83812 Camping Horgásztanya, Petöfi út 53, 7937 Boldogasszonyfa [(73) 702003; csukabeno@ciromail.hu; www.horgasztanya.hu] Take rte 67 S fr Kaposvár. Immed after vill of Boldogasszonyfa turn L, site sp on rvside. Sm, hdg pitch, pt sl, shd; wc; chem disp (wc); shwrs inc; EHU (10A); rest; bar; fishing; quiet;CKE/CCI. "Simple, rural site; conv Pécs & border area; rec use own facs." ♦ ltd. 1 May-30 Sep.   2012*

"I like to fill in the reports as I travel from site to site"

You'll find report forms at the back of this guide, or you can fill them in online at www.caravanclub.co.uk/europereport.

BOZSOK see Köszeg B1

⊞ **BUDAPEST** B2 (10km N Urban) 47.57434, 19.05179 Római Camping, Szentendrei útca 189, 1031 Budapest [(1) 3887167; fax 2500426; info@romaicamping.hu; www.romaicamping.hu] Fr Gyor/Budapest m'way M1/E50 foll rte 11 twd Szentendre/Esztergom for approx 9km. Turn R at site sp. Site adj Római Fürdő rlwy stn. Med, mkd pitch, shd; wc; chem disp; shwrs inc; EHU (16A) HUF600; lndry (inc dryer); shop 500m; rest, snacks; BBQ; playgrnd; htd pool; playgrnd; waterslide; TV; dogs HUG590; train 300m; phone; Eng spkn; poss noisy; ccard not acc; CKE/CCI. "V conv for city." HUF 10613   2013*

BUDAPEST B2 (13km N Urban) 47.60451, 19.06931 Mini Camping, Királyok út 307, 1039 Budapest [(6) 302003752] N fr Budapest on rte 11 dir Szentendre, 3.5km past Roman ruins turn R just after Shell stn. Cont E for 1km & turn N at 'give way' sp & site sp. Site in 1.3km (sp poss obscured by trees). Sm, mkd pitch, pt shd; wc; chem disp; shwrs inc; EHU (10A) inc; lndry rm; shop 300m; rest adj; BBQ; playgrnd; pool 1km; dogs HUF400; boat, bus or tram to Budapest; poss cr; quiet; CKE/CCI. "Gd security; sh walk to Danube; 40 mins by public transport to city cent; helpful staff; quiet, pleasant oasis in scruffy area." 1 May-30 Sep. HUF 5604   2011*

BUDAPEST B2 (14km N Rural) 47.6013, 19.0191 Jumbo Camping, Budakalászi út 23, 2096 Üröm [tel/fax (26) 351251; jumbo@campingbudapest.com; www.jumbocamping.hu] Best app fr N on rd 10 or 11. Fr M1 take Zsámbék exit thro Perbál to join rd 10 & turn W twd Budapest. After Pilisvörösvar turn L in 8km sp Üröm Site well sp. Med, hdg pitch, hdstg, pt sl, terr, pt shd; wc; chem disp; shwrs inc; EHU (6-10A) inc; lndry; shop 500m; rest 300m; snacks; bar; playgrnd; htd pool high ssn; TV; 10% statics; dogs; bus to Budapest fr vill; Eng spkn; adv bkg; quiet. "Highly rec; v helpful owners; clean, modern facs; immac, family-run site." 1 Apr-31 Oct. HUF 12453   2012*

⊞ **BUDAPEST** B2 (10km E Urban) 47.50421, 19.15834 Camping Arena, Pilisi Str 7, 1106 Budapest [06 30 29 691 29; info@campingbudapest.hu; www.budapestcamping.hu] Leave M0 at exit 60 Kistarcsa & foll Rd 3 twd city centre for 7.5km. Turn L just bef rlwy bdge. Site 200m on R. Sm, hdg pitch, pt shd; wc; chem disp; mv service pnt; shwrs; EHU (16A); lndry (inc dryer); cooking facs; wifi; 10% statics; dogs; bus 400m; metro 1km; Eng spkn; adv bkg; CCI. "Some rlwy & aircraft noise; supmkt 400m; shopping arcade 1km; rec all day travel card for metro, trams & busses; vg." ♦ ltd. HUF 5800   2014*

BUDAPEST B2 (5km SE Urban) 47.47583, 19.08305 Haller Camping, 27 Haller útca, 1096 Budapest [(20) 3674274; info@hallercamping.hu; www.hallercamping.hu] Fr S on M5 twd Budapest cent. At ring rd foll dir Lagnymanyosi Hid (bdge). Bef bdge by lge shopping cent (Lurdy-Ház) turn R. Site sp. Or fr SE on rd 4 sp airport/Cegléd, turn R 100m bef new church steeple on L, foll sp Haller Piac. Med, hdstg, pt shd; wc; chem disp; mv service pnt; shwrs inc; EHU (16A) inc; lndry; lge shoping cent 500m; rest adj; snacks; BBQ; wifi; dogs free; phone; tram & bus 100m; poss cr; Eng spkn; adv bkg; quiet; red long stay/CKE/CCI. "V friendly; vg security; gd, clean san facs; tram stop opp site; conv for city cent; v helpful staff." ♦ ltd. 10 May-30 Sep. HUF 8985   2013*

⊞ **BUDAPEST** B2 (5km NW Urban) 47.51645, 18.9741 Zugligeti Niche Camping, Zugligeti út 101, 1121 Budapest [tel/fax (1) 2008346; camping.niche@t-online.hu; www.campingniche.hu] Fr W approx 12km bef Budapest exit M1/E60/E75 N'wards sp Budakesi. Foll sp Budakeszi & Budapest - bumpy, rough rd. Clear sp for Zugligeti. Or fr W on M1 foll sp Budapest cent & Moszkva Tér. Keep to NW side of Moszkva, site clearly sp. Site nr new Tesco. Sm, terr, pt sl, shd; wc; chem disp; mv service pnt; shwrs inc; EHU (6A) HUF1200; gas adj; lndry; shop 700m; rest, snacks; bar; playgrnd; pool 3km; wifi; dogs HUF600; bus to city; Eng spkn; adv bkg; red long stay/CKE/CCI. "Site converted former tram terminus; gd, modern san facs; ltd facs LS; gd security; friendly, helpful owners; buffet breakfast inc in price; pitches for twin-axles (rec check in adv)." ♦ HUF 7390   2011*

HUNGARY

⊞ **BUK** *B1* (4.1km E Rural) *47.38433, 16.79051* **Romantik Camping, Thermál Krt 12, 9740 Bükfürdő [(94) 558050; fax 558051; info@romantikcamping.com; www.romantik camping.com]** Fr Sopron on rte 84 twd Lake Balaton for approx 45km, foll sp & exit Bükfürdő. After service stn turn R then cont for 5km sp Thermalbad & site. Lge, pt shd; htd wc; chem disp; mv service pnt; shwrs inc; EHU (10-16A) metered; lndry; shop; rest; bar 100m; playgrnd; pool high ssn; thermal cent 500m; tennis 500m; bike hire; entmnt; 10% statics; dogs €2; adv bkg; quiet; ccard acc; red long stay/CKE/CCI. "Quiet and peaceful an ideal place to unwind." ♦ HUF 5604   2015*

CEGLED *B3* (7km NW Rural) *47.2009, 19.73553* **Thermalcamping Cegléd, Fürdo út 27-29, 2700 Cegléd [tel/fax (53) 501177; camping@cegleditermal.hu; http://cegleditermal.hu]** On rd 4/E60 dir Budapest, foll sp thermal pool & aquapark. Med, hdg/mkd pitch, pt shd; htd wc; chem disp; mv service pnt; baby facs; serviced pitches; shwrs inc; EHU (6-10A) HUF750; lndry; shop; rest, snacks 100m; cooking facs; playgrnd; htd, covrd pool & spa complex adj; 30% statics; dogs HUF1000; phone; bus; quiet; ccard acc; red CKE/CCI. "Highly rec, clean site; superb thermal facs - open late at night." ♦ 15 Apr-15 Oct. HUF 3400   2010*

⊞ **CSERKESZOLO** *C3* (800m S Urban) *46.86386, 20.2019* **Thermal Camping Cserkeszölö, Beton út 5, 5465 Cserkeszölö [(6) 56568450; fax 56568464; hotelcamping@ cserkeszolo.hu]** On rte 44 bet Kecksemet & Kunszentmárton. Site sp in Cserkeszölö. Lge, pt shd; htd wc; chem disp; mv service pnt; sauna; shwrs inc; EHU (10A) inc; lndry; shop 200m; rest, snacks; BBQ; cooking facs; 2 pools (1 htd, covrd); paddling pool; waterslide; tennis; games area; 10% statics; dogs; phone; bus 200m; poss cr; quiet; CKE/CCI. "Use of sw pools & thermal pools inc in site fee; gd." HUF 6226   2011*

DOMOS *B2* (500m E Rural) *47.7661, 18.91495* **Dömös Camping, Dömös Dunapart, 2027 Dömös [(33) 482319; fax 414800; info@domoscamping.hu; www.domoscamping.hu]** On rd 11 fr Budapest, site on R on ent Dömös, adj Rv Danube. Med, hdg pitch, pt shd; wc; chem disp; shwrs inc; EHU (10A) HUF950; lndry (inc dryer); rest, snacks; bar; cooking facs; playgrnd; pool; paddling pool; wifi; TV rm; dogs HUF500; phone; bus to Budapest; poss cr; Eng spkn; adv bkg; some rd & rlwy noise; red long stay/CKE/CCI. "Delightful site with views Danube bend; spacious pitches - lower ones poss subject to flooding; excel, clean facs & rest." ♦ 1 May-15 Sep. HUF 4200   2011*

⊞ **DUNAFOLDVAR** *C2* (2km NE Rural) *46.81227, 18.92664* **Kék-Duna Camping, Hösök Tere 23, 7020 Dunaföldvár [tel/fax (75) 541107; ddifzrt@freemail.hu]** Fr rndabt S of Dunafoldvar turn twd town cent. At traff lts turn R down to rv, then turn L, under green bdge & foll towpath 300m to site. Sm, shd; wc; shwrs inc; EHU (16A) inc; lndry; shop high ssn & 500m; rest; BBQ; 2 pools adj (1 covrd); paddling pool; watersports; fishing; tennis; bike hire; adv bkg; quiet; 10% red CKE/CCI. "Pleasant position o'looking Danube; adequate, clean san facs but dated; gd touring base Transdanubia." HUF 4100   2010*

EGER *B3* (12km N Rural) *47.98935, 20.32951* **Öko-Park Panzió Kemping, Borsod út 9, 3323 Eger-Szarvaskö [tel/fax (36) 352201; info@oko-park.hu; www.oko-park.hu]** Fr Eger N on rd 25. On app vill 500m fr vill name sp, turn R (sp parking) into car park. Cross sm wooden bdge at back of sq. Sm, hdg/mkd pitch, pt shd; htd wc; chem disp; baby facs; shwrs inc; EHU (16A) inc; lndry; shop adj, rest, snacks; bar; playgrnd; wifi; TV; 5% statics; dogs; phone; bus; Eng spkn; adv bkg; rd & rlwy noise; ccard acc. "Well-laid out; well-managed site; clean facs; lge o'fits stop in car park & walk in; friendly owner; vg." ♦ 15 Mar-15 Nov. HUF 5600   2010*

EGER *B3* (2km SW Urban) *47.89396, 20.36992* **Tulipán Camping, Szépasszonyvölgy 71, 3300 Eger [tel/fax (36) 311542; info@tulipancamping.com; www.tulipancamping.com]** Enter Eger fr S on rte 25 & foll sp to site. Med, mkd pitch, pt shd; wc; chem disp; shwrs inc; EHU (10A) HUF700; shop 500m; rest; bar; snacks; htd pool; phone; dogs HUF400; poss cr; Eng spkn; adv bkg. "Clean, modern san facs; sm pitches; sh walk to local wine cellars; v interesting town; painting of Council of Trent on library ceiling is a must; waterlogged after heavy rain; pleasant site." 15 Mar-15 Oct. HUF 2980   2010*

"We must tell The Club about that great site we found"

Get your site reports in by mid-August and we'll do our best to get your updates into the next edition.

ERD *B2* (3km E Urban) *47.39388, 18.93638* **Flamingo Camping, Fürdö út 4, 2030 Érd [(23) 375328; flamingocamp@t-online.hu]** Fr Vienna on M1, then M0, exit at Diósd/Érd & foll sp to site on rd 70. Med, pt shd; htd wc; chem disp; shwrs inc; EHU (6A) HUF1000; lndry; shop 200m; rest, snacks; bar; cooking facs; pool high ssn; tennis; TV rm; few statics; dogs HUF1000; bus 50m; rlwy stn 1km; quiet; red long stay/CKE/CCI. "Conv Budapest (12km)." 1 Apr-1 Nov. HUF 5000   2010*

ESZTERGOM *B2* (1km W Urban) *47.7910, 18.73165* **Gran Camping, Nagy-Duna Sétány 3, 2501 Esztergom [(33) 402513; fax 411953; fortanex@t-online.hu; www.grancamping-fortanex.hu]** Fr rte 11 site well sp into town. Fr cent turn twds Danube along street to old bdge, foll sp to site on rv bank. Med, mkd pitch, pt shd; wc; chem disp; shwrs inc; EHU (20A) HUF400; shop high ssn; rest, snacks; bar; BBQ; playgrnd; htd pool; rv cruises; tennis; games area; wifi; 5% statics; dogs HUF500; bus; poss cr; Eng spkn; quiet; red long stay/CKE/CCI. "Basilica worth a visit; poss youth groups; gd clean facs." 1 May-30 Sep. HUF 4200   2011*

FERTOD *B1* (8km W Urban) *47.62116, 16.78513* **Termál Camping, Fürdö út 1, 9437 Hegykö [tel/fax (99) 376818; termalkemping@freemail.hu; www.termalkemping.hu]** Fr Sopron on rd 85 turn N at km 60.2 to Hegykö, site in 4.5km on S side of main rd, sp. Sm, pt shd; wc; chem disp; shwrs inc; EHU (6A) HUF600; lndry; shop, rest, snacks 500m; htd, covrd pool 500m; no statics; dogs free; poss cr; ccard acc; CKE/CCI. "Economical NH; excel spa complex adj; Lake Fertőd & Esterházy Palace worth visit." 15 Apr-15 Oct. HUF 2700   2009*

FONYOD *C1* (6km SW Rural) *46.73312, 17.53198* **Napsugár Camping, Wekerle út 5, 8644 Fonyód-Bétatelep [(85) 361211; fax 361024; napsugar@balatontourist.hu; www.balatontourist.hu]** On NW side of rte 7/E71 on S side of Lake Balaton, sp. V lge, hdg pitch, shd; wc; chem disp; shwrs inc; EHU (16A) inc; lndry; shop & 1km; rest, snacks adj; playgrnd; rocky beach adj; 5% statics; dogs; rd & rlwy noise; ccard acc. 1 May-15 Sep. HUF 5604   2010*

GYENESDIAS see Keszthely *C1*

⊞ **GYULA** *C4* (2km E Urban) *46.64538, 21.29851* **Thermál Camping & Motel, Szlésö út 16, 5700 Gyula [(66) 463704; fax 463551; gyulacamping@t-online.hu; www.gyula camping.hu]** Site sp on every app rd to Gyula. Med, some hdstg, shd; wc; chem disp; shwrs inc; EHU (16A) inc (poss no earth); shop & 500m; lndry; shop 500m; rest 200m; snacks; cooking facs; thermal baths 1.5km; tennis; dogs HUF500; adv bkg; quiet; CKE/CCI. "Site 5km fr Romanian border." HUF 4100   2010*

⊞ **HAJDUSZOBOSZLO** *B4* (2km N Urban) *47.45756, 21.39396* **Thermál Camping, Böszörményi út 35A, 4200 Hajdúszoboszló [tel/fax (52) 558552; thermalcamping@ hungarospa-rt.hu; www.hungarospa.hu]** Fr W on rte 4/ E573 thro town, site sp on L. Fr Debrecen, turn R 500m past Camping Hadjdútourist on lakeside. Lge, hdg pitch, pt shd; wc; chem disp; mv service pnt; shwrs inc; EHU (12A) inc; gas 1km; lndry; shop, rest high ssn; snacks; BBQ; cooking facs; playgrnd; htd, covrd pool & thermal baths adj; paddling pool; waterslide; TV rm; dogs HUF440; phone; poss cr; Eng spkn; no adv bkg; quiet; ccard acc; red CKE/CCI. "Pleasant site; sm naturist island in lake." HUF 6435   2010*

HEGYKO see Fertöd *B1*

HEVIZ see Keszthely *C1*

JASZAPATI *B3* (1.5km S Urban) *47.50537, 20.14012* **Tölgyes Strand Camping, Gyöngyvirág u 11, 5130 Jászapáti [(57) 441187; fax 441008; info@tolgyesstrand.hu; www.tolgyesstrand.hu]** Fr Budapest E on M3, exit at Hatvan & take rd 32 to Jászberény then foll rd 31 to Jászapáti. Site sp fr town cent. Med, mkd pitch, pt shd; wc; chem disp; mv service pnt; shwrs; EHU (10A) lndry (inc dryer); rest, snacks; bar; playgrnd; 2 pools (1 htd, covrd); tennis 200m; games area; bike hire; internet; TV rm; some statics; dogs; site clsd 1 Nov to mid-Dec; adv bkg; quiet. "Gd, modern facs." 1 Apr-30 Nov.
                                                 2009*

KESZTHELY *C1* (8.5km N Rural) *46.80803, 17.21248* **Camping Panoráma, Köz 1, 8372 Cserszegtomaj [(83) 314412; fax 330215; matuska78@freemail.hu; www.panorama camping.com]** Exit Keszthely by direct rd to Sümeg. After turn to Hévíz (Thermal Spa). Clearly sp on R of side rd. Med, terr, pt shd; htd wc; chem disp; shwrs €0.90; EHU (16A) €2.50; lndry; shops 200m; rest; lake sw 2km; TV; 30% statics; dogs €1; phone; quiet; red CKE/CCI. "Conv Lake Balaton area; v friendly & clean; remedial massage avail; gd views." 1 Apr-31 Oct. HUF 4000   2015*

⊞ **KESZTHELY** *C1* (18km N Rural) *46.89442, 17.23166* **Camping St Vendal, Fö út Hrsz 192/3, 8353 Zalaszántó [tel/fax (83) 370147; camping.stvendel@freemail.hu; www.szallas.net/st.vendel-camping]** Fr N on rd 84 turn dir Bazsi/Hévíz at Sümeg. Site at ent to town. Fr S take Sümeg/ Hévíz off rd 71 bef Keszthely & foll sp Sümeg & Zalaszántó. Sm, pt shd; htd wc; chem disp; shwrs inc; EHU (6A) HUF540 long lead poss req'd; lndry; rest, snacks; bar; BBQ; cooking facs; internet; TV rm; dogs HUF250; quiet; CKE/CCI. "Friendly welcome; gd walking/cycling; conv for thermal lake at Heviz & Lake Balaton but without crowds, noise of lakeside sites; delightful site in orchard - awkward for lge o'fits; spotless facs; lovely peaceful site." HUF 9293   2013*

KESZTHELY *C1* (1km E Rural) *46.76797, 17.25936* **Camping Castrum Keszthely, Móra Ferenc u 48, 8360 Keszthely [(83) 312120; fax 314422; keszthely@castrum.eu; www.castrum-group.hu]** Clearly sp W fr Budapest. Fr all other dir take rd 71 out of town; 300m past church turn twd Lake Balaton. Lge, hdg pitch, pt shd; wc; chem disp; shwrs inc; EHU (6-15A) HUF900; shop & 200m; lndry; rest, snacks; playgrnd; pool; paddling pool; lake & watersports 300m; tennis; TV; dogs HUF900; phone; poss cr; adv bkg; some rlwy noise. "Attractively laid-out with excel facs; rlwy runs close to site; friendly staff; Festetics Palace & gardens worth visit." ♦ 1 Apr-31 Oct. HUF 5200 (CChq acc)   2010*

KESZTHELY *C1* (8km NW Rural) *46.78393, 17.19575* **Kurcamping Castrum, Tópart, 8380 Héviz [(83) 343198; fax 540263; heviz@castrum.eu; www.castrum-group.hu]** Fr Keszthely foll sp to Héviz & site 700m to E, opp Héviz thermal lake. Lge, mkd pitch, pt shd; htd wc; chem disp; mv service pnt; 20% serviced pitches; shwrs inc; EHU (6-16A) €3; lndry; shop; rest; bar; htd pool adj; lake sw adj; sat TV; dogs €4; poss cr; Eng spkn; adv bkg; quiet; CKE/CCI. "Lake fed by hot springs so gd for sw; casino adj; easy cycle ride/walk into lovely spa town & cycle path to Keszthely; excel san facs; excursions Budapest fr gate; v nice site; gd location to explore by foot or bike." 1 Mar-31 Dec. HUF 3113   2013*

⊞ **KOSZEG** *B1* (500m N Urban) *47.39336, 16.54291* **Gyöngyvirág Camping, Bajcsy-Zsilinszky út. 6, 9730 Köszeg [(94) 360454; fax 360574; info@gyongyvirag panzio.hu; www.gyongyviragpanzio.hu]** Foll sp in town cent to site adj hotel. Sm, pt shd; htd wc (cont); shwrs inc; EHU (10A) HUF400; shop 200m; BBQ; playgrnd; quiet; no ccard acc; red low stay. "Superb, welcoming, orchard site; clean, modern facs; site diff in wet weather; access diff lge o'fits; nature reserve adj town; gd walking; sh walk to one of prettiest towns in Hungary." HUF 3300   2010*

HUNGARY

MANFA D2 (18km NE Rural) 46.23372, 18.30844 **Campsite Mare Vara, Varvolgyi utca 2, 7332 Magyaregregy [tel/fax (72) 420126; info@camping-marevara.com; www.camping-marevara.com]** Fr Pecs head N on 6. Turn L onto Cseresznyes ut, which then becomes Komlo-Zobakpuszta. In 6.8km turn R onto Varvolgyi u. Site in 120m. Sm, pt sl, pt shd; htd wc; chem disp; fam bthrm; shwrs inc; EHU (10A) inc; lndry (inc dryer); snacks; bar; BBQ; pool; games area; wifi; 1% statics; dogs; Eng spkn; adv bkg; quiet; CKE/CCI. "Dutch owners, warm welcome; ample space to pitch; almost an orchard setting; vg." ♦ ltd. 15 Apr-30 Sep. HUF 5499   2015*

MATRAFURED B3 (4km N Rural) 47.84416, 19.95725 **Mátra Camping Sástó, Farkas út 4, 3232 Mátrafüred [tel/fax (37) 374025; info@matrakemping.hu; www.matrakemping.hu]** Take rte 24 N fr Gyöngyös. Site on L 2km after Mátrafüred. Med, some hdstg, pt sl, pt shd; wc; shwrs inc; EHU (10A) inc; shop, rest, snacks, bar adj; cooking facs; TV; some statics; dogs HUF500; phone adj; poss cr; ccard acc. "Site pt of controlled sports complex; vg secure site." 15 Apr-10 Oct. HUF 3500   2010*

MEZOKOVESD B3 (5km W Rural) 47.7969, 20.5291 **Autóscamping Zsóry, Zsóry-fürdő, 3400 Mezökövesd [tel/fax (49) 411436; zsoryamping@freemail.hu; www.zsory-camping.lhcom.hu]** Fr W leave M3/E71 at exit Eger/Füzesabony for 3km N twd Eger. Turn E onto rd 3 sp Miskolc, site on L in 8km. Lge, hdg pitch, pt shd; wc; chem disp; mv service pnt; baby facs; shwrs inc; EHU (16A) HUF550; lndry; shop 500m; rest, snacks; bar; cooking facs; playgrnd; htd, covrd thermal pool 500m; some statics; dogs HUF330; phone; Eng spkn; quiet; ccard acc; redCKE/CCI. "Thermal baths adj; helpful staff; nr National Park." 1 May-30 Sep. HUF 3200   2011*

"I need an on-site restaurant"

We do our best to make sure site information is correct, but it is always best to check any must-have facilities are still available or will be open during your visit.

MISKOLC A3 (14km W Rural) 48.09623, 20.62128 **Camping Lillafüred, Erzsébet Sétány 39, 3517 Miskolc-Lillafüred [(46) 333146; kovatt@lillacamp.hu; http://kovatt.lillacamp. hu]** Fr Miskolc take rd to Lillafüred. After passing under 2 low bdges (max height 3.4m) site sp on L. Sm, hdg/mkd pitch, pt shd; wc; own san; chem disp (wc); shwrs inc; EHU (16A) HUF500; shop in vill; rest in hotel nrby; cooking facs; dogs; phone; bus 1km; adv bkg; quiet. "Basic site; gd mkd walks; friendly owner; not suitable lge o'fits; 1km to narr gauge rlwy; NH." ♦ ltd. 1 May-30 Sep. HUF 3700   2009*

MOSONMAGYAROVAR B1 (1km E Urban) 47.87718, 17.27874 **Termál Aqua Camping, Kigyó út 1, 9200 Mosonmagyaróvár [tel/fax (96) 579168; aquahotel@t-online.hu; www.tha.hu]** Foll sp fr town cent to Termál Hotel Aqua; site in grnds, just behind lge thermal baths. Sm, hdg/mkd pitch, shd; htd wc; chem disp; mv service pnt; shwrs inc; EHU €3; lndry; shop 1km; rest, snacks; bar; BBQ; cooking facs; htd, covrd thermal & sw pool adj; dogs €2; bus, train 1km; phone; Eng spkn; quiet. "Vg site; price inc ent to thermals & sauna." 1 Apr-30 Oct. HUF 9028   2009*

⊞ **MOSONMAGYAROVAR** B1 (3km SE Urban) 47.84224, 17.28591 **Camping Kis-Duna, Gabonarakpart 6, 9200 Mosonmagyaróvár [tel/fax (96) 216433; www.hotels.hu/kis_duna]** Site on L of M1 Mosonmagyaróvár-Győr in grnds of motel & rest, 15km fr border. Sm, some hdstg, unshd; wc; chem disp; shwrs inc; EHU (16A) HUF500; lndry; shop 1km; rest; thermal pool 2.5km; TV; dogs HUF500. "Gd, clean, facs; rest gd but busy; gd alt to Bratislava site (Slovakia); ideal NH." HUF 3150   2011*

NESZMELY B2 (4km E Rural) 47.74421, 18.40258 **Éden Camping, Dunapart, 2544 Neszmély [(33) 474183; fax 474327; eden@mail.holop.hu; www.edencamping.com]** Site sp on rte 10 bet Neszmély & Süttő, on rvside. Lge, hdg pitch, pt shd; htd wc; chem disp; mv service pnt; baby facs; shwrs inc; EHU (6-10A) HUF500; lndry (inc dryer); shop; rest, snacks; bar; playgrnd; pool high ssn; rv sw adj; canoeing; watersports; boat & bike hire; tennis 3km; games area; entmnt; excursions; 10% statics; dogs HUF470; phone; bus 500m; Eng spkn; adv bkg; some rd/rlwy noise; ccard acc; red CKE/CCI. "V pleasant, tranquil site in gd location; helpful staff." ♦ 1 Apr-31 Oct. HUF 4310   2010*

ORFU D2 (2km SW Rural) 46.14638, 18.13750 **Panoráma Camping, Dollar út 1, 7677 Orfü [tel/fax (72) 378434; campingorfu@freemail.hu; www.panoramacamping.hu]** Rte 66 fr Pécs dir Kaposvár. In Magyarszék take rd to Orfü & at lake turn R & foll rd down W side of lake. Site shortly bef end of lake. Lge, mkd pitch, terr, pt shd; wc; chem disp; shwrs inc; EHU (6A) HUF700; lndry; shop; snacks; playgrnd; pool, tennis, watersports 1km; lake sw 500m; tennis; bike hire; games area; TV; some statics; phone; quiet on higher terr; ccard acc; 10% red CKE/CCI. "Lovely situation; twin-axles on lower terr only; site badly in need of refurb; gd base for Pécs." 1 May-30 Sep. HUF 3900   2010*

OZD A3 (12km E Rural) 48.21281, 20.40603 **Camping Amedi, Rákóczi út 181, 3658 Borsodbóta [tel/fax (48) 438468; info@campingamedi.hu; www.camping amedi.hu]** Fr Budapest N on M3/E71, exit at Hatvan N onto rd 21. At Kisterenye turn R onto rd 23 dir Ózd. In Ózd foll sp Borsodbóta for 12km to site. Sm, mkd pitch, pt shd; wc; shwrs inc; EHU (10A) €3.75; lndry; supmkt 500m; rest 6km; bar; BBQ; cooking facs; pool; bike hire; games area; entmnt; some statics; dogs €2; adv bkg; quiet. "Peaceful, Dutch-owned site." 15 Apr-15 Oct. HUF 5448   2010*

PANNONHALMA *B2* (500m E Urban) *47.54916, 17.75777*
Panoráma Camping, Fenyvesalja 4/A, 9090 Pannonhalma
[(96) 471240; fax 470561; akosprikkel@axelero.hu]
Fr Györ take rte 82 twd Veszprém. After approx 20km turn L
on sm loop rd to vill of Pannonhalma. Site at top of v steep
slope, low gear needed. Med, hdg pitch, terr, pt shd; htd wc;
chem disp (wc); shwrs inc; EHU (10A) HUF800; lndry rm; shop
300m; rest in vill; snacks; TV rm; dogs HUF450; adv bkg; quiet;
red CKE/CCI. "Panoramic views; v helpful owners; clean facs;
levelling blocks req; conv for visit to basilica; diff app but site
worth it; little Eng spkn" 1 May-31 Oct. HUF 5650   2015*

⊞ **PAPA** *B1* (2km N Urban) *47.33797, 17.47367*
Termál Camping Pápa, Várkert út 7, 8500 Pápa
[tel/fax 36 89 320 735; info@thermalkemping.hu;
www.thermalkemping.hu] Fr 83 exit at Gyori Way. Foll
sp. Lge, hdg/mkd pitch, hdstg, pt shd; htd wc; chem disp;
mv service pnt; baby facs; shwrs; EHU (16A); gas; lndry rm
(inc dryer); shop 1km; rest; snacks; bar; BBQ; cooking facs;
playgrnd; htd pool adj; paddling pool; sw thermal adj; games
area; games rm; entmnt; wifi; 20% statics; dogs €2; phone;
bus 500m; twin axles; Eng spkn; quiet; adv bkg; red LS; CCI.
"Onsite kids club; boccia; basketball; archery; disco adj; thermal
baths with indoor & outdoor pools, slides; excel; well managed
site; gd area for long stay & touring; very helpful staff." ◆
HUF 7390   2014*

⊞ **PECS** *D2* (3km ENE Urban) *46.08352, 18.26358* **Familia
Privat Camping, Gyöngyösi Istvan út 6, 7627 Pécs
[(72) 327034]** On rte 6 fr Budapest (N side) well sp fr city
o'skts. Tight ent for lge o'fits. Sm, pt sl, terr, hdstg, pt shd; htd
wc; chem disp; shwrs inc; EHU (10A) inc (long lead req); lndry;
shop 800m; adv bkg; quiet. "V congested site; arr early to
ensure pitch; OK NH." HUF 4200   2010*

REVFULOP see Balatonszepezd *C1*

SAROSPATAK *A4* (2km NE Rural) *48.33274, 21.58245*
**Tengerszem Camping, Herceg Ferenc ut 2, 3950
Sárospatak [(47) 312744; fax 323527; info@tengerszem-
camping.hu; www.tengerszem-camping.hu]** NW fr Tokaj
on R38; then NE on R37 to Sárospatak; foll camp sp. Med, hdg
pitch, pt shd; wc; mv service pnt; shwrs; EHU (10A) inc; shop;
rest, snacks; playgrnd; pool; tennis; games area; TV; rlwy noise;
CKE/CCI. "Refurbished thermal sw baths next door; gd site for
mountains." 15 Apr-15 Oct. HUF 4000   2010*

⊞ **SARVAR** *B1* (2km SE Urban) *47.24671, 16.9473* **Sárvár
Thermal Camping, Vadkert út 1, 9600 Sárvár [(95) 320292;
fax 523612; info@thermalcamping.com; www.thermal
camping.com]** E fr Szombathely via rtes 86 & 88. Site on
Sopron-Lake Balaton rte 84. Med, some hdstg, pt shd; htd
wc; chem disp; mv service pnt; sauna; baby facs; private san
facs avail; shwrs; EHU (16A) €3; lndry; shop; rest, snacks adj;
BBQ; cooking facs; playgrnd; htd thermal pools adj; paddling
pool; waterslide; lake fishing; tennis 500m; wifi; dogs €2;
poss cr; 10% statics; ccard acc; quiet; red long stay; CKE/CCI.
"Barrier clsd 1330-1500; free ent to spa & fitness cent adj." ◆
HUF 10274 (CChq acc)   2010*

SIOFOK *C2* (4km NE Urban) *46.92838, 18.10245*
**Balatontourist Camping Aranypart, Szent László út 183-
185, 8604 Siófok [(84) 353399; fax 352801; aranypart@
balatontourist.hu; www.balatontourist.hu]** Fr Budapest
on M7 take exit Siófok onto rd 70. Site sp at Balatonszabadi
rlwy stn. V lge, hdg pitch, pt shd; wc; chem disp; mv service
pnt; shwrs inc; EHU (10A) inc; lndry; shop; rest, snacks; bar;
BBQ; cooking facs; playgrnd; lake sw, fishing adj; waterslide;
bike hire; tennis 500m; games area; wifi; entmnt; TV rm;
15% statics; dogs HUF950; phone; poss cr; Eng spkn; adv
bkg; quiet; CKE/CCI. "Price varies according to pitch size;
well-maintained, attractive site." ◆ 22 Apr-11 Sep. HUF 6700
(CChq acc)   2011*

> ## "Satellite navigation makes touring much easier"
>
> Remember most sat navs don't know if
> you're towing or in a larger vehicle – always
> use yours alongside maps and site directions.

⊞ **SOPRON** *B1* (8km SE Rural) *47.6525, 16.6575*
**Kurcamping Castrum Balf-Sopron, Fürdö Sor 59-61, 9494
Balf [(99) 339124; fax (83) 314422; castrum.sopronbalf@
rlan.hu; www.sopron-balf-castrum.hu]**
On rte 84 S of Sopron turn E sp Balf. In 2km turn N sp Sopron
& foll sps. Site at W end Balf vill. Med, hdg/mkd pitch, pt shd;
htd wc (cont); chem disp; sauna; shwrs inc; EHU (6A) HUF800;
lndry (inc dryer); shops 350m; rest 250m; pool & 250m; bike
hire; TV; dogs €2.50; phone; Eng spkn; rd noise; ccard acc;
CKE/CCI. "Thermal baths avail; Tesco hypmkt on app to Sopron
6km, with ATM; pitches uneven; ltd facs LS & poss unkempt;
poss cold shwrs but new owners (2010) plan refurb; site in
need of maintenance; overpriced NH." HUF 4730   2010*

SZENTES *C3* (2km W Urban) *46.65052, 20.24812* **Thermál
Camping Szentes (Szentesi Üdülökozpont), Csallány
Gáborport 4, 6600 Szentes [tel/fax (63) 400123; udulohazak@
udulokozpont-szentes.hu; www.udulokozpont-szentes.hu]**
Fr N fr Csongrád on rte 451, site on R at ent to town in park,
int'l camping sp. Sm, pt shd; wc; chem disp (wc); shwrs inc;
EHU (16A) HUF1000; shop 1km; rest, snacks, bar in park; 4 htd
pools; tennis; horseriding; dogs HUF600; phone; poss cr; Eng
spkn; quiet; ccard acc; CKE/CCI. "Attractive park; thermal
pools open to day visitors; helpful staff." ◆ 1 Apr-30 Sep.
HUF 4300   2010*

SZILVASVARAD *A3* (1km S Rural) *48.09615, 20.38783*
**Hegyi Camping, Egri út 36, 3348 Szilvásvárad
[tel/fax (36) 355207; hegyi.camping@axelero.hu;
www.hegyicamping.com]** App fr Eger, site sp just bef
vill. Turn R at petrol stn. Med, pt sl, pt shd; wc; chem disp;
shwrs inc; EHU (16A) inc; lndry; shop 1km; rest; bar; cooking
facs; internet; TV; 40% statics; phone; poss noisy; ccard acc;
red CKE/CCI. "Lipizzaner horse stud farm nr; conv touring
Bükk National Park; conv narr gauge rlwy into Szalajka
Valley; gd rests within 10 mins walk; facs inadequate & tired;
poss school parties on site; friendly staff." 1 May-15 Oct.
HUF 4000   2010*

SZOLNOK B3 (850m SE Urban) 47.16666, 20.18915 **Tiszaligeti Motel & Camping, Tiszaligeti Sétány 34, 5000 Tiszaligeti [tel/fax (56) 424403; tiszaligetimotel@gmail.com; www.tiszaligetimotel.hu]** Leave rte 4 onto rd 442 sp Martfü, but foll sp 'Centrum' into Szolnok. Bef bdge look for sps to turn L & foll rd for 800m, site on L. Med, pt shd; wc; chem disp (wc); shwrs inc; EHU HUF700; shop 2km; rest; BBQ; playgrnd; pool 300m; canoeing, tennis nr; bike hire; some statics; dogs HUF1500; phone; bus; poss cr; quiet; CKE/CCI. "Pleasant location; vg, modern facs." 1 May-30 Sep. HUF 3200   2009*

TAHITOTFALU B2 (200m E Rural) 47.75117, 19.08043 **Duna Camping, Kemping út 1, 2022 Tahitótfalu [(26) 385216; fax (33) 412294; juhaszjozsef@mailbox.hu]** In cent Tahitótfalu at km 30.3 on rte 11 to Budapest, site sp. Med, shd; wc; chem disp; shwrs inc; EHU (10A) inc; lndry; shops adj; rest, snacks; bar; BBQ; playgrnd; boating; TV; 20% statics; dogs; poss noisy; ccard acc. "Beautiful situation on Danube bend; Szentendre worth visit; basic site; NH only." 15 Apr-15 Oct. HUF 4359   2009*

TAKSONY B2 (6km S Rural) 47.28711, 19.09990 **Camping Rukkel-tó Waterpark, Rukkel-tó 1, 2335 Taksony [(70) 3860852; rukkel@waterpark.hu; www.waterpark.hu]** Exit M0/E71 onto rd 51 dir Taksony & Dunavarsány. Waterpark sp 6km S of Taksony dir Bugyi. Med, mkd pitch, pt shd; wc; shwrs; EHU; lndry; rest, snacks; bar; playgrnd; pools; waterslides; boat hire; no dogs; quiet. "Clean site adj waterpark; excel." 1 May-7 Sep. HUF 4800   2009*

TAMASI C2 (1km S Urban) 46.62577, 18.28734 **Thermál Camping, Hársfa út 1, 7090 Tamási [tel/fax (74) 471738; camping@tamasistrand.hu; www.tamasikemping.hu]** Site & thermal baths sp on rd 65 adj motel. Med, pt shd; wc; shwrs inc; EHU (10A) HUF575 (long lead req); lndry; shop 500m; rest 200m; htd pool; dogs HUF67; 10% statics; phone; CKE/CCI. "Security gate; free access to lge thermal pool complex; vg; perfect location for spa next door; nice town and surrounding area." 1 May-15 Oct. HUF 5099   2013*

TATABANYA B2 (14km N Rural) 47.6679, 18.3090 **Fényes Camping, Környei út 24, 2890 Tata [(34) 481208; fax 588144; fenyes@fenyesfurdo.hu; www.fenyesfurdo.hu]** Exit junc 67 fr M1 to Tata town cent; foll sp for 3km E to site. Lge, shd; wc; own san rec; shwrs inc; EHU; shop; rest; playgrnd; 3 pools; games area; dogs HUF500; Eng spkn; CKE/CCI. "Tata interesting town; fair site set in lge park." 1 May-15 Sep. HUF 1800   2009*

TOKAJ A4 (1km NE Rural) 48.12306, 21.41806 **Tiszavirág Camping, Horgász út 11a, 3910 Tokaj [tel/fax (06) 709344175; tiszavir@axelero.hu; www.tokaj.hu]** Fr town cent turn E over rv on rte 38 sp Nyiregyháza. Camp ent 100m over bdge on L. Med, shd; wc; chem disp; shwrs inc; EHU (10A) HUF450; lndry; shops 300m; bar; fishing; dogs HUF400; poss cr; quiet. "On rv bank; wine cellars in walking dist; ltd facs on Sun." 1 Apr-30 Oct. HUF 4200   2015*

⊞ **TOROKBALINT** B2 (1km S Rural) 47.43305, 18.90027 **Fortuna Camping, Dózsa György út 164, 2045 Törökbálint [(23) 335364; fax 339697; fortunacamping@axelero.hu; www.fortunacamping.hu]** Fr M1 or M7 take exit for Törökbálint & foll camp sp to Törökbálint. Leave on rd sp Erd, rd bends L, go under m'way into vill. At T-junc site sp, turn R, rd swings L; site ent halfway up hill on L. Med, some hdg pitch, sl, terr, pt shd, htd wc; chem disp; baby facs; shwrs inc; EHU (4-16A) €2; lndry; shop 1.5km; hypmkt 5km; rest high ssn; playgrnd; 2 pools (1 htd, covrd); dogs €2; phone; bus to city 1km; Eng spkn; CKE/CCI. "Friendly, helpful, family-run site adj vineyards, but untidy; gd, clean san facs; gd security; variable elec supply & san facs block poss poorly lit; bus/tram tickets to Budapest fr site; excursions arranged; excel rest; ltd facs LS." ♦ HUF 5604   2011*

⊞ **TURISTVANDI** A4 (1km SW Rural) 48.04710, 22.64300 **Vizimalom Camping, Malom út 3, 4944 Túristvándi [(44) 721082; turvizimalom@freemail.hu; www.turvizimalom.hu]** Fr Fehérgyarmat foll rd 491 NE for 4km to Penyige, turn L to Túristvándi. After approx 12km site on R adj 18thC water mill on Rv Túr. Sm, some hdstg, pt shd; wc; shwrs; EHU (10A); shop 500m; rest, snacks; bar; BBQ; playgrnd; canoeing; games area; games rm; TV; internet; dogs; quiet. "Excel location; no hdstg." HUF 4670   2010*

> # "There aren't many sites open at this time of year"
>
> If you're travelling outside peak season remember to call ahead to check site opening dates – even if the entry says 'open all year'.

UROM see Budapest B2

VAJTA C2 (1km N Rural) 46.72859, 18.65587 **Aucost Holiday Parc, Termálsor 1, 7041 Vajta [tel/fax (25) 229700 or 0031 0416 543258 (N'lands); holiday@aucost.nl; www.aucost.nl]** Take rd 63 S fr Cece dir Szekszárd, site on R bef Vajta. Med, mkd pitch, pt sl, pt shd; wc; chem disp; shwrs inc; EHU €1.95; lndry; shop 1km; rest 1km; bar; playgrnd; thermal pool; 400m; games rm; internet; TV; 10% statics; dogs €1; Eng spkn; adv bkg; quiet. "Friendly, helpful Dutch owners; gd birdwatching area; vg site." 18 Apr-14 Sep. HUF 7472   2009*

ZALAKAROS C1 (3km S Rural) 46.53165, 17.12443 **Kurcamping Castrum, Ady Endre út, 8754 Galambok [tel/fax (93) 358610; zalakaros@castrum.eu; www.castrum-group.hu]** Fr rte 7 N dir Zalakaros, site sp. Med, hdg/mkd pitch, pt shd; htd wc; chem disp; sauna; shwrs inc; EHU (6A) inc; lndry; shop, rest 1km; snacks; bar; BBQ; htd, covrd pool; thermal complex 2km; wifi; some statics; dogs; bus; quiet; ccard acc; CKE/CCI. ♦ 1 Mar-31 Oct. HUF 7783 (CChq acc)   2010*

ZALASZANTO see Keszthely C1

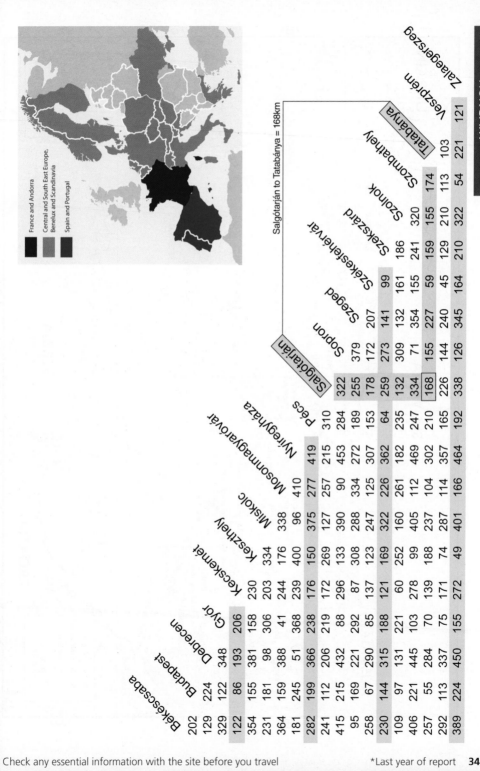

Salgótarján to Tatabánya = 168km

France and Andorra

Central and South East Europe, Benelux and Scandinavia

Spain and Portugal

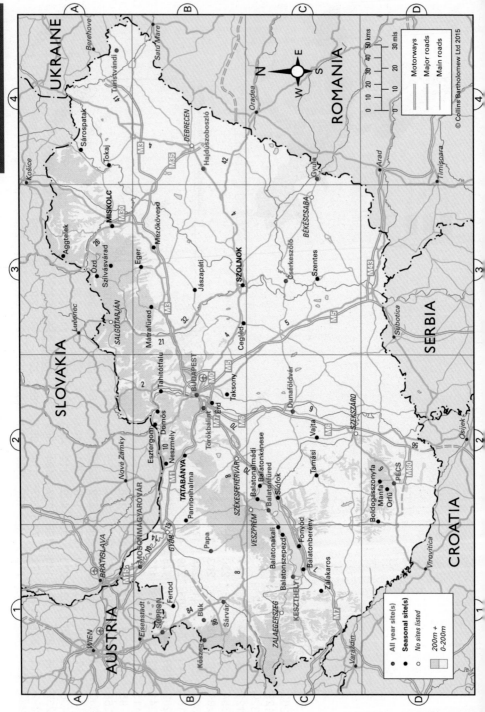

Italy
Country Introduction

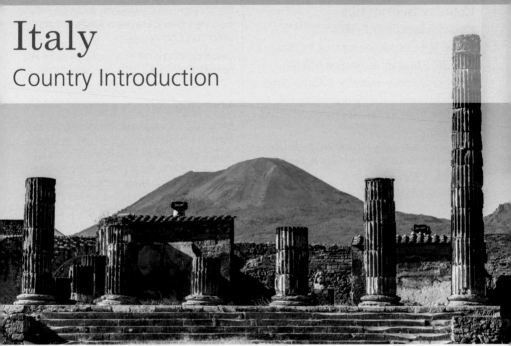

Pompeii

Welcome to Italy

One of the greatest cultural jewels in Europe's crown has to be Italy. It is a country alive with art and fashion that is envied across the world, and boasts some of the most extraordinary architectural masterpieces in existence. Alongside the grandeur is a country with great natural diversity, from the snow-capped Alps in the north to the stunning Mediterranean coastline. The variety of local customs and traditions encountered through the different regions are always captivating.

Country highlights

Italy is often considered the fashion capital of the world, and leather working has often been at the forefront of its fashion industry. The Italian tanning industry is considered a world leader and there are many products available from bags to belts which showcase this skill.

Italy is also a country of celebration, with hundreds of festivals and carnivals taking place. One of the most famous is the Carnival of Venice, where traditional masks and costumes are worn by attendees.

Major towns and cities

- Rome – this remarkable city is known as the "Capital of the World".
- Milan – a global centre of fashion and known for its exquisite galleries.
- Turin – famous for its baroque architecture and monuments.
- Naples – boasting a wealth of historical buildings from a variety of periods.

Attractions

- Venice – one of the world's most beautiful cities and boasting a wealth of historic sites.
- Santa Maria del Fiore, Florence – one of the most recognisable cathedrals that houses several important works of art.
- Pompeii – the remains of an ancient Roman town in the shadow of Mount Vesuvius.
- Cinque Terre – five beautiful and traditional villages that lie on the Italian Riviera.

Find out more

www.enit.it
Tel: 0039 (0) 06 49 711 Italian Tourist Board

Country Information

Population (approx): 61.7 million

Capital: Rome (population approx 4.3 million)

Area: 301,318 sq km (inc Sardinia & Sicily)

Bordered by: France, Switzerland, Austria, Slovenia

Terrain: Mountainous in the north descending to rolling hills in the centre; some plains and coastal lowlands

Climate: Predominantly Mediterranean climate, alpine in the far north, hot and dry in the south

Coastline: 7,600km

Highest Point: Monte Bianco (Mont Blanc) 4,810m

Language: Italian, German (in the northern Alps)

Local Time: GMT or BST + 1, i.e. 1 hour ahead of the UK all year

Currency: Euros divided into 100 cents; £1 = €1.42, €1 = £0.71 (September 2015)

Emergency numbers: Police 113; Fire brigade 115; Ambulance 118

Public Holidays 2016: Jan 1, 6; Mar 27, 28; Apr 25; May 1; Jun 2; Aug 15; Nov 1; Dec 8, 25, 26.

Each locality also celebrates its patron saint's day. School summer holidays run from mid June to mid September

Camping and Caravanning

There are approximately 2,000 organised and supervised campsites in Italy. They are usually well signposted and are open from April to September. Advance booking is recommended in high season, especially by the lakes and along the Adriatic coast. About 20% of campsites are open all year including some in the mountains and around large towns. Campsites organised by the Touring Club Italiano (TCI) and the Federcampeggio are particularly well equipped.

In general pitch sizes are small at about 80 square metres and it may be difficult to fit a large outfit plus an awning onto a pitch. You will frequently find that hot water is supplied to showers only, for which you will be charged. Published opening and closing dates may be unreliable - phone ahead if travelling during the low season.

It is not compulsory to have a Camping Key Europe (CKE) or Camping Card International (CCI), but it is recommended as a means of identification. If for any reason details are missing from the CKE or CCI a site will insist on holding a visitor's passport instead.

Casual camping is not recommended and is not permitted in national parks or in state forests.

Motorhomes

Many local authorities permit motorhomes to park overnight in specially designated places known as 'Camper Stops' or 'Aree di Sosta' and a list of their locations and the services provided are contained in a number of publications and on a number of websites including the French 'Guide Officiel Aires de Service Camping-Car' published by the Fédération Française de Camping et de Caravaning, www.ffcc.fr. You will also find a list of 'Camper Stops' on www.turismoitinerante.com

Cycling

Transportation of bicycles

An overhanging load must be indicated by an aluminium square panel (panello) measuring 50cm x 50cm with reflective red and white diagonal stripes. The load must not exceed 30% of the length of the vehicle, may only overhang at the rear and the regulation applies to a car or caravan carrying bicycles at the rear or windsurf boards on the roof. A fine may be imposed for failure to display the approved sign which is made by Fiamma and in the UK may be purchased from or ordered through motorhome or caravan dealers/accessory shops. For a list of Fiamma stockists please see www.fiamma.com.

At night, outside built up areas, cyclists must wear a reflective jacket and must ride in single file.

Electricity and Gas

Current at campsites varies between 2 and 16 amps and often it is very low, offering a maximum of only 4 amps across the whole site. Many sites have CEE connections. Plugs have three round pins in line.

Campingaz cylinders are generally available, except in the south of Italy, Sardinia and Sicily where exchange may be difficult outside of marinas and holiday resorts.

Entry Formalities

British and Irish passport holders may stay in Italy for up to three months without a visa.

Regulations for Pets

All dogs, including those temporarily imported, must be on a leash at all times. It is advisable to carry a muzzle as the police/authorities can insist on your dog wearing one if they consider your dog to be dangerous. Some sites and some public transport operators insist that all dogs are muzzled at all times - check local requirements on arrival.

A domestic animal may be transported in a car provided it does not distract the driver. More than one animal may be transported provided they are kept in the rear of the car, separated from the driver by bars, or kept in special cages.

Medical Services

Ask at a pharmacy (farmacia) for the nearest doctor registered with the state health care scheme (SSN) or look in the telephone directory under 'Unita Sanitaria Locale'. The services of a national health service doctor are normally free of charge.

A European Health Insurance Card (EHIC) entitles you to emergency treatment and medication at local rates and to hospital treatment under the state healthcare scheme. Any charges you do incur are non-refundable in Italy but you may be able to make a claim on your return to the UK. Dental treatment is expensive and you will be charged the full fee.

Emergency services (Guardia Medica) are available at weekends and at night and there are first aid posts at major train stations and airports. Staff at pharmacies can advise on minor ailments and at least one pharmacy remains open 24 hours in major towns.

Opening Hours

Banks – Mon-Fri 8.30am-1.30pm & 3pm-4pm.

Museums – Check locally as may vary. The Vatican museums and Sistine Chapel are not open to visitors Sun. Visitors under 18 or over 60 are admitted free to State museums on production of a passport.

Post Offices – Mon-Fri 8.30am-2pm/5.30pm, Sat 8.30am-12 noon.

Shops – Mon-Sat 8.30am/9am-1pm & 3.30pm/4pm-7.30pm/8pm. In southern Italy and tourist areas shops may stay open later. There is no lunch time closing in large cities. Shops are closed half a day each week (variable by region).

Safety and Security

Most visits to Italy are trouble free and, in general, levels of crime are low, but visitors should take care on public transport and in crowded areas where pickpockets and bag snatchers may operate. In Rome take particular care around the main railway station, Roma Termini, and on the bus to and from St Peter's Square. Also take care in and around railway stations in large cities. Be particularly wary of groups of children who may try to distract your attention while attempting to steal from you. Do not carry your passport, credit cards and cash all together in one bag or pocket and only carry what you need for the day. Do not wear expensive jewellery, particularly in the south of Italy.

Take care in bars and don't leave drinks unattended. Recently there have been cases of drinks being spiked. Check prices before ordering food and insist on seeing a priced menu. Be particularly careful when ordering items, such as lobster, which are charged by weight.

When driving in towns keep your car windows shut and doors locked and never leave valuables on display. Around Rome and Naples moped riders may attempt to snatch bags from stationary cars at traffic lights. Always lock your vehicle and never leave valuables in it, even if you will only be away for a short time or are nearby. Avoid leaving luggage in cars for any length of time or overnight.

Increasingly robberies are taking place from cars at rest stops and service stations on motorways. Treat offers of help with caution, for example with a flat tyre, particularly on the motorway from Naples to Salerno, as sometimes the tyre will have been punctured deliberately.

Do not be tempted to enter or bathe in Italy's many fountains – there are heavy fines if you do. Dress conservatively when visiting places of worship, i.e. cover shoulders and upper arms and do not wear shorts. Avoid queues in the peak season by visiting early in the morning.

The authorities are making strenuous efforts to stamp out the illegal production and sale of counterfeit goods. Illegal traders operate on the streets of all major cities, particularly tourist cities such as Florence and Rome. You are advised not to buy from them at the risk of incurring a fine.

Italy shares with the rest of Europe a general threat from terrorism. Attacks could be indiscriminate and against civilian targets in public places, including tourist sites. There continue to be isolated cases of domestic terrorism by extreme left wing and secessionist groups, aimed primarily at official Italian targets.

British Embassy

VIA XX SETTEMBRE 80A, I-00187 ROMA RM
Tel: 06 4220 0001 (24 hour emergency number)
www.ukinitaly.fco.gov.uk/en

British Consulate-General
VIA SAN PAOLO 7, I-20121 MILANO MI
Tel: 02 7230 01
There is also a British Consulates in Naples.

Irish Embassy
VILLA SPADA, VIA GIACOMO MEDICI
1 - 00153 ROMA
Tel: 06 5852 381
www.embassyofireland.it
There is also an Irish Honorary Consulate in Milan.

Documents

Driving Licence
The standard pink UK paper driving licence is recognised in Italy but holders of the old-style green UK licence are recommended to change it for a photocard licence. Alternatively an International Driving Permit may be purchased from the AA, the RAC or selected Post Offices.
Vehicle(s)
You must be able to present to the police on demand your vehicle and insurance documents, i.e. vehicle registration certificate (V5C), insurance certificate and MOT certificate (if applicable) and, if you are not the owner of your vehicle(s), authorisation for its use from the owner.

Money

There are few bureaux de change, so change cash at a bank.

Major credit cards are widely accepted including at petrol stations, but not as widely as in some other European countries. Automatic cash machines (Bancomat) are widespread. Carry your credit card issuers'/banks' 24-hour UK contact numbers in case of loss or theft of your cards.

Motoring in Italy
Alcohol

The maximum permitted level of alcohol is 50 milligrams in 100 millilitres of blood, i.e. less than in the UK (80 milligrams). For drivers with less than three years' driving experience, the limit is zero. It is advisable to adopt the 'no drink and drive' rule at all times as penalties are severe.

Breakdown Service

The motoring organisation, Automobile Club d'Italia (ACI) operates a breakdown service 24 hours a day throughout Italy, including San Marino and Vatican City. Telephone 803116 from a landline or mobile phone. ACI staff speak English. This number also gives access to the ACI emergency information service, operated by multi-lingual staff, for urgent medical or legal advice. You may also use the emergency phones placed every 2km on motorways.

On all roads, including motorways, standard charges are made for assistance and/or recovering a vehicle weighing up to 2,500kg to the nearest ACI garage. Higher charges apply at night, over weekends and public holidays and for towing to anywhere other than the nearest ACI garage. Vehicles over 2,500kg also incur higher charges. Payment is required in cash.

Road police, 'Polizia Stradale', constantly patrol all roads and motorways and can assist when vehicles break down.

Congestion Charge in Milan

In January 2012 a new congestion charge scheme in Milan was introduced to replace the old Pollution Charge (Ecopass). The new scheme is more restrictive than the old Ecopass scheme. To access the historical centre (Area C) from 7.30am – 7.30pm on Monday, Tuesday, Wednesday and Friday and from 7.30am- 6pm on Thursday you must pay a fee of €5 a day.

You can buy a ticket for entrance from parking meters, newsagents and some ATM points or online at www.areac.it – tickets must then be activated on the day before you plan to drive into the area. You can activate the ticket via text message or telephone. Visit the above website address to find out more. Petrol vehicles classed as Euro 0 and diesel vehicles in classes Euro 0 - 3 are not allowed to enter Area C at all during the above times.

Essential Equipment

Lights
It is compulsory for all vehicles to have dipped headlights at all times when driving outside built-up areas, on motorways and major roads, when driving in tunnels and when visibility is poor, e.g. in rain or snow. Bulbs are more likely to fail with constant use so you are advised to carry spares.

Reflective Jackets/Waistcoats
If your vehicle is immobilised on the carriageway outside a built-up area at night, or in poor visibility, you must wear a reflective jacket or waistcoat when getting out of your vehicle. This rule also applies to passengers who may leave the vehicle, for example, to assist with a repair. Keep the jackets to hand inside your vehicle, not in the boot.

Warning Triangle
At night a warning triangle must be used to give advance warning of any vehicle parked outside a built-up area near a bend, or on a hill if rear side lights have failed, or in fog. Place the triangle at least 50 metres behind the vehicle (100 metres on motorways). Failure to use a triangle may result in a fine.

Child Restraint System
Children travelling in UK registered vehicles must be secured according to UK legislation.

Winter Driving
In the area of Val d'Aosta vehicles must be equipped with winter tyres or snow chains must be carried between 15 October and 15 April. This rule may apply in other areas and over other periods as conditions dictate.

Fuel

Unleaded petrol is sold from pumps marked 'Super Unleaded' or 'Super Sensa Piombo'. Diesel is called 'gasolio' and LPG is known as 'gas auto' or 'GPL'.

Fuel is sold 24 hours a day on motorways but elsewhere petrol stations may close for an extended lunch break and overnight from approximately 7pm. Opening hours are clearly displayed, as are the addresses of the nearest garages which are open.

Major credit cards are accepted, but possibly not in rural areas, so always carry some cash. Look for the 'Carta Si' sign. Recent visitors report that many petrol stations in rural areas and on major routes between towns are now unmanned and automated. Payment may be made with bank notes but the machines will usually only accept credit cards issued by Italian banks.

Low Emission Zones

Many Italian cities and towns operate low emission zones. They often affect all vehicles, but rules vary from city to city. For more information visit www.lowemissionzones.eu.

Overtaking

On roads with three traffic lanes, the middle lane is reserved for overtaking, but overtaking is only allowed if a vehicle travelling in the opposite direction is not already in the middle lane.

When pulling out to overtake on motorways check for cars travelling at well over the maximum speed limit of 130km/h (81 mph).

Parking

In major towns there are parking zones where payment is required and these are indicated by blue road signs. Pay either at a machine with coins or buy a card from local tobacconists or newspaper shops and display it inside your vehicle. Some cities also have green zones where parking is prohibited on working days during the morning and afternoon rush hours.

Parking against the traffic flow and parking on the pavement are not allowed. Illegally parked vehicles may be clamped or towed away.

Priority

In general, priority must be given to traffic coming from the right except if indicated by road signs. At traffic lights a flashing amber light indicates that traffic must slow down and proceed with caution, respecting the priority rules.

Roads

The road network is of a high standard and main and secondary roads are generally good. Many main roads are winding and hilly but provide a more interesting route than the motorways. Stopping places for refreshments may be few and far between in some areas.

Standards of driving may be erratic, especially overtaking, and lane discipline poor; some roads have a particularly bad reputation for accidents. Those where special vigilance is called for include the Via Aurelia between Rome and Pisa, which is mostly two lane and is extremely busy at weekends, the A12 to the north with its series of tunnels and curves, the A1 between Florence and Bologna, the Rome ring road, roads around Naples and Palermo, and mountain roads in the south and in Sicily.

Road Signs and Markings

Road signs conform to international standards. White lettering on a green background indicates motorways (autostrada), whereas state and provincial roads outside built-up areas have white lettering on a blue background.

Other frequently encountered signs include the following:

Snow chains required · Horizontal traffic light

Carabinieri (police) · Ecopass zone (Milan)

Italian	English Translation
Attenzione	Caution
Autocarro	Lorries
Coda	Traffic jam
Curva pericolosa	Dangerous bend
Destra	Right
Deviazione	Diversion
Divieto di accesso	No entry
Divieto di sorpasso	No overtaking
Divieto di sosta	No parking
Ghiaia	Gravel
Incidente	Accident
Incrocio	Crossroads
Lavori in corso	Roadworks ahead
Pericoloso	Danger
Rallentare	Slow down
Restringimento	Narrow lane
Senso unico	One-way street
Senso vietato	No entry
Sinistra	Left
Sosta autorizzata	Parking permitted (times shown)
Sosta aietata	No parking
Svolta	Bend
Uscita	Exit
Vietato ingresso veicili	No entry for vehicles

A single or double unbroken line in the centre of the carriageway must not be crossed.

Speed Limits

	Open Road (km/h)	Motorway (km/h)
Car Solo	90-110	130
Car towing caravan/trailer	70	80
Motorhome under 3500kg	90-110	130
Motorhome 3500-7500kg	80	100

Motorhomes over 3,500kg are restricted to 80 km/h (50 mph) outside built-up areas and 100 km/h (62 mph) on motorways.

Speed on some sections of Italian motorways is electronically controlled. When you leave a motorway at a toll booth electronic tills calculate the distance a vehicle has travelled and the journey time. The police are automatically informed if speeding has taken place, and fines are imposed.

In bad weather the maximum speed is 90 km/h (56 mph) on roads outside built-up areas and 110 km/h (68 mph) on motorways.

The transportation or use of radar detectors is prohibited.

Traffic Jams

During the summer months, particularly at weekends, the roads to the Ligurian and Adriatic coasts and to the Italian lakes are particularly busy, as are the narrow roads around the lakes. Travelling mid week may help a little. Bottlenecks are likely to occur on the A1 north-south motorway at stretches between Milan and Bologna, Rioveggio and Incisa and on the ring road around Rome. Other traffic jams occur on the A14 to the Adriatic coast; on the A4 between Milan and Brescia caused by heavy traffic to Lakes Iseo and Garda; the A11 Florence to Pisa (before the A12 junction); the A12 Rome to Civitavecchia; the A23 Udine to Tarvisio and before the tunnels on the A26 between Alessandria and Voltri.

Italians traditionally go on holiday during the first weekend of August when traffic density is at its worst. Rush hour traffic jams regularly occur on the ring roads for Milan, Rome and Naples.

Violation of Traffic Regulations

The police may impose on the spot fines, which are particularly heavy for speeding and drink and/or drug related driving offences. Payment is required in cash and a receipt must be given. It can take up to a year for notice of a traffic violation and resulting fine to reach the owner of a foreign registered vehicle.

Motorways

There are approximately 6,500km of motorway (autostrade) in Italy. Tolls (pedaggio) are levied on most of them.

On some motorways, tolls are payable at intermediate toll booths for each section of the motorway used. On a few others the toll must be paid on entering the motorway.

Tolls

Category A Cars with height from front axle less than 1.30m.

Category B Motor vehicles with 2 axles with height from front axle over 1.30m including motorhomes.

Category C Motor vehicles with 3 axles, e.g. car plus caravan.

Category D Motor vehicles with 4 axles, e.g. car plus twin-axle caravan.

To calculate the tolls payable and find traffic and motorway services information see www.autostrade.it which allows you to enter your route and class of vehicle.

Tolls can prove to be expensive especially over long distances.

Toll Payment

Cash (euro only), debit and credit cards are accepted. Credit cards are also accepted for payment in the Fréjus, Mont-Blanc and Grand St Bernard tunnels. However, visitors advise that on some stretches of motorway automated pay desks which accept credit cards will only do so for solo vehicles. If you are towing a caravan it is advisable to have cash available as you may need to pass through the manned white channel for cash payments.

The prepaid Viacard, available in values of €25, €50 and €75, is also accepted on the majority of motorways and is obtainable from motorway toll booths, service areas and PuntoBlu points of sale along the motorways. The card may be used for any vehicle. When leaving a motorway on which the Viacard is accepted (use the blue or white lanes – do not use the yellow 'Telepass' lanes), insert your entry ticket and card into the machine or give them to the attendant who will deduct the amount due. A Viacard is valid until the credit expires and may be used on a subsequent visit to Italy but cannot be refunded. Viacards are not accepted on Sicilian motorways.

Touring

Italy's great cities, with their religious, artistic and historic treasures, are high on the short break list and are worthy destinations in their own right. Visitors over 65 often qualify for reduced or free entrance to museums and other attractions, so carry your passport as proof of age.

In Rome an Archaeological Card is available, valid for up to seven days, offering entry (ahead of any queues) to many of the most famous sites, together with discounts on guided tours. The cards are available from participating sites and museums.

Smoking is not permitted in public places including restaurants and bars.

In bars prices shown are for drinks taken standing at the bar. Prices are higher if you are seated at a table. In restaurants a service or cover charge is usually added to the bill but it is customary to add 50 cents or €1 per person if you are happy with the service provided. Not all restaurants accept credit cards; check before ordering.

The east coast of Italy has many holiday resorts with fine, sandy beaches, from Ravenna, to Pescara and beyond. However, most beaches in Italy are commercially managed and unless a campsite or hotel has its own private beach, be prepared to pay to enjoy a day by the sea. By law a part of every beach must have free access, but usually it is the least attractive part.

Many parts of Italy lie on a major seismic fault line and tremors and minor earthquakes are common. Visitors climbing Mount Etna should follow the marked routes and heed the advice of guides. There is also ongoing low-intensity volcanic activity on the island of Stromboli.

Visitors to Venice should note that parts of the city are liable to flood in late autumn and early spring.

There are more than 40 World Heritage Sites in Italy (more than any other country) including the historic centres of Florence, Siena, Naples, Pienza, Urbino and the Vatican City.

The Vatican museums and Sistine Chapel are closed on Sundays, except on the last Sunday of the month. When visiting art galleries in Florence, in particular the Uffizi and Accademia, you are advised to buy timed tickets in advance, either online or in person. Otherwise you will encounter very long queues.

There are numerous ferry services transporting passengers and vehicles between Italy and neighbouring countries. Major ports of departure for Croatia, Greece and Turkey are Ancona, Bari, Brindisi, Trieste and Venice. Services also operate to Corsica from Citavecchia, Genoa, Livorno, Porto Torres (Sardinia), Santa Teresa di Gallura (Sardinia) and Savona.

For further information contact:

VIAMARE LTD
SUITE 108, 582 HONEYPOT LANE
STANMORE
MIDDX HA7 1JS
Tel: 020 8206 3420, Fax: 020 8206 1332
www.viamare.com
Email: ferries@viamare.com

If you are planning a skiing holiday contact the Italian State Tourist Board for advice on safety and weather conditions before travelling. Off-piste skiing is highly dangerous and all safety instructions should be followed meticulously in view of the dangers of avalanches in some areas. Italy has introduced a law requiring skiers and snowboarders to carry tracking equipment if going off-piste. The law also obliges children up to 14 years of age to wear a helmet. There are plans for snowboarders to be banned from certain slopes, check local news for updates.

Public Transport & Local Travel

Traffic is restricted or prohibited at certain times in the historical centre of most Italian cities in order to reduce congestion and pollution levels, and you are advised to use out of centre car parks and public transport. The boundaries of historic centres are usually marked with signs displaying the letters ZTL (zona traffico limitato). A crossed hammer on the sign means the restriction does not apply on Sundays and public holidays. Do not pass the ZTL sign as your registration number is likely to be caught on camera and notice of a fine – or fines if you cross more than one ZTL zone – will probably be sent to your home address. Fines are around €100 each time you enter a ZTL.

In addition many northern Italian regions have banned traffic in town and city centres on Sundays. Buses and taxis are permitted to operate.

Public transport is usually cheap and efficient. All the major cities have extensive bus networks and

Messina, Milan, Padova, Rome and Turin also have trams. At present only Rome and Milan have an extensive underground network and Perugia has recently inaugurated a 'minimetro'. Bus and metro tickets cannot be purchased on board and must be obtained prior to boarding from newsagents, tobacconists, ticket kiosks or bars. Books of tickets and daily, weekly and monthly passes are also available for purchase.

Validate your ticket when using public transport at the yellow machines positioned at the entrance to platforms in railway stations, in the entrance hall of metro stations and on board buses and trams. Officials patrol all means of public transport and will issue an on the spot fine if you do not hold a validated ticket. Tickets for buses and the metro tend to be time limited (75 minutes) and it is therefore necessary to complete your journey within the allotted time and purchase a new ticket for any additional travel.

Only use taxis which are officially licensed. They will have a neon taxi sign on the roof and are generally white or yellow. Also ensure that the meter in the taxi has been reset before starting your journey. Fares are quite high and there are additional charges for luggage and pets, at night and on public holidays. A tip is expected (up to 10%) and this is sometimes already added to the fares for foreigners.

Car ferry services operate between Venice and the Lido, the Italian mainland and the Aeolian Islands, Sardinia, Sicily, Elba and Capri, Corsica (France) and on Lakes Maggiore, Como and Garda. Parking in Venice is very difficult; instead park at a mainland car park and use a bus or ferry to the city. However, be aware that thieves may operate in car parks in Mestre. Driving and parking in Naples are not recommended in any circumstances.

Cars towing caravans are prohibited at all times from using the S163 south of Naples because it is narrow and has many bends. Motorhomes are prohibited in summer between Positano and Vietri-a-Mare.

Venice

⊞ **AGEROLA** *3A3* (3.5km SE Urban) *40.62537, 14.56761* **Camping Beata Solitudo, Piazza Generale Avitabile 4, San Lazzaro, 80051 Agerola (NA) [tel/fax 081 8025048; beatasol@tiscalinet.it; www.beatasolitudo.it]** Exit A3/S145 at Castellammare-di-Stabia & foll dirs S on S366 to Agerola. Turn L sp San Lazzaro, site in vill sq - narr access rds. Do not app via Amalfi coast rd. Sm, terr, shd; wc (cont); chem disp; mv service pnt; shwrs inc; EHU (3A) inc; lndry rm; shop, rest, snacks, bar in vill; sm playgrnd; shgl beach 16km; wifi; 70% statics; dogs free; bus adj; poss cr; Eng spkn; adv bkg; quiet; red CKE/CCI. "Vg access to Amalfi coast via bus; site at 650m - sea views; v helpful owner; bungalows & hostel accomm avail in restored castle building on site; vg but suitable m'vans only." € 20.00   2009*

⊞ **ALBA** *1B2* (1km SW Urban) *44.68507, 8.01019* **Camping Village Alba, Corso Piave 219, San Cassiano, 12051 Alba (CN) [0173 280972; fax 288621; info@albavillagehotel.it; www.albavillagehotel.it]** Fr A21 exit Asti Est onto S231 to Alba ring rd. Take Corso Piave dir Roddi & Castiglione Falletto, site sp (Campo Sportivo) on L - red block. Or fr A6 exit at SP662 & foll sp Cherasco & Marene, then at rndabt foll sp Pollenza, then Roddi. Fr Roddi site sp dir Alba. Med, hdg/mkd pitch, pt shd; htd wc; chem disp; mv service pnt outside site; shwrs inc; EHU (16A) €2.50; lndry; shop 150m; rest; bar; BBQ; htd pool adj; paddling pool; sports cent adj; bike hire; games area; internet; some statics/apartmnts; dogs free; bus; Eng spkn; adv bkg; quiet; ccard acc; red CKE/CCI. "Excel, friendly, clean site; open country to rear; vg facs; conv Barolo vineyards; attractive town & area." ♦ € 38.00   2014*

ALBENGA *1B2* (2km E Rural/Coastal) *44.08277, 8.21611* **Camping Baciccia, Via Torino 19, 17023 Ceriale (SV) [0182 990743; fax 993839; info@campingbaciccia.it; www.campingbaciccia.it]** Exit A10 for Albenga, turn L onto SS1 Via Aurelia dir Savona for 3km. Turn L inland at traff lts bef Famiglia Supmkt in Ceriale, site in 200m on L, sp. Med, mkd pitch, pt sl, pt shd; htd wc (some cont); chem disp; mv service pnt; serviced pitches; baby facs; shwrs inc; EHU (6A) inc; gas; lndry; shop; supmkt nr; rest, snacks; bar; BBQ; playgrnd; pool high ssn; paddling pool; public shgl beach 600m, private beach nrby; tennis 500m; bike hire; horseriding 2km; golf 10km; wifi; entmnt; TV rm; 5% statics; dogs €4; bus to private beach; sep car park; poss cr; Eng spkn; adv bkg; quiet; ccard acc; red long stay/LS/CKE/CCI. "Family-run site; ltd touring pitches; narr site rds & ent & sm pitches; friendly owners; gd san facs & pool; busy w/ends; lovely pool & café; conv many historical attractions." 1 Apr-3 Nov & 1 Dec-10 Jan. € 50.00 (3 persons)   2013*

ALBENGA *1B2* (5km NW Rural) *44.08472, 8.21027* **Camping Bella Vista, Via Campore 23, 17030 Campochiesa-d'Albenga (SV) [0182 540213; fax 554925; info@campingbellavista.it; www.campingbellavista.it]** Exit A10 at Borghetto S Spirito & foll sp Ceriale. In Ceriale turn R at 3rd traff lts, R at next traff lts & foll site sp. Med, hdg/mkd pitch, terr, pt shd; htd wc (some cont); chem disp; mv service pnt; baby facs; shwrs inc; EHU (3-6A) €2.50 (poss rev pol); lndry; shop; rest, snacks; bar; BBQ; htd pool; paddling pool; beach 1.5km; games rm; internet; entmnt; 30% statics; dogs €6.50; phone; bus 900m; poss cr; Eng spkn; adv bkg; quiet. "Pleasant, friendly, clean, Dutch family-run site; helpful staff; narr site rds; mostly sm pitches; owner will site c'van with tractor on request; poss diff lge o'fits." ♦ ltd. 15 Mar-15 Nov & 15 Dec-15 Jan. € 33.50   2011*

ALBEROBELLO *3A4* (1.5km N Rural) *40.80194, 17.25055* **Camping Dei Trulli, Via Castellana Grotte, Km 1.5, 70011 Alberobello (BA) [0804 323699; fax 322145; info@campingdeitrulli.it; www.campingdeitrulli.com]** Fr Alberobello, site sp on R. Lift barrier to ent if clsd. Med, mkd pitch, hdstg, pt shd; wc; mv service pnt opp; shwrs €0.50; EHU (6A) €2.50; shop &1.5km; rest, snacks; bar; 2 pools high ssn; bike hire; wifi; entmnt; phone; Eng spkn; ccard acc; red long stay/CKE/CCI. "Gd touring base; some pitches sm due to trees; ltd, basic facs LS; hot water to shwrs only; site run-down." 1 Apr-30 Sep. € 42.50   2014*

⊞ **ALBEROBELLO** *3A4* (1km S Rural) *40.77507, 17.24040* **Camping Bosco Selva, 27 Via Bosco Selva, 70011 Alberobello (BA) [080 4323726; fax 4323863; info@campingboscoselva.it; www.campingboscoselva.it]** Sp fr S172/S239 Alberobello ring rd. Med, some hdstg, pt sl, shd; wc; chem disp; mv service pnt; shwrs inc; EHU (2A) inc; lndry; shop 1km; rest; bar; wifi; Eng spkn; quiet; red LS; CKE/CCI. "In heart of 'Trulli' region of sm beehive-shaped houses; wooded site; friendly owner; vg facs; v nice site; tennis courts; walks in forest adj." € 37.00   2014*

ALBINIA see Orbetello *1D4*

AMEGLIA see Sarzana *1C2*

⊞ **ANGHIARI** *1D3* (600m S Urban) *43.53666, 12.05204* **Agrturism Vel della Pieve, Via della Fossa, 8 - 52031(AR) [tel/fax 0575 788593; info@agriturismovaldellapieve.it; www.agriturismovaldellapieve.it]** Fr N on the SP47 turn L on to Via della Fossa rd to the site. Sm, hdstg, pt shd; htd wc; chem disp; mv service pnt; shwrs; fam bthrm; EHU (6A) inc; gas 1km; lndry (inc dryer); shop 1/2 Km; rest 1/2 Km; snacks 1/2 Km; playgrnd; htd pool; wifi; dogs; Eng spkn; adv bkg; CKE/CCI. € 25.00   2013*

⊞ **ANTERSELVA DI SOPRA/ANTHOLZ OBERTAL** *2E1* (500m NE Rural) *46.86450, 12.10966* **Camping Anterselva/ Antholz, Obertal 34, 39030 Anterselva-di-Sopra/Antholz-Obertal (BZ) [0474 492204; fax 492444; info@camping-antholz.com; www.camping-antholz.com]** E fr Brunico on S49. Turn N at Rasun & Antholz valley; cont 12km, well sp, app not steep. Site is 2km N of Antholz. Med, pt sl, unshd; htd wc; chem disp; mv service pnt; baby facs; shwrs inc; EHU (4A) inc; gas; lndry; shop; rest snacks; bar; playgrnd; tennis 500m; bike hire; wifi; TV; dogs €3; bus nr; adv bkg; quiet. ♦ € 25.00   2009*

AOSTA *1B1* (1km N Rural) *45.74666, 7.31897* **Camping Ville d'Aoste, Viale Gran San Bernardo 67, Loc Les Fourches, 11100 Aosta (AO) [0165 361360]** 1st site on L off old rd fr Aosta to Grand St Bernard tunnel rte S27. Nr Hotel Rayon du Soleil. Sm, pt shd; wc (some cont); chem disp; mv service pnt; shwrs inc; EHU (4-10A) inc; gas; lndry; shop; snacks; bar; playgrnd; TV; phone; train at Saraillon; some rd noise; ccard acc; CKE/CCI. "Interesting town with many Roman historic remains; excel mountain views; uncr, even in high ssn; clean & friendly site; unrel opening dates." 9 Jul-31 Oct. € 17.40   2014*

AOSTA *1B1* (4km E Rural) *45.74088, 7.39355* **Camping Aosta, Villaggio Clou 29, 11020 Quart (AO) [tel/ fax 0165 765602; info@campingaosta.com]** Site 1km fr Villefranche at Quart on SS26. Med, pt sl, terr, shd; wc (some cont); chem disp; shwrs inc; mv service pnt; EHU (6A) inc; lndry; sm shop; supmkt 2km; rest; bar; playgrnd; pool 5km; bike hire; mainly statics; phone; rlwy noise. "Ltd touring pitches; poorly-maintained site; NH only." 15 May-15 Sep. € 21.00   2012*

⊞ **AOSTA** *1B1* (3km SE Rural) *45.73338, 7.36006* **Camping Les Iles, Loc Les Iles 17, 11020 Pollein (AO) [tel/fax 0165 53154; camping_les_iles@hotmail.it]** Fr N exit A5 Aosta Est sp St Christophe/Pollein, go under a'strada, cross Rv Dora, site sp. Med, pt shd; wc; chem disp; mv service pnt; shwrs; EHU metered; snacks; bar; playgrnd; tennis; some statics; dogs €3; bus nr; some rd noise; ccard acc; CKE/CCI. "Beautiful location; conv Mont Blanc & St Bernard tunnels." ♦ € 29.00   2009*

AOSTA *1B1* (5km SW Rural) *45.71706, 7.26161* **Camping Monte Bianco, St Maurice 15, 11010 Sarre (AO) [tel/fax 0165 258514; info@campingmontebianco.it; www.campingmontebianco.it]** Fr A5/E25 exit Aosta W twd Aosta, site on R, well sp. Fr Mont Blanc tunnel on S26 site on R at Sarre 500m past St Maurice sp. W fr Aosta, site on L 100m past boundary sp St Maurice/Sarre, yellow sp. Turn into site poss tight for lge o'fits. Sm, terr, pt shd; wc (some cont); chem disp; mv service pnt; shwrs €0.50; EHU (6-10A) €2.80; gas; lndry rm; shop adj; supmkt 800m; rest 200m; bar 100m; playgrnd; pool 4km; phone; Eng spkn; adv bkg; quiet; red long stay LS; CKE/CCI. "Sm, gd, family-run site set in orchard on rv; friendly, helpful; excel tourist info; beautiful alpine scenery & walks; last tunnel is close to exit when coming fr Mont Blanc do not rely on Sat Nav to restart in time." 15 May-30 Sep. € 23.50   2015*

AOSTA *1B1* (4km W Rural) *45.72190, 7.26985* **Camping International Touring, Fraz. Arensod 10, 11010 Sarre (AO) [tel/fax 0165 257061; campingtouring@libero.it; www.campingtouring.com]** Exit A5/E25 Aosta West, site sp fr rd S26. Lge, pt shd; wc (some cont); own san rec; chem disp; mv service pnt; shwrs inc; EHU (3-6A) €2.80; gas; lndry; sm supmkt 100m; rest, snacks; bar; playgrnd; pool high ssn; tennis; 10% statics; dogs €1; poss cr; quiet; 10% red CKE/ CCI. "Lovely scenery; conv for Val d'Aosta with historical castles; somewhat run down site; NH only." 15 May-15 Sep. € 24.50   2009*

AQUILEIA *2E1* (300m NE Rural) *45.77786, 13.36943* **Camping Aquileia, Via Gemina 10, 33051 Aquileia (UD) [0431 91042; fax 30804; info@campingaquileia.it; www.campingaquileia.it]** Fr A4/E70 take Grado/Palmanova exit & foll sp Grado on SS352. Turn L at traff lts at ent to Aquileia. Site in 400m on R. Fr SS14 turn onto SS352, site sp. Med, shd; wc (some cont); chem disp; mv service pnt; shwrs inc; EHU (6A) inc; lndry rm; supmkt adj; rest, snacks; playgrnd; pool; paddling pool; some statics; dogs €3; bus 300m; quiet; red long stay; ccard acc; CKE/CCI. "Excel site; lge pitches; 10 mins walk thro Roman ruins to magnificent, unique basilica & mosaics; poss noisy concerts July festival week; gd, friendly site; great site." 1 May-30 Sep. € 30.50   2013*

AQUILEIA *2E1* (3km S Coastal) *45.72640, 13.39860* **Camping Village Belvedere Pineta, Via Martin Luther King, 33051 Belvedere-di-Grado (UD) [0431 91007; fax 918641; info@belvederepineta.it; www.belvederepineta.it]** Fr Venezia/Trieste a'strada, exit for Palmanova & foll Grado sp on S352 to Aquileia. Drive thro Belvedere, & site is nr lagoon. Slow app to site due to uneven surface. V lge, mkd pitch, shd; wc; chem disp; mv service pnt; baby facs; shwrs inc; EHU (3-6A) inc; gas; lndry (inc dryer); supmkt; rest, snacks; bar; BBQ; playgrnd; pool; paddling pool; waterslide; sand beach adj; watersports; tennis; games area; games rm; bike hire; excursions; entmnt; golf 5km; 50% statics; dogs €7.50; rlwy stn 10km at Cervignano; adv bkg; quiet; red long stay/snr citizens; CKE/CCI. "Wooded site - poss mosquitoes; steamer trips fr Grado; gd touring base, inc Venice; red for Seniors; excel site with v clean san facs." ♦ 1 May-30 Sep. € 59.00 (CChq acc)   2013*

ARCO *1D1* (1km N Rural) *45.92694, 10.8925* **Camping Arco, Loc Prabi, Via Legionari Cecoslovacchia 12, 38062 Arco (TN) [0464 517491; fax 515525; arco@arcoturistica.com; www.arcoturistica.com]** Fr N foll sp Arco Centre at rndabt at start of ring rd & turn R immed after x-ing rv bdge. Fr S foll ring rd sp Trento. Turn L at Camping/Prabi (climbing area) sp. Lge, shd; wc (some cont); chem disp; mv service pnt; shwrs inc; EHU (4A) inc; gas; lndry; shop; rest 300m; snacks adj; bar; playgrnd; pool adj; tennis; games area; bike hire; wifi; 10% statics; dogs €4; quiet; ccard acc. "V busy site; v clean." ♦ 21 Mar-8 Nov. € 28.00   2009*

ARCO *2D1* (6km SSW Coastal) *45.87614, 10.86779* **Camping Bellavista, Via Gardesana, 31 - Arco [0464 505644; fax 505166; www.camping-bellavista.it]** Fr A22 take exit for Roveretto Sud-Lago di Garda; at rndabt take 4th exit twrds Riva Del Garda; in 3km turn L onto SS240. After town cent in 8km take L into site bef lakeside tunnel, just after Lidl supmkt on L. Med, mkd pitch, shd; wc; chem disp; mv service pnt; baby facs; fam bthrm; shwrs; EHU (3A) inc; lndry (inc dryer); shop; rest; snacks; takeaway; bar; bbq; pool; lakeside beach; bike hire; wifi; dogs €3.50; phone; public transport 100m; twin axles; poss cr; Eng spkn; noisy (fr deliveries at adj supmkt & busy rd); "V busy but v pleasant site; direct access to beach; excel, immac san facs; vg & reasonable rest; next to supmkt; town cent 5 min walk along lakeside path; vg touring area for northern towns of lake Garda; excel site." ♦ 1 Apr-30 Oct. € 33.50   2014*

ARENZANO see Genova *1C2*

⊞ **AREZZO** *1D3* (10km SW Rural) *43.44982, 11.78990* **Camping Villaggio Le Ginestre, Loc Ruscello 100, 52100 Arezzo [0575 363566; fax 366949; info@campingle ginestre.it; www.campingleginestre.it]** Ont A1 sp Arezzo. Foll sp to Battifolle & Ruscello, proceed for 2km to rdbt, turn L to Ruscello and foll signs to site which will be on the L. Med, some hdstg, terr, pt sl, pt shd; htd wc; chem disp; mv service pnt; shwrs inc; EHU (5-10A) inc; lndry; shop 500m; rest, snacks; bar; playgrnd; pool; tennis; games area; games rm; 5% statics; dogs; bus; site clsd Jan; poss cr; adv bkg; ccard acc; CKE/ CCI. "Pleasant, grassy site with views; friendly owner; gd rest; trains fr Arezzo to Florence, Rome etc; gd touring base." ♦ € 41.00   2013*

ARONA 1B1 (7km N Rural) 45.81583, 8.54992 **Camping Solcio, Via al Campeggio, 28040 Solcio-de-Lesa (NO) [0322 7497; fax 7566; info@campingsolcio.com; www.campingsolcio.com]** Foll S33 N fr Arona, thro Meina campsite on R of rd app Solcio; well sp, adj boatyard. Med, mkd pitch, pt shd; htd wc (some cont); chem disp; mv service pnt; baby facs; shwrs inc; EHU (6A) inc; gas; lndry (inc dryer); shop & 1km; rest, snacks; bar; BBQ; lake sw & shgl beach adj; fishing; watersports; wifi; entmnt; 40% statics; dogs €7.80; phone; rlwy noise; poss cr; Eng spkn; adv bkg; red LS/long stay; CKE/CCI. "Gd site adj lake; some sm pitches; premium for lakeside pitches; gd rest; gd cent for area; conv Stresa; friendly; highly rec; beach has permanent wooden parasols; immac san facs." 8 Mar-20 Oct. € 55.00 (3 persons) (CChq acc)   2014*

⊞ **ARONA** 1B1 (2km S Rural) 45.73741, 8.57651 **Camping Lago Azzurro, Via Enrico Fermi 2, 28040 Dormelletto (NO) [tel/fax 0322 497197; info@campinglagoazzurro.it; www.campinglagoazzurro.it]** Exit A8/A26/E62 dir Castelletto Ticino onto SS33. Site 1km N of Dormelletto, on W shore of lake. Rec app fr Dormelletto, not Arona. Med, hdg/mkd pitch, shd; wc (some cont); mv service pnt; shwrs €0.70; EHU (3A) €3.50; lndry; shop; rest 1km; snacks; bar; pool high ssn; tennis; private shgl beach; boating; tennis adj; games area; entmnt; sat TV; 50% statics; dogs €4; phone; poss cr; adv bkg; quiet but motor boats noisy w/end, noisy entmnt high ssn. "Facs stretched high ssn due tented teenage vill on site; sm pitches." ◆ € 29.50   2010*

ARONA 1B1 (2km S Urban) 45.73648, 8.57564 **Camping Röse, Via Fermi 3, 28040 Dormelletto (NO) [0322 497979; fax 498970; info@campingrose.it; www.campingrose.it]** Site 2km N of Dormelletto, on W shore of lake. Rec app fr Dormelletto, not Arona. Med, some mkd pitch, shd; wc (some cont); chem disp; shwrs; EHU (3A) €3; gas; lndry; shop; rest adj; snacks; bar; playgrnd; beach adj; fishing; watersports; 80% statics; dogs €5; adv bkg; ccard acc; quiet. "Friendly site; inadequate shwrs; lake ferry boats at Arona." ◆ 1 Apr-12 Oct. € 26.00   2010*

⊞ **ARONA** 1B1 (5km S Rural) 45.72825, 8.57966 **Camping Lido Holiday Inn, Via Marco Polo 1, 28040 Dormelletto (NO) [0322 497047; fax 019646; info@campingholidayinn. com; www.campingholidayinn.com]** Exit A8/A26/E62 at Castelletto Ticino dir Arona, foll sp Dormelletto. Lido sp on R. Lge, hdg/mkd pitch, pt sl, pt shd; wc; chem disp; mv service pnt; baby facs; shwrs inc; EHU (3A) €4.50; gas; lndry; shop; rest, snacks; bar; BBQ; playgrnd; pool; lake sw & shgl beach; tennis; golf 8km; 30% statics; dogs €5; phone; train 400m; Eng spkn; adv bkg; quiet; red CKE/CCI. "Basic facs; lakeside pitch; gd rest." ◆ € 39.00   2015*

ARSIE 1D1 (1km S Rural) 45.96333, 11.76027 **Camping Al Lago, Via Campagna 14, 32030 Rocca di Arsie (BL) [0439 58540; fax 58471; info@campingallago.bl.it; www.campingallago.bl.it]** Fr Trento on S47, turn E dir Feltre/Belluno rd SS50B, take 1st exit after long tunnel. Fr Belluno on S50 & S50B take Arsié exit & foll site sp. Med, pt shd; wc; chem disp (wc); shwrs inc; EHU (3A) inc; gas 2.5km; shop 3km; rest high ssn; bar; playgrnd; lake sw adj; 15% statics; dogs; phone; poss cr; adv bkg; quiet; ccard acc; CKE/CCI. "Excel, well-run, clean, tidy site in unspoilt area of historical & cultural interest; simple facs, basic but clean; boat hire locally; ent clsd 1400-1530 & 0000-0800; passport req to register." 1 Apr-4 Oct. € 23.00   2009*

ARSIE 1D1 (3km S Rural) 45.96777, 11.76583 **Gajole - Quiet & Lake Camping, Loc Soravigo, 32030 Arsie (BL) [tel/fax 0439 58505; info@campinggajole.it; www.campinggajole.it]** Fr S47 take S50bis dir Feltre, Belluno. Turn 1st R after long tunnel, site well sp. Med, hdstg, pt sl, terr, pt shd; wc (some cont); chem disp; mv service pnt; shwrs inc; EHU (4A) inc; lndry; shop; snacks; bar; lake sw 200m; 50% statics; dogs; Eng spkn; quiet. "Excel, peaceful site." ◆ ltd. 1 Apr-30 Sep. € 22.00   2009*

⊞ **ASCOLI PICENO** 2E3 (200m Urban) 42.85274, 13.58182 **Parking De Gasperc, Viale A De Gasperi, Ascoli Piceno** Foll signs in town ctr. Sm, hdstg, unshd; own san rec; shops 200m; train 500. "C'van parking only; NH; historic town." € 1.00   2014*

⊞ **ASSISI** 2E3 (1km SE Rural) 43.06605, 12.63056 **Camping Fontemaggio, Via Eremo delle Carceri, 24 Assisi 06081 (PG) [075 813636 or 812317; fax 813749; info@fontemaggio.it]** Fr Perugia on S75, turn L onto rd SS147 twd Assisi; keeping Assisi walls on L past coach car park & foll sp to Porta Nuova. In sq at front of gate turn R & foll sp to Eremo delle Carceri, Foligno & Cmp Fontemaggio. Foll sp 1km to sq in front of next gate, turn R (sharp hairpin), site sp 800m on R at gate with narr arch, site 800m on R. Diff long, winding uphill app; recep in hotel. Pls do not use SatNav. Lge, terr, hdstg, pt shd; htd wc (some cont); chem disp; mv service pnt; some serviced pitches; shwrs inc; EHU (6A) inc (long lead rec); gas; lndry rm; shop (high ssn) & 1km; rest; snacks (high ssn); bar; htd pool 3km; TV cab/sat; some statics; dogs; phone; poss cr; Eng spkn; adv bkg; quiet; ccard acc; CKE/CCI. "Lovely, spacious site in olive grove; views; footpath to attractive town; steep site rds diff when wet; order bread at hotel recep; firefly displays on site; facs tired; great rest." ◆ € 25.50   2015*

ASSISI 2E3 (3km W Rural) 43.07611, 12.57361 **Camping Assisi (Formaly Internazionale), Via San Giovanni Campiglione 110, 06081 Assisi (PG) [075 816813; fax 812335; info@campingassisi.it; www.campingassisi.com]** Fr Perugia SS75 to Ospedalicchio, then SS147 twd Assisi. Site well sp on R bef Assisi. Fr Assisi take SS147 to Perugia. Site on L in 3km adj Hotel Green. Lge, mkd pitch, shd; wc (mainly cont); chem disp; mv service pnt; shwrs inc; EHU (3A) €2 (rev pol), 6A avail; gas; lndry (inc dryer); shop & supmkt 3km; rest; pizzeria; bar; playgrnd; pool high ssn; tennis; 40% statics; dogs €2; phone; bus; car wash; poss cr; Eng spkn; adv bkg rec high ssn; quiet; ccard acc; red LS; CKE/CCI. "Helpful staff; minibus to Assisi; lovely, tidy, clean site; busy even in LS; immac san facs; gd rest; sm pitches; caves at Genga worth visit; excel; 10% red on next site if pt of same chain." ◆ ltd. 20 Mar-2 Nov. € 42.00   2014*

ASTI 1B2 (2km NW Rural) 44.94087, 8.18726 **Camping Umberto Cagni, Loc Valmanera 152, 14100 Asti [0141 271238; info@campingcagniasti.it; www.campingcagniasti.it]** Leave A21 at Asti E. Foll sp to Asti. At beg of town cntre with Asti Service Stn on L; turn R foll sp to camping site. Med, pt sl, shd; wc (mainly cont); shwrs; EHU €3; shop; rest, snacks; bar; games area; entmnt; 50% statics; dogs €2; poss cr & noisy; 10% red CKE/CCI. "Fair NH/sh stay; friendly staff; not suitable lge o'fits; poss travellers; gates clsd 1300-1500." 1 Apr-30 Sep. € 23.50   2012*

BAIA DOMIZIA see Marina di Minturno *2F4*

BALISIO DI BALLABIO see Lecco *1C1*

BARBERINO VAL D'ELSA see Poggibonsi *1D3*

BARDOLINO *1D2* (1.2km N Rural) *45.56388, 10.71416*
**Camping La Rocca, Loc San Pietro, Via Gardensana 37,
37011 Bardolino (VR) [045 7211111; fax 7211300;
info@campinglarocca.com; www.campinglarocca.com]**
Exit A22/E45 Affi/Lago di Garda Sud & foll SR249 sp Bardolino.
Camp 1st site on both sides of rd exit town at km 53/IV. V lge,
shd; wc (some cont); chem disp; mv service pnt; shwrs inc;
EHU (10A) inc; lndry; shop; rest, snacks; bar; BBQ; playgrnd;
pool; paddling pool; shgl beach adj; lake sw; fishing; bike hire;
TV rm; 15% statics; dogs €5.90; phone; poss cr; Eng spkn; no
adv bkg; some rd noise (rd thro site); ccard acc; red CKE/CCI.
"Pleasant, popular site; gd views; avoid field nr lake; lakeside
walk to Garda or Bardolino 20mins; mkt Thurs Bardolino, Fri
Garda; red snr citizens." ♦ Easter-6 Oct. € 52.00   2013*

BARDOLINO *1D2* (1.5km N Rural) *45.55944, 10.71666*
**Camping Serenella, Loc Mezzariva 19, 37011 Bardolino
(VR) [045 7211333; fax 7211552; serenella@camping-
serenella.it; www.camping-serenella.it]** Site on R SR249.
Lge, pt sl, pt shd; wc; chem disp; mv service pnt; shwrs inc;
EHU (6A) inc; lndry (inc dryer); shop; rest, snacks; bar; playgrnd;
pool; paddling pool; lake sw; boat launching; waterski; games
rm; bike hire; entmnt; 50% statics; no dogs; poss v cr; Eng
spkn; no ccard acc. "Bus to Verona; lakeside walk to Garda
or Bardolino; excel, clean facs; sm pitches poss diff lge o'fits
- check bef pitching; vg supmkt, rest." ♦ ltd. 1 Apr-18 Oct.
€ 36.50   2009*

BARDOLINO *1D2* (800m N Rural) *45.5570, 455570*
**Camping Continental, Loc Reboin, 37011 Bardolino (VR)
[045 7210192; fax 7211756; continental@campingarda.it;
www.campingarda.it/continental]** Exit A22/E45 Lago di
Garda Sud onto SR249. Site bet km 52/III & 52IV. Lge, shd; wc
(some cont); mv service pnt; shwrs inc; EHU (3A) inc; lndry (inc
dryer); shop; rest, snacks; bar; playgrnd; lake sw & beach adj;
car wash; 50% statics; dogs not acc end Jun-end Aug; poss cr;
adv bkg; quiet. ♦ 16 Apr-9 Oct. € 33.60   2011*

BARDOLINO *1D2* (2km S Rural) *45.52525, 10.72977*
**Camping Cisano/San Vito, Via Peschiera 48, 37011 Cisano
(VR) [045 6229098; fax 6229059; cisano@camping-cisano.it;
www.camping-cisano.it]** Sites on S boundary of Cisano,
on SE shore of Lake Garda. V lge, mkd pitch, terr, sl, shd;
wc; chem disp; mv service pnt; shwrs inc; EHU (4A) inc; gas;
lndry (inc dryer); supmkt; rest, snacks; bar; pool; paddling
pool; waterslide; private beach & lake sw adj; waterskiing;
windsurfing; canoeing; tennis; games area; bike hire; entmnt;
TV rm; statics; no dogs; Eng spkn; quiet; red LS. "Two lovely,
clean, lakeside sites run as one - San Vito smaller/quieter;
helpful staff; san facs in need of refurb; some pitches diff
access & chocks req; passport req at site check-in; Verona
Opera excursions arranged high ssn; gd; v popular; helpful
staff; gd walking/cycling; gd rest." ♦ 29 Mar-12 Oct.
€ 66.00   2014*

BARDOLINO *1D2* (500m S Rural) *45.54275, 10.72513*
**Camping Europa, Loc Mandracci, Via Santa Cristina 12,
37011 Bardolino (VR) [045 7211089; fax 7210073; europa@
campingarda.it; www.campingarda.it]** N fr Peschiera on
SR249, site on W side of rd opp 2nd Bardolino 50 km/h sp at
S of vill, adj lge petrol stn & Hotel du Lac. Med, mkd pitch,
pt shd; wc; chem disp; shwrs inc; EHU (6A) inc; lndry (inc
dryer); shop; rest 500m; snacks; bar; lake sw & watersports
adj; TV; 40% statics; no dogs Jul & Aug; adv bkg; rd noise.
"Lovely lakeside setting; helpful staff." ♦ 1 Apr-9 Oct.
€ 32.50   2010*

⊞ **BARDONECCHIA** *1A2* (5km SW Rural) *45.04954, 6.66510*
**Camping Bokki, Loc Pian del Colle, 10052 Bardonecchia
(TO) [tel/fax 0122 99893; info@bokki.it; www.bokki.it]**
Fr A32 ent Bardonecchia & foll sp Melezet. After Melezet foll
rd uphill for 1.5km. Bokki is 2nd site on R. Med, mkd pitch, pt
sl, pt shd; htd wc; chem disp; mv service pnt; baby facs; fam
bthrm; shwrs inc; EHU (2A) inc; lndry; shop 3km; rest, snacks;
bar; playgrnd; lake sw adj; TV rm; 95% statics; dogs €1; phone;
Eng spkn; adv bkg; quiet; CKE/CCI. "Helpful owners; beautiful
location; conv Fréjus tunnel; diff ent to v sm sloping, uneven
pitch; no red in LS." € 31.00   2014*

BAROLO *1B2* (1km W Rural) *44.61246, 7.92106* **Camping
Sole Langhe, Piazza della Vite e Del Vino, Frazione
Vergne, 12060 Barolo (CN) [0173 560510; fax 386819;
info@solelanghe.com; www.campingsolelanghe.it]**
Fr S exit A6 E sp Carru. At Carru turn N onto SP12 & foll sp
Barolo. Site sp on ent Barolo. Sm, hdg pitch, pt shd; wc; chem
disp; mv service pnt; shwrs inc; EHU (6A) inc; lndry; shop; rest;
snacks, bar 1km; BBQ; playgrnd; games area; dogs; Eng spkn;
quiet. "Lovely orchard site in cent Barolo wine region; v helpful
owner." 1 Mar-30 Nov. € 32.00   2014*

⊞ **BARREA** *2F4* (500m S Rural) *41.74978, 13.99128*
**Camping La Genziana, Loc Tre Croci 1, 67030 Barrea (AQ)
[tel/fax 0864 88101; pasettanet@tiscalinet.it;
www.campinglagenzianapasetta.it]** Fr S83 to S end Lago di
Barrea, thro Barrea S, site immed on L on uphill L-hand bend.
Med, mkd pitch, terr, pt shd; wc; chem disp; mv service pnt;
shwrs; EHU (3A) €2.60; lndry; sm shop; rest 300m; bar; BBQ;
playgrnd; sand beach & lake sw 3km; dogs €3; bus; Eng spkn;
adv bkg; quiet. "Knowledgeable owner; delightful site but
unrel hot water & poor facs; excel area cycling; trekking, skiing;
ltd shops Barrea 10 mins walk; conv Abruzzi National Park."
€ 26.40   2009*

⊞ **BASTIA MONDOVI** *1B2* (1km N Rural) *44.44871, 7.89417*
**Camping La Cascina, Loc Pieve 3, 12060 Bastia-Mondovi
(CN) [tel/fax 0174 60181; info@campinglacascina.it;
www.campinglacascina.it]** Fr Cuneo on S564 turn R at
rndabt adj to Rv Tanaro sp to Bastìa Mondovi, site on R in
500m. Lge, pt shd; wc; chem disp; mv service pnt; shwrs inc;
EHU (6A) €2.50; lndry; shop; rest 1km; bar; playgrnd; pool;
games area; 90% statics; phone; site clsd Sep; poss cr; Eng
spkn; ccard acc; CKE/CCI. "Touring vans on edge of sports
field; conv wine vills; hot water poss erratic; v busy w/end high
ssn." ♦ 1 Jan-2 Sep & 22 Sep-31 Dec. € 35.50   2013*

BAVENO see Stresa *1B1*

ITALY

BELLAGIO *1C1* (1.8km S Rural) *45.97093, 9.25381* **Clarke Camping, Via Valassina 170/C, 22021 Bellagio, Como [031 951325; info@villa-magnolia.co.uk; www.bellagio-camping.com]** Fr Como, on arr in Bellagio foll sp Lecco to R, foll site sps uphill. Narr rds & site ent. Med, terr, pt shd; wc (some cont); chem disp; mv service pnt; shwrs inc; EHU €2; shop 500m; rest, snacks, bar 1.5km; lake sw 1.5km; no dogs; ferries, water taxis 1.5km; quiet; wifi; ccards & chq's not acc. "Friendly British owner; views over lake; uphill walk fr town to campsite; town is on lakeside; site & app not suitable lge o'fits; no twin-axles; beautiful, peaceful site; basic san facs but clean; use vehicle ferry fr Cadenabbis or Varenne €20 for m'van & 2 people, then foll dirs." 15 May-15 Sep. € 33.00   2013*

BELLARIA *2E2* (3km N Coastal) *44.16606, 12.43563* **Camping Delle Rose, Via Adriatica 29, 47043 Gatteo-a-Mare (FC) [0547 86213; fax 87583; info@villaggiorose.com; www.villaggiorose.com]** Exit A14/E55 dir Rimini Nord onto S16. Exit S16 at Gatteo a Mare, turn R at junc, over rndabt. Site on L in 100m at km 186. Lge, mkd pitch, shd; wc (some cont); chem disp; mv service pnt; shwrs inc; EHU (6A) €3; gas; lndry; shop; rest, snacks; bar; playgrnd; pool; paddling pool; sand beach 300m; games area; entmnt; TV; 30% statics; dogs €8.10 (sm only); free shuttle bus to beach; poss cr; Eng spkn; adv bkg; quiet, some rlwy & rd noise; ccard acc; red CKE/CCI. "Easy reach San Marino & Urbino." ♦ 24 Apr-20 Sep. € 36.00   2009*

⊞ **BELLARIA** *2E2* (2km NE Coastal) *44.16076, 12.44836* **Happy Camping Village, Via Panzini 228, San Mauro a Mare, 47814 Bellaria (RN) [0541 346102; fax 346408; info@happycamping.it; www.happycamping.it]** Fr A14 exit Rimini Nord onto S16 N. Turn off dir San Mauro Mare & Bellaria Cagnona, foll sp Aquabell Waterpark. Over rlwy x-ing, turn R, site on L. Lge, mkd pitch, hdstg, pt sl, pt shd; wc (some cont); chem disp; mv service pnt; baby facs; fam bthrm; shwrs inc; EHU (8-10A) €3.50; gas; lndry (inc dryer); shop; rest, snacks; bar; playgrnd; pool; paddling pool; sand beach adj; tennis; games area; games rm; wifi; TV; 40% statics; dogs €6; phone; poss cr & noisy; ltd Eng spkn; adv bkg; red LS; CKE/CCI. "Conv Rimini, San Marino; variable size pitches; clean, private beach; pool clsd 1300-1530 & after 1900; lge shopping cent & cinema complex 2km; Bellaria pleasant resort with port & marina." € 39.00   2012*

BELLARIA *2E2* (1.5km NW Coastal/Urban) *44.16235, 12.44231* **Camping Green, Via Vespucci 8, 47030 San Mauro-Mare (FO) [tel/fax 0541 341225; info@campinggreen.it; www.campinggreen.it]** Exit A14/E55 at Rimini Nord onto S16. Foll sp N to San Mauro-Mare, site sp. Med, shd; wc; chem disp; mv service pnt; shwrs inc; EHU (6A) €2.50; gas; lndry; shop 200m; rest 100m; playgrnd; sand beach adj; watersports; bike hire; wifi; some statics; dogs €4; poss cr; quiet but some rlwy noise. "Excel, family-run, friendly site." ♦ 9 Apr-24 Sep. € 27.50   2011*

BELVEDERE DI GRADO see Aquileia *2E1*

BERGAMO *2C1* (25km N Rural) *45.78866, 9.94705* **Camping La Tartufaia, Via Nazionale 2519, 24060 Ranzanico al Lago di Endine [tel/fax 39 035 819 259; info@latartufaia.com; www.latartufaia.com]** Fr A4 Milan-Venice, exit at Seriate. Take SS42 dir Lovere. Campsite on L past Ranzanico exit. Med, mkd pitch, hdstg, terr, pt shd; wc; chem disp; mv service pnt; shwr; EHU (6A) inc; gas; lndry (inc dryer); shop 50m; rest; snacks; bar; BBQ; pool; beach adj; sw adj; games rm; wifi; dogs; bus adj; twin axles; Eng spkn; ccard acc; red LS; CCI. "Excel site; beautiful views over lake & mountains; gd bus conns; footpath around lake; v friendly & helpful owners." ♦ 25 Apr-21 Sep. € 42.50   2014*

BEVAGNA *2E3* (4.5km SW Rural) *42.91236, 12.58622* **Camping Pian di Boccio, Via Pian de Boccio 10, 06031 Bevagna [0742 360 164; fax 360 391; info@piandiboccio.com; www.piandiboccio.com]** Fr Foligno to Bevagna in c'van strt on S316 & turn R after 3km, foll signs. In car - just past Bevagna 1st rd on the R past the bdge. Med, hdg pitch, pt sl, hdstg, terr, shd; wc; chem disp; mv service pnt; shwrs; EHU (6A); lndry; rest; bar; playgrnd; htd pool; paddling pool; games area; games rm; wifi; dogs; phone; bus 2km; Eng spkn; adv bkg; quiet. "Excel site; beautiful location; conv for Assis and historic hill towns; dated san facs." ♦ ltd. 1 Apr-30 Sep. € 26.50   2015*

"I like to fill in the reports as I travel from site to site"

You'll find report forms at the back of this guide, or you can fill them in online at www.caravanclub.co.uk/europereport.

BIBIONE *2E1* (6km W Coastal) *45.63055, 12.99444* **Camping Village Capalonga, Viale della Laguna 16, 30020 Bibione-Pineda (VE) [0431 438351 or 0431 447190 LS; fax 438370 or 0431 438986 LS; capalonga@bibionemare.com; www.capalonga.com]** Well sp approx 6km fr Bibione dir Bibione Pineda. V lge, shd; wc (some cont); chem disp; mv service pnt; baby facs (on request); shwrs inc; EHU (10A) inc; gas; lndry; shop; rest, snacks; bar; BBQ; playgrnd; pool; private Blue Flag sand beach adj; watersports; fishing; tennis; archery; bike hire nrby; horseriding 6km; golf 10km; games rm; excursions; various activities; wifi; entmnt; TV; 25% statics; no dogs; no o'fits over 10m high ssn; phone; adv bkg; quiet; ccard acc; red LS. "Well-organised site; gd for families; extra for pitches on beach; spacious, clean san facs; rest o'looking lagoon; voracious mosquitoes!" ♦ 24 Apr-21 Sep. € 52.00 SBS - Y15   2011*

⊞ **BOBBIO** *1C2* (1.5km S Rural) *44.75340, 9.38456* **Camping PonteGobbo Terme, Via San Martino 4, 29022 Bobbio (PC) [0523 936927 or 0523 936068; fax 960610; camping. pontegobbe@iol.it; www.campingpontegobbo.com]** Heading twd Genova on S45 turn L on long bdge & immed R. Site sp. Lge, pt sl, shd; htd wc (some cont); chem disp; shwrs €0.50; EHU (4A) €2; gas; shop & 1km; bar; playgrnd; games area; entmnt; TV; 40% statics; phone; sep car park; No dogs; Eng spkn; no adv bkg; quiet; ccard acc; red LS/CKE/CCI. "Trout-fishing in rv; gd scenery; lovely town; hot water to shwrs only; rvside walks and cycling." ♦ € 21.50   2013*

BOGLIASCO see Genova *1C2*

BOLOGNA *1D2* (2km NE Rural) *44.52333, 11.37388*
Centro Turistico Campeggio Città di Bologna, Via Romita 12/4a, 40127 Bologna [051 325016; fax 325318; info@hotelcamping.com; www.hotelcamping.com] Access is fr A14 Bologna to Ancona. Leave at junc 7 sp Fiera & Via Stalingrado. Can be accessed fr the parallel 'Tangenziale' at same junc. Sp at 1st junc after toll. Med, mkd pitch, pt shd; htd wc; chem disp; mv service pnt; shwrs inc; EHU (6A) inc; lndry (inc dryer); shop; supmkt nrby; rest, snacks; bar; BBQ (charcoal/gas); playgrnd; pool; fitness cent; games rm; wifi; TV rm; dogs €2; no o'fits over 15m on hdstg & over 9m on grass; bus to city; site clsd 20 Dec-9 Jan; Eng spkn; adv bkg; some rd & aircraft noise; ccard acc; red LS/long stay/CKE/CCI. "Conv Bologna Trade Fair & Exhibition cent; friendly, helpful staff; excel, clean san facs; excel pool; tourist pitches at rear nr san facs block; gd bus service fr ent into city; access to pitches poss diff lge o'fits; Sat Nav dir may take you down narr rds; poss lots mosquitoes; excel site." ♦ 26 Jan-19 Dec. € 44.00 SBS - Y14   2014*

BOLSENA *1D3* (2km S Rural) *42.62722, 11.99444* **Camping Village Lido di Bolsena, Via Cassia, Km 111, 01023 Bolsena (VT) [0761 799258; fax 796105; info@bolsenacamping.it; www.bolsenacamping.it]** Fr S on a'strada A1 foll sp Viterbo & Lago di Bolsena, then take SR2 N to site; sp. Fr N exit A1 at Orvieto onto SS71 to Bolsena. At traff lts in cent of town turn L, site on R in approx 2km. V lge, pt shd; wc; chem disp; mv service pnt; private bthrms avail; shwrs €0.50; EHU (3A) inc (poss rev pol); gas; lndry (inc dryer); shop; rest, snacks; bar; playgrnd; pool; private sand beach adj; lake sw; watersports; tennis; bike hire; games area; entmnt; some statics; phone; sep car park; Eng spkn; adv bkg; quiet; ccard not acc. "Beautiful lakeside location; gd size pitches; all facs excel; cycle path around lake to town; sm dogs acc; charge for pool." 20 Apr-30 Sep. € 44.50   2014*

BOLSENA *1D3* (1.8km SW Rural) *42.63039, 11.99802*
Camping Le Calle, Via Cassia, Km 111.2, 01023 Bolsena (VT) [0761 797041] On S2 bet Lido Camping Vill & Camping Blu, ent by Fornacella rest. Sm, mkd pitch, pt shd; wc; chem disp; mv service pnt; shwrs inc; EHU (6A) inc; lndry rm; rest adj; lake sw & beach adj; dogs €2; adv bkg; quiet; CKE/CCI. "Family-run CL-type 'Agrituristico' site; friendly, helpful owners offer own produce inc wine & olive oil; vg san facs; foot/cycle path to Bolsena; excel sm site." ♦ 1 Mar-31 Oct. € 17.00   2015*

BOLSENA *1D3* (6km W Rural) *42.65340, 11.93120* **Camping Valdisole, Via Cassia, Km 117, 01023 Bolsena (VT) [tel/ fax 0761 797064 or 03349 952575 LS; valdisolecamping@ virgillio.it; www.campingvaldisole.com]** Fr N on A1 exit Orvieta & foll S71 to junc with S74; turn R twd San Lorenzo Nuovo. Then take S2 (Via Cassia) to site on R, 10km after San Lorenzo Nuovo. Fr S exit at Orte onto S204 sp Viterbo, then S2 Via Cassia N dir Montefiascone & Bolsena. Thro town & site in approx 500m after g'ge. Lge, mkd pitch, shd; wc (cont); chem disp; shwrs inc; EHU (8A) inc (check pol); gas; lndry; shop; rest, snacks; pizzeria adj; bar; BBQ; playgrnd; lake sw & (black) sand beach; fishing; watersports; horseriding 5km; golf 500m; guided walks 5km; wifi; games/TV rm; dogs; Eng spkn; adv bkg rec Jul/Aug; poss noisy high ssn; ccard acc; red LS/CKE/CCI. "Beautiful location; charming owners; lge grassed pitches, shd or sunny (poss dusty high ssn); vg san facs; easy transport Rome, Siena & Orvieto; rallies welcome; mkt Tues." ♦ 1 May-30 Sep. € 33.00   2009*

BOLZANO/BOZEN *1D1* (10km S Rural) *46.42982, 11.34357*
Camping-Park Steiner, Kennedystrasse 32, 39055 Laives/ Leifers (BZ) [0471 950105; fax 593141; info@campingsteiner. com; www.campingsteiner.com] Fr N take Bolzano/Bozen-Sud exit fr A22/E45 & pick up rd S12 twd Trento to site; site on R on ent Laives at N edge of vill. Fr S leave A22 at junc for Egna onto rd S12 dir Bolzano. Poorly sp. Lge, hdg/mkd pitch, pt sl; shd; htd wc; (some cont) chem disp; mv service pnt; baby facs; shwrs inc; EHU (6A) inc; gas; lndry; shop; rest, snacks; pizzeria; bar; playgrnd; 2 pools (1 covrd); bike hire; wifi; TV; some statics; dogs €5, no dogs hg ssn; phone; Eng spkn; adv bkg rec; some rd & rlwy noise; CKE/CCI. "Pleasant, well-run, excel site on edge of Dolomites; attractive pitches; helpful staff; gd clean, modern san facs; gates clsd 1300-1500 & 2200-0700; beautiful area; vg walking; well stocked shop; highly rec; easy 5 min walk into town; excel rest; busy in high ssn; excel value transport passes fr TO." ♦ 5 Apr-31 Oct. € 37.00   2014*

⊞ **BOLZANO/BOZEN** *1D1* (2km NW Rural) *46.50333, 11.3000* **Camping Moosbauer, Via San Maurizio 83, 39100 Bolzano [0471 918492; fax 204894; info@moosbauer.com; www.moosbauer.com]** Exit A22/E45 at Bolzano Sud exit & take S38 N dir Merano (keep L after toll booths). After tunnel take 1st exit sp Eppan & hospital, & turn L at top of feeder rd sp Bolzano. After approx 2km at island past 08 G'ge turn L & foll site sp. Site on R in 1km by bus stop on S38, sp. Med, hdg/ mkd pitch, hdstg, pt sl, pt shd; htd wc; chem disp; mv service pnt; serviced pitches; baby facs; shwrs inc; EHU (5A) inc; lndry; shop; rest, snacks; bar; playgrnd; htd pool; games rm; cab/ sat TV; entmnt; dogs €4; bus; poss cr; Eng spkn; adv bkg; quiet but some rd noise; CKE/CCI. "Popular, well-maintained, attractive site; gd welcome fr friendly owners; pitches narr; excel, modern san facs; gate shut 1300-1500; bus service adj for archaeological museum (unique ice man); gd cent for walks in Dolomites." ♦ ltd. € 34.00   2012*

⊞ **BOMBA** *2F4* (2km W Rural) *42.0175, 14.36138*
Campeggio Isola Verde, Via del Lago 2, 66042 Bomba (CH) [0872 860475; fax 860450; isolaverde@tin.it; www.isolaverdeonline.it] Exit A14 at Val di Sangro exit & take S652 for Bomba. Site clearly sp. Med, some hdstg, terr, pt shd; wc; chem disp; shwrs inc; EHU (10A) inc; shop; rest, snacks; bar; playgrnd; pool; lake sw & beach; tennis; bike hire; entmnt; 50% statics; dogs; bus/train 500m; Eng spkn; adv bkg; quiet; ccard acc. "Excel position above lake in beautiful countryside; gd base winter sports; excel rest." € 38.00   2011*

BORGO SAN LORENZO *1D3* (7km SE Rural) *43.93087, 11.46426*
Camping Vicchio Ponte, Via Costoli 16, 50039 Vicchio [055 8448306; fax 579405; info@campingvecchioponte.it; www.campingvecchioponte.it] On SP551 adj to sw pool in Vicchio. Med, pt shd; wc (cont); chem disp; mv service pnt; shwrs inc; EHU (4A) inc; lndry rm; shop, rest, bar in vill; htd pool adj; dogs; train to Florence 1km; poss cr; Eng spkn; quiet; CKE/CCI. "Simple, municipal site." 1 Jun-15 Sep. € 24.00   2009*

ITALY

BORGO SAN LORENZO *1D3* (5km W Rural) *43.96144, 11.30918*
**Camping Mugello Verde, Via Massorondinaio 39, 50037 San
Piero-a-Sieve (FI) [055 848511; fax 8486910; mugelloverde@
florencecamping.com; www.florencecamping.com]**
Exit A1 at Barberino exit & foll Barberino sp twd San Piero-a-
Sieve & Borgo San Lorenzo. Turn S on S65 twd Florence. Site
sp immed after Cafaggiolo. Lge, sl, terr, pt shd; htd wc (some
cont); chem disp; mv service pnt; shwrs inc; EHU (6A) inc; gas;
lndry (inc dryer); shop; rest, snacks; bar; playgrnd; pool (bathing
caps req); tennis; bike hire; wifi; entmnt; 50% statics; bus/
train; no adv bkg; quiet; ccard acc; red LS; CKE/CCI. "Hillside
site; bus to Florence high ssn (fr vill LS) or 20 mins drive; hard
grnd diff for awnings; poss long walk to recep & shop; helpful,
friendly staff; refurbed, gd, clean san facs; avoid early Jun -
Italian Grand Prix!." ♦ 15 Mar-30 Oct. € 42.00   2014*

BOTTAI see Firenze *1D3*

BRACCIANO *2E4* (3km N Rural) *42.1300, 12.17333* **Kwan
Village Roma Flash Sporting, Via Settevene Palo 42,
00062 Bracciano [tel/fax 0699 805458 or 3389 951738 LS;
info@romaflash.it; www.romaflash.it]**
Fr A1 exit at Magliano Sabina dir Civita Castellana. Then foll
sp Nepi, Sutri, Trevignano & Bracciano. Sp on lakeside rd N of
Bracciano. Lge, mkd pitch, pt shd; wc (some cont); chem disp;
mv service pnt; baby facs; sauna; shwrs inc; EHU (6A) inc; lndry
(inc dryer); shop high ssn; rest, snacks; bar; BBQ (charcoal, gas);
playgrnd; pool; lake sw & free beach; fitness cent; watersports;
fishing; horseriding 4km; tennis; bike hire; games rm; wifi;
entmnt; TV; 5% statics; dogs €5.50; no o'fits over 12m; shuttle
bus to Bracciano; bus/train to Rome; sep car park; Eng spkn;
quiet; ccard acc; red LS. "Attractive, well-kept lakeside site;
clean, modern san facs; conv Rome." ♦ 1 Apr-29 Sep. € 42.00
(CChq acc) SBS - Y16   2012*

BRACCIANO *2E4* (8km N Rural) *42.14673, 12.26905*
**Camping Internazionale Lago di Bracciano, Via Del
Pianoro 4, 00069 Trevignano-Romano (RM) [0699 85032;
fax 826781; robertocarrano@tin.it; www.camping-inter-
lagodibracciano.com]** Fr SS2 exit at Lake Bracciano & cont
twd Trevignano then Anguillara. Site on lakeside at end of
lane. Lge, pt shd; wc (some cont); chem disp; mv service pnt;
shwrs; EHU (3-6A) inc; lndry (inc dryer); shop; rest, snacks;
cooking facs; playgrnd; paddling pool; bike hire; games area;
internet; TV rm; 20% statics; dogs €3.70; adv bkg; quiet; ccard
acc. "Set in Due Laghi Nature Park; peaceful." 1 Apr-30 Sep.
€ 28.00   2009*

BRACCIANO *2E4* (1.5km SE Rural) *42.10505, 12.18595*
**Camping Porticciolo, Via Porticciolo, 00062 Bracciano
[06 99803060; fax 99803030; info@porticciolo.it;
www.porticciolo.it]** Avoid town cent. Fr Rome circular rd
take S2 dir Viterbo, then Anguillara & dir Bracciano. Keep to
lakeside; at traff lts turn twds town & after rlwy bdge turn
immed R & foll site sp. Avoid town cent. Med, hdg/mkd pitch,
shd; wc; chem disp; shwrs €0.50; EHU (3-6A) €3.40-5; lndry;
shop; rest, snacks; bar; playgrnd; shgl beach & lake adj; sand
beach 15km; sailing; watersports; wifi; 10% statics; dogs
€4.50; sep car park Jul/Aug; site bus to stn; excursions; Eng
spkn; adv bkg; quiet; red LS/long stay; ccard acc; CKE/CCI.
"Lovely position on lakeside; gd base for touring; frequent
trains to Rome fr Bracciano; new, modern san facs; lge pitches;
haphazard site layout; vg." ♦ 1 Apr-30 Sep. € 26.00   2010*

BRESSANONE/BRIXEN *1D1* (1km SE Rural) *46.73472, 11.64555*
**Camping Löwenhof, Brennerstrasse 60, 39040 Varna/Vahrn
(BZ) [0472 836216; fax 801337; info@loewenhof.it;
www.loewenhof.it]** On main Brenner rd SS12 at 481km
mark, on R at minor rd junc adj hotel; easily seen fr main rd.
Sm, mkd pitch, wc; shwrs inc; EHU (4A) €2; lndry; shop &
2km; rest, snacks; bar; htd pool; paddling pool; hotel sauna,
solarium, whirlpool & steambaths avail for use; tennis; games
rm; bike hire; dogs €5 (not acc Jul/Aug); poss cr; Eng spkn; adv
bkg; quiet but rd noise behind hotel; red LS/long stay/CKE/CCI.
"Vg." 1 Apr-30 Oct. € 33.00   2009*

BRIATICO *3B4* (W Coastal) *38.72378, 16.02538*
**Villaggio Camping L'Africano, 89817 Briatico (VV)
[tel/fax 0699 805458; info@villaggiocampinglafricano.
it; www.villaggiocampinglafricano.it]** Exit A3/E45 or S18
at Pizzo onto S522 W dir Tropea, site sp. Lge, pt shd; wc; mv
service pnt; shwrs inc; EHU €3; lndry; shop high ssn; rest high
ssn; rest, snacks; bar; pool; paddling pool; sand beach 200m;
games area; entmnt; TV rm; some statics; dogs €2; adv bkg;
quiet. 1 Apr-31 Oct. € 31.50   2009*

BRUNICO/BRUNECK *1D1* (10km E Rural) *46.77600, 12.03688*
**Camping Residence Corones, Niederrasen 145, 39030
Rasun-di-Sotto/Niederrasen (BZ) [0474 496490; fax 498250;
info@corones.com; www.corones.com]** On SS49 dir Rasun,
turn N to site to Antholz, bear L in front of Gasthof, over
bdge turn L, site in 400m. Med, pt shd; wc; chem disp; mv
service pnt; serviced pitches; sauna; shwrs inc; private bthrms
avail; EHU (3A) metered; gas; lndry; shop; rest, snacks; bar;
playgrnd; htd pool; paddling pool; tennis; games area; bike
hire; solarium; some statics; dogs €4.20; phone; Eng spkn; adv
bkg; quiet; ccard acc (poss not in rest); red LS. "Gd cent for
walking & skiing - outings arranged; superb facs, inc in winter;
conv day visit to Dolomites; helpful owner & staff; excel." ♦
1 Dec-19 Apr & 20 May-25 Oct. € 33.00   2013*

BRUNICO/BRUNECK *1D1* (8km W Rural) *46.80805, 11.81305*
**Camping Gisser, Via Val Pusteria 26, San Sigismondo,
39030 Chienes/Kiens (BZ) [0474 569605; fax 569657;
camping@hotelgisser.it; www.hotelgisser.it]**
On SS49 at 20.8km post in San Sigismondo. Lge, pt sl, pt
shd; wc; shwrs inc; EHU (5A) €2; lndry; shop 100m; rest,
snacks; bar; htd pool; canoeing; dogs €2.50; no adv bkg;
quiet. "NH en rte Venice; ltd facs LS & basic." 1 May-15 Oct.
€ 22.00   2009*

CALCERANICA AL LAGO see Levico Terme *1D1*

⊞ **CANAZEI** *1D1* (500m SE Rural) *46.47326, 11.77586*
**Camping Marmolada, Via Pareda 60, 38032 Canazei (TN)
[0462 601660; fax 601722; campingmarmolada@virgilio.it;
www.campingmarmolada.com]** On R bank of Rv Avisio on
rd S641. Sp fr cent of Canazei. Lge, hdstg, pt shd; wc; chem
disp; shwrs; EHU (4A) €3; lndry (inc dryer); snacks; bar; BBQ;
htd pool adj; 45% statics; dogs €3; winter ski cent; poss cr;
Eng spkn; no adv bkg ess high ssn; poss noisy high ssn; ccard
acc. "Opp cable car & stn; gd for walking/skiing; excel views all
round; vg san facs; 10 min walk to town." € 36.00   2010*

CANAZEI *1D1* (2km W Rural) *46.47479, 11.74067* **Camping Miravalle, Strèda de Greva 39, 38031 Campitello-di-Fassa (TN) [0462 750502; fax 751563; info@campingmiravalle.it; www.campingmiravalle.it]** In vill cent on rte 48 site sp down side rd. Lge, sl, unshd; wc; chem disp; mv service pnt; baby facs; shwrs inc; EHU (6A) inc (poss rev pol), extra €2 for 6A; lndry; shop 100m; rest, snacks; 100m; bar; dogs €4; poss cr; Eng spkn; adv bkg; quiet; ccard acc; CKE/CCI. "Excel new san facs 2015; conv cable car." ♦ 1 Jan- 30 Mar, 1 Jun-30 Sep & 1 Dec-31 Dec. € 37.00   2015*

CANNIGIONE see Arzachena (Sardinia) *1C4*

CANNOBIO *1C1* (1km N Rural) *46.07791, 8.69345* **Villaggio Camping Bosco, Punta Bragone, 28822 Cannobio (VB) [0323 71597; fax 739647; bosco@boschettoholiday.it; www.boschettoholiday.it/bosco]** On W side of lakeshore rd bet Cannobio & Swiss frontier. Sh steep app to site & hairpin bend fr narr rd, unsuitable for car/c'van o'fits & diff for m'vans. Med, terr, pt shd; wc; chem disp; shwrs €0.50; EHU (3A) €3.50; gas; lndry; shop; BBQ; bar; playgrnd; private shgl beach; lake sw; dogs €3.50; Eng spkn; adv bkg - ess in high ssn; quiet; CKE/CCI. "All pitches with magnificent lake view; beautiful town; hot water to shwrs only." ♦ 1 Apr-30 Sep. € 28.50 (CChq acc)   2011*

CANNOBIO *1C1* (1.5km N Urban) *46.07136, 8.69366* **Camping Campagna, Via Casali Darbedo, 20-22 - 28822 Cannobio (VB) [0323 70100; fax 72398 or 0323 71190; info@campingcampagna.it; www.campingcampagna. it]** Brissago-Cannobio rd, site on L on ent town. Med, shd; wc; mv service pnt; shwrs inc; EHU (6-10A) €4.; gas; lndry; shop; rest, snacks; bar; shgl beach; some statics; dogs €5.; poss cr; Eng spkn; adv bkg; quiet. "Steamer trips on Lake Maggiore; vg Sunday mkt in Cannobio; vg, modern facs; friendly staff; clean; friendly staff; fabulous views of lake." ♦ 15 Mar-15 Nov. € 47.00   2013*

CANNOBIO *1C1* (200m N Rural) *46.06515, 8.6905* **Camping Riviera, Via Casali Darbedo 2, 28822 Cannobio (VB) [tel/fax 0323 71360; riviera@riviera-valleromantica.com; www.riviera-valleromantica.com]** N of Cannobio twd Switzerland on main rd. Over rv at o'skts of town, site ent on R in 30m; sp. Lge, hdg/mkd pitch, shd; wc; chem disp; mv service pnt; private san facs some pitches; shwrs inc; EHU (4A) €4; gas; lndry; shop; rest, snacks; bar; playgrnd; private shgl beach & lake sw adj; boat hire; windsurfing; some statics; dogs €4.50; poss cr; adv bkg. "Popular, peaceful, well-maintained site bet rv & lake; extra for lakeside pitch; gd sailing; v helpful staff." ♦ 1 Apr-18 Oct. € 47.00   2013*

CANNOBIO *1C1* (500m N Urban) *46.06678, 8.69507* **Camping Del Sole, Via Sotto i Chiosi 81/A, 28822 Cannobio (VB) [0323 70732; fax 72387; info@campingsole.it; www.campingsole.it]** Fr S fr A26 foll Verbania sp then sp Cannobio or Locarno. Ent vill, over cobbles, 2nd R in 750m. Bef rv bdge immed sharp R under main rd, site on L after quick R turn. Fr N ent Cannobio, 1st L after x-ing rv, then as above. Lge, hdg/mkd pitch, hdstg, pt shd; wc; chem disp; mv service pnt; shwrs inc; EHU (4A) €3; gas; lndry; supmkt 150m; rest; snacks; bar; playgrnd; pool; shgl beach & lake sw 250m; wifi; 60% statics; dogs €3; poss cr; Eng spkn; poss noisy; red long stay/LS; CKE/CCI. "Attractive vill & lake frontage; friendly, family-run site; poss tight access some pitches; lovely pool area; cramped pitches; diff to park m'van; dated clean san facs; close to town; fair." 1 Mar-2 Nov. € 31.00   2014*

CANNOBIO *1C1* (1.5km SW Rural) *46.05756, 8.67831* **Camping Valle Romantica, Via Valle Cannobina, 28822 Cannobio (VB) [tel/fax 0323 71249; valleromantica@ riviera-valleromantica.com; www.riviera-valleromantica. com]** Turn W on S o'skirts of Cannobio, sp Valle Cannobina. In 1.5km at fork keep L. Site immed on R. On ent site cont to bottom of hill to park & walk back to recep. Lge, hdg/mkd pitch, pt sl, terr, pt shd; wc; chem disp; mv service pnt; shwrs inc; EHU (4-6A) €4; lndry; shop; rest, snacks; bar; playgrnd; pool; golf 12km; 25% statics; dogs €4; adv bkg; quiet. "Vg; some sm pitches; particularly helpful staff; narr site rds poss diff m'vans; masses of flowers; beautiful situation; footpath to town, poss cr high ssn." ♦ 24 Mar-30 Sep. € 32.00   2011*

CA'NOGHERA see Mestre *2E2*

CAORLE *2E2* (3km SW Coastal) *45.57388, 12.81166* **Centro Vacanze Pra' delle Torri, Via Altanea 201, 30021 Caorle (VE) [0421 299063; fax 299035; torri@vacanze-natura.it; www.pradelletorri.it]** Fr A4 exit dir Santo Stino di Livenza, then foll sp Caorle & Porto Santa Margherita. by-pass town & cont on coast rd. Site clearly sp on L. V lge, shd, mkd pitch, serviced pitch; wc (some cont); mv service pnt; chem disp; baby facs; shwrs inc; EHU (5A) inc; lndry; shop; snacks; rest; shop; htd pool complex; sand beach; boat hire; windsurfing; tennis; bike hire; games area; car wash; internet; entmnt; 30% statics; phone; no dogs; poss cr; adv bkg (min 3 nts); quiet; red snr citizens; ccard acc. "Extensive, excel sport & entmnt facs for children; lge water park inc; entmnt inc; excel family holiday cent." ♦ 4 Apr-27 Sep. € 42.00   2009*

CAORLE *2E2* (5km SW Coastal) *45.56694, 12.79416* **Camping Villaggio San Francesco, Via Selva Rosata 1, Duna Verde, 30020 Porto-Santa-Margherita (VE) [0421 299333; fax 299284; info@villaggiostrancesco.com; www.villaggiosfrancesco.com]** Fr A4/E70 exit Santo Stino di Livenza, then dir Caorle. By-pass town & cont on coast rd, site sp on L. V lge, shd; wc (some cont); chem disp; mv service pnt; baby facs; shwrs inc; EHU (6A) inc; gas; lndry (inc dryer); shop; 3 rests; snacks; bar; 5 pools; waterslide; private beach adj; boat hire; windsurfing; waterskiing; tennis; games area; games rm; bike hire; solarium; internet; entmnt; TV; 60% statics; dogs €3; phone; min 2 nights' stay; poss cr; quiet; ccard not acc; red snr citizens/CKE/CCI. "Excel family facs." ♦ 24 Apr-25 Sep. € 44.60 (CChq acc)   2009*

CAPALBIO *1D3* (8km S Coastal) *42.38086, 11.44660* **Campeggio di Capalbio, Strada del Chiarone, Loc Graticciala, 58010 Capalbio (GR) [0564 890101; fax 890437; mauro.ricci@ilcampeggiodicapalbio.it; www.ilcampeggiodicapalbio.it]** Exit SS1 heading S twd Rome at sp Chiarone Scalo twd sea. Cross rlwy, site sp. Lge, mkd pitch, pt sl, shd; wc (some cont); mv service pnt; shwrs; EHU (3-5A); gas; lndry (inc dryer); shop; rest, snacks; bar; BBQ; playgrnd; sand beach adj; bike hire; games area; entmnt; 70% statics; no dogs; sep car park; poss cr; adv bkg; quiet; ccard acc. "Narr lanes, diff for lge o'fits without mover." 10 Apr-4 Oct. € 47.00   2011*

CAPANNOLE see Montevarchi *1D3*

CAPRAROLA 2E4 (6km NW Rural) 42.33504, 12.20488 **Camping Natura, Loc Sciente Le Coste, 01032 Caprarola (VT) [tel/fax 0761 612347; info@camping-natura.com; www.camping-natura.com]** Fr Viterbo take Via Cimina sp Ronciglione. After approx 19km bef Ronciglione turn R sp Nature Reserve Lago di Vico, in 200m turn R, site sp on R in 3km. Med, mkd pitch, pt shd; wc; chem disp; mv service pnt; shwrs; EHU (4A) €3; shop; rest, snacks; bar; lake sw adj; dogs €3; quiet; red LS; ccard acc. "Friendly site; guided walks in nature reserve; run down LS & ltd facs." Easter-30 Sep. € 18.00   2012*

CARLAZZO see Porlezza 1C1

CAROVIGNO 3A4 (5km N Coastal) 40.76643, 17.67850 **Camping Villaggio Lamaforca, SS379, Km 25, Contrada da Mindelli, 72012 Carovigno (BR) [0831 968496; fax 968070; informazioni@lamaforca.it; www.lamaforca.it]** Exit SS379 sp Torre Pozella, site sp. Lge, pt shd; wc; mv service pnt; baby facs; shwrs inc; EHU inc; lndry; shop; rest, snacks; bar; playgrnd; pool; paddling pool; waterslide; sand beach adj; bike hire; games rm; TV rm; 70% statics; dogs €2.50; phone; adv bkg; quiet; ccard acc; red LS/snr citizens. "Conv Brindisi, Ostuni." ♦ 1 Apr-18 Sep. € 39.00   2009*

CASAL BORSETTI see Marina di Ravenna 2E2

CASALBORDINO 2F4 (7km NE Coastal) 42.20018, 14.60897 **Camping Village Santo Stefano, S16, Km 498, 66020 Marina-di-Casalbordino (CH) [0873 918118; fax 918193; info@campingsantostefano.com; www.campingsanto stefano.com]** Exit A14 Vasto N onto S16 dir Pescara, site at km 498 on R. Med, mkd pitch, shd; wc; chem disp; shwrs inc; EHU (6A) inc; shop; rest, snacks; bar; playgrnd; pool; paddling pool; beach adj; entmnt; 10% statics; no dogs; Eng spkn; adv bkg; quiet but some rlwy noise; CKE/CCI. "Pleasant, well-maintained, family-run site; sm pitches; beautiful private beach & pool area; gd rest." 24 Apr-12 Sep. € 41.00   2014*

> ## "We must tell The Club about that great site we found"
> Get your site reports in by mid-August and we'll do our best to get your updates into the next edition.

CA'SAVIO see Punta Sabbioni 2E2

⊞ **CASSA, LA** 1B2 (600m N Rural) 45.18689, 7.51599 **Camping Club Le Betulle (Naturist), Via Lanzo 33, 10040 La Cassa (TO) [011 9842962; fax 9842819; info@lebetulle. org; www.lebetulle.org]** Exit Turin by-pass at Collegno & foll sp Pianezza. In 200m bear R at traff lts sp San Gillio & La Cassa. In La Cassa foll sp Fiano, site on L. Site is 25km fr Turin cent. Lge, hdstg, pt sl, pt shd; htd wc (some cont); chem disp (wc); baby facs; fam bthrm; shwrs inc; EHU (16A) inc; lndry; shop 600m; rest, snacks; bar; playgrnd; pool; TV rm; 90% statics; dogs €2; poss cr; Eng spkn; adv bkg; INF card. "Friendly staff." € 38.00   2011*

CASSONE see Malcesine 1D1

⊞ **CASTEL DEL PIANO** 1D3 (500m S Urban) 42.88454, 11.53646 **Camping Residence Amiata, Via Roma 15, Montoto, 58033 Castel-del-Piano (GR) [0564 956260; fax 955107; info@amiata.org; www.amiata.org]** Fr Siena on S223 to Paganico. Turn L (via overpass) twd Castel del Piano. On reaching town, turn R, sp Ospedale (Hospital). Strt over rndabt site on R up hill (1km). Lge, hdg/mkd pitch, hdstg, shd; htd wc; chem disp; mv service pnt; baby facs; shwrs; EHU (3-6A) inc; gas; lndry (inc dryer); shop & 1km; rest, snacks; bar; BBQ; playgrnd; pool 3km; games area; solarium; TV rm; some statics; dogs €2.70; poss cr; Eng spkn; adv bkg; quiet; ccard acc; red long stay; red CKE/CCI. "Friendly owners; dated san facs; lovely views; excel touring base medieval towns & vills." ♦ € 22.00 (CChq acc)   2010*

CASTELDIMEZZO see Pesaro 2E3

CASTELLETTO SOPRA TICINO see Sesto Calende 1B1

CASTELLINA IN CHIANTI see Poggibonsi 1D3

CASTELSANTANGELO SUL NERA 2E3 (4km S Rural) 42.88223, 13.18181 **Camping Monte Prata, Loc. Schianceto, 62030 Castel S Angelo Sul Nera [07 37 97 00 62 or 33 32 95 18 60 (mob); sostare@ campingmonteprata.it; www.campingmonteprata.it]** Fr SP209 Muccia-Visso. Thro Visso on the Strada Provinciale 134 twds Castelsantangelo Sur Nera. Aft vill slight R onto SP 136. Campsite on L after vill of Gualdo. Med, mkd pitch, hdstg, terr, pt shd; htd wc; chem disp; mv service pnt; shwrs inc; EHU; lndry (inc dryer); shop; rest; snacks; bar; BBQ; playgrnd; games area; 0% statics; dogs; Eng spkn; quiet; ccard acc. "Gd site; excel position nr top of Monte Prata; guided walks & other excursions fr site in Nat Park." ♦ 15 Jun-15 Sep. € 29.50   2014*

CASTIGLIONE DEL LAGO 2E3 (6km N Rural) 43.18028, 12.0163 **Camping Badiaccia, Via Pratovecchio 1, 06061 Castiglione-del-Lago (PG) [0759 659097; fax 659019; info@badiaccia.com; www.badiaccia.com]** Leave A1 m'way at Val-di-Chiana exit & foll sp for Castiglione-del-Lago. Site on L immed past Shell g'ge. Lge, mkd pitch, sl, pt shd; wc (cont); chem disp; mv service pnt; baby facs; shwrs inc; EHU (4A) inc; gas; lndry (inc dryer); shop; rest, snacks; bar; BBQ; playgrnd; 2 pools; lake sw; boat & bike hire; windsurfing; tennis; games area; wifi; 10% statics; dogs €2.50; adv bkg ess; quiet; red 7+ days. "Refurbished san facs; gd site." ♦ 1 Apr-30 Sep. € 25.00   2010*

CASTIGLIONE DEL LAGO 2E3 (500m N Rural) 43.13460, 12.04383 **Camping Listro, Via Lungolago, Lido Arezzo, 06061 Castiglione-del-Lago (PG) [tel/fax 075 951193; listro@listro.it; www.listro.it]** Fr N A1 Val di Chiana exit 75 bis Perugia, site clearly sp on N edge of town on lakeside. Med, mkd pitch, pt shd; wc; chem disp; mv service pnt; shwrs inc; EHU (3A) inc (poss rev pol); gas; lndry; shop & 500m; rest 200m; snacks; bar; playgrnd; pool nr; private sand beach & lake sw adj; tennis nr; bike hire; poss cr; Eng spkn; adv bkg; rd noise; ccard acc; red long stay/LS; CKE/CCI. "On W shore of Lake Trasimeno; facs stretched when site full; v helpful staff; bus to Perugia; rlwy stn 1km for train to Rome; 'tree fluff' a problem in spring." ♦ ltd. 1 Apr-30 Sep. € 18.70   2011*

Leading Camping in Europe

From the Scandinavian North to the deep South, on white sandy beaches or in the mountains – you'll find Leading Campings always at the nicest spots in continental Europe.

LeadingCampings means **first class camping** and it shows: spacious pitches, fully equipped. Flawless sanitary blocks at highest level. Pools, wellness and sports facilities. Well trained animation teams, gastronomy and leisure programs: all leading.

And, well, children are especially welcome.

We are looking forward welcoming you.

Get your personal LeadingCard at any LeadingCamping and profit from all its benefits. Visit us on internet, you are welcome!
www.leadingcampings.com

LeadingCampings · Kettelerstr. 26 · D-40593 Düsseldorf
info@leadingcampings.com · **www.leadingcampings.com**

LeadingCampings

CASTIGLIONE DELLA PESCAIA *1D3* (2km N Coastal) *42.77361, 10.84398* **Camping Maremma Sans Souci, Strada delle Collacchie, Casa Mora, 58043 Castiglione-della-Pescaia (GR) [0564 933765; fax 935759; info@maremmasanssouci.it; www.maremmasanssouci.it]** Exit SS1 Via Aurelia at Follonica onto SS322, site at km post 12, sp. Lge, mkd pitch, shd; wc; chem disp; mv service pnt; shwrs; EHU (3A) inc; lndry; shop; rest, snacks; bar; no BBQ; sand beach adj; TV; dogs €2 (not acc Jun-Aug); phone; sep car park; Eng spkn; adv bkg ess Jul-Aug; ccard acc; red LS. "Most pitches diff lge o'fits; lovely location; direct access to beach; poss mosquito problem." ♦ 1 Apr-31 Oct. € 43.00 (CChq acc)   2011*

CASTIGLIONE DELLA PESCAIA *1D3* (6km W Coastal) *42.77760, 10.79384* **Camping Village Baia Azzurra, Via delle Rocchette, 58043 Castiglione-della-Pescaia (GR) [0564 941092; fax 941242; info@baiaazzurra.it; www.baiaazzurra.it]** Fr Castiglione della Pescaia on S322, turn L sp Rocchette, site on R in 3km. Med, mkd pitch, shd; wc (some cont); chem disp; shwrs inc; EHU (3A) inc; gas; lndry; shop; rest nr; snacks; bar; no BBQ; playgrnd; pool high ssn; paddling pool; private sand beach adj; tennis; bike hire; wifi; entmnt; TV; 10% statics; dogs €6; phone; sep car park; bus; poss cr; Eng spkn; adv bkg; quiet; ccard acc; red LS. "Beautiful location; 24 hr security." ♦ 15 Apr-17 Oct. € 54.00 (CChq acc)   2011*

CAVALLINO *2E2* (2.5km S Coastal) *45.45710, 12.50702* **Camping Village Vela Blu, Via Radaelli 10, 30013 Cavallino (VE) [041 968068; fax 5371003; info@velablu.it; www.velablu.it]** Site sp on leaving Ca'ballarin. Lge, mkd pitch, pt shd; wc; chem disp; mv service pnt; 50% serviced pitches; baby facs; shwrs inc; EHU (6A) inc; lndry (inc dryer); shop; rest, snacks; bar; BBQ; playgrnd; private beach adj; bike hire; wifi; entmnt; sat TV; 50% statics; dogs €4.50; phone; poss cr; Eng spkn; adv bkg; ccard acc; red long stay/snr citizens; CKE/CCI. "Well-kept site; excel san facs; excel rest; gd facs for children; gd beach; bus/ferry tickets to Venice fr recep; friendly site." ♦ 30 Apr-30 Sep. € 33.00 (CChq acc)   2009*

CAVALLINO *2E2* (2.5km S Coastal) *45.46726, 12.53006* **Union Lido Park & Resort, Via Fausta 258, 30013 Cavallino (VE) [041 968080 or 2575111; fax 5370355; info@unionlido.com; www.unionlido.com]** Exit a'strada A4 (Mestre-Trieste) at exit for airport or Quarto d'Altino & foll sp for Jesolo & then Punta Sabbiono; site on L 2.5km after Cavallino. V lge, mkd pitch, shd; htd wc; chem disp; mv service pnt; 60% serviced pitches; baby facs; sauna; shwrs inc; EHU (6A) inc; gas; lndry (inc dryer); 30 shops & supmkt; 7 rests; snacks; bars; playgrnd; pools & children's lagoon with slides; dir access private beach; tennis; gym; golf; fishing; boating; horseriding; watersports; bike hire; skating rink; hairdressers; babysitting; wifi; entmnt; sat TV some pitches; late arr (after 2100) o'night parking area with EHU; church; banking facs; 1st aid cent; Italian lessons; wellness cent; 50% statics; no dogs; Eng spkn; adv bkg; ccard acc. "Variable pitch size & price; min stay 7 days in high ssn; some pitches soft sand (a spade useful!); many long-stay campers; no admissions 1230-1500 (poss busy w/end); excursions; varied entmnt programme high ssn inc firework displays; well-organised, well-run; clean facs; no need to leave site; worth every penny! excel." ♦ 30 Apr-26 Sep. € 48.00   2010*

See advertisement on previous page

CAVALLINO *2E2* (5km SW Coastal) *45.45638, 12.4960* **Camping Enzo Stella Maris, Via delle Batterie 100, 30010 Cavallino-Treporti (VE) [041 966030; fax 5300943; info@enzostellamaris.com; www.enzostellamaris.com]** Exit A4 at sp for airport. Foll sp Jesolo, Cavallino, Punta Sabbioni rd SW. Site sp after Ca'Ballarin. Lge, mkd pitch, pt shd; wc; chem disp; mv service pnt; baby facs; serviced pitches; shwrs inc; EHU (6A) inc; gas; lndry; shop; rest, snacks; bar; no BBQ; playgrnd; htd pool; sand beach adj; fitness rm; games area; wifi; entmnt; TV rm; 25% statics; no dogs; phone; clsd 1230-1600 & 2300-0700; poss cr; Eng spkn; no adv bkg; quiet; ccard acc; red snr citizens/long stay; CKE/CCI. "Well-run, friendly, family-owned site; excel facs; beware mosquitoes; indoor htd pool; wellness cent." ♦ 12 Apr-18 Oct. € 54.00   2014*

CAVALLINO *2E2* (5km SW Coastal) *45.45666, 12.50066* **Camping-Village Cavallino, Via delle Batterie, 164 - 30013 Cavallino-Treporti (VE) [041 966133; fax 5300827; info@campingcavallino.com www.baiaholiday.com]** Foll rd Jesolo/Cavallino, lge sp at L turn into camp. V lge, hdstg, pt shd; wc; chem disp; mv service pnt; serviced pitches; shwrs inc; EHU (6A) inc; lndry; supmkt; shop; rest, snacks; bar; playgrnd; 2 pools; sand beach adj; waterskiing; golf 2km; internet; entmnt; 25% statics; dogs €8; poss cr; adv bkg - ess in high ssn; quiet; red snr citizens. "Lovely, wooded, well-organised, clean site; gd facs; poss mosquito prob." ♦ 24 Mar-31 Oct. € 46.00   2011*

CAVALLINO *2E2* (6km SW Coastal) *45.44872, 12.47116* **Camping Dei Fiori, Via Vettor Pisani 52, 30010 Cavallino-Treporti (VE) [041 966448; fax 966724; fiori@vacanze-natura.it; www.deifiori.it]** Fr Lido di Jesolo foll sp to Cavallino; site on L approx 6km past Cavallino & bef Ca'Vio. Lge, mkd pitch, shd; wc; chem disp; mv service pnt; serviced pitch; shwrs inc; EHU (5A) inc (poss rev pol); gas; lndry; shop; supmkt; rest, snacks; bar; playgrnd; pool; sand beach adj; hydro massage; games area; entmnt; internet; no dogs; Eng spkn; adv bkg ess Jul/Aug; quiet; ccard acc; red snr citizens/long stay. "V clean & quiet even in Aug; excel facs & amenities; conv water bus stop at Port Sabbioni; 3/5 day min stay med/high ssn; highly rec; excel." ♦ 19 Apr-30 Sep. € 43.50   2009*

CA'VIO see Cavallino *2E2*

CAVRIGLIA see Montevarchi *1D3*

CECINA *1D3* (5km E Rural) *43.30043, 10.58153* **Camping Valle Gaia, La Casetta, Via Cecinese 87, 56040 Casale-Marittimo (PI) [0586 681236; fax 683551; info@vallegaia.it; www.vallegaia.it]** Fr Cecina E on S68 foll sp Guardistallo & Casale Marittimo, site poorly sp - look for Robin Hood rest. Med, hdg pitch, pt shd; wc; chem disp; baby facs; shwrs inc; EHU (6A) inc; gas; lndry; shop; rest, snacks; bar; BBQ; playgrnd; 2 pools; tennis; games area; bike hire; entmnt; TV rm; 10% statics; dogs €3; phone; poss cr; Eng spkn; adv bkg; quiet; red CKE/CCI. "Best site in area; scenic location; gd sized pitches; excel, modern facs; helpful staff; excursions arranged; conv Siena, San Gimignano, Pisa." ♦ 4 Apr-10 Oct. € 29.60   2009*

CECINA *1D3* (5km S Rural) *43.25388, 10.55291* **Camping Le Capanne, SS Aurelia, Km 273, 57020 Marina-di-Bibbona (LI) [0586 600064; fax 600198; info@campinglecapanne.it; www.campinglecapanne.it]** Fr E side of rd SS1 fr La California to Marina di Bibbona, sp at km 273. Lge, shd; wc (some cont); chem disp; mv service pnt; shwrs inc; EHU (3A) inc; gas; lndry; shop; rest, snacks; bar; playgrnd; pool; paddling pool; beach 1.5km; tennis; games area; bike hire; entmnt; 10% statics; dogs €8.20; adv bkg; quiet; ccard acc; red LS. 24 Apr-30 Sep. € 38.00   2009*

⊞ **CECINA** *1D3* (2km W Urban/Coastal) *43.30464, 10.48809* **Camping Bocca di Cecina, Via Guado alle Vacche 2, 57023 Marina-di-Cecina (LI) [0586 620509; fax 621326; bocca. cecina@tin.it; www.ccft.it]** Fr Livorno ignore 1st sp to Cecina Mare Centu. At cent of Marina di Cecina turn R, site bef rv bdge. Lge, shd; wc; shwrs; EHU (2A); gas; lndry; shop; rest high ssn; snacks; bar; beach; windsurfing; tennis; games area; many statics; no dogs; sep car park; poss cr; ccard acc. "Lovely situation." € 29.00   2009*

CECINA *1D3* (3km NW Coastal) *43.31850, 10.47440* **Camping Mareblu, Via dei Campilunghi, Mazzanta, 57010 San Pietro-in-Palazzi (LI) [0586 629191; fax 629192; info@campingmareblu.com; www.campingmareblu.com]** Fr S on SS1 exit sp Cecina Nord & foll dir Mazzanta, site sp. Fr N exit sp Vada then Mazzanta. Lge, hdg/mkd pitch, pt shd; wc (some cont); chem disp; mv service pnt; shwrs inc; EHU (3A) inc; gas; lndry (inc dryer); shop; rest, snacks; bar; BBQ (gas only); playgrnd; pool; paddling pool; sand beach adj; wifi; 10% statics; dogs free (not acc Jul & Aug); phone; sep car park; ATM; poss cr; Eng spkn; adv bkg; red LS; ccard acc; red CKE/CCI. "Lge pitches; gd facs & pool area; car must be parked in sep car park; well-organised, friendly site." ♦ 26 Mar-15 Oct. € 37.00 (CChq acc)   2011*

CECINA *1D3* (6km NW Coastal) *43.33206, 10.46021* **Camping Molino a Fuoco, Via Cavalleggeri 32, 57018 Vada (LI) [0586 770150; fax 770031; info@campingmolinoafuoco.com; www.campingmolinoafuoco.com]** Sp fr SS1 Aurelia at cent of vill of Vada, adj Camping Rada Etrusca. Lge, shd; wc (some cont); chem disp; mv service pnt; baby facs; shwrs inc; EHU (4A) inc; lndry (inc dryer); shop; rest, snacks; bar; BBQ; playgrnd; shgl beach adj; games area; bike hire; wifi; 30% statics; dogs €2 (not acc Jul/Aug); sep car park; phone; poss cr; ccard acc; red LS. "Pleasant site; helpful staff; gd san facs." ♦ 2 Apr-16 Oct. € 34.00   2010*

CERIALE see Albenga *1B2*

CERVIA *2E2* (1.5km S Coastal) *44.24760, 12.35901* **Camping Adriatico, Via Pinarella 90, 48015 Cervia (RA) [0544 71537; fax 72346; info@campingadriatico.net; www.camping adriatico.net]** On SS16 S fr Cervia twd Pinarella, turn L at km post 175, over rlwy line & take 1st R, site sp. Lge, shd; wc (some cont); chem disp; mv service pnt; baby facs; shwrs inc; EHU (6A) inc; lndry; shop; rest, snacks; bar; playgrnd; htd pool; paddling pool; sand beach 600m; fishing; tennis 900m; golf 5km; entmnt; TV rm; 40% statics; dogs €6; Eng spkn; adv bkg; ccard acc; red CKE/CCI. "V pleasant site; friendly staff; gd san facs." ♦ 21 Apr-15 Sep. € 34.00 (CChq acc)   2010*

CERVO see Diano Marina *1B3*

⊞ **CESENATICO** *2E2* (1.5km N Coastal) *44.21545, 12.37983* **Camping Cesenatico, Via Mazzini 182, 47042 Cesenatico (FC) [0547 81344; fax 672452; info@campingcesenatico.it; www.campingcesenatico.com]** Travelling S on S16 look for Esso g'ge on R on app Cesenatico. Take 2nd L after Erg g'ge, over rlwy x-ing, site on L, sp. V lge, mkd pitch, hdstg, pt shd; htd wc (some cont); chem disp; mv service pnt; shwrs inc; EHU (4A) €3.60; gas; lndry; shop; snacks; rest; bar; playgrnd; htd pool; private sand beach adj; tennis; games area; entmnt; hairdresser; medical cent; wifi; entmnt; TV; 80% statics; dogs €8.70; phone; poss cr; Eng spkn; adv bkg; ccard acc; red long stay/LS/CKE/CCI. "Many long stay winter visitors; gd touring base; unspoilt seaside resort with canal (designed by Da Vinci), port & marina; excel; in easy walking/cycling dist fr Cesenatico." ♦ € 55.00 (CChq acc)   2014*

CESENATICO *2E2* (2km N Coastal) *44.21584, 12.37798* **Camping Zadina, Via Mazzini 184, 42047 Cesenatico (FC) [0547 82310; fax 702381; info@campingzadina.it; www.campingzadina.it]** Leave A14 at Cesena Sud; foll sp Cesenático; after 10.5km turn R at T-junc onto SS16; after 2km fork L over level x-ing; site on L. Lge, mkd pitch, pt terr, pt shd; wc; chem disp; mv service pnt; shwrs inc; EHU (6A) inc; gas; lndry; shop; rest, bbq; snacks; bar; playgrnd; private sand beach; entmnt; wifi; fishing; 80% statics; dogs €7; train 1.5km; Eng spkn; sep car park; poss cr; adv bkg; noisy in high ssn; ccard not acc; red LS. "Sea water canal runs thro site; pitches poss tight lge o'fits; gd." ♦ ltd. 20 Apr-21 Sep. € 56.00   2014*

CHATILLON see St Vincent *1B1*

CHIENES/KIENS see Brunico/Bruneck *1D1*

CHIOGGIA *2E2* (2km E Coastal) *45.20533, 12.29856* **Camping Adriatico, Lungomare Adriatico 82, 30019 Sottomarina (VE) [041 492907; fax 5548567; info@campingadriatico.com; www.campingadriatico.com]** Fr rd S309 foll sp for Sottomarina Lido, foll dual c'way on sea front, site on L. Med, mkd pitch, shd; wc (cont); chem disp; mv service pnt; some serviced pitches; shwrs inc; EHU (6A) inc (some rev pol); gas; lndry; shop; rest, snacks; bar; playgrnd; pool; sand beach adj; sailing; watersports; TV; 30% statics; phone; dogs (not acc Jun-Aug); poss v cr; quiet; some traff noise; adv bkg; Eng spkn; red long stay; ccard acc; red LS; CKE/CCI. "Water bus to Venice; Chioggia worth visit; money exchange." ♦ 4 Apr-20 Sep. € 32.50   2009*

CHIOGGIA *2E2* (2km E Urban/Coastal) *45.19027, 12.30361* **Camping Miramare, Via A. Barbarigo 103, 30015 Sottomarina (VE) [tel/fax 041 490610; campmir@tin.it; www.miramarecamping.com]** Fr SS309 foll sp Sottomarina. In town foll brown sp to site. Lge, mkd pitch, pt shd; wc; chem disp; mv service pnt; shwrs inc; EHU (6A) inc; gas; lndry; shop; rest, snacks; bar; playgrnd; pool; private sand beach; games area; wifi; entmnt; 75% statics; dog €3.50; poss cr; adv bkg; ccard acc; CKE/CCI. "Busy site - field across rd quieter; friendly staff; gd entmnt facs for children; cycle tracks to picturesque Chioggia; site 10 min walk fr ferry point and beach or free shuttle bus service until mid Sept; free sun umbrella for the beach fr rec." ♦ 18 Apr-23 Sep. € 35.00   2015*

ITALY

CHIOGGIA *2E2* (3km SE Coastal) *45.18138, 12.3075* **Kawan Village Camping Oasi, Via A. Barbarigo 147, 30019 Sottomarina (VE) [041 5541145; fax 490801; info@campingoasi.com; www.campingoasi.com]** Exit SS309/E55 sp Sottomarina, Chioggia & foll Viale Mediterraneo twd coast. Site sp on R - last one along Via Barbarigo. Med, hdg/mkd pitch, pt shd; wc (some cont); chem disp; mv service pnt; baby facs; shwrs inc; EHU (6A) inc; lndry (inc dryer); shop; rest, snacks; bar; BBQ; playgrnd; pool; paddling pool; private sand beach adj; watersports; games area; tennis; bike hire; wifi; entmnt; TV; 50% statics; dogs €3; phone; poss cr; adv bkg; quiet; ccard acc; red LS. "Pleasant, welcoming site; vg facs; excel beach; water bus to Venice." ♦ 25 Mar-30 Sep. € 34.00 (CChq acc)   2011*

"I need an on-site restaurant"

We do our best to make sure site information is correct, but it is always best to check any must-have facilities are still available or will be open during your visit.

⊞ **CHIUSA/KLAUSEN** *1D1* (650m E Rural) *46.64119, 11.57332* **Camping Gamp, Via Griesbruck 10, 39043 Chiusa/Klausen (BZ) [0472 847425; fax 845067; info@camping-gamp.com; www.camping-gamp.com]** Exit A22 Chiusa/Klausen & bear L at end of slip rd (sp Val Gardena). Site on L at rd fork 800m, sp. Sm, mkd pitch, pt shd; htd wc; chem disp; shwrs inc; mv service pnt; baby facs; EHU (6A) €2.60; lndry; shop & 500m; rest, snacks; bar; playgrnd; pool; table tennis; htd ski & boot rm; internet; sat TV; dogs €3.50; phone; sep m'van o'night facs; Eng spkn; some rd & rlwy noise; CKE/CCI. "Excel cent for mountain walks; Chiusa attractive town; immac facs, sep m'van o'night area; busy site; some pitches sm for lge o'fits; discount with Camping Euro card." ♦ € 34.00   2014*

CIRO MARINA *3B4* (2km N Coastal) *39.38526, 17.14255* **Camping Villaggio Punta Alice, 88811 Ciro-Marina (KR) [0962 31160; fax 373823; info@puntalice.it; www.puntalice. it]** Fr N on S106 twd Crotone, exit Cirò Marina. Cross rlwy line, foll site sp thro town (rds narr) to site. Lge, mkd pitch, pt shd; wc; chem disp; mv service pnt; shwrs inc; EHU (6A) inc; lndry; shop; rest, snacks; bar; playgrnd; pool; private sand/shgl beach; games area; bike hire; entmnt; cinema; TV rm; 50% statics; dogs €5.50; phone; sep car park high ssn; poss cr; Eng spkn; poss noisy; CKE/CCI. "Vg, clean site; friendly staff; excel rest." ♦ 1 Apr-30 Sep. € 44.00   2010*

CISANO see Bardolino *1D2*

CITTA DI CASTELLO *2E3* (3km W Rural) *43.45142, 12.22205* **Camping La Montesca, Loc Montesca, 06012 Città di Castello (PG) [0758 558566; fax 520786; info@lamontesca.it; www.lamontesca.it]** W fr SS3bis on winding rd; foll sp to town cent then sm brown site sp. Med, hdg/mkd pitch, terr, pt shd; wc; shwrs; EHU (6A) inc; lndry; shop & 3km; rest, bar high ssn; pool; entmnt; dogs; quiet; red CKE/CCI. "Superb views; ltd, sm touring pitches, but made welcome; poor san facs (2009); beautiful town." ♦ 15 Apr-20 Sep. € 27.00   2009*

COGNE *1B1* (3km SW Rural) *45.58764, 7.34157* **Camping Lo Stambecco, Frazione Valnontey, 11012 Cogne (AO) [0165 74152; infotiscali@campeggiolostambecco.it; www.campeggiolostambecco.it]** On Aosta-Mont Blanc rd (S26) heading W, after Sarre turn L to Cogne. In Cogne turn R sp Valnontey (Gran Paradiso). Site on L at ent to Valnontey vill. Use easier 2nd ent opp car park. Long 10% app fr S26. Med, pt sl, pt shd; wc (some cont); chem disp; mv service pnt; shwrs inc; EHU (3A) €2; gas; lndry; shop 3km; bar; 20% statics; Eng spkn; poss cr; quiet; ccard not acc; CKE/CCI. "In magnificent Gran Paradiso National Park; botanic garden highly rec; gd facs; excel walks." 20 May-20 Sep. € 22.00   2011*

COLTANO see Pisa *1C3*

COMACCHIO *2E2* (1km SE Coastal) *44.70130, 12.23810* **Kawan Village Florenz, Via Alpi Centrali 199, 44020 Lido-degli-Scacchi (FE) [0533 380193; fax 313166; info@campingflorenz.com; www.campingflorenz.com]** Fr a'strade Ferrara-Comacchio take exit dir Porto Garibaldi, site sp on coast rd. V lge, hdg pitch, pt shd; wc (some cont); chem disp; mv service pnt; baby facs; shwrs inc; EHU (3A) inc; gas; lndry; shop; rest, snacks; playgrnd; pool; paddling pool; sand beach adj; beauty cent; bike hire; games area; golf 5km; wifi; entmnt; TV rm; 60% statics; dogs €5.90; poss cr; quiet; ccard acc; red snr citizens; CKE/CCI. ♦ 1 Apr-1 Nov. € 37.60 (CChq acc)   2011*

COMACCHIO *2E2* (2km SE Coastal) *44.68944, 12.23833* **Camping Spiaggia e Mare, S.P. Ferrara-Mare 4, 44029 Porto Garibaldi (FE) [0533 327431; fax 325620; info@camping spiaggiamare.it; www.campingspiaggiamare.it]** Fr a'strada Ferrara-Comacchio take exit dir Porto Garibaldi, then S on S309 dir Ravenna. In 1km take sliprd on R to Porto Garibaldi. Strt over traff lts, site on L just bef RH bend. Fr S take slip rd on R at km 27 sp, then as above. Lge, mkd pitch, pt shd; wc (mainly cont); chem disp; mv service pnt; shwrs inc; EHU inc (6A) inc; gas; lndry; supmkt; rest, snacks; bar; playgrnd; 2 pools; paddling pool; sand beach adj; watersports; games area; bike hire; wifi; entmnt; 50% statics; dogs €6.30; poss cr; poss noisy; red snr citizens. "Excel beach; excel sw pool; active fishing port." ♦ 10 Apr-20 Sep. € 38.70   2009*

COMO *1C1* (5km S Urban) *45.78385, 9.06034* **International Camping-Sud, Breccia, Via Cecilio, 22100 Como [tel/fax 031 521435; campingint@hotmail.com; www.camping-internazionale.it]** Fr E to Como, on SS35 Milano rd foll sp a'strada Milano; site on Como side of rndabt at junc S35 & S432; ent/exit diff unless turn R. Or take 2nd exit off m'way after border (Como S), site sp. Med, pt sl, pt shd; wc; shwrs inc; EHU (4-6A) €2.50 (rev pol); gas; lndry; shop; supmkt nr; rest, snacks; bar; playgrnd; pool; bike hire; golf 5km; dogs €2; poss cr; no adv bkg; rd noise; red LS; ccard acc. "Conv NH for m'way." 1 Apr-31 Oct. € 24.00   2014*

ITALY

⊞ **CORIGLIANO CALABRO** *3A4* (7km N Coastal) *39.70333,
16.52583* **Camping Onda Azzurra, Contrada Foggia, 87064
Corigliano-Calabro (CS) [tel/fax 0983 851157; info@onda-
azzurra.it; www.onda-azzurra.it]** On SS106-bis Taranto to
Crotone rd, after turn off for Sibari, cont S for 6km. Turn L at
4 lge sp on 1 notice board by lge sep building, 2km to site on
beach. Lge, mkd pitch, shd; htd wc; chem disp; mv service pnt;
shwrs inc; EHU (6-10A) €3-4; lndry; shop; rest (all year); snacks;
bar; playgrnd; sand beach adj; tennis; bike hire; 10% statics;
dogs €3; adv bkg; ccard acc; red long stay/CKE/CCI. "Excel,
well-run site all ssns - facs open all yr; popular long stay; clean
facs; lge pitches; water not drinkable; v friendly helpful owner;
popular in winter; special meals Xmas/New Year; site conv
Sybaris & Rossano; high standard site; excel friendly welcome;
free acitivities LS." ♦ € 45.00   2014*

⊞ **CORIGLIANO CALABRO** *3A4* (8km N Coastal) *39.68141,
16.52160* **Camping Il Salice, Contrada da Ricota Grande,
87060 Corigliano-Calabro (CS) [0983 851169; fax 851147;
info@salicevacanze.it; www.salicevacanze.it]**
Exit A3 dir Sibari onto SS106 bis coast rd dir Crotone. At 19km
marker after water tower on L, turn L sp Il Salice - 1.5km to
new access rd to site on L. Site sp easily missed. Lge, mkd pitch,
hdstg, pt sl, pt shd; htd wc (cont); chem disp; mv service pnt;
serviced pitches; baby facs; fam bthrm; shwrs inc; EHU (3-6A)
inc; gas; lndry; shop & 2km; rest, snacks; bar; BBQ; playgrnd;
pool; sand beach adj; watersports; tennis; games area; games
rm; bike hire; TV; 70% statics; dogs €4; phone; poss cr; Eng
spkn; red LS; CKE/CCI. "Narr rds thro vill to site - care needed
when busy; v popular, well-run winter destination; haphazard
siting in pine trees; clean, private beach; modern san facs; ltd
facs LS; big price red LS; scenic area." ♦ € 48.00   2012*

⊞ **CORIGLIANO CALABRO** *3A4* (10km N Coastal) *39.69130,
16.52233* **Camping Thurium, Contrada Ricota Grande,
87060 Ricota Grande (CS) [tel/fax 0983 851101;
info@campingthurium.com; www.campingthurium.com]**
Exit SS106 at km stone 21. Site sp on gd app rd for 2km. Rd
narr and bumpy in places. Do not foll SatNav. Lge, mkd pitches,
pt shd; mv chem disp; mv service pnt; shwrs (€0.35); EHU inc
(3-6A); lndry (inc dryer); shop; snacks; rest; bar; gas; playgrnd;
pool; paddling pool; sand beach adj; tennis; games area; bike
hire; windsurfing lessons; entmnt; wifi; 20% statics; dogs
(€4.80); twin axles; Eng spkn; CKE/CCI. "Vg well-run site; site
rdways narr on corner, tight for lge o'fits; fair." ♦ ltd. € 65.00
(CChq acc)   2014*

CORTENO GOLGI see Edolo *1D1*

CORTINA D'AMPEZZO *2E1* (1.5km SE Rural) *46.52241,
12.13413* **Camping Rocchetta, Via Campo 1, 32043
Cortina-d'Ampezzo (BL) [tel/fax 0436 5063; camping@
sunrise.it; www.campingrocchetta.it]** Fr Cortina on SS51
dir Belluno & Venice, site sp. Fr Belluno on S51 on app Cortina
turn L, brown sp at junc, site sp. Lge, shd; htd wc (some cont);
chem disp; mv service pnt; shwrs inc; EHU (3A) inc; lndry (inc
dryer); shop; rest adj; bar; pool 2km; 10% statics; dogs €1;
poss cr; Eng spkn; adv bkg; quiet; ccard acc; red LS; CKE/CCI.
"Gd, clean facs; 30 min walk to Cortina; mountain views."
1 Jun-20 Sep & 3 Dec-3 Apr. € 26.00   2010*

CORTINA D'AMPEZZO *2E1* (3.5km S Rural) *46.51858,
12.1370* **Camping Dolomiti, Via Campo di Sotto,
32043 Cortina-d'Ampezzo (BL) [0436 2485; fax 5403;
campeggiodolomiti@tin.it; www.campeggiodolomiti.it]**
2km S of Cortina turn R off S51. Site beyond Camping
Cortina & Rocchetta. Lge, mkd pitch, pt shd; htd wc; shwrs
inc; chem disp; EHU (4A) inc (check earth); gas; lndry; shop;
rest 1km; bar; playgrnd; htd pool; games area; games rm;
wifi; 10% statics; dogs; phone; bus; poss cr; Eng spkn; no adv
bkg; quiet; red LS; ccard acc. "Superb scenery in mountains,
gd walks; cycle rte into Cortina; helpful owner; beautiful
setting; choice of open meadow or shd woodland pitches." ♦
1 Jun-20 Sep. € 24.00   2014*

COURMAYEUR *1A1* (6.2km NE) *45.83293, 6.99095*
**Campsite Grandes Jorasses, Via per la Val Ferret 53,
11013 Courmayeur (Valle d'Aosta) [0165 869708;
info@grandesjorasses.com; www.grandesjorasses.com]**
Foll the brown 'Val Ferret' signs bet Courmayeur and the Mont
Blanc tunnel, and the campsite is located a few km on the L
of the rd. Med, hdstg, pt shd; wc; chem disp; mv service pnt;
shwrs (50c); lndry; shop on site; rest; snacks; bar; games rm;
wifi; CKE/CCI. "Beautiful site at the foot of Mt Blanc; nature
trails thro forest; trekking expeditions arranged; gd rest." ♦ ltd.
20 Jun-15 Sep. € 30.00   2014*

⊞ **COURMAYEUR** *1A1* (6km SE Rural) *45.76333, 7.01055*
**Camping Arc en Ciel, Loc Feysoulles, 11017 Morgex (AO)
[0165 809257; fax 807749; info@campingarcenciel.it;
www.campingarcenciel.it]** Fr A5/E25 take Morgex exit,
turn L to vill & foll sp dir Dailley. Site in 1km on L, sp. Fr tunnel
take SS25 to Morgex, then as above. Med, terr, pt shd; wc;
chem disp; shwrs inc; EHU (4-6A) €1.50; lndry; shop; rest,
snacks; bar; rafting; mountain climbing; ski lift 8km; ski bus;
30% statics; dogs €1; sep car park; site clsd 6 Nov-8 Dec; poss
cr; adv bkg; quiet; ccard acc; red CKE/CCI. "Gd, clean san facs;
views Mont Blanc fr some pitches; vg; views of the mountains
marvellous." € 21.50   2011*

> ## "Satellite navigation makes touring much easier"
>
> Remember most sat navs don't know if
> you're towing or in a larger vehicle – always
> use yours alongside maps and site directions.

CREMONA *1C2* (2.5km SW Rural) *45.11978, 10.0088*
**Camping Parco al Po, Via Lungo Po Europa 12,
26100 Cremona [0372 21268; fax 27137; info@camping
cremonapo.it; www.campingcremonapo.it]**
Exit A21 at Castelvetro or Cremona onto S10 ring rd. Site
well sp fr ring rd, adj to sports complex nr rvside. If lost foll
sp Paziena, then site. Lge, mkd pitch, pt shd; wc (some cont);
chem disp; mw service pnt; shwrs €0.50; EHU (4A) inc; lndry
(inc dryer); shop 1km; bar; snacks; rest; rv sw 1km; bike hire;
20% statics; dogs €2; phone; poss cr; Eng spkn; adv bkg;
ccard acc; quiet. "In spacious park; some pitches gloomy due
excessive shading; san facs dated; gates locked 1400-1530;
gd rest; interesting town; mosquitoes; muddy; poor." ♦
1 Apr-25 Nov. € 29.00   2011*

CUNEO *1B2* (3km SW Rural) *44.36443, 7.51483* **Camping Communale Bisalta, Via San Maurizio 33, 12010 San Rocco-Castagnaretta (CN) [tel/fax 0171 491334; campingbisalta@libero.it]** App Cuneo on S20 fr S fr Col de Tende (France) dir. On o'skts of town turn L at traff lts by cemetary, foll site sp. Lge, shd; wc; chem disp; mv service pnt; shwrs inc; EHU (3A) inc; lndry; shop; rest 1km; snacks; bar; BBQ; cooking facs; pool; tennis; bike hire; 85% statics; dogs; 10% red long stay/CKE/CCI. "Pleasant site; friendly atmosphere; fair facs poss stretched high ssn; gd touring base." ♦ € 21.50   2009*

CUPRA MARITTIMA *2F3* (1km W Urban/Coastal) *43.02054, 13.84925* **Villaggio Verde Cupra, Via Lazio 26, 63012 Cupra-Marittima (AP) [0735 777411; fax 777666; info@verdecupra.it; www.verdecupra.it]** Fr N leave A14 dir Pedaso, then S on SS16 in dir Pescara. In 10km site sp in town on R. Med, mkd pitch, pt shd; wc; shwrs inc; EHU (4A) inc; gas 2km; lndry; shop; rest, snacks; bar; playgrnd; pool; beach 1km; tennis; bike hire; entmnt; TV rm; phone; poss cr; some Eng spkn; adv bkg; poss noisy; CKE/CCI. "Helpful owner & staff; quite a climb up a hill to the site." ♦ ltd. 1 Apr-31 Oct. € 33.00   2011*

DEIVA MARINA *1C2* (1km NE Rural) *44.22520, 9.53250* **Villaggio Turistico Arenella, Loc Arenella, 19013 Deiva-Marina (SP) [0187 825259; info@campingarenella.it; www.campingarenella.it]** Exit A12/E80 Deiva Marina. In approx 6.8km site sp on R, easy access. Med, hdstg, terr, pt shd; wc (some cont); chem disp; mv service pnt; shwrs inc; EHU (3A) €2; lndry; shop; rest, snacks; bar; BBQ; beach 2.2km; wifi; 40% statics; dogs; phone; bus to stn (trains to Cinque Terre) high ssn; Eng spkn; adv bkg; quiet; red LS/CKE/CCI. "Pleasant site with stream running thro it; helpful staff; vg." ♦ ltd. 1 May-31 Oct & 5-31 Dec. € 33.00   2010*

⊞ **DEIVA MARINA** *1C2* (3km E Rural) *44.22630, 9.55013* **Camping La Sfinge, Loc Gea 5, 19013 Deiva-Marina (SP) [tel/fax 0187 825464; info@campinglasfinge.com; www.campinglasfinge.com]** Fr a'strada A12 exit Deiva Marina, site on R in approx 4.5km Med, hdg/mkd pitch, hdstg, terr, pt shd; wc (cont); mv service pnt; chem disp; serviced pitches; shwrs inc; EHU (3A) inc; gas; lndry; shop; rest, snacks; bar; playgrnd; shgl beach 3km (free bus high ssn); entmnt; fishing; watersports; trekking; internet; 50% statics; dogs €2; phone; bus to beach/stn high ssn; sep car park; poss cr; Eng spkn; adv bkg ess high ssn; quiet; 10% red 5+ days; red LS; ccard acc; 10% red CKE/CCI. "Excel san facs; v popular inc LS - rec arr early; gd, clean site; ltd touring pitches & some sm/ diff for lge o'fits; conv Genova, Pisa, Portofino, Cinque Terre, marble quarry at Carrara; gd walking." ♦ € 31.50   2010*

DEIVA MARINA *1C2* (3km E Coastal) *44.22476, 9.55146* **Villaggio Camping Valdeiva, Loc Ronco, 19013 Deiva-Marina (SP) [0187 824174; fax 825352; camping@valdeiva. it; www.valdeiva.it]** Fr A12 exit Deiva Marina, site sp on L in approx 4km by town sp. Med, mkd pitch, hdstg, pt sl, pt shd; wc (some cont); chem disp; shwrs inc; EHU (3-6A) inc; lndry; shop; rest, snacks; bar; BBQ; playgrnd; pool; shgl beach 3km; wifi; entmnt; sat TV; 90% statics; dogs; phone; bus to stn; sep car park high ssn; poss cr; Eng spkn; adv bkg ess high ssn; ccard acc; red LS; CKE/CCI. "Free minibus to stn - conv Cinque Terre or Portofino; helpful, friendly staff; gd rest; excel walking; v quiet LS & shwrs ltd." 1 Jan-31 Oct & 5 Dec-31 Dec. € 43.00 (3 persons)   2013*

DEIVA MARINA *1C2* (1km SE Coastal) *44.21473, 9.51874* **Camping Fornaci al Mare, Loc Fornaci, 19014 Framura (SP) [tel/fax 0187 816295]** Foll 1-way to L in town, sp La Spezia-A'strada, over narr bdge. Site immed S of rv bdge. Med, pt sl, pt shd; wc (some cont); chem disp; mv service pnt; shwrs €0.50; EHU (2A) inc; shop, rest, snacks, bar nr; beach adj; 80% statics; no dogs; train nr; phone; poss cr; rlwy noise; CKE/ CCI. "Not suitable lge o'fits; v friendly; san facs dated; sh walk to stn for Cinque Terra towns, some railyway noise." ♦ ltd. 1 Apr-31 Oct. € 25.00   2011*

⊞ **DEMONTE** *1B2* (1.5km N Rural) *44.32260, 7.29222* **Campeggio Il Sole, Frazione Perosa 3/B, 12014 Demonte (CN) [0334 1132724; fax 0171 955630; erikamelchio@ virgilio.it; www.ghironda.com]** Fr lge town sq on S21 go E for 100m, fork L & in 100m turn L. Pass 2 churches on L, turn L, then R over rv into Via Colle dell'Urtica to N. Foll this rd uphill for 1.2km, turn L at T-junc & in 300m L at T-junc again. Site on R. Town cent side rds v narr with arches & app rd narr & steep in places. Sm, mkd pitch, unshd; wc; chem disp; mv service pnt; shwrs €1; EHU €2; lndry rm; rest; bar; BBQ; playgrnd; dogs; quiet. "Lovely, peaceful site in mountains; vg value rest." ♦ ltd. € 17.00   2013*

DEMONTE *1B2* (1.5km W Rural) *44.31357, 7.27275* **Camping Piscina Demonte, Loc Bagnolin, 12014 Demonte (CN) [338 2464353; fax 011 2274301; info@campingdemonte.com; www.campingdemonte.com]** App only fr Borgo on S21, 500m after Demonte turn L, foll sp. Med, pt shd; wc; chem disp; shwrs €0.60; EHU (6A) €1.50; gas; lndry; shop, rest 1.5km; bar; pool; 90% statics; dogs €1.60; poss cr; adv bkg; quiet; ccard acc; CKE/CCI. "Gd NH bef Col d'Larche; helpful, friendly owner; gd mountain scenery." 15 Jun-15 Sep. € 16.50   2013*

DESENZANO DEL GARDA *1D2* (5km SE Rural) *45.46565, 10.59443* **Camping San Francesco, Strada V San Francesco, 25015 Desenzano-del-Garda (BS) [030 9110245; fax 9902558; booking@campingsanfrancesco.com; www.campingsanfrancesco.com]** E fr Milan on A4 a'strada take exit Sirmione & foll sp twd Sirmione town; join S11 twd Desenzano & after Garden Center Flowers site 1st campside on R after rndabt; site sp twd lake bet Sirmione & Desenzano. Or fr Desenzano, site just after Rivoltella. Lge, mkd pitch, pt sl, shd; wc; chem disp; baby facs; shwrs inc; EHU (6A) inc; gas; lndry (inc dryer); shop; rest, snacks; bar; BBQ (charcoal/gas); playgrnd; pool; lake sw & shgl beach; boat hire; windsurfing; sailing; canoe hire; fishing; tennis; games area; bike hire; golf 10km; wifi; entmnt; TV rm; 50% statics; dogs free; no o'fits over 6m high ssn; phone; recep clsd 1300-1500 & no vehicle movement; poss cr; Eng spkn; adv bkg; noisy entmnt high ssn; ccard acc; red LS; CKE/CCI. "Lovely lakeside pitches for tourers (extra); muddy if wet; poss diff lge o'fits due trees; helpful staff; well managed site; gd position on edge of lake; handy for local bus; excel site; v clean facs; gd rest." ♦ 1 Apr-30 Sep. € 51.00   2014*

Tell us about the sites you visit

DIANO MARINA *1B3* (4km NE Coastal) *43.92177, 8.10831*
Camping del Mare, Via alla Foce 29, 18010 Cervo (IM)
[0183 400130 or 0183 405556; fax 402771; info@camping
delmare-cervo.com; www.campingdelmare-cervo.com]
Exit A10/E80 at San Bartolomeo/Cervo onto Via Aurelia. Turn
L at traff lts twd Cervo. Sp adj rv bdge. R turn acute - long
o'fits app fr NE. Med, hdg/mkd pitch, hdstg, shd; wc; chem
disp; baby facs; shwrs; EHU (6A) €2; gas; lndry; shop; snacks;
shgl beach adj; internet; TV; 40% statics; dogs; phone; Eng
spkn; adv bkg rec Jun-Aug; quiet; ccard acc. "Immac site;
spacious pitches; friendly, helpful staff; picturesque beach &
perched vill (Cervo); easy walk San Bartolomeo; gd mkts; highly
rec site; pitches close together; office closes 1200-1500." ♦
23 Mar-15 Oct. € 50.00   2014*

DIANO MARINA *1B3* (4km NE Urban/Coastal) *43.92345,
8.10924* **Camping Lino**, Via Nazario Sauro 4, 18010 Cervo
(IM) [0183 400087; fax 400089; info@campinglino.it;
www.campinglino.it] Exit A10 dir San Bartolomeo al Mare.
Inside Cervo boundary where main coast rd N bends L to pass
under rlwy. Turn R clearly sp. Site ent visible fr rd. Med, mkd
pitch, shd; wc (some cont); chem disp; fam bthrm; serviced
pitches; shwrs; EHU (6A) metered; gas; lndry; shop; rest 100m;
snacks; playgrnd; bike hire; internet; 10% statics; dogs; adv bkg;
red LS; quiet. "Lge pitches completely shd; vans manhandled
onto pitch fr ent; sw & boating for children in lagoon; clean, tidy
site, but regimented; minimum stay 3 nights; various pitch sizes
& prices; park outside bef checking in as diff to turn once inside
site." ♦ 1 Apr-20 Oct. € 43.00 (4 persons)   2009*

"There aren't many sites open at this time of year"

If you're travelling outside peak season
remember to call ahead to check site opening
dates – even if the entry says 'open all year'.

DIANO MARINA *1B3* (4km NE Urban/Coastal) *43.92384, 8.11100*
Camping Miramare, Via Nazario Sauro 12, 18010 Cervo (IM)
[tel/fax 0183 400285; info@campingmiramare.im.it;
www.campingmiramare.im.it] In Cervo where coastal main rd
bends L under rlwy bdge, turn R 50m beyond Camping Lino. Sm,
mkd pitch, shd; wc; chem disp; shwrs inc; EHU (4A) €2; lndry;
shop; rest 100m; snacks; bar; shgle beach adj; 10% statics;
dogs; phone; poss cr; quiet but some rlwy noise. "Pleasant,
family-run site." 1 Apr-3 Oct. € 43.00 (3 persons)   2010*

⊞ **DIANO MARINA** *1B3* (500m W Urban/Coastal) *43.90667,
8.07097* **Camping Oasi Park**, Via Sori 5, 18013 Diano-
Marina (IM) [tel/fax 0183 497062; oasi-park@libero.it;
www.oasipark.it] On W o'skts Diano Marina, cross rlwy bdge
& immed turn R. Foll rd to L past Camping Marino. In 200m
turn L, site 200m ahead. M'vans only. Lge, hdstg, terr, pt shd;
wc (cont); own san; chem disp; mv service pnt; shwrs €1; EHU
(8A) €2; gas; lndry; shop 200m; playgrnd; sand beach 500m;
20% statics; dogs; phone; bus, train 500m; poss v cr; Eng spkn;
quiet; ccard acc; CKE/CCI. "Conv pleasant town & gd beaches;
helpful owner; awnings not allowed." € 15.00   2009*

DIMARO *1D1* (1km W Rural) *46.32611, 10.86222* **Dolomiti
Camping Village**, Via Gole 105, 38025 Dimaro (TN)
[0463 974332; fax 973200; info@campingdolomiti.com;
www.campingdolomiti.com]** Site sp on S42 nr rv bdge.
Med, terr, pt shd; wc; chem disp; sauna; baby facs; shwrs inc;
EHU (5A) €1.30 or metered; gas; lndry (inc dryer); shop; rest,
snacks; bar; playgrnd; 2 htd pools (1 covrd); tennis; canoeing;
bike hire; ski lift 1.5km; free skibus; mountain biking; extreme
sports; wifi; entmnt; TV; 25% statics; dogs €4 (not acc Jul/
Aug); sep car park high ssn; gate clsd 1300-1500; quiet;
ccard acc; red long stay/CKE/CCI. "Helpful staff; gd facs;
some pitches poss diff lge o'fits & m'vans; excel walking." ♦
20 May-25 Sep & 3 Dec-15 Apr. € 33.40   2010*

⊞ **DIMARO** *1D1* (11km W Rural) *46.30980, 10.74010*
Camping Cevedale, Via di Sotto Pilla 4, 38026 Fucine-di-
Ossana (TN) [tel/fax 0463 751630; info@campingcevedale.
it; www.campingcevedale.it] Exit A22 at San Michele sull'
Adige onto SS43/SS42 twd Dimaro & Fucine. Foll sp Ossana
& site over bdge. Lge, mkd pitch, terr, pt shd; htd wc (some
cont); chem disp; mv service pnt; shwrs; EHU (3A) inc; lndry
(inc dryer); shop 500m; snacks; bar; playgrnd; games area; ski
shuttle bus; internet; TV rm; 30% statics; no dogs; adv bkg;
quiet; ccard acc. "Excel, clean san facs; beautiful area." ♦
€ 32.00   2011*

⊞ **DOBBIACO/TOBLACH** *2E1* (2km W Rural) *46.73431,
12.19362* **Camping International Olympia**, Via Pusteria 1,
39034 Dobbiaco/Toblach (BZ) [0474 972147; fax 972713;
info@camping-olympia.com; www.camping-olympia.it]
Trun off S49 at E end of Villabassa/Niederdorf by-pass, sp
'camping'. Site 1km E of Villabassa. Lge, mkd pitch, pt shd; wc;
chem disp; mv service pnt; some serviced pitches; sauna; shwrs
inc; EHU (6A) inc; gas; lndry; shop; rest, snacks; bar; playgrnd;
pool; paddling pool; bike hire; solarium; ski school; entmnt; TV;
30% statics; dogs €4.50; Eng spkn; adv bkg; quiet; ccard acc;
CKE/CCI. "Vg, luxurious facs; magnificent views; cycle tracks;
gd walks; sm zoo; excel." ♦ € 31.00   2010*

⊞ **EDOLO** *1D1* (1.5km W Rural) *46.17648, 10.31333*
Camping Adamello, Via Campeggio 10, Loc Nembra,
25048 Edolo (BS) [tel/fax 0364 71694; info@camping
adamello.com; www.campingadamello.com]
On rd 39 fr Edolo to Aprica; after 1.5km turn sharp L down
narr lane by rest; camping sp on rd; diff app. Med, pt sl, terr,
pt shd; wc; chem disp; shwrs inc; EHU (6A) €1.50; lndry; shop;
rest, snacks 1km; bar; 50% statics; dogs €3; poss cr; quiet; no
ccard acc. "Useful NH; beautiful mountain site; steep rds all
round; v diff app fr W; quiet for couples; nothing for children."
♦ € 27.00   2011*

ELBA ISLAND *1C3* Sites on Elba Island are listed together
at the end of the Italy site entry pages.

ERACLEA MARE see Lido di Jesolo *2E2*

ITALY

⊞ **FALZE DI PIAVE** *2E1* (700m S Rural) **Parking Le Grave, Via Passo Barca, 31010 Falze-di-Piave (TV) [0339 2348523; fax 0438 86896; belleluigi@libero.it; www.legrave.it]** Fr A27 exit Conegliano & turn R onto SP15 then SS13 to Susegana. At Ponte-della-Priula turn onto SP34 to Falze-di-Piave. Fr town cent turn L just past war memorial into Via Passo Barca, site on R. Sm, unshd; no wc or shwrs; chem disp; mv service pnt; EHU(4A) inc; BBQ; playgrnd; quiet. "CL-type site in delightful area; friendly, helpful owner; gd walking/cycling; wine tasting last w/end May." € 10.00   2011*

FERIOLO see Verbania *1B1*

⊞ **FERRARA** *1D2* (2km NE Rural) *44.85303, 11.63328* **Campeggio Comunale Estense, Via Gramicia 76, 44100 Ferrara [tel/fax 0532 752396; campeggio.estense@free internet.it or idem@libero.it]** Exit A13 Ferrara N. After Motel Nord Ovest on L turn L at next traff lts into Via Porta Catena. Rd is 500m fr city wall around town; foll brown/yellow sps - well sp fr all dirs. Med, pt shd; htd wc (some cont); chem disp; mv service pnt; shwrs inc; EHU (6A) €3; lndry; shops, rest 200m; pool in park nrby; bike hire; golf adj; some stored c'vans; dogs €1.50; site clsd early-Jan to end-Feb; Eng spkn; quiet; ccard acc €50+; 10% red CKE/CCI. "Peaceful, well-kept, clean site; helpful staff; lge pitches; ltd privacy in shwrs; interesting town; gd cycle tracks round town; rlwy stn in town for trains to Venice; gd NH." ♦ 1 Jan-7 Jan / 22 Feb-31 Dec. € 32.00   2013*

"That's changed – Should I let The Club know?"

If you find something on site that's different from the site entry, fill in a report and let us know. See www.caravanclub.co.uk/europereport.

FIANO ROMANO *2E4* (2km W Rural) *42.15167, 12.57670* **Camping I Pini, Via delle Sassete 1/A, 00065 Fiano-Romano [0765 453349; fax 1890941; ipini@camping.it; www.camping. it/roma/ipini]** Fr A1/E35 exit sp Roma Nord/Fiano Romano (use R-hand lane for cash toll), foll sp Fiano at rndabt. Take 1st exit at next rndabt sp I Pini & stay on this rd for approx 2km. Take 2nd exit at next rndabt, L at T-junc under bdge, site sp on R. Med, hdg/mkd pitch, pt sl, terr, pt shd; htd wc; chem disp; mv service pnt; shwrs inc; EHU (6A) inc (poss rev pol); lndry (inc dryer); shop; rest, snacks; bar; BBQ; playgrnd; pool; paddling pool; tennis; bike hire; horseriding nrby; fishing; wifi; entmnt; games rm; TV; 60% statics (tour ops); dogs €2; no o'fits over 10m high ssn; phone; bus; poss cr; Eng spkn; adv bkg rec high ssn; quiet, but noisy nr bar; ccard acc; red LS/CKE/CCI. "Well-run, clean, excel san facs; helpful, friendly staff; excel rest; access poss diff lge o'fits; kerbs to all pitches; most pitches slope badly side to side req double height ramps; excursions by coach inc daily to Rome or gd train service; super site." ♦ 18 Apr-21 Sep. € 56.00 SBS - Y13   2014*

FIE/VOLS *1D1* (3km N Rural) *46.53334, 11.53335* **Camping Alpe di Siusi/Seiser Alm, Loc San Constantino 16, 39050 Fiè-allo-Sciliar/Völs-am-Schlern (BZ) [0471 706459; fax 707382; info@camping-seiseralm.com; www.camping-seiseralm.com]** Leave Bolzano on SS12 (not A22) sp Brixen & Brenner. After approx 7km take L fork in tunnel mouth sp Tiers, Fiè. Foll rd thro Fiè, site in 3km dir Castelrotto, sp on L. Lge, mkd pitch, hdstg, terr, unshd; htd wc; chem disp; mv service pnt; baby facs; sauna; shwrs inc; EHU (16A) metered; lndry (inc dryer); shop; rest, snacks; bar; playgrnd; golf 1km; sat TV; wifi; 20% statics; dogs €4.50; bus; phone; site clsd 5 Nov to 20 Dec; poss cr; Eng spkn; adv bkg; quiet; CKE/CCI. "Well-organised site with gd views; impressive, luxury undergrnd san facs block; private san facs avail; vg walking/skiing; an amazing experience; v popular site; efficiently run!" 1 Jan-2 Nov & 20 Dec-31 Dec. € 47.00   2014*

⊞ **FIESOLE** *1D3* (1km NE Rural) *43.80666, 11.30638* **Camping Panoramico, Via Peramonda 1, 50014 Fiesole (FI) [055 599069; fax 59186; panoramico@florencecamping.com; www.florencecamping.com]** Foll sp for Fiesole & Camping Panoramico fr Florence; site on R. Rd to Fiesole v hilly & narr thro busy tourist area. Lge, terr, pt shd; wc; chem disp; shwrs inc; EHU (3A) inc; gas; lndry; shop; bar; rest in high ssn; playgrnd; pool; internet; 20% statics; dogs free; poss cr; Eng spkn; quiet; ccard acc. "Access v diff - more suitable tenters; site soggy in wet; ltd water points; Florence 20 mins bus but 1.5km steep walk to stop; excel views; excel site." ♦ € 39.00   2012*

FIGLINE VALDARNO *1D3* (20km SW Rural) *43.53847, 11.41380* **Camping Orlando in Chianti, Localita Caffggiolo, 52022 Cavriglia [tel/fax 055 967 422; info@campingorlandoinchianti. it; www.campingorlandoinchianti.it]** Fr A1 Firenze-Roma, exit Incisa. Foll Figline Val d'Arno. Dir Greve in Chianti, exit at Lucolena, then foll signs to 'Piano Orlando Parco Cavriglia'. Med, mkd pitch, hdstg, pt sl, shd; wc; chem disp; mv service pnt; shwrs inc; EHU (16A); lndry; BBQ; shop; rest; snacks; bar; pool; 10% statics; poss cr; Eng spkn; adv bkg; quiet; CCI. "Vg site; excel priced rest; rural; v friendly staff." ♦ 12 Apr-19 Oct. € 48.50   2014*

FIGLINE VALDARNO *1D3* (2.5km W Rural) *43.61111, 11.44940* **Camping Norcenni Girasole Club, Via Norcenni 7, 50063 Figline-Valdarno (FI) [055 915141; fax 9151402; girasole@ ecvacanze.it; www.ecvacanze.it]** Fr a'strada A1, dir Rome, take exit 24 (sp Incisa SS69) to Figline-Valdarno; turn R in vill & foll sp to Greve; site sp Girasole; steep app rd to site with some twists for 3km. V lge, some hdg pitch, terr, pt shd; wc (some cont); chem disp; mv service pnt; baby facs; private bthrm extra; sauna; shwrs inc; EHU (6A) inc; gas; lndry (inc dryer); shop; rest, snacks; bar; BBQ; playgrnd; 2 pools (1 covrd); paddling pool; jacuzzi; tennis; games area; horseriding; bike hire; fitness cent; games rm; wifi; entmnt; TV; dogs free; twin-axles acc (rec check in adv); stn 1.5km; bus to Florence; excursions; initial cash payment to smart card req for all expenses on site (cash not acc); busy at w/end in ssn & poss v cr; Eng spkn; adv bkg; ccard acc; red LS/long stay; CKE/ CCI. "Excel, well-run site; some pitches sm; steep site rds poss diff lge o'fits; steel pegs rec; upper level pool area excel for children; site clsd 1330-1530; poss long walk to san facs block; site hilly; wine tasting trips; gd touring base." ♦ 1 Apr-13 Oct. € 45.50 SBS - Y07   2011*

ITALY

FINALE LIGURE *1B2* (1.5km N Rural) *44.18395, 8.35349*
**Eurocamping Calvisio, Via Calvisio 37, 17024 Finale-Ligure
(SV) [019 600491; fax 601240; info@eurocampingcalvisio.it;
www.eurocampingcalvisio.it]** On SS1 Savona-Imperia, turn
R at ent to Finale-Ligure; sp to site in Calvisio vill. Med, hdg/
mkd pitch, shd; wc (some cont); chem disp; shwrs €0.50; EHU
(6A) inc; lndry (inc dryer); shop; rest, snacks; bar; playgrnd;
pool high ssn; paddling pool; sand beach 2km; solarium; wifi;
entmnt; 80% statics; dogs; sep car park high ssn; poss cr; adv
bkg; quiet; ccard acc; red LS. "Security guard at night; clean,
well-maintained san facs." ♦ Easter- 5 Nov. € 54.50   2010*

"I like to fill in the reports
as I travel from site to site"

You'll find report forms at the back of
this guide, or you can fill them in online
at www.caravanclub.co.uk/europereport.

⊞ **FIRENZE** *1D3* (3km NE Urban) *43.79066, 11.29005* **Camp
& Ostello Municipal Villa di Camerata, Viale Augusto
Righi 2/4, 50100 Firenze [055 601451; fax 610300; firenze@
ostellionline.org]** Exit a'strada at Firenze Sud. Foll any sp for
Fiesole several km fr a'strada. Rd crosses Rv Arno at Ponte G da
Verrazzano, then cross rlwy & cont along Via Lungo L'Affrico.
Watch for camp sp/Youth Hostel sp (Ostello) on L at rndabt
into Viale Augusto Righi. Turn L, site is 50m on R in Youth
Hostel grnds. V poor sp around Florence & poss diff to find.
Med, pt sl, pt shd, mkd pitch, hdstg; wc; chem disp; mv service
pnt; shwrs inc; EHU (5A) inc; lndry; shop 700m; rest 700m;
snacks; bar; bus; poss cr; Eng spkn; adv bkg; noisy; red CKE/
CCI. "Bus to Florence every 20 mins (tickets fr hostel office);
access to Youth Hostel facs LS; hot water to shwrs only - other
san facs basic but clean; gd local rest; poss unkempt LS."
€ 30.00   2009*

⊞ **FIRENZE** *1D3* (3km SE Urban) *43.76183, 11.26801* **Camping
Michelangelo, Viale Michelangelo 80, 50125 Firenze
[055 6811977; fax 689348; michelangelo@evacanze.it;
www.ecvacanze.it]** Exit a'strada A1/E35 at Firenze Certosa or
Firenze Sud; foll sp for Piazzale Michelangelo; site on L (N) in
approx 6km, 200m past Piazzale (lge view point); steep site ent.
Lge, some hdstg, pt sl, pt shd; wc (mainly cont); chem disp;
mv service pnt; shwrs inc; EHU (2-5A) inc; gas; lndry; supmkt
high ssn; rest 1km; snacks; bar; playgrnd; bike hire; golf 10km;
wifi; 30% statics; dogs €2; phone; bus; poss v cr; Eng spkn;
quiet; ccard acc (€103 min); CKE/CCI. "Views over city fr some
pitches; noise fr jukebox & bar at top end of site high ssn; cr,
busy, backpacker site but well-run; gd rests walking dist; bus
(tickets fr recep); v conv to visit city on foot; arr early for gd
pitch; diff sl pitches in wet weather; check for suitable place
bef booking in; care using light switches; old san facs in poor
condition; few pitches suitable c'vans & most diff for m'vans."
€ 37.70   2011*

FIRENZE *1D3* (24km SE Rural) *43.70138, 11.40527*
**Camping Village Il Poggetto, Strada Provinciale Nr1
Aretina Km14, 50067 Troghi [tel/fax 055 8307323; info@
campingilpoggetto.com; www.campingilpoggetto.com]**
Fr S on E35/A1 a'strada take Incisa exit & turn L dir Incisa.
After 400m turn R dir Firenze, site in 5km on L. Fr N on A1
exit Firenze-Sud dir Bagno a Ripoli/S. Donato; go thro S.
Donato to Troghi, site on R, well sp. Narr, hilly app rd & sharp
turn - app fr S easier. Lge, hdg/mkd pitch, pt sl, pt terr, pt
shd; wc (some cont); chem disp; mv service pnt; baby facs;
private san facs avail; shwrs inc; EHU (7A) inc (poss rev pol);
gas; lndry; shop; rest, snacks; bar; playgrnd; 2 pools; bike hire;
table tennis; internet; 5% statics; dogs €2.20; phone; bus adj;
money change; poss cr; Eng spkn; adv bkg ess high ssn; quiet
but some m'way noise; red long stay; ccard acc over €200;
10% red CKE/CCI (LS). "Superb, picturesque, family-run site
in attractive location inc vineyard; clean, modern facs; lovely
pool; bus to Florence 45mins - tickets fr recep; trains fr Incisa
Valdarno (free parking at stn); excursions; gd rest; LS offers for
long stay (7+ days); vg site; helpful staff; lge o'fits come fr S."
♦ 1 Apr-15 Oct. € 35.00   2015*

⊞ **FIRENZE** *1D3* (3km SW Rural) *43.72146, 11.21861* **Camping
Internazionale Firenze, Via San Cristofano 2, 50029 Bottai
(FI) [055 2374704; fax 2373412; internazionale@florence
camping.com; www.florencecamping.com]** Exit A1/E35 for
Firenze/Certosa & foll sp twds Florence. Site well sp in 1.4km.
Fairly steep climb on narr, v congested app rd. Med, pt sl, terr,
pt shd; wc; shwrs; chem disp; mv service pnt; EHU (6A) inc
(rev pol); gas; lndry; shop; rest, snacks; bar; playgrnd; pool;
internet; entmnt; 50% statics; dogs; bus; poss cr; Eng spkn;
rd noise; ccard acc. "Conv Florence, Siena; gates clsd 0000-
0700; vg, clean facs; friendly recep; touring pitches on hilltop
only - levelling poss diff; site diff in wet weather; poss cr." ♦
€ 34.00   2011*

FLORENCE see Firenze *1D3*

FOCE DI VARANO see Rodi Garganico *2G4*

FOLLONICA *1D3* (6km E Rural) *42.91291, 10.85253*
**Camping Vallicella, Loc Vallicella, 58020 Scarlino (GR)
[0566 37229; fax 37232; info@vallicellavillage.com;
www.vallicellavillage.com]** Fr E80, S1 Via Aurelia exit for
Scarlino-Scalo, foll sp Scarlino & site. Lge, hdg/mkd pitch,
terr, pt shd; wc (some cont); chem disp; mv service pnt; baby
facs; private san facs avail; shwrs inc; EHU (4-6A) inc; lndry
(inc dryer); shop; rest, snacks; bar; playgrnd; pool;
paddling pool; sand beach 6km; tennis; bike & boat hire;
tennis; archery; horseriding 3km; golf 10km; wifi; TV rm;
40% statics; dogs €4.50; sep car park; adv bkg; quiet; ccard
acc. ♦ 23 Apr-1 Oct. € 35.00 (CChq acc)   2011*

⊞ **FOLLONICA** *1D3* (3km NW Coastal) *42.94339, 10.71522*
**Camping Parco Vacanze Il Veliero, Isole Eolie, 58022
Follonica (GR) [0566 260099; fax 260100; ilveliero@
sivacanze.it; www.sivacanze.it]** Exit SS1 Follonica Nord S
onto SP152 Pratoranieri, site sp. Lge, pt shd; wc; chem disp; mv
service pnt; private san facs on pitches; sauna; shwrs; EHU inc;
lndry; shop; rest, snacks; bar; playgrnd; pool; paddling pool;
sand beach 1km; tennis; bike hire; golf 12km; some statics; adv
bkg; quiet. € 50.00   2009*

FOLLONICA *1D3* (5km NW Coastal) *42.95029, 10.68681*
Camping Village Pappasole, Loc Torre Mozza, Via di
Carbonifera 14, 57020 Vignale-Riotorto (LI) [0565 20414 or
20420; fax 20346; info@pappasole.it; www.pappasole.it]
Fr SS1 take Follonica Nord exit onto SS322 & foll sp twd
Piombino. After approx 1km turn L twd Torre Mozza onto
overpass over m'way. Site in 1km. V lge, hdg/mkd pitch, hdstg,
pt shd; wc; chem disp; mv service pnt; baby facs; private san
facs + kitchen avail; shwrs inc; EHU (3-10A) inc; gas; lndry (inc
dryer); shop; rest, snacks; bar; BBQ; playgrnd; pool; sand beach
adj; watersports; tennis; bike hire; games area; wifi; entmnt;
70% statics; dogs €9; phone; poss cr; Eng spkn; adv bkg; rd
& rlwy noise & poss noisy at w/end; ccard acc; red long stay/
LS; CKE/CCI. "Excel site; helpful staff; vg beach; lots of tourist
info." ◆ 3 Apr-16 Oct. € 56.50   2010*

FONDOTOCE see Verbania *1B1*

⊞ **FORNI DI SOPRA** *2E1* (2km E Rural) *46.42564, 12.56928*
Camping Tornerai, Stinsans. Via Nazionale, 33024 Forni-
di-Sopra (UD) [0433 88035] Site sp on SS52 Tolmezzo-Pieve
di Cadore rd, 2km E of Forni-di-Sopra (approx 35km by rd
fr Pieve-di-Cadore). Sm, pt sl, pt shd; wc (cont); chem disp (wc);
EHU (2A) €1 (extra for 6A) (long lead poss req); 50% statics;
dogs €2; poss cr; Eng spkn; quiet; ccard acc. "Conv CL-type
site for Forni-di-Sopra chairlift & Passo-della-Mauria; gd san
facs." € 20.00   2009*

FUCINE DI OSSANA see Dimaro *1D1*

FUSINA see Venezia *2E2*

GALLIPOLI *3A4* (4km SE Coastal) *39.99870, 18.02590*
Camping Baia di Gallipoli, Litoranea per Santa Maria di
Leuca, 73014 Gallipoli (LE) [0833 273210 or 338 8322910 l/s;
fax 275405 or 340 7632095 l/s; info@baiadigallipoli.com;
www.baiadigallipoli.com] Fr Brindisi/Lecce take S101 to
Gallipoli. Exit at sp Matino-Lido Pizzo & foll sp to site, on coast
rd bet Gallipoli & Sta Maria di Leuca. V lge, pt shd; htd wc;
chem disp; mv service pnt; shwrs inc; EHU (6A) inc; lndry (inc
dryer); shop; rest, snacks; bar; BBQ; playgrnd; pool; paddling
pool; sand beach 800m (free shuttle bus); tennis; games area;
wifi; entmnt; excursions; TV rm; statics; dogs (sm only) €3; sep
car park; quiet; ccard acc. ◆ 1 Apr-15 Sep. € 64.00   2014*

GEMONA DEL FRIULI *2E1* (12km NW Rural) *46.32570, 13.06317*
Camping Val del Lago, Loc Alesso, Via Tolmezzo 54, 33010
Trasaghis (UD) [0432 979164; fax 979455]
Exit A23 sp Gemona-del-Friuli onto S13 N. Foll sp for Alesso,
Trasaghis & Lago di Cavazzo. Site adj Camping Lago dei Tre
Comuni. Sm, mkd pitch, shd; wc; chem disp; shwrs inc; EHU
inc (poss rev pol); shop 2km; rest, snacks; bar; lake sw adj;
statics; dogs €3; Eng spkn; quiet. "Superbly situated; friendly
owner; gd facs." 1 Apr-30 Sep. € 24.00   2009*

GENOA see Genova *1C2*

GENOVA *1C2* (10km E Rural/Coastal) *44.38085, 9.07215*
Camping Genova Est, Via Marconi, Loc Cassa, 16031
Bogliasco (GE) [tel/fax 010 3472053; info@camping-
genova-est.it; www.camping-genova-est.it] Sp fr SS1 (Via
Aurelia) in both dir. Exit A12/E80 Genova/Nervi exit & foll La
Spezia sp to Bogliasco, look for sp on wall on L. V steep narr
access, unsuitable without high power/weight ratio. Med, terr,
pt shd; wc; mv service pnt; shwrs; EHU (5A) €2.70; gas; lndry;
shop; rest, snacks, bar high ssn; BBQ; playgrnd; shgl beach
1.5km; dogs €2; bus; sep car park; Eng spkn; quiet; ccard acc.
"Narr pitches; manhandling vans poss req; upper facs better
than lower; steep footpath to Bogliasco; adv bkg rec during
boat show in Oct." 15 Mar-20 Oct. € 25.00   2010*

⊞ **GENOVA** *1C2* (9km W Urban/Coastal) *44.43055, 8.81364*
Camping Villa Doria, Via al Campeggio Villa Doria 15,
16156 Pegli [tel/fax 010 6969600; villadoria@camping.it]
Take SS1 coast rd W fr Genova to cent Pegli, past airport thro
dock waterfront & look out for brown site sp on R by bus stop
at traff lts. Foll narr & steep app to site - care needed. Site sp
on wall on R round blind L-hand bend. Or exit A26 sp Pegli,
turn W & foll site sp. Sm, mkd pitch, pt sl, unshd; htd wc (some
cont); chem disp; mv service pnt; shwrs inc; EHU (3-10A) inc;
gas; lndry (inc dryer); shop; rest 1km; snacks; bar; playgrnd;
beach 1km; solarium; TV; dogs; phone; bus; sep car park; site
clsd Jan; poss cr; Eng spkn; ccard acc; CKE/CCI. "Friendly,
helpful owner; conv trains to Genoa & La Spezia; not rec for lge
o'fits due narr access rd & o'hanging branches; footpath to vill;
gd site but needs some TLC." ◆ € 30.00   2010*

⊞ **GENOVA** *1C2* (15km W Coastal) *44.41437, 8.70475*
Caravan Park La Vesima, Via Aurelia, Km 547, 16100
Arenzano (GE) [010 6199672; fax 6199686; info@
caravanparklavesima.it; www.caravanparklavesima.it]
E of Arenzano on coast rd, clearly sp. Or leave A10 at Arenzano
& go E on coast rd. Med, mkd pitch, hdstg, unshd; htd wc
(cont); chem disp; baby facs; fam bthrm; shwrs €0.50; EHU
(3A) inc (poss rev pol); gas; lndry; shop high ssn & 3km; rest,
snacks, bar high ssn; private shgl beach adj; 90% statics; no
dogs; poss cr; Eng spkn; adv bkg; rd, rlwy noise; CKE/CCI.
"Useful LS NH/sh stay; gd security; gd, clean san facs; v cr,
noisy high ssn; some pitches sm; vg site." € 32.60   2012*

GIANO DELL'UMBRIA *2E3* (1km SW Rural) *42.82932,
12.57178* Camping Pineta Di Giano, Via Monte Cerreto,
25 06030 Giano Dell'Umbria [39 07 42 93 00 40 or
39 34 03 76 23 43; fax 34 92 43 69 72; info@pinetadigiano.
com; www.pinetadigiano.com] N fr Spoleto on S418 twds
Montefalco. Turn L after Mercatello. Site well sp (brown) to
Griano dell'Umbria. Site just outside vill. Sm, mkd pitch, hdstg,
terr, shd; htd wc; shwr inc; EHU (3A); shop 1km; rest; snacks;
bar; htd pool; 60% statics; dogs; quiet. "Gd site; off beaten
track, v quiet in pine forest surrounded by long dist trails; v
conv for Spoleto." 1 Apr-30 Sep. € 18.00   2014*

GIGNOD see Aosta *1B1*

GIOVINAZZO *2H4* (1km NW Coastal) *41.19167, 16.65769*
Camping La Baia, Loc Trincea, 70054 Giovinazzo (BA)
[tel/fax 0803 945165; camping.labaia@libero.it;
www.campinglabaia.it] Well sp fr S16bis onto S16, then no
sp. Turn L at traff lts sp 'Lungomare', then L at end. Cont for
1km, site on L. Med, mkd pitch, some hdstg; pt shd; wc (mainly
cont); shwrs €0.50; EHU (6A) €3; lndry; shop 1km; snacks;
bar; shgl beach adj; 40% statics; dogs €3; poss noisy (rd &
disco adj); ccard acc; red CKE/CCI. "Attractive town & close
to cathedral town of Trani & 13thC Castel de Monte; no sea
views; gd NH." ♦ 1 May-30 Sep. € 26.00   2010*

GIULIANOVA LIDO *2F3* (2.9km N Coastal) *42.77790, 13.95613*
Camping Don Antonio (formerly Baviera Holiday Ovest),
Lungamare Zara Nord 127, 64022 Giulianova-Lido (TE)
[085 8008928; fax 8004420; baviera@camping.it;
www.campingbaviera.it] Exit A14/E55 dir Giulianova, site sp
at Lido, 2km N of Giulianova, sp adj Camping Holiday. Med,
mkd pitch, pt shd; wc; serviced pitches; shwrs inc; EHU (6A)
inc; lndry; shop, rest, snacks in Cmp Holiday adj; pool; sand
beach adj; playgrnd; games area; tennis adj; watersports;
entmnt; excursions; sep car park high ssn; statics; dogs free
(not acc Jul/Aug); adv bkg; quiet but some rlwy noise; red LS/
snr citizens; ccard acc; red CKE/CCI. "Excel family site; lots to
do in area." ♦ 16 May-13 Sep. € 42.00   2011*

> **"We must tell The Club about
> that great site we found"**
>
> Get your site reports in by mid-August
> and we'll do our best to get your updates
> into the next edition.

GIULIANOVA LIDO *2F3* (2.9km N Coastal) *42.77790,
13.95588* Camping Village Holiday, Lungamare Zara,
64022 Giulianova-Lido (TE) [085 8000053; fax 8004420;
holiday@camping.it; www.villaggioholiday.it] Exit A14/
E55 dir Giulianova, site sp at Lido, adj Baviera Camping. Lge,
pt shd; wc (some cont); chem disp; mv service pnt; serviced
pitches; shwrs inc; EHU (6A) €1.86; lndry; supmkt; rest, snacks;
bar; playgrnd; pool; sand beach adj; watersports; tennis; games
area; entmnt;TV; sep car park; 20% statics; dogs free (not acc
Jul/Aug); poss cr; adv bkg; quiet but some rlwy noise & tannoy;
ccard acc; red LS; red CKE/CCI. "Excel family site; sm pitches;
site clsd 1400-1600." ♦ 24 Apr-20 Sep. € 42.00   2009*

GIULIANOVA LIDO *2F3* (500m S Coastal) *42.73510, 13.98095*
Camping Stork, Viale Del Mare 11, 64020 Cologna-Spiaggia
(TE) [0858 937076; fax 937542; info@campingstork.com;
www.campingstork.com] Fr a'strada foll sp on SS80 to
Giulianova; at junc with SS16 turn R for 300m, turn L at traff
lts, site sp. V lge, mkd pitch, shd; wc; chem disp; mv service
pnt; baby facs; shwrs inc; EHU (6A) inc; lndry; supmkt; rest,
snacks; bar; playgrnd; pool; paddling pool; sand beach adj;
watersports; tennis; games area; bike hire; wifi; entmnt; TV;
cash machine; 40% statics; dogs €2.50; phone; sep car park
high ssn; adv bkg; ccard acc; red long stay. ♦ 19 Apr-13 Sep.
€ 38.50 (CChq acc)   2011*

GIUNCUGNANO *1C2* (2km W Rural) *44.20680, 10.23520*
Camping Argegna, Via Argegna, 55030 Giuncugnano (LU)
[0583 611182; fax 611536; info@toscanacampclub.com;
www.toscanacampclub.com] Exit A1 at Aulla. After bdge
turn R; at rndabt foll sp Fivizzano. Approx 5km bef Fivizzano
turn R onto rd SR445; foll sp Lucca to Carpinelli Pass, site sp in
4km on L - foll rd (approx 4m wide) to site. NB Fr Giuncugnano
rte to site narr & winding for 20km; poor surface in parts. Sm,
mkd pitch; shd; wc; mv service pnt; shwrs; EHU €2.20; lndry;
shop; rest, snacks, bar 100m; BBQ; cooking facs; games area;
WiFi; TV rm; some statics; dogs; adv bkg; quiet. "Peaceful
site in lovely, little-known, interesting area." 1 May-15 Oct.
€ 26.00   2011*

GLURNS/GLORENZA see Mals/Malles Venosta *1D1*

GOLDRAIN *1D1* (1km SW Urban) *46.61762, 10.81859*
Camping Cevedale, Via Val Venosta 59, 39021 Goldrain
[0473 742132; info@camping-cevedale.com;
www.camping-cevedale.com] SS38 Merano-Silandro, pass
Latsch/Laces to rndabt sp Goldrain/Martelltal, sp on R (do
not confuse vill of Lasa/Laas). Med, hdg pitch, pt shd; wc;
chem disp; mv service pnt; baby facs; shwrs; EHU (6A); lndry
(inc dryer); shop; BBQ; htd & cov pool; wifi; dogs €4; phone;
bus/train 50m; Eng spkn; adv bkg; quiet. "Excel site." ♦ ltd.
15 Mar-7 Nov. € 35.50   2015*

GOREGLIA ANTELMINELLI *1D2* (750m N Rural) *44.06642,
10.52879* Camping Pian d'Amora, Via Crocifisso, Loc.
Pian d'Amora, 55025 Coreglia Antelminelli [0583 78334;
info@campingpiandamora.nl; www.campingpiandamora.
nl] Fr A11 at Lucca foll sp Val Gaifagnama SS12. After 30km
at Piano di Coreglia turn N on minor rd 7km to Coreglia
Antelminelli. Site top of town. Sm, terr, shd; wc; chem disp; mv
service pnt; shwrs; EHU (10A); lndry; rest; bar; playgrnd; htd/
covrd pool; wifi; Eng spkn; adv bkg; quiet. "Beautiful historic
hill top town, 5 min walk; gd walking area; conv Lucca; sm
c'vans rec; excel." ♦ ltd. 15 Apr-1 Oct. € 35.50   2015*

GRADO *2E1* (2km E Coastal) *45.67848, 13.42021* Camping
Al Bosco, Loc La Rotta, 34073 Grado (GO) [043 180485; fax
181008; info@campingalbosco.it; www.campingalbosco.it]
Site in dunes E of Grado. App via narr rd, ent 3.6km, sp. Lge,
pt shd; wc; shwrs €0.30; EHU (3A) inc; lndry (inc dryer); shop;
rest, snacks; bar; playgrnd; sand beach 500m; bike hire; no
dogs; poss cr; adv bkg ess Jul/Aug; ccard acc. "Poss long walk
to facs; reasonable site." 1 May-15 Sep. € 28.00   2009*

GRAVEDONA *1C1* (3km NE Rural) *46.15438, 9.33701*
Camping Le Vele, 244 Via Case Sparse, 22013 Domaso
[0344 965049; fax 536107; levele@domaso.it; www.levele.
domaso.it] Site sp fr SS340. Med, mkd pitch, pt shd; htd wc;
chem disp; mv service pnt; sauna; shwrs inc; EHU (3A) inc;
lndry (inc dryer); shop nr; rest, snacks; bar; BBQ; playgrnd; htd
pool; lake sw & beach adj; watersports; fitness cent; internet;
15% statics; dogs free; bus 200m; adv bkg; quiet; ccard acc.
"Clean, well-run site; excel san facs; vg situation - direct access
to lake; sm pitches." 26 Mar-24 Oct. € 38.00   2010*

ITALY

GRAVEDONA *1C1* (2km SW Rural) *46.1255, 9.2842* **Camping La Breva, Via Cimitero 19, Loc Cossognini, 22014 Dongo (CO) [tel/fax 034 480017; info@campinglabreva.com; www.campinglabreva.com]** On E o'skts Dongo on SS340, site sp. Rec app fr Colico - avoid Julier Pass fr N if towing. Med, mkd pitch, some hdstg, pt sl, pt shd; htd wc (some cont); chem disp; mv service pnt; shwrs €0.80; EHU (6A) €1.50; gas; shop 500m; snacks; bar; BBQ; playgrnd; pool 2km; shgl beach adj; lake sw; 5% statics; no dogs; phone; sep car park; poss cr; Eng spkn; adv bkg; red long stay. "Clean, well-run, family-owned site; v helpful staff; pitches tight for lge o'fits; gd location next to lake; san facs basic diff to fill van with water or empty; elec usage poss poor." ♦ ltd. 1 Mar-31 Oct. € 26.00   2011*

GRAVEDONA *1C1* (2km SW Rural) *46.13268, 9.28954* **Camping Magic Lake, Via Vigna del Lago 60, 22014 Dongo (CO) [tel/fax 034 480282; camping@magiclake.it; www.magiclake.it]** Site sp on S340d adj Lake Como. Sm, pt sl, pt shd; htd wc; chem disp; mv service pnt; baby facs; shwrs inc; EHU (6A) inc; lndry; shop adj; snacks; bar; BBQ; playgrnd; lake sw adj; TV; 40% statics; dogs €3; bus 100m; poss cr; Eng spkn; adv bkg; quiet; red long stay; CKE/CCI. "Excel, friendly, family-run site; walk, cycle to adj vills along lake; excel facs; v.clean mod facs, cycle/kayak hire on site, cycle repairs on site." ♦ 8 Apr-11 Oct. € 38.00   2013*

GROSSETO *1D3* (10km SW Coastal) *42.71390, 11.00870* **Camping Cieloverde, Via della Trappola 180, 58046 Marina-di-Grosseto (GR) [0564 321611; fax 30178; info@cieloverde.it; www.cieloverde.it]** Fr Grosseto take SS322 twd Marina-di-Grosseto, then twd Principina-a-Mare. Site on R. V lge, pt shd; wc; private san facs avail; baby facs; shwrs inc; EHU (3-6A) inc; lndry (inc dryer); supmkt; rest, snacks; bar; BBQ; sand beach 800m (free shuttle); watersports; tennis 500m; games area; bike hire; wifi; entmnt; cinema; TV rm; some statics; adv bkg; ccard acc. "Conv Maremma Nature Reserve; some pitches for RVs." ♦ 9 May-20 Sep. € 49.00 (CChq acc)   2009*

GROSSETO *1D3* (12km SW Coastal) *42.74598, 10.94936* **Camping Le Marze, Strada Statale 322 della Collacchie, Le Marze, 58046 Marina-di-Grosseto (GR) [0564 35501; fax 744503; lemarze@boschettoholiday.it; www.boschetto holiday.it/lemarze]** Fr E80/SS1 S fr Livorno foll dual c'way round Grosseto by-pass. Leave at 4th exit Grossetto Sud; cont dir Grosseto for 5km on SP154; look for sp Marina on L & foll rd for 9km; at traff lts turn R onto SP158 sp Castiglione-della-Pescia, site on R in approx 5km. Lge, shd; wc (cont); chem disp; mv service pnt; baby facs; shwrs inc; EHU (3A) inc; gas; lndry (inc dryer); sm shop; rest; pizzeria; bar; BBQ areas (gas/elec); playgrnd; pool; private beach 1km; bike hire; fishing 500m; games rm; cinema; wifi; entmnt; TV; dogs €4.50; no o'fits over 7m; sep car park; 15% statics; adv bkg; quiet; red facs LS; ccard acc; red long stay/LS; CKE/CCI. "Site in pine forest; excel staff; vg san facs; some pitches uneven & poss tight lge o'fits, espec when site busy; free standing pool not suitable unsupervised childen; poss mosquitoes; excursions Elba, Florence, Rome, Siena." ♦ 1 Apr-7 Oct. € 49.00   2011*

GROTTAMMARE see Martinsicuro *2F3*

GUBBIO *2E3* (3.5km SW Rural) *43.32105, 12.56778* **Camping Citta di Gubbio, Frazione. Cipolleto 49, 06024 Gubbio (PG) [075 9272037; fax 9276620; info@gubbiocamping.com; www.gubbiocamping.com]** Fr E3 take 1st Gubbio exit onto Gubbio by-pass & take Perugia rd. Fork R in 500m beside garden cent into narr lane, site 1.5km on R. Fr Perugia on S298 site sp on L 4km bef Gubbio at bottom of hill at Ponte d'Assi, well sp. Med, pt shd; wc; chem disp; shwrs; EHU (3A) €3; lndry; shop, rest, snacks, bar 3.5km; playgrnd; pool; paddling pool; tennis; games area; bike hire; dogs €2.50; phone; Eng spkn; adv bkg; quiet; red long stay; ccard acc; red CKE/CCI. "Excel, friendly, spacious site; clean facs; Gubbio sm medieval city well worth a visit." ♦ 1 Apr-15 Sep. € 29.50   2011*

⊞ **GUBBIO** *2E3* (1.2km W) *43.35213, 12.56704* **Camping Parking Gubbio, Via Bottagnone 06024 Area Communale P4 [07 59 22 06 93]** Head NW on SR298 twd Via Bruno Buozzi, at rndbt take 2nd exit onto Viale Parruccini cont for 500m, take 1st exit at rndabt onto Viale Leonardo da Vinci, after 250m turn L onto Via Botagore. Sm; pt shd; no san facs; chem disp; mv service pnt; gd NH. "Only campervan parking allowed; historical town worth a visit." € 5.00   2014*

IDRO *1D1* (2km NE Rural) *45.7540, 457540* **Azur Ferienpark Idro Rio Vantone, Via Vantone 45, 25074 Idro (BS) [0365 83125; fax 823663; idro@azur-camping.de; www.idrosee.eu]** Fr Brescia, take S237 N. At S tip of Lago d'Idro, turn E to Idro. thro Crone, on E shore of lake, thro sh tunnel, site 1km on L, last of 3 sites. Lge, shd; wc; chem disp; mv service pnt; baby facs; serviced pitches; shwrs; EHU (6-16A) €2.50; lndry; gas; shop; rest, snacks; bar; playgrnd; paddling pool; tennis; lake adj; boat hire; windsurfing; games area; bike hire; internet; entmnt; TV rm; dogs €2.80; phone; poss cr; bkg; quiet; ccard acc; 5% red CKE/CCI. "Idyllic on lakeside with beautiful scenery; superb san facs; excel." ♦ 20 Mar-31 Oct. € 52.00   2013*

IMER *1D1* (1km E Rural) *46.14805, 11.79666* **Camping Calavise, Villaggio Sass Maor 36, Loc Pezze, 38050 Imer (TN) [tel/fax 0439 67468; info@campingcalavise.it; www.campingcalavise.it]** Fr Trento on S47 then N on S50 - take care as narr in places. Turn R at traff lts in Imer in front hotel Al Bivio to site in 1km. Med, mkd pitch, terr, pt shd; wc (mainly cont); chem disp; shwrs inc; EHU (2A) inc; lndry; shop 500m; rest, snacks 1km; bar; playgrnd; pool; wifi; TV rm; 80% statics; dogs €3; bus 1km; poss cr; Eng spkn; adv bkg; quiet; CKE/CCI. "V helpful owner; beautiful area; excel walking in National Park; easy 10km cycle track along rv; vg." ♦ 1 Jun-30 Sep & 8 Dec-30 Apr. € 22.50   2010*

⊞ **IMPERIA** *1B3* (1km SW Coastal) *43.86952, 7.99810* **Camping de Wijnstok, Via Poggi 2, 18100 Porto-Maurizio (IM) [tel/fax 0183 64986; info@campingdewijnstok.com; www.campingdewijnstok.com]** Exit A10/E80 Imperia W twds sea, take coast rd SS1 Via Aurelia dir San Remo. At km 651/1 turn R at Poggi, site sp. Med, shd; wc (some cont); chem disp; shwrs €0.70; EHU (3A) €2; gas; lndry; shop 200m; snacks; bar; shgl beach 500m; wifi; TV; 80% statics; phone; sep car park; site clsd mid-Dec to mid-Jan; quiet but some rd noise; ccard acc. "Shabby facs ltd LS; sm pitches diff for lge o'fits; sh walk to town; NH only." ♦ € 25.00   2010*

⊞ **IMPERIA** *1B3* (2km SW Coastal) *43.87152, 8.00362*
Camping Eucalyptus, Via D'Annunzio 32, 18100 Imperia
[tel/fax 0183 61534; info@campingeucalyptus.com;
www.campingeucalyptus.com] Exit A10 Imperia W. Turn
L after tolls. Site well sp. Diff access lge o'fits - rec site ent via
2nd gate 100m beyond 1st. Med, hdstg, pt terr, shd; wc; chem
disp; mv service pnt; shwrs inc; EHU (6A) €1.50; lndry; gas; bar;
rest 100m; shop 200m; sand beach 500m; wifi; some statics;
dogs; Eng spkn; red LS; CKE/CCI. "Quiet on terr pitches away
fr rd; each pitch set in own garden & site in grnds of villa;
interesting owner; mosquitoes." € 26.00   2010*

⊞ **IMPERIA** *1B3* (2km SW Coastal) *43.87244, 7.99997*
Camping Parco La Pineta, Via Tommaso Littardi 68, 18100
Imperia [0183 61498] Exit A10 Imperia W. Turn L after tolls.
Site well sp. Med, hdstg, terr, pt shd; wc; chem disp; shwrs
€1; EHU (3A) €2; lndry rm; shop & 200m; rest by beach; sand
beach adj; 95% statics; poss cr; Eng spkn; ccard not acc; quiet.
"Site in grnds of 17thC house; a few sm touring pitches - no
rm for awnings; clean san facs; pleasant owners; smart town
30 mins walk; gd." ♦ ltd. € 26.00   2009*

ISEO *1C1* (1km NE Rural) *45.66527, 10.06277* **Camping Quai,**
Via Antonioli 73, 25049 Iseo (BS) [tel/fax 030 9821610;
info@campingquai.it; www.campingquai.it]
Fr Brescia-Boario Terme rd by-passing Iseo, take NE exit; look
for 'Camping d'Iseo' sp on corner. After 200m cross rlwy, site
sp (sps obscured - go slow). Site adj Punta d'Oro on lakeside.
Med, mkd pitch, shd; wc (some cont); chem disp; mv service
pnt; shwrs inc; EHU (4A) inc (poss rev pol); lndry; shop, rest
1km; snacks; bar; BBQ; playgrnd; shgl beach & lake sw adj;
watersports; games area; boat-launching; 25% statics; dogs;
phone; bus, train 1km; sep car park; poss cr; Eng spkn; adv
bkg; some rd noise; ccard acc; red long stay/snr citizens. "Well-
kept; lake views fr some pitches; helpful manager; some noise
fr nrby rlwy." ♦ ltd. 18 Apr-21 Sep. € 41.00   2014*

ISEO *1C1* (500m NE Rural) *45.66416, 10.05722* **Camping**
Iseo, Via Antonioli 57, 25049 Iseo (BS) [tel/fax 030 980213;
info@campingiseo.it; www.campingiseo.it] Fr A4 exit
sp Rovato & immed foll brown sp Lago d'Iseo. Site well sp in vill.
Med, some hdg pitch, pt shd; wc (some cont); chem disp; mv
service pnt; baby facs; fam bthrm; some serviced pitches; shwrs
inc; EHU (6-10A) inc; gas; lndry; shop; rest 300m; snacks; bar;
playgrnd; beach adj; windsurfing; games area; bike hire; golf 3km
(red for campers); wifi; entmnt; some statics; dogs €3.50; phone;
poss v cr; Eng spkn; adv bkg; quiet; red CKE/CCI. "V scenic;
friendly, welcoming owner; well-organised, smart site; sm pitches;
extra for lakeside pitches; well-maintained, clean facs but ltd;
cruises on lake; many rests nr; excel; site next to a rlwy line, poss
sm noise; sm pitches." ♦ 1 Apr-1 Nov. € 39.00   2011*

ISEO *1C1* (500m NE Rural) *45.66388, 10.05638* **Camping**
Punta d'Oro, Via Antonioli 51-53, 25049 Iseo (BS)
[tel/fax 030 980084; info@camping-puntadoro.com;
www.puntadoro.com] Fr Brescia-Boario Terme into Iseo, look
for `Camping d'Iseo' sp on corner; after 200m cross rlwy, 1st R
to site in 400m on lakeside. Med, pt sl, pt shd; wc; chem disp;
mv service pnt; shwrs inc; EHU (4A) inc; lndry; shop 500m; rest
500m; snacks; bar; playgrnd; shgl beach; lake sw; boating; golf
6km; wifi; dogs €3.50; poss v cr high ssn; Eng spkn; some rlwy
noise; red snr citizens; CKE/CCI. "Strictly-run but friendly site;
gd security; beautiful area; friendly family run site cheerful and
eager to help." ♦ Easter-19 Oct. € 32.00   2011*

ISEO *2F2* (1km E Urban) *45.66700, 10.06766* **Camping**
Covelo, Via Covelo 18, 25049 Iseo [tel/fax 030 982 13 05;
info@campingcovelo.it; www.campingcovelo.it]
Fr A4 Bergamo-Brescia, take exit Palazzolo/SP469. Cont Onto
SP12. At rndabt take 2nd exit SPxi. Take 3rd exit at next rndabt
and foll sp to camp. Med, pt shd; wc; chem disp; shwrs; EHU
(6A); lndry (inc dryer); shops; rest; snacks; bar; playgrnd; sw adj;
games area; wifi; dogs €3.50; poss cr; Eng spkn; adv bkg; ccard
acc. "Excel site; v well run; adj to lake; beautiful views; range of
watersports; v helpful staff." 17 Apr-2 Nov. € 40.00   2014*

ISEO *1C1* (1.5km W Rural) *45.65689, 10.03739* **Camping Del**
Sole, Via per Rovato 26, 25049 Iseo (BS) [030 980288; fax
9821721; info@campingdelsole.it; www.campingdelsole.it]
Exit Brescia-Milan at Rivato-Lago d'Iseo exit & foll sp to Iseo.
At complex rd junc with rndabts on Iseo o'skirts, site
ent on L (lge sp). Site bet lakeside & rd, bef API petrol stn on
R. Lge, mkd pitch, shd; wc; chem disp; mv service pnt; htd
private bthrms avail; shwrs; EHU (6A) inc; lndry (inc dryer);
supmkt; rest, snacks; bar; playgrnd; htd pool; paddling pool;
shgl beach & lake sw; tennis; waterskiing; bike hire; games
area; wifi; entmnt; TV rm; 75% statics; dogs €3; sep car park;
poss cr; Eng spkn; adv bkg; quiet; ccard acc. "Glorious views;
excel facs; well-run, pleasant, popular lakeside site; pitches
poss closely packed; ltd waste/water disposal; narr site rds." ♦
15 Apr-25 Sep. € 41.00 (CChq acc)   2011*

ISEO *1C1* (1.5km W Rural) *45.65690, 10.03429* **Camping**
Sassabanek, Via Colombera 2, 25049 Iseo (BS)
[030 980300; fax 9821360; sassabanek@sassabanek.it;
www.sassabanek.it] On periphery of Iseo by lakeside. Lge,
pt shd; wc (some cont); chem disp; mv service pnt; sauna;
shwrs inc; EHU (3A) inc; gas; lndry; shop; rest, snacks; bar;
BBQ; playgrnd; pool; paddling pool; boating; windsurfing;
tennis; bike hire;TV; 50% statics; no dogs; phone; sep car
park; adv bkg; quiet; ccard acc. "Clean facs; sh walk to pretty
lakeside & vill; helpful staff; gd NH/sh stay." ♦ 1 Apr-30 Sep.
€ 35.00   2010*

ISPRA see Sesto Calende *1B1*

LAIVES/LEIFERS see Bolzano/Bozen *1D1*

⊞ **LAVENA** *1C1* (9km SW Rural) *45.95960, 8.86340*
International Camping di Rimoldi Claudio, Via Marconi
18, 21037 Lavena-Ponte-Tresa (VA) [0332 550117;
fax 551600; info@internationalcamping.com;
www.internationalcamping.com] On rte S233 going SW
into Italy fr Switzerland, turn SE after border twd Lavena-Ponte-
Tresa. Going twd Switzerland fr Italy on same rte turn R twd
vill. Site sp in vill. Med, pt sl, hdg pitch; pt shd; wc (some cont);
shwrs; EHU (2-6A) €1.50; lndry; supmkt opp; rest, snacks; bar;
playgrnd; sand beach on lake; mainly statics; poss cr; adv bkg;
quiet; ACSI card acc; CKE/CCI. "On smallest, most W bay of
Lake Lugano; excel facs; friendly, helpful staff; wall around site
so no lake views." € 40.50   2013*

ITALY

LAZISE *1D2* (1.5km N Urban) *45.50807, 10.73166* **Camp Municipale, Via Roma 1,37017 Lazise (VR) [045 7580020; fax 7580549; camping.municipale@comune.lazise.vr.it; www.comune.lazise.vr.it]** N on S249 fr Peschiera, thro Pacengo & Lazise, at rndabt cont on S249 then turn L into Via Roma. Site sp at end of rd. Care req in 100m, sharp R turn; site ent pt hidden. Med, hdg/mkd pitch, pt shd; wc; chem disp; mv service pnt; shwrs inc; EHU (10A) inc; lndry; shop 250m; rest, snacks, bar adj; lake sw & beach adj; 5% statics; dogs €3; Eng spkn; quiet; ccard acc. "Gd touring cent; some pitches v muddy; gd, clean facs; friendly staff; avoid arr bef 1500 Wed (mkt on app rd); easy walk along lake to interesting sm town."
♦ ltd. 22 Mar-2 Nov. € 32.00   2012*

LAZISE *1D2* (1km S Urban) *45.49722, 10.73694* **Camping Spiaggia d'Oro, Loc Bottona, Via Sentieri 1, 37017 Lazise (VR) [045 7580007; fax 7580611; info@campingspiaggia doro.com; www.campingspiaggiadoro.com]** Fr A4/E70 exit dir Peschiera & take SR249 N; site sp. Fr Innsbruck on A22 exit Lago di Garda S. At rndabt take SR450 for Peschiera, then in 8km exit to Lazise. V lge, mkd pitch, pt sl, pt shd; wc; chem disp; mv service pnt; shwrs inc; EHU (3-5A) inc (rev pol on 3A); gas; lndry; shop & supmkt; snacks; bar; playgrnd; 3 pools; sandy private beach & sw adj; boat hire; dogs €7; quiet; Eng spkn; ccard not acc; CKE/CCI. "Helpful staff; lovely location nr historic walled town; gd facs."
♦ 27 Mar-15 Oct. € 49.40   2009*

LAZISE *1D2* (1.5km S Rural) *45.49277, 10.73305* **Camping La Quercia, Loc Bottona, 37017 Lazise (VR) [045 6470577; fax 6470243; laquercia@laquercia.it; www.laquercia.it]** Exit A22/E45 at Affi/Lago di Garda Sud or exit A4/E70 at Peschiera-del-Garda. Site on SR249, on SE shore of lake. V lge, hdg/mkd pitch, pt sl, shd; htd wc; chem disp; mv service pnt; baby facs; fam bathrm; shwrs inc; EHU (6A) inc; gas; lndry (inc dryer); shops; rest, snacks; bar; playgrnd; pool; paddling pool; waterslide; jacuzzi; private sand beach; watersports; tennis; games area; gym; wifi; entmnt; 15% statics; dogs €6.90; phone; vehicle safety checks for cars/m'vans; poss cr; adv bkg. "Superb site for family holidays; many excel sports & leisure facs; some pitches on lakeside; easy walk to town along beach; highly rec." ♦ 1 Apr-4 Oct. € 61.00   2012*

"I need an on-site restaurant"

We do our best to make sure site information is correct, but it is always best to check any must-have facilities are still available or will be open during your visit.

⊞ **LAZISE** *1D2* (2km S Urban) *45.47912, 10.72635* **Camping Amici di Lazise, Loc Fossalta Nuova, Strada del Roccolo 8, 37017 Lazise (VR) [045 6490146; fax 6499448; daniela@campingamicidilazise.it]** S fr Lazise, immed bef high rest with Greek columns (bef Gardaland) take side rd on R, site on R. Med, pt shd; wc (some cont); mv service pnt; some serviced pitches; shwrs inc; EHU (6A) inc; lndry; shop; rest; bar; playgrnd; pool; paddling pool; shgl beach 300m; entmnt; 40% statics; dogs €4.50; poss cr; Eng spkn; adv bkg; quiet; red LS. "Gd." ♦ € 32.00   2011*

LAZISE *1D2* (2.5km S Rural) *45.4825, 10.72861* **Camping Piani di Clodia, Loc Bagatta, 37017 Lazise (VR) [045 7590456; fax 7590939; info@pianidiclodia.it; www.pianidiclodia.it]** Site on SR249 just bef Camping Fossalta. V lge, mkd pitch, pt sl, terr, pt shd; wc (some cont); chem disp; 25% serviced pitch; shwrs inc; EHU (10A); lndry; shop & 2km; rest, snacks; bar; playgrnd; 5 pools; private shgl beach adj; tennis; games area; bike hire; solarium; 10% statics; dogs €9; bus; Eng spkn; adv bkg; red long stay/ LS; ccard acc; red LS; CKE/CCI. "Excel clean facs; superb pools; ideal for families; v helpful staff; some pitches poss diff lge o'fits." ♦ 24 Mar-14 Oct. € 46.00   2009*

See advertisement inside the front cover

LAZISE *1D2* (900m S Rural) *45.49861, 10.7375* **Camping Du Parc, Via Gardesana, 110 I, 37017 Lazise (VR) [045 7580127; fax 6470150; duparc@campingduparc.com; www.campingduparc.com]** Site on W side of lakeside rd SR249. Lge, pt sl, hdg pitch, pt shd; wc; chem disp; mv service pnt; shwrs; EHU (5A) inc (rev pol); lndry; shop; rest, snacks; bar; playgrnd; pool; waterslides; sand beach & lake sw; watersports; boat & bike hire; gym; entmnt; 15% statics; dogs €5.70; poss cr at w/end; Eng spkn; adv bkg; red LS; ccard acc; red LS. "Sh walk to old town & ferry terminal; lovely lakeside position; excel, well-maintained site; vg san facs; gd size pitches, some on lake - long walk to water point; vg pizzeria & pool; quiet LS; ideal for families; gd security; Magic of Europe discount; vg; site improved every year; most pitches have water & drain." ♦ 15 Mar-31 Oct. € 48.00   2015*

⊞ **LECCE** *3A4* (10km W Rural) *40.36417, 18.09889* **Camping Lecce Namaste, 73100 Lecce [0832 329647; info@camping-lecce.it; www.camping-lecce.it]** Fr Lecce ring rd exit junc 15 W dir Novoli, in 5km immed after (abandoned) sm petrol stn turn R at sp Namaste. App rd to site potholed/gravelled. Site may appear clsd - sound horn for attention. Sm, some hdstg, pt shd; wc; shwrs inc; EHU (10A) inc; shop 2km; beach 16km; bus to Lecce; quiet. "Gd, clean site but dated facs; conv for Baroque city of Lecce & coast around heel of Italy." € 21.00   2015*

LECCO *1C1* (5.8km S) *45.81555, 9.39969* **Camping Village Riviera, Via Foppaola 113, 23852, Garlate [0341 680346; info@campingvillageriviera.com; www.campingvillageriviera.com]** Head S on SS36, take exit Pescate/Lecco, cont strt, at rndbt take 3rd exit onto Via Roma, over rndbt, cont onto Via Statale, turn L onto Via Foppaola, site on L. Sm, hdg pitch, pt shd; wc; shwrs; chem disp; EHU (10A); lndry; playgrnd; games rm; wifi; TV in bar; bus; Eng spkn. "Lake location with free kayak, pedalo, gym, playgrnd & pool." ♦ ltd. € 26.00   2014*

LECCO *1C1* (4km W Rural) *45.81730, 9.34307* **Camping Due Laghi, Via Isella 34, 23862 Civate (LC) [tel/fax 0341 550101; erealin@tin.it; www.duelaghicamping.com]** S side of Lecco-Como rd on lake. Use slip rd mkd Isella/Civate. Turn L at T-junc, then L over bdge; foll v narr app rd to site, sp. Med, pt sl, shd; wc (cont); shwrs inc; EHU (4A) inc; gas; lndry; shop; rest, snacks; bar; pool; paddling pool; games area; mainly statics; dogs €3; quiet; Eng spkn. "Unkempt site; gd, modern san facs; app to site is v narr." 1 Apr-30 Sep. € 36.00   2014*

You can now fill in site reports online

LECCO *1C1* (9km NW Rural) *45.92138, 9.28777* **Camping La Fornace, Via Giuseppe Garibaldi, 52 23865 Oliveto-Lario (LC) [tel/fax 031 969553; lafornace@libero.it; www.lafornace.it]** Fr Lecco SP583 twd Bellagio. Site on R at '37km' sp. Fr Bellagio on SP583 site on L 100m after Onno boundary sp. V sharp L turn at yellow sp. App diff for lge o'fits, narr app rd. Sm, mkd pitch, hdstg, pt sl, pt shd; wc (male cont); chem disp; mv service pnt; shwrs inc; EHU (5A) inc; shop; rest, snacks; bar; beach & lake sw adj; games rm; dogs; poss cr; adv bkg; quiet; red LS; CKE/CCI. "Peaceful, lakeside site but poss loud music fr bar until sm hrs; delightful setting; simple, clean facs." 1 Apr-30 Sep. € 22.00   2013*

LENNO see Menaggio *1C1*

"Satellite navigation makes touring much easier"

Remember most sat navs don't know if you're towing or in a larger vehicle – always use yours alongside maps and site directions.

LEVANTO *1C2* (1km NE Coastal) *44.17364, 9.62550* **Camping Cinque Terre, Sella Mereti, 19015 Levanto (SP) [tel/fax 0187 801252; info@campingcinqueterre.it; www.campingcinqueterre.it]** Clearly sp fr cent of Lèvanto. Fr E turn L off SS1 to Lèvanto, sp Carradano, site on R bef town. Sm, hdg/mkd pitch, terr, shd; htd wc (mainly cont); chem disp; mv service pnt; shwrs €2; EHU (3A) inc; gas; lndry; shop 500m; rest 500m; snacks; bar; sm playgrnd; shgl/sand beach 1km; games rms; wifi; TV; no dogs high ssn; sep car park; bus to beach high ssn; poss cr; adv bkg; quiet; ccard not acc; red LS; CKE/CCI. "Excel, friendly, family-run site; gd, modern san facs; steep ent, but site level; quiet and secluded; helpful staff; some rd noise; sm pitches." ◆ ltd. Easter-30 Sep. € 35.00   2013*

⊞ **LEVANTO** *1C2* (4km NE Rural) *44.17561, 9.63665* **Camping San Michele, Localita' Busco, 19015 Levanto (SP) [tel/fax 0187 800 449; info@campingsanmichele.net; www.campingsanmichele.net]** Head S on SS566 dir Carrodano Inferiore-Levanto. At 2nd rndabt take 3rd exit, then turn L onto Localita Albero D'Oro. Campsite on the R after 2.3km. Lge, hdstg, terr, pt shd, wc (cont), chem disp; shwrs; snacks; bar; scooter hire; poss cr; Eng spkn. "Helpful staff; fair site; clean but tired facs." € 29.00   2014*

LEVANTO *1C2* (1km E Coastal) *44.17505, 9.62289* **Camping Pian di Picche, Pian di Picche, 19015 Levanto (SP) [tel/fax 0187 800597; piandipicche@libero.it]** Clearly sp fr cent of Lèvanto. Fr E turn L off SS1 to Lèvanto, sp Carradano, site on R bef town; adj Camping Cinque Terre. Med, hdg pitch, terr, pt shd; wc (some cont); chem disp; shwrs €0.50; EHU (3A) inc; gas; lndry; sm shop; rest 200m; bar; BBQ; shgl beach 800m; TV; dogs; sep car park high ssn; Eng spkn; quiet; ccard acc. "Basic facs; access to site/pitches diff - narr rds; early arr rec in Aug; conv Cinque Terre vills; friendly, helpful staff." ◆ 1 Apr-30 Sep. € 34.00   2010*

⊞ **LEVANTO** *1C2* (400m SE Coastal/Urban) *44.16656, 9.61366* **Camping Acqua Dolce, Via Guido Semenza 5, 19015 Levanto (SP) [0187 808465; fax 807365; mail@ campingacquadolce.com; www.campingacquadolce.com]** Site sp fr town cent, app rd to Levanto steep & winding. Site ent steep. Pls do not use SatNav fr town. Med, mkd pitch, hdstg, terr, shd; wc (some cont); chem disp; mv service pnt; serviced pitches; shwrs inc; EHU (6A) €2.50 (rev pol); lndry; shops adj; rest, snacks; bar; playgrnd; pool 250m; sand beach 300m; dogs; phone; sep car park; site clsd mid-Jan to end Feb; poss cr; Eng spkn; adv bkg; ccard acc; red LS. "Site ent poss diff; sm pitches; vg, modern san facs but unisex; o'fits parked v close high ssn; not rec c'vans over 6m; gd touring base Cinque Terre vills; gd walks fr site; lovely, clean beach; easy walk to boat terminal & rlwy stn." ◆ € 38.50   2015*

LEVICO TERME *1D1* (1km S Rural) *46.00638, 11.28944* **Camping Jolly, Via Pleina 5, 38056 Levico-Terme (TN) [0461 706934; fax 700227; mail@campingjolly.com; www.campingjolly.com]** Foll sp to Levico fr A22 or SS12 onto SS27; site sp. Lge, mkd pitch, shd; wc; chem disp; mv service pnt; serviced pitches; baby facs; shwrs inc; EHU (6A) inc; gas; lndry (inc dryer); shop & 500m; rest 200m; snacks; bar; BBQ; playgrnd; pool high ssn; paddling pool; shgl beach 200m; golf 7km; internet; entmnt; 30% statics; dogs €5; poss cr; adv bkg; quiet; red snr citizens. "Health spa nr; vg." ◆ 1 Apr-10 Oct. € 38.00   2011*

"There aren't many sites open at this time of year"

If you're travelling outside peak season remember to call ahead to check site opening dates – even if the entry says 'open all year'.

LEVICO TERME *1D1* (5km SW Rural) *46.00392, 11.25838* **Camping Spiaggia, Viale Venezia 12, 38050 Calceranica al Lago (TN) [tel/fax 0461 723037; info@campingspiaggia.net; www.campingspiaggia.net]** Foll sp to Levico fr Trento; after exit rd turn L & in 400m turn L foll sp to site. Site after Camping Jolly on S side of lake. Med, hdg/mkd pitch, pt shd; wc; chem disp; mv service pnt; private san facs avail; shwrs inc; EHU inc; playgrnd; private shgl beach & lake sw (across rd); some statics; dogs €3; poss cr; Eng spkn; quiet. "Gd site; new san facs (2015) & private bthrms." 10 Apr-27 Sep. € 22.50   2015*

LEVICO TERME *1D1* (6km SW Urban) *46.00574, 11.24698* **Camping Penisola Verde, Via Penisola Verde, 5 38050 Galceranica Al Lago [0461 723272; fax 1820746; info@penisolaverde.it; www.penisolaverde.it]** Exit Trento-Padova SS47 either end of lake for Calceranica. Turn W in vill at camping sp, over rlwy x-ing and immed L to lakeside site. Med, mkd pitch, hdstg, pt shd; wc; chem disp; mv service pnt; shwrs inc; EHU (6A); lndry (inc dryer); rest; café; snacks; bar; BBQ; playgrnd; beach, lake sw; games area; wifi; 10% statics; dogs €3; train 200m; bus 100m; twin axles; poss cr; Eng spkn; adv bkg; quiet; red in LS. "Mountain views across lake; beach has sep area for sw, fishing & boating; excel." 9 May-13 Sep. € 36.00   2015*

ITALY

LEVICO TERME *1D1* (2km W Rural) *46.00444, 11.28527*
**Camping Due Laghi, Loc Costa 3, 38056 Levico-Terme (TN)
[0461 706290; fax 707381; info@campingclub.it;
www.campingclub.it]** E fr Trento on S47 to Levico Terme;
L at junc & in 100m turn L up Trento slip rd & foll sp to site
immed on R on lake. Lge, pt shd; wc (some cont); chem disp;
mv service pnt; baby facs; sauna; shwrs inc; EHU (3-6A) inc;
gas; lndry (inc dryer); shop; rest, snacks; bar; BBQ; htd pool;
paddling pool; shgl beach 500m; tennis; games area; bike
hire; wifi; entmnt; TV rm; 5% statics; dogs €4; phone; poss cr;
Eng spkn; adv bkg; some rd noise; ccard acc; red long stay/snr
citizens. "Friendly, helpful owner; clean facs; individ washrms
avail; scenic area & pretty town." ♦ 14 Apr-11 Sep. € 34.00
(CChq acc)   2011*

LEVICO TERME *1D1* (5km W Rural) *46.00194, 11.25527*
**Camping Al Pescatore, Via dei Pescatori 1, 38050
Calceranica-al-Lago (TN) [0461 723062; fax 724212;
trentino@campingpescatore.it; www.campingpescatore.it]**
Exit Trento-Padova rd (SS47) either end of lake for Calceranica.
Turn W in vill over rlwy x-ing & R on to lakeside. Site sp in
300m. Lge, pt shd; wc; chem disp; mv service pnt; shwrs inc;
EHU (3A) inc; lndry (inc dryer); shop; rest, snacks 200m; bar;
pool; paddling pool; shgl beach & lake sw adj; wifi; entmnt;
10% statics; dogs €3; poss cr; quiet. "Vg, modern san facs;
lovely lakeside location; cycle rtes fr site." ♦ 7 May-11 Sep.
€ 32.50   2011*

LEVICO TERME *1D1* (5km W Rural) *46.00458, 11.26034*
**Camping Mario Village, Via Lungolago 4, 38052 Caldonazzo
(TN) [0461 723341; fax 723106; direzione@campingmario.
com; www.campingmario.com]** Exit A22 onto SS47 E. Past
Pergine foll sp Calceranica & Caldonazzo. Site on lakeside.
Med, mkd pitch, pt sl, pt shd; wc; chem disp; mv service pnt;
baby facs; shwrs inc; EHU (6A) inc; gas; lndry; shop; rest,
snacks adj; bar; playgrnd; pool; solarium; lake sw; games
area; wifi; entmnt; some statics; dogs €3; phone; poss cr;
Eng spkn; adv bkg; quiet; red LS. "Lovely location; mountain
views; cycle paths; vg, modern san facs." ♦ 1 May- 13 Sep.
€ 25.00   2009*

LIDO DELLE NAZIONI see Comacchio *2E2*

LIDO DI JESOLO *2E2* (5.8km NE Coastal) *45.52862, 12.69693*
**Campsite Parco Capraro, Via Corer 2 ramo, 4 30016 Lido
di Jesolo [0421 961073; fax 362994; info@parcocapraro.it;
www.parcocapraro.it]** Fr Jesolo head NE on Via Roma Destra
twrds Via Giotto da Bondone. Cont onto Via Loghetto, then
onto Via Cà Gamba, L onto Via Corer. Site on L. Lge, pt shd;
wc, chem disp; mv service pnt; baby facs; shwrs; EHU (16A);
lndry (inc dryer); shop; rest; café; bar; takeaway; bar; bbq;
playgrnd; htd pool; games rm; bike hire; entmnt; wifi; tv in bar;
dogs; public transport 1km; twin axles; Eng spkn; quiet. "Vg;
v well kept family site; path thro sm pine forest leads to beach
& bus stop to cent of town; vg rest/bar; superb sw pool."
1 Mar-28 Sep. € 44.50   2014*

LIDO DI JESOLO *2E2* (300m W Coastal) *45.48425, 12.58762*
**Jesolo International Club Camping, Via Alberto da
Guissano 1, 30017 Lido-di-Jesolo (VE) [0421 971826;
fax 972561; info@jesolointernational.it; www.jesolo
international.it]** Site at W end of Lido-di-Jesolo, twd
Cavallino. V lge, mkd pitch, shd; wc; serviced pitches; chem
disp; mv service pnt; shwrs inc; EHU (10A) inc; gas; lndry; shop;
rest, snacks; bar; playgrnd; pool; paddling pool; sand beach
adj; watersports; tennis; boat hire; games area; golf 3km; wifi;
entmnt; sat TV; 10% statics; no dogs; site boat to Venice; sep
car par; poss cr; quiet; ccard acc; red long stay/LS. "Superb site;
many activities." ♦ 1 May-30 Sep. € 50.00   2010*

LIDO DI JESOLO *2E2* (6km NW Coastal) *45.55356, 12.76705*
**Portofelice Camping Village, Viale dei Fiori, 30020 Eraclea-
Mare (VE) [0421 66441; fax 66021; info@portofelice.it;
www.portofelice.it]** Exit A4 sp Caorle. In Caorle foll coast rd
S to Eraclea-Mare, site sp. V lge, hdg/mkd pitch, shd; wc; chem
disp; baby facs; some serviced pitches; shwrs inc; EHU (6A) inc;
gas; lndry; shop; rest, snacks; bar; playgrnd; pools; paddling
pool; sand beach 400m; tennis; games area; golf 6km; entmnt;
50% statics; no dogs; phone; bus; sep car park; poss cr; Eng
spkn; adv bkg; ccard acc; red long stay/snr citizens. "Excel pool
complex." ♦ ltd. 9 May-16 Sep. € 41.00   2009*

LIDO DI SAVIO see Cervia *2E2*

LIGNANO SABBIADORO *2E1* (2km NE Urban) *45.68196,
13.12580* **Camping Sabbiadoro, Via Sabbiadoro 8, 33054
Lignano-Sabbiadoro (UD) [0431 71455; fax 721355;
campsab@lignano.it; www.campingsabbiadoro.it]**
Fr Latisano strt rd 20km to Lignano. Bear L & foll sp to
Sabbiadoro. After 3km thro pine trees on edge of town
turn R. Rndabt with BP g'ge after 400m. Site opp. V lge, pt
shd; shwrs; wc; EHU (4A) inc; lndry; shop; rest, snacks; bar;
playgrnd; htd pool; paddling pool; tennis; bike hire; games
area; internet; some statics; dogs €2; adv bkg; ccard acc; quiet.
"Vg; fine beach for children 20 mins walk." ♦ 4 Apr-18 Oct.
€ 35.50   2009*

LIMONE SUL GARDA *1D1* (650m S Rural) *45.80555, 10.7875*
**Camping Garda, Via 4 Novembre, 25010 Limone-sul-
Garda (TN) [tel/fax 0365 954550; horstmann.hotel@tin.it]**
Site sp fr SS45b. Sm, mkd pitch, hdstg, pt sl, terr, pt shd; wc
(cont); chem disp; shwrs €0.25; EHU (3A) €1; lndry; shop
250m; rest, snacks high ssn; pool; paddling pool; shgl beach &
lake sw; bike hire; 10% statics; dogs €4; poss cr; Eng spkn; adv
bkg; quiet; CKE/CCI. "Splendid views; v friendly owner; clean,
well-kept site adj to lake; excel pool; tired facs but ok (2014)."
♦ 1 Apr-31 Oct. € 38.00   2015*

⊞ **LIVORNO** *1C3* (10km S Coastal) *43.48119, 10.33327*
**Camping Village Miramare, Via del Littorale 220, 57100
Antignano (LV) [0586 580402; fax 587462; contact@
campingmiramare.com; www.campingmiramare.com]**
Fr Livorno foll SS1 in dir Grossetto/Rome. Site on R just after
2nd rd tunnel. Med, hdg pitch, hdstg, pt shd; wc (cont); chem
disp; mv service pnt; shwrs inc; EHU (10A) inc; lndry; shop &
5km; rest, snacks; bar; BBQ; playgrnd; pool; paddling pool; shgl
beach adj; wellness cent; entmnt; internet; TV; 10% statics;
bus; phone; no dogs; quiet but some rlwy noise; adv bkg; Eng
spkn; red long stay; ccard acc. "Extra for beachside pitches; ltd
space/access for twin-axle vans; conv visits Pisa, Siena, Florence
& wine areas; lovely setting." ♦ € 52.00   2009*

LUCCA 1D3 (800m NW Urban) 43.85000, 10.48583 Camper Il Serchio, Via del Tiro a Segno 704, Santa Anna, 55100 Lucca (LU) [tel/fax 0583 317385; info@ camperilserchio.it; www.camperilserchio.it] Sp fr main rds to Lucca & fr town. Med, hdg/mkd pitch, hdstg, pt shd; wc; chem disp; mv service pnt; shwrs inc; EHU (5A) inc; lndry (inc dryer); rest nr; BBQ; playgrnd; pool €5; tennis, games area opp; bike hire; wifi; dogs; bus; poss cr; adv bkg; quiet but disco noise nrby; "Attractive pitches; mainly for m'vans - not suitable lge car/c'van o'fits or lge tents; vg site."
♦ € 25.00   2012*

"That's changed – Should I let The Club know?"

If you find something on site that's different from the site entry, fill in a report and let us know. See www.caravanclub.co.uk/europereport.

LUINO 1C1 (6km N Rural) 46.04189, 8.73279 Camping Lido Boschetto Holiday, Via Pietraperzia 13, 21010 Maccagno (VA) [tel/fax 0332 560250; lido@boschettoholiday.it; www.boschettoholiday.it/lido] On E shore of Lake Maggiore on SS394 bet Bellinzona & Laveno. Fr Luino pass under 2 rlwy bdges & foll sp L twd lake, site clearly sp. Med, pt shd; wc; shwrs inc; chem disp; mv service pnt; EHU (3-4A) €3.50; (poss rev pol); lndry; shop; snacks adj; playgrnd; lake sw & beach adj; watersports; some statics; dogs €3; adv bkg; quiet; ccard acc; CKE/CCI. "Hydrofoil/ferries fr vill to all parts of lake; trains to Locarno." 1 Apr-30 Sep. € 29.00 (CChq acc)   2011*

MACCAGNO see Luino 1C1

MAGIONE 2E3 (10km S Rural) 43.08140, 12.14340 Camping Polvese, Via Montivalle, 06060 Sant' Arcangelo-sul-Trasimeno (PG) [075 848078; fax 848050; polvese@ polvese.com; www.polvese.com] Fr A1 exit dir Lake Trasimeno to Castiglione-del-Lago, then S599 to San Arcangelo. Med, mkd pitch, pt shd; wc (cont); chem disp; mv service pnt; shwrs inc; EHU (10A) inc; gas; lndry; shop; snacks; bar; playgrnd; 2 pools; paddling pool; sand beach adj; watersports; lake fishing; bike hire; games area; wifi; entmnt; 40% statics; dogs €2; phone; poss cr; adv bkg; quiet; red long stay; CKE/CCI. "Gd touring base for Umbria; lakeside pitches avail; helpful staff." ♦ 1 Apr-30 Sep. € 22.00 (CChq acc)   2012*

MAGIONE 2E3 (5km SW Rural) 43.12422, 12.16700 Camping Riva Verde, Loc Trasiemeno, Via Ghandi 5/7, 06063 San Feliciano (PG) [tel/fax 075 8479351; info@ rivaverdecamping.com; www.rivaverdecamping.com] Exit SS75 at Magione, foll SS599 twd Chiusi. In 4km R on SP316 to San Feliciano & foll to site at N end of vill on lakeside. Med, shd; wc; shwrs; EHU inc; shops 1km; bar; rest; BBQ; pool adj high ssn; lake sw; waterskiing; games area; entmnt; lge new pool (2011), many statics; no dogs; sep car park; poss cr; adv bkg; quiet. "Excel for touring Umbria; individual washrms; lovely lake views; hot water to shwrs only; diff for lge o'fits." ♦ 1 Apr-30 Sep. € 22.00   2011*

MAGIONE 2E3 (6km SW Rural) 43.08835, 12.15630 Camping Villaggio Italgest, Via Martiri di Cefalonia, 06060 Sant' Arcangelo-sul-Trasimeno (PG) [075 848238 or 848292; fax 848085; camping@italgest.com; www.italgest.com] Fr Magione, take SS599 on S edge of Lake Trasimeno; site sp to R on app to Sant' Arcangelo. Lge, mkd pitch, pt shd; wc (some cont); chem disp; mv service pnt; baby facs; shwrs inc; EHU (6A) inc; gas; lndry (inc dryer); shop; rest, snacks; bar; cooking facs; playgrnd; pool; paddling pool; waterslides; lake sw & private sand beach adj; fishing; watersports; tennis; boat, bike hire; games area; games rm; wifi; entmnt; sat TV rm; 60% statics; dogs €2.50; sep car park; poss cr esp w/end; Eng spkn; adv bkg (dep); ccard acc; CKE/CCI. "High standard, well-maintained site; mosquitoes poss a prob; friendly owner; helpful staff; clean facs; noisy nr disco & recep; quiet LS; highly rec." ♦ 20 Apr-30 Sep. € 28.50   2009*

MALCESINE 1D1 (Urban) 45.76583, 10.81096 Camping Villaggio Turistico Priori, Via Navene 31, 37018 Malcesine (VR) [045 7400503; fax 6583098; antpriori@katamail.com; www.appartement-prioriantonio.it] Well sp in town cent. Take care if app fr N. Sm, mkd pitch, hdstg, pt sl, terr, pt shd; wc; chem disp; shwrs inc; EHU (3A) inc; lndry; shop adj; rest, snacks, bar adj; lake sw & shgl beach 200m; no dogs; phone; poss cr; some rd noise; adv bkg; Eng spkn; CKE/CCI. "Vg; conv all amenities & Monte Baldo funicular." 15 Apr-16 Oct. € 24.00   2011*

MALCESINE 1D1 (2km N Rural) 45.7850, 10.82027 Camping Tonini, Via Gardesana 378, Loc Campagnola, 37018 Malcesine (VR) [tel/fax 0457 401341; info@campingtonini. com; www.campingtonini.com] Site sp on SS249 on lakeside, sp at gate. Med, mkd pitch, terr, pt sl, pt shd; wc; chem disp; mv service pnt; shwrs inc; EHU (6A) €2; lndry; sm shop; rest, snacks, bar 2km; shgl beach thro tunnel; dogs €2; poss cr; Eng spkn; some rd noise; CKE/CCI. "In beautiful position, walking dist town; gd sized pitches; clean, modern san facs; gd views; friendly owner; gd cent mountain walking/biking & windsurfing; excel." ♦ ltd. 1 Apr-5 Oct. € 25.00   2009*

MALCESINE 1D1 (3km N Rural) 45.78971, 10.82609 Camping Martora, Campagnola, Martora 2, 37018 Malcesine (VR) [045 4856733; fax 4851278; martora@ martora.it; www.martora.it] On E side of lake on rd SS249 at km 86/11. Ent up concrete rd bet iron gates at 'Prinz Blau' sp. Med, mkd pitch, pt sl, pt shd; wc; chem disp; shwrs; EHU (4A) inc; gas 200m; rest 100m; lake sw, windsurfing adj; wifi; 10% statics; poss cr; adv bkg; quiet. "Lakeside cycle path to town." 1 Apr-3 Oct. € 27.00   2011*

MALCESINE 1D1 (5km S Rural) 45.7300, 10.78333 Camping Bellavista, Via Gardesana 4, Loc Vendemme, 37010 Cassone (VR) [tel/fax 045 7420244; info@camping bellavistamalcesine.com; www.campingbellavistamalcesine. com] 1km S of Cassone on R of rd SS249. Steep access rd. Lge, terr, pt shd; wc; mv service pnt; shwrs; EHU (5A) inc (poss rev pol); gas; lndry; shop; rest adj; bar; playgrnd; shgl beach & lake sw; no dogs; poss cr; adv bkg; quiet. "Ltd facs LS; footpath along lake shore; lovely views over lake; on arr park 20m past STOP sp at recep; v clean san facs." € 31.00   2009*

⊞ **MALS/MALLES VENOSTA** *1D1* (1km S Rural) *46.68416, 10.55055* **Mals Camping, Bahnhofstrasse/Via Stazione 51, 39024 Mals (BZ) [0473 835179; fax 845172; info@camping mals.it; www.campingmals.it]** Exit A12 to Landeck. In Landeck take 1st exit at rndabt over rv bdge, then turn L & foll sp Reschen Pass. On app Mals do not take any of L turns into town (v narr streets); stay on main rd until traff lts then turn R twd stn. Site in 500m on L. Sm, hdg/mkd pitch, terr, pt shd; htd wc; chem disp; mv waste; shwrs inc; EHU (16A) inc; gas; lndry; shop 500m; snacks; bar; playgrnd; htd, covrd pool, tennis nr; bike hire adj; wifi; dogs €3; bus/train 250m; skibus 100m; Eng spkn; adv bkg; quiet; ccard acc; CKE/CCI. "Gd walking, cycling area, free ent to local pools; vg, high-quality, modern site." ♦ ltd. € 32.00   2009*

MALS/MALLES VENOSTA *1D1* (3km S Rural) *46.67305, 10.5700* **Campingpark Gloria Vallis, Wiesenweg 5, 39020 Glurns/Glorenza (BZ) [0473 835160; fax 835767; info@gloriavallis.it; www.gloriavallis.it]** Sp on rd S41 E of Glorenza. Med, mkd pitch, terr, unshd; htd wc; chem disp; mv service pnt; baby facs; shwrs inc; EHU (10A) inc; gas; lndry; shop; snacks; bar; playgrnd; pool 1km; tennis; games area; entmnt; 5% statics; dogs €4; phone; o'night parking place for m'vans; Eng spkn; adv bkg; quiet; ccard acc; CKE/CCI. "Excel mountain views; dog shwr rm; higher prices in winter." ♦ 1 Apr-31 Oct. € 35.00   2009*

MALS/MALLES VENOSTA *1D1* (3km S Rural) *46.67023, 10.55305* **Stadt-Camping im Park (Municipal), 39026 Glurns/Glorenza (BZ) [0473 835160; fax 845767]** Fr W (Ofenpass) on rd 28/S41 at Glorenza take v sharp L turn immed after bdge & bef town walls. Site 500m along v narr rd, not suitable lge/wide o'fits. Sp 'MV Parking' fr town but all units acc. NB Height restriction fr S (S40) 2.8m; fr N (Mals) 3.4m. Sm, pt sl, pt shd; wc; chem disp; mv service pnt; shwrs €0.50; EHU (10A) €2.50; shop, rest, snacks, bar 400m; dogs; CKE/CCI. "Spacious, tranquil CL-type site; beautiful views; easy walking, cycling; attractive medieval town with all facs; v clean san facs; owner calls in evening." 1 Apr-30 Oct. € 12.00   2010*

MANERBA DEL GARDA *1D2* (1.5km N Rural) *45.56194, 10.56472* **Camping La Rocca, Via Cavalle 22, 25080 Manerba-del-Garda (BS) [0365 551738; fax 552045; info@laroccacamp.it; www.laroccacamp.it]** Fr Desenzano-Salo rd SS572 turn E at sp Manerba. Site sp fr Manerba. Be careful to head for 'Camping La Rocca' & not 'La Rocca'. Sh, steep app rd, site on R. Lge, pt shd; wc (some cont); chem disp; mv service pnt; shwrs inc; EHU (4A) inc; shop; rest 200m; snacks; bar; playgrnd; pool & paddling pool; shgl beach & lake sw adj; tennis; games area; bike hire; wifi; 20% statics; €4.50; adv bkg; quiet; "Excel site & facs; some pitches with lake views, some with low olive trees - care req; amusing, helpful owner; highly rec." 1 Apr-30 Sep. € 35.00   2010*

MANERBA DEL GARDA *1D2* (1.5km N Rural) *45.56333, 10.56611* **Camping San Biagio, Via Cavalle 19, 25080 Manerba-del-Garda (BS) [0365 551549; fax 551046; info@campingsanbiagio.net; www.campingsanbiagio.net]** Fr S572 rd turn E at sp Manerba, site sp 1.5km N fr Manerba. Lge, mkd pitch, hdstg, terr, shd; htd wc; baby facs; shwrs inc; EHU (16A) metered; lndry (inc dryer); shop; rest, snacks; bar; BBQ; playgrnd; shgl beach & lake sw; wifi; dogs €5; poss cr; Eng spkn; adv bkg; quiet; ccard acc. "Terr pitches with views over Lake Garda; v clean, modern san facs; easily got twin axle into lge pitch (reserved); excel." ♦ ltd. 1 Apr-30 Sep. € 45.00   2011*

MANERBA DEL GARDA *1D2* (2km N Rural) *45.56138, 10.55944* **Camping Rio Ferienglück, Via del Rio 37 Pianarolli, 25080 Manerba-del-Garda (BS) [0365 551450 summer 0365 551075 winter; fax 551044; info@campingrioferiengluck. com; www.gardalake.it/rioferiengluck]** Fr S572 rd turn E at traff lts sp Manerba Centro. At TO turn L down hill & at petrol stn turn R into Viale Degli Alpini. At next rndabt turn L & foll site sp. Site 1.5km N of Manerba opp Hotel Zodiaco. Lge, mkd pitch, pt shd; wc (some cont); chem disp; mv service pnt; shwrs inc; EHU (6A) €3; gas; lndry (inc dryer); shop; rest nr; snacks; bar; BBQ; playgrnd; htd pool; paddling pool; shgl beach & lake sw adj; watersports; wifi; some statics; dogs €2; Eng spkn; no adv bkg; quiet; CKE/CCI. "Excel, family-run lakeside site with lge, level, grass pitches; welcoming vill nr; cent for Garda sightseeing; conv for train to Venice & Milan; beautiful area; cr but delightful situation." ♦ 23 Mar-20 Oct. € 40.50   2013*

MANERBA DEL GARDA *1D2* (1km SE Rural) *45.53040, 10.55487* **Camping Sivino's, Via Gramsci 78, 25080 Manerba-del-Garda (BS) [0365 552767; fax 550678; info@sivinos.it; www.campingsivinos.it]** Exit A4/E70 to Desenzano & foll sp dir Salo. In Moniga-del-Garda turn R at traff lts to vill sq & foll sp to Sivino's. Med, mkd pitch, pt shd; wc; chem disp; shwrs inc; EHU (6A) inc; gas 3km; lndry; shops 1km; rest, snacks, bar at adj holiday vill; lake sw & shgl beach adj; 5% statics; dogs €8; phone; bus 500m; poss cr; Eng spkn; adv bkg; quiet. "Beautiful site; excel facs; dir access to lake; extra for superior lakeside pitches; noise poss high ssn due parties/discos nrby; this pt of lake poss v windy - extra storm straps ess." ♦ 1 Apr-30 Sep. € 43.00   2009*

MANERBA DEL GARDA *1D2* (1km S Rural) *45.53916, 10.55555* **Camping Zocco, Via del Zocco 43, 25080 Manerba-del-Garda (BS) [0365 551605; fax 552053; info@campingzocco.it; www.campingzocco.it]** Fr Desenzano rd N twd Riva. In 5km take minor rd to Manerba. Shortly after Irish pub turn R dir Moniga-del-Garda, thro vill & foll site sp. Lge, mkd pitch, terr, shd; wc (some cont); some serviced pitches; baby facs; fam bthrm; shwrs inc; EHU (4A) inc; gas; lndry; shop; rest; bar; playgrnd; pool; paddling pool; beach & lake sw adj; tennis; games area; wifi; entmnt; 60% statics; dogs €4; ccard acc; red long stay/LS/CKE/CCI. "Beautiful situation; excel pool complex." ♦ 4 Apr-20 Sep. € 30.60   2009*

MANERBA DEL GARDA *1D2* (3km S Rural) *45.52555, 10.54333* **Camping Fontanelle, Via del Magone 13, 25080 Moniga-del-Garda (BS) [0365 502079; fax 503324; info@campingfontanelle.it; www.campingfontanelle.it]**
Exit A4 m'way dir Desenzano del Garda & foll sp Salo. In 10km arr at Moniga del Garda take 2nd exit off 1st rndabt twd Salo, then 1st R into Via Roma sp Moniga Centro. Immed after 'Api' g'ge on L turn R into into Via Caccinelli; at end of this narr rd turn R into del Via del Magone; site on L by lake. Access poss diff lge o'fits due narr vill streets. Lge, mkd pitch, sl, terr, pt shd; wc; chem disp; mv service pnt; baby facs; shwrs inc; EHU (6A) inc; gas; lndry (inc dryer); shop; supmkt; rest, snacks; bar; BBQ (gas/charcoal only); playgrnd; pool; paddling pool; lake sw & shgl beach; watersports; boat trips; fishing; tennis; golf 5km; horseriding 8km; bike hire 2km; wifi; entmnt; games/TV rm; 20% statics; dogs €7; no o'fits over 6.5m high ssn; phone; poss cr nr lake; Eng spkn; adv bkg; ccard acc; red LS/snr citizens; extra for lakeside pitches; CKE/CCI. "Vg site; excursions to Venice, Florence, Verona; friendly, helpful staff; excel san facs; levellers needed all pitches; pitches poss tight lge o'fits due trees; mkt Mon; lovely site." ♦ 18 Apr-26 Sep. € 40.00 SBS - Y01   2011*

MANERBA DEL GARDA *1D2* (3.5km S Rural) *45.52006, 10.52945* **Camping Piantelle, Via San Michele 2, 25080 Moniga-del-Garda (BS) [0365 502013; fax 502637; info@piantelle.com; www.piantelle.com]**
Fr Desenzano take SP572 sp Salo. In Moniga turn R twd lake & foll site sp. Lge, hdg/mkd pitch, some terr, pt shd; wc; chem disp; some serviced pitches; EHU (6A) inc; lndry; shop; rest, snacks; bar; playgrnd; pool; paddling pool; lake sw & beach adj; watersports; games area; gym; wifi; entmnt; TV; 25% statics; dogs €7.50; extra for lakeside pitches; Eng spkn; adv bkg; quiet; red LS/snr citizens. "Friendly, helpful staff; gd touring base; excel, well-kept, well-managed site & facs; sep area for v lge o'fits; site produces own olive oil." ♦ 1 Apr-26 Sep. € 35.00   2009*

⊞ **MANERBA DEL GARDA** *1D2* (2km SW Rural) *45.53186, 10.52741* **Camping Trevisago, Via Prato Negro 10, 25080 Moniga-del-Garda (BS) [tel/fax 0365 502252; info@trevisago.com; www.trevisago.com]**
Fr Desenzano take SP572 sp Salo. In Moniga foll brown sp. Med, hdg/mkd pitch, pt shd; wc (some cont); chem disp; shwrs €1; EHU (10A) €2.50; lndry; shop; rest, snacks; bar; playgrnd; pool; paddling pool; lake beach 1km; watersports; TV; 80% statics; dogs €2.50 (not acc mid-July to end Aug); phone; bus 400m; poss cr high ssn w/end; Eng spkn; adv bkg; quiet; CKE/CCI. "Owner v helpful; well-maintained facs; mountain views; gd." € 30.50   2010*

⊞ **MANFREDONIA** *2G4* (10.5km SSW Coastal) *41.55477, 15.88794* **Camping Lido Salpi, SS159 delle Saline Km 6,200, 71043 Manfredonia [tel/fax 0884 571160; lidosalpi@alice.it; www.lidosalpi.it]** Head S on A14, exit at Foggia dir Manfredonia/SS89. Take ramp to Manfredonia Sud and cont strt. Turn R onto SS159, site on the R. Sm, mkd pitch, pt shd; wc; chem disp; mv service pnt; shwrs €0.50; EHU (6A) €2; lndry (inc dryer); shop; rest; café; bar; bbq; beach; wifi; 10% statics; dogs; ltd bus 0.5km; twin axles; Eng spkn; red LS. "V well located for San Giovanni Rotondo & Gargano; gd o'night stop fr A14; some pitches awkward for lge o'fits due to trees & site furniture; gd site." ♦ ltd. € 31.00 (CChq acc)   2014*

MARCIALLA CERTALDO see Poggibonsi *1D3*

MARINA DI BIBBONA see Cecina *1D3*

MARINA DI CAMEROTA *3A4* (4km N Coastal) *40.02650, 15.32583* **Camping Nessuno, Via Mingardo 3, 84059 Marina-di-Camerota (SA) [tel/fax 0974 931457; info@villaggionessuno.com; www.villaggionessuno.com]**
On coast rd N twd Palinuro, site on L 1.5km after series of sh tunnels. NB Height restriction 3.3m & width 2.3m at Lentiscosa. Lge, mkd pitch, pt shd, terr, shd; wc; chem disp; mv service pnt; shwrs inc; EHU (3A) inc; gas; lndry; shop & 1km; rest; bar; playgrnd; sand beach adj; games area; cash machine; entmnt; 10% statics; dogs; phone; sep car park; poss cr; Eng spkn; no adv bkg; some rd noise; ccard acc. "On sand in pine forest; dir access to beach; most pitches reasonable size; friendly, helpful staff." ♦ ltd. 29 May-5 Sep. € 46.00   2010*

MARINA DI CAULONIA *3B4* (1km NE Coastal) *38.35480, 16.48375* **Camping Calypso, Contrada Precariti, 89040 Marina-di-Caulonia (RC) [tel/fax 0964 82028; info@villaggiocalypso.com; www.villaggiocalypso.com]**
On o'skts of Marina-di-Caulonia on S106. Med, mkd pitch, shd; wc (mainly cont); mv service pnt; chem disp; baby facs; shwrs €0.50; EHU (2A) €3.50; lndry; shop; rest, snacks; bar; playgrnd; sand beach adj; games area; tennis 500m; games area; entmnt; TV rm; wifi; 5% statics; dogs €2.50; phone; sep car park high ssn; Eng spkn; ccard acc; CKE/CCI. "Superb sandy beach; gd (if dated) facs; close to early Byzantine church at Stilo & medieval hill vill of Gerace." 1 Apr-30 Sep. € 28.50   2013*

MARINA DI EBOLI see Paestum *3A3*

MARINA DI GROSSETO see Grosseto *1D3*

MARINA DI MASSA *1C3* (1km N Coastal) *44.0250, 10.07388* **Camping Giardino, Via delle Pinete 382, Loc Partaccia, 54037 Marina-di-Massa (MS) [0585 869291; fax 240781; info@campinggiardino.com; www.campinggiardino.com]**
On coast rd bet Marina-di-Massa & Marina-di-Carrara, sp. Lge, shd; wc (some cont); chem disp; mv service pnt; shwrs; EHU (3A) (check pol); gas; lndry; shop; rest 200m; snacks; bar; playgrnd; pool adj; paddling pool; sand beach 100m; 50% statics; dogs (not Jun-Aug); phone; sep car park; poss cr; adv bkg; rd noise; ccard acc; red LS. "Spacious pitches LS; conv NH for A12." ♦ 1 Apr-26 Sep. € 38.00   2010*

MARINA DI MINTURNO *2F4* (6km SE Coastal) *41.20731, 13.79138* **Camping Villlagio Baia Domizia, Via Pietre Bianche, 81030 Baia-Domizia (CE) [0823 930164; fax 930375; info@baiadomizia.it; www.baiadomizia.it]**
Exit A1 at Cassino onto S630, twd Minturno on S7 & S7quater, turn off at km 2, then foll sp Baia Domizia, site in 1.5km N of Baia-Domizia. V lge, hdg pitch, shd; wc (some cont); chem disp; mv service pnt; baby facs; shwrs inc; EHU (5-10A) inc (poss rev pol); gas; lndry; shop; rest, snacks; bar; 2 pools; sand beach adj; boat hire; windsurfing; tennis; games area; bike hire; entmnt; TV; no dogs; poss cr; quiet; ccard acc; red LS. "Excel facs; 30/7-16/8 min 7 night stay; site clsd 1400-1600 but adequate parking area; top class site with all facs; gd security." ♦ 30 Apr-20 Sep. € 45.40   2009*

MARINA DI MINTURNO 2F4 (3km S Coastal) 41.22891, 13.75482 **Camping Golden Garden, Via Dunale 74, 04020 Marina-di-Minturno (LT) [tel/fax 0771 614985; servizio. clienti@goldengarden.it; www.goldengarden.it]** S on S7 Via Appia; bef x-ing Rv Garigliano turn R foll N bank of rv almost to mouth. Turn R, site on L in 300m. Or fr Gaeta (16km S) foll old S7 Via Appia, thro Scauri, turn R at traff lts after km 153 sp, Bar Marina on corner, foll sp. Med, mkd pitch, pt shd; wc; chem disp; shwrs inc; EHU (4A) inc; gas 5km; lndry; shop 5km; bar; sand beach adj; waterskiing; games area; solarium; entmnt; 50% statics; dogs €5; phone; sep car park; poss cr; Eng spkn; adv bkg; ccard acc; red LS. "Gd sand beach; slightly run down area." ♦ 30 Apr-5 Sep. € 35.00   2010*

MARINA DI MONTENERO 2F4 (1km NW Coastal) 42.06500, 14.77700 **Centro Vacanze Molise, SS Adriatica, Km 525, 86036 Montenero di Bisaccia [tel/fax 0873 803570 or 3385 408323 (mob); info@campingmolise.it; www.campingmolise.it]** Exit A14 at Vasto Sud to SS16 dir S. On R Centro Commerciale Costa Verde, site opp on L. Med, mkd pitch, pt shd; wc (some cont); chem disp; mv service pnt; shwrs inc; EHU (3A) inc; gas; lndry; shop opp; rest, snacks; bar; private sand beach adj; tennis; games area; dogs €1; phone; bus; poss cr; Eng spkn; adv bkg; poss noisy high ssn; CKE/CCI. "Excel site; helpful staff; vg beach; Aqualand Water Park nr; Tremiti Isands rec; gd touring base; conv for m'way A14." ♦ 1 Jun-8 Sep. € 33.00   2015*

MARINA DI PISA 1C3 (6km S Coastal) 43.64720, 10.29603 **Camping Village St Michael, Via della Bigattiera 24, 56018 Tirrenia (PI) [050 33103; fax 33041; info@campingstmichael.com; www.campingstmichael.com]** Fr A12/E80 exit Pisa Sud & foll sp Tirrenia. In vill turn N twd Marina di Pisa, sp along coast rd to R. Lge, hdg pitch, pt shd; wc (some cont); chem disp; shwrs €0.50; EHU (3A) inc; gas; lndry; shop; rest, snacks; bar; playgrnd; private sand beach 600m; games area; golf 1.5km; entmnt; TV; 25% statics; no dogs; bus to Pisa & Livorno 600m; phone; poss cr; quiet; ccard acc. "Nr Livorno for ferries to Sardinia & Corsica; helpful staff." ♦ 1 Jun-15 Sep. € 29.00   2009*

MARINA DI RAVENNA 2E2 (6km N Coastal) 44.55895, 12.27995 **Camping Adria, Via Spallazzi 30, 48010 Casal-Borsetti (RA) [0544 445217; fax 442014; adria@camping.it; www.villaggiocampingadria.it]** Fr Ravenna take SS309 N for 17km, then at km 13 R (E) to sea & Casal-Borsetti & foll camp sp. Lge, pt shd; wc (some cont); chem disp; baby facs; shwrs inc; EHU (4A) inc; gas; lndry (inc dryer); shop; rest, snacks; bar; BBQ; playgrnd; pool; paddling pool; private beach 200m; wifi (recep area); entmnt; TV rm; 75% statics; dogs €4; phone; bus; poss cr; Eng spkn; adv bkg; ccard acc; red LS; CKE/CCI. "Conv Venice/gd NH bet Ancona & Venice; 1st class beach; new pool complex; many interesting buildings." ♦ 16 Apr-15 Sep. € 30.60 (CChq acc)   2011*

MARONE 1C1 (1km S Rural) 45.73166, 10.09361 **Campeggio Riva di San Pietro, Via Cristini 9, 25054 Marone (BS) [tel/fax 030 9827129; info@rivasanpietro.it; www.rivasanpietro.it]** Site well sp on lakeside on L of SS510 on app Marone dir Pisogne. Turn sharp L, site adj Camping Breda. Med, mkd pitch, pt shd; wc (some cont); chem disp; mv service pnt; baby facs; shwrs inc; EHU (4A) inc; gas; lndry; shop; rest, snacks, bar 150m; playgrnd; 2 pools; lake sw; boat hire; windsurfing; canoeing; solarium; bike hire; 30% statics; dogs €3; sep car park; poss v cr; Eng spkn; adv bkg (ess high ssn); rd/rlwy noise; red long stay; ccard acc; CKE/CCI. "Welcoming, helpful owners; poss v cr & cramped, even LS; gd dog exercise area." ♦ ltd. 1 May-30 Sep. € 31.00   2009*

MARTINSICURO 2F3 (10km N Coastal) 42.97238, 13.87748 **International Camping Don Diego, Lungomare De Gasperi 124, 63013 Grottammare (AP) [0735 581285; fax 583166; info@dondiegocamping.it; www.campingdondiego.it]** Exit A14/E55 dir Grottammare, site bet San Bernadetto & Grottammare off SS16 coast rd, well sp. Lge, shd; wc (some cont); shwrs inc; EHU (6A) €3.50; gas; lndry; shop; rest, snacks, bar; no BBQ; playgrnd; beach adj; games area; internet; entmnt; 50% statics; no dogs; adv bkg; quiet; ccard acc; red LS; CKE/CCI. "Gd facs; vg." ♦ 29 May-12 Sep. € 44.50   2010*

MASSA LUBRENSE see Sorrento 3A3

> # "I like to fill in the reports as I travel from site to site"
> You'll find report forms at the back of this guide, or you can fill them in online at www.caravanclub.co.uk/europereport.

⊞ **MATERA** 3A4 (2km S Rural) 40.65305, 16.60694 **Azienda Agrituristica Masseria del Pantaleone, Contrada Chiancalata 27, 75100 Matera (MT) [0835 335239; fax 240021; info@agriturismopantaleonematera.it; www.agriturismopantaleonematera.it]** Do not use SatNav. Fr S on SS7 take Matera Sud exit, site 2km on L, not well sp. Opp Ospedale Madonna delle Grazie. Sm, all hdstg, terr, pt shd; wc; chem disp; mv service pnt; shwrs €1; EHU (16A) inc; rest; bar; BBQ; dogs; Eng spkn; quiet; CKE/CCI. "Conv Matera - World Heritage site; helpful owners provide transport to/fr Matera cent." € 12.00   2013*

MATTINATA 2G4 (2km Coastal) 41.70510, 16.06681 **Camping Mattinata, Contrada Funni, 71030 Mattinata (FG) [tel/fax 0884 550313; mattinata@camping.it]** Exit a'strada A14 at Foggia, sp Manfredonia. Fr Manfredonia on SS89 foll sp to Mattinata. Turn twds sea at km 145.8 & foll sp 'Lido'. Tight turn R into site fr W. Lge, pt shd; wc; shwrs €0.50; EHU (4A) €2.07; gas; lndry; shop; snacks; bar; playgrnd; sand/shgl beach adj; watersports; tennis; entmnt; 30% statics; no dogs; sep car park; poss cr; adv bkg; quiet. 25 May-25 Sep. € 39.00 (3 persons)   2009*

MENAGGIO *1C1* (500m N Rural) *46.02516, 9.23996*
**Camping Europa, Loc Leray, Via dei Cipressi 12, 22017
Menaggio (CO) [344 31187; europamenaggio@hotmail.it]**
On ent Menaggio fr S (Como) on S240 turn R & foll
'Campeggio' sp along lakeside prom. On ent fr N turn L at
'Campeggio' sp, pass site ent & turn in boatyard. Sm, mkd
pitch, terr, pt shd; wc; shwrs €70 for 5 mins; EHU; shop; rest
300m; snacks; bar; lake sw; boat hire; bike hire; 80% statics;
dogs; poss v cr; Eng spkn; adv bkg; rd noise; CKE/CCI. "V
sm pitches cramped high ssn; narr site rds diff for lge o'fits;
old-fashioned facs but clean; poor security; helpful owner;
m'vans rec to arr full of water & empty of waste; hardly any rd
noise, Menaggio delightful place; v friendly." 1 Apr-30 Sep.
€ 22.50   2013*

"We must tell The Club about that great site we found"

Get your site reports in by mid-August
and we'll do our best to get your updates
into the next edition.

MENAGGIO *1C1* (6km S Urban) *45.96937, 9.19298*
**Camping La'vedo, Via degli Artigiani 1, 22016 Lenno (CO)
[0344 56288; www.campinglavedo.it]** Fr Como foll S340
along W shore of lake, site SE of Lenno 200m fr lake, adj to
supmkt. Sm, pt sl, pt shd; wc (cont); chem disp; mv service pnt;
shwrs €0.50; EHU (3A) inc; lndry; shop adj; rest opp; bar; BBQ;
games area; entmnt; 25% statics; dogs; rd noise; CKE/CCI.
"Picturesque, friendly site in sm town; basic facs; 15 mins to
boat stn for other towns on lake; great care needed on S340 -
v narr & busy rd." ♦ 1 Apr-30 Sep. € 20.00   2013*

MERANO/MERAN *1D1* (5km E Rural) *46.67144, 11.20091*
**Camping Hermitage, Via Val di Nova 29, 39012 Meran
[0473 232191; fax 256407; info@einsiedler.com;
www.einsiedler.com]** Exit SS38 at Meran Süd & foll sp twds
Merano to Meran 2000 past Trautmannsdorf. Site sp. Med,
mkd pitch, hdstg, terr, pt shd; wc; chem disp; mv service pnt;
fam bthrm; sauna; shwrs; EHU (10-16A); lndry (inc dryer);
rest; café; snacks; bar; BBQ; pool; bike hire; wifi; dogs €3;
phone; public transport 100m; twin axles; adv bkg; quiet, some
daytime traff noise. "Tennis; all serviced pitches; mountain
views; hotel facs avail to campers; forest walk; ACSI site;
excel." 28 Mar-1 Nov. € 34.00   2015*

⊞ **MERANO/MERAN** *1D1* (1km S Urban) *46.66361,
11.15638* **Camping Merano, Via Piave/Piavestrasse 44,
39012 Merano/Meran (BZ) [0473 231249; fax 235524;
info@meran.eu]** Exit S38 at Meran Sud & foll rd into town.
Brown site sps to Camping & Tennis (no name at main juncs
in town cent). Site ent mkd 'Camping Tennis'. Site also sp
fr N. Med, hdstg, pt shd; wc; chem disp; mv service pnt; shwrs
inc; EHU (6A) €2.40; shop opp; supmkt 500m; rest, snacks,
bar adj; htd pool; tennis adj; dogs €3.30; phone; poss cr;
some rd noise; red long stay days; CKE/CCI. "Sh walk to town
cent; fine site surrounded by spectacular mountain scenery;
helpful staff; pitches soft after rain; gd clean san facs; helpful
staff; 10% surcharge for 1 night; excel thermal baths."
€ 36.00   2015*

MERANO/MERAN *1D1* (15.4km S Rural) *46.59861, 11.14527*
**Camping Völlan, Zehentweg 6, 39011 Völlan/Foiana
[0473 568056; fax 557249; info@camping-voellan.com;
www.camping-voellan.com]** Leave S38 dual c'way (Merano-
Bolzano) S of Merano sp Lana. Drive thro Lana, turn uphill sp
Gampenpass. Turn R sp Foliana/Völlan & foll sp to site. Sm,
mkd pitch, terr, pt shd; wc; chem disp; mv service pnt; some
serviced pitches; shwrs €0.50; EHU (4A) €2.50; lndry (inc dryer);
shop; rest 800m; playgrnd; pool; golf 6km; 10% statics; dogs
€3; phone; Eng spkn; quiet; CKE/CCI. "Long drag up to site fr
Lana, but worth it; beautiful situation o'looking Adige Valley;
excel facs & pool; barriers clsd 1300-1500 & 2200-0700; v
helpful owners; some pitches with steep acc & tight for lge
units." 19 Mar-7 Nov. € 34.00   2014*

MESTRE *2E2* (3km E Urban) *45.48098, 12.27516* **Venezia
Camping Village, Via Orlanda 8/C, 30170 Mestre/Venezia
(VE) [041 5312828; fax 5327618; info@veneziavillage.it;
www.veneziavillage.it]** On A4 fr Milan/Padova take exit
SS11 dir Venice. Exit SS11 for SS14 dir Trieste & airport. 200m
after Agip g'ge on R watch for sp and take 1st exit R fr rdbt
bet two major dealerships. Keep in R lane all way to site. Med,
mkd pitch, pt shd; wc; chem disp; mv service pnt; shwrs inc;
EHU (6A) inc (poss rev pol); gas; lndry (inc dryer); shop high
ssn; rest, snacks; bar; playgrnd; pool 3km; sand beach 6km;
rv sw 2km; wifi; TV; 20% statics; dogs €2; phone; buses to
Venice; poss cr & noisy high ssn; Eng spkn; adv bkg; red long
stay/CKE/CCI. "V conv Venice - tickets/maps fr recep; clean,
well-run site; popular with m'vans; friendly, helpful owners;
pitches poss cramped when site full; mosquitoes; new recep,
bar/rest, shop, wellness area & toilet block (2011); excel."
22 Feb-9 Nov & 26 Dec-31 Dec. € 44.70   2014*

MESTRE *2E2* (4km E Urban) *45.48425, 12.28227* **Camping
Rialto, 16 Via Orlanda, Loc Campalto, 30175 Mestre (VE)
[tel/fax 041 5420295; rialto@camping.it;
www.campingrialto.com]** Fr A4 take Marco Polo Airport exit,
then fork R onto SS14 dir Venice. Site on L 1km past Campalto
opp lge car sales area, well sp. Do not enter Mestre. Med, pt
shd; wc (mainly cont); chem disp; mv service pnt; shwrs inc;
EHU (15A) €1.50; lndry; shop; dogs €3; phone; wifi; bus to
Venice; poss cr; Eng spkn; adv bkg; some rd noise; red CKE/
CCI. "Site in need of refurb but v conv Venice; bus tickets
fr recep; friendly, helpful staff; vg san facs; vg rest; rec."
20 Feb-6 Mar / 1 Apr-20 Oct. € 39.60   2014*

⊞ **MESTRE** *2E2* (7km SW Urban) *45.47138, 12.21166*
**Camping Jolly delle Querce, Via G De Marchi 7, 30175
Marghera (VE) [tel/fax 041 920312; campingjolly@
ecvacanze.it; www.ecvacanze.it]** App fr Milan, exit A4/
E70 immed after toll, sp Mestre/Ferrovia/Marghera, then onto
SS309 at rndabt sp Chioggia, then 1st R, site sp on R. Lge, shd;
wc; chem disp; shwrs; EHU (4A) inc (rev pol); gas; lndry; shop;
snacks; bar; pool; paddling pool; 80% statics; dogs free; poss
cr; v noisy fr adj airport & m'way. "Bus to Venice 15 min walk;
excel modern facs block." € 62.00   2015*

ITALY

⊞ **MILANO** *1C2* (8km W Urban) *45.47390, 9.08233*
Camping Citta di Milano, Via Gaetano Airaghi 61, 20153
Milano [0248 207017; fax 202999; info@campingmilano.it;
www.campingmilano.it] Fr E35/E62/A50 Tangentiale Ovest
ring rd take Settimo-Milanese exit & foll sp San Siro along
Via Novara (SS11). Turn R in 2km at Shell petrol stn, then R
at traff lts in 500m & L to site in 600m. Site ent at Gardaland
Waterpark, poorly sp. Lge, hdstg, mkd pitch, pt shd; wc; chem
disp; mv service pnt; shwrs inc; EHU (6A) inc; lndry; shop 500m;
rest, snacks; bar; waterspark adj; dogs €3.50; phone; bus
500m; poss cr; Eng spkn; no adv bkg; rd, aircraft noise, disco
at w/end & waterpark adj; ccard acc; red LS/CKE/CCI. "Gd
san facs; noise fr adj concerts high ssn; conv bus/metro Milan;
penned animals for kid to enjoy; gd security; peacocks roaming
site." ♦ € 44.00   2013*

MISURINA see Cortina d'Ampezzo *2E1*

⊞ **MODENA** *1D2* (3km N Urban) *44.65429, 10.86884* **Camping
International, Via Cave di Ramo 111, 41100 Modena
(MO) [059 332252 or 06771259 (mob); fax 823235; info@
internationalcamping.org; www.internationalcamping.org]**
Exit A1/E35/E45 to Modena Nord; after toll stn turn 1st L &
immed L again at rndabt, then R; site nr motel rest adj to toll
booth. Alt rte fr city cent: take S9 Via Emilia fr cent sp dir
Milan; camp sp clear on R of main rd; turn R; foll sp. Med,
mkd pitch, pt shd; wc (cont); chem disp; mv service pnt; shwrs
inc; EHU (6-10A) €3 (poss rev pol); gas; lndry; ice shop; rest,
snacks; bar; playgrnd; pool; dogs €2; phone; poss cr; Eng spkn;
rd noise; ccard not acc; CKE/CCI. "Easy to find; poss travellers;
parts of site waterlogged after heavy rain; facs clean but
inadequate for size of site high ssn; conv for m'way; call mob
no, if arr LS; mosquitoes NH only." ♦ ltd. € 27.00   2009*

⊞ **MODENA** *1D2* (2km SE Urban) *44.61361, 10.94444*
**Camper Club Mutina, Strada Collegarola 76A, 41100
Modena (MO) [059 4557043; fax 39 1782732524;
camperclub.mutina@tiscali.it; www.camperclubmutina.it]**
Exit A1 Modena Sud onto SP623 dir 'Centro'. In approx 4km
site sp on L (also sp Camper Mkt). Site adj rugby club. M'vans
only. Sm, hdstg, unshd; htd wc (cont); chem disp; mv service
pnt; shwrs inc; EHU (6A) inc; gas; lndry rm; BBQ; wifi; bus
1km; vehicle-washing facs; red CKE/CCI. "Vg facs; easy access
to Modena; phone first if car+c'van - poss acc, gd security,
mini-bus to city, cycle path to city 60m, v friendly site."
€ 15.00   2011*

MOLINA DI LEDRO see Pieve di Ledro *1D1*

⊞ **MOLVENO** *1D1* (1km SW Rural) *46.13916, 10.95916*
**Camping Spiaggia Lago di Molveno, Via Lungolago 25,
38018 Molveno (TN) [0461 586978; fax 586330;
info@campingmolveno.it; www.campingmolveno.it]**
Fr Molveno head S on W side of lake, 1km on L. Lge, shd,
mkd pitch; wc; shwrs inc; chem disp; mv service pnt; EHU
(5A) inc; gas 1km; lndry; shop; rest, snacks; bar; lake sw;
windsurfing; tennis; games area; bike hire; ski school; hiking;
TV; 60% statics; dogs €4; phone; poss cr w/end; Eng spkn;
quiet; ccard acc; red LS. "Beautiful vill & mountains; well-
maintained, high quality, friendly, busy site; clean san facs; vg."
€ 35.00   2009*

MONFALCONE *2E1* (8km SE Coastal) *45.77241, 13.6245*
**Camping Mare Pineta, Via Sistiana 60/D, 34019 Sistiana
(TS) [040 299264; fax 299265; info@marepineta.com;
www.baiaholiday.com]** Well sp on SS14 on NW o'skirts of
Sistiana. V lge, pt sl, terr, shd; wc (mainly cont); mv service pnt;
some serviced pitches; shwrs inc; EHU (3A) inc; lndry; shop;
rest, snacks; bar; playgrnd; pool; beach 600m; tennis; bike
hire; solarium; 30% statics; dogs €8; quiet; ccard acc; red long
stay/CKE/CCI. "Free bus to beach; overlkg Adriatic & Bay of
Trieste; site tight for lge m'vans." ♦ 1 Apr-15 Oct. € 40.00
(CChq acc)   2011*

MONFALCONE *2E1* (9km SE Rural/Coastal) *45.76742,
13.64214* **Camping Alle Rose, Via Sistiana 24/D, 34013
Sistiana (TS) [040 299457]** Exit A4 at Sistiana exit & foll sp
Sistiana. On app to vill turn R at T-junc, pass supmkt set back
on R & look for blue site sp on L bef shops. Narr ent poss diff
lge o'fits. Sm, shd; wc (some cont); shwrs; EHU (6A) inc; gas
adj; rest 200m; shgl beach 1km; dogs; bus to Trieste 300m;
Eng spkn; quiet. "Shops & rests in walking dist; sand beach at
Monfalcone; friendly, helpful owner; lovely spot - like a gd CL."
10 May-30 Sep. € 21.00   2010*

MONIGA DEL GARDA see Manerba del Garda *1D2*

⊞ **MONOPOLI** *2H4* (5km S Coastal) *40.91333, 17.34387*
**Camping Atlantide, Contrada Lamandia 13E, 70043
Capitolo Monopoli (BA) [080 801212; fax 4120238;
demattia@residenceatlantide.it; www.residenceatlantide.
it]** On SS379 (Bari-Brindisi coast rd), 3km S of Monopoli,
fr SS16 (Adriatica) take exit Capitolo. Lge, mkd hdstg pitch,
pt sl, terr, pt shd; wc; chem disp; mv service pnt; serviced
pitches; shwrs; EHU (6A) inc (poss rev pol); lndry; shop 2km;
rest; bar; pool; tennis; games area; rocky waterfront adj; golf
5km; entmnt; 40% statics; dogs €4 on leash (not acc Aug);
bus adj; adv bkg; Eng spkn; poss noisy; ccard acc; red LS/CKE/
CCI. "Friendly owner; gd, clean site; basic facs LS; hot water to
shwrs only; gd size pitches; disco every Sat high ssn until v late;
Conv Roman ruins & UNESCO site; excel seafood rest 1km; site
& area highly rec; conv Bari ferries; gd rest." € 41.00   2013*

MONTECATINI TERME *1D3* (3km N Rural) *43.90505,
10.79190* **Camping Belsito, Via delle Vigne 1/A, Loc Vico,
51016 Montecatini-Terme (PT) [tel/fax 0572 67373;
info@campingbelsito.it; www.campingbelsito.it]**
Fr Montecatini-Terme foll sp to Montecatini-Alto for 3km; site
sp fr rd junc nr vill. NB Steep app with hairpins but OK with
care & balanced o'fit. Med, mkd pitch, some hdstg, pt sl, pt
shd; wc (some cont); chem disp; mv service pnt; 50% serviced
pitch; private bthrms some pitches - extra charge; shwrs inc;
EHU (6A) €1.50 (check pol); lndry (inc dryer); sm shop; rest; bar;
BBQ; playgrnd; htd pool; games rm; internet; TV; 10% statics;
dogs; phone; bus; Eng spkn; adv bkg ess; quiet; ccard acc;
red LS/long stay/CKE/CCI. "Superb, well-kept site; excel facs;
beautiful situation in high grnd o'looking Tuscan hills/valleys;
helpful staff; conv for Florence, Pisa & Lucca; gate clsd 1300-
1500; excel pool & rest; traditional Easter lunch at camp rest
was outstanding." ♦ ltd. 1 Apr-30 Sep. € 33.00   2011*

MONTESE *1D2* (3km S Rural) *44.25569, 10.93254* **Camping Ecochiocciola, Via Testa 80, 41055 Maserno-di-Montese (MO) [059 980065; fax 980025; info@ecochiocciola.com; www.ecochiocciola.com]** Exit A1 Modena Sud onto S623 dir Vignola, then rd P4. At Verica turn L to Montese & foll sp 'Chiocciola' to Maserno & site. Med, mkd pitch, pt sl, pt shd; wc (mainly cont); mv service pnt; shwrs inc; EHU (6A) inc; shop 200m; rest; bar; BBQ; pool high ssn; tennis; games rm; TV; 30% statics; dogs €5; bus 100m; sep car park; site clsd 5 Nov-5 Dec; Eng spkn; quiet; CKE/CCI. "Beautiful setting; friendly owner knowledgeable about local ecology; excel cent for walking; ltd touring pitches suitable sm m'vans only; gd rest." ♦ ltd. 4 Apr-2 Nov & Xmas/New Year. € 35.00   2010*

MONTEVARCHI *1D3* (10km S Rural) *43.44500, 11.61855* **Camping La Chiocciola, Via G Cesare, 52020 Capannole (AR) [tel/fax 055 995776; info@campinglachiocciola.com; www.campinglachiocciola.com]** Exit A1 at Valdarno & foll sp Levane. In Levane strt on at traff lts sp Bucine, site on R in 7km. NB Do not ent Bucine - narr rds. Med, hdg/mkd pitch, terr, pt shd; wc; chem disp; mv service pnt; all serviced pitch; shwrs inc; EHU (6A) inc; gas; lndry; hypmkt 13km; rest adj; playgrnd; htd pool adj; statics inc tour ops; dogs €2; poss v cr; Eng spkn; adv bkg (rec book in Jan for Jul/Aug); ccard acc; noise of barking dogs; CKE/CCI. "Excel for Tuscany, Florence & Siena easy drive; vg, clean san facs; lge pitches; site v cr early ssn - rec book mkd pitch; vg pool." ♦ ltd. 1 Mar-25 Oct. € 40.00   2011*

MONTEVARCHI *1D3* (21km W Rural) *43.53820, 11.41079* **Camping Piano Orlando, Loc Cafaggiolo, 52022 Cavriglia (FI) [tel/fax 055 967422; info@campingchianti.com; www.campingchianti.com]** Fr Montevarchi take P408 to Cavriglia & foll sp for Castelnuovo-dei-Sabbiono. Site is 5km W of Castelnuovo, sp. Steep, narr rd. Easier rte on R222, turn E at Greve-in-Chianti & foll sp. Med, mkd pitch, pt sl, shd; wc; chem disp; mv service pnt; shwrs inc; EHU (3A) inc; gas; lndry; shop; rest, snacks; bar; pool; 10% statics; dogs; phone; poss cr; Eng spkn; ccard acc. "Site high on Monti di Chianti, surrounded by forests; 500m fr ent of Parco di Cavriglia; gd walking." 1 Mar-31 Oct. € 30.00 (CChq acc)   2009*

⊞ **MONTOPOLI IN VAL D'ARNO** *1D3* (1km N Rural) *43.67611, 10.75333* **Kawan Toscana Village, Via Fornoli 9, 56020 Montópoli (PI) [0571 449032; fax 449449; info@toscanavillage.com; www.toscanavillage.com]** Bet Pisa & Florence; exit Fi-Pi-Li dual c'way at Montópoli, foll site sps. Turn L bef Montópoli vill - site well sp. Med, mkd pitch, terr, pt shd; htd wc (some cont); chem disp; mv service pnt; some serviced pitches; baby facs; shwrs inc; EHU (10A) €2.50; gas; lndry (inc dryer); shop; supmkt 4km; rest, snacks; bar; BBQ; playgrnd; pool high ssn; bike hire; golf 7km; wifi; TV rm; 15% statics; dogs; phone; train 3km; poss cr; Eng spkn; adv bkg req; some rd noise; ccard acc; red long stay; CKE/CCI. "Helpful staff; gravel site rds, steep in places; some v sm pitches; spotless facs; gd food in rest; gd pool; well organised; excel for Florence, Pisa & Tuscany; walking dist to Montopoli; beautiful surroundings; reasonably priced rest." ♦ € 43.50 (CChq acc)   2013*

MONZA *1C2* (4km N Urban) *45.62305, 9.28027* **Camping Autodromo, Autodromo Nazionale Monza 20900 [tel/fax 039 339 2665523; segreteria@campeggiomonza.it; www.monzanet.it/eng/campeggi.aspx]** Fr E exit A4 at Agrate-Brianza; fr W A4 exit Sesto San Giovanni onto S36. Foll sp to Autodromo/Biassono, then to site in Parco Reale complex. NB: Do not go to Monza Centro or exit main rd to Autodromo as no access to site; site clearly sp by g'ge. Lge, shd; wc (cont); own san rec; mv service pnt; shwrs €0.50; EHU (5A) €6; lndry (inc dryer); shop; rest adj; snacks; bar; playgrnd; pool adj; games area; 10% statics; dogs; phone; bus to Milan nr; poss cr; Eng spkn; no adv bkg; quiet except during racing. "Day ticket for all transport; bus 200m fr gate to Sesto FC (rlwy stn, bus terminal & metro line 1) - fr there take metro to Duomo; poor facs; NH/sh stay only for racing." ♦ 31 Aug - 9 Sep. € 60.00   2013*

MORGEX see Courmayeur *1A1*

MUGGIA see Trieste *2F1*

NARNI *2E3* (6km S Rural) *42.48459, 12.51516* **Camping Monti del Sole, Strada Borgaria 22, 05035 Narni (TR) [tel/fax 0744 796336; montisole@libero.it; www.camping montidelsole.it]** Fr Narni on S3 dir Rome, then foll sp Borgheria, R in 1km. Diff rd to site. Med, shd; wc (some cont); chem disp; mv service pnt; shwrs inc; EHU (5A) inc; lndry; rest high ssn; snacks; bar; pool high ssn; paddling pool; tennis; games area; 20% statics; no dogs; phone; adv bkg; quiet. "Beautiful wooded site in heart of Umbria; off-the-beaten-track; lge pitches; dated san facs, but clean; friendly, welcoming owner; conv Rome, Perugia, Spoleto." ♦ 1 Apr-30 Sep. € 27.50   2010*

NATURNO/NATURNS *1D1* (500m S Rural) *46.6475, 11.00722* **Camping Adler, Via Lido 14, 39025 Naturno (BZ) [0473 667242; fax 668346; info@campingadler.com; www.campingadler.com]** Fr E on SS38 turn L at rndabt into Naturno, L at traff lts & foll sp to site. Fr W after passing thro tunnel bypass, turn R at rndabt then as above. Med, mkd pitches, pt shd; htd wc; chem disp; mv service pnt; baby facs; shwrs inc; EHU (4-6A) €3.90; lndry (inc dryer); shop, rest 200m; snacks; food 300m; wifi; TV; 10% statics; dogs €2.50; bus/ train 500m; twin axles; poss cr; Eng spkn; adv bkg; quiet; ccard acc; CKE/CCI. "Well-kept site; conv town cent; gd hill walks; friendly staff; off clsd 1230-1500; cable car nrby; excel." ♦ 15 Mar-15 Nov. € 33.00   2015*

⊞ **NICOTERA** *3B4* (3km S Coastal) *38.50755, 15.92666* **Camping Villaggio Mimosa, Mortelletto, 89844 Nicotera Marina (VV) [tel/fax 0963 81397; info@villaggiomimosa. com]** Exit A3/E45 at Rosarno exit. Cross S18 & site sp dir San Ferdinando Porto. Foll sp on SP50 for approx 7km. Sm, mkd pitch, pt shd (reed matting); wc; chem disp; mv service pnt; hot shwrs; EHU (12A); lndry; gas; shop; rest, snacks; bar; BBQ; playgrnd; pool; paddling pool; sand beach adj; boat hire; windsurfing; tennis; games area; bike hire; entmnt; wifi; 40% statics; dogs; twin axles; Eng spkn; CKE/CCI. "Some pitches have tight corners for lge o'fits; gd site." ♦ ltd. € 54.00 (CChq acc)   2014*

NORBELLO *3A1* (7km NW Rural) *40.17472, 8.77305* **Camping Villaggio Nuragheruiu, Loc Sant' Ignacio, 09070 Norbello [0785 825101; info@nuragheruiu.it; www.nuragheruiu.it]** Fr SS131 take Norbello/Sant' Ignacio exit; site in 4km. Lge, mkd pitch, some hdstg, pt sl, pt shd; wc; chem disp; mv service pnt; shwrs inc; EHU (5A) inc; lndry; shop; rest, snacks; bar; BBQ; playgrnd; pool; paddling pool; games area; bike hire; wifi; entmnt; TV; some statics; dogs €3.50; Eng spkn; adv bkg; quiet; ccard acc; red CKE/CCI. "Gd touring base." ♦ 1 May-30 Sep. € 39.00 (CChq acc) 2010*

OLIVETO LARIO see Lecco *1C1*

OLMO, L' see Perugia *2E3*

⊞ **OPI** *2F4* (3km E Rural) *41.77914, 13.86282* **Camping Il Vecchio Mulino, Via Marsicana, Km 52, 67030 Opi (AQ) [tel/fax 0863 912232; ilvecchiomulino@tiscalinet.it; www.campingvecchiomulino.it]** Turn off A1 twd Frosinone, 35km NE on S214 to Sora, 40km E on S509 to Opi, 5km E on S83 twd Villetta Barrea. Site on R. Med, pt shd; htd wc (some cont); chem disp; mv service pnt; shwrs inc; EHU (8A) inc; lndry; shop 3km; rest, snacks; bar; BBQ; playgrnd; games area; some statics; dogs; phone; Eng spkn; adv bkg rec Jul/Aug; quiet; ccard acc; CKE/CCI. "Wonderful walking country; excel rest; lovely site but facs stretched if site full." ♦ € 28.50 2010*

ORA/AUER *1D1* (NE Urban) *46.34779, 11.29980* **Camping Markushof, Via Truidn 1, 39040 Ora/Auer (BZ) [0471 810025; fax 810603; info@campingmarkushof.it; www.hotelmarkushof.it]** Exit A22 at Bolzano Sud onto SS12, then S to Ora. Site on main rd, sp. Sm, mkd pitch, some hdstg, unshd; wc; chem disp; mv service pnt; some serviced pitches; EHU (16A) inc; lndry (inc dryer); shop adj; rest, snacks; bar adj; playgrnd; htd pool; paddling pool; some statics; dogs €4; quiet; CKE/CCI. "Pt of hotel complex; excel facs." ♦ 1 Apr-20 Oct. € 27.00 2010*

ORBETELLO *1D4* (5.5km N Coastal) *42.46341, 11.18597* **Camping Village Obertello, Strada Gianella 166, 58015 Orbetello [0564 820 201; fax 821 198; info@orbetellocamping village.com; www.orbetellocampingvillage.it]** Fr SS1 Aurelia take exit Albinia. Cont twds Porto Santo Stefano. Campsite on L after 5km. V lge, mkd pitch, pt shd; wc; chem disp; mv service pnt; baby facs; shwrs; EHU (6A); lndry (inc dryer); shop; rest; snacks; bar; BBQ; cooking facs; playgrnd; htd pool; paddling pool; beach adj; games area; bike hire; entmnt; wifi; tv; quiet; Eng spkn; adv bkg; CCI. ♦ 19 Apr-27 Sep. € 62.00 2014*

ORBETELLO *1D4* (7km N Coastal) *42.49611, 11.19416* **Argentario Camping Village, Torre Saline, 58010 Albinia (GR) [0564 870302; fax 871380; info@argentariocamping village.com; www.argentariocampingvillage.com]** Turn W off Via Aurelia at 150km mark, sp Porto S. Stefano, site on R, clearly sp in 500m. Ignore sps Zona Camping. Lge, mkd pitch; shd; wc; mv service pnt; shwrs inc; EHU (6A) inc; lndry; rest, snacks; bar; shop; playgrnd; pool & paddling pool; sand/shgl beach; boat hire; games area; 90% statics; no dogs; phone; sep car park; poss cr; adv bkg; quiet. "Better suited for campervans and tent; san facs due for upgrade; excel rest; easy access to beach." ♦ 1 Apr-30 Sep. € 42.00 2012*

ORBETELLO *1D4* (8km N Coastal) *42.53258, 11.18593* **Camping Il Gabbiano, SS Aurelia, Km 154.2, 58010 Albinia (GR) [tel/fax 0564 870202; info@ilgabbianocampingvillage. com; www.ilgabbianocampingvillage.com]** On W side of Via Aurelia at km stone 154. Lge, mkd pitch, shd; wc; shwrs inc; EHU (3A) inc; gas; lndry; shop; rest, snacks; bar; BBQ; playgrnd; private sand beach adj; entmnt; 90% statics; no dogs Jul/Aug; sep car park high ssn; poss cr; adv bkg; poss noisy; red LS. "Vg; v clean facs." ♦ 1 Apr-13 Sep. € 37.50 2010*

ORIAGO see Venezia *2E2*

⊞ **ORTA SAN GIULIO** *1B1* (4km N Rural) *45.83117, 8.39664* **Camping La Punta di Crabbia, Via Crabbia 2, 28028 Pettenasco (NO) [tel/fax 0323 89117; infotiscali@ campingpuntacrabbia.it; www.campingpuntacrabbia.it]** Site situated on L (E) of rd 229 fr Omegna to Orta, 1.5km N of Pettenasco. Steep access rd to site. Med, sl, shd; wc (cont); chem disp; mv service pnt; shwrs; EHU (6A) €2.50; lndry; ice shop & 3km; rest 700m; snacks; bar; lake adj; windsurfing; solarium; 90% statics; dogs €4; quiet; Eng spkn; ccard not acc; red LS. "Gd view of lake fr some pitches but with rd noise; v helpful recep." € 24.00 2009*

ORTA SAN GIULIO *1B1* (500m N Rural) *45.80125, 8.42093* **Camping Orta, Via Domodossola 28, Loc Bagnera, 28016 Orta San Giulio (NO) [tel/fax 0322 90267; info@campingorta.it; www.campingorta.it]** Fr Omegna take rd on SS229 for 10km to km 44.5 sp Novara. Site both sides of rd 500m bef rndabt at Orta x-rds. Recep on L if heading S; poor access immed off rd. Med, pt sl, pt terr, pt shd; htd wc (some cont); chem disp; shwrs €0.20; EHU (3-6A) €2.50; gas; lndry (inc dryer); shop; rest 500m; bar; playgrnd; lake sw adj; waterskiing; wifi; dogs €4; Eng spkn; adv bkg; rd noise; ccard not acc; red LS. "Popular site in beautiful location; sm pitches; narr site rds & tight corners; arr early for lakeside pitch (extra charge); slipway to lake; friendly, helpful owner; Orta a gem; noise fr Beach Club at night; €4.50 for lakeside pitches." ♦ 1 Mar-31 Dec. € 45.50 2013*

ORTA SAN GIULIO *1B1* (E Rural) *45.79785, 8.42087* **Camping Cusio Lyons Edda, Via Giovanni Bosco 5, 28016 Orta San Giulio (NO) [tel/fax 0322 90290; cusio@tin.it; www.campingcusio.it]** S fr Omegna, turn L at traff lts (sp Miasino) & site on L in 100m. Access via steep, rough track. Med, pt sl, pt shd; wc; shwrs; EHU €2.70; gas; lndry; shop 150m; snacks; bar; sm pool; beach 2km; tennis; games rm; internet; some statics; dogs €3.70; quiet. "Views over Lake Orta; gd, clean facs; conv for walk into town." 1 Apr-30 Nov. € 27.60 2009*

ORTONA *2F4* (5km NW Coastal) *42.37623, 14.37394* **Camping Torre Mucchia, Loc Lido Riccio, 66026 Ortona (CH) [0859 196298; taoceti@supereva.it]** Exit SS16 at Ortona. In 500m turn sharp L & site sp. Med, shd; wc; shwrs; EHU inc; gas; lndry; shops 300m; snacks; bar; sand beach 200m; dogs; sep car park; adv bkg; quiet; CKE/CCI. "Sm, friendly, family-run site but poss scruffy." Easter-15 Sep. 2009*

⊞ **ORVIETO** *2E3* (500m S Urban) *42.72379, 12.13162* **Aree di Sosta Parcheggio Funicolare, Via della Direttissima, 05018 Orvieto (TR) [0763 300161 or 338 6843153 or 328 0644317; renzo.battistelli@hotmail.com; www.orvietoonline.com]** At Orvieto foll sp rlwy stn & funicular parking. Site on L just beyond funicular parking & behind rlwy stn. Foll sp 'Parcheggio Camper'. Sm, mkd pitch, hdstg, unshd; htd wc; chem disp; shwrs inc; EHU (10A) inc; lndry (inc dryer); shops 500m; rest, snacks, bar 200m; dogs; phone; bus, train 200m; rlwy noise; CKE/CCI. "M'vans only but c'vans poss acc LS; conv A1; gd san facs." ♦ € 15.00   2013*

OSTRA *2E3* (200m SW Rural) *43.61032, 13.15351* **Camping 'L Prè, Viale Matteotti 45, 60010 Ostra (AN) [tel/fax 071 68045; info@lpre.it; www.lpre.it]** Exit A14 at Senigallia onto S360. After approx 10km turn R to Ostra. Sp in vill. Sm, terr, pt shd; wc (some cont); chem disp; shwrs inc; EHU (3A) €2.50; shop 300m; rest 100m; sand beach 10km; games rm; dogs; red long stay. "Gd san facs; v friendly owners; lovely, quiet, simple site with easy access Ancona, Esini Valley; beautiful views over valley; gd for cyclists; gd place to relax after Venice." 1 Apr-30 Sep. € 24.50   2014*

OSTUNI *3A4* (9km NE Coastal) *40.76602, 17.65044* **Camping Cala dei Ginepri, Contrada da Montanaro, SS 379, Km 23.500, 72017 Ostuni (BR) [tel/fax 0831 330402; info@caladeiginepri.com; www.caladeiginepri.com]** Fr SS379 exit Cala dei Ginepri & foll sp to site. Lge, hdg/mkd pitch, shd; htd wc; mv service pnt; htd private san facs on pitches; shwrs inc; EHU inc; lndry; shop; rest, snacks; bar; pool; sand beach 700m; watersports; bike hire; entmnt; TV rm; some statics; adv bkg; quiet. "Gd touring base." 1 May-12 Sep. € 38.00   2009*

OTRANTO *3A4* (1.5km NW Urban/Coastal) *40.16665, 18.47620* **Camping Mulino d'Acqua, Via Santo Stefano, 73028 Otranto (LE) [0836 802191; fax 802196; mulino. camping@anet.it; www.mulinodacqua.it]** Clearly sp on S611 coast rd. Lge, pt sl, pt shd; wc (cont); chem disp; mv service pnt; baby facs; shwrs €0.50; EHU (6A) €3; gas; lndry; shop; rest, snacks; bar; pool; sand beach adj; playgrnd; tennis; games area; bike hire; entmnt; TV; statics; dogs €6; sep car park; adv bkg; quiet; ccard acc; red LS. 21 May-12 Sep. € 56.00   2010*

PACENGO see Peschiera del Garda *1D2*

PADENGHE SUL GARDA see Desenzano del Garda *1D2*

PAESTUM *3A3* (N Coastal) *40.42780, 14.98244* **Camping Villaggio Ulisse, Via Ponte di Ferro, 84063 Paestum (SA) [tel/fax 0828 851095; info@campingulisse.com; www.campingulisse.com]** Foll site sp in cent Paestum, well sp. Lge, unmkd pitch, shd; wc (some cont); shwrs inc; EHU (3A) inc; lndry; shop; rest, snacks; bar; playgrnd; sand beach adj; games area; 80% statics; dogs; poss cr; quiet; CKE/CCI. "Direct access to beach; gd, clean, friendly site." ♦ 1 Apr-30 Sep. € 35.00   2012*

PAESTUM *3A3* (9km N Coastal) *40.49248, 14.94196* **Camping Villaggio Paestum, Loc Foce Sele, 84025 Marina-di-Eboli (SA) [tel/fax 0828 691003; info@campingpaestum. it; www.campingpaestum.it]** Fr Salerno/Battipaglia foll sp S to Paestum, turn R at site sp, site 150m on L after T-junc with coast rd. Lge, shd; htd wc (some cont); chem disp; mv service pnt; shwrs inc; EHU (6A) inc; lndry; shop; rest, snacks; bar; playgrnd; pool; paddling pool; sand beach 300m; tennis; games area; wifi; TV rm; dogs; phone; poss cr; adv bkg; poss noisy at w/end; ccard acc; CKE/CCI. "Gd rest & pool; sm pitches; Greek temples at Paestum superb." ♦ 15 Apr-15 Sep. € 36.00   2010*

PAESTUM *3A3* (5km WNW Coastal) *40.42896, 14.98214* **Campsite Athena, Via Ponte di Ferro, 84063 Paestum [0828 851105; fax 724809; vathena@tiscali.it; www.campingathena.com]** Site 50km S of Salerno. Foll a'strada to Battipaglia onto main rd to Paestum. Head S on SS18. At rndabt take 1st exit onto SP276, then at next rndabt take 1st exit onto Via della Repubblica. Go thro 1 rndabt, turn L onto SP175, at rndabt take 1st exit onto Via Marittima, L onto Via Poseidonia and 1st L onto Via Ponte di Ferro. Site on R. Med, pt shd; wc; chem disp; mv service pnt; shwrs; EHU (5A); lndry; shop; rest; snacks; takeaway; bar; wifi; dogs; train 2.5km; twin axles; Eng spkn; red LS; CKE/CCI. "Gd site, direct access to beach." ♦ ltd. 1 Apr-30 Oct. € 51.00   2014*

⊞ **PAESTUM** *3A3* (5km NW Coastal) *40.41330, 14.99140* **Camping Villaggio Dei Pini, Via Torre, 84063 Paestum (SA) [0828 811030; fax 811025; info@campingvillaggiodeipini. com; www.campingvillaggiodeipini.com]** Site 50km S of Salerno in vill of Torre-de-Paestum. Foll a'strada to Battipaglia onto main rd to Paestum, site sp bef Paestum on rd S18, foll to beach. Med, hdg/mkd pitch, shd; wc (mainly cont); chem disp; mv service pnt; shwrs inc; EHU (6A) inc; lndry; shop; rest, snacks; bar; BBQ; playgrnd; private sand beach adj; games area; internet; entmnt; 30% statics; no dogs Jul/Aug; phone; adv bkg; quiet LS; red LS; ccard acc; CKE/CCI. "Historical ruins nr; narr access rd fr vill due parked cars; lge o'fits may grnd at ent; some sm pitches - c'vans manhandled onto pitches; pleasant site by beach; gd rest; helpful owner; rec." ♦ ltd. € 51.00 (4 persons)   2014*

⊞ **PALMI** *3B4* (4km N Coastal) *38.39194, 15.86555* **Camping San Fantino, Via San Fantino 135, Loc Taureana, 89015 Lido-di-Palmi (RC) [tel/fax 0966 479729 or 334 3015485 (mob); info@campingsanfantino.it; www.campingsanfantinopalmi.it]** Leave A3/E45 at Palmi exit & take S18 N dir Gioia. After 4km turn L sp Taureana, site well sp. Lge, hdstg, terr, shd; wc; chem disp; shwrs; EHU (4A) €2 (rev pol); gas; lndry; shop; rest; bar; playgrnd; sand beach 400m; 20% statics; Eng spkn; 20% statics; adv bkg; quiet; CKE/CCI. "Site on cliff top with path to beach; gd views fr some pitches; conv NH bef Sicily ferry; gd rest; rough site rds - care needed; path to beach locked LS." ♦ € 28.00   2014*

PASSIGNANO SUL TRASIMENO 2E3 (1km E Rural)
43.18338, 12.15085 **Camping Kursaal, Viale Europa 24,
06065 Passignano-sul-Trasimeno (PG) [075 828085; fax
827182; info@campingkursaal.it; www.campingkursaal.
it]** Fr Perugia on S75 to Lake Trasimeno. Exit at Passignano-
Est twd lake; site on L past level x-ing adj hotel, well sp. Med,
hdg/mkd pitch, pt sl, pt shd; wc; chem disp; mv service pnt;
baby facs; shwrs inc; EHU (6A) €2 (poss rev pol); lndry (inc
dryer); shop; rest, snacks; bar; playgrnd; pool; private shgl
lake beach; bike hire; wifi; TV; dogs €1.50; phone; poss v cr;
Eng spkn; adv bkg ess; some rlwy noise; red LS; ccard acc; red
CKE/CCI. "Pleasant site in gd position; vg rest; some pitches
have lake view; ltd space & pitches tight; gd clean site." ♦
10 Apr-31 Oct. € 43.00   2014*

PASSIGNANO SUL TRASIMENO 2E3 (2km E Rural) *43.18176,
12.16517* **Camping Europa, Loc San Donato 8, 06065
Passignano-sul-Trasimeno (PG) [tel/fax 075 827405;
info@camping-europa.it; www.camping-europa.it]**
Fr A1 E on SS75 bis twd Perugia; exit SS75 at Passignano Est
& cont E on smaller parallel rd for 2km. Site on R via subway
under rlwy. Med, pt shd; wc (some cont) chem disp; mv
service pnt; shwrs inc; EHU (6A) inc; gas; lndry; shop; rest,
snacks; bar; playgrnd; pool; private sand beach by lake; boat
hire; watersports; games area; bike hire; wifi; 20% statics;
bus; Eng spkn; quiet; some rlwy noise; ccard acc. "Well-run,
clean, friendly, gd value site; san facs in need of renovation; ltd
(plunge-type pool); conv Assisi, Perugia, lake trips to islands."
♦ 28 Mar-10 Oct. € 23.00   2009*

PASSIGNANO SUL TRASIMENO 2E3 (800m E Rural)
43.18397, 12.15089 **Camping La Spiaggia, Via Europe 22,
06065 Passignano-sul-Trasimeno (PG) [tel/fax 075 827246;
info@campinglaspiaggia.it; www.campinglaspiaggia.it]**
Exit A1 at Bettolle-Valdichiana & foll sp Perugia for 30km. Exit
at Passignano Est & foll sp to site. Sm, mkd pitch, shd; htd
wc (some cont); chem disp; mv service pnt; baby facs; fam
bthrm; shwrs inc; EHU (6A/10A) inc; lndry; shop 800m; rest,
snacks; bar; BBQ; playgrnd; pool; lake & sand beach adj; slip
for boats; beach for dogs; nursery; table tennis; games area;
bike hire; wifi; sat TV; dogs €2; phone; bus/train 800m; poss cr;
Eng spkn; adv bkg; quiet; ccard acc; red long stay/LS. "Lovely
lakeside site; friendly owner; lge pitches; excel san facs but hot
water variable; gd rest; interesting lakeside town; 800m fr the
historic cent of Passignano; excel touring base for hill towns."
♦ 27 Mar-13 Oct. € 29.00   2013*

PEGLI see Genova *1C2*

⊞ **PEIO** *1D1* (1.5km S Rural) *46.35833, 10.68138* **Camping
Panoramico Val di Sole, Via Dossi di Cavia, 38020 Peio
(TN) [0463 753177; fax 753176; info@valdisolecamping.it;
www.valdisolecamping.it]** Travelling W fr Dimaro on SS42
twd Tonale Pass, turn R into Val-de-Peio thro Cogolo twd Peio-
Fonti. Site in 1.8km on R. Med, mkd pitch, terr, pt shd; htd wc
(some cont); chem disp; mv service pnt; baby facs; shwrs inc;
EHU (3A) inc; lndry (inc dryer); shop; rest 2km; snacks high ssn;
bar; playgrnd; 60% statics; dogs €2; phone; bus 300m; site
clsd end May & Nov; poss cr Aug; quiet; ccard acc; red CKE/
CCI. "Excel for mountain walking in Stelvio National Park."
♦ ltd. € 23.50   2009*

PERTICARA 2E3 (2km N Rural) *43.89608, 12.24302* **Camping
Perticara, Via Serra Masini 10/d, 61017 Perticara (PS)
[0541 927602; fax 927707; info@campingperticara.com;
www.campingperticara.com]** Fr A14 at Rimini take S258 to
Novafeltria. Foll sp Perticara & site. Steep, hairpins on pt of rte.
Med, hdg/mkd pitch, hdstg, terr, unshd; htd wc; chem disp;
mv service pnt; baby facs; serviced pitches; shwrs inc; EHU
(10A) inc; gas; lndry; shop & 2km; snacks; bar; playgrnd; pool;
paddling pool; wifi; entmnt; TV rm; 5% statics; dogs; phone;
bus; poss cr; Eng spkn; adv bkg; quiet; ccard acc; red LS; CKE/
CCI. "Clean, well-maintained, scenic site; hospitable Dutch
owners; many activities arranged; immac san facs; poss diff
egress to SW (hairpins with passing places) - staff help with 4x4
if necessary; rough terrain; excel; well run." 13 May-20 Sep.
€ 37.00   2015*

PERUGIA 2E3 (8km NW Rural) *43.12030, 12.31328* **Camping
Paradis d'Eté, Colle della Trinita, Strada Fontana 29/H,
06074 Perugia [075 5173121; fax 0755 176056; jnlagu@tin.it;
www.wel.it/cparadis]** Exit Perugia-Firenze a'strada A1 at
Ferro-di-Cavallo exit to N. At traff lts turn L (W) & foll rd parallel
to a'strada for approx 1km. Turn R at camp sp, & site 3km up
steep hill on R. Sm, pt sl, terr, shd; wc; mv service pnt; shwrs
inc; EHU (6A) €1.50; lndry; shop; supmkt 3km; snacks; bar;
playgrnd; pool; games rm; dogs; bus to Perugia; quiet; ccard
acc; CKE/CCI. "Peaceful site; steep incline in & out of site;
dated facs, but clean." 1 Mar-31 Aug. € 29.00   2009*

PESARO 2E3 (10km N Coastal) *43.95993, 12.80136* **Camping
Paradiso, Via Rive del Faro 2, 61010 Casteldimezzo (PS)
[tel/fax 0721 208579; info@campingparadiso.it;
www.campingparadiso.it]** Turn of SS16 at Colombare,
turn in vill (by bank). Steep & narr - best turn by church N of
vill. Site sp. Med, terr, shd; wc (some cont); chem disp; shwrs
inc; EHU (6A) inc; lndry; shop; rest adj; snacks; bar; playgrnd;
sand & shgl beach adj; internet; 10% statics; dogs €2.50;
phone; poss cr; adv bkg; some rlwy noise; red LS; ccard acc.
"Gd views; beach down v steep cliff rd." ♦ 1 Mar-31 Dec.
€ 35.50   2010*

⊞ **PESCASSEROLI** 2F4 (500m S Rural) *41.79888, 13.79222*
**Camping Sant' Andrea, Via San Donato, 67032 Pescasseroli
(AQ) [tel/fax 0863 912725 or 335 5956029 (mob); info@
campingsantandrea.com; www.campingsantandrea.com]**
Site sp on R bet Pescasseroli & Opi. If gate clsd ent thro side
gate & turn key to open main gate. Sm, mkd pitch, pt shd;
htd wc (some cont); chem disp; mv service pnt; shwrs inc; EHU
(10A) inc; shop, rest, snacks, bar in town; playgrnd; statics in
sep area; dogs; phone; CKE/CCI. "Beautiful, open pitches in
lovely area; clean facs but ltd high ssn." € 15.00   2013*

PESCHICI 2G4 (10km E Coastal) *41.94361, 16.04855*
**Villaggio Camping Internazionale Manacore, 71010
Manacore (FG) [0884 911020; fax 911049; manacore@
grupposaccia.it; www.grupposaccia.it]** Coast rd thro town
of Peschici to Vieste, site sp. If app fr W, do NOT enter town.
Turn R twd Vieste; at rndabt in 2km turn L, sp Manacore. V lge,
pt sl, pt shd; wc; chem disp; mv service pnt; shwrs inc; private
bthrms avail; EHU (3A) inc; gas; lndry; shop; rest, snacks; bar;
playgrnd; sand beach; boat hire; windsurfing; tennis; bike hire;
games area; entmnt; 25% statics; dogs; sep car park high ssn;
poss cr; no adv bkg; quiet; ccard acc; CKE/CCI. "Magnificent
scenery; excel for boats & sw; excel facs." ♦ 1 May-11 Oct.
€ 49.00   2010*

You can now fill in site reports online

PESCHICI *2G4* (5km SE Rural) *41.93815, 16.04963* **Camping La Gemma, Loc Baia di Manaccora, 71010 Peschici (FG) [0884 911010; fax 962777; info@la-gemma.it; www.la-gemma.it]** Exit A14 at Poggio Imperiale onto SS89 E to Peschici. Turn off & foll sp to Manaccora & site. Med, shd; htd wc; mv service pnt; shwrs; EHU; lndry; shop; rest, snacks; bar; playgrnd; pool; paddling pool; sand beach 300m; watersports; fishing; tennis; entmnt; internet; TV rm; some statics; adv bkg; quiet. 1 Apr-1 Oct. € 26.50   2009*

PESCHICI *2G4* (1.5km S Coastal) *41.94237, 16.03054* **Centro Turistico San Nicola, Punta San Nicola, 71010 Peschici (FG) [0884 964024; fax 964025; sannicola@sannicola.it; www.sannicola.it]** Site clearly sp on S89 bet Peschici & Vieste. V lge, mkd pitch, sl, terr, pt shd; wc (some cont); chem disp; mv service pnt; shwrs inc; EHU (5A) inc; gas; lndry; shop; rest, snacks; sand beach; windsurfing; tennis; gym; entmnt & some statics; no dogs high ssn; adv bkg; noisy; ccard acc; red long stay/CKE/CCI. "Excel for families; lovely site in beautiful location; surface water on pitches after heavy rain." ♦ 1 Apr-15 Oct. € 37.00   2009*

PESCHIERA DEL GARDA *1D2* (1km N Urban) *45.44780, 10.70195* **Camping del Garda, Via Marzan 6, 37019 Castelnuovo-del-Garda (VR) [045 7550540; fax 6400711; info@camping-delgarda.com; www.campingdelgarda.it]** Exit A4/E70 dir Peschiera onto SR249 dir Lazise. Turn L in 500m dir Lido Campanello, site in 1km on L on lakeside. V lge, shd; wc (mainly cont); chem disp; mv service pnt; shwrs inc; EHU (4A) inc; gas; lndry; shop; rest, snacks; bar; playgrnd; 3 pools; shgl beach; lake sw; tennis; games area; entmnt; 60% statics; no dogs; phone; adv bkg; quiet. "Busy, well-organised site; helpful staff, discount snr citizens." ♦ 1 Apr-30 Sep. € 51.00   2011*

PESCHIERA DEL GARDA *1D2* (1km N Rural) *45.46722, 10.71638* **Eurocamping Pacengo, Via del Porto 13, 37010 Pacengo (VR) [tel/fax 045 7590012; info@eurocampingpacengo.it; www.eurocampingpacengo.it]** On SS249 fr Peschiera foll sp to Gardaland, Pacengo in 14km. Turn L at traff lts in cent of vill, site on L. Lge, mkd pitch, sl, pt shd; wc (some cont) chem disp (wc); mv service pnt; shwrs €0.30; EHU (4A) inc; lndry; shop & 500m; rest, snacks; bar; playgrnd; pool adj; lake sw, boat-launching adj; entmnt; 25% statics; dogs €2.40; phone; poss cr; Eng spkn; adv bkg; quiet; CKE/CCI. "Well-equipped site on shore Lake Garda; helpful staff; some sm pitches; espec gd end of ssn; excel rest; conv Verona." ♦ 10 Apr-22 Sep. € 41.60   2014*

PESCHIERA DEL GARDA *1D2* (2.5km N Rural) *45.45480, 10.70200* **Camping Gasparina, Loc Cavalcaselle, 37014 Castelnuovo-del-Garda (VR) [045 7550775; fax 7552815; info@gasparina.com; www.gasparina.com]** On SS249 dir Lazise, turn L at site sp. Lge, mkd pitch, sl, pt shd; wc; chem disp; mv service pnt; shwrs inc; EHU (3A) inc; gas; lndry; shop; rest, snacks; bar; playgrnd; pool; lake adj; games area; entmnt; some statics; dogs; poss cr; adv bkg; poss noisy; ccard acc; "Popular, busy site; variable pitch sizes; lake views some pitches; long lead req." 1 Apr-30 Sep. € 35.00   2013*

PESCHIERA DEL GARDA *1D2* (6km NE Rural) *45.46472, 10.71416* **Camping Le Palme, Via del Tronchetto 2, 37017 Pacengo (VR) [045 7590019; fax 7590554; info@lepalmecamping.it; www.lepalmecamping.it]** A4/E70 exit at Peschiera onto SS249, sp Lazise. Site sp bef Pacengo in approx 5km. Lge, mkd pitch, terr, pt shd; wc; chem disp; serviced pitches; baby facs; shwrs inc; EHU (6A) inc; lndry (inc dryer); shop; rest 300m; snacks; bar; playgrnd; htd pool; paddling pool; waterslide; lake sw & shgl beach adj; wifi; 40% statics; dogs €4.60; Eng spkn; adv bkg; ccard acc; red LS. "Well-maintained site; excel, clean facs; extra for lakeside pitches; helpful staff; sh walk to vill; 4 theme parks nr; excel." ♦ 27 Mar-26 Oct. € 37.00   2015*

PESCHIERA DEL GARDA *1D2* (1km W Urban) *45.44222, 10.67805* **Camping Bella Italia, Via Bella Italia 2, 37019 Peschiera del Garda (VR) [045 6400688; fax 6401410; info@camping-bellaitalia.it; www.camping-bellaitalia.it]** Fr Brescia or Verona on SP11 to Peschiera del Garda, site sp on lakeside. Fr Brescia or Verona on A4/E70 exit at Peschiera on to SP11 in dir of Brescia, site on R in about 2km. V lge, slight sl, shd; wc; chem disp; mv service pnt; baby facs; shwrs inc; EHU (16A); gas; lndry (inc dryer); shop; 2 rests; snacks; bar; BBQ; playgrnd; pool; paddling pool; waterslides; lake sw adj; windsurfing; tennis; games area; bike hire; archery; wifi; entmnt; many static tents; no dogs; bus to Verona; poss cr; Eng spkn; adv bkg rec; poss noisy high ssn; red LS; CKE/CCI. "Busy, popular site, nr theme park, Aqua World, Verona; suits all ages; v clean; rests gd & gd price; gd recep for satellite & wifi." ♦ 16 Mar-26 Oct. € 56.50   2013*

PESCHIERA DEL GARDA *1D2* (6km W Coastal) *45.45120, 10.66557* **Camping Wien, Loc. Fornaci, 37019 Peschiera (VR) [045 7550379; fax 7553366; info@campingwien.it]** On Verona-Brescia rd (not a'strada) W of Peschiera, turn R at San Benedetto, turn R 400m after traff lts, site has 2 ents 100m apart. Med, mkd pitch, hdstg, pt sl, shd; wc; chem disp; mv service pnt; shwrs inc; EHU inc (3A); gas; lndry; ice; shop; rest; snacks; bar; playgrnd; pool; shgl beach adj; games area; entmnt; boating; fishing; 50% statics; dogs; phone; bus adj; Eng spkn; adv bkg; poss cr; quiet; ccard not acc; red long stay; CKE/CCI. "Wonderful pool o'looking Lake Garda; walking/cycle path into town; vg site." ♦ 18 Apr-30 Sep. € 52.00   2014*

PESCHIERA DEL GARDA *1D2* (700m W Rural) *45.44555, 10.69472* **Camping Butterfly, Lungo Lago Garibaldi 11, 37019 Peschiera (VR) [045 6401466; fax 7552184; info@campingbutterfly.it; www.campingbutterfly.it]** Fr A4/E70 exit twd Peschiera for 2km. At x-rds with bdge on L, strt over & foll rv to last site after RH bend at bottom. Lge, shd; wc (some cont); shwrs; EHU inc; gas; lndry; shop; rest, snacks; bar; playgrnd; pool; paddling pool; lake sw; entmnt; 75% statics; dogs €5; poss cr; adv bkg; quiet except w/end; ccard acc. "Busy holiday site; conv town & lake steamers; sm pitches; clean san facs; adv bkg rec." ♦ 9 Mar-10 Nov. € 50.00 (4 persons)   2013*

PESCHIERA DEL GARDA *1D2* (2km NW Urban) *45.44825, 10.66978* **Camping San Benedetto, Strada Bergamini 14, 37019 San Benedetto (VR) [045 7550544; fax 7551512; info@campingsanbenedetto.it; www.campingsan benedetto.it]** Exit A4/E70 dir Peschiera-del-Garda, turn N at traff lts in cent of vill, site on lake at km 274/V111 on rd S11. Lge, pt sl, shd; wc; mv service pnt; shwrs inc; EHU (3A) inc; lndry; shop; rest, snacks; bar; playgrnd; pool; paddling pool; lakeside shgl beach nr; boat hire; windsurfing; canoeing; bike hire; games area; entmnt; 30% statics; dogs; poss cr; adv bkg; quiet; red snr citizens. "Pleasant, well-run; sm harbour; site clsd 1300-1500; excel modern rest beside lake." 28 Mar-4 Oct. € 35.00   2014*

PETTENASCO see Orta San Giulio *1B1*

PEVERAGNO see Cuneo *1B2*

"I need an on-site restaurant"

We do our best to make sure site information is correct, but it is always best to check any must-have facilities are still available or will be open during your visit.

PIENZA *1D3* (7km E Rural) *43.08089, 11.71159* **Camping Il Casale, 64 53026 Pienza (SI) [tel/fax 0578 755109, 333 4250705 (mob); podereilcasale@libero.it]** Fr Pienza dir Montepulciano on S146, turn R in 4km onto sm, gritted track sp Monticchiello (sm, brown sp easily missed). Site in 3km on L sp Podereilcasale. Fr Montepulciano dir Pienza rd to L sp Il Borghetto (Fago). Sm, pt shd; pt sl; wc; shwrs inc; EHU (16A) inc; shop; rest; bar; playgrnd; lake adj; dogs; phone; poss cr; Eng spkn; adv bkg; quiet; ccard acc. "8 pitches only for c'vans/mvans; simple farm site; price inc breakfast; panoramic views; rec phone to check availability; v friendly owners, site fees inc breakfast." ♦ 1 Apr-15 Nov. € 26.00   2013*

PIEVE DI LEDRO *1D1* (3km E Rural) *45.87805, 10.76777* **Camping Al Sole, Loc Besta, Via Maffei 127, 38060 Molina-di-Ledro (TN) [tel/fax 0464 508496; info@camping alsole.it; www.campingalsole.it]** Exit A22 at Rovereto S onto SS240 twd Riva-del-Garda then Vall di Ledro & Molina, site sp on Lake Ledro. Lge, mkd pitch, pt shd; wc; shwrs inc; EHU (3A) inc; lndry (inc dryer); shop; rest, snacks; bar; playgrnd; pool; lake sw & beach adj; watersports; tennis adj; wifi; entmnt; TV rm; 10% statics; dogs; adv bkg; quiet. "Peaceful site; busy but clean & well-ordered; some lake view pitches; gd outdoor activities." ♦ 1 Apr-30 Sep. € 31.00   2010*

PIEVE DI LEDRO *1D1* (500m S Rural) *45.88361, 10.73157* **Camping Al Lago, Via Alzer 7-9, 38060 Pieve-di-Ledro (TN) [tel/fax 0464 591250; info@camping-al-lago.it; www.camping-al-lago.it]** Exit A22 W onto SS240 to Riva-del-Garda, then cont on SS240 to Pieve-di-Lago. Turn L into Via Alzer & foll sp to site (after Cmp Azzuro). Med, mkd pitch, some hdstg, pt shd; wc (some cont); chem disp; mv service pnt; shwrs; EHU (3A) inc; lndry (inc dryer); shop 500m; rest 250m; snacks; bar; BBQ; playgrnd; lake sw adj; fishing; tennis; games area; bike & canoe hire; wifi; entmnt; TV; 10% statics; dogs; Eng spkn; adv bkg; quiet; ccard acc; CKE/CCI. "Vg site; gd walking area." ♦ ltd. 2 Apr-10 Oct. € 30.00   2010*

PIEVE DI LEDRO *1D1* (Rural) *45.88527, 10.73138* **Camping Azzurro, Via Alzer, 38060 Pieve-di-Ledro (TN) [0464 508435 or 591276; fax 508150; info@campingazzurro.net; www.campingazzurro.net]** Fr Riva-del-Garda foll sp Val di Ledro on S240. Ent vill on by-pass, at x-rds turn L, site on L in 200m on lakeside. Med, mkd pitch, some hdstg, shd; wc; chem disp; mv service pnt; shwrs inc; EHU (2-6A) inc; lndry; supmkt adj; rest 100m; snacks; playgrnd; pool; lake sw; fishing; watersports; internet nr; 50% statics; dogs €5; bus nr; adv bkg; quiet; red LS. "Attractive vill; cycle track around lake; friendly staff; well-run site." ♦ 1 May-30 Sep. € 30.00 (CChq acc)   2011*

⊞ **PIEVE TESINO** *1D1* (6km N Rural) *46.11361, 11.61944* **Villaggio Camping Valmalene, Loc Valmalene, 38050 Pieve-Tesino (TN) [0461 594214; fax 592654; info@valmalene.com; www.valmalene.com]** Fr Trento E for 50km on S47. Turn N at Strigno to Pieve-Tesino, site sp. Med, mkd pitch, pt shd; htd wc; mv service pnt; sauna; private bthrms avail; baby facs; shwrs; EHU inc; lndry; shop; supmkt 6km; rest, snacks; bar; playgrnd; htd pool; padding pool; tennis; bike hire; games area; fitness rm; internet; some statics; dogs €4; site clsd Nov; adv bkg rec; quiet; ccard acc. "Gd base for summer & winter hols." ♦ € 27.00   2009*

PINETO *2F3* (9km S Coastal) *42.5675, 14.0925* **Camping Europe Garden, Via Belvedere 11, 64028 Silvi-Marina (TE) [085 930137; fax 932846; info@europegarden.it; www.europegarden.it]** Exit A14/E55 for Atri/Pineto or Pescara N onto coast rd SS16, bet Silvi-Marina & Pineto, turn W away fr coast at Europe Garden at km 5 & site sp. Lge, terr, shd; wc (some cont); mv service pnt; baby facs; shwrs inc; EHU (5A) €2.50; gas; lndry; shop; hypmkt 2km; rest, snacks; bar; playgrnd; pool; paddling pool; sand beach adj; tennis; archery; bike hire; entmnt; 90% statics; no dogs; sep car park high ssn; Eng spkn; adv bkg; ccard acc; red CKE/CCI. "Well laid-out; steep slopes; tractor help for c'vans avail; sm pitches diff for l'ge u'fits; site muddy in wet weather; panoramic views; pleasant staff; conv Appenines, Atri walled town & Abruzzo National Park." 1 May-1 Sep. € 36.50 (CChq acc)   2009*

PINZOLO *1D1* (5km N Rural) *46.18535, 10.78027* **Camping Faè, 38080 Sant' Antonio-di-Mavignola (TN) [tel/fax 0465 507178; campingfae@campiglio.it; www.campiglio. it/campingfae]** Site well sp on SS239 bet Pinzolo & Madonna-di-Campiglio. Med, mkd pitch, terr, pt shd; htd wc (some cont); chem disp; mv service pnt; shwrs inc; EHU (6A) inc; lndry; shop 1km; bar; BBQ; playgrnd; games rm; TV; 40% statics; dogs; bus adj; poss cr; adv bkg; quiet; ccard acc; red LS. "Well-run, family owned site; clean san facs; gd walking." ♦ 1 Jun-30 Sep & 1 Dec-30 Apr. € 31.50   2009*

PISA *1C3* (1km N Urban) *43.72416, 10.3830* **Camp Torre Pendente, Viale delle Cascine 86, 56122 Pisa [050 561704; fax 561734; info@campingtorrependente.com; www.campingtorrependente.com]** Exit A12/E80 Pisa Nord onto Via Aurelia (SS1). After 8km & after x-ing rlwy bdge, turn L after passing Pisa sp at traff lts. Site on L, sp. Lge, mkd pitch, pt shd; wc; mv service pnt; chem disp; baby facs; fam bthrm; shwrs inc; EHU (5A) inc (poss rev pol); gas; lndry (inc dryer); shop; supmkt 400m; rest; pizzeria; snacks; bar; BBQ; playgrnd; pool; sand beach 10km; bike hire; wifi; TV rm; dogs €1.60; phone; poss cr; Eng spkn; no adv bkg; ccard acc over €100; red long stay; CKE/CCI. "Gd base Pisa; leaning tower 15 mins walk; immac, modern, well-maintained san facs; private san facs avail; pitches typically 50sqm; poss tight lge o'fits due narr site rds & corners; many pitches shd by netting; site rds muddy after rain; friendly staff; excel, well-run site; 300m fr Pisa San Rossore rlwy stn, trains to Lucca etc." ♦ 1 Apr-2 Nov. € 37.00   2015*

"Satellite navigation makes touring much easier"

Remember most sat navs don't know if you're towing or in a larger vehicle – always use yours alongside maps and site directions.

⊞ **PISA** *1C3* (500m N Urban) **Camper Parking, Via Pietrasantina, 56100 Pisa** On Via Aurelia SS1 fork R app Pisa, then turn E approx 1km N of Arno Rv, sp camping. After 1km turn L into Via Pietrasantina. Site on R behind lge Tamoil petrol stn, sp coach parking. Max height under rlwy bdge 3.30m. C'vans acc. Lge, hdstg, unshd; own san ess; mv service pnt; no EHU; shop; rest, snacks, bar 100m; dogs; bus adj; quiet. "Excel NH; parking within walking dist of leaning tower; water & waste inc; plenty of space; san facs open at café opp during day." ♦ € 12.00   2012*

PISA *1C3* (7km S Rural) *43.63083, 10.36277* **Agricampeggio Lago Le Tamerici, Via della Sofina 6, 56121 Coltano (PI) [050 989007; info@lagoletamerici.it; www.lagoletamerici.it]** S fr Pisa on SS1 Via Aurelia, turn L sp Coltano, then Lago Le Tamerici. Or fr S on SS206 foll sp Coltano etc. Sm, hdg/mkd pitch, pt shd; wc; chem disp; mv service pnt; EHU (10A) inc; lndry (inc dryer); shop; rest, snacks; bar; BBQ; playgrnd; pool; lake fishing; canoe & bike hire; games area; adv bkg; quiet."V friendly." ♦ 12 Mar-16 Oct. € 28.00   2011*

PISOGNE *1C1* (200m N Rural) *45.80611, 10.1050* **Camping Eden, Loc Goia, Via Piangrande 3/A, 25055 Pisogne (BS) [tel/fax 0364 880500; info@campeggioeden.com; www.campeggioeden.com]** Exit P510 at Pisogne Sud, over rlwy line, site sp. Med, mkd pitch, shd; wc; shwrs inc; EHU (2A) €1.30; lndry; shop 200m; rest, snacks 100m; playgrnd; sand beach; watersports; tennis; some statics (sep area); dogs €1.50; adv bkg; quiet. "Lovely, wooded site; excel facs." ♦ 1 May-15 Sep. € 24.50   2010*

PISTOIA *1D3* (10km S Rural) *43.84174, 10.91049* **Camping Barco Reale, Via Nardini 11, 51030 San Baronto-Lamporecchio (PT) [0573 88332; fax 856003; info@barcoreale.com; www.barcoreale.com]** Leave A11 at Pistoia junc onto P9 & foll sp to Vinci, Empoli & Lamporecchio to San Baronto. In vill turn into rd by Monti Hotel & Rest, site sp. Last 3km steep climb. Lge, mkd pitch, pt sl, terr, shd; wc; chem disp; mv service pnt; 30% serviced pitch; baby facs; shwrs inc; EHU (3-6A) inc (poss rev pol); gas; lndry; shop; rest, snacks; bar; playgrnd; pool; games area; bike hire; internet; wifi; entmnt; dogs; phone; Eng spkn; adv bkg ess; quiet; red long stay/LS; ccard acc; red long stay; CKE/CCI. "Excel site in Tuscan hills; helpful staff; gd touring base; excel mother & baby facs; vg rest; poss diff access some pitches but towing help provided on request; unsuitable lge o'fits; well-organised walking & bus trips; excel pool." ♦ 1 Apr-30 Sep. € 57.40   2014*

See advertisement inside the front cover

PIZZO *3B4* (6km N Coastal) *38.72213, 16.15104* **Camping Villaggio Pinetamare, 88812 Pizzo (VV) [0963 264067; fax 534871; info@villaggiopinetamare.it]** Exit A3/E45 dir Pizzo. Fr Pizzo go N on S18 twd Santa Eufemia-Lamezia, km 392; site sp. Lge, mkd pitch, hdstg, shd; wc (some cont); chem disp; shwrs inc; EHU (6A) €3.50; gas; lndry rm; shop; rest, snacks; bar; playgrnd; 3 pools; private sand/shgl beach adj; windsurfing; tennis; entmnt & no dogs; Eng spkn; adv bkg; ccard acc; CKE/CCI. "Vg family site under pine trees." 15 Jun-15 Sep. € 37.00   2009*

"There aren't many sites open at this time of year"

If you're travelling outside peak season remember to call ahead to check site opening dates – even if the entry says 'open all year'.

POGGIBONSI *1D3* (12km N Rural) *43.58198, 11.13801* **Camping Panorama Del Chianti, Via Marcialla 349, 50020 Marcialla-Certaldo (FI) [tel/fax 0571 669334; info@campingchianti.it; www.campingchianti.it]** Fr Florence-Siena a'strada exit sp Tavarnelle. On reaching Tavernelle turn R sp Tutti Direzione/Certaldo & foll by-pass to far end of town. Turn R sp to Marcialla, in Marcialla turn R to Fiano, site in 1km. NB Some steep hairpins app site fr E. Med, mkd pitch, hdstg, terr, pt shd; wc (some cont); chem disp; mv service pnt; shwrs inc; EHU (3A) inc; shop, rest, snacks, bar 800m; sm pool; bike hire; dogs €2; phone; adv bkg; Eng spkn; quiet; red long stay; ccard not acc; CKE/CCI. "Gd tourist info (in Eng); sports facs in area; cultural sites; helpful staff; friendly owner; san facs clean - hot water to shwrs only; 4 excel rests nr; panoramic views; midway bet Siena & Florence; popular site - arr early to get pitch; facs need updating." 21 Mar-31 Oct. € 36.00 (CChq acc)   2014*

ITALY

ITALY

⊞ **POMPEI** *3A3* (1km S Urban) *40.74638, 14.48388* **Camping Spartacus, Loc Pompei Scavi, Via Plinio 127, 80045 Pompei (NA) [tel/fax 081 8624078; staff@campingspartacus.it; www.campingspartacus.it]** Fr N on A3 exit Pompei Ovest. At T-junc turn L & site on R just after passing under rlwy bdge. Fr S exit Pompei Est & foll sp Pompei Scavi (ruins). SatNav may lead to low bdge. Sm, mkd pitch, shd; wc; chem disp; mv service pnt; shwrs inc; EHU (5A) €2.3.(poss rev pol); gas; lndry; supmkt 400m; rest, snacks, bar in high ssn; internet; TV rm; poss v cr; Eng spkn; adv bkg; some rd/rlwy noise; ccard acc; red LS/CKE/CCI. "Nice, family-run, welcoming site, 50m fr historical ruins; conv train to Naples, boats to Capri; stray dogs poss roam site & ruins; v popular with students high ssn; best of 3 town sites; gd site for exploring area; friendly owners; clean san facs.; poss cr high ssn; steep access rd. " ♦ € 34.00　　2015*

PORLEZZA *1C1* (4km E Rural) *46.04074, 9.16827* **Camping Ranocchio, Via Al Lago 7,22010 Loc Piano di Porlezza, Carlazzo (CO) [tel/fax 0344 70385; campingranocchio@ngi.it]** On main rd bet Menaggio & Porlezza. Ent in vill of Piano on S side. Sp. Steep app in Lugano with hairpin bends; 15% gradient. V narr rd fr Lugano - clsd to c'vans at peak times. Lge, terr, shd, pt sl; wc; chem disp; mv service pnt; baby facs; shwrs €0.50; EHU inc; gas; lndry (inc dryer); shop adj; rest 50m; snacks; bar; playgrnd; pool; paddling pool; lake sw & fishing; horseriding 2km; wifi; TV rm; dogs €2; Eng spkn; quiet; CKE/CCI. "Friendly recep; gd for exploring Como & Lugano; steamer trips on both lakes; lovely site; v attractive site; helpful recep; excel corner shop." ♦ 1 Apr-30 Sep. € 32.00　2013*

PORTESE see San Felice Del Benaco *1D2*

PORTO CESAREO *3A4* (6.5km NE Coastal) *40.29077, 17.82711* Camping Porto Cesareo, Via Torre Lapillo-Torre Columena, Km 0.7, 73010 Porto-Cesareo (LE) [tel/fax 0833 565312; info@portocesareocamping.it; www.portocesareocamping. it] S fr Manduria or N fr Nardo on SP359, foll sp Porto Cesareo & site. Med, hdg/mkd pitch, shd; wc; chem disp; mv service pnts; shwrs inc; EHU (4A) inc; lndry; shop & 1km; rest, snacks; bar; BBQ; playgrnd; pool; sand beach 400m; bike hire; games area; wifi; entmnt; TV rm; 15% statics; dogs free; Eng spkn; adv bkg; quiet; ccard acc. "Scenic, well-maintained site; vg, modern san facs; lovely pool; bus transfer to beach - gd snorkelling area; friendly, helpful staff." ♦ 1 Jun-12 Sep. € 32.00　　2010*

PORTO RECANATI *2F3* (4km N Coastal) *43.47123, 13.64150* Camping Bellamare, Lungomare Scarfiotti 13, 62017 Porto-Recanati (MC) [071 976628; fax 977586; info@bellamare.it; www.bellamare.it] Exit A14/E55 Loreto/Porto-Recanati; foll sp Numana & Sirolo; camp on R in 4km on coast rd. Lge, unshd; wc; chem disp; shwrs; EHU (6A) €3; gas; lndry; shop; rest, snacks; bar; playgrnd; pool; paddling pool; sand & shgl beach (shelves steeply); bike hire; games area; games rm; entmnt; internet; some statics; no dogs; phone; Eng spkn; ccard acc; red LS; CKE/CCI. "V well-run site; NH tarrif of €19 (inc elec) for a pitch at the edge of the site but ok; beach access." ♦ 23 Apr-30 Sep. € 42.50　　2011*

⊞ **PORTO RECANATI** *2F3* (7.7km NW Urban) *43.44155, 13.61446* **Area Attrezzata Camper Loreto, Via Maccari, 60025 Loreto [07 19 77 748; info@prolocoloreto.com]** Fr A14 S of Ancona, exit at Loreto. Fr town ctr foll sp to campsite. Med, mkd pitch, hdstg, unshd; wc; mv service pnt; shwrs inc; EHU inc; dogs; quiet. "M'van NH; conv for Basilica, beach & Ancona ferries; clean & well run; occasional c'vans allowed if not busy; vg site." € 12.00　　　2014*

PORTO SAN GIORGIO *2F3* (1km S Coastal) *43.15905, 13.80823* **Camping Spinnaker, Via Campofiloni, Santa Maria-a-Mare 27, 63023 Fermo (AP) [0734 53412; fax 53737; info@vacanzespinnaker.it; www.vacanze spinnaker.it]** Exit A14 at junc for Porto-San Giorgio onto S16 S, foll site sp. V lge, mkd pitch, pt shd; wc; chem disp; mv service pnt; baby facs; shwrs inc; EHU €3; lndry; shop; rest, snacks; bar; playgrnd; pool; waterslide; sand beach adj; watersports; tennis; games area; bike hire; entmnt; cash machine; some statics; dogs €3 (sm only); poss cr; adv bkg. 16 May-13 Sep. € 44.00　　　　2009*

PORTO SANTA MARGHERITA see Caorle *2E2*

> ## "That's changed – Should I let The Club know?"
>
> If you find something on site that's different from the site entry, fill in a report and let us know. See www.caravanclub.co.uk/europereport.

PORTOFERRAIO *1C3* (9km E Rural) *42.80072, 10.36452* Rosselba Le Palme, Loc. Ottone 3, 57037 Elba Portoferraio [0565 933 101; fax 933 041; info@rosselbalepalme.it; www.rosselbalepalme.it] Fr ferry terminal foll signs 'tutti direzioni'. At 3rd rndabt head twds Porto Azzurro. Take L fork to Bagnaia. Site sp. Sm, hdg pitch, terr, pt shd; wc; chem disp; mv service pnt; shwrs inc; EHU (6A); lndry rm; shop; rest; snacks; bar; playgrnd; pool; sand beach 0.5km; entmnt; wifi; 80% statics; bus adj; twin axles; Eng spkn; adv bkg; quiet; CCI. "Ferry service fr Piombino every 1/2 hr; statics enhance site facs." 20 Apr-6 Oct. € 49.00　　　2014*

⊞ **POZZA DI FASSA** *1D1* (1km SE Rural) *46.42015, 11.70730* **Caravan Garden Vidor, Loc Vidor 5, 38036 Pozza-di-Fassa (TN) [0462 763247; fax 764780; info@campingvidor.it; www.campingvidor.it]** Exit A22 at Ora/Auer onto SS48 to Pozza-di-Fassa cent, turn R (E) over bdge dir Val di Nicolo, site in 2km on L on rvside. Other rds in area clsd to c'vans. Med, mkd pitch, hdstg, terr, pt shd; htd wc (some cont); chem disp; mv service pnt; baby facs; fam bthrm; sauna; shwrs inc; EHU (2-16A) metered; gas (fixed supply to some pitches); lndry (inc dryer); shop; rest adj & 2km; snacks; bar; BBQ; playgrnd; htd pool; paddling pool; sh tennis; cable car 1km; wifi; TV rm; 30% statics; dogs €4.50; phone; site clsd Nov; poss cr; Eng spkn; adv bkg; quiet; ccard acc; CKE/CCI. "Beautiful location; friendly, family-run site; excel views & facs; above hubbub of main valley; gd walking." ♦ € 31.00　　　2010*

POZZA DI FASSA *1D1* (500m SW Rural) *46.42638,*
11.68527 **Camping Rosengarten, Via Avisio 15, 38036
Pozza-di-Fassa (TN) [0462 763305; fax 762247; info@
catinacciorosengarten.com; www.catinacciorosengarten.
com]** Fr S SS48 site sp just after San Giovanni. Lge, hdstg, pt
shd; wc; chem disp; mv service pnt; shwrs inc; EHU (2A) inc
(extra for higher amperage); lndry; shop 500m; rest, snacks
adj; bar; pool 300m; ski lift 1km; ski bus; wifi; 30% statics;
dogs €4; site clsd Oct; poss cr; Eng spkn; adv bkg ess; quiet;
10% red 14+ days; ccard acc; CKE/CCI. "Superb scenery;
helpful staff; luxury san facs; free taxi (2010) to Vigo di
Fassa cable car; excel site; v convly sited for access to vill &
public transport; 20 min walk to Buffaure cable car; off clsd
1230-1500." 1 Jan-30 Apr, 1 Jun-15 Oct, 1 Dec-31 Dec.
€ 32.00   2015*

PRAIA A MARE *3A4* (2km S Coastal) *39.87654, 15.78867*
**Camping Villaggio Turistico La Mantinera, Contrada de
Mantinera, 87028 Praia-a-Mare (CS) [0985 779023;
fax 779009; lamantinera@tiscali.it; www.lamantinera.it]**
On old coast rd, exit SS18 at sp to Praia. Fr N thro town on L;
fr S immed at bottom of hill on R. Lge, hdg/mkd pitch, shd,
all serviced pitches; wc; shwrs inc; EHU (7A) inc; rest (Jul/
Aug); bar; snacks; shop; lndry rm; playgrnd; shgl beach 750m;
pool; boat hire; windsurfing; tennis; bike hire; 30% statics;
no dogs high ssn; poss cr; adv bkg; noisy disco & traff; ccard
acc; 10% red CKE/CCI. "Individual tree-lined bays with
own water & EHU; free transport to beach; tours to Naples,
Pompei & organised activities." ♦ 30 Apr-30 Sep. € 42.00
(3 persons)   2009*

PRAIA A MARE *3A4* (500m S Coastal) *39.88198, 15.78529*
**International Camping Village, Lungomare F. Sirimarco,
87028 Praia-a-Mare (CS) [tel/fax 0985 72211; reception@
campinginternational.it; www.campinginternational.it]**
On beach rd just bef rocky island. Lge, hdg/mkd pitch, hdstg,
shd; wc (some cont); chem disp; mv service pnt; shwrs inc;
EHU (5A) inc; lndry; shop, rest, bar high ssn; BBQ; playgrnd;
paddling pool; private shgl beach adj; tennis; games area;
entmnt; some statics; dogs; phone; rlwy noise; ccard acc;
red LS. "Welcoming, clean site; hot water to shwrs only." ♦
23 Apr-30 Sep. € 38.50   2009*

PRATO ALLO STELVIO *1D1* (500m E Rural) *46.61777,*
10.59555 **Camping Sägemühle, Dornweg 12, 39026
Prato-allo-Stélvio (BZ) [0473 616078; fax 617120; info@
campingsaegumuehle.com; www.campingsaegumuehle.
com]** Fr rd S40 turn E at Spondigna onto rd S38 dir Stélvio,
site sp in vill. Med, hdg/mkd pitch, hdstg, pt sl, pt shd; htd wc;
chem disp; mv service pnt; baby facs; fam bthrm; sauna; shwrs
inc; EHU (16A) inc; lndry (inc dryer); shop 200m; rest; bar;
playgrnd; 2 pools (1 htd, covrd); paddling pool; games area;
ski lift 10km; skibus; wifi; TV; phone; dogs €4; adv bkg; quiet;
10% red LS; ccard acc; CKE/CCI. "Excel, well-run site; gd,
clean facs; helpful staff; gd walking area in National Park; conv
for the reschen pass Austria Italy; all pitches fully serviced."
1 Jan-9 Nov & 16 Dec-31 Dec. € 55.00   2014*

PRATO ALLO STELVIO *1D1* (500m NW Rural) *46.62472,*
10.59388 **Camping Kiefernhain, Via Pineta 37, 39026
Prato-allo-Stélvio (BZ) [0473 616422; fax 617277;
kiefernhain@rolmail.net; www.camping-kiefernhain.it]**
Fr rd S40 turn SW at Spondigna onto rd S38 dir Stélvio, site
sp in vill. Lge, mkd pitch, pt shd; wc; chem disp; mv service
pnt; baby facs; private bthrms avail; shwrs inc; EHU (6A)
€2.50; lndry; shop; rest 300m; snacks; bar; BBQ; playgrnd; htd
pool; waterslide; sports cent adj; dogs €4; phone; dog shwr;
wifi; Eng spkn; adv bkg rec high ssn; quiet; red long stay.
"V modern, clean san facs; superb views; facs stretched high
ssn; vg value." ♦ 1 May-4 Oct. € 52.50   2014*

PRECI *2E3* (3km NW Rural) *42.88808, 13.01483* **Camping Il
Collaccio, 06047 Castelvecchio-di-Preci (PG) [0743 665108;
fax 939094; info@ilcollaccio.com; www.ilcollaccio.com]**
S fr Assisi on S75 & S3, turn off E sp Norcia, Cascia. Then foll
sp for Visso on S209. In approx 30km turn R for Preci, then
L, site sp. Rte is hilly. Med, mkd pitch, terr, pt shd; htd wc
(some cont); chem disp; mv service pnt; baby facs; shwrs inc;
EHU (6A) inc (long lead poss req); lndry; shop & 2km; rest,
snacks; bar; playgrnd; 2 pools; tennis; games area; horseriding;
paragliding; bike hire; TV rm; 20% statics; dogs; phone; Eng
spkn; adv bkg; quiet; ccard acc; red CKE/CCI. "Beautiful
views; well-maintained, clean site; pleasant rest; maganificent
pool area; sm pitches; gd walking in Monti Sibillini National
Park; conv Assisi & historic hill towns; excel; well run." ♦
1 Apr-30 Sep. € 35.00   2015*

PREDAZZO *1D1* (2.5km E Rural) *46.31027, 11.63138*
**Camping Valle Verde, Loc Ischia 2, Sotto Sassa, 38037
Predazzo (TN) [tel/fax 0462 502394; info@campingvalle
verde.it; www.campingvalleverde.it]** Exit A22 dir Ora onto
rd S48 dir Cavalese/Predazzo. Fr Predazzo take SS50 W, turn R
in 1.5km, site on L in 500m. Med, mkd pitch, pt sl, pt shd; htd
wc (some cont); chem disp; mv service pnt; shwrs inc; EHU (6A)
€2; lndry (inc dryer); rest, snacks; bar; BBQ; playgrnd; rv sw
1km; games area; wifi; 5% statics; dogs €3.50; mini train adj;
bus 0.5km; twin axles; poss cr; Eng spkn; adv bkg; quiet; red
low stay/snr citizens; ccard acc. "Excel; bus & cable car rides;
walks, cycle tracks & mountain climbs nrby; beautiful site." ♦
1 May-1 Oct. € 32.00   2015*

PUNTA MARINA TERME see Ravenna *2E2*

PUNTA SABBIONI *2E2* (2km N Coastal) *45.43773, 12.43881*
**Camping Marina di Venezia, Via Montello 6, 30010
Punta-Sabbioni (VE) [041 5300955; fax 966036; camping@
marinadivenezia.it; www.marinadivenezia.it]**
Exit A4 dir Marco Polo Airport, foll dir Jesolo. At Jesolo where
rd splits, bear R dir Cavallino/Punta-Sabbioni. Site well sp. V
lge, hdg/mkd pitch, pt shd; wc; chem disp; shwrs inc; EHU (6A)
inc; gas; lndry; shops & supmkt; rest, snacks; bar; playgrnd;
2 pools; sand beach adj; boat hire; windsurfing; tennis; bike
hire; solarium; games area; 5% statics; dogs €3.50; phone;
bus fr site to waterbus to Venice; adv bkg rec; quiet; ccard acc;
red LS/snr citizen. "Lge pitches; high quality site, wonderfully
equipped and well run; min stay 2 nts (7 nts Jul/Aug); excel,
clean facs; some pitches avail v lge o'fits; superb pool complex;
pleasant, helpful staff; within easy reach of Venice; highly rec."
♦ 16 Apr-30 Sep. € 44.00 (CChq acc)   2011*

PUNTA SABBIONI *2E2* (2km NE Coastal) *45.44560, 12.46100* Campéole Camping Ca'Savio, Via di Ca'Savio 77 - 30013 Cavallino Treporti Ca'Savio (VE) [041 966017 or 041 966 570 (mob); fax 5300707; info@casavio.it; www.casavio.it or www.campeole.com] Fr Lido di Jesolo head twd Punta-Sabbioni; at x-rds/rndabt in cent of Ca'Savio turn L twd beach (La Spiaggia) for 800m; turn L into site just bef beach. Or at L turn at rndabt - rd poss clsd at night - cont to Punta-Sabbioni, turn L at sp to beach; L at T-junc, then R at x-rds. V lge, hdg/mkd pitch, shd; wc (some cont); chem disp; mv service pnt; baby facs; shwrs; EHU (5A) inc (check pol); gas; lndry (inc dryer); supmkt; rest; pizzeria; snacks; bar; playgrnd; pool; paddling pool; direct access to adj sandy beach; water sports; canoeing/kayaking; fishing; games area; archery; bike hire; wifi; entmnt; games rm; TV; 50% statics; no dogs; no o'fits over 7m high ssn; phone; bus to Venice ferry; ccard acc; red LS; CKE/CCI. "Well laid-out, well-run, busy site - noisy high ssn; helpful staff; conv Venice by ferry fr Punta Sabbioni; excel, clean san facs; facs ltd LS; long, narr pitches; access poss diff lge o'fits; gd supmkt; min 3 nights stay high ssn; barriers clsd 1300-1500." ♦ 26 Apr-27 Sep. € 38.50 (CChq acc) SBS - Y02   2013*

PUNTA SABBIONI *2E2* (700m S Coastal) *45.44141, 12.42127* Parking Dante Alighieri, Lungomare Dante Alighieri 26, 30010 Punta-Sabbioni (VE) Take rd Jesolo to Punta-Sabbioni, pass all camps & go to end of peninsula. Turn L at boat piers & foll rd alongside beach; site on L just bef Camping Miramare. Sm, pt shd; wc; chem disp; mv service pnt; shwrs inc; EHU (8A) inc; shop, rest, snacks, bar 500m; bus 500m; dogs; poss cr; Eng spkn; quiet. "M'vans only; friendly, helpful owner; 10 min walk for boats to Venice; vg." € 23.00   2012*

PUNTA SABBIONI *2E2* (1.6km SSW Coastal) *45.44035, 12.4211* Camping Miramare, Lungomare Dante Alighieri 29, 30013 Punta-Sabbioni (VE) [041 966150; fax 5301150; info@camping-miramare.it; www.camping-miramare.it] Take rd Jesolo to Punta-Sabbioni, pass all camps & go to end of peninsula. Turn L at boat piers & foll rd alongside beach; site 500m on L. Med, hdg/mkd pitch, pt shd; htd wc; chem disp; mv service pnt; shwrs inc; EHU (6A) inc (rev pol); gas; lndry; shop; rest & pizzeria adj; playgrnd; internet; statics; dogs €4 (only sm dogs allowed); phone; bus to beach 2km & ferry; min 3 nights stay high ssn; Eng spkn; quiet; ccard acc (min €100); red LS/snr citizens. "Excel, well-organised, helpful, friendly family-owned site - 10 mins walk for Venice (tickets fr recep) - can leave bikes at terminal; gd security; new pt of site v pleasant wooded area; clean facs; poss mosquito problem; superior to many other sites in area; min stay 2 nights Jul/Aug; don't miss camping supmkt on way in - an Aladdin's cave; avoid dep on Sat due traffic; Magic of Italy site; highly rec, reasonable mob home rentals; excel staff." ♦ 29 Mar-1 Nov 23 Mar-3 Nov. € 37.00   2015*

⊞ **PUNTA SABBIONI** *2E2* (1km Rural) *44.44278, 12.42260* Al Batèo, via Lungomare Dante Alighieri 19/A, 30013 Cavallino Treporti Venice [040 5301 455 or 041 5301 564; info@albateo.it; www.albateo.it] Take rd Jesolo to Punta Sabbioni and go to end of the peninsula. Turn L at boat piers and foll rd along side beach. Site 300 on L. Sm, hdg pitch, shd; htd wc; chem disp; mv service pnt; shwrs inc; lndry; shop; dogs; bus; Eng spkn; adv bkg; quiet. "M'vans only; gd value; Vapporetti to Venice 300m." € 25.00   2014*

QUART see Aosta *1B1*

RAPALLO *1C2* (2km N Urban) *44.35805, 9.2100* Camping Miraflores, Via Savagna 10, 16035 Rapallo (GE) [0185 263000; fax 260938; info@campingmiraflores.it; www.campingmiraflores.it] Exit A12/E80 at Rapallo. In 100m fr toll gate sharp L across main rd, sharp L again, site sp 200m on R. Site almost immed beside toll gate but not easily seen. Sp fr town. Med, hdg/mkd pitch, hdstg, terr, pt shd; wc (some cont); chem disp; mv service pnt; shwrs €0.60; EHU (3A) €1.80; gas; lndry rm; shop 300m; rest 200m; snacks; bar; playgrnd; pool; 10% statics; dogs free; bus 200m to stn & town cent; sep car park; poss cr; rd noise; ccard acc; red LS/CKE/CCI. "Excel htd pool adj; gd, modern san facs; grass pitches for tents, earth only for m'vans & c'vans; v noisy & dusty as under m'way; v friendly staff; ferries to Portofino fr town; conv NH; rec phone ahead if lge o'fit." ♦ 1 Mar-31 Dec. € 26.50   2011*

RAPALLO *1C2* (2.5km W Urban) *44.35691, 9.1992* Camping Rapallo, Via San Lazzaro 4, 16035 Rapallo (GE) [tel/fax 0185 262018; campingrapallo@libero.it; www.campingrapallo.it] Exit A12/E80 dir Rapallo, turn immed R on leaving tolls. Site sp in 500m on L at bend (care), over bdge then R. Narr app rd. Site sp. Med, hdg/mkd pitch, pt shd; wc (some cont); chem disp; mv service pnt; shwrs inc; EHU (3A) €2.20; gas; lndry; supmkt 500m; rest 200m; bar; htd pool; shgl beach 2.5km; bike hire; 10% statics; dogs; bus (tickets fr recep); poss cr; Eng spkn; adv bkg; some daytime rd noise; ccard acc; CKE/CCI. "Clean, family-run site; conv Portofino (boat trip) & train to Cinque Terre; beautiful coastlline; shwrs clsd during day but hot shwrs at pool; v busy public hols - adv bkg rec; awkward exit, not suitable for lge o'fits; NH only." 13 Mar-15 Nov. € 32.50   2014*

RASUN DI SOTTO/NIEDERRASEN see Brunico/Bruneck *1D1*

RAVENNA *2E2* (9km E Coastal) *44.43147, 12.30034* Camping Villaggio dei Pini, Via della Fontana, 48020 Punta-Marina-Terme (RA) [0544 437115; fax 531863; villaggiodeipini@gestionecampeggi.it; www.gestionecampeggi.it] Foll sp to Punta Marina fr S67; in cent of Punta-Marina take sm rd S; site at end of rd on L. Lge, pt shd; wc (some cont); chem disp; mv service pnt; shwrs inc; EHU (5A) inc; gas; lndry; shop; rest, snacks; bar; playgrnd; beach adj; bike hire; entmnt; 90% statics; no dogs; phone; clsd 1400-1600 & 0000-0700; poss v cr; quiet; ccard acc. "Conv for mosaics; pitches v sm." ♦ 23 Apr-13 Sep. € 31.00   2010*

RAVENNA *2E2* (10.6km E Coastal) *44.43335, 12.29680* Camping Park Adriano, Via dei Campeggi 7, 48122 Punta-Marina-Terme (RN) [0544 437230; fax 438510; info@adrianocampingvillage.com; www.campingadriano.com] Fr S309 Ravenna-Venezia rd foll sp to Lido Adriano. Site at N end of Lido. Lge, shd; wc; chem disp; mv service pnt; shwrs inc; EHU (5A) inc (poss rev pol/no earth); lndry (inc dryer); shop; rest, snacks; bar; BBQ; playgrnd; pool; paddling pool; beach 300m; bike hire; golf 10km; wifi; entmnt; TV rm; 70% statics; dogs €3; bus to Ravenna; ATM; Eng spkn; adv bkg; poss noisy disco; ccard acc; red snr citizens/CKE/CCI. "Site in pine forest; excel san facs; sh walk to beach." ♦ 20 Apr-18 Sep. € 43.00 (CChq acc)   2015*

RHEMES ST GEORGE *1B1* (Rural) *45.64966, 7.15150*
Camping Val di Rhemes, Loc Voix 1, 11010 Rhêmes-St
George (AO) [tel/fax 0165 907648; info@campingvaldi
rhemes.com; www.campingvaldirhemes.com]
Fr S26 or A54/E25 turn S at Introd dir Rhêmes-St George &
Rhêmes-Notre-Dame; site on R in 10km past PO; app is diff
climb with hairpins. Med, pt sl, pt shd; htd wc (some cont);
chem disp; mv service pnt; shwrs; EHU (2-6A) €2; lndry dryer;
shop; bar; wifi; Eng spkn; ccard acc; playgrnd; 10% statics;
dogs €2.50; adv bkg; quiet; CCI. "Peaceful, family-run
site; nr Gran Paradiso National Park; gd walking; excel." ♦
1 Jun-10 Sep. € 35.60   2014*

RICCIONE *2E3* (1km SE Coastal) *43.9850, 12.67916*
Camping Riccione, Via Marsala 10, 47838 Riccione (RN)
[0541 690160; fax 690044; info@campingriccione.it;
www.campingriccione.it] Exit A14/E55 onto SS16 thro
Riccione ignoring numerous other camp sp & look for site sp.
Turn L and site in 150m on R. Lge, shd; wc; mv service pnt;
some serviced pitches; shwrs inc; EHU (5A) inc; gas; lndry;
shop; rest, snacks; bar; playgrnd; pool & paddling pool; sand
beach 500m; tennis; games area; bike hire; solarium; wifi;
sat TV; 10% statics; dogs (not acc mid-Jul to mid-Aug); poss
cr; adv bkg; traff noise (rd, rlwy & air); ccard acc; redCKE/
CCI. "Pitch acc poss diff due to trees." ♦ 18 Apr-21 Sep.
€ 47.00   2011*

RICCIONE *2E3* (2km S Coastal) *43.98610, 12.68806* **Camping
Alberello, Viale Torino 80, 47838 Riccione (RN) [tel/fax
0541 615248; direzione@alberello.it; www.alberello.it]**
Exit A14/E55 dir Riccione on SS16. Site is sp off this rd dir
Misano Adriatico, twds sea. Lge, hdg/mkd pitch, shd; wc;
shwrs inc; EHU (4A) €2.50; gas; lndry; shop; rest, snacks; bar;
playgrnd; sand beach adj; games area; golf 1km; entmnt; TV
rm; no dogs; car wash; no adv bkg; quiet but rlwy/rd noise.
"Gd for families." ♦ 9 Apr-28 Sep. € 33.00   2009*

RIVA DEL GARDA *1D1* (2.5km E Rural) *45.88111, 10.86194*
Camping Monte Brione, Via Brione 32, 38066 Riva-del-
Garda (TN) [0464 520885; fax 520890; info@camping
brione.com; www.campingbrione.com] Exit A22 Garda
Nord onto SS240 to Torbole & Riva; on app to Riva thro open-
sided tunnel; immed R after enclosed tunnel opp Marina; site
ent 700m on R. Med, mkd pitch, terr, pt shd; wc (some cont);
chem disp; mv service pnt; shwrs inc; EHU (6A) inc; gas; lndry;
shop; rest 200m; snacks; bar; BBQ; playgrnd; htd pool; shgl
beach & lake sw 500m; watersports; bike hire; solarium; wifi;
dogs €4; barriers clsd 1300-1500 & 2300-0700; Eng spkn;
adv bkg; quiet; ccard acc;CKE/CCI. "Olive groves adj; pleasant
site with lge pitches; gd, modern san facs." ♦ 1 Apr-30 Sep.
€ 28.50   2009*

⊞ **RIZZOLO** *1C2* (3km S Rural) *44.88957, 9.70181* **Camping
Cascinotta, 29019 Rizzolo (Postal address: San Giorgio-
Piacentino (PC)) [0523 530113; fax 530451;
rose@cittadellerose.it; www.cittadellerose.it]**
Site is 10km S of San Giorgio-Piacentino on rd fr Rizzolo to
Ponte-dell'Ollio. Med, mkd pitch, pt terr, pt shd; wc; chem
disp; mv service pnt; shwrs inc; EHU €2; lndry; bar; BBQ;
playgrnd; 5% statics; dogs; adv bkg;CKE/CCI. "Site attached
to religious sanctuary & pilgrimage cent; set in parkland;
vg touring base." € 24.00   2009*

⊞ **ROCCARASO** *2F4* (2km NE Rural) *41.84194, 14.10277*
Camping Del Sole, Piana del Leone, Via Pietransieri, 67037
Roccaraso (AQ) [0864 62532 or 0864 62571; fax 619329;
albergodelsole@libero.it; www.villaggiodelsole.com]
Turn E fr S17 at sp Petransieri & site on R in 2km. Med, pt sl,
pt shd; wc; chem disp; shwrs inc; EHU inc (poss no earth - long
lead rec); gas; lndry; shop 2km; rest; bar; playgrnd; sw 2km; ski
school; 50% statics; dogs (sm only); bus; quiet; ccard acc;CKE/
CCI. "Excel & conv National Park; ltd facs LS; unrel opening,
suggest phone to confirm." ♦ € 26.00   2013*

RODI GARGANICO *2G4* (7.5km E Rural) **Camping Village
Valle D'Oro, Via degli Ulivi, Loc Aia del Cervone, 71010
San Menaio (FG) [tel/fax 0884 991580; info@campingvalle
doro.it; www.campingvalledoro.it]**
Exit A14 at Poggio Emperiate onto S89 E dir Peschici & Vieste
thro Rodi Garganico. At San Menaio turn R twd Vico del
Gargano for 4km, site on R, well sp. Sm, terr, pt shd; htd
wc; chem disp; shwrs inc; EHU (3A) €2.50; lndry rm; shop;
rest, snacks; bar; playgrnd; sm pool; sand beach 4km; games
area; dogs; poss cr; Eng spkn; adv bkg; quiet; red LS;CKE/CCI.
"Pleasant site in olive trees away fr busy coastal sites; friendly,
welcoming, helpful owners; vg rest; shuttle bus to beach high
ssn; Vico-del-Gargano interesting town." ♦ ltd. 1 Jun-15 Sep.
€ 23.50   2009*

RODI GARGANICO *2G4* (4km W Coastal) *41.91209, 15.72950*
Camping 5 Stelle, C da Pagliai dei Combattenti, Km
34.500, 71010 Foce-di-Varano (FG) [tel/fax 0884 917583;
info@camping5stelle.it; www.camping5stelle.it]
Exit A14 at Poggio-Imperiale E twd Vieste. Turn N at
Sannicandro & foll sp Torre-Mileto, Porto-Capoiale & Isola-
Varano. Site sp. Lge, pt shd; wc; chem disp; mv service pnt;
private bthrms some pitches; baby facs; shwrs; EHU (5A) €2.50;
lndry; shop; rest, snacks; bar; BBQ; playgrnd; pool; paddling
pool; sand beach adj; lake fishing; tennis; bike hire; games
area; entmnt; TV rm; 20% statics; dogs €3; poss cr; quiet;
ccard acc; red LS. ♦ 1 Apr-30 Sep. € 49.00 (CChq acc)   2011*

⊞ **ROMA** *2E4* (8km N Urban) *41.95618, 12.48240* **Camping
Village Flaminio, Via Flaminia Nuova 821, 00189 Roma
[06 3332604 or 3331429; fax 3330653; info@village
flaminio.com; www.villageflaminio.com]**
Exit GRA ring rd at exit 6 & proceed S along Via Flaminia twd
Roma Centrale. In 3km where lanes divide keep to L-hand
lane (R-hand land goes into underpass). Cross underpass, then
immed back to R-hand lane & slow down. Site on R 150m, sp
as Flaminio Bungalow Village. No vehicular access to site fr S or
exit to N. Lge, pt sl, pt shd; htd wc; chem disp; mv service pnt;
shwrs inc; EHU (3-12A) inc; gas; lndry (inc dryer); shop; supmkt
200m; rest, snacks; bar; playgrnd; pool (sw caps req); bike hire;
wifi; TV rm; some statics; phone; bus (cross v busy rd); train nr;
site clsd mid-Jan to end Feb; poss cr; no adv bkg; red long stay/
LS; ccard acc (min €155). "Well-run site; excel, clean san facs;
poss long walk fr far end of site to ent (site transport avail);
poss dusty pitches; take care sap fr lime trees; cycle/walking
track to city cent nrby; train 10 mins walk (buy tickets on site);
local excursions pick-up fr site (tickets fr recep)." ♦ € 57.00
(CChq acc)   2013*

ITALY

ROMA 2E4 (9km N) 42.00353, 12.45283 **Happy Village & Camping, Via Prato della Corte 1915, 00123 Roma [06 33626401 or 06 33614596; fax 33613800; info@happy camping.net; www.happycamping.net]** Take exit 5 fr Rome ring rd sp Viterbo. Site sp on ring rd, fr N & S on dual c'way Rome/Viterbo at 1st exit N of ring rd. Lge, pt terr, pt shd; wc; chem disp; mv service pnt; shwrs inc; EHU (6A) inc; gas; lndry; shop; rest, snacks; bar; BBQ; playgrnd; pool high ssn; some statics; dogs free; train into Rome; poss cr; adv bkg; poss noisy; ccard acc; red CKE/CCI. "Friendly, busy site in hills; sm pitches; vg rest; mini bus shuttle to train stn; gd site; v nice well kept site; steep access rd." ♦ 1 Mar-6 Jan. € 25.00   2015*

ROMA 2E4 (19km N Urban) 43.00976, 12.50566 **Camping Tiber, Via Tiberina, Km 1.4, 00188 Roma [06 33610733; fax 33612314; info@campingtiber.com; www.campingtiber. com]** Fr Florence, exit at Rome Nord-Fiano on A1 & immed after tolls turn S on Via Tibernia, site sp. Fr any dir on Rome ring rd take exit 6 N'bound on S3 Via Flaminia. Site 1km S of Prima Porta. Lge, pt shd; wc; mv service pnt; shwrs inc; EHU (4-6A) inc (long lead req & poss rev pol); gas; lndry (inc dryer); shop; rest, snacks; bar; pool high ssn; games area; wifi; some statics; dogs; free bus to metro stn; Eng spkn; quiet; ccard acc; red long stay/CKE/CCI. "Ideal for city by metro (20 mins) & bus; helpful staff; recep 0700-2300; modern san facs; some lge pitches; poss ant/mosquito prob; Magic of Europe discount; perfectly comfortable; excel, well-run site; quiet on outer edges, but no wifi; discount fr 'We love camping'." ♦ 1 Apr-31 Oct. € 37.00   2014*

ROMA 2E4 (10km SW Rural) 41.77730, 12.39605 **Camping Fabulous, Via Cristoforo Colombo, Km 18, 00125 Acilia (RM) [06 5259354; fax 83517789; fabulous@ecvacanze.it; www.ecvacanze.it]** Exit junc 27 fr Rome ring rd into Via C Colombo. At 18km marker turn R at traff lts, site 200m on R. V lge, mkd pitch, pt sl, shd; htd wc; baby facs; shwrs inc; EHU (6-10A) inc; lndry; shop; rest, snacks; bar; BBQ; playgrnd; pool; paddling pool; waterslide; sand beach 12km; tennis; games area; entmnt; quiet at night; 80% statics; dogs €1.50; phone; bus on main rd; Eng spkn; adv bkg; ccard acc; CKE/ CCI. "Set in pinewoods; gd sh stay." ♦ ltd. 12 Mar-31 Oct. € 35.00   2009*

⊞ **ROMA** 2E4 (4km W Urban) 41.88741, 12.40468 **Roma Camping, Via Aurelia 831, Km 8.2, 00165 Roma [06 6623018; fax 66418147; campingroma@ecvacenze.it]** Site is on Via Aurelia approx 8km fr Rome cent on spur rd on S side of main dual c'way opp lge Panorama Hypmkt. Fr GRA ring rd exit junc 1 Aurelio & head E sp Roma Cent & Citta del Vaticano. In approx 3km take spur rd on R 50m bef covrd pedestrian footbdge x-ing dual c'way & 250m bef flyover, sp camping; site gates on R (S) in 100m. W fr Rome take spur rd 8km fr cent sp camping just after Holiday Inn & just bef Panorama Hypmkt. At top turn L (S) over flyover & immed R sp camping; site gates on L in 200m. V lge, hdstg, terr, pt shd; wc (some cont); baby facs; shwrs inc; EHU (4-6A) inc; lndry; supmkt opp; rest, snacks; bar; playgrnd; pool high ssn; games area; wifi; 75% statics; dogs €1.50; bus to city; poss cr; Eng spkn; rd noise; ccard acc; red LS/CKE/CCI. "Gd, clean site; excel san facs & pool; friendly staff; popular site - rec arr early; rec not leave site on foot after dark; rest open all year; conv walk to hypermkt." ♦ € 55.00   2013*

ROME see Roma 2E4

ROSETO DEGLI ABRUZZI 2F3 (3km S Coastal) 42.65748, 14.03568 **Eurcamping Roseto, Lungomare Trieste Sud 90, 64026 Roseto-degli-Abruzzi (TE) [085 8993179; fax 8930552; info@eurcamping.it; www.eurcamping.it]** Fr A14 exit dir Roseto-degli-Abruzzi to SS16. At rndabt turn R, next L & under rlwy bdge to promenade. Turn R at sea front, site at end of promenade. Med, shd, hdg/mkd pitch; wc; chem disp; mv service pnt; shwrs inc; EHU (3A) inc; lndry (inc dryer); shop; rest, snacks; bar; playgrnd; pool; paddling pool; private sand & shgl beach adj; tennis; bike hire; games area; wifi; 20% statics; dogs €5; poss cr; Eng spkn; adv bkg; quiet but some rlwy noise; red LS; CKE/CCI. "Phone to check if open LS; gates close 2300; pitches poss flood after heavy rainfall; Roseto excel resort." ♦ 1 May-24 Oct. € 43.50   2015*

⊞ **ST VINCENT** 1B1 (10km N Rural) 45.78729, 7.60361 **Camping Dalai Lama Village, Loc Promiod, 11024 Châtillon (AO) [0166 548688; fax 549921; info@dalailama village.com; www.dalailamavillage.com]** Exit A5/E25 at Châtillon & take R46 N to Antey-St André. In cent of town fork R over sm bdge & climb for approx 5km to site, sp. Care needed lge m'vans. Lge, mkd pitch, pt shd; htd wc; chem disp; mv service pnt; sauna; shwrs inc; EHU inc; lndry; rest, snacks; bar; playgrnd; htd, covrd pool; games area; games rm; gym; entmnt; 50% statics; dogs €4; adv bkg; quiet. "Stunning views; superb, peaceful site & san facs; vg bar/ rest terr; highly rec; diff narr rd for lge o'fits, 1km single track without passing places, excep views, 80% statics, shwrs not incl or pool/sauna €29 for session." ♦ € 39.00   2011*

⊞ **SALBERTRAND** 1A2 (1km SW Rural) 45.06200, 6.86821 **Camping Gran Bosco, SS24, Km 75, Monginevro, 10050 Salbertrand (TO) [0122 854653; fax 854693; info@campinggranbosco.it; www.campinggranbosco.it]** Leave A32/E70 (Torino-Fréjus Tunnel) at Oulx Ouest junc & foll SS24/SS335 sp Salbertrand. Site sp 1.5km twd Salbertrand at km 75. Fr S (Briançon in France) on N94/SS24 to Oulx cent, foll SS24 thro town & foll sp Salbertrand, then as above. Lge, pt shd; htd wc (mainly cont); chem disp; mv service pnt; shwrs; EHU (3-6A) inc; gas; lndry; shop; rest 1km; snacks; bar; playgrnd; tennis; games area; entmnt; 80% statics (sep area); some rd & rlwy noise; ccard acc. "Beautiful setting; excel NH bef/after Fréjus Tunnel or pass to/fr Briançon; gates open 0830-2300; excel, modern, clean san facs; sm pitches; grnd soft in wet - no hdstg." € 29.00   2012*

SALSOMAGGIORE TERME 1C2 (3km E Rural) 44.80635, 10.00931 **Camping Arizona, Via Tabiano 42, 43039 Tabiano-Salsomaggiore Terme (PR) [0524 565648; fax 567589; info@camping-arizona.it; www.camping-arizona. it]** Exit A1 for Fidenza & foll sps for Salsomaggiore fr Co-op supmkt, to Tabiano; sp on S side of rd. Not rec to attempt to find site fr S9 fr Piacenza. Lge, pt sl, shd; wc (some cont); chem disp (wc); mv service pnt; shwrs inc; EHU (3A) inc (rev pol); lndry (inc dryer); shop; rest, snacks; bar; playgrnd; 4 pools high ssn; 2 waterslides; jacuzzi; fishing; tennis; games rm; games area; bike hire; golf 7km; wifi; entmnt; 30% statics; dogs €3; phone; sep car park; bus to Salsomaggiore; phone; quiet; red LS; ccard not acc. "Vg site; friendly, helpful staff; interesting, smart spa town; excel touring base; gd for families; san facs vg; best campsite shop; vg rest." ♦ 1 Apr-7 Oct. € 47.00   2014*

SALTO DI FONDI see Terracina 2E4

SAN BARONTO LAMPORECCHIO see Pistoia *1D3*

SAN CANDIDO/INNICHEN see Dobbiaco/Toblach *2E1*

SAN FELICE DEL BENACO *1D2* (1km N Rural) *45.59972, 10.54972* **Camping Eden, Via Preone 45, 25010 Portese (BS) [0365 62093; fax 559311; mail@camping-eden.it; www.camping-eden.it]** Best app fr Salo (N), foll lakeside twd Porto Portese. Site ent up steep slope on R. Lge, hdg/ mkd pitch, hdstg, terr, shd; wc; chem disp; mv service pnt; baby facs; shwrs inc; EHU (3A) inc; lndry; shop; rest, snacks; bar; playgrnd; pool; lake sw & shgl beach adj; golf 3km; 85% statics; dogs €10; phone; Eng spkn; adv bkg; quiet; red LS/snr citizen; CKE/CCI. "Beach down steep rd opp site; 10 mins walk to boat terminal for lake; steep steps to san facs; manhandling req to get c'vans onto pitches; site not rec lge o'fits." ♦ 11 Apr-27 Sep. € 42.00   2009*

SAN FELICE DEL BENACO *1D2* (1km E Rural) *45.58500, 10.56583* **Camping Fornella, Via Fornella 1, 25010 San Felice-del-Benaco (BS) [0365 62294; fax 559418; fornella@ fornella.it; www.fornella.it]** N fr Desenzano on S572 twd Salo. Turn R to San Felice-del-Benaco, over x-rds & take 2nd R turn at sp to site. R into app rd, L into site. Rd narr but accessible. Avoid vill cent, site sp (with several others) fr vill by-pass just bef g'ge. Lge, pt sl, terr, pt shd; htd wc (some cont); chem disp; mv service pnt; baby facs; shwrs inc; EHU (6A) inc; gas; lndry (inc dryer); shop; rest, snacks; bar; BBQ (charcoal); playgrnds; pool; paddling pool; sw & shgl beach on lake; fishing; boat hire & windsurfing; bike hire; tennis; games area; entmnt; games rm; wifi; entmnt; TV (in bar); 20% statics; dogs €7; no o'fits over 7m high ssn; sep car park; recep 0800-1200 & 1400-2000; poss v cr; Eng spkn; adv bkg; quiet; ccard acc; extra for lge pitches & lakeside pitches; red LS & snr citizens LS; CKE/CCI. "Family-run site in vg location by Lake Garda; park outside until checked in; excel pool; excursions to Venice, Florence & Verona opera; excel rest; gd san facs." ♦ 1 May-20 Sep. € 49.50 SBS - Y11   2014*

> **"I like to fill in the reports as I travel from site to site"**
> You'll find report forms at the back of this guide, or you can fill them in online at www.caravanclub.co.uk/europereport.

SAN FELICE DEL BENACO *1D2* (1km SE Rural) *45.57861, 10.55388* **Camping Ideal Molino, Via Gardiola 1, 25010 San Felice-del-Benaco (BS) [0365 62023; fax 559395; info@campingmolino.it; www.campingmolino.it]** Site approx 6km S of Salo on W shore of lake. Foll sp Porto & San Felice. Site 1km past San Felice; narr app. Med, mkd pitch, pt shd; wc; chem disp; baby facs; shwrs inc; EHU (4A) inc; gas; lndry; shop; rest; bar; playgrnd; shgl beach; boat hire; fishing; 30% statics; no dogs; phone; adv bkg rec; quiet; red LS/snr citizens. "Steamer trips on lake; some v sm pitches; excel lakeside rest." ♦ 24 Mar-30 Sep. € 38.60   2009*

SAN FELICE DEL BENACO *1D2* (1km NW Rural) *45.59517, 10.53313* **Camping Villaggio Weekend, Via Vallone della Selva 2, 25010 San Felice-del-Benaco (BS) [0365 43712; fax 42196; info@weekend.it; www.weekend.it]** Well sp fr Desenzano. Ignore 1st sp San Felice-del-Benaco, turn R at rndabt to vill then 2nd L. Do not app fr Riva-del-Garda end of lake - narr tunnels. Nearest town Salo. Lge, mkd pitch, terr, shd; wc; chem disp; some serviced pitches; baby facs; shwrs inc; EHU (6A) inc; lndry (inc dryer); supmkt; rest, snacks; bar; BBQ; playgrnd; pool; paddling pool; waterslide; lake sw & scuba diving; bike hire; games area; wifi; entmnt; 20% statics; dogs €7.50; poss cr; Eng spkn; adv bkg ess; quiet; ccard acc; red LS; CKE/CCI. "Excel, family site in olive grove; excel entmnt; bathing caps req in pool; views of lake & mountains fr some pitches; low branches some pitches diff for m'vans; some sm pitches - lge avail; tight corners poss diff lge o'fits; office clsd 1300-1500." ♦ 16 Apr-25 Sep. € 52.00   2010*

⊞ **SAN GIOVANNI ROTONDO** *2G4* (700m SE Rural) **Aree di Sosta Vacanze di Cerbo, Contrada Coppa Mazzanelle, 71013 San Giovanni-Rotondo (FG) [0882 453900]** Fr A14 exit onto SS272 dir San Marco-in-Lamis. Foll sp to San Giovanni-Rotondo. On town o'skts at rndabt turn R dir Foggia. Site on R bef next rndabt - 1km down narr lane. Fr S fr Foggia foll sp Manfredonia then San Giovanni. On o'skts of town turn L at rndabt, site in 50m. Sm, all hdstg, pt sl, unshd; wc; chem disp; mv service pnt; shwrs inc; EHU (10A) metered (poss rev pol/no earth); shop 500m; rest; bar; htd pool 8km; sand beach 20km; dogs; poss cr; Eng spkn; adv bkg; noisy dogs in area; CKE/CCI. "V popular with m'vanners; off beaten track in scenic area; ltd san facs; minibus to town cent; conv Gargano National Park & Forest of Umbra." ♦ € 15.00   2010*

SAN LORENZO DI SEBATO see Brunico/Bruneck *1D1*

⊞ **SAN MARINO** *2E3* (4km N Rural) *43.95990, 12.46090* **Centro Vacanze San Marino, Strada San Michele 50, 47893 Cailungo, Repubblica di San Marino [0549 903964; fax 907120; info@centrovacanzesanmarino.com; www.centrovacanzesanmarino.com]** Exit A14 at Rimini Sud, foll rd S72 to San Marino. Pass under 2 curved footbdges, then 800m after 2nd & 13km after leaving a'strada, fork R. Cont uphill for 1.5km then turn R at Brico building, site sp. Steep long-haul climb. Lge, hdg pitch, hdstg, terr, pt shd; htd wc; chem disp; mv service pnt; serviced pitch; shwrs inc; EHU (6A) inc (poss rev pol); lndry; sm shop, rest high ssn; snacks; bar; BBQ; cooking facs; playgrnd; htd pool; paddling pool; tennis; games area; bike hire; solarium; mini-zoo; wifi; sat TV; some statics; dogs €5; bus; poss v cr; Eng spkn; adv bkg; quiet; red 7+ days; ccard acc; CKE/CCI. "V busy at w/end - rec arr early; superb hill fort town; excel rest & pool; sm pitches; conv Rimini 24km; excel, clean site; bus calls at site ent for San Marino." ♦ € 53.00 (CChq acc) SBS - Y04   2014*

SAN MENAIO see Rodi Garganico *2G4*

SAN MICHELE ALL'ADIGE *1D1* (3km SW Rural) *46.16789, 11.11452* **Camping Moser, Via Nazionale 64, 38015 Nave San Felice (TN) [0461 870248]** 12km N of Trento on SS12. Sm, mkd pitch, shd; wc; chem disp; shwrs; EHU inc; shop in vill; rest; bar; dogs; bus 500m; poss cr; Eng spkn; adv bkg; rd & rlwy noise; ccard acc. "Gd, friendly NH; site run by Hotel Moser (well sp on S12); scruffy & run down but busy; new san facs block almost completed (2014)." 1 May-31 Oct. € 18.00   2015*

SAN PIERO A SIEVE see Borgo San Lorenzo *1D3*

⊞ **SAN REMO** *1B3* (2.5km W Coastal) *43.80244, 7.74506* **Camping Villaggio Dei Fiori, Via Tiro a Volo 3, 18038 San Remo (IM) [0184 660635; fax 662377; info@villaggio deifiori.it; www.villaggiodeifiori.it]** Fr A10/E80 take Arma-di-Taggia exit & foll sp San Remo Centro. At SS1 coast rd turn R sp Ventimiglia. At 2.5km look for red/yellow Billa supmkt sp on R; 50m past sp take L fork, site on L in 50m. Fr W on A10 take 1st exit dir San Remo - winding rd. Turn R & site on L after Stands supmkt. Fr Ventimiglia on SS1, 150m past San Remo boundary sp turn sharp R (poss diff lge o'fits) to site. Lge, some hdg/mkd pitch, all hdstg, pt terr, pt shd; htd wc (some cont); chem disp; mv service pnt; baby facs; fam bthrm; shwrs inc; EHU (3-6A) €4-7; lndry (inc dryer); supmkt 200m; rest, snacks; bar; BBQ; playgrnd; htd pool; shgl beach adj; tennis; games area; bike hire; wifi; entmnt; 60% statics; no dogs; train to Monaco & bus San Remo nr; poss cr; Eng spkn; adv bkg rec high ssn; rd & fairgrnd noise; red long stay/LS; ccard acc.; CKE/ CCI "Gd location; well-kept, tidy, paved site; vg, clean facs; beach not suitable for sw; some pitches superb sea views (extra charge), some sm; lge o'fits not acc high ssn as sm pitches; vg rest; conv Monaco; gates locked at night." ♦ ltd. € 67.00 (4 persons)   2013*

SAN ROCCO CASTAGNARETTA see Cuneo *1B2*

⊞ **SAN VALENTINO ALLA MUTA** *1D1* (700m N Rural) *46.7700, 10.5325* **Camping Thöni, Landstrasse 83, 39020 St Valentin-an-der-Haide, Graun [0473 634020; thoeni.h@ rolmail.net; www.camping-thoeni.it]** N twd Austrian border site on L on edge of vill on S edge of Lago di Resia. Sm, pt sl, unshd; htd wc; chem disp; shwrs inc; EHU (6A) €1.50; shop, rest, snacks, bar 300m; pool 7km; dogs; site clsd Nov; quiet. "Conv sh stay/NH en rte Austria; cycle rte around lake; scenic area; off open 0900-1000 & 1700-1800; numbered pitches." € 22.50   2015*

SAN VINCENZO *1D3* (8km S Coastal) *43.02815, 10.5345* **Camping Park Albatros, Pineta di Torre Nuova, 57027 San Vincenzo (LI) [0565 701018; fax 703589; albatros@ camping.it; www.camping.it/toscana/albatros]** Fr N exit SS1 San Vincenzo Nord, fr S exit Sud. As app town foll sp Piombino on SP23 Via Della Principessa, just after 7km post turn L on reaching pine wood, site sp. V lge, pt shd; wc; chem disp; mv service pnt; baby facs; shwrs; EHU (5A) inc; lndry; gas; shop; rest, snacks; bar; playgrnd; pool complex; sand beach 900m; games area; bike hire; wifi; entmnt; 40% statics; dogs €3; phone; poss cr; Eng spkn; loud music in pool area all day; ccard acc; red LS. "Gd, improving, busy site; lge pitches; gd, modern san facs; excel pool complex." ♦ 24 Apr-25 Sep. € 47.70   2010*

SANT' ANTONIO DI MAVIGNOLA see Pinzolo *1D1*

SANT' ARCANGELO SUL TRASIMENO see Magione *2E3*

SANTA MARIA DI MERINO see Vieste *2G4*

SANTA TERESA GALLURA *1C4* (1km W Urban) *41.21938, 9.18372* **Camping Gallura Village, Loc Li Lucianeddi, 07028 Santa Teresa Gallura [078 975 55 80; fax 974 19 32; info@galluravillage.it]** Fr Santa Teresa Gallura on SP90. Site 1km on L. Med, mkd pitch, unshd; wc; chem disp; shwrs inc; shop 0.5km; snacks; rest; bar; playgrnd; pool; paddling pool; games area; entmnt; wifi; bike hire; 50% statics; dogs; Eng spkn; ccard acc. "Fair site; power point at each plot; gd NH for ferry to Corsica." 1 Mar-30 Oct. € 52.00   2014*

SARDINIA Campsites in towns in Sardinia are listed together at the end of the Italian site entry pages.

⊞ **SARNANO** *2E3* (3km SSW Rural) *43.01743, 13.28358* **Quattro Stagioni, Contrada Brilli, 62028 Sarnano [0733 651147; fax 651104; quattrostagioni@camping.it; www.camping4stagioni.it]** A14 exit Civitanova Marche. M'way to Macerata as far as Sarnano exit. In Sarnano turn R at sq, foll main rd. Site approx 3km outside Sarnano to the W. Sm, mkd pitch, pt sl, pt shd; wc; chem disp; mv service pnt; shwrs; EHU; lndry; shop; rest; café; snacks; bar; bbq; playgrnd; pool; paddling pool; games area; wifi; 60% statics; dogs; twin axles; Eng spkn; adv bkg; red LS; CKE/CCI. "Fair site." ♦ ltd. € 41.00   2014*

SARRE see Aosta *1B1*

SARZANA *1C2* (8km S Rural/Coastal) *44.07638, 9.97027* **Camping River, Loc Armezzone, 19031 Ameglia (SP) [0187 65920; fax 65183; info@campingriver.com; www.campingriver.com]** Exit A12 at Sarzana & foll sp Ameglia & Bocca di Magra on SP432. In 7km turn L into Via Crociata to site (blue sp). Narr app rd with few passing places. Lge, mkd pitch; pt shd; wc (mainly cont); chem disp; mv service pnt; sauna; shwrs inc; EHU (3-6A) inc; lndry (inc dryer); supmkt 700m; rest, snacks; pizzeria; bar; playgrnd; 2 pools; paddling pool; beach 2km; rv fishing; tennis 200m; games area; boat & bike hire; horseriding 200m; golf driving range; wifi; entmnt; TV rm; 50% statics; dogs €3; bus to beach; poss cr; adv bkg; red LS. "Gd touring base Cinque Terre; pleasant, helpful staff; vg, well-situated site; gd shop & rest; nice location by rv; dated facs; gd pools." ♦ 12 Apr-4 Oct. € 43.00 (3 persons) (CChq acc)   2014*

SASSELLO *1B2* (5km NE Rural) *44.49672, 8.52794* **Club Naturista Costalunga (Naturist), 17046 Sassello (SV) [tel/ fax 019 720004; info@costalunga.com; www.costalunga. org]** Fr A10 exit at Albissola & turn L after toll booth sp Sassello. In Sassello bear R sp Palo & Urbe, in 5km turn L at site sp, site on L in 500m. Sm, hdstg, pt sl, terr, pt shd; wc; chem disp; shwrs inc; EHU (6A) €3; lndry; shop 5km; pre-ordered snacks; playgrnd; pool; TV rm; 30% statics; dogs €2; bus 500m; adv bkg; quiet; ccard not acc; red long stay; INF card. "Friendly, helpful owners; views fr some pitches; gd." 1 Apr-30 Sep. € 25.00   2011*

⊞ **SASSO MARCONI** *1D2* (17km SW Rural) *44.30097, 11.18694* **Centro Naturista Ca'Le Scope (Naturist), Loc San Martino/La Quercia, 40043 Marzabotto (BO) [tel/fax 051 932328; calescope@virgilio.it; www.calescope.com]** Fr A1 exit at Rioveggio, turn R after toll booth. In 200m turn R onto S325 sp Bologna. In 3.5km turn sharp L sp Quercia, over rv & foll rd for 4km (narr & uneven in parts - care req). Turn L at x-rds sp to site, site in 1.5km on L. Med, hdg/mkd pitch, hdstg, pt sl, pt shd; wc (some cont); chem disp (wc); baby facs; shwrs inc; EHU (6A) €3.15; gas; lndry; basic shop; rest, snacks; bar; playgrnd; pool; internet; TV rm; 50% statics; dogs; train 6km; poss cr; Eng spkn; adv bkg; quiet; ccard acc; INF card. "Spectacular views over Monte Sole National Park; friendly Dutch owners; site rds steep in parts - care req."
€ 31.00   2011*

SAVONA *1B2* (10km NE Rural) *44.38105, 8.50151* **Camping Dolce Vita, Via Riobasco 62, 17040 Stella-San Giovanni (SV) [tel/fax 019 703269 or 03939 836543 (mob); campingdolcevita@libero.it; www.campingdolcevita.it]** Foll sp Albisola off Genoa-Savona a'strada, Turn L in town onto rd SS334 dir Sassello. Site in 5km on L on rd twd mountains. Site sp faces S only; if app fr N look for flags. Sm, pt shd; wc; mv service pnt; chem disp; shwrs €1; EHU (4-8A) €3; gas; lndry; shop 2.5km; rest, snacks; bar; playgrnd; pool; beach 5.5km; TV; 75% statics; dogs €3; Eng spkn; no adv bkg; quiet; CKE/CCI. "Sm touring pitches unsuitable lge o'fits; v busy at w/end; gd welcome; poss untidy LS; gd NH." ♦ 1 Jan-20 Oct.
€ 31.00   2009*

SAVONA *1B2* (1km SW Coastal) *44.29014, 8.45211* **Camping Charly, Via Nizza 93/R, Zinola, 17100 Savona (SV) [0198 62265; fax 0192 63427; info@campingcharly.it; www.campingcharly.it]** Take SS1 fr Savona twd Sportorno. Site in vicinity of Zinola bet AGIP & BP g'ges on dual c'way. Med, shd; wc; shwrs €0.50; EHU (5A) inc; shop; snacks; bar; pool; paddling pool; sm sand beach across rd; 50% statics; no dogs; poss cr; Eng spkn; adv bkg; some rd & rlwy noise at night; red LS; CKE/CCI. "Hot water to shwrs only."
15 Apr-14 Sep. € 30.00   2009*

SAVONA *1B2* (2km SW Coastal) *44.29079, 8.45331* **Camping Vittoria, Via Nizza 111/113, Zinola, 17100 Savona (SV) [019 881439; www.campingvittoria.com]** Exit Savona heading SW, site on L on seashore immed bef Shell petrol stn behind bar Vittoria. Med, unshd; wc (some cont); shwrs; EHU €2; shops adj; rest adj; bar; private sand beach adj; 90% statics; poss v cr; Eng spkn; adv bkg; quiet; CKE/CCI. "Excel location with views; busy site; helpful, friendly owner; pitches adj beach; clean, simple facs; ltd sm touring pitches."
1 Apr-30 Sep. € 35.00   2013*

SAVONA *1B2* (13km SW Coastal) *44.22731, 8.40795* **Camping Rustia, Via La Torre 4, 17028 Spotorno (SV) [019 745042 or 019 741446; info@campingrustia.it; www.campingrustia.it]** Exit A10/E80 for Spotorno, site sp on app rd to m'way. V steep app rd. C'vans returning to m'way use ent at Albissola Marina. Lge, shd; wc; shwrs €1; EHU (3A) €3; shop; bar; rest, snacks 300m; sand beach 600m; 30% statics; dogs; poss cr; no adv bkg; Eng spkn; ccard acc. "Site diff for lge o'fits due narr paths & many trees - manhandling necessary onto pitches; gd san facs; gates locked at night; busy, well laid out site; helpful staff." ♦
1 Mar-30 Sep. € 32.00   2015*

SCARLINO see Follonica *1D3*

SENIGALLIA *2E3* (1km S Coastal) *43.70416, 13.23805* **Villaggio Turistico Camping Summerland, Via Podesti 236, 60019 Senigallia (AN) [tel/fax 071 7926816; info@campingsummerland.it; www.campingsummerland.it]** Exit A14/E55 onto SS16 to Senigallia S. Site on R after lge car park at side of rd. Lge, shd; wc (cont); mv service pnt; baby facs; shwrs; EHU (5A) €2.50; gas; lndry; shop; rest, snacks; bar; playgrnd; 2 pools & paddling pool; beach 200m; tennis; games area; entmnt; TV rm; some statics; no dogs Jul/Aug; sep car park; poss cr; adv bkg. ♦ 1 Jun-15 Sep. € 42.00   2012*

SESTO CALENDE *1B1* (1km N Rural) *45.72988, 8.61989* **Camping La Sfinge, Via Angera 1, 21018 Sesto-Calende (VA) [0331 924531; fax 922050; info@campeggiolasfinge.it; www.campeggiolasfinge.it]** Take rd fr Sesto-Calende to Angera. Site 1km on L bef junc for Sant' Anna. Med, mkd pitch, shd; wc (mainly cont); shwrs; EHU; gas; lndry; shop 1km; snacks; bar; playgrnd; pool; boating; games area; 90% statics; dogs €4; poss cr; quiet; ccard acc. "Friendly owners; gd lakeside location; poss mosquitoes; poor facs; lovely pool; excel position for lake Maggiore; within reach of gd shops and rest." ♦ 1 Jan-30 Oct. € 39.00   2014*

"We must tell The Club about that great site we found"

Get your site reports in by mid-August and we'll do our best to get your updates into the next edition.

SESTO CALENDE *1B1* (4km N Rural) *45.74892, 8.59698* **Camping Okay Lido, Via per Angera 115, Loc Lisanza, 21018 Sesto Calende (VA) [tel/fax 0331 974235; campingokay@camping-okay.com; www.camping-okay.com]** Exit A8 at Sesto Calende onto SP69 N dir Angera, site sp. Med, mkd pitch, terr, pt shd; wc; chem disp; mv service pnt; private san facs avail; baby facs; shwrs €0.60; EHU (6A) €3; lndry; supmkt 3km; rest, snacks; bar; playgrnd; htd pool; paddling pool; lake sw; watersports; games area; games rm; wifi; entmnt; TV rm; some statics; dogs €5; Eng spkn; adv bkg; quiet. "Friendly, welcoming site; NH pitches by lakeside; gd NH for Amsterdam ferry." ♦ 21 Mar-11 Oct. € 36.00   2014*

SESTO CALENDE *1B1* (7.5km N Rural) *45.82712, 8.62722* **International Camping Ispra, Via Carducci, 21027 Ispra (VA) [0332 780458; fax 784882; info@internationalcampingispra.it; www.internationalcampingispra.it]** Site 1km NE of Ispra on E side of lake. Med, pt terr, shd; wc (cont); own san; shwrs €0.20; EHU (6A) €3; lndry; shop; rest, snacks; bar; BBQ; playgrnd; pool (sw caps req); beach & lake sw; boating; fishing; games area; TV rm; 90% statics; dogs €6; poss cr; Eng spkn; adv bkg; quiet; red LS; CKE/CCI. "Gd views of lake - muddy beach; vg rest; nice, peaceful site; friendly, helpful staff." 16 Mar-1 Nov. € 42.00   2013*

ITALY

⊞ **SESTO/SEXTEN** *2E1* (3km SE Rural) *46.66806, 12.39935* **Caravan Park Sexten, St. Josefstr. 54, 39030 Sexten / Moos [0474 710444; fax 710053; info@caravanparksexten. it; www.caravanparksexten.it]** Fr S49 take S52 SE fr San Candido thro Sexten & Moos. After sh, steep climb site on W of S52 midway bet Moos & Kreuzberg pass. Lge, mkd pitch, pt sl, pt shd; wc; chem disp; mv service pnt; serviced pitches; sauna; private bthrms avail; shwrs inc; EHU (16A) metered; gas; lndry; shop; rest; bar; playgrnd; pool; paddling pool; solarium; tennis; wintersports; internet; entmnt; beauty & wellness treatments; TV; dogs €6; poss cr; Eng spkn; adv bkg ess high ssn; quiet; CKE/CCI. "Excel, clean facs; Waldbad worth visit; rock climbing wall; lovely scenery; mountain walks; v popular & busy site; v well managed & equipped; rest worth a visit." ♦ € 57.00 SBS - Y03   2014*

See advertisement inside the front cover

⊞ **SETTIMO VITTONE** *1B1* (2.5km N Rural) *45.56474, 7.81668* **Camping Mombarone, Torre Daniele, 10010 Settimo-Vittone (TO) [0125 757907; fax 757396; info@campingmombarone.it; www.campingmombarone.it]** On E side of Ivrea-Aosta rd (SS26), 100m S of Pont-St Martin. Exit A5 at Quincinetto, turn R onto SP69 across bdge, R at end onto SP26 & site on L in 150m. (App fr S, sp at ent but if overshoot go on 100m to rndabt to turn). Tight ent off busy rd. Med, pt sl, pt shd; wc; chem disp; shwrs inc; EHU (6A) €2.50; lndry down 400m; rest adj; snacks; bar; sm pool; games area; wifi; 80% statics; poss v cr & noisy high ssn; ccard not acc; red CKE/CCI. "Gd base Aosta valley; superb views; Quincinetto medieval vill walking dist; lovely, grassy, well-kept site; ltd space for tourers; v pleasant, helpful owner who speaks gd Eng, friendly welcome; san facs immac; gd NH; rlwy stn nrby." ♦ € 29.50   2014*

"I need an on-site restaurant"

We do our best to make sure site information is correct, but it is always best to check any must-have facilities are still available or will be open during your visit.

SIBARI *3A4* (4km E Coastal) *39.77944, 16.47889* **Camping Villaggio Pineta di Sibari, 87070 Sibari (CS) [0981 74135; fax 74302; info@pinetadisibari.it; www.pinetadisibari.it]** Exit A3 at Frascineto onto SS106, then exit at Villapiana-Scalo. Site sp on beach. Lge, pt shd; wc; mv service pnt; shwrs inc; EHU (4A) inc; lndry; shop; rest, snacks; bar; playgrnd; sand beach adj; tennis; bike hire; internet; entmnt; TV rm; 20% statics; dogs €5; poss cr; poss noisy; ccard acc. "Vg beach; site in pine forest; noisy bar/music; gd touring base; watch out for low bdge on app." ♦ 17 Apr-22 Sep. € 56.50   2014*

SICILY Campsites in towns in Sicily are listed together at the end of the Italian site entry pages.

SIENA *1D3* (7.4km N Urban) *43.33750, 11.33055* **Camping Siena Colleverde, Via Scacciapensieri 47, 53100 Siena [0577 334080; fax 334005; info@sienacamping.com; www.sienacamping.com]** Site sp ('Camping' or symbol) on all app to Siena, foll sp for 'Ospedale' (hospital). Use exit Siena Nord & foll site sp, but take care as some sp misleadingly positioned. Lge, hdg/mkd pitch, hdstg, pt sl, terr, pt shd; htd wc; chem disp; mv service pnt; shwrs inc; EHU (10A) inc; gas; lndry; shop; rest, snacks; bar; playgrnd; pool high ssn; wifi; TV rm; dogs; phone; bus; poss cr; Eng spkn; adv bkg; some rd noise; CKE/CCI. "Attractive location; gd views old town wall fr upper pitches (no shd); excel touring base; upgraded, well-run site - gd, well kept; modern san facs; easy access by bus to town fr site ent; excel; pt of 'We Love Camping' group; some lge unmkd pitches." ♦ 1 Mar-31 Dec. € 37.00   2015*

SIENA *1D3* (21km W Rural) *43.2815, 11.21905* **Camping La Montagnola, Strada della Montagnola 139, 53100 Sovicille (SI) [tel/fax 0577 314473; info@campingla montagnola.it; www.campinglamontagnola.it]** Fr N on S2 or S on S223 site well sp fr junc with S73. Avoid Siena town cent. Med, mkd pitch, hdstg, terr, pt shd; wc; chem disp; mv service pnt; shwrs inc; EHU (6A) inc; gas; lndry; shop & 5km; rest 800m; snacks; bar; playgrnd; games area; wifi; 7% statics; dogs free; phone; bus to Siena; sep car park; poss cr; adv bkg rec; Eng spkn; quiet; ccard acc (over €50); red CKE/CCI. "Super site; sm pitches; sharp stone chippings on hdstg pitches; v clean facs; vg refuge fr summer heat in wooded hills; facs poss stretched high ssn & rubbish bins o'flowing; gd walks fr site (booklet fr recep); Magic of Italy disc, conv bus service to Siena fr site." 1 Apr-30 Sep. € 29.00   2015*

SILVI MARINA see Pineto *2F3*

SIRMIONE *2G2* (3km E Coastal) *45.45738, 10.64025* **Tiglio, Loc. Punta Grò, 25019 Sirmione [tel/fax 030 990 4009; info@campingtiglio.it]** A4 Milan-Verona, exit Sirmione. 1st exit at rndabt onto SP13. 1st exit at next rndabt. Turn L twds Via San Martino. 1st exit at rndabt onto Via Verona. Foll sp to camp. Lge, mkd pitch, shd; wc; mv service pnt; shwrs inc; EHU inc (4A); rest; snacks; bar; BBQ; playgrnd; 50% statics; bus adj; twin axles; poss cr; Eng spkn; adv bkg; ccard acc; CKE/CCI. "Gd site; noisy & busy but friendly; on bus rte to Verona." 16 Apr-30 Sep. € 39.00   2014*

SIRMIONE *1D2* (3km S Rural) *45.46845, 10.61028* **Camping Sirmione, Via Sirmioncino 9, 25010 Colombare-di-Sirmione (BS) [030 99 04 665; fax 91 90 45; info@camping-sirmione.it; www.camping-sirmione.it]** Exit S11 at traff lts sp Sirmione, in 500m R at site sp. Lge, mkd pitch, pt sl, some hdstg, pt shd; wc (cont); mv service pnt; shwrs; EHU (6A) inc; lndry; shop; rest, snacks; bar; pool; paddling pool; lake sw; private beach; watersports; games area; 30% statics; dogs; poss cr; adv bkg; quiet; ccard acc. "Excel lakeside site; facs poss stretched when site busy; excel rest, bar, pool & san facs; lovely walk to Sirmione; highly rec." ♦ 25 Mar-5 Oct. € 54.00   2014*

SISTIANA see Monfalcone *2E1*

SOLCIO DE LESA see Arona *1B1*

ITALY

SORICO *1C1* (500m E Rural) *46.17152, 9.39302* **Camping La Riva, Via Poncione 3, 22010 Sorico (CO) [tel/fax 0344 94571; info@campinglariva.com; www.campinglariva.com]** Fr Lecco take SS36 twd Colico & Sondrio. At end of tunnels fork L sp Como & Menaggio. At end of dual c'way turn L onto S340 to Sorico sp Como & Menaggio. Cross bdge & site 500m down lane on L bef cent Sorico, sp Cmp Poncione & La Riva. Easiest app on SS36 on E side of lake (pt dual c'way). Rd on W side narr & congested. Med, mkd pitch, pt shd; wc (some cont); chem disp; mv service pnt; shwrs €0.80; EHU (6A) inc; gas 50m; lndry; sm shop; rest nr; snacks; bar; BBQ; playgrnd; pool; sw & rv/lakeside beach adj; canoeing; waterskiing; fishing; bike & boat hire; games/TV rm; dogs €4 (must be kept on lead); no o'fits over 7.5m high ssn; phone; Eng spkn; quiet; wifi; 50% statics; red LS; CKE/CCI. "Excel, family-run site; gd views of lake & mountains; clean, well-kept & tidy; immac san facs; v warm welcome; less commercialised than some other sites in area; cycle track to vill; poss mosquito problem in Jun; v tidy clean site; friendly helpful owners; rd fr Lugano to Como not adv for c'vans." ♦ 1 Apr-2 Nov. € 54.00 SBS - Y12   2013*

⊞ **SORRENTO** *3A3* (3km N Coastal) *40.63541, 14.41758* **Camping I Pini, Corso Italia 242, 80063 Piano-di-Sorrento (NA) [081 8786891; fax 8788770; info@campingipini.com; www.campingipini.com]** S fr Naples on A3; Exit A3 sp Castellammare di Stabia & take SS145 sp to Sorrento; pass thro vill of Meta; site on R immed over bdge; lge sp on main rd. Med, hdg/mkd pitch, pt sl, pt shd; wc; chem disp; mv service pnt; shwrs inc; EHU (4A) inc; shops 500m; rest; snacks; bar; pool (in winter htd & open fr 0830-1500); beach 1km; 50% statics; dogs; bus 50m; Eng spkn; adv bkg; quiet; ccard acc; red long stay/LS; CKE/CCI. "Spacious site in mountains bet 2 vills; pool restricted to campers; sh walk to public transport to sites of interest; best site in Sorrento to avoid narr gridlocked rds; old, tired facs (2013); tight narr pitches." ♦ € 47.50   2014*

SORRENTO *3A3* (5km NE Coastal) *40.65953, 14.41835* **Camping Sant Antonio, Via Marina d'Equa 20/21, Seiano, 80069 Vico-Equense (NA) [tel/fax 081 8028570 or 081 8028576; info@campingsantantonio.it; www.campingsantantonio.it]** Fr A3 exit at Castellamare-di-Stabia. Foll sp for Sorrento; app Vico-Equense take L fork thro tunnel, at end of viaduct R to Seiano-Spaggia. Last site of 3 on L down narr twisting rd after 1km (poss v congested). Access to pitches poss diff due to trees. Med, pt sl, shd; wc; chem disp; shwrs €0.50; EHU (5A) inc; gas; lndry rm; shop; rest, snacks; bar; shgl beach 100m; boat hire; excursions; solarium; some statics; dogs €3 (not allowed Aug); phone; bus adj, train 800m; poss cr; Eng spkn; adv bkg; quiet; ccard acc; 10% red CKE/CCI. "Ideal base Amalfi coast, Capri, Naples; lovely harbour adj; v helpful, friendly staff; bus & train tickets avail fr site; gd rest." ♦ ltd. 15 Mar-31 Oct. € 32.50   2013*

SORRENTO *3A3* (5km NE Coastal) *40.66022, 14.42048* **Camping Seiano Spiaggia, Marina Aequa, Seiano, 80069 Vico-Equense [tel/fax 081 8028560; info@campingseiano.it; www.campingseiano.it]** Fr A3 exit at Castellammare-di-Stabia & foll sp Sorrento. On app Vico-Equense take L fork thro tunnel & turn R at end of viaduct to Seiano-Spiaggia. Site on L in 800m. Med, mkd pitch, terr, shd; htd wc; chem disp; shwrs €0.50; EHU (6A) inc; gas; shop; rest, snacks adj; bar; BBQ; pool 200m; sand/shgl beach adj; no statics; dogs; bus, train to Sorrento nrby; Eng spkn; adv bkg; quiet but some rd noise at front of site; red long stay/CKE/CCI. "Clean, well-maintained site; helpful, welcoming staff; conv sightseeing base." ♦ 1 Apr-30 Sep. € 27.50   2009*

SORRENTO *3A3* (5km NE Coastal) *40.65990, 14.42153* **Villaggio Turistico Azzurro, Via Marina Aequa 9, 80066 Seiano-di-Vico-Equense (NA) [081 8029984; fax 8029176; info@villaggioazzurro.net; www.villaggioazzurro.net]** Fr A3 exit sp Castellammare-di-Stabia, foll sp Sorrento. App Vico-Equense take L fork thro tunnel. At end of viaduct turn R to Seiano-Spaggia. Site on L in 800m down steep, narr, twisting rd - poss congested espec at w/ends & used by buses. Sm, mkd pitch, shd; wc (some cont); chem disp; mv service pnt; shwrs €0.50; EHU (6A) inc; lndry (inc dryer); shop; rest, snacks; bar; BBQ; playgrnd; shgl beach 400m; bike hire; some statics; dogs; bus to stn high ssn; ferry; Eng spkn; adv bkg; rd noise; ccard acc; red long stay/CKE/CCI. "Conv Naples, Pompei etc; v helpful owner; site in orange grove & pitching poss diff lge o'fits due trees; vg." 1 Mar-1 Dec. € 30.00   2009*

SORRENTO *3A3* (10km S Coastal) *40.58389, 14.35220* **Camping Nettuno, Via A Vespucci, Marina-del-Cantone, 80068 Massa-Lubrense (NA) [081 8081051; fax 8081706; info@villaggionettuno.it; www.villaggionettuno.it]** Fr Castellammare to Sorrento rd, turn L in Meta dir Positano. Site well sp in dir St Agate, then Marina-del-Cantone. Tortuous rd to site & steep, diff ent to site. Sm, shd; wc (some cont); chem disp; mv service pnt; shwrs inc; EHU (3A) €2.50; gas; lndry; shop; rest, snacks; bar; BBQ; shgl/rock beach adj; diving cent; boat hire; tennis; internet; entmnt; TV rm; some statics; phone; Eng spkn; quiet; ccard acc. "Lovely situation; sea views fr some pitches (extra cost); v muddy when wet; san facs need refurb (2009); ltd/primitive water & drainage facs; coastal walks; gd public transport; 10% red on next site if pt of same chain." ♦ ltd. 1 Mar-2 Nov. € 32.00   2009*

SORRENTO *3A3* (1.5km SW Coastal) *40.62555, 14.36583* **Camping Nube d'Argento, Via Capo 21, 80067 Sorrento (NA) [081 8781344; fax 8073450; info@nubedargento.com; www.nubedargento.com]** Exit a'strada for Castellamare. Foll sp to Sorrento. At 1-way system foll sp out of Sorrento dir Massa Lubrense on SS148. On exit Sorrento site ent on R. App diff; rec head approx 500m beyond ent to wide rd, make 'U' turn & rtn to site. Driving thro town cent diff. Med, pt sl, terr, pt shd; wc (some cont); chem disp (wc); mv service pnt; shwrs inc; EHU (4-6A) inc; gas; lndry; shop; rest, snacks; bar; playgrnd; pool; boat hire; entmnt; TV; 15% statics; dogs; phone; bus/train; Eng spkn; no adv bkg; rd noise; ccard acc; red LS/CKE/CCI. "Some excel pitches with sea views, others v sm; steep, narr rds thro site, obstacles, o'hanging trees & tight bends - suitable sm o'fits only; pitches muddy after rain; san facs old & basic; hot water to shwrs only; site nr sewage plant; friendly & helpful staff; excel rest; sh walk to town; red facs LS." 20 Dec-10 Jan & 15 Mar-10 Nov. € 41.00   2010*

ITALY

SORRENTO *3A3* (2km W Coastal) *40.62818, 14.35816*
Camping Villaggio Santa Fortunata, Via Capo 39, 80067
Capo-de-Sorrento (NA) [081 8073579 or 081 8073574;
fax 8073590; info@santafortunata.com; www.santa
fortunata.com] Only app fr a'strada, exit Castellamare.
Foll sp into Sorrento then sp Massa-Lubrense. Site poorly sp
fr Sorrento on R, gd wide ent. V lge, mkd/hdg pitch, pt sl,
terr, shd; wc (some cont); chem disp; mv service pnt; shwrs
inc; EHU (6A) inc; gas; lndry; shop; rest, snacks; bar; playgrnd;
rocky beach; pool high ssn; internet; entmnt; TV; 50% statics;
dogs free; phone; bus adj; sep car park; poss cr; Eng spkn; red
long stay/CKE/CCI. "Gd, clean facs; pitches sm for lge o'fits
(7m+) & poss dusty; bus fr gate, ticket fr recep; boat trips to
Capri fr site beach; noisy nr gd rest, disco & 18-30 tours; many
scruffy statics; facs dated; steep access & tight hairpins to some
pitches; friendly, vg site." ♦ ltd. 1 Apr-15 Oct. € 42.00   2014*

SORSO see Porto Torres (SARDINIA) *3A1*

SOTTOMARINA see Chioggia *2E2*

SOVICILLE see Siena *1D3*

SPERLONGA *2E4* (1km SE Coastal) *41.25514, 13.44625*
Camping Villaggio Nord-Sud, Via Flacca, Km 15.5, 04029
Sperlonga (LT) [0771 548255; fax 557240; info@camping
nordsud.it; www.campingnordsud.it] Site on seaward side
of S213 at km post 15.9. Lge sp visible fr both dirs. Lge, mkd
pitch, hdstg, shd; wc (mainly cont); chem disp; shwrs inc; EHU
(4A) inc; lndry; shop, rest high ssn; snacks; bar; private sand
beach; windsurfing; tennis; fitness rm; games area; entmnt;
some statics; no dogs; adv bkg; quiet; red LS. "Mostly statics
but great location; pleasant site; picturesque beach." ♦
1 Apr-31 Oct. € 48.00   2010*

⊞ **SPOLETO** *2E3* (2.2km NE Urban) *47.73820, 12.74312*
Parcheggio a Pagamento "Ponzianina", Via del Tiro a
Segno 12622 [07 43 21 81] N on Viale Giacomo Matteotti
twd Viale Martiri della Resistenza, take 1st L onto Viale Martiri
della Resistenza, over rndbt, turn R onto SS418, turn L onto
Piazza Vittoria/SS418 and cont for 80m; turn R onto Via
Cacciatore delle Alpi cont 350m; L onto Viale Trento e Trieste,
then R onto Via del Tiro a Segno, site in 230m. Sm; no facs;
paid parking site only. "200m escalator to the top of historic
town and Cathedral; gd NH; m'vans only." € 5.00   2014*

SPOTORNO see Savona *1B2*

STELLA SAN GIOVANNI see Savona *1B2*

STIA *1D3* (5km N Rural) *43.83028, 11.70061* **Camping Falterona,**
Loc Montalto, 52017 Stia (AR) [tel/fax 0575 582360;
info@campingfalterona.it; www.campingfalterona.it]
E fr Florence on R69 to Pontassieve, then R70 to Poppi. Turn
N onto R310 to Stia then foll dir Forli to Papiano & site. Med,
some hdstg, terr, pt shd; wc (some cont); chem disp; mv service
pnt; shwrs; EHU (3A) €1.50; shop; snacks; bar; BBQ; playgrnd;
sm pool; games area; Eng spkn; quiet. "Beautiful area; vg
walking." 29 May-5 Sep. € 21.50   2010*

STRESA *1B1* (3.4km NW Urban) *45.91246, 8.50410* **Camping**
Parisi, Via Piave 50, 28831 Baveno (VB) [tel/fax 0323 924160;
campingparisi@tiscalinet.it; www.campingparisi.it]
Exit A26 at Baveno, after x-ing bdge on o'skirts Baveno, turn L
off main rd bet Hotel Simplon & Agip g'ge & foll sp. Fr Stresa
drive thro Baveno. At end of prom, take R fork at Dino Hotel
up a minor 1-way rd (poss congested by parked cars); foll Parisi
sp. Med, pt sl, pt shd; wc; chem disp; mv service pnt; shwrs inc;
EHU (6A) €3.50; lndry; shop, supmkt 500m; rest, snacks 500m;
bar adj, playgrnd; lake sw; sm shgl beach adj; boat-launching;
fishing; wifi; 10% statics; dogs €4; bus; phone; poss cr; Eng
spkn; adv bkg; quiet but w/end evening noise fr adj lido; red
CKE/CCI. "Well-managed site on Lake Maggiore; fine views;
extra for lakeside pitches; frequent lake steamers nr site; gd
rests adj; long hose rec for m'van fill up; sm pitches; busy at
w/end; sw in lake - supervise children; many repeat visitors;
clean facs; welcoming recep; conv base for visiting Borromeo
Islands." ♦ ltd. 25 Mar-30 Sep. € 34.00   2015*

STRESA *1B1* (4km NW Rural) *45.91185, 8.48913* **Camping**
Tranquilla, Via Cave 2, Oltrefuime, 28831 Baveno (VB)
[tel/fax 0323 923452; info@tranquilla.com;
www.tranquilla.com] Fr N go into Baveno & turn R 200m
past Hotel Splendide; fr S turn L immed after x-ing bdge.
Foll brown sp to site up steep hill 1km. Med, hdg/mkd pitch,
some hdstg, pt sl, terr, pt shd; wc (some cont); chem disp; mv
service pnt; serviced pitch; shwrs inc; EHU (6A) €2.60; lndry
(inc dryer); shops 1km; rest 400m; bar; shgl lake beach 800m;
pool; watersports; bike hire; entmnt at w/end; 25% statics;
dogs €2.50; train to Milan 2km; car wash; Eng spkn; adv bkg;
quiet; red long stay/snr citizens/CKE/CCI. "Clean, comfortable,
well-managed, pleasant, family-owned site; v helpful staff;
excel rest; sm pitches; conv Lake Maggiore; day trip by train to
Milan." 15 Mar-15 Oct. € 26.00   2011*

STRESA *1B1* (6km NW Urban) *45.90323, 8.50807*
Camping Calaverde, Sempione 24, 28831 Baveno (VB)
[0323 922721; info@calaverde.it] Fr Stresa N on S33, site
ent on R 100m after 87km post. Tight, concealed ent. Sm, pt
shd; wc, chem disp; shwrs inc; EHU inc; lndry rm; shop opp;
bar; lake & private shgl beach adj; quiet but some rd/rlwy
noise; Eng spkn; dogs; phone; quiet. "Helpful, friendly owner;
clean site; boat-launching; gd size pitches; lake steamer 2km."
€ 26.00   2014*

TERLAGO see Trento *1D1*

⊞ **TERMOLI** *2F4* (6km SE Coastal) *41.93861, 15.08194*
Camping La Pineta, Contrada Ramitelli 5/A, 86042
Campomarino-Lido (CB) [0875 539402; fax 538143;
info@lapinetacamping.it; www.lapinetacamping.it]
Leave a'strada A14 at Termoli onto SS16 dir Foggia. After
approx 2km turn sp Lido-di-Campomarino; cross over rlwy
bdge twds sea, foll site sp. Lge, pt shd; wc (some cont); shwrs;
EHU (3A) €3; gas; lndry; shop; rest, snacks; bar; sand beach adj;
tennis; games area; entmnt; 80% statics; no dogs Jul/Aug; poss
cr; some rd & rlwy noise; red LS; CKE/CCI. "Friendly, family-
run site; site grubby & gloomy LS; tight turns & narr pitches
poss diff lge o'fits; pitches boggy after rain; gd san facs; hot
water only in shwrs; beach access; v friendly staff; NH only."
€ 29.00   2011*

TERNI *2E3* (7km E Rural) *42.54801, 12.71878* **Camping Marmore, Loc Campacci, 05100 Cascata-delle-Marmore (TN) [tel/fax 0744 67198; camping.marmore@hotmail.it; www.campinglemarmore.com]** E fr Terni on S79 dir Marmore & Rieti. Foll site sp. Med, hdstg, pt sl, shd; htd wc (some cont); chem disp; shwrs inc; EHU inc; water free; shop on site & 1km; rest; bar; rv sw adj; watersports on lake nrby; games rm; 90% statics; dogs €4; phone; poss cr; Eng spkn; quiet. "Spectacular waterfalls adj & mountain scenery; gd; Casacata Hydro elec, well worth visiting." ♦ 1 Apr-30 Sep. € 25.00   2013*

TERRACINA *2E4* (4km W Coastal) *41.28285, 13.19610* **Camping Internazionale Badino (Naturist), Via Badino, Km 4.8, Porto Badino, 04019 Terracina (LT) [tel/fax 0773 764430]** Fr Latina on S148 (SS Mediana) foll sp Port Badino & site. Med, mkd pitch, pt shd; wc; shwrs €1; chem disp; EHU (1.5A) inc; gas; lndry; shop, rest 100m; bar; sand beach adj; games area; solarium; no dogs Jul/Aug; quiet. ♦ 1 Apr-15 Oct. € 35.00   2009*

⊞ **TONARA** *3A1* (200m N Rural) *40.02851, 9.17578* **Camping Sa Colonia, Via Muggianeddu 4, 08039 Tonara (NU) [03921 282340; info@campingsacolonia.it; www.campingsacolonia.it]** Fr S fr Cagliari on SS128/SS295, site sp. Sp rte unsuitable lge car + c'van o'fits or v lge m'vans. Avoid town cent streets - v narr & steep. Med, mkd pitch, terr, shd; wc; chem disp (wc); shwrs; EHU (5A) inc; shop in town; rest; bar; playgrnd; Eng spkn; quiet. CKE/CCI. "Mountain scenery; rds gd but steep, twisty & slow." € 15.00   2010*

TORBOLE *1D1* (350m N Urban) *45.8725, 10.87361* **Camping Al Porto, Via Al Cor, 38069 Tórbole (TN) [tel/fax 0464 505891; info@campingalporto.it; www.campingalporto.it]** On ent Tórbole fr S take rd twd Riva-del-Garda for approx 600m. Petrol stn & car park on R, turn L into narr lane after shops; site sp. Med, mkd pitch, pt shd; wc (some cont); chem disp; mv service pnt; shwrs inc; EHU (5A) inc; lndry; shops 300m; rest 100m; snacks; bar; BBQ; playgrnd; lake sw & shgl beach 100m; watersports; dogs €2.50; poss cr; quiet; red long stay/LS; CKE/CCI. "Excel san facs; excel site; secure; helpful staff; vill has many rest & sportling locations." ♦ 14 Mar-2 Nov. € 33.00   2014*

TORRE DEL LAGO PUCCINI see Viareggio *1C3*

TOSCOLANO MADERNO *1D1* (N Urban) *45.63777, 10.61277* **Camping Toscolano, Via Religione 88, 25088 Toscolano-Maderno (BS) [0365 641584; fax 642519; toscolano@ hg-hotels.com; www.hghotels.com]** Site at lakeside bet Gargnano & Maderno. Narr archway on app. Lge, pt shd; wc (some cont); shwrs inc; EHU (3A) inc; gas; lndry; shop; rest, snacks; bar; playgrnd; pool; paddling pool; shgl beach & lake sw; tennis; games area; golf 5km; entmnt; 50% statics; dogs €3.50; poss v cr; adv bkg rec. ♦ 1 Apr-30 Sep. € 34.50   2010*

TRAFOI *1D1* (900m S Rural) *46.54332, 10.50750* **Camping Trafoi, Drei Brunnen Weg 1, 39020 Trafoi [tel/fax 0473 611533; info@camping-trafoi.com; www.camping-trafoi.com]** Fr SS40 turn SW at Spondigna onto SS38 dir Stelvio to Trafoi. Site thro vill sp on L. Sm, pt sl, pt shd; wc; chem disp; mv service pnt; shwrs; EHU (4A); lndry; shop; BBQ; dogs €3; bus 500m; Eng spkn; quiet. "Excel cycle rtes, mountaineering; chair lift for skiing; excel." ♦ ltd. 15 Jun-15 Sep. € 30.00   2015*

TRASAGHIS see Gemona del Friuli *2E1*

TRENTO *1D1* (12km NW Rural) *46.11111, 11.04805* **Camping Laghi di Lamar, Via alla Selva Faeda 15, 38070 Terlago (TN) [0461 860423; campeggio@laghidilamar.com; www.laghidilamar.com]** Head W fr Trento for 10km on SS45b dir Riva-del-Garda/Brescia. Turn R twd Monte-Terlago; site sp on R. Last section via SS45 v steep. Med, terr, pt shd; wc (some cont); chem disp; mv service pnt; shwrs inc; EHU (6A) inc; gas; lndry (inc dryer); shop; rest 100m; rest, snacks; bar; BBQ; playgrnd; pool; lake sw 700m; games area; games rm; bike hire; wifi; TV; 30% statics; dogs €2.50; phone; Eng spkn; quiet; ccard acc; red snr citizens/CKE/CCI. "Excel site." ♦ 1 Apr-15 Oct. € 27.50   2010*

> ## "Satellite navigation makes touring much easier"
>
> Remember most sat navs don't know if you're towing or in a larger vehicle – always use yours alongside maps and site directions.

TREPORTI see Cavallino *2E2*

⊞ **TRIESTE** *2F1* (5.5km N Rural) *45.67974, 13.78387* **Camping Obelisco, Strada Nuova Opicina 37, 34016 Opicina (TS) [tel/fax 040 212744; info@campeggiobelisco. it; www.campeggiobelisco.it]** Sp fr S58. Med, hdstg, pt sl, terr, shd; wc (cont); own san; mv service pnt; shwrs inc; EHU €2.50; rest, snacks; bar 1km; playgrnd; 95% statics; dogs €2.50; Eng spkn; quiet; CKE/CCI. "V steep, narr, twisting ent/exit to site - suitable sm c'vans only & diff in wet; excel views Trieste harbour; interesting tram ride into city fr obelisk; demanding up hill walk to top of site, both Turkish & European wcs." € 18.00   2011*

TROGHI see Firenze *1D3*

TROPEA *3B4* (7km NE Coastal) *38.70610, 15.97024* **Villaggio Camping Sambalon, Via del Mare, 89868 Marina-di-Zambrone (VV) [0963 392828; fax 45385; info@sambalon. com; www.sambalon.com]** Fr N exit A3 at Pizzo Calabro onto S522 dir Tropea for 20km. Foll sp Marina di Zambrone & site. Med, mkd pitch, some hdstg, pt shd; wc; mv service pnt; shwrs; EHU; lndry; shop on site & 1km; rest, snacks; bar; playgrnd; sand beach adj; wifi; entmnt; TV; some statics; dogs; adv bkg; quiet. 20 May-23 Sep. € 46.50   2012*

UGENTO *3A4* (6km S Coastal) *39.87331, 18.14261* **Camping Riva di Ugento, Loc Fontanelle, 73059 Ugento (LE) [0833 933600; fax 933601; info@rivadiugento.it; www.rivadiugento.it]** Fr Bari take Brindisi rd to Lecce, then SS101 to Gallipoli, then SR274 twd Sta Maria di Leuca & exit at Ugento. Turn R at traff lts on SS91, site well sp. V lge, mkd pitch, shd; htd wc (some cont); mv service pnt; shwrs inc; EHU (3A) inc; gas; lndry (inc dryer); shop; rest, snacks; bar; BBQ; playgrnd; pool; paddling pool; sand beach adj; watersports; tennis; boat & bike hire; games area; horseriding 1km; wifi; TV rm; cinema; excursions; 10% statics; no dogs; no adv bkg; ccard acc. "Excel beach; some pitches at water's edge; tranquil site." ♦ 15 May-30 Sep. € 45.00   2011*

URBINO *2E3* (2.5km E Rural) *43.73055, 12.65710* **Camping Pineta, Via Ca' Mignore, 5, 61029 San Donato (PS) [0722 4710; fax 4734; campeggiopinetaurbino@email.it; www.camping-pineta-urbino.it]** Site sp fr rndabout just below city walls on S423 fr Pesaro. Med, terr, pt shd; wc (mainly cont); chem disp (wc); shwrs inc; EHU (4-6A) inc (long lead poss req); lndry; shop in ssn; supmkt 1km; rest, bar 2km; pool; sand beach 20km; dogs €3; bus to town (ltd); Eng spkn; adv bkg red Jul/Aug; quiet; ccard acc; red long stay/LS. "Lovely setting on hill o'looking Urbino; v interesting area; sm, steep, tight pitches unsuitable lge o'fits; tired, old facs poss stretched; gd pool." Easter-30 Sep. € 50.00   2010*

⊞ **URBISAGLIA** *2E3* (5km NE Rural) *43.21136, 13.41544* **Centro Agrituristico La Fontana, Via Selva 8, Abbadia-di-Fiastra, 62010 La Fontana (MC) [tel/fax 0733 514002]** Fr SP77 turn S to Abbadia-di-Fiastra onto SP78. On reaching Abbadia turn L & immed R, then uphill above Monastery for 2km & foll sp to site on R just after sharp RH bend. Sm, terr, pt shd; wc; chem disp; mv service pnt; shwrs inc; EHU (6A) inc; rest, snacks; bar; BBQ; playgrnd; sand beach 35km; TV cab/sat; quiet. "Fair sh stay/NH; CL-type site on farm; not suitable lge o'fits; attactive countryside; v helpful owners." ♦ € 21.00   2012*

VADA see Cecina *1D3*

VALLECROSIA *1B3* (1km W Coastal) *43.78411, 7.63368* **Camping Vallecrosia, Lungomare Marconi 149, 18019 Vallecrosia (IM) [tel/fax 0184 295591; info@camping vallecrosia.com; www.campingvallecrosia.com]** Fr SS1 Via Aurelia cont W dir Bordighera & Vallecrosia, foll sp. Site on seafront. Fr A10 exit at Ventimiglia & take SS1 dir San Remo, foll site sp. Do not take m'way exits at San Remo or Bordighera as rds unsuitable c'vans & m'vans. Sm, mkd pitch, hdstg, pt shd; htd wc; chem disp; mv service pnt; shwrs inc; EHU (6A) €3; lndry; shop; rest, snacks, bar 200m; playgrnd; shgl beach 100m; wifi; 25% statics; dogs €3; phone; quiet; CKE/CCI. "Lovely, well-spaced site; excel beach opp with beach bar; popular with windsurfers; helpful staff; v clean san facs; longer vans may req manhandling onto mkd pitches; ideal NH bet Italy & France." ♦ 1 Apr-30 Sep. € 30.00   2010*

VALSAVARENCHE *1B1* (5km S Rural) *45.54889, 7.21250* **Camping Gran Paradiso, Loc Plan de la Pesse 1, 11010 Valsavarenche (AO) [tel/fax 0165 905801; campinggran paradiso@libero.it; www.campinggranparadiso.it]** Exit A5 Aosta Ovest onto S26 W dir Monte Bianco. In 3km at Villeneuve turn S & foll sp Valsavarenche for approx 18km. Approx 5km after passing cent of Degioz site sp just bef rd crosses rv. Sm, mkd pitch, terr, shd; wc; chem disp; mv service pnt; fam bthrm; shwrs inc; EHU (3A) €2; lndry (inc dryer); snacks; bar; BBQ; cooking facs; games area; games rm; dogs; phone; Eng spkn; adv bkg; quiet. "Well-situated, scenic site for hiking, canyoning, rafting; guided walks; excel." ♦ ltd. 1 Jun-30 Sep. € 18.00   2010*

VARIGOTTI see Finale Ligure *1B2*

⊞ **VENEZIA** *2E2* (18km SW Coastal) *45.41916, 12.25666* **Camping Fusina, Via Moranzani 79, 30030 Fusina (VE) [041 5470055; fax 5470050; info@campingfusina.com; www.campingfusina.com]** Exit A4 at sp Ravenna/Chiogga onto SS309 S, & foll sp to site. Take care when turning into rd leading to Fusina as L-hand turning lane used by locals for o'taking. Lge, pt shd; htd wc; chem disp; mv service pnt; shwrs inc; EHU (6A) inc (poss rev pol); gas; lndry; shop; rest, snacks; bar; playgrnd; boat hire; games area; wifi; entmnt; TV rm; 50% statics; dogs free; poss cr; no adv bkg; some ship & aircraft noise + noise fr bar & adj indus complex; ccard acc; red CKE/CCI. "Pleasant, busy site; some pitches o'looking lagoon; many backpackers, educational groups & 18-30s; gd san facs; gd public transport/boat dir to Venice; ferry to Greece adj; helpful staff; poss mosquitoes; some pitches diff due trees & soft when wet; ltd facs LS & poss travellers." € 35.00   2015*

> ## "There aren't many sites open at this time of year"
>
> If you're travelling outside peak season remember to call ahead to check site opening dates – even if the entry says 'open all year'.

VENEZIA *2E2* (16km W Rural) *45.45222, 12.18305* **Camping Serenissima, Via Padana 334/A, 30176 Malcontenta [041 5386498 or 041 921850; fax 920286; info@camping serenissima.it; www.campingserenissima.it]** Exit A4 at Oriago/Mira exit. At 1st rndabt foll sp Ravenna/Venezia; at next rndabt take 1st exit sp Padova/Riviera del Brenta (SR11) twd Oriago. Rv on L, site on R in approx 2km. Med, mkd pitch, pt shd; htd wc (some cont); chem disp; mv service pnt; shwrs inc; EHU (16A) inc; gas; lndry; shop; supmkt 5km; rest, snacks; bar; playgrnd; pool 3km; sand beach 10km; bike & boat hire; wifi; 25% statics; dogs free; phone; poss cr; gd Eng spkn; adv bkg; quiet; ccard acc; red snr citizens; CKE/CCI. "Bus to Venice/Padua - buy tickets on site; friendly, helpful owners; efficient recep; some sm pitches; excel, v clean san facs; poss mosquitoes; conv Padova; highly rec for Venice; vg." ♦ 14 Apr-7 Nov. € 33.00   2014*

VENEZIA (VENICE) See also sites listed under Cavallino, Lido di Jesolo, Mestre and Punta Sabbioni.

VERBANIA *1B1* (6km NE Rural) *45.97659, 8.63385* **Camping La Sierra, Corso Belvedere, 337 - 28823 Ghiffa (VB) [0333 7815534; info@campinglasierra.it; www.camping lasierra.it]** Fr Verbania N on SS34 dir Cannobio, site on L just after exit fr Ghiffa. Sm, mkd pitch, hdstg, terr, pt shd; wc; chem disp; shwrs inc; EHU (6A) inc; lndry; shop 1km; rest, snacks; bar; BBQ; playgrnd; shgl beach adj; fishing; watersports; 8% statics; dogs €3; bus; phone; poss cr; Eng spkn; adv bkg; rd noise; CKE/CCI. "Vg site; views of lake; steep walk to sans facs fr upper terraces." 1 Mar-1 Nov. € 33.00   2013*

VERBANIA *1B1* (4km W Rural) *45.95365, 8.47698* **Camping La Quiete, Via Turati 72, Lago di Mergozzo, 28924 Fondotoce (VB) [0323 496013; fax 496139; info@camping laquiete.it; www.campinglaquiete.it]** Exit A26 at Gravellona Toce onto SS34 to Fondotoce, then SP54 to Lago di Mergozzo. Site on E edge Lago di Mergozzo, sp. Lge, mkd pitch, pt shd; wc; chem disp; mv service pnt; shwrs; EHU (6A) €3; lndry; shop; rest; bar; lake sw adj; canoing; fishing; windsurfing; games area; games rm; golf 2km; some statics; dogs €5.50; some Eng spkn; adv bkg rec; quiet; ccard not acc. "Lovely site with view of alps & lake; extra for lakeside pitches; friendly, welcoming owner; excel." 1 Apr-30 Sep. € 27.00   2010*

VERBANIA *1B1* (6km W Rural) *45.93731, 8.48615* **Camping Conca d'Oro, Via 42 Martiri 26, 28835 Feriolo di Baveno (VB) [0323 28116; fax 28538; info@concadoro.it; www.concadoro.it]** Foll S33 NW fr Stresa, thro Bavena to Feriolo. At traff lts in Feriolo fork R, sp Verbania & in 800m immed over rv bdge, turn R into site. Clearly sp. Lge, mkd pitch, pt sl, shd; wc; chem disp; mv service pnt; shwrs inc; EHU (6A) inc; lndry; supmkt; rest, snacks; bar; playgrnd; private sand beach adj; windsurfing; games area; bike hire; internet; entmnt; 10% statics; dogs €5 (not acc Jul/Aug); Eng spkn; adv bkg; quiet; ccard acc; CKE/CCI. "Helpful staff; gd, clean, modern san facs; discount for local services; extra for lakeside pitches; excel site." ♦ 29 Mar-29 Sep. € 48.00   2013*

VERBANIA *1B1* (6km W Urban) *45.93283, 8.48266* **Camping Orchidea, Via 42 Martiri, 28835 Feriolo (VB) [0323 28257; fax 28573; info@campingorchidea.it; www.camping orchidea.it]** Exit A26/E62 sp Baveno onto SS33 dir Verbania. Past traff lts in Feriolo to site on R in 500m. Lge, pt shd; wc; mv service pnt; baby facs; shwrs; EHU (6A) €2.60; gas; lndry; shop; rest, snacks; bar; playgrnd; sand beach & lake sw adj; bike hire; wifi; 25% statics; dogs €5; poss cr; adv bkg ess high ssn; quiet but rd noise; ccard acc. "Beautiful situation at lake end, splendid views; lake shore walk to vill; 3 gd rests in 10 mins walk; boats fr Stresa to Locarno; sm pitches." 1 Mar-1 Oct. € 32.00   2009*

VERBANIA *1B1* (9km NW Urban) *45.96111, 8.45694* **Camping Lago delle Fate, La Quartina, Via Pallanza 22, 28802 Mergozzo (VB) [0323 80326; fax 800916; info@lagodellefate.com; www.lagodellefate.com]** 1km E of vill of Mergozzo which is 2nd L after exit Gravellona on S34 to Verbania. Med, hdstg, pt shd; wc (cont); chem disp; shwrs; EHU (6A); gas; lndry; rest 100m; snacks; bar; BBQ; shgl beach; lake sw; boat hire; wifi; 10% statics; twin axles; poss cr; Eng spkn; adv bkg; CKE/CCI. "Extra charge for lakeside pitches, slightly bigger with superb views; gd sh stay; town, 5 min walk; gd walking & cycling." ♦ ltd. 2 Apr-4 Oct. € 43.00   2015*

VERONA *1D2* (1.5km N Rural) *45.44985, 11.00415* **Camping San Pietro, Via Castel San Pietro 2, 37100 Verona [tel/fax 045 592037; info@campingcastelsanpietro.com; www.campingcastelsanpietro.com]** Exit A4/E70 to San Martino-Buon-Albergo & foll S11 dir Verona cent, site sp adj Castel San Pietro. Sm, mkd pitch, hdstg, shd; wc (cont); chem disp (wc); shwrs inc; no EHU; lndry; shop; rest 500m; snacks; bar; BBQ; wifi; no dogs; some statics; bus 1km; no vehicles/o'fits over 7m; adv bkg ess; some rd noise. "Basic site in park, more suited to tents or sm m'vans only - no EHU; beautiful views over city; easy walk to town cent, but many steps; poor & ltd san facs." ♦ 2 May-30 Sep. € 41.00   2014*

⊞ **VERONA** *1D2* (1km NE Urban) *45.45150, 10.95456* **Camper Park Verona, Via Eraclea, 37100 Verona [0348 7328589; camperparkverona@libero.it]** Fr W on SR11 Corso Milano, site sp to L behind Esselunga supmkt; sp. Sm, unshd; EHU; water fill. "New m'van parking area; v conv town cent." 2012*

⊞ **VERONA** *1D2* (14.7km W Rural) *45.44557, 10.83447* **Camping El Bacàn, Via Verona 11, 37010 Palazzolo di Sona (VR) [348 9317204; fax 045 6080708; info@el-bacan.it; www.el-bacan.it]** Exit A4 onto A22 N & foll sp for Brescia (W) on SR11. Site in 7km on R, sp 150m bef site ent. Sm, hdg/mkd pitch, pt shd; wc (cont); chem disp; EHU (16A) inc; lndry; shop (farm produce); rest, snacks, bar 2km; BBQ; playgrnd; internet; TV; dogs; bus 1km; Eng spkn; adv bkg; quiet, some rd noise; cc acc; CKE/CCI. "Charming, pleasant site on working farm; conv Verona, Lake Garda; helpful, friendly owner & staff; excel farm shop; highly rec; easy access; vg." ♦ € 23.00   2015*

VIAREGGIO *1C3* (2km S Coastal) *43.85133, 10.25963* **Camping Viareggio, Via Comparini 1, 55049 Viareggio (LU) [0584 391012; fax 395462; info@campingviareggio.it; www.campingviareggio.it]** Fr sea front at Viareggio, take rd on canal sp Livorno; after x-ing canal bdge turn L (but not immed on canal) & 2nd R to site in 2km. Lge, shd; wc (some cont); chem disp; mv service pnt; baby facs; shwrs €0.50; EHU (4A) (poss rev pol); gas; lndry; shop; rest; bar; playgrnd; pool €3; beach 800m; games area; TV; internet; phone; dogs €4 (not permitted Aug); adv bkg; quiet; red LS/CKE/CCI. "Gd site & facs; hot water to shwrs only; cycle rte/footpath to town." ♦ 1 Apr-4 Oct. € 32.00   2014*

VIAREGGIO *1C3* (4km S Rural) *43.82693, 10.27182* **Camping Dei Tigli, Viale del Tigli 54, 55048 Torre-del-Lago Puccini (LU) [0584 359182; fax 341278; info@campingdeitigli.com; www.campingdeitigli.com]** Leave A11/12 at Viareggio, foll rd parallel to a'strada sp Torre-del-Lago-Puccini & after 6km turn R twd Torre. When thro town turn L at traff lts, over rlwy, L at rndabt & foll brown camp sp. V lge, hdg pitch, pt shd; wc; chem disp (wc); shwrs €0.50; EHU (5A) inc; gas; lndry; shop; rest, snacks; bar; BBQ; sand beach 1.2km; entmnt; 50% statics; dogs €6 (only small); phone; poss cr w/end; Eng spkn; adv bkg; quiet but poss disco noise high ssn; ccard acc; red long stay/ CKE/CCI. "Pleasant, friendly site; facs old but clean; sep area for tourers; cycle path to town cent." 1 Apr-30 Sep. € 35.00 (3 persons) (CChq acc)   2011*

ITALY

VIAREGGIO *1C3* (5km S Coastal) *43.82920, 10.2727* **Camping Italia, Viale dei Tigli 52, 55048 Torre-del-Lago Puccini (LU) [0584 359828; fax 341504; info@campingitalia.net; www.campingitalia.net]** Fr A12 N exit sp Viareggio, fr S exit Pisa N onto SS1 & turn twd Torre del Lago at S junc, site well sp thro vill. Do not turn L at vill cent but cont for 2km N, then L at rlwy bdge. At rndabt turn L, site on R in 250m. Avoid Viareggio town cent. Med, shd; wc (some cont); chem disp; mv service pnt; shwrs €0.50; EHU (6A) €1.30; gas; lndry (inc dryer); shop; rest, snacks; bar; lge playgrnd; pool; sand beach 1.5km; tennis; bike hire; wifi; entmnt; TV rm; some statics (sep area); no dogs Jun-Aug; sep car park; Eng spkn; adv bkg; noisy w/ends high ssn; ccard acc; red LS; "Vg for Lucca - Puccini's birthplace; bus tickets fr site for Pisa & Lucca; some pitches diff for lge o'fits due trees & low branches; gd clean facs; poss problem with mosquitoes." ♦ 16 Apr-25 Sep. € 42.50   2014*

"That's changed – Should I let The Club know?"

If you find something on site that's different from the site entry, fill in a report and let us know. See www.caravanclub.co.uk/europereport.

VIAREGGIO *1C3* (6km S Rural) *43.83105, 10.2707* **Camping Europa, Viale dei Tigli, 55048 Torre-del-Lago Puccini (LU) [0584 350707; fax 342592; info@europacamp.it; www.europacamp.it]** Exit A12/E80 at Pisa Nord exit, foll sp dir Viareggio to Torre-del-Lago & turn L. Site well sp fr vill cent. Lge, shd; wc (some cont); shwrs €0.40; EHU (3A) inc (poss rev pol); gas; lndry; shop on site & 2km; rest, snacks; bar; playgrnd; pool; paddling pool; sand beach 1km; tennis; games area; bike hire; entmnt; 50% statics; dogs €2 (not acc Jul/Aug); poss cr; Eng spkn; adv bkg; quiet; ccard acc; red long stay/CKE/CCI. "Excel, clean, tidy site in regional coastal park; facs poss stretched when site full; helpful, friendly staff; poss mosquitoes; 1km to bus to Pisa, Lucca, Florence." ♦ Easter-1 Oct. € 33.00   2011*

VICCHIO see Borgo San Lorenzo *1D3*

VICENZA *1D2* (5km E Urban) *45.5175, 11.60222* **Camping Vicenza, Strada Pelosa 239, 36100 Vicenza [0444 582311; fax 582434; info@campingvicenza.it; www.ascom.vi.it/camping]** Exit A4 Vicenza Est dir Torri di Quartesole; turn R immed after toll; site on L 300m fr Vicenza exit, hidden behind Viest Quality Inn. Fr city foll sp Padua & a'strada; sp. Med, pt sl, pt shd; wc (some cont); chem disp; mv service pnt; baby facs; shwrs inc; EHU (3A) inc (rev pol); lndry; shops 1km; rest, snacks 500m; bar; BBQ; playgrnd; tennis; bike hire; internet; entmnt; bus; Eng spkn; adv bkg; rd noise; 10% red long stay; ccard acc; red CKE/CCI. "Cycle path to interesting town; poss ant problem; functional site." ♦ ltd. 1 Apr-30 Sep. € 32.00   2013*

VICO EQUENSE see Sorrento *3A3*

VIESTE *2G4* (2km N Coastal) *41.89901, 16.14964* **Camping Punta Lunga, Loc Defensola, 71019 Vieste (FG) [0884 706031 or 0884 706032; fax 706910; puntalunga@ puntalonga.com; www.puntalunga.it]** N fr Vieste 1.5km fr end of long beach, turn R at traff lts down narr lane. Site sp. Lge, mkd pitch, pt terr, pt shd; htd wc (some cont); chem disp; mv service pnt; baby facs; shwrs inc; EHU (3-5A) inc; gas; lndry; shop; rest, snacks; playgrnd; beach adj; windsurfing; canoeing; bike hire; wifi; entmnt; TV; 15% statics (sep area); no dogs; phone; bus; sep car park; Eng spkn; adv bkg; quiet; ccard acc; red LS/CKE/CCI. "Friendly, helpful staff; well-run site on lovely cove; tight pitches - beware pitch marker posts; v clean facs; rec use bottled water; beautiful coastal area; gd rest; lovely cove; excel beaches." 30 May-15 Sep. € 49.00   2014*

VIESTE *2G4* (2km S Coastal) *41.85914, 16.17405* **Camping Adriatico, Lungomare. Enrico Mattei 110, 71019 Vieste (FG) [tel/fax 0884 700954; info@campingadriatico.it; www.campingadriatico.it]** S fr Vieste on coast rd SP53, site on both sides of rd. Med, mkd pitch, pt shd; wc (cont); chem disp; mv service pnt; shwrs inc; EHU (6A) inc; lndry; shop; rest, snacks; bar; BBQ; playgrnd; sand beach adj; windsurfing; games area; wifi; some statics; phone; bus; poss cr; Eng spkn; adv bkg; red LS. "Vg family-run site." ♦ ltd. 1 Apr-31 Oct. € 33.50   2014*

VIGNALE RIOTORTO see Follonica *1D3*

VILLANOVA D'ALBENGA see Albenga *1B2*

⊞ **VIPITENO/STERZING** *1D1* (1km S Urban) *46.88737, 11.43098* **Autoporto, 00098 Vipiteno [0472 760620; info@hotel-brenner.com]** S fr Brenner Pass approx 17km, take exit immed bef toll booths Vipiteno & foll sp 'Autoporto'. Site well sp fr toll booth - 500m. Can also be accessed fr SS12. Push button on site barrier if office clsd. Med, hdstg, pt shd; wc; mv service pnt; shwrs; EHU inc; shop, rest adj. "Excel NH for c'vans or m'vans; conv Austrian border; all facs in services." € 15.00   2015*

VIVERONE *1B2* (3km S Rural) *45.40544, 8.05313* **Camping Internazionale del Sole, Loc Comuna 45, 13886 Viverone (BI) [tel/fax 0161 98169; www.campeggiodelsole.com]** Exit A5/A4 m'way network at junc for Cavaglia/Santhia. Foll S143 to Cavaglia approx 4km. At Cavaglia join S228 for Viverone/Ivrea. Immed after Viverone town sp turn L at rndabt. After 2km site sp strt on past hotel on R, recep on L. Lge, terr, pt sl, pt shd; wc (some cont); chem disp; shwrs €1; EHU (3A) €1.50; lndry; shop; rest, snacks; bar; playgrnd; lake sw; boating & fishing in lake; games rm; 90% statics; poss cr; adv bkg; poss noisy; red CKE/CCI. "Conv Aosta Valley, National Park & mountain resorts below Matterhorn; lovely situation by lake but facs minimal for such a lge site, espec LS; NH only." 1 Apr-30 Sep. € 21.50   2010*

VIVERONE *1B2* (1km SW Rural) *45.41644, 8.04874*
Camping Rocca, Via Lungo Lago 35, 13040 Viverone (BI)
[tel/fax 0161 98416; laroccaviverone@hotmail.com;
www.la-rocca.org] On lakeside sp fr S228. Not well sp. Sm,
pt shd; wc (mainly cont); chem disp; mv service pnt; shwrs
€0.50; EHU (2A) €1.80; shop 1km; rest, snacks; bar; playgrnd;
lake sw & beach adj; 50% statics; phone; CKE/CCI. "Somewhat
tatty (06/09); NH only." ♦ 1 Apr-30 Sep. € 22.00   2011*

VOLLAN/FOIANA see Merano/Meran *1D1*

"I like to fill in the reports as I travel from site to site"

You'll find report forms at the back of this guide, or you can fill them in online at www.caravanclub.co.uk/europereport.

VOLTERRA *1D3* (1km NW Rural) *43.41271, 10.8509* **Camping
Le Balze, Via di Mandringa 15, 56048 Volterra (PI)**
[tel/fax 0588 87880; campinglebalze@hotmail.it;
www.campinglebalze.com] Take Pisa rd (S68) fr town; site
clearly sp ('Camping' or symbol) after 1km. Watch out for R
turn at sharp L corner. Med, pt sl, terr, pt shd; wc (some cont);
chem disp; shwrs inc; EHU (6A) inc; gas; lndry; shop; supmkt
300m; rest 150m; bar; pool; paddling pool; dogs free; bus
adj; poss cr; Eng spkn; no adv bkg; quiet; ccard acc; CKE/CCI.
"Beautifully situated with views of Volterra & hills; gd, modern
san facs; select own pitch; easy walk to town; Etruscan walls
just outside site; excel site." ♦ 1 Apr-15 Oct. € 38.00   2012*

ZAMBRONE see Tropea *1B4*

ELBA ISLAND

CAPOLIVERI *1C3* (3km NW Coastal) *42.75810, 10.36070*
**Camping La Calanchiole, Loc Calanchiole, 57031 Capoliveri
(LI) [0565 933488; fax 940001; info@lecalanchiole.it;**
www.lecalanchiole.it] Fr Portoferraio, take rd twd Porto
Azzuro & Marina de Campo. Then foll sp Capoliveri, site sp.
Lge, mkd pitch, pt shd; wc (some cont); chem disp; mv service
pnt; shwrs; EHU (3A) inc; lndry (inc dryer); rest, snacks; bar;
BBQ; paddling pool; private sand beach; watersports; boat &
bike hire; tennis; wifi; entmnt; some statics; adv bkg; quiet;
ccard acc. ♦ 1 Apr-31 Oct. € 53.50 (CChq acc)   2011*

SARDINIA

AGLIENTU *1C4* (6km N Coastal) *41.12701, 9.07071* **Camping
Village Saragosa, Pineta di Vignola-Mare, 07020 Aglientu
(SS) [079 602077; fax 602037; info@campingsaragosa.it;**
www.campingsaragosa.it] Take coastal rd SW fr Santa
Teresa Gallura (ferries fr Corsica) to Vignola Mare - approx
20km, site sp. Lge, shd; wc; mv service pnt; shwrs; EHU (3A)
inc; lndry; shop; rest, snacks; bar; playgrnd; sand beach adj;
games area; entmnt; 50% statics; dogs €4; phone; poss
cr; Eng spkn; adv bkg; ccard acc; red LS. "Direct access to
superb beach; some pitches adj beach." ♦ 1 May-30 Sep.
€ 37.00   2010*

ALGHERO *3A1* (1.5km N Coastal) *40.57916, 8.31222*
Camping La Mariposa, Via Lido 22, 07041 Alghero (SS)
[079 9950480; fax 984489; info@lamariposa.it;
www.lamariposa.it] N fr Alghero on coast rd dir Fertilia.
Site on L just beyond pool. Lge, pt sl, hdstg, terr, pt shd; wc;
chem disp; mv service pnt; shwrs €0.50; EHU (6-10A) €3;
gas; lndry; shop; rest, snacks; bar; BBQ; private sand beach
adj; watersports; bike hire; games rm; wifi; entmnt; TV; dogs;
20% statics; dogs; bus nr; sep car park; Eng spkn; ccard acc;
red CKE/CCI. "Lovely wooded site; gd clean facs; gd security;
friendly staff; boat fr Alghero to caves at Cape Caccia or by rd
+ 625 steps." 1 Apr-15 Oct. € 46.00   2011*

ALGHERO *3A1* (6km NW Coastal) *40.59474, 8.29088*
**Camping Calik, 07040 Fertilia (SS) [tel/fax 079 930111;
info@campeggiocalik.it; www.campeggiocalik.it]**
Fr Alghero W on coast rd, site bet rndabt & rv bdge 500m bef
Fertilia on R. Med, shd; wc; chem disp; shwrs inc; EHU (3A);
lndry; shop; rest, snacks; bar; playgrnd; sand beach 200m;
entmnt; 50% statics; dogs €3; bus at gate; poss cr; adv bkg;
ccard acc. "Well-situated by rv with easy access to beach; cycle
track to Fertilia." 15 Mar-30 Sep. € 35.50   2009*

ALGHERO *3A1* (12km NW Coastal) *40.64110, 8.18960*
**Camping Torre del Porticciolo, Loc Porticciolo, 07041
Alghero (SS) [079 919007; fax 919212; info@torredel
porticciolo.it; www.torredelporticciolo.it]**
N fr Alghero sp S127 to Capo Caccia; in 18km site sp R at
T-junc then L in 300m. V lge, shd; wc (some cont); private
san facs avail; shwrs inc; EHU (4A) inc; gas; lndry; shop; rest,
snacks; bar; BBQ; playgrnd; sand beach; pool; paddling pool;
watersports; tennis; games area; games rm; wifi; entmnt;
TV; some statics; dogs €6; quiet; adv bkg; ccard acc; CKE/
CCI. "Excel; close to Grotto di Nettuno; beautiful area."
1 May-10 Oct. € 45.00 (CChq acc)   2011*

ARBOREA *3A1* (2km NW Coastal) *39.81667, 8.55337*
**Camping Village S'Ena Arrubia, Strada Ovest 29, 09092
Arborea (OR) [tel/fax 0783 809011; info@senarrubia.it;**
www.senarrubia.it] Fr N on SS131 dir Oristano at km 94.5
foll sp Oristano-Sorgono. In 2km foll sp Oristano-Fenosu, then
Santa Giusta (Oristano-Sud) to site. Lge, mkd pitch, pt sl, shd;
wc; mv service pnt; shwrs inc; EHU €3; lntte; shop; rest, snacks;
bar; BBQ; playgrnd; pool; sand beach nr; lake sw & fishing;
watersports; tennis; bike & boat hire; games area; entmnt;
some statics; adv bkg; red snr citizens. "Wooded site; excel
touring base; gd modern san facs; cycle rtes." 10 May-30 Sep.
€ 41.00   2011*

ITALY

ITALY

ARZACHENA *1C4* (7km NW Coastal) *41.13156, 9.44064*
Camping Centro Vacanze Isuledda, 07020 Cannigione (OT)
[0789 86003; fax 86089; info@isuledda.it; www.isuledda.it]
Fr S125 foll sp Cannigione, site 3km N of Cannigione, sp on R.
V lge, mkd pitch, pt shd; wc (some cont); chem disp; mv service
pnt; shwrs; EHU (4A); lndry (inc dryer); shop; rest; bar; BBQ;
sand beach adj; watersports; boat & bike hire; fitness/beauty
rm; wifi; entmnt; TV; some statics; no dogs; adv bkg; quiet;
ccard acc. 1 Apr-30 Oct. € 54.00   2011*

⊞ **CAGLIARI** *3B1* (1km SE Urban) *39.21129, 9.12883* **Camper**
Cagliari Park, 13 Via Stanislao Caboni, 09125 Cagliari
[346 7245766 or 070 303147 or 0328 3348847 (mob);
fax 070 303147; info@campercagliaripark.it;
www.campercagliaripark.it] Well sp on main rds into
Cagliari. Sm, unshd; wc; chem disp; mv service pnt; EHU (10A)
€4; lndry nr; bus 200m; Eng spkn; CKE/CCI. "Gd secure site;
v helpful owner; walking dist historical cent, rests etc; c'vans
enquire 1st." € 21.00   2014*

CASTIADAS *3B2* (4km E Coastal) *39.24450, 9.56980*
Villaggio Camping Capo Ferrato, Via delle Ginestre, Loc
Costa Rei-Monte Nai, 09040 Castiadas (CA) [070 991012;
fax 885653; info@campingcapoferrato.it; www.camping
capoferrato.it] Fr Cagliari take coastal rd E twd Villasimius,
then N to Monte Nai, site sp. Or fr Cagliari take S125 to San
Priamo, then S to Monte Nai & site. Med, pt shd; wc; chem
disp; mv service pnt; shwrs inc; EHU (2-6A) €2.30-3.40; lndry;
shop; supmkt 500m; rest, snacks; bar; BBQ; playgrnd; sand
beach adj; windsurfing 100m; tennis; bike hire; horseriding
3km; games area; wifi; entmnt; TV; 10% statics; Eng spkn;
adv bkg; quiet; ccard acc. "Welcoming, family-run site; might
be diff for lge o'fits; Discover Sardinia theme weeks end Jun
& beg Sep; conv Capo Carborana Nature Park." 1 Apr-2 Nov.
€ 44.00   2011*

> ## "We must tell The Club about that great site we found"
> Get your site reports in by mid-August and we'll do our best to get your updates into the next edition.

CUGLIERI *3A1* (15km S Rural) *40.07083, 8.49055* **Camping**
Bella Sardinia - Village Europa, Loc Torre del Pozzo,
09073 Cuglieri (OR) [0785 38058; info@bellasardinia.it;
www.bellasardinia.it] S fr Olbia on SS131 dir Alghero, foll
sp to Caglieri on SS15, then S on SS292, site sp in 15km. Lge,
mkd pitch, pt shd; wc (some cont); chem disp; mv service pnt;
shwrs; EHU (3A); lndry; shop; rest, snacks; bar; BBQ; playgrnd;
pool; paddling pool; tennis; games area; games rm; wifi;
entmnt; TV; some statics; adv bkg; quiet; ccard acc. "Pleasant,
forested site." 9 Apr-15 Oct. € 44.00 (CChq acc)   2010*

DORGALI *3A2* (7km W Coastal) *40.28486, 9.63370* **Camping**
Villaggio Calagonone, Via Collodi 1, 08022 Cala-Gonone
(NU) [0784 93165; fax 93255; info@campingcalagonone.it;
www.campingcalagonone.it] Fr S125 turn E twd Cala
Gonone, thro tunnel. Site sp on L of main rd. Med, terr, shd;
wc; chem disp; mv service pnt; EHU (6A) €5; shop; rest, snacks;
bar; BBQ; playgrnd; pool; sand/shgl beach 400m; tennis;
games area; 30% statics; dogs €5; phone; poss cr; adv bkg;
ccard acc. "Beautiful situation in pine forest on edge of pretty
town; nrby coves & grottoes accessible by boat or on foot." ♦
1 Apr-3 Nov. € 63.00   2014*

⊞ **NARBOLIA** *3A1* (6km W Coastal) *40.06956, 8.48375*
Camping Nurapolis, Loc Is Arenas, 09070 Narbolia (OR)
[0783 52283 or 348 8080839(mob); fax 52255;
info@nurapolis.it; www.nurapolis.it] Fr Oristano take sp to
Cuglier on rd SS292i. Site sp fr rd approx 5km fr S. Caterina-di-
Pittinura. Lge, pt shd; wc; shwrs; EHU (3A) €3; gas; shop; rest,
snacks; bar; sand beach adj; tennis; entmnt; watersports; dogs;
poss cr; adv bkg; ccard acc; red CKE/CCI. "Site in pine forest;
many sports, guided walks Easter to Oct; v pleasant owners."
♦ € 26.50   2014*

ORISTANO *3A1* (5km W Coastal) *39.90388, 8.53111*
Camping Spinnaker, Via del Pontile, Marina-di-Torre
Grande, 09170 Oristano [0783 22074; fax 22071;
info@campingspinnaker.com; www.spinnakervacanze.com]
Fr Cagliari on S131 exit at Sta Giusta & foll sp Oristano &
Torre-Grande. Med, mkd pitch, pt shd; htd wc; mv service pnt;
baby facs; shwrs €0.50; EHU €3; lndry; shop; rest, snacks; bar;
BBQ; playgrnd; pool; paddling pool; beach 200m; watersports;
fishing; tennis 500m; bike & boat hire; entmnt; TV rm; some
statics; dogs €3; adv bkg; quiet. "Easy access to Sinis Peninsula
for birdwatching & Tharros archaeological site." ♦ ltd.
1 Apr-30 Sep. € 46.00 (CChq acc)   2009*

PALAU *1C4* (500m N Coastal) *41.18586, 9.37700* **Villagio**
Camping Acapulco, Loc Punta Palau 07020 Palau
[0789 709497; fax 706380; info@campingacapulco.com;
www.campingacapulco.com] Take rd S133 SE fr Sta Teresa-
Gallura (ferry fr Corsica) sp Palau/Olbia, site sp in Palau. Med,
mkd pitch, terr, some hdstg, pt shd; wc (some cont); chem
disp; shwrs inc; EHU (4A) €3; lndry (inc dryer); shop 500m; rest,
snacks; pizzeria; bar; BBQ; playgrnd; sand beach adj; boat-
launching; watersports; wifi; entmnt; TV; 30% statics; phone;
sep car park; Eng spkn; no adv bkg; ccard acc; quiet. "Superb
situation; vg Mexican rest; helpful staff; vg site." 1 Mar-31 Oct.
€ 36.00   2009*

PALAU *1C4* (400m E Coastal) *41.17916, 9.39333* **Villagio**
Camping Baia Saraceno (Part Naturist), Punta Nera, 07020
Palau (SS) [0789 709403; fax 709425; info@baiasaraceno.
com; www.baiasaraceno.com] Take rd S133 SE fr Sta Teresa-
Gallura (ferry fr Corsica) sp Palau/Olbia, site sp dir Capo d'Orso.
Lge, mkd pitch, pt shd; wc (some cont); chem disp; mv service
pnt; shwrs inc; EHU (3A) €3; gas; lndry (inc dryer); supmkt
high ssn; rest, snacks; pizzeria; bar; BBQ; playgrnd; beach adj;
watersports; boat-launching; wifi; entmnt; 25% statics; no
dogs; sep area & beach for naturists; no adv bkg; ccard acc.
"Superb situation on water's edge; helpful, friendly staff; vg
rest; site busy in ssn; ferry to La Maddalena islands; conv day
trips to Corsica." ♦ 1 Mar-31 Oct. € 40.00   2009*

ITALY

PALAU *1C4* (5km SE Coastal) *41.16116, 9.40300*
Camping Capo d'Orso, Loc Le Saline, 07020 Palau (SS) [0789 702007; fax 702006; info@capodorso.it; www.capodorso.it] Site sp on coast rd dir Arzachena. Lge, mkd pitch, pt sl, terr, shd; wc (some cont); chem disp; mv service pnt; shwrs; EHU (3A) €3; gas; lndry; shop; rest, snacks; pizzeria; bar; playgrnd; pool; private sand beach adj; boat hire; sailing & diving school; watersports; tennis; bike hire; games area; games rm; entmnt; TV; 50% statics; dogs; phone; bus (high ssn); extra for pitches adj beach high ssn; sep car park high ssn; poss cr; Eng spkn; adv bkg; quiet; CKE/CCI. "Excel family site in beautiful position; vg facs." 15 May-30 Sep. € 41.00   2009*

PORTO SAN PAOLO *3A2* (2km S Coastal) *40.85870, 9.64296*
Camping Tavolara, Loc Porto Taverna, 07020 Loiri-Porta San Paolo (SS) [0789 40166; fax 480778; info@camping-tavolara.it; www.camping-tavolara.it] On SS125, sp. Med, hdg/mkd pitch, shd; wc (mainly cont); mv service pnt; shwrs inc; EHU (3-6A) €3.50; lndry; shop & 2km; rest, snacks; bar; playgrnd; sand beach 500m; tennis; bike hire; entmnt; 50% statics; dogs €3; phone; site clsd Dec & early Jan; Eng spkn; adv bkg; ccard acc; red CKE/CCI. "Friendly staff; conv ferries & boat trips." 20 Apr-15 Oct. € 59.50   2014*

PORTO TORRES *3A1* (7km E Coastal) *40.81607, 8.48541*
Camping Golfo dell'Asinara-Cristina, Loc Platamona, 07037 Sorso (SS) [079 310230; fax 310589; info@camping asinara.it; www.campingasinara.it] Foll coast rd SP81 E fr Porto-Torres to site. Sp. Lge, pt shd; wc; mv service pnt; shwrs; EHU (4A) €4; gas; lndry; shop; rest, snacks; bar; playgrnd; pool; sand beach adj; tennis; games area; bike hire; 40% statics; no dogs; sep car park; poss cr; quiet; ccard acc; red long stay/CKE/CCI. "Gd position." ♦ 1 May-30 Sep. € 34.00   2010*

PULA *3B1* (4km Coastal) *38.95778, 8.96930* Camping Cala d'Ostia, Localita Cala d'Ostia, 09010 Pula [39 070 921470; fax 070 921471; info@campingcaladostia.com; www.campingcaladostia.com] Fr Cagliari, take SS195 past Pula. Foll the rd along the seafront about 1km, sp to site. Lge, pt shd; wc; mv service pnt; fam bthrm; shwrs; EHU (13A); bar; BBQ; beach; games rm; wifi; dogs; bus adj; twin axles; poss cr; Eng spkn; CCI. "Fair site; busy in high ssn; beautiful coastline; lovely area." ♦ ltd. Apr-Sep. € 35.00   2014*

⊞ **PULA** *3B1* (4km S Coastal) *38.96779, 8.97799*
Camping Flumendosa, Santa Margherita, Km 33.800, 09010 Pula (CA) [070 9208364; fax 9249282; info@ campingflumendosa.it; www.campingflumendosa.it] Fr Cagliari take SS195 past Pula, sp. Turn L, foll track for 500m to site ent. Med, hdstg, pt shd; wc; chem disp; mv service pnt; shwrs €0.50; EHU (3A) €3; gas; lndry; shop; rest 1km; snacks; bar; playgrnd; sand beach; boat & bike hire; windsurfing; waterskiing; canoeing; golf 4km; 20% statics; dogs €2.50; sep car park; poss cr; Eng spkn; adv bkg; quiet; ccard acc; red LS. "Beautiful coastline; excel for children; sand flies abound." ♦ € 27.00   2011*

SANT' ANTIOCO *3B1* (12km SW Coastal) *39.00691, 8.38752*
Tonnara Camping, Cala Sapone, 09017 Sant' Antioco (CA) [0781 809058; fax 809036; mail@camping-tonnara.it; www.campingtonnara.co.uk] Fr Cagliari take S130 & then S126. Site on W coast of Isola-di-S. Antiocio. Lge, hdg/mkd pitch, shd; wc; mv service pnt; shwrs; EHU (6A) inc; gas; lndry; shop; rest; bar; pool; sand/shgl beach; tennis; games area; scuba-diving school; sep car park; dogs €6; phone; bus 100m; poss cr; adv bkg; quiet; ccard acc; red LS. "Delightful, peaceful site in gd location; some narr lanes." 1 Apr-30 Sep. € 49.00   2011*

SINISCOLA *3A2* (7km E Coastal) *40.57853, 9.77306* Camping Selema, Thiria Soliana, 08029 Santa Lucia-di-Siniscola (NU) [tel/fax 0784 819068; info@selemacamping.com; www.selemacamping.com] Sp fr coast rd S125. Lge, mkd pitch, pt sl, terr, pt shd; wc; chem disp; mv service pnt; shwrs inc; EHU (6A) €4.50; lndry; shop; rest, snacks; bar; playgrnd; pool; paddling pool; sand beach adj; tennis; games area; horseriding; bike hire; wifi; 30% statics; poss cr; adv bkg; red LS; CKE/CCI. "Excel clean facs; site in pine forest; might be diff for lge o'fits if cr." 1 Apr-31 Oct. € 45.50   2011*

"I need an on-site restaurant"

We do our best to make sure site information is correct, but it is always best to check any must-have facilities are still available or will be open during your visit.

TEULADA *3B1* (7km SW Coastal) *38.92669, 8.71153*
Camping Proturismo Portu Tramatzu, 09019 Teulada (CA) [0709 283027; fax 283028; coop.proturismo@libero.it] Sp fr Teulada on SP71 & fr coast rd. Med, terr, pt shd; wc; mv service pnt; shwrs; EHU (5A) inc; gas; lndry; shop; rest, snacks, bar high ssn; BBQ; playgrnd; sand beach adj; games area; entmnt; some statics; dogs €3; sep car park high ssn; Eng spkn; adv bkg; red CKE/CCI. "Vg." ♦ Easter-31 Oct. € 33.00   2010*

TORTOLI *3A2* (5km E Coastal) *39.90810, 9.67830* Camping Orri, Loc Orri, 08048 Tortoli (NU) [0782 624695; fax 624685; camping.orri@tiscali.it; www.campingorri.it] E fr Tortoli to Arbatax, site sp along coast rd. Med, shd; wc (some cont); chem disp; mv service pnt; shwrs inc; EHU (4A) €2.50; lndry; shop; rest, snacks; bar; BBQ; playgrnd; pool; paddling pool; sand beach adj; lake fishing; bike hire; games area; horseriding 1km; entmnt; TV rm; statics; dogs; adv bkg; quiet; red CKE/CCI. "Eng spkn." ♦ 1 May-20 Sep. € 42.00   2011*

VALLEDORIA *1B4* (1km W Coastal) *40.93333, 8.81694*
Camping La Foce, Via Ampurias 1, 07039 Valledoria (SS) [079 582109; fax 582191; info@foce.it; www.foce.it] Fr Porto Torres N via Castelsardo to Valledoria, site sp twd sea. Lge, shd; wc (some cont); chem disp; mv service pnt; shwrs inc; EHU (4A) €1.50; gas; lndry (inc dryer); shop; rest, snacks; bar; no BBQ; playgrnd; pool; paddling pool; sand beach adj; fishing; canoeing; watersports; tennis; bike hire; games aea; wifi; 10% statics; dogs €3; sep car park; poss cr; adv bkg; ccard acc. 25 Apr-30 Sep. € 35.00 (CChq acc)   2011*

SICILY

⊞ **ACIREALE** *3C4* (1.5km NE Coastal) *37.62015, 15.17320* **La Timpa International Camping, Via Santa Maria La Scala, 25 -Cap 95024 Acireale (CT) [095 7648155; fax 7640049; info@campinglatimpa.com; www.campinglatimpa.com]** Exit A18/E45 onto rd S114 dir Acireale. Foll sp for Santa Maria La Scala; site on L after 1.5km; steep & diff access rds. Med, pt shd; wc; shwrs free; EHU (6A) €3.50; lndry; shop high ssn; rest, snacks; bar; playgrnd; beach adj; 60% statics; dogs €4 (not acc Jul/Aug); sep car park; poss noisy; ccard acc; red CKE/CCI. "Site in orchard, surfaced in black volcanic ash; hot & cold shwrs; chem displ; trips to Etna; lift down to rocky beach; sh, steep walk to vill & harbour." ♦ € 25.50   2013*

⊞ **AGRIGENTO** *3C3* (4km SE Coastal) *37.24395, 13.61423* **Camping Internazionale Nettuno, Via Lacco Ameno 3, San Leone, 92100 Agrigento [tel/fax 0922 416268 or 0922 416983; info@campingnettuno.com; www.camping nettuno.com]** Fr Agrigento to San Leone on SS115, foll rd SE out of San Leone alongside beach until sharp L away fr beach. Turn immed R into lane, site on R. Med, hdg pitch, hdstg, terr, pt shd; wc (some cont); chem disp; mv service pnt; shwrs inc; EHU (6A) €2.50 (rev pol); gas; lndry; shop; rest, snacks; bar; BBQ; sand beach adj; wifi; entmnt; TV rm; 15% statics; dogs free; phone; poss cr; adv bkg; ccard acc; red long stay/CKE/CCI. "Bus to temples at Agrigento; peaceful, unspoilt beach; steep slope to pitches - towed c'vans rec to keep to upper levels if poss; gd rest; take care low branches." ♦ ltd. € 27.00   2013*

"Satellite navigation makes touring much easier"

Remember most sat navs don't know if you're towing or in a larger vehicle – always use yours alongside maps and site directions.

⊞ **AGRIGENTO** *3C3* (8km S Coastal/Urban) *37.26936, 13.58299* **Camping Valle dei Templi, Viale Emporium, 92110 San Leone [tel/fax 0922 411115; info@campingvelle deitempli.com; www.campingvalledeitempli.com]** Sp S of Agrigento, foll sp San Leone, site on L bef beach. Lge, some hdstg, pt sl, terr, pt shd; wc; chem disp; mv service pnt; shwrs inc; EHU (6A) €3; lndry; shop adj; rest, snacks; bar; beach 800m; tennis; bike hire; 20% statics; dogs; phone adj; bus; site clsd 8 Dec-15 Jan; poss cr; Eng spkn; adv bkg; ccard acc; red long stay/CKE/CCI. "Gd modern facs; no potable water on site; bus to temples fr site ent." ♦ € 26.50   2009*

⊞ **AVOLA** *3C4* (4km N Coastal) *36.93631, 15.17462* **Camping Sabbiadoro, Via Chiusa di Carlo 45, 96012 Avola (SR) [tel/fax 0931 822415; info@campeggiosabbiadoro.com; www.campeggiosabbiadoro.com]** Fr N exit A18/E45 at Cassibile onto S115 dir Avola, site sp in 4km. Last 500m on narr, winding rd. Med, mkd pitch, terr, pt sl, shd; wc; chem disp; mv service pnt; shwrs €0.50; EHU (2A) €4; lndry; shop & 2km; snacks; bar; dir access to sand beach; horseriding; wifi; 20% statics; dogs; phone; sep car park Jul-Aug; adv bkg; quiet; ccard acc. "V attractive site with clean, ltd facs; rec visit Noto; well run; poss muddy pitches after heavy rain." € 59.00   2014*

⊞ **BRUCOLI** *3C4* (E Coastal) *37.28191, 15.18941* **Camping Baia del Silenzio, Campolato Basso, 96010 Brucoli (SR) [0931 981881; fax 982288; www.baiadelsilenzio.net]** Sp fr Brucoli stn level x-ing, E of rd SS114. Lge, mkd pitch, pt sl, shd; wc (some cont); chem disp; mv service pnt; shwrs inc; EHU (2A) €8; lndry; shop; rest, snacks; bar; sm sandy/rocky beach adj; tennis; 20% statics; dogs €5 (not acc Jul/Aug); phone; sep car park high ssn; adv bkg; poss noisy; ccard acc; red LS; CKE/CCI. "Clean, well-maintained site with gd facs; conv Siracusa, Catania & Mt Etna." ♦ ltd. € 43.00   2009*

CAPO D'ORLANDO *3B3* (1km W Coastal) *38.12866, 14.70936* **Camping Santa Rosa, Via Trazzera Marina 761, 98071 Capo-d'Orlando (ME) [0941 901723; info@camping santarosa.com; http://campingsantarosa.it]** Fr S113 fr Palermo in Capo d'Orlando cross over rlwy line at level x-ing or carry on to end of town & acc 'lungomare' at E end. Site well sp. Med, hdg pitch, pt shd; wc; chem disp; mv service pnt; shwrs inc; EHU (6A) €3; lndry rm; shop; rest; bar; playgrnd; pool; sand/shgl beach adj; TV rm; 20% statics; phone; poss cr; rec CKE/CCI. "Pleasant, friendly, simple site." 15 Jun-15 Sep. € 27.50   2010*

CASTELLAMMARE DEL GOLFO *3C3* (1km E Coastal) *38.02393, 12.89348* **Nausicaa Camping, C/da Spiaggia-Plaia, Loc Forgia, 91014 Castellammare-del-Golfo (TP) [0924 33030; fax 35173; info@nausicaa-camping.it; www.nausicaa-camping.it]** Site 1km E fr Castellammare on R of rte 187. Well sp. Awkward ent for lge o'fits as steep ramp. Sm, mkd pitch, hdstg, pt shd; wc; chem disp; shwrs inc; EHU €3; gas; lndry rm; shop; rest 100m; snacks; playgrnd; sand beach adj; tennis; some statics; quiet; ccard acc; CKE/CCI. "Nr Roman temple at Segesta; gd 1st stop fr Palermo if touring historical sites." 1 Mar-31 Oct. € 42.00   2009*

CASTELLAMMARE DEL GOLFO *3C3* (4.5km NW Coastal) *38.05596, 12.83868* **Camping Baia di Guidaloca, Corso Garibaldi, 91014 Scopello (TP) [tel/fax 0924 541262 or 0924 32359 or 339 1581927 l/s; giovannitod@libero.it; www.campinguidaloca.com]** Fr SS187 foll sp bet km 34 & 33 dir Scopello, site sp on L. Med, pt shd; wc; chem disp; shwrs inc; EHU (3A) €2.50; shop 2km; rest 2km; snacks; bar; sand beach adj; 10% statics; phone; dogs leashed; bus; sep car park high ssn; poss cr; adv bkg; quiet; CKE/CCI. "Conv Zingaro nature reserve - v beautiful; vg." 1 Apr-30 Sep. € 27.00   2013*

⊞ **CASTELVETRANO** *3C3* (12km SE Rural) *37.59764, 12.84269* **Camping Maggiolino, Contrada Garroffo, 91022 Marinella di Selinunte (TP) [tel/fax 0924 46044; info@campingmaggiolino. it; www.campingmaggiolino.it]** Exit SS115 (Castelvetrano-Sciacca) at sp to Selinunte, site on L bef Selinunte. Sm, pt shd, hdstg; wc; shwrs; EHU (3A) €2; shop 1km; lndry; snacks; bar; playgrnd; sand beach 1.5km; tennis; bike hire; dogs; Eng spkn; quiet; ccard acc; red CKE/CCI. "Ideal for Greek city of Selinunte, temples, etc; not suitable lge o'fits." ♦ € 21.00   2009*

⊞ **CASTELVETRANO** *3C3* (13km SE Coastal) *37.59571, 12.84139*
**Camping Athena, Loc Marinella, Contrada Garraffo, 91022
Castelvetrano (TP) [tel/fax 0924 46132; info@campingathena
selinunte.it; www.campingathenaselinunte.it]**
Exit SS115 (Castelvetrano-Sciacca) at sp to Selinunte, site on
L bef Selinunte. Sm, some hdstg, pt shd; wc; mv service pnt;
shwrs inc; EHU (10A) inc; lndry; shop 1km; rest, snacks; bar;
BBQ; sand beach 800m; dogs; phone; ccard acc; red CKE/CCI.
"Can take lger o'fits than Maggiolino site; conv temples at
Selinunte; excel facs; gd rest adj." € 18.00   2012*

CEFALU *3B3* (3km W Coastal) *38.02703, 13.98283* **Camping
Costa Ponente, C de Ogliastrillo, 90015 Cefalù (PA)
[0921 420085; fax 424492]** Fr Palermo E twd Cefalù, on rd
SS113 at km stone 190.3, site sp. Lge, hdstg, terr, shd; wc
(some cont); chem disp; shwrs; EHU rev pol (3A) €5; gas; lndry
rm; shop & 4km; rest high ssn; snacks; bar; pool; paddling
pool; sand beach (down steep steps); tennis; 10% statics;
dogs €3.50 (not acc Aug); bus nr; sep car park (high ssn); poss
cr; no adv bkg; poss noisy; ccard acc; 5% red CKE/CCI. ♦
1 Apr-31 Oct. € 30.00   2012*

CEFALU *3B3* (3km W Rural) *38.02700, 13.98247*
**Camping Sanfilippo, Ogliastrillo SS113, 90015 Cefalù
[tel/fax 0921 420 184; info@campingsanfilippo.com;
www.campingsanfilippo.com]** Fr Palermo E twds Cafalu
on rd SS113. Med, mkd pitch, hdstg, terr, shd; wc; chem
disp; mv service pnt; shwrs; EHU (4A) inc; lndry; shop; snacks;
BBQ; playgrnd; beach 150m; games area; games rm; wifi;
50% statics; dogs €3.50; bus 300m; twin axles; poss cr;
Eng spkn; adv bkg; quiet; no ccard acc; CCI. "Vg site." ♦
1 Apr-31 Oct. € 42.50   2014*

⊞ **DONNALUCATA** *3C3* (3km SE Rural/Coastal) *36.74767,
14.66314* **Camping Club Piccadilly, Via Mare Adriatico,
Contrada da Spinasanta, 97010 Donnalucata (RG) [tel/fax
0932 938704; info@club-piccadilly.it; www.club-piccadilly.
it]** Site sp fr coast rd bet Donnalucata & Cava d'Aliga. Med,
mkd pitch, hdstg, pt shd; wc; chem disp; mv service pnt; shwrs
€1; EHU (6A) €4; gas 2km; lndry; shop 2km; rest, snacks, 2km
bar; playgrnd; htd, covrd pool 15km; sand beach adj; internet;
TV rm; dogs €2; poss cr; Eng spkn; adv bkg; red long stay; CKE/
CCI. "Gd touring base; excursions to Malta high ssn; v friendly
owner sells own wine; lovely quiet seaside site; strongly rec;
poss cr in Aug." ♦ € 33.00   2014*

⊞ **FINALE** *3B3* (500m W Coastal) *38.02305, 14.15388*
**Camping Rais Gerbi, di Triscele Tu.Rist Srl - Finale di
Pollina (PA) S.S.113 Km. 172,9 [0921 426570; fax 426577;
camping@raisgerbi.it; www.raisgerbi.it]**
Direct access fr SS113 immed after bdge W of Finale. Lge, hdg/
mkd pitch, mainly hdstg, terr, pt shd; wc; chem disp; mv service
pnt; shwrs inc; EHU (6A) €5.; lndry; shop; rest, snacks; bar;
BBQ; playgrnd; pool; private shgl beach 600m; tennis; games
area; bike hire; horseriding 200m; internet; internet; TV rm;
13% statics; dogs free; phone; bus; poss cr; Eng spkn; adv bkg
(min 10 day stay); quiet but some rlwy noise; ccard acc; red
long stay/CKE/CCI. "Gd touring base Cefalu & N coast; friendly,
helpful staff; excel, clean site & facs." ♦ € 41.00   2013*

MAZARA DEL VALLO *3C3* (1km E Coastal) *37.63630, 12.61722*
**Sporting Club Camping, Contrada da Bocca Arena,
91026 Mazara-del-Vallo (TP) [tel/fax 0923 947230; info@
sportingcampingvillage.com; www.sportingclubvillage.com]**
Site 1km fr S115, clearly sp (brown) fr all dirs. Lge, pt shd; wc
(some cont); chem disp; mv service pnt; shwrs inc; EHU (6A)
€5; lndry; shop; rest, snacks; bar; BBQ; playgrnd; pool; beach
500m; tennis; games area; games rm; entmnt; 5% statics;
dogs; bus 500m; dogs €4; poss cr; Eng spkn; red long stay/
LS; ccard acc; CKE/CCI. "Interesting area." ♦ 1 Apr-1 Oct.
€ 32.00   2009*

⊞ **MENFI** *3C3* (6km S Coastal) *37.56500, 12.96416* **Camping
La Palma, Contrada Fiore, Via delle Palme 29, 92013 Menfi
(AG) [tel/fax 0925 78392; campinglapalma@libero.it;
www.campinglapalma.com]** Foll sp fr SS115 past Menfi
to coast. Med, shd; hdstg; wc; chem disp; shwrs; EHU €4.50;
EHU 16 A; gas; lndry; rest, snacks; bar; shop; bbq; playgrnd;
sand beach adj; quiet; entmnt; wifi; tv; 10% statics; dogs;
bus 1.5km; twin axles; poss cr; eng spkn; adv bkg; CKE/CCI.
"Lovely, unspoilt quiet beach (blue flag) with dunes; v helpful
owner & staff; family run site; excel." ♦ ltd. € 29.50   2014*

MESSINA *3B4* (12km W Coastal) *38.25920, 15.46779*
**Camping Il Peloritano, Contrada Tarantonia, Km
28, 98161 Rodia-Messina (ME) [tel/fax 090 348496;
il_peloritano@yahoo.it; www.peloritanocamping.it]**
Fr Messina on A20 take exit Villafranca. Turn R onto rd S113
dir Rodia, site 2km on R. Fr Palermo exit sp Rometta, under
m'way & turn R, site on R in approx 5km. Med, mkd pitch,
pt sl, pt shd; htd wc; chem disp; mv service pnt; shwrs €0.50;
EHU (6A) €4; gas; lndry; shop; rest, snacks; bar; playgrnd; htd,
covrd pool; sand beach; wifi; entmnt; excursions; dogs; phone;
bus; poss cr; Eng spkn; adv bkg; quiet; red long stay/CKE/CCI.
"Local bus to Messina; site in olive grove; low trees & tight ent
poss diff lge o'fits; old but clean san facs; conv Messina ferry;
vg." ♦ 1 Mar-31 Oct. € 27.00   2009*

⊞ **MILAZZO** *3B4* (2km N Coastal) *38.26090, 15.24335*
**Camping Villaggio Riva Smeralda, Strada Panoramica 64,
98057 Milazzo (ME) [090 9282980; fax 9287791;
info@rivasmeralda.it; www.rivasmeralda.it]** Clearly sp in
Milazzo; foll sp Capo-di-Milazzo. Diff app. Med, hdstg, pt sl,
terr, shd; wc; chem disp; mv service pnt; shwrs; EHU (6A) €3;
lndry rm; shop; rest, snacks; bar; BBQ; playgrnd; paddling pool;
rocky beach adj; entmnt; 5% statics; poss cr; Eng spkn; adv
bkg; twin axles acc; poss noisy; CKE/CCI. "Gd base for trips
to adj isles; site a bit run down; 1 in 5 sl access to pitches, ltd
turning space; best for sm m'vans; diving cent on site; excel;
v nice site with beautiful views of sea; pitches tight; extremely
helpful owners; €3 a night to leave camper to go to Aeolian
Islands." ♦ € 43.50   2014*

MILAZZO *3B4* (4km N Coastal) *38.26222, 15.24387* **Villaggio
Turistico Cirucco, Strada Panoramica 66, Capo di Milazzo,
98057 Milazzo (ME) [090 9284746; fax 9287384;
info@cirucco.it; www.cirucco.it]** Foll Capo di Milazzo sp
fr Milazzo, site sp adj Camping Riva Smeralda. Diff, narr app.
Med, hdstg, pt sl, terr, pt shd; wc; chem disp; mv service pnt;
shwrs inc; EHU (6A); shop; rest, snacks; bar; playgrnd; private
shgl beach 100m; internet; entmnt; 30% statics; sep car park
high ssn; poss cr; Eng spkn; red long stay. "Insufficient san
facs; private beach down steps; barrier clsd 1400-1600; gd
base Stromboli." 1 Apr-31 Oct. € 35.00   2009*

ITALY

⊞ **NICOLOSI** *3C3* (1km N Rural) *37.62303, 15.00854*
Camping Etna, Via Goethe s/n, Monti Rossi, 95030 Nicolosi (CT) [tel/fax 095 914309; campingetna@tiscali.it]
Fr Nicolosi on SP92 foll sp Etna Sud, turn L just bef Titanic rest. Site on L in pinewood, sp. Med, mkd pitch, terr, shd; wc; chem disp; mv service pnt; EHU (6A) inc; lndry; shop 1km; rest 500m; snacks; bar; BBQ; playgrnd; pool; paddling pool; entmnt; TV rm; 50% statics; dogs; poss cr; Eng spkn; poss noisy; CKE/CCI. "Gd, modern san facs; friendly staff; v conv Etna." ♦ ltd. € 23.00   2010*

⊞ **OLIVERI** *3B4* (1.5km N Coastal) *38.12913, 15.05813*
Camping Villaggio Marinello, Via del Sole, 17 Contrada Marinello, 98060 Oliveri (ME) [0941 313000 or 0941 526038; fax 313702; marinello@camping.it or villaggiomarinell@gmail.com; www.camping.it/sicilia/marinello or www.villaggiomarinello.it] Exit A20 Falcone dir Oliveri, site well sp. Lge, hdg/mkd pitch, hdstg, pt shd; wc; chem disp; mv service pnt; shwrs inc; EHU (6A) inc; lndry; shop; rest high ssn; snacks bar; playgrnd; sand/shgl beach adj; watersports; tennis; excursions; 20% statics; dogs free (not acc Jul/Aug); phone; train; poss cr; Eng spkn; quiet but some rlwy noise; red CKE/CCI. "Basic, clean, well-managed site; excel but shelving beach; helpful staff." ♦ € 46.00   2013*

PALERMO *3B3* (12km NW Coastal) *38.19686, 13.24455*
Camping La Playa, Viale Marino 55 - 90040 Isola delle Femmine (PA) [tel/fax 091 8677001; campinglaplaya@virgilio.it; www.laplayacamping.it] On Palermo-Trapani rd take A29 exit Isola-delle-Femmine & foll sp. Med, hdstg, pt shd; wc; chem disp; mv service pnt; shwrs €0.50; EHU (6A) inc; gas; lndry (inc dryer); shop; rest, snacks; bar; BBQ; playgrnd; sand beach adj; dogs; Eng spkn; adv bkg; quiet; ccard acc; red CKE/CCI. "V helpful staff; bus into Palermo hourly; barrier clsd 1400-1600; v clean, well-managed, busy site; manager well versed on local info." 21 Mar-15 Oct. € 47.00   2013*

> **"There aren't many sites open at this time of year"**
> If you're travelling outside peak season remember to call ahead to check site opening dates – even if the entry says 'open all year'.

⊞ **PIAZZA ARMERINA** *3C3* (4km SE Rural) *37.20239, 14.23155* **Camping Agriturismo Agricasale, C da Ciavarini, 94015 Piazza-Armerina (EN) [tel/fax 0935 686034; www.agricasale.it]** In Piazza-Armerina town foll sp twd Mirabella but at rndabt with stone cross bear R (red fox sign) & foll red fox down nar rd to wooded site. Park with care. Sm, pt sl, pt shd; wc; chem disp; mv service pnt; shwrs inc; EHU (4A) inc; lndry; shop 4km; rest; bar; BBQ; playgrnd; pool; TV rm; dogs; poss cr; Eng spkn; adv bkg; quiet; CKE/CCI. "Excel site close Palazzo Romana mosaics; pony-trekking, archery & other activities high ssn; all inc rate of €50 avail per day inc excel banquet; site run down." ♦ € 15.00   2014*

⊞ **PUNTA BRACCETTO** *3C3* (Coastal/Urban) *36.81722, 14.46583* **Camping Luminoso, Viale dei Canalotti, 97017 Punta Braccetto - Santa Croce Camerina (RG) [0932 918401; fax 918455; info@campingluminoso.com; www.campingluminoso.com]** W fr Marina di Ragusa on SP80/SC25 coast rd. Site sp. Med, mkd pitch, hdstg, shd; wc; chem disp; mv service pnt; private bathrms avail; shwrs; EHU (6A) €5; lndry; shop & 400m; rest, snacks; bar; direct access to private sand beach adj; bike hire; wifi; child entmnt; TV; dogs free; adv bkg rec high ssn; ccard acc; red LS/CKE/CCI. "Well-run site in gd location; easy access to pitches - suitable lge o'fits/m'vans; excel; modern, immac facs; spacious level hdstg pitches; reliable wifi; helpful English manager; direct access to sandy beach; mob shops call daily; ideal long stay in winter." ♦ ltd. € 61.00 (CChq acc)   2014*

⊞ **PUNTA BRACCETTO** *3C3* (Coastal/Urban) *36.81713, 14.46736* **Camping Scarabeo, Via dei Canaletti 120, Punta-Braccetto, 97017 Santa Croce Camerina (RG) [0932 918096; fax 918391; info@scarabeocamping.it; www.scarabeocamping.it]** W fr Marina di Ragusa on SP80/SC25 coast rd. Site sp. Sm, mkd pitch, hdstg, pt sl, pt shd; wc; chem disp; mv service pnt; private bthrm €4; shwrs €0.60; EHU (3-6A) €3.50-4.50; lndry (inc dryer); shop & 4km; rest, snacks 600m, bar nr; BBQ; direct access to sand beach adj; wifi; child entmnt; 5% statics; dogs €2.50; phone; poss cr; Eng spkn; adv bkg; quiet; red long stay; CKE/CCI. "Beautiful situation; well-maintained, friendly, family-run site; gd, clean, modern facs; vg security; friendly, helpful staff; excel." ♦ € 37.50   2011*

⊞ **PUNTA BRACCETTO** *3C3* (4km SW Coastal) *36.81661, 14.46895* **Camping Baia Dei Coralli, Punta Braccetto, 97017 Santa Croce Camerina [0932 91 81 92; fax 91 82 82; info@baiadeicoralli.it; www.baiadeicoralli.it]** Fr Agrigento take SS115 twds Sircusa to Gela. Turn L onto SP14, cont onto SP13. At rndabt take 3rd exit onto SP20, R onto SP85, L twd Strada Regionale 25. R onto Strada Regionale 24. Campsite on L. Lge, hdg pitch, hdstg, unshd; wc; chem disp; mv service pnt; shwrs inc; EHU (6A); lndry; rest; snacks; bar; BBQ; playgrnd; pool; sand beach; entmnt; wifi; tv rm; dogs; bus; twin axles; Eng spkn; adv bkg; quiet; ccard acc; red LS; CCI. "Excel site; v busy in summer." ♦ € 30.00   2014*

⊞ **SAN VITO LO CAPO** *3B3* (1km E Coastal) *38.17395, 12.74795* **Camping La Pineta, Via del Secco 88, 91010 San Vito-lo-Capo (TP) [0923 972818; fax 974070; info@campinglapineta.it; www.campinglapineta.it]** Foll sp fr town. Lge, mkd pitch, hdstg, pt sl, shd; htd wc; chem disp; mv service pnt; shwrs €0.50; EHU (6A) €5; lndry; shop; rest; bar; BBQ; playgrnd; pool; paddling pool; sand beach 1km; bike hire; games area; wifi; entmnt; 30% statics; phone; site clsd Nov; Eng spkn; ccard acc; red LS/CKE/CCI. "Gd, clean site; easy walk to vill." ♦ € 38.00 (CChq acc)   2009*

⊞ **SAN VITO LO CAPO** *3B3* (3km S Coastal) *38.15067, 12.73184* **El Bahira Camping Village, Contrada Salinella, 91010 San Vito-lo-Capo (TP) [0923 972577; fax 972552; info@elbahira.it; www.elbahira.it]** W fr Palermo on A29 dir Trapani. Exit at Castellammare del Golfo onto SS187, then turn N onto SP16 sp San Vito-lo-Capo. At Isolidda foll site sp. Lge, mkd pitch, shd; wc (some cont); chem disp; EHU (6A) inc; lndry; shops; rest, snacks; bar; pizzeria; BBQ; playgrnd; pool (sw caps req); paddling pool; sand/shgl beach adj; watersports; tennis; games area; games rm; entmnt; excursions; TV; some statics; phone; bus nr; sep car park; Eng spkn; ccard acc; quiet; CKE/CCI. "Excel, secure site in vg location; gd facs for families; san facs tired need updating (2014)." ◆ € 55.40   2014*

⊞ **SECCAGRANDE** *3C3* (Coastal) *37.43833, 13.2450* **Kamemi Camping Village, Contrada Camemi Superiore, 92016 Seccagrande-di-Ribera (AG) [tel/fax 0925 69212; info@kamemicamping.it; www.kamemicamping.it]** Foll sp fr S115 to Seccagrande & site. Med, hdstg, pt shd; wc; shwrs inc; EHU (6A) €5; lndry; rest, snacks; bar; 2 pools; sand beach 1km; tennis; games area; entmnt; 40% statics; dogs free; sep car park high ssn; Eng spkn; adv bkg. ◆ € 57.00 (CChq acc)   2014*

SFERRACAVALLO see Palermo *3B3*

⊞ **SIRACUSA** *3C4* (4km SW Rural) *37.03841, 15.25063* **Camping Agritourist Rinaura, Strada Laganelli, Loc Rinaura, SS115, 96100 Siracusa [tel/fax 0931 721224; marinas@sistenia.it]** S fr Siracusa on S115 twd Avola. Turn R 300m past Hotel Albatros then immed R after rlwy x-ing. Narr lane to site in 300m. Lge, pt shd; wc; chem disp (wc); shwrs €0.60; EHU (16A) €3; shop high ssn; rest 2km; bar; playgrnd; sand beach 2km; bike hire; phone; bus 1km; poss cr; Eng spkn; adv bkg; noise fr nrby hol camp; red long stay/CKE/CCI. "CL-type site in lge orchard; basic but adequate san facs; rather neglected LS; helpful owners." ◆ € 27.00   2014*

⊞ **TAORMINA** *3C4* (10km NE Coastal) *37.93159, 15.35560* **Camping La Focetta Sicula, Via Torrente Agro, 98030 Sant' Alessio Siculo (ME) [0942 751657; fax 756708; info@lafocetta.it; www.lafocetta.it]** A'strada fr Messina to Catania, exit Roccalumera. SS114 thro Sta Teresa-di-Riva to vill of Sant' Alessio-Siculo. Sp at beg of vill. NB Many towns poorly sp. Med, mkd pitch, pt shd; wc; mv service pnt; chem disp; shwrs €0.50; EHU (3A) €3 gas; lndry; shop; rest, snacks; bar; playgrnd; sand beach; games area; bike hire; wifi; entmnt; dogs free; sep car park; poss cr; quiet; red long stay/LS/CKE/CCI. "Popular winter site; v helpful owner." € 36.50   2014*

TAORMINA *3C4* (12km S Coastal) *37.74928, 15.20616* **Camping Mokambo, Via Spiaggia 211, Fondachello, 95016 Máscali (CT) [095 938731; fax 934369; info@camping mokambo.it; www.campingmokambo.it]** Exit A18/E45 at Fiumefreddo & take S114 sp Catania. In Máscali turn L twd Fondachello. At Fondachello turn R & foll site sp, site 1km on R. Med, pt shd; wc; chem disp; shwrs €0.50; EHU (3A) €2.80; rest, snacks; BBQ; playgrnd; beach adj; games area; wifi; 10% statics; no dogs Jul/Aug; Eng spkn; quiet; ccard acc; red CKE/CCI. "V pleasant site, gd views Etna; conv beach & Taormina." ◆ 1 Apr-30 Sep. € 25.00   2009*

⊞ **TAORMINA** *3C4* (7km SW Coastal) *37.8047, 15.2444* **Camping Internazionale Almoetia, Via San Marco 19, 95011 Calatabiano (CT) [tel/fax 095 641936; info@campingalmoetia.it; www.campingalmoetia.it]** Exit a'strada dir Giardini Naxos. Turn S onto S114 dir Catania, foll sp L onto Via San Marco, site clearly sp. Med, pt shd; wc (some cont); chem disp; shwrs inc; EHU (6A) €2.50; gas; lndry; shop & 1.5km; rest, snacks; bar; BBQ; shgl beach 500m; bike hire; tennis; canoeing; TV rm; dogs; phone; poss cr; adv bkg; quiet but noise fr bar in eve; red LS/long stay; CKE/CCI. "Conv Etna, Taormina; surrounded by orchards; used by tour groups in motor hotels; site well kept; excel facs; lovely beach nrby." ◆ ltd. € 27.00   2012*

Legend

- France and Andorra
- Central and South East Europe, Benelux and Scandinavia
- Spain and Portugal

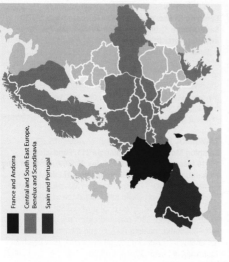

Milano (Milan) to Venezia (Venice) = 274km

Distance chart (distances in km). Origin cities are listed across the top/bottom; destination cities down the diagonal.

Cities (both axes): Ancona, Aosta, Bari, Bologna, Bolzano, Brindisi, Como, Cortina d'Ampezzo, Desenzano del Garda, Firenze (Florence), Foggia, Genova (Genoa), Grosseto, Imperia, L'Aquila, La Spezia, Livorno, Messina, Milano (Milan), Napoli (Naples), Otbetello, Palermo, Parma, Perugia, Pescara, Piacenza, Pisa, Ravenna, Reggio di Calabria, Roma (Rome), Salerno, Siena, Siracusa (Syracuse), Taranto, Torino (Turin), Trento, Trieste, Venezia (Venice), Verona, Vicenza.

Selected readable values from the chart (origin → destination, km):

Origin (Ancona)	km
Ancona – Aosta	619
Ancona – Bari	467
Ancona – Bologna	220
Ancona – Bolzano	573
Ancona – Brindisi	475
Ancona – Como	529
Ancona – Cortina d'Ampezzo	385
Ancona – Desenzano del Garda	262
Ancona – Firenze	343
Ancona – Foggia	508
Ancona – Genova	324
Ancona – Grosseto	622
Ancona – Milano	411
Ancona – Napoli	308
Ancona – Roma	286
Ancona – Venezia	364
Ancona – Verona	354
Ancona – Vicenza	360

Top-right cluster (readable):

Pair	km
Verona – Vicenza	52
Venezia – Vicenza	73
Venezia – Verona	115
Trieste – Vicenza	213
Trieste – Verona	253
Trento – Vicenza	144
Trento – Verona	103
Torino – Verona	292
Torino – Vicenza	342
Milano – Venezia	274

ABRUZZO

Chieti
L'Aquila
Pescara
Teramo

BASILICATA

Matera
Potenza

CALABRIA

Catanzaro
Cosenza
Crotone
Reggio di Calabria
Vibo Valentia

CAMPANIA

Avellino
Benevento
Caserta
Napoli
Salerno

EMILIA-ROMAGNA

Bologna
Ferrara
Forli
Modena
Parma
Piacenza
Ravenna
Reggio Emilia
Rimini

FRIULI-VENEZIA GIULIA

Gorizia
Pordenone
Trieste
Udine

LAZIO

Frosinone
Latina
Rieti
Roma
Viterbo

LIGURIA

Genova
Imperia
La Spezia
Savona

LOMBARDIA

Bergamo
Brescia
Como
Cremona
Lecco
Lodi
Mantova
Milano
Pavia
Sondrio
Varese

MARCHE

Ancona
Ascoli Piceno
Macerata
Pesaro e Urbino

MOLISE

Campobasso
Isernia

PIEMONTE

Alessandria
Asti
Biella
Cuneo
Novara
Torino
Verbano-Cusio-Ossola
Vercelli

PUGLIA

Bari
Brindisi
Foggia
Lecce
Taranto

SARDEGNA

Cagliari
Nuoro
Oristano
Sassari

SICILIA

Agrigento
Caltanissetta
Catania
Enna
Messina
Palermo
Ragusa
Siracusa
Trapani

TOSCANA

Arezzo
Firenze
Grosseto
Livorno
Lucca
Massa Carrara
Pisa
Pistoia
Prato
Siena

TRENTINO-ALTO ADIGE

Bolzano
Trento

UMBRIA

Perugia
Terni

VALLE D'AOSTA

Aosta/Aoste

VENETO

Belluno
Padova
Rovigo
Treviso
Venezia
Verona
Vicenza

419

Map I

Map 2

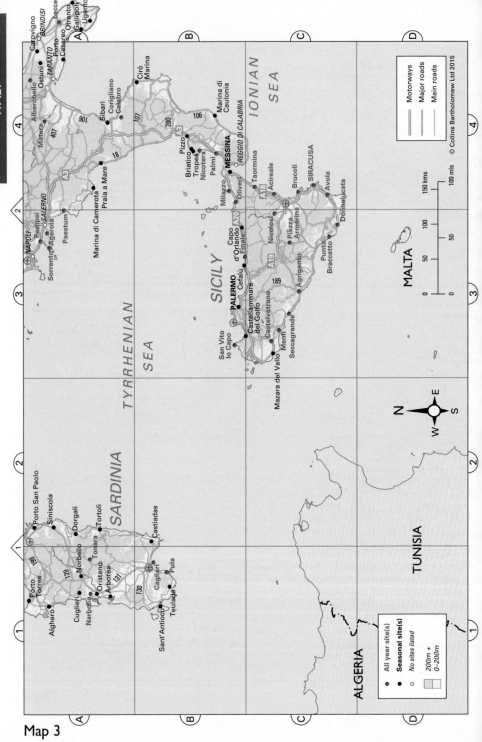

ITALY

Map 3

422

Luxembourg
Country Introduction

Vianden Castle, Luxembourg

Welcome to Luxembourg

Although a tiny country just over 50 miles long, Luxembourg is one of the world's economic powerhouses. Luxembourg City is famous for its stunning, medieval old town and for the number of notable museums and galleries that it boasts.

Most of the country is rural, and the landscape varies from the micro-gorges of Müllerthal to the vineyards of the Moselle wine region. It is a beautiful country with plenty packed in to its borders.

Country highlights

Luxembourg cuisine is heavily influenced by its neighbours and in particular has many Germanic flavourings. Judd mat Gaardebounen, which is a smoked collar of pork with broad beans, is a particularly popular meal and is widely recognised as one of the country's national dishes.

The Festival of Wiltz is an annual affair that celebrates some of the most talented international musicians. With its open air setting and castle backdrop, it attracts large audiences each year and is considered to be a cultural highlight.

Major towns and cities

- Luxembourg City – this fascinating capital lies in the heart of Europe.
- Esch-sur-Alzette – this city has the longest shopping street in the country.
- Diekirck – a city with charming old streets.
- Dudelange – a cultural centre with lots to see.

Attractions

- Mullerthal Trail – explore 112km of varied landscape, from pastures to canyons and forests to rock formations.
- Vianden Castle, Vianden – a grand building that originates from the 10th century and which dominates the landscape.
- National Museum of Art and History, Luxembourg City – enjoy a fascinating range of exhibitions from archaeology to fine arts.
- Holy Ghost Citadel, Luxembourg City – a majestic fortress with stunning views.

Find out more

www.visitluxembourg.lu
Tel: 0035 (0) 24 28 28 21 Luxembourg Tourist Office

Country Information

Population (approx): 521,000

Capital: Luxembourg City (population approx 107,000)

Area: 2,586 sq km

Bordered by: Belgium, France, Germany

Terrain: Rolling hills to north with broad, shallow valleys; steep slope to Moselle valley in south-east

Climate: Temperate climate without extremes of heat or cold; mild winters; warm, wet summers; July and August are the hottest months; May and June have the most hours of sunshine.

Highest Point: Kneiff 560m

Languages: French, German, Lëtzebuergesch (Luxembourgish)

Local Time: GMT or BST + 1, i.e. 1 hour ahead of the UK all year

Currency: Euros divided into 100 cents; £1 = €1.42, €1 = £0.71 (September 2015)

Emergency numbers: Police 113; Fire brigade 112; Ambulance 112. Operators speak English

Public Holidays 2016: Jan 1; Mar 28; May 1, 5, 16; Jun 23 (National Day); Aug 15; Nov 1; Dec 25, 26.

There are other dates such as Luxembourg City Fete and 2 Nov which are not official holidays but many businesses, banks and shops may close. School summer holidays run from mid-July to mid-September.

Camping and Caravanning

There are approximately 120 campsites in Luxembourg; most are open from April to October. Apart from in the industrial south, campsites are found all over the country. The Ardennes, the river banks along the Moselle and the Sûre and the immediate surroundings of Luxembourg City are particularly popular.

Casual/wild camping is only permitted with a tent, not a caravan, but permission must first be sought from the landowner.

Motorhomes

Many campsites have motorhome amenities and some offer Quick Stop overnight facilities at reduced rates.

Electricity and Gas

Most campsites have a supply of between 6 and 16 amps and many have CEE connections. Plugs have two round pins. The full range of Campingaz cylinders is widely available.

Entry Formalities

British and Irish passport holders may stay for up to three months without a visa.

Medical Services

Emergency medical treatment is available on presentation of a European Health Insurance Card (EHIC) but you will be charged both for treatment and prescriptions. Refunds can be obtained from a local sickness insurance fund office, Caisse de Maladie des Ouvriers (CMO). Emergency hospital treatment is normally free apart from a non-refundable standard daily fee.

Opening Hours

Banks – Mon-Fri 8.30am-12 noon & 1.30pm-4.30pm.Some stay open to 6pm and open Sat 9am-12 noon.

Museums – Tue-Sun 10am-6pm, Thurs late opening 5pm-8pm (check locally); most close Mon.

Post Offices – Mon-Fri 8am-12 noon & 1.30pm-4.30pm/5pm; the central post office in Luxembourg City is open 7am-7pm Mon to Fri & 7am-5pm Sat.

Shops – Mon-Sat 9am/10am-6pm/6.30pm. Some close for lunch and Mon mornings. Large malls may be open to 8pm or 9pm.

Safety and Security

There are few reports of crime but visitors should take the usual commonsense precautions against pickpockets. Do not leave valuables in your car.

Luxembourg shares with the rest of Europe an underlying threat from terrorism. Attacks could be indiscriminate and against civilian targets in public places, including tourist sites.

British Embassy
BOULEVARD JOSEPH II, L-1840 LUXEMBOURG
Tel: 22 98 64
www.ukinluxembourg.fco.gov.uk

Irish Embassy
Résidence Christina (2nd floor)

28 ROUTE D'ARLON, L-1140 LUXEMBOURG
Tel: 450 6101
www.embassyofireland.lu

Documents
Passport
When driving it is easy to cross into neighbouring countries without realising it. Although you are unlikely to be asked for it, you must have your valid passport with you.

Vehicle(s)
Drivers of foreign-registered vehicles must be able to produce on demand a current driving licence, vehicle registration document (V5C) insurance certificate, insurance certificate and MOT certificate (if applicable).

Money
Major credit cards are widely accepted although there are often minimum amount requirements. Cash machines are widespread. Carry your credit card issuers'/banks' 24-hour UK contact numbers in case of loss or theft of your cards.

Motoring in Luxembourg
Alcohol
The maximum permitted level of alcohol is 50 milligrams in 100 millilitres of blood, i.e. lower than that permitted in the UK (80 milligrams). For drivers who have held a driving licence for less than two years the permitted level is 20 milligrams i.e. virtually nil. Breath tests are compulsory following serious road accidents and road offences.

Breakdown Service
A 24-hour breakdown service 'Service Routier' is operated by the Automobile Club De Grand-Duche de Luxembourg (ACL) on all roads, telephone 26000. Operators speak English. Payment by credit card is accepted.

Essential Equipment
Warning Triangle
A warning triangle must be used if the vehicle is immobilised on the roadway.

Lights
The use of dipped headlights in the daytime is recommended for all vehicles.

Reflective Jacket/Waistcoat
It is compulsory to wear a reflective jacket when getting out of your vehicle on a motorway or main road. Pedestrians walking at night or in bad visibility outside built-up areas must also wear one.

Child Restraint System
Children under the age of 3 years old must be seated in an approved child restraint system.

Children from the ages of 3 to 17 and/or under the height of 1.5m must be seated in an appropriate restraint system. If they are over 36kg in weight they can use a seat belt but only if they are in the rear of the vehicle.

Rear-facing child restraint systems are not allowed on seats with front airbags unless the airbag has been deactivated.

Tyres
Vehicles are required to have M&S (Mud and Snow) marked tyres fitted when driving in wintery conditions (frost, snow, ice etc.). This regulation applies to all drivers, regardless of where the vehicle is registered.

Fuel
Petrol stations are generally open from 8am to 8pm with 24 hour service on motorways. Most accept credit cards and many have automatic pumps operated with a credit card.

It is illegal to carry petrol in a can.

LPG is available at a handful of petrol stations – see www.mylpg.eu and use the drop down menu listed under LPG stations.

Overtaking
When overtaking at night outside built-up areas it is compulsory to flash headlights.

Parking

Parking is prohibited where there are yellow lines or zigzag white lines. Blue zone parking areas exist in Luxembourg City, Esch-sur-Elzette, Dudelange and Wiltz. Parking discs are obtainable from the ACL, police stations, tourist offices and shops. Parking meters operate in Luxembourg City. The police will clamp or remove illegally parked vehicles.

There are free car parks two to three kilometres outside Luxembourg City and Esch-sur-Elzette from which regular buses leave for the city.

If there is no public lighting when parking on a public road sidelights are required to be switched on.

Priority

Where two roads of the same category intersect, traffic from the right has priority. In towns give priority to traffic coming from the right, unless there is a 'priority road' sign (yellow diamond with white border) indicating that the driver using that road has right of way.

Road Signs and Markings

Road signs and markings conform to international standards and are shown in French and German. Traffic lights pass from red immediately to green (no red and amber phase). A flashing amber light allows traffic to turn in the direction indicated, traffic permitting. In Luxembourg City some bus lanes and cycle lanes are marked in red.

Speed Limits

	Open Road (km/h)	Motorway (km/h)
Car Solo	90	130
Car towing caravan/trailer	75	90
Motorhome under 3500kg	90	130
Motorhome 3500-7500kg	90	130

The top speed of 130 km/h (80 mph) for solo cars is reduced to 110 km/h (68 mph) in wet weather. The speed limit for drivers who have held a licence for less than a year is 90 km/h (56 mph) on motorways and 75 km/h (47 mph) outside built-up areas. In some residential areas called 'Zones de Rencontre' the maximum permitted speed is 20 km/h (13 mph).

Traffic Jams

Many holidaymakers travel through Luxembourg in order to take advantage of its cheaper fuel. Queues at petrol stations often cause traffic congestion, in particular along the 'petrol route' past Martelange (N4 in Belgium), at Dudelange on the A3/E25 at the Belgium-Luxembourg border, and at the motorway junction near Steinfort on the A6.

Other bottlenecks occur, particularly during weekends in July and August, at the junctions on the A1/E44 near Gasperich to the south of Luxembourg City, and the exit from the A3/E25 at Dudelange. To avoid traffic jams between Luxembourg City and Thionville (France), leave the western ring road around Luxembourg and take the A4 to Esch-sur-Alzette and then the D16. When past Aumetz join the N52 which then connects to the A30 to Metz.

The website www.cita.lu provides webcam views of all motorways and information on traffic flow.

Violation of Traffic Regulations

Police officers may impose on the spot fines for infringement of regulations. These must be settled in cash and a receipt given. Non-residents of Luxembourg are liable to receive penalty points for serious infringements of traffic law.

Motorways

There are approximately 152km of motorways, all of which are toll-free for private vehicles. Motorway service areas are situated at Capellen on the A6 near Mamer, at Pontpierre on the A4, and at Berchem near Bettenbourg on the A3.

Emergency telephones are situated every 1.5km along main roads and motorways and link motorists to the 'Protection Civile'.

Touring

Luxembourg is the only Grand Duchy in the world and measures a maximum of 81km (51 miles) from north to south and 51km (32 miles) from east to west. The fortifications and old town of Luxembourg City have been designated as a UNESCO World Heritage site.

Smoking is not allowed in bars and restaurants. A service charge is usually added to restaurant bills and it is normal practice to leave a little extra if the service is good.

The Luxembourg Card is valid for one, two or three days, and entitles the holder to free public transport, admission to numerous museums and tourist attractions, and discounts on sightseeing trips. It is available from tourist offices, campsites, hotels, information and public transport offices as well as from participating attractions. You can also buy it online at www.ont.lu.

There are many marked walking trails throughout the country – see www.hiking-in-luxembourg. co.uk for full details. A Christmas market is held in the pedestrianised Place d'Armes in Luxembourg City. Others are held in towns and villages throughout the country.

French is the official language, but Luxembourgish is the language most commonly used. English is widely spoken in Luxembourg City, but less so elsewhere.

Public Transport & Local Travel

A transport network ticket (billet réseau) is available at railway stations throughout the country and at the airport. It allows unlimited travel on city buses, trains and country coaches for one day (until 8am the next morning) throughout Luxembourg. Public transport maps can be downloaded from the Luxembourg Tourist Office website, www.luxembourg.co.uk.

Luxembourg is a compact city and walking around it is easy and pleasant. It is served by an efficient network of buses. You can buy bus tickets valid either for two hours (billet de courte durée) or one day (billet de longue durée). A discount is offered on a block of 10 tickets. Tickets must be validated at the machines on buses and train platforms. Dogs are allowed free of charge on city buses. People over 65 years of age may qualify for travel concessions; show your passport as proof of age.

ALZINGEN see Luxembourg City *C3*

BERDORF see Echternach *C3*

BETTENDORF *C2* (1km SE Rural) *49.87262, 6.22137*
Camping Um Wirt, 12 Rue de la Gare, L-9353 Bettendorf [tel 808386; fax 26804792; info@campingumwirt.lu; campingumwirt.lu] Foll the N17/N19 Diekirch/Echternach. Turn R and foll camping signs in Bettendorf. Med, pt shd or shd; wc; chem disp; shwrs; EHU (10A); lndry; rest/café; bar; playgrnd; rv adj; games area; games rm; entmnt; wifi; 70% statics; dogs €2.50; Eng spkn; adv bkg; red LS; bowling green; trampoline; tennis court; sports field; "Vg site; gd walking & cycling; open plan, grassy site." 1 Apr-15 Oct. € 25.00   2013*

BORN SUR SURE *C3* (500m NE Rural) *49.76081, 6.51672*
Camping Officiel Born-Sûre, 9 Rue du Camping, 6660 Born-sur-Sûre [tel/fax 730144; syndicat@gmx.lu; www.camping-born.lu] E along E44 sp Trier; leave immed bef ent Germany. On N10 go N sp Echternach; ignore Sat Nav & drive to end of vill, site sp. Med, mkd pitch, pt shd; wc; chem disp; shwrs inc; EHU (6A); lndry; supmkt 8km; rest, snacks; bar; BBQ; htd pool 8km; fishing; boating; 70% statics; dogs €2.50; wifi; phone; Eng spkn; adv bkg; some rd noise; ccard acc; CKE/CCI. "Gd, clean site; all tourers on rvside; if barrier clsd find contact in bar; excel." ◆ 1 Apr-1 Oct. € 16.00   2014*

CLERVAUX *B2* (16km SW Rural) *49.97045, 5.93450* **Camping Kaul, Rue Joseph Simon, 9550 Wiltz [tel 950359; fax 957770; icamping@campingkaul.lu; www.campingkaul. lu]** Turn N off rd 15 (Bastogne-Ettelbruck) to Wiltz, foll sp N to Ville Basse & Camping. Lge, mkd pitch, unshd; htd wc; chem disp; mv service pnt; baby facs; fam bthrm; shwrs €0.50; EHU (6-10A) €2.50-2.75; gas; lndry; shop high ssn & 500m; snacks; playgrnd; pool adj; waterslides; tennis; dogs €1.50; poss cr; quiet; adv bkg. "Gd site; pitches tight for awnings if site full; excel san facs & take-away; local children use playgrnd." ◆ 1 Apr-31 Oct. € 28.00   2014*

CLERVAUX *B2* (400m W Rural) *50.05471, 6.02391* **Camping Officiel de Clervaux, 33 Klatzewe, 9714 Clervaux [tel 920042; fax 929728; campingclervaux@internet.lu; www.camping-clervaux.lu]** Site sp fr town cent & fr all dirs at foot of Abbey Hill; some sharp bends. Med, hdg/mkd pitch, pt shd; htd wc; chem disp; mv service pnt; baby facs; shwrs €1; EHU (10A) €2.50; gas; lndry (inc dryer); shop & 1km; snacks; BBQ; playgrnd; htd pool; tennis 200m; games area; internet; TV; 50% statics; dogs €2; phone; poss cr; Eng spkn; some rlwy noise; CKE/CCI. "Friendly, helpful staff; pleasant town; gd walking; trains to Liège & L'bourg City; rv on site unfenced; 5 mins walk town; vg." ◆ 1 Apr-15 Oct. € 17.00   2010*

DIEKIRCH *C2* (10km E Rural) *49.86852, 6.26430* **Camping de la Rivière, 21 Rue de la Sûre, 9390 Reisdorf [tel/fax 836398; campingreisdorf@pt.lu; www.campingreisdorf.com]** Fr Diekirch take N19 (sp Echternach) for 10km to where rd crosses Rv Sûre. Site on L after bdge. Med, mkd pitch, pt shd; htd wc; chem disp; shwrs €1.10; EHU (6-10A) metered; gas; lndry (inc dryer); shop adj; rest, snacks; bar; playgrnd; internet; 20% statics; dogs €1.50; bus; poss cr; Eng spkn; quiet; red CKE/CCI. "Lovely site in beautiful countryside; excel for walking/cycling; helpful, friendly owners; gd touring base." ◆ ltd. Feb - Nov. € 15.00   2013*

DIEKIRCH *C2* (500m SE Urban) *49.86635, 6.16513* **Camping de la Sûre, 34 Route de Gilsdorf, 9234 Diekirch [tel 809425; fax 802786; tourisme@diekirch.lu; www.diekirch.lu]** Fr town cent take N14 twds Larochette, then 1st L after x-ing rv bdge. Well sp. Lge, mkd pitch, pt shd; htd wc; chem disp; baby facs; shwrs €1; EHU (10A) €2.50; lndry; shop 500m; bar; playgrnd; pool 200m; 50% statics; dogs €2; m'van o'night area outside gates; Eng spkn; adv bkg; quiet; ccard acc; red CKE/CCI. "Nice welcome; excel, clean facs; pleasant rvside site 5 mins walk fr town cent; vg touring base, Battle of Bulge Museum nrby." ◆ 1 Apr-30 Sep. € 20.50   2012*

> ## "I like to fill in the reports as I travel from site to site"
> You'll find report forms at the back of this guide, or you can fill them in online at www.caravanclub.co.uk/europereport.

DIEKIRCH *C2* (900m S Rural) *49.86768, 6.16984* **Camping op der Sauer, Route de Gilsdorf, L 9234 Diekirch [tel 808590; fax 809470; info@campsauer.lu; www.campsauer.lu]** On rd 14 to Larochette, on S o'skts of Diekirch. 1st L after x-ing rv bdge, site well sp on L past Camping de la Sûre and behind sports facs. Lge, mkd pitch, pt shd; htd wc; chem disp; shwrs inc; EHU (6A) €3; gas; lndry; shop & 400m; rest, snacks; bar; playgrnd; pool 400m; dogs €2.50; bus 800m; Eng spkn; adv bkg; CKE/CCI. "On banks Rv Sûre; sh walk/cycle to town; spacious site; friendly owners; ltd facs LS; gd, basic site; helpful recep; clean san facs with plenty of hot water; vet is 20 mins walk." 1 Mar-31 Oct. € 21.00   2015*

ECHTERNACH *C3* (2km SE Rural) *49.79681, 6.43122* **Camping Alferweiher, Alferweiher 1, 6412 Echternach [tel/fax 720271; info@camping-alferweiher.lu; www.camping-alferweiher.lu]** Fr S on N10 on ent Echternach turn R at sp (pictogram fishing/camping) then L at sp to Alferweiher. Lge, mkd pitch, pt shd; htd wc; chem disp; mv service pnt; baby facs; shwrs inc; EHU (10A) €2.75; gas; lndry; shop; snacks; bar; playgrnd; bike hire; TV rm; entmnt; dogs €2; poss cr; Eng spkn; adv bkg; quiet; CKE/CCI. "Gd walking; office open 0900-1300 & 1400-1800; if shut site yourself - el boxes not locked; hot water in individ cubicles in san facs block only - other basins cold water." ◆ 23 Apr-15 Sep. € 20.00   2010*

ECHTERNACH *C3* (1km NW Rural) *49.81716, 6.41058*
**Camping Officiel, 5 Rue de Diekirch, 6430 Echternach
[tel 720272; fax 26720747; info@camping-echternach.lu;
www.camping-echternach.lu]** Fr Luxembourg City cont thro
Echternach on N10 sp Diekirch & Ettelbruck. Site clearly sp on L
overlkg rd & rv; diff exit fr site. Lge, hdg/mkd pitch, terr, pt shd;
wc; chem disp; mv service pnt; baby facs; shwrs inc; EHU (16A)
€2.50; lndry (inc dryer); shops 500m; playgrnd; pool; rv/lake
sw; fishing; 10% statics; dogs €2; bus to Luxemb'g City 500m;
Eng spkn; adv bkg; some rd noise; ccard acc; red LS. "Music
festival Jun/Jul; gd walks; gd rests in town; rvside cycle path."
♦ 15 Mar-30 Oct. € 17.00   2011*

ECHTERNACH *C3* (6km NW Rural) *49.81904, 6.34694*
**Camping Bon Repos, 39 Rue de Consdorf, 6551 Berdorf [tel
790631; fax 799571; irma@bonrepos.lu; www.bonrepos.lu]**
In cent Echternach at x-rds take Vianden rd, then in 2km turn
L to Berdorf thro vill twds Consdorf. Site nr cent vill on L adj
Camping Belle-Vue. Fr Luxembourg thro Consdorf to Berdorf,
site on R on ent to vill, clearly sp. Med, hdg/mkd pitch, terr, pt
sl, pt shd; htd wc; chem disp; baby facs; shwrs inc; EHU (16A)
€2.80 (poss rev pol); gas; lndry; shop adj; rest & bar 100m;
playgrnd; pool 5km; games rm; wifi; TV; no dogs; bus 100m;
Eng spkn; adv bkg; quiet; red long stay; CKE/CCI. "Clean, tidy
site - best in area; clean facs; helpful, friendly owners; some
pitches sm; forest walks fr site; conv for trips to Germany."
1 Apr74 Nov. € 18.00   2013*

⊞ **ESCH SUR ALZETTE** *B3* (2km E Rural) *49.48761, 5.98554*
**Camping Gaalgebierg, 4001 Esch-sur-Alzette [tel 541069;
fax 549630; gaalcamp@pt.lu; www.gaalgebierg.lu]**
Sp in cent of town, turn L dir Kayl. Under rlwy bdge sharp R,
up steep hill. Lge, hdstg, terr, shd; htd wc; baby facs; shwrs inc;
EHU (16A) €1.50 but elec for heating metered & restricted in
bad weather; lndry; shop; snacks; bar; playgrnd; pool 2km; TV
conn all pitches; mainly statics; bus 1km; train to Luxembourg
city; Eng spkn; quiet; ccard acc; CKE/CCI. "V clean san facs; gd
walks; park & sm zoo adj site; well-kept site; poss boggy when
wet." ♦ € 20.70   2013*

ESCH SUR SURE *B2* (7km NE Rural) *49.91420, 6.00098*
**Camping Toodlermillen, 1 Op der Millen, 9181 Tadler-
Moulin [tel 839189; fax 899236; keisera@gms.lu;
www.toodlermillen.lu]** Fr Ettelbrück on N15 twd Esch-sur-
Sûre, turn E onto N27 dir Goebelsmühle. Site is 4km on R.
Med, mkd pitch, unshd; htd wc; chem disp; baby facs; shwrs
€1; EHU (6A) €3; lndry; shop, rest, bar adj; playgrnd; BBQ;
rv fishing; canoeing; 20% statics; dogs €3; Eng spkn. "V
helpful owner; beautiful area; excel san facs." 15 Apr-15 Oct.
€ 22.50   2010*

ESCH SUR SURE *B2* (1km SE Rural) *49.90693, 5.94220*
**Camping Im Aal, 7 Rue du Moulin, 9650 Esch-sur-Sûre
[tel 839514; fax 899117; info@camping-im-aal.lu;
www.camping-im-aal.lu]** Fr N turn R off N15 onto N27 sp
Esch-sur-Sûre. Pass thro sh tunnel, site on L in 500m on banks
of Rv Sûre. Lge, hdg/mkd pitch, pt sl, pt shd; htd wc; chem
disp; shwrs inc; EHU (6A) €2; lndry (inc dryer); shop & 500m;
bar; playgrnd adj; fishing; 30% statics; dogs €2; site clsd 1
Jan-14 Feb; Eng spkn; quiet; red CKE/CCI. "Well-kept, clean
site; gd welcome; gd, modern facs; some rvside pitches; walks
along towpath in a woods; gd for wheelchair users; gd fishing,
walking; gd NH & longer." ♦ 13 Feb-20 Dec. € 22.00 2015*

ETTELBRUCK *B2* (4km E Rural) *49.85043, 6.13461* **Camping
Gritt, 2 Rue Gritt, 9161 Ingeldorf [tel 802018; fax 802019;
apeeters@pt.lu; www.campinggritt.lu]** On N15 fr Bastogne
turn R at rndabt in Ettelbrück sp Diekirch, go under A7 sp
Diekirch. In 3km at end of elevated section foll slip rd sp
Diekirch, Ettelbrück, Ingeldorf. At rndabt take 2nd exit sp
Ingledorf, site on R over narr rv bdge. Fr Diekirch on N7 fork L
twd Ingeldorf. Site on L over rv bdge. Lge, mkd pitch, pt shd;
htd wc; chem disp; baby facs; mv service pnt; shwrs inc; EHU
(6A) €2.80; gas; lndry; supmkt 1.5km; snacks; bar; BBQ; rv
sw 1.5km; playgrnd; fishing, canoe hire, tennis nrby; ltd wifi;
entmnt; games/TV rm; 30% statics; dogs €2; twin-axles acc (rec
check in advy); bus/train to Luxembourg City; recep 0900-1800
high ssn; poss cr; Eng spkn; adv bkg; quiet; red for groups; red
LS/CKE/CCI. "Peaceful site; helpful, welcoming Dutch owners;
lge pitches with open aspect; gd, modern san facs; pitching
still OK after heavy rain; on banks of Rv Sûre (swift-flowing
& unfenced); gd walking & sightseeing; rest vg; vg site." ♦
1 Apr-30 Oct. € 28.40 SBS - H07   2014*

ETTELBRUCK *B2* (1.5km W Rural) *49.84600, 6.08193*
**Camping Ettelbruck (formerly Kalkesdelt), 88 Chemin
du Camping, 9022 Ettelbrück [tel 812185; fax 819839;
ellen.ringelberg@gmx.de; www.campingettelbruck.com]**
Exit Ettelbrück on Bastogne rd N15. Site visible as app town;
approx 200m fr town cent fork L into lane, turn R at sp at foot
of hill, steep & narr rd. Site sp fr town. Lge, mkd pitch, terr,
pt shd; htd wc; chem disp; mv service pnt; baby facs; shwrs
inc; EHU (16A) €2.90; lndry; shop; rest, snacks; bar; playgrnd;
pool 3km; TV; 15% statics; dogs €2.50; phone; poss cr; Eng
spkn; adv bkg; quiet; CKE/CCI. "Gd, well-maintained, friendly,
family-run site in woods; excel san facs; lge pitches; gd walks;
train to Luxembourg city fr town; excel site." ♦ 14 Apr-1 Nov.
€ 29.00   2015*

⊞ **ETTELBRUCK** *B2* (10km NW Rural) *49.87748, 5.99288*
**Camping Fuussekaul, 4 Fuussekaul, 9156 Heiderscheid
[tel 268888; fax 26888828; info@fuussekaul.lu]** Take N15
fr Bastogne twd Ettelbrück, site 1.5km past Heiderscheid on
R. Lge, pt sl, pt shd; htd wc; chem disp; mv service pnt; sauna;
shwrs €1; EHU (10A) inc; gas; lndry; shop high ssn; rest, snacks;
bar; playgrnd; 2 pools; waterslide; lake sw 8km; tennis; games
area; archery; internet; entmnt; 30% statics; dogs €2; bus; poss
cr; adv bkg; quiet; red long stay. "Vg site." € 35.00   2009*

GREVENMACHER *C3* (800m N Urban) *49.68302, 6.44891*
**Camping La Route du Vin, 32 Route de Thionville, 6791
Grevenmacher [tel 750234 or 758275; fax 758666; sitg@
pt.lu; www.grevenmacher.lu]** Fr E44/A1 exit junc 14 onto
N1 to Grevenmacher. After 1km turn R at T-junc opp Esso
g'ge. Site sp in town, ent off rndabt. Med, mkd pitch, pt sl, pt
shd; wc; chem disp; shwrs inc; EHU (6A) €2; lndry; shop, rest,
snacks 500m; bar; pool adj; games area; games rm; tennis;
child entmnt; wifi; 60% statics; dogs €1; Eng spkn; adv bkg;
quiet, some rlwy noise; CKE/CCI. "Easy walk to town cent;
wine festival in Sep; pleasant, well kept site; excel new san
facs (2015); boat trips; rvside walks; excel base for touring
Moselle & Luxembourg; views; excel." ♦ 1 Apr-30 Sep.
€ 14.40   2015*

HEIDERSCHEID see Ettelbrück *B2*

INGELDORF see Ettelbrück *B2*

⊞ **KAUTENBACH** *B2* (1km E Rural) *49.95387, 6.02730*
**Camping Kautenbach, An der Weierbaach, 9663
Kautenbach [tel 950303; fax 950093; info@camping
kautenbach.lu; www.campingkautenbach.lu]**
Travelling E fr Bastogne on N84, approx 5km after
Luxembourg border take N26 to Wiltz & foll sp to
Kautenbach/Kiischpelt. In 10km turn L over bdge into vill,
site sp 800m. Lge, mkd pitch, pt shd; htd wc; chem disp;
shwrs inc; baby facs; EHU (6A) inc; gas; lndry; shop; rest,
snacks; bar; BBQ; playgrnd; entmnt; bike hire; wifi; TV rm;
20% statics; phone; dogs; site clsd 21 Dec-14 Jan; Eng
spkn; adv bkg; quiet but some rlwy noise; ccard acc. "Gd
for walking & mountain biking; long site along beautiful,
secluded rv valley." ♦ € 22.00   2009*

See advertisement opposite

KOCKELSCHEUER see Luxembourg City *C3*

LAROCHETTE *C3* (2km W Rural) *49.78525, 6.21010* **Camping
Birkelt, 1 Um Birkelt, 7633 Larochette [tel 879040; fax
879041; info@camping-birkelt.lu; www.camping-birkelt.lu]**
Fr Diekirch take N14 to Larochette; turn R in town on
CR118 (N8), foll sp for Mersch. At top of hill foll site sp.
Fr Luxembourg take N7 foll sp for Mersch & Ettelbruck (ignore
Larochette sp bef Mersch). Turn R bef rv bdge at Mersch onto
CR118 & foll rd to o'skts of town. Site on R beyond municipal
sports cent - fairly steep, winding app rd. Lge, hdg/mkd pitch,
pt sl, pt shd; htd wc; chem disp; mv service pnt; serviced
pitch; baby facs; sauna; shwrs inc; EHU (16A) inc; gas; lndry
(inc dryer); shop; rest, snacks; bar; BBQ (gas/charcoal only);
playgrnd; 2 pools (1 htd, covrd); paddling pool; tennis; fitness
rm; horseriding; fishing, canoeing, golf 5km; bike hire; games
rm; games area; games rm; wifi; entmnt; TV rm; 50% statics;
dogs €2.50; no o'fits over 9m; poss cr; Eng spkn; ccard acc; red
LS; CKE/CCI. "Excel, well-kept, busy site in pleasant wooded
hilltop location; friendly, helpful staff; ideal for families; gd
san facs, poss stretched high ssn; access poss diff lge o'fits,
care req; late arr report to rest/bar; gd bar & rest, open in LS;
under new ownership." ♦ 15 Mar-1 Nov. € 46.40 (CChq acc)
SBS - H08   2014*

LAROCHETTE *C3* (7km W Rural) *49.78521, 6.16596*
**Europacamping Nommerlayen, Rue Nommerlayen, 7465
Nommern [tel 878078; fax 879678; nommerlayen@vo.lu;
www.nommerlayen-ec.lu]** N7 Luxembourg to Diekirch.
At Mersch N8 E dir Larochette & Nommern. Site is 1km S
of Nommern. Lge, hdg/mkd pitch, terr, pt shd; htd wc; mv
service pnt; chem disp; baby facs; sauna; shwrs inc; private
bthrms avail; EHU (2A) inc (16A €3.75); gas; lndry (inc dryer);
shop; rest, snacks; bar; playgrnd; htd pool; paddling pool;
tennis, games area; games rm; bike hire; wifi; entmnt; TV;
10% statics; dogs €2.85; phone; Eng spkn; adv bkg; quiet;
red LS/snr citizens. "Superb site & facs." ♦ 1 Feb-1 Dec.
€ 40.00   2011*

See advertisement opposite

⊞ **LIELER** *B2* (500m SW Rural) *50.12365, 6.10509* **Camping
Trois Frontières, Hauptstroos 12, 9972 Lieler [tel 998608;
fax 979184; info@troisfrontieres.lu; www.troisfrontieres.lu]**
Fr N7/E421 turn E sp Lieler, site sp. Med, mkd pitch; pt shd;
htd wc; chem disp; mv service pnt; baby facs; shwrs; EHU
(6A) €2.75; lndry (inc dryer); rest, snacks; bar; playgrnd; pool;
paddling pool; bike hire; games rm; games area; wifi; entmnt;
TV; some statics; dogs €2.20; adv bkg; quiet. "V pleasant
site; gd touring base; site under new ownership (2014); ACSI
registered; discount in LS." € 32.00   2014*

LUXEMBOURG CITY *C3* (7km S Rural) *49.57220, 6.10857*
**Camping Kockelscheuer, 22 Route de Bettembourg, 1899
Kockelscheuer [tel 471815; fax 401243; caravani@pt.lu;
www.ccclv.lu/site/index.php/en]** Fr N on A6 then A4 exit
junc 1 sp Leudelange/Kockelscheuer, at top of slip rd turn L N4.
After about 1.5km turn R N186 sp Bettemburg/Kockelscheuer
& foll camp sp. Foll sp 'Park & Ride', site is 1st R. Fr S exit
A3 junc 2 sp Bettembourg & Kockelscheuer. In 700m turn R
dir Kockelscheuer & in 3km turn L & foll site sp, rd numberd
CR196. Lge, some hdg/mkd pitch, pt terr; pt shd; htd wc; chem
disp; mv service pnt; shwrs inc; EHU (10-16A) metered (check
pol); gas; lndry (inc dryer); shop; rest adj; snacks; bar; playgrnd;
pool 4km; sports complex adj; internet; sat TV; dogs free; bus
to city 400m (tickets fr site recep); office & gates clsd 1200-
1400 & 2230-0700; Eng spkn; adv bkg; some rd & aircraft
noise during day; ccard not acc; LS weekly rate for snr citizens;
10% red CKE/CCI. "Rec arr early afternoon as popular; well-
run, clean, pretty site; helpful, pleasant staff; gd san facs; pitch
access on lower level needs care; gd size pitches on terr; poss
boggy after rain; gd dog walks nrby; useful NH for Zeebrugge;
excel site." ♦ 12 Aprr-31 Oct. € 19.50   2014*

LUXEMBOURG CITY *C3* (9km S Rural) *49.56907, 6.16010*
**Camping Bon Accueil, 2 Rue du Camping, 5815 Alzingen
[tel/fax 367069; www.camping-alzingen.lu]**
Fr Luxembourg city take A3/E25 S, exit junc 1 sp Hespérange.
Cont thro town to Alzingen, site sp on R after Mairie, well sp.
Med, hdg/mkd pitch, some hdstg, pt shd; htd wc; chem disp;
mv service pnt; baby facs; shwrs inc; EHU (16A) inc (poss rev
pol); gas; lndry; shop, rest; snacks; bar; BBQ; playgrnd; pool
3km; games area; wifi; dogs €3; phone; bus to city adj; twin
axles; Eng spkn; adv bkg; poss cr; quiet; ccard acc; CCI/ACSI.
"Pleasant, open, clean, tidy site; gd size pitches; friendly staff;
vg, clean, modern san facs; hot water metered; lovely gardens
adj; clsd 1200-1400 - ltd waiting space; excel base for city;
spotlessly clean; vg site; rec arrive early." ♦ 1 Apr-15 Oct.
€ 16.00   2015*

LUXEMBOURG CITY *C3* (14km W Rural) *49.63012, 6.04761*
**Camping Mamer, 4 Rue de Mersch, 8251 Mamer
[tel/fax 312349; campingmamer@hotmail.com;
www.campingmamer.tk]** App Luxembourg on A6/E25. Exit
m'way at Mamer junc on N6. Pass thro Mamer vill, turn L in
1km at 2nd rndabt, site sp. Bef m'way viaduct turn R into site.
Med, pt sl, pt shd; htd wc; chem disp; shwrs inc; EHU (6A) inc
(poss rev pol); gas; shops 1.5km; hypmkt nr; rest, snacks; bar;
playgrnd; dogs; poss v cr; Eng spkn; adv bkg; CKE/CCI. "V
pleasant site; helpful owners; easy access to city; bus into city
fr hypmkt; o'night/late arr area in gravel car park under m'way
(noisy); poss long walk to facs; many o'nighters."
1 Apr-30 Sep. € 18.00   2010*

MAMER see Luxembourg City *C3*

Camping Kautenbach

An der Weierbaach
L-9663 Kautenbach, Luxembourg

Tel.:(+352) 950303
info@campingkautenbach.lu • www.campingkautenbach.lu

ZENsational Our location is unique! Come camp in a snug valley, surrounded by forested hills. The banks of the calm CLERF River offer ample opportunities for peace and tranquillity.

Open from 20 January till 20 December

NOMMERN see Larochette *C3*

OBEREISENBACH *C2* (2.6km N Rural) *50.01640, 6.13680* **Camping Kohnenhof, Maison 1, 9838 Obereisenbach [tel 929464; fax 929690; kohnenho@pt.lu; www.campingkohnenhof.lu]** Fr N on N7/E421 turn E onto N10 at Marbourg, foll rd S to Kohnenhof, site sp on rvside. Med, mkd pitch, pt sl, terr, pt shd; htd wc; chem disp; mv service pnt; baby facs; shwrs inc; EHU (6A) inc; gas; lndry; shop; hypmkt 10km; rest, snacks; bar; BBQ; playgrnd; htd pool 12km; rv sw adj; boating; tennis 4km; games area; bike hire; golf 18km; wifi; TV rm; 5% statics; dogs €3; phone; poss cr; Eng spkn; adv bkg rec; red LS; CKE/CCI. "Clean site in lovely setting; gd walking & interesting town; self-operated ferry on site to cross rv to forest; vg touring base; excel." 20 Mar-9 Nov. € 28.00 (CChq acc)   2011*

REMICH See also sites listed under Nennig in Germany, map ref 3A2.

"We must tell The Club about that great site we found"

Get your site reports in by mid-August and we'll do our best to get your updates into the next edition.

REMICH *C3* (4km S Rural) *49.5106, 6.36302* **Camping Le Port, 5447 Schwebsange [tel 23664460; fax 26 66 53 05; commune@wellenstein.lu or info@camping-port.lu]** Fr Remich take N10 S on W bank of Moselle. Site 1km E of Schwebsange. Or fr S leave A13 at junc 13 onto N10. Site sp. Lge, mkd pitch, pt shd; wc; chem disp; mv service pnt; serviced pitch; shwrs inc; EHU (10A) inc; gas; lndry; shop 4km; bar; playgrnd; pool 4km; marina & rv activities; 80% statics; dogs; Eng spkn; poss cr; adv bkg rec high ssn; rd, rv & port noise; debit cards acc (no ccards); CKE/CCI. "Busy transit site for Austria/Italy; clean facs; helpful staff; office open 1830-2030; sep area for m'vans on far side of port; red facs LS; gd cycle rtes fr site." ♦ 1 Apr-31 Oct. € 18.00   2014*

SCHWEBSANGE see Remich *C3*

⊞ **SEPTFONTAINES** *B3* (2.5km NE Rural) *49.69274, 5.98514* **Camping Simmerschmelz, Rue de Simmerschmelz 1, 8363 Septfontaines [tel 307072; fax 308210; info@campingsimmer.lu; www.campingsimmer.lu]** Head NE fr Arlon sp Mersch. In 4km at Gaichel (Bel/Lux frontier) foll valley of Rv Eisch thro Hobscheid, Septfontaines & in 2km at rd junc turn R. Site on L in 100m. Or fr E25 m'way exit at Windhof. Head N to Koerich & onto Septfontaines, as above. Med, pt sl, pt shd; htd wc; chem disp; shwrs inc; EHU (6A) €2.50; gas; lndry; shop high ssn; snacks; pool high ssn; TV; 40% statics; dogs €3; phone; Eng spkn; adv bkg; quiet. "Pleasant site in valley - wet in winter; 1 hdstg pitch; helpful owner." € 21.00   2009*

Leading Campings

alan rogers

BEST 2015 CAMPING ADAC CampingKeur

Europacamping Nommerlayen
L-7465 Nommern
www.nommerlayen-ec.lu
(00352) 878078

LUXEMBOURG

TROISVIERGES *B2* (400m S Urban) *50.11908, 6.00251*
**Camping Walensbongert, Rue de Binsfeld, 9912
Troisvierges [tel 997141; fax 26957799; wbongert@pt.lu;
www.walensbongert.lu]** Fr Belgium on E42/A27 exit at
junc 15 St Vith on N62 sp Troisvierges. Site sp. Med, hdg/mkd
pitch, pt shd; htd wc; chem disp; mv service pnt; baby facs;
shwrs inc; EHU (16A) €2.50; lndry (inc dryer); shop 500m;
rest 500m; snacks; bar; pools adj; paddling pool; tennis;
games rm; 10% statics; dogs €2; phone; train 1km; Eng spkn;
adv bkg; quiet; ccard acc; red LS; CKE/CCI. "Pretty town;
gd hiking; charming, helpful owners." ♦ ltd. 1 Apr-30 Sep.
€ 19.50   2014*

VIANDEN *C2* (1km E Urban) *49.93213, 6.21554* **Camping op
dem Deich, Rue Neugarten, 9420 Vianden [tel 834375;
fax 834642; info@campingopdemdeich.lu;
www.campingopdemdeich.lu]** Fr Diekirch take N19 E for
3km. Turn L on N17 to Vianden. Site sp 500m fr town cent twd
Bitburg. Lge, mkd pitch, hdstg, unshd; htd wc; chem disp; baby
facs; shwrs; EHU (16A) €2.20; lndry (inc dryer); shops 500m;
BBQ; playgrnd; pool 2km; fishing; games rm; wifi; some statics;
dogs €1.50; phone; poss cr; quiet. "Some rvside pitches; excel
scenery; sh walk along rv to lovely old town & castle."
1 Apr-11 Oct. € 17.00   2010*

VIANDEN *C2* (2km SE Rural) *49.92673, 6.21990* **Camping
du Moulin, Rue de Bettel, 9415 Vianden [tel/fax 834501;
info@campingdumoulin.lu; www.campingdumoulin.lu]**
Fr Diekirch take N17 dir Vianden. In 8km at Fouhren take
rd N17B sp Bettel then sp Vianden. Site on R behind yellow
Vianden sp. Lge, mkd pitch, pt shd; htd wc; chem disp; mv
service pnt; baby facs; shwrs; EHU (10-16A) €2.20; lndry; shop;
rest, bar; playgrnd; pool 2km; rv adj; wifi; cab TV; dogs €1.50;
phone; Eng spkn; quiet; CKE/CCI. "Lovely location; spacious
pitches, some on rv bank; gd, modern san facs; superb
children's san facs." 24 Apr-5 Sep. € 17.00   2011*

WASSERBILLIG *C3* (350m N Urban) *49.71536, 6.50592*
**Camping Schützwiese, 41 Rue des Romains, 6649
Wasserbillig [tel/fax 740543; info@camping-schuetzwiese.
eu]** Fr A1/E44 exit 14, B49 sp Trier, site sp 150m fr frontier
bdge. Med, pt sl, pt shd; wc; chem disp; mv service pnt;
shwrs inc; EHU (6A) €2; shops adj; rest 4km; tennis 500m;
40% statics; dogs €1.50; poss cr; adv bkg ess; quiet.
1 Apr-31 Oct. € 11.50   2009*

WASSERBILLIG *C3* (2km SW Rural) *49.70241, 6.47717*
**Camping Mertert, Rue du Parc, 6684 Mertert
[tel/fax 748174]** On E of rte 1 (Wasserbillig-Luxembourg),
clearly sp in both dir. Immed R after rlwy x-ing. Site on rv. Med,
some mkd pitch, shd; htd wc; chem disp; baby facs; shwrs;
EHU (10A) inc; lndry; shops 250m; playgrnd; pool 4km; sm
boating pond; 70% statics; buses & trains nr; adv bkg; quiet;
ccard not acc. "Grassed tourer area open fr Apr, but owner
allows pitching on tarmac rd adj office; excel, clean facs; scruffy
statics area; recep clsd 1300-1500; vg." ♦ ltd. 15 Apr-15 Oct.
€ 12.50   2013*

WEISWAMPACH *B2* (2km W Rural) *50.13806, 6.06335*
**Camping du Lac, Klackepëtzn, 9990 Weiswampach
[tel 9972811; fax 9972812; camping.weiswampach@pt.lu;
http://camping.weiswampach.lu]**
Foll N7/E421 fr Luxembourg. Site sp on L 500m fr vill of
Weiswampach. Lge, hdg/mkd pitch, terr, pt shd; htd wc; chem
disp; mv service pnt; baby facs; fam bthrm; shwrs €0.50; EHU
(10A) €1.90; gas; lndry (inc dryer); shop; supmkt 1km; rest,
snacks; bar; BBQ; cooking facs; playgrnd; lake sw adj; fishing;
watersports; entmnt; TV; 50% statics; dogs €1.80; phone;
poss cr; Eng spkn; adv bkg; quiet; red long stay/CKE/CCI.
"Wonderful site on edge of 2 lakes; gd facs; warm welcome."
♦ 1 Apr-31 Oct. € 16.40   2010*

WILTZ see Clervaux *B2*

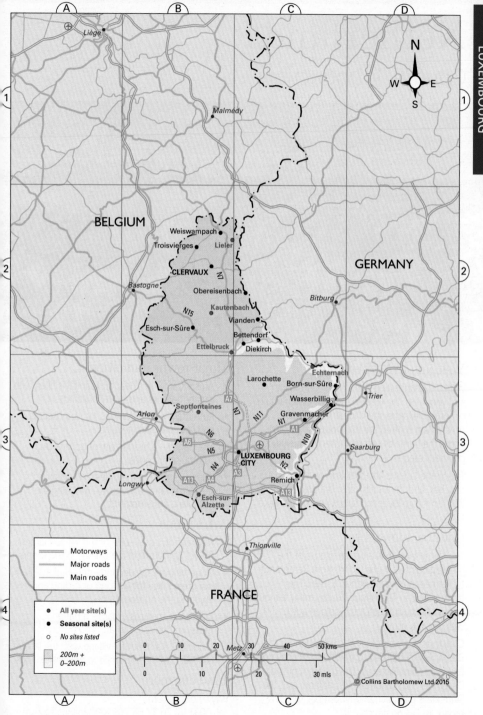

N

W E

S

BELGIUM

GERMANY

Liège

Malmédy

Weiswampach
Troisvierges   Lieler
CLERVAUX
N7
Bastogne
Obereisenbach
N15   Kautenbach
Vianden
Esch-sur-Sûre   Bettendorf
Ettelbruck   Diekirch

Bitburg

Larochette
Born-sur-Sûre
Wasserbillig
Septfontaines   Gravenmacher
Arlon   A7   N7   N11   N1
A1
N6   N10
A6   N5
N4   LUXEMBOURG   N2
CITY
A13   A4   A3
Longwy   Remich
Esch-sur-
Alzette

Echternach

Trier

Saarburg

A13

Thionville

FRANCE

Motorways
Major roads
Main roads

• All year site(s)
• Seasonal site(s)
○ No sites listed

200m +
0–200m

0   10   20   30   40   50 kms
Metz

0   10   20   30 mls

© Collins Bartholomew Ltd 2015

Netherlands
Country Introduction

Kinderdijk

Welcome to Netherlands

With a flat landscape that's covered in tulips and windmills, the Netherlands is an enchanting country to explore and is ideal for cyclists. Amsterdam is often the main draw for tourists, and is the home of several museums, including one dedicated to Van Gogh.

The Netherlands is also well known for its beaches, and the Dutch coast is a great place to visit for nature lover and sports enthusiasts alike.

Country highlights

The Netherlands has produced some of the greatest painters in the world, from Rembrandt to Vermeer and Van Gogh to Escher. The Mauritschuis in The Hague houses many famous works of art from the Dutch golden age and is well worth a visit.

Christmas is a time of great celebration for the Dutch, with Sinterklaas a traditional holiday figure based on Saint Nicholas. The giving of gifts on December 5th is a long-held tradition, as is the Sinterklaas parade in mid-November, which is broadcast live on national TV.

Major towns and cities

- Amsterdam – this beautiful capital is filled with canals, galleries and pretty buildings.
- Rotterdam – a city famous for its museums and landmark architecture.
- The Hague – a historic city of political and cultural significance.
- Leiden – home of the oldest university in the Netherlands and known for being the birthplace of Rembrandt.

Attractions

- Keukenhof, Lisse – one of the world's largest flower gardens and a must-see in the spring.
- Hoge Veluwe, Gelderland – this National Park is a great place for walking or cycling and enjoying the outdoors.
- Rijksmuseum, Amsterdam – a national museum dedicated to arts and history.
- Kinderdijk - a beautiful village with the largest collection of old windmills in the Netherlands.

Find out more

www.holland.com
Tel: 0031 (0) 70 37 05 705 Netherlands Tourism

Country Information

Population (approx): 16.8 million

Capital: Amsterdam (population approx 825,000)

Area: 33,939 sqkm

Bordered by: Belgium, Germany

Terrain: Mostly coastal lowland and reclaimed land (polders) dissected by rivers and canals; hills in the south-east

Climate: Temperate maritime climate; warm, changeable summers; cold/mild winters; spring is the driest season

Coastline: 451km

Highest Point: Vaalserberg 322m

Language: Dutch

Local Time: GMT or BST + 1, i.e. 1 hour ahead of the UK all year

Currency: Euro divided into 100 cents; £1 = €1.42, €1 = £0.71 (September 2015)

Emergency numbers: Police 112; Fire brigade 112; Ambulance 112. Operators speak English

Public Holidays 2016: Jan 1; Mar 27, 28; Apr 27; May 5, 15, 16; Dec 25, 26

School summer holidays vary by region, but are roughly early/mid July to end August/early September

Camping and Caravanning

There are approximately 2,500 officially classified campsites which offer a wide variety of facilities. Most are well equipped with modern sanitary facilities and they generally have a bar, shop and leisure facilities.

A number of sites require cars to be parked on a separate area away from pitches and this can present a problem for motorhomes. Some sites allow motorhomes to park on pitches without restrictions, but others will only accept them on pitches if they are not moved during the duration of your stay. Check before booking in.

A tourist tax is levied at campsites of approximately €1.00 per person per night. It is not generally included in the prices quoted in the Site Entry listings which follow this chapter.

The periods over, and immediately after, the Ascension Day holiday and the Whitsun weekend are very busy for Dutch sites and you can expect to find many of them full. Advance booking is highly recommended.

Casual/wild camping is prohibited as is overnight camping by the roadside or in car parks. There are overnight parking places specifically for motorhomes all over the country – see the website of the Camper Club Nederland, www.campervriendelijk.nl and look under 'camperplaatsen NL' or write to CCN at Postbus 115, 7480 AC Haaksbergen, tel:(0)634 492 913. Alternatively see www.campercontact.nl or email cnn@camperclubnetherland.nl

Many campsites also have motorhome amenities and some offer Quick Stop overnight facilities at reduced rates.

Cycling

There are twice as many bicycles as cars in the Netherlands and as a result cyclists are catered for better than in any other country. There are 15,000 km of well-maintained cycle tracks in both town and country, all marked with red and white road signs and mushroom-shaped posts indicating the quickest and/or most scenic routes. Local tourist information centres (VVV) sell maps of a wide range of cycling tours and cycling fact sheets and maps are available from the Netherlands Board of Tourism in London. Motorists should expect to encounter heavy cycle traffic, particularly during rush hours.

Obligatory separate bicycle lanes for cyclists are indicated by circular blue signs displaying a white bicycle. Small oblong signs with the word 'fietspad' or 'rijwielpad' indicate optional bicycle lanes. White bicycles and dotted white lines painted on the road surface indicate cycle lanes which may be used by motor vehicles providing they do not obstruct cyclists. Cycle lanes marked by continuous white lines are prohibited for use by motor vehicles.

Cyclists must obey traffic light signals at crossroads and junctions; elsewhere, where no traffic lights are in operation, they must give way to traffic from the right.

Cycle tracks are also used by mobility scooters and mopeds. Pedestrians should be especially cautious when crossing roads, especially on zebra crossings. Look out for both cyclists and riders of mopeds, who often ignore traffic rules as well as red lights. In Amsterdam in particular, many cyclists do not use lights at night.

Transportation of Bicycles

Bicycles may be carried on the roof of a car providing the total height does not exceed 4 metres. They may also be carried at the rear providing the width does not extend more than 20cm beyond the width of the vehicle.

Electricity and Gas

Most campsites have a supply ranging from 4 to 10 amps and almost all have CEE connections. Plugs have two round pins.

The full range of Campingaz cylinders is available.

Entry Formalities

British and Irish passport holders may stay in the Netherlands for up to three months without a visa.

Medical Services

Pharmacies (apotheek) dispense prescriptions whereas drugstores (drogisterij) sell only over-the-counter remedies, amongst other items. Pharmacies may require a photocopy of the details on your European Health Insurance Card (EHIC). You will need to show your EHIC to obtain treatment by a doctor contracted to the state health care system (AGIS Zorgverzekeringen) and you will probably have to pay a fee. You will be charged for emergency dental treatment. Charges for prescriptions vary. Treatment refunds are obtained from AGIS.

Inpatient hospital treatment is free provided it is authorised by AGIS. Local state health insurance fund offices can give advice on obtaining emergency medical services and provide names and addresses of doctors, health centres and hospitals. Tourist Information offices also keep lists of local doctors.

Opening Hours

Banks – Mon-Fri 9am-4pm/5pm (some open Sat).

Museums – Tue-Fri 10am-5pm; Sat & Sun 11am/1pm-5pm.

Post Offices – Mon-Fri 9am-5pm; some Sat 9am-12 noon/1.30pm.

Shops – Mon-Fri 8am/8.30am-6pm/8pm; Sat 8am/8.30am-4pm/5pm; late night shopping in many towns on Thursday or Friday to 9pm. Shops close one day or half day in the week in addition to Sunday.

Safety and Security

In relative terms there is little crime but visitors should take the usual precautions in central Amsterdam (particularly in and around Central Station), in Rotterdam and The Hague. As in many large cities, pickpocketing and bag snatching are more common. Pickpockets operate on trams, especially on numbers 2 and 5 in Amsterdam.

Ensure you keep your valuables safely with you at all times and do not leave them unattended or hanging on the back of a chair. Bicycle theft is a common occurrence in the major cities.

Fake, plain clothes policemen carrying badges are in action pretending to be investigating counterfeit money and false credit cards. Dutch police do not have badges and plain clothes police will rarely carry out this kind of inspection. Always ask for identity, check it thoroughly and do not allow yourself to be intimidated. Call 0900 8844 to contact the nearest police station if you are concerned or suspicious.

Several deaths occur each year due to drowning in canals. Take particular care when driving, cycling or walking alongside canals.

Avoid confrontation with anyone offering to sell you drugs and stay away from quiet or dark alleys, particularly late at night.

There have been incidences of drinks being spiked in city centre locations. Always be aware of your drink and do not leave it unattended. Young women and lone travellers need to be especially vigilant in these situations.

The Netherlands shares with the rest of Europe a general threat from terrorism. Attacks could be indiscriminate and against civilian targets in public places, including tourist sites.

British Embassy

LANGE VOORHOUT 10, 2514 ED THE HAAG
Tel: (070) 4270427
www.ukinnl.fco.gov.uk

British Consulate-General
KONINGSLAAN 44,1075 AE AMSTERDAM
Tel: (020) 6764343

Irish Embassy
SCHEVENINGSEWEG 112, 2584 AE THE HAGUE
Tel: (070) 3630993
www.embassyofireland.nl

Documents

Passport
Everyone from the age of 14 is required to show a valid identity document to police officers on request and you should, therefore, carry your passport at all times.

Vehicle(s)
When driving carry your driving licence, vehicle registration certificate (V5C), insurance certificate and MOT certificate, if applicable. If driving a vehicle that does not belong to you, carry a letter of authority from the owner.

Money

Money may be exchanged at main border crossing posts, major post offices, banks, VVV tourist information offices and some ANWB offices. Other bureaux de change may not give such favourable rates.

The major credit and debit cards are widely accepted but supermarkets will not generally accept credit cards. As a precaution carry enough cash to cover your purchases as you may find that debit cards issued by banks outside the Netherlands are not accepted. Cash machines are widespread.

Motoring in the Netherlands

The Dutch drive assertively and are not renowned for their road courtesy. Pedestrians should be very careful when crossing roads, including on zebra crossings.

Accidents

All accidents which cause injuries or major damage must be reported to the police. Drivers involved in an accident must exchange their identity details and their insurance company contact information.

Alcohol

The maximum permitted level of alcohol is 50 milligrams in 100 millilitres of blood, i.e. lower than that permitted in the UK (80 milligrams). Penalties for driving under the influence of alcohol can be severe. A lower level of 20 milligrams applies to drivers who have held a driving licence for less than five years. It is wisest to adopt a 'no drinking and driving' rule.

Breakdown Service

There are emergency telephones every 2km on all motorways and they are directly linked to the nearest breakdown centre.

ANWB, the motoring and leisure organisation, has a road patrol service which operates 24 hours a day on all roads. Drivers requiring assistance may call the 'Wegenwacht' road patrol centre by telephoning 088 2692888. Alternatively call the ANWB Emergency Centre on (070) 3141414. Operators speak English.

Charges apply for breakdown assistance and towing is charged according to distance and time of day. Members of clubs affiliated to the AIT/FIA, such as The Caravan Club, incur lower charges. Payment by credit card is accepted. In some areas the ANWB Wegenwacht has contracts with local garages to provide assistance to its members and affiliates.

Essential Equipment

Lights
The use of dipped headlights during the day is recommended.

Child Restraint System
Children under the age of 18 years, measuring less than 1.35m, must be seated in an approved child restraint adapted to their size (ECE 44/03 or 44/04 safety approved). Children under 3 years old are able to travel in the front if they are seated in a rear facing child seat with the airbag deactivated, and under no circumstances are they allowed to travel in a car with no child restraint system fitted.

Fuel

Unleaded petrol is available from green pumps marked 'Loodvrije Benzine'. LPG (autogas) is widely available along main roads and motorways.

Petrol stations along motorways and main roads and in main towns are open 24 hours, except in parts of the north of the country where they close at 11pm. Credit cards are accepted but some all night petrol stations only have automatic pumps which may operate with bank notes only.

Low Emission Zones

Low Emission Zones are in operation in 16 cities in the Netherlands. Restrictions only apply to freight vehicles over 3500kg, however currently all foreign vehicles are able to enter the Low Emission Zone without any restrictions. Check www.lowemissionzones.eu before you travel.

Parking

Parking meters or discs are in use in many towns allowing parking for between 30 minutes and two or three hours; discs can be obtained from local shops. A sign 'parkeerschijf' indicates times when a disc is compulsory. Paid parking is expensive and there are insufficient parking spaces to meet demand. Clamping and towing away of vehicles are commonplace and fines are high. Check signs for the precise times you are allowed to park, particularly on main roads in Amsterdam.

Priority

Yellow diamond shaped signs with a white border indicate priority roads. In the absence of such signs drivers must give way to all traffic approaching from the right. At the intersection of two roads of the same class where there are no signs, traffic from the right has priority.

At junctions marked with a 'priority road ahead' sign, a stop sign or a line of white painted triangles ('shark's teeth') across the road, drivers must give way to all vehicles on the priority road, including bicycles and mopeds.

Be particularly careful when using roundabouts as on some you have the right of way when on them, but on others you must give way to vehicles entering the roundabout, i.e. on your right.

Trams have priority at the intersection of roads of equal importance, but they must give way to traffic on priority roads. If a tram or bus stops in the middle of the road to allow passengers on and off, you must stop. Buses have right of way over all other vehicles when leaving bus stops in built-up areas.

Roads

Roads are generally good and well maintained, but are overcrowded and are frequently subject to strong winds. Most cities have a policy of reducing the amount of nonessential traffic within their boundaries. Narrowing roads, obstacles, traffic lights and speed cameras are often in place to achieve this.

Road Signs and Markings

National motorways are distinguished by red signs, and prefixed with the letter A, whereas European motorways have green signs and are prefixed E. Dual carriageways and other main roads have yellow signs with the letter N and secondary roads are prefixed B.

In general road signs and markings conform to international standards. The following are some road signs which may also be seen:

Cycle path   Cycle route

District   Hard shoulder open
Numbers   as rush-hour lane

Dutch	English Translation
Afrit	Exit
Doorgaand verkeer gestremd	No throughway
Drempels	Humps
Langzaam rijden	Slow down
Omleiding	Detour
Oprit	Entrance
Ousteek u lichten	Switch on lights
Parkeerplaats	Parking
Pas op!	Attention
Stop-verbod	No parking
Wegomlegging	Detour
Werk in uitvoering	Road works
Woonerven	Slow down (in built-up area)

A continuous central white line should not be crossed even to make a left turn.

Speed Limits

	Open Road (km/h)	Motorway (km/h)
Car Solo	80-100	130*
Car towing caravan/trailer	80-90	90
Motorhome under 3500kg	80-100	130*
Motorhome 3500-7500kg	80	80

*Unless otherwise indicated.

Be vigilant and observe the overhead illuminated lane indicators when they are in use, as speed limits on motorways are variable. Speed cameras, speed traps and unmarked police vehicles are widely used. Radar detectors are illegal, with use resulting in a heavy fine.

Motorhomes over 3,500kg are restricted to 50 km/h (31 mph) in built-up areas and to 80 km/h (50 mph) on all other roads.

The beginning of a built up area is indicated by a rectangular blue sign with the name of the locality in white. The end of a built up area is indicated by the same sign with a white diagonal lines across it.

Traffic Jams

The greatest traffic congestion occurs on weekdays at rush hours around the major cities of Amsterdam, Den Bosch, Eindhoven, Rotterdam, Utrecht, The Hague and Eindhoven.

Summer holidays in the Netherlands are staggered and, as a result, traffic congestion is not too severe. However during the Christmas, Easter and Whitsun holiday periods, traffic jams are common and bottlenecks regularly occur on the A2 (Maastricht to Amsterdam), the A12 (Utrecht to the German border) and on the A50 (Arnhem to Apeldoorn). Roads to the Zeeland coast, e.g. the A58, N57 and N59, may become congested during periods of fine weather.

Many Germans head for the Netherlands on their own public holidays and the roads are particularly busy during these periods.

Violation of Traffic Regulations

Police are empowered to impose on-the-spot fines (or confiscate vehicles) for violation of traffic regulations and fines for speeding can be severe. If you are fined always ask for a receipt.

Motorways

There are over 2,750 kilometres of toll-free motorway. There are rest areas along the motorways, most of which have a petrol station and a small shop. Tolls are charged on some bridges and tunnels, notably the Westerschelde Toll Tunnel. This road tunnel links Terneuzen (north of Gent) and Ellewoutsdijk (south of Goes) across the Westerschelde. It provides a short, fast route between Channel ports and the road network in the west of the country. The tunnel is 6.6km long (just over 4 miles) and the toll for a car + caravan (maximum height 3m measured from front axle) is €7.45 and for a motorhome €7.45 height under 2.5m) or €18.20 (height over 3m) (all prices for 2015). Credit cards are accepted. For more information go to www.westerscheldetunnel.nl.

NETHERLANDS

Touring

The southern Netherlands is the most densely populated part of the country but, despite the modern sprawl, ancient towns such as Dordrecht, Gouda, Delft and Leiden have retained their individuality and charm. Rotterdam is a modern, commercial centre and a tour of its harbour – the busiest in Europe – makes a fascinating excursion. The scenery in the north of the country is the most typically Dutch – vast, flat landscapes, largely reclaimed from the sea, dotted with windmills. Some of the most charming towns and villages are Marken, Volendam and Alkmaar (famous for its cheese market). Aalsmeer, situated south of Amsterdam, stages the world's largest daily flower auction.

It is worth spending time to visit the hilly provinces in the east such as Gelderland, known for its castles, country houses and its major city, Arnhem, which has many links with the Second World War. Overijssel is a region of great variety and the old Hanseatic towns of Zwolle and Kampen have splendid quays and historic buildings. Friesland is the Netherland's lake district.

An Amsterdam Card entitles you to free admission to many of the city's famous museums, including the Rijksmuseum and Van Gogh Museum, and to discounts in many restaurants, shops, attractions and at Park & Ride car parks. It also entitles you to discounts on tours as well as free travel on public transport and a free canal cruise. The Card is valid for one, two or three days and is available from tourist information offices, some Shell petrol stations, Canal Bus kiosks, Park & Ride car parks and some hotels. Alternatively purchase online from www.iamsterdamcard.com.

Service charges are included in restaurant bills and tips are not necessary. Smoking is not permitted in bars or restaurants.

Spring is one of the most popular times to visit the Netherlands, in particular the famous Keukenhof Gardens near Lisse, open from 24 March to 16 May in 2016, see www.keukenhof.nl. Visitors enjoy a display of over seven million flowering bulbs, trees and shrubs. Special events take place here at other times of the year, including a National Bulb Market in October.

Public Transport

There is an excellent network of buses and trams, together with metro systems in Amsterdam (called the GVB), Rotterdam and The Hague. An electronic card 'OV Chipkaart' is gradually replacing the previous system of 'Strippenkaart' which were strips of 15 or 45 tickets valid throughout the country.

OV-Chip cards can be bought at vending machines at stations or ticket offices and on board buses and trams and are available for periods from one hour to seven days allowing unlimited travel on trams, buses and the metro. Children under 12 and people over the age of 65 qualify for reduced fares (show your passport as proof of age). See www.gvb.nl for more information.

Tickets must be validated before travel either at the yellow machines on trams and at metro stations or by your bus driver or conductor.

In Amsterdam canal transport includes a regular canal shuttle between Centraal Station and the Rijksmuseum. A 'circle tram' travels from Centraal Station through the centre of Amsterdam past a number of local visitor attractions, such as Anne Frank's house, the Rijksmuseum, Van Gogh museum and Rembrandthuis.

There are Park & Ride facilities at most railway stations. Secure parking is also offered at 'transferiums', a scheme offering reasonably priced guarded parking in secure areas on the outskirts of major towns with easy access by road and close to public transport hubs. Transferiums have heated waiting rooms and rest rooms as well as information for travellers, and some even have a shop.

Frequent car ferry services operate on routes to the Frisian (or Wadden) Islands off the north west coast, for example, from Den Helder to Texel Island, Harlingen to Terschelling Island and Holwerd to Ameland Island. Other islands in the group do not allow cars but there are passenger ferry services. In the summer island-hopping round tickets are available to foot passengers and cyclists and are popular for exploring the country.

AARDENBURG see Sluis *A4*

AERDT see Zevenaar *C3*

ALKMAAR *B2* (9km N Rural) *52.69425, 4.77080* **Camping DroomPark Molengroet, Molengroet 1, 1723 PX Noord-Scharwoude [(0226) 393444; fax 391426; info@molengroet.nl; www.molengroet.nl]** Fr Amsterdam, Haarlem take A9 to end at rndabt, then onto Ring Alkmaar & foll sp Schagen. Take N245 sp Schagen (dual carr'way). Exit at km post 25.2 W sp Geestmeerambacht. Site sp on R. Lge, hdg/mkd pitch, unshd; htd wc; chem disp; mv service pnt; baby facs; fam bthrm; some serviced pitches; private san facs some pitches; shwrs inc; EHU (4-10A) inc; gas; lndry (inc dryer); shop; rest, snacks; bar; BBQ; htd pool; sand beach 10km; lake sw 300m; entmnt; bike hire; sat TV; 50% statics; dogs €3; sep car park; free bus to cheese mkt (Fri) & beach (Sat); Holland Tulip Parcs site; adv bkg; quiet; ccard acc. "Located in recreation park with lge lake; site bus to cheese mkt & beach; modern, clean san facs." Easter-31 Oct. € 26.00 (CChq acc)   2009*

⊞ **ALKMAAR** *B2* (7km W Rural) *52.63100, 4.69500* **Camping Hoeve Engeland, Egmondermeer 9, 1934 PN Egmond aan den Hoef [(072) 5116370; rus.jan@tiscali.nl]** Take A9 to Alkmaar & take N9 ring rd W. Take 1st L turn after rlwy viaduct at traff lts opp ING bank. Foll sm rd past garden cent, site in approx 250m - sp on gate. Sm, pt shd; htd wc; shwrs inc; EHU (16A) inc (poss rev pol); beach 8km; bus 1km; poss cr; Eng spkn; adv bkg; quiet. "CL-style farm site; clean (ltd) facs; mosquitoes; gd cycling to historic Alkmaar & coastal dunes; gd cycling area; friendly, helpful owner." 15 Mar-15 Oct. € 15.00   2013*

> ## "I like to fill in the reports as I travel from site to site"
> You'll find report forms at the back of this guide, or you can fill them in online at www.caravanclub.co.uk/europereport.

ALKMAAR *B2* (2.6km NW Rural) *52.64205, 4.72407* **Camping Alkmaar, Bergerweg 201, 1817 ML Alkmaar [(072) 5116924; info@campingalkmaar.nl; www.campingalkmaar.nl]** Fr W ring rd (Martin Luther Kingweg) foll Bergen sp, bear R at T-junc & site 150m on L. Site well sp. Med, mkd pitch, hdstg, pt shd; htd wc; chem disp; mv service pnt; fam bthrm; shwrs €0.50; EHU (4-10A) inc; lndry; shop 1km; BBQ; playgrnd; pool adj; sand beach 6km; golf 2km; cab TV; some statics; dogs €3; bus at gate; poss cr; Eng spkn; adv bkg; quiet; ccard acc; red CKE/CCI. "Clean, friendly site; sm pitches; buses to town; 10 mins walk to cent; cheese mkt on Friday in ssn." ♦ ltd. 20 Mar-1 Oct. € 27.00   2015*

ALMERE *C3* (7km W Rural) *52.35688, 5.22505* **Camping Waterhout, Archerpad 6, 1324 ZZ Almere [(036) 5470632; fax 5470634; info@waterhout.nl; www.waterhout.nl]** Exit A6 junc 4, site sp fr slip rd on S edge Weerwater. Med, mkd pitch, shd; wc; chem disp; baby facs; fam bthrm; shwrs €0.50; EHU (10A) inc; lndry (inc dryer); shop; rest, snacks; bar; playgrnd; sand beach & lake sw adj; entmnt; TV rm; 30% statics; dogs €2.50; phone; bus 200m; poss cr; Eng spkn; adv bkg; quiet; red CKE/CCI. "Well laid-out site; conv Amsterdam by bus or train - 30 mins; Almere ultra-modern city." 4 Apr-19 Oct. € 25.00   2014*

AMELAND ISLAND *C1* Sites on Ameland Island are listed together at the end of the Netherlands site entry pages.

AMERSFOORT *C3* (11km S Rural) *52.07975, 5.38151* **Vakantiepark De Heigraaf, De Haygraeff 9, 3931 ML Woudenberg [(033) 2865066; info@heigraaf.nl; www.heigraaf.nl]** Exit A12 at Maarn junc 21 or junc 22 & foll sp to site on N224, 2km W of Woudenberg. V lge, mkd pitch, pt shd; htd wc; chem disp; mv service pnt; baby facs; shwrs €0.50; EHU (4-6A) inc; lndry (inc dryer); shop; rest, snacks; bar; playgrnd; lake sw 150m; wifi; entmnt; 50% statics; no dogs; phone; bus 500m; Eng spkn; adv bkg; quiet. "Vg, well-managed site; modern san facs; well run site, does not accept Visa." ♦ 1 Apr-31 Oct. € 20.00   2012*

AMSTELVEEN see Amsterdam *B3*

Reception open from 09:00 till 22:00

Meeuwenlaan 138 • 1022 AM Amsterdam
tel. +31 (0)20 - 636 88 55
mail: vliegenbos@noord.amsterdam.nl

www.vliegenbos.com

Camping Vliegenbos

Check any essential information with the site before you travel   *Last year of report   **441**

AMSTERDAM *B3* (12km N Rural) *52.43649, 4.91445* **Camping Het Rietveen, Noordeinde 130, 1121 AL Landsmeer [(020) 4821468; fax 4820214; info@campinghetrietveen.nl; www.campinghetrietveen.nl]** Fr A10 ring rd exit junc 117. At junc off slip rd turn L dir Landsmeer, site sp. Sm, mkd pitch, mkd pitch; wc; chem disp; mv service pnt; shwrs inc; EHU (10A) inc; shop, rest, bar 500m; lake sw & fishing; tennis; bike hire; dogs free; phone adj; bus to Amsterdam 200m; poss cr; Eng spkn; adv bkg; quiet; CKE/CCI. "Vg, pretty lakeside site, like lge CL, in well-kept vill; no recep - site yourself & owner will call; sep field avail for rallies; excel touring base; city 30 mins by bus; san facs inadequate." 1 Mar-30 Nov. € 34.00   2014*

AMSTERDAM *B3* (5km NE Urban) *52.38907, 4.92532*
Camping Vliegenbos, Meeuwenlaan 138, 1022 AM Amsterdam [(020) 6368855; fax 6322723; vliegenbos@ noord.amsterdam.nl; www.vliegenbos.com]
Fr A10 Amsterdam ring rd, take exit S116 Amsterdam Noord, at 2nd slip rd turn R sp Noord over rndabt, turn L at next rndabt, then immed sharp R, L onto service rd, site sp. Lge, hdstg, pt sl, pt shd; htd wc; chem disp; mv service pnt; baby facs; shwrs inc; EHU (6A) inc; gas; lndry; shop; rest 2km; snacks; bar; pool 1.5km; no dogs; phone; bus to city nr; poss cr; Eng spkn; poss noisy tent campers; ccard acc. "Sm pitches mainly for tents; ltd EHU; m'vans & c'vans park outside barrier; friendly staff; bus tickets to city cent fr recep; cycle path to city cent via free ferry; modern san facs." ♦ 1 Apr-1 Oct. € 28.50   2013*

See advertisement on previous page

⊞ **AMSTERDAM** *B3* (6km E Urban) *52.36555, 4.95829*
Camping Zeeburg, Zuider Ijdijk 20, 1095 KN Amsterdam [(020) 6944430; fax 6946238; info@campingzeeburg.nl; www.campingzeeburg.nl] Fr A10 ring rd exit at S114 & foll site sps. Lge, unshd; wc; chem disp; mv service pnt; shwrs €0.80; EHU (6-10A) inc; gas; lndry; shop; snacks; bike hire; internet; some statics; dogs €3; bus/tram to city nr; poss cr; adv bkg. "Used mainly by tents in summer, but rest of year suitable for c'vans; conv city cent." € 28.00   2011*

AMSTERDAM *B3* (12km SE Urban) *52.31258, 4.99035*
Gaasper Camping, Loosdrechtdreef 7, 1108 AZ Amsterdam-Zuidoost [(020) 6967326; fax 6969369; info@gaaspercamping.nl; www.gaaspercamping.nl] Fr A2 take A9 E sp Amersfoort. After about 5km take 3rd exit sp Gaasperplas/Weesp S113. Cross S113 into site, sp. Lge, hdg/mkd pitch, some hdstg, pt shd; htd wc; chem disp; mv service pnt; serviced pitches; shwrs metered; EHU (10A) €3.50 (care needed); gas; lndry; shop; rest, snacks; bar; playgrnd; 20% statics; dogs €2.50; metro 5 mins walk (tickets fr site recep); poss cr; Eng spkn; quiet but some rd & air traffic noise; CKE/CCI. "Immac site set in beautiful parkland; well-run with strict rules; night guard at barrier (high ssn); vans must be manhandled onto pitch (help avail); high ssn arr early to ensure pitch - no adv bkg for fewer than 7 nights; poss cold shwrs & ltd shop LS; gd security; well run site; conv for metro; adv bkg rec in high ssn." 1 Jan-6 Jan, 15 Mar-1 Nov, 27 Dec-31 Dec. € 33.50   2014*

AMSTERDAM *B3* (15km SW Rural) *52.29366, 4.82316*
Camping Het Amsterdamse Bos, Kleine Noorddijk 1, 1187 NZ Amstelveen [(020) 6416868; fax 6402378; info@ campingamsterdam.com; www.campingamsterdamsebos. com] Foll A10 & A4 twd Schiphol Airport. Fr junc on A4 & A9 m'way, take A9 E twd Amstelveen; at next exit (junc 6) exit sp Aalsmeer. Foll Aalsmeer sp for 1km bearing R at traff lts then at next traff lts turn L over canal bdge onto N231. In 1.5km turn L at 2nd traff lts into site. Fr S exit A4 junc 3 onto N201 dir Hilversum (ignore other camp sps). Turn L onto N231 dir Amstelveen, at rd junc Bovenkirk take N231 dir Schiphol, site on R in 200m, sp. V lge, pt shd; htd wc; chem disp; mv service pnt; shwrs €0.80; EHU (10A) €4.50; gas; lndry; shop; supmkt nr; rest, snacks; bar; waterpark nr; wifi; 20% statics; dogs €3; bus to city; poss cr; Eng spkn; adv bkg; some aircraft noise; ccard acc; CKE/CCI. "Conv Amsterdam by bus - tickets sold on site; poss migrant workers resident on site; san facs stretched high ssn; gd walking & cycling paths; spectacular daily flower auctions at Aalsmeer; conv bulbfields." ♦ 15 Mar-31 Oct. € 30.50   2014*

AMSTERDAM *B3* (13km W Rural) *52.39548, 4.75308* **Camping Parc Spaarnwoude (formerly Houtrak), Zuiderweg 2, 1105 NA Halfweg [(020) 4972796; fax (087) 7844089; info@campinghoutrak.nl; www.parcspaarnwoude.nl]** Fr A9 dir Haarlem exit onto A200 sp Halfweg. In 1.5km sp for Spaarnwoude, go L under A200, over rlwy x-ing & take 4th on L. Site on R in 100m. Fr Amsterdam N202, Spaarnwoude & site sp. Sm, mkd pitch, pt shd; htd wc; chem disp; mv service pnt; baby facs; shwrs €0.50; EHU (6A) €2.20; lndry; playgrnd; pool 11km; internet; TV; dogs €5; poss cr; noise fr aircraft. "Under flightpath into Schiphol airport; min stay 3 nights Aug." 1 Apr-31 Oct. € 17.40   2009*

⊞ **ANNEN** *D2* (3.7km S Rural) *53.03017, 6.73912* **De Baldwin Hoeve, Annerweg 9, 9463 TB Eext [05 92 27 16 29; baldwinhoeve@hetnet.nl; www.baldwinhoeve.nl]** Fr N34 take Annen exit. Turn R onto Anlooerweg. At rndabt take R dir Eext. Bef underpass take sm service rd on L to campsite. Sm, mkd pitch, unshd; wc; chem disp; shwrs; EHU (10A); BBQ; dogs; bus adj; twin axles; Eng spkn; adv bkg; quiet; CCI. "CL type farm site with excel san facs; friendly owners; some rd noise; horses & other livestock; lg group accomodation avail; vg." € 51.00   2014*

APELDOORN *C3* (10km N Rural) *52.29066, 5.94520* **Camping De Helfterkamp, Gortelseweg 24, 8171 RA Vaassen [(0578) 571839; fax 570378; info@helfterkamp.nl; www.helfterkamp.nl]** Leave A50 junc 26; foll sp to Vaassen; site sp on ent to town - 2.5km W of Vaassen. Med, mkd pitch, pt shd; htd wc; chem disp; baby facs; fam bthrm; shwrs €0.50; EHU (16A) metered (poss rev pol); gas; lndry; shop; playgrnd; lake sw 1.5km; bike hire; 40% statics; dogs €1.75; phone; Eng spkn; adv bkg ess high ssn; quiet; wifi; ccard acc; 10% red long stay; CKE/CCI. "Excel, immac, well-maintained, busy site in beautiful woodland area; key for shwrs & hot water; v friendly owners; conv for Apeldoorn/Arnhem areas & De Hooge Veluwe National Park; gd walking/cycling." 22 Feb-31 Oct. € 33.50   2014*

APELDOORN C3 (16km N Rural) 52.31366, 5.92705
**Recreatiecentrum De Wildhoeve, Hanendorperweg 102,
8166 JJ Emst [(0578) 661324; fax 662965; info@wildhoeve.nl;
www.wildhoeve.nl]** Exit 26 fr A50, site sp 3.5km W of
Emst. Lge, mkd pitch, pt shd; htd wc; chem disp; mv service
pnt; serviced pitches; fam bthrm; baby facs; shwrs; EHU
(6A); gas; lndry (inc dryer); shop; rest, snacks; bar; playgrnd;
2 pools (1 htd, covrd); paddling pool; waterslide; games
area; tennis; bike hire; wifi; TV; 20% statics; no dogs; sep
car park; Holland Tulip Parcs site; adv bkg. ♦ 1 Apr-30 Sep.
€ 32.00   2011*

See advertisement inside the front cover

⊞ **APELDOORN** C3 (10km S Rural) 52.15096, 6.02197
**Camping De Vinkenkamp, Vinkenkamp 10, 7364 CD Lieren
[(055) 5051253; info@vinkenkamp.nl; www.vinkenkamp.nl]**
Exit A1 junc 20 Apeldoorn Sud & foll sp Loenen-Eerbeek. Site
sp. Med, mkd pitch, pt shd; htd wc; chem disp; mv service
pnt; baby facs; shwrs inc; EHU (6-16A) inc; gas; lndry; shop;
snacks; bar; playgrnd; entmnt; TV; some statics; dogs €1.70;
Eng spkn; quiet; ccard acc. "Beautiful pt of Holland; excel site."
€ 22.50   2010*

APELDOORN C3 (27km SW Rural) 52.15040, 5.74080 **Camping
De Harskamperdennen, Houtvester van 't Hoffweg 25,
3775 KB Kootwijk [(0318) 456272; fax 457695;
info@harskamperdennen.nl; www.harskamperdennen.nl]**
Exit A1/E30 at junc 17 dir Harskamp, site sp on L in 6km. Lge,
shd; htd wc; chem disp; mv service pnt; baby facs; shwrs €0.50;
EHU (4-6A) inc; gas; lndry; playgrnd; games area; bike hire; TV;
no dogs; phone; sep car park; quiet; ccard acc. "All pitches in
sm glades in forest; military base nr & explosions heard fr time
to time, otherwise peaceful; neat, tidy site; friendly staff." ♦
1 Apr-25 Oct. € 26.00   2009*

APPELSCHA D2 (4.5km S Rural) 52.92134, 6.34447
**Boscamping Appelscha, Oude Willem 3, 8426 SM
Appelscha [(0516) 431391; info@boscampingappelscha.nl;
www.campingalkenhaer.nl]** A28 junc 31 sp Drachten. Turn
L onto N381. About 13km turn L onto Oude Willem then
take 3rd R, site on L. Lge, mkd pitch, pt shd; wc; chem disp;
mv service pnt; baby facs; shwrs; EHU (16A); lndry (inc dryer);
snacks; takeaway; playgrnd; paddling pool; wifi; 60% statics;
Eng spkn; quiet; CKE/CCI. "Neat, friendly, well run site; many
walking, cycling & riding trails in nrby national park; vg site."
1 Apr-1 Oct. € 33.50   2014*

ARNHEM C3 (6km W Rural) 51.99365, 5.82203 **Camping
Aan Veluwe (formerly De Bilderberg), Sportlaan 1,
6861 AG Oosterbeek [(0224) 563109; fax 563093;
info@aannoordzee.nl; www.aanveluwe.nl]** Fr S
fr Nijmegen, cross new bdge at Arnhem. Foll Oosterbeek sp
for 5km, cont past memorial in Oosterbeek, in 1km turn R at
rndabt, 500m L to site. Or fr A50 exit junc 19 onto N225 twd
Osterbeek/Arnhem. In 3km at rndabt turn L, site on L in 500m.
Med, pt sl, pt shd; htd wc; chem disp; shwrs inc; EHU (16A) inc;
gas; shop; bar; playgrnd; pool 3km; adv bkg; few statics; dogs
€1.80; sep car park; quiet; red for long stays. "Conv Airborne
Museum & Cemetery & Dutch Open Air Museum; sports club
bar open to site guests; shwr facs for each pitch; lovely walks."
29 Mar-13 Oct. € 28.00   2014*

ARNHEM C3 (5km NW Rural) 52.0072, 5.8714 **Camping
Warnsborn, Bakenbergseweg 257, 6816 PB Arnhem
[(026) 4423469; fax 4421095; info@campingwarnsborn.nl;
www.campingwarnsborn.nl]** Fr Utrecht on E35/A12, exit
junc 25 Ede (if coming fr opp dir, beware unnumbered m'way
junc 200m prior to junc 25). Take N224 dual c'way twd
Arnhem & foll sp Burgers Zoo, site sp. Beware oncoming traff
& sleeping policeman nr site ent. Med, pt shd; htd wc; chem
disp, mv service pnt; baby facs; fam bthrm; shwrs €0.60; EHU
(6A) inc; gas; lndry; sm shop & 3km; rest 1km; BBQ; playgrnd;
internet; 5% statics; dogs €3; phone; bus 100m; poss cr; Eng
spkn; adv bkg; quiet; ccard acc; red long stay/CKE/CCI. "Excel,
spacious, clean, well-maintained, wooded site; san facs clean;
friendly, helpful family owners & staff; airborne museum &
cemetery; cycle rtes direct fr site; conv Hooge Veluwe National
Park & Kröller-Müller museum (Van Gogh paintings); super site
but busy." ♦ ltd. 1 Apr-1 Nov. € 21.50   2015*

ARNHEM C3 (9km NW Rural) 52.03192, 5.86652 **Droompark
Hooge Veluwe, Koningsweg 14, Schaarsbergen, 6816 TC
Arnhem [(026) 4432272 or (088) 0551500; fax 4436809;
hoogeveluwe@droomparken.nl; www.hoogeveluwe.nl]**
Fr Utrecht A12/E35, Oosterbeck exit 25 & foll sp for Hooge
Veluwe to site in 4km on R. Lge, pt shd; htd wc; chem disp;
mv service pnt; baby facs; fam bthrm; serviced pitches; shwrs
inc; EHU (6-16A) inc; gas; lndry; shop; rest, snacks; bar;
playgrnd; 2 pools (1 htd, covrd); paddling pool; games area;
entmnt; dogs €3.50; 50% statics in sep area; sep car park;
some rd noise; poss cr; adv bkg; Eng spkn; ccard acc. "Vg,
espec for children; excel site; lots of facs; helpful staff; care
needed turning into site area; great value; vg clean san facs; gd
rest; conv for Arnhem area, m'way & Ijmuiden ferry port." ♦
28 Mar-26 Oct. € 39.00   2014*

ASSEN D2 (16km NW Rural) 53.07783, 6.44870 **Camping
de Norgerberg, Langeloërweg 63. 9331 VA Norg
[(0592) 612281; info@norgerberg.nl; www.norgerberg.nl]**
Fr Leeuwarden, N31 S to junc 30(20km). Then N381 sp Emmen
for 10km, L twrds Waskemeer/Norg on N917. Turn L at Norg
onto N373. Site on L in 1km. Med, hdg/mkd pitch, pt shd; htd
wc; chem disp, mv service pnt; baby facs; shwrs inc; EHU (10A);
gas; lndry (inc dryer); supmkt; rest; snacks; bar; BBQ; playgrnd;
pool 1km; games area & rm; entmnt; internet; wifi; tv rm; dogs
€2.30; bus adj; Eng spkn; adv bkg; quiet; red LS; CCI. "Vg
cycling trails including forest; easy access to town, rest & shops;
excel." ♦ 27 Mar-1 Nov. € 28.00   2015*

BARENDRECHT see Rotterdam B3

BEERZE see Ommen D2

BEILEN D2 (7km E Rural) 52.85285, 6.59010 **Camping
De Valkenhof, Beilerstraat 13a, 9431 GA Westerbork
[(0593) 331546; fax 333278; info@camping-de-valkenhof.nl;
www.camping-de-valkenhof.nl]** Exit A28 junc 30 Beilen, dir
Westerbork, site sp to W of Westerbork. Lge, some hdstg, pt
shd; htd wc; chem disp; mv service pnt; baby facs; fam bthrm;
shwrs inc; EHU (6A) inc; gas; lndry (inc dryer); supmkt high ssn;
snacks; BBQ; playgrnd; htd pool; paddling pool; waterslide;
games area; bike hire; wifi; cab TV; 20% statics; dogs €4.35;
sep car park; Holland Tulip Parcs site; Eng spkn; adv bkg; quiet.
"Gd walking area." 1 Apr-1 Oct. € 25.00   2011*

BEILEN *D2* (10km S Rural) *52.80166, 6.52501* **Camping De Otterberg, Drijberseweg 36A, 9418 TL Wijster [(0593) 562362; fax 562941; info@otterburg.nl; www.otterberg.nl]** Take A28 Hoogeveen-Assen exit Dwingeloo/Wijster. In Wijster turn R & foll sps approx 1.5km dir Dribjer. Lge, mkd pitch, pt shd; htd wc; fam bthrm; baby facs; chem disp; shwrs €0.20; EHU (6A) inc; gas; lndry (inc dryer); shop; snacks; rest; playgrnd; pool; tennis; bike hire; TV; 60% statics; dogs €3; phone; poss cr; Eng spkn; adv bkg. "Helpful, friendly site adj National Park; gd, modern san facs." ♦ 1 Apr-1 Oct. € 25.00   2010*

BELT SCHUTSLOOT see Meppel *C2*

BERG EN TERBLIJT see Valkenburg aan de Geul *C4*

BERGEIJK see Eersel *C4*

BERGEN OP ZOOM *B4* (5km NE Rural) *51.51122, 4.31652* **Camping De Heide, Bemmelenberg 12, 4614 PG Bergen op Zoom [(0164) 235659 or 253522; fax 254377; info@campingdeheide.nl; www.campingdeheide.nl]** Exit A58 at Bergen op Zoom Noord, foll sp to town until De Heide sps are picked up. Lge, hdg pitch, pt shd; wc; chem disp; mv service pnt; baby facs; fam bthrm; serviced pitch; shwrs €0.50; EHU (4A) €2.50; gas; lndry; shop; rest, snacks; playgrnd; pool; sand beach 3km; TV; 75% statics; dogs €3; phone; adv bkg; quiet; red snr citizens; CKE/CCI. "Gd NH." ♦ 1 Apr-26 Sep. € 30.00   2009*

BERGEN OP ZOOM *B4* (5km SE Rural) *51.46913, 4.32236* **Camping Uit en Thuis, Heimolen 56, 4625 DD Bergen op Zoom [(0164) 233391; fax 238328; info@campinguitenthuis.nl; www.campinguitenthuis.nl]** Exit A4/E312 at junc 29 sp Huijbergen & foll site sp. Lge, hdg pitch, pt shd; htd wc; chem disp; mv service pnt; baby facs; fam bthrm; shwrs €0.50; EHU (4-6A) €2; lndry; rest, snacks; bar; playgrnd; tennis; games area; TV; 75% statics; dogs €2.80; poss cr; Eng spkn; adv bkg; quiet; red long stay; red CKE/CCI. "Spacious site in woodland; gd cycle paths to pleasant town; sep mv places; vg site." ♦ 1 Apr-31 Oct. € 21.00   2015*

BERLICUM see 'S-Hertogenbosch *C3*

BIDDINGHUIZEN see Harderwijk *C3*

BILTHOVEN see Utrecht *B3*

BLADEL *C4* (1.6km S Rural) *51.35388, 5.22254* **Mini-Camping De Hooiberg, Bredasebaan 20, 5531 NB Bladel [(0497) 369619 or 06 54341822 (mob); info@minicampingdehooiberg.nl; www.minicampingdehooiberg.nl]** Exit A67 junc 32 onto N284 to Bladel, turn L at traff lts to Bladel-Zuid, site on L in 2km. Sm, pt shd; htd wc; chem disp; shwrs inc; EHU (6A) inc; lndry (inc dryer); dogs free; bus adj; sep car park; Eng spkn; adv bkg; quiet. "Gd, quiet site; clean san fac; v friendly owner; farm shop selling local produce adj; 10 mins fr A67; conv NH & for Eindhoven & Efteling theme park." ♦ ltd. 15 Mar-31 Oct. € 15.00   2014*

BLADEL *C4* (3km S Rural) *51.34325, 5.22740* **Camping De Achterste Hoef, Troprijt 10, 5531 NA Bladel [(0497) 381579; fax 387776; info@achterstehoef.nl; www.achterstehoef.nl]** Fr A67 exit junc 32 onto N284 to Bladel, then Bladel-Zuid, site sp. V lge, pt shd; htd wc; chem disp; mv service pnt; baby facs; fam bthrm; private san facs avail; shwrs; EHU (6A) inc; lndry (inc dryer); supmkt; rest, snacks; bar; playgrnd; 2 pools (1 htd, covrd); paddling pool; waterslide; tennis; games area; games rm; bike hire; wifi; entmnt; 70% statics; dogs; adv bkg; ccard acc. ♦ 4 Apr-26 Oct. € 48.40 (CChq acc)   2014*

BOURTANGE *D2* (1km NW Rural) *53.01014, 7.18494* **NCC Camping 't Plathuis, Bourtangerkanaal Noord 1, 9545 VJ Bourtange [(0599) 354383; fax 354388; info@plathuis.nl; www.plathuis.nl]** Exit A47 junc 47 onto N368 sp Blijham to Vlagtwedde. Turn L onto N365 to Bourtange, site sp on R. Med, pt shd, htd wc; chem disp; mv service pnt; baby facs; fam bthrm; shwrs €0.50; EHU (6A) inc (extra for 10A); gas; lndry; shop; snacks; bar; playgrnd; lake sw; fishing; games area; cycle canoe hire; wifi; 50% statics; dogs; phone; bus; adv bkg; quiet; red CCI. "Site adj historic fortress town 2km fr German border; sm marina at ent; pt of site belongs to NCC (CC members welcome at red rates but must phone ahead); gd, clean facs; friendly, helpful owners; vg." ♦ 1 Apr-31 Oct. € 17.50   2010*

BREDA *B3* (11km E Rural) *51.58270, 4.90721* **Camping D'n Mastendol, Oosterhoutseweg 7-13, 5121 RE Rijen [(0161) 222664; fax 222669; info@mastendol.nl; www.mastendol.nl]** Take main rd fr Breda twd Tilburg (not m'way). After 9km turn L, on rd sp Oosterhout 9km; camp 500m on L. Lge, pt shd; htd wc; chem disp; mv service pnt; baby facs; shwrs €0.75; EHU (10A) inc; lndry; shops 2km; snacks; bar; playgrnd; pool; TV; 90% statics; dogs €3; phone; rd noise; ccard acc. "Conv touring base; pitches in pine woods; friendly staff." ♦ 21 Mar-31 Oct. € 23.00   2010*

BREDA *B3* (16km SE Rural) *51.49334, 4.89964* **Camping RCN De Flaasbloem, Flaasdijk 1, 4861 RC Chaam [(0161) 491654; fax 492054; flaasbloem@rcn.nl; www.rcn.nl/centra/deflaasbloem]** A58 Breda-Tilberg, exit junc 14 for Chaam. Fr vill on Alphen rd, site sp. V lge, mkd pitch, pt sl, pt shd; htd wc; chem disp; mv service pnt; baby facs; fam bthrm; shwrs inc; EHU (10A) inc; gas; lndry (inc dryer); shop; supmkt; rest, snacks; playgrnd; 2 pools (1 htd, covrd) lake sw & beach; wifi; TV; 75% statics; dogs €4.75; adv bkg; quiet, but poss noisy w/end; Eng spkn; CKE/CCI. "Cycling cent in flat woodland; many sports facs; many facs for children; well-run site." ♦ 1 Apr-31 Oct. € 28.00   2010*

BREDA *B3* (8km W Rural) *51.56488, 4.69628* **Camping Liesbos, Liesdreef 40, 4838 GV Breda [(076) 5143514; fax 5146555; info@camping-liesbos.nl; www.camping-liesbos.nl]** Fr A16 take exit 16 dir Etten-Leur. Fr A58/E312 take exit 18; site sp. Lge, pt shd; wc; chem disp; mv service pnt; shwrs €0.75; EHU (6A) inc; gas; lndry; shop; rest, snacks; bar; playgrnd; pool; paddling pool; tennis; bike hire; TV; 95% statics; dogs €2.50; phone; poss v cr; quiet; ccard acc. "Narr site rds; sm pitches; v clean san facs; NH only." 1 Apr-1 Oct. € 20.00   2009*

NETHERLANDS

⊞ **BRESKENS** *A4* (7km W Coastal) *51.40360, 3.51310*
**Molecaten Park Napoleon Hoeve, Zandertje 30, 4511 RH
Breskens [(0117) 383838 or 381428; fax 383550; camping@
napoleonhoeve.nl; www.napoleonhoeve.nl]** Fr S on N58
twd Breskens, turn L onto N675 dir Groede. Approx 500m
bef Groede turn N onto Noordweg twd coast, then L into
Zandertje. Site sp on coast rd. Lge, mkd pitch, unshd; htd wc;
chem disp; mv service pnt; baby facs; private san facs avail;
shwrs €0.50; fam bthrm; EHU (10A) inc; gas; lndry; supmkt;
rest; snacks; bar; playgrnd; 2 pools (1 htd, covrd); sand
beach adj; sep naturist beach; tennis; bike hire; entmnt; TV;
60% statics; dogs €3.90; phone; adv bkg; ccard acc. "Friendly,
family site; excel facs; gd bar, rest & children's play area." ♦
€ 37.00   2010*

"We must tell The Club about that great site we found"

Get your site reports in by mid-August
and we'll do our best to get your updates
into the next edition.

BRIELLE *B3* (12km NE Urban) *51.90969, 4.18533* **Camping
De Krabbeplaat, Oude Veerdam 4, 3231 NC Brielle
[(0181) 412363; fax 412093; info@krabbeplaat.nl;
www.krabbeplaat.com]** Exit A15 fr Rotterdam junc 12 onto
N57. Foll sp Brielse Maas-Noord, then site sp. Site sp fr N57.
Lge, hdg/mkd pitch, pt shd; wc; chem disp; mv service pnt;
baby facs; shwrs inc; EHU (4-10A) inc; gas; lndry (inc dryer);
shop; rest, snacks; bar; playgrnd; rv adj; tennis; games area;
bike & boat hire; wifi; cab TV; 70% statics; no dogs; phone;
ferry to Brielle; poss cr; Eng spkn; adv bkg; ccard acc; CKE/
CCI. "Gd for families; easy access to rv." ♦ 1 Apr-24 Oct.
€ 24.00   2010*

BRIELLE *B3* (13km NE Coastal) *51.91379, 4.18218* **NCC
Camping De Lepelaar, Brielse Veerweg, 3231 NA Brielle
[(0181) 417338; www.ncc.nl]** Fr Rotterdam foll A15/N15 W
dir Europoort. Exit junc 12 at Brielle, over Hartelkanaal & at
end sliprd exit Brielse Maas Noord. Turn L on Staaldiepseweg,
in 2.3km L into Brielse Veerweg, sp Voetveer Brielle. Site 2nd
on R. Sm, mkd pitch, pt shd; htd wc; chem disp; shwrs inc;
EHU (4A) €2.75; lndry; shop, rest, snacks, bar 9km; BBQ;
playgrnd; lake sw & beach 500m; dogs; phone; poss cr; adv
bkg req; quiet; CKE/CCI. "Excel site; CC members welcome,
but must pre-book; ferry to Brielle (high ssn) 200m." ♦ ltd.
1 Apr-31 Oct. € 10.00   2009*

BRIELLE *B3* (1km E Urban) *51.90666, 4.17527* **Camping de
Meeuw, Batterijweg 1, 3231 AA Brielle [(0181) 412777;
fax 418127; info@demeeuw.nl; www.demeeuw.nl]**
On A15/N57 foll sp to Brielle. Turn R after passing thro town
gates & foll sp to site. Lge, pt shd; wc; chem disp; mv service
pnt; fam bthrm; baby facs; shwrs inc; EHU (6A) €2 (poss rev
pol); gas; lndry; shop; rest, snacks; bar; playgrnd; pool 2km;
sand beach; bike hire; entmnt; 70% statics; dogs €3.75;
phone; Eng spkn; red CKE/CCI. "Historic fortified town;
attractive area for tourers; conv Europoort ferry terminal; gd
NH/sh stay." 1 Apr-31 Oct. € 22.50   2009*

BROEKHUIZENVORST see Horst *C4*

BURGH HAAMSTEDE *A3* (3km NW Coastal) *51.71478, 3.72219*
**Camping Ginsterveld, Maireweg 10, 4328 GR Burgh-
Haamstede (Zeeland) [(0111) 651590; fax 653040;
info@ginsterveld.nl or ginsterveld@ardoer.com;
www.ardoer.com/en/camping/ginsterveld]** SP fr Burgh-
Haamstede. Foll R107. Lge, pt shd, wc, chem disp, child/
baby facs, shwrs, EHU (6A) inc; lndry, shop, rest, snack bar,
take away, BBQ; playgrnd, paddling pool, sandy beach 2Km,
games area, bicycles, entmnt ssn, wifi, 50% statics, Eng spkn,
adv bkg acc, red LS, "Excel cycling & walking fr site, vg." ♦
22 Mar-27 Oct. € 46.00   2013*

⊞ **CALLANTSOOG** *B2* (2.5km NE Coastal) *52.84627, 4.71549*
**Camping Tempelhof, Westerweg 2, 1759 JD Callantsoog
[(0224) 581522; fax 582133; info@tempelhof.nl;
www.tempelhof.nl]** Fr A9 Alkmaar-Den Helder exit
Callantsoog, site sp to NE of vill. Lge, mkd pitch, pt shd;
htd wc; mv service pnt; chem disp; mv service pnt; serviced
pitches; baby facs; fam bthrm; sauna; private bthrms avail;
shwrs inc; EHU (10A) inc; gas; lndry; rest, snacks, bar high
ssn; playgrnd; htd, covrd pool; paddling pool; sand beach
1km; tennis; games area; gym; bike hire; wifi; entmnt; sat TV;
50% statics; dogs €3.50; phone; adv bkg. "Superb, well-run
site & facs; ACSI Card acc." ♦ € 39.00   2013*

See advertisement inside the front cover

CALLANTSOOG *B2* (3km NE Coastal) *52.84143, 4.71909*
**NCC Camping De Ooster Nollen, Westerweg 8, 1759 JD
Callantsoog [(0224) 581281 or 561351; fax 582098;
info@denollen.nl; www.denollen.nl]** N fr Alkmaar on A9;
turn L sp Callantsoog. Site sp 1km E of Callantsoog. Lge, mkd
pitch, pt shd; htd wc; chem disp; mv service pnt; baby facs;
shwrs inc; EHU (10A) inc; gas; lndry (inc dryer); shop; rest,
snacks; bar; playgrnd; pool 400m; sand beach 1.5km; bike
hire; games area; wifi; entmnt; TV; 40% statics; dogs €3;
phone; Eng spkn; adv bkg; quiet; ccard acc; 10% red long
stay; CKE/CCI. "Nature area nr; cheese mkt." 1 Apr-31 Oct.
€ 25.50   2009*

CHAAM see Breda *B3*

DE KOOG see Den Burg (Texel Island) *B2*

DE KOOG *B2* (500m E Rural) *53.09610, 4.76500* **De Luwe
Boshoek (Texel Island), Kamperfoelieweg 3, 1796 MT De
Koog [02 22 31 73 90]** Fr ferry take 501 to De Koog. Sp after
ref point 17. R at De Zwaluw Hotel. Site on L after 100m. Med,
mkd pitch, unshd; htd wc; chem disp; fam bthrm; shwr inc;
EHU (16A); lndry (inc dryer); shop 0.5km; BBQ; sandy beach
1km; 10% statics; dogs; quiet. "Excel; gd base to stay; bike
hire 0.5 km." ♦ 15 Mar-1 Nov. € 28.00   2014*

DE VEENHOOP see Drachten *C2*

NETHERLANDS

VERSATILE AND SURPRISING

vakantiepark
DelftseHout
verrassend veelzijdig

Korftlaan 5
2616 LJ - Delft
The Netherlands

+31 15 213 00 40
info@delftsehout.nl
www.delftsehout.nl

DEIL C3 (2km SE Rural) 51.87040, 5.26047 **Camping De Kijfakkers, Hooiweg 6A, 4158 LE Deil [(0345) 651203; fax 651000; famdeheus@kijfakker.nl; www.kijfakker.nl]** Fr A2 exit junc 15 onto N327 E sp Geldermalsen. Turn R at 1st rndabt, L at T-junc into Hooiweg, site on L in 500m, sp. Sm, hdg/mkd pitch, unshd; htd wc; chem disp; shwrs inc; EHU (6A) inc; lndry (inc dryer); shop, rest, snacks, bar 3km; BBQ; pool 2km; TV; dogs €1; bus 3km; poss cr; Eng spkn; adv bkg rec; quiet. "CL-type site on farm (cattle, horses); gd cycling, walking espec along Rv Linge; gd touring base." 15 Mar-31 Oct. € 13.50   2010*

DELFT B3 (4km NE Urban) 52.01769, 4.37945 **Camping Delftse Hout, Korftlaan 5, 2616 LJ Delft [(015) 2130040; fax 2131293; info@delftsehout.nl; www.delftsehout. nl]** Fr Hook of Holland take N220 twd Rotterdam; after Maasdijk turn R onto A20 m'way. Take A13 twd Den Haag at v lge Kleinpolderplein interchange. Take exit 9 sp Delft (Ikea on R). Turn L under m'way (3.2m height limit) & immed R at 1st traff lts; then site sp. Pls do not use SatNav fr Hook. Lge, hdg/mkd pitch, some hdstg, pt shd; htd wc; chem disp; mv service pnt; baby facs; fam bthrm; shwrs inc; EHU (10A) inc; gas; lndry (inc dryer); shop; rest, snacks; bar; BBQ; playgrnd; htd pool; paddling pool; watersports; fishing nrby; bike hire; golf 5km; wifi; entmnt; games/TV rm; 50% statics; dogs €3.25; no o'fits over 7.5m; phone; bus to Delft; Holland Tulip Parcs site; Eng spkn; some rd noise; ccard acc; red LS/long stay/snr citizens/CKE/CCI. "Located by pleasant park; gd quality, secure, busy site with excel facs; helpful, friendly staff; little shd; sm pitches poss diff lge o'fits; excursions by bike & on foot; easy access Delft cent; sm m'van o'night area outside site; mkt Thur; excel; site clean & well maintained; gd rest; vg play areas for kids." ♦ 27 Mar-1 Nov. € 33.00 SBS - H06   2015*

See advertisement

DELFT B3 (9.4km SW Rural) 51.95450, 4.28833 **Hoeve Bouwlust, Oostgaag 31, 3155 CE Maasland [(0105) 912775; info@hoevebouwlust.nl; www.hoevebouwlust.nl]** Fr Hofh on A20 turn N at junc 7. Go thro Maasland on N468. Site on L in 3km. Sm, hdg pitch, pt shd; wc; chem disp; mv service pnt; shwrs; EHU; lndry (inc dryer); rest; café; bbq; playgrnd; wifi; 10% statics; bus adj; twin axles; Eng spkn; adv bkg; CKE/CCI. "Lots of outdoor activities inc tandem, boating & scotters; v friendly & helpful owners; vg site." 1 Apr-31 Oct. € 17.50   2014*

DEN HELDER B2 (3.5km SW Coastal) 52.93672, 4.73377 **Camping de Donkere Duinen, Jan Verfailleweg 616, 1783 BW Den Helder [(0223) 614731; fax 615077; info@donkereduinen.nl; www.donkereduinen.nl]** Fr S turn L off N9 sp Julianadorp (Schoolweg), strt over at x-rds in Julianadorp (Van Foreestweg). Turn R at t-junc onto N502, site on L in approx 4km. Lge, pt shd; wc; chem disp; mv service pnt; baby facs; shwr inc; EHU (4-16A) inc; gas; lndry; shops 3km; playgrnd; sand beach 800m; tennis; bike hire; wifi; 10% statics; dogs €2.75; poss cr; Eng spkn; adv bkg (fee); quiet; ccard acc (matercard only); CKE/CCI. "V helpful owner; excel walking/cycling; ferry to Texel ls; lge naval museum & submarine." 17 Apr-3 Sep. € 33.50   2014*

You can now fill in site reports online

NETHERLANDS

DENEKAMP D3 (4km NE Rural) 52.39190, 7.04890 **Camping De Papillon, Kanaalweg 30, 7591 NH Denekamp [(0541) 351670; fax 355217; info@depapillon.nl; www.depapillon.nl]** Fr A1 take exit 32 onto N342 Oldenzaal-Denekamp, dir Nordhorn, site sp just bef German border. Lge, pt shd; htd wc; chem disp; mv service pnt; baby facs; fam bthrm; shwrs €0.20; EHU (4A) inc; gas; lndry; shop; rest, snacks; bar; playgrnd; 2 pools (1 htd & covrd); lake sw; tennis; bike hire; TV; 12% statics; dogs €4.50; phone; quiet; red long stay/LS. "Super, clean site; friendly, helpful owners; man-made lake." ♦ 1 Apr-1 Oct. € 24.70   2012*

See advertisement inside the front cover

DEVENTER C3 (4km S Urban) 52.24992, 6.14634 **Camp Municipal De Worp, De Worp 12, 7419 AD Deventer [(0570) 613601; deventer@stadscamping.eu; www.stadscamping.eu]** Fr N on N337 on o'skts of Deventer foll 'Centrum' sp to W of town cent. Go over rv bdge on N344 dir Apeldoorn, site immed on R. sp. Or fr A1 exit junc 22 dir Twello, turn R onto N344, site on L just bef rv bdge on ent Deventer. Med, pt shd; htd wc; chem disp (wc); baby facs; fam bthrm; shwrs €1; EHU (4-6A) €2.50; lndry; playgrnd; 10% statics; dogs €2.50; phone; Eng spkn; quiet; CKE/CCI. "Foot passenger ferry over rv to Deventer cent adj site; lovely, interesting old town; Terwolde windmill worth visit; refurbished san facs but inadequate if site full." 1 Apr-30 Sep. € 16.50   2011*

"I need an on-site restaurant"

We do our best to make sure site information is correct, but it is always best to check any must-have facilities are still available or will be open during your visit.

⊞ **DIEREN** C3 (2.5km NW Rural) 52.06908, 6.07705 **De Jutberg Vakantiedorp, Jutberg 78, 6957 DP Laag-Soeren [03 13 61 92 20; jutberg@ardoer.com; www.ardoer.com/ jutberg]** Fr A12 take exit 27 onto the A348. Turn L on the N348 into Dieren. Turn L at petrol stn, cont for 2.7km. Foll sp to site. V lge, mkd pitch, pt sl, shd; htd wc; chem disp; baby facs; shwrs inc; EHU (6A); lndry; shop; rest; snacks; bar; BBQ; playgrnd; htd covrd pool; games area; games rm; entmnt; wifi; dogs; Eng spkn; adv bkg; quiet; CCI. "Hugh pitches, fully serviced; v lively but not noisy; excursions for adults & kids in summer; wet weather diversions; excel san facs; extensive cycle paths thro countryside & forest; excel site." € 42.50   2014*

DIEVER D2 (1km N Rural) 52.86684, 6.32004 **Camping Diever, Haarweg 2, 7981 LW Diever [tel/fax (0521) 591644; camping.diever@hetnet.nl; www.campingdiever.nl]** Fr A32 exit 4 dir Havelte & Diever. In Diever take dir Zorgvlied/ Wateren, site sp. Lge, mkd pitch; pt sl, shd; htd wc; chem disp; fam bthrm; baby facs; shwrs €0.50; EHU (10A) €2.75; gas; lndry; shop; snacks; playgrnd; pool 5km; bike hire; internet; TV; some statics; dogs €2.25; phone; sep car park; Eng spkn; adv bkg; quiet. "Pleasant, densely wooded site." 1 Apr-1 Oct. € 16.60   2009*

DIEVER D2 (4km S Rural) 52.82405, 6.31650 **Camping Wittelterbrug, Wittelterweg 31, 7986 PL Wittelte [(0521) 598288; fax 598250; info@wittelterbrug.nl; www.wittelterbrug.nl]** N of Meppel on N371 for approx 12km. Site on R over narr canal bdge. Med, hdg pitch, pt shd; wc; chem disp; mv service pnt; serviced pitch; baby facs; shwrs €0.60; EHU (10A) inc; gas; lndry; shop & 5km; rest, snacks; bar; playgrnd; covrd pool; paddling pool; bike hire; entmnt; TV; 65% statics; dogs €3.60; phone; Eng spkn; adv bkg; quiet. "Lovely family-run site; facs excel." 1 Apr-31 Oct. € 19.50   2009*

DIFFELEN see Hardenberg D2

DOETINCHEM D3 (4km SE Rural) 51.94628, 6.33550 **Camping De Wrange, Rekhemseweg 144, 7004 HD Doetinchem [(0314) 324852; info@dewrange.nl; www.dewrange.nl]** Leave A18 at exit 4 dir Doetinchem Oost, then L dir Doetinchem. In 500m turn R at water tower, foll site sp. Lge, mkd pitch, unshd; htd wc; chem disp; mv service pnt; baby facs; fam bthrm; shwrs €0.70; EHU (4-6A) €3; gas; lndry; shop; rest, snacks; bar; BBQ; playgrnd; htd pool; paddling pool; bike hire; entmnt; TV; 75% statics; dogs €3; phone; sep car park; poss cr; Eng spkn; adv bkg; quiet; CKE/CCI. ♦ ltd. 1 Apr-31 Oct. € 16.50   2009*

DOKKUM C2 (400m E Urban) 53.32611, 6.00468 **Camping Harddraverspark, Harddraversdijk 1a, 9101 XA Dokkum [(0519) 294445; fax 571402; info@campingdokkum.nl; www.campingdokkum.nl]** Best app fr E fr ring rd N361 onto Harddraversdijk alongside rv, site sp. Do not app thro town - narr rds. Med, hdg/mkd pitch, some hdstg, pt shd; wc; chem disp; mv service pnt; shwrs €0.50; EHU (6A) €2.50; gas; lndry; shop, rest, snacks, bar 400m; playgrnd; tennis; dogs €2; wifi; Eng spkn; quiet. "Excel location in cent of pleasant town; conv for ferry to Ameland Island (12km)." 1 Apr-31 Oct. € 19.00   2015*

DOMBURG A3 (2km SE Rural) 51.55578, 3.51516 **Camping Westhove, Zuiverseweg 2, 4363 RJ Aagtekerke [(0118) 581809; fax 582502; westhove@ardoer.com; www.ardoer.com]** Fr Middelburg thro Oostkapelle, site sp on L twds Domburg. Lge, mkd pitch, pt shd; htd wc; chem disp; mv service pnt; baby facs; shwrs inc; EHU (4A) inc; lndry; shop; rest, snacks; bar; playgrnd; htd, covrd pool; sand beach 2km; bike hire; entmnt; TV; 25% statics; dogs (not acc Jul/ Aug); phone; sep car park; Eng spkn; quiet; ccard acc; CKE/ CCI. "Gd pool; easy walk/cycle to Domburg & beach." ♦ 27 Mar-25 Oct. € 35.00 (3 persons)   2009*

DORDRECHT B3 (3km SE Rural) 51.80738, 4.71862 **Camping Het Loze Vissertje, Loswalweg 3, 3315 LB Dordrecht [(078) 6162751; info@campinghetvissertje.nl; www.camping hetvissertje.nl]** Fr Rotterdam across Brienenoord Bdge foll sp Gorinchem & Nijmegen A15. Exit junc 23 Papendrecht & turn R onto N3 until exit Werkendam. Turn R & foll sp 'Het Vissertje'. Sm, pt shd; wc; chem disp; shwrs €0.50; EHU (6A) inc; wifi; 20% statics; dogs €1; Eng spkn; quiet; red long stay. "Lovely, delightful site; friendly, helpful manager; modern, clean san facs; gd cycle rtes nr; vg; easy acc to town on local train." 1 Apr-31 Oct. € 21.00   2014*

⊞ **DORDRECHT** *B3* (17km W Rural) *51.79279, 4.53679*
**Camping De Fruitgaarde, Polderdijk 47, 3299 LL Maasdam
[(078) 6765176; www.campercontact.nl]** Exit A16 junc
20 onto N217 W dir Puttershoek & Maasdam thro Kiltunnel
(toll). Fork L onto N491 then foll rd round W side of polder
dir Binnenmaas & Westmaas. Site sp on L, 1km W of
Maasdam. Sm, hdstg, pt shd; htd wc; chem disp; mv service
pnt; baby facs; shwrs inc; EHU (16A) €2; lndry; shop 6km;
rest; snacks 1km; bar; playgrnd; pool 4km; sw adj; dogs;
bus 1km; Eng spkn; quiet. "Site in orchard; helpful owner;
water bus, Kinderdijk windmills, historic towns nrby." ♦ ltd.
€ 14.00   2012*

DRACHTEN *C2* (7km SE Rural) *53.07095, 6.13672* **Camping
Het Koningsdiep, De Mersken 2, 9247 WK Ureterp
[(0512) 381844; info@campinghetkoningsdiep.nl;
www.campinghetkoningsdiep.nl]** Exit A7/E22 at junc 30
onto N381 dir Oosterwolde. In 1km after Azeven indus est
turn R into Selmien West, then in 1km turn L into Selmien/De
Mersken, site sp. Sm, pt shd; htd wc; chem disp; fam bthrm;
shwrs inc; EHU (10A) inc; lndry rm; shop 2.5km; rest, snacks,
bar 2.5km; BBQ; horseriding; dogs; Eng spkn; adv bkg; quiet;
CKE/CCI. "Vg, friendly site on working stud farm; gd walking;
gd touring base." ♦ 1 Apr-28 Oct. € 20.00   2009*

DRACHTEN *C2* (10km W Rural) *53.09696, 5.94695* **Camping
De Veenhoop Watersport & Recreatie, Eijzengapaed 8,
9215 VV De Veenhoop [(0512) 462289; fax 461057;
info@de-veenhoop.nl; www.de-veenhoop.nl]**
Exit A7 junc 28 dir Nij Beets, foll De Veenhoop sp to site. Or
exit A32 junc 13 & turn W for approx 6km via Aldeboarn. Turn
L at Pieter's Rest to De Veenhoop, site on L bef sm bdge. Med,
pt shd; htd wc; chem disp; shwrs €0.50; EHU (6-10A) €3; lndry;
shops 5km; rest 200m; BBQ; sm playgrnd; lake sw; boat hire;
50% statics; dogs; bus adj; Eng spkn; adv bkg; quiet. "Excel,
peaceful, friendly site; clean & well-maintained; excel sailing,
cycling, walking; well situated for lakes & N N'lands; gd NH."
1 Apr-31 Oct. € 14.50   2010*

DRACHTEN *C2* (14km W Rural) *53.12556, 5.98391* **Camping
de Stjelp, It West 48, 9216 XE Oudega [(0512) 372270; fax
371053; stjelp@camping-de-stjelp.nl; www.camping-de-
stjelp.nl]** W fr Drachten on N31. Turn L at Nijega then bear
R to Oudega. Site at W end of vill at bungalow no. 1920. Sm,
mkd pitch, unshd; wc; chem disp; shwrs inc; EHU (4A) metered;
lndry rm; shop, snacks, bar 1km; BBQ; lake sw & beach 3km;
bike hire; dogs €1; quiet; CKE/CCI. "Attractive farm site,
friendly owners; conv Friesland canals & lakes; cycle rtes; vg
touring base." ♦ ltd. 14 Apr-15 Oct. € 13.60   2011*

⊞ **DRIMMELEN** *B3* (2km E Rural) *51.70690, 4.82290* **Camping
Biesbosch Marina, Marinaweg 50, 4924 AD Drimmelen
[(0162) 685795; fax 681675; info@campingbiesboschmarina.nl;
www.campingbiesboschmarina.nl]** Exit A59 junc 32 at Made
& foll sp Drimmelen & site. Med, mkd pitch, unshd; htd wc;
chem disp; mv service pnt; baby facs; fam bthrm; serviced
pitches; shwrs inc; EHU (16A) inc; gas; lndry (inc dryer); shop;
rest, snacks; bar; BBQ; playgrnd; lake sw & sand beach; sailing
lessons; boat, canoe, bike hire; games area; wifi; some statics;
dogs €3 (max 1); Holland Tulip Parcs site; adv bkg; quiet; ccard
acc; red long stay. "Superb site; access to all facs by electronic
key; lge, well-drained pitches; excel touring base & conv NH
Hook of Holland." € 30.50   2009*

DRONTEN *C2* (3km W Rural) *52.52099, 5.69189* **Camping en
Horecacentrum 't Wisentbos, De West 1, 8251 ST Dronten
[(0321) 316606; info@wisentbos.nl; www.wisentbos.nl]**
E fr Lelystad on N309, site well sp. Sm, some hdstg, pt shd;
htd wc; chem disp; mv service pnt; baby facs; shwrs €0.50;
EHU (10A) inc; lndry; rest, snacks; bar; playgrnd; beach &
fishing lake adj; 80% statics; dogs €1.55; bus adj; Eng spkn;
adv bkg; quiet; ccard acc (not Visa). "Wooded area; friendly,
helpful staff; sep area for m'vans; excel." 1 Apr-31 Oct.
€ 15.00   2009*

⊞ **DWINGELOO** *D2* (2km SE Rural) *52.82216, 6.39258*
**Camping De Olde Bârgen, Oude Hoogeveensedijk 1,
7991 PD Dwingeloo [(0521) 597261; fax 597069;
info@oldebargen.nl; www.oldebargen.nl]** Exit A28 Zwolle/
Assen rd at Spier, turn W sp Dwingeloo, site clearly sp in
wooded area. Sm, mkd pitch, pt shd; wc; chem disp; fam
bthrm; shwrs inc; EHU (4-6A) inc; lndry; shop 800m; playgrnd;
pool 1.5km; few statics; wifi; dogs €2; adv bkg; Eng spkn;
quiet; CKE/CCI. "Excel, well-run site on N side Dwingelderveld
National Park; gd for walkers & cyclists; v friendly, helpful
owners; delightful, quiet site." ♦ € 27.70   2014*

⊞ **ECHT** *C4* (9km E Rural) *51.12075, 5.96888* **Camping
Biej De Vogel, Heinsbergerweg 15, 6065 NK Montfort
[(0475) 541522; info@campingbiejdevogel.nl;
www.campingbiejdevogel.nl]** Exit A2/E25 junc 44 dir
Roermond, turn R to Montfort & go thro town to fork & statue.
Turn L up narr rd, then strt over x-rds, farm approx 1km on L.
Sm, mkd pitch, pt shd; wc; chem disp; shwrs €1; EHU (10-16A)
€1.75; lndry; shop 2km; pool 2km; dogs; phone; Eng spkn;
adv bkg; quiet; bef long stay. "Excel CL-type site - 15 pitches."
€ 12.00   2009*

ECHT *C4* (5km SE Rural) *51.09213, 5.91116* **Camping
Marisheem, Brugweg 89, 6102 RD Echt [(0475) 481458;
fax 488018; info@marisheem.nl; www.marisheem.nl]**
Exit A2 Maastricht-Eindhoven junc 45 dir Echt. In Echt foll sp
Koningsbosch, site down side rd on L. Lge, mkd pitch, pt shd;
htd wc; chem disp; mv service pnt; shwrs; EHU (6-10A) inc; gas;
lndry; shop; rest, snacks; bar; htd pool; playgrnd; 60% statics;
no dogs; quiet; Eng spkn; red LS; CKE/CCI. "Vg, well-organised
site; vg pool; helpful staff; gd train service to Maastricht."
1 Apr-30 Sep. € 31.00 (4 persons)   2011*

EDAM *B2* (2km NE Coastal) *52.52457, 5.06478* **Camping
Strandbad Edam, Zeevangszeedijk 7A, 1135 PZ Edam
[(0299) 371994; fax 371510; info@campingstrandbad.nl;
www.campingstrandbad.nl]** Foll N247 Amsterdam-Hoorn;
after sp for Edam foll site sp. At traff lts in Edam keep on
N247 past bus stn on R, then R at next rndabt. Last 100m to
site is single track opp marina. Access thro public car park.
Lge, pt shd; htd wc; chem disp; mv service pnt; baby facs;
fam bthrm; shwrs €1; EHU (10A) €2.90; gas; lndry; shop;
rest, snacks; bar; playgrnd; pool 3km; paddling pool; sand
beach adj; watersports; bike hire; wifi; TV; 40% statics; no
dogs; phone; poss cr; Eng spkn; adv bkg; quiet; ccard acc; red
long stay. "Walking dist Edam; landing stage for boats; excel
san facs; sm, poss cramped pitches high ssn." 1 Apr-30 Sep.
€ 20.00   2010*

NETHERLANDS

EDAM *B2* (14km S Rural) *52.42787, 5.07387* **Camping-Jachthaven Uitdam, Zeedijk 2, 1154 PP Uitdam [(020) 4031433; fax 4033692; info@campinguitdam.nl; www.campinguitdam.nl]** Fr Amsterdam foll N247 (Amsterdam-Hoorn), at 10km turn R sp Marken/Monickendam across canal. After 5km turn R at camping sp to site on L after 2km. Lge, pt shd; htd wc; chem disp; mv service pnt; baby facs; shwrs €0.90; EHU (4-6A) inc; gas; lndry; shop; rest, snacks; bar; playgrnd; pool 5km; paddling pool; sand beach adj; fishing; boating; bike hire; entmnt; TV; 50% statics; dogs €5; phone; poss cr; Eng spkn; adv bkg; 20% red LS; ccard acc; CKE/CCI. "Exposed location LS; no water supply nr touring pitches; bus 2km to Amsterdam cent; water taxi to Volendam; excel cycle tracks." 1 Mar-31 Oct. € 23.70   2009*

> "Satellite navigation makes touring much easier"
>
> Remember most sat navs don't know if you're towing or in a larger vehicle – always use yours alongside maps and site directions.

EERSEL *C4* (4km SE Rural) *51.33635, 5.35552* **Camping De Paal, De Paaldreef 14, 5571 TN Bergeijk [(0497) 571977; fax 577164; info@depaal.nl; www.depaal.nl]** Fr A67/E34 Antwerp/Eindoven exit junc 32 sp Eersel & bear R onto N284 & stay in R-hand lane. At rndabt take 1st exit onto Eijkereind. In 500m after rndabt turn L at traffic lts & foll rd around R & L bend. Take R turn sp Bergeijk after lge church (sm sp on sharp L bend). After approx 5km turn L into site rd. V lge, pt shd, htd wc (some cont); chem disp; mv service pnt; baby facs; sauna; fam bthrm; shwrs inc; EHU (6A) inc; gas; BBQ (gas/charcoal); lndry (inc dryer); shop; rest & snacks (high ssn); bar; playgrnds; 2 htd pools (1 covrd); paddling pool; fitness cent; sand beach, lake sw 7km; watersports 10km; fishing; excursions; sm children's zoo; tennis; bike hire; horseriding 500m; wifi; entmnt; games rm/TV rm (sat TV); recep 0900-1800; 10% statics; dogs €5; no o'fits over 8m high ssn; no twin-axles; phone; sep cark park; poss cr; ccard not acc; red LS. "Excel, family-run site set in woodland; espec gd for young children; lge pitches in groups with sep sm play areas; cent play areas; conv Efteling theme park, Hilvarenbeek safari park, Oisterwijk bird park; mkt Mon & Tue pm." ♦ 1 Apr-25 Oct. € 49.00 SBS - H04   2011*

See advertisement inside the front cover

EERSEL *C4* (9km S Rural) *51.29155, 5.29475* **Camping De Zwarte Bergen, Zwarte Bergendreef 1, 5575 XP Luyksgestel [(0497) 541373; fax 542673; info@zwartebergen.nl; www.zwartebergen.nl]** Fr Eindhoven foll sps to Bergeyk & Luyksgestel; site sp on main rd 2km S of Luyksgestel. V lge, mkd pitch, pt sl, shd; htd wc; chem disp; mv service pnt; some serviced pitches; baby facs; shwrs inc; EHU (6-16A) inc; gas; lndry; shop; rest, snacks; bar; playgrnd; pool; paddling pool; 60% statics; phone; sep car park; poss cr & noisy; Eng spkn; adv bkg; CKE/CCI. "Vg; well organised; ample facs but ltd LS; welcoming staff." ♦ 1 Apr-30 Sep. € 28.50   2009*

⊞ **EINDHOVEN** *C4* (14km SE Rural) *51.37393, 5.55206* **Camping Heezerenbosch, Heezerenbosch 6, 5591 TA Heeze [(040) 2263811; fax 2262422; info@heezerenbosch.nl; www.heezerenbosch.nl]** Exit m'way A56 at junc 34 & foll sp Heeze. Foll rd to town, site sp fr town limits, 2km W of cent. V lge, pt shd; htd wc (cont); chem disp; mv service pnt; baby facs; shwrs inc; EHU (4A) inc; gas; lndry; shop; rest, snacks; bar; playgrnd; pool; waterslide; lake sw adj; tennis; games area; bike hire; TV; 95% statics; dogs €1.50; phone; adv bkg; quiet; red LS. "Low ssn site charges per day, ie 1 night's stay costs 2 days' fees; tourers in open field with elec & water - san facs some dist; helpful, friendly staff; busy, poss noisy site; grnd poss boggy LS." € 30.00   2009*

EINDHOVEN *C4* (16km S Rural) *51.32887, 5.46160* **Recreatiepark Brugse Heide, Maastrichterweg 183, 5556 VB Valkenswaard [(040) 2018304; fax 2049312; info@brugseheide.nl; www.brugseheide.nl]** S fr Eindhoven, exit Waalre; take N69 Valkenswaard; drive thro to rndabt, turn L. At next rndabt strt ahead, at next rndabt turn R, foll sp Achel. Site on L in 1km. Lge, mkd pitch, shd; htd wc; all serviced pitches; chem disp; mv service pnt; baby facs; shwrs inc; EHU (6A) inc; gas; lndry (inc dryer); shop 2km; snacks; bar; BBQ; playgrnd; htd pool; paddling pool; bike hire; wifi; entmnt; TV; 40% statics; dogs; phone; Eng spkn; adv bkg (no dep); quiet (can be v noisy w/end); ccard acc; red LS. "Excel, friendly site; gd NH en rte Germany." ♦ Easter-31 Oct. € 23.00 (4 persons)   2010*

ELBURG *C2* (2.6km SE Rural) *52.44294, 5.84318* **Natuurkamping Landgoed Old Putten, Zuiderzeestraatweg Oost 65, 8081 LB Elburg [(0525) 681938; fax 681325; info@oldputten.nl; www.oldputten.nl]** Fr A28 exit junc 16 dir 't Harde & Elburg. Foll sp on Zuiderzeestraatweg. Sm, mkd pitch, pt shd; wc; chem disp; baby facs; shwrs inc; EHU (4A) €2; lndry; shops 500m; pool; tennis; 20% statics; sep car park; phone. 1 Apr-1 Oct. € 16.50   2009*

ELLEWOUTSDIJK *A4* (1km W Coastal) *51.38801, 3.82226* **NCC Camping Zuudschorre, P J Israelweg 3, 4437 NE Ellewoutsdijk [(0113) 548598; www.ncc.nl]** Exit A58 junc 35 at 's-Gravenpolder & foll sp S to Ovezande. Turn L dir Oudelande & foll sp Ellewoutsdijk. At statue turn L thro vill onto dyke, turn L & site sp 200m on L. Sm, hdg pitch, pt shd; htd wc; chem disp; shwrs inc; EHU (4A) €2.75; lndry; shop & 1km playgrnd; rv sw adj; dogs; bus; quiet. "Lovely setting on Schelde estuary nr charming vill; gd touring base Goes & Middelburg; well-maintained, friendly site; members only - CC members welcome but must pre-book." ♦ ltd. 1 Apr-31 Oct. € 10.00   2009*

EMMEN *D2* (6km N Rural) *52.82861, 6.85714* **Vakantiecentrum De Fruithof, Melkweg 2, 7871 PE Klijndijk [(0591) 512427; fax (0591 513572; info@fruithof.nl; www.fruithof.nl]** On N34 N fr Emmen dir Borger, turn R sp Klijndijk, foll site sp. Lge, hdg/mkd pitch, pt shd; htd wc; chem disp; mv service pnt; serviced pitches; baby facs; fam bthrm; shwrs inc; EHU (6A) inc; gas; lndry; shop & 5km; rest, snacks; bar; BBQ; playgrnd; htd pool; paddling pool; lake sw & beach adj; tennis; games area; bike hire; entmnt; TV; 50% statics; dogs; Eng spkn; adv bkg; red LS/long stay; CKE/CCI. "Excel." Easter-29 Sep. € 28.00   2009*

EMST see Apeldoorn *C3*

NETHERLANDS

ENKHUIZEN C2 (1km N Coastal) 52.70888, 5.28830
**Camping De Vest, Noorderweg 31, 1601 PC Enkhuizen
[(0228) 321221; fax 312211; info@campingdevest.nl;
www.campingdevest.nl]** When N302 turns R at traff lts,
keep strt on to T-junc. Foll site sp to R, site on R in 50m.
Sm, pt shd; wc; chem disp; shwrs; EHU (4A) inc; sand beach
800m; 25% statics; dogs; poss cr; Eng spkn; adv bkg; ccard
not acc. "Gates clsd 2300-0800; easy walk to town cent; lively
jazz festival last w/end in May; facs old but well-kept - poss
stretched when site full." Easter-30 Sep. € 18.50   2011*

ENKHUIZEN C2 (1km SE Coastal) 52.7098, 5.2956 **Camping
Enkhuizer Zand, Kooizandweg 4, 1601 LK Enkhuizen
[(0228) 317289; fax 312211; info@campingenkhuizerzand.nl;
www.campingenkhuizerzand.nl]** Sp in town. Lge, pt shd;
htd wc; chem disp; mv service pnt; baby facs; shwrs inc; EHU
(4A) inc; lndry; shop; snacks; playgrnd; htd, covrd pool adj;
sand beach & lake sw; boating; tennis adj; TV; 70% statics;
dogs €3.50; phone; sep car park; poss cr; poss noisy; CKE/CCI.
"Modern san facs; Zuider Zee museum 1km; deer park." ♦
1 Apr-30 Sep. € 23.50   2009*

⊞ **ENSCHEDE** D3 (6km E Urban) 52.21034, 6.95127 **Euregio
Camping de Twentse Es, Keppelerdijk 200, 7534 PA
Enschede [(053) 4611372; fax 4618558; info@twentse-es.nl;
www.twentse-es.nl]** Fr Germany, cross border at Gronau on
B54/N35; twd Enschede. In 2.5km turn R into Oostweg, then
in 2km turn R into Gronausestraat, then in 800m turn R into
Esmarkelaan. Foll rd thro residential area, turn L at end, site on
R. Not rec to foll Sat Nav due rd building, rec foll rd signs. Lge,
pt shd; htd wc; chem disp; shwrs inc; EHU (10A) inc; gas; lndry;
shop; rest, snacks; bar; playgrnd; pool; paddling pool; games
area; bike hire; wifi; entmnt; TV rm; 70% statics; dogs free; adv
bkg; quiet; ccard acc; red CKE/CCI. "Excel site; modern facs."
♦ ltd. € 27.00   2013*

ERICHEM see Tiel C3

⊞ **EXLOO** D2 (2km SE Rural) 52.86841, 6.88496 **Camping
Exloo, Valtherweg 37, 7875 TA Exloo [05 91 54 91 47 or
05 91 56 40 14; info@campingexloo.nl; www.camping
exloo.nl]** N34 fr Groningen, exit Exloo. Turn R after vill twd
Valthe. Site 2km on L. Sm, pt shd; wc; chem disp; mv service
pnt; fam bthrm; shwrs; EHU (6A); lndry; BBQ; wifi; TV rm;
dogs €1; twin axles; Eng spkn; adv bkg; quiet; CCI. "Friendly
recreation rm; vg site." € 14.00   2014*

GENDT C3 (1km E Rural) 51.87599, 5.98900 **Waalstrand
Camping, Waaldijk 23, 6691 MB Gendt [(0481) 421604;
fax 422053; info@waalstrand.nl; www.waalstrand.nl]**
Exit A15 to Bemmel, then Gendt. In Gendt foll sp to site on
Rv Waal. Med, mkd pitch, terr, unshd; wc; chem disp; baby
facs; fam bthrm; EHU (6A) inc; gas; lndry; snacks, bar adj;
playgrnd; pool; rv beach adj; tennis; bike hire; wifi; cab TV inc;
50% statics; dogs €3; poss cr; Eng spkn; adv bkg; quiet but
some noise fr rv traff. "Excel, well-kept site; clean, modern san
facs; interesting rv traff; v friendly owners; lovely position; gd
walks." 1 Apr-30 Sep. € 28.00   2015*

GIETHOORN see Meppel C2

GOES A3 (10km NW Rural) 51.54685, 3.81339 **Camping
De Veerhoeve, Veerweg 48, 4471 NC Wolphaartsdijk
[(0113) 581155; fax 581944; info@deveerhoeve.nl;
www.deveerhoeve.nl]** Off N256 Zierikzee to Goes rd foll
sp Wolphaartsdijk. Site is last of 3 on this rd. Lge, mkd pitch,
some hdstg, pt shd; htd wc; chem disp; mv service pnt;
serviced pitches; baby facs; fam bthrm; shwrs €0.50; EHU
(10A) inc; gas; lndry (inc dryer); shop; snacks; playgrnd; pool
8km; watersports cent adj; windsurfing; sport fishing; diving;
sailing; tennis; games area; bike hire; wifi; 50% statics; dogs
€4; phone; Holland Tulip Parcs site; poss cr; Eng spkn; adv
bkg ess; quiet; ccard acc; CKE/CCI. "By nature reserve & lovely
lake Veerse Meer." ♦ 1 Apr-30 Oct. € 26.00 (4 persons)
(CChq acc)   2009*

GOES A3 (12km NW Rural) 51.54200, 3.78000 **de Heerlijkheid
van Wolphaartsdijk - Formaly Minicamping Janse,
Muidenweg 10, 4471 NM Wolphaartsdijk [(0113) 581584 or
06 12612728 (mob); fax 581111; info@heerlijkheid
wolphaartsdijk.nl; www.heerlijkheidwolphaartsdijk.nl]**
Off N256 Zierikzee to Goes rd foll sp Jachthaven
Wolphaartsdijk. Shortly after vill turn L twd windmill. Turn R
at mini rndabt (ignore camping sp by L turn) sp Arnemuiden,
strt on at next rndabt, then L at next rndabt; site on L in 1km
on lakeside - ent thro farm gate. Sm, hdg pitch, pt shd; wc;
chem disp; shwrs inc; EHU (6-16A) €2.50; lndry; playgrnd;
lake sw & beach adj; windsurfing; sailing; dogs €0.50; bus
1km; Eng spkn; quiet; CKE/CCI. "CL-type, farm site; modern
san facs; friendly owners; bird reserve opp; excel cycling; rec."
15 Mar-31 Oct. € 24.50   2013*

GOOR D3 (10km N Rural) 52.29639, 6.61444 **Camping 't
Schuttenbelt, Vloodweg 7, 7468 RS Enter [0547 381472;
schuttenbelt@3onnet.nl]** Leave A1 at exit 28 twds Enter;
site sp bef Enter. Sm, mkd pitch, pt shd; wc; chem disp;
baby facs; shwrs inc; EHU (10A) inc; lndry; snacks; bar; BBQ;
playgrnd; pool; entmnt; dogs (extra charge); quiet. "Gd facs
with excel pitches; beautiful cycling & walking; gd site." ♦
15 Apr-20 Sep. € 19.00   2011*

GORINCHEM B3 (6km NE Rural) 51.84524, 5.03995 **Camping
Het Lingebos, Haarweg 6, 4214 KL Vuren [(0183) 630631;
fax 637185; info@lingebos.nl; www.lingebos.nl]**
Exit A15 exit junc 28 Gorinchem E sp Lingebos. Site at end of
lge recreation area. Lge, pt shd; wc; chem disp; mv service pnt;
baby facs; shwrs inc; EHU (4A) €2.50; lndry; sm shop & 4km;
rest, snacks; playgrnd; pool 5km; lake sw; fishing; canoeing;
bike hire; games area; few statics; dogs €3.50; phone; sep
car park; poss cr; Eng spkn; adv bkg; quiet but some m'way
noise; red long stay; CKE/CCI. "Pt grass, pt wooded; paved
rdways; muddy when wet; gd rest; excel." ♦ 1 Apr-30 Sep.
€ 19.00   2009*

GORINCHEM B3 (13km E Rural) 51.81845, 5.12563
**Camping De Zwaan, Waaldijk 56, 4171 CG Herwijnen
[(0418) 582354]** Exit A15 at junc 29 dir Herwijnen. In
Herwijnen turn R at T-junc sp Brakel. Turn L in 500m
(Molenstraat). At T-junc turn R (Waaldijk), site on L in 150m
on Rv Waal. Sm, pt shd; wc; chem disp; shwrs €0.50; EHU
(4A) inc; shop 1km; playgrnd; rv adj; 75% statics; poss cr;
adv bkg rec; Eng spkn; quiet but some boat noise; CKE/CCI.
"Helpful owners; ltd but clean facs; 66 m fr Amsterdam ferry."
15 Apr-15 Oct. € 13.00   2012*

⊞ **GOUDA** *B3* (2km E Urban) *52.01226, 4.71544* **Klein Amerika Parking, 2806 Gouda** 500m fr Gouda town cent, sp off Blekerssingel/Fluwelensingel. There are 3 designated parking spaces for m'vans in car park at Klein Amerika supervised by Gouda City Council. Max stay 3 days. Chem disp, water, rubbish bins, all free. Public wc (sm fee). Normal car parking fees applicable. € 7.00   2009*

⊞ **GOUDA** *B3* (10km E Rural) *52.01719, 4.82943* **Camping De Mulderije, Hekendorpsebuurt 33, 3467 PA Hekendorp [(0348) 563233 or 06 20680521 (mob); demulderije@wxs.nl; www.demulderije.com]** Exit A12 junc 14 Woerden onto N204 S. In 5km turn R to Oudewater N228. Cont dir Hekendorp & in approx 2km site sp on R. Narr rd to site. Sm, hdstg, pt shd; wc; chem disp; shwrs inc; EHU (6A) inc; lndry rm; shop, rest, snacks, bar 2km; dogs free; quiet. "Vg, clean, friendly site in nature reserve; cycle or boat to Gouda; facs clean attractive position; gd base; narr rd to site not suitable for lge o'fits; no passing places; do not use Sat Nav." ◆ ltd. € 16.00   2013*

⊞ **GRIJPSKERKE** *A3* (500m SE Rural) *51.53200, 3.56700* **Mini-Camping Het Munniken Hof, Jacob Catsweg 4, 4364 TE Grijpskerke [(0118) 591659; fax 594826]** Fr S via Westerschelde Tunnel to Middelburg, N on N57 & foll sp L dir Domburg & Grijpskerke. At vill sp take 1st R (opp windmill). In 300m 1st R, site on R 200m. Sm, pt shd; htd wc; chem disp; shwrs inc; EHU (6A) inc; lndry; shop, rest, snacks, bar 1km; playgrnd; sand beach 7km; dogs €0.50; sep car park; poss cr; Eng spkn; adv bkg; quiet. "Pleasant farm site; excel for cyling; vg touring base; v helpful owners." Easter-31 Oct. € 17.50   2009*

GROEDE see Breskens *A4*

⊞ **GROENLO** *D3* (3km SE Rural) *52.03680, 6.63185* **Camping Marveld, Elshofweg 6, 7141 DH Groenlo [(0544) 466000; fax 465295; info@marveld.nl; www.marveld.nl]** Fr Groenlo take N319 dir Winterswijk, site well sp. V lge, mkd pitch, pt shd; htd wc; chem disp; mv service pnt; baby facs; fam bthrm; private san facs some pitches; sauna; shwrs €0.20; EHU (6A) inc; gas; lndry (inc dryer); shop; rest, snacks; bar; BBQ; playgrnd; htd, covrd pools; paddling pool; lake fishing; bike hire; games area; wifi; entmnt; TV rm; 60% statics; dogs €2.50; phone; sep car park; Holland Tulip Parcs site; poss cr; adv bkg; Eng spkn; ccard acc (surcharge); CKE/CCI. "Huge leisure complex; something for everyone; immac." € 22.60 (CChq acc)   2009*

⊞ **GRONINGEN** *D2* (6km SW Urban) *53.20128, 6.53577* **Camping Stadspark, Campinglaan 6, 9727 KH Groningen [(050) 5251624; fax 5250099; info@campingstadspark.nl; www.campingstadspark.nl]** Take exit 36-A (dir Drachten) and foll 'Stadspark'. In the park go to the L and foll the sp. Fr Drachten/Winsum, take exit 36. Med, shd; wc; chem disp; mv service pnt; fam bthrm; shwrs €0.45; EHU (6A) €2.50 (poss rev pol); gas; lndry (inc dryer); shop in ssn; snacks; bar; playgrnd; pool 3km; bike hire; internet; TV; 20% statics; dogs €2; phone; sep car park; poss cr; Eng spkn; adv bkg; quiet; ccard not acc. "Municipal site adj parkland with gd sports facs; park & ride into town; plenty of space, tents & vans mixed; extensive cycle paths; car park adj to each set of pitches; gd san facs; well run site; interesting town; friendly helpful staff." 15 Mar-15 Oct. € 24.00   2015*

GULPEN *C4* (1.5km S Rural) *50.80720, 5.89430* **Panorama Terrassencamping De Gulperberg, Berghem 1, 6271 NP Gulpen [(043) 4502330; fax 4504609; info@gulperberg.nl; www.gulperberg.nl]** Fr Maastricht on N278 twd Aachen. At 1st traff lts in Gulpen turn sharp R & foll site sp for 2km (past sports complex). Narr final app. Lge, mkd pitch, some hdstg, terr, pt shd; htd wc; chem disp; baby facs; fam bthrm; shwrs inc; EHU (6A) inc; gas; lndry (inc dryer); shop; rest, snacks; bar; BBQ; playgrnd; pool; paddling pool; bike hire; games area; wifi; cab/sat TV; 10% statics; dogs €3; phone; Holland Tulip Parcs site; poss cr; Eng spkn; adv bkg; quiet; red snr citizens; CKE/ CCI. "Nr 3 nations boundary visitor cent & Maastricht with gd walking/views; mkd cycle rtes & footpaths; modern, clean facs - poss long walk; some tourers sited on top terr - long way fr shop & recep; beautiful views; v popular site, poss cr even in LS; excel." 1 Apr-30 Oct. € 25.60 (CChq acc)   2010*

GULPEN *C4* (2km SW Rural) *50.80688, 5.87175* **Camping Osebos, Reijmerstokkerdorpsstraat, 6271 PP Gulpen [(043) 4501611; info@osebos.nl; www.osebos.nl]** W fr Gulpen on N278 dir Maastricht in 1km turn L, site sp. Lge, mkd pitch, terr, unshd; htd wc; chem disp; mv service pnt; baby facs; fam bthrm; shwrs inc; EHU (6A) inc; gas; lndry (inc dryer); shop; rest, snacks; bar & 1.5km; playgrnd; pool; games rm; entmnt; 20% statics; dogs €3; bus; poss cr; Eng spkn; adv bkg; quiet; red long stay. "Excel, popular site; rec book ahead." ◆ 1 Apr-27 Nov. € 24.00   2010*

⊞ **HAARLEM** *B3* (4km E Rural) *52.37700, 4.67500* **Camping De Liede, Lieoever 68, 2033 AD Haarlem [(023) 5358666; fax 5405613; kampeerbedrijfdeliede@hetnet.nl; www.campingdeliede.nl]** Fr Amsterdam on A9 foll sp Haarlem onto A200. On A200 at 1st traff lts turn L, then L again, site sp. Med; wc; chem disp; shwrs; EHU (4A) €3; gas; lndry; shop; rest; beach 11km; 20% statics; phone; bus 700m; poss cr; Eng spkn; adv bkg; CKE/CCI. "Site in 2 parts both sides of rd." € 17.00   2011*

HAARLEM *B3* (12km SW Rural) *52.32006, 4.56698* **Camping Vogelenzang, Tweede Doodweg 17, 2114 AP Vogelenzang [(023) 5847014; fax 5849249; camping@ vogelenzang.nl; www.vogelenzang.nl]** Foll site sp on rd N206. V lge, hdg/mkd pitch, pt shd; htd wc; chem disp; mv service pnt; baby facs; shwrs €0.50; EHU (4A) inc; lndry (inc dryer); shop; rest, snacks; bar; playgrnd; pools; paddling pool; sand beach 4km; games rm; golf 7km; TV; 50% statics; no dogs; adv bkg; quiet; ccard acc; CKE/CCI. "Gd screening & hedging make site appear much smaller than it is; overflow field has EHU & wc; gd san facs; vg." ◆ 1 Apr-15 Sep. € 25.00   2010*

HALFWEG see Amsterdam *B3*

HARDENBERG *D2* (10km SW Rural) *52.52246, 6.54563* **NCC Camping De Rolle, Grote Esweg 96, 7795 DD Diffelen [(0523) 251556; hardenberg@ncc.nl; www.ncc.nl]** Fr N34 turn S onto N36 dir Almelo. After 5km turn L sp Marienberg, then L in 300m; after x-ring rv take 1st L, site 1km on L, sp. Sm, mkd pitch, pt shd; htd wc; chem disp; shwrs inc; EHU (4A) €4.75; shop 3km; rest 1km; snacks, bar 3km; playgrnd; htd, covrd pool 8km; dogs; poss cr; adv bkg; quiet. "CC members welcome but must pre-book (phone ahead bet 1700 & 1800); excel walking, cycling country; historic towns in area; v friendly; vg." 1 Apr-31 Oct. € 10.00   2009*

HARDERWIJK C3 (7km N Rural) 52.38500, 5.62860 **Camping Flevostrand, Strandweg 1, 8256 RZ Biddinghuizen [(0320) 288480; fax 288617; info@flevostrand.nl; www.molecaten.nl/flevostrand]** Foll A28 dir Amersfoort-Zwolle past Utrecht. At junc 13 turn off onto N302 Harderwijk; cont on N302 over lake bdge; turn R onto N306 sp Veluwemeer & 'Walibi World'; foll rd along lakeside for 1.5km to site on R. V lge, mkd pitch, pt shd; htd wc; chem disp; mv service pnt; fam bthrm; baby facs; sauna; shwrs inc; EHU (6A) inc; gas; lndry (inc dryer); shop; rest, snacks; bar; BBQ; playgrnds; 2 htd pools (1 covrd); paddling pool; marina; sand beach & lake sw; free sailing & surfing lessons; waterskiing; bike & boat hire; horseriding; tennis; two theme parks nrby; organised child activities; entmnt; games rm; wifi; TV; 60% statics; dogs €3.90; no o'fits over 8.5m high ssn; various pitch prices; phone; sep car park; poss cr; adv bkg; quiet; ccard acc; red LS; CKE/CCI. "Full marina facs on Veluwemeer for all types of boating; vg." 1 Apr-1 Nov. € 31.00   2011*

HARDERWIJK C3 (12km NE Rural) 52.39470, 5.73230 **Camping De Hooghe Bijsschel, Randmeerweg 8, 8071 SH Nunspeet [(0341) 252406; fax 262565; info@hooghebijsschel.nl; www.molecaten.nl/nl/de-hooghe-bijsschel]** Fr A28/E232 exit junc 14 & turn L at rndabt. Go strt over next 3 rndbts foll sp Nunspeet then turn L at 4th rndabt sp Hulshorst, then R at next rndabt sp Veluwemeer. Site on R after 3km (after sharp L-hand bend). Lge, mkd pitch, pt sl, pt shd; htd wc (some cont); chem disp; mv service pnt; serviced pitches; baby facs; fam bthrm; shwrs; EHU (6A) inc; gas; lndry (inc dryer); sm shop; supmkt nr; rest, snacks; bar; BBQ; playgrnd; htd pool; lake sw & sand beach adj; gd watersports; fishing; tennis; bike hire; horseriding 2km; wifi; entmnt; games/TV rm; 60% statics; dogs €3.90 (1 only per pitch); no o'fits over 7.5m; phone; sep car park; recep 0900-2100 high ssn 0900-1700 LS; adv bkg; quiet; ccard acc; red LS. "Excel, spacious pitches; shop at w/end only LS with ltd stock; rec use new san facs block nr rest/pool; gd walking/cycling." 28 Mar-29 Sep. € 34.50   2014*

HARDERWIJK C3 (25km SW Rural) 52.27155, 5.43550 **Camping Flevo-Natuur (Naturist), Wielseweg 3, 3896 LB Zeevolde [(036) 5228880; fax 5228664; info@flevonatuur.nl; www.flevonatuur.nl]** Fr A28 Harderwijk exit junc 13 onto N302, L onto N305, foll sp Zeevolde & site. V lge, mkd pitch, pt shd; htd wc; chem disp; mv service pnt; sauna; shwrs €0.50; EHU (4A) inc (poss rev pol); gas; lndry; shop; rest, snacks; bar; htd, covrd pool; lake sw; games area; TV; 50% statics; dogs; phone; sep car park; Eng spkn; adv bkg; red long stay. "Excel pool complex." 28 Mar-25 Oct. € 23.40   2009*

HARICH see Lemmer C2

⊞ **HARLINGEN** C2 (10km NE Urban) 53.18979, 5.55392 **Recreatiepark Bloemketerp, Burg J Dijkstraweg 3, 8801 PG Franeker [(0517) 395099; fax 395150; info@bloemketerp.nl; www.bloemketerp.nl]** In Franeker town cent, adj sw pool. Med, hdg/mkd pitch, pt shd; htd wc; chem disp; mv service pnt; baby facs; shwrs €0.50; EHU (6-10A) inc; lndry (inc dryer); shop; rest, snacks; bar; playgrnd; pool; bike hire; sat TV; phone; quiet; Eng spkn; ccard acc; CKE/CCI. "Pleasant site; gd train link to Harlingen." ♦ € 22.50   2010*

HARLINGEN C2 (2km SW Coastal) 53.16253, 5.41653 **Camping De Zeehoeve, Westerzeedijk 45, 8862 PK Harlingen [(0517) 413465; fax 416971; info@zeehoeve.nl; www.zeehoeve.nl]** Leave N31 N'bound at sp Kimswerd. At rndabt turn L under N31 & foll site sp. Site on R in 1.6km. Lge, pt shd; htd wc; chem disp; mv service pnt; baby facs; fam bthrm; shwrs €0.50; EHU (6A) inc; gas; lndry (inc dryer); shop 1km; rest, snacks; bar; playgrnd; beach adj; fishing; watersports; bike hire; games area; wifi; entmnt; TV; 30% statics; dogs €3.50; phone; Eng spkn; ccard acc (surcharge). "Roomy, well-maintained, open site; clean facs; easy walk to town & harbour; interesting area; vg." ♦ 1 Apr-15 Oct. € 21.50   2011*

HATTEM see Zwolle C2

HAVELTE D2 (1km SE Rural) 52.76820, 6.24987 **Campsite Jelly's Hoeve, Raadhuislaan 2, 7971 CT Havelte [(052) 1342808; fax 1340475; info@jellyshoeve.nl; www.jellyshoeve.nl]** Take exit 4 on A32. Then N371 twrds Havelte/Diever. After 4km cross the bdge and take immed R, foll rd for 1km. Turn L at canal bdge, bear R & after 75m turn R. Site on R after 100m. Sm, hdg/mkd pitch, pt shd; wc; chem disp; shwrs €0.60; EHU (10A) €2; lndry (inc dryer); BBQ; games area; wifi; dogs €2; bus 5km; twin axles; Eng spkn; quiet. "Plenty of walks & cycle tracks; excel." ♦ ltd. 1 Apr-30 Sep. € 21.00   2015*

HEERDE C3 (5km SW Rural) 52.37764, 6.00601 **Camping De Klippen, De Klippenweg 4, 8181 PC Heerde [(0578) 696690; fax 560258]** Exit A50 junc 28 or 29 & head twd Heerde. Site sp on ent vill on L. Foll sp to De Klippen & also Mussenkamp site. Med, mkd pitch, pt shd; wc; chem disp; shwrs €0.45; EHU (4A); lndry; shops 3km; playgrnd; 60% statics; phone; v quiet; CKE/CCI. "Excel site; immac facs; ltd space for tourers - phone ahead." ♦ ltd. 1 Apr-31 Oct. € 11.50   2009*

HEERENVEEN C2 (8km S Rural) 52.90814, 5.91828 **Camping De Frije Fries, Schoterweg 2, 8462 TD Rotstergaast [(0513) 636178 or 06 53367727 (mob); fax 647084; info@gebrdevries.nl]** Exit A32 at junc 11 onto N924 W. In 2.5km turn L sp Rotstergaast, site on R in 4km. Sm, pt shd; wc; chem disp (wc); shwrs €0.50; lndry; shop; BBQ; Eng spkn; quiet. "Vg, friendly site; gd cycling." 15 Mar-1 Nov. € 9.50   2009*

HEERLEN C4 (8km SW Rural) 50.85213, 5.93594 **Camping Colmont, Colmontweg 2, 6367 HE Voerendaal [(045) 5620057; fax 5620058; markpot@colmont.nl; www.colmont.nl]** Fr A76 take exit 6 Voerendaal; foll sp Ubachsberg; site sp. Med, pt sl, pt shd; htd wc; chem disp; mv service pnt; baby facs; shwrs inc; EHU (4-6A) €2; gas; lndry; shop; rest, snacks; bar; BBQ; playgrnd; htd pool; games area; bike hire; TV; 30% statics; dogs €2; phone; poss cr; adv bkg (fee); quiet; CKE/CCI. "Gd size pitches; friendly owner." ♦ 2 Apr-25 Sep. € 19.00   2010*

HEEZE see Eindhoven C4

HEILOO see Alkmaar B2

HELDEN *C4* (2km E Rural) *51.31813, 6.0235* **Camping De Heldense Bossen, De Heldense Bossen 6, 5988 NH Helden [tel/fax 07 73 07 24 76; heldensebossen@ardoer.com; www.deheldensebossen.nl]** Fr A67 Eindhoven-Venlo, take exit 38 (Helden). Turn R onto N277 twds Maasbreeseweg. Cont onto N562. Fr Helden dir Kessel. Turn L after 1km. Campsite 1km further on. V lge, mkd pitch, pt shd; wc; chem disp; mv service pnt; baby facs; shwrs; EHU (10A); lndry (inc dryer); shop; rest; snacks; bar; BBQ; playgrnd; htd covrd pool; waterslide; paddling pool; games area; bike hire; wifi; 65% statics; dogs 26DKK; twin axles; poss cr; Eng spkn; adv bkg; CCI. "Excel site." ♦ ltd. 29 Mar-26 Oct. € 45.00   2014*

HELLEVOETSLUIS *B3* (2km W Coastal) *51.82918, 4.11606* **Camping 't Weergors, Zuiddijk 2, 3221 LJ Hellevoetsluis [(0181) 312430; fax 311010; weergors@pn.nl; www.weergors.nl]** Via m'way A20/A4 or A16/A15 dir Rotterdam-Europoort-Hellevoetsluis; take N15 to N57, exit Hellevoetsluis, site sp. Lge, hdg/mkd pitch, some hdstg, unshd; htd wc; chem disp; mv service pnt; baby facs; shwrs €0.15/min; EHU (16A) €2.80; gas; lndry (inc dryer); shop; rest; bar; BBQ; playgrnd; paddling pool; lake fishing; tennis; games area; bike hire; wifi; TV rm; 60% statics; dogs €1.60; sep car park; Holland Tulip Parcs site; poss cr; Eng spkn; quiet; ccard acc. "Delta works 6km worth visit; bird sanctuary adj; flat site; gd san facs; v friendly, helpful staff; excel rest; gd walking/cycling; excel site; charming owners." ♦ 1 Apr-31 Oct. € 19.50 (CChq acc)   2013*

HENGELO *D3* (7km W Rural) *52.25451, 6.72704* **Park Camping Mooi Delden, De Mors 6, 7491 DZ Delden [(074) 3761922; fax 3767539; info@parkcamping.nl; www.parkcamping.nl]** Exit A35 junc 28 onto N346 dir Delden. Fr Delden-Oost, site sp. Site ent is R-hand of 2 via barrier (use intercom on arr.) If you have a high vehicle take the turning after Delden-Oost to avoid low rail bdge (2.3m); turn L immed aft lge rv bdge & foll site sp. Med, mkd pitch, pt shd; htd wc; chem disp; baby facs; fam bthrm; shwrs; EHU (6-10A) €3.40 (poss rev pol); lndry; shop & 1km; snacks; bar; playgrnd; pool; tennis; 50% statics; dogs €3.15; poss cr; Eng spkn; adv bkg; quiet. "Ideal for touring beautiful pt of Holland; sports complex adj; pleasant, well-kept site; clean facs." ♦ 1 Apr-1 Oct. € 18.60   2011*

HERKENBOSCH see Roermond *C4*

⊞ **HEUMEN** *C3* (2km NW Rural) *51.76890, 5.82140* **Camping Heumens Bos, Vosseneindseweg 46, 6582 BR Heumen [(024) 3581481; fax 3583862; info@heumensbos.nl; www.heumensbos.nl]** Take A73/E31 Nijmegen-Venlo m'way, leave at exit 3 sp Heumen/Overasselt. Do not re-cross m'way. After 500m turn R at camp sp. Site on R in approx 1.5km, 1km S of Heumen. V lge, hdg/mkd pitch, shd; htd wc (some cont); chem disp; mv service pnt; baby facs; fam bthrm; shwrs €0.50; EHU (6A) inc; gas; lndry (inc dryer); sm supmkt; rest; snacks; bar; BBQ; playgrnd; 2 pools (1 htd); paddling pool; jacuzzi; lake sw, sandy beach 2km; fishing 2km; watersports 6km; tennis; games area; bike hire; horseriding 100m; activities/entmnt in ssn; wifi; games/TV rm; 60% statics in sep area; dogs €4; no o'fits over 14m; eng spkn; adv bkg; quiet; phone; sep car park; extra €3 for m'vans; adv bkg; noise fr bar high ssn; ccard acc; red LS; CCI. "Excel, busy, family-run site; modern san facs; lots to do on site & in area - info fr recep; ideal for Arnhem; WW2 museums nr; mkt Sat & Mon in Nijmegen." ♦ € 36.00 SBS - H01   2014*

HILVARENBEEK *B3* (7km N Rural) *51.52839, 5.12398* **Safaripark Beekse Bergen, Beekse Bergen 1, 5081 NJ Hilvarenbeek [(013) 5491100; fax 5366716; info@beeksebergen.nl; www.safaripark.nl]** Exit A58 m'way junc 10 onto N269, site sp. Lge, pt shd; htd wc; chem disp; mv service pnt; baby facs; fam bthrm; shwrs inc; EHU (6-10A) inc; gas; lndry (inc dryer); shop; rest; snacks; bar; BBQ; playgrnds; covrd pool; paddling pool; tennis; games area; bike hire; internet; entmnt; TV; 30% statics; dogs; phone; adv bkg; ccard acc. "Free ent to adj Safari & Adventure Parks; excel facs; excel value - all sports inc in price." ♦ 1 Apr-15 Oct. € 30.60   2010*

"There aren't many sites open at this time of year"

If you're travelling outside peak season remember to call ahead to check site opening dates – even if the entry says 'open all year'.

⊞ **HOEK** *A4* (7km W Rural) *51.31464, 3.72618* **Braakman Holiday Island, Middenweg 101, 4542 PN Hoek [(0115) 481730; fax 482077; info@braakman.nl; www.braakman.nl]** Sp fr N61. V lge, mkd pitch, pt shd; htd wc; chem disp; mv service pnt; shwrs €0.50; fam bthrm; baby facs; serviced pitches; EHU (4A) inc; gas; lndry; shop; rest; snacks; bar; playgrnd; sub-tropical pool; lake beach; sailing; tennis; squash; entmnt; cab TV; 50% statics; dogs €5; phone; poss cr; Eng spkn; adv bkg; ccard acc;. "Excel for families; extensive recreation facs; conv Bruges/Antwerp; extra for lake view pitches." € 30.00   2009*

HOEK VAN HOLLAND *B3* (1.5km N Urban) *51.98953, 4.12767* **Camping Hoek van Holland, Wierstraat 100, 3151 VP Hoek van Holland [(0174) 382550; fax 310210; info@campinghoekvanholland.nl; www.campinghoekvanholland.nl]** Fr ferry foll N211/220 Rotterdam. After 2.4km turn L, 50m bef petrol stn on R, sp 'Camping Strand', site 400m on R. Lge, mkd pitch, hdstg, pt shd; htd wc; chem disp; baby facs; shwrs inc; EHU (6A) inc; gas; lndry; shop; rest; snacks; bar; playgrnd; pool; sand beach nr; tennis; bike hire; entmnt; TV; 60% statics; no dogs; phone; bus; sep car park; poss v cr; Eng spkn; quiet; CKE/CCI. "Open 0800-2300; modern san facs but poss inadequate when site full & long walk fr m'van area; conv ferry." ♦ 14 Mar-11 Oct. € 28.00 (4 persons)   2009*

HOEK VAN HOLLAND *B3* (3km N Coastal) *51.99685, 4.13347* **Camping Jagtveld, Nieuwlandsedijk 41, KV 2691 'S-Gravenzande [(0174) 413479; fax 422127; info@jagtveld.nl; www.jagtveld.nl]** Fr ferry foll N211/220 sp Rotterdam. After 3.2km, turn L at junc with traff lts gantry into cul-de-sac. Site 200m on L. Med, unshd; wc; chem disp; shwrs inc; shop; EHU (16A) poss rev pol €2; gas; lndry; shop; snacks; playgrnd; sand beach 400m; entmnt; mostly statics; no dogs; phone; sep car park; poss cr; Eng spkn; quiet. "Ideal for ferry port; conv Den Haag & Delft; gd, clean, level, family-run site; diff when wet; helpful owners; excel 8km long beach." 1 Apr-1 Oct. € 33.50   2014*

HOENDERLOO see Apeldoorn *C3*

NETHERLANDS

HORST *C4* (12km NE Rural) *51.50657, 6.15603*
**Recreatiepark Kasteel Ooijen, Blitterswijckseweg 2,
5871 CE Broekhuizenvorst [(077) 4631307; fax 4632765;
info@kasteelooijen.nl; www.kasteelooijen.nl]** N fr Venlo
on A72/73 turn R at junc 11 Horst twd Lottum. At T-junc
turn L twd Broekhuizen & Broekhuizenvorst, site sp on R. Lge,
hdg/mkd pitch, pt shd; htd wc; chem disp; mv service pnt;
90% serviced pitches; baby facs; fam bthrm; EHU (4-10A)
inc; gas; lndry; shop; rest, snacks; bar; playgrnd; pool; tennis;
games area; cab/sat TV; entmnt; 30% statics; dogs €1; phone;
Eng spkn; adv bkg; quiet; ccard acc; CKE/CCI. "Gd facs; helpful
staff; special area for families with children; gardens at Arcen
worth visit." ♦ 27 Mar-31 Oct. € 24.50   2009*

IJHORST see Meppel *C2*

JULIANADORP *B2* (3km N Coastal) *52.90667, 4.72499* **Camping
't Noorder Sandt, Noordersandt 2, 1787 CX Julianadorp
[(0223) 641266; fax 645600; info@noordersandt.com;
www.noordersandt.com]** On ent Den Helder on N9 turn L
sp Julianadorp. Foll sp to site. V lge, mkd pitch, pt shd; htd
wc; chem disp; mv service pnt; baby facs; shwrs €0.50; EHU
(10A) inc; lndry; shop; snacks; playgrnd; covrd pool; waterslide;
sand beach 600m; tennis; games area; cab TV; 30% statics;
dogs €3.50; phone; adv bkg; quiet; ccard acc; red long stay.
"Excel, friendly site; gd facs for children; excel pool; breakfast avail
& bread baked daily; gd foot & cycle paths; conv Alkmaar."
28 Mar-25 Oct. € 34.00   2009*

"That's changed – Should I let The Club know?"

If you find something on site that's different from
the site entry, fill in a report and let us know. See
www.caravanclub.co.uk/europereport.

KAATSHEUVEL *B3* (3km E Rural) *51.66086, 5.05484* **Mini-
Camping De Hoefstal, Horst 7A, 5171 RA Kaatsheuvel
[(0416) 273344; fax 284614; info@dehoefstal.com;
www.dehoefstal.com]** Turn S off A59 at junc 37 Waalwijk
& foll sp Kaatsheuvel & Loonen/Drunense Duinen, site sp.
Strt ahead at windmil, site on L in 250m. Sm, pt shd; wc;
chem disp; shwrs €0.50; EHU (4A) inc; lndry (inc dryer); rest;
playgrnd; Eng spkn; poss cr; adv bkg rec; some rd noise. "V
clean facs; friendly, helpful owner; cycle path to Efteling theme
park." 1 Apr-31 Oct. € 11.00   2009*

KAATSHEUVEL *B3* (4km E Rural) *51.66300, 5.07100*
**Boerderij Camping, Van Loon's Hoekske, Van
Haestrechtstraat 17a, 5171 RB Kaatsheuvel [(0416) 335758
or 06 20935679 (mob); vanloonshoekske@kpnplanet.nl;
www.vanloonshoekske.nl]** Exit A59 junc 37 Waalwijk & foll
sp Kaatsheuvel & Park de Loose Drunense Duinen. At windmill
turn L, site 1km on L, sp. Sm, mkd pitch, unshd; wc; chem
disp; shwrs inc; EHU (10A) inc; BBQ; rest, snacks, bar 1km;
playgrnd; Eng spkn; quiet. "Vg CL-type site on working farm."
1 Apr-31 Oct. € 15.00   2009*

KAMPERLAND *A3* (1km NW Rural) *51.57902, 3.69795*
**Camping De Molenhoek, Molenweg 69a, 4493 NC
Kamperland [(0113) 371202; molenhoek@zeelandnet.nl;
www.demolenhoek.com]** Site sp fr N255. V lge, mkd pitch,
pt shd; htd wc; chem disp; mv service pnt; baby facs; shwrs
€0.50; EHU (6A) inc; gas; lndry (inc dryer); shop; supmkt 800m;
rest, snacks; bar; playgrnd; htd tropical pool complex; paddling
pool; sand beach 2.5km; games area; games rm; bike hire; wifi;
entmnt; TV; 75% statics; dogs €5; Eng spkn; adv bkg; quiet.
"Excel, spacious, family site; gd, clean san facs; gd touring
base." ♦ 1 Apr-30 Oct. € 34.00   2010*

⊞ **KATWIJK AAN ZEE** *B3* (2km N Coastal) *52.21137, 4.41019*
**Camping De Noordduinen, Campingweg 1, 2221 EW
Katwijk [(071) 4025295; fax 4033977; info@noordduinen.nl;
www.noordduinen.nl]** Fr A44 Wassenaar-Amsterdam, exit 8
Katwijk, onto N206. Leave at Katwijk Noord (fr S) or Katwijk
ann Zee (fr N), R at rndabt & go over 6 sets of traff lts, immed
R then L. Lge, hdg/mkd pitch, terr, unshd; htd wc; chem disp;
mv service pnt; serviced pitches; baby facs; shwrs inc; EHU
(10A) €4.50 (poss rev pol); lndry (inc dryer); shop; rest, snacks;
bar; BBQ (gas/elec); playgrnd; 2 pools (1 htd/covrd); paddling
pool; sand beach adj; tennis; wifi; cab TV; 60% statics; no
dogs; sep car park; Holland Tulip Parcs site; poss cr; Eng spkn;
adv bkg (dep); ccard acc; red LS/snr citizens. "Friendly, helpful
management; clean facs; gd security; poss cr; 'comfort' pitches
avail at extra cost." ♦ € 31.50   2011*

KATWIJK AAN ZEE *B3* (6km E Rural) *52.19990, 4.45625*
**Camping Koningshof, Elsgeesterweg 8, 2331 NW Rijnsburg
[(071) 4026051; fax 4021336; info@koningshofholland.nl;
www.koningshofholland.nl]** Fr A44 (Den Haag/Wassenaar-
Amsterdam) exit junc 7 (Rijnsburg-Oegstgeest). In Rijnsburg
cont twd Noordwijk. Foll blue & white sps thro Rijnsburg,
across a bdge & then R twd Voorhout. Site in 2km. Lge, hdg/
mkd pitch, hdstg, pt shd; htd wc (some cont); chem disp; mv
service pnt; baby facs; shwrs inc; EHU (16A) inc; gas; lndry
(inc dryer); shop; rest, snacks; bar; BBQ; playgrnd; 2 pools
(1 htd, covrd); paddling pool; sand beach 5km; fishing; bike
hire; tennis; games rm; wifi; entmnt; TV cab/sat; 20% statics;
dogs €3; o'fits over 8m high ssn by request; phone; sep
car park for some pitches; recep 0900-1230 & 1330-2000
high ssn; Holland Tulip Parcs site; Eng spkn; adv bkg; quiet;
red long stay LS/snr citizens; CKE/CCI. "Vg, well-run, busy,
friendly site; gd for families; excel rest; excel facs & pool;
useful tour base for bulb fields; mkt Tues; well maintained;
close to beaches and town; rec cash as few cards acc." ♦
15 Mar-14 Nov. € 35.00 SBS - H03   2012*

See advertisement opposite

KATWIJK AAN ZEE *B3* (1km S Coastal) *52.19319, 4.38986*
**Camping De Zuidduinen, Zuidduinseveg 1, 2225 JS
Katwijk [(071) 4014750; fax 4077097; info@zuidduinen.nl;
www.zuidduinen.nl]** Fr A44 turn off at junc 8 onto N206
to Katwijk & foll 'Zuid-Blvd' sps. Site sp. Lge, mkd pitch,
unshd; htd wc; chem disp; mv service pnt; baby facs; shwrs
inc; EHU (4A) €3.50; gas; lndry (inc dryer); shop; snacks; bar;
no BBQ; playgrnd; sub-tropical pool 2km in Katwijk; sports
& organised activities; tennis nr; bike hire; wifi; cab TV; tour
boats; tourist mkt; 50% statics; no dogs; phone; sep secure
car park; adv bkg; quiet; ccard acc; red LS/snr citizens. "In
dunes conservation area; well-run, peaceful site; excel facs." ♦
1 Apr-30 Sep. € 32.50 (4 persons)   2011*

KLIJNDIJK see Emmen *D2*

KOOTWIJK see Apeldoorn *C3*

KORTGENE *A3* (500m S Rural) *51.55446, 3.80483* **Camping Villa Park de Pardakreek, Havenweg 1, NL 4484, N Beevland [0113-302051; fax 0113-3302280; paardekreek@ ardoer.com; www.ardoer.com/nl/camping/paardekreek]** Take the N256 to Zierikzee, exit Kortgene foll sps to camp. Med, mkd/hdg pitch, pt shd; wc; chem disp; mv service pnt; fam bthrm; baby facs; shwrs; EHU (16A); lndry; shop; rest; snacks, bar; BBQ; playgrnd; sw pool; water playgrnd; sauna; adj lake; games rm; wifi; 40% statics; dogs; bus 0.5km; Eng spkn; quiet; CKE/CCI. "Excel site; boat slipway & storage; adj Lake Veerse Meer; many places to visit." ♦ 27 Mar-1 Nov. € 43.00   2015*

⊞ KOUDUM *C2* (2km S Rural) *52.90290, 5.46625* **Kawan Village De Kuilart, De Kuilart 1, 8723 CG Koudum [(0514) 522221; fax 523010; info@kuilart.nl; www.kuilart.nl]** Fr A50 exit sp Lemmer/Balk. Foll N359 over Galamadammen bdge, site sp. Lge, mkd pitch, pt shd; htd wc; mv service pnt; fam bthrm; baby facs; private bthrms some pitches; 90% serviced pitches; sauna; shwrs €0.35; EHU (6-16A) €1.50-3.60; gas; lndry (with dryer); supmkt; rest, snacks; bar; playgrnd; 2 pools (1 htd, covrd); waterslide; sailing; watersports; marina; games area; wifi; entmnt; TV & cinema rm; 50% statics; ltd dogs €3.35 (adv bkg rec); phone; sep car park; poss cr; Eng spkn; adv bkg; Holland Tulip Parcs site; CKE/CCI. ♦ € 26.00 (CChq acc)   2011*

KOUDUM *C2* (7.5km S Rural) *52.87526, 5.43887* **Camping Martinus, De Soal 6, 8584 VS Hemelum [tel/fax (0514) 581970 or 06 54632485 (mob); pieterzeldenrust@ wanadoo.nl]** W fr Lemmer or E fr Koudum on N359. Turn L sp Hemelum, thro vill into De Soal rd. Site on R in 1.5km. Sm, pt shd; htd wc; chem disp; shwrs inc; shop 1.5km; rest; no statics; dogs €1.25; Eng spkn; quiet. "Friendly, helpful owners; excel cycling; gd." 1 Mar-31 Oct. € 10.00   2009*

KRAGGENBURG *C2* (2km N Rural) *52.67566, 5.89224* **Camping De Voorst, Leemringweg 33, 8317 RD Kraggenburg [(0527) 252524; devoorst@vdbrecreatie.nl; www.vdbrecreatie.nl]** Exit A6 junc 13 onto N352 sp Nagele & Ens. In Ens turn L at 1st traff lts (still N352) & foll sp Kraggenburg. Site sp at 1st rndabt. Lge, mkd pitch, some hdstg, pt shd; wc; chem disp; mv service pnt; shwrs €0.50; EHU (4A) inc; lndry (inc dryer); rest adj; snacks; bar; BBQ; playgrnd; htd pool; paddling pool; waterslide; tennis; games area; bike hire; wifi; TV; 30% statics; dogs €2; bus; Eng spkn; quiet; CKE/CCI. "Excel." 1 Apr-30 Sep. € 19.00   2010*

"I like to fill in the reports as I travel from site to site"

You'll find report forms at the back of this guide, or you can fill them in online at www.caravanclub.co.uk/europereport.

A carefree stay in Holland

CAMPING	CARAVANNING	CHALETS

Recreatiecentrum De Zuidduinen
Zuidduinseweg 1, 2225 JS Katwijk
info@zuidduinen.nl
www.zuidduinen.nl
tel: 071-4014750
fax: 071-4077097

Recreatiecentrum De Noordduinen
Campingweg 1, 2221 EW Katwijk
info@noordduinen.nl
www.noordduinen.nl
tel: 071-4025295
fax: 071-4033977

Recreatiecentrum Koningshof
Elsgeesterweg 8, 2231 NW Rijnsburg
info@koningshofholland.nl
www.koningshofholland.nl
tel.: 071-4026051
fax: 071-4021336

DE ZUIDDUINEN   Holland.   DE NOORDDUINEN   HOLLAND TULIP PARCS   KONINGSHOF

NETHERLANDS

LANDSMEER see Amsterdam *B3*

⊞ **LAUWERSOOG** *D1* (500m SE Coastal) *53.40250, 6.21740* **Camping Lauwersoog, Strandweg 5, 9976 VS Lauwersoog [(0519) 349133; fax 349195; info@lauwersoog.nl; www.lauwersoog.nl]** Fr N355 Leeuwarden-Groningen rd, take N361 Dokkum exit. Foll rd to Lauwersoog, site sp. V lge, unshd; htd wc; chem disp; mv service pnt; serviced pitches; baby facs; shwrs; EHU (10A) inc; gas; lndry (inc dryer); shop, rest, snacks; bar; playgrnd; pool; tennis; bike hire; wifi; entmnt; TV; 50% statics; dogs €4.75; phone; sep car park; Holland Tulip Parcs site; poss v cr; Eng spkn; adv bkg; quiet; ccard acc; CKE/CCI. "Excel, well-maintained site; vg rest; gd facs." ♦ € 38.00 (CChq acc) 2014*

LEEUWARDEN *C2* (7km E Rural) *53.21644, 5.88714* **Camping De Kleine Wielen, De Groene Ster 14, 8926 XE Leeuwarden [(0511) 431660; fax 432584; info@dekleinewielen.nl; www.dekleinewielen.nl]** E fr Leeuwarden on N355 twds Groningen; in 5km look on S side for site sp. Lge, pt shd; htd wc; chem disp; mv service pnt; baby facs; shwrs €0.40; EHU (4A) €3.25; gas; lndry; shop; snacks; playgrnd; sand beach; lake sw; watersports; fishing; entmnt; TV; 60% statics; dogs €2.40; phone; adv bkg; some rd noise; ccard acc; CKE/CCI. "Beautiful location; helpful staff; sep area for tourers; vg." ♦ 1 Apr-1 Oct. € 14.60 2009*

LEEUWARDEN *C2* (7km W Rural) *53.19484, 5.73785* **Minicamping Van Harinxma, Marssummerdyk 7, 9033 WD Deinnum [0031 (0) 58 215 04 98; Info@minicamping-van-Harinxma.nl; www.minicamping-van-harinxma.nl]** Fr S: take N31/N32 twrds Leeuwarden. Turn L on N31 sp Harlingen, turn R to Masum-Harlingen, and imm R sp Ritsumazijl. Foll rd turn L at T- junc, then fork L into no thro rd. Site on L. Sm, med, hdg pitch, pt shd; wc; chem disp; shwrs; EHU (6A); lndry; snacks; playgrnd; billiards; tv; dogs; twin-axle; Eng spkn; adv bkgs; CKE/CCI. "Vg; fishing fr site." 15 Mar-15 Oct. € 12.00 2012*

LEIDEN *B3* (8km N Rural) *52.20984, 4.51370* **Camping De Wasbeek, Wasbeeklaan 5b, 2361 HG Warmond [(071) 3011380; dewasbeek@hetnet.nl]** Exit A44 junc 4 dir Warmond; in 200m turn L into Wasbeeklaan, then R in 50m. Site sp. Sm, pt shd; wc; chem disp; shwrs €0.70; lndry; shop, rest, snacks, bar 1km; BBQ; pool 2km; sand beach 8km; 40% statics; dogs free; bus 500m; sep car park; Eng spkn; adv bkg; quiet but some aircraft noise. "Attractive, lawned site close to bulb fields; m'vans by arrangement; twin-axles not acc; friendly, helpful staff; gd cycling (track to Leiden); fishing; boating; birdwatching; lovely sm tidy site; nice area." 1 Apr-1 Oct. € 26.00 2014*

LELYSTAD *C2* (11km SW Rural) *52.48570, 5.41720* **Camping 't Oppertje, Uilenweg 11, 8245 AB Lelystad [(0320) 253693; info@oppertje.nl; www.oppertje.nl]** Exit A6 junc 10 & take Larserdreef dir Lelystad. In 3km turn L into Buizerdweg & foll sp to site. Med, mkd pitch, pt shd; htd wc; chem disp; mv service pnt; baby facs; fam bthrm; shwrs €0.50; EHU (10A) €3; lndry; shop 5km; snacks; bar; BBQ; playgrnd; lake sw & beach adj; fishing; 20% statics; no dogs; sep car park; Eng spkn; quiet; red LS/CKE/CCI. "Pleasant site in nature reserve; friendly, helpful staff; modern san facs; cycle track adj; excel." ♦ 1 Apr-1 Oct. € 17.00 2010*

LEMMER *C2* (9km NW Rural) *52.87929, 5.62082* **Camping De Tjasker, Iwert 17, 8563 AM Wijckel [(0514) 605869; info@campingdetjasker.nl; www.campingdetjasker.nl]** Fr Lemmer take N359 sp Balk, in approx 7km turn R at c'van sp. Sm, unshd; wc; chem disp; shwrs inc; EHU (4-6A) €2.20; lndry; shops 4km; playgrnd; dogs; sep car park; adv bkg; quiet. "Sm farm site with gd facs; gd for exploring Friesland with easy cycling & walking." 15 Mar-1 Oct. € 11.00 2009*

LEMMER *C2* (12km NW Rural) *52.89993, 5.64208* **Camping De Jerden, Lytse Jerden 1, 8556 XC Sloten [(0514) 531389; fax 531837; info@campingdejerden.nl; www.campingdejerden.nl]** Exit A6 at Lemmer onto N359 sp Balk. In 9km foll sp Wijckel & Slotten. In 3km turn R into Heerenhoogweg, L into Lytse Jerden, site along canal on L. Sm, hdg/mkd pitch, unshd; htd wc; chem disp; shwrs €0.50; EHU (16A) €3; lndry (inc dryer); shop 500m; rest, bar in vill; playgrnd; lake sw 500m; sand beach; boat & bike hire; games area; dogs €2; phone; adv bkg; Eng spkn; CKE/CCI. "Lovely site in excel position; gd touring base; clean facs; lge pitches." 1 Apr-1 Nov. € 17.00 2009*

LEMMER *C2* (14km NW Rural) *52.92019, 5.57494* **Camping Zwinzicht, Trophornsterweg 2, 8571 MX Harich [tel/fax (0514) 604512 or 06 12145209 (mob); info@zwinzicht.nl; www.zwinzicht.nl]** Fr N359 turn N dir Balk & Woudsend onto N928. Site sp 2km N of Harich. Sm, hdg/mkd pitch, pt shd; htd wc; chem disp; EHU (6A) inc; lndry; shop 2km; rest 1km; BBQ; playgrnd; games rm; no statics; dogs €1.75; sep car park; Eng spkn; quiet; red LS. "Vg." 1 Apr-2 Oct. € 14.00 2009*

LIEREN see Apeldoorn *C3*

LISSE *B3* (6km S Rural) *52.22175, 4.55418* **Camping De Hof van Eeden, Hellegatspolder 2, 2160 AZ Lisse [(0252) 221573; fax 235200; info@dehofvaneeden.nl; www.dehofvaneeden.nl]** Exit A44 junc 3 & turn N onto N208 dir Lisse. Turn R at rest on R bef 1st set traff lts into narr rd, foll rd to end (under A44) to site. Sm, unshd; wc; chem disp (wc); shwrs €0.50; EHU (16A) inc; rest; playgrnd; wifi; 90% statics; Eng spkn; rlwy noise. "Gd CL-type site, space for 10 tourers - rec phone or email bef arr; interesting location by waterway & lifting rlwy bdge; conv Keukenhof; helpful owners." 15 Apr-15 Oct. € 17.50 2014*

LOCHEM *D3* (4km SW Rural) *52.14251, 6.38210* **Camping Landgoed Ruighenrode, Ploegdijk 2, 7241 SC Lochem [(0573) 253618; fax 253535; info@landgoedruighenrode.nl; www.landgoedruighenrode.nl]** Site sp fr N346 dir Zutphen. V lge, shd; htd wc; chem disp; mv service pnt; baby facs; fam bthrm; shwrs inc; EHU (4-6A) inc; gas; lndry (inc dryer); shop; rest, snacks; bar; playgrnd; pool complex 1km; lake sw; tennis; bike hire; games rm; entmnt; TV; 60% statics; dogs €2; phone; adv bkg; quiet; CKE/CCI. "Pleasant wooded site." 1 Apr-30 Oct. € 25.00 2011*

LUTTENBERG see Nijverdal *D3*

LUYKSGESTEL see Eersel *C4*

MAASDAM see Dordrecht *B3*

Tell us about the sites you visit

⊞ **MAASTRICHT** *C4* (10km E Rural) *50.84399, 5.78307*
**Camping Mooi Bemelen, Gasthuis 3, 6268 NN Bemelen
[(043) 4071321 or 4072327; fax 4072535;
info@mooibemelen.nl; www.mooibemelen.nl]**
A2 as far as Maastricht, turn L at the 1st traff lts and then
foll the signs to Bemelen. In Bemelen there are signs to the
campsite. Lge, pt shd; wc; chem disp; child/baby facs; EHU (4A)
€4; lndry rm; gas; shop; rest, snacks; htd pool; playgrnd; games
area; games rm; dog €4; adv bkg; quiet. "Fine surroundings;
gd for children; excel site." € 33.70   2013*

MAURIK *C3* (2km NE Rural) *51.97605, 5.43020* **Recreatiepark
Eiland van Maurik, Rijnbandijk 20, 4021 GH Maurik
[(0344) 691502; fax 692248; receptie@eilandvanmaurik.nl;
www.eilandvanmaurik.nl]** Exit A15 junc 33 at Tiel onto B835
N & foll sp to Maurik & site on rvside. Or exit A2 junc 13 at
Culembourg onto N320 to Maurik. Lge, pt shd; htd wc; chem
disp; mv service pnt; baby facs; fam bthrm; shwrs €0.50; EHU
(10A) inc; gas; lndry; shop; rest, snacks; bar; playgrnd; tennis;
fishing; watersports; games area; covrd play area; horseriding;
entmnt; wifi; TV; 50% statics; dogs €4; Holland Tulip Parcs
site; Eng spkn; adv bkg; quiet. ♦ 1 Apr-1 Oct. € 43.00
(CChq acc)   2014*

MEDEMBLIK *B2* (1km S Rural) *52.75900, 5.10873* **Camping
& Lodge Arado, Brakeweg 61, 1671 LP Medemblik
[(0227) 541671; info@arado.nl; www.arado.nl]**
Exit A7/E22 junc 11 onto N239 dir Medemblik. Go strt over
rndabt & turn R onto N240 dir Enkhuizen. Site on R in 2km.
Sm, unshd; wc; chem disp; shwrs inc; EHU (16A) inc; lndry;
shop 2km; cooking facs; internet; TV; dogs free; Eng spkn; adv
bkg; CKE/CCI. "Vg CL-type site; friendly owners; easy access
to pleasant town & yachting harbour; excel san facs; comf
lounge." ♦ 1 Mar-1 Dec. € 22.50   2011*

MEERKERK *B3* (4km NW Rural) *51.93635, 4.96601* **Camping de
Victorie, Broeksweg 75-77, 4231 VD Meerkerk [(0183) 351516
or 352741; fax 351234; info@campingdevictorie.nl;
www.campingdevictorie.nl]** Leave m'way A27 10km N of
Gorinchem at junc 25 Noordeloos/Meerkerk; take N214 twd
Noordeloos. Turn R after Noordeloos sp SVR Camping & after
1.5km turn R. After 4km turn L at T-junc, site on L. NB: Not rec
to tow thro Meerkerk due narr rds. Med, mkd pitch, pt shd;
wc; chem disp; shwrs €0.50; EHU (4A) inc; gas; lndry; shop
4km; playgrnd; bike hire; beach 35km; rv sw 3km; 50% statics;
dogs €0.50; Eng spkn; sep car park; quiet; adv bkg; ccard
acc; CKE/CCI. "Well-run farm site; HQ of SVR organisation
(mem'ship avail); helpful staff; sep areas 60+ & families with
children; poss boggy after rain; poss long walk to san facs; gd
for touring old world Holland; fruit festival in Tiel mid Sep."
1 Apr-30 Sep. € 10.00   2010*

MEERSSEN *C4* (1.6km ESE Rural) *50.87851, 5.77112* **Camping
Meerssen, Houthemerweg 95, 6231 KT Meerssen
[(0433) 654743; fax 654745; info@campingmeerssen.nl;
www.campingmeerssen.nl]** Fr Eindhoven A2, take exit 51,
foll Valkenburg sp. Take A79 to Hellen exit 2 Meerssen. L at
junc after 400m, site on R. Sm, mkd, pt shd; wc; chem disp;
mv service pnt; shwrs inc; EHU (6A); gas; lndry (inc dryer); shop
1km; rest 1km; snacks 1km; bar 1km; bbq; wifi; 2% statics;
dogs; twin axles; poss cr; Eng spkn; quiet; no ccard acc; red
LS. "Nice, peaceful & relaxing site; v popular with Dutch
people; cent for touring the area; excel site." 1 Apr-30 Sep.
€ 34.50   2014*

MEPPEL *C2* (11km W Rural) *52.69395, 6.08130* **Camping
de Kettingbrug, Veneweg 270, 7946 LW Wanneperveen
[(0522) 281207; fax 282657; info@dekettingbrug.nl;
www.dekettingbrug.nl]** N on A28/A32 & exit junc 3 Meppel
N onto N375 dir Giethoorn for approx 8km. Turn R onto N334
after x-ing lifting bdge & look for site sp in approx 4km. Sm,
hdg/mkd pitch, pt shd; htd wc; chem disp; shwrs; EHU
(10A) €3; gas; lndry; shop 300m; playgrnd; lake sw & grass
beach adj; watersports; statics in sep area across rd; dogs
€1.50; bus; phone; poss cr; Eng spkn; adv bkg; quiet. "Excel,
family-run site; ltd touring pitches, some on lakeside; gd views;
conv Giethoorn by cycle rte." 1 Apr-15 Oct. € 19.00   2010*

"We must tell The Club about that great site we found"

Get your site reports in by mid-August
and we'll do our best to get your updates
into the next edition.

MEPPEL *C2* (13km W Rural) *52.67261, 6.05973* **NCC
Camping 't Hoogland, Vaste Belterweg 4, 8066 PT Belt-
Schutsloot [(038) 3866313; www.ncc.nl]**
Exit A32 junc 3 at Meppel Noord onto N375 sp Genemuiden.
At T-junc after bdge turn R onto N334 sp Giethoorn, in 2km
turn L sp Belt-Schutsloot. In vill turn R into Kerklaan then in
200m L into Belterweg, site on R. Do not app fr W - sharp
turn onto narr bdge. Med, mkd pitch, unshd; wc; chem disp;
shwrs inc; EHU (4A) €2.75; lndry; shop, rest, snacks, bar adj;
playgrnd; htd, covrd pool; lake sw adj; boating; watersports;
dogs; phone; adv bkg; quiet. "Lovely area; historic towns &
vills; friendly staff; CC members welcome but must pre-book."
♦ ltd. 1 Apr-31 Oct. € 12.50   2009*

MEPPEL *C2* (15km W Rural) *52.72164, 6.07484*
**Passantenhaven Zuiderkluft, Jonenweg, 8355 LG
Giethoorn [(0521) 362312]** Turn off N334 sp Dwarsgracht,
over lifting bdge, 1st L over bdge, 1st L again, site on R. Sm,
unshd; wc; chem disp; mv service pnt; shwrs €0.50; EHU (10A)
metered; lndry; drinking water €0.50; Eng spkn; m'vans only;
quiet. "Site run by VVV (tourist board) for m'vans only; ltd EHU;
walking dist fr delightful vill on water." € 10.00   2009*

MEPPEL *C2* (15km NW Rural) *52.72100, 6.06300* **Mini-
Camping Van de Werfe Hoeve, Jonenweg 11, 8355 CN
Giethoorn [tel/fax (0521) 360492]** In Giethoorn turn L at
Smost bdge sp Dwarsgracht & Jonen, immed L to foll rd on L
side of canal - narr rd. Site on L in 500m. Sm, unshd; wc; chem
disp; shwrs; EHU (4A) inc; gas 1km; shops 1km; no statics; dogs
€0.50; poss cr; Eng spkn; adv bkg; quiet; ccard not acc. "Facs
clean; boat hire nrby; gd cycle tracks & footpaths; bike hire
avail locally." € 15.00   2009*

NETHERLANDS

MIDDELBURG *A4* (8km N Rural) *51.55005, 3.64022* **Mini Camping Hoekvliet, Meiwerfweg 3, 4352 SC Gapinge [(0118) 501615; copgapinge@zeelandnet.nl; www.hoekvliet.nl]** Fr Middelburg turn R off N57 at traff lts sp Veere & Gapinge, site sp after Gapinge vill. Sm, mkd pitch, some hdstg, pt shd; wc; chem disp; mv service pnt; shwrs inc; EHU (6A) inc; lndry (inc dryer); BBQ; rest, snacks, bar 2km; playgrnd; sand beach 5km; TV cab; bike hire; 20% statics; dogs €1; sep car park; Eng spkn; quiet; CKE/CCI. "Superb little (25 o'fits) farm site; excel, modern san facs; helpful owner." ♦ ltd. 1 Apr-31 Oct. € 21.00   2011*

MIDDELBURG *A4* (7km NE Rural) *51.53863, 3.65394* **Minicamping Trouw Vóór Goud, Veerseweg 66, 4351 SJ Veere [(0118) 501373; info@trouwvoorgoud.nl; www.trouwvoorgoud.nl]** Take Veere rd N out of Middelburg. Site on L in 4km, bef lge g'ge, sp 'Minicamping'. 1.5km SW of Veere. Sm, pt shd; wc; chem disp; shwrs inc; EHU (6A) €1.75; lndry; playgrnd; sand beach 6km; some statics; dogs €0.80; Eng spkn; quiet. "Excel facs; friendly, tidy, spacious, CL-type site; walking dist Veere." 15 Mar-31 Oct. € 14.00   2010*

MIDWOLDA *D2* (2km W Urban) *53.18900, 6.99053* **Camping de Bouwte, Hoofdweg 20A, 9681 AH Midwolda [05 97 59 17 06; fax 97 59 19 63; info@campingdebouwte. nl; www.campingdebouwte.nl]** Via A7 dir Groningen-Winschoten or via N33 Assen-Delfzil, then onto A7. Exit 45 Scheemda-Midwolda. Foll camping signs. Turn R at traff lts, site on R in 500m. Med, pt shd; wc; chem disp; baby facs; shwrs; EHU (10A); lndry (inc dryer); shop; rest; bar; BBQ; playgrnd; sw lake; games area; games rm; bike hire; entmnt; wifi; TV rm; 50% statics; dogs €1.75; phone; bus adj; twin axles; poss cr; Eng spkn; adv bkg; CCI. "Vg walking/cycling area with mkd rtes; horse riding 1km; WWll Museum in vill; watersports on Oldambtmeer 2km; vg site." ♦ 6 Jan-20 Dec. € 24.00   2014*

MONTFORT see Echt *C4*

NIEUWVLIET *A4* (2km NW Rural) *51.37425, 3.44862* **Camping De Waag, Sint Jansdijk 8, 4504 PB Nieuwvliet [(0117) 371666; dewaag@zeelandnet.nl; www.camping dewaag.nl]** S fr Westerschelde Tunnel onto N61 & N58 dir Breskens. S of Breskens turn W sp Groede & Cadzand. In 6.5km beyond Groede at 2nd sp Nieuwvliet turn R; foll camp sp to site on R in 1.3km. Med, pt shd; wc; chem disp; baby facs; shwrs €0.50; EHU (6A) €2.50; lndry (inc dryer); shop; playgrnd; pool 1.5km; sand beach 1.5km; games area; wifi; entmnt; TV; 40% statics; dogs €1.20; phone; quiet; adv bkg. "Helpful owners; gd for sm children; conv Bruges, Zeeland & Zeebrugge." 23 Apr-1 Oct. € 14.70   2010*

⊞ **NIEUWVLIET** *A4* (3km NW Coastal) *51.3872, 3.4398* **Vakantiepark De Pannenschuur, Zeedijk 19, 4504 PP Nieuwvliet [(0117) 372300; fax 371415; info@pannenschuur.nl; www.roompotparken.nl/parken/ pannenschuur]** Fr Westerschelde Tunnel take N58. Foll sp Groede & Cadzand, thro Groede & in 3km turn R sp Nieuwvliet Strand, foll sp Pannenschuur. V lge, pt shd; htd wc; chem disp; mv service pnt; baby facs; fam bthrm; sauna; shwrs; EHU (6A) inc; gas; lndry (inc dryer); shop; rest, snacks; bar; playgrnd; covrd pool; sand beach 500m; tennis; bike hire; wifi; TV; 70% statics; phone; sep car park; adv bkg; quiet; ccard acc. "Vg touring base for N & S Zeeland, Sluis, Bruges, Ghent." ♦ € 44.40   2010*

NIJVERDAL *D3* (2km SW Rural) *52.34980, 6.45458* **Camping De Noetselerberg, Holterweg 116, 7441 DK Nijverdal [(0548) 612665; fax 611908; info@camping-noetselerberg.nl; www.camping-noetselerberg.nl]** Exit A1 at junc 28. Foll N347 dir Rijssen & Nijverdal. Turn L at rndabt down Noetselerbergweg, site sp. Lge, hdg/mkd pitch, pt shd; htd wc; chem disp; mv service pnt; fam bthrm; baby facs; shwrs; EHU (4-6A) inc; gas; lndry; shop; rest, snacks; bar; playgrnd; 2 pool (1 htd, covrd); bike hire; entmnt; TV; 30% statics; phone; sep car park; quiet; adv bkg; Eng spkn. "Beautiful area; gd cycle tracks; friendly, helpful staff; excel." ♦ 3 Apr-25 Oct. € 34.00   2009*

NOORD SLEEN see Emmen *D2*

NOORDWIJK AAN ZEE *B3* (5km N Rural) *52.27102, 4.47686* **Camping De Carlton, Kraaierslaan 13, 2204 AN Noordwijk aan Zee [(0252) 372783; fax 370299; info@campingcarlton.nl; www.campingcarlton.nl]** Fr N206 take Noordwijkerhout turn off, foll sp to town & drive thru to rndabt. Take R exit sp Congrescentrum Leeuwenhorst, then take 1st L & foll site sp. Med, mkd pitch, pt shd; htd wc; chem disp; mv service pnt; shwrs €0.50; EHU (4A) inc; lndry (inc dryer); shops 1km; rest, snacks, bar; playgrnd; pool; bike hire; TV; 40% statics; phone; sep car park; poss cr; Eng spkn; quiet; ccard acc; CKE/ CCI. "Conv Keukenhof; gd clean site; friendly owners." ♦ 1 Apr-1 Nov. € 26.60   2009*

NOORDWIJK AAN ZEE *B3* (5km N Rural/Coastal) *52.26817, 4.46981* **Camping De Duinpan, Duindamseweg 6, 2204 AS Noordwijk aan Zee [(0252) 371726; fax 344112; contact@ campingdeduinpan.nl; www.campingdeduinpan.com]** Exit A44 at junc 3 dir Sassenheim then foll sp Noordwijkerhout. At 5th rndabt (Leeuwenhorst Congress building) turn R then L. Site sp. Med, mkd pitch, unshd; htd wc; chem disp; mv service pnt; shwrs €0.50; EHU (10A) inc; gas; lndry; rest, snacks, bar adj; playgrnd; pool 2.5km; bike hire; wifi; 60% statics; phone; sep car park; ccard acc; CKE/CCI. "Conv for tulip fields in ssn." 15 Mar-31 Oct. € 29.50   2013*

See advertisement opposite

⊞ **NOORDWIJK AAN ZEE** *B3* (2km NE Rural) *52.24874, 4.46358* **Camping op Hoop van Zegen, Westeinde 76, 2211 XR Noordwijkerhout [(0252) 375491; info@camping ophoopvanzegen.nl; www.campingophoopvanzegen.nl]** Exit A44 junc 6 dir Noordwijk aan Zee. Cross N206 & turn R in 1km into Gooweg dir Leeuwenhorst. In 1km turn L into Hoogweg & foll sp to site. Med, hdg/mkd pitch, unshd; htd wc; chem disp; mv service pnt; baby facs; fam bthrm; shwrs; EHU (6A) €2.25; lndry (inc dryer); shop 2km; playgrnd; sand beach 2.5km; bike hire; games area; dogs €3; phone; poss cr; adv bkg rec when Keukenhof open; Eng spkn; quiet; ccard acc; CKE/ CCI. "Gd site; modern san facs; conv bulb fields, beaches." € 18.00   2013*

NOORDWIJKERHOUT see Noordwijk aan Zee *B3*

NUNSPEET see Harderwijk *C3*

Camping De Duinpan

Camping de Duinpan
Duindamseweg 6
2204 AS Noordwijk

Tel. +31 (0)252 - 37 17 26
Mail: contact@campingdeduinpan.nl
Web: www.campingdeduinpan.com

NETHERLANDS

Come and enjoy a wonderful holiday with us.

⊞ OIRSCHOT *C3* (1km N Rural) *51.51684, 5.30854* **Camping De Bocht, Oude Grintweg 69, 5688 MB Oirschot [(0499) 550855; info@campingdebocht.nl; www.campingdebocht.nl]** Fr A58/E312 take exit 8 to Oirschot. Site in 4km on Boxtel rd. Site sp. Med, hdg pitch, shd; htd wc; chem disp; baby facs; shwrs €0.50; EHU (10A) €3; gas; lndry (inc dryer); rest, snacks; bar; playgrnd; pool high ssn; paddling pool; bike hire; wifi; entmnt; TV; 60% statics; dogs €2.50; phone; poss cr; adv bkg; quiet; Eng spkn. "Gd touring base; gd for families; pleasant town." € 21.70   2011*

"I need an on-site restaurant"

We do our best to make sure site information is correct, but it is always best to check any must-have facilities are still available or will be open during your visit.

OMMEN *D2* (8km E Rural) *52.51033, 6.51564* **Camping de Roos, Beerzerweg 10, 7736 PJ Beerze-Ommen [(0523) 251234; fax 251903; info@camping-de-roos.nl; www.camping-de-roos.nl]** Fr N34 at Ommen turn S onto N347. Cross rv & immed turn E. Site on L in Beerze. Lge, pt shd; htd wc; chem disp; baby facs; shwrs inc; EHU (6A) €2.70; gas; lndry; shop; snacks; playgrnd; lake & rv sw adj; boating; fishing; bike hire; 10% statics; no dogs; phone; sep car park; quiet; ccard acc; red LS. "Excel family site; lots of play space." 2 Apr-3 Oct. € 17.00   2010*

OMMEN *D2* (6km W Rural) *52.51911, 6.36461* **Resort de Arendshorst, Arendshorsterweg 3A, 7731 RC Ommen [(0529) 453248; fax (0059) 453045; info@resort-de-arendshorst.nl; www.resort-de-arendshorst.nl]** W fr Ommen on N34/N340 turn L at site sp, then 500m along lane past farm, site on rvside. Lge, mkd pitch, pt shd; htd wc; chem disp; serviced pitches; baby facs; shwrs €0.20; EHU (10A) inc; gas; lndry; shop; rest, snacks; bar; no BBQ; playgrnd; pool 3km; paddling pool; sw in canal; games area; bike hire; TV rm; wifi; 50% statics; dogs; phone; Eng spkn; adv bkg (fee); quiet; red 7+ days/snr citizens; CKE/CCI. "Beautiful area; many cycle rtes; gd children's facs." 1 Apr-31 Oct. € 28.50 SBS - H02   2009*

OOSTERBEEK see Arnhem *C3*

OOSTERHOUT *B3* (3km NW Rural) *51.65358, 4.82736* **Mini-Camping Vrachelen, Vrachelsestraat 48, 4911 BJ Den Hout [(0162) 454032; fax 430680; jan@pheninckx.nl; www.pheninckx.nl]** Leave A59 at junc 32 S twd Oosterhout West. At 1st rndabt foll sp Oosterhout, at next rndabt turn R sp Den Hout & site. Site on R in 400m. Sm, mkd pitch, unshd; htd wc; chem disp; shwrs inc; EHU (6A) inc; shop; playgrnd; TV; many statics; poss cr; Eng spkn; quiet; red LS; CKE/CCI. "Perfect level lawn in mkt garden; farm produce for sale; v helpful, friendly owners; pitches have hdstg for awnings; highly rec." 15 Mar-1 Nov. € 15.00   2011*

OOSTKAPELLE *A3* (1km SW Rural) *51.56253, 3.54627* **Zeeland Camping Ons Buiten, Aagtekerkseweg 2A, 4356 RJ Oostkapelle [(0118) 581813; fax 583771; onsbuiten@ardoer.com; www.ardoer.com/nl/camping/ons-buiten]** Fr Middelburg foll sps to Domburg; Oostkapelle vill 4km bef Domburg, on ent foll 1-way system, foll sps to site, 400m fr cent. Lge, mkd pitch, pt shd (in orchard); htd wc; chem disp; mv service pnt; private bthrms some pitches; baby facs; fam bthrm; shwrs inc; EHU (6A) inc; gas; lndry (inc dryer); shop; rest, snacks; playgrnd; covrd pools; sand beach 3.5km; tennis; bike hire; wifi; entmnt; TV; 10% statics; phone; sep car park; no dogs; adv bkg; quiet. "Friendly staff; ideal for sm children." ♦ 1 Apr-1 Nov. € 40.50   2010*

OOSTWOUD see Enkhuizen *C2*

OPENDE *D2* (3km SE Rural) *53.16465, 6.22275* **NCC Camping de Watermolen, Openderweg 26, 9865 XE Opende [tel/fax (0594) 659144; info@campingdewatermolen.nl; www.campingdewatermolen.nl]** Exit A7 junc 32 dir Kornhorn. In Noordwijk turn L at church & in 3 km turn R into Openderweg. Site in 700m on L. Med, hdstg, pt shd; htd wc; chem disp; mv service pnt; fam bthrm; shwrs €0.50; EHU (16A) €2.50; lndry (inc dryer); shops 4km; rest; bar; BBQ; playgrnd; pool; lake sw; internet; wifi; tv rm; some statics; dogs €2.50; phone; adv bkg; twin axles; ccard acc; quiet; CKE/CCI. "Friendly owners; pt of site for NCC members - CC members welcome but must book ahead; brilliant site with lakes to walk around & woods; hide for bird watching; excel." 1 Apr-30 Sep. € 33.00   2014*

OPENDE *D2* (3km S Rural) *53.15262, 6.19175* **Camping 't Strandheem, Parkweg 2, 9865 VP Opende [(0594) 659555; fax 658592; info@strandheem.nl; www.strandheem.nl]** E22/A7 Amsterdam to Groningen m'way take Frieschepalen exit 31. Foll N358 to Suirhesterveen; site sp. Lge, mkd pitch, some hdstg, pt shd; htd wc; mv service pnt; chem disp; serviced pitches; some pitches individ san facs; baby facs; fam bthrm; shwrs inc; EHU (10A) €2.50; gas; lndry (inc dryer); shop; rest, snacks; bar; playgrnd; htd, covrd pool; sand beach 5km; wifi; entmnt; 30% statics; dogs €4.25; poss cr; Eng spkn; adv bkg; quiet; Holland Tulip Parcs site; CKE/CCI. "Lge pitches; friendly owners; gd well-run site." ♦ 1 Apr-30 Sep. € 25.50 (CChq acc) 2011*

OTTERLO *C3* (2km S Rural) *52.08657, 5.76934* **Camping De Wije Werelt, Arnhemseweg 100-102, 6731 BV Otterlo [(0318) 591201; fax 592101; info@wijewerelt.nl; www.wijewerelt.nl]** Exit A50 junc 22 dir Hoenderlo & N304 to Otterlo. Site on R after Camping de Zanding. Lge, mkd pitch, unshd; htd wc; chem disp; mv service pnt; baby facs; fam bthrm; shwrs inc; EHU (6-10A) inc; lndry; shop; rest, snacks; bar; playgrnd; pool; paddling pool; games area; 40% statics; dogs €4; phone; Eng spkn; adv bkg; quiet; ccard acc. "Excel, well-run site; immac san facs; vg for families; conv Arnhem." 27 Mar-31 Oct. € 33.00 2009*

OTTERLO *C3* (1km SW Rural) *52.09310, 5.77762* **Camping De Zanding, Vijverlaan 1, 6731 CK Otterlo [(0318) 596111; fax 596110; info@zanding.nl; www.zanding.nl]** Leave A1 at exit 17 onto N310 thro Otterlo, or junc 19 onto N304. Foll camp sp to site. Fr A50 exit junc 22 dir Hoenderloo & N304 to Otterlo. V lge, mkd pitch, some hdstg, pt shd; htd wc; chem disp; mv service pnt; serviced pitches; baby facs; shwrs inc; EHU (4-10A) inc; gas; lndry (inc dryer); rest; shop; playgrnd; lake sw & sand beach; tennis; wifi; entmnt; TV; 45% statics; dogs €3.50; Holland Tulip Parcs site; poss cr; Eng spkn; adv bkg ess hol periods; red LS; ccard acc; CKE/CCI. "Peaceful, wooded site; modern, well-organised & well laid-out; friendly, helpful staff; gd for families; excel facs; conv National Park, Kröller Müller museum; excel." ♦ 26 Mar-31 Oct. € 35.00 (CChq acc) 2011*

OUDEGA see Drachten *C2*

OUDEMIRDUM *C2* (2km N Rural) *52.86005, 5.54450* **Camping De Wigwam, Sminkewei 7, 8567 HB Oudemirdum [(0514) 571223; fax 571725; camping@dewigwam.nl; www.dewigwam.nl]** Exit A6 junc 17 onto N359 to Balk. Approx 3km beyond Balk turn L at sp Oudemirdum & foll site sp in woodland N of vill. Lge, mkd pitch, pt shd; wc; chem disp; baby facs; shwrs €0.75; EHU (16A) inc; gas; lndry; snacks; playgrnd; lake sw & sand beach 3km; bike hire; golf adj; wifi; TV; 60% statics (sep area); dogs €2.70; Eng spkn; quiet; ccard acc; red snr citizens/LS. "Close to Ijsselmeer; lge pitches; gd cycling area; easy walk to pleasant vill; charge for all hot water." 1 Apr-1 Nov. € 17.00 2010*

OUDEMIRDUM *C2* (500m N Rural) *52.85436, 5.53147* **Boskampeerterrein De Waps, Fonteinwei 14, 8567 JT Oudemirdum [tel/fax (0514) 571437; waps@planet.nl; www.dewaps.nl]** Fr Lemmer take N359 twd Balk. In 12km turn L sp Oudemirdum, site sp fr church in vill. Med, hdg/mkd pitch, pt shd; htd wc; chem disp; shwrs inc; baby facs; fam bthrm; EHU (10A) inc; lndry; shop 500m; rest, snacks; bar; playgrnd; sand beach 3km; games area; bike hire; entmnt; 25% statics; dogs €2; phone; Eng spkn; quiet; ccard acc. "In pine forest; excel walks; clean facs; friendly staff." 1 Apr-31 Oct. € 24.00 2009*

PANNINGEN *C4* (4km NW Rural) *51.34894, 5.96111* **Beringerzand Camping, Heide 5, 5981 NX Panningen [07 73 07 20 95; fax 73 07 49 80; info@beringerzand.nl; www.beringerzand.nl]** Fr A67 exit at junc 38 twd S, dir Koningslust/Panningen. Site is 3km NW Panningen, down narr lane thro asparagus fields. Med, mkd pitch, pt shd; wc; chem disp; mv service pnt; shwrs; EHU (10A); lndry (inc dryer); shop; snacks; bar; BBQ; playgrnd; htd pool; covrd pool; waterslide; paddling pool; games area & rm; bike hire; wifi; dogs €4.85 max 2 per pitch; twin axles acc; Eng spkn; adv bkg. ♦ 28 Mar-7 Nov. € 45.00 2014*

"Satellite navigation makes touring much easier"

Remember most sat navs don't know if you're towing or in a larger vehicle – always use yours alongside maps and site directions.

PETTEN *B2* (1km N Coastal) *52.77057, 4.65908* **Camping Corfwater, Strandweg 3, 1755 LA Petten [(0226) 381981; fax 383371; camping@corfwater.nl; www.corfwater.nl]** On A9 N of Alkmaar, foll sp for Petten. Thro vill, site behind sea wall. Lge, mkd pitch, unshd; htd wc; chem disp; mv service pnt; baby facs; fam bthrm; shwrs inc; EHU (6A) inc; gas; lndry; shop; no BBQ; playgrnd; pool 3km; sand beach adj; 20% statics; no dogs; phone; sep car park; Eng spkn; quiet; ccard acc; CKE/CCI. "Vg site; busy in high ssn." ♦ 1 Apr-31 Oct. € 26.00 2011*

RAVENSTEIN *C3* (500m E Urban) *51.79600, 5.65500* **NCC Camping De Pollepel, Bleek 5, 5371 AP Ravenstein [(0486) 413849; info@ncc.nl; www.ncc.nl]** Fr N exit A50 junc 17 dir Ravenstein, strt on at rndabt into Ravenstein. Fr S exit A50 junc 17 turn R at rndabt into Ravenstein. Foll sp for NCC camping; pass sm marina on RH side; turn L into Walstraat; then L immed after car park, site ent 50m thro gates. Sm, mkd pitch, pt shd; htd wc; chem disp; shwrs inc; EHU (4A) £2.75; lndry; shop, rest, snacks, bar 500m; playgrnd; htd, covrd pool 4km; rv sw adj; TV rm; train 3km; poss cr; adv bkg; some rd noise. "Beautiful site; located in cent picturesque fortress town on Rv Maas; gd cycling, walking; interesting area; CC members welcome but must phone ahead." 1 Apr-31 Oct. € 12.00 2011*

REEUWIJK see Gouda *B3*

RENESSE *A3* (1km N Coastal) *51.73917, 3.77611*
Camping Duinhoeve, Scholderlaan 8, 4328 EP Renesse
[(0111) 461309; fax 462760; info@campingduinhoeve.nl;
www.campingduinhoeve.nl] On rd 102 fr Renesse to
Haamstede, turn R on ent to Haamstede bef T-junc. Last site
on long picturesque lane. Lge, hdg/mkd pitch, pt shd; htd wc;
chem disp; mv service pnt; baby facs; shwrs inc; EHU (4-6A)
inc; gas; lndry; shop; rest, snacks; bar; playgrnd; sand beach
nr; games area; bike hire; TV; 20% statics; dogs €3.50; poss
cr; adv bkg; quiet; ccard acc. "Charming area; Delta works
worth visit; wide dunes on sea shore." ♦ 1 Feb-31 Oct.
€ 28.00   2009*

RENSWOUDE *C3* (2km NE Rural) *52.08435, 5.55069* **Camping
de Grebbelinie, Ubbeschoterweg 12, 3927 CJ Renswoude**
[(0318) 591073; info@campingdegrebbelinie.nl;
www.campingdegrebbelinie.nl] Head NW on Dorpsstraat/
N224, at rndabt take 1st exit onto Barneveldsestraat, turn R
onto Bekerweg, R onto Ubbeschoterweg then turn L. Site on
the R. Med, unshd; htd wc; chem disp; baby facs; fam bthrm;
shwrs inc; EHU; lndry; shops 2km; rest 2km; snacks 2km; bar
2km; playgrnd; games area; internet; wifi; dogs €1.75; bus
2km; Eng spkn; adv bkg; quiet; CKE/CCI. "Friendly owners;
excel cycling with cycle rte adj; conv for Arnhem & Utrecht;
peaceful site on former farm; in open countryside; excel value
for money." 21 Mar-18 Oct. € 27.00   2014*

RETRANCHEMENT see Sluis *A4*

RIJEN see Breda *B3*

RIJNSBURG see Katwijk aan Zee *B3*

> "There aren't many sites
> open at this time of year"
>
> If you're travelling outside peak season
> remember to call ahead to check site opening
> dates – even if the entry says 'open all year'.

ROCKANJE *A3* (2km NW Coastal) *51.88000, 4.05422*
Molecaten Park Waterbos, Duinrand 11, 3235 CC Rockanje
[(0181) 401900; fax 404233; info@waterboscamping.nl;
www.waterboscamping.nl] Site clearly sp fr Rockanje vill.
Lge, hdg pitch, pt shd; htd wc; chem disp; mv service pnt;
baby facs; private san facs avail; shwrs €0.50; EHU (6A) inc;
lndry; shop; rest, snacks; bar; sand beach/dunes 1km;
entmnt; cab/sat TV; 80% statics; phone; no dogs; phone; poss
cr; adv bkg; quiet;CKE/CCI. "Lovely base for Voorne area."
1 Apr-1 Oct. € 19.00   2009*

ROERMOND *C4* (8km W Rural) *51.19186, 5.94955* **Resort
Marina Oolderhuuske, Oolderhuuske 1, 6041 TR Roermond**
[(0475) 588686; fax 582652; info@oolderhuuske.nl;
www.oolderhuuske.nl] Exit N280 1km fr Roermond sp De
Weerd & foll sp to Marina Oolderhuuske. Med, mkd pitch,
unshd; htd wc; chem disp; mv service pnt; baby facs; shwrs inc;
EHU (6A) €2.50; gas; lndry (inc dryer); shop; rest, snacks; bar;
playgrnd; htd, covrd pool; paddling pol; lake sw adj; boating;
fishing; watersports; tennis; games area; golf driving range;
bike hire; wifi; 75% statics; dogs €4; Eng spkn; quiet; red long
stay. "Facs v clean; mkt Wed/Sat; gd site in gd weather." ♦
1 Apr-31 Oct. € 33.00 (4 persons)   2010*

ROERMOND *C4* (15km W Rural) *51.20947, 5.83008* **Camping
Geelenhoof, Grathemerweg 16, 6037 NR Kelpen-Oler
(Limburg)** [(0495) 651858; info@geelenhoof.nl;
www.geelenhoof.nl] 1km S of Kelpen-Oler; bet Roermond
& Weert; exit N280 foll sp; well mkd. Med, hdg/mkd pitch, pt
shd; htd wc; chem disp; mv service pnt; baby facs; shwrs inc;
EHU (6A) €3; rest, snacks; bar; playgrnd; games area; games
rm; dogs (on request) €2.50; Eng spkn; adv bkg; quiet;CKE/
CCI. "Cars not to be parked with c'van; vg site." 1 Apr-4 Nov.
€ 29.00   2013*

ROOSENDAAL *B3* (7km S Rural) *51.49430, 4.48536*
Camping Zonneland, Turfvaartsestraat 6, 4709 PB Nispen
[(0165) 365429; info@zonneland.nl; www.zonneland.nl]
Take A58 exit 24 onto N262 dir Nispen. Foll site sps. Lge,
some hdstg, shd; wc; chem disp; mv service pnt; shwrs €0.50;
EHU (4-10A) €2; lndry; shop; supmkt 4km; snacks; bar; pool;
playgrnd; entmnt; 80% statics; no dogs; phone; Eng spkn; adv
bkg; quiet; ccard acc. 1 Mar-15 Oct. € 19.00   2012*

⊞ **ROTTERDAM** *B3* (14km SE Rural) *51.83454, 4.54673*
Camping De Oude Maas, Achterzeedijk 1A, 2991 SB
Barendrecht [(078) 6772445; fax 6773013;
www.campingdeoudemaas.nl] Leave A29 (Rotterdam-
Bergen op Zoom) junc 20 Barendrecht, foll sp for Heerjansdam,
site sp, Fr A16 (Breda-Dordrecht) foll Europort sp, then
Zierikzee, Barendrecht, site sp. Lge, pt shd; htd wc; chem disp;
mv service pnt; baby facs; fam bthrm; shwrs inc; EHU (10A)
inc; lndry; shop; snacks; playgrnd; TV; 80% statics in sep area;
dogs; phone; quiet; ccard acc. "Excel site on Rv Maas inc sm
marina & joins rec park; excel facs; some pitches rough & long
way fr facs; ferry fr site in ssn; check recep opening time if
planning dep bef midday (espec Sun) for return of deposit &
barrier key; entry via new ent past old." ♦ € 25.00   2012*

⊞ **ROTTERDAM** *B3* (3km W Urban) *51.93100, 4.44200*
Stadscamping Rotterdam, Kanaalweg 84, 3041 JE Rotterdam
[(010) 4153440; fax 4373215; info@stadscamping-rotterdam.nl;
www.stadscamping-rotterdam.nl] Adj to junc of A13 & A20,
take slip rd sp Rotterdam Centrum & Camping Kanaalweg sp
to site. Dist fr m'way 2.5km with 3 L turns. Lge, pt shd; wc;
chem disp; baby facs; shwrs inc; EHU (6A) €3.75; gas; lndry;
shop; snacks; bar; internet; pool 500m; dogs €2; bus; poss cr;
adv bkg; quiet but rds; rlwy adj; ccard acc. "Gd bus service to
city cent; few water taps." ♦ € 34.70   2014*

RUINEN *D2* (2km N Rural) *52.77570, 6.37170* **Camping Ruinen, Oude Benderseweg 11, 7963 PX Ruinen [(0522) 471770; fax 472614; info@camping-ruinen.nl; www.camping-ruinen.nl]** Exit A28 junc 28 sp Ruinen & foll sp to site; narr lanes. Lge, mkd pitch, some hdstg, pt shd; htd wc; chem disp; mv service pnt; baby facs; fam bthrm; shwrs inc; EHU (6A) inc; gas; lndry (inc dryer); supmkt high ssn; rest, snacks; playgrnd; htd pool; paddling pool; waterslide; tennis; bike hire; wifi; entmnt; cab TV; 30% statics; dogs €3.35; sep car park; Holland Tulip Parcs site; Eng spkn; adv bkg; quiet. "V pleasant site." ♦ 1 Apr-1 Oct. € 25.00   2011*

RUURLO *D3* (5km SE Rural) *52.06778, 6.50236* **Camping de Meibeek, Bekkenwal 2,7261 RG Ruurlo [(0573) 491236; info@campingdemeibeek.nl; www.campingdemeibeek.nl]** Site on N319, sp. Med, hdg/mkd pitch, pt shd; htd wc; chem disp; mv service pnt; baby facs; shwrs €0.50; EHU (6A) metered; lndry (inc dryer); rest, snacks; bar; playgrnd; pool; fishing nr; tennis 3km; golf 10km; games area; wifi; entmnt; 50% statics; dogs; Eng spkn; adv bkg; quiet. "Friendly, enthusiastic young owners; excel." 1 Apr-31 Oct. € 20.00   2009*

SCHIMMERT *C4* (600m E Rural) *50.90746, 5.83122* **Camping Mareveld, Mareweg 23, 6333 BR Schimmert South Limburg [(045) 4041269; fax 4042148; info@mareveld.nl; www.campingmareveld.nl]** A76 exit Spaubeek, turn R twd Schimmert. 2nd on the L in Schimmert. Campsite sp. Sm, pt shd; wc; chem disp; baby facs; shwrs, EHU (6A) €2.10; rest/café; bar; playgrnd; htd pool; games area; wifi; tv in bar; 80% statics; dog €1.75; poss cr; Eng spkn; adv bkg; popular with families; red LS. "Gd cycling/walking fr site; gd site; open plan, grassy site." 1 Apr-31 Dec. € 30.00   2014*

> ## "That's changed – Should I let The Club know?"
>
> If you find something on site that's different from the site entry, fill in a report and let us know. See www.caravanclub.co.uk/europereport.

⊞ **SEVENUM** *C4* (5km SW Rural) *51.38310, 5.97590* **Camping De Schatberg, Midden Peelweg 1, 5975 MZ Sevenum [(077) 4677777; fax 4677799; receptie@schatberg.nl; www.schatberg.nl]** Fr A2/A67 exit junc 38 for Helden; foll sp Sevenum & site by sm lake. V lge, shd; htd wc; chem disp; mv service pnt; fam bthrm; baby facs; private san facs some pitches; sauna; shwrs inc; EHU (6-10A) inc; gas; lndry (inc dryer); shop; rest, snacks; bar; playgrnd; 2 pools (1 htd, covrd); paddling pool; waterslide; jacuzzi; lake sw & sand beach; watersports; fishing; tennis; games area; bike hire; entmnt; TV; 60% statics; dogs (in sep area); phone; Holland Tulip Parcs site; Eng spkn; adv bkg; quiet; CKE/CCI. "Excel leisure facs, espec for children; vg site but impersonal; tourers pitched amongst statics; Venlo Sat mkt worth visit." ♦ € 41.00 (4 persons) (CChq acc)   2011*

'S-HEERENBERG *D3* (3km W Rural) *51.87795, 6.21125* **Camping Brockhausen, Eltenseweg 20, 7039 CV Stokkum [(0314) 661212; fax 668563; info@brockhausen.nl; www.brockhausen.nl]** Fr A12 exit junc sp 's-Heerenberg, cont past 's-Heerenberg sp & pick up sp to Stokkum & site on L. Med, mkd pitch, pt shd; htd wc; chem disp; mv service pnt; baby facs; shwrs metered; EHU (4-6A) inc; lndry (inc dryer); shop 3km; playgrnd; cab TV; 40% statics; dogs €3.45; Eng spkn; adv bkg; quiet. "V clean, eco-friendly site; facs charged on electronic key; friendly, helpful staff; lovely area walking, cycling; excel." ♦ 1 Apr-31 Oct. € 24.00   2012*

'S-HERTOGENBOSCH *C3* (10km E Rural) *51.6938, 5.4148* **Camping de Hooghe Heide, Werstkant 17, 5258 TC Berlicum [(073) 5031522; fax 5037351; info@hoogheheide. nl; www.hoogheheide.nl]** Fr A59/A2 circular rd around 's-Hertogenbosch exit junc 21 dir Berlicum. Foll sp Berlicum & site. Site is NE of Berlicum. Med, mkd pitch, pt shd; wc; chem disp; baby facs; shwrs inc; EHU (10A) €3; lndry; shop; snacks; playgrnd; pool; paddling pool; games area; TV; 70% statics; dogs €4.25; phone; poss cr/noisy high ssn; Eng spkn; adv bkg ess; quiet; CKE/CCI. "Nice, peaceful wooded site; narr site rds for lge o'fits; tourers on open field; excel." ♦ 1 Apr-16 Oct. € 26.50   2010*

SINT OEDENRODE *C3* (2km N Rural) *51.57741, 5.44648* **Camping De Kienehoef, Zwembadweg 37, 5491 TE Sint Oedenrode [(0413) 472877; fax 477033; info@kienehoef.nl; www.kienehoef.nl]** Exit A50 junc 9; go twds Sint Oedenrode; foll sp to Centrum at rndabt; foll sp. Lge, hdg/mkd pitch, some hdstg, pt shd; htd wc; chem disp; mv service pnt; fam bthrm; baby facs; shwrs inc; EHU (6A) inc; gas; lndry (inc dryer); shop; rest, snacks; bar; BBQ; playgrnd; htd, covrd pool; paddling pool; lake sw; fishing; tennis; bike hire; wifi; entmnt; TV rm; 50% statics; no dogs; phone; sep car park; Holland Tulip Parcs site; Eng spkn; adv bkg; ccard acc; CKE/CCI. "Lovely CL type site; vg facs; 1.5 miles fr lovely sm town with plenty of shops & rests." 1 Apr-25 Sep. € 30.00 (CChq acc)   2011*

⊞ **SINT OEDENRODE** *C3* (3km N Rural) *51.57800, 5.4400* **NCC Camping 't Roois Klumpke, Vliegden 1, 5491 VS Sint Oedenrode [(0413) 474702; www.ncc.nl]** Exit A2 junc 26 to Sint Oedenrode; site sp on Schijndel rd - 100m bef Camping Kienehoef turn R onto Vliegden, site 400m on L. Med, mkd pitch, pt shd; htd wc; chem disp; shwrs inc; EHU (4A) €2.75; lndry; BBQ; Eng spkn; poss cr; Eng spkn; adv bkg; quiet; CKE/CCI. "Members only - CC members welcome but must pre-book; shop, rest, snacks avail at Camping de Kienehoef." ♦ ltd. € 11.00   2009*

SINT OEDENRODE *C3* (3.7km SE Urban) *51.54780, 5.48703* **Camping De Graspol, Bakkerpad 17, 5492 TL Sint Oedenrode [(0413) 474133 or (0653) 224220; info@campingdegraspol.nl; www.campingdegraspol.nl]** Fr A50 take exit St Oedenrode, dir Nijnsel. Foll sp to site. Med, mkd pitch, pt shd; htd wc; chem disp; mv service pnt; baby facs; shwrs; EHU (16A) gas; lndry (inc dryer); BBQ; bike hire; fishing; games rm; wifi; TV; dogs; Eng spkn; quiet; ACSI. "Well kept; gd for NH or longer; warm welcome." 1 Mar-1 Oct. € 25.00   2015*

NETHERLANDS

SLUIS *A4* (800m N Rural) *51.31395, 3.38863* **Camping De Meidoorn, Hoogstraat 68, 4524 LA Sluis [tel/fax (0117) 461662; info@campingdemeidoorn.eu; www.campingdemeidoorn.eu]** Fr Zeebrugge, ignore 1st turn L to Sluis, cont to rndabt sp Sluis 1km. At windmill keep R (do not go to town cent). After LH bend turn R, foll sps. Lge, pt shd; htd wc; chem disp; mv service pnt; baby facs; shwrs €0.50; EHU (6A) €3; gas; shop; rest, snacks; bar; playgrnd; tennis; TV; 80% statics; dogs €1.75; phone; Eng spkn; red CKE/CCI. "Bus to Bruges and Breskens fr rear site ent." ♦ 1 Apr-1 Nov. € 33.40   2013*

"I like to fill in the reports as I travel from site to site"

You'll find report forms at the back of this guide, or you can fill them in online at www.caravanclub.co.uk/europereport.

SLUIS *A4* (5km SE Rural) *51.28682, 3.43580* **Camping de Oliepot, Draaibrugseweg 8, 4527 PA Aardenburg [(0117) 491518; fax 493286; s.van.male@agroweb.nl; www.oliepot.nl]** Fr Knokke take N376 onto Sluis by-pass N58; turn R onto N251 Aardenburg. At next rndat in 1km turn L sp Draaibrug & immed R onto service rd. Site on L in 1km. Sm, mkd pitch, pt shd; wc; chem disp; shwrs €0.50; EHU (4-16A) €1.65-6.30; lndry; shop 1km; playgrnd; pool 3km; sand beach 6km; no statics; dogs €1.30; Eng spkn; adv bkg rec high ssn; quiet; ccard not acc; CKE/CCI. "V well-run site, clean & tidy; friendly, helpful owners; conv Bruges & Ghent." 1 Apr-30 Sep. € 11.00   2009*

SNEEK *C2* (2km E Urban) *53.03557, 5.67630* **Jachthaven Camping De Domp, De Domp 4, 8605 CP Sneek [(0515) 412559; fax 439846; www.dedomp.nl]** Fr cent of Sneek on Leeuwarden rd, turn R sp De Domp. Med, pt shd; htd wc; chem disp; mv service pnt; serviced pitches; baby facs; shwrs €0.50; EHU (6A) inc; gas; lndry; rest, snacks; bar; supmkt nr; playgrnd; boating; sep car park; dogs; adv bkg; Eng spkn. "Many canals in Sneek; marina on site; easy walk to pleasant town; gd cycling cent." ♦ 1 Apr-1 Nov. € 18.00   2009*

STADSKANAAL *D2* (1km W Urban) *52.99079, 6.94159* **Camping 't Nije Hof, Spoorstraat 29b, 9503 AM Stadskanaal [599 658 892; info@nijehof.nl; www.nijehof.nl]** Fr Groningen take exit 44 off A7 Winschoten onto N33 dir Pekela; take N366 dir Stadskanaal & foll this rd until junc & take exit Stadskanaal (N) onto Van Boekerenweg; drive strt on for several km and pass hospial; turn L after hospital at traff lts island onto Handlestraat, which becomes Postraat; rd alongside canal, turn R over bdge sp Drouwener; take 1st R into Spoorstraat; pass over rlwy lines and immed sharp L into site. Sm, pt shd; htd wc; chem disp; baby facs; shwrs inc; EHU inc; lndry; playgrnd; 15% statics; dogs €1.50; adv bkings; quiet; CKE/CCI. "Pleasant quiet site; friendly owners; pay on arr; handy for exploring Dolmen on Dutch/German border." Apr-Sep. € 17.50   2011*

STEENBERGEN *B3* (5km NW Rural) *51.60887, 4.27303* **Camping De Uitwijk, Dorpsweg 136, 4655 AH De Heen [(0167) 560000; fax 560010; info@de-uitwijk.nl; www.de-uitwijk.nl]** Fr N259 at Steenbergen turn W onto N257 dir Zierikzee. In 2km turn N thro De Heen & turn R at T-junc. Site recep on R, site on L. Do not take c'van to recep, but ent site, park on R & walk back. Med, mkd pitch, pt shd; htd wc; chem disp; mv service pnt; baby facs; shwrs inc; EHU (4-10A) inc; lndry (inc dryer); shop 4km; rest, snacks; bar; playgrnd; games rm; wifi; entmnt; sat TV; 60% statics; dogs €3.20; bus 750m; poss cr; Eng spkn; adv bkg; CKE/CCI. "Pleasant, well run, quiet site adj marina; friendly staff; excel; excel cycle rtes; conv for ferry." 23 Mar-28 Sep. € 26.00   2014*

STEENWIJK *C2* (8km NE Rural) *52.84123, 6.17674* **Camping de Moesberg, Hoofdweg 14, 8383 EG Nijensleek [(0521) 381563; fax 383285; info@moesberg.nl; www.moesberg.nl]** Exit A32 junc 6 at Steenwijk N onto N855 sp Frederiksoord & Vledder; thro Nijensleek, site on L. Med, mkd pitch, unshd; htd wc; chem disp; mv service pnt; baby facs; shwrs inc; EHU (10A) inc; lndry rm; shop 2km; rest adj; bar; playgrnd; pool 3km; wifi; sat TV; 10% statics; dogs; poss cr; Eng spkn; adv bkg; quiet. "Paved patio area at each pitch; helpful, friendly owners; gd rest adj." 28 Mar-31 Oct. € 23.00   2009*

TERSCHELLING ISLAND *C1* Sites on Terschelling Island are listed together at the end of the Netherlands site entry pages.

TEXEL ISLAND *B2* Sites on Texel Island are listed together at the end of the Netherlands site entry pages.

THORN *C4* (1km SW Rural) *51.1596, 5.8340* **Camping Viverjerbroek, Kessenicherweg 20, 6017 AA Thorn [(0475) 561914; fax 565565; info@campingthorn.com]** Take junc 41 of A2, foll sp to Thorn. Turn R in vill down Wilhelminalaan, R into Holstraat, foll rd to site. Sm, hdg/mkd pitch, pt shd; wc; chem disp; shwrs €1; EHU (4A) inc (rev pol); shop 500m; rest; bar; BBQ; lake sw & sand beach 1km; watersports; playgrnd; 80% statics; dogs; phone; adv bkg; quiet; CKE/CCI. "Nr attractive vill; conv m'way; site run down (May 2010); NH only." 1 Apr-30 Oct. € 17.50   2010*

TIEL *C3* (7km NW Rural) *51.89964, 5.35948* **Camping de Vergarde, Erichemseweg 84, 4117 GL Erichem [(0344) 572017; fax 572229; info@devergarde.nl; www.devergarde.nl]** Exit A15 at Tiel-West junc 32; foll sp Erichem & site. Lge, mkd pitch, pt shd; htd wc; chem disp; mv service pnt; serviced pitches; baby facs; fam bthrm; shwrs; EHU (10A) inc; gas; lndry; shop; rest, snacks; bar; playgrnd; htd pool; fishing; tennis; bike hire; horseriding; children's farm; entmnt; internet; TV; 60% statics; dogs €3.75; poss cr; Eng spkn; quiet; red LS; ccard acc; CKE/CCI. "Gd facs." ♦ 1 Apr-18 Oct. € 27.50   2010*

TUITJENHORN *B2* (4km SE Rural) *52.73495, 4.77612*
**Campingpark de Bongerd, Bongerdlaan 3, 1747 CA
Tuitjenhorn [(0226) 391481; fax 394658; info@bongerd.nl;
www.bongerd.nl]** N fr Alkmaar on N245, exit at Dirkshorn
& foll sp to site. V lge, mkd pitch, pt shd; htd wc; chem disp;
baby facs; shwrs inc; EHU (10A) inc; gas; lndry (inc dryer);
shop; rest, snacks; bar; BBQ; playgrnd; 2 htd pools (1 covrd);
paddling pool; waterslide; lake fishing; tennis; games area;
bike hire; wifi; entmnt; 60% statics; dogs €1.90; Eng spkn; adv
bkg; ccard acc; quiet. "Excel, attractive family site; vg facs." ♦
8 Apr-30 Sep. € 43.00   2014*

UDEN *C3* (14km E Rural) *51.66309, 5.77641* **Mini
Camping Boszicht, Tipweg 10, 5455 RC Wilbertoord
[(0485) 451565 or (06) 12957217; fax (0845) 471522;
boszicht-wilbertoord@planet.nl; www.boszichtcamping.nl]**
Fr 's-Hertogenbosch on N279 dir Helmond. At Veghel turn
L onto N265. Bef Uden turn R onto N264 to Wilbertoord
in 11km. Sm, hdg/mkd pitch, unshd; wc; shwrs; EHU (6A)
metered; shops; rest in vill; playgrnd; games area; dog €2;
quiet; "Family-run farm site in woodland; conv Arnhem,
Nijmegen." 20 Mar-19 Oct. € 14.50   2013*

"We must tell The Club about that great site we found"

Get your site reports in by mid-August
and we'll do our best to get your updates
into the next edition.

UITDAM see Edam *B2*

UTRECHT *B3* (10km NE Rural) *52.13123, 5.22024*
**Camping Bospark Bilthoven, Burg van der Borchlaan 7,
3722 GZ Bilthoven [(030) 2286777; fax 2293888;
info@bosparkbilthoven.nl; www.bosparkbilthoven.nl]**
Exit A28/E30 Utrecht-Amersfoort at exit sp De Bilt & strt to
Bilthoven. Approx 3km after leaving m'way (400m S of level
x-ing) turn R sp De Bospark Bilthoven. At edge of town foll sps
twd lge brown tower & golf course. Site on L. V lge, pt shd; htd
wc; chem disp; mv service pnt; baby facs; fam bthrm; serviced
pitches; shwrs inc; EHU (4-6A) inc (poss rev pol); gas; lndry;
shop 1km; snacks; bar; playgrnd; htd pool; TV; 60% statics;
dogs €3.50; phone; poss cr; Eng spkn; adv bkg; quiet but some
noise fr air base. "Helpful management; 20 mins walk to stn
for trains to Utrecht cent." ♦ 1 Apr-31 Oct. € 25.70   2012*

UTRECHT *B3* (14km E Rural) *52.09272, 5.28287* **Camping
de Krakeling, Woudensbergseweg 17, 3707 HW Zeist
[(030) 6915374; fax 6920707; allurepark@dekrakeling.nl;
www.dekrakeling.nl]** Fr A12 exit junc 20 Driebergen/Zeist.
In Zeist foll dir Woudenberg, site sp. V lge, hdg/mkd pitch,
pt shd; htd wc; chem disp; mv service pnt; baby facs; shwrs
€0.50; EHU (6-10A) €2.50; lndry; shop; rest, snacks, bar w/
end only LS; playgrnd; pool 3km; lake sw 5km; tennis; internet
free; cab TV; 90% statics; dogs free; phone; adj nature reserve;
bus; adv bkg. "Gd touring base Amsterdam/Utrecht; friendly;
excel, clean facs; recep open 0900-1700, clsd for lunch." ♦
28 Mar-29 Sep. € 28.40   2013*

VAALS *C4* (1km N Rural) *50.78159, 6.00694* **Camping
Hoeve de Gastmolen, Lemierserberg 23, 6291 NM Vaals
[(043) 3065755; fax 3066015; info@gastmolen.nl;
www.gastmolen.nl]** Fr A76 exit at Knooppunt Bocholtz onto
N281 SW to join N278, turn L twd Aachen. Site on L just bef
1st rndabt as ent Vaals. Med, hdg/mkd pitch, pt sl, pt shd;
wc; chem disp; shwrs €0.50; EHU (4A) €2.70; lndry; shops
500m; rest 500m; snacks; playgrnd; 10% statics; dogs €2.70;
bus 500m; sep car park; poss cr; Eng spkn; adv bkg rec; quiet;
CKE/CCI. "Sm rural site; conv Aachen; vg san facs; diff in wet
- tractor avail; mosquitoes; 'Drielandenpunt' 4km, in walking
dist (where Netherlands, Germany & Belgium meet); excel."
15 Apr-31 Oct. € 35.50   2014*

VAASSEN see Apeldoorn *C3*

VALKENBURG AAN DE GEUL *C4* (2km N Rural) *50.88013,
5.83466* **Familie Camping De Bron, Stoepertweg 5,
6301 WP Valkenburg [(045) 4059292; fax 4054281;
info@camping-debron.nl; www.camping-debron.nl]**
Fr A79 exit junc 4 dir Hulsberg. Take 3rd exit fr rndabt onto
N298, across next rndabt, then L onto N584, site sp. Fr A76
exit junc 3 dir Schimmert, foll sp Valkenburg & site. Lge, mkd
pitch, pt shd; htd wc; chem disp; mv service pnt; baby facs;
shwrs inc; EHU (4-6A) €3-4.50; lndry; shop; rest, snacks; bar;
playgrnd; pool; games area; bike hire; entmnt; internet; TV;
30% statics; dogs €3.50; phone; adv bkg; CKE/CCI. "Vg, well
laid-out site; gd facs; muddy in wet weather; 2 pools with lots
of equipment for kids; statics hidden away in the greenery;
helpful staff." ♦ 1 Apr-20 Dec. € 42.50   2014*

VALKENBURG AAN DE GEUL *C4* (6km E Rural) *50.84990,
5.87320* **Camping Vinkenhof, Engwegen 2A, 6305
PM Schin op Geul [(043) 4591389; fax 4591780;
info@campingvinkenhof.nl; www.campingvinkenhof.nl]**
Exit E2 Eindhoven-Maastricht at Meersen/Valkenburg about
6km bef Maastricht; foll rd E to Valkenburg. In town take
rd E to Schin op Geul & foll camping sps. Med, mkd pitch,
unshd; htd wc; serviced pitches; chem disp; baby facs; serviced
pitches; shwrs €0.75; EHU (6A) inc; gas; lndry; shop 1km; rest
adj; snacks; playgrnd; pool; bike hire; TV rm; 5% statics; dogs
€3; phone; site clsd 20 Dec-14 Jan; Eng spkn; quiet; CKE/CCI.
"Gd walking country; well-kept, friendly site." 1 Mar-4 Jan.
€ 26.50   2010*

VALKENBURG AAN DE GEUL *C4* (5km SE Rural) *50.85042,
5.88120* **Camping Schoonbron, Valkenburgerweg 128,
6305 EA Schin op Geul [(043) 4591209; fax 4591486; info@
schoonbron.nl; www.schoonbron.nl]** E fr Valkenburg on
N595 to Schin op Geul. Site opp Camping Vinkenhof, just after
Esso g'ge on L. Clearly sp, but ent pt hidden by RH bend in rd.
V lge, mkd pitch, pt sl, pt shd; htd wc; chem disp; mv service
pnt; baby facs; fam bthrm; shwrs inc; EHU (4A) inc; lndry (inc
dryer); shop; rest, snacks; bar; playgrnd; covrd, htd pool; games
area; wifi; entmnt; TV; 60% statics; dogs €3.25; Eng spkn;
quiet; ccard not acc; CKE/CCI. "Clean, modern facs; friendly
staff; vg." ♦ 15 Mar-31 Oct. € 24.00   2009*

You can now fill in site reports online

VALKENBURG AAN DE GEUL *C4* (3km S Urban) *50.85972, 5.83138* **Stadscamping Den Driesch, Heunsbergerweg 1, 6301 BN Valkenburg [(043) 6012025; fax 6016139; info@campingdendriesch.nl; www.campingdendriesch.nl]** Fr A2 dir Maastricht exit sp Valkenburg-Cauberg. Foll sp Valkenburg N590 & take turning sp Sibbe-Margraten. At rndabt foll sp Valkenburg, pass coal mine & turn R in 250m into sm, sl, unmkd ent. Steep turn off main rd into ent. NB L turn into site diff - proceed to rndabt at top of hill & return downhill to site. Med, mkd pitch, hdstg, pt sl, terr, pt shd; htd wc; chem disp; mv service pnt; shwrs €0.70; EHU (10A) inc; lndry; shop on site & 500m; rest 500m; snacks; no BBQs; htd, covrd pool 1km; bike hire; 10% statics; dogs €3; phone; Eng spkn; adv bkg; quiet; ccard acc; CKE/CCI. "Castle & caves adj; other attractions nr; gd Xmas mkts in caves; easy access Maastricht by bus/train; vg." Easter-21 Dec. € 28.00   2009*

VALKENBURG AAN DE GEUL *C4* (1km SW Rural) *50.85672, 5.81891* **Camping De Cauberg, Rijksweg 171, 6325 AD Valkenburg [(043) 6012344; info@campingdecauberg.nl; www.campingdecauberg.nl]** Exit A79 sp Valkenburg, foll Sibbe & Margraten sp to town cent. Take R fork in town sp De Cauberg, site on R at top of hill just past end Valkenburg sp. Med, mkd pitch, pt sl, shd; htd wc; chem disp; baby facs; shwrs inc; EHU (10A) inc; lndry; shop, rest, snacks; playgrnd; htd pool 1km; internet; 10% statics; dogs €3.10; bus; phone; site clsd 1-15 Nov; Eng spkn; adv bkg; quiet; red long stay; CKE/CCI. "Excel pool 1km; excel, modern, clean san facs; friendly, helpful owner; conv Maastricht; many rests, cafes in Valkenburg." 1 Jan-5 Jan 14 Mar-31 Oct & 14 Nov-31 Dec. € 34.00   2014*

"I need an on-site restaurant"

We do our best to make sure site information is correct, but it is always best to check any must-have facilities are still available or will be open during your visit.

VALKENBURG AAN DE GEUL *C4* (7km W Rural) *50.86057, 5.77237* **Camping Oriëntal, Rijksweg 6, 6325 PE Berg en Terblijt [(043) 6040075; info@campingoriental.nl; www.campingoriental.nl]** Fr A2/E25 exit onto N278 E & in 1km turn L onto N590 sp Berg en Terblijt & Valkenburg. Cont on N590, site on R in 4km at start of vill. Lge, mkd pitch, pt shd; htd wc; chem disp; mv service pnt; serviced pitch inc TV at extra cost; baby facs; serviced pitches (inc cab TV); shwrs; EHU (6A) inc (poss rev pol); gas; lndry; shop; rest 500m; snacks; bar; supmkt; playgrnd; htd, covrd pool; paddling pool; games area; wifi; 10% statics; dogs €3.50; phone; bus to Maastricht adj; Eng spkn; adv bkg; quiet; red LS; red LS; CKE/CCI. "Immac, well-run site; some areas flood in heavy rain; gd entmnt for young children; conv Maastricht." ♦ Easter-30 Oct. € 27.00   2013*

VALKENSWAARD see Eindhoven *C4*

VEERE see Middelburg *A4*

VENLO *C4* (22km N Rural) *51.45989, 6.17120* **Camping Landhuis De Maashof, Veerweg 9, 5973 NS Lottum [07 74 63 19 24; fax 74 63 24 72; info@demaashof.nl; www.demaashof.nl]** Fr A67 Eindhoven - Venlo, take exit 12 onto A73. Then exit 11 twd Horst/Melderslo. Foll sp to Lottum. Foll sp to campsite. Med, pt shd; wc; chem disp; shwr; lndry; snacks; BBQ; playgrnd; wifi; dogs €1.20; bus 800m; twin axles; poss cr; Eng spkn; adv bkg; quiet; CCI. "Cycling, rv bank walks; rose gdn exhibition in vill; lots of rv traff & ferries; working windmill & castle nrby." 1 Apr-30 Sep. € 20.00   2014*

⊞ **VENLO** *D4* (3.5km S Rural) *51.34823, 6.18548* **Camping/ Restaurant De Kraal, Kaldenkerkerweg 186, 5915 PP Venlo [(077) 3514116; fax 3546164; kraal@dekraal.nl; www.dekraal.nl]** Fr rndabt by Venlo rlwy stn, take Kaldenkerkerweg SE for 2km; rest adj petrol stn. Sm, hdstg, pt shd; own san; chem disp; mv service pnt; EHU inc; rest, snacks; bar; adv bkg. "CL-type site behind excel rest; nature park; watersports; walking; cycling; excel NH; m'vans only." € 6.00   2009*

VENLO *D4* (10km NW Rural) *51.42029, 6.10675* **Camping Californië, Horsterweg 23, 5971 ND Grubbenvorst [(077) 3662049; fax 3662997; info@limburgsecamping.nl; www.limburgsecamping.nl]** Exit A73 at Grubbenvorst junc 12 dir Sevenum, site sp. Med, pt shd; htd wc; chem disp; mv service pnt; shwrs inc; EHU (4-10A); lndry; playgrnd; Eng spkn; quiet. "Pleasant, peaceful, warm welcome; unisex shwrs; CL style site with grass cut reg." 15 Mar-15 Oct. € 26.60   2014*

VIERHUIZEN *D1* (300m E Rural) *53.36011, 6.29505* **Camping Lauwerszee, Hoofdstraat 49, 9975 VR Vierhuizen [05 95 40 16 57; info@camping-lauwerszee.nl; www.camping-lauwerszee.nl]** Fr A7/E22 Amsterdam-Groningen take exit 33 Oude Riet onto N388 Grijpskerk. Turn L on N355 then R onto N388. 2.5km after Zoutcamp turn L to Vierhuizen. Site on R in 1km. Med, hdg/mkd pitch, pt shd; wc; chem disp; mv service pnt; shwrs; EHU (6A); lndry (inc dryer); rest; bar; BBQ; playgrnd; bike hire; wifi; dogs; bus 0.5km; twin axles; Eng spkn; adv bkg; quiet; CCI. "Sep field with lge pitches avail for CC memb at red price; helpful owner; vg." ♦ ltd. 1 Apr-1 Nov. € 24.00   2014*

VLISSINGEN *A4* (2.5km N Urban) *51.4684, 3.5546* **Camping De Lange Pacht, Boksweg 1, 4384 NP Vlissingen [tel/fax (0118) 460447; delangepacht@zeelandnet.nl]** Fr E on A58 to Vlissingen, then onto N288 & foll sp Kouderkerke. At rndabt at end built-up area turn L into Lammerenburgweg/Jacoba van Beierenweg then L tinto Vlamingstraat & foll to Boksweg & site. Sm, mkd pitch, pt shd; htd wc; chem disp; shwrs inc; EHU (4-6A) inc; lndry (inc dryer); shops 500m; BBQ; sand beach & pool 3km; sand beach 2km; wifi; 40% statics; dogs; phone; sep car park; adv bkg; quiet; CKE/CCI. "Clean, friendly site." 1 Apr-31 Oct. € 20.50   2010*

VORDEN *D3* (5km SE Rural) *52.08379, 6.35510* **'t Lebbink, Lindense Enkweg 1, 7251 NH Vorden [(0575) 556680; harmsen@tlebbink.nl; www.tlebbink.nl]** Fr Vordon N316 S for 1.6km. L onto Lindeseweg for 3km to Linde. L just bef windmill along access rd to campsite on R. Med, hdg/mkd pitch, pt shd; wc; chem disp; shwrs; EHC (6-16A); lndry; BBQ; bike hire; wifi; dogs; twin axles; adv bkg; quiet; CKE/CCI. "On numbered cycle rte & walking rte; vg." ♦ ltd. 15 Mar-1 Nov. € 16.00   2015*

NETHERLANDS

VUREN see Gorinchem *B3*

WASSENAAR *B3* (3km NE Rural) *52.15269, 4.43361* **Camping Maaldrift, Maaldriftseweg 9, 2241 BN Wassenaar [(070) 5113688; fax 5170980; campingmaaldrift@hotmail. com]** Fr Hoek take N211/E30 to A4, then A12 & N44. Turn 1st L after Wassenaar & immed R onto rd parallel with main rd. Site sp on L in approx 2km. Sm, mkd pitch, pt shd; wc; chem disp; baby facs; shwrs €0.75; EHU (6A) €2.25; lndry (inc dryer); shop; snacks; bar; BBQ; playgrnd; pool 5km; sand beach 8km; 60% statics; dogs €1.25; phone; Eng spkn; quiet. "Excel, quiet base away fr cr commercial sites; narr site rds; lge pitches; clean, modern san facs." 1 Apr-30 Sep. € 16.00   2010*

⊞ **WASSENAAR** *B3* (1km NW Rural) *52.14638, 4.38750* Camping Duinrell, Duinrell 1, 2242 JP Wassenaar [tel/fax (070) 5155147 or (070) 5155255; touroperator@ duinrell.nl; www.duinrell.nl] Fr Rotterdam in dir Den Haag on A13/E19, then on A4/E19 foll sp for Amsterdam. On A4 keep R onto A12 in dir Voorburg/Den Haag. At end m'way turn R onto N44 sp Wassenaar. In 8km turn L at traff lts immed bef Mercedes g'ge, foll site sp. On arr at site foll sp to campsite not coach park. Not rec to arrive mid-afternoon/early evening due to heavy traff leaving amusement park. V lge, hdg/mkd pitch, pt shd; htd wc; chem disp; mv service pnt; baby facs; serviced pitches; sauna; private san facs avail; shwrs inc; EHU (6A) inc; gas; lndry (inc dryer); shop; rest, snacks; bar; BBQ; playgrnd; 2 pools (1 covrd); paddling pool; waterslide; sand beach 3km; fishing, horseriding nrby; tennis; bike hire; free ent adj amusement park; golf 1km; games rm; internet; wifi; entmnt; TV; 30% statics; dogs €6; no o'fits over 7.75m high ssn; phone; sep car park for some pitches; poss cr; Eng spkn; adv bkg; quiet; red LS/snr citizens; ccard acc. "Popular, busy site; some pitches poss diff access, check bef siting; superb, modern facs; tropical indoor pool; vg security; excel." ♦ € 33.50 SBS - H13   2011*

See advertisement

WEERSELO *D3* (2km N Rural) *52.36530, 6.84285* **Camping De Molenhof, Kleijsenweg 7, 7667 RS Reutum [(0541) 661165 or 661201; fax 662032; info@demolenhof.nl; www.demolenhof.nl]** Exit A1 junc 33 dir Oldenzaal then Tubbergen. At Weerselo, foll site sp. Lge, pt shd; htd wc; chem disp; mv service pnt; baby facs; fam bthrm; shwrs inc; EHU (10A) inc; gas; lndry (inc dryer); shop; rest, snacks; bar; BBQ; playgrnd; 2 pools (1 htd, covrd); waterslide; fishing; tennis; covrd play area; bike hire; golf 10km; wifi; entmnt; TV rm & cab TV to pitches; 25% statics; dogs €3; Holland Tulip Parcs site; Eng spkn; adv bkg; quiet; ccard acc. "Spacious pitches; spotlessly clean." ♦ 16 Apr-2 Oct. € 39.00 (CChq acc)   2013*

"Satellite navigation makes touring much easier"

Remember most sat navs don't know if you're towing or in a larger vehicle – always use yours alongside maps and site directions.

WEERSELO *D3* (2km NW Rural) *52.35930, 6.83740* **Camping De Veldmeijer, Oude Almelosedijk 4, 7595 LJ Weerselo [(0541) 662195; info@develdmeijer.nl; www.develdmeijer. nl]** Exit A1/E30 dir Oldenzaal then N343 dir Tubbergen. After Weerselo foll 'Mini-Camping' sp. Sm, pt shd; htd wc; chem disp; shwrs inc; EHU (6A) inc; lndry (inc dryer); shop, snacks 1km; playgrnd; pool nrby; wifi; 25% statics; Eng spkn; adv bkg; quiet. "Welcoming owners; excel facs; lge pitches; gd cycling; vg." ♦ ltd. 1 Apr-31 Oct. € 16.00   2009*

WEERT *C4* (9km SE Rural) *51.22480, 5.79916* **Camping Landgoed Lemmenhof, Kampstraat 10, 6011 RV Ell Limburg [(0495) 551277; fax 551797; info@lemmenhof.nl; www.lemmenhof.nl]** Exit A2 junc 40 dir Kelpen. In 2km at traff lts turn R; in 50m turn R dir Ell. In 2km immed bef vill sp & De Prairie Cafe turn R into Kempstraat, site in 200m. Sm, hdg/mkd pitch, unshd; htd wc; chem disp; shwrs inc; EHU (10A) inc; lndry; shop 500m; rest, bar 200m; playgrnd; dogs €0.70; Eng spkn; adv bkg; quiet; CKE/CCI. "Vg; B&B & apartments avail; v friendly helpful owners and friendly local caravaners on site." ♦ 15 Mar-31 Oct. € 18.60   2013*

★★★★✦
classification
LIMITLESS PLEASURE AT CAMPING DUINRELL!

• "Super" pitches from about 80 m² -100 m² with modern facilities and sanitary buildings.
• A free amusement park (April - October).
• Tropical Tiki Pool, fun water paradise with spectacular water attractions.
• Woods and dunes, sea and beach, Den Haag and Scheveningen nearby.
• Entertainment programm in summer.
• Luxury bungalows (4/5/6/7 pers.) and Lodge tents (6 pers.) for hire.

www.duinrell.nl
m.duinrell.nl
0031 70 5155 255

WiFi €

Duinrell
WASSENAAR

Duinrell, puts spring in your step!

2242 JP Wassenaar, Holland

NETHERLANDS

WEIDUM see Leeuwarden C2

WESTERBORK see Beilen D2

⊞ **WEZUPERBRUG** D2 (300m E Rural) 52.84030, 6.72370 **Rekreatiepark 't Kuierpadtien, Oranjekanaal Noordzijde 10, 7853 TA Wezuperbrug [(0591) 381415; fax 382235; info@kuierpad.nl; www.kuierpad.nl]** Fr A28 m'way exit 31 dir Emmen onto N381. Take exit Zweeloo & turn L immed. Go under viaduct twd Wezuperbrug via Wezup. In Wezuperbrug go over bdge, turn R, site sp. V lge, pt shd; htd wc; chem disp; mv service pnt; baby facs; fam bthrm; shwrs inc; EHU (6A) inc; gas; lndry (inc dryer); shop, rest, snacks; bar; playgrnd; htd, covrd pool; paddling pool; waterslide; lake sw & boating; tennis; games rm; bike hire; wifi; entmnt; TV; 30% statics; dogs €5; phone; sep car park; Holland Tulip Parcs site; quiet. "Excel site; great for kids; vg pool & extensive sports facs; can get busy; some pitches diff to access, narr & steep ent to pitch espec nr the water." ♦ € 53.00   2014*

WIER C2 (700m S Rural) 53.25033, 5.62216 **Tuincamping De Brinkhoeve, Gernierswei 19, 9043 VN Wier [(0518) 462287; info@debrinkhoeve.com; www.debrinkhoeve.com]** Exit A31 junc 21 dir Menaldum, then dir St Jacobiparochie. Site on this rd 6km fr Menaldum on Gernierswei, not in Wier. Sp locally as 'Theeschenkerij Wier'. Sm, pt shd; htd wc; chem disp; baby facs; shwrs inc; EHU (6A) €2; lndry; rest, snacks; BBQ; playgrnd; dogs €1.50; bus 50m; poss cr; Eng spkn; adv bkg rec. "Friendly, nothing too much trouble; like a high quality CL; beautiful gardens; cycle rtes adj." 1 Apr-15 Oct. € 17.00   2011*

WIERINGERWERF B2 (1km N Rural) 52.85757, 5.02361 **Camping Land Uit Zee, Oom Keesweg 12A, 1771 ME Wieringerwerf [tel/fax (0227) 601893; campinglanduitzee@hetnet.nl; www.campinglanduitzee. nl]** Fr A7/E22 exit junc 13 Wieringerwerf & foll site sp N thro town 200m, site on R. Sm, hdg pitch, pt shd; wc; chem disp; mv service pnt; shwrs €0.80; EHU (6A) €2.25; gas; shop; playgrnd; bike hire; TV; 10% statics; dogs €1.55; Eng spkn; adv bkg; quiet; CKE/CCI. "Friendly, welcoming owners; gd base for cycling; nrby town Medemblick worth visit; run down statics, unclean facs & travellers (Apr 2010)." 1 Apr-12 Sep. € 11.50   2010*

WIJCKEL see Lemmer C2

WIJSTER see Beilen D2

WILBERTOORD see Uden C3

⊞ **WINSCHOTEN** D2 (2km N Urban) 53.15315, 7.02728 **Stadscamping De Burcht, Bovenburen 46A, 9675 HG Winschoten [(0597) 413290; fax 414467; info@camping deburcht.nl; www.campingdeburcht.nl]** Exit E22/A7 junc 47 Winschoten exit & foll sp to site on edge of town. Sm, hdg pitch, pt shd; wc; chem disp; shwrs inc; EHU (4A) €2.60; lndry; shop 500m; playgrnd; pool 1km; 15% statics; dogs €1.50; quiet; CKE/CCI. "Gd site for cyclists; pay site fees on arr; vg NH/ sh stay." € 16.00   2009*

WINTERSWIJK D3 (5km N Rural) 52.00878, 6.73850 **Poelhuis Boerderijcamping, Poolserweg 3, 7104 DC Winterswijk [(0543) 569246; info@poelhuis.nl; www.poelhuis.nl]** N on Meddoseweg to Meddo, R on Wandersweg to x-rds, Poolserweg, L and site on R in 500m. Sm, mkd pitch, hdstg, pt shd; wc; chem disp; shwrs; EHU (6A); lndry; BBQ; games rm; bike hire; wifi; tv rm; Eng spkn; adv bkg; quiet; CKE/ CCI. "Numbered cycle rte; close to German border; flamingo nature park with walking rtes; vg." ♦ ltd. 15 Mar-31 Oct. € 18.00   2015*

WOERDEN B3 (4km NE Rural) 52.09280, 4.88530 **Camping Batenstein, Van Helvoortlaan 37, 3443 AP Woerden [(0348) 421320; fax 409691; campingbatenstein@planet.nl; www.camping-batenstein.nl]** Fr A12 exit junc 14 sp Woerden. Twd cent of town, L at rndabt, R at next rndabt, thro rlwy tunnel. L at traff lts, L again at next traff lts, R at camping sp. Ent narr & sm sp. Med, pt shd; wc; chem disp; mv service pnt; baby facs; sauna; shwrs €0.60; EHU (6-10A) inc; gas; lndry (inc dryer); shops 1km; snacks; playgrnd; htd, covrd pool; paddling pool; waterslide; games area; wifi; 75% statics; dogs €1.50; phone; bus 750m; Eng spkn; sep car park; poss cr; adv bkg; quiet but some noise fr pool during day; ccard acc; red long stay; CKE/CCI. "Gd touring base; el conn by site staff only (locked boxes); san facs cramped but gd quality & clean; conv for ferries." 28 Mar-26 Oct. € 30.50   2014*

> ## "There aren't many sites open at this time of year"
>
> If you're travelling outside peak season remember to call ahead to check site opening dates – even if the entry says 'open all year'.

WOLPHAARTSDIJK see Goes A3

WONS C2 (2.5km S Rural) 53.06569, 5.42389 **Mini-Camping DeWeeren, Weersterweg 35, 8747 NR Wons [(0515) 231374 or 06 18498048 (mob); deweeren@hetnet.nl]** Exit A7 junc 16 dir Makkum. Site on L in 2km. Sm, pt shd; htd wc; chem disp; shwrs inc; EHU (10A) inc; lndry; shop, rest, snacks, bar 2km; BBQ; playgrnd; bike hire; dogs €0.50; sep car park; quiet. "Gd." 1 Apr-31 Oct. € 13.50   2009*

WORKUM C2 (5km NE Rural) 52.99216, 5.49391 **Minicamping De Klompen, Nummer 19, 8775 XD Nijhuizum [(0515) 541597; info@minicampingdeklompen.nl; www.minicampingdeklompen.nl]** On N359 thro Workumturn R sp Nijhuizum. In vill turn L & foll site sp to end of rd, 2km. Sm, unshd; htd wc; chem disp; shwrs €0.50; EHU (10A) €2; lndry; shop, rest, snacks, bar 3km; BBQ; lake & watersports nr; dogs €1; sep car park; Eng spkn; quiet. "Gd, v hospitable owners; san facs v clean; communal rm if rainy day; peaceful; rural dairy farm." € 14.00   2011*

WOUDENBERG see Amersfoort C3

AMELAND ISLAND

⊞ **BUREN** C1 (1km N Coastal) 53.45355, 5.80460 **Camping Klein Vaarwater, Klein Vaarwaterweg 114, 9164 ME Buren [(0519) 542156; fax 542655; info@kleinvaarwater.nl; www.kleinvaarwater.nl]** Take ferry fr Holwerd to Nes on Ameland Island. Turn R at rndabt twd Buren & strt on to supmkt. At 3-lane intersection turn L twd beach rd & site. Med, mkd pitch, pt shd; htd wc; chem disp; mv service pnt; baby facs; fam bthrm; shwrs; EHU (16A); gas; lndry (inc dryer); supmkt; ATM; rest, snacks; bar; BBQ; playgrnd; htd, covrd pool; paddling pool; waterslide; sand beach 800m; tennis; 10-pin bowling; games area; fitness rm; wifi; entmnt; TV; 75% statics; no dogs; Holland Tulip Parcs site; poss cr; adv bkg; red LS. "Nature park adj; site in dunes & forest." ♦ € 20.00   2011*

ZANDVOORT B3 (5km N Coastal) 52.40415, 4.55180 **Kennemer Duincamping De Lakens, Zeeweg 60, 2051 EC Bloemendaal aan Zee [(023) 5411570; fax 5411579; delakens@ kennemerduincampings.nl; www.kennemerduincampings.nl]** Site sp N of Zaandvoort on coast rd, site in sand dunes. V lge, unshd; htd wc; chem disp; mv service pnt; baby facs; shwrs inc; EHU (4-10A) inc; gas; lndry; shop; rest, snacks; playgrnd; pool 4km; sand beach 200m; windsuring 2km; games area; horseriding 300m; internet; TV rm; 50% statics; no dogs; poss cr; Eng spkn; adv bkg rec high ssn; ccard acc; quiet. "V busy May/June public holidays; gd facs; excel walking, cycling fr site; welcoming helpful staff; excel spar shop; gd position in National Park; gd for sightseeing in Amsterdam, Haarlem, Aalsmeer flower mkt as well as outdoor pursuits." ♦ 28 Mar-26 Oct. € 53.00   2014*

ZEELAND see Uden C3

⊞ **ZEEWOLDE** C3 (4km S Rural/Coastal) 52.30300, 5.53400 **NCC Camping de Distel, Dasselaarweg 53, 3896 LT Zeewolde [(036) 5221575; zeewolde@ncc.nl; www.ncc.nl]** Exit A28 junc 9 at Nijkerk onto N301 sp Zeewolde. After 4km turn R onto N705 dir Zeewolde. After 5.6km turn R sp NCC Camping. In 300m turn R & foll site sp. Site on L at white stones. Lge, mkd pitch, pt shd; htd wc; chem disp; mv service pnt; baby facs; shwrs inc; EHU (4A) €3; lndry; shop; playgrnd; sand beach 500m; watersports; dogs; bus 4km; poss cr; adv bkg; quiet, "Warm, friendly atmosphere; members only - open to CC members, but must pre-book; conv Amsterdam 1hr by rd." ♦ € 12.00   2009*

ZEIST see Utrecht B3

ZEVENAAR C3 (8km S Rural) 51.89666, 6.07041 **Camping De Rijnstrangen, Beuningsestraat 4, 6913 KH Aerdt [(0316) 371941 or (0612) 559464; info@derijnstrangen.nl; www.derijnstrangen.nl]** Exit A12 junc 29 onto N 336 Elten & Lobith. At sp Aerdt turn R onto dyke (narr) & cont approx 1.5km to church. Turn L in 100m, site on R (500m W of Aerdt). Sm, hdg/mkd pitch, pt shd, hdstg; htd wc; chem disp; mv service pnt; fam bthrm; shwrs; EHU (6A); lndry; shop 2km; BBQ; cooking facs; games rm; bike hire; wifi; twin axles; poss cr; Eng spkn; adv bkg; quiet; CKE/CCI. "Friendly, welcoming owners; gd cycling area with numbered rte; excel htd facs; excel." ♦ ltd. 1 Mar-1 Nov. € 21.00   2015*

ZEVENHUIZEN see Gouda B3

ZIERIKZEE A3 (2km N Rural) 51.65683, 3.91242 **Camping 't Uulof, Zandweg 37, 4301 TA Zierikzee [(0111) 414614; info@tuulof.nl; www.campingtuulof.nl]** SE fr Serooskerke on N59. In 9km just bef traff lts turn L. Site 300m on R; sp fr N59. Sm, pt shd; wc; chem disp; serviced pitches; shwrs €2; EHU (6A) inc; shop 1km; gas 1km; lndry; pool 2km; sand beach 13km; 25% statics; dogs €1; Eng spkn; some rd noise; CKE/ CCI. "Lovely site on farm - produce avail; excel san facs, pt unisex; helpful, friendly owner; interesting town, steamer trips; easy cycling to town; peaceful site, friendly & welcoming, lovely home-grown veg." 1 Apr-1 Oct. € 15.50   2013*

ZIERIKZEE A3 (5km N Rural) 51.68048, 3.89847 **Mini-Camping Appelgaerd, Zandweg 6, 4321 TA Kerkwerve [(0614) 489332; info@appelgaerd.nl; www.appelgaerd.nl]** Fr Zierikzee take N59 dir Serooskerke. Immed turn R onto Zandwek. Cont for 3km, site on L bef vill of Kerkwerve. Sm, lge, hdg pitch, pt shd; wc; chem disp; mv service pnt; shwrs; EHU (6A) inc; bbq; playgrnd; beach 4km; wifi; dogs; bus 250m; twin axles; Eng spkn; adv bkg; quiet. "Gd cycling, walking & bird watching area; excel site." ♦ ltd. 1 Apr-30 Oct. € 20.00   2014*

ZIERIKZEE A3 (1km SW Coastal) 51.64660, 3.91133 **Camping Kloet, Eerst Weegje 3, 4301 SL Zierikzee [(0111) 414214; fax (0114) 421200; info@campingkloet.nl; www.camping kloet.nl]** Fr S on N256 cross Zeelandbrug & turn L onto N59 twd Zierikzee. After rndabt turn L sp 'Parking'. Site on L after 2nd rndabt. Sm, htd pitch, pt shd; wc; chem disp; mv service pnt; shwrs inc; EHU (4A) inc; lndry; shop, rest, bar 1km; playgrnd; games rm; TV; no dogs; bus 1km; Eng spkn; adv bkg; quiet; CKE/CCI. "Attractive, historic town in walking dist; excel area for cycling; gd birdwatching." 1 Apr-1 Nov. € 28.00   2011*

ZOETERMEER B3 (4km W Rural) 52.06716, 4.44862 **Camping De Drie Morgen, Voorweg 155, 2716 NJ Zoetermeer [(079) 3515107; fax 3512084; mail@dedriemorgen.nl; www.dedriemorgen.nl]** Fr Den Haag take A12/E30 sp Zoetermeer. Exit junc 6 sp Zoetermeer cent. In 1.5km turn L onto Amertaweg. In 2km foll sp to Mini-Camping. At rndabt turn R onto Voorweg, site on R. Sm, unshd; wc; chem disp; mv service pnt; shwrs inc; EHU (6A) €1.75; farm shop; playgrnd; dogs; sep car park; Eng spkn; adv bkg; quiet. "A working farm; gd touring base; pleasant staff; peaceful; busy in ssn." 1 Apr-31 Oct. € 14.50   2013*

TERSCHELLING ISLAND

⊞ **OOSTEREND** C1 (200m N Rural) 53.40562, 5.37947 **Camping 't Wan Tij, Oosterend 41, 8897 HX Oosterend [(0562) 448522; fax 4433495; info@wantij-terschelling.nl; www.wantij-terschelling.nl]** Fr Harlingen to Terschelling by ferry. Take rd to Oosterend, site ent on L 250m after vill sp, past bus stop & phone box. Sm, mkd pitch, pt shd; htd wc; chem disp; shwrs €0.50; EHU (6A) €3 (poss rev pol); lndry; shop 3km; rest, snacks, bar 100m; cooking facs; playgrnd; sand beach 2km; internet; TV; dogs €1.75; bus adj; Eng spkn; adv bkg; quiet; CKE/CCI. "Gd area for birdwatching; many cycle/ foot paths across dunes; horsedrawn vehicles for conducted tours; Elvis memorabilia 2km at Heartbreak Hotel - rest on stilts; excel site." ♦ ltd. € 15.00   2010*

TEXEL ISLAND

DEN BURG *B2* (8km NW Rural) *53.10346, 4.77107*
Camping Om de Noord, Boodtlaan 50, 1796 BG De Koog
[(0222) 327842; fax 327167; info@texelcampings.nl;
www.texelcampings.nl] Fr ferry take rd to De Koog; site sp
on R of rd on N of town dir De Cocksdorp. Med, mkd pitch,
pt shd; htd wc; mv service pnt; chem disp; fam bthrm; baby
facs; private san facs avail; shwrs inc; EHU (16A) inc; lndry (inc
dryer); playgrnd; pool 1.5km; sand beach 2km; games area;
wifi; 10% statics; dogs €4; phone; poss cr; quiet; ccard acc;
CKE/CCI. "Excel site adj nature reserve; walks in heathland;
conv touring Texel; friendly owners." ♦ 1 Apr-31 Oct.
€ 38.60   2010*

ZUIDWOLDE *D2* (2km S Rural) *52.65822, 6.42726* **NCC**
Camping De Krententerp, Ekelenbergweg 2, 7921 RH
Zuidwolde DR [(0528) 372847; www.ncc.nl] Fr S fr Zwolle
exit A28 junc 22 dir Dedemsvaart. Turn L at Balkbrug onto
N48, then L at junc Alteveer-Linde to site. Sm, mkd pitch, shd;
htd wc; chem disp; shwrs inc; EHU (4A) €2.75 (long lead poss
req); lndry; shop, rest, snacks, bar 2km, playgrnd; htd, covrd
pool 2km; dogs; bus 200m; poss cr; adv bkg; quiet. "Peaceful
site; friendly, helpful staff; CC members welcome; phone
ahead bet 1700 & 1800; excel cycling, walking; Zuidwolde
beautiful town." 1 Apr-31 Oct. € 11.00   2009*

ZUNDERT *B4* (5km NW Rural) *51.49492, 4.60208* **Camping**
Internationaal Priem, Rucphenseweg 51, 4882 KB Zundert
[(076) 5972632; fax 5971923; info@internationaalpriem.nl;
www.internationaalpriem.nl] S fr Breda on N263 to
Zundert. Take N638 dir Rucphen, camp on S of rd, opp
abbey. Sm, hdg pitch, pt shd; wc; chem disp; shwrs €0.50;
EHU (4A) inc; gas; lndry; rest in ssn; playgrnd; entmnt; TV rm;
75% statics (sep area); dogs €3.50; phone; Eng spkn; adv bkg;
quiet; ccard acc; red long stay; CKE/CCI. "Well-established,
mature site; friendly." 1 Apr-31 Oct. € 17.50   2009*

ZWOLLE *C2* (5km NE Urban) *52.53690, 6.12954* **Camping**
De Agnietenberg, Haersterveerweg 27, 8034 PJ Zwolle
[(038) 4531530; fax 4542084; info@campingagnietenberg.
nl; www.campingagnietenberg.nl] N fr Zwolle on A28 exit
junc 20 Zwolle Oost & turn R at end of slip rd then immed L.
In 400m turn L at traff lts into Haersterveerweg & foll site sp.
Lge, mkd pitch, pt shd; htd wc; chem disp; mv service pnt;
baby facs; shwrs €0.50; EHU (10A); lndry; shop, rest, snacks,
bar; BBQ; playgrnd; pool; lake beach & sw adj; fishing; tennis;
wifi; entmnt; TV; 60% statics; dogs €3.50; Eng spkn; quiet;
ccard acc (Mastercard only). "Excel, family site in pleasant area;
gd walking, cycling, water recreation; cars parked in sep areas;
single track rd to site." 1 Apr-31 Oct. € 26.00   2014*

"That's changed – Should I let The Club know?"

If you find something on site that's different from
the site entry, fill in a report and let us know. See
www.caravanclub.co.uk/europereport.

ZWOLLE *C2* (10km SW Rural) *52.45566, 6.04016* **Molecaten**
Park De Leemkule, Leemkuilen 6, 8051 PW Hattem
[(038) 4441945; fax 4446280; info@leemkule.ne;
www.leemkule.nl] Exit A50 junc 29 dir Wezep; foll sp
Hattem/Wapenveld, site on L after 3km. Lge, shd; htd wc;
chem disp; baby facs; shwrs inc; EHU (10A) inc; gas; lndry;
shop; rest, snacks; bar; playgrnd; 2 pools (1 htd, covrd);
paddling pool; tennis; bike hire; games area; entmnt;
20% statics; no dogs; phone; sep car park; adv bkg; quiet;
ccard acc. 1 Apr-1 Nov. € 25.00   2009*

NETHERLANDS

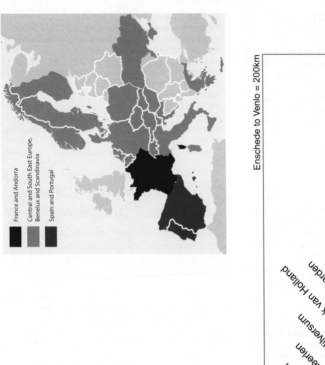

Legend:
- France and Andorra
- Central and South East Europe, Benelux and Scandinavia
- Spain and Portugal

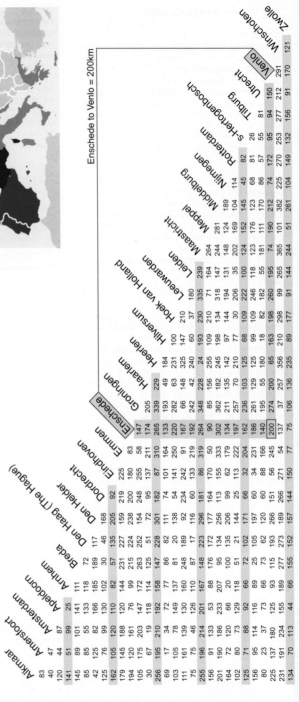

Enschede to Venlo = 200km

Distance chart (distances in km). Cities along the bottom/left axis: Alkmaar, Amersfoort, Amsterdam, Apeldoorn, Arnhem, Breda, Den Haag (The Hague), Den Helder, Dordrecht, Eindhoven, Emmen, Enschede, Groningen, Haarlem, Heerlen, Hilversum, Hoek van Holland, Leeuwarden, Leiden, Maastricht, Meppel, Middelburg, Nijmegen, Rotterdam, s-Hertogenbosch, Tilburg, Utrecht, Venlo, Winschoten, Zwolle.

From \ To	Alkmaar	Amersfoort	Amsterdam	Apeldoorn	Arnhem	Breda	Den Haag	Den Helder	Dordrecht	Eindhoven	Emmen	Enschede	Groningen	Haarlem	Heerlen	Hilversum	Hoek van Holland	Leeuwarden	Leiden	Maastricht	Meppel	Middelburg	Nijmegen	Rotterdam	s-Hertogenbosch	Tilburg	Utrecht	Venlo	Winschoten
Amersfoort	47																												
Amsterdam	44	87																											
Apeldoorn	120	101	141																										
Arnhem	111	99	133	30																									
Breda	118	55	166	57	72																								
Den Haag (The Hague)	82	76	72	135	117	46																							
Den Helder	81	120	92	168		205	168																						
Dordrecht	135	188	144	205	223	57	30	92																					
Eindhoven	227	161	76	159	86	148	159	219	225																				
Emmen	170	203	147	238	172	231	227	219	180	83																			
Enschede	50	19	118	200	134	224	238	200	255	58	310																		
Groningen	333	210	192	248	256	263	256	248	137	310	87	205																	
Haarlem	156	34	72	154	147	154	255	154	182	174	147	339	229																
Heerlen	245	105	149	252	86	21	72	95	301	133	265	193	49	184															
Hilversum	142	139	130	263	82	248	256	182	228	101	133	133	63	231	100														
Hoek van Holland	210	46	126	51	30	87	263	118	301	164	220	148	325	147	210	180													
Leeuwarden	30	196	201	125	95	148	51	51	111	141	167	66	240	60	37	239													
Leiden	206	133	53	72	21	72	82	66	82	250	192	242	228	242	230	335	281												
Maastricht	35	186	233	17	62	102	111	60	86	91	264	66	348	264	335	180	264	24											
Meppel	206	72	66	189	206	105	164	60	170	219	90	228	156	244	71	210	164	281	193										
Middelburg	30	80	73	277	144	277	172	60	177	133	85	205	198	318	147	194	124	202	104	114									
Nijmegen	77	71	116	151	134	151	177	151	134	50	302	133	245	131	206	189	104	170	86	57	82								
Rotterdam	257	95	73	189	25	193	134	266	95	179	134	167	142	35	148	74	26	55	81	172									
s-Hertogenbosch	70	23	37	277	113	266	99	266	72	62	162	192	211	202	30	169	123	95	253	132									
Tilburg	200	137	125	155	99	151	206	151	206	113	257	264	257	206	176	206	181	94	277	156									
Utrecht	65	191	234	152	206	189	144	189	144	222	197	197	70	210	123	35	170	81	150	212	91								
Venlo	163	74	155	152	144	277	157	277	144	204	162	200	125	180	181	206	145	212	382	225	104								
Winschoten	198	190	189	151	277	273	266	266	25	32	186	140	129	125	111	77	123	170	94	170	291								
Zwolle	134	70	113	66	155	152	157	144	150	77	75	136	235	89	177	144	244	51	261	104	149	132	91	156	132	121			

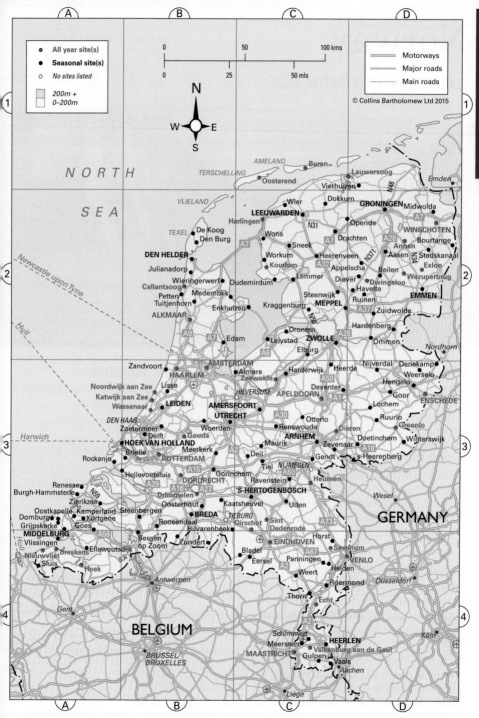

Legend

- ● All year site(s)
- ● Seasonal site(s)
- ○ No sites listed

200m +
0–200m

0   50   100 kms
0   25   50 mls

N
W   E
S

Motorways
Major roads
Main roads

© Collins Bartholomew Ltd 2015

NORTH

SEA

AMELAND
TERSCHELLING
Buren
Oosterend
Lauwersoog
Emden
Vierhuizen
VLIELAND
Wier
Dokkum
GRONINGEN Midwolda
LEEUWARDEN
Harlingen
N31
Opende
WINSCHOTEN
TEXEL
De Koog
Den Burg
Wons
Sneek
Drachten
A7
Annen
Bourtange
DEN HELDER
A7
Workum
Heerenveen
N371
Assen
Stadskanaal
Julianadorp
Koudum
Appelscha
Beilen
Exloo
Wieringerwerf
Oudemirdum
Lemmer
Diever
Dwingeloo
Wezuperbrug
Callantsoog
Medemblik
Steenwijk
Havelte
EMMEN
Petten
Tuitjenhorn
Enkhuizen
Kraggenburg
MEPPEL
Ruinen
Zuidwolde
ALKMAAR
A9
A7
Edam
Dronten
Hardenberg
A28
Lelystad
ZWOLLE
Ommen
Nordhorn
Zandvoort
AMSTERDAM
Elburg
Noordwijk aan Zee
HAARLEM
Almere
Zeewolde
Harderwijk
Heerde
Nijverdal
Denekamp
Weerselo
Katwijk aan Zee
Lisse
HILVERSUM
Deventer
Hengelo
Wassenaar
LEIDEN
APELDOORN
Goor
ENSCHEDE
DEN HAAG
AMERSFOORT
UTRECHT
Lochem
Zoetermeer
Woerden
A30
Otterlo
Ruurlo
Groenlo
HOEK VAN HOLLAND
Maurik
Renswoude
Dieren
Doetinchem
Winterswijk
Rockanje
Brielle
ROTTERDAM
Meerkerk
Deil
ARNHEM
Zevenaar
's-Heerenberg
Hellevoetsluis
A15
Gorinchem
Tiel
NIJMEGEN
A18
Renesse
A29
DORDRECHT
Ravenstein
Heumen
Burgh-Hammstede
N59
Drimmelen
'S-HERTOGENBOSCH
Wesel
Zierikzee
A16
Oosterhout
Kaatsheuvel
Uden
Oostkapelle
Kamperland
Steenbergen
BREDA
A73
Domburg
Kortgene
Roosendaal
TILBURG
Sint
Oedenrode
Grijpskerke
Goes
A58
Hilvarenbeek
Oirschot
Horst
MIDDELBURG
Bergen
op Zoom
Zundert
EINDHOVEN
Sevenum
Vlissingen
Eflewoutsdijk
Bladel
A67
VENLO
Nieuwvliet
Breskens
Eersel
Panningen
Helden
Sluis
Hoek
Weert
Roermond
Düsseldorf
Antwerpen
Thorn
Echt
Köln
Gent
Schimmert
HEERLEN
BELGIUM
Meerssen
Valkenburg aan de Geul
MAASTRICHT
Gulpen
Vaals
BRUSSEL/
BRUXELLES
Aachen
Liège

Newcastle upon Tyne
Hull
Harwich

GERMANY

471

Norway
Country Introduction

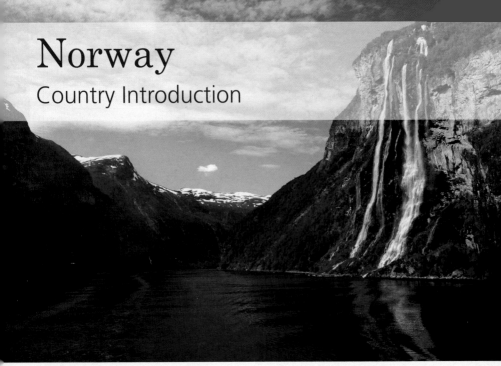

Seven Sister's Waterfall, Geirangerfjord

Welcome to Norway

Home to soaring fjords, glaciers and polar bears juxtaposed with cosmopolitan cities and vibrant festivals, Norway truly is a remarkable country. The natural landscape must rank as one of the most beautiful in the world, it is easy to see why people become entranced.

With a rich culture spanning centuries from the ancient Vikings to the present day, and plenty of legends, folklore and fairytales in between, Norway is a magical place that invariably delights and inspires its visitors.

Country highlights

The Nobel Peace Prize has, since its inception, been awarded in Oslo by the Norwegian Nobel Committee. Oslo City Hall, where the ceremony is held, is now one of Norway's most famous buildings.

As a country steeped in myths and legends, Norway has a vibrant heritage of story-telling. Trolls are some of the most talked about fairytale creatures, and statues, books and pictures of them can be found all over the country.

Major towns and cities

- Oslo – Norway's capital city hosts numerous festivals throughout the year.
- Bergen – a colourful and peaceful city surrounded by mountains.
- Trondheim – home to the world's most northerly medieval cathedral.
- Drammen – a city with plenty of attractions such as the oldest brewery in Norway.

Attractions

- Heddal Stave Church, Notodden – Norway's largest medieval wooden church.
- Geirangerfjord, Sunnmøre – one of Norway's most breathtaking fjords and a UNESCO site.
- Jostedal Glacier, Sogn og Fjordane – Europe's largest glacier and an outstanding natural environment.
- The Royal Palace, Oslo - take a tour through some of the most beautiful state rooms during the summer months.

Find out more

www.visitnorway.com
Tel: 0047 (0) 22 00 25 00 Norway Tourist Office

Country Information

Population (approx): 5.1 million

Capital: Oslo (population approx 648,000)

Area: 328,878 sqkm

Bordered by: Finland, Russia, Sweden

Terrain: Mostly high plateaux and mountain ranges broken by fertile valleys; deeply indented coastline; arctic tundra in the north

Climate: Moderate climate along coastal areas thanks to the Gulf Stream; more extreme inland with snowy/rainy winters; arctic conditions in the northern highlands; summers can be unpredictable and May and June can be cool

Coastline: 25,148km (including islands and fjords)

Highest Point: Galdhøpiggen 2,469m

Language: Norwegian; Sami in some areas

Local Time: GMT or BST + 1, i.e. 1 hour ahead of the UK all year

Currency: Krone (NOK) divided into 100 øre; £1 = NOK 12.84, NOK 10 = £0.78 (September 2015)

Emergency numbers: Police 112, with mobile phone 911; Fire brigade 110; Ambulance 113. From a mobile phone dial 112 for any service.

Public Holidays 2016: Jan 1; Mar 24, 25, 27, 28; May 1, 5, 15, 16, 17; Dec 25, 26.

School summer holidays run from mid-June to mid-August.

Camping and Caravanning

There are more than 1,000 campsites in Norway which are classified 1 to 5 stars and which are generally open between June and mid August. A camping guide listing 300 sites is available from the Norwegian Automobile Association, Norges Automobilforbund (NAF), see www.nafcamp.no. The Norwegian Tourist Board also distributes a camping guide free of charge – see www.camping.no. Most 3 star sites and all 4 and 5 star sites have sanitary facilities for the disabled and all classified sites have cooking facilities.

Many sites do not open until mid-June and do not fully function until the beginning of July, particularly if the winter has been prolonged. Sites with published opening dates earlier than June may not open on time if the weather has been particularly bad and if, for example, there has

been heavy rain and flooding near rivers or lakes where campsites are situated. Campsites which are open all year will usually have very limited facilities for most of the year outside the short holiday season.

Facilities vary; in main tourist centres there are large, well-equipped sites with good sanitary facilities, grocery shops, leisure facilities and attendants permanently on duty. Sites are generally maintained to a high standard of cleanliness. In more remote areas, sites are small and facilities can be very simple.

Many small campsites have no chemical disposal point. Roadside notice boards at the entrance to each local area (kommune) indicate campsites, chemical disposal points (normally sited at petrol stations) and other local amenities. These disposal facilities are usually coin-operated and have instructions in English. It is understood that in some areas in the north, there may be no adequate arrangements for the disposal of waste water, either on site or in the immediate area, and you are advised to make enquiries when arriving at a campsite.

The Camping Key Europe, which replaced the Camping Card Scandinavia (CCS) in 2012, may be required at some sites. You can buy the Camping Key Europe on arrival at your first site for around NOK 160, and will be issued with a temporary card. Alternatively, you can order the card before you travel for NOK 130 (2015 prices) from www.camping.no/en/cke and click on 'Bestillig av Kort' where you can then select to view the order form in English. If ordering in advance allow at least three weeks for the card to arrive.

There are many sites on the E6 to the North Cape, seldom more than 30km apart. These sites may be subject to road noise. Caravans are allowed to stay at the North Cape but no facilities are available – see Nordkapp later in this chapter and in the Site Entry listing.

In the short summer season campsites can be crowded and facilities stretched and you are recommended to arrive before 3pm (many sites have a latest arrival time of 4pm) in order to have a better choice of pitches and have the opportunity to erect an awning.

Casual/wild camping is not actively encouraged but the Norwegian 'Right of Access' allows visitors to explore the countryside freely, except for cultivated land, farmland, gardens, nurseries, etc. Off-road driving is not allowed. Visitors must respect nature and take their rubbish away with them when they leave. Open fires (which include Primus stoves) are prohibited in forests or on open land between 15 April and 15 September.

Motorhomes

Many towns provide parking places for motorhomes close to city centres, known as Bobil Parks, which are open in June, July and August. In general these parking areas provide limited facilities and car and caravan outfits are not permitted. Details, where known, are listed in the Site Entry pages.

Apart from at campsites, motorhome service points are reported to be few and far between and are generally to be found at petrol stations, where water refill may also be available.

Cycling

Cyclists are fairly well catered for and some areas, such as Vestfold, Rogaland and the Lillehammer area, have a well-developed network of cycle paths. Some old roads have been converted into cycle paths in the mountains and along western fjords. Paths run through magnificent scenery in the Lofoten and Vesterålen Islands in particular, and from Haugastøl in the Hardangervidda National Park to Flåm. A number of tunnels are prohibited to cyclists, but local detours are generally signposted. Information is available at www.cyclingnorway.no

Electricity and Gas

Campsites usually have a minimum 10 amp supply. Plugs are the continental type and have two round pins plus two earth strips. Some sites do not yet have CEE connections. It is recommended that you take an extension cable of at least 50 metres.

There are often problems with both polarity and the earthing of the electrical supply on some sites. Due to its geology and mountainous nature, Norway's electricity supply network is quite different from that found elsewhere in Europe. There is no national grid and electricity systems vary from place to place throughout the country.

Any polarity testing system is likely to give false readings. It is understood that progress is being made to improve and standardise the electrical supply throughout the country but you should exercise caution and, if in any doubt, ask site staff to demonstrate the integrity of the earthing system before connecting.

Propane gas cylinders are generally widely available from Esso and Statoil petrol stations. You will need to buy an appropriate adaptor, available from camping shops or Statoil garages. AGA AS dealers will allow you to sell back propane cylinders within six months of purchase prior to leaving Norway at approximately 80% of the purchase price. It is understood that Statoil garages no longer buy them back. Some Statoil garages and AGA AS dealers will exchange Swedish Primus propane cylinders for their Norwegian version but will not accept other foreign propane cylinders. There is no refund for the adaptor.

Gas supplies can be conserved by taking advantage of the kitchens and/or cooking facilities available at classified campsites, and using electrical hook-ups at every opportunity.

Entry Formalities

Holders of British and Irish passports may visit Norway for up to three months without a visa.

Regulations for Pets

For details of the regulations regarding the import of pets into Norway, see website www.mattilsynet.no (English option) or contact the Norwegian Embassy in London.

Medical Services

British visitors are entitled to the same basic emergency medical and dental treatment as Norwegian citizens, on production of a UK passport or European Health Insurance Card (EHIC), but you will have to pay the standard fees. Ensure you consult a doctor who has a reimbursement arrangement with the NAV (Norwegian Employment and Welfare Organisation). Hotels and tourist offices have lists of local doctors and dentists.

You will have to pay in full for most prescribed medicines which are available from pharmacies (apotek). Emergency in-patient hospital treatment at public hospitals, including necessary medication, is free of charge but you will have to pay for out-patient treatment. NAV Health Service Agencies will reimburse any payments that are refundable.

It is recommended to have insect repellent devices as mosquitos and midges may be a nuisance at certain times of the year, especially near lakes.

Opening Hours

Banks – Mon-Fri 8am-3.30pm and some open until 5pm on Thurs.

Museums – 9am/10am-4pm/5pm; no regular closing day.

Post Offices – Mon-Fri 8am/8.30am-4pm/5pm; Sat 8am-1pm.

Shops – Mon-Fri 9am-4pm/5pm (Thurs until 6pm/8pm); Sat 9am/10am-1pm/3pm. Some supermarkets and shopping centres are open longer and some open Sun.

Safety and Security

Norway is considered to have lower crime rates than some other European countries, even in the large cities, however you should always take the usual precautions against pickpockets and petty theft, especially in crowded areas. Do not leave valuables in your car.

Following some recent incidents of robbery, the police are warning motorists with caravans, motorhomes and trailers not to stop in lay-bys overnight. The Norwegian Automobile Association, Norges Automobilforbund (NAF), has also sent out warnings to campsites urging campers to be careful.

If you plan to go off the beaten track or out to sea you should take local advice about weather conditions, have suitable specialist equipment and respect warning signs. Because of Norway's northerly latitude the weather can change rapidly, producing sudden arctic conditions on exposed mountains – even in summer. The winter is long (it can last well into April) and temperatures can drop to minus 25° celcius and below, plus any wind chill factor.

Norway shares with the rest of Europe an underlying threat from terrorism. Attacks could be indiscriminate and against civilian targets in public places, including tourist sites.

British Embassy
THOMAS HEFTYES GATE 8, OSLO
Tel: 23 13 27 00
www.ukinnorway.fco.gov.uk/en/
Irish Embassy
HAAKON VIIS GATE 1, N-0244 OSLO
Tel: 22 01 72 00
www.embassyofireland.no

Customs Regulations

Border Posts
Borders with Sweden and Finland may be crossed on all main roads and Customs posts are usually open day and night.

Storskog on the E105, east of Kirkenes, is the only border crossing for tourist traffic from Norway into Russia (visa required).

Duty-Free Import Allowances
Norway is not a member of the EU and therefore it is possible to import goods duty-free into the country from the EU. Duty-free allowances are not particularly generous and are strictly enforced. Visitors may import the following:

200 cigarettes or 250gm tobacco

1 litre spirits and 1½ litres wine

or 1 litre spirits and 3.5 litres beer
or 3 litres wine and 2 litres beer

or 5 litres beer

Goods to the value of NOK 6,000 (including alcohol and tobacco products)

Visitors must be aged 20 years and over to import spirits and 18 years and over for wine, beer and cigarettes.

Food and Medicines

Up to 10kg (combined weight) of meat, meat products and cheese can be imported into Norway from EU countries for personal consumption. The import of potatoes is not permitted but you can take in up to 10kg of fruit, berries and other vegetables. Visitors may only take in medicines for their own personal use with a covering letter from a doctor stating their requirements.

Money

Travellers may import or export currency up to the equivalent of NOK 25,000 in Norwegian and/or foreign notes and coins. Any amount above this must be declared to Customs.

Refund of VAT on Export

Some shops have a blue and red sign in their window indicating that visitors may, on presentation of a passport, purchase goods free of VAT. For visitors from the UK the purchase price of individual items (exclusive of VAT) must be at least NOK 250. Shop assistants will issue a voucher and on departure from Norway visitors must present goods and vouchers at a tax-free counter situated on ferries, at airports and at main border crossings where a refund of 11-18% will be made.

Documents

Vehicle(s)

Carry your vehicle registration document (V5C), insurance certificate and MOT certificate (if applicable). If driving a borrowed vehicle carry a letter of authority from the owner.

Money

Norway is expensive; bring or have electronic access to plenty of money, especially if you are intending to eat and drink in restaurants and bars.

Bank opening hours are shorter than in the UK, especially in summer, but cash machines are widespread. Bureaux de change are found in banks, post offices, airports, stations, hotels and some tourist offices.

The major credit cards are widely accepted (although some supermarkets and petrol stations do not accept credit cards) and may be used at cash machines (minibanks) throughout the country. In remote areas banks and cash machines may be few and far between.

It is advisable to carry your passport or photocard driving licence if paying with a credit card as you may well be asked for photographic proof of your identity.

Carry your credit card issuers'/banks' 24-hour UK contact numbers in case of loss or theft of your cards.

Motoring in Norway
Alcohol

Norwegian law is very strict: do not drink and drive. Fines and imprisonment await those who exceed the legal limit of 20 milligrams of alcohol in 100 millilitres of blood, which is considerably lower than that permitted in the UK (80 milligrams), and equates to virtually zero for at least 12 hours before driving. Random roadside breath tests are frequent.

If you are involved in a road accident which causes damage to property or vehicles or injuries you should not drink any alcohol for six hours following the accident as the police may wish to carry out blood alcohol tests.

If purchasing medicines in Norway you should be aware that some containing alcohol should be avoided if you intend to drive. These are marked with a red triangle.

Breakdown Service

Norges Automobilforbund (NAF) operates a 24-hour breakdown service nationwide. Call 08505 from a landline or 0926 08505 from a mobile phone. Emergency yellow telephones have been installed on difficult stretches of road.

NAF Veipatrulje (road patrols) operates from mid-June to mid-August on difficult mountain passes and in remote areas but in Oslo, Stavanger and Bergen, they operate all year round.

If you're a member of The Caravan Club show your Club membership card in order to benefit from special NAF rates for breakdown assistance. Some breakdown vehicles have credit card payment terminals; otherwise payment for services is required in cash.

Essential Equipment

Warning Triangle

An warning triangle must be used if the vehicle has broken down, punctures or is involved in an accident, and could cause danger to other road users.

Lights

The use of dipped headlights is compulsory at all times, regardless of weather conditions. Bulbs are more likely to fail with constant use and it is recommended that you carry spares.

Reflective Jacket/Waistcoat

Owners of vehicles registered in Norway are required to carry a reflective jacket to be worn if their vehicle is immobilised on the carriageway following a breakdown or accident. This legislation does not yet apply to foreign registered vehicles but you are strongly advised to carry at least one such jacket. Passengers who leave the vehicle, for example to assist with a repair, should also wear one.

Child Restraint System

Children of four years and under 135cm must be seated in a special child restraint system. If in a rear facing system on the front seat, the airbag must be deactivated. A child between 135-150cm should use a booster seat with an adult seatbelt.

All child restraints must conform to ECE R44-03 or 04 regulations.

Winter Driving

Vehicles with a total weight of 3,500kg or more must carry chains during the winter season, regardless of road conditions. Checks are often carried out.

Generally spiked tyres can be used from 1st November to the first Sunday after Easter. In an effort to discourage the use of spiked tyres in Bergen, Oslo and Trondheim a tax is levied on vehicles equipped with them. For vehicles up to 3,500kg the tax is NOK 30 for one day and NOK 400 for a month. For vehicles over 3,500kg the fee is doubled. Daily permits are available from vending machines along major roads into the city marked 'Frisk luft i byen'. Vehicles over 3,500 kg must be equipped with winter tyres on all axles between 15th November and 31st March.

Fuel

Prices vary not only according to region (they are slightly higher in the north and in mountainous areas) but also according to the manner in which fuel is sold. Prices can also vary on different days and fuel tends to be cheaper on Sunday and Monday. There are automatic petrol pumps where payment is made by credit card or bank notes.

Petrol stations are generally open from 7am to 10pm on weekdays, but may close early. Petrol stations maybe scarce, particularly in the north. In cities some petrol stations remain open 24 hours.

Unleaded petrol is dispensed from pumps marked 'Blyfri'. Not all petrol stations stock diesel. If you fill up with it, ensure that you use the correct pump and do not inadvertently fill with 'Afgift Diesel' (red diesel for agricultural vehicles). LPG is available at a limited number of outlets – see www.visitnorway.com for a list.

Mountain Passes

If you're visiting in the autumn, winter or spring you should check that any mountain passes you intend to use are open. Some high mountain roads close during the winter, the duration of the closure depending on weather conditions, but many others remain open all year. Other passes may close at short notice, at night or during periods of bad weather.

The Norwegian Tourist Board can provide a list, for guidance purposes, of roads which usually close in winter, or contact the Road User Information Centre (Vegtrafikksentralen) which will provide information about roads, road conditions, mountain passes, tunnels, border crossings, etc. The Centre is open round the clock all year, telephone 02030 within Norway or (0047) 91 50 20 30 from abroad. Alternatively a list of roads that are closed in winter or which have limited accessibility can be found at www.vegvesen.no/en/Traffic and click on Truckers' Guide, or email firmapost@vegvesen.no.

Yellow emergency telephones are installed on mountain passes.

Parking

A white line on the edge of the carriageway indicates a parking restriction. Do not park on main roads if visibility is restricted or where there is a sign 'All Stans Førbudt' (no stopping allowed). If you do so you may have your vehicle towed away. Parking regulations in towns are very strict and offences are invariably subject to fines. Pay and display car parks are in use in the main towns.

Priority

Priority roads (main roads) are indicated by a road sign bearing a yellow diamond on a white background. A black diagonal bar through the sign indicates the end of the priority rule. If you are not travelling on a priority road then vehicles coming from the right have priority. Traffic already on a roundabout has priority and trams always have priority.

Narrow roads have passing places (møteplass) to allow vehicles to pass. The driver on the side of the road where there is a passing place must stop for an oncoming vehicle. However heavy goods vehicles tend to take right of way on narrow roads, especially if travelling uphill, and it may be necessary to reverse to a passing place to allow one to pass.

Roads

The standard of roads is generally good but stretches of major roads may be bumpy and rutted as a result of use by heavy freight traffic. Caravanners in particular should take care to avoid wheels being caught in ruts.

Some roads are narrow, especially in the mountains, and may not have a central yellow line. State roads are shown in red on maps and are asphalted but may not have kerbs and may, therefore, easily become cracked and rutted. Many roads have barriers mounted close to the side of the road.

Secondary roads have a gravel surface that can be tricky when wet and may be in poor condition for some weeks during and after the spring thaw.

Do not assume that roads with an E prefix are necessarily major roads - sections of the E39, for example, are still single-track with passing places. The E6 road is asphalted all the way to the Swedish border in the south and to Kirkenes in the north. You may encounter reverse camber on both left and right-hand bends.

Some roads in the fjord region have many hairpin bends and can be challenging. Roads may narrow to a single carriageway and single-track bridges often appear without any advance warning.

Gradients on main highways are generally moderate, not over 10%, but the inside of hairpin bends may be much steeper than this. There is a gradient of 20% on the E68 from Gudvangen (on the southern tip of the Sognefjord) to Stalheim, but a tunnel under the steepest section of the Stalheim road eliminates this difficult section.

Maps showing roads closed to caravans and those only recommended for use by experienced caravanners, together with rest stops, may be obtained from the Norwegian Tourist Board, Norwegian local road authority offices and from the NAF.

Because of the nature of the country's roads – and the beauty of the scenery – average daily mileage may be less than anticipated. Major repairs to roads and tunnels take place during the summer months and traffic controls may cause delays. Ferries make up an integral part of a number of routes, particularly when travelling north along the coast, which also causes slow progress.

Care should be taken to avoid collisions with elk, deer and reindeer, particularly at dawn and dusk. Accidents involving any kind of animal must be reported to the police.

A number of roads are closed in winter, including the E69 to the North Cape, due to snow conditions; some do not open until late May or early June.

Road Signs and Markings

European highways are prefixed with the letter E and are indicated by signs bearing white letters and figures on a green background, national highways (Riksvei or Stamvei) are indicated by black figures prefixed Rv on a yellow background and local, county roads (Fylkesvei) by black figures on a white background. County road numbers do not generally appear on maps.

Lines in the middle of the carriageway are yellow. Bus, cycle and taxi lanes are marked in white.

Some signs have been introduced, for example a square blue sign showing a car and '2+' in white means that cars carrying more than two people can use bus lanes. Square signs indicate the presence of speed cameras, small rectangular signs indicate the exit numbers on highways and main roads, and a number of triangular signs with a yellow background indicate a temporary danger. Signs advising maximum speeds on bends, obstructions, etc, should be respected.

In addition to international road signs, the following signs may also be seen:

Norwegian	English Translation
All stans førbudt	No stopping allowed
Arbeide pa vegen	Roadworks ahead
Enveiskjøring	One-way traffic
Ikke møte	No passing, single line traffic
Kjør sakte	Drive slowly
Løs grus	Loose chippings
Møteplass	Passing place
Omkjøring	Diversion
Rasteplass	Lay-by

Speed Limits

	Open Road (km/h)	Motorway (km/h)
Car Solo	80	90-100
Car towing caravan/trailer	80	80
Motorhome under 3500kg	80	90-100
Motorhome 3500-7500kg	80	80

Drivers should pay close attention to speed limits, which are in general significantly lower than in the UK. Fines for exceeding speed limits are high and often have to be paid on the spot. Radar detectors are illegal.

In residential areas the speed limit may be as low as 30 km/h (18 mph). Frequent speed controls are in operation. Ramps and speed control bumps are not always signposted.

Vehicles over 3,500kg are restricted to 80 km/h (50 mph) on motorways and highways, regardless of signs showing higher general limits.

Towing

Drivers of cars and caravans with a combined length of more than 12.4 metres must check from the list of national highways and/or municipal roads may not be allowed on some routes.

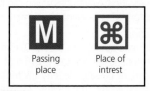

You can check this information with the Road User Information Centre (Vegtrafikksentralen), tel: 02030 within Norway or (0047) 91 50 20 30 from abroad, www.vegvesen.no/en/Traffic and click on Truckers' Guide, or from the Norwegian Tourist Board or NAF. For a motorhome the maximum length is 12 metres (12.4 metres for those registered before September 1997).

Any vehicle towing must have extended towing mirrors fitted.

Some secondary roads have a maximum width of less than 2.55 metres. If your caravan is wider than 2.3 metres and more than 50cm wider than your car, white reflectors must be mounted on the front of your car mirrors. More information is available from the Road User Information Centre.

It is understood that the Rv55 from Sogndal to Lom and the Rv63 north from Geiranger are not suitable for caravans exceeding 5 metres in length, or those without an adequate power/weight ratio.

Traffic Jams

Roads in general are rarely busy but the roads in and around the cities of Oslo, Bergen, Kristiansand and Trondheim suffer traffic jams during rush hours and at the beginning and end of the holiday season.

The E6 Oslo-Svinesund road at the border with Sweden and the E18 Oslo-Kristiansand road are generally busy during the June to August holiday period. During the summer you should also expect delays at ferry terminals.

Tunnels

The road network includes approximately 950 tunnels, most of which can be found in the counties of Hordaland and Sogn og Fjordane in western Norway. Most tunnels are illuminated and about half are ventilated. There are emergency telephones at the entrance to tunnels and inside them. Tunnels also have refuges which can be used by motorists in the event of an emergency.

Laersdal Tunnel
The Lærsdal road tunnel links the Rv50 from just east of Aurlandsvangen to the E16 east of Lærdalsoyri, by-passing the ferry link from Gudvangen to Lærsdal. The toll-free 24.5km long tunnel is illuminated and ventilated throughout and has a number of caverns at regular intervals which act as turning points and, it is reported, help dispel any feelings of claustrophobia. An alternative route is to take the Rødnes tunnel and then the Rv53, but this involves a steep climb beyond Øvre Ardal.

Lofoten and Vesterålen Islands
The Lofoten Islands can be reached by ferries from Bodø & Skutvik and the Vesteralen Islands can be reached by road (E10) west of Narvik. The individual islands of the Lofoten and Vesterålen groups are connected to each other by bridge or tunnel and the two groups of islands are linked by the E10 Lofast route from Gullesfjordbotn in Vesterålen to Fiskebøl in Lofoten. This route was formerly only possible by ferry.

Oslo Tunnel
A 3km long toll-free tunnel runs from east to west Oslo.

Violation of Traffic Regulations

The police are empowered to impose and collect on-the-spot fines for infringement of traffic regulations.

Motorways

There are 300km of 4 lane motorways signposted by the prefix A, which are situated around the towns of Bergen and Oslo. In addition there are category B motorways with 2 lanes.

There are normally no emergency telephones on motorways.

Motorway Tolls

There are many toll roads throughout the country and most have an electronic toll system. Vehicles are categorised as follows:

Class 1 – Motorcycles

Class 2 – Car, with or without trailer, with a total weight less than 3,500kg and maximum length of 6m.

Class 3 – Vehicle with or without trailer and a total weight of more than 3,500kg or between 6m and 12.4m in length.

Payment

If you have not registered your credit card under the Visitors' Payment scheme (see below) you would normally pass through tolls in the lanes marked 'Mynt/Coin' or 'Manuell'. You either pay manually or at a coin machine – keep a supply of small change handy as it is understood that the machines do not issue change. Most toll roads have a facility for credit card payment. Drivers of vehicles over 3,500kg must, if there is one, drive through the 'Manuell' lane.

Don't be tempted to pass through unmanned tolls without paying, as checks are made. However, many toll road operators have installed fully automatic toll stations – AutoPASS – where a sign indicates that you should not stop. Drivers without an AutoPASS can stop and pay at a nearby Esso stations (following the 'KR-Service' signs) within three days of being eligible to pay a toll, or they will receive an invoice by post at their home address. This also applies to drivers of foreign-registered vehicles.

Visitors' Payment

Alternatively, and more conveniently, there is now a 'Visitors' Payment' system for which you register and pay NOK 300 (vehicles below 3,500kg) or NOK 1,000 (over 3,500kg) by credit card. You specify how long your account is to be operative (maximum three months) and it is then automatically debited when you pass a pay point. Three months after your 'Visitors' Payment' has expired your account will be credited with any balance remaining. See www.autopass.no (English option) for more information and to open an account.

This system means you can drive through all toll roads in the AutoPASS lane and pay automatically at toll stations and pay points where there is no option for manual payment. You do not need an AutoPASS tag which is designed for residents and long-stay visitors and for which you have to enter into a contract.

City Tolls

Toll ring roads are in place around major cities charging drivers to take their vehicles into city centres (charge applied one-way only). For example, the toll for the use of the Oslo ring road for an outfit under 6 meters and under 3,500kg is NOK32 whilst an outfit between 6.01-12 meters and over 3,500kg is NOK96 depending on the weight and length of your vehicle (2015).

Other Tolls

Because of the mountainous terrain and the numerous fjords and streams, there are many bridges and tunnels where tolls are normally payable. Tunnels may be narrow and unlit and care is needed when suddenly entering an unlit tunnel from bright daylight. Alternative routes to avoid tolls can be full of obstacles which are not marked on a map, e.g. narrow stretches with sharp turns and/or poor road surface, and are best avoided.

Svinesund Bridge

There is a 700 metre long bridge linking Norway and Sweden on the E6 at Svinesund (Sweden) – the busiest border crossing between the two countries. Tolls are NOK20 for vehicles up to 3,500kg and NOK100 for vehicles over 3,500kgs (2015 prices).

Touring

International ferry services operate between Norway and Denmark, Germany, Iceland and Sweden. Routes from Harwich to Denmark and Newcastle to the Netherlands are in operation as gateways to Europe and, in addition, a daily overnight ferry service connects Copenhagen and Oslo.

A green 'i' sign indicates a tourist information office which is open all year with extended opening hours in summer, whereas a red sign means that the office is only open during the summer season.

Norwegians take their school and industrial holidays from the middle of June to the middle of August; travelling outside this season will ensure that facilities are less crowded and more economically priced. Winter brings the inevitable snowfall with some of the most reliable snow conditions in Europe. The winter sports season is from November to April.

Alta, on the coast north of the Arctic Circle, boasts the most extensive prehistoric rock carvings in Europe and has been declared a UNESCO World Heritage Site. Other World Heritage Sites include Geirangerfjord, Nærøyfjord, Bryggen in Bergen and the wooden buildings in Røros.

City cards are available for Oslo and Bergen, giving unlimited free travel on public transport, free public parking and free or discounted admission to museums and tourist attractions. They can be bought from tourist information centres, hotels and campsites in or near the city, from some kiosks or online at www.visitoslo.com or www.visitbergen.com.

Wine and spirits are only available from special, state-owned shops (vinmonopolet) usually found in larger towns, and are expensive, as are cigarettes. Beer is available from supermarkets. Smoking in bars, restaurants and public places is prohibited. Tipping is not expected in restaurants.

English is widely spoken, often fluently, by virtually everyone under the age of 60.

The Midnight Sun and Northern Lights

The best time to experience the midnight sun is early or high summer. The sun does not sink below the horizon at the North Cape (Nordkapp) from the second week in May to the last week in July.

Midsummer Night's Eve is celebrated all over the country with thousands of bonfires along the fjords.

You can hope to see the Northern Lights (Aurora Borealis) between November and February depending on weather conditions. You need to go north of the Arctic Circle, which crosses Norway, just south of Bodø on the Nordland coast. Occasionally the Northern Lights may be seen in southern Norway, again depending on weather conditions.

North Cape (Nordkapp)

A tunnel links the island of Magerøya, on which the North Cape is situated, to the mainland.

North Cape is open from the beginning of May until the end of September. It is possible to visit in winter; contact the Nordkapp Tourist Office, www.nordkapp.no or tel: (0047) 78 47 70 30. A charge of NOK 255 per adult and NOK 90 per child (2015) is payable to enter the North Cape Hall area. This is a tourist centre where there are exhibitions, displays, restaurants, shops and a post office, as well as an area of hardstanding for parking. This charge covers a stay of up to 48 hours. More information is given in the campsite entry for Nordkapp or on the website www.nordnorge.com. There are no cash machines at North Cape but credit cards are accepted in shops and restaurants, as are euros and sterling.

The true northernmost point of Norway is in fact at Knivskjellodden on a peninsular to the west of North Cape which is marked by a modest monument and a wooden box where you can record your name in a log book. It is possible to walk the 18km round trip from a car park on the E69 to Knivskjellodden but the walk should not be undertaken lightly. Later you can claim a certificate to mark your achievement from the tourist office in Honningsvåg by quoting the reference number of your signed entry in the log book.

The Order of Bluenosed Caravanners

Visitors to the Arctic Circle from anywhere in the world may apply for membership of the Order of Bluenosed Caravanners, which will be recognised by the issue of a certificate by the International Caravanning Association (ICA). For further details contact David Hirst on 01422 372390, or email: david.hirst118@gmail.com and attach a photograph of yourselves and your outfit under any Arctic Circle signpost, together with the date and country of crossing and the names of those who made the crossing. This service is free to members of the ICA (annual membership £20); the fee for non-members is £5. Coloured plastic decals for your outfit, indicating membership of the Order, are also available at a cost of £4. Cheques should be payable to the ICA. See www.icacaravanning.org.

Public Transport

The public transport network is excellent and efficient with bus routes extending to remote villages. For economical travel buy a 24 hour bus pass (campsites often sell them), valid when stamped for the first time. Many train routes run through very scenic countryside and special offers and discounts mean that train travel is reasonably priced. Only Oslo has a metro system. Trams operate in Bergen and Trondheim.

Using domestic public ferry services is often the quickest way of travelling around Norway and from place to place along the coast and within fjords. Most operate from very early in the morning until late at night. Booking is not normally necessary except in the height of the holiday season when there may be long queues to the more popular destinations. However, internal ferries can be expensive in high season and you may wish to plan your route carefully in order to avoid them.

The ultimate ferry journey is the Norwegian steamer trip (hurtigrute) up the coast from Bergen to Kirkenes. A daily service operates in both directions and the steamer stops at about 30 ports on the way. The round trip lasts eleven days.

The scenic round trip from Bergen or Oslo, 'Norway in a Nutshell', takes you through some of the most beautiful scenery in the country. It combines rail, boat and coach travel on the scenic Bergen railway, the breathtaking Flåm Railway, and takes in the Aurlandsfjord, the narrow Naerøyfjord and the steep Stalheimskleiva. Further details are available from the Norwegian Tourist Board.

You can safely hail a taxi off the street or take one from a taxi stand. Most drivers speak English and all taxis are equipped for taking payment by credit card.

ALESUND *1B1* (1km N Coastal) *62.47571, 6.15688* **Ålesund Bobilsenter, Storgata 39, 6015 Ålesund (Møre og Romsdal)** Foll coast to N of town cent & m'van sps; well sp. Sm, hdstg, unshd; wc; mv service pnt; shwrs; EHU; some traff noise; motor c'vans only Ccard acc. "No on-site warden; site on water's edge adj sea wall; conv town cent; v nice facs in wonderful location." May-Sep. NOK 200   2014*

ALESUND *1B1* (3km E Urban/Coastal) *62.46986, 6.19839* **Volsdalen Camping, Sjømannsveien, 6008 Ålesund (Møre og Romsdal) [tel 70 12 58 90; fax 70 12 14 94; v.camp@online.no; www.volsdalencamping.no]** Foll Rv136 two Centrum, ignore 1st camping sp (Prinsen), take 2nd site sp Volsdalsberga to exit R, up slip rd. At top turn L over E136 then immed R, site on L. Sm, mkd pitch, hdstg, terr, unshd; htd wc; chem disp; mv service pnt; shwrs NOK10; EHU (10A) NOK30 (no earth); gas; lndry; shop on site & 500m; rest, snacks high ssn; cooking facs; TV rm; 40% statics; dogs; bus 600m; poss cr; Eng spkn; adv bkg; quiet; ccard acc; red long stay. "Stunning location; some pitches o'looking fjord; sm pitches not suitable lge o'fits high ssn; 75% travellers; site unkempt; new san facs being built (2013); rec NH; only site for c'van nr Alesund, so adv bkg strongly advised; town 30 min walk." ◆ 1 May-1 Sep. NOK 250   2014*

ALTA *2G1* (6km NE Coastal) *70.00000, 23.48283* **Solvang Camping & Ungdomssenter, 9505 Alta (Finnmark) [tel 78 43 04 77; fax 78 44 30 20; post@solvangcamping.no; www.solvangcamping.no]** E along E6 fr Alta dir Rafsbotn, sp. Sm, unshd; wc; chem disp; shwrs; EHU; lndry; snacks; cooking facs; beach adj; TV rm; some statics; phone; Eng spkn; adv bkg; quiet; CKE/CCI. "Gd NH in lovely area." 1 Jun-30 Aug.   2009*

⊞ **ALTA** *2G1* (6km S Rural) *69.92904, 23.26136* **Alta River Camping, Steinfossveien 5, 9518 Øvre Alta (Finnmark) [tel 78 43 43 53; fax 78 43 69 02; post@alta-river-camping. no; www.alta-river-camping.no]** Fr E6 (by-passing Alta), take E93 S sp Kautokeino. Site clearly sp on L (opp information board). Med, pt shd; htd wc; chem disp; mv service pnt; sauna; shwrs NOK10; EHU (10-16A) NOK30; lndry; shop; cooking facs; playgrnd; ltd wifi; TV; Eng spkn; adv bkg; quiet; ccard acc; CKE/CCI. "Excel facs; o'looks salmon rv; pitches not mkd and close together, some hdstg; elec point poss no earth; facs dated but clean; elec poss no earth." ◆ NOK 279   2014*

⊞ **ALTA** *2G1* (7km S Rural) *69.92735, 23.27075* **Alta Strand Camping & Apartments, Stenfossveien 29, 9518 Øvre Alta (Finnmark) [tel 78 43 40 22; fax 78 43 42 40; mail@altacamping.no; www.altacamping.no]** Fr E6 (W of Alta) take Rv93 S sp Kautokeino. Three sites adj in 3km on L, clearly sp, Strand is last one. Sm, pt shd; htd wc; chem disp; mv service pnt; sauna; shwrs inc; EHU (10A) NOK40 (poss no earth); lndry; shop 5km; snacks; bar; BBQ; cooking facs; playgrnd; wifi; some statics; phone; car wash; Eng spkn; adv bkg; ccard acc; CKE/CCI. "Gd for visiting rock carvings; midnight sun visible fr nrby Alta museum; vg." NOK 190   2010*

⊞ **ALVDAL** *1C2* (5km NE Rural) *62.13115, 10.56896* **Gjelten Bru Camping, 2560 Alvdal (Hedmark) [tel 62 48 74 44; fax 62 48 70 20; www.nafcamp.com/gjelten-camping]** Fr Rv3 join rd 29 at Alvdal. Cross rv opp general store to site on rv bank. Sm, mkd pitch, pt shd; wc; chem disp; mv service pnt; baby facs; shwrs NOK5; EHU (10A) NOK40; lndry (inc dryer); playgrnd; games area; fishing; dogs; Eng spkn; quiet. "V pleasant site; friendly owner." NOK 160   2010*

AMOT *1B3* (400m SW Rural) *59.5725, 7.99158* **Camping Groven, Ytre Vinje, 3890 Åmot (Telemark) [tel 35 07 14 21; fax 35 07 10 87; grovenc@online.no; www.grovencamping.no]** Fr Åmot take Rv37 N, site 200m on R. Med, terr, pt shd; htd wc; chem disp; mv service pnt; baby facs; sauna; shwrs NOK5; EHU (10A) NOK30; lndry; shop; playgrnd; pool 100m; winter skiing; TV rm; phone. "Attractive scenery; walking tours arranged; clean, rustic site." 20 May-1 Oct. NOK 150   2009*

ANDALSNES *1B1* (3km S Rural) *62.55223, 7.70394* **Åndalsnes Camping & Motell, 6300 Åndalsnes (Møre og Romsdal) [tel 71 22 16 29; fax 71 22 63 60; epost@ andalsnes-camping.no; www.andalsnes-camping.com]** Foll E136 to o'skirts of Åndalsnes. Foll sp Ålesund x-ing rv bdge twd W & L immed. Lge, pt shd; wc; chem disp; mv service pnt; shwrs NOK15; EHU (10-16A) NOK40 (check earth); lndry; shop; rest, snacks; fishing; boating; wifi; TV; ccard acc; red CKE/CCI. "Excel facs; rvside, excel mountain scenery; nr Troll Rd & Wall; nice site; grnd can be soft; poss long lead req (poss no earth); gd cent site." ◆ 1 May-30 Sep. NOK 242   2014*

ANDALSNES *1B1* (11km S Rural) *62.4940, 7.75846* **Trollveggen Camping, Horgheimseidet, 6300 Åndalsnes (Møre og Romsdal) [tel 71 22 37 00; fax 71 22 16 31; post@trollveggen.com; www.trollveggen.com]** Sp on W side of E136, dir Dombås. Sm, mkd pitch, terr, pt shd; htd wc; chem disp; mv service pnt; baby facs; fam bthrm; shwrs NOK25; EHU (16A) NOK40; lndry (inc dryer); kiosk; rest 5km; BBQ; cooking facs; playgrnd; fishing; golf 10km; bike hire; wifi; statics; dogs; Eng spkn; adv bkg; quiet; ccard acc. "Friendly, family-run site; excel touring base; outstanding scenery; at foot of Trollveggen wall - shd fr late afternoon; ideal site for walking in Romsal; on Trollsteig classic rte." ◆ ltd. 10 May-19 Sep. NOK 258   2014*

ANDALSNES *1B1* (23km NW Rural Coastal) *62.58720, 7.53004* **Saltkjelsnes Camping, N-6350 Eidsbygda [tel 71 22 39 00; fax 71 22 12 00; camping@saltkjelsnes.no; www.saltkjelsnes.no]** FV64 twds Molde, site on L sp Eidsbyga. Sm, pt sl, terr, pt shd; htd wc; chem disp; mv service pnt; shwrs; EHU (10a) 40 NOK; lndry; shop 10km; BBQ; cooking facs; wifi; boat hire; fishing; 60% statics; dogs; twin axles; poss cr; Eng spkn; quiet. "Lovely location; site small & space ltd, but 1st class facs; Rodven Stavkirke 10km; vg." 1 Apr-1 Oct. NOK 287   2015*

AURLAND see Flåm *1B2*

NORWAY

BALESTRAND *1B2* (1km S Coastal) *61.20220, 6.53140*
Sjøtun Camping, 6899 Balestrand (Sogn og Fjordane)
[tel/fax 57 69 12 23; camping@sjotun.com; www.sjotun.
com] Fr Dragsvik ferry or fr W on by-pass; foll int'l site sp. Sm,
pt sl, unshd; htd wc; chem disp (wc); mv service pnt; shwrs inc;
EHU (16A) NOK25; lndry; shop, rest, snacks 1km; BBQ; cooking
facs; shgl beach 1km; few statics; dogs; phone; Eng spkn; adv
bkg; quiet; red long stay; CKE/CCI. "Neat, well-kept site with
gd view of Sognefjord; poss diff if wet due grass pitches."
1 Jun-28 Feb & 15 Apr-1 Oct. NOK 317   2014*

BALLANGEN *2F2* (3.6km E Coastal) *68.3383, 16.85776*
Ballangen Camping, 8540 Ballangen (Nordland)
[tel 76 92 76 90; fax 76 92 76 92; ballcamp@c2i.net;
www.ballangen-camping.no] Sp on N side of E6 fr Narvik,
beside fjord. Lge, mkd pitch, pt shd; htd wc; chem disp; mv
service pnt; sauna; shwrs inc; EHU (10A) NOK40; lndry (inc
dryer); shop; rest, snacks; playgrnd; htd pool; paddling pool;
waterslide; shgl fjord beach; tennis; games area; wifi; TV; some
statics; dogs; Eng spkn; ccard acc; CKE/CCI. "Pleasant site adj
fjord; friendly owners; gd facs - ltd san facs high ssn; gd rest;
foot/cycle path to town." ◆ 14 Mar-1 Oct. NOK 200   2010*

BARDU see Setermoen *2F2*

⊞ **BEITOSTOLEN** *1C2* (1km S Rural) *61.24128, 8.92068*
Beitostølen Hytter & Camping (OP151), Finntøppvegen
2, 2953 Beitostølen (Oppland) [tel 61 34 11 00 or
95 70 35 05; fax 61 34 15 44; info@beitocamp.no;
www.beitocamp.no] Fr S on Rv51, site on L. Lge, hdstg, pt
sl, unshd; htd wc; chem disp; mv service pnt; sauna; baby facs;
fam bthrm; shwrs NOK10; EHU (13A) NOK30; lndry (inc dryer);
shop adj; rest BBQ; cooking facs; playgrnd; htd, covrd pool
1km; canoe & bike hire; wifi; 90% statics (sep area); dogs; Eng
spkn; quiet; ccard acc; CKE/CCI. "Wintersports, horseriding
nrby; gd walking; excel site." ◆ NOK 200   2010*

BERGEN *1A3* (21km E Rural) *60.37381, 5.45768* **Lone**
Camping, Hardangerveien 697, 5268 Haukeland (Horda-
Rogaland) [tel 55 39 29 60; fax 55 39 29 79; booking@
lonecamping.no; www.lonecamping.no]
Fr N on E39 until junc with E16. foll sp Voss to rndabt junc
with Rv580 sp Nesttun. Foll Rv580 S for approx 5km, site sp
on L. Fr S on E39 until Nesttun, foll Rv580 N sp Indre Arna
for approx 6km, site sp on R. Rte approx is sm bureau adj g'ge or,
if unmanned, in g'ge. Do NOT go into Bergen city cent. Site
is 20km by rd fr Bergen. Lge, pt sl, pt shd, some hdstg; wc;
chem disp; mv service pnt; shwrs NOK10 (no earth); EHU (16A)
NOK40; gas; lndry; shop; supmkt adj; snacks; playgrnd; lake
sw, fishing & boating; wifi; TV rm; some statics; phone; bus
to Bergen; site clsd 5 Nov-19 Dec & New Year; poss v cr; Eng
spkn; quiet; red 3+ days; ccard acc; CKE/CCI. "Well-organised;
helpful staff; peaceful lakeside setting; superb views; lakeside
pitches diff when wet; bus at camp ent for Bergen (35 mins)."
2 Jan-20 Dec. NOK 294   2014*

BERGEN *1A3* (17km SE Rural) *60.35220, 5.43520* **Bratland**
Camping, Bratlandsveien 6, 5268 Haukeland (Hordaland)
[tel 55 10 13 38 & 92 61 52 00 (mob); fax 55 10 53 60;
post@bratlandcamping.no; www.bratlandcamping.no]
Fr N on E39 until junc with E16, foll sp Voss to rndabt junc with
Rv580 sp Nesttun. Foll Rv580 S for approx 4km; site sp on L.
Fr Voss on E16, emerge fr tunnel to rndabt, turn L onto Rv580.
Then as above. Site 16km by rd fr Bergen. Sm, some hdstg,
unshd; wc; chem disp; mv service pnt; shwrs inc; EHU
(10A) NOK40; lndry (inc dryer); shop; cooking facs; wifi; TV rm;
10% statics; bus to Bergen at site ent; poss cr; Eng spkn; rd
noise; ccard acc; CKE/CCI. "Clean, family-run site; gd, modern
san facs; v helpful owners; conv Bergen, nrby stave church &
Grieg's home." ◆ 1 May-15 Sep. NOK 286   2014*

BERGEN *1A3* (7jn SSE Urban) *60.35405, 5.35962*
Bergenshallen, Vilhelm Bjerknes Vei 24, 5081 Bergen
[tel 47 55 30 88 50; www.visitnorway.com]
Head SW on E39. Exit onto E39 twrds Stavanger/Rv580,
take exit. At rndabt take 3rd exit onto Mindeallé. Turn R to
stay on Mindeallé, go thro 1 rndabt, cont onto Rv582. Thro 1
rndabt then at next rndabt take 2nd exit onto Fv252. Turn R
onto Hagerups vei, cont onto Vilhelm Bjerknes'vei. Turn L and
site is on the R. Sm, hdstg, unshd; own san rec; mv service pnt;
EHU (on some pitches); dogs inc; train adj. "28 spaces for MV's
only; arrive early; adj to Bergen light Rail - 15 mins to city cent;
only fasc are water, emptying toilet & waste disposal; excel
location for visiting Bergen; no shwrs or wc." 1 May-31 Aug.
NOK 150   2014*

BERLEVAG *2H1* (600m E Coastal) *70.85716, 29.09933*
Berlevåg Camping & Apartments, Havnagata 8, 9980
Berlevåg (Finnmark) [tel 78 98 16 10; post@berlevag-
pensjonat.no; www.berlevag-pensjonat.no]
Leave E6 at Tanabru, foll Rv890 to Berlevåg. Site sp at beg
of vill. Sm, unshd; htd wc; chem disp; mv service pnt; shwrs
NOK10; EHU (16A) NOK40; lndry (inc dryer); shop 500m; BBQ;
cooking facs; playgrnd; beach; library & lounge; wifi; TV rm;
phone; Eng spkn; adv bkg; ccard acc; CKE/CCI. "Busy fishing
port on edge of Barents Sea; museum, glassworks, WW2
resistance history; v helpful staff as site is also TO; site will open
outside Jun-Sep on request if contacted ahead; rec arr early;
excel site." ◆ 1 Jun-30 Sep. NOK 160   2009*

BIRISTRAND see Lillehammer *1C2*

BIRTAVARRE *2G1* (700m S Rural) *69.49051, 20.82976*
Camping Birtavarre (TR34), 9147 Birtavarre (Troms)
[tel/fax 77 71 77 07; mail@birtavarrecamping.com;
www.birtavarrecamping.com] On E6 Olderdalen to
Nordkjsobotn, sp. Or foll sp fr vill. Med, unshd; wc; chem disp;
mv service pnt; baby facs; shwrs NOK10; EHU NOK45; lndry;
shop 1km; snacks; cooking facs; fjord sw; Eng spkn; some rd
noise; ccard acc; CKE/CCI. "Basic site; ok for NH."
1 May-15 Oct. NOK 195   2014*

NORWAY

⊞ **BO** *1C3* (5km N Rural) *59.44425, 9.06318* **Bø Camping (TE5), Lifjellvegen 51, 3800 Bø (Telemark) [tel 35 95 20 12; fax 35 95 34 64; bocamping@bo.online.no; www.bocamping.com]** Fr Bø cent on Rv36 dir Folkestad; take rd on L to Lifjell, site sp; 500m fr Bø Sommarland amusement park. Med, hdstg, pt shd; htd wc; chem disp; shwrs; EHU NOK30; gas; lndry; snacks; shop; playgrnd; pool; paddling pool; fishing; solarium; TV; 20% statics; phone; poss cr; Eng spkn; adv bkg; ccard acc; CKE/CCI. NOK 180   2009*

BO *1C3* (9km SE Rural) *59.38478, 9.18171* **Teksten Camping AS, Strannavegen 140, 3810 Gvary [tel 35 95 55 96; fax 35 95 54 40; teksten@barnascamping.no; www.barnascamping.no]** On 36 dir Skien. Go thro Gvarv. Site sp on L. 700m fr main rd by rv. Med, mkd pitch, terr, pt shd; htd wc; chem disp; mv service pnt; fam bthrm; lndry; cooking facs; playgrnd; sw adj; sand; games area; games rm; 30% statics; twin axles; poss cr; Eng spkn; adv bkg; quiet; ccard acc; CKE/CCI. "Vg site for children." 1 May-9 Sep. NOK 258   2015*

⊞ **BODO** *2F2* (2km SE Rural) *67.2695, 14.42483* **Camping Bodøsjoen, Båtstøveien 1, 8013 Bodø (Nordland) [tel 75 56 36 80; fax 75 56 46 89; bodocamp@yahoo.no; www.bodocamp.no]** Fr E on Rv80 at Bodø sp, turn L at traff lts by Esso g'ge sp airport & camping. L at next rndabt, foll camping sp. Lge, pt sl, unshd; wc; chem disp; shwrs inc; EHU (10A) NOK20 (no earth); lndry; shop 1km; rest 2km; beach; bus 1km; boat hire; fishing excursions; bus 250m; Eng spkn; aircraft noise; CKE/CCI. "Conv Lofoten ferry; superb views; midnight sun (Jun-Jul); Mt Rønvik 3.2km fr camp." ◆ NOK 252   2014*

⊞ **BODO** *2F2* (28km SE Coastal) *67.23545, 14.62125* **Saltstraumen Camping, Knapplund, 8056 Saltstraumen (Nordland) [tel 75 58 75 60; fax 75 58 75 40; saltstraumen@ pluscamp.no; www.saltstraumen-camping.no]** Fr Bodø take Rv80 for 19km; turn S onto rte 17 at Løding; site sp in Saltstraumen. Site is 33km by rd fr Bodø. Med, hdstg, unshd; htd wc; chem disp; mv service pnt; shwrs inc; EHU (16A) NOK30; gas; lndry (inc dryer); shop adj; rest adj; cooking facs; playgrnd; fishing; cycling; boating; TV; phone; poss cr; Eng spkn; quiet; ccard acc; CKE/CCI. "5 min walk to Mælstrom, the 'angler's paradise'; v busy high ssn - rec arr early." ◆ ltd. NOK 200   2014*

BOSBERG see Trondheim *2E3*

BOVERDALEN see Lom *1C2*

⊞ **BREMSNES** *1B1* (6km W Coastal) *63.08043, 7.59535* **Skjerneset Brygge Camping, Ekkilsøy, 6530 Averøy (Møre og Romsdal) [tel 71 51 18 94; fax 71 51 18 15; info@ skjerneset.com; www.skjerneset.com]** Foll sp to Ekkilsøya Island on Rv64 (off Averøy Island). Site on R over bdge. Sm, some hdstg, pt shd; htd wc; chem disp; mv service pnt; shwrs inc; EHU (10-16A) NOK30; lndry; sm shop; cooking facs; boat hire; fishing; sat TV; apartments to rent; quiet. "Charming, clean, peaceful site adj working harbour; beautiful outlook; basic san facs; waterside pitches - unfenced deep water in places; museum adj." NOK 200   2015*

BRIKSDALSBRE see Olden *1B2*

⊞ **BRONNOYSUND** *2E3* (14km SW Coastal) *65.39340, 12.09920* **Torghatten Camping, 8900 Torghatten (Nordland) [tel 75 02 54 95; fax 75 02 58 89; pkha@online. no; www.rv17.no/torghatten-camping/]** Fr Rv17 onto Rv76 to Brønnøysund, foll sp Torghatten. Site at base of Torghatten mountain. Sm, pt sl, unshd; wc; chem disp; mv service pnt; shwrs inc; EHU (16A) NOK30; lndry; shop; snacks; bar; playgrnd; sea water pool & beach adj; bus; phone; Eng spkn; quiet. "Take care speed humps in/out Brønnøysund; vg." ◆ ltd. NOK 140   2009*

⊞ **BRUFLAT** *1C2* (10km SE Rural) *60.82932, 9.75050* **Etna Familiecamping, Maslangrudvegen 50, 2890 Etnedal [tel 61 12 17 55 or 94 81 90 56 (mob); info@etnacamping.no; www.etnacamping.no]** Fr Gjovik, W on 33 past Dokka. Site on R approx 2 km past 251. Downhill to ent. Lge, pt sl, terr, pt shd; htd wc; chem disp, dedicated pnt; mv service pnt; fam bthrm; shwrs; lndry; snacks; pool; games rm; tv rm; 20% statics; twin axles; Eng spkn; adv bkg; quiet; ccard acc; CKE/CCI. "Relaxing site; sep area for touring; may need long lead, some still 2 pin; vg." ◆ ltd. NOK 276   2015*

BUD *1B1* (1km SE Coastal) *62.9040, 6.92866* **PlusCamp Bud (MR11), 6430 Bud (Møre og Romsdal) [tel 71 26 10 23 or 97 70 05 44 (mob); fax 71 26 11 47; bud@pluscamp.no; www.budcamping.no]** Site on Rv664, sp fr Bud. Med, pt sl, unshd; htd wc; chem disp; mv service pnt; baby facs; shwrs NOK10; EHU (16A) NOK40; lndry (inc dryer); shop; snacks; cooking facs; playgrnd; sand beach & sw adj; boat hire; fishing; TV rm; wifi; 50% statics; dogs; Eng spkn; quiet; ccard acc; CKE/ CCI. "Waterfront site with beautiful views; 20 min walk to vill shops/rest; gd facs; gd location for start of Atlantic Highway, National Tourist Rte & for cycling; vg site." ◆ 20 Apr-1 Oct. NOK 270   2015*

BURFJORD *2G1* (11km N Rural) *70.02728, 22.08860* **Alteidet Camping, Alteidet, 9161 Burfjord (Troms) [tel 78 48 75 59; fax 77 76 93 51; alteidetcamp@hotmail.com]** On W of E6, midway bet Burfjord & Langfjordbotn. Med, pt sl, unshd; wc; chem disp; baby facs; sauna; shwrs NOK10; EHU (10A) NOK40; lndry; kiosk; shops 5km; bar; cooking facs; playgrnd; TV; dogs; phone; poss cr; adv bkg; quiet; Eng spkn. "Attractive by rv & fjord; excl base to visit glacier." 15 Jun-15 Aug. NOK 140   2009*

⊞ **BYGLANDSFJORD** *1B4* (3km N Rural) *58.68895, 7.80322* **Neset Camping, 4741 Byglandsfjord (Aust-Agder) [tel 37 93 40 50; fax 37 93 43 93; post@neset.no; www.neset.no]** N on Rv9 fr Evje, thro Byglandsfjord, site on L. Lge, pt sl, unshd; htd wc; chem disp; mv service pnt; fam bthrm; sauna; shwrs NOK5; EHU (10A) NOK30; gas; lndry (inc dryer); shop; snacks; rest; BBQ; cooking facs; playgrnd; lake sw & beach adj; fishing; windsurfing; boat & bike hire; wifi; TV rm; 40% statics; dogs; Eng spkn; adv bkg; quiet; ccard acc. "Wonderful site on lakeside; elk safaris; walks; ww rafting nrby; check elec earth." ◆ NOK 304 (CChq acc)   2014*

BYRKJELO *1B2* (250m S Rural) *61.73026, 6.50843* **Byrkjelo Camping & Hytter, 6826 Byrkjelo (Sogn og Fjordane) [tel 91 73 65 97; fax 57 86 71 54; mail@byrkjelo-camping.no; www.byrkjelo-camping.tefre.com]** Fr S site ent on L as ent town, clearly sp. Sm, some hdstg, pt shd, wc; chem disp; baby facs; fam bthrm; shwrs NOK5; EHU (10A) NOK30; lndry; shop, snacks adj; rest 500m; cooking facs; playgrnd; htd pool; paddling pool; fishing; cycling; solarium; wifi; 25% statics; phone; Eng spkn; adv bkg; quiet but some rd noise; ccard acc; CKE/CCI. "Horseriding, mountain & glacier walking; excel, well kept site; great facs." ◆ 30 Mar-20 Sep. NOK 190   2014*

DALEN (TELEMARK) *1B3* (500m SW Rural) *59.44223, 8.00758* **Buøy Camping (TE20), Buøyvegen, 3880 Dalen (Telemark) [tel 35 07 75 87; fax 35 07 77 01; info@dalen camping.com; www.dalencamping.com]** Fr E134 at Høydalsmo take Rv45 twd Dalen (approx 20km, 12% gradient). Of fr E134 at Åmot take Rv38 to Dalen (no gradient). Site in cent of Dalen on Rv45, well sp. Med, pt shd; htd wc; chem disp; mv service pnt; baby facs; shwrs inc; EHU (16A) NOK35; gas; lndry; shop; rest; cooking facs; playgrnd; leisure cent 500m; bike hire; wifi; TV; 60% statics; dogs; phone; Eng spkn; quiet; ccard acc; CKE/CCI. "Site on island; gd family base; gd walking." 1 May-28 Aug. NOK 240   2010*

DALSGRENDA see Mo i Rana *2F2*

DOMBAS *1C2* (6km S Rural) *62.02991, 9.17586* **Bjørkhol Camping, 2660 Dombås (Oppland) [tel 61 24 13 31; post@ bjorkhol.no; www.bjorkhol.no]** Site on E6. Sm, pt sl, pt shd; htd wc; chem disp; mv service pnt; shwrs NOK5; EHU (10A) NOK40 (long lead poss req); lndry; shop; rest, snacks, bar 6km; cooking facs; playgrnd; 10% statics; dogs; phone; Eng spkn; adv bkg; quiet; CKE/CCI. "A well-kept, friendly, family-owned, basic site; excel mountain walking in area." 1 May-1 Sep. NOK 150   2013*

DRAMMEN *1C3* (25km SE Coastal) *59.60003, 10.40383* **Homannsberget Camping, Strømmveien 55, 3060 Svelvik (Vestfold) [tel 33 77 25 63 or 91 30 98 52 (mob); post@homannsberget.no; www.homannsberget.no]** Head SW on E18, take exit 25 twr Svelvik/RV319, at rndabt take 3rd exit onto E134. At next rndabt take 1st exit onto Bjørnsons gate/Rv282. Turn L onto Havnegata/Rv319. Cont on Rv319, go thro 1 rndabt. Site on the L. Med, mkd pitch, unshd; mv service pnt; shwr NOK5; EHU; lndry (inc dryer); shop; bar; playgrnd; beach adj; games area; wifi; twin axles; poss cr; adv bkg; quiet; ccard acc; CKE/CCI. "Vg site; train stn within 20 mins; site is also a strawberry farm & orchard." 1 May-1 Sep. NOK 245   2014*

EDLAND *1B3* (6km E Rural) *59.72378, 7.69712* **Velemoen Camping, 3895 Edland Vinje i Telemark [tel 35 07 01 09 or 90 89 40 49 (mob); fax 35 07 02 15; velemoen@frisurf. no; www.velemoen.no]** Fr E site on L off E134 bef Edland; Fr W site is on R, 8km after Haukeligrend on Lake Tveitevatnet. Sm, pt sl, shd; wc; baby facs; no chem disp/mv service pnt; shwrs; EHU; lndry; shops 1km; cooking facs; playgrnd; lake sw adj; sat TV; some statics; dogs; Eng spkn; quiet; no ccard acc. "V helpful owner; immac san facs; beautiful lakeside/mountain location; on S side of Hardangervidda National Park; on main E-W rte Oslo-Bergen." ◆ 15 May-1 Oct. NOK 150   2013*

⊞ **EGERSUND** *1A4* (4km N Rural) *58.4788, 5.9909* **Steinsnes NAF Camping, Jærveien 190, Tengs, 4370 Egersund (Horda-Rogaland) [tel 97 40 09 66; fax 51 49 40 73; post@steinsnescamping.no; www.steinsnescamping.no]** Site located S of Rv44 & on bank of rv; rv bdge at Tengs Bru. Med, mkd pitch, unshd; wc; chem disp; mv service pnt; shwrs NOK5; EHU (4A) NOK35; lndry; shops adj; snacks adj; bar 2km; BBQ; playgrnd; sand beach 8km; horseriding school adj; phone; poss cr; Eng spkn; adv bkg; quiet but some rd noise; ccard acc; CKE/CCI. "Spectacular rapids 1km (salmon leaping in July); on North Sea cycle rte; conv ferry to Denmark or Bergen; vg." ◆ NOK 230   2013*

EIDFJORD *1B3* (7km SE Rural) *60.42563, 7.12318* **Sæbø Camping (HO11), 5784 Øvre-Eidfjord (Hordaland) [tel 53 66 59 27 or 55 10 20 48; scampi@online.no; www.saebocamping.com]** Site N of Rv7 bet Eidfjord & Geilo, 2nd on L after tunnel & bdge; clearly sp. Med, pt shd; htd wc; chem disp; mv service pnt; fam bthrm; shwrs NOK10; EHU (10A) NOK30 (earth fault); lndry (inc dryer); shop; rest, snacks 500m; cooking facs; playgrnd; boating; quiet; CKE/CCI. "Vg; beautiful lakeside setting; adj to excel nature cent with museum/shop/theatre; clean san facs; helpful staff; gd location for walking & cycling." ◆ 1 May-30 Sep. NOK 248   2014*

⊞ **ELVERUM** *1D2* (2km S Rural) *60.86701, 11.55623* **Elverum Camping, Halvdan Gransvei 6, 2407 Elverum (Hedmark) [tel 62 41 67 16; fax 62 41 68 17; booking@ elverumcamping.no; www.elverumcamping.no]** Site sp fr Rv20 dir Kongsvinger. Lge, pt shd; htd wc; chem disp; mv service pnt; shwrs inc; EHU (10A) NOK40; lndry; shop, rest, snacks, bar 2km; BBQ; playgrnd; 20% statics; phone; dogs; adv bkg; Eng spkn; quiet. "Vg; museum of forestry adj; rlwy museum at Hamar (30km)." NOK 200   2009*

⊞ **FAGERNES** *1C2* (600m S Rural) *60.98189, 9.23125* **Camping Fagernes, Tyinvegen 23, 2900 Fagernes (Oppland) [tel 61 36 05 10; fax 61 36 07 51; post@fagernes-camping.no; www.fagernes-camping.no]** Site on N side of Fagernes on E16. Lge, some hdg pitch, pt sl, pt shd; htd wc; chem disp; mv service pnt; baby facs; shwrs NOK12; EHU (10-16A) NOK30; lndry; shop; rest, snacks; bar; cooking facs; playgrnd; lake sw; activity cent; cycling; skiing; fishing; car wash; TV; 90% statics; dogs; phone; poss cr; Eng spkn; quiet LS; ccard acc; CKE/CCI. "Helpful owner; ltd water pnts; Valdres folk museum park adj highly rec; fjord views; excel new san facs & site refurbished (2015); vg." ◆ NOK 275   2015*

FARSUND *1A4* (6km S Rural) *58.0663, 6.7957* **Lomsesanden Familiecamping, Loshavneveien 228, 4550 Farsund (Vest-Agder) [tel 38 39 09 13; e-vetlan@online.no; www.lomsesanden.no]** Exit E39 at Lyngdal onto Rv43 to Farsund & foll camp sps. (NB Rv465 fr Kvinesdal not suitable for c'vans.) Med, pt shd; wc; chem disp; baby facs; shwrs NOK10; EHU (10A) NOK45; lndry; shop; playgrnd; dir access sand beach adj; fishing; TV; 95% statics; dogs; Eng spkn; adv bkg rec; quiet; ccard acc. "Gd site in beautiful location." 1 May-15 Sep. NOK 185   2009*

⊞ **FAUSKE** *2F2* (15km NE Coastal) *67.34618, 15.59533*
Strømhaug Camping, Strømhaugveien 2, 8226 Straumen (Nordland) [tel 75 69 71 06; fax 75 69 76 06; mail@ stromhaug.no; www.stromhaug.no] N fr Fauske on E6, turn off sp Straumen, site sp. Sm, pt sl, pt shd; htd wc; chem disp; mv service pnt; shwrs NOK10; EHU (6-10A) inc; lndry; shop, rest, snacks, bar adj; cooking facs; playgrnd; fishing; boating; TV; Eng spkn; red 7+ days. "Site on rv bank; salmon-fishing in Aug." ◆ NOK 239   2013*

⊞ **FAUSKE** *2F2* (5km S Urban) *67.23988, 15.41961* **Fauske Camping & Motel, Leivset, 8201 Fauske (Nordland) [tel 75 64 84 01; fax 75 64 84 13; fausm@online.no]** Fr S site on R of E6, approx 6km fr exit of Kvenflåg rd tunnel, & 2km bef Finneid town board. Fr N site on L approx 1km after rv bdge. Sm, pt sl, pt shd; wc; mv service pnt; baby facs; shwrs NOK10; EHU (10A) NOK40; lndry; shop 2km; snacks; cooking facs; playgrnd; sw 2km; fishing; cycling; wifi; dogs; poss cr; some Eng spkn; adv bkg; some rd noise; ccard acc. "Vg; phone ahead LS to check open." NOK 165   2009*

FAUSKE *2F2* (3km SW Rural/Coastal) *67.24541, 15.3360*
Lundhøgda Camping, Lundeveien, 8200 Fauske (Nordland) [tel 75 64 39 66; fax 75 64 92 49; post@ lundhogdacamping.no; www.lundhogdacamping.no] Site on Rv80 fr Fauske dir Bodø, sp. Sm, sl, pt shd; htd wc; chem disp; mv service pnt; shwrs NOK10; EHU (16A) NOK40; lndry; shops 3km; rest 2km; snacks; cooking facs; playgrnd; beach 300m; bike hire; TV rm; 40% statics; poss cr; Eng spkn; quiet; ccard acc; CKE/CCI. "On high open grnd on headland but lower slopes boggy; gd views; helpful, friendly staff." 15 Jun-15 Aug. NOK 150   2009*

⊞ **FJAERLAND** *1B2* (4km N Rural) *61.42758, 6.76211*
Bøyum Camping, 5855 Fjærland (Sogn og Fjordane) [tel 57 69 32 52; fax 57 69 29 57; kfodne@frisurf.no; www.fjaerland.org/boyumcamping] On Rv5 Sogndal to Skei. Shortly after end of toll tunnel on L, well sp. Sm, pt hdstg, unshd; htd wc; chem disp; mv service pnt; shwrs NOK5-10; EHU NOK30; lndry; ltd shop; snacks; cooking facs; playgrnd; wifi; TV rm; 30% statics; phone; poss cr; Eng spkn; adv bkg; quiet; ccard acc; CKE/CCI. "Adj glacier museum, conv for glacier & fjord trips; beautiful location nr fjord (no views); visit Mundal for 2nd hand books; helpful owner; superb, clean site." ◆ NOK 150   2009*

FLAKK see Trondheim *1C1*

FLAM *1B2* (10km NE Rural) *60.90006, 7.20618* **Lunde Camping, 5745 Aurland (Sogn og Fjordane) [tel 57 63 34 12; fax 57 63 31 65; lunde.camping@alb.no; www.lunde-camping.no]** Fr N exit E16 at rndabt immed after S end of 25km tunnel turn for Aurland. R S exit E16 8km fr Flam at rndabt sp Aurland. Site on S side of rd, sp. Steep ent. Med, pt shd; htd wc; chem disp; mv service pnt; shwrs NOK10; EHU (16A) NOK10 (rev pol); lndry; shops 1.4km; cooking facs; dogs; phone; Eng spkn; some rd noise; ccard acc; CKE/CCI. "Much quieter than site in Flåm; clean facs; superb setting with views; gd walking." Easter & 1 May-1 Oct. NOK 250   2011*

FLAM *1B2* (1km WNW Urban) *60.86296, 7.10985* **Flåm Camping, Nedre Brekkevegen 12, 5743 Flåm (Sogn og Fjordane) [tel 57 63 21 21; camping@flaam-camping.no; www.flaam-camping.no]** Fr Lærdal Tunnel cont on E16 thro 2 more tunnels. At end of 2nd tunnel (Fretheim Tunnel) turn L immed to Sentrum. Turn L at x-rds, site on L. Med, hdstg, pt sl, terr, pt shd; htd wc; chem disp; mv service pnt; serviced pitches; baby facs; shwrs NOK10; EHU (10A) inc; lndry (inc dryer); shop; supmkt nrby; rest, snacks & bar 500m; BBQ; cooking facs; playgrnd; bike hire; watersports; boating; fishing; dogs free; no o'fits over 8.5m; phone; poss cr; Eng spkn; quiet but noise fr rd & cruise ships during day; ccard acc; red long stay; CKE/CCI. "Well-kept, friendly, busy, family-run site; excel san facs; conv mountain walks, excel location for Flambana rlwy, Aurlandsvangen 7km - gd shops; gd cycling base; excel." ◆ 1 Mar-31 Oct. NOK 300   2015*

⊞ **FLEKKEFJORD** *1A4* (6km ESE Rural) *58.28868, 6.7173*
Egenes Camping (VA7), 4400 Flekkefjord (Vest-Agder) [tel 38 32 01 48; fax 38 32 01 11; post@egenescamping.no; www.egenes.no] Located N of E39 dir Seland. Med, mkd pitch, pt shd; htd wc; chem disp; mv service pnt; baby facs; shwrs NOK10; EHU (5A) NOK40; lndry; shop; snacks; playgrnd; TV; 75% statics; phone; ccard acc; red CKE/CCI. "Ltd facs LS; overflow car park area with facs for tourers 0.5km; poss cr; lovely situation." ◆ NOK 250   2014*

"I like to fill in the reports as I travel from site to site"

You'll find report forms at the back of this guide, or you can fill them in online at www.caravanclub.co.uk/europereport.

⊞ **FLORO** *1A2* (2km E Coastal) *61.59420, 5.07244*
Pluscamp Krokane (SF15), Strandgt 30, 6900 Florø (Sogn og Fjordane) [tel 57 75 22 50; fax 57 75 22 60; post@ krocamp.no; www.krocamp.no] On Rv5 Forde to Florø, on ent town turn L at rndabt sp Krokane, then immed R & foll rd to coast. Turn L, pass marina to site, sp. Steep ent/exit. Sm, hdstg, pt sl, pt shd; htd wc; chem disp; mv service pnt; baby facs; fam bthrm; shwrs NOK10; EHU (10A) NOK30; lndry; shop 2km; rest, snacks, bar 2km; playgrnd; htd, covrd pool 1km; sand beach adj; boat hire; fishing; internet; 80% statics; phone; bus; Eng spkn; quiet; CKE/CCI. "V sm area for tourers; Florø interesting fishing town with boat trips etc." ◆ NOK 130   2010*

FORDE *1A2* (3km E Rural) *61.44940, 5.89008* **Førde Gjestehus & Camping (SF94), Kronborgvegen 44, Havstad, 6800 Førde (Romsdal Sogn og Fjordane) [tel 46 80 60 00; post@fordecamping.no; www.fordecamping.no]** Site is on NE o'skirts Forde. At rndabt on E39at Havstad foll sp 'Hospital', site on R in 1km; well sp. Med, mkd pitch, some hdstg, pt shd; htd wc; chem disp; mv service pnt; shwrs inc; baby facs; fam bthrm; EHU (16A) inc; lndry; shop; rest; cooking facs; playgrnd; rv sw adj; TV rm; some statics; phone; Eng spkn; adv bkg; quiet; ccard acc; CKE/CCI. "Pleasant, peaceful site." ◆ ltd. 1 Jan-29 Feb & 15 Apr-1 Oct. NOK 304   2013*

FREDRIKSTAD *1C4* (4km SE Coastal) *59.20116, 10.96263*
Fredrikstad Motel & Camping (OF20), Torsnesveien 16, 1630 Fredrikstad (Østfold) [tel 69 32 03 15; fax 69 32 36 66; eivind.enger@hotelcity.no; www. fredrikstadmotel.no] Fr S on Rv110 at rndabt bef lge span bdge (TO at bdge) foll sp Gamlebyen/Torsnes, site on L. Or foll brown sps for old city. Med, hdstg, pt sl, pt shd; htd wc; chem disp; baby facs; fam bthrm; shwrs inc; EHU (10A) NOK50; lndry; shop; cooking facs; playgrnd; pool 100m; beaches adj; bike hire; TV; dogs; adv bkg; quiet but poss noise fr late arr fr ferry; CKE/CCI. "Guided tours to craft indus; sh walk to lovely walled city; v cr water festival (2nd w/end July)." ♦
1 Jun-31 Aug. NOK 200   2011*

FREDRIKSTAD *1C4* (16km SE Coastal) *59.13942, 11.03855*
Bevo Camping, Bevoveien 31, 1634 Gamle Fredrikstad [tel 69 34 92 15; info@bevo.no; www.bevo.no] Avoid app fr Fredrikstad. Fr E6 junc 4, take RV110 (Fredrikstad) then L on RV111 & L on RV107 (Torsnesveien). Foll signs to campsite. Sm, mkd pitch, pt shd; wc; chem disp; shwrs 10kr; EHU; lndry rm; shop; snacks; sw sand beach adj; poss cr; quiet; CCI. "Isolated site on Oslo Fjord; 15 mins to Gamle Frederikstad by car." 28 Apr-8 Sep. NOK 260   2014*

⊞ **GAUPNE** *1B2* (2km S Rural) *61.40056, 7.30076* **Sandvik Camping (SF20), 6868 Gaupne (Sogn og Fjordane) [tel 57 68 11 53; fax 57 68 16 71; sandvik@pluscamp.no; www.pluscamp.no/sandvik]** Site sp N of Rv55 (Sogndal/ Lom) after leaving Gaupne. Med, pt shd; htd wc; chem disp; baby facs; shwrs NOK10; EHU (16A) (poss earth fault); lndry (inc dryer); shop; snacks; rest 500m; bar; playgrnd; games area; TV; quiet; ccard acc. "Vg; ltd facs early ssn & poss stretched if site full; lovely, peaceful site; gd touring base." ♦ ltd.
NOK 150   2009*

⊞ **GEILO** *1B3* (2km NE Urban) *60.54251, 8.23495* **Breie Hytter & Camping, Lauvrudvegen 11, 3580 Geilomoen, Geilo [tel 32 09 04 12 or 97 16 46 01 (mob); fax 32 09 10 44; post@breiehytter.no; www.breiehytter.no]** Fr Geilo take RV7 twds Gol & Sundre. Site sp, take R into Lauvrudvegen. Sm, unshd; wc; chem disp; shwr; EHU inc; shop 1.5km; rest 1.5km; bar 1.5km; 30% statics; quiet; CCI. "Vg for long or sh stays; pleasant, well kept site in residential area; helpful owner." NOK 170   2014*

⊞ **GEILO** *1B3* (2km NE Rural) *60.54422, 8.23637* **Øen Turistsenter & Geilo Vandrerhjem, Lienvegen 139, 3580 Geilo [tel 32 08 70 60; fax 32 08 70 66; post@oenturist.no; www.oenturist.no]** Fr Geilo on Rv.7 twds Gol. Turn L onto Lienvegen & site. Med, hdg/gravel pitch, pt sl, pt shd; wc; sauna; shwrs inc; EHU (10A) 30 NOK; lndry (inc dryer); rest; BBQ; cooking facs; wifi; 30% statics; dogs; Eng spkn; quiet; some rd noise; CKE/CCI. "Vg site". NOK 230   2015*

⊞ **GEILO** *1B3* (600m S Rural) *60.52915, 8.20705* **Geilo Camping, Skurdalsveien 23, 3580 Geilo (Buskerud) [tel 32 09 07 33; fax 32 09 11 56; post@geilocamping.no; www.geilocamping.no]** Fr W on Rv7 at rndabt in town cent turn R (S) onto Rv40 sp Kongsberg, site on R in 300m by rv. Sm, mkd pitch, hdstg, some terr, pt shd; wc; chem disp; shwrs NOK10; EHU (10A) NOK30; lndry (inc dryer); shop; snacks; rv beach adj; fishing; 70% statics; bus 300m; Eng spkn; quiet; ccard acc. "Mountain views; walking & fishing cent; poss muddy after heavy rain; san facs tired." NOK 220   2009*

GEIRANGER *1B1* (350m S Rural) *62.09998, 7.20421* **Camping Geiranger, 6216 Geiranger (Møre og Romsdal) [tel/fax 70 26 31 20; post@geirangercamping.no; www.geirangercamping.no]** Site on fjord edge in vill. On Rv63 Eidsdal-Geiranger take lower rd thro vill to site on R & on both sides of rv. Rv63 not suitable for c'vans - steep hill & hairpins, use ferry fr Hellesylt. Lge, pt sl, unshd; wc; chem disp; mv service pnt; shwrs NOK10; ltd EHU (16A) NOK35; lndry (inc dryer); BBQ; cooking facs; wifi; dogs; poss cr; Eng spkn; quiet but noise of waterfall; ccard acc; no adv bkgs; CKE/ CCI. "Busy site in superb location, gd touring base, gd boat trips on fjord, facs (inc EHU) ltd if site full; gd facs." ♦
10 May-20 Sep. NOK 270   2015*

GEIRANGER *1B1* (2km NNW Rural) *62.11548, 7.18437* **Grande Hytteutleige og Camping, 6216 Geiranger (Møre og Romsdal) [tel 70 26 30 68; office@grande-hytteutleige. no; www.grande-hytteutleige.no]** Head N on Rv63, in 2.3km turn L at the foot of zigzags, then 1st R. Site on the L. Sm, pt sl; htd wc; shwr 15 NOK; EHU (16A); lndry; cooking facs; internet; wifi; Eng spkn; quiet; ccard acc. "Friendly staff; conv for Fjord cruise, vg site." May-Oct. NOK 250   2014*

⊞ **GOL** *1C2* (3km S Rural) *60.70023, 9.00416* **Gol Campingsenter (BU17), Heradveien 7, 3550 Gol (Buskerud) [tel 32 07 41 44; fax 32 07 53 96; gol@pluscamp.no; www.golcamp.no]** Ent on R of Rv7 fr Gol twd Nesbyen. Lge, pt sl, unshd; htd wc; chem disp; mv service pnt; baby facs; fam bthrm; sauna; shwrs inc; EHU (16A) inc; lndry (inc dryer); gas; shop; supmkt 2km; rest, snacks; bar; cooking facs; playgrnd; htd pool; padding pool; rv sw 2km; games area; wifi; TV rm; poss noisy; ccard acc; CKE/CCI. "Excel; lge extn with full facs across main rd - modern & clean." ♦ NOK 245 (4 persons)   2010*

> ## "We must tell The Club about that great site we found"
> Get your site reports in by mid-August and we'll do our best to get your updates into the next edition.

⊞ **GOL** *1C2* (2km SW Rural) *60.69161, 8.91909* **Personbråten Camping, 3550 Gol (Buskerud) [tel 32 07 59 70; leif.personbraten@c2i.net]** Fr Gol to Geilo on Rv7, on L on rvside. Med, pt shd; wc; chem disp (wc); shwrs inc; EHU (10A); lndry; BBQ; cooking facs; playgrnd; fishing; cycling; rv sw 1km; adv bkg; Eng spkn; CKE/CCI. "On rvside; v pleasant; poss noise fr rd & rv; honesty box if office unmanned; excel NH."   2009*

GRANLI see Kongsvinger *1D3*

GRANVIN *1B2* (11km NE Rural) *60.59220, 6.80680* **Camping Espelandsdalen, 5736 Granvin (Hordaland) [tel 56 52 51 67; fax 56 52 59 62; post@espelandsdalencamping.no; www.espelandsdalencamping.no]** Fr Granvin on Rv13, take Rv572 sp Espelandsdalen, narr rd. Sm, pt sl, unshd; htd wc; chem disp; shwrs NOK5; EHU (10A) NOK35; shops 13km; cooking facs; playgrnd; lake sw; some statics; dogs; adv bkg; quiet. "Ideal for Ulvik & Voss area." 1 May-1 Sep. NOK 130   2009*

⊞ **GRIMSBU** *1C2* (N Rural) *62.15546, 10.17198* **Grimsbu Turistsenter, 2582 Grimsbu (Oppland) [tel 62 49 35 29; fax 62 49 35 62; mail@grimsbu.no; www.grimsbu.no]**
On Rv29 11km E of Folldal, well sp. Med, pt sl, pt shd; htd wc; chem disp; mv service pnt; sauna; private san facs avail; shwrs NOK10; EHU (16A) NOK30; lndry (inc dryer); shop, rest, snacks; BBQ; cooking facs; playgrnd; lake sw 1.5km; rv fishing; bike & boat hire; fitness rm; wifi; TV rm; Eng spkn; adv bkg; quiet; ccard acc. "Family-run site; beautiful situation." ◆ NOK 243 (3 persons) (CChq acc)   2014*

⊞ **GRIMSTAD** *1B4* (5km NE Coastal) *58.36888, 8.63722* **Moysand Familiecamping, Moy, 4885 Grimstad (Aust-Agder) [tel 91 19 75 94; mail@moysand-familiecamping. no; www.moysand-familiecamping.no]** Exit A18 junc 78 onto Rv420 E twd Fevik. Foll site sp on rd to Riksveien, site 2km after Riksveien. Lge, mkd pitch, pt shd; htd wc; baby facs; private san facs avail; shwrs; EHU metered; lndry (inc dryer); shop; supmkt 5km; rest; BBQ; cooking facs; playgrnd; fishing; boat hire; TV; some statics; dogs; adv bkg; quiet. ◆ NOK 190   2010*

⊞ **GRONG** *2E3* (2km S Rural) *64.4604, 644604* **Langnes Camping, 7870 Grong (Nord-Trøndelag) [tel 47 68 83 33; langnescamping@hero.no; www.nafcamp.com/langnes-camping]** N on E6 turn off S of bdge over rv on by-pass, site sp. Med, mkd pitch, some hdstg, unshd; htd wc; chem disp; mv service pnt; shwrs NOK10; EHU (10A) NOK35; lndry (inc dryer); snacks; rest 3km; BBQ; cooking facs; playgrnd; rv sw & beach nr; rv fishing; drying rm for skiers; games area; games rm; wifi; TV; some statics; Quick Stop pitches; Eng spkn; adv bkg; quiet. "Helpful staff; pleasant, family-run site; free phone to owner if site clsd; gd facs." ◆ NOK 140   2011*

⊞ **GUDVANGEN** *1B2* (1km SW Rural) *60.87206, 6.82873* **Vang Camping, 5747 Gudvangen (Sogn og Fjordane) [tel/fax 57 63 39 26; post@vang-camping.no; www. vang-camping.no]** At S end of of Nærøy Fjord on E16 at edge of vill. Sm, some hdstg, unshd; wc; chem disp/mv service pnt at Shell g'ge 1km; shwrs NOK5; EHU (16A) NOK30 (poss no earth); lndry; shop 1km; rest 1km at ferry; Eng spkn; quiet but some rd noise; no ccard acc; CKE/CCI. "Immac site in beautiful valley with waterfalls; spectacular scenery; cruises on adj fjord; bus to Flam; poor san facs (2015)." 1 May-15 Sep. NOK 225   2015*

HALSA *2E2* (2.6km W Coastal) *66.73930, 13.51661* **Furøy Camping, Furøy 6, 8178 Halsa (Nordland) [tel 75 75 05 25; fax 75 75 03 36; post@furoycamp.no; www.furoycamp.no]** Foll Rv17 S fr Ornes, at Forøy ferry x-ing strt on, foll rd sp to site. Sm, pt sl; htd wc; chem disp; shwrs NOK10; EHU (16A) NOK25; lndry; kiosk; shop 1km; rest; bar; BBQ; cooking facs; shgl beach adj; fishing; boat hire; some statics; dogs; phone; Eng spkn; adv bkg; quiet. "Lovely position; arr early for prime pitch, site fills up quickly after 1730 high ssn; archaeological site adj; 15km Svartisen glacier; san facs stretched when site full." ◆ 1 May-30 Sep. NOK 175   2009*

HAMALVOLL see Os I Osterdalen *1D1*

HAMMERFEST *2G1* (1km E Urban) *70.65890, 23.71335* **Storvannet Camping, Storvannsveien 103, 9615 Hammerfest (Finnmark) [tel 78 41 10 10; storvannet@ yahoo.no]** Descend into & cont thro town. Turn R immed after x-ing rv bdge. Site at top of Storvannet lake nr mouth of Rv Storelva. Sp. Med, some hdstg; pt sl; unshd; htd wc; chem disp; shwrs NOK10; EHU NOK40; lndry (inc dryer); shop 3km; rest 3km; BBQ; cooking facs; sw adj; fishing; dogs; poss cr; Eng spkn; quiet; 10% red +3 days; CKE/CCI. "Vg; by attractive lake; 2km out of town." ◆ 1 Jun-15 Sep. NOK 230   2014*

HAMRESANDEN see Kristiansand *1B4*

HARRAN *2E3* (300m S Rural) *64.55916, 12.48376* **Harran Camping, 7873 Harran (Nord-Trøndelag) [tel 74 33 29 90; harrancamping@gmail.com]** Site E of E6 N of Grong in cent Harran behind Statoil filling stn. Med, pt shd; wc; chem disp; mv service pnt; baby facs; fam bthrm; shwrs NOK10; EHU (10A) NOK50; gas; lndry (inc dryer); shop & rest 500m; BBQ; playgrnd; fishing; TV; phone; Eng spkn; quiet but some rd noise. "Pleasant site; lovely location." ◆ 1 May-15 Sep. NOK 150   2009*

HAUGE *1A4* (5km NE Rural) *58.36166, 6.30944* **Bakkaåno Camping, Bakkaveien, Fidje 4380 Hauge i Dalane (Rogaland) [tel 51 47 78 52 or 930 50 219 (mob); visit@bakkaanocamping.no; www.bakkaanocamping.no]** Heading E fr Hauge on Rv44, over rv & immed turn L & foll site sp. Site on L, recep on R over golf course at white house. Rd narr. Med, pt shd; wc; chem disp; mv service pnt; shwrs NOK1; EHU (5A) NOK30; shop; cooking facs; sw & fishing adj; 80% statics; Eng spkn; quiet. "Sep area for tourers; friendly, welcoming owners." ◆ ltd. Easter-30 Sep. NOK 220   2013*

HAUKELAND see Bergen *1A3*

⊞ **HEIDAL** *1C2* (11km W Rural) *61.73005, 9.12070* **Jotunheim Feriesenter, N2676 Heidal [tel 61 23 49 50; post@jotunheim enferiesenter.no; www.jotunheimenferiesenter.no]** Fr Rv51 turn E at Randsverk onto rd 267. Site on R in approx 2km. Med, pt sl, pt shd; htd wc; chem disp; baby facs; shwrs NOK10; EHU (12A) NOK45; lndry (inc dryer); shop 8km; snacks; BBQ; cooking facs; playgrnd; games area; internet; TV; dogs; Eng spkn; adv bkg; quiet; ccard acc; CKE/CCI. "Beautiful surroundings & walks; friendly owners; vg site." ◆ NOK 190   2010*

HELLESYLT *1B1* (400m S Coastal) *62.08329, 6.87224* **Hellesylt Camping, 6218 Hellesylt (Møre og Romsdal) [tel 90 20 68 85; fax 70 26 52 10; postmottak@hellesylt turistsenter.no; www.hellesyltturistsenter.no]** Site on edge of fjord, sp fr cent of vill dir Geiranger. Sm, unshd; htd wc; chem disp; mv service pnt; shwrs NOK10; EHU (10A) NOK30; lndry (inc dryer); sm shop; supmkt 100m, rest adj; shgl beach; wifi; 40% statics; dogs; Eng spkn; adv bkg; quiet; no ccard acc; CKE/CCI. "Conv ferry to Geiranger; adj fjord surrounded by mountains - great views; gd rest in local hotel; beautiful church nr." ◆ ltd. 15 Apr-30 Sep. NOK 140   2014*

NORWAY

HJERKINN *1C1* (2km E Rural) *62.22148, 9.57801* **Camping Hjerkinn Fjellstue, 2661 Hjerkinn (Oppland) [tel 61 21 51 00; fax 61 21 51 01; fjellstue@hjerkinn.no; www.hjerkinn.no]** At Hjerkinn on E6 turn E onto Rv29 to Folldal for 1km. Site at hotel on L. Med, terr, unshd; wc; chem disp; sauna; shwrs NOK10; EHU (10A) inc; lndry (inc dryer); shop 1.5km; jacuzzi; rest, snacks; bar; horseriding school adj; wifi; 30% statics; dogs; no adv bkg; quiet; ccard acc. "O'looks magnificent mountains; walks of historical interest on Old King's Rd; excel." ◆ 1 Jun-1 Oct. NOK 200   2009*

HONEFOSS *1C3* (8km NW Rural) *60.19441, 10.15145* **Elvenga Camping, Elvengveien 3, 3518 Hønefoss (Boskerud) [tel 32 14 43 70; fax 32 13 14 27; elvanga-camp@hotmail.com]** Fr Hønefoss head twds Gol on Rv7; site on R in approx 10km. Sm, pt shd; wc; chem disp; baby facs; shwrs NOK10; EHU NOK30; lndry (inc dryer); shop; snacks; bar; playgrnd; TV; Eng spkn; some traff noise; CKE/CCI. ◆ ltd. 1 May-15 Sep. NOK 150   2009*

HONNINGSVAG *2H1* (8km NW Coastal) *71.02625, 25.89091* **Nordkapp Camping, 9751 Honningsvåg (Finnmark) [tel 78 47 33 77; fax 78 47 11 77; post@nordkappcamping. no; www.nordkappcamping.no]** En rte Nordkapp on E69, site clearly sp. Sm, unshd; htd wc; chem disp; shwrs NOK5; EHU (16A) NOK35; lndry; shop & 10km; snacks; dogs NOK10; quiet; ccard acc; red CKE/CCI. "Gd." ◆ 1 May-30 Sep. NOK 180   2009*

HORTEN *1C3* (3km S Rural/Coastal) *59.39776, 10.47582* **Rørestrand Camping, Parkveien 34, 3186 Horten (Vestfold) [tel 33 07 33 40; fax 33 07 47 90]** Fr Horten foll Rv19 for 500m S to rndabt, then foll sp. Sm, sl, unshd; htd wc; chem disp; baby facs; shwrs NOK10; EHU (10A) NOK40; lndry (inc dryer); shop; snacks; playgrnd; games area; 90% statics; dogs; phone; poss cr; Eng spkn; quiet; ccard acc; CKE/CCI. "Conv NH en rte Oslo; facs stretched high ssn." ◆ ltd. 1 May-15 Sep. NOK 205   2010*

HOVAG see Kristiansand *1B4*

IFJORD *2H1* (60m N Rural) *70.46294, 27.10636* **Nilsen Gjestgiveri & Camping, Lebesby, 9740 Ifjord (Finnmark) [tel 78 49 98 17 or 90 88 28 14 (mob); fax 78 49 98 57; halvdanhansen@hotmail.com]** Behind petrol stn at junc of Rv98 and Rv888; recep in café/petrol stn/shop. Sm, hdstg, pt shd; htd wc; sauna; shwrs NOK10; EHU (10A) inc; snacks; wifi; 10% statics. "Remote area; basic site & facs; conv NH." 1 Jun-31 Aug. NOK 150   2009*

INNHAVET *2F2* (8km S Rural) *67.90618, 15.87368* **Tømmerneset Camping, Tømmernes, 8260 Innhavet (Nordland) [tel 75 77 29 55; fax 75 77 29 65; to.ca@online. no]** Sp on L fr E6 nr Rv835 to Steigen. Med, pt sl, pt shd; wc; chem disp; mv service pnt; sauna; shwrs NOK10; EHU (5A) inc; lndry (inc dryer); snacks; cooking facs; playgrnd; solarium; TV; Eng spkn; adv bkg; quiet; CKE/CCI. "Vg; rock carvings adj to site; museum of Vikings & Iron Age; canoes avail on adj lake." 1 Jun-31 Aug. NOK 170   2009*

⊞ **JORPELAND** *1A3* (5km SE Rural) *58.99925, 6.0922* **Preikestolen Camping (RO17), Preikestolvegan 97, 4100 Jørpeland (Horda-Rogaland) [tel 47 48 19 39 50; fax 51 74 80 77; info@preikestolencamping.com; www.preikestolencamping.com]** Fr S exit Rv13 to Preikestolen to R, site sp. Rd narr in places, care needed. Med, mkd pitch, hdstg, unshd; wc; chem disp; mv service pnt; shwrs inc; EHU (16A) NOK40; lndry; shop & 10km; rest, snacks; bar; playgrnd; rv sw adj; games area; dogs; phone; bus to Preikestolen parking; poss cr; adv bkg; Eng spkn; quiet; red long stay; ccard acc; CKE/CCI. "Marvellous views; poss walk to Pulpit Rock but not easy; conv Stavanger by ferry; excel facs; esp shwrs; midge repellent ess." ◆ NOK 392   2014*

⊞ **KARASJOK** *2H1* (1km SW Rural) *69.46888, 25.48908* **Camping Karasjok, Kautokeinoveien, 9730 Karasjok (Finnmark) [tel 78 46 61 35; fax 78 46 66 97; karasjokcamping@runbox.no or booking@karacamp.no]** Sp in town; fr x-rds in town & N of rv bdge take Rv92 W dir Kautokeino, site 900m on L. Sm, pt shd; htd wc; chem disp; mv service pnt 1km; shwrs NOK5; EHU (10A) NOK40; lndry (inc dryer); shops 1km; playgrnd; wifi; Eng spkn; adv bkg; v quiet; ccard acc; CKE/CCI. "Youth hostel & cabins on site; gd, clean site & facs; lge pitches suitable RVs & lge o'fits; sh walk to Sami park & museum." ◆ NOK 211   2014*

⊞ **KAUTOKEINO** *2G1* (2.5km S Rural) *68.99760, 23.03662* **Arctic Motell & Kautokeino Camping, Suomaluodda 16, 9520 Kautokeino (Finnmark) [tel 78 48 54 00; fax 78 48 75 05; samicamp@me.com; www.kauto.no]** Well sp fr Rv93. Sm, pt sl, unshd; htd wc; shwrs NOK10; EHU NOK30; lndry; shop; rest; 20% statics; poss cr; Eng spkn; quiet. "No chem disp; Juhls silver gallery worth visit; gd, friendly site; san facs being improved (2009)." NOK 180   2009*

⊞ **KILBOGHAMN** *2E2* (3km S Coastal) *66.50667, 13.21608* **Hilstad Camping, 8752 Kilboghamn (Nordland) [tel 75 09 71 86; fax 75 09 71 01; post@polarcamp.com or booking@polarcamp.com; www.polarcamp.com]** N on Rv17 sp to L just bef Kilboghamn ferry. Sm, hdstg, terr, unshd; wc; chem disp; shwrs inc; EHU (10A); lndry; shop; rest, snacks; bar; playgrnd; shgl beach adj; fishing; 40% statics; phone; poss cr; Eng spkn; quiet. "Superb location on Arctic Circle; ltd san facs in high ssn; fishing/boat trips arranged." NOK 235   2014*

KINSARVIK *1B3* (10km N Rural) *60.44128, 6.77941* **Ringøy Camping (HO39), 5780 Kinsarvik (Hordaland) [tel 53 66 39 17; fax 53 66 32 05; torleivr@kinsarvik.net; www.ringoy-camping.no]** Site on Rv13 halfway bet Kinsarvik & Brimnes. Do not use 1st access if app fr Brimnes (v tight turn). Sm, sl, pt terr, unshd; wc; chem disp; mv service pnt; shwrs NOK10; EHU (10A) NOK30 (long lead req); BBQ; cooking facs; fishing; boating; dogs; no adv bkg; quiet. "Delightful meadowland site alongside Hardanger Fjord; no recep - site yourself, owner calls bet 1900 & 2100." 1 Jun-15 Sep. NOK 120   2009*

⊞ **KINSARVIK** *1B3* (500m SW Rural/Coastal) *60.37426, 6.71866* **Kinsarvik Camping, RV13, 5780 Kinsarvik (Hordaland) [tel 53 66 32 90; evald@kinsarvikcamping.no; www.kinsarvikcamping.no]** Fr SW edge of vill on rv. At Esso g'ge foll sp uphill fr cent of Kinsarvik. Sm, pt shd; wc; chem disp, mv service pnt at Esso g'ge; baby facs; fam bthrm; shwrs NOK10; EHU (10A) NOK30 (poss no earth); lndry; sm shop 400m; snacks; cooking facs; playgrnd; fishing; TV; 80% statics; bus 400m; quiet; CKE/CCI. "Wonderful views over Hardanger Fjord." NOK 284   2013*

KIRKENES *2H1* (8km SW Rural) *69.69911, 29.95000* **Kirkenes Camping, Maggadalen, Ekveien 19, 9912 Hesseng (Finnmark) [tel 78 99 80 28; fax 78 99 23 03; eiri-ols@ online.no]** Sp W of Hesseng on E6. Sm, hdstg, pt sl, pt shd; htd wc; chem disp; mv service pnt; shwrs NOK10; EHU (10A) inc; lndry (inc dryer); playgrnd; fishing; hiking; TV; some statics; dogs; Eng spkn; CKE/CCI. "Conv for Kirkenes & Russian border; helpful staff; gd site." 1 Jun-1 Sep. NOK 190   2010*

⊞ **KOLVEREID** *2E3* (13km S Coastal) *64.82530, 11.58628* **Kvisterø Kystcamping, 7970 Kolvereid (Nord-Trøndelag) [tel 74 39 67 37; info@kvisteroe.com; www.kvisteroe.com]** Fr Rv17 just N of Foldereid take Rv770 S to Kolvereid. After Kolvereid foll sp ferries (Geisnes/Lund), site sp 1km fr ferries & Hoflesja. Sm, some mkd pitch, some hdstg, unshd; htd wc; chem disp; shwrs inc; EHU (16A) NOK40; lndry; shop 1km; snacks; cooking facs; playgrnd; shgl beach adj; fishing; boat hire; games rm; wifi; 40% statics; dogs; phone; Eng spkn; adv bkg; quiet; ccard acc; CKE/CCI. "Vg site; beautiful views." ♦ ltd. NOK 150   2009*

⊞ **KONGSBERG** *1C3* (7km N Rural) *59.71683, 9.61133* **Pikerfoss Camping, Svendsplassveien 2, 3614 Kongsberg (Buskerud) [tel 32 72 49 78 or 91 19 07 41; mail@pikerfoss. no or erikfred@online.no; www.pikerfoss.no]** Fr E134 in Kongsberg turn N bef x-ring rv & go N bet rv (on L) & rlwy line (on R) on Bærvergrendveien. Site on R just after x-ing rlwy line. Sm, mkd pitch, pt shd; htd wc; chem disp; shwrs inc; EHU (10A) NOK30; lndry; shop, rest, snacks, bar 6km; playgrnd; 75% statics; Eng spkn; quiet; ccard acc. "Modern, clean facs; lge pitches; facs stretched high ssn; excel." NOK 160   2014*

KONGSVINGER *1D3* (10km S Rural) *60.11786, 12.05208* **Sigernessjøen Familiecamping, Strenelsrud Gård, Arko-Vegen, 2210 Granli (Hedmark) [tel 62 82 72 05; fax 62 82 72 04; post@golfcamping.no; www.golfcamping. no]** On N side of Rv2 Kongsvinger to Swedish border, well sp. Med, pt sl, pt shd; htd wc; chem disp; baby facs; shwrs inc; EHU (10A) NOK40; lndry (inc dryer); playgrnd; lake sw adj; golf adj; wifi; 30% statics; Eng spkn; quiet. "Gd." 1 May-30 Sep. NOK 250   2010*

KOPPANG *1D2* (3km W Rural) *61.57163, 11.01745* **Camping Koppang, 2480 Koppang (Hedmark) [tel 62 46 02 34; fax 62 46 12 34; info@koppangcamping.no; www.koppang camping.no]** Fr Rv3, 25km S of Atna, turn onto Rv30; site on L soon after Shell stn & immed bef rv bdge. Med, pt sl, pt shd; wc; chem disp; baby facs; shwrs NOK10; EHU (16A) NOK25; gas; lndry (inc dryer); shop; snacks; rest 100m; cooking facs; playgrnd; fishing; wifi; TV; some statics; dogs; Eng spkn; adv bkg; quiet; no ccard acc. ♦ ltd. 1 May-30 Sep. NOK 175   2010*

KRISTIANSAND *1B4* (12km NE Coastal) *58.19011, 8.08283* **Hamresanden Camping, Hamresandveien 3, 4656 Hamresanden (Vest-Agder) [tel 38 14 42 80; fax 38 14 42 81; info@hamresanden.com; www.hamresanden.com]** Fr E18 foll sp Kjevik airport then Hamresanden & site. Lge, pt shd; htd wc; chem disp; fam bthrm; shwrs NOK15; EHU (10A) inc; lndry; rest, snacks; bar; cooking facs; playgrnd; htd pool; waterslides; sand beach & sw adj; watersports; tennis; boat & bike hire; games area; TV; 10% statics; dogs; bus; poss cr; Eng spkn; noise fr airport; ccard acc. ♦ 1 May-30 Sep. NOK 295   2014*

⊞ **KRISTIANSAND** *1B4* (2.7km E Coastal) *58.14701, 8.0303* **Camping Roligheden, Framnesveien, 4632 Kristiansand (Vest-Agder) [tel 38 09 67 22; fax 38 09 11 17; roligheden@roligheden.no; www.roligheden.no]** Sp fr E18 on N side of town. Lge, pt sl, pt shd; wc; chem disp; mv service pnt; shwrs NOK40; EHU (25A) NOK40; lndry; supmkt 400m; rest adj; playgrnd; sand beach adj; 5% statics; bus; poss cr; Eng spkn; quiet; ccard acc; red CKE/CCI. "Conv for ferry & exploring Kristiansand & district; 40 min walk to town; poss travellers; NH/sh stay only; site v run down; lovely coastal walks." 31 May-1 Sep. NOK 300   2014*

⊞ **KRISTIANSAND** *1B4* (12km E Rural) *58.12187, 8.06568* **Kristiansand Feriesenter, Dvergsnesveien 571, 4639 Kristiansand (Vest-Agder) [tel 38 04 19 80; fax 38 04 19 81; post@kristiansandferiesenter.no; www.dvergsnestangen.no]** Turn S off E18 jnc 91, 6km E of Kristiansand after Varoddbrua onto Rv401, cont for 5.5km foll sps to site. Rd narr last 3km. Lge, mkd pitch, sl, shd; htd wc; chem disp; mv service pnt; baby facs; shwrs NOK12 pre paid; EHU (16A) inc; lndry; shop; snacks; cooking facs; playgrnd; sw in fjord but rocky; fishing; boat hire; TV; phone; poss cr; quiet; ccard acc; CKE/CCI. "Gd NH; conv for ferry (20 mins); beautiful location; helpful, friendly staff." ♦ NOK 417   2014*

⊞ **KRISTIANSAND** *1B4* (23km E Coastal) *58.12551, 8.2310* **Skottevik Feriesenter (AA1), Hæstadsvingen, 4770 Høvåg (Aust-Agder) [tel 37 26 90 30; fax 37 26 90 33; post@skottevik.no; www.skottevik.no]** Fr Kristiansand, take E18 E, turn onto Rv401 twd Høvåg; site sp. Lge, pt shd; wc; chem disp; mv service pnt; private bathrms avail; shwrs NOK10; EHU (10A) NOK45; gas; lndry; shop; snacks & bar high ssn; rest 3km; playgrnd; htd pool; paddling pool; beach; 9-hole golf course; wifi; entmnt; poss cr; Eng spkn; adv bkg; quiet; ccard acc; CKE/CCI. "Beautiful area." ♦ NOK 205   2013*

⊞ **KRISTIANSUND** *1B1* (3km N Rural) *63.12543, 7.74106* **Atlanten Motel & Camping, Dalaveien 22, 6501 Kristiansund (Møre og Romsdal) [tel 71 67 11 04; fax 71 67 24 05; resepsjonen@atlanten.no; www.atlanten.no]** Fr Atlantic Rd (Atlanterhavsveien) & Bremsnes-Kristiansund ferry, foll sp on leaving ferry 5km to site. Med, terr, hdstg, pt shd; htd wc; chem disp; mv service pnt; baby facs; shwrs inc; EHU (6A) NOK40; lndry; shops; BBQ; cooking facs; playgrnd; pool 300m; shgl beach 2km; dogs; phone; Eng spkn; adv bkg; quiet; ccard acc; CKE/CCI. "Conv Kristiansund & fjords; boat trips to Grip Is with Stave Church; site clsd 20-31 Dec." ♦ NOK 170   2014*

KROKELVDALEN see Tromsø *2F1*

NORWAY

KROKSTRANDA *2F2* (300m SE Rural) *66.46233,
15.09344* **Krokstrand Camping, Saltfjellveien 1573,
8630 Krokstranda (Nordland) [tel/fax 75 16 60 74;
toverakvaag@msn.com]** Nr Krokstrand bdge on E6, 18km
S of Artic Circle & approx 50km N of Mo i Rana. Med, pt sl,
pt shd; htd wc; chem disp; mv service pnt; baby facs; shwrs
NOK5-10; EHU (10A) NOK30; lndry (inc dryer); shop; rest;
snacks bar; cooking facs; playgrnd; fishing; 20% statics; phone;
train; Eng spkn; adv bkg; ccard acc; quiet; CKE/CCI. "Conv
Polar Circle Cent; gd." 1 Jun-1 Sep. NOK 280   2014*

KVAM *1C2* (600m E Rural) *61.66663, 9.69380* **Kirketeigen
Camping (OP18), Bygdahusvegen 11, 2642 Kvam (Oppland)
[tel 61 21 60 90; fax 61 21 60 91; post@kirketeigen.no;
www.kirketeigen.no]** On E6, sp fr both dirs. Sm, pt shd;
wc; EHU inc; lndry; kiosk; games area; covr'd pool, tennis
nrby; 80% statics; some rlwy noise. "Conv Peer Gynt rd, war
museum." 15 May-1 Sep. NOK 210   2009*

KVANNDAL see Granvin *1B2*

KVISVIKA *1B1* (8km NE Coastal) *63.10910, 8.07875*
**Magnillen Camping, 6674 Kvisvika (Møre og Romsdal)
[tel 71 53 25 59; jarl-mo@online.no; www.magnillen.no]**
Fr W turn L off E39 approx 5km after Vettafjellet (N); thro
Kvisvika & after another 9km turn L into site; sp. Sm, unshd;
wc; chem disp; mv service pnt; serviced pitches; shwrs NOK10;
EHU (10A) NOK30; gas; lndry; shop 8km; snacks; BBQ;
playgrnd; lake sw & sand beach adj; boat hire; 50% statics; Eng
spkn; adv bkg; quiet; ccard acc; red long stay; CKE/CCI. "Site
adj sm harbour; gd views." ♦ ltd. NOK 130   2009*

LAERDALSOYRI *1B2* (800m NW Rural/Coastal) *61.10056,
7.47031* **Lærdal Ferie & Fritidspark, Grandavegen 5,
6886 Lærdal (Sogn og Fjordane) [tel 57 66 66 95;
fax 57 66 87 81; info@laerdalferiepark.com; www.laerdal
feriepark.com]** Site on N side of Lærdal off Rv5/E16 adj
Sognefjord. Med, unshd; htd wc; chem disp; mv service pnt;
baby facs; fam bthrm; shwrs NOK5; EHU NOK40 (poss no
earth); lndry (inc dryer); shop; supmkt 400m; rest high ssn;
snacks; bar; BBQ; cooking facs; playgrnd; shgl beach adj; boat
& bike hire; tennis; games area; games rm; golf 12km; wifi;
TV rm; dogs; phone; Eng spkn; quiet; ccard acc; red long stay/
CKE/CCI. "Modern, clean, gd value site; excel san & cooking
facs; lovely location adj fjord ferry terminal & nr attractive vill;
gd touring base; friendly, helpful owners - will open on request
outside dates shown; nice site next to Fjord." ♦
27 Mar-25 Oct. NOK 291 (CChq acc)   2014*

LAKSELV *2G1* (1km E Rural) *70.05100, 25.00860* **Solstad
Camping, 9700 Lakselv (Finnmark) [tel 78 46 14 04;
fax 78 46 12 14]** Fr N thro town & cont on E6, at rndabt take
Rv98. Site on R in 500m. Sm, shd; wc; chem disp at Esso g'ge
in town; sauna; shwrs inc; EHU inc; lndry rm; shops 1km;
cooking facs; dogs; phone; Eng spkn; quiet; ccard acc. "Poss
poor/red facs LS; mosquitoes; last site bef Tana Bru; NH only."
30 May-30 Sep. NOK 180   2009*

LANGFJORDBOTN *2G1* (1km S Rural) *70.02781, 22.2817*
**Altafjord Camping, 9545 Langfjordbotn (Finnmark)
[tel/fax 78 43 28 24; post@altafjord-camping.no;
www.altafjord-camping.no]** On E6, 600m S of exit to
Bognelv, site adj to fjord across E6, sp. Dist by rd fr Alta 80km.
Med, hdstg, terr, unshd; htd wc; chem disp; mv service pnt; chem
disp; sauna; shwrs NOK5; EHU (16A); gas; lndry; shops adj;
cooking facs; sand & shgl beach; fjord sw & fishing; bike hire;
TV rm; 50% statics; dogs; phone; poss cr; Eng spkn; no adv
bkg; quiet; ccard acc. "Friendly owner; excel views; boat hire;
mountaineering." 1 Jun-1 Sep.   2009*

⊞ **LARVIK** *1C4* (1km S Urban) *59.04902, 10.03330* **Larvic
Bobilparkering, Tollerudden, Larvik (Vestfold)**
Fr E18 exit at Rv303 twd Larvik. At rndabt take 1st exit onto
Strandpromenaden. Sm, hdstg, unshd; EHU (3A); BBQ;
0% statics; dogs. "Gd; parking lot for m'vans; NH only."
NOK 120   2014*

LARVIK *1C4* (13km S Rural/Coastal) *58.97381, 9.96795*
**Kjærstranda Familiecamping, 3294 Stavern
(Vestfold) [tel 33 19 57 50 or 91 77 12 01 (mob);
fax 33 19 57 50; kjaerstr@online.no; www.kjarstranda.no]**
Fr Larvik W on Rv303 & turn L (S) on Rv301 to Stavern; thro
Stavern for approx 6km; then L to Skarabakken; 2nd site on L.
Lge, unshd; wc; chem disp; mv service pnt; baby facs; shwrs
NOK15; EHU (8A) NOK45; lndry (inc dryer); shop 6km; snacks;
playgrnd; beach adj; TV; 75% statics; dogs; Eng spkn; CKE/CCI.
"Fair sh stay/NH." 1 May-1 Sep. NOK 215   2009*

⊞ **LARVIK** *1C4* (37km SSW Coastal) *59.00872, 9.70290*
**Rognstranda Camping, Rognsveien 146, 3960 Stathelle
(Vestfold) [tel 35 97 39 11 or 92 04 56 61 (mob); post@
rognstrandacamping.no; www.rognstrandacamping.no]**
Fr Larvik head SW on E18 for 34km. Turn L onto Tangvallveien,
R onto Rognsveien. After 1.4km turn L. Take site 2nd L and
1st R. Site on L. Lge, pt sl, unshd; htd wc; mv service pnt; shwr;
EHU (2 pin); lndry (inc dryer); shop; sandy beach adj; twin axles;
poss cr; Eng spkn; adv bkg; CKE/CCI. "Coastal walks; v clean
modern facs; 2 areas for sh stay; site popular with MH for NH;
vg." NOK 320   2014*

LARVIK *1C4* (14km SW Coastal) *58.98061, 9.92904* **Trane
Camping, Hummerbakken, 3294 Stavern (Vestfold)**
Exit E18 onto Rv303 (Larvik); foll Rv302 (sp Helgeroa); in
13km, turn L onto Rv301 (sp Stavern); in 2km, R nr church
(Hummerbakken); site on R in 2km. Sm, unshd; wc; chem disp;
shwrs; EHU (10A); lndry; playgrnd; 30% statics; phone; Eng spkn;
CKE/CCI. "Site yourself if recep clsd." ♦ ltd. Jun-Sep.   2009*

⊞ **LILLEHAMMER** *1C2* (3km S Urban) *61.10275, 10.46278*
**Camping Lillehammer, Dampsagveien 47, 2609
Lillehammer (Oppland) [tel 61 25 33 33; fax 61 25 33 65;
resepsjon@lillehammer-camping.no; www.lillehammer-
camping.no]** Exit E6 at Lillehammer Sentrum. Turn 1st R at
1st rndabt, foll rd around Strandtorget shopping cent, cont
approx 1.5km along lakeside rd. Med, mkd pitch, some hdstg,
unshd; wc; chem disp; mv service pnt; baby facs; shwrs NOK10;
EHU (10A) inc (check earth); gas; lndry lnc dryer); shop 2km;
playgrnd; pool 2km; internet; TV rm; statics; dogs; phone;
poss cr; Eng spkn; adv bkg; quiet; ccard acc; red CKE/CCI.
"Excel san facs, site adj Lake Mjøsa; gd views, conv town &
skiing areas; site adj to c'van cent, spare parts etc; excel." ♦
NOK 240   2009*

LILLESAND *1B4* (1km NE Rural) *58.2560, 8.3896* **Tingsaker Familiecamping, Øvre Tingsaker, 4790 Lillesand (Aust-Agder) [tel 37 27 04 21; fax 37 27 01 47; post@tingsakercamping.no; www.tingsakercamping.no]** E18 take 1st R at Texaco petrol stn past turn for Lillesand. Med, pt sl, unshd; htd wc; chem disp; shwrs NOK10; EHU (10A) NOK35; lndry; shop; snacks; playgrnd; sand beach; boating; bike hire; TV; poss cr; adv bkg; quiet; ccard acc. "Gd situation, friendly owner; rather cramped." ♦ 1 May-31 Aug. NOK 255   2010*

LOEN *1B2* (1km SW Rural) *61.86753, 6.85032* **Lo-Vik Camping, 6878 Loen (Sogn og Fjordane) [tel 57 87 76 19; fax 57 87 78 11; lo-vik@c2i.net; www.lo-vik.no]** On lake side of Rv60. Med, unshd; htd wc; chem disp; shwrs NOK5; EHU (10-16A) NOK35; lndry; shop & 300m; rest adj; snacks; playgrnd; pool in hotel opp; sw adj; TV rm; 50% statics; dogs; poss cr; Eng spkn; adv bkg; some rd noise; red long stay; CKE/CCI. "Beautiful views; field adj to fjord exclusively for tourers." ♦ 20 May-15 Sep. NOK 160   2009*

LOFOTEN ISLANDS Campsites in towns in the Lofoten Islands are listed together at the end of the Norwegian site entry pages.

LOM *1C2* (70m E Rural) *61.83812, 8.56969* **Camping Nordal Turistsenter, 2686 Lom (Oppland) [tel 61 21 93 00; fax 61 21 93 01; booking@nordalturistsenter.no; www.nordalturistsenter.no]** In cent Lom at x-rds R of Rv15. Ent by rndabt bet Esso stn & recep. Site at foot of Sognefjell Pass. Med, pt shd; htd wc; chem disp; mv service pnt; baby facs; fam bthrm; sauna; shwrs inc; EHU (10A) (no earth); lndry; shop adj; rest; snacks adj; bar; cooking facs; playgrnd; TV rm; some statics; dogs; Eng spkn; adv bkg; ccard acc; CKE/CCI. "Split level site; bottom level quiet; top level adj to recep - often noisy due to rd noise & w/end coach parties; gd, modern san facs; mosquitoes troublesome in hot weather; busy tourist area; pleasant site; nice vill." 15 May-30 Sep. NOK 356   2015*

"I need an on-site restaurant"

We do our best to make sure site information is correct, but it is always best to check any must-have facilities are still available or will be open during your visit.

LOM *1C2* (7.5km NW Rural) *61.87050, 8.45096* **Gjeilo Camping, 2690 Skjåk (Oppland) [tel 61 21 30 32; s.gjeilo@ online.no]** Site on R of Rv15 fr Lom, sp. Med, pt sl, pt shd; htd wc; chem disp; shwrs NOK5; EHU (10A) NOK25; lndry (inc dryer); shop 3.5km; snacks; cooking facs; playgrnd; lake sw & sand beach adj; kayak hire; 20% statics; phone; Eng spkn; adv bkg; quiet; CKE/CCI. "Undulating site on lake; gd." 1 Jun-1 Sep. NOK 120   2010*

LOM *1C2* (14km NW Rural) *61.87923, 8.33326* **Storøya Camping, Rv15, 2690 Skjåk (Oppland) [tel 61 21 43 51; post@storoyacamping.com; www.storoyacamping.com]** Site clearly sp N of Rv15. Sm, pt shd; htd wc; shwrs; EHU (10A); some statics; quiet. "Friendly, little site with basic facs; excel san facs (2014)." 15 May-15 Sep. NOK 200   2014*

LOM *1C2* (15km NW Rural) *61.72099, 8.34857* **Bøverdalen Vandrerhjem & Galdesand Camping, 2687 Bøverdalen (Oppland) [tel/fax 61 21 20 64]** On Rv55 S of junc with Rv15. Site sp in vill just bef Co-op shop. Sm, pt shd, unshd; wc; shwrs; chem disp; EHU; lndry; rest; Eng spkn; quiet. "Immac site." Opens May 21. NOK 120   2009*

LUNDE *1C3* (750m W Rural) *59.29844, 9.09041* **Telemark Kanalcamping, Slusevegen 21, 3825 Lunde [tel 91 57 54 21; post@kanalcamping.no; www.kanal camping.no]** Fr Rv 359 foll sp to Lunde slues. Site on L 1km fr centre of Lunde. Med, open plan, hdstg, sl, unshd; wc; chem disp; mv service pnt; fam bthrm; shwr 10 NOK; EHU (16A); BBQ; lake adj; boat hire; wifi; dogs; bus/train 1km; twin axles; Eng spkn; adv bkg; CKE/CCI. "Site on Telemark canal; lovely position; gd cycling/walking; site & san facs being developed, current san facs adequate (2015); vg." ♦ ltd. Mar-Sep. NOK 210   2015*

LUSTER see Skjolden *1B2*

MAJAVATN *2E3* (500m S Rural) *65.16238, 13.3659* **Majavatn Camping, 8683 Majavatn (Nordland) [tel 47 28 94 69; marianne@majavatncamping.no; www.majavatncamping.no]** S on E6 fr Trofors for approx 45km, site on R on lakeside. Sm, pt sl, pt shd; htd wc; fam bthrm; shwrs NOK15; EHU (10A) NOK20; lndry rm; BBQ; cooking facs; lake sw; fishing; boating; Eng spkn; rd & rlwy noise. "Rlwy stn nr; few touring pitches - rec arr early." ♦ ltd. 1 Jun-31 Aug. NOK 100   2009*

MALMEFJORDEN see Molde *1B1*

MALVIK *1D1* (2km E Rural) *63.43243, 10.70778* **Storsand Gård Camping (ST68), 7563 Malvik (Sør-Trøndelag) [tel 73 97 63 60; fax 73 97 73 46; post@storsandcamping.no; www.storsandcamping.no]** On N side of E6 N, site sp. Rec use E6 toll rd fr S, 2nd exit after tunnel. Many lge speed humps on local rd Rv950, care needed. Lge, unshd; wc; chem disp; shwrs NOK10; EHU (16A); lndry; shop; cooking facs; playgrnd; shgl beach; fishing; games area; TV; some statics; phone; poss cr; rlwy noise. ♦ ltd. 15 May-1 Sep. NOK 364   2015*

⊞ **MALVIK** *1D1* (2km W Coastal) *63.44064, 10.63978* **Vikhammer Camping, Vikhammerløkka 4, 7560 Vikhammer [tel 73 97 61 64; vikcampi@online.no; www.vikhammer.no]** E fr Trondheim on E6. Immed bef toll plaza take ramp sp Vikhammer/Ransheim & turn R, then foll sp Vikhammer. After approx 6km at traff lts cont strt on Rv950 to rndabt & take 3rd exit sp motel & site. Fr N exit E6 after airport sp Hell, then Malvik/Hommelvik. Then take Rv950 to site. NB Many lge speed humps on Rv950, care req. Sm, terr, unshd; htd wc; chem disp; mv service pnt; shwrs inc; EHU (16A) NOK30; shop 1km; rest; bar; BBQ; wifi; 75% statics; dogs; phone; bus adj; Eng spkn; adv bkg; rd & rlwy noise; ccard acc; CKE/CCI. "Insuffiicient san facs; site muddy after rain; migrant workers in statics." ♦ NOK 258   2014*

MANDAL *1B4* (3.5km N Rural) *58.04213, 7.49436* **Sandnes Camping, Holumsveien 133, 4516 Mandal (Vest-Agder) [tel 38 26 51 51 or 98 88 73 66; sandnescamping@online.no; www.sandnescamping.com]** On E39 Kristiansand to Stavanger. Turn N onto Rv455, site on R 1.4km. Med, some hdstg, pt shd; htd wc; chem disp; mv service pnt; baby facs; shwrs NOK10; EHU (16A) NOK40 (poss rev pol); lndry; shop, rest, snacks, bar in Mandal; cooking facs; BBQ; sand beach 2.5km; rv sw & beach nr; fishing; boating; 5% statics; dogs; wifi NOK20; phone; Eng spkn; adv bkg; quiet; CKE/CCI. "Excel, well-kept site; friendly, helpful owners; superb scenery; nature trails thro adj pine forest; Mandal pretty town with longest sandy beach in Norway, conv Kristiansand ferry & Lindesnes, Norway's most S point." ♦ 1 May-1 Sep. NOK 260   2014*

MAURANGER see Odda *1A3*

⊞ **MAURVANGEN** *1C2* (100m SW Rural) *61.48838, 8.84176* **Maurvangen Hyttegrend Camping, Besseggen Fjellpark, 2680 Maurvangen VÅGÅ (Oppland) [tel 61 23 89 22; fax 61 23 89 58; post@maurvangen.no; www. maurvangen.no]** At rv bdge turn off Rv51. Foll sp. Med, pt hdstg, pt sl, pt shd; wc; mv service pnt; chem disp; baby facs; fam bthrm; shwrs NOK15; EHU (10A) inc; lndry; shop; rest, snacks; BBQ; cooking facs; playgrnd; lake sw 5km; fishing; cycling; TV; phone; Eng spkn; adv bkg; quiet; CKE/CCI. "White water rafting; gd views; rd 51 poss clsd Nov to mid-May; gd hill-walking cent." ♦ NOK 180   2013*

MELHUS *1C1* (8km NW Coastal) *63.32635, 10.21564* **Øysand Camping (ST38), Øysandan, 7224 Melhus (Sør-Trøndelag) [tel 72 87 24 15 or 92 08 71 74 (mob); fax 72 85 22 81; post@oysandcamping.no; www.oysandcamping.no]** Fr Melhus, N on E6; then L (W) onto E39; site sp. Med, mkd pitch, unshd; wc; chem disp (wc); shwrs NOK15; EHU (10A) NOK50; lndry; shop; rest, snacks; bar; BBQ; cooking facs; playgrnd; lake sw, fishing, boating & beach adj; games area; wifi; statics; dogs; phone; poss cr; Eng spkn; noise fr daytrippers; ccard acc; red long stay; CKE/CCI. "Fair site with gd views; facs stretched if full; next to Fjord; beach open to day trippers; barrier clsd at night." ♦ ltd. 1 May-1 Sep. NOK 240   2014*

MEVIK see Ornes *2E2*

MO I RANA *2F2* (17km SW Rural) *66.23307, 13.89178* **Yttervik Camping, Sørlandsveien 874, 8617 Dalsgrenda (Nordland) [tel 75 16 45 65 or 90 98 73 55 (mob); fax 75 16 92 57; ranjas@online.no; www.yttervikcamping.no]** Sp S of Mo i Rana, on W side of E6, cross sm bdge over rlwy - diff for long o'fits. Sm, mkd pitch, hdstg, unshd; htd wc; chem disp; shwrs NOK5; EHU (16A) NOK40 (no earth); lndry; sm shop; rest; playgrnd; fishing; 50% statics; dogs; poss cr; Eng spkn; adv bkg; quiet; ccard acc; CKE/CCI. "Pleasant location on edge fjord; friendly owners; clean, well-run site." 1 Jun-15 Sep. NOK 180   2010*

MOLDE *1B1* (15km N Coastal) *62.81468, 7.22528* **Bjølstad Camping, 6445 Malmefjorden [tel 71 26 56 56 or 47 23 79 62 (mob); post@bjolstad.no; www.bjolstad.no]** E fr Molde on E39 turn L by airport & foll Rv 64 N. Turn L sp Lindset, site on L in 1km. Sm, pt sl, pt shd; wc; chem disp; mv service pnt; shwrs NOK10; EHU (10A) NOK30; shop 1km; BBQ; cooking facs; playgrnd; shgl beach adj; boat hire; dogs; Eng spkn; quiet. "Vg site on fjord edge; views." 1 Jun-30 Sep. NOK 170   2009*

⊞ **MOLDE** *1B1* (4km E Rural) *62.74258, 7.2333* **Camping Kviltorp, Fannestrandveien 140, 6400 Molde (Møre og Romsdal) [tel 71 21 17 42 or 47 90 14 83 05 (mob); fax 71 21 10 19; kviltorp.camping@online.no; www. kviltorpcamping.no]** On app fr S, Rv64 (toll) turn L onto E39/Rv62, site on L, sp. Nr airport. Med, pt sl, pt shd; htd wc; baby facs; shwrs NOK10; EHU (10A) NOK35; gas; lndry; shop & adj; rest, snacks; playgrnd; pool 3km; fjord sw adj; fishing; boating; solarium; TV; phone; Eng spkn; aircraft & rd noise; ccard acc; CKE/CCI. "Conv Molde; adj Romsdal Fjord (some pitches avail on fjord-side); wonderful mountain views; excel, clean facs; poor security - site open to rd on 1 side; helpful owners; gd site; cycle track into Molde." ♦ NOK 260   2015*

MORGEDAL *1B3* (300m S Rural) *59.47478, 8.42138* **Morgedal Camping, 3848 Morgedal (Telemark) [tel 35 05 41 52; morgedalcamping@kviteseid.online.no; www.morgedalcamping.no]** W of Seljord, adj E134, sp. Med, pt shd; wc; chem disp; shwrs NOK10; EHU (16A) NOK30; lndry (inc dryer); shop 500m; BBQ; cooking facs; lake sw & fishing; boating; 5% statics; dogs; Eng spkn; quiet; CKE/CCI. "Vg site; conv Heddal stave church; on site lgest wooden bowl in world!" 14 May-15 Sep. NOK 150   2009*

⊞ **MOSJOEN** *2E3* (2km E Rural) *65.83453, 13.21971* **Mosjøen Camping & Hotel, Kippermoen, 8657 Mosjøen (Nordland) [tel 75 17 79 00; fax 77 17 79 01; post@ mosjoenhotell.no or mosjoen_camping@hotmail.com; www.mosjoencamping.no]** E6 by-passes town, well sp on W side of E6 by rndabt. Fr S only mkd by flag 500m bef rndabt at start Mosjøen bypass. Med, terr, pt shd; htd wc; chem disp (wc); mv service pnt; shwrs inc; baby facs; EHU (10A) NOK30; lndry; shop 1km; rest, snacks; bar; playgrnd; pool; bowling alley; entmnt; TV; wifi; dogs; phone; poss cr; Eng spkn; adv bkg; rd noise; ccard acc; CKE/CCI. "Clean, v basic san facs; gd site; gd kitchen facs and san facs, friendly staff." ♦ NOK 264   2014*

⊞ **NAMSOS** *2E3* (4km E Rural) *64.47393, 11.57796* **Namsos Camping, 7800 Namsos (Nord-Trøndelag) [tel 74 27 53 44; fax 74 27 53 93; namsos@pluscamp.no; www.pluscamp.no]** Fr Namsen bdge turn E on Rv17. Site on R in 1.5km beside airfield & lake. Sm, hdstg, pt shd; htd wc; chem disp; mv service pnt; fam bthrm; shwrs NOK5; EHU (16A) NOK35; lndry; shop; snacks; playgrnd; boating; TV; 60% statics; phone; no dogs; Eng spkn; quiet; ccard acc; CKE/CCI. "Well-equipped site." ♦ NOK 215   2009*

NARVIK *2F2* (2km NE Rural) *68.4506, 17.45851* **Camping Narvik, Rombaksveien 75, 8517 Narvik (Nordland) [tel 76 94 58 10; fax 76 94 14 20; narvikcamping@narvik camping.com; www.narvikcamping.com]** Sp on E6, site by rd. Med, terr, unshd; wc; chem disp; baby facs; fam bthrm; sauna; shwrs NOK20; EHU (6-10A) inc (no earth); lndry; shop; rest; BBQ; TV; phone; poss cr; Eng spkn; adv bkg; rd/rlwy noise; ccard acc; red CKE/CCI. "Facs 'tired' & stretched high ssn (may need to share electrics) & poss unkempt; no privacy in shwrs; walk/cycle to town, 20 mins; 3-level site, chem disp 3rd level only; poor NH/sh stay only." ♦ 1 Mar-30 Sep. NOK 211   2014*

NES I ADAL *1C3* (12km SE Rural) *60.49379, 10.07103* **Sperillen Camping, Skagnes, 3524 Nes I Ådal (Buskerud) [tel/fax 32 14 32 00; sperillc@start.no; www.sperillen camp.no]** Site sp on E15, 45km N of Hønefoss. Med, mkd pitch, unshd; htd wc; chem disp; fam bthrm; shwrs inc; EHU (10A) NOK40; lndry; shop; cooking facs; playgrnd; lake sw & beach; 90% statics; poss cr; Eng spkn; quiet; CKE. "Lovely lakesite position; friendly owner; gd facs for children; RVs acc; if coming out of ssn, give 7 days' notice & owner will open site." ♦ 1 May-1 Oct. NOK 200   2009*

⊞ **NESBYEN** *1C3* (4km N Rural) *60.59881, 9.07928* **Sutøya Feriepark, Hallingdal, 3540 Nesbyen (Buskerud) [tel 32 07 13 97; fax 32 07 01 11; sutferie@online.no; www.sutoyaferiepark.no]** On E side of Rv7, sp. Lge, mkd pitch, terr, pt shd; wc; chem disp; shwrs NOK10; EHU (10A) NOK35; lndry (inc dryer); sm shop; rest, snacks; playgrnd; rv adj; trout-fishing; skibus; wifi; 40% statics; Eng spkn; quiet; ccard acc; red CKE/CCI. NOK 170 (4 persons)   2009*

⊞ **NESNA** *2E2* (700m N Coastal) *66.20273, 13.02278* **Nesna Feriecamp & Motell, Sjåberget 3, 8700 Nesna (Nordland) [tel 75 05 65 40; fax 75 05 66 97; nesnafer@online.no; www.arctic-circle-coast.no]** Foll rds E12 & Rv17 fr Mo i Rana to Nesna & foll site sp on ent vill. Med, pt sl, unshd; htd wc; chem disp; mv service pnt; shwrs; EHU (10A); lndry (inc dryer; shop high ssn; rest, snacks 200m; cooking facs; playgrnd; pool 300m; beach; waterslide; bike hire; games area; wifi; TV rm; quiet; ccard acc; CKE/CCI. "Lovely scenery; boat trips to islands & viewing puffins; trip to Træna a must." ♦   2010*

NESTTUN see Bergen *1A3*

NORDKAPP *2H1* **See also Skarsvåg.**

⊞ **NORDKAPP** *2H1* (400m S Rural/Coastal) *71.16795, 25.78174* **Nordkapphallen Carpark, 9764 Nordkapp (Finnmark) [tel 78 47 68 60; fax 78 47 68 61; nordkapphallen@rica.no; www.rica.no]** N on E69. Hdstg, pt sl, unshd; wc (0100-1100); own san; rest; bar; shop; 1 Nov-1 Apr private vehicles not permitted - buses in convoy (daily) only. "Max stay 48 hrs; no other o'night or site charges; price inc visit to Nordkapp Cent; no facs; v exposed gravel surface; excel for viewing midnight sun." NOK 235 (per person)   2010*

NORDKJOSBOTN *2G1* (200m S Rural) *69.21623, 19.55530* **Bjørnebo Camping, Sentrumsveien 10, 9040 Nordkjosbotn (Troms) [tel 77 72 81 61]** Fr junc of E6 & E8 (Tromsø) 200m S turn L twd Nordkjosbotn, site 200m on L. Sm, pt shd; htd wc; chem disp; baby facs; shwrs NOK10; EHU (16A) NOK30; lndry; shop adj; snacks; bar; playgrnd; TV; dogs; phone; Eng spkn. "Conv for day trip to Tromsø; friendly owners." ♦ 5 Jun-15 Aug. NOK 200   2014*

NOTODDEN *1C3* (1km W Rural) *59.55850, 9.24878* **Notodden Bobilcamp, Nesøya 11, 3674 Notodden** 1km W of Notodden on the E134. Sm, hdstg, pt shd, wc; chemp disp; mv service pnt; shwrs; bus/tram 1km. "City run stop over; low charge for all facs except electric; no one on site, owner calls in evening." NOK 150   2014*

NOTODDEN *1C3* (4km W Rural) *59.56592, 9.20805* **Notodden Camping, Reshjemveien 46, 3670 Notodden (Telemark) [tel 35 01 33 10; fax 35 01 85 87; notcamp@ notoddencamping.com; www.notoddencamping.com]** On E134 by airfield. Med, unshd; wc; baby facs; shwrs NOK10; EHU (10A) NOK30; lndry; shops adj; snacks; playgrnd; TV; statics; poss cr; Eng spkn; quiet but some airfield noise; red CKE/CCI. "Heddal Stave church 10 mins drive; NH only." ♦ ltd. 1 Jul-1 Sep. NOK 230   2009*

⊞ **ODDA** *1A3* (2km S Rural) *60.0533, 6.5426* **Odda Camping, Jordalsveien 29, 5750 Odda (Hordaland) [tel 41 32 16 10; fax 53 64 12 92; post@oddacamping.no; www.oddacamping.no]** Sp on Rv13; adj sports complex, nr lakeside. Med, pt shd; htd wc; mv service pnt; private san facs avail; shwrs NOK10; EHU (16A) NOK40; lndry (with dryer); shop 1km; rest 1km; BBQ; lake fishing; watersports; bike hire; games area; dogs; Eng spkn; quiet. "Beautiful area; nr Hardanger Fjord; watersports with canoes for hire; owner owns a guesthouse where you can use wifi & organise trips." ♦ NOK 150   2011*

ODDA *1A3* (19km W Rural) *60.11795, 6.27405* **Sundal Camping, Sunndal, 5476 Mauranger (Hordaland) [tel 53 48 41 86; fax 53 48 18 20; sundal.camping@c2i.net; www.sundalcamping.no]** W fr Odda thro Folgefonn Tunnel. Site sp. Or fr ferry at Løfallstrand, take Rv551 approx 22km NE along side of fjord dir Gjerde. Med, pt sl, terr, pt shd; wc; chem disp; mv service pnt; shwrs; EHU (10A) NOK30; lndry; shop; rest, snacks; bar; playgrnd; shgl beach adj; fishing; boat hire; games area; 50% statics; poss cr Jul/Aug; Eng spkn; adv bkg; CKE/CCI. "Beautiful location; fisherman's paradise; walk fr site to Bondhus Glacier & Fureberg Waterfall." ♦ ltd. 1 Apr-31 Oct. NOK 110   2009*

OLDEN *1B2* (10km S Rural) *61.75823, 6.81173* **Camping Oldevatn, Sunde, 6788 Olden (Sogn og Fjordane) [tel/fax 57 87 59 15; post@oldevatn.com; www.oldevatn.com]** Turn S off Rv60 in Olden, sp Briksdal, site on R immed after rd crosses lake. Sm, terr, unshd; htd wc; chem disp; mv service pnt; baby facs; fam bthrm; shwrs NOK10; EHU (16A) NOK30; lndry; rest 11km; snacks; bar 11km; cooking facs; playgrnd; lake sw & boating; bike hire; TV rm; few statics; dogs free; phone; bus 50m; Eng spkn; quiet; red CKE/CCI. "Lovely lakeside setting; 11km fr base of glacier; well-kept, clean site & facs." ♦ 1 May-30 Sep. NOK 200   2010*

OLDEN *1B2* (22km S Rural) *61.66513, 6.81600* **Camping Melkevoll Bretun, Oldedalen, 6792 Briksdalsbre (Sogn og Fjordane) [tel 57 87 38 64; fax 57 87 38 90; post@melkevoll.no; www.melkevoll.no]** Take rte to Briksdal glacier to end of rd. Med, hdg pitch, terr, unshd; htd wc; chem disp; mv service pnt; baby facs; sauna; shwrs NOK10; EHU (25A) NOK30; lndry; shop; snacks; cooking facs; playgrnd; internet; phone; Eng spkn; quiet; ccard acc. "Walks to glacier; excel views glaciers some pitches; excel." 15 Apr-15 Oct. NOK 170   2013*

⊞ **OLDERFJORD** *2G1* (1km N Rural) *70.48121, 25.06321* **Olderfjord Hotel Russenes Camping, 9713 Russenes (Finnmark) [tel 78 46 37 11; fax 78 46 37 91; olderfj@online.no; www.olderfjord.no]** N fr Olderfjord on E69. Site on L. Med, pt sl, pt shd; wc; shwrs NOK10; EHU NOK20; gas; lndry; shop; rest, snacks; cooking facs; playgrnd; beach adj; fishing; boating; TV; bus 500m; Eng spkn; ccard acc; CKE/CCI. "Gd facs but untidy area & poss stretched; space ltd - rec arr early; conv N Cape tunnel." NOK 150   2009*

⊞ **OPPDAL** *1C1* (2.6km NE Rural) *62.60649, 9.73028* **Solly Camping, Gorsetråket, 7340 Oppdal (Sør-Trøndelag) [tel 72 42 44 16; anug@online.no]** Site sp on E6. Sm, pt shd; wc; chem disp 10km; mv service pnt; shwrs inc; EHU (10A) inc; lndry; shop; rest, snacks, bar 2km; BBQ; sm playgrnd; htd pool 2km; games area 1km; internet; TV; dogs; bus nr; train 2km; poss cr; Eng spkn; adv bkg; quiet; CKE/CCI. "Nr Dovrefjell National Park; rv rafting nrby; gd walking & cycle paths; ski area in winter; v pleasant site; gd NH." NOK 150   2013*

⊞ **OPPDAL** *1C1* (4.5km NE Rural) *62.61537, 9.74172* **Camping Imi Stølen, 7340 Oppdal (Sør-Trøndelag) [tel 72 42 13 70; fax 72 42 08 70; post@imi-stolen.no; www.imi-stolen.no]** N of Oppdal on E6, site sp on L. Sm, mkd pitch, terr, unshd; wc; baby facs; fam bthrm; shwrs NOK10; EHU NOK40; lndry rm; shop; snacks; playgrnd; TV; Eng spkn; quiet. ♦ NOK 160   2009*

⊞ **OPPDAL** *1C1* (6.5km S Rural) *62.54779, 9.62911* **Granmo Camping, 7340 Oppdal (Sør-Trøndelag) [tel/fax 72 42 41 47; grancamp@online.no]** On E6 Oppdal to Dombas rd, well sp by Rv Driva. Med, unshd; htd wc; shwrs; EHU (10A); lndry; shop 6km; cooking facs; playgrnd; 15% statics; adv bkg; Eng spkn; quiet; CKE/CCI. "Simple site; pleasant location; friendly staff; gd hillwalking."   2009*

⊞ **OPPDAL** *1C1* (13km SW Rural) *62.49886, 9.58853* **Magalaupe Camping, 7340 Oppdal (Sør-Trøndelag) [tel/fax 72 42 46 84 or 99 25 99 93 (mob); anja.moene@gmail.com; www.magalaupe.no]** On W side of E6 Dombås to Trondheim rd, sp on side of Rv Driva. Med, pt sl, unshd; htd wc; chem disp; mv service pnt; sauna; shwrs NOK10; EHU (10-16A) NOK20; lndry; shop; supmkt 11km; snacks; bar; cooking facs; playgrnd; fishing; bike hire; TV rm; some statics; dogs; Eng spkn; quiet. "Sh walk to waterfalls; musk oxen safaries run by owner; excel; facs satisfactory; quiet site." NOK 158   2015*

⊞ **ORNES** *2E2* (7km NW Rural) *66.91327, 13.62995* **Reipa Camping, N 8146 Reipa [tel 75 75 57 74 or 95 48 19 53; post@reipacamping.com; www.reipacamping.com]** Head NE on Havneveien twd Chr. Tidemanns vei/Rv17, then turn R onto Havneveien/Fv456. Sm; htd wc; chem disp; mv service pnt; shwrs inc; EHU inc (16A); playgrnd; internet; wifi; dogs; Eng spkn; adv bkg; ccard acc; CKE/CCI. "Gd NH on classic Rv17." NOK 230   2014*

⊞ **OS I OSTERDALEN** *1D1* (2km NE Rural) *62.50430, 11.25938* **Røste Hyttetun & Camping, 2550 Os I Østerdalen (Sør-Trøndelag) [tel 62 49 70 55; fax 62 49 70 86; post@rostecamping.no; www.rostecamping.no]** Sp on Rv30. Sm; wc; chem disp; shwrs NOK10; EHU NOK40; lndry (inc dryer); cooking facs; playgrnd; fishing 150m; TV rm; some statics; quiet. NOK 150   2010*

OS I OSTERDALEN *1D1* (10km SW Rural) *62.44696, 11.11960* **Camping Hummelfjell, 2550 Håmålvoll (Hedmark) [tel 62 49 72 58]** Sp on Rv30. Sm, pt shd; wc; chem disp; baby facs; shwrs NOK10; EHU NOK35; lndry; cooking facs; playgrnd; TV rm; quiet. 15 May-15 Sep. NOK 150   2009*

OSEN *2E3* (1km NW Coastal) *64.29993, 10.49976* **Osen Fjordcamping, 7740 Steinsdalen [tel 72 57 79 00 or 41 14 68 02 (mob); booking@osen-fjordcamping.no; www.osen-fjordcamping.no]** Fr Rv17 about halfway bet Namsos & Steinkjer take rd 715 W for approx 40km to sea, site sp. Med, unshd; wc; chem disp; sauna; shwrs NOK10; EHU NOK30; shop, rest in town; playgrnd; beach adj; wifi; 50% statics; dogs; bus adj; Eng spkn; quiet. "Vg." ♦ 1 May-31 Aug. NOK 165   2009*

OSLO *1C3* (5km SE Urban) *59.8984, 10.7734* **Ekeberg Camping, Ekebergveien 65, 1181 Oslo [tel 22 19 85 68; fax 22 67 04 36; mail@ekebergcamping.no; www.ekebergcamping.no]** Fr Göteborg to Oslo on E6 leave 2km bef Oslo; sp Ekeberg, foll sp to site. Fr S on E6 just after passing thro Oslo ent toll take slip rd sp Ekeberg; camp sp about 6km, up 10% hill. V lge, sl, unshd; wc; chem disp; mv service pnt; shwrs NOK10; baby facs; ltd EHU (6-10A) inc (long lead poss req & poss rev pol); gas; lndry (inc dryer); shop; supmkt 1km; rest 200m; snacks; bar; playgrnd; dogs; internet; bus/tram to city - tickets fr site recep; poss cr; Eng spkn; no adv bkg; ccard acc; CKE/CCI. "Insufficient EHU & leads running across rds; area without hook-ups flatter & quieter; use san facs block taps for fresh water; easy access to Oslo cent & places of interest; avoid site during annual children's football tournament end Jul/beg Aug - queues for pitches & facs v stretched; poss itinerant workers on site; recep open 0730-2300; helpful staff." ♦ 1 Jun-1 Sep. NOK 355 (4 persons)   2013*

OSLO *1C3* (10km S Rural/Coastal) *59.83554, 10.77676* **Oslo Fjordcamping, Ljanbruksveien 1, 1250 Oslo [tel 22 75 20 55; fjordcamping@yahoo.no; www.oslofjordcamping.no]** S on E18 to exit for Rv155 & sp Fjordcamping, site in 100m. Sm, pt sl, pt shd; wc; chem disp; mv service pnt; shwrs inc; EHU inc (check earth & long lead poss req); lndry; shop; snacks; BBQ; playgrnd; sand/shgl beach 300m; 20% statics; dogs; phone; bus adj; poss cr; Eng spkn; little rd noise; ccard acc; CKE/CCI. "V easy access by bus to Oslo; gd site but poss run down LS & poss travellers; run down, basic san facs; site muddy in wet; NH only." 1 May-30 Sep. NOK 290 (4 persons)   2009*

OSLO *1C3* (5km W Urban) *59.91802, 10.67554* **Sjølyst Marina Campervan Parking, Drammensveien 160, Sjølyst Båtopplag, 0273 Oslo [tel/fax 22 50 91 93; post@bobilparkering.no; www.bobilparkering.no]** Fr E exit E18 at junc after Bygdøy (museums) junc. At rndabt take last exit, go under E18 & into site. Fr W leave E18 at Sjølyst junc, at bottom of slip rd turn R into site. Sm, hdstg, unshd; own san rec; chem disp; mv service pnt; shwrs NOK10; EHU inc; snacks; BBQ; dogs; bus adj; clsd 2300-0700; Eng spkn; quiet. "Gd, basic site, pt of marina; m'vans only - pay at machine; san facs clsd o'night; 30 min walk city cent." ◆ 1 Jun-15 Sep. NOK 150   2011*

⊞ **OSLO** *1C3* (9km NW Urban) *59.9623, 10.6429* **NAF Camping Bogstad, Ankerveien 117, Røa, 0766 Oslo [tel 22 51 08 00; fax 22 51 08 50; bogstad@naf.no; www.bogstadcamping.no]** Fr N on E16 cont to E18 & turn E twd Oslo. After approx 7km exit & proceed N twds Røa and Bogstad. Site sp adj Oslo golf club. V lge, some mkd pitch, pt sl, pt shd; htd wc; chem disp; mv service pnt; shwrs NOK10 (swipe card fr recep); EHU (10A) NOK50 (long lead poss req); lndry (inc dryer); shop adj; snacks; lake nr; 25% statics; dogs; poss v cr; Eng spkn; adv bkg; bus to Oslo 100m; wifi; ccard acc; CKE/CCI. "Beautiful area with walking trails; avoid area of site with statics & many itinerant workers (behind recep), far end OK with lake views; modern, clean san facs; helpful staff; recep open 24 hrs; conv Oslo cent; bus stop nrby, bus every 10 mins; 30 mins to cent; gd." ◆ NOK 335   2014*

OTTA *1C2* (2km W Rural) *61.77223, 9.50653* **Otta Camping & Motell, Ottadalen 580, 2670 Otta (Oppland) [tel 61 23 03 09; fax 61 23 38 19; post@ottacamping.no; www.ottacamping.no]** Exit E6 twd Vagamo, 2km; turn L over 2 bdges, then R down track by rv. Med, pt shd; htd wc; chem disp; baby facs; shwrs NOK5; EHU (10A) NOK30; lndry; shop; rest 1km; playgrnd; bike hire; sw; TV; dogs; phone; Eng spkn; adv bkg; rd & rv noise; red LS; ccard acc. "Conv for local sightseeing; lovely site; gd facs; gd views of rv." ◆ 1 May-15 Oct. NOK 140   2009*

OVRE EIDFJORD see Eidfjord *1B3*

⊞ **OYSTESE** *1A3* (2.4km SSW Coastal) *60.36828, 6.18969* **Hardanger Feriesenter, Hardangerfjordvegen 341, 5600 Norheimsund [tel 92 05 09 55; booking@hardanger feriesenter.no; www.hardanger-resort.com]** Directly at Rv7 in Kvam, app 2.5km E of Norheimsund on the shores of Hardangerfjord. Sm, pt sl, unshd; wc; mv service pnt; shwrs (5 NOK); EHU (10A); lndry (inc dryer); rest; BBQ; cooking facs; beach; 50% statics; dogs; poss cr high ssn; Eng spkn; quiet; CKE/CCI. "Boat hire & pier on site; vg". NOK 250   2015*

⊞ **PORSGRUNN** *1C4* (5km SE Rural) *59.11183, 9.71208* **Camping Olavsberget, Nystrandveien 64, 3944 Porsgrunn (Vestfold) [tel/fax 35 51 12 05]** Leave E18 at Eidanger onto Rv354 N; foll camp sp for 1km; site on L. Fr Porsgrunn foll Rv36 S; just bef E18 junc turn L; foll sp as above. Med, pt sl, unshd; wc; shwrs; EHU (16A) NOK30 (no earth); lndry (inc dryer); sm shop; supmkt 1km; snacks; sand beach adj with diving boards; 60% statics; poss cr; rd noise; no ccard acc; clsd 2300-0700; wifi; Eng spkn; CKE/CCI. "Well-run site; public access to beach thro site; gd walks in wood; visits to Maritime Brevik & mineral mine, Porsgrunn porcelain factory & shop, Telemark Canal inc boat tour." ◆ NOK 200   2014*

RAMFJORDBOTN see Sakariasjord *2F1*

⊞ **RANDSVERK** *1C2* (800m NE Rural) *61.73016, 9.08155* **Randsverk Camping, Fjellvegen 1972 Randsverk (Oppland) [tel 61 23 87 45; fax 61 23 93 61; randsverk. kiosk@c2i.net; www.randsverk-camping.no]** Heading S on Rv51, 20km fr junc with Rv15, site on L on ent vill of Randsverk. Med, hdstg, sl, terr, unshd; htd wc; chem disp; mv service pnt; shwrs; EHU (10A) inc (long lead poss req); lndry (inc dryer); shop 26km; rest, snacks; BBQ; cooking facs; playgrnd; wifi; twin axles; Eng spkn; poss cr; quiet. "V scenic rds; excel area for walking or driving excursions; excel san facs; vg site in area." NOK 270   2015*

⊞ **RISOR** *1C4* (18km SW Coastal) *58.69083, 9.16333* **Sørlandet Feriecenter, Sandnes, 4950 Risør [tel 37 15 40 80; sorferie@online.no; www.sorlandet-feriesenter.no]** Fr N take E18 to Sørlandsporten then Rv416 to Risør, then Rv411 to Laget. Foll sp Sørlandet. Fr S exit E18 at Tvedestrand & cont to Laget, then foll site sp. Site is 20km by rd fr Risør. Med, mkd pitch, pt shd; htd wc; chem disp; baby facs; private san facs avail; shwrs; EHU inc; lndry (inc dryer); shop; supmkt 1km; rest; bar; cooking facs; playgrnd; sand beach; watersports; boat & bike hire; tennis 1km; fitness rm; games rm; wifi; cab TV; some statics; dogs; adv bkg; Eng spkn; quiet. ◆ NOK 317 (CChq acc)   2014*

⊞ **RISOR** *1C4* (10km W Coastal) *58.72592, 9.07783* **Risør Resort Moen Camping, 4950 Risor [tel 37 15 50 91; fax 37 15 50 92; karen@moen-camping.no; www.moen-camping.no]** Fr E18 S, L onto 416 twds Risor. Site sp on L. Med, unshd; htd wc; baby facs; fam bthrm; shwrs inc; lndry (inc dryer); snacks; BBQ; cooking facs; playgrnd; sand beach; games area; wifi; tv rm; 90% statics; dogs; poss cr; Eng spkn; ccard acc; CCI. "Well cared for, popular site; EHU & water widely spaced; volleyball; boat hire." NOK 400   2014*

⊞ **RODBERG** *1C3* (6.5km SE Rural) *60.23533, 9.0040* **Fjordgløtt Camping, Vrenne, 3630 Rødberg (Buskerud) [tel 32 74 13 35 or 97 15 96 53 (mob); fax 32 74 16 90; info@fjordglott.net; www.fjordglott.net]** Fr Rødberg on Rv40 dir Kongsberg, take R turn sp Vrenne, cross bdge & foll sp past power stn. Med, mkd pitch, terr, pt shd; htd wc; chem disp; 75% serviced pitches; baby facs; sauna; shwrs NOK10; EHU (16A) NOK30; lndry; shop; snacks; playgrnd; lake sw; fishing; 40% statics; phone; Eng spkn; quiet; ccard acc; CKE/CCI. "Lovely views of fjord; excel facs; well kept." ◆ NOK 240   2014*

RODBERG *1C3* (5km W Rural) *60.26106, 8.87418* **Persgård Camping, Nore og Uvdal, 3630 Rødberg (Buskerud) [tel 32 24 32 54]** Site fr Rv40. Sm, unshd; wc; chem disp; shwrs NOK10; EHU NOK30; sand beach & lake sw adj; 20% statics; quiet. "Beautiful setting; basic, clean facs; gd." ◆ ltd. Jul-Sep. NOK 100   2009*

RODBERG *1C3* (10km W Rural) *60.26602, 8.78878* **Uvdal Resort, N-3632 Uvdal (Buskerud) [tel 32 74 31 08; fax 99 22 82 10; aud@uvdalresort.no; www.uvdalresort. no]** Fr Rodberg, take Rv40 W for about 9km. Site on R. Sm; htd wc; chem disp; mv service pnt; shwr 5nok; EHU (16A) 30nok; lndry (inc dryer); snacks; playgrnd; games area; Eng spkn; ccard acc; CKE/CCI. "Family run; level site by rv; fishing & kayaking; vg site." 1 May-30 Sep. NOK 190   2014*

NORWAY

ROGNAN *2F2* (5km S Rural) *67.06150, 15.37120* **Medby Camping, 8250 Rognan (Nordland) [tel 75 69 03 15; fax 75 69 07 09]** S on E6, foll sp Medby. Sm, unshd; htd wc; chem disp; mv service pnt; shwrs inc; EHU NOK20; lndry rm; shop, rest, bar, shop 5km; cooking facs; Eng spkn; quiet. "Lovely, peaceful, CL-type site; gd." 1 Jun-1 Sep. NOK 120   2009*

⊞ **ROLDAL** *1B3* (500m E Rural) *59.83103, 6.82888* **Røldal Hyttegrend & Camping, Kyrkjevegen 49, 5760 Røldal (Hordaland) [tel 53 64 71 33; fax 53 64 39 41; adm@roldal-camping.no; www.roldal-camping.no]** Fr E on E134 turn L on ent vill, site sp. Sm, pt shd; htd wc; chem disp; mv service pnt; baby facs; shwrs NOK10; baby facs; fam bthrm; EHU (10A) NOK30; gas; lndry; shop; snacks; cooking facs; playgrnd; rv sw adj; wifi; TV rm; 20% statics; dogs; phone; Eng spkn; adv bkg; ccard acc; red CKE/CCI. "Gd walking, angling." ◆ ltd. NOK 206   2014*

⊞ **ROLDAL** *1B3* (500m S Rural) *59.83178, 6.82014* **Saltvold Camping, Kirkeveien 34, 5760 Røldal (Hordaland) [tel 53 64 72 45; gulleik@online.no]** Fr W on E134 turn R at 2nd camping sp (immed after 1st camping sp). Site at bottom of hill just bef stave church. Med, pt sl, unshd; wc; chem disp; shwrs NOK5; EHU (10A) NOK40; lndry; shop, rest, snacks 100m; 20% statics; Eng spkn; quiet; red CKE/CCI. "Mountain views." NOK 135 (4 persons)   2009*

⊞ **ROLDAL** *1B3* (1km SW Rural) *59.83012, 6.81061* **Seim Camping, 5760 Røldal (Horda-Rogaland) [tel/fax 53 64 73 71 or 97 53 35 17 (mob) or 90 91 90 63 (mob); seim@seimcamp.no; www.seimcamp.no]** App fr SW on E134, site sp at ent town. Turn R off main rd & R again. Med, pt sl, pt shd; htd wc; chem disp; baby facs; fam bthrm; shwrs NOK5; EHU (20A) NOK40; lndry; shop, rest, snacks, bar 200m; playgrnd; fishing; boating; dogs; Eng spkn; CKE/CCI. "Gd walks; beautiful views; prehistoric burial mounds & museum on site; poss rd noise." ◆ ltd. NOK 193   2014*

⊞ **ROLDAL** *1B3* (100m W Rural) *59.83227, 6.81843* **Skysstasjonen Hytter & Camping, Kyrkjevegen 24, 5760 Røldal (Hordaland) [tel 53 64 73 85; fax 53 64 73 44; roldal@roldalstunet.no; www.skysstasjonen.no]** Fr E on E134 turn L down into vill bef petrol stn. Site ent opp supmkt. Med, some hdstg, pt sl, pt terr, pt shd; htd wc; chem disp; sauna; shwrs NOK10; EHU (10A) NOK35; lndry (inc dryer); shop adj; rest, snacks; cooking facs; internet; TV; 50% statics; dogs; phone; quiet; CKE/CCI. "Vg site in beautiful, sheltered rvside location; wintersports." ◆ NOK 160   2009*

ROROS *1D1* (550m S Urban) *62.57078, 11.38295* **Idrettsparken Hotel & Camping, Øra 25, 7374 Røros (Sør-Trøndelag) [tel 72 41 10 89; fax 72 41 23 77; ihotell@online.no; www.idrettsparken.no]** Heading twd Trondheim on Rv30 to Røros cent, turn L at rndabt into Peter Møllersvei, over rlwy line, L again & foll sp to site. Sm, unshd; htd wc; shwrs NOK10; EHU (16A) NOK35; shops & pool nr; quiet. "Tours of museums & mines; nature reserve & nature park nr; no chem disp - use dump point at fire stn on Rv30; fair NH." ◆ ltd. 1 May-30 Sep. NOK 300   2014*

RORVIK *2E3* (2km NE Coastal) *64.8729, 11.2609* **Nesset Camping, Engan, 7900 Rørvik (Nord-Trøndelag) [tel 74 39 06 60]** Fr cent of Rørvik on Rv770, foll sp to site. Med, hdg pitch, hdstg, pt sl, terr, pt shd; htd wc; chem disp; shwrs NOK10; EHU (10A); sw adj; some statics; Eng spkn; quiet. "Many pitches with fjord view; facs stretched high ssn; beware of speed bumps on app rd." May-Sep. NOK 250   2014*

RUNDE ISLAND *1A1* **Sites on Runde Island are listed together at the end of the Norway site entry pages.**

RYSSTAD *1B4* (550m S Rural) *59.0908, 7.5402* **Sølvgarden Feriesenter, 4748 Rysstad (Aust-Agder) [tel 37 93 61 30; fax 37 93 61 09; post@rysstadferie.no; www.rysstadferie.no]** Site sp on E side of Rv9, S of junc of Rv9 & Rv45. Sm, some hdg/mkd pitch, pt sl, pt shd; htd wc; chem disp; shwrs NOK10; EHU (10A) NOK35; lndry (inc dryer); shop; rest, snacks; bar; cooking facs; BBQ; playgrnd; rv sw adj; fishing; canoeing; bike hire; wifi; TV rm; some statics; dogs; phone; Eng spkn; ccard acc; CKE/CCI. "Pleasant site; beautiful setting; modern san facs." ◆ 1 May-1 Oct. NOK 320   2010*

SAKARIASJORD (RAMFJORDBOTN) *2F1* (1km NE Rural) *69.51665, 19.24845* **Camping Ramfjord, Sørbotn, 9027 Ramfjordbotn (Troms) [tel 77 69 21 30; fax 77 69 22 60; post@ramfjordcamp.no; www.ramfjordcamp.no]** Approx 27km S of Tromsø on E8, clearly sp. Sm, unshd; wc; chem disp; mv service pnt; baby facs; shwrs NOK5; EHU (10A) NOK50; gas; lndry; shop; snacks; cooking facs; playgrnd; shgl beach adj; TV; 75% statics; dogs; phone; poss cr; Eng spkn; adv bkg ess; quiet; ccard acc; red CKE/CCI. "Facs ltd when cr; superb views of fjord; conv Tromsø." ◆ 1 Jun-15 Aug. NOK 170   2009*

SALTSTRAUMEN see Bodø *2F2*

⊞ **SANDANE** *1A2* (2km SW Coastal) *61.76743, 6.19605* **Gloppen Camping, 6823 Sandane (Sogn og Fjordane) [tel 57 86 62 14; fax 57 86 81 05; post@gloppen-camping.no; www.gloppen-camping.no]** Fr town cent on rd E39 take Rv615 sp Rygg & Hyen. Site on R at fjordside. Med, mkd pitch, hdstg, unshd; htd wc; chem disp; mv service pnt; shwrs NOK10; EHU (16A) NOK30; lndry; rest, snacks, bar 2km; BBQ; cooking facs; playgrnd; pool high ssn; beach adj; fishing; boat trips; tennis; golf 3km; TV rm; 70% statics; phone; quiet; ccard acc; CKE/CCI. "Day trips to Briksdal Glacier; gd." ◆ NOK 200   2011*

SETERMOEN *2F2* (21km SW Rural) *68.73231, 18.09285* **Solbakken Camping, Sollidveien, Salangsdalen, 9360 Bardu (Troms) [tel 77 18 41 34]** On W side of E6, foll sp up hill. Sm, pt sl, terr, unshd; htd wc; shwrs NOK10; cooking facs; games area; 70% statics; some Eng spkn; quiet. "Poss bleak, windswept but gd views; warden calls evenings; gd NH." May-Sep.   2009*

Tell us about the sites you visit

⊞ **SJOHOLT** *1B1* (9km NE Rural) *62.52022, 6.91722* **Camping Ørskog Fjellstova, 6249 Ørskog (Møre og Ronsdal) [tel 70 27 03 03; fax 70 27 00 60; post@fjellstova.no; www.fjellstova.no]** Site sp on E39, 50km E of Ålesund & 25km W of Molde. Med, hdstg, unshd; htd wc; chem disp; shwrs inc; EHU (10A) NOK30; rest, snacks; BBQ; 5% statics; bus; Eng spkn; quiet; ccard acc. "Dutch owners; gd site mainly for winter use; gd for fishing, cross country, skiing." NOK 150   2011*

⊞ **SKARNES** *1D3* (10km SW Rural) *60.19910, 11.58054* **Sanngrund Camping, Oslovegen 910, 2100 Skarnes (Hedmark) [tel 62 96 46 60; fax 62 96 46 69; booking@ sanngrund.no; www.sanngrund.no]** Fr Skarnes foll Rv2 S; site sp on L. Sm, mkd pitch, pt shd; htd wc; chem disp; mv service pnt; baby facs; shwrs inc; EHU inc; lndry; shop 10km; rest, snacks; BBQ; cooking facs; playgrnd; rv sw & fishing adj; TV; 50% statics; poss cr; Eng spkn; rd noise; CKE. "Conv NH to/fr Oslo (approx 70km); pleasant rest; fair site." ♦ ltd. NOK 235   2010*

> ## "Satellite navigation makes touring much easier"
>
> Remember most sat navs don't know if you're towing or in a larger vehicle – always use yours alongside maps and site directions.

SKARSVAG *2G1* (1km SW Coastal) *71.1073, 25.81238* **Kirkeporten Camping, 9763 Skarsvåg (Finnmark) [tel 90 96 06 48; fax 78 47 52 47; kipo@kirkeporten.no; www.kirkeporten.no]** Foll E69 fr Honningsvåg for 20km to Skarsvåg junc; site sp at junc & on L after 2km immed bef vill. Sm, hdstg, pt sl, unshd; htd wc; chem disp; mv service pnt; sauna; shwrs inc; EHU (16A) NOK25; lndry (inc dryer); rest, snacks; bar; TV; wifi; poss cr; Eng spkn; adv bkg; quiet; ccard acc; CKE/CCI. "Site on edge sm fishing vill 10km fr N Cape, ringed by mountains; exposed location; claims to be world's most N site; helpful, knowledgeable owner; vg rest; clean facs but stretched if site full; poss reindeer on site; highly rec; arr early; work being done to extend camping area (2014)." ♦ 15 May-15 Sep. NOK 220   2014*

SKIBOTN *2G1* (400m N Coastal) *69.39397, 20.26797* **NAF Camping Skibotn, 9143 Skibotn (Troms) [tel 77 71 52 77]** On W of E6 400m N of town. Sm, pt sl, unshd; wc; chem disp; shwrs NOK10 (10 mins); EHU (10A) NOK25; gas; lndry; cooking facs; fishing; Eng spkn. "NH only, dir access to beach on fjord; poss traffic noise fr E6." 1 Jun-31 Aug. NOK 200   2014*

SKIBOTN *2G1* (1km SE Rural) *69.38166, 20.29528* **Olderelv Camping (TR30), 9048 Skibotn (Troms) [tel 77 71 54 44 or 91 13 17 00 (mob); fax 77 71 51 62; firmapost@olderelv.no; www.olderelv.no]** W of E6 1km N of junc at E8. Lge, mkd pitch, pt sl, pt shd; wc; chem disp; sauna; baby facs; shwrs NOK10; EHU (10A) inc; lndry (inc dryer); shop; snacks; cooking facs; playgrnd; solarium; wifi; 80% statics; dogs free; phone; quiet; ccard acc. "Well-maintained & clean; dryest area of Troms; gd walking." ♦ 15 May-15 Sep. NOK 220   2009*

SKJAK see Lom *1C2*

SKJOLDEN *1B2* (3km E Rural) *61.48453, 7.6505* **Vassbakken Camping, RV 55, 6876 Skjolden (Romsdal SogneFjord) [tel 57 68 61 88 or 57 68 67 00; fax 57 68 61 85; info@vassbakken.com; www.skjolden.com/vassbakken]** Site on Rv55. Sm, pt shd; wc; chem disp; mv service pnt; baby facs; sauna; shwrs NOK10; EHU (10A) NOK30; lndry; sm shop & 3km; rest, snacks; playgrnd; lake sw & fishing adj; wifi; TV; phone; Eng spkn; no adv bkg; ccard acc. "Mountain setting; waterfall ad, gd walking & fishing; ltd facs until June." 1 May-20 Sep. NOK 254   2013*

SKJOLDEN *1B2* (350m E Rural) *61.48977, 7.60709* **Nymoen Leirplass, 6876 Skjolden (Sogn og Fjordane) [tel 57 68 66 03; fax 57 68 67 33; nymoen@skjolden.com; www.skjolden.com/nymoen]** Fr Lom on rd 55 site on R behind petrol stn. Fr Sogndal on exit Skjolden after 2nd bdge site on L. Sm, unshd; wc; chem disp; mv service pnt; shwrs NOK10; EHU (16A) NOK25; gas; lndry (inc dryer); shops adj & 500m; cooking facs; lake sw 500m; fishing; poss cr; adv bkg; quiet; ccard acc. "Beautiful situation on lakeside; fine views; walk to vill & Lustrafjorden." 1 May-1 Oct. NOK 159   2010*

SNASA *2E3* (19km SW Rural) *64.17503, 12.08652* **Strindmo Gård Camping, Strindmo, 7760 Snåsa (Nord-Trøndelag) [tel/fax 74 16 39 12]** Fr Snåsa take Rv763 twds Steinkjer; site is sp on L in approx 15km. Sm, hdstg, pt sl, pt shd; htd wc; chem disp; shwrs NOK10; EHU NOK35; lndry; cooking facs; playgrnd; rv sw adj; boat & bike hire; Eng spkn; adv bkg; some rlwy noise; CKE/CCI. "V friendly, welcoming, family-owned site; immac san facs; site has own hydro-elec generating plant open for inspection; midges!" 1 Apr-1 Oct. NOK 160   2009*

SOGNDALSFJORA *1B2* (15km NE Rural) *61.30738, 7.21500* **Lyngmo Camping (SF16), Lyngmovegen 12, 6869 Hafslo (Sogn of Fjordane) [tel 57 68 43 66; fax 57 68 39 29; lyngmo@lyngmoinfo.com; www.lyngmoinfo.com]** Fr Rv55 Sogndal-Gaupne turn L at sp Galden. Immed turn R at camping sp & foll gravel rd down to site on lakeside. Sm, pt sl, unshd; wc; chem disp; mv service pnt; baby facs; shwrs; EHU; lndry rm; cooking facs; lake sw & fishing; some statics; phone; Eng spkn; quiet; ccard acc; CKE/CCI. "Beautiful location; steep hill to san facs block." 19 Jun-24 Aug.   2014*

⊞ **SOGNDALSFJORA** *1B2* (4.5km SE Coastal) *61.2118, 7.12106* **Camping Kjørnes, 6856 Sogndal (Sogn og Fjordane) [tel 57 67 45 80 or 975 44 156 (mob); fax 57 67 33 26; camping@kjornes.no; www.kjornes.no]** Fr W foll sp in Sogndal for Kaupanger/Lærdal (Rv5) over bdge. Fr E (Rv55) turn L at T-junc with rd 5 over bdge. Site on R; sharp R turn into narr lane (passing places); site ent on R in approx 500m. Med, pt sl, terr, pt shd; wc; chem disp; shwrs NOK10; EHU (10-16A) NOK30 (no earth); lndry; shops; rest, snacks 3.5km; cooking facs; playgrnd; beach adj; boat launching; fishing; wifi; some statics; phone; poss cr; Eng spkn; adv bkg; rd noise; ccard acc; CKE/CCI. "Useful for ferries; stunning location on edge of fjord; superb san facs, the best!; excel site; v highly rec." ♦ ltd. NOK 316   2015*

SOGNDALSFJORA *1B2* (100m S Rural) *61.22490, 7.10218*
**Stedje Camping, Kyrkjevegen 2, 6851 Sogndal
(Sogn og Fjordane) [tel 57 67 10 12; fax 57 67 11 90;
post@scamping.no; www.scamping.no]** W fr Hella to
Sogndal, turn L off Rv55 adj Shell petrol stn, site clearly sp, narr
ent. Med, sl, pt shd; htd wc; chem disp; mv service pnt; baby
facs; shwrs NOK10; EHU (16A) NOK40 (check earth); lndry;
shop; snacks; playgrnd; lake sw & beach 500m; watersports;
solarium; bike hire; wifi; TV; Eng spkn; quiet; CKE/CCI. "1st
gd site after Vangsnes-Hella ferry - in orchard; poss poor facs
early ssn; poss v diff in wet for lge m' vans; conv visit to 12th C
Urnes stave church." ♦ 1 Jun-31 Aug. NOK 140   2014*

SOLA *1A4* (8km SW Coastal) *58.86713, 5.56485* **Ølberg
Camping & Friområde, Ølberg Havneveg 93, Ræg, 4054
Tjelta [tel 51 65 43 75; post@jarenfri.no; www.jarenfri.no]**
Fr Stavanger or Sandnes take rds Rv209 & Rv210 to Sola airport
& then foll sps for campsite along Fv380. Med, pt sl, unshd;
wc; chem disp; mv service pnt; shwrs NOK10; EHU (10A)
NOK45; lndry (inc dryer); snacks; BBQ; cooking facs; playgrnd;
sand beach adj; games area; bike hire; 30% statics; dogs free;
phone; bus 500m; Eng spkn; adv bkg; quiet; CKE/CCI. "Adj
pretty beach & sm harbour; gd walking & cycling; v relaxed,
seaside site; vg, clean & well-run." ♦ ltd. 10 May-31 Aug.
NOK 180   2010*

SPANGEREID *1A4* (8km S Coastal) *57.99593, 7.09003*
**Lindesnes Camping, Lillehavn, 4521 Spangereid
(Vest-Agder) [tel 38 25 88 74 or 91 60 22 76 (mob);
fax 38 25 88 92; gabrielsen@lindesnescamping.no;
www.lindesnescamping.no]** Fr E39 at Vigeland turn S
onto Rv460 sp Lindesnes lighthouse (Fyr). Approx 8km after
vill of Spangereid turn L sp Lillehavn, site sp. Sm, pt sl, pt
shd; htd wc; chem disp; mv service pnt; shwrs NOK10; EHU
(16A) NOK40; lndry; BBQ; cooking facs; dogs; phone; poss cr;
Eng spkn; adv bkg; quiet; ccard acc; CKE/CCI. "Excel, clean,
well-run site; pitches not mkd adv early arr." 1 Apr-30 Sep.
NOK 210   2013*

STABBURSNES see Lakselv *2G1*

STAVANGER *1A3* (3.5km SW Rural) *58.9525, 5.71388*
**Mosvangen Camping, Henrik Ibsens Gate, 4021 Stavanger
(Rogaland) [tel 51 53 29 71; fax 51 87 20 55; info@
mosvangencamping.no; www.mosvangencamping.no]**
Fr Stavanger foll sp E39/Rv510; site well sp. Fr Sandnes on E39
exit Ullandhaug; foll camp sp. Med, some hdstg, sl, pt shd; wc;
chem disp; mv service pnt; shwrs NOK10; EHU (10A) NOK40
(no earth & poss intermittent supply); lndry (inc dryer); kiosk;
shop 500m; rest 1km; cooking facs; playgrnd; lake sw adj; sand
beach 10km; dogs; phone; bus; poss v cr; Eng spkn; quiet but
some rd noise; ccard acc; CKE/CCI. "Excel for wooden city of
Stavanger; easy, pleasant walk to town cent; soft grnd in wet
weather; facs well used but clean but stretched when site full;
helpful manager; excel rustic type of site; bus to cent nr ent."
♦ 1 Apr-1 Oct. NOK 210   2014*

STAVERN see Larvik *1C4*

⊞ **STEINKJER** *2E3* (14km N Rural) *64.10977, 11.57816*
**Føllingstua Camping, Haugåshalla 6, 7732 Steinkjer
(Nord-Trøndelag) [tel 74 14 71 90; fax 74 14 71 88;
post@follingstua.no; www.follingstua.com]** N on E6, site
on R, well sp. Sm, mkd pitch, hdstg, pt shd; htd wc; chem
disp; mv service pnt; shwrs NOK20; EHU (16A) NOK50; lndry;
shop 11km; rest, snacks; bar; BBQ; playgrnd; lake & beach adj;
fishing; boating; TV rm; 60% statics; dogs; bus 200m; poss cr;
adv bkg; quiet. "Excel san facs down 10 steps; some lakeside
pitches." ♦ NOK 190   2010*

STOREN *1C1* (1.5km NE Rural) *63.04465, 10.29078*
**Vårvolden Camping (ST17), Volløyan 3A, 7290 Støren
(Sør-Trøndelag) [tel/fax 72 43 20 24; varvolden.camping@
gauldalen.no]** Leave E6 for Støren & foll site sp. Sm, unshd;
htd wc; chem disp; mv service pnt; baby facs; fam bthrm;
shwrs; EHU (16A); lndry (inc dryer); shop 500m; rest, snacks
1km; cooking facs; playgrnd; 20% statics; dogs; Eng spkn;
CKE/CCI. "Vg." ♦ 15 May-1 Sep. NOK 202   2013*

STOREN *1C1* (2km E Rural) *63.04083, 10.29333* **Camping
Støren, Frøsetøren 1, 7290 Støren (Sør-Trøndelag) [tel/
fax 72 43 14 70; post@storencamping.no; www.gaula.no]**
Located at Støren off E6 on sm app rd dir Røros, nr Rv Gaula.
Low bdge at ent to site 3.3m. Med, mkd pitch, pt shd; htd wc;
chem disp; baby facs; shwrs NOK10; EHU (10-16A) NOK30;
lndry (inc dryer); shop; snacks; playgrnd; TV; mainly statics;
phone. "Gd salmon rv, permit needed." ♦ 1 Jun-31 Aug.
NOK 125   2010*

STORFORSHEI *2F2* (6km N Rural) *66.37946, 14.60366*
**Camping Skogly Overnatting, Saltfjellveien 931, Skogly,
8630 Storforshei (Nordland) [tel 97 66 74 68; post@
skoglyovernatting.com]** N fr Mo i Rana for 30km, site on L of
E6. Sm, hdstg, unshd; htd wc; chem disp (wc); baby facs; shwrs
inc; EHU NOK40; cooking facs; Eng spkn; quiet. "Excel facs;
helpful owner." ♦ ltd. 1 May-20 Sep. NOK 180   2013*

⊞ **STORJORD** *2F2* (1km Rural) *66.81317, 15.40055* **Saltdal
Turistsenter, 8255 Storjord (Nordland) [tel 75 68 24 50;
fax 75 68 24 51; firmapost@saltdal-turistsenter.no;
www.saltdal-turistsenter.no]** Site is 35km S of Rognan
by-pass on E6, 700m N of junc of Rv77, adj filling stn. Med,
mkd pitch, some hdstg, terr, pt shd; htd wc; chem disp; mv
service pnt; shwrs NOK10; EHU (10A) NOK25; lndry; shop, rest,
snacks; BBQ; cooking facs; playgrnd; 99% statics; wifi; phone;
Eng spkn; adv bkg; quiet; CKE/CCI. "M'way-style service
stn & lorry park; tightly packed cabins & statics; 10 pitches
only for tourers; excel rv walks fr site; beautiful area; NH
only; secure barrier; clean facs, could be stretched if full." ♦
NOK 263   2014*

STORSLETT *2G1* (11km NE Coastal) *69.83880, 21.21058*
**Fosselv Camping, Straumfjord, 9151 Storslett (Troms)
[tel 77 76 49 29; fax 77 76 76 09; fosselv.camping@c2i.net;
www.fosselv-camping.no]** Sp fr E6. Sm, pt sl, pt shd; wc;
chem disp; mv service pnt; shwrs; EHU (10A) NOK50; lndry;
cooking facs; playgrnd; shgl beach adj; Eng spkn; rd noise;
CKE. "Lovely fjord setting; poss reindeer on site in evening."
10 May-25 Oct. NOK 150   2009*

STRAUMEN see Fauske *2F2*

STRYN *1B2* (10km E Rural) *61.93347, 6.88640* **Mindresunde Camping (SF43), 6783 Stryn (Sogn og Fjordane) [tel 57 87 75 32 or 41 56 63 16 (mob); fax 57 87 75 40; post@ mindresunde.no; www.mindresunde.no]** 2nd site on Rv15 on N side of rd. Sm, mkd pitch, pt sl, unshd; htd wc; chem disp; mv service pnt; baby facs; fam bthrm; shwrs NOK10; EHU inc (earth prob); lndry; shop; snacks; playgrnd; shgl beach; TV; car wash; Eng spkn; adv bkg; little rd noise; CKE/CCI. "Well-kept, pleasant site; many pitches on lake; friendly staff; site yourself; vg views; excel facs; conv Geiranger, Briksdal glacier & Strynefjellet summer ski cent; gd walking." ♦ 1 Apr-1 Nov. NOK 220   2014*

STRYN *1B2* (12km E Rural) *61.9314, 6.92121* **Strynsvatn Camping, Meland, 6783 Stryn (Sogn og Fjordane) [tel 57 87 75 43; fax 57 87 75 65; camping@strynsvatn.no; www.strynsvatn.no]** On Rv15 Lom to Stryn, on L. Sm, terr, unshd; wc; chem disp; mv service pnt; sauna; shwrs NOK10; EHU (10A) inc (poss earth fault); lndry (inc dryer); shop; snacks; playgrnd; lake adj; TV; 20% statics; Eng spkn; adv bkg; quiet; ccard acc; CKE/CCI. "Superb site; excel facs & v clean, gd views/walking; v friendly owners." ♦ 1 Apr-30 Sep. NOK 210   2010*

TANA *2H1* (5km SE Rural) *70.1663, 28.2279* **Tana Familiecamping, Skiippagurra, 9845 Tana (Finnmark) [tel 78 92 86 30; fax 78 92 86 31; tana@famcamp.net]** On ent Tana fr W, cross bdge on E6, heading E sp Kirkenes; site on L in approx 4km. Sm, pt sl, unshd; htd wc; chem disp; mv service pnt; sauna; shwrs inc; EHU (16A); lndry (inc dryer); rest; BBQ; playgrnd; Eng spkn; ccard acc; quiet. 1 May-1 Oct.   2010*

⊞ **TINN AUSTBYGD** *1B3* (8km S Rural) *59.98903, 8.81665* **Sandviken Camping (TE13), 3650 Tinn Austbygd (Telemark) [tel 35 09 81 73; fax 35 09 41 05; kontakt@ sandviken-camping.no; www.sandviken-camping.no]** Site is off Rv364 on L after passing thro Tinn Austbygd. Med, pt shd; htd wc; chem disp; mv service pnt; fam bthrm; sauna; shwrs NOK10; EHU (10A) NOK35 (check earth); gas; lndry; shop high ssn; BBQ; cooking facs; playgrnd; lake sw; games rm; games area; boat hire; TV rm; some statics; dogs; phone; poss cr; Eng spkn; CKE/CCI. "Superb, peaceful location at head of Lake Tinnsjø; sh walk thro woods to shops & bank; conv for museum at Rjukan heavy water plant." ♦ NOK 205   2009*

TJOTTA *2E3* (8km N Coastal) *65.87313, 12.46579* **Offersøy Camping, 8860 Tjøtta (Nordland) [tel 75 04 64 11; fax 75 04 63 72; post@kystferie.no; www.kystferie.no]** At end of Rv17 take L & cont 8km. Site well sp. Sm, hdstg, pt sl, pt shd; htd wc; shwrs inc; EHU NOK40; lndry; BBQ; cooking facs; playgrnd; beach adj; boat hire & launching; wifi; 80% statics; dogs; poss cr; Eng spkn; quiet. "Conv for ferry; gd." ♦ 15 Jun-15 Aug. NOK 170   2009*

TJOTTA *2E3* (26km N Rural) *65.94692, 12.46255* **Sandnessjøen Camping, Steiro, 8800 Sandnessjøen, Norge [tel 97 56 20 50 or 75 04 54 40; post@ssj.no; www.ssj.no]** Head NW on Rv17 twrds Parkveien. Site is on R. Sm, Pt sl, unshd; htd wc; chem disp; shwrs inc; EHU; lndry (inc dryer); bbq; cooking facs; dogs; Eng spkn; some aircraft noise; ccard acc. "Excel san facs; fjord views; gd hiking & fishing; excel site." ♦ 1 May-31 Aug. NOK 250   2014*

TRETTEN *1C2* (9km N Rural) *61.38504, 10.26019* **Krekke Camping (OP33), Sør Fåvang, 2634 Fåvang (Oppland) [tel 61 28 45 71; fax 61 28 46 71]** On W side of E6 about 1km N of Mageli Camping, on lakeside. Med, pt sl, unshd; wc; chem disp; mv service pnt; baby facs; shwrs; EHU inc; lndry; playgrnd; beach adj; 20% statics; quiet. "Site yourself, warden calls; beautiful views." 1 May-1 Oct.   2009*

TREUNGEN *1B4* (18km N Rural) *59.15560, 8.50611* **Søftestad Camping, Nissedal, 3855 Treungen (Aust-Agder) [tel 41 92 76 20]** N fr Kristiansand on Rv41 to Treungen, then alongside E edge of Nisser Water to Nissedal, site sp. Sm, shd; wc; chem disp; baby facs; shwrs 10nok; EHU (10A) inc; lndry; BBQ; playgrnd; phone; bus adj; Eng spkn; adv bkg; quiet; red long stay; CKE/CCI. "Close to Telemarken heavy water plant; beautiful alt rte N fr Kristiansand - rd suitable for towed c'vans; gorgeous views over lake." ♦ ltd. 1 May-1 Sep. NOK 162   2014*

TROGSTAD *1D3* (6km N Rural) *59.68888, 11.29275* **Olberg Camping, Olberg, 1860 Trøgstad (Østfold) [tel 99 37 45 08; fax 69 82 85 55; froesol@online.no]** Fr Mysen on E18 go N on Rv22 for approx 20km dir Lillestrøm. Site is 2km 2 of Båstad. Sm, hdg pitch, pt shd; htd wc; chem disp; shwrs; baby facs; EHU (10-16A) NOK35; lndry (ind dryer); kiosk; snacks; BBQ; playgrnd; pool; beach 3km; fishing; tennis 200m; ice-skating; TV; phone; Eng spkn; adv bkg; quiet; ccard acc; red long stay/CKE/CCI. "Site on lge, working farm with elk safaris; local bread & crafts; farm museum; conv Oslo (40km); v helpful staff; gd for NH or longer." ♦ 1 May-1 Oct. NOK 200   2014*

⊞ **TROMSO** *2F1* (27km NE Coastal) *69.77765, 19.38273* **Skittenelv Camping, Ullstindveien 736, 9022 Krokelvdalen (Troms) [tel 46 85 80 00; fax 77 69 00 50; post@skittenelv camping.no; www.skittenelvcamping.no]** Fr S end of Tromsø Bdge on E8, foll sps to Kroken & Oldervik. Site on N side of rd Fv53. Med, some hdstg, unshd; htd wc; chem disp; sauna; shwrs NOK10; EHU (10A) NOK50; lndry (inc dryer); shop; snacks; BBQ; playgrnd; htd pool; paddling pool; waterslide; fishing; games rm; wifi; TV; some statics; dogs free; quiet; ccard acc; red CKE/CCI. "Beautiful situation on edge of fjord; arctic sea birds; some facs dated but nice; location o'looking Fjord." ♦ NOK 258   2014*

⊞ **TROMSO** *2F1* (4km E Rural) *69.64735, 19.01505* **Tromsø Camping, 9020 Tromsdalen (Troms) [tel 77 63 80 37; fax 77 63 85 24; post@tromsocamping.no; www.tromso camping.no]** At rndabt on edge of Tromsø take 2nd exit under E8 bdge. Shortly turn R & foll sp. Do not cross narr bdge but turn R then fork L to site. Sm, unshd; wc; chem disp; shwrs inc; mv service pnt; EHU (10-16A) NOK50; lndry (inc dryer); shops 1.5km; snacks; playgrnd; wifi; dogs; poss cr; Eng spkn; some noise fr stadium; CKE. "V busy site; facs poss stretched when cr, esp EHU - improvements in hand; surrounded by fast rv after rain; poss mkt traders on site; rec visit to Arctic church at midnight." NOK 230   2010*

⊞ **TRONDHEIM** *1C1* (2km SW Urban) *63.42556, 10.38137* **Parking Øya Stadium, 7030 Trondheim** N on E6, foll sp for St Olevs Hospital. Parking is beyond hospital at side of Øya Stadium running track. Sm. "Free parking; gets busy; MV's only; no facs; o'night parking allowed; 10 min easy walk to cent of Trondheim; excel."   2014*

TRONDHEIM *1C1* (14km W Rural) *63.45004, 10.20230*
Flakk Camping (ST19), 7070 Flakk (Sør-Trøndelag)
[tel 72 84 39 00; contact@flakk-camping.no; www.flakk-camping.no] Fr N on E6 to Trondheim cent, then foll sp Fosen onto Rv715 W; site sp & adj Flakk ferry terminal; fr S to Trondheim take Rv707 to site & ferry. Med, pt sl, unshd; wc; chem disp; mv service pnt; baby facs; shwrs inc; EHU (10A) NOK40 (check earth); lndry; shop 5km; supmkt 8km; dogs; bus to city; poss cr; Eng spkn; adv bkg; ccard acc; CKE/CCI. "V well-kept site; clean facs; pleasant view over fjord; parts poss muddy after rain; site by ferry terminal (Need to be on R), some ferry noise at night; helpful owner; no earth on elec." ♦ 1 May-1 Sep. NOK 338   2014*

⊞ **TRYSIL** *1D2* (2km N Rural) *61.30400, 12.27459*
Camping Klara, Storvegen, 2420 Trysil (Hedmark)
[tel 62 45 13 63; fax 62 45 47 98; klaracamping@trysil.com; www.klaracamping.no] By Rv26 by Rv Trysilelva, 6km N of Nybergsund, opp hotel. Med, pt sl, pt shd; wc; chem disp; shwrs NOK10; EHU NOK30; lndry (inc dryer); shop; snacks; bar; cooking facs; playgrnd; fishing; boating; quiet; CKE/CCI. NOK 170   2010*

ULSVAG *2F2* (100m N Rural) *68.11583, 15.86611* **Ulsvåg Camping, 8276 Ulsvåg (Nordland) [tel 75 77 15 73; fax 75 77 12 81; post@gjestgiveriet.net; www.ulvsvag-gjestgiveri.no]** At junc of rd E6 & Rv81 to Skutvik at Hotel Gjestgiveri on N side of junc. Med, hdstg, pt shd; wc; chem disp; mv service pnt; serviced pitches; shwrs NOK5; EHU (10A) inc; lndry; shop adj; rest, snacks; bar; shgl beach & lake sw adj; wifi; dogs; poss cr; Eng spkn; adv bkg; quiet; ccard acc; CKE/CCI. "Conv ferries Lofoten Is; beautiful setting & views; gd walking area; useful NH." ♦ ltd. NOK 200   2010*

ULSVAG *2F2* (3km NE Coastal) *68.13273, 15.89699*
Sorkil Fjordcamping, Sorkil 8276 [tel 75 77 16 60 or 41 66 08 42 (mob); kontakt@sorkil.no; www.sorkil.no] Head NE fr Ulsvag on E6, turn R in abt 2.7km onto site. Sm, mkd pitch, pt sl, unshd; htd wc; chem disp; shwr; wc x1; EHU (16A) NOK40; lndry NOK30; lndry rm; BBQ; beach adj; wifi; eng spkn; quiet. "Lovely site S of ferry; adj Fjord excel for midnight sun and fishing." 1 May-30 Sep.   2014*

ULVIK *1B2* (1km SW Rural) *60.56485, 6.90741* **Ulvik Fjordcamping, Sponheim, 5730 Ulvik (Hordaland) [tel 91 17 96 70; post@ulvikcamping.no]** Fr ferry at Bruravik take rd to Ulvik. Site on R in 9km. Fr Granvin, site visible on descending to Ulvik. Sm, pt sl, pt shd; wc; chem disp; shwrs NOK10; EHU (10A) inc; gas; lndry; shops 500m; hotel rest adj; snacks; playgrnd; shgl beach; some statics; Eng spkn; adv bkg; quiet; CKE/CCI. "On fjord edge; spectacular scenery; picturesque vill; Osa waterfall 10km, Solsævatnet Lake 10km; immac facs; gd walking; recep in hotel opp." 1 May-31 Aug. NOK 185   2009*

UTVIKA *1C3* (500m N Rural) *60.02972, 10.26316* **Utvika Camping (BU14), Utstranda 263, 3531 Utvika (Buskerud) [tel/fax 32 16 06 70; post@utvika.no; www.utvika.no]** Site on loop rd fr E16 N of Nes twd Hønefoss. Site sp but sp opp site ent v sm. Med, pt sl, pt shd; wc; chem disp; baby facs; shwrs NOK10; EHU (10A) NOK30; lndry; playgrnd; lake sw adj; cab TV; 50% statics; Eng spkn; quiet. "Conv Oslo (40km) & better than Oslo city sites; busy, friendly site." ♦ 1 May-1 Oct. NOK 225   2009*

VADSO *2H1* (18km W Rural) *70.11935, 29.33155* **Vestre Jakobselv Camping, Lilledalsveien 6, 9801 Vestre Jakobselv (Finnmark) [tel 78 95 60 64; s.jankila@imf.no; www.vj-camping.no]** E fr Tana for approx 50km on E6/ E75 dir Vadsø, site sp, 1km N of Vestre Jakobselv. Sm, hdstg, pt shd; wc; chem disp; mv service pnt; shwrs inc; EHU (10A) NOK40; lndry; shop 1km; rest, snacks; cooking facs; 10% statics; dogs; bus 1km; Eng spkn; quiet; ccard acc; red CKE/CCI. "Conv Vadsø & Vardø - interesting towns." ♦ ltd. 15 May-15 Aug. NOK 150   2009*

VAGAMO *1C2* (1km S Rural) *61.86950, 9.10291* **Smedsmo Camping, Vågåvegen 80, 2680 Vågåmo (Oppland) [tel 61 23 74 50; fax 61 23 74 14; smedsmo@online.no]** Behind petrol stn on Rv15 twd Lom. Med, pt shd; wc; chem disp; mv service pnt; baby facs; fam bthrm; shwrs NOK10; EHU (10A) NOK40; lndry; shop; snacks at g'ge; playgrnd; TV; some statics; dogs; Eng spkn; ccard acc; CKE/CCI. "Gd touring base; pay at petrol stn." ♦ 1 May-30 Sep. NOK 190   2009*

VALLE *1B3* (12km N Rural) *59.2441, 7.4753* **Flateland Camping & Hyttesenter, 4747 Valle (Aust-Agder) [tel 95 00 55 00; flateland.camping@broadpark.no; www.flatelandcamping.no]** On W side of Rv9 to Bykle, 1km N of junc with Rv45 Dalen. Med, pt sl, pt shd; htd wc; chem disp; mv service pnt; shwrs NOK10; EHU (10A) NOK30; lndry (inc dryer); shop 600m; BBQ; cooking facs; playgrnd; rv adj; boat hire; wifi; 20% cabins; dogs; Eng spkn; quiet; ccard acc; CKE/CCI. "Pleasant; site yourself; fee collected pm; water trampolin; rvside walks; climbing; excel site." 1 Jun-1 Sep. NOK 160   2014*

VALLE *1B3* (16km N Rural) *59.27153, 7.46030* **Sanden Såre Bobilpark, 4747 Valle (Aust-Agder) [tel 37 93 68 49; td.lunden@online.no; www.setesdal.com]** On Rv9, sp. Sm, mkd pitch, hdstg, pt sl, shd; htd wc; chem disp; mv service pnt; serviced pitches; shwrs inc; EHU inc; lndry rm; rv adj; TV; quiet. "M'vans & c'vans, but poss diff lge o'fits; honesty box for payment; lovely setting." NOK 150   2009*

⊞ **VANGSNES** *1B2* (N Rural/Coastal) *61.17483, 6.63729* **Solvang Camping & Motel, 6894 Vangsnes (Sogn og Fjordane) [tel 57 69 66 20; fax 57 69 67 55; post@solvang camping.com; www.solvangcamping.com]** Site at end of peninsula, on S side of Sognefjord on Rv13, immed overlkg ferry terminal. Sm, sl, pt shd; wc; fam bthrm; baby facs; shwrs inc; EHU NOK30; lndry; shops adj & 300m; rest, snacks; bar; playgrnd; pool; lake sw; fishing; boating; TV; some noise fr ferries. "Wonderful views; useful sh stay/NH for x-ing Sognefjord; delightful." NOK 185   2010*

VANGSNES *1B2* (3km S Rural) *61.14515, 6.62330* **Tveit Camping (SF32), 6894 Vangsnes (Sogn og Fjordane) [tel 57 69 66 00; fax 57 69 66 70; tveitca@online.no; www.tveitcamping.no]** On Rv13; sp. Sm, terr, pt shd; htd wc; chem disp; mv service pnt; baby facs; shwrs NOK10; EHU (10A) NOK25; lndry (inc dryer); kiosk; shop, rest, snacks 3.5km; playgrnd; boating; boat & bike hire; internet; TV; 30% statics; dogs; phone; quiet; red long stay/CKE/CCI. "Sw poss off rocky shore; views of Sognefjord." ♦ 1 May-1 Oct. NOK 160   2010*

NORWAY

⊞ **VASSENDEN** *1A2* (2km SW Rural) *61.48785, 6.08366* **PlusCamp Jølstraholmen, 6847 Vassenden (Sogn og Fjordane) [tel 57 72 89 07; fax 57 72 75 05; jostraholmen@ pluscamp.no; www.jolstraholmen.no]** On R of E39, site is 2km SW of Vassenden at Statoil petrol stn. Med, hdg pitch, terr, pt sl, pt shd; htd wc; mv service pnt; chem disp; baby facs; shwrs NOK6; EHU (10-16A) NOK40; lndry (inc dryer); shop; rest, snacks; BBQ; playgrnd; paddling pool; rv & lake sw & fishing; ski lift 500m; cab TV; 70% statics; dogs; Eng spkn; no adv bkg; quiet; ccard acc; red CKE/CCI. "Rv flows thro site; gd facs; friendly site; ltd facs for tourers; NH." ♦ NOK 180   2010*

⊞ **VEGA** *2E3* (6km S Rural) *65.64353, 11.95110* **Vega Camping, 8980 Vega [tel 47 94 35 00 80; post@vegacamping.no; www.vegacamping.no]** Fr Fv90 head NW, take 1st L onto Fv90, turn L twd Fv84, turn R onto Fv84. After 1.6km turn L, then take 2nd L. Site in 450m. Sm, unshd; htd wc; chem disp; shwrs 20NOK; EHU (16A) inc; cooking facs; sw lake; 0% statics; dogs; Eng spkn; quiet; cash only. "Island ideal for cycling/walking; Elder Duck cent; beautiful location; excel site." NOK 230   2014*

VESTERALEN ISLANDS Campsites in towns in the Vesteralen Islands are listed together at the end of the Norwegian site entry pages.

VIKEDAL *1A3* (1km S Coastal) *59.49320, 5.90702* **Camping Søndenaastranden, Søndenå, 5583 Vikedal (Rogaland) [tel 52 76 03 29; fax 53 76 62 63; gunnar@halvorsen-regnskap.no]** Sp on Rv46. Lge, mkd pitch, unshd; wc; chem disp; shwrs NOK10; EHU (6A); lndry (inc dryer); shop adj; snacks; bar; cooking facs; playgrnd; shgl beach adj; fishing; boat launching facs; 60% statics; Eng spkn; no ccard acc; CKE/CCI. 1 Apr-1 Oct.   2010*

"There aren't many sites open at this time of year"

If you're travelling outside peak season remember to call ahead to check site opening dates – even if the entry says 'open all year'.

VIKERSUND *1C3* (4km NE Rural) *59.97766, 10.02036* **Natvedt Gård & Camping, Øst-Modumveien, 3370 Vikersund (Buskerud) [tel 32 78 73 55; natvedt@frisurf.no]** On Rv35 Hokksund-Hønefoss; in Vikersund R onto Rv284 sp Sylling to site 3km after lake bdge. Clearly sp on L. Med, pt sl, pt shd; chem disp; mv service pnt; shwrs; EHU (4A) NOK35; lndry (inc dryer); sm shop on site & 3km; rest 4km; playgrnd; lake sw; phone; poss cr; quiet. "Hilly - not suitable for handicapped." 1 May-15 Sep. NOK 170   2010*

VIKHAMMER see Malvik *1D1*

VIKOYRI *1B2* (180m N Rural) *61.08884, 6.57721* **Vik Camping, 6891 Vikøyri (Sogn og Fjordane) [tel 57 69 51 25; grolilje@ hotmail.com]** Sp in cent of Vikøyri dir Ligtvor; 67km N of Voss on Rv13. Sm, unshd; htd wc; chem disp; shwrs; EHU (10A) (no earth); lndry; shop 200m; dogs; quiet; Eng spkn; CKE/CCI. "Conv for ferry fr Vangsnes, easier access than other sites; gd NH." ♦ 10 May-30 Sep.   2009*

VIKSDALEN *1A2* (12km SE Rural) *61.32628, 6.26926* **Hov Camping, Eldalsdalen, 6978 Viksdalen (Sogn og Fjordane) [tel 57 71 79 37 or 911 88 466 (mob); fax 57 71 79 55; ottarhov@c2i.net; www.viksdalen.no/hov-hyttegrend]** Fr Dragsvik N on Rv13, site is approx 9km S of junc with Rv610, sp. Sm, hdstg, unshd; htd wc; baby facs; shwrs NOK10; EHU (8-10A)inc; lndry (inc dryer); shop; playgrnd; fishing; bike hire; Eng spkn; quiet; ccard acc; CKE/CCI. "Attractive site with boating on lake; wcs by parking area; all other facs 150m; remote area." ♦ 1 Apr-30 Sep. NOK 180   2013*

VOSS *1A2* (300m S Rural) *60.62476, 6.42235* **Voss Camping, Prestegardsmoen 40, 5700 Voss (Hordaland) [tel/fax 56 51 15 97 or 90 18 11 20; post@vosscamping.no; www.vosscamping.no]** Exit town on E16 & camping sp; by lake nr cent of Voss; app fr W on E16, site visible by lake on R; 2nd turn on R in town to site in 300m. Sm, mkd pitch, hdstg, terr, pt shd; htd wc; shwrs NOK10; EHU (10A) NOK45; lndry; shop 500m; snacks; playgrnd; htd pool; watersports; beach/lake adj; boat & bike hire; few statics; phone; poss v cr; Eng spkn; no adv bkg; ccard acc; CKE/CCI. "Excel cent for fjords; cable car stn in walking dist; tourist bureau; most pitches hdstg gravel but narr/sm." 1 Jan-1 Oct. NOK 225   2014*

LOFOTEN ISLANDS

FREDVANG see Ramberg *2E2*

KABELVAG see Svolvær *2F2*

KLEPPSTAD see Svolvær *2F2*

⊞ **LAUKVIK** *2F2* (300m N Coastal) *68.38991, 14.42216* **Skippergaarden Camping, 8315 Laukvik [tel/fax 97 10 66 36; laukvikcamping@gmail.com; www.skippergaarden.no]** Approx 26km N of Svolvær in Laukvik; sp fr E10. Sm, some hdstg, pt shd; wc; chem disp; mv service pnt; shwrs NOK20; EHU (16A) NOK25; lndry; shop, rest 200m; playgrnd; few statics; poss cr; Eng spkn; quiet. "Sh walk to view point for midnight sun; pleasant site with 'local' atmosphere; site in need of attention (2014) but is adequate." NOK 200   2014*

RAMBERG *2E2* (7km W Rural) *68.0975, 13.1619* **Strand & Skærgårdscamping, 8387 Fredvang [tel 76 09 42 33 or 76 09 41 12; fax 76 09 41 12; mail@fredvangcamping.no; www.fredvangcamp.no]** Foll Fredvang sp fr E10; site sp in vill cent. Sm, unshd; htd wc; mv service pnt; shwrs NOK10; EHU (16A) NOK25; lndry; kiosk; cooking facs; sand beach adj; boat hire & launching; sat TV; Eng spkn; quiet; CKE/CCI. "View of midnight sun; surrounded by sand beach, sea & mountains; peaceful; gd san facs; friendly." 20 May-31 Aug. NOK 200   2014*

SORVAGEN *2E2* (3km N Coastal) *67.90017, 13.04656* **Moskenes Camping, 8392 Sørvågen [tel 99 48 94 05]** Fr ferry turn L, then immed R opp terminal exit, site up sh unmade rd, sp. Med, hdstg, terr, unshd; htd wc; chem disp; mv service pnt; EHU (10A) NOK10; lndry; shop 2km; snacks 1km; no statics; Eng spkn; quiet. "Excel NH." May-Sep. NOK 180   2009*

STAMSUND *2F2* (15km N Rural/Coastal) *68.20429, 13.88580*
Brustranda Sjøcamping, Rolfsfjord, 8356 Leknes
[tel 76 08 71 00; fax 76 08 71 44; post@brustranda.no;
www.brustranda.no] Take E10 W fr Svolvaer ferry for approx
19km. After 3rd bdge turn L onto Rv815. Site on L in 22km
at petrol stn. Sm, pt shd; wc; chem disp; shwrs NOK10; EHU
(10A) NOK40 (poss rev pol); lndry; shop 16km; snacks; shgl
beach adj; sand beach 2km; fishing; boat hire; 30% statics;
dogs; Eng spkn; quiet. "Idyllic setting; mountain views; v
helpful staff; san facs stretched when site full; highly rec."
1 Jun-31 Aug. NOK 160   2009*

SVOLVAER *2F2* (15km W Coastal) *68.20573, 14.42576*
Sandvika Fjord & Sjøhuscamping (N09), Ørsvågveien 45,
8310 Kabelvåg [tel 76 07 81 45; fax 76 07 87 09;
post@sandvika-camping.no; www.sandvika-camping.no]
Sp on S of E10; app lane thro 1 other site. Lge, mkd pitch, terr,
unshd; wc; chem disp; mv service pnt; fam bthrm; sauna; shwrs
NOK10; EHU (16A) NOK35 (poss rev pol); lndry (inc dryer); shop,
rest high ssn; snacks; playgrnd; pool; boating; fishing; bike hire;
wifi; TV; phone; bus nr; currency exchange; poss cr; Eng spkn;
quiet; ccard acc. "Ideal for trip thro Lofoten Islands; conv Svolvær
main fishing port; vg; beautiful views; helpful staff; san facs
stretched in high ssn." ♦ 15 Apr-30 Sep. NOK 258   2014*

SVOLVAER *2F2* (19km W Coastal) *68.22356, 14.21471*
Lofoten Bobilcamp, Lyngvær, 8333 Kleppstad
[tel 76 07 87 80 or 76 07 87 81; fax 76 07 82 10; post@
lofoten-bobilcamping.no; www.lofoten-bobilcamping.no]
On E10 at SW side of island; approx 3km S of Kleppstad. Fr E
fr Kabelvåg 13km on E10. Site on L approx 1km after rd turns
N. Med, terr, unshd; htd wc; chem disp; mv service pnt; shwrs
NOK10; EHU (10-16A) NOK35; lndry; shop, rest 10km; BBQ;
cooking facs; playgrnd; sand beach adj; boat hire; salmon/trout
pond; sat TV; dogs; poss cr; Eng spkn; quiet; red long stay.
"Vg; on edge of fjord; facs poss stretched if site full."
1 May-30 Sep. NOK 110   2009*

RUNDE ISLAND

RUNDE *1A1* (1km NE Coastal) *62.39717, 5.65624* **Runde**
Camping & Hostel, 6096 Runde (Møre og Romsdal)
[tel 90 74 43 43; runde@hihostels.no; www.runde.no]
Fr S via E39 Volda & Ørsta, thro Eiksundsambandet Tunnel, then
25km by rd to Runde. On reaching Runde Island turn R along
coast, site sp. Fr N take ferry fr Sulesund (nr Ålesund) to Hareid,
then 45km by rd, site sp. Sm, hdstg, unshd; htd wc; chem disp;
shwrs; EHU (16A); lndry; shop; snacks 300m; BBQ; cooking facs;
wifi; beach adj; dogs; phone; o'night area for m'vans; Eng spkn;
adv bkg; quiet; ccard acc; CKE/CCI. "Lge bird colonies on island;
boat trips organised; helpful owner." 1 May-30 Sep.   2010*

⊞ **RUNDE** *1A1* (4km NW Rural/Coastal) *62.40416, 5.62525*
Camping Goksøyr, 6096 Runde (Møre og Romsdal)
[tel 70 08 59 05 or 924 12 298 (mob); fax 70 08 59 60;
camping@goksoyr.no; www.goksoeyr-camping.com]
Take causeway/bdge to Runde Island. Turn R off bdge & foll rd
round island, thro tunnel. Rd ends 1km after site. Sm, hdstg,
unshd; wc; chem disp; mv service pnt; shwrs NOK10; EHU
(16A) NOK30; lndry; shop; snacks; fishing; bike hire; phone;
Eng spkn; adv bkg; quiet; CKE/CCI. "Excel birdwatching (inc
puffins); site on water's edge; boat trips avail; basic facs poss
inadequate when site full; owner helps with pitching; vg."
NOK 190   2014*

VESTERALEN ISLANDS

ANDENES *2F1* (3km SW Coastal) *69.30390, 16.06621*
Andenes Camping, Bleiksveien 34, 8480 Andenes [tel
47 41 34 03 88; fax 47 76 11 56 10; camping@whalesafari.
no; www.andenescamping.no] Site on L of Rv82, sp. Sm,
some hdstg, unshd; htd wc; chem disp; mv service pnt; shwrs
NOK10; EHU (16A) inc (check earth); shop 250m; cooking facs;
sand beach adj; Eng spkn; some rd noise; CKE/CCI. "Nice,
sandy beaches; conv whale safari, summer ferry to Gryllefjord
& Bleiksøya bird cliff; gd for midnight sun; beautiful location;
whale trips." 1 Jun-30 Aug. NOK 200200   2014*

ANDENES *2F1* (21km SW Coastal) *69.20410, 15.84674*
Stave Camping & Hot Pools, Stave 8489 Nordmela [tel
92 60 12 57; info@stavecamping.no; www.stavecamping.
no] Head S on Storgata/Rv82 twds Stadionveien, cont to foll
Rv82, turn R onto Fv976, bear L onto Laksebakkveien, cont
onto Fv976; site on L. Sm, pt unshd; htd wc; chem disp; shwr
20NOK; EHU (16A) 40NOK; nearest shop 18km; cooking facs;
beach adj; wifi; Eng spkn; ccard acc. "Excel for midnight sun,
hot tubs 250NOK pn." 17 May-1 Sep. NOK 230   2014*

⊞ **GULLESFJORDBOTN** *2F2* (1km NW Coastal) *68.53213,*
15.72611 **Gullesfjordbotn Camping, Våtvoll, 8409**
Gullesfjordbotn [tel 77 09 11 10; fax 77 09 11 11; post@
gullesfjordcamping.no; www.gullesfjordcamping.no]
Fr S on E10 then rd 82. At rndabt just bef Gullesfjordbotn
take 2nd exit to site, well sp. Sm, hdstg, unshd; htd wc; chem
disp; mv service pnt; sauna; shwrs NOK10; EHU (16A) NOK50;
lndry (inc dryer); shop; snacks high ssn; cooking facs; sw &
shgl beach adj; fishing; boat hire; phone; poss cr; Eng spkn;
ccard acc; CKE/CCI. "On edge of fjord; liable to flood after
heavy rain; mountain views; gd san facs; friendly owners."
NOK 150   2009*

⊞ **HARSTAD** *2F2* (5km S Coastal) *68.77231, 16.57878*
Harstad Camping, Nessevegen 55, 9411 Harstad
[tel 77 07 36 62; fax 77 07 35 02; postmaster@harstad-
camping.no; www.harstad-camping.no] Sp fr E10/Rv83.
Med, pt sl, unshd; wc; chem disp; shwrs NOK10; EHU (16A)
inc; shop; snacks 1km; rest 5km; playgrnd; fishing; boating;
quiet; ccard acc; CKE/CCI. "San facs poss stretched high ssn;
lovely situation." ♦ NOK 260 (6 persons)   2009*

⊞ **RISOYHAMN** *2F1* (13km S Coastal) *68.88408, 15.60304*
Andøy Friluftssenter & Camping, Buksnesfjord, 8484
Risøyhamn [tel/fax 76 14 88 04; post@andoy-
friluftssenter.no; www.andoy-friluftssenter.no] Exit E10
onto Rv82 sp Sortland; in 31km at bdge to Sortland do not
cross bdge but cont N on Rv82 sp Andenes. Site on R in 38km
at Buknesfjord. Sm, hdstg, pt sl, unshd; htd wc; chem disp;
shwrs inc; EHU (10A) NOK50; lndry; rest, snacks; playgrnd; lake
sw; fishing; 50% statics; Eng spkn; adv bkg; quiet; ccard acc;
CKE/CCI. "Lake fishing; guided mountain walks; easy access
for whale-watching; v clean facs; gourmet meals." ♦ ltd.
NOK 150   2009*

⊞ **SORTLAND** *2F2* (2km NW Rural) *68.70286, 15.3919*
**Camping Sortland & Motel, Vesterveien 51, 8400 Sortland
[tel 76 11 03 00; fax 76 12 25 78; hj.bergseng@sortland-
camping.no; www.sortland-camping.no]**
Exit E10 onto Rv82 sp Sortland; in 31km turn L over bdge to
Sortland, L again at end bdge. Site sp in approx 1km immed
past church. Foll rd uphill for 1km, site on R. Med, hdstg, pt
shd; wc; chem disp; baby facs; fam bthrm; shwrs NOK10; EHU
(16A) NOK30; gas; lndry; shop; snacks; cooking facs; playgrnd;
skiing; cycling; walking; fishing; boating; solarium; gym; wifi;
TV; phone; poss cr; Eng spkn; quiet; ccard acc; CKE/CCI.
"Basic, clean site; helpful staff; gd base to tour islands; facs
stretched when full." NOK 250   2014*

STO *2F1* (150m N Coastal) *69.01891, 15.12215* **Stø
Bobilcamp, 8438 Stø [tel 76 13 25 30; fax 76 13 25 31;
loleinan@frisurf.no; www.stobobilcamp.com]**
Site sp fr cent of Stø. Sm, hdstg, unshd; htd wc; chem disp;
mv service pnt; shwrs NOK10; EHU (16A) NOK30; shop; rest;
cooking facs; fishing; bike hire; some statics; poss cr; quiet;
Eng spkn. "View of midnight sun; 10min walk to whale boat
safari; coastal walks, Queen Sonja's walk fr site, v scenic but
poss strenuous; facs stretched high ssn; site open to public for
parking." ◆ ltd. 15 May-1 Sep. NOK 130   2009*

NORWAY

▲ see map 2

Map 1

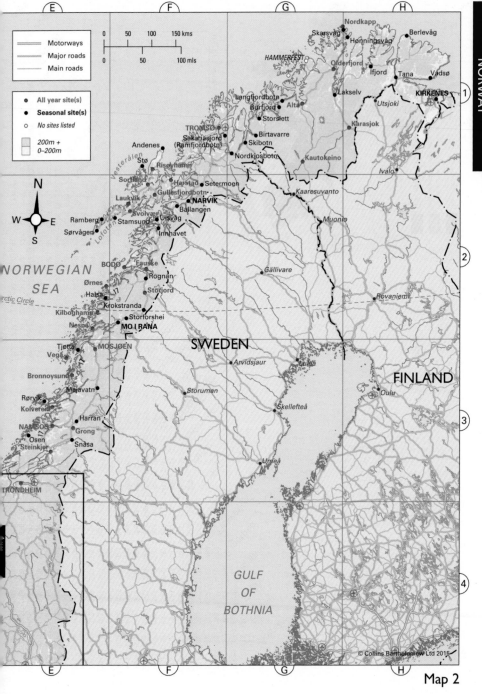

Map 2

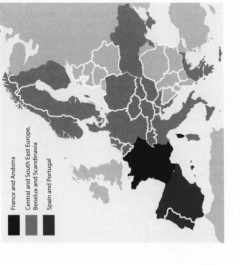

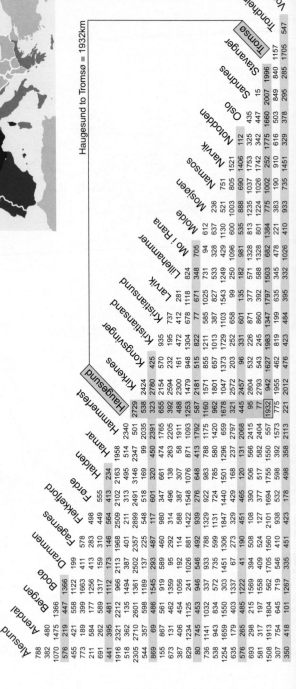

Kraków

Poland
Country Introduction

Welcome to Poland

Poland is a country with a deep sense of history, cultural identity and resilience that has been built over thousands of years. The historic and beautiful centre of Kraków is a must see, while the engaging and fascinating museums of Warsaw are also a fantastic experience.

For those looking for relaxation, the Polish countryside is peaceful and unspoilt. There are many hiking trails scattered around the country taking you alongside rivers, through thick forests and around mountains.

Country highlights

Amber, sometimes called the gold of the Baltic, has been crafted in Poland for centuries. Amber products are still produced and sold with the best place to shop being Cloth Hall in the heart of Kraków.

Poland has been producing vodka since the early Middle Ages, and is the birthplace of this spirit. The vodka distilled in Poland is considered some of the finest in the world and vodka tasting events are held around the country.

Major towns and cities

- Warsaw – Poland's capital and the largest city in the country.
- Kraków – a charming and beautiful place that has retained its historic feel.
- Łódź - the high street is one of the longest in the world.
- Wrocław – a city with plenty of landmarks and wonderful buildings.

Attractions

- Main Square, Kraków – a bustling, medieval market square filled with historic buildings and monuments.
- Białowieża Forest – the remains of a primeval forest, home to European bison, ancient oaks and a magical beauty.
- Wieliczka Salt Mine – discover a fascinating mix of history, art and industry in one of Poland's oldest salt mines.

Find out more

www.poland.travel

Tel: 0048 (0) 22 53 67 070 Polish Tourist Office

Country Information

Population (approx): 38.3 million

Capital: Warsaw (population approx 1.7 million)

Area: 312,685 sq km

Bordered by: Belarus, Czech Republic, Germany, Lithuania, Russia, Slovakia, Ukraine

Terrain: Mostly flat plain with many lakes; mountains along southern border

Climate: Changeable continental climate with cold, often severe winters and hot summers; rainfall spread throughout the year; late spring and early autumn are the best times to visit

Coastline: 440km

Highest Point: Rysy 2,499m

Language: Polish

Local Time: GMT or BST + 1, i.e. 1 hour ahead of the UK all year

Currency: Zloty (PLN) divided into 100 groszy; £1 = PLN 5.89; PLN10 = £1.70 (September 2015)

Emergency numbers: Police 997; Fire brigade 998; Ambulance 999. Call 112 for any service.

Public Holidays 2016: Jan 1, 6; Mar 27, 28; May 1, 3 (Constitution Day), 15, 26; Aug 15; Nov 1, 11 (Independence Day); Dec 25, 26.

School summer holidays run from the last week of June to the end of August.

Camping and Caravanning

There are around 250 organised campsites throughout Poland, with the most attractive areas being the Mazurian lake district and along the coast. Campsites are usually open from the beginning of May or June to the middle or end of September, but the season only really starts towards the end of June. Until then facilities may be very limited and grass may not be cut, etc.

You can download details of approximately 160 sites (including GPS co-ordinates) from the website of the Polish Federation of Camping & Caravanning, www.pfcc.eu.

Campsites are classified into two categories. Category one sites provide larger pitches and better amenities, but it may still be advisable to use your own facilities. There are also some basic sites which are not supervised and are equipped only with drinking water, toilets and washing facilities. Sites may be in need of modernisation but, on the whole, sanitary facilities are clean although they may provide little privacy. Some new sites are being built to higher standards. A site may close earlier than its published date if the weather is bad.

Many sites are not signposted from main roads and may be difficult to find. It is advisable to obtain a large scale atlas or good maps of the areas to be visited and not rely on one map covering the whole of Poland.

Casual/wild camping is not recommended and is prohibited in national parks (except on organised sites) and in sand dunes along the coast.

Cycling

There are several long-distance cycle routes using a combination of roads with light motor traffic, forest trails or tracks along waterways. There are some cycle lanes on main roads where cyclists may not ride two or more abreast.

Electricity and Gas

The current on most campsites is 10 amps. Plugs have two round pins. There are some CEE connections.

It is understood that both propane and butane supplies are widely available, but cylinders are not exchangeable and it may be necessary to refill. The Caravan Club does not recommend this practice and you should aim to take enough gas to last during your stay. Some campsites have kitchens which you may use to conserve your gas supplies.

Entry Formalities

British and Irish passport holders may visit Poland for up to three months without a visa. At campsites reception staff should undertake any required registration formalities with local authorities.

Medical Services

For simple complaints and basic advice consult staff in a pharmacy (apteka). Some English may be spoken. In general, medical facilities are comparatively inexpensive and of a good standard. Medical staff are well qualified. English is not always widely spoken and you may face language difficulties.

You will need a European Health Insurance Card (EHIC) to obtain emergency treatment from doctors, dentists and hospitals contracted to the state health care system, the NFZ. Reimbursements for any charges that you incur can be claimed from the NFZ office in Warsaw. You will have to pay a proportion of the cost of prescriptions, which is not refundable in Poland.

Private health clinics offering a good standard of medical care can also be found in large cities.

Opening Hours

Banks – Mon-Fri 9am-4pm; Sat 9am-1pm.

Museums – Tue-Sun 10am-5pm; closed Mon.

Post Offices – Mon-Fri 8am-6pm; Sat 8am-2pm (on rota basis).

Shops – Mon-Fri 11am-8pm; Sat 9am-2pm/4pm; food shops open and close earlier; supermarkets open until 9pm/10pm.

Safety and Security

Most visits to Poland are trouble free and violent crime is rare, but there is a risk of robbery in tourist areas, particularly near hotels, at main railway stations and on public transport. Passengers are most at risk when boarding and leaving trains or trams. Avoid walking alone at night, particularly in dark or poorly-lit streets or in public parks.

Some tourists have been the target of a scam in which men claiming to be plain clothes police officers ask visitors to show their identity documents and bank cards, and then ask for their PIN(s).

Theft of and from vehicles is common so do not leave vehicle documentation or valuables in your car. Foreign registered cars may be targeted, especially in large, busy supermarket car parks.

Cases have been reported of vehicles with foreign number plates being stopped by gangs posing as police officers, either claiming a routine traffic control or at the scene of fake accidents, particularly in rural and tourist areas. If in doubt, when flagged down keep all doors and windows locked, remain in your vehicle and ask to see identification. The motoring organisation, PZM, advises that any car or document inspection performed outside built-up areas can only be carried out by uniformed police officers and at night these officials must use a police patrol car. Although police officers do not have to be in uniform within built-up areas, they must always present their police identity card. More details are available to motorists at Polish road borders.

An emergency helpline has been set up to assist visitors who have been victims of crime or who require assistance tel: 0800 200300 (freephone) or +48 608 599999 (mobile number). The helpline operates from 1 June to 30 September between 10am and 10pm.

Do not leave drinks or food unattended or accept drinks from strangers. There has been a small number of reports of drinks being spiked and of visitors having their valuables stolen whilst drugged.

British Embassy
UL KAWALERII 12
00-468 WARSZAWA
Tel: (022) 3110000
www.ukinpoland.fco.gov.uk

Irish Embassy
UL MYSIA 5, 00-496 WARSZAWA
Tel: (022) 5642200
www.embassyofireland.pl.

Border Posts

Customs posts are open 24 hours a day throughout the year. Cars crossing the eastern borders, especially to Lithuania and Belarus, are usually intensively scrutinised by the Polish authorities in an effort to combat widespread smuggling of stolen cars. Travellers should ensure all documents are in order.

Borders may be busy at weekends with cross border shoppers, and in particular the crossing from Germany via Frankfurt-on-Oder can be heavily congested on Saturday mornings.

Documents

Driving Licence

The standard pink UK paper driving licence is recognised, but if you hold the old style green UK licence or a Northern Irish licence issued prior to 1991 you are advised to update it to a photocard licence in order to avoid any local difficulties.

Passport

You should carry your passport with you at all times.

Vehicle(s)

You must carry your original vehicle registration certificate (V5C), insurance documentation and MOT certificate (if applicable) at all times. You may be asked for these if you are stopped by the police and, in particular, when crossing borders. If you do not own the vehicle(s) you will need a letter of authority from the owner, together with the vehicle's original documentation.

Money

Cash can easily be obtained from ATMs in banks and shopping centres. ATMs offer an English option.

Major credit cards are widely accepted in hotels, restaurants and shops but you may find that supermarkets do not accept them. Take particular care with credit/debit cards and don't lose sight of them during transactions.

Sterling and euros are readily accepted at exchange bureaux but Scottish and Northern Irish bank notes are not generally recognised and you may have difficulties trying to exchange them.

Carry your credit card issuers'/banks' 24-hour UK contact numbers in case of loss or theft of your cards.

Motoring in Poland

Poland is a major east to west route for heavy vehicles and driving can be hazardous. There are few dual carriageways and even main roads between large towns can be narrow and poorly surfaced. Slow moving agricultural and horse-drawn vehicles are common in rural areas. Street lighting is weak even in major cities.

Local driving standards are poor and speed limits, traffic lights and road signs are often ignored. Drivers rarely indicate before manoeuvring and you may encounter aggressive tailgating, overtaking on blind bends and overtaking on the inside. Take particular care on national holiday weekends when there is a surge in road accidents.

It is not advisable to drive a right hand drive vehicle alone for long distances or to drive long distances at night. At dusk watch out for cyclists riding without lights along the edge of the road or on its shoulder.

Hitchhikers use an up and down motion of the hand to ask for a lift. This may be confused with flagging down.

Accidents

A driver involved in an accident must call the police, obtain an official record of damages and forward it to the insurance company of the Polish driver involved (if applicable), for example, the Polish National Insurance Division (PZU) or the Polish Insurance Association (WARTA). Members of AIT/FIA affiliated clubs, such as The Caravan Club, can obtain help from the touring office ('Autotour') of the Polish motoring organisation, Polski Zwiazek Motorowy (PZM), tel: (022) 8496904 or (022) 8499361.

If people are injured, you must call an ambulance or doctor. By law, it is an offence for a driver not to obtain first aid for accident victims or to leave the scene of an accident. In such circumstances the authorities may withdraw a tourist's passport and driving licence, vehicle registration certificate or even the vehicle itself and the penalties can be a prison sentence and a fine.

Alcohol

There is zero tolerance for drink-driving; the permitted level of alcohol is 20 milligrams in 100 millilitres of blood, which in practice equates to zero. At the request of the police or if an accident has occurred a driver must undergo a blood test which, if positive, may lead to a prison sentence, withdrawal of driving licence and a fine. Penalty points will be notified to the authorities in the motorist's home country.

Breakdown Service

The toll free telephone number for breakdown assistance throughout the country is 981.

The PZM runs a breakdown service covering the entire country 24 hours a day. Members of AIT and FIA affiliated clubs, such as The Caravan Club, should call the PZM Emergency Centre on (022) 5328433. Staff speak English. Roadside assistance must be paid for in cash.

Essential Equipment

Fire extinguisher
It is compulsory to carry a fire extinguisher on board all vehicles.

First aid kit
It is not compulsory to have a first aid kit but it is recommended.

Lights
Dipped headlights must be used at all times. Bulbs are more likely to fail with constant use and you are recommended to carry spares. In bad visibility use your horn to indicate that you are going to overtake.

Warning Triangles
You must use a warning triangle when a vehicle is stationary on a road in poor visibility (less than 100 metres) and if the vehicle is likely to obstruct traffic. On a normal road the triangle must be placed between 30 and 50 metres behind the vehicle and must be clearly visible to oncoming traffic; on a motorway, it must be placed 100 metres behind the vehicle. Hazard warning lights may be used in addition to, but not instead of, a triangle.

Child Restraint System
Children under the age of 12 years old and under the height of 1.5m must use a suitable restraint system that has been adapted to their size. It is prohibited to place a child in a rear facing seat in the front of the vehicle if the car is equipped with airbags.

Fuel

The usual opening hours for petrol stations are from 8am to 7pm; many on main roads and international routes and in large towns are open 24 hours. Credit cards are widely accepted. LPG (Autogas) is widely available from service stations.

Parking

There are parking meters in many towns and signs display parking restrictions or prohibitions. There are many supervised car parks charging an hourly rate. Illegally parked cars causing an obstruction may be towed away and impounded, in which case the driver will be fined. Wheel clamps are in use.

Sidelights must be used when parking in unlit streets during the hours of darkness.

Priority

Priority should be given to traffic coming from the right at intersections of roads of equal importance, however vehicles on rails always have priority. At roundabouts traffic already on a roundabout has priority.

Give way to buses pulling out from bus stops. Trams have priority over other vehicles at all times. Where there is no central reservation or island you should stop to allow passengers alighting from trams to cross to the pavement.

Roads

All roads are hard surfaced and the majority of them are asphalted. However, actual road surfaces may be poor; even some major roads are constructed of cement or cobbles and heavily rutted. Average journey speed is about 50 km/h (31 mph).

Some roads, notably those running into Warsaw, have a two metre wide strip on the nearside to pull onto in order to allow other vehicles to overtake. Oncoming lorries expect other motorists to pull over when they are overtaking.

Overtake trams on the right unless in a one-way street.

Road Signs and Markings

Road signs and markings conform to international standards. Motorway and national road numbers are indicated in red and white, and local roads by yellow signs with black numbering. Signs on motorways are blue with white lettering and on main roads they are green and white.

The following road signs may be seen:

Polish	English Translation
Rondzie	Roundabout
Wstep szbroniony	No Entry
Wyjscie	Exit

You may also encounter the following:

Paid parking between 7am and 6pm **Residential area- predestrians have priority** **Toll road**

Rutted road **Winding road** **Emergency vehicles**

Crossroads and road junctions may not be marked with white 'stop' lines, and other road markings in general may be well worn and all but invisible, so always take extra care.

Speed Limits

	Open Road (km/h)	Motorway (km/h)
Car Solo	90	140
Car towing caravan/trailer	70	80
Motorhome under 3500kg	90	140
Motorhome 3500-7500kg	70	80

In built up areas the speed limit is 50 km/h (31 mph) between 5am and 11pm, and 60 km/h (37 mph) between 11pm and 5am.

For vehicles over 3,500kg all speed limits are the same as for a car and caravan outfit. In residential zones indicated by entry/exit signs, the maximum speed is 20 km/h (13 mph). The use of radar detectors is illegal.

Traffic Lights

Look out for a small, non-illuminated green arrow under traffic lights, which permits a right turn against a red traffic light if the junction is clear.

Violation of Traffic Regulations

Motorists must not cross a road's solid central white line or even allow wheels to run on it. Radar speed traps are frequently in place on blind corners where speed restrictions apply. Police are very keen to enforce traffic regulations with verbal warnings and/or on the spot fines. Fines are heavy and drivers of foreign registered vehicles will be required to pay in cash. Always obtain an official receipt.

Motorways and Tolls

There are approximately 1420km of motorways in Poland. Tolls are levied on sections and vary in price, for example, the A1 Rusocin to Nowe Marzy is PLN 41.80 (2015 prices) for a car towing a caravan weighing under 3500kg.

An electronic toll system is in place for vehicles which weigh over 3,500kg, including motorhomes and car and caravan combinations if the total weight is over 3,500kg. These vehicles will need to be equipped with an electronic device called a viaBOX. Visit www.viatoll.pl/en and select the 'Trucks' option for details of toll costs for motorhomes and car/caravan combinations weighing over 3500kg.

An electronic option is also available for vehicles and car/caravan combinations which weigh under 3500kg - go to the above website and choose the 'Cars' options for details.

There are emergency telephones every 2km along motorways. Recent visitors report that newer stretches of motorway have rest areas with chemical disposal and waste water disposal facilities.

Touring

Poland's climate does not permit the production of wine, the national drinks being varieties of vodka and plum brandy. It is usual to leave a tip of between 10 to 15%.

There are over 9,000 lakes in Poland, mostly in the north. The regions of Western Pomerania, Kaszubia and Mazuria are a paradise for sailing enthusiasts, anglers and nature lovers. In order to protect areas of great natural beauty, national parks and nature reserves have been created, two of the most interesting of which are the Tatra National Park covering the whole of the Polish Tatra mountains, and the Slowinksi National Park with its 'shifting' sand dunes.

There are 14 UNESCO World Heritage sites including the restored historic centres of Warsaw and Kraków, the medieval, walled town of Toruń and Auschwitz Concentration Camp. Other towns worth a visit are Chopin's birthplace at Zelazowa Wola, Wieliczka with its salt mines where statues and a chapel are carved out of salt, and Wrocław.

White and brown signs placed strategically in cities and near sites of interest pinpoint architectural and natural landmarks, places of religious worship, etc. Each sign includes not only information on the name of and distance to a particular attraction, but also a pictogram of the attraction, e.g. Jasna Góra monastery. Themed routes, such as the trail of the wooden churches in the Małopolska Region (south of Kraków), are marked in a similar way.

A Warsaw Tourist Card and a Kraków Tourist Card are available, both valid for up to three days and offering free travel on public transport and free entry to many museums, together with discounts at selected restaurants and shops and on sightseeing and local excursions. Buy the cards from tourist information centres, travel agents or hotels.

The Polish people are generally friendly, helpful and polite. English is becoming increasingly widely spoken in major cities.

Public Transport & Local Travel

For security reasons recent visitors recommend using guarded car parks such as those in Warsaw on the embankment below the Old Town, in the Palace of Culture and near the Tomb of the Unknown Soldier.

Problems have been reported involving overcharging by non-regulated taxi drivers. Use only taxis from official ranks whose vehicles have the name and telephone number of the taxi company on the door and on the roof (beside the occupied/unoccupied light). They also display a rate card in the window of the vehicle. Taxis with a crest but no company name are not officially registered.

There are frequent ferries from Gydnia, Swinoujscie and Gdansk to Denmark, Germany and Sweden. There are no car ferry services on internal waters but passenger services operate along the Baltic Coast, on the Mazurian lakes and on some rivers, for example, between Warsaw and Gdansk.

There is a metro system in Warsaw linking the centre to the north and south of the city. It is possible to buy a daily or weekly tourist pass which is valid for all means of public transport – bus, tram and metro. Buy tickets at newspaper stands and kiosks displaying a sign 'bilety'. Tickets must be punched before travelling at the yellow machines at the entrance to metro stations or on board buses and trams. You will incur an on the spot fine if you are caught travelling without a valid ticket.

AUSCHWITZ see Oświęcim *D3*

BAKOW see Kluczbork *C2*

BARANOWO see Poznań *B2*

BIALOWIEZA *B4* (3km W Rural) *52.69395, 23.83088* **Camping U Michała (No. 124), ul Krzyże 11, 17-230 Białowieża [(085) 6812703]** Exit Bielsk Podlaski onto rd 689; cont past Hajnówka for 17m; site on R at end of vill. Sm, mkd pitch, pt shd; wc; chem disp; shwrs inc; EHU (16A); lndry; playgrnd; bike hire; poss cr; quiet. "Gd san facs." ♦ 15 Apr-30 Sep. PLN 50 2011*

⊞ **BIALYSTOK** *B4* (8km N Rural) *53.19364, 23.19364* **Camping Hotel Jard, ul Białostocka 94, 16-010 Wasilków [(085) 7185240; fax 7185511; www.jard.pl]** On L of rte 19 when on app Wasilków fr Białystok. Sm, pt sl, pt shd; own san rec; shwrs inc; EHU (10A) PLN8; shop 2km; rest; bar; ccard acc. "Fair NH; simple site - only one for some dist." PLN 34 2009*

BIELSKO BIALA *D3* (6km S Rural) *49.78031, 19.05318* **Camping Ondraszek (No. 57), ul Pocztowa 43, 43-309 Bielsko-Biała [(033) 8146425; fax 8143601; kemping57ondraszek@op.pl; www.tkkfblonia.ovh.org]** Fr E462 ent Bielsk0-Biała & foll sp Szczyrk. Site sp on R after Park Hotel. Cont uphill to T-junc, L to gates. Site on edge of town in park. Sm, hdg pitch, pt sl, pt shd; wc; chem disp; mv service pnt; shwrs inc; EHU; shops 1.5km; rest adj; bar; BBQ; playgrnd; pool & sports facs adj; quiet. "Pretty, well-kept site in woods; daytime noise fr neighbouring sports facs; conv Oswięcim (Auschwitz)." ♦ 15 Apr-30 Sep. PLN 54 2010*

BIELSKO BIALA *D3* (6km SW Rural) *49.78148, 19.02281* **Camping Pod Dębowcem (No. 99), ul Karbowa 15, 43-316 Bielsko-Biała [(033) 8216181 or (0604) 144186 (mob); 99@camping.org.pl; www.camping.bielsko.com.pl]** Rd 1/E75 out of Bielsko-Biała to Cieszyn or fr B942 foll sp 'Szyndzielnia' (cable car) to site. Med, mkd pitch, some hdstg, terr, pt sl, pt shd; wc; chem disp; shwrs inc; EHU (6A) PLN10; lndry; snacks; bar; BBQ; playgrnd; TV; dogs; no adv bkg; quiet; CKE/CCI. "Conv Czech border." ♦ 1 May-31 Oct. PLN 48 2010*

BOGACZEWO see Gizycko *A3*

CHMIELNO see Kartuzy *A2*

⊞ **CZESTOCHOWA** *C3* (4km W Urban) *50.81122, 19.09131* **Camping Oleńka (No. 76), ul Oleńki 10, 42-200 Częstochowa [tel/fax (034) 3606066; camping@mosir.pl; www.mosir.pl]** Fr A1/E75 foll sp Jasna Góra monastery, pick up sm white camping sp to site. Lge, pt shd; wc; chem disp; shwrs inc; EHU (20A); lndry; shops nrby; rest; bar; playgrnd; pool 2km; internet; TV; 20% statics; dogs; phone; Eng spkn; no adv bkg; quiet; ccard acc; red CKE/CCI. "Guided tours; monastery worth visit; gd NH/sh stay nr Jasna Góra & Black Madonna painting; poor security; san facs unclean & poorly maintained (6/09)." ♦ PLN 84 2009*

DZIWNOW *A1* (3km E Coastal) *54.03404, 14.79978* **Camping Wiking (No. 194), ul Wolności 3, 72-420 Dziwnówek [tel/fax (091) 3813493; camping@campingwiking.pl; www.campingwiking.pl]** Foll rd 102 thro Dziwnówek twd Dziwnów. Site on R in 400m (past ent to diff site). Med, pt sl, shd; wc; chem disp; baby facs; shwrs PLN15; EHU PLN13.50 (poss rev pol); lndry; shop; rest, snacks; bar; BBQ; playgrnd; sw & sand beach adj; some statics; dogs PLN7; bus; poss cr; CKE/CCI. "Fair sh stay/NH; gd security." ♦ 1 May-10 Sep. PLN 60 2009*

ELBLAG *A3* (1km W Urban) *54.15349, 19.39403* **Camping Elbląg (No. 61), ul Panieńska 14, 82-300 Elbląg [tel/fax (055) 6418666; camping@camping61.com.pl; www.camping61.com.pl]** Fr rd 7/E77 fr Gdańsk, take slip rd into Elbląg. At traff lts bdge over canal turn L, site on R, well sp fr ring rd. Sm, pt shd; wc; chem disp; shwrs; EHU (16A) PLN8; lndry; rest 500m; snacks 400m; playgrnd; wifi; dogs; red LS/long stary/CKE/CCI. "Helpful staff; old san facs clean but poss stretched high ssn; conv turn for 'shiplift' canal." 29 Apr-30 Sep. PLN 51 2011*

ELK *A3* (3km SW Urban) *53.81545, 22.35215* **Camping Plaża Miejska (No. 62), ul Parkowa 2, 19-300 Ełk [(087) 6109700; fax 6102723; mosir@elk.com.pl; www.mosir.elk.com.pl]** Fr town cent on rd 16 take rd 65/669 dir Białystok. After 200m cross rv & immed turn R, site 100m on L. Sm, mkd pitch, hdstg, pt shd; htd wc; shwrs inc; EHU (10A) inc; shop 500m; snacks; bar; cooking facs; lake sw & sand beach 200m; quiet; CKE/CCI. "Gd security; well-maintained, clean site adj town cent & attractive lake; gd touring base lake district." ♦ 1 Jun-1 Sep. PLN 65 2011*

FROMBORK *A3* (1km E Rural/Coastal) *54.35877, 19.69572* **Camping Frombork (No. 12), ul Braniewska, 14-530 Frombork [(0506) 803151; kontakt@campingfrombork.pl; www.campingfrombork.pl]** Fr Frombork on rd 504 dir Braniewo, site on L. Med, pt shd; wc; chem disp & mv service pnt at car wash; shwrs inc; EHU inc; lndry; shop 1km; bar; BBQ; playgrnd; sand beach 2km; games area; dogs; quiet. "Pleasant, basic site; san facs tatty but clean (2009); pleasant countryside." 1 May-30 Sep. PLN 60 2013*

GAJ see Krakow *D3*

GDANSK *A2* (9km E Coastal) *54.37021, 18.72938* **Camping Stogi (No. 218), ul Wydmy 9, 80-656 Gdańsk [(058) 3073915; fax 3042259; jan@camping-gdansk.pl; www.kemping-gdansk.pl]** E fr Gdańsk on rd 7 (E77) for approx 2km, then L foll sp for Stogi. Then foll tram rte no. 8 to Stogi Plaza/Beach. Site is 100m fr tram terminus, well sp. Med, hdstg; wc; chem disp; shwrs inc; EHU (10-16A) PLN11; lndry; shop; snacks; bar; BBQ; playgrnd; sand beach adj; games area; wifi; 75% statics; tram 100m; poss cr & poss noise fr school parties; CKE/CCI. "Basic site, more a holiday camp for school groups; ltd facs LS; close to huge, clean beach; gd security; vg site; sep area for m'vans; san facs upgraded (2013)." 25 Apr-5 Oct. PLN 89 2013*

GIZYCKO *A3* (13km S Rural) *53.96750, 21.77666* **Camping Echo (No. 55), Mazurska 48, 11-511 Rydzewo-Miłki [(087) 4211186; olanowakowska84@gmail.com; www.mazury.info.pl/echo]** Fr Giżycko rd 63 dir Orzysz; in Ruda foll sp to R Rydzewo & site on lakeside. Sm, pt shd; wc; shwrs inc; EHU (16A) PLN9; lndry; shop; rest 1km; snacks high ssn; BBQ; sand beach; lake sw; dogs PLN5; Eng spkn; quiet. "Vg; gd, modern san facs; ideal for touring Masurian Lake District." 1 May-30 Sep. PLN 50   2010*

GIZYCKO *A3* (3km W Urban) *54.03413, 21.76002* **Camping Zamek (No. 1), ul Moniuszki 1, 11-500 Giżycko [(087) 4283410; info@cmazur.pl; www.cmazur.pl]** Fr Olsztyn on rte 59 ent town. After junc with rte 592 fr Kętrzyn bear R to town cent & swing bdge. Site on R bef swing bdge over canal adj Hotel Zamek. NB Swing bdge 2.5T weight & 2m height limit, do not app site thro town. Sm, hdg pitch, pt sl, pt shd; wc; chem disp; shwrs PLN10; EHU (16A) PLN8; lndry; shop 500m; rest, snacks; bar; cooking facs; lake 500m; wifi; dogs PLN10; rlwy noise & poss noisy until 2300 as disco adj; CKE/CCI. "Adj boat marina & nr beautiful lakes/ forests." ♦ 1 May-30 Sep. PLN 41   2011*

> ## "I like to fill in the reports as I travel from site to site"
> You'll find report forms at the back of this guide, or you can fill them in online at www.caravanclub.co.uk/europereport.

⊞ **JELENIA GORA** *C2* (2km SE Urban) *50.89638, 15.74266* **Auto-Camping Park (No. 130), ul Sudecka 42, 58-500 Jelenia Góra [tel/fax (075) 7524525; campingpark@interia.pl; www.camping.karkonosz.pl]** In town foll sp to Karpacz on rd 367. Site 100m fr hotel. Well sp. Med, some hdstg, pt terr, pt shd; wc in recep building; shwrs inc; EHU (6-10A) PLN10 (poss rev pol); lndry; shops 100m; rest 200m; snacks; pool, tennis & sports facs 500m; wifi; TV; 20% statics; dogs PLN5; adv bkg; quiet but some rd noise; ccard acc; red CKE/CCI. "Conv Karkanosze mountains & Czech border; well-run, clean, neat site nr hotel with gd, modern facs; 20 min walk to pleasant town; staff friendly, helpful & obliging; conv NH; gd facs." ♦ PLN 53   2015*

JELENIA GORA *C2* (7km SW Urban) *50.86566, 15.6644* **Camping Słoneczna Polana, ul Rataja 9, 58-560 Cieplici [tel/fax (075) 7552566; info@camping-polen.pl; www.camping-polen.pl]** Fr SW on rd 3/E65 twd Jelenia Góra; after Wojcieszyce, then o'head power lines, turn R to Cieplice & watch for church spire strt ahead. Take care at level x-ing, turn R at T-junc to site on L after 1km where rd crosses stream. Fr N app Jelenia Góra on rd 297 & rd 30, turn R on rd 3/E65 sp Szklarska Poręba. After about 3km app x-rds at Wojcieszyce. Turn L to Cieplice, then as above. Med, mkd pitch, pt shd; wc; chem disp; mv service pnt; shwrs inc; EHU (6-10A) (adaptors free) PLN10; lndry (inc dryer); shop 300m; rest, snacks; playgrnd; pool; paddling pool; thermal baths nr; games rm; wifi; sat TV; some statics; dogs PLN5; poss cr; Eng spkn; adv bkg; quiet; ccard not acc; red LS/snr citizens; CKE/CCI. "Excel Dutch-run site; barrier clsd 2200-0700; Cieplici attractive spa; v helpful staff; bus stop outside gates." 1 May-30 Sep. PLN 67   2013*

KARPACZ *D2* (3km N Rural) *50.80428, 15.76776* **Camping Wiśniowa Polana (No. 142), Miłków 40A, 58-535 Mlłków [tel/fax (0510) 111415; camping-milkow@karkonosz.pl; www.camping-milkow.karkonosz.pl]** Fr Jelenia Góra to Kowary on rte 367, turn R at junc with rte 366 at Kowary, site on E of Miłków by rv. Med, some hdstg, pt shd; wc; chem disp (wc); mv service pnt; shwrs inc; EHU (10A) PLN10; lndry; shop 500m; snacks; bar; BBQ; playgrnd; pool; paddling pool; fishing; games area; internet; dogs PLN5; quiet; red snr citizens/CKE/ CCI. "Well-kept, guarded site & facs; v friendly staff; 7km fr chairlift onto mountain ridge; gd walking - map fr recep." ♦ 1 May-30 Sep. PLN 55   2013*

⊞ **KARTUZY** *A2* (9km W Rural) *54.31983, 18.11736* **Camping Tamowa (No. 181), Zawory 47A, 83-333 Chmielno [tel/fax (058) 6842535; camping@tamowa.pl; www.tamowa.pl]** Fr Gdańsk take rd 7 & rd 211 to Kartuzy, cont for approx 4km on 211. Turn L for Chmielno; site sp fr vill on lakesite along narr, bumpy app rd. Med, terr, unshd; wc; chem disp; sauna; shwrs PLN2; EHU (10-16A) inc; shop 1km; snacks; bar; BBQ; playgrnd; lake sw adj; boat & bike hire; little Eng spkn; quiet; CKE/CCI. "Attractive, well-kept site in beautiful location; friendly owner; not suitable lge o'fits; v nice site; shop 0.5m." PLN 54   2012*

KATOWICE *D3* (4km SE Rural) *50.24355, 19.04795* **Camping Dolina Trzech Statow (No. 215), ul Murckowska 1, 40-266 Katowice [tel/fax (032) 2565939]** Exit A4 at junc Murckowska & foll sp on rd 86 Sosnowiec. In 500m turn R & foll site sp. Med, pt sl, shd; htd wc; shwrs inc; EHU (16A) PLN2.50/kwh; shop 1km; rest adj; snacks; bar; cooking facs; playgrnd; lake; tennis; dogs PLN5; Eng spkn; adv bkg; quiet; ccard acc; red CKE/CCI. "V clean facs but basic & little privacy; vg." ♦ 1 May-30 Sep. PLN 42   2010*

KAZIMIERZ DOLNY *C3* (2km N Rural) *51.33106, 21.95879* **Campsite Pielak, Pulawska 82, 24-120 Kazimierz Dolny (Lubelskie) [(069) 1047409]** Site sp on the S824 300m N of the town. Sm, pt sl, pt shd; wc; chem disp; shwrs; EHU (16A); lndry; BBQ; Wifi; bus o'side. "Very friendly owners; walking dist to town; close to rv; open grassy site." ♦ ltd. 1 May-30 Oct. PLN 61   2013*

⊞ **KLODZKO** *D2* (13km W Urban) *50.41502, 16.51335* **Camping Polanica-Zdroj (No. 169), ul Sportowa 7, 57-320 Polanica-Zdrój [(074) 8681210; fax 8681211; osir. polanica@neostrada.pl; www.osir.polanica.net/pl]** Foll sp fr rd 8/E67. Site is 1km N of Polanica-Zdrój. Med, pt shd; htd wc; shwrs inc; EHU (6A) PLN9.50; shop & 500m; snacks; rest; tennis; many statics adj; dogs PLN5; poss cr; Eng spkn; quiet; ccard acc; CKE/CCI. "Well-run site; clean san facs; helpful warden; easy walk to pleasant spa town - many rests/ cafés; wifi free in recep." PLN 49   2014*

KLUCZBORK *C2* (5km E Rural) *50.96486, 18.27743* **Camping Bąków (No. 23), ul Kluczborska, 46-233 Bąków [(077) 4180586; osir@kluczbork.pl; www.osir.kluczbork.pl]** On rd 11 Kluczbork to Olesno. Sp on L of rd. Med, mkd pitch, shd; wc; shwrs inc; EHU (10A) PLN5; lndry; rest, snacks; bar; playgrnd; pool; TV; 50% statics; quiet; CKE/CCI. "No privacy in shwrs; site poss open outside dates shown; campfires in evening; excel value." 1 May-30 Sep. PLN 23   2009*

KOLOBRZEG *A2* (1km NE Coastal) *54.18131, 15.59566*
Camping Baltic (No. 78), ul 4 Dywizji, 78-100 Kołobrzeg
[tel/fax (094) 3524569 or (0606) 411954 (mob); baltic78@
post.pl; www.camping.kolobrzeg.pl] Nr Solny Hotel on NE
edge of town over rlwy x-ing; sp fr rndabt in vill. Med, pt shd;
wc; chem disp; mv service pnt; shwrs; shops 500m; EHU (10-
16A) PLN10; shop, rest adj; snacks; bar; playgrnd; sand beach
800m; TV; dogs PLN3; phone; poss cr; Eng spkn; adv bkg; rd &
rlwy noise; ccard acc; red long stay/CKE/CCI. "V helpful staff;
easy walk/cycle to town; well kept site with spotless facs; easy
walk into town." ◆ 15 Apr-15 Oct. PLN 103   2013*

KRAKOW *D3* (5km N Urban) *50.09454, 19.94127* **Camping**
Clepardia (No. 103), ul Pachońskiego 28A, 31-223 Kraków
[(012) 4159672; fax 6378063; clepardia@gmail.com;
www.clepardia.com.pl] Fr Kraków cent take rd 7/E77 N twds
Warsaw for 3km. Turn L onto rd 79 'Opolska' & foll sp 'Domki
Kempingowe - Bungalows'. Fr A4/E40 exit onto E462 then S
on rd 79 'Pasternik' thro to 'J Conrada & foll sp. Site is nr lge
Elea supmkt & Clepardia Basen (sw pools). Med, mkd pitch, pt
shd; wc; chem disp; shwrs inc; EHU (6A) PLN12; lndry; supmkt,
rest 300m; pool adj; wifi; dogs free; phone; bus nr; poss cr;
Eng spkn; no adv bkg; aircraft noise; red LS/CKE/CCI. "Busy
site with tightly packed pitches - rec arr bef 1700 high ssn to
secure pitch; excel, clean, modern san facs; ltd EHU if site full;
muddy in wet weather; friendly, helpful staff; gd security; well
maintained." 2 Apr-24 Oct. PLN 70   2014*

KRAKOW *D3* (8km S Urban) *50.01546, 19.92525*
Camping Krakowianka (No. 171), ul Żywiecka
Boczna 2, 30-427 Kraków [tel/fax (012) 2681135 or
(012) 2681417 (phone fax); hotel@krakowianka.com.pl
or hotel@krakowianka.info; www.krakowianka.com.pl]
Exit A4 at Wezel Opatkowice & head N on E77 twd city cent
for approx 3km. After passing Carrefour supmkt on R, turn
L at next traff lts & foll site sp. Lge, pt shd; wc; chem disp;
shwrs; EHU (16A) inc; lndry; supmkt 400m; rest 1.5km; snacks;
playgrnd; pool adj; games area; TV; some statics; dogs; wifi;
phone; tram; car wash. "Ltd, basic facs; conv tram to town;
shwrs in hotel v clean & plenty hot water; gd site; nice snack/
bar." 1 May-30 Sep. PLN 50   2013*

KRAKOW *D3* (15km S Rural) *49.9625, 19.89277* **Korona**
Camping (No. 241), ul Myślenicka 32, 32-031 Gaj
[tel/fax (012) 2701318; biuro@corona-korona.com.pl;
www.camping-korona.com.pl] Site on E77, well sp fr all
dirs. NB dangerous main rd - rec app fr S cont twd Kraków for
approx 2km, then turn at x-rds, back to site. When leaving site
& travelling N, drive about 5km S, take R turn after speed limit
warnings, cross rd by bdge, then back N. Med, mkd pitch, terr,
pt shd; wc; chem disp; mv service pnt; shwrs inc; EHU (10-16A)
PLN12; lndry; shop; snacks; bar; BBQ; playgrnd; games area;
dogs PLN4; bus to city at gate; poss cr; Eng spkn; adv bkg; rd
noise; red long stay/CKE/CCI. "Friendly, family-run site; clean
facs need modernising (2010); lower pt of site unrel in wet." ◆
1 May-15 Sep. PLN 65   2011*

⊞ **KRAKOW** *D3* (7km SW Rural) *50.04638, 19.88111*
Camping Smok (No. 46), ul Kamedulska 18, 30-252
Kraków [tel/fax 48 12 429 88 00; info@smok.krakow.pl;
www.smok.krakow.pl] Fr Kraków W ring rd site sp as No
46. Fr S 1st exit immed after x-ing rv onto rd 780 twd Kraków.
Med, pt sl, shd; wc; chem disp; mv service pnt; shwrs inc;
EHU (5-10A) PLN12; lndry; sm shop; supmkt 4km; rest 1km;
playgrnd; lake sw & windsurfing 6km; dogs PLN5; poss v cr;
some Eng spkn; adv bkg (rec for upper pitches); quiet but some
rd noise; red long stay/CKE/CCI. "On rd to Auschwitz; salt mine
at Wieliczka; friendly, well-kept site; spotless san facs; lower
field (m'vans) poss muddy after rain - tractor tow avail; poss
rallies on site; gd tour base; frequent bus to Krakow connects
with trams to cent; cycle rte to cent; gd security; tours with
pick-up fr site; excel; v helpful and friendly." PLN 85   2014*

KRETOWINY see Morąg *A3*

LEBA *A2* (2km N Coastal) *54.76150, 17.53833* **Camping**
Morski (No. 21), ul Turystyczna 3, 84-360 Łeba
[tel/fax (059) 8661380; camp21@op.pl; www.camping21.
interleba.pl] N fr Łębork on E214. Take foll sp Camping
Raphael & pass rlwy stn on L, over rv bdge twd sea. Site sp.
Lge, hdg/mkd pitch, pt shd; htd wc; chem disp; mv service pnt;
baby facs; shwrs inc; EHU (10A) PLN12; lndry (inc dryer); shop
adj; rest; bar; BBQ; cooking facs; playgrnd; sand beach 150m;
tennis; wifi; TV; dogs PLN8; phone; poss cr, adv bkg; CKE/CCI.
"Nice, well-run site in gd position; modern san facs; pleasant
resort; excel; Lacka sand dunes worth a visit." ◆
1 May-30 Sep. PLN 94 (CChq acc)   2013*

LEBA *A2* (2km NE Urban) *54.76580, 17.57145* **Camping**
Przymorze Nr. 48, ul. Nadmorska 9, 84-360 Leba
[059 866 5016; fax 866 1304; biuro@camping.leba.pl;
www.camping.leba.pl] Take DW214 dir Leba, at rndabt take
1st exit onto aleja swietego Jakuba. Turn R onto Nadmorska &
foll sp to camp. Lge, mkd pitch, pt shd; htd wc; chem disp; mv
service pnt; shwrs inc; EHU; lndry; shop; rest; BBQ; playgrnd;
sandy beach 0.5km; wifi; tv rm; 10% statics; dogs; phone;
bus adj; poss cr; Eng spkn; quiet; ccard acc; CCI. "Excel site;
shops & rest in walking dist; interesting harbour with fresh fish
for sale; windsurfing; lovely sandy beach." ◆ 1 May-30 Sep.
PLN 110   2014*

LEBA *A2* (1km SW Urban) *54.75705, 17.55178* **Camping**
Marco Polo (No. 81), ul Wspólna 6, 84-360 Łeba
[(059) 8662333; marcopolo@leba.info; www.marcopolo.
leba.info] App fr S, foll camping sp L fr main rd. Pass rlwy stn,
immed L alongside rlwy, site on R. Med, hdg/mkd pitch, unshd;
wc; chem disp; shwrs; EHU (16A) PLN10; lndry rm; shop;
snacks; bar; BBQ; sand beach 700m; games area; some statics;
poss cr; Eng spkn; CKE/CCI. "Conv Slowinksi National Park
sand dunes." 1 Jun-30 Sep. PLN 44   2010*

LEBA *A2* (1km W Rural) *54.7572, 547572* **Camping Rafael**
(No. 145), ul Turystyczna 4, 84-360 Łeba [(059) 8661972;
campingrafael@campingrafael.pl; www.campingrafael.pl]
Fr town cent, site well sp. Med, pt shd; wc; chem disp; shwrs;
EHU (16A) PLN12; lndry; shop high ssn; snacks, bar high ssn;
playgrnd; sand beach 500m; wifi; TV; 5% statics; site open
all year for statics, poss also for tourers; dogs PLN5; CKE/CCI.
"Nice site, but san facs poor (2011); easy walk to town; conv
beaches." 1 Jun-31 Aug. PLN 55   2011*

LEGNICA C2 (13km SE Rural) 51.14216, 16.24006 **Camping Legnickie Pole (No. 234), Ul Henryka Brodatego 7, 59-241 Legnickie Pole [(076) 8582397; fax 8627577; osir.legnica@ wp.pl; www.osir.legnica.pl]** Fr A4/E40 fr Görlitz take exit dir Legnickie Pole/Jawor, foll sp to vill & site. Sharp L turn after leaving main rd. Site sp on S o'skirts of Legnica on E65 & fr m'way. Sm, pt shd; wc; shwrs inc; EHU (10A) inc; shop 500m; snacks; bar; playgrnd; dogs PLN8; poss cr; no adv bkg; CKE/CCI. "Helpful, friendly welcome; clean, basic facs (hot water to shwrs only); poss diff after heavy rain; gd NH on way S; pleasant vill." ♦ 1 May-30 Sep. PLN 53   2015*

"We must tell The Club about that great site we found"

Get your site reports in by mid-August and we'll do our best to get your updates into the next edition.

LODZ C3 (9km NE Rural) 51.81591, 19.50273 **Camping Na Rogach (No. 167), ul Łupkowa 10/16, 91-527 Łódź [(042) 6306111; hotel.spt@hotel.spt.com.pl; www.hotelspt.com.pl]** Turn L off rte N14 (to Warsaw) 100m bef Peugeot dealer. Site not well sp. Call at adj hotel recep bef ent site. Sm, hdg/mkd pitch, hdstg, unshd; wc; shwrs inc; EHU (16A) inc; shop opp; playgrnd; rest adj; few statics; dogs PLN6; quiet. "Gd NH; facs run down but clean (2009); o'night coach parties." 15 May-30 Sep. PLN 50   2011*

LUBLIN C4 (8km S Rural) 51.19186, 22.52725 **Camping Graf Marina (No. 65), ul Kręźnicka 6, 20-518 Lublin [tel/fax (081) 7441070; info@graf-marina.pl; www.graf-marina.pl]** Take rd 19 S & cross rlwy line; lge parking area after 1.8km then L after 300m (no sp but leads to Zemborzyce); in 5km cross rlwy then L at T-junc; site on R in 5km on lakeside. Med, hdg/mkd pitch, unshd; wc; own san; shwrs inc; EHU (10A); shop 3km; rest; sand beach & lake sw adj; statics; Eng spkn; quiet but rd & rlwy noise; CKE/CCI. "Marina adj; sailing; fishing; site run down (early ssn 2011); sodden after rain." 1 May-30 Sep. PLN 71   2011*

MALBORK A2 (2km N Urban) 54.04741, 19.03938 **Camping Nogat (No. 197), ul Parkowa 3, 82-200 Malbork [tel/fax (055) 2722413; hotel@osirmalbork.pl; www.osir-malbork.e-tur.com.pl]** Fr Gdańsk on 1/E75 thro Tczew & join rd 22. At Malbork 1st L after main bdge over Rv Nogat. Site adj stadium & Hotel Parkowa. Well sp. Sm, pt shd; wc; chem disp; shwrs inc; EHU (10A) PLN12; Indry; supmkt 1.5km; snacks; bar; cooking facs; playgrnd; fishing; canoeing; tennis; games rm; TV; dogs PLN8; phone; quiet; CKE/CCI. "Recep at Hotel Parkowa; gd san facs; excel." ♦ 15 Apr-15 Oct. PLN 56   2011*

MIEDZYZDROJE A1 (2km W Coastal) 53.92241, 14.43505 **Camping Gromada (No. 24), ul Polna 134, 72-510 Międzyzdroje [(091) 3280275; fax 3280610; dwgrazyna@ poczta.onet.pl; www.nadmorze.pl/polenamiotowe24]** Fr Świnoujście take rd 3/E65 twd Szczecin. After 12km turn L twd Międzyzdroje. Foll sm camping sp fr town cent. Lge, pt shd; wc; chem disp; shwrs ltd; EHU (10A) PLN9; Indry; shop; snacks; bar; BBQ; playgrnd; beach 1km; TV; poss cr; quiet; CKE/CCI. "Gd NH." 1 May-30 Sep. PLN 49   2009*

MIELNO A2 (800m E Coastal) 54.26272, 16.07245 **Camping Rodzinny (No. 105), ul Chrobrego 51, 76-032 Mielno [(094) 3189385; fax 3475008; recepcja@campingrodzinny. pl; www.campingrodzinny.pl]** Fr Koszalin W on rd 11, turn N onto rd 165 to Mielno turn R at rdbt then 1 1/2 km & foll site sp. Site on L thro narr gate bet gardens - easy to miss. Sm, pt shd; htd wc; chem disp; EHU (6A) PLN1.50; Indry; shop; BBQ; cooking facs; playgrnd; sand beach 500m; games rm; internet; some statics; dogs PLN5; poss cr; some Eng spkn; adv bkg; quiet; CKE/CCI. "Easy walk to town; secure, well-kept, family-owned site; gd san facs; Gd site local to beach and shops; friendly owners." ♦ 15 Apr-15 Nov. PLN 88   2013*

MIKOLAJKI A3 (1.5km SW Rural) 53.7954, 21.56471 **Camping Wagabunda (No. 2), ul Leśna 2, 11-730 Mikołajki [tel/fax (087) 4216018; wagabunda-mikolajki@ wagabunda-mikolajki.pl; www.wagabunda-mikolajki.pl]** Exit town by rd 16 dir Mrągowo & site sp to L. Med, pt sl, unshd; wc; shwrs inc; EHU (16A) PLN13; Indry; shop & 1.5km; rest, snacks; shgl beach 2km; lake sw 400m; games area; TV; 50% statics; dogs PLN2.50; phone; poss cr; adv bkg; quiet; no ccard acc; twin-axles extra charge; Eng spkn; red LS/CKE/CCI. "Pleasant site nr nice town; san facs adequate but need update (2011); conv Masurian Lakes & historical sites; vg site; 10 min walk into town." ♦ 1 May-30 Sep. PLN 82   2013*

MORAG A3 (11km E Rural) 53.90373, 20.02753 **Camping Kretowiny (No. 247), Kretowiny29, 14-300 Morag [(089) 7582440 or (697) 523402 (mob); pensjonat@narie.pl; www.narie.pl]** Fr cent Morąg foll rd 527 S twd Olsztyn but bef exit town, fork L at sp Żabi Róg/Kretowiny. Site sp on Lake Jezioro Narie. Med, hdg pitch, pt shd; wc; chem disp; shwrs; EHU (6A) PLN8; Indry; shop; rest; bar; playgrnd; lake sw; fishing; watersports; tennis; games area; games rm; quiet; CKE/CCI. "On shore of lge, lovely lake with sw, boating, fishing; pleasant, attractive site." ♦ 1 May-30 Sep. PLN 34   2013*

🏕 **MRAGOWO** A3 (11km N Rural) 53.94278, 21.32001 **Camping Seeblick, Ruska Wieś 1, 11-700 Mrągowo [tel/fax (089) 7413155; marian.seeblick@gmail.com; www.campingpension.de]** Fr Mrągowo N on rd 591 dir Ketrzyn, site sp. Med, terr, pt shd; htd wc; chem disp; shwrs inc; EHU inc; Indry rm; shop 500m; rest; bar; lake sw; boating; tennis; games area; entmnt; quiet. "Gd but ltd san facs; lots for kids to do; shop nrby; little Eng spkn." PLN 50   2012*

🏕 **NIEDZICA** D3 (2km SE Urban) 49.40477, 20.33411 **Camping Polana Sosny (No. 38), Osiedle Na Polanie Sosny, 34-441 Niedzica [tel/fax (018) 2629403; polana. sosny@niedzica.pl; www.niedzica.pl]** Fr cent Morąg foll rd 969 fr Nowy Targ. At Dębno turn R & foll sp to border (lake on L). At 11km pass castle & 1st dam on L twds 2nd Dunajec dam. Site sp. Sm, mkd pitch, unshd; htd wc; chem disp; shwrs; fam bthrm; EHU inc; Indry/ shop 1.5km; rest adj; snacks; bar; cooking facs; rv adj; watersports; games area; phone; quiet but noise fr dam; adv bkg; quiet; red long stay; CKE/CCI. "Beautiful, well-maintained site in superb location; friendly, helpful staff; clean, modern san facs; excel walks in mountains; 2km to Slovakian border; vg touring base." ♦ PLN 42   2010*

NOWY SACZ D3 (400m N Urban) 49.61975, 20.71548
Camping Dom Turysty Nowy Sącz (No. 87), ul Nadbrzeżna 40, 33-300 Nowy Sącz [tel/fax (018) 4415012; apazdyk@gmail.com] Fr W on rd 28 cross Rv Dunajec & in 2km at rndabt turn L into rd 75. Site on L. Sm, mkd pitch, some hdstg, pt shd; wc; chem disp; shwrs; EHU (16A); lndry; shops 1km; snacks; bar; BBQ; quiet; CKE/CCI. "Close to Slovakian border & lakes."
♦ 1 May-30 Sep. PLN 23   2010*

OLSZTYN A3 (8km W Rural) 53.78686, 20.40170 Agro Camping, ul Młodzieżowa 1, 11-041 Olsztyn [(089) 5238666] Fr Olsztyn W on rd 16 for approx 5km, turn N thro Łupstych & foll site sp. Sm, pt sl, pt shd; wc; shwr; some Eng spkn; quiet. "Lovely position on Lake Ukiel; CL-type site with facs."
1 May-30 Sep.   2009*

⊞ **OSWIECIM** D3 (4km S Rural) 50.02262, 19.19891 Centre for Dialogue & Prayer in Auschwitz, ul Maksymiliana Kolbego 1, 32-600 Oświęcim [(033) 8431000; fax 8431001; biuro@centrum-dialogu.oswiecim.pl; www.centrum-dialogu.oswiecim.pl] 700m fr Auschwitz 1 museum car park on parallel rd to S, on forecourt of hotel-like building. Sm, hdstg, unshd; wc; shwrs inc; EHU inc; shops 2km; rest; BBQ; phone; Eng spkn; rd noise; CKE/CCI. "Conv Auschwitz museum & Auschwitz-Birkenau (3km); clean, modern, site; gd, clean san facs, similar quality to UK CC sites; friendly, helpful staff; v nice site; excel facs; a gem of a site; highly rec." ♦
PLN 80   2015*

⊞ **OSWIECIM** D3 (2km W Urban) 50.02895, 19.20054 Parking Przy Museum Auschwitz, 32-600 Oświęcim Foll sp to Auschwitz museum fr rd 933. Parking area is on opp side of rd (away fr main car park) by TO. M'vans only. Sm; EHU (6A) PLN7; shop; rest, snacks; bar; internet; water PLN6; dogs; quiet. "NH only permitted; ltd EHU; allow 4 hrs for museum tour; basically a big car park with a few elec points; internet at TO or wifi at pizza rest." PLN 40   2014*

PIECKI A3 (2km N Rural) 53.77938, 21.33583 Camping Piecki (No. 269), ul Zwycięstwa 60, 11-710 Piecki [tel/fax (089) 7421025; owpttk@post.pl; www.owpttk.pl] Site sp bet Mrągowo & Piecki on rd 59. No sps except sm sp at ent. In Masurian Lake District 3km to W of Piecki. NB Ent tight lge o'fits. Med, pt sl, pt shd; wc; chem disp (wc); shwrs inc; EHU (10A) PLN12; lndry; shop, rest & snacks 5km; bar; BBQ; playgrnd; lake sw; watersports; games area; TV; 10% statics; dogs PLN10; bus adj; Eng spkn; adv bkg; poss noisy high ssn due school parties; CKE/CCI. "San facs poor; NH only."
1 May-30 Sep. PLN 50   2011*

POLANICA ZDROJ see Kłodzko D2

⊞ **POZNAN** B2 (5km E Urban) 52.40343, 16.98399 Camping Malta (No. 155), ul Krańcowa 98, 61-036 Poznań-Malta [(061) 8766203; fax 8766283; camping@malta.poznan.pl; www.poznan.pl] Fr A2/E30 Poznań bypass leave at rte 2/11 dir Poznań. Turn R at traff Its onto rte 5/E261 sp Malta, Zoo & camping, site sp. Sm, hdg pitch, pt shd; htd wc; chem disp; shwrs inc; EHU (16A) inc; lndry; shop; snacks; bar; shop 1km; lake adj; many statics; tram to city; Eng spkn; quiet but loud disco across lake at w/end; ccard acc; red CKE/CCI. "Clean tidy site on lake with sports but poss unkempt pitches LS; 6 tram stops to Poznań Sq; vg 24-hr security; helpful staff; site amongst sports facs by lake." ♦ PLN 108   2014*

PRZEWORSK D4 (1km W Urban) 50.06138, 22.48361 Camping Pastewnik (No. 221), ul Łańcucka 2, 37-200 Przeworsk [(016) 6492300; fax 6492301; zajazdpastewnik@hot.pl; www.pastewnik.prv.pl] On N side of N4/E40, sp. Sm, pt shd; wc; shwrs inc; EHU (10A) PLN10; lndry; shop adj; rest, snacks; bar; playgrnd; Eng spkn; rd noise; ccard acc; CKE/CCI. "Conv NH/sh stay with motel & rest; Łańcut Castle & Carriage Museum 25km; elec v dubious, no socket circuit breakers." 1 May-30 Sep. PLN 112   2013*

ROWY A2 (750m S Coastal) 54.65940, 17.04926 Camping Prymorze (No. 156), ul Bałtycka 6, 76-212 Rowy [tel/fax (059) 8141940; biuro@przymorze.com.pl; www.przymorze.com.pl] Fr Ustka on coast rd, site on rd into Rowy. Med, pt shd; wc; shwrs inc; EHU (16A) inc; lndry; shop; snacks; bar; cooking facs; playgrnd; pool 300m; TV; dogs €2; phone; quiet. "Sm fishing port; gd facs; helpful staff." ♦ ltd.
1 May-31 Aug. PLN 75   2009*

⊞ **RUCIANE NIDA** A3 (8km N Rural) 53.68668, 21.54713 Camping Nad Zatoka (No. 9), Wygryny 52, 12-220 Ruciane Nida [(087) 4231597 or (502) 328111 (mob); fax 4236342; zbigre@orange.pl; www.ter-lid.com.pl] Fr rte 58 N onto rd 610 NE twds Piecki for 4km. Turn R for Wygryny 2km, foll sp in vill. Sm, pt sl, unshd; wc; chem disp; mv service pnt; shwrs inc; EHU (16A) PLN10; lndry; shop 300m; rest, bar nrby; BBQ; playgrnd; sand beach; lake sw; canoe & bike hire; dogs PLN6; poss cr; quiet. "Private site in field on lakeside; beautiful scenery; vg san facs; excel." PLN 50   2013*

RYDZEWO MILKI see Giżycko A3

SANDOMIERZ C3 (1km E Urban) 50.68010, 21.75502 Camping Browarny (No. 201), ul Żwirki I Wigury 1, 27-600 Sandomierz [(015) 8332703; fax 8323050; wmajsak@poczta.fm; www.majsak.pl] Fr S on rd 79, cross rv bdge, site on L. Sm, pt shd; wc; chem disp; mv service pnt; shwrs inc; EHU (16A) PLN10; lndry; shop in town; rest nr; bar; BBQ; cooking facs; playgrnd; games rm; dogs; wifi; phone; bus adj; poss cr; Eng spkn; adv bkg; some rd noise; CKE/CCI. "Attractive sm town in walking dist; vg site; helpful staff." ♦ Easter-30 Oct.
PLN 42   2012*

SIERAKOW B2 (2km SE Rural) 52.63324, 16.09870 Camping Sieraków Owir (No. 109), ul Poznańska 28, 64-410 Sieraków [(061) 2952868; recepcja@owir.sierakow.pl; www.sierakow.pl] Fr rd 182 in town cent, SE on ul Ponzańska on L, opp hotel. Not well sp. Med, pt sl, shd; wc; chem disp (wc); shwrs inc; EHU (5A) PLN5; lndry rm; shop 200m; rest 300m; snacks; bar & 300m; htd covrd pool; lake sw & beach 300m; boating; TV rm; 5% statics; phone; poss cr & noisy w/end; CKE/CCI. "Poss pop concerts on beach in summer; gd san facs; site poss diff lge o'fits due tall trees." ♦
20 Jun-30 Sep.   2009*

SLAWA C2 (1km NW Rural) 51.88145, 16.05817 Camping Słoneczny (No. 261), ul Odrodzonego Wojska Polskiego 19, 67-410 Sława [tel/fax (068) 3566452; osir.slawa@wp.pl; www.osir.slawa.pl] Site sp on lakeside. Sm, mkd pitch, pt shd; wc; chem disp; EHU; lndry; snacks; lake sw; waterslide; fishing; games area; bike hire; some statics; adv bkg; quiet; CKE/CCI. "Beautiful location; friendly, helpful owners; san facs unclean (6/09)." 1 May-30 Sep. PLN 50   2009*

SOPOT *A2* (2km N Urban) *54.46136, 18.5556* **Camping Kamienny Potok (No. 19), ul Zamkowa Góra 25, 220-474 and 27-468 Sopot [tel/fax (058) 5500445; kempingnr19@ wp.pl; www.kemping19.cba.pl]** Fr Gdańsk rte 27 twds Sopot. Site on R just behind Shell petrol stn. Fr N on rte 6/E28 turn S at Gdynia, onto new section of E28, for 7.5km. Turn L onto rte 220 by 'Euromarket' for 5km. Turn R onto rte 27 (S) twd Gdańsk & site nr Shell g'ge on opp c'way. Lge, mkd pitch, pt shd; wc; chem disp; shwrs inc; EHU (2-20A) PLN10; lndry; shop 500m; snacks; bar; playgrnd; TV; phone; poss cr; rd & rlwy noise; ccard acc; red CKE/CCI. "Pleasant site; friendly & helpful staff; frequent trains for Gdansk 250m; modern, clean san facs; gd security; gd walking/cycling track into town; busy site; upgrades in process (2012)." 1 May-30 Sep. PLN 72   2012*

STEGNA *A2* (2km N Coastal) *54.34186, 19.1176* **Camping Stegna No. 159, ul Morska 26, 82-103 Stegna [(055) 2478303; fax 2478034; camp@camp.pl; www.camp.pl]** Fr Stegna vill on rte 501 turn N at church onto Morska. Site on R, sp. Sm, shd; wc; chem disp; shwrs inc; EHU (10A) PLN8; lndry; shop 300m; rest, snacks, bar 100m; playgrnd; sand beach 400m; 10% statics; dogs PLN4; Eng spkn; adv bkg; quiet. "Friendly, family-run site; gd security; gd base Gdansk 30km; rec." 1 May-30 Sep. PLN 56   2009*

STETTIN see Szczecin *B1*

STRZESZYNEK see Poznań *B2*

SULECIN *B1* (4km S Rural) *52.40911, 15.11761* **Camping Marina (No. 50), Ostrów 76, 69-200 Sulęcin [tel/fax (957) 552294 or (171) 3704553; przemyslaw-gula@wp.pl; www.camping-marina.eu]** Cross border fr Frankfurt-an-Oder & take rd 2 to Torzym (35km). In Torzym turn L onto rd 138 dir Sulęcin; thro Tursk & site in 3km. Med, mkd pitch, pt shd; wc; mv service pnt; shwrs; EHU €2; lndry; supmkt 4km; snacks; bar; playgrnd; lake sw; fishing; bike hire; wifi; TV rm; some statics; dogs €1; adv bkg; quiet; red CKE/CCI. "Gd, modern san facs; gd walking/cycling; pleasant, relaxing site; conv Berlin." ♦ 1 Apr-31 Oct. PLN 63   2013*

SUWALKI *A3* (11km SE Rural) *54.0767, 23.0742* **Kajaki Camping Pokoje, 16-412 Stary Folwark 44, Wigry [(087) 5637789; wigry@wigry.info; www.wigry.info]** Fr Suwalki take 653 dir Sejny. In about 11km turn R in Stary Folwark at PTTK sp. Site on R in approx 100m. Sm, unshd; wc; chem disp; shwrs inc; EHU (10A) inc; lndry; BBQ; lake sw & kayaking nrby; wifi; Eng spkn; quiet. "Nr lake in National Park; kayaking fr site; vg site." 1 May-30 Sep. PLN 40   2011*

SWIECIE *B2* (1km S Urban) *53.40321, 18.45574* **Camping Zamek (No. 54), ul Zamkowa 10, 86-100 Świecie [tel/fax (052) 3311726 or 604 993 070; recepcja@camping-zamek.pl; www.camping-zamek.pl]** S fr Gdańsk on E75 take rd 1 to Chełmno & Świecie. Cross Rv Wisła & L at x-rds in Świecie cent; site sp at traff lts. Med, shd; wc; own san rec; shwrs; EHU (10A); lndry; shop; bar; playgrnd; games area; fishing; 50% statics; dogs; phone; quiet. "Interesting town & churches; helpful staff; in castle grnds (tower visible fr rd); if gate clsd, ring bell on L; new tolet block (2012)." 1 May-15 Sep. PLN 25   2012*

⊞ **SWINOUJSCIE** *A1* (2km N Coastal) *53.91709, 14.25693* **Camping Relax (No. 44), ul Słowackiego 1, 72-600 Świnoujście [(097) 3213912; relax@osir.uznam.net.pl; www.camping-relax.com.pl]** Fr E rd 3/E65 cross rv on free ferry. Fr town cent N for 500m. No vehicle border x-ing fr W. V lge, shd; wc; shwrs inc; EHU (16A) PLN10; lndry; shops 500m; snacks; cooking facs; playgrnd; beach 200m; games rm; wifi; phone; quiet; adv bkg; ccard acc. "Nice town; gd beach; gd walking; site popular with families; red snr citizens." PLN 65   2012*

⊞ **SZCZECIN/STETTIN** *B1* (8km SE Rural) *53.39505, 14.63640* **Marina Camping (No. 25), ul Przestrzenna 23, 70-800 Szczecin-Dabie [tel/fax (091) 4601165; camping.marina@ pro.onet.pl; www.campingmarina.pl]** Fr E28/A6 take A10 sp Szczecin. Immed after rlwy bdge turn R sp Dąbie. At traff lts in cent Dąbie turn L, site on R in approx 2km on lake. Med, pt shd; htd wc; mv service pnt; baby facs; shwrs; EHU (6A) inc; lndry (inc dryer); shop 2km; supmkt 3km; rest, snacks; bar; lake sw; boat hire; tennis; games area; dog; wifi; bus to Stettin; poss cr; noise fr late arr & early deps; red CKE/CCI. "Pleasant, lakeside site; clean, modern san facs but inadequate if site full; bus tickets fr recep; helpful staff; vg site on lake side." PLN 106 (CChq acc)   2014*

⊞ **TARNOW** *D3* (2km N Rural) *50.02320, 20.98813* **Camping Pod Jabłoniami (No. 202), ul Piłsudskiego 28a, 33-100 Tarnów [(014) 6215124; fax 6522933; recepcja@camping. tarnow.pl; www.camping.tarnow.pl]** E fr Kraków on E40, foll sp to Tarnów 'Centrum'. Turn L by Tesco & foll sp to site. Sm, pt sl, pt shd; wc; chem disp; shwrs inc; EHU (16A) PLN10; lndry; supmkt 2km; rest, bar 1km; BBQ; playgrnd; pool adj; wifi; TV; poss cr; Eng spkn; some rd noise; red CKE/CCI. "Walk to attractive town; vg site." ♦ ltd. PLN 85   2013*

TORUN *B2* (2km S Urban) *53.00138, 18.60472* **Camping Tramp (No. 33), ul Kujawska 14, 87-100 Toruń [tel/fax (056) 6547187; tramp@mosir.torun.pl; www.mosir.torun.pl]** Cross bdge S of town & take 1st L at traff lts, site sp in 500m on rvside. Med, shd; wc; chem disp; shwrs; EHU (10A) inc; lndry; shop 500m; rest 1.5km; snacks; bar; games area; some statics; dogs PLN4.50; continual traffic noise & poss noise fr bar; red CKE/CCI. "Noisy, busy site but reasonable; walking dist fr interesting old town across bdge; gd security; NH/sh stay only." ♦ 1 May-30 Sep. PLN 62   2010*

UCIECHOW *C2* (1km E Rural) *50.75561, 16.69412* **Camping Forteca, ul. Wroclawska 12, 58-211 Uciechów (Dolnoslaskie) [(074) 8323008; info@campingforteca.nl; www.campingforteca.nl]** Fr cent of Dzierzoniów foll rd 384 twds Lagiewniki and Wroclaw for 4km. In cent of Uciechów go ahead at crossrds. After 400m turn R down gravel track sp to rest and parking. Sm, pt sl; wc; chem disp; child/baby facs; shwrs; EHU (16A) 15 ZL; rest, bar; BBQ; lake adj; wifi; 10% appartments; dog 5 ZL; twin axle; Eng spkn; adv bkg acc; CKE/CCI. "Pitches surround lake where sw; fishing and boating permitted; new clean toilet block; helpful, friendly family owners; lovely peaceful site LS; open plan, grassy site." 1 Apr-1 Oct. PLN 88   2013*

USTKA *A2* (1.6km SE Urban) *54.57655, 16.88088* **Camping Morski (No. 101), ul Armii Krajowej 4, Przewloka, 76-270 Ustka [tel/fax (059) 8144789 or 8144426; cam_mor@pro. onet.pl; www.camping-morski.afr.pl]** Fr Koszalin & Sławno to Słupsk on rd 6/E28 turn L to Ustka. Foll main rd which bears R & foll camping sp to R. After 200m turn R at rndabt & camp on L after 300m. Sm, pt shd; wc; shwrs; EHU (6A) inc; lndry; shop 500m; rest adj; snacks; bar; BBQ; playgrnd; beach 1.3km; tennis; dogs; quiet; red long stay/CKE/CCI. "Seaside resort with gd shopping & fishing port; vg for children; gd cycling; gd nh; 30 min walk to town." ♦ 1 May-30 Sep. PLN 60   2013*

WALCZ *B2* (17km N Rural) *53.37965, 16.49992* **Camping Zdbice, 78-611 Wałcz [tel/fax (067) 2581677]** Fr N on rd 22 at Szwecja turn R at sp Zdbice, site sp. Site on L bef vill of Zdbice. Med, pt sl, unshd; wc; chem disp (wc); shwrs; EHU; bar; lake sw adj; statics; quiet. "Pleasant site on lakeside; facs basic but adequate; at site ent, stop to register & ask owner to open gate at 2nd ent - main ent has diff turn & overhanging branches; if arr late - phone number displayed on barrier." 1 May-30 Sep. PLN 49   2010*

WARSZAWA *B3* (13km SE Urban) *52.17798, 21.14727* **Camping Wok (No. 90), ul Odrębna 16, 04-867 Warszawa [(022) 6127951; fax 6166127; wok@campingwok. warszawa.pl; www.campingwok.warszawa.pl]** Fr city cent or fr W on E30, take bdge on E30 over Rv Wisła to E side of rv. Then take rte 801 for approx 8km (dual c'way). At rndabt double back for 600m & take 3rd R into Odrębna. Site 200m on R. Sm, shd; htd wc; chem disp; mv service pnt; baby facs; shwrs inc; EHU (10-16A) PLN15; gas; lndry; shop 700m; rest 1km; snacks; bar; BBQ; cooking facs; playgrnd; games area; internet; TV; bus/tram adj; Eng spkn; adv bkg; quiet; ccard acc; red CKE/CCI. "Lovely little site; v secure; spotless, modern san facs; helpful staff." 1 Apr-31 Oct. PLN 85   2012*

"I need an on-site restaurant"

We do our best to make sure site information is correct, but it is always best to check any must-have facilities are still available or will be open during your visit.

WARSZAWA *B3* (4km W Urban) *52.2144, 20.96575* **Majawa Camping (No. 123), ul Bitwy Warszawskiej 19/20, 02-366 Warszawa-Szcześliwice [(022) 8229121; fax 8237244; biuro@majawa.pl; www.majawa.pl]** Fr W on E30/rd 2 at junc with E67/rd 8 rd goes S thro tunnel under rlwy then strt on under new over-pass. Site on R in 100m. On E67/rd 8 fr Wrocław app concrete monument 3m high in middle of tramway; turn L at traff lts. Hotel Vera on R, site on L. Fr cent of Warsaw, take rd no. 7/8 700m twds Katowice. Not v well sp fr cent of town. Ent & exit diff due v busy rd. Sm, pt shd; wc; chem disp; shwrs inc; EHU (6A) PLN15; lndry rm; shop 300m; rest 100m; BBQ; tennis; some statics; phone; bus 500m; poss cr; Eng spkn; ccard acc; red CKE/ CCI. "Easy access to Warsaw & Royal Castle; gd meals at adj bowling alley or Vera hotel; poss lge rallies on site; friendly; poor condition but well positioned to get into city." 1 May-30 Sep. PLN 152   2014*

WARSZAWA *B3* (17km W Rural) *52.23066, 20.79196* **Campsite Kaputy 222, Sochaczewska 222, 05-850 Kreczki, (Mazowieckie) [(022) 1100061; biuro@camping222.pl; www.camping222.pl]** Head S on SS36, take exit Pescate twd Pescate/Lecco/Malgrate/SS583/Bellagio/Calco, cont strt; at rndabt take 3rd exit via Roma, go thro 1 rndabt; cont onto Via Statale, turn L onto Via Foppaola, site on L. Med, mkd pitch, htd wc; chem disp; mv service pnt; shwr; EHU 15PLN; lndry; bread on site; Wifi 10PLN; dogs 5PLN; public transport adj; Eng spkn; quiet; CCI. "Fishing lake on site; NH or visit to Warsaw; excel san facs; clean, spacious site & easy to find." ♦ 15 Apr-31 Oct. PLN 95   2014*

WEGORZEWO *A3* (4km SE Rural) *54.18647, 21.77018* **Camping Rusałka (No. 175), ul Lesna 2, 11-600 Węgorzewo [(087) 4272191; fax 4272049; camp.175@wp.pl; www.cmazur.pl]** Fr rte 63 fr Giżycko to Węgorzewo turn W approx 3km SW of Węgorzewo. Foll sp to site. Lge, pt shd; wc; chem disp (wc); shwrs inc; EHU PLN8; lndry; shops 2km; snacks; bar; playgrnd; lake sw adj; fishing; sailing; many statics; dogs; quiet. "Lovely pt of Lake District; delightful situation; all facs at top of steep hill." 1 May-30 Sep. PLN 48   2012*

WIELICZKA *D3* (1.5km SE Urban) *49.98273, 20.07611* **Motel Camping Wierzynka, ul Wierzynka 9, 32-020 Wieliczka [tel/fax (012) 2783614; motel@nawierzynka.pl; www. nawierzynka.pl]** Site sp fr E40/rte 4 about 2km fr salt mine. Sm, some hdstg, pt sl, pt shd; wc; shwrs; EHU (10A) PLN10 (rev pol); shop 1.5km; rest, snacks; bar; bike hire; wifi; bus to Krakow; train 1km; poss cr; Eng spkn; quiet; ccard acc (fee); CKE/CCI. "10 pitches in pleasant setting; helpful staff; facs basic but clean; shwrs erratic; 2km fr salt mines; vg site, local to salt mines; shwr portacabin, but clean." 1 May-30 Sep. PLN 80   2014*

WROCLAW *C2* (4km NE Urban) *51.11722, 17.09138* **Stadion Olimpijski Camp (No. 117), ul Padarewskiego 35, 51-620 Wrocław [tel/fax (071) 3484651]** Fr A4 into Wrocław foll N8 sp Warszawa thro city. On N8 dir Warszawa, pass McDonalds, at fork in rd take Sienkiewicza to end, then Rozyckiego to stadium, site on R. If poss foll sp 'stadion' to camp; head for lighting towers of sports stadium if seen thro trees. Lge, pt shd; wc; shwrs inc; EHU (16A) PLN7.50; lndry rm; shops, rest adj; snacks; bar; BBQ; playgrnd; pool 700m; 10% statics; dogs; tram nr; phone; poss cr; no adv bkg; poss noise fr stadium; red CKE/CCI. "San facs basic but clean; site in need of modernisation (2010); gd security; v conv for city but NH only; run down." 1 May-15 Oct. PLN 72   2014*

⊞ **ZAKOPANE** *D3* (4km NE Rural) *49.32415, 19.98506* **Camping Harenda (No. 160), Oś Harenda 51B, 34-500 Zakopane [tel/fax (018) 2014700; harenda51b@gmail.com; www.harenda.tatrynet.pl]** On main rd to Zakopane fr N, after town sp turn R into petrol stn with McDonalds. Cont to R, pass Cmp Ustep on L then turn L over rv bdge to site in 200m on R. Med, pt sl, pt shd; htd wc; shwrs inc; chem disp; mv service pnt; EHU (10A) PLN10 (long lead req); lndry; shop 100m; rest; BBQ; playgrnd; dogs; wifi; poss cr; Eng spkn; no adv bkg; some train noise & barking dogs; red CKE/CCI. "Gd views Tatra mountains fr site; superb walking; poss rallies on site; poss unkempt LS; laundry done at modest cost; vg rest; rafting (not white water) on Dunajec Rv; Nowy Targ rec; lower site poss muddy in wet weather." PLN 52   2014*

ZAKOPANE *D3* (4km NE Rural) *49.32229, 19.98550* **Camping Ustup (No. 207), ul Ustup K/5, 34-500 Zakopane-Ustup [(0605) 950007; camping.ustup@gmail.com]** Turn R off Kraków-Zakopane rd 47 at petrol stn/McDonalds just after 1st town sp. Turn R again immed (also sp Cmg Harenda), site on L in 200m. Sm, pt sl, unshd; wc; chem disp; baby facs; shwrs inc; EHU (10A) inc; shop adj; rest opp; playgrnd; bus to town cent; poss cr; adv bkg; quiet; CKE/CCI. "Ideal cent for Tatra region; mountain views; excel, family-run site; v welcoming, friendly & helpful owner (ltd Eng); vg, clean san facs; grassy pitches; coach tours arranged fr adj g'ge info desk." 1 May-5 Oct. PLN 94   2014*

⊞ **ZAKOPANE** *D3* (3km SE Urban) *49.2830, 19.9690* **Camping Pod Krokwia (No. 97), ul Żeromskiego 26, 34-500 Zakopane [tel/fax (018) 2012256; camp@podkrokwia.pl; www.pod krokwia.pl]** Sp fr town cent. Fr N 2nd exit at 1st rndbt; strt over at 2nd rndbt; turn R at 3rd rndabt, then R in 250m. Site on L. Lge, hdstg, pt sl, shd; wc; chem disp; shwrs inc; EHU (10A) inc; lndry; shop 500m; rest, snacks; bar nr; BBQ; cooking facs; playgrnd; pool, tennis adj; bus to Kraków; ski slopes & cable cars; rafting on rapids; wifi; TV; dogs PLN5; phone; poss cr; Eng spkn; quiet; CKE/CCI. "Lge tent area; few mkd pitches; poss scruffy LS; poor san facs; conv town cent; muddy when set; conv Tatra Mountains; mountain walks; town v touristy; vg loc; ltd facs; free gas stove." PLN 65.4   2012*

⊞ **ZAMOSC** *C4* (1km SW Rural) *50.71919, 23.23908* **Camping Duet (No. 253), ul Królowej Jadwigi 14, 22-400 Zamość [tel/fax (084) 6392499; duet@virgo.com.pl; www.duet.virgo.com.pl]** Fr Zamość cent W on rd 74, site on R bef Castorama. Sm, pt shd; wc; chem disp (wc); shwrs inc; EHU PLN12; shop opp; rest, snacks; bar; pool 150m; some statics; dogs; poss cr; quiet; CKE/CCI. "Walk to attractive town; fair sh stay/NH." PLN 31   2011*

⊞ **ZGORZELEC** *C1* (1km N Urban) *51.15957, 15.00069* **Camping Zgorzelec, ul Lubańska 1a, 59-900 Zgorzelec [(075) 7752436; ardi@op.pl]** Ent Zgorzelec fr Germany & foll rd sp Zagan. Turn L at traff lts at BP g'ge INTO Lubanska rd sp 351 site on R after 560m, bef downwards hill. Only sp is at camp gate. Sm, pt sl, unshd; wc; EHU inc; CKE/CCI. "Conv NH." PLN 60   2012*

ZIELONA GORA *C2* (4km NE Urban) *51.95338, 15.53037* **Leśny Camping (No. 52), ul Sulechowska 39, 65-022 Zielona Góra [tel/fax (068) 3253636; hotel.lesny@op.pl]** Fr N on E65 fr Swebodzin, L to cent of town & immed L again. Hotel Lesny is sp. Go to recep for key. Sm, pt shd; wc; chem disp; shwrs; EHU (10A); lndry; shop 1km; rest; cooking facs; playgrnd; games area; adv bkg; ccard acc; CKE/CCI. ♦ ltd. 1 May-30 Oct.   2010*

ZLOCIENIEC *B2* (13km SW Rural) *53.46123, 15.91964* **Inter Nos Island Camping (No. 110), ul Błędno 1, 78-520 Złocieniec [(094) 3631190 or (0602) 554348 (mob); m.moser@inter-nos.pl; www.inter-nos.pl]** Fr Stettin E on rd 10 to Stargard Szczeciński then rd 20 to Drawsko Pomorski. In Drawsko take rd sp Lubieszewo & foll site sps W to lakeside. Access to site on island by ferry. Med, pt shd; wc; chem disp; sauna; shwrs; EHU €1.50; lndry rm; shop; rest, snacks; bar; BBQ; playgrnd; lake sw & beach; watersports; tennis; bike hire; horseriding; TV rm; dogs; adv bkg; quiet. "Scenic area." ♦ 1 May-30 Sep. PLN 71 (CChq acc)   2009*

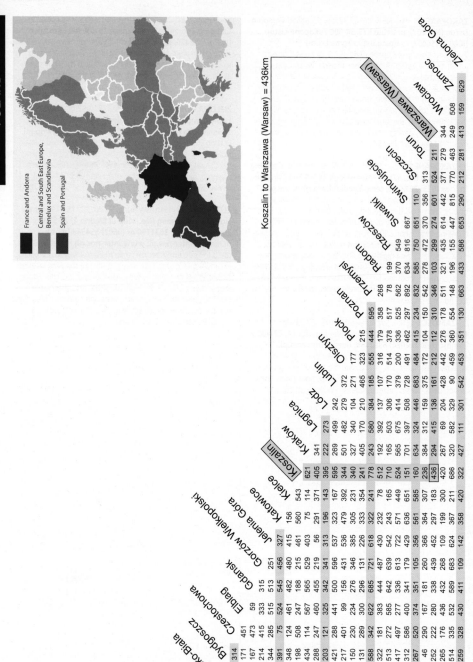

France and Andorra

Central and South East Europe, Benelux and Scandinavia

Spain and Portugal

Koszalin to Warszawa (Warsaw) = 436km

Warszawa (Warsaw)

Zielona Góra · Zamosc · Wrocław · Toruń · Szczecin · Świnoujście · Suwałki · Rzeszów · Radom · Przemyśl · Poznań · Płock · Olsztyn · Lublin · Łódź · Legnica · Kraków · Koszalin · Kielce · Katowice · Jelenia Góra · Gorzów Wielkopolski · Gdańsk · Elbląg · Częstochowa · Bydgoszcz · Bielsko-Biała · Białystok · Biała Podlaska

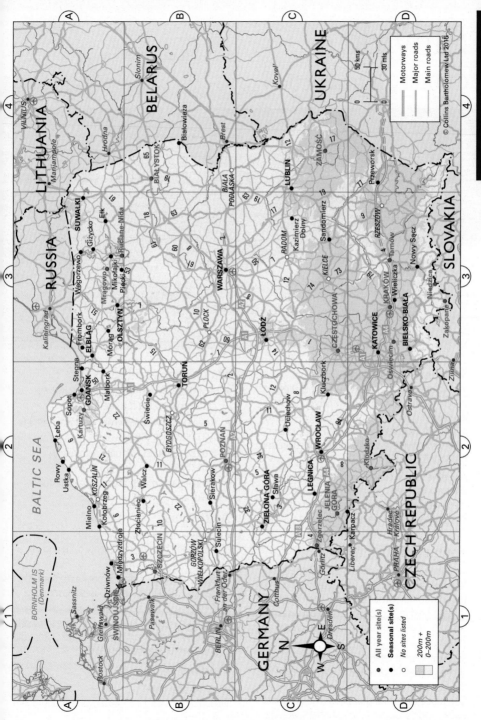

POLAND

© Collins Bartholomew Ltd 2016

Slovakia
Country Introduction

Bratislava Castle

Welcome to Slovakia

Well known for the sheer volume of castles to be found, Slovakia is a country rich in culture. It retains much of its sense of tradition, both in its beautiful medieval towns such as Levoča or Bardejov and in the small villages dotted around the countryside.

A relatively small country with an untamed and diverse wilderness, Slovakia is a great place for those wanting to experience new and different landscapes on a daily basis.

Country highlights

Slovakia has a rich tradition of folklore, and festivals celebrating local folk customs are found throughout the country. The oldest of these is held in Východná, and showcases parades, music, costumes and local crafts.

There are several speciality foods found in Slovakia, one of which is bryndza, a creamy sheep's cheese known for its strong smell. It is the main ingredient of Bryndzové Halušky, a dish made of potato dumplings, bryndza and bacon and considered the national speciality.

Major towns and cities

- Bratislava – a unique capital with a hill-top castle overlooking the city.
- Košice – the well-preserved historical centre is full of heritage sites.
- Prešov – a tourist favourite with many attractions.
- Žilina – packed with museums and historic buildings.

Attractions

- Tatras National Park – with a rich variety of flora and fauna there is plenty to discover in this gorgeous landscape.
- Spiš Castle – the sprawling remains of a 12th century castle that now houses a fascinating museum.
- Nedbalka Gallery, Bratislava – admire the works of major modern artists from Slovakia from the 19th century to the present day.

Find out more

www.slovakia.travel
Tel:0042 (0) 14 84 13 61 46 Slovakia Tourist Board

Country Information

Population (approx): 5.4 million

Capital: Bratislava (population approx 500,000)

Area: 49,036 sq km

Bordered by: Austria, Czech Republic, Hungary, Poland, Ukraine

Terrain: Rugged mountains in the centre and north; lowlands in the south

Climate: Continental climate; warm, showery summers; cold, cloudy, snowy winters; best months to visit are May, June and September

Highest Point: Gerlachovský štít 2,655m

Languages: Slovak, Hungarian, German

Local Time: GMT or BST + 1, i.e. 1 hour ahead of the UK all year

Currency: Euros divided into 100 cents; £1 = €1.42, €1 = £0.71 (September 2015)

Emergency numbers: Police 112; Fire brigade 112; Ambulance 112

Public Holidays 2016: Jan 1, 6; Mar 25, 28; May 1, 8; Jul 5; Aug 29; Sep 1, 15; Nov 1, 17; Dec 24, 25, 26.

School summer holidays are from the beginning of July to the end of August

Camping and Caravanning

There are approximately 175 campsites (Kemping or Autocamp) situated near tourist resorts and classified into four categories. Sites are normally open from 15 June until 15 September, although some may open in May and a handful are open all year. The season is slow to get going and sites which claim to open in May may not do so or there may be only minimal facilities.

Campsites' standards are variable and facilities may be basic. Many consist mainly of cabins and chalets in various states of repair, while others form part of the facilities offered by hotels, guest houses or leisure/thermal spa complexes.

Casual/wild camping is not permitted; it is prohibited to sleep in a caravan or motorhome outside a campsite.

Campsite prices and the cost of living in general are still relatively low. Some of the prices shown in the campsite entries that follow have been directly converted from prices previously shown in koruna (crowns) and rounded up. You may find actual prices somewhat higher now that the official currency is the euro. Prices charged include a tourist tax.

Cycling

There are a number of long distance cycle tracks throughout the country (visit the website www.slovakia.travel for more information) including alongside the River Danube between Bratislava and the Gabčikovo Dam.

Cyclists must ride in single file on the right hand side of the road or may use the verge outside built up areas. Children under 10 years of age may not ride on the road unless accompanied by a person over 15 years of age.

Electricity and Gas

Usually the current on campsites varies between 10 and 16 amps. Plugs have two round pins. Some campsites, but not all, have CEE connections.

It is not possible to purchase Campingaz International or any other of the gas cylinders normally available in the UK. Sufficient supplies for your stay should be taken with you. Many sites have communal kitchen facilities which enable visitors to make great savings on their own gas supply.

Entry Formalities

Holders of valid British and Irish passports may visit Slovakia for up to three months without a visa. There are no registration formalities for short stay visitors.

All foreign visitors are required to show proof of medical insurance cover on entry.

Medical Services

Medical facilities are variable. Whereas the standard of care from doctors is good and medical equipment is constantly improving, many hospitals suffer from a lack of maintenance. The biggest problem you will probably encounter is language, as nurses and ancillary workers may not speak English.

SLOVAKIA

There is a reciprocal health care agreement with the UK for urgent medical treatment and you should present a European Health Insurance Card (EHIC). Emergency treatment is from doctors and dentists contracted to the Slovak health insurance system, but you will be asked for payment and follow on costs could be considerable. Hospital patients are required to make a financial contribution towards costs.

Charges incurred are not refundable in Slovakia.

A 24 hour first aid service exists in all provincial and district towns, as well as in some small communities. For minor ailments, the first call should be to a pharmacy (lekáren) where staff are qualified to give advice and may be able to prescribe drugs normally available only on prescription in the UK.

Hepatitis A immunisation is advised for long stay travellers to rural areas, and those who plan to travel outside tourist areas.

Opening Hours

Banks – Mon-Fri 8am-3pm/5pm.

Museums – Tue-Sun 10am-5pm; closed Mon.

Post Offices – Mon-Fri 8am-6pm; Sat 8am-1pm.

Shops – Mon-Fri 7am-6pm; Sat 7am-12 noon. Hypermarkets usually open Sun.

Food Shops - Mon-Fri 7am-6pm; Sat 7am-12pm. Department Stores - Mon-Sat 9am-9pm

Safety and Security

Most visits to Slovakia are trouble free. However, there is a risk of being a victim of petty theft, particularly in Bratislava, and pickpocketing is common at the main tourist attractions and in some bars where foreigners are easily identified.

When placing your jacket on the back of a chair in a restaurant make sure you don't leave valuables in the pockets. Don't put handbags on the floor or under chairs, where they may be vulnerable to theft. There have been occurrences in Bratislava of visitors being offered 'spiked' drinks and subsequently being robbed.

Visitors entering Slovakia via the border crossings on the D2 and D4 motorways should be extremely vigilant. While you leave your vehicle to buy petrol or a motorway vignette, a tyre may be deliberately damaged. Once you are back on the road and have driven a few kilometres other motorists will flag you down under the pretext of offering assistance. In these circumstances you should stay in your vehicle with the doors locked and call the police (dial 112) or the emergency service of the Slovensky Autoturist Klub (SATC) on18124 or (02) 68249211.

Robberies from parked cars are on the increase. Cameras, mobile phones and tablets are as attractive as cash and credit cards; don't leave them or other valuables unattended.

If you intend to ski or hike in the Slovak mountains you are recommended to have sufficient insurance to cover rescue costs should the Slovak Mountain Rescue (HZS) be called out. Take heed of any instructions issued by HZS; if you ignore their advice you may be liable to a heavy fine.

Taking photos of anything that could be perceived as a military establishment or of security interest may result in problems with the authorities.

Slovakia shares with the rest of Europe an underlying threat from terrorism. Attacks, although unlikely, could be indiscriminate and against civilian targets, including places frequented by tourists.

British Embassy
PANSKA 16, 81101 BRATISLAVA
Tel: (02) 59982000
www.ukinslovakia.fco.gov.uk/en/

Irish Embassy
MOSTOVA 2, 81102 BRATISLAVA
Tel: (02) 32338700
www.embassyofireland.sk

Documents
Passport

Carry your passport at all times as it is an offence to be without it and you may be fined and held in custody for up to 24 hours. Keep a photocopy of the details page separately. Ensure your passport is in a presentable state as the authorities can refuse you entry if it is worn or damaged or looks as if it may have been tampered with.

Vehicle(s)

You should carry your vehicle registration certificate (V5C), at all times together with your driving licence, insurance certificate and your vehicle's MOT certificate (if applicable). Fines may be imposed by police patrols if you cannot produce these documents on request.

Money

Exchange kiosks, although legal, offer poor exchange rates and there is a risk of being robbed by thieves loitering nearby. Scottish and Northern Irish bank notes will not be exchanged in Slovakia.

Cash machines which accept UK debit or credit cards are common but do not rely on finding one in remote areas. Shops, particularly in the main tourist areas, increasingly accept credit cards but are sometimes reluctant to accept cards issued by foreign banks. If you intend to pay for something by card do check first that the shop will accept it and that it can be read. You are also recommended to check your statements carefully for transactions you did not make.

Motoring in Slovakia

The standard of driving is not high and sometimes aggressive with drivers going too fast, especially in bad weather, pushing into dangerously small gaps, tailgating and overtaking dangerously. Drive defensively and allow yourself more 'thinking time'. Beware particularly of oncoming cars overtaking on your side of the road (especially on bends and hills).

Accidents

If your vehicle is damaged when you enter Slovakia the border authorities must issue a certificate confirming the visible damage. While in the country if an accident causes bodily injury or material damage exceeding a value of approximately €4,000 it must be reported to the police immediately. If a vehicle is only slightly damaged both drivers should complete a European Accident Report. In the case of foreign motorists driving vehicles registered abroad, it is advisable to report the accident to the police who will issue a certificate which will facilitate the exportation of the vehicle.

Alcohol

Don't drink and drive. Slovakia has a policy of zero tolerance for drinking or consuming drugs before driving. There is no permitted level of alcohol in the bloodstream. Police carry out random breath tests and you will be heavily penalised if there is any trace of alcohol in your system.

Breakdown Service

The motoring organisation, Slovensky Autoturist Klub (SATC), operates an emergency centre which can be contacted 24 hours a day by dialling (0)18124 or (02) 68249211. Operators speak English.

Essential Equipment

First aid kit

A first aid kit is compulsory in all vehicles.

Lights

All vehicles must use dipped headlights at all times.

Reflective Jacket/Waistcoat

If your vehicle is immobilised on the carriageway outside a built up area, or if visibility is poor, you must wear a reflective jacket or waistcoat when getting out of your vehicle. Passengers who leave the vehicle, for example, to assist with a repair, should also wear one.

Sat Nav/GPS Device

A GPS device must not be placed in the middle of the windscreen. The driver's view must not be impeded.

Warning Triangles

Carry a warning triangle which, in an emergency or in case of breakdown, must be placed at least 100 metres behind your vehicle on motorways and highways, and 50 metres behind on other roads.
The triangle may be placed closer to the vehicle in built-up areas. Drivers may use hazard-warning lights until the triangle is in position.

In case of breakdown, vehicles left on the edge of the carriageway will be towed away after three hours by the organisation in charge of the motorway or road at the owner's expense.

Child Restraint System

Children under the age of 12 years and anyone under 1.5m in height must not travel in the front seat of a vehicle. Child restraint seats must be used for any children weighing less than 36kg.

Winter Driving

In winter equip your vehicle(s) for severe driving conditions and fit winter tyres, which are compulsory when roads are covered in snow or ice. Carry snow chains and use them when there is enough snow to protect the road surface.

Fuel

Diesel is sold in service stations with the sign 'TT Diesel' or 'Nafta'. LPG is widely available and is sold under the name ECO Auto-gas or ECO Car-Gas – see www.lpg.szm.sk/slovensko_5.pdf for a list of outlets. If driving a vehicle converted to use LPG you must be in possession of a safety certificate covering the combustion equipment in your vehicle.

Some service stations on international roads and in main towns are open 24 hours but in other areas they may close by 6pm. Credit cards are generally accepted. Service stations may be hard to find in rural areas.

Parking

Visitors are warned to park only in officially controlled parking areas since cars belonging to tourists may be targeted for robbery. There are many restrictions on parking in Bratislava and fines are imposed. Wheel clamps are used in main towns and vehicles may be towed away.

Continuous white/yellow lines along the carriageway indicate that parking is prohibited and broken white/yellow lines indicate parking restrictions.

Priority

At uncontrolled crossroads or intersections not marked by a priority sign, priority must be given to vehicles coming from the right. Drivers must not enter an intersection unless the exit beyond the crossing is clear.

Drivers must slow down and, if necessary, stop to allow buses and trams to move off from stops and to allow buses to merge with general traffic at the end of a bus lane. A tram turning right and crossing the line of travel of a vehicle moving on its right has priority once the driver has signalled his intention to turn. Trams must be overtaken on the right but do not overtake near a tram refuge.

Roads

Roads are relatively quiet and are generally well maintained. They often follow routes through towns and villages, resulting in sharp bends and reduced speed limits.

Many main roads, although reasonably good, have only a single carriageway in each direction making overtaking difficult. Road markings may be difficult to see in bad weather.

In winter, north-south routes through Slovakia can be challenging as they pass through mountain ranges. The passes of Donovaly (Ružomberok to Banská Bystrica), Veľký Šturec (Martin to Banská Bystrica), and Čertovica (Liptovský Mikuláš to Brezno) are the most frequented. Slow moving vehicles travelling uphill should pull over at suitable stopping places to allow vehicles behind to pass.

Road Signs and Markings

Road signs and markings conform to international standards. The following signs may also be seen:

Slovak	English Translation
Dialkova premavka	By-pass
Hnemocnica	Hospital
Jednosmerny premavka	One-way traffic
Obchadzka	Diversion
Průjezd zakázaný	Closed to all vehicles
Zákaz parkovania	No parking
Zákaz vjazdu	No entry

Signs indicating motorways are red and white and signs on motorways or semi-motorways have a green or blue background; on other roads signs have a blue background.

Speed Limits

	Open Road (km/h)	Motorway (km/h)
Car Solo	90	130
Car towing caravan/trailer	90	90
Motorhome under 3500kg	90	130
Motorhome 3500-7500kg	80	90

Motorhomes over 3,500kg are restricted to 80/90 km/h (56 mph) on motorways and to 80 km/h (50 mph) on other main roads and dual carriageways. Do not exceed 30 km/h (18 mph) when approaching and going over level crossings.

Speed limits are strictly enforced. Carrying and/or use of radar detectors is prohibited.

Traffic Lights

A green arrow together with a red or amber light indicates that drivers may turn in the direction indicated by the arrow provided they give way to other traffic and to pedestrians. A green arrow accompanied by an amber light in the form of a walking figure means that pedestrians have right of way.

Violation of Traffic Regulations

Police are empowered to collect on the spot fines for contravention of driving regulations. An official receipt should be obtained.

Motorways

There are 432km of motorways. Bratislava has direct motorway connections with Prague and Vienna and a new motorway is planned to connect it with Budapest.

Emergency phones are placed along motorways and callers are connected directly to the police.

Vehicles using motorways and selected highways must display a vignette (windscreen sticker), which may be purchased at border crossings, petrol stations and post offices. Charges for vehicles up to 3,500kg with or without a caravan or trailer are as follows (2015 prices): €10 for a period of 10 days and €14 for one month. Fines are payable for non-display and old stickers must be removed. The road from the Austrian border crossing at Berg to Bratislava is free of charge.

Motorhomes over 3,500kg are considered private vehicles and can buy the above vignettes as long as you are able to show the Vehicle Registration Certificate (V5) and it shows that the vehicle has fewer than 9 seats. Without the V5, drivers of vehicles over 3,500kg must pay motorway tolls by means of an electronic toll collection unit fitted to their vehicle. Tolls vary according to distance driven, vehicle weight and emissions classification. For information see www.emyto.sk or telephone 00421 235 111111.

Touring

Smoking is not allowed on the premises where food is served and a partial smoking ban is in force in some bars and cafés which have a dedicated area for smokers. A tip of between 5 to 10% is usual in restaurants. It is normal to give taxi drivers a small tip by rounding up fares to the nearest 50 cents.

Mains water is heavily chlorinated and may cause stomach upsets. Bottled water is available.

The highest peaks of the Tatras mountains are covered with snow for approximately four months of the year and offer ample scope for winter sports. There are plenty of cableways and ski-lifts.

There are a number of UNESCO World Heritage sites in Slovakia including the town of Bardejov, the mining centre of Banská Štiavnica, the 'gingerbread houses' of Vlkolínec village, Spiš Castle, wooden churches in the Carpathian mountains and the caves of Aggtelek Karst and Slovak Karst.

Slovakia has over a thousand curative mineral and thermal springs, together with extensive deposits of high quality healing peat and mud reputed to cure a variety of diseases and ailments. Visitors from all over the world attend these spas every year.

The Bratislava City Card valid for one, two or three days, offers discounts and benefits at approximately 60 attractions and at restaurants and cafés. In addition, it offers free access to public transport and a free one hour walking tour of the Old Town. The card can be obtained at tourist information centres, at the central railway station and at hotels.

In general Slovakia does not cater for the physically handicapped. For example, it is normal for cars to park on the pavement and dropped kerbs are perceived as helping drivers to achieve this without damaging tyres or suspension! Public transport invariably requires large steps to be climbed and bus and tram drivers tend to accelerate from stops at great speed, catching passengers by surprise. Access to most buildings is by steps, rather than ramps. However effort is now being taken to make buildings more accessible.

German is the most common second language, English is not widely understood or spoken.

Public Transport

From April to September hydrofoil services operate from Bratislava to Vienna and Budapest.

In Bratislava bus, trolley bus and tram tickets are valid for periods of up to 60 minutes, extending to up to 90 minutes at night and weekends. Buy them from kiosks and yellow ticket machines. Alternatively you can buy tickets valid for one or several city zones for a fixed period, e.g. 24, 48 or 72 hours or for seven days. Ensure that you validate your ticket on boarding the bus or tram.

Passengers aged 70 and over travel free; carry your passport as proof of age. You must buy a ticket for dogs travelling on public transport and they must be muzzled. You must also purchase a ticket for large items of luggage. For more information see www.imhd.zoznam.sk/ba.

Tatres

⊞ **BANSKA BYSTRICA** *B2* (11km W Rural) *48.7540, 487540* **Autocamping Tajov, 97634 Tajov [(048) 4197320; kukis@slovanet.sk; www.velkydvor.sk/en]** Fr Tajov dir Kordíky. Site well sp 2km NW of Tajov. Sm, pt sl, unshd; htd wc; chem disp; shwrs inc; EHU (6-10A) inc; shop; snacks; bar; rest 300m; playgrnd; wifi; TV; statics; bus; quiet; red CKE/CCI. "Lovely setting in wooded valley; friendly welcome." € 16.00   2011*

BRATISLAVA *C1* (9km NE Urban) *48.18801, 17.18488* **Autocamping Zlaté Piesky, Senecká Cesta 12, 82104 Bratislava [(02) 44257373 or 44450592; fax 44257373; kempi@netax.sk; www.intercamp.sk]** Exit D1/E75 junc sp Zlaté Piesky. Site on S side of rd 61 (E75) at NE edge of Bratislava. Look for pedestrian bdge over rd to tram terminus, ent thro adj traff lts. If x-ing Bratislava foll sp for Žilina. In summer a 2nd, quieter, drier site is opened. For 1st site turn L when ent leisure complex; for 2nd site carry strt on then turn R. Med, shd; wc; shwrs inc; EHU (10A) €3 (long lead poss req); shop; supmkt (Tesco) 300m; rest, snacks; bar; playgrnd; sw & pedalos on lake; fishing; tennis; golf 10km; entmnt; dogs €2; phone; tram to city; poss cr; Eng spkn; v noisy fr adj m'way & bar; red CKE/CCI. "Basic site on lge leisure complex; no privacy in shwrs; ltd hot water; muddy in wet; security guard at night & secure rm for bikes etc but reg, major security problems as site grnds open to public; helpful, friendly staff; interesting city." 1 May-15 Oct. € 13.00   2010*

BREZNO *B3* (6km SE Rural) *48.79501, 19.72867* **Camping Sedliacky Dvor, Hliník 7, 97701 Brezno [(048) 911 078 303; info@sedliackydvor.com; www.sedliackydvor.com]** Fr cent of Brezno at traff lts nr Hotel Dumbier take rd 530/72 SE sp Tisovec. In approx 5km cross rlwy line & ent vill of Rohozná. At end of vill turn L after Camping sp. Site in 500m. Sm, pt shd; wc; shwrs; EHU (10A) €3.25; lndry; cooking facs; pool; games area; wifi; dogs €1; Eng spkn; adv bkg; quiet. "Excel site in lovely orchard setting; welcoming Dutch owners; camp fires in evening; excel facs." 15 Apr-31 Oct. € 22.50   2013*

CEROVO *C2* (8km E Rural) *48.25228, 19.21783* **Camping Lazy, Cerovo 163, 96252 Cerovo [(090) 8590837; info@minicamping.eu; www.campinglazy.eu]** S fr Zvolen on rd 66 dir Krupina. S of Krupina turn L onto rd 526 to Bzovik. After church in Bzovik turn R sp Kozí Vrbovok, Trpin & Litava. Cont thro Litava (agricultural co-operative, Družtvo, on R) & cont for approx 5km to T-junc with bus shelter & turn R. Do not foll sp Cerovo on R but cont to forest & look out for sm lane & site sp to R. Sm, pt sl, pt shd; wc; chem disp; shwrs; EHU (4-6A) €2.50; lndry; some statics (equipped tents); dogs free; quiet. "Site on working farm; ideal for nature lovers, hikers, dog owners; pleasant, helpful owners; v clean, modern facs." 1 May-30 Sep. € 16.00   2013*

DEMANOVSKA DOLINA see Liptovský Mikuláš *B3*

KOSICE *B4* (8km S Rural) *48.68746, 21.25583* **Autocamping Salaš Barca, Alejová ul, 04001 Košice [(055) 6233397; fax 6258309; www.autocamping.szm.sk]** Access only avail E'bound on E571/E50/E58. Fr W foll sp Miskolc E571/E50/E58. Site on R 2km after clover leaf junc. Fr N or E foll sp E50/E571 Rožňava W-bound past camp to clover leaf junc & return E-bound on E571/E50/E58. Fr S (Hung border) on ent Košice turn L under ring rd sp Spišská Nová Ves & Rožňava (E571). After approx 2.5km take airport/Rožňava exit over clover leaf & back down E-bound ringrd (E571). Site on R. Sm, unshd; wc; shwrs inc; EHU (10A) inc; shop 1km; rest; snacks, bar 1km; cooking facs; sand/shgl beach & rv sw 1km; pool 1km; 50% workers' chalets; tram 500m; Eng spkn; rd noise; CKE/CCI. "Old but clean facs; ltd LS; recep sells tram tickets; 24hr security; gd touring base, but run down (2009); Košice delightful city." 15 May-15 Oct. € 19.00   2009*

⊞ **LEVOCA** *B3* (5km N Rural) *49.04982, 20.58727* **Autocamping Levočská Dolina, 05401 Levoča [(053) 4512705 or 4512701; fax 4513689; rzlevoca@pobox.sk]** Site on E side of minor rd 533 running N fr E50 at Dolina to Levočská Dolina. Steep ent; ltd access lge o'fits. Med, sl, pt shd; wc; chem disp; shwrs inc; EHU (16A) €3; lndry; shop 3km; rest, snacks; bar; playgrnd; ski lift 2.5km; TV; dogs €1.50; Eng spkn; quiet; CKE/CCI. "Diff in wet weather due v sl grnd; friendly staff; interesting old town; Spišský Hrad castle worth visit; walks in forests around site." € 15.00   2009*

> ## "I like to fill in the reports as I travel from site to site"
> You'll find report forms at the back of this guide, or you can fill them in online at www.caravanclub.co.uk/europereport.

LIPTOVSKY MIKULAS *B3* (6km NW Rural) *49.11108, 19.54608* **Autocamp Liptovský Trnovec, 03222 Liptovský Trnovec [(044) 5598459; fax 5598458; atctrnovec@atctrnovec.sk; www.atctrnovec.sk]** E fr Ružomberok on R18/E50 exit on R584 to Liptovský Mikuláš. Site on N side of Lake Liptovský Mara. Med, unshd; wc; chem disp; shwrs inc; EHU (6A) €2.50; lndry; shop; rest, bar in ssn; playgrnd; lake sw; boating; bike hire; internet; 10% statics; dogs €2; Eng spkn; quiet; red CKE/CCI. "Excel; lovely site in beautiful location." ♦ 1 May-31 Oct. € 13.50   2010*

⊞ **LIPTOVSKY MIKULAS** *B3* (11km NW Rural) *49.13608, 19.5125* **Resort Villa Betula (formerly Penzión), 03223 Liptovský Sielnica [(907) 812327; villabetula@villabetula.sk; www.villabetula.sk]** Fr rd 18/E50 exit onto R584 to Liptovský Mikuláš, site on N of lake 6km past Autocamp. Med, unshd; wc; chem disp; sauna; baby facs; shwrs inc; EHU (10A) inc; rest; bar; playgrnd; lake sw adj; bike hire; jacuzzi; wifi; dogs €7; phone; Eng spkn; quiet; ccard acc; CKE/CCI. "Family-friendly, gem of a site in wonderful area of lakes, mountains & forest; welcoming, helpful owners; v clean & well-kept; vg rest; site at rear of hotel; excel for long or sh stay." € 26.00   2015*

LIPTOVSKY SIELNICA see Liptovský Mikuláš *B3*

LIPTOVSKY TRNOVEC see Liptovský Mikuláš *B3*

NITRIANSKE RUDNO *B2* (1km N Rural) *48.80457, 18.47601*
Autocamping Nitrianske Rudno, 97226 Nitrianske Rudno [(046) 5455403; info@camping-nrudno.sk; www.camping-nrudno.sk] E fr Bánovce & Dolné Vestenice on rd 50, turn N onto rd 574. Site on shore of Lake Nitrianske Rudno, sp in vill. Med, pt shd; wc; shwrs; EHU €2.50; lndry; snacks; bar; cooking facs; playgrnd; lake sw; watersports; games area; internet; entmnt; some statics; dogs €1; adv bkg; quiet; red CKE/CCI. "Welcoming, helpful owner; pleasant location." 1 Jun-30 Sep. € 8.70   2009*

> ## "We must tell The Club about that great site we found"
> Get your site reports in by mid-August and we'll do our best to get your updates into the next edition.

PREŠOV *B4* (13km W Rural) *49.00386, 21.08145*
Autokemping A Motorest Kemp, Chminianske Nová Ves, District Prešov 082 33 [0517 795190 or 0905 191056 mob; kemppo@kemppo.sk; www.kemppo.sk] Fr W on Rte 18/D1/E50, take exit twd Vit'az/Hrabkov, site on R. Sm pt shd; wc shwrs inc; gas; EHU €4; lndry with campers kitchen; shop, rest, snacks, bar, BBQ; cooking facs; plygrnd; games area; dog €2; twin axles acc; Eng spkn; quiet; ccard acc; CKE/CCI. "Site behind motorest Kemp on Rte 18; recep in rest; 5 chalets for rent on site; fair site." Feb-Dec. € 15.00   2014*

ROZNAVA *B3* (6km E Rural) *48.64920, 20.59796*
Autocamping Krásnohorské, Hradná 475, 04941 Krásnohorské Podhradie [(058) 7325457; fax 7921332] E fr Rožňava on rd 50/E571 foll sp Krásnohorské Podhradie. Site under shadow of castle. Sm, pt shd; wc; shwrs; mainly huts. "Lovely setting in pine woods; primitive facs but plenty of hot water; conv for cave visits." € 10.00   2012*

SENEC *C1* (1.5km SE Urban) *48.21386, 17.41088*
Autocamping Slnečné Jazerá (Die Sonnenseen), Mierové Námestie 19, 90301 Senec [(02) 45924081; fax 45923080; info@slnecnejazerasenec.sk; www.slnecnejazerasenec.sk] Fr D1/E75 take junc exit for Senec onto rd 503, site sp. Lge, pt shd; wc; shwrs inc; EHU (16A) inc; lndry; shop; supmkts in town; rest, snacks; playgrnd; aqua park nr; sand beach; lake sw; boating; tennis; cycling; TV; entmnt; no dogs; phone; bus/train to Bratislava nr; poss cr; noise fr disco, rd & rlwy. "Gd alt to Bratislava site." 15 Jun-15 Sep. € 19.00   2011*

TAJOV see Banská Bystrica *B2*

TATRANSKA LOMINICA *B3* (2.6km S Rural) *49.14974, 20.27968* **Camping Rijo (formerly Jupela), Dolny Smokovec, 3705981 Vysoke Tatry [(421) 911 616530; rijocamping@rijocamping.eu; www.rijocamping.eu]** Fr Tatranska Lominca travel W on 537 take L turn twrds Nova Lesna. Foll sp to site. Sm, pt shd; wc; chem disp; shwrs; EHU 16A €3.50; snacks; bar; BBQ; playgrnd; adv bkg. "Beautiful location nr to mountain torrent; conv for walking in Takranska; basic clean san facs; lovely spot; walks and scenice drives." 7 May-16 Sept. € 13.00   2013*

⊞ **TATRANSKA LOMNICA** *B3* (2.5km ESE Rural) *49.15830, 20.30979* Intercamp Tatranec, 05960 Tatranská Lomnica [(052) 4467092; fax 4467082; hoteltatranec@hoteltatranec.com] NE fr Poprad on rd 67, after 8km turn L over level x-ing, thro Vel'ká Lomnica twds Tatranská Lomnica on rd 540. Site on L. Lge, pt sl, unshd; wc; chem disp; shwrs inc; EHU (6A) inc; lndry; shop & 4km; rest; bar; playgrnd; wifi; entmnt; Eng spkn; adv bkg; quiet; red CKE/CCI. "Superb views of High Tatras; conv cable car, train etc; excel base for walking & holiday resort; hotel adj; poor, dated facs & ltd privacy." € 18.50   2015*

TERCHOVA *B2* (3km SW Rural) *49.24779, 18.98866*
Autocamp Belá, Nižné Kamence, 01305 Belá [(041) 5695135; camp@bela.sk; www.camping.bela.sk] Fr Zilina foll rd 583 twd Terchová. Site on L 3km after vill of Belá. Med, pt shd; wc; chem disp; mv service pnt; shwrs €0.30; EHU (10A) €3; lndry rm; shop; rest, snacks; BBQ; cooking facs; playgrnd; tennis; 10% statics; dogs €1; rd noise. "Delightful rvside site; gd welcome; clean, modern san facs; conv walking in Malá Fatra mountains." 1 May-15 Oct. € 11.50   2011*

TRENCIN *B2* (2km N Urban) *48.90011, 18.04076*
Autocamping Na Ostrove, Ostrov, 91101 Trenčín [(032) 7434013; autocamping.tn@mail.pvt.sk; http://web.viapvt.sk/auto camping.tn] Fr SW on rd 61/E75 cross rv at Hotel Tatra, 1st L dir Sihot, go under rlwy bdge. 1st L, then immed 1st L again, then R at stadium, cross canal to island, site on L. Sm, unshd; wc; chem disp; shwrs inc; 25% serviced pitches; EHU (10A) €3; lndry; shop in town; snacks; bar; cooking facs; pool 500m; 90% statics; dogs €1.50; poss cr; some Eng spkn; some noise fr rlwy & sports stadium; CKE/CCI. "Popular NH en rte Poland, rec arr early high ssn; on rvside in run down pt of town adj sports stadium; adj delightful town with fairy-tale castle; poss waterlogged in wet; facs old but clean - some lack privacy." 1 May-15 Sep. € 18.00   2013*

ZVOLEN *B2* (6km NW Rural) *48.60611, 19.10175* **Autocamp Kováčová, Kúpeľná ul, 96237 Kováčová [(045) 5445220; fax 5445363; recent@recent.sk]** Fr E77/66 dir Banská Bystrica turn at sp Kováčová. In vill foll site sp. Med, pt sl, pt shd; wc; chem disp (wc); shwrs inc; EHU €2.50; lndry rm; shop 500m; snacks; bar; BBQ; cooking facs; htd pool adj; TV rm; 40% statics; Eng spkn; quiet; CKE/CCI. "Clean site but run down (6/09); friendly owner." 26 May-2 Sep. € 11.40   2009*

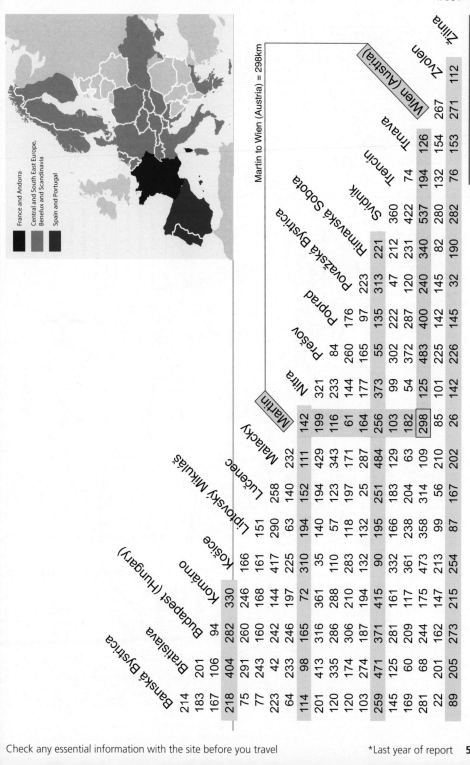

Martin to Wien (Austria) = 298km

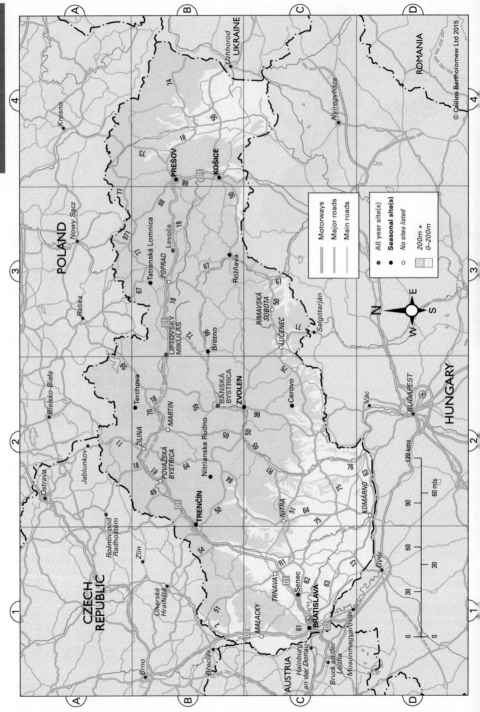

Slovenia
Country Introduction

Lake Bled, Slovenia

Welcome to Slovenia

Equipped with an extraordinarily pretty landscape, Slovenia is deeply in tune with its natural surroundings and is one of the greenest countries in Europe. Outdoor pursuits are wholeheartedly embraced here and are top of the list when it comes to attractions.

There is also plenty to see and do for history fans to see and do - this small country boasts around 500 castles and manor houses. Not to be missed are the hilltop castles of Bled, Ljubljana and Predjama.

Country highlights

Slovenia is one of the world's most biologically diverse countries, and despite its small size is home to an estimated total of 45,000 – 120,000 species.

Slovenia is also a key centre for winter sports, with major competitions and events held in the country on a regular basis. Kanin, the highest ski centre in Slovenia, offers the opportunity to ski to neighbouring Italy.

Major towns and cities

- Ljubljana – a charming capital with an old-world feel.
- Maribor – this vibrant city holds many events throughout the year.
- Celje – an ancient settlement with Celtic and Roman origins.
- Kranj – a lively city with a castle and 14th century church.

Attractions

- Bled Castle – a medieval castle overlooking the popular Lake Bled, and one of the most visited attractions in the country.
- Tivoli Park, Ljubljana - home to botanical gardens and a contemporary history museum.
- Škocjan Caves – an extraordinary series of caves renowned as a natural treasure.
- Predjama Castle, Postojna – a gothic castle built 700 years ago into the mouth of a cave.

Find out more

www.slovenia.info

Tel: 0038 (0) 61 58 98 550 Slovenian Tourist Board

Country Information

Population (approx): 2 million

Capital: Ljubljana (population approx 280,000)

Area: 20,273 sqkm

Bordered by: Austria, Croatia, Hungary, Italy

Coastline: 46.6km

Terrain: Coastal strip on the Adriatic; alpine mountains in west and north; many rivers and forests

Climate: Mediterranean climate on the coast; hot summers and cold winters in the plateaux and valleys in the east; spring and early autumn are the best times to visit

Highest Point: Triglav 2,864m

Languages: Slovenian; Serbo-Croat

Local Time: GMT or BST + 1, i.e. 1 hour ahead of the UK all year

Currency: Euros divided into 100 cents; £1 = €1.42, €1 = £0.71 (September 2015)

Emergency numbers: Police 113; Fire brigade 112; Ambulance 112. Operators speak English

Public Holidays 2016: Jan 1; Feb 8; Mar 27, 28; Apr 27; May 1, 2, 15; Jun 25; Aug 15; Oct 31; Nov 1; Dec 25, 26.

School summer holidays are from the last week in June to the end of August

Camping and Caravanning

There are over 60 organised campsites in Slovenia rated one to five stars. They are usually open from May to October but a few are open all year. Standards of sites and their sanitary facilities are generally good. Campsites on the coast consist mostly of statics and can be overcrowded during the peak summer season. Casual/wild camping is not permitted.

Cycling

There are some cycle lanes which are also used by mopeds. Cyclists under the age of 15 must wear a safety helmet.

Transportation of Bicycles

An overhanging load which exceeds one metre at the rear of a vehicle must be indicated by a red flag or red panel measuring 30cm square. At night the overhanging load must be indicated by a red light and a reflector. Loads may only project rearwards; they must not overhang the sides of vehicles.

Electricity and Gas

Usually the current on campsites varies between 6 and 16 amps. Plugs have two round pins. Hook-up points on most campsites conform to CEE standards.

Campingaz cylinders cannot be purchased or exchanged. Recent visitors report that it is possible to have gas cylinders refilled at premises on Verovškova Ulica 70, Ljubljana. The company's name is Butan-Plin. However, The Caravan Club does not recommend this practice and you should aim to take enough gas to last during your stay.

Entry Formalities

All foreign nationals must register with the police within three days of arrival in Slovenia. Campsites carry out registration formalities, but if you are staying with friends or family you or your host will need to visit the nearest police station to register your presence in the country.

British and Irish passport holders may stay in Slovenia for up to three months without a visa. For longer stays contact the Slovenian Embassy for further information.

Medical Services

British visitors may obtain emergency medical, hospital and dental treatment from practitioners registered with the public health service, Health Institute of Slovenia (HIIS) on presentation of a European Health Insurance Card (EHIC). You will have to make a contribution towards costs which will not be refunded in Slovenia. Full fees are payable for private medical and dental treatment.

Health resorts and spas are popular and the medical profession uses them extensively for treatment of a wide variety of complaints.

Opening Hours

Banks – Mon-Fri 9am-12 noon & 2pm-5pm; closed Sat/Sun

Museums – Tues-Sun 9/10am-5/6pm. Most closed Mon.

Post Offices – Mon-Fri 8am-6pm; Sat 8am-12 noon.

Shops – Mon-Fri 8am-7pm/9pm; Sat 8am-1pm.

Safety and Security

Slovenia is relatively safe for visitors but the usual sensible precautions should be taken against pickpockets in large towns and cities.
Do not leave valuables in your car.

Western Slovenia is on an earthquake fault line and is subject to occasional tremors.

If you are planning a skiing or mountaineering holiday, contact the Slovenian Tourist Board for advice on weather and safety conditions before travelling. You should follow all safety instructions meticulously, given the danger of avalanches in some areas. Off-piste skiing is highly dangerous.

There is a low threat from terrorism but attacks could be indiscriminate and against civilian targets, including places frequented by tourists.

British Embassy
4TH FLOOR, TRG REPUBLIKE 3, 1000 LJUBLJANA
Tel: (01) 2003910
www.ukinslovenia.fco.gov.uk/en

Irish Embassy
PALACA KAPITELJ, 1st floor
POLJANSKI NASIP 6
1000 Ljubljana
Tel: (01) 3008970
www.embassyofireland.si

Documents

Driving Licence
All European countries recognise the EU format paper UK driving licence introduced in 1990. However, it is a legal requirement to show your driving license with a form of photographic identification, such as your passport, if your driving licence does not include a photograph.

Passport
Carry a copy of your passport at all times as a form of identification.

Vehicle(s)
You should carry your vehicle documentation, i.e. vehicle registration certificate (V5C), insurance certificate, MOT certificate (if applicable) and driver's licence.

If you are driving a hired or borrowed vehicle, you must be in possession of a letter of authorisation from the owner or a hire agreement.

Money

Cash machines are widespread and the major credit cards are widely accepted. Carry your credit card issuers'/banks' 24-hour UK contact numbers in case of loss or theft of your cards.

Motoring in Slovenia

Accidents

Any visible damage to a vehicle entering Slovenia must be certified by authorities at the border. All drivers involved in an accident while in the country should inform the police and obtain a written report (Potrdilo). Drivers of vehicles which have been damaged will need to present this police report to Customs on departure.

Alcohol

The maximum permitted level of alcohol is 50 milligrams in 100 millilitres of blood, i.e. lower than what is permitted in the UK (80 milligrams). If a driver is under the age of 21 or has held a driving licence for less than three years the permitted level of alcohol is zero. The police carry out tests at random.

Breakdown Service

The motoring organisation, Avto-Moto Zveza Slovenije (AMZS), operates a 24 hour breakdown service which can be contacted by telephoning 1987. On motorways, using a mobile phone, call the AMZS Alarm Centre in Ljubljana on (01) 5305353 or use the emergency telephones and ask for AMZS assistance.

Charges apply for repairs or towing, plus supplements at night, weekends and on public holidays. Credit cards are accepted.

Essential Equipment

First aid kit
Although a first aid kit is not compulsory in all vehicles, it is recommended.

Lights
Dipped headlights are compulsory at all times, regardless of weather conditions. Bulbs are more likely to fail with constant use and you are required to carry spares. Hazard warning lights must be used when reversing.

Reflective Jacket/Waistcoat
In the event of vehicle breakdown on a motorway, anyone who leaves the vehicle must wear a reflective jacket.

Child Restraint System
Children under 12 years of age and under the height of 1.5 metres must use a suitable child restraint system for their size and age.

Warning Triangles
Vehicles towing a trailer must carry two warning triangles (single vehicles require only one). In the event of a breakdown to vehicle and trailer combinations, one triangle must be placed at the rear of the towed vehicle and another at the front of the towing vehicle at a distance which ensures maximum safety and visibility.

At night, drivers must always use hazard warning lights or a torch in addition to the warning triangles.

Winter Driving
From 15 November to 15 March, and beyond those dates during winter weather conditions (snowfalls, black ice, etc), private cars and vehicles up to 3,500kg must have winter tyres on all four wheels or, alternatively, carry snow chains. Minimum tread depth of tyres is 3mm.

Fuel

Petrol stations are generally open from 7am to 8pm Monday to Saturday. Many near border crossings, on motorways and near large towns are open 24 hours. Credit cards are accepted. It is understood that few petrol stations sell LPG.

Parking

Parking meters are used in towns. In city centres white lines indicate that parking is permitted for a maximum of two hours between 7am and 7pm, a parking ticket must be purchased from a machine. Blue lines indicate places where parking is allowed free of charge for up to 30 minutes. Vehicles parked illegally may be towed away or clamped.

Priority

At intersections drivers must give way to traffic from the right, unless a priority road is indicated. The same rule applies to roundabouts, i.e. traffic entering a roundabout has priority.

Roads

Slovenia has a well-developed road system, and international and main roads are in good condition. Secondary roads may still be poorly maintained and generally unlit. Minor roads are often gravelled and are known locally as 'white roads'. Road numbers are rarely mentioned on road signs and it is advisable to navigate using place names in the direction you are travelling.

Roadside verges are uncommon, or may be lined with bollards which make pulling over difficult. Where there is a hard shoulder it is usual for slow vehicles to pull over to allow faster traffic to overtake.

The capital, Ljubljana, can be reached from Munich, Milan, Vienna and Budapest in less than five hours. There are numerous border crossings for quick and trouble free entry into Slovenia.

Care should be taken, especially on narrow secondary roads, where tailgating and overtaking on blind bends are not unknown. Drive defensively and take extra care when driving at night. Be prepared for severe weather in winter.

Information on roads may be obtained by telephoning the AMZS Information Centre on (01) 5305300.

Road Signs and Markings

Road signs conform to international standards. Motorway signs have a green background and national road signs a blue background. On your travels you may see the following signs:

Mountain pass

School area

Toll: Vignette/card or cash

Speed Limits

	Open Road (km/h)	Motorway (km/h)
Car Solo	90-110	130
Car towing caravan/trailer	90	100
Motorhome under 3500kg	90-110	130
Vehicle over 3500-7500kg	80	80

Motorhomes over 3,500kg are restricted to 80 km/h (50 mph) on open roads, including motorways. Other speed limits are the same as for solo cars.

There is an increasing number of areas where speed is restricted to 30 km/h (18 mph) and these are indicated by the sign 'Zone 30'. In bad weather when visibility is reduced to 50 metres the maximum speed limit is 50 km/h (31 mph).

Traffic Jams

Slovenia is a major international through-route and bottlenecks do occur on the roads to and from Ljubljana, such as the E61/A2 from Jesinice and the E57 from Maribor. Traffic queues can be expected from May to August on the roads around Lake Bled and to the Adriatic and on the E70/A1 motorway near the Razdrto toll station and near Kozina and Koper. Tailbacks also occur at border posts near the Karawanken Tunnel, Ljubelj

and Šentilj/Spielfeld particularly at weekends. The motoring organisation, AMZS, provides traffic information in English – telephone (01) 5305300 or see their website www.amzs.si.

Violation of Traffic Regulations

The police have powers to stop drivers and levy heavy on-the-spot fines, including penalties for speeding, driving under the influence of alcohol and for using mobile phones without properly installed wireless headsets (bluetooth). Jaywalking is an offence and you could be fined if caught. Fines must be paid in local currency and you should obtain an official receipt.

Motorways

There are about 620km of motorways (avtoceste) and expressways (hitre ceste) with more under construction. For more information about motorways see the website www.dars.si.

There are service areas and petrol stations along the motorways and emergency telephones are situated every 2km.

Emergency corridors are compulsory on motorways and dual carriageways. Drivers are required to create a precautionary emergency corridor to provide access for emergency vehicles whenever congestion occurs. Drivers in the left-hand lane must move as far over to the left as possible, and drivers in the central and right-hand lanes must move as far over to the right as possible.

Motorway Tolls

Drivers of vehicles weighing up to 3,500kg must purchase a vignette (windscreen sticker) for use on motorways and expressways. Caravans/trailers don't need an additional vignette and the weight of the caravan/trailer isn't taken into account. The vignette is available from petrol stations in Slovenia, neighbouring countries and at border posts. The cost of a 7 day vignette is €15, 1 month is €30 and an annual is €110 (2015 charges). For vehicles over 3,500kg tolls are payable with cash or credit card.

Karawanken Tunnel

The 8km Karawanken Tunnel links the E61/A11 in Austria and E61/A2 in Slovenia. The toll is €7.00

for car and caravan or motorhome up to 3,500kg and €10.50 for a motorhome over 3,500kg (2015 charges).

Touring

A 10% tip is usual in restaurants and for taxi drivers.

The capital, Ljubljana, is a gem of a city with many Baroque and Art Nouveau influences. The works of the world renowned architect Jože Plecnik are among the finest urban monuments in the city. A Ljubljana Card is available for one, two or three days and offers free travel on city buses, tourist boat trips, the city funicular, guided tours and the tourist train to Ljubljana Castle, plus free admission to museums together with discounts at a wide range of shops, restaurants and bars. You can buy the card at the main bus and railway stations, hotels and tourist information centres or from www.visitljubljana.si.

The largest cave in Europe is situated at Postojna, south west of Ljubljana and is a 'must' for tourists. Also worth visiting are the mountains, rivers and woods of Triglav National Park, which covers the major part of the Julian Alps, together with the oldest town in Slovenia, Ptuj, and the city of Maribor. In Lipica guided tours are available around the stud, home to the world famous Lipizzaner horses.

There is a hydrofoil service between Portorož and Venice from April to November.

Slovenian is the official language although Serbo-Croat is widely spoken. Most Slovenians speak at least one other major European language and many, especially the young, speak English.

Public Transport

There is an extensive bus network in Ljubljana. Buy a yellow 'top-up' Urbana card for a one-off payment of €2 from news-stands, tobacconists, tourist information offices or the central bus station and add credit (between €1 and €50) at the same locations or at the green Urbanomati machines around the city. When boarding a bus simply touch the card to one of the card readers at the front of the bus and €1.20 will be deducted allowing 90 minutes of unlimited travel regardless of how many changes you make. Taxis are generally safe, clean and reliable. Fares are metered. For longer distances ordering a taxi by phone will attract lower rates.

Izola

ANKARAN see Koper *D1*

BLED *B2* (4km SE Rural) *46.35527, 14.14833* **Camping Šobec, Šobčeva Cesta 25, 4248 Lesce [(04) 5353700; fax 5353701; sobec@siol.net; www.sobec.si]** Exit rte 1 at Lesce, site sp. Lge, pt shd, pt sl; wc; chem disp; mv service pnt; shwrs; EHU (16A) €3.70 (poss long lead req); lndry; shop, rest, snacks; bar; playgrnd; rv pool; many sports & activities; bike hire; internet; TV; wifi; dogs €3.50; bus 2km; Eng spkn; ccard acc; red 7+ days/CKE/CCI. "Excel, tranquil rvside site in wooded area surrounded by rv; friendly staff; lge pitches; clean san facs; gd rest; gd walking/cycling; real camping atmosphere, plenty of space; def rec; beautiful area." ♦ 15 Apr-30 Sep. € 41.00   2013*

BLED *B2* (6km SE Urban) *46.34772, 14.17284* **Camping Radovljica, Kopališka 9, 4240 Radovljica [(04) 5315770; fax 5301229; pkrad@plavalnicklub-radovljica.si]** Exit A1/E61 junc Bled/Bohinj, site in cent of Radovljica bet bus & train stn sp Camping & Sw. Med, pt sl, pt shd; wc; chem disp; shwrs inc; EHU (16A) inc; shop 500m; rest 300m; snacks adj; bar; playgrnd; pool adj; paddling pool; bike hire; fitness rm; wifi; 10% statics; dogs; poss cr; quiet; red long stay. "Vg; security gate; vg, clean san facs; gd NH; friendly staff." 1 Jun-15 Sep. € 38.00   2013*

BLED *B2* (4km SW Rural) *46.36155, 14.08066* **Camping Bled, Kidričeva 10c, SI 4260 Bled [04 5752000; fax 5752002; info@camping-bled.com; www.camping-bled.com]** Fr Ljubljana take E16/A2 & exit dir Bled/Lesce. At rndabt take 2nd exit for Bled & cont along rd 209. In Bled take rd around lake on L (lake on R), site sp - winding rd. Lge, some mkd pitch, pt sl, pt shd; wc; chem disp; mv service pnt; baby facs; shwrs inc; EHU (16A) inc (long lead req some pitches - fr recep); gas; lndry (inc dryer); shop, rest adj; snacks; bar; BBQ; playgrnd; shgl beach; lake sw adj; spa cent nrby; fishing; white water rafting; paragliding; horseriding; bike hire; games area; wifi; entmnt; games rm; TV rm; dogs €3; twin-axles acc (rec check in adv); m'van & car wash; dog shwrs; bus to Ljubljana adj; Eng spkn; fairly quiet but some rlwy noise; ccard acc; red long stay/LS/snr citizens/CKE/CCI. "Beautifully situated nr lake; busy, popular, well-run site; well-drained in bad weather altho lower pitches poss muddy; modern, clean san facs, stretched in ssn; helpful, efficient staff; conv Vintgar Gorge, Bled Castle, Lake Bohinj, Dragna Valley; excel walking/cycling around lake; excel rest." ♦ 1 Apr-15 Oct. € 31.50 SBS - X03   2015*

See advertisement

SAVA CAMPING

Camping Bled***

www.camping-slovenia.com

SPRING AND AUTUMN SPECIAL OFFERS

At one with nature in the heart of the Julian Alps.
Enjoy the view of the tiny island on the lake.

ALL INCLUSIVE

Buffet breakfast and dinner + pitch + swimming pools ticket

Terme 3000 from € 26.40 person/night
Terme Ptuj from € 26.00 person/night
Terme Banovci from € 25.00 person/night
Terme Lendava from € 24.00 person/night

Terme 3000** • Terme Ptuj**** • Terme Lendava*** • Terme Banovci*****

Check any essential information with the site before you travel   *Last year of report

SLOVENIA

BOHINJSKA BISTRICA *B1* (11km W Rural) *46.27902, 13.83606* Autocamp Zlatarog, Ukanc 2, 4265 Bohinjsko Jezero [(04) 5723482; fax 5723064; info@aaturizem.com; www.aaturizem.com] On rte 1 exit at Lesce or Jesenice for Bled & Bohinj. Clearly sp fr Bohinj, further 5km on L side of lake. Lge, some mkd pitch, sl, shd; wc; chem disp; shwrs; EHU (6A) €5 (long lead req); gas; lndry; shop adj; rest adj (high ssn); snacks; playgrnd; beach adj; lake sw; 50% statics; dogs €3; bus; sep car park high ssn; Eng spkn; adv bkg; ccard acc; red LS/long stay/CCI. "Excel walking, watersports; sm, uneven pitches & rather cramped site, but beautiful lakeside location; facs stretched high ssn; poss long walk to facs; site grnd rough to walk on (2011); poor security LS; gd touring base; cable car nr to Mount Vogel." 15 May-30 Sep. € 26.00   2011*

⊞ **BOHINJSKA BISTRICA** *B1* (800m NW Rural) *46.27438, 13.94798* Camping Danica Bohinj, Triglavska 60, 4264 Bohinjska Bistrica [(04) 5721702; fax 5723330; info@camp-danica.si; www.camp-danica.si] Site on o'skts of vill clearly sp. Med, pt shd; wc; chem disp; mv service pnt; shwrs; EHU (6A) inc (long lead poss req); gas; lndry; shops 500m; rest, snacks; bar; tennis; entmnt; lake sw 6km; canoe & kayak hire; fly-fishing; wifi; 10% statics; dogs €2; Eng spkn; quiet; ccard acc; red long stay/CCI. "Excel site, spacious, open, attractive site in beautiful valley; gd walking & climbing; gd, clean san facs but poss stretched high ssn; conv bus to Ljubljana & Lake Bohinji." € 38.00   2014*

"I like to fill in the reports as I travel from site to site"

You'll find report forms at the back of this guide, or you can fill them in online at www.caravanclub.co.uk/europereport.

BOHINJSKO JEZERO see Bohinjska Bistrica *B1*

BOVEC *B1* (1km E Rural) *46.33659, 13.55803* Autocamp Polovnik, Ledina 8, 5230 Bovec [(05) 3896007; fax 3896006; kamp.polovnik@siol.net; www.kamp-polovnik.com] Sp on rd 206 down fr Predil Pass (1,156m - 14% gradient) fr Italy - do not turn into vill. Site 200m after turn to Bovec. Sm, pt shd; wc; chem disp; shwrs €0.50; EHU (16A) €2.50 (poss rev pol); lndry (inc dryer); shop adj; rest, snacks; bar; BBQ; tennis; fishing; wifi; poss cr; no adv bkg; quiet; ccard acc; CKE/CCI. "Helpful staff; clean facs; muddy when wet; friendly staff." 1 Apr-15 Oct. € 30.00   2013*

BOVEC *B1* (9km E Rural) *46.33527, 13.64416* Camping Soča, Soča 8, 5232 Soča [(05) 3889318; fax 3881409; kamp. soca@siol.net] Sp on S side of rd 206 in national park, nr turning for Lepena approx 3km bef Soča vill. Lge, pt terr, pt shd; htd wc; chem disp; mv service pnt; shwrs inc; EHU (6A) inc; lndry; shop, rest 2km; snacks; bar; BBQ; playrnd; rv & shgl beach adj; TV rm; 50% statics (sep area); dogs €1; poss cr; Eng spkn; quiet; red long stay. "Beautiful situation in rv valley; gd, modern san facs; gd walking, rafting; gd touring base Triglav National Park; excel; braziers and wood avail; walking and cycling tracks fr site." ♦ ltd. 1 Apr-31 Oct. € 35.00   2013*

⊞ **BREZICE** *C3* (5km S Rural) *45.89138, 15.62611* Camping Terme Čatež, Topliška Cesta 35, 8251 Čatež ob Savi [(07) 4936700; fax 6207804; info@terme-catez.si; www.terme-catez.si] Exit E70 at Brežice, foll brown sp to Terme Čatež, then site sp. Lge, mkd pitch, pt shd; htd wc; chem disp; mv service pnt; sauna; baby facs; shwrs inc; EHU (10A) inc; gas; lndry (inc dryer); supmkt; rest, snacks; bar; BBQ area; playgrnd; thermal water complex, inc 10 outdoor & 3 indoor pools, waterfalls & whirlpools, etc; paddling pool; fishing; golf 7km; boating; canoeing; tennis; fitness studio; games area; bike hire; games rm; wifi; entmnt; TV; 50% statics (sep area); dogs €4; poss cr; wifi; Eng spkn; adv bkg; ccard acc; red LS; CKE/CCI. "Site in lge thermal spa & health resort; many sports, leisure & health facs; shops 2km; select own pitch - best at edge of site; gd family site; conv Zagreb; san facs dated (2013); not value for money." ♦ € 67.00 SBS - X05   2013*

CATEZ OB SAVI see Brežice *C3*

KAMNIK *B2* (1km NE Urban) *46.22724, 14.61902* Kamp Resnik, Nevlje 1a, 1240 Kamnik [(01) 8317314; fax 8318192; info@kampresnik.com; www.kampresnik.com] Fr Ljubljana foll rd sp Celje then turn N for Kamnik. Fr Kemnik by-pass (E side of rv) bear R thro 2 sets traff lts, site 200m on L just after sports cent - site ent not obvious, turn bef zebra x-ing opp pub. Fr E on rd 414, site sp. Med, pt shd; wc (some cont); chem disp; mv service pnt; shwrs; EHU (10A) €3; gas; lndry; shops 500m; rest, snacks 100m; bar; playgrnd; pool adj; thermal spa, golf course nr; 5% statics; dogs; bus; Eng spkn; adv bkg; some daytime rd noise; ccard acc; red CKE/CCI. "Conv Ljubljana & Kamnik Alps; basic, v old facs (2010); friendly staff; pleasant, well-kept NH." 1 May-30 Sep. € 17.00   2013*

⊞ **KOBARID** *B1* (1km NE Rural) *46.25070, 13.58664* Kamp Koren, Drežniške Ravne 33, 5222 Kobarid [(05) 3891311; fax 3891310; info@kamp-koren.si; www.kamp-koren.si] Turn E fr main rd in town, site well sp dir Drežnica. Med, pt shd; htd wc (some cont); chem disp; mv service pnt; shwrs inc; EHU (16A) €4; shop; lndry; snacks; rest 500m; playgrnd; bike hire; canoeing; internet; TV rm; dogs €2; Eng spkn; quiet; ccard acc; red LS/long stay/CKE/CCI. "Vg, clean facs but stretched; friendly, helpful staff; pitches cramped; pleasant location in beautiful rv valley; excel walk to waterfall (3hrs); WW1 museum in town." ♦ € 23.00   2011*

KOPER *D1* (7km N Coastal) *45.57818, 13.73573* Camping Adria, Jadranska Zesta 25, 6280 Ankaran [(05) 6637350; fax 6637360; camp@adria-ankaran.si; www.adria-ankaran.si] Fr A1/E70/E61 onto rd 10 then rd 406 to Ankaran. Or cross Italian border at Lazzaretto & foll sp to site in 3km. Site sp in vill. Lge, mkd pitch, shd; wc; chem disp; mv service pnt; sauna; private san facs avail; shwrs inc; EHU (10A) €3; lndry (inc dryer); shop; supmkt adj; rest, snacks; bar; BBQ; playgrnd; 2 pools (1 Olympic-size); waterslide; beach adj; tennis; bike hire; wifi; entmnt; 60% statics; dogs €4; bus 500m; ccard acc. "Old town of Koper worth a visit; Vinakoper winery rec N of site on dual c'way; poss noisy groups high ssn; insect repellent req; clean san facs but red LS; gd rest; vg." ♦ 14 Apr-14 Oct. € 46.00   2013*

⊞ **KRANJSKA GORA** *B1* (14km E Rural) *46.46446, 13.95773*
Camping Kamne, Dovje 9, 4281 Mojstrana
[tel/fax (04) 5891105; info@campingkamne.com;
www.campingkamne.com] Sp fr rd 201 bet Jesenice &
Kranjska Gora, 2km E of Mojstrana. Do not go thro vill of
Dovje. Sm, terr, pt shd; some hdstg; htd wc; chem disp; mv
service pnt; shwrs €0.50; EHU (6A) €2.50-3.50; lndry (inc
dryer); shop 1km; rest 1.5km; snacks; bar; playgrnd; sm pool;
fishing; hiking; tennis; bike hire; TV rm; 10% statics; dogs €2;
bus to Kranjska Gora fr site; Eng spkn; quiet but some rd noise;
red long stay/CKE/CCI. "Conv Triglav National Park & border;
views Mount Triglav; warm welcome; ltd san facs stretched
high ssn; friendly helpful staff; gd cycling along old rlwy track."
♦ € 19.00   2013*

⊞ **LENDAVA** *B4* (2km S Rural) *46.55195, 16.45875* **Camping
Terme Lendava (Part Naturist),** Tomšičeva 2a, 9220
Lendava [(02) 5774400; fax 5774412; info@terme-lendava.
si; www.terme-lendava.si] Site well sp, adj hotel complex.
Med, pt shd; htd wc; chem disp; mv service pnt; private bthrms
avail; sauna; shwrs inc; EHU (16A) €4.; lndry; shop 200m; rest,
snacks; bar; no BBQ; playgrnd; 2 pools (1 htd, covrd); naturist
pool; paddling pool; waterslide; tennis; games area; bike hire;
fitness rm; internet; TV rm; some statics; dogs €3; adv bkg;
ccard acc. "Conv Hungarian & Croatian borders; use of spa inc;
unisex san facs." € 45.00   2013*

LESCE see Bled *B2*

⊞ **LJUBLJANA** *C2* (5km N Urban) *46.09752, 14.51870*
Ljubljana Resort, Dunajska Cesta 270, 1000 Ljubljana
[(01) 5890130; fax 5890129; ljubljana.resort@gpl.si;
www.ljubljanaresort.si] Fr Maribor take A1 twd Ljubljana,
at junc Zadobrova take Ljubljana ring rd twd Kranj & exit junc
3 sp Lj - Ježica, Bežigrad. At x-rds turn R twd Črnuče along
Dunajska Cesta, turn R 100m bef rlwy x-ing. Fr N (Jesenica/
Karawanken tunnel) exit A2/E66 at junc 13 sp Ljubljana Črnuče
& foll rd for 3.5km; at rndabt junc with Dunajska Cesta rd turn
R (1st exit); site on L in 200m. Lge, hdg/mkd pitch, pt shd; htd
wc; chem disp; mv service pnt; shwrs inc; EHU (10A) €4.50;
lndry/dishwash area; lndry (inc dryer); shop; supmkt 900m;
rest, snacks; bar; BBQ (gas/elec, sep area); playgrnd; htd pool
complex adj; whirlpools; paddling pool; naturist sunbathing adj
pool; rv fishing; tennis; bike hire; horseriding 500m; archery;
fitness club; wifi; entmnt; games rm; some statics; dogs €3;
phone; bus to city at site ent (tickets at recep); some rlwy noise;
ccard acc; red LS/CKE/CCI. "Busy site by rv; gd rest; red facs
LS; pitches nr hotel poss noisy due late-night functions; some
pitches muddy when wet; conv for city; cycle to city cent fr
site." ♦ € 58.00 SBS - X04   2014*

LUCE OB SAVINJI *B2* (1km N Rural) *46.36092, 14.73637*
Autocamp Šmica, Luče 4, 3334 Luče [(03) 5844330;
fax 5844333; camp.smica@siol.net; www.camp-smica.com]
Fr rd 428, site sp on rvside. Sm, pt shd; wc; shwrs inc; EHU
(16A) €2.50; gas; lndry; BBQ; playgrnd; tennis; wifi; 5% statics;
dogs; phone; bus 400m; poss cr; Eng spkn; adv bkg; quiet; red
long stay; CKE/CCI. "Ideal base for mountaineering, hiking,
watersports etc; vg." ♦ ltd. 1 May-30 Sep. € 13.00   2009*

⊞ **MARIBOR** *B3* (5km SW Urban) *46.5355, 15.60508*
Camping Centre Kekec, Pohorska ulica 35c, 2000 Maribor
[040 665 732; info@cck.si or bernard@cck.si; www.cck.si]
Fr S on A1 exit Maribor Jug; foll rd until you see Bauhaus
shopping cent on the R, turn L at this x-rd; turn R after approx
400m; turn L after approx 100m; site on L after approx 3km
opp the Merano Hotel. Sm, mkd pitch, hdstg, pt sl, terr,
unshd; htd wc; chem disp; mv service pnt; baby facs; shwrs;
EHU (25A) €3; lndry; rest & bar 250m; BBQ; wifi; dogs €1.50;
Eng spkn; adv bkg; ccard acc; CKE/CCI. "Rec for larger o'fits
as lge pitches avail but care with narr ent rd; v nice site."
€ 35.00   2013*

MOJSTRANA see Kranjska Gora *B1*

MOZIRJE *B3* (6km SW Rural) *46.30930, 14.91593* **Camping
Savinja,** Spodnje Pobrežje 11, 3332 Rečica ob Savinji
[tel/fax (035) 835472; www.sloveniaholidays.com]
SW fr Velenje for 14km to Mozirje. Then foll sp to Pobrežje for
4km, over bdge. Site is sp in vill down lane opp house no 11.
Med, pt shd; wc; chem disp; shwrs; EHU (16A) €3; lndry; shop;
fishing; dogs €1; quiet; CKE/CCI. "Scenic Savinja & Logarska
Dolina valleys; ideal walking & cycling; clean facs; lovely,
peaceful, simple site." 1 May-30 Sep. € 12.00   2010*

⊞ **NAZARJE** *B2* (7km W Rural) *46.31166, 14.90916*
Camping Menina, Varpolje 105, 3332 Rečica ob Savinji
[(03) 5835027; fax 35835027; info@campingmenina.com;
www.campingmenina.com] Fr rte E57 bet Ljubljana & Celje,
turn N twd Nazarje, then dir Ljubno for 3km. Site sp. Med,
mkd pitch, some hdstg, shd; wc; chem disp; mv service pnt;
shwrs inc; EHU (6-16A) €3; lndry (inc dryer); rest, snacks; bar;
playgrnd; lake sw adj; bike hire; wifi; 10% statics; dogs €3; Eng
spkn; adv bkg; quiet; red CKE/CCI. "Helpful owners; delightful
site in woodland; v ltd facs in winter." € 20.00   2010*

NOVA GORICA *C1* (7km SE Rural) *45.94182, 13.71761*
Camping Lijak - Mladovan Farm, Ozeljan 6A, 5261 Šempas
[(05) 3088557; fax 53079619; camp.lijak@volja.net;
www.camplijak.com] Fr Nova Gorica take rd 444 twd
Ljubljana/Ajdovščina. Site on L bef turn-off to Ozeljan. Sm, pt
shd; htd wc; chem disp; shwrs inc; EHU (10A) €3 (poss long
lead req); shop 1km; snacks; BBQ; wifi; some statics; dogs €1;
phone; bus; Eng spkn; slight rd noise; red LS. "Farm site in
wine-growing area; weekly wine tasting; hang-gliding area,
enthusiasts use site; friendly owner; gd san facs."
15 Mar-31 Oct. € 35.50   2013*

PODCETRTEK see Rogaška Slatina *B3*

⊞ **PORTOROZ** *D1* (4km NE Coastal) *45.52536, 13.60754*
Autocamp Strunjan, Strunjan 23, 6320 Portorož
[(05) 6782076; amd-piran@siol.net; www.amdpiran-
drustvo.si] Fr Koper on rd 111 at 6.5km marker turn R at
traff lts sp Strunjan. In 50m turn L, site in L in 200m, well sp.
Med, pt shd; wc; chem disp; shwrs inc; EHU (6A) inc; lndry rm;
shop 300m; bar; shgl beach 500m; 95% statics; dogs; phone;
bus adj; Eng spkn; rd noise; rec CKE/CCI. "Open all yr for
m'vans, but ltd pitches; excel san facs; friendly staff." ♦ ltd.
€ 19.00   2010*

SLOVENIA

SLOVENIA

PORTOROZ *D1* (3km S Coastal) *45.50138, 13.59388*
Camping Lucija, Obala 77, 6320 Portorož [(05) 6906000; fax 6906900; camp@metropolgroup.si; www.metropol group.si] Fr Koper (N) on rd 111, turn R at traff lts in Lucija. Take next L, then 2nd L into site. Nr Metropol Hotel, site sp. Lge, pt shd; wc; mv service pnt; serviced pitches; shwrs inc; EHU (6-10A) €4.50; lndry; shop; rest; bar; beach adj; bike hire; 60% statics; dogs €5; poss cr; Eng spkn; quiet; ccard acc; red CKE/CCI. "Conv Piran old town by bike or bus; sea views; sep area for tourers, extra for beach pitch; sm pitches; vg facs." ♦ 1 Apr-3 Oct. € 33.00   2010*

POSTOJNA *C2* (5km NW Rural) *45.80551, 14.20470* Camping Pivka Jama, Veliki Otok 50, 6230 Postojna [(05) 7203993; fax 7265348; avtokamp.pivka.jama@siol.net; www.venus-trade.si] Fr N or S Exit A1/E61 strt over traff lts, R at rdbt then bear L at next, foll sp to caves grotto (Postojnska Jama). Pass caves on R & then foll signs for Predjama Castle. 3km after caves site sp. Narr, winding app rd. Lge, hdstg, pt sl, terr, hdstg, shd; htd wc; chem disp; mv service pnt; shwrs inc; EHU (6A) €3.70 (rev pol); lndry; shop; rest, snacks; bar; cooking facs; playgrnd; pool; paddling pool; tennis; 50% statics; dogs; poss v cr; Eng spkn; adv bkg; quiet but noisy nr sw pool; ccard acc; red LS CKE/CCI. "Gd forest site; gd rest with live Tirolean music; gd san facs; used as transit to Croatia, open 24 hrs; caves 4km a must visit (take warm clothing!)." 1 Apr-31 Oct. € 23.00   2011*

⊞ **PREBOLD** *B3* (200m N Rural) *46.24027, 15.08790*
Camping Dolina, Dolenja Vas 147, 3312 Prebold [(03) 5724378; fax 5742591; camp@dolina.si; www.dolina. si] On A1/E57 turn R 16km fr Celje sp Prebold & foll sp, site on N edge of vill. Sm, unshd; wc; chem disp; shwrs (inc); EHU (6-10A) €3.30; gas; lndry; shop 400m; rest in hotel 800m; htd pool; bike hire; dogs €2; poss cr; quiet; red long stay; CKE/CCI. "Gd clean facs but no changing area in shwrs; helpful, friendly owner; conv Savinja valley; gd walking." € 18.50   2010*

PREBOLD *B3* (350m N Rural) *46.23832, 15.09266* Camping Park, Latkova Vas 227, 3312 Prebold [(03) 7001986; info@ campingpark.si; www.campingpark.si] Fr A1/E57 or rd 5 exit at Prebold. Foll site sp for 400m, cross Rv Savinja & site on L. Sm, shd; htd wc; chem disp; shwrs inc; EHU (6A) inc; lndry; shops 2km; rest; bar; BBQ; games area; some Eng spkn; adv bkg; quiet; 10% red CKE/CCI. "V pleasant, well-kept site but ltd facs; pleasant walks by rv; helpful owners own adj hotel; gd walking & cycling." 1 Apr-31 Oct. € 20.00   2012*

⊞ **PTUJ** *B4* (3km NW Rural) *46.42236, 15.85478* Autokamp Terme Ptuj, Pot V Toplice 9, 2250 Ptuj [(02) 7494100; fax 7494520; info@terme-ptuj.si; www.terme-ptuj.si] S fr Maribor on A4 or rd 1/E59; turn L onto rd 2 sp Ptuj (exit junc 2 fr A4); on app Ptuj foll sp Golf/Terme Camping to L off rd 2; site after leisure complex on Rv Drava. Diff to find when app fr SW on rd 432. Med, pt shd; htd wc; chem disp; mv service pnt; sauna; steam rm; shwrs inc; EHU (10A) €4; gas; lndry (inc dryer); shop 2km; rest, snacks, bar; BBQ; playgrnd; htd, covrd pools/spa; waterslide; games area; tennis; fitness rm; bike hire; golf 1km; internet; statics; dogs €4; phone; weekly bus to Vienna; poss cr; Eng spkn; red LS/long stay/snr citizens/ CKE/CCI. "Helpful staff; clean san facs, poss stretched high ssn; pitches muddy in wet; superb water park free to campers; lovely area; castle & monastery in Ptuj old town worth a visit; new san facs (2013)." ♦ ltd. € 58.00   2013*

RECICA OB SAVINJI see Mozirje *B3*

ROGASKA SLATINA *B3* (12km S Rural) *46.16499, 15.60495* Camping Natura Terme Olimia, Zdraviliška Cesta 24, 3254 Podčetrtek [(03) 8297000; fax 5829024; info@terme-olimia. com; www.terme-olimia.com] Fr Celje take rte E dir Rogaška Slatina. Turn S sp Podčetrtek just bef Rogaška. Site on L (waterchutes) alongside Rv Solta on Croatian border in approx 10km. Sm, unshd; htd wc; chem disp; mv service pnt; sauna; shwrs inc; EHU (10-16A) €3.20; lndry; shop high ssn; rest 800m; snacks; bar; playgrnd; 2 htd pools (1 covrd); paddling pool; waterslide; fitness rm; tennis; bike hire; horseriding 2km; golf 4km; wifi; TV rm; phone; adv bkg; ccard acc; red CKE/CCI. "Aqualuna Thermal Pk adj; vg walking country with wooded hillsides." ♦ 15 Apr-15 Oct. € 32.00 (CChq acc)   2011*

SKOFJA LOKA *B2* (12km E Rural) *46.17455, 14.41720* Camping Smlednik (Part Naturist), Dragočajna 14a, 1216 Smlednik [(01) 3627002; camp@dm-campsmlednik.si; www.dm-campsmlednik.si] Fr Ljubljana N on E61 take turning W onto rd 413 sp Zapoge & Zbilje. After Valburg & bef x-ing rv turn R to Dragočajna & site. Lge, terr, pt shd; wc; chem disp; shwrs inc; EHU (6-10A) €3-4; shop; snacks; bar; BBQ; canoeing; tennis; many statics; dogs €1; Eng spkn; quiet; CKE/CCI. "Pleasant rvside location; steep site; sep sm naturist site; shwrs poss only warm as solar powered; ltd facs LS; poss muddy when wet." 1 May-15 Oct. € 24.00   2013*

"We must tell The Club about that great site we found"

Get your site reports in by mid-August and we'll do our best to get your updates into the next edition.

SOCA see Bovec *B1*

VELENJE *B3* (2km NW Rural) *46.36832, 15.08864* Autocamp Jezero, Cesta Simona Blatnika 26, 3320 Velenje [(03) 5866466; mastodontbar@gmail.com] Exit A1/E57 at Velenje & cont to 2nd traff lts, then turn R. Turn L at 3rd traff lts & foll site sp. Site on lakeside. Med, mkd pitch, pt shd; wc; chem disp; mv service pnt; shwrs; EHU (10A) inc; lndry; supmkt 2km; rest 300m; snacks; playgrnd; lake sw; watersports; tennis; games area; fitness rm; internet; some statics; dogs €1.50; quiet. "Lovely location but nr coal-powered power stn; poss unkempt LS; Velenje coal mining museum worth visit 1km; san facs need refurb (2015); poor." ♦ 1 May-30 Sep. € 22.00   2015*

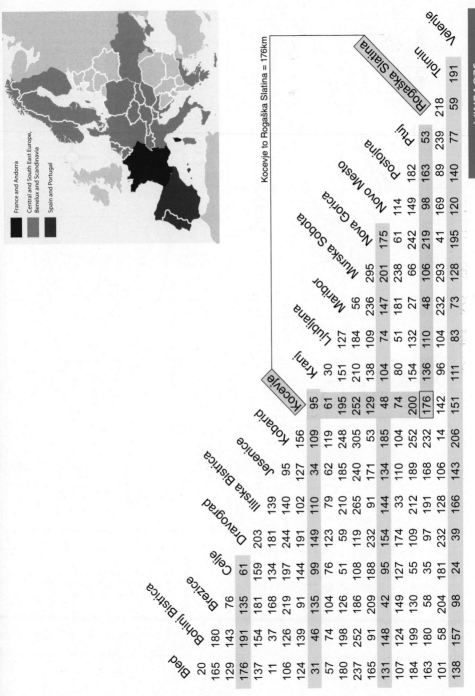

Kocevje to Rogaška Slatina = 176km

France and Andorra
Central and South East Europe, Benelux and Scandinavia
Spain and Portugal

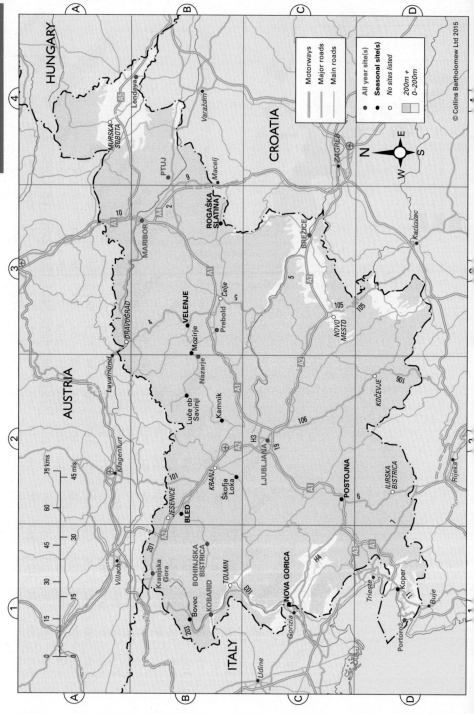

Map legend:

- Motorways
- Major roads
- Main roads

● All year site(s)
● Seasonal site(s)
○ No sites listed

200m +
0–200m

© Collins Bartholomew Ltd 2015

Countries and places labelled on map:

HUNGARY
AUSTRIA
ITALY
CROATIA

Lendava
MURSKA SOBOTA
PTUJ
Varaždin
Macelj
ROGAŠKA SLATINA
MARIBOR
BREŽICE
ZAGREB
Karlovac
DRAVOGRAD
Lavamünd
VELENJE
Mozirje
Prebold
Celje
NOVO MESTO
Nazarje
Luče ob Savinji
Kamnik
KOČEVJE
Klagenfurt
LJUBLJANA
POSTOJNA
ILIRSKA BISTRICA
Rijeka
JESENICE
KRANJ
Škofja Loka
Villach
Kranjska Gora
BLED
BOHINJSKA BISTRICA
TOLMIN
KOBARID
Bovec
NOVA GORICA
Gorizia
Udine
Trieste
Koper
Buje
Portorož

Scale:
0 15 30 45 60 75 kms
0 15 30 45 mils

N
W — E
S

Sweden
Country Introduction

Drottningholm Palace, Sweden

Welcome to Sweden

Renowned for combining simple beauty with functionality, Sweden is one of the design capitals of the world. This is shown in everything from gothic cathedrals and baroque palaces to its more modern creations.

As one of Europe's largest, least populated countries Sweden has a lot of green space to enjoy. An extensive network of national parks and trails mean even the most remote parts of the country are easily accessible.

Country highlights

Due to its shorter summers, Sweden makes the most of the long days by packing as many events into them as possible. One of these is a crayfish party, which is a traditional summertime eating and drinking celebration.

Sweden is also celebrated for its rich variety of children's literature, with Astrid Lindgren's Pippi Longstocking, or Pippi Långstrump, one of the most well-known creations.

Major towns and cities

- Stockholm – a dynamic capital city which is the home of the Nobel Prize.
- Gothenburg – this port city has plenty of history on show.
- Malmö – a green city with plenty of beautiful parks.
- Uppsala – this city has ancient roots and boast a dominating cathedral and castle.

Attractions

- Vasa Museum, Stockholm – featuring a fantastically preserved shipwreck from the 17th century, this one-of-a-kind museum has something for everyone.
- Sigtuna – the oldest town in Sweden, boasting a picturesque medieval centre filled with restaurants, shops and cafés.
- Drottningholm Palace – A residence of the Swedish royal family, this stunning palace has beautiful gardens and an exquisite interior.

Find out more

www.visitsweden.com

Tel: 0046 (0) 87 89 10 00 Swedish Tourist Office

Country Information

Population (approx): 9.6 million

Capital: Stockholm (population 915,000 approx)

Area: 450,000 sqkm

Bordered by: Finland, Norway

Terrain: Mostly flat or gently rolling lowlands; mountains in the west

Climate: Cold, cloudy winters, sub-arctic in the north; cool/warm summers. The best time to visit is between May and September; August can be hot and wet. Be prepared for occasional sub-zero temperatures and snowfalls, even in summer months

Coastline: 3,218km

Highest Point: Kebnekaise 2,104m

Language: Swedish

Local Time: GMT or BST + 1, i.e. 1 hour ahead of the UK all year

Currency: Krona (SEK) divided into 100 öre; £1 = SEK 13.48, SEK 100 = £7.42 (September 2015)

Emergency Numbers: Police 112 (or 11414 for non-emergency calls); Fire Brigade 112; Ambulance 112. Operators speak English

Public Holidays 2016: Jan 1, 6; Mar 25, 27, 28; May 1, 5, 15; Jun 6, 25; Nov 5; Dec 25, 26.

School summer holidays are from early June to the second or third week of August

Camping and Caravanning

Camping and caravanning are very popular, but because summer is short the season is brief - from May to late August/early September, although winter caravanning is increasing in popularity. High season on most sites ends around the middle of August when prices and site office opening hours are reduced or sites close altogether. There are more than 1,000 campsites, about 350 of which remain open during the winter particularly in mountainous regions near to ski resorts. Those that are open all year may offer fewer or no facilities from mid-September to April and advance booking may be required.

In late June and July advance booking is recommended, especially at campsites along the west coast (north and south of Göteborg), on the islands of Öland and Gotland and near other popular tourist areas.

Approximately 500 campsites are members of the SCR (Svenska Campingvärdars Riksfärbund – Swedish Campsite Owners' Association), which are classified from 1 to 5 stars. Visitors wishing to use these sites must have a Camping Key Europe card. You can buy the Camping Key Europe at campsites for around €20 and you will be given a temporary card, or you can order it in advance from www.camping.se/en for 150 SEK (2015 prices). If ordering in advance you should allow at least 3 weeks for delivery.

Most Swedes use electric hook-ups so caravanners using their battery may obtain a pitch which is on a less congested part of the site. Also aim to arrive by mid afternoon to get a better pitch, since many Swedes arrive late. It is reported that hand basins on sites often do not have plugs so it is advisable to carry a flat universal plug when touring.

Many sites have a 'Quick Stop' amenity which provides safe, secure overnight facilities on, or adjacent to, a site. This normally includes the use of sanitary facilities. 'Quick Stop' rates are about two thirds of the regular camping rate if you arrive after 9pm and leave before 9am.

Casual/wild camping is normally permitted (except in National Parks and recreational areas), however for security reasons it is not recommended to spend the night in a vehicle on the roadside or in a public car park. Instead use the 'Quick Stop' amenity at campsites. In any event local parking rules and signposting should always be observed.

Alternatively there are around 150 organised 'ställplatser' mainly intended for motorhomes but generally car and caravan outfits may also use them for an overnight stay at the discretion of the site's manager. For a list of 'ställplatser' see www. campinggladje.se/resa.

Most designated rest areas along highways are owned and managed by the Vägverket (Swedish Roads Administration) which, although not officially ranked as 'ställplatser', offer adequate parking space and various facilities for motorhomes staying overnight. A map showing these rest areas is available at local tourist offices.

Cycling

The network of cycle lanes in Sweden is growing rapidly and many cycle routes are named and signposted. In some cases cycle lanes are combined with foot paths.
See www.svenska-cykelsallskapet.se.

The 'Sverigeleden' cycle trail covers the whole country and connects all major ports and cities. The 190km cycle route along the Göta Canal from Sjötorp on Lake Vänern to Mem on the Baltic coast is relatively flat and hence a very popular route.

The wearing of a safety helmet is compulsory for children up to the age of 15 and is recommended for everyone.

Electricity and Gas

On campsites the current is usually 10 amps or more and round two-pin plugs are used. CEE connections are becoming standard.

Propane (gasol) is the gas most widely obtainable at more than 2,000 Primus dealers; you will need to buy an appropriate adaptor. It is understood that it is possible to sell back your propane cylinder at the end of your holiday and outlets will also exchange the corresponding Norwegian Progas cylinders. Recent visitors report that major distributors will refill cylinders but they must be of a recognised make/type and in perfect condition. The Caravan Club does not recommend the refilling of cylinders.

Butane gas is available from a number of outlets including some petrol stations. It is understood that Campingaz 904 and 907 cylinders are available but recent visitors report that they may be difficult to find, and virtually impossible in the north of the country. For more information on butane suppliers contact the Swedish Campsite Owners' Association (SCR) by email: info@scr.se

Ensure that you are well-equipped with gas if venturing north of central Sweden as it may be difficult to find an exchange point. Many sites have communal kitchen facilities which enable visitors to make great savings on their own gas supply.

Entry Formalities

Holders of valid British and Irish passports may visit Sweden for up to three months without a visa.

Regulations for Pets

In order to protect the countryside and wildlife, dogs are not allowed to run off the lead from 1 March to 20 August and at other times in certain areas.

Dogs travelling directly from the UK and Ireland must be microchipped and have an EU pet passport. For more information please visit www.jordbruksverket.se (english option) and go to the 'Animals' section.

Medical Services

Health care facilities are generally very good and most medical staff speak English. The general practitioner system does not apply; instead visit the nearest hospital clinic (Akutmottagning or Värdcentral) and present your passport and European Health Insurance Card (EHIC). You will be charged a fee for the clinic visit (free for anyone under 20) plus a daily standard charge if it is necessary to stay in hospital. These charges are non-refundable in Sweden.

Prescriptions are dispensed at pharmacies (apotek) which are open during normal shopping hours. Emergency prescriptions can be obtained at hospitals. Dental surgeons or clinics (tandläkare or folktandvård) offer emergency out-of-hours services in major cities but you may have to pay the full cost of treatment.

The use of mosquito repellent is recommended, particularly from mid June to September when mosquitos are most common. Mosquitos are generally more often encountered in the north of Sweden rather than the south.

Visitors to remote areas should consider the relative inaccessibility of the emergency services. In northern Sweden mobile phone coverage does not generally extend beyond main roads and the coast.

Opening Hours

Banks – Mon-Fri 9.30am-2pm/3pm and until 5.30pm one day a week in larger towns. Many banks do not handle cash after 3pm and some banks will not handle cash at all.

Museums – Check locally, opening hours can vary.

Post Offices – Post offices no longer exist. Mail

is dealt with at local shops, kiosks and petrol stations; opening hours vary.

Shops – Mon-Fri 9am-6pm; Sat 9am-1pm/2pm/3pm; supermarkets may open until 8pm and Sun. Shops generally close early the day before a public holiday.

Safety and Security

Petty crime levels are much lower than in most other European countries but you should take the usual commonsense precautions. Pickpocketing is common in the summer months in major cities where tourists may be targeted for their passports and cash.

In recent years there have been incidents of 'highway robbery' from motorhomes parked on the roadside, especially on the west coast between Malmö and Gothenburg.

Sweden shares with the rest of Europe an underlying threat from terrorism. Attacks could be indiscriminate and against civilian targets in public places, including tourist sites.

British Embassy
SKARPÖGATAN 6-8,115 93 STOCKHOLM
Tel: (08) 6713000
www.ukinsweden.fco.gov.uk/en/
Irish Embassy
Hovslagargatan 5, 111 48 STOCKHOLM
Tel: (08) 54504040
www.embassyofireland.se

Customs Regulations

Visitors arriving from an EU country via a non-EU country (e.g. Norway) may bring quantities of tobacco and alcohol obtained in EU countries, plus the amounts allowed duty-free from non-EU countries. However, you must be able to produce proof of purchase for goods from EU countries and goods must be for your personal use.

Border Posts

There are approximately 40 Customs posts along the Swedish/Norwegian border. They are situated on all main roads and are normally open Mon to Fri from 8.30am - 4pm/5pm.

Travellers with dutiable goods must cross the land borders during hours when the Customs posts are open. However, travellers without dutiable goods may cross the border outside Customs post opening hours.

The main border posts with Finland are at Haparanda, Övertornea, Pajala and Karesuando.

Documents

Driving Licence
A UK driving licence is only valid when it bears a photograph of the holder, i.e. a photocard licence, or when it is carried together with photographic proof of identity, such as a passport.

Money

Foreign currency may be exchanged in banks and bureaux de change.

Major credit cards are widely used both for major and minor transactions and cash machines (Bankomat or Minuten) are widespread. It is advisable to carry your passport or photocard driving licence if paying with a credit card as you may be asked for photographic proof of identity.

Motoring in Sweden

Accidents

In the case of an accident it is not necessary to call the police unless there are injuries to drivers or passengers and/or vehicles are badly damaged, but drivers are required to give their details to the other persons involved before leaving the accident scene. A driver leaving the scene of an accident without following this procedure may be fined.

If you are involved in an accident with a possible third party claim, you are strongly recommended to report the accident to the national Swedish insurance bureau which will act as claims agent. Contact Trafikförsäkringsforeningen in Stockholm, tel: 08 522 78100, info@ tff.se, www.tff.se.

Accidents involving wild animals (e.g. elk, reindeer, bear, wolf, etc) must be reported to the police immediately by calling 112 or 11414 and the spot where the accident took place must be marked by putting up reflective tape or anything clearly noticeable so that the police can find it easily.

Collisions must be reported even if the animal involved is not injured. After reporting the accident and marking out the place, a driver may leave. Accidents involving smaller animals (badgers, foxes, etc) need not be reported.

Alcohol

Penalties for driving a motor vehicle under the influence of alcohol are extremely severe. The police carry out random breath tests. If the level of alcohol exceeds 20 milligrams in 100 millilitres of blood a fine will be imposed and driving licence withdrawn. This level is considerably lower than that permitted in the UK (80 milligrams) and equates to virtually zero. A level exceeding 100 milligrams is considered to be severe drink driving for which a jail sentence of up to two years may be imposed and licence withdrawn.

Breakdown Service

The motoring organisation, Motormännens Riksförbund (known as the 'M'), does not operate a breakdown service. It does, however, have an agreement with 'AssistanceKåren' (a nationwide road service company) which operates a 24-hour, all-year service and can be contacted free on (020) 912912 or 08 6275757 from a foreign-registered mobile phone. Phone boxes are becoming quite scarce and it is advisable to carry a mobile phone. There are normally no emergency telephones along motorways or dual carriageways. Charges for assistance and towing vary according to day and time and payment by credit card is accepted.

Essential Equipment

Warning Triangle
It is compulsory for foreign registered vehicles to carry a warning triangle. They should be placed as a distance of 50 meters behind the vehicle on ordinary roads and 100 meters on motorways.

Lights
Dipped headlights are compulsory at all times, regardless of weather conditions. Bulbs are more likely to fail with constant use and you are recommended to carry spares. Fog lights may be used when visibility is poor but they must not be used together with dipped headlights.

Vehicles parked or stopped on a poorly lit road at night, including dawn, dusk and bad weather, must have their parking lights switched on.

Child Restraint System
Children under the height of 135cm must be seated in a child restraint or child seat. A child aged 15 or over, or 135cm in height or taller, can use normal seat belts in the car.

Children under the height of 140cm are only allowed in the front seat if the passenger seat airbag has been deactivated.

Winter Driving
The winter months are periods of severe cold and you should be prepared for harsh conditions. The fitting of winter tyres is compulsory for vehicles from 1st December to 31st March in the event of severe winter road conditions, i.e. the road is covered with ice or snow, or if the road is wet and the temperature is around freezing point. Trailers towed by these vehicles must also be equipped with winter tyres. These regulations apply to foreign registered vehicles.

Fuel

Petrol stations are usually open from 7am to 9pm. Near motorways and main roads and in most cities they may remain open until 10pm or even for 24 hours. Outside large towns garages seldom stay open all night but most have self-service pumps (possibly not for diesel) which accept credit cards. In the far north filling stations may be few and far between so keep your tank topped up. Credit cards are accepted.

LPG (known as gasol) is sold at a very limited number of petrol stations mainly located in central and southern Sweden.

Low Emission Zones

There are Low Emission Zones (Miljözen) in Sweden. Please see www.lowemissionzones.eu for the most up-to-date information.

Overtaking

Take care when overtaking long vehicles. A typical long-distance Swedish truck is a six-wheeled unit towing a huge articulated trailer, i.e. a very long load.

Many roads in Sweden have wide shoulders or a climbing lane to the right of the regular lane and these permit drivers of slow moving vehicles or wide vehicles to pull over to allow other traffic to pass. These climbing lanes and shoulders should not be used as another traffic lane.

Parking

Parking meters and other parking restrictions are in use in several large towns. Vehicles must be parked facing the direction of the flow of traffic. Wheel clamps are not in use but illegally parked vehicles may be towed away and, in addition to a parking fine, a release fee will be charged.

In an area signposted 'P' parking is permitted for a maximum of 24 hours, unless otherwise stated.

Priority

Vehicles driving on roads designated and signposted (with a yellow diamond on a black background) as primary roads always have priority. On all other roads, as a general rule, vehicles coming from the right have priority, unless signs indicate otherwise. This rule is sometimes ignored however, especially by vehicles on roads regarded as major roads but not signposted as such.

At most roundabouts signs indicate that traffic already on the roundabout has priority, i.e. from the left.

Give trams priority at all times. Where there is no refuge at a tram stop, you must stop to allow passengers to board and alight from the tram.

Roads

The condition of national and country roads is good although some minor roads may be covered with oil-gravel only. Road surfaces may be damaged following the spring thaw, and some may be closed or have weight restrictions imposed during that period. Gradients are generally slight and there are no roads that need to be avoided for vehicles towing a caravan.

Road repairs tend to be intensive during the short summer season. Information on major roadworks and road conditions on E roads and major national roads can be obtained from www.trafikverket.se.

There is a good road link with Norway in the far north of Sweden. The Kiruna-Narvik road is open all year from Kiruna to the border. It is a wide road with no steep gradients.

There is generally little or no heavy goods traffic on roads during the Christmas, Easter and midsummer holidays or on the days preceding these holidays so good progress can be made.

Road Signs and Markings

Road signs and markings conform to international standards. Road markings are white. The middle of the road is indicated by broken lines with long intervals. Warning lines (usually on narrow roads) are broken lines with short intervals which indicate that visibility is limited in one or both directions; they may be crossed when overtaking. Unbroken lines should not be crossed at any time.

National roads (riksvägar) have two-digit numbers and country roads (länsvägar) have three-digit numbers. Roads which have been incorporated into the European road network – E roads – generally have no other national number.

Direction and information signs for motorways and roads which form part of the European road network are green. Signs for national roads and the more important country roads are blue. Signs for local roads are white with black numerals.

In some towns traffic restrictions, including weight restrictions, may apply at certain times and these are signposted. The following are some other signs that you may see:

Passing place

Additional stop sign

Accident

Swedish	English Tanslation
Enkelriktat	One way
Farlig kurva	Dangerous bend
Grusad väg	Loose chippings
Höger	Right
Ingen infart	No entrance
Parkering förbjuden	No parking
Vänster	Left

Speed Limits

	Open Road (km/h)	Motorway (km/h)
Car Solo	60-100	90-120
Car towing caravan/trailer	70-80	80
Motorhome under 3500kg	60-100	90-120
Motorhome 3500-7500kg	70-100	90-120

Speed limits are no longer based on the category of road but on the quality and safety level of the roads themselves. As a result limits may vary from one town to another and along stretches of the same road. It is advisable, therefore, to pay close attention to road signs as speed limits are strictly enforced. If in doubt, or if no speed limit is indicated, you are advised to keep to 70 km/h (44 mph) until you see a speed limit sign.

Outside built-up areas, including expressways, speeds up to 100 km/h (62 mph) may be permitted according to road signs, providing a lower maximum speed is not applicable for certain vehicle categories. Vehicles with trailers must never exceed 80 km/h (49mph). On motorways the maximum permitted speed is 110 or 120 km/h (68 or 74 mph). During the winter a speed limit of 90 km/h (56 mph) is in force on some motorways and dual carriageways. This limit is signposted.

In most residential areas and during certain periods in areas near schools, speed is limited to 30 km/h (18 mph) according to road signs. Periods indicated in black mean Monday to Friday, those in black in brackets mean Saturday and the eves of public holidays, and those indicated in red mean Sunday and public holidays.

Speed limits for motorhomes under 3,500kg and privately registered motorhomes over 3,500kg are the same as for solo cars.

Speed cameras are in use on many roads. The use of radar detectors is not permitted.

Traffic Lights

A green arrow indicates that traffic may proceed with caution in the direction of the arrow but pedestrians must be given priority. A flashing amber light indicates that a crossing/turning must be made with caution.

Violation of Traffic Regulations

Police are authorised to impose and collect fines for violation of minor traffic offences which must be paid at a bank, normally within two to three weeks. Offences, which may qualify for a fine include driving without lights in daylight, speeding, lack of a warning triangle or nationality plate (GB or IRL) or a dirty or missing number plate.

If a fine is not paid and the driver is a resident of another EU country, notice of the fine will be forwarded to the authorities in the driver's country of residence.

Jaywalking is not permitted; pedestrians must use official crossings.

Motorways

There are approximately 1,900 kms of motorway and 560 kms of semi-motorway or dual carriageway, all confined to the south of the country and relatively free of heavy traffic by UK standards. There are no service areas or petrol stations on motorways; these are situated near the exits and are indicated on motorway exit signs. Please note that there are no petrol stations close to the 110km long Uppsala to Gälve motorway.

Tolls

Tolls for private vehicles have now been introduced. The Motala by-pass (on road 50m in central Sweden) the toll will be 5 SEK and for the Sundsvall by-pass (on E4 in northern Sweden) the toll will be 9 SEK.

Toll Bridges

The Øresund Bridge links Malmö in Sweden with Copenhagen in Denmark and means that it is possible to drive all the way from mainland Europe by motorway. The crossing is via a 7.8 km bridge to the artificial island of Peberholm and a 4 km tunnel. Tolls (payable in cash, including EUR, SEK or DKK or by credit card) are levied on the Swedish side and are as follows for single journeys (2015 prices subject to change)

Vehicle(s)	Price
Solo car or motorhome up to 6 metres	€ 52
Car + caravan/trailer or motorhome over 6 metres	€ 104

Vehicle length is measured electronically and even a slight overhang over six metres will result in payment of the higher tariff.

Speed limits apply in the tunnel and on the bridge, and during periods of high wind the bridge is closed to caravans. Bicycles are not allowed. Information on the Øresund Bridge can be found on www.oeresundsbron.com.

Svinesund Bridge

There is a 700 metre long bridge linking Sweden and Norway on the E6, at Svinesund. Tolls are SEK24 (NOK20) for light vehicles and SEK120 (NOK100) for vehicles over 3,500kgs (2015).

Touring

Ferry services connect Sweden with Denmark, Estonia, Finland, Germany, Latvia, Lithuania, Norway and Poland; some services only operate in the summer. Full details are available from Visit Sweden, www.visitsweden.com. Scheduled car ferry services also operate between the mainland and the island of Gotland during the summer season.

In the south and centre the touring season lasts from May to September. In the north it is a little shorter, the countryside being particularly beautiful at each end of the season. Campsites are most crowded over the midsummer holiday period and during the Swedish industrial holidays in the last two weeks of July and first week of August. Tourist attractions may close before the end of August or operate on reduced opening hours.

Sweden has 15 UNESCO World Heritage sites and 29 national parks which, together with nature reserves, cover eight percent of the country. Information on national parks and nature reserves is available on www.naturvardsverket.se.

Inland, particularly near lakes, visitors should be armed with spray-on, rub-on and electric plug-in insect repellent devices as mosquitoes and midges are a problem.

Discount cards are available in Stockholm and Gothenburg offering free public transport and free admission to many museums and other attractions, plus free boat and canal sightseeing trips. Buy the cards at tourist information offices, hotels, kiosks, some campsites and online – see www.stockholmtown.com or www.goteborg.com.

Local tourist offices are excellent sources of information and advice; look for the blue and yellow 'i' signs. Information points at lay-bys at the entrance to many towns are good sources of street maps.

A good-value 'dagens rätt' (dish of the day) is available in most restaurants at lunchtime. A service charge is usually included in restaurant bills but an additional small tip is normal if you have received good service.

The most popular alcoholic drink is lager, available in five strengths. Wines, spirits and strong beer are sold only through the state-owned 'Systembolaget' shops, open from Monday to Friday and on Saturday morning, with branches all over the country. Light beer can be bought from grocery shops and supermarkets. The minimum age for buying alcoholic drinks is 20 years at Systembolaget and 18 years in pubs, bars and licensed restaurants.

It is not permitted to smoke in restaurants, pubs or bars or in any place where food and drinks are served.

The Midnight Sun and Northern Lights

The Midnight Sun is visible north of the Arctic Circle from about the end of May until the middle of July.

The Northern Lights (Aurora Borealis) are often visible during the winter from early evening until midnight. They are seen more frequently the further north you travel. The best viewing areas in Sweden are north of the Arctic Circle between September and March.

The Order of Bluenosed Caravanners

Visitors to the Arctic Circle from anywhere in the world may apply for membership of the Order of Bluenosed Caravanners which will be recognised by the issue of a certificate by the International Caravanning Association (ICA).

For more information contact David Hirst on telephone 01422 372390, or email: david.hirst118@gmail.com and attach a photograph of yourselves and your outfit under any Arctic Circle signpost, together with the date and country of crossing and the names of those who made the crossing. This service is free to members of the ICA (annual membership £20); the fee for non-members is £5. Coloured plastic decals for your outfit, indicating membership of the Order, are also available at a cost of £4. Cheques should be payable to the ICA. See www.icacaravanning.org.

Public Transport & Local Travel

Stockholm has an extensive network of underground trains (T-bana), commuter trains, buses and trams. Underground station entrances are marked with a blue 'T' on a white background. You can buy single tickets for one of three zones at the time of your journey, or save money by buying tickets in advance. A discount applies if you are aged 65 or over. Single tickets and prepaid tickets are valid for one hour after beginning your journey. Travel cards offer reduced price public transport throughout the Greater Stockholm area for periods of 1, 3, 7 or 30 days, regardless of zone – see www.sl.se (click on 'Visitor') for details of routes, fares and tickets.

For information on public transport systems in Göteborg and Malmö, see www.vasttrafik.se and www.skanetrafiken.se.

Stockholm is built on an archipelago of islands and island hopping ferries operate all year. You can buy single tickets or an island hopping pass for use on the Waxholmsbolaget and Cinderella fleet of ferries.

Confirm your taxi fare before setting off in the vehicle. Some companies have fixed fares which vary according to the day of the week and time of day. A full price list must be on display. Payment by credit card is generally accepted. It is usual to round up the fare shown on the meter by way of a tip.

Sweden is a country of lakes, rivers and archipelagos and, as a result, there are over 12,000 bridges. Road ferries, which form part of the national road network, make up the majority of other crossings; no bookings are necessary or possible. Most ferries are free of charge and services are frequent and crossings very short.

A congestion charge was introduced in Stockholm in 2007. Drivers of foreign-registered vehicles are exempt from the charge. For more information go to www.visitstockholm.com. In some other towns traffic restrictions may apply during certain periods and these are signposted.

When giving directions Swedes will often refer to distances in 'miles'. A Swedish 'mile' is, in fact, approximately ten kilometres. All road signs are in kilometres so if a Swede tells you it is 3 miles to a town, expect the journey to be around 30km.

⊞ **AHUS** *2F4* (1km NE Urban/Coastal) *55.94118, 14.31286*
Regenbogen Camp (L27), Kolonivägen 59, 29633 Åhus
[(044) 249530; fax 243523; ahus@regenbogen-camp.se;
www.regenbogen-camp.se] Take rd 118 fr Kristianstad SE
twd Åhus. Site well sp fr ent to town. Lge, mkd pitch, hdstg,
pt shd; htd wc; chem disp; mv service pnt; baby facs; sauna;
shwrs inc; EHU (10A) SEK29; lndry (inc dryer); shop; rest, bar
500m; BBQ; playgrnd; htd pool 300m; sand beach 150m; some
statics; dogs; site clsd 3 Nov-16 Dec; poss cr; Eng spkn; quiet;
ccard acc; CKE. "Gd base for walking, cycling, watersports;
excel fishing; famous area for artists." ♦ SEK 260   2011*

ALINGSAS *2E2* (4km W Rural) *57.92575, 12.48708* **Lövekulle**
Camping, 44144 Alingsås [(0322) 12372; lovekulle@telia.com;
www.lovekulle.com] Foll sp fr E20. Sm, mkd pitch, some
hdstg, unshd; htd wc; chem disp; mv service pnt; shwrs; EHU
(10A); lndry; shop; snacks; playgrnd; sw; fishing; games area;
10% statics; Eng spkn; quiet; CKE/CCI. "Pleasant situation by
lake; clean san facs." ♦ 1 May-30 Sep. SEK 185   2010*

ALMHULT *2F3* (2km N Rural) *56.56818, 14.13217* **Sjöstugans**
Camping (G5), Campingvägen, Bökhult, 34394 Älmhult
[(0476) 71600; fax 15750; info@sjostugan.com;
www.sjostugan.com] Fr Växjö SW on rd 23, at rndabt turn W
to Älmhult. Fr town cent turn N on Ljungbyvägen, site in 1.5km
on lakeside, well sp. Sm, pt sl, pt shd; htd wc; chem disp; mv
service pnt; baby facs; shwrs; EHU (10A) SEK40; lndry (inc
dryer) shop & 1.5km; rest, snacks; bar; cooking facs; playgrnd;
lake & sand beach adj; canoe hire; wifi; some statics; dogs; Eng
spkn; quiet; ccard acc; CKE. "Some lakeside pitches; well-kept
site; 1st Ikea store opened here in 1958; gd." 1 May-30 Sep.
SEK 165   2009*

> "I like to fill in the reports
> as I travel from site to site"
> You'll find report forms at the back of
> this guide, or you can fill them in online
> at www.caravanclub.co.uk/europereport.

⊞ **ALVDALEN** *1B4* (W Urban) *61.22789, 14.03007* **Älvdalens**
Camping (W2), Ribbholmsvägen 26, 79631 Älvdalen
[tel/fax (0251) 12344; kontakt@alvdalenscamping.se;
www.alvdalenscamping.se] Fr S & Mora take rd 70 N; in
Älvdalen, 200m after church turn L (W) to site; pt of sports &
leisure cent; well sp. Lge, hdstg, pt shd; htd wc; chem disp; mv
service pnt; baby facs; fam bthrm; shwrs inc; EHU (10A) SEK40;
lndry (inc dryer); shop, rest, snacks 500m; BBQ; cooking facs;
playgrnd; htd, covrd pool, waterslide, ice rink nr; bike hire; wifi;
TV; dogs; Eng spkn; quiet; ccard acc; CKE. "Sh walk to town
cent; gd facs." ♦ SEK 175   2011*

⊞ **AMAL** *2E2* (1km SE Urban) *59.0465, 12.7236* **Örnäs**
Camping (P2), Gamla Örnäsgatan, 66222 Åmål
[(0532) 17097; fax 71624; ornascamping@amal.se;
www.amal.se] Leave rd 45 to Åmål, site sp. Sm, some hdstg,
pt sl, terr, pt shd; htd wc; chem disp; mv service pnt; sauna;
shwrs SEK5; EHU (10A) inc; lndry (inc dryer); shop, rest 1km;
snacks; bar; playgrnd; sand beach/lake adj; fishing; tennis; boat
& bike hire; wifi; some statics; dogs; Eng spkn; red 7 days; ccard
acc; CCS. "Gd views Lake Vänern." ♦ ltd. SEK 250   2011*

ANASET *1C3* (1km S Rural) *64.26834, 21.04120* **Lufta Camping**
(AC15), Galgbacken 1, 91594 Ånäset [(0934) 20488;
fax 20215; info@luftacamping.se; www.luftacamping.se]
Exit E4 at Int'l Camp sp at Ånäset. Site immed S of Ånäset &
300m W of E4. Med, pt sl, pt shd; htd wc; chem disp; mv service
pnt; sauna; shwrs; EHU (10A) SEK50; lndry; shop 500m; rest,
snacks; bar; playgrnd; htd pool adj; waterslide; games area; bike
hire; fishing; wifi; TV; some statics; Eng spkn; ccard acc; CKE.
"Beautiful setting." ♦ 1 May-30 Sep. SEK 130   2009*

ANGELHOLM *2E4* (2km W Coastal) *56.2540, 12.8336*
Råbocka Camping (L12), Råbockavägen 101, 26263
Ängelholm [(0431) 10543 or 430600; fax 16144;
rabockacamping@telia.com; www.rabockacamping.se]
Fr E6 foll sps to Ängelholm, site 2km fr town cent. Lge, mkd
pitch, pt shd; wc; chem disp; mv service pnt; baby facs; shwrs
SEK10; EHU (10A) SEK50; lndry; shop; snacks; bar; playgrnd;
sand beach; TV; 10% statics; poss cr; Eng spkn; adv bkg; ccard
acc; CKE. "Excel, busy site; gd beach & nature park nrby." ♦
16 Apr-11 Sep. SEK 275   2009*

⊞ **ARBOGA** *2G1* (13km S Rural) *59.28134, 15.90509*
Herrfallets Camping (U14), 73293 Arboga [(0589) 40110;
fax 40133; reception@herrfallet.se; www.herrfallet.se]
Foll sp fr E20/E18, turn off at Sätra junc twd Arboga, cross rv.
Foll sp to Herrfallet/Västermo. Med, mkd pitch, pt shd; htd wc;
chem disp; 50% serviced pitches; mv service pnt; baby facs;
sauna; shwrs SEK10; EHU (10A) SEK40; lndry (inc dryer); shop;
rest; bar; BBQ; playgrnd; lake sw & beach; boating; bike hire;
wifi; entmnt; dogs; phone; quiet; ccard acc; CKE/CCI. "Lovely
spot on edge Lake Hjälmaren." ♦ SEK 190   2010*

ARBOGA *2G1* (1km SW Rural) *59.38863, 15.82713*
Krakaborgs Camping, Örebrovägen 2A 24B, 73221
Arboga [(0589) 12670; fax 17425; www.arboga.se]
Fr E18 exit sp Arboga. On ent town at rndabt foll site sp, site
on L. Sm, pt shd; htd wc; chem disp; baby facs; shwrs; EHU
(10A) SEK35; lndry; shop; snacks; cooking facs; playgrnd; TV;
dogs; phone; adv bkg; quiet. 1 Jun-31 Oct. SEK 150   2009*

ARJANG *2E1* (25km SE Rural) *59.30295, 12.44474*
Camping Grinsby, Grindsbyn 100, Sillerud, 67295 Årjäng
[(0573) 42022; fax 40175; campgrinsby@telia.com]
On E18 SE fr Årjäng & Sillerud, turn L at site sp. Site in 2km
on Stora Bör lake. Med, some hdstg, terr, pt shd; htd wc; chem
disp; mv service pnt; baby facs; shwrs SEK10; EHU (10A)
SEK40; lndry (inc dryer); shop; BBQ; cooking facs; playgrnd;
sand beach & lake sw adj; boat & bike hire; games rm; some
statics; dogs; phone; Eng spkn; adv bkg; quiet; ccard acc; CKE/
CCI. "A 'wilderness' site in beautiful setting; many walking
paths; friendly, helpful staff; vg san facs." ♦ ltd.
15 May-31 Aug. SEK 150   2010*

⊞ **ARJANG** *2E1* (3km S Rural) *59.36756, 12.14036* **Årjäng Camping (S13), Strand Sommarvik, 67291 Årjäng [(0573) 12060; fax 12048; booking@sommarvik.se; www.sommarvik.se]** Foll sp fr E18/rd 172. Site sp in Årjäng. At T-junc foll sp Stugby & site sp on R 400m up hill, steep in parts but strt. Lge, pt sl, pt shd; htd wc; mv service pnt; baby facs; sauna; shwrs SEK10; EHU (10A) inc; gas; lndry (inc dryer); shop; rest, snacks; bar; cooking facs; playgrnd; htd pool high ssn; paddling pool; lake sw & beach; fishing; boating; boat & bike hire; games area; tennis 1.5km; wifi; entmnt; TV rm; 50% statics; dogs; phone; Quickstop o'night facs; quiet; CKE. "Gd family site." ♦ SEK 200   2011*

⊞ **ARJEPLOG** *1C2* (1.5km W Rural) *66.05007, 17.86298* **Kraja Camping (BD1), Krajaudden, 93090 Arjeplog [(0961) 31500; fax 31599; arjeplog@kraja.se; www.kraja.se]** NW fr Arvidsjaur thro Arjeplog vill to site on R. Med, pt shd; htd wc; chem disp; baby facs; sauna; shwrs; EHU (10A) SEK40; lndry (inc dryer); shop; rest; bar; cooking facs; playgrnd; htd pool; paddling pool; sand beach; lake sw 4km; fishing; boating; TV; many statics; dogs; phone; poss cr; quiet; CKE. "Gd cent for local Lapp area." ♦ SEK 195   2010*

ASA *2E3* (S Coastal) *57.34906, 12.12200* **Åsa Camping (N3), Stora Badviksvägen 10, 43031 Åsa [(0340) 219590; info@ asacamping.com; www.asacamping.com]** On E6/E20 S fr Göteborg take exit rd sp Åsa. On app Åsa site sp on R. Med, unshd wc; chem disp; mv service pnt; baby facs; shwrs SEK5; EHU (10A) SEK40; lndry (inc dryer); shop & adj; rest; bar; playgrnd; sand beach nr; games area; games rm; golf; fishing; wifi; TV; 80% statics; dogs; phone; adv bkg; quiet; ccard acc; CKE. "Well-organised, family site but dominated by statics; avoid pitches nr access rd & facs block." ♦ 22 Apr-11 Sep. SEK 200   2009*

⊞ **ASARNA** *1B3* (9km S Rural) *62.56340, 14.38786* **Kvarnsjö Camp, Kvarnsjö 696, 84031 Åsarna [tel/fax (0682) 22016; info@kvarnsjocamp.com; www.kvarnsjocamp.com]** Fr N on E45 3km after Åsarna turn R onto rd 316 dir Klövsjo. In 8km turn L sp Cmp Kvarnsjö. In 8km cross rlwy, thro vill, site on L in 1km. Fr S 9km after Rätan turn L dir Klövsjo. In 1.5km bear R at Y-junc site in 4km. Sm, hdstg, terr, unshd; wc; chem disp; mv service pnt; sauna; shwrs inc; EHU (10A) SEK40; lndry; shop 16km; dogs; Eng spkn; adv bkg; quiet. CKE/CCI. "CL-type family-run site o'looking woods & mountains; excel walking, fishing; boating, fresh bread/breakfast in high sssn." SEK 130   2011*

ASKIM see Göteborg *2E3*

BARSEBACK *2E4* (1km W Coastal) *55.77030, 12.92621* **Barsebäckstrand Camping (M19), Kustvägen 125, 24657 Barsebäck [(046) 776079; info@barsebackstrand.se; www.barsebackstrand.se]** Fr S exit E6 junc 23 sp 'Center Syd' & foll sp Barsebäck thro vill. Turn L at T-junc, site in 2km, sp. Fr N exit junc 24 & foll coast rd 'Kustvägen' to site in 5km. Med, mkd pitch, terr, unshd; htd wc; chem disp; mv service pnt; shwrs inc; EHU (10A) SEK40; lndry rm; shop 4km; rest, snacks; cooking facs; playgrnd; beach & sw adj; 40% statics; dogs free; poss cr; Eng spkn; adv bkg; quiet; CKE. "Vg site; excel rest." ♦ 26 Apr-1 Sep. SEK 250   2013*

⊞ **BENGTSFORS** *2E2* (12km SE Rural) *58.95271, 12.25201* **Laxsjöns Camping & Friluftsgård (P3), 66010 Dals Långed [(0531) 30010; fax 30555; office@laxsjons.se; www.laxsjon.se]** Fr Bengtsfors S on rd 172; 4km after x-ing Dalsland Canal at Billingsfors turn L twd Dals Långed; after 1km site on Lake Laxsjön on L; sp. Ent 4.5m. Lge, mkd pitch, pt sl, pt shd; htd wc; chem disp; sauna; shwrs SEK5; EHU (10A) SEK40; lndry (inc dryer); shop; rest in ssn; playgrnd; htd pool; lake sw adj; canoe hire; waterskiing; sailing; fishing; bus 200m/1km; Quickstop o'night facs; Eng spkn; adv bkg; quiet; ccard acc; red 7+ days; CKE. "Vg for quiet holiday & watersports; friendly staff; rec." ♦ SEK 190   2010*

BERGKVARA *2G4* (1km E Coastal) *56.39043, 16.09061* **Dalskärs Camping (H15), Dalskärvägen11, 385 40 Bergkvara [(0709) 415567; info@dalskarscamping.se; www.dalskarscamping.se]** Exit E22 in Bergkvara twd Dalskärsbadet, site sp. Med, mkd pitch, pt shd; wc; chem disp; mv service pnt; baby facs; sauna; shwrs SEK5; EHU SEK40; lndry; shop; rest; bar; htd pool; paddling pool; sand beach adj; boat & bike hire; games area; wifi; some statics; dogs free; phone; Eng spkn; quiet; ccard acc. "Gd family site; san facs adequate; excel rest; scenic location." ♦ 24 Apr-11 Sep. SEK 220   2013*

⊞ **BOCKSJO** *2F2* (5km NW Rural) *58.68058, 14.59911* **Stenkällegårdens Camping Tiveden, 54695 Stenkällegården [(0505) 60015; fax 60085; stenkallegarden@swipnet.se; www.stenkallegarden.nu]** N on rd 49 fr Karlsborg, turn L at Bocksjö, site sp on L in 2km. Pt of rte single track with passing places. Med, mkd pitch, pt sl, terr, pt shd; htd wc; chem disp; mv service pnt; baby facs; sauna; shwrs SEK10, EHU (10A) SEK40; lndry (inc dryer); shop; rest; cooking facs; BBQ; playgrnd; lake sw; fishing; boat hire; TV rm; 30% statics; dogs; site clsd last 2 weeks Apr & 1st 2 weeks Oct; Eng spkn; quiet; ccard acc; CKE. "Gd cycling; mkd walking trails; spacious, sheltered site; clean san facs; skiing on site in winter; Tividen National Park 5km." ♦ SEK 170   2009*

BOLLNAS *1C4* (3km E Rural) *61.3475, 16.43245* **Vevlingestrands Camping (X24), Vevlinge 3680, 82150 Bollnäs [(0278) 12684; info@vevlingestrand.com; www.vevlingestrand.com]** Fr Söderhamn take rd 50 twds Bollnäs; turn L at town edge & foll sp for Vevlinge & Segersta. In 600m foll sp Vevlingestrand to site; well sp. Med, mkd pitch, sl, unshd; wc; chem disp; baby facs; shwrs; EHU (10A) SEK40; lndry; shop; rest, snacks; cooking facs; playgrnd; lake sw & private beach adj; fishing; games area; Eng spkn; quiet; CKE. "Lovely lakeside setting; pleasant site." 1 May-30 Sep. SEK 150   2009*

BORENSBERG *2G2* (1.5km S Rural) *58.55663, 15.27911* **Strandbadets Camping, 59030 Borensberg [(0141) 40385; info@strandbadetscamping.se; www.strandbadets camping.se]** Site sp off rd 36. Med, pt shd; wc; mv service pnt; baby facs; shwrs; EHU (10A) SEK40; lndry; shop, rest in vill; snacks; cooking facs; playgrnd; lake sw & beach; fishing; few statics; quiet; CKE. "Gd base for Östergötland & Lake Vättern area; cycle rte along Göta Canal." 22 Apr-11 Sep. SEK 190   2013*

BROMMA see Stockholm *2H2*

DALS LANGED see Bengtsfors *2E2*

SWEDEN

SWEDEN

DEGERFORS *2F2* (1.5km N Rural) *59.25145, 14.4595* **Degernäs Camping (T7), 69335 Degerfors [(0586) 44999; reception@ degernascamping.se; www.degernascamping.se]** Fr rd 204, take rd 243 twds lake, site sp. Med, pt sl, pt shd; htd wc; chem disp; mv service pnt; baby facs; sauna; shwrs inc; EHU (10A) SEK50; lndry (inc dryer); shop; rest; snacks 2km; playgrnd; lake beach; fishing; boating; bike hire; TV; 50% statics; poss cr; no adv bkg; quiet; ccard acc; CKE. ♦ 1 May-18 Sep. SEK 160   2011*

⊞ **DOROTEA** *1C3* (500m SW Rural) *64.26003, 16.39606* **Doro Camping, Storgatan 1A, 91070 Dorotea [(0942) 10238; fax 10779; reception@dorocamp.com; www.dorocamp.com]** Site on E side of E45. Med, pt sl, pt shd; wc; chem disp; sauna; baby facs; shwrs inc; EHU (10A) SEK50; lndry (inc dryer); shop; snacks; cooking facs; lake sw; playgrnd; fishing; golf; hiking; internet; some statics; site clsd Nov; poss cr; Eng spkn; quiet. ♦ ltd. SEK 135   2010*

⊞ **ED** *2E2* (2km E Rural) *58.89931, 11.93486* **Gröne Backe Camping (P8), Södra Moränvägen 64, 66832 Ed [(0534) 10144; fax 10145; gronebackecamping@telia.com]** App Ed on rd 164/166, site sp on Lake Lilla Le. Med, pt sl, shd; wc; chem disp; sauna; baby facs; shwrs SEK5; EHU (10A) SEK40; lndry (inc dryer); shops, rest, snacks 300m; playgrnd; lake sw; bike hire; wifi; quiet; ccard acc; CKE. "Excel for boating." SEK 180   2009*

EKSHARAD *2F1* (1km E Rural) *60.1760, 13.5090* **Byns Camping (S3), Slätta, 68050 Ekshärad [(0563) 40885; fax 30196; info@bynscamping.eu; www.bynscamping.eu]** Turn E off rd 62 at x-rds by church, site sp on rv bank. Sm, pt shd; htd wc; chem disp; baby facs; shwrs SEK5; EHU (10A) SEK35; lndry (inc dryer); shop; snacks; cooking facs; playgrnd; bike hire; phone; v quiet; ccard acc; CKE. "Pleasant site." ♦ 27 May-31 Aug. SEK 140   2010*

⊞ **EKSJO** *2F3* (1km E Rural) *57.66766, 14.98923* **Eksjö Camping (F13), Prästängsvägen 5, 57536 Eksjö [(0381) 39500; fax 14096; info@eksjocamping.se; www.eksjocamping.se]** Site sp fr town cent on rd 33 twd Västervik, on lakeside. Med, shd; wc; chem disp; mv service pnt; baby facs; shwrs; EHU (10A) SEK45; lndry (inc dryer); shop; rest, snacks; bar; playgrnd; covrd pool 100m; lake sw adj; fishing; boating; bike hire; wifi; 10% statics; dogs; phone; poss cr; no adv bkg; quiet; ccard acc; CKE. "Gd cent glass region; attractive countryside & old town." ♦ SEK 140   2009*

ELDSBERGA see Halmstad *2E3*

⊞ **ENKOPING** *2H1* (6km S Rural) *59.59334, 17.07146* **Bredsand Camping & Stugby, Bredsandsvägen 22, 74948 Enköping [(0171) 80011; bredsand@nordiccamping.se; www.nordiccamping.se]** Fr E18 or rd 55 foll sp to site, well sp on Lake Mälaren. Med, mkd pitch, pt sl, pt shd; htd wc; chem disp; mv service pnt; baby facs; shwrs inc; EHU (10A) SEK50; lndry (inc dryer); supmkt 4km; rest, snacks; lake sw & beach adj; 50% statics; dogs; quiet; CKE. "Vg site." SEK 287   2015*

ESKILSTUNA *2G2* (10km N Rural) *59.45138, 16.43700* **Mälarbadens Camping (D15), Mälarbadsvägen, 64436 Torshälla [(016) 343187; fax 343559; campingmalarbaden@ gmail.com]** Fr Eskilstuna on E20 turn N to Torshälla & foll site sp N twds lake. Sm, hdg pitch, pt sl, pt shd; wc; chem disp; baby facs; EHU (13A) SEK35; lndry (inc dryer); shop; rest, snacks; cooking facs; playgrnd; lake sw & beach 1km; sports stadium nr; 60% statics; dogs; phone; Eng spkn; adv bkg; quiet; CKE/CCI. "Vg, clean, peaceful site; gd security; gd for children." 1 May-15 Sep. SEK 195   2011*

FALKENBERG *2E3* (10km SE Coastal) *56.8234, 12.60955* **Ugglarps Camping (N30), Strandkantsvägen 2, 31169 Ugglarp [(0346) 43889; info@ugglarp.nu; www.ugglarp.nu]** Exit E6 junc 48, foll sp Slöinge, then site sp. Lge, mkd pitch, terr, pt shd; htd wc; chem disp; mv service pnt; baby facs; some serviced pitches; shwrs inc; EHU (16A) inc; lndry (inc dryer); shop; rest, snacks; bar; BBQ; cooking facs; playgrnd; beach adj; games rm; wifi; 15% statics; dogs; phone; Eng spkn; adv bkg; quiet; red LS; CKE. "Gd san facs." ♦ 21 Apr-11 Sep. SEK 340   2011*

FALKENBERG *2E3* (3km S Coastal) *56.88315, 12.51495* **Skrea Camping (N12), Strandvägen, 31142 Falkenberg [(0346) 17107; fax 15840; info@skreacamping.se; www.skreacamping.se]** Turn off E20/E6 at junc 50 to Falkenberg S, foll sp Skrea Strand to site. Lge, mkd pitch, pt shd; htd wc; chem disp; mv service pnt; baby facs; shwrs SEK2; EHU (10-16A) SEK45; gas; lndry (inc dryer); shop & 500m; rest 200m; BBQ; playgrnd; paddling pool; sand beach 250m; windsurfing; golf 5km; wifi; entmnt; sat TV; 20% statics; dogs; phone; Quickstop o'night facs; barrier clsd 2300-0600; poss cr; adv bkg; ccard acc; CKE. "Vg site; gd san facs." ♦ 20 Apr-4 Sep. SEK 295   2009*

FALKENBERG *2E3* (10km NW Coastal) *56.95551, 12.36641* **Rosendals Camping Morup (N26, Rosendalsvägen 22, 31198 Glommen [(0346) 97300; fax 97302; info@rosendals camping.se; www.rosendalscamping.se]** Fr N on E6 exit junc 52 sp Morup/Glommen. Foll rd to x-rds by school (ent to Glommen vill). Turn R sp Morup & site on R in 3km at minor rds. Fr Falkenberg take rd sp Glommen at traff lts nr docks; foll 11km along coast rd to x-rds at ent to Glommen vill. Go across x-rds sp Morup & foll rd as above. Med, pt shd; wc; chem disp; baby facs; sauna; shwrs; EHU (6A) SEK30; lndry (inc dryer); shop; playgrnd; beach 5km; bike hire; 60% statics; dogs; Quickstop o'night facs; quiet; ccard acc; CKE. "Site yourself & owner calls." ♦ 1 Apr-11 Sep. SEK 190   2009*

⊞ **FALKOPING** *2F2* (1km W Rural) *58.17595, 13.52726* **Mössebergs Camping & Stugby (R7), Lidgatan 4, 52132 Falköping [(0515) 17349; mossebergscamping@telia.com]** Exit rd 184 at Falköping; foll Int'l Camping sps or sps to Mösseberg; site also sp fr rds 46 & 47 & in town. Site on plateau overlkg town. Med, mkd pitch, pt shd; wc; mv service pnt; baby facs; sauna; shwrs SEK5; EHU SEK40; lndry (inc dryer); cooking facs; shops 1km; playgrnd; pool 400m; lake sw 400m; wifi; some statics; dogs; phone; quiet; ccard acc; CKE. ♦ SEK 150   2009*

⊞ **FILIPSTAD** 2F1 (1km N Rural) 59.72035, 14.15899
Munkeberg Camping (S5), Skillervägen, 68233 Filipstad
[tel/fax (0590) 50100; alterschwede@telia.com;
www.munkeberg.com] Fr Karlstad take rd 63 to Filipstad.
In town foll sp for rd 246 twd Hagfors, site sp in town. Med,
pt sl, pt shd; htd wc; chem disp; shwrs inc; EHU (10A) SEK30;
lndry (inc dryer); shop 1km; snacks; playgrnd; lake sw; boating;
fishing; wifi; some statics; dogs; adv bkg; quiet; CKE/CCI.
"Beautiful lakeside site; gd for touring old mining district." ♦
SEK 160   2009*

FINNERODJA 2F2 (5km W Rural) 58.92808, 14.33558
Skagern Camping (T26), 69593 Finnerödja [tel/fax
(0506) 33040; camp.skagern@telia.com] S fr Örebro & Laxå
on E20, vill is sp. Med, mkd pitch, sl, pt shd; htd wc; chem disp;
mv service pnt; sauna; baby facs; shwrs; EHU (10A) inc; lndry
(inc dryer); shop; BBQ; playgrnd; sand beach/lake; boat hire;
fishing; games area; games rm; wifi; TV; 75% statics; dogs;
Quickstop o'night facs; Eng spkn; quiet; ccard acc; CKE/CCI.
"Vg site; levelling blocks req." 1 May-30 Sep. SEK 230   2011*

FJALLBACKA 2E2 (3.5km N Coastal) 58.63125, 11.27283
Långsjö Camping (O12), Långesjö Vikarna 22, 45071
Fjällbacka [(0525) 12116; info@langsjocamping.se;
www.langsjocamping.se] Exit E6 at junc 103 & foll rd 163
to Fjällbacka. Site sp in vill, narr ent. Sm, pt shd; wc; chem
disp; mv service pnt; baby facs; shwrs SEK5; EHU (10A) SEK45;
lndry (inc dryer); shop; snacks; BBQ; cooking facs; playgrnd;
beach adj; fishing; bike hire; games area; games rm; wifi;
entmnt; some statics; dogs; poss cr; Eng spkn; quiet; ccard
acc; CKE/CCI. "Gd site; beautiful vill." ♦ 1 May 13 Sep.
SEK 250   2009*

FROSON see Östersund 1B3

⊞ **GADDEDE** 1B2 (1km NE Rural) 64.50400, 14.14900
Gäddede Camping & Stugby, Sagavägen 9, 83090 Gäddede
[(0672) 10035; fax 10511; info@gaddedecamping.com;
www.gaddedecamping.se] On ent Gäddede cent on rd 342,
turn R & site in 500m on R, sp. Med, mkd pitch, pt shd; htd wc;
chem disp; shwrs SEK5; EHU (10A) SEK50; lndry; shop
500m; rest 100m; playgrnd; htd pool; paddling pool; canoe
hire; fishing; games area; games rm; TV; 40% statics; dogs;
poss cr; Eng spkn; adv bkg; quiet; ccard acc; CKE/CCI. "Gd
touring base 'Wilderness Way'." ♦ SEK 211   2014*

GAMLEBY 2G2 (1km SE Coastal) 57.88475, 16.41373
Hammarsbadets Camping (H2), Hammarsvägen 10,
59432 Gamleby [(0493) 10221; fax 12686; info@campa.se;
www.campa.se] On E22 Kalmar-Norrköping, foll sp to site
2km off main rd. Med, mkd pitch, terr, pt shd; wc; chem
disp; mv service pnt; baby facs; sauna; shwrs SEK5; EHU (10A)
SEK45; lndry (inc dryer); shop; rest, snacks; bar; playgrnd; pool;
sand beach adj; lake sw; boat & bike hire; tennis; wifi; some
statics; dogs; phone; Quickstop o'night facs; quiet; ccard acc;
CKE/CCI. "Clean, well-kept, relaxing site." 30 Apr-13 Sep.
SEK 190   2009*

GAVLE 2H1 (10km NE Coastal) 60.72946, 17.29145
Engesbergs Camping & Stugby, Solviksvägen 7, 80595
Gävle [(026) 99025; fax 99347; info@engesbergscamping.
se; www.engesbergscamping.se] Site sp along coast rd to
Bönan. Lge, pt sl, pt shd; wc; chem disp; mv service pnt; shwrs
inc; EHU (10A) SEK40 or metered; shop; snacks; playgrnd;
statics; dogs; poss cr; quiet; ccard acc; CKE. "Lovely site, mostly
in trees." ♦ 1 May-1 Oct. SEK 150   2009*

⊞ **GESUNDA** 1B4 (2km N Rural) 60.90100, 14.58500
Solleröns Camping (W60), Levsnäs, 79290 Sollerön
[(0250) 22230; fax 22268; info@sollerocamping.se;
www.sollerocamping.se] Fr Gesunda take bdge to Sollerön
Island in Lake Siljan. Site immed on R on reaching island; clearly
visible fr bdge. Lge, pt sl, pt shd; wc; chem disp; mv service pnt;
baby facs; sauna; shwrs inc; EHU (10A) SEK30; lndry (inc dryer);
shop; rest, snacks; bar; playgrnd; lake sw adj; canoe & boat
hire; tennis; wifi; poss cr; adv bkg; quiet; ccard acc; CKE/CCI.
"Beautiful outlook to S across lake; gd base for Dalarna folklore
area; gd site & facs; every 7th day is free." ♦ SEK 190   2011*

GLAVA 2E1 (10km S Rural) 59.4768, 12.68526 **Sölje**
Camping (S61), Tångeberg, 67020 Glava [(0570) 464141;
fax 464142; solje.camping@telia.com] Fr Arvika take rd 175
S. Just bef Stömne (approx 30km) turn R sp Sulvik. Foll sp at
Sölje x-rds. Sm, pt sl, unshd; wc; chem disp; mv service pnt;
baby facs; sauna; shwrs SEK5; EHU SEK40; lndry (inc dryer);
kiosk; cooking facs; playgrnd; lake sw adj, fishing; boat & bike
hire; games area; wifi; entmnt; some statics; dogs; CKE. "Idyllic
lakeside location; peaceful - a real find." ♦ 1 Jun-31 Aug.
SEK 140   2011*

GLOMMEN see Falkenberg 2E3

⊞ **GOTEBORG** 2E3 (4km E Rural) 57.7053, 12.0286
Lisebergsbyn Kärralund (O39), Olbersgatan 1,
41655 Göteborg [(031) 840200; fax 840500; lisebergsbyn@
liseberg.se; www.liseberg.se] Exit E6/E20 junc 71 onto
rd 40 E & foll sp Lisebergsbyn, site well sp. Lge, pt sl, terr, pt
shd; wc; chem disp; mv service pnt; fam bthrm; baby facs;
shwrs inc; EHU (10A) inc; gas; lndry (inc dryer); shop (open
only once a week LS); supmkt nrby; playgrnd; wifi; TV; phone;
tram 400m; poss cr/noisy high ssn; Eng spkn; adv bkg rec; red
LS; ccard acc; red LS & Sun-Fri; CKE. "Boat trips arranged; vg,
well-run site; LS arr early to obtain barrier key; poss travellers
on site; cycle path to Liseberg amusement park & town cent."
SEK 450   2013*

GOTEBORG 2E3 (15km NW Coastal) 57.7434, 11.7566
Göteborgs Camping Lilleby (O40), Lillebyvägen 100,
42353 Torslanda [(031) 562240; fax 562246; lillebycamping@
gmail.com; www.goteborgscamping.se] Fr S on E6 pass thro
Tingstads Tunnel in Göteborg & immed turn W onto R155 &
foll sp Torslanda. Site sp fr N on E6; immed S of Kungälv, exit
W at sps for Säve; foll sp to Torslanda; site sp. Med, mkd pitch,
pt shd; wc; chem disp; mv service pnt; shwrs inc; EHU SEK50;
gas; lndry (inc dryer); shop; cooking facs; playgrnd; sw at rocky
beach 250m with waterchute; bus adj; poss cr; Eng spkn; poss
noisy in ssn; ccard acc; CKE. "V attractive area; meadowland;
clean & pleasant with gd bus nr ent; avoid arr or dep rush hr
- traffic fr Volvo factory; facs stretched in ssn; friendly, helpful
staff." 1 Jun-28 Aug. SEK 200   2010*

GOTHENBURG see Göteborg 2E3

GRANNA *2F2* (9km S Rural) *57.92446, 14.32341*
Vätterledens Camping (F4), Vättersmålen 7, 56393 Gränna
[(036) 52167; vatterledenscamping@glocalnet.net;
www.vatterledenscamping.se] Site sp off E4 bet Jönköping
& Gränna, behind a motel. Sm, pt sl, unshd; htd wc; chem disp;
mv service pnt; baby facs; shwrs inc; EHU (10A) SEK40; lndry
(inc dryer); rest, snacks, bar 200m; wifi; TV rm; some statics;
Eng spkn; quiet; CKE. "Ltd facs but clean; helpful owner;
pitches waterlogged after rain, but tractor avail; gd NH."
1 May-14 Aug. SEK 150   2011*

GRANNA *2F2* (500m NW Rural) *58.02783, 14.45821*
Grännastrandens Familjecamping (F3), Hamnen, 56300
Gränna [(0390) 10706; fax 41260; info@grannacamping.se;
www.grannacamping.se] In cent of Gränna down rd twd
Lake Vättern, sp Visingsö Island. Lge, unshd; wc; chem disp;
mv service pnt; baby facs; shwrs; EHU (10A) metered + conn
fee; lndry (inc dryer); shop; rest adj; playgrnd; lake sw & beach;
wifi; sat TV; some cottages; dogs; poss v cr; CKE. "Ballooning
cent of Sweden; Visingsö Island, Brahehus ruined castle, glass-
blowing 3km; vg site; gd location; gd san facs, excel camp
kitchen." ♦ 30 Apr-3 Oct. SEK 260   2014*

⊞ **GREBBESTAD** *2E2* (1km S Coastal) *58.6832, 586832*
Grebbestads Familjecamping (O10), Rörvik, 45795
Grebbestad, Sverige [(0525) 61211; fax 14319; info@
grebbestadfjorden.com; www.grebbestadfjorden.com]
Exit E6 at Tanumshede sp Grebbestad; foll rd thro vill, past
harbour; site on R approx 500m after harbour. Lge, mkd
pitch, pt sl, unshd; wc; chem disp; mv service pnt; baby facs;
sauna; shwrs inc; EHU (10A) SEK50; lndry (inc dryer); sm shop
& 500m; snacks; cooking facs; htd pool 1km; sand beach
150m; games area; wifi; mainly statics; phone; dogs; poss cr;
Eng spkn; adv bkg; quiet; ccard acc; CKE. "Well-maintained
site 500m fr busy fishing/yachting harbour; meadowland;
excel mv services; helpful staff; vg facs, lge cr noisy site." ♦
SEK 350   2013*

GRYT *2G2* (2km E Coastal) *58.17378, 16.85228* **KustCamp**
Ekön (E27), Ekövägen, 61042 Gryt [(0123) 40283;
fax 12686; ekon@campa.se; www.campa.se]
Exit E2 sp Valdemarsvik, then rd 212 twd Gryt. Approx 2 km
after Gryt turn R into Ekövägen. Foll site sp. Med, unshd; htd
wc; chem disp; mv service pnt; baby facs; shwrs inc; EHU (10A)
SEK45; lndry (inc dryer); shop; rest, snacks; BBQ; cooking
facs; playgrnd; beach adj; canoe & boat hire; games area;
internet; 30% statics; dogs; poss cr; Eng spkn; quiet; ccard
acc; CKE/CCI. "Gd walking & cycling; gd." ♦ 1 Apr-13 Sep.
SEK 160   2009*

⊞ **HALMSTAD** *2E3* (10km S Coastal) *56.59033, 12.94430*
Gullbrannagården Camping (N27), 31031 Eldsberga
[tel/fax (035) 42180; mail@gullbrannagarden.se;
www.gullbrannagarden.se] Fr S site sp on E6. Lge, pt sl, pt
shd; wc; chem disp; mv service pnt; baby facs; shwrs inc; EHU
SEK45; lndry; shop; snacks; cooking facs; playgrnd; sand beach
500m; games rm; wifi; entmnt; 60% statics; dogs; poss cr;
Eng spkn; adv bkg; quiet. "Christian-run site; church & bible
classes; alcohol discouraged; OK for those of like mind." ♦
SEK 290   2009*

HAMBURGSUND *2E2* (1KM S Coastal) *58.54075, 11.28240*
Rorviks Camping, Rorviksangen 15 45747 Hamburgsund
[05 25 33 573; info@rorvikscamping.se; www.rorviks
camping.se] Take exit 103 on the E6 (bet Tatum V-Munkedal).
Foll 163 W to Kville. Turn L to Hamburgsund, cont S 1km.
Campsite on R. Lge, mkd pitch, hdstg, pt shd; wc; chem disp; mv
service pnt; fam bthrm; shwr (5kr); EHU (10A) inc; lndry (inc dryer);
shop; BBQ; cooking facs; games area; entmnt; 10% statics; dogs;
bus 1km; twin axles; Eng spkn; adv bkg; CCI. "Quiet, low key site
in a great area; vg." 1 May-31 Aug. SEK 350   2014*

⊞ **HAMMARSTRAND** *1C3* (1km E Rural) *63.12030, 16.34330*
Hammarstrands Camping (Z6), Koppelhällsvägen 18, 84070
Hammarstrand [(0696) 10302; info@goragunda.com;
www.goragunda.com] Exit rd 87 N twd Hammarstrand onto
rd 323. Cross rv bdge & take 1st R & 1st R again; site along gravel
track in 1km. Sm, pt shd; wc; chem disp; shwrs; EHU (10A) SEK30;
lndry (inc dryer); shop 1km; rest, snacks; bar; cooking facs; playgrnd;
htd pool; sand beach 200m; games area; wifi; TV; some statics;
dogs free; bus 1km; Eng spkn; adv bkg; quiet; ccard acc; red long
stay; CKE/CCI. "Pleasant Dutch owners; gd site with basic, clean
facs; views across rv; ideal NH." ♦ ltd. SEK 150   2011*

⊞ **HAPARANDA** *1D2* (15km N Rural) *65.9620, 24.0378*
Kukkolaforsen Camping (BD27), Kukkolaforsen 184,
95391 Haparanda [(0922) 31000; fax 31030; info@
kukkolaforsen.se; www.kukkolaforsen.se] On rd 99 on
banks of Rv Tornionjoki. Med, pt shd; htd wc; chem disp;
baby facs; sauna; shwrs inc; EHU (10A) SEK40; lndry; shop;
rest, snacks; bar; playgrnd; fishing; bike hire; TV; statics;
phone; adv bkg; ccard acc; CKE. "Friendly staff; rv rapids."
SEK 210   2010*

"We must tell The Club about
that great site we found"

Get your site reports in by mid-August
and we'll do our best to get your updates
into the next edition.

HARNOSAND *1C3* (2.5km NE Coastal) *62.64451, 17.97123*
Sälstens Camping (Y21), Sälsten 22, 87133 Härnösand
[tel/fax (0611) 18150; salsten.camping@telia.com]
On Gulf of Bothnia, E of town & on S side of inlet; exit off E4;
foll sp for Härnösand town cent, then intn'l camping sp; then
site. Sm, mkd pitch, terr, pt shd; htd wc; chem disp; shwrs inc;
EHU (10A) SEK30; lndry (inc dryer); shop; playgrnd; beach; wifi;
TV; Eng spkn; quiet; CKE. "Folk museum in town; excel site."
♦ ltd. 15 May-31 Aug. SEK 220   2014*

⊞ **HARNOSAND** *1C3* (8km SW Rural) *62.58648, 17.79083*
Antjärns Camping & Stugby (Y28), Antjärn 113, 87191
Härnösand [(0611) 74150; contact@antjarnscamping.com;
www.antjarnscamping.com] Fr E4 approx 30km N of
Sundsvall, turn R at Antjärns & site sp, site on R in 300m.
Sm, pt sl, unshd; htd wc; chem disp; sauna; shwrs inc; EHU
(10A) SEK25; lake sw; fishing; wifi; sat TV; dogs; adv bkg;
some rd noise; ccard acc; CKE/CCI. "Beautiful lakeside
setting; lovely town; pleasant owners; immac, modern facs."
SEK 160   2009*

HEBERG see Falkenberg 2E3

⊞ **HEDE** 1B3 (10km E Rural) 62.40899, 13.67394
Sonfjällscampen, Hedeviken 753, 84093 Hede
[tel/fax (0684) 12130; info@sonfjallscampen.se;
www.sonfjallscampen.se] Sp in vill of Hedivikens S of rd
84 on lakeside. Sm, pt shd; htd wc; chem disp; shwrs; EHU
(10A) SEK30; lndry; shops adj; sand beach; fishing; boat hire;
60% statics; adv bkg; quiet; red facs LS; ccard acc; CKE.
"Pleasant stay; helpful owner; gd facs; conv Sånfjallet National
Park." SEK 130   2009*

HEDESUNDA 2G1 (5km SE Rural) 60.35000, 17.02100
Sandsnäs Camping, Övägen 68, 81040 Hedesunda
[tel/fax (0291) 44123; info@hedesundacamping.se;
www.hedesundacamping.se] Exit rd 67 L at sp Hedesunda.
Foll camp sp thro Hedesunda; past church, cont about 4km to
Hedesunda Island. Sm, pt shd; htd wc; chem disp; shwrs inc;
EHU (6A) SEK30; gas; lndry (inc dryer); shop 3km; rest, snacks;
cooking facs; playgrnd; sand beach & lake sw adj; boat hire;
fishing; TV; poss cr at w/end; Eng spkn; quiet; red 16+ days;
CKE. "Peaceful, lakeside site; organised activities in ssn; helpful
staff." ♦ 15 Apr-15 Nov. SEK 175   2010*

HEDEVIKEN see Hede 1B3

⊞ **HELSINGBORG** 2E4 (5km S Coastal) 56.0034, 12.7300
Campingplatsen Råå Vallar (M3), Kustgatan, 25270 Råå
[(042) 182600; fax 107681; raavallar@nordiccamping.se;
www.nordiccamping.se] Exit E6 into Helsingborg onto rd
111 to Råå, foll sp to camp. Lge, pt shd; htd wc; baby facs;
sauna; shwrs inc; EHU (10A) SEK50; gas; lndry (inc dryer);
shop; rest, snacks; bar; playgrnd; pool; paddling pool; sand
beach; fishing; sports cent 2km; golf 5km; wifi; some statics;
phone; Quickstop o'night facs; poss cr; ccard acc; CKE/CCI.
"Excel, secure site with gd facs; friendly staff; excursions to
Copenhagen via Helsingør or Landskrona; town bus excursions
to King's Summer Palace daily; boat trips to glass works at
Hyllinge." ♦ SEK 368   2013*

HJO 2F2 (600m N Rural) 58.30986, 14.30311 **Hjo Camping**
(R11), Karlsborgsvägen, 54432 Hjo [(0503) 31052;
fax 13264; campinghjo@hotmail.com; www.hjocamping.se]
Sp fr town cent on lakeside. Med, mkd pitch; wc; chem
disp; mv service pnt; baby facs; shwrs inc; EHU (10A) SEK40;
lndry (inc dryer); shop; bar; cooking facs; playgrnd; htd pool;
lake adj; fishing; games area; wifi; some statics; Eng spkn;
ccard acc; CKE. "Delightful wooden town; gd." 1 Apr-1 Oct.
SEK 180   2010*

HOGANAS 2E4 (8km N Rural) 56.27061, 12.52981 **FirstCamp**
Mölle (M1), Kullabergsvägen, 26042 Mölle [(042) 347384;
fax 347729; molle@firstcamp.se; www.firstcamp.se]
Site is S of Mölle at junc of rds 11 & 111, at foot of Kullaberg.
Lge, pt sl, unshd; htd wc; chem disp; mv service pnt; sauna;
shwrs inc; EHU (10A) inc; lndry (inc dryer); shop; rest, snacks;
bar; cooking facs; playgrnd; beach 1.5km; fishing; games
area; walking; golf; wifi; entmnt; 10% statics; dogs; Quickstop
o'night facs; Eng spkn; quiet; ccard acc. "Steep slope to san
facs; Krapperups Castle & park sh walk fr site; excel outdoor
activities." ♦ 1 Feb-14 Nov. SEK 275   2010*

HOGANAS 2E4 (2km S Coastal) 56.18194, 12.55805 **Camping**
Lerbergets (M2), Lerbergsvägen 108, 26352 Lerberget
[(042) 331400; camping@lerberget.se; www.lerbergets
camping.se] Exit E20 at junc 33 W to Höganäs, then turn S
along coast rd. Site in 2km bef Viken. Med, shd; wc; chem
disp; mv service pnt; baby facs; shwrs inc; EHU SEK45; gas;
lndry (inc dryer); shop, rest 1km; playgrnd; sand beach adj;
bike hire; internet; 80% statics; bus adj; Eng spkn; quiet; ccard
acc; CKE/CCI. "Lovely coast; access to site by phoning for code
to open box with gate-opener (same code for shwr); gd." ♦
1 Apr-25 Sep. SEK 200   2009*

HOVA 2F2 (8.7km NE Coastal) 58.90998, 14.28995
Otterbergets Bad & Camping, 54891 Hova [050633 127
or 0738064 935; info@otterbergetscamping.com;
www.otterbergetscamping.com] Fr Laxa take E20 rd; site
sp approx 4km fr Hova; drive 2 km thro woods to site. Med,
mkd pitch, pt shd; wc; chem disp; baby facs; shwrs (metered);
EHU (10A) SEK 40; lndry; snacks; BBQ; playgrnd; sauna; beach
adj; 10% statics; poss cr; Eng spkn; adv bking; quiet; red LS.
"Attractive site with private access to lake; events held such
as fishing competition & trade fairs (when site may be busy); v
helpful Dutch owners." ♦ 15 Apr-18 Nov. SEK 240   2015*

⊞ **HOVMANTORP** 2G3 (1.6km W Urban) 56.7839, 15.13081
Gökaskratts Campingplats (G11), Bruksallén, 36051
Hovmantorp [(0478) 40807; fax 40822; jonnan.s@live.se]
On Lake Rottnen S of town. Med, mkd pitch, pt shd; htd wc;
chem disp; baby facs; shwrs; EHU (10A) inc; lndry (inc dryer);
shop; rest; playgrnd; lake sw adj; fishing; boating; bike hire;
wifi; TV; 10% statics; phone; Quickstop o'night facs; poss cr;
quiet; ccard acc; CKE. "Conv rlwy stn for Gothenborg/Kalmar."
♦ SEK 200   2011*

HULT 2G3 (1km N Rural) 57.65583, 15.12435 **Movänta**
Camping (F14), Badvägen 4, 57592 Hult [(0381) 30028;
fax 30166; info@movantacamping.se; www.movanta
camping.se] Fr Eksjö rd 33 E to Hult, turn L into vill, foll sp to
lakeside. Med, mkd pitch, some hdstg, pt shd; htd wc; chem
disp; mv service pnt; baby facs; shwrs; EHU (10A) SEK40; lndry
(inc dryer); shop; snacks; bar; playgrnd; lake sw adj; fishing;
sailing; wifi; TV; some statics; dogs; phone; Quickstop o'night
facs; Eng spkn; quiet; ccard acc; CKE. "Conv Eksjö & Skurugata
canyon." ♦ 29 Apr-25 Sep. SEK 185   2011*

⊞ **JARNA** 2H2 (2km E Coastal) 59.09801, 17.64825 **Farstanäs**
Camping, Farsta 1, 15391 Järna [(08551) 50215; fax 50650;
info@farstanashf.se; www.vatterledenscamping.se]
Exit E4 junc 141 for Järna, E fr m'way site sp past filling
stn about 6km fr exit. Lge, pt sl, pt shd; wc; mv service
pnt; baby facs; shwrs; EHU (10A) SEK40; lndry; shop; rest,
snacks; bar; playgrnd; pool; sand beach & sw; fishing; boat
hire; 25% statics; dogs; phone; poss cr; quiet; CKE. "Conv
Södertälje & Stockholm on m'way; superb wooded location."
♦ SEK 250   2011*

JOKKMOKK *1C2* (3km SE Rural) *66.59453, 19.89145*
Jokkmokk Camping Center (BD4), Notudden, 96222
Jokkmokk [(0971) 12370; fax 12476; campingcenter@
jokkmokk.com; www.jokkmokkcampingcenter.com]
Sp fr rd 45. In Jokkmokk take rd 97 E, site in 3km on N side
of rd situated bet rv & rd. Lge, mkd pitch, pt shd; htd wc;
chem disp; mv service pnt; sauna; shwrs inc; EHU (10A) SEK40
(poss rev pol); lndry (inc dryer); sm shop & 3km; rest, snacks;
bar; playgrnd; 3 htd pools high ssn; waterslide; lake sw adj;
fishing; bike hire; internet; some statics; dogs; Eng spkn; adv
bkg; ccard acc; quiet; CKE. "Friendly, clean, well-maintained
site 5km inside Arctic Circle; gd area for Sami culture; excel
playgrnd; lakeside setting, gd pool." ♦ 20 May-31 Aug.
SEK 195   2011*

⊞ **JONKOPING** *2F3* (2.5km E Urban) *57.7876, 14.2195*
Swecamp Villa Björkhagen (F6), Friggagatan 31, 55454
Jönköping [(036) 122863; fax 126687; info@villa
bjorkhagen.se; www.villabjorkhagen.se]
Fr N exit E4 junc 99 or fr S exit E4 junc 98a & foll sp Rosenlund/
Elmia & site sp nr exhibition cent. Site on Lake Vättern. Lge,
mkd pitch, pt sl, pt shd; htd wc; chem disp; mv service pnt;
baby facs; sauna; shwrs inc; EHU (10A) SEK35; lndry (inc dryer)
shop; rest; bar; playgrnd; htd, covrd pool complex, waterslide
300m; lake sw 500m; fishing; bike hire; wifi; entmnt; sat TV;
50% statics; dogs; phone; Quickstop o'night facs; poss v cr;
quiet; ccard acc; CKE. "Gd rest; prone to flooding after heavy
rain; some facs run down & site untidy (2010); site charges
increase considerably during exhibitions & site v full; pitches
well mkd; easy walk into town along sea front." ♦ SEK 265
(CChq acc)   2014*

JONKOPING *2F3* (15km S Rural) *57.66245, 14.18407*
Lovsjöbadens Camping (F7), Hyltena, 55592
Jönköping [(036) 182010; info@lovsjocamping.se;
www.lovsjocamping.se] Exit E4 at Hyltena, site sp on lakeside.
Sm, mkd pitch, terr, pt sl; wc; chem disp; baby facs; shwrs inc;
EHU (10-16A) SEK30; lndry (inc dryer); snacks; BBQ; cooking facs;
lake sw; boat & bike hire; games rm; wifi; TV; some statics; dogs;
Eng spkn; adv bkg; quiet; ccard acc; CKE. "V friendly owners; vg
site by sm lake; busy in high ssn; sm sw beach; rowing boats for
hire." ♦ 15 May-15 Sep. SEK 260   2015*

KALMAR *2G3* (2km S Coastal) *56.64975, 16.32705*
Stensö Camping (H12), Stensövägen, 39247 Kalmar
[(0480) 88803; fax 420476; info@stensocamping.se;
www.stensocamping.se] Fr E22 foll sp Sjukhus (hosp) then
camping sp - this avoids town cent. Lge, some mkd pitch, pt sl,
shd; wc; chem disp; mv service pnt; baby facs; shwrs inc; EHU
(10A) SEK40 (check pol); lndry (inc dryer); shop; rest, snacks;
bar; cooking facs; playgrnd; pool 1km; sand beach adj; fishing;
boating; cycling; wifi; some statics; phone; Quickstop o'night
facs; Eng spkn; ccard acc; CKE. "Conv Öland Island (over bdge);
glass factories in vicinity; walking dist to town; helpful, friendly
staff; new clean san facs (2014); excel."
♦ 27 Mar-30 Sep. SEK 264   2014*

KAPPELLSKAR *2H1* (500m W Rural) *59.72046, 19.05045*
Camping Kapellskär (B9), Riddersholm 985, 76015 Gräddö
[(0176) 44233] Fr Norrtälje take E18 E sp Kapellskär. At ferry
sp turn R, site in 1km, sp. Last 700m on unmade rd. Med,
mkd pitch, some hdstg, terr, pt shd; htd wc; chem disp; mv
service pnt; baby facs; shwrs inc; EHU (10A) SEK40; lndry
(inc dryer); shop; rest 1.5km; snacks; bar; playgrnd; bike hire;
games area; 60% statics; dogs; Eng spkn; adv bkg; quiet; ccard
acc; CKE. "Conv for ferry terminal; fair site." 1 May-29 Sep.
SEK 272   2015*

KARESUANDO *1D1* (2km SE Rural) *68.43396, 22.51577*
Karesuando Camping, Laestadiusvagen 185, 98016
Karesuando [(0981) 20139; fax 20381; karesuando.
camping@hotmail.com; www.karesuando.se/foretag/
camping/camping.htm] Travelling N on E45, in town cont
past bdge to Finland onto rd 99 for approx 2km; site on L. App
fr Finland, turn L after x-ing bdge; cont on 99 for 2km. Sm,
unshd; wc; chem disp; mv service point; sauna; shwrs; EHU
(10A) inc; lndry; cafe; snacks; BBQ; playgrnd; rv adj; games
area; 50% statics; dogs; twin axles; poss cr; Eng spkn; adv
bkg; quiet; CKE/CCI. "Model Sami vill on site; cash point in PO;
poss mosquito prob; canoe hire avail; gd view of midnight sun
on rv; unmkd pitches, fills up quickly." ♦ ltd. 15 May-15 Sep.
SEK 200   2014*

KARLSBORG *2F2* (1km N Rural) *58.5453, 14.50075*
Karlsborgs Camping (R12), Norra Vägen 3, 54633 Karlsborg
[(0505) 44916; fax 44912; info@karlsborgscamping.se;
www.karlsborgscamping.se] Heading N on rd 49 300m N of
Göta canal on L of rd on Lake Bottensjö. Med, shd; wc; chem
disp; mv service pnt; baby facs; shwrs SEK5; EHU (10A) SEK40;
gas; lndry (inc dryer); shops adj; rest, snacks; bar; cooking
facs; playgrnd; sand beach on lake; fishing; boating; wifi; TV;
dogs; phone; poss noisy at w/end; ccard acc; CKE. "Gd touring
base in beautiful location; gd fishing." ♦ 24 Apr-30 Sep.
SEK 180   2010*

KARLSHAMN *2F4* (3km SE Coastal) *56.15953, 14.89085*
Kolleviks Camping (K7), Kolleviksvägen, 37430 Karlshamn
[(0454) 19280; fax 16280; kollevik@karlshamn.se;
www.karlshamn.se] Fr E22 dir Karlshamn & Hamnar
(harbour), then site well sp. Med, mkd pitch, pt sl, pt shd; htd
wc; chem disp; mv service pnt; baby facs; shwrs SEK5; EHU
(10A) SEK45; lndry (inc dryer); shop; rest, snacks; playgrnd;
pool 1km; sand beach adj; canoeing; 25% statics; Quickstop
o'night facs; Eng spkn; adv bkg; quiet; ccard acc; red long
stay/LS; CKE. "Helpful owner; attractive location inc harbour;
gd base for area; ltd facs LS; well-kept site; facs tired, poss
stretched when busy." ♦ 26 Apr-14 Sep. SEK 155   2012*

KARLSKRONA *2G4* (4km N Coastal) *56.20158, 15.60546*
Skönstaviks Camping (K12), Ronnebyvägen, 37191
Karlskrona [(0455) 23700; fax 23792; info@skonstavik
camping.se; www.skonstavikcamping.se]
Rd 15/E22 fr Malmö, camp sp on app to Karskrona. Lge, pt sl,
pt shd; htd wc; chem disp; mv service pnt; baby facs; shwrs;
EHU (10A) SEK45; lndry; rest, snacks; bar; shop; playgrnd;
sm sand beach; bike hire; fishing; boating; wifi; entmnt; TV;
10% statics; dogs; Quickstop o'night facs; quiet; ccard acc;
CKE. ♦ 1 Apr-31 Aug. SEK 225   2011*

KARLSKRONA *2G4* (2km NE Coastal) *56.1729, 15.5675*
Dragsö Camping (K10), Dragsövägen 14, 37137
Karlskrona [(0455) 15354; fax 15277; info@dragso.se;
www.dragso camping.se] Foll app to town cent, taking
m'way. At end of m'way foll sp to Dragsö. Site sp - on its own
island. Lge, mkd pitch, pt shd; htd wc; mv service pnt; baby
facs; sauna; shwrs; EHU (10A) inc; lndry (inc dryer); kiosk;
supmkt, rest 3km; snacks; bar; playgrnd; beach adj; fishing;
boating; bike hire; wifi; entmnt; TV rm; some statics; dogs;
Quickstop o'night facs; poss v cr; CKE. "Sea bathing; rocky
cliffs; scenic beauty; gd." ◆ 1Apr-10 Oct. SEK 323   2013*

⊞ **KARLSTAD** *2F1* (6km W Rural) *59.37428, 13.38958* **First**
Camp Karlstad-Skutberget (S10), Skutbergsvägen, 65346
Karlstad [(054) 535120; fax 535121; karlstad@firstcamp.se;
www.firstcamp.se] Sp 1km S of E18, on Lake Vänern, also
sp on rd 61 fr N. Lge, unshd; htd wc; mv service pnt; baby
facs; sauna; shwrs; EHU (10A); lndry (inc dryer); shop; rest
adj; snacks; bar; BBQ; cooking facs; playgrnd; sand & shgl
beach 500m; fishing; sailing; bike hire; fitness rm; sport facs
adj; wifi; TV; dogs; Quickstop o'night facs; quiet; CKE. ◆
SEK 317   2011*

⊞ **KARLSTAD** *2F1* (9km W Rural) *59.36233, 13.35891*
Swecamp Bomstad-Badens (S9), Bomstadsvägen 640,
65346 Karlstad [(054) 535068; fax 535375; info@bomstad-
baden.se; www.bomstadbaden.se] 2km S of E18 on Lake
Vänern. Foll sp thro woods. Lge, pt sl, shd; wc; chem disp; mv
service pnt; baby facs; shwrs SEK10; EHU (10A) SEK50; lndry
(inc dryer); shop; supmkt 4km; snacks; bar; BBQ; playgrnd;
pool; sand beach; lake sw; fishing; canoeing; bike hire; wifi;
entmnt; statics; phone; adv bkg; CKE. "Excel base; beautiful
site in trees; gd walks on mkd trails." ◆ SEK 290   2013*

⊞ **KATRINEHOLM** *2G2* (2km S Rural) *58.9696, 16.21035*
Djulöbadets Camping (D6), Djulögatan 51, 64192
Katrineholm [tel/fax (0150) 57242; djulocamping@
hotmail.com; www.djulocamping.se] At Norrköping on E4
cont twd Stockholm for about 3km, turn L onto rd 55 N twd
Katrineholm. Camping site sp in 2km. Lge, hdstg, pt sl; wc;
mv service pnt; baby facs; shwrs SEK1; EHU (10A) SEK35; gas;
lndry (inc dryer); shop 2km; rest 2km; snacks; playgrnd; lake
sw; boating; fishing; games area; bike hire; wifi; poss cr; adv
bkg; quiet; ccard acc; CKE. "On lakeside in lge park; well-run,
friendly site." ◆ SEK 140   2009*

⊞ **KIL** *2F1* (6km N Rural) *59.54603, 13.34145* **Frykenbadens**
Camping (S17), Stubberud, 66591 Kil [(0554) 40940;
fax 41010; info@frykenbaden.se; www.frykenbaden.se]
Fr Karlstad take rd 61 to Kil, site clearly sp on lakeside. Lge,
pt sl, pt shd; wc; chem disp; mv service pnt; baby facs; sauna
SEK5; shwrs; EHU (10A) SEK40; lndry (inc dryer); shop; snacks;
bar; playgrnd; lake sw; fishing; boat-launching; bike hire; wifi;
TV; phone; Quickstop o'night facs; quiet; adv bkg; CKE. "Very
clean, spacious waterfront site." ◆ SEK 237   2013*

KINNA *2E3* (3km SE Rural) *57.47400, 12.70415* **DreamCamp**
Hanatorp (P14), Öresjövägen 26, 51131 Örby [(0320) 48312;
fax 49314; info@dreamcamp.se; www.dreamcamp.se]
3.2km E of junc rds 41 & 156, site sp 650m along rd to
Öxabäck. Lge, mkd pitch, hdstg, pt shd; wc; chem disp; mv
service pnt; baby facs; shwrs SEK5; EHU (10A) SEK40; gas;
lndry (inc dryer); shop; rest, snacks; bar; playgrnd; htd, covrd
pool 8km; lake sw adj; boat & bike hire; golf 8km; wifi; TV;
20% statics; dogs; phone; Quickstop o'night facs; adv bkg;
quiet; red long stay; ccard acc; CKE/CCI. "Variable pitch price;
excel." ◆ 21 Apr-18 Sep. SEK 220   2010*

⊞ **KIRUNA** *1C1* (500m N Urban) *67.8604, 20.2405* **Ripan**
Hotel & Camping, Campingvägen 5, 98135 Kiruna
[(0980) 63000; fax 63040; info@ripan.se; www.ripan.se]
Site sp fr town cent. Med, unshd, mkd pitch, hdstg; htd wc;
chem disp; sauna; shwrs SEK20; EHU (10A) inc; lndry; shop
500m; rest; bar; playgrnd; htd pool; cab TV; poss cr; quiet;
Eng spkn; ccard acc. "No privacy in shwrs; easy walk to town;
public footpath thro site (top end) - poss v noisy & disruptive;
trips to Kirunavaara Deep Mine fr tourist info office." ◆
SEK 275   2014*

KLIPPAN *2F4* (1.5km E Urban) *56.13461, 13.16213*
Elfdalens Camping (L25), Vedbyvägen 69, 26437 Klippan
[tel/fax (0345) 14678; elfdalens.camping@telia.com]
E fr Helsingborg on rd 21. Take E exit to Klippan & foll local
sps. Med, pt shd; wc; chem disp; sauna; shwrs inc; EHU (6A)
SEK30; lndry (inc dryer); shop 300m; snacks; cooking facs;
playgrnd; wifi; 5% statics; phone; bus 3km; Eng spkn; quiet;
CKE. "Vg, friendly site; gd touring base; gd walking." ◆
1 Apr-15 Sep. SEK 130   2009*

KOLMARDEN *2G2* (2km SE Coastal) *58.6597, 586597* **First**
Camp Kolmården (E3), 61834 Kolmården [(011) 398250;
fax 397081; kolmarden@firstcamp.se; www.firstcamp.se]
Fr E4 NE fr Norrköping take 1st Kolmården exit sp Kolmården
Djur & Naturpark. Site on sea 2km bef Naturpark. Lge, pt terr,
pt shd; htd wc; chem disp; mv service pnt; baby facs; sauna;
shwrs SEK5; EHU (10A); lndry (inc dryer); shop; kiosk; rest,
snacks; bar; cooking facs; playgrnd; beach adj; waterslide; boat
& bike hire; entmnt; TV rm; wifi; 10% statics; dogs; phone;
ccard acc; CKE. "Gd site; nr to Kilmarden zoo & aquarium; well
mkd pitches." ◆ 17 Apr-30 Sep. SEK 383   2014*

KUNGALV *2E2* (1km SE Rural) *57.86211, 11.99613*
Kungälvs Vandrarhem & Camping (O37), Färjevägen 2,
44231 Kungälv [(0303) 18900; fax (303) 19295; info@
kungalvsvandrarhem.se; www.kungalvsvandrarhem.se]
Exit E6 junc 85 or 86 & foll sp Kungälv cent, then sp 'Bohus
Fästning'. Site sp. Sm, mkd pitch, some hdstg, shd; htd wc;
chem disp; mv service pnt; baby facs; shwrs inc; EHU (12A)
SEK40; lndry (inc dryer); shop; rest, snacks; bar; gas BBQ;
playgrnd; wifi; some statics; dogs; bus adj; Eng spkn; quiet;
ccard acc; red long stay; CC1. "Site adj Bonus Fästning (fort)
& Kungälv Church (17th C) on rv bank; find pitch & check in
at recep 0800-1000 & 1700-1900; door code fr recep for san
facs; gd NH." ◆ ltd. 15 Apr-30 Sep. SEK 250   2014*

KUNGSBACKA 2E3 (5km SE Rural) 57.42492, 12.15860
Silverlyckans Camping, Varbergsvägen 875, 43433 Fjärås
[(0300) 541349; www.silverlyckan.eu] Exit E6/E20 junc 58
dir Åsa. Site in 400m on L. Med, pt sl, unshd; htd wc; chem
disp; mv service pnt (refill only); shwrs SEK5; EHU (10A) SEK30;
lndry; shop, rest, snacks 3km; cooking facs; playgrnd; htd pool
3km; sand beach 4km; 10% statics; dogs; bus adj; Eng spkn;
adv bkg; quiet. "Vg site; rec visit Tjolöholms Slott (castle)."
1 May-15 Sep. SEK 180   2014*

KUNGSHAMN 2E2 (10km NE Rural/Coastal) 58.37825,
11.33095 **Örns Camping (O67), Håle 2, 45691 Kungshamn**
[(0523) 34335; fax 34409; kjell.andersson@ornscamping.com;
www.ornscamping.com] Exit E6 junc 101 onto rd 162/171
twd Kungshamn; 7km after Nordens Ark turn L sp Kungshamn
S. In 3km turn L twd Bohus Malmön, site on R in approx 2km
(thru vill). Lge, mkd pitch, pt shd; wc; chem disp; mv service
pnt; baby facs; shwrs SEK5; EHU SEK50; lndry (inc dryer); shop;
playgrnd; beach adj; wifi; sat TV; statics; dogs; Eng spkn; quiet;
ccard acc. "Beautiful area; gd coastal walks, fishing, boating."
♦ ltd. 1 May-30 Sep. SEK 220   2011*

KVIDINGE see Klippan 2F4

LACKEBY 2G3 (6km SE Coastal) 56.75718, 16.37700
Kalmar Camping (H73), Rafshagen 430, 38031 Läckeby
[(0480) 60464; fax 60424; info@kalmarcamping.se;
www.kalmarcamping.se] On E22 10km N of Kalmar, turn
R approx 500m N of junc with rd 125 to Läckeby & foll sp for
Rafshagen & site. Med, mkd pitch, pt sl, pt shd; htd wc; chem
disp; mv service pnt; baby facs; shwrs inc; EHU (10A) SEK40;
lndry (inc dryer); rest, snacks; bar; BBQ; cooking facs; playgrnd;
shgl beach adj; fishing; boat hire; games area; TV; some statics;
dogs; Eng spkn; quiet; ccard acc. "Gd site; pleasant area; gd
cycling area; lakeside site amongst trees, helpful owners; trips
across Oland bdge to island, san facs excel." ♦ 1 Mar-31 Oct.
SEK 210   2011*

LANDSKRONA 2E4 (4km N Rural) 55.90098, 12.8042
Borstahusens Camping (M5), Campingvägen, 26161
Landskrona [(0418) 10837; fax 22042; bengt@borstahusens
camping.se; www.borstahusenscamping.se] Exit E6/E20 at
'Landskrona N' & foll sp for Borstahusen 4.5km fr E6/D20. Lge;
htd wc; chem disp; shwrs inc; baby facs; EHU (10A) SEK40;
lndry (inc dryer); shop; snacks 200m; playgrnd; htd pool 2km;
tennis; bike hire; game reserve; golf; wifi; TV rm; 75% statics;
phone; poss v cr; ccard acc; CKE/CCI. "Gd, pleasant site on
edge of Kattegat; sm pitches; boat to Ven Island fr town." ♦
21 Apr-11 Sep. SEK 320   2015*

LIDHULT 2F3 (15km NE Rural) 56.89671, 13.64343 **Lökna**
Camping & Stugby, Lökna Norregård 8, 34010 Lidhult
[(035) 92026; fax 92120; lokna-camping@telia.com;
www.loknacamping.com] Fr rd 25 Ljungby to Halmstad
turn N to Odensjö. In Odensjö turn R by church dir Lökna, site
in 5km on well-maintained dirt rd, sp. Sm, mkd pitch, hdstg,
pt shd; htd wc; chem disp; mv service pnt; sauna; shwrs inc;
EHU (16A) SEK30; lndry (inc dryer); sm shop; BBQ; cooking
facs; playgrnd; lake sw adj; fishing; watersports; some statics;
dogs; Eng spkn; adv bkg rec high ssn; quiet; ccard not acc.
"Wonderful lake views; excel, relaxing site; no shops nr."
21 Apr-13 Sep. SEK 200   2010*

⊞ **LIDKOPING** 2F2 (3km N Rural) 58.51375, 13.14008
Krono Camping (R3), Läckögaten, 53154 Lidköping
[(0510) 26804; fax 21135; info@kronocamping.com;
www.kronocamping.com] On Lake Vänern nr Folkparken,
on rd to Läckö; at Lidköping ring rd foll int'l camping sp. Lge,
pt shd; serviced pitch; wc; chem disp; mv service pnt; baby
facs; some serviced pitches; shwrs inc; EHU (10A) inc; gas; lndry
(inc dryer); shop; rest 300m; playgrnd; htd pool 300m; lake sw
300m; watersports; wifi; cab TV (via el hook-up); quiet; ccard
acc; CKE. "V clean, friendly, well-run site; open pinewoods on
lakeside; interesting area." ♦ SEK 412   2015*

LIMHAMN see Malmo 2E4

⊞ **LINKOPING** 2G2 (4km NW Rural) 58.42140, 15.56230
Glyttinge Camping (E28), Berggårdsvägen 6, 58437
Linköping [(013) 174928; fax 175923; glyttinge@nordic
camping.se; www.nordiccamping.se] Exit fr E4 sp Linköping
N; foll sp to Centrum & camping sp. Lge, hdg pitch, pt shd;
htd wc; chem disp; mv service pnt; baby facs; fam bthrm;
shwrs inc; EHU (10A) SEK50; gas; lndry (inc dryer); shop; rest;
playgrnd; pool adj; bike hire; fishing; boating; internet; TV;
Quickstop o'night facs; quiet; ccard acc; red LS; CKE. "Lovely
site but inadequate san facs for size; gd touring base; easy
cycle ride to town cent; recep only mornings only LS - no access
if arr later than 1pm." ♦ SEK 180   2010*

LIT 1B3 (1km E Rural) 63.31928, 14.8651 **Lits Camping/**
Little Lake Hill Canoe Centre, 83030 Lit [(0642) 10247;
fax 10103; ove.djurberg@swipnet.se; www.litscamping.
com] On rd 45, sp. Med, pt sl, pt shd; wc; chem disp; mv
service pnt; baby facs; sauna; shwrs inc; EHU (10A) SEK35;
lndry; shop, rest 1km; cooking facs; playgrnd; canoeing;
fishing; tennis; bike hire; wifi; some statics; phone; adv bkg;
quiet; ccard acc; CKE. "Pleasant site, gd alt to cr sites in
Östersund high ssn." ♦ 29 May-30 Sep. SEK 155   2009*

LJUNGBY 2F3 (1km N Urban) 56.84228, 13.95251 **Ljungby**
Camping Park, Campingvägen 1, 34134 Ljungby
[tel/fax (0372) 10350; reservation@ljungby-semesterby.se;
www.ljungby-semesterby.se] Exit E4 at Ljungby N, site sp.
Med, shd; htd wc; chem disp; shwrs inc; EHU (10A) SEK35;
lndry (inc dryer); shop; rest (Jun-Aug); playgrnd; htd pool adj;
paddling pool; cycling; poss cr in ssn; ccard acc; CKE. "Adv bkg
ess high ssn; NH only rec LS." 1 May-31 Aug. SEK 215   2009*

LJUNGBY 2F3 (14km NW Rural) 56.90406, 13.77996
SweCamp Sjön Bolmen Camping (G27), Bolmstad Mjälen,
34196 Ljungby [(0372) 92051; fax 92351; swecamp@
bolmencamping.se] Exit E4 at sp Ljungby N, turn L at top of
slip rd & 1st L over E4 sp Ljungby. Foll sp to Bolmsö & site sp
to Sjön Bolmen. Med, mkd pitch, pt shd; htd wc; chem disp;
mv service pnt; baby facs; shwrs inc; EHU (10A) SEK40; lndry;
shop; rest; playgrnd; lake sw fr pontoon; boating; games area;
bike hire; TV; 5% statics; dogs; phone; poss cr; Eng spkn; quiet;
ccard acc; CKE. ♦ 1 Jun-31 Aug. SEK 210   2011*

⊞ **LJUSDAL** *1B3* (3km W Rural) *61.83894, 16.04059* **Ljusdals Camping (X21), Ramsjövägen 56, 82730 Ljusdal [(0651) 12958; info@ljusdalscamping.se; www.ljusdalscamping.se]** Leave Ljusdal on Rv83 dir Ånge, site on R in 3km. Med, pt shd; htd wc; chem disp; mv service pnt; sauna; shwrs inc; EHU (10A) SEK40; lndry (inc dryer); rest, snacks; bar; cooking facs; playgrnd; lake sw & beach adj; games area; bike hire; wifi; entmnt; some statics; dogs; Eng spkn; adv bkg; ccard acc; CKE. ♦ SEK 255   2014*

LODERUP *2F4* (5km S Coastal) *55.38181, 14.12795* **Löderups Strandbad Camping (M12), Östanvägen, 27645 Löderup [(0411) 526311; fax 526613; www.loderupsstrandbads camping.se]** Rd 9 fr Ystad, after Nybrostrand turn R sp Kaseberga, site sp. Lge, mkd pitch, pt shd; wc; chem disp; baby facs; shwrs SEK10; EHU SEK40; lndry (inc dryer); shop 400m; rest 1km; snacks nr; playgrnd; sand beach adj; TV; 50% statics; dogs; phone; quiet; poss cr; Eng spkn; ccard acc; CKE. "Site in dunes adj nature reserve; facs poss stretched high ssn; uneven grnd; gd birdwatching, rambling; nr historical sites." ♦ ltd. 21 Apr-27 Sep. SEK 180   2009*

"I need an on-site restaurant"

We do our best to make sure site information is correct, but it is always best to check any must-have facilities are still available or will be open during your visit.

LOMMA see Malmö *2E4*

⊞ **LULEA** *1D2* (8km W Coastal) *65.59565, 22.07221* **First Camp Luleå (BD18), Arcusvägen 110, 97594 Luleå [(0920) 60300; fax 60315; lulea@firstcamp.se; www.firstcamp.se/lulea]** Exit E4 on R 500m N of Luleälv Rv bdge. Foll sp 'Arcus' (recreation complex). V lge, mkd pitch, pt shd; htd wc; chem disp; mv service pnt; baby facs; sauna; shwrs inc; EHU (10A) inc; lndry (inc dryer); shop; rest, snacks; bar; cooking facs; playgrnd; htd pool complex 700m; sand beach adj; tennis 300m; bike hire; wifi; TV; dogs; phone; car wash; Eng spkn; adv bkg; quiet; ccard acc; CKE. "Excel family site; many sports facs; san facs poss stretched high ssn; suitable RVs & twin-axles; adj rlwy museum." ♦ SEK 365   2014*

MALMO *2E4* (11km N Coastal) *55.68873, 13.05756* **Habo-Ljung Camping (M23), Södra Västkustvägen 12, 23434 Lomma [(040) 411210; fax 414310; info@ haboljungcamping.se; www.haboljungcamping.se]** Turn off E6 dir Lomma, head N for Bjärred, site on L. Lge, pt shd; htd wc (cont); chem disp; mv service pnt; baby facs; shwrs inc; EHU (10A) SEK40; lndry (inc dryer); shop; snacks; BBQ; cooking facs; playgrnd; sand beach adj; entmnt; 5% statics; phone; poss cr; Eng spkn; poss noisy; ccard acc; CKE. "Conv NH; vg; location for wind & kite surfing; 20 min walk along beach to town." ♦ ltd. 15 Apr-15 Sep. SEK 280   2014*

⊞ **MALMO** *2E4* (7km SW Urban) *55.5722, 12.90686* **Malmö Camping & Feriesenter (M8), Strandgatan 101, Sibbarp, 21611 Limhamn [(040) 155165; fax 159777; malmocamping@ malmo.se; www.malmo.se/malmocamping]** Fr Öresund Bdge take 1st exit & foll sp Limhamn & Sibbarp, then int'l campsite sp. Fr N on E6 round Malmö until last exit bef bdge (sp), then as above. Fr Dragør-Limnhamn ferry turn R on exit dock. Site in 1km on R, nr sea, in park-like setting. V lge, pt sl, pt shd; htd wc; chem disp; mv service pnt; baby facs; shwrs inc; EHU (10A) inc (poss rev pol); gas; lndry (inc dryer); shops; rest, snacks; cooking facs; playgrnd; pool 400m; sand beach 250m; windsurfing; bike hire; wifi; TV rm; phone; bus to Malmo; poss cr; no adv bkg; quiet; ccard acc; CKE. "Easy cycle to town cent; facs poss stretched high ssn; v busy city site; well-laid out but poss long walk to san facs; conv Öresund Bdge." ♦ SEK 290   2010*

⊞ **MALUNG** *2F1* (1km W Rural) *60.68296, 13.70243* **Malungs Camping (W22), Bullsjövägen, 78200 Malung [(0280) 18650; fax 18615; campingen@malung.se; www.malungscamping.se]** Fr Stöllet take rd 45 to Malung, site sp. Lge, pt shd; htd wc; chem disp; baby facs; shwrs inc; EHU (10A) SEK40; lndry (inc dryer); shop; snacks; playgrnd; pool; fishing; boating; bike hire; internet; TV; car wash; Quickstop o'night facs; quiet; ccard acc; CKE. ♦ SEK 160   2009*

⊞ **MARIESTAD** *2F2* (2km NW Rural) *58.7154, 13.79516* **Ekuddens Camping (R2), 54245 Mariestad [(0501) 10637; fax 18601; andreas.appelgren@mariestad.se or ekudden@ nordiccamping.se; www.ekuddenscamping.se]** Fr E20 take turn off twd Mariestad. At 1st rndabt foll ring rd clockwise until site sp on Lake Vänern. Lge, shd; wc; mv service pnt; sauna; shwrs inc; EHU (10A) SEK40; gas; lndry (inc dryer); shop; rest; bar; playgrnd; htd pool; beach; golf 2km; bike hire; dogs; phone; Quickstop o'night facs; ccard acc; CKE. "Gd views fr lakeside pitches; friendly, helpful staff; gd san facs." ♦ SEK 294   2014*

MARKARYD *2F3* (500m N Urban) *56.46475, 13.60066* **Camping Park Sjötorpet (G4), Strandvägen 4, 28531 Markaryd [(0433) 10316; fax 12391; reservation@ sjotorpet-roc.se; www.sjotorpet-roc.se]** E4 fr Helsingborg (ferry) site is bet E4 N turn to Markaryd & rd 117, sp. Narr app. Sm, pt sl, pt shd; htd wc; shwrs inc; chem disp; mv service pnt; baby facs; EHU (10A) SEK40; lndry (inc dryer); shop; rest, snacks; bar; cooking facs; playgrnd; lake sw; fishing; boating; bike hire; wifi; some statics; dogs; phone; poss cr; Eng spkn; quiet; ccard acc; CKE. "Excel san & cooking facs; well-run site; helpful staff." ♦ 1 Apr-31 Oct. SEK 210   2011*

MARSTRAND *2E2* (1.4km NE Coastal) *57.89380, 11.60510* **Marstrands Camping (036), Långedalsvägen 16, 44030 Marstrand [(0303) 60584; fax 60440; info@ marstrandcamping.se; www.marstrandscamping.se]** Exit A6 dir Kungsälv/Marstrand & foll rd 168 to Marstrand. Site sp on Koön Island. App rd to site v narr. Med, pt sl, pt shd; htd wc; chem disp; mv service pnt; baby facs; shwrs; EHU (10A) SEK45; lndry; shop; cooking facs; playgrnd; shgl beach; wifi; TV; 50% statics; dogs; poss v cr; adv bkg; quiet; ccard acc; CKE. "Ferry to Marstrand Island." ♦ 15 Apr-30 Sep. SEK 310   2015*

SWEDEN

MELLBYSTRAND 2E3 (1km N Coastal/Urban) 56.51961, 12.94628 **Marias Camping (N18), Norra Strandvägen 1, 312 60 Mellbystrand [(0430) 28585; fax 27321; info@mariascamping.se; www.mariascamping.se]** 20km N of Båstad, exit junc 41 fr E6 W onto rd 24, site sp off coast rd N. Lge, hdg/mkd pitch, pt shd; htd wc; chem disp (wc); mv service pnt; baby facs; shwrs; EHU inc; lndry (inc dryer); shop; rest; snacks; bar; cooking facs; playgrnd; sand beach adj; games rm; internet; TV; dogs; bus 500m; Eng spkn; adv bkg; quiet; CKE. "Vg site beside dunes; beautiful beach." ◆ ltd. 21 Apr-26 Aug. SEK 320   2013*

⊞ **MELLERUD** 2E2 (4km SE Coastal) 58.68933, 12.51711 **Mellerud SweCamp Vita Sandar (P13), 46421 Mellerud [(0530) 12260; fax 12934; mail@vitasandarscamping.se; www.vitasandarscamping.se]** Fr S on rd 45 take Dalslandsgatan Rd on R & foll sp. Fr N turn L twd Sunnanåhamn, Vita Sandar. Med, pt shd; htd wc; chem disp; mv service pnt; sauna; shwrs SEK5; baby facs; EHU (10A) SEK50; lndry (inc dryer); shop; rest, snacks; bar; cooking facs; playgrnd; htd pool; waterslides; sand beach & lake sw; boat & bike hire; fishing; tennis; games area; wifi; TV rm; 20% statics; dogs; Quickstop o'night facs; poss cr; quiet; ccard acc; red LS; CKE/CCI. "Pleasant family site in pine trees; excel sw." ◆ SEK 420   2013*

MELLERUD 2E2 (2km W Rural) 58.71288, 12.43231 **Kerstins Camping (P21), Hålsungebyn 1, 46494 Mellerud [tel/fax (0530) 12715; epost@kerstinscamping.se; www.kerstinscamping.se]** Fr Mellerud on rd 166 dir Bäckefors & Ed, site sp. Sm, pt shd; htd wc (cont); chem disp; mv service pnt; baby facs; shwrs inc; EHU (10A) SEK45; lndry (inc dryer); shop; BBQ; cooking facs; playgrnd; games rm; TV rm; some statics; dogs; phone; Eng spkn; adv bkg; quiet; CKE. "Pleasant area; excel." ◆ 3 May-26 Aug. SEK 175   2011*

MOLLE see Höganäs 2E4

MOLNDAL see Göteborg 2E3

⊞ **MORA** 1B4 (500m N Urban) 61.00853, 14.53178 **Mora Parkens Camping, Parkvägen 1, 79231 Mora [(0250) 27600; fax 12785; info@moraparken.se; www.moraparken.se]** Fr SW site sp on rd 45. Or foll sp in town cent; site in 400m. Recep in adj hotel. Lge, mkd pitch, pt sl, pt shd; htd wc; chem disp; mv service pnt; baby facs; shwrs inc; EHU (10A) inc; lndry (inc dryer); shops 500m; rest 300m; covrd, htd pool; paddling pol; waterslide; fishing; sports facs; games rm; TV; wifi; some statics; Quickstop o'night facs; Eng spkn; no adv bkg; quiet; ccard acc; CKE. "Excel site; ltd facs LS & poss unclean; suitable RVs & twin-axles; conv for bear sanctuary at Orsa." ◆ SEK 165   2009*

NJURUNDABOMMEN 1C3 (5km E Coastal) 62.26828, 17.45181 **Bergafjärdens Camping & Havsbad (Y29), Bergafjärden, 86286 Njurundabommen [(060) 34598; fax 34841; info@bergafjarden.nu; www.bergafjarden.nu]** Clearly sp on E4 at Njurundabommen. Lge, shd; wc; chem disp; mv service pnt; baby facs; shwrs SEK5; EHU (6A) SEK40; lndry (inc dryer); shop; snacks; bar; playgrnd; sand beach; lake sw; bike hire; wifi; TV; some statics; dogs; phone; quiet; ccard acc; CKE. ◆ 9 May-18 Sep. SEK 180   2011*

NORA 2G1 (1km N Rural) 59.52576, 15.04386 **Trängbo Camping (T1), 713280 Nora [(0587) 12361; fax 311389; info@trangbocamping.se; www.trangbocamping.se]** Site sp fr sq in cent of town, on rd 244 fr Hällefors to Örebro. Med, pt sl, pt shd; htd wc; chem disp; mv service pnt; baby facs; shwrs; EHU (10A) SEK35; lndry (inc dryer); shop & 1km; playgrnd; lake sw; boating; fishing; nature trails; bike hire; games area; wifi; some statics; ccard acc; quiet; CKE. ◆ 1 May-30 Sep. SEK 190   2011*

NORA 2G1 (3km N Rural) 59.5342, 15.0405 **Gustavsberg Camping (Naturist), NF Bergslagens Solsport, 71322 Nora [(073) 6425282; info@gustavsbergscamping.com; www.gustavsbergscamping.com]** Fr Örebro take rd N to Nora, site sp fr Nora cent past Trängbo Camping, just outside vill limits on R. Sm, mkd pitch, pt shd; htd wc; chem disp; fam bthrm; sauna; shwrs inc; EHU (10A) SEK35; lndry; shop, rest, snacks, bar 3km; BBQ; cooking facs; playgrnd; lake sw adj; fishing; games area; TV rm; 20% statics; dogs; phone; Eng spkn; adv bkg; quiet; ccard acc; red for INF cardholders. "Gd family site; all facs unisex; many preserved buildings & antique shops in Nora." ◆ 1 Jun-31 Aug. SEK 145   2009*

⊞ **NORDMALING** 1C3 (200m W Rural/Coastal) 63.57546, 19.45881 **SweCamp Rödviken (AC43), Rödviksvägen 93, 91431 Nordmaling [tel/fax (0930) 31250; info@rundviksrederi.se]** Site off E4, well sp. Med, unshd; wc; chem disp; mv service pnt; shwrs inc; EHU (16A) SEK45; lndry (inc dryer); shop; rest; snacks adj; bar; cooking facs; playgrnd; htd pool; paddling pool; sand beach; rv fishing; sports & ice rink adj; bike hire; some statics; dogs; Quickstop o'night facs; quiet; ccard acc; CKE. ◆ SEK 170   2009*

NORRFJARDEN 1D2 (8km SE Rural/Coastal) 65.35521, 21.58571 **Borgaruddens Camping (BD31), Borgaruddsvägen, 94521 Norrfjärden [(0911) 203518; borgarudden.nif@telia.com]** Site on E side of E4. Med, mkd pitch, htd wc; chem disp; mv service pnt; baby facs; shwrs inc; EHU (10A) SEK40; lndry (inc dryer); snacks; cooking facs; playgrnd; pool; shgl beach adj; wifi; 10% statics; phone; Eng spkn; quiet; ccard acc; CKE. "Conv unique parish vills Luleå, Piteå & Skellefteå." ◆ 1 Jun-31 Aug. SEK 170   2011*

NORRKOPING 2G2 (2km W Urban) 58.59138, 16.14080 **Himmelstalunds Camping (E4), Utställningsvägen, 60234 Norrköping [(011) 171190; fax 170987; info@norrkopingscamping.com; www.norrkopingscamping.com]** Exit Norrköping S fr E4, foll sp sports cent & site. Lge, pt sl, pt shd; htd wc; chem disp; mv service pnt; baby facs; serviced pitches; shwrs inc; EHU (10A) SEK40; lndry (dryer); shop; snacks; cooking facs; playgrnd; htd pool & sports facs 200m; bike hire; wifi; TV; 10% statics; phone; quiet; ccard acc; CKE. ◆ 15 Apr-15 Oct. SEK 160   2009*

NOSSEBRO 2E2 (500m N Urban) 58.19195, 12.72161 **Nossebrobada Camping (R22), Marknadsgatan 4, 46530 Nossebro [(0512) 57043; fax 57042; info@nossebrobadet.se; www.nossebrobadet.se]** N fr Alingsås on E20; exit N to Nossebro, site in 16km. Clearly sp. Sm, pt sl, unshd; wc; mv service pnt; sauna; shwrs; EHU inc; lndry (inc dryer); shop 500m; playgrnd; 2 pools (1 covrd); fishing; boat hire; sports grnd adj; bike hire; some statics; dogs; quiet. "Vg NH; stream thro site." ◆ 25 Apr-31 Aug. SEK 200   2013*

You can now fill in site reports online

NYKOPING *2G2* (8km SE Coastal) *58.71970, 17.09182*
**Strandstuvikens Bad & Camping (D10), 61192 Nyköping
[tel/fax (0155) 97810; lilian@bissarna.se; www.
strandstuviken camping.com]** On E4 dir Nyköping foll
sp town cent then 'Hamnen' (harbour) & turn R onto rd 53
sp Arno. In approx 3km turn L onto minor rd & foll site sp.
Med, mkd pitch, pt shd; htd wc; chem disp; mv service pnt;
baby facs; fam bthrm; EHU (10A) SEK50; lndry; shop; snacks;
cooking facs; playgrnd; sand beach adj; TV; some statics;
Eng spkn; quiet; CKE/CCI. "Gd site; gd walking, cycling." ◆
1 May-15 Sep. SEK 150   2009*

**"Satellite navigation makes
touring much easier"**
Remember most sat navs don't know if
you're towing or in a larger vehicle – always
use yours alongside maps and site directions.

⊞ **NYNASHAMN** *2H2* (1km NW Coastal) *58.90717,
17.93805* **Nicksta Camping (B8), Nickstabadsvägen 17,
14943 Nynäshamn [(08) 52012780; fax 52015317; info@
nickstacamping.se; www.nickstacamping.se]** Fr Stockholm
on Rv 73 to Nynäshamn. Foll site sp, turning R at ICA supmkt,
then immed L (sp poss cov'rd by hedge.) Med, pt sl, pt shd; htd
wc; chem disp; mv service pnt; baby facs; shwrs inc; EHU (10A)
SEK50; lndry (inc dryer); shop 700m; snacks; cooking facs;
playgrnd; beach adj; waterslide; games area; bike hire; wifi;
some statics; dogs; train 600m; site clsd mid-Dec to mid-Jan;
Quickstop o'night facs; Eng spkn; CKE. "Gd site; ferries to
Gotland & Poland." ◆ SEK 165   2009*

**OLAND ISLAND Campsites in towns on Öland Island
are listed together at the end of the Swedish site entry
pages.**

OREBRO *2G2* (1km S Rural) *59.2554, 15.18955* **Gustavsviks
Camping (T2), Sommarrovägen, 70229 Örebro
[(019) 196950; fax 196961; camping@gustavsvik.com;
www.gustavsvik.com]** Foll sp fr E18/E20 & rd 51 to site. V
lge, mkd pitch, pt sl, pt shd; htd wc; chem disp; some serviced
pitches; mv service pnt; baby facs; fam bthrm; shwrs inc; EHU
(10A) SEK80 inc sat TV (poss rev pol); gas; lndry (inc dryer);
shop; kiosk; rest, snacks; bar; BBQ; cooking facs; playgrnd;
2 pools (1 htd, covrd); waterslide; paddling pool; lake sw
& beach adj; golf nr; gym; solarium; wifi; entmnt; cab TV;
10% statics; dogs; phone; bus; Eng spkn; quiet; ccard acc;
CKE. "Excel family site; superb facs; gentle stroll to town; v
highly rec." ◆ 15 Apr-6 Nov. SEK 295   2010*

⊞ **ORSA** *1B4* (1km W Rural) *61.12090, 14.59890* **Orsa
SweCamp (W3), Timmervägen 1, 79421 Orsa [(0250) 46200;
fax 46260; info@orsagronklitt.se; www.orsacamping.se]**
Sp fr town cent & fr rd 45. V lge, pt shd; htd wc; shwrs inc;
baby facs; sauna; EHU (10A) SEK50; mv service pnt; lndry (inc
dryer); shops 500m; rest; bar; cooking facs; playgrnd; 4 htd
pools high ssn; waterslide; sand beach & lake sw; fishing;
canoe & bike hire; tennis; wifi; entmnt; sat TV; 5% statics;
phone; quiet; CKE. "Excel countryside; bear reserve 15km; gd
general facs but ltd LS." ◆ SEK 215 (CChq acc)   2010*

OSKARSHAMN *2G3* (3km SE Coastal) *57.2517, 16.49206*
**Gunnarsö Camping (H7), Östersjövägen 103, 57263
Oskarshamn [tel/fax (0491) 13298; gunnarso@
oskarshamn.se; www.oskarshamn.se]**
Fr E22 Dir Oskarshamn, site sp on Kalmar Sound. Med, pt
shd; htd wc; chem disp; mv service pnt; baby facs; sauna;
shwrs SEK5; EHU (10A) SEK35; lndry (inc dryer); shop; snacks;
playgrnd; 2 pools; watersports; wifi; TV; 40% statics; dogs;
phone; adv bkg; quiet; ccard acc; CKE. "Beautiful location;
many pitches with gd views; gd walking/cycling." ◆
1 May-18 Sep. SEK 175   2009*

OSTERFARNEBO *2G1* (1.5km S Rural) *60.29937, 16.80614*
**Färnebofjärdens Camping, Berreksvägen 19, 46291
Österfärnebo [0736 505334 (mob); farnebocamping@
hotmail.com; www.farnebocamping.se]** Fr rd 67 turn W
at Gysinge onto rd 272 dir Österfärnebo. In 5km turn L sp By
at football grnd, site in 2km, sp. Med, mkd pitch, unshd; wc;
shwrs; EHU (10A) SEK40; lndry; lake sw; fishing; boat hire;
20% statics; quiet. "Pleasant site; conv National Park."
1 Jun-30 Sep. SEK 130   2010*

⊞ **OSTERSUND** *1B3* (3km S Rural) *63.15955, 14.6731*
**Östersunds Camping (Z11), Krondikesvägen
95, 83146 Östersund [(063) 144615; fax 144323;
ostersundscamping@ostersund.se; www.ostersund.se]**
At Odensala on lakeside, well sp fr E14. Lge, mkd pitch; pt sl;
htd wc; chem disp; mv service pnt; baby facs; sauna; shwrs
SEK5; EHU (10A) SEK50 (poss rev pol); lndry (inc dryer); shop;
rest; bar; cooking facs; playgrnd; pool; paddling pool; tennis;
wifi; cab TV; 80% statics; dogs; phone; poss cr; quiet; ccard
acc; CKE. "Gd NH; v helpful staff." ◆ SEK 278   2013*

⊞ **PAJALA** *1D1* (1.5km SE Rural) *67.20381, 23.4084*
**Pajala Camping (BD8), Tannavägen 65, 98431 Pajala
[tel/fax (0978) 74180; pajalacamping@gmail.com]**
Site sp fr rd 99. Med, mkd pitch, hdstg, pt shd; htd wc; chem
disp; mv service pnt; baby facs; sauna; shwrs inc; EHU (10A)
SEK30; lndry (inc dryer); shop; snacks; cooking facs; playgrnd;
tennis; bike hire; wifi; TV rm; dogs; bus 1.5km; Eng spkn;
adv bkg; quiet; ccard acc; red long stay; CKE. "Clean, well-
presented site; delightful owner; salmon-fishing in rv in ssn
(mid-Jun approx)." ◆ SEK 190   2011*

RAMVIK *1C3* (1km S Rural) *62.79911, 17.86931* **Snibbens
Camping (Y19), Snibben 139, 87016 Ramvik
[tel/fax (0612) 40505; info@snibbenscamping.com;
www.snibbenscamping.com]** Fr S on E4, 23km N of
Härnösand; after high bdge sighted take slip rd dir Kramfors;
site sp in 2.5km on L just bef Ramvik. Med, mkd pitch, pt sl, pt
shd; htd wc; chem disp; mv service pnt; baby facs; shwrs inc;
EHU (16A) SEK20; lndry (inc dryer); shop 1km; rest, snacks; bar;
cooking facs; playgrnd; lake sw & beach adj; fishing; boat hire;
wifi; TV rm; some statics; bus; poss cr; Eng spkn; quiet; ccard
acc; CKE. "Helpful owners; delightful site with lakeside setting;
v peaceful even when busy; spotless facs & lovely camp kitchen
with seating areas inside & out; conv Höga Kusten suspension
bdge; delightful site in beautiful surroundings." ◆
6 May-11 Sep. SEK 212   2013*

SWEDEN

⊞ **RATTVIK** 1B4 (1km N Rural) 60.89103, 15.13115
**Enåbadets Camping (W7), Enåbadsvägen 8, 79532 Rättvik
[(0248) 56111; fax 12660; info@enan.se; www.enan.se]**
Site sp on N o'skts of town fr Tourist Info board, on rd 70.
Lge, shd; wc; chem disp; mv service pnt; serviced pitches; baby
facs; sauna; shwrs inc; EHU (10A) SEK50; lndry (inc dryer);
shop; rest, snacks; bar; cooking facs; playgrnd; pool; lake adj;
wifi; entmnt; TV; 10% statics; phone; poss cr; quiet; ccard acc;
CKE. "Gd base for touring potteries & local vills; wooded." ◆
SEK 190   2010*

RATTVIK 1B4 (1km W Rural) 60.88891, 15.10881
**Siljansbadets Camping (W8), Långbryggevägen 4, 79532
Rättvik [(0248) 56118; fax 51689; camp@siljansbadet.com;
www.siljansbadet.com]** Fr S on rd 70 thro Rättvik. Immed
outside town turn L at rndabt, site sp on Lake Siljan. Height
restriction 3.5m. V lge, mkd pitch, pt shd; wc; chem disp;
baby facs; shwrs inc; EHU (10A) SEK50; lndry (inc dryer); shop
& 500m; rest & 500m; bar; cooking facs; playgrnd; lake sw &
sand beach; boat hire; wifi; TV rm; 15% statics; dogs; bus/train;
poss cr; Eng spkn; quiet; ccard acc. "Lovely scenic location;
conv town cent." ◆ 26 Apr-6 Oct. SEK 330   2015*

RORBACK 1D2 (Coastal) 65.80030, 22.59516 **Rörbäcks
Camping & Havsbad (BD79), Rörbäck 79, 95592 Råneå
[tel/fax (0924) 35047; info@rorbackscamping.se]**
Off E4 approx 10km SW of junc with E10, at Jämtöfjärden foll
sp S to coast, site well sp. Sm, mkd pitch, hdstg, pt shd; htd
wc; chem disp; serviced pitches; sauna; shwrs inc; baby facs;
EHU (10A) inc; lndry; rest, snacks; BBQ; cooking facs; playgrnd;
sand beach adj; fishing; canoe hire; TV; phone; poss cr; Eng
spkn; adv bkg; ccard acc; CKE. "Cosy, clean site on water's
edge in a wood; vg facs." ◆ 1 Jun-31 Aug. SEK 200   2009*

ROSTANGA 2F4 (500m SW Rural) 55.99656, 13.28050
**Röstånga Camping (M20), Blinkarpsvägen 3, 26024
Röstånga [(0435) 91064; fax 91652; info@rostangacamping.
se; www.rostangacamping.se]** Site sp in Röstånga along
rd 108. Med, pt shd; htd wc; chem disp; mv service pnt; fam
bthrm; baby facs; private san facs avail; shwrs inc; EHU (10A)
SEK40; lndry (inc dryer); shop high ssn; rest 300m; snacks;
bar; BBQ; cooking facs; htd pool; paddling pool; waterslide;
lake fishing; canoeing; tennis; games area; games rm; wifi;
entmnt; TV rm; 15% statics; dogs; Eng spkn; adv bkg; quiet;
ccard acc; CKE. "Pleasant family site; some pitches by stream;
superb pool; conv Söderåsens National Park." ◆ 21 Apr-2 Oct.
SEK 220   2010*

ROXENBADEN 2G2 (S Rural) 58.54135, 15.62292 **Sandviks
Camping, Stjärnorp, 59078 Roxenbaden [tel/fax (013) 61470;
sandvik@caravanclub.se]** Fr E4 Jönköping to Linköping turn
onto rd 36 & foll sp Göta Canal, Berg. Site sp in Berg & is 3km
E of Stjärnorp. Med, mkd pitch, terr, pt shd; wc; chem disp;
shwrs inc; EHU (10A) SEK50; lndry (inc dryer); shop; playgrnd;
lake sw & sand/shgl beach adj; 30% statics; dogs; phone;
bus at gate; Eng spkn; quiet; ccard acc; CKE/CCI. "Well-kept,
relaxing site; interesting area; gd walks." ◆ 15 Apr-15 Sep.
SEK 180   2010*

RYD see Urshult 2F3

⊞ **SAFFLE** 2F2 (6km S Rural) 59.08326, 12.88616 **Duse Udde
Camping (S11), 66180 Säffle [(0533) 42000; fax 42002;
duseudde@krokstad.se; www.duseudde.se]**
Site sp fr rd 45. Med, pt sl, shd; wc; mv service pnt; baby
facs; sauna; shwrs SEK10; EHU (10A) SEK50; lndry (inc dryer);
shop; rest high ssn; snacks; bar; playgrnd; watersports; pool
6km; beach; lake sw; bike hire; wifi; entmnt; bus; 20% statics;
phone; dogs; Quickstop o'night facs; quiet; ccard acc; red long
stay; CKE. "Place to relax; useful base for Värmland area with
nature walks." ◆ SEK 180   2010*

SALA 2G1 (6km N Rural) 59.95473, 16.5168 **Silvköparens
Camping (U2), Gamla Riksväg 70, 73397 Sala [tel/fax
(0224) 59003; silvkoparen@caravanclub.se; www.sala.se]**
Site on rd 70 bet Sala & Avesta, sp. Med, pt shd; htd wc; chem
disp; shwrs inc; EHU (10A); lndry (inc dryer); shop adj & 6km;
snacks; playgrnd; lake sw adj; boating; canoeing; cycling; TV;
some statics; dogs; phone; poss cr; Eng spkn; quiet; ccard
acc; CKE. "Sala silver mine & museum; Sätra Brunn spa; lovely
situation." ◆ 30 Apr-18 Sep. SEK 205   2011*

SANDARNE see Söderhamn 1C4

⊞ **SARNA** 1B3 (1km S Rural) 61.69281, 13.14696 **Särna
Camping (W32), Särnavägen 6, 79090 Särna [(0253) 10851;
fax 32055; camping@sarnacamping.se; www.sarnacamping.
se]** Turn R off rd 70 opp fire stn. Med, terr, pt shd; wc; chem
disp; mv service pnt; sauna; shwrs SEK5; EHU (10A) SEK35;
lndry (inc dryer); shop, rest, snacks 200m; playgrnd; shgl beach;
bike hire; poss cr; adv bkg; quiet. "Beautiful setting o'looking
lake; pleasant town." ◆ SEK 160   2010*

"There aren't many sites open at this time of year"

If you're travelling outside peak season
remember to call ahead to check site opening
dates – even if the entry says 'open all year'.

⊞ **SIMRISHAMN** 2F4 (2km N Coastal) 55.57021, 14.33611
**Tobisviks Camping (L14), Tobisvägen, 27294 Simrishamn
[(0414) 412778; fax 412771; hakan@fritidosterlen.se;
www.fritidosterlen.se]** By sea at N app to town. Lge, pt
shd; wc; chem disp; mv service pnt; shwrs SEK1/min; EHU
(10A) SEK50; lndry (inc dryer); shop 400m; rest 2km; htd pool;
watersports; TV; phone; ccard acc; CKE. SEK 210   2010*

SKANOR 2E4 (2km SE Coastal) 55.39750, 12.86555 **Ljungens
Camping (M9), Strandbadsvägen, 23942 Falsterbo
[(040) 471132; fax 470955; camping@telia.com; www.mamut.
net/ljungenscamping]** Fr E6/E22 exit to W sp Höllviken onto
rd 100. Foll sp Skanör/Falsterbo. Site sp on L at rndabt at ent
to town, dir Falsterbo. Lge, mkd pitch, some hdstg, pt shd;
htd wc; chem disp; mv service pnt; baby facs; shwrs SEK5;
EHU (10A) SEK40; lndry (inc dryer); shop; snacks high ssn;
BBQ; cooking facs; playgrnd; sand beach 200m; wifi; TV;
50% statics; dogs; bus; Eng spkn; no adv bkg; aircraft noise
(under flight path Copenhagen airport) ccard acc; CKE. "Conv
Viking Vill museum; nature reserve adj; gd birdwatching;
cycling; vg." ◆ 1 Mayr-1 Oct. SEK 220   2011*

SKARHOLMEN see Stockholm *2H2*

⊞ **SKELLEFTEA** *1C2* (1.5km N Rural) *64.76156, 20.97513*
**Skellefteå Camping (AC18), Mossgaten, 93170 Skellefteå
[(0910) 735500; fax 701890; skellefteacamping@skelleftea.
se; www.skelleftea.se/skellefteacamping]** Turn W off E4;
well sp behind g'ge. Also sp as Camping Stugby. Lge, mkd pitch,
pt sl, unshd; htd wc; chem disp; mv service pnt; sauna; shwrs
inc; EHU (10A) SEK60; lndry (inc dryer); shop; rest, snacks 100m;
bar 1km; BBQ; cooking facs; playgrnd; htd pool; waterslide; sand
beach 5km; fishing; tennis 150m; bike hire; games area; wifi; TV
rm; 10% statics; dogs; phone; poss cr; Eng spkn; quiet; ccard
acc; CKE. "Friendly, clean site in pine trees on sheltered inlet;
lge pitches suitable RVs & twin-axles; Nordanå Cultural Cent &
Bonnstan Church Vill in walking dist; if site clsd book in at Statoil
stn 500m S on E4 at rndabt. Exc san facs, lgr camp kitchen,
helpful staff, lge supmkt nrby." ♦ SEK 230   2011*

SKELLEFTEA *1C2* (7km NE Coastal) *64.77681, 21.11993*
**Bovikens Havsbad Camping (AC60), 93140 Skellefteå
[tel/fax (0910) 54000; cecilia@bovikenshavsbad.se;
www.bovikenscamping.se]** Site sp off E4, site in 5km. Med,
mkd pitch, pt shd; wc; chem disp; baby facs; shwrs inc; EHU;
lndry (inc dryer); snacks; playgrnd; sand beach adj; tennis nr; TV
rm; some statics; dogs; poss cr; Eng spkn; adv bkg; quiet; ccard
acc; CKE. "Gd family site by secluded beach; friendly owner;
excel birdwatching; avoid shwr cubicles with elec heaters nr
floor level; v nice!" ♦ 16 May-14 Sep. SEK 360   2014*

SLAGNAS *1C2* (550m E Urban) *65.58458, 18.17284*
**Slagnäsforsens Camping, Campingvägen 5, 93091 Slagnäs
[tel/fax (0960) 650093; info@slagnascamping.com;
www.slagnascamping.com]** On rd 45 bet Sorsele &
Arvidsjaur, nr bdge over Skellefteälvan. Sm, pt sl, unshd; wc;
chem disp; sauna; shwrs inc; EHU (10A) inc; lndry; shop; rest
700m; cooking facs; playgrnd; dogs; no adv bkg; quiet; CKE.
"Gd." 1 May-30 Sep. SEK 150   2009*

SODERALA see Söderhamn *1C4*

SODERHAMN *1C4* (10km SE Coastal) *61.24843, 17.19506*
**Stenö Havsbad Camping (X9), Stenövägen, 82022 Sandarne
[(0270) 60000; fax 60005; steno@nordiccamping.se;
www.nordiccamping.se]** Exit E4 at sp Bollnäs-Sandarne (S
of Söderhamn turn), foll sp Sandarne at Östansjö, turn L at
camping sp. Lge, shd; wc; chem disp; baby facs; mv service
pnt; shwrs inc; EHU (10A) SEK50; lndry (inc dryer); shop; rest,
snacks; bar; cooking facs; playgrnd; pool 12km; sand beach;
games area; wifi; TV rm; some statics; phone; bus; poss cr; adv
bkg; quiet; ccard acc; CKE. "Adj nature reserve." ♦
1 May-31 Oct. SEK 150   2009*

⊞ **SODERHAMN** *1C4* (10km W Rural) *61.29318, 16.8266*
**Moheds Camping (X6), Mohedsvägen 59, 82692 Söderala
[(0270) 425233; fax 425326; info@mohedscamping.se;
www.mohedscamping.se]** Take Söderhamn exit fr E4 onto rd
50 twds Bollnäs; site sp after approx 10km. Med, hdstg, pt sl, pt
shd; wc; chem disp; mv service pnt; sauna; shwrs SEK5; baby facs;
EHU (10A) SEK35; lndry (inc dryer); shop; snacks; bar; playgrnd;
pool; lake beach, fishing, boating & sw adj; tennis; cycling; wifi;
TV; many statics; phone; poss cr; Eng spkn; adv bkg; quiet; ccard
acc; CKE. "Skydiving in nrby airfield; attractive coastline; sh walk
to bus to town; busy site." ♦ SEK 165   2011*

SODERKOPING *2G2* (1km N Rural) *58.49163, 16.30618*
**Skeppsdockans Camping (E34), Dockan 1, 61421
Söderköping [(0121) 21630; korskullenscamp@hotmail.com;
www.soderkopingscamping.se]** On E22 immed N of canal
bdge. Sm, mkd pitch, unshd; htd wc; shwrs inc; EHU SEK40;
lndry (inc dryer); rest & shops 1km; cooking facs; canal sw; bike
hire; TV; Eng spkn; quiet; ccard acc; CKE. "On side of Gota
Canal with constant boating traffic, but peaceful." ♦ 30 Apr-
2 Oct. SEK 200   2013*

SODERKOPING *2G2* (1km E Urban) *58.4770, 16.33471*
**Korskullen Camping (E17), Skönbergagaten 50, 61421
Söderköping [(0121) 21621; korskullencamp@hotmail.com]**
On E22 in town cent. Sm, hdg pitch, pt shd; wc; chem disp;
shwrs; EHU SEK40; lndry (inc dryer); shop adj; rest; bar;
playgrnd; TV; some statics; dogs; Eng spkn; quiet but some rd
noise; ccard acc; CKE. "Well-maintained san facs."
6 May-18 Sep. SEK 180   2011*

SOLLENTUNA see Stockholm *2H2*

SOLLERON see Gesunda *1B4*

⊞ **SORSELE** *1C2* (400m W Rural) *65.53428, 17.52663* **Sorsele
Camping (AC21), Fritidsvägen, Näset, 92070 Sorsele
[(0952) 10124; fax 10625; info@lapplandskatan.nu;
www.lapplandskatan.nu]** N on rd 45/363 fr Storuman to
Arvidsjaur. In Sorsele vill turn W for 500m; site sp. Med, unshd;
htd wc; chem disp; baby facs; shwrs; EHU (16A) SEK35; lndry
(inc dryer); shop 200m; playgrnd; pool; beach; canoeing;
fishing; hiking; bike hire; wifi; TV; some statics; dogs; phone;
poss cr; quiet; ccard acc; CKE. "Nature reserve; interesting
ancient Lapp vill; friendly, welcoming; attractive site." ♦
SEK 183   2014*

STENKALLEGARDEN see Bocksjö *2F2*

STOCKEN *2E2* (700m S Coastal) *58.14786, 11.42143* **Stocken
Camping, 101, 474 92 Ellös [0304 511 00; info@stocken.nu;
www.stocken.nu]** Foll rd 160 (sp Orust); at Varekil turn L onto
rd 178 (sp Ellös); in approx 15km turn L (sp Stocken) & foll sp
to site (on L just bef vill). Lge, mkd pitch, pt sl, unshd; wc; chem
disp; MV service pnt; baby facs; shwrs metered; EHU (10-16A)
metered; lndry; shop; rest, snacks; bar; BBQ; playgrnd; beach
500m; games area; games rm; TV; 20% statics; dogs; bus adj;
adv bking; quiet; cc acc; red long stay. "Beautiful coastline; gd
walks; vg site." 9 Apr-2 Oct. SEK 285   2011*

⊞ **STOCKHOLM** *2H2* (15km N Rural) *59.43821, 17.99223*
**Rösjöbadens Camping (B1), Lomvägen 100, 19256
Sollentuna [(08) 962184; fax 929195; info@rosjobaden.se;
www.rosjobaden.se]** Take E18 m'way N fr Stockholm, sp
Norrtälje. Pass Morby Centrum on L after 7km. Take Sollentuna
exit, turn L & foll Sollentuna rd 265/262 for approx 5km. At
2nd set of traff lts with pylons adj, turn R on sm rd, clear
sp to site. Lge, pt sl, pt shd; wc; chem disp; mv service pnt;
baby facs; shwrs SEK10; EHU (10A) SEK45; lndry (inc dryer);
shops; snacks; playgrnd; fishing; boating; lake sw fr pontoons;
sat TV; some statics; dogs; bus; Quickstop o'night facs; Eng
spkn; quiet; CKE. "Conv Morby Centrum, lge shopping cent,
petrol, metro to city; pleasant walks in woods & lakeside." ♦
SEK 215   2011*

SWEDEN

STOCKHOLM *2H2* (10km SW Rural) *59.29558, 17.92300*
Bredäng Camping (A4), Stora Sällskapetväg, 12731
Skärholmen [(08) 977071; fax 7087262; bredangcamping@
telia.com; www.bredangcamping.se] Exit E4/E20 to
Bredäng junc 152 & foll sp to site. Lge, mkd/hdstg pitch nr ent
otherwise grass/unmkd, pt shd; htd wc; chem disp; serviced
pitches; mv service pnt; baby facs; sauna; shwrs inc; EHU (16A)
SEK40; lndry; shop; rest, snacks; bar; cooking facs; playgrnd;
lake & beach adj; bike hire; battery-charging; metro 700m;
Quickstop o'night facs; poss cr; quiet; ccard acc; red snr
citizens/LS. "Facs ltd LS & poss stretched in ssn; helpful staff;
overspill 3km at Sätra Camping; conv for Stockholm; shopping
cent & metro with free car park about 700m; access to
Stockholm also poss by lake steamer fr pier (high ssn) - 10 min
walk; well-run site." ♦ 28 Mar-6 Oct. SEK 325   2014*

STOCKHOLM *2H2* (2.5km W Urban) *59.32021, 18.03198*
Långholmens Motorcaravan Park (A11), Skutskepparvägen,
11733 Stockholm [(08) 6691890; info@autocamper-
stockholm.se; www.autocamper-stockholm.se]
Fr N foll sp Södermalm fr E4. Immed after x-ing Västerbron
(bdge) foll 'Autocamper' sp. Site under S end of bdge. Fr S foll
sp Södermalm, then sp Långholmen & site. Med, mkd pitch,
hdstg, unshd; wc; chem disp; mv service pnt; shwrs inc; EHU
(10A) SEK30; lndry (inc dryer); rest, bar, shop 300m; bike hire;
TV; adv bkg; Eng spkn; recep open 0700-2200; m'vans only;
security fence; constant rd noise; ccard acc; CKE. "Site under
flyover but conv city cent." 27 May-4 Sep. SEK 190   2009*

⊞ **STOCKHOLM** *2H2* (10km W Rural) *59.33731, 17.90105*
Ängby Campingplats (A3), Blackebergsvägen 25,
16850 Bromma [(08) 370420; fax 378226; reservation@
angbycamping.se; www.angbycamping.se]
On E4 fr Stockholm take rd 275 W twd Vällingby. At rndabt
turn L for rd 261 dir Ekerö, then R sp Sodra Ängby, site sp.
Med, mkd pitch, pt sl, pt shd; wc; chem disp; mv service pnt;
sauna; shwrs SEK5; baby facs; EHU SEK35; lndry (inc dryer);
shop; rest, snacks; bar; sand beach & lake sw adj; waterslide;
tennis; wifi; cab TV; some statics; dogs; phone; train; poss v cr;
Eng spkn; ltd facs LS; ccard acc; CKE/CCI. "Sh walk to metro
stn - 20 mins to city; gd situation; walk/cycle to Drottningsholm
Palace; some sm pitches; poss diff pitching for lge o'fits; lack
of privacy in shwrs; san facs stretched high ssn & need update;
workers living on site; site poss muddy after rain; helpful staff."
♦ SEK 322   2013*

STODE *1C3* (200m W Rural) *62.41585, 16.57015* **Stöde**
Camping (Y39), Kälsta 107, 86013 Stöde [(0691) 10180;
stodecampingstode@hotmail.com; www.stodecamping.
com] Fr S on rd 305 site on L after x-ing rv bdge. Fr Sundsvall
on E14 turn S onto rd 305, site on R after underpass. Sm, mkd
pitch, pt sl, pt shd; htd wc; chem disp; mv service pnt; baby
facs; fam bthrm; EHU (16A) SEK30; lndry (inc dryer); shop
500m; snacks; playgrnd; htd pool & sports facs adj; paddling
pool; lake sw adj; fishing; boat hire; tennis; TV rm; some statics;
dogs; phone; Eng spkn; adv bkg; quiet; red long stay; CKE/CCI.
"Well-kept, friendly site." 15 May-30 Oct. SEK 140   2011*

STORUMAN *1C2* (200m NW Rural) *65.10022, 17.11427*
Storumans Camping (AC5), Lokgränd 3, 92331 Storuman
[(0951) 14300; storumanscamping@storuman.se;
www.storuman.se] On Lake Storuman, site sp fr rd 45/E12.
Med, pt shd; wc; chem disp; mv service pnt; sauna; baby facs;
shwrs inc; EHU (10A) SEK50; lndry (inc dryer); shop; rest, snacks
200m; playgrnd; lake sw & beach adj; watersports; boat hire;
tennis; bike hire; TV; quiet; ccard acc; CKE. "Ltd facs LS." ♦
1 Apr-30 Sep. SEK 165   2011*

⊞ **STROMSTAD** *2E2* (3km S Coastal) *58.91350, 11.20531*
Camping Lagunen (O3), Skärsbygdsvägen 40, 45297
Strömstad [(0526) 755000; fax 12367; info@lagunen.se;
www.lagunen.se] On Uddevalla rd 176 out of Strömstad.
Site on L. Lge, pt sl, pt shd; wc; mv service pnt; baby facs;
shwrs; EHU inc; lndry (inc dryer); shop; rest, snacks; bar;
cooking facs; playgrnd; beach adj; boat & bike hire; wifi; TV rm;
some statics; dogs; poss cr; adv bkg; quiet; ccard acc; red LS.
SEK 280   2013*

⊞ **STROMSTAD** *2E2* (5km S Coastal) *58.9039, 11.20011*
Daftö Feriecenter (O4), Dafter 2511, 45297 Strömstad
[(0526) 26040; fax 26250; info@dafto.com; www.dafto.com]
Fr Uddevalla E6 exit at sp Strömstad, turn L at sp approx 6km
on R. Fr Oslo exit E6 sp Strömstad; foll ring rd 176 round E
side town; foll sp Daftö; site on R. V lge, pt sl, pt shd; wc;
mv service pnt; some serviced pitches; baby facs; sauna;
shwrs inc; EHU (10A) SEK50; lndry (inc dryer); shop; rest,
snacks high ssn; bar; cooking facs; playgrnd; htd pool; sand
beach; lake sw; boating; canoeing; fishing; games area; wifi;
entmnt; 15% statics; Quickstop o'night facs; site clsd Xmas
to 8 Jan; poss cr; adv bkg ess in ssn; quiet; ccard acc; CKE.
"Holiday complex with many children's activities; busy at w/
end; quiet during wk; views fr some pitches." ♦ SEK 425
(5 persons)   2010*

STROMSTAD *2E2* (12km S Coastal) *58.8832, 11.14253*
Bofors Camping (O62), Korsnäs Tjärnö 2821, 45296
Strömstad [(0526) 25036; birgittahyft@hotmail.com;
www.boforscamping.com] Fr S exit E6 L at sp Strömstad;
after 5km turn L at sp Tjarnö 7km (pass Camp Daftö on R);
after 5km turn R at sp Befors Camping 2; site on L. Fr N exit
E6 R of Strömstad; foll as above. Lge, mkd pitch, pt sl, pt
shd; wc; chem disp; shwrs SEK5; EHU (10A) SEK35; lndry (inc
dryer); shop; sand beach adj; fishing; boat-launching facs;
wifi; 60% statics; dogs; Eng spkn; adv bkg; quiet; ccard acc.
"Attractive rocky coast with sandy bays; v busy - rec adv bkg."
1 May-15 Sep. SEK 245   2011*

STROMSTAD *2E2* (4km NW Coastal) *58.95741, 11.14763*
Seläters Camping (O48), Norrkärr, 45290 Strömstad
[(0526) 12290; fax 12238; info@selater.se; www.selater.se]
Exit E6 at sp Strömstad; foll sps to Seläter; site on R. V lge,
mkd pitch, pt shd; wc; mv service pnt; baby facs; shwrs inc;
EHU (10A) SEK50; lndry (inc dryer); shop; rest; playgrnd; beach
800m; watersports; tennis 500m; golf 1km; wifi; 10% statics;
bus; phone; dogs; Quickstop o'night facs; CKE. "Pleasant
countryside; well-run site." ♦ 1 Apr-30 Sep. SEK 250   2010*

⊞ **STROMSUND** *1B3* (1km SW Rural) *63.84651, 15.53378* Strömsunds Camping (Z3), Näsviken, 83324 Strömsund [(0670) 16410; fax 13705; turism@stromsund.se or stromsund.turistbyra@stromsund.se; www.stromsund.se/ stromsundscamping] W of rd 45, over bdge S of main town on lakeside. Lge, pt sl, pt shd; htd wc; chem disp; mv service pnt; baby facs; shwrs SEK5; EHU (10A) SEK30; lndry (inc dryer); shop adj, rest, snacks; cooking facs; playgrnd; pool; paddling pool; fishing; bike & boat hire; wifi; 10% statics; dogs; phone; quiet; cccard acc; CKE. "In 2 parts: W side has main facs but E quieter; go to g'ge adj when site office clsd." ♦ SEK 223   2014*

SUNDSVALL *1C3* (4km SE Urban/Coastal) *62.3585, 17.37016* Fläsians Camping & Stugor (Y26), Norrstigen 15, 85468 Sundsvall [(060) 554475; fax 569601; bernt.ostling@gmail. com] Clear sps on E4 in both dirs; site on E coast side of rd. Med, mkd pitch, terr, pt shd; htd wc; chem disp; mv service pnt; baby facs; shwrs inc; EHU (10A) SEK35; lndry (inc dryer); shop on site & 2km; rest; cooking facs; playgrnd; sand beach adj; fishing; poss cr; quiet; adv bkg; Eng spkn; ccard acc; CKE. "Sea view all pitches; gd access even in wet; suitable RVs & twin-axles; if recep clsd, site yourself & pay later; helpful staff; some traff noise; sw pools in Sundsvall; clean san facs." ♦ 15 May-31 Aug. SEK 200   2013*

⊞ **SVEG** *1B3* (700m S Rural) *62.03241, 14.36496* Svegs Camping (Z32), Kyrkogränd 1, 84232 Sveg [(0680) 13025; fax 10337; info@svegscamping.se] Just S of traff lts at junc rds 45 & 84. Opp Statoil at rear of rest, well sp. Med, mkd pitch, pt shd; htd wc; chem disp; shwrs inc; EHU (16A) SEK25; lndry (inc dryer); rest, bar nrby; snacks; playgrnd; pool 500m; bike hire; games area; TV; some statics; dogs; phone; some rd noise; ccard acc; CKE. "Gd for sh stay/NH; many cabins used as long stay family units." SEK 264   2014*

⊞ **TIMMERNABBEN** *2G3* (1.5km S Rural/Coastal) *56.94405, 16.46708* Camping Timmernabben, Varvsvägen 29, 38052 Timmernabben [(0499) 23809; fax 23871; timmernabben-camp@telia.com] Turn off E22, site sp. Med, mkd pitch, pt sl, shd; htd wc; chem disp; baby facs; shwrs; EHU (10A) inc; lndry (inc dryer); BBQ; playgrnd; shgl beach adj; tennis; games area; internet; Eng spkn; quiet. CKE/CCI. "Tranquil site; delightful views; gd walking & windsurfing; paths on site not wheelchair-friendly." SEK 266   2009*

TIVED *2F2* (2km N Rural) *58.79855, 14.5371* Camping Tiveden (T24), Baggekärr 2, 69597 Tived [(0584) 474083; fax 474044; info@campingtiveden.com; www.campingtiveden.com] Fr Karlsborg N on rd 202 to Undernäs. Turn R dir Tived, site on L in 2km. Med, mkd pitch, pt shd; wc; chem disp; mv waste; baby facs; shwrs SEK5; EHU (10A) SEK40; lndry (inc dryer); shop 2km; snacks; playgrnd; sand beach 15km; lake sw adj; boat & bike hire; fishing; dogs; some statics; poss cr; Eng spkn; quiet; CKE/CCI. "Friendly owners; gd walks; conv Tiveden National Park & Göta Canal; excel." ♦ 1 Apr-30 Sep. SEK 145180   2011*

TOMELILLA *2F4* (800m N Urban) *55.54578, 13.95856* Väla Camping, Folkets Park, Parkgatan 4, 27380 Tomelilla [(0417) 18110; fax 14400; www.tomelilla.se/en/turism/] Fr Ystad take rd 19 NE to Tomelilla; foll sp in town cent; recep at sw pool kiosk. Sm, mkd pitch, pt sl, pt shd; wc; chem disp; sauna; shwrs; EHU (10A) SEK30; lndry; shop & snacks 500m; BBQ; cooking facs; playgrnd; htd pool adj; some statics; dogs; Eng spkn; quiet; CKE. "Well-situated for historic sites, coastal towns; some traff noise at rush hrs." 1 Jun-1 Sep. SEK 125   2009*

TOREKOV *2E3* (1km N Coastal) *56.43540, 12.63700* FirstCamp Båstad (L9), Flymossavägen 5, 26093 Torekov [tel/fax (0431) 364525; torekov@firstcamp.se; www.firstcamp.se] Exit E6 onto rd 115 & head for Torekov, site on R bef Torekov. Lge, pt sl, pt shd; htd wc; chem disp; mv service pnt; baby facs; fam bthrm; sauna; shwrs inc; EHU (10A); lndry (inc dryer); shop; rest, snacks; bar; cooking facs; playgrnd; pool; beach adj; fishing; watersports; bike hire; games rm; golf; wifi; cab TV; 10% statics; bus 800m; poss v cr high ssn; CKE. "Gd sea fishing; pitches cramped high ssn; Båstad picturesque town." ♦ 15 Apr-25 Sep. SEK 383   2010*

⊞ **TORSBY** *2F1* (20km N Rural) *60.30529, 13.04200* Abbas Stugby & Camping, Nötön 1, 68594 Torsby [(0560) 30360; fax 30361; info@abbasstugby.se; www.abbasstugby.se] N fr Torsby on E45 for approx 20km, turn L after Vägsjöfors at site sp. Sm, pt sl, pt shd; htd wc; chem disp; baby facs; shwrs inc; EHU (10A) SEK40; lndry (inc dryer); rest, snacks; bar; BBQ; cooking facs; playgrnd; lake sw adj; games area; bike & boat hire; wifi; entmnt; some statics; dogs; Eng spkn; adv bkg; quiet; ccard acc; CKE. "Vg site." SEK 160   2009*

TORSBY *2F1* (5km S Rural) *60.09168, 13.03045* Torsby Camping Svenneby (S21), Bredviken, 685 33 Torsby [(0560) 71095; info@torsbycamping.se; www.torsby camping.se] On shore of Lake Fryken, sp fr rd 45. Med; wc; chem disp; mv service pnt; baby facs; sauna; shwrs SEK5; EHU (10A) inc; lndry (inc dryer); shop; rest, snacks; bar; playgrnd; lake sw; watersports; wifi; entmnt; TV; 80% statics; dogs; quiet; red long stay; ccard acc; CKE/CCI. 1 May-15 Sep. SEK 260   2014*

TORSLANDA see Göteborg *2E3*

⊞ **TRANAS** *2F2* (3km E Rural) *58.03548, 15.0309* Hättebadens Camping (F1), Hätte, 57382 Tranås [(0140) 17482; fax 68404; hattebaden@tranas.se; www.hattecamping.se] On W edge Lake Sommen on rd 131, sp. Med, mkd pitch, pt shd; wc; mv service pnt; baby facs; shwrs; EHU (10A) SEK40; lndry (inc dryer); sm shop, rest, snacks adj; bar; playgrnd; lake sw; fishing; boating; bike hire; wifi; 20% statics; dogs; phone; Quickstop o'night facs; Eng spkn; ccard acc; CKE/ CCI. "Generous pitches; spacious site; gd, clean facs." ♦ SEK 180   2009*

⊞ **TRELLEBORG** *2E4* (2.5km E Coastal) *55.3638, 13.20933* Camping Dalabadet, Dalköpingestrandväg 2, 23132 Trelleborg [(0410) 14905; fax 45068] Bet sea shore & rd 9 (Trelleborg-Ystad), E of town. Foll sp fr town. Med, shd; htd wc; chem disp; mv service pnt; baby facs; sauna; shwrs inc; EHU (10A) SEK30; lndry; shop, rest nr; cooking facs; playgrnd; beach; tennis; cab TV; 20% statics; dogs; phone; ccard acc; CKE. "Conv for ferries; gd." ♦ SEK 200   2009*

TROLLHATTAN *2E2* (1km N Urban) *58.29206, 12.29848*
Trollhättans Camping Hjulkvarnelund (P7),
Kungsportsvägen 7, 46139 Trollhättan [(0520) 30613;
fax 32961; folketspark.trollhattan@telia.com; www.
trollhattansfp.se/camping] Foll rd 45, site sp adj rv/canal.
Med, pt sl, pt shd; wc; chem disp; mv service pnt; baby facs;
shwrs inc; EHU (10A) SEK40; lndry (inc dryer); shops 1km;
playgrnd; htd pool 300m; tennis; cycles; dogs; poss cr; Eng
spkn; no adv bkg; some train & rd noise; CKE. "Access to
Trollhätte Canal; beautiful, spacious wooded site; easy walk to
town & impressive gorge/waterfall; modern, clean san facs poss
stretched high ssn." ♦ 2 May-4 Sep. SEK 150   2011*

⊞ **TROLLHATTAN** *2E2* (5km S Rural) *58.23946, 12.23605*
Stenrösets Camping (P25), Assarebo Stenröset 2, 46198
Trollhättan [(0520) 70710; fax 70811; stenroset.camping@
telia.com; www.stenrosetscamping.se] Site visible & sp
fr rd 45. Sm, sl, pt shd; htd wc (cont); mv service pnt; baby
facs; shwrs inc; EHU (10A) SEK30; lndry (inc dryer); shop;
BBQ; cooking facs; playgrnd; wifi; 5% statics; dogs; phone;
quiet; Eng spkn; adv bkg; some rd noise; red long stay; ccard
acc; CKE. "Helpful owners; conv Göteborg (60km); scenic
surroundings & interesting area." ♦ SEK 170   2009*

TROSA *2H2* (3km S Coastal) *58.87288, 17.57431* **Trosa Havsbad**
Camping (D12), Rävuddsvägen 40, 61922 Trosa [(0156) 12494;
info@trosahavsbad.se; www.trosahavsbad.se] Exit E4 at junc
138 onto rd 218 twd Trosa, site sp dir harbour. Lge, pt sl, pt
shd; htd wc; baby facs; chem disp; mv service pnt; shwrs; EHU
(10A) SEK40; lndry (inc dryer); shops 3km; snacks; playgrnd;
sand beach; lge sailing marina; fishing; tennis; cycling; wifi;
30% statics; dogs; phone; poss cr; quiet; CKE. ♦
17 Apr-26 Sep. SEK 200   2010*

TYLOSAND see Halmstad *2E3*

⊞ **UDDEVALLA** *2E2* (9.5km W Rural) *58.3306, 583306* **Unda**
Camping (O30), Unda 149, 45194 Uddevalla [(0522) 86347;
fax 86392; info@undacamping.se; www.undacamping.se]
Exit E6 junc 96 Uddevalla N onto rte 44 twd Uddevalla
Centrum. Site sp in 1km on R. Lge, pt sl, pt shd; htd wc; chem
disp; mv service pnt; baby facs; shwrs SEK5; EHU (10A)
SEK50; lndry (inc dryer); shop; rest; bar; cooking facs; playgrnd;
pool; beach sw; fishing; boat & bike hire; wifi; TV; many statics;
phone; o'flow area when full; Quickstop o'night facs; adv bkg;
ccard acc; CKE. "Lovely situation in nature reserve; recep hrs
erratic LS; cr in high ssn." ♦ SEK 310   2015*

⊞ **UDDEVALLA** *2E2* (15km W Coastal) *58.31470, 11.72310*
Hafsten SweCamp Resort (O28), Hafsten 120, 45196
Uddevalla [(0522) 644117; fax 644480; info@hafsten.se;
www.hafsten.se] Fr S take rd 160 thro Island of Orust, 1km
N of bdge turn E at site sp for 4km. Fr N, turn W off E6 at junc
96 onto rd 161 sp Lysekil/Fiskebäcksil, after 8km at Rotviksbro
rndabt turn onto rd 160 twd Orust. Turn L (E) in 2km, sp as
above. App rd narr with passing places. Lge, pt shd, pt sl, terr;
htd wc; chem disp; mv service pnt; baby facs; sauna; shwrs
SEK5; EHU (10A) inc; gas; lndry (inc dryer); shop; snacks; bar;
cooking facs; playgrnd; sand beach adj; fishing; tennis; boat &
bike hire; pedalos; horseriding; wifi; TV rm; 50% statics; dogs;
phone; bus 4km; Quickstop o'night facs; poss cr & noisy high
ssn; ccard acc; CKE. "Excel location; helpful staff; gd facs block;
steel or rock pegs req for awnings; o'flow field used in high ssn
- no facs." ♦ SEK 315 (CChq acc)   2009*

ULRICEHAMN *2F3* (2km S Rural) *57.77055, 13.40173* **Camping**
Skotteksgården (P34), Gamla Marbäcksvägen, 52390
Ulricehamn [(0321) 13184; fax 35185; skotteksgarden@
telia.com; www.skottek.cc] On rd 40 take dir Centrum. Foll
sp Skotteksgården to Tranemo. Sm, mkd pitch, hdstg, unshd;
htd wc; mv service pnt; serviced pitches; baby facs; fam bthrm;
sauna; shwrs inc; EHU (10A) SEK45; lndry (inc dryer); shop on site
& 1.5km; rest, snacks; cooking facs; playgrnd; lake sw adj;
fishing; bike & boat hire; 10% statics; dogs; phone; quiet;
ccard acc; CKE. "Friendly, helpful owner; cycle path adj." ♦
15 Apr-15 Oct. SEK 195   2009*

⊞ **ULRICEHAMN** *2F3* (12km S Rural) *57.67870, 13.37535*
Vegby Camping (P35), Storgatan 2, 52011 Vegby
[(0321) 72912; fax 72562; vegbycamping@hotmail.com;
www.vegbycamping.com] Fr Ulricehamn take rd 157 on
rd 157. Turn R at Gällstad & foll sp for Vegby & site. Med, terr,
unshd; wc; chem disp; mv service pnt; baby facs; sauna; shwrs
inc; EHU (10A) SEK35; lndry (inc dryer); shop; snacks; cooking
facs; playgrnd; pool nr; lake sw; fishing; wifi; TV; Eng spkn;
quiet; ccard acc; red LS; CKE/CCI. "Vg site; lake views fr all
pitches; cycle rtes nr." SEK 190   2009*

⊞ **UMEA** *1C3* (5km NE Coastal) *63.84210, 20.33815*
FirstCamp Umeå (AC12), Nydalasjön 2, 90654 Umeå
[(090) 702600; fax 702610; umea@firstcamp.se;
www.firstcamp.se] Sp fr E4 to N of town on lakeside. Lge,
mkd pitch, pt shd; wc; chem disp; mv service pnt; 30% serviced
pitches; shwrs inc; EHU (10A) inc; lndry (inc dryer); shop;
snacks; playgrnd; htd pool complex; waterslide; lake sw 500m;
tennis; games area; games rm; wifi; some statics; bus; ccard
acc; CKE. "Attractive site; lge pitches suitable RVs & twin-axles;
excel service block; conv E4." ♦ SEK 260   2009*

⊞ **UPPSALA** *2H1* (1.5km N Urban) *59.87133, 17.61923*
Fyrishov Camping (C12), Idrottsgatan 2, 75333 Uppsala
[(018) 7274960; fax 244333; info@fyrishov.se;
www.fyrishov.se] Exit E4 Uppsala N; in 300m at rndabt foll
sp Strangnas, Sala. In 2.25km exit via slip rd sp Bjorklinge,
Fyrishov. At rndabt foll sp Fyrishov, in 1.6km at traff lts turn R
& immed R. Site in Fyrishov Park adj sw & sports complex. Med,
unshd; wc; chem disp; mv service pnt; shwrs SEK5; EHU (10A)
SEK45; lndry (inc dryer); shop adj; rest adj; snacks; playgrnd;
pool adj (sports complex behind pool); bus; poss cr; no adv
bkg; ccard acc; CKE. "Within easy access of city cent; fair NH."
♦ ltd. SEK 180   2010*

URSHULT *2F3* (1km N Rural) *56.54476, 14.80703*
Urshults Camping (G7), Sirkövägen 19, 36013 Urshult
[(0477) 20243; fax 48046; info@urshult-camping.com;
www.urshult-camping.com] Rd 30 S fr Växjö, turn W
onto rd 120 at Tingsryd. In 10km at Urshult turn R, site sp
on lakeside. Med, pt shd; htd wc; chem disp; mv service pnt;
baby facs; shwrs; EHU (10A) SEK45; lndry (inc dryer); shop;
snacks; cooking facs; playgrnd; lake sw adj; 10% statics; dogs;
Eng spkn; quiet; CKE. "Well-run site; nr Kurrebo gardens &
museum; vg." ♦ 25 Apr-25 Oct. SEK 165   2009*

URSHULT *2F3* (10km NW Rural) *56.58466, 14.69491* **Getnö Gård Naturcamping (G24), Lake Åsnen Resort, 36010 Ryd [(0477) 24011; fax 24049; info@getnogard.se; www.getnogard.se]** W fr Urshult on rte 120 to junc with rte 126; turn NW onto rte 126, site in 7km via Ålshult to Getnö Gård. Site on shore Lake Åsnen. Med, mkd pitch, pt sl, pt shd; htd wc; chem disp; mv service pnt; baby facs; shwrs inc; EHU (10A) SEK45; lndry (inc dryer); shop; rest, snacks; bar; cooking facs; playgrnd; lake & private shgl beach adj; fishing; canoe hire; some statics; dogs; phone; poss cr; Eng spkn; adv bkg; red long stay; quiet; CKE. "Beautiful location in private nature reserve; well-kept facs." ◆ ltd. 1 May-10 Oct. SEK 195   2009*

VADSTENA *2F2* (4km NE Rural) *58.46448, 14.9334* **Vadstena Camping (E9), Vätterviksbadets, 59230 Vadstena [(0143) 12730; info@vadstenacamping.se; www.vadstena camping.se]** On rd 50, 3km N of Vadstena by Lake Vattern. Lge, mkd pitch, pt shd; wc; chem disp; mv service pnt; sauna; shwrs inc; EHU (10A) SEK50; lndry (inc dryer); shop; snacks; cooking facs; playgrnd; htd pool 3km; waterslide; sand beach & lake adj; fishing; tennis; wifi; 20% statics; dogs; poss cr; Eng spkn; adv bkg; ccard acc; red LS; CKE. "Many local attractions; vg family site; cycle path to town; gd birdwatching nrby; lakeside site with beach." ◆ 1 May-12 Sep. SEK 346   2015*

VAGGERYD *2F3* (500m N Rural) *57.50973, 14.1327* **Hjortsjöns Camping (F8), Badplatsvägen, 56731 Vaggeryd [(0393) 12262; hjortsjonscamping@vaggeryd.se; www.hjortsjonscamping.com]** Site is at E side of lake; take turning at N app to Vaggeryd. Med, mkd pitch, pt sl, pt shd; wc; chem disp; baby facs; shwrs; EHU (10A) SEK40; lndry (inc dryer); shop; snacks; cooking facs; playgrnd; lake sw; fishing & boating adj; dogs; phone; quiet; CKE. "Lakeside site with woodland walks; gd touring base." ◆ 16 May-18 Sep. SEK 150   2009*

VANERSBORG *2E2* (3km N Coastal) *58.4122, 12.3208* **Ursands Camping (P6), Ursandsvägen, 46221 Vänersborg [(0521) 18666; ursandscamping@telia.com; www.ursands camping.se]** On rd 45 heading N over rv bdge to site on R in 2km; sp fr bdge. Med, shd; wc; baby facs; mv service pnt; shwrs SEK7; EHU (10A) SEK40; lndry (inc dryer); shop high ssn; rest; bar; cooking facs; playgrnd; sand beach & lake sw; fishing; boating; bike hire; wifi; TV; Quickstop o'night facs; poss cr; adv bkg; quiet; ccard acc; CKE. "Pleasant, family site." ◆ 23 Apr-12 Sep. SEK 205   2010*

VARBERG *2E3* (8km N Coastal) *57.1826, 12.22076* **Kärradals Camping (N7), Torpavägen 21, 43295 Varberg [(0340) 622377 or (0708) 975806 (mob); fax 623576; brink@karradalscamping.se; www.karradalscamping.se]** Fr S exit E6 junc 55 Varberg N & foll sp Tångeberg & Kärradal. Fr N exit junc 56 & foll sp Värö & Åskloster, then Kärradal & site. Lge, mkd pitch, pt shd; wc; chem disp; mv service pnt; baby facs; shwrs SEK1; EHU SEK40; lndry (inc dryer); shop; rest, snacks; bar; cooking facs; playgrnd; sand beach 500m; games area; bike hire; wifi; TV rm; 80% statics; dogs; phone; poss cr; Eng spkn; rlwy noise; ccard acc; CKE/CCI. "Rec arrive early afternoon high ssn; o'flow field has minimal san facs, but clean." ◆ 23 Apr-5 Sep. SEK 340   2013*

VARBERG *2E3* (5km NW Coastal) *57.1165, 12.21426* **Getteröns Camping (N6), Valvikavägen 1-3, 43293 Varberg [(0340) 16885; fax 10422; info@getteronscamping.se; www.getteronscamping.se]** Exit E6/E20 junc 54 Varberg Centrum, then W dir Getterön, site sp. V lge, mkd pitch, unshd; htd wc; mv service pnt; baby facs; sauna; shwrs; EHU (6A) SEK45; lndry (inc dryer); snacks; shop adj; playgrnd; sand beach 200m; fishing; bike hire; wifi; entmnt; 50% statics; dogs; phone; poss cr; ccard acc; CKE. "Conv ferry to Denmark; Varberg pleasant town; lge nature reserve nr; gd beach walk; clean san facs; well laid-out site." ◆ 25 Apr-14 Sep. SEK 290   2015*

VARNAMO *2F3* (500m N Rural) *57.19055, 14.04615* **Värnamo Camping (F10), Prostsjön, 33183 Värnamo [(0370) 16660; fax 47150; info@varnamocamping.se]** Exit E4 Värnamo N, foll site sp. Site is 2km W of E4. Med, pt shd; wc; mv service pnt; baby facs; shwrs SEK5; EHU (10A) SEK40; lndry (inc dryer); shop high ssn; rest, snacks 500m; cooking facs; playgrnd; lake sw; fishing; boating; cycling; games rm; wifi; TV; 20% statics; dogs; phone; quiet; red CKE. "NH only; not particularly welcoming." ◆ 1 May-15 Sep. SEK 230   2010*

⊞ **VASTERVIK** *2G3* (3km SE Coastal) *57.73823, 16.66846* **Camping Lysingsbadets (H3), Lysingsvägen, 593 53 Västervik [(0490) 258000; fax 254855; lysingsbadet@ vastervik.se; www.lysingsbadet.se]** On coast 3km SE of town. Fr E22 foll sp around S ring rd; on app to Västervik. Site well sp fr E22. V lge, pt shd; htd wc; chem disp; mv service pnt; serviced pitches; sauna; shwrs inc; EHU (10A) inc; lndry (inc dryer); shop; 2 rests high ssn; snacks; bar; cooking facs; playgrnd; htd pool; waterslide; sand beach adj; boat & bike hire; tennis; golf; wifi; entmnt; some statics; dogs; o'night area for m'vans; ccard acc. "Lovely, family site in landscaped, coastal woodland; easy access to islands by wooden footbdge fr site." ◆ SEK 455   2013*

VATTERSMALEN see Gränna *2F2*

VAXHOLM *2H1* (2km W Coastal) *59.40508, 18.3047* **Waxholm Strand & Camping (B6), Eriksövägen, 18521 Vaxholm [(08) 54130101; info@waxholmstrand.com; www.vaxholmstrand.com]** On rd 274 turn R immed after x-ing bdge to Vaxholm Island, foll sp 'Eriksö Camping'. Med, mkd pitch, pt sl, unshd; wc; chem disp; mv service pnt; shwrs inc; EHU SEK40; lndry (inc dryer); shop 1km; rest, snacks; playgrnd; sand beach adj; wifi; some statics; dogs; phone; adv bkg; quiet; ccard acc; CKE. "35 mins drive fr Stockholm; boat trips, bike hire, ferry terminal Vaxholm-Stockholm 3.3km." ◆ 30 Apr-25 Sep. SEK 210   2015*

⊞ **VAXJO** *2F3* (5km N Rural) *56.92216, 14.81905* **Växjö SweCamp Evedal (G16), 35263 Växjö [(0470) 63034; fax 63122; evedals.camping@telia.com; www.evedals camping.com]** Sp fr Växjö on E23. Med, pt shd; htd wc; chem disp; baby facs; sauna; shwrs inc; EHU (10A) SEK50; lndry (inc dryer); shop; rest adj; playgrnd; sand beach; watersports; bike hire; wifi; TV; some statics; dogs; quiet; red 7+ days; ccard acc; CKE. "Ideal for children; in lakeside park in cent of glass industry; Kroneberg castle adj; Småland Museum in Växjö." SEK 225   2011*

VEGBY see Ulricehamn *2F3*

VENJAN *1B4* (1km E Rural) *60.9537, 13.93021* **Venjans Camping, Moravägen, 79293 Venjan [(0250) 62310; fax 62350; info@venjanscamping.se; www.venjanscamping. se]** Fr E45 turn W 3km N of junc of E45/64. Site in 18km, sp. Sm, mkd pitch, pt shd; htd wc; chem disp; mv service pnt; shwrs SEK5; EHU (10A) SEK35; lndry; shop 1km; playgrnd; lake sw & sand beach adj; fishing; boat hire; dogs; phone; Eng spkn; adv bkg; quiet; CKE. ♦ 1 Jun-31 Aug. SEK 130   2010*

VILHELMINA *1C2* (1.5km SE Rural) *64.62131, 16.67846* **Saiva Camping (AC4), Baksjön 1, 91231 Vilhelmina [(0940) 10760; info@saiva.se; www.saiva.se]** Sp on E site of rd 45. Med, pt shd; htd wc; chem disp; baby facs; shwrs SEK1; EHU (10A) SEK30; lndry (inc dryer); shop; snacks; playgrnd; lake beach; tennis; bike hire; wifi; TV; some statics; dogs; phone; poss cr; quiet; ccard acc; CKE. "Gd; excel san facs in log style cabins, v helpful staff, lovely lakeside setting." ♦
20 May-1 Oct. SEK 160   2011*

⊞ **VILHELMINA** *1C2* (5km NW Rural) *64.64998, 16.59240* **Kolgärdens Camping, Lövhöjden 16, 91292 Vilhelmina [(0940) 10304; kolgarden@vilhelmina.ac; www.kolgarden.se]** Site sp fr E45 N of Vilhelmina. Sm, pt shd; htd wc; chem disp; mv service pnt; sauna; shwrs inc; EHU (10A) SEK35; lndry; shop 5km; cooking facs; fishing; internet; TV rm; 50% statics; dogs; Eng spkn; quiet. "Wonderful lakeside location; clean san facs; helpful, pleasant owner; highly rec." ♦ ltd. SEK 145   2011*

VINSLOV *2F4* (500m N Rural) *56.10988, 13.91245* **Vinslövs Camping (L2), Troed Nelsongatan 18, 28834 Vinslöv [(070) 2077679; info@vinslovscamping.se]** Site sp of rte 21. Sm, mkd pitch, pt shd; wc; chem disp; shwrs inc; EHU (6A) SEK40; lndry (inc dryer) shop 500m; cooking facs; rest, snacks, bar 500m; playgrnd; htd pool adj; 20% statics; dogs; bus 500m; quiet; CKE. ♦ 1 Apr-30 Sep. SEK 120   2010*

⊞ **VITTSJO** *2F4* (1km N Rural) *56.35106, 13.66541* **Vittsjö Camping, Campingvägen 1, 28022 Vittsjö [(0451) 22489; v.turistforening@telia.com; www.vittsjocamping.se]** Well sp on N edge of vill on rd 117 by Lake Vittsjö, approx 20km N of Hässleholm. Sm, mkd pitch, hdstg, pt shd; htd wc; chem disp; mv service pnt; baby facs; shwrs inc; EHU (16A); lndry; shop & 2km; rest 2km; snacks; cooking facs; playgrnd; lake sw adj; bike hire; wifi; 40% statics; dogs; Eng spkn; quiet; CKE. "Family-run site; security barrier; gd." SEK 160   2010*

YSTAD *2F4* (3km E Coastal) *55.43286, 13.8650* **Camping Sandskogens (M15), Österleden, 27160 Ystad [(0411) 19270; fax 19169; info@sandskogenscamping.se; www.sandskogenscamping.se]** On N side of rd 9. Lge, mkd pitch, shd; wc; chem disp; mv service pnt; baby facs; shwrs SEK5; EHU (10A) SEK40; lndry (inc dryer); shop; rest 400m; playgrnd; paddling pool; sand beach 100m; wifi; TV; some statics; dogs; phone; no adv bkg; rlwy noise; ccard acc; CKE. "On Baltic coast; cycle path to beautiful town; mkd walks nrby; gd site, well-managed site; extremely helpful Eng spkn staff; high ssn expect queues checking in; CKE card req; metered shwrs; Wallander tv series studios nr site, tours avail." ♦
17 Apr-21 Sep. SEK 325   2014*

OLAND ISLAND

BORGHOLM *2G3* (12km S Coastal) *56.7933, 16.5664* **Ekerums Camping & Stugor SweCamp (H26), 38792 Borgholm [(0485) 564700; fax 564701; info@ekerum.nu; www.ekerum.nu]** Cross land bdge fr Kalmar, turn N, site sp on rd 136 bet Färjestaden & Borgholm. V lge, shd; htd wc; chem disp; mv service pnt; baby facs; shwrs inc; EHU (10A) inc; lndry (inc dryer); shop; rest, snacks; bar; cooking facs; playgrnd; 2 htd pools; waterslide; sand/shgl beach adj; fishing; boating; golf 1km; bike hire; tennis 1km; wifi; TV rm; 20% statics; dogs; phone; Quickstop o'night facs; quiet; CKE. "Excel family site; private san facs avail; Borgholm castle worth visit." ♦
11 Apr-2 Oct. SEK 300 (CChq acc)   2009*

BYXELKROK *2G3* (1km N Coastal) *57.33013, 17.01211* **Neptuni Camping (H41), Småskogsvägen 2, 38075 Byxelkrok [(0485) 28495 or 070 5428495 (mob); neptuni. camping@telia.com; www.neptunicamping.se]** Fr S on rd 136 thro Böda, at Byxelkrok turn R past harbour for 200m. Site on R. Med, pt shd; wc; chem disp; mv service pnt; shwrs SEK5; EHU (16A) SEK40; lndry (inc dryer); shop; playgrnd; beach adj; games area; dogs; phone; Eng spkn; quiet; ccard acc; CKE. "Conv touring base N Öland, sh walk to harbour, rest & supmkt." ♦ 30 Apr-31 Aug. SEK 170   2009*

> ## "That's changed – Should I let The Club know?"
>
> If you find something on site that's different from the site entry, fill in a report and let us know. See www.caravanclub.co.uk/europereport.

⊞ **DEGERHAMN** *2G4* (12km S Rural) *56.23778, 16.4530* **Ottenby Vandrarhem & Camping (H57), Ottenby 106, 38065 Degerhamn [(0485) 662062; fax 662161; info@ ottenbyvandrarhem.se; www.ottenbyvandrarhem.se]** Rd 36 S to Ottenby, bear R for 4km, site on R at youth hostel. Sm, unshd; htd wc; chem disp; mv service pnt; baby facs; shwrs inc; EHU (10A) SEK40; lndry (inc dryer); shop 5km; cooking facs; htd pool; paddling pool; bike hire; 10% statics; dogs free; phone; quiet; ccard acc. "On edge Ottenby nature reserve; excel walks & birdwatching - ssn geared to bird migration; poss noise fr late arr & early risers as no barrier; World Heritage Site on S pt of island." ♦ SEK 210   2014*

FARJESTADEN *2G3* (1km N Coastal) *56.68681, 16.48253* **Krono Camping Saxnäs/Öland (H25), Södra Saxnäs, 38695 Färjestaden [(0485) 35700; info@kcsaxnas.se; www.kcsaxnas.se]** Cross Öland Bdge fr Kalmar on rd 137, take exit for Öland Zoo/Saxnäs. Site sp. Lge, mkd pitch, pt shd; wc; chem disp; mv service pnt; baby facs; 25% serviced pitches; shwrs inc; EHU (10A) inc (poss rev pol); lndry; shop; rest; bar; playgrnd; shgl beach adj; games area; sat TV inc; some statics; dogs; phone; adv bkg; poss noisy high ssn; ccard acc; red LS; CKE. "Öland is beautiful island with 400 19thC windmills." ♦ 12 Apr-2 Oct. SEK 350   2011*

LOTTORP *2G3* (3km N Coastal) *57.17876, 17.03746* **Sonjas Camping (H39), John Emils Gata 43, 38074 Löttorp [(0485) 23212; fax 23255; info@sonjascamping.se; www.sonjascamping.oland.com]** Fr Kalmar over bdge to Öland Island, take rd 136 N thro Borgholm. Cont to Löttorp, site sp. Lge, mkd pitch, pt shd; htd wc; chem disp; mv service pnt; fam bthrm; baby facs; sauna; shwrs SEK5; EHU (10A) SEK45; lndry (inc dryer); shop; rest, snacks; bar; cooking facs; playgrnd; htd pool; paddling pool; sand beach adj; fishing; tennis; bike hire; wifi; entmnt; 10% statics; adv bkg; quiet. CKE. "Vg beach; excel family site; vg touring base." ♦ 21 Apr-4 Oct. SEK 250 (6 persons) 2010*

MELLBODA *2G3* (500m E Coastal) *57.23891, 17.0698* **Böda Hamns Camping (H43), Bödahamnsvägen 42, 38074 Mellböda [(0485) 22043; fax 22457; info@bodahamns camping.se; www.bodahamnscamping.se]** N fr Borgholm for 52km on rte 136 twd Mellböda & Böda, turn R twd Böda Hamn, site nr harbour. Lge, mkd pitch, pt shd; chem disp; mv service pnt; shwrs; EHU (10A) SEK40; lndry (inc dryer); shop; rest, snacks; bar; BBQ; cooking facs; playgrnd; sand beach adj; games area; wifi; some statics; dogs free; phone; Eng spkn; quiet; ccard acc. "Sep area of beach for dogs; vg site." ♦ 29 Apr-3 Oct. SEK 160 2010*

MORBYLANGA *2G3* (1km N Coastal) *56.52163, 16.37725* **Mörbylånga Camping, Kalvhagen 1, 38062 Mörbylånga [tel/fax (0485) 40591; info@morbylangacamping.se; www.morbylangacamping.se]** Site sp off rd 136 in Mörbylånga. Med, unshd; wc; chem disp; mv service pnt; baby facs; shwrs inc; EHU SEK40; lndry; shop; rest, snacks; bar; cooking facs; sand beach adj; fishing; games area; bike hire; sat TV; some statics; dogs; phone; Eng spkn; red LS; ccard acc; CKE. "Pleasant, relaxing, family-run site with open view; unusual & interesting island." ♦ 15 May-1 Oct. SEK 190 2009*

SWEDEN

Map 1

⊞ Site open all year

Tell us about the sites you visit

▲ see map 1

Map 2

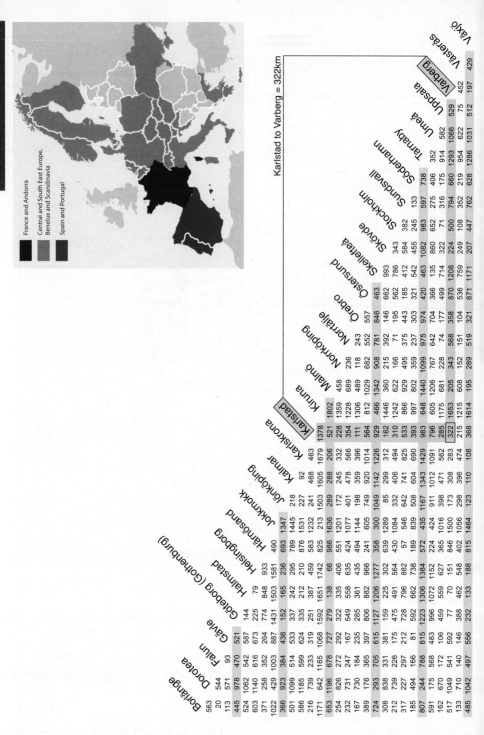

Switzerland
Country Introduction

Zürich, Switzerland

Welcome to Switzerland

A country of mountains, lakes and natural beauty, Switzerland's high alpine peaks make it one of the world's top destinations for winter sports.

Inside the cities, you will find a world that compliments the outstanding landscape while providing a modern and vibrant outlook on life.

There is an endless supply of places to visit and experience, with mouth-watering chocolates and cuckoo clocks just the tip of the cultural iceberg.

Country highlights

Switzerland is renowned for being a hub for winter sports enthusiasts, but there are also a variety of traditional competitions such as Schwingen, a type of Swiss wrestling and Hornussen, a strange mixture of golf and baseball, which are still practiced today.

Switzerland also produces a delicious variety of food, with cheese being one of its specialities. Types such as Emmental and Gruyère are used to make fondue, which is often associated with the skiing culture of the Alps.

Major towns and cities

- Zürich – there are tons of museums and cultural sites in this metropolitan capital.
- Geneva – this breathtaking city is one of the world's most diverse.
- Basel – a world-leading city of culture and arts.
- Lausanne – this city has a stunning view of Lake Geneva and the Alps.

Attractions

- Jungfraujoch – admire unrivalled views of the Alps from the highest railway station in Europe, located 3,43 metres above sea level.
- Château de Chillon, Veytaux – an island castle on Lake Geneva, set in a stunning backdrop.
- Kapellbrücke, Lucerne – Europe's oldest wooden covered bridge and one of Switzerland's main attractions.
- Rhine Falls, Shaffhausen – discover the breathtaking sight of Europe's largest waterfall.

Find out more

www.myswitzerland.com

Tel: 0041 (0) 80 01 00 20 029 Swiss Tourist Office

Country Information

Population: 8 million

Capital: Bern (population 128,848)

Area: 41,285 sq km

Bordered by: Austria, France, Germany, Italy, Liechtenstein

Terrain: Mostly mountainous; Alps in the south, Jura in the north-west; central plateau of rolling hills, plains and large lakes

Climate: Temperate climate varying with altitude; cold, cloudy, rainy or snowy winters; cool to warm summers with occasional showers

Highest Point: Dufourspitze 4,634m

Languages: French, German, Italian, Romansch

Local Time: GMT or BST + 1, i.e. 1 hour ahead of the UK all year

Currency: Swiss Franc (CHF) divided into 100 centimes (also called 'rappen' or 'centesimi' in German/Italian areas of the country); £1 = CHF 1.51, CHF 10 = £6.63 (September 2015)

Emergency numbers: Police 117; Fire brigade 118; Ambulance 144 or 112 for any service

Public Holidays 2016: Jan 1, 2*, 6*; Mar 19*; 25*, 28*; May 1*, 5, 15, 16*, 26*; Aug 1 (National Day), 15*; Sep 18*, Nov 1*; Dec 8*, 25, 26*

*These public holidays are not necessarily celebrated throughout Switzerland and individual cantons may have additional holidays.

School summer holidays vary by canton but are approximately from early July to mid/end August.

Camping and Caravanning

There are approximately 340 campsites available to touring caravanners, with around 100 sites remaining open in winter. Some sites may be nearly full with statics, with only a small area for tourers.

There are 27 Touring Club Suisse (TCS) sites and affiliated sites classified into five categories according to amenities available. All TCS campsites have a service station with facilities for emptying sanitary tanks. For further information and current rates see www.reisen-tcs.ch.

The Swiss Camp Sites Association (VSC/ACS) produces a camping and road map covering approximately 180 sites, including charges and classification. See www.swisscamps.ch. To download a guide to more than 40 campsites, including those open in winter, in the Bernese Oberland region of Switzerland see www.camping-bo.ch

The Swiss are environmentally conscious with only limited scope for removing waste. Recycling is vigorously promoted and it is normal to have to put rubbish in special plastic bags obtainable from campsites. A 'rubbish charge' or 'entsorgungstaxe' of approximately CHF 3 per person per day is commonly charged.

A visitors' tax, varying according to the area, is levied in addition to the site charges.

The rules on casual/wild camping differ from canton to canton. It may be tolerated in some areas with the permission of the landowner or local police, or in motorway service areas, but local laws – particularly on hygiene – must not be contravened. For reasons of security The Caravan Club recommends that overnight stops should always be at recognised campsites.

Cycling

Switzerland has 9,000 km of cycle trails, including nine national cycle routes, which have been planned to suit all categories of cyclist from families to sports cyclists. Maps of cycle routes are available from www.schweizmobil.ch. Routes are marked by red and white signs. The problem of strenuous uphill gradients can be overcome by using trails routed near railway lines. Most trains will transport bicycles and often bicycles are available for hire at stations. Switzerland Tourism can provide more information.

Children under the age of 6 may only cycle on the road if accompanied by a person over 16 years of age.

Transportation of Bicycles

Bicycles may be carried on the roof of a car providing they are attached to an adequate roof rack and providing the total height does not exceed 4 metres. Bicycles carried on special carriers at the rear of a vehicle can exceed the width of the vehicle by 20 cm on each side, but the total width must not exceed 2 metres. The rear lights and number plate must remain visible and the driver's view must not be obstructed.

Electricity and Gas

Usually current on campsites varies between 4 and 16 amps. Plugs have two or, more usually, three round pins. Some campsites have CEE connections. Some may lend or hire out adaptors – but do not rely on it – and it may be advisable to purchase an appropriate adaptor cable with a Swiss 3-pin plug. Adaptors are readily available in local supermarkets.

The full range of Campingaz cylinders is available from large supermarkets.

Entry Formalities

Holders of valid British or Irish passports may enter Switzerland without a visa for a period of up to 3 months.

Medical Services

There are reciprocal emergency health care arrangements with Switzerland for EU citizens. A European Health Insurance Card (EHIC) will enable you to get reduced cost for emergency treatment in a public hospital but you will be required to pay the full cost of treatment and apply afterwards for a refund from the Department for Work & Pensions on your return to the UK. Ensure that any doctor you visit is registered with the national Swiss Health Insurance Scheme. Dental treatment is not covered.

You will have to pay 50% of the costs of any medically-required ambulance transport within Switzerland and/or Liechtenstein, including air ambulance. There is a fixed charge for in-patient treatment in a public hospital.

If you are planning to participate in sports activities, such as skiing and mountaineering, your personal holiday insurance should be extended to cover these activities and should also include cover for mountain rescue and helicopter rescue costs.

Opening Hours

Banks – Mon-Fri 8.30am-4.30pm (some close for lunch; late opening once a week to 5.30pm/6pm in some towns).

Museums – Check locally as times vary.

Post Offices – Mon-Fri 7.30am-12pm & 13.45pm-6pm (no lunch break in main towns); Sat 7.30am-11am.

Shops – Mon-Fri 8am/8.30am-6.30pm/7pm (closed lunch time) & Sat 8am-4pm/7pm (sometimes lunch time closing); shops close early on the eve of a public holiday. Food shops may be closed on religious and public holidays.

Safety and Security

Most visits to Switzerland and Liechtenstein are trouble-free and the crime rate is low. However, petty theft is on the increase and you should be alert to pickpockets, confidence tricksters and thieves in city centres, railway stations and other public places.

You should be aware of the risks involved in the more hazardous sports activities and take note of weather forecasts and conditions, which can change rapidly in the mountains. You should be well-equipped; do not undertake the activity alone, study the itinerary and inform someone of your plans. Off-piste skiers should follow the advice given by local authorities and guides; to ignore such advice could put yourselves and other mountain users in danger.

Switzerland and Liechtenstein share with the rest of Europe an underlying threat from terrorism. Attacks could be indiscriminate and against civilian targets in public places, including tourist sites.

British Embassy

THUNSTRASSE 50, CH-3005 BERN
Tel: 031 3597700
www.ukinswitzerland.fco.gov.uk/en

Irish Embassy

KIRCHENFELDSTRASSE 68, CH-3000 BERN 6
Tel: 031 3521442
www.embassyofireland.ch

Customs Regulations

Alcohol and Tobacco

Switzerland is not a member of the EU and visitors aged 17 years and over may import the following items duty-free:

200 cigarettes or 50 cigars or 250 g tobacco

2 litres of alcoholic drink up to 15% proof
1 litre of alcoholic drink over 15% proof

All goods are duty free up to a total combined value of CHF300, including alcohol and tobacco products.

Caravans and Motorhomes
Caravans registered outside Switzerland may be imported without formality up to a height of 4 metres, width of 2.55 metres and length of 12 metres (including towbar). The total length of car + caravan/trailer must not exceed 18.75 metres.

Food
From EU countries you may import per person 1 kg of meat and/or meat products (excluding game). This is applicable as of 1st July 2014.

Refund of VAT on Export

A foreign visitor who buys goods in Switzerland in a 'Tax-Back SA' or 'Global Refund Schweiz AG' shop may obtain a VAT refund (7.6%) on condition that the value of the goods is at least CHF 300 including VAT. Visitors should complete a form in the shop and produce it, together with the goods purchased, at Customs on leaving Switzerland. See www.globalrefund.com for more information.

Documents

Vehicle(s)

Carry your original vehicle registration certificate (V5C), MOT certificate (if applicable) and insurance documentation at all times. Recent visitors report that drivers may be asked to produce proof of vehicle ownership at the border and failure to do so may mean that entry into Switzerland is refused. If you are driving a vehicle which does not belong to you, you should be in possession of a letter of authorisation from the owner.

Money

Prices in shops are often displayed in both Swiss francs and euros. Major credit cards are widely accepted, although you may find small supermarkets and restaurants do not accept them. Recent visitors report that some retail outlets may accept only one kind of credit card (MasterCard or VISA), not both, and it may be advisable to carry one of each. You may occasionally find that a surcharge is imposed for the use of credit cards.

Carry your credit card issuers'/banks' 24-hour UK contact numbers in case of loss or theft of your cards.

Motoring in Switzerland
Accidents

In the case of accidents involving property damage only, when drivers decide not to call the police, a European Accident Statement must be completed.

In the case of injury or of damage to the road, road signs, lights etc, the police must be called.

Alcohol

The maximum permitted level of alcohol is 50 milligrams in 100 millilitres of blood, i.e. lower than that permitted in the UK (80 milligrams). A lower limit of 10 milligrams in 100 millilitres applies for new drivers of up to three years. A blood test may be required after an accident, and if found positive, the penalty is either a fine or a prison sentence, plus withdrawal of permission to drive in Switzerland for at least two months. Police carry out random breath tests.

Breakdown Service

The motoring and leisure organisation Touring Club Suisse (TCS) operates a 24-hour breakdown service, 'Patrouille TCS'. To call for help throughout Switzerland and Liechtenstein, dial 140. On motorways use emergency phones and ask for TCS.

Members of clubs affiliated to the AIT, such as The Caravan Club, who can show a current membership card will be charged reduced rates for breakdown assistance and towing, according to the time of day and/or the distance towed. Payment by credit card is accepted.

Essential Equipment

Lights

Dipped headlights are compulsory at all times, even during the day. Bulbs are more likely to fail with constant use and you are recommended to carry spares.

Nationality Plate (GB or IRL Stickers)

Strictly-speaking, it is necessary to display a conventional nationality plate or sticker when driving outside EU member states, even when vehicle number plates incorporate the GB or IRL Euro-symbol. However, the Swiss authorities have adopted a commonsense approach and confirm that it is not necessary to display a separate GB or IRL sticker if your number plates display the GB or IRL Euro-symbol. If your number plates do not incorporate this symbol then you will need a separate sticker.

Warning Triangles

All vehicles must be equipped with a warning triangle which has to be within easy reach and not in the boot.

Child Restraint System

Vehicles registered outside of Switzerland that are temporarily imported into the country, have to comply with the country of registration with regards to safety belt equipment and child restraint regulations. All children up to 12 years of age must be placed in an approved UN ECE 44.03 regulation child restraint, unless they measure more than 150cm and are over seven years old.

Winter Driving

Alpine winters often make driving more difficult. You should equip your vehicle(s) with winter tyres and snow chains and check road conditions prior to departure.

A sign depicting a wheel and chains indicates where snow chains are required for the mountain road ahead.

Snow chains are compulsory in areas where indicated by the appropriate road sign. They must be fitted on at least two drive wheels.

Fuel

Prices of petrol vary according to the brand and region, being slightly cheaper in self-service stations. Credit cards are generally accepted.

On motorways, where prices are slightly higher, some service stations are open 24 hours and others are open from 6am to 10pm or 11pm only, but petrol is available outside these hours from automatic pumps where payment can be made by means of bank notes or credit cards.

There are 44 outlets (August 2015) selling LPG (GPL) – see www.jaquet-ge.ch for a list of outlets and a map showing their location.

Mountain Roads and Tunnels

One of the most attractive features of Switzerland for motorists is the network of finely engineered mountain passes, ranging from easy main road routes to high passes that may be open only from June to October. In the Alps most roads over passes have been modernised; only the Umbrail Pass, which is not recommended for caravans, is not completely tarred. Passes have a good roadside telephone service for calling aid quickly in the event of trouble.

A blue rectangular sign depicting a yellow horn indicates a mountain postal road and the same sign with a red diagonal stripe indicates the end of the postal road. On such roads, vehicles belonging to the postal services have priority.

During certain hours, one-way traffic only is permitted on certain mountain roads. The hours during which traffic may proceed in either or both directions are posted at each end of the road. The TCS road map of Switzerland, scale 1:300,000, indicates this type of road.

Speed must always be moderate on mountain passes, very steep roads and roads with numerous bends. Drivers must not travel at a speed which would prevent them from stopping within the distance they can see ahead.

When it is difficult to pass oncoming vehicles, the heavier vehicle has priority.

Slow-moving vehicles are required by law to use the lay-bys provided on alpine roads to allow the free flow of faster traffic. This is the case where a car towing a caravan causes a queue of vehicles capable of a higher speed.

Parking

Parking in cities is difficult and it is worth using the numerous Park & Ride schemes which operate around major towns and cities. Illegal parking of any kind is much less tolerated in Switzerland than in any of its neighbours and fines are common for even minor violations.

Pay and display car parks and parking meters are used throughout the country and permitted parking time varies from 15 minutes to 2 hours. Feeding meters is not allowed. Wheel clamps are not used, but vehicles causing an obstruction may be removed to a car pound.

You may park in a 'blue zone' for limited periods free of charge providing you display a parking disc in your vehicle. These are available from petrol stations, kiosks, restaurants and police stations. Parking in a marked red zone is free for up to 15 hours with a red parking disc obtainable from police stations, tourist offices, etc.

Parking on pavements is not allowed. Do not park where there is a sign 'Stationierungsverbot' or 'Interdiction de Stationner'. Continuous or broken yellow lines and crosses at the side of the road and any other yellow markings also indicate that parking is prohibited.

Priority

In general, traffic (including bicycles) coming from the right has priority at intersections but drivers approaching a roundabout must give way to all traffic already on the roundabout, i.e. from the left, unless otherwise indicated by signs. However, vehicles on main roads – indicated by a yellow diamond with a white border or a white triangle with a red border and an arrow pointing upwards – have priority over traffic entering from secondary roads.

Please be aware sometimes pedestrians have right of way and will expect vehicles to stop for them.

Roads

Switzerland has some 72,000 kilometres of well-surfaced roads, from motorways to local municipal roads, all well-signposted. Four-wheel drive vehicles must not be driven off road without the permission of the local authority.

During daylight hours outside built-up areas you must sound your horn before sharp bends where visibility is limited. After dark this warning must be given by flashing your headlights.

Dial the following numbers for information:

162: Weather information

163: Road conditions, mountain passes, access to tunnels and traffic news

187: In winter, avalanche bulletins; in summer, wind forecasts for Swiss lakes

It is also possible to obtain updated information on road conditions via teletext in larger motorway service areas.

Motorway Tax

To be able to use national roads (motorways and semi-motorways) in Switzerland, motor vehicles and trailers up to a total weight of 3,500kg must have a vehicle sticker (vignette). The ticket is valid for 14 months from 1st December every year and costs CHF40 (2015). An additional fee is charged for caravans and trailers. The sticker allows multiple re-entry into Switzerland during the period of validity.

If you enter a motorway or semi-motorway without a sticker you will be fined CHF200 and also the cost of the sticker. The stickers can be bought from custom offices, petrol stations or TCS offices in Switzerland or alternatively they can be purchased from the UK before travelling by calling the Swiss Travel Centre on 0207 420 4934.

Heavy Vehicle Tax

Vehicles (including motorhomes) over 3,500kg must pay a heavy vehicle tax on entry into Switzerland which is applicable for all roads. This charge applies for every day you are in Switzerland and your vehicle is on the road. For a 10-day pass (valid for a year) you self-select the days that your vehicle is on the road and, therefore, you are not penalised if your motorhome is parked at a campsite and not driven on a public road. This heavy vehicle tax applies to any Swiss road and replaces the need for a motorway vignette.

This particular tax is only payable at the border on entry into Switzerland and if there is any doubt about the exact weight of your vehicle it will be weighed. An inspection may be carried out at any time and is likely at the exit border. Failure to pay the tax can result in an immediate fine.

Road Signs and Markings

Road signs and markings conform to international standards.

White lettering on a green background indicates motorways, whereas state and provincial main roads outside built-up areas have white lettering on a blue background. This is the reverse of the colouring used in France and Germany and may initially cause confusion when driving from one country to the other. Road signs on secondary roads are white with black lettering.

The following are some road signs which you may encounter:

Postal vehicles have priority

Parking disc compulsory

Slow lane

One-way street with a two-way cycle lane

Speed Limits

	Open Road (km/h)	Motorway (km/h)
Car Solo	80-100	120
Car towing caravan/trailer	80	80
Motorhome under 3500kg	80-100	120
Motorhome 3500-7500kg	80	80

The fundamental rule, which applies to all motor vehicles and bicycles, is that you must always have the speed of your vehicle under control and must adapt your speed to the conditions of the road, traffic and visibility. On minor secondary roads without speed limit signs speed should be reduced to 50 km/h (31 mph) where the road enters a built-up area. The speed limit in residential areas is 30 km/h (18 mph). Speeding fines are severe.

When travelling solo the speed limit on dual carriageways is 100 km/h (62 mph) and on motorways, 120 km/h (74 mph) unless otherwise

indicated by signs. On motorways with at least three lanes in the same direction, the left outside lane may only be used by vehicles which can exceed 80 km/h (50 mph).

Motorhomes with a laden weight of under 3,500 kg are not subject to any special regulations. Those over 3,500 kg may not exceed 80 km/h (50 mph) on motorways.

In road tunnels with two lanes in each direction, speed is limited to 100 km/h (62 mph); in the St Gotthard tunnel and San Bernardino tunnels the limit is 80 km/h (50 mph).

It is illegal to transport or use radar detection devices. If your GPS navigation system has a function to identify the location of fixed speed cameras, this must be deactivated.

Traffic Jams

Traffic congestion occurs near tunnels in particular, during the busy summer months, at the St Gotthard tunnel on Friday afternoons and Saturday mornings. When congestion is severe and in order to prevent motorists coming to a standstill in the tunnel, traffic police stop vehicles before the tunnel entrance and direct them through in groups.

Other bottlenecks occur on the roads around Luzern (A2) and Bern (A1, A6 and A12), the border crossing at Chiasso (A2), the A9 around Lausanne and between Vevey and Chexbres, and the A13 BellinzonaSargans, mainly before the San Bernardino tunnel.

Traffic Lights

Outside peak rush hours traffic lights flashing amber mean proceed with caution.

Violation of Traffic Regulations

The police may impose and collect on-the-spot fines for minor infringements. In the case of more serious violations, they may require a deposit equal to the estimated amount of the fine. Fines for serious offences are set according to the income of the offender. Drivers of foreign-registered vehicles may be asked for a cash deposit against the value of the fine

Motorways

There are 1,700 km of motorways and dual carriageways. To use these roads motor vehicles and trailers up to a total weight of 3,500kg must display a vignette. Motorists using roads to avoid motorways and dual carriageways may find it necessary to detour through small villages, often with poor signposting. In addition, due to a diversion, you may be re-routed onto roads where the motorway vignette is required.

If you have visited Switzerland before, make sure you remove your old sticker from your windscreen.

There are emergency telephones along the motorways.

Touring

The peak season for winter sports is from December to the end of April in all major resorts. February and March are the months with the most hours of winter sunshine and good snow for skiing. Summer skiing is also possible in a few resorts. Information on snow conditions, including avalanche bulletins, is available in English from www.slf.ch.

Besides being famous for watches, chocolate and cheese, the Swiss have a fine reputation as restaurateurs, but eating out can be expensive. Local beers are light but pleasant and some very drinkable wines are produced.

There are a number of UNESCO World Heritage Sites in Switzerland including the three castles of Bellinzona, Bern Old Town, the Monastery of St John at Müstair, the Jungfrau, the Aletsch Glacier and the Bietschhoorn region.

Liechtenstein is a principality of 160 sq km sharing borders with Switzerland and Austria. The capital, Vaduz, has a population of approximately 5,500 and German is the official language. The official currency is the Swiss franc. There are no passport or Customs controls on the border between Switzerland and Liechtenstein.

Public Transport & Local Travel

Some towns are inaccessible by road, e.g. Zermatt and Wengen, and can only be reached by train or tram.

The Swiss integrated transport system is well known for its efficiency, convenience and punctuality. Co-ordinated timetables ensure fast, trouble-free interchange from one means of transport to another. Yellow post buses take travellers off the beaten track to the remotest regions. As far as railways are concerned, in addition to efficient inter-city travel, there is an extensive network of mountain railways, including aerial cableways, funiculars and ski-lifts.

Half-fare tickets are available for attractions such as cable cars, railways and lake steamers. In addition, Switzerland Tourism offers a public transport map and a number of other useful publications. See www.swisstravelsystem.com.

All visitors to campsites and hotels in Interlaken are issued with a pass allowing free bus and train travel in the area.

A ferry operates on Lake Constance (Bodensee) between Romanshorn and Friedrichshafen (Germany) saving a 70km drive. The crossing takes 40 minutes. Telephone 071 4667888 for more information; www.bodensee-schiffe.ch. A frequent ferry service also operates between Konstanz and Meersburg on the main route between Zürich, Ulm, Augsburg and Munich (Germany); information is available on a German telephone number, 0049 7531 8030; www.stadtwerke.konstanz.de. The crossing takes 20 minutes. Principal internal ferry services are on Lake Lucerne between Beckenried and Gersau, www.autofaehre.ch, and on Lake Zürich between Horgen and Meilen, www.faehre.ch. All these services transport cars and caravans.

AARBURG *A2* (1km SW Rural) *47.31601, 7.89488*
Camping Wiggerspitz, Hofmattstrasse 40, 4663 Aarburg
[062 7915810; fax 7915811; info@camping-aarburg.ch;
www.camping-aarburg.ch] Exit A1/A2/E35 junc 46 sp
Rothrist/Olten, foll sp to site. Med, mkd pitch, pt shd; htd wc;
chem disp; mv service pnt; shwrs CHF1; EHU (6A) CHF3 (rev
pol), long lead req; gas; lndry; shop; rest 500m; snacks; bar;
BBQ; htd pool adj; 25% statics; dogs CHF1; phone; rlwy noise;
red CKE/CCI. "Conv Luzern, Zürich, Bern; picturesque, walled
town; excel, clean site; friendly warden; excel san facs; site is
popular so rec adv bkg." 1 May-15 Sep. CHF 29.00   2015*

ADLISWIL *A3* (7km S Urban) *47.26384, 8.56056* **Camping
Sihlwald, 8135 Langnau-am-Albis [044 7200434; camping.
sihlwald@gmx.ch]** Turn off Zürich-Luzern rd dir Adliswil, site
sp on L by Forsthaus rest. Med, pt shd; htd wc; chem disp;
shwrs; EHU inc; gas; lndry; shop; rest, snacks; bar; playgrnd;
pool 4km; dogs CHF4; poss cr; Eng spkn; adv bkg; quiet, but
some rd noise; red CKE/CCI. "Pretty setting by rv; conv Luzern,
Zürich & Bern; pitches furthest fr rv unrel in wet; excel, clean
facs; helpful staff." 15 Apr-15 Oct. CHF 28.00   2009*

AESCHI see Spiez *C2*

AGNO see Lugano *D3*

AIGLE *C2* (1km N Rural) *46.32385, 6.96206* **Camping de la
Piscine, Ave des Glariers 1, 1860 Aigle [tel/fax 024 4662660]**
Turn W off N9 (Aigle-Lausanne) at N edge of Aigle, site sp. Foll
rd for 400m, site past pool on L. Med, pt shd; wc; chem disp;
mv service pnt; shwrs inc; EHU (4A) CHF3.50 (adaptor avail);
gas; lndry; sm shop; snacks; bar; playgrnd; pool; tennis; fishing;
bike hire; some statics; dogs CHF4; poss cr; Eng spkn; adv bkg;
quiet but a little rlwy noise; ccard acc; red CKE/CCI. "V helpful
owner; vg, well-maintained site; pleasant town & gd touring
base; outlook on to vineyards; easy flat walk into town, about
10 mins." 6 Apr-30 Sep. CHF 35.00   2013*

⊞ **AIGLE** *C2* (16km NE Rural) *46.34030, 7.01550* **Camping
du Soleil, Route du Suchet, 1854 Leysin [024 4943939;
fax 4942121; info@camping-leysin.ch; www.camping-
leysin.ch]** Take rd 20 Aigle to Le Sépey, exit at Le Sépey for
Leysin, 6 hairpin bends to site. On ent vill pass g'ge on L, in
50m turn L into app rd to lge sports cent. In 100m turn R into
narr access rd & bear L; site opp Hotel du Soleil. NB: Fr Aigle
dist by rd 16km, last 5km up winding, steep but gd rd. Med, pt
sl, pt shd; htd wc; chem disp; baby facs; shwrs inc; EHU (16A)
metered (adaptor avail); gas; lndry (inc dryer); shops, rest nr;
bar; BBQ; playgrnd; covrd pool adj; tennis adj; bike hire; games
area; games rm; horseriding, winter & summer skiing; sports
cent & skating rink (all year) 100m; TV; many statics; dogs
CHF3; quiet; ccard acc; red CKE/CCI. "Mainly winter ski resort
but magnificent views; 15 min walk (uphill) to shops etc; conv
cablecar; navette 100m; ski & boot rm; friendly, helpful staff;
mkt Thu; used by school groups." ♦ CHF 37.00   2011*

⊞ **ALTDORF** *B3* (2km N Rural) *46.89256, 8.62800*
**Remo-Camp Moosbad, Flüelerstrsse 122, 6460 Altdorf
[041 8708541; fax 8708161]** Exit A2 at Altdorf junc 36. Foll
sp Altdorf to rndabt & turn R. Site 200m on L adj cable car &
sports cent. Sm, pt shd; wc; chem disp; mv service pnt; shwrs
CHF1; EHU (10A) CHF3 (adaptor loan); lndry (inc dryer); shop
& 200m; rest; bar; BBQ; public pool, waterslide & rest adj;
80% statics; dogs €1; phone; poss cr; Eng spkn; some rd &
rlwy noise; ccard not acc; CKE/CCI. "Ideal windsurfing; useful
NH en rte Italy; friendly welcome; excel san facs; excel rest;
superb views; gd base for train trip over St Gotthard pass;
plenty to see & do in Altdorf; bus & cable car combos avail."
CHF 39.00   2014*

ALTDORF *B3* (5km N Rural) *46.91497, 8.62257* **Camping
Windsurfing Urnersee, Unterer Winkel 11, 6454 Flüelen-See
[041 8709222; fax 8709216; info@windsurfing-urnersee.ch;
www.windsurfing-urnersee.ch]** On N4 & Axenstrasse, site sp
on ent Flüelen. Steep app, not rec for lge or heavy o'fits. Med,
terr, pt shd; wc; chem disp; shwrs CHF1; EHU CHF3.50; shop;
rest; bar; htd, covrd pool 2km; shgl beach; lake sw; fishing;
watersports; bike hire; tennis; no dogs; poss cr; adv bkg; quiet
but some rlwy noise; Eng spkn. "Excel watersports."
1 Apr-30 Oct. CHF 36.00   2011*

ANDEER see Thusis *C4*

> ### "I like to fill in the reports
> ### as I travel from site to site"
> You'll find report forms at the back of
> this guide, or you can fill them in online
> at www.caravanclub.co.uk/europereport.

ANDELFINGEN *A3* (1km NE Rural) *47.59698, 8.68376*
**TCS Camping Rässenwies, Alte Steinerstrasse 1, 8451
Kleinandelfingen [079 2383535; raessenwies@tcs-ccz.ch;
www.tcs-ccz.ch]** On N4 Schaffhausen-Winterthur rd, site
well sp in Kleinandelfingen, on Rv Thur. Sm, unshd; wc;
shwrs; EHU CHF3.50; gas; lndry; shop pool 1km; fishing; dogs
CHF3.50; quiet. "Beautiful area; v friendly." 20 Mar-4 Oct.
CHF 43.00   2013*

ARBON *A4* (2km NW Rural) *47.52449, 9.42049* **Camping
Buchorn, Philosophenweg 17, 9320 Arbon [071 4466545;
fax 4464834; info@camping-arbon.ch; www.camping-
arbon.ch]** Fr N on Kreuzlingen-Romanshorn rd 13, 8km after
Romanshorn, site sp at ent to Arbon, on lakeside. Med, mkd
pitch, pt shd; wc; chem disp; mv service pnt; baby facs; shwrs;
EHU CHF3; gas; lndry (inc dryer); sm shop; rest, snacks; BBQ;
playgrnd; paddling pool; lake sw; fishing; watersports; boat
hire; tennis; games rm; wifi; TV; no dogs; poss cr; adv bkg;
quiet but some rlwy noise; ccard acc. "Pleasant location;
clean site; helpful owner; steamer trips fr Arbon." ♦ ltd.
Easter-1 Oct. CHF 38.00   2010*

BASEL *A2* (10km S Urban) *47.49963, 7.60283* **Camping Waldhort, Heideweg 16, 4153 Basel-Reinach [061 7116429; fax 7139835; info@camping-waldhort.ch; www.camping-waldhort.ch]** Fr Basel foll m'way sp to Delémont & exit m'way at Reinach-Nord exit; at top of slip rd, turn R & L at 1st traff lts (about 300m). Site on L in approx 1km at curve in rd with tramway on R, sp. Basel best app off German m'way rather than French. Lge, mkd pitch, pt shd; wc; chem disp; mv service pnt; baby facs; shwrs inc; EHU (6A) inc; gas; lndry; shop; rest 500m; snacks; playgrnd; pool; paddling pool; 50% statics; dogs CHF3; tram 500m (tickets fr recep); poss cr; Eng spkn; adv bkg; m'way noise; ccard acc; 10% red CKE/CCI. "Rec arr early in high ssn; helpful staff; gd sized pitches; m'van pitches sm; excel san facs; gates clsd 2200-0700; site muddy when wet; excel art museums in Basel." ◆ 1 Mar-29 Oct. CHF 47.00   2013*

⊞ **BASEL** *A2* (17km S Rural) *47.45806, 7.63545* **TCS Camping Uf der Hollen, Auf der Hollen, 4146 Hochwald [061 7511398; fax 7120240; info@tcscampingbasel.ch; www.tcscampingbasel.ch]** Exit A18 at Reinach-Sud dir Dornach, S thro Dornach dir Hochwald, uphill thro forest to site. Med, mkd pitch, pt shd; htd wc; chem disp; shwrs CHF0.50; EHU CHF3; lndry; playgrnd; htd, covrd pool 10km; games area; 90% statics; adv bkg; quiet; red CKE/CCI. "Gd views; peaceful, pleasant site." ◆ CHF 27.00   2010*

BEATENBERG see Interlaken *C2*

BELLINZONA *C3* (2.6km N Urban) *46.21186, 9.03831* **TCS Camping Bosco di Molinazzo, Via San Gottardo 131, 6500 Bellinzona [091 8291118; fax 8292355; camping. bellinzona@tcs.ch; www.campingtcs.ch]** Fr A13 exit Bellinzona Nord, foll rd over rv & rlwy bdgs. In approx 200m on R, immed after rd to Gorduno, site sp in 200m down ramp to R just bef Shell g'ge. Med, sl, pt shd; wc; chem disp; mv service pnt; baby facs; shwrs; EHU (6A) CHF4; gas; lndry (inc dryer); shop; rest, snacks; bar; BBQ; playgrnd; pool; tennis; rv adj; bike hire; golf; wifi; TV; 20% statics; dogs CHF4; poss v cr; adv bkg; rd & rlwy noise; ccard acc; red CKE/CCI. "Pleasant & attractive city; gd NH en rte Italy; san facs stretched high ssn & site overcr; early arr site yourselves & report later - instructions on barrier." ◆ 1 Apr-9 Oct. CHF 63.00   2013*

BERN *B2* (4km S Rural) *46.93285, 7.45569* **Camping Eichholz, Strandweg 49, 3084 Wabern [031 9612602; fax 9613526; info@campingeichholz.ch; www.camping eichholz.ch]** Exit A1/A12 & take 2nd turn-off sp Bern/Bümplitz dir Belp & airport. Turn L under A12 & foll sp Wabern & site. Lge, hdstg, shd; wc; chem disp; mv service pnt; shwrs CHF3.50; EHU (rev pol) CHF3.50; gas; lndry; shop; supmkt nr; rest, snacks; bar; BBQ; playgrnd; pool 2km; fishing; tennis; bike hire; wifi; tram; poss cr; Eng spkn; adv bkg; poss v noisy; ccard acc. "Walk to Bern by rv (steep climb); clean, modern san facs; helpful staff." ◆ 20 Apr-30 Sep. CHF 44.00   2013*

BERN *B2* (15km SW Rural) *46.89301, 7.33408* **Freizeitzentrum Thörishaus, Strandheimstrasse 20, 3174 Thörishaus [031 8890271; fax 8890296; sense.giardino@ hispeed.ch]** Exit m'way Bern-Fribourg at Flamatt. Strt at 1st rndabt, R at 2nd sp Thörishaus. Site on R in 150m. Med, pt shd; wc; shwrs inc; EHU (10A) CHF3.50; gas; lndry; shop; rest, snacks; bar; playgrnd; pool 4km; tennis; fishing; 80% statics; sep car park; Eng spkn; adv bkg; ccard acc; 10% red CKE/ CCI. "Conv Bern; gd cycle paths; vg site." ◆ 1 Apr-31 Oct. CHF 26.00   2009*

⊞ **BERN** *B2* (6km NW Rural) *46.96375, 7.38420* **TCS Camping Bern-Eymatt, Wohlenstrasse 62C, 3032 Hinterkappelen [031 9011007; fax 9012591; camping. bern@tcs.ch; www.campingtcs.ch/bern]** Fr E on A1 exit junc 33 sp Bern-Bethlehem; foll sp for Wohlen & site. In 200m turn R at bottom of hill into site on shores Wohlensee. Fr W take Brunnen-Bern exit, then sp to Wohlen. Access for lge o'fits poss diff. Lge, some hdstg, pt shd; htd wc; chem disp; mv service pnt; baby facs; shwrs inc; EHU (6A) inc; gas; lndry; shop; rest, snacks; bar; BBQ (charcoal/gas); playgrnd; htd pool; paddling pool; fishing; bike hire; games area; wifi; entmnt; TV/games rm; many statics; dogs CHF5; no o'fits over 8m high ssn; bus to Bern nrby; sep car park; poss cr; ccard acc; red LS; CKE/CCI. "Recep 0830-1100 & 1700-2000 high ssn, but site yourself; various pitch sizes; clean facs; gd value rest; helpful staff; daily mkt in Bern; 2 supmkt nrby; excel." ◆ CHF 42.00   2012*

BERNHARDZELL see St Gallen *A4*

BIEL/BIENNE *B2* (6km SW Rural) *47.10779, 7.21886* **Camping Sutz am Bielersee, Kirchrain 40, 2572 Sutz [032 3971345; fax 3972061; mail@camping-sutz.ch; www.camping-sutz.ch]** Exit A1/E25 Biel cent on rd twd Neuchâtel. Turn L at Biel o'skts, foll sp to Ipsach-Täuffelen along E side of lake. Site sp after Ipsach on R at edge of lake. Lge, unshd; wc; chem disp; baby facs; shwrs inc; EHU (10A) inc; gas; lndry; shop; rest 2km; lake sw; fishing; tennis; 90% statics; Eng spkn; adv bkg; quiet; ccard acc. "Gd, modern san facs; extra lge pitches avail; friendly staff; cycle path adj." ◆ 1 Apr-31 Oct. CHF 39.00   2009*

BIEL/BIENNE *B2* (20km SW Rural) *47.08556, 7.11726* **Camping Prêles AG, Route de la Neuveville 61, 2515 Prêles [032 3151716; fax 3155160; info@camping-jura.ch; www.camping-jura.ch]** App Biel fr N on rd 6 approx 2km bef town; immed after emerging fr 2nd long tunnel turn R then L sp Orvin. Cont thro Orvin to Lamboing, in Lamboing turn L dir La Neuveville to Prêles. Drive strt thro vill & look out for tent sp beyond vill when descending hill. App fr S on rd 5 poss via Neuveville or Twann but steep climb, tight bends & narr vill streets. Lge, pt sl, shd; wc; chem disp; mv service pnt; baby facs; shwrs CHF0.50; EHU (10A) CHF3.50; gas; lndry; sm shop; rest, snacks; BBQ; playgrnd; htd pool; watersports 5km; tennis; bike hire; horseriding; games rm; entmnt; dogs CHF2; some statics; sep car park high ssn; adv bkg; v quiet; ccard acc; red long stay; CKE/CCI. "Nice scenery & gd views; peaceful site surrounded by woods & meadows; recep clsd 1130-1400 & after 1800." ◆ 1 Apr-15 Oct. CHF 46.00   2012*

BLUMENSTEIN see Thun *B2*

BONIGEN see Interlaken *C2*

SWITZERLAND

BOURG ST PIERRE *D2* (500m N Rural) *45.95265, 7.20740*
**Camping du Grand St Bernard, 1946 Bourg-St Pierre
[tel/fax 027 7871411; grand-st-bernard@swisscamps.ch;
www.campinggrand-st-bernard.ch]** Fr Martigny S to Grand
St Bernard Tunnel. Site well sp in cent of vill. Med, unshd; wc;
chem disp; shwrs; EHU (4A) CHF3.50; gas; lndry; shop 200m;
rest, snacks, bar adj; htd pool adj; dogs; Eng spkn; quiet; ccard
acc; CKE/CCI. "Conv St Bernard Tunnel; gd views."
15 May-15 Oct. CHF 28.00   2009*

BOUVERET, LE see Villeneuve *C1*

BRENZIKOFEN see Thun *B2*

BRIENZ *B2* (2km SE Rural) *46.75069, 8.04838* **Camping
Seegartli, 3855 Brienz [033 9511351]** Fr Interlaken take N8
sp Luzern/Brienz. Take Brienz exit, ignore sp to site to R & take
L in 1km bef Esso stn, sp Axalp. Site in 500m on R immed after
passing under rlwy. Site on E shore of lake, next to sawmill.
Sm, pt sl, pt shd; wc; chem disp; mv service pnt; shwrs CHF1;
EHU (10A) CHF3; lndry; shop; lake sw; watersports; fishing;
tennis; Eng spkn; quiet CKE/CCI. "Beautiful lakeside situation;
well-kept site; friendly owner; lakeside pitches boggy in wet
weather; long hose req for m'van fill-up; arr bef noon in ssn;
no dogs." 1 Apr-31 Oct. CHF 33.00   2011*

BRIENZ *B2* (3km SE Urban) *46.74811, 8.04769* **Camping
Aaregg, Seestrasse 22, 3855 Brienz [033 9511843;
fax 9514324; mail@aaregg.ch; www.aaregg.ch]**
Fr Interlaken take N8 sp Luzern/Brienz. Take Brienz exit, ignore
sp to site to R & take L in 1km bef Esso stn, sp Axalp. Site in
500m on R after passing under rlwy. Site on E shore of lake,
next to sawmill. Med, mkd pitch, hdstg, pt shd; htd wc; chem
disp; mv service pnt; some serviced pitches; shwrs inc; EHU
(10A) CHF5; lndry; shop; rest, snacks; bar; pool 500m; lake
sw adj; internet; dogs CHF4; phone; rlwy stn nr; poss cr; Eng
spkn; adv bkg rec (lge dep req); quiet; ccard acc; red long stay/
LS; CKE/CCI. "Excel, busy site on lakeside; lakeside pitches sm
& poss cr; ideal touring base; min stay 9 nights on best pitches
high ssn; excel, modern san facs; many attractions nrby."
1 Apr-31 Oct. CHF 42.00 SBS - S02   2009*

BRIG *C2* (3km E Rural) *46.31500, 8.01369* **Camping Tropic,
Simplonstrasse 11, 3901 Ried bei Brig [027 9232537]**
On Brig-Domodossola rd on Swiss side of Simplon Pass.
Fr Brig, exit Simplon rd at sp Ried-Brig Termen. Site on L in
500m. Fr Simplon foll sp to Ried-Brig, site in vill. Med, sl, pt
shd; wc; shwrs CHF1; EHU CHF3; gas; lndry; shop; playgrnd;
pool 2km; TV; Eng spkn; rd noise. "Useful CL-type NH to/fr
Italy; welcoming & helpful owners; superb scenery; san facs
adequate." 1 Jun-15 Sep. CHF 24.00   2012*

BRIG *C2* (1km S Rural) *46.30838, 7.99338* **Camping
Geschina, Geschinastrasse 41, 3900 Brig [tel/fax
027 9230688; www.geschina.ch]** Foll sps twd Simplon
Pass, site on R at 700m, behind pool at rv bdge. Best app
fr Glis. Med, pt sl, pt shd; wc; chem disp; shwrs inc; EHU
(10A) CHF2.50; gas; lndry; shop; snacks; bar; playgrnd; pool
adj; fishing; dogs CHF2; poss cr; Eng spkn; adv bkg; quiet;
red long stay/CKE/CCI. "Friendly, well-kept, family-run site;
vg san facs; superb mountain & glacier views; ideal for Rhône
Valley & Simplon Pass; sh walk to town." 1 Apr-15 Oct.
CHF 29.00   2011*

⊞ **BRUNNEN** *B3* (5km E Rural) *46.99030, 8.63394* **Camping
Ferienhof Rüti, Rüti 4, 6443 Morschach [41 8205309; fax
8205313; info@ferienhof-rueti.com; www.ferienhof-rueti.
ch]** N4/E41 S thro Brunnen tunnel, take next L sp Morschach,
thro vill & site on R bef cable car. Sm, mkd pitch, pt sl, pt shd;
htd wc; chem disp; shwrs inc; EHU (6a) inc; shop; BBQ (gas/
charcoal); playgrnd; lake sw nrby; games area; games rm;
wifi; TV; dogs; bus adj; Eng spkn; quiet; ccard acc; CKE/CCI.
"Panoramic views; on hobby farm with donkeys, mini-pigs,
hens etc; excel site, quiet." CHF 28.00   2013*

BRUNNEN *B3* (1km NW Rural) *46.99775, 8.59346* **Camping
Hopfreben, 6440 Brunnen [041 8201873; www.camping-
brunnen.ch]** A4/E41 exit Brunnen-Nord, dir Weggis, site sp
on lakeside. Med, pt shd; wc; chem disp; mv service pnt; shwrs
CHF1; EHU (6A) CHF3 (adaptor avail/long cable req); lndry;
shop; rest 1km; snacks; bar; playgrnd; pool 200m; lake sw
500m; boat launch; bike hire; 20% statics; dogs CHF3; poss cr
w/end; adv bkg; quiet but some daytime noise fr gravel barges/
lorries adj; CKE/CCI. "Delightful location." 15 Apr-24 Sep.
CHF 39.00   2011*

BRUNNEN *B3* (1km NW Rural) *47.00076, 8.59149*
**Camping Urmiberg, Gersauerstrasse 75, 6440 Brunnen
[tel/fax 041 8203327; fragen@campingurmiberg.ch;
www.campingurmiberg.ch]** Exit A4 Brunnen Nord dir
Weggis. Site sp opp Urmiberg cable car stn. Med, pt shd; htd
wc; chem disp; shwrs inc; EHU (10A) CHF2.30; lndry; shop;
rest, snacks; bar; playgrnd; lake sw adj; 40% statics; dogs
CHF2; phone; poss cr; Eng spkn; adv bkg; quiet. "Peaceful,
clean, family-run site; wonderful views." 1 Apr-15 Oct.
CHF 27.00   2013*

BUCHS *B4* (500m W Rural) *47.16663, 9.46524* **Camping
Werdenberg, 9470 Buchs [081 7561507; fax 7565090;
verkehrsvereinbuchs@bluemail.ch; www.werdenberg.ch]**
Fr bdge over Rv Rhine at Buchs on rd 16 dir Werdenberg &
Grabs. Turn L at parking/camping sp, thro car park to site.
Sm, unshd; wc; chem disp; shwrs CHF1; EHU (16A) CHF4;
gas; lndry (inc dryer); shops nr; htd pool 2km; lake sw adj;
dogs CHF2; adv bkg; quiet but church bells adj every 15 mins.
"Vg, attractive setting by lake with views of old town &
castle; friendly owners; gd base for Liechtenstein, Appenzell
& Vorarlberg; walking; plenty of activities mini-golf etc; extra
charge for vans over 5m; gd for families." ♦ 1 Apr-31 Oct.
CHF 34.00   2012*

BULLE *C2* (8km N Rural) *46.67545, 7.08478* **Camping du
Lac, 1643 Gumefens [026 9152162; fax 9152168; info@
campingdulac-gruyere.ch; www.campingdulac-gruyere.ch]**
Fr S on N12 exit junc 4 for Bulle. At T-junc turn N for Riaz.
Foll rd thro Riaz & Vuippens. Site on R 500m after Gumefens
turning. Fr N exit junc 5 Rossens & foll dir Bulle. In 7km turn
L twd lake & site. Med, mkd pitch, unshd; wc; chem disp; mv
service pnt; shwrs CHF0.50; EHU (6A) CHF2.50; gas; lndry;
shop; rest, snacks; bar; playgrnd; private beach; watersports;
bike hire; 60% statics; no dogs; site open w/ends May & Sep;
Eng spkn; adv bkg; quiet; ccard not acc; red long stay/CKE/
CCI. "Lovely lakeside site, mountain views; helpful owner; sm
pitches not suitable lge o'fits; exit to main rd sh & steep."
1 Jul-31 Aug. CHF 27.00   2010*

⊞ **BULLE** *C2 (10km NW Rural) 46.67373, 7.02492* **Camping La Forêt, Route de Montiollin, 1642 Sorens [026 9151882; fax 9150363; info@camping-la-foret.ch; www.camping-la-foret.ch]** Fr S exit N12 Bulle dir Fribourg. In 6km turn L uphill to Sorens & site in 2km on L twd Malessert, sp. Lge, pt sl, pt shd; wc; chem disp; mv service pnt; shwrs CHF1; EHU CHF3 (adaptor avail); lndry; shop; rest, snacks; bar; playgrnd; pool; tennis; bike hire; 80% statics; dogs CHF2; Eng spkn; adv bkg; quiet; red long stay. ♦ CHF 24.00   2009*

BUOCHS *B3 (1km N Rural) 46.97950, 8.41860* **TCS Camping Sportzentrum, Seefeldstrasse, 6374 Buochs-Ennetbürgen [041 6203474; fax 6206484; camping.buochs@tcs.ch; www.campingtcs.ch]** Fr W on N2 m'way, exit junc 33 Stans-Süd & bear L. Foll sp Buochs. At 1st x-rds in Buochs, turn L to Ennetbürgen, in approx 1km R twd lake, sp. Fr E exit junc 34 for Buochs, turn L onto Beckenriederstrasse; at x-rds in cent of town turn R dir Ennetbürgen & foll sp as above. Med, mkd pitch, pt shd; wc; chem disp; mv service pnt; shwrs inc; EHU (4A) CHF3.50 (adaptor avail); gas; lndry (inc dryer); supmkt adj; rest, snacks; bar; playgrnd; pool adj; lake sw adj; fishing; tennis; bike hire; games rm; wifi; TV rm; 60% statics in sep area; dogs CHF5; Eng spkn; quiet but some light aircraft noise; ccard acc; red LS/CKE/CCI. "Gd NH twd Italy; helpful staff; well-maintained facs; fine views; boat trip tickets sold on site; ferry close by; if recep clsd find own pitch & sign in later; pitches not draining well after heavy rains; v friendly staff; picturesque site." 1 Apr-3 Oct. CHF 62.00   2013*

BURGDORF *B2 (1.4km SE Rural) 47.05241, 7.63350* **TCS Camping Waldegg, Waldeggweg, 3400 Burgdorf [078 8718780; www.campingtcs.ch]** Exit Bern-Basel N1 m'way at sp Kirchberg. Site in Burgdorf clearly sp. App over narr (2.7m) humpback bdge. Med, pt shd; wc; chem disp; mv service pnt; shwrs inc; EHU (10A) CHF4; lndry rm; shops 300m; rest 100m; playgrnd; pool 200m; fishing; tennis; golf; wifi; dogs; adv bkg; quiet. "Conv Bern; old town of Burgdorf v interesting; friendly staff; clean san facs; gd NH." 1 Apr-31 Oct. CHF 24.00   2010*

CHABLE, LE *D2 (4km SE Rural) 46.05488, 7.24563* **Camping La Sasse, Chemin de la Sasse 11, 1947 Champsec [078 8277342; patricia.gabbud@netplus.ch]** Fr Martigny E on rd 21 & cont dir Verbier. Ent Le Châble & turn R at traff lts. Site on R in 5km. Sm, unshd; wc; chem disp; shwrs CHF1; EHU CHF4; lndry; shop, rest 1km; bar; 50% statics; adv bkg; quiet. "Rustic site; ltd facs; superb location." 15 May-31 Oct. CHF 20.00   2009*

⊞ **CHAUX DE FONDS, LA** *B1 (15km SW Rural) 47.06568, 6.69856* **Camping Lac des Brenets, 2416 Les Brenets [032 9321618; fax 9321639; campinglesbrenets@kfnmail.ch; www.camping-brenets.ch]** Take rd 20 fr La Chaux-de-Fonds to Le Locle, foll sp Les Brenets. Foll twisting rd downhill to lake, turn & ascend to rest site on R. NB Diff L turn on descent. Med, hdstg/grass, terr, unshd; htd wc; chem disp; mv service pnt; shwrs inc; baby facs; EHU (12A) CHF4; gas; lndry; shop, rest, snacks, bar high ssn; sm pool; lake sw adj; tennis; 80% statics; dogs CHF3; adv bkg; quiet; Eng spkn; red long stay; ccard acc; CKE/CCI. "Gd site o'looking Lac des Brenets & Rv Doubs; beautiful views; watch/clock museum 3km; friendly owner; ltd recep hrs, site yourself; sm pitches; excel rest; scenic touring & walking area." ♦ CHF 34.00   2015*

CHESSEL see Villeneuve *C1*

⊞ **CHUR** *B4 (2.6km W Rural) 46.85605, 9.50435* **Camping Au Chur, Felsenaustrasse 61, Obere Au, 7000 Chur [081 2842283; fax 2845683; info@camping-chur.ch; www.camping-chur.ch]** Site sp fr Chur Süd a'bahn exit, foll sp with tent pictogram (easily missed). Lge, pt shd; htd wc; chem disp; mv service pnt; baby facs; shwrs inc; EHU (10A) CHF3.50; gas; lndry; shop; rest 400m; snacks; bar; playgrnd; htd pool 200m; tennis; games area; wifi; TV; 65% statics; dogs CHF3; bus nr; poss cr; Eng spkn; ccard acc; red CKE/CCI. "Well-ordered, clean site; sm area for tourers; sm pitches; gd, modern facs; v soft when wet; helpful, friendly owners; interesting, old town." ♦ CHF 33.00   2010*

CLARO see Bellinzona *C3*

COLOMBIER see Neuchâtel *B1*

CORCELETTES LA POISSINE see Yverdon *B1*

CRANS MONTANA see Sierre *C2*

CUGNASCO see Locarno *C3*

CULLY see Lausanne *C1*

CUREGLIA see Lugano *D3*

DISENTIS MUSTER *C3 (1.6km S Rural) 46.69620, 8.85270* **TCS Camping Fontanivas, Via Fontanivas 9, 7180 Disentis-Mustèr [081 9474422; fax 9474431; camping.disentis@tcs.ch; www.campingtcs.ch]** Fr Disentis S twd Lukmanier Pass for 2.5km. Site on L. Lge, pt shd; htd wc; chem disp; mv service pnt; baby facs; shwrs inc; EHU (6-10A) CHF4; gas; lndry (inc dryer); shop, rest, snacks; bar; BBQ; cooking facs; playgrnd; pool 2.5km; lake sw; tennis; bike hire; wifi; TV rm; 25% statics; dogs CHF6; Eng spkn; adv bkg; quiet; ccard acc; CKE/CCI. "Excel san facs; historic old town; gd walks." ♦ 23 Apr-26 Sep. CHF 36.00   2009*

DUDINGEN see Fribourg *B2*

EGLISAU *A3 (9km E Rural) 47.57900, 8.58169* **TCS Camping Steubisallmend, 8416 Flaach [052 3181413; fax 3182683; camping.flaach@tcs.ch; www.campingtcs.ch]** Fr S (Zürich) on A51 to Bülach at end of m'way, then N4 N to Eglisau. Cross rv & cont twd Schaffhausen. Turn R dir Rüdlingen & Flaach. Site 2km W of Flaach; turn N at Rest Ziegelhütte. Steep access rd needs care. Lge, shd; wc; chem disp; mv service pnt; shwrs inc; EHU (4A) CHF4; gas; lndry; shops; rest 500m; snacks; bar; playgrnd; pool; fishing; bike hire; 75% statics; dogs CHF6; poss cr; Eng spkn; adv bkg; ccard acc; red CKE/CCI. "Well situated on Rv Rhine; lower area subject to flood in wet." ♦ Easter- 4 Oct. CHF 39.00   2009*

EGNACH see Romanshorn *A4*

SWITZERLAND

ERLACH *B2* (500m N Rural) *47.04649, 7.09812* **Camping Erlach, Stadtgraben 23, 3235 Erlach [032 3381646; fax 3381656; camping@erlach.ch; www.erlach.ch]** Fr any dir foll sp for sm town of Ins; fr there foll sp Erlach. In Erlach turn L dir Le Landeron, then R twd Hotel du Port; turn L at hotel, site 200m on L by pier. Med, mkd pitch, shd; wc; chem disp; mv service pnt; baby facs; shwrs CHF1; EHU inc; gas; lndry (inc dryer); freezer; shop; rest, 200m; snacks; bar; playgrnd; pool 3km; lake sw & beach; tennis; games area; bike hire; entmnt; TV; 60% statics; dogs CHF3; poss cr; Eng spkn; adv bkg rec; quiet; ccard acc; red CKE/CCI. "Scenic area; gd for walking & sightseeing; pleasure steamers on lake; gd, superb modern san facs; charming site; sep car park - no cars on pitch; busy, friendly; rec." 31 Mar-15 Oct. CHF 55.00   2015*

"We must tell The Club about that great site we found"

Get your site reports in by mid-August and we'll do our best to get your updates into the next edition.

ESCHENZ *A3* (1.7km W Rural) *47.64467, 8.85985* **Camping Hüttenberg, 8264 Eschenz [052 7412337; fax 7415671; info@huettenberg.ch; www.huettenberg.ch]** Fr Schaffhausen dir Kreuzlingen on rd 13, in Eschenz turn R over level x-ing up hill, site sp. Lge, some hdstg, terr, unshd; htd wc; chem disp; mv service pnt; shwrs inc; EHU (6-10A) CHF3; lndry; shop; rest, snacks; bar; playgrnd; pool; paddling pool; internet; 80% statics; dogs CHF3; phone; bus 1km; train 2km; o'night area for m'vans; poss cr; Eng spkn; adv bkg; quiet; ccard acc; red LS; CKE/CCI. "Beautiful site with stunning views over Untersee; Stein am Rhein & Rhine Falls a must; gd, modern san facs; ltd space for tourers." ♦ ltd. 9 Apr-18 Oct. CHF 33.00   2009*

ESTAVAYER LE LAC *B1* (3km NE Rural) *46.86042, 6.86332* **Camping La Ferme de la Corbière, 1470 Estavayer-le-Lac [026 6633619; fax 6631638; info@corbiere.ch; www.corbiere.ch]** Fr Yverdon foll sp Estavayer-le-Lac. On app Estavayer foll sp Lac de Neuchâtel to pick up site sp. Med, pt shd; wc; shwrs; EHU (10A) inc (adaptor avail & long lead poss req); shop 3km; BBQ; playgrnd; lake sw adj (steep climb); shgle beach; wifi; dogs; adv bkg; quiet; CKE/CCI. "Delightful, quiet alt to busy lakeside sites; helpful owner; CL-type with basic facs; hostel in farm buidings adj; used by lge youth/school tent groups." CHF 31.00   2009*

EVOLENE *C2* (800m S Rural) *46.11080, 7.49656* **Camping Evolène, 1983 Evolène [027 2831104; fax 2833255; info@camping-evolene.ch; www.camping-evolene.ch]** Fr Sion take rd to Val d'Hérens. As app Evolène take L fork to avoid vill cent. Proceed to Co-op on L, turn sharp R & 1st L to site. Site sp. Sm, unshd; htd wc; chem disp; mv service pnt; shwrs CHF1; EHU (10A) CHF4; gas; lndry; shop & 400m; rest adj; bar; playgrnd; cycle, x-country ski & snowboard hire; 5% statics; dogs CHF3; Eng spkn; quiet; ccard acc; ACSI; CKE/CCI. "Mountain scenery; well-kept site; vg san facs; attentive owners; sh walk to vill cent, poss cr." 15 May-15 Oct. CHF 43.00   2012*

FAIDO *C3* (2.4km SE Rural) *46.47134, 8.81771* **Camping Gottardo, 6764 Chiggiogna [tel/fax 091 8661562; schroeder.camp@vtxmail.ch]** Exit A2/E35 at Faido, site on R in 500m, sp immed bef Faido. Med, terr, pt shd; htd wc; chem disp; shwrs CHF0.50; EHU (6A) CHF4; gas; lndry; sm shop & 2km; rest, snacks; bar; playgrnd; sm pool; few statics; dogs CHF2; phone; bus 400m; train 1.5km; poss v cr; Eng spkn; quiet but some rlwy noise; red long stay. "On main rd fr Italian lakes to St Gotthard Pass; interesting vill; poss diff for lge o'fits, espec upper terrs (rec pitch bef white building); excel facs; gd bar & rest - home cooking inc bread, pastries; friendly, helpful staff; access to pitches v ltd in snowy conditions; excel NH." 1 Mar-1 Nov. CHF 40.00   2014*

⊞ **FIESCH** *C2* (2km N Rural) *46.41016, 8.13871* **Camping Eggishorn, Fieschertalstrasse, 3984 Fiesch [027 9710316; fax 9710317; info@camping-eggishorn.ch; www.camping-eggishorn.ch]** Fr N19 turn into Fiesch, site sp in town. Med, mkd pitch, pt shd; htd wc; chem disp; mv service pnt; baby facs; shwrs inc; EHU (16A) CHF4; gas; lndry (inc dryer); shop 500m; rest, snacks; bar; BBQ; playgrnd; htd, covrd pool; fishing; games area; games rm; wifi; TV; 25% statics; dogs CHF3; bus, train 600m; poss cr; Eng spkn; quiet; ccard acc; CKE/CCI. "Beautiful situation - views all dirs; cable cars nr for Aletsch glacier; excel walking; well-kept site; highly rec." ♦ CHF 43.00   2011*

FILISUR *C4* (2.6km W Rural) *46.67176, 9.67408* **Camping Islas, 7477 Filisur [081 4041647; fax 4042259; info@campingislas.ch; www.campingislas.ch]** Fr Tiefencastel take dir Albula. At Filisur foll camping sp. Long, single track rd to site. Med, some hdstg, unshd; htd wc; chem disp; shwrs inc; EHU (10A) CHF2; gas; lndry (inc dryer); shop; supmkt 1.5km; rest; bar; BBQ; playgrnd; pool; fishing; wifi; TV; 70% statics; dogs free; phone; train 1.5km; adv bkg; ccard acc; Eng spkn; quiet. "Gd touring base; informal management; euros acc; train to Davos free with guest card supplied; excel san facs." ♦ 1 Apr-31 Oct. CHF 52.00   2013*

"I need an on-site restaurant"

We do our best to make sure site information is correct, but it is always best to check any must-have facilities are still available or will be open during your visit.

FLAACH see Eglisau *A3*

FLEURIER *B1* (1.4km NW Rural) *46.90643, 6.57508* **Camping Val de Travers, Belle Roche 15, 2114 Fleurier [tel/fax 032 8614262; camping.fleurier@tcs.ch; www.camping-val-de-travers.ch]** On Pontarlier (France) to Neuchâtel rd, site sp in Fleurier to L at start of vill. Med, pt shd; wc; chem disp; mv service pnt; shwrs; EHU (4A) CHF3; gas; lndry; shop; rest; bar; playgrnd; htd pool 2km; rv fishing; tennis; games area; bike hire; 15% statics; dogs CHF3; Eng spkn; adv bkg; quiet; ccard acc. "Helpful owners; wild chamois on rocks behind site visible early morning; vg." 17 Apr-26 Sep. CHF 28.00   2009*

FOREL see Vevey *C1*

SWITZERLAND

FOULY, LA *D2* (700m N Rural) *45.93693, 7.09548* **Camping des Glaciers, 1944 La Fouly-Val Ferret [027 7831735; fax 7833605; info@camping-glaciers.ch; www.camping-glaciers.ch]** Exit Martigny-Grand St Bernard rd at Orsières. Cont thro Val Ferret to vill of La Fouly. At end of vill turn R, site in 500m. V steep rd for 13km fr Orsières. Lge, terr, pt sl, pt shd; wc; chem disp; mv service pnt; baby facs; shwrs inc; EHU CHF3.50; gas; lndry; shop 500m; rest 500m; playgrnd; tennis 300m; games area; fishing; horseriding; wifi; TV; dogs CHF2; Eng spkn; adv bkg; quiet; ccard acc; CKE/CCI. "Lovely site; excel facs; excel walking, climbing cent; lovely views." 15 May-30 Sep. CHF 30.00   2009*

FRIBOURG *B2* (13km N Rural) *46.87827, 7.19121* Camping Schiffenensee, Schiffenen 15, 3186 Düdingen [026 4933486; fax 4933474; info@camping-schiffenen.ch; www.camping-schiffenen.ch] Exit A12 Bern-Fribourg at Düdingen & foll rd for Murten (sp). Ent poss tight lge o'fits. Lge, mkd pitch, pt shd; wc; chem disp; shwrs CHF1; EHU (10A) CHF3; lndry; shop; rest, snacks; bar; pool; paddling pool; lake adj; tennis; 80% statics; dogs CHF3; bus; poss cr; Eng spkn; adv bkg; quiet; ccard not acc; CKE/CCI. 1 Apr-31 Oct. CHF 27.00   2009*

FRUTIGEN see Kandersteg *C2*

GAMPEL see Leuk *C2*

GAMPELEN see Neuchâtel *B1*

GENEVE *C1* (8km NE Urban) *46.24465, 6.19433* **TCS Camping Pointe à la Bise, Chemin de la Bise, 1222 Vésenaz [022 7521296; fax 7523767; camping.geneve@tcs.ch; www.campingtcs.ch]** Fr Geneva take S lakeside rd N5 sp Evian to Vésanez 4km. Turn L on Rte d'Hermance (D25) at traff lts & foll sp to site in 1km. Med, pt shd; wc; chem disp; mv service pnt; baby facs; shwrs inc; EHU (4-10A) CHF4.50 (adaptor on loan); gas; lndry; shop; rest, snacks; bar; playgrnd; paddling pool; lake sw; fishing; bike hire; wifi; TV; 60% statics; dogs CHF5; bus to Geneva; poss cr; Eng spkn; ccard acc; red CKE/CCI. "Pleasant site; excel lake & mountain excursions; helpful staff; muddy when wet." 1 Apr-3 Oct. CHF 46.00   2010*

GENEVE *C1* (9km W Rural) *46.20111, 6.06621* **Geneva City Camping (previously Camping du Bois de Bay), 19 Route du Bois de Bay, 1242 Geneve [022 3410505; fax 3410606; info@geneva-camping.ch; www.geneva-camping.ch]** Fr A1 exit sp Bernex, then foll sp to Vernier, site sp. Lge, hdg pitch, pt shd; htd wc; chem disp; mv service pnt; baby facs; shwrs inc; EHU (6A) CHF4.50; gas; lndry (inc dryer); shop; snacks; bar; BBQ; playgrnd; tennis 2km; wifi; 40% statics; dogs CHF3.50; bus 2km; Eng spkn; some aircraft noise; ccard acc; red CKE/CCI. "V friendly; modern san facs; park & ride bus to city; don't be put off by indus site outside site." ♦ 1 Mar-31 Dec. CHF 43.00 (CChq acc)   2012*

GORDEVIO see Locarno *C3*

GRAFSCHAFT see Ulrichen *C3*

GRINDELWALD *C2* (2km SE Rural) *46.62061, 8.04400* **Camping Gletscherdorf, Lochenbodenweg, 3818 Grindelwald [033 8531429; fax 8533129; info@gletscherdorf.ch; www.gletscherdorf.ch]** Exit N6 at Interlaken & then dir Grindelwald. Turn R just after church at end of main rd thro town at sp Gletscher/Schlucht & down steep descent for 500m, camp on R, sharp R turn to ent. Med, mkd pitch, hdstg, pt sl, unshd; wc; chem disp; mv service pnt; shwrs inc; EHU (10A) CHF4; gas; lndry; shop; rest 500m; covrd pool 1km; 60% statics; no dogs; poss cr; Eng spkn; adv bkg; quiet; ccard acc; CKE/CCI. "Sh walk to glacier; ideal base for walking; views of Eiger; site yourself & pay later - recep clsd 1000-1730; excel san facs, but ltd; friendly." 1 May-20 Oct. CHF 34.00   2011*

> ## "Satellite navigation makes touring much easier"
>
> Remember most sat navs don't know if you're towing or in a larger vehicle – always use yours alongside maps and site directions.

⊞ **GRINDELWALD** *C2* (1.5km W Rural) *46.62211, 8.01550* **Camping Eigernordwand, 3818 Grindelwald [033 8534227 or 8553322 winter; camp@eigernordwand.ch; www.eigernordwand.ch]** At 1st rndabt at ent to town turn R, site sp, no. 27. Med, pt sl, pt shd; htd wc; chem disp; mv service pnt; serviced pitch; shwrs inc; EHU (10A) CHF5 (poss rev pol); gas; lndry; shop; rest, snacks; bar; playgrnd; pool 1km; games area; TV; 60% statics; no dogs; bus 1km; site clsd mid-Apr to mid-May; higher winter prices; poss cr; quiet; ccard acc; red long stay. "Superb position at base of Eiger N wall; relaxed atmosphere; friendly, helpful staff; uphill walk to town; ski in/ski out; excel." ♦ CHF 34.00   2010*

⊞ **GRUYERES** *C2* (6km S Rural) *46.56080, 7.08740* **Camping Haute Gruyère, Chemin du Camping 18, 1667 Enney [tel/fax 026 9212260; camping.enney@bluewin.ch; www.camping-gruyere.ch]** Well sp fr N (Gruyères) but not by name - foll TCS sp, not well sp fr S. Site E of rd fr Bulle to Château d'Oex, 1km S of Enney vill. Beware trains on x-ing at turn in. Med, unshd; htd wc; chem disp; mv service pnt; fam bthrm; shwrs inc; EHU (6-10A) CHF4.50 (adaptor on loan); gas; lndry (inc dryer); shops 1km; rest, snacks; bar; playgrnd; lake sw 10km; fishing; bike hire; entmnt; TV; 50% statics; dogs CHF4; poss cr; adv bkg; quiet; 10% red long stay; ccard acc. "Friendly owners; vg, modern san facs; sm area for tourers; bread to order; mainly level cycle rte to Gruyeres." CHF 45.00 (CChq acc)   2015*

⊞ **GSTAAD** *C2* (2km NW Rural) *46.48119, 7.27269* **Camping Bellerive, Bellerivestrasse 38, 3780 Gstaad [033 7446330; fax 7446345; bellerive.camping@bluewin.ch; www.bellerivecamping.ch]** App fr Saanen turn R bef Gstaad, sp. Sm, mkd pitch, some hdstg, pt shd; htd wc; chem disp; mv service pnt; shwrs CHF1; EHU (12A) CHF2.70; gas; lndry (inc dryer); playgrnd; pool 700m; tennis; fishing; skiing; internet; TV; 60% statics; dogs CHF2.70; Eng spkn; adv bkg; rlwy noise. "Gd touring, walking, wintersports; rvside site; sm pitches; buy Gstaad Card for rd, rail & mountain transport." CHF 29.00   2011*

GSTEIG BEI GSTAAD see Gstaad *C2*

GUDO *C3* (2km W Rural) *46.17080, 8.93170* **Camping Isola, Via al Gaggioletto 3, 6515 Gudo [091 8593244; fax 8593344; campeggio.isola@ticino.com; www.camping-isola.ch]** Exit A2 at Bellinzona Sud dir Bellinzona (47), turn L at major traff lts sp Locarno. Cross rv & m'way, cont thro Gudo, site on L in 500m, sharp L into site v narr rd, poorly sp. Lge, hdg/mkd pitch, pt shd; htd wc; chem disp; mv service pnt; baby facs; shwrs inc; EHU (10A) CHF40; lndry; shop; rest, snacks; bar; playgrnd; htd pool; paddling pool; 95% statics; dogs CHF4; site clsd mid-Dec to mid-Jan; quiet. "Delightful, well-kept site; NH pitches poor with inadequate elec supply; easy access fr main rd; mainly statics creating cr; v sm pitches not suitable for lge o'fits." 15 Jan-15 Dec. CHF 75.00 2013*

GUMEFENS see Bulle *C2*

GWATT see Thun *B2*

HASLIBERG GOLDERN *B3* (500m SW Rural) *46.73727, 8.19588* **Camping Hofstaff-Derfli, Hoffstatt, 6085 Hasliberg-Goldern [033 9713707; fax 9713755; welcome@ derfli.ch; www.derfli.ch]** Fr Brünig pass foll sp for Hasliberg. After cable car at Twing foll rd to Gasthof & turn R down narr rd opp. Site well sp. Sm, mkd pitch, pt shd; htd wc; chem disp; mv service pnt; baby facs; shwrs inc; EHU (10A) metered; gas; lndry (inc dryer); shop & 2km; rest, snacks, bar 500m; playgrnd; hot tub; bike hire; games area; games rm; wifi; TV; 20% statics; dogs CHF2; phone; bus 500m; Eng spkn; adv bkg; quiet. "Excel, beautiful site; vg summer walking/winter sports; gd size pitches." ♦ 15 Dec-30 Apr & 15 May-31 Oct. CHF 34.00 2010*

HAUDERES, LES *D2* (2km N Rural) *46.09303, 7.50560* **Camping Molignon, Route de Molignon 183, 1984 Les Haudères [027 2831240; fax 2831331; info@molignon.ch; www.molignon.ch]** Fr Sion take rd to Val d'Hérens, turn R 2.5km after Evolène. Site sp. Rd fr Sion steep, twisting & narr in places. Med, mkd pitch, terr, pt shd; wc; mv service pnt; chem disp; baby facs; shwrs inc; EHU (10A) CHF3.80; gas; lndry; shop; rest, snacks; bar; playgrnd; htd pool; ski lift 3km; TV; 15% statics; dogs CHF3.20; phone; Eng spkn; adv bkg; quiet; ccard acc; red CKE/CCI. "V friendly owner; ideal for mountain climbing & walking; beautiful location." CHF 46.00 2014*

HINTERKAPPELEN see Bern *B2*

HORW see Luzern *B3*

INNERTKIRCHEN *C3* (500m N Rural) *46.70669, 8.22619* **Camping Grund, Grundstrasse 44, 3862 Innertkirchen [tel/fax 033 9714409; info@camping-grund.ch; www.camping-grund.ch]** App fr Susten or Grimsel Pass, turn L at camping sp immed on ent vill. Foll further sp for 1km. Sm, pt shd; htd wc; chem disp; mv service pnt; shwrs CHF1; EHU (6A) CHF3; gas; lndry (inc dryer); shops 200m; BBQ; playgrnd; htd covrd pool 6km; tennis; fishing; horseriding; games rm; dogs CHF2; adv bkg; quiet; 10% red long stay. "V helpful & friendly; gd cent for mountains." CHF 29.00 2011*

INNERTKIRCHEN *C3* (2km E Rural) *46.70700, 8.24219* **Camping Bauernhof-Wyler, Sustenstrasse 32, 3862 Innertkirchen [033 9718451; camping-wyler@bluewin.ch; www.camping-wyler.com]** App fr Innertkirchen dir Sustenpass, take care hairpin bends. Turn R on ent vill & foll sp. Sm, pt sl, unshd; wc; chem disp; shwrs CHF1; EHU (10A) CHF2.50 (long lead poss req); lndry (inc dryer); BBQ; playgrnd; tennis; fishing; games rm; horseriding; 20% statics; dogs CHF2; phone nr; adv bkg; Eng spkn; quiet. "Picturesque location; pleasant owner; CL-type site." ♦ ltd. 1 Apr-31 Oct. CHF 27.00 2009*

INNERTKIRCHEN *C3* (1.5km NW Rural) *46.70938, 8.21519* **Camping Aareschlucht, Hauptstrasse 34, 3862 Innertkirchen [033 9715332; fax 9715344; campaareschlucht@bluewin.ch; www.camping-aareschlucht.ch]** On Meiringen rd out of town on R. Sm, pt shd; htd wc; chem disp; shwrs CHF1; EHU (6-10A) CHF3; gas; lndry (inc dryer); shop & rests nr; BBQ; playgrnd; pool 5km; games rm; 30% statics; dogs CHF2; adv bkg; Eng spkn; sep car park; quiet, but some rd noise; ccard acc; Red CKE/CCI. "Excel site; clean facs; gd walking; gd touring base Interlaken, Jungfrau region; conv Grimsel & Susten passes; rv walk to town." 1 May-31 Oct. CHF 24.00 2011*

INTERLAKEN, Sites in the Interlaken area are identified by numbers sp fr the N8. Foll the appropriate number to your site as folls: Manor Farm 1, Alpenblick 2, Hobby 3, Lazy Rancho 4, Jungfrau 5, Interlaken-Ost 6, Jungfraublick 7, Oberoi 8, Seeblick 10, Du Lac 15, Bauernhof Wang 19. *

INTERLAKEN *C2* (5km NE Rural) *46.70761, 7.91330* **Camp au Lac, 3852 Ringgenberg [033 8222616; fax 8234360]** Fr Ringgenberg to Brienz, site sp on R when exit Ringgenberg. Cont under rlwy viaduct to site. Med, pt sl, pt shd; wc; chem disp (wc); mv service pnt; shwrs CHF1; EHU (6A) CHF3 (long cable poss req); lndry rm; shop & 1km; rest (clsd Mon,Tue LS); bar; pool 2km; 25% statics; dogs CHF2; bus; poss cr; Eng spkn; adv bkg; quiet; ccard acc; red LS; CKE/CCI. "Excel site; private access to lake; magnificent setting." ♦ CHF 36.00 2009*

INTERLAKEN (NO. 1) *C2* (8km W Rural) *46.68004, 7.81669* **Camping Manor Farm, Seestrasse 201, 3800 Interlaken-Thunersee [033 8222264; fax 8222279 or 033 8232991; manorfarm@swisscamps.ch or info@ manorfarm.ch; www.manorfarm.ch]** Fr W on A8 exit junc 24 Interlaken West & foll sp Thun & Gunten. At rndabt take 2nd exit twd Thun, sp Gunten; pass Camping Alpenblick on R, then site on L after bdge. V lge, mkd pitch, pt shd; chem disp; mv service pnt; wc; baby facs; serviced pitches; shwrs inc; EHU (6A) inc (adaptor avail); gas; lndry (inc dryer); shop; 2 rests adj; snacks; bar; BBQ (charcoal/gas); playgrnd; paddling pool; private beach/lake sw adj; boat & bike hire; steamer boat trips; excursions; cable car & chairlift nrby; watersports; fishing; golf 300m; horseriding 3km; wifi; entmnt; games/TV rm; 25% statics; dogs CHF5; o'fits over 8m by request; money exchange; variable pitch price; poss cr; Eng spkn; adv bkg (bkg fee); quiet, rd noise some pitches; ccard acc; red LS; CKE/CCI. "Site on banks of Lake Thun; excel views; gd sized pitches; helpful staff; immac san facs; excel facs for children; local bus pass provided free; gd walking; if staying on Super pitch, water hose with pressurised valve fitting req; site v easy to find; v pleasant and well looked after; if taking an awning a storm strap req." ♦ CHF 66.00 2013*

SWITZERLAND

⊞ **INTERLAKEN (NO. 2)** *C2* (5km W Rural) *46.67969, 7.81764*
Camping Alpenblick, Seestrasse 130, 3800 Unterseen-
Interlaken [033 8227757 or 8231470; fax 8216045;
info@camping-alpenblick.ch; www.camping-alpenblick.ch]
Fr W on A8 exit junc 24 Interlaken West & foll sp Thun &
Gunten. At rndabt take 2nd exit twd Thun, sp Gunten. Site
adj Motel Neuhaus & Rest Strandbad on Gunten-Thun rd.
Lge, mkd pitch, pt shd; htd wc; chem disp; mv service pnt;
baby facs; shwrs inc; EHU (10A) CHF4.50; gas; lndry (inc
dryer); shop, rest, snacks; BBQ; pool 3km; playgrnd; lake sw
adj; watersports; fishing; golf adj; wifi; 30% statics; dogs
CHF3; phone; bus fr site ent; stn 3km; Eng spkn; ccard acc
(surcharge); red LS/long stay/CKE/CCI. "In beautiful situation;
mountain views; excel, modern facs; bread baked on site; lake
steamers fr hotel opp; gd walks nr; free bus pass to town;
cycle rte to Interlaken; CHF1 to fill m'van water tank; adv bkg
attracts surchage; site next to shooting club, poss noisy." ♦
CHF 55.00   2014*

INTERLAKEN (NO. 3) *C2* (4km W Rural) *46.68400, 7.82961*
Camping Hobby, Lehnweg 16, 3800 Unterseen-Interlaken
[033 8229652; fax 8229657; info@campinghobby.ch;
www.campinginterlaken.ch or www.campinghobby.ch]
On N8 fr Thun at E end of lake exit junc to Unterseen on rd
70. In 200m past petrol stn, turn L into narr lane; site sp. Site
next to Camping Lazy Rancho. Or fr Interlaken turn R by side
of Landhotel Golf opp g'ge, foll No.3 sp. Med, pt shd, some
hdstg; htd wc; chem disp; mv service pnt; baby facs; shwrs
CHF0.50; EHU (10A) CHF4.50 (adaptor avail); gas; lndry (inc
dryer); shop, rest, snacks 400m; BBQ; playgrnd; paddling pool;
shgl beach & lake sw 1.5km; golf 1km; wifi; 25% statics; dogs;
Eng spkn; adv bkg; quiet but some noise fr shooting range
at w/end; ccard not acc; red LS; CKE/CCI. "Gd for touring
Interlaken, Jungfrau region & Bernese Oberland; wonderful
views of Eiger & other mountains; v clean facs; friendly staff."
♦ 1 Apr-30 Sep. CHF 50.00   2011*

INTERLAKEN (NO. 4) *C2* (4.2km W Rural) *46.68555, 7.83083*
Camping Lazy Rancho, Lehnweg 6, 3800 Unterseen-
Interlaken [033 8228716; fax 8231920; info@lazyrancho.ch;
www.lazyrancho.ch] Fr W on app to Interlaken, exit A8/
A6 junc 24 sp Interlaken West. Turn L at slip rd rndabt then
at rndabt take a sharp R turn (foll camping sp Nos. 3-5); at
Migrol petrol stn foll sp for Lazy Rancho 4 (narr rd on L just bef
Landhotel Golf); it is 2nd site. Cent of Interlaken best avoided
with c'vans or lge m'vans. Rec arr bef 1900 hrs. Med, hdg/
mkd pitch, some hdstg, pt shd; htd wc; some serviced pitches;
chem disp; mv service pnt; baby facs; shwrs inc; EHU (10A) inc
(adaptors provided); gas; lndry (inc dryer); shop; cooking facs;
bar; BBQ; playgrnd; sm pool; watersports, fishing nrby; bike
hire; tennis 2.5km; horseriding 500m; fitness cent/spa; games
rm; wifi; sat TV; 30% statics; dogs CHF3; no o'fits over 7.5m
high ssn; phone; Eng spkn; quiet but some noise fr shooting
range at w/end; ccard acc; red LS; CKE/CCI. "Superb views
Eiger, Monch & Jungfrau; ideal for touring Interlaken, Bernese
Oberland; friendly, caring, helpful owners; sm pitches; recep
0900-1200 & 1330-2100 high ssn; 5 mins to bus stop nr Cmp
Jungfrau; ask about Swiss red fare rlwy services - excel value;
immac, outstanding, well-maintained site & facs; brilliant site"
♦ 1 May-27 Sep. CHF 57.00 SBS - S01   2014*

INTERLAKEN (NO. 5) *C2* (2km W Rural) *46.68688, 7.83411*
Jungfrau Camp, Steindlerstrasse 60, 3800 Unterseen-
Interlaken [tel/fax 033 8225730; info@jungfraucamp.ch;
www.campinginterlaken.ch or www.jungfraucamp.ch]
Leave N8 at exit Unterseen. In approx 600m turn R at rndabt &
foll sp to site. Med, pt shd; htd wc; chem disp (ltd); mv service
pnt; baby facs; fam bthrm; shwrs CHF1; EHU (10A) CHF4.50; gas;
lndry (inc dryer); shop; rest, snacks; bar; playgrnd; pool; lake sw
1.5km; tennis; 40% statics; dogs CHF4; bus adj; poss cr; Eng
spkn; adv bkg; quiet some noise fr shooting range at w/end;
red LS. "Visits to all Bernese Oberland vills; views of Jungfrau,
Mönch & Eiger; town in walking dist; excel, relaxing, well-run
site; high standard san facs." 1 Jun-15 Sep. CHF 46.00   2013*

INTERLAKEN (NO. 6) *C2* (1.1km N Rural) *46.69256,*
7.8689 **TCS Camping Interlaken-Ost, Brienzstrasse 24,**
3800 Interlaken [033 8224434; fax 8224456; camping.
interlaken@tcs.ch; www.campinginterlaken.ch]
Exit N8 at Ringenberg & foll sp for Brienz/Luzern. After viaduct
turn L & site sp in 100m. Awkward bends on app. Med, mkd
pitch, pt shd; wc; chem disp; mv service pnt; shwrs; EHU (8A)
CHF4; gas; lndry (inc dryer); shop in ssn; rest; bar; playgrnd;
pool 300m; sand beach 2km; wellness facs; wifi; 20% statics;
dogs CHF5; train opp; poss cr high ssn; Eng spkn; some rd
noise; ccard acc; red CKE/CCI. "Gd cent for Bernese Oberland;
excel walking; helpful staff; easy access to town; lively entmnt
on lake cruises; concerts." 1 Apr-10 Oct. CHF 44.00   2011*

INTERLAKEN (NO. 8) *C2* (4km S Rural) *46.66161, 7.86500*
Camping Oberei, Obereigasse 9, 3812 Wilderswil-
Interlaken [tel/fax 033 8221335; oberei8@swisscamps.ch;
www.campinginterlaken.ch or www.campingwilderswil.ch]
Fr Interlaken by-pass take rd sp Grindelwald & Lauterbrunnen
to Wilderswil. Site sp 800m past stn on R in vill. Narr ent. Med,
mkd pitch, pt sl, pt shd; htd wc; chem disp; baby facs; shwrs
CHF1; EHU (6A) CHF3; gas; lndry (inc dryer); shop; rest, snacks
in vill; pool 3km; TV rm; dogs CHF2; bus adj, bus/train nr; poss
cr; Eng spkn; adv bkg; quiet; ccard not acc; CKE/CCI. "Well-
managed, relaxing, family-run site in superb scenic location;
helpful owners; grnd sheets supplied if wet/muddy; blocks
provided; gd, clean facs; gd touring cent; easy walk to rlwy
stn; guest card gives free local train & bus travel; excel rec high
ssn." 1 May-15 Oct. CHF 48.00   2013*

INTERLAKEN (NO. 10) *C2* (700m N Rural) *46.69125, 7.89353*
TCS Camping Seeblick, Campingstrasse 14, 3806 Bönigen
[033 8221143; fax 8221162; camping.boenigen@tcs.ch;
www.campingtcs.ch] Fr A8 exit junc 26 Interlaken-Ost dir
Bönigen; on ent vill turn L, site sp on Lake Brienz. Med, some
hdstg, shd; htd wc; chem disp; mv service pnt; baby facs; shwrs
inc; EHU (6A) CHF4; gas; lndry (inc dryer); shop; rest 600m;
snacks; bar; playgrnd; htd pool, paddling pool 200m; lake sw;
fishing; boating; golf 4km; wifi; entmnt; TV rm; 10% statics;
dogs CHF5; phone; Eng spkn; quiet; ccard acc; red LS/CKE/
CCI. "Ideal for fishing or boating; v helpful, friendly owner;
clean facs; excel site; excel position walking & cycling into
Interlaken." ♦ 28 Mar- 6 Oct. CHF 49.00   2013*

SWITZERLAND

INTERLAKEN (NO. 15) *C2* (9km ENE Rural) *46.71141, 7.96886*
Camping du Lac, Schorren, 3807 Iseltwald [079 3533021;
info@campingdulac.ch; www.campingdulac.ch]
Leave N8 at Iseltwald. Site sp fr N8, on Lake Brienz adj hotel.
Sm, mkd pitch, terr, unshd; wc; chem disp; shwrs inc; EHU
CHF4.50; lndry (inc dryer); shop; lakeside rest adj; paddling
pool; lake beach & sw 200m; fishing; watersports; mountain
biking; internet; TV rm; 80% statics; dogs CHF4; bus 300m;
Eng spkn; adv bkg; quiet; red LS. "Peaceful site in superb
location; friendly owner; vg, modern facs; access poss diff lge
o'fits; touring pitches in cent of statics; vg." 1 May-30 Sep.
CHF 46.00   2011*

INTERLAKEN (NO. 19) *C2* (13km W Rural) *46.69025, 7.78469*
Camping auf dem Bauernhof Wang, 3803 Beatenberg
[033 8412105; fax 8412185; camping-wang@gmx.ch;
www.naturpur.ch/camping-wang] Exit m'way at junc
Unterseen & foll sp to Beatenberg; 300m after church turn L
& site sp. GPS rte not rec - use these dirs. Sm, terr, pt shd; wc;
chem disp; shwrs inc; EHU CHF3; lndry; playgrnd; htd, covrd
pool, tennis 1km; wifi; some statics; dogs CHF2; bus 300m;
adv bkg; quiet; red LS. "Vg, peaceful, beautiful site in superb
location; gd san facs; owner helpful; excel hiking country; conv
Interlaken." 20 Apr-15 Oct. CHF 31.00   2011*

"There aren't many sites
open at this time of year"
If you're travelling outside peak season
remember to call ahead to check site opening
dates – even if the entry says 'open all year'.

ISELTWALD see Interlaken *C2*

⊞ **KANDERSTEG** *C2* (15km N Rural) *46.58188, 7.64150*
Camping Grassi, 3714 Frutigen [033 6711149; fax 6711380;
campinggrassi@bluewin.ch; www.camping-grassi.ch]
Exit rd to Kandersteg at Frutigen-Dorf & in 400m L to site in
500m. Med, pt shd; htd wc; chem disp; mv service pnt; baby
facs; shwrs inc; EHU (10A) CHF3; gas; lndry; shops; rest 500m;
playgrnd; htd covrd pool 1km; fishing; tennis; bike hire; wifi;
TV; 50% statics; dogs CHF1.50; phone; Eng spkn; adv bkg;
red long stay. "Walking rte dir fr site to spectacular pedestrian
suspension bdge; 10 min walk to town." CHF 41.00   2014*

⊞ **KANDERSTEG** *C2* (1.3km NE Rural) *46.49800, 7.68519*
Camping Rendez-Vous, 3718 Kandersteg [033 6751534;
fax 6751737; rendez-vous.camping@bluewin.ch;
www.camping-kandersteg.ch] In middle of Kandersteg
turn E dir Sesselbahn Öschinensee; site sp. Med, some hdstg,
pt sl, terr, pt shd; htd wc; chem disp; mv service pnt; shwrs
CHF1; EHU (10A) (adaptors avail); gas; lndry (inc dryer); shop;
rest, snacks; bar; BBQ; htd pool 800m; bike hire; games rm;
wifi; dogs CHF3; Eng spkn; adv bkg; quiet; ccard acc; CKE/
CCI. "Excel, well-supervised site; chair-lift adj; excel walking."
CHF 49.00   2014*

KRATTIGEN see Spiez *C2*

KREUZLINGEN *A3* (8km SE Rural) *47.62182, 9.26602*
Camping Ruderbaum, Ruderbaum 3, 8595 Altnau-am-
Bodensee [071 6952965; camping@ruderbaum.ch;
www.ruderbaum.ch] Fr Kreuzlingen foll main lakeside rd 13
twd Romanshorn. After passing sp for Altnau, at rndabt turn
L, cross rlwy, site on L. Lge, pt sl, pt shd; htd wc; chem disp;
mv service pnt; shwrs; EHU CHF3.50; lndry; shop; rest, snacks,
bar adj; shgl beach & lake adj sw; 80% statics; dogs €2.50;
train adj; Eng spkn; quiet; some rlwy noise; CKE/CCI. "Sep
area for tourers sloping down to lake - poss diff when wet; gd
site in beautiful setting; helpful staff; lakeside walks & cycling;
landing stage for Lake Constance ships; gd." ◆ 1 Apr-31 Oct.
CHF 29.00   2010*

LANDERON, LE *B2* (300m S Rural) *47.05216, 7.06975*
Camping des Pêches, Route du Port, 2525 Le Landeron
[032 7512900; fax 7516354; info@camping-lelanderon.ch;
www.camping-lelanderon.ch] A5 fr Neuchâtel, exit Le
Landeron or La Neuveville; foll site sp. Med, mkd pitch, pt shd;
wc; chem disp; mv service pnt; 20% serviced pitches; baby
facs; shwrs CHF1; EHU (15A) CHF3.50; gas; lndry; shop; rest;
bar; playgrnd; htd pool 100m; fishing; tennis; bike hire; TV rm;
60% statics; sep car park; poss cr; Eng spkn; adv bkg; noisy;
ccard acc; red CKE/CCI. "Sep touring section on busy site;
walks by lake & rv; interesting old town." ◆ ltd. 1 Apr-15 Oct.
CHF 32.00   2009*

LANDQUART *B4* (3km E Rural) *46.97040, 9.59620* TCS
Camping Neue Ganda, Ganda 21, 7302 Landquart
[081 3223955; fax 3226864; camping.landquart@tcs.ch;
www.campingtcs.ch] Exit A13/E43 dir Landquart, site sp on
rd to Davos. Lge, pt sl, pt shd; htd wc; chem disp; mv service
pnt; fam bthrm; baby facs; shwrs inc; EHU (6-10A) CHF4;
gas; lndry (inc dryer); shop; snacks; bar; BBQ; cooking facs;
playgrnd; rv fishing; canoeing; tennis 300m; games rm; bike
hire; wifi; entmnt; 60% statics; dogs CHF4; rd noise; ccard acc;
red CKE/CCI. "Immac san facs; excel site; v helpful owner &
staff; poss uneven pitches, mainly grass; if recep clsd find pitch
& sign in later; many mkd walks fr site." ◆
10 Dec-28 Feb & 19 Mar-17 Oct. CHF 46.00   2015*

LANGNAU AM ALBIS see Adliswil *A3*

LANGWIESEN see Schaffhausen *A3*

LAUSANNE *C1* (9km E Rural) *46.48973, 6.73786* **Camping
de Moratel, Route de Moratel 2, 1096 Cully [021 7991914;
camping.moratel@bluewin.ch]** Fr Lausanne-Vevey lakeside
rd (not m/way), turn R to Cully; sp thro town; site on R on lake
shore. Ent not sp. Sm, hdg/mkd pitch, hdstg, pt shd; wc; chem
disp; mv service pnt; shwrs inc; EHU (3-5A) metered (adaptor
provided); gas; lndry; shop; snacks; bar; pool 3km; lake sw;
fishing; boating; 80% statics; bus, train, ferry; poss cr; adv bkg;
some rlwy noise. "Vg value; attractive, clean site with beautiful
views; rec adv bkg for lakeside pitch; friendly staff; siting poss
diff for lge o'fits; gd location for best pt Lake Geneva; ex san
facs." 20 Mar-20 Oct. CHF 23.00   2011*

SWITZERLAND

LAUTERBRUNNEN

in the Valley of
72 Waterfalls

Mountain Holiday Park

Camping Jungfrau
Schweiz · Switzerland

www.camping-jungfrau.ch

– Very modern facilities
– Family-friendly, children's playground
– Hiking & skiing areas of the
  Jungfrau region
– Restaurant, grocery shop, ...
– Specially adapted for motorhomes
– Bungalows, caravans, B&B
– Winter season sites, free ski bus

Open the whole year round!

WiFi Zone
Hotspot
swisscom

Eiger   Mönch   Jungfrau

CAMPING JUNGFRAU AG, CH-3822 LAUTERBRUNNEN, Berner Oberland, Phone +41 (0)33 856 20 10
info@camping-jungfrau.ch, www.camping-jungfrau.ch, GPS: 3822 Lauterbrunnen, Weid 406, N 46:35.314, E 07:54.504
facebook.com/CampingJungfrau   twitter.com/CampingJungfrau

⊞ **LAUSANNE** *C1* (3km W Rural) *46.51769, 6.59766*
**Camping de Vidy, Chemin du Camping 3, 1007 Lausanne
(Genferseegebiet) [021 6225000; fax 6225001;
info@clv.ch; www.clv.ch]** Leave A1 at Lausanne Süd/Ouchy
exit; take 4th exit at rndabt (Rte de Chavannes); in 100m filter
L at traff lts & foll site sp to L. Site adj to HQ of Int'l Olympic
Organisation, well sp all over Lausanne. Lge, mkd pitch, pt
shd; htd wc (some cont); chem disp; mv service pnt; baby facs;
shwrs inc; EHU (10A) inc; gas; lndry (inc dryer); shop; rest,
snacks; bar; BBQ; playgrnd; lake beach adj; watersports; tennis
1km; bike hire; sports & recreation area adj; games rm; wifi;
TV; many statics in sep area; recep 0800-2100 high ssn; dogs
CHF2; no o'fits over 8m high ssn; bus to Lausanne 400m; chem
disp up steps; Eng spkn; adv bkg; quiet; ccard acc; CKE/CCI.
"Excel lakeside site in attractive park; friendly staff; sm pitches;
gd san facs; gd train service to Geneva; conv m'way; free bus
passes for unltd bus & Metro tavel in Lausanne; facs need
updating (2013); gd cycling." ♦ CHF 47.00   2013*

⊞ **LAUTERBRUNNEN** *C2* (1km SE Rural) *46.59100, 7.91311*
**Camping Schützenbach, Witimatte 204B, 3822 Lauterbrunnen
[033 8551268; fax 8551275; info@schutzenbach.ch;
www.schutzenbach.ch]** S fr Interlaken, site sp after
Lauterbrunnen. Med, pt sl, terr, pt shd; htd wc; chem disp; mv
service pnt; shwrs CHF0.50; EHU (15A) CHF4 (poss rev pol);
gas; lndry (inc dryer); shop & 300m; snacks; bar; playgrnd; pool
400m; fishing; tennis; 60% statics; dogs CHF3; bus at site ent;
rlwy stn nr; site clsd 6 Nov-9 Dec; Eng spkn; adv bkg; quiet
but some noise fr nrby helipad & hostel adj; ccard acc. "Clean,
modern san facs; site used by coach camping parties & lge
groups; friendly owners." CHF 26.00   2010*

⊞ **LAUTERBRUNNEN** *C2* (1km S Rural) *46.58788, 7.91030*
**Camping Jungfrau, Weid 406, 3822 Lauterbrunnen
[033 8562010; fax 8562020; info@camping-jungfrau.ch;
www.camping-jungfrau.ch]** S o'skirts of Lauterbrunnen sp at
R fork, site in 500m. Lge, some hdstg, terr, pt shd; htd wc; chem
disp; mv service pnt; baby facs; some serviced pitches; shwrs inc;
EHU (15A) CHF2.5 (metered in winter; poss rev pol); gas; lndry
(inc dryer); supmkt; rest, snacks; bar; playgrnd; pool 600m; tennis;
bike hire; wifi; TV; 30% statics; dogs CHF3; phone; sep car park
when site full; ski-bus; ATM; poss cr; Eng spkn; adv bkg rec; quiet;
ccard acc; red/long stay/CKE/CCI. "Friendly, helpful welcome; fine
scenery, superb situation in vertical walled valley; rlwy tickets sold;
close to town & rlwy stn to high alpine resorts; ski & boot rm;
1st class rest (clsd Sun & Mon in winter); navette inc; superb facs;
clean; shop gd; excel site." ♦ CHF 58.00   2014*

See advertisement

⊞ **LAUTERBRUNNEN** *C2* (3.6km S Rural) *46.56838,
7.90869* **Camping Breithorn, Sandbach, 3824 Stechelberg
[033 8551225; fax 8553561; breithorn@stechelberg.ch;
www.campingbreithorn.ch]** Up valley thro Lauterbrunnen,
300m past Trümmelbach Falls to ent on R. Med, unshd; wc;
chem disp; mv service pnt; shwrs inc; EHU (10A); gas; lndry (inc
dryer); shop; rest 200m; BBQ; sm playgrnd; pool 3km; tennis;
fishing; 60% statics; dogs CHF1; phone; Eng spkn; adv bkg;
quiet; red CKE/CCI. "Quiet site in lovely area; arr early high
ssn; fine scenery & gd touring base; friendly helpful owners;
frequent trains, funiculars & cable cars fr Lauterbrunnen stn
(4km); Schilthorn cable car 1.5km; excel cent for mountain
walking & cycling; excel, clean facs." CHF 27.50   2015*

LAUTERBRUNNEN *C2* (6km S Rural) *46.54619, 7.90100* Camping Rütti, 3824 Stechelberg [033 8552885; fax 8552611; campingruetti@stechelberg.ch; www.campingruetti.ch] Fr Interlaken thro Lauterbrunnen, past Trümmelbach Falls, site on R at end of valley. Med, pt sl, pt shd; wc; chem disp; shwrs; EHU (10A) CHF3; gas; lndry (inc dryer); shop, rest, bar 200m; playgrnd; fishing; tennis; bike hire; games rm; 10% statics; phone; dogs CHF2.50; bus 200m; poss cr; Eng spkn; adv bkg rec; quiet; CKE/CCI. "Frequent buses to Lauterbrunnen stn; gd walking/cycling; superb site." 1 May-30 Sep. CHF 31.00   2009*

⊞ **LENK** *C2* (5km SE Rural) *46.42819, 7.47788* Camping Hasenweide, Hasenweide 1, Oberried, 3775 Lenk im Simmental [033 7332647; fax 7332973; info@camping-hasenweide.ch; www.camping-hasenweide.ch] Take rd S fr Zweisimmen to Lenk, thro Lenk vill twd Oberreid for 4.5km, ignore 1st site on R, site at end of rd on L. Sm, pt sl, pt shd; htd wc; chem disp; shwrs inc; EHU (6A) CHF3 (poss long lead req); lndry (inc dryer); sm shop & 5km; rest adj; BBQ; games rm; internet; 75% statics; dogs CHF2; phone; bus to town; site clsd mid-Oct to mid-Nov; Eng spkn; quiet. "Mostly statics but some rm for tourers, otherwise field outside; poss long walk to san facs; ideal cent walking & skiing; beautiful location at foot of waterfall; vg." CHF 30.00   2009*

⊞ **LENZERHEIDE** *C4* (3km S Rural) *46.69873, 9.55813* Camping St Cassian, 7083 Lenz bei Lenzerheide [081 3842472; fax 3842489; camping.st.cassian@bluewin.ch] Fr Chur exit m'way Chur Süd & foll sp Lenzerheide. 2km past Lenzerheide site clearly sp on L. Fr S 1km past Lenz on R. NB Long, hard climb & hairpin bet Lenzerheide & Chur. Med, hdstg, pt sl, terr, shd; wc; all serviced pitches; mv service pnt; chem disp; shwrs CHF1; EHU (10A) CHF3; gas; lndry; shop 3km; rest adj; playgrnd; lake sw 2km; wifi; 90% statics; dogs CHF2; phone; poss cr; some Eng spkn; adv bkg; quiet; CKE/CCI. "Site in conifer woodland; non-glaciated area gd for walking, touring, mountain biking; mountain views; rec arr early to secure pitch." ◆ ltd. CHF 31.00   2009*

LENZERHEIDE *C4* (700m SW Rural) *46.72331, 9.55468* TCS Camping Gravas, Voa Nova 6, 7078 Lenzerheide/Lai [081 3842335; fax 3842306; camping.lenzerheide@tcs.ch; www.campingtcs.ch] Exit A13 at Chur-Süd onto rd 3 dir Lenzerheide (20km). Site sp fr cent of Lenzerheide. Long, hard climb to site with hairpin. Lge, shd; htd wc; chem disp; shwrs; EHU (6-10A) CHF4.50; gas; lndry (inc dryer); shops adj; pool 1km; lake sw 1.2km; 60% statics; dogs CHF5; poss cr; Eng spkn; adv bkg; rd noise; ccard acc; CKE/CCI. "Many sports & activities in Lenzerheide; excel walking; sm pitches." 2 Dec-11 Apr & 28 May-2 Nov. CHF 35.00   2010*

LEUK *C2* (15km N Rural) *46.38119, 7.62361* Camping Sportarena, 3954 Leukerbad [027 4701037; fax 4703707; info@sportarenatop.ch; www.sportarenatop.ch] Exit A9 at Susten & foll sp N to Leukerbad, site sp. Med, some hdstg, pt sl, pt terr, pt shd; htd wc; chem disp; mv service pnt; shwrs inc; EHU (10A) CHF5; lndry; shop 500m; rest, snacks; bar; BBQ; htd, covrd pool 200m; thermal pools nr; sports cent adj; games area; TV rm; 20% statics; dogs CHF2; poss cr; Eng spkn; adv bkg; quiet. "Beautiful situation; pleasant, helpful staff; attractive little town; cable cars; walks; vg." ◆ ltd. 1 May-31 Oct. CHF 30.00   2012*

LEUK *C2* (12km E Rural) *46.30667, 7.74117* Camping Rhône, 3945 Gampel [027 9322041; info@campingrhone.ch; www.campingrhone.ch] Fr rd A9/E62 exit dir Gampel, site well sp on R bank of Rv Rhône. Lge, pt shd; wc; chem disp; mv service pnt; baby facs; shwrs inc; EHU CHF3.20; gas; lndry; shop high ssn; rest high ssn; bar; playgrnd; htd pool & paddling pool; tennis; golf; fishing; 30% statics; dogs CHF3; poss cr; adv bkg; quiet. "Superb location & touring base; gd walking, cycling; driest pt of Switzerland." ◆ 1 Apr-31 Oct. CHF 23.00   2009*

LEUK *C2* (4km SE Rural) *46.29780, 7.65936* Camping Gemmi 'Agarn', Briannenstrasse 4, 3952 Susten [tel/fax 027 4731154 or 4734295; info@campgemmi.ch; www.campgemmi.ch] Foll A9/E27 SE; then nr Martigny take A9/E62 to Sierre; then take E62 thro Susten. After 2km, by Hotel Relais Bayard, take R lane (Agarn, Feithieren), ignoring sp Camping Torrent, & foll Alte Kantonstrasse sp Agarn. Turn R at site sp into Briannenstrasse; site in 200m. Med, mkd pitch, pt sl, pt shd; wc; chem disp; mv service pnt; serviced pitches; indiv san facs some pitches; shwrs inc; EHU (16A) inc; gas; lndry (inc dryer); shop; rest, snacks; bar; BBQ (gas/elec); playgrnd; pool 600m; golf, tennis, bike hire; horseriding nrby; wifi; sat TV; 5% statics; dogs CHF3; no o'fits over 9m high ssn; Eng spkn; adv bkg; quiet; various pitch prices; ccard acc; red LS; CKE/CCI. "Outstanding site; friendly, helpful, hardworking owners; private bthrms avail; gd stop on way Simplon Pass; barrier clsd 2200-0800; excel walking; conv A9." 12 Apr-11 Oct. CHF 40.00 SBS - S12   2011*

"That's changed – Should I let The Club know?"

If you find something on site that's different from the site entry, fill in a report and let us know. See www.caravanclub.co.uk/europereport.

LEUK *C2* (3km S Urban) *46.29911, 7.63738* Camping Bella-Tola, Waldstrasse 57, 3952 Susten [027 4731491; fax 4733641; info@bella-tola.ch; www.bella-tola.ch] E fr Sierre turn R at ent to Susten, after bdge over Illgraben & foll sp for 1.5km. NB Acute turn off main rd; v steep hill & bad rd surface. Lge, mkd pitch, sl, pt shd; wc; chem disp; mv service pnt; baby facs; shwrs inc; EHU (10A) CHF3.60; gas; lndry; shop; rest, snacks; bar; BBQ; playgrnd; htd pool; lake sw & shgl beach; games rm; wifi; TV; 25% statics; dogs CHF2.70; phone; bus 1.6km; poss cr; adv bkg; noisy at w/end; ccard acc; red LS. 11 May-30 Sep. CHF 49.00   2011*

LEUK *C2* (3.7km SW Rural) *46.30702, 7.61101* Camping du Monument de Finges, Alter Kehr 33, 3952 Susten [027 473 18 27; camping.monument@hotmail.com; www.campingmonument.ch] Fr Visp twds Sion, foll E62 (blue sp); site sp on R approx 3km after passing thro Susten. Lge, hdg, mkd pitch, pt sl, pt shd; wc; chem disp; shwrs; EHU (10A); lndry; BBQ; playgrnd; pool; 10% statics; dogs; twin axles; quiet; CKE/CCI. "Lovely, well maintained sw pool; site partly in pine forest & in lge grassy fields; spacious open pitches; mountain views; walking tracks fr site; gd site." 1 May-21 Sep. CHF 50.00   2014*

LEYSIN see Aigle *C2*

⊞ **LIGNIERES** *B2* (700m NE Rural) *47.08545, 7.07093*
Camping Fraso Ranch, Chemin du Grand-Marais, 2523
Lignières [032 7514616; fax 7514614; camping.fraso-
ranch@bluewin.ch; www.camping-lignieres.ch]
Fr A5 exit dir Le Landeron. In Le Landeron turn L sp Lignières. In
5km (do not go into vill) keep strt to site on R in further 2km.
Bef Lignières keep R & foll camp sp. Lge, pt shd; wc; chem
disp; mv service pnt; baby facs; sauna; shwrs CHF0.50; EHU
(10A) CHF3.50; gas; lndry; shop; cooking facs; playgrnd; htd
pool; paddling pool; jacuzzi; tennis; games area; 90% statics
(sep area); dogs CHF1.50; sep car park; site clsd 1 Nov-20 Dec;
gates clsd 1230-1400; Eng spkn; ccard acc; red CKE/CCI. "V
well-organised, tidy site." ♦ CHF 31.00   2009*

LOCARNO see also sites under Tenero *C3*

LOCARNO *C3* (14km E Rural) *46.16978, 8.91396* **Park-
Camping Riarena, Via Campeggio, 6516 Cugnasco
[091 8591688; fax 8592885; camping.riarena@bluewin.ch;
www.camping-riarena.ch]** Exit A2/E35 Bellinzona-Süd & foll
sp dir airport. Bear R at rndabt & foll site sp to Gudo, site on R
in 2km. Med, mkd pitch, shd; wc; chem disp; mv service pnt;
shwrs inc; EHU (10A) CHF5 (adaptor avail); gas; lndry; shop;
rest, snacks; bar; playgrnd; pool & 2 paddling pools; games
area; bike hire; wifi; entmnt; dogs CHF4; bus 0.5km; twin axles;
Eng spkn; adv bkg; quiet; ccard acc (CHF100+); red long stay.
"Friendly, family-run site; excursions arranged; gd cycle rtes;
gate shut 1300-1500; clean san facs; dusty site; beware acorn
drop September; vg." ♦ 21 Mar-17 Oct. CHF 53.00   2014*

LOCARNO *C3* (2km S Urban) *46.15587, 8.80258* **Camping
Delta, Via Respini 7, 6600 Locarno [091 7516081;
fax 7512243; info@campingdelta.com; www.campingdelta.
com]** Fr cent of Locarno make for prom & foll sp to Lido. Site
in 400m past Lido on L. Fr Simplon Pass SS337 fr Domodossola
to Locarno clsd to trailer c'vans; narr rd with many bends. Site
well sp fr m'way. Lge, hdg/mkd pitch, pt shd; wc; chem disp;
mv service pnt; shwrs; EHU (10A) CHF5; gas; lndry (inc dryer);
shop; rest, snacks; bar; playgrnd; pool & lake sw 300m; bike
& kayak hire; fitness rm; wifi; no dogs; poss cr; Eng spkn;
adv bkg to end Mar; quiet; no radios or musical instruments
allowed; red LS/snr citizens. "No access for vehicles 2200-0700;
superb location walking dist Locarno; excel facs but long walk
fr S end of site; premium for lakeside pitches." 1 Mar-31 Oct.
CHF 82.00   2013*

LOCARNO *C3* (9km NW Rural) *46.22436, 8.74395* **TCS
Camping Bella Riva, 6672 Gordévio [091 7531444; fax
7531764; camping.gordevio@tcs.ch; www.campingtcs.ch]**
Fr W end of an A13 tunnel under Locarno foll sp Centovalle &
Valle Maggia. In 3km turn R to Valle Maggia. Stay on rd which
bypasses Gordévio (approx 5km), site on L. Lge, pt shd; wc;
chem disp; mv service pnt; baby facs; shwrs; EHU inc (10A)
CHF4.50; gas; lndry; shop; rest, snacks; playgrnd; pool; rv sw
& beach; fishing; tennis; bike hire; wifi; TV; 30% statics; dogs
CHF5; sep car park; poss cr; Eng spkn; adv bkg; quiet; ccard
acc; red CKE/CCI. "Attractive region; well-run site; lge tent area
adj; bus to vill nr site." 1 Apr-15 Oct. CHF 54.00   2012*

LUCERNE see Luzern *B3*

LUGANO *D3* (10km N Rural) *46.06921, 8.93675* **Camping
Taverne Nord, 6807 Taverne [tel/fax 091 9451198;
taverne67@bluewin.ch; http://campeggiotaverne.ch]**
Exit A2/E35 at Rivera or Lugano Nord onto N2. Foll sp for
Bellinzona to Taverne. Site ent clearly sp nr long bdge. Med,
pt shd; wc; chem disp; mv service pnt; shwrs CHF1; EHU (6A)
CHF4 (poss rev pol); shop; bar; rest 200m; playgrnd; pool
high ssn; tennis; 20% statics; dogs CHF2.50; poss cr; adv bkg;
rlwy & factory noise; red long stay. "Basic NH site in pleasant
situation by shallow stream; Lugano beautiful." 1 Apr-15 Oct.
CHF 25.00   2011*

⊞ **LUGANO** *D3* (12km N Rural) *46.09036, 8.91626* **Camping
Palazzina, La Cuntrada, 6805 Mezzovico [091 9461467;
fax 9463061]** Exit A2/E35 at Rivera. R at T-junc dir Lugano; site
on L in approx 3.5km. Med, pt shd; wc; chem disp; shwrs; EHU
(10A) CHF4; gas; shop; rest, snacks; bar; playgrnd; pool 1km;
TV; 80% statics; dogs CHF2; adv bkg; rd & rlwy noise; ccard
acc. "Helpful owner." CHF 34.00   2011*

LUGANO *D3* (12km S Urban) *45.92861, 8.97670* **Camping
Monte Generoso, 6818 Melano [091 6498333; fax 6495944;
camping@montegeneroso.ch; www.montegeneroso.ch]**
S fr Lugano on N2/E35 m'way; exit immed after tunnel sp
Bissone & Chiasso. Cross lake & foll sp Chiasso (blue sps) thro
Caroggio. Site on R after rlwy stn. Or fr Como & S on m'way,
take exit sp Bissone & Melide bef x-ing lake; foll sp Melano.
Med, mkd pitch, pt sl, pt shd; wc; chem disp; shwrs CHF0.50;
EHU (6A) CHF4; gas; lndry; shop & 1km; snacks; bar; playgrnd;
pool 2km; shgl lake beach adj; boating; tennis; games area;
boating; TV; 20% statics; dogs CHF5; Eng spkn; adv bkg;
50% statics; quiet but rd & rlwy noise; ccard acc; red LS.
"Wonderful lakeside location; vg san facs; 500m to rlwy stn for
Lugano; gd." 26 Mar-24 Oct. CHF 46.00   2009*

LUGANO *D3* (14km S Rural) *45.92273, 8.97981* **Camping
Paradiso-Lago, Via Pedreta, 6818 Melano [091 6482863;
fax 6482602; campingparadiso@bluewin.ch; www.
camping-paradiso.ch]** Fr N2/E35 exit after tunnel sp Bissone,
foll sp to Bissone. Turn R to site 1km bef Melano, app rd
under m'way & rlwy bdges. Lge, mkd pitch, pt sl, pt shd; wc;
chem disp; shwrs inc; EHU (6A) CHF5 inc; gas; lndry; shop;
rest, snacks; bar; BBQ; playgrnd; pool 2km; lake sw adj;
watersports; beach; tennis; 40% statics; no dogs; phone; poss
cr; adv bkg; rlwy & rd noise, poss noise bar & fr dog-training
site adj; ccard acc; CKE/CCI. "Pleasant surroundings; premium
for lakeside pitches; sep car park high ssn; excel site; avoid
pitches nr off; euros acc mtn rlwy stn 3m." 30 Mar-15 Nov.
CHF 43.00   2011*

LUGANO *D3* (6km W Rural) *45.99565, 8.90593* **Camping
Eurocampo, Via Molinazzo 9, 6982 Agno [091 6052114; fax
6053187; eurocampo@ticino.com; www.eurocampo.ch]**
Exit A2/E34 Lugano N & foll sp airport and Agno. In Agno turn
L, then over rlwy x-ing & rnadbt. Turn R down narr lane to
site. Lge, pt shd; wc; chem disp; mv service pnt; shwrs; EHU
CHF3.50 (poss rev pol); gas; lndry; shop; rest; bar; htd pool
200m; paddling pool; lake sw adj; TV rm; 95% statics; dogs
free; phone; train 500m; poss cr; Eng spkn; adv bkg; quiet.
"Gd site but facs need upgrade; site built in 60's, no changes
since; NH only." 1 Apr-31 Oct. CHF 56.00   2014*

LUGANO *D3* (6km W Rural) *45.99523, 8.90417* **Camping La Palma, Via Molinazzo 21, 6982 Agno [79 2415343 or 91 6052561; www.lugano-tourism.ch]** N2 exit for Lugano & foll sp airport/camping. Site on L ent Agno. Make U-turn at rndabt & turn R. Narr lane ent. Lge, pt shd; wc (cont); own san rec; chem disp; mv service pnt; shwrs CHF0.50; EHU (6A) CHF4; gas; lndry; shop & 1km; rest high ssn & 2km; snacks; bar; BBQ; shgl beach adj; lake sw; TV; 30% statics; dogs CHF4; train; some daytime aircraft noise; CKE/CCI. "Beautiful lakeside location; gd, clean modern san facs; conv Lugano; Swiss adaptor CHF8; friendly, helpful owner; handy for supmkt, bike path and train stn." 18 Apr-1 Nov. CHF 60.00   2014*

> ## "I like to fill in the reports as I travel from site to site"
> You'll find report forms at the back of this guide, or you can fill them in online at www.caravanclub.co.uk/europereport.

⊞ **LUGANO** *D3* (6km W Rural) *45.99534, 8.90845* **Lugano (formerly TCS Camping La Piodella), Via alla Force 14, 6933 Muzzano-Lugano [091 9947788 or 091 9858070 LS; fax 9946708; camping.muzzano@tcs.ch; www.campingtcs.ch/muzzano]** Leave A2 at Lugano Nord & foll sp Ponte Tresa & airport. In Agno turn L at traff island; foll camping sp. In 800m, just after La Piodella town sp, look for sm sp at rd junc with tent symbol & TCS sticker. NB This may appear to direct you to your R but you must make a 180° turn & take slip rd along R-hand side of rd you have just come along - app rd to site. Lge, some mkd pitch, pt shd; wc; own san rec; mv service pnt; baby facs; serviced pitch; shwrs inc; EHU (10A) inc (long lead poss req - avail fr recep); gas; lndry (inc dryer); shop & 800m; rest, snacks; bar; BBQ; playgrnd; htd pool & paddling pool; sand beach by lake; watersports; boating & horseriding 6km; fishing; tennis; games area; wifi; entmnt; games/TV rm; some statics; dogs CHF5.50; no cats; o'fits over 7.5m high ssn; sep car park; poss cr; Eng spkn; adv bkg; day/eve aircraft noise; ccard acc; red LS/CKE/CCI. "Idyllic location; pitches nr lake higher price; gd welcome; helpful staff; modern san facs; access to pitches poss diff lge o'fits; local train to Lugano 1km, or easy drive; ideal for Ticino Lakes; barrier clsd 1200-1400." ♦ CHF 71.00 SBS - S10   2012*

LUGANO *D3* (7km W Rural) *45.9927, 8.9006* **Camping Golfo del Sole, 6982 Agno [091 6054802; fax 6054306; info@golfodelsole.ch; www.golfodelsole.ch]** Exit A2 Lugano Nord & foll sp Ponte Tresa & airport. In Agno at junc, turn R dir Ponte Tresa & Varese. Site sp in 500m, turn L immed bef nightclub. Sm, pt shd; wc; chem disp; shwrs CHF1; EHU (4A) CHF4 (adaptor avail); gas; lndry rm; shop 500m; playgrnd; lake sw & beach; fishing; tennis; 25% statics; phone; bus/train to Lugano; extra charge for lakeside pitch; poss cr; Eng spkn; adv bkg; quiet. "Beautiful setting; friendly owner." 15 Mar-17 Oct. CHF 38.00   2009*

LUNGERN see Meiringen *C3*

LUTSCHENTAL see Grindelwald *C2*

⊞ **LUZERN** *B3* (3km E Rural) *47.0500, 8.33833* **Camping International Lido, Lidostrasse 19, 6006 Luzern [041 3702146; fax 3702145; luzern@camping-international.ch; www.camping-international.ch]** Fr bdge on lake edge in city cent foll sp Küssnacht & Verkehrshaus. Turn R off Küssnacht rd at traff lts by transport museum (sp Lido), site 50m on L beyond lido parking. Fr A2/E35 exit Luzern Centrum. Lge, mkd pitch, hdstg (mv pitch poss diff), pt shd; htd wc; chem disp; mv service pnt; shwrs inc; EHU (10A) CHF5 (poss rev pol; adaptors avail); gas; lndry (inc dryer); shop & 400m; rest 1km; snacks; bar; BBQ; playgrnd; pool adj (May-Sep); lake sw & sand beach adj; boat trips; boat-launch; wifi; 10% statics; dogs CHF4; phone; bus; lake ferry 200m; recep open 0830-1200 & 1400-1800 high ssn; money exchange; poss v cr high ssn; Eng spkn; adv bkg rec; ccard acc; red snr citizens/LS/CKE/CCI. "Various sizes/prices pitches; ltd touring pitches cr in peak ssn, early arr rec; recep in bar LS; clean, well-maintained facs stretched high ssn; helpful staff; pleasant lakeside walk to Luzern; conv location; excel rest in Wurzenbach; transport museum worth a visit; well-run site." ♦ ltd. CHF 45.00   2014*

LUZERN *B3* (9km E Rural) *47.06164, 8.40239* **Camping Vierwaldstättersee, Luzernerstrasse 271, 6402 Merlischachen [041 8500804; fax 8505041; welcome@seecamping.ch; www.seecamping.ch]** Exit A2/E35 junc 26 to Luzern; exit Luzern dir Merlischachen & Küssnacht. Site on R 500m bef Merlischachen on lakeside, well sp. Med, unshd; htd wc; chem disp; mv service pnt; shwrs inc; EHU (6A) CHF4; gas; shops 500m; rest, snacks, bar & lake sw adj; pool 6km; 10% statics; no dogs; bus adj; phone 500m; Eng spkn; adv bkg; some rd noise; ccard not acc; red long stay/CKE/CCI. "Beautiful lakeside location; wonderful views; excel facs; excel." 1 Apr-30 Sep. CHF 38.00   2011*

> ## "We must tell The Club about that great site we found"
> Get your site reports in by mid-August and we'll do our best to get your updates into the next edition.

LUZERN *B3* (5km S Rural) *47.01201, 8.31113* **TCS Camping Steinibachried, Seefeldstrasse, 6048 Horw [041 3403558; fax 3403556; camping.horw@tcs.ch; www.campingtcs.ch]** Fr A2/E336 exit Horw & foll sp. After x-ing rlwy turn R twd lake in 200m, site sp. Lge, mkd pitch, unshd; wc; chem disp; shwrs (inc) CHF1; EHU inc (4A) CHF4 (adaptor on loan); gas; lndry (inc dryer); shop; rest, snacks; bar; playgrnd; lake sw 200m; games rm; 30% statics; dogs CHF5; bus; sep car park; poss cr; Eng spkn; adv bkg; quiet but daytime factory noise; ccard acc; red long stay/CKE/CCI. "Excel facs; beautiful location but car park adj high-rise flats; vg." ♦ 4 Apr-7 Oct. CHF 41.00   2014*

MADULAIN *C4* (300m N Rural) *46.58764, 9.94004* **Camping Madulain, Via Vallatscha, 7523 Madulain [tel/fax 081 8540161; mail@campingmadulain.ch; www.campingmadulain.ch]** Sp fr N27 at foot of Albula Pass. Sm, pt sl, terr, pt shd; htd wc; chem disp; shwrs inc; EHU (10A) CHF2; lndry rm; shop, rest, snacks, bar 1.5km; wifi; 70% statics; Eng spkn; bus/train adj, some noise. "Simple CL-type site; excel san facs; helpful owner." 19 Dec-10 Apr & 27 May-18 Oct. CHF 35.00   2015*

SWITZERLAND

MARTIGNY D2 (1km S Urban) 46.09788, 7.07953 TCS
Camping Les Neuvilles, Route du Levant 68, 1920
Martigny [027 7224544; fax 7223544; camping.martigny@
tcs.ch; www.campingtcs.ch]
Exit A9/E62 dir Grand St Bernard to Martigny. Camping
poorly sp fr town; foll Expo sp, ent past cemetary. (SatNav
poss inacurate). Lge, mkd pitch, some hdstg, unshd; htd wc;
chem disp; mv service pnt; baby facs; shwrs inc; EHU (6-10A)
CHF4.50; gas; lndry (inc dryer); shop & 500m; rest, snacks; bar;
playgrnd; plunge pool; fishing; tennis; bike hire; wifi; TV rm;
65% statics; dogs CHF5; poss cr; Eng spkn; adv bkg; quiet, but
some rd noise; ccard acc; red CKE/CCI. "Excel san facs; conv
Valais & Mont Blanc area; Martigny pleasant town; gd cycling."
♦ 1 Apr-31 Oct. CHF 39.00   2012*

MATTEN see Interlaken C2

MAUR see Zürich A3

MEIERSKAPPEL B3 (1km S Rural) 47.12175, 8.44670
Campingplatz Gerbe, Landiswilerstrasse, 6344
Meierskappel [041 7904534; info@swiss-bauernhof.ch;
www.swiss-bauernhof.ch] Exit A4/E41 at Küssnacht & foll sp
N to Meierskappel. Bef ent Meierskappel turn L into farm ent
for site (sp.) Med, pt sl, pt shd, htd wc; chem disp; mv service
pnt; baby facs; shwrs inc; EHU (10A) CHF3.50 (poss rev pol);
lndry (inc dryer); shop; rest, snacks; bar; BBQ; playgrnd; htd,
covrd pool; wifi; 5% statics; dogs CHF2.50; poss cr; quiet; CKE/
CCI. "Vg, basic farm site, poor facs (unisex), in need of refurb;
lge field - choose own pitch; conv Luzerne & Zürich." ♦ ltd.
1 Mar-1 Nov. CHF 25.00   2015*

⊞ **MEIRINGEN** C3 (2km W Rural) 46.72538, 8.17088
Camping Balmweid, Balmweidstrasse 22, 3860 Meiringen
[033 9715115; info@camping-meiringen.ch;
www.camping-meiringen.ch] Turn R off A6 Breinz-
Innertkirchen rd immed after rndabt at BP petrol stn. Site on
L after 200m. Lge, mkd pitch, hdstg, terr, pt shd; htd wc;
chem disp; mv service pnt; 20% serviced pitches; baby facs;
fam bthrm; shwrs inc; EHU (10A) CHF4.50; gas; lndry (inc
dryer); shops & 2km; rest, snacks; bar; BBQ; playgrnd; pool;
ski lift 1km; games rm; wifi; TV; 65% statics; dogs CHF2; adv
bkg; quiet; ccard acc; red CKE/CCI. "Ideal base for Sherlock
Holmes fans (Reichenbach Falls) & 3 passes tour; gd cycle track
into town; site unattractive & rather run down (2010)." ♦
CHF 35.00   2010*

MEIRINGEN C3 (1.5km NW Rural) 46.73431, 8.17139
Alpencamping, Brünigstrasse 47, 3860 Meiringen
[033 9713676; fax 9715278; info@alpencamping.ch;
www.alpencamping.ch] Leave A8, then take rd11/6 twd
Brünig Pass. On entering Meiringen, at 1st rndabt foll camp
sp L to site. Med, unshd; htd wc; chem disp; mv service pnt;
baby facs; shwrs inc; EHU (10A) CHF5.50; gas; lndry (inc dryer);
shop; rest, snacks nrby; BBQ; cooking facs; playgrnd; pool nr;
internet; entmnt; 30% statics; dogs CHF3; bus 200m; train
1.3km; site clsd Nov; Eng spkn; adv bkg; CKE/CCI. "Meeting
point of alpine passes; friendly, family-run site; excel, modern
san facs; vg walking/cycling; beautiful site with gd views." ♦
1 Jan-31 Oct & 1 Dec-31 Dec. CHF 55.00   2015*

⊞ **MEIRINGEN** C3 (14km NNW Rural) 46.78499, 8.15157
Camping Obsee, Campingstrasse 1, 6078 Lungern
[041 6781463; fax 6782163; camping@obsee.ch;
www.obsee.ch] S fr Luzern on N8 to Sachseln. Exit m'way
for rte 4 to Brienz; thro Lungern; R at end of vill & site on R
on lakeside. Best app fr Luzern - turn fr Interlaken diff for lge
o'fits. Lge, pt sl, pt shd; htd wc; chem disp; mv service pnt;
shwrs CHF2; EHU CHF3; gas; lndry (inc dryer); shops 1km; rest,
snacks; playgrnd; paddling pool; lake sw; fishing; tennis; games
rm; entmnt; TV; 95% statics; dogs CHF3; poss cr; quiet; Eng
spkn. "Well-kept site in beautiful situation - ski cent; cable
rlwy adj; 10 mins walk to vill; sm adv for tourers; vg rest; easy
access by rd or train to attractions; Swiss adaptor & poss long
lead for elec." ♦ CHF 42.00   2013*

MELANO see Lugano D3

MENDRISIO D3 (8km NW Rural) 45.88921, 8.94841 TCS
Camping Parco al Sole, Via Ala Caraa 2, 6866 Meride
[091 6464330; fax 6460992; camping.meride@tcs.ch;
www.campingtcs.ch] Fr A2/E35 exit Mendrisio, then foll sp
Rancate & Serpiano. Steep climb. Site on L to S of vill. Med,
some hdstg, pt sl, pt shd; wc; chem disp; mv service pnt; baby
facs; shwrs inc; EHU (4A) CHF4.50; gas; lndry (inc dryer); shop
2km; rest, snacks; bar; playgrnd; htd pool; paddling pool;
fishing lake; wifi; entmnt; TV rm; 20% statics; dogs CHF5;
sep car park; poss v cr; Eng spkn; adv bkg; v quiet; ccard acc.
"Attractive, peaceful setting away fr traffic; Unesco World
Heritage vill; pitches uneven in parts & v sm, some surrounded
by other pitches - make sure you can get off with o'fit; site clsd
to arr 1100-1700; conv Milan by train." ♦ 23 Apr-26 Sep.
CHF 37.00   2010*

MERIDE see Mendrisio D3

MERLISCHACHEN see Luzern B3

MEZZOVICO see Lugano D3

MONTANA see Sierre C2

MORGES C1 (2km S Rural) 46.50360, 6.48760 Morges
(formerly TCS Camping Le Petit Bois), Promenade
du Petit-Bois 15, 1110 Morges [021 8011270 or
091 9858070 LS; fax 8033869 or 091 9946708 LS; camping.
morges@tcs.ch; www.campingtcs.ch/morges]
Exit A1/E25 at Morges Ouest, then foll sp to lake. Site well sp
on Lake Léman N shore adj pool. Lge, hdg/mkd pitch, pt shd;
wc; chem disp; mv service pnt; baby facs; shwrs; EHU (10A)
inc (adaptor/long lead avail); gas; lndry (inc dryer); shop; rest;
bar; BBQ; htd pool in complex 200m (high ssn) inc;
lake sw adj; watersports; boating; bike hire; tennis 500m;
wifi; entmnt; games/TV rm; 50% statics; dogs CHF3-5; no
o'fits over 7/8m high ssn; m'van o'night/late arr area; poss
cr; adv bkg; Eng spkn; quiet, but rd/rlwy noise some pitches;
ccard acc; red LS/CKE/CCI. "Pleasant site but sm pitches;
pleasant, helpful staff; clean san facs; conv Lausanne, Geneva
& some Alpine passes; tulip festival Apr; easy walk to town &
stn; cycle path around lake; vg." ♦ 4 Apr-4 Oct. CHF 53.00
SBS - S14   2012*

SWITZERLAND

MOSEN *B3* (100m W Rural) *47.24497, 8.22451* **Camping Seeblick, Seestrasse, 6295 Mosen [tel/fax 041 9171666; infos@camping-seeblick.ch; www.camping-seeblick.ch]** Fr Lenzburg or Luzern on rd 26 turn E in Mosen at rlwy stn, immed L into site ent. Med, hdg/mkd pitch, some hdstg, pt sl, pt shd; wc; chem disp; mv service pnt; shwrs CHF0.50; EHU (10A) CHF3; gas; lndry (inc dryer); shop; rest adj; snacks; BBQ; playgrnd; lake sw adj; fishing; paddling pool; boating; games rm; 60% statics; dogs CHF3; poss cr; quiet; red CKE/CCI. "Pleasant site conv Luzern & Zürich; excel shop & san facs; helpful owner." ♦ 1 Mar-31 Oct. CHF 27.00   2011*

MURG *B3* (500m N Rural) *47.11543, 9.21445* **Camping Murg am Walensee, 8877 Murg [081 7381530; info@camping-murg.ch; www.murg-camping.ch]** Exit A3 junc 47 dir Murg, site sp on lake. Med, pt shd; wc; chem disp; shwrs CHF1; EHU (10A) CHF3.70; shop & 200m; rest 300m; lake sw & beach adj; 30% statics; dogs CHF4.50; phone; poss cr; adv bkg ess high ssn; quiet. "Spectacular outlook at water's edge; sm pitches; beautiful setting; boat trips adj; cable car 4km; vg." 1 Apr-15 Oct. CHF 49.00   2014*

MUZZANO see Lugano *D3*

"I need an on-site restaurant"

We do our best to make sure site information is correct, but it is always best to check any must-have facilities are still available or will be open during your visit.

NEUCHATEL *B1* (13km NE Rural) *47.00198, 7.04145* **TCS Camping Fanel, Seestrasse 50, 3236 Gampelen [032 3132333; fax 3131407; camping.gampelen@tcs.ch; www.campingtcs.ch]** Foll TCS camping sp fr turning off N5 in Gampelen - approx 4km fr vill, on lakeside. V lge, mkd pitch, pt shd; wc; chem disp; mv service pnt; 20% serviced pitch; shwrs; EHU (4-6A) CHF 3.50-4.50 (adaptor on loan); gas; lndry (inc dryer); shop; rest; bar; BBQ; playgrnd; htd pool; lake sw & beach; watersports; fishing; tennis; golf; archery; wifi; entmnt; 80% statics; dogs CHF5; wifi; Eng spkn; adv bkg; 10% red 3+ days; ccard acc; CKE/CCI. "In nature reserve; office/barrier clsd 1200-1400; office & shop hrs vary with ssn; gd, modern facs; helpful staff; Euros also acc." ♦ 1 Apr-2 Oct. CHF 48.00   2012*

NEUCHATEL *B1* (7km SW Rural) *46.96727, 6.87029* **Camping Paradis-Plage, La Saunerie, 2013 Colombier [032 8412446; fax 8414305; info@paradisplage.ch; www.paradisplage.ch]** Take Lausanne rd out of Neuchâtel; after tunnel exit at int'chge sp Auvenier, Colombier. Foll Colombier sp thro traff lts. Ent L over tram rails past Inn Des Alleens. Lge, shd; wc; chem disp; mv service pnt; shwrs inc; EHU (10A) CHF4; gas; lndry; shop; rest, snacks; playgrnd; paddling pool; lake sw; fishing; watersports; tennis; 60% statics; dogs CHF2; adv bkg; some m'way noise; red long stay. "Gd walks/cycling; v pleasant site." ♦ 1 Mar-31 Oct. CHF 41.00   2009*

NOVILLE see Villeneuve *C1*

OTTENBACH see Zürich *A3*

PONTRESINA MORTERATSCH see St Moritz *C4*

PRELES see Biel/Bienne *B2*

⊞ **PRESE, LE** *C4* (500m N Rural) *46.29490, 10.08010* **Camping Cavresc, 7746 Le Prese [tel/fax 081 8440259; camping.cavresc@bluewin.ch; www.campingsertori.ch]** S fr Pontresina on N29 site sp on L 5km S of Poschiavo adj Lake Poschiavo. Med, shd; htd wc; chem disp; mv service pnt; shwrs CHF0.50; EHU (10A) CHF4; gas; lndry; shop adj; rest, snacks; bar; BBQ; playgrnd; sm pool; htd, covrd pool 5km; lake 300m; games area; TV; dogs CHF2; bus/train adj; poss cr; adv bkg; quiet; ccard acc; red long stay; CKE/CCI. "Stunning scenery; walking/cycling rtes; excel; friendly owners." ♦ CHF 36.00   2015*

RANDA see Zermatt *D2*

RARON see Visp *C2*

RECKINGEN see Ulrichen *C3*

REINACH see Basel *A2*

RINGGENBERG see Interlaken *C2*

ROLLE *C1* (1km E Rural) *46.46192, 6.34613* **Camping Aux Vernes, Chemin de la Plage, 1180 Rolle [tel/fax 021 8251239; reception@campingrolle.ch; www.campingrolle.ch]** Fr A1/E25/E62 exit Rolle, site sp dir Lausanne. Lge, shd; wc; chem disp; mv service pnt; baby facs; shwrs; EHU (4A) CHF3.50 (loan of adaptor); gas; lndry (inc dryer); shop; snacks; bar; BBQ; playgrnd; shgl beach & lake sw; boating; watersports; fishing; 20% statics; dogs CHF3; phone; poss cr; Eng spkn; adv bkg; quiet; ccard acc; red long stay/CKE/CCI. "Gd base Geneva, Gruyères, Chillon Castle; attractive site." 1 Apr-1 Oct. CHF 39.00   2011*

ROMANSHORN *A4* (5km SE Rural) *47.53620, 9.39885* **Camping Seehorn (formerly Wiedehorn), Wiedehorn, 9322 Egnach [071 4771006; fax 4773006; info@seehorn.ch; www.seehorn.ch]** Site is 2km E of Egnach, dir Arbon. Med, pt sl, pt shd, mkd, serviced pitch; wc; chem disp; shwrs inc; EHU (16A) CHF2.50; gas; lndry; shop; rest, snacks; bar; playgrnd; fishing; TV; 60% statics; dogs CHF4; phone; sep car park high ssn; adv bkg; quiet. "Direct access Lake Constance; statics sep; vg facs." 1 Mar-27 Oct. CHF 53.00   2013*

⊞ **SAANEN** *C2* (300m S Urban) *46.48738, 7.26406* **Camping Beim Kappeli, Campingstrasse, 3792 Saanen [033 7446191; fax 7446184; info@camping-saanen.ch; www.camping-saanen.ch]** On edge of vill bet rv & light rlwy. Site sp fr town cent. Med, pt shd; htd wc; shwrs CHF0.50; EHU (6-13A) CHF4; lndry; shop 1km; playgrnd; pool adj; tennis; fishing; 50% statics; dogs CHF3; site clsd Nov; poss cr; Eng spkn; quiet; ccard acc. "Beautiful walks; neat site; excel, clean facs; buy Gstaad card vg value." CHF 36.00   2012*

SAAS FEE *D2* (4.6km NE Rural) *46.11588, 7.93819* **Camping am Kapellenweg, 3910 Saas-Grund [027 9574997; fax 9573316; camping@kapellenweg.ch; www.kapellenweg. ch]** Fr Visp, take Saas Fee rd to Saas Grund, cont twd Saas Almagell, site on R after 1km. Sm, pt sl, pt shd; wc; chem disp; shwrs inc; EHU CHF3; gas; lndry; shop & 1km; snacks; golf; fishing; dogs CHF2.50; Eng spkn; red LS. "Ideal for walking; family-run site; clean san facs; beautiful scenery; if recep clsd, site yourself; bus or walk (50 mins) into town; excel site." ♦ 1 May-12 Oct. CHF 63.00   2014*

SAAS FEE *D2* (5km NE Rural) *46.11368, 7.94136* **Camping Mischabel, Unter den Bodmen, 3910 Saas-Grund [tel/fax 027 9571608; mischabel@hotmail.com]** Fr Visp take Saas Fee rd to Saas Grund & cont twd Saas Almagell for 1.2km. Med, pt shd; wc; chem disp; shwrs inc; EHU (10A) CHF3; lndry; shop & 1km; rest, snacks; bar; pool 1km; boating; fishing; TV; dogs CHF2.50; poss cr; Eng spkn; adv bkg; quiet; CKE/CCI. "Lovely scenery; gd walking; helpful, friendly staff." 1 Jun-30 Sep. CHF 63.00   2013*

⊞ **SAAS FEE** *D2* (5km E Rural) *46.11150, 7.94238* **Camping Schönblick, 3910 Saas-Grund [tel/fax 027 9572267; schoenblick@campingschweiz.ch]** Fr Visp take Saas Fee rd to Saas Grund & cont twd Saas Almagell for 1.5km. Site on R over rv. Sm, hdstg, unshd; htd wc; shwrs CHF1; EHU (10A) CHF3; gas; lndry; shop 1km; rest, snacks; bar; playgrnd; pool 1km; fishing; tennis; winter & summer skiing; horseriding; TV; 25% statics; adv bkg; open Oct-May with adv bkg only; quiet; ccard acc. "Site ideal for walking & mountain scenery; navette 50m; facs ltd LS." CHF 64.00   2013*

SAAS GRUND see Saas Fee *D2*

ST GALLEN *A4* (9km N Rural) *47.46191, 9.36371* **Camping St Gallen-Wittenbach, Leebrücke, 9304 Bernhardzell [071 2984969; fax 2985069; campingplatz.stgallen@ccc-stgallen.ch; www.ccc-stgallen.ch]** Exit A1/E60 St Fiden. L in Wittenbach cent at site sp. Cross Rv Sitter on sharp R bend, turn sharp R at sp. Med, some hdstg, pt shd; wc; chem disp; baby facs; shwrs inc; EHU (6A) CHF4 (adaptor loan); gas; lndry (inc dryer); basic shop & 2km; snacks; bar; BBQ; playgrnd; htd, covrd pool nr; canoeing; bike hire; golf 10km; TV; 30% statics; dogs CHF3; bus; poss cr; Eng spkn; adv bkg; quiet; ccard acc; red CKE/CCI. "Gd base for S shore of Bodensee; pleasant rvside setting; friendly staff." 10 Apr-2 Oct. CHF 28.00   2010*

ST MARGRETHEN *A4* (3km E Rural) *47.45114, 9.65650* **Strandbad Camping Bruggerhorn, 9430 St Margrethen [071 7442201; fax 7442757]** Exit N1/E60 dir St Margrethen, site well sp. Med, pt shd; wc; chem disp; shwrs inc; EHU (10A) CHF2.50 (adaptor avail); gas; lndry; shop; rest 500m; snacks; playgrnd; 2 pools; lake sw; sports cent adj; tennis; no dogs; poss cr; Eng spkn; adv bkg; quiet; red CKE/CCI. "Picturesque, clean site; vg shwrs; helpful staff." 1 Apr-31 Oct. CHF 34.00   2009*

ST MORITZ *C4* (5km NE Rural) *46.50988, 9.87936* **TCS Camping Punt Muragl, Via da Puntraschigna 56, 7503 Samedan [tel/fax 081 8428197; camping.samedan@tcs.ch; www.campingtcs.ch]** Site on S side of rd fr Celerina to Pontresina, adj to rndabt at junc rds 27 & 29. Med, shd; htd wc; mv service pnt; chem disp; shwrs inc; EHU (6-10A) CHF4 (metered in winter); gas; lndry; shop; rest 300m; snacks; bar; playgrnd; pool & lake 3km; fishing; tennis; skiing; entmnt; 30% statics; dogs CHF5; adv bkg; quiet; ccard acc. "Excel for mountains & Engadine; close rlwy stns & funicular; walking rtes thro forest; clean, spacious facs; enquire about public transport travel card." 26 Nov-18 Apr & 21 May-10 Oct. CHF 40.00   2011*

ST MORITZ *C4* (13km SE Rural) *46.46132, 9.93568* **Camping Plauns, Via da Bernina, 7504 Pontresina-Morteratsch [081 8426285; fax 8345136; plauns@bluewin.ch; www.campingplauns.ch]** On Bernina Pass rd 4km SE of Pontresina, turn R at camp sp. If app fr St Moritz or Samedan, keep to Pontresina by-pass, do not turn L where sp Pontresina. Lge, pt sl, pt shd; htd wc; chem disp; mv service pnt; shwrs CHF0.50; EHU (6-13A) CHF3.50 (adaptor avail & long lead poss req); gas; lndry; shop; rest 1km; snacks; playgrnd; pool 4km; ski lift 3km; ski bus; golf 4km; internet; some statics; dogs CHF4; phone; poss cr; some Eng spkn; adv bkg 2 weeks or more only (non-return fee); quiet; ccard acc; CKE/CCI. "Idyllic site in forest clearing; magnificent scenery; v clean, modern san facs; conv Morteratsch Glacier, Bernina Pass, St Moritz; walking dist rlwy & rest; cable rlwys, funiculars, chair lifts; high walks; glacier excursions." ♦ 25 May-15 Oct & 15 Dec-15 Apr. CHF 38.00   2011*

SALGESCH see Sierre *C2*

SAMEDAN see St Moritz *C4*

⊞ **SAVOGNIN** *C4* (700m NW Rural) *46.59777, 9.59083* **Camping Julia, Veia Sandeilas 10, 7460 Savognin [081 6841444; camping.julia@savogninbergbahnen.ch; www.savogninbergbahnen.ch]** S on rd 3, clearly sp adj Cube Hotel. Sm, hdstg, unshd; htd wc; chem disp; shwrs inc; EHU (16A) CHF2.50; lndry (inc dryer); shop 400m; rest, snacks; bar adj; rv sw & shgl beach adj; 80% statics; dogs CHF1; bus 500m; Eng spkn; adv bkg; quiet; ccard acc; CKE/CCI. "Not particularly attractive site but superb facs; adj chairlift & postbus use free; best for smaller o'fits; gd NH Julier Pass." ♦ CHF 31.00   2010*

SCHAFFHAUSEN *A3* (18km ESE Rural) *47.66216, 8.84034* **Camping Wagenhausen, Hauptstrasse 82, 8260 Wagenhausen [052 7414271; fax 7414157; campingwagenhausen@bluewin. ch; www.campingwagenhausen.ch]** Turn R off Stein-am-Rhein/Schaffhausen rd, site sp. Med, pt shd; wc; chem disp; serviced pitches; shwrs CHF1; EHU (10A) CHF3; gas; lndry; shop; rest; bar; playgrnd; pool; paddling pool; fishing; games area; TV rm; 80% statics; dogs CHF4; poss cr; Eng spkn; quiet; ccard acc. "Vg; direct access to Rv Rhine; rvside footpath." ♦ 1 Apr-31 Oct. CHF 33.00   2009*

SWITZERLAND

SCHAFFHAUSEN *A3* (3km SE Rural) *47.68763, 8.65461* **TCS Camping Rheinwiesen, Hauptstrasse, 8246 Langwiesen [052 6593300; fax 6593355; camping.schaffhausen@tcs.ch; www.campingtcs.ch/schaffhausen]** Fr N, S & W on A4/E41 exit Schaffhausen & foll sp 'Kreuzlingen' on rd 13. Fr E on rd 13 pass under rlwy bdge to Langwiesen about 3km bef Schaffhausen; site sp at Feuerthalen (tent sign only - no site name) down narr rd on L on Rv Rhine. Med, mkd pitch, pt shd; wc; chem disp; mv service pnt; baby facs; shwrs inc; EHU (4A) inc (adaptor avail); gas; lndry (inc dryer); shop; rest, snacks; bar; BBQ (gas & charcoal); playgrnd; children's pool; covrd pool 4km; rv beach & sw; fishing; horseriding 3km; wifi; games/TV rm; 30% statics; no dogs; no o'fits over 7m high ssn; phone; Eng spkn; adv bkg; quiet but some rd/rlwy noise; ccard acc; red LS; CKE/CCI. "Excel site in beautiful location; conv Rhine Falls & Lake Constance; pitches on rvside (rv v fast-moving & unfenced); clean, adequate san facs; grass pitches poss muddy after rain; poss tight access to pitches; gd facs sm children; gd cycling." 24 Apr-7 Oct. CHF 41.00   2012*

SCHWYZ *B3* (7km NW Rural) *47.04761, 8.59173* **Camping Buchenhof, Seebad, 6422 Steinen [041 8321429; www.camping-buchenhof.ch]** Fr N4 exit dir Goldau, then R dir Lauerz. Bef lake take R fork sp Steinen, over m'way bdge; site sp Seebad. Med, mkd pitch, some hdstg, pt sl, unshd; wc; chem disp; shwrs CHF1; EHU (4A) CHF2; gas; lndry; shop; rest, snacks; BBQ; playgrnd; lake sw & beach; fishing; boat hire; tennis; 50% statics; dogs CHF2; Eng spkn; quiet but rlwy noise; CKE/CCI. "Mountain scenery; gd facs." ♦ 1 Apr-31 Oct. CHF 44.00   2010*

SEMPACH *B3* (1.5km S Rural) *47.12447, 8.18924* **TCS Camping Sempach, Seelandstrasse, 6204 Sempach Stadt [041 4601466 or 091 9858070; fax 4604766 or 091 9946708 LS; camping.sempach@tcs.ch; www.campingtcs.ch/sempach]** Fr Luzern on A2 take exit sp Emmen N, Basel, Bern. Join E35 & cont on this rd to exit at Sempach sp. Site well sp. Lge, mkd pitch, unshd; htd wc; chem disp; mv service pnt; baby facs; private san facs avail; shwrs inc; EHU (13A) inc (adaptor avail); gas; lndry (inc dryer); shop; rest; BBQ (gas/charcoal only); playgrnd; paddling pool; shgl beach & lake sw adj; watersports; fishing; golf 5km; bike hire; tennis; wifi; entmnt; games/TV rm; 60% statics; dogs CHF5; no o'fits over 9m high ssn; sep car parks high ssn; poss cr; Eng spkn; adv bkg; quiet; ccard acc; red LS/CKE/CCI. "Excel location on Sempacher See, 10 mins drive fr m'way & attractive town; sm pitches; helpful staff; rest & beach open to public; water & bins far fr many pitches; poss tight parking; ltd facs LS; lakeside walk to Sempach." ♦ 4 Apr-7 Oct. CHF 56.00 SBS - S08   2011*

SIERRE *C2* (3km NE Rural) *46.30215, 7.56420* **Camping Swiss Plage, Campingweg 3, 3970 Salgesch [027 4556608 or 4816023; fax 4813215; info@swissplage.ch; www.swissplage.ch]** Fr A9/E62 exit at Sierre, turn L & go over bdge, Foll sp Salgesch & Site. Fr town site well sp. Lge, shd; wc; chem disp; mv service pnt; shwrs CHF1; EHU (10A) CHF3.60; gas; lndry; shop; rest, snacks; bar; playgrnd; pool 2km; lake sw; tennis; dogs CHF3.50; Eng spkn; adv bkg ess for long stay; quiet; ccard acc. "Pleasant site in lovely location." Easter-1 Nov. CHF 34.00   2011*

SIERRE *C2* (2km E Rural) *46.29362, 7.55777* **Camping Bois de Finges, Route du Bois de Finges, 3960 Sierre [027 4550284; fax 4553351]** Exit A9 Sierre-Est dir Sierre, site in 500m E of Rhône bdge. Med, mkd pitch, terr, shd; wc; chem disp; mv service pnt; shwrs; EHU (4A) CHF3.50; gas; lndry; shop; snacks; bar; playgrnd; htd pool; tennis nr; lake fishing 1.5km; TV; 10% statics; dogs CHF5; phone; Eng spkn; adv bkg; quiet; red LS/long stay; ccard acc. "Lovely wooded site; slopes/terr poss diff; warm welcome." 1 May-30 Sep. CHF 35.00   2011*

SIERRE *C2* (15km NW Rural) *46.30426, 7.48308* **Camping La Moubra, Impasse de la Plage 2, 3962 Crans-Montana [027 4812851; fax 4810551; moubra@campings.ch; www.campingmoubra.ch]** Fr Sierre take rd to Chermignon & Montana. In Montana turn L sp La Moubra; site in 3km by lake. Med, pt shd; wc; mv service pnt; shwrs; EHU (10A) CHF4; gas; lndry; rest 300m; snacks; bar; pool 500m; lake sw; tennis; boating; fishing; watersports; golf; 20% statics; dogs CHF3; Eng spkn; adv bkg; quiet; ccard acc. "Ski & boot rm; navette adj; frozen lake - start of x-country skiing; well-maintained site in gd position; lovely situation, quiet, E to reach mountain; gd walking & cycling on site." 16 May-15 Oct & 15 Dec-18 Apr. CHF 60.00   2011*

SILVAPLANA *C4* (600m SW Rural) *46.45671, 9.79316* **Camping Silvaplana, 7513 Silvaplana [tel/fax 081 8288492; reception@campingsilvaplana.ch; www.campingsilvaplana.ch]** Exit by-pass rd at S junc for Silvaplana (opp camp site). In 100m after g'ge turn R & site sp via underpass, on lakeside. When app fr Julier Pass foll sp for Maloja Pass as above. Lge, pt sl, pt shd; wc; chem disp; mv service pnt; shwrs CHF1.10; EHU (16A) CHF3.50; gas; lndry; shop & 300m; playgrnd; pool 3km; lake sw; watersports; fishing; tennis; wifi; many statics in sep area; dogs CHF3; poss cr; Eng spkn; no adv bkg; quiet; ccard acc. "V beautiful location; gd walking; hiking; climbing; vg watersports & windsurfing; excel facs for m'vans; 2.5% surcharge on ccard." 13 May-20 Oct. CHF 45.00   2013*

"Satellite navigation makes touring much easier"

Remember most sat navs don't know if you're towing or in a larger vehicle – always use yours alongside maps and site directions.

⊞ **SION** *C2* (9km SW Rural) *46.20578, 7.27855* **Camping du Botza, Route du Camping 1, 1963 Vétroz [027 3461940 or 079 2203575 (mob); fax 3462535; info@botza.ch; www.botza.ch]** Exit A9/E62 junc 25 S'wards over a'bahn. Site adj Vétroz indus est, foll sp 'CP Nr.33'. Lge, mkd pitch, pt shd; wc; chem disp; mv service pnt; baby facs; serviced pitches; shwrs inc; EHU (10A) CHF3.70; gas; lndry; shop; rest, snacks; bar; playgrnd; free htd pool high ssn; paddling pool; fishing; tennis; squash; golf 8km; wifi; entmnt; 30% statics; dogs CHF3.50; adv bkg; quiet; ccard acc; red LS. "Superb site conv m'way & ski resorts; excel facs; gd security; organised excursions; vg rest; fine mountain views; cycle track along Rhone nrby; some noise fr nrby airport." ♦ CHF 47.00   2014*

SOLOTHURN *B2* (2km SW Rural) *47.19883, 7.52288* **TCS Camping Lido Solothurn, Glutzenhofstrasse 5, 4500 Solothurn [tel/fax 032 6218935 or 091 9858070 LS; camping.solothurn@tcs.ch; www.campingtcs.ch/solothurn]** Exit A5 dir Solothurn W, cross rv bdge. At traff lts turn L & foll sp to site (new rd 2009). Lge, mkd pitch, pt shd; htd wc; chem disp; mv service pnt; baby facs; 10% serviced pitches; shwrs inc; EHU (13A) inc; gas; lndry (inc dryer); shop; rest, snacks; bar; BBQ; cooking facs; playgrnd; htd pool adj; paddling pool; fishing; tennis 200m; bike & boat hire; golf 100m; games area; wifi; entmnt; games/TV rm; 20% statics; dogs CHF5; no o'fits over 12m high ssn; bus 200m; Eng spkn; adv bkg; quiet; ccard acc; red LS; CKE/CCI. "Gd touring base by Rv Aare; lge pitches; excel facs; helpful staff; 20 mins walk to picturesque town; excel cycling paths." ◆ 28 Feb-29 Nov. CHF 58.00 SBS - S13   2013*

SORENS see Bulle *C2*

⊞ **SPIEZ** *C2* (6km SE Rural) *46.65880, 7.71688* **Camping Stuhlegg, Stueleggstrasse 7, 3704 Krattigen [033 6542723; fax 6546703; campstuhlegg@bluewin.ch; www.camping-stuhlegg.ch]** 13km fr Interlaken on hillside on S side of Lake Thun. Advise app fr Spiez. Fr Spiez rlwy stn heading SE turn R over rlwy bdge; foll sp Leissigen & Krattigen for 5km. In Krattigen after modern church turn R (low gear), site 500m on R. To avoid going thro Spiez town, leave Bern-Interlaken m'way at junc 19. Foll dir to Aeschi. At rndabt in Aeschi turn L to Krattigen. Turn L after 1m opp wood yard into Stuhleggstrasse. Site in 300 yds. Lge, pt sl, terr, pt shd; htd wc; chem disp; mv service pnt; baby facs; shwrs CHF1; EHU (10A) CHF4 (some rev pol); gas; lndry (inc dryer); sm shop; rest 300m; snacks; bar; playgrnd; htd pool; entmnt; 60% statics; dogs CHF3; sdki bus; phone; site clsd last week Oct to end Nov; adv bkg; quiet; ccard acc; red LS/long stay/CKE/CCI. "Excel well-kept, well run site; immac facs; helpful friendly staff; recep clsd 1300-1500; mountain views; gd dog-walking in area; scenic rtes fr site; free bus service with Guest Card; gd rest; bread can be ordered." CHF 43.00   2014*

SPIEZ *C2* (6km S Rural) *46.65311, 7.70030* **Camping Panorama-Rossern, Scheidgasse, 3703 Aeschi [033 6544377; postmaster@camping-aeschi.ch; www.camping-aeschi.ch]** Leave N6 Thun to Interlaken rd at Spiez junc on main rd, foll sp Spiezwieler. In Spiezwieler turn L at g'ge sp Aeschi. Strt on at x-rds in Aeschi town cent. Site on R immed after fire stn. Med, pt sl, pt terr, pt shd; wc; chem disp; shwrs CHF1; EHU CHF3 (adaptor avail); lndry; sm shop & shops 2km; playgrnd; 40% statics; dogs CHF1; bus; quiet; poss cr. "Views of Blümlisalp, Niesen; some cars parked away fr vans due terraces." 15 May-15 Oct. CHF 30.00   2011*

⊞ **SPLUGEN** *C3* (700m W Rural) *46.55003, 9.31662* **Camping auf dem Sand, Untere Allmend, 7435 Splügen [081 6641476; fax 6641460; camping@splugen.ch; www.campingsplugen.ch]** Exit A13/E61 (Chur-San Bernardino) & take slip rd sp Splügen. Foll rd thro vill, site at end. Med, unshd; wc; chem disp; mv service pnt; shwrs inc; EHU (10A) CHF3; gas; lndry; shop 800m; playgrnd; tennis; fishing; wifi; 70% statics; dogs CHF3; adv bkg; quiet; red CKE/CCI. "Conv for San Bernardino Tunnel." CHF 45.00   2011*

STECHELBERG see Lauterbrunnen *C2*

SUMVITG *C3* (900m SW Rural) *46.72439, 8.92968* **Camping Garvera, Campadi alla Staziun, 7175 Sumvitg [081 9431922; info@garvera.ch; www.garvera.ch]** Fr Chur on rd 19, site well sp in Sumvitg. Sm, terr, pt shd; htd wc; chem disp; shwrs inc; EHU (10A) CHF4; lndry; shop 500m; rest; bar; dogs CHF4; bus/train adj; Eng spkn; quiet - some daytime rlwy noise; red LS. "Excel, clean, well cared for site; friendly, helpful owners, who run nrby rest; beautiful area; gd walking; excel facs, inc a natural spring water pond; highly rec." ◆ ltd. 1 May-1 Oct. CHF 34.00   2015*

⊞ **SUR EN** *B4* (400m NE Rural) *46.81859, 10.36594* **Camping Sur En, 7554 Sur En (Graubünden) [079 0111147; fax 081 8663767; wb@sur-en.ch; www.sur-en.ch]** Visible in valley fr rd 27. Steep access. Sm, unshd; htd wc; chem disp; mv service pnt; shwrs inc; EHU (6-10A) CHF3; (long lead poss req; warden has adaptors); lndry (inc dryer); shop; rest (ccard not acc); snacks; bar; BBQ; playgrnd; sm pool; ski lift 7km; free ski bus; 30% statics in sep area; dogs CHF3; Eng spkn; no adv bkg; quiet; ccard acc (surcharge); CKE/CCI. "Superb facs in out-of-the-way spot; great atmosphere for nature lovers/walkers/cyclists; gd for dog walking but tick treatment ess." CHF 49.00   2013*

⊞ **SURCUOLM** *B3* (700m N Rural) *46.76053, 9.14324* **Panorama Camping Surcuolm, 7138 Surcuolm [081 9333223; fax 9333224; info@camping-surcuolm; www.camping-surcuolm.ch]** Fr N19 to Ilanz & in Ilanz foll sp Valata & Obersaxen. In Valata turn L to Surcuolm, site on L. This is only rec rte - steep climbs. Med, pt sl, unshd; htd wc; chem disp; mv service pnt; shwrs CHF0.50; EHU (16A) metered; lndry (inc dryer); shop; rest, snacks nr; bar; playgrnd; ski lift nr; wifi; 10% statics; dogs CHF3; bus 500m; adv bkg; quiet. "Mountain views; popular winter site; quiet in summer; excel facs." CHF 41.00   2012*

SURSEE *B2* (2km NW Rural) *47.17505, 8.08685* **Camping Sursee Waldheim, Baslerstrasse, 6210 Sursee [041 9211161; fax 9211160; info@camping-sursee.ch; www.camping-sursee.ch]** Exit A2 at junc 20 & take L lane onto rd 24 dir Basel/Luzern. Turn R at traff lts, foll rd 2 turn R at 2nd rndabt dir Basel to site. Med, shd; wc; chem disp; shwrs CHF0.50; EHU (10A) CHF3; gas; lndry; shop; rest in town; snacks; bar; playgrnd; lake sw 1.5km; 60% statics; dogs CHF1; poss cr; Eng spkn; quiet but poss noisy at w/end; CKE/CCI. "Pretty site; excel san facs; gd train service to Luzern; sh walk to town cent; popular NH; gd touring base." 1 Apr-30 Sep. CHF 35.00   2013*

SUSTEN see Leuk *C2*

SUTZ see Biel/Bienne *B2*

TAGERWILEN *A3* (800m NW Rural) *47.65928, 9.12341* **Restaurant Werkhof Oase, Hauptstrasse 12, 8274 Tägerwilen [071 6691717; oasecamping@hotmail.com]** Fr Kreuzlingen take rd 13 twds Schaffhausen. Site on L on o'skirts of Tägerwilen. Sm, hstg, unshd; wc; chem disp; mv service pnt; shwrs inc; EHU (10A) CHF4; lndry (inc dryer); shop 3km; rest, snacks; bar; lake sw & beach 2km; wifi; dogs; Eng spkn; quiet; red LS. "Sm m'van site, but c'vans acc if rm; v friendly owners; conv Lake Constance." Jan-Oct. CHF 20.00   2010*

TASCH see Zermatt *D2*

TAVERNE see Lugano *D3*

TENERO *C3* (1km S Urban) *46.16921, 8.8538* **Camping Lago Maggiore, Via Lido 4, 6598 Tenero [091 7451848; fax 7454318; info@clm.ch; www.clm.ch]**
Fr A2 take Bellinzona S exit & foll sp Locarno. In about 12km take Tenero exit, at end slip rd foll sp to site. C'vans not permitted on rd S337 fr Domodossola to Locarno. If app fr Simplon Pass cont S of Domodossola & take S34 up W shore of lake. Lge, pt shd; wc; chem disp; mv service pnt; shwrs inc; EHU (adaptor avail) inc; gas; lndry (inc dryer); shop; rest; bar; BBQ; playgrnd; lake sw, pools for adults & children; watersports; fishing; tennis; TV; no dogs; adv bkg; Eng spkn; quiet; ccard acc. "Beautiful region; extra for pitches nr lake; vg." 15 Mar-31 Oct. CHF 58.00 (5 persons) 2010*

⊞ **TENERO** *C3* (1km SW Urban) *46.17292, 8.84808* **Camping Miralago, Via Roncaccio 20, 6598 Tenero [091 7451255; fax 7452878; info@camping-miralago.ch; www.camping-miralago.ch]** Turn L off A13 Bellinzona/Locarno rd at Tenero & foll camping sps. Med, mkd pitch, unshd; htd wc; chem disp; mv service pnt; baby facs; shwrs CHF1; EHU (10A) inc; lndry (inc dryer); shop; rest, snacks; bar; BBQ; playgrnd; htd pool; paddling pool; sand beach & lake sw adj; games area; wifi; dogs CHF3; bus adj; poss cr; Eng spkn; adv bkg; quiet; ccard acc; red LS/CKE/CCI. "Beautiful area; ltd facs LS; lake steamer pier lakefront camping; sm pitches with no privacy hdgs; fairly new san facs; beautiful location, no rd noise." ◆ CHF 117.00 2014*

TENERO *C3* (1km W Rural) *46.1770, 8.84185* **Camping Lido Mappo, Via Mappo, 6598 Tenero [091 7451437; fax 7454808; camping@lidomappo.ch; www.lidomappo.ch]**
Fr A2 take Bellinzona Sud exit & foll sp Locarno. In about 12km take Tenero exit, at end slip rd foll sp to site on lakeside. Lge, shd; htd wc; chem disp; mv service pnt; baby facs; shwrs; EHU (10A) inc; gas; lndry (inc dryer); supmkt; rest, snacks; bar; BBQ; playgrnd; lake sw; sand/shgl beach; fishing; boating; watersports; bike hire; wifi; entmnt; TV; no dogs; phone; adv bkg; poss cr; Eng spkn; quiet, but some noise fr local airfield; ccard acc. "Extra for lakeside pitch; cycle rte to Locarno; v helpful staff." ◆ 14 Mar-31 Oct. CHF 53.00 2010*

TENERO *C3* (1km W Rural) *46.17575, 8.84515* **Camping Tamaro, Via Mappo, 6598 Tenero [091 7452161; fax 7456636; info@campingtamaro.ch; www.camping tamaro.ch]** Fr N2 take Bellinzona Süd exit dir Locarno. In about 12km take Tenero exit, at end slip rd foll sp to site. Lge, unshd; htd wc; chem disp; mv service pnt; baby facs; shwrs inc; EHU (10A) CHF4; gas; lndry; shops; adv bkg; rest; bar; lake sw; beach; watersports; fishing; tennis; 30% statics; no dogs; phone; bus; boat to Locarno; adv bkg; Eng spkn; red LS/long stay; debit card acc. "Excel site; helpful staff; extra for lakeside pitches; tight corners & high kerbs on site rd - manhandling poss req; ferry to Locarno fr site." ◆ 6 Mar-1 Nov. CHF 56.00 2009*

THORISHAUS see Bern *B2*

THUN *B2* (9km N Rural) *46.81368, 7.60829* **Camping Wydeli, Wydeli 60, 3671 Brenzikofen [031 7711141; fax 7711181; info@camping-brenzikofen.ch; www.camping-brenzikofen. ch]** Fr A6 take Kiesen exit; foll sp Konolfingen-Langnau to Oppligen; site sp. Med, pt shd; wc; chem disp; shwrs; EHU CHF 2.50; gas; lndry; shop; rest, snacks; bar; playgrnd; pool; paddling pool; fishing; tennis; horseriding; 60% statics; dogs; Eng spkn; adv bkg. 1 May-30 Sep. CHF 28.00 2009*

"There aren't many sites open at this time of year"

If you're travelling outside peak season remember to call ahead to check site opening dates – even if the entry says 'open all year'.

THUN *B2* (3km S Rural) *46.72753, 7.62778* **TCS Camping Thunersee, Gwattstrasse 103a, 3645 Gwatt [033 3364067; fax 3364017; camping.gwatt@tcs.ch; www.thunersee.ch]**
Fr A6 take Thun-Süd exit & foll sp to Gwatt; on reaching Thun-Speiz main rd turn L, site on R in 500m. Well sp on rte 6 in Gwatt on lake side of rd. Med, unshd, wc; chem disp; mv service pnt; shwrs inc; EHU (4A) CHF3.50 (adaptor on loan); gas; lndry; shop; rest, snacks; bar; pool 1km; shgl beach; lake sw adj; watersports; fishing; mooring for boats; tennis; 40% statics; dogs CHF5; bus to Thun; sep car park; poss cr; Eng spkn; adv bkg; quiet; ccard acc; red long stay; red CKE/ CCI. "Walks by lake; mkd cycle ways; superb views; pretty site; office/barrier clsd 1130-1400; helpful management; gd san facs." ◆ 3 Apr-11 Oct. CHF 41.00 2010*

THUN *B2* (11km W Rural) *46.74514, 7.52014* **Camping Restaurant Bad, 3638 Blumenstein [033 3562954; k.wenger@bad-blumenstein.ch; www.bad-blumenstein.ch]**
Fr A6 exit Thun Nord dir Wattenwil & Blumenstein; site sp in vill. Sm, pt sl, unshd; wc; shwrs CHF0.50/2mins; EHU CHF3; rest & bar (Wed-Sun); pool 3km; fishing; wifi; bus, train nr; Eng spkn; adv bkg; quiet; red long stay/LS; CKE/CCI. "Basic, CL-type site - v pleasant, but v ltd; gd." 1 May-30 Sep. CHF 25.00 2009*

THUSIS *C4* (2km E Rural) *46.69945, 9.44547* **Camping Viamala, Pantunweg 1, 7430 Thusis [tel/fax 081 6512472; info@camping-thusis.ch; www.camping-thusis.ch]**
Turn off A13 Chur-San Bernardino rd dir Thusis, site well sp. Med, deeply shd; wc; chem disp; shwrs inc; EHU CHF3; gas; lndry; shop; rest 500m; snacks; bar; playgrnd; pool adj; tennis; games area; fishing; 20% statics; dogs; phone; Eng spkn; adv bkg; CKE/CCI. "Gd cent for mountains; beautiful situation." 1 May-30 Sep. CHF 27.00 2010*

⊞ **THUSIS** *C4* (12km S Rural) *46.60580, 9.42630* **Camping Sut Baselgia, 7440 Andeer [081 6611453; fax 6307077; camping.andeer@bluewin.ch; www.campingandeer.ch]**
On N edge of vill of Andeer. Exit N13 at Zillis for Andeer; site sp. Med, pt shd; wc; chem disp; shwrs inc; EHU (10A) CHF3; gas; lndry (inc dryer); shop; snacks; bar; 2 pools adj (1 htd, covrd); paddling pool; tennis; bike hire; games rm; wifi; 90% statics; dogs CHF2; site clsd Nov; quiet; ccard acc. "Beautiful location; helpful owner; gd NH." CHF 33.00 2011*

SWITZERLAND

TRIESEN see Vaduz (Liechtenstein) *B4*

ULRICHEN *C3* (1km SE Rural) *46.50369, 8.30969* **Camping Nufenen, 3988 Ulrichen [027 9731437; info@camping-nufenen.ch; www.camping-nufenen.ch]**
On NE end of Ulrichen turn R on Nufenen pass rd. After rlwy & rv x-ing (1km), site on R. Med, pt shd; wc; chem disp; shwrs CHF0.50; EHU (8A) CHF3.50; lndry; shop; snacks 500m; rest 1km; pool 6km; tennis 2km; 50% statics; dogs CHF2; phone; poss cr; adv bkg; quiet; red long stay/CKE/CCI. "Pleasantly situated, mountainous site with gd local facs; gd walking; san facs basic but clean; recep clsd 1230-1400." ♦ ltd.
1 Jun-30 Sep. CHF 26.00   2009*

ULRICHEN *C3* (8km SW Rural) *46.46480, 8.24469* **Camping Augenstern, 3988 Reckingen [027 9731395; info@campingaugenstern.ch; www.campingaugenstern.ch]**
On Brig-Gletsch rd turn R in Reckingen over rlwy & rv; site sp. Med, unshd; wc; chem disp; mv service pnt; shwrs CHF1; EHU (10A) CHF4.50; lndry; shop; rest, snacks; bar; htd pool adj; golf; fishing; 20% statics; dogs CHF2; quiet; red CKE/CCI. "Nr Rv Rhône & mountains." 14 May-16 Oct & 10 Dec-13 Mar. CHF 28.00   2009*

UNTERSEEN see Interlaken *C2*

UTTWIL see Romanshorn *A4*

⊞ **VADUZ (LIECHTENSTEIN)** *B4* (7km S Rural) *47.0866, 9.52666* **Camping Mittagspitze, Saga 29, 9495 Triesen [3923677; fax 3923680; info@campingtriesen.li; www.campingtriesen.li]** On rd 28 bet Vaduz & Balzers, sp. Poss diff for lge o'fits. Med, some hdstg, terr, pt shd; wc; chem disp; shwrs inc; EHU (6A) CHF5; gas; lndry; shop on site & 3km; rest; beergarden; BBQ; playgrnd; pool high ssn; fishing; fitness trail; many statics; dogs CHF4; poss cr; Eng spkn; quiet; ccard acc. "Pretty site in lovely location; excl touring base; site yourself; recep open 0800-0830 & 1900-1930 only; steep, diff access to pitches & slippery when wet; gd rest." CHF 33.00   2009*

VALLORBE *B1* (700m SW Urban) *46.71055, 6.37472* **Camping Pré Sous Ville, 10 Rue des Fontaines, 1337 Vallorbe [021 8432309; yvan.favre@vallorbe.com]**
Foll camping sp in town. Med, mkd pitch, pt shd; wc; chem disp; mv service pnt; shwrs inc; EHU (10A) CHF5; gas; lndry; rest, snacks adj; bar; playgrnd; htd pool adj; fishing; tennis; games area; 20% statics; dogs; Eng spkn; quiet; red CKE/CCI. "Gd, clean facs; gd size pitches; site yourself if warden absent; conv for Vallée de Joux, Lake Geneva & Jura; views down valley." ♦ 15 Apr-15 Oct. CHF 25.00   2009*

⊞ **VERS L'EGLISE** *C2* (3km W Rural) *46.35530, 7.12705* **TCS Camping La Murée, 1865 Les Diablerets [079 4019915; dagonch@bluewin.ch; www.camping-caravaningvd.com]**
Fr N9 exit Aigle. In 8km at Le Sepey turn R dir Vers-l'Eglise & Les Diablerets; site on R at ent to vill. Med, pt sl, terr; htd wc; shwrs; chem disp; EHU (6A) CHF3; gas; lndry; playgrnd; pool 3km; fishing; tennis; wifi; 40% statics; quiet. CHF 21.00   2009*

VESENAZ see Genève *C1*

VETROZ see Sion *C2*

⊞ **VEVEY** *C1* (12km NW Rural) *46.52864, 6.76556* **Camping Les Cases, Chemin des Cases 2, 1606 Forel [021 7811464; fax 7813126; www.campingforel.ch]** Exit A9/E62 Chexbres & foll Lac de Bret & turn L sp Savigny, then immed L. Site 100m on R, 1km S of Forel. Sm, pt sl, unshd; wc; chem disp; mv service pnt; shwrs CHF1; EHU (13A) CHF4; gas; lndry; supmkt; rest, snacks; bar; playgrnd; pool; paddling pool; waterslide; fishing; games area; wifi; TV; 75% statics; dogs CHF2; adv bkg; red long stay. "Sep touring area; gd." ♦ CHF 29.00   2010*

⊞ **VILLENEUVE** *C1* (6km SW Rural) *46.35638, 6.89916* **Camping au Grand-Bois, Chemin au Grand Bois 6, 1846 Chessel [024 4814225; fax 4815113; au.grand-bois@bluewin.ch; www.augrandbois.ch]** Fr N9 Montreux-Aigle, take Villeneuve exit, at end of slip rd turn N twds Villeneuve. At 1st traff lts turn L twds Noville, site on R in 4km. Lge, pt shd; wc; chem disp; mv service pnt; shwrs CHF1; EHU (10A) CHF3 (adaptor avail); lndry; shop 3km; playgrnd; htd pool; sand beach 6km; 80% statics; adv bkg; red long stay/CKE/CCI. "Gd cent for Geneva & pt of Alps; clean, peaceful site; poss travellers." ♦ CHF 24.00   2009*

⊞ **VILLENEUVE** *C1* (5km W Rural) *46.39333, 6.89527* **Camping Les Grangettes, Rue des Grangettes, 1845 Noville [021 9601503; fax 9602030; noville@treyvaud.com; www.les-grangettes.ch]** Fr N9 Montreux-Aigle rd, take Villeneuve exit, at end slip rd turn N twds Villeneuve. At 1st traff lts turn L to Noville, turn R by PO, site sp. Narr app rd. Med, mkd pitch, unshd; htd wc; chem disp; mv service pnt; shwrs; EHU (10A) CHF4; lndry; shop on site & 3km; rest, snacks; bar; pool 3km; lake sw; fishing; boating; 80% statics; dogs CHF3; phone; sep car park; Eng spkn; quiet. "Beautifully situated on SE corner Lake Geneva o'looking Montreux; sep tourer area; poss noisy in high ssn." ♦ CHF 50.00   2014*

VILLENEUVE *C1* (12km W Rural) *46.38666, 6.86055* **Camping Rive-Bleue, Bouveret-Plage, 1897 Le Bouveret [024 4812161; fax 4812108; info@camping-rive-bleue.ch; www.camping-rive-bleue.ch]** Fr Montreux foll sp to Evian to S side of Lake Geneva. Turn R after sp 'Bienvenue Bouveret'. Foll camp sp to Aqua Park. Site on R approx 1km fr main rd. Lge, mkd pitch, pt shd; wc; chem disp; mv service pnt; shwrs inc; EHU (10A) CHF4.20 (adaptor avail - check earth); gas; lndry; rest & snacks adj; shop; playgrnd; pool adj; waterslide; lake sw; watersports; tennis; 20% statics; dogs CHF2.60; wifi; sep car park; Eng spkn; adv bkg; quiet; CKE/CCI. "Well-maintained, well-ordered, completely flat site in lovely setting on lake; friendly staff; water/waste pnts scarce; vg facs but red LS; 15 mins walk to vill with supmkt; conv ferries around Lake Geneva; cars must be parked in sep public car park; gd cyling area; free bicycles for 4 hrs fr vill; 1st class san block." 1 Apr-12 Oct. CHF 43.00   2014*

VIRA GAMBAROGNO see Locarno *C3*

VISP *C2* (7km W Rural) *46.30280, 7.80188* **Camping Santa Monica, Kantonstrasse, Turtig, 3942 Raron [027 9342424; fax 9342450; santamonica@rhone.ch; www.santa-monica.ch]** Turn R off Sion-Brig rd after Turtig, just after sm rndabt. Lge, pt shd; wc; chem disp; mv service pnt; private san facs avail; shwrs CHF1; EHU (16A) CHF4; gas; lndry; shop 250m; snacks; htd pool; tennis; fishing; 50% statics; dogs CHF3.80 (1 only); Eng spkn; adv bkg; quiet, but some rd noise; red LS. "Recep clsd lunchtime, but no barrier so site yourself." 10 Apr-18 Oct. CHF 30.00   2009*

⊞ **VISP** *C2* (7.6km W Rural) *46.30288, 7.79530* **Camping Simplonblick, 3942 Raron [027 9343205; fax 9675012; simplonblick@bluewin.ch; www.camping-simplonblick.ch]** Site on S of rd 9. Fr Visp site past junc to Raron thro g'ge forecourt. Lge, pt shd; wc; chem disp; shwrs inc; EHU CHF4 (adaptor loan); gas; lndry; rest; bar; playgrnd; pool; paddling pool; dogs CHF4; Eng spkn; adv bkg; quiet; ccard acc. "Vg rest; friendly, welcoming staff; recep clsd 1200-1500 fr end Aug." CHF 35.00   2011*

VISP *C2* (1.6km NW Rural) *46.29730, 7.87269* **Camping Schwimmbad Mühleye, 3930 Visp [027 9462084; fax 9463469; info@camping-visp.ch; www.camping-visp.ch]** Exit main rd E2 at W end of town bet Esso petrol stn & rv bdge at Camping sp. Site nr pool. Lge, pt shd; wc; chem disp; shwrs; EHU (13A) CHF3.50; gas; lndry; shops 500m; snacks; bar; playgrnd; lge pool adj; tennis; fishing; 20% statics; dogs CHF2; Eng spkn; some noise fr rlwy & sometimes rifle range; red long stay/LS/CKE/CCI. "Gd for Zermatt & Matterhorn; recep at sw pool ent; gd value espec LS; suitable lge o'fits." 10 Mar-31 Oct. CHF 35.00   2015*

"That's changed – Should I let The Club know?"

If you find something on site that's different from the site entry, fill in a report and let us know. See www.caravanclub.co.uk/europereport.

VITZNAU *B3* (500m SE Rural) *47.00683, 8.48621* **Camping Vitznau, Altdorfstrasse, 6354 Vitznau [041 3971280; fax 3972457; info@camping-vitznau.ch; www.camping-vitznau.ch]** On E edge of Vitznau, sp. Fr Küssnacht twd Brunnen turn L at RC church with tall clock tower. Lge, terr, hdstg, pt shd; wc; chem disp; mv service pnt; shwrs inc; EHU (15A) CHF4 (adaptors on loan); gas; lndry; shop & 500m; bar; pool; lake sw & beach 500m; tennis; 40% statics; dogs CHF5; Quickstop o'night facs CHF20; poss cr; Eng spkn; adv bkg rec; quiet; card acc; red LS; ccard acc; red long stay; CKE/CCI. "Excel, v clean, family-run site; friendly owner will help with pitching; max c'van length 7m high ssn; sm pitches; some site rds tight & steep; recep closes 1830 hrs; fine views lakes & mountains; many activities inc walking; gd dog-walking; conv ferry terminal, cable cars & mountain rlwy (tickets avail on site); gd saving by using 'tell-pass'; lake steamer to Luzern 500m; gd pool, sm shop." ♦ ltd. 27 Mar-17 Oct. CHF 54.00   2013*

WABERN see Bern *B2*

WAGENHAUSEN see Schaffhausen *A3*

WALENSTADT *B3* (1km SW Rural) *47.11688, 9.30086* **See Camping, Ziegelhütte, 8880 Walenstadt [081 7351896 or 7351212; fax 7351841; kontakt@see-camping.ch; www.see-camping.ch]** Fr Zürich on A3 turn R at Walenstadt sp, turn L & go thro town. Foll camping sp 2km, turn R into site. Med, pt shd; htd wc; chem disp; mv service pnt; shwrs inc; EHU (16A) CHF3; lndry; shop; snacks; playgrnd; lake sw adj; TV; quiet but some train noise; 75% statics; phone; no dogs; sep car park; no adv bkg; Eng spkn; red long stay; CKE/CCI. "Beautiful area; wonderful lake views." 1 May-30 Sep. CHF 38.00   2010*

⊞ **WILDBERG IM TOSSTAL** *A3* (1km NE Rural) *47.43500, 8.82862* **Camping in der Weid, Wildbergerstrasse, 8489 Wildberg-im-Tösstal [052 3853388; seiler.camping@bluewin.ch; www.campingwildberg.ch]** Leave N1/E17 at Winterthur-Ohringen to cent Winterthur. Turn R onto N15 sp Turbenthal. Wildberg sp on ent Turbenthal, turn R, site on L in 1km. Steep access rd. Med, hdstg, pt sl, terr, pt shd; htd wc; chem disp; mv service pnt; shwrs CHF0.50; EHU (6A) CHF1.50; lndry; shop; rest, snacks; bar; BBQ; playgrnd; pool 2km; paddling pool; games area; TV; 90% statics; dogs CHF2; Eng spkn; adv bkg; aircraft noise. "Gd NH for Zürich; ltd space for tourers; friendly, helpful staff; gd for children." ♦ CHF 26.00   2010*

WILDERSWIL see Interlaken *C2*

⊞ **WINTERTHUR** *A3* (3km N Rural) *47.51965, 8.71655* **Camping am Schützenweiher, Eichliwaldstrasse 4, 8400 Winterthur [tel/fax 052 2125260; campingplatz@win.ch; www.campingwinterthur.ch]** Fr A1/E60 exit Winterthur-Ohringen dir Winterthur, turn R & foll site sp, site adj police stn in about 200m. Sm, shd; htd wc; chem disp; shwrs CHF1; EHU CHF3; gas; lndry; shops adj; rest; playgrnd; pool 3km; 8% statics; dogs CHF4; phone; poss cr; Eng spkn; some m'way noise; red CKE/CCI. "Helpful owner; office open 1900-2000 to register & pay; find own pitch outside these hrs; sm pitches; NH only." CHF 28.00   2010*

YVERDON *B1* (3km N Rural) *46.80284, 6.63399* **Camping Le Pécos, Rue du Pécos, 1422 Grandson [024 4454969; fax 4462904; vd24@campings-ccyverdpn.ch; www.campings-ccyverdon.ch]** Foll rd 5 dir Neuchâtel. Site is 800m SW fr Grandson town cent, lakeside site, sp VD24. Med, mkd pitch, hdstg, pt shd; htd wc; chem disp; mv service pnt; baby facs; fam bthrm; shwrs CHF1; EHU (10A) CHF6 (adaptor avail); gas; lndry rm; shop; rest, snacks; bar; playgrnd; lake sw adj; wifi; 70% statics; dogs CHF3; phone; extra for lakeside pitches; poss cr; Eng spkn; adv bkg; quiet but some rlwy noise; CKE/CCI. "Clean san facs; friendly owners; sm pitches." ♦ 1 Apr-30 Sep. CHF 30.00   2010*

YVONAND see Yverdon *B1*

SWITZERLAND

ZERMATT *D2* (6km N Rural) *46.06450, 7.77500* **Camping Alphubel, 3929 Täsch (Wallis) [027 9673635; welcome@ campingtaesch.ch; www.campingtaesch.ch]** Turn down R-hand slip rd over level x-ing & bdge after rlwy stn in Täsch, & foll sp to site. S bend bdge poss diff for lge o'fits at app. Med, unshd; htd wc; chem disp; mv service pnt; shwrs inc; EHU (10A) CHF5 (long lead poss req); lndry; shops 200m; rest adj; htd pool 1km; tennis; fishing; dogs CHF2; recep clsd 1200-1400; poss cr; Eng spkn; no adv bkg; quiet but rlwy noise; ccard not acc. "Conv for frequent train to Zermatt fr vill; superb scenery & walking; helpful owner; vg, modern san facs; excel." 8 May-14 Oct. CHF 49.00   2013*

ZERMATT *D2* (8km N Rural) *46.08600, 7.78219* **Camping Attermenzen, 3928 Randa [027 9672555 or 9671379; fax 9676074; sommercamping@oberwallis.ch or wintercamping@oberwallis.ch; www.camping-randa.ch]** Fr A9/E62 turn S in Visp dir Zermatt. Site on L after approx 30km 2km S of Randa vill bef Tasch. Med, pt sl, unshd; wc; shwrs inc; EHU (5A) CHF4 (adaptors avail); gas; lndry; shop; rest, snacks; bar; playgrnd; dogs CHF2; shuttle bus to Zermatt; site clsd Jan; poss cr; Eng spkn; quiet; CKE/CCI. "Winter c'vanning; main clientele climbers; excel san facs; humourous owner." 15 Jun-15 Sep & 1 Nov-30 Apr. CHF 24.00   2009*

ZERNEZ *C4* (1km SW Rural) *46.69716, 10.08718* **Camping Cul, 7530 Zernez [tel/fax 081 8561462; info@camping-cul.ch; www.camping-cul.ch]** Fr N foll sp for St Moritz to edge of town, sp thro woodyard to site. Fr S sp on L on reaching town. Med, mkd pitch, pt shd; wc; chem disp; mv service pnt; shwrs inc; EHU (8A) CHF2.50; lndry; shop & 500m; rest high ssn; playgrnd in town; 5% statics; dogs CHF2; poss cr; adv bkg; quiet; 10% red CKE/CCI. "Roomy, clean, pretty, well-organised site surrounded by mountains; friendly staff; excel san facs; barrier clsd 1200-1300; conv Swiss National Park & train to St Moritz; conv Livigno (Italy) for tax-free shopping; easy walk into town along Rv Inn & many walking trails." 15 May-31 Oct. CHF 32.00   2009*

ZUG *B3* (2km E Rural) *47.17806, 8.49438* **TCS Camping Zugersee, Chamer Fussweg 36, 6300 Zug [041 7418422; fax 7418430; camping.zug@tcs.ch; www.campingtcs.ch]** Fr A4/E41 take A4a Zug-West, site sp on R in 3km on lakeside. Fr Zug take Luzern rd for 2km. Site on L under rlwy. Med, mkd pitch, pt shd; htd wc; chem disp; mv service pnt; shwrs inc; EHU (4A) CHF4; gas; lndry (inc dryer); shop; rest, snacks; bar; playgrnd; pool 3km; lake sw; fishing; tennis; games area; bike hire; 40% statics; dogs CHF5; phone; poss cr; Eng spkn; rlwy noise; ccard acc; red CKE/CCI. "Easy walk to town." 30 Mar-7 Oct. CHF 36.00   2011*

ZURICH *A3* (4km S Rural) *47.33633, 8.54167* **Camping Seebucht, Seestrasse 559, 8038 Zürich-Wollishofen [044 4821612; fax 4821660; 2008@camping-zurich.ch; www.camping-zurich.ch]** Fr city foll rd 3 (twd Chur) on S side of lake; foll camping sp. Lge, hdstg, pt shd; wc; chem disp; mv service pnt; shwrs CHF2; EHU (6A) CHF5; gas; lndry; shop; rest, snacks; bar; BBQ; playgrnd; pool 3km; lake sw; watersports; fishing; tennis; 80% statics; dogs CHF5; bus; poss cr & noisy; Eng spkn; rd & rlwy noise. "Parking in Zürich v diff, use bus; sm area for tourers; conv NH, v sm pitches." ♦ 1 May-30 Sep. CHF 39.00   2012*

ZURICH *A3* (20km SW Rural) *47.27970, 8.39570* **Camping Reussbrücke, Muristrasse 32, 8913 Ottenbach [044 7612022; fax 7612042; reussbruecke8913@bluewin.ch; www.camping-ottenbach.ch]** Exit Basel-Zürich m'way at Lenzburg. Foll sps to Zug/Luzern to Muri. Turn L foll sps twd Affoltern thro Birri. Site on L past rv bdge at Ottenbach. Fr Zürich, take rd to Luzern via Birmensdorf. At Affoltern R sp Muri to site on R in 4.5km at Ottenbach, bef rv bdge. Lge, pt shd; wc; shwrs; chem disp; mv service pnt; EHU (10A) CHF4; gas; lndry (inc dryer); shop; rest, snacks; playgrnd; pool; fishing; bike hire; 75% statics; dogs CHF3.50; poss cr; Eng spkn; adv bkg; quiet; ccard acc; CKE/CCI. "Excel san facs; friendly welcome; in beautiful area; sep car pk partly outside gates." 26 Mar-15 Oct. CHF 34.00   2011*

> ## "I like to fill in the reports as I travel from site to site"
> You'll find report forms at the back of this guide, or you can fill them in online at www.caravanclub.co.uk/europereport.

⊞ **ZWEISIMMEN** *C2* (1km N Rural) *46.56338, 7.37691* **Camping Fankhauser, Ey Gässli 2, 3770 Zweisimmen [033 7221356; fax 7221351; info@camping-fankhauser.ch; www.camping-fankhauser.ch]** N6 exit Spiez, then foll sp Zweisimmen. On o'skts of town turn L at camping sp immed bef Agip petrol stn, site on L immed after rlwy x-ing. Med, pt sl; htd wc; chem disp; mv service pnt; shwrs CHF0.50; EHU (10A) CHF3.50 or metered; lndry; shop 1km; rest, snacks, bar 1km; BBQ; playgrnd; pool 800m; fishing; golf; 90% statics; dogs free; phone; Eng spkn; adv bkg; some rlwy noise & glider tow planes at w/end; CKE/CCI. "Gd NH." CHF 28.00   2011*

⊞ **ZWEISIMMEN** *C2* (1km N Rural) *46.56219, 7.37780* **Camping Vermeille, Ey Gässli 2, 3770 Zweisimmen [033 7221940; fax 7723625; info@camping-vermeille.ch; www.camping-vermeille.ch]** Fr N6 exist Spiez & foll sp Zweisimmen. Pass Camping Fankhauser. Site sp almost opp Aldi supmkt. Med, pt shd; htd wc; chem disp; mv service pnt; baby facs; shwrs; EHU (10A) CHF3.50; gas; lndry (inc dryer); shop; rest 300m; snacks; BBQ; cooking facs; playgrnd; htd pool; fishing; tennis; bike hire; games rm; golf; wifi; TV; 70% statics; dogs CHF2; Eng spkn; adv bkg; quiet; ccard acc; red CKE/CCI. "Well-run site; friendly, helpful staff; clsd 1200-1400; cable car to top of mountains; many walks & excursions; easy walk to vill/rlwy stn; cycle track to vill & up valley." ♦ CHF 33.00   2009*

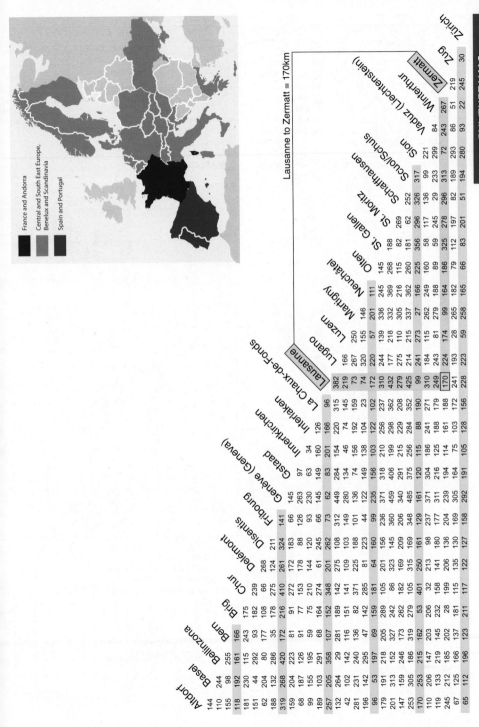

France and Andorra

Central and South East Europe, Benelux and Scandinavia

Spain and Portugal

Lausanne to Zermatt = 170km

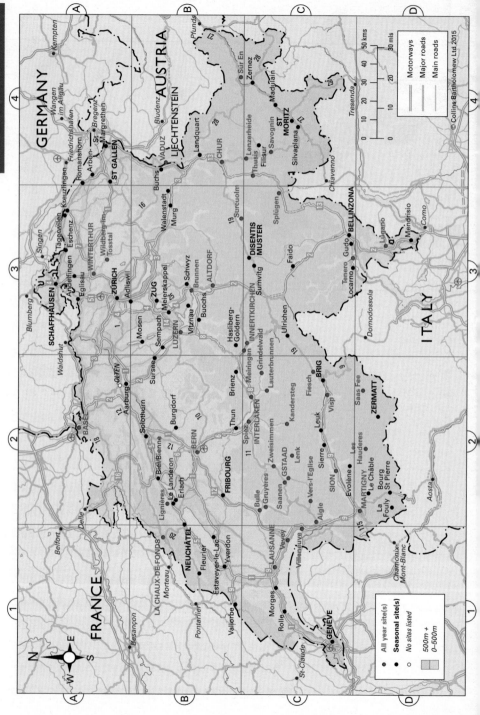

CLUB INSURANCE

Protect your adventure

Why choose Club insurance?

- Club know-how ensures great cover
- Created with your touring needs in mind
- Superb value for money
- Friendly call handlers
- The aftercare you expect from The Club

I'm delighted with the service, the premium is very competitive and the online quote system was so easy   Sara Reynolds, member, Cheshire

Get a quote today
www.caravanclub.co.uk/insure or call

Caravan Insurance	01342 336610	
Overseas Holiday Insurance	01342 336633	
Gadget Insurance	01342 489163	
Key Cover	01342 489162	

Lines are open Mon-Fri 8.45am-5.30pm

Motorhome & Car Insurance	0345 504 0334
Home Insurance	0345 504 0335
Pet Insurance	0345 504 0336

Lines are open Mon-Fri 8.30am-7.00pm & Sat 9.00am-1.00pm & Sun 10.00am-4.00pm. Service provided by Devitt Insurance Services Ltd.

Mayday UK Breakdown & Recovery   0800 731 0112

Mon-Fri 8.00am-8.00pm, Sat 9.00am-5.00pm & Sun 10.00am-4.00pm. Service provided by GreenFlag.

THE CARAVAN CLUB

Calls may be recorded. Motorhome and car insurance new business is not available for drivers aged over 80.

Wish you
were here?

FREE
Venture Abroad
brochure

TAKE YOUR ADVENTURE ABROAD

Join today to book your overseas holiday
Visit www.caravanclub.co.uk/overseas
or call us on 01342 488717

- Over 250 Club-inspected campsites in 16 countries
- Family friendly and peaceful sites
- The best ferry rates, guaranteed
- Insurance designed for caravanners and motorhomers

THE
**CARAVAN
CLUB**

Site Report Form

If campsite is already listed, complete only those sections of the form where changes apply
or alternatively use the Abbreviated Site Report form on the following pages.

Sites not reported on for 5 years may be deleted from the guide

Year of guide used	20.........	Is site listed?	Listed on page no.	Unlisted	Date of visit	......./......../........

A – CAMPSITE NAME AND LOCATION

Country		Name of town/village site listed under *(see Sites Location Maps)*				
Distance & direction from centre of town site is listed under *(in a straight line)*		....................km	eg N, NE, S, SW	Urban	Rural	Coastal
Site open all year?	Y / N	Period site is open *(if not all year)*	................/................ to ..../................			
Site name				Naturist site		Y / N
Site address						
Telephone			Fax			
E-mail			Website			

B – CAMPSITE CHARGES

Charge for outfit + 2 adults in local currency	PRICE	EL PNTS inc in this price?	Y / N	Amps ....

C – DIRECTIONS

Brief, specific directions to site (in km) *To convert miles to kilometres multiply by 8 and divide by 5 or use Conversion Table in guide*	
GPS	Latitude...*(eg 12.34567)* Longitude...*(eg 1.23456 or -1.23456)*

D – CAMPSITE DESCRIPTION

SITE size ie number of pitches	Small Max 50	SM	Medium 51-150	MED	Large 151-500	LGE	Very large 500+	V LGE	Unchanged
PITCH size	*eg small, medium, large, very large, various*								Unchanged
Pitch features if NOT open-plan/grassy		Hedged	HDG PITCH	Marked or numbered	MKD PITCH	Hardstanding or gravel	HDSTG		Unchanged
If site is NOT level, is it		Part sloping	PT SL	Sloping	SL	Terraced	TERR		Unchanged
Is site shaded?		Shaded	SHD	Part shaded	PT SHD	Unshaded	UNSHD		Unchanged

E – CAMPSITE FACILITIES

WC	Heated	HTD WC	Continental	CONT	Own San recommended	OWN SAN REC
Chemical disposal point	CHEM DISP			Dedicated point		WC only
Motorhome waste discharge and water refill point				MV SERVICE PNT		
Child / baby facilities (bathroom)	CHILD / BABY FACS			Family bathroom		FAM BTHRM
Hot shower(s)	SHWR(S)			Inc in site fee?	Y / N	Price...................*(if not inc)*
ELECTRIC HOOK UP *if not included in price above*	EL PNTS			Price.........................		Amps................................
Supplies of bottled gas	GAS			On site	Y / N	Or in .... Kms
Launderette / Washing Machine	LNDTTE		Inc dryer Y / N		LNDRY RM *(if no washing machine)*	

You can also complete forms online: www.caravanclub.co.uk/europereport

CUT ALONG DOTTED LINE

F – FOOD & DRINK

Shop(s) / supermarket	SHOP(S) / SUPMKT	On site		or		.... kms
Bread / milk delivered	TRADSMN					
Restaurant / cafeteria	REST	On site		or		.... kms
Snack bar / take-away	SNACKS	On site		or		.... kms
Bar	BAR	On site		or		.... kms
Barbecue allowed	BBQ	Charcoal		Gas	Elec	Sep area
Cooking facilities	COOKING FACS					

G – LEISURE FACILITIES

Playground	PLAYGRND					
Swimming pool	POOL	On site		or ....km	Heated	Covered
Beach	BEACH	Adj		or ....km	Sand	Shingle
Alternative swimming *(lake)*	SW	Adj		or ....km	Sand	Shingle
Games /sports area / Games room	GAMES AREA	GAMES ROOM				
Entertainment in high season	ENTMNT					
Internet use by visitors	INTERNET	Wifi Internet		WIFI		
Television room	TV RM	Satellite / Cable to pitches		TV CAB / SAT		

H – OTHER INFORMATION

% Static caravans / mobile homes / chalets / cottages / fixed tents on site				.............% STATICS
Dogs allowed	DOGS	Y / N	Price per night .... *(if allowed)*	
Phone	PHONE	On site	Adj	
Bus / tram / train	BUS / TRAM / TRAIN	Adj	or .... km	
Twin axles caravans allowed?	TWIN AXLES Y / N	Possibly crowded in high season		POSS CR
English spoken	ENG SPKN			
Advance bookings accepted	ADV BKG	Y / N		
Noise levels on site in season	NOISY QUIET	If noisy, why?		
Credit card accepted	CCARD ACC	Reduction low season		RED LOW SSN
Camping Key Europe or Camping Card International accepted in lieu of passport	CKE/CCI	INF card required *(If naturist site)*		Y / N
Facilities for disabled	Full wheelchair facilities ♦	Limited disabled facilities		♦ ltd

I – ADDITIONAL REMARKS AND/OR ITEMS OF INTEREST

Tourist attractions, unusual features or other facilities, eg waterslide, tennis, cycle hire, watersports, horseriding, separate car park, walking distance to shops etc	YOUR OPINION OF THE SITE:	
	EXCEL	
	VERY GOOD	
	GOOD	
	FAIR	POOR
	NIGHT HALT ONLY	

Your comments & opinions may be used in future editions of the guide, if you do not wish them to be used please tick ....

J – MEMBER DETAILS

ARE YOU A:	Caravanner		Motorhomer		Trailer-tenter?	
NAME:				MEMBERSHIP NO:		
				POST CODE:		
DO YOU NEED MORE BLANK SITE REPORT FORMS?		YES			NO	

Please use a separate form for each campsite and do not send receipts. Owing to the large number of site reports received, it is not possible to enter into correspondence. Please return completed form to:

**The Editor, Overseas Touring Guides, East Grinstead House
East Grinstead, West Sussex RH19 1UA**

Please note that due to changes in the rules regarding freepost we are no longer able to provide a freepost address for the return of Site Report Forms. You can still supply your site reports free online by visiting www.caravanclub.co.uk/europereport. We apologise for any inconvenience this may cause.

Site Report Form

**If campsite is already listed, complete only those sections of the form where changes apply
or alternatively use the Abbreviated Site Report form on the following pages.**

Sites not reported on for 5 years may be deleted from the guide

Year of guide used	20.........	Is site listed?	Listed on page no.		Unlisted	Date of visit	......./......./.........

A – CAMPSITE NAME AND LOCATION

Country		Name of town/village site listed under *(see Sites Location Maps)*			
Distance & direction from centre of town site is listed under *(in a straight line)*		...................km	eg N, NE, S, SW	Urban	Rural	Coastal

Site open all year?	Y / N	Period site is open *(if not all year)*	................/................ to ..../................		

Site name			Naturist site	Y / N

Site address	

Telephone		Fax	
E-mail		Website	

B – CAMPSITE CHARGES

Charge for outfit + 2 adults in local currency	PRICE		EL PNTS inc in this price?	Y / N	Amps ....

C – DIRECTIONS

Brief, specific directions to site (in km) *To convert miles to kilometres multiply by 8 and divide by 5 or use Conversion Table in guide*	
GPS	Latitude..*(eg 12.34567)* Longitude..*(eg 1.23456 or -1.23456)*

D – CAMPSITE DESCRIPTION

SITE size ie number of pitches	Small Max 50	SM	Medium 51-150	MED	Large 151-500	LGE	Very large 500+	V LGE	Unchanged
PITCH size	eg small, medium, large, very large, various								Unchanged
Pitch features if NOT open-plan/grassy		Hedged	HDG PITCH	Marked or numbered	MKD PITCH	Hardstanding or gravel	HDSTG		Unchanged
If site is NOT level, is it		Part sloping	PT SL	Sloping	SL	Terraced	TERR		Unchanged
Is site shaded?		Shaded	SHD	Part shaded	PT SHD	Unshaded	UNSHD		Unchanged

E – CAMPSITE FACILITIES

WC	Heated	HTD WC	Continental	CONT	Own San recommended		OWN SAN REC	
Chemical disposal point		CHEM DISP		Dedicated point			WC only	
Motorhome waste discharge and water refill point				MV SERVICE PNT				
Child / baby facilities (bathroom)		CHILD / BABY FACS		Family bathroom			FAM BTHRM	
Hot shower(s)		SHWR(S)		Inc in site fee?	Y / N	Price...................*(if not inc)*		
ELECTRIC HOOK UP *if not included in price above*		EL PNTS		Price.........................		Amps.........................		
Supplies of bottled gas		GAS		On site	Y / N	Or in .... Kms		
Launderette / Washing Machine		LNDTTE	Inc dryer Y / N		LNDRY RM *(if no washing machine)*			

You can also complete forms online: www.caravanclub.co.uk/europereport

CUT ALONG DOTTED LINE

F – FOOD & DRINK

Shop(s) / supermarket	SHOP(S) / SUPMKT	On site		or		.... kms	
Bread / milk delivered	TRADSMN						
Restaurant / cafeteria	REST	On site		or		.... kms	
Snack bar / take-away	SNACKS	On site		or		.... kms	
Bar	BAR	On site		or		.... kms	
Barbecue allowed	BBQ	Charcoal		Gas		Elec	Sep area
Cooking facilities	COOKING FACS						

G – LEISURE FACILITIES

Playground	PLAYGRND						
Swimming pool	POOL	On site		or ....km		Heated	Covered
Beach	BEACH	Adj		or ....km		Sand	Shingle
Alternative swimming *(lake)*	SW	Adj		or ....km		Sand	Shingle
Games /sports area / Games room	GAMES AREA	GAMES ROOM					
Entertainment in high season	ENTMNT						
Internet use by visitors	INTERNET	Wifi Internet		WIFI			
Television room	TV RM	Satellite / Cable to pitches		TV CAB / SAT			

H – OTHER INFORMATION

% Static caravans / mobile homes / chalets / cottages / fixed tents on site					................% STATICS
Dogs allowed	DOGS	Y / N	Price per night .... *(if allowed)*		
Phone	PHONE	On site	Adj		
Bus / tram / train	BUS / TRAM / TRAIN	Adj	or .... km		
Twin axles caravans allowed?	TWIN AXLES Y / N	Possibly crowded in high season		POSS CR	
English spoken	ENG SPKN				
Advance bookings accepted	ADV BKG	Y / N			
Noise levels on site in season	NOISY	QUIET	If noisy, why?		
Credit card accepted	CCARD ACC	Reduction low season		RED LOW SSN	
Camping Key Europe or Camping Card International accepted in lieu of passport	CKE/CCI	INF card required *(If naturist site)*		Y / N	
Facilities for disabled	Full wheelchair facilities	♦	Limited disabled facilities		♦ ltd

I – ADDITIONAL REMARKS AND/OR ITEMS OF INTEREST

Tourist attractions, unusual features or other facilities, eg waterslide, tennis, cycle hire, watersports, horseriding, separate car park, walking distance to shops etc	YOUR OPINION OF THE SITE:
	EXCEL
	VERY GOOD
	GOOD
	FAIR / POOR
	NIGHT HALT ONLY

Your comments & opinions may be used in future editions of the guide, if you do not wish them to be used please tick ....

J – MEMBER DETAILS

ARE YOU A:	Caravanner	Motorhomer	Trailer-tenter?	
NAME:		MEMBERSHIP NO:		
		POST CODE:		
DO YOU NEED MORE BLANK SITE REPORT FORMS?		YES	NO	

Please use a separate form for each campsite and do not send receipts. Owing to the large number of site reports received, it is not possible to enter into correspondence. Please return completed form to:

The Editor, Overseas Touring Guides, East Grinstead House
East Grinstead, West Sussex RH19 1UA

Please note that due to changes in the rules regarding freepost we are no longer able to provide a freepost address for the return of Site Report Forms. You can still supply your site reports free online by visiting www.caravanclub.co.uk/europereport. We apologise for any inconvenience this may cause.

Abbreviated Site Report Form

Use this abbreviated Site Report Form if you have visited a number of sites and there are no changes (or only small changes) to their entries in the guide. If reporting on a new site, or reporting several changes, please use the full version of the report form. **If advising prices,** these should be for an outfit, and 2 adults for one night's stay. **Please indicate high or low season prices and whether electricity is included.**

Remember, if you don't tell us about sites you have visited, they may eventually be deleted from the guide.

Year of guide used	20.........	Page No.	....	Name of town/village site listed under			
Site Name					Date of visit	.... /....... /.......	
GPS	Latitude...(eg 12.34567)			Longitude...(eg 1.23456 or -1.23456)			
Site is in: Andorra / Austria / Belgium / Croatia / Czech Republic / Denmark / Finland / France / Germany / Greece / Hungary / Italy / Luxembourg / Netherlands / Norway / Poland / Portugal / Slovakia / Slovenia / Spain / Sweden / Switzerland							
Comments:							
Charge for outfit + 2 adults in local currency	High Season	Low Season	Elec inc in price?		Y / N	............amps	
			Price of elec (if not inc)			............amps	

Year of guide used	20.........	Page No.	....	Name of town/village site listed under			
Site Name					Date of visit	.... /....... /........	
GPS	Latitude...(eg 12.34567)			Longitude...(eg 1.23456 or -1.23456)			
Site is in: Andorra / Austria / Belgium / Croatia / Czech Republic / Denmark / Finland / France / Germany / Greece / Hungary / Italy / Luxembourg / Netherlands / Norway / Poland / Portugal / Slovakia / Slovenia / Spain / Sweden / Switzerland							
Comments:							
Charge for outfit + 2 adults in local currency	High Season	Low Season	Elec inc in price?		Y / N	............amps	
			Price of elec (if not inc)			............amps	

Year of guide used	20.........	Page No.	....	Name of town/village site listed under			
Site Name					Date of visit	.... /....... /........	
GPS	Latitude...(eg 12.34567)			Longitude...(eg 1.23456 or -1.23456)			
Site is in: Andorra / Austria / Belgium / Croatia / Czech Republic / Denmark / Finland / France / Germany / Greece / Hungary / Italy / Luxembourg / Netherlands / Norway / Poland / Portugal / Slovakia / Slovenia / Spain / Sweden / Switzerland							
Comments:							
Charge for car, caravan & 2 adults in local currency	High Season	Low Season	Elec inc in price?		Y / N	............amps	
			Price of elec (if not inc)			............amps	

Please fill in your details and send to the address on the reverse of this form.
You can also complete forms online: www.caravanclub.co.uk/europereport

CUT ALONG DOTTED LINE

Year of guide used	20.........	Page No.	....	Name of town/village site listed under	
Site Name				Date of visit	.... / .... / ....
GPS	Latitude..(eg 12.34567) Longitude..(eg 1.23456 or -1.23456)				

Site is in: Andorra / Austria / Belgium / Croatia / Czech Republic / Denmark / Finland / France / Germany / Greece / Hungary / Italy / Luxembourg / Netherlands / Norway / Poland / Portugal / Slovakia / Slovenia / Spain / Sweden / Switzerland

Comments:

Charge for outfit + 2 adults in local currency	High Season	Low Season	Elec inc in price?	Y / N	.............amps
			Price of elec (if not inc)		.............amps

Year of guide used	20.........	Page No.	....	Name of town/village site listed under	
Site Name				Date of visit	.... / .... / ....
GPS	Latitude..(eg 12.34567) Longitude..(eg 1.23456 or -1.23456)				

Site is in: Andorra / Austria / Belgium / Croatia / Czech Republic / Denmark / Finland / France / Germany / Greece / Hungary / Italy / Luxembourg / Netherlands / Norway / Poland / Portugal / Slovakia / Slovenia / Spain / Sweden / Switzerland

Comments:

Charge for outfit + 2 adults in local currency	High Season	Low Season	Elec inc in price?	Y / N	.............amps
			Price of elec (if not inc)		.............amps

Year of guide used	20.........	Page No.	....	Name of town/village site listed under	
Site Name				Date of visit	.... / .... / ....
GPS	Latitude..(eg 12.34567) Longitude..(eg 1.23456 or -1.23456)				

Site is in: Andorra / Austria / Belgium / Croatia / Czech Republic / Denmark / Finland / France / Germany / Greece / Hungary / Italy / Luxembourg / Netherlands / Norway / Poland / Portugal / Slovakia / Slovenia / Spain / Sweden / Switzerland

Comments:

Charge for outfit + 2 adults in local currency	High Season	Low Season	Elec inc in price?	Y / N	.............amps
			Price of elec (if not inc)		.............amps

Your comments & opinions may be used in future editions of the guide, if you do not wish them to be used please tick ....

Name ....

Membership No. ....

Post Code ....

Are you a Caravanner / Motorhomer / Trailer-Tenter?

Do you need more blank Site Report forms?   YES / NO

Please return completed forms to:
The Editor – Overseas Touring Guides
East Grinstead House
East Grinstead
West Sussex
RH19 1FH
Please note that due to changes in the rules regarding freepost we are no longer able to provide a freepost address for the return of Site Report Forms. You can still supply your site reports free online by visiting www.caravanclub.co.uk/europereport.
We apologise for any inconvenience this may cause.

You can also complete forms online: www.caravanclub.co.uk/europereport

Abbreviated Site Report Form

Use this abbreviated Site Report Form if you have visited a number of sites and there are no changes (or only small changes) to their entries in the guide. If reporting on a new site, or reporting several changes, please use the full version of the report form. **If advising prices,** these should be for an outfit, and 2 adults for one night's stay. **Please indicate high or low season prices and whether electricity is included.**

Remember, if you don't tell us about sites you have visited, they may eventually be deleted from the guide.

Year of guide used	20..........	Page No.	....	Name of town/village site listed under	
Site Name					Date of visit .... /....... /........
GPS	Latitude..(eg 12.34567) Longitude..(eg 1.23456 or -1.23456)				

Site is in: Andorra / Austria / Belgium / Croatia / Czech Republic / Denmark / Finland / France / Germany / Greece / Hungary / Italy / Luxembourg / Netherlands / Norway / Poland / Portugal / Slovakia / Slovenia / Spain / Sweden / Switzerland

Comments:

Charge for outfit + 2 adults in local currency	High Season	Low Season	Elec inc in price?	Y / N	............amps
			Price of elec (if not inc)		............amps

Year of guide used	20..........	Page No.	....	Name of town/village site listed under	
Site Name					Date of visit .... /....... /........
GPS	Latitude..(eg 12.34567) Longitude..(eg 1.23456 or -1.23456)				

Site is in: Andorra / Austria / Belgium / Croatia / Czech Republic / Denmark / Finland / France / Germany / Greece / Hungary / Italy / Luxembourg / Netherlands / Norway / Poland / Portugal / Slovakia / Slovenia / Spain / Sweden / Switzerland

Comments:

Charge for outfit + 2 adults in local currency	High Season	Low Season	Elec inc in price?	Y / N	............amps
			Price of elec (if not inc)		............amps

Year of guide used	20..........	Page No.	....	Name of town/village site listed under	
Site Name					Date of visit .... /....... /........
GPS	Latitude..(eg 12.34567) Longitude..(eg 1.23456 or -1.23456)				

Site is in: Andorra / Austria / Belgium / Croatia / Czech Republic / Denmark / Finland / France / Germany / Greece / Hungary / Italy / Luxembourg / Netherlands / Norway / Poland / Portugal / Slovakia / Slovenia / Spain / Sweden / Switzerland

Comments:

Charge for car, caravan & 2 adults in local currency	High Season	Low Season	Elec inc in price?	Y / N	............amps
			Price of elec (if not inc)		............amps

Please fill in your details and send to the address on the reverse of this form.
You can also complete forms online: www.caravanclub.co.uk/europereport

CUT ALONG DOTTED LINE

Year of guide used	20.........	Page No.	....	Name of town/village site listed under	
Site Name				Date of visit	.... /....... /.......
GPS	Latitude...(eg 12.34567) Longitude...(eg 1.23456 or -1.23456)				

Site is in: Andorra / Austria / Belgium / Croatia / Czech Republic / Denmark / Finland / France / Germany / Greece / Hungary / Italy / Luxembourg / Netherlands / Norway / Poland / Portugal / Slovakia / Slovenia / Spain / Sweden / Switzerland

Comments:

Charge for outfit + 2 adults in local currency	High Season	Low Season	Elec inc in price?	Y / N	............amps
			Price of elec (if not inc)		............amps

Year of guide used	20.........	Page No.	....	Name of town/village site listed under	
Site Name				Date of visit	.... /....... /.......
GPS	Latitude...(eg 12.34567) Longitude...(eg 1.23456 or -1.23456)				

Site is in: Andorra / Austria / Belgium / Croatia / Czech Republic / Denmark / Finland / France / Germany / Greece / Hungary / Italy / Luxembourg / Netherlands / Norway / Poland / Portugal / Slovakia / Slovenia / Spain / Sweden / Switzerland

Comments:

Charge for outfit + 2 adults in local currency	High Season	Low Season	Elec inc in price?	Y / N	............amps
			Price of elec (if not inc)		............amps

Year of guide used	20.........	Page No.	....	Name of town/village site listed under	
Site Name				Date of visit	.... /....... /.......
GPS	Latitude...(eg 12.34567) Longitude...(eg 1.23456 or -1.23456)				

Site is in: Andorra / Austria / Belgium / Croatia / Czech Republic / Denmark / Finland / France / Germany / Greece / Hungary / Italy / Luxembourg / Netherlands / Norway / Poland / Portugal / Slovakia / Slovenia / Spain / Sweden / Switzerland

Comments:

Charge for outfit + 2 adults in local currency	High Season	Low Season	Elec inc in price?	Y / N	............amps
			Price of elec (if not inc)		............amps

Your comments & opinions may be used in future editions of the guide, if you do not wish them to be used please tick ....

Name ....

Membership No. ....

Post Code ....

Are you a Caravanner / Motorhomer / Trailer-Tenter?

Do you need more blank Site Report forms?   YES / NO

Please return completed forms to:
The Editor – Overseas Touring Guides
East Grinstead House
East Grinstead
West Sussex
RH19 1FH
Please note that due to changes in the rules regarding freepost we are no longer able to provide a freepost address for the return of Site Report Forms. You can still supply your site reports free online by visiting www.caravanclub.co.uk/europereport.
We apologise for any inconvenience this may cause.

You can also complete forms online: www.caravanclub.co.uk/europereport

Index

Index